CALIFORNIA

McDougal Littell
LITERATURE
AMERICAN LITERATURE

Built for CALIFORNIA

Full Standards Correlation

Table of Contents

Student Guide

Embedded Standards Support

McDougal Littell
EVANSTON, ILLINOIS · BOSTON · DALLAS

ART CREDITS

COVER, TITLE PAGE

La Maison noire, East Hampton. New York (1964), Jeanloup Sieff. © The Estate of Jeanloup Sieff.

Consultants *Janet Allen* Photo by Duane McCubrey; *Arthur Applebee* Photo by Mark Schmidt; *Jim Burke* Photo by Bruce Forrester; *Douglas Carnine* © McDougal Littell; *Yvette Jackson* Photo by Howard Gollub; *Robert T. Jiménez* Photo by Tamra Stallings; *Judith A. Langer* Photo by Mark Schmidt; *Robert J. Marzano* Photo by Robert J. Marzano; *Donna M. Ogle* © McDougal Littell; *Carol Booth Olson* © Dawson & Associates Photography; *Carol Ann Tomlinson* © Gitchell's Studio; *David M. Considine* Photo by Bill Caldwell; *Larkin Pauluzzi* Photo by Gabriel Pauluzzi; *Lisa K. Scheffler* Photo by Steven Scheffler; *Mary Lou McCloskey* Photo by Michael Romeo; *Lydia Stack* Photo by Monica Ani; *William McBride* Photo by William McBride.

Student and Teacher Resource Covers *McDougal Littell Literature, La Maison noire,* East Hampton. New York (1964), Jeanloup Sieff. © The Estate of Jeanloup Sieff.; *Universal Access Guide* © Blend Images/Punchstock; *Resource Manager* © Brand X Pictures; *Easy Planner DVD-Rom* © Frances L. Fruit. Used under license from Shutterstock, Inc.; *MediaSmart* © Jim Arbogast/Getty Images; Illustration © Cliff Nielson; Courtesy Democratic National Committee; © Solstice Photography/Brand X/Corbis; *Best Practices Toolkit cover,* teen reading © Punchstock; teens with map © Yellow Dog Productions/Getty Images; teacher at chalkboard © Corbis; *background* © Getty Images; *Standards Lesson File* Photograph by Sharon Hoogstraten; *Power Presentations* Cyrill Kourachov/ShutterStock; © Andersen Ross/Getty Images; *Test Generator* © Comstock Images/Jupiter Images; *Grammar for Writing* Ryan Aldrich/McDougal Littell; *Pronunciation Guide* © Johanna Goodyear. Used under license from Shutterstock, Inc.; *The Tragedy of Romeo and Juliet* Cover illustration by Curtis Parker; *Audio Anthology* © Rob Melnychuk/Getty Images; *Assessment File* Photograph by Sharon Hoogstraten.

T1 © Brand X Pictures; **T4** McDougal Littell In-House Art except *Linda Valdez* Photo by Linda Valdez; *Lynda Zimmerman* Photo by Lynda Zimmerman; **T5** © Carolina K. Smith/ShutterStock; **T6–T7** Photograph by Ed-Imaging; **T6** *from WriteSmart, Cool Hand (2005),* Gil Mayers. Mixed media. Photo © Gilbert Mayers/SuperStock; **T8–T9** Photograph by Ed-Imaging; **T8** *Mandan Offering the Buffalo Skull.* Edward S. Curtis Collection. © McCormick Library of Special Collections, Northwestern University Library; **T9** *Coyote Survivor,* John Nieto. Serigraph, 29" x 22". © John Nieto; **T25** *top Thomas Jefferson* (1805), Gilbert Stuart. Oil on panel, 36 1/8" x 21". National Portrait Gallery, Smithsonian Institution, Washington, D.C.: gift of the Regents of the Smithsonian Institution, the Thomas Jefferson Memorial Foundation, and the Enid and Crosby Kemper Foundation; owned jointly with Monticello. Photo © National Portrait Gallery, Smithsonian Institution/Art Resource, New York; *bottom* © Pat and Chuck Blackley; **T26** The Granger Collection, New York; **T27** *top left Thomas Jefferson* (1805), Gilbert Stuart. Oil on panel, 36 1/8" x 21". National Portrait Gallery, Smithsonian Institution, Washington, D.C.: gift of the Regents of the Smithsonian Institution, the Thomas Jefferson Memorial Foundation, and the Enid and Crosby Kemper Foundation; owned jointly with Monticello. Photo © National Portrait Gallery, Smithsonian Institution/Art Resource, New York; *bottom left* © Pat and Chuck Blackley; *right* The Granger Collection, New York.

BACK COVER
© Brand X Pictures.

ISBN 13: 978-0-618-98385-8   ISBN 10: 0-618-98385-6

Printed in China.

1 2 3 4 5 6 7 8 9—DSC—12 11 10 09 08

SENIOR PROGRAM CONSULTANTS

JANET ALLEN
Reading and Literacy Specialist, Lecturer, Consultant, and Author. Creator of the "It's Never Too Late for Literacy" institutes.

ARTHUR N. APPLEBEE
Leading Professor, School of Education at the University at Albany, State University of New York; Director of the Center on English Learning and Achievement

JIM BURKE
Lecturer and Author; Teacher of English at Burlingame High School, Burlingame, California.

DOUGLAS CARNINE
Professor of Education at the University of Oregon; Director of the Western Region Reading First Technical Assistance Center.

YVETTE JACKSON
Executive Director of the National Urban Alliance for Effective Education

ROBERT T. JIMÉNEZ
Professor of Language, Literacy, and Culture at Vanderbilt University

JUDITH A. LANGER
Distinguished Professor at the University at Albany, State University of New York; Director of the Center on English Learning and Achievement; Director of the Albany Institute for Research in Education.

ROBERT J. MARZANO
Senior Scholar at Mid-Continent Research for Education and Learning (McREL); Associate Professor at Cardinal Stritch University in Milwaukee, Wisconsin; President of Marzano & Associates

DONNA M. OGLE
Professor of Reading and Language at National-Louis University in Chicago, Illinois

CAROL BOOTH OLSON
Senior Lecturer in the Department of Education at the University of California, Irvine; Director of the UCI site of the National Writing Project.

CAROL ANN TOMLINSON
Professor of Educational Research, Foundations, and Policy at the University of Virginia; Co-Director of the University's Institutes on Academic Diversity.

MEDIA SPECIALISTS

DAVID M. CONSIDINE
Professor of Instructional Technology and Media Studies at Appalachian State University in North Carolina

LARKIN PAULUZZI
Teacher and Media Specialist; trainer for the New Jersey Writing Project

LISA K. SCHEFFLER
Specialist Teacher and Media

ENGLISH LEARNER SPECIALISTS

MARY LOU McCLOSKEY
Director of Teacher Development and Curriculum Design for Educo in Atlanta, Georgia

LYDIA STACK
International ESL consultant

CURRICULUM SPECIALIST

WILLIAM L. McBRIDE
Curriculum Specialist; Lecturer and Author

CALIFORNIA TEACHER ADVISORY PANEL

JORDANA BENONE
Teacher
North High School
Torrance, CA

NANCY HIMEL
Teacher
Board member of CATE
Paramount High School
Paramount, CA

JAN SAMMONS
Teacher, Reading Specialist
Joaquin Moraga
Intermediate School
Moraga, CA

TERESA BUNNER
English Department Chair
Monterey Trail High School
Elk Grove, CA

GAIL KIDD
Department Chair,
Language Arts Testing
& Standards Coordinator
Center Middle School
Azusa, CA

RUTH ELLEN SCHMUTZ
Professional Development
Secondary Specialist: ELA
Moreno Valley USD
Moreno Valley, CA

HOPPY CHANDLER
Teacher
San Diego City Schools
San Diego, CA

BETH LEDERACH
Teacher
Clovis High School
Clovis, CA

JOSEPH STAUB
Resource Specialist Teacher
Thomas Starr King
Middle School
Los Angeles, CA

DAWN CHARTSCHLAA
English Teacher
Oakland Technical
High School
Oakland, CA

TONI MCELROY
ELA Secondary
Content Coach
Oakland Unified SD
Oakland, CA

LINDA VALDEZ
Educational Consultant
Oxnard Union High School District
Oxnard, CA

QUEANA GIVENS
Secondary Language
Arts Coordinator
Imperial County Ed
El Centro, CA

SAMANTHA MO
English Literature and
Composition Teacher
OCHSA
Santa Ana, CA

ARLENE WALKER
Teacher, Department Chair
Chaparral Middle School
Diamond Bar, CA

LIZ HARRINGTON
Teacher, Language Arts
Department Chair
Jefferson Middle School
San Gabriel, CA

PAGE MURPHY
English Language
Arts Teacher
Talbert Middle School
Huntington Beach, CA

LYNDA ZIMMERMAN
Teacher
El Camino High School
South San Francisco, CA

CALIFORNIA

McDougal Littell
LITERATURE
AMERICAN LITERATURE

Where Great
Lessons Begin

Great Lessons Begin with You.

You teach. You inspire. We help.

We help you with support for every standard, every selection, and every student.

WriteSmart CD-ROM
A state-specific, interactive writing instruction tool with a rubric generator.

Resource Manager
Provides all-in-one support for essential skills and standards.

Standards Lesson File
Gives you a fast, organized approach to teaching every California standard.

CONSULTANT'S CORNER

Bob Marzano
McDougal Littell provides maximum support to teachers in terms of instructional strategies and addressing California state standards. Used well, this literature series can dramatically enhance student achievement while maximizing teacher creativity.

Great Lessons Begin with
Your Students.

They wonder. They question. We help.

We help your students become active readers, writers, and thinkers.

The **Student's Edition** helps engage and motivate students with a vibrant mix of selections.

COYOTE and the BUFFALO

Retold by Mourning Dove

BACKGROUND "Coyote and the Buffalo" is one of many traditional stories featuring the Animal People, a race of supernatural beings believed by the Okanogan to have been the first inhabitants of the world. The Animal People had magical powers and could alter their shapes. When human beings appeared on the earth, the Animal People were changed into different animal species. Coyote, one of the most important Animal People, is thought to have made the world habitable for humans by killing monsters and bringing fire and salmon.

ANALYZE VISUALS
Describe the painting on page 45. How is the use of color significant? Does the color treatment cause this coyote to reflect the traits of a trickster? Explain your answer.

No buffalo ever lived in the *Swah-netk'-qhu* country. That was Coyote's fault. If he had not been so foolish and greedy, the people beside the *Swah-netk'-qhu* would not have had to cross the Rockies to hunt the *quas-peet-za* (curled-hairs).

This is the way it happened:

Coyote was traveling over the plains beyond the big mountains. He came to a flat. There he found an old buffalo skull. It was the skull of Buffalo Bull. Coyote always had been afraid of Buffalo Bull. He remembered the many times Bull Buffalo had scared him, and he laughed upon seeing the old skull there on the flat. "Now I will have some fun," Coyote remarked. "I will have revenge for the

10 times Buffalo made me run."

He picked up the skull and threw it into the air; he kicked it and spat on it; he threw dust in the eye sockets. He did these things many times, until he grew tired. Then he went his way. Soon he heard a rumbling behind him. He thought it was thunder, and he looked at the sky. The sky was clear. Thinking he must have imagined the sound, he walked on, singing. He heard the rumbling again, only

TRICKSTER TALES
In the first paragraph, the tale's narrator pronounces Coyote "foolish and greedy." Based on lines 5–13, what other character traits would you attribute to this trickster?

1. *Swah-netk'-qhu* (shwa-ni't'kawai: the Salish name for the Columbia River and its waterfall.

2. *quas-peet-za* (kawa-piit'za): a Salish word for buffalo.

44 UNIT 1: EARLY AMERICAN WRITING

Coyote Services: John Nieto.
Serigraph, 20" x 32".

Media Studies

- Stagecoach, The Lone Ranger Smoke Signals
- Illustrations Inspired by Poe
- American Landscapes
- Gatsby Era Ads
- Zora Neale Hurston
- Cesar Chavez News Reports
- The Crucible
- An Occurrence at Owl Creek Bridge

MediaSmart DVD-ROM Helps promote critical thinking through analysis of a variety of media.

CONSULTANT'S CORNER

Janet Allen

In choosing to work on writing a literature program, I found a home with McDougal Littell because all our decisions could be based on students' needs and teachers' expertise. It was a perfect match for my interests and experience.

Carol Ann Tomlinson

Students come to us as a mixed set. They don't learn in the same ways, aren't motivated by the same things, and don't function at the same pace or depth. What I've always cared about is how teachers can help diverse learners succeed by teaching flexibly......that flexibility is built into this program.

Great Lessons Begin with
McDougal Littell Literature.

Teacher Resources

Time-saving, easy-to-use teacher resources make lesson planning and preparation simple.

Core Teacher Resources include:

- **Teacher's Edition**
- **EasyPlanner CD-Rom**
- **Resource Manager**

- **WriteSmart CD-ROM**
  A state-specific, interactive writing instruction tool with a rubric generator.

- **MediaSmart DVD-ROM**
  Helps promote critical thinking through analysis of a variety of media.

Best Practices Toolkit
Support for classroom management and differentiation, including professional development articles and over 200 graphic organizer transparencies.

Targeted Instruction for the California Standards

Standards Lesson File
Stand-alone lessons ensure standards mastery.

Assessment File
Opportunities to assess student progress with a comprehensive array of tests including diagnostic, progress monitoring, and summative assessments.

Electronic Resources

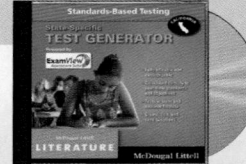

Power Presentations
A collection of dynamic classroom presentation materials including leveled discussion questions, graphic organizers, and interactive vocabulary practice.

McDougal Littell Assessment System and Test Generator
Provides program assessment tests, scoring, and reporting.

Student Resources

A complete program of technology and print resources provides support for differentiated student learning.

Core Student Resources include:

- **Student Edition**
- **eEdition online and DVD-ROM**
- **Grammar for Writing**
- **Grammar for Writing Workbook**
  Supports systematic, student-friendly instruction in all aspects of grammar, usage, and mechanics.

Novels
Over 700 novels, works of nonfiction, and plays promote independent learning and reading.

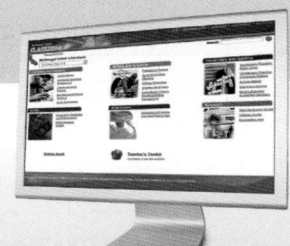

Multi-Language Academic Glossary Online
Facilitates comprehension of academic vocabulary with key terms and definitions in 8 languages.

Classzone.com
Provides a wealth of interactive resources for literature, reading, writing, grammar, vocabulary, spelling, and assessment.

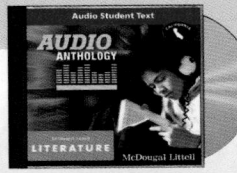

Audio Anthology CD
Enables students to hear pronunciation, phrasing, and interpretations of all selections as they follow along in their textbook.

Correlation to California Standards

McDougal Littell *Literature* provides comprehensive instruction in all domains of the California Language Arts Standards. The chart below lists the Grade 11 standards and indicates where each standard is taught in the Student's Edition, Teacher's Edition, and relevant ancillaries. These references will provide a systematic, standards-based approach to instruction, practice, reteaching, and assessment.

READING

 1.0 Word Analysis, Fluency, and Systematic Vocabulary Development

Standards	Primary Citations	Supporting Citations
Vocabulary and Concept Development **1.1** Trace the etymology of significant terms used in political science and history.	**STUDENT'S/TEACHER'S EDITION** 108, 242	**STUDENT'S/TEACHER'S EDITION** 960, 1030, R74 **PRINT COMPONENTS** **Resource Manager:** Unit 1: 181, 375; Unit 5: 273, 397 **Standards Lesson File:** Vocabulary and Spelling: 49–58, 59–66, 67–74, 85–90, 229–237 **Targeted Instruction:** 1–2
1.2 Apply knowledge of Greek, Latin, and Anglo-Saxon roots and affixes to draw inferences concerning the meaning of scientific and mathematical terminology.	**STUDENT'S/TEACHER'S EDITION** 326, 425, 472, 686, 736, 866, 1171	**STUDENT'S/TEACHER'S EDITION** 86, 232, 273, 391, 1016, R73, R74 **PRINT COMPONENTS** **Resource Manager:** Unit 1: 133; Unit 2: 157, 203, 279; Unit 4: 103, 161; Unit 5: 86, 372; Unit 6: 118, 119 **Standards Lesson File:** Vocabulary and Spelling: 39–47, 49–58, 59–66, 67–74, 75–83, 85–90 **Targeted Instruction:** 3–4
1.3 Discern the meaning of analogies encountered, analyzing specific comparisons as well as relationships and inferences.	**STUDENT'S/TEACHER'S EDITION** 252, 272, 865, 1157, 1158	**STUDENT'S/TEACHER'S EDITION** 222–223, R16 **PRINT COMPONENTS** **Resource Manager:** Unit 1: 345, 346, 353; Unit 3: 109, 110, 114; Unit 6: 187, 188, 195 **Standards Lesson File:** Vocabulary and Spelling: 207–215; Literature: 317–324 **Targeted Instruction:** 5–6

NOTES: Targeted Instruction stands for *Targeted Instruction for California Standards.*

The Student's Edition is also available online and on DVD-ROM. The Teacher's Edition is available on DVD-ROM.

Universal Access Guide correlation is available separately.

2.0 Reading Comprehension (Focus on Informational Materials)

Standards	Primary Citations	Supporting Citations
Structural Features of Informational Materials **2.1** Analyze both the features and the rhetorical devices of different types of public documents (e.g., policy statements, speeches, debates, platforms) and the way in which authors use those features and devices.	**STUDENT'S/TEACHER'S EDITION** 224–231, 562–568, 1192–1199	**STUDENT'S/TEACHER'S EDITION** 222–223, R16 **PRINT COMPONENTS** **Resource Manager:** Unit 1: 345, 346, 353; Unit 3: 109, 110, 114; Unit 6: 187, 188, 195 **Standards Lesson File:** Literature: 333–341; Reading and Informational Texts: 191–201, 333–341, 391–395 **Targeted Instruction:** 7–8
Comprehension and Analysis of Grade-Level-Appropriate Text **2.2** Analyze the way in which clarity of meaning is affected by the patterns of organization, hierarchical structures, repetition of the main ideas, syntax, and word choice in the text.	**STUDENT'S/TEACHER'S EDITION** 50–59, 234–241, 254–261, 328–332, 358–359, 1222–1229, 1230–1235	**STUDENT'S/TEACHER'S EDITION** 89, 1059, 1071, R8–R12, R33 **PRINT COMPONENTS** **Resource Manager:** Unit 1: 69, 70, 76, 371, 372, 377, 417, 418, 422; Unit 2: 51, 52, 53; Unit 6: 255, 256, 257, 258, 260, 273, 274, 277 **Standards Lesson File:** Literature: 383–391, 421–429; Reading and Informational Texts: 203–210, 211–218, 219–226, 227–240, 241–249, 251–260, 261–271, 273–280, 281–290, 291–303 **Targeted Instruction:** 9–10
2.3 Verify and clarify facts presented in other types of expository texts by using a variety of consumer, workplace, and public documents.	**STUDENT'S/TEACHER'S EDITION** 1281, R15–R18	**STUDENT'S/TEACHER'S EDITION** 1269, 1271–1277 **PRINT COMPONENTS** **Resource Manager:** Unit 7: 17, 18, 22, 25 **Standards Lesson File:** Reading and Informational Texts: 45–54, 343–352, 363–375, 377–386, 387–395 **Targeted Instruction:** 11–12
2.4 Make warranted and reasonable assertions about the author's arguments by using elements of the text to defend and clarify interpretations.	**STUDENT'S/TEACHER'S EDITION** 234–241, 868–874, 1144–1157, 1172–1175	**STUDENT'S/TEACHER'S EDITION** R19–R24 **PRINT COMPONENTS** **Resource Manager:** Unit 1: 369, 370, 377; Unit 5: 107, 108, 110; Unit 6: 91, 92, 97, 135, 136, 140 **Standards Lesson File:** Reading and Informational Texts: 91–100, 325–332, 343–352, 353–361 **Targeted Instruction:** 13–14

Standards	Primary Citations	Supporting Citations
2.5 Analyze an author's implicit and explicit philosophical assumptions and beliefs about a subject.	**STUDENT'S/TEACHER'S EDITION** 98–108, 262–272, 333, 360–367, 370–380, 382–389, 394–400, 450–451, 570–575, 562–568, 744–753, 1066–1071, 1160–1170, 1247	**STUDENT'S/TEACHER'S EDITION** 61, 755, 1048–1056, 1058–1064, 1214–1221 **PRINT COMPONENTS** **Resource Manager:** Unit 1: 175, 176, 183, 437, 438, 439, 445; Unit 2: 125, 126, 133, 153, 154, 159, 177, 179, 180, 182; Unit 3: 111, 112, 113; Unit 4: 199, 200, 205; Unit 5: 483, 484, 485; Unit 6: 115, 116, 121, 235, 236, 240 **Standards Lesson File:** Literature: 431–439 **Targeted Instruction:** 15–16
Expository Critique **2.6** Critique the power, validity, and truthfulness of arguments set forth in public documents; their appeal to both friendly and hostile audiences; and the extent to which the arguments anticipate and address reader concerns and counterclaims (e.g., appeal to reason, to authority, to pathos and emotion).	**STUDENT'S/TEACHER'S EDITION** 118–126, 222–223, 224–231, 234–241, 244–252, 1144–1157	**STUDENT'S/TEACHER'S EDITION** R19 **PRINT COMPONENTS** **Resource Manager:** Unit 1: 219, 220, 225, 353, 369, 370, 377, 393, 394, 401; Unit 6: 91, 92, 97 **Standards Lesson File:** Reading and Informational Texts: 325–332, 343–352, 353–361, 387–395 **Targeted Instruction:** 17–18

 ## 3.0 Literary Response and Analysis

Standards	Primary Citations	Supporting Citations
Structural Features of Literature **3.1** Analyze characteristics of subgenres (e.g., satire, parody, allegory, pastoral) that are used in poetry, prose, plays, novels, short stories, essays, and other basic genres.	**STUDENT'S/TEACHER'S EDITION** 32, 78, 310–325, 427–435, 445, 801	**STUDENT'S/TEACHER'S EDITION** 457–471, 785 **PRINT COMPONENTS** **Resource Manager:** Unit 2: 27, 28, 35, 221, 222, 229; Unit 4: 73, 74, 81 **Standards Lesson File:** Literature: 107–114, 115–123, 125–134, 307–315 **Targeted Instruction:** 19–20
Narrative Analysis of Grade-Level-Appropriate Text **3.2** Analyze the way in which the theme or meaning of a selection represents a view or comment on life, using textual evidence to support the claim.	**STUDENT'S/TEACHER'S EDITION** 744–753, 756–757, 852–857, 1002–1015, 1230–1235	**STUDENT'S/TEACHER'S EDITION** 392–393, 593, 911, 951, 959, 999, 1135, 1142 **PRINT COMPONENTS** **Resource Manager:** Unit 1: 197, 198, 205; Unit 4: 61, 62, 65; Unit 5: 367, 368, 375; Unit 6: 277 **Standards Lesson File:** Literature: 97–106 **Targeted Instruction:** 21–22

Standards	Primary Citations	Supporting Citations
3.3 Analyze the ways in which irony, tone, mood, the author's style, and the "sound" of language achieve specific rhetorical or aesthetic purposes or both.	**STUDENT'S/TEACHER'S EDITION** 88–96, 78–85, 310–325, 328–332, 334–339, 340–345, 370–380, 402–424, 506–507, 508–519, 524–534, 538–548, 634–647, 658, 691, 710–735, 738–743, 758–764, 790–801, 858–865, 888–893, 896–902, 920–927, 928–934, 968–975, 988–999, 1018–1029, 1032–1044, 1046–1047, 1048–1056, 1058–1064, 1066–1070, 1114–1120, 1202–1203, 1222–1229, 1230–1235, 1242–1246	**STUDENT'S/TEACHER'S EDITION** 358, 359, 632–633, 921, 1052 **PRINT COMPONENTS** **Resource Manager:** Unit 1: 151, 152, 219, 220, 225; Unit 2: 53, 67, 68, 69, 70, 71, 85, 86, 89, 151, 152; Unit 3: 27, 28, 29, 30, 31, 45, 46, 49, 65, 66, 70; Unit 4: 29, 30, 38, 157, 158, 163, 177, 225, 226, 269, 270, 277; Unit 5: 81, 82, 89, 151, 152, 155, 171, 172, 175, 229, 230, 301, 302, 309, 343, 344, 351, 391, 392, 399, 415, 416, 420, 439, 440, 442, 459, 460, 464, 481, 482, 486; Unit 6: 27, 28, 32, 255, 256, 260, 273, 274, 277, 309, 310, 313 **Standards Lesson File:** Literature: 343–351, 383–391, 401–409, 411–419, 421–429 **Targeted Instruction:** 23–24
3.4 Analyze ways in which poets use imagery, personification, figures of speech, and sounds to evoke readers' emotions.	**STUDENT'S/TEACHER'S EDITION** 110–117, 346–356, 437–443, 506–507, 523, 524–534, 703, 838–845, 852–857, 892–893, 912–918, 1114–1120, 1236–1241	**STUDENT'S/TEACHER'S EDITION** 519, 535, 880–887, 919 **PRINT COMPONENTS** **Resource Manager:** Unit 1: 197, 198, 199, 200, 201; Unit 2: 103, 104, 107; Unit 5: 27, 28, 29, 43, 44, 45, 46, 47, 61, 62, 63, 64, 65, 133, 134, 171, 172, 175, 209, 210, 213; Unit 6: 27, 28, 29, 30, 291, 292, 295, 309, 310, 313 **Standards Lesson File:** Literature: 181–190, 191–200, 201–208, 209–216, 247–256, 257–265, 267–275, 277–285 **Targeted Instruction:** 25–26
3.5 Analyze recognized works of American literature representing a variety of genres and traditions: a. Trace the development of American literature from the colonial period forward. b. Contrast the major periods, themes, styles, and trends and describe how works by members of different cultures relate to one another in each period. c. Evaluate the philosophical, political, religious, ethical, and social influences of the historical period that shaped the characters, plots, and settings.	**STUDENT'S/TEACHER'S EDITION** 19–27, 66–67, 75, 128–129, 130–209, 212–217, 297–305, 495–501, 456–471, 619–627, 632–633, 672–685, 703, 756–757, 766–785, 825–833, 894–895, 920–927, 1093–1101, 1122–1131, 1202–1203, 1247	**STUDENT'S/TEACHER'S EDITION** 4–5, 26–27, 28–29, 306–307, 502–503, 834–835, 628–629, 1102–1103 **PRINT COMPONENTS** **Resource Manager:** Unit 1: 27–30, 32, 103–106, 111, 243, 244, 249, 315–318, 320; Unit 2: 275, 276, 281; Unit 4: 97, 98, 105, 247, 248, 253; Unit 6: 51, 52, 54 **Standards Lesson File:** Literature: 97–106, 237–245, 421–429, 431–439 **Targeted Instruction:** 27–28
3.6 Analyze the way in which authors through the centuries have used archetypes drawn from myth and tradition in literature, film, political speeches, and religious writings (e.g., how the archetypes of banishment from an ideal world may be used to interpret Shakespeare's tragedy *Macbeth*).	**STUDENT'S/TEACHER'S EDITION** 42–49, 1002–1015	**STUDENT'S/TEACHER'S EDITION** 327 **PRINT COMPONENTS** **Resource Manager:** Unit 1: 47, 48, 52; Unit 5: 363, 367, 368, 375 **Standards Lesson File:** Literature: 297–305 **Targeted Instruction:** 29–30

Standards	Primary Citations	Supporting Citations
3.7 Analyze recognized works of world literature from a variety of authors: a. Contrast the major literary forms, techniques, and characteristics of the major literary periods (e.g., Homeric Greece, medieval, romantic, neoclassic, modern). b. Relate literary works and authors to the major themes and issues of their eras. c. Evaluate the philosophical, political, religious, ethical, and social influences of the historical period that shaped the characters, plots, and settings.	**STUDENT'S/TEACHER'S EDITION** 66–67, 68–75, 78–85, 392–393, 520–523, 1132–1135	**STUDENT'S/TEACHER'S EDITION** 4–5, 28–29, 306–307, 205–203, 628–629, 834–835 **PRINT COMPONENTS** **Resource Manager:** Unit 1: 103, 104, 111, 127, 128, 135 **Standards Lesson File:** Literature: 115–123, 135–145, 147–157, 217–226, 227–229, 231–235, 237–245 **Targeted Instruction:** 31–32
Literary Criticism **3.8** Analyze the clarity and consistency of political assumptions in a selection of literary works or essays on a topic (e.g., suffrage, women's role in organized labor). (Political approach)	**STUDENT'S/TEACHER'S EDITION** 758–765, 766–785, 790–801, 838–845, 846–851, 852–857, 858–865, 1144–1157, 1160–1170, 1172–1175, 1180–1190, 1192–1199	**STUDENT'S/TEACHER'S EDITION** 121, 756–757, 803 **PRINT COMPONENTS** **Resource Manager:** Unit 4: 247, 248, 253; Unit 6: 113, 114, 115, 116, 121, 135, 136, 137, 138 **Standards Lesson File:** Literature: 431–493 **Targeted Instruction:** 33–34
3.9 Analyze the philosophical arguments presented in literary works to determine whether the authors' positions have contributed to the quality of each work and the credibility of the characters. (Philosophical approach)	**STUDENT'S/TEACHER'S EDITION** 360–367, 370–380, 382–389, 392–393, 396–400, 1144–1157, 1160–1170, 1172–1175, 1180–1190, 1192–1199	**STUDENT'S/TEACHER'S EDITION** 109, 358–359, 401, 858–865, 1201 **PRINT COMPONENTS** **Resource Manager:** Unit 2: 125, 126, 153, 154, 159; Unit 6: 89, 90, 92, 113, 114, 115, 116, 121, 135, 136, 137, 138, 140, 165, 166 **Standards Lesson File:** Literature: 431–439 **Targeted Instruction:** 35–36

WRITING

 1.0 Writing Strategies

Organization and Focus **1.1** Demonstrate an understanding of the elements of discourse (e.g., purpose, speaker, audience, form) when completing narrative, expository, persuasive, or descriptive writing assignments.	**STUDENT'S/TEACHER'S EDITION** 276–282, 474–480, 598–604, 804–810, 1072–1078, 1248–1254	**STUDENT'S/TEACHER'S EDITION** 87, 243, 369, 391, 426, 437, 444, 569, 687, 1121, 1159, 1191, 1201, 1213 **PRINT COMPONENTS** **Resource Manager:** Unit 1: 136, 455–460; Unit 2: 291–296; Unit 3: 177–182; Unit 4: 257–292; Unit 5: 495–500; Unit 6: 98, 323–328 **Standards Lesson File:** Writing, Research, and Study Skills: 23–31 **Targeted Instruction:** 37–38 **TECHNOLOGY** Write*Smart*

Standards	Primary Citations	Supporting Citations
1.2 Use point of view, characterization, style (e.g., use of irony), and related elements for specific rhetorical and aesthetic purposes.	**STUDENT'S/TEACHER'S EDITION** 559, 599–603, 737, 1057	**STUDENT'S/TEACHER'S EDITION** 77, 327, 426, 444, 669, 687, 765, 867, 919, 935, 988, 1017, 1065, 1071, 1213, R34 **PRINT COMPONENTS** **Resource Manager:** Unit 2: 36; Unit 4: 164, 229; Unit 5: 214, 352, 376, 443 **Standards Lesson File:** Literature: 23–29, 87–96, 343–351, 353–362; Writing, Research, and Study Skills: 405–416 **Targeted Instruction:** 39–40 **TECHNOLOGY** **Write*Smart***
1.3 Structure ideas and arguments in a sustained, persuasive, and sophisticated way and support them with precise and relevant examples.	**STUDENT'S/TEACHER'S EDITION** 1175, 1201, 1248–1253, 1276–1282, 1289–1298	**STUDENT'S/TEACHER'S EDITION** 233, 369, 391, 911, 961, 1031, 1065, 1121, 1159 **PRINT COMPONENTS** **Resource Manager:** Unit 1: 455–460, 462; Unit 2: 135, 161; Unit 6: 323–328, 330; Unit 7: 30 **Standards Lesson File:** Reading and Informational Texts: 325–332, 333–341, 353–361; Writing, Research, and Study Skills: 317–327, 371–382, 383–393, 395–408 **Targeted Instruction:** 41–42 **TECHNOLOGY** **Write*Smart***
1.4 Enhance meaning by employing rhetorical devices, including the extended use of parallelism, repetition, and analogy; the incorporation of visual aids (e.g., graphs, tables, pictures); and the issuance of a call for action.	**STUDENT'S/TEACHER'S EDITION** 276–282, 391, 569, 1001, 1159	**STUDENT'S/TEACHER'S EDITION** 233, 282, R5–R7, R38–R39 **PRINT COMPONENTS** **Resource Manager:** Unit 1: 11, 345, 346, 455–460, 462; Unit 2: 161; Unit 3: 115; Unit 5: 352; Unit 6: 98 **Standards Lesson File:** Writing, Research, and Study Skills: 89–98, 317–327, 395–403; Reading and Informational Texts: 333–341; Literature 317–324 **Targeted Instruction:** 43–44 **TECHNOLOGY** **Write*Smart***
1.5 Use language in natural, fresh, and vivid ways to establish a specific tone.	**STUDENT'S/TEACHER'S EDITION** 444, 559, 569, 765, 867, 919, 977, 1065, 1121, 1191	**STUDENT'S/TEACHER'S EDITION** 935, 1017 **PRINT COMPONENTS** **Resource Manager:** Unit 2: 248; Unit 3: 93, 115; Unit 4: 229; Unit 5: 90, 214, 310; Unit 6: 33, 171 **Standards Lesson File:** Writing, Research, and Study Skills: 405–416, 427–432, 453–465, 467–476 **Targeted Instruction:** 45–46 **TECHNOLOGY** **Write*Smart***

Standards	Primary Citations	Supporting Citations
Research and Technology **1.6** Develop presentations by using clear research questions and creative and critical research strategies (e.g., field studies, oral histories, interviews, experiments, electronic sources).	**STUDENT'S/TEACHER'S EDITION** 1179, 1268–1277, 1281, 1285–1300	**STUDENT'S/TEACHER'S EDITION** 1251, R47 **PRINT COMPONENTS** **Resource Manager:** Unit 6: 323–327; Unit 7: 15–18, 25, 30 **Standards Lesson File:** Writing, Research, and Study Skills: 489–497, 499–509, 511–523, 521–532, 533–545, 547–559, 561–570, 571–583; Media Studies, Speaking, and Listening: 287–294 **Targeted Instruction:** 47–48 **TECHNOLOGY** Write*Smart*
1.7 Use systematic strategies to organize and record information (e.g., anecdotal scripting, annotated bibliographies).	**STUDENT'S/TEACHER'S EDITION** 279, 1278–1280, 1284–1301, 1299	**STUDENT'S/TEACHER'S EDITION** R48–R49, 1268 **PRINT COMPONENTS** **Resource Manager:** Unit 1: 455, 456; Unit 7: 27, 29, 30 **Standards Lesson File:** Reading and Informational Texts: 149–160; Writing, Research, and Study Skills: 571–580, 591–599, 633–644, 645–656; Media Studies, Speaking, and Listening: 163–176 **Targeted Instruction:** 49–50 **TECHNOLOGY** Write*Smart*
1.8 Integrate databases, graphics, and spreadsheets into word-processed documents.	**STUDENT'S/TEACHER'S EDITION** 1302–1303	**STUDENT'S/TEACHER'S EDITION** 1272–1273, R46 **PRINT COMPONENTS** **Resource Manager:** Unit 7: 17, 29 **Standards Lesson File:** Writing, Research, and Study Skills: 395–403 **Targeted Instruction:** 51–52 **TECHNOLOGY** Write*Smart*
Evaluation and Revision **1.9** Revise text to highlight the individual voice, improve sentence variety and style, and enhance subtlety of meaning and tone in ways that are consistent with the purpose, audience, and genre.	**STUDENT'S/TEACHER'S EDITION** 479, 559, 603, 669, 809, 867, 977, 1001, 1065, 1121, 1191, 1213, 1253	**STUDENT'S/TEACHER'S EDITION** 87, 243, 391, 559, 569, 687, 919, 1017, 1077, R26–R27 **PRINT COMPONENTS** **Resource Manager:** Unit 1: 136, 378; Unit 2: 296; Unit 3: 93, 115; Unit 4: 289; Unit 5: 90, 310, 352, 376, 465; Unit 6: 33, 171, 219, 328 **Standards Lesson File:** Writing, Research, and Study Skills: 79–87, 89–98, 227–233, 405–416, 467–476 **Targeted Instruction:** 53–54 **TECHNOLOGY** Write*Smart*

2.0 Writing Applications (Genres and Their Characteristics)

Standards	Primary Citations	Supporting Citations
2.1 Write fictional, autobiographical, or biographical narratives: a. Narrate a sequence of events and communicate their significance to the audience. b. Locate scenes and incidents in specific places. c. Describe with concrete sensory details the sights, sounds, and smells of a scene and the specific actions, movements, gestures, and feelings of the characters; use interior monologue to depict the characters' feelings. d. Pace the presentation of actions to accommodate temporal, spatial, and dramatic mood changes. e. Make effective use of descriptions of appearance, images, shifting perspectives, and sensory details.	**STUDENT'S/TEACHER'S EDITION** 327, 474–480, 598–604, 1017	**STUDENT'S/TEACHER'S EDITION** 867, 1001, 1180, 1191, R34–R35 **PRINT COMPONENTS** **Resource Manager:** Unit 5: 376, 433; Unit 6: 171 **Standards Lesson File:** Writing, Research, and Study Skills: 235–243, 329–337, 361–373, 477–487 **Targeted Instruction:** 55–56 **TECHNOLOGY** **Write***Smart*
2.2 Write responses to literature: a. Demonstrate a comprehensive understanding of the significant ideas in works or passages. b. Analyze the use of imagery, language, universal themes, and unique aspects of the text. c. Support important ideas and viewpoints through accurate and detailed references to the text and to other works. d. Demonstrate an understanding of the author's use of stylistic devices and an appreciation of the effects created. e. Identify and assess the impact of perceived ambiguities, nuances, and complexities within the text.	**STUDENT'S/TEACHER'S EDITION** 804–810, 1072–1078	**STUDENT'S/TEACHER'S EDITION** 61, 109, 211, 217, 275, 333, 357, 391, 473, 535, 569, 595, 705, 737, 755, 787, 803, 875, 902, 911, 977, 1031, 1247 **PRINT COMPONENTS** **Resource Manager:** Unit 2: 217; Unit 3: 104; Unit 5: 411, 455, 495, 500 **Standards Lesson File:** Writing, Research, and Study Skills: 307–315; Literature: 373–381 **Targeted Instruction:** 57–58 **TECHNOLOGY** **Write***Smart*
2.3 Write reflective compositions: a. Explore the significance of personal experiences, events, conditions, or concerns by using rhetorical strategies (e.g., narration, description, exposition, persuasion). b. Draw comparisons between specific incidents and broader themes that illustrate the writer's important beliefs or generalizations about life. c. Maintain a balance in describing individual incidents and relate those incidents to more general and abstract ideas.	**STUDENT'S/TEACHER'S EDITION** 474–480	**STUDENT'S/TEACHER'S EDITION** 77, 221, 401, 549, 867, 1213, 1247 **PRINT COMPONENTS** **Resource Manager:** Unit 2: 269, 291–296, 298; Unit 5: 433 **Standards Lesson File:** Writing, Research, and Study Skills: 223–233, 329–337 **Targeted Instruction:** 59–60 **TECHNOLOGY** **Write***Smart*

Standards	Primary Citations	Supporting Citations
2.4 Write historical investigation reports: a. Use exposition, narration, description, argumentation, or some combination of rhetorical strategies to support the main proposition. b. Analyze several historical records of a single event, examining critical relationships between elements of the research topic. c. Explain the perceived reason or reasons for the similarities and differences in historical records with information derived from primary and secondary sources to support or enhance the presentation. d. Include information from all relevant perspectives and take into consideration the validity and reliability of sources. e. Include a formal bibliography.	**STUDENT'S/TEACHER'S EDITION** 1284–1301	**STUDENT'S/TEACHER'S EDITION** 61, 1201, 1268–1283 **PRINT COMPONENTS** **Resource Manager:** Unit 7: 14–21, 28–30 **Standards Lesson File:** Writing, Research, and Study Skills: 489–497, 533–545 **Targeted Instruction:** 61–62 **TECHNOLOGY** **Write*Smart***
2.5 Write job applications and résumés: a. Provide clear and purposeful information and address the intended audience appropriately. b. Use varied levels, patterns, and types of language to achieve intended effects and aid comprehension. c. Modify the tone to fit the purpose and audience. d. Follow the conventional style for that type of document (e.g., résumé, memorandum) and use page formats, fonts, and spacing that contribute to the readability and impact of the document.	**STUDENT'S/TEACHER'S EDITION** R40, R41, R42	**STUDENT'S/TEACHER'S EDITION** R26–R27 **PRINT COMPONENTS** **Standards Lesson File:** Writing, Research, and Study Skills: 339–349 **Targeted Instruction:** 63–64 **TECHNOLOGY** **Write*Smart***
2.6 Deliver multimedia presentations: a. Combine text, images, and sound and draw information from many sources (e.g., television broadcasts, videos, films, newspapers, magazines, CD-ROMs, the Internet, electronic media-generated images). b. Select an appropriate medium for each element of the presentation. c. Use the selected media skillfully, editing appropriately and monitoring for quality. d. Test the audience's response and revise the presentation accordingly.	**STUDENT'S/TEACHER'S EDITION** 602, 1255, 1302–1303	**STUDENT'S/TEACHER'S EDITION** R88–R89 **PRINT COMPONENTS** **Resource Manager:** Unit 3: 183; Unit 6: 329; Unit 7: 29 **Standards Lesson File:** Media Studies, Speaking, and Listening: 149–162, 163–176, 177–189 **Targeted Instruction:** 65–66 **TECHNOLOGY** **Write*Smart***

WRITTEN AND ORAL ENGLISH LANGUAGE CONVENTIONS

 1.0 Written and Oral English Language Conventions

Standards	Primary Citations	Supporting Citations
1.1 Demonstrate control of grammar, diction, and paragraph and sentence structure and an understanding of English usage.	**STUDENT'S/TEACHER'S EDITION** R50–R52, R56–R69 **Grammar for Writing:** 4–5, 6–23, 24–47, 48–75, 76–103, 104–129, 130–151, 152–179, 180–199, 200–221, 222–239, 240–263	**STUDENT'S/TEACHER'S EDITION** 211, 233, 327, 426, 444, 549, 737, 765, 787, 911, 961, 1031, 1057, 1159 **PRINT COMPONENTS** **Resource Manager:** Unit 2: 36, 134, 206, 248; Unit 3: 71; Unit 4: 229, 254; UNIT 5: 196, 276, 400, 443; Unit 6: 98 **Standards Lesson File:** Writing, Research, and Study Skills: 79–87, 111–120, 121–131, 133–143, 427–432; Grammar 1–8, 9–18, 29–39, 41–50, 51–62, 63–73, 19–28, 165–174 **Targeted Instruction:** 67–68
1.2 Produce legible work that shows accurate spelling and correct punctuation and capitalization.	**STUDENT'S/TEACHER'S EDITION** R53–R55, R76 **Grammar for Writing:** 200–221, 222–239, 240–259, 286–287	**STUDENT'S/TEACHER'S EDITION** 480, 1078 **PRINT COMPONENTS** **Resource Manager:** Writing, Research, and Study Skills: 43–54, 67–78, 213–221, 477–487; Grammar: 195–205 **Standards Lesson File:** Writing, Research, and Study Skills: 43–54, 67–78, 213–221, 477–487; Grammar: 195–205 **Targeted Instruction:** 69–70
1.3 Reflect appropriate manuscript requirements in writing.	**STUDENT'S/TEACHER'S EDITION** 1295, 1296, 1299–1300, 1301, R40–R43	**STUDENT'S/TEACHER'S EDITION** 1290 **PRINT COMPONENTS** **Resource Manager:** Writing, Research, and Study Skills: 591–599; Media Studies, Speaking, and Listening: 203–209, 219–228 **Standards Lesson File:** Writing, Research, and Study Skills: 213–221, 591–599; Media Studies, Speaking, and Listening: 203–209, 219–228 **Targeted Instruction:** 71–72

LISTENING AND SPEAKING

 1.0 Listening and Speaking Strategies

Standards	Primary Citations	Supporting Citations
Comprehension **1.1** Recognize strategies used by the media to inform, persuade, entertain, and transmit culture (e.g., advertisements; perpetuation of stereotypes; use of visual representations, special effects, language).	**STUDENT'S/TEACHER'S EDITION** 62–65, 446–449, 964–967, 1176–1179	**STUDENT'S/TEACHER'S EDITION** 738–743, 1201, R88–R95 **PRINT COMPONENTS** **Resource Manager:** Unit 1: 87–89; Unit 2: 259–261; Unit 5: 287–289; Unit 6: 151–153 **Standards Lesson File:** Media Studies, Speaking, and Listening: 9–14, 15–19, 21–27, 43–47, 81–87, 89–97, 99–105, 117–124 **Targeted Instruction:** 73–74 **TECHNOLOGY** *MediaSmart*
1.2 Analyze the impact of the media on the democratic process (e.g., exerting influence on elections, creating images of leaders, shaping attitudes) at the local, state, and national levels.	**STUDENT'S/TEACHER'S EDITION** 1176–1179	**STUDENT'S/TEACHER'S EDITION** 707, 1201, R89 **PRINT COMPONENTS** **Resource Manager:** Unit 4: 142; Unit 6: 151–153 **Standards Lesson File:** Media Studies, Speaking, and Listening: 15–19 **Targeted Instruction:** 75–76 **TECHNOLOGY** *MediaSmart*
1.3 Interpret and evaluate the various ways in which events are presented and information is communicated by visual image makers (e.g., graphic artists, documentary filmmakers, illustrators, news photographers).	**STUDENT'S/TEACHER'S EDITION** 62–65, 446–449, 596–597, 706–709, 876–879, 980–987, 1176–1179	**STUDENT'S/TEACHER'S EDITION** 595, R90–R91, R94–R95 **PRINT COMPONENTS** **Resource Manager:** Unit 1: 87–89; Unit 2: 259–261; Unit 3: 171; Unit 4: 141–143; Unit 5: 121–123, 323–326; Unit 6: 151–153 **Standards Lesson File:** Media Studies, Speaking, and Listening: 21–27, 43–47, 99–105, 107–116, 117–124, 141–147 **Targeted Instruction:** 77–78 **TECHNOLOGY** *MediaSmart*
Organization and Delivery of Oral Communication **1.4** Use rhetorical questions, parallel structure, concrete images, figurative language, characterization, irony, and dialogue to achieve clarity, force, and aesthetic effect.	**STUDENT'S/TEACHER'S EDITION** 535, R80–R85	**STUDENT'S/TEACHER'S EDITION** 222–223, 803 **PRINT COMPONENTS** **Resource Manager:** Unit 1: 42, 213, 341 **Standards Lesson File:** Media Studies, Speaking, and Listening: 191–201 **Targeted Instruction:** 79–80

Standards	Primary Citations	Supporting Citations
1.5 Distinguish between and use various forms of classical and contemporary logical arguments, including: a. Inductive and deductive reasoning b. Syllogisms and analogies	**STUDENT'S/TEACHER'S EDITION** R20–R21	**STUDENT'S/TEACHER'S EDITION** 222–223, 252, 272, 865, 1157, R75 **PRINT COMPONENTS** **Standards Lesson File:** Media Studies, Speaking, and Listening: 191–201, 257–265 **Targeted Instruction:** 81–82
1.6 Use logical, ethical, and emotional appeals that enhance a specific tone and purpose.	**STUDENT'S/TEACHER'S EDITION** 119–126, 222–223, 245–252, 1201, R82, R94	**PRINT COMPONENTS** **Resource Manager:** Unit 1: 213, 393, 394 **Standards Lesson File:** Media Studies, Speaking, and Listening: 191–201 **Targeted Instruction:** 83–84
1.7 Use appropriate rehearsal strategies to pay attention to performance details, achieve command of the text, and create skillful artistic staging.	**STUDENT'S/TEACHER'S EDITION** 283, 811, 1079, 1303	**STUDENT'S/TEACHER'S EDITION** 535, 875, R81 **PRINT COMPONENTS** **Resource Manager:** Unit 1: 461; Unit 4: 293; Unit 5: 501; Unit 7: 29 **Standards Lesson File:** Media Studies, Speaking, and Listening: 203–209, 219–228, 249–256, 257–265, 267–276 **Targeted Instruction:** 85–86
1.8 Use effective and interesting language, including: a. Informal expressions for effect b. Standard American English for clarity c. Technical language for specificity	**STUDENT'S/TEACHER'S EDITION** 221, R80, R82	**STUDENT'S/TEACHER'S EDITION** 535, 859–865, 1208, 1213, 1270, 1271 **PRINT COMPONENTS** **Resource Manager:** Unit 6: 208, 219 **Standards Lesson File:** Media Studies, Speaking, and Listening: 191–201, 203–209 **Targeted Instruction:** 87–88
1.9 Use research and analysis to justify strategies for gesture, movement, and vocalization, including dialect, pronunciation, and enunciation.	**STUDENT'S/TEACHER'S EDITION** R81–R82	**STUDENT'S/TEACHER'S EDITION** 535 **PRINT COMPONENTS** **Resource Manager:** Unit 1: 461; Unit 5: 501 **Standards Lesson File:** Media Studies, Speaking, and Listening: 191–201, 267–276 **Targeted Instruction:** 89–90
1.10 Evaluate when to use different kinds of effects (e.g., visual, music, sound, graphics) to create effective productions.	**STUDENT'S/TEACHER'S EDITION** 605, 811, 879, 1179	**STUDENT'S/TEACHER'S EDITION** 283, 401, 1143, R81 **PRINT COMPONENTS** **Resource Manager:** Unit 1: 461; Unit 3: 183; Unit 4: 293; Unit 5: 124; Unit 6: 154 **Standards Lesson File:** Media Studies, Speaking, and Listening: 149–162, 163–176, 177–189, 191–201 **Targeted Instruction:** 91–92

Standards	Primary Citations	Supporting Citations
Analysis and Evaluation of Oral and Media Communications **1.11** Critique a speaker's diction and syntax in relation to the purpose of an oral communication and the impact the words may have on the audience.	**STUDENT'S/TEACHER'S EDITION** R82–R87 **PRINT COMPONENTS** **Targeted Instruction:** 93–94	**STUDENT'S/TEACHER'S EDITION** 811, 1079, 1303
1.12 Identify logical fallacies used in oral addresses (e.g., attack *ad hominem*, false causality, red herring, overgeneralization, bandwagon effect).	**STUDENT'S/TEACHER'S EDITION** R20, R22–R23 **PRINT COMPONENTS** **Targeted Instruction:** 95–96	**STUDENT'S/TEACHER'S EDITION** 281 **PRINT COMPONENTS** **Standards Lesson File:** Reading and Informational Texts: 315–324; Media Studies, Speaking, and Listening: 257–265
1.13 Analyze the four basic types of persuasive speech (i.e., propositions of fact, value, problem, or policy) and understand the similarities and differences in their patterns of organization and the use of persuasive language, reasoning, and proof.	**STUDENT'S/TEACHER'S EDITION** R19–R24	**STUDENT'S/TEACHER'S EDITION** 224–231 **PRINT COMPONENTS** **Standards Lesson File:** Media Studies, Speaking, and Listening: 257–265 **Targeted Instruction:** 97–98
1.14 Analyze the techniques used in media messages for a particular audience and evaluate their effectiveness (e.g., Orson Welles' radio broadcast "War of the Worlds").	**STUDENT'S/TEACHER'S EDITION** 62–65, 218–219, 596–597, 738–743, 946–967	**STUDENT'S/TEACHER'S EDITION** 595, 1071, R90–R95 **PRINT COMPONENTS** **Resource Manager:** Unit 1: 87–89, 331; Unit 3: 171; Unit 5: 287–289 **Standards Lesson File:** Media Studies, Speaking, and Listening: 21–27, 29–33, 35–41, 43–47, 49–55, 57–64, 65–73, 75–79, 81–87, 89–97, 99–105, 107–116, 117–124, 125–131, 133–140 **Targeted Instruction:** 99–100 **TECHNOLOGY** **Media*Smart***

2.0 Speaking Applications (Genres and Their Characteristics)

Standards	Primary Citations	Supporting Citations
2.1 Deliver reflective presentations: a. Explore the significance of personal experiences, events, conditions, or concerns, using appropriate rhetorical strategies (e.g., narration, description, exposition, persuasion). b. Draw comparisons between the specific incident and broader themes that illustrate the speaker's beliefs or generalizations about life. c. Maintain a balance between describing the incident and relating it to more general, abstract ideas.	**STUDENT'S/TEACHER'S EDITION** R84	**STUDENT'S/TEACHER'S EDITION** 401, 474–480, 1247, R84 **PRINT COMPONENTS** **Standards Lesson File:** Media Studies, Speaking, and Listening: 203–209 **Targeted Instruction:** 101–102
2.2 Deliver oral reports on historical investigations: a. Use exposition, narration, description, persuasion, or some combination of those to support the thesis. b. Analyze several historical records of a single event, examining critical relationships between elements of the research topic. c. Explain the perceived reason or reasons for the similarities and differences by using information derived from primary and secondary sources to support or enhance the presentation. d. Include information on all relevant perspectives and consider the validity and reliability of sources.	**STUDENT'S/TEACHER'S EDITION** 1302, 1303	**STUDENT'S/TEACHER'S EDITION** 401, 595 **PRINT COMPONENTS** **Standards Lesson File:** Media Studies, Speaking, and Listening: 219–228 **Targeted Instruction:** 103–104

Standards	Primary Citations	Supporting Citations
2.3 Deliver oral responses to literature: a. Demonstrate a comprehensive understanding of the significant ideas of literary works (e.g., make assertions about the text that are reasonable and supportable). b. Analyze the imagery, language, universal themes, and unique aspects of the text through the use of rhetorical strategies (e.g., narration, description, persuasion, exposition, a combination of those strategies). c. Support important ideas and viewpoints through accurate and detailed references to the text or to other works. d. Demonstrate an awareness of the author's use of stylistic devices and an appreciation of the effects created. e. Identify and assess the impact of perceived ambiguities, nuances, and complexities within the text.	**STUDENT'S/TEACHER'S EDITION** 810–811, 935	**STUDENT'S/TEACHER'S EDITION** 221, 275, 357, 803, R85 **PRINT COMPONENTS** **Standards Lesson File:** Media Studies, Speaking, and Listening: 229–238 **Targeted Instruction:** 105–106

Standards	Primary Citations	Supporting Citations
2.4 Deliver multimedia presentations: a. Combine text, images, and sound by incorporating information from a wide range of media, including films, newspapers, magazines, CD-ROMs, online information, television, videos, and electronic media-generated images. b. Select an appropriate medium for each element of the presentation. c. Use the selected media skillfully, editing appropriately and monitoring for quality. d. Test the audience's response and revise the presentation accordingly.	**STUDENT'S/TEACHER'S EDITION** 811, 879, 1179, 1255, 1302–1303	**STUDENT'S/TEACHER'S EDITION** R88–R95 **PRINT COMPONENTS** **Resource Manager:** Unit 5: 124; Unit 6: 154 **Standards Lesson File:** Media Studies, Speaking, and Listening: 149–162, 163–176, 177–189 **Targeted Instruction:** 107–108 **TECHNOLOGY** **Media**Smart
2.5 Recite poems, selections from speeches, or dramatic soliloquies with attention to performance details to achieve clarity, force, and aesthetic effect and to demonstrate an understanding of the meaning (e.g., Hamlet's soliloquy "To Be or Not to Be").	**STUDENT'S/TEACHER'S EDITION** 357, 935, 1079, 1143	**STUDENT'S/TEACHER'S EDITION** 875, R84–R85 **PRINT COMPONENTS** **Resource Manager:** Unit 1: 62; Unit 3: 42; Unit 5: 501 **Standards Lesson File:** Media Studies, Speaking, and Listening: 267–276 **Targeted Instruction:** 109–110

Language Arts Content/Alignment to Standards

McDougal Littell Literature provides lessons for mastering the California English-Language Arts Content Standards. The student edition provides comprehensive coverage of the standards.

Standards Correlation for the Teacher

The correlation chart beginning on page T12 of this Teacher's Edition provides a detailed listing of where the standards are covered in the student and teacher editions and key ancillaries.

Standards Listing for the Student

A complete list of the California English–Language Arts Content Standards is provided in the front matter of the Student's Edition, along with an explanation of what the students will need to learn to master each standard. Students and their parents can use these pages to familiarize themselves with the standards.

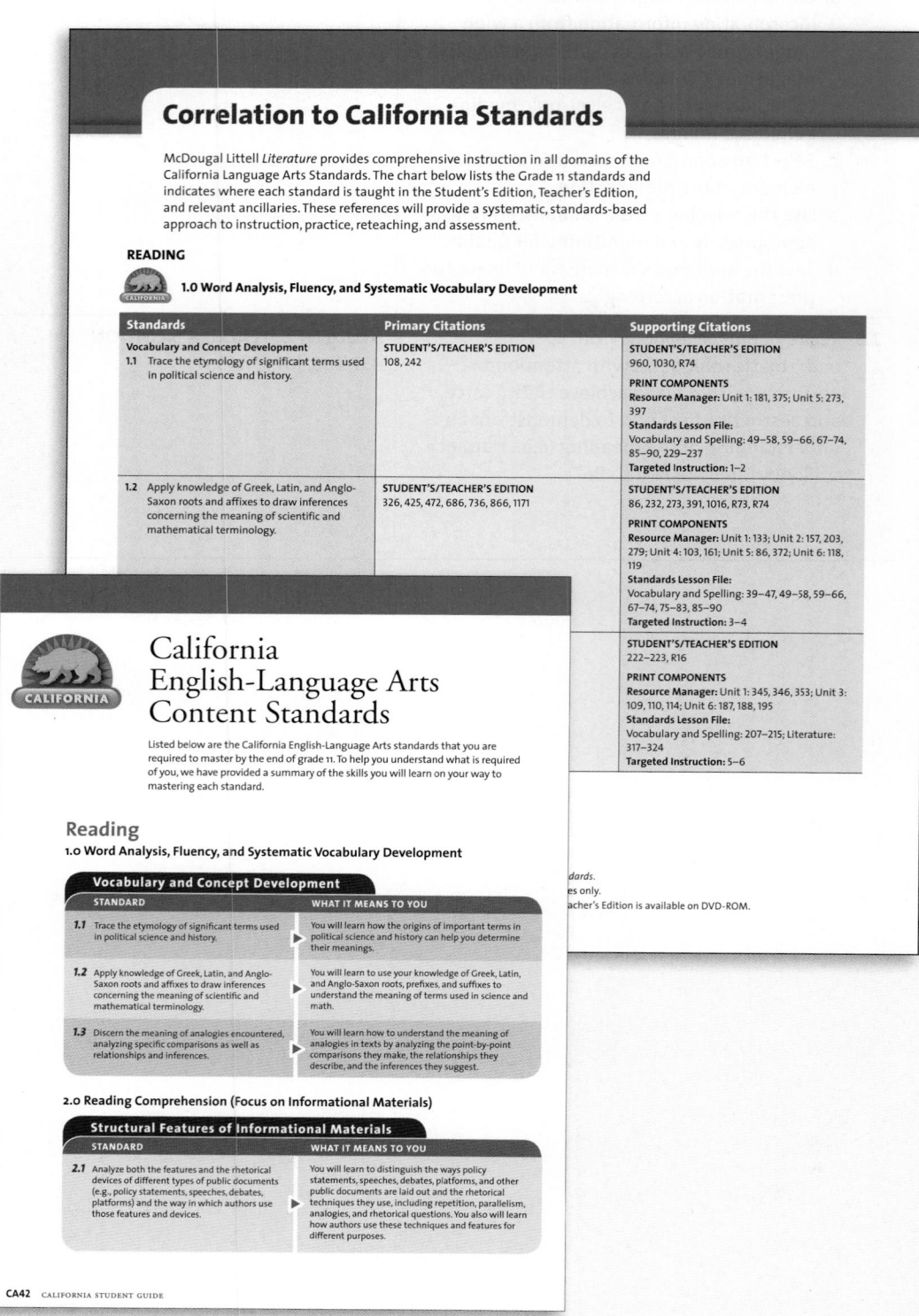

Correlation to California Standards

McDougal Littell *Literature* provides comprehensive instruction in all domains of the California Language Arts Standards. The chart below lists the Grade 11 standards and indicates where each standard is taught in the Student's Edition, Teacher's Edition, and relevant ancillaries. These references will provide a systematic, standards-based approach to instruction, practice, reteaching, and assessment.

READING

1.0 Word Analysis, Fluency, and Systematic Vocabulary Development

Standards	Primary Citations	Supporting Citations
Vocabulary and Concept Development 1.1 Trace the etymology of significant terms used in political science and history.	STUDENT'S/TEACHER'S EDITION 108, 242	STUDENT'S/TEACHER'S EDITION 960, 1030, R74 **PRINT COMPONENTS** **Resource Manager:** Unit 1: 181, 375; Unit 5: 273, 397 **Standards Lesson File:** Vocabulary and Spelling: 49–58, 59–66, 67–74, 85–90, 229–237 **Targeted Instruction:** 1–2
1.2 Apply knowledge of Greek, Latin, and Anglo-Saxon roots and affixes to draw inferences concerning the meaning of scientific and mathematical terminology.	STUDENT'S/TEACHER'S EDITION 326, 425, 472, 686, 736, 866, 1171	STUDENT'S/TEACHER'S EDITION 86, 232, 273, 391, 1016, R73, R74 **PRINT COMPONENTS** **Resource Manager:** Unit 1: 133; Unit 2: 157, 203, 279; Unit 4: 103, 161; Unit 5: 86, 372; Unit 6: 118, 119 **Standards Lesson File:** Vocabulary and Spelling: 39–47, 49–58, 59–66, 67–74, 75–83, 85–90 **Targeted Instruction:** 3–4
		STUDENT'S/TEACHER'S EDITION 222–223, R16 **PRINT COMPONENTS** **Resource Manager:** Unit 1: 345, 346, 353; Unit 3: 109, 110, 114; Unit 6: 187, 188, 195 **Standards Lesson File:** Vocabulary and Spelling: 207–215; Literature: 317–324 **Targeted Instruction:** 5–6

...dards.
...es only.
...acher's Edition is available on DVD-ROM.

California English-Language Arts Content Standards

Listed below are the California English-Language Arts standards that you are required to master by the end of grade 11. To help you understand what is required of you, we have provided a summary of the skills you will learn on your way to mastering each standard.

Reading

1.0 Word Analysis, Fluency, and Systematic Vocabulary Development

Vocabulary and Concept Development

STANDARD	WHAT IT MEANS TO YOU
1.1 Trace the etymology of significant terms used in political science and history.	You will learn how the origins of important terms in political science and history can help you determine their meanings.
1.2 Apply knowledge of Greek, Latin, and Anglo-Saxon roots and affixes to draw inferences concerning the meaning of scientific and mathematical terminology.	You will learn to use your knowledge of Greek, Latin, and Anglo-Saxon roots, prefixes, and suffixes to understand the meaning of terms used in science and math.
1.3 Discern the meaning of analogies encountered, analyzing specific comparisons as well as relationships and inferences.	You will learn how to understand the meaning of analogies in texts by analyzing the point-by-point comparisons they make, the relationships they describe, and the inferences they suggest.

2.0 Reading Comprehension (Focus on Informational Materials)

Structural Features of Informational Materials

STANDARD	WHAT IT MEANS TO YOU
2.1 Analyze both the features and the rhetorical devices of different types of public documents (e.g., policy statements, speeches, debates, platforms) and the way in which authors use those features and devices.	You will learn to distinguish the ways policy statements, speeches, debates, platforms, and other public documents are laid out and the rhetorical techniques they use, including repetition, parallelism, analogies, and rhetorical questions. You also will learn how authors use these techniques and features for different purposes.

CA42 CALIFORNIA STUDENT GUIDE

Standards for Planning and Instruction

Resource Manager lesson plans list the standards that will be taught in each lesson, so you can prepare your instruction accordingly.

The standards taught in each lesson are listed on the Teacher Edition page and on the Student Edition page at the beginning of the lesson. The bear icon denotes that a standard is taught on the page.

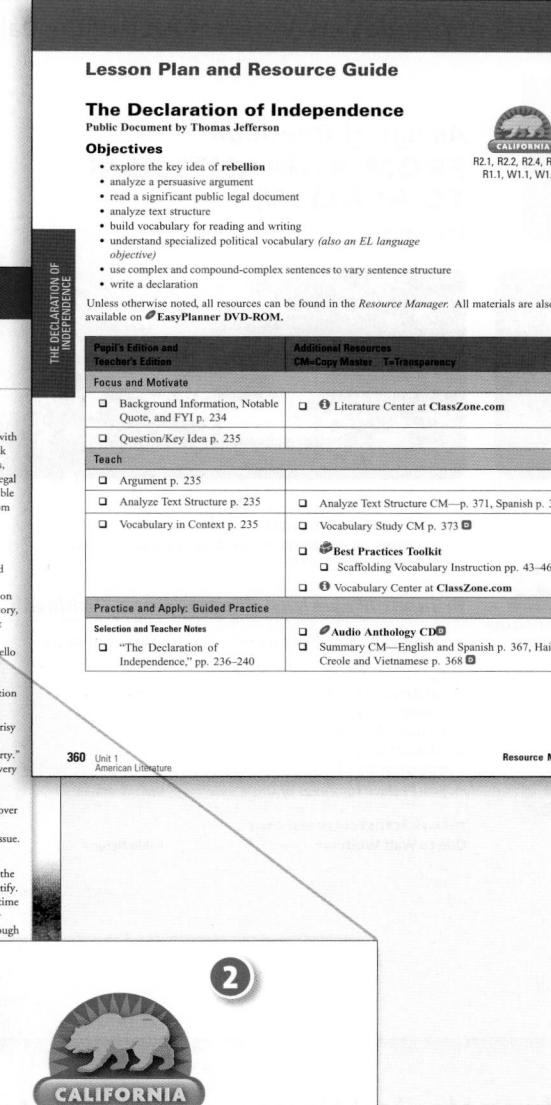

Lesson Plan and Resource Guide

The Declaration of Independence
Public Document by Thomas Jefferson

Objectives
- explore the key idea of **rebellion**
- analyze a persuasive argument
- read a significant public legal document
- analyze text structure
- build vocabulary for reading and writing
- understand specialized political vocabulary *(also an EL language objective)*
- use complex and compound-complex sentences to vary sentence structure
- write a declaration

R2.1, R2.2, R2.4, R2.6, R1.1, W1.1, W1.9

Unless otherwise noted, all resources can be found in the *Resource Manager.* All materials are also available on **EasyPlanner DVD-ROM.**

Pupil's Edition and Teacher's Edition	Additional Resources CM=Copy Master T=Transparency
Focus and Motivate	
❑ Background Information, Notable Quote, and FYI p. 234	❑ ❶ Literature Center at **ClassZone.com**
❑ Question/Key Idea p. 235	
Teach	
❑ Argument p. 235	
❑ Analyze Text Structure p. 235	❑ Analyze Text Structure CM—p. 371, Spanish p. 372
❑ Vocabulary in Context p. 235	❑ Vocabulary Study CM p. 373
	❑ **Best Practices Toolkit** ❑ Scaffolding Vocabulary Instruction pp. 43–46
	❑ ❶ Vocabulary Center at **ClassZone.com**
Practice and Apply: Guided Practice	
Selection and Teacher Notes	❑ ✎ **Audio Anthology CD**
❑ "The Declaration of Independence," pp. 236–240	❑ Summary CM—English and Spanish p. 367, Haitian Creole and Vietnamese p. 368

360 Unit 1
American Literature

Resource Manager

Copyright © McDougal Littell/Houghton Mifflin Company.

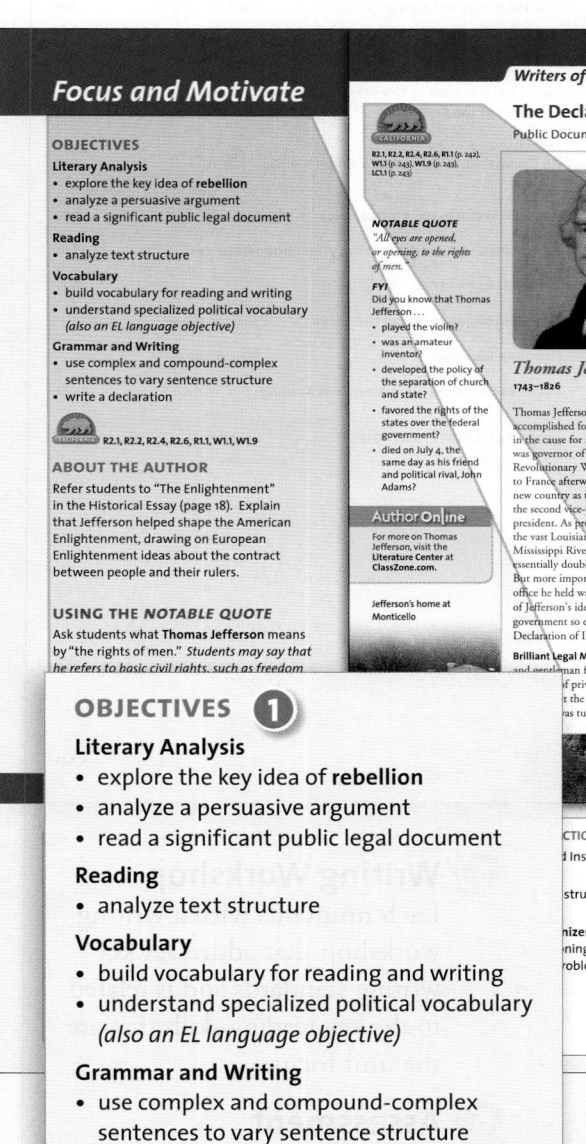

Focus and Motivate

OBJECTIVES

Literary Analysis
- explore the key idea of **rebellion**
- analyze a persuasive argument
- read a significant public legal document

Reading
- analyze text structure

Vocabulary
- build vocabulary for reading and writing
- understand specialized political vocabulary *(also an EL language objective)*

Grammar and Writing
- use complex and compound-complex sentences to vary sentence structure
- write a declaration

R2.1, R2.2, R2.4, R2.6, R1.1, W1.1, W1.9

ABOUT THE AUTHOR
Refer students to "The Enlightenment" in the Historical Essay (page 18). Explain that Jefferson helped shape the American Enlightenment, drawing on European Enlightenment ideas about the contract between people and their rulers.

USING THE NOTABLE QUOTE
Ask students what Thomas Jefferson means by "the rights of men." *Students may say that he refers to basic civil rights, such as freedom*

Writers of the Revolution

The Declaration of Independence
Public Document by Thomas Jefferson

R2.1, R2.2, R2.4, R2.6, R1.1 (p. 242),
W1.1 (p. 243), W1.9 (p. 243),
LC1.1 (p. 243)

NOTABLE QUOTE
"All eyes are opened, or opening, to the rights of men."

FYI
Did you know that Thomas Jefferson . . .
- played the violin?
- was an amateur inventor?
- developed the policy of the separation of church and state?
- favored the rights of the states over the federal government?
- died on July 4, the same day as his friend and political rival, John Adams?

Author Online
For more on Thomas Jefferson, visit the **Literature Center at ClassZone.com.**

Jefferson's home at Monticello

Thomas Jefferson
1743–1826

Thomas Jefferson was one of the most accomplished founding fathers. Active in the cause for independence, he was governor of Virginia during the Revolutionary War and U.S. minister to France afterward. He also served the new country as the first secretary of state, the second vice-president, and the third president. As president, he acquired the vast Louisiana Territory west of the Mississippi River to the Rocky Mountains, essentially doubling the size of the country. But more important than any political office he held was the lasting impact of Jefferson's ideals of liberty and self-government so eloquently expressed in the Declaration of Independence.

Brilliant Legal Mind The son of a surveyor and gentleman farmer, Jefferson was born to a life of privilege in rural Virginia. He went to the College of William and Mary and was tutored in the law and

practiced successfully before entering politics at age 26. As a member of the colonial Virginia legislature, he fell in with a group of radicals, among them Patrick Henry. Lacking Henry's oratorical gifts, Jefferson distinguished himself by his legal writing. Significantly, Jefferson's indelible mark on American life came largely from the many legal documents and laws he wrote promoting democracy.

Passion for Learning Jefferson had an insatiable curiosity about the world and often indulged in what he called his "canine appetite for reading." In addition to devouring works on the classics, history, law, science, and philosophy, he taught himself architecture from books. He designed his elaborate estate at Monticello and the buildings of the University of Virginia, which he also founded as the embodiment of his principles of education and individual freedom.

The Issue of Slavery Charges of hypocrisy on the issue of slavery have tarnished Jefferson's image as the "apostle of liberty." In his early writings, he denounced slavery and tried unsuccessfully to include the issue in the Declaration. Yet Jefferson always owned slaves—as many as 600 over the course of his lifetime—and in later years, he remained undecided on this issue.

A Quintessential American Jefferson's problematic stand on slavery mirrored the nation's, which took a long time to rectify. In the end, Jefferson was a man of his time who had a noble vision for the country and the genius to articulate it, even though he did not always live up to his ideals.

PRACTICES TOOLKIT
d Instruction
struction

Organizers/Strategies
ning • Classifica-
roblem and Solution

Reading Support
✎ Audio Anthology CD*

Technology
❶ Literature, Vocabulary, and Writing Centers at ClassZone.com
✎ Write*Smart* CD

OBJECTIVES ❶

Literary Analysis
- explore the key idea of **rebellion**
- analyze a persuasive argument
- read a significant public legal document

Reading
- analyze text structure

Vocabulary
- build vocabulary for reading and writing
- understand specialized political vocabulary *(also an EL language objective)*

Grammar and Writing
- use complex and compound-complex sentences to vary sentence structure
- write a declaration

R2.1, R2.2, R2.4, R2.6, R1.1, W1.1, W1.9

❶ For the Teacher
In the Teacher Edition, the standards taught in the lesson are listed on the first page of the lesson, under the list of objectives.

❷ For the Student
In the Student Edition, the standards appear at the beginning of the lesson and on the post-reading pages where relevant.

Program Organization

The McDougal Littell Literature program is organized to provide a logical and systematic approach to mastering the standards. The instructional design allows teachers to efficiently and effectively provide a coherent sequence of content, well-structured lessons, and clusters of skills and standards that represent each of the California ELA strands.

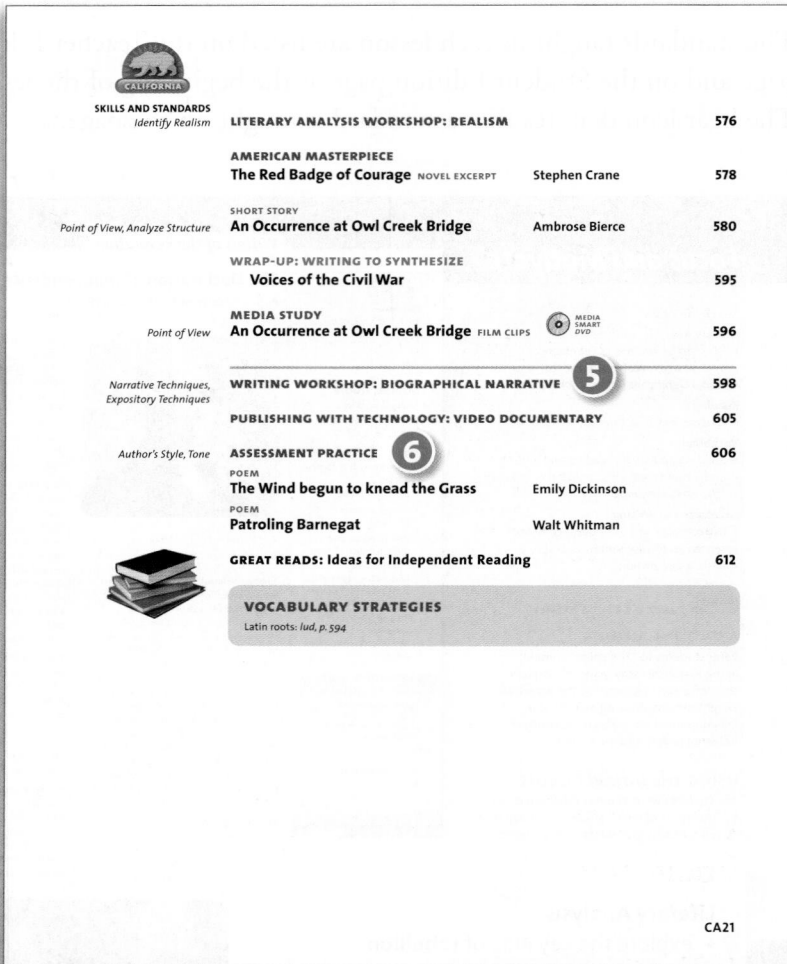

① **Chronological Units**
Each unit presents clusters of selections that are representative of the literary periods. Key skills are highlighted in each lesson.

② **Unit Introduction**
Each unit begins with an essay on the significant events, key people, and ideas of the period that will be presented in the unit.

③ **Literary Analysis Workshop**
Throughout each unit are workshops that highlight the forms and characteristics of literary movements.

④ **Lessons**
Selections encompass a diverse array of authors, titles, and genres, including classic texts and new classics.

⑤ **Writing Workshop**
Each unit ends with a writing workshop that addresses key writing standards and is related to the key reading skills that are the unit focus.

⑥ **Assessment**
An Assessment Practice concludes every unit.

How a Lesson Is Structured

The weekly lessons are structured in an easy-to-use format that provides a clear path of instruction and application for both the teacher and the student.

① Focus and Motivate

Each lesson begins with a list of skills objectives related to the standards. Author background information is included on the Student Edition page.

② Teach

The prereading page of each lesson provides students with instruction and definitions of key academic vocabulary. Throughout the lesson, the Teacher's edition provides background information, important teaching tips, and discussion prompts to successfully engage students and lead them toward mastery of the standards. Each lesson also includes an Essential Question that gets the conversation started with your students.

③ Practice and Apply

The post-reading pages of every lesson provide opportunities for practice, application, and progress-monitoring. A full page of vocabulary practice appears with major fiction and nonfiction selections, followed by a full page of writing and grammar instruction—directly tied to the skills taught with the selection.

④ Assess and Reteach

Opportunities for assessment and reteaching of all the skills and standards taught are provided at the end of every lesson.

Assessment

McDougal Littell Literature incorporates a comprehensive set of resources for assessing student knowledge and performance before, during, and after instruction. Our ongoing program assessment evaluates student success and informs future instruction.

Guide to Assessment

- **Teacher's Guide to Assessment** describes the types of assessment in the program and suggests effective ways to structure assessment.
- **Diagnostic Assessment** assesses students' mastery of reading, writing, grammar, and vocabulary skills and standards.
- **Selection Tests A and B/C** check student comprehension of literary selections and key skills.

Unit and Benchmark Tests

- **Unit tests** allow you to assess students' mastery of reading, writing, grammar, and vocabulary skills and standards.
- **Benchmark tests** allow you to assess students' mastery of the skills and standards four times a year.

The skills covered in these assessments match a spiraled curriculum in order to review skills and standards of previous grades and to prepare students for upcoming grades and state tests.

Grammar Assessment

- **Daily Skills Practice Transparencies**
- **Grammar Pretests**
- **Mastery Tests**

California Standards-Based Assessment

- **CST Diagnostic and Practice Tests**
- **CAHSEE Diagnostic Test**

ACT and SAT practice is available online.

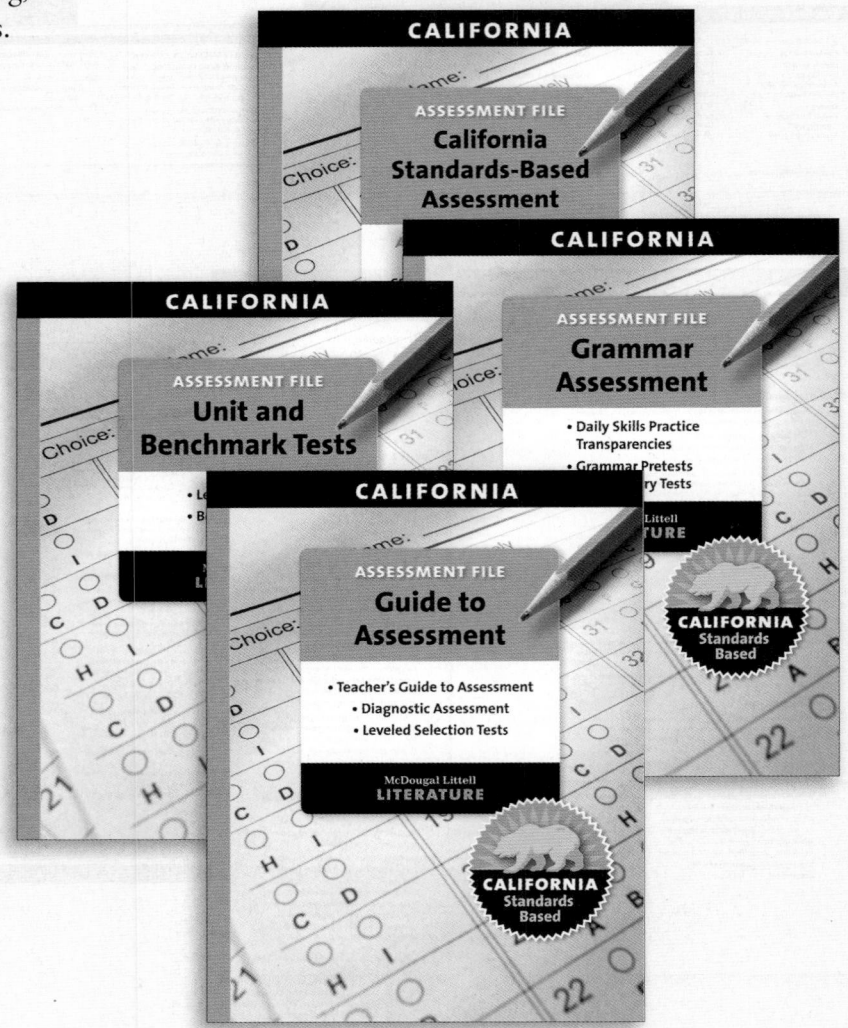

Custom Tests for Specific Needs

The McDougal Littell Test Generator on CD-ROM powered by ExamView® Assessment Suite provides computer-generated tests of all the assessment available in the Assessment File. When necessary, the teacher may also customize tests to specific standards for reteaching purposes. The McDougal Littell Assessment System is an online source of all program assessments including leveled selection and unit tests and benchmark tests.

Together these resources provide the following:

TEST Generate selection, unit, and benchmark tests from the Assessment File.

SCORE Get itemized individual and class results in minutes by scanning completed tests into MLAS.

REPORT Inform future instruction with standards-based reports.

RETEACH Address reteaching with lessons from the Standards Lesson File.

Reteach

The **Standards Lesson File** provides hundreds of ready-made lessons, with leveled models, for reteaching the standards and skills required for mastery.

The **Targeted Instruction for the California Standards** booklet provides direct instruction on each of the standards and can be used for reteaching and review of standards mastery.

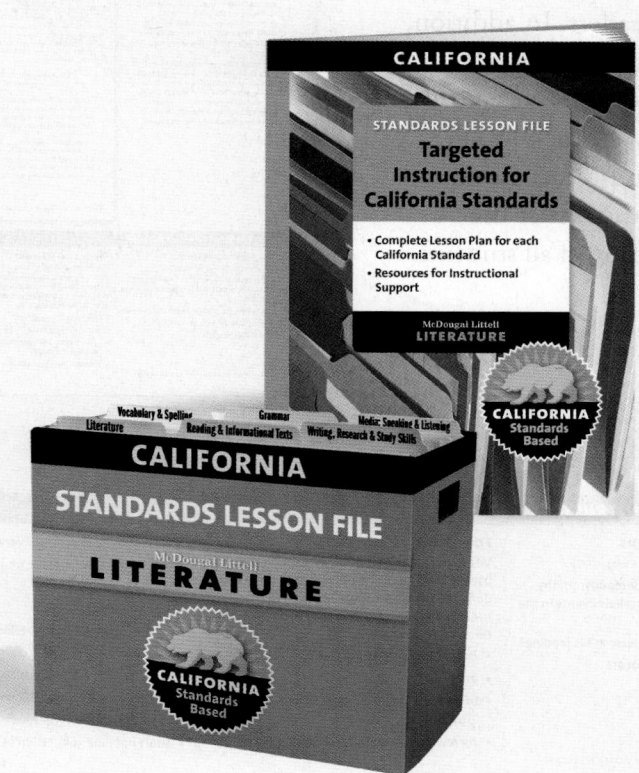

Universal Access

The goal of the McDougal Littell Literature program is to ensure all students have access to quality instruction that will help them master the California content standards. With a variety of research-based instructional tools, the core program provides many opportunities to meet the needs of advanced learners, English learners, and strategic learners.

① Tiered Discussion Prompts

One of the unique features of the program is the tiered discussion prompts, which encourage discussion from all students.

② Scaffolded Instruction

The Teacher's Edition provides universal access to the core curriculum for all students beginning with instruction at the point of use on each page of a lesson. Daily teaching notes provide reading and vocabulary support for English learners and strategic readers. In addition, extension and challenge activities for Advanced learners are also provided with each lesson. Background information is provided to assist the understanding of all students.

① Lines 497–527
TIERED DISCUSSION PROMPTS

Use these prompts to help students understand the story within the story and the connections between these two tales:

Recall What causes the narrator to pause in his reading of the story of the "Mad Trist"?
Possible answer: During his first pause, the narrator hears the sound of cracking and

---

② DIFFERENTIATED INSTRUCTION

FOR STRATEGIC READERS

ⓘ Targeted Passage [Lines 497–507]

In this passage, the narrator reads from the "Mad Trist," a story that parallels events in the narrative.

- Why does the narrator pause in his reading?
- What does the narrator hear?
- How does he react?

FOR ENGLISH LEARNERS

Vocabulary: Outdated Forms Explain that Poe used many words and phrases that were seldom used in his time and are even more rarely used today. Have students substitute modern terms for the outdated ones.

- *hold parley* (line 490), "talk"
- *in sooth* (lines 490–491), "truly"
- *of an obstinate and maliceful turn* (line 491), "stubborn and mean"
- *therewith* (line 494), "with that"

- *sore enraged* (line 509), "very angry"
- *in the stead thereof* (line 510), "instead"
- *sate* (line 511), "sat"
- *slayeth* (line 515), "kills"
- *withal* (line 518), "also; besides"
- *had fain* (line 518), "was obliged"
- *whereof* (line 519), "of which"
- *tarried not* (line 548), "did not wait"
- *clangorous* (line 553), "loud"
- *Said I not* (line 565), "Didn't I say"

FOR ADVANCED LEARNERS/AP

Synthesize The theme of burial alive was a favorite of Poe's. He used it in several stories, including "The Cask of Amontillado" and "The Premature Burial." Why do you think an author would turn to this same macabre topic again and again? *Possible answers: The topic is frightening, and so it helped Poe achieve his intended effect on the reader; the topic may have reflected an obsessive fear in Poe.* Ask students to research Poe to find evidence that either verifies or refutes their responses. Have them discuss their findings as a group and then share their conclusions with the class.

420 UNIT 2: AMERICAN ROMANTICISM

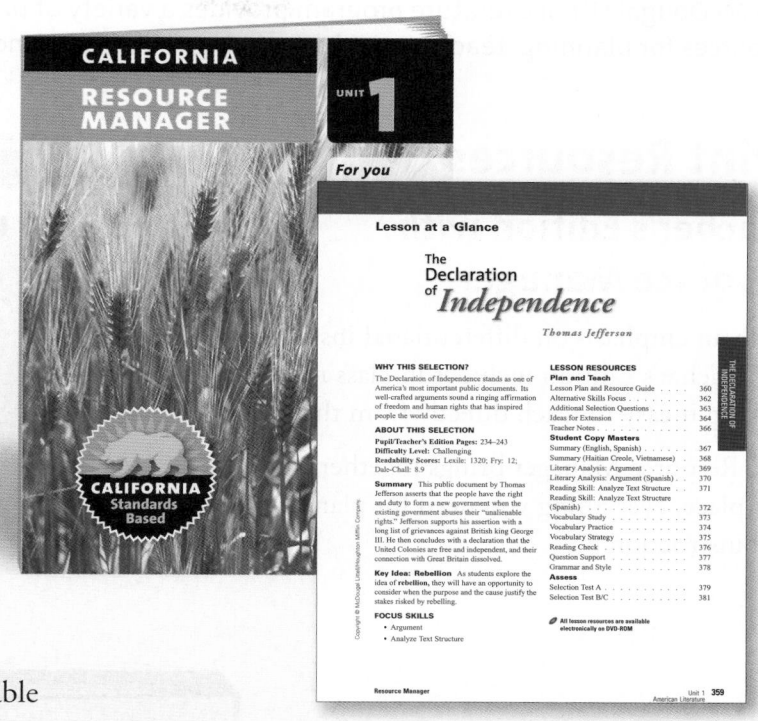

Resource Manager

The Resource Manager contains all the support materials needed to plan and teach selections in conjunction with the Teacher's Edition, including lesson plans, selection summaries in four languages, ideas for extension, skills pages, and leveled selection tests. It also includes a Big Questions Transparency book with a complete collection of Big Questions throughout the anthology.

eEdition Online and DVD-ROM

An interactive edition of the Student Edition, available on DVD-ROM or online, features one- and two-page views; audio summaries; vocabulary in four languages; vocabulary games; and search, highlighting, and note-taking features, plus a "508 compliant" Accessible Version for the visually impaired.

Audio Anthology CD

Full selections from the anthology on audio allow students to hear pronunciation, phrasing, and interpretation of written text.

Multilanguage Academic Glossary

On ClassZone.com, McDougal Littell's online resource, teachers and students can access a Multilanguage Glossary of 250 academic terms in eight languages in addition to English: Arabic, Chinese, Haitian Creole, Hmong, Portuguese, Russian, Spanish, and Vietnamese.

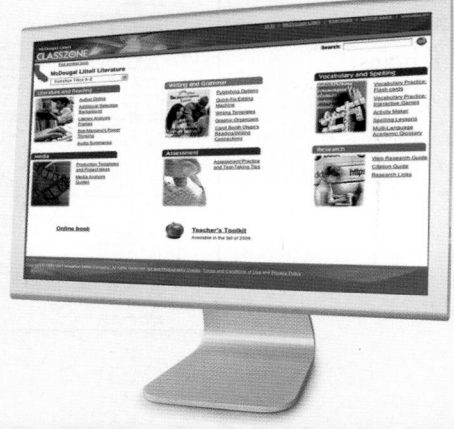

Instructional Planning and Support

The McDougal Littell Literature program provides a variety of print and technology resources for planning, teaching, and reteaching skills and standards.

Print Resources

Teacher's Edition *with* Resource Manager

With an emphasis on differentiated instruction, the Teacher's Edition includes in-class notes, making it easy to teach directly from the page.

The Resource Manager brings together, all in one place, everything you need for planning and instruction.

Best Practices Toolkit

Part One: The Art of Instruction
Includes articles with ready-to-use classroom activities from the program's consultant team, including Janet Allen, Carol Booth Olson, Jim Burke, Robert Marzano, and Carol Ann Tomlinson.

Part Two: Skills, Strategies, and Transparencies
Areas covered include reading, organizing and summarizing information, writing, literary analysis, vocabulary, and notetaking. Includes over 160 transparencies.

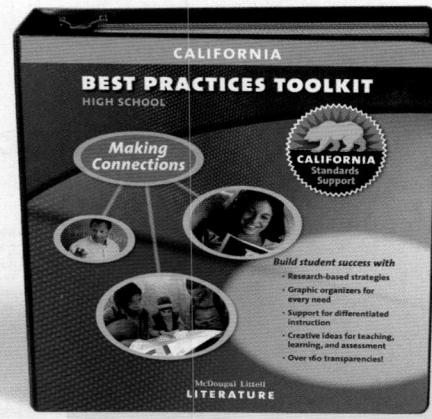

PROGRAM CONSULTANTS

Janet Allen

Carol Booth Olson

Jim Burke

Yvette Jackson

Robert J. Marzano

Carol Ann Tomlinson

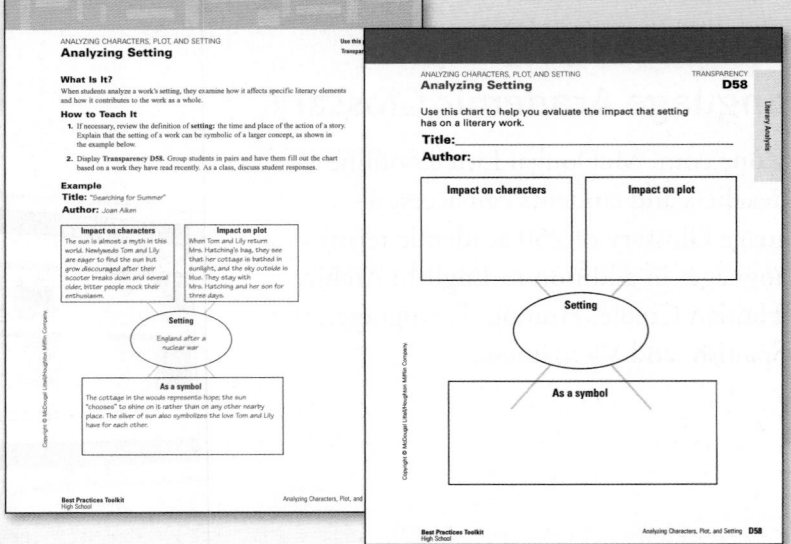

Technology Resources

EasyPlanner DVD-ROM

Includes program resources all on one disc for easy, at-home planning, a full Teacher's Edition, and resources from

- Assessment File
- Best Practices Toolkit
- Resource Manager
- Standards Lesson File

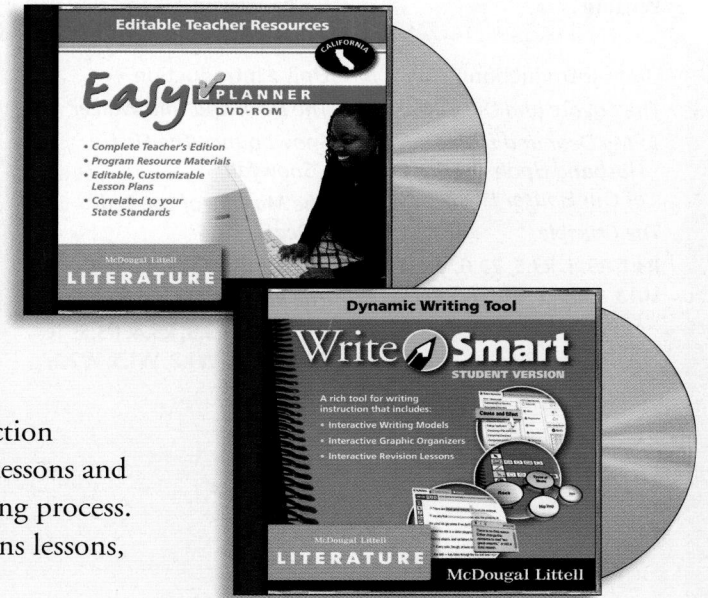

WriteSmart CD-ROM

This interactive software for writing instruction includes a collection of ready-made writing lessons and support for students at all steps of the writing process. Includes interactive student models, revisions lessons, model bank, and a rubric generator.

MediaSmart DVD-ROM

MediaSmart provides the real media—film clips, commercials, documentaries, and news—that are needed to complete the media studies in the Student Edition. It also includes guided viewing and questions that allow students in-depth media analysis and further practice in critical thinking skills.

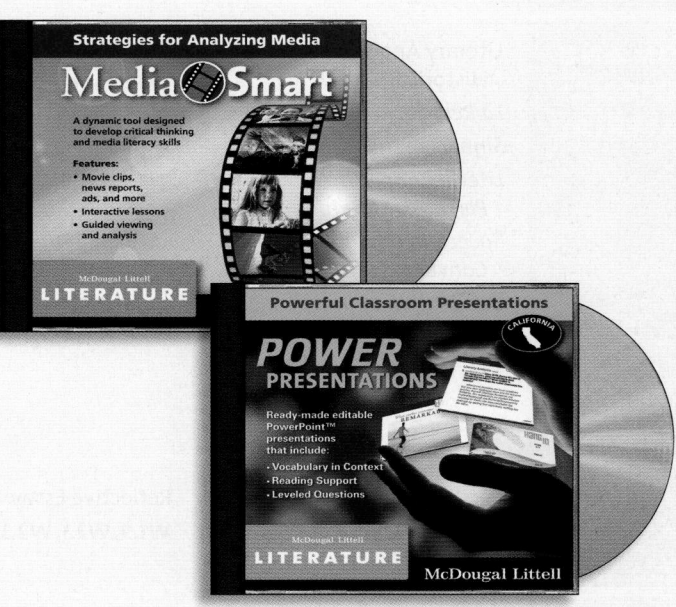

Power Presentations DVD-ROM

Editable PowerPoint™ presentations of materials from the Resource Manager includes the Big Question activity, tiered discussion prompts, after-reading question support, additional selection questions, vocabulary games, and writing workshops.

180-Day Path

To ensure that your students meet all the instructional requirements and master their grade-level standards during the school year, we have prepared a "180-Day Path."

For a full listing of state standards see page T12.

	UNIT 1 Early American Writing	UNIT 2 American Romanticism	UNIT 3 From Romanticism to Realism	UNIT 4 Reagionalism and Naturalism
LITERATURE	Unit 1 Introduction *The Coyote and the Buffalo* *To My Dear and Loving Husband Upon the Burning of Our House/ Huswifery* *The Crucible* **R3.1, R3.4, R3.5, R3.6, W2.2, LC1.1**	Unit 2 Introduction *The Devil and Tom Walker* *Snowbound/ The First Snowfall* *The Masque of the Red Death* *The Minister's Black Veil* *The Raven* **R1.2, R3.1, R3.3, R3.4, R3.5, R3.6, W1.1, W1.2, W1.5, W2.1, LC1.1**	Unit 3 Introduction Literary Analysis Workshop: Form and Content in Poetry *I Hear America Singing/ Song of Myself/ The Noiseless Patient Spider/ Beat! Beat! Drums!* *Because I could not stop for Death/ Success is counted sweetest/ Much Madness.../ My life is closed.../ The Soul.../ I heard a fly.../ My life had stood...* Literary Analysis Workshop: Realism *An Occurrrence at Owl Creek Bridge* **R1.2, R3.2, R3.3, R3.4, R3.5, R3.7**	Unit 4 Introduction *Literary Analysis Workshop: Setting in Regional Literature* *The Notorious Jumping Frog of Calaveras County* *The Outcasts of Poker Flat* *A Wagner Matinee* *The Law of LIfe* *The Yellow Wallpaper* **R1.2, R2.5, R3.1, R3.2, R3.3, R3.5, R3.8, W1.1, W1.2, W1.9, W2.2, LC1.1**
NONFICTION AND INFORMATIONAL MATERIAL	Literary Analysis Workshop: Historical Narratives *La Relación* *Sinners in the Hands...* Literary Analysis Workshop: Persuasive Rhetoric *Speech in the Virginia Convention* *Declaration of Independence* *The Crisis* **R1.1, R2.1, R2.2, R2.4, R2.6, R3.3, R3.5, W1.1, W1.2, W1.3, W1.4, W1.9, LC1.1, LS1.5**	*Self-Reliance / Nature* *Walden/ Civil Disobedience* *On Civil Disobedience* **R2.5, R3.3, R3.7, W1.1, W1.3, W1.4, W1.9, W2.2, LC1.1**	*The Narrative of the LIfe of Frederick Douglass, an American Slave* *The Gettysburg Address/ The Emancipation Proclamation* **R2.1, R2.5, R3.3, W1.1, W1.5, W1.9, W2.2, W2.3, LC1.1**	
WRITING	Persuasive Essay **W1.3, W1.4, W1.7**	Reflective Essay **W1.9, W2.1, W2.3**	Biographical Narrative **W1.9, W2.1, W2.6**	Literary Analysis **W1.9, W2.2**
SPEAKING, LISTENING, AND MEDIA	Persuasive Speech **LS1.7, LS1.10** Media Study **LS1.1, LS1.3 LS1.14**		Video Documentary **W2.6, LS1.10**	Power Presentation **LS2.4**

CALIFORNIA

McDougal Littell
LITERATURE
AMERICAN LITERATURE

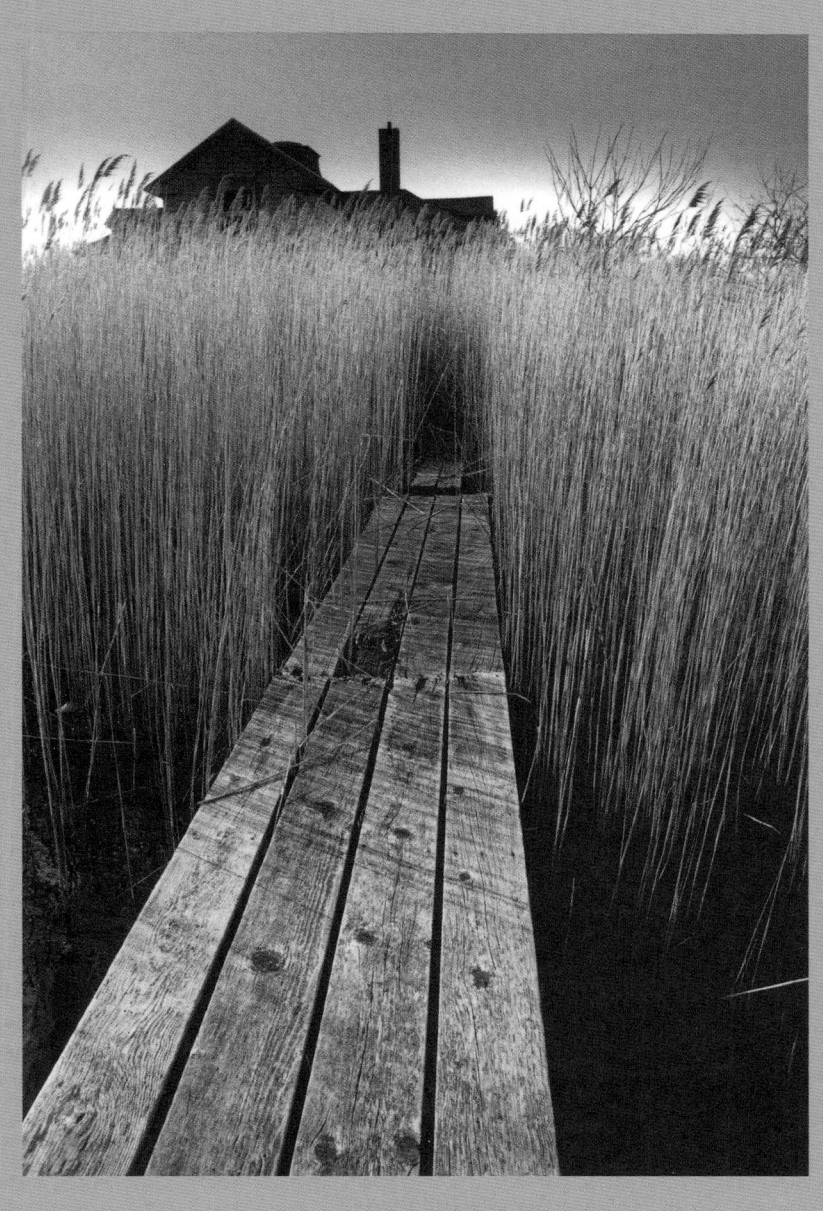

ACKNOWLEDGMENTS

INTRODUCTORY UNIT

Scribner: From *The Great Gatsby* by F. Scott Fitzgerald. Copyright 1925 by Charles Scribner's Sons. Copyright renewed 1953 by Frances Scott Fitzgerald Lanahan. Reprinted with permission of Scribner, an imprint of Simon & Schuster Adult Publishing Group.

Continued on page R168

ART CREDITS

COVER, TITLE PAGE

La Maison noire, East Hampton, New York, 1965, Jeanloup Sieff. © The Estate of Jeanloup Sieff. *Big Sur and Bixby Creek Bridge above the Pacific Ocean* © Photographer's Choice/Punchstock

Continued on page R172

ISBN 13: 978-0-618-98861-7   ISBN 10: 0-618-98861-0

Printed in the United States of America.

1 2 3 4 5 6 7 8 9—DJM—12 11 10 09 08

CALIFORNIA

McDougal Littell
LITERATURE

Janet Allen

Arthur N. Applebee

Jim Burke

Douglas Carnine

Yvette Jackson

Robert T. Jiménez

Judith A. Langer

Robert J. Marzano

Mary Lou McCloskey

Donna M. Ogle

Carol Booth Olson

Lydia Stack

Carol Ann Tomlinson

Big Sur and Bixby Creek Bridge above the Pacific Ocean © Photographer's Choice/Punchstock

McDougal Littell
EVANSTON, ILLINOIS • BOSTON • DALLAS

SENIOR PROGRAM CONSULTANTS

JANET ALLEN Reading and Literacy Specialist; creator of the popular "It's Never Too Late"/"Reading for Life" Institutes. Dr. Allen is an internationally known consultant who specializes in literacy work with at-risk students. Her publications include *Tools for Content Literacy; It's Never Too Late: Leading Adolescents to Lifelong Learning; Yellow Brick Roads: Shared and Guided Paths to Independent Reading; Words, Words, Words: Teaching Vocabulary in Grades 4–12;* and *Testing 1, 2, 3 . . . Bridging Best Practice and High-Stakes Assessments.* Dr. Allen was a high school reading and English teacher for more than 20 years and has taught courses in both subjects at the University of Central Florida. She directed the Central Florida Writing Project and received the Milken Foundation National Educator Award.

ARTHUR N. APPLEBEE Leading Professor, School of Education at the University at Albany, State University of New York; Director of the Center on English Learning and Achievement. During his varied career, Dr. Applebee has been both a researcher and a teacher, working in institutional settings with children with severe learning problems, in public schools, as a staff member of the National Council of Teachers of English, and in professional education. Among his many books are *Curriculum as Conversation: Transforming Traditions of Teaching and Learning; Literature in the Secondary School: Studies of Curriculum and Instruction in the United States;* and *Tradition and Reform in the Teaching of English: A History.* He was elected to the International Reading Hall of Fame and has received, among other honors, the David H. Russell Award for Distinguished Research in the Teaching of English.

JIM BURKE Lecturer and Author; Teacher of English at Burlingame High School, Burlingame, California. Mr. Burke is a popular presenter at educational conferences across the country and is the author of numerous books for teachers, including *School Smarts: The Four Cs of Academic Success; The English Teacher's Companion; Reading Reminders; Writing Reminders;* and *ACCESSing School: Teaching Struggling Readers to Achieve Academic and Personal Success.* He is the recipient of NCTE's Exemplary English Leadership Award and was inducted into the California Reading Association's Hall of Fame.

DOUGLAS CARNINE Professor of Education at the University of Oregon; Director of the Western Region Reading First Technical Assistance Center. Dr. Carnine is nationally known for his focus on research-based practices in education, especially curriculum designs that prepare instructors of K-12 students. He has received the Lifetime Achievement Award from the Council for Exceptional Children and the Ersted Award for outstanding teaching at the University of Oregon. Dr. Carnine frequently consults on educational policy with government groups, businesses, communities, and teacher unions.

YVETTE JACKSON Executive Director of the National Urban Alliance for Effective Education. Nationally recognized for her work in assessing the learning potential of underachieving urban students, Dr. Jackson is also a presenter for the Harvard Principal Center and is a member of the Differentiation Faculty of the Association for Supervision and Curriculum Development. Dr. Jackson's research focuses on literacy, gifted education, and cognitive mediation theory. She designed the Comprehensive Education Plan for the New York City Public Schools and has served as their Director of Gifted Programs and Executive Director of Instruction and Professional Development.

ROBERT T. JIMÉNEZ Professor of Language, Literacy, and Culture at Vanderbilt University. Dr. Jiménez's research focuses on the language and literacy practices of Latino students. A former bilingual education teacher, he is now conducting research on how written language is thought about and used in contemporary Mexico. Dr. Jiménez has received several research and teaching honors, including two Fulbright awards from the Council for the International Exchange of Scholars and the Albert J. Harris Award from the International Reading Association. His published work has appeared in the *American Educational Research Journal, Reading Research Quarterly, The Reading Teacher, Journal of Adolescent and Adult Literacy,* and *Lectura y Vida.*

JUDITH A. LANGER Distinguished Professor at the University at Albany, State University of New York; Director of the Center on English Learning and Achievement; Director of the Albany Institute for Research in Education. An internationally known scholar in English language arts education, Dr. Langer specializes in developing teaching approaches that can enrich and improve what gets done on a daily basis in classrooms. Her publications include *Getting to Excellent: How to Create Better Schools* and *Effective Literacy Instruction: Building Successful Reading and Writing Programs.* She was inducted into the International Reading Hall of Fame and has received many other notable awards, including an honorary doctorate from the University of Uppsala, Sweden, for her research on literacy education.

ROBERT J. MARZANO Senior Scholar at Mid-Continent Research for Education and Learning (McREL); Associate Professor at Cardinal Stritch University in Milwaukee, Wisconsin; President of Marzano & Associates. An internationally known researcher, trainer, and speaker, Dr. Marzano has developed programs that translate research and theory into practical tools for K-12 teachers and administrators. He has written extensively on such topics as reading and writing instruction, thinking skills, school effectiveness, assessment, and standards implementation. His books include *Building Background Knowledge for Academic Achievement; Classroom Management That Works: Research-Based Strategies for Every Teacher;* and *What Works in Schools: Translating Research Into Action.*

DONNA M. OGLE Professor of Reading and Language at National-Louis University in Chicago, Illinois; Past President of the International Reading Association. Creator of the well-known KWL strategy, Dr. Ogle has directed many staff development projects translating theory and research into school practice in middle and secondary schools throughout the United States and has served as a consultant on literacy projects worldwide. Her extensive international experience includes coordinating the Reading and Writing for Critical Thinking Project in Eastern Europe, developing integrated curriculum for a USAID Afghan Education Project, and speaking and consulting on projects in several Latin American countries and in Asia. Her books include *Coming Together as Readers; Reading Comprehension: Strategies for Independent Learners; All Children Read;* and *Literacy for a Democratic Society.*

CAROL BOOTH OLSON Senior Lecturer in the Department of Education at the University of California, Irvine; Director of the UCI site of the National Writing Project. Dr. Olson writes and lectures extensively on the reading/writing connection, critical thinking through writing, interactive strategies for teaching writing, and the use of multicultural literature with students of culturally diverse backgrounds. She has received many awards, including the California Association of Teachers of English Award of Merit, the Outstanding California Education Research Award, and the UC Irvine Excellence in Teaching Award. Dr. Olson's books include *Reading, Thinking, and Writing About Multicultural Literature* and *The Reading/Writing Connection: Strategies for Teaching and Learning in the Secondary Classroom.*

CAROL ANN TOMLINSON Professor of Educational Research, Foundations, and Policy at the University of Virginia; Co-Director of the University's Institutes on Academic Diversity. An internationally known expert on differentiated instruction, Dr. Tomlinson helps teachers and administrators develop effective methods of teaching academically diverse learners. She was a teacher of middle and high school English for 22 years prior to teaching at the University of Virginia. Her books on differentiated instruction have been translated into eight languages. Among her many publications are *How to Differentiate Instruction in Mixed-Ability Classrooms* and *The Differentiated Classroom: Responding to the Needs of All Learners.*

ENGLISH LEARNER SPECIALISTS

MARY LOU McCLOSKEY Past President of Teachers of English to Speakers of Other Languages (TESOL); Director of Teacher Development and Curriculum Design for Educo in Atlanta, Georgia. Dr. McCloskey is a former teacher in multilingual and multicultural classrooms. She has worked with teachers, teacher educators, and departments of education around the world on teaching English as a second and foreign language. She is author of *On Our Way to English, Voices in Literature, Integrating English,* and *Visions: Language, Literature, Content.* Her awards include the Le Moyne College Ignatian Award for Professional Achievement and the TESOL D. Scott Enright Service Award.

LYDIA STACK International ESL consultant. Her areas of expertise are English language teaching strategies, ESL standards for students and teachers, and curriculum writing. Her teaching experience includes 25 years as an elementary and high school ESL teacher. She is a past president of TESOL. Her awards include the James E. Alatis Award for Service to TESOL (2003) and the San Francisco STAR Teacher Award (1989). Her publications include *On Our Way to English; Wordways: Games for Language Learning;* and *Visions: Language, Literature, Content.*

CURRICULUM SPECIALIST

WILLIAM L. McBRIDE Curriculum Specialist. Dr. McBride is a nationally known speaker, educator, and author who now trains teachers in instructional methodologies. A former reading specialist, English teacher, and social studies teacher, he holds a Masters in Reading and a Ph.D. in Curriculum and Instruction from the University of North Carolina at Chapel Hill. Dr. McBride has contributed to the development of textbook series in language arts, social studies, science, and vocabulary. He is also known for his novel *Entertaining an Elephant,* which tells the story of a burned-out teacher who becomes re-inspired with both his profession and his life.

MEDIA SPECIALISTS

DAVID M. CONSIDINE Professor of Instructional Technology and Media Studies at Appalachian State University in North Carolina. Dr. Considine has served as a media literacy consultant to the U.S. government and to the media industry, including Discovery Communications and Cable in the Classroom. He has also conducted media literacy workshops and training for county and state health departments across the United States. Among his many publications are *Visual Messages: Integrating Imagery into Instruction,* and *Imagine That: Developing Critical Viewing and Thinking Through Children's Literature.*

LARKIN PAULUZZI Teacher and Media Specialist; trainer for the New Jersey Writing Project. Ms. Pauluzzi puts her extensive classroom experience to use in developing teacher-friendly curriculum materials and workshops in many different areas, including media literacy. She has led media literacy training workshops in several districts throughout Texas, guiding teachers in the meaningful and practical uses of media in the classroom. Ms. Pauluzzi has taught students at all levels, from Title I Reading to AP English IV. She also spearheads a technology club at her school, working with students to produce media and technology to serve both the school and the community.

LISA K. SCHEFFLER Teacher and Media Specialist. Ms. Scheffler has designed and taught media literacy and video production curriculum, in addition to teaching language arts and speech. Using her knowledge of mass communication theory, coupled with real classroom experience, she has developed ready-to-use materials that help teachers incorporate media literacy into their curricula. She has taught film and television studies at the University of North Texas and has served as a contributing writer for the Texas Education Agency's statewide viewing and representing curriculum.

CALIFORNIA TEACHER ADVISORY PANEL

JORDANA BENONE
Teacher
North High School
Torrance, CA

NANCY HIMEL
Teacher
Board member of CATE
Paramount High School
Paramount, CA

JAN SAMMONS
Teacher, Reading Specialist
Joaquin Moraga
Intermediate School
Moraga, CA

TERESA BUNNER
English Department Chair
Monterey Trail High School
Elk Grove, CA

GAIL KIDD
Department Chair,
Language Arts Testing
& Standards Coordinator
Center Middle School
Azusa, CA

RUTH ELLEN SCHMUTZ
Professional Development
Secondary Specialist: ELA
Moreno Valley USD
Moreno Valley, CA

HOPPY CHANDLER
Teacher
San Diego City Schools
San Diego, CA

BETH LEDERACH
Teacher

**Clovis High School
Clovis, CA**

JOSEPH STAUB
Resource Specialist Teacher
Thomas Starr King
Middle School
Los Angeles, CA

DAWN CHARTSCHLAA
English Teacher
Oakland Technical
High School
Oakland, CA

TONI MCELROY
ELA Secondary
Content Coach
Oakland Unified SD
Oakland, CA

LINDA VALDEZ
Educational Consultant
Oxnard Union
High School District
Oxnard, CA

QUEANA GIVENS
Secondary Language
Arts Coordinator
Imperial County Ed
El Centro, CA

SAMANTHA MO
English Literature and
Composition Teacher
OCHSA
Santa Ana, CA

ARLENE WALKER
Teacher, Department Chair
Chaparral Middle School
Diamond Bar, CA

LIZ HARRINGTON
Teacher, Language Arts
Department Chair
Jefferson Middle School
San Gabriel, CA

PAGE MURPHY
English Language
Arts Teacher
Talbert Middle School
Huntington Beach, CA

LYNDA ZIMMERMAN
Teacher
El Camino High School
South San Francisco, CA

TEACHER ADVISORS

These are some of the many educators from across the country who played a crucial role in the development of the tables of contents, the lesson design, and other key components of this program:

Virginia L. Alford, MacArthur High School, San Antonio, Texas

Yvonne L. Allen, Shaker Heights High School, Shaker Heights, Ohio

Dave T. Anderson, Hinsdale South High School, Darien, Illinois

Kacy Colleen Anglim, Portland Public Schools District, Portland, Oregon

Beverly Scott Bass, Arlington Heights High School, Fort Worth, Texas

Jordana Benone, North High School, Torrance, California

Patricia Blood, Howell High School, Farmingdale, New Jersey

Marjorie Bloom, Eau Gallie High School, Melbourne, Florida

Edward J. Blotzer, Wilkinsburg Junior/Senior High School, Wilkinsburg, Pennsylvania

Stephen D. Bournes, Evanston Township High School, Evanston, Illinois

Barbara M. Bowling, Mt. Tabor High School, Winston-Salem, North Carolina

Kiala Boykin-Givehand, Duval County Public Schools, Jacksonville, Florida

Laura L. Brown, Adlai Stevenson High School, Lincolnshire, Illinois

Cynthia Burke, Yavneh Academy, Dallas, Texas

Hoppy Chandler, San Diego City Schools, San Diego, California

Gary Chmielewski, St. Benedict High School, Chicago, Illinois

Delorse Cole-Stewart, Milwaukee Public Schools, Milwaukee, Wisconsin

Kathy Dahlgren, Skokie, Illinois

Diana Dilger, Rosa Parks Middle School, Dixmoor, Illinois

L. Calvin Dillon, Gaither High School, Tampa, Florida

Dori Dolata, Rufus King High School, Milwaukee, Wisconsin

Jon Epstein, Marietta High School, Marietta, Georgia

Helen Ervin, Fort Bend Independent School District, Sugarland, Texas

Sue Friedman, Buffalo Grove High School, Buffalo Grove, Illinois

Chris Gee, Bel Air High School, El Paso, Texas

Paula Grasel, The Horizon Center, Gainesville, Georgia

Christopher Guarraia, Centreville High School, Clifton, Virginia

Rochelle L. Greene-Brady, Kenwood Academy, Chicago, Illinois

Michele M. Hettinger, Niles West High School, Skokie, Illinois

Elizabeth Holcomb, Forest Hill High School, Jackson, Mississippi

Jim Horan, Hinsdale Central High School, Hinsdale, Illinois

James Paul Hunter, Oak Park-River Forest High School, Oak Park, Illinois

Susan P. Kelly, Director of Curriculum, Island Trees School District, Levittown, New York

Beverley A. Lanier, Varina High School, Richmond, Virginia

Pat Laws, Charlotte-Mecklenburg Schools, Charlotte, North Carolina

Diana R. Martinez, Treviño School of Communications & Fine Arts, Laredo, Texas

Natalie Martinez, Stephen F. Austin High School, Houston, Texas

Elizabeth Matarazzo, Ysleta High School, El Paso, Texas

Carol M. McDonald, J. Frank Dobie High School, Houston, Texas

Amy Millikan, Consultant, Chicago, Illinois

Terri Morgan, Caprock High School, Amarillo, Texas

Eileen Murphy, Walter Payton Preparatory High School, Chicago, Illinois

Lisa Omark, New Haven Public Schools, New Haven, Connecticut

Kaine Osburn, Wheeling High School, Wheeling, Illinois

Andrea J. Phillips, Terry Sanford High School, Fayetteville, North Carolina

Cathy Reilly, Sayreville Public Schools, Sayreville, New Jersey

Mark D. Simon, Neuqua Valley High School, Naperville, Illinois

Scott Snow, Sequin High School, Arlington, Texas

Jane W. Speidel, Brevard County Schools, Viera, Florida

Cheryl E. Sullivan, Lisle Community School District, Lisle, Illinois

Anita Usmiani, Hamilton Township Public Schools, Hamilton Square, New Jersey

Linda Valdez, Oxnard Union High School District, Oxnard, California

Nancy Walker, Longview High School, Longview, Texas

Kurt Weiler, New Trier High School, Winnetka, Illinois

Elizabeth Whittaker, Larkin High School, Elgin, Illinois

Linda S. Williams, Woodlawn High School, Baltimore, Maryland

John R. Williamson, Fort Thomas Independent Schools, Fort Thomas, Kentucky

Anna N. Winters, Simeon High School, Chicago, Illinois

Tonora D. Wyckoff, North Shore Senior High School, Houston, Texas

Karen Zajac, Glenbard South High School, Glen Ellyn, Illinois

Cynthia Zimmerman, Mose Vines Preparatory High School, Chicago, Illinois

Lynda Zimmerman, El Camino High School, South San Francisco, California

Ruth E. Zurich, Brown Deer High School, Brown Deer, Wisconsin

CALIFORNIA

OVERVIEW
California Student's Edition

LESSONS WITH EMBEDDED STANDARDS INSTRUCTION

Look for the California symbol throughout the book. It highlights targeted objectives to help you succeed on your test.

Walt Disney Concert Hall © Core Imagery/Alamy Ltd.

CALIFORNIA

CONTENTS IN BRIEF

Online LITERATURE CLASSZONE.COM

LITERATURE AND READING CENTER
- Author Biographies
- Additional Selection Background
- Literary Analysis Frames
- Power Thinking Activities

WRITING AND GRAMMAR CENTER
- Writing Templates and Graphic Organizers
- Publishing Options
- Grammar Arcade

MEDIA CENTER
- Production Templates
- Analysis Guides

VOCABULARY CENTER
- Vocabulary Strategies and Practice
- Vocabulary Flip Cards
- Multi-Language Glossary of Academic Vocabulary

RESEARCH CENTER
- Web Research Guide
- Citation Guide

 ASSESSMENT CENTER
- Assessment Practice and Test-Taking Tips
- SAT/ACT Practice and Tips

MORE TECHNOLOGY

eEdition
- Interactive Selections
- Audio Summaries

WriteSmart
- Writing Prompts and Templates
- Interactive Student Models
- Interactive Graphic Organizers
- Interactive Revision Lessons
- Rubric Generator

MediaSmart
- Media Lessons
- Interactive Media Studies

EssaySmart
- Online Essay Analyzer

An Emerging Nation
EARLY AMERICAN WRITING
1600–1800

SKILLS AND STANDARDS

VOCABULARY STRATEGIES

Specialized vocabulary, *p. 60*

Etymologies, *p. 76*

Latin roots: *nom, p. 86*

Multiple meanings, *p. 97*

Words from French, *p. 108*

Synonyms, *p. 119*

Connotation, *p. 127*

Context clues, *p. 210*

Words from gods and mythology, *p. 232*

Political words, *p. 242*

Words from Middle English, *p. 253*

Latin roots: *fic, p. 273*

Celebrating the Individual
AMERICAN ROMANTICISM
1800–1855

SKILLS AND STANDARDS

American Gothic

VOCABULARY STRATEGIES

Latin roots: *spec, p. 326*
Words with multiple affixes, *p. 368*
Prefixes: *ab-* and *per-, p. 390*

Greek roots: *path, p. 425*
Affixes and spelling changes, *p. 436*
Latin roots: *ambi, p. 472*

An Age of Transition
FROM ROMANTICISM TO REALISM

1855–1870

SKILLS AND STANDARDS

Form and Meaning, Traditional and Organic Forms, Free Verse

Free Verse, Analyze Tone

CA19

VOCABULARY STRATEGIES

Latin roots: *lud, p. 594*

Capturing the American Landscape
REGIONALISM AND NATURALISM

1870–1910

CA22

CA23

A Changing Awareness
THE HARLEM RENAISSANCE AND MODERNISM

1910–1940

UNIT 5 CONTINUED

The New Poetry

SKILLS AND STANDARDS

Journalism as Literature

VOCABULARY STRATEGIES

Greek roots: *cosm* or *cosmo, p. 866*
Words from the Jazz Age, *p. 960*
Words from Italian, *p. 976*

Nouns and figurative verbs, *p. 1000*
Latin roots: *med* and its meanings, *p. 1016*
Etymologies, *p. 1030*

New Perspectives
CONTEMPORARY LITERATURE

1940–PRESENT

A Mosaic of American Voices

VOCABULARY STRATEGIES

Analogies, *p. 1158*   Idioms, *p. 1200*
Greek prefixes: *syn-, p. 1171*

Investigation and Discovery
THE POWER OF RESEARCH

SKILLS AND STANDARDS
Use Reference Materials and Technology, Evaluate Sources

Research, Synthesis

Selections by Genre

DRAMA

Features

LITERARY ANALYSIS WORKSHOPS

 LITERATURE CENTER at ClassZone.com

WRITING WORKSHOPS

 WriteSmart

SPEAKING, LISTENING, AND VIEWING

 MEDIA CENTER at ClassZone.com

WRAP-UPS

MEDIA STUDIES

MediaSmart DVD

VOCABULARY STRATEGIES

GRAMMAR AND STYLE

STUDENT GUIDE TO ACADEMIC SUCCESS

STUDENT GUIDE

Joshua Tree National Park © Jupiterimages Corporation

CA39

Understanding California's English-Language Arts Content Standards

What are the English-Language Arts Content Standards?

The English-Language Arts Content Standards for California Public Schools indicate the skills you will need to master by the end of your grade level. These skills will help you be better prepared for your future classes and goals. Your teacher uses the standards to provide a course of instruction that will help you develop the skills and knowledge you are expected to have by the end of grade 11.

How will I learn the English-Language Arts Content Standards?

Your textbook is closely aligned to the English-Language Arts Content Standards, so that every time you learn or practice a skill, you are mastering one of the standards. Each unit, each selection, and each workshop in your textbook connects to one or more of the standards, which are listed on the following pages.

The English-Language Arts Content Standards are divided into four domains, or groups of skills: Reading, Writing, Written and Oral English Language Conventions, and Listening and Speaking. Some of these domains are divided into strands as shown.

Reading (R)
1.0 Word Analysis, Fluency, and Systematic Vocabulary Development
2.0 Reading Comprehension (Focus on Informational Materials)
3.0 Literary Response and Analysis

Writing (W)
1.0 Writing Strategies
2.0 Writing Applications (Genres and Their Characteristics)

Written and Oral English Language Conventions (LC)
1.0 Written and Oral English Language Conventions

Listening and Speaking (LS)
1.0 Listening and Speaking Strategies
2.0 Speaking Applications (Genres and Their Characteristics)

These strands are further divided into substrands and standards. The standards describe the skills you must learn to master the domains. California uses a special code to identify the domain, strand, and standard.

CALIFORNIA STANDARD DECODER

W 1.3

Indicates that this standard is from the Writing domain

Identifies the standard
Structure ideas and arguments in a sustained, persuasive, and sophisticated way and support them with precise and relevant examples.

Identifies the strand
1.0 Writing Strategies

California English-Language Arts Content Standards

Listed below are the California English-Language Arts standards that you are required to master by the end of grade 11. To help you understand what is required of you, we have provided a summary of the skills you will learn on your way to mastering each standard.

Reading

1.0 Word Analysis, Fluency, and Systematic Vocabulary Development

Vocabulary and Concept Development

STANDARD	WHAT IT MEANS TO YOU
1.1 Trace the etymology of significant terms used in political science and history.	You will learn how the origins of important terms in political science and history can help you determine their meanings.
1.2 Apply knowledge of Greek, Latin, and Anglo-Saxon roots and affixes to draw inferences concerning the meaning of scientific and mathematical terminology.	You will learn to use your knowledge of Greek, Latin, and Anglo-Saxon roots, prefixes, and suffixes to understand the meaning of terms used in science and math.
1.3 Discern the meaning of analogies encountered, analyzing specific comparisons as well as relationships and inferences.	You will learn how to understand the meaning of analogies in texts by analyzing the point-by-point comparisons they make, the relationships they describe, and the inferences they suggest.

2.0 Reading Comprehension (Focus on Informational Materials)

Structural Features of Informational Materials

STANDARD	WHAT IT MEANS TO YOU
2.1 Analyze both the features and the rhetorical devices of different types of public documents (e.g., policy statements, speeches, debates, platforms) and the way in which authors use those features and devices.	You will learn to distinguish the ways policy statements, speeches, debates, platforms, and other public documents are laid out and the rhetorical techniques they use, including repetition, parallelism, analogies, and rhetorical questions. You also will learn how authors use these techniques and features for different purposes.

Comprehension and Analysis of Grade-Level-Appropriate Text

STANDARD	WHAT IT MEANS TO YOU
2.2 Analyze the way in which clarity of meaning is affected by the patterns of organization, hierarchical structures, repetition of the main ideas, syntax, and word choice in the text.	You will learn to examine how a writer organizes information, structures text, and uses language devices, such as repetition of main ideas, syntax, and word choice, in order to make text understandable and clear.
2.3 Verify and clarify facts presented in other types of expository texts by using a variety of consumer, workplace, and public documents.	You will learn how to use information from many kinds of business, government, and consumer documents to help you confirm and clarify facts in nonfiction and informational text.
2.4 Make warranted and reasonable assertions about the author's arguments by using elements of the text to defend and clarify interpretations.	You will learn how to state your opinion or interpretation of an author's arguments by supporting your statements with quotations, facts, and examples from the text.
2.5 Analyze an author's implicit and explicit philosophical assumptions and beliefs about a subject.	You will learn strategies that will help you distinguish and examine an author's implied and stated philosophical assumptions and beliefs about a subject.

Expository Critique

STANDARD	WHAT IT MEANS TO YOU
2.6 Critique the power, validity, and truthfulness of arguments set forth in public documents; their appeal to both friendly and hostile audiences; and the extent to which the arguments anticipate and address reader concerns and counterclaims (e.g., appeal to reason, to authority, to pathos and emotion).	You will learn how to judge the strength, validity, and truthfulness of the arguments presented in public documents. You also will learn ways that arguments appeal to different kinds of audiences, and how far the arguments anticipate and meet reader concerns and responses.

3.0 Literary Response and Analysis

Structural Features of Literature

STANDARD	WHAT IT MEANS TO YOU
3.1 Analyze characteristics of subgenres (e.g., satire, parody, allegory, pastoral) that are used in poetry, prose, plays, novels, short stories, essays, and other basic genres.	You will learn to distinguish and examine the elements of satire, parody, allegory, and pastoral in a variety of forms and genres, including poetry, prose, plays, novels, short stories, and essays.

Narrative Analysis of Grade-Level-Appropriate Text

STANDARD	WHAT IT MEANS TO YOU
3.2 Analyze the way in which the theme or meaning of a selection represents a view or comment on life, using textual evidence to support the claim.	You will learn to examine a literary selection to determine how its theme or meaning expresses a specific view or comment on life, and you will learn how to find evidence for its theme or meaning within the text.

STANDARD	WHAT IT MEANS TO YOU
3.3 Analyze the ways in which irony, tone, mood, the author's style, and the "sound" of language achieve specific rhetorical or aesthetic purposes or both.	You will learn to examine how authors use irony, tone, mood, style, and language to convey specific ideas, attitudes, and images.
3.4 Analyze ways in which poets use imagery, personification, figures of speech, and sounds to evoke readers' emotions.	You will learn to examine ways poets call forth readers' emotions by using imagery, personification, sound devices, and figurative language, such as metaphors and similes.

3.5 Analyze recognized works of American literature representing a variety of genres and traditions:
  a. Trace the development of American literature from the colonial period forward.
  b. Contrast the major periods, themes, styles, and trends and describe how works by members of different cultures relate to one another in each period.
  c. Evaluate the philosophical, political, religious, ethical, and social influences of the historical period that shaped the characters, plots, and settings.
	You will learn to recognize and examine important works of American literature in various genres and traditions. You will discover how American literature developed from the colonial period to the present, and how to contrast major periods, themes, styles, and trends. You will also learn to recognize and describe the ways those works relate to works by members of different cultures in the same period and determine how various influences of the historical period shaped the characters, plots, and settings.

3.6 Analyze the way in which authors through the centuries have used archetypes drawn from myth and tradition in literature, film, political speeches, and religious writings (e.g., how the archetypes of banishment from an ideal world may be used to interpret Shakespeare's tragedy *Macbeth*).	You will learn to identify and examine how authors have used archetypes from antiquity to the present.

3.7 Analyze recognized works of world literature from a variety of authors:
  a. Contrast the major literary forms, techniques, and characteristics of the major literary periods (e.g., Homeric Greece, medieval, romantic, neoclassic, modern).
  b. Relate literary works and authors to the major themes and issues of their eras.
  c. Evaluate the philosophical, political, religious, ethical, and social influences of the historical period that shaped the characters, plots, and settings.
	You will learn to examine important works of world literature by different kinds of authors, contrasting major literary forms, techniques, and characteristics of the major literary periods, and relating these works and authors to the major themes and issues of their eras. You will also learn to evaluate various influences of the historical period that shaped the characters, plots, and settings.

Literary Criticism

STANDARD	WHAT IT MEANS TO YOU
3.8 Analyze the clarity and consistency of political assumptions in a selection of literary works or essays on a topic (e.g., suffrage, women's role in organized labor). (Political approach)	You will learn how to examine and assess how an author conveys a set of political assumptions in a literary work on a specific topic.
3.9 Analyze the philosophical arguments presented in literary works to determine whether the authors' positions have contributed to the quality of each work and the credibility of the characters. (Philosophical approach)	You will learn ways to examine the philosophical arguments in literary works in order to determine whether the authors' positions add to the quality of each work and make the characters more believable.

Writing

1.0 Writing Strategies

Organization and Focus

STANDARD	WHAT IT MEANS TO YOU
1.1 Demonstrate an understanding of the elements of discourse (e.g., purpose, speaker, audience, form) when completing narrative, expository, persuasive, or descriptive writing assignments.	You will learn how to consider purpose, speaker, audience, and form when developing a variety of writing assignments.
1.2 Use point of view, characterization, style (e.g., use of irony), and related elements for specific rhetorical and aesthetic purposes.	You will learn to use literary devices, such as point of view, characterization, and style elements, in your writing to achieve a specific purpose.
1.3 Structure ideas and arguments in a sustained, persuasive, and sophisticated way and support them with precise and relevant examples.	You will learn how to organize arguments in a thorough, convincing, and sophisticated manner, and to support your arguments with accurate and relevant examples.
1.4 Enhance meaning by employing rhetorical devices, including the extended use of parallelism, repetition, and analogy; the incorporation of visual aids (e.g., graphs, tables, pictures); and the issuance of a call for action.	You will learn ways to select and use rhetorical devices, such as parallelism, repetition, and analogy, in your writing. You will also learn ways to include graphs, tables, pictures, and similar visual elements that help convey information efficiently, and you will learn how to enhance meaning with a call for action.
1.5 Use language in natural, fresh, and vivid ways to establish a specific tone.	You will learn how to select and use words and phrases to create a desired tone in your writing.

Research and Technology

STANDARD	WHAT IT MEANS TO YOU
1.6 Develop presentations by using clear research questions and creative and critical research strategies (e.g., field studies, oral histories, interviews, experiments, electronic sources).	You will learn to focus research questions and to develop and use field studies, oral histories, interviews, experiments, and electronic sources to produce presentations.
1.7 Use systematic strategies to organize and record information (e.g., anecdotal scripting, annotated bibliographies).	You will learn techniques to organize and record information systematically, using methods such as anecdotal scripting and annotated bibliographies.
1.8 Integrate databases, graphics, and spreadsheets into word-processed documents.	You will learn to effectively incorporate databases, graphics, and spreadsheets into writing created in word processing software.

Evaluation and Revision

STANDARD	WHAT IT MEANS TO YOU
1.9 Revise text to highlight the individual voice, improve sentence variety and style, and enhance subtlety of meaning and tone in ways that are consistent with the purpose, audience, and genre.	You will learn how to revise your writing in order to emphasize and develop your own personal voice, improve sentence variety, refine style, and enhance meaning and tone so that they appropriately match the purpose, audience, and genre of your writing.

2.0 Writing Applications (Genres and Their Characteristics)

STANDARD	WHAT IT MEANS TO YOU

2.1 Write fictional, autobiographical, or biographical narratives:
  a. Narrate a sequence of events and communicate their significance to the audience.
  b. Locate scenes and incidents in specific places.
  c. Describe with concrete sensory details the sights, sounds, and smells of a scene and the specific actions, movements, gestures, and feelings of the characters; use interior monologue to depict the characters' feelings.
  d. Pace the presentation of actions to accommodate temporal, spatial, and dramatic mood changes.
  e. Make effective use of descriptions of appearance, images, shifting perspectives, and sensory details.
	You will learn to write stories about yourself, other people, or fictional characters that relate a sequence of significant events in specific settings. You also will learn to use sensory details and interior monologue to convey the actions and feelings of characters. You will learn how to pace the action of a scene in order to appropriately depict mood, and you will learn how to use devices, such as description, imagery, shifting perspectives, and sensory details.

2.2 Write responses to literature:
  a. Demonstrate a comprehensive understanding of the significant ideas in works or passages.
  b. Analyze the use of imagery, language, universal themes, and unique aspects of the text.
  c. Support important ideas and viewpoints through accurate and detailed references to the text and to other works.
  d. Demonstrate an understanding of the author's use of stylistic devices and an appreciation of the effects created.
  e. Identify and assess the impact of perceived ambiguities, nuances, and complexities within the text.
	You will learn to write an opinion or thoughts about literary works or passages, showing your thorough understanding of their significant ideas. You will learn how to examine literary and style devices, including imagery, language, and theme, and discuss them when analyzing the work, using detailed references from the text to support your own viewpoint about the literary work. You will learn to recognize and evaluate the impact of ambiguities, subtleties, and complxities within the text.

STANDARD	WHAT IT MEANS TO YOU

2.3 Write reflective compositions:

   a. Explore the significance of personal experiences, events, conditions, or concerns by using rhetorical strategies (e.g., narration, description, exposition, persuasion).

   b. Draw comparisons between specific incidents and broader themes that illustrate the writer's important beliefs or generalizations about life.

   c. Maintain a balance in describing individual incidents and relate those incidents to more general and abstract ideas.

You will learn how to write compositions that explore your personal experiences or concerns and to convey them using narrative, descriptive, expository, and persuasive strategies. You will also learn to make comparisons between specific incidents and more general themes and discuss these ideas with a balanced approach that allows you to relate the specific to the general.

2.4 Write historical investigation reports:

   a. Use exposition, narration, description, argumentation, or some combination of rhetorical strategies to support the main proposition.

   b. Analyze several historical records of a single event, examining critical relationships between elements of the research topic.

   c. Explain the perceived reason or reasons for the similarities and differences in historical records with information derived from primary and secondary sources to support or enhance the presentation.

   d. Include information from all relevant perspectives and take into consideration the validity and reliability of sources.

   e. Include a formal bibliography.

You will learn to write a report about a historical period, event, or literary work, and discuss it using strategies such as exposition, narration, description, or argumentation in order to support your main proposition. You will learn how to research historical records on a single event and examine the relationships between elements of the research topic. You also will learn to explain the apparent reason(s) for similarities and differences in historical records by citing information taken from primary and secondary sources. You will learn how to assess the validity and reliability of sources and include information from all relevant viewpoints, citing your sources in a formal bibliography.

2.5 Write job applications and résumés:

   a. Provide clear and purposeful information and address the intended audience appropriately.

   b. Use varied levels, patterns, and types of language to achieve intended effects and aid comprehension.

   c. Modify the tone to fit the purpose and audience.

   d. Follow the conventional style for that type of document (e.g., résumé, memorandum) and use page formats, fonts, and spacing that contribute to the readability and impact of the document.

You will learn how to write effective job applications and résumés that will provide clear and relevant information to your intended audience. You will learn to vary the language and how to modify the tone of your writing appropriately both for maximum comprehension and to fit your purpose. You will also learn the correct style for each type of document, including page formats, fonts, and spacing, to improve your document's readability and strengthen its impact.

2.6 Deliver multimedia presentations:

   a. Combine text, images, and sound and draw information from many sources (e.g., television broadcasts, videos, films, newspapers, magazines, CD-ROMs, the Internet, electronic media-generated images).

   b. Select an appropriate medium for each element of the presentation.

   c. Use the selected media skillfully, editing appropriately and monitoring for quality.

   d. Test the audience's response and revise the presentation accordingly.

You will learn how to prepare and deliver powerful multimedia presentations that incorporate text, images, and sounds from a variety of sources, including television broadcasts, videos, newspapers, CD-ROMs, and the Internet. You will learn how to pick an appropriate medium for each presentation element, to use your chosen media effectively, to test how your audience responds, and then to revise your presentation as needed.

Written and Oral English Language Conventions

1.0 Written and Oral English Language Conventions

STANDARD	WHAT IT MEANS TO YOU
1.1 Demonstrate control of grammar, diction, and paragraph and sentence structure and an understanding of English usage.	You will learn to effectively use and demonstrate an understanding of grammar, diction, paragraph and sentence structure, and English usage.
1.2 Produce legible work that shows accurate spelling and correct punctuation and capitalization.	You will learn to create writing that can be read easily, and uses correct spelling, punctuated, and capitalization.
1.3 Reflect appropriate manuscript requirements in writing.	You will learn to prepare manuscript so that it meets specific requirements.

Listening and Speaking

1.0 Listening and Speaking Strategies

Comprehension

STANDARD	WHAT IT MEANS TO YOU
1.1 Recognize strategies used by the media to inform, persuade, entertain, and transmit culture (e.g., advertisements; perpetuation of stereotypes; use of visual representations, special effects, language).	You will learn to identify the media's use of language; visual, sound, and editing techniques; and special effects to inform, persuade, entertain, and transmit messages about the culture, such as in creating and presenting advertisements and perpetuating stereotypes.
1.2 Analyze the impact of the media on the democratic process (e.g., exerting influence on elections, creating images of leaders, shaping attitudes) at the local, state, and national levels.	You will learn how to examine the media's effects on an audience in regard to shaping people's attitudes, creating images of leaders, and influencing local, state, and national elections.
1.3 Interpret and evaluate the various ways in which events are presented and information is communicated by visual image makers (e.g., graphic artists, documentary filmmakers, illustrators, news photographers).	You will learn to determine and critique the ways images, including those in photos, drawings, and film, affect the way information is conveyed and impact people's thoughts and emotions.

Organization and Delivery of Oral Communication

STANDARD	WHAT IT MEANS TO YOU
1.4 Use rhetorical questions, parallel structure, concrete images, figurative language, characterization, irony, and dialogue to achieve clarity, force, and aesthetic effect.	You will learn how to engage your audience by employing a variety of rhetorical and literary techniques, including rhetorical questions and figurative language, in clear, forceful, and expressive speeches.

1.5 Distinguish between and use various forms of classical and contemporary logical arguments, including:
  a. Inductive and deductive reasoning
  b. Syllogisms and analogies
	You will learn how to use techniques of classical and contemporary logical arguments, such as inductive and deductive reasoning, syllogisms, and analogies, to effectively convey your message to an audience.

1.6 Use logical, ethical, and emotional appeals that enhance a specific tone and purpose.	You will learn to use persuasive techniques that appeal to your audience's reasoning, beliefs, and feelings, and to support your tone and purpose.

STANDARD	WHAT IT MEANS TO YOU
1.7 Use appropriate rehearsal strategies to pay attention to performance details, achieve command of the text, and create skillful artistic staging.	You will learn to use rehearsal strategies that will help you refine performance details, master your text, and skillfully stage your performance.

1.8 Use effective and interesting language, including:
   a. Informal expressions for effect
   b. Standard American English for clarity
   c. Technical language for specificity
	You will discover how to incorporate language that effectively serves the purpose of your presentation, including informal expressions for effect when appropriate, Standard American English to convey ideas clearly, and technical language when necessary for specific details.

1.9 Use research and analysis to justify strategies for gesture, movement, and vocalization, including dialect, pronunciation, and enunciation.	You will learn how to research and analyze strategies that will support your use of verbal and nonverbal techniques in a presentation.
1.10 Evaluate when to use different kinds of effects (e.g., visual, music, sound, graphics) to create effective productions.	You will learn how to judge when visual, music, sound, or graphic effects can be used most effectively in your presentations.

Analysis and Evaluation of Oral and Media Communications

STANDARD	WHAT IT MEANS TO YOU
1.11 Critique a speaker's diction and syntax in relation to the purpose of an oral communication and the impact the words may have on the audience.	You will learn to analyze a speaker's oral delivery and to evaluate how well the diction and syntax serve the purpose of the communication and impact the audience.
1.12 Identify logical fallacies used in oral addresses (e.g., attack *ad hominem*, false causality, red herring, overgeneralization, bandwagon effect).	You will learn to recognize and examine a variety of logical mistakes often found in oral presentations.
1.13 Analyze the four basic types of persuasive speech (i.e., propositions of fact, value, problem, or policy) and understand the similarities and differences in their patterns of organization and the use of persuasive language, reasoning, and proof.	You will learn to recognize and examine the four basic types of persuasive speech and discover how they are alike and different in their structures and uses of persuasive language, reasoning, and proof.
1.14 Analyze the techniques used in media messages for a particular audience and evaluate their effectiveness (e.g., Orson Welles' radio broadcast "War of the Worlds").	You will learn to recognize and examine techniques in media messages, such as images, text, and sound, that target a specific audience, and you will learn how to assess their effectiveness in creating an impact on the audience.

2.0 Speaking Applications (Genres and Their Characteristics)

STANDARD	WHAT IT MEANS TO YOU
2.1 Deliver reflective presentations: *a.* Explore the significance of personal experiences, events, conditions, or concerns, using appropriate rhetorical strategies (e.g., narration, description, exposition, persuasion). *b.* Draw comparisons between the specific incident and broader themes that illustrate the speaker's beliefs or generalizations about life. *c.* Maintain a balance between describing the incident and relating it to more general, abstract ideas.	You will learn how to deliver oral presentations that explore your personal experiences or concerns and to convey them using narrative, descriptive, expository, and persuasive strategies. You will also learn to make comparisons between specific incidents and more general themes and discuss these ideas with a balanced approach that allows you to relate the specific to the general.
2.2 Deliver oral reports on historical investigations: *a.* Use exposition, narration, description, persuasion, or some combination of those to support the thesis. *b.* Analyze several historical records of a single event, examining critical relationships between elements of the research topic. *c.* Explain the perceived reason or reasons for the similarities and differences by using information derived from primary and secondary sources to support or enhance the presentation. *d.* Include information on all relevant perspectives and consider the validity and reliability of sources.	You will learn to prepare an oral report about a historical period, event, or literary work, and discuss it using strategies such as exposition, narration, description, argumentation in order to support your thesis. You will learn how to research historical records on a single event and examine the relationships between elements of the research topic. You also will learn to explain the apparent reason(s) for similarities and differences in historical records by citing information taken from primary and secondary sources. You will learn how to assess the validity and reliability of sources and include information from all relevant viewpoints.
2.3 Deliver oral responses to literature: *a.* Demonstrate a comprehensive understanding of the significant ideas of literary works (e.g., make assertions about the text that are reasonable and supportable). *b.* Analyze the imagery, language, universal themes, and unique aspects of the text through the use of rhetorical strategies (e.g., narration, description, persuasion, exposition, a combination of those strategies). *c.* Support important ideas and viewpoints through accurate and detailed references to the text or to other works. *d.* Demonstrate an awareness of the author's use of stylistic devices and an appreciation of the effects created. *e.* Identify and assess the impact of perceived ambiguities, nuances, and complexities within the text.	You will learn to prepare and deliver an oral presentation of your opinion or thoughts about literary works or passages, showing your thorough understanding of their significant ideas and supporting your assertions with evidence from the text. You will learn how to examine literary and style devices, including imagery, language, and theme, and discuss them when analyzing the work, using detailed references from the text to support your own viewpoint about the literary work. You will learn to recognize and evaluate the impact of ambiguities, subtleties, and complexities within the text.

STANDARD	WHAT IT MEANS TO YOU

2.4 Deliver multimedia presentations:
 	
   a. Combine text, images, and sound by incorporating information from a wide range of media, including films, newspapers, magazines, CD-ROMs, online information, television, videos, and electronic media-generated images.
 	
   b. Select an appropriate medium for each element of the presentation.
 	
   c. Use the selected media skillfully, editing appropriately and monitoring for quality.
 	
   d. Test the audience's response and revise the presentation accordingly.
	You will learn how to prepare and deliver powerful multimedia presentations that incorporate text, images, and sounds from a variety of sources, including television broadcasts, videos, newspapers, CD-ROMs, and the Internet. You will learn how to pick an appropriate medium for each presentation element, to use your chosen media effectively, to test how your audience responds, and then to revise your presentation as needed.

2.5 Recite poems, selections from speeches, or dramatic soliloquies with attention to performance details to achieve clarity, force, and aesthetic effect and to demonstrate an understanding of the meaning (e.g., Hamlet's soliloquy "To Be or Not to Be").	You will learn how to give dramatic interpretations of poems, speech selections, or dramatic soliloquies, using performance techniques, such as voice modulation, tone, and gestures to clearly and powerfully convey the meaning and drama of the work.

CALIFORNIA

Academic Vocabulary

In this grade level, you will be required to use a variety of skills. The vocabulary on these pages includes terms for skills you will typically be asked to use in lessons and tests, and to master the standards. Knowing these terms and what they mean will help you to complete assignments accurately, develop critical thinking skills, and master the standards.

Interpret

Defining the Skill

To **interpret** is to explain the meaning of something. In order to interpret an element of literature, you must first determine what it is, then what it represents, and finally its significance to the text as a whole.

Applying the Skill

The following is an excerpt from a poem about the planned destruction of a ship that fought in the War of 1812. Use the strategies listed below to interpret a symbol used in the poem.

HOW TO INTERPRET

STRATEGY ❶ Look for a person, place, or object that stands for something beyond itself. Here the symbol is the condemned warship, "Old Ironsides." Once you identify a symbol, note how the writer describes it. In this passage, what thoughts and feelings are conveyed by the ship's worn pieces?

STRATEGY ❷ Note details that relate to the symbol. What might the symbol mean in context? In this poem, also pay attention to the writer's sardonic tone. This tone and the descriptions reveal that the ship has a strong personal meaning for the poem's speaker.

> *from* ❶ **Old Ironsides**
> by Oliver Wendell Holmes
>
> ❷ Ay, tear her tattered ensign down!
>   Long has it waved on high,
> And many an eye has danced to see
>   That banner in the sky;
> ❷ Beneath it rung the battle shout,
>   And burst the cannon's roar;–
> ❶ The meteor of the ocean air
>   Shall sweep the clouds no more.

MAKE A CHART FOR INTERPRETING

Use a chart to help you identify and understand how to interpret a symbol.

Symbol	Clues from the text	Meaning
The ship "Old Ironsides"	"Ay, tear her tattered ensign down!" (sardonic tone) "The meteor of the ocean air Shall sweep the clouds no more."	The ship represents dramatic memories of our country's history.

Analyze

Defining the Skill

To **analyze** something is to examine it in detail by separating it into parts and studying the relationships among those parts. You can then form your own ideas about the subject of your analysis. In literature, you are often asked to analyze elements of a text, such as a character's behavior and how it affects the plot or the importance of setting to a story.

Applying the Skill

In the story passage below, the narrator describes the ocean where four men are shipwrecked. Use the strategies listed below to analyze the importance of this setting to the story.

HOW TO ANALYZE

STRATEGY ❶ Note the details used to describe the setting in the text.

STRATEGY ❷ Note the story action, as well as the character description in relation to the setting.

STRATEGY ❸ Use your own experience and background to form ideas about the setting as you think about the importance of setting to the story.

from **The Open Boat**
by Stephen Crane

❷ None of them knew the color of the sky. Their eyes glanced level, and were fastened upon the waves that swept toward them. ❶ These waves were the hue of slate, save for the tops, which were of foaming white, and all of the men knew the colors of the sea. ❶ The horizon narrowed and widened, and dipped and rose, and at all times its edge was jagged with waves that seemed thrust up in points like rocks.

❶ Many a man ought to have a bathtub larger than the boat which here rode upon the sea. These waves were most wrongfully and barbarously abrupt and tall, and each froth top was a problem in small boat navigation. . . .

MAKE A CHART FOR ANALYZING

Using a chart can help you analyze details of the setting and explain their relevance.

Description of Setting	Effect of Setting on Story	Importance of Setting to Story
slate-colored waves with foaming white tops sweep toward the men jagged horizon a tiny boat at sea waves look like rocks dangerously tall and abrupt waves	Navigating the huge waves, to prevent their tiny boat from sinking and reach safety, completely absorbs the attention and energy of the men in the boat	The threatening setting is an important part of the story action and character development. The many changing features of the sea will have a strong impact on what the characters think and feel and the events of the plot.

Evaluate

Defining the Skill

To **evaluate** is to examine something carefully and then make a judgment about its value. Sometimes you will be asked to evaluate an aspect of literature. For example, you may be asked to evaluate a character's believability or the consistency of a story. In a nonfiction text, you may be asked to evaluate information, which means you will need to decide whether or not the information is relevant, interesting, or reasonable.

Applying the Skill

The following paragraph is from an essay about nature's effect on people, particularly the writer. Use the strategies listed below to evaluate whether or not the details adequately support the main idea.

HOW TO EVALUATE

STRATEGY ❶ Identify and examine the excerpt's main idea. Note the language used in the first sentence to express the main idea. How does the writer feel about nature?

STRATEGY ❷ Note words, phrases, or sentences that support the main idea. Are the supporting examples relevant, accurate, and reasonable? Do the details presented clearly support the writer's main idea?

STRATEGY ❸ Note words, phrases, or sentences that fail to support the main idea. Are there any irrelevant or inaccurate details?

from **Nature**
by Ralph Waldo Emerson

❶ Nature is a setting that fits equally well a comic or a mourning piece. ❷ In good health, the air is a cordial of incredible virtue. Crossing a bare common, in snow puddles, at twilight, under a clouded sky, without having in my thoughts any occurrence of special good fortune, ❷ I have enjoyed a perfect exhilaration. I am glad to the brink of fear. ❷ In the woods too, a man casts off his years, as the snake his slough, and at what period soever of life, is always a child. ❷ In the woods, is perpetual youth. Within these plantations of God, a decorum and sanctity reign, . . .

MAKE A DIAGRAM FOR EVALUATING

Using a diagram can help you organize and examine the information you want to evaluate for accuracy and relevance.

Main Idea:	Details That Support:	Evaluation of Accuracy and Relevance:
Nature greatly stimulates, refreshes, and inspires people.	• Fresh air in nature greatly promotes health. • Walking outdoors is exhilarating. • In the woods, people feel young and are at peace.	The writer provides strong, relevant personal examples that support the main idea.

Compare and Contrast

Defining the Skill

To **compare** means to look at the ways in which two or more subjects are alike. To **contrast** means to examine the ways two or more subjects are different. Tests often ask you to compare and contrast characters in a story or ideas and opinions in nonfiction.

Applying the Skill

The following passage describes Koskoosh and his granddaughter Sit-cum-to-ha, two Native American characters in a short story set in Alaska. Use the strategies listed below to help you compare and contrast these two characters.

HOW TO COMPARE AND CONTRAST

STRATEGY ❶ Look for aspects of the characters that may be compared or contrasted. This excerpt describes actions and qualities that help you compare and contrast Koskoosh and Sit-cum-to-ha.

STRATEGY ❷ To compare, look for aspects the two characters have in common.

STRATEGY ❸ To contrast, look for words and phrases that signal that the two characters differ, for example, *but* and *not*.

> *from* **The Law of Life**
> by Jack London
>
> Old Koskoosh listened greedily. ❶ Though his sight had long since faded, his hearing was still acute, and the slightest sound penetrated to the glimmering intelligence which yet abode behind his withered forehead, but which no longer gazed forth upon the things of the world. Ah! that was Sit-cum-to-ha, shrilly anathematizing the dogs as she cuffed and beat them into the harness. ❷ Sit-cum-to-ha was his daughter's daughter, ❸ but she was too busy to waste a thought upon her broken grandfather, sitting alone there in the snow, forlorn and helpless. Camp must be broken. The long trail waited while the short day refused to linger. ❸ Life called her, and the duties of life, not death. And he was very close to death now. . . .

MAKE A MATRIX FOR COMPARING AND CONTRASTING

Making a comparison/contrast matrix can help you identify similarities and differences. The matrix below shows points of comparison between Koskoosh and Sit-cum-to-ha from the excerpt you just read.

Points of Comparison	Subject 1: Koskoosh	Subject 2: Sit-cum-to-ha	Same/Different
Tribal and family membership	grandfather	granddaughter	same
Activity	sitting alone in the snow, listening	busy breaking camp: cursing, beating dogs	different
Use of senses	faded sight, acute hearing	sees and hears	different
Life stage	near death	in the midst of duties of life	different

Test Practice STRATEGIES

What are the ACT and SAT*?

High school juniors often need to take standardized tests, especially if they are considering going to college. This section will introduce you to the formats used by two of the most common standardized tests you may take: the ACT and the SAT. Studying these formats and completing the practice items will help prepare you for the tests and make you a more confident test taker.

HOW THE TESTS COMPARE

ACT	SAT
Required for admission at many colleges	Required for admission at many colleges
Tests achievement in English, reading, science reasoning, and math	Tests critical reading skills, math, and writing
Tests grammar skills	Tests grammar skills
Tests vocabulary skills	Places more emphasis on vocabulary
Multiple choice with an optional essay	Mostly multiple choice with an essay and 10 student-determined math questions
Does not penalize guessing, so answer every question	Penalizes guessing, so skip a question if you cannot eliminate any answer choices
Scores range from 1 to 36 for each of the four tests; a composite score, which is the average of the four test scores, can also range from 1–36	Scores range from 200 to 800 for each of the three sections

* SAT is a registered trademark of the College Board, which was not involved in the production of, and does not endorse, this product.

Focus on the English, Reading, and Writing Sections of the ACT and the SAT

HOW ENGLISH SKILLS ARE COVERED ON THE ACT

Reading Test

Multiple-choice questions. Includes 4 readings in these subject areas: social sciences, natural sciences, fiction, humanities

Requires you to demonstrate ability to

- understand literal meaning and make inferences
- identify main ideas and details
- understand cause and effect/sequence of events
- compare and contrast
- use context to find meaning of words and phrases
- analyze voice and techniques

English

Multiple-choice questions. Covers **usage and mechanics**

- punctuation
- grammar and usage
- sentence structure

Covers **rhetorical skills**

- strategy
- organization
- style

Writing Test (Optional)

Essay prompt identifies two positions on an issue. You are asked to take a position and support it in an essay. You will have thirty minutes to plan and write your essay.

HOW ENGLISH SKILLS ARE COVERED ON THE SAT

The Critical Reading Section

Includes two types of multiple-choice questions: sentence-completion and passage-based reading questions

Sentence-completion questions test your vocabulary and understanding of how sentence parts work together

Passage-based reading questions test your understanding of what is stated or implied by the passage. These questions require you to

- understand literal meaning, including vocabulary
- make inferences (extended reasoning)
- identify main ideas and details
- understand cause and effect
- follow the logic of an argument
- recognize tone

Writing Section

This part of the test begins with an essay. You will be asked to present and support your response on a specific topic.

You will also be asked to answer multiple-choice questions that test your ability to

- improve sentences
- identify sentence errors
- improve paragraphs

Test-Taking Strategies

Stay calm when you are faced with a test. These tips will help you approach any test with confidence.

STEPS TO TAKE BEFORE ANY TEST

- **Be prepared.** Know what you need to take with you to the test (for example, identification, a registration ticket, and #2 pencils). Get your things together the night before you take the test.

- **Be on time.** Know where the testing center is and how long it will take you to get there. Plan to arrive a few minutes early.

- **Know the format.** Find out what the test will cover and what format it will have. The ACT and the SAT are both mostly multiple-choice tests. The SAT has a written essay and the ACT has an optional written essay.

- **Practice.** You may want to take a practice test to familiarize yourself with the question types and format of the test. If you get nervous about taking tests, practice may help you relax and feel more confident.

- **Review the Test-Taking Handbook that is part of this textbook.** Pages R96–R103 provide a handy reference along with many helpful strategies and tips.

STEPS TO TAKE DURING ANY TEST

- **Read directions.** Be sure you understand what you are being asked to do.

- **Fill in the answer sheet carefully.** Follow directions for filling in the answer sheet. Avoid unnecessary marks. If you skip a question, make sure you skip that item on the answer sheet.

- **Manage your time.** Many tests tell you about how much time to spend on each section. Try resetting your watch to noon just before you begin the test so that during the test, you can tell at a glance how much time you have spent.

- **Answer easy questions first.** Look over the test once and answer any questions you know quickly. Skip questions when you are unsure of the answers. Then go back and spend more time on the questions you skipped.

- **Check your answers if you have time.** Look over your work. Make sure you have filled in the answer sheet correctly. See if you can answer any questions you skipped. Usually your first answer is correct, so do not change answers unless you have a good reason, such as realizing that you misread a question.

Testing Tips for the ACT and the SAT

Keep a positive attitude. Take the test seriously, but remember it is only one piece of the information used to assess your ability or achievement. If you are nervous, take a few deep breaths and remember that you have prepared yourself for success on the test.

FOR THE ACT

- **Answer every question.** You earn points for each correct answer. There is no penalty for incorrect answers, so if you do not know the answer to a question, try to narrow down the choices and make your best guess. Even if you are unable to narrow down the choices, you should still guess.

- **Complete the test.** Because there is no penalty for incorrect answers, it is in your best interest to answer every question. If you manage your time well, you should be able to complete the test. If you are running out of time, try to quickly answer any remaining questions.

- **Know that the optional writing test is last.** If you choose to take the writing test, remember to take some time to plan your response in the beginning and to do a final check at the end.

FOR THE SAT

- **Try to narrow down choices.** You earn points for each correct answer. You lose a fraction of a point for each incorrect answer. If you cannot eliminate any responses, leave the question blank. If you can eliminate even one answer, you may want to guess.

- **Complete as much of the test as you can.** The more questions you answer correctly, the better your score will be. However, many students do not have time to answer every question. Try not to linger on any one question, and do not panic if you think you will not be able to answer all of the questions.

- **Be prepared to write first.** The essay writing test is first, while the multiple-choice writing question section is last. (The other test sections in between appear in random order, and are not the same for each test-taker.)

Reading Comprehension Tips and Strategies

The ACT and the SAT both require you to read passages and answer multiple-choice questions about them.

The questions will not require you to have any other outside knowledge of the subject. Instead, they will focus on what is stated directly in the text or what you can infer from the text. Questions in these tests are designed to assess your ability to identify the main idea, read for details, understand the author's intent, and make sense of vocabulary, among other skills.

GENERAL TIPS FOR READING COMPREHENSION QUESTIONS

Before You Read

- **Scan the questions and answer choices first.** This will help you focus your reading.

- **Read shorter passages first.** Leave longer passages until later. If you do not understand a passage, move on to the next one. Go back and reread the skipped passage if you have time.

- **Examine the title.** Quickly preview the passage to locate any helpful text features, such as headings.

As You Read

- **Read the passage carefully.** It is important that you read each sentence rather than skim the text. Make sure you understand relationships between and among ideas.

- **Identify main ideas and key supporting details.** Mentally summarize what you learn from each paragraph or section.

- **Look for transitional words and phrases.** Words such as *later, because, in addition to,* and *instead of* can help you determine relationships among sentences, paragraphs, and sections.

When You Answer the Questions

- **Refer to the passage.** Correct answers must be based on what is in the passage, not on other information you may know about the subject.

- **Reread, if necessary.** If a question asks about a particular section of the reading passage, you may find it helpful to quickly review it or even reread it.

- **Do not spend too much time on any one question.** Remember, you do not have to answer questions in sequential order.

STRATEGIES FOR THE ACT READING TEST

- **Focus on the reading.** You may want to make notes about important ideas in the passage either in the test booklet or on scratch paper, if provided.

- **Manage your time.** Try to save time to review your work and to return to any questions you may have skipped.

- **Start with topics you know best.** ACT reading passages cover a variety of subjects. If you feel more confident about one subject than another, begin with a passage about that subject. Then move on to other subjects.

- **Read all of the answer choices.** Make sure the answer choice you select is the one that *best* answers what the question is asking.

STRATEGIES FOR THE SAT CRITICAL READING TEST

- **Answer the sentence-completion questions first.** These questions take less time than the passage-based reading questions because you can read the sentences more quickly than a passage. Make sure you leave time for the passage-based reading questions.

- **For two-part answers, test the logic of one part of each answer.** If you have a sentence-completion question with two blanks, test the logic of the first word/phrase. Eliminate any answer that does not make sense. Then test the second part of the remaining answers.

Example: Afraid of causing _____, the committee put together a program that was too _____ to generate much response.

(A) controversy, bland

(B) interest, diverse

(C) discord, questionable

(D) appeal, general

(E) disinterest, controversial

When you test just the first word of each answer, you can eliminate *B* and *D* because logically, the committee would not be afraid of causing interest or appeal in a program. Then test the remaining answers using both parts. *A* makes more sense than *C* or *E* because a questionable or controversial program is more likely to generate a response than a bland one. Even if you cannot decide between *A*, *C*, and *E*, eliminating two answers improves your chances of guessing correctly.

- **Do not worry if you cannot answer every question.** If you are unable to eliminate at least one answer choice, it is best not to guess on the SAT.

Reading Comprehension Practice

Both the SAT and the ACT require you to read passages and answer multiple-choice questions about them. Use the models below for practice. The strategies in the margins will guide you as you read the passages and answer the questions.

ACT MODEL

DIRECTIONS: Read the following passage. Then answer questions 1 through 6. You may refer to the passage as often as necessary.

HISTORY: The following passage is taken from an informational article about World War I.

The Great War

War Affects the Home Front

By the time the United States joined the Allies, the war had been going on for nearly three years in Europe. In those three years, Europe had lost more men in battle than in all the wars of the previous three centuries. The Great War, as the conflict came to be known, affected everyone. It touched not
5   only the soldiers in the trenches, but civilians as well. It affected not just military institutions, but also political, economic, and social institutions.

Governments Wage Total War

World War I soon became a total war. This meant that countries devoted all their resources to the war effort. In Britain, Germany, Austria, Russia, and
10   France, all the resources of each government were dedicated to winning the conflict.

In each country, the government took control of the economy. Factories were told what products to produce and how many of each. Numerous facilities were converted to munitions factories where weapons and
15   ammunition were manufactured. Nearly every able-bodied civilian was put to work. Unemployment in many European countries nearly disappeared.

So many goods were in short supply that governments turned to rationing. Under this system, people could buy only small amounts of those items that were needed for the war effort. Eventually, rationing covered a
20   wide range of goods, from metals to butter and shoe leather.

Governments also suppressed antiwar activity—sometimes by force. In addition, they censored news about the war. Many leaders feared that honest reporting of the war would turn people against it. Governments also used propaganda—persuasive information designed to promote their goals and
25   opinions—to keep up morale and support for the war.

SAT/ACT

STRATEGIES
FOR THE READING PASSAGE

Look for the main idea.
The title and opening paragraph will often help you identify the main idea of a passage.

Use subheadings.
These help you understand how the article is organized and find information quickly.

Use context clues.
Look for restatement, examples, or other clues that help you understand the meaning of unfamiliar words. This paragraph explains what *propaganda* means.

The War's Impact on Women

Total war meant that governments turned to women for help as never before. Thousands of women replaced men in factories, offices, and shops. Women built tanks and weapons, plowed fields, paved streets, and ran hospitals. They
30 also kept troops supplied with food, clothing, and weapons. The propaganda effort sought to glorify women's part in the war effort. In reality, much of the women's work was dangerous and low paying.

Although most women left the work force when the war ended, their work for the war effort set an important precedent.

Now answer questions 1 through 6 on a separate sheet of paper. Base your answers on the article "The Great War."

SAT/ACT

STRATEGIES FOR
ANSWERING THE QUESIONS

Eliminate incorrect answer choices. If you are not sure of an answer, eliminate answer choices that you know are incorrect.

1 **According to the author, the Great War affected:**

   A. soldiers and civilians.

   B. military personnel and institutions around the world.

   C. American and European society at large.

   D. women most of all.

2 **Which heading would be most appropriate for the fifth paragraph (lines 21–25) of the article?**

   F. Propaganda and Media

   G. Keeping Up Morale

   H. Crack Down! Controlling Anti-War Activity

   J. Governments Control Images of War

3 **In the third paragraph (lines 12–16) the author states, "Numerous facilities were converted to munitions factories where weapons and ammunition were manufactured." After the war, these factories most likely were:**

   A. destroyed.

   B. converted again to produce something else.

   C. run by women.

   D. converted to housing for returning soldiers.

4 **Which of the following conclusions can reasonably be drawn from the article?**

   F. Women would become soldiers if there was another war.

   G. Female workers were as productive as male workers.

   H. Many men would lose their jobs to women.

   J. Women would have a difficult time keeping their jobs or getting new jobs once men returned from war.

Refer back to the text. If the question refers you to a specific part of the passage, reread that section.

5 **In the fourth paragraph, the word *rationing* means:**

A. limiting how much of a resource people can buy.

B. replacing one material with another that is less in demand.

C. making people wait in long lines to get their goods.

D. producing only goods needed for the war effort.

6 **The main idea of the section "The War's Impact on Women" is that:**

F. the war did not affect women very much.

G. people finally recognized women as heroes.

H. women played an important role in the war.

J. during the war, women were subjected to great danger.

SAT/ACT

STRATEGIES
FOR THE READING PASSAGE

SAT MODEL

Put it in context. Descriptions or explanations that appear before the passage may provide context for the passage or help you focus your reading by identifying a main idea or asking a question.

DIRECTIONS: Read the following passage. Then answer questions 7 through 9. You may refer to the passage as often as necessary.

The following passage is from President Lincoln's Second Inaugural Address. He delivered the speech on March 4, 1865, while the Civil War was still raging.

Lincoln's Second Inaugural Address

Fellow countrymen: At this second appearing to take the oath of the presidential office, there is less occasion for an extended address than there was at the first. Then a statement, somewhat in detail, of a course to be pursued, seemed fitting and proper. Now, at the expiration of four years,
5 during which public declarations have been constantly called forth on every point and phase of the great contest which still absorbs the attention and engrosses the energies of the nation, little that is new could be presented. The progress of our arms, upon which all else chiefly depends, is as well known to the public as to myself; and it is, I trust, reasonably satisfactory
10 and encouraging to all. With high hope for the future, no prediction in regard to it is ventured.

On the occasion corresponding to this four years ago, all thoughts were anxiously directed to an impending civil war. All dreaded it—all sought to avert it. While the inaugural address was being delivered from this place,
15 devoted altogether to saving the Union without war, insurgent agents were in the city seeking to destroy it without war—seeking to dissolve the Union, and divide effects, by negotiation. Both parties deprecated war; but one of them would make war rather than let the nation survive; and the other would accept war rather than let it perish. And the war came.

Recognize sequence of events. Notice tense, past or present, and words that identify time to help you understand the sequence of events.

Now answer questions 7 through 9 on a separate sheet of paper. Base your answers on the excerpt from Lincoln's *Second Inaugural Address*.

7 **What was the purpose of Lincoln's previous inaugural address?**
(A) to avert war while saving the Union
(B) to arouse the nation's continued support for war
(C) to gain support for war to save the Union
(D) to highlight the dangers the nation had faced during the war
(E) to restate that war was not an option

8 **In line 16, "deprecated" most nearly means**
(A) denounced
(B) predicted
(C) desired
(D) desisted
(E) predicated

9 **Based on the first paragraph of the speech (lines 1–11), you can infer that**
(A) Lincoln will show how the country has changed.
(B) Lincoln will not talk long because the country is at peace.
(C) Lincoln will summarize the war's past and outline its future.
(D) Lincoln's address will be shorter than his first address.
(E) Lincoln's address will be less hopeful than his first address.

Now turn to page CA78 and see how well you did.

Vocabulary Strategies and Practice

Both the ACT and the SAT test your vocabulary.

In the ACT, vocabulary is covered in the Reading Test. You are asked to determine the meaning of words in context.

The SAT asks you to find the meaning of words in context in the passage-based reading questions. Sentence-completion questions also test your word knowledge.

BUILDING YOUR VOCABULARY SKILLS

- **Use a dictionary.** When you read or write, have a dictionary handy and be sure to look up any unfamiliar words.

- **Keep a word list.** Write down any words and their definitions that you are learning. Although neither test is a rote test of vocabulary, it does make sense to expand your vocabulary.

- **Read and write often.** Both skills improve your vocabulary. Make the effort to use precise language whenever you write.

- **Review the Vocabulary and Spelling Handbook.** Pages R72–R79 provide a handy reference along with the many helpful strategies and tips. Also review the glossaries on pages R104–R138.

WHEN YOU ANSWER QUESTIONS

- **Use context clues.** Other words in the sentence or passage can help you figure out unfamiliar words.

- **Break unfamiliar words into parts.** Even if you have not seen a certain word before, you may recognize a prefix, suffix, or a root within it. This can help you eliminate some answers.

VOCABULARY PRACTICE

Choose the response that best completes each sentence.

1. Discovering the secluded beach was _____; if we hadn't taken a wrong turn we never would have found it.
   (A) treacherous   (B) serendipitous   (C) spontaneous   (D) isolated
   (E) auspicious

2. The careful investigators _____ examined the scene for _____ pieces of evidence.
   (A) doggedly . . . superfluous   (B) scrupulously . . . obvious
   (C) scurrilously . . . anticipated   (D) perfunctorily . . . essential
   (E) meticulously . . . minute

Grammar, Usage, and Style Tips and Strategies

The English Test on the ACT and the multiple-choice part of the writing section on the SAT cover grammar, usage, and style issues.

BUILDING YOUR GRAMMAR SKILLS

- **Look for ways to improve your grammar and usage.** Ask your teacher for helpful books and other resources. When you take a practice SAT or ACT test, read any explanations provided, even if you answered correctly.

- **Read and write often.** Both activities improve your grammar skills. For example, offer to proofread a friend's paper and ask him or her to proofread yours. When you read a newspaper or magazine, be on the lookout for errors—and for proper grammar, usage, and style.

- **Review the Grammar Handbook.** Pages R50–R71 provide a handy reference along with many helpful tips.

WHEN YOU ANSWER QUESTIONS

- **Know the answer format for each test.** Both tests may include answer choices that indicate the item in question is correct. On SAT multiple-choice questions for the writing section, choice A repeats the original phrasing. (Other SAT section questions include "No error" as choice E.) On the ACT, many questions have "NO CHANGE" as the first choice.

- **Use grammar clues.** For fill-in-the-blank items, choose answers that match the verb tense and pronouns used in the rest of the sentence. For example, if you are asked to complete the sentence, "Tomorrow he _____ the achievement award," you would choose *will accept,* not *accepted* or *accepting*.

- **Try to formulate an answer as you read.** If you are asked to choose the best version of a sentence or a new part of a sentence, think about how you would write the sentence before looking at the choices. Then look for a sentence similar to your answer.

- **Choose the best answer.** If more than one answer seems right, choose the answer that seems clearest to you.

ACT English Test Practice

On the ACT, you will be asked to read certain passages and find errors in underlined sections. Remember that some underlined sections will not have errors. You will have a choice of "NO CHANGE" for sections that are correct as written.

You will also be asked general questions about each passage's purpose and organization. These questions refer to the passage as a whole, not to any one section.

DIRECTIONS: Read the passage and choose the answer that you think is best.

The Appalachian Trail

> **Notice style and tone.** The answers you choose should fit the style and tone of the passage.

The Appalachian Trail (A.T.) is a marked footpath of a little over 2100 miles connecting Mt. Katahdin in Maine and Springer Mountain in Georgia. The A.T. itself passes through fourteen states.

[1]

Millions of people will have hiked part

[2]

of the A.T. each year. Most of these people hike a small piece of the trail on a day hike or short trip. Section hikers aim to hike the whole trail in pieces over time. Thru-

[3]

hikers make up a very small portion of the people on the trail each year. They attempt to hike from Georgia to Maine, or vice versa, in one season. A complete thru-hike typically takes about five to seven months to complete. In recent years, more people are attempting thru-hikes, but only about

[4]

20% complete the entire trail.

> **Keep reading.** Although each question is based on a specified part of the passage, you may need to read beyond the marked section to decide which answer is correct.

1.
  A. NO CHANGE
  B. Along the way, the path
  C. The A.T. path
  D. Between the two end points, the path

2.
  F. NO CHANGE
  G. will hike
  H. hike
  J. had hiked

3.
  A. NO CHANGE
  B. sections but not in the same year
  C. parts but each part at a different time
  D. little bits and pieces not all at once

4.
  F. NO CHANGE
  G. yet 20% finish
  H. but hardly anybody finishes
  J. and now it's about 20% who complete the trail

Question 5 asks about the passage as a whole.

5. The writer intends to continue the article. Which sentence would make the best transition to talking about the challenges of thru-hiking the A.T.?

A. Care to guess why the numbers are so low?

B. The allure of the trail is great, but the challenges are, too.

C. The low completion rate is indicative of the numerous rigors of the trail.

D. That so few finish isn't surprising given the difficulties of a thru-hike.

Now turn to page CA78 to see how well you did.

SAT Multiple-Choice Writing Practice

The multiple-choice questions in the writing section of the SAT are similar to the questions in the ACT English test in that they assess the same types of skills. However, the SAT includes more variety in the format of questions meant to assess those skills.

In some questions, several parts of a sentence will be underlined. You will be asked to choose the part of the sentence that contains an error. If the sentence is correct, choose "No error."

In another type of question, you will be asked to choose the best wording to replace the underlined section of a sentence.

A third type of question asks you to read a passage. Questions following the passage ask you about sentence structure, word choice, organization, or development of ideas.

IDENTIFYING SENTENCE ERRORS

DIRECTIONS: Select the part of the sentence that contains an error. *If* the sentence is correct, select choice *E*.

1. <u>Until we know</u> the extent of the damage, <u>we can not</u> <u>begun</u> to determine

    when the school <u>will reopen</u>. <u>No error</u>

    A   B   C   D   E

2. The rail-trail committee <u>wants</u> to pave the section of trail from Main

    Street to Cooper Street <u>but,</u> <u>it has been</u> blocked by abutting land owners

    <u>who want</u> to take control of the land and by conservation groups who

    want to protect the wooded area. <u>No error</u>

IMPROVING SENTENCES

DIRECTIONS: Select the best answer from the choices given.

3. **Most people understand the effects of gravity, <u>but without being able to explain how it works.</u>**

    (A) but without being able to explain how it works.
    (B) but are being unable to explain how it works.
    (C) though they can't explain how it works.
    (D) and they can't explain how it works.
    (E) without explaining how it works.

4. **<u>Although many people associate tomatoes with Italian cooking, tomatoes were only introduced to Italy in the sixteenth century.</u>**

    (A) Although many people associate tomatoes with Italian cooking, tomatoes were only introduced to Italy in the sixteenth century.
    (B) Many people associate tomatoes with Italian cooking, while tomatoes were only introduced to Italy in the sixteenth century.
    (C) Although many people associate tomatoes with Italian cooking, they were introduced to Italy in the sixteenth century.
    (D) Although people associate tomatoes with Italian cooking, tomatoes were not becoming introduced to Italy until recently.
    (E) Although tomatoes were only introduced to Italy in the sixteenth century, they are associated with Italian cooking by many people.

IMPROVING PARAGRAPHS

DIRECTIONS: Read the passage and choose the best answer for the questions that follow.

(1) Zora Neale Hurston died with little fanfare in 1960. (2) She died in poverty in a nursing home and was buried in an unmarked grave. (3) About a decade later, her writings were rediscovered. (4) Since the 1970s, her works have grown in popularity, and her works are taught in many high school and college classes in the United States. (5) How did such a change in fortune come about?

5. **Which is the best way to combine sentences 1 and 2?**
- **(A)** Zora Neale Hurston died with little fanfare in 1960. She died in poverty in a nursing home and was buried in an unmarked grave.
- **(B)** Zora Neale Hurston died with little fanfare in 1960 and in poverty in a nursing home and was buried in an unmarked grave.
- **(C)** In 1960, Zora Neale Hurston died and was buried in an unmarked grave.
- **(D)** Zora Neale Hurston died with little fanfare in 1960, and she died in poverty in a nursing home and was buried in an unmarked grave.
- **(E)** In poverty and with little fanfare in 1960, Zora Neale Hurston died in a nursing home and was buried in an unmarked grave.

6. **Which of the following would be the best information to provide in the next paragraph of this essay?**
- **(A)** more information about Hurston's death
- **(B)** the cause of Hurston's death
- **(C)** details about Hurston's early life
- **(D)** information about Hurston's success
- **(E)** how Hurston gained, lost and regained popularity

Now turn to pages CA78–CA79 to see how well you did.

Taking Essay Tests

Essay tests assess your ability to develop a point of view on a topic and to write about it in a clear, logical manner. The SAT includes an essay test. The ACT includes the option of taking an essay test. Knowing how to write an essay in a limited amount of time will help you on future tests and in many classes.

Essay tests are usually timed. For the SAT, you will have 25 minutes to write your essay. For the ACT, you will have 30 minutes. Because time is short, you will need to manage your time carefully to complete your essay. The following writing plan will help.

PREWRITING

Spend about 5 minutes thinking through your essay.

- Read the prompt carefully and restate it in your own words.

- Brainstorm ideas first, then identify the position you will take.

- Note reasons and examples you will use to support your position.

- Think of any arguments for the opposing position that you may want to address.

- Quickly organize your ideas by making a simple outline or by numbering your ideas in the order you will use them.

WRITING

Spend about 18-20 minutes writing your essay.

- Create a strong introduction. Consider the purpose and audience for your response. State your position clearly.

- Develop the body of your essay. Add additional paragraphs to explain and support your position. Each paragraph should focus on one idea. Include a strong topic sentence and supporting details for each paragraph.

- Write a closing paragraph that summarizes your ideas or draws a conclusion. Explain why the reader should accept your solution, explanation, or argument.

REVIEWING

Spend your remaining time proofreading your essay.

- Correct errors in grammar, punctuation, and spelling.

- Change wording if you can improve your sentences or paragraphs.

- Make other minor additions or changes that will improve your essay.

Essay Tips and Strategies

Good essays have a clear point of view, use specific details and examples to support a position, are well-organized, use correct and varied sentences, use precise and varied vocabulary, and are generally free of errors in grammar, usage, and mechanics.

Use these strategies to help you write a successful essay.

- **Follow directions.** Read the directions carefully. Find out whether you are allowed to use scrap paper or your test book to write down ideas. Follow directions about where to write your essay and how long it should be.

- **Stay on topic.** Read the writing prompt carefully. Make sure you understand what you are being asked to take a position on. Essays written off-topic generally do not score well. For the SAT, essays written off-topic receive a score of 0.

- **Choose a specific viewpoint.** Many essays ask you to take a clear stand on a topic. State your position in your introductory paragraph. Make sure all examples and reasons are related to your point of view.

- **Be precise.** Avoid generalities. Use specific statistics, information, or examples. For example, instead of writing "Everyone thinks going to school year-round is a bad idea," try writing "The majority of the teachers in our district recently voted against a plan to move to a year-round school schedule."

- **Choose your words carefully.** Use precise and varied words to convey your ideas. You can vary your word choice without using complex words or words that you do not know well. It is better to use simple but precise words you know instead of complicated language that does not express your meaning.

- **Write neatly.** Readers need to be able to understand your handwriting to score your essay. Write as legibly as possible. If you need to correct an error or make a change, use a single, clear line to cross out anything you want to delete. Write "new text" clearly in the margin or above where the change should be inserted. Follow any specific instructions given on the test for making corrections.

Building Your Writing Skills

The more you write, the better prepared you will be for writing a timed essay on the SAT or ACT. Take advantage of writing opportunities at school and in your community. For example, most essay tests ask you to explain or defend a position. Writing an editorial or a letter to the editor is good practice in this regard. For a handy writing guide, use the Writing Handbook in this textbook on pages R26–R43. It provides a wealth of information about the writing process and strategies and tips for effective writing.

ACT Essay Model

ACT essay questions include prompts that describe an issue and ask you to write about your perspective. Each prompt provides two perspectives. You can support either perspective or take a different view. The prompt below is typical of an ACT essay question.

> Some schools are adding volunteering to the list of requirements for graduation, saying that volunteering allows students to give back to their communities while gaining hands-on experience in a number of fields. Others claim that there isn't enough time to meet academic requirements even without the volunteering requirement. Do you think volunteering should be a requirement for graduation?
>
> In your essay, take a position on this question. You may write about either one of the two points of view given, or you may take a different point of view. Use specific reasons and examples to support your position.

State your position. The essay opens with a clear statement of the writer's position.

Volunteering should be encouraged, but not required for graduation. While volunteering offers many benefits, it should be done voluntarily and it should not overshadow academic pursuits at school.

Use specific examples. Use specific experiences, information, or other evidence to support generalizations.

Volunteering is a wonderful thing. I feel good about volunteering at the local animal shelter. I've learned about animals and am considering studying to be a veterinarian. I've also used my computer skills to help keep records and my people skills when working with potential pet adopters. I choose to volunteer, because I learn from my experience, not because I have to do it for school.

I already have plenty to do for school. Studying for tests, researching papers, and keeping up with my assigned reading all take time. We currently have enough academic requirements for graduation in math, science, English, social studies, health, and even physical education. We don't need another requirement.

Write a strong conclusion. Restate your position in the last paragraph of your essay.

Students should be able to choose what activities they do outside of school. Most schools make it easy for students to play sports or join clubs. If schools think volunteering is important, they should help students find opportunities. Encourage volunteering, but keep it voluntary. After all, volunteering means giving your time and talents freely. It does not mean being forced to do so.

ACT Essay Practice

Focus on the question. The question at the end of the prompt is the one you must answer in your essay. Make sure every part of your response relates to the question.

Some school administrators support the use of vending machines as a way to generate money for school programs. Other people are concerned that the foods sold in vending machines are unhealthy and submit students to unnecessary marketing. In your opinion, should high schools allow vending machines for student use?

In your essay, take a position on this question. You may write about either of the two points of view given, or take a different point of view. Use specific reasons and examples to support your position.

Be specific. Choose examples and reasons that support your position. Consider using examples and reasons to counter the opposing side of the argument, too.

On your own paper, write an essay in response to the question. You have 30 minutes.

SAT Essay Model

SAT essay questions also ask you to state and support a point of view. The writing prompts contain excerpts and assignments asking you to take a position on the issue. You must write your essay in the allotted space. The prompt below is typical of an SAT essay question.

Be specific. Choose examples and reasons that support your position. Consider using examples and reasons to counter the opposing side of the argument, too.

Modern technology purports to bring us closer together. We can move from place to place with greater ease and speed or send a message instantaneously around the globe with the push of a button. Yet we often fail to communicate with the people right in front of us. We chat on cell phones while our companions wait. We seem to spend more time with the computer than with the ones we love. Technology provides the means to communicate with others, but we still have to make the effort.

Adapted from Roman Urmeev, *The Advancement of Isolation: Personal Technology in the 21st Century*

Assignment: Has modern technology improved communication? Plan and write an essay in which you develop your point of view on this issue. Support your position with reasoning and examples taken from your reading, studies, experiences, or observations.

On your own paper, write an essay in response to the quesion. You have 25 minutes.

Modern technology has definitely improved communication. People can easily communicate with people all over the world whenever it's convenient for them. Before the Internet, email, and cell phones, communication was more difficult, time consuming, and expensive.

Personally, I've found modern technology makes my life easier. I can call friends from anywhere, anytime with my cell phone. My phone also allows my friends to get in touch with me. My mom bought me the phone to improve communication. I call her if I'm going to be late, to let her know when I've arrived where I said I was going, or to ask for permission to go somewhere. In fact, I often call my mom for a little chat or a quick question. In some ways, I think I talk with my mom more than the average teen did before cell phones.

I also use the computer to communicate. I can send instant messages to friends while doing other work. I can email requests for information during off-hours when I couldn't make a phone call.

Sure, some people misuse our new technology. It is rude to chat on your phone while somebody is standing next to you. It's wrong to spend so much time emailing or messaging that you don't even see your friends or family. Most people I know don't do that, or don't do it too much, anyway.

I think the possible etiquette issues of modern communication technology are far outstripped by the benefits of fast, convenient connections.

Use more than one example. Provide two or three strong examples to support your main idea.

Address counter-arguments. Look at the other side of the issue. In addition to supporting your position, point out weaknesses in the opposing view.

SAT Essay Practice

Be consistent. Make sure you stick to the assigned topic. Essays written on any other topic will receive a score of zero.

Helen Keller said, "Life is either a daring adventure, or nothing.... Security is mostly a superstition. It does not exist in nature."

Assignment: Is it better to live life as an adventure or to seek security? Plan and write an essay in which you develop your point of view on this issue. Support your position with reasoning and examples taken from your reading, studies, experiences, or observations.

Use space wisely. On the SAT, you must use only the space provided for the essay. Write on every line, leave small margins, and make sure your handwriting is legible.

On your own paper, write an essay in response to the question. You have 25 minutes.

ACT/SAT Practice Answer Key with Explanations

Read all the explanations, even those for questions you answered correctly. The explanations include tips that can help you when you take other tests.

READING COMPREHENSION PRACTICE

1. The correct answer is *C*. The main idea of the piece is that the war affected the military and civilians in all aspects of life. Some of the other choices are accurate, but answer *C* is best.

2. The correct answer is *J*. "Governments Control Images of War" is focused by mentioning the role of government and broad enough that it addresses morale and censorship.

3. The correct answer is *B*. Since the factories had been operating before the war, it is logical that they would be converted back to their original functions.

4. The correct answer is *G*. By replacing men, women proved that they could handle any job. If they had not been as productive as male workers, the war effort would have failed.

5. The correct answer is *A*. *B* and *C* are occasional effects of rationing. The next sentence explains what rationing is .

6. The correct answer is *H*. While women were heroes in some cases, the article refers to propaganda selling women as heroes. Women were subjected to dangerous jobs, but that is a detail, not a main idea. The main idea is that women helped their country in a time of need in ways they had not helped before.

7. The correct answer is *A*. Lincoln wanted to save the Union, but he also wanted to avoid war. This idea is most clearly stated in the second paragraph: "While the inaugural address was being delivered from this place, devoted altogether to saving the Union without war...."

8. The correct answer is *A*. Both sides spoke out against, or denounced, war.

9. The correct answer is *D*. Lincoln begins by saying, "At this second appearing to take the oath of the presidential office, there is less occasion for an extended address than there was at the first." He has less to say because people are aware of the state of the country.

VOCABULARY PRACTICE

1. The correct answer is *B*. Answer *D* better describes the beach than the discovery. The other choices are inappropriate.

2. The correct answer is *E*. Answer *C* does not make sense. Answer *D* is incorrect because investigators would not work perfunctorily. The second parts of the other choices do not make sense.

ACT ENGLISH TEST PRACTICE

1. The correct answer is *B*. The pronoun *itself* is unnecessary in the original wording. The word *path* in answer *C* is redundant.

2. The correct answer is *H*. The sentence and rest of the passage require the present tense.

3. The correct answer is *A*. The original wording states the idea most clearly and concisely.

4. The correct answer is *F*. The other choices are either awkward or too informal and imprecise.

5. The correct answer is *D*. Answer *B* conveys the right idea, but answer *D* provides a smoother transition from the previous paragraph.

SAT MULTIPLE-CHOICE WRITING PRACTICE

1. The correct answer is *C*. The verb form is incorrect; it should be *begin*.

2. The correct answer is *B*. The comma should come before the conjunction in this sentence.

3. The correct answer is *C*. Answers *C* and *D* are similar, but answer *C* correctly uses *though* to show a contrast.

4. The correct answer is *A*. The sentence is best as written. In answer *B*, the word *while* does not logically connect the two parts of the

sentence. The antecedent of the pronoun *they* is unclear in answer *C*. The verb form *were not becoming* in answer *D* is incorrect. Answer *E* contains passive language.

5. The correct answer is *A*. Answers *B, D* and *E* have misplaced phrases that make them awkward or confusing. Answer *C* does not provide the necessary context to understand the rest of the passage.

6. The correct answer is *E*. The paragraph asks about the rise of Zora Neal Hurston's popularity after her works were virtually ignored for many years. It makes the most sense to talk about the process of her rediscovery: how she gained initial success, then fell from public notice before being rediscovered, in that order.

ACT ESSAY PRACTICE

Practice Essay Model

In my opinion, vending machines should be allowed in schools. Schools always need money, and if vending machines provide that, why keep them out?

Students benefit from a variety of school programs, like extracurricular activities and field trips. They also benefit from resources such as up-to-date materials in the library. Money from vending machines can help schools provide these resources.

Some people disagree. They think that vending machines give students access to unhealthy foods. One response to this is to stock only healthy foods: water instead of soda, yogurt instead of candy bars. However, if students really want junk food, they will likely bypass the vending machine. Having healthy options is wise, but if the machines are there to generate money, the most popular items must be stocked.

Part of why schools get money is because they are marketing products. Schools may minimize the impact of the marketing by using generic vending machines or restricting the size of logos on the machines. We are bombarded with marketing everywhere else. Is it so terrible to have it in schools, too?

If schools did not get anything from vending machines, I would be less convinced that they belong in schools. Since schools may make thousands of dollars a year off contracts with soft drink and snack companies, I think the benefit is worth the price. For schools concerned with students' health, offering a variety of foods, including healthy options, seems like a fair compromise.

SAT ESSAY PRACTICE

Practice Essay Model

I agree with Helen Keller that "Life is either a daring adventure, or nothing. . . . Security is mostly a superstition. It does not exist in nature." Worrying too much about what might happen to us simply hampers our ability to live life to the fullest.

Taking risks and pushing ourselves beyond our limits is what makes us grow. For example, I'm afraid of heights. This year my soccer team did a ropes course to teach us to work together and stretch beyond what we thought we could do. The last activity involved climbing thirty-five feet to a small platform and crossing a rope bridge to another platform. Looking up I thought, "There's no way can I do this."

If I lived a life of security, I would have dropped out. Instead, I embraced the "daring adventure." The climb seemed to take forever. I stopped once, paralyzed with fear, but my teammates urged me on. The instructor reminded me that I had safety equipment on, so I took a deep breath and kept going. I finally made it across. I was trembling and practically crying when I finished, but I was proud of myself.

As my example shows, being daring doesn't have to mean taking foolish risks. I had safety equipment, but still stepped outside my comfort zone. Going beyond our feelings of security makes life challenging and rewarding.

When I look back on my life, I don't want to regret things I didn't do because I was too scared. At the same time, I don't want my life cut short by a stupid risk. When a risk seems worthy, I may take some steps to protect myself, but I will continue to take risks and enjoy the adventure of my life.

Exploring American Literature

INTRODUCING
THE ESSENTIALS

- Literary Essentials Workshop
- Writing Essentials Workshop

IN CONGRESS, JULY

A DECLARAT

BY THE REPRESENTATIVES of

UNITED STATES OF AM

IN GENERAL CONGRESS ASSE

WHEN in the Course of human Events, it becomes neceſſary for one People to diſſolve the Polit
with another, and to aſſume among the Powers of the Earth, the ſeparate and equal Station to
Nature's God entitle them, a decent Reſpect to the Opinions of Mankind requires that they ſhould
to the Separation.

We hold theſe Truths to be ſelf-evident, that all Men are created equal, that they are e
unalienable Rights, that among theſe are Life, Liberty, and the Purſuit of Happineſs—That to
inſtituted among Men, deriving their juſt Powers from the Conſent of the Governed, that whenever any Form of Go
Ends, it is the Right of the People to alter or to aboliſh it, and to inſtitute new Government, laying its Foundati
its Powers in ſuch Form, as to them ſhall ſeem moſt likely to effect their Safety and Happineſs. Prudence, indeed, w
eſtabliſhed ſhould not be changed for light and tranſient Cauſes; and accordingly all Experience hath ſhewn, that Mank
Evils are ſufferable, than to right themſelves by aboliſhing the Forms to which they are accuſtomed. But when a long T
ing invariably the ſame Object, evinces a Deſign to reduce them under abſolute Deſpotiſm, it is their Right, it is their D
and to provide new Guards for their future Security. Such has been the patient Sufferance of theſe Colonies; and ſuch
them to alter their former Syſtems of Government. The Hiſtory of the preſent King of Great-Britain is a Hiſtory of
having in direct Object the Eſtabliſhment of an abſolute Tyranny over theſe States. To prove this, let Facts be ſubmitted t
He has refuſed his Aſſent to Laws, the moſt wholeſome and neceſſary for the public Good.

For help using this Introductory Unit, see

R RESOURCE MANAGER—Introductory Unit
　　p. 1

About the Art The images on this spread are, clockwise from right, a photograph of civil rights activist Martin Luther King Jr. (see page 1147); a still from director Nicholas Hytner's 1996 film adaptation of Arthur Miller's *The Crucible*, with Winona Ryder and Daniel Day-Lewis (see page 149); an excerpt from the Declaration of Independence, July 4, 1776; a collage of American citizens by Jane Sterrett; poet Emily Dickinson (see page 524); *Kindred Spirits*, 1849, a painting by Asher Durand (see page 300).

Insights and Perspectives

The introductory unit provides an overview of the major movements in American literature, essential strategies for literary criticism, and the writing process that students will study in later units.

Begin by reading aloud the introduction, **Insights and Perspectives.** Then read aloud the topics on pages 2 and 3 and the paragraphs that follow them. Use these notes to prompt exploration of the ideas.

Explore BIG IDEAS

Challenge students to give examples of "the American dream." Who seems to be achieving the American dream in today's generations? In what ways? Encourage students to cite examples of the ways in which previous generations of Americans sought out the dream.

Build CULTURAL LITERACY

Call on volunteers to answer the two questions in the paragraph. Supplement students' ideas with this information:

- Mark Twain, born Samuel Clemens in 1835, secured his place as a great American novelist with works such as *The Adventures of Tom Sawyer* and *The Adventures of Huckleberry Finn.*

- The witch trials of 1692 in Salem, Massachusetts, comprise the setting of *The Crucible,* a 1953 play by Arthur Miller. The drama can be considered a work of courage because it warns against mass hysteria and injustice, issues that Miller himself had to confront during the McCarthy era.

About the Art *The Mayflower in Plymouth Harbor* (1882), oil painting by William Formby Halsall (see page 18); photograph of author Mark Twain (see page 634).

Insights and Perspectives

America's literature comes from all of us and belongs to everyone. It began with the lore of the Native Americans, then appeared in the journals of settlers, the letters of Civil War soldiers, and the tales of Mark Twain. Fast forward another century, and it lives in the books of John Steinbeck and shines from the poems of Gwendolyn Brooks.

Why does American literature matter? Not only does it keep us connected to the past, but it also gives us insights into the events and issues that challenge the nation today. The literature in this book can help you . . .

Explore BIG IDEAS

Why do we explore new horizons? What is the American dream? Today's generations aren't the first to grapple with questions about freedom, progress, exploration, and injustice. Some ideas and issues are timeless, as you'll discover when you read the dramatic accounts of early explorers and F. Scott Fitzgerald's fiction.

Build CULTURAL LITERACY

There are some questions that all Americans should be able to answer. In the area of American literature, such questions include: Who is Mark Twain? Why was *The Crucible* a work of great courage? By reading American literature, you become aware of the pioneering authors and literary milestones that are a part of the American heritage.

Introductory Unit Resources

 RESOURCE MANAGER
Note Taking pp. 2–4

BEST PRACTICES TOOLKIT
Graphic Organizers/Strategies
Venn Diagram • Y Chart • Cluster Diagram

Technology
ℹ ClassZone.com

Connect HISTORY and Literature

Whether it's the Gettysburg Address or the poetry of the Harlem Renaissance, all works of American literature are products of the events and ideas that inspired their authors. By examining history and literature together, you can gain a deeper understanding of how the country changed over the centuries, and what makes its people unique.

Appreciate a LEGACY

Trailblazers in their times, Margaret Fuller and Martin Luther King Jr. fought for equal rights—a fight that still continues. Learning about the great writers, thinkers, and ideas of the past helps you better appreciate how we all continue to build on what we learned from them.

OBJECTIVES

- understand the interrelation of major literary movements with historical events and developments
- identify critical lenses for focusing on literature
- review the use of primary sources

Literature in Context

The timeline on pages 4 and 5 provides a chronological overview of the literary movements the students will be studying this year.

Read aloud the introductory paragraph. Ask students to suggest ways in which recent or modern events have shaped contemporary literature. For example, how has the Internet influenced literary forms? Has technology been the subject of recent literary works that students have read? What major events do they think may affect the attitudes of contemporary writers?

READING SKILL

READ A TIMELINE

Call on volunteers to identify the three horizontal sections of the timeline:

- *Top:* Names, dates, and authors of major U.S. literary movements
- *Middle:* Picture of a representative person, place, or event in the time period
- *Bottom:* Key historical events that occurred during the same periods as the literary movements

Explain that by scanning down the vertical columns of the timeline, students can see the major authors and events of any single period.

Literary Essentials Workshop

Literature in Context

The growth of the Internet, the discovery of a new medical treatment, a declaration of war, a decision of the Supreme Court—consider how events like these affect your attitudes, your outlook, your politics. They shape the attitudes of writers, as well, who then express their ideas in stories, poems, speeches, blogs, and public documents. In the same way, the writing of every time period reflects its unique historical context. By reading it, you can transport yourself back through time and gain perspective on people and events you could never otherwise experience.

LITERARY MOVEMENTS IN CONTEXT

NATIVE AMERICAN EXPERIENCE 1200 B.C.–1600	PURITAN AGE/ COLONIAL PERIOD 1600–1700	REVOLUTIONARY PERIOD/AGE OF REASON 1750–1800	ROMANTICISM/ AMERICAN GOTHIC 1800–1855	TRANSCENDENTALISM 1840–1860
• Sioux • Okanogan • Iroquois • Kiowa	• William Bradford • Anne Bradstreet • Edward Taylor	• Ben Franklin • Thomas Jefferson • Thomas Paine	• Henry Wadsworth Longfellow • Edgar Allan Poe	• Ralph Waldo Emerson • Henry David Thoreau • Margaret Fuller

1200 B.C.–1600 Native American cultures flourish. **1492** Christopher Columbus lands in the Bahamas.	**1607** British settlers establish colony in Jamestown, Virginia. **1692** Witch trials take place in Salem, Massachussetts.	**1776** American colonies declare independence. **1788** U.S. Constitution is ratified.	**1803** Louisiana Purchase doubles the country's size. **1808** United States bans slave trade. **1812** War of 1812 spurs Industrial Revolution.	**1846** Mexican-American War begins. **1848** Gold discoveries in California lead to first gold rush. **1857** Supreme Court's Dred Scott decision denies slaves basic rights.

DIFFERENTIATED INSTRUCTION

FOR STRATEGIC READERS

Understanding a Timeline Model reading the timeline by using the column *Modernism.* Run your finger down the column while identifying the information in each row. Then provide student practice by using the third column to elicit information about the Revolutionary period or Age of Reason:

- What literary movement was occurring from 1750 to 1800? *Answer: The Age of Reason*

- What chief American authors expressed their views during this period? *Answer: Ben Franklin, Thomas Jefferson, Thomas Paine*

- What major political event happened in 1788? *Answer: The U.S. Constitution was ratified.*

Literary Movements

Think about how certain types of music reflect the times in which they were written. Some folk songs, for example, can remind listeners of an earlier time of protest. Similarly, the literature of each historical period has a unique flavor. Subject matter, style, form, and attitude all combine to create a **literary movement,** such as **realism** or **regionalism.** While not all writers fit neatly into specific categories, it is still helpful to know the major movements that have defined the nation's literature. By studying these movements in context, you can see not only the overlap between them, but also better appreciate the writers and works from particular time periods.

REALISM 1855–1900	REGIONALISM/ NATURALISM 1870–1910	MODERNISM 1910–1945	HARLEM RENAISSANCE 1920–1930	CONTEMPORARY LITERATURE 1940–PRESENT
• Stephen Crane • Ambrose Bierce	• Mark Twain • Willa Cather • Jack London	• T. S. Eliot • Ernest Hemingway • Ezra Pound	• Langston Hughes • Zora Neale Hurston • Countee Cullen	• Kurt Vonnegut Jr. • John Steinbeck • Rita Dove • Amy Tan
1861–1865 North and South fight in Civil War. **1865** 13th Amendment abolishes slavery. **1879** Thomas Edison invents the light bulb.	**1889** Oklahoma is opened for settlement, triggering a land rush. **1903** Wright brothers achieve first airplane flight.	**1917** United States enters World War I. **1920** 19th Amendment is passed, giving women the right to vote.	**1919** Race riots erupt in 25 American cities. **1929** The Wall Street stock market crashes and the Great Depression begins.	**1941** Japanese bomb Pearl Harbor, bringing United States into World War II. **1965** U.S. combat troops enter Vietnam War. **2001** Terrorists attack World Trade Center and Pentagon.

FOR STRATEGIC READERS

Note Taking For students who need help with note-taking, hand out the copy master. After discussing **Literary Movements** with students, have them complete the copy master. Follow this procedure for the sections of the Literary Essentials Workshop beginning on pages 6 and 9.

RESOURCE MANAGER—Copy Master
Note Taking p. 2

Literary Movements

Read aloud and discuss the paragraph on page 5. Then suggest a song that was widely popular five or more years ago, and invite a volunteer to sing a few bars. Brainstorm with students what memories the song inspires. Can they recall what was happening in the nation or the world at large at that time? Was the mood of the times reflected in the music? Encourage volunteers to provide other examples of how art is influenced by political and social events of the time.

QUESTIONS

Ask students to study the literary timeline to answer these questions:

1. Who were key authors of the Harlem Renaissance? ***Answer:*** *Langston Hughes, Zora Neale Hurston, Countee Cullen*

2. Did major literary movements overlap one another? Give examples. ***Possible answer:*** *Yes. Examples of overlapping movements are romanticism (1800–1855) and transcendentalism (1840–1860), and transcendentalism and realism (1855–1900).*

3. What historical events influenced the trend of realism in literature? ***Possible answer:*** *The crisis of the Civil War and the turmoil of its aftermath caused authors to turn their attention to starkly realistic issues. The new Industrial Age that followed Edison's invention of the light bulb also generated a spirit of realism.*

Using Critical Lenses

Determine Readiness Discuss the concepts on the page with students. Then read aloud these observations of literature and ask students to identify what critical lens the writer used to examine the subjects:

- The myth "The World on the Turtle's Back" expresses the respect that the Iroquois have for the balance of nature. (*cultural lens*)

- After reading Edgar Allan Poe's haunting tale "The Masque of the Red Death," one is not surprised to learn that Poe himself experienced a life marked by pain and loss. (*biographical lens*)

- Washington Irving's use of sensory language contributes to the images of darkness and decay in "The Devil and Tom Walker." (*literary lens*)

- The Declaration of Independence, written by Thomas Jefferson in 1776, expressed the ideals of freedom and equality for which the American Revolution was fought. (*historical lens*)

Discuss and Review Divide students into small groups and ask them to select a literary work of their choice or one of these works: a Ray Bradbury science fiction story, a short story by O. Henry, "The Raven" by Edgar Allan Poe, or *The Grapes of Wrath* by John Steinbeck. Ask students to make observations of the literature using at least two different critical lenses. Afterwards, invite each group to share their observations with the class.

Using Critical Lenses

Have you ever looked through a prism or camera lens and seen the world in an entirely new way? Critical lenses, or lenses of the mind, can affect your perception—and your reading—in a similar manner. They allow you to notice details you might otherwise have missed, and can lead you to unexpected insights about a writer and his or her work. Use the following lenses, as well as others you might develop, to see beyond your own personal perspective.

THE LENSES	QUESTIONS TO ASK	
LITERARY LENS The literary lens is the one you're used to using with literature. It focuses your attention on the author's style and on such elements as plot, setting, character, and theme.	• What is unique about this author's style? • How do the plot, characters, and setting help to communicate the author's message? • How are language and imagery used to support the theme?	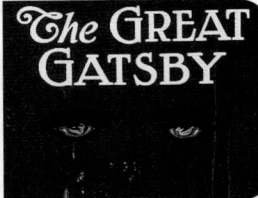
HISTORICAL AND CULTURAL LENSES Historical and cultural lenses force you to consider how elements of history and culture may have influenced the author and the writing.	• What was going on in the country at the time this work was written? • What attitudes, trends, and priorities characterized the times? • How are those events and attitudes, and the author's reactions to them, reflected in the writing?	
BIOGRAPHICAL LENS The biographical lens draws you into the arena of an author's personal life. By considering a writer's heritage, experiences, and economic circumstances, you are able to "read into" a piece of literature with far more insight.	• What were some key events and people in the author's life? • What were his or her social and economic circumstances? • Did culture and heritage play a strong role in shaping the author's attitudes?	
OTHER LENSES • psychological • social • political • philosophical/moral	• What motivations might be influencing a character's behavior? (psychological) • Are the characters' choices, behavior, and actions ethical and honest? (philosophical/moral)	

DIFFERENTIATED INSTRUCTION

FOR ENGLISH LEARNERS

Vocabulary Support Establish the concept of using different lenses for different reasons and outcomes by asking students how the lenses of sunglasses, binoculars, and microscopes change the view of the outside world and why these lenses are used.

MODEL: CRITICAL LENSES

The Great Gatsby is a novel set in the 1920s. World War I had just ended, and the country was embarking on a time of great self-indulgence, eager to forget what it had just experienced. In this scene, the narrator describes an outing with his friendly but mysterious neighbor, Jay Gatsby. Read the passage twice—with and without lenses.

from
The **Great** Gatsby

Novel by **F. Scott Fitzgerald**

At nine o'clock, one morning late in July, Gatsby's gorgeous car lurched up the rocky drive to my door and gave out a burst of melody from its three-noted horn. It was the first time he had called on me, though I had gone to two of his parties, mounted in his hydroplane, and, at his urgent invitation, made
5 frequent use of his beach.

"Good morning, old sport. You're having lunch with me today and I thought we'd ride up together."

He was balancing himself on the running board of his car with that resourcefulness of movement that is so peculiarly American—that comes,
10 I suppose, with the absence of lifting work or rigid sitting in youth and, even more, with the formless grace of our nervous, sporadic games. This quality was continually breaking through his punctilious manner in the shape of restlessness. He was never quite still; there was always a tapping foot somewhere or the impatient opening and closing of a hand.
15 He saw me looking with admiration at his car.

"It's pretty, isn't it, old sport!" He jumped off to give me a better view. "Haven't you ever seen it before?"

I'd seen it. Everybody had seen it. It was a rich cream color, bright with nickel, swollen here and there in its monstrous length with triumphant hat-
20 boxes and supper-boxes and tool-boxes, and terraced with a labyrinth of wind-shields that mirrored a dozen suns. Sitting down behind many layers of glass in a sort of green leather conservatory, we started to town.

I had talked with him perhaps half a dozen times in the past month and found, to my disappointment, that he had little to say. So my first impression,
25 that he was a person of some undefined consequence, had gradually faded and he had become simply the proprietor of an elaborate road-house next door.

And then came that disconcerting ride. We hadn't reached West Egg Village before Gatsby began leaving his elegant sentences unfinished and slapping himself indecisively on the knee of his caramel-colored suit.
30 "Look here, old sport," he broke out surprisingly, "what's your opinion of me, anyhow?"

Close Read

1. **Literary Lens** What do the details in lines 1–5 tell you about Gatsby and his relationship with the narrator?

2. **Cultural Lens** Reread the boxed text. What is the narrator's attitude toward Americans of this time period? What reality might this attitude be reflecting?

3. **Psychological Lens** Private cars were not common in the 1920s. Why might Gatsby not only want to own a car, but also insist on such a luxurious one?

MODEL: CRITICAL LENSES
Close Read
Possible answers:

1. *Lines 1–5 reveal that Gatsby is a wealthy man who enjoys displaying and sharing his status and privilege. The text says, "It was the first time [Gatsby] had called on me," which suggests that Gatsby and the narrator are not close friends. Some readers may infer that Gatsby, in addition to amassing material possessions, may "collect" acquaintances and followers. Perhaps the narrator is one of them.*

2. *The narrator describes Gatsby's "resourcefulness of movement" as a result of leading a carefree, charmed life. The narrator seems to be suggesting that young Americans in this time period have grown up without having had to abide by strict rules or do much hard work. Perhaps this reflects society's attitude toward privileged youth after World War I.*

3. *Gatsby probably wants to own a luxurious car to attract the admiration of friends and acquaintances. For Gatsby, the car may also serve as a status symbol of wealth and privilege. The narrator says, "I'd seen it. Everybody had seen it," which suggests just how much attention the car gets. Perhaps Gatsby is an insecure person who measures his self-worth in material possessions.*

FOR ENGLISH LEARNERS

Vocabulary: Cognates Share or elicit the Spanish cognates for these words. Invite students who speak other Latin-based languages to identify the cognates in their own languages and to share them with other students.

- lens *(lente)*
- psychology *(psicología)*
- cultural *(cultural)*
- literary *(literario)*

Close Read

Possible answers:

4. *Gatsby informs the narrator that he is the son of wealthy people from the Middle West, that his family is dead, and that, like his ancestors, he was educated at Oxford. These "facts" point to the cultural value placed on wealth and education, especially education in prestigious schools.*

5. *Fitzgerald uses these techniques to develop Gatsby as a character who is mysterious, friendly, insecure, impatient, materialistic, and eager to impress:*

- *describes Gatsby's movements and clothing (lines 8–9, 13–14, 28–29)*
- *includes Gatsby's speech and actions (lines 6–7, 34–42)*
- *provides the narrator's reactions to and statements about Gatsby (lines 23–26, 46–47)*

Close Read

Possible answers:

1. *After Fitzgerald achieved success as a writer, he and his wife "embarked on a flamboyant, high-spending life," much like Gatsby's. Fitzgerald's own pursuit of success may have given him insight into a person who is insecure, materialistic, and eager to impress.*

2. *Like Gatsby, Fitzgerald pursued and valued a life of "wealth and privilege." Still, Fitzgerald would probably resist categorizing himself with Gatsby. Gatsby claimed that his wealth was inherited, whereas Fitzgerald earned his own wealth through work, talent, and perseverance. In parts of the excerpt, Fitzgerald takes on a gently amused, slightly mocking tone toward Gatsby's words and actions. The narrator thinks Gatsby has "little to say" and that he is not as well-educated as he claims to be.*

A little overwhelmed, I began the generalized evasions which that question deserves.

"Well, I'm going to tell you something about my life," he interrupted.

35 "I don't want you to get a wrong idea of me from all these stories you hear."

So he was aware of the bizarre accusations that flavored conversation in his halls.

"I'll tell you God's truth." His right hand suddenly ordered divine retribution to stand by. "I am the son of some wealthy people in the

40 Middle West—all dead now. I was brought up in America but educated at Oxford, because all my ancestors have been educated there for many years. It is a family tradition."

He looked at me sideways—and I knew why Jordan Baker had believed he was lying. He hurried the phrase "educated at Oxford," or swallowed it, or

45 choked on it, as though it had bothered him before. And with this doubt, his whole statement fell to pieces, and I wondered if there wasn't something a little sinister about him, after all.

"What part of the Middle West?" I inquired casually.

"San Francisco."

50 "I see."

Close Read

4. Cultural Lens What "facts" about himself and his background does Gatsby provide? What does this tell you about the cultural values of the time?

5. Literary Lens What techniques has Fitzgerald used in this excerpt to create the intriguing character of Jay Gatsby?

Now read the biographical information about F. Scott Fitzgerald and answer the questions. Refer back to the excerpt from *The Great Gatsby* as needed.

F. Scott Fitzgerald

Born in 1896 of southern and Irish heritage, Francis Scott Key Fitzgerald began writing in his early teens. Encouraged by a mentor at school, Fitzgerald pursued

5 his dream of becoming a writer, quickly neglecting his studies in the process. He served in the army during World War I, and convinced he was going to die, dashed off an autobiographical novel. A few years—and

10 several revisions—later, he sold his novel, titled *Tender Is the Night*, and became an overnight success. One week after the novel's publication, Fitzgerald married a southern belle, Zelda Sayre. He and his wife embarked on a flamboyant, high-spending life, although their extravagance and

15 Zelda's illnesses kept Fitzgerald constantly in debt. Fitzgerald died in 1940, impoverished, after spending his lifetime in pursuit of wealth and privilege.

Close Read

1. Biographical Lens How might Fitzgerald's own experiences have influenced his characterization of Gatsby?

2. Biographical Lens What similarities do you see between Fitzgerald's and Gatsby's values? What was Fitzgerald's attitude toward these values? Why do you think so?

Reading American Literature

The varied formats and distinctive language that make American literature unique can also make it a challenge. In addition to applying the reading strategies you've always used, you will need to develop more advanced strategies.

CONSIDER THE CONTEXT

American literature includes not only short stories, novels, essays, and poems, but also a vast array of **primary sources**—historical documents, letters, and journals, for example. To gain the most from all these reading experiences, ask the following questions as you read:

- What is the format? How might this affect the content and language?
- What was the writer's purpose? In what ways might the purpose have affected the writer's choice of details or presentation of ideas?
- Who was the writer's audience? How might it have impacted what was written?
- What was the writer's perspective? Does the work reflect his or her biases or viewpoint?

BASIC READING STRATEGIES
- Preview
- Set a Purpose
- Connect
- Use Prior Knowledge
- Predict
- Visualize
- Monitor
- Make Inferences

SOURCE AND FORMAT	WRITER'S PURPOSE	POSSIBLE PURPOSES FOR READING
Chronicle "Of Plymouth Plantation" (William Bradford)	To record the experiences of Plymouth's first settlers	• To gain a sense of how the settlers lived • To understand the settlers' attitudes toward the Native Americans as well as their biases and beliefs
Speech "To the American Equal Rights Association" (Sojourner Truth)	To make a case for women's rights	• To understand the cultural and social influences affecting African Americans and women • To gain insight into one woman's perspective

LEARN THE LANGUAGE

The literature in this book is presented in the language of its time and place. This language may include words we no longer use; words that have different meanings today; dialect; and unfamiliar sentence constructions, conventions, and style. Use these reminders and strategies to help you break the time barrier:

- Remember that language that sounds dauntingly formal may not always be complicated or serious. These works were written by people just like you, and often express straightforward ideas, and even humor.
- Dialects have their own rules of grammar and pronunciation, which you can figure out from context clues. Read passages aloud until you become more familiar with the words and structure.
- Complex sentence structures are made up of simple parts. Break down difficult sentences, then restate them more simply, rearranging them, if necessary.

DIFFERENTIATED INSTRUCTION

FOR STRATEGIC READERS

Basic Reading Strategies Use these tips to review or model the strategies listed on page 9:

- **Preview** Get the gist of a selection before reading by scanning the title, headings, subheadings, captions, and illustrations.
- **Set a Purpose** Before starting a selection ask, "What is my reason for reading?"
- **Connect** While reading, continually make connections between the text and your personal knowledge and experience.

- **Use Prior Knowledge** Before reading, recall what you know; then compare it with new information as you read.
- **Predict** Make guesses about what happens next to help you understand and remember.
- **Visualize** Look for sensory details that help you "see" the characters and action.
- **Monitor** While you read, ask yourself if you're "getting it." If not, you can reread, read ahead, or ask for help.
- **Make Inferences** Use text clues to figure out things that the writer does not state.

Reading American Literature

CONSIDER THE CONTEXT

Read aloud the introduction at the top of the page. Then call on volunteers to read the instruction and examples of **Consider the Context.** Provide practice by asking students to apply the bulleted questions to one or two commonly known works, such as the Declaration of Independence or a sports article from the local newspaper.

LEARN THE LANGUAGE

Ask students to translate these difficult passages into their own words:

- **"Formal" Language** (page 264, from *The Autobiography* by Benjamin Franklin, lines 1–2)

    It was about this time I conceived the bold and arduous project of arriving at moral perfection.

- **Dialect** (page 1043, "The Life You Save May Be Your Own" by Flannery O'Connor, lines 333–335)

    "My mother was a angel of Gawd," Mr. Shiftlet said in a very strained voice. "He took her from heaven and giver to me and I left her." His eyes were instantly clouded over with a mist of tears.

- **Complex Sentence Structures** (page 230, "Speech in the Virginia Convention" by Patrick Henry, lines 56–60)

    "If we wish to be free—if we mean to preserve inviolate those inestimable privileges for which we have been so long contending—if we mean not basely to abandon the noble struggle in which we have been so long engaged, and which we have pledged ourselves never to abandon until the glorious object of our contest shall be obtained, we must fight!"

CHECK UNDERSTANDING

Have students define *primary source* in their own words. Then ask them to give an example of a primary source they have read.

OBJECTIVES

- identify thinking skills that contribute to effective writing
- understand steps in the writing process
- become familiar with the key traits of effective writing

Focus on Thinking Skills

Read aloud the introductory paragraph and discuss the **Thinking Skill** chart with students. Suggest that many writers find that thinking skills are enhanced by the use of graphic organizers. Explore with students how they might visually represent the thinking skills of **comparison, analysis, synthesis,** and **evaluation.** For example, a Venn Diagram or Y Chart can help writers organize their thinking about the similarities and differences of two or more subjects. A Cluster Diagram can effectively display the parts of an analysis.

BEST PRACTICES TOOLKIT—Transparencies
Venn Diagram p. A26
Y Chart p. A27
Cluster Diagram p. B18

Writing Essentials Workshop

Critical Thinking and Writing

Good writing is much more than a process of gathering and organizing information. It is also a powerful tool—a way of clarifying concepts, exploring opinions, and adding something new to the world of ideas. That is what every writer represented in this book knew, and it's what you can discover as well. It's time to begin seriously analyzing and honing your thinking, then challenging yourself to express your thoughts in increasingly sophisticated ways.

Focus on Thinking Skills

Author Ambrose Bierce once said, "Good writing is clear thinking made visible." In other words, before you can write well, you have to think well. By challenging yourself to higher levels of thinking, you can give your writing increased depth and sophistication.

THINKING SKILL	HOW TO APPLY IT	
COMPARISON Juxtaposing ideas and weighing their similarities and differences	• How does realism differ from romanticism? • How did Martin Luther King Jr.'s protest strategies differ from Malcolm X's?	
ANALYSIS Breaking down subjects and examining their component parts	• What makes E.E. Cummings's style unique? • What characteristics make Nathaniel Hawthorne's *The Scarlet Letter* an American Gothic novel?	**anyone lived in a pretty how town** E. E. Cummings
SYNTHESIS Drawing from ideas in multiple sources to answer a question or arrive at a conclusion	• What messages do an Iroquois myth and Okanogan folk tale have for teenagers in the 21st century? • How do the unique cultural experiences of authors like César Chávez and Amy Tan contribute to American literature?	
EVALUATION Using established criteria to make judgments about subjects or ideas	• Does Stephen Crane create a realistic portrayal of war in *The Red Badge of Courage*? • How effective is the movie *The Crucible* at recreating Arthur Miller's drama?	

10 EXPLORING AMERICAN LITERATURE

DIFFERENTIATED INSTRUCTION

FOR STRATEGIC READERS

Note Taking Use the Writing Essentials Workshop to introduce students to thinking skills that contribute to effective writing, graphic organizers that facilitate this thinking, and steps in the writing process. If students need help in note taking, hand out the copy master for them to complete.

 RESOURCE MANAGER—Copy Masters
Note Taking pp. 3–4

FOR ENGLISH LEARNERS

Language: Skill Words Discuss the meanings of these terms from the chart:

- *comparison:* the process of examining two or more things to see how they are alike and how they are different
- *analysis:* the breaking down of a subject into parts
- *synthesis:* the combining of different ideas to come up with a new, unified whole
- *evaluation:* the act of thinking something over in order to judge its importance or value

The Writing Process

As you complete the **Writing Workshops** in this book, you'll follow the process that suits your own working style. Use this model as a starting point.

What To Do	What It Looks Like
1. Analyze the prompt. Underline key words that indicate the content, format, audience, and purpose of your writing. If you are developing your own topic, make sure your goals are both clear and challenging.	**WRITING PROMPT** Society has viewed and treated women differently from men throughout history. Write <u>an essay analyzing how two women from different centuries or cultures have responded to these biased social attitudes</u> in their works. *I will be writing an essay analyzing works of two women. Since the audience isn't specified, I assume I'm writing for my teacher and classmates.*
2. Choose your subjects. Decide which authors and literary works you want to examine. Consider whether they will provide you with enough material for a rich analysis.	*It would be interesting to explore how Sojourner Truth and Sandra Cisneros responded to social biases. Both women explore issues of equality in "Speech to the American Equal Rights Association" and "Straw into Gold: The Metamorphosis of the Everyday."*
3. Explore what you know. Use a chart or other graphic organizer to explore your key ideas and make sure your subject choices are sound.	**Sojourner Truth**: 18th-century black slave; abused by white owners; not given same freedoms as black men. **Both**: social minorities; defy society's expectations; describe their own lives. **Sandra Cisneros**: 20th-century Latina; left home as an unmarried woman; treated differently from brothers.
4. Develop a thesis. In a sentence or two, state the main point you want to make about the works and their authors. You can use this statement to guide your writing and revise it as you draft so it is clear, specific, and able to be supported.	*Born centuries apart, Sojourner Truth and Sandra Cisneros suffered social discrimination. Sojourner Truth's "Speech to the American Equal Rights Association" and Cisneros's "Straw into Gold" reflect both society's attitudes toward women of their times and the authors' strength in defying those attitudes.*

FOR DEVELOPING WRITERS

Concept Support Draw a flow chart on the board to help students visualize the writing process. Work with students to fill in the chart with key words, definitions, and details.

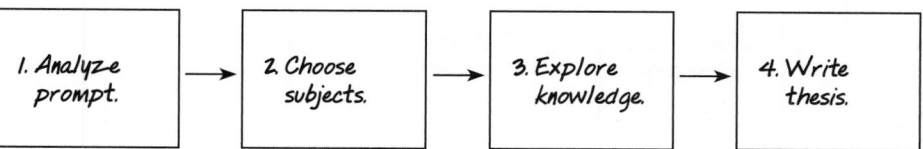

1. Analyze prompt. → 2. Choose subjects. → 3. Explore knowledge. → 4. Write thesis.

The Writing Process

Ask volunteers to read aloud the first four steps in the **Writing Process** and discuss the corresponding example for each step.

1. **Analyze the prompt.** Provide additional practice for students in analyzing a prompt by writing the following prompt on the board, without underlines. Call on volunteers to underline key words and to identify the format, audience, and purpose of the writing suggested by the prompt.

   WRITING PROMPT <u>Compare and contrast</u> literature of the 19th-century antislavery movement with literature of the 1960s civil rights movement. Point out important <u>similarities and differences</u> you see between works by <u>Douglass, Lowell,</u> and <u>Harper</u>, and later works by <u>Moody</u> and <u>Randall.</u>

   Possible answer: I will point out similarities and differences between the literature of two different movements. My audience is my teacher and classmates.

2. **Choose your subjects.** Refer again to the prompt you wrote on the board. Ask students what subjects they would write about. *Possible answer: In this case, the writing prompt clearly specifies the subjects I should write about—Douglass, Lowell, and Harper of the 19th century and Moody and Randall of the 1960s.*

3. **Explore what you know.** Suggest that using a graphic organizer can help students explore and organize their prior knowledge. Ask students to suggest graphic organizers that have proven especially helpful to them.

4. **Develop a thesis.** Review with students that a thesis statement is a sentence that explains what a paper will be about. Explain that a thesis statement can guide their research and help them sort out relevant and irrelevant information on their topic.

Have volunteers read aloud steps 5–8 and corresponding examples. Use these questions to prompt discussion of students' own experiences with the writing process:

5. **Gather evidence.** How do you organize the quotations and details you cite from a piece so that you can clearly and accurately document them in your writing?

6. **Plan your structure.** What methods have you found helpful for planning and organizing your writing? Do you prefer to work from an outline or a graphic organizer? Explain.

7. **Create a draft.** Do you work through a draft in one sitting? While drafting, do you stop and correct errors? What traps have you found helpful to avoid during this stage of the writing process?

8. **Revise your writing.** Do you find a peer reader helpful? Explain. How do you decide that your writing is ready to turn in, send out, or publish?

What To Do	What It Looks Like	
5. Gather evidence. Find evidence from the works to support your statements. Choose strong quotations and details and clearly explain how they illustrate your ideas.	*Sojourner Truth's speech* "I have been forty years a slave and forty years free, and would be here forty years more to have equal rights for all."	*"Straw into Gold"* "I've managed to do a lot of things ... which many others didn't think I was capable of either. Especially because I am a woman, a Latina ..."
6. Plan your structure. Make an informal outline to help you organize your ideas. Consider beginning—or ending—with your most important point, and make sure there is a logical progression in your presentation. You might want to try several structures and decide which works best.	*Introduction* *Historical background (Sojourner Truth, Sandra Cisneros)* *Message (Sojourner Truth, Sandra Cisneros)* *Style of communication (Sojourner Truth, Sandra Cisneros)* *Conclusion (changing attitudes toward women)*	
7. Create a draft. Get your ideas down on paper, following the structure you have outlined. As you draft, **cite evidence** that supports your ideas. Feel free to alter your approach as your ideas develop. You'll eventually want to hook readers with a strong beginning, but don't worry about getting it perfect at this point.	*Sojourner Truth was a slave born at the end of the 18th century; Sandra Cisneros is a mid-20th-century Latina. Although worlds apart, both women defied discrimination and documented their struggles in their works.*	
8. Revise your writing. Read your draft critically, and enlist the help of a peer reader. Consider these questions: • How clearly have I expressed my ideas? • Is my structure logical? • Do my examples support my points? • Have I added new insights and drawn conclusions? • Do I have an engaging introduction and a solid conclusion? Make necessary changes and proofread the final product.	*Sojourner Truth dealt with ongoing oppression as a black woman, as reflected in her statement, "so much good luck to have slavery partly destroyed; not entirely."* *How does the quote show her oppression?* *Good question. I'll substitute this quote instead: "I have done a great deal of work; as much as a man, but did not get so much pay."*	

DIFFERENTIATED INSTRUCTION

FOR DEVELOPING WRITERS

Concept Support Work with students to complete steps 5–8 of their writing process charts.

5. Gather evidence. → 6. Plan structure. → 7. Create draft. → 8. Revise writing.

Analyze a Student Model

Read the beginning of one student's essay, noting the comments in the margins.

Sruba Desai
Randolph High School

Similar Struggles, Different Worlds

What could Sojourner Truth, a slave born at the end of the 18th century, and Sandra Cisneros, a mid-20th-century Latina, have in common? Although their heritage and times were strikingly different, both women faced discrimination and described their experiences in their works. Comparing

5   their lives and messages shows both the social inequality women have had to face throughout history and the way strong individuals can rise above it.

Sojourner Truth was born in New York more than 60 years before the Emancipation Proclamation freed the slaves. Although she ran away to freedom decades earlier, she still suffered under the unequal treatment afforded

10 American blacks, especially black women. She summarized this history in her 1867 "Speech to the American Equal Rights Association": "I have been forty years a slave and forty years free, and would be here forty years more to have equal rights for all. I suppose I am kept here because something remains for me to do; I suppose I am yet to help to break the chain."

15 Sojourner Truth did help break that chain of inequality; and a century and a half later, Sandra Cisneros was born into an America in which women had continued struggling for and finally earned the right to vote. Like Sojourner Truth, Cisneros grew up in poverty, but she also straddled two cultures—Mexican and American—moving back and forth between

20 the two and not belonging fully to either. Despite social advances for women, she experienced biased attitudes similar to those Sojourner Truth faced. She explains these in her essay "Straw into Gold: The Metamorphosis of the Everyday": "In our culture men and women don't leave their father's house except by way of marriage. I crossed my father's threshold with

25 nothing carrying me but my own two feet. . . . To make matters worse, I left before any of my six brothers had ventured away from home. I broke a terrible taboo."

KEY TRAITS IN ACTION

Hooks readers with an intriguing question and states the **thesis** clearly and concisely.

Supports the main idea about the time in which Sojourner Truth lived with a strong **quotation** from her speech.

Includes cultural and biographical information about Cisneros that clearly shows the influences on her as a writer.

A quotation from Cisneros's work provides **evidence** to illustrate the biographical information.

Exhibits a logical **structure,** discussing one writer's life and times and then the other's.

INTRODUCING THE ESSENTIALS   **13**

Analyze a Student Model

Call attention to the *KEY TRAITS IN ACTION* in the side column of the essay. Review with students the six key traits that are important characteristics of any piece of writing: ideas, organization, voice, word choice, sentence fluency, and conventions.

Read aloud the student model. Then invite students to examine it more closely by providing these discussion prompts:

- Restate the first sentence as a declarative sentence. Which version is a more interesting hook? Why? *Possible answer: A question is a more interesting hook because it gets readers thinking through their own ideas about the topic.*

- What main idea is supported by the quotation from Sojourner Truth in lines 11–14? *Possible answer: Sojourner Truth lived during a time of strong discrimination against African Americans.*

- What cultural and biographical details does the writer provide that help the reader understand Cisneros? *Possible answer: She grew up in poverty (line 18); she "experienced biased attitudes" because she was bicultural (line 21).*

- What does Cisneros compare in her quotation, lines 23–27? *Possible answer: She compares the different treatments of men and women in Mexican culture when she says that she "broke a terrible taboo" by leaving home before her brothers did.*

DIFFERENTIATED INSTRUCTION

FOR DEVELOPING WRITERS

Concept Support: Organization Help clarify the organization of the essay by supplying students with this graphic organizer. Call attention to the first sentence in the third paragraph of the essay. Note that because the sentence mentions both Sojourner Truth and Sandra Cisneros, it acts as a transition between the two subjects.

1st paragraph
States the thesis, the main idea of the essay.

↓

2nd paragraph
Tells about the first subject, Sojourner Truth.

↓

3rd paragraph
Tells about the second subject, Sandra Cisneros.

Preview Unit Goals

This page presents an overview of the skills and strategies covered in this unit. Explain to students that they can get more from their reading by previewing. Then ask them to skim the page to preview the skills that they will learn. Note that each strand or category of skill is color-coded on this page and throughout the unit.

Model the strategy of copying the Academic Vocabulary and writing a preliminary definition for each term. Suggest that students use a journal or a notebook for this purpose. Encourage them to use the terms in discussions and in writing. Also urge students to revisit each term throughout the unit and to refine its meaning.

ADDITIONAL UNIT GOALS

These skills will be taught in this unit but are not the major focus of the unit:

Literary Analysis
- Analyze slave narrative, chronicle, sermon, poetry, essay, speech, letter
- Analyze a sermon for purpose, audience, and context

Reading
- Predict and summarize
- Draw conclusions (about characters)
- Analyze main ideas and details
- Make inferences (about author)
- Analyze text structure

Writing and Grammar
- Write to analyze and synthesize
- Add descriptive details
- Use appropriate word choice and sentence structure to create realistic dialogue
- Use a variety of sentence types

Speaking, Listening, and Viewing
- Examine how media influence viewers' perceptions of reality
- Debate
- Deliver an informal speech
- Present an issue and lead a discussion

Vocabulary
- Use a dictionary etymology to understand word origin and history
- Use word connotations
- Use context clues
- Use the Latin roots *nom* and *fic*

CALIFORNIA

Included in this unit: R1.1, R1.2, R2.1, R2.2, R2.4, R2.5, R2.6, R3.1, R3.3, R3.4, R3.5, R3.6, W1.1, W1.2, W1.3, W1.4, W1.7, W1.9, W2.2, W2.3, LC1.1, LS1.1, LS1.3, LS1.5, LS1.7, LS1.10, LS1.14, LS2.3

Preview Unit Goals

LITERARY ANALYSIS	• Analyze the influence of historical context • Identify and analyze cultural characteristics • Analyze figurative language and descriptive details • Identify characteristics of creation myth, folk tale, memoir, historical narrative, drama, and autobiography • Analyze diction and tone
READING	• Develop strategies for reading older texts • Analyze and evaluate elements of an argument • Analyze persuasive techniques and rhetorical devices • Analyze and evaluate primary sources
WRITING AND GRAMMAR	• Write a persuasive speech • Use prepositional phrases and adverb clauses as modifiers • Understand and use compound and compound-complex sentences
SPEAKING, LISTENING, AND VIEWING	• Deliver a persuasive speech • Analyze how media influence cultural values and stereotypes • Evaluate film techniques • Compare a film and a play
VOCABULARY	• Determine the meaning of multiple-meaning words • Understand and use specialized vocabulary
ACADEMIC VOCABULARY	• argument • primary source • persuasion • historical context • rhetorical devices • cultural characteristics

Online LITERATURE
CLASSZONE.COM

Literature and Reading Center
Writing Center
Vocabulary Center

DIFFERENTIATED INSTRUCTION

FOR ENGLISH LEARNERS

Academic Vocabulary Use the copy master to help students learn the Academic Vocabulary.

1. Read aloud each Academic Vocabulary term and have students locate it on their copy masters.

2. Discuss the meaning or example shown on the copy master, and complete the chart as a class.

3. Have students work in small groups to complete the remaining activities.

Additional Academic Vocabulary Use the copy master to help students learn academic words they will use in subsequent lessons and on the Assessment Practice. Follow the same procedure as for the Academic Vocabulary copy master.

 RESOURCE MANAGER—Copy Masters
Academic Vocabulary p. 11
Additional Academic Vocabulary p. 12

Mourning
Dove

Early American Writing

1600–1800
AN EMERGING NATION

- The Native American Experience
- Exploration and the Early Settlers
- The Puritan Tradition
- Writers of the Revolution

15

For help in planning this unit, see

R RESOURCE MANAGER UNIT 1
pp. 1–13

INTRODUCE THE UNIT

Call students' attention to the pictures on this page. Explain that the large picture, *Declaration of Independence,* is a painting by John Trumbull. Tell students that they will be reading the Declaration of Independence later in this unit.

Ask students if they know the writer, Mourning Dove, shown in the smaller picture on the page. Point out that Mourning Dove is the pen name of Christine Quintasket (c. 1888–1936), one of the first female Native American novelists. Explain that Mourning Dove helped to preserve traditional stories of the Okanogan and other Native American cultures. Tell students that they will read her story "Coyote and the Buffalo" in this unit. Also note that students can read more about Mourning Dove on page 42.

About the Art American artist John Trumbull (1756–1843) captured numerous prominent historical figures in his well-known oil painting *Declaration of Independence,* including Thomas Jefferson, John Adams, Benjamin Franklin, and John Hancock. The painting reflects the artist's intention to commemorate the significant historical event and to depict nearly 50 of the men involved in the creation of the Declaration. In actuality, not all of the individuals shown were present at the same time, and 15 men who did sign the Declaration do not appear in the painting.

Unit Resources

PRINT RESOURCES

- **R** RESOURCE MANAGER UNIT 1
- BEST PRACTICES TOOLKIT
- **S** STANDARDS LESSON FILE
- INTERACTIVE READER & WRITER
- CALIFORNIA ASSESSMENT FILE
- GRAMMAR FOR WRITING

TECH RESOURCES

- EasyPlanner DVD-ROM
- Write*Smart* CD-ROM
- ClassZone.com
- Audio Anthology CD
- Multi-Language Academic Vocabulary Online

- eEdition DVD-ROM & Online
- McDougal Littell Assessment System
- Test Generator CD-ROM
- Media*Smart* DVD-ROM
- Literature in Context DVD-ROM

	Unit 1 Introduction pp. 16–31 • Questions of the Times • Historical Essay • Timeline • Legacy of Early America	Literary Analysis Workshops • Historical Narratives pp. 66–67 • American Drama pp. 128–129 • Persuasive Rhetoric pp. 222–223	The World on the Turtle's Back Iroquois Creation Myth pp. 32–41 Lexile: 850 Fry: 6 Dale-Chall: 5.2	Coyote and the Buffalo Folk Tale pp. 42–49 Lexile: 710 Fry: 6/7 Dale-Chall: 5.4	Themes Across Time: from The Way to Rainy Mountain Memoir pp. 50–60 Lexile: 1000 Fry: 8 Dale-Chall: 6.4	Media Study: Changing Views of Native Americans Film Clips pp. 62–65
Literary Analysis	Historical and Cultural Context of Early American Writing pp. 18–29 R3.5 Perspectives of Early American Writing pp. 18–27 R3.5	Characteristics of Historical Narrative p. 66 R3.5 Conventions of Drama pp. 128–129	Creation Myths pp. 33, 34, 37, 40, 41 R3.1, R3.5	Trickster Tales pp. 43, 44, 46, 48, 49 R3.1, R3.6	Memoir pp. 51, 52, 57, 58, 59	
Reading and Informational Texts	Build Context for Reading pp. 16–17 Use Prior Knowledge pp. 16–17 Connect pp. 16–17, 28–29, 30–31 Preview p. T18 Take Notes pp. 19–27 Read a Timeline pp. 28–29	Strategies for Reading Primary Sources pp. 66–67 R3.5 Identify Primary Source pp. 66–67 R3.5 Identify and Analyze Persuasive Techniques and Rhetorical Devices pp. 222–223 R2.1, R2.6 Identify and Analyze Elements of an Argument pp. 222–223 R2.6, LS1.5	Strategies for Reading Folk Literature pp. 33, 36, 38, 39, 41 R3.5	Predict pp. 43, 47, 49	Analyze Structure pp. 51, 54, 56, 59 R2.2	
Vocabulary		Academic Vocabulary pp. 66–67, 128–129, 222–223			Word Acquisition pp. 51, T51, 60 Context Clues p. T51 Specialized Vocabulary (Science) p. 60	Academic Vocabulary (Film and TV) p. 63
Writing, Grammar, and Style						
Speaking, Listening, Viewing, and Media	Discuss pp. 16–17, T18–T31 Analyze Visuals pp. 22, 27	Discuss pp. T66–T67, T128–T129, T222–T223	Discuss pp. T32, 33, T34–T40, 41 Analyze Visuals pp. 34, T39	Discuss pp. T42, 43, T44–T48, 49 Analyze Visuals pp. 44, T47	Discuss pp. T50, 51, T52–T58, 59 Analyze Visuals pp. 52, 57	Discuss pp. 62, 65 Analyze Ways Media Transmits Values and Stereotypes and Influences Viewers' Perceptions pp. 62–65 LS1.1, LS1.14 Create an Image Award p. 65 LS1.3

from **La Relación** Report pp. 68–77	from **The Interesting Narrative of the Life of Olaudah Equiano** Slave Narrative pp. 78–87	from **The General History of Virginia** Historical Narrative pp. 88–97	from **Of Plymouth Plantation** Chronicle pp. 98–108	**To My Dear and Loving Husband/ Upon the Burning of Our House/ Huswifery** Poetry pp. 110–117	from **Sinners in the Hands of an Angry God** Sermon pp. 118–127
Lexile: 1010 *Fry: 10* *Dale-Chall: 6.3*	*Lexile: 1220* *Fry: College* *Dale-Chall: 6.9*	*Lexile: 1680* *Fry: 8* *Dale-Chall: 8.0*	*Lexile: 1370* *Fry: 10* *Dale-Chall: 6.7*		*Lexile: 1210* *Fry: 9* *Dale-Chall: 6.6*
Historical Context pp. 69, 72, 74, 75 R3.5	Slave Narrative pp. 79, 80, 83, 84, 85 R3.1	Narrator pp. 89, 92, 94, 96 R3.3	Cultural Characteristics pp. 99, 100, 103, 105, 107 R2.5	Figurative Language pp. 111, 112, 115, 116,117 R3.4	Sermon pp. 119, 120, 122, 125, 126
Strategies for Reading a Primary Source pp. 69, 70, 73, 75 R3.5	Analyze Details pp. 79, 82, 83, 85 R3.3	Strategies for Reading Older Texts pp. 89, 90, 92, 95, 96	Summarize pp. 99, 102, 106, 107	Clarify Meaning in Older Poetry pp. 111, 112, 114, 115, 116, 117	Identify and Analyze Emotional Appeals pp. 119, 122, 124, 125, 126 R2.6, R3.3
Word Acquisition pp. 69, T69, 76 Context Clues p. T69 Etymologies p. 76	Word Acquisition pp. 79, T79, 86 Context Clues p. T79 Latin Roots (*nom*) p. 86 R1.2	Word Acquisition pp. 89, T89, 97 Context Clues p. T89 Words with Multiple Meanings p. 97	Word Acquisition pp. 99, T99, 108 Context Clues p. T99 Words from French p. 108 R1.1		Word Acquisition pp. 119, T119, 127 Context Clues p. T119 Connotation p. 127
Writing Prompt p. 77 W1.2 Prepositional Phrases as Modifiers pp. 74, 77 W1.9, LC1.1	Writing Prompt p. 87 W1.1 Adverb Clauses as Modifiers pp. 83, 87 W1.9, LC1.1				
Discuss pp. 69, T70–T74, 75 Analyze Visuals p. 70	Discuss pp. T78, 79, T80–T84, 85 Analyze Visuals p. 80	Discuss pp. T88, 89, T90–T95, 96 Analyze Visuals pp. 90, T93	Discuss pp. T98, 99, T100–T106, 107 Analyze Visuals pp. 100, T102, 105	Discuss pp. T110, 111, T112–T116, 117 Analyze Visuals p. 112	Discuss pp. T118, 119, T120–T125, 126 Analyze Visuals pp. 120, T123, T124

UNIT 1
Standards

SKILLS STRAND	*Linked Selections*			*Speech in the Virginia Convention* Speech pp. 224–233	*The Declaration of Independence* Public Document pp. 234–243
	Themes Across Time: The Crucible Drama pp. 130–211	*The Crucible and McCarthyism* Online Article, Newspaper Article, Memoir pp. 212–217	*Media Study: from The Crucible* Film Clip pp. 218–220	Lexile: 990 Fry: 9 Dale-Chall: 7.4	Lexile: 1320 Fry: 12 Dale-Chall: 8.9
Literary Analysis	Conventions of Drama pp. 131, T132, T135, T137, T138, T142, T144, T146, T151, T155, 159, T160, T162, T167, T171, T172, 175, T176, T179, T186, T189, T190, 195, T198, T206, 209			Rhetorical Devices pp. 225, 226, 228, 230, 231 R2.1	Argument pp. 235, 236, 238, 240, 241 R2.4, R2.6
Reading and Informational Texts	Draw Conclusions About Characters pp. 131, T135, T139, T140, T144, T145, T146, T147, T151, T153, 159, T163, T164, T168, 175, T179, T183, T185, T187, T189, 195, T196, T198, T200, T202, T204, 209	Understand Historical Context pp. 212, 213, 214, 215, 216, 217 R3.5 Synthesize p. 217 R3.5, W2.2	Read a Movie Review p. 220	Strategies for Reading a Persuasive Speech pp. 225, 228, 230, 231	Analyze Text Structure pp. 235, 238, 239, 240, 241 R2.1, R2.2
Vocabulary	Word Acquisition pp. 131, T131, 210 Context Clues pp. T131, 210			Word Acquisition pp. 225, T225, 232 Context Clues p. T225 Words from Gods and Mythology p. 232 R1.2	Word Acquisition pp. 235, T235, 242 Context Clues p. T235 Etymology of Specialized Vocabulary (Politics and Government) p. 242 R1.1
Writing, Grammar, and Style	Writing Prompt p. 211 W2.2 Word Choice and Inverted Sentences in Realistic Dialogue pp. T142, T166, T182, T202, 211 LC1.1			Writing Prompt p. 233 W1.1, W1.3, W1.4 Variety in Sentence Types pp. 228, 233 LC1.1	Writing Prompt p. 243 W1.1 Variety in Sentence Structures (Complex and Compound-Complex Sentences) pp. 240, 243 W1.9, LC1.1
Speaking, Listening, Viewing, and Media	Discuss pp. T130, 131, T132–T158, 159, T160–T174, 175, T176–T194, 195, T196–T208, 209 Scene Selection p. 149 Setting and Characters (Staging) p. 193 Analyze Visuals pp. T133, T143, T168, T177, T197	Discuss pp. 212, T213–T216, 217	Discuss pp. 218–219, T220 Compare Dialogue in a Play and a Film p. 219 LS1.14 Evaluate Film Techniques p. 219 LS1.14	Discuss pp. T224, 225, T226–T230, 231 Analyze Visuals pp. 226, T229	Discuss pp. T234, 235, T236–T240, 241 Analyze Visuals pp. 236, T239

Standards Designations R = Reading W = Writing LC = Language Conventions LS = Listening and Speaking T = Teacher's Edition page

from *The Crisis* Essay pp. 244–253	*Letter to the Reverend Samson Occom/Letter to John Adams* Letters pp. 254–261	from *Benjamin Franklin's Autobiography* Autobiography pp. 262–274	*Wrap-Ups* • The Native American Experience p. 61 • Exploration and Early Settlers p. 109 • The Puritan Tradition p. 221 • Writers of the Revolution p. 275	*Writing Workshop: Persuasive Essay* pp. 276–283
Lexile: 1180 Fry: 10 Dale-Chall: 7.5	Lexile: 1230 Fry: 9 Dale-Chall: 7.9	Lexile: 1390 Fry: 8 Dale-Chall: 7.2		
Persuasive Techniques pp. 245, 246, 248, 249, 250, 252 R2.6	Diction pp. 255, 256, 260, 261 R2.2	Characteristics of Autobiography pp. 263, 264, 268, 270, 272		
Analyze Main Ideas and Support pp. 245, 248, 251, 252	Strategies for Reading Primary Sources pp. 255, 256, 258, 260, 261	Make Inferences About the Author pp. 263, 266, 267, 269, 272 R2.5 Review: Connect p. 269 Read Aphorisms p. 271 Read a Magazine Article p. 274		Analyze a Persuasive Essay pp. 277–278, 282
Word Acquisition pp. 245, T245, 253 Context Clues p. T245 Words from Middle English p. 253		Word Acquisition pp. 263, T263, 273 Context Clues p. T263 Latin Roots (*fic*) p. 273 R1.2		
			Write to Synthesize p. 61 R2.5, W2.2 Write to Evaluate p. 109 W2.2 Write to Analyze p. 221 W2.2, W2.3 Write to Persuade p. 275 W2.2, LS2.3	Write a Persuasive Essay pp. 276–282 W1.3, W1.7 Faulty Reasoning pp. 281, 282 Parallel Structure p. 282 W1.4, LC1.1
Discuss pp. T244, 245, T246–T251, 252 Analyze Visuals pp. 246, 249, 251	Discuss pp. T254, 255, T256–T260, 261 Analyze Visuals pp. 256, 258	Discuss pp. T262, 263, T264–T270, T271, 272, T274 Analyze Visuals pp. 264, T270	Discuss Internet Research p. 61 Debate p. 109 Deliver a Speech pp. 221, 275	Discuss pp. 276–278, 282 Present a Persuasive Speech p. 283 LS1.7, LS1.10

Skills Assessed on the Unit 1 Test:

Literary Analysis
- Analyze the influence of historical context
- Identify and analyze rhetorical devices
- Analyze diction

Reading and Informational Texts
- Analyze descriptive details
- Identify and analyze a primary source
- Identify and analyze persuasive techniques
- Identify, analyze, and evaluate elements of an argument

Vocabulary
- Understand and use specialized vocabulary (politics and government)
- Determine the intended meanings of words with multiple meanings

Writing, Grammar, and Style
- Write a persuasive essay
- Use prepositional phrases and adverb clauses as modifiers
- Understand and use complex and compound-complex sentences
- Vary sentence types
- Additional writing and grammar skills

For additional lesson planning help, see **Easy Planner DVD-ROM.**

UNIT 1 *Assessment*

	ASSESS PRIOR KNOWLEDGE Diagnostic	ONGOING ASSESSMENT Reteaching
BEGINNING OF UNIT		
Unit Opener	Preview Unit Goals, **TE** p. 14	
UNIT LESSONS		
Before every lesson	Big Question activity, **SE** Preteach vocabulary, **TE**	Check Understanding, **TE**
During every lesson		Annotations, **SE** Check Understanding, **TE** Tiered Discussion Prompts, **TE**
After every lesson		Post Reading pages, **SE** Assess and Reteach, **TE** Reading Check, **RM** Selection Tests A and B/C, **AF**
END OF UNIT		
Writing Workshop	Checklist, **SE** p. 282 Rubric for Evaluation, **RM** p. 460	Assess and Reteach, **TE** p. 282
Speaking & Listening	Criteria, **TE** p. 283	For reteaching options, see **TE** p. 283
Assessment	Assessment Practice, **SE** pp. 284–289	Unit Test, **AF** **MLAS**

For systematic instruction of grammar, use *Grammar for Writing*.

Key to Abbreviations:
SE = Student's Edition
TE = Teacher's Edition
RM = Resource Manager
AF = Assessment File
MLAS = McDougal Littell Assessment System

Universal Access

	Strategic Reader	Benchmark	Advanced Learner	English Learner	Students with Disabilities
SE STUDENT'S EDITION					
Vocabulary strategy instruction	✔	✔	✔	✔	✔
Instructional annotations	✔	✔	✔	✔	✔
English/Spanish glossary				✔	
TE TEACHER'S EDITION					
Skill annotation support	✔	✔	✔	✔	✔
Tiered discussion prompts	✔	✔	✔	✔	✔
Differentiated instruction	✔	✔	✔	✔	✔
R RESOURCE MANAGER					
Selection summaries in four languages	✔	✔	✔		✔
Skill copy masters in English and Spanish	✔			✔	
Vocabulary preteaching and support	✔			✔	✔
Additional leveled selection questions	✔	✔	✔	✔	✔
Question support	✔	✔	✔	✔	✔
Writing support	✔	✔	✔	✔	✔
Extension activities		✔	✔		
AF ASSESSMENT FILE					
Leveled selection and unit tests	✔	✔	✔	✔	✔
S STANDARDS LESSON FILE					
Leveled and reteaching copy masters	✔	✔	✔	✔	✔
BEST PRACTICES TOOLKIT					
Strategy bank	✔	✔	✔	✔	✔
Graphic organizers	✔	✔	✔	✔	✔
TECHNOLOGY					
WriteSmart Rubrics and student models	✔	✔	✔	✔	✔
Audio Anthology CD	✔			✔	✔
CLASSZONE					
Instructional centers	✔	✔	✔	✔	✔
Audio summaries of selections	✔			✔	✔
Multilanguage glossary				✔	

Questions of the Times

Read aloud the questions on pages 16 and 17 and the paragraphs that follow them. Open the discussion of each idea by having students respond to the questions that conclude each paragraph. Use these notes to prompt further exploration of the ideas.

Who owns the LAND?

Challenge students to give reasons why one group of people should have more rights to land than another. Discuss whether the argument of "they were here first" is sufficient grounds to merit ownership forever.

What makes an EXPLORER?

Encourage students to suggest additional motivators—both internal and external—that would cause people "to seek out the unknown" despite the various risks of doing so. Extend the discussion by asking what character traits modern-day explorers are likely to share with early explorers.

UNIT

1

Questions of the Times

DISCUSS With your whole class or in small groups, discuss these questions. Keep them in mind as you read the selections in this unit and consider how **Early American Writers** tried to answer them.

Who owns the LAND?

For thousands of years, Native Americans regarded themselves as caretakers, not owners, of the land. The Europeans who began arriving in North America, however, saw things differently. They laid claim to the land and aggressively defended it from Native Americans—and from one another. In the end, the British claim overpowered all others. Yet the question remains: What entitles people to claim land as their own?

What makes an EXPLORER?

America's early explorers traveled for many reasons: to gain glory for themselves or for their countries, to find gold or other riches, to discover new routes for travel and trade. Yet none of these motivators alone seems enough to make the uncertainties of exploration—unknown destinations, unknown rewards, unknown dangers—worth the risk. What is it that causes people to seek out the unknown?

16

Are people basically GOOD?

Puritan settlers believed that human beings were sinful creatures doomed to a fiery eternity unless saved by the grace of God. Yet others who came to North America celebrated the powers of reason and proclaimed the goodness and intrinsic worth of humans. Are people destined always to struggle against their basest instincts? Or are they fundamentally good—and capable of becoming even better?

Who has the right to RULE?

For centuries, European kings and queens had ruled because it was believed that they had a God-given right to do so. But in the Age of Enlightenment, people began to question basic assumptions about government. In America, a popular uprising put a new kind of government to the test: democracy. With this experiment, the young American nation was asking: Who really has the right to rule?

IN CONGRESS, JULY 4, 1776.

A DECLARATION
BY THE REPRESENTATIVES OF THE
UNITED STATES OF AMERICA
IN GENERAL CONGRESS ASSEMBLED.

Are people basically GOOD?

Prompt students to explain which early American group would be more likely to agree with their views—the Puritans or the settlers who celebrated the powers of reason.

Who has the right to RULE?

Have students identify the fundamental differences between a system based on "a God-given right" to rule and a system based on democracy. Challenge students to explain why one system is superior to the other in terms of reflecting the will of the people governed.

- understand the historical and cultural context of early American writing
- understand historical perspectives that make up early American writing
- take notes by charting main ideas and details

 R3.5

To provide a motivating introduction to this unit and to give students a sense of time and place for early American writing, see

 Literature in Context DVD

The following essay (pages 18–27) provides students with a historical context for the Unit 1 reading selections. It presents a brief overview of significant events occurring during the time period, 1600–1800, and introduces key people, places, and ideas of the times.

To get started, read and discuss the opening paragraph on page 18. Call students' attention to the various groups mentioned: explorers, settlers, colonists, revolutionaries. Ask students to review the role that each of these groups played in the creation of "an entirely new country and unique way of life." Discuss the kinds of challenges that early settlers faced, and ask why writers of the time would have wanted to record them.

READING STRATEGY

◼ PREVIEW

Have students preview the historical essay by reading the **KEY IDEAS** and by skimming the heads, boldfaced terms, and **Taking Notes** side-column features. Ask volunteers to summarize what the essay is about.

About the Art *The Mayflower in Plymouth Harbor* (1882) is an oil painting by artist William Formby Halsall (1841–1919). Born in England, Halsall himself later immigrated to the United States, where he studied art at the Lowell Institute in Boston. Later, he became a sailor and went to sea for seven years. This painting shows the English ship that carried the Pilgrims to Plymouth, Massachusetts, in 1620.

Early American Writing
1600–1800

An Emerging Nation

For many people, early America was an experiment in hope. Explorers seeking adventure, settlers searching for religious freedom, colonists building communities, revolutionaries designing a new government—all embraced their challenges with a sense of faith and purpose. Writers of the day recorded and interpreted the extraordinary experiences of these ordinary people. They and their fellow colonists imagined and created an entirely new country and unique way of life.

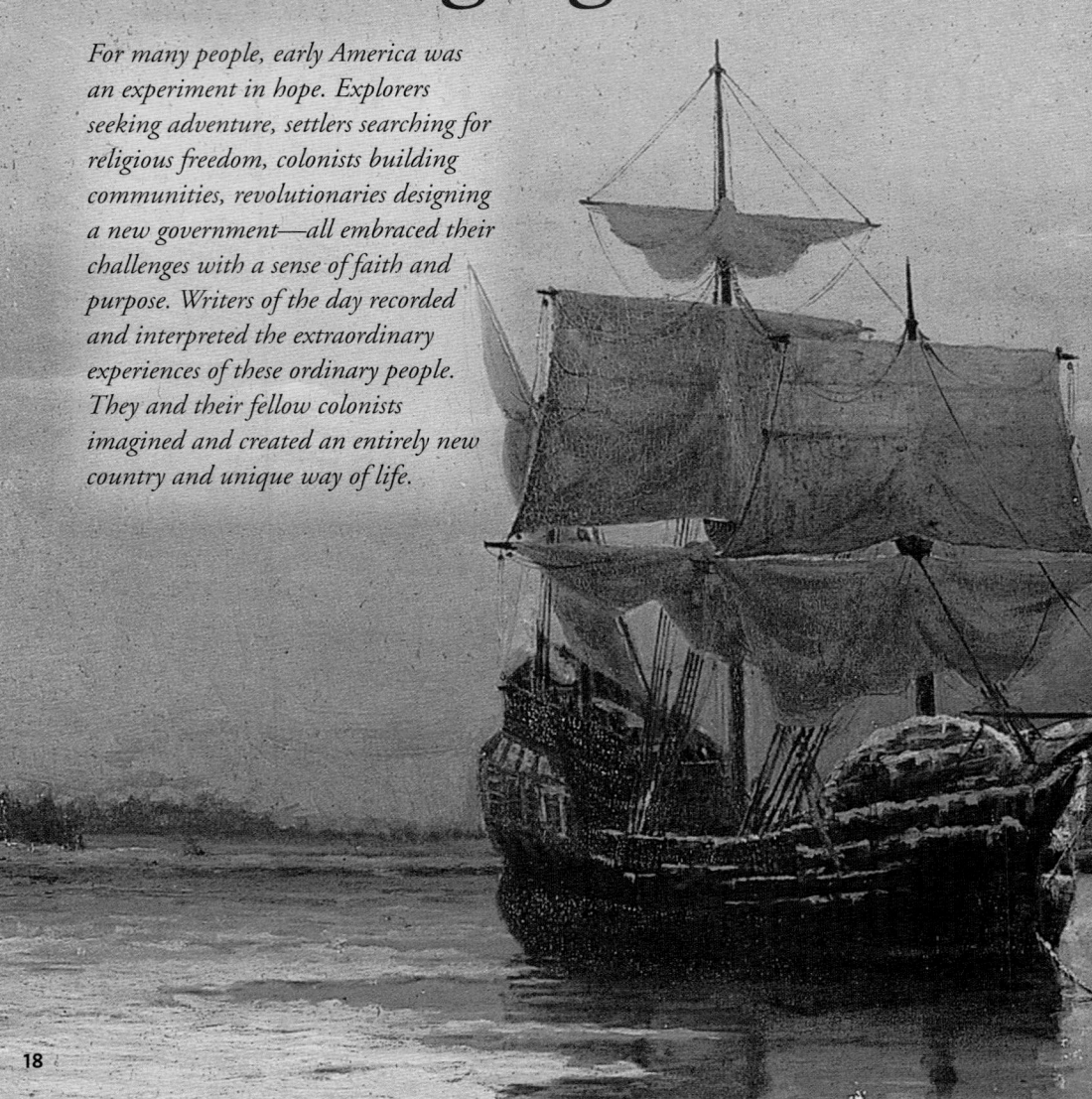

18

DIFFERENTIATED INSTRUCTION

FOR STRATEGIC READERS
Preteach Academic Vocabulary

- *colony,* "a group of people who settle in a new country but retain ties to their home"
- *colonist,* "a person who lives in a colony"
- *chronicle,* "to write a historical account"
- *self-rule,* "government of a group by its own members"
- *subject,* "a person under the control of a sovereign power"
- *parliament,* "England's lawmaking body"
- *export,* "to send (goods) out of one's country"
- *import,* "to bring (goods) in from another country"
- *raw materials,* "materials in their natural state that can be used to manufacture products"

Use this copy master to help students take notes on the essay, pages 18–27:

 RESOURCE MANAGER—Copy Master
    Note Taking p. 16

Early American Writing: Historical Context

KEY IDEAS Early American literature captures a nation in its infancy. From the first interactions between Native Americans and Europeans to the stirring cries of the Revolutionary War, writers chronicled the tensions and the triumphs of the day.

The Meeting of Two Worlds

Explorers and early settlers forged a life for themselves in America that was completely foreign to what they had known in their home countries. In fact, so extraordinary were their experiences that the earliest American writers concentrated mainly on describing and trying to make sense out of their challenging new environment and the unfamiliar people with whom they shared it. In diaries, letters, and reports back home, they recorded a historical turning point: when the world of the Europeans first intersected with that of the Native Americans.

Unknown to Europeans, people had been living in the Americas for at least tens of thousands of years, adapting to its diverse environments, forming communities, establishing trading networks, and building working cities. Millions of people lived in the Americas on the eve of the arrival of the Europeans—as many as lived in Europe at the time.

The earliest writers chronicled how the Europeans and Native Americans viewed one another and the North American land. In 1634, for example, **William Wood** of Massachusetts Bay Colony noted that the Native Americans "took the first ship they saw for a walking island, the mast to be a tree, the sail white clouds." **William Bradford,** governor of Plymouth Plantation, in turn described North America as "a hideous and desolate wilderness, full of wild beasts and wild men." The land, however, was neither desolate nor hideous, and the Native Americans were usually cooperative—at least until they began to be forced off their land by European colonists.

From Colony to Country

The first permanent colony was established at **Jamestown** in 1607. By 1733, English colonies stretched all along the Atlantic coast. Once rooted in North American soil, the colonies became increasingly self-reliant and practiced local self-rule.

LOYALTY TO ENGLAND The first colonists thought of themselves as English subjects, even though they did not have representatives in the British parliament. They supported England economically by exporting raw materials to the homeland and importing Britain's manufactured goods.

Britain, in turn, protected its territory. It sent soldiers to fight during the **French and Indian War** (1759–1763), when France allied with a

The Mayflower in Plymouth Harbor, (1882), William Formby Halsall. © Pilgrim Hall Museum, Plymouth, Massachusetts.

> ▶ **TAKING NOTES**
>
> **Outlining** As you read this introduction, use an outline to record the main ideas about the characteristics and the literature of the period. You can use article headings, boldfaced terms, and the information in these boxes as starting points. (See page R49 in the **Handbook** for more help with outlining.)
>
> *Early American Writing*
> I. Historical Context
>   A. The Meeting of Two Worlds
>   1. Early writers described land and people.
>   2. Native Americans had well-established communities when Europeans arrived.
>   3. Writers chronicled Native American and European views of one another.
>   B. From Colony to Country

ADDITIONAL BACKGROUND
For more on Early American Writing, visit **The Literature Center** at ClassZone.com.

Early American Writing: Historical Context

KEY IDEAS This section of the essay (pages 19–20) tells how the earliest American writers described the strange new environment of the Americas and the first encounters between Europeans and Native Americans. The text also explains the establishment of English colonies in North America and the subsequent rebellion of these colonies against England, resulting in the birth of the United States of America.

TIERED DISCUSSION PROMPTS

Use these prompts to help students understand the ideas in **The Meeting of Two Worlds:**

Summarize What was life like in the Americas prior to the arrival of the Europeans? *Possible answer: Native Americans enjoyed a well-established way of life informed by the tens of thousands of years they had spent adapting to their environment.*

Analyze How do the William Wood and William Bradford quotations illustrate the clash of cultures that occurred when Europeans and Native Americans first met? *Possible answer: The quotations show how unfamiliar each group was with the other's way of life. The Native Americans had apparently never before seen a ship, while the Europeans viewed North America as "a hideous and desolate wilderness."*

Evaluate Were Wood and Bradford fair in their assessment of the landscape and population of North America? *Possible answer: Their lack of experience with the land and people of North America made Wood and Bradford unqualified to fairly assess either. While Wood's description of the Native Americans' reaction to the ship is relatively unbiased, it is unfair of Bradford to call them "wild men" before getting to know them. The passage also suggests that Bradford is unfair in his inaccurate depiction of the American landscape as "hideous and desolate."*

FOR ENGLISH LEARNERS

Set a Purpose After introducing the *KEY IDEAS,* ask students to look for details as they read about how English colonization of North America led to the birth of the United States.

FOR ADVANCED LEARNERS/AP*

Brainstorm Have students brainstorm a list of "the tensions and the triumphs of the day" that writers would have been most likely to chronicle. Which items on the list proved to have historical significance, and why?

* AP is a registered trademark of the College Entrance Examination Board. Use of the trademark does not constitute production, participation, sponsorship, or endorsement by the College Board.

CHECK UNDERSTANDING

Have students describe the significance of these names:

- Jamestown
- French and Indian War
- Declaration of Independence
- Constitution of the United States

About the Art The illustration of the Boston Tea Party is from an engraving (c. 1845) commemorating the dumping of tea into Boston Harbor by colonists in 1773. The skull and crossbones drawing is a cartoon inspired by the Stamp Act. It appeared in 1765 in the *Pennsylvania Journal,* a newspaper that shut down in protest of the Stamp Act.

Cultural Influences

KEY IDEAS This section of the essay (pages 20–21) explains who the Puritans were and describes their beliefs and values. The text points out positive aspects of Puritanism, such as hard work and thrift, as well as negative aspects, such as intolerance.

TIERED DISCUSSION PROMPTS

Use these prompts to discuss **Puritan Beliefs:**

Recall Why did many Puritans leave England and come to America? *Possible answer: Many Puritans left England in order to be free to worship as they pleased without fear of persecution.*

Analyze How does Winthrop's notion of the "City upon a hill" reflect the Puritan notion of the "elect"? *Possible answer: "A City upon a hill" is a fitting metaphor for the Puritan community. Puritans believed that God chose them to be above all others, and to set an example of Christian piety for people to look up to and emulate.*

---

number of Native American groups to drive the British out of North America. After many defeats, England brought in new military leaders and made its own alliance with Native Americans—the powerful Iroquois. After a long and costly war, the victorious Great Britain claimed all of North America east of the Mississippi River.

A BREAK WITH ENGLAND When Great Britain tried to tax the colonists to recover some of the money spent on the war, however, it ended up losing far more than its war costs. Fired by cries of "No taxation without representation," the colonists protested British control—in both fiery words and bold actions. With each new act of British "tyranny," writers for colonial newspapers and pamphlets stirred the hearts and minds of the colonists to support independence.

The colonies declared themselves to be "free and independent" in 1776 and fought and defeated one of the greatest military powers on earth to turn their declaration into a reality. The remarkable minds of **Benjamin Franklin, Thomas Jefferson,** and other colonial thinkers put timeless words to this experiment in the form of the **Declaration of Independence** and the **Constitution of the United States.** When the Constitution was approved in 1788, the United States of America was born.

British parliament imposed the Stamp Act and the Tea Act to gain revenue from the colonies. Instead, these acts incited revolt. The Boston Tea Party was but one of many skirmishes leading to the Revolutionary War.

Cultural Influences

KEY IDEAS Religion was the most influential cultural force on writers of this period. Puritan values and beliefs directed people's everyday lives as well as the formation of an American society.

Puritan Beliefs

Many of the settlers in the 1600s were Puritans. **Puritans** were a group of English Protestants who had sought to "purify" the Church of England and return to simpler ways of worshiping. Their efforts had been most unwelcome in England, however, and many left the country for America to escape persecution.

Puritan settlers believed themselves chosen by God to create a new order in America. **John Winthrop,** for example, wrote in 1630 that "we must consider that we shall be as a City upon a hill. The eyes of all people are upon us." Puritans' values directed every aspect of their lives. They saw human struggle with sin as a daily mission and believed, above all else, that the Bible would help them through the torments of human weakness. Although they felt that humans were essentially sinful, they believed that some, the "elect," would be spared from eternal punishment by God's grace.

DIFFERENTIATED INSTRUCTION

FOR ENGLISH LEARNERS

Analyze Puritanism Have students paraphrase the *KEY IDEAS.* After they read the section, ask them to list positive and negative aspects of Puritanism:

Positive	Negative
hard workers	inflexible
thrifty	intolerant
responsible	

FOR STRATEGIC READERS

Preteach Academic Vocabulary

- *alliance,* "a union or agreement between groups or nations for mutual benefit"
- *tyranny,* "unfair use of power"
- *persecution,* "mistreatment because of one's beliefs"
- *ideal,* "a perfect example of something; a goal to which people aspire"
- *democracy,* "government that is run by the people"

Hard work, thrift, and responsibility were therefore seen as morally good, a sign that God was working within. The thriving settlements and financial success that grew from these qualities were thought to be a mark of God's approval. However, Puritanism had a dark side as well. Puritans tended to be inflexible in their religious faith and intolerant of viewpoints other than their own. In one famous case, the Salem witchcraft trials, a whole community fell victim to the hysteria of the witch-hunt, ending with more than 20 people dead by execution.

Ideas of the Age

KEY IDEAS In the 1700s, both Enlightenment ideals and Puritan values contributed to the country's thirst for independence.

The Enlightenment

In the 1700s, there was a burst of intellectual energy taking place in Europe that came to be known as the **Enlightenment**. Enlightenment thinkers had begun to question previously accepted truths about who should hold the power in government. Their thinking pointed the way to a government by the people—one in which people consent to government limitations in exchange for the government's protection of their basic rights and liberties.

American colonists adapted these Enlightenment ideals to their own environment. The political writings of **Benjamin Franklin, Thomas Paine,** and **Thomas Jefferson** shaped the **American Enlightenment** and began to eclipse even the most brilliant European thought. Enlightenment ideals prompted action and gave colonists a philosophical footing for their revolution. "I know not what course others may take," **Patrick Henry** thundered to the delegates at the second Virginia Convention in 1775, "but as for me, give me liberty, or give me death!"

> **A Voice from the Times**
>
> *We hold these truths to be self-evident, that all men are created equal, that they are endowed by their Creator with certain unalienable Rights, that among these are Life, Liberty, and the pursuit of Happiness.*
>
> —Thomas Jefferson
> from the Declaration
> of Independence

The Great Awakening

At the same time, many people began to worry that Puritan values were being lost. Preachers such as **Jonathan Edwards** called for people to rededicate themselves to the original Puritan vision, and a new wave of religious enthusiasm began to rise. This movement, called the **First Great Awakening,** united colonists who were in other ways diverse. Across the colonies, people began to feel joined in the belief that a higher power was helping Americans set a new standard for an ethical life.

While the Enlightenment and the Great Awakening emphasized opposing aspects of human experience—reason and emotionalism, respectively—they had similar consequences. Both caused people to question traditional authority, eventually leading colonists to break from Britain's control and embrace democracy.

CHECK UNDERSTANDING

Ask students how Puritan values contributed to the success of the settlements.

Ideas of the Age

KEY IDEAS This section of the essay describes the Enlightenment in 18th-century Europe and explains how the colonists adapted the Enlightenment's concepts as a philosophical basis for the American Revolution. The text also describes the new wave of religious enthusiasm known as the Great Awakening.

TIERED DISCUSSION PROMPTS

Use these prompts to help students understand the ideas in **Ideas of the Age:**

Summarize What is the author's definition of "a government by the people"? ***Possible answer:*** *In "a government by the people," the citizens agree to abide by government laws and rules. In return, the government promises to protect the citizens' rights and freedoms.*

Analyze How did the Enlightenment concepts that had their roots in Europe affect the American colonists' relationship with Britain? ***Possible answer:*** *The Enlightenment led European thinkers to question traditional concepts of government and pointed the way toward government by the people. As American colonists adapted Enlightenment ideas, they too questioned traditional authority, causing them to reject British control and move toward democratic government.*

Synthesize In what way did the Enlightenment and the Great Awakening produce similar results? ***Possible answer:*** *Both led people to question traditional authority.*

FOR STRATEGIC READERS

Ideals of the Enlightenment Emphasize to students that the Enlightenment was a movement in Europe in which new ideas about government "enlightened," or gave new knowledge or insight to, the people. Discuss with students how ideals of the Enlightenment are evident in Patrick Henry's quote. ***Possible answer:*** *Personal liberty was valued above all else.*

FOR ADVANCED LEARNERS/AP

Research the Enlightenment Have students learn more about the Enlightenment: its leaders, ideals and principles, methods, and impact. Have students make informal oral presentations to the class, sharing their findings and explaining why this period in history is also known as the Age of Reason.

Early American Literature

KEY IDEAS This section of the essay (pages 22–27) focuses on early American writing. The text describes

- Native American oral literature
- historical narratives written by explorers, early settlers, and colonists
- sermons, histories, and poetry of Puritan writers
- political pamphlets that fueled the American Revolution
- the Declaration of Independence and the Constitution
- contributions of women writers of the time

ANALYZE VISUALS

Possible answer: The sculpture represents the natural world playing a vital role in the world of humans. It suggests that people have a close, respectful relationship with nature.

About the Art *Raven and the First Men,* a seven-foot-tall sculpture carved by Canadian sculptor Bill Reid (1920–1998), reflects the artist's lifelong interest in Haida art and cultural tradition. The Haida are Native Americans who live on islands off the west coast of North America. Reid's mother was of Haida descent.

TIERED DISCUSSION PROMPTS

Use these prompts to help students understand the ideas in **The Native American Experience:**

Interpret From the perspective of the Native American holy woman, how is oral tradition more meaningful than the written word? *Possible answer: Oral tradition requires each person to learn and remember historical and cultural information. The written word requires only that someone read what another person has recorded.*

Evaluate Why is preservation through oral tradition more vulnerable to loss than preservation through written works? *Possible answer: Oral tradition requires people to remember and accurately communicate to others their history, legends, and myths. Written works preserve such information on the printed page, creating a lasting record.*

Early American Literature

KEY IDEAS Early American writing is as varied as early Americans themselves. Native Americans, explorers, settlers, and revolutionaries all contributed their own perspectives to our knowledge of this literary period.

The Native American Experience

When the Europeans arrived, there were more than 300 different Native American cultures in North America with strongly differing customs and about 200 different languages spoken. Yet wherever they lived—in the smoky longhouses of the Northeastern woodlands, the well-defended cliff dwellings of the desert Southwest, the cedar-scented lodges of the Pacific Northwest—one activity was common to all: storytelling.

The Native North American cultures did not have a written language. Instead, a group's history, legends, and myths were entrusted to memory and faithfully passed from generation to generation through **oral tradition.** In the words of one Native American holy woman, "When you write things down you don't have to remember them. But for us it is different. . . . [A]ll that we are, all that we have ever been, all the great names of our heroes and their songs and deeds are alive within each of us. . . living in our blood."

▶ *For Your Notes*
NATIVE AMERICANS
- were culturally diverse
- had an oral tradition
- had many different genres of spoken literature
- explored common themes, such as a reverence for nature and the worship of many gods

ANALYZE VISUALS
This modern depiction of a Haida creation story shows the Raven (a popular cultural hero in many Native American myths and legends) opening a shell to release the first humans into the world. What relationship between humans and the natural world does this sculpture suggest?

Raven and the First Men (1980), Bill Reid. Yellow cedar. University of British Columbia Museum of Anthropology, Vancouver, Canada.

DIFFERENTIATED INSTRUCTION

FOR STRATEGIC READERS
Oral Tradition Emphasize that before written language was invented, people around the world used oral tradition to preserve their literature. Today, oral tradition has been largely replaced by print and electronic media.

Vocabulary Support
- *oral tradition,* "the practice of storytelling to pass a group's memories, histories, and stories from one generation to the next"
- *legendary histories,* "stories passed down from earlier times and popularly regarded as true"

LITERARY STYLE The forms of Native American oral literature are rich and varied. Creation stories, ways to explain how the universe and humans came into being, can be found in every Native American culture. Other forms include legendary histories tracing the migration of peoples or the deeds of great leaders, fairy tales, lyrics, chants, children's songs, healing songs, and dream visions.

Tragically, much of this literature did not survive after so many Native Americans fell to European diseases. Some groups lost as many as 90 percent of their people, all of whom had a share in preserving the traditional stories. The surviving works, however, show that diverse Native American groups explored common themes in their spoken literature, including a reverence for nature and the worship of many gods.

Exploration and the Early Settlers

While Native American literature offers us a glimpse into the ways and values of America's indigenous peoples, much of our understanding of pre-colonial America comes from the first-person accounts of its early explorers, settlers, and colonists. The journals, diaries, letters, logs, and historical narratives of those first Europeans to view the American landscape describe in vivid detail its many sights and wonders, as well as its dangers and challenges.

THE EXPLORERS The first of these writings were the journals and letters of **Christopher Columbus,** which recounted his four voyages to the Americas begun in 1492. Columbus's adventures opened the door to a century of Spanish expeditions in the Americas. Incapable of visualizing the historical significance of his travels, however, he died disappointed, convinced that he had barely missed the cities of gold described by Marco Polo. His fascinating journals provide a vivid record of the most significant journeys of his time.

Just over 50 years later came *La Relación.* This report by **Álvar Núñez Cabeza de Vaca,** one of the four survivors of the 600-man Narváez expedition, chronicled his eight years of wandering through Florida, Texas, and Mexico. In it he describes the landscape and people he encountered, as well as animals that were new to Europeans. The French and Dutch also sent explorers such as **Samuel de Champlain,** the "Father of New France," who in the early 1600s wrote vivid accounts of New England and the Iroquois.

EARLY SETTLERS The early English settlers described their difficult and amazing new lives in letters, reports, and chronicles to friends and family back home. Their writings helped people in England imagine what life might be like in America. One of the most influential writings was *A Brief and True Report of the New Found Land of Virginia,* by **Thomas Harriot,** which faithfully captured the area's natural resources, the ways of life of the Native Americans, and the potential for building a successful colony. It was published in 1588 and was accompanied by illustrations that helped thousands upon thousands of English readers form their first clear picture of North America.

▶ *For Your Notes*

EXPLORERS

- Columbus's journals chronicle his four voyages to the Americas.

- Cabeza de Vaca's *La Relación* tells of his failed expedition.

- Samuel de Champlain wrote accounts of New England and the Iroquois.

EARLY SETTLERS

- Settlers described the new land for those still in Europe.

- Accounts helped English readers visualize North America.

COLONISTS

- Writers focused on the story of the new settlements and their larger purpose.

- Equiano, an enslaved African, described his unjust treatment.

Synthesize How did the arrival of the Europeans affect the preservation of Native American literature? ***Possible answer:*** *When Native Americans were exposed to European diseases, as many as 90 percent of them died. The death of so many Native Americans left fewer people to remember and, thereby, to preserve the oral tradition of their literature.*

ADDITIONAL BACKGROUND

Marco Polo (1254–1324) was an Italian traveler famous for his accounts of China. Columbus consulted Polo's writings when planning his voyage to reach Asia.

CHECK UNDERSTANDING

Ask students what accounts left by early explorers and settlers contribute to our understanding of precolonial America.

FOR STRATEGIC READERS

Preteach Academic Vocabulary

- *longhouse,* "a long rectangular dwelling of some Native Americans, such as the Iroquois"

- *migration,* "movement from one region or country to another"

- *indigenous,* "originating in a region; natural"

- *expedition,* "a journey undertaken for a particular purpose, such as exploration"

FOR ADVANCED LEARNERS/AP

Explore Harriot's Work Have students locate (via the Internet or a library) and read portions of Thomas Harriot's *A Brief and True Report of the New Found Land of Virginia.* Discuss Harriot's observations and descriptions of Native Americans. If pictures accompany the text, discuss how they contribute to the students' knowledge of the time.

Use this prompt to help students discuss colonial histories:

Analyze In what ways do the writings of Captain John Smith, William Bradford, John Winthrop, and Olaudah Equiano reflect their different perspectives and purposes?

Possible answer: Smith wrote vivid, "sometimes-embroidered" accounts of life in the early colonies, which attracted settlers to Virginia. Bradford and Winthrop wrote more seriously, reflecting on "their role in God's plan for a better society." Equiano recounted his capture and brutal treatment, offering readers insight into the life of a slave.

A modern reconstruction of the original Jamestown, Virginia, settlement

COLONIAL HISTORIES As the colonies took root, writing began to focus less on pure description and more on the story of the growth of the colonies. In contrast to the carefully accurate Harriot, for example, **Captain John Smith** wrote sometimes-embroidered accounts of the history of Virginia and New England. By force of his vivid and engaging writing, he created an enduring record of life in the early colonies and an intriguing self-portrait of a man proud of his great deeds and eager to gain recognition. His accounts were also instrumental in attracting settlers to Virginia, thus ensuring the eventual success of that colony.

Other writers who documented the history of the New England settlements wrote in a plainer style and with a more serious purpose. **William Bradford,** longtime governor of Plymouth, and **John Winthrop Sr.,** who served as governor of Massachusetts, reflected upon what they saw as their role in God's plan for a better society. But not all who wrote narrative histories saw the colonists' efforts as following God's plan. **Olaudah Equiano** described his harsh capture from his African home and the brutal and "un-Christian" treatment he received as a slave in the West Indies.

The Puritan Tradition

Puritan writers had their own purposes for recording history. They believed writing should be useful, a tool to help readers understand the Bible and guide them in their daily lives. For this reason, logic, clarity, and order were more prized in writing than beauty or adornment. One Puritan compared adorned writing to stained-glass windows. "The paint upon the glass may feed the fancy, but the room is not well lighted by it." Using a familiar, down-to-earth metaphor such as this to make a deeper point is a common feature of Puritan writing. The direct, powerful, plain language of much of American literature owes a debt to the Puritans.

> **A Voice from the Times**
>
> *So as there died sometimes two or three of a day . . . , that of one hundred and odd persons, scarce fifty remained.*
>
> **—William Bradford**
> from *Of Plymouth Plantation*

▶ *For Your Notes*

PURITAN WRITERS

- believed writing should be useful and clear
- wrote histories, sermons, scientific works, and essays
- delivered sermons contrasting good and evil
- wrote poems with religious themes

DIFFERENTIATED INSTRUCTION

FOR STRATEGIC READERS
Preteach Academic Vocabulary

- *sermon,* "a public talk about religious or moral matters, usually given by a member of the clergy"
- *treatise,* "a formal piece of writing about a particular subject"
- *meditation,* "a formal speech or writing, often about sacred matters, intended to express the author's thoughts or to guide others"

FOR ADVANCED LEARNERS/AP

Joint-Stock Companies While Spanish and French rulers funded their colonies directly, British rulers granted charters for colonies to groups of investors called joint-stock companies. Have students research the joint-stock companies that financed the colonies in Virginia and New England and discuss how they may have affected the composition of the histories of those settlements.

SERMONS AND OTHER WRITINGS The works of Puritan writers, such as **Cotton Mather** and **Jonathan Edwards,** include histories of the colonies and fiery sermons on the dangers of sinful ways. Along with histories and sermons, Cotton Mather chronicled the disturbing Salem witch trials, where 20 people were condemned to death in an atmosphere of mass hysteria. He also wrote about scientific matters, including inoculation for smallpox.

Like Mather, Jonathan Edwards wrote on a variety of subjects, including the flying (or ballooning) spiders he had observed as a boy. His account of these spiders is considered the first natural history essay on that subject. A spider makes another, very different kind of appearance in Edwards's best-known work, his sermon "Sinners in the Hands of an Angry God." In that sermon he warns his listeners that God "holds you over the pit of hell, much as one holds a spider, or some loathsome insect over the fire."

Imagine the scene when Edwards first delivered this sermon: the congregation quaking in fear from Edwards's vivid descriptions of hellfire and a vengeful god. "Sinners in the Hands of an Angry God," while perhaps more fiery than most, is typical of the Puritan sermon. Melodramatic contrasts between good and evil, vivid imagery, powerful language, and strong moral lessons characterized this form of literature.

PURITAN POETRY Most Puritan writers composed "plain" sermons, histories, and treatises, but poetry was the means of expression for others. In fact, the first book issued in the North American colonies was the the *Bay Psalm Book* in 1640, in which the Bible's psalms were rewritten to fit the rhythms of familiar Puritan hymns.

Puritan poets such as **Anne Bradstreet** and **Edward Taylor** viewed poetry primarily as a means of exploring the relationship between the individual and God. Bradstreet's poems reflect her wide learning, deep faith, and love for her husband and children. They also provide insight into the position of women in the male-dominated Puritan society. Her book of poetry, *The Tenth Muse Lately Sprung Up in America* (1650), was the first work by a North American woman to be published. Minister Edward Taylor, possibly considered the best-known Puritan poet, wrote most of his poems as aids for his meditations. His poetry, like much Puritan writing, uses vivid images from nature and from everyday life as a way to help readers grasp the spiritual world beyond.

> ## A Voice from the Times
> *I made seeking salvation the main business of my life.*
> —Jonathan Edwards

Evangelical preacher George Whitefield was a key figure in the revival movement of America's "Great Awakening."

TIERED DISCUSSION PROMPTS

Use these prompts to help students understand the ideas in **The Puritan Tradition:**

Analyze The essay quotes a Puritan as saying, "The paint upon the glass may feed the fancy, but the room is not well lighted by it." Explain how this quotation represents the Puritans' approach to writing. *Possible answer: The quotation conveys this idea by noting the Puritans' preference for things that are simple and functional (plain glass) over things that are decorative and fancy (stained-glass windows).*

Synthesize On page 21 you learned that the Puritans were practical people who valued "hard work, thrift, and responsibility." How do the writings of Cotton Mather and Jonathan Edwards reflect an interest in practical as well as spiritual matters? *Possible answer: In addition to writing religious sermons, Mather and Edwards documented practical observations and historical events that help readers better understand life in the Puritan colonies. Examples include Mather's writing about the Salem witch trials and smallpox inoculation, and Edwards's writing about the spiders he remembered from childhood.*

Evaluate In what ways do the works of Puritan poets Anne Bradstreet and Edward Taylor provide insight into the Puritan way of life? *Possible answer: In addition to focusing on the Puritan ideals of faith and family, Bradstreet's poetry helps readers see the world from the perspective of a woman living in a "male-dominated Puritan society." Taylor uses familiar images "from nature and from everyday life" to explore spirituality. In this way, his poetry reflects the Puritan belief that "writing should be useful, a tool to help readers understand the Bible and guide them in their daily lives."*

FOR STRATEGIC READERS

Taking Notes Have students record the main ideas about the Puritan writing tradition (pages 24–25) in outline form. Then ask students to exchange papers and evaluate each other's work. Tell them to offer specific suggestions for possible improvement.

Sample notes:

Puritans
- Puritans believed writing should be useful.
- They prized reason, logic, clarity, and order.

Sermons and Other Writing
- Cotton Mather chronicled Salem witch trials.
- Jonathan Edwards wrote fiery sermons.

Puritan Poetry
- Puritan poetry was a means of exploring the relationship between the individual and God.
- Outstanding poets included Anne Bradstreet and Edward Taylor.

WRITERS OF THE
REVOLUTION

- expressed the ideas of the Enlightenment

- concentrated on political writing

- used pamphlets to spread ideas

- focused on natural law and human rights

- played a key role in the creation of a new nation

TIERED DISCUSSION PROMPTS

Use these prompts to help students understand the ideas in **Writers of the Revolution:**

Interpret The essay writer describes pamphlets as "the fuel of the revolution." What does the writer mean by this phrase? *Possible answer: The political writing in pamphlets was widely read and discussed. It helped to ignite the discontent that people were feeling about British rule and added to the movement for independence.*

Synthesize To what extent do you think that modern-day Internet communication serves the same purpose as the political pamphlets of the 1700s? Explain your answer. *Possible answer: Much as the political pamphlets of the 1700s spread ideas to thousands of people, Internet communication today reaches a vast number of people and disseminates political ideas all over the world. On the other hand, Internet communication can be so common that important information may not stand out as easily as it did with the pamphlets.*

Writers of the Revolution

It is curious to consider now, but some of the most famous figures of the American Revolution lived at the same time as Puritans such as Jonathan Edwards. As products of the Enlightenment, however, revolutionary writers focused their energies on matters of government rather than religion.

PAMPHLETS AND PROPAGANDA Many of the gifted minds of this period were drawn to political writing as the effort to launch a grand experiment in government took shape in North America. The most important outlet for the spread of these political writings was the pamphlet. Between 1763 and 1783, about two thousand pamphlets were published. These inexpensive "little books" became the fuel of the revolution, reaching thousands of people quickly and stirring debate and action in response to growing discontent with British rule.

Through these pamphlets the words that would define the American cause against Great Britain became the currency of the day, and the debate about independence grew louder and louder. One such pamphlet, *Common Sense,* by **Thomas Paine,** helped propel the colonists to revolution. Though

Soldier of the Revolution (1876), George Willoughby Maynard. Oil on canvas, 51″ × 39″. Photo © Christie's Images Ltd.

26

A Voice from the Times

These are the times that try men's souls: The summer soldier and the sunshine patriot will, in this crisis, shrink from the service of his country; but he that stands it NOW, *deserves the love and thanks of man and woman.*

—Thomas Paine
from *The Crisis*

DIFFERENTIATED INSTRUCTION

FOR ADVANCED LEARNERS/AP

Revolutionary vs. Puritan Writing [small-group option] The essay writer points out that the political revolutionaries of the Enlightenment were contemporaries of devout Puritans, such as the famous Puritan reformer Jonathan Edwards. Though they wrote for different purposes, both groups used writing to appeal to their readers' emotions and sense of responsibility. Have students incorporate what they have learned so far about the Enlightenment and Puritan tradition into a discussion in which they compare and contrast political and religious writing in colonial America. Encourage students to go beyond the obvious contrasts in search of comparisons.

expressing the views of the rational Enlightenment, Paine also agreed with the Puritan belief that America had a special destiny to be a model to the rest of the world. At the end of his stirring essay, he says that freedom had been hunted down around the globe and calls on America to "receive the fugitive," to give freedom a home, and to welcome people from around the world to its free society.

WRITING THAT LAUNCHED A NATION Thomas Jefferson also wrote pamphlets, but his great contribution to American government, literature, and the cause of freedom throughout the world is the **Declaration of Independence,** in which he eloquently articulated the **natural law** that would govern America. This natural law is the idea that people are born with rights and freedoms and that it is the function of government to protect those freedoms.

Eleven years later, after the Revolutionary War had ended, delegates from all but one state gathered at the Philadelphia State House—in the same room in which the Declaration of Independence had been signed—in order to discuss forming a new government. The delegates included many outstanding leaders of the time, such as **Benjamin Franklin, Alexander Hamilton,** and **George Washington.** Four months later, they emerged with perhaps the country's most important piece of writing: the **Constitution of the United States of America.** Although Washington said at the time, "I do not expect the Constitution to last for more than 20 years," it was indeed flexible enough to last through the centuries to come.

VOICES OF THE PEOPLE Statesmen were not the only ones to contribute to the discussion of the day, however. In that age of political writing, even poetry sometimes examined political and social themes. Among the finest is the work of former slave **Phillis Wheatley.** In her poems and letters, Wheatley wrote of the "natural rights" of African-Americans and pointed out the discrepancy between the colonists' "cry for freedom" and their enslavement of fellow human beings.

Another voice calling for the rights of all citizens was **Abigail Adams,** whose husband John became the nation's second president. In letters written while the couple was apart, Adams encouraged her husband to include the rights of women in the nation's founding documents.

Wheatley, Adams, and other women writers join the Native Americans, colonists, Puritans, and patriots who came before them to give us an understanding of the dreams and values that shaped our nation. All contributed their voices and ideals to building this "city upon a hill."

The "Father of American Portraiture"
Many colonial artists earned their livings with portraits, which were in high demand. Gilbert Stuart was among the best of colonial portrait painters. Because he painted the likenesses of virtually all the notable men and women of the period (including the first five American presidents), he earned himself the moniker "The Father of American Portraiture" by his contemporaries.

Painting the President One of Stuart's favorite subjects was the first president of the United States, George Washington. His 104 likenesses of Washington inform the image most of us have of our first president. In fact, one of his paintings became the basis for the one-dollar bill.

Stuart was known to chat with his subjects as they sat for his paintings. By entertaining them during the long hours of posing, he hoped to capture an unguarded, fresh expression on their faces. The serious George Washington, however, found Stuart's chat annoying. The artist says of Washington, "An apathy seemed to seize him, and a vacuity spread over his countenance, most appalling to paint." Nevertheless, in *George Washington (Vaughan portrait)*, 1795, shown here, Stuart was able to capture Washington's imposing presence by placing his head high in the design and adding a crimson glow around it.

THE ARTISTS' GALLERY

American artist Gilbert Stuart (1755–1828) painted about 1000 pictures during his career, almost all of which were portraits. His numerous paintings of the first president are categorized according to their owners. Thus, the work depicted on page 27, painted in 1795, is *George Washington (Vaughan portrait)*. It was bought by Samuel Vaughan, an English merchant and close friend of Washington.

Activity Ask students what qualities of George Washington they think Gilbert Stuart was trying to capture in this portrait. ***Possible answer: Stuart wanted to capture Washington's dignity and self-confidence.***

TIERED DISCUSSION PROMPTS

Use this prompt to help students understand the ideas in **Writers of the Revolution:**

Analyze The essay explains that in the Declaration of Independence, Jefferson argues that "people are born with rights and freedoms and that it is the function of government to protect those freedoms." How was this belief reflected in the writings of Phillis Wheatley and Abigail Adams? ***Possible answer: In her poetry and letters, Wheatley wrote about the rights of African Americans and the unfairness of their enslavement. Adams's letters spoke out for the rights of women.***

CHECK UNDERSTANDING

Identify a few relevant events or figures related to each of these topics:

- The Native American Experience
- Exploration and the Early Settlers
- The Puritan Tradition
- Writers of the Revolution

FOR STRATEGIC READERS
Preteach Academic Vocabulary

- *propaganda,* "ideas, opinions, or information spread to further a cause"
- *rational,* "relating to or based on reason"
- *delegate,* "a person who has the authority to act for others; representative"
- *patriot,* "a person who loves and supports his or her country"

FOR ADVANCED LEARNERS/AP

Synthesize Point out that the final sentence of the essay refers back to John Winthrop's words in the last paragraph on page 20. Ask students to review that paragraph. Then have them discuss to what extent America today still views itself as a "city upon a hill." Encourage students to support their responses with specific reasons and information.

Connecting Literature, History, and Culture

OBJECTIVES

- read a timeline
- make connections among the perspectives and events of literature, history, and culture

READING SKILL

READ A TIMELINE

Point out that each of the three horizontal sections of the timeline—*American Literary Milestones, Historical Context,* and *World Culture and Events*—displays a sequence of events that occurred between 1600 and 1800. By looking at the vertical columns on the timeline, students can see which events were going on at approximately the same time.

Have students locate, for example, each of these events on the timeline between 1630 and 1635:

- **1630** William Bradford published *Of Plymouth Plantation.* (See *American Literary Milestones.*)
- **1632** Construction of the Taj Mahal began. (See *World Culture and Events.*)
- **1635** North America's first public school was founded. (See *Historical Context.*)

Ask students to identify events that occurred between 1787 and 1790. *Answer: The U.S. Constitution was approved in 1787. Olaudah Equiano's narrative was published in 1789. That same year, the storming of the Bastille began the French Revolution.*

Connecting Literature, History, and Culture

Early American writing reflects the growing pains of a new nation but also reveals much about trends occurring elsewhere in the world. Use this timeline and the questions on page 29 to find connections between literature, history, and culture.

AMERICAN LITERARY MILESTONES

1600

1624 John Smith publishes *The General History of Virginia.*

1630 William Bradford describes his journey across the Atlantic and pilgrims' settlement in *Of Plymouth Plantation.*

1640 *Bay Psalm Book* is the first book to be printed in America. ▶

1650

1650 Anne Bradstreet's poems, collected as *The Tenth Muse Lately Sprung Up in America,* are published in London.

1682 Mary Rowlandson publishes *The Sovereignty and Goodness of God,* an account of her captivity at the hands of Algonquian Indians.

1693 Cotton Mather publishes *The Wonders of the Invisible World* in defense of the Salem witch trials.

HISTORICAL CONTEXT

1600

1607 The first permanent English settlement is founded in Jamestown, Virginia.

1619 The first enslaved Africans arrive in North America at Jamestown.

1620 The *Mayflower* pilgrims establish the Massachusetts Bay Colony at Plymouth. ▶

1635 North America's first public school is founded in Boston.

1650

1676 The Puritans' victory in King Philip's War ends Native American resistance in New England colonies.

1682 William Penn founds the colony of Pennsylvania.

1688 Quakers voice opposition to slavery.

1692 Salem witch trials show atmosphere of mass hysteria. ▶

WORLD CULTURE AND EVENTS

1600

1615 Inquisition condemns Italian scientist Galileo Galilei for supporting Copernicus's theory.

1616 Shakespeare dies.

1632 Indian emperor Shah Jahan begins construction of Taj Mahal. ▶

1650

1652 Dutch found Cape Town on the southern tip of South Africa.

1687 Isaac Newton publishes *Philosophiae naturalis principia mathematica,* considered to be the most important work of the Scientific Revolution.

1694 Japanese poet Matsuo Bashō, known for revitalizing the haiku form, dies.

DIFFERENTIATED INSTRUCTION

FOR STRATEGIC READERS

Understanding a Timeline Explain that the timeline runs chronologically (in time order) from left to right across the page. Each of the four columns represents a 50-year period between 1600 and 1800. The three parallel rows of the timeline represent events occurring simultaneously. By comparing the three rows, readers can better understand what events in literature, history, and culture were taking place at about the same time.

MAKING CONNECTIONS

- Religion played a central role in America during this period. What works written at this time might support this observation?
- While American writers of this period worked mostly in nonfiction and poetry, groundbreaking novels were being written elsewhere in the world. Name one.
- The Revolutionary War was a defining event in American history. What other country held a bloody revolution during this period?

1700

1704 The *Boston Newsletter,* the first American newspaper, is established. ▶

1722 Benjamin Franklin uses humor to criticize the Puritan establishment in his first published work, *The Dogood Papers.*

1741 Jonathan Edwards delivers a sermon called "Sinners in the Hands of an Angry God." The sermon typifies the religious movement known as the Great Awakening.

1750

1774 Abigail Adams writes first entry in what is published as *Familiar Letters of John Adams and His Wife, Abigail.*

1776 Thomas Paine's widely read pamphlet *Common Sense* passionately argues the case for independence.

1776 George Washington invites Phillis Wheatley to visit after receiving from her a poem and letter.

1789 Olaudah Equiano's *Interesting Narrative of . . . Olaudah Equiano* details harsh treatment of captive Africans. ▶

1700

1720 The colonial population reaches about a half million; Boston's population is about 12,000.

1739 The religious revival known as the Great Awakening (1739–1742) begins.

1744 The six nations of the Iroquois Confederation (whose tribe-mark is shown here) cede Ohio Valley territory north of the Ohio River to Britain. ▶

1750

1773 The Boston Tea Party marks a violent rejection of Britain's taxation policies. The Revolutionary War begins two years later. ▶

1776 July 4: Second Continental Congress adopts the Declaration of Independence.

1781 British defeat at Yorktown ends the American Revolution.

1787 U.S. Constitution is approved.

1700

1721 Johann Sebastian Bach composes the *Brandenburg Concertos.*

1725 Peter the Great, czar of Russia, dies.

1726 Jonathan Swift publishes *Gulliver's Travels.* ▶

1750

1752 Calcutta's population reaches 120,000.

1762 Catherine the Great, an "enlightened despot," becomes empress of Russia.

1784 The Indian sacred text the *Bhagavad-Gita* is translated into English for the first time.

1789 Storming of the Bastille incites the French Revolution.

1791 The classic Chinese novel *Dream of the Red Chamber* is published.

MAKING CONNECTIONS

Possible answers:

- Bay Psalm Book *(1640)*, The Sovereignty and Goodness of God *(1682)*, "Sinners in the Hands of an Angry God" *(1741)*
- Gulliver's Travels *(1726)*, Dream of the Red Chamber *(1791)*
- *France (1789)*

ADDITIONAL QUESTIONS

1. About three decades after Boston's population reached 12,000, a city in India attained a population ten times as great. Name the city. ***Answer:*** *Calcutta*

2. Fifty years after the English writer Jonathan Swift published *Gulliver's Travels*, an American writer published a pamphlet that encouraged the colonists to revolt against England. Who was the writer? What was the name of the pamphlet? ***Answers:*** *Thomas Paine;* Common Sense

FOR ADVANCED LEARNERS/AP

Making Additional Connections Ask students to choose one of the four time periods shown in the timeline and to research online, in encyclopedias, or in history texts other events that occurred during the 50-year time span. Challenge students to identify events for each category: *American Literary Milestones, Historical Context,* and *World Culture and Events.* Have students prepare and present brief oral reports, summarizing significant events and discussing their connection to events shown in the timeline or discussed in class.

OBJECTIVE

- to connect the legacy of early American culture and writing to present times

An American Work Ethic

Have students read the paragraph. (You may also want to ask students to review the section on Puritan beliefs on pages 20–21 of the historical essay.) Discuss the legacy of Puritan attitudes and values. Point out that the idea of hard work leading to success is communicated to children at an early age when they are told to study hard to get good grades.

DISCUSS Explore with students the kinds of rewards that work can provide. Elicit responses from the class, and list them on the board. ***Possible answer:*** *Work can be a source of personal satisfaction, a way to socialize with others, a means of increasing self-esteem.* Then ask the other **DISCUSS** questions. Extend the discussion by asking students how much the success of individuals can be attributed to such factors as these:

- hard work
- who you know
- luck
- perseverance
- taking risks

Encourage students to support their opinions with clear reasons.

UNIT 1

The Legacy of Early America

An American Work Ethic

Shunning frivolous pleasures that would distract them from thoughts of God, Puritans instead trained their energy on hard, useful work. That hard work often led to material success, which was in turn seen as a sign of God's favor. Many Americans today also believe in the intrinsic value of hard work—as well as the idea that hard work leads to financial success.

DISCUSS With your class, discuss whether work in and of itself is something to value. What does work provide? In your opinion, does work indeed lead to success? What other factors might be involved?

DIFFERENTIATED INSTRUCTION

FOR STRATEGIC READERS
Vocabulary Support

- *legacy,* "something passed on from an ancestor or predecessor"
- *ethics,* "moral principles or values"
- *frivolous,* "not serious; silly"
- *intrinsic,* "essential; inherent; basic"

FOR ADVANCED LEARNERS/AP
Reflect on Working Ask students to consider how our view of work changes as we age. For example, how might a high school student's concept of hard work differ from that of a child? from that of an adult? Whose concept might be closer to the Puritan work ethic? Ask students to write an essay exploring changes in our view of work as we grow older and reflecting on the reasons for these changes. Then have students share their essays with the class.

Government by the People

Democracy is surely the most significant legacy of the early American period. Reacting against the monarchy they had left behind and embracing Enlightenment ideals, the framers of the Constitution ensured that governmental power would be shared by the people. The people would elect representatives to carry out their will, and a system of checks and balances would ensure that no one person could rule over all. More than two centuries later, the system still stands.

TAKE ACTION Contact your local representative or senator and ask for support on a current issue that affects you. For example, you may wish to discuss the condition of your local parks or the lack of an after-school center in your area. Contact information can be found at www.congress.org.

The Power of Political Writing

During the early American period, political writing served as an agent for change. Thomas Paine's *Common Sense,* for example, furthered the case for American independence. Later, when the army suffered several brutal defeats and many soldiers were deserting, Paine wrote a series of articles called *The Crisis.* These articles inspired greater public support for the war and convinced many soldiers to reenlist. Today, political writers of all stripes are working in nearly every form—hardcover, softcover, editorial, blog, newsmagazine—to influence our current political landscape.

WRITE AND DISCUSS Catalog the political writing you encounter over the course of one week. Make a list that includes the formats, the topics covered, and your response to each. Then, with a small group, discuss the issues that are motivating today's political writers. Are these writers changing the public debate, or merely recording it?

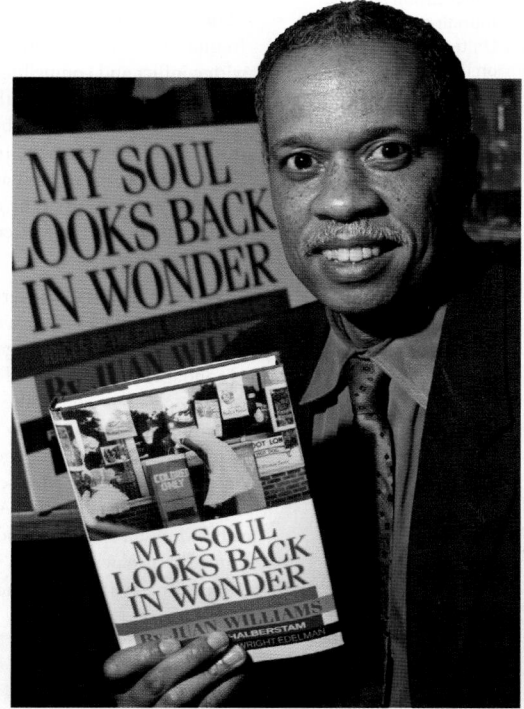

Journalist Juan Williams

FOR STRATEGIC READERS

Vocabulary Support To support instruction, clarify the meaning of these words:

- *motivate,* "encourage to act; inspire"
- *monarchy,* "a government controlled by a monarch, such as a king or queen"
- *framer,* "a person who plans or shapes something"

FOR ADVANCED LEARNERS/AP

Write to a Newspaper Have students choose an issue they feel strongly about and express their views in a letter to the editor of a local newspaper. Encourage students to take a definite position and to support their position with specific reasons and facts.

Government by the People

Have students read the paragraph. Ask volunteers to summarize the text, explaining in their own words the concept of a representative form of government.

TAKE ACTION Have students work in pairs to brainstorm local or state issues that affect them directly. Suggest they choose an issue that they can realistically address. For example, improving a local park is realistic; reducing the school week to four days is probably not. Whether students choose to contact their representative by phone, e-mail, or mail, tell them to be polite and respectful and to express their ideas clearly and specifically. Ask students to share their responses with the class.

The Power of Political Writing

Have students read the paragraph. Discuss how political writing can instigate change. Elicit or provide the various writing purposes and goals mentioned in the paragraph: "furthered the case for . . . independence," "inspired . . . support for the war," "convinced . . . soldiers to reenlist," "influence . . . political landscape." Ask students in what other ways political writing can affect how people think or act. ***Possible answer:*** *Political speeches influence voters.*

Point out that political writing is generally a form of persuasive writing that reflects the author's point of view. Explain that some forms of political writing are obvious, while others are more subtle. Elicit examples of both. ***Possible answer:*** *obvious—editorials, letters to the editor; more subtle—magazine articles, newspaper columns.* Then discuss how political writing is targeted to specific audiences.

WRITE AND DISCUSS Assign students the activity. Extend the discussion of their findings by exploring the similarities and differences among written pieces that address local, national, and international issues.

OBJECTIVES

Literary Analysis
- explore the key idea of **origin**
- analyze characteristics of a creation myth
- read a creation myth

Reading
- develop strategies for reading folk literature

CALIFORNIA R3.1, R3.5

ABOUT THE IROQUOIS

Have students read page 32 and summarize the key points. Students should recognize that

- the Iroquois passed down myths such as "The World on the Turtle's Back" through oral tradition, as discussed on page 22 of the historical essay
- the term *Iroquois* refers to six separate Native American groups
- cultural similarities helped to unify the Iroquois nations

USING THE *NOTABLE QUOTE*

- This quotation comes from a paper entitled "Native Oral Traditions" by Larry Evers and Paul Pavich, scholars of Native American literature.
- Have students paraphrase the quotation and discuss its meaning. Elicit that the quote underscores the role of creation myths and other stories in helping to establish and preserve people's way of life and their sense of history and tradition.

CALIFORNIA R3.1, R3.5

The World on the Turtle's Back
Iroquois Creation Myth

NOTABLE QUOTE
"[Native American] stories . . . remind the people of who and what they are, why they are in this particular place, and how they should continue to live here."

FYI
Did you know that . . .
- both the U.S. Constitution and the founding charter of the United Nations are based on ideas found in the Iroquois constitution, known as "The Great Binding Law"?
- Iroquois women had many more rights than colonial American women?
- more than 50,000 Iroquois live in the United States today?

BUILDING BACKGROUND
To learn more about the Iroquois, visit the **Literature Center** at ClassZone.com.

The totem, or tribal symbol, of the Iroquois

"The World on the Turtle's Back" is an Iroquois (ĭr′ə-kwoi′) creation story filled with conflict and compelling characters. The Iroquois passed down this story from one generation to the next by telling it in elaborate performances. In the 1800s, David Cusick, an Iroquois author, recorded one version of the story in print. Today, more than 25 written versions of the story exist.

The Power of Unity The term *Iroquois* refers to six separate Native American groups—the Seneca, Cayuga, Oneida, Onondaga, Mohawk, and Tuscarora. Five of these groups—all but the Tuscarora—once resided in what is now New York State. They continually waged war with one another, putting themselves at risk of attack from neighboring Algonquin tribes. Troubled by the bloodshed, a Huron named Deganawidah (də-gä′nə-wē′-də) joined forces with an Onondaga chief

named Hiawatha (hī′ə-wŏth′ə) to end the fighting. Sometime between 1570 and 1600, they formed the Iroquois League, a confederacy empowered to negotiate treaties with foreign nations and to resolve conflicts among the five nations. In 1722, the Tuscarora, from North Carolina, joined the league. For the next 175 to 200 years, the Iroquois managed to dominate other Native American groups and to remain free of both British and French rule.

The Iroquois Way of Life The league's effectiveness stemmed in part from the nations' shared culture. The groups spoke similar languages, held similar beliefs, and followed similar ways of life. They lived in longhouses made of pole frames covered with elm bark, and they built fences around their villages for protection. Up to 50 people occupied each longhouse, and 300 to 600 people lived in each village. Villages were governed by a chief or chiefs, who received advice from a council of adult males. Groups of women gathered wild fruits and nuts and cultivated corn, beans, and squash. In addition to waging war, the men traded, hunted, fished, and built the longhouses.

The Iroquois Through Time During the American Revolution, the Iroquois nations disagreed about whether to support the rebelling colonists or Great Britain. This dispute severely weakened the Iroquois League. Today, the league shows renewed vigor as it fights for environmental protection and increased recognition by the U.S. government.

RESOURCE MANAGER UNIT 1

Plan and Teach pp. 17–24

Literary Analysis
Summary pp. 25†*, 26‡*
Creation Myths pp. 27, 28†*
Question Support p. 32*

Reading
Reading Folk Literature pp. 29, 30†*
Reading Check p. 31

Assessment
Selection Tests A, B/C pp. 33*, 35*
Test Generator CD

BEST PRACTICES TOOLKIT

Differentiated Instruction
pp. 31–38*
Scaffolding Instruction
pp. 43–46*

Graphic Organizers/Strategies
Word Questioning • Two-Column Chart

Reading Support
Audio Anthology CD*

Technology
Literature Center at ClassZone.com
WriteSmart CD

---

* Resources for Differentiation   † Also in Spanish   ‡ In Haitian Creole and Vietnamese

LITERARY ANALYSIS: CREATION MYTHS

A **myth** is a traditional story, usually involving supernatural beings or events, that explains how some aspect of human nature or the natural world came to be. **Creation myths** are a specific kind of myth that typically

- describes how the universe, the earth, and life began
- explains the workings of the natural world
- supports and validates social customs and values
- guides people through the trials of living

As you read "The World on the Turtle's Back," note the supernatural explanation it offers of the world's origin. Think about how this myth serves the functions listed here.

READING STRATEGY: READING FOLK LITERATURE

You're probably already familiar with different types of **folk literature**, which includes folk tales, myths, fables, and legends passed orally from one generation to the next. The creation myth you are about to read is another example of folk literature. Using the following strategies as you read will help you not only understand and appreciate the myth's message but also glean information about the culture it comes from:

- Read the myth aloud, or imagine a storyteller's voice as you read silently.
- Note mysteries of nature and details about creation that the myth explains.
- Make inferences about the social values or customs taught through the characters and situations.
- Look for details that reveal other aspects of Iroquois culture.

As you read, use a chart like the one shown to record your notes and observations about the three kinds of information you find in this myth.

Details About Creation/Nature	Social Values or Customs	Other Cultural Details
Before the earth was created, humans and animals "of the kind that are around us now" did not exist.		

How do we make SENSE of our world?

KEY IDEA Since the beginning of time, people of all cultures have gathered to discuss one of life's biggest questions: how was the world created? The Iroquois creation myth you're about to read offers one answer to this question about the **origin** of the world.

DISCUSS What different accounts of creation—biblical narratives, scientific theories, or stories from other cultures, for example—have you heard or read? With a small group of classmates, summarize as many of these accounts as you know.

33

How do we make SENSE of our world?

Have students read the question and **KEY IDEA**. Ask them why people are eager to understand the **origin** of their world. Extend the exploration by having groups complete the **DISCUSS** activity.

SKILLS FOCUS

LITERARY ANALYSIS	R3.1, R3.5

● CREATION MYTHS

Have students summarize any creation myths they know about. For instance, one version of an African creation myth describes how a cosmic egg hatches. Spirits emerge from the egg and then create humankind.

Ask students why different cultures have different creation myths. ***Possible answer: Creation myths reflect a culture's physical environment. Thus, a desert society might envision the world's origin differently from people who live beside the ocean.***

CHECK UNDERSTANDING Ask students what kinds of questions a creation myth is likely to answer.

READING STRATEGY

◼ READING FOLK LITERATURE

Provide familiar examples of different types of folk literature, such as the Paul Bunyan folk tales, any of the ancient Greek myths, or Aesop's fables. Encourage students to provide additional examples. Discuss why folk literature is popular.

R RESOURCE MANAGER—Copy Master Reading Folk Literature p. 29 (for student use while reading the selection)

DIFFERENTIATED INSTRUCTION

FOR STRATEGIC READERS
Concept Support: Reading Folk Literature
Explain that folk literature typically teaches life lessons. For example, the story of King Midas and the golden touch presents a lesson about greed. The Greek myth of Arachne warns against boastfulness. All the fables of Aesop contain morals. By providing lessons with which listeners and readers can identify, folk literature transmits values and beliefs that are important to a culture or society.

SUMMARY

This Iroquois creation myth describes how the earth is formed. Before the earth's creation, a vast ocean lies beneath the Sky-World of the gods. When a woman falls through the floor of the Sky-World, birds set her down upon a great sea turtle. A muskrat brings her soil from the ocean bottom, which the woman uses to make the land. She gives birth to a daughter who, in turn, bears twin boys. The boys—one honest, the other devious—struggle against each other, each playing a part in creating and ruling the world.

LITERARY ANALYSIS

Ⓐ CREATION MYTHS

Answers will vary. Students should cite details both from this myth and from the creation accounts they've heard or read. Some students may recognize similarities between the beginning of this myth and the biblical story of Adam and Eve, who tasted the fruit of the tree of knowledge in the Garden of Eden. Eve encouraged Adam to taste the fruit against his better judgment.

The **World** on the **Turtle's Back**

IROQUOIS

ANALYZE VISUALS
Examine the painting on page 35. How does the artist use light and color to emphasize the division between the Sky-World and the void below it?

In the beginning there was no world, no land, no creatures of the kind that are around us now, and there were no men. But there was a great ocean which occupied space as far as anyone could see. Above the ocean was a great void of air. And in the air there lived the birds of the sea; in the ocean lived the fish and the creatures of the deep. Far above this unpeopled world, there was a Sky-World. Here lived gods who were like people—like Iroquois.

In the Sky-World there was a man who had a wife, and the wife was expecting a child. The woman became hungry for all kinds of strange delicacies, as women do when they are with child. She kept her husband busy almost to distraction finding ① **Targeted Passage**
10 delicious things for her to eat.

In the middle of the Sky-World there grew a Great Tree which was not like any of the trees that we know. It was tremendous; it had grown there forever. It had enormous roots that spread out from the floor of the Sky-World. And on its branches there were many different kinds of leaves and different kinds of fruits and flowers. The tree was not supposed to be marked or mutilated by any of the beings who dwelt in the Sky-World. It was a sacred tree that stood at the center of the universe. Ⓐ

The woman decided that she wanted some bark from one of the roots of the Great Tree—perhaps as a food or as a medicine, we don't know. She told her husband this.
20 He didn't like the idea. He knew it was wrong. But she insisted, and he gave in. So he dug a hole among the roots of this great sky tree, and he bared some of its roots. But the floor of the Sky-World wasn't very thick, and he broke a hole through it. He was terrified, for he had never expected to find empty space underneath the world.

Ⓐ **CREATION MYTHS**
So far, how is this myth similar to and different from other accounts of creation you've heard or read? Explain your answer, citing details.

Sky Woman (1936), Ernest Smith. Courtesy of the Rochester Museum and Science Center, Rochester, New York.

DIFFERENTIATED INSTRUCTION

FOR ALL STUDENTS

Provide these independent projects to extend the lesson:

- Prepare a visual representation of a memorable scene from the myth.
- Write a poem describing life in the Sky-World.

For further details on these projects, see

R RESOURCE MANAGER
Ideas for Extension pp. 22–23

FOR STRATEGIC READERS

In combination with the *Audio Anthology CD*, use one or more Targeted Passages (pp. 34, 36, 37, 38, 40) to ensure that students focus on key story events and concepts. Targeted Passages are also good for English learners.

① **Targeted Passage [Lines 1–17]**

This passage introduces the mythical setting and the woman who is a key character. It also describes the sacred Great Tree.

ANALYZE VISUALS

Possible answer: The artist paints the Sky-World in bright, sunny yellow. In contrast, the void below the Sky-World is dark, its only light coming through the hole from the world above.

About the Art In paintings such as *Sky Woman*, Seneca artist and craftsman Ernest Smith (1907–1975) recorded the traditions and customs of the Iroquois people. Through his clear and clean style, Smith worked to preserve the memory of cultural details that he feared might otherwise be forgotten. The painting on page 35 vividly depicts the events described at the beginning of "The World on the Turtle's Back."

CULTURAL CONNECTION

Myths About Twins This Iroquois creation myth centers on the rivalry between twins. In fact, twins play a central role in the legends and myths of many Native American cultures, including those of the Great Plains and the desert Southwest. The Navajo, for example, tell the story of Changing Woman and the Hero Twins, a myth of how twins rid the world of monsters, making it safe for the Navajo people. Invite students to identify stories from other cultures in which twins play an important role. Encourage them to look for common themes.

- What is the setting of this myth?
- Who lives in the Sky-World?
- What two characters are introduced?
- What is special about the Great Tree?

FOR ENGLISH LEARNERS

Key Academic Vocabulary Use Word Questioning to teach these words: *enormous* (line 13), *finally* (line 55), *approach* (line 86), *conflict* (line 103), *domain* (line 176).

 BEST PRACTICES TOOLKIT—Transparency
Word Questioning p. E9

Prereading For prereading instruction for English learners, see

 BEST PRACTICES TOOLKIT
Scaffolding Reading Instruction pp. 43–46

FOR ADVANCED LEARNERS/AP

AP exercises in the bottom channel provide additional challenge for students. Use these suggestions for small groups or individuals.

ADDITIONAL GUIDELINES

For more help with differentiation and tips for classroom management, see

 BEST PRACTICES TOOLKIT
Differentiated Instruction pp. 31–38

Lines 33–67
REINFORCE *KEY IDEA*: ORIGIN

Discuss How does the great sea turtle's role in the **origin** of the world explain the title of the story? *Possible answer: The turtle takes the falling woman on his back (lines 38–41), where she remains afloat in the ocean. The woman places dirt from the ocean bottom on the turtle's back and plants the roots from the Great Tree in the soil. In time, the "earth began to grow" and "the plants grew on the earth" (lines 65–67). Thus, the world formed on the turtle's back.*

B FOLK LITERATURE

Possible answer: The animals play a significant role in the myth, helping and supporting the woman. They are depicted as wise and resourceful, suggesting that the Iroquois had a respectful, even reverential, attitude toward animals.

If students need help . . .

- Have students review lines 33–41. Discuss how the sea creatures respond to the woman's situation.

- Have students reread lines 46–62. Talk about how the animals help the woman.

- Discuss how the creatures' actions and reactions reveal the Iroquois' positive feelings toward animals.

But his wife was filled with curiosity. He wouldn't get any of the roots for her, so she set out to do it herself. She bent over and she looked down, and she saw the ocean far below. She leaned down and stuck her head through the hole and looked all around. No one knows just what happened next. Some say she slipped. Some say that her husband, fed up with all the demands she had made on him, pushed her.

30 So she fell through the hole. As she fell, she frantically grabbed at its edges, but her hands slipped. However, between her fingers there clung bits of things that were growing on the floor of the Sky-World and bits of the root tips of the Great Tree. And so she began to fall toward the great ocean far below.

The birds of the sea saw the woman falling, and they immediately consulted with each other as to what they could do to help her. Flying wingtip to wingtip they made a great feathery raft in the sky to support her, and thus they broke her fall. But of course it was not possible for them to carry the woman very long. Some of the other birds of the sky flew down to the surface of the ocean and called up the ocean creatures to see what they could do to help. The great sea turtle came and agreed to receive her on his back. The birds placed her gently

40 on the shell of the turtle, and now the turtle floated about on the huge ocean with the woman safely on his back.

The beings up in the Sky-World paid no attention to this. They knew what was happening, but they chose to ignore it.

When the woman recovered from her shock and terror, she looked around her. All that she could see were the birds and the sea creatures and the sky and the ocean.

And the woman said to herself that she would die. But the creatures of the sea came to her and said that they would try to help her and asked her what they could do. She told them that if they could find some soil, she could plant the roots stuck between her fingers, and from them plants would grow. The sea

50 animals said perhaps there was dirt at the bottom of the ocean, but no one had ever been down there so they could not be sure.

If there was dirt at the bottom of the ocean, it was far, far below the surface in the cold deeps. But the animals said they would try to get some. One by one the diving birds and animals tried and failed. They went to the limits of their endurance, but they could not get to the bottom of the ocean. Finally, the muskrat said he would try. He dived and disappeared. All the creatures waited, holding their breath, but he did not return. After a long time, his little body floated up to the surface of the ocean, a tiny crumb of earth clutched in his paw. He seemed to be dead. They pulled him up on the turtle's back and they sang and prayed

60 over him and breathed air into his mouth, and finally, he stirred. Thus it was the muskrat, the Earth-Diver, who brought from the bottom of the ocean the soil from which the earth was to grow. **B**

The woman took the tiny clod of dirt and placed it on the middle of the great sea turtle's back. Then the woman began to walk in a circle around it, moving in the direction that the sun goes. The earth began to grow. When the earth was big

② **Targeted Passage**

B FOLK LITERATURE
Reread lines 46–62 and consider the role that "all the creatures" play in this myth. What does this suggest about the Iroquois' attitude toward animals?

DIFFERENTIATED INSTRUCTION

FOR STRATEGIC READERS

② Targeted Passage [Lines 29–49]

This passage explains how the first woman comes to the world and how animals help her. It also sets up the explanation for the creation of soil and plants in the world.

- How does the woman leave the Sky-World? What does she hold between her fingers?

- Which animals help the woman? How?

- Predict how the myth may explain the beginning of plants on the earth.

FOR ADVANCED LEARNERS/AP

Analyze Symbolism Have students discuss the symbolism of the Great Tree. Then ask them to recall or research the symbolism associated with trees (for example, the tree of knowledge in the Garden of Eden) and share their findings with the class. Challenge students to identify literary works that use tree symbolism, such as Shel Silverstein's *The Giving Tree*.

enough, she planted the roots she had clutched between her fingers when she fell from the Sky-World. Thus the plants grew on the earth.

To keep the earth growing, the woman walked as the sun goes, moving in the direction that the people still move in the dance rituals. She gathered roots and
70 plants to eat and built herself a little hut. After a while, the woman's time came, and she was delivered of a daughter. The woman and her daughter kept walking in a circle around the earth, so that the earth and plants would continue to grow. They lived on the plants and roots they gathered. The girl grew up with her mother, cut off forever from the Sky-World above, knowing only the birds and the creatures of the sea, seeing no other beings like herself.

One day, when the girl had grown to womanhood, a man appeared. No one knows for sure who this man was. He had something to do with the gods above. Perhaps he was the West Wind. As the girl looked at him, she was filled with terror, and amazement, and warmth, and she fainted dead away. As she lay on the ground,
80 the man reached into his quiver, and he took out two arrows, one sharp and one blunt, and he laid them across the body of the girl, and quietly went away.

When the girl awoke from her faint, she and her mother continued to walk around the earth. After a while, they knew that the girl was to bear a child. They did not know it, but the girl was to bear twins.

Within the girl's body, the twins began to argue and quarrel with one another. There could be no peace between them. As the time approached for them to be born, the twins fought about their birth. The right-handed twin wanted to be born in the normal way, as all children are born. But the left-handed twin said no. He said he saw light in another direction, and said he would be born that
90 way. The right-handed twin beseeched him not to, saying that he would kill their mother. But the left-handed twin was stubborn. He went in the direction where he saw light. But he could not be born through his mother's mouth or her nose. He was born through her left armpit, and killed her. And meanwhile, the right-handed twin was born in the normal way, as all children are born.

The twins met in the world outside, and the right-handed twin accused his brother of murdering their mother. But the grandmother told them to stop their quarreling. They buried their mother. And from her grave grew the plants which the people still use. From her head grew the corn, the beans, and the squash—"our supporters, the three sisters."[1] And from her heart grew the sacred tobacco, which
100 the people still use in the ceremonies and by whose upward-floating smoke they send thanks. The women call her "our mother," and they dance and sing in the rituals so that the corn, the beans, and the squash may grow to feed the people. **C**

But the conflict of the twins did not end at the grave of their mother. And, strangely enough, the grandmother favored the left-handed twin.

The right-handed twin was angry, and he grew more angry as he thought how his brother had killed their mother. The right-handed twin was the one who did everything just as he should. He said what he meant, and he meant what he said.

---

1. **the three sisters:** Corn, beans, and squash—the Iroquois' staple food crops—were grown together. The bean vines climbed and were supported by the corn stalks; squash, which spread across the ground and kept weeds from growing, was planted around the bean plants.

③ Targeted Passage

C CREATION MYTHS
Creation myths often contain **symbols**—people, places, and things that stand for something beyond themselves. Reread lines 97–102. What might the twins' mother symbolize?

Lines 85–106
TIERED DISCUSSION PROMPTS

Use these prompts to help students understand the events leading up to the twins' birth and the effects of their birth:

Recall How is the twins' mother related to the woman who fell from the Sky-World? How are the twins related to her? ***Answer: The twins' mother is the adult daughter of the woman who fell from the Sky-World. The twins are the woman's grandchildren.***

Analyze What causes the death of the twins' mother? What positive effect results from her death? What negative effect? ***Possible answers: The stubborn left-handed twin wants to go toward the light he sees, so he is born through her left armpit, which kills her. A positive effect is that useful plants grow from the mother's grave. A negative effect is that the right-handed twin blames his brother for killing their mother.***

Synthesize The author writes that there "could be no peace between" the unborn twins (line 86). Symbolically, what might this conflict between the twins represent? ***Possible answer: It might represent the "birth" of the struggle between good and evil in the world.***

LITERARY ANALYSIS

C CREATION MYTHS
Possible answer: The twins' mother might symbolize Mother Earth, the development of agriculture, or the geological formation of the earth.

FOR STRATEGIC READERS
③ Targeted Passage [Lines 66–86]

This passage explains how plants began to grow on the earth and how the birth of the first twins brought conflict to the earth.

- From where do the roots come that the woman plants in the world?

- Who visits the girl after she has grown to womanhood? How does she respond?

- What do the twins do as they begin to grow?

FOR ENGLISH LEARNERS
Related Vocabulary Stress that the conflict between the twins takes many forms, which are signified in the author's choice of words. Teach these closely related words from page 37: *argue* (line 85), *quarrel* (line 85), *fought* (line 87), *kill* (line 90), *murdering* (line 96), *conflict* (line 103).

FOLK LITERATURE

Possible answer: *The right-handed twin is characterized as more admirable. He is truthful and direct, while the left-handed twin is untruthful and devious. This characterization suggests that the Iroquois valued honesty and straightforwardness.*

If students need help . . . Review lines 105–112, and help students use a Two-Column Chart to compare the qualities of the twins.

🧰 BEST PRACTICES TOOLKIT—Transparency Two-Column Chart p. A25

Lines 117–142
TIERED DISCUSSION PROMPTS

Use these prompts to help students understand the role of the twins in creating a balanced world:

Connect What examples in nature can you think of that suggest "a balanced and orderly world" (line 137)? *Accept all reasonable responses.*

Analyze How do the opposing efforts of the twins create balance in the world? ***Possible answer:*** *Each twin uses his powers to counterbalance the other's creations. For example, one twin makes deer and squirrels, while the other twin creates predators who kill these animals (lines 119–125). Similarly, one twin makes life-sustaining berries and fruits, while the other creates briars and poisonous plants (lines 129–132).*

Evaluate How effective is the author in showing how the twins achieved a natural balance in the newly created world? Explain. *Accept all reasonable responses.*

He always told the truth, and he always tried to accomplish what seemed to be right and reasonable. The left-handed twin never said what he meant or meant
110 what he said. He always lied, and he always did things backward. You could never tell what he was trying to do because he always made it look as if he were doing the opposite. He was the devious one. **D**

These two brothers, as they grew up, represented two ways of the world which are in all people. The Indians did not call these the right and the wrong. They called them the straight mind and the crooked mind, the upright man and the devious man, the right and the left.

The twins had creative powers. They took clay and modeled it into animals, and they gave these animals life. And in this they contended with one another. The right-handed twin made the deer, and the left-handed twin made the
120 mountain lion which kills the deer. But the right-handed twin knew there would always be more deer than mountain lions. And he made another animal. He made the ground squirrel. The left-handed twin saw that the mountain lion could not get to the ground squirrel, who digs a hole, so he made the weasel. And although the weasel can go into the ground squirrel's hole and kill him, there are lots of ground squirrels and not so many weasels. Next the right-handed twin decided he would make an animal that the weasel could not kill, so he made the porcupine. But the left-handed twin made the bear, who flips the porcupine over on his back and tears out his belly.

And the right-handed twin made berries and fruits of other kinds for his
130 creatures to live on. The left-handed twin made briars and poison ivy, and the poisonous plants like the baneberry and the dogberry, and the suicide root with which people kill themselves when they go out of their minds. And the left-handed twin made medicines, for good and for evil, for doctoring and for witchcraft.

And finally, the right-handed twin made man. The people do not know just how much the left-handed twin had to do with making man. Man was made of clay, like pottery, and baked in the fire. . . .

The world the twins made was a balanced and orderly world, and this was good. The plant-eating animals created by the right-handed twin would eat up all the vegetation if their number was not kept down by the meat-eating animals,
140 which the left-handed twin created. But if these carnivorous animals ate too many other animals, then they would starve, for they would run out of meat. So the right- and the left-handed twins built balance into the world.

As the twins became men full grown, they still contested with one another. No one had won, and no one had lost. And they knew that the conflict was becoming sharper and sharper, and one of them would have to vanquish the other.

And so they came to the duel. They started with gambling. They took a wooden bowl, and in it they put wild plum pits. One side of the pits was burned black, and by tossing the pits in the bowl and betting on how these would fall, they gambled against one another, as the people still do in the New Year's

D FOLK LITERATURE
Reread lines 95–112. Which twin is characterized as being more admirable? What does this characterization tell you about Iroquois values?

④ Targeted Passage

DIFFERENTIATED INSTRUCTION

FOR STRATEGIC READERS

④ **Targeted Passage [Lines 113–142]**

This passage describes the twins' role in achieving balance in the world.

- Paraphrase this sentence: "These two brothers, as they grew up, represented two ways of the world which are in all people."

- What are some of the living things that each twin created?

- What was a positive effect of the twins' opposing efforts?

FOR ENGLISH LEARNERS

Related Vocabulary Examine these words related to the conflict between the twins: *contested* (line 143), *won* and *lost* (line 144), *vanquish* (line 145), *duel* (line 146), *battle* (line 153), *succumb* (line 157), *weak point* (line 160), *destroyed* (line 168).

Detail of *Sky Woman* (1936), Ernest Smith. Courtesy of the Rochester Museum and Science Center, Rochester, New York.

150 rites.[2] All through the morning they gambled at this game, and all through the afternoon, and the sun went down, the game was done, and neither one had won.

So they went on to battle one another at the lacrosse[3] game. And they contested all day, and the sun went down, and the game was done. And neither had won.

And now they battled with clubs, and they fought all day, and the sun went down, and the fight was done. But neither had won. **E**

And they went from one duel to another to see which one would succumb. Each one knew in his deepest mind that there was something, somewhere, that would vanquish the other. But what was it? Where to find it?

160 Each knew somewhere in his mind what it was that was his own weak point. They talked about this as they contested in these duels, day after day, and somehow the deep mind of each entered into the other. And the deep mind of the right-handed twin lied to his brother, and the deep mind of the left-handed twin told the truth.

On the last day of the duel, as they stood, they at last knew how the right-handed twin was to kill his brother. Each selected his weapon. The left-handed twin chose a mere stick that would do him no good. But the right-handed twin

E FOLK LITERATURE
Reread lines 146–156. Note in your chart the information about Iroquois customs and rituals you learn from these lines.

---

2. **New Year's rites:** various ceremonies to get ready for the New Year. They often included community confession of sins, the replenishing of hearths in the homes, and sacred dances, as well as the gambling ritual.

3. **lacrosse:** a game of Native American origin wherein participants on two teams use long-handled sticks with webbed pouches to maneuver a ball into the opposing team's goal.

ANALYZE VISUALS

Activity Ask students what ideas this detail from the painting on page 35 emphasizes.

Possible answer: *The detail emphasizes the importance of the turtle and, by extrapolation, of other animals in the creation myth of the Iroquois.*

READING STRATEGY

E FOLK LITERATURE

Possible answer:

Details About Creation/ Nature	Social Values or Customs	Other Cultural Details
	The Iroquois gambled and played lacrosse. They held ceremonies to prepare for the New Year.	

FOR ADVANCED LEARNERS/AP

Analyze Tone and Style [small-group option] Have students work in small groups to discuss the author's tone and style. Have them analyze the sentence variety, diction, and author's viewpoint. Then have them consider these questions:

- Does the author reveal any personal feelings about the Iroquois' beliefs, or does the author remain totally neutral?
- Is the author's tone and style appropriate for the subject?

- In what ways might the author have changed the style and tone of the selection? How would these changes have affected the readers' response to the selection?

Encourage groups to exchange their conclusions.

picked out the deer antler, and with one touch he destroyed his brother. And the left-handed twin died, but he died and he didn't die. The right-handed twin
170 picked up the body and cast it off the edge of the earth. And some place below the world, the left-handed twin still lives and reigns.

When the sun rises from the east and travels in a huge arc along the sky dome, which rests like a great upside-down cup on the saucer of the earth, the people are in the daylight realm of the right-handed twin. But when the sun slips down in the west at nightfall and the dome lifts to let it escape at the western rim, the people are again in the domain of the left-handed twin—the fearful realm of night.

Having killed his brother, the right-handed twin returned home to his grandmother. And she met him in anger. She threw the food out of the cabin onto the ground and said that he was a murderer, for he had killed his brother. He grew
180 angry and told her she had always helped his brother, who had killed their mother. In his anger, he grabbed her by the throat and cut her head off. Her body he threw into the ocean, and her head, into the sky. There, "Our Grandmother, the Moon" still keeps watch at night over the realm of her favorite grandson. **F**

The right-handed twin has many names. One of them is Sapling. It means smooth, young, green and fresh and innocent, straightforward, straight-growing, soft and pliable, teachable and trainable. These are the old ways of describing him. But since he has gone away, he has other names. He is called "He Holds Up the Skies," "Master of Life," and "Great Creator."

The left-handed twin also has many names. One of them is Flint. He is called
190 the devious one, the one covered with boils. Old Warty. He is stubborn. He is thought of as being dark in color.

These two beings rule the world and keep an eye on the affairs of men. The right-handed twin, the Master of Life, lives in the Sky-World. He is content with the world he helped to create and with his favorite creatures, the humans. The scent of sacred tobacco rising from the earth comes gloriously to his nostrils.

In the world below lives the left-handed twin. He knows the world of men, and he finds contentment in it. He hears the sounds of warfare and torture, and he finds them good.

In the daytime, the people have rituals which honor the right-handed twin.
200 Through the daytime rituals, they thank the Master of Life. In the nighttime, the people dance and sing for the left-handed twin. ❧

F CREATION MYTHS
The transformation of a character is a common element of mythology, often used to explain natural phenomena. Consider the natural feature explained in lines 172–183. How does this myth explain the fact that the moon is visible mainly at night?

5 Targeted Passage

LITERARY ANALYSIS

F CREATION MYTHS

Possible answer: According to the myth, when the twin hurled the grandmother's head into the sky, she transformed into the moon, which "keeps watch at night over the realm of her favorite grandson" (line 183).

Extend the Discussion Why do you suppose the grandmother favors the left-handed twin (see also line 104)?

SELECTION WRAP–UP

REFLECT A creation myth is usually meant to answer questions about how the world was created and to describe how life began. Ask students to consider how well "The World on the Turtle's Back" accomplishes these goals.

⭐ **CRITIQUE**

- Have students evaluate the story. Discuss which parts were most and least interesting. Ask whether the story would have been more or less effective if told in a more conventional manner.

- After completing the After Reading questions on page 41, have students revisit their responses and tell whether they have changed their opinions.

DIFFERENTIATED INSTRUCTION

FOR STRATEGIC READERS

5 Targeted Passage [Lines 192–201]

This passage summarizes the twins' shared role in ruling the world.

- Which twin lives in the Sky-World?

- Which twin controls "the world below"?

- How do the people show their appreciation of both twins?

FOR ADVANCED LEARNERS/AP

Analyze and Evaluate Have students reflect on the effectiveness of "The World on the Turtle's Back" as a myth. Does this version accomplish what a creation myth should? Or does the story raise as many questions as it answers and leave too many questions unanswered? Have students express their opinions in an essay, supporting their views with specific ideas and details. Ask volunteers to share their essays with the class.

Comprehension

R3.1, R3.5

1. **Recall** How do the animals help the woman who fell from the sky?

2. **Recall** What roles do the grandmother and her daughter play in the earth's creation?

3. **Summarize** What is the outcome of the battles between the twins?

Literary Analysis

4. **Compare and Contrast** How does this myth compare with the accounts of the world's origin you summarized before you read? Use a Venn diagram to record the differences and similarities between "The World on the Turtle's Back" and one of the accounts you discussed.

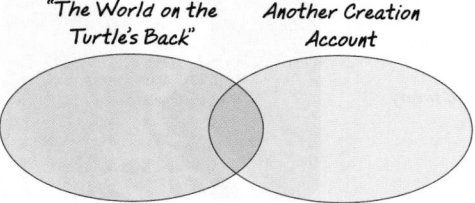

"The World on the Turtle's Back"   Another Creation Account

5. **Analyze a Creation Myth** Reread lines 105–112. Summarize the differences between the right-handed twin and the left-handed twin. Why do you think the Iroquois honor both twins? What elements of human nature are explained by "The World on the Turtle's Back"?

6. **Draw Conclusions from Folk Literature** Folk literature often transmits information about a people's culture and way of life. Review the details you noted in your chart as you read. From this myth, what did you learn about the Iroquois'

   • attitude toward nature?
   • view of their gods?
   • important food, games, and rituals?
   • beliefs about good and evil?

7. **Synthesize Cultural Ideas** How would you relate the Iroquois reverence for both the right-handed and left-handed twins to your own concept of good and evil? Explain your response, citing details and description from the text.

Literary Criticism

8. **Critical Interpretations** Creation stories often serve many purposes. According to Larry Evers and Paul Pavich, scholars of Native American literature, such stories "remind the people of who and what they are, why they are in this particular place, and how they should continue to live here." Do you think that "The World on the Turtle's Back" fulfills these functions? Explain, citing evidence from the text to support your interpretation.

6. ● **SKILLS FOCUS Reading Folk Literature** *The Iroquois respect nature. They see animals as worthy of admiration; they respect the balance of nature. The Iroquois believe the world was created by a higher power; they speak of their gods with reverence. Corn, beans, and squash are essential to the Iroquois; lacrosse is a key game and competition is important; the Iroquois perform ceremonies to get ready for the New Year. The Iroquois believe good and evil together create a balanced world.*

7. *Students should recognize that the Iroquois view neither twin as wholly good or wholly evil and give thanks to each for his creations.*

8. *Students may say that the myth explains where the Iroquois came from, suggests why humans feel conflicting impulses and emotions, and serves as a guide for living by teaching reverence both for the gods and for nature.*

Practice and Apply

After Reading

Use these copy masters to check understanding and provide extra support:

R RESOURCE MANAGER—Copy Masters
   Reading Check p. 31
   Creation Myths p. 27
   Question Support p. 32

   Additional selection questions are provided for teachers on page 21.

ANSWERS

1. *The birds break the woman's fall; the turtle carries her on its back; the muskrat brings back soil from the ocean floor.*

2. *The woman and her daughter make the earth grow by walking around the soil. The daughter gives birth to twins, who eventually rule the earth.*

3. *The left-handed twin is defeated but reigns in the underworld, while the right-handed twin rules from the Sky-World.*

Possible answers:

4. *Answers will vary. Encourage students to be specific.*

5. ● **SKILLS FOCUS Creation Myths** *The right-handed twin tells the truth and acts in a "right and reasonable" way. He creates edible berries and herbivorous animals. The left-handed twin lies, does things "backward," and acts deviously. He creates poisonous plants and carnivorous animals. The Iroquois honor both twins because they recognize "crooked" and "straight," predators and prey as necessary to a balanced world. The myth explains why humans have both virtuous and devious impulses.*

Assess and Reteach

Assess

R RESOURCE MANAGER—Copy Masters
   Selection Test A pp. 33–34
   Selection Test B/C pp. 35–36

🖴 Test Generator CD

Reteach

S STANDARDS LESSON FILE
   Literature Lessons 30, 31: Symbol and Symbolism; Archetypes
   Reading Lesson 8: Making Inferences

Focus and Motivate

OBJECTIVES

Literary Analysis
- explore the key idea of **villains**
- analyze characteristics of a trickster tale
- read a trickster tale

Reading
- predict

 CALIFORNIA R3.1, R3.6

ABOUT THE AUTHOR

Have students read page 42 and summarize key points about Mourning Dove. Point out that, as explained in the historical essay (pages 22–23), folk tales such as "Coyote and the Buffalo" were passed down through oral tradition. By recording such stories, Mourning Dove helped to preserve them during a time when the power of oral tradition had weakened.

USING THE *NOTABLE QUOTE*

Discuss the meaning of the quotation from **Mourning Dove.** She says that "every person [has] a mission." Ask what Mourning Dove may have seen as her own "mission." *Students should note that Mourning Dove wanted to preserve the Okanogan culture and the tales of the storytellers she admired.*

Selection Resources

The Native American Experience

 CALIFORNIA R3.1, R3.6

Coyote and the Buffalo

Folk Tale Retold by Mourning Dove

NOTABLE QUOTE
"Everything on the earth has a purpose, every disease an herb to cure it, and every person a mission. This is the Indian theory of existence."

FYI
Did you know that Mourning Dove . . .
- was born in a canoe while her mother was crossing a river in Idaho?
- learned to read English by poring over melodramatic dime-store novels?
- was the first woman ever elected to the Colville tribal council?

Author Online

For more on Mourning Dove, visit the **Literature Center** at **ClassZone.com.**

Mourning Dove
c. 1885–1936

Mourning Dove is the pen name of Christine Quintasket (kwən-tăs′kət), who triumphed over adversity to become one of the first female Native American novelists. As a child, Quintasket was enthralled by the traditional stories told by her elders. As an adult, she worked to preserve these tales. By publishing stories that recount the history of her people, she carried on the work of the storytellers she so admired.

Determined to Write Quintasket grew up on the Colville Reservation in Washington State with her mother, the daughter of a Colville chief, and her father, an Okanogan. When Quintasket was 14, her mother died, leaving her to run the household and help raise her younger siblings. Despite her many responsibilities, Quintasket pushed herself to learn to write in English. She later attended secretarial school to learn how to type and business school to hone her grammar and writing

skills. She drafted a novel in 1912 but put it away for several years until she met Lucullus McWhorter, a Native American–rights activist, who offered to edit it.

Battling Stereotypes Published in 1927, Mourning Dove's novel, *Cogewea, the Half-Blood,* is credited with breaking down the stereotype of Native Americans as stoic, or unfeeling. "It is all wrong, this saying that Indians do not feel as deeply as whites," the author asserted. "We do feel, and by and by some of us are going to make our feelings appreciated, and then will the true Indian character be revealed."

Chronicling Her Culture After *Cogewea* was published, Mourning Dove began to record traditional stories of the Okanogan and other Colville tribes. A migrant worker, she picked fruit ten hours a day but managed to do her writing at night. *Coyote Stories,* from which "Coyote and the Buffalo" is taken, was published in 1933. "Coyote and the Buffalo" is a folk tale once told by Okanogan storytellers in Salish, their native language. Mourning Dove's retelling includes Salish words and place names. This story and others like it help keep the Okanogan culture alive today.

Mourning Dove's Legacy In addition to preserving her people's culture, Mourning Dove worked hard to promote their welfare. She fought for their rights in court, started organizations supporting Native American crafts, and paved the way for female participation on tribal councils. Worn down by chronic illness and fatigue, the writer and activist died in 1936.

42

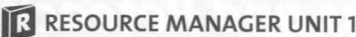 **RESOURCE MANAGER UNIT 1**

Plan and Teach pp. 37–44
Literary Analysis
Summary pp. 45†*, 46‡*
Trickster Tales pp. 47, 48†*
Question Support p. 52*
Reading
Predict pp. 49, 50†*
Reading Check p. 51

Assessment
Selection Tests A, B/C pp. 53*, 55*
 Test Generator CD

 BEST PRACTICES TOOLKIT

Differentiated Instruction pp. 31–38*
Scaffolding Instruction pp. 43–46*
Graphic Organizers/Strategies
Character Analysis Chart

Reading Support
 Audio Anthology CD*

Technology
ℹ️ Literature Center at **ClassZone.com**
WriteSmart CD

---

* Resources for Differentiation   † Also in Spanish   ‡ In Haitian Creole and Vietnamese

LITERARY ANALYSIS: TRICKSTER TALES

You already know that a folk tale is a simple story passed orally from one generation to the next. **Trickster tales** are a type of folk tale that features an animal or human character who typically engages in deceit, violence, and magic. Often, trickster tales are mythic, explaining how some aspect of human nature or the natural world came to be. The opening lines of "Coyote and the Buffalo" announce what this trickster tale will explain.

No buffalo ever lived in the Swah-netk'-qhu *country. That was Coyote's fault.*

Tricksters are **archetypal characters**—character types that can be found in literary works from different cultures throughout the ages. As you read this tale, notice how the coyote demonstrates the trickster's contradictory qualities: he is foolish yet clever, greedy yet helpful, immoral yet moral.

READING STRATEGY: PREDICT

Tricksters are often schemers or scoundrels—they don't usually act as other characters do. Using your background knowledge of this character's contradictory qualities, as well as text clues, can help you **predict** upcoming story events. As you read, use a chart like the one shown to record Coyote's key traits and unusual behavior. Pause occasionally to predict what will happen next.

Coyote's Traits and Behavior	My Predictions
Coyote is "foolish and greedy"; it is his fault there are no buffalo in Swah-netk'-qhu country.	This story will reveal that Coyote did something reckless or unwise to scare away the buffalo.

Why do we root for the "BAD GUY"?

KEY IDEA Wherever they go, they ignore the rules. They stir up trouble. And yet we admire and love them despite—or maybe because of—their bad behavior. Many societies have famous **villains** or trickster figures, who both infuriate and inspire the people around them.

QUICKWRITE Think about movies or books in which the villain is more compelling than the hero. What qualities does such a villain typically display? Which of these traits contribute most to his or her appeal? Record your responses in a short paragraph.

43

Why do we root for the "BAD GUY"?

Introduce the question, and have students read the **KEY IDEA**. Have students think about the different types of **villains** they have encountered in books and movies and on TV. Which ones are mischievous? Which are evil? Then have students complete the **QUICKWRITE**.

SKILLS FOCUS

LITERARY ANALYSIS   R3.1, R3.6

TRICKSTER TALES

Explain that the archetypal trickster character takes many forms. For example, in Native American oral tradition, it may be a coyote or raven. In African tales, it may be a hare or spider, while in Japan it may be a fox. No matter what the form, the trickster usually exhibits contradictory qualities. He may be both creative and destructive, wise yet childlike. Ask students why they think trickster characters have appealed to people through the ages and in so many different cultures. *Possible answer: The trickster embodies the contradictory qualities of human beings.*

CHECK UNDERSTANDING Ask students to explain why a trickster character might be both likable and unlikable at the same time.

READING STRATEGY

PREDICT

Point out to students that, even without realizing it, they often make predictions about a character based on their knowledge of the character's qualities and on text clues. For example, once they have identified the villain in a movie, they may anticipate what he or she will do next. Elicit examples of predictions students have made about characters in books and movies.

 RESOURCE MANAGER—Copy Master
    Predict p. 49 (for student use while reading the selection)

DIFFERENTIATED INSTRUCTION

FOR STRATEGIC READERS

Concept Support: Trickster Tales Explain that trickster tales are usually grouped in cycles. That is, they consist of a series of stories focusing on the adventures of the trickster character. Each story involves a particular incident or situation to which the trickster responds, often leading to a violent or absurd conclusion. Among the best-known trickster tales in the United States are those of the sly Brer Rabbit, a character who originated in African folk tales.

Practice and Apply

SUMMARY

This folk tale, retold by Mourning Dove, tells how Coyote angers Buffalo Bull, who then chases him. Coyote saves himself by offering to make Buffalo Bull new horns to replace his worn, old ones. Grateful, Buffalo Bull gives Coyote a magical cow that will always provide him with meat, so long as he does not kill it. Nevertheless, Coyote kills the cow, only to have birds eat the meat and an old woman steal the bones. Coyote tries to get another cow from Buffalo Bull but is refused, which explains why "No buffalo ever lived in the *Swah-netk'-qhu* country."

LITERARY ANALYSIS

Ⓐ TRICKSTER TALES

Possible answer: *Based on lines 5–13, Coyote seems vengeful and childish.*

If students need help . . . Have them use a Character Analysis Chart to make inferences about the trickster.

 BEST PRACTICES TOOLKIT—Transparency Character Analysis Chart p. D5

COYOTE
and the
BUFFALO

Retold by Mourning Dove

BACKGROUND "Coyote and the Buffalo" is one of many traditional stories featuring the Animal People, a race of supernatural beings believed by the Okanogan to have been the first inhabitants of the world. The Animal People had magical powers and could alter their shapes. When human beings appeared on the earth, the Animal People were changed into different animal species. Coyote, one of the most important Animal People, is thought to have made the world habitable for humans by killing monsters and bringing fire and salmon.

ANALYZE VISUALS
Describe the painting on page 45. How is the use of color significant? Does the color treatment cause this coyote to reflect the **traits** of a trickster? Explain your answer.

No buffalo ever lived in the *Swah-netk'-qhu*[1] country. That was Coyote's fault. If he had not been so foolish and greedy, the people beside the *Swah-netk'-qhu* would not have had to cross the Rockies to hunt the *quas-peet-za*[2] (curled-hairs).

This is the way it happened:

Coyote was traveling over the plains beyond the big mountains. He came to a flat. There he found an old buffalo skull. It was the skull of Buffalo Bull. Coyote always had been afraid of Buffalo Bull. He remembered the many times Bull Buffalo had scared him, and he laughed upon seeing the old skull there on the flat.

"Now I will have some fun," Coyote remarked. "I will have revenge for the
10 times Buffalo made me run."

He picked up the skull and threw it into the air; he kicked it and spat on it; he threw dust in the eye sockets. He did these things many times, until he grew tired. Then he went his way. Soon he heard a rumbling behind him. He thought it Ⓐ was thunder, and he looked at the sky. The sky was clear. Thinking he must have imagined the sound, he walked on, singing. He heard the rumbling again, only

Ⓞ **Targeted Passage**

Ⓐ **TRICKSTER TALES**
In the first paragraph, the tale's narrator pronounces Coyote "foolish and greedy." Based on lines 5–13, what other **character traits** would you attribute to this trickster?

---

1. **Swah-netk'-qhu** (shwǝ-nĭt'kwǝ): the Salish name for the Columbia River and its waterfall.
2. **quas-peet-za** (kwǝs-pēt'zä): a Salish word for buffalo.

44 UNIT 1: EARLY AMERICAN WRITING

Coyote Survivor, John Nieto.
Serigraph, 29″ × 22″.

DIFFERENTIATED INSTRUCTION

FOR ALL STUDENTS

Provide these independent projects to extend the lesson:

- Improvise imagined conversations between Coyote and Buffalo Bull or between Coyote and the old woman.

- Write all or part of an original trickster tale.

For further details on these activities, see

Ⓡ **RESOURCE MANAGER**
Ideas for Extension pp. 42–43

FOR STRATEGIC READERS

In combination with the *Audio Anthology CD,* use one or more Targeted Passages (pp. 44, 46, 47, 48) to ensure that students focus on key story events and concepts. Targeted Passages are also good for English learners.

Ⓞ **Targeted Passage [Lines 1–13]**

This passage introduces Coyote and Buffalo Bull and sets up the conflict between them. It also announces what the tale will explain.

ANALYZE VISUALS

Possible answer: The painting uses intense primary colors to create an electric image, giving an unearthly, magical feel to the picture. This color treatment is appropriate for a trickster, who may be associated with supernatural powers and spirit helpers.

About the Art In pictures such as *Coyote Survivor*, American artist John Nieto (b. 1936) uses strong colors and bold strokes to create striking images with depth and detail. He chooses common subjects, but presents them in a way that gives viewers a fresh, more powerful understanding of them.

BACKGROUND

Columbia River The *Swah-netk'-qhu* (line 1) is the Columbia River in the Pacific Northwest. This river drains an extensive area that includes parts of present-day Oregon, Washington, Idaho, Montana, Nevada, Wyoming, and Utah.

- According to the opening lines of the story, what was Coyote's fault? What qualities of Coyote made this problem happen?

- What does Coyote find? How does he treat it?

- How does Coyote feel about Buffalo Bull?

FOR ENGLISH LEARNERS

Prereading For prereading instruction for English learners, see

 BEST PRACTICES TOOLKIT
Scaffolding Reading Instruction pp. 43–46

FOR ADVANCED LEARNERS/AP

AP exercises in the bottom channel provide additional challenge for students. Use these suggestions for small groups or individuals.

ADDITIONAL GUIDELINES

For more help with differentiation and tips for classroom management, see

 BEST PRACTICES TOOLKIT
Differentiated Instruction pp. 31–38

Lines 20–40
TIERED DISCUSSION PROMPTS

Use these prompts to help students understand the interaction between Coyote and Buffalo Bull:

Connect Have you ever tried to talk your way out of a tough situation? How does that experience help you understand how Coyote feels? *Accept all reasonable responses.*

Analyze Review the trickster traits on page 42. Which of these traits are evident in these lines? Cite examples to support your answer. *Possible answer: Coyote twice resorts to magic through his link to supernatural powers. First,* Squas-tenk', *his spirit helper, puts trees in the path of Coyote (lines 20–21). Later, Coyote obtains a "loaded and lighted" pipe from his "medicine-power" (lines 34–35).*

Synthesize How does Coyote use his wiles to try to manipulate Buffalo Bull? *Possible answer: Coyote addresses Buffalo Bull as "friend" (line 29) and offers to smoke his pipe with him (line 35). Then he addresses him as "my uncle" (line 39), trying to flatter him. Next, he offers to make him new horns, because the bull's old ones are "dull and worn." He suggests that with new horns, Buffalo Bull can kill his enemy Young Buffalo (lines 39–40).*

LITERARY ANALYSIS

Ⓑ TRICKSTER TALES

Possible answer: These lines explain why buffalo bulls have "heavy horns with sharp points."

---

much closer and louder. Turning around, he saw Buffalo Bull pounding along after him, chasing him. His old enemy had come to life!

    Coyote ran, faster than he thought he could run, but Buffalo gained steadily. Soon Buffalo was right at his heels. Coyote felt his hot breath.

20   "Oh, *Squas-tenk',*[3] help me!" Coyote begged, and his power answered by putting three trees in front of him. They were there in the wink of an eye. Coyote jumped and caught a branch of the first tree and swung out of Buffalo's way. Buffalo rammed the tree hard, and it shook as if in a strong wind. Then Buffalo chopped at the trunk with his horns, first with one horn and then the other. He chopped fast, and in a little while over went the tree, and with it went Coyote. But he was up and into the second tree before Buffalo Bull could reach him. Buffalo soon laid that tree low, but he was not quick enough to catch Coyote, who scrambled into the third and last tree.

    "Buffalo, my friend, let me talk with you," said Coyote, as his enemy hacked
30 away at the tree's trunk. "Let me smoke my pipe. I like the *kinnikinnick.*[4] Let me smoke. Then I can die more content."

    "You may have time for one smoke," grunted Bull Buffalo, resting from his chopping.

    Coyote spoke to his medicine-power, and a pipe, loaded and lighted, was given to him. He puffed on it once and held out the pipe to Buffalo Bull.

    "No, I will not smoke with you," said that one. "You made fun of my bones. I have enough enemies without you. Young Buffalo is one of them. He killed me and stole all my fine herd."

    "My uncle,"[5] said Coyote, "you need new horns. Let me make new horns for
40 you. Then you can kill Young Buffalo. Those old horns are dull and worn."

    Bull Buffalo was pleased with that talk. He decided he did not want to kill Coyote. He told Coyote to get down out of the tree and make the new horns. Coyote jumped down and called to his power. It scolded him for getting into trouble, but it gave him a flint knife and a stump of pitchwood.[6] From this stump Coyote carved a pair of fine heavy horns with sharp points. He gave them to Buffalo Bull. All buffalo bulls have worn the same kind of horns since. Ⓑ

    Buffalo Bull was very proud of his new horns. He liked their sharpness and weight and their pitch-black color. He tried them out on what was left of the pitchwood stump. He made one toss and the stump flew high in the air, and he
50 forgave Coyote for his mischief. They became good friends right there. Coyote said he would go along with Buffalo Bull to find Young Buffalo.

    They soon came upon Young Buffalo and the big herd he had won from Buffalo Bull. Young Buffalo laughed when he saw his old enemy, and he walked out to meet him. He did not know, of course, about the new horns. It was not much of a fight,

---

3. ***Squas-tenk'*** (skwəs-tĭnk'): a Salish word referring to Coyote's spirit helper.

4. ***kinnikinnick*** (kĭn'ĭ-kĭ-nĭk'): the Salish word for the bearberry shrub. The Okanogan toasted bearberry leaves and then crumbled them and mixed them with tobacco for pipe smoking.

5. **my uncle:** Terms like *uncle, brother, sister,* and *cousin* were sometimes used as a sign of respect. Here, Coyote is using the term to flatter Buffalo Bull.

6. **pitchwood:** the sap-filled wood of a pine or fir tree.

❷ Targeted Passage

Ⓑ TRICKSTER TALES
This trickster tale is **mythic** in that it explains how something came to be—in this case, the lack of buffalo in a certain geographic area. What second mythic explanation is offered in lines 39–46?

DIFFERENTIATED INSTRUCTION

FOR STRATEGIC READERS
❷ Targeted Passage [Lines 36–46]

This passage describes how Coyote slyly wins Buffalo Bull's approval.

- Why is Buffalo Bull angry at Coyote?
- How does Coyote gain Buffalo Bull's friendship?
- Why does Buffalo Bull want revenge against Young Buffalo?

FOR ADVANCED LEARNERS/AP
Native American Spirit Helpers "Coyote and the Buffalo" refers to Coyote's "power," or spirit helper, in lines 20, 34, and 43. Have students research spirit helpers in Native American literature and art. Ask students to share their findings with the class.

that fight between Young Buffalo and Buffalo Bull. With the fine new horns, Buffalo Bull killed the other easily, and then he took back his herd, all his former wives and their children. He gave Coyote a young cow, the youngest cow, and he said:

"Never kill her, *Sin-ka-lip'*![7] Take good care of her and she will supply you with meat forever. When you get hungry, just slice off some choice fat with a flint
60 knife. Then rub ashes on the wound and the cut will heal at once." **C**

Coyote promised to remember that, and they parted. Coyote started back to his own country, and the cow followed. For a few suns he ate only the fat when he was hungry. But after awhile he became tired of eating fat, and he began to long for the sweet marrow-bones and the other good parts of the buffalo. He smacked his lips at the thought of having some warm liver.

───────────────────

7. **Sin-ka-lip'** (sĭng'kə-lĭp'): the Salish name for Coyote; it means "imitator."

Buffalo, John Nieto. Acrylic, 30″× 40″.

C PREDICT
Consider what you know about the **archetypal** trickster character and think about Coyote's behavior thus far. How do you think Coyote will respond to Buffalo Bull's instructions? Give reasons for your prediction.

READING STRATEGY

C PREDICT

Possible answer: Coyote seems to play by his own rules and is unlikely to follow anyone else's. Trickster characters are also greedy, so just slicing off some fat may not satisfy Coyote. Coyote may disregard Buffalo Bull's instructions and get into trouble.

If students need help . . . Have them use the chart introduced on page 43 to list Coyote's behavior and students' predictions about it.

Coyote's Traits and Behavior	My Predictions
Coyote seems to play by his own rules and is unlikely to follow anyone else's. Trickster characters are also greedy, so just slicing off some fat may not satisfy Coyote.	Coyote will disregard Buffalo Bull's instructions and get into trouble.

ANALYZE VISUALS

Activity Ask students how the picture helps them visualize Buffalo Bull. *Possible answer: The picture captures the buffalo's large size and sharp horns.*

FOR STRATEGIC READERS

③ **Targeted Passage** [Lines 55–61]

This passage describes how Buffalo Bull rewards Coyote with a magical cow.

- How do the new horns help Buffalo Bull?
- How does Buffalo Bull thank Coyote?
- What warning does Buffalo Bull give Coyote?

FOR ENGLISH LEARNERS

Language: Idioms Clarify these idioms from the story: *in the wink of an eye* (line 21), "very quickly"; *at once* (line 60), "right away"; *gave up* (line 84), "stopped"; *set out* (line 90), "began with a certain purpose."

REINFORCE KEY IDEA: VILLAINS

Discuss Which of the two is more of a **villain**: the old woman or Coyote? Explain your answer. *Possible answer: The old woman is more of a villain than Coyote. She not only flatters and deceives Coyote but also steals from him. Then she taunts him by shouting, "do you want this?" (line 83)*

LITERARY ANALYSIS

D TRICKSTER TALES

Possible answer: The old woman also plays the role of the trickster; she is clever and deceitful.

SELECTION WRAP–UP

REFLECT Early in the story, Coyote uses flattery to try to talk his way out of trouble with Buffalo Bull. At the end, the old woman uses flattery to deceive Coyote. Ask students what message about flattery the story may be conveying.

★ CRITIQUE

- Have students evaluate the story. Ask them which parts of the story they found most entertaining, and why.

- After completing the After Reading questions on page 49, have students revisit their responses and tell whether they have changed their opinions.

"Buffalo Bull will never know," Coyote told himself, and he took his young cow down beside a creek and killed her.

As he peeled off the hide, crows and magpies came from all directions. They settled on the carcass and picked at the meat. Coyote tried to chase them away, 70 but there were too many of them. While he was chasing some, others returned and ate the meat. It was not long until they had devoured every bit of the meat.

"Well, I can get some good from the bones and marrow-fat," Coyote remarked, and he built a fire to cook the bones. Then he saw an old woman walking toward him. She came up to the fire.

"Sin-ka-lip','" she said, "you are a brave warrior, a great chief. Why should you do woman's work? Let me cook the bones while you rest."

Vain Coyote! He was flattered. He believed she spoke her true mind. He stretched out to rest and he fell asleep. In his sleep he had a bad dream. It awoke him, and he saw the old woman running away with the marrow-fat and the boiled 80 grease. He looked into the cooking-basket. There was not a drop of soup left in it. He chased the old woman. He would punish her! But she could run, too, and she easily kept ahead of him. Every once in awhile she stopped and held up the marrow-fat and shouted: *"Sin-ka-lip','* do you want this?" **D**

Finally Coyote gave up trying to catch her. He went back to get the bones. He thought he would boil them again. He found the bones scattered all around, so he gathered them up and put them into the cooking-basket. Needing some more water to boil them in, he went to the creek for it, and when he got back, there were no bones in the basket! In place of the bones was a little pile of tree limbs!

Coyote thought he might be able to get another cow from Buffalo Bull, so he 90 set out to find him. When he came to the herd, he was astonished to see the cow he had killed. She was there with the others! She refused to go with Coyote again, and Buffalo Bull would not give him another cow. Coyote had to return to his own country without a buffalo.

That is why there never have been any buffalo along the *Swah-netk'-qhu.* ❧

④ Targeted Passage

D TRICKSTER TALES
Who else, besides Coyote, plays the role of a trickster in this tale? Explain which of the trickster's qualities this character exhibits.

DIFFERENTIATED INSTRUCTION

FOR STRATEGIC READERS

④ Targeted Passage [Lines 66–81]

In this passage, the trickster himself is tricked, losing every part of his buffalo.

- What does Coyote do that Buffalo Bull told him not to?

- What becomes of the meat and the marrow-fat?

- How does the old woman trick Coyote?

- Which of Coyote's qualities makes it possible for the old woman to trick him?

FOR ADVANCED LEARNERS/AP

Analyze Tone Have students describe and discuss the tone of "Coyote and the Buffalo." Ask why the tone is appropriate for a folk tale and whether a more serious tone would or would not have worked equally well. Extend the discussion by asking students to compare the tone of this tale with that of other folk tales they have read.

Comprehension

1. **Recall** Why is Buffalo Bull so enraged at Coyote at the beginning of the story?

2. **Recall** How does Coyote convince Buffalo Bull to spare his life?

3. **Summarize** According to the story, why don't buffalo live in the *Swah-netk'-qhu* country?

Literary Analysis

4. **Analyze Predictions** Review the chart you completed as you read. How accurate were your predictions? Did the fact that the trickster is a somewhat familiar **archetypal character** make it easier to predict Coyote's actions, or did his behavior surprise you? Explain your answer, referring to both your chart and the selection.

5. **Interpret Trickster Tales** Trickster tales endure, in part, simply because they are fun to read. But they also often serve to teach a lesson or moral. What does "Coyote and the Buffalo" teach or explain? Support your answer with specific lines from the story.

6. **Draw Conclusions** Trickster tales, like other forms of folk literature, offer readers insight into a society's way of life. What information about the following aspects of Okanogan culture did you glean from this tale?

   • traits or qualities the Okanogan admired as well as those they disapproved of
   • the traditional role of women in Okanogan society
   • Okanogan rituals and religious beliefs

7. **Make Judgments** Review the paragraph you wrote earlier about famous or compelling villains and tricksters. What qualities does Coyote have in common with these characters? In your opinion, is Coyote an admirable character? Explain, citing evidence from the text to support your opinion.

Literary Criticism

8. **Critical Interpretations** Critic Paul Rodin has argued that a trickster "is at one and the same time creator and destroyer, giver and negator, he who dupes others and who is always duped himself.... He possesses no values, moral or social, is at the mercy of his passions and appetites." Identify the ways in which Coyote fits this definition of a trickster. Cite evidence from the selection to support your answer.

 R3.1, R3.6

cooked and men waged war (lines 75–76). The Okanogan smoked pipes; Coyote has a spirit helper, who both assists and scolds him; Buffalo Bull comes back from the dead, so the Okanogan may have believed in reincarnation.

7. Students may note that, like many well-known villains from movies and literature, Coyote is clever, manipulative, and deceitful.

8. Students may say that Coyote is both creator (he creates Buffalo Bull's new horns) and destroyer (he kills the young cow). He is greedy (he kills the cow, though he doesn't need to) and generous (he helps Buffalo Bull). He is cunning (he talks Buffalo Bull out of killing him) and foolish (he is duped by the old woman).

Practice and Apply

After Reading

Use these copy masters to check understanding and provide extra support:

R RESOURCE MANAGER—Copy Masters
Reading Check p. 51
Trickster Tales p. 47
Question Support p. 52

Additional selection questions are provided for teachers on page 41.

ANSWERS

1. *Buffalo Bull, who has come back to life, is enraged because Coyote had been desecrating his skull.*

2. *Coyote convinces Buffalo Bull to spare his life by offering to make Buffalo Bull new horns to use for killing Young Buffalo.*

3. *Coyote disobeyed Buffalo Bull and killed the cow Buffalo Bull had given him. Buffalo Bull refused to replace the cow. As a result, Coyote has to return to his own land without a buffalo.*

Possible answers:

4. ■ **SKILLS FOCUS Predict** *Answers will vary. Students should support their responses with evidence from their charts and details from the selection.*

5. ● **SKILLS FOCUS Trickster Tales** *This tale teaches that it pays to befriend one's enemy, that greed will be punished, and that a person can usually be tricked only once before wising up. Students should support their answers with lines from the story.*

6. *The Okanogan admired cleverness, quick thinking, and helpfulness; they disapproved of greediness and vanity. The Okanogan followed strict gender roles—women*

Assess and Reteach

Assess

R RESOURCE MANAGER—Copy Masters
Selection Test A pp. 53–54
Selection Test B/C pp. 55–56

◉ Test Generator CD

Reteach

S STANDARDS LESSON FILE
Literature Lesson 31: Archetypes
Reading Lesson 1: Predicting

Focus and Motivate

OBJECTIVES

Literary Analysis
- explore the key idea of **heritage**
- analyze characteristics of a memoir
- read a memoir

Reading
- analyze text structure

Vocabulary
- build vocabulary for reading and writing
- understand and use specialized vocabulary
  (also an EL language objective)

CALIFORNIA R2.2

ABOUT THE AUTHOR

Have students read page 50 and summarize important points of Momaday's biography. Emphasize that in his search for his identity, the author finds "the key to self-understanding in awareness of the past." Point out that the selection reflects Momaday's strong link to his Native American heritage.

USING THE *NOTABLE QUOTE*

Discuss with students the meaning of the quotation by **N. Scott Momaday.** Ask whether they agree that it is not a good idea to "let yourself be determined by others," and why or why not. *Students should recognize that the quotation suggests the importance of developing one's own identity rather than allowing other people to define one as a person.*

Selection Resources

R2.2
CALIFORNIA

from The Way to Rainy Mountain
Memoir by N. Scott Momaday

NOTABLE QUOTE
"Ask yourself how you would like to be known. Don't let yourself be determined by others."

FYI
Did you know that N. Scott Momaday . . .
- rode the bus 28 miles to and from school as a teenager?
- taught both middle school and high school on the Jicarilla reservation in New Mexico before becoming a professional writer?
- won the Pulitzer Prize, the most prestigious U.S. literary award, for his very first novel?

Author Online
For more on N. Scott Momaday, visit the **Literature Center** at **ClassZone.com.**

N. Scott Momaday
born 1934

"The most important question one can ask is 'Who am I?'" N. Scott Momaday (mŏm'ə-dā') has asserted. "People tend to define you. As a child, you can't help that, but as you grow older, the goal is to garner enough strength to insist on your own definition of yourself." In his writing, Momaday focuses on the search for identity, and he locates the key to self-understanding in awareness of the past.

Native American Roots Momaday developed a deep sense of his own roots early on. His father, a successful artist and a member of the Kiowa (kī'ə-wô') tribe, routinely told him Kiowa folk tales. His mother, an accomplished writer of French, English, and Cherokee ancestry, instructed him in traditional ways. Momaday grew up on reservations in the Southwest and often spent his summers with his grandparents and other Kiowa relatives in Oklahoma.

The Making of a Writer Growing up on reservations, Momaday developed a reverence for the land and a strong Native American identity. "I saw people," he recalls, "who were deeply involved in their traditional life, in the memories of their blood. They had, as far as I could see, a certain strength and beauty that I find missing in the modern world at large." The lives of these people, together with the Southwestern landscape, inspired Momaday to begin writing at an early age. With the encouragement of his parents, Momaday began composing poetry. Years of hard work and determination paid off when he was awarded a poetry fellowship by Stanford University in 1959.

Voice of the Kiowa In both his poetry and prose, Momaday pays tribute to Native American storytelling traditions and culture. His first novel, *House Made of Dawn,* tells the story of one man's struggle to recover his identity after a stint in the U.S. Army. Original in both theme and structure, the novel was awarded the Pulitzer Prize in 1969. In one of his most popular works, *The Way to Rainy Mountain,* Momaday mixes Kiowa myths, legends, and history with autobiographical details. In addition to his poetry and fiction, Momaday has published essays and articles on preserving the environment. He says, "Writing is a way of expressing your spirit. So there's much more to it than the question of material success. You are out to save your soul after all, and be the best thing that you can be."

 RESOURCE MANAGER UNIT 1

Plan and Teach pp. 57–64

Literary Analysis
Summary pp. 65†*, 66‡*
Memoir pp. 67, 68†*
Question Support p. 76*

Reading
Analyze Structure pp. 69, 70†*
Reading Check p. 75

Vocabulary
Study p. 71*
Practice p. 72
Strategy p. 73

Assessment
Selection Tests A, B/C pp. 77*, 79*
Test Generator CD

 BEST PRACTICES TOOLKIT

Differentiated Instruction
pp. 31–38*

Scaffolding Instruction
pp. 43–46*

Graphic Organizers/Strategies
New Word Analysis

Reading Support
Audio Anthology CD*

Technology
Literature and Vocabulary Centers at **ClassZone.com**

Write*Smart* CD

---

*Resources for Differentiation   † Also in Spanish   ‡ In Haitian Creole and Vietnamese

LITERARY ANALYSIS: MEMOIR

A **memoir** is a form of autobiographical writing in which a person shares personal experiences along with observations of significant events or people. Memoirs give readers insight into the impact of historical events on people's lives. They can also be elegantly written texts containing elements such as a distinctive tone, rich sensory details, and symbols.

As you read M. Scott Momaday's memoir, note passages in which he shares strictly personal experiences as well as sections in which he comments on larger historical events.

READING SKILL: ANALYZE STRUCTURE

Writers usually arrange their information using a **structure** that helps the reader see how the ideas are related. Momaday interweaves three distinct strands throughout his memoir:

• geographical details about the landscape
• historical details about the rise and fall of the Kiowa
• personal details about his grandmother, Aho

As you read, use a chart like the one shown to record details about each topic. Jot down what you learn about each topic, and consider how the three separate strands are related.

The Landscape	The Kiowa	Momaday's Grandmother

VOCABULARY IN CONTEXT

Momaday used the following words in this exploration of his heritage. To test your knowledge, substitute one vocabulary word for the boldfaced word or phrase in each sentence.

WORD LIST		
enmity	opaque	solstice
inherently	pillage	tenuous
luxuriant	preeminently	
nocturnal	profusion	

1. My mother's garden yields an **abundance** of flowers.
2. The feuding brothers eyed each other with **hostility**.
3. There is something **intrinsically** funny about seeing pictures of my father as a teenager.
4. The summer reunion is held on the **longest day of the year**.

Explore the Key Idea

What is your HERITAGE?

KEY IDEA What makes you who you are? Part of the answer lies in your **heritage,** or the beliefs, traditions, and culture passed down to you from preceding generations. Think of the things you have gained or learned from older relatives—the recipe for your favorite meal, perhaps, or a sense of humor, or an attitude toward hardship. How have the things you've learned helped shape who you are today? In the selection that follows, N. Scott Momaday offers his own perspective on the importance of heritage.

INTERVIEW Interview one of your classmates about his or her heritage. Ask your subject about a family tradition, an important belief or value, or a story about his or her family's roots. Find out if your classmate thinks heritage has affected his or her identity.

51

What is your HERITAGE?

Lead into the **KEY IDEA** by asking the question. Explore the ways in which **heritage** influences a person as a child growing up and later as an adult. Then have students do the **INTERVIEW** activity.

SKILLS FOCUS

LITERARY ANALYSIS

● MEMOIR

Have students read **Voice of the Kiowa** on page 50. Point out that in his memoir Momaday blends his knowledge of the history, myths, and legends of the Kiowa with personal thoughts and feelings. Explain that it is the integration of personal observations and experiences with factual information that makes a memoir unique. Ask students why a memoir might, as a result, be more interesting to read than a historical account of events. ***Possible answer:*** *A memoir provides the author's personal insight into the people, places, and events described.*

READING SKILL R2.2

■ ANALYZE STRUCTURE

Elicit or explain that *structure* refers to the organization that holds a work together. Provide some familiar examples, such as the use of chronological order in a historical narrative or spatial order in a descriptive essay. Discuss how a clear structure aids comprehension.

CHECK UNDERSTANDING Ask students to describe the structure of other works they have read, such as articles, essays, and stories.

 RESOURCE MANAGER—Copy Master
   Analyze Structure p. 69 (for student use while reading the selection)

VOCABULARY

▲ VOCABULARY IN CONTEXT

DIAGNOSE WORD KNOWLEDGE To determine preteaching needs, have all students complete Vocabulary in Context. ***Answers:***
1. *profusion,* 2. *enmity,* 3. *inherently,*
4. *solstice*

PRETEACH VOCABULARY Preteach vocabulary with this copy master. Read each item aloud.

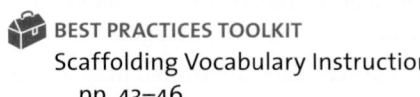 **RESOURCE MANAGER**—Copy Master
   Vocabulary Study p. 71

MORE VOCABULARY SUPPORT
For additional activities and guidelines, see

 BEST PRACTICES TOOLKIT
   Scaffolding Vocabulary Instruction
      pp. 43–46
   Vocabulary Center at **ClassZone.com**

Practice and Apply

SUMMARY

In this memoir, an excerpt from *The Way to Rainy Mountain*, N. Scott Momaday describes his pilgrimage to visit his grandmother's grave near Rainy Mountain, an old landmark of the Kiowa in Oklahoma. The author weaves together descriptive details of his ancestral lands, historical information about his people, the Kiowa, and personal recollections of his grandmother, Aho.

LITERARY ANALYSIS

Ⓐ MEMOIR

Possible answer: *This descriptive, almost poetic writing expresses and elicits more emotion than a scientific description would. Such imagery-laden phrases as "the prairie is an anvil's edge" (lines 4–5) and "the steaming foliage seems almost to writhe in fire" (lines 7–8) help the reader bring to mind vivid pictures of the land described. Sentences like "Loneliness is an aspect of the land" (lines 10–11) help convey a wistful, reflective tone.*

Extend the Discussion How does the rhythm of the opening paragraph contribute to the tone of the words?

THE WAY TO
Rainy Mountain

N. Scott Momaday

BACKGROUND In the 1600s, after a bitter dispute between two chiefs, a band of Kiowa moved from what is now Montana to South Dakota's Black Hills. In around 1785, the Kiowa migrated farther south to escape attacks by neighboring tribes, settling in what is now western Kansas and Oklahoma. With their Comanche allies, the Kiowa ruled the southern Great Plains for a century. One of the last tribes to be defeated by the U.S. government, the Kiowa surrendered in 1875 and were forced onto a reservation in Oklahoma, where members of the tribe still live today.

ANALYZE VISUALS
Examine the portrait on page 53, and consider the photographer's use of high-contrast lighting. What **traits** are suggested by this emphasis of light and shadow? Do you think the subject might look stronger or more vulnerable in a different kind of light? Explain your answer.

A single knoll[1] rises out of the plain in Oklahoma, north and west of the Wichita Range. For my people, the Kiowas, it is an old landmark, and they gave it the name Rainy Mountain. The hardest weather in the world is there. Winter brings blizzards, hot tornadic winds arise in the spring, and in summer the prairie is an anvil's edge. The grass turns brittle and brown, and it cracks beneath your feet. There are green belts along the rivers and creeks, linear groves of hickory and pecan, willow and witch hazel. At a distance in July or August the steaming foliage seems almost to writhe in fire. Great green and yellow grasshoppers are everywhere in the tall grass, popping up like corn to sting the flesh, and tortoises crawl about
10 on the red earth, going nowhere in the plenty of time. Loneliness is an aspect of the land. All things in the plain are isolate; there is no confusion of objects in the eye, but one hill or one tree or one man. To look upon that landscape in the early morning, with the sun at your back, is to lose the sense of proportion. Your imagination comes to life, and this, you think, is where Creation was begun. Ⓐ

I returned to Rainy Mountain in July. My grandmother had died in the spring, and I wanted to be at her grave. She had lived to be very old and at last infirm.

① Targeted Passage

Ⓐ MEMOIR
Note the **descriptive language** in the opening paragraph. How might a reader respond differently to this type of writing than to a more scientific description of the Oklahoma plains?

---

1. **knoll** (nōl): a small round hill.

Edward S. Curtis Collection.
Library of Congress.

DIFFERENTIATED INSTRUCTION

FOR ALL STUDENTS

Provide these independent projects to extend the lesson:

- Prepare a visual representation of one of Momaday's descriptive passages.
- Make a poster-sized annotated map of the Kiowa migration.

For further details on these projects, see

R RESOURCE MANAGER
Ideas for Extension pp. 62–63

FOR STRATEGIC READERS

In combination with the *Audio Anthology CD*, use one or more Targeted Passages (pp. 52, 54, 56) to ensure that students focus on key events and concepts. Targeted Passages are also good for English learners.

① Targeted Passage [Lines 1–16]

This passage explains what and where Rainy Mountain is, describes the region, and tells why the author is returning there.

ANALYZE VISUALS

Possible answer: The photographer's emphasis of light and shadow suggests a reflective melancholy, especially when coupled with the subject's wide eyes and somber expression. Had the photographer used a brighter, more direct light, the subject's features would have been more sharply delineated, and she might have looked stronger. On the other hand, dimmer light would have further softened her features, making her appear more vulnerable.

BACKGROUND

The Sun Dance Ceremony The Sun Dance was important not only to the Kiowa, but also to numerous other Plains Indian tribes. Have students do research to learn more about the Sun Dance. Ask students to share their findings in an oral presentation to the class.

- What is Rainy Mountain? Where is it located?
- With what group of people does the author associate himself?
- Describe the environment of Rainy Mountain.
- Why does the author return to Rainy Mountain?

FOR ENGLISH LEARNERS

Key Academic Vocabulary Use New Word Analysis to teach these words: *range* (line 2), *crucial* (line 29), *culture* (line 35), *evolve* (line 35), *approach* (line 144).

 BEST PRACTICES TOOLKIT—Transparency New Word Analysis p. E8

Prereading For prereading instruction for English learners, see

 BEST PRACTICES TOOLKIT Scaffolding Reading Instruction pp. 43–46

FOR ADVANCED LEARNERS/AP

AP exercises in the bottom channel provide additional challenge for students. Use these suggestions for small groups or individuals.

ADDITIONAL GUIDELINES

For more help with differentiation and tips for classroom management, see

 BEST PRACTICES TOOLKIT Differentiated Instruction pp. 31–38

Tai-me and the Sun Dance Tai-me was a small, decorated human figure considered sacred by the Kiowa. It played a central role in the Sun Dance, a religious tribal ceremony. Many other Plains Indian cultures, including the Lakota and Crow, practiced the Sun Dance. The federal prohibition of the Sun Dance expired in 1935, and many Native American groups have since renewed the practice.

READING SKILL

B ANALYZE STRUCTURE

Possible answers: The lines describing the Kiowa (lines 36–51) convey historical information, while the lines referring to Momaday's grandmother (lines 35–36, 52–57) provide more personal details. References to Momaday's grandmother—for example, "Her name was Aho," "lived out her long life," "She could tell of the Crows"—signal personal details, as does the phrase that begins the final sentence on the page (lines 55–57): "I wanted to see . . . ."

If students need help . . . Work with students to fill in the prereading chart introduced on page 51 with details from these lines. Help them distinguish historical information from personal details.

The Landscape	The Kiowa	Momaday's Grandmother
	• Mountain people	• Name: Aho
	• Language not identified	• Lived near Rainy Mountain
	• Began migration in late 1600s	• No experience with the Crows or the Black Hills

---

Her only living daughter was with her when she died, and I was told that in death her face was that of a child.

20   I like to think of her as a child. When she was born, the Kiowas were living the last great moment of their history. For more than a hundred years they had controlled the open range from the Smoky Hill River to the Red, from the headwaters of the Canadian to the fork of the Arkansas and Cimarron. In alliance with the Comanches, they had ruled the whole of the southern Plains. War was their sacred business, and they were among the finest horsemen the world has ever known. But warfare for the Kiowas was **preeminently** a matter of disposition rather than of survival, and they never understood the grim, unrelenting advance of the U.S. Cavalry. When at last, divided and ill-provisioned, they were driven onto the Staked Plains in the cold rains of autumn, they fell into panic. In Palo Duro Canyon they abandoned their crucial stores to **pillage** and had nothing then 30   but their lives. In order to save themselves, they surrendered to the soldiers at Fort Sill[2] and were imprisoned in the old stone corral that now stands as a military museum. My grandmother was spared the humiliation of those high gray walls by eight or ten years, but she must have known from birth the affliction of defeat, the dark brooding of old warriors.

Her name was Aho, and she belonged to the last culture to evolve in North America. Her forebears came down from the high country in western Montana nearly three centuries ago. They were a mountain people, a mysterious tribe of hunters whose language has never been positively classified in any major group. In the late seventeenth century they began a long migration to the south and east. 40   It was a journey toward the dawn, and it led to a golden age. Along the way the Kiowas were befriended by the Crows,[3] who gave them the culture and religion of the Plains. They acquired horses, and their ancient nomadic spirit was suddenly free of the ground. They acquired Tai-me, the sacred Sun Dance doll, from that moment the object and symbol of their worship, and so shared in the divinity of the sun. Not least, they acquired the sense of destiny, therefore courage and pride. When they entered upon the southern Plains they had been transformed. No longer were they slaves to the simple necessity of survival; they were a lordly and dangerous society of fighters and thieves, hunters and priests of the sun. According to their origin myth, they entered the world through a hollow log. From one point 50   of view, their migration was the fruit of an old prophecy, for indeed they emerged from a sunless world.

Although my grandmother lived out her long life in the shadow of Rainy Mountain, the immense landscape of the continental interior lay like memory in her blood. She could tell of the Crows, whom she had never seen, and of the Black Hills, where she had never been. I wanted to see in reality what she had seen more perfectly in the mind's eye, and traveled fifteen hundred miles to begin my pilgrimage. **B**

---

2. **Fort Sill:** a U.S. army post established in 1869 in the Indian Territory (now Oklahoma).

3. **Crows:** a group of Native Americans who once inhabited the region between the Platte and Yellowstone rivers in the northern Great Plains. The Crows are now settled in Montana.

54   UNIT 1: EARLY AMERICAN WRITING

preeminently
(prē-ĕm′ə-nnənt-lē)
adv. above all; most importantly

pillage (pĭl′ĭj) *n.* the act of looting or plundering by force

② Targeted Passage

B ANALYZE STRUCTURE
Reread lines 35–57. Which lines convey historical information? Which offer more personal details? Identify the key words or phrases that allowed you to distinguish between the two types of information.

DIFFERENTIATED INSTRUCTION

FOR STRATEGIC READERS

② Targeted Passage [Lines 32–57]

This passage provides background about Momaday's grandmother, introduces the idea of the Sun Dance, and explains the motivation for Momaday's journey.

• Who is Aho?

• What was Tai-me? Why was it important to the Kiowa?

• Why does the author go on a "pilgrimage"?

FOR ADVANCED LEARNERS/AP

Myth and History Ask students to analyze the style of lines 36–51. In what ways does it read like myth? In what ways does it read like history? How effective is it for Momaday to combine both?

Yellowstone, it seemed to me, was the top of the world, a region of deep lakes and dark timber, canyons and waterfalls. But, beautiful as it is, one might have the
60 sense of confinement there. The skyline in all directions is close at hand, the high wall of the woods and deep cleavages of shade. There is a perfect freedom in the mountains, but it belongs to the eagle and the elk, the badger and the bear. The Kiowas reckoned their stature by the distance they could see, and they were bent and blind in the wilderness.

Descending eastward, the highland meadows are a stairway to the plain. In July the inland slope of the Rockies is **luxuriant** with flax and buckwheat, stonecrop and larkspur. The earth unfolds and the limit of the land recedes. Clusters of trees, and animals grazing far in the distance, cause the vision to reach away and wonder to build upon the mind. The sun follows a longer course in the day, and the sky is
70 immense beyond all comparison. The great billowing clouds that sail upon it are shadows that move upon the grain like water, dividing light. Farther down, in the land of the Crows and Blackfeet,[4] the plain is yellow. Sweet clover takes hold of the hills and bends upon itself to cover and seal the soil. There the Kiowas paused on their way; they had come to the place where they must change their lives. The sun is at home on the plains. Precisely there does it have the certain character of a god. When the Kiowas came to the land of the Crows, they could see the dark lees of the hills at dawn across the Bighorn River, the **profusion** of light on the grain shelves, the oldest deity ranging after the **solstices.** Not yet would they veer southward to the caldron of the land that lay below; they must wean their blood
80 from the northern winter and hold the mountains a while longer in their view. They bore Tai-me in procession to the east.

A dark mist lay over the Black Hills, and the land was like iron. At the top of a ridge I caught sight of Devil's Tower upthrust against the gray sky as if in the birth of time the core of the earth had broken through its crust and the motion of the world was begun. There are things in nature that engender an awful quiet in the heart of man; Devil's Tower is one of them. Two centuries ago, because they could not do otherwise, the Kiowas made a legend at the base of the rock. My grandmother said:

Eight children were there at play, seven sisters and their brother. Suddenly the boy
90 *was struck dumb; he trembled and began to run upon his hands and feet. His fingers became claws, and his body was covered with fur. Directly there was a bear where the boy had been. The sisters were terrified; they ran, and the bear after them. They came to the stump of a great tree, and the tree spoke to them. It bade them climb upon it, and as they did so it began to rise into the air. The bear came to kill them, but they were just beyond its reach. It reared against the tree and scored the bark all around with its claws. The seven sisters were borne into the sky, and they became the stars of the Big Dipper.*

---

4. **Blackfeet:** a group of Native Americans who once inhabited a region now occupied by parts of Montana and the Canadian provinces of Alberta and Saskatchewan.

luxuriant (lŭg-zhŏŏr′ē-ənt) *adj.* characterized by abundant growth

profusion (prə-fyōō′zhən) *n.* abundance; lavishness

solstice (sŏl′stĭs) *n.* either of two days of the year when the sun is farthest from the celestial equator; the summer solstice is the longest day of the year, and the winter solstice is the shortest.

THE WAY TO RAINY MOUNTAIN **55**

Lines 58–80
TIERED DISCUSSION PROMPTS

Use these prompts to help students understand and appreciate Momaday's use of descriptive language:

Connect When you are surrounded by tall mountains or high buildings, do you feel closed in? Do you prefer wide open spaces? Explain your reasons. *Accept all reasonable responses.*

Analyze How does Momaday help readers visualize the change in surroundings during the Kiowas' journey? *Possible answer: Momaday contrasts the "confinement" of the woods with the openness of the plains. He explains that in the Yellowstone region the "skyline in all directions is close at hand," and he mentions "the high wall of the woods and deep cleavages of shade" (lines 60–61). In contrast, he captures the openness of the plains with these details: "trees, and animals grazing far in the distance" (lines 67–68); "the sky is immense beyond all comparison" (lines 69–70); and a "profusion of light on the grain shelves" (lines 77–78).*

Evaluate How effectively does Momaday use language to paint a vivid picture in this passage? Explain. *Accept all thoughtful responses.*

FOR STRATEGIC READERS

Paraphrase Have students read lines 58–64 and lines 65–81 aloud. Discuss how the author uses poetic language and rhythm to describe the terrain. Then help students paraphrase the lines. Ask students how Momaday's description differs from the kind of description they might find in a history textbook. Ask which approach they prefer, and why.

FOR ADVANCED LEARNERS/AP

Analyze Creation Myth Ask students how the creation myth found in lines 89–97 fulfills the characteristics described on page 33. Have them compare and contrast the creation myth found in lines 89–97 with other myths they have read in *The Native American Experience,* noting particularly the roles of men, women, animals, and nature. Have students present their findings to the class.

REINFORCE *KEY IDEA:* HERITAGE

Discuss What does Momaday's discussion of the Kiowa legend suggest about the author's feelings regarding his **heritage?** *Possible answer: Momaday not only recalls the Kiowa legend that his grandmother told him but also chooses to include it in detail, which suggests that his heritage means a great deal to him.*

READING SKILL

C ANALYZE STRUCTURE

Possible answer: Momaday may mean that as long as the legend continues to be passed down through oral tradition (discussed on page 22 of the historical essay), the Kiowa can take comfort in knowing that their ancestors are looking down on them from the heavens. Seeing the Big Dipper can remind the Kiowa of their heritage and inspire cultural pride. The inclusion of the legend adds depth to the personal elements of the memoir by drawing readers into Kiowa history and culture, which Momaday feels so much a part of.

From that moment, and so long as the legend lives, the Kiowas have kinsmen in the night sky. Whatever they were in the mountains, they could be no more. 100 However **tenuous** their well-being, however much they had suffered and would suffer again, they had found a way out of the wilderness. **C**

My grandmother had a reverence for the sun, a holy regard that now is all but gone out of mankind. There was a wariness in her, and an ancient awe. She was a Christian in her later years, but she had come a long way about, and she never forgot her birthright. As a child she had been to the Sun Dances; she had taken part in those annual rites, and by them she had learned the restoration of her people in the presence of Tai-me. She was about seven when the last Kiowa Sun Dance was held in 1887 on the Washita River above Rainy Mountain Creek. The buffalo were gone. In order to consummate the ancient sacrifice—to impale the 110 head of a buffalo bull upon the medicine tree—a delegation of old men journeyed into Texas, there to beg and barter for an animal from the Goodnight herd.[5] She was ten when the Kiowas came together for the last time as a living Sun Dance culture. They could find no buffalo; they had to hang an old hide from the sacred tree. Before the dance could begin, a company of soldiers rode out from Fort Sill under orders to disperse the tribe. Forbidden without cause the essential act of their faith, having seen the wild herds slaughtered and left to rot upon the ground, the Kiowas backed away forever from the medicine tree. That was July 20, 1890, at the great bend of the Washita. My grandmother was there. Without bitterness, and for as long as she lived, she bore a vision of deicide.[6]

120 Now that I can have her only in memory, I see my grandmother in the several postures that were peculiar to her: standing at the wood stove on a winter morning and turning meat in a great iron skillet; sitting at the south window, bent above her beadwork, and afterwards, when her vision failed, looking down for a long time into the fold of her hands; going out upon a cane, very slowly as she did when the weight of age came upon her; praying. I remember her most often at prayer. She made long, rambling prayers out of suffering and hope, having seen many things. I was never sure that I had the right to hear, so exclusive were they of all mere custom and company. The last time I saw her she prayed standing by the side of her bed at night, naked to the waist, the light of a kerosene lamp moving 130 upon her dark skin. Her long, black hair, always drawn and braided in the day, lay upon her shoulders and against her breasts like a shawl. I do not speak Kiowa, and I never understood her prayers, but there was something **inherently** sad in the sound, some merest hesitation upon the syllables of sorrow. She began in a high and descending pitch, exhausting her breath to silence; then again and again—and always the same intensity of effort, of something that is, and is not, like urgency in the human voice. Transported so in the dancing light among the shadows of her room, she seemed beyond the reach of time. But that was illusion; I think I knew then that I should not see her again.

---

5. **Goodnight herd:** a herd of Southern Plains bison established in the 1870s by Charles and Molly Goodnight for the purpose of preserving the animals from extinction.

6. **a vision of deicide** (dē′ə-sīd′): a picture in her mind of the killing of a god.

56 UNIT 1: EARLY AMERICAN WRITING

---

tenuous (tĕn′yōō-əs) *adj.* having little substance or strength; flimsy

C ANALYZE STRUCTURE
Reread lines 98–101. What does Momaday mean when he says that "the Kiowas have kinsmen in the night sky"? How does the inclusion of this legend add depth to the personal elements of this memoir?

❸ Targeted Passage

inherently (ĭn-hîr′ənt-lē) *adv.* related to part of something's inmost nature

---

DIFFERENTIATED INSTRUCTION

FOR STRATEGIC READERS

❸ Targeted Passage [Lines 102–119]

This passage describes Aho's experience with the Sun Dance ritual.

- How did Aho develop her reverence for the sun?

- What were the Sun Dances?

- What sacrifice was part of the Sun Dance?

- Why did the Kiowa stop holding the annual Sun Dance ritual?

- How did Aho react to the stopping of the Sun Dance ritual?

FOR ADVANCED LEARNERS/AP

Analyze Tone Have students reflect on the author's tone in *The Way to Rainy Mountain* as he recounts the Kiowa history in lines 19–34 and 105–118. Ask students to write one or two paragraphs summarizing Momaday's apparent feelings toward the Kiowa and their struggle to survive. Have volunteers share their summaries with the class.

ANALYZE VISUALS
In your opinion, does this photograph convey the same **mood** that Momaday evokes in his autobiography? Explain your answer, citing details from both the photograph and the text.

Mandan Offering the Buffalo Skull, Edward S. Curtis, photographer. McCormick Library of Special Collections, Northwestern University Library.

Houses are like sentinels in the plain, old keepers of the weather watch. There,
140 in a very little while, wood takes on the appearance of great age. All colors wear soon away in the wind and rain, and then the wood is burned gray and the grain appears and the nails turn red with rust. The windowpanes are black and **opaque;** you imagine there is nothing within, and indeed there are many ghosts, bones given up to the land. They stand here and there against the sky, and you approach them for a longer time than you expect. They belong in the distance; it is their domain. **D**

Once there was a lot of sound in my grandmother's house, a lot of coming and going, feasting and talk. The summers there were full of excitement and reunion. The Kiowas are a summer people; they abide the cold and keep to themselves, but when the season turns and the land becomes warm and vital they cannot
150 hold still; an old love of going returns upon them. The aged visitors who came to my grandmother's house when I was a child were made of lean and leather, and they bore themselves upright. They wore great black hats and bright ample shirts

opaque (ō-pāk′) *adj.* not allowing light to pass through

D MEMOIR
Reread lines 120–145. What words and phrases give you an indication of Momaday's **tone,** or attitude toward his subject matter?

FOR ENGLISH LEARNERS
Related Vocabulary Discuss how Momaday uses carefully chosen words and phrases to convey the image of old houses on the prairie. Make sure students understand any unfamiliar words.

- *like sentinels* ["someone standing guard"] . . . *old keepers of the weather watch* (line 139)
- *great age* (line 140)
- *wood is burned gray* (line 141)

- *nails turn red with rust. The windowpanes are black and opaque* ["allowing no light to come through"] (line 142)
- *nothing within . . . ghosts, bones* (line 143)
- *belong in the distance; it is their domain* ["area"] (line 145)

ANALYZE VISUALS
Possible answer: The photograph does seem to convey the same mood that Momaday evokes in the text. In the picture, a lone Native American holds a buffalo skull reverentially toward the heavens, perhaps in a prayer of thanks. Momaday's memoir expresses a similar feeling of reverence—for his grandmother and for the Kiowa culture. The text makes reference to the Kiowa Sun Dance (lines 43, 105–113), a religious ceremony, and to the grandmother's "reverence for the sun" (line 102). Momaday also notes that he remembers his grandmother "most often at prayer" (lines 125–126).

LITERARY ANALYSIS

D MEMOIR
Possible answer: Phrases that suggest Momaday's somber and pensive tone include: "Now that I can have her only in memory" (line 120); "She made long, rambling prayers out of suffering and hope" (line 126); "there was something inherently sad in the sound . . . syllables of sorrow" (lines 132–133); "I think I knew then that I should not see her again" (lines 137–138); "you imagine there is nothing within, and indeed there are many ghosts" (line 143).

If students need help . . . Discuss the tone and the reasons behind it. Remind students that the memoir includes memories of Momaday's grandmother and recollections of the troubled times of the Kiowa.

REINFORCE *KEY IDEA:* HERITAGE

Discuss How do Momaday's memories of his grandmother's house help to define his link with his **heritage?** *Possible answer: Moma-day's remembrance of traditions and cultural details shows how meaningful these early experiences were. He recalls how visitors to his grandmother's house dressed and talked, the "prayer meetings, and great nocturnal feasts" (line 162), and "the singing of the old people" (line 164).*

LITERARY ANALYSIS

ⓔ MEMOIR

Possible answer: The house might sym-bolize the old, weathered state of Kiowa strength and culture. Like the house, Kiowa culture was once vital and alive; although it is not what it once was, it continues to in-spire people like Momaday. The house may also represent Aho herself, who "had lived to be very old and at last infirm" (line 16). The house too had once been full of life, but now holds a "funeral silence" (line 168), just as Aho is silent.

SELECTION WRAP–UP

REFLECT Have students think about Moma-day's relationship with his grandmother. In what lasting ways did the relationship affect him?

⭐ CRITIQUE

- Have students evaluate Momaday's blend of history and personal recollection. Ask whether combining the two is effective or distracting, and why.

- After completing the After Reading ques-tions on page 59, have students revisit their responses and tell whether they have changed their opinions.

---

that shook in the wind. They rubbed fat upon their hair and wound their braids with strips of colored cloth. Some of them painted their faces and carried the scars of old and cherished **enmities.** They were an old council of warlords, come to remind and be reminded of who they were. Their wives and daughters served them well. The women might indulge themselves; gossip was at once the mark and compensation of their servitude. They made loud and elaborate talk among themselves, full of jest and gesture, fright and false alarm. They went abroad in
160 fringed and flowered shawls, bright beadwork and German silver. They were at home in the kitchen, and they prepared meals that were banquets.

enmity (ĕn′mĭ-tē) *n.* hostility; hatred

There were frequent prayer meetings, and great **nocturnal** feasts. When I was a child I played with my cousins outside, where the lamplight fell upon the ground and the singing of the old people rose up around us and carried away into the darkness. There were a lot of good things to eat, a lot of laughter and surprise. And afterwards, when the quiet returned, I lay down with my grandmother and could hear the frogs away by the river and feel the motion of the air.

nocturnal (nŏk-tûr′nəl) *adj.* occurring at night

Now there is a funeral silence in the rooms, the endless wake of some final word. The walls have closed in upon my grandmother's house. When I returned
170 to it in mourning, I saw for the first time in my life how small it was. It was late at night, and there was a white moon, nearly full. I sat for a long time on the stone steps by the kitchen door. From there I could see out across the land; I could see the long row of trees by the creek, the low light upon the rolling plains, and the stars of the Big Dipper. Once I looked at the moon and caught sight of a strange thing. A cricket had perched upon the handrail, only a few inches away from me. My line of vision was such that the creature filled the moon like a fossil. It had gone there, I thought, to live and die, for there, of all places, was its small definition made whole and eternal. A warm wind rose up and purled like the longing within me. ⓔ
180 The next morning I awoke at dawn and went out on the dirt road to Rainy Mountain. It was already hot, and the grasshoppers began to fill the air. Still, it was early in the morning, and the birds sang out of the shadows. The long yellow grass on the mountain shone in the bright light, and a scissortail hied[7] above the land. There, where it ought to be, at the end of a long and legendary way, was my grandmother's grave. Here and there on the dark stones were ancestral names. Looking back once, I saw the mountain and came away. ◌

ⓔ MEMOIR
Think about how Momaday contrasts his grandmother's house as it was during his childhood visits with how it is now. What might this house **symbolize?**

---

7. **a scissortail hied:** a fork-tailed bird of the Southwest hied, or hurried.

DIFFERENTIATED INSTRUCTION

FOR ENGLISH LEARNERS
Related Vocabulary In contrast to the lively imagery of the two preceding paragraphs, lines 168–170 group together words per-taining to death. Teach these interrelated words, and then discuss with students how they work together to create a somber mood:

- *funeral,* "relating to a funeral—a ceremo-ny held for someone who has died"

- *silence,* "quiet; hush"

- *wake,* "a watch over the body of a dead person before burial"

- *final,* "last; concluding"

- *mourning,* "sorrow or grief for a person's death"

Comprehension

R2.2

1. **Recall** Where is Rainy Mountain, and why does Momaday return there?

2. **Clarify** What two natural phenomena are explained by the Kiowa legend about the seven sisters and their brother ?

3. **Summarize** What important events in Kiowa history does Momaday recount?

Literary Analysis

4. **Draw Conclusions** In your opinion, what is the most important insight Momaday gains about his **heritage** during his pilgrimage from Yellowstone to his grandmother's grave at Rainy Mountain? Support your opinion with evidence from the text.

5. **Understand Memoirs** Reread lines 52–101. What does Momaday's account of the Kiowa's migration offer you that a description in a history book might not? Explain, citing specific lines of the selection that support your answer.

6. **Analyze Structure** Review the chart you created as you read, and summarize the geographical, historical, and personal details that Momaday includes in each of the three strands. How are they related? Describe the impact of Momaday's technique of weaving the three strands together.

7. **Examine Author's Style** Although best known as a novelist, Momaday is also an accomplished poet. In what way might this selection be described as poetic? In a chart like the one shown, record examples of the poetic elements Momaday uses in his memoir. Use your completed chart to explain what you think these stylistic choices add to the selection. (Refer to the **Glossary of Literary Terms** on page R104 if needed.)

Poetic Elements		
Alliteration	Consonance	Imagery
"The grass turns brittle and brown ..."		

Literary Criticism

8. **Critical Interpretations** Teacher and scholar Kenneth M. Roemer has argued that "in *The Way to Rainy Mountain*, M. Scott Momaday links the survival of his people to their ability to remember, preserve and pass on stories." Do you agree that a culture's survival rests on this ability? Explain, using evidence from this selection to support your opinion.

THE WAY TO RAINY MOUNTAIN **59**

7. *The selection is poetic in Momaday's use of language, imagery, and rhythm (for example, lines 1–14). Examples of poetic elements include* **alliteration:** *"The grass turns brittle and brown" (line 5), "the eagle and the elk, the badger and the bear" (line 62);* **consonance:** *"luxuriant with flax" (line 66);* **imagery:** *"the prairie is an anvil's edge" (lines 4–5), "the steaming foliage seems almost to writhe in fire" (lines 7–8), "the highland meadows are a stairway to the plain" (line 65).*

8. *Students may say that preserving stories enables people to maintain their cultural identity and in so doing helps the culture to survive. The Kiowa culture, for example, survives in part because its stories and myths—such as the one on page 55— continue to be passed on, giving them the confidence and fortitude to overcome adversity.*

Practice and Apply

After Reading

Use these copy masters to check understanding and provide extra support:

RESOURCE MANAGER—Copy Masters
Reading Check p. 75
Memoir p. 67
Question Support p. 76

Additional selection questions are provided for teachers on page 61.

ANSWERS

1. *Rainy Mountain is located on a plain in Oklahoma, north and west of the Wichita Range. Momaday returns to Rainy Mountain to visit his grandmother's grave.*

2. *The legend explains the creation of Devil's Tower and the stars of the Big Dipper.*

3. *Momaday recounts the Kiowa's migration from western Montana to Oklahoma; their coming together for the final Sun Dance; and their surrender to the U.S. Cavalry at Fort Sill.*

Possible answers:

4. *Students may say that Momaday learns to appreciate his grandmother's abiding influence on him. He learns the importance of place in maintaining identity, the establishment of a harmonious relationship with the natural world, and the preservation of traditions and culture.*

5. ● **SKILLS FOCUS Memoir** *Momaday's account offers a more emotional look at the Kiowas' migration. His description feels more authentic and personal than a mere reporting of facts. Supporting lines include lines 73–81 and 98–101.*

6. ■ **SKILLS FOCUS Analyze Structure** *Students should recognize that the three strands complement one another in presenting an informative, yet personalized, account of the events and experiences described. The resulting impact is to create a memoir that serves as a moving tribute both to the Kiowa and to Momaday's grandmother.*

ANSWERS

Vocabulary in Context

VOCABULARY PRACTICE

1. *nocturnal*
2. *solstice*
3. *enmity*
4. *tenuous*
5. *preeminently*

6. *pillage*
7. *luxuriant*
8. *profusion*
9. *opaque*
10. *inherently*

📘 RESOURCE MANAGER—Copy Master
Vocabulary Practice p. 72

VOCABULARY IN WRITING

Encourage students to list several possible locations, events, or persons and choose the one they think they can best describe using the vocabulary words. Remind students to include their own feelings or reactions regarding the location, event, or person.

VOCABULARY STRATEGY: SPECIALIZED VOCABULARY (*also an EL language objective*)

For words with more than one dictionary meaning, encourage students to consider all the possibilities before deciding on one.

***Answers:* 1.** *c,* **2.** *a,* **3.** *d,* **4.** *e,* **5.** *b; eccentric also has a non-technical meaning: "odd or unconventional."*

📘 RESOURCE MANAGER—Copy Master
Vocabulary Strategy p. 73

ℹ️ Vocabulary Center at **ClassZone.com**
Additional Vocabulary Activities

Assess and Reteach

Assess

📘 RESOURCE MANAGER—Copy Masters
Selection Test A pp. 77–78
Selection Test B/C pp. 79–80

💿 Test Generator CD

Reteach

📘 STANDARDS LESSON FILE
Literature Lesson 45: Author's Perspective
Informational Text Lesson 2: Sequence and Chronological Order
Vocabulary Lesson 19: Multiple-Meaning Words

Vocabulary in Context

VOCABULARY PRACTICE

Choose the vocabulary word that answers each riddle.

1. I refer to things that do not happen in daylight.
2. I represent extremes of time, both shortest and longest.
3. I am the opposite of friendship.
4. I describe something uncertain or insubstantial.
5. I mean the same thing as *chiefly*.
6. I am the act of looting by force.
7. I am an adjective that could describe a field filled with wildflowers.
8. I am a noun indicating an abundance of wildflowers.
9. Air filled with dense fog is one example of what I am.
10. One of my meanings is "essentially."

VOCABULARY IN WRITING

Which location, event, or person in this account do you find most memorable? Using three or more vocabulary words, write a brief description of the person, place, or event, including your own response to it. You might start this way.

> **EXAMPLE SENTENCE**
> The final Sun Dance of the Kiowa had only a **tenuous** connection with earlier rituals.

VOCABULARY STRATEGY: SPECIALIZED VOCABULARY

The Kiowa recognize the importance of seasonal events such as the solstices. There are a number of terms that describe other natural phenomena relating Earth to the sun and the moon. Some of these terms have only technical meanings, but others are also used in more general ways.

PRACTICE Match each term with its definition. Use a dictionary if you need help. Then choose the term that also has a nontechnical meaning, and write a definition for it.

1. apogee
2. equinox
3. diurnal
4. perigee
5. eccentric

a. two dates each year when day and night are of equal length
b. having a noncircular planetary orbits such as Earth's
c. point when the moon is farthest from Earth
d. relating to the daily rotation of Earth
e. point when the moon is closest to Earth

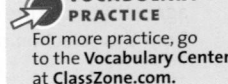

VOCABULARY PRACTICE
For more practice, go to the **Vocabulary Center** at **ClassZone.com.**

DIFFERENTIATED INSTRUCTION

FOR ENGLISH LEARNERS

Task Support: Vocabulary Practice Help students use the riddles in conjunction with suffixes of the listed words to determine parts of speech and figure out the answers. For example, explain that -*ly* is an adverb suffix—as in *chiefly* and *essentially*—so the answers to items 5 and 10 will also be adverbs. Similarly, -*sion* is a noun suffix, which will help students determine the answer to item 8.

FOR ADVANCED LEARNERS/AP

Vocabulary in Writing Ask students to use as many vocabulary words as they can in a paragraph about the moon and the earth.

Native American Values

Stereotypes have long characterized the portrayal of Native Americans in our culture. Early explorers' and settlers' lack of knowledge about Native American ways colored their written accounts, while later writers indulged in blatant "cowboys and Indians" stereotyping. Yet by reading the literature written by Native American groups, both past and present, one can move past the stereotypes to gain a clearer understanding of the Native American experience.

Writing to Synthesize

Make a list of the things you have in common with the Native Americans you've read about in this section—the things that connect us all as people. Then write one paragraph describing something that Native Americans valued in the past that many people still value today and one paragraph describing something they found objectionable with which you might also agree.

Consider

- the theme of each selection
- passages that shed light on traditional Native American values
- characters who are portrayed as "good" or "bad" and what they reveal about the culture

Extension Online

RESEARCH Historically, many university and professional sports teams have employed Native American mascots. In recent years, this practice has come under attack. With a partner, go online to **research** images of three such mascots and print them to share with the class. Also find out what routines or traditions each mascot has performed. Then, as a class, discuss why people might find such mascots offensive. As you discuss, be sure to take into account what you learned from your reading.

R2.5, W2.2

The Buffalo Chase with Bow (1832), George Catlin. The Granger Collection, New York.

61

Wrap-Up: The Native American Experience

This Wrap-Up provides students with an opportunity to revisit ideas about Native Americans from the literature in this section. What stereotypes of Native Americans were presented? What authentic facts and images about native cultures emerged from the writings of Native Americans? Encourage students to examine their own views in light of insights gained from the selections.

Writing to Synthesize

- Review with students that *synthesizing* means combining ideas and facts with other information and prior knowledge in order to better understand a subject or develop new ideas. Those new ideas help break down old misunderstandings and stereotypes.

- To help students write their two paragraphs, direct them to think about the selections they have read and brainstorm things that the Native Americans valued (for example, the natural world and its creatures; such qualities as cleverness and courage) and things that they found objectionable (for example, greediness and vanity).

Extension Online

- If students are researching online, suggest that they use key words such as *Native American mascots*, *Indian mascots*, or *sports mascots*.

- Direct students to organize their research and thoughts by creating a Three-Column Journal, using the headings *Mascot*, *Routines or Traditions*, and *Possible Objections*. To help students think about possible objections, suggest that they consider their research in light of the seriousness with which Native Americans regarded totems and ceremonies.

 BEST PRACTICES TOOLKIT—Transparency
Three-Column Journal p. B10

DIFFERENTIATED INSTRUCTION

FOR DEVELOPING WRITERS

Writing Support Help students get started by directing them to relevant passages in the selections. For example, students might draw on lines 117–142 and 192–201 of "The World on the Turtle's Back" to write about how Native Americans valued "a balanced and orderly world." Or they might draw on lines 58–67 and 72–83 of "Coyote and the Buffalo" and lines 106–116 of "The World on the Turtle's Back" to write about deceitfulness and right and wrong.

FOR ENGLISH LEARNERS

Writing Topic Sentences To help students create topic sentences for their paragraphs, provide sentence starters such as these:

- Like many people today, Native Americans of the past valued _____.

- One thing that Native Americans of the past found objectionable that I also find offensive is _____.

Tell students to find details in the selections to support each of their topic sentences.

OBJECTIVES

Media Literacy

- explore the key idea of **stereotypes**
- view film clips to understand how the mass media reinforce stereotypes and create new ones
- create image awards to honor film and television performances that overcome stereotypes

 LS1.1, LS1.14, LS1.3

SUMMARIES

The three clips explore the portrayal of Native Americans in film and TV.

Stagecoach A stagecoach crosses a vast, dry valley and is attacked by Native Americans.

"The Lone Ranger" Tonto gets a smoke signal message from his Cheyenne friends asking to see him. He leaves after he assures the Lone Ranger that he'll check in with the Indian agent on the reservation.

Smoke Signals On a train, one modern Native American gives a friend tips on how to act like a "real Indian."

How do media shape PERCEPTIONS?

To emphasize the importance of the **KEY IDEA,** take a student poll of weekly TV hours watched. Use the poll results to demonstrate the potential power of the media to reinforce **stereotypes** or otherwise manipulate the perceptions of its viewers. Brainstorm ideas that are shaped by media even today, such as physical appearance or materialism.

BACKGROUND

For director Chris Eyre and writer Sherman Alexie, both Native Americans, the most important mission for *Smoke Signals* was to confront the oversimplified stereotypes of Native Americans that had been built by "The Lone Ranger" and other 20th-century westerns. Their film reveals the complexity of their culture and puts Native American film on the cinematic map.

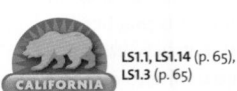

Media Study

Changing Views of Native Americans

Film Clips on **MediaSmart DVD**

 CALIFORNIA
LS1.1, LS1.14 (p. 65),
LS1.3 (p. 65)

How do media shape PERCEPTIONS?

KEY IDEA In this unit, Native American voices from the past and present reveal their way of life and worldview. In contrast, many 20th-century films about the Old West lacked this Native American perspective, often reinforcing inaccurate **stereotypes** and creating new ones. In this lesson, you will watch three film clips that present images of Native Americans from three different time periods.

Background

How the Western Won America's fascination with the Old West began with late 19th-century dime-novel westerns. These low-priced, fast-paced stories were typically set in the frontier between the mid-1800s and the turn of the century. Alongside dime novels arose Wild West shows. These colorful, outdoor spectacles featured frontier figures, such as Buffalo Bill, Sitting Bull, and Annie Oakley, and staged reenactments of battles. Both dime novels and Wild West shows presented simplistic morality tales. To establish order and perhaps justify the taking of Native American lands and lives, the so-called good guys—cowboys and settlers—had to overcome the alleged bad guys— rampaging Indians or marauding outlaws. Thus was born a source for stereotyping that would endure in other forms.

At the start of the 20th century, as the motion picture industry evolved, the western film genre burst onto the screen. While Hollywood filmmakers glorified the frontier by shooting in spectacular locations, they recycled the simple formulas of the earlier western forms and perpetuated some of the inaccurate images.

By the mid-1900s, as TV became commonplace, westerns dominated both big and small screens. At the peak of the western's golden age, over 20 westerns were televised each week, exposing viewers to themes and images that went unquestioned. It didn't seem to matter if an Indian's costume wasn't historically accurate or if his or her language wasn't realistic. Little was said about the effects of western expansion on Native American life and culture. The Hollywood images took hold in the minds of viewers. Aware of this, filmmakers of more recent times have made deliberate efforts to bring more authentic portrayals to the screen.

62

Media Study Resources

 RESOURCE MANAGER UNIT 1

Plan and Teach pp. 81–84

Media Analysis
Summary pp. 85†*, 86‡*
Viewing Guide p. 87
Close Viewing p. 88
Media Activity p. 89
Produce Your Own Media p. 90

STANDARDS LESSON FILE
Media Lesson 3: Influence of Media on Society
Media Lesson 7: Evaluating Films and TV Shows

ⓘ Media Center at **ClassZone.com**

MEDIA VIEWING
⌀ Media*Smart* DVD

---

* Resources for Differentiation † Also in Spanish ‡ In Haitian Creole and Vietnamese

Media Literacy: Images in Mass Media

The **western** is a film and TV genre that portrays the early days of the American frontier. In many TV shows and movies, particularly classic westerns, the film and TV industry depended on **stereotypes,** oversimplified or inaccurate representations of people. Stereotypes can create misconceptions, especially when there are no alternative portrayals to displace them. Use your knowledge of characterization and film techniques to help you spot these stereotypes.

STRATEGIES FOR ANALYZING FILM AND TELEVISION STEREOTYPES

A Character's Appearance	Look for how actors are costumed and how make-up is applied. Keep in mind that most often, little historical research was done to present Native Americans accurately. Costumes and language were often a mix of different tribes.	
A Character's Dialogue	Focus on how characters speak. Which characters speak dialogue in complete sentences? Which speak in simple words or phrases? Stereotypical characters are usually depicted as being somehow outside of the mainstream culture and as holding a different set of values.	
A Character's Actions	Ask yourself: Do characters behave according to a stereotype? Are the actions more negative than positive? Notice how **lighting** and **music** reinforce these impressions. How does the director film the actions? Be aware of camera placement. • **Low-angle shots** position the camera to look up at an object or a person. Such shots convey an imposing or powerful presence. • **High-angle shots** position the camera to look down, often conveying helplessness.	
Other Characters' Responses to the Character	Notice how other characters react to the individual. Do **close-up shots** reveal expressions of tolerance, condescension, or superiority? In what ways do the dialogue and the acting convey how the character is regarded?	

MEDIA STUDY: TEACHING OPTIONS

Teaching Option 1: The Basics (1–2 Days)
1. Begin the Media Study using the material provided on pages 62–63.
2. Show the Introduction on Media*Smart*. Then show the First Viewing. As they watch, have students use the Viewing Guide on page 64, along with the corresponding copy master on page 87 of the Resource Manager. Discuss their responses.
3. Return to the pupil book for the extension activities on page 65.

Teaching Option 2: In-Depth Study (2–3 Days)
1. Begin the Media Study using pages 62–63.
2. Show the Introduction and First Viewing from Media*Smart*. Then continue on Media*Smart* with the Media Lessons, using the teacher notes available in the Resources section.
3. Show the Guided Analysis presentation. Have students record their observations on the Student Viewing Guide available in the Resources section of Media*Smart*.
4. Return to the pupil book, page 65.

Teach

Media Literacy

Ask volunteers to describe the plot of a familiar film western or to invent a likely plot from their knowledge of the genre. Have them identify stereotypical characters (good guy, bad guy, beautiful woman), settings (wild west, prairie, western cow town), and typical plots. In particular, challenge students to identify ways in which Native Americans are stereotypically misrepresented in westerns. Then discuss the chart on page 63.

- **A Character's Appearance** To clarify how costuming and makeup can influence viewers' perceptions, describe two characters: one has ragged pants, a dirty headscarf, and a scarred cheek; the other has a clean white hat, a neat mustache, and shiny boots. Ask students what the appearances convey.

- **A Character's Dialogue** Read this aloud:

  Guide: See far mountain. Smoke in sky. Me help Cherokee brothers.

  Cowboy: Ride safely, my friend. Help your friends with great courage.

  Discuss how the contrast in syntax creates a stereotypical portrayal of the "white man's helper" and the cowboy. How does the limited English of the guide influence viewers' perceptions?

- **A Character's Actions** To enforce the importance of action and camera angle, have students imagine directing a scene in which Native Americans react to a threat. Ask how they would show the Native Americans as either powerful and brave or nervous and helpless. Contrast the results.

- **Other Characters' Responses to the Character** Note that a film may show positive, trustful reactions to Native American characters or hostile, suspicious reactions. Discuss how such reactions reinforce stereotypes.

 Media*Smart* DVD

Practice and Apply

VIEWING GUIDE

1. To prepare students for viewing, explain that the three clips portray Native Americans differently. Encourage students to pay attention to these elements:

   - the **appearance** of the Native American characters, such as their facial expressions, costuming, and grooming

   - **dialogue** that conveys the intelligence or loyalty of Native Americans

   - **actions** and camera **shots** that suggest power or helplessness in Native American and other characters

   - **characters' reactions** that convey a positive or negative perception of Native Americans

2. Students may find stereotypical characterizations of Native Americans offensive. Ask them to identify what **stereotypes** are portrayed in the clips. Explain that the frightening Indian attack portrayed in *Stagecoach* was a characteristic scene in many classic westerns. "The Lone Ranger," while portraying Native Americans as helpers, nonetheless cast them in limited roles.

 RESOURCE MANAGER—Copy Masters
   Viewing Guide p. 87
   Close Viewing p. 88
   Media Activity p. 89

Use this resource with the Viewing Guide:

MediaSmart DVD

ANSWERS

FIRST VIEWING: Comprehension

1. *The travelers begin firing their guns.*

2. *According to Victor, Native Americans should live up to the ignorant preconceived notions of outsiders by looking stoic and threatening.*

CLOSE VIEWING: Media Literacy

Possible answers:

3. *The striking musical rhythms and the low-angle camera shots underscore the stereotypically threatening presence of the Native Americans. High-angle shots make the white travelers appear vulnerable and unassuming.*

⊙ MediaSmart DVD
- **Film 1:** *Stagecoach*
- **Director:** John Ford
- **Genre:** Movie Western
- **Running Time:** 2 minutes

- **Film 2:** *The Lone Ranger*
- **Genre:** TV Western
- **Running Time:** 2 minutes

- **Film 3:** *Smoke Signals*
- **Director:** Chris Eyre
- **Rating:** PG-13
- **Genre:** Drama
- **Running Time:** 2.5 minutes

Viewing Guide for
Changing Views of Native Americans

Watch the first two clips to explore how Native Americans were portrayed during the glory days of the western. The scene from *Stagecoach* (1939) brings two groups into direct contact. In the clip from *The Lone Ranger* TV series (1949–1957), the two main characters prepare to take action. Watch the third clip to see a more recent Native American portrayal—one that challenges the old Hollywood images. In *Smoke Signals* (1998), friends Victor and Thomas engage in lively conversation during a road trip.

To critically analyze the clips, view them more than once. Examine the portrayals, and answer these questions.

NOW VIEW

FIRST VIEWING: Comprehension

1. **Recall** In *Stagecoach*, what do the travelers do as soon as they spot the Native Americans?

2. **Summarize** Think about Victor in *Smoke Signals*. Summarize his view of the acceptable look and behavior for "Indian" males.

CLOSE VIEWING: Media Literacy

3. **Identify Film Techniques** Consider how the use of music and the **high-** and **low-angle** shots contribute to characterization in the beginning of the *Stagecoach* clip. How might the effect reinforce **stereotypes?**

4. **Analyze Stereotypes** In *The Lone Ranger* clip, the character Tonto might be considered an improvement over past portrayals of Native Americans. However, what might still be **stereotypical** about this character?

5. **Analyze Characters** Recall how Victor in *Smoke Signals* describes "real Indian" behavior. Might their portrayal be perceived as a step forward? Why or why not?

6. **Evaluate Characterization** *Smoke Signals* director Chris Eyre has said, "I'm interested in telling stories about Indians who are normal, everyday people." How effectively do the character portrayals in the scene from his film counter the stereotypes in *Stagecoach* and *The Lone Ranger*? Base your opinion on the modern-day setting in *Smoke Signals* and on the characterizations of Thomas and Victor.

---

4. *Tonto's style of speech is depicted as simplistic, and he displays a stoic demeanor. Viewed superficially, Tonto's actions place him in a subservient position to his counterpart, the Lone Ranger.*

5. *It is a step forward because Victor's description and the conversation of the characters involve humor as well as a consciousness of how mainstream society thinks a "real Indian" ought to behave.*

6. *The characters effectively counter stereotypes, since the young men appear in modern clothing and a modern setting. Also, Victor and Thomas act like typical teenagers, not stereotypical Native Americans.*

Write or Discuss

Compare Portrayals What impressions of Native Americans do you get from each clip? At the time each portrayal was first presented, how might it have affected perceptions of Native Americans? Write a comparison of the three clips you've viewed. Consider:

- the portrayals of individuals or groups
- the techniques of camera position, lighting, and music
- the fact that *Smoke Signals* was written and directed by Native Americans

LS1.1, LS1.14

Produce Your Own Media

Create an Image Award Consider any films or TV shows that you think rise above the simplistic techniques of stereotyping. What character portrayals or story lines strike you as complex and true to life? How sensitively are different social groups portrayed? As a class, create a name for the award and devise basic criteria for judging the pieces. After brainstorming choices with a partner, present your nominees to the class and choose one award winner.

HERE'S HOW Follow these guidelines as you plan your presentation:

- As you brainstorm choices, ask yourself: In what aspects has this work succeeded while others have missed the mark? What impact might the choice have on viewers' perceptions over time?
- As you present each of your films or shows, explain the reasons it was nominated. The choice that meets (or exceeds) most of the criteria wins the image award.

LS1.3

MEDIA TOOLS
For help with devising the image award criteria, visit the **Media Center** at **ClassZone.com.**

Tech Tip
Use presentational software to show the title and attributes of each nominee.

Further Exploration

Hold a Native American Film Festival According to Native American filmmaker Bird Runningwater, "Filmmaking provides a new way to merge a strong oral tradition of storytelling with technology and, in the process, revitalize ourselves." Research Native American films and reviews. If possible, rent movies to view as a group, and then critique them in a panel discussion.

Conduct a Native American Film Study Savage warrior. Noble savage. Sage protector of the earth. One hundred years of moviemaking hasn't begun to cover the complexity and diversity of Native American cultural groups. Research westerns ranging from the 1950s to the present. What historical inaccuracies are evident? In contemporary works, have attempts to present more positive depictions fully succeeded?

Write or Discuss

Compare Portrayals In their comparisons, students should include examples of characters' appearance, dialogue, and actions to support their points. For example, Tonto speaks in broken English while Victor and Thomas speak fluently. To support their analysis, have students imagine watching the clips in 1939, in the 1950s, and in 1998 as they consider the portrayal of Native Americans.

Produce Your Own Media

Rubric: Create Image Awards A strong image award should have

- at least five points of criteria for judging
- a catchy title
- a coherent presentation explaining the nomination of at least three films or shows
- an accurate understanding of each film's impact on viewer perceptions

R RESOURCE MANAGER—Copy Master
Produce Your Own Media p. 90

Further Exploration

Hold a Native American Film Festival Have students work in small groups to identify Native American films. Compile a master list and then assign a film to each group. Have the group view its assigned film, select a two-minute clip to share with the class, and prepare a discussion and critique.

Conduct a Native American Film Study To answer the questions, have students research and analyze at least one film. Have them write a short essay, using examples from the film or films to support their analysis.

MEDIA STUDY WRAP-UP

Have students summarize what they have learned about how media can create or reinforce **stereotypes.** Urge students to use examples of how dialogue, appearances, actions, and reactions contribute to this process.

RETEACH

S STANDARDS LESSON FILE

Media Lesson 3: Influence of Media on Society

Media Lesson 7: Evaluating Films and TV Shows

OBJECTIVES

- develop strategies for reading primary sources
- identify the characteristics of historical narrative
- identify, analyze, and evaluate a primary source

R3.5

Recording the American Experience

Primary and Secondary Sources Discuss the key distinctions between the two kinds of sources. Then have students use a Two-Column Chart to classify these examples as primary or secondary sources, and ask volunteers to explain their answers:

- the handwritten will of a European settler in Virginia, dated 1610 *(primary)*
- an encyclopedia article entitled "Puritans" *(secondary)*
- the *Mayflower Compact,* an agreement written and signed by passengers on the Mayflower in 1620 *(primary)*
- a book entitled *Massachusetts Before the Pilgrims,* written in 1975 *(secondary)*
- a record of births and deaths kept by the residents of a village in colonial Virginia *(primary)*

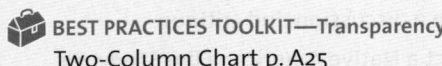 BEST PRACTICES TOOLKIT—Transparency
  Two-Column Chart p. A25

Bringing the Past to Life

Reading Primary Sources Offer these additional strategies for reading historical narratives:

- Reread and paraphrase unfamiliar ideas.
- Restate the main idea in your own words.
- Visualize what the author describes.
- Predict what will happen next.
- Connect the narrative to what you know.
- Ask questions about the narrative.
- Make a timeline of the events described.

Review the excerpts on page 66, clarifying text as needed. Ask students to describe sensory images evoked by the passages. Then help them identify the main idea of each passage.

R3.5

Historical Narratives

If you wanted to know what life was like for someone 400 years ago, where could you get the information? History books could give you a general account, but what if you wanted to know the details of someone's daily life or what it was like to actually be at an important historical event? In American literature, there are many personal accounts that have been published and passed down through the centuries that give unique perspectives on the events of the past.

Recording the American Experience

Europeans began voyages by ship to the Americas in the late 15th century and reported news of their explorations and settlement. These historical narratives of the survivors told gripping adventure stories, written down in journals and letters, of the the first Europeans' experiences of coming to America. **Historical narratives** are accounts of real-life historical experiences, written by either a person who experienced those events or someone

Indian Summer, Regis François Gignoux. © Christie's Images/Corbis.

who studied or observed them. In many cases, the narratives became important historical documents that now exist as our principal record of events. Historical narratives can be divided into two categories:

- **Primary sources** are materials written by people who were either participants in or observers of the events written about. Letters, diaries, journals, speeches, autobiographies, and interviews are all primary sources.

- **Secondary sources** are records of events written by people who were not directly involved in the events. Two typical examples of secondary sources are biographies and histories.

Bringing the Past to Life

Primary sources offer valuable insights into the thinking and culture of a given time period. Use these strategies to bring the information to life:

- Determine a document's origin.
- Try to understand the **perspective** and **motives** of the writer.
- Note **sensory details** that depict people, places, and events.
- Identify customs, values, or conditions of the **culture** or **time period.**

DIFFERENTIATED INSTRUCTION

For general guidelines on differentiating instruction, see

 BEST PRACTICES TOOLKIT
  Differentiated Instruction pp. 31–38

FOR STRATEGIC READERS

Note Taking For students who are unfamiliar with historical narratives or need help with note taking, hand out the copy master before discussing each page. Explain to students that they will be learning many terms

relating to historical narratives in this workshop. Discuss the boldfaced terms on this spread as students record notes on their copy masters.

 RESOURCE MANAGER—Copy Master
  Note Taking p. 91

Álvar Núñez Cabeza de Vaca was one of many explorers who sailed to the New World after Christopher Columbus. The historical narrative *La Relación* (page 70) was Cabeza de Vaca's report to the king of Spain. Note the personal **perspective** he provides in this excerpt about one night in his crossing of the Atlantic Ocean.

> When night fell, only the navigator and I remained able to tend the barge. Two hours after dark he told me I must take over; he believed he was going to die that night.
>
> **—Álvar Núñez Cabeza de Vaca, *La Relación***

In 1620, the Puritans survived a journey across the Atlantic in the *Mayflower* and landed at Cape Cod. In 1630, William Bradford, Plymouth Colony's second governor, began writing *Of Plymouth Plantation* (page 100), a chronicle of his colony's experiences. Notice the use of **sensory details** in Bradford's description of the colony's first winter.

> The weather was very cold and it froze so hard as the spray of the sea lighting on their coats, they were as if they had been glazed.
>
> **—William Bradford, *Of Plymouth Plantation***

As the American colonies expanded from the 16th through the 18th centuries, the slave trade expanded as well. Olaudah Equiano was one of the millions of Africans captured and transported to the Americas. He survived this ordeal and published his autobiography in 1789. These lines from his autobiography describe the conditions below the decks of a slave ship and his first reaction to what he saw.

> When I looked round the ship too, and saw a large furnace of copper boiling, and a multitude of black people of every description chained together, every one of their countenances expressing dejection and sorrow, I no longer doubted of my fate.
>
> **—Olaudah Equiano, *The Interesting Narrative of the Life of Olaudah Equiano***

THE SLAVE NARRATIVE

The **slave narrative** is an American literary genre that portrays the daily life of slaves as written by the slaves themselves after gaining their freedom. Some 6,000 slave narratives are known to exist. The Reverend Ephraim Peabody wrote in 1849 about three recently published slave narratives:

> *We place these volumes without hesitation among the most remarkable productions of the age—remarkable as being pictures of slavery by the slave, remarkable as disclosing under a new light the mixed elements of American civilization, and not less remarkable as a vivid exhibition of the force and working of the native love of freedom in*
> *the individual mind.*
>
> **–The Reverend Ephraim Peabody**

Probably the most influential example of the genre is the autobiography of Frederick Douglass, *Narrative of the Life of Frederick Douglass, an American Slave*, published in 1845.

Close Read

Describe what you think were the writer's motives for recording the events in the first two **primary source** examples on this page.

Close Read

Point out details that are particularly vivid. Describe how you would visualize the scene.

THE SLAVE NARRATIVE

Explain that between 1760 and 1865, about 100 slave narratives were published in the United States, including that of Olaudah Equiano. Slave narratives played a crucial role in winning people over to the cause of abolitionism by informing them about the horrors of slave trade. Other slave narratives include:

- *My Bondage and My Freedom* (1855): Frederick Douglass's expanded autobiography
- *Narrative of William W. Brown, A Fugitive Slave* (1847): written by William Wells Brown, the first African American to publish a novel
- *The Narrative of Sojourner Truth* (1850): dictated by abolitionist and women's rights leader Sojourner Truth

During the 1930s, the Federal Writers' Project gathered several volumes' worth of oral histories from 2,500 former slaves. Invite students to share their feelings as to why these narratives are still important.

Close Read

Possible answer: *Both writers described harrowing experiences. They probably wanted to describe to their readers what difficult hardships they had to endure.*

If students need help . . . Ask these questions to help students infer the writers' motives:

- How would you feel if you had lived through the experience the writer is describing?
- Why would you want others to know about it?

Close Read

Possible answer: *Vivid details include "large furnace of copper boiling," "multitude of black people of every description chained together," "every one of their countenances expressing dejection and sorrow." Students may visualize the scene as cramped, dark, hot, and frightening.*

FOR ENGLISH LEARNERS

Language: Skill Words Students who speak Romance languages should know cognates for *primary, secondary, source,* and *narrative*. Ask students to say and explain cognates from their home languages. Then have volunteers say and explain the English words, repeating the pronunciations as needed. Review the definitions on page 66.

FOR ADVANCED LEARNERS/AP

Compare and Contrast Style [paired option] Review that style is not what is said so much as how it is said. Components include word choice, figurative language, and sentence structure or length. Have students work in pairs to read the three narrative excerpts on page 67, and then compare and contrast the three writers' styles. Then have students write a brief passage in the style of one of these writers.

Focus and Motivate

OBJECTIVES

Literary Analysis
- explore the key idea of why some **survive**
- analyze the influence of historical context
- read an eyewitness report

Reading
- use strategies for reading primary sources

Vocabulary
- build vocabulary for reading and writing
- use etymology to understand word origin and history *(also an EL language objective)*

Grammar and Writing
- use prepositional phrases to add details
- write a journal entry

 CALIFORNIA R3.5, W1.2, W1.9, LC1.1

ABOUT THE AUTHOR

After students have read about Cabeza de Vaca, ask a volunteer to use a map to locate the places mentioned in the text: Tampa Bay, Mexico, the Gulf Coast, and Galveston Island. Then point out that the excerpt students are about to read recounts events described in **Disaster Strikes.**

USING THE *NOTABLE QUOTE*

Ask students why **Cabeza de Vaca** might have "lessened" (understated) rather than exaggerated the events and details in his account. *Students should recognize that incredible events do not have to be exaggerated and that grotesque survival details should probably be understated.*

CALIFORNIA

R3.5, W1.2 (p. 77), W1.9 (p. 77), LC1.1 (p. 77)

NOTABLE QUOTE

"Better than to exaggerate, I have lessened in all things."

FYI
Did you know that Cabeza de Vaca . . .

- recorded the only accounts of some now-extinct Native American groups?
- was the first European to cross North and South America?
- was accompanied by an enslaved African named Esteban?

Author Online

For more on Álvar Núñez Cabeza de Vaca, visit the **Literature Center** at ClassZone.com.

---

from La Relación
Report by Álvar Núñez Cabeza de Vaca

Álvar Núñez Cabeza de Vaca
c. 1490–1557

In 1536, Spanish slave hunters raiding in northern Mexico were startled by a strange sight: a Spaniard "strangely dressed and in company with Indians." Long given up for dead, Álvar Núñez Cabeza de Vaca had survived one of the most disastrous expeditions in the history of the Spanish conquest to become the first European to cross North America.

Conquering Hero Cabeza de Vaca came from a family of Spanish *conquistadors,* or conquerors. He had been a soldier for nearly 20 years when, in 1527, he joined an expedition to Spanish North America. Appointed by the king of Spain, he became treasurer and second in command, assigned the task of colonizing the territory north and east of the Gulf of Mexico.

Disaster Strikes Led by Pánfilo de Narváez, the expedition sailed with five ships and 600 men. Two ships were lost in a hurricane; 200 men drowned or deserted. After landing in Tampa Bay, Narváez sent his ships north and ordered 300 men to march to New Spain (present-day Mexico), which he guessed to be a few weeks away. Months later, the ships were gone and the desperate landing party was eating its horses to survive. Using horsehide and nails made from melted armor, they built five barges and sailed along the Gulf Coast from Florida to Texas, hoping to reach Spanish settlements in northern Mexico. Two barges and 80 men washed up on or near Galveston Island. Ultimately, only Cabeza de Vaca and three other men survived.

Cabeza de Vaca survived by adapting to his new surroundings. For six years, he lived with dozens of Native American groups in various roles—as a captive, a trader, and a well-known healer. In 1534, the four survivors escaped, setting out across the desert in search of New Spain. In 1536, they finally reached their goal. A year later, Cabeza de Vaca returned to Spain, where he wrote his account of the expedition, *La Relación* (The Account), as a report to the king.

Conqueror No More The king rewarded Cabeza de Vaca by appointing him governor of a South American colony, where his humane treatment of Native Americans may have cost him his job. By 1545, he had been ousted from his position and convicted on a corruption charge in Spain. Exiled to Africa, Cabeza de Vaca was eventually pardoned. In 1552, he returned to Spain to end his days as a judge.

Selection Resources

 RESOURCE MANAGER UNIT 1

Plan and Teach pp. 93–100

Literary Analysis
Summary pp. 101†*, 102‡*
Historical Context pp. 103, 104†*
Question Support p. 111*

Reading
Reading a Primary Source pp. 105, 106†*
Reading Check p. 110

Vocabulary
Study p. 107*
Practice p. 108
Strategy p. 109

Grammar and Writing
Add Necessary Details p. 112

Assessment
Selection Tests A, B/C pp. 113*, 115*
Test Generator CD

BEST PRACTICES TOOLKIT

Differentiated Instruction pp. 31–38*

Scaffolding Instruction pp. 43–46*

Graphic Organizers/Strategies
Definition Mapping • Cluster Diagram • Sensory Notes

Reading Support
Audio Anthology CD*

Technology
Literature, Vocabulary, and Writing Centers at **ClassZone.com**
Write*Smart* CD

---

 * Resources for Differentiation   † Also in Spanish   ‡ In Haitian Creole and Vietnamese

• LITERARY ANALYSIS: HISTORICAL CONTEXT

When you read historical works, you may notice statements that seem strange or even offensive. These remarks might be a reflection of the work's **historical context**—the ideas and details from the author's time that influence the written work.

It was amazing to see these wild, untaught savages howling like brutes in compassion for us.

The author's statement reflects views about Indians that most people of his time shared. To familiarize yourself with the historical context of *La Relación*, read the author biography on page 68 and the background information on page 70. Then, as you read the work, note details that reflect this context.

• READING STRATEGY: READING A PRIMARY SOURCE

Unlike a history book, *La Relación* is an eyewitness report of events. Such **primary sources** give us special insight into historical events. When using these sources, consider

- the intended audience
- the author's role in events
- where and when the document was written

As you read, complete a chart like the one shown. Consult the author biography and background information as needed.

Questions	Answers
What do I know about the author and his times?	
What details tell me about life in 16th-century North America?	
What is the relationship between the author and his audience?	
What is the author's role in the events he describes?	

▲ VOCABULARY IN CONTEXT

The following words help bring this explorer's account to life. Choose a synonym for each word from the numbered terms.

WORD LIST		
cauterize	ingratiate	locomotion
embody	inundate	tarry

1. movement   3. burn   5. flood
2. personify   4. seek favor   6. delay

What's the STORY behind the GLORY?

KEY IDEA Dreams of wealth, glory, and conquest lured adventurers to the Americas, but few were prepared for the harsh reality that awaited them. For every hero who claimed a fortune, there were hundreds of others who died trying. Often, the greatest prize of all was living to tell the tale. What enabled some to **survive** while others failed?

DISCUSS In a small group, share stories you've read or heard that describe a person's struggle to survive in desperate circumstances, such as a shipwreck, war, or a natural disaster. Then make a list of traits that those people or characters exhibit. Decide what qualities seem essential in a survivor.

69

What's the STORY behind the GLORY?

Lead into the **KEY IDEA** by asking the question. After the class speculates about why some people **survive** an ordeal while others perish, tell students to consider their answers as they complete the *DISCUSS* activity.

SKILLS FOCUS

LITERARY ANALYSIS R3.5

• HISTORICAL CONTEXT

Have students read **Conqueror No More** on page 68 and the background information on page 70. Ask them what they can infer about the views most Spanish conquistadors of Cabeza de Vaca's time period held about Native Americans. What can they infer about the author's views?
Possible answer: Most Spanish conquistadors of Cabeza de Vaca's time period viewed Native Americans as inferior people to be conquered, their riches plundered. Though a conqueror, Cabeza de Vaca treated Native Americans more humanely and respectfully than his own culture thought was appropriate.

CHECK UNDERSTANDING Ask students to give an example of a book, movie, or TV show that reflects the ideas and values of its time period but seems outdated today.

READING STRATEGY R3.5

■ READING A PRIMARY SOURCE

Refer students to the three bulleted items in the instruction. Then have them reread the author biography to identify Cabeza de Vaca's intended audience, his role in the events he describes, and where and when his report was written. *Possible answer: Cabeza de Vaca's intended audience is the king of Spain; the author is a participant in the events he describes; his report was written in Spain around 1537.*

R RESOURCE MANAGER—Copy Master
Reading a Primary Source p. 105
(for student use while reading the selection)

VOCABULARY

▲ VOCABULARY IN CONTEXT

DIAGNOSE WORD KNOWLEDGE To determine preteaching needs, have all students complete Vocabulary in Context. *Answers:*
1. *locomotion,* **2.** *embody,* **3.** *cauterize,*
4. *ingratiate,* **5.** *inundate,* **6.** *tarry*

PRETEACH VOCABULARY Preteach vocabulary with this copy master. Read each item aloud.

R RESOURCE MANAGER—Copy Master
Vocabulary Study p. 107

MORE VOCABULARY SUPPORT
For additional activities and guidelines, see

🧰 BEST PRACTICES TOOLKIT
Scaffolding Vocabulary Instruction
pp. 43–46
ℹ️ Vocabulary Center at **ClassZone.com**

SUMMARY

This excerpt from the report *La Relación* opens with Cabeza de Vaca and his dying men adrift on a barge. They wash ashore on Galveston Island, where the Karankawa Indians welcome and feed them. When the conquistadors embark again, their barge capsizes, and the starving survivors return to shore. The Karankawas care for them again, but when disease spreads throughout the island, the Native Americans make the Spaniards serve as medicine men.

READING STRATEGY

A PRIMARY SOURCE

Possible answer: *The author relates frightening details in a calm, objective tone. He does not describe his own reactions or fear. Cabeza de Vaca may have chosen this tone to present himself as a calm, clear-thinking leader to his audience: the king.*

If students need help . . . Work with them to answer the third question in the pre-reading chart introduced on page 69. Then have students use the answer to infer that Cabeza de Vaca's choice of tone reflects his desire to present himself to the king as a calm, clear-thinking leader.

Questions	Answers
What is the relationship between the author and his audience?	The author's audience is the king of Spain. The author is reporting to his ruler and "boss"— the person who controls his career and future.

La Relación

Álvar Núñez Cabeza de Vaca

BACKGROUND In the 1500s, Spanish conquistadors took to the seas to claim new land for Spain. Seeking gold and silver, they explored unfamiliar territory and encountered Native American cultures they did not understand. By the time Cabeza de Vaca sailed, Spaniards had conquered the Aztecs of Mexico and the Inca of Peru, two of the most advanced civilizations in the Americas. Millions of Native Americans would die in this often brutal cultural encounter. In *La Relación,* Cabeza de Vaca finds himself unexpectedly at the mercy of the people he came to conquer.

At this point in the account, Narváez's barge has abandoned the rest, and Cabeza de Vaca's barge has joined one commanded by two other officers. The next three chapters describe the shipwreck of Cabeza de Vaca's barge on Galveston Island and the crew's encounter with the Karankawa Indians who lived there.

ANALYZE VISUALS
What **details** in the image convey the desperate situation of the shipwrecked men?

A Sinking and a Landing

Our two barges continued in company for four days, each man eating a ration of half a handful of raw corn a day. Then the other barge was lost in a storm. Nothing but God's great mercy kept us from going down, too.

It was winter and bitterly cold, and we had suffered hunger and the heavy beating of the waves for many days. Next day, the men began to collapse. By sunset, all in my barge had fallen over on one another, close to death. Few were any longer conscious. Not five could stand. When night fell, only the navigator and I remained able to tend the barge. Two hours after dark he told me I must take over; he believed he was going to die that night. **A**

10 So I took the tiller. After midnight I moved over to see if he were dead. He said no, in fact was better, and would steer till daylight. In that hour I would have welcomed death rather than see so many around me in such a condition. When I had returned the helm to the navigator, I lay down to rest—but without much rest, for nothing was farther from my mind than sleep.

Near dawn I seemed to hear breakers resounding; the coast lying low, they roared louder. Surprised at this, I called to the navigator, who said he thought we

① Targeted Passage

A **PRIMARY SOURCE**
Describe the **tone** of lines 4–9. In what ways might the author's choice of tone be influenced by his intended **audience?**

Illustration by Tom McNeely.

DIFFERENTIATED INSTRUCTION

FOR ALL STUDENTS

Expert Groups Encourage students to become subject experts by selecting and researching one of these topics:

- Spanish territories in the 1500s
- Cabeza de Vaca's South American explorations
- other accounts of living with Native Americans, such as Mary Rowlandson's captivity narrative

FOR STRATEGIC READERS

In combination with the *Audio Anthology CD,* use one or more Targeted Passages (pp. 70, 73, 74) to ensure that students focus on key events and concepts. Targeted Passages are also good for English learners.

① Targeted Passage [Lines 1–14]

This passage introduces students to the conflict Cabeza de Vaca and his men face in this excerpt.

REINFORCE *KEY IDEA:* SURVIVE

Discuss What do these lines suggest that people need to **survive** in desperate circumstances? *Possible answer: People need hope. As soon as the almost-dead men see land, they revive a bit and become more hopeful (lines 21–24). They act as if they believe they have a chance at survival.*

LITERARY ANALYSIS

Ⓑ HISTORICAL CONTEXT

Possible answer: Christianity was the central feature of the Spaniards' cultural identity; the Spaniards assumed that all Europeans were Christians, and that all people should be.

---

were coming close to land. We sounded and found ourselves in seven fathoms.[1] The navigator felt we should stay clear of the shore till daylight; so I took an oar and pulled it on the shore side, wheeling the stern to seaward about a league[2] out.

20   As we drifted into shore, a wave caught us and heaved the barge a horseshoe-throw [about 42 feet] out of the water. The jolt when it hit brought the dead-looking men to. Seeing land at hand, they crawled through the surf to some rocks. Here we made a fire and parched some of our corn. We also found rain water. The men began to regain their senses, their **locomotion,** and their hope.

This day of our landing was November 6.

locomotion
(lō′kə-mō′shən) *n.* the power to move from place to place

What Befell Oviedo with the Indians

After we ate, I ordered Lope de Oviedo, our strongest man, to climb one of the trees not far off and ascertain the lay of the land. He complied and found out from the treetop that we were on an island. [This was Galveston Island.] He also said that the ground looked as if cattle had trampled it and therefore that this

30   must be a country of Christians. Ⓑ

I sent him back for a closer look, to see if he could find any worn trails, but warned him not to risk going too far. He went and came upon a path which he followed for half a league to some empty huts. The Indians were gone to shoal-flats[3] [to dig roots]. He took an earthen pot, a little dog, and a few mullets[4] and started back.

We had begun to worry what might have happened to him, so I detailed another two men to check. They met him shortly and saw three Indians with bows and arrows following him. The Indians were calling to him and he was gesturing them to keep coming. When he reached us, the Indians held back

40   and sat down on the shore.

Half an hour later a hundred bowmen reinforced the first three individuals. Whatever their stature, they looked like giants to us in our fright. We could not hope to defend ourselves; not half a dozen of us could even stand up.

The Inspector [Solís] and I walked out and greeted them. They advanced, and we did our best to placate and **ingratiate.** We gave them beads and bells, and each one of them gave us an arrow in pledge of friendship. They told us by signs that they would return at sunrise and bring food, having none then.

Ⓑ HISTORICAL CONTEXT
In the 1500s, "Christians" was used as a synonym for Europeans. What does this suggest about how the Spaniards saw the world?

ingratiate (ĭn-grā′shē-āt′) *v.* to gain another's favor by deliberate effort

The Indians' Hospitality Before and After a New Calamity

As the sun rose next morning, the Indians appeared as they promised, bringing an abundance of fish and of certain roots which taste like nuts, some bigger than

50   walnuts, some smaller, mostly grubbed from the water with great labor.

That evening they came again with more fish and roots and brought their women and children to look at us. They thought themselves rich with the little bells and beads we gave them, and they repeated their visits on other days.

---

1. **We sounded . . . fathoms:** We measured the depth of the water and found it to be about 42 feet. (A fathom is equal to 6 feet, or 1.83 meters.)
2. **league:** a unit of distance; Cabeza de Vaca probably used the Spanish league, equal to 3.1 miles (5 kilometers).
3. **shoal-flats:** stretches of level ground under shallow water.
4. **mullets:** certain edible fish.

DIFFERENTIATED INSTRUCTION

FOR STRATEGIC READERS

Summarize Point out the subheads in the excerpt, and explain that they summarize the events that take place during this section of the report. Ask students to briefly summarize the events described under "What Befell Oviedo with the Indians."

FOR ADVANCED LEARNERS/AP

Analyze and Research [paired option] Have student pairs find examples in the selection that show Cabeza de Vaca's Christian faith and beliefs. *Examples: "God's great mercy" (line 3), "The Lord willed" (line 73), "we prayed for mercy and pardon" (line 75), "Our method . . . was to . . . pray earnestly to God our Lord" (lines 122–123).* Then have students research some of the main beliefs of Christians during this time

period, recording their findings in a Cluster Diagram. For example, what did Christians believe prayer accomplished? How did they believe they should treat strangers? Did they believe in healing? After students finish the selection, have them identify actions of Cabeza de Vaca that did—or did not—reflect his Christian beliefs.

 BEST PRACTICES TOOLKIT—Transparency Cluster Diagram p. B18

Being provided with what we needed, we thought to embark again. It was a struggle to dig our barge out of the sand it had sunk in, and another struggle to launch her. For the work in the water while launching, we stripped and stowed our clothes in the craft.

Quickly clambering in and grabbing our oars, we had rowed two crossbow shots from shore when a wave **inundated** us. Being naked and the cold intense, 60 we let our oars go. The next big wave capsized the barge. The Inspector and two others held fast, but that only carried them more certainly underneath, where they drowned.

A single roll of the sea tossed the rest of the men into the rushing surf and back onto shore half-drowned.

We lost only those the barge took down; but the survivors escaped as naked as they were born, with the loss of everything we had. That was not much, but valuable to us in that bitter November cold, our bodies so emaciated we could easily count every bone and looked the very picture of death. I can say for myself that from the month of May I had eaten nothing but corn, and that sometimes 70 raw. I never could bring myself to eat any of the horse-meat at the time our beasts were slaughtered; and fish I did not taste ten times. On top of everything else, a cruel north wind commenced to complete our killing. **C**

The Lord willed that we should find embers while searching the remnants of our former fire. We found more wood and soon had big fires raging. Before them, with flowing tears, we prayed for mercy and pardon, each filled with pity not only for himself but for all his wretched fellows.

At sunset the Indians, not knowing we had gone, came again with food. When they saw us looking so strangely different, they turned back in alarm. I went after them calling, and they returned, though frightened. I explained to them by signs 80 that our barge had sunk and three of our number drowned. They could see at their feet two of the dead men who had washed ashore. They could also see that the rest of us were not far from joining these two.

The Indians, understanding our full plight, sat down and lamented for half an hour so loudly they could have been heard a long way off. It was amazing to see these wild, untaught savages howling like brutes in compassion for us. It intensified my own grief at our calamity and had the same effect on the other victims.

When the cries died down, I conferred with the Christians about asking the Indians to take us to their homes. Some of our number who had been to New Spain warned that the Indians would sacrifice us to their idols.[5] But death being 90 surer and nearer if we stayed where we were, I went ahead and beseeched the Indians. They were delighted. They told us to **tarry** a little while, then they would do as we wished.

Presently thirty of them gathered loads of wood and disappeared to their huts, which were a long walk away; while we waited with the remainder until near nightfall. Then, supporting us under our arms, they hurried us from one

---

5. **New Spain . . . their idols:** New Spain included what is now the southwest United States, Mexico, Central America north of Panama, and some West Indian islands. In Mexico, conquistadors had encountered Aztecs who practiced human sacrifice.

inundate (ĭn′ŭn-dāt′) *v.* to cover with water; to overwhelm

C PRIMARY SOURCE
Reread lines 68–71. What does the author's reponse to his current situation tell you about his usual diet?

② **Targeted Passage**

tarry (tăr′ē) *v.* to delay

READING STRATEGY

C PRIMARY SOURCE

Possible answer: The author does not normally eat horse meat (line 70), and he could not bring himself to do so, even though he is starving.

Lines 54–86
TIERED DISCUSSION PROMPTS
Use these prompts to help students consider the Spanish conquistadors' decision to try to leave the island:

Connect Have you ever failed to solve a difficult problem or predicament and then confronted the same situation again? How did you respond? *Accept all reasonable responses.*

Intepret Why do you think the men decide to embark again and leave the island so soon? *Possible answer: The men feel refreshed by the food the Indians have given them. They feel a bit hopeful and think that they have enough strength to sail again. They may also feel that the Indians might not continue to be welcoming, so they should leave while they still can.*

Evaluate Do you think the conquistadors' decision to leave was a good one? Why or why not? *Possible answers: No: The men were obviously still weak (lines 54–56), and the Indians showed no unfriendly signs. The men had only a barge to sail on; they should have waited until they had built a more seaworthy vessel. Yes: The men needed to try to leave the island, where they thought they would become unwelcome. This was the best time to leave—before any hostility developed.*

FOR STRATEGIC READERS

② **Targeted Passage [Lines 77–92]**

This passage introduces the conflict the conquistadors face after their barge capsizes.

• Why do the Indians return with food?

• Why do the conquistadors look "so strangely different" to the Indians?

• How do the Indians respond to the conquistadors' plight?

• Why are some of the conquistadors afraid to go to the Indians' homes?

FOR ENGLISH LEARNERS

Vocabulary: Idioms Help students use context clues to determine the meanings of these idioms: *brought . . . to* (lines 21–22), "brought back to consciousness"; *regain their senses* (line 24), "feel better"; *came upon* (line 32), "discovered"; *held fast* (line 61), "held on tightly"; *On top of everything else* (line 71), "Along with everything else that happened"; *as a matter of fact* (line 119), "actually."

D GRAMMAR AND STYLE

Analyze Details These prepositional phrases give readers more information about the setting of the excerpt and help readers understand the men's experience. Ask students to identify other prepositional phrases in the report that provide important details. *Possible answers: "to land," "in seven fathoms" (line 17); "for half a league," "to some empty huts" (line 33); "of the sea," "into the rushing surf" (line 63)*

Lines 106–109
REINFORCE KEY IDEA: SURVIVE

Discuss What does the Karankawas' insistence that the Spaniards serve as medicine men tell you about their desire to **survive?** *Possible answer: Despite their generosity to the Spaniards, the Karankawas are willing to refuse to give them food unless they help them overcome the sickness that is threatening their survival.*

LITERARY ANALYSIS

E HISTORICAL CONTEXT

Possible answer: Both the Spanish and the Karankawas believed in a power beyond themselves that is capable of healing (lines 109–113, 122–125).

SELECTION WRAP-UP

SUMMARIZE Have students sum up Cabeza de Vaca's encounter with the Karankawas.

⭐ CRITIQUE

- Have students explain what part of the excerpt they found most surprising, encouraging, or upsetting—and why.

- After completing the After Reading questions on page 75, have students revisit their responses and tell whether they have changed their opinions.

---

to another of the four big fires they had built along the path. At each fire, when we regained a little warmth and strength, they took us on so swiftly our feet hardly touched ground. **D**

100 Thus we made their village, where we saw they had erected a hut for us with many fires inside. An hour later they began a dance celebration that lasted all night. For us there was no joy, feasting, or sleep, as we waited the hour they should make us victims.

In the morning, when they brought us fish and roots and acted in every way hospitably, we felt reassured and somewhat lost our anxiety of the sacrificial knife.

Cabeza de Vaca learned that men from one of the other barges had also landed on the island, bringing the number of Europeans there to about 90. In a matter of weeks, all but 16 of them died of disease, which spread to the Karankawas and killed half of them as well. Some of the Karankawas wanted to put the remaining Europeans to death but were dissuaded by Cabeza de Vaca's host. Cabeza de Vaca and his men were later forced to act as healers.

How We Became Medicine-Men
The islanders wanted to make physicians of us without examination or a review of diplomas. Their method of cure is to blow on the sick, the breath and the laying-on of hands supposedly casting out the infirmity. They insisted we should do this too and be of some use to them. We scoffed at their cures and at the idea we knew how to heal. But they withheld food from us until we complied. An Indian told
110 me I knew not whereof I spoke in saying their methods had no effect. Stones and other things growing about in the fields, he said, had a virtue whereby passing a pebble along the stomach could take away pain and heal; surely extraordinary men like us **embodied** such powers over nature. Hunger forced us to obey, but disclaiming any responsibility for our failure or success.

An Indian, falling sick, would send for a medicine-man, who would apply his cure. The patient would then give the medicine-man all he had and seek more from his relatives to give. The medicine-man makes incisions over the point of the pain, sucks the wound, and **cauterizes** it. This remedy enjoys high repute among the Indians. I have, as a matter of fact, tried it on myself with good results. The
120 medicine-men blow on the spot they have treated, as a finishing touch, and the patient regards himself relieved.

Our method, however, was to bless the sick, breathe upon them, recite a *Pater noster* and *Ave Maria,*[6] and pray earnestly to God our Lord for their recovery. When we concluded with the sign of the cross, He willed that our patients should directly spread the news that they had been restored to health. **E**

In consequence, the Indians treated us kindly. They deprived themselves of food to give to us, and presented us skins and other tokens of gratitude. ❦

Translated by Cyclone Covey

---

6. ***Pater noster*** (pä′tər nŏs′tər) **and *Ave Maria*** (ä′vä mə-rē′ə): the Lord's Prayer ("Our Father") and the Hail Mary, named for the prayers' opening words in Latin.

74   UNIT 1: EARLY AMERICAN WRITING

D GRAMMAR AND STYLE
Reread lines 93–98. Note how the author uses **prepositional phrases**, such as "until near nightfall" and "along the path," to add important details about where and when events are happening.

embody (ĕm-bŏd′ē) *v.* to represent in human form

③ Targeted Passage

cauterize (kô′tə-rīz′) *v.* to burn or sear to destroy diseased tissue

E HISTORICAL CONTEXT
In Cabeza de Vaca's time, no one had good knowledge of what caused disease. Reread lines 105–125. In what ways did the Spanish and the Karankawas have similiar ideas about healing?

DIFFERENTIATED INSTRUCTION

FOR STRATEGIC READERS
③ Targeted Passage [Lines 115–127]
This passage shows how the Spanish and the Karankawas resolved their relationship.

- What do the Karankawa medicine men do to "heal" their patients?

- What does Cabeza de Vaca think of the Indians' remedies after he has tried them?

- When the conquistadors serve as medicine men, how do they "heal" their patients?

- How do the Karankawas respond?

FOR ADVANCED LEARNERS/AP
Analyze Have small groups discuss these questions and share their findings:

- What preconceived notions did the Spanish have about the Indians?

- Did the Karankawas' actions support the conquistadors' preconceived notions?

- How much are the preconceived notions a person holds based on historical context rather than personal experience? Give some examples that support your theory.

Comprehension

1. **Summarize** What was life like for the Spaniards on the barges?

2. **Recall** What happened to Cabeza de Vaca's men when they tried to leave Galveston Island?

3. **Clarify** Why did the Karankawas enlist the Spaniards as healers?

Literary Analysis

4. **Make Inferences** Based on the events and reactions Cabeza de Vaca describes, what appears to be the Karankawas' view of the Spaniards? Cite details to support your answer.

5. **Examine Character Traits** What qualities of a **survivor** does Cabeza de Vaca demonstrate in each situation?

   • approaching Galveston Island (lines 10–17)
   • meeting the Karankawas (lines 41–46)
   • asking the Karankawas for help (lines 89–91)
   • adopting a new healing practice (lines 118–119)

6. **Evaluate a Primary Source** Review the information you collected about *La Relación* as you read. In what ways would you consider this account a valuable and reliable source of information? What are its shortcomings? Explain your conclusions.

7. **Make Generalizations About Historical Context** To understand the historical context of a work, you need to consult sources outside of the work for information. Identify three passages from *La Relación* that reflect ideas, values, or events from the author's time. Then, using the footnotes to the text and the background information on page 70 as sources, explain the historical context of each example. Based on your results, what generalizations can you make about 16th-century Spanish perspectives? Create a chart to organize your notes.

Examples from Text	Information from Other Sources
•	
•	•
•	•
	•

Generalizations About Historical Context
•
•
•

Literary Criticism

8. **Biographical Context** Later in life, Cabeza de Vaca spoke out against the enslavement of Native Americans. How might his experiences as a captive, trader, and healer among the Karankawas and other groups have influenced his position? Explain your answer, citing evidence from the text.

8. *He saw how compassionate and generous the Native Americans were (lines 46–47, 48–50, 77–92, 99–102). He appreciated the Indians' culture and humanity (lines 115–121). His captivity showed him that slavery was unjust (lines 105–110).*

Practice and Apply

After Reading

Use these copy masters to check understanding and provide extra support:

R RESOURCE MANAGER—Copy Masters
   Reading Check p. 110
   Historical Context p. 103
   Question Support p. 111

   Additional selection questions are provided for teachers on page 97.

ANSWERS

1. *The Spaniards were lost at sea, starving to death, and freezing.*

2. *A wave capsized their barge. Three men drowned; the others washed ashore, naked and having lost all their supplies.*

3. *They believed the Spaniards to be extraordinary men with power over nature.*

Possible answers:

4. *The Karankawas are curious about the Spaniards (lines 51–52). They think the Spaniards have magical powers (lines 112–113). They are unafraid of the Spaniards and feel empathy for them (lines 83–101).*

5. ***approaching Galveston Island:*** *recognizes the signs of land and acts quickly to verify;* ***meeting the Karankawas:*** *finds ways to communicate with the inhabitants, despite his fear;* ***asking the Karankawas for help:*** *asks for needed help despite the Spaniards' fear;* ***adopting a new healing practice:*** *under threat, complies with the Indians' commands*

6. ■ **SKILLS FOCUS** **Reading a Primary Source** *Reliable: The author uses a calm tone and gives detailed observations;* ***Unreliable:*** *The author has personal motives and makes cultural assumptions that can distort his interpretation of events (lines 41–43, 88–89).*

7. ● **SKILLS FOCUS** **Historical Context** *Students should cite passages and source material that lead to valid generalizations, as shown here.* ***Text Example:*** *Spanish conquistadors were afraid that Indians would sacrifice them to their idols (lines 88–89).* ***Other Sources:*** *Footnote on page 73 supports idea; background information says conquistadors encountered Native American cultures they didn't understand.* ***Generalization:*** *In the 16th century, Spanish explorers feared and misunderstood Native Americans.*

ANSWERS

Vocabulary in Context

VOCABULARY PRACTICE

1. *(d) connection*   4. *(d) weep*
2. *(c) ingratiate*   5. *(a) obtain*
3. *(c) wind*   6. *(d) construct*

RESOURCE MANAGER—Copy Master
Vocabulary Practice p. 108

VOCABULARY IN WRITING

Have students review lines 4–9, 41–47, and 51–52. Urge them to recall the condition of Cabeza de Vaca and his men and how the Karankawas reacted to them. These details will help students infer how the Karankawas might have described the Spanish conquistadors.

VOCABULARY STRATEGY: ETYMOLOGIES
(also an EL language objective)

- Explain to students that etymologies can help them recognize related words and therefore figure out their meanings.

- Note that students' answers may vary slightly based on the dictionary they use.

Possible answers:

1. *Italian*

2. kunosoura, *meaning "dog's tail"; "focal point or center of attention"*

3. *The word comes from the name of a character, Mrs. Malaprop, who misuses words in Richard Brinsley Sheridan's 18th-century play* The Rivals.

4. *Latin, Old French, and Middle English*

RESOURCE MANAGER—Copy Master
Vocabulary Strategy p. 109

Vocabulary Center at ClassZone.com
Additional Vocabulary Activities

Vocabulary in Context

VOCABULARY PRACTICE

Choose the word that is not related in meaning to the other words.

WORD LIST
cauterize
embody
ingratiate
inundate
locomotion
tarry

1. (a) transit, (b) locomotion, (c) movement, (d) connection
2. (a) inane, (b) incompetent, (c) ingratiate, (d) inept
3. (a) deluge, (b) inundate, (c) wind, (d) overwhelm
4. (a) cauterize, (b) sear, (c) singe, (d) weep
5. (a) obtain, (b) dawdle, (c) tarry, (d) linger
6. (a) embody, (b) personify, (c) actualize, (d) construct

VOCABULARY IN WRITING

How do you suppose Cabeza de Vaca's men looked to the Karankawas when they first met? Write a brief description of the crew from the Karankawas' point of view. Include two or more vocabulary words. You could start like this.

> **EXAMPLE SENTENCE**
> The strangers on shore seemed to **embody** pure misery.

VOCABULARY STRATEGY: ETYMOLOGIES

The **etymology** of a word, or its origin and history, can provide insight into the word's meaning. Information about a word's etymology will often appear near the beginning or end of a dictionary entry, as in the following example:

cau•ter•ize (kô'tə-rīz') *tr.v.* **-ized, -iz•ing, -iz•es 1.** To burn or sear with a cautery. **2.** To deaden, as to feelings or moral scruples. [Middle English *cauterizen*, from Late Latin *cautērizāre*, to cauterize, brand, from Latin *cautērium*, cautery.] —**cau•ter•i•za•tion** (-tər-ĭ-zā'shən) *n.*

PRACTICE Use a dictionary to answer these questions.

1. From what language did *oratorio* enter English?
2. From which Greek word is *cynosure* derived? What is the word's current meaning?
3. What is the origin of the word *malaprop*?
4. Through which languages can the history of *querulous* be traced?

VOCABULARY PRACTICE
For more practice, go to the **Vocabulary Center** at **ClassZone.com**.

DIFFERENTIATED INSTRUCTION

FOR ADVANCED LEARNERS/AP

Vocabulary Strategy Have pairs select five words from Cabeza de Vaca's account and research each word's etymology. Then have them use the five words in a paragraph about some aspect of the report. Have pairs share their etymologies and paragraphs with the class.

Reading-Writing Connection

W1.2

GRAMMAR AND STYLE

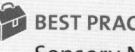

W1.9, LC1.1

ADD NECESSARY DETAILS Review the **Grammar and Style** note on page 74. Cabeza de Vaca uses numerous details throughout his account to help readers visualize his amazing journey. **Prepositional phrases** include details about what happens, as well as where, when, and how. Read this example from *La Relación*:

> *A single roll of the sea tossed the rest of the men into the rushing surf and back onto shore half-drowned.* (lines 63–64)

PRACTICE Rewrite each sentence, adding prepositional phrases that modify the boldfaced words. Follow the directions in parentheses. An example has been done for you.

> **EXAMPLE**
>
> The barges, filled with half-starved men, **drifted** for days. (Tell where they drifted.)
>
> *The barges, filled with half-starved men, drifted on the stormy seas for days.*

1. They told us they **would return** and bring us food. (Tell when they will return.)

2. We **traveled** through the woods to the **village.** (Add two phrases. Tell how long they traveled and where the village was located.)

3. We waited anxiously for **news.** (Tell what kind of news was expected.)

WRITING TOOLS
For prewriting, revision, and editing tools, visit the **Writing Center** at ClassZone.com.

FOR DEVELOPING WRITERS

Writing Support

• Help students get started by asking, When did you experience this moment? What were you exploring?

• Work with students to translate several details from their Sensory Notes organizer into sentences that describe their journey.

• Limit the length of the assignment to two paragraphs.

Reading-Writing Connection

WRITING PROMPT

Encourage students to use a Sensory Notes organizer to help them record vivid and meaningful descriptions that they have either experienced or imagined.

 BEST PRACTICES TOOLKIT—Transparency
Sensory Notes p. B9

For writing support, see

ℹ️ Writing Center at **ClassZone.com**

GRAMMAR AND STYLE

Remind students that a prepositional phrase begins with a preposition (such as *of, on, in, against,* and *for*) and includes the object of the preposition and any words that modify the object. It does not include a verb. For more on adding details with prepositional phrases, see **Grammar Handbook,** page R65.

Possible answers:

1. *They told us they would return **in the morning** and bring us food.*

2. *We traveled **for three hours** through the woods to the village **in their territory**.*

3. *We waited anxiously for news **about the missing men**.*

🇷 RESOURCE MANAGER—Copy Master
Add Necessary Details p. 112

Assess and Reteach

Assess

🇷 RESOURCE MANAGER—Copy Masters
Selection Test A pp. 113–114
Selection Test B/C pp. 115–116

💿 Test Generator CD

Reteach

🇸 STANDARDS LESSON FILE
Research Lesson 5: Using Primary Sources
Vocabulary Lesson 25: Etymologies

Focus and Motivate

OBJECTIVES

Literary Analysis
- explore the key idea of **slavery**
- analyze a slave narrative
- read a slave narrative

Reading
- analyze descriptive details

Vocabulary
- build vocabulary for reading and writing
- use the Latin root *nom* to unlock meaning (also an EL language objective)

Grammar and Writing
- use adverb clauses to add descriptive details
- write a personal letter

CALIFORNIA R3.1, R3.3, R1.2, W1.1, W1.9, LC1.1

ABOUT THE AUTHOR

After students have read about Equiano, have them create a timeline of his life, from his capture as a slave to his writing of his narrative. Discuss his extraordinary personal journey. Then point out that the excerpt details the events described in **Ocean Crossings.**

USING THE *NOTABLE QUOTE*

Ask students how **Olaudah Equiano's** habit of remembering every new thing he saw may have affected his narrative. *Possible answer: Equiano would have remembered important events and details, and so been able to create a vivid and fairly accurate narrative.*

CALIFORNIA
R3.1, R3.3, R1.2 (p. 86), W1.1 (p. 87), W1.9 (p. 87), LC1.1 (p. 87)

from The Interesting Narrative of the Life of Olaudah Equiano

Slave Narrative by Olaudah Equiano

NOTABLE QUOTE
"Every new thing that I observed I treasured up in my memory."

FYI
Did you know that Olaudah Equiano . . .
- was a best-selling author in Britain?
- owned slaves in Central America?
- married an English woman and raised two daughters?
- died a wealthy man?

Author Online
For more on Olaudah Equiano, visit the **Literature Center** at **ClassZone.com.**

Olaudah Equiano
c. 1745–1797

Soldier, sailor, North Pole explorer—Olaudah Equiano led a remarkable life by the standards of any age. Writing as a former slave in the 1700s, Equiano left powerful testimony on the brutality of enslavement that became the model for a new genre, the slave narrative.

Ocean Crossings According to his autobiography, Equiano was born a chief's son in the Ibo (or Igbo) culture of present-day Nigeria. When he was 11, he was captured and sold as a slave to a series of African masters before making the miserable journey to the Americas known as the Middle Passage. Sold in the West Indies to British navy officer Michael Pascal, Equiano returned to sea with his new owner, who renamed him Gustavus Vassa.

Equiano spent years fighting for Britain, hoping to be freed for good service.

Instead, in 1762 he was sold again, to Quaker merchant Robert King, who trained him in business. In 1766, after 21 years as a slave, Equiano bought back his freedom, moved to London, and promptly launched his business career. But by 1773, he was at sea again, first on an expedition to find a northwest passage, and later traveling to Central America and Turkey.

Turning Points In the late 1770s, Equiano returned to London where he got involved in antislavery efforts and converted to Christianity. In 1789, as public debate over abolishing the slave trade began in Britain, Equiano wrote, self-published, and promoted his narrative. Equiano's life story exposed the cruelty of the slave trade and made him an important public figure. He died in 1797, just ten years before Britain abolished the slave trade.

Historians Look More Closely Equiano's narrative includes a wealth of specific details, most of which check out against other sources. But, in 1999, English professor Vincent Carretta uncovered two documents that suggested Equiano was not born in Africa: his baptismal record from England and a ship's passenger list, both of which identify Equiano's birthplace as South Carolina. Historians continue to debate the evidence and how, if at all, it changes the value of *The Interesting Narrative.* Carretta himself points out that even if the narrative is based on the oral accounts of other slaves, its descriptions still provide a valuable portrait of early African life and the Middle Passage.

Diagram of the cargo hold of a fully loaded slave ship

Selection Resources

---

* Resources for Differentiation   † Also in Spanish   ‡ In Haitian Creole and Vietnamese

● LITERARY ANALYSIS: SLAVE NARRATIVE

Few of us can imagine what slavery was really like. **Slave narratives,** the life stories of people who survived slavery, help us understand the grim realities of this experience.

Olaudah Equiano wrote *The Interesting Narrative* at a time when many Africans remembered their lives before enslavement. Like other 18th-century slave narratives, his work

- portrays the culture shock of a newly captured African
- focuses criticism on slave traders, not slave owners
- includes religious and moral appeals against slavery

As you read, note how the author develops these topics.

■ READING SKILL: ANALYZE DETAILS

Equiano's readers had little contact with slavery. He chose powerful **descriptive details** to bring the experience to life.

The closeness of the place, and the heat of the climate, added to the number in the ship, which was so crowded that each had scarcely room to turn himself, almost suffocated us.

To reach his readers, Equiano uses

- **sensory details,** ones that appeal to the five senses
- descriptions of his own reactions
- **anecdotes,** brief stories that support his points

As you read, use a chart like the one shown to record effective examples of each kind of detail.

Sensory Details	Reactions	Anecdotes

▲ VOCABULARY IN CONTEXT

Equiano used the following words in his argument against slavery. Restate each phrase, using a different word or words for the boldfaced term.

1. **copious** amounts of rain, causing a flood
2. the **nominal** boss, but with no real authority
3. her **countenance** betraying her fear
4. cruel rulers acting without worry or **scruple**
5. to our **consternation,** revealed all our plans
6. deadly effects of **pestilential** beetles

Explore the Key Idea

What does it mean to be a SLAVE?

KEY IDEA From the 1500s to the 1800s, millions of Africans were enslaved to work in the Americas. Their experiences have been documented in books and portrayed in films. What do you know about the realities of **slavery?**

TEST YOURSELF Decide whether each statement is true or false. Think about the facts or impressions that helped you choose your answer.

SLAVERY: *Fact or Fiction*

1. Slavery was a common practice in Africa.
   ☐ TRUE   ○ FALSE

2. No Africans participated willingly in the slave trade.
   ☐ TRUE   ○ FALSE

3. Most enslaved Africans were brought to North America.
   ☐ TRUE   ○ FALSE

4. Captured Africans were packed like cargo into slave ships.
   ☐ TRUE   ○ FALSE

5. Slave traders typically sold families as a single group.
   ☐ TRUE   ○ FALSE

Teach

What does it mean to be a SLAVE?

Ask the question. After students read the **KEY IDEA**, have them consider the question at the end of the paragraph. Have students complete **TEST YOURSELF,** then invite them to share and explain their answers about **slavery.**

SKILLS FOCUS

LITERARY ANALYSIS   R3.1

● SLAVE NARRATIVE

Have students read **Ocean Crossings** on page 78. Ask them to describe aspects of the culture shock Equiano would have faced in his first days as a slave. *Possible answer: He would have faced separation from his family at age 11, recognition that Africans had enslaved him, a miserable journey, and abrupt change from a chief's son to a slave.*

CHECK UNDERSTANDING Ask students if Equiano was always a slave. Have them discuss how his history may have influenced his slave narrative.

READING SKILL   R3.3

■ ANALYZE DETAILS

Have students read the first paragraph of **Ocean Crossings.** Ask what descriptive phrases hint at details Equiano will develop in his narrative. *Possible answer: "miserable journey" and "sold in the West Indies"*

R RESOURCE MANAGER—Copy Master
Analyze Details p. 129 (for student use while reading the selection)

▲ VOCABULARY IN CONTEXT

DIAGNOSE WORD KNOWLEDGE To determine preteaching needs, have all students complete Vocabulary in Context. *Possible answers:* **1.** *plentiful,* **2.** *so-called,* **3.** *facial expression,* **4.** *second thought,* **5.** *grave concern,* **6.** *lethal*

PRETEACH VOCABULARY Preteach vocabulary with this copy master. Read each item aloud.

R RESOURCE MANAGER—Copy Master
Vocabulary Study p. 131

MORE VOCABULARY SUPPORT
For additional activities and guidelines, see

🧰 **BEST PRACTICES TOOLKIT**
Scaffolding Vocabulary Instruction pp. 43–46
ℹ Vocabulary Center at **ClassZone.com**

SUMMARY

This excerpt from Equiano's slave narrative details his horrendous journey on a slave ship as a captured 11-year-old boy. It opens with Equiano being forced aboard the slave ship, then recounts the inhumane conditions of the journey, including the floggings he receives for not eating. After surviving the ocean journey, Equiano and other Africans are sold as slaves. Many are cruelly separated from family members.

Lines 4–5
REINFORCE *KEY IDEA:* SLAVERY

Discuss What does the way in which Equiano was treated when he was carried on board the ship tell you about **slavery?** *Possible answer: Slavery was dehumanizing and cruel. Equiano was "handled" and "tossed" as if he were an inanimate object and not a person.*

LITERARY ANALYSIS

Ⓐ SLAVE NARRATIVE

Possible answer: Equiano describes this experience from an African's point of view. Most Europeans would be startled to hear themselves and their culture described as a "world of bad spirits" (lines 5–6)—as if their culture is strange, hostile, and horrible. They would also be surprised to think that their physical attributes were perceived as abnormal (lines 6–8).

If students need help . . . Point out that Equiano is describing Europeans. Ask students how they would feel if someone described them as part of a "world of bad spirits."

THE INTERESTING NARRATIVE
of the Life of Olaudah Equiano

OLAUDAH EQUIANO

BACKGROUND As European colonies in the Americas expanded, so did the slave trade. Slaves were captured in Africa, then taken by ship to the West Indies—a journey called the Middle Passage. For two months, Africans lay tightly chained in storage compartments with hardly enough air to breathe. Millions died from bad food, harsh treatment, disease, and despair. Olaudah Equiano is one of the few to describe this horrific journey.

When Olaudah Equiano was 11 years old, he and his sister were kidnapped while the adults in his village were working in the fields. After being forced to travel for several days, Equiano and his sister were separated. For the next six or seven months, Equiano was sold several times to African masters in different countries. He was eventually taken to the west coast of Africa and carried aboard a slave ship bound for the West Indies.

The first object which saluted my eyes when I arrived on the coast, was the sea, and a slave ship, which was then riding at anchor, and waiting for its cargo. These filled me with astonishment, which was soon converted into terror, when I was carried on board. I was immediately handled, and tossed up to see if I were sound, by some of the crew; and I was now persuaded that I had gotten into a world of bad spirits, and that they were going to kill me. Their complexions, too, differing so much from ours, their long hair, and the language they spoke (which was very different from any I had ever heard), united to confirm me in this belief. Ⓐ
Indeed, such were the horrors of my views and fears at the moment, that, if ten
10 thousand worlds had been my own, I would have freely parted with them all to

ANALYZE VISUALS
Describe the mood of this painting. What does the image reveal about the conditions on board a slave ship?

① Targeted Passage

Ⓐ **SLAVE NARRATIVE**
Note Equiano's use of **first-person point of view** in lines 1–8. In what ways might this description be startling to Equiano's mostly European audience?

Detail of *The Slave Ship* (1956), Robert Riggs. N.A. Courtesy of Les Mansfield, Cincinnati, Ohio.

DIFFERENTIATED INSTRUCTION

FOR ALL STUDENTS

Provide these independent projects to extend the lesson:

- Write a poem.
- Discuss how injustices are exposed today.
- Create a visual representation.

For further details on these projects, see

Ⓡ RESOURCE MANAGER
Ideas for Extension pp. 122–123

FOR STRATEGIC READERS

In combination with the *Audio Anthology CD,* use one or more Targeted Passages (pp. 80, 83, 84) to ensure that students focus on key events and concepts. Targeted Passages are also good for English learners.

① Targeted Passage [Lines 1–8]

This passage enables students to feel the author's fear and recognize his predicament.

- What is the cargo the slave ship is waiting for?
- How does Equiano feel while on the slave ship?
- What does Equiano think is going to happen to him?

have exchanged my condition with that of the meanest slave[1] in my own country. When I looked round the ship too, and saw a large furnace of copper boiling, and a multitude of black people of every description chained together, every one of their **countenances** expressing dejection and sorrow, I no longer doubted of my fate; and, quite overpowered with horror and anguish, I fell motionless on the deck and fainted. When I recovered a little, I found some black people about me, who I believed were some of those who had brought me on board, and had been receiving their pay; they talked to me in order to cheer me, but all in vain. I asked them if we were not to be eaten by those white men with horrible looks, red faces,

20 and long hair. They told me I was not, and one of the crew brought me a small portion of spirituous liquor in a wine glass; but, being afraid of him, I would not take it out of his hand. One of the blacks, therefore, took it from him and gave it to me, and I took a little down my palate, which, instead of reviving me, as they thought it would, threw me into the greatest **consternation** at the strange feeling it produced, having never tasted any such liquor before. Soon after this, the blacks who brought me on board went off, and left me abandoned to despair. **B**

I now saw myself deprived of all chance of returning to my native country, or even the least glimpse of hope of gaining the shore, which I now considered as friendly; and I even wished for my former slavery in preference to my present

30 situation, which was filled with horrors of every kind, still heightened by my ignorance of what I was to undergo. I was not long suffered to indulge my grief; I was soon put down under the decks, and there I received such a salutation in my nostrils as I had never experienced in my life; so that, with the loathsomeness of the stench, and crying together, I became so sick and low that I was not able to eat, nor had I the least desire to taste anything. I now wished for the last friend, death, to relieve me; but soon, to my grief, two of the white men offered me eatables; and, on my refusing to eat, one of them held me fast by the hands, and laid me across, I think, the windlass,[2] and tied my feet, while the other flogged[3] me severely. I had never experienced anything of this kind before, and, although not

40 being used to the water, I naturally feared that element the first time I saw it, yet, nevertheless, could I have got over the nettings,[4] I would have jumped over the side, but I could not; and besides, the crew used to watch us very closely who were not chained down to the decks, lest we should leap into the water; and I have seen some of these poor African prisoners most severely cut, for attempting to do so, and hourly whipped for not eating. This indeed was often the case with myself. In a little time after, amongst the poor chained men, I found some of my own nation, which in a small degree gave ease to my mind. I inquired of these what was to be done with us? They gave me to understand, we were to be carried to these white people's country to work for them. I then was a little revived, and thought, if

50 it were no worse than working, my situation was not so desperate; but still I feared

---

1. **the meanest slave:** the poorest or most wretched slave.
2. **windlass** (wĭnd'ləs): a device for raising and lowering a ship's anchor.
3. **flogged:** beat with a whip or rod.
4. **nettings:** networks of small ropes on the sides of a ship that were used for various purposes, such as stowing sails. On slave ships, the nettings helped keep the slaves from jumping overboard.

countenance
(koun'tə-nəns) *n.*
appearance, especially the expression of the face

consternation
(kŏn'stər-nā'shən) *n.*
a state of paralyzing dismay; fear

B ANALYZE DETAILS
Reread lines 1–26. What details reinforce Equiano's impression that he has been captured by bad spirits?

READING SKILL

B ANALYZE DETAILS

Possible answer: The details that reinforce Equiano's fear that he has been captured by bad spirits include the strange appearance and unfamiliar language of the men on the ship (lines 6–8); the boiling furnace (line 12); the miserable, chained Africans (lines 13–15); and the fearful feelings he experiences after drinking the liquor (lines 21–25).

If students need help . . . Work with them to use the prereading chart introduced on page 79. Help students list the sensory details Equiano describes and his reactions. Point out the sense to which each detail appeals.

Sensory Details	Reactions
men's strange language (hearing)	felt he was being captured by bad spirits
miserable, chained Africans (sight)	felt overcome with fear and fainted

Lines 27–50
TIERED DISCUSSION PROMPTS

Use these prompts to have students consider Equiano's situation:

Connect How have you or someone you know reacted to a seemingly hopeless situation? *Accept all reasonable responses.*

Interpret Why might Equiano feel grief at the offer of food? *Possible answer: Food makes Equiano's survival more likely and he longs for death at this point (lines 35–36).*

Synthesize Based on what you know about slavery and Equiano's experiences so far, will Equiano's situation become not "so desperate" (line 50) when he reaches "the white people's country" (line 49)? Explain. *Possible answer: No. He will most likely continue to be mistreated by slave owners. Being "owned" by someone will always make him feel desperate and debased.*

DIFFERENTIATED INSTRUCTION

FOR STRATEGIC READERS

Visualize Direct students to the diagram on page 78. Explain that it was used by British abolitionists in 1789 to bring home the horror of the slave trade to the British public. It shows 482 slaves packed together in a ship. Have students use this image to help them visualize the ship that Equiano traveled on. As they read, ask them to note details in Equiano's narrative that would support this image (lines 77–85).

FOR ENGLISH LEARNERS

Vocabulary: Outdated Forms Have students reread these lines and substitute these definitions for the outdated terms:

- *gave me to understand* (line 48), "explained that"
- *how comes it* (line 61), "how can it be"
- *made ready* (line 72), "got ready (to sail)"
- *they thought fit* (line 92), "they wanted"

I should be put to death, the white people looked and acted, as I thought, in so savage a manner; for I had never seen among any people such instances of brutal cruelty; and this not only shown towards us blacks, but also to some of the whites themselves. One white man in particular I saw, when we were permitted to be on deck, flogged so unmercifully with a large rope near the foremast,[5] that he died in consequence of it; and they tossed him over the side as they would have done a brute. This made me fear these people the more; and I expected nothing less than to be treated in the same manner. I could not help expressing my fears and ap-
60 prehensions to some of my countrymen; I asked them if these people had no country, but lived in this hollow place (the ship)? They told me they did not, but came from a distant one. "Then," said I, "how comes it in all our country we never heard of them?" They told me because they lived so very far off. I then asked where were their women? had they any like themselves? I was told they had. "And why," said I, "do we not see them?" They answered, because they were left behind. I asked how the vessel could go? They told me they could not tell; but that there was cloth put upon the masts by the help of the ropes I saw, and then the vessel went on; and the white men had some spell or magic they put in the water when they liked, in order to stop the vessel. I was exceedingly amazed at this account, and really thought they were spirits. I therefore wished much to be from amongst them, for I expected they
70 would sacrifice me; but my wishes were vain—for we were so quartered that it was impossible for any of us to make our escape. . . . **D**

At last, when the ship we were in, had got in all her cargo, they made ready with many fearful noises, and we were all put under deck, so that we could not see how they managed the vessel. But this disappointment was the least of my sorrow. The stench of the hold while we were on the coast was so intolerably loathsome, that it was dangerous to remain there for any time, and some of us had been permitted to stay on the deck for the fresh air; but now that the whole ship's cargo were confined together, it became absolutely **pestilential.** The closeness of the place, and the heat of the climate, added to the number in the ship, which
80 was so crowded that each had scarcely room to turn himself, almost suffocated us. This produced **copious** perspirations, so that the air soon became unfit for respiration, from a variety of loathsome smells, and brought on a sickness among the slaves, of which many died. . . . This wretched situation was again aggravated by the galling[6] of the chains. . . . The shrieks of the women, and the groans of the dying, rendered the whole a scene of horror almost inconceivable. Happily perhaps, for myself, I was soon reduced so low here that it was thought necessary to keep me almost always on deck; and from my extreme youth I was not put in fetters. In this situation I expected every hour to share the fate of my companions, some of whom were almost daily brought upon deck at the point of death, which I began
90 to hope would soon put an end to my miseries. . . . **E**

One day they had taken a number of fishes; and when they had killed and satisfied themselves with as many as they thought fit, to our astonishment who

---

5. **foremast** (fôr′məst): the mast (tall pole that supports sails and rigging) nearest the forward end of a sailing ship.
6. **galling:** rubbing or chafing, enough to produce sores.

THE INTERESTING NARRATIVE OF THE LIFE OF OLAUDAH EQUIANO   **83**

C GRAMMAR AND STYLE
Reread lines 54–57. Note how Equiano uses **adverb clauses,** such as "when we were permitted to be on deck," to modify verbs and adverbs in the sentence.

D SLAVE NARRATIVE
Look back at lines 48–52. What does Equiano's reaction reveal about the way he regards slavery?

pestilential
(pĕs′tə-lĕn′shəl) *adj.* deadly; poisonous

copious (kō′pē-əs) *adj.* in large amounts; abundant

2 Targeted Passage

E ANALYZE DETAILS
What details in lines 75–85 does Equiano use to describe conditions below decks?

C GRAMMAR AND STYLE

Analyze Details Equiano's use of adverb clauses allows his sentences to provide more detailed information. This phrase, for example, tells readers that the Africans are seldom allowed on deck. Ask students to identify other adverb clauses in Equiano's narrative and list the extra details these provide. Examples include "When I looked round the ship too" (line 12); "When I recovered a little" (line 16); "when we had a smooth sea and moderate wind" (lines 98–99).

LITERARY ANALYSIS

D SLAVE NARRATIVE

Possible answer: Equiano doesn't object to being forced to work for the Europeans (slavery) nearly as much as he objects to the cruel treatment by his captors (lines 50–53).

Extend the Discussion What does Equiano's viewpoint tell you about his view of work?

READING SKILL

E ANALYZE DETAILS

Possible answer: Details that describe the conditions below decks include "The stench of the hold" (line 75), "The closeness of the place" (lines 78–79), "the heat" (line 79), "copious perspirations" (line 81), "loathsome smells" (line 82), the sick slaves and the rubbing chains (lines 82–84), and "The shrieks of the women, and the groans of the dying" (lines 84–85).

FOR STRATEGIC READERS

2 Targeted Passage [Lines 78–90]

This passage shows readers how repulsive the conditions below deck are and how Equiano reacts to the conditions.

- What nearly suffocates the slaves?
- What causes many slaves to die?
- Why is Equiano brought on deck?

FOR ADVANCED LEARNERS/AP

Research Context Refer students to the **BACKGROUND** on page 80 and note that Equiano is traveling the Middle Passage. Clarify that the selection focuses on Equiano's personal experience rather than the overall journey. Have pairs learn more about the Middle Passage, such as its exact route, its usual duration, and the origin of its name. Invite pairs to map the Middle Passage and share findings with the class.

were on deck, rather than give any of them to us to eat, as we expected, they tossed the remaining fish into the sea again, although we begged and prayed for some as well as we could, but in vain; and some of my countrymen, being pressed by hunger, took an opportunity, when they thought no one saw them, of trying to get a little privately; but they were discovered, and the attempt procured them some very severe floggings. One day, when we had a smooth sea and moderate wind, two of my wearied countrymen who were chained together (I was near
100 them at the time), preferring death to such a life of misery, somehow made through the nettings and jumped into the sea; immediately, another quite dejected fellow, who, on account of his illness, was suffered to be out of irons, also followed their example; and I believe many more would very soon have done the same, if they had not been prevented by the ship's crew, who were instantly alarmed. . . .

During the rest of his voyage to the West Indies, Equiano continued to endure hardships. After the ship anchored on the coast of Barbados, Equiano and the other slaves were brought ashore and herded together in a slave merchant's yard to be sold.

We were not many days in the merchant's custody, before we were sold after their usual manner, which is this: On a signal given (as the beat of a drum), the buyers rush at once into the yard where the slaves are confined, and make choice of that parcel[7] they like best. The noise and clamor with which this is attended, and the eagerness visible in the countenances of the buyers, serve not a little to
110 increase the apprehension of terrified Africans, who may well be supposed to consider them as the ministers of that destruction to which they think themselves devoted. In this manner, without **scruple,** are relations and friends separated, most of them never to see each other again. I remember, in the vessel in which I was brought over, in the men's apartment, there were several brothers, who, in the sale, were sold in different lots; and it was very moving on this occasion, to see and hear their cries at parting. O, ye **nominal** Christians! might not an African ask you—Learned you this from your God, who says unto you, Do unto all men as you would men should do unto you? Is it not enough that we are torn from our country and friends, to toil for your luxury and lust of gain? Must every tender
120 feeling be likewise sacrificed to your avarice? Are the dearest friends and relations now rendered more dear by their separation from their kindred, still to be parted from each other, and thus prevented from cheering the gloom of slavery, with the small comfort of being together, and mingling their sufferings and sorrows? Why are parents to lose their children, brothers their sisters, or husbands their wives? Surely, this is a new refinement in cruelty, which . . . thus aggravates distress, and adds fresh horrors even to the wretchedness of slavery. ∾ 🅕

❸ **Targeted Passage**

scruple (skrōō′pəl) *n.* feeling of uneasiness or guilt that keeps a person from doing something

nominal (nŏm′ə-nəl) *adj.* in name but not in reality

🅕 **SLAVE NARRATIVE**
What point is Equiano making in lines 116–118? To what emotions is he appealing?

---

7. **parcel:** a group of slaves offered for sale as one "package."

Lines 91–98
REINFORCE *KEY IDEA:* SLAVERY

Discuss What does this anecdote say about how the Africans are treated under **slavery?**
Possible answer: *The anecdote suggests that they are treated worse than animals; they are not even worthy of food scraps. The men throw their leftover scraps of food overboard rather than give them to the slaves.*

LITERARY ANALYSIS

🅕 SLAVE NARRATIVE

Possible answer: *Equiano's point is that it is against the men's Christian religion to treat people the way they are treating the Africans. He is appealing to the readers' personal and spiritual emotions and their thoughts about basic human decency. He is pointing out how unjust this treatment is.*

SELECTION WRAP–UP

SUMMARIZE Have students sum up Equiano's introduction to slavery.

⭐ CRITIQUE

- Have students describe what aspects of Equiano's narrative might have had the most powerful impact on 18th-century readers. Remind students to support their answers with specific details from the text.

- After completing the After Reading questions on page 85, have students revisit their responses and tell whether they have changed their opinions.

DIFFERENTIATED INSTRUCTION

FOR STRATEGIC READERS

❸ **Targeted Passage [Lines 105–116]**

This passage explains what happened to the slaves once they reached shore.

- How are the slaves sold?

- How does Equiano characterize the slave buyers?

- Which of the slave buyers' actions does Equiano consider the most immoral?

After Reading

Comprehension

1. **Recall** Who has brought Equiano to the slave ship?

2. **Recall** What does Equiano think will happen to him when he is brought on board ship?

3. **Clarify** What does Equiano mean when he refers to "nominal Christians"?

Literary Analysis

4. **Analyze Descriptive Details** Review the chart you made while reading. Identify the details that had the strongest impact on you as a reader. Why were those details so effective?

5. **Make Inferences About Cultural Context** Equiano portrays himself as an African encountering Europeans for the very first time. By describing his shocked and confused responses to the men of this different culture, Equiano reveals clues about African beliefs and customs. In each example, what inferences can you make about the narrator's cultural context?

   • his fears of white men (lines 18–20)
   • how he responds to fellow Africans (lines 20–23)
   • his questions about the ship (lines 59–68)
   • his reactions to cruelty around him (lines 50–57 and 91–95)

6. **Compare and Contrast** Like Cabeza de Vaca, Equiano describes a journey to the Americas. In what ways does his narrative resemble *La Relación?* Identify at least two similarities and two differences.

7. **Synthesize Information** Review your answers to the quiz about **slavery** that you took before reading Equiano's narrative. What facts or details in his account most surprised you? Correct your quiz answers to reflect what you learned.

8. **Evaluate a Slave Narrative** Some historians have questioned whether Equiano's narrative is authentic. Read the information on this debate in the author's biography on page 78. Based on the issues raised, what you have learned about slave narratives, and your own reading, make an argument for or against the historical value of Equiano's account. Support your answer with details.

Literary Criticism

9. **Biographical Context** In 1775, just 14 years before writing his life story, Equiano bought slaves to work on his Central American plantation. He explained his actions by saying he did what he could "to comfort the poor creatures, and render their condition easy." Do you find this explanation consistent with the views of slavery put forth in *The Interesting Narrative?* Cite evidence from the text to support your answer.

THE INTERESTING NARRATIVE OF THE LIFE OF OLAUDAH EQUIANO **85**

8. ● **SKILLS FOCUS** Slave Narrative *For: The account tells how slaves were treated and proves that slavery was wrong.* **Against:** *If he did not take the journey, the details may not be correct.*

9. *Yes, when he said this Equiano thought slavery was acceptable, but that slaves must be treated humanely. His narrative is more about the inhuman treatment of slaves than a criticism of slavery itself.*

Practice and Apply

After Reading

Use these copy masters to check understanding and provide extra support:

RESOURCE MANAGER—Copy Masters
Reading Check p. 134
Slave Narrative p. 127
Question Support p. 135

Additional selection questions are provided for teachers on page 121.

ANSWERS

1. *The Africans who captured Equiano brought him to the slave ship.*

2. *He believes he will be killed and eaten by the white men.*

3. *Slave traffickers are Christians in name only, not in their actions.*

Possible answers:

4. ■ **SKILLS FOCUS** **Analyze Details** *the floggings Equiano received (lines 37–39); the conditions below deck (lines 75–90); the slaves committing suicide (lines 99–104); the way the slaves were sold (lines 105–113). These details appeal to readers' senses and enable them to visualize slavery's horrors.*

5. *He has never seen white men and finds them strange and unattractive. Though he was sold by Africans, he still trusts them and is reassured by their presence. He has never seen a ship and knows nothing of life on other continents. He is not used to seeing people treated so cruelly.*

6. *Similarities: Both men encounter cultures that are unfamiliar to them. Both describe how they survive great hardships and show curiosity about their new environment. Differences: Cabeza de Vaca makes his journey as a conqueror and not a captive. He does not suffer the physical cruelty that Equiano suffers.*

7. *Accept all reasonable responses, but students should refer to specific quiz answers and cite specific facts or details from the selection.*

THE INTERESTING NARRATIVE OF THE LIFE OF OLAUDAH EQUIANO **85**

ANSWERS

Vocabulary in Context

VOCABULARY PRACTICE

1. *(a) a sad expression*
2. *(b) a serious accident*
3. *(c) a 20-inch snowfall*
4. *(a) a contagious disease*
5. *(a) an attack of conscience*
6. *(c) a leader with no real power*

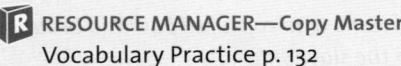 **RESOURCE MANAGER**—Copy Master
Vocabulary Practice p. 132

VOCABULARY IN WRITING

Have students reread lines 105–116 and consider Equiano's observations before they begin writing. Tell students that their chosen words should have negative connotations or emotional connections.

VOCABULARY STRATEGY: THE LATIN ROOT *nom* *(also an EL language objective)*

• For each item, help students use their knowledge of the root and context clues to determine word meaning.

• Have students consider the meanings of the common prefixes *de-* and *mis-* to help them build meanings for *denomination* and *misnomer*.

Possible answers:

1. *nominate*
2. *misnomer*
3. *nomenclature*
4. *denomination*
5. *ignominious*

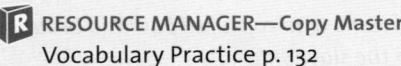 **RESOURCE MANAGER**—Copy Master
Vocabulary Strategy p. 133

ⓘ Vocabulary Center at **ClassZone.com**
Additional Vocabulary Activities

Vocabulary in Context

VOCABULARY PRACTICE

Choose the letter of the phrase that defines or is related to the boldfaced word.

1. **countenance:** (a) a sad expression, (b) a well-toned body, (c) a cash register
2. **consternation:** (a) a freight ship, (b) a serious accident, (c) a peace treaty
3. **copious:** (a) a nest of baby birds, (b) a xerographic machine, (c) a 20-inch snowfall
4. **pestilential**: (a) a contagious disease, (b) a cooking implement, (c) a vegetarian meal
5. **scruple:** (a) an attack of conscience, (b) a two-handed card game, (c) a ruffle on a skirt
6. **nominal:** (a) a stretch limousine, (b) a word derived from a foreign language, (c) a leader with no real power

VOCABULARY IN WRITING

Imagine yourself as an observer at a slave auction in early America. Using three or more vocabulary words, write a brief description of what you might have observed. Here is a sample beginning.

> **EXAMPLE SENTENCE**
>
> On the **countenance** of every prisoner to be sold at the auction was an expression of terror and panic.

R1.2

VOCABULARY STRATEGY: THE LATIN ROOT *nom*

The vocabulary word *nominal* contains the Latin root *nom,* which means "name." This root is found in a number of English words. To understand words with *nom,* use context clues as well as your knowledge of the root.

PRACTICE Choose the word from the word web that best completes each sentence. Consider what you know about the Latin root *nom* and other word parts shown. If necessary, consult a dictionary.

1. The president decided to _____ a young woman to fill the job.
2. It is a real_____ to call this stringy meat "tenderloin."
3. Scientific _____ often makes use of Latin words.
4. The 20-dollar bill is a _____ that is frequently counterfeited.
5. After that _____ defeat, he was ashamed to show his face.

VOCABULARY PRACTICE
For more practice, go to the **Vocabulary Center** at **ClassZone.com.**

DIFFERENTIATED INSTRUCTION

FOR STRATEGIC READERS

Vocabulary Practice Clarify that not all of the choices are definitions of the boldfaced words. Some are examples. For example, *consternation* means "fear," and "a serious accident" could cause fear. *Copious* means "a large amount," and a "twenty-inch snowfall" is an example of a large amount.

FOR ADVANCED LEARNERS/AP

Vocabulary Strategy Have pairs find five more words in the dictionary that use the Latin root *nom.* Ask them to create a word web like the one on page 86 and write five sentences with context clues and a space for each word. Have pairs exchange their sentences and word webs and try to fill in the correct words based on the context clues.

Reading-Writing Connection

 W1.1

SELF-CHECK

A successful letter will . . .

• be written in the first person, using the pronouns *I* or *me*

• address a familiar audience

• include language appropriate to the audience

• conform to standard letter-writing formats

GRAMMAR AND STYLE

 W1.9, LC1.1

ADD DESCRIPTIVE DETAILS Review the **Grammar and Style** note on page 83. Equiano uses elaborate and richly detailed sentences to describe his experiences. Some of the details are contained in **adverb clauses,** as in this example:

> *These filled me with astonishment, which was soon converted into terror,* when *I was carried on board.* (lines 2–4)

In this sentence, the adverb clause modifies *filled,* describing when the action occurred. Adverb clauses also help answer the questions *where, why, how,* or *to what degree.* Like other **subordinate clauses,** adverb clauses include a subject and a predicate, but they cannot stand alone as independent sentences. They are often introduced with words such as *as if, because, since, so that, until, while, when,* or *where.*

PRACTICE Add adverb clauses to the following sentences to modify the boldfaced words, as instructed in parentheses. A sample answer has been done for you.

> **EXAMPLE**
>
> He **saw** the ship for the first time. (Tell when he saw it.)
>
> *He saw the ship for the first time when he arrived at the harbor.*

1. The men on the ship **had been captured.** (Tell why they were captured.)

2. The prisoners **were kept** in the ship's hold. (Tell how long they were kept there.)

3. Many slaves **became** ill. (Add two details. Tell why and when the slaves became ill.)

WRITING TOOLS
For prewriting, revision, and editing tools, visit the **Writing Center** at **ClassZone.com.**

FOR DEVELOPING WRITERS

Task Support: Writing Prompt

• Work with students to complete an Observation Chart. After they describe their experience or scene, help them identify descriptive words to convey it vividly.

• Urge students to identify their audience before they begin to write. This decision can help them choose the correct tone and words for their letters.

• Review the personal letter format, including date, salutation, and closing.

• Be sure that students include at least two paragraphs in their letters. Encourage them to exchange letters and explain how the first-person narration affected the descriptions of an experience or scene.

Reading-Writing Connection

WRITING PROMPT

Remind students that Equiano's excellent use of detailed descriptions allows readers to understand his experience. Encourage students to use an Observation Chart to explore vivid details of the experience or scene they want to convey in their letters.

BEST PRACTICES TOOLKIT—Transparency
Observation Chart p. C7

For writing support, see
Writing Center at **ClassZone.com**

GRAMMAR AND STYLE
Possible answers:

1. The men on the ship had been captured **so that they could be sold as slaves.**

2. The prisoners were kept in the ship's hold **until the ship reached its destination.**

3. **Because conditions on the ship were so poor,** many slaves became ill **as they set sail.**

RESOURCE MANAGER—Copy Master
Add Descriptive Details p. 136

For more on using adverb clauses to add detail, see page R67 of the **Grammar Handbook.**

Assess and Reteach

Assess

RESOURCE MANAGER—Copy Masters
Selection Test A pp. 137–138
Selection Test B/C pp. 139–140

Test Generator CD

Reteach

STANDARDS LESSON FILE
Vocabulary Lesson 7: Latin Roots

Focus and Motivate

OBJECTIVES

Literary Analysis
- explore the key idea of **leadership**
- analyze narrator
- read a historical narrative

Reading
- understand techniques for reading aloud a persuasive speech

Vocabulary
- build vocabulary for reading and writing
- analyze multiple-meaning words (also an EL language objective)

CALIFORNIA R3.3

ABOUT THE AUTHOR

After students have read about John Smith, have them consider whether "boastful bully" or "early American hero" is a more apt description and to keep the question in mind as they read his narrative. Point out that the first Jamestown colonists dreamed of making easy fortunes by finding gold. Many were gentlemen unused to hard labor. Their arrival also coincided with a severe drought. As a result, about half the colonists died that first year.

USING THE *NOTABLE QUOTE*

Ask students what the quote suggests about **John Smith's** ideas on how to build a colony and the underlying conflict between Smith and the other colonists. *Possible answer: Smith considered hard work a requirement for a successful colony. Other colonists may not have shared his work ethic, leading to conflict.*

Selection Resources

CALIFORNIA R3.3

from The General History of Virginia

Historical Narrative by John Smith

NOTABLE QUOTE
"He that will not work, shall not eat."

FYI
Did you know that John Smith . . .
- coined the name "New England"?
- offered to accompany the Pilgrims—who chose Miles Standish instead?
- wrote a how-to manual on establishing colonies?
- left the Jamestown colony after two years and never went back?

Author Online
For more on John Smith, visit the **Literature Center** at **ClassZone.com**.

Replicas of Jamestown ships

John Smith
c. 1580–1631

The author of one of the earliest works of American literature continues to inspire widely varied reactions among historians. Called a boastful bully by some and an early American hero by others, John Smith created a legend around himself that lasts to this day.

Great Adventures At age 16, Smith left England to become a soldier for hire and occasional pirate. In 1605, after traveling to Austria, Turkey, and North Africa, he returned to England. Smith's military experience made him a good leader in the eyes of the Virginia Company, the group of investors hoping for huge profits from their New World venture. They hired him to help run the Jamestown colony, where he arrived in 1607.

Struggles for Control Conflicts broke out in Jamestown almost immediately. The first president died and the next two were deposed; colonists mutinied and deserted the colony, living in the nearby woods. Smith took control of the colony in 1608. As he tells it, he focused on survival—safety, shelter, and food—and led forcefully, pushing settlers of all social levels to work as hard as he did. History tells us a slightly different story: Smith was nearly executed for the deaths of two colonists on an expedition he led. It also tells us, however, that Jamestown thrived under his command and fell into greed, chaos, and starvation after his departure in 1610.

Fact or Fiction? Shortly after arriving in Virginia, John Smith was captured by the Powhatan Indians. Smith writes several times of his 1607 capture and of being brought before the tribe's leader, Powhatan. Only in the final version, the 1624 *General History of Virginia*, does Smith mention his rescue by Powhatan's daughter Pocahontas, who would have been ten years old at the time. The story may have been an attempt by Smith to cash in on Pocahontas's later fame: she had visited England in 1616 and become a celebrity.

In the meantime, Smith had fallen on hard times. After one early success, his attempts to colonize New England were dismal failures. Smith wanted to prove that hard work was the smartest way to develop a colony, but he never got his chance. He made his living from tales of his adventurous life and died unemployed in London in 1631.

88

R RESOURCE MANAGER UNIT 1

Plan and Teach pp. 141–148

Literary Analysis
Summary pp. 149†*, 150‡*
Narrator pp. 151, 152*†
Question Support p. 159*

Reading
Reading Older Texts pp. 153, 154†*
Reading Check p. 158

Vocabulary
Study p. 155*
Practice p. 156
Strategy p. 157

Assessment
Selection Tests A, B/C pp. 161*, 163*
Test Generator CD

BEST PRACTICES TOOLKIT

Differentiated Instruction pp. 31–38*

Scaffolding Instruction pp. 43–46*

Graphic Organizers/Strategies
Word Squares • Analysis Frame: Persuasion

Reading Support
Audio Anthology CD*

Technology
Literature and Vocabulary Centers at **ClassZone.com**
WriteSmart CD

---

* Resources for Differentiation   † Also in Spanish   ‡ In Haitian Creole and Vietnamese

● LITERARY ANALYSIS: NARRATOR

A **narrator** is the voice that tells a story. The voice an author chooses shapes the way readers perceive the events described. Most nonfiction authors write about themselves in the **first person.** John Smith writes about himself mostly in the **third person,** using a voice that sounds like an objective observer.

As you read, notice how Smith uses the narrator to portray himself and his role in events. Consider how the third-person point of view affects your perceptions of the account.

■ READING STRATEGY: READING OLDER TEXTS

Reading centuries-old texts can be like reading a foreign language. Here are some strategies you can use to confront common difficulties in reading older texts:

- Replace unclear pronouns with names.
- Simplify difficult **syntax** (word order) by paraphrasing. For a difficult sentence, first establish who is doing what. Then sort out the meaning in the phrases and clauses.
- Use footnotes or side notes to translate **archaic expressions,** words and phrases no longer in use.
- Focus on key details by setting a purpose for reading.

In this case, your purpose for reading is to make sense of the conflicts among the Jamestown colonists. Use a chart like the one shown to take notes about these key individuals.

Individuals	Connection to Smith	Actions
President Wingfield		
Captain Kendall		
Robinson and Emry		
George Cassen		

▲ VOCABULARY IN CONTEXT

Choose words from the list to complete the phrases below.

WORD LIST	depose	industry	mollify
	entreaty	interim	

1. a corrupt leader whom they voted to _____
2. a peacemaker trying to _____ the unruly crowd
3. a desperate _____ for our assistance
4. admired by co-workers for her _____

What makes a LEADER?

KEY IDEA In some societies, like 17th-century Britain, leaders were chosen on the basis of their social status. But men used to luxury and privilege didn't thrive in the Jamestown colony, where hard work and scarce supplies were facts of daily life. In this context, where leaders needed common sense and determination to succeed, a new standard of **leadership** emerged.

DISCUSS Working with a small group, brainstorm examples of strong leaders who demonstrate different leadership styles. Use your examples to debate the pros and cons of each style. Is any one style best in all situations?

What makes a LEADER?

Lead into the question and **KEY IDEA** by asking students to brainstorm a list of qualities helpful for effective **leadership.** Extend the **DISCUSS** activity by asking them which of the qualities on their list is essential for any leader in any situation.

SKILLS FOCUS

LITERARY ANALYSIS R3.3

● NARRATOR

Read aloud these two statements:

1. Captain Brown employed strict discipline and economy to lead his expedition through the hard winter.

2. I was forced to employ strict discipline and economy to lead this expedition through that hard winter.

Ask students which statement seems more objective and which seems more immediate. How does the narrator's point of view affect students' response? *Possible answer: Statement 1 seems more objective because the narrator speaks in the third person. Statement 2 seems more immediate because the narrator speaks in the first person.*

CHECK UNDERSTANDING Ask students to write a statement by a narrator describing his own experience in Brown's expedition.

READING STRATEGY

■ READING OLDER TEXTS

To orient students to the selection, do a preview together. Point out the footnotes and side notes that translate archaic language and paraphrase difficult syntax, as well as the questions that focus on important aspects of the narrative as an "older text."

📄 RESOURCE MANAGER—Copy Master
Reading Older Texts p. 153 (for student use while reading the selection)

VOCABULARY

▲ VOCABULARY IN CONTEXT

DIAGNOSE WORD KNOWLEDGE To determine preteaching needs, have all students complete Vocabulary in Context. *Answers: 1. depose, 2. mollify, 3. entreaty, 4. industry*

PRETEACH VOCABULARY Preteach vocabulary with this copy master. Read each item aloud.

📄 RESOURCE MANAGER—Copy Master
Vocabulary Study p. 155

MORE VOCABULARY SUPPORT
For additional activities and guidelines, see

💼 BEST PRACTICES TOOLKIT
Scaffolding Vocabulary Instruction
   pp. 43–46
ℹ️ Vocabulary Center at **ClassZone.com**

SUMMARY

This excerpt from John Smith's historical narrative describes Jamestown colony's struggle for survival and Smith's leadership conflicts. During an excursion to find food, Smith is captured by the Powhatan Indians, but Chief Powhatan's daughter Pocahontas saves him from execution. After a ceremony, Powhatan gives Smith control of a village and promises to think of him as a son, in return for cannons and a millstone. After he returns to Jamestown, Smith is accused of causing two men's deaths but ends up punishing his accusers and strengthening his authority.

READING STRATEGY

Ⓐ OLDER TEXTS

Possible answer: Paraphrase: If we'd been as free from every sin as we were from gluttony and drunkenness, we could have been declared saints, but not our president, because he took oatmeal, wine, oil, brandy, eggs—everything but the common food supply—for his own use. Smith's joke is to suggest that the men avoided the sins of gluttony and drunkenness out of virtuous restraint, when in fact they were starving. His joke also points out that the president's greediness is making them suffer.

If students need help . . . Work with them to understand how Smith's joke reveals the colonists' conflict with their president. Then have students complete the first row of the prereading chart introduced on page 89.

Individuals	Connection to Smith	Actions
President Wingfield	first president of colony	took colonists' food and drink

THE GENERAL HISTORY OF VIRGINIA

John Smith

BACKGROUND The Jamestown colony was modeled after a military expedition, transplanting about 100 hardy men into the Virginia wilderness in May 1607. Five members of Jamestown's ruling council—Edward Wingfield, Bartholomew Gosnold, John Ratcliffe, George Kendall, and John Smith—soon found themselves wrestling for control of the colony. As Smith's account opens, the colonists' ships have returned to England for supplies, leaving the men to survive on their own.

ANALYZE VISUALS
Which details of this map do not seem realistic? Explain what helps you distinguish accurate details from fictitious ones.

The Struggle for Jamestown

Being thus left to our fortunes, it fortuned that within ten days, scarce ten amongst us could either go or well stand, such extreme weakness and sickness oppressed us. And thereat none need marvel if they consider the cause and reason which was this: While the ships stayed, our allowance was somewhat bettered by a daily proportion of biscuit which the sailors would pilfer to sell, give, or exchange with us for money, sassafras, furs, or love. But when they departed, there remained neither tavern, beer-house, nor place of relief but the common kettle. Had we been as free from all sins as [we were free from] gluttony and drunkenness we might have been canonized
10 for saints, but our President [Edward Wingfield] would never have been admitted for engrossing to his private, oatmeal, sack, oil, aqua vitae, beef, eggs, or what not but the kettle; that indeed he allowed equally to be distributed, and that was half a pint of wheat and as much barley boiled with water for a man a day, and this, having fried some twenty-six weeks in the ship's hold, contained as many worms as grains so that we might truly call it rather so much bran than corn; our drink was water, our lodgings castles in the air. Ⓐ

❶ Targeted Passage

6 sassafras: A kind of tree believed to have medical properties.

8 common kettle: food that was available to everyone.

11 engrossing to his private: taking for his private use; **sack:** wine; **aqua vitae:** brandy.

Ⓐ OLDER TEXTS
Using the side notes, restate lines 8–12 in modern English. What joke is Smith making?

Arrival of the English in Virginia (1585–1588), Theodore de Bry. Engraving © Giraudon/Art Resource, New York.

DIFFERENTIATED INSTRUCTION

FOR ALL STUDENTS

Expert Groups Encourage students to become subject experts by selecting and researching one of these topics relating to the founding of the Jamestown colony:

- who the Jamestown colonists were and why they founded the colony

- how the site for Jamestown was chosen and the fort constructed

- how Chief Powhatan was a powerful leader in his own right

FOR STRATEGIC READERS

In combination with the *Audio Anthology CD*, use one or more Targeted Passages (pp. 90, 92, 94, 95) to ensure that students focus on key events and concepts. Targeted Passages are also good for English learners.

❶ Targeted Passage [Lines 1–8]

This passage establishes the dire situation faced by the new Jamestown settlers.

Pasquenoke

Dasamonquepeuc

Roanoac

Trinety harbor

AN

ANALYZE VISUALS

Possible answer: The sea monster and the wrecked, partially submerged ships do not seem realistic. These features represent dangers that the artist likely created to add drama to his engraving. The geographical features, by contrast, appear to be based on a cartographer's work and are likely to be more accurate.

About the Art In 1590 the Flemish publisher and engraver Theodore de Bry (1528–1598) illustrated a natural history of Virginia by Thomas Hariot. Hariot was a scientist and a member of Sir Walter Raleigh's expedition to Roanoke, Virginia, in 1585. De Bry illustrated Hariot's book with his own engravings, based on drawings by John White, an artist who had also been on the expedition. *Arrival of the English in Virginia* is an original engraving by de Bry that appears at the beginning of Hariot's book, whose English title is *A Briefe and True Report of the New Found Land of Virginia.*

BACKGROUND

Algonquian Neighbors The Jamestown settlers would never have survived the grim conditions John Smith describes if not for their Native American neighbors. The Powhatan Confederacy, a group of six Algonquian tribes under Powhatan's authority, traded corn and other food to the starving settlers in return for copper and iron implements. Over time, cultural differences led to misunderstanding and conflict. The Algonquian people believed that land could not be bought or sold; it belonged to the entire group. The English, by contrast, recognized individual ownership. This difference, along with the new settlers' belief in the superiority of their culture, led to many clashes.

- What is the condition of the men who stay in Jamestown after the ships return to England?

- How much time has passed since the ships left?

- Why was the men's condition better while the ships were there?

FOR ENGLISH LEARNERS

Key Academic Vocabulary Use Word Squares to teach these words: *proportion* (line 5), *sufficient* (line 20), *authority* (line 49), *conclude* (line 57), *aid* (line 87)

 BEST PRACTICES TOOLKIT—Transparency Word Squares p. E10

Prereading For prereading instruction for English learners, see

 BEST PRACTICES TOOLKIT Scaffolding Reading Instruction pp. 43–46

FOR ADVANCED LEARNERS/AP

AP exercises in the bottom channel provide additional challenge for students. Use these suggestions for small groups or individuals.

ADDITIONAL GUIDELINES

For more help with differentiation and tips for classroom management, see

 BEST PRACTICES TOOLKIT Differentiated Instruction pp. 31–38

B OLDER TEXTS

Possible answer: *The pronoun* his *in line 27 refers to Smith, who is responsible for healing Martin and Ratcliffe.*

If students need help . . . Point out Smith's name at the beginning of the sentence, followed by the pronoun *his.* Have students reread the sentence, substituting *Smith's* for *his.*

LITERARY ANALYSIS

C NARRATOR

Possible answer: *Expressed in the third person, Smith's claims sound like the observations of a neutral third party; as a result, they seem more credible. If he had written the account in the first person, his claims would have appeared boastful.*

If students need help . . . Have them listen as you reread the lines, substituting *me* for *Captain Smith* (line 37), *my* for *his* (lines 37 and 40), *myself* for *himself* (lines 39 and 41), and *I* for *he* (line 40).

Extend the Discussion How reliable is John Smith's account of his own rise to power and use of power? Which details should the reader be skeptical about? Why?

Lines 42–55
REINFORCE *KEY IDEA:* LEADERSHIP

Discuss What do John Smith's actions in this passage reveal about his attitude toward **leadership**? *Possible answer: Smith's efforts to provide food show his belief that a leader must take responsibility for the colony's survival. His own hard work shows his belief that a leader should set a good example. His action against Kendall presents him as a forceful leader who will not tolerate challenges to his authority.*

With this lodging and diet, our extreme toil in bearing and planting palisades so strained and bruised us and our continual labor in the extremity 20 of the heat had so weakened us, as were cause sufficient to have made us as miserable in our native country or any other place in the world.

From May to September, those that escaped lived upon sturgeon and sea crabs. Fifty in this time we buried; the rest seeing the President's projects to escape these miseries in our pinnace by flight (who all this time had neither felt want nor sickness) so moved our dead spirits as we **deposed** him and established Ratcliffe in his place (Gosnold being dead), Kendall deposed. Smith newly recovered, Martin and Ratcliffe were by his care preserved and relieved, and the most of the soldiers recovered with the skillful diligence of Master Thomas Wotton our surgeon general. **B**

30 But now was all our provision spent, the sturgeon gone, all helps abandoned, each hour expecting the fury of the savages, when God, the patron of all good endeavors, in that desperate extremity so changed the hearts of the savages that they brought such plenty of their fruits and provision as no man wanted.

The new President [Ratcliffe] and Martin, being little beloved, of weak judgment in dangers, and less **industry** in peace, committed the managing of all things abroad to Captain Smith, who, by his own example, good words, and fair promises, set some to mow, others to bind thatch, some to build houses, others to thatch them, himself always bearing the greatest task 40 for his own share, so that in short time he provided most of them lodgings, neglecting any for himself. . . . **C**

A Surprise Attack

Smith, perceiving (notwithstanding their late misery) not any regarded but from hand to mouth, (the company being well recovered) caused the pinnace to be provided with things fitting to get provision for the year following, but in the **interim** he made three or four journeys and discovered the people of Chickahominy, yet what he carefully provided the rest carelessly spent.

Wingfield and Kendall, living in disgrace strengthened themselves with the sailors and other confederates to regain their former credit and authority, 50 or at least such means aboard the pinnace (being fitted to sail as Smith had appointed for trade), to alter her course and to go for England.

Smith, unexpectedly returning, had the plot discovered to him, much trouble he had to prevent it, till with the store of saker and musket shot he forced them [to] stay or sink in the river: which action cost the life of Captain Kendall.

These brawls are so disgustful, as some will say they are better forgotten, yet all men of good judgment will conclude it were better their baseness should be manifest to the world, than the business bear the scorn and shame of their excused disorders.

---

19 **palisades:** walls made of tall, pointed wooden stakes.

24 **pinnace:** a small sailing ship.

depose (dĭ-pōz′) *v.* to remove from rule

B OLDER TEXTS
Reread lines 27–28. **Clarify** the pronoun referent for the word *his* in line 27. Who is responsible for healing Martin and Ratcliffe?

industry (ĭn′də-strē) *n.* hard work; diligence

37 **abroad:** outside the palisades.

C NARRATOR
Reread lines 35–41. Do Smith's claims sound more or less credible than they would if stated by a **first-person narrator?** Give reasons for your answer.

interim (ĭn′tər-ĭm) *n.* period in between; interval

46 **Chickahominy** (chĭ′kə-hä′mə-nē): a river in Virginia.

② Targeted Passage

52 **discovered:** revealed.
53 **saker:** cannon shot.

55 **Captain Kendall:** Kendall was executed for mutiny in 1607.

57–59 **it were . . . disorders:** It is better to reveal the troublemakers than to have the "business" of the colony get a bad name.

DIFFERENTIATED INSTRUCTION

FOR STRATEGIC READERS

② Targeted Passage [Lines 42–59]

This passage describes a plot against Smith and Smith's response.

- What is Smith doing while Wingfield and Kendall are plotting against him?
- What does Smith do when he discovers the plot?
- What happens to Kendall?
- According to Smith, why has he revealed this plot?

FOR ENGLISH LEARNERS

Vocabulary: Outdated Forms Point out examples of words that are now outdated or used differently today from the way they were used 400 years ago. Ask students to use a dictionary to find and apply current meanings for these words to the selection context: *fair* (line 38), "hopeful"; *asunder* (line 76), "into pieces"; *dolefulest* (line 119), "most terrible"; *quartered* (line 125), "stayed in"; *betimes* (line 129), "early"; *hath* (line 156), "has."

Illustration of Jamestown Fort, Virginia, about 1608. Getty Images.

60   The President and Captain Archer not long after intended also to have abandoned the country, which project also was curbed and suppressed by Smith.

    The Spaniard never more greedily desired gold than he [Smith] victual, nor his soldiers more to abandon the country than he to keep it. But [he found] plenty of corn in the river of Chickahominy, where hundreds of savages in divers places stood with baskets expecting his coming.

    And now the winter approaching, the rivers became so covered with swans, geese, ducks, and cranes that we daily feasted with good bread, Virginia peas, pumpkins, and putchamins, fish, fowl, and divers sort of wild
70 beasts as fast as we could eat them, so that none of our tuftaffety humorists desired to go for England.

    But our comedies never endured long without a tragedy, some idle exceptions being muttered against Captain Smith for not discovering the head of Chickahominy river and [he being] taxed by the Council to be too slow in so worthy an attempt. The next voyage he proceeded so far that with much labor by cutting of trees asunder he made his passage, but when his barge could pass no farther, he left her in a broad bay of danger of shot, commanding none should go ashore till his return, himself with two English and two savages went up higher in a canoe, but he was not long absent but
80 his men went ashore, whose want of government gave both occasion and opportunity to the savages to surprise one George Cassen whom they slew and much failed not to have cut off the boat and all the rest.

60 Captain Archer: Gabriel Archer had abandoned the colony and then returned. He did not support Smith.

63 victual: food.

69 putchamins: persimmons.
70 tuftaffety humorists: unreliable lace-wearers

73 exceptions: objections.

80–82 whose want . . . the rest: the men's lack of discipline in going ashore led to the surprise attack on Cassen; only by some failure on the attackers' side did the others survive.

ANALYZE VISUALS

Activity Ask students what this illustration of Jamestown Fort around the time of its founding shows about the conditions of the settlement. Does it support the information in John Smith's account? *Possible answer: The illustration shows that the fort was small, isolated, and primitive. It supports John Smith's account of the harsh conditions encountered by the colonists.*

Lines 60–82
TIERED DISCUSSION PROMPTS

Use these prompts to help students understand John Smith's ongoing challenges:

Connect How do you respond when people criticize you or oppose your ideas? *Accept all thoughtful answers.*

Interpret What seems to be John Smith's main problem in getting the settlement to run smoothly? Why are there mutterings against him? *Possible answer: Several members of the colony are vying for more power and trying to remove Smith from office; they hinder his cause through plots to undermine him or failure to obey his orders. Their mutterings are criticisms that grow out of their desire to question Smith's authority and methods (lines 60–62, 72–75).*

Evaluate How believable is Smith's suggestion that he was unfairly blamed for not finding the head of the Chickahominy and was responsible for George Cassen's death? *Some students may say that Smith's explanation is plausible. Others may argue that he showed a lack of leadership and foresight in both cases and is reacting defensively.*

FOR ADVANCED LEARNERS/AP

Analyze the Art of Persuasion [small-group option] Smith presents persuasive arguments to defend his actions and leadership. Ask small groups to identify Smith's specific claims; then have them analyze his supporting evidence. Using the Analysis Frame: Persuasion as their guide, have students consider the logic and clarity of his conclusions. How does Smith deal with opposing arguments? Invite groups to create an analysis chart of Smith's claims.

Claim: *Wingfield was inept and selfish.*
Reason 1: *did not provide for the colony*
Evidence:

Have groups share their findings with the class. Then invite all students to discuss whether Smith was successful in proving his claims.

  BEST PRACTICES TOOLKIT—Transparency
Analysis Frame: Persuasion pp. D21, D44

D NARRATOR

Possible answer: The narrator (Smith) includes these details to exonerate himself: He has no idea that his men were attacked, as he is 20 miles away hunting for food to supply the fort (lines 83–84); Smith himself is attacked by an overwhelming force of 200 Native Americans (line 86); during this heroic struggle, he is wounded and taken prisoner (lines 87–90).

If students need help . . . Clarify lines 84–85: Smith means that he assumes the two men were slain while sleeping by the canoes, not that he ordered them to be slain.

Lines 91–123
TIERED DISCUSSION PROMPTS

Use these prompts to help students understand how John Smith intended the scene at Powhatan's court to affect readers:

Summarize What happens to Smith after he is taken prisoner? *Possible answer: Smith's captors take him to Powhatan, their chief (lines 91–92). They let him wash his hands and eat (lines 101–104). They prepare to execute him, but Powhatan's daughter Pocahontas convinces them to spare Smith's life (lines 105–110). Powhatan later agrees to free Smith, give him control of a village, and esteem him as a son in exchange for two cannons and a grindstone (lines 115–123).*

Analyze How does Smith present himself to the reader in this scene? *Possible answer: Smith presents himself as a strong leader who can calmly survive a harrowing ordeal and still effectively deal with the Powhatans.*

Evaluate Thus far, do you think Smith's account is realistic? Explain. *Students may say that Smith's details and his survival support this account. Others may say that Smith shows himself so positively that the story is suspect.*

Smith little dreaming of that accident, being got to the marshes at the river's head twenty miles in the desert, had his two men [Robinson and Emry] slain (as is supposed) sleeping by the canoe, while himself by fowling sought them victual, who finding he was beset with 200 savages, two of them he slew, still defending himself with the aid of the savage his guide, whom he bound to his arms with his garters and used him as a buckler, yet he was shot in his thigh a little, and had many arrows that stuck in his
90 clothes but no great hurt, till at last they took him prisoner. . . . **D**

At Powhatan's Court

At last they brought him to Werowocomoco, where was Powhatan, their Emperor. Here more than two hundred of those grim courtiers stood wondering at him, as [if] he had been a monster, till Powhatan and his train had put themselves in their greatest braveries. Before a fire upon a seat like a bedstead, he sat covered with a great robe made of raccoon skins and all the tails hanging by. On either hand did sit a young wench of sixteen or eighteen years and along on each side [of] the house, two rows of men and behind them as many women, with all their heads and shoulders painted red, many of their heads bedecked with the white down of birds, but every
100 one with something, and a great chain of white beads around their necks.

At his entrance before the King, all the people gave a great shout. The Queen of Appomattoc was appointed to bring him water to wash his hands, and another brought him a bunch of feathers, instead of a towel, to dry them; having feasted him after their best barbarous manner they could, a long consultation was held, but the conclusion was, two great stones were brought before Powhatan; then as many as could, laid hands on him, dragged him to them, and thereon laid his head and being ready with their clubs to beat out his brains, Pocahontas, the King's dearest daughter, when no **entreaty** could prevail, got his head in her arms and laid her own upon
110 his to save him from death, whereat the Emperor was contended he should live to make him hatchets, and her bells, beads, and copper, for they thought him as well of all occupations as themselves. For the King himself will make his own robes, shoes, bows, arrows, pots; plant, hunt, or do anything so well as the rest.

Two days after, Powhatan, having disguised himself in the most fearfulest manner he could, caused Captain Smith to be brought forth to a great house in the woods and there upon a mat by the fire to be left alone. Not long after, from behind a mat that divided the house, was made the most dolefulest noise he ever heard; then Powhatan more like a devil than a man,
120 with some two hundred more as black as himself, came unto him and told him now that they were friends, and presently he should go to Jamestown to send him two great guns and a grindstone for which he would give him the country of Capahowasic and forever esteem him as his son Nantaquoud.

So to Jamestown with twelve guides Powhatan sent him. That night they quartered in the woods, he still expecting (as he had done all this long time of his imprisonment) every hour to be put to one death or other, for all

84 desert: wilderness; **85–86 by fowling . . . victual:** hunted birds to find them food.

88 garters: shirtlaces; **buckler:** shield.

D NARRATOR
Reread lines 83–90. What details does the narrator include that suggest Smith is not responsible for the deaths of the two men?

94 greatest braveries: fanciest clothes.

102 the Queen of Appomattoc (ăp′ə-mǎt′ək): the leader of the nearby village of Appomattoc.

3 Targeted Passage

entreaty (ĕn-trē′tē) *n.* plea

112 as well . . . themselves: The Indians thought Smith had varied skills as they did.

122–123 the country of Capahowasic (căp′ə-hou′ə-sĭk′) **. . . Nantaquoud** (nŏn′tə-kwōōd′): Powhatan would give Smith control of a nearby village and also promised to think as highly of him as he did of his own son.

DIFFERENTIATED INSTRUCTION

FOR STRATEGIC READERS

3 Targeted Passage [Lines 101–114]

This passage describes John Smith's imprisonment by the Powhatans and rescue by Pocahontas.

- What happens to Smith right after he is brought to see the king?

- Why do the Powhatans bring out two huge rocks?

- Who saves Smith's life? How?

FOR ENGLISH LEARNERS

Vocabulary: Multiple-Meaning Words Remind students that some words have more than one meaning in English. Ask volunteers to suggest different meanings for the word *down*. Then refer them to its use in line 99. Help students use context clues to define *down* as "the soft, fluffy under-feathers of birds." Repeat this procedure with *plenty* (line 150), "abundance or bounty"; and *crossed* (line 154), "obstructed or interfered with."

their feasting. But almighty God (by His divine providence) had **mollified** the hearts of those stern barbarians with compassion. The next morning betimes they came to the fort, where Smith having used the savages with

130 what kindness he could, he showed Rawhunt, Powhatan's trusty servant, two demi-culverins and a millstone to carry [to] Powhatan; they found them somewhat too heavy, but when they did see him discharge them, being loaded with stones, among the boughs of a great tree loaded with icicles, the ice and branches came so tumbling down that the poor savages ran away half dead with fear. But at last we regained some conference with them and gave them such toys and sent to Powhatan, his women, and children such presents as gave them in general full content. **E**

Now in Jamestown they were all combustion, the strongest preparing once more to run away with the pinnace; which, with the hazard of his life,

140 with saker falcon and musket shot, Smith forced now the third time to stay or sink.

Some, no better than they should be, had plotted with the President the next day to have him put to death by the Levitical law, for the lives of Robinson and Emry; pretending the fault was his that had led them to their ends; but he quickly took such order with such lawyers that he laid them by the heels till he sent some of them prisoners for England.

Now every once in four or five days, Pocahontas with her attendants brought him so much provision that saved many of their lives, that else for all this had starved with hunger.

150 His relation of the plenty he had seen, especially at Werowocomoco, and of the state and bounty of Powhatan (which till that time was unknown), so revived their dead spirits (especially the love of Pocahontas) as all men's fear was abandoned.

Thus you may see what difficulties still crossed any good endeavor; and the good success of the business being thus oft brought to the very period of destruction; yet you see by what strange means God hath still delivered it. ✿

mollify (mŏl′ə-fī′) *v.* to soothe; to reduce in intensity

131 demi-culverins (dĕm′ē-kŭl′vər-ĭnz): large cannons.

E OLDER TEXTS
Reread lines 128–137. **Paraphrase** this passage to clarify its meaning. What does Smith do to keep his promise to Powhatan?

143 Levitical law: According to the Book of Leviticus in the Bible, "He that killeth any man shall surely be put to death."

④ **Targeted Passage**

FOR STRATEGIC READERS

④ **Targeted Passage [Lines 138–156]**

This passage concludes the narrative by showing additional challenges Smith faces after his harrowing return to Jamestown.

- What new difficulty does John Smith face upon his return to Jamestown?

- What was the result of the plot against Smith?

- According to Smith, why are the settlers' fears relieved after his return?

FOR ADVANCED LEARNERS/AP

Synthesize The historical essay says that Smith's "accounts were . . . instrumental in attracting settlers to Virginia" (page 30, paragraph 1). Read this text to students. Then point out that Smith employs many literary elements used by fiction writers, such as characterization, plot, suspense, tone, and mood. Have student pairs list qualities of Smith's writing that might have inspired immigration to North America. Then ask them to share their findings with the class.

E OLDER TEXTS

Possible answer: *Paraphrase: The next morning Smith and his 12 Powhatan guides got to the fort, where Smith treated them well and showed Rawhunt, Powhatan's servant, two large cannons and a millstone to take back to his chief. Smith fired the cannons, which had been loaded with stones, into a tree covered with icicles, and the falling ice and branches startled the Indians, making them run away in fear. But they returned, and Smith sent them with enough presents for Powhatan and his women and children to keep them all satisfied. Smith keeps his promise to Powhatan by giving him the cannons and millstone.*

Lines 138–149
REINFORCE *KEY IDEA:* LEADERSHIP

Discuss What **leadership** qualities does Smith project in this passage? ***Possible answer:*** *Smith projects presence of mind, determination, and strength by disproving the charges against him and even imprisoning some of his accusers.*

SELECTION WRAP–UP

SUMMARIZE Have students summarize the difficulties John Smith faced at Jamestown.

⭐ CRITIQUE

- Ask students to evaluate whether John Smith was an effective leader.

- After completing the After Reading questions on page 96, have students revisit their responses and tell whether they have changed their opinions.

Practice and Apply

After Reading

Use these copy masters to check understanding and provide extra support:

R RESOURCE MANAGER—Copy Masters
Reading Check p. 158
Narrator p. 151
Question Support p. 159

Additional selection questions are provided for teachers on page 145.

ANSWERS

1. *The Jamestown colonists have deposed the previous president.*

2. *Kendall tries to steal the colony's ship and sail for England.*

3. *Smith is attacked by Powhatan Indians while exploring the Chickahominy River.*

4. *Smith is sentenced to death but saved by Pocahontas's intervention. A ceremony confirms him as Powhatan's ally.*

Possible answers:

5. *Leaders deserve special treatment; leaders should provide for the future; leaders should stick to their goals even if those they lead want to give up; leaders should possess the skills that others have and participate in all necessary work.*

6. ■ SKILLS FOCUS **Reading Older Texts**
   Smith has a motive to portray Wingfield as corrupt and incompetent because Smith helped depose him (line 25). Smith's actions get Kendall, Cassen, Robinson, and Emry killed, actions that he justifies to clear his name (lines 52–59, 80–85).

7. *Monarchs rule Smith's England and other European countries. He assumes that all cultures are like his own.*

8. **Smith's Version:** *He is not responsible for George Cassen's death because he told his men to stay put. They disobeyed, inviting attack. He is not responsible for Robinson's and Emry's deaths. They were slain because they fell asleep. Smith fought 200 warriors before his capture.* **Accusations Against Him:** *Smith failed to find the head of the river. He is at fault in the deaths of Cassen, Robinson, and Emry because he left them vulnerable.*

9. ● SKILLS FOCUS **Narrator** *The details of Jamestown life and Native American culture are probably credible, as Smith has no motive to lie. Smith's reliability as narrator is suspect when retelling his own actions or conflicts in Jamestown. His statements are self-serving: to show his merits as a leader and assert his innocence in the face of accusations.*

10. *Wingfield's report would highlight his own good efforts and diminish or criticize Smith's. He might offer a different account of the distribution of supplies (lines 11–12), his intention to flee (lines 24, 49–50), and Smith's characterization of mutiny.*

R3.3
CALIFORNIA

Comprehension

1. **Recall** Why does Ratcliffe become the leader of Jamestown?

2. **Recall** What leads to the killing of Captain Kendall?

3. **Clarify** How does Smith become Powhatan's captive?

4. **Summarize** What happens to Smith during his stay with Powhatan?

Literary Analysis

5. **Draw Conclusions About Attitudes** In each example, what conclusions can you draw about each man's idea of **leadership?**
   - Wingfield's distribution of supplies (lines 10–14)
   - Smith's criticism of the colonists (lines 42–47)
   - Smith's determination in dire circumstances (lines 63–64)
   - Powhatan's assumption about Smith's abilities (lines 111–114)

6. **Interpret Older Texts** Review the character chart you made. Consider Smith's connection to each character. What motives might have influenced Smith's portrayal of his fellow colonists? Cite details to support your answer.

7. **Make Inferences About Historical Context** Reread lines 91–102. Notice that Smith uses the terms *Emperor, King, Queen,* and *courtiers* to describe Native American tribal structures. What does this tell you about the time and place in which he lived?

8. **Examine a Historical Narrative** Smith's account of his explorations along the Chickahominy River is filled with details that suggest he is a hero. But if you read closely, he reveals that he was severely criticized for the way he performed. Reread lines 72–90, and record the conflicting information in a chart like the one shown. What accusations is Smith defending himself against?

Smith's Version	Accusations Against Him

9. **Evaluate Narrator** Consider Smith's use of **third-person point of view** as well as the **motives** that influenced his writing. Given these factors, is Smith a credible narrator? Evaluate the reliability of Smith's narrative as a source on the following topics. Give reasons for your answers.
   - daily life in Jamestown
   - Native American culture
   - Smith's own actions
   - conflicts in Jamestown

Literary Criticism

10. **Different Perspectives** If Wingfield had written a report, how might it have differed from Smith's description of these events? Cite details to support your answer.

Vocabulary in Context

VOCABULARY PRACTICE

Decide whether the words in each pair are synonyms or antonyms.

1. depose/appoint
2. interim/gap
3. mollify/anger
4. industry/diligence
5. entreaty/plea

WORD LIST
depose
entreaty
industry
interim
mollify

VOCABULARY IN WRITING

Write a brief explanation of the animosity and hard feelings that sprang up among members of Smith's expedition. Use two or more vocabulary words in your explanation. You might begin like this.

> **EXAMPLE SENTENCE**
> Within Smith's expedition it was not uncommon to **depose** a leader or blame others for one's problems.

VOCABULARY STRATEGY: MULTIPLE MEANINGS

Many words have more than one meaning. To make sense of what you read, you need to make sure you understand which meaning a writer intends. This is particularly true with words that are used as more than one part of speech, or with words that occur in older texts. For example, the noun *industry* usually refers to a specific branch of manufacture or trade. Smith uses it to mean "dedication to a task."

PRACTICE Determine the meaning of each boldfaced word as it is used in the sentence. Refer to a dictionary if you need to.

1. Was John Smith a **contemporary** of Olaudah Equiano?
2. The **gravity** of the situation required the presence of several police officers.
3. What **accommodations** have the two leaders managed to reach?
4. The governor intends to **commute** several prisoners' sentences.
5. At this point we cannot **countenance** any more delays.
6. The hotel employees **agitated** for better working conditions.

VOCABULARY PRACTICE
For more practice, go to the **Vocabulary Center** at **ClassZone.com**.

DIFFERENTIATED INSTRUCTION

FOR ENGLISH LEARNERS

Task Support: Vocabulary Practice Remind students that synonyms are words that have the same or almost the same meanings. Antonyms are words that have opposite meanings. Refer students back to the prereading vocabulary activity on page 89. Have them try to put both words in each pair into the context sentence. Explain that if both words in a pair fit the context, they are synonyms. If only one fits, the words are antonyms.

FOR ADVANCED LEARNERS/AP

Vocabulary in Writing Have students write a news account that might have appeared in an English newspaper circa 1608 about Jamestown, using the words on the word list.

ANSWERS

Vocabulary in Context

VOCABULARY PRACTICE

1. *antonyms*
2. *synonyms*
3. *antonyms*
4. *synonyms*
5. *synonyms*

R RESOURCE MANAGER—Copy Master
Vocabulary Practice p. 156

VOCABULARY IN WRITING

Suggest that students consider which words lend themselves best to the topic. They might also begin by using the words in general statements about Smith and then adjusting them to fit the topic.

VOCABULARY STRATEGY: MULTIPLE MEANINGS *(also an EL language objective)*

Point out to students that with multiple-meaning words, they have to use their judgment to determine which meaning is correct. Suggest that students follow these steps:

- Substitute the meaning you think fits.
- Ask whether that meaning makes sense.
- If not, try substituting another meaning.
- Continue until a meaning makes sense.

Possible answers:

1. *person who lived at the same time*
2. *seriousness*
3. *reconciliation of differences; settlement*
4. *change to something less severe*
5. *approve of; tolerate*
6. *attempted to arouse public feeling*

R RESOURCE MANAGER—Copy Master
Vocabulary Strategy p. 157

i Vocabulary Center at **ClassZone.com**
Additional Vocabulary Activities

Assess and Reteach

Assess

R RESOURCE MANAGER—Copy Masters
Selection Tests A, B/C pp. 161–162, 163–164
O Test Generator CD

Reteach

S STANDARDS LESSON FILE
Literature Lesson 45
Vocabulary Lesson 19

Focus and Motivate

OBJECTIVES

Literary Analysis
- explore the key idea of **hardship**
- analyze cultural characteristics
- read a chronicle

Reading
- summarize

Vocabulary
- build vocabulary for reading and writing
- use dictionary etymology to understand words with French language origins *(also an EL language objective)*

 R2.5, R1.1

ABOUT THE AUTHOR

Before students read about William Bradford, tell them that his religious devotion deeply inspired his actions and writing. During reading, help them connect this devotion and the traits Bradford showed as a young man—determination, idealism, independence, and zeal—with his ability to lead in adulthood. As students read the author biography, point out how Bradford's faith and resolve contributed to the survival of Plymouth colony.

USING THE *NOTABLE QUOTE*

Invite volunteers to speculate on what the quote reveals about **William Bradford's** character and beliefs. *Students should appreciate Bradford's supreme optimism and self-confidence, and link it to his religious faith.*

R2.5, R1.1 (p. 108) CALIFORNIA

from Of Plymouth Plantation
Chronicle by William Bradford

William Bradford
c. 1590–1657

NOTABLE QUOTE
"The difficulties were many, but not invincible."

FYI
Did you know that William Bradford . . .
- lost his first wife to drowning shortly after the *Mayflower* landed?
- sold one of his farms to help pay Plymouth Colony's debts?
- was elected governor of Plymouth 30 times?

Author Online
For more on William Bradford, visit the **Literature Center** at ClassZone.com.

Plymouth Plantation today

Long before there were holiday legends of Pilgrims and Indians, a group of English Puritans set off to create a new, pure society in the North American wilderness. Their leader was William Bradford.

Early Rebel Born into a time of religious upheaval in England, Bradford joined the crusade for religious reform at age 12. He was inspired by the ideals of the Puritans, a Protestant religious group that wanted to purify the Church of England and create simpler, more democratic ways to worship. By 17, Bradford had joined the radical Puritans known as Separatists, who called for a total break with the official church.

Not surprisingly, the Separatists clashed with the king of England, who also headed the church. Emigration to North America offered the hope of freedom, and Bradford helped plan and finance the voyage across the Atlantic. In 1620, Bradford and his wife, Dorothy, left behind their four-year-old son to join nearly 40 other Separatists on the ship *Mayflower*. Facing the journey with typical resolve, Bradford described the group as "pilgrims," or religious wanderers, the name we use for them today.

A Natural Leader Although the Pilgrims initiated the voyage, they made up fewer than half of the ship's 102 passengers. During the long, difficult journey, disagreements broke out among the group, and Bradford took decisive action. He helped craft the Mayflower Compact, often called the first U.S. Constitution. Signed by the 41 men on board, the compact was an agreement to work together for the good of the entire group. And they kept their promise. In April 1621, when the *Mayflower* returned to England, not one colonist left Plymouth Colony—a tribute to Bradford's sound leadership.

Bradford was also effective in forging alliances with local Native American tribes such as the Wampanoag (wäm′pə-nō′ăg), a union of tribes led by Massasoit (măs′ə-soit′). The Wampanoag, who had lost 80 percent of their people to smallpox shortly before the Pilgrims' arrival, faced their own struggle to survive. Out of mutual need, Bradford and Massasoit created a strong alliance that lasted throughout their lifetimes.

Historian in the Making With a historian's instinct, Bradford saved many documents from the trip's planning phase. During his 30 years as governor, he continued to document the challenges of the growing colony, which owed its survival to his energy, vision, and expert diplomacy. His chronicle, *Of Plymouth Plantation,* is our best history of these adventurous times.

98

Selection Resources

---

* Resources for Differentiation   † Also in Spanish   ‡ In Haitian Creole and Vietnamese

LITERARY ANALYSIS: CULTURAL CHARACTERISTICS

Many texts, especially those about community life, reflect the **cultural characteristics** of the communities they describe, such as their shared beliefs, values, and goals. *Of Plymouth Plantation* is a record of the Pilgrims' efforts to create a model Puritan society. In it, William Bradford describes the outcome of an Indian attack.

Thus it pleased God to vanquish their enemies and give them deliverance; and by His special providence so to dispose that not any one of them were either hurt or hit....

Bradford's description makes it clear that the Pilgrims see the victory as a gift from God. As you read, consider what else Bradford's descriptions and sometimes subtle word choice reveal about Puritan ideals.

READING STRATEGY: SUMMARIZE

When you **summarize**, you restate the **main ideas** and the most important **details** of what you read. This process will help you sift through Bradford's long, complex sentences for key information.

This excerpt from *Of Plymouth Plantation* has five sections. As you read each section, record

- the date or time of year events occur
- a one- or two-sentence summary of the section

> **Section:** *Their Safe Arrival at Cape Cod*
> **Time of Year:**
> **Summary:**

▲ VOCABULARY IN CONTEXT

The following boldfaced words help tell the story of the founding of Plymouth Colony. Use context clues to guess the meaning of each word, then write a brief definition.

1. found **solace** in the peaceful woodland setting
2. her survival was an act of **providence**
3. will **tender** her resignation in a letter
4. chose a **rendezvous** convenient for everyone
5. tried to **procure** enough food for the family
6. an illness **feigned** in order to avoid work

When does HARDSHIP *unite us?*

KEY IDEA Hard times can bring people together or tear them apart. For example, in a blackout after a serious storm, people could respond by sharing supplies or by stealing what they need from unprotected homes. When does facing **hardship** become a source of strength and unity rather than one of distrust and division?

DISCUSS Working with a small group, list events you know from history or from the news that imposed great hardships on a community. Compare situations that had a unifying effect with those that divided the community. Identify factors that may account for the different responses.

99

When does HARDSHIP *unite us?*

Read the question and **KEY IDEA** with students. Using the blackout example, help students consider when facing **hardship** creates unity and when it creates division. Have students incorporate their responses to complete the *DISCUSS* activity.

SKILLS FOCUS

> **LITERARY ANALYSIS** R2.5
>
> ● **CULTURAL CHARACTERISTICS**
>
> Share this example of a diary entry:
>
> Dear Diary, For dinner at Jenny's house, I had veggie burgers, tofu salad, and a fruit cup. Jenny told me she's never eaten a hamburger! When I got home, I was so hungry that I made myself a baloney sandwich. Your friend, Elisa
>
> Ask students what Elisa's diary entry shows about Jenny's family's values. ***Possible answer:*** *Jenny's family members are vegetarians. For health or religious reasons, they do not believe in eating meat.*
>
> **CHECK UNDERSTANDING** Have students contrast Elisa's and Jenny's values.

> **READING STRATEGY**
>
> ■ **SUMMARIZE**
>
> Ask students to summarize **Early Rebel** on page 98. ***Possible answer:*** *As a youth with strong convictions, Bradford joined the Puritan Separatists, who broke with the Church of England. In 1620, he and his wife sailed with the Pilgrims for North America on the Mayflower, in search of religious freedom.*
>
> **CHECK UNDERSTANDING** Call on volunteers to summarize **A Natural Leader** and **Historian in the Making.**
>
> 📕 RESOURCE MANAGER—Copy Master
>   Summarize p. 177 (for student use while reading the selection)

VOCABULARY

▲ VOCABULARY IN CONTEXT

DIAGNOSE WORD KNOWLEDGE To determine preteaching needs, have all students complete Vocabulary in Context. ***Possible answers:*** **1.** *comfort;* **2.** *divine care;* **3.** *offer;* **4.** *meeting place;* **5.** *get, obtain;* **6.** *pretended*

PRETEACH VOCABULARY Preteach vocabulary with this copy master. Read each item aloud.

📕 RESOURCE MANAGER—Copy Master
Vocabulary Study p. 179

MORE VOCABULARY SUPPORT
For additional activities and guidelines, see

💼 BEST PRACTICES TOOLKIT
Scaffolding Vocabulary Instruction pp. 43–46
ℹ️ Vocabulary Center at **ClassZone.com**

SUMMARY

This excerpt from William Bradford's chronicle opens with the Pilgrims' winter arrival in the Cape Cod wilderness. A search party explores the land and survives a surprise Indian attack. Conditions are dire, and many in the group starve or fall ill. Finally, the local Indians help them find food and ways to survive. They meet Squanto and his chief Massasoit, with whom they make a friendly pact and share a feast of thanksgiving.

LITERARY ANALYSIS

Ⓐ CULTURAL CHARACTERISTICS

Possible answer: *It reveals that the Pilgrims credited God for saving them and for watching over and protecting them.*

If students need help . . . Direct their attention to the phrases "fell upon their knees" (lines 4–5) and "blessed the God of Heaven" (line 5). Make sure they understand that the Pilgrims gave their thanks for bringing them across the Atlantic Ocean, saving them from danger, and setting them on firm ground.

Lines 5–13
REINFORCE *KEY IDEA:* HARDSHIP

Discuss What **hardships** do the Pilgrims face on their voyage across the ocean? What new dangers confront them when they first arrive on Cape Cod? *Possible answer: Bradford mentions the "vast and furious ocean" (lines 5–6), referring to the dangers of a voyage across the Atlantic: storms, gales, waves, hunger, and cold weather. The Pilgrims arrive in poor condition with no shelter or friends who could help them adjust (lines 12–13).*

Of Plymouth Plantation

William Bradford

> **BACKGROUND** By the time the Pilgrims landed at Cape Cod, the local Native American tribes had had 100 years of contact and conflict with European explorers. Squanto, who became the Pilgrims' interpreter, had learned English when he was kidnapped by an English expedition in 1605. The Nauset Indians, who attacked the Pilgrims shortly after their arrival, had survived years of skirmishes with English explorers, including a 1609 battle with John Smith of Jamestown fame. Keep these events in mind as you read Bradford's account.

Their Safe Arrival at Cape Cod

But to omit other things (that I may be brief) after long beating at sea they[1] fell with that land which is called Cape Cod; the which being made and certainly known to be it, they were not a little joyful. . . .

Being thus arrived in a good harbor, and brought safe to land, they fell upon their knees and blessed the God of Heaven who had brought them over the vast and furious ocean, and delivered them from all the perils and miseries thereof, again to set their feet on the firm and stable earth, their proper element. . . . Ⓐ

But here I cannot but stay and make a pause, and stand half amazed at this poor people's present condition; and so I think will the reader, too, when he
10 well considers the same. Being thus passed the vast ocean, and a sea of troubles before in their preparation (as may be remembered by that which went before), they had now no friends to welcome them nor inns to entertain or refresh their weatherbeaten bodies; no houses or much less towns to repair to, to seek for

---

1. **they:** Bradford refers to the Pilgrims in the third person, even though he is one of them.

100 UNIT 1: EARLY AMERICAN WRITING

ANALYZE VISUALS
Describe the landscape that awaits the travellers. What emotional response might they have had to this sight?

Ⓐ **CULTURAL CHARACTERISTICS**
Reread lines 4–7. What does this paragraph reveal about the way Puritans viewed God?

The Landing of the Pilgrims (1803–1806), Michael Felice Corne. Tempera on canvas. Pilgrim Hall Museum. Plymouth, Massachusetts.

DIFFERENTIATED INSTRUCTION

FOR ALL STUDENTS

Provide these independent projects to extend the lesson:

- Research and present findings about daily life in Europe in the 1600s.
- Write a character sketch of William Bradford.

For further details on these projects, see

R RESOURCE MANAGER
Ideas for Extension pp. 170–171

FOR STRATEGIC READERS

In combination with the *Audio Anthology CD*, use one or more Targeted Passages (pp. 102, 104, 105, 106) to ensure that students focus on key events and concepts. Targeted Passages are also good for English learners.

Possible answer: *The landscape in this painting is cold, bare, and foreboding. The Pilgrims' response to such a setting would have been fearful and uncertain, because of known and unknown dangers. However, they would have also been grateful to have arrived and optimistic because of their faith.*

About the Art Michael Felice Corne (1752–1815) painted this scene nearly 200 years after the Pilgrims' landing. It was based on a 1799 engraving by Samuel Hall. Corne had not read William Bradford's account of the landing, so he did not know that the Pilgrims met no Native Americans for the first four months after their arrival.

BACKGROUND

Mayflower Compact Before William Bradford and his charges ever set foot in North America, they faced challenges that threatened the success of their venture. Their ship had arrived in territory that was outside the authority of the colonial charter granted to them in England. In addition, some non-Pilgrims questioned the Pilgrim leader's command. The Mayflower Compact created a civil government and pledged loyalty to the British king. Laws approved by the majority were binding on Pilgrims and non-Pilgrims alike. The document became a landmark of American democratic government.

FOR ENGLISH LEARNERS

Key Academic Vocabulary Use New Word Analysis to teach these words: *brief* (line 1), *civil* (line 29), *principal* (line 57), *couple* (line 67), *Encounter* (line 99).

 BEST PRACTICES TOOLKIT—Transparency
New Word Analysis p. E8

Prereading For prereading instruction for English learners, see

 BEST PRACTICES TOOLKIT
Scaffolding Reading Instruction pp. 43–46

FOR ADVANCED LEARNERS/AP

AP exercises in the bottom channel provide additional challenge for students. Use these suggestions for small groups or individuals.

ADDITIONAL GUIDELINES

For more help with differentiation and tips for classroom management, see

 BEST PRACTICES TOOLKIT
Differentiated Instruction pp. 31–38

succor.[2] It is recorded in Scripture as a mercy to the Apostle and his shipwrecked company, that the barbarians showed them no small kindness in refreshing them,[3] but these savage barbarians, when they met with them (as after will appear) were readier to fill their sides full of arrows than otherwise. And for the season it was winter, and they that know the winters of that country know them to be sharp and violent, and subject to cruel and fierce storms, dangerous to travel to known
20 places, much more to search an unknown coast. Besides, what could they see but a hideous and desolate wilderness, full of wild beasts and wild men—and what multitudes there might be of them they knew not. Neither could they, as it were, go up to the top of Pisgah[4] to view from this wilderness a more goodly country to feed their hopes; for which way soever they turned their eyes (save upward to the heavens) they could have little **solace** or content in respect of any outward objects. For summer being done, all things stand upon them with a weatherbeaten face, and the whole country, full of woods and thickets, represented a wild and savage hue. If they looked behind them, there was the mighty ocean which they had passed and was now as a main bar and gulf to separate them from all the civil
30 parts of the world. . . . **B**

Targeted Passage

solace (sŏl′ĭs) *n.* comfort in sorrow or distress

B SUMMARIZE
Reread lines 16–30. What challenges confronted the colonists when they arrived at Cape Cod?

---

2. **to seek for succor:** to look for help or relief.

3. **It is . . . refreshing them:** a reference to the Biblical account of the courteous reception given to Paul ("the Apostle") and his companions by the inhabitants of Malta (Acts 27:41–28:2).

4. **Pisgah:** the mountain from whose peak Moses saw the Promised Land (Deuteronomy 34:1–4).

The First Winter of the Pilgrims in Massachusetts, 1620 (1800s). Colored engraving. The Granger Collection, New York.

B SUMMARIZE

Possible answer: The colonists faced fierce weather, unsettled wilderness without comforts, and the expectation of hostile inhabitants.

If students need help . . . Direct them to lines 17–18 to identify the season. Help them list nouns and descriptive words that portray the colonists' surroundings. Then work with them to complete the first section of the chart from page 99.

Section: Their Safe Arrival
Time of Year: Winter
Summary: The Pilgrims reached land and thanked God. They faced fierce weather, wilderness, no comforts, and the expectation of hostile inhabitants.

ANALYZE VISUALS

Activity Ask students what the colored engraving shows about the Pilgrims' first winter. Does it accurately reflect William Bradford's account? *Possible answer: The engraving shows primitive and desperate conditions confronting the Pilgrims: freezing cold, minimal shelter, and a lack of all comforts. It accurately reflects William Bradford's account (lines 17–28).*

DIFFERENTIATED INSTRUCTION

FOR STRATEGIC READERS

① Targeted Passage [Lines 16–22]

This passage establishes the setting and the challenges the Pilgrims confront.

- What kind of weather do the Pilgrims face in the new land?

- How do the Pilgrims expect the Native Americans to respond to them?

- How does the land appear?

FOR ADVANCED LEARNERS/AP

Research Relations with Native Americans

The Pilgrims' relations with Native Americans were both hostile and friendly. To provide background, have students research the importance of

- the Nauset and Wampanoag tribes
- Native American allies Samoset, Squanto, Hobbamock, and Massasoit
- the Pilgrim leader Miles Standish

Encourage small groups to present oral reports of their findings.

The First Encounter

Being thus arrived at Cape Cod the 11th of November, and necessity calling them to look out a place for habitation (as well as the master's and mariners' importunity); they having brought a large shallop[5] with them out of England, stowed in quarters in the ship, they now got her out and set their carpenters to work to trim her up; but being much bruised and shattered in the ship with foul weather, they saw she would be long in mending. Whereupon a few of them **tendered** themselves to go by land and discover those nearest places, whilst the shallop was in mending; . . .

40 After this, the shallop being got ready, they set out again for the better discovery of this place, and the master of the ship desired to go himself. So there went some thirty men but found it to be no harbor for ships but only for boats. There was also found two of their [the Indians'] houses covered with mats, and sundry of their implements in them, but the people were run away and could not be seen. Also there was found more of their corn and of their beans of various colors; the corn and beans they [the English] brought away, purposing to give them [the Indians] full satisfaction when they should meet with any of them as, about some six months afterward they did, to their good content.[6]

And here is to be noted a special **providence** of God, and a great mercy to this poor people, that here they got seed to plant them corn the next year, or else they

50 might have starved, for they had none nor any likelihood to get any till the season had been past, as the sequel did manifest.[7] Neither is it likely they had had this, if the first voyage had not been made, for the ground was now all covered with snow and hard frozen; but the Lord is never wanting unto His in their greatest needs; let His holy name have all the praise. **C**

The month of November being spent in these affairs, and much foul weather falling in, the 6th of December they sent out their shallop again with ten of their principal men and some seamen, upon further discovery, intending to circulate that deep bay of Cape Cod. The weather was very cold and it froze so hard as the spray of the sea lighting on their coats, they were as if they had been

60 glazed. . . . [The next night they landed and] made them a barricado[8] as usually they did every night, with logs, stakes, and thick pine boughs, the height of a man, leaving it open to leeward,[9] partly to shelter them from the cold and wind (making their fire in the middle and lying round about it) and partly to defend them from any sudden assaults of the savages, if they should surround them; so being very weary, they betook them to rest. But about midnight they heard a hideous and great cry, and their sentinel called "Arm! arm!" So they bestirred them and stood to their arms and shot off a couple of muskets, and then the noise

---

tender (těn'dər) *v.* to offer formally

providence (prŏv'ĭ-dəns) *n.* an instance of divine care

C CULTURAL CHARACTERISTICS
Reread lines 48–54. What belief helps Bradford justify taking the corn?

---

5. **shallop** (shăl'əp): an open boat usually used in shallow waters.
6. **purposing . . . content:** intending to repay the Nauset Indians for the corn and beans they took, as they in fact did, to the Indians' satisfaction, six months later.
7. **as the sequel did manifest:** as the events that followed proved to be the case.
8. **barricado** (băr'ĭ-kä'dō): a barrier for defense.
9. **to leeward:** on the side sheltered from the wind.

TIERED DISCUSSION PROMPTS

Use these prompts to help students understand the colonists' first contact with Native American culture on Cape Cod Bay:

Connect When have you met new people you knew nothing about? How were they like, or not like, what you expected? *Accept all thoughtful responses.*

Interpret What do the Pilgrims learn from the Indians' abandoned homes? How does this information differ from their fears and expectations? *Possible answer: The Pilgrims learn that Native Americans are civilized and possess the tools for survival in New England (lines 41–45). They had expected and feared savage and barbarian cultures (lines 15–16).*

Synthesize What does this encounter suggest about the Pilgrims' intentions toward the Native Americans? *Possible answer: It suggests that their intentions are honest and that they hope to deal peacefully with the Native Americans (lines 45–47).*

LITERARY ANALYSIS

C CULTURAL CHARACTERISTICS

Possible answer: Bradford's justification for taking the corn was his belief that God sent the corn to them, answering their needs.

If students need help . . . Paraphrase the paragraph with them, breaking the two sentences into phrases and making sure that they understand the meaning of each phrase.

FOR ENGLISH LEARNERS

Vocabulary: Outdated Forms Help students use context to define these outdated forms: *they knew not* (line 22), "they did not know"; *more goodly* (line 23), "more promising or hopeful"; *which way soever* (line 24), "where ever"; *save* (line 24), "except"; *hue* (line 28), "appearance"; *Being thus arrived* (line 31), "Having arrived"; *whilst* (line 37), "while"; *being got ready* (line 39), "made ready for use"; *sundry* (line 42), "an assortment"; *purposing* (line 45), "planning, expecting"; *betook* (line 65), "decided to"; *Arm! arm!* (line 66), "Get your guns"; *bestirred* (line 66), "woke up"; *stood to their arms* (line 67), "stood with their guns ready."

TIERED DISCUSSION PROMPTS

Use these prompts to help students understand the Pilgrims' first direct encounter with Native Americans:

Summarize How do the Indians approach the Pilgrims? How do the Pilgrims respond? *Possible answer: The Indians attack and the Pilgrims fight back. The Indians retreat.*

Analyze The Pilgrims' expectations about Indian behavior were probably typical of the historical period. How would 17th-century European readers likely have responded to this passage? *Possible answer: European readers probably would have been fascinated and terrified by the attack and impressed with the outcome.*

Evaluate Why do you think that Bradford wanted to create this effect? How effective is Bradford in reaching his goal? *Possible answer: He probably wanted his European readers to recognize how dangerous the Pilgrims' situation was, so that they might better appreciate God's "special providence so to dispose that not any one of them were either hurt or hit" (lines 94–95). His description is highly effective, including vivid action and sensory details, as in lines 80–81.*

Lines 100–114

REINFORCE *KEY IDEA:* HARDSHIP

Discuss How did the Pilgrims react to **hardship** during the Starving Time? What was the effect of their response? *Possible answer: They responded to adversity by pulling together, risking their lives for one another, and maintaining their optimism. Despite their efforts, only half of their group survived the winter.*

---

ceased. They concluded it was a company of wolves or such like wild beasts, for one of the seamen told them he had often heard such a noise in Newfoundland.

70 So they rested till about five of the clock in the morning; for the tide, and their purpose to go from thence, made them be stirring betimes. So after prayer they prepared for breakfast, and it being day dawning it was thought best to be carrying things down to the boat. But some said it was not best to carry the arms down, others said they would be the readier, for they had lapped them up in their coats from the dew; but some three or four would not carry theirs till they went themselves. Yet as it fell out, the water being not high enough, they laid them down on the bank side and came up to breakfast.

But presently, all on the sudden, they heard a great and strange cry, which they knew to be the same voices they heard in the night, though they varied 80 their notes; and one of their company being abroad came running in and cried, "Men, Indians! Indians!" And withal, their arrows came flying amongst them. Their men ran with all speed to recover their arms, as by the good providence of God they did. In the meantime, of those that were there ready, two muskets were discharged at them, and two more stood ready in the entrance of their **rendezvous** but were commanded not to shoot till they could take full aim at them. And the other two charged again with all speed, for there were only four had arms there, and defended the barricado, which was first assaulted. The cry of the Indians was dreadful, especially when they [the Indians] saw their men [the English] run out of the rendezvous toward the shallop to recover their arms, the Indians wheeling 90 about upon them. But some running out with coats of mail on, and cutlasses in their hands, they [the English] soon got their arms and let fly amongst them [the Indians] and quickly stopped their violence. . . .

Thus it pleased God to vanquish their enemies and give them deliverance; and by His special providence so to dispose that not any one of them were either hurt or hit, though their arrows came close by them and on every side [of] them; and sundry of their coats, which hung up in the barricado, were shot through and through. Afterwards they gave God solemn thanks and praise for their deliverance, and gathered up a bundle of their arrows and sent them into England afterward by the master of the ship, and called that place the First Encounter. . . .

② Targeted Passage

rendezvous (rän′dā-vōō) *n.* a gathering place

The Starving Time

100 But that which was most sad and lamentable was, that in two or three months' time half of their company died, especially in January and February, being the depth of winter, and wanting houses and other comforts; being infected with the scurvy[10] and other diseases which this long voyage and their inaccommodate condition had brought upon them. So as there died some times two or three of a day in the foresaid time, that of 100 and odd persons, scarce fifty remained. And of these, in the time of most distress, there was but six or seven sound persons who to their great commendations, be it spoken, spared no pains night nor day, but with abundance of toil and hazard of their own health fetched them wood, made them fires, dressed them meat, made their beds, washed their loathsome clothes,

---

10. **scurvy** (skûr′vē): a disease caused by lack of vitamin C.

DIFFERENTIATED INSTRUCTION

FOR STRATEGIC READERS

② Targeted Passage [Lines 78–95]

This passage describes the Pilgrims' violent first meeting with Native Americans.

- What happens after the Pilgrims hear the strange cry?
- What do the Pilgrims do to protect themselves?
- What weapons do the Indians have?
- How many Pilgrims are hurt?

FOR ADVANCED LEARNERS/AP

Analyze the Effect of Disease Have students research smallpox and scurvy, focusing on the physical effects and impact on the settlers and Native Americans in the time of early European settlement in the Americas. Have students write a one-page essay exploring how disease played a role in European settlement of the Americas and domination over Native Americans. Ask students to share their essays with the class.

The First Thanksgiving (1914), Jennie Augusta Brownscombe. © Burstein Collection/Corbis.

110 clothed and unclothed them. . . . In a word, did all the homely and necessary offices for them which dainty and queasy stomachs cannot endure to hear named; and all this willingly and cheerfully, without any grudging in the least, showing herein their true love unto their friends and brethren; a rare example and worthy to be remembered. Two of these seven were Mr. William Brewster, their reverend Elder, and Myles Standish, their Captain and military commander, unto whom myself and many others were much beholden in our low and sick condition. And yet the Lord so upheld these persons as in this general calamity they were not at all infected either with sickness or lameness. . . . **D**

Indian Relations

All this while the Indians came skulking about them, and would sometimes show
120 themselves aloof off, but when any approached near them, they would run away; and once they [the Indians] stole away their [the colonists'] tools where they had been at work and were gone to dinner. But about the 16th of March, a certain Indian came boldly amongst them and spoke to them in broken English, which they could well understand but marveled at it. At length they understood by discourse with him, that he was not of these parts, but belonged to the eastern parts where some English ships came to fish, with whom he was acquainted and could name sundry of them by their names, amongst whom he had got his language. He became profitable to them in acquainting them with many things concerning the state of the country in the east parts where he lived, which was
130 afterwards profitable unto them; as also of the people here, of their names, number and strength, of their situation and distance from this place, and who was chief amongst them. His name was Samoset. He told them also of another Indian whose name was Squanto, a native of this place, who had been in England and could speak better English than himself.

ANALYZE VISUALS
Contrast the scenery in this image with the landscape on page 102. How has the view of nature changed?

D CULTURAL CHARACTERISTICS
Reread lines 106–114. What values are demonstrated by the seven colonists' responses to their ailing companions?

3 Targeted Passage

ANALYZE VISUALS

Possible answer: The scenery is congenial rather than foreboding; fertile rather than bare; warm and comfortable rather than cold and miserable. Nature in this scene welcomes and nourishes the Pilgrims—as if it is a facet of divine protection.

About the Art This painting by the American artist Jennie Augusta Brownscombe presents an idyllic view of the Pilgrims' first Thanksgiving. A descendent of a *Mayflower* passenger, Brownscombe created many nostalgic scenes of colonial history, which earned her quick success during her lifetime.

LITERARY ANALYSIS

D CULTURAL CHARACTERISTICS

Possible answer: The colonists' responses to the Starving Time reflect their dedication to the welfare of the group, sacrifice, and willingness to face hardships.

If students need help . . . Help them complete a concept web of actions taken by individuals on behalf of the group.

Extend the Discussion How does Bradford explain the Pilgrims' survival during the Starving Time?

FOR STRATEGIC READERS

3 Targeted Passage [Lines 119–134]

This passage describes the Pilgrims' evolving relationship with the local Native Americans.

- What are the Pilgrims' relations with the Indians after their illness?
- Who comes to speak with the Pilgrims?
- What does he do for the Pilgrims?
- Who does he tell them about?

FOR ENGLISH LEARNERS

Comprehension: Self-Monitor As students read lines 114–118, have them use context to define difficult words or phrases and restate inverted text in subject-verb sequence. Urge students to check their comprehension by paraphrasing. *Possible answer: William Brewster (an Elder) and Myles Standish (their captain) were two of the seven men who helped the sick. We owe them a lot for their help when we were sick. The Lord protected these men, so they didn't become sick or crippled.*

E SUMMARIZE

Possible answer: The Pilgrims met a Native American named Samoset who spoke English and aided them (lines 122–132); he arranged a meeting between the Pilgrims and Chief Massasoit (lines 135–139).

If students need help... Remind them that a good summary should explain only the main ideas and important details of a passage. Review that the main idea will be supported by all of the details in the passage or paragraph.

Extend the Discussion How did the treaty with Massasoit contribute to the colony's survival?

SELECTION WRAP–UP

SUMMARIZE Have students sum up the events and actions that contributed to the eventual success of Plymouth Plantation.

★ CRITIQUE

- Ask students to evaluate William Bradford's leadership of the Puritan settlement on a scale of 1 to 10. Have them support their evaluations.

- After completing the After Reading questions on page 107, have students revisit their responses and tell whether they have changed their opinions.

Being, after some time of entertainment and gifts dismissed, a while after he came again, and five more with him, and they brought again all the tools that were stolen away before, and made way for the coming of their great Sachem,[11] called Massasoit. Who, about four or five days after, came with the chief of his friends and other attendance, with the aforesaid Squanto. With whom, after friendly
140 entertainment and some gifts given him, they made a peace with him (which hath now continued this 24 years) in these terms: **E**

1. That neither he nor any of his should injure or do hurt to any of their people.
2. That if any of his did hurt to any of theirs, he should send the offender, that they might punish him.
3. That if anything were taken away from any of theirs, he should cause it to be restored; and they should do the like to his.
4. If any did unjustly war against him, they would aid him; if any did war against them, he should aid them.
150 5. He should send to his neighbors confederates to certify them of this, that they might not wrong them, but might be likewise comprised in the conditions of peace.[12]
6. That when their men came to them, they should leave their bows and arrows behind them.

After these things he returned to his place called Sowams,[13] some 40 miles from this place, but Squanto continued with them and was their interpreter and was a special instrument sent of God for their good beyond their expectation. He directed them how to set their corn, where to take fish, and to **procure** other commodities, and was also their pilot to bring them to unknown places for their
160 profit, and never left them till he died.

First Thanksgiving

They began now to gather in the small harvest they had, and to fit up their houses and dwellings against winter, being all well recovered in health and strength and had all things in good plenty. For as some were thus employed in affairs abroad, others were exercised in fishing, about cod and bass and other fish, of which they took good store, of which every family had their portion. All the summer there was no want; and now began to come in store of fowl, as winter approached, of which this place did abound when they came first (but afterward decreased by degrees). And besides waterfowl there was great store of wild turkeys, of which they took many, besides venison, etc. Besides they had about a peck a meal a week
170 to a person, or now since harvest, Indian corn to that proportion. Which made many afterwards write so largely of their plenty here to their friends in England, which were not **feigned** but true reports. ℘

E SUMMARIZE
Reread lines 122–141. What events led to the treaty with Massasoit?

procure (prō-kyŏŏr') *v.* to get by special effort; to obtain

④ Targeted Passage

feigned (fānd) *adj.* not real; pretended **feign** *v.*

---

11. **Sachem** (sā'chəm): chief.
12. **He should send ... peace:** Massasoit was to send representatives to other tribes to let them know about the treaty with the Pilgrims.
13. **Sowams** (sō'əmz): near the site of present-day Barrington, Rhode Island.

DIFFERENTIATED INSTRUCTION

FOR STRATEGIC READERS

④ Targeted Passage [Lines 155–172]

This passage illustrates the productive relationship between the Pilgrims and Squanto and the successful outcome of the Pilgrims' first year on Cape Cod.

- How does Squanto help the Pilgrims?
- How does the summer go for the Pilgrims?
- What resources do they find?
- How do the Pilgrims describe their condition?

FOR ADVANCED LEARNERS/AP

Evaluate Ask students to review the research they completed for the activity **Research Relations with Native Americans** on page 102. Then ask them to write one or two paragraphs evaluating Bradford's presentation of the role of Native Americans in the survival of Plymouth colony. What key details did he include? distort? omit? Ask students to read their papers to the class.

Comprehension

1. **Recall** What happens to the colonists during "the starving time"?

2. **Recall** Who is Squanto?

3. **Clarify** In what ways did the Wampanoag help the colonists survive?

Literary Analysis

4. **Make Inferences About Cultural Characteristics** Bradford's **word choice** and his choice of details provide subtle clues to Puritan beliefs. Reread Bradford's account of the arrival at Cape Cod (lines 4–30). What does his description reveal about Puritan attitudes toward nature? Use a chart like the one shown to gather evidence and make inferences.

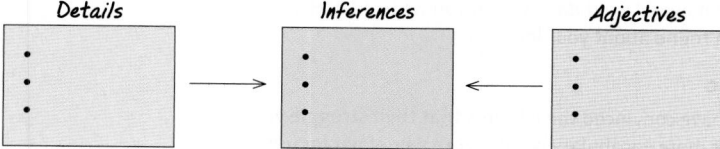

5. **Analyze Outcomes** Using the **summary** chart you created as you read, review the events of the first year at Plymouth. How did events change the colonists'

   - prospects for survival?
   - impressions of Native Americans?
   - attitude toward the region?
   - sense of providence?

6. **Analyze Form** A **chronicle** is a chronological, objective account of historical events. What features of Bradford's narrative might have changed had he written a personal account of his experiences?

7. **Make Judgments** Review the terms of the treaty between the Plymouth colonists and the Wampanoag (lines 142–154). Notice which terms apply to both parties equally and which do not. In your opinion, is the treaty fair? Explain your answer.

8. **Evaluate Motivations** Which of the following most contributed to the colonists' willingness to face **hardships** together? Support your answer with details from Bradford's account and from the historical background provided.

   - Puritan values
   - landscape and climate
   - fears of Indian attack
   - the events of "the starving time"

Literary Criticism

9. **Different Perspectives** How might a Wampanoag historian's version of events differ from Bradford's? Choose an episode from *Of Plymouth Plantation* and cite specific details that might change to reflect this different perspective.

---

7. *Some students may say it is not fair because the terms aren't mutual (lines 142–145, 153–154). Others may argue that it is fair, because the weaker Pilgrims required greater protections.*

8. *Students should support a chosen factor with historical background and appropriate details from the text. These should not contradict the chronicle's facts.*

9. *Students should identify a specific part of the narrative and cite appropriate details.*

Practice and Apply

After Reading
Use these copy masters to check understanding and provide extra support:

R RESOURCE MANAGER—Copy Masters
Reading Check p. 182
Cultural Characteristics p. 175
Question Support p. 183

Additional selection questions are provided for teachers on page 169.

ANSWERS

1. *Half of the group dies from disease, malnutrition, and lack of shelter.*

2. *Squanto is a Native American who was captured and taken to England, and so has learned to speak English. He becomes the Pilgrims' interpreter (lines 133–134, 155–157).*

3. *The Wampanoag teach the Pilgrims how to plant corn, where to fish and find resources, and how to get around the area. Their peace treaty secures the Pilgrims from Native American attack (lines 158–160).*

Possible answers:

4. ● **SKILLS FOCUS Cultural Characteristics**
Details: calls land a hideous wilderness: no friends, no inns, no houses, no towns, wild beasts and men, terrible weather
Adjectives: vast and furious (sea), sharp and violent (winter); cruel and fierce storms, wild and savage (beasts and men)
Inferences: Nature is dangerous, people need towns, the Pilgrims face terrible weather and huge odds.

5. ■ **SKILLS FOCUS Summarize** *Prospects: After suffering malnutrition, cold, and disease, the colony thrives and prepares for winter. Region: With Squanto's help, they learn to use the land for sustenance and profit. Native Americans: After initial fear and worry, they develop ties and view them as divine instruments. Providence: Through the worst times, they find signs of divine favor in survival and success.*

6. *He might have talked more about personal feelings and reactions, used the first-person point of view, and provided only details he witnessed.*

Vocabulary in Context

VOCABULARY PRACTICE

1. *go to a store*
2. *bogus*
3. *no*
4. *an unexpected victory*
5. *someone whose grandmother has just died*
6. *write a letter to the election board*

 RESOURCE MANAGER—Copy Master
Vocabulary Practice p. 180

VOCABULARY IN WRITING

Suggest that students use the example sentence as a topic sentence. They can then write two or more supporting sentences using the vocabulary words to give examples of positive events.

VOCABULARY STRATEGY: WORDS FROM FRENCH *(also an EL language objective)*

Emphasize that knowledge of a word's French etymology is a useful tool for remembering its English meaning. Students should note changes from the original to current English meaning.

Possible answers: 1. *to let do/letting people do as they wish;* **2.** *face to face/in relation to;* **3.** *outside the work/appetizer;* **4.** *nobility obliges/rank creates duty to those with less;* **5.** *false step/social blunder;* **6.** *stroke of mercy/finishing stroke or decisive event;* **7.** *spirit of group/group spirit;* **8.** *know how to do/ability to do the right thing*

 RESOURCE MANAGER—Copy Master
Vocabulary Strategy p. 181

ℹ️ **Vocabulary Center at ClassZone.com**
Additional Vocabulary Activities

Assess and Reteach

Assess

 RESOURCE MANAGER—Copy Masters
Selection Test A pp. 185–186
Selection Test B/C pp. 187–188

💿 **Test Generator CD**

Reteach

⑤ **STANDARDS LESSON FILE**
Study Skills Lesson 13: Summarizing
Reading Lesson 4: Recognizing Main Idea and Details
Vocabulary Lesson 25: Etymologies

Vocabulary in Context

VOCABULARY PRACTICE

Show you understand the vocabulary words by answering these questions.

1. If you wanted to **procure** something, would you go to a store or go swimming?
2. If someone's sorrow is **feigned,** is it genuine or bogus?
3. Is a **rendezvous** a good place to be alone?
4. What would be a sign of **providence**—an unexpected victory or a deadly accident?
5. Who would be in more need of **solace**—a person who has just won a race or someone whose grandmother has just died?
6. To **tender** yourself as a mayoral candidate, would you write a letter to the election board or tell a friend about your idea?

WORD LIST
feigned
procure
providence
rendezvous
solace
tender

VOCABULARY IN WRITING

What experiences might have convinced the Pilgrims that their struggle was worthwhile? Using two or more vocabulary words, write a brief paragraph identifying a few positive things that happened. Here is a sample beginning.

> **EXAMPLE SENTENCE**
> *Despite many hardships, several events did provide* **solace** *for the Pilgrims.*

VOCABULARY STRATEGY: WORDS FROM FRENCH

Rendezvous is one of a number of words in English that comes directly from French. The meaning of some French words and terms may change slightly in English; *rendezvous*, for example, means "present yourself" in French. Other terms keep the same meaning. If you are not sure of the meaning of a French term when you hear or read it, it is a good idea to check a dictionary.

PRACTICE Create a three-column chart with these headings: *Term, Original Meaning,* and *Meaning in English.* Then, using a dictionary that contains etymologies, fill in the chart for each of the following terms.

1. laissez faire
2. vis-à-vis
3. hors d'oeuvre
4. noblesse oblige
5. faux pas
6. coup de grâce
7. esprit de corps
8. savoir-faire

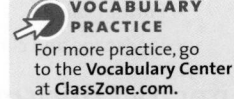 R1.1
CALIFORNIA

🔊 **VOCABULARY PRACTICE**
For more practice, go to the **Vocabulary Center** at **ClassZone.com**.

DIFFERENTIATED INSTRUCTION

FOR ENGLISH LEARNERS

Task Support: Vocabulary Strategy Ask Spanish speakers to share words or phrases that are similar to the French terms that have entered English. Then have all English learners use the French terms in a sentence or describe an example of the term.

FOR ADVANCED LEARNERS/AP

Words from French Encourage students to find and define other words that have entered English from French. Students should add to the chart additional examples such as *au contraire, bonjour, cause célèbre, crêpe, fait accompli,* and *entourage.* Have students learn the correct pronunciations, then share the words and their definitions with the class.

Personal Accounts of Exploration and Settlement

The selections in this section not only provide information about life in early America but are also sources of insight into the personal challenges and moral conflicts that shaped so much of our colonial culture. Because they are all firsthand accounts, the reader's understanding of the events, places, and people described is colored by the very personal feelings of each writer. Their fears, opinions, and doubts help bring this long-past world to life, as shown here.

> *"In that hour, I would have welcomed death rather than see so many around me in such a condition."*
> —**Álvar Núñez Cabeza de Vaca**

> *"I was soon put down under the decks, and there I received a salutation in my nostrils as I had never experienced in my life; so that, with the loathsomeness of the stench, and crying together, I became so sick and low that I was not able to eat.*
> —**Olaudah Equiano**

> *"That night they quartered in the woods, he still expecting (as he had done all this long time of his imprisonment) every hour to be put to one death or other, for all their feasting."*
> —**Captain John Smith**

> *"Besides, what could they see but a hideous and desolate wilderness, full of wild beasts and wild men—and what multitudes there might be of them they knew not."*
> —**William Bradford**

Pocahontas rescues John Smith.

Extension

SPEAKING & LISTENING In a group of four students **debate** the following statement:

The narrators of the selections in this section are unreliable because of their personal and emotional involvement in the events and experiences they relate.

CALIFORNIA   W2.2

Writing to Evaluate

Review the selections beginning on page 68 and choose the one that gives you the most complete picture of an event, experience, or person. In a brief essay, describe the elements that help bring that selection to life.

Consider

• which selection had the greatest impact on you

• descriptive details, images, and dialogue that enhance meaning and aid visualization

• what the writer's personal feelings and opinions add to your understanding and interest in the work

FOR DEVELOPING WRITERS

Writing Support Offer students this thesis sentence frame to begin their essays:

The firsthand account that gave me the most complete picture of _____ was "_____."

Then have students list two reasons. Tell them to develop one paragraph for each reason, using details, images, and dialogue from their chosen selection.

FOR ENGLISH LEARNERS

Writing Support Review these terms from the writing assignment:

• *descriptive details,* "details that tell how a thing looks, sounds, tastes, feels, or smells"

• *images,* "mental pictures created for readers, usually with descriptive details"

• *dialogue,* "the exact words of a character"

• *visualization,* "the process of picturing a description or text in your mind"

Wrap-Up: *Exploration and the Early Settlers*

This Wrap-Up provides students with an opportunity to consider the unique views of early American life offered in the personal accounts of participants in that life. Urge students to keep in mind the prejudices and purposes of these first American writers.

Writing to Evaluate

Review with students that *evaluating* involves forming opinions and judgments based on evidence, information, and personal insight. These critical tools allow students to make meaningful assessments of a work's value, interest, and reliability, as well as to place its historical information in the context of the writer's personal feelings and opinions.

Suggest that after students answer the first bulleted question, they freewrite some reasons *why* one account particularly affected them. Then they can turn to the text to find details, images, and dialogue to support their reasons.

Extension

• List the writers and selections on the board. Discuss each one, asking students whether the writer was believable or not.

• Ask students to brainstorm reasons that support or contradict the debate statement, then list these reasons in a T Chart.

• Suggest that students recall each writer's audience and purpose as they prepare to debate the statement.

• After groups complete their debate, invite them to share the results with the class.

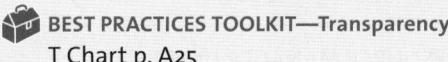 **BEST PRACTICES TOOLKIT—Transparency** T Chart p. A25

Focus and Motivate

OBJECTIVES

Literary Analysis
- explore the key idea of what we **value**
- analyze figurative language
- read poetry

Reading
- clarify meaning in older poetry

 R3.4

ABOUT THE POETS

Anne Bradstreet After students have read about Bradstreet, explain that the title of her book is an allusion to the nine Muses (goddesses of the arts and sciences) in Greek mythology. Bradstreet later became famous for personal meditations such as the two poems that students are about to read.

Edward Taylor After students have read about Taylor, tell them that the discovery of his manuscripts is considered one of the most important "finds" in American literary history. Ask students to consider why Taylor, like Bradstreet, did not attempt to publish his poetry.

USING THE *NOTABLE QUOTES*

Ask students what **Bradstreet** sees as the difference between "authority" and "wisdom." *Possible answer: Authority is merely power; wisdom is what gives power its ability to do good.* Then ask students what **Taylor** implies about his beliefs. *Possible answer: His day-to-day emotions fall short of his intellectual beliefs.*

Selection Resources

Anne Bradstreet
1612–1672

NOTABLE QUOTE
"Authority without wisdom is like a heavy axe without an edge, fitter to bruise than polish."

To My Dear and Loving Husband *and* Upon the Burning of Our House, July 10th, 1666
Poetry by Anne Bradstreet

Anne Bradstreet was essentially the first notable American poet, man or woman. Considering that Puritan women were not encouraged to improve their minds—let alone express their ideas—this achievement is remarkable.

Coming to America Anne Dudley Bradstreet was born in England and raised on an estate, which her father managed for the Earl of Lincoln. With access to the earl's library, she received a good education. In 1628, 16-year-old Anne married Simon Bradstreet. Two years later, the young couple sailed for Massachusetts.

After her privileged upbringing, Anne Bradstreet was not prepared for the harsh living conditions of colonial America. Her religious faith helped her endure these hardships—as did writing poetry.

Personal Poetry Bradstreet focused primarily on the realities of her life—her husband, her eight children, and her house. In 1650, without her knowledge, Bradstreet's brother-in-law had some of her verses published in London in a volume titled *The Tenth Muse Lately Sprung Up in America*. It was the first book of poetry ever published by an American colonist.

Edward Taylor
1642?–1729

NOTABLE QUOTE
"Oh! That I ever felt what I profess. / 'Twould make me then the happi'st man alive."

Huswifery
Poetry by Edward Taylor

For over 200 years, the work of Edward Taylor, one of colonial America's most inventive poets, remained unread. His poetry did not come to light until the 1930s when his long-forgotten manuscripts were discovered in the Yale University Library.

Frontier Parson and Poet Born in England, Taylor came to America in 1668 to escape religious persecution in his homeland. In 1671, after graduating from Harvard University, Taylor became the minister of a church in Westfield, Massachusetts. He held that position until his death 58 years later.

The wilderness town of Westfield presented many challenges to the highly

intellectual Taylor. But he undertook his roles as farmer, physician, and minister with energy. He even called his flock to worship by beating a drum.

Like Anne Bradstreet—a volume of whose work he owned—Taylor wrote his poetry to glorify God. He found his subjects in human life, nature, and everyday activities. His poems on these topics served as a form of worship.

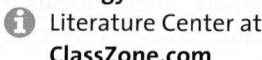

Author On|ine

For more on Anne Bradstreet and Edward Taylor, visit the **Literature Center** at **ClassZone.com**.

110

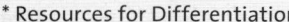 **RESOURCE MANAGER UNIT 1**

Plan and Teach pp. 189–196

Literary Analysis
Figurative Language pp. 197, 198†*
Question Support p. 201*

Reading
Clarify Meaning in Older Poetry
  pp. 199, 200†*

Assessment
Selection Tests A, B/C
  pp. 203*, 205*
 Test Generator CD

BEST PRACTICES TOOLKIT

Differentiated Instruction
  pp. 31–38*

Graphic Organizers/Strategies
Two-Column Chart

Reading Support
 Audio Anthology CD*

Technology
 Literature Center at
  ClassZone.com
 Write*Smart* CD

* Resources for Differentiation   † Also in Spanish

LITERARY ANALYSIS: FIGURATIVE LANGUAGE

Like all poets, Puritan poets used **figurative language** to communicate ideas beyond the literal meaning of words. Figurative language helped the Puritan poets convey ideas about their religious faith and their personal lives. As you read, look for the following types of figurative language, also called **figures of speech,** in the poems by Anne Bradstreet and Edward Taylor:

- A **metaphor** is a figure of speech that directly compares two unlike things without using *like* or *as*. (*Our house is our nest.*)

- An **extended metaphor** is one that draws the comparison out and compares the two things at length and in many ways. (*Our house is our nest; we fly away only to return to its snug protection.*)

- **Personification** is a figure of speech in which an object, animal, or idea is given human characteristics. (*Our house wraps our family in a warm embrace.*)

- **Hyperbole** is a figure of speech in which the truth is exaggerated for emphasis. (*Our house means more to us than all the money in the world.*)

READING STRATEGY: CLARIFY MEANING IN OLDER POETRY

When reading works from the Puritan era, it is important to stop and **clarify meaning** by rereading and restating difficult passages as needed in order to fully appreciate the literature. Be aware of the following as you read the Puritan poets:

- **Archaic language**—words that were once in common use but that are now considered old-fashioned or out-of-date

- **Inverted syntax**—sentence structure in which the expected order of words is reversed

As you read each poem, use a chart like the one shown to record and restate examples of archaic language and inverted syntax.

"Upon the Burning of Our House"	
Archaic Language	Inverted Syntax
"blest" (blessed)	"when rest I took" (when I took rest)

What do you VALUE *most?*

KEY IDEA The things that we **value** in life may be actual objects or they may be less tangible. For instance, a person might prize a favorite CD or jacket. On the other hand, the gift of family may outweigh more material possessions. The Puritan poets you are about to read valued family life and their religious faith above all things. What do you prize most in your life?

QUICKWRITE Imagine that a reality show has offered you the chance to win a million dollars. The catch is that you will have to give up an object, a person, or a belief that you truly value. Assume that you are not willing to make the sacrifice. Write a brief letter to explain why you must turn down the money.

111

What do you VALUE *most?*

Read the question aloud, and then discuss the **KEY IDEA** as a class. Ask students to brainstorm a list of things, people, or ideas that they **value** greatly and then to choose one as the subject of their *QUICKWRITE.*

SKILLS FOCUS

LITERARY ANALYSIS R3.4

● FIGURATIVE LANGUAGE

Write these lines on the board:

> Our burning house was a ghost,
> Moaning in mournful despair;
> Its memories gasping for breath,
> Its bones turned to smoky air.

Have students identify the figurative language in the stanza. ***Possible answer:*** *"Our burning house was a ghost" is a metaphor, and the whole stanza is an extended metaphor. "Moaning" and "Its memories gasping for breath" are examples of personification.*

CHECK UNDERSTANDING Have students present original examples of two of the figures of speech discussed on this page.

READING STRATEGY

■ CLARIFY MEANING IN OLDER POETRY

Write these examples of inverted syntax on the board, and ask students to rewrite them using normal English word order:

- From the flames ran I away. *(I ran away from the flames.)*

- My words on deaf ears fall. *(My words fall on deaf ears.)*

Explain that in past centuries, poets often inverted normal English word order to conform to a meter or rhyme scheme. However, people usually did not use inverted syntax in everyday speech.

R **RESOURCE MANAGER**—Copy Master
Clarify Meaning in Older Poetry p. 199 (for student use while reading the selections)

DIFFERENTIATED INSTRUCTION

FOR STRATEGIC READERS

Concept Support: Archaic Language To prepare students for some of the most common archaic language that they will encounter in the poems, write these two groups of words on the board: (1) *hast, hath, art, shalt, doth, didst* and (2) *thou, thee, thy, thine, ye.* Explain that the first group consists of older forms of the verbs *have, has, are, shall, does,* and *did.* Then explain that the second group contains older pronouns in place of which we now use *you* (*thou* and *thee*), *your* (*thy*) and *yours*

(*thine*). *Ye* was originally a plural form of *you,* and was also used when addressing someone of superior rank.

SUMMARY

The speaker in this poem describes her love for her husband and the value that she places upon his love for her. She concludes by saying that they will be rewarded in heaven for their love.

LITERARY ANALYSIS

Ⓐ FIGURATIVE LANGUAGE

Possible answer: Bradstreet uses hyperbole to emphasize how she values her husband's love, which is more precious to her than "whole mines of gold" and "all the riches" of the East, and that her own love is so strong that "rivers cannot quench" it.

READING STRATEGY

Ⓑ CLARIFY MEANING

Possible answer: Restatement: Then while we live, let's persevere in love so well that when we have died, we may live forever. These lines suggest a connection between earthly love and eternal life. By loving greatly in life, the speaker and her husband will be rewarded with everlasting life in heaven.

If students need help . . . Work with them to paraphrase these lines by restating the archaic language and untangling the inversions. Make sure students understand that "when we live no more" can be reworded as "when we aren't living anymore" and that "we may live ever" can be reworded as "we will be able to live forever."

To My Dear and Loving Husband

Anne Bradstreet

If ever two were one, then surely we.
If ever man were loved by wife, then thee;
If ever wife was happy in a man,
Compare with me, ye women, if you can.
5 I prize thy love more than whole mines of gold
Or all the riches that the East doth hold.
My love is such that rivers cannot quench, Ⓐ
Nor ought but love from thee, give recompense.[1]
Thy love is such I can no way repay,
10 The heavens reward thee manifold, I pray.
Then while we live, in love let's so persevere[2]
That when we live no more, we may live ever. Ⓑ

Ⓐ **FIGURATIVE LANGUAGE**
Reread lines 5–7. How does the poet use **hyperbole** in these lines to emphasize her feelings for her husband?

Ⓑ **CLARIFY MEANING**
Use conventional word order to restate the **inverted syntax** in lines 11–12. What relationship do the lines suggest between earthly love and eternal life?

ANALYZE VISUALS
Many Puritan women stitched samplers like the one shown here. The samplers often depicted nature scenes or stories from the Bible. What values are suggested by the subject matter of the sampler?

---

1. **recompense** (rĕk′əm-pĕns′): payment in return for something, such as a service.

2. **persevere**: In Bradstreet's time, *persevere* would have been pronounced pûr-sĕv′ər, which rhymes with *ever*.

DIFFERENTIATED INSTRUCTION

For general guidelines on differentiating instruction, see

 BEST PRACTICES TOOLKIT
Differentiated Instruction pp. 31–38

FOR STRATEGIC READERS
Options for Reading: Audio Recording

- Have students listen to the poems on the *Audio Anthology CD* (also recommended for English learners) while they read along in their texts. Ask students to notice the emotional tone of each speaker.

- For "Upon the Burning of Our House," ask students to notice the shift that occurs in line 37, when the speaker begins to address herself directly.

ANALYZE VISUALS

Possible answer: The man and woman shown working together suggest the value of family life and the virtue of honest labor. The tree and bird convey the value of appreciating nature and its bounty. The apple tree may allude to the biblical account of Adam and Eve in the Garden of Eden and thus may suggest the value of religious faith.

About the Art The sampler is a pillow cover made of silk and wool. The lettering reveals that it was stitched by Abigail Gould in 1796, when she was 12 years old. Like Bradstreet, Gould probably never intended her simple work to be put on display—as it is today at Boston's Museum of Fine Arts.

BACKGROUND

Puritan Belief Calvinist in their theology, Puritans believed in the absolute sovereignty of God—the idea that God is in complete control of events and ultimately works all things out for a believer's good. Anne Bradstreet reveals that belief by interpreting her personal subject matter through a religious lens. In her poems, every event, no matter how trivial, carries a divine message; each blessing or loss reveals God's will and an opportunity for spiritual growth. Bradstreet's poetry helps us understand the Puritan belief that individual events are part of God's master plan.

FOR STRATEGIC READERS

Clarify Meaning

- Explain the meaning of these archaic words from the poem: *ought* (line 8), "anything"; *manifold* (line 10), "in many ways."

- Point out that many of Bradstreet's constructions omit words that are understood. For example, in line 1 the word *are* is left out at the end: "If ever two were one, then surely we [are]." Similarly, in line 2, the words *I love* are omitted: "If ever man were loved by wife, then [I love] thee." Work with students to add omitted words to lines 4 and 7. **Possible answers:** *Compare yourselves with me, ye women, if you can (line 4); My love is such that rivers cannot quench it (line 7).*

FOR ADVANCED LEARNERS/AP

Research Archaic Pronouns and Verbs Explain that English once had two types of second-person pronouns: the familiar singular forms *thou, thee, thy,* and *thine* plus the polite or plural forms *you/ye* and *yours.* The familiar forms were used to address friends, family members (as in Bradstreet), or God (as in Taylor). Have student pairs do research to see how the forms of *you* have changed over time. Suggest that students create a chart to summarize their research.

SUMMARY

After her beloved home is destroyed in a fire, the poem's speaker grieves over her devastating loss but recognizes that true wealth, and her true home, are in heaven.

READING STRATEGY

C CLARIFY MEANING

Possible answer: *Paraphrase: In the silence of night, I was sleeping and did not expect something bad to happen. I awoke to a loud noise and a voice pitifully shrieking "Fire!" I pray that no person ever hears such a frightening sound. Bradstreet conveys her fear by contrasting the silence and peace of sleep with the terror of waking to cries of "Fire!"*

Lines 13–20
REINFORCE *KEY IDEA:* VALUE

Discuss According to the speaker, why shouldn't she place too high a **value** on personal property? *Possible answer: She should not place too high a value on personal property because it is not really hers; it belongs to God (line 17).*

Upon the Burning of Our House,
July 10th, 1666

Anne Bradstreet

In silent night when rest I took
For sorrow near I did not look
I wakened was with thund'ring noise
And piteous shrieks of dreadful voice.
5 That fearful sound of "Fire!" and "Fire!"
Let no man know is my desire. **C**

I, starting up, the light did spy,
And to my God my heart did cry
To strengthen me in my distress
10 And not to leave me succorless.[1]
Then, coming out, beheld a space
The flame consume my dwelling place.

And when I could no longer look,
I blest His name that gave and took,[2]
15 That laid my goods now in the dust:
Yea, so it was, and so 'twas just.
It was His own, it was not mine,
Far be it that I should repine;[3]

---

1. **succorless** (sŭk′ər-lĭs): without help or relief.
2. **I . . . took:** an allusion to Job 1:21 in the Bible—"The Lord gave, and the Lord hath taken away; blessed be the name of the Lord."
3. **repine:** to complain or fret; to long for something.

C CLARIFY MEANING
Paraphrase lines 1–6 to clarify their meaning. How does the poet use contrast to convey a sense of fear?

DIFFERENTIATED INSTRUCTION

FOR STRATEGIC READERS

Clarify Meaning Work with students to add items to the chart introduced on page 111. Have them use a dictionary to clarify the meaning of archaic words. Suggest that students substitute the modern meanings of any archaic words that appear in the examples of inverted syntax.

"Upon the Burning of Our House"	
Archaic Language	Inverted Syntax
line 16: "Yea" (Yes); "twas" (it was)	line 2: "For sorrow near I did not look" (I did not look near for sorrow)
line 19: "bereft" (deprived)	line 7: "I, starting up, the light did spy" (Starting up, I did spy [spied] the light)

line 39: "mold'ring" (decaying)	line 21: "When by the ruins oft I past" (When often I passed by the ruins)

He might of all justly bereft,
20 But yet sufficient for us left.
When by the ruins oft I past,
My sorrowing eyes aside did cast,
And here and there the places spy
Where oft I sat and long did lie:

25 Here stood that trunk and there that chest,
There lay that store I counted best.
My pleasant things in ashes lie,
And them behold no more shall I.
Under thy roof no guest shall sit,
30 Nor at thy table eat a bit.

No pleasant tale shall e'er be told,
Nor things recounted done of old.
No candle e'er shall shine in thee,
Nor bridegroom's voice e'er heard shall be.
35 In silence ever shalt thou lie;
Adieu, Adieu, all's vanity.[4] **D**

Then straight I 'gin my heart to chide,[5]
And did thy wealth on earth abide?
Didst fix thy hope on mold'ring dust?
40 The arm of flesh didst make thy trust?
Raise up thy thoughts above the sky
That dunghill mists away may fly. **E**

Thou hast an house on high erect,
Framed by that mighty Architect,
45 With glory richly furnishéd,
Stands permanent though this be fled.
It's purchaséd and paid for too
By Him who hath enough to do. **F**

A price so vast as is unknown
50 Yet by His gift is made thine own;
There's wealth enough, I need no more,
Farewell, my pelf,[6] farewell my store.
The world no longer let me love,
My hope and treasure lies above.

---

4. **all's vanity:** an allusion to Ecclesiastes 1:2 in the Bible—"All is vanity," meaning that all is temporary and meaningless.

5. **chide:** to scold mildly so as to correct or improve.

6. **pelf:** wealth or riches, especially when dishonestly acquired.

D FIGURATIVE LANGUAGE
What does the use of **personification** in lines 29–36 reveal about the speaker's feelings for her house?

E CLARIFY MEANING
Use contemporary vocabulary to restate the **archaic language** in lines 37–40. What does the speaker chide, or scold, herself for?

F FIGURATIVE LANGUAGE
Reread lines 43–48. What two things does Bradstreet compare in the **metaphor** in these lines?

LITERARY ANALYSIS

D FIGURATIVE LANGUAGE

Possible answer: Through the use of personification—addressing her house as if it were alive—the speaker reveals her emotional attachment to the house and the memories that were made there.

READING STRATEGY

E CLARIFY MEANING

Possible answer: Restatement: Did I think that my only wealth was in my earthly possessions? Did I put all my hope in this pile of decaying dust? Was it this house, built by man, in which I put my trust? The speaker chides herself for placing too much value upon earthly possessions.

If students need help . . . Point out that the questions in lines 38–40 are rhetorical questions; no answer is expected because the answer is obvious. Elicit that *no* is the answer to each question.

Extend the Discussion How would you change each question into a statement in which the speaker confirms her faith?

LITERARY ANALYSIS

F FIGURATIVE LANGUAGE

Possible answer: Bradstreet's metaphor compares a temporary earthly home with an eternal home in heaven (a home built and paid for by God and furnished with glory).

FOR STRATEGIC READERS
Comprehension Support Have students reread the poem, looking for answers to these questions:

• What vivid memories does the speaker have of the house that has been destroyed?

• What events had the speaker hoped to experience in that house?

• How does the speaker envision the house that will be hers after her death?

FOR ADVANCED LEARNERS/AP
Write a Journal Entry Have students think about the events of the poem and draw inferences based on textual evidence. Then ask them to imagine that the speaker is a close friend of theirs. Have students write and share a journal entry about the night her house burned down and how she responded to the tragedy. Encourage them to include their feelings about the speaker and her family. Offer students the option of imagining that the speaker is the poet.

In this poem, the speaker develops an extended metaphor in which he asks God to transform him so that he can become all that God wants him to be.

READING STRATEGY

G CLARIFY MEANING

Possible answer: These lines describe the activity of using a spinning wheel to make yarn for weaving.

LITERARY ANALYSIS

H FIGURATIVE LANGUAGE

Possible answer: The extended metaphor compares the transformation of wool to cloth and clothing to the speaker's relationship with God, who transforms him.

Lines 1–18
TIERED DISCUSSION PROMPTS

Use these prompts to help students explore the poem's theme:

Connect Describe a time when you wanted to change something about yourself. *Students should connect to the speaker's desire for personal transformation.*

Interpret Why does the speaker ask God to make him a spinning wheel (line 1) and a loom (lines 7)? *Possible answer: The speaker wants God to change him so that he will be an instrument that God controls completely.*

Synthesize How do the speaker's requests reflect Taylor's Puritan beliefs? *Possible answer: They reflect the Puritan belief that God controls everything.*

SELECTION WRAP-UP

SYNTHESIZE Ask students to explain what modern readers might best connect to in each of these poems, and why.

Huswifery   Edward Taylor

Make me, O Lord, Thy spinning wheel complete.
Thy holy word my distaff[1] make for me.
Make mine affections Thy swift flyers[2] neat,
And make my soul Thy holy spool to be.
5 My conversation make to be Thy reel,
And reel the yarn thereon spun of Thy wheel. **G**

Make me Thy loom then, knit therein this twine:
And make Thy holy spirit, Lord, wind quills:[3]
Then weave the web Thyself. The yarn is fine.
10 Thine ordinances make my fulling mills.[4]
Then dye the same in heavenly colors choice,
All pinked[5] with varnished flowers of paradise.

Then clothe therewith mine understanding, will,
Affections, judgment, conscience, memory;
15 My words and actions, that their shine may fill
My ways with glory and Thee glorify.
Then mine apparel shall display before Ye
That I am clothed in holy robes for glory. **H**

G CLARIFY MEANING
Huswifery means "housekeeping." What housekeeping activity is being described in lines 1–6?

H FIGURATIVE LANGUAGE
What **extended metaphor** does Taylor use throughout the poem to express his relationship to God?

1. **distaff:** staff on a spinning wheel for holding the wool or flax to be spun.
2. **flyers:** parts of spinning wheels that twist fibers into yarn.
3. **quills:** rods or spindles used to wind and hold yarn.
4. **fulling mills:** machines that beat and process woven cloth to make it denser and more compact.
5. **pinked:** decorated.

DIFFERENTIATED INSTRUCTION

FOR STRATEGIC READERS

Explore Metaphorical Details To create his extended metaphor, Taylor provides several interrelated comparisons. Work with students to complete a Two-Column Chart, such as the one begun here, that identifies the two terms in each comparison. Discuss the finished charts, making sure students understand that the details show that the speaker wants to serve God completely, in every way.

Everyday Object	Compared to . . .
"spinning wheel" (line 1)	"me" (the speaker)
"my distaff" (line 2)	"Thy holy word"
"flyers" (line 3)	"mine affections"
"spool" (line 4)	"my soul"
"reel" (line 5)	"My conversation"

 BEST PRACTICES TOOLKIT—Transparency
Two-Column Chart p. A25

Comprehension

1. **Recall** In "To My Dear and Loving Husband," what does the speaker value more than gold?

2. **Recall** When the speaker in "Upon the Burning of Our House" wakes up to find her house on fire, what is her initial reaction?

3. **Clarify** The speaker in Taylor's "Huswifery" compares himself to a loom. Who or what is compared to the weaver?

Literary Analysis

4. **Clarify Meaning** Review the examples of **archaic language** and **inverted syntax** you recorded as you read the poems. How would you restate lines 19–20 of "Upon the Burning of Our House": "He might of all justly bereft, / But yet sufficient for us left"?

5. **Draw Conclusions** Use details from the two poems by Anne Bradstreet to explain what she reveals about her

   • marriage   • religious beliefs   • daily life

6. **Make Inferences** What did Bradstreet **value** more than her house? How did this help her accept the loss of her house by fire?

7. **Analyze Figurative Language** How do the "holy robes for glory" mentioned in line 18 of "Huswifery" complete the poem's **extended metaphor**?

8. **Evaluate Description** Why do you think Taylor used a typical Puritan housekeeping activity to express his religious faith?

9. **Compare Literary Works** What do the poems by Bradstreet and Taylor have in common? What distinguishes one poet's work from the other's? In a chart like the one shown, compare and contrast the poets' work, noting the religious views expressed, the formality of each poet's **style,** and the personality revealed. Use specific details from the poems to complete the chart.

	Bradstreet	Taylor
Religious Views		
Style		
Personality		

Literary Criticism

10. **Examine Social Context** The Puritans strongly disapproved of women writers. A Puritan minister even wrote a letter to his sister in England saying, "Your printing of a book, beyond the custom of your sex, doth rankly smell." In spite of this disapproval, do you think the Puritan community would have considered any aspects of Anne Bradstreet's poetry praiseworthy? Explain your answer.

has described. These robes allow the speaker to glorify God and "display" the spiritual character of a person whose ultimate destiny is heaven.

8. Taylor's housekeeping imagery is something that Puritans understood well. It also reflects Puritan beliefs by suggesting that God is present in everyday activities.

9. *Religious Views:* Both poets have a deep religious faith; both look to God for help. *Style:* Bradstreet uses more accessible language; Taylor's style is more formal; both use figurative language, but Taylor's

is more complex and extended; both poets also use archaic language and inverted syntax. *Personality:* Bradstreet provides personal details and insights into her emotions, making her seem human and real; Taylor is personal but offers little insight into his life, making him seem more remote.

10. *Yes, Puritans probably would have approved of Bradstreet's glorification of God and her reconciliation to the loss of material possessions. No, they might have thought it inappropriate for her poetry to focus on her personal life.*

Practice and Apply

After Reading
Use these copy masters to check understanding and provide extra support:

R RESOURCE MANAGER—Copy Masters
Figurative Language p. 197
Question Support p. 201

Additional selection questions are provided for teachers on page 193.

ANSWERS

1. *Bradstreet values her husband's love more than gold.*

2. *The speaker initially prays to God for strength and help.*

3. *God is compared with the weaver.*

Possible answers:

4. ■ **SKILLS FOCUS Clarify Meaning in Older Poetry** *God is entitled to take everything away but will meet our needs.*

5. *"To My Dear and Loving Husband": Lines 1–4 suggest a strong, loving marriage.* **"Upon the Burning of Our House":** *Lines 19–20 and 49–54 reveal a strong faith in God; lines 25–34 suggest a happy and sociable daily life.*

6. *More than her house, Bradstreet valued her faith in God, whom she trusted to meet her needs and grant her an eternal home in heaven. This faith helped her accept her loss and recognize that material possessions are relatively unimportant.*

7. ● **SKILLS FOCUS Figurative Language** *The image of the "holy robes" completes the poem's extended metaphor by showing the garment that is the finished product of the clothing-making process the speaker*

Assess and Reteach

Assess

R RESOURCE MANAGER—Copy Masters
Selection Test A pp. 203–204
Selection Test B/C pp. 205–206

💿 Test Generator CD

Reteach

S STANDARDS LESSON FILE
Literature Lesson 27: Simile and Metaphor
Literature Lesson 29: Personification
Literature Lesson 44: Style and Syntax
Study Skills Lesson 12: Paraphrasing

Focus and Motivate

OBJECTIVES

Literary Analysis
- explore the key idea of **morality**
- analyze a sermon
- read a sermon

Reading
- analyze emotional appeals

Vocabulary
- build vocabulary for reading and writing
- use word connotations to help unlock meaning (*also an EL language objective*)

CALIFORNIA R2.6, R3.3

ABOUT THE AUTHOR

After students read the biography, emphasize that Edwards's focus on emotion does not mean that he rejected careful thought. As they read the excerpt from his sermon, have them note how he structures his argument. Also, be prepared to discuss the term "born again" (a personal commitment of faith instead of reliance upon church membership or good deeds) and encourage students to see how Edwards explains the concept.

USING THE *NOTABLE QUOTE*

Ask students what childlike qualities **Jonathan Edwards** is referring to in the context of this comment. *Possible answer: Edwards is referring to the relative simplicity and helplessness of a child. He wishes to depend upon God's help and be as ready as a child to learn.*

Selection Resources

R2.6, R3.3
CALIFORNIA

from Sinners in the Hands of an Angry God
Sermon by Jonathan Edwards

NOTABLE QUOTE
"[I wish] to lie low before God, as in the dust; that I might be nothing, and that God might be all, that I might become as a little child."

FYI
Did you know that Jonathan Edwards . . .
- wrote a paper on spiders at age 11?
- died as a result of a smallpox inoculation?
- was the grandfather of Aaron Burr, vice-president under Thomas Jefferson?

Author Online

For more on Jonathan Edwards, visit the **Literature Center** at **ClassZone.com.**

Jonathan Edwards
1703–1758

When Jonathan Edwards delivered a sermon, with its fiery descriptions of hell and eternal damnation, people listened. Edwards believed that religion should be rooted in emotion rather than reason. Although 19th-century editors tried to tone down his style, Edwards is recognized today as a masterful preacher. In fact, he is considered by many to be America's greatest religious thinker.

A Spiritual Calling Born in East Windsor, Connecticut, Edwards was a child prodigy and entered what is now Yale University at the age of 12. While a graduate student there, Edwards experienced a spiritual crisis that led to what he later described as "religious joy." He came to believe that such an intense religious experience was an important step toward salvation.

In 1722, after finishing his education, Edwards followed the path of his father and grandfather and became a Puritan minister. In 1726, Edwards began assisting his grandfather, who was the minister at the parish church in Northampton, Massachusetts. When his grandfather died three years later, Edwards became the church's pastor.

Religious Revivalist Edwards soon became an effective preacher. In 1734 and 1735, he delivered a series of sermons that resulted in a great number of conversions. The converts believed they had felt God's grace and were "born again" when they accepted Jesus Christ.

Edwards's sermons helped trigger the Great Awakening, a religious revival that swept through New England from 1734 to 1750. The movement grew out of a sense among some Puritan ministers that their congregations had grown too self-satisfied. Delivered at the height of the Great Awakening, "Sinners in the Hands of an Angry God" is the most famous of Edwards's nearly 1,200 sermons.

Last Years Although Edwards inspired thousands, his church dismissed him in 1750 because he wanted to limit membership to those who had undergone conversion. A year later, Edwards went to Stockbridge, Massachusetts, where he became a missionary in a Native American settlement. In 1757, he accepted an appointment as president of what is now Princeton University.

By the time of Edwards's death the following year, the extremism of the Great Awakening had been rejected. However, his vision of humanity suspended, like a spider, over the burning pit of hell still maintains its emotional impact.

 RESOURCE MANAGER UNIT 1

Plan and Teach pp. 207–214

Literary Analysis
Summary pp. 215†*, 216‡*
Sermon pp. 217, 218†*
Question Support p. 225*

Reading
Analyze Emotional Appeals
pp. 219, 220†*
Reading Check p. 224

Vocabulary
Study p. 221*
Practice p. 222
Strategy p. 223

Assessment
Selection Tests A, B/C
pp. 227*, 229*
Test Generator CD

 BEST PRACTICES TOOLKIT

Differentiated Instruction
pp. 31–38*

Scaffolding Instruction
pp. 43–46*

Graphic Organizers/Strategies
Open Mind

Reading Support
Audio Anthology CD*

Technology
Literature and Vocabulary Centers at **ClassZone.com**
Write*Smart* CD

---

* Resources for Differentiation   † Also in Spanish   ‡ In Haitian Creole and Vietnamese

LITERARY ANALYSIS: SERMON

A **sermon** is a form of religious persuasion in which a speaker exhorts listeners to behave in a more spiritual and moral fashion. Like all sermons, Jonathan Edwards's is shaped by

- **purpose**—why Edwards delivers the sermon
- **audience**—whom Edwards is addressing
- **context**—when and where Edwards delivers the sermon

As you read Edwards's sermon, look for passages that reveal his purpose, his audience, and the context for his delivery.

READING SKILL: ANALYZE EMOTIONAL APPEALS

Emotional appeals are messages designed to persuade an audience by creating strong feelings rather than by providing facts and evidence. Writers often use **tone, imagery,** and **figurative language** to make these types of emotional appeals:

- **appeal to fear,** which taps into people's fear of losing their safety or security
- **appeal to pity,** which takes advantage of people's sympathy and compassion for others
- **appeal to vanity,** which relies on people's desire to feel good about themselves

As you read, use a chart like the one shown to record examples of language used to appeal to the audience's emotions.

Examples	Emotional Appeals
"arrows of death fly unseen"	appeals to fear by creating anxiety, unease

VOCABULARY IN CONTEXT

Jonathan Edwards uses the listed words to help convey his spiritual message. Choose a word from the list that is a synonym for each of the numbered words.

WORD LIST	abhor	deliverance	mitigation
	abominable	discern	whet
	appease	incense	
	ascribe	induce	

1. detest
2. easing
3. sharpened
4. anger greatly
5. attribute

What keeps you IN LINE?

KEY IDEA A sense of **morality** probably keeps you from cheating on a test. In other words, you know cheating is wrong. But there are other reasons for behaving morally. Some people are anxious to please. Others fear the consequences of breaking the rules. Jonathan Edwards uses fear to get his point across in the sermon you're about to read. Is fear the best motivator?

ROLE-PLAY With a partner, take turns role-playing a conversation with a child who has been stealing. Your mission is to persuade him or her to stop. Before you begin, consider how best to keep the child in line. For example, you might frighten or shame the child or appeal to his or her pride.

119

What keeps you IN LINE?

Read the question and the **KEY IDEA**. Call on volunteers to name other factors that might keep people from violating standards of **morality** and to comment upon the idea of fear as a motivator. Suggest that students choose the most persuasive factor from the discussion as the tactic they use in the *ROLE-PLAY* activity.

SKILLS FOCUS

LITERARY ANALYSIS

● **SERMON**

Read this example aloud:

> You who gossip about your neighbors— your tongues will shrivel even as you speak. End your gossiping ways!

Have students suggest a purpose, audience, and context for the example. *Possible answer: purpose: to warn people to stop gossiping; audience: townspeople; context: a church or revival meeting.*

CHECK UNDERSTANDING Ask students to identify the purpose, audience, and context for some advertisements that they have read or seen.

READING SKILL   R2.6, R3.3

■ **ANALYZE EMOTIONAL APPEALS**

Have students reread the example in the previous note and then identify its chief emotional appeal. *Answer: an appeal to fear.*

R RESOURCE MANAGER—Copy Master
Analyze Emotional Appeals p. 219 (for student use while reading the selection)

VOCABULARY

▲ VOCABULARY IN CONTEXT

DIAGNOSE WORD KNOWLEDGE To determine preteaching needs, have all students complete Vocabulary in Context. Check students' answers and confirm their understanding of the synonyms. *Answers:*
1. *abhor,* **2.** *mitigation,* **3.** *whet,* **4.** *incense,* **5.** *ascribe*

PRETEACH VOCABULARY Preteach vocabulary with this copy master. Read each item aloud.

R RESOURCE MANAGER—Copy Master
Vocabulary Study p. 221

MORE VOCABULARY SUPPORT
For additional activities and guidelines, see

 BEST PRACTICES TOOLKIT
Scaffolding Vocabulary Instruction pp. 43–46

ⓘ Vocabulary Center at **ClassZone.com**

SUMMARY

In this sermon excerpt, Jonathan Edwards describes God's great anger toward sinners—people who may attend church and appear religious but who have not experienced a personal conversion. He warns sinners that at any moment, God may send them to hell, whose torments Edwards describes in vivid detail. He concludes, however, with an offer of hope, urging sinners to come to faith in Christ.

LITERARY ANALYSIS

Ⓐ SERMON

Possible answer: *The audience probably responded with curiosity about which people "now in this congregation" Edwards might have in mind and with some anxiety or dismay about what more he might say.*

If students need help . . . Have them begin an Open Mind diagram that captures what might be going through listeners' minds as they hear Edwards's words.

> Is he saying that I'm a worm or insect?
> I don't want to go to hell!
> Could God be angry with me?

Extend the Discussion Why do you think Edwards says that God is "a great deal more angry" with some audience members than with people who have already gone to hell?

 BEST PRACTICES TOOLKIT—Transparency Open Mind p. D9

Sinners in the Hands
of an
Angry God

Jonathan Edwards

> **BACKGROUND** Jonathan Edwards delivered his sermon "Sinners in the Hands of an Angry God" in 1741 to a congregation in Enfield, Connecticut. Edwards read the sermon, as he always did, in a composed style, with few gestures or movements. However, the sermon had a dramatic effect on his parishioners, many of whom wept and moaned. Some even considered suicide.

We find it easy to tread on and crush a worm that we see crawling on the earth; so it is easy for us to cut or singe a slender thread that any thing hangs by; thus easy is it for God when he pleases to cast his enemies down to hell. . . .

They[1] are now the objects of that very same *anger* and wrath of God, that is expressed in the torments of hell. And the reason why they do not go down to hell at each moment, is not because God, in whose power they are, is not then very angry with them; as angry as he is with many miserable creatures now tormented in hell, who there feel and bear the fierceness of his wrath. Yea, God is a great deal more angry with great numbers that are now on earth; yea, doubtless, with many
10 that are now in this congregation, who it may be are at ease, than he is with many of those who are now in the flames of hell. Ⓐ

---

1. **they:** Earlier in the sermon, Edwards refers to all "unconverted men," whom he considers God's enemies. Unconverted men are people who have not been "born again," meaning that they have not accepted Jesus Christ.

Fire, allegory (1566), Giuseppe Arcimboldo. Painted for Emperor Maximillian II. Limewood, 66.5 cm × 51 cm. Inv. 1585. Kunsthistorisches Museum, Vienna. © Erich Lessing/Art Resource, New York.

ANALYZE VISUALS
This painting by Italian artist Giuseppe Arcimboldo presents an **allegory** of fire. What lesson or message does the painting seem to suggest about the meaning of fire?

❶ Targeted Passage

Ⓐ SERMON
Reread lines 8–11. Notice that Edwards directly addresses his **audience** in these lines. How do you imagine the audience responded to these words?

DIFFERENTIATED INSTRUCTION

FOR ALL STUDENTS

Provide these independent projects to extend the lesson:

- Plan and present an interview with Jonathan Edwards.
- Write a letter as if you had been part of Edwards's audience.

For further details on these projects, see

Ⓡ RESOURCE MANAGER
Ideas for Extension pp. 212–213

FOR STRATEGIC READERS

In combination with the *Audio Anthology CD*, use one or more Targeted Passages (pp. 120, 122, 125) to ensure that students focus on key concepts in the selection. Targeted Passages are also good for English learners.

❶ Targeted Passage [Lines 1–5]

This introductory passage sets up the idea that God can and will judge sinners.

B EMOTIONAL APPEALS

Possible answer: Edwards appeals to fear by using vivid images of the fires of hell, such as these: "The wrath of God burns against them" (line 14–15); "the flames do now rage and glow" (lines 16–17); and "the pit hath opened its mouth under them" (line 18).

C EMOTIONAL APPEALS

Possible answer: These loaded terms have negative connotations: "the fiery pit" and "sentenced" (line 28); "dreadfully provoked" (line 29); and "suffering," "executions," and "the fierceness of his wrath in hell" (line 30).

If students need help . . . Write the words *cheap, inexpensive, flame,* and *inferno* on the board. Elicit that *cheap* and *inferno* are synonyms for *inexpensive* and *flame* but that they have negative connotations. Have students suggest examples of other words with negative connotations.

D SERMON

Possible answer: Edwards is delivering this sermon for the purpose of urging those "that were never born again" (lines 43–44) to undergo "a great change of heart" (line 42) so that they will not face God's anger.

So that it is not because God is unmindful of their wickedness, and does not resent it, that he does not let loose his hand and cut them off. God is not altogether such an one as themselves, though they may imagine him to be so. The wrath of God burns against them, their damnation does not slumber; the pit is prepared, the fire is made ready, the furnace is now hot, ready to receive them; the flames do now rage and glow. The glittering sword is **whet,** and held over them, and the pit hath opened its mouth under them. . . . B

20 Unconverted men walk over the pit of hell on a rotten covering, and there are innumerable places in this covering so weak that they will not bear their weight, and these places are not seen. The arrows of death fly unseen at noonday; the sharpest sight cannot **discern** them. God has so many different unsearchable ways of taking wicked men out of the world and sending them to hell, that there is nothing to make it appear, that God had need to be at the expense of a miracle, or go out of the ordinary course of his providence, to destroy any wicked man, at any moment. . . .

So that, thus it is that natural men[2] are held in the hand of God, over the pit of hell; they have deserved the fiery pit, and are already sentenced to it; and God is dreadfully provoked, his anger is as great towards them as to those that are actually

30 suffering the executions of the fierceness of his wrath in hell; and they have done nothing in the least to **appease** or abate that anger, neither is God in the least bound by any promise to hold them up one moment; the devil is waiting for them, hell is gaping for them, the flames gather and flash about them, and would fain[3] lay hold on them, and swallow them up; the fire pent up in their own hearts is struggling to break out: and they have no interest in any Mediator,[4] there are no means within reach that can be any security to them. In short, they have no refuge, nothing to take hold of. . . . C

The bow of God's wrath is bent, and the arrow made ready on the string, and justice bends the arrow at your heart, and strains the bow, and it is nothing but

40 the mere pleasure of God, and that of an angry God, without any promise or obligation at all, that keeps the arrow one moment from being made drunk with your blood. Thus all you that never passed under a great change of heart, by the mighty power of the Spirit of God upon your souls; all you that were never born again, and made new creatures, and raised from being dead in sin, to a state of new, and before altogether unexperienced light and life, are in the hands of an angry God. However you may have reformed your life in many things, and may have had religious affections, and may keep up a form of religion in your families and closets,[5] and in the house of God, it is nothing but his mere pleasure that keeps you from being this moment swallowed up in everlasting destruction. . . . D

50 The God that holds you over the pit of hell, much as one holds a spider, or some loathsome insect over the fire, **abhors** you, and is dreadfully provoked: his

---

2. **natural men:** people who have not been born again.
3. **would fain:** would rather.
4. **Mediator:** Jesus Christ, who mediates, or is the means of bringing about, salvation.
5. **closets:** private rooms for meditation.

whet (hwĕt) *adj.* sharpened **whet** *v.*

B EMOTIONAL APPEALS
Reread lines 14–18. What **imagery** does Edwards use to appeal to fear in these lines?

discern (dĭ-sûrn') *v.* to perceive or recognize something

appease (ə-pēz') *v.* to bring peace, quiet, or calm to; to soothe

C EMOTIONAL APPEALS
Loaded language, or words with strong emotional associations, can be used to influence an audience's attitude. What examples of loaded language do you see in lines 27–30?

2 Targeted Passage

D SERMON
Note that Edwards reveals the **purpose** of his sermon in lines 42–46. Why is he delivering this sermon?

abhor (ăb-hôr') *v.* to regard with disgust

DIFFERENTIATED INSTRUCTION

FOR STRATEGIC READERS

2 Targeted Passage [Lines 38–49]

In this passage, Edwards declares that nothing but conversion will allow people to escape God's wrath.

- Why does God have a bow and arrows? Why hasn't he used them yet?

- Name two things that Edwards says will happen to people who are born again.

- What terrible fate awaits some people who only seem to be religious? Why?

FOR ENGLISH LEARNERS

Vocabulary: Prefixes As you point out the word *Unconverted* in line 19, explain that the prefix *un-,* meaning "not," gives a clue to the meaning of the word. Have students find *unsearchable* (line 22) and *unexperienced* (line 45) on the page. Point out that, although these words are outdated and are not used in modern English, the prefix helps the reader determine the meaning. Brainstorm with students for additional examples of words with this prefix.

Babylon Burning. From the *Apocalypse of Saint John* (Revelations 18). Luther Bible, First Edition. 1530. Private collection. Photo © Art Resource, New York.

ANALYZE VISUALS

Activity How is the burning of Babylon relevant to Edwards's warnings to his listeners? *Possible answer: The burning of Babylon is relevant because it shows God's fiery judgment. The angels indicate that the fire was an act of God. The people in the image seem not to have known that judgment was close at hand. Edwards tells his listeners that they could face such a judgment at any moment.*

About the Art In Protestant thought, the city of Babylon symbolized immoral living and a disregard for the things of God. According to the New Testament book of Revelation, Babylon would find its final destruction in divine fire. This woodcut, by Lucas Cranach the Elder (1472–1553), depicts that scene; Cranach created it for the Bible that Martin Luther translated into German. Like Edwards's sermon, the image uses the motif of fire to show the severity of God's anger against sinners.

wrath towards you burns like fire; he looks upon you as worthy of nothing else, but to be cast into the fire; he is of purer eyes than to bear to have you in his sight; you are ten thousand times more **abominable** in his eyes, than the most hateful venomous serpent is in ours. You have offended him infinitely more than ever a stubborn rebel did his prince; and yet it is nothing but his hand that holds you from falling into the fire every moment. It is to be **ascribed** to nothing else, that you did not go to hell the last night; that you was suffered[6] to awake again in this world, after you closed your eyes to sleep. And there is no other reason to be
60 given, why you have not dropped into hell since you arose in the morning, but that God's hand has held you up. There is no other reason to be given why you have not gone to hell, since you have sat here in the house of God, provoking his pure eyes by your sinful wicked manner of attending his solemn worship.

abominable
(ə-bŏm′ə-nə-bəl) *adj.*
thoroughly detestable

ascribe (ə-skrīb′) *v.* to attribute to a specified cause or source

---

6. **you was suffered:** you were permitted.

Lines 42–57
REINFORCE *KEY IDEA:* MORALITY

Discuss According to Edwards, is **morality** enough to save a person from judgment? What does he indicate is needed? *Possible answer: Morality is not enough. Edwards says that even a person who has made personal reforms and who has "religious affections" is subject to "everlasting destruction." Such a fate, he says, awaits "all you that never passed under a great change of heart . . . that were never born again" (lines 42–46), indicating that a complete conversion experience is needed.*

FOR STRATEGIC READERS

Concept Support Edwards's sermon is filled with figurative language, so pause from time to time to check students' understanding. Revisit the chart introduced on page 119, offering advice as students record and analyze examples of emotional appeals and figurative language in the sermon.

Examples	Emotional Appeals
"made drunk with your blood" (lines 41–42)	appeals to fear by creating an image of a painful death
"swallowed up in everlasting destruction" (line 49)	appeals to fear by personifying hell as a hungry beast

E EMOTIONAL APPEALS

Possible answer: The comparison might make the listener feel superior to the spider (an appeal to vanity) but also very aware of the vulnerability of the spider as it dangles over a fire (an appeal to fear).

Lines 66–74
TIERED DISCUSSION PROMPTS

Use these prompts to help students explore Edwards's use of suspense:

Analyze Who is Edwards alluding to when he refers to a Mediator (line 71)? Why doesn't he explain here that the Mediator can save them? *Possible answer: Edwards is referring to Jesus Christ. He does not explain here how sinners can be saved because he is building suspense; he wants listeners to feel the desperation of their situation.*

Evaluate Do you think that this description achieves its purpose? Why or why not? *Possible answer: Yes. The description makes the listener feel the need for an escape.*

ANALYZE VISUALS

Activity How is the hell in the painting similar to or different from the hell that Edwards describes? *Possible answer: Both are full of fire. The flames seen through the gaping doorway seem to tell viewers that hell is ready to receive them, too.*

About the Art Flemish painter Hendrik met de Bles (c. 1510–1550) frequently explored religious themes. This image vividly suggests what Edwards describes as hell's "exquisite horrible misery" (line 77).

Yea, there is nothing else that is to be given as a reason why you do not this very moment drop down into hell. **E**

   O sinner! Consider the fearful danger you are in: it is a great furnace of wrath, a wide and bottomless pit, full of the fire of wrath, that you are held over in the hand of that God, whose wrath is provoked and **incensed** as much against you, as against many of the damned in hell. You hang by a slender thread, with the
70 flames of divine wrath flashing about it, and ready every moment to singe it, and burn it asunder;[7] and you have no interest in any Mediator, and nothing to lay hold of to save yourself, nothing to keep off the flames of wrath, nothing of your own, nothing that you ever have done, nothing that you can do, to **induce** God to spare you one moment. . . .

   It is *everlasting* wrath. It would be dreadful to suffer this fierceness and wrath of Almighty God one moment; but you must suffer it to all eternity. There will be no end to this exquisite[8] horrible misery. When you look forward, you shall see a long forever, a boundless duration before you, which will swallow up your

---

7. **burn it asunder** (ə-sŭn′dər): burn it into separate parts or pieces.
8. **exquisite** (ĕk′skwĭ-zĭt): intensely felt.

Detail of *Hell*, Hendrik met de Bles, Kunsthistorisches Museum, Vienna. © Erich Lessing/Art Resource, New York.

E EMOTIONAL APPEALS
Notice the use of the **simile**, or comparison, in lines 50–65. In what way does comparing the audience to a spider appeal to both fear and vanity?

incense (ĭn-sĕns′) v. to cause to be extremely angry

induce (ĭn-dōōs′) v. to succeed in persuading someone to do something

---

DIFFERENTIATED INSTRUCTION

FOR ENGLISH LEARNERS

Vocabulary: Suffixes Help students use this suffix chart to define the words *Mediator* (line 71); *dreadful* and *fierceness* (line 75); *boundless* (line 78); *merciless* (line 82); and *inexpressible* and *inconceivable* (line 87).

Suffix	Meaning
-able, -ible	capable of being
-er, -or	a person who
-ful	full of
-ness	the quality or act of
-less	without
-tion	a thing that

FOR ADVANCED LEARNERS/AP

Synthesize Point out the contrast between the emotionally charged sermon text and the fact that Edwards delivered the sermon by reading it aloud in a plain way. Then challenge students to deliver a few paragraphs as they think Edwards might have done—with enough emotion to show his sincerity but not so much that the message is overpowered by theatrics. After students have presented parts of the sermon, invite insights and comments about the impact of Edwards's language.

thoughts, and amaze your soul; and you will absolutely despair of ever having
80 any **deliverance**, any end, any **mitigation**, any rest at all. You will know certainly that you must wear out long ages, millions of millions of ages, in wrestling and conflicting with this almighty merciless vengeance; and then when you have so done, when so many ages have actually been spent by you in this manner, you will know that all is but a point to what remains. So that your punishment will indeed be infinite. Oh, who can express what the state of a soul in such circumstances is! All that we can possibly say about it, gives but a very feeble, faint representation of it; it is inexpressible and inconceivable: For "who knows the power of God's anger?"[9]

How dreadful is the state of those that are daily and hourly in the danger of
90 this great wrath and infinite misery! But this is the dismal case of every soul in this congregation that has not been born again, however moral and strict, sober and religious, they may otherwise be. . . . **F**

> And now you have an extraordinary opportunity, a day wherein Christ has thrown the door of mercy wide open, and stands in the door calling and crying with a loud voice to poor sinners; a day wherein many are flocking to him, and pressing into the kingdom of God. Many are daily coming[10] from the east, west, north, and south; many that were very lately in the same miserable condition that you are in, are now in a happy state, with their hearts filled with love to him who has loved them, and washed them from their sins in his own blood, and rejoicing
> 100 in hope of the glory of God. How awful is it to be left behind at such a day! To see so many others feasting, while you are pining and perishing! To see so many rejoicing and singing for joy of heart, while you have cause to mourn for sorrow of heart, and howl for vexation of spirit! How can you rest one moment in such a condition? . . . **G**
>
> Therefore, let every one that is out of Christ, now awake and fly from the wrath to come. . . . ❧

---

9. **"who knows . . . anger?":** an allusion to Psalm 90:11 in the Bible—"Who knoweth the power of thine anger?"

10. **Many . . . coming:** a reference to the hundreds of people who were being converted during the Great Awakening.

deliverance (dĭ-lĭv′ər-əns)
n. rescue from danger

mitigation (mĭt-ĭ-gā′shən)
n. lessening of something that causes suffering

F SERMON
Keep in mind that Edwards delivers his sermon in the **context** of his own time and place. In lines 90–92, in what way does he acknowledge the Puritan heritage of his listeners?

3 Targeted Passage

G EMOTIONAL APPEALS
Reread lines 93–104 and note the change in **tone.** How might the change in tone appeal to the audience's pity and vanity?

LITERARY ANALYSIS

F SERMON

Possible answer: Edwards acknowledges the Puritan heritage of his listeners in the words "moral and strict, sober and religious," which refer to core values of the Puritan lifestyle.

READING SKILL

G EMOTIONAL APPEALS

Possible answer: The invitational tone might appeal to the audience's vanity if listeners felt proud to think that Christ is inviting them to enter the kingdom of God; it might appeal to self-pity if listeners imagined themselves to be those whom Edwards describes as missing out on the blessings of salvation.

Lines 96–100
REINFORCE *KEY IDEA:* **MORALITY**

Discuss What does Edwards imply about **morality** in the kingdom of God? *Possible answer:* Edwards implies that such morality can be practiced only by those whose sins have been cleansed and that it is based on love for God.

SELECTION WRAP—UP

SUMMARIZE Have students sum up Edwards's message by completing this sentence: *You need to _____ because _____.*

FOR STRATEGIC READERS

3 Targeted Passage [Lines 93–106]

In this passage, Edwards explains how his listeners can avoid the fires of hell.

- What is the "extraordinary opportunity" that Edwards refers to in line 93?

- What two types of people does Edwards describe in lines 100–104? What creates the difference between them?

- What call to action does Edwards make at the end of his sermon?

FOR ADVANCED LEARNERS/AP

Evaluate a Presentation By the end of this sermon, Edwards has described what sinners stand to lose and what they stand to gain. Have students write a brief essay in which they explain both concepts and evaluate Edwards's effectiveness in presenting them. Invite students to compare their responses in small groups.

Practice and Apply

After Reading

Use these copy masters to check under-standing and provide extra support:

RESOURCE MANAGER—Copy Masters
Reading Check p. 224
Sermon p. 217
Question Support p. 225

Additional selection questions are provided for teachers on page 211.

ANSWERS

1. *All humans suffer the threat of being snatched out of life and cast into hell at any moment.*

2. *To save themselves, sinners must have "a great change of heart" and be "born again."*

3. *Edwards uses the image of fire—in particular, fire over which someone holds a disgusting insect.*

Possible answers:

4. ■ SKILLS FOCUS **Analyze Emotional Appeals** *The language helps listeners to feel God's wrath and to imagine what it might be like to suffer the torments of hell.*

5. ● SKILLS FOCUS **Sermon** *Edwards felt that his listeners had grown complacent in their Puritan heritage. The terror in his message probably reflects his deep concern for them and his desire to grab their attention.*

6. *God: all-powerful, holy, and angry (as in lines 8–11 and 52–55); Christ: merciful, and humanity's only hope for salvation (as in lines 93–100); humanity: made of miserable creatures who, unconverted, are worth no more in God's eyes than loathsome insects (as in lines 50–51).*

7. *Yes, because those who took the message to heart and were born again would start living a life that pleased God. No, because a fear-induced change of behavior might not be rooted in true conversion and because Edwards says that improved morality only cannot appease God's anger (lines 46–49, 93–100).*

8. *Eternal Life: Edwards: terrifying vision of hell (lines 14–18) and welcoming vision of the kingdom of God (lines 93–100); Bradstreet: a heavenly home, provided by God ("House," lines 43–50).*

   God's Relation to People: Edwards: God is angry at sinners, who have rebelled against

---

R2.6, R3.3

Comprehension

1. **Recall** According to Jonathan Edwards's sermon, what is a constant threat to all human beings?

2. **Clarify** In Edwards's view, what must sinners do to save themselves?

3. **Summarize** What key image does Edwards use to frighten his audience?

Literary Analysis

4. **Analyze Emotional Appeals** Review the examples of words, phrases, and images you recorded as you read. How does this language effectively appeal to the audience's emotions and get Edwards's message across?

5. **Analyze the Sermon** Why do you think Edwards felt it was necessary to terrify his Puritan **audience** into action?

6. **Draw Conclusions** How would you describe Jonathan Edwards's view of the following? Cite specific examples for each.

   • God • Christ • humanity

7. **Make Judgments** Do you believe that Edwards's sermon resulted in improving the **morality** of his congregation? Explain why or why not.

8. **Compare Literary Works** Use a chart like the one shown to compare some of Jonathan Edwards's and Anne Bradstreet's attitudes and beliefs. Cite specific details from their writings to support your ideas.

	Edwards	Bradstreet
Eternal Life		
God's Relation to People		
Religious Beliefs		
Human Frailty		

Literary Criticism

9. **Historical Context** In the 18th century, many people died at a much younger age than they do today. How might awareness of the fragility of life have affected people's receptiveness to Edwards's sermon?

Him (lines 50–57), but offers salvation through Christ (lines 93–96); Bradstreet: God supplies people's needs ("House," lines 19–20 and 51–54).

Religious Beliefs: Edwards and Bradstreet— *God is all-powerful and central to human life and endeavor.*

Human Frailty: Edwards: *Humans are at God's mercy and cannot save themselves (lines 42–49); Bradstreet: Every human possession belongs to God, who gives or takes according to divine purposes ("House," lines 13–18).*

9. *Edwards's imagery of immediate danger and impending doom probably would have found fertile ground among people for whom death was a common occurrence.*

Vocabulary in Context

VOCABULARY PRACTICE

Decide whether the boldfaced words make the statements true or false.

1. If a movie is said to be **abominable,** you should expect to hate it.
2. A good way to **appease** a friend is to criticize her.
3. Feeding the hungry would result in the **mitigation** of their suffering.
4. If you **discern** a difference between two documents, you notice that they are not alike.
5. A person who **abhors** you is probably a close friend.
6. When you **ascribe** a motive to a crime, you explain why someone did it.
7. One way to **incense** someone is to say something complimentary.
8. If you have trouble cutting a steak, it might help to **whet** your knife.
9. An example of **deliverance** is the rescue of passengers from a sinking ship.
10. If I **induce** you to help me do a hard job, I have managed to persuade you.

WORD LIST
abhor
abominable
appease
ascribe
deliverance
discern
incense
induce
mitigation
whet

VOCABULARY IN WRITING

How would people today react to a sermon like Edwards's? Using at least four vocabulary words, briefly explain your opinion and why you feel as you do. You might start like this.

> **EXAMPLE SENTENCE**
> I think that hearing a sermon like Edwards's would **induce** people to think seriously about their lives.

VOCABULARY STRATEGY: CONNOTATION

Though some words may have the same definition, their **connotations,** or shades of meaning, can vary. In Edwards's sermon, for example, the word *incense* (page 124) suggests a stronger feeling than *anger.* Being aware of words' shades of meaning can strengthen your writing as well as your reading comprehension.

PRACTICE Choose a more intense word from the following list to replace the boldfaced word in each sentence.

> antipathy   disconsolate   induce   momentous   negligible

1. Nothing could **persuade** him to run for president.
2. Getting a college degree was a very **important** event in Mom's life.
3. They expressed their **dislike** for the new law with a huge protest march.
4. Because I enjoyed my job so much, I was **sad** when I lost it.
5. The wishes of the stockholders had a **slight** effect on the board's decision.

> **VOCABULARY PRACTICE**
> For more practice, go to the **Vocabulary Center** at ClassZone.com.

DIFFERENTIATED INSTRUCTION

FOR ENGLISH LEARNERS

Task Support: Vocabulary Strategy Help students find and define the base word for these vocabulary words with suffixes: *abominable, deliverance, mitigation, momentous,* and *disconsolate.* Then have them use the chart on page 130 and a dictionary to combine the base word's definition with the definition of the suffix to define the vocabulary word.

FOR ADVANCED LEARNERS/AP

Vocabulary in Writing Have students use at least four vocabulary words as they write a one-paragraph summary of "Sinners in the Hands of an Angry God."

ANSWERS

Vocabulary in Context

VOCABULARY PRACTICE

1. *true*   5. *false*   8. *true*
2. *false*   6. *true*   9. *true*
3. *true*   7. *false*   10. *true*
4. *true*

> **R** RESOURCE MANAGER—Copy Master
> Vocabulary Practice p. 222

VOCABULARY IN WRITING

Ask students to write a one-sentence reaction to Edwards's sermon. Then have them write sentences using words from the word list that relate to their feelings. Invite volunteers to share sample sentences.

VOCABULARY STRATEGY: CONNOTATION
(also an EL language objective)

Have students experiment with shades of meaning by replacing the bracketed words in this sentence with more powerful words:

> The doors [rattled] as a [strong] [wind] [blew] against the [old] house.

Possible answers:

1. *induce*   4. *disconsolate*
2. *momentous*   5. *negligible*
3. *antipathy*

> **R** RESOURCE MANAGER—Copy Master
> Vocabulary Strategy p. 223

> **ℹ** Vocabulary Center at **ClassZone.com**
> Additional Vocabulary Activities

Assess and Reteach

Assess

> **R** RESOURCE MANAGER—Copy Masters
> Selection Tests A, B/C pp. 227–228, 229–230
> **⊘** Test Generator CD

Reteach

> **S** STANDARDS LESSON FILE
> **Reading Lesson 3:** Determining Author's Purpose
> **Informational Text Lesson 15:** Persuasive Techniques
> **Vocabulary Lesson 17:** Denotation and Connotation

Literary Analysis Workshop

American Drama

Have you ever gone to the theater or a movie and felt as if life were unfolding before you? Dramas that realistically portray events have a way of hitting a nerve. American playwrights, in particular, are known for writing dramas that reveal the truth of our everyday experience, and sometimes our not-so-everyday experience.

The Rise of American Drama

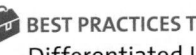 R3.5

Though drama is one of the oldest forms of literature, it was one of the last of the literary genres to develop in the United States. The Puritans in New England regarded theatrical performances as frivolous, so few plays were staged in the 1600s. During the 18th and 19th centuries, drama gradually became an accepted form of entertainment. However, most of the plays performed in the United States were imported from Europe or were adapted from novels.

Eugene O'Neill's *The Iceman Cometh* became an American classic.

In 1920 the Broadway production of Eugene O'Neill's *Beyond the Horizon* marked a turning point in presenting true-to-life characters who were struggling to understand their lives. Building on O'Neill's achievement, American playwrights Thornton Wilder, Lillian Hellman, Tennessee Williams, and Arthur Miller created dramas in the 1930s and 1940s that met with critical and popular success. Following World War II, American dramatists Edward Albee and Lorraine Hansberry made significant contributions to the theater. Arthur Miller's 1953 *The Crucible* (page 134) is an example of a modern drama that portrays events from Puritan times.

Conventions of Drama

The two main types of drama are tragedy and comedy. A **tragedy** recounts the downfall of a main character, and a **comedy** is light and humorous in tone, usually ending happily. Many dramas combine elements of both. In addition, most dramas follow similar conventions, or rules, in how they are presented. An understanding of basic dramatic conventions can help you imagine the performance as you read.

PLOT AND STRUCTURE

The **plot** in drama, as in fiction, introduces events and character interactions that produce a **conflict,** or struggle between opposing forces. The conflict builds as the action intensifies throughout the play's **acts** and **scenes,** finally reaching a peak and then resolution. Each scene serves as a building block in the stages of the plot: **exposition, rising action, climax, falling action,** and **resolution.**

DIFFERENTIATED INSTRUCTION

For general guidelines on differentiating instruction, see

 BEST PRACTICES TOOLKIT
Differentiated Instruction pp. 31–38

FOR STRATEGIC READERS

Note Taking For students who need help with note taking, hand out the note-taking copy master before discussing this page. Explain to students that they will be learning many terms relating to drama in this

workshop. Discuss the major terms on this spread *(tragedy, comedy, plot, conflict, act, scene, protagonist, antagonist, foil, cast of characters, dialogue, monologue, soliloquy, aside, stage directions)* as students record notes on the copy master.

RESOURCE MANAGER—Copy Master
Note Taking p. 231

TYPES OF CHARACTERS

Drama has many of the same types of characters that are found in fiction. The **protagonist** is the central character of the play. This character is at the center of the conflict and often undergoes radical changes during the course of the play. The **antagonist** often opposes the protagonist, giving rise to the central conflict of the play. Some plays also include a **foil,** a minor character who provides a striking contrast to another character. Interplay among these characters heightens the dramatic tension as the play develops. The names of all a play's characters are listed in the **cast of characters** at the beginning of the play.

SPEECH DEVICES

In drama, the playwright develops the story line through the characters' actions and dialogue. Virtually everything of consequence—from the plot details to the character revelations—flows from **dialogue,** or conversation between characters. Other **speech devices** used by playwrights include

- **monologue:** a long speech spoken by a single character to the audience or another character
- **soliloquy:** a reflective speech in which a character speaks his or her private thoughts aloud, unheard by other characters.
- **aside:** a short speech or comment that is delivered by a character to the audience, but that is not heard by other characters who are present

STAGE AND SETTING

Stage directions are the italicized instructions in a play. The playwright includes the stage directions in order to describe the setting, props, lighting, scenery, sound effects, and costumes. Stage directions also describe the entrances and exits of characters and how the characters look, speak, and react to events or to others. These stage directions from *The Crucible* describe the stage set at the beginning of Act Four.

> (*A cell in Salem jail, that fall.*)
>
> (*At the back is a high barred window; near it, a great, heavy door. Along the walls are two benches.*)
>
> (*The place is in darkness but for the moonlight seeping through the bars. It appears empty. Presently footsteps are heard coming down a corridor beyond the wall, keys rattle, and the door swings open. Marshal Herrick enters with a lantern.*)
>
> —Arthur Miller, ***The Crucible***

Close Read

Why is the description of the cell important to this scene? What effect does it have on the **mood** the scene evokes?

Types of Characters Share the Greek etymology of *protagonist* and *antagonist*:

- The prefix *prot(o)-* means "first" or "leading."
- The prefix *ant(i)-* means "against."
- The root *agon* means "contest."

Elicit that a conflict is like a contest, that the protagonist is the leading character, and that the antagonist acts against him or her.

Speech Devices To distinguish the terms *monologue, soliloquy,* and *aside,* ask a student to come to the front of the room. Then follow these steps:

1. Read the definition of *monologue* aloud while looking at the student. Explain that what you have just performed is similar to a monologue because you were the only character speaking.

2. Step away from the student and read the definition of *aside* aloud while shielding your mouth from him or her but not from the class. Explain that you have just performed an aside.

3. Have the student sit down. Read the definition of *soliloquy* aloud to yourself, in a reflective manner. Explain that you have just performed a soliloquy.

Stage and Setting Ask students to describe what they visualize as they read the passage from *The Crucible.*

Close Read

Possible answer: The description is important because some action (following Herrick's entrance) seems about to occur in the cell. Details such as the heavy door and moonlight cutting into the darkness create a grim but mysterious mood.

FOR ENGLISH LEARNERS

Language: Skill Words Because of the large number of skill words presented on these two pages, reassure students that they will find and learn these words again as they read *The Crucible.* Ask students to explain any of the words they know from prior reading. Then focus on the remaining words. Work with students to preview the beginning of *The Crucible,* finding the stage directions, the cast of characters, and the opening dialogue.

FOR ADVANCED LEARNERS/AP

Compare and Contrast Genres Ask students to write and share responses to these questions:

- Suppose that one writer presents a story in a novel and another writer presents the same story in a play. When reading both texts, what differences would you find?
- What can drama do that fiction cannot do? What can fiction do that drama cannot do?

OBJECTIVES

Literary Analysis
- explore the key idea of **hysteria**
- identify and analyze conventions of drama
- read a drama

Reading
- draw conclusions about characters

Vocabulary
- build vocabulary for reading and writing
- use context clues to help determine word meaning *(also an EL language objective)*

Grammar and Writing
- use appropriate word choice and sentence structure to create realistic dialogue
- use writing to analyze literature

 CALIFORNIA R3.2, W2.2, LC1.1

ABOUT THE PLAYWRIGHT

After students read the biography, call on volunteers to share what they know about the Cold War era. Then discuss the connection between it and *The Crucible*.

USING THE *NOTABLE QUOTE*

Discuss how tolerance, a key issue in *The Crucible*, involves "the question of right or wrong."
Possible answer: *During the Salem witch trials and the anti-Communist investigations, people had to evaluate the "rightness" and "wrongness" of opposing views. In both cases, some people went against prevailing views.*

 Themes Across Time

The Crucible
Drama by Arthur Miller

R3.5, W2.2 (p. 211), **LC1.1** (p. 211)

NOTABLE QUOTE
"I don't see how you can write anything decent without using as your basis the question of right or wrong."

FYI
Did you know that Arthur Miller . . .
- was once rejected by the University of Michigan because of low grades?
- was once married to film star Marilyn Monroe?
- wrote *Death of a Salesman* in six weeks?

Author Online

For more on Arthur Miller, visit the **Literature Center** at **ClassZone.com**.

Arthur Miller
1915–2005

Arthur Miller once paid playwright Edward Albee a compliment, saying that his plays were "necessary." Albee replied: "I will go one step further and say that Arthur's plays are 'essential.'" Miller's plays explore family relationships, morality, and personal responsibility. Many critics consider him the greatest American dramatist of the 20th century.

A Born Playwright Miller was born in New York City in 1915 into an upper-middle-class family. However, the family's comfortable life ended in the 1930s when Miller's businessman father was hit hard by the Great Depression. Unable to afford college, Miller worked in a warehouse to earn tuition money. He eventually attended the University of Michigan.

While in college, Miller won several awards for his plays. These successes inspired him to pursue a career in the theater. His first Broadway hit, *All My Sons*

(1947), was produced when Miller was still in his early 30s. However, it was his masterpiece *Death of a Salesman* that made Miller a star. The play won a Pulitzer Prize in 1949 and earned rave reviews from both critics and the public.

Dramatic Years Miller's rise to fame occurred during a difficult period in American history. In the 1940s and 1950s, a congressional committee was conducting hearings to identify suspected Communists in American society. Miller himself was called before the congressional committee and questioned about his activities with the American Communist Party. Although Miller admitted that he had attended a few meetings years earlier, he refused to implicate others. For his refusal, he was cited for contempt of Congress—a conviction that was later overturned.

The hearings provided the inspiration for his 1953 play *The Crucible,* set during the Salem, Massachusetts, witch trials of 1692. Miller wrote the play to warn against mass hysteria and to plead for freedom and tolerance.

The Curtain Closes In the 1970s, Miller's career declined a bit. The plays he wrote did not earn the critical or popular success of his earlier work. In the 1980s and 1990s, however, he enjoyed a resurgence with revivals of *Death of a Salesman* on Broadway. He even directed a production of the play in Beijing.

To the end of his life, Miller continued to write. "It is what I do," he said in an interview. "I am better at it than I ever was. And I will do it as long as I can."

 RESOURCE MANAGER UNIT 1

Plan and Teach pp. 233–240, 255–260, 271–276, 287–292

Literary Analysis
Summary pp. 241†*, 242‡*, 261†*, 262‡*, 277†*, 278‡*, 293†*, 294‡*
Conventions of Drama pp. 243, 244†*, 263, 264†*, 279, 280†*, 295, 296†*
Question Support pp. 249*, 266*, 282*, 300*

Reading Draw Conclusions pp. 245, 246†*
Reading Check pp. 248, 265, 281, 299
Vocabulary Study p. 247*, Practice p. 297, Strategy p. 298
Grammar and Style
Use Realistic Dialogue p. 301
Assessment Selection Tests A, B/C pp. 251*, 253*, 267*, 269*, 283*, 285*, 303*, 305*
Test Generator CD

BEST PRACTICES TOOLKIT

Differentiated Instruction pp. 31–38*
Scaffolding Instruction pp. 43–46*
Graphic Organizers/Strategies
Sequence Chain • New Word Analysis • Two-Column Chart • Jigsaw Reading • Spider Map • Venn Diagram • Storyboard • Reporter's Questions • Y Chart

Reading Support
Audio Anthology CD*

Technology
Literature, Vocabulary, and Writing Centers at **ClassZone.com**
Write*Smart* CD

---

* Resources for Differentiation   **† Also in Spanish**   **‡ In Haitian Creole and Vietnamese**

LITERARY ANALYSIS: CONVENTIONS OF DRAMA

Drama is literature in play form. It is meant to be performed and seen. However, an understanding of dramatic conventions can help you picture the performance when you read a script. As you read *The Crucible*, be aware of these drama conventions:

- **Stage directions,** which Miller uses not only to describe settings and characters but also to provide historical background in the form of expository mini-essays
- **Dialogue,** the lifeblood of drama, which moves the plot forward and reveals character traits
- **Types of characters**—heroes, villains, and foils—which Miller uses to heighten the tension of his drama
- **Plot,** which is driven by **conflict** that builds throughout each act

READING SKILL: DRAW CONCLUSIONS ABOUT CHARACTERS

Characters in drama reveal their personality traits through their words and actions. The descriptions in the stage directions can also provide insight into these characters. As you read *The Crucible*, **draw conclusions** about the play's main characters. Record their important traits and the evidence that reveals these traits in a chart like the one shown. Be sure to add characters to the chart as you encounter them.

	Abigail Williams	John Proctor	Reverend John Hale
Traits	proud	assertive	
Evidence			

▲ VOCABULARY IN CONTEXT

Arthur Miller uses the words shown here to help convey the atmosphere of the Salem witch trials. Place them in the following categories: words that describe character traits, words that describe actions, and words that are concepts.

WORD LIST		
adamant	corroborate	immaculate
ameliorate	deference	imperceptible
anarchy	deposition	iniquity
conciliatory	dissembling	subservient
contentious	effrontery	trepidation

Explore the Key Idea

What fuels a MOB?

KEY IDEA Visualize a mob of people rampaging through the streets, whipped into a frenzy by **hysteria.** The fear, anger, and panic produced by hysteria can make otherwise reasonable people do irrational things. In *The Crucible*, for example, the hysteria created by the Salem witch trials makes neighbor turn against neighbor.

DISCUSS What makes people act as a mob? What are some of the results of mob action? Think about news reports or historical accounts of mobs that you've come across. In a small group, discuss what caused these mobs to form and how they behaved.

131

Teach

What fuels a MOB?

Ask the question. As students read the **KEY IDEA**, ask them to think about the difference between a mob and a crowd. After groups complete the **DISCUSS** activity, invite students to share their ideas about **hysteria** and mob behavior.

SKILLS FOCUS

LITERARY ANALYSIS

● CONVENTIONS OF DRAMA

Share this example:

Beth (*shouting offstage where rushing water is heard*). Don't worry, Jenny! I'll save you!

Have students use the stage directions and dialogue to identify what type of character Beth is. ***Possible answer:*** *Beth is a heroic character.*

CHECK UNDERSTANDING Have students review dramatic conventions on page 131.

READING SKILL

■ DRAW CONCLUSIONS ABOUT CHARACTERS

Have students draw a conclusion about Beth's personality. ***Possible answer:*** *Beth is brave and caring.*

RESOURCE MANAGER—Copy Master Draw Conclusions About Characters p. 245 (for use while reading the selection)

VOCABULARY

▲ VOCABULARY IN CONTEXT

PRETEACH VOCABULARY To preteach vocabulary for *The Crucible*, use the Vocabulary Study copy master. Supply these definitions as needed for Acts One and Two:

- Act One, line 30: **dissembling** (dĭ-sĕm′blĭng) *n.* disguising the truth; **dissemble** *v.*
- line 156: **deference** (dĕf′ər-əns) *n.* respect and honor due to a superior or elder
- page 141: **corroborate** (kə-rŏb′ə-rāt′) *v.* to support with evidence

- line 289: **trepidation** (trĕp′ ĭ-dā′shən) *n.* alarm; dread
- line 310: **subservient** (səb-sûr′vē-ənt) *adj.* acting like a servant
- page 147: **iniquity** (ĭ-nĭk′wĭ-tē) *n.* wickedness; immorality
- line 686: **anarchy** (ăn′ər-kē) *n.* condition of lawlessness and disorder
- Act Two, line 225: **ameliorate** (ə-mēl′yə-rāt′) *v.* to improve

RESOURCE MANAGER—Copy Master Vocabulary Study p. 247

MORE VOCABULARY SUPPORT
For additional activities and guidelines, see

BEST PRACTICES TOOLKIT
Scaffolding Vocabulary Instruction pp. 43–46

ⓘ Vocabulary Center at **ClassZone.com**

131

SUMMARY

In this play, Arthur Miller traces the **hysteria** in Salem, Massachusetts, in 1692, as several girls begin to accuse their neighbors of associating with the Devil. Suspicion and ill will spread as the townspeople bring up current disputes and past grudges, implicate one another in the charge of witchcraft, and witness court proceedings against those so charged. By the time the witch trials end, Salem has been forever stained.

LITERARY ANALYSIS

● CONVENTIONS OF DRAMA

All the characters in a drama usually are presented in a list at the beginning of the play. If you were watching this play in a theater, which character would you expect to see first on the stage? *Answer: Reverend Samuel Parris would be first on the stage, because the cast is listed in the order of appearance.*

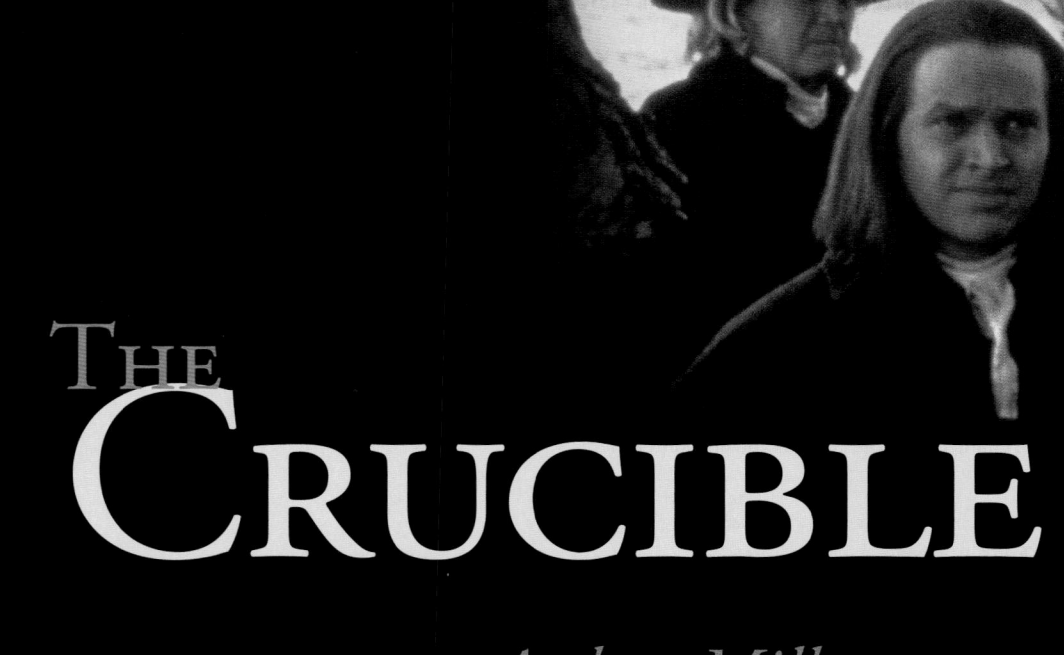

THE CRUCIBLE

Arthur Miller

132

DIFFERENTIATED INSTRUCTION

FOR ALL STUDENTS

Expert Groups Encourage students to become subject experts by selecting and re-searching one of these topics relating to the Salem witch trials of 1692:

- Massachusetts and Salem politics in the 1690s
- the first accusations of witchcraft in Salem in winter 1692
- examinations and trials for witchcraft in Salem in spring and summer 1692

FOR STRATEGIC READERS

In combination with the *Audio Anthology CD,* use one or more Targeted Passages (pp. 133, 143, 152, 158) to ensure that students focus on key story events and concepts. Targeted Passages are also good for English learners.

① Targeted Passage [*BACKGROUND*]

This passage introduces the play's historical context and Miller's approach to the culture and troubled tone of Salem in that era.

BACKGROUND *The Crucible* is based on the witch trials that took place in the Puritan community of Salem, Massachusetts, in 1692. At these trials, spectral evidence—the testimony of a church member who claimed to have seen a person's spirit performing witchcraft—was enough to sentence the accused to death. Miller studied the court records of the trials to gain insight into his characters—all of whom were real people—and get a feel for the Puritan way of speaking. Above all, he wanted to capture the mood of a time when no one was safe.

 Targeted Passage

CAST OF CHARACTERS
(*in order of appearance*)

Reverend Samuel Parris	Mrs. Ann Putnam	Ezekiel Cheever
Betty Parris	Thomas Putnam	Marshal Herrick
Tituba	Mercy Lewis	Judge Hathorne
Abigail Williams	Mary Warren	Martha Corey
John Proctor	Rebecca Nurse	Deputy Governor Danforth
Elizabeth Proctor	Giles Corey	Girls of Salem
Susanna Walcott	Reverend John Hale	Sarah Good
	Francis Nurse	

133

BACKGROUND

A Metaphorical Title Arthur Miller chose wisely when he gave this play its title. Literally, a *crucible* is a container that can withstand high heat. A crucible most often is associated with the melting of metal, allowing for impurities in the metal to be identified and removed. Metaphorically, *crucible* refers to a severe test—a test that puts great stress upon people, revealing their weaknesses and strengths. As students will see, the situation that Miller develops in *The Crucible* will put great stress upon the characters. The stress, like a fire, will burn away characters' pretenses and bring their true natures to light. Which characters will be shattered by the experience? Which will be purified? Urge students to keep these questions in mind as they read.

ANALYZE VISUALS

Activity Ask students how this photograph suggests the atmosphere of suspicion alluded to in the **BACKGROUND** note. *Possible answer: The photograph suggests suspicion because it shows a group of men who appear ready to judge others. Visually, the men are intimidating: They stand close together, wearing stern expressions that suggest a united front in a matter of great seriousness.*

- What events provide the historical basis for this play?
- What is "spectral evidence"?
- Why was no one safe in Salem during the time period covered in the play?
- Are the characters in the play purely fictional, or are they based on real people?

FOR ENGLISH LEARNERS

Prereading For prereading instruction for English learners, see

 BEST PRACTICES TOOLKIT
Scaffolding Reading Instruction pp. 43–46

FOR ADVANCED LEARNERS/AP

AP exercises in the bottom channel provide additional challenge for students. Use these suggestions for small groups or individuals.

ADDITIONAL GUIDELINES

For more help with differentiation and tips for classroom management, see

BEST PRACTICES TOOLKIT
Differentiated Instruction pp. 31–38

Practice and Apply

Get Into the Act
SUMMARY

Act One opens with Reverend Parris praying for his sick daughter, Betty. An essay explains the historical setting; then Parris reveals that the illness is thought to be due to bewitchment. Among the townspeople who discuss the matter is John Proctor, who had an affair with Parris's niece, Abigail. Reverend Hale comes to purge the town of witches; but in the conversations that follow, innocent people are accused of witchcraft.

Resources for Act One

ACT *One*

An Overture

(*A small upper bedroom in the home of* Reverend Samuel Parris, *Salem, Massachusetts, in the spring of the year 1692.*

There is a narrow window at the left. Through its leaded panes the morning sunlight streams. A candle still burns near the bed, which is at the right. A chest, a chair, and a small table are the other furnishings. At the back a door opens on the landing of the stairway to the ground floor. The room gives off an air of clean spareness. The roof rafters are exposed, and the wood colors are raw and unmellowed.

As the curtain rises, Reverend Parris *is discovered kneeling beside the bed, evidently in prayer. His daughter,* Betty Parris, *aged ten, is lying on the bed, inert.*)

At the time of these events Parris was in his middle forties. In history he cut a villainous path, and there is very little good to be said for him. He believed he was being persecuted wherever he went, despite his best efforts to win people and God to his side. In meeting, he felt insulted if someone rose to shut the door without first asking his permission. He was a widower with no interest in children, or talent with them. He regarded them as young adults, and until this strange crisis he, like the rest of Salem, never conceived that the children were anything but thankful for being permitted to walk straight, eyes slightly lowered, arms at the sides, and mouths shut until bidden to speak.

His house stood in the "town"—but we today would hardly call it a village. The meeting house[1] was nearby, and from this point outward—toward the bay or inland—there were a few small-windowed, dark houses snuggling against the raw Massachusetts winter. Salem had been established hardly forty years before. To the European world the whole province was a barbaric frontier inhabited by a sect of fanatics who, nevertheless, were shipping out products of slowly increasing quantity and value.

No one can really know what their lives were like. They had no novelists—and would not have permitted anyone to read a novel if one were handy. Their creed forbade anything resembling a theater or "vain enjoyment." They did not celebrate Christmas, and a holiday from work meant only that they must concentrate even more upon prayer.

Which is not to say that nothing broke into this strict and somber way of life. When a new farmhouse was built, friends assembled to "raise the roof," and there would be special foods cooked and probably some potent cider passed around. There was a good supply of ne'er-do-wells in Salem, who dallied at the shovelboard[2] in Bridget Bishop's tavern. Probably more than the creed, hard work kept the morals of the place from spoiling, for the people were forced

---

1. **meeting house:** the most important building in the Puritan community, used both for worship and for meetings.
2. **shovelboard:** a game in which a coin or disc is shoved across a board by hand.

---

* Resources for Differentiation   † Also in Spanish   ‡ In Haitian Creole and Vietnamese

Daniel Day-Lewis as John Proctor

● CONVENTIONS OF DRAMA

What information do the opening stage directions provide? *Possible answer: The stage directions describe the set (a small, simply furnished bedroom in Parris's house) and identify the play's setting (Salem, Massachusetts, in the spring of 1692). They also identify the characters on stage (Parris and Betty, his ten-year-old daughter) and provide direction about what these characters should be doing (Parris, kneeling in prayer; Betty, lying motionless in bed).*

◾ DRAW CONCLUSIONS ABOUT CHARACTERS

What have you learned about Reverend Parris by the end of the first paragraph? *Possible answer: His praying, seen in the stage directions, suggests that Parris loves and is worried about Betty, his daughter. In the first paragraph of the mini-essay, however, Miller says that Parris has "no interest in children" and does not understand them. Miller suggests that the motive for Parris's concern is self-centered fear.*

If students need help . . . Work with them to use the chart introduced on page 131 to draw a conclusion about Reverend Parris. Help them cite evidence to support their ideas.

DIFFERENTIATED INSTRUCTION

FOR STRATEGIC READERS

Preview Ask students to listen carefully as you read the Summary aloud. Then help them begin a Sequence Chain to organize the plot events in *The Crucible*.

> *Betty Parris is ill—perhaps bewitched.*
>
> ↓
>
> [ ]
>
> ↓

BEST PRACTICES TOOLKIT—Transparency
Sequence Chain p. B21

FOR ENGLISH LEARNERS

Culture: Clarify Explain that the word *creed* in the third paragraph refers to a religious group's statement of beliefs. Invite students to respond to Miller's statement that the Puritans, a Christian sect, did not include a Christmas celebration in their culture; then explain that the Puritans felt that the ways in which most people celebrated the holiday were overindulgent and heathen. Urge students to consider these questions as they read *The Crucible:*

- Which characters in the play show the strongest support for Puritan beliefs and behavior? Which characters seem to find the Puritan way of life difficult?

- What evidence in the play suggests that there can be divisions even among people with a common culture?

- Why might having a common culture make it easier for problems to spread? for problems to be solved?

Use these prompts to help students explore the importance of the Salem residents' interest in each other's personal lives:

Connect Have you ever encountered someone who pried into what you were doing? How did the experience affect you? *Accept all responses.*

Interpret Why does a constant interest in other people's business have the potential to make people suspicious of each other? *Possible answer: People may become suspicious because they imagine that someone is spying on them. Similarly, they may become suspicious because they think that they know the whole truth about someone they have spied on and then rush to judgment, when they probably know only a part of the story.*

Synthesize On the basis of your own experiences and what you know about the play so far, do you think that "minding other people's business" is an example of unity, which keeps a community safe, or an example of a judgmental mindset, which breeds intolerance? *Accept all thoughtful responses.*

---

to fight the land like heroes for every grain of corn, and no man had very much time for fooling around.

That there were some jokers, however, is indicated by the practice of appointing a two-man patrol whose duty was to "walk forth in the time of God's worship to take notice of such as either lye about the meeting house, without attending to the word and ordinances, or that lye at home or in the fields without giving good account thereof, and to take the names of such persons, and to present them to the magistrates, whereby they may be accordingly proceeded against." This predilection for minding other people's business was time-honored among the people of Salem, and it undoubtedly created many of the suspicions which were to feed the coming madness. It was also, in my opinion, one of the things that a John Proctor would rebel against, for the time of the armed camp had almost passed, and since the country was reasonably—although not wholly—safe, the old disciplines were beginning to rankle. But, as in all such matters, the issue was not clear-cut, for danger was still a possibility, and in unity still lay the best promise of safety.

The edge of the wilderness was close by. The American continent stretched endlessly west, and it was full of mystery for them. It stood, dark and threatening, over their shoulders night and day, for out of it Indian tribes marauded from time to time, and Reverend Parris had parishioners who had lost relatives to these heathen.

The parochial snobbery of these people was partly responsible for their failure to convert the Indians. Probably they also preferred to take land from heathens rather than from fellow Christians. At any rate, very few Indians were converted, and the Salem folk believed that the virgin forest was the Devil's last preserve, his home base and the citadel of his final stand. To the best of their knowledge the American forest was the last place on earth that was not paying homage to God.

For these reasons, among others, they carried about an air of innate resistance, even of persecution. Their fathers had, of course, been persecuted in England. So now they and their church found it necessary to deny any other sect its freedom, lest their New Jerusalem[3] be defiled and corrupted by wrong ways and deceitful ideas.

They believed, in short, that they held in their steady hands the candle that would light the world. We have inherited this belief, and it has helped and hurt us. It helped them with the discipline it gave them. They were a dedicated folk, by and large, and they had to be to survive the life they had chosen or been born into in this country.

The proof of their belief's value to them may be taken from the opposite character of the first Jamestown settlement, farther south, in Virginia. The Englishmen who landed there were motivated mainly by a hunt for profit. They had thought to pick off the wealth of the new country and then return rich to England. They were a band of individualists, and a much more ingratiating group than the Massachusetts men. But Virginia destroyed them. Massachusetts tried to kill off the Puritans, but they combined; they set up a communal society which, in the beginning, was little more than an armed camp with an autocratic and very devoted leadership. It was, however, an autocracy by consent, for they were united from top to bottom by a commonly held ideology whose perpetuation was the reason and justification for all their sufferings. So their self-denial, their purposefulness, their suspicion of all vain pursuits, their hard-handed justice, were altogether perfect instruments for the conquest of this space so antagonistic to man.

But the people of Salem in 1692 were not quite the dedicated folk that arrived on the *Mayflower*. A vast differentiation had taken place, and in their own time a revolution had unseated the royal government and substituted a junta which was at this

---

3. **New Jerusalem:** in Christianity, a heavenly city and the last resting place of the souls saved by Jesus. It was considered the ideal city, and Puritans modeled their communities after it.

DIFFERENTIATED INSTRUCTION

FOR STRATEGIC READERS

Concept Support Make sure students understand the symbolic importance of the forest. Point to details in the left column that indicate that the Puritans thought that only they had true belief in God. Help students make the connection between the forest, the Native Americans (who sometimes attacked from the forest and who generally were not Christians), and the Devil. Elicit that the forest represented things that are mysterious and evil.

FOR ENGLISH LEARNERS

Related Vocabulary Make sure students understand that some charges of witchcraft originated in a desire for revenge rather than in a fear of Satan. Discuss these interrelated terms from the concluding paragraph of the mini-essay:

- *Long-held hatreds,* "Bitter resentments toward others that people refuse to resolve"

- *vengeance,* "harmful, punishing action taken against someone who has harmed you"

- *Land-lust,* "A deep desire to own a neighbor's land"

- *constant bickering,* "arguing continuously about unimportant matters"

- *cry witch,* "to accuse someone of being a witch"

- *Old scores,* "Complaints or resentment that people have had for a long time"

- *envy of the miserable,* "the jealousy that unhappy people feel toward happy people" moment in power.[4] The times, to their eyes, must have been out of joint, and to the common folk must have seemed as insoluble and complicated as do ours today. It is not hard to see how easily many could have been led to believe that the time of confusion had been brought upon them by deep and darkling forces. No hint of such speculation appears on the court record, but social disorder in any age breeds such mystical suspicions, and when, as in Salem, wonders are brought forth from below the social surface, it is too much to expect people to hold back very long from laying on the victims with all the force of their frustrations.

The Salem tragedy, which is about to begin in these pages, developed from a paradox. It is a paradox in whose grip we still live, and there is no prospect yet that we will discover its resolution. Simply, it was this: for good purposes, even high purposes, the people of Salem developed a theocracy, a combine of state and religious power whose function was to keep the community together, and to prevent any kind of disunity that might open it to destruction by material or ideological enemies. It was forged for a necessary purpose and accomplished that purpose. But all organization is and must be grounded on the idea of exclusion and prohibition, just as two objects cannot occupy the same space. Evidently the time came in New England when the repressions of order were heavier than seemed warranted by the dangers against which the order was organized. The witch-hunt was a perverse manifestation of the panic which set in among all classes when the balance began to turn toward greater individual freedom.

When one rises above the individual villainy displayed, one can only pity them all, just as we shall be pitied someday. It is still impossible for man to organize his social life without repressions, and the balance has yet to be struck between order and freedom.

The witch-hunt was not, however, a mere repression. It was also, and as importantly, a long overdue opportunity for everyone so inclined to express publicly his guilt and sins, under the cover of accusations against the victims. It suddenly became possible—and patriotic and holy—for a man to say that Martha Corey had come into his bedroom at night, and that, while his wife was sleeping at his side, Martha laid herself down on his chest and "nearly suffocated him." Of course it was her spirit only, but his satisfaction at confessing himself was no lighter than if it had been Martha herself. One could not ordinarily speak such things in public.

Long-held hatreds of neighbors could now be openly expressed, and vengeance taken, despite the Bible's charitable injunctions. Land-lust which had been expressed before by constant bickering over boundaries and deeds, could now be elevated to the arena of morality; one could cry witch against one's neighbor and feel perfectly justified in the bargain. Old scores could be settled on a plane of heavenly combat between Lucifer and the Lord; suspicions and the envy of the miserable toward the happy could and did burst out in the general revenge.

＊ ＊ ＊ ＊ ＊

1   (Reverend Parris *is praying now, and, though we cannot hear his words, a sense of his confusion hangs about him. He mumbles, then seems about to weep; then he weeps, then prays again; but his daughter does not stir on the bed.*

   The door opens, and his Negro slave enters. Tituba *is in her forties.* Parris *brought her with him from Barbados, where he spent some years as a merchant before entering the ministry. She enters as one does who*
10 *can no longer bear to be barred from the sight of her beloved, but she is also very frightened because her slave sense has warned her that, as always, trouble in this house eventually lands on her back.*)

   Tituba (*already taking a step backward*). My Betty be hearty soon?

---

4. **a junta** (hŏŏn´tə) **. . . power:** *Junta* is a Spanish term meaning "a small, elite ruling council." The reference here is to the group that led England's Glorious Revolution of 1688–1689.

● **CONVENTIONS OF DRAMA**

Lines 19–27 are a blend of stage directions and dialogue. Which words does Parris speak in these lines? *Answer: Parris says, "Out of my sight! Out of my— . . . Oh, my God! God help me! . . . Betty. Child. Dear child. Will you wake, will you open up your eyes! Betty, little one . . . ."*

Lines 57–59
REINFORCE *KEY IDEA:* HYSTERIA

Discuss What role do you think rumor has in the creation of **hysteria** in a community? *Possible answer: Rumor may be the first step in the creation of a hysterical response. Rumors often consist of falsehoods that are embellished in ways that trigger people's fears and then are taken as fact as the rumor spreads. The fear or fanaticism triggered by rumors can contribute to a community's frenzied response to an issue.*

Parris. Out of here!

Tituba (*backing to the door*). My Betty not goin' die . . .

20 **Parris** (*scrambling to his feet in a fury*). Out of my sight! (*She is gone.*) Out of my—(*He is overcome with sobs. He clamps his teeth against them and closes the door and leans against it, exhausted.*) Oh, my God! God help me! (*Quaking with fear, mumbling to himself through his sobs, he goes to the bed and gently takes* Betty's *hand.*) Betty. Child. Dear child. Will you wake, will you open up your eyes! Betty, little one . . .

(*He is bending to kneel again when his niece,* Abigail Williams, *seventeen, enters—a strikingly beautiful girl,* 30 *an orphan, with an endless capacity for **dissembling.** Now she is all worry and apprehension and propriety.*)

Abigail. Uncle? (*He looks to her.*) Susanna Walcott's here from Doctor Griggs.

Parris. Oh? Let her come, let her come.

Abigail (*leaning out the door to call to* Susanna, *who is down the hall a few steps*). Come in, Susanna.

(Susanna Walcott, *a little younger than* Abigail, *a nervous, hurried girl, enters.*)

Parris (*eagerly*). What does the doctor say, child?

40 **Susanna** (*craning around* Parris *to get a look at* Betty). He bid me come and tell you, reverend sir, that he cannot discover no medicine for it in his books.

Parris. Then he must search on.

Susanna. Aye, sir, he have been searchin' his books since he left you, sir. But he bid me tell you, that you might look to unnatural things for the cause of it.

Parris (*his eyes going wide*). No—no. There be no unnatural cause here. Tell him I have sent for Reverend Hale of Beverly, and Mr. Hale will surely con-50 firm that. Let him look to medicine and put out all thought of unnatural causes here. There be none.

Susanna. Aye, sir. He bid me tell you. (*She turns to go.*)

Abigail. Speak nothin' of it in the village, Susanna.

Parris. Go directly home and speak nothing of unnatural causes.

Susanna. Aye, sir. I pray for her. (*She goes out.*)

Abigail. Uncle, the rumor of witchcraft is all about; I think you'd best go down and deny it yourself. The parlor's packed with people, sir. I'll sit with her.

60 **Parris** (*pressed, turns on her*). And what shall I say to them? That my daughter and my niece I discovered dancing like heathen in the forest?

Abigail. Uncle, we did dance; let you tell them I confessed it—and I'll be whipped if I must be. But they're speakin' of witchcraft. Betty's not witched.

Parris. Abigail, I cannot go before the congregation when I know you have not opened with me. What did you do with her in the forest?

Abigail. We did dance, uncle, and when you leaped 70 out of the bush so suddenly, Betty was frightened and then she fainted. And there's the whole of it.

Parris. Child. Sit you down.

Abigail (*quavering, as she sits*). I would never hurt Betty. I love her dearly.

Parris. Now look you, child, your punishment will come in its time. But if you trafficked with[5] spirits in the forest I must know it now, for surely my enemies will, and they will ruin me with it.

Abigail. But we never conjured spirits.

80 **Parris.** Then why can she not move herself since midnight? This child is desperate! (Abigail *lowers her eyes.*) It must come out—my enemies will bring it out. Let me know what you done there. Abigail, do you understand that I have many enemies?

Abigail. I have heard of it, uncle.

Parris. There is a faction that is sworn to drive me from my pulpit. Do you understand that?

Abigail. I think so, sir.

Parris. Now then, in the midst of such disruption, 90 my own household is discovered to be the very center of some obscene practice. Abominations are done in the forest—

---

5. **trafficked with:** met with.

DIFFERENTIATED INSTRUCTION

FOR STRATEGIC READERS

Paraphrasing Puritan English Have students reread lines 47–51. Then model how to paraphrase lines 47–48: *No—no. Nothing supernatural is happening here.* Ask students to paraphrase lines 50–51. ***Possible answer:** The doctor should keep looking for the right medicine and forget the idea that there is a supernatural cause [for Betty's condition]. There is no such cause.*

FOR ENGLISH LEARNERS

Vocabulary: Outdated Forms Remind students that Miller crafted authentic language for his characters that differs from modern English. Provide these terms and definitions for students. Then have them paraphrase the lines in more modern English.

• *bid me come* (line 41), "asked me to come"

• *let you tell* (line 63), "please tell"

• *witched* (line 65), "bewitched," "possessed"

• *opened with me* (line 67), "told me the truth"

Winona Ryder as Abigail Williams

READING SKILL

■ DRAW CONCLUSIONS ABOUT CHARACTERS

What do the stage directions in line 73 tell you about how Abigail is feeling? Explain. *Possible answer: The stage directions describe Abigail as "quavering," or shaking. She seems anxious about her cousin Betty's health and nervous about discussing what she and Betty did in the forest.*

READING SKILL

■ DRAW CONCLUSIONS ABOUT CHARACTERS

Parris expresses concern for his daughter, but his comments to Abigail suggest that he has another motive for wanting to know what happened in the forest. What does his conversation with Abigail suggest about his personality? *Possible answer: The conversation suggests that Parris is self-interested, concerned mainly about his reputation in the village. He also may be difficult to get along with, because he is on the verge of losing his job (lines 86–87). He may be pressuring Abigail for a full, truthful report so that he can counter charges that enemies may make against him.*

FOR ENGLISH LEARNERS

Key Academic Vocabulary Use New Word Analysis to teach these words: *capacity* (line 30), *consult* (line 541), *contract* (line 594), *plus* (line 603), *definite* (line 754), *process* (line 953).

 BEST PRACTICES TOOLKIT—Transparency New Word Analysis p. E8

FOR ADVANCED LEARNERS/AP

Analyze Dialogue and Stage Directions Have students reread Parris's conversation with Abigail in lines 57–151, envisioning Parris's movement around the stage, tone of voice, and so on. Then ask pairs of students to collaborate on a detailed set of stage directions that present their ideas in the form of instructions to an actor. Students might consider questions such as these:

- How do Parris's tone and gestures change when he talks about his enemies (beginning at line 78)?
- When Parris talks about Abigail's "name in the town" (beginning at line 127), does he move closer to her, or farther away?

After students have presented a reading that illustrates their stage directions, discuss whether Miller's limited stage directions make the actor's work more difficult or free him to interpret the role as he wishes.

■ DRAW CONCLUSIONS ABOUT CHARACTERS

What conclusions can you draw about Abigail's character, given Parris's remarks and her responses in lines 131–147? *Possible answer: The reader can conclude that Abigail is a proud young woman. She refuses work that she considers too lowly and is quick to defend herself against the charge of being "soiled" (lines 137–139 and 149–151). Abigail also may be a troublemaker: Since Goody Proctor fired her, no one else has wanted to hire her (lines 140–145).*

Lines 158–166
REINFORCE *KEY IDEA:* HYSTERIA

Discuss How might comments like the ones that Mrs. Putnam makes in these lines contribute to a sense of **hysteria** among the townsfolk? *Possible answer: Mrs. Putnam's comments repeat a rumor, and rumors often fuel hysteria. If the rumor is true, there may be cause for fear, because supernatural powers are at work. If the rumor is untrue, such comments are still dangerous because people sometimes believe the worst, even if they suspect that the information is false. Such willingness to think irrationally can lead to hysterical behavior.*

Abigail. It were sport, uncle!

Parris (*pointing at* Betty). You call this sport? (*She lowers her eyes. He pleads.*) Abigail, if you know something that may help the doctor, for God's sake tell it to me. (*She is silent.*) I saw Tituba waving her arms over the fire when I came on you. Why was she doing that? And I heard a screeching and gibberish
100 coming from her mouth. She were swaying like a dumb beast over that fire!

Abigail. She always sings her Barbados songs, and we dance.

Parris. I cannot blink what I saw, Abigail, for my enemies will not blink it. I saw a dress lying on the grass.

Abigail (*innocently*). A dress?

Parris (*It is very hard to say*). Aye, a dress. And I thought I saw—someone naked running through the trees!

110 **Abigail** (*in terror*). No one was naked! You mistake yourself, uncle!

Parris (*with anger*). I saw it! (*He moves from her. Then, resolved*) Now tell me true, Abigail. And I pray you feel the weight of truth upon you, for now my ministry's at stake, my ministry and perhaps your cousin's life. Whatever abomination you have done, give me all of it now, for I dare not be taken unaware when I go before them down there.

120 **Abigail.** There is nothin' more. I swear it, uncle.

Parris (*studies her, then nods, half convinced*). Abigail, I have fought here three long years to bend these stiff-necked people to me, and now, just now when some good respect is rising for me in the parish, you compromise my very character. I have given you a home, child, I have put clothes upon your back—now give me upright answer. Your name in the town—it is entirely white, is it not?

Abigail (*with an edge of resentment*). Why, I am sure
130 it is, sir. There be no blush about my name.[6]

---

6. **There be . . . my name:** There is nothing wrong with my reputation.
7. **Goody:** short for *Goodwife*, the Puritan equivalent of *Mrs.*

Parris (*to the point*). Abigail, is there any other cause than you have told me, for your being discharged from Goody[7] Proctor's service? I have heard it said, and I tell you as I heard it, that she comes so rarely to the church this year for she will not sit so close to something soiled. What signified that remark?

Abigail. She hates me, uncle, she must, for I would not be her slave. It's a bitter woman, a lying, cold, sniveling woman, and I will not work for such a woman!

140 **Parris.** She may be. And yet it has troubled me that you are now seven month out of their house, and in all this time no other family has ever called for your service.

Abigail. They want slaves, not such as I. Let them send to Barbados for that. I will not black my face for any of them! (*with ill-concealed resentment at him*) Do you begrudge my bed, uncle?

Parris. No—no.

Abigail (*in a temper*). My name is good in the vil-
150 lage! I will not have it said my name is soiled! Goody Proctor is a gossiping liar!

(*Enter Mrs. Ann Putnam. She is a twisted soul of forty-five, a death-ridden woman, haunted by dreams.*)

Parris (*as soon as the door begins to open*). No—no, I cannot have anyone. (*He sees her, and a certain* **deference** *springs into him, although his worry remains.*) Why, Goody Putnam, come in.

Mrs. Putnam (*full of breath, shiny-eyed*). It is a marvel. It is surely a stroke of hell upon you.

160 **Parris.** No, Goody Putnam, it is—

Mrs. Putnam (*glancing at* Betty). How high did she fly, how high?

Parris. No, no, she never flew—

Mrs. Putnam (*very pleased with it*). Why, it's sure she did. Mr. Collins saw her goin' over Ingersoll's barn, and come down light as bird, he says!

Parris. Now, look you, Goody Putnam, she never—

DIFFERENTIATED INSTRUCTION

FOR ADVANCED LEARNERS/AP

Analyze Stage Directions Ask students to focus on the description of Mrs. Putnam that appears in the stage directions in lines 152–153. Have students write a description or draw an illustration to indicate what they think Mrs. Putnam looks like. Have students compare descriptions or drawings to see if there are any common elements. Then instruct students to write a brief character sketch about Mrs. Putnam's life and personal-

ity, based on Miller's stage directions. (For example, why might she have a "twisted soul"? What cause would she have to be "death-ridden" and "haunted by dreams"?) Invite students to share their ideas with the class; then urge them to keep reading to see whether their ideas are verified as the story unfolds.

(*Enter* Thomas Putnam, *a well-to-do, hard-handed landowner, near fifty.*) Oh, good morning, Mr. Putnam.

170 **Putnam.** It is a providence the thing is out now! It is a providence. (*He goes directly to the bed.*)

Parris. What's out, sir, what's—?

(*Mrs. Putnam goes to the bed.*)

Putnam (*looking down at* Betty). Why, *her* eyes is closed! Look you, Ann.

Mrs. Putnam. Why, that's strange. (*to* Parris) Ours is open.

Parris (*shocked*). Your Ruth is sick?

180 **Mrs. Putnam** (*with vicious certainty*). I'd not call it sick; the Devil's touch is heavier than sick. It's death, y'know, it's death drivin' into them, forked and hoofed.

Parris. Oh, pray not! Why, how does Ruth ail?

Mrs. Putnam. She ails as she must—she never waked this morning, but her eyes open and she walks, and hears naught, sees naught, and cannot eat. Her soul is taken, surely.

(Parris *is struck.*)

190 **Putnam** (*as though for further details*). They say you've sent for Reverend Hale of Beverly?

Parris (*with dwindling conviction now*). A precaution only. He has much experience in all demonic arts, and I—

Mrs. Putnam. He has indeed; and found a witch in Beverly last year, and let you remember that.

Parris. Now, Goody Ann, they only thought that were a witch, and I am certain there be no element of witchcraft here.

200 **Putnam.** No witchcraft! Now look you, Mr. Parris—

Parris. Thomas, Thomas, I pray you, leap not to witchcraft. I know that you—you least of all, Thomas, would ever wish so disastrous a charge laid upon me. We cannot leap to witchcraft. They will howl me out of Salem for such corruption in my house.

---

8. **fought the Indians at Narragansett:** The Puritans fought a series of battles against the Narragansett Indians over territory that both groups had settled on.

A word about Thomas Putnam. He was a man with many grievances, at least one of which appears justified. Some time before, his wife's brother-in-law, James Bayley, had been turned down as minister of Salem. Bayley had all the qualifications, and a two-thirds vote into the bargain, but a faction stopped his acceptance, for reasons that are not clear.

Thomas Putnam was the eldest son of the richest man in the village. He had fought the Indians at Narragansett,[8] and was deeply interested in parish affairs. He undoubtedly felt it poor payment that the village should so blatantly disregard his candidate for one of its more important offices, especially since he regarded himself as the intellectual superior of most of the people around him.

His vindictive nature was demonstrated long before the witchcraft began. Another former Salem minister, George Burroughs, had had to borrow money to pay for his wife's funeral, and, since the parish was remiss in his salary, he was soon bankrupt. Thomas and his brother John had Burroughs jailed for debts the man did not owe. The incident is important only in that Burroughs succeeded in becoming minister where Bayley, Thomas Putnam's brother-in-law, had been rejected; the motif of resentment is clear here. Thomas Putnam felt that his own name and the honor of his family had been smirched by the village, and he meant to right matters however he could.

Another reason to believe him a deeply embittered man was his attempt to break his father's will, which left a disproportionate amount to a stepbrother. As with every other public cause in which he tried to force his way, he failed in this.

So it is not surprising to find that so many accusations against people are in the handwriting of Thomas Putnam, or that his name is so often found as a witness **corroborating** the supernatural testimony, or that his daughter led the crying-out at the most opportune junctures of the trials, especially when—But we'll speak of that when we come to it.

Lines 190–205
TIERED DISCUSSION PROMPTS

Use these prompts to help students understand the characters' growing concerns about witchcraft:

Connect Think about a time when you or someone you know tried but failed to change someone's opinion. How might it feel to have your argument rejected—and to know that the other person continues to hold a view that you do not? *Students should note the frustration and possible suspicion that both parties might feel in such a situation.*

Analyze Why does Parris speak "with dwindling conviction now" (line 192)? *Possible answer: Parris realizes that people know that he has asked Reverend Hale to come to Salem (lines 190–191). The realization may weaken his confidence that witchcraft is not involved in the girls' condition.* Why does Parris try to change the Putnams' view about witchcraft at this point? *Possible answer: Parris wants to win the Putnams to his side before Hale arrives, to minimize the chance that he will be forced to leave Salem (lines 201–205).*

Synthesize On the basis of what you have learned about these characters so far, what do you think is the significance of Mrs. Putnam's observation that Reverend Hale "found a witch in Beverly last year" (lines 195–196)? *Possible answer: The observation is significant because it foreshadows the finding of witches in Salem.*

FOR STRATEGIC READERS

Explore Cause and Effect Help students grasp the key points of Miller's discussion of Thomas Putnam. Summarize the main idea—namely, that Putnam will be a "problem" character because he has complaints against many people of Salem. Then work with students to complete a cause-and-effect diagram that notes Putnam's chief complaints and their effect.

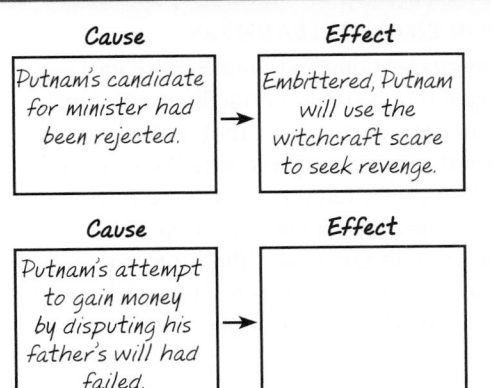

Cause		Effect
Putnam's candidate for minister had been rejected.	→	Embittered, Putnam will use the witchcraft scare to seek revenge.

Cause		Effect
Putnam's attempt to gain money by disputing his father's will had failed.	→	

FOR ENGLISH LEARNERS

Vocabulary: Multiple-Meaning Words Explain that some words have more than one meaning and that students must determine the appropriate definition for a given use. Have students use a dictionary and context clues to figure out the meaning of *sport* (line 93), *dumb* (line 101), *compromise* (line 125), *white* (line 128), *discharged* (line 132), *cold* (line 138), *element* (line 198), *pray* (line 201).

● CONVENTIONS OF DRAMA

According to the stage directions in lines 206–208, why does Putnam continue to talk about witches? ***Possible answer: Putnam continues to talk because he wants to cause Parris's downfall in the community. Putnam seeks revenge because his relative was not chosen to be the town's minister.***

Extend the Discussion Given this information, how might you interpret Putnam's advice to Parris in lines 249–251 and 272–276?

◆ GRAMMAR AND STYLE

Use Realistic Dialogue Miller used examples of writing from the late 17th century as models for his writing; he wanted the characters' language and sentence structures to sound realistic for that time period. Reread lines 272–282. What repeated phrase sounds dated? ***Answer: "Let you" (lines 272, 277).*** What word choice adds to the realism in line 281? ***Answer: the contraction "d'y'hear."*** In what sense is "Now look you, sir" (line 272) an example of an inverted sentence? ***Possible answer: Speakers of modern English would probably say, "Now [you] look, sir."***

Putnam (*At the moment he is intent upon getting* Parris, *for whom he has only contempt, to move toward the abyss*). Mr. Parris, I have taken your part in all contention here, and I would continue; but I cannot
210 if you hold back in this. There are hurtful, vengeful spirits layin' hands on these children.

Parris. But, Thomas, you cannot—

Putnam. Ann! Tell Mr. Parris what you have done.

Mrs. Putnam. Reverend Parris, I have laid seven babies unbaptized in the earth. Believe me, sir, you never saw more hearty babies born. And yet, each would wither in my arms the very night of their birth. I have spoke nothin', but my heart has clamored intimations.[9] And now, this year, my Ruth, my only—I see her turning
220 strange. A secret child she has become this year, and shrivels like a sucking mouth were pullin' on her life too. And so I thought to send her to your Tituba—

Parris. To Tituba! What may Tituba—?

Mrs. Putnam. Tituba knows how to speak to the dead, Mr. Parris.

Parris. Goody Ann, it is a formidable sin to conjure up the dead!

Mrs. Putnam. I take it on my soul, but who else may surely tell us what person murdered my babies?

230 **Parris** (*horrified*). Woman!

Mrs. Putnam. They were murdered, Mr. Parris! And mark this proof! Mark it! Last night my Ruth were ever so close to their little spirits; I know it, sir. For how else is she struck dumb now except some power of darkness would stop her mouth? It is a marvelous sign, Mr. Parris!

Putnam. Don't you understand it, sir? There is a murdering witch among us, bound to keep herself in the dark. (Parris *turns to* Betty, *a frantic terror rising*
240 *in him*.) Let your enemies make of it what they will, you cannot blink it more.

Parris (*to* Abigail). Then you were conjuring spirits last night.

Abigail (*whispering*). Not I, sir—Tituba and Ruth.

Parris (*turns now, with new fear, and goes to* Betty, *looks down at her, and then, gazing off*). Oh, Abigail, what proper payment for my charity! Now I am undone.

Putnam. You are not undone! Let you take hold
250 here. Wait for no one to charge you—declare it yourself. You have discovered witchcraft—

Parris. In my house? In my house, Thomas? They will topple me with this! They will make of it a— (*Enter* Mercy Lewis, *the Putnams' servant, a fat, sly, merciless girl of eighteen.*)

Mercy. Your pardons. I only thought to see how Betty is.

Putnam. Why aren't you home? Who's with Ruth?

Mercy. Her grandma come. She's improved a little,
260 I think—she give a powerful sneeze before.

Mrs. Putnam. Ah, there's a sign of life!

Mercy. I'd fear no more, Goody Putnam. It were a grand sneeze; another like it will shake her wits together, I'm sure. (*She goes to the bed to look.*)

Parris. Will you leave me now, Thomas? I would pray a while alone.

Abigail. Uncle, you've prayed since midnight. Why do you not go down and—

Parris. No—no. (*to* Putnam) I have no answer for
270 that crowd. I'll wait till Mr. Hale arrives. (*to get* Mrs. Putnam *to leave*) If you will, Goody Ann . . .

Putnam. Now look you, sir. Let you strike out against the Devil, and the village will bless you for it! Come down, speak to them—pray with them. They're thirsting for your word, Mister! Surely you'll pray with them.

Parris (*swayed*). I'll lead them in a psalm, but let you say nothing of witchcraft yet. I will not discuss it. The cause is yet unknown. I have had enough con-
280 tention since I came; I want no more.

Mrs. Putnam. Mercy, you go home to Ruth, d'y'hear?

Mercy. Aye, mum.

(Mrs. Putnam *goes out.*)

---

9. **clamored intimations** (klăm'ərd ĭn'tə-mā'shənz): nagging suspicions.

DIFFERENTIATED INSTRUCTION

FOR ENGLISH LEARNERS

Language: Conversational English Patterns
Explain that some contractions in the text, especially contractions that replace the final *g* in the *-ing* ending, recreate the sound of informal, excited speech. Point out these examples: *layin'* (line 211), *nothin'* (line 218), *pullin'* (line 221), *beatin'* (line 296), *comin'* (line 299), *talkin'* (line 312), *callin'* (line 313), *hangin'* (line 317), *dancin'* (line 319).

Parris (*to* Abigail). If she starts for the window, cry for me at once.

Abigail. I will, uncle.

Parris (*to* Putnam). There is a terrible power in her arms today. (*He goes out with* Putnam.)

Abigail (*with hushed* **trepidation**). How is Ruth sick?

290 **Mercy.** It's weirdish, I know not—she seems to walk like a dead one since last night.

Abigail (*turns at once and goes to* Betty, *and now, with fear in her voice*). Betty? (Betty *doesn't move. She shakes her.*) Now stop this! Betty! Sit up now!

(Betty *doesn't stir.* Mercy *comes over.*)

Mercy. Have you tried beatin' her? I gave Ruth a good one and it waked her for a minute. Here, let me have her.

Abigail (*holding* Mercy *back*). No, he'll be comin' up.

300 Listen, now; if they be questioning us, tell them we danced—I told him as much already.

Mercy. Aye. And what more?

Abigail. He knows Tituba conjured Ruth's sisters to come out of the grave.

Mercy. And what more?

Abigail. He saw you naked.

Mercy (*clapping her hands together with a frightened laugh*). Oh, Jesus!

(*Enter* Mary Warren, *breathless. She is seventeen,*
310 *a* **subservient**, *naive, lonely girl.*)

Mary Warren. What'll we do? The village is out! I just come from the farm; the whole country's talkin' witchcraft! They'll be callin' us witches, Abby!

Mercy (*pointing and looking at* Mary Warren). She means to tell, I know it.

Mary Warren. Abby, we've got to tell. Witchery's a hangin' error, a hangin' like they done in Boston two year ago! We must tell the truth, Abby! You'll only be whipped for dancin', and the other things!

320 **Abigail.** Oh, *we'll* be whipped!

Mary Warren. I never done none of it, Abby. I only looked!

(2)

Villagers gathering to gossip

THE CRUCIBLE: ACT ONE **143**

BACKGROUND

The Execution of Goody Glover Mary Warren's comment in lines 317–318 may refer to the execution of Ann "Goody" Glover, an Irish washerwoman who was hanged as a witch in Boston in 1688. Glover's case was widely publicized in an influential book published in 1689 *Memorable Providences, Relating to Witchcrafts and Possessions* by the famous Boston minister, Cotton Mather. Scholars have discovered that the "real" Samuel Parris actually kept a copy of Mather's book in his library.

Targeted Passage

ANALYZE VISUALS

Activity Take a close look at this photograph from the 1996 film version of *The Crucible*. From what you can see of the body language and facial expressions of the people, what do you think is the mood of this crowd? Does it match the mood of the text? Explain. ***Possible answer:*** *The mood seems tense; the people seem nearly frantic. Distressed expressions appear on many faces; and some people seem to be weeping, praying, or crying out. Their bodies turn in all directions, and everyone seems to be talking at once; these details contribute to the agitated mood.*

FOR STRATEGIC READERS

(2) **Targeted Passage [Lines 309–322]**

This passage reveals the growing speculation and the girls' differing responses to it.

- According to Mary, who is talking about witchcraft?

- On the basis of Mercy's comment, what do you think the girls had planned to do? Why is that plan not working?

- What does Mary want the girls to do? Why? How will that plan benefit her?

Concept Support Direct students to the departure of Mrs. Putnam (line 283) and of Reverend Parris and Mr. Putnam (line 288). Elicit that when Abigail and Mercy are left alone, they immediately start talking about Betty and the overall situation. As you discuss the scene (lines 289–372), lead students to grasp (1) the increasingly frantic tone of their comments and (2) their mutual accusations, which foreshadow even greater accusations as the play continues.

■ DRAW CONCLUSIONS ABOUT CHARACTERS

What new conclusions can you draw about Abigail, given her comments in lines 353–364? *Possible answer: Abigail is a take-charge person, for she dominates the conversation. Her threats to harm the other girls if they do not support her story (lines 355–363) reveal that she is intimidating to the point of being cruel.*

If students need help . . . Work through the passage, sentence by sentence. Help students choose at least one revealing comment to add to the chart on page 131.

Extend the Discussion How did Abigail's parents die? How might that information affect your thinking about her personality?

● CONVENTIONS OF DRAMA

On the basis of Miller's mini-essay, what role do you think John Proctor will play: hero, villain, major figure, minor figure, foil (character used as a contrast to another character)? Explain. *Possible answer: Proctor will be a major character, perhaps even the hero. Miller indicates that Proctor has integrity and is strong and even-tempered. These traits could be called "heroic." Furthermore, Miller says that Proctor has "a sharp and biting way with hypocrites" and that he is "not easily led." These traits could put him in conflict with major figures in the story.*

Mercy (*moving menacingly toward* Mary). Oh, you're a great one for lookin', aren't you, Mary Warren? What a grand peeping courage you have!

(Betty, *on the bed, whimpers.* Abigail *turns to her at once.*)

Abigail. Betty? (*She goes to* Betty.) Now, Betty, dear, wake up now. It's Abigail. (*She sits* Betty *up and* 330 *furiously shakes her.*) I'll beat you, Betty! (Betty *whimpers.*) My, you seem improving. I talked to your papa and I told him everything. So there's nothing to—

Betty (*darts off the bed, frightened of* Abigail, *and flattens herself against the wall*). I want my mama!

Abigail (*with alarm, as she cautiously approaches* Betty). What ails you, Betty? Your mama's dead and buried.

Betty. I'll fly to Mama. Let me fly! (*She raises her arms as though to fly, and streaks for the window, gets* 340 *one leg out.*)

Abigail (*pulling her away from the window*). I told him everything; he knows now, he knows everything we—

Betty. You drank blood, Abby! You didn't tell him that!

Abigail. Betty, you never say that again! You will never—

Betty. You did, you did! You drank a charm to kill John Proctor's wife! You drank a charm to kill Goody Proctor!

Abigail (*smashes her across the face*). Shut it! Now 350 shut it!

Betty (*collapsing on the bed*). Mama, Mama! (*She dissolves into sobs.*)

Abigail. Now look you. All of you. We danced. And Tituba conjured Ruth Putnam's dead sisters. And that is all. And mark this. Let either of you breathe a word, or the edge of a word, about the other things, and I will come to you in the black of some terrible night and I will bring a pointy reckoning that will shudder you.[10] And you know I can do it; I saw 360 Indians smash my dear parents' heads on the pillow next to mine, and I have seen some reddish work done at night, and I can make you wish you had never seen the sun go down! (*She goes to* Betty *and roughly sits her up.*) Now, you—sit up and stop this!

(*But* Betty *collapses in her hands and lies inert on the bed.*)

Mary Warren (*with hysterical fright*). What's got her? (Abigail *stares in fright at* Betty.) Abby, she's going to die! It's a sin to conjure, and we—

370 **Abigail** (*starting for* Mary). I say shut it, Mary Warren!

(*Enter* John Proctor. *On seeing him,* Mary Warren *leaps in fright.*)

Proctor was a farmer in his middle thirties. He need not have been a partisan of any faction in the town, but there is evidence to suggest that he had a sharp and biting way with hypocrites. He was the kind of man—powerful of body, even-tempered, and not easily led—who cannot refuse support to partisans without drawing their deepest resentment. In Proctor's presence a fool felt his foolishness instantly—and a Proctor is always marked for calumny[11] therefore.

But as we shall see, the steady manner he displays does not spring from an untroubled soul. He is a sinner, a sinner not only against the moral fashion of the time, but against his own vision of decent conduct. These people had no ritual for the washing away of sins. It is another trait we inherited from them, and it has helped to discipline us as well as to breed hypocrisy among us. Proctor, respected and even feared in Salem, has come to regard himself as a kind of fraud. But no hint of this has yet appeared on the surface, and as he enters from the crowded parlor below it is a man in his prime we see, with a quiet confidence and an unexpressed, hidden force. Mary Warren, his servant, can barely speak for embarrassment and fear.

---

10. **bring . . . shudder you:** inflict a terrifying punishment on you.

11. **marked for calumny** (kǎl′əm-nē): singled out to have lies told about him.

DIFFERENTIATED INSTRUCTION

FOR ADVANCED LEARNERS/AP

Synthesize "In Proctor's presence," Miller writes, "a fool felt his foolishness instantly— and a Proctor is always marked for calumny therefore." Ask students to reflect upon those comments and to consider situations that they have experienced or read about in which they think that "a Proctor" has been present. Then have students write and share a paragraph that responds to these questions:

- What is "a Proctor"?
- What traits does a person need to make a fool feel his foolishness instantly?
- Why is this kind of person "marked for calumny" (in other words, lied about in an effort to destroy his reputation)?

Mary Warren. Oh! I'm just going home, Mr. Proctor.

Proctor. Be you foolish, Mary Warren? Be you deaf? I forbid you leave the house, did I not? Why shall I pay you? I am looking for you more often than my cows!

Mary Warren. I only come to see the great doings in the world.

Proctor. I'll show you a great doin' on your arse one
380 of these days. Now get you home; my wife is waitin' with your work! (*Trying to retain a shred of dignity, she goes slowly out.*)

Mercy Lewis (*both afraid of him and strangely titillated*). I'd best be off. I have my Ruth to watch. Good morning, Mr. Proctor.

(*Mercy sidles out. Since* Proctor's *entrance,* Abigail *has stood as though on tiptoe, absorbing his presence, wide-eyed. He glances at her, then goes to* Betty *on the bed.*)

Abigail. Gah! I'd almost forgot how strong you are,
390 John Proctor!

Proctor (*looking at* Abigail *now, the faintest suggestion of a knowing smile on his face*). What's this mischief here?

Abigail (*with a nervous laugh*). Oh, she's only gone silly somehow.

Proctor. The road past my house is a pilgrimage to Salem all morning. The town's mumbling witchcraft.

Abigail. Oh, posh! (*Winningly she comes a little closer, with a confidential, wicked air.*) We were dancin' in the woods last night, and my uncle leaped in on us.
400 She took fright, is all.

Proctor (*his smile widening*). Ah, you're wicked yet, aren't y'! (*A trill of expectant laughter escapes her, and she dares come closer, feverishly looking into his eyes.*) You'll be clapped in the stocks before you're twenty. (*He takes a step to go, and she springs into his path.*)

Abigail. Give me a word, John. A soft word. (*Her concentrated desire destroys his smile.*)

Proctor. No, no, Abby. That's done with.

Abigail (*tauntingly*). You come five mile to see a silly
410 girl fly? I know you better.

Proctor (*setting her firmly out of his path*). I come to see what mischief your uncle's brewin' now. (*with final emphasis*) Put it out of mind, Abby.

Abigail (*grasping his hand before he can release her*). John—I am waitin' for you every night.

Proctor. Abby, I never give you hope to wait for me.

Abigail (*now beginning to anger—she can't believe it*). I have something better than hope, I think!

Proctor. Abby, you'll put it out of mind. I'll not be
420 comin' for you more.

Abigail. You're surely sportin' with me.

Proctor. You know me better.

Abigail. I know how you clutched my back behind your house and sweated like a stallion whenever I come near! Or did I dream that? It's she put me out, you cannot pretend it were you. I saw your face when she put me out, and you loved me then and you do now!

Proctor. Abby, that's a wild thing to say—

430 **Abigail.** A wild thing may say wild things. But not so wild, I think. I have seen you since she put me out; I have seen you nights.

Proctor. I have hardly stepped off my farm this sevenmonth.

Abigail. I have a sense for heat, John, and yours has drawn me to my window, and I have seen you lookin' up, burning in your loneliness. Do you tell me you've never looked up at my window?

Proctor. I may have looked up.

440 **Abigail** (*now softening*). And you must. You are no wintry man. I *know* you, John. I know you. (*She is weeping.*) I cannot sleep for dreamin'; I cannot dream but I wake and walk about the house as though I'd find you comin' through some door. (*She clutches him desperately.*)

Proctor (*gently pressing her from him, with great sympathy but firmly*). Child—

Abigail (*with a flash of anger*). How do you call me child!

■ **DRAW CONCLUSIONS ABOUT CHARACTERS**

Reread the stage directions in lines 391–404. What does Proctor's facial expression reveal about his attitude toward Abigail as he first addresses her? *Possible answer: Proctor's smiling (lines 391–392 and 401) reveals that he is familiar with Abigail. The nature of that familiarity becomes clear in the dialogue that develops between them.*

Lines 401–428
TIERED DISCUSSION PROMPTS

Use these prompts to help students understand Abigail and Proctor's relationship:

Summarize Why does Abigail grow angry with Proctor? *Possible answer: Abigail wants physical intimacy with Proctor (beginning at line 402). She grows angry because he repeatedly refuses her advances (lines 408, 413, 416, 419–420, and 422).*

Analyze What caused Abigail to lose her job with the Proctors? *Possible answer: Abigail lost her job because she and Proctor had an affair. Proctor's wife ("she," line 427) learned of it, or suspected it, and sent Abigail away.*

Synthesize Why might Abigail resist Proctor's decision to end their affair? *Possible answer: Abigail has shown herself to be a quick-tempered young woman who tries to make others do what she wants. She has also displayed a streak of vindictiveness, so she may seek revenge against Proctor.*

FOR STRATEGIC READERS
Paraphrase Remind students that some of the characters' ways of speaking may seem awkward or out of date to speakers of modern English. Have students work in pairs to paraphrase Proctor's first words (lines 374–376). After volunteer pairs have shared their paraphrases with the class, discuss which version allows them to read more expressively.

FOR ENGLISH LEARNERS
Language: Conversational English Patterns
Discuss these words and phrases that Miller includes to add to the conversational feel of the dialogue on these pages: *you're a great one for lookin'* (lines 323–324); *shut it* (lines 349, 350, and 370); *Gah!* (line 389); *she's . . . gone silly* (lines 393–394); *Oh, posh!* (line 397); *aren't y'!* (line 402); *I'll not be comin' for you* (lines 419–420).

■ DRAW CONCLUSIONS ABOUT CHARACTERS

As Proctor responds to Abigail's insults about Elizabeth in lines 457–463, what do his words and the stage directions suggest about his view of his marriage? Cite evidence to explain your response. **Possible answer:** *Proctor's order that Abigail be quiet (lines 458–459) and his threat to see her punished (line 463) suggest that he wants to protect Elizabeth and their marriage. The stage directions (lines 458 and 463) verify that he indeed is angry—not only with Abigail for insulting Elizabeth, but with himself, as well (probably for having indulged in the affair in the first place).*

● CONVENTIONS OF DRAMA

Miller's mini-essays create two worlds: the world inhabited by the play's characters, and the world that contains him and his readers. Notice how this time Miller begins by speaking of "we," as if he and his readers are talking behind the characters' backs. Is Miller's strategy of inviting the reader into his confidence effective? Why or why not? **Possible answers:** *Yes, the strategy is effective, for it is exciting to be taken into the playwright's confidence. No, the fact that the mini-essays shift the play's focus might cause some readers to lose contact with the plot and characters.*

450 **Proctor.** Abby, I may think of you softly from time to time. But I will cut off my hand before I'll ever reach for you again. Wipe it out of mind. We never touched, Abby.

Abigail. Aye, but we did.

Proctor. Aye, but we did not.

Abigail (*with a bitter anger*). Oh, I marvel how such a strong man may let such a sickly wife be—

Proctor (*angered—at himself as well*). You'll speak nothin' of Elizabeth!

460 **Abigail.** She is blackening my name in the village! She is telling lies about me! She is a cold, sniveling woman, and you bend to her! Let her turn you like a—

Proctor (*shaking her*). Do you look for whippin'?

(*A psalm is heard being sung below.*)

Abigail (*in tears*). I look for John Proctor that took me from my sleep and put knowledge in my heart! I never knew what pretense Salem was, I never knew the lying lessons I was taught by all these Christian women and their covenanted[12] men! And now you 470 bid me tear the light out of my eyes? I will not, I cannot! You loved me, John Proctor, and whatever sin it is, you love me yet! (*He turns abruptly to go out. She rushes to him.*) John, pity me, pity me!

(*The words "going up to Jesus" are heard in the psalm, and* Betty *claps her ears suddenly and whines loudly.*)

Abigail. Betty? (*She hurries to* Betty, *who is now sitting up and screaming.* Proctor *goes to* Betty *as* Abigail *is trying to pull her hands down, calling* "Betty!")

Proctor (*growing unnerved*). What's she doing? Girl, 480 what ails you? Stop that wailing!

(*The singing has stopped in the midst of this, and now* Parris *rushes in.*)

Parris. What happened? What are you doing to her? Betty! (*He rushes to the bed, crying,* "Betty, Betty!" Mrs. Putnam *enters, feverish with curiosity, and with her* Thomas Putnam *and* Mercy Lewis. Parris, *at the*

bed, *keeps lightly slapping* Betty's *face, while she moans and tries to get up.*)

Abigail. She heard you singin' and suddenly she's up 490 and screamin'.

Mrs. Putnam. The psalm! The psalm! She cannot bear to hear the Lord's name!

Parris. No. God forbid. Mercy, run to the doctor! Tell him what's happened here! (*Mercy Lewis* rushes out.)

Mrs. Putnam. Mark it for a sign, mark it!

(Rebecca Nurse, *seventy-two, enters. She is white-haired, leaning upon her walking-stick.*)

Putnam (*pointing at the whimpering* Betty). That is a notorious sign of witchcraft afoot, Goody Nurse, 500 a prodigious sign!

Mrs. Putnam. My mother told me that! When they cannot bear to hear the name of—

Parris (*trembling*). Rebecca, Rebecca, go to her, we're lost. She suddenly cannot bear to hear the Lord's—

(Giles Corey, *eighty-three, enters. He is knotted with muscle, canny, inquisitive, and still powerful.*)

Rebecca. There is hard sickness here, Giles Corey, so please to keep the quiet.

Giles. I've not said a word. No one here can testify I've 510 said a word. Is she going to fly again? I hear she flies.

Putnam. Man, be quiet now!

(*Everything is quiet.* Rebecca *walks across the room to the bed. Gentleness exudes from her.* Betty *is quietly whimpering, eyes shut.* Rebecca *simply stands over the child, who gradually quiets.*)

A nd while they are so absorbed, we may put a word in for Rebecca. Rebecca was the wife of Francis Nurse, who, from all accounts, was one of those men for whom both sides of the argument had to have respect. He was called upon to arbitrate disputes as though he were an unofficial judge, and

---

12. **covenanted** (kŭv′ə-nən-tĭd): In Puritan religious practice, the men of a congregation would make an agreement, or covenant, to govern the community and abide by its beliefs and practices.

DIFFERENTIATED INSTRUCTION

FOR ENGLISH LEARNERS

Language: Cognates Point out the English word *dispute*, meaning "quarrel," which appears as *disputes* in the final line on page 146. Explain that the word derives from Latin and is similar to the Spanish *disputa*, the Italian *disputa*, and the French *dispute*. Have students who speak Latin-based languages suggest cognates for these English words that appear in the next paragraph: *suggestion, systematic, campaign, proportions.*

FOR ADVANCED LEARNERS/AP

Evaluate Plot Has Miller made it clear whether he wants the audience to believe that Betty (and, by extension, Ruth) truly is possessed by a demonic force? Have students work alone to make two lists: one stating reasons why the audience is meant to think that the girls are bewitched, and the other giving evidence that contradicts this view. Then have partners debate the question and report on the outcome.

Rebecca also enjoyed the high opinion most people had for him. By the time of the delusion,[13] they had three hundred acres, and their children were settled in separate homesteads within the same estate. However, Francis had originally rented the land, and one theory has it that, as he gradually paid for it and raised his social status, there were those who resented his rise.

Another suggestion to explain the systematic campaign against Rebecca, and inferentially against Francis, is the land war he fought with his neighbors, one of whom was a Putnam. This squabble grew to the proportions of a battle in the woods between partisans of both sides, and it is said to have lasted for two days. As for Rebecca herself, the general opinion of her character was so high that to explain how anyone dared cry her out for a witch—and more, how adults could bring themselves to lay hands on her—we must look to the fields and boundaries of that time.

As we have seen, Thomas Putnam's man for the Salem ministry was Bayley. The Nurse clan had been in the faction that prevented Bayley's taking office. In addition, certain families allied to the Nurses by blood or friendship, and whose farms were contiguous with the Nurse farm or close to it, combined to break away from the Salem town authority and set up Topsfield, a new and independent entity whose existence was resented by old Salemites.

That the guiding hand behind the outcry was Putnam's is indicated by the fact that, as soon as it began, this Topsfield-Nurse faction absented themselves from church in protest and disbelief. It was Edward and Jonathan Putnam who signed the first complaint against Rebecca; and Thomas Putnam's little daughter was the one who fell into a fit at the hearing and pointed to Rebecca as her attacker. To top it all, Mrs. Putnam—who is now staring at the bewitched child on the bed—soon accused Rebecca's spirit of "tempting her to **iniquity**," a charge that had more truth in it than Mrs. Putnam could know.

---

13. **the time of the delusion:** the era of the witchcraft accusations and trials.

14. **wardens:** officers appointed to keep order.

Mrs. Putnam (*astonished*). What have you done?

(*Rebecca, in thought, now leaves the bedside and sits.*)

Parris (*wondrous and relieved*). What do you make of it, Rebecca?

520 **Putnam** (*eagerly*). Goody Nurse, will you go to my Ruth and see if you can wake her?

Rebecca (*sitting*). I think she'll wake in time. Pray calm yourselves. I have eleven children, and I am twenty-six times a grandma, and I have seen them all through their silly seasons, and when it come on them they will run the Devil bowlegged keeping up with their mischief. I think she'll wake when she tires of it. A child's spirit is like a child, you can never catch it by running after it; you must stand

530 still, and, for love, it will soon itself come back.

Proctor. Aye, that's the truth of it, Rebecca.

Mrs. Putnam. This is no silly season, Rebecca. My Ruth is bewildered, Rebecca; she cannot eat.

Rebecca. Perhaps she is not hungered yet. (*to Parris*) I hope you are not decided to go in search of loose spirits, Mr. Parris. I've heard promise of that outside.

Parris. A wide opinion's running in the parish that the Devil may be among us, and I would satisfy them that they are wrong.

540 **Proctor.** Then let you come out and call them wrong. Did you consult the wardens[14] before you called this minister to look for devils?

Parris. He is not coming to look for devils!

Proctor. Then what's he coming for?

Putnam. There be children dyin' in the village, Mister!

Proctor. I seen none dyin'. This society will not be a bag to swing around your head, Mr. Putnam. (*to Parris*) Did you call a meeting before you—?

Putnam. I am sick of meetings; cannot the man turn

550 his head without he have a meeting?

Proctor. He may turn his head, but not to Hell!

Rebecca. Pray, John, be calm. (*Pause. He defers to her.*) Mr. Parris, I think you'd best send Reverend

THE CRUCIBLE: ACT ONE 147

READING SKILL

■ **DRAW CONCLUSIONS ABOUT CHARACTERS**

In what sense do Rebecca Nurse's words in lines 522–530 set her character apart from the others? *Possible answer: Rebecca Nurse's words show that she is calm in the presence of Betty. She uses past experience and reason, rather than hearsay and emotion, to think about the girl's illness.*

If students need help . . . Model the use of a Two-Column Chart to list and compare traits.

Rebecca	Other Salemites
bases reasoning on firsthand experience	base reasoning on hearsay
understanding	fearful

 BEST PRACTICES TOOLKIT—Transparency Two-Column Chart p. A25

Lines 532–552
REINFORCE *KEY IDEA*: HYSTERIA

Discuss What do these comments from Rebecca and Proctor suggest about the likelihood of their being caught up in a **hysteria** over witchcraft? *Possible answer: Their comments suggest that they are unlikely to join in the hysteria. Rebecca urges Reverend Parris not to search for "loose spirits" (lines 535–536) and advises Proctor to calm down (line 552). Proctor pushes for more open discussion of the matter (lines 540–542 and 546–548).*

FOR STRATEGIC READERS

Comprehension Support Point out that the relationship between Francis and Rebecca Nurse and Thomas Putnam is complicated and unfriendly. Using the mini-essay on this page, help students review the main reasons for the families' conflict.

LAND: Francis Nurse had a land war with a Putnam relative (past); Putnam may be among those in Salem who resent his social status (present).

MINISTRY: The Nurses successfully opposed Bayley, Putnam's choice for minister (past); Putnam may be among those in Salem who resent the Nurses' creation of Topsfield (present).

WITCHCRAFT: Rebecca Nurse is generally well respected (present), but Thomas Putnam's daughter and wife will accuse her of attacking them with witchcraft (future).

TIERED DISCUSSION PROMPTS

Use these prompts to help students explore Parris's character in greater detail:

Recall What does Reverend Parris complain about in these lines? *Answer: Parris complains that he is not properly supplied with firewood (lines 594–597 and 600–602), that he lives in relative poverty (lines 609–611), that he has not been awarded the deed to his house (lines 618–619), and that his congregation is too quick to fire its ministers (lines 624–629).*

Analyze What do Parris's complaints suggest about how he thinks of himself? Explain. *Possible answer: The complaints suggest that Parris is a proud man. He feels that he deserves the firewood, a better salary, home ownership, and greater job security—perhaps because of his education (line 604–606) or his status as a servant of God (lines 627–629).*

Synthesize How might Parris's attitude harm his ability to deal effectively with the witchcraft scare? *Possible answer: Parris's prideful comments suggest that his attention may be divided; that is, at the same time that he is trying to deal with the witchcraft scare, he also is trying to defend himself and his ministry.*

Hale back as soon as he come. This will set us all to arguin' again in the society, and we thought to have peace this year. I think we ought rely on the doctor now, and good prayer.

Mrs. Putnam. Rebecca, the doctor's baffled!

560 **Rebecca.** If so he is, then let us go to God for the cause of it. There is prodigious danger in the seeking of loose spirits. I fear it, I fear it. Let us rather blame ourselves and—

Putnam. How may we blame ourselves? I am one of nine sons; the Putnam seed have peopled this province. And yet I have but one child left of eight—and now she shrivels!

Rebecca. I cannot fathom that.

Mrs. Putnam (*with a growing edge of sarcasm*). But I must! You think it God's work you should never 570 lose a child, nor grandchild either, and I bury all but one? There are wheels within wheels in this village, and fires within fires!

Putnam (*to* Parris). When Reverend Hale comes, you will proceed to look for signs of witchcraft here.

Proctor (*to* Putnam). You cannot command Mr. Parris. We vote by name in this society, not by acreage.

Putnam. I never heard you worried so on this society, Mr. Proctor. I do not think I saw you at Sabbath meeting since snow flew.

580 **Proctor.** I have trouble enough without I come five mile to hear him preach only hellfire and bloody damnation. Take it to heart, Mr. Parris. There are many others who stay away from church these days because you hardly ever mention God any more.

Parris (*now aroused*). Why, that's a drastic charge!

Rebecca. It's somewhat true; there are many that quail to bring their children—

Parris. I do not preach for children, Rebecca. It is not the children who are unmindful of their obliga590 tions toward this ministry.

Rebecca. Are there really those unmindful?

Parris. I should say the better half of Salem village—

Putnam. And more than that!

Parris. Where is my wood? My contract provides I be supplied with all my firewood. I am waiting since November for a stick, and even in November I had to show my frostbitten hands like some London beggar!

Giles. You are allowed six pound a year to buy your wood, Mr. Parris.

600 **Parris.** I regard that six pound as part of my salary. I am paid little enough without I spend six pound on firewood.

Proctor. Sixty, plus six for firewood—

Parris. The salary is sixty-six pound, Mr. Proctor! I am not some preaching farmer with a book under my arm; I am a graduate of Harvard College.

Giles. Aye, and well instructed in arithmetic!

Parris. Mr. Corey, you will look far for a man of my kind at sixty pound a year! I am not used to this 610 poverty; I left a thrifty business in the Barbados to serve the Lord. I do not fathom it, why am I persecuted here? I cannot offer one proposition but there be a howling riot of argument. I have often wondered if the Devil be in it somewhere; I cannot understand you people otherwise.

Proctor. Mr. Parris, you are the first minister ever did demand the deed to this house—

Parris. Man! Don't a minister deserve a house to live in?

620 **Proctor.** To live in, yes. But to ask ownership is like you shall own the meeting house itself; the last meeting I were at you spoke so long on deeds and mortgages I thought it were an auction.

Parris. I want a mark of confidence, is all! I am your third preacher in seven years. I do not wish to be put out like the cat whenever some majority feels the whim. You people seem not to comprehend that a minister is the Lord's man in the parish; a minister is not to be so lightly crossed and contradicted—

630 **Putnam.** Aye!

Parris. There is either obedience or the church will burn like Hell is burning!

Proctor. Can you speak one minute without we land in Hell again? I am sick of Hell!

DIFFERENTIATED INSTRUCTION

FOR STRATEGIC READERS

Concept Support Miller complicates the plot by revealing conflicts between various Salemites. Have students work in pairs or small groups to summarize the conflict that exists between these characters:

- Rebecca vs. Mrs. Putnam (regarding Salem's sick children)
- Putnam vs. Proctor (regarding Proctor's spiritual condition)
- Proctor vs. Parris (regarding Parris's preaching)
- Giles vs. Parris (regarding Parris's salary and benefits)

Urge students to watch for ways in which these and other interpersonal conflicts grow and how they fuel the hysteria over possible witchcraft in Salem.

Scene Selection

The film scenes pictured here show
a meeting between John Proctor and
Abigail that never took place in the play,
and the girls dancing in the forest, which
occurs before the play begins. Why do
you think such scenes were left out of the
original play? Identify the advantages and
disadvantages of presenting these scenes
in the film version.

BEHIND THE CURTAIN

Scene Selection Point out that film directors
often consider the text of the play a starting point and feel free to omit or add scenes,
depending upon the story elements that they
want to emphasize. For example, adding the
scene between Proctor and Abigail clarifies
their relationship. Similarly, dramatizing the
scene in the forest shows the audience that
the girls' actions are deeply important to
the story. Note that film directors also may
add a scene primarily because it lends itself
to visual representation. ***Possible answer:***
*Miller might have chosen to avoid these scenes
because of the difficulty of staging scenes that
take place outdoors. An advantage of staging
scenes that contain such action and emotion is
that they become powerful scenes to view on
a large movie screen. A disadvantage is that
when directors present the scenes, the readers
or spectators lose the chance to create their
own visualizations of the characters and their
actions.*

FOR ADVANCED LEARNERS/AP

Create an Original Scene Ask students to
review the play and choose a scene that is
only referred to, not dramatized on stage.
Here are a few examples:

- a scene between Abigail and Elizabeth
  Proctor in which Abigail loses her job

- a scene showing Ruth Putnam and her
  mysterious illness

- a scene from the past that Miller describes
  in one of the informative mini-essays

Have students, either individually or in small
groups, write a dramatization of the chosen
scene. Remind them to include dialogue
for the characters and any stage directions
necessary to bring the scene to life. After
volunteers perform their scenes, discuss
whether each scene would contribute to or
distract from the action of the play.

Lines 638–654
TIERED DISCUSSION PROMPTS

Use these prompts to help students understand the hostility between Parris and Proctor, which here boils to the surface:

Connect Have you ever been in a situation in which someone blurted out a confession or other piece of secret information? What happened as a result of the revelation? *Accept all responses.*

Analyze What can you infer about Proctor's personality and attitudes from his remark in line 646? *Possible answer: Proctor is not easily led by others. He does not like people who abuse power in an attempt to control others. He is not afraid to say what he thinks, even if his words seem rebellious.*

Synthesize What do you think Rebecca means when she says, "You are another kind, John" (line 653)? Explain. *Possible answer: Proctor seems willing to go against the group's view; he would rather live by his own code of ethics than follow a minister who he thinks is in the wrong. Rebecca probably is referring to Proctor's individualism—a trait that she views as dangerous, which is why she urges him to make peace with Parris.*

Parris. It is not for you to say what is good for you to hear!

Proctor. I may speak my heart, I think!

Parris (*in a fury*). What, are we Quakers?[15] We are not Quakers here yet, Mr. Proctor. And you may tell
640 that to your followers!

Proctor. My followers!

Parris (*Now he's out with it*). There is a party in this church. I am not blind; there is a faction and a party.

Proctor. Against you?

Putnam. Against him and all authority!

Proctor. Why, then I must find it and join it.

(*There is shock among the others.*)

Rebecca. He does not mean that.

Putnam. He confessed it now!

650 **Proctor.** I mean it solemnly, Rebecca; I like not the smell of this "authority."

Rebecca. No, you cannot break charity[16] with your minister. You are another kind, John. Clasp his hand, make your peace.

Proctor. I have a crop to sow and lumber to drag home. (*He goes angrily to the door and turns to* Corey *with a smile.*) What say you, Giles, let's find the party. He says there's a party.

Giles. I've changed my opinion of this man, John.
660 Mr. Parris, I beg your pardon. I never thought you had so much iron in you.

Parris (*surprised*). Why, thank you, Giles!

Giles. It suggests to the mind what the trouble be among us all these years. (*to all*) Think on it. Wherefore is everybody suing everybody else? Think on it now, it's a deep thing, and dark as a pit. I have been six time in court this year—

Proctor (*familiarly, with warmth, although he knows he is approaching the edge of* Giles' *tolerance with this*).
670 Is it the Devil's fault that a man cannot say you good

morning without you clap him for defamation?[17] You're old, Giles, and you're not hearin' so well as you did.

Giles (*He cannot be crossed*). John Proctor, I have only last month collected four pound damages for you publicly sayin' I burned the roof off your house, and I—

Proctor (*laughing*). I never said no such thing, but I've paid you for it, so I hope I can call you deaf without charge. Now come along, Giles, and help
680 me drag my lumber home.

Putnam. A moment, Mr. Proctor. What lumber is that you're draggin', if I may ask you?

Proctor. My lumber. From out my forest by the riverside.

Putnam. Why, we are surely gone wild this year. What **anarchy** is this? That tract is in my bounds, it's in my bounds, Mr. Proctor.

Proctor. In your bounds! (*indicating* Rebecca) I bought that tract from Goody Nurse's husband five
690 months ago.

Putnam. He had no right to sell it. It stands clear in my grandfather's will that all the land between the river and—

Proctor. Your grandfather had a habit of willing land that never belonged to him, if I may say it plain.

Giles. That's God's truth; he nearly willed away my north pasture but he knew I'd break his fingers before he'd set his name to it. Let's get your lumber home, John. I feel a sudden will to work coming on.

700 **Putnam.** You load one oak of mine and you'll fight to drag it home!

Giles. Aye, and we'll win too, Putnam—this fool and I. Come on! (*He turns to* Proctor *and starts out.*)

Putnam. I'll have my men on you, Corey! I'll clap a writ on you!

(*Enter* Reverend John Hale *of Beverly.*)

---

15. **Quakers:** a radical English religious sect—much hated by the Puritans—who often "spoke their heart" during their religious meetings.

16. **break charity:** break off; end the relationship.

17. **clap . . . defamation** (děf'ə-mā'shən): imprison him for slander.

DIFFERENTIATED INSTRUCTION

FOR STRATEGIC READERS

Vocabulary Support Have students reread the lines containing these unusual terms. After you define each one, have students paraphrase the lines.

- *a party in this church* (lines 642–643), "a group of church members who have organized to gain power (in opposition to the existing authority)"

- *iron* (line 661), "firmness (in speaking out with criticism)"

- *in my bounds* (line 687), "on my property"

- *clap a writ* (lines 704–705), "issue a warrant or court order"

FOR ADVANCED LEARNERS/AP

Research Land Ownership Have students work in pairs to research the laws and traditions of land ownership at this time in colonial America. Students should locate information about who could own land, how land was transferred from one person to another (inheritance, buying and selling, and so on), and how land disputes were settled. Ask students to prepare and share a paragraph or bulleted list that presents their main points.

Rob Campbell as Reverend Hale

Mr. Hale is nearing forty, a tight-skinned, eager-eyed intellectual. This is a beloved errand for him; on being called here to ascertain witchcraft he felt the pride of the specialist whose unique knowledge has at last been publicly called for. Like almost all men of learning, he spent a good deal of his time pondering the invisible world, especially since he had himself encountered a witch in his parish not long before. That woman, however, turned into a mere pest under his searching scrutiny, and the child she had allegedly been afflicting recovered her normal behavior after Hale had given her his kindness and a few days of rest in his own house. However, that experience never raised a doubt in his mind as to the reality of the underworld or the existence of Lucifer's many-faced lieutenants. And his belief is not to his discredit. Better minds than Hale's were—and still are—convinced that there is a society of spirits beyond our ken. One cannot help noting that one of his lines has never yet raised a laugh in any audience that has seen this play; it is his assurance that "We cannot look to superstition in this. The Devil is precise." Evidently we are not quite certain even now whether diabolism is holy and not to be scoffed at. And it is no accident that we should be so bemused.

Like Reverend Hale and the others on this stage, we conceive the Devil as a necessary part of a respectable view of cosmology.[18] Ours is a divided empire in which certain ideas and emotions and actions are of God, and their opposites are of Lucifer. It is as impossible for most men to conceive of a morality without sin as of an earth without "sky." Since 1692 a great but superficial change has wiped out God's beard and the Devil's horns, but the world is still gripped between two diametrically opposed

---

18. **cosmology** (kŏz-mŏl′ə-jē): a branch of philosophy dealing with the structure of the universe.

■ DRAW CONCLUSIONS ABOUT CHARACTERS

Reread the first 16 lines of Miller's mini-essay. What character traits of Reverend Hale's can you add to the prereading chart introduced on page 131? What evidence supports your ideas? ***Possible answer:*** *One of Hale's traits is "intelligent" (for Miller describes Hale as an "intellectual" who is a "specialist" and a man of learning); another is "focused" (for Miller says that Hale enters "eager-eyed" into his "beloved" mission).*

● CONVENTIONS OF DRAMA

How does Miller draw attention to the fact that this drama is something separate from the "real world"? ***Possible answer:*** *Miller makes the distinction clear by referring to "one of his [Hale's] lines," to "any audience that has seen this play," and to "the others on this stage."*

FOR ENGLISH LEARNERS

Vocabulary Support Point out that the words *will, willing,* and *willed* all occur within lines 692–699. Have Jigsaw groups of mixed language ability investigate the meanings and usages of these words. Ask them to report their findings and explain each word in the context of the passage.

🧰 **BEST PRACTICES TOOLKIT**
Jigsaw Reading p. A1

Related Vocabulary As students read and discuss this mini-essay, point out and clarify Miller's use of terminology that refers to forces of good and evil, as in these examples: *Lucifer; society of spirits; superstition; diabolism; holy; God's beard and the Devil's horns; diametrically opposed absolutes; arch-fiend; Old Boy; moral right . . . diabolical malevolence.*

Mini-Essay
TIERED DISCUSSION PROMPTS

Use these prompts to help students grasp some of Miller's points in this mini-essay:

Restate According to the paragraph that begins this page, why is the Devil a "weapon"? *Possible answer: Miller calls the Devil a "weapon" because, in his view, churches and religious governments have repeatedly used people's fear of the Devil to force obedience to their authority.*

Analyze How is the "political inspiration of the Devil" at work in Salem? *Possible answer: Various Salemites—Reverend Parris and the Putnams, for example—are using belief in demonic activity to gain or hold power.* Does Miller seem to think that this approach will work for long? How can you tell? *Possible answer: Miller seems to think that the approach ultimately will not work. He says that the fact that each side in a conflict can accuse the other of "alliance with Hell" makes it hard for him to believe in the "political inspiration of the Devil."*

Evaluate Compare this mini-essay to other mini-essays in *The Crucible* so far. In your opinion, is this mini-essay as helpful as the others? Why or why not? *Possible answer: While some students may find this essay interesting and provocative, others may find it tedious. The previous mini-essays provided information about the setting and characters, but here Miller primarily discusses religious and political philosophy. Except for its beginning and end, where Miller describes Reverend Hale, the mini-essay is perhaps more distracting than helpful.*

absolutes. The concept of unity, in which positive and negative are attributes of the same force, in which good and evil are relative, ever-changing, and always joined to the same phenomenon—such a concept is still reserved to the physical sciences and to the few who have grasped the history of ideas. When it is recalled that until the Christian era the underworld was never regarded as a hostile area, that all gods were useful and essentially friendly to man despite occasional lapses; when we see the steady and methodical inculcation into humanity of the idea of man's worthlessness—until redeemed—the necessity of the Devil may become evident as a weapon, a weapon designed and used time and time again in every age to whip men into a surrender to a particular church or church-state.

Our difficulty in believing the—for want of a better word—political inspiration of the Devil is due in great part to the fact that he is called up and damned not only by our social antagonists but by our own side, whatever it may be. The Catholic Church, through its Inquisition,[19] is famous for cultivating Lucifer as the arch-fiend, but the Church's enemies relied no less upon the Old Boy to keep the human mind enthralled. Luther[20] was himself accused of alliance with Hell, and he in turn accused his enemies. To complicate matters further, he believed that he had had contact with the Devil and had argued theology with him. I am not surprised at this, for at my own university a professor of history—a Lutheran, by the way—used to assemble his graduate students, draw the shades, and commune in the classroom with Erasmus.[21] He was never, to my knowledge, officially scoffed at for this, the reason being that the university officials, like most of us, are the children of a history which still sucks at

the Devil's teats. At this writing, only England has held back before the temptations of contemporary diabolism. In the countries of the Communist ideology, all resistance of any import is linked to the totally malign capitalist succubi,[22] and in America any man who is not reactionary in his views is open to the charge of alliance with the Red hell. Political opposition, thereby, is given an inhuman overlay which then justifies the abrogation of all normally applied customs of civilized intercourse. A political policy is equated with moral right, and opposition to it with diabolical malevolence. Once such an equation is effectively made, society becomes a congerie of plots and counterplots, and the main role of government changes from that of the arbiter to that of the scourge of God.

The results of this process are no different now from what they ever were, except sometimes in the degree of cruelty inflicted, and not always even in that department. Normally the actions and deeds of a man were all that society felt comfortable in judging. The secret intent of an action was left to the ministers, priests, and rabbis to deal with. When diabolism rises, however, actions are the least important manifests of the true nature of a man. The Devil, as Reverend Hale said, is a wily one, and, until an hour before he fell, even God thought him beautiful in Heaven.[23]

The analogy, however, seems to falter when one considers that, while there were no witches then, there are Communists and capitalists now, and in each camp there is certain proof that spies of each side are at work undermining the other. But this is a snobbish objection and not at all warranted by the facts. I have no doubt that people *were* communing with, and even worshiping, the Devil in Salem,

---

19. **Inquisition:** a former tribunal in the Roman Catholic Church dedicated to the discovery and punishment of heresy.
20. **Luther:** Martin Luther (1483–1546), the German theologian who led the Protestant Reformation.
21. **Erasmus** (ĭ-răz′məs): Desiderius Erasmus (1466?–1536), a Dutch scholar who sought to restore Christian faith by a study of the Scriptures and classical texts.
22. **succubi** (sŭk′yə-bī): demons that assume female form. Demons that assume male form are called incubi (ĭn′kyə-bī).
23. **The Devil . . . beautiful in Heaven:** According to Christian belief, Lucifer was God's favorite angel until the angel rebelled and was cast out of Heaven.

DIFFERENTIATED INSTRUCTION

FOR STRATEGIC READERS

3 Targeted Passage [Column 2, first 16 lines]

In this passage, Miller explains how a fear similar to the one that gripped Salem is possible in the world today.

- What political system demonizes capitalism?
- Why is it useful for governments to cast their political opponents as diabolical?
- If a political position is claimed as "moral," what happens to those who oppose this position?

FOR ADVANCED LEARNERS/AP

Research Political Systems Have students work in small groups to research the basic beliefs of the Communist political system as it existed in the 1950s and capitalism as it has been practiced in the United States. Instruct them to create a chart or other graphic aid that shows why each side would equate the other with the Devil. Work with students to create a format for sharing and discussing their findings.

and if the whole truth could be known in this case, as it is in others, we should discover a regular and conventionalized propitiation of the dark spirit. One certain evidence of this is the confession of Tituba, the slave of Reverend Parris, and another is the behavior of the children who were known to have indulged in sorceries with her.

There are accounts of similar *klatches* in Europe, where the daughters of the towns would assemble at night and, sometimes with fetishes, sometimes with a selected young man, give themselves to love, with some bastardly results. The Church, sharp-eyed as it must be when gods long dead are brought to life, condemned these orgies as witchcraft and interpreted them, rightly, as a resurgence of the Dionysiac forces[24] it had crushed long before. Sex, sin, and the Devil were early linked, and so they continued to be in Salem, and are today. From all accounts there are no more puritanical mores in the world than those enforced by the Communists in Russia, where women's fashions, for instance, are as prudent and all-covering as any American Baptist would desire. The divorce laws lay a tremendous responsibility on the father for the care of his children. Even the laxity of divorce regulations in the early years of the revolution was undoubtedly a revulsion from the nineteenth-century Victorian immobility of marriage and the consequent hypocrisy that developed from it. If for no other reasons, a state so powerful, so jealous of the uniformity of its citizens, cannot long tolerate the atomization of the family. And yet, in American eyes at least, there remains the conviction that the Russian attitude toward women is lascivious. It is the Devil working again, just as he is working within the Slav[25] who is shocked at the very idea of a woman's disrobing herself in a burlesque show. Our opposites are always robed in sexual sin, and it is from this unconscious conviction that demonology gains both its attractive sensuality and its capacity to infuriate and frighten.

Coming into Salem now, Reverend Hale conceives of himself much as a young doctor on his first call. His painfully acquired armory of symptoms, catchwords, and diagnostic procedures are now to be put to use at last. The road from Beverly is unusually busy this morning, and he has passed a hundred rumors that make him smile at the ignorance of the yeomanry in this most precise science. He feels himself allied with the best minds of Europe—kings, philosophers, scientists, and ecclesiasts of all churches. His goal is light, goodness and its preservation, and he knows the exaltation of the blessed whose intelligence, sharpened by minute examinations of enormous tracts, is finally called upon to face what may be a bloody fight with the Fiend himself.

(*He appears loaded down with half a dozen heavy books.*)

Hale. Pray you, someone take these!

710 **Parris** (*delighted*). Mr. Hale! Oh! it's good to see you again! (*taking some books*) My, they're heavy!

Hale (*setting down his books*). They must be; they are weighted with authority.

Parris (*a little scared*). Well, you do come prepared!

Hale. We shall need hard study if it comes to tracking down the Old Boy. (*noticing* Rebecca) You cannot be Rebecca Nurse?

Rebecca. I am, sir. Do you know me?

Hale. It's strange how I knew you, but I suppose you 720 look as such a good soul should. We have all heard of your great charities in Beverly.

Parris. Do you know this gentleman? Mr. Thomas Putnam. And his good wife Ann.

Hale. Putnam! I had not expected such distinguished company, sir.

---

24. **Dionysiac** (dī′ə-nĭs′ē-ăk′) **forces:** forces associated with Dionysus, the Greek god of wine and ecstasy.

25. **Slav:** a generic reference to Russians and other Slavic-speaking peoples of Eastern Europe who were under the control of the Soviet Union.

◼ DRAW CONCLUSIONS ABOUT CHARACTERS

Compare the concluding paragraph of this mini-essay to the opening paragraph on page 151. How would you describe Hale's view of himself and his goal in Salem?
Possible answer: *Hale views himself as a great intellect, equal to Europe's best thinkers and superior to the average villager (whom he finds rather humorous). Hale's goal is to restore Salem to a great spiritual state, and he will do anything—even fight the Devil—to succeed in that goal.*

FOR STRATEGIC READERS

Vocabulary Support As Miller waxes philosophical in his mini-essays, his diction becomes more difficult. Discuss the meanings of some or all of these terms from this page:

- *propitiation*, "an act that calms or pleases someone"
- *klatches*, "gatherings"
- *fetishes*, "objects believed to have magical power"
- *resurgence*, "return," "revival"
- *mores*, "accepted standards of behavior"
- *prudent*, "careful to avoid danger"
- *laxity*, "looseness"
- *atomization*, "breakup"
- *yeomanry*, "farmers (as a group)"
- *tracts*, "religious writings"

Lines 707–758
TIERED DISCUSSION PROMPTS

Use these prompts to help students explore the initial impression of Reverend Hale:

Recall What heavy items has Reverend Hale brought with him to Salem, and why? *Answer: Hale has brought several heavy books with him; they are reference sources that he might consult as he conducts his investigation (lines 707–716).*

Analyze What evidence suggests that Hale may not be as quick to believe a charge of witchcraft as some of the Salemites seem to be? *Possible answer: Proctor calls Hale "a sensible man" (line 741), suggesting that Hale will apply reason to the situation. Furthermore, even when Hale is presented with reports of Betty Parris's bewitchment, he says that he will not proceed in the investigation unless the people promise to accept his ruling if he rules against bewitchment (lines 754–756).*

Synthesize Do you think that Hale will maintain his "sensible" attitude as the story unfolds? Why or why not? *Possible answer: Hale's "sensible" attitude may be shaken if hysteria rises in the community or if he witnesses repeated manifestations of possible demonic power.*

Putnam (*pleased*). It does not seem to help us today, Mr. Hale. We look to you to come to our house and save our child.

Hale. Your child ails too?

730 **Mrs. Putnam.** Her soul, her soul seems flown away. She sleeps and yet she walks . . .

Putnam. She cannot eat.

Hale. Cannot eat! (*Thinks on it. Then, to* Proctor *and* Giles Corey.) Do you men have afflicted children?

Parris. No, no, these are farmers. John Proctor—

Giles Corey. He don't believe in witches.

Proctor (*to* Hale). I never spoke on witches one way or the other. Will you come, Giles?

Giles. No—no, John, I think not. I have some few
740 queer questions of my own to ask this fellow.

Proctor. I've heard you to be a sensible man, Mr. Hale. I hope you'll leave some of it in Salem.

(Proctor *goes.* Hale *stands embarrassed for an instant.*)

Parris (*quickly*). Will you look at my daughter, sir? (*leads* Hale *to the bed*) She has tried to leap out the window; we discovered her this morning on the highroad, waving her arms as though she'd fly.

Hale (*narrowing his eyes*). Tries to fly.

Putnam. She cannot bear to hear the Lord's name,
750 Mr. Hale; that's a sure sign of witchcraft afloat.

Hale (*holding up his hands*). No, no. Now let me instruct you. We cannot look to superstition in this. The Devil is precise; the marks of his presence are definite as stone, and I must tell you all that I shall not proceed unless you are prepared to believe me if I should find no bruise of hell upon her.

Parris. It is agreed, sir—it is agreed—we will abide by your judgment.

Hale. Good then. (*He goes to the bed, looks down*
760 *at* Betty. *To* Parris.) Now, sir, what were your first warning of this strangeness?

Parris. Why, sir—I discovered her—(*indicating* Abigail) and my niece and ten or twelve of the other girls, dancing in the forest last night.

Hale (*surprised*). You permit dancing?

Parris. No, no, it were secret—

Mrs. Putnam (*unable to wait*). Mr. Parris's slave has knowledge of conjurin', sir.

Parris (*to* Mrs. Putnam). We cannot be sure of that,
770 Goody Ann—

Mrs. Putnam (*frightened, very softly*). I know it, sir. I sent my child—she should learn from Tituba who murdered her sisters.

Rebecca (*horrified*). Goody Ann! You sent a child to conjure up the dead?

Mrs. Putnam. Let God blame me, not you, not you, Rebecca! I'll not have you judging me any more! (*to* Hale) Is it a natural work to lose seven children before they live a day?

780 **Parris.** Sssh!

(Rebecca, *with great pain, turns her face away. There is a pause.*)

Hale. Seven dead in childbirth.

Mrs. Putnam (*softly*). Aye. (*Her voice breaks; she looks up at him. Silence.* Hale *is impressed.* Parris *looks to him. He goes to his books, opens one, turns pages, then reads. All wait, avidly.*)

Parris (*hushed*). What book is that?

Mrs. Putnam. What's there, sir?

790 **Hale** (*with a tasty love of intellectual pursuit*). Here is all the invisible world, caught, defined, and calculated. In these books the Devil stands stripped of all his brute disguises. Here are all your familiar spirits—your incubi and succubi; your witches that go by land, by air, and by sea; your wizards of the night and of the day. Have no fear now—we shall find him out if he has come among us, and I mean to crush him utterly if he has shown his face! (*He starts for the bed.*)

Rebecca. Will it hurt the child, sir?

800 **Hale.** I cannot tell. If she is truly in the Devil's grip we may have to rip and tear to get her free.

Rebecca. I think I'll go, then. I am too old for this. (*She rises.*)

Parris (*striving for conviction*). Why, Rebecca, we may open up the boil of all our troubles today!

DIFFERENTIATED INSTRUCTION

FOR ADVANCED LEARNERS/AP

Analyze Metaphor Have students reread Parris's comment in lines 804–805. Instruct them to write a brief paragraph that explains the metaphor that Parris uses and that paraphrases the line. Then ask students to create a few original metaphors that would convey the same idea. As you lead a discussion about the metaphor, call on volunteers to share their original examples of figurative language.

Rebecca. Let us hope for that. I go to God for you, sir.

Parris (*with trepidation—and resentment*). I hope you do not mean we go to Satan here! (*slight pause*)

810 **Rebecca.** I wish I knew. (*She goes out; they feel resentful of her note of moral superiority.*)

Putnam (*abruptly*). Come, Mr. Hale, let's get on. Sit you here.

Giles. Mr. Hale, I have always wanted to ask a learned man—what signifies the readin' of strange books?

Hale. What books?

Giles. I cannot tell; she hides them.

Hale. Who does this?

Giles. Martha, my wife. I have waked at night many 820 a time and found her in a corner, readin' of a book. Now what do you make of that?

Hale. Why, that's not necessarily—

Giles. It discomfits me! Last night—mark this—I tried and tried and could not say my prayers. And then she close her book and walks out of the house, and suddenly—mark this—I could pray again!

Old Giles must be spoken for, if only because his fate was to be so remarkable and so different from that of all the others. He was in his early eighties at this time, and was the most comical hero in the history. No man has ever been blamed for so much. If a cow was missed, the first thought was to look for her around Corey's house; a fire blazing up at night brought suspicion of arson to his door. He didn't give a hoot for public opinion, and only in his last years—after he had married Martha—did he bother much with the church. That she stopped his prayer is very probable, but he forgot to say that he'd only recently learned any prayers and it didn't take much to make him stumble over them. He was a crank and a nuisance, but withal a deeply innocent and brave man. In court once, he was asked if it were true that he had been frightened by the strange behavior of a hog and had then said he knew it to be the Devil in an animal's shape. "What frighted you?" he was asked. He forgot everything but the word "frighted," and instantly replied, "I do not know that I ever spoke that word in my life."

Hale. Ah! The stoppage of prayer—that is strange. I'll speak further on that with you.

Giles. I'm not sayin' she's touched the Devil, now, 830 but I'd admire to know what books she reads and why she hides them. She'll not answer me, y' see.

Hale. Aye, we'll discuss it. (*to all*) Now mark me, if the Devil is in her you will witness some frightful wonders in this room, so please to keep your wits about you. Mr. Putnam, stand close in case she flies. Now, Betty, dear, will you sit up? (*Putnam comes in closer, ready-handed. Hale sits Betty up, but she hangs limp in his hands.*) Hmmm. (*He observes her carefully. The others watch breathlessly.*) Can you hear me? I am 840 John Hale, minister of Beverly. I have come to help you, dear. Do you remember my two little girls in Beverly? (*She does not stir in his hands.*)

Parris (*in fright*). How can it be the Devil? Why would he choose my house to strike? We have all manner of licentious people in the village!

Hale. What victory would the Devil have to win a soul already bad? It is the best the Devil wants, and who is better than the minister?

Giles. That's deep, Mr. Parris, deep, deep!

850 **Parris** (*with resolution now*). Betty! Answer Mr. Hale! Betty!

Hale. Does someone afflict you, child? It need not be a woman, mind you, or a man. Perhaps some bird invisible to others comes to you—perhaps a pig, a mouse, or any beast at all. Is there some figure bids you fly? (*The child remains limp in his hands. In silence he lays her back on the pillow. Now, holding out his hands toward her, he intones.*) In nomine Domini Sabaoth sui filiique ite ad infernos.[26] (*She does not stir.* 860 *He turns to* Abigail, *his eyes narrowing.*) Abigail, what sort of dancing were you doing with her in the forest?

---

26. **In nomine ... infernos** *Latin:* "In the name of the Father and Son, get thee back to Hell."

LITERARY ANALYSIS

● **CONVENTIONS OF DRAMA**
Where does Miller position his mini-essay about Giles Corey? How does the placement affect the dialogue? *Possible answer: Miller places this mini-essay in the middle of Giles's comments about his wife. Miller's remarks function as an aside, and he picks up the dialogue right where he left off.*

If students need help . . . Ask them to imagine that this mini-essay is being presented as part of the play. Review the speech devices listed in the Literary Analysis Workshop (page 129) and discuss which one best fits this situation.

Extend the Discussion Reread lines 814–831, but skip over the mini-essay this time. How might your understanding of Giles's character be different if you did not possess the information found in the mini-essay?

FOR STRATEGIC READERS

Comprehension Support Ask students to think about whether Miller intended Giles's remarks to be humorous. Have volunteers read lines 814–831 with different expressions, depending on whether they intend to emphasize humor. Discuss why Miller might add humor to this scene. (Later, when students learn Giles's fate, have them come back to this scene and discuss whether the seeming humor may also have a deeper irony.)

REINFORCE *KEY IDEA*: HYSTERIA

Discuss How does Reverend Hale help create the **hysteria** about witches that is starting to sweep through Salem? *Possible answer: Hale helps create hysteria by asking leading questions that plant ideas for responses in the minds of Abigail and Tituba. He also pressures them so much that they feel trapped and start looking to shift the attention onto someone else.*

Abigail. Why—common dancing is all.

Parris. I think I ought to say that I—I saw a kettle in the grass where they were dancing.

Abigail. That were only soup.

Hale. What sort of soup were in this kettle, Abigail?

Abigail. Why, it were beans—and lentils, I think, and—

Hale. Mr. Parris, you did not notice, did you, any living thing in the kettle? A mouse, perhaps, a spider, a frog—?

870 **Parris** (*fearfully*). I—do believe there were some movement—in the soup.

Abigail. That jumped in, we never put it in!

Hale (*quickly*). What jumped in?

Abigail. Why, a very little frog jumped—

Parris. A frog, Abby!

Hale (*grasping Abigail*). Abigail, it may be your cousin is dying. Did you call the Devil last night?

880 **Abigail.** I never called him! Tituba, Tituba . . .

Parris (*blanched*). She called the Devil?

Hale. I should like to speak with Tituba.

Parris. Goody Ann, will you bring her up? (*Mrs. Putnam exits.*)

Hale. How did she call him?

Abigail. I know not—she spoke Barbados.

Hale. Did you feel any strangeness when she called him? A sudden cold wind, perhaps? A trembling below the ground?

890 **Abigail.** I didn't see no Devil! (*shaking Betty*) Betty, wake up. Betty! Betty!

Hale. You cannot evade me, Abigail. Did your cousin drink any of the brew in that kettle?

Abigail. She never drank it!

Hale. Did you drink it?

Abigail. No, sir!

Hale. Did Tituba ask you to drink it?

Abigail. She tried, but I refused.

Hale. Why are you concealing? Have you sold your-
900 self to Lucifer?

Abigail. I never sold myself! I'm a good girl! I'm a proper girl!

(*Mrs. Putnam enters with* Tituba, *and instantly* Abigail *points at* Tituba.)

Abigail. She made me do it! She made Betty do it!

Tituba (*shocked and angry*). Abby!

Abigail. She makes me drink blood!

Parris. Blood!!

Mrs. Putnam. My baby's blood?

910 **Tituba.** No, no, chicken blood. I give she chicken blood!

Hale. Woman, have you enlisted these children for the Devil?

Tituba. No, no, sir, I don't truck with no Devil!

Hale. Why can she not wake? Are you silencing this child?

Tituba. I love me Betty!

Hale. You have sent your spirit out upon this child, have you not? Are you gathering souls for the Devil?

920 **Abigail.** She sends her spirit on me in church; she makes me laugh at prayer!

Parris. She have often laughed at prayer!

Abigail. She comes to me every night to go and drink blood!

Tituba. You beg *me* to conjure! She beg *me* make charm—

Abigail. Don't lie! (*to* Hale) She comes to me while I sleep; she's always making me dream corruptions!

Tituba. Why you say that, Abby?

930 **Abigail.** Sometimes I wake and find myself standing in the open doorway and not a stitch on my body! I always hear her laughing in my sleep. I hear her singing her Barbados songs and tempting me with—

Tituba. Mister Reverend, I never—

Hale (*resolved now*). Tituba, I want you to wake this child.

DIFFERENTIATED INSTRUCTION

FOR STRATEGIC READERS

Explore Stage Directions Point out that except for line 878, there are no stage directions describing Hale's interrogation of Abigail. Have students work in pairs and read lines 885–908 aloud, choosing the facial expressions, vocal tones, and gestures that seem most appropriate for the dialogue. Have students make suggestions for stage directions that Miller could have included in these lines.

FOR ADVANCED LEARNERS/AP

Analyze Motive This scene is important to the plot because it sheds light on Abigail's motives. Have students reread the exchange between Abigail, Hale, and Tituba in lines 905–937. Then instruct students to write a brief character analysis that answers these questions:

- What does Abigail say Tituba made her do?

- Why does Abigail accuse Tituba of witchcraft?

- Why would Abigail single out Tituba instead of one of the other girls?

Encourage students to make a connection between Abigail's behavior and the general atmosphere in the town. Invite students to discuss their analyses with the class.

Tituba. I have no power on this child, sir.

Hale. You most certainly do, and you will free her from it now! When did you compact with the Devil?

940 **Tituba.** I don't compact with no Devil!

Parris. You will confess yourself or I will take you out and whip you to your death, Tituba!

Putnam. This woman must be hanged! She must be taken and hanged!

Tituba (*terrified, falls to her knees*). No, no, don't hang Tituba! I tell him I don't desire to work for him, sir.

Parris. The Devil?

Hale. Then you saw him! (*Tituba weeps.*) Now
950 Tituba, I know that when we bind ourselves to Hell it is very hard to break with it. We are going to help you tear yourself free—

Tituba (*frightened by the coming process*). Mister Reverend, I do believe somebody else be witchin' these children.

Hale. Who?

Tituba. I don't know, sir, but the Devil got him numerous witches.

Hale. Does he! *It is a clue.* Tituba, look into my eyes.
960 Come, look into me. (*She raises her eyes to his fearfully.*) You would be a good Christian woman, would you not, Tituba?

Tituba. Aye, sir, a good Christian woman.

Hale. And you love these little children?

Tituba. Oh, yes, sir, I don't desire to hurt little children.

Hale. And you love God, Tituba?

Tituba. I love God with all my bein'.

Hale. Now, in God's holy name—

970 **Tituba.** Bless Him. Bless Him. (*She is rocking on her knees, sobbing in terror.*)

Hale. And to His glory—

Tituba. Eternal glory. Bless Him—bless God . . .

Hale. Open yourself, Tituba—open yourself and let God's holy light shine on you.

Tituba. Oh, bless the Lord.

Hale. When the Devil comes to you does he ever come—with another person? (*She stares up into his face.*) Perhaps another person in the village? Some-
980 one you know.

Parris. Who came with him?

Putnam. Sarah Good? Did you ever see Sarah Good with him? Or Osburn?

Parris. Was it man or woman came with him?

Tituba. Man or woman. Was—was woman.

Parris. What woman? A woman, you said. What woman?

Tituba. It was black dark, and I—

Parris. You could see him, why could you not see
990 her?

Tituba. Well, they was always talking; they was always runnin' round and carryin' on—

Parris. You mean out of Salem? Salem witches?

Tituba. I believe so, yes, sir.

(*Now Hale takes her hand. She is surprised.*)

Hale. Tituba. You must have no fear to tell us who they are, do you understand? We will protect you. The Devil can never overcome a minister. You know that, do you not?

1000 **Tituba** (*kisses Hale's hand*). Aye, sir, oh, I do.

Hale. You have confessed yourself to witchcraft, and that speaks a wish to come to Heaven's side. And we will bless you, Tituba.

Tituba (*deeply relieved*). Oh, God bless you, Mr. Hale!

Hale (*with rising exaltation*). You are God's instrument put in our hands to discover the Devil's agents among us. You are selected, Tituba, you are chosen to help us cleanse our village. So speak utterly,
1010 Tituba, turn your back on him and face God—face God, Tituba, and God will protect you.

Tituba (*joining with him*). Oh, God, protect Tituba!

Hale (*kindly*). Who came to you with the Devil? Two? Three? Four? How many?

Lines 959–997
TIERED DISCUSSION PROMPTS

Use these prompts to help students explore this crucial scene:

Connect Have you ever known someone who claimed to do or see something that he or she might not really have done or seen? How would that memory help you identify with this scene? *Students may suggest that such a memory would help them sympathize with Tituba, who is distressed at the intense questioning and who makes questionable claims out of desperation.*

Analyze What are Hale and Parris trying to get Tituba to do, and why? *Possible answer: Hale and Parris are trying to get Tituba to name the witches to whom she has referred (lines 957–958).* How do the approaches of the two ministers differ? *Possible answer: Although Hale is firm, he treats Tituba kindly and points her to God instead of condemning her outright. Parris, however, is curt and demanding.*

Evaluate How effective is Miller in creating suspense in this scene? Explain. *Possible answer: Miller is very effective in creative suspense in this scene. Since the questioning of Tituba is drawn out, suspense builds as readers and audience members wait to discover how far the questioning will go and what it will reveal.*

FOR ENGLISH LEARNERS

Culture: Clarify Remind students that Tituba is not a native speaker of English (line 886); thus, it is not surprising to hear her speak in dialect, reflecting her upbringing in the culture of Barbados. Have students express in standard English these comments that Tituba makes: "I give she chicken blood!" (lines 910–911); "I love me Betty!" (line 917); "She beg *me* make charm—" (lines 925–926); "Why you say that, Abby?" (line 929); "No, no, don't hang Tituba! I tell him I don't desire to work for him, sir" (lines 945–947); "Mister Reverend, I do believe somebody else be witchin' these children" (lines 953–955); " . . . the Devil got him numerous witches" (lines 957–958).

REINFORCE *KEY IDEA*: HYSTERIA

Hysteria feeds on fear, anger, and panic. How are the seeds of **hysteria** sown in these lines?

Possible answer: Hale seems to have convinced Tituba and the girls that they are doing God's will by naming others who associate with the Devil. Furthermore, the more afraid these characters become of being persecuted themselves, the more willing they are to implicate others. Thus, panic and hidden anger (such as Tituba's for Parris) cause them to act irrationally. Even if the accusations are calculated and totally false, the emotional scene in which they are made encourages the growth of hysteria.

SELECTION WRAP–UP

REFLECT Ask students to think about the conflicts that are emerging between various Salemites. How do these conflicts contribute to the growing atmosphere of suspicion and hysteria in the play?

⭐ CRITIQUE

- Ask students to think about the events that have led up to the climax of Act One and to decide whether they think that the confessions from Tituba and the girls are believable. Why or why not?

- After completing the After Reading questions on page 159, have students revisit their responses and tell whether they have changed their opinions.

(Tituba *pants, and begins rocking back and forth again, staring ahead.*)

Tituba. There was four. There was four.

Parris (*pressing in on her*). Who? Who? Their names, their names!

1020 **Tituba** (*suddenly bursting out*). Oh, how many times he bid me kill you, Mr. Parris!

Parris. Kill me!

Tituba (*in a fury*). He say Mr. Parris must be kill! Mr. Parris no goodly man, Mr. Parris mean man and no gentle man, and he bid me rise out of my bed and cut your throat! (*They gasp.*) But I tell him "No! I don't hate that man. I don't want kill that man." But he say, "You work for me, Tituba, and I make you free! I give you pretty dress to wear, and put 1030 you way high up in the air, and you gone fly back to Barbados!" And I say, "You lie, Devil, you lie!" And then he come one stormy night to me, and he say, "Look! I have *white* people belong to me." And I look—and there was Goody Good.

Parris. Sarah Good! **Targeted Passage** ④

Tituba (*rocking and weeping*). Aye, sir, and Goody Osburn.

Mrs. Putnam. I knew it! Goody Osburn were midwife to me three times. I begged you, Thomas, did 1040 I not? I begged him not to call Osburn because I feared her. My babies always shriveled in her hands!

Hale. Take courage, you must give us all their names. How can you bear to see this child suffering? Look at her, Tituba. (*He is indicating* Betty *on the bed.*) Look at her God-given innocence; her soul is so tender; we must protect her, Tituba; the Devil is out and preying on her like a beast upon the flesh of the pure lamb. God will bless you for your help.

(Abigail *rises, staring as though inspired, and cries out.*)

1050 **Abigail.** I want to open myself! (*They turn to her, startled. She is enraptured, as though in a pearly light.*) I want the light of God, I want the sweet love of Jesus! I danced for the Devil; I saw him; I wrote in his book; I go back to Jesus; I kiss His hand. I saw Sarah Good with the Devil! I saw Goody Osburn with the Devil! I saw Bridget Bishop with the Devil!

(*As she is speaking,* Betty *is rising from the bed, a fever in her eyes, and picks up the chant.*)

Betty (*staring too*). I saw George Jacobs with the
1060 Devil! I saw Goody Howe with the Devil!

Parris. She speaks! (*He rushes to embrace* Betty.) She speaks!

Hale. Glory to God! It is broken, they are free!

Betty (*calling out hysterically and with great relief*). I saw Martha Bellows with the Devil!

Abigail. I saw Goody Sibber with the Devil! (*It is rising to a great glee.*)

Putnam. The marshal, I'll call the marshal!

(Parris *is shouting a prayer of thanksgiving.*)

1070 **Betty.** I saw Alice Barrow with the Devil!

(*The curtain begins to fall.*)

Hale (*as* Putnam *goes out*). Let the marshal bring irons!

Abigail. I saw Goody Hawkins with the Devil!

Betty. I saw Goody Bibber with the Devil!

Abigail. I saw Goody Booth with the Devil!

(*On their ecstatic cries, the curtain falls.*)

DIFFERENTIATED INSTRUCTION

FOR STRATEGIC READERS

④ **Targeted Passage [Lines 1050–1077]**

In this passage, the climax of Act One, accusations boost the plot complexity and emotional intensity of the play.

- Whose example finally compels Betty to rise and speak? What does she say?

- Why does Betty cry out "with great relief"? Why does Hale seem relieved?

- Why does Hale want the marshal to come with "irons"? Which Salemites do you think the marshal will visit?

Comprehension

R3.5

1. **Recall** What is the cause for concern in the Parris household?

2. **Clarify** What has occurred between John Proctor and Abigail Williams before the time in which the play begins?

3. **Summarize** Why does Reverend Hale come to Salem?

Literary Analysis

4. **Infer Character Motives** Reread lines 1017–1056 at the end of Act One. Why do you think Tituba and Abigail admit to having practiced witchcraft? Why do they name others?

5. **Draw Conclusions About Characters** Review the **traits** you recorded in your chart for the characters you have encountered so far. How would you describe the most important character traits of the following?

   • Abigail Williams   • John Proctor   • Reverend Hale

6. **Make Predictions** Based on what you have learned about Abigail in Act One, whom do you think she might accuse as the play goes on? Cite specific evidence to support your answer.

7. **Identify Beliefs** What do the characters in the play believe about witches? List their beliefs in a concept web like the one shown.

8. **Connect Setting and Mood** The setting of a literary work refers to the time and place in which the action occurs. How do you think Miller uses setting to help create mood in Act One?

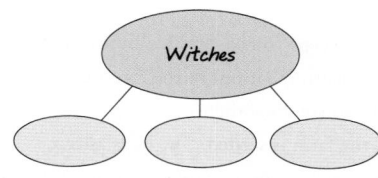

9. **Analyze Conventions of Drama** Review the **stage directions** that take the form of mini-essays in Act One. What insights about America after the Second World War does Miller convey? Use details from the mini-essays in your answer.

Literary Criticism

10. **Author's Style** The mini-essays in Act One are not usually included in a stage production of *The Crucible*. Why do you think this is so? Why do you think Miller included them in his drama?

against Elizabeth Proctor, who thwarted Abigail's plans to be with Proctor.

7. (1) exist and are the Devil's agents, (2) can control people and harm children, and (3) can take the form of animals

8. All of Act One takes place in a small bedroom in Parris's house, a room that Miller describes as having "an air of clean spareness." The unchanging setting creates a feeling of entrapment; its simplicity underscores the feeling that this will be a place where moral absolutes will be discussed.

9. ● **SKILLS FOCUS** Conventions of Drama
Miller discusses the Puritan traits of discipline and hypocrisy, which modern America has inherited. He also discusses the relationship between America's political policy and religious beliefs, Americans' fear of Communism, and Americans' mistrust of the Soviet Union.

10. Including the mini-essays would disrupt the action of the play. Miller probably included them to help the director, actors, and readers understand the play's characters and time period.

Practice and Apply

After Reading

Use these copy masters to check understanding and provide extra support:

R RESOURCE MANAGER—Copy Masters
   Reading Check p. 248
   Conventions of Drama p. 243
   Question Support p. 249

   Additional selection questions are provided for teachers on page 237.

ANSWERS

1. *Reverend Parris's daughter, Betty, lies in bed in a mysterious trance. Parris is concerned that witchcraft may be the cause.*

2. *Proctor and Abigail have had an illicit affair.*

3. *Hale comes to determine whether Betty's condition is the result of witchcraft. If so, he intends to fight the Devil.*

Possible answers:

4. *Tituba and Abigail admit it because the pressure is so great, but they name others in order to deflect blame from themselves.*

5. ■ **SKILLS FOCUS** Draw Conclusions About Characters

   Abigail Williams: willful, self-centered, controlling, devious, and vengeful

   John Proctor: intelligent, skeptical, and courageous

   Reverend Hale: intellectual, devout, and firm yet compassionate

6. *Abigail might accuse the Proctors. Her threats (lines 353–364) reveal a vindictive nature; and she might want revenge against John Proctor, who has rejected her, and*

Assess and Reteach

Assess

R RESOURCE MANAGER—Copy Masters
   Selection Test A pp. 251–252
   Selection Test B/C pp. 253–254

💿 Test Generator CD

Reteach

S STANDARDS LESSON FILE
   Literature Lessons 1–2: Characters
   Literature Lesson 6: Conflict
   Literature Lessons 23–24: Elements of Drama
   Reading Lesson 9: Drawing Conclusions

Practice and Apply

Get Into the Act

SUMMARY

As Act Two begins, John and Elizabeth Proctor express concern about the growth of the witchcraft scare. Then they argue: Elizabeth urges her husband to expose Abigail as a fraud, and the two revisit his affair with her. Mary Warren brings news of further arrests and the possible implication of Elizabeth. Reverend Hale arrives and interviews the couple; and when the marshal arrests Elizabeth, Proctor condemns the desire for vengeance that is driving events, and he vows to save his wife.

LITERARY ANALYSIS

● CONVENTIONS OF DRAMA

Use the stage directions to explain what happens between Elizabeth and Proctor in lines 33–34. Why does he feel "a certain disappointment"? ***Possible answer:*** *Proctor kisses Elizabeth, she "receives his kiss" (line 33), and he returns to his seat at the table. He feels disappointment because she has not returned his kiss; he feels the distance between them.*

Extend the Discussion Why do you think that Elizabeth does not respond to her husband's kiss with a kiss of her own?

ACT *Two*

(*The common room of* Proctor's *house, eight days later.*

At the right is a door opening on the fields outside. A fireplace is at the left, and behind it a stairway leading upstairs. It is the low, dark, and rather long living room of the time. As the curtain rises, the room is empty. From above, Elizabeth *is heard softly singing to the children. Presently the door opens and* John Proctor *enters, carrying his gun. He glances about the room as he comes toward the fireplace, then halts for an instant as he hears her singing. He continues on to the fireplace, leans the gun against the wall as he swings a pot out of the fire and smells it. Then he lifts out the ladle and tastes. He is not quite pleased. He reaches to a cupboard, takes a pinch of salt, and drops it into the pot. As he is tasting again, her footsteps are heard on the stair. He swings the pot into the fireplace and goes to a basin and washes his hands and face.* Elizabeth *enters.*)

Elizabeth. What keeps you so late? It's almost dark.

Proctor. I were planting far out to the forest edge.

Elizabeth. Oh, you're done then.

Proctor. Aye, the farm is seeded. The boys asleep?

Elizabeth. They will be soon. (*And she goes to the fireplace, proceeds to ladle up stew in a dish.*)

Proctor. Pray now for a fair summer.

Elizabeth. Aye.

Proctor. Are you well today?

10 **Elizabeth.** I am. (*She brings the plate to the table, and, indicating the food.*) It is a rabbit.

Proctor (*going to the table*). Oh, is it! In Jonathan's trap?

Elizabeth. No, she walked into the house this afternoon; I found her sittin' in the corner like she come to visit.

Proctor. Oh, that's a good sign walkin' in.

Elizabeth. Pray God. It hurt my heart to strip her, poor rabbit. (*She sits and watches him taste it.*)

20 **Proctor.** It's well seasoned.

Elizabeth (*blushing with pleasure*). I took great care. She's tender?

Proctor. Aye. (*He eats. She watches him.*) I think we'll see green fields soon. It's warm as blood beneath the clods.

Elizabeth. That's well.

(Proctor *eats, then looks up.*)

Proctor. If the crop is good I'll buy George Jacob's heifer. How would that please you?

30 **Elizabeth.** Aye, it would.

Proctor (*with a grin*). I mean to please you, Elizabeth.

Elizabeth (*It is hard to say*). I know it, John.

(*He gets up, goes to her, kisses her. She receives it. With a certain disappointment, he returns to the table.*)

Proctor (*as gently as he can*). Cider?

Elizabeth (*with a sense of reprimanding herself for having forgot*). Aye! (*She gets up and goes and pours a glass for him. He now arches his back.*)

160 UNIT 1: EARLY AMERICAN WRITING

Resources for Act Two

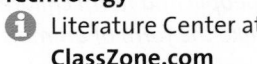 **RESOURCE MANAGER UNIT 1**

Plan and Teach pp. 255–260

Literary Analysis
Summary pp. 261†, 262‡*
Conventions of Drama
    pp. 263, 264†*
Question Support p. 266*

Reading
Reading Check p. 265

Assessment
Selection Tests A, B/C
    pp. 267*, 269*
⊘ Test Generator CD

BEST PRACTICES TOOLKIT

Differentiated Instruction
    pp. 31–38*

Graphic Organizers/Strategies
Two-Column Chart • New Word
Analysis • Spider Map
• Jigsaw Reading • Sequence
Chain

Reading Support
⊘ Audio Anthology CD*

Technology
ⓘ Literature Center at
    ClassZone.com
⊘ Write*Smart* CD

Joan Allen as Elizabeth Proctor

Lines 20–32
TIERED DISCUSSION PROMPTS

Use these prompts to help students explore the relationship between John and Elizabeth Proctor:

Connect Think of a time when you have done something in hopes of making someone happy, only to have your effort fail. How does that experience help you understand Proctor's feelings when Elizabeth fails to respond to his attempts to make her feel better? *Accept all responses that make an effort to connect to Proctor's unsuccessful compliments and offers of gifts.*

Analyze Why does Proctor make a point of saying, "I mean to please you, Elizabeth" (line 31)? *Possible answer: Proctor probably wants Elizabeth to know that he is trying to make up for his past infidelity.* What do the stage directions in that same line suggest about Proctor's efforts? *Possible answer: The stage directions, which instruct the actor to grin, probably mean that Proctor is grinning in hopes that he can coax a smile out of Elizabeth.*

Synthesize On the basis of how Proctor and Elizabeth act in this scene, how do you think each of them feels about the other? *Possible answer: Proctor wants to put their troubles behind them, and he tries to be affectionate and agreeable with Elizabeth. Elizabeth is still hurt and perhaps angry with him; she cannot or will not forgive him.*

DIFFERENTIATED INSTRUCTION

For general guidelines on differentiating instruction, see

 BEST PRACTICES TOOLKIT
Differentiated Instruction pp. 31–38

FOR STRATEGIC READERS

In combination with the *Audio Anthology CD*, use one or more Targeted Passages (pp. 162, 164, 169, 170, 173, 174) to ensure that students focus on key story events and concepts. Targeted Passages are also good for English learners.

Preview Ask students to listen carefully as you read the Summary aloud. Have them use a Two-Column Chart to identify key details in Act Two of *The Crucible*.

BEST PRACTICES TOOLKIT—Transparency
Two-Column Chart p. A25

Character	Action
Proctor	argues with Elizabeth; condemns the vengeful spirit in Salem
Elizabeth	argues with Proctor
Mary Warren	brings news of arrests; notes possible implication of Elizabeth
Hale	questions the Proctors
the marshal	arrests Elizabeth

● CONVENTIONS OF DRAMA

Miller reveals more about the Proctors' attitudes toward each other in the stage directions. Elizabeth worries that her husband was in Salem, and *"He knows what she means"* (line 65). Of what concern is John Proctor aware? ***Possible answer:*** *Proctor is aware of Elizabeth's concern that he might have gone to Salem to see Abigail.*

If students need help . . . Relate the stage directions in lines 60 and 65.

- Discuss what Miller means by the comment "and yet she must" in the stage directions for line 60.

- Point out that Miller leaves part of the comment unstated but implied. Elicit that Elizabeth's description (*doesn't want friction, and yet she must,* line 60) refers to her need to express her sadness and her mistrust of her husband.

Lines 106–116
REINFORCE *KEY IDEA:* HYSTERIA

Discuss In Elizabeth's mind, what is the only way to bring the rising **hysteria** in Salem to an end? Why is that solution a problem for Proctor? ***Possible answer:*** *Elizabeth says that her husband must reveal that Abigail had admitted to him that witchcraft played no role in what was going on (lines 108–109). Doing so is a problem because Proctor also would have to reveal that Abigail made that admission when he and she had been alone together.*

Proctor. This farm's a continent when you go foot
40 by foot droppin' seeds in it.

Elizabeth (*coming with the cider*). It must be.

Proctor (*drinks a long draught, then, putting the glass down*). You ought to bring some flowers in the house.

Elizabeth. Oh! I forgot! I will tomorrow.

Proctor. It's winter in here yet. On Sunday let you come with me, and we'll walk the farm together; I never see such a load of flowers on the earth. (*With good feeling he goes and looks up at the sky through the open doorway.*) Lilacs have a purple smell. Lilac is the
50 smell of nightfall, I think. Massachusetts is a beauty in the spring!

Elizabeth. Aye, it is.　　　　**Targeted Passage** ①

(*There is a pause. She is watching him from the table as he stands there absorbing the night. It is as though she would speak but cannot. Instead, now, she takes up his plate and glass and fork and goes with them to the basin. Her back is turned to him. He turns to her and watches her. A sense of their separation rises.*)

Proctor. I think you're sad again. Are you?

60 **Elizabeth** (*She doesn't want friction, and yet she must*). You come so late I thought you'd gone to Salem this afternoon.

Proctor. Why? I have no business in Salem.

Elizabeth. You did speak of going, earlier this week.

Proctor (*He knows what she means*). I thought better of it since.

Elizabeth. Mary Warren's there today.

Proctor. Why'd you let her? You heard me forbid her go to Salem any more!

70 **Elizabeth.** I couldn't stop her.

Proctor (*holding back a full condemnation of her*). It is a fault, it is a fault, Elizabeth—you're the mistress here, not Mary Warren.

Elizabeth. She frightened all my strength away.

Proctor. How may that mouse frighten you, Elizabeth? You—

Elizabeth. It is a mouse no more. I forbid her go, and she raises up her chin like the daughter of a

prince and says to me, "I must go to Salem, Goody
80 Proctor; I am an official of the court!"

Proctor. Court! What court?

Elizabeth. Aye, it is a proper court they have now. They've sent four judges out of Boston, she says, weighty magistrates of the General Court, and at the head sits the Deputy Governor of the Province.

Proctor (*astonished*). Why, she's mad.

Elizabeth. I would to God she were. There be fourteen people in the jail now, she says. (Proctor *simply looks at her, unable to grasp it.*) And they'll be tried,
90 and the court have power to hang them too, she says.

Proctor (*scoffing, but without conviction*). Ah, they'd never hang—

Elizabeth. The Deputy Governor promise hangin' if they'll not confess, John. The town's gone wild, I think. She speak of Abigail, and I thought she were a saint, to hear her. Abigail brings the other girls into the court, and where she walks the crowd will part like the sea for Israel. And folks are brought before them, and if they scream and howl and fall to the floor—the
100 person's clapped in the jail for bewitchin' them.

Proctor (*wide-eyed*). Oh, it is a black mischief.

Elizabeth. I think you must go to Salem, John. (*He turns to her.*) I think so. You must tell them it is a fraud.

Proctor (*thinking beyond this*). Aye, it is, it is surely.

Elizabeth. Let you go to Ezekiel Cheever—he knows you well. And tell him what she said to you last week in her uncle's house. She said it had naught to do with witchcraft, did she not?

110 **Proctor** (*in thought*). Aye, she did, she did. (*now, a pause*)

Elizabeth (*quietly, fearing to anger him by prodding*). God forbid you keep that from the court, John. I think they must be told.

Proctor (*quietly, struggling with his thought*). Aye, they must, they must. It is a wonder they do believe her.

Elizabeth. I would go to Salem now, John—let you go tonight.

DIFFERENTIATED INSTRUCTION

FOR STRATEGIC READERS

① **Targeted Passage [Lines 82–104]**

This passage reveals that the search for witches in Salem is getting out of control.

- Why has a court been set up in Salem?
- Who is the leader of the girls who claim to be bewitched?
- What system is used to determine whether the accused people are witches?

- Do Proctor and Elizabeth believe that the accused are witches? How can you tell?

FOR ENGLISH LEARNERS

Vocabulary: Multiple-Meaning Words Direct students' attention to the word *court* in lines 80 and 81. Explain that *court* can be a verb, meaning "to attempt to gain someone's favor or love," or a noun, referring to "a place where accused people are judged." Elicit that *court* is a noun in these lines. Then have small groups use a dictionary and context clues to explore

these other words from this page: *fault* (line 72), *mad* (line 86), *tried* (line 89), *wild* (line 94), *clapped* (line 100), *black* (line 101), *wonder* (line 116).

Proctor. I'll think on it.

120 **Elizabeth** (*with her courage now*). You cannot keep it, John.

Proctor (*angering*). I know I cannot keep it. I say I will think on it!

Elizabeth (*hurt, and very coldly*). Good, then, let you think on it. (*She stands and starts to walk out of the room.*)

Proctor. I am only wondering how I may prove what she told me, Elizabeth. If the girl's a saint now, I think it is not easy to prove she's fraud, and 130 the town gone so silly. She told it to me in a room alone—I have no proof for it.

Elizabeth. You were alone with her?

Proctor (*stubbornly*). For a moment alone, aye.

Elizabeth. Why, then, it is not as you told me.

Proctor (*his anger rising*). For a moment, I say. The others come in soon after.

Elizabeth (*quietly—she has suddenly lost all faith in him*). Do as you wish, then. (*She starts to turn.*)

Proctor. Woman. (*She turns to him.*) I'll not have 140 your suspicion any more.

Elizabeth (*a little loftily*). I have no—

Proctor. I'll not have it!

Elizabeth. Then let you not earn it.

Proctor (*with a violent undertone*). You doubt me yet?

Elizabeth (*with a smile, to keep her dignity*). John, if it were not Abigail that you must go to hurt, would you falter now? I think not.

Proctor. Now look you—

Elizabeth. I see what I see, John.

150 **Proctor** (*with solemn warning*). You will not judge me more, Elizabeth. I have good reason to think before I charge fraud on Abigail, and I will think on it. Let you look to your own improvement before you go to judge your husband any more. I have forgot Abigail, and—

Elizabeth. And I.

Proctor. Spare me! You forget nothin' and forgive nothin'. Learn charity, woman. I have gone tiptoe in this house all seven month since she is gone. I have 160 not moved from there to there without I think to please you, and still an everlasting funeral marches round your heart. I cannot speak but I am doubted, every moment judged for lies, as though I come into a court when I come into this house!

Elizabeth. John, you are not open with me. You saw her with a crowd, you said. Now you—

Proctor. I'll plead my honesty no more, Elizabeth.

Elizabeth (*now she would justify herself*). John, I am only—

170 **Proctor.** No more! I should have roared you down when first you told me your suspicion. But I wilted, and, like a Christian, I confessed. Confessed! Some dream I had must have mistaken you for God that day. But you're not, you're not, and let you remember it! Let you look sometimes for the goodness in me, and judge me not.

Elizabeth. I do not judge you. The magistrate sits in your heart that judges you. I never thought you but a good man, John—(*with a smile*)—only somewhat 180 bewildered.

Proctor (*laughing bitterly*). Oh, Elizabeth, your justice would freeze beer![1] (*He turns suddenly toward a sound outside. He starts for the door as* Mary Warren *enters. As soon as he sees her, he goes directly to her and grabs her by her cloak, furious.*) How do you go to Salem when I forbid it? Do you mock me? (*shaking her*) I'll whip you if you dare leave this house again! (*Strangely, she doesn't resist him, but hangs limply by his grip.*)

190 **Mary Warren.** I am sick, I am sick, Mr. Proctor. Pray, pray, hurt me not. (*Her strangeness throws him off, and her evident pallor and weakness. He frees her.*) My insides are all shuddery; I am in the proceedings all day, sir.

---

1. **your justice . . . beer:** Alcoholic beverages freeze at very low temperatures, so Proctor is sarcastically calling his wife cold-hearted.

READING SKILL

■ DRAW CONCLUSIONS ABOUT CHARACTERS

Reread lines 149–164. What character traits do Elizabeth and Proctor reveal in this dialogue? *Possible answer: Elizabeth reveals that she is suspicious of Proctor and increasingly bold in her willingness to confront him about his affair. Proctor reveals that he is defensive about his actions and angry about Elizabeth's inability or unwillingness to forgive him.*

If students need help . . .

- Work with them to enter more information about Elizabeth and Proctor in the chart introduced on page 131.
- Remind them to record evidence in the chart to support their information. Invite suggestions about quotations or other evidence that students might glean from this passage.

FOR ENGLISH LEARNERS

Key Academic Vocabulary Use New Word Analysis to teach these words: *evident* (line 192), *compensate* (line 199), *aware* (line 452), *restrain* (line 518), *image* (line 556), *define* (line 571).

 BEST PRACTICES TOOLKIT—Transparency New Word Analysis p. E8

FOR ADVANCED LEARNERS/AP

Analyze Dialogue Have students discuss Proctor's outburst in lines 170–176. Encourage them to try reading it aloud a few times to get a feel for the emotions that Proctor expresses in these lines. Then ask students to write a brief essay analyzing the passage in the light of these questions:

- How did Elizabeth find out about his affair with Abigail?

- What does Proctor think about himself?

- What does he mean by the phrase "roared you down" (line 170)? How might his relationship with Elizabeth be different at this moment if he had "roared [her] down" earlier?

- What are his criticisms of Elizabeth?

As students share their essays, ask them what they think it would take for the Proctors to resolve their conflict.

■ DRAW CONCLUSIONS ABOUT CHARACTERS

Miller provides clues about Mary Warren's character by describing her directly and by showing how other characters react to her. Reread lines 199–217. What do the stage directions suggest about how Mary feels after her day in court? *Possible answer: The stage directions suggest that Mary feels tired, upset, anxious, and overwhelmed by what is happening.*

If students need help . . . Have them meet in small groups, using a Spider Map to consider Mary's emotions. Remind them to record both stage directions that relate to Mary's emotions and lines that describe how other characters react to her.

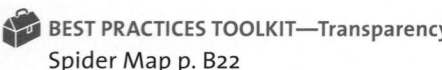

BEST PRACTICES TOOLKIT—Transparency
Spider Map p. B22

Proctor (*with draining anger—his curiosity is draining it*). And what of these proceedings here? When will you proceed to keep this house, as you are paid nine pound a year to do—and my wife not wholly well?

(*As though to compensate,* Mary Warren *goes to* 200 Elizabeth *with a small rag doll.*)

Mary Warren. I made a gift for you today, Goody Proctor. I had to sit long hours in a chair, and passed the time with sewing.

Elizabeth (*perplexed, looking at the doll*). Why, thank you, it's a fair poppet.[2]

Mary Warren (*with a trembling, decayed voice*). We must all love each other now, Goody Proctor.

Elizabeth (*amazed at her strangeness*). Aye, indeed we must.

210 **Mary Warren** (*glancing at the room*). I'll get up early in the morning and clean the house. I must sleep now. (*She turns and starts off.*)

> Proctor. Mary. (*She halts.*) Is it true? There be fourteen women arrested?
>
> **Mary Warren.** No, sir. There be thirty-nine now— (*She suddenly breaks off and sobs and sits down, exhausted.*)
>
> **Elizabeth.** Why, she's weepin'! What ails you, child?
>
> **Mary Warren.** Goody Osburn—will hang!
>
> 220 (*There is a shocked pause, while she sobs.*)
>
> **Proctor.** Hang! (*He calls into her face.*) Hang, y'say?
>
> **Mary Warren** (*through her weeping*). Aye.
>
> **Proctor.** The Deputy Governor will permit it?
>
> **Mary Warren.** He sentenced her. He must. (*to* **ameliorate** *it*) But not Sarah Good. For Sarah Good confessed, y'see.
>
> **Proctor.** Confessed! To what?
>
> **Mary Warren.** That she—(*in horror at the memory*) —she sometimes made a compact with Lucifer,
> 230 and wrote her name in his black book—with her blood—and bound herself to torment Christians till God's thrown down—and we all must worship Hell forevermore.

2. **fair poppet:** pretty doll.

(*pause*)

Proctor. But—surely you know what a jabberer she is. Did you tell them that?

Mary Warren. Mr. Proctor, in open court she near to choked us all to death.

Proctor. How, choked you?

240 **Mary Warren.** She sent her spirit out.

Elizabeth. Oh, Mary, Mary, surely you—

Mary Warren (*with an indignant edge*). She tried to kill me many times, Goody Proctor!

Elizabeth. Why, I never heard you mention that before.

Mary Warren. I never knew it before. I never knew anything before. When she come into the court I say to myself, I must not accuse this woman, for she sleep in ditches, and so very old and poor. But 250 then—then she sit there, denying and denying, and I feel a misty coldness climbin' up my back, and the skin on my skull begin to creep, and I feel a clamp around my neck and I cannot breathe air; and then (*entranced*) I hear a voice, a screamin' voice, and it were my voice—and all at once I remembered everything she done to me!

Proctor. Why? What did she do to you?

Mary Warren (*like one awakened to a marvelous secret insight*). So many time, Mr. Proctor, she come to 260 this very door, beggin' bread and a cup of cider— and mark this: whenever I turned her away empty, she *mumbled*.

Elizabeth. Mumbled! She may mumble if she's hungry.

Mary Warren. But *what* does she mumble? You must remember, Goody Proctor. Last month—a Monday, I think—she walked away, and I thought my guts would burst for two days after. Do you remember it?

Elizabeth. Why—I do, I think, but—

Mary Warren. And so I told that to Judge Hathorne, 270 and he asks her so. "Sarah Good," says he, "what curse do you mumble that this girl must fall sick after turning you away?" And then she replies

② Targeted Passage

DIFFERENTIATED INSTRUCTION

FOR STRATEGIC READERS

② Targeted Passage [Lines 213–233]

This passage reveals the extremes to which the community is willing to go to eliminate witchcraft and the desperation of the women charged with the crime.

- How many women have been arrested?
- What is the punishment if a person is found guilty of witchcraft? How can a person avoid that punishment?

- How does Mary feel about what happened to Goody Osburn and Goody Good?

FOR ADVANCED LEARNERS/AP

Research and Evaluate [small-group option] Point out that Mary's personal experience in court has convinced her that the evidence presented against the accused women is reliable. Ask students to reread Mary's account of what happened in court (lines 246–256) and to consider this question:

What reason other than Goody Good's "witchcraft" might have caused Mary to experience the symptoms that she describes in lines 249–256? Ask students to do some research to support their answers (including some research about "false memory syndrome"). Have students share their findings and see if they can reach a consensus about the validity of Mary's experience.

(*mimicking an old crone*) "Why, your excellence, no curse at all. I only say my commandments;[3] I hope I may say my commandments," says she!

Elizabeth. And that's an upright answer.

Mary Warren. Aye, but then Judge Hathorne say, "Recite for us your commandments!" (*leaning avidly toward them*) and of all the ten she could not say a
280 single one. She never knew no commandments, and they had her in a flat lie!

Proctor. And so condemned her?

Mary Warren (*now a little strained, seeing his stubborn doubt*). Why, they must when she condemned herself.

Proctor. But the proof, the proof!

Mary Warren (*with greater impatience with him*). I told you the proof. It's hard proof, hard as rock, the judges said.

Proctor (*pauses an instant, then*). You will not go to
290 court again, Mary Warren.

Mary Warren. I must tell you, sir, I will be gone every day now. I am amazed you do not see what weighty work we do.

Proctor. What work you do! It's strange work for a Christian girl to hang old women!

Mary Warren. But, Mr. Proctor, they will not hang them if they confess. Sarah Good will only sit in jail some time (*recalling*) and here's a wonder for you; think on this. Goody Good is pregnant!

300 **Elizabeth.** Pregnant! Are they mad? The woman's near to sixty!

Mary Warren. They had Doctor Griggs examine her, and she's full to the brim. And smokin' a pipe all these years, and no husband either! But she's safe, thank God, for they'll not hurt the innocent child. But be that not a marvel? You must see it, sir, it's God's work we do. So I'll be gone every day for some time. I'm—I am an official of the court, they say, and I—(*She has been edging toward offstage.*)

310 **Proctor.** I'll official you! (*He strides to the mantel, takes down the whip hanging there.*)

Mary Warren (*terrified, but coming erect, striving for her authority*). I'll not stand whipping any more!

Elizabeth (*hurriedly, as Proctor approaches*). Mary, promise now you'll stay at home—

Mary Warren (*backing from him, but keeping her erect posture, striving, striving for her way*). The Devil's loose in Salem, Mr. Proctor; we must discover where he's hiding!

320 **Proctor.** I'll whip the Devil out of you! (*With whip raised he reaches out for her, and she streaks away and yells.*)

Mary Warren (*pointing at Elizabeth*). I saved her life today!

(*Silence. His whip comes down.*)

Elizabeth (*softly*). I am accused?

Mary Warren (*quaking*). Somewhat mentioned. But I said I never see no sign you ever sent your spirit out to hurt no one, and seeing I do live so closely with
330 you, they dismissed it.

Elizabeth. Who accused me?

Mary Warren. I am bound by law, I cannot tell it. (*to Proctor*) I only hope you'll not be so sarcastical no more. Four judges and the King's deputy sat to dinner with us but an hour ago. I—I would have you speak civilly to me, from this out.

Proctor (*in horror, muttering in disgust at her*). Go to bed.

Mary Warren (*with a stamp of her foot*). I'll not be
340 ordered to bed no more, Mr. Proctor! I am eighteen and a woman, however single!

Proctor. Do you wish to sit up? Then sit up.

Mary Warren. I wish to go to bed!

Proctor (*in anger*). Good night, then!

Mary Warren. Good night. (*Dissatisfied, uncertain of herself, she goes out. Wide-eyed, both,* Proctor *and* Elizabeth *stand staring.*)

Elizabeth (*quietly*). Oh, the noose, the noose is up!

Proctor. There'll be no noose.

---

3. **commandments:** the Ten Commandments in the Bible.

Lines 277–288
REINFORCE *KEY IDEA:* HYSTERIA

Discuss Mary Warren explains that Goody Good was condemned when she could not recite the Ten Commandments. How might this method of judgment indicate that Salem's **hysteria** over witches is growing? *Possible answer: Mary asserts that Goody Good's inability to recite the Ten Commandments is "hard proof, hard as rock" (line 287) that she's a witch, when really such a lapse is not proof at all. The leap of judgment that it takes to connect the two ideas is an indication of hysteria—that is, hysteria is causing people to make life-and-death judgments against their neighbors based on nothing more than an elderly woman's faulty memory (which might be the result of the stress of the situation).*

FOR STRATEGIC READERS
Comprehension Support Point out the word *noose* in lines 348–349. Explain that a *noose* is the loop of rope used to hang someone and that Elizabeth and Proctor use the word to refer to Elizabeth's execution, should she be convicted. Have students paraphrase these two lines, using modern English, so that it reads something like this: *Elizabeth. Oh, they'll hang me, they'll hang me for sure!* *Proctor. No one is going to hang you.*

FOR ENGLISH LEARNERS
Language: Verb Tenses Explain that Mary Warren sometimes uses the present tense when describing past events, as in these examples: "she come into the court" (line 247); "I say to myself" (lines 247–248); "I never see no sign" (line 328). Elicit that *came, said,* and *saw,* respectively, are the standard verb forms in these examples. Then have pairs of students locate other uses of the present tense to relate a past event.

FOR ADVANCED LEARNERS/AP
Analyze Conflict Ask students to consider these questions as they reread lines 323–344:

- How has Mary's defense of Elizabeth in court changed the power dynamics among Mary, Elizabeth, and Proctor?
- How does that change reflect the upheaval throughout the community?

Have students summarize their analysis in a paragraph that they share with the class.

Use Realistic Dialogue Reread lines 354–356. How does Miller make this exchange realistic for the time of its setting? *Possible answer: Miller chooses era-specific words and expressions ("cry me out") and an inverted sentence ("Sit you down") to make this exchange realistic.*

Lines 378–384
TIERED DISCUSSION PROMPTS

Use these prompts to discuss Elizabeth's thoughts about why Abigail has accused her:

Restate Retell in your words what Elizabeth says about Abigail in lines 382–384. *Possible answer: Abigail wouldn't accuse me unless she had a lot to gain. She wants to get rid of me so that she can be with you.*

Analyze How and why does Elizabeth try to show that she is different from Goody Good and Goody Osburn? *Possible answer: Elizabeth notes the flaws of the women (lines 381–382) and sets herself above them both to make her point that Abigail has a different reason for accusing her.*

Evaluate How effective is this passage in deepening our understanding of Elizabeth and Abigail? Explain. *Possible answer: The passage is very effective. It shows that Elizabeth is perceptive, realistic, and smart; it also reveals the mean-spirited, dishonest side of Abigail's personality by suggesting that to get what she wants, she would have a person executed on false charges.*

---

350 **Elizabeth.** She wants me dead. I knew all week it would come to this!

Proctor (*without conviction*). They dismissed it. You heard her say—

Elizabeth. And what of tomorrow? She will cry me out until they take me!

Proctor. Sit you down.

Elizabeth. She wants me dead, John, you know it!

Proctor. I say sit down! (*She sits, trembling. He speaks quietly, trying to keep his wits.*) Now we must be wise, 360 Elizabeth.

Elizabeth (*with sarcasm, and a sense of being lost*). Oh, indeed, indeed!

Proctor. Fear nothing. I'll find Ezekiel Cheever. I'll tell him she said it were all sport.

Elizabeth. John, with so many in the jail, more than Cheever's help is needed now, I think. Would you favor me with this? Go to Abigail.

Proctor (*his soul hardening as he senses . . .*). What have I to say to Abigail?

370 **Elizabeth** (*delicately*). John—grant me this. You have a faulty understanding of young girls. There is a promise made in any bed—

Proctor (*striving against his anger*). What promise!

Elizabeth. Spoke or silent, a promise is surely made. And she may dote on it now—I am sure she does— and thinks to kill me, then to take my place.

(*Proctor's anger is rising; he cannot speak.*)

Elizabeth. It is her dearest hope, John, I know it. There be a thousand names; why does she call 380 mine? There be a certain danger in calling such a name—I am no Goody Good that sleeps in ditches, nor Osburn, drunk and half-witted. She'd dare not call out such a farmer's wife but there be monstrous profit in it. She thinks to take my place, John.

Proctor. She cannot think it! (*He knows it is true.*)

Elizabeth (*"reasonably"*). John, have you ever shown her somewhat of contempt? She cannot pass you in the church but you will blush—

Proctor. I may blush for my sin.

390 **Elizabeth.** I think she sees another meaning in that blush.

Proctor. And what see you? What see you, Elizabeth?

Elizabeth (*"conceding"*). I think you be somewhat ashamed, for I am there, and she so close.

Proctor. When will you know me, woman? Were I stone I would have cracked for shame this seven month!

Elizabeth. Then go and tell her she's a whore. Whatever promise she may sense—break it, John, break it.

400 **Proctor** (*between his teeth*). Good, then. I'll go. (*He starts for his rifle.*)

Elizabeth (*trembling, fearfully*). Oh, how unwillingly!

Proctor (*turning on her, rifle in hand*). I will curse her hotter than the oldest cinder in hell. But pray, begrudge me not my anger!

Elizabeth. Your anger! I only ask you—

Proctor. Woman, am I so base? Do you truly think me base?

Elizabeth. I never called you base.

410 **Proctor.** Then how do you charge me with such a promise? The promise that a stallion gives a mare I gave that girl!

Elizabeth. Then why do you anger with me when I bid you break it?

Proctor. Because it speaks deceit, and I am honest! But I'll plead no more! I see now your spirit twists around the single error of my life, and I will never tear it free!

Elizabeth (*crying out*). You'll tear it free—when you 420 come to know that I will be your only wife, or no wife at all! She has an arrow in you yet, John Proctor, and you know it well!

(*Quite suddenly, as though from the air, a figure appears in the doorway. They start slightly. It is Mr. Hale. He is different now—drawn a little, and there is a quality of deference, even of guilt, about his manner now.*)

DIFFERENTIATED INSTRUCTION

FOR ENGLISH LEARNERS

Vocabulary: Outdated Forms Discuss these examples of outdated uses of the verb *to be:*

> *Be* for *is* and *are:* lines 379, 380, 383
> *Were* for *was:* line 491

Make sure that students understand the meaning of each example, and encourage them to be alert to additional examples as they continue to read.

Hale. Good evening.

Proctor (*still in his shock*). Why, Mr. Hale! Good
430 evening to you, sir. Come in, come in.

Hale (*to* Elizabeth). I hope I do not startle you.

Elizabeth. No, no, it's only that I heard no horse—

Hale. You are Goodwife Proctor.

Proctor. Aye; Elizabeth.

Hale (*nods, then*). I hope you're not off to bed yet.

Proctor (*setting down his gun*). No, no. (Hale *comes
further into the room. And* Proctor, *to explain his
nervousness.*) We are not used to visitors after dark,
but you're welcome here. Will you sit you down, sir?

440 **Hale.** I will. (*He sits.*) Let you sit, Goodwife Proctor.

(*She does, never letting him out of her sight. There is
a pause as* Hale *looks about the room.*)

Proctor (*to break the silence*). Will you drink cider,
Mr. Hale?

Hale. No, it rebels[4] my stomach; I have some further
traveling yet tonight. Sit you down, sir. (Proctor
sits.) I will not keep you long, but I have some
business with you.

Proctor. Business of the court?

450 **Hale.** No—no, I come of my own, without the
court's authority. Hear me. (*He wets his lips.*) I know
not if you are aware, but your wife's name is—
mentioned in the court.

Proctor. We know it, sir. Our Mary Warren told us.
We are entirely amazed.

Hale. I am a stranger here, as you know. And in my
ignorance I find it hard to draw a clear opinion of
them that come accused before the court. And so
this afternoon, and now tonight, I go from house
460 to house—I come now from Rebecca Nurse's house
and—

Elizabeth (*shocked*). Rebecca's charged!

Hale. God forbid such a one be charged. She is,
however—mentioned somewhat.

Elizabeth (*with an attempt at a laugh*). You will never
believe, I hope, that Rebecca trafficked with the Devil.

Hale. Woman, it is possible.

Proctor (*taken aback*). Surely you cannot think so.

Hale. This is a strange time, Mister. No man may
470 longer doubt the powers of the dark are gathered
in monstrous attack upon this village. There is too
much evidence now to deny it. You will agree, sir?

Proctor (*evading*). I—have no knowledge in that line.
But it's hard to think so pious a woman be secretly
a Devil's bitch after seventy year of such good prayer.

Hale. Aye. But the Devil is a wily one, you cannot
deny it. However, she is far from accused, and I
know she will not be. (*pause*) I thought, sir, to put
some questions as to the Christian character of this
480 house, if you'll permit me.

Proctor (*coldly, resentful*). Why, we—have no fear
of questions, sir.

Hale. Good, then. (*He makes himself more comfortable.*) In the book of record that Mr. Parris keeps, I
note that you are rarely in the church on Sabbath Day.

Proctor. No, sir, you are mistaken.

Hale. Twenty-six time in seventeen month, sir. I must
call that rare. Will you tell me why you are so absent?

Proctor. Mr. Hale, I never knew I must account to
490 that man for I come to church or stay at home. My
wife were sick this winter.

Hale. So I am told. But you, Mister, why could you
not come alone?

Proctor. I surely did come when I could, and when
I could not I prayed in this house.

Hale. Mr. Proctor, your house is not a church; your
theology must tell you that.

Proctor. It does, sir, it does; and it tells me that a
minister may pray to God without he have golden
500 candlesticks upon the altar.

Hale. What golden candlesticks?

---

4. **rebels:** upsets.

◼ DRAW CONCLUSIONS ABOUT CHARACTERS

Think about Proctor's comments on this page. Why would it be reasonable to conclude that Proctor is an independent thinker? *Possible answer: Proctor is an independent thinker because he prefers to focus directly on God rather than on the rules and wishes of Reverend Parris. In particular, Proctor's decision not to have his youngest son baptized by Parris (lines 514–520) violates the rules for Puritan behavior but honors his conscience.*

If students need help . . . Discuss the importance of Proctor's comment about not seeing any "light of God" in Reverend Parris (lines 519–520). Help students link that comment to Proctor's bitterness over the fact that Parris replaced the pewter candlesticks with golden ones (lines 502–511).

ANALYZE VISUALS

Activity Study how the characters are positioned in the photo and what they are doing. What do their positions and activities reveal about the Proctor family? *Possible answer: The characters' positions reveal the distance between Elizabeth and Proctor by showing Elizabeth looking on from outside the group. The activity of reading, especially of Proctor reading to his sons, reveals that the household values thinking and education.*

Proctor. Since we built the church there were pewter candlesticks upon the altar; Francis Nurse made them, y'know, and a sweeter hand never touched the metal. But Parris came, and for twenty week he preach nothin' but golden candlesticks until he had them. I labor the earth from dawn of day to blink of night, and I tell you true, when I look to heaven and see my money glaring at his elbows—it hurt my
510 prayer, sir, it hurt my prayer. I think, sometimes, the man dreams cathedrals, not clapboard meetin' houses.

Hale (*thinks, then*). And yet, Mister, a Christian on Sabbath Day must be in church. (*pause*) Tell me— you have three children?

Proctor. Aye. Boys.

Hale. How comes it that only two are baptized?

Proctor (*starts to speak, then stops, then, as though unable to restrain this*). I like it not that Mr. Parris should lay his hand upon my baby. I see no light
520 of God in that man. I'll not conceal it.

Hale. I must say it, Mr. Proctor; that is not for you to decide. The man's ordained, therefore the light of God is in him.

Proctor (*flushed with resentment but trying to smile*).

What's your suspicion, Mr. Hale?

Hale. No, no, I have no—

Proctor. I nailed the roof upon the church, I hung the door—

Hale. Oh, did you! That's a good sign, then.

530 **Proctor.** It may be I have been too quick to bring the man to book,[5] but you cannot think we ever desired the destruction of religion. I think that's in your mind, is it not?

Hale (*not altogether giving way*). I—have—there is a softness in your record, sir, a softness.

Elizabeth. I think, maybe, we have been too hard with Mr. Parris. I think so. But sure we never loved the Devil here.

Hale (*nods, deliberating this. Then, with the voice of*
540 *one administering a secret test*). Do you know your Commandments, Elizabeth?

Elizabeth (*without hesitation, even eagerly*). I surely do. There be no mark of blame upon my life, Mr. Hale. I am a convenanted Christian woman.

Hale. And you, Mister?

Proctor (*a trifle unsteadily*). I—am sure I do, sir.

---

5. **bring the man to book:** judge the man.

John Proctor and his sons

DIFFERENTIATED INSTRUCTION

FOR ADVANCED LEARNERS/AP

Research: Church Membership Some scholars believe that a key aspect of the background to the Salem witch trials was the fear of certain leaders in the community that Puritan values no longer influenced citizens in the way that they once did. Challenge students to research what church membership once meant in terms of the rights and privileges it provided for Puritans in Massachusetts, and why, by the 1690s, a lapse of membership might have

reminded Puritan elders that the original ideals of the "city upon a hill" had begun to fade. Ask students to summarize their findings and present them to the class.

Hale (*glances at her open face, then at* John, *then*). Let you repeat them, if you will.

Proctor. The Commandments.

550 **Hale.** Aye.

Proctor (*looking off, beginning to sweat*). Thou shalt not kill.

Hale. Aye.

Proctor (*counting on his fingers*). Thou shalt not steal. Thou shalt not covet thy neighbor's goods, nor make unto thee any graven image. Thou shalt not take the name of the Lord in vain; thou shalt have no other gods before me. (*with some hesitation*) Thou shalt remember the Sabbath Day and keep it holy. (*Pause.*

560 *Then.*) Thou shalt honor thy father and mother. Thou shalt not bear false witness. (*He is stuck. He counts back on his fingers, knowing one is missing.*) Thou shalt not make unto thee any graven image.

Hale. You have said that twice, sir.

Proctor (*lost*). Aye. (*He is flailing for it.*)

Elizabeth (*delicately*). Adultery, John.

Proctor (*as though a secret arrow had pained his heart*). Aye. (*trying to grin it away—to* Hale) You see, sir, between the two of us we do know them

570 all. (Hale *only looks at* Proctor, *deep in his attempt to define this man.* Proctor *grows more uneasy.*) I think it be a small fault.

Hale. Theology, sir, is a fortress; no crack in a fortress may be accounted small. (*He rises; he seems worried now. He paces a little, in deep thought.*)

Proctor. There be no love for Satan in this house, Mister.

Hale. I pray it, I pray it dearly. (*He looks to both of them, an attempt at a smile on his face, but his misgiv-*

580 *ings are clear.*) Well, then—I'll bid you good night.

Elizabeth (*unable to restrain herself*). Mr. Hale. (*He turns.*) I do think you are suspecting me somewhat? Are you not?

Hale (*obviously disturbed—and evasive*). Goody Proctor, I do not judge you. My duty is to add what I may to the godly wisdom of the court. I pray you

both good health and good fortune. (*to* John) Good night, sir. (*He starts out.*)

Elizabeth (*with a note of desperation*). I think you
590 must tell him, John.

Hale. What's that?

Elizabeth (*restraining a call*). Will you tell him?

(*Slight pause.* Hale *looks questioningly at* John.)

Proctor (*with difficulty*). I—I have no witness and cannot prove it, except my word be taken. But I know the children's sickness had naught to do with witchcraft.

Hale (*stopped, struck*). Naught to do—?

Proctor. Mr. Parris discovered them sportin' in the
600 woods. They were startled and took sick.

(*pause*)

Hale. Who told you this?

Proctor (*hesitates, then*). Abigail Williams.

Hale. Abigail!

Proctor. Aye.

Hale (*his eyes wide*). Abigail Williams told you it had naught to do with witchcraft!

Proctor. She told me the day you came, sir.

Hale (*suspiciously*). Why—why did you keep this?
610 **Proctor.** I never knew until tonight that the world is gone daft with this nonsense.

Hale. Nonsense! Mister, I have myself examined Tituba, Sarah Good, and numerous others that have confessed to dealing with the Devil. They have *confessed* it.

Proctor. And why not, if they must hang for denyin' it? There are them that will swear to anything before they'll hang; have you never thought of that?

Hale. I have. I—I have indeed. (*It is his own suspi-*
620 *cion, but he resists it. He glances at* Elizabeth, *then at* John.) And you—would you testify to this in court?

Proctor. I—had not reckoned with goin' into court. But if I must I will.

Hale. Do you falter here?

Targeted Passage ③

FOR STRATEGIC READERS

③ **Targeted Passage** [Lines 594–623]

In this passage, both Hale and Proctor come to a new understanding of the situation.

- What news from Proctor shocks Hale? Why is Hale suspicious about its accuracy?
- How does Proctor explain his silence?
- Why does Hale consider his interviews with other Salemites effective? How does Proctor explain Hale's effectiveness?

- What does Hale suspect, though he fights the suspicion?

FOR ENGLISH LEARNERS

Vocabulary: Outdated Forms Discuss these terms from the dialogue that rarely appear in modern English:

- *Thou shalt* (lines 551–563), "You will"
- *pray it dearly* (line 578), "hope so very much"
- *naught* (lines 596, 598, 607), "nothing"
- *daft* (line 611), "crazy"
- *reckoned with* (line 622), "planned on"

Lines 578–595
TIERED DISCUSSION PROMPTS

Use these prompts to help students explore the characterization in this critical scene:

Summarize What does Elizabeth see in Hale's behavior that makes her desperate for Proctor to reveal what he knows about Abigail? *Possible answer: Elizabeth sees that Hale is "obviously disturbed" by the Proctors' answers to his questions and "evasive" in declaring that he supports her (line 584). She also sees that although Hale attempts to smile, "misgivings are clear" on his face (lines 579–580).*

Analyze Elizabeth nearly begs Proctor to tell Hale about Abigail. Why do you think Elizabeth doesn't reveal the information herself? *Possible answer: Elizabeth defers to her husband; she would never reveal something about him without his consent. Furthermore, it is Proctor rather than Elizabeth who would have firsthand knowledge of the conversation with Abigail.*

Evaluate Do you find Proctor's weakness in this scene believable? Why or why not? *Possible answer: Proctor's weakness—that is, his reluctance to give information that might save his wife—is believable. Readers and audience members understand and sympathize with Proctor's desire to protect himself and his wife from scandal.*

TIERED DISCUSSION PROMPTS

Use these prompts to help students understand Elizabeth's defense before Reverend Hale:

Connect Have you or someone you know ever had to put up a defense against a false accusation? How does that experience help you understand Elizabeth's risky response to Hale's concern that she does not believe in witches? *Accept all responses that attempt to connect to Elizabeth's self-defense.*

Interpret When Proctor comes to her defense during the questioning, Elizabeth cries out, "Question Abigail Williams about the Gospel, not myself!" (lines 661–662). What does she mean? *Possible answer: Elizabeth is implying that she knows the Bible and lives according to its teachings, whereas Abigail, whom everyone seems to consider above reproach, is the one who needs lessons in Christian morality (because of her lies and her illicit interest in Proctor).*

Synthesize Consider what you have learned about Elizabeth in this passage. Do you think that she will make a favorable impression in court? Why or why not? *Possible answer: Elizabeth probably will make an unfavorable impression because she is willing to speak her mind even though she voices an unpopular—and, in the mind of the court, perhaps heretical—view of witchcraft.*

Proctor. I falter nothing, but I may wonder if my story will be credited in such a court. I do wonder on it, when such a steady-minded minister as you will suspicion such a woman that never lied, and cannot, and the world knows she cannot! I may
630 falter somewhat, Mister; I am no fool.

Hale (*quietly—it has impressed him*). Proctor, let you open with me now, for I have a rumor that troubles me. It's said you hold no belief that there may even be witches in the world. Is that true, sir?

Proctor (*He knows this is critical, and is striving against his disgust with* Hale *and with himself for even answering*). I know not what I have said, I may have said it. I have wondered if there be witches in the world—although I cannot believe they come among
640 us now.   **Targeted Passage** ④

Hale. Then you do not believe—

Proctor. I have no knowledge of it; the Bible speaks of witches, and I will not deny them.

Hale. And you, woman?

Elizabeth. I—I cannot believe it.

Hale (*shocked*). You cannot!

Proctor. Elizabeth, you bewilder him!

Elizabeth (*to* Hale). I cannot think the Devil may own a woman's soul, Mr. Hale, when she keeps an
650 upright way, as I have. I am a good woman, I know it; and if you believe I may do only good work in the world, and yet be secretly bound to Satan, then I must tell you, sir, I do not believe it.

Hale. But, woman, you do believe there are witches in—

Elizabeth. If you think that I am one, then I say there are none.

Hale. You surely do not fly against the Gospel, the Gospel—

660 **Proctor.** She believe in the Gospel, every word!

Elizabeth. Question Abigail Williams about the Gospel, not myself!

(Hale *stares at her.*)

Proctor. She do not mean to doubt the Gospel, sir, you cannot think it. This be a Christian house, sir,

---

a Christian house.

Hale. God keep you both; let the third child be quickly baptized, and go you without fail each Sunday in to Sabbath prayer; and keep a solemn, quiet
670 way among you. I think—

(Giles Corey *appears in doorway.*)

Giles. John!

Proctor. Giles! What's the matter?

Giles. They take my wife.

(Francis Nurse *enters.*)

Giles. And his Rebecca!

Proctor (*to* Francis). Rebecca's in the *jail!*

Francis. Aye, Cheever come and take her in his wagon. We've only now come from the jail, and
680 they'll not even let us in to see them.

Elizabeth. They've surely gone wild now, Mr. Hale!

Francis (*going to* Hale). Reverend Hale! Can you not speak to the Deputy Governor? I'm sure he mistakes these people—

Hale. Pray calm yourself, Mr. Nurse.

Francis. My wife is the very brick and mortar of the church, Mr. Hale (*indicating* Giles) and Martha Corey, there cannot be a woman closer yet to God than Martha.

690 **Hale.** How is Rebecca charged, Mr. Nurse?

Francis (*with a mocking, half-hearted laugh*). For murder, she's charged! (*mockingly quoting the warrant*) "For the marvelous and supernatural murder of Goody Putnam's babies." What am I to do, Mr. Hale?

Hale (*turns from* Francis, *deeply troubled, then*). Believe me, Mr. Nurse, if Rebecca Nurse be tainted, then nothing's left to stop the whole green world from burning. Let you rest upon the justice of the court; the court will send her home, I know it.

700 **Francis.** You cannot mean she will be tried in court!

Hale (*pleading*). Nurse, though our hearts break, we cannot flinch; these are new times, sir. There is a misty plot afoot so subtle we should be criminal to cling to old respects and ancient friendships. I have seen too many frightful proofs in court—the Devil

---

DIFFERENTIATED INSTRUCTION

FOR STRATEGIC READERS

④ **Targeted Passage [Lines 672–695]**

This passage shows that even the most upstanding citizens of Salem are not safe from the charge of witchcraft.

- With what crime is Rebecca Nurse charged?

- Why is it so surprising that Rebecca Nurse and Martha Corey have been accused?

- How does Elizabeth characterize the town after learning of these arrests? Why does she direct her comment to Reverend Hale?

Comprehension Support Explain that Hale expresses his disbelief that Rebecca Nurse could be "tainted," or guilty of association with the Devil (lines 696–698). Then read this comment aloud: "if Rebecca Nurse be tainted, then nothing's left to stop the whole green world from burning." Help students restate Hale's comment in their own words, as in this example: *If Rebecca Nurse is guilty of witchcraft, then no one is safe from accusation.*

is alive in Salem, and we dare not quail to follow wherever the accusing finger points!

Proctor (*angered*). How may such a woman murder children?

710 **Hale** (*in great pain*). Man, remember, until an hour before the Devil fell, God thought him beautiful in Heaven.

Giles. I never said my wife were a witch, Mr. Hale; I only said she were reading books!

Hale. Mr. Corey, exactly what complaint were made on your wife?

Giles. That bloody mongrel Walcott charge her. Y'see, he buy a pig of my wife four or five year ago, and the pig died soon after. So he come dancin' in

720 for his money back. So my Martha, she says to him, "Walcott, if you haven't the wit to feed a pig properly, you'll not live to own many," she says. Now he goes to court and claims that from that day to this he cannot keep a pig alive for more than four weeks because my Martha bewitch them with her books!

(*Enter* Ezekiel Cheever. *A shocked silence.*)

Cheever. Good evening to you, Proctor.

Proctor. Why, Mr. Cheever. Good evening.

Cheever. Good evening, all. Good evening, Mr. Hale.

730 **Proctor.** I hope you come not on business of the court.

Cheever. I do, Proctor, aye. I am clerk of the court now, y'know.

(*Enter* Marshal Herrick, *a man in his early thirties, who is somewhat shamefaced at the moment.*)

Giles. It's a pity, Ezekiel, that an honest tailor might have gone to Heaven must burn in Hell. You'll burn for this, do you know it?

Cheever. You know yourself I must do as I'm told.

740 You surely know that, Giles. And I'd as lief[6] you'd not be sending me to Hell. I like not the sound of it, I tell you; I like not the sound of it. (*He fears* Proctor, *but starts to reach inside his coat.*) Now believe me, Proctor, how heavy be the law, all its tonnage

---

6. **as lief** (lēf): rather.

I do carry on my back tonight. (*He takes out a warrant.*) I have a warrant for your wife.

Proctor (*to* Hale). You said she were not charged!

Hale. I know nothin' of it. (*to* Cheever) When were she charged?

750 **Cheever.** I am given sixteen warrant tonight, sir, and she is one.

Proctor. Who charged her?

Cheever. Why, Abigail Williams charge her.

Proctor. On what proof, what proof?

Cheever (*looking about the room*). Mr. Proctor, I have little time. The court bid me search your house, but I like not to search a house. So will you hand me any poppets that your wife may keep here?

Proctor. Poppets?

760 **Elizabeth.** I never kept no poppets, not since I were a girl.

Cheever (*embarrassed, glancing toward the mantel where sits* Mary Warren's *poppet*). I spy a poppet, Goody Proctor.

Elizabeth. Oh! (*going for it*) Why, this is Mary's.

Cheever (*shyly*). Would you please to give it to me?

Elizabeth (*handing it to him, asks* Hale). Has the court discovered a text in poppets now?

Cheever (*carefully holding the poppet*). Do you keep
770 any others in this house?

Proctor. No, nor this one either till tonight. What signifies a poppet?

Cheever. Why, a poppet—(*He gingerly turns the poppet over.*) a poppet may signify—Now, woman, will you please to come with me?

Proctor. She will not! (*to* Elizabeth) Fetch Mary here.

Cheever (*ineptly reaching toward* Elizabeth). No, no, I am forbid to leave her from my sight.

Proctor (*pushing his arm away*). You'll leave her out
780 of sight and out of mind, Mister. Fetch Mary, Elizabeth. (Elizabeth *goes upstairs.*)

Hale. What signifies a poppet, Mr. Cheever?

THE CRUCIBLE: ACT TWO **171**

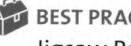

● CONVENTIONS OF DRAMA

The characters become more agitated and the dialogue moves quickly as the plot now becomes more complicated. How does Abigail use the poppet to create further conflict between herself and Elizabeth? *Possible answer:* *Abigail has sabotaged the poppet, knowing that Mary would give it to Elizabeth; then she injured herself to implicate Elizabeth falsely.*

If students need help . . .

- Review with them the action discussed in this scene involving Mary, Abigail, and the poppet, especially lines 799–810.

- Help students fill in a Sequence Chain to understand the steps leading to Elizabeth's being charged with the stabbing of Abigail.

```
┌─────────────────────────────────────┐
│ Mary Warren sews a poppet in court.  │
└─────────────────────────────────────┘
                  ↓
┌─────────────────────────────────────┐
│ Abigail sticks a needle into the     │
│ poppet.                              │
└─────────────────────────────────────┘
                  ↓
┌─────────────────────────────────────┐
│ Mary gives the poppet to Elizabeth.  │
└─────────────────────────────────────┘
                  ↓
┌─────────────────────────────────────┐
│ Abigail falls to the ground with     │
│ a needle in her belly.               │
└─────────────────────────────────────┘
                  ↓
┌─────────────────────────────────────┐
│ Abigail claims that Elizabeth's      │
│ "spirit" put the needle into her.    │
└─────────────────────────────────────┘
                  ↓
┌─────────────────────────────────────┐
│ Elizabeth is arrested.               │
└─────────────────────────────────────┘
```

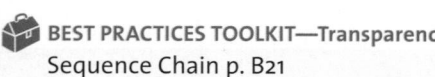 **BEST PRACTICES TOOLKIT—Transparency** Sequence Chain p. B21

Cheever (*turning the poppet over in his hands*). Why, they say it may signify that she—(*He has lifted the poppet's skirt, and his eyes widen in astonished fear.*) Why, this, this—

Proctor (*reaching for the poppet*). What's there?

Cheever. Why (*He draws out a long needle from the poppet.*) it is a needle! Herrick, Herrick, it is a
790 needle!

(*Herrick comes toward him.*)

Proctor (*angrily, bewildered*). And what signifies a needle!

Cheever (*his hands shaking*). Why, this go hard with her, Proctor, this—I had my doubts, Proctor, I had my doubts, but here's calamity. (*to Hale, showing the needle*) You see it, sir, it is a needle!

Hale. Why? What meanin' has it?

Cheever (*wide-eyed, trembling*). The girl, the Wil-
800 liams girl, Abigail Williams, sir. She sat to dinner in Reverend Parris's house tonight, and without word nor warnin' she falls to the floor. Like a struck beast, he says, and screamed a scream that a bull would weep to hear. And he goes to save her, and, stuck two inches in the flesh of her belly, he draw a needle out. And demandin' of her how she come to be so stabbed, she (*to Proctor now*) testify it were your wife's familiar spirit[7] pushed it in.

Proctor. Why, she done it herself! (*to Hale*) I hope
810 you're not takin' this for proof, Mister!

(*Hale, struck by the proof, is silent.*)

Cheever. 'Tis hard proof! (*to Hale*) I find here a poppet Goody Proctor keeps. I have found it, sir. And in the belly of the poppet a needle's stuck. I tell you true, Proctor, I never warranted to see such proof of Hell, and I bid you obstruct me not, for I—

(*Enter Elizabeth with Mary Warren. Proctor, seeing Mary Warren, draws her by the arm to Hale.*)

Proctor. Here now! Mary, how did this poppet come
820 into my house?

Mary Warren (*frightened for herself, her voice very small*). What poppet's that, sir?

Proctor (*impatiently, pointing at the doll in* Cheever's *hand*). This poppet, this poppet.

Mary Warren (*evasively, looking at it*). Why, I—I think it is mine.

Proctor. It is your poppet, is it not?

Mary Warren (*not understanding the direction of this*). It—is, sir.

830 **Proctor.** And how did it come into this house?

Mary Warren (*glancing about at the avid faces*). Why—I made it in the court, sir, and—give it to Goody Proctor tonight.

Proctor (*to Hale*). Now, sir—do you have it?

Hale. Mary Warren, a needle have been found inside this poppet.

Mary Warren (*bewildered*). Why, I meant no harm by it, sir.

Proctor (*quickly*). You stuck that needle in yourself?

840 **Mary Warren.** I—I believe I did, sir, I—

Proctor (*to Hale*). What say you now?

Hale (*watching* Mary Warren *closely*). Child, you are certain this be your natural memory? May it be, perhaps, that someone conjures you even now to say this?

Mary Warren. Conjures me? Why, no, sir, I am entirely myself, I think. Let you ask Susanna Walcott—she saw me sewin' it in court. (*or better still*) Ask Abby, Abby sat beside me when I made it.

850 **Proctor** (*to Hale, of* Cheever). Bid him begone. Your mind is surely settled now. Bid him out, Mr. Hale.

Elizabeth. What signifies a needle?

Hale. Mary—you charge a cold and cruel murder on Abigail.

Mary Warren. Murder! I charge no—

Hale. Abigail were stabbed tonight; a needle were found stuck into her belly—

---

7. **familiar spirit:** the spirit or demon, most usually in the form of an animal such as a black cat, that was a companion and helper to a witch.

DIFFERENTIATED INSTRUCTION

FOR STRATEGIC READERS

Comprehension Support Have students reread the exchange between Hale and Mary Warren in lines 842–849. Point out that Hale's question, "May it be, perhaps, that someone conjures [bewitches] you even now to say this?" (lines 843–845) attempts to influence Mary's answer. Discuss with students whom Hale means by "someone"—the Devil? Abigail? Elizabeth?

Elizabeth. And she charges me?

Hale. Aye.

860 **Elizabeth** (*her breath knocked out*). Why—! The girl is murder! She must be ripped out of the world!

Cheever (*pointing at* Elizabeth). You've heard that, sir! Ripped out of the world! Herrick, you heard it!

Proctor (*suddenly snatching the warrant out of* Cheever's *hands*). Out with you.

Cheever. Proctor, you dare not touch the warrant.

Proctor (*ripping the warrant*). Out with you!

Cheever. You've ripped the Deputy Governor's warrant, man!

870 **Proctor.** Damn the Deputy Governor! Out of my house!

Hale. Now, Proctor, Proctor!

Proctor. Get y'gone with them! You are a broken minister.

Hale. Proctor, if she is innocent, the court—

Proctor. If *she* is innocent! Why do you never wonder if Parris be innocent, or Abigail? Is the accuser always holy now? Were they born this morning as clean as God's fingers? I'll tell you what's walking
880 Salem—vengeance is walking Salem. We are what we always were in Salem, but now the little crazy children are jangling the keys of the kingdom, and common vengeance writes the law! This warrant's vengeance! I'll not give my wife to vengeance!

Elizabeth. I'll go, John— **Targeted Passage** ⑤

Proctor. You will not go!

Herrick. I have nine men outside. You cannot keep her. The law binds me, John, I cannot budge.

Proctor (*to* Hale, *ready to break him*). Will you see
890 her taken?

Hale. Proctor, the court is just—

Proctor. Pontius Pilate! God will not let you wash your hands of this![8]

Elizabeth. John—I think I must go with them. (*He cannot bear to look at her.*) Mary, there is bread

enough for the morning; you will bake, in the afternoon. Help Mr. Proctor as you were his daughter—you owe me that, and much more. (*She is fighting her weeping. To* Proctor.) When the children wake,
900 speak nothing of witchcraft—it will frighten them. (*She cannot go on.*)

Proctor. I will bring you home. I will bring you soon.

Elizabeth. Oh, John, bring me soon!

Proctor. I will fall like an ocean on that court! Fear nothing, Elizabeth.

Elizabeth (*with great fear*). I will fear nothing. (*She looks about the room, as though to fix it in her mind.*) Tell the children I have gone to visit someone sick.

(*She walks out the door,* Herrick *and* Cheever *behind*
910 *her. For a moment,* Proctor *watches from the doorway. The clank of chain is heard.*)

Proctor. Herrick! Herrick, don't chain her! (*He rushes out the door. From outside.*) Damn you, man, you will not chain her! Off with them! I'll not have it! I will not have her chained!

(*There are other men's voices against his.* Hale, *in a fever of guilt and uncertainty, turns from the door to avoid the sight;* Mary Warren *bursts into tears and sits weeping.* Giles Corey *calls to* Hale.)

920 **Giles.** And yet silent, minister? It is fraud, you know it is fraud! What keeps you, man?

(Proctor *is half braced, half pushed into the room by two deputies and* Herrick.)

Proctor. I'll pay you, Herrick, I will surely pay you!

Herrick (*panting*). In God's name, John, I cannot help myself. I must chain them all. Now let you keep inside this house till I am gone! (*He goes out with his deputies.*)

(Proctor *stands there, gulping air. Horses and a wagon*
930 *creaking are heard.*)

Hale (*in great uncertainty*). Mr. Proctor—

Proctor. Out of my sight!

Hale. Charity, Proctor, charity. What I have heard in

---

8. **Pontius** (pŏn′tē-əs) **Pilate . . . hands of this:** the Roman governor who presided over the trial and sentencing of Christ. Pilate publicly washed his hands to absolve himself of responsibility for Christ's death.

Lines 894–908
TIERED DISCUSSION PROMPTS

Use these prompts to help students explore Elizabeth's departure:

Connect Have you ever tried to act strong in a difficult situation? Do you think that you were successful? Do you think that others noticed your attempt? *Accept all responses.*

Interpret Why is it significant that when Elizabeth realizes that she must leave her home, she immediately gives a set of ordinary household orders? *Possible answer: Elizabeth's orders are significant because they underscore her central role in her family—that of manager of the home and chief caretaker of the children. She is also trying to maintain a sense of normalcy for others as she herself faces great danger.*

Synthesize Given what you have learned about Proctor and Elizabeth, who do you think is better equipped to handle a court appearance? Explain. *Possible answer: Elizabeth seems better equipped to handle the upcoming challenge. Although she is afraid, she makes herself stand up and face the future; Proctor, however, has been reluctant to get involved because of his past relationship with Abigail.*

FOR STRATEGIC READERS

⑤ **Targeted Passage [Lines 876–884]**

In this passage, Proctor's outburst points to a key idea in *The Crucible*.

- According to Proctor, what does a person gain by accusing others of witchcraft?

- Why does Proctor say that the children have all the power in Salem now? What evidence might he offer to prove this claim?

- Who does Proctor think are the truly guilty people in Salem? Why are they guilty?

FOR ADVANCED LEARNERS/AP

Analyze Character [paired option] Point out that Reverend Hale is "in a fever of guilt and uncertainty" and cannot watch as Proctor protests the chaining of Elizabeth (lines 916–918). Ask students to write a soliloquy in which Hale expresses his thoughts and feelings in this scene, drawing upon his experiences in Salem thus far and perhaps speculating about his future involvement there. Invite students to share and compare soliloquies in small groups.

REINFORCE *KEY IDEA:* HYSTERIA

How has **hysteria** created a situation that causes Proctor to say, "Now Hell and Heaven grapple on our backs, and all our old pretense is ripped away" (lines 996–998)? *Possible answer: Hysteria in the community has created a situation in which people's basest potential is being revealed and even encouraged. Now the Salemites must decide whether to continue along the destructive path that their hysteria has created (Hell) or to treat the accusations fairly and without fear (Heaven).*

SELECTION WRAP–UP

REFLECT Have students consider how far the girls' accusations reach by the end of Act Two. What does the Salemites' willingness to support the girls' accusations reveal about Salem's people? about its leaders?

★ CRITIQUE

- Remind students that although Abigail does not appear in this act, her presence is undeniable. Have students identify and explain the moment in Act Two in which they felt Abigail's presence most strongly.

- After completing the After Reading questions on page 175, have students revisit their responses and tell whether they have changed their opinions.

---

her favor, I will not fear to testify in court. God help me, I cannot judge her guilty or innocent—I know not. Only this consider: the world goes mad, and it profit nothing you should lay the cause to the vengeance of a little girl.

Proctor. You are a coward! Though you be ordained
940 in God's own tears, you are a coward now!

Hale. Proctor, I cannot think God be provoked so grandly by such a petty cause. The jails are packed—our greatest judges sit in Salem now—and hangin's promised. Man, we must look to cause proportionate. Were there murder done, perhaps, and never brought to light? Abomination? Some secret blasphemy that stinks to Heaven? Think on cause, man, and let you help me to discover it. For there's your way, believe it, there is your only way, when such
950 confusion strikes upon the world. (*He goes to* Giles *and* Francis.) Let you counsel among yourselves; think on your village and what may have drawn from heaven such thundering wrath upon you all. I shall pray God open up our eyes.

(Hale *goes out.*)   **Targeted Passage** Ⓖ

Francis (*struck by* Hale's *mood*). I never heard no murder done in Salem.

Proctor (*He has been reached by* Hale's *words*). Leave me, Francis, leave me.

960 **Giles** (*shaken*). John—tell me, are we lost?

Proctor. Go home now, Giles. We'll speak on it tomorrow.

Giles. Let you think on it. We'll come early, eh?

Proctor. Aye. Go now, Giles.

Giles. Good night, then.

(Giles Corey *goes out. After a moment.*)

Mary Warren (*in a fearful squeak of a voice*). Mr. Proctor, very likely they'll let her come home once they're given proper evidence.

970 **Proctor.** You're coming to the court with me, Mary. You will tell it in the court.

Mary Warren. I cannot charge murder on Abigail.

Proctor (*moving menacingly toward her*). You will tell the court how that poppet come here and who stuck the needle in.

Mary Warren. She'll kill me for sayin' that! (Proctor *continues toward her.*) Abby'll charge lechery on you, Mr. Proctor!

Proctor (*halting*). She's told you!

980 **Mary Warren.** I have known it, sir. She'll ruin you with it, I know she will.

Proctor (*hesitating, and with deep hatred of himself*). Good. Then her saintliness is done with. (Mary *backs from him.*) We will slide together into our pit; you will tell the court what you know.

Mary Warren (*in terror*). I cannot, they'll turn on me—

(Proctor *strides and catches her, and she is repeating,* "I cannot, I cannot!")

990 **Proctor.** My wife will never die for me! I will bring your guts into your mouth but that goodness will not die for me!

Mary Warren (*struggling to escape him*). I cannot do it, I cannot!

Proctor (*grasping her by the throat as though he would strangle her*). Make your peace with it! Now Hell and Heaven grapple on our backs, and all our old pretense is ripped away—make your peace! (*He throws her to the floor, where she sobs,* "I cannot, I cannot . . ."
1000 *And now, half to himself, staring, and turning to the open door.*) Peace. It is a providence, and no great change; we are only what we always were, but naked now. (*He walks as though toward a great horror, facing the open sky.*) Aye, naked! And the wind, God's icy wind, will blow!

(And she is over and over again sobbing, "I cannot, I cannot, I cannot," as the curtain falls.)

DIFFERENTIATED INSTRUCTION

FOR STRATEGIC READERS

Ⓖ Targeted Passage [Lines 934–954]

This passage reveals Hale's stubbornness, despite his concern about the way that Salem is handling its witchcraft scare.

- To whom does Hale refer when he says that the "the vengeance of a little girl" could not have caused the town's frenzy?

- Why does Proctor call Hale a coward?

- Why does Hale think that such terrible events are happening in Salem? Does he think that witchcraft is the only explanation?

Comprehension Support As students reread Proctor's threat in lines 990–992, point out the word "goodness." Elicit or explain that Proctor uses the word to refer to Elizabeth; she is the "goodness" that he will not allow to be executed. Have students suggest other terms that Proctor could use to refer to his wife, based on what they have learned about Elizabeth in Act Two.

Comprehension

1. **Recall** Why does Elizabeth want John to go to Salem?

2. **Clarify** Why does Hale come to the Proctors' home?

3. **Summarize** What proof leads to Elizabeth's arrest?

Literary Analysis

4. **Form Opinions** Do you think Reverend Hale believes that Elizabeth Proctor is practicing witchcraft? Support your opinion with specific details.

5. **Draw Conclusions About Characters** Review the **traits** you recorded in your chart for Elizabeth Proctor. How would you describe her character?

6. **Analyze Conventions of Drama** What does **dialogue** reveal about the complicated relationship between John and Elizabeth in the following scenes?

   • Elizabeth learns that John was alone with Abigail (lines 132–138)
   • Elizabeth asks John to break his unspoken promise to Abigail (lines 398–422)
   • John threatens Mary Warren (lines 990–1005)

7. **Analyze Dramatic Irony** Dramatic irony occurs when readers know more about a situation than a character does. Why is John struck by Hale's declaration that "some secret blasphemy" (lines 946–947) has caused all of the confusion?

8. **Make Judgments About a Character** How would you judge John's behavior so far? Cite evidence from the play to support your judgment.

9. **Compare Characters** Compare the following characters and determine which one has the greatest faith in the court proceedings. What accounts for their differing attitudes?

   • John Proctor   • Hale   • Cheever

Literary Criticism

10. **Historical Context** Miller wrote that during the anti-Communist hearings, "I saw accepted the notion that conscience was no longer a private matter but one of state administration." How does this notion apply to the witch-hunts in Salem?

R3.5

CALIFORNIA

Practice and Apply

After Reading

Use these copy masters to check understanding and provide extra support:

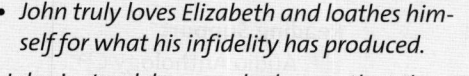 **RESOURCE MANAGER**—Copy Masters
   Reading Check p. 265
   Conventions of Drama p. 263
   Question Support p. 266

   Additional selection questions are provided for teachers on page 259.

ANSWERS

1. *to tell the Salem court that its cases are based on Abigail's fraudulent testimony*

2. *to determine the Christian character of their household*

3. *a doll with a needle in it, linked to Abigail's claim that Elizabeth's spirit stabbed her*

Possible answers:

4. *Yes; he is "struck by the proof" of the poppet (line 811). No; he thinks she is a good woman—so much so that he turns away in "guilt and uncertainty" when she is arrested (line 917).*

5. ■ **SKILLS FOCUS Draw Conclusions About Characters** *Elizabeth is virtuous, honest, and courageous, yet defensive of her position as the wronged wife and cold toward John.*

6. ● **SKILLS FOCUS Conventions of Drama**
   • *There still is much tension between John and Elizabeth over Abigail.*
   • *John feels that Elizabeth does not trust him, and Elizabeth feels that John is not honest about his feelings.*

Assess and Reteach

Assess

RESOURCE MANAGER—Copy Masters
   Selection Test A pp. 267–268
   Selection Test B/C pp. 269–270
   Test Generator CD

Reteach

STANDARDS LESSON FILE
   Literature Lessons 1–2: Characters
   Literature Lesson 6: Conflict
   Literature Lessons 23–24: Elements of Drama
   Reading Lesson 9: Drawing Conclusions

   • *John truly loves Elizabeth and loathes himself for what his infidelity has produced.*

7. *John is struck because he knows that the "secret blasphemy" might be his adultery.*

8. *So far, John appears weak and defensive. He hesitates to expose Abigail, and he is angry that Elizabeth is disappointed in him. However, by the end of Act Two, he agrees to appear in court and rages against Elizabeth's arrest.*

9. *Proctor: He thinks the proceedings are unjust, for he knows Abigail's motives.*
   Hale: He wants to believe the proceedings

are just. Hale probably has the greatest faith in the proceedings because he set them in motion.

   Cheever: He believes the proceedings are just because he is a court official.

10. *The notion applies to the witch-hunts because personal principles no longer seem to matter in Salem. For example, Proctor's decision not to attend church due to his moral convictions arouses suspicion. The court is interested in the perception of guilt, even guilt based on far-fetched accusations.*

Practice and Apply

Get Into the Act

SUMMARY

In Act Three, Proctor brings Mary Warren to the court, where Giles Corey and Francis Nurse also are trying to defend their wives. There, Mary confesses that Abigail and the other girls are frauds. When Abigail accuses Mary of bewitching her, Mary turns from Proctor and rejoins the girls. Proctor admits his infidelity, but Elizabeth denies it to save his reputation. The girls make hysterical accusations against Proctor; when he is arrested, Reverend Hale quits in disgust.

LITERARY ANALYSIS

● CONVENTIONS OF DRAMA

These stage directions describe the setting of Act Three. Who is on stage as the act opens? Of whose presence is the audience aware? Explain. ***Possible answer:*** *As the act opens, the stage is empty. The audience is aware of the presence of Judge Hathorne and Martha Corey, whose voices are heard offstage. They are in the meeting house, to the right of the vestry, the room that the set represents.*

If students need help . . .

- Call on volunteers to locate details about the set and characters in the stage directions.

- Use the stage directions to help students sketch the room.

Act *Three*

(*The vestry room of the Salem meeting house, now serving as the anteroom*[1] *of the General Court.*

As the curtain rises, the room is empty, but for sunlight pouring through two high windows in the back wall. The room is solemn, even forbidding. Heavy beams jut out, boards of random widths make up the walls. At the right are two doors leading into the meeting house proper, where the court is being held. At the left another door leads outside.

There is a plain bench at the left, and another at the right. In the center a rather long meeting table, with stools and a considerable armchair snugged up to it.

Through the partitioning wall at the right we hear a prosecutor's voice, Judge Hathorne's, *asking a question; then a woman's voice,* Martha Corey's, *replying.*)

Hathorne's Voice. Now, Martha Corey, there is abundant evidence in our hands to show that you have given yourself to the reading of fortunes. Do you deny it?

Martha Corey's Voice. I am innocent to a witch. I know not what a witch is.

Hathorne's Voice. How do you know, then, that you are not a witch?

Martha Corey's Voice. If I were, I would know it.

10 **Hathorne's Voice.** Why do you hurt these children?

Martha Corey's Voice. I do not hurt them. I scorn it!

Giles' Voice (*roaring*). I have evidence for the court!

(*Voices of townspeople rise in excitement.*)

Danforth's Voice. You will keep your seat!

Giles' Voice. Thomas Putnam is reaching out for land!

Danforth's Voice. Remove that man, Marshal!

Giles' Voice. You're hearing lies, lies!

(*A roaring goes up from the people.*)

20 **Hathorne's Voice.** Arrest him, excellency!

Giles' Voice. I have evidence. Why will you not hear my evidence?

(*The door opens and* Giles *is half carried into the vestry room by* Herrick.)

Giles. Hands off, damn you, let me go!

Herrick. Giles, Giles!

Giles. Out of my way, Herrick! I bring evidence—

Herrick. You cannot go in there, Giles; it's a court!

(*Enter* Hale *from the court.*)

30 **Hale.** Pray be calm a moment.

Giles. You, Mr. Hale, go in there and demand I speak.

---

1. **vestry room . . . anteroom:** A vestry room is a room in a church used for nonreligious meetings or church business. An anteroom is a waiting room or a room that leads into another.

176   UNIT 1: EARLY AMERICAN WRITING

Resources for Act Three

---

* **Resources for Differentiation**   † **Also in Spanish**   ‡ **In Haitian Creole and Vietnamese**

Paul Scofield as Deputy Governor Danforth

THE CRUCIBLE: ACT THREE **177**

ANALYZE VISUALS

Activity Explain that students will meet Judge Danforth on the next page (line 41). Have students use this photograph to form an initial impression of Danforth's personality. *Possible answer: The picture suggests that Judge Danforth is a serious, stern man. The character in the photograph seems powerful and intimidating and his expression is stern. The camera angle reinforces this impression.*

Lines 10–25
REINFORCE *KEY IDEA:* HYSTERIA

Discuss What details indicate that there is some degree of **hysteria** in the meeting room, which the audience cannot see? *Possible answer: The outcry of the townspeople in what should be an orderly court (lines 13 and 19) signals possible hysteria, as do the shouts of Giles Corey and Judge Hathorne's attempts to remove him and settle the room.*

DIFFERENTIATED INSTRUCTION

For general guidelines on differentiating instruction, see

 BEST PRACTICES TOOLKIT
Differentiated Instruction pp. 31–38

FOR STRATEGIC READERS

In combination with the *Audio Anthology CD*, use one or more Targeted Passages (pp. 178, 181, 184, 189, 192, 194) to ensure that students focus on key story events and concepts. Targeted Passages are also good for English learners.

Preview Read the Summary aloud. Have students fill in a cause-and-effect diagram:

Cause → *Effect*

| Proctor is defending his wife. | He brings Mary Warren to tell the court the truth. |

FOR ENGLISH LEARNERS

Key Academic Vocabulary Use New Word Analysis to teach these words: *deny* (line 4), *submit* (line 79), *precise* (line 348), *legal* (line 377), *attitude* (line 799), *remove* (line 959).

 BEST PRACTICES TOOLKIT—Transparency
New Word Analysis p. E8

Lines 77–96
TIERED DISCUSSION PROMPTS

Use these prompts to help students grasp the difficulty that some Salemites have in making their voices heard:

Connect Have you or someone you know ever been unable to make a person listen to you? How did it feel to be ignored? Did you finally succeed in being heard? *Accept all reasonable responses.*

Analyze How are Hale's attempts to help Giles and Francis hindered? Why else might these men be frustrated? *Possible answers: In both of Hale's attempts (lines 77–78 and 88–89), Danforth responds by insisting that they follow legal procedure. Hathorne urges Danforth to have the men arrested (lines 93–94). They might be frustrated because this is the third day that they have tried but failed to be heard (lines 84–85); they also may fear that while they are waiting for Danforth to review a written plea (lines 95–96), their wives will be executed.*

Synthesize Do you think that the judges will be sympathetic to the husbands' efforts to save their wives? Why or why not? *Possible answers: The judges probably will not be sympathetic. In this passage, Giles receives an unsympathetic, formulaic answer: He should "submit his evidence in proper affidavit" (lines 79–80). In addition, Danforth shows a lack of sympathy when he wonders why Francis is in "such uproar" over his wife's condemnation (lines 90–91).*

Hale. A moment, sir, a moment.

Giles. They'll be hangin' my wife!

(*Judge Hathorne enters. He is in his sixties, a bitter, remorseless Salem judge.*)

Hathorne. How do you dare come roarin' into this court! Are you gone daft, Corey?

Giles. You're not a Boston judge yet, Hathorne.
40 You'll not call me daft!

(*Enter Deputy Governor Danforth and, behind him, Ezekiel Cheever and Parris. On his appearance, silence falls. Danforth is a grave man in his sixties, of some humor and sophistication that does not, however, interfere with an exact loyalty to his position and his cause. He comes down to Giles, who awaits his wrath.*)

Danforth (*looking directly at Giles*). Who is this man?

Parris (*to Giles*). Giles Corey, sir, and a more **contentious**—

Giles (*to Parris*). I am asked the question, and I am
50 old enough to answer it! (*to Danforth, who impresses him and to whom he smiles through his strain*) My name is Corey, sir, Giles Corey. I have six hundred acres, and timber in addition. It is my wife you be condemning now. (*He indicates the courtroom.*)

Danforth. And how do you imagine to help her cause with such contemptuous riot?[2] Now be gone. Your old age alone keeps you out of jail for this.

Giles (*beginning to plead*). They be tellin' lies about my wife, sir, I—

60 **Danforth.** Do you take it upon yourself to determine what this court shall believe and what it shall set aside?

Giles. Your Excellency, we mean no disrespect for—

Danforth. Disrespect indeed! It is disruption, Mister. This is the highest court of the supreme government of this province, do you know it?

Giles (*beginning to weep*). Your Excellency, I only said she were readin' books, sir, and they come and take her out of my house for—

Danforth (*mystified*). Books! What books?

---

70 **Giles** (*through helpless sobs*). It is my third wife, sir; I never had no wife that be so taken with books, and I thought to find the cause of it, d'y'see, but it were no witch I blamed her for. (*He is openly weeping.*) I have broke charity with the woman, I have broke charity with her. (*He covers his face, ashamed. Danforth is respectfully silent.*)

Hale. Excellency, he claims hard evidence for his wife's defense. I think that in all justice you must—

Danforth. Then let him submit his evidence in
80 proper affidavit. You are certainly aware of our procedure here, Mr. Hale. (*to Herrick*) Clear this room.

Herrick. Come now, Giles. (*He gently pushes Corey out.*)

Francis. We are desperate, sir; we come here three days now and cannot be heard.

Danforth. Who is this man?

Francis. Francis Nurse, Your Excellency.

Hale. His wife's Rebecca that were condemned this morning.

90 **Danforth.** Indeed! I am amazed to find you in such uproar. I have only good report of your character, Mr. Nurse.

Hathorne. I think they must both be arrested in contempt, sir.

Danforth (*to Francis*). Let you write your plea, and in due time I will—

Francis. Excellency, we have proof for your eyes; God forbid you shut them to it. The girls, sir, the girls are frauds.

100 **Danforth.** What's that?

Francis. We have proof of it, sir. They are all deceiving you.

(*Danforth is shocked, but studying Francis.*)

Hathorne. This is contempt, sir, contempt!

Danforth. Peace, Judge Hathorne. Do you know who I am, Mr. Nurse?

①
Targeted Passage

---

2. **contemptuous** (kən-tĕmp′chōō-əs) **riot:** disrespectful, outrageous behavior.

DIFFERENTIATED INSTRUCTION

FOR ALL STUDENTS

Preteach Vocabulary Students will encounter the following vocabulary words in Act Three. Supply them with these definitions as needed:

- line 48: **contentious** (kən-tĕn′shəs) *adj.* quarrelsome

- line 150: **deposition** (dĕp′ə-zĭsh′ən) *n.* a written statement by a witness

- line 278: **imperceptible** (ĭm′pər-sĕp′tə-bəl) *adj.* extremely slight; barely noticeable

- line 486: **effrontery** (ĭ-frŭn′tə-rē) *n.* disrespectful and insulting boldness

- line 518: **immaculate** (ĭ-măk′yə-lĭt) *adj.* without stain; pure

R RESOURCE MANAGER—Copy Master Vocabulary Study p. 247

FOR STRATEGIC READERS

① Targeted Passage [Lines 47–69]

This passage illustrates the fact that any comment can arouse suspicion in Salem.

- Why has Giles Corey come to court?

- Does Giles think that the court knows the truth? How can you tell?

- As he talks to Judge Danforth, what emotions rise to the surface? Explain.

- Why does Giles feel he is responsible for his wife's situation?

Francis. I surely do, sir, and I think you must be a wise judge to be what you are.

Danforth. And do you know that near to four hun-
110 dred are in the jails from Marblehead to Lynn,[3] and upon my signature?

Francis. I—

Danforth. And seventy-two condemned to hang by that signature?

Francis. Excellency, I never thought to say it to such a weighty judge, but you are deceived.

(*Enter* Giles Corey *from left. All turn to see as he beck-ons in* Mary Warren *with* Proctor. Mary *is keeping her eyes to the ground;* Proctor *has her elbow as though*
120 *she were near collapse.*)

Parris (*on seeing her, in shock*). Mary Warren! (*He goes directly to bend close to her face.*) What are you about here?

Proctor (*pressing* Parris *away from her with a gentle but firm motion of protectiveness*). She would speak with the Deputy Governor.

Danforth (*shocked by this, turns to* Herrick). Did you not tell me Mary Warren were sick in bed?

Herrick. She were, Your Honor. When I go to fetch
130 her to the court last week, she said she were sick.

Giles. She has been strivin' with her soul all week, Your Honor; she comes now to tell the truth of this to you.

Danforth. Who is this?

Proctor. John Proctor, sir. Elizabeth Proctor is my wife.

Parris. Beware this man, Your Excellency, this man is mischief.

Hale (*excitedly*). I think you must hear the girl, sir,
140 she—

Danforth (*who has become very interested in* Mary Warren *and only raises a hand toward* Hale). Peace. What would you tell us, Mary Warren?

(Proctor *looks at her, but she cannot speak.*)

Proctor. She never saw no spirits, sir.

Danforth (*with great alarm and surprise, to* Mary). Never saw no spirits!

Giles (*eagerly*). Never.

Proctor (*reaching into his jacket*). She has signed a
150 **deposition,** sir—

Danforth (*instantly*). No, no, I accept no deposi-tions. (*He is rapidly calculating this; he turns from her to* Proctor.) Tell me, Mr. Proctor, have you given out this story in the village?

Proctor. We have not.

Parris. They've come to overthrow the court, sir! This man is—

Danforth. I pray you, Mr. Parris. Do you know, Mr. Proctor, that the entire contention of the state
160 in these trials is that the voice of Heaven is speaking through the children?

Proctor. I know that, sir.

Danforth (*thinks, staring at* Proctor, *then turns to* Mary Warren). And you, Mary Warren, how came you to cry out people for sending their spirits against you?

Mary Warren. It were pretense, sir.

Danforth. I cannot hear you.

Proctor. It were pretense, she says.

170 **Danforth.** Ah? And the other girls? Susanna Walcott, and—the others? They are also pretending?

Mary Warren. Aye, sir.

Danforth (*wide-eyed*). Indeed. (*Pause. He is baffled by this. He turns to study* Proctor's *face.*)

Parris (*in a sweat*). Excellency, you surely cannot think to let so vile a lie be spread in open court!

Danforth. Indeed not, but it strike hard upon me that she will dare come here with such a tale. Now, Mr. Proctor, before I decide whether I shall hear you
180 or not, it is my duty to tell you this. We burn a hot fire here; it melts down all concealment.

Proctor. I know that, sir.

---

3. **Marblehead . . . Lynn:** two coastal towns in Massachusetts, near Salem.

THE CRUCIBLE: ACT THREE   **179**

LITERARY ANALYSIS

● **CONVENTIONS OF DRAMA**

In lines 121–133, what does Miller's dialogue reveal about Mary Warren's participation in the court proceedings? ***Possible answer:*** *The dialogue reveals that Mary has not been at court for at least a week. Herrick says that she was sick (lines 129–130); Giles says that she has been "strivin' with her soul all week" (line 131).*

Extend the Discussion Why do you think that Mary has stayed away from court?

READING SKILL

■ **DRAW CONCLUSIONS ABOUT CHARACTERS**

When Mary Warren confirms Proctor's claim that the girls have been lying in court, Judge Danforth is described as "wide-eyed" and "baffled" (line 173). Why would he be reluctant to believe what he has just heard? ***Possible answer:*** *Danforth would be reluctant because he, too, has found the girls to be convincing in court. If Proctor and Mary are right and the girls indeed are frauds, then Danforth and his court will look foolish for having been duped.*

FOR ENGLISH LEARNERS

Language: Conversational English Patterns
Explain that a pattern of speaking, such as the use of the verb *be*, can be used to show whether a character is more or less educated. Note these examples:

• "It is my wife you be condemning now" (lines 53–54)

• "They be tellin' lies about my wife" (lines 58–59)

• "His wife's Rebecca that were condemned" (line 88)

• "Mary Warren were sick in bed" (line 128)

Have pairs of students identify other examples on these two pages and throughout the play.

FOR ADVANCED LEARNERS/AP

Analyze Dialogue Direct students' attention to this comment from Judge Danforth: "We burn a hot fire here; it melts down all conceal-ment" (lines 180–181). Have students write and share a statement that explains (1) what the statement means in its immediate context and (2) how the statement relates to the title of the play.

Lines 215–241
TIERED DISCUSSION PROMPTS

Use these prompts to help students explore Proctor's attempts at self-defense:

Recall Why does Proctor avoid church and sometimes plow on Sunday? *Possible answer: Proctor avoids church because he dislikes Reverend Parris (line 221). He sometimes plows on Sunday because he feels that he must work whenever he can to make his farm successful (lines 227–229).*

Interpret How can you give both a positive and a negative interpretation to Proctor's responses to the disclosures that he stays away from church and sometimes works on Sunday? *Possible answer: Proctor's responses can be interpreted positively if the reader considers them honest expressions of his beliefs and actions. Proctor is not a hypocrite. On the other hand, his responses can be judged negatively because they violate the rules that govern Puritan behavior.*

Evaluate How easy is it for readers to sympathize with Proctor as he answers Danforth's questions? Explain. *Possible answer: It is quite easy to sympathize with Proctor, for the reader probably shares Proctor's dislike of Parris. The reader probably also supports Proctor's desire to support his family, even if supporting his family sometimes means plowing on a Sunday.*

Danforth. Let me continue. I understand well, a husband's tenderness may drive him to extravagance in defense of a wife. Are you certain in your conscience, Mister, that your evidence is the truth?

Proctor. It is. And you will surely know it.

Danforth. And you thought to declare this revelation in the open court before the public?

190 **Proctor.** I thought I would, aye—with your permission.

Danforth (*his eyes narrowing*). Now, sir, what is your purpose in so doing?

Proctor. Why, I—I would free my wife, sir.

Danforth. There lurks nowhere in your heart, nor hidden in your spirit, any desire to undermine this court?

Proctor (*with the faintest faltering*). Why, no, sir.

Cheever (*clears his throat, awakening*). I—Your
200 Excellency.

Danforth. Mr. Cheever.

Cheever. I think it be my duty, sir—(*kindly, to* Proctor) You'll not deny it, John. (*to* Danforth) When we come to take his wife, he damned the court and ripped your warrant.

Parris. Now you have it!

Danforth. He did that, Mr. Hale?

Hale (*takes a breath*). Aye, he did.

Proctor. It were a temper, sir. I knew not what I did.

210 **Danforth** (*studying him*). Mr. Proctor.

Proctor. Aye, sir.

Danforth (*straight into his eyes*). Have you ever seen the Devil?

Proctor. No, sir.

Danforth. You are in all respects a Gospel Christian?

Proctor. I am, sir.

Parris. Such a Christian that will not come to church but once in a month!

Danforth (*restrained—he is curious*). Not come to
220 church?

Proctor. I—I have no love for Mr. Parris. It is no secret. But God I surely love.

Cheever. He plow on Sunday, sir.

Danforth. Plow on Sunday!

Cheever (*apologetically*). I think it be evidence, John. I am an official of the court, I cannot keep it.

Proctor. I—I have once or twice plowed on Sunday. I have three children, sir, and until last year my land give little.

230 **Giles.** You'll find other Christians that do plow on Sunday if the truth be known.

Hale. Your Honor, I cannot think you may judge the man on such evidence.

Danforth. I judge nothing. (*Pause. He keeps watching* Proctor, *who tries to meet his gaze.*) I tell you straight, Mister—I have seen marvels in this court. I have seen people choked before my eyes by spirits; I have seen them stuck by pins and slashed by daggers. I have until this moment not the slightest reason to
240 suspect that the children may be deceiving me. Do you understand my meaning?

Proctor. Excellency, does it not strike upon you that so many of these women have lived so long with such upright reputation, and—

Parris. Do you read the Gospel, Mr. Proctor?

Proctor. I read the Gospel.

Parris. I think not, or you should surely know that Cain were an upright man, and yet he did kill Abel.[4]

Proctor. Aye, God tells us that. (*to* Danforth) But
250 who tells us Rebecca Nurse murdered seven babies by sending out her spirit on them? It is the children only, and this one will swear she lied to you.

(Danforth *considers, then beckons* Hathorne *to him.* Hathorne *leans in, and he speaks in his ear.* Hathorne *nods.*)

---

4. **Cain . . . Abel:** According to the Book of Genesis in the Bible, Cain and Abel were the sons of Adam and Eve, the first humans.

DIFFERENTIATED INSTRUCTION

FOR STRATEGIC READERS

Concept Support Discuss the stage directions that describe Cheever in lines 199, 202, and 225: He is "awakening" as he addresses Danforth, and he speaks "kindly" and "apologetically" to Proctor as he gives evidence against him. Explain that it is difficult to understand Cheever's actions: He sounds sympathetic to Proctor, yet he says things that could be very damaging to Proctor. Invite students to offer their impressions of Cheever.

FOR ENGLISH LEARNERS

Language: Pronoun Referents Explain that there are two different referents for the pronoun *it* in lines 225–226: "I think *it* [the fact that Proctor plowed on Sunday] be evidence, John. I am an official of the court, I cannot keep *it* [the evidence]." Then have students work in mixed-language groups to identify referents for the pronoun *it* in lines 202–209 and the pronoun *they* in lines 309–313.

Hathorne. Aye, she's the one.

Danforth. Mr. Proctor, this morning, your wife send me a claim in which she states that she is pregnant now.

260 **Proctor.** My wife pregnant!

Danforth. There be no sign of it—we have examined her body.

Proctor. But if she say she is pregnant, then she must be! That woman will never lie, Mr. Danforth.

Danforth. She will not?   **Targeted Passage** ②

Proctor. Never, sir, never.

Danforth. We have thought it too convenient to be credited. However, if I should tell you now that I will let her be kept another month; and if she begin to

270 show her natural signs, you shall have her living yet another year until she is delivered—what say you to that? (*John Proctor is struck silent.*) Come now. You say your only purpose is to save your wife. Good, then, she is saved at least this year, and a year is long. What say you, sir? It is done now. (*In conflict,* Proctor *glances at* Francis *and* Giles.) Will you drop this charge?

Proctor. I—I think I cannot.

Danforth (*now an almost **imperceptible** hardness in his voice*). Then your purpose is somewhat larger.

280 **Parris.** He's come to overthrow this court, Your Honor!

Proctor. These are my friends. Their wives are also accused—

Danforth (*with a sudden briskness of manner*). I judge you not, sir. I am ready to hear your evidence.

Proctor. I come not to hurt the court; I only—

Danforth (*cutting him off*). Marshal, go into the court and bid Judge Stoughton and Judge Sewall declare recess for one hour. And let them go to the tavern, if they will. All witnesses and prisoners are

290 to be kept in the building.

Herrick. Aye, sir. (*very deferentially*) If I may say it, sir, I know this man all my life. It is a good man, sir.

Danforth (*It is the reflection on himself he resents*). I am sure of it, Marshal. (Herrick *nods, then goes out.*) Now,

what deposition do you have for us, Mr. Proctor? And I beg you be clear, open as the sky, and honest.

Proctor (*as he takes out several papers*). I am no lawyer, so I'll—

Danforth. The pure in heart need no lawyers.

300 Proceed as you will.

Proctor (*handing* Danforth *a paper*). Will you read this first, sir? It's a sort of testament. The people signing it declare their good opinion of Rebecca, and my wife, and Martha Corey. (Danforth *looks down at the paper.*)

Parris (*to enlist* Danforth's *sarcasm*). Their good opinion! (*But* Danforth *goes on reading, and* Proctor *is heartened.*)

Proctor. These are all landholding farmers, mem-

310 bers of the church. (*delicately, trying to point out a paragraph*) If you'll notice, sir—they've known the women many years and never saw no sign they had dealings with the Devil.

(Parris *nervously moves over and reads over* Danforth's *shoulder.*)

Danforth (*glancing down a long list*). How many names are here?

Francis. Ninety-one, Your Excellency.

Parris (*sweating*). These people should be sum-

320 moned. (Danforth *looks up at him questioningly.*) For questioning.

Francis (*trembling with anger*). Mr. Danforth, I gave them all my word no harm would come to them for signing this.

Parris. This is a clear attack upon the court!

Hale (*to* Parris, *trying to contain himself*). Is every defense an attack upon the court? Can no one—?

Parris. All innocent and Christian people are happy for the courts in Salem! These people are gloomy for

330 it. (*to* Danforth *directly*) And I think you will want to know, from each and every one of them, what discontents them with you!

Hathorne. I think they ought to be examined, sir.

Lines 309–333
REINFORCE *KEY IDEA:* HYSTERIA

Discuss How do Parris and Hathorne respond when they see the petition presented in support of Elizabeth, Martha, and Rebecca? How does their response contribute to the **hysteria** sweeping through Salem and nearby communities? *Possible answer: Parris and Hathorne respond by insisting that everyone who signed the petition be summoned before the court and examined (lines 319–321 and 333). Their response contributes to the hysteria because it shows that even the judges are acting upon illogical personal opinions by wanting to bring before the court everyone with an unpopular opinion. As Reverend Hale protests, "Is every defense an attack upon the court?" (lines 326–327).*

FOR STRATEGIC READERS

② **Targeted Passage [Lines 265–279]**

This passage focuses on Proctor's true reasons for coming before the court.

- What offer does Danforth make to Proctor regarding Elizabeth's freedom?

- How does Proctor respond?

- Why does Proctor choose not to drop his charges against Abigail and the other girls?

- How does his refusal affect Elizabeth?

FOR ADVANCED LEARNERS/AP

Analyze Dialogue Invite students to think about Hale's question in lines 326–327: "Is every defense an attack upon the court?" Discuss what might happen to a nation—to a government and to its citizens—when the answer to Hale's question is "yes." Have students work in groups to discuss modern cases, drawn from history or personal experience, in which criticism of power has proven dangerous.

REINFORCE *KEY IDEA:* HYSTERIA

Discuss In this passage, how does Danforth try to keep potential **hysteria** under control? Do you think that he will succeed? Why or why not? *Possible answer: Danforth tries to control potential hysteria by speaking calm, reassuring words to Francis (lines 336–337, 344–345, and 351–353). As long as he is dealing with Salemites on an individual basis, Danforth may succeed. In this passage, however, he also calls for 91 more people to be brought into court to testify (lines 337–339); and the more people who are added to the highly emotional proceedings, the greater the chance that hysteria will spread.*

◆ GRAMMAR AND STYLE

Use Realistic Dialogue Reread lines 395–401. How does Miller make Danforth's words sound as though they actually might have been spoken in the late 17th century? *Possible answer: Miller chooses era-specific terms (such as "cry witchery," line 397) and an inverted sentence ("What say you to that," line 401) to make this dialogue realistic.*

Danforth. It is not necessarily an attack, I think. Yet—

Francis. These are all covenanted Christians, sir.

Danforth. Then I am sure they may have nothing to fear. (*hands* Cheever *the paper*) Mr. Cheever, have warrants drawn for all of these—arrest for examination. (*to* Proctor) Now, Mister, what other informa-
340 tion do you have for us? (Francis *is still standing, horrified.*) You may sit, Mr. Nurse.

Francis. I have brought trouble on these people; I have—

Danforth. No, old man, you have not hurt these people if they are of good conscience. But you must understand, sir, that a person is either with this court or he must be counted against it, there be no road between. This is a sharp time, now, a precise time—we live no longer in the dusky afternoon
350 when evil mixed itself with good and befuddled the world. Now, by God's grace, the shining sun is up, and them that fear not light will surely praise it. I hope you will be one of those. (Mary Warren *suddenly sobs.*) She's not hearty,[5] I see.

Proctor. No, she's not, sir. (*to* Mary, *bending to her, holding her hand, quietly*) Now remember what the angel Raphael said to the boy Tobias.[6] Remember it.

Mary Warren (*hardly audible*). Aye.

Proctor. "Do that which is good, and no harm shall
360 come to thee."

Mary Warren. Aye.

Danforth. Come, man, we wait you.

(Marshal Herrick *returns, and takes his post at the door.*)

Giles. John, my deposition, give him mine.

Proctor. Aye. (*He hands* Danforth *another paper.*) This is Mr. Corey's deposition.

Danforth. Oh? (*He looks down at it. Now* Hathorne *comes behind him and reads with him.*)

Hathorne (*suspiciously*). What lawyer drew this,
370 Corey?

Giles. You know I never hired a lawyer in my life, Hathorne.

Danforth (*finishing the reading*). It is very well phrased. My compliments. Mr. Parris, if Mr. Putnam is in the court, will you bring him in? (Hathorne *takes the deposition, and walks to the window with it.* Parris *goes into the court.*) You have no legal training, Mr. Corey?

Giles (*very pleased*). I have the best, sir—I am thirty-
380 three time in court in my life. And always plaintiff, too.

Danforth. Oh, then you're much put-upon.

Giles. I am never put-upon; I know my rights, sir, and I will have them. You know, your father tried a case of mine—might be thirty-five year ago, I think.

Danforth. Indeed.

Giles. He never spoke to you of it?

Danforth. No, I cannot recall it.

Giles. That's strange, he give me nine pound dam-
390 ages. He were a fair judge, your father. Y'see, I had a white mare that time, and this fellow come to bor-row the mare—(*Enter* Parris *with* Thomas Putnam. *When he sees* Putnam, Giles' *ease goes; he is hard.*) Aye, there he is.

Danforth. Mr. Putnam, I have here an accusation by Mr. Corey against you. He states that you coldly prompted your daughter to cry witchery upon George Jacobs that is now in jail.

Putnam. It is a lie.

400 **Danforth** (*turning to* Giles). Mr. Putnam states your charge is a lie. What say you to that?

Giles (*furious, his fists clenched*). A fart on Thomas Putnam, that is what I say to that!

Danforth. What proof do you submit for your charge, sir?

Giles. My proof is there! (*pointing to the paper*) If Jacobs hangs for a witch he forfeit up his property—that's law! And there is none but Putnam with the

---

5. **hearty:** well.

6. **what the angel said . . . Tobias:** In the Book of Tobit in the Apocrypha, Tobit's son Tobias cured his father's blindness with the help of the angel Raphael.

DIFFERENTIATED INSTRUCTION

FOR STRATEGIC READERS

Vocabulary Support Discuss these terms, pointing out that some words have other meanings in other contexts:

- *drew* (line 369), "prepared"
- *plaintiff* (line 380), "person who brings a case before a court of law"
- *put-upon* (line 382), "victimized"
- *tried a case* (lines 384–385), "presided over and made a judgment about a court case"
- *ease* (line 393), "relaxed attitude"

FOR ADVANCED LEARNERS/AP

Debate a Viewpoint Ask students to reread lines 344–354, especially Danforth's claim that "a person is either with this court or he must be counted against it." Divide students into two groups to debate Danforth's "all or nothing" philosophy. One side should support Danforth and the other should disagree with him, but each side should offer clear reasons to support its position.

coin to buy so great a piece. This man is killing his
410 neighbors for their land!

Danforth. But proof, sir, proof.

Giles (*pointing at his deposition*). The proof is there! I
have it from an honest man who heard Putnam say
it! The day his daughter cried out on Jacobs, he said
she'd given him a fair gift of land.

Hathorne. And the name of this man?

Giles (*taken aback*). What name?

Hathorne. The man that give you this information.

Giles (*hesitates, then*). Why, I—I cannot give you his
420 name.

Hathorne. And why not?

Giles (*hesitates, then bursts out*). You know well why
not! He'll lay in jail if I give his name!

Hathorne. This is contempt of the court, Mr. Danforth!

Danforth (*to avoid that*). You will surely tell us the
name.

Giles. I will not give you no name. I mentioned my
wife's name once and I'll burn in hell long enough
430 for that. I stand mute.

Danforth. In that case, I have no choice but to arrest
you for contempt of this court, do you know that?

Giles. This is a hearing; you cannot clap me for contempt of a hearing.

Danforth. Oh, it is a proper lawyer![7] Do you wish
me to declare the court in full session here? Or will
you give me good reply?

Giles (*faltering*). I cannot give you no name, sir, I
cannot.

440 **Danforth.** You are a foolish old man. Mr. Cheever,
begin the record. The court is now in session. I ask
you, Mr. Corey—

Proctor (*breaking in*). Your Honor—he has the story
in confidence, sir, and he—

Parris. The Devil lives on such confidences! (*to Danforth*) Without confidences there could be no conspiracy, Your Honor!

Hathorne. I think it must be broken, sir.

Danforth (*to* Giles). Old man, if your informant tells
450 the truth let him come here openly like a decent
man. But if he hide in anonymity I must know
why. Now sir, the government and central church
demand of you the name of him who reported
Mr. Thomas Putnam a common murderer.

Hale. Excellency—

Danforth. Mr. Hale.

Hale. We cannot blink it more. There is a prodigious
fear of this court in the country—

Danforth. Then there is a prodigious guilt in the
460 country. Are *you* afraid to be questioned here?

Hale. I may only fear the Lord, sir, but there is fear
in the country nevertheless.

Danforth (*angered now*). Reproach me not with
the fear in the country; there is fear in the country
because there is a moving[8] plot to topple Christ in
the country!

Hale. But it does not follow that everyone accused
is part of it.

Danforth. No uncorrupted man may fear this court,
470 Mr. Hale! None! (*to* Giles) You are under arrest in
contempt of this court. Now sit you down and take
counsel with yourself, or you will be set in the jail
until you decide to answer all questions.

(Giles Corey *makes a rush for* Putnam. Proctor *lunges
and holds him.*)

Proctor. No, Giles!

Giles (*over* Proctor's *shoulder at* Putnam). I'll cut
your throat, Putnam, I'll kill you yet!

Proctor (*forcing him into a chair*). Peace, Giles,
480 peace. (*releasing him*) We'll prove ourselves. Now
we will. (*He starts to turn to* Danforth.)

---

7. **Oh . . . lawyer:** Oh, he thinks he is a real lawyer.

8. **moving:** active.

READING SKILL

■ DRAW CONCLUSIONS ABOUT CHARACTERS

Reread lines 438–442. What conclusion
can you draw from Giles's refusal to name
the man who has implicated Putnam?
*Possible answer: The reader can conclude
that Giles is an honorable person who will
not betray a confidence, even though he
himself will suffer for his silence.*

Extend the Discussion Do you agree with
Danforth's assessment that Giles is "a foolish old man" (line 440)? Why or why not?

Lines 463–466
REINFORCE *KEY IDEA:* HYSTERIA

Discuss In this passage, Danforth's references
to "fear in the country" indicate that he recognizes the spreading **hysteria** in the community.
What does he think is the cause of that fear?
*Possible answer: Danforth thinks that the fear
is an emotional response to either a recognized
or an instinctive fear that there is a plot to
undermine Christianity in the community.* Consider what else has been said in the dialogue
on this page. Do you think that Danforth is
correct? Why or why not? *Possible answer:
Danforth probably is not correct. It may be
more likely that the cause of the hysteria is fear
over the way that some people are taking advantage of the situation to ruin their neighbors'
reputations and take their possessions.*

FOR STRATEGIC READERS

Explore Plot and Character Development
Have students reread lines 457–470.

- Point out that this scene is a key moment in
the development of the plot. Help students
summarize Hale's opinion of the court and
Danforth's defense of it.

- Explain that this scene also contributes
to character development. Help students
identify the crucial shift in Hale's position.
Also discuss what Danforth's angry words
reveal about his own position.

FOR ADVANCED LEARNERS/AP

Synthesize Encourage students to reflect
upon Giles's responses to Danforth in lines
411–430. Then ask them to write a brief paragraph explaining how this scene connects
to the themes of *The Crucible* and to Miller's
own views. Students may choose to reread
the mini-essays found earlier in the play or to
do brief research online for more information
about Miller's views on and experiences of
McCarthyism.

Lines 501–525
TIERED DISCUSSION PROMPTS

Use these prompts to help students explore Hale's thoughts and feelings:

Connect Have you ever tried to help someone who was unknowingly heading toward danger? What was that experience like, and what challenges did you face? *Accept all thoughtful responses that apply to Hale's situation.*

Analyze What will it mean if Proctor is right about Abigail and the other girls? Why does Hale want Proctor to hire a lawyer to make his case? *Possible answer: If Proctor is right, then innocent people have been sentenced to die. Hale wants Proctor to hire a lawyer because such a charge is a matter of life or death—for the accused and perhaps even for Proctor. Hale is concerned that "a farmer" will not have the skill to present "a claim so weighty" (lines 511–512).*

Evaluate How well does Miller convey the intensity of Hale's feelings in this scene? Cite evidence. *Possible answer: Miller successfully conveys Hale's concern. Hale comes forth "in a trembling state" (line 506), and he implores Danforth to stop the proceedings "in God's name" (line 512). After signing Rebecca Nurse's death warrant, his "hand shakes yet as with a wound" (line 524) because he realizes the seriousness of the situation—and perhaps because he suspects that Proctor may be right.*

Giles. Say nothin' more, John. (*pointing at* Danforth) He's only playin' you! He means to hang us all!

(Mary Warren *bursts into sobs.*)

Danforth. This is a court of law, Mister. I'll have no **effrontery** here!

Proctor. Forgive him, sir, for his old age. Peace, Giles, we'll prove it all now. (*He lifts up* Mary's *chin.*) You cannot weep, Mary. Remember the angel, what he say
490 to the boy. Hold to it, now; there is your rock. (Mary *quiets. He takes out a paper, and turns to* Danforth.) This is Mary Warren's deposition. I—I would ask you remember, sir, while you read it, that until two week ago she were no different than the other children are today. (*He is speaking reasonably, restraining all his fears, his anger, his anxiety.*) You saw her scream, she howled, she swore familiar spirits choked her; she even testified that Satan, in the form of women now in jail, tried to win her soul away, and then when she refused—

500 **Danforth.** We know all this.

Proctor. Aye, sir. She swears now that she never saw Satan; nor any spirit, vague or clear, that Satan may have sent to hurt her. And she declares her friends are lying now.   **Targeted Passage** ③

(Proctor *starts to hand* Danforth *the deposition, and* Hale *comes up to* Danforth *in a trembling state.*)

Hale. Excellency, a moment. I think this goes to the heart of the matter.

Danforth (*with deep misgivings*). It surely does.

510 **Hale.** I cannot say he is an honest man; I know him little. But in all justice, sir, a claim so weighty cannot be argued by a farmer. In God's name, sir, stop here; send him home and let him come again with a lawyer—

Danforth (*patiently*). Now look you, Mr. Hale—

Hale. Excellency, I have signed seventy-two death warrants; I am a minister of the Lord, and I dare not take a life without there be a proof so **immaculate** no slightest qualm of conscience may doubt it.

520 **Danforth.** Mr. Hale, you surely do not doubt my justice.

Hale. I have this morning signed away the soul of Rebecca Nurse, Your Honor. I'll not conceal it, my hand shakes yet as with a wound! I pray you, sir, this argument let lawyers present to you.

Danforth. Mr. Hale, believe me; for a man of such terrible learning you are most bewildered—I hope you will forgive me. I have been thirty-two year at the bar, sir, and I should be confounded were I
530 called upon to defend these people. Let you consider, now—(*to* Proctor *and the others*) And I bid you all do likewise. In an ordinary crime, how does one defend the accused? One calls up witnesses to prove his innocence. But witchcraft is *ipso facto,*[9] on its face and by its nature, an invisible crime, is it not? Therefore, who may possibly be witness to it? The witch and the victim. None other. Now we cannot hope the witch will accuse herself; granted? Therefore, we must rely upon her victims—and they do testify, the
540 children certainly do testify. As for the witches, none will deny that we are most eager for all their confessions. Therefore, what is left for a lawyer to bring out? I think I have made my point. Have I not?

Hale. But this child claims the girls are not truthful, and if they are not—

Danforth. That is precisely what I am about to consider, sir. What more may you ask of me? Unless you doubt my probity?[10]

Hale (*defeated*). I surely do not, sir. Let you consider
550 it, then.

Danforth. And let you put your heart to rest. Her deposition, Mr. Proctor.

(Proctor *hands it to him.* Hathorne *rises, goes beside* Danforth, *and starts reading.* Parris *comes to his other side.* Danforth *looks at* John Proctor, *then proceeds to read.* Hale *gets up, finds position near the judge, reads too.* Proctor *glances at* Giles. Francis *prays silently, hands pressed together.* Cheever *waits placidly, the*

---

9. **ipso facto** *Latin:* by that very fact.
10. **doubt my probity:** question my integrity.

DIFFERENTIATED INSTRUCTION

FOR STRATEGIC READERS
③ **Targeted Passage [Lines 526–543]**

This passage presents the philosophy that allows the witch hunt to continue unchecked.

- What does Danforth think of Hale's request for more caution from the court?

- How are the accused supposed to defend themselves against charges of witchcraft?

- Why does Danforth think that there is no need for Proctor to enlist a lawyer's help?

sublime official, dutiful. Mary Warren sobs once.

560 John Proctor *touches her head reassuringly. Presently* Danforth *lifts his eyes, stands up, takes out a kerchief and blows his nose. The others stand aside as he moves in thought toward the window.*)

Parris (*hardly able to contain his anger and fear*). I should like to question—

Danforth (*his first real outburst, in which his contempt for* Parris *is clear*). Mr. Parris, I bid you be silent! (*He stands in silence, looking out the window. Now, having established that he will set the gait.*) Mr. Cheever, will

570 you go into the court and bring the children here? (Cheever *gets up and goes out upstage.* Danforth *now turns to* Mary.) Mary Warren, how came you to this turnabout? Has Mr. Proctor threatened you for this deposition?

Mary Warren. No, sir.

Danforth. Has he ever threatened you?

Mary Warren (*weaker*). No, sir.

Danforth (*sensing a weakening*). Has he threatened you?

580 **Mary Warren.** No, sir.

Danforth. Then you tell me that you sat in my court, callously lying, when you knew that people would hang by your evidence? (*She does not answer.*) Answer me!

Mary Warren (*almost inaudibly*). I did, sir.

Danforth. How were you instructed in your life? Do you not know that God damns all liars? (*She cannot speak.*) Or is it now that you lie?

Judge Danforth questioning Mary Warren

■ DRAW CONCLUSIONS ABOUT CHARACTERS

As you read this page, pay attention to Danforth's dialogue and the description of his demeanor. What traits describing Danforth can you add to the prereading chart from page 131? Be sure to include evidence supporting your response.

Possible answer: Danforth is powerful and controlling. He takes charge of the situation, angrily overruling Parris (lines 567–570), and he is aggressive in his interrogation of Mary Warren (lines 576–588).

If students need help . . . Point out the term *set the gait* in the stage directions (line 569). Explain that the term usually refers to riding a horse. A rider who "sets the gait," or pace, at which the horse moves is controlling the movement of the animal. Discuss how the dialogue on this page illustrates what this phrase means when it is applied to Danforth.

FOR ENGLISH LEARNERS

Vocabulary Support Help students use context clues to determine the meanings of these phrases:

- *Hold to* (line 490), "Remember"
- *goes to the heart of the matter* (lines 507–508), "addresses the most important point"
- *put your heart to rest* (line 551), "be calm and unworried"

- *It does not escape me* (lines 616–617), "I am not forgetting"
- *search your heart* (line 782), "think about this very carefully"
- *put her out* (line 858), "dismissed her"
- *struck me true/struck me false* (lines 969 and 975), "impressed me as being a truthful person"/"impressed me as being a liar"

FOR ADVANCED LEARNERS/AP

Synthesize a Narrative Have students examine the photograph and then write a first-person narrative from the point of view of one of the girls watching Judge Danforth and Mary Warren. Urge them to use details from the text as well as what they already have learned about Danforth and Mary. Also challenge students to write in a style that mimics Miller's representation of Puritan speech. Call on volunteers to read their finished narratives aloud to the class.

Lines 605–630
REINFORCE *KEY IDEA:* HYSTERIA

Discuss As Danforth speaks to the other girls, how does he try to urge them away from speaking and acting in response to **hysteria**? *Possible answer: Danforth warns the girls to think carefully about what they have said. He urges them not to focus upon their feelings or imagination but to remember the facts—namely, that the charge of witchcraft could result in people's deaths (lines 618–620) and that the Bible condemns liars (lines 615–616).*

LITERARY ANALYSIS

● CONVENTIONS OF DRAMA

Review lines 632–662. How would you describe the atmosphere that Miller creates in this scene through his use of dialogue? Why is Proctor eventually "furious" (line 661)? *Possible answer: Miller creates an atmosphere of barely controlled chaos by having many characters speak in rapid order. (Seven characters either make accusations or give evidence.) This confusion allows logic and truth to be twisted, and Proctor becomes furious as he sees an irrational argument against Elizabeth develop.*

Mary Warren. No, sir—I am with God now.

590 **Danforth.** You are with God now.

Mary Warren. Aye, sir.

Danforth (*containing himself*). I will tell you this—you are either lying now, or you were lying in the court, and in either case you have committed perjury and you will go to jail for it. You cannot lightly say you lied, Mary. Do you know that?

Mary Warren. I cannot lie no more. I am with God, I am with God.

(*But she breaks into sobs at the thought of it, and the* 600 *right door opens, and enter* Susanna Walcott, Mercy Lewis, Betty Parris, *and finally* Abigail. Cheever *comes to* Danforth.)

Cheever. Ruth Putnam's not in the court, sir, nor the other children.

Danforth. These will be sufficient. Sit you down, children. (*Silently they sit.*) Your friend, Mary Warren, has given us a deposition. In which she swears that she never saw familiar spirits, apparitions, nor any manifest of the Devil. She claims as well that 610 none of you have seen these things either. (*slight pause*) Now, children, this is a court of law. The law, based upon the Bible, and the Bible, writ by Almighty God, forbid the practice of witchcraft, and describe death as the penalty thereof. But likewise, children, the law and Bible damn all bearers of false witness. (*slight pause*) Now then. It does not escape me that this deposition may be devised to blind us; it may well be that Mary Warren has been conquered by Satan, who sends her here to distract our 620 sacred purpose. If so, her neck will break for it. But if she speak true, I bid you now drop your guile and confess your pretense, for a quick confession will go easier with you. (*pause*) Abigail Williams, rise. (Abigail *slowly rises.*) Is there any truth in this?

Abigail. No, sir.

Danforth (*thinks, glances at* Mary, *then back to* Abigail). Children, a very auger bit[11] will now be turned into your souls until your honesty is proved. Will either of you change your positions now, or do 630 you force me to hard questioning?

Abigail. I have naught to change, sir. She lies.

Danforth (*to* Mary). You would still go on with this?

Mary Warren (*faintly*). Aye, sir.

Danforth (*turning to* Abigail). A poppet were discovered in Mr. Proctor's house, stabbed by a needle. Mary Warren claims that you sat beside her in the court when she made it, and that you saw her make it and witnessed how she herself stuck her needle into it for safe-keeping. What say you to that?

640 **Abigail** (*with a slight note of indignation*). It is a lie, sir.

Danforth (*after a slight pause*). While you worked for Mr. Proctor, did you see poppets in that house?

Abigail. Goody Proctor always kept poppets.

Proctor. Your Honor, my wife never kept no poppets. Mary Warren confesses it was her poppet.

Cheever. Your Excellency.

Danforth. Mr. Cheever.

Cheever. When I spoke with Goody Proctor in that 650 house, she said she never kept no poppets. But she said she did keep poppets when she were a girl.

Proctor. She has not been a girl these fifteen years, Your Honor.

Hathorne. But a poppet will keep fifteen years, will it not?

Proctor. It will keep if it is kept, but Mary Warren swears she never saw no poppets in my house, nor anyone else.

Parris. Why could there not have been poppets hid 660 where no one ever saw them?

Proctor (*furious*). There might also be a dragon with five legs in my house, but no one has ever seen it.

Parris. We are here, Your Honor, precisely to discover what no one has ever seen.

---

11. **auger** (ô′gər) **bit:** drill.

186   UNIT 1: EARLY AMERICAN WRITING

DIFFERENTIATED INSTRUCTION

FOR ENGLISH LEARNERS
Related Vocabulary Danforth's speech to the children sets up the crucial battle that pits Mary and Proctor against Abigail and her supporters (the girls, Hathorne, and Parris). To ensure that students understand Danforth's difficult vocabulary and syntax, teach these related terms:

- *the penalty thereof* (line 614), "the punishment for that offense"

- *bearers of false witness* (lines 615–616), "liars"

- *devised to blind us* (lines 617–618), "created to fool us"

- *distract our sacred purpose* (lines 619–620), "make us forget that we are doing God's work"

- *guile* (line 621), "trickery"

- *pretense* (line 622), "deception"

Proctor. Mr. Danforth, what profit this girl to turn herself about? What may Mary Warren gain but hard questioning and worse?

Danforth. You are charging Abigail Williams with a marvelous cool plot to murder, do you understand
670 that?

Proctor. I do, sir. I believe she means to murder.

Danforth (*pointing at* Abigail, *incredulously*). This child would murder your wife?

Proctor. It is not a child. Now hear me, sir. In the sight of the congregation she were twice this year put out of this meetin' house for laughter during prayer.

Danforth (*shocked, turning to* Abigail). What's this? Laughter during—!

Parris. Excellency, she were under Tituba's power at
680 that time, but she is solemn now.

Giles. Aye, now she is solemn and goes to hang people!

Danforth. Quiet, man.

Hathorne. Surely it have no bearing on the question, sir. He charges contemplation of murder.

Danforth. Aye. (*He studies* Abigail *for a moment, then.*) Continue, Mr. Proctor.

Proctor. Mary. Now tell the Governor how you danced in the woods.

Parris (*instantly*). Excellency, since I come to Salem
690 this man is blackening my name. He—

Danforth. In a moment, sir. (*to* Mary Warren, *sternly, and surprised*) What is this dancing?

Mary Warren. I—(*She glances at* Abigail, *who is staring down at her remorselessly. Then, appealing to* Proctor.) Mr. Proctor—

Proctor (*taking it right up*). Abigail leads the girls to the woods, Your Honor, and they have danced there naked—

Parris. Your Honor, this—

700 **Proctor** (*at once*). Mr. Parris discovered them himself in the dead of night! There's the "child" she is!

Danforth (*It is growing into a nightmare, and he turns, astonished, to* Parris). Mr. Parris—

Parris. I can only say, sir, that I never found any of them naked, and this man is—

Danforth. But you discovered them dancing in the woods? (*Eyes on* Parris, *he points at* Abigail.) Abigail?

Hale. Excellency, when I first arrived from Beverly, Mr. Parris told me that.

710 **Danforth.** Do you deny it, Mr. Parris?

Parris. I do not, sir, but I never saw any of them naked.

Danforth. But she have *danced*?

Parris (*unwillingly*). Aye, sir.

(*Danforth, as though with new eyes, looks at* Abigail.)

Hathorne. Excellency, will you permit me? (*He points at* Mary Warren.)

Danforth (*with great worry*). Pray, proceed.

Hathorne. You say you never saw no spirits, Mary,
720 were never threatened or afflicted by any manifest of the Devil or the Devil's agents.

Mary Warren (*very faintly*). No, sir.

Hathorne (*with a gleam of victory*). And yet, when people accused of witchery confronted you in court, you would faint, saying their spirits came out of their bodies and choked you—

Mary Warren. That were pretense, sir.

Danforth. I cannot hear you.

Mary Warren. Pretense, sir.

730 **Parris.** But you did turn cold, did you not? I myself picked you up many times, and your skin were icy. Mr. Danforth, you—

Danforth. I saw that many times.

Proctor. She only pretended to faint, Your Excellency. They're all marvelous pretenders.

Hathorne. Then can she pretend to faint now?

Proctor. Now?

THE CRUCIBLE: ACT THREE **187**

READING SKILL

■ **DRAW CONCLUSIONS ABOUT CHARACTERS**

Hathorne looks at Mary Warren "with a gleam of victory" (line 723) during his interview with her. Why does Hathorne respond to her in this way? What do his feelings of "victory" reveal about him? ***Possible answer:*** *Hathorne responds "with a gleam of victory" because he thinks that he has caught her in a lie: He reminds her that she used to faint when she pretended to see spirits. His "gleam of victory" may indicate that he enjoys manipulating people.*

Extend the Discussion Why would Hathorne be so committed to taking the side of Abigail and the other girls? What does your answer say about his ability to serve as a judge in this case?

FOR ENGLISH LEARNERS

Vocabulary: Multiple-Meaning Words Explain that some words have multiple meanings. Point out that *keep* means "to retain possession of" in line 651 but also can mean "to stay in good condition." Have Jigsaw groups of mixed language ability investigate the multiple meanings of *keep* or *kept* in lines 651, 654, and 656 and then report their findings.

 BEST PRACTICES TOOLKIT
Jigsaw Reading p. A1

Lines 738–759
TIERED DISCUSSION PROMPTS

Use these prompts to help students understand Mary Warren's dilemma:

Connect Have you ever failed to do something when the need arose—something that you had done before or that you were sure you could do? How does that experience help you understand Mary Warren's position in front of the judges? *Accept all responses that relate to Mary's anxiety and confusion when she can't faint on cue.*

Analyze Why is Mary unable to faint when Parris asks her to do so? *Possible answer: She says that she has "no sense of it now" (line 750); she searches "for the emotion of it" (line 758) but cannot find it. Mary's earlier fake fainting spells were induced by the emotion of the others.*

Synthesize Consider what you have learned about Mary Warren up to this point. Why is placing great importance upon her testimony an effective way of creating suspense? *Possible answer: The method of creating suspense is effective because the reader knows that Mary is an unstable character and may not be confident enough to stand by her confession.*

Parris. Why not? Now there are no spirits attacking her, for none in this room is accused of witchcraft.
740 So let her turn herself cold now, let her pretend she is attacked now, let her faint. (*He turns to* Mary Warren.) Faint!

Mary Warren. Faint?

Parris. Aye, faint. Prove to us how you pretended in the court so many times.

Mary Warren (*looking to* Proctor). I—cannot faint now, sir.

Proctor (*alarmed, quietly*). Can you not pretend it?

Mary Warren. I—(*She looks about as though searching*
750 *for the passion to faint.*) I—have no *sense* of it now, I—

Danforth. Why? What is lacking now?

Mary Warren. I—cannot tell, sir, I—

Danforth. Might it be that here we have no afflicting spirit loose, but in the court there were some?

Mary Warren. I never saw no spirits.

Parris. Then see no spirits now, and prove to us that you can faint by your own will, as you claim.

Mary Warren (*stares, searching for the emotion of it, and then shakes her head*). I—cannot do it.

760 **Parris.** Then you will confess, will you not? It were attacking spirits made you faint!

Mary Warren. No, sir, I—

Parris. Your Excellency, this is a trick to blind the court!

Mary Warren. It's not a trick! (*She stands.*) I—I used to faint because I—I thought I saw spirits.

Danforth. *Thought* you saw them!

Mary Warren. But I did not, Your Honor.

Hathorne. How could you think you saw them
770 unless you saw them?

Mary Warren. I—I cannot tell how, but I did. I—I heard the other girls screaming, and you, Your Honor, you seemed to believe them, and I—It were only sport in the beginning, sir, but then the whole world cried spirits, spirits, and I—I promise you, Mr. Danforth, I only thought I saw them but I did not.

(Danforth *peers at her.*)

Parris (*smiling, but nervous because* Danforth *seems to be struck by* Mary Warren's *story*). Surely Your Excel-
780 lency is not taken by this simple lie.

Danforth (*turning worriedly to* Abigail). Abigail. I bid you now search your heart and tell me this—and beware of it, child, to God every soul is precious and His vengeance is terrible on them that take life without cause. Is it possible, child, that the spirits you have seen are illusion only, some deception that may cross your mind when—

Abigail. Why, this—this—is a base question, sir.

Danforth. Child, I would have you consider it—

790 **Abigail.** I have been hurt, Mr. Danforth; I have seen my blood runnin' out! I have been near to murdered every day because I done my duty pointing out the Devil's people—and this is my reward? To be mistrusted, denied, questioned like a—

Danforth (*weakening*). Child, I do not mistrust you—

Abigail (*in an open threat*). Let *you* beware, Mr. Danforth. Think you to be so mighty that the power of Hell may not turn *your* wits? Beware of it! There is—(*Suddenly, from an accusatory attitude, her face*
800 *turns, looking into the air above—it is truly frightened.*)

Danforth (*apprehensively*). What is it, child?

Abigail (*looking about in the air, clasping her arms about her as though cold*). I—I know not. A wind, a cold wind, has come. (*Her eyes fall on* Mary Warren.)

Mary Warren (*terrified, pleading*). Abby!

Mercy Lewis (*shivering*). Your Honor, I freeze!

Proctor. They're pretending!

Hathorne (*touching* Abigail's *hand*). She is cold, Your Honor, touch her!

810 **Mercy Lewis** (*through chattering teeth*). Mary, do you send this shadow on me?

DIFFERENTIATED INSTRUCTION

FOR ADVANCED LEARNERS/AP

Analyze Motivation Point out that Abigail dramatically shifts attention away from herself in lines 796–805. Have students discuss these questions:

- What techniques does Abigail use to redirect the attention of the court?

- Why does she deflect interest in herself?

Have students write a brief paragraph analyzing Abigail's motives and share their responses with the class.

Mary Warren. Lord, save me!

Susanna Walcott. I freeze, I freeze!

Abigail (*shivering visibly*). It is a wind, a wind!

Mary Warren. Abby, don't do that!

Danforth (*himself engaged and entered by* Abigail). Mary Warren, do you witch her? I say to you, do you send your spirit out? **Targeted Passage** ④

(*With a hysterical cry* Mary Warren *starts to run.* 820 Proctor *catches her.*)

Mary Warren (*almost collapsing*). Let me go, Mr. Proctor, I cannot, I cannot—

Abigail (*crying to Heaven*). Oh, Heavenly Father, take away this shadow!

(*Without warning or hesitation,* Proctor *leaps at* Abigail *and, grabbing her by the hair, pulls her to her feet. She screams in pain.* Danforth, *astonished, cries,* "What are you about?" *and* Hathorne *and* Parris *call,* "Take your hands off her!" *and out of it all comes* 830 Proctor's *roaring voice.*)

Proctor. How do you call Heaven! Whore! Whore!

(Herrick *breaks* Proctor *from her.*)

Herrick. John!

Danforth. Man! Man, what do you—

Proctor (*breathless and in agony*). It is a whore!

Danforth (*dumbfounded*). You charge—?

Abigail. Mr. Danforth, he is lying!

Proctor. Mark her! Now she'll suck a scream to stab me with, but—

840 **Danforth.** You will prove this! This will not pass!

Proctor (*trembling, his life collapsing about him*). I have known her, sir. I have known her.

Danforth. You—you are a lecher?

Francis (*horrified*). John, you cannot say such a—

Proctor. Oh, Francis, I wish you had some evil in you that you might know me! (*to* Danforth) A man will not cast away his good name. You surely know that.

12. **every scrap and tittle:** every tiny bit.

Danforth (*dumbfounded*). In—in what time? In what place?

850 **Proctor** (*his voice about to break, and his shame great*). In the proper place—where my beasts are bedded. On the last night of my joy, some eight months past. She used to serve me in my house, sir. (*He has to clamp his jaw to keep from weeping.*) A man may think God sleeps, but God sees everything, I know it now. I beg you, sir, I beg you—see her what she is. My wife, my dear good wife, took this girl soon after, sir, and put her out on the highroad. And being what she is, a lump of vanity, sir—(*He* 860 *is being overcome.*) Excellency, forgive me, forgive me. (*Angrily against himself, he turns away from the* Governor *for a moment. Then, as though to cry out is his only means of speech left.*) She thinks to dance with me on my wife's grave! And well she might, for I thought of her softly. God help me, I lusted, and there *is* a promise in such sweat. But it is a whore's vengeance, and you must see it; I set myself entirely in your hands. I know you must see it now.

Danforth (*blanched, in horror, turning to* Abigail). 870 You deny every scrap and tittle[12] of this?

Abigail. If I must answer that, I will leave and I will not come back again!

(Danforth *seems unsteady.*)

Proctor. I have made a bell of my honor! I have rung the doom of my good name—you will believe me, Mr. Danforth! My wife is innocent, except she knew a whore when she saw one!

Abigail (*stepping up to* Danforth). What look do you give me? (Danforth *cannot speak.*) I'll not have such 880 looks! (*She turns and starts for the door.*)

Danforth. You will remain where you are! (Herrick *steps into her path. She comes up short, fire in her eyes.*) Mr. Parris, go into the court and bring Goodwife Proctor out.

Parris (*objecting*). Your Honor, this is all a—

LITERARY ANALYSIS

● **CONVENTIONS OF DRAMA**
Reread lines 825–842. How does the fight between Proctor and Abigail signal a turning point in the play? *Possible answer: The close physical clash between Proctor and Abigail shows that there is some terrible connection between them. It foreshadows the revelation of their affair, which will be a turning point because it dooms Proctor and also might doom Abigail.*

If students need help . . . Discuss Proctor's outburst, "How do you [dare you] call Heaven!" (line 831). Elicit or explain that Proctor thinks that Abigail is such a base person that she has given up her right to ask for heavenly help.

READING SKILL

■ **DRAW CONCLUSIONS ABOUT CHARACTERS**
Reread lines 841–847. What traits describing Proctor can you add to the prereading chart from page 131? What evidence reveals these traits? *Possible answer: Proctor is volatile ("Without warning or hesitation, Proctor leaps at Abigail" [lines 825–826]), honest (in front of the court and his friends, he reveals his affair with Abigail [lines 835–853]), and self-critical ("Oh, Francis, I wish you had some evil in you that you might know me!" [lines 845–846]).*

FOR STRATEGIC READERS
④ **Targeted Passage [Lines 850–868]**

In this passage, Proctor reveals the true reason that Abigail persists in her charges of witchcraft.

• Why is Proctor overcome with emotion? How does he show his emotion?

• What does he say motivates Abigail to lie about his wife?

• How does Proctor hope the court will react to his revelations?

FOR ENGLISH LEARNERS
Vocabulary: Cognates Point out that the Spanish word *pasión* is spelled and pronounced almost like the English word *passion* (line 750). Help students understand these words with Spanish cognates: *emotion/emoción* (line 758), *illusion/ilusión* (line 786), *deception/decepción* (line 786), *conviction/convicción* (lines 1052–1053), *denounce/denunciar* (line 1160), *proceedings/procedimientos* (line 1161).

● CONVENTIONS OF DRAMA

Skim through lines 920–958, focusing on the stage directions. Through what gestures does Elizabeth communicate her anxiety about Danforth's questions? Explain. *Possible answers: Several times, Elizabeth communicates anxiety by trying to glance at her husband, hoping to find a clue from him about how she should respond to Danforth's questions (lines 921–922, 930, and 952). She is reluctant to look at Danforth because she knows that however she answers his questions, she may hurt her husband. She also wets her lips "to stall for time" (line 927) because she is nervous about speaking.*

Extend the Discussion In what sense is Danforth's gesture in line 953 an attempt to override Elizabeth's anxiety? Why is it a powerful action?

Danforth (*sharply to* Parris). Bring her out! And tell her not one word of what's been spoken here. And let you knock before you enter. (*Parris goes out.*) Now we shall touch the bottom of this swamp. (*to* Proctor) Your wife, you say, is an honest woman.

Proctor. In her life, sir, she have never lied. There are them that cannot sing, and them that cannot weep—my wife cannot lie. I have paid much to learn it, sir.

Danforth. And when she put this girl out of your house, she put her out for a harlot?[13]

Proctor. Aye, sir.

Danforth. And knew her for a harlot?

Proctor. Aye, sir, she knew her for a harlot.

Danforth. Good then. (*to* Abigail) And if she tell me, child, it were for harlotry, may God spread His mercy on you! (*There is a knock. He calls to the door.*) Hold! (*to* Abigail) Turn your back. Turn your back. (*to* Proctor) Do likewise. (*Both turn their backs—Abigail with indignant slowness.*) Now let neither of you turn to face Goody Proctor. No one in this room is to speak one word, or raise a gesture aye or nay. (*He turns toward the door, calls.*) Enter! (*The door opens. Elizabeth enters with* Parris. Parris *leaves her. She stands alone, her eyes looking for* Proctor.) Mr. Cheever, report this testimony in all exactness. Are you ready?

Cheever. Ready, sir.

Danforth. Come here, woman. (*Elizabeth comes to him, glancing at* Proctor's *back.*) Look at me only, not at your husband. In my eyes only.

Elizabeth (*faintly*). Good, sir.

Danforth. We are given to understand that at one time you dismissed your servant, Abigail Williams.

Elizabeth. That is true, sir.

Danforth. For what cause did you dismiss her? (*Slight pause. Then* Elizabeth *tries to glance at* Proctor.) You will look in my eyes only and not at your husband. The answer is in your memory and you need no help to give it to me. Why did you dismiss Abigail Williams?

Elizabeth (*not knowing what to say, sensing a situation, wetting her lips to stall for time*). She—dissatisfied me. (*pause*) And my husband.

Danforth. In what way dissatisfied you?

Elizabeth. She were—(*She glances at* Proctor *for a cue.*)

Danforth. Woman, look at me! (*Elizabeth does.*) Were she slovenly? Lazy? What disturbance did she cause?

Elizabeth. Your Honor, I—in that time I were sick. And I—My husband is a good and righteous man. He is never drunk as some are, nor wastin' his time at the shovelboard, but always at his work. But in my sickness—you see, sir, I were a long time sick after my last baby, and I thought I saw my husband somewhat turning from me. And this girl—(*She turns to* Abigail.)

Danforth. Look at me.

Elizabeth. Aye, sir. Abigail Williams—(*She breaks off.*)

Danforth. What of Abigail Williams?

Elizabeth. I came to think he fancied her. And so one night I lost my wits, I think, and put her out on the highroad.

Danforth. Your husband—did he indeed turn from you?

Elizabeth (*in agony*). My husband—is a goodly man, sir.

Danforth. Then he did not turn from you.

Elizabeth (*starting to glance at* Proctor). He—

Danforth (*reaches out and holds her face, then*). Look at me! To your own knowledge, has John Proctor ever committed the crime of lechery? (*In a crisis of indecision she cannot speak.*) Answer my question! Is your husband a lecher!

Elizabeth (*faintly*). No, sir.

Danforth. Remove her, Marshal.

---

13. **for a harlot:** as a woman of low morals.

DIFFERENTIATED INSTRUCTION

FOR STRATEGIC READERS

Comprehension Support Explain that Danforth's "Now we shall touch the bottom of this swamp" (line 889) is a metaphor. This type of figurative language makes a comparison between two things that at first do not seem comparable. Clarify students' understanding by asking these questions:

• What is being referred to as a "swamp"?

• What does Danforth mean by "touch the bottom"?

FOR ADVANCED LEARNERS/AP

Analyze Character Relationships [small-group option] Note that as Danforth has Elizabeth brought into the room, he gives equally stern instructions to Abigail and to Proctor (lines 903–907). Have students trace Danforth's dealings with Abigail throughout Act Two. Challenge students to identify the point at which the relationship changes most dramatically and to offer a reason for that change.

960 **Proctor.** Elizabeth, tell the truth!

Danforth. She has spoken. Remove her!

Proctor (*crying out*). Elizabeth, I have confessed it!

Elizabeth. Oh, God! (*The door closes behind her.*)

Proctor. She only thought to save my name!

Hale. Excellency, it is a natural lie to tell; I beg you, stop now before another is condemned! I may shut my conscience to it no more—private vengeance is working through this testimony! From the begin-
970 ning this man has struck me true. By my oath to Heaven, I believe him now, and I pray you call back his wife before we—

Danforth. She spoke nothing of lechery, and this man has lied!

Hale. I believe him! (*pointing at* Abigail) This girl has always struck me false! She has—

(Abigail, *with a weird, wild, chilling cry, screams up to the ceiling.*)

Abigail. You will not! Begone! Begone, I say!

Danforth. What is it, child? (*But* Abigail, *pointing*
980 *with fear, is now raising up her frightened eyes, her awed face, toward the ceiling—the girls are doing the same—and now* Hathorne, Hale, Putnam, Cheever, Herrick, *and* Danforth *do the same.*) What's there? (*He lowers his eyes from the ceiling, and now he is frightened; there is real tension in his voice.*) Child! (*She is transfixed—with all the girls, she is whimpering open-mouthed, agape at the ceiling.*) Girls! Why do you—?

Mercy Lewis (*pointing*). It's on the beam! Behind the rafter!

990 **Danforth** (*looking up*). Where!

Abigail. Why—? (*She gulps.*) Why do you come, yellow bird?

Proctor. Where's a bird? I see no bird!

Abigail (*to the ceiling*). My face? My face?

Proctor. Mr. Hale—

Danforth. Be quiet!

Proctor (*to* Hale). Do you see a bird?

Danforth. Be quiet!!

Abigail (*to the ceiling, in a genuine conversation with*
1000 *the "bird," as though trying to talk it out of attacking her*). But God made my face; you cannot want to tear my face. Envy is a deadly sin, Mary.

Mary Warren (*on her feet with a spring, and horrified, pleading*). Abby!

Abigail (*unperturbed, continuing to the "bird"*). Oh, Mary, this is a black art[14] to change your shape. No, I cannot, I cannot stop my mouth; it's God's work I do.

Mary Warren. Abby, I'm *here!*

Proctor (*frantically*). They're pretending, Mr.
1010 Danforth!

Abigail (*Now she takes a backward step, as though in fear the bird will swoop down momentarily*). Oh, please, Mary! Don't come down.

Susanna Walcott. Her claws, she's stretching her claws!

Proctor. Lies, lies.

Abigail (*backing further, eyes still fixed above*). Mary, please don't hurt me!

Mary Warren (*to* Danforth). I'm not hurting her!

Danforth (*to* Mary Warren). Why does she see this
1020 vision?

Mary Warren. She sees nothin'!

Abigail (*now staring full front as though hypnotized, and mimicking the exact tone of* Mary Warren's *cry*). She sees nothin'!

Mary Warren (*pleading*). Abby, you mustn't!

Abigail and All the Girls (*all transfixed*). Abby, you mustn't!

Mary Warren (*to all the girls*). I'm here, I'm here!

Girls. I'm here, I'm here!

1030 **Danforth** (*horrified*). Mary Warren! Draw back your spirit out of them!

Mary Warren. Mr. Danforth!

---

14. **a black art:** sorcery.

Lines 999–1032
REINFORCE *KEY IDEA:* HYSTERIA

Why does Mary Warren's desperation build toward **hysteria** as she suffers Abigail's persistent attacks? *Possible answer: Mary's desperation builds because she has no control over her own fate. She is powerless to stop the girls' attack on her.* Who else in this scene appears to become infected by the **hysteria** in the room? Explain. *Possible answer: Judge Danforth seems infected by hysteria, as evidenced by his horrified command that Mary withdraw her spirit from the girls and Mary's shock that he would say such a thing (lines 1030–1032).*

FOR STRATEGIC READERS
Comprehension: Text Structure Point out the transition that occurs immediately after Hale expresses his support of Proctor and suspicions of Abigail: Abigail screams, "You will not! Begone! Begone, I say!" (line 978) Explain that this outburst shifts attention away from the issue of Abigail's honesty. Help students use a Storyboard to trace the changing action in this scene.

BEST PRACTICES TOOLKIT—Transparency
Storyboard p. C11

FOR ADVANCED LEARNERS/AP
Analyze Character Behavior Have students review the scene in which Elizabeth is asked to incriminate her husband. Point out that she must choose between two noble impulses: honesty and loyalty. Then have students work in small groups to discuss her choices and her decision. Invite group representatives to share with the class the negative and positive aspects of Elizabeth's honesty and loyalty.

TIERED DISCUSSION PROMPTS

Use these prompts to help students explore the girls' roles as tormentors:

Summarize When the girls speak as a group, what do they say? Why? *Possible answer: As a group, the girls repeat everything that Mary Warren says. They are trying to make onlookers believe that Mary is directing demonic power against them.*

Interpret How do the girls behave as Mary grows increasingly upset? *Possible answer: As Mary grows more upset, the girls torment her more mercilessly. Mary tries to talk to them, but they continue to mock her, ignoring her pleas (lines 1048–1050).*

Synthesize What causes might explain the girls' behavior? Which cause do you think has the best textual support? *Possible answer: The girls might be under the influence of demonic powers, but the slim evidence for that cause has become suspect by now. There is stronger evidence for the possibility that Abigail has coached them; for example, the girls do not start mimicking Mary Warren until Abigail has done so first (lines 1022–1024). The girls' behavior also might result from hysteria; in this scene, even Judge Danforth is carried away by the emotional charge in the room (lines 1038–1039 and following). Perhaps the best explanation for the girls' behavior is a combination of hysteria and coaching from Abigail.*

Girls (*cutting her off*). Mr. Danforth!

Danforth. Have you compacted with the Devil? Have you?

Mary Warren. Never, never!

Girls. Never, never!

Danforth (*growing hysterical*). Why can they only repeat you?

1040 **Proctor.** Give me a whip—I'll stop it!

Mary Warren. They're sporting.[15] They—!

Girls. They're sporting!

Mary Warren (*turning on them all hysterically and stamping her feet*). Abby, stop it!

Girls (*stamping their feet*). Abby, stop it!

Mary Warren. Stop it!

Girls. Stop it!

Mary Warren (*screaming it out at the top of her lungs, and raising her fists*). Stop it!!

1050 **Girls** (*raising their fists*). Stop it!!

(Mary Warren, *utterly confounded, and becoming overwhelmed by* Abigail's—*and the girls'*—*utter conviction, starts to whimper, hands half raised, powerless, and all the girls begin whimpering exactly as she does.*)

Danforth. A little while ago you were afflicted. Now it seems you afflict others; where did you find this power?

Mary Warren (*staring at* Abigail). I—have no power.

Girls. I have no power.

1060 **Proctor.** They're gulling you,[16] Mister!

Danforth. Why did you turn about this past two weeks? You have seen the Devil, have you not?

Hale (*indicating* Abigail *and the girls*). You cannot believe them!

Mary Warren. I—   **Targeted Passage** ⑤

Proctor (*sensing her weakening*). Mary, God damns all liars!

Danforth (*pounding it into her*). You have seen the Devil, you have made compact with Lucifer, have 1070 you not?

Proctor. God damns liars, Mary!

(Mary *utters something unintelligible, staring at* Abigail, *who keeps watching the "bird" above.*)

Danforth. I cannot hear you. What do you say? (Mary *utters again unintelligibly.*) You will confess yourself or you will hang! (*He turns her roughly to face him.*) Do you know who I am? I say you will hang if you do not open with me!

Proctor. Mary, remember the angel Raphael—do 1080 that which is good and—

Abigail (*pointing upward*). The wings! Her wings are spreading! Mary, please, don't, don't—!

Hale. I see nothing, Your Honor!

Danforth. Do you confess this power! (*He is an inch from her face.*) Speak!

Abigail. She's going to come down! She's walking the beam!

Danforth. Will you speak!

Mary Warren (*staring in horror*). I cannot!

1090 **Girls.** I cannot!

Parris. Cast the Devil out! Look him in the face! Trample him! We'll save you, Mary, only stand fast against him and—

Abigail (*looking up*). Look out! She's coming down! (*She and all the girls run to one wall, shielding their eyes. And now, as though cornered, they let out a gigantic scream, and* Mary, *as though infected, opens her mouth and screams with them. Gradually* Abigail *and the girls leave off, until only* Mary *is left there, staring* 1100 *up at the "bird," screaming madly. All watch her, horrified by this evident fit.* Proctor *strides to her.*)

Proctor. Mary, tell the Governor what they—(*He has hardly got a word out, when, seeing him coming for her, she rushes out of his reach, screaming in horror.*)

---

15. **sporting:** playing a game.

16. **gulling you:** deceiving you.

DIFFERENTIATED INSTRUCTION

FOR STRATEGIC READERS

⑤ **Targeted Passage [Lines 1055–1064]**

This passage reveals who holds the most power in this court.

- What does Danforth ask Mary Warren about power? Why does he think that she has power?

- How does Mary respond? Why?

- What do Proctor and Hale tell Danforth?

- Is Hale still a friend of the court? How can you tell?

Concept Support Point out some of the ways in which Arthur Miller creates frenzy in this critical scene:

- The din in the courtroom is palpable as the girls shout incessantly.

- Danforth grows "hysterical" (line 1038) and Mary "hysterically" stamps her feet and screams (lines 1043 and 1048–1049).

- That Mary becomes "overwhelmed" (line 1052) is proof that things are out of control.

Setting and Characters

The same scene presented on stage and produced in a film may look very different. Compare these stage and film versions of the scene in which Abigail and the girls claim to see Mary Warren's spirit flying overhead. What differences do you see? What can the film version show you about the setting and characters that a stage version cannot?

THE CRUCIBLE: ACT THREE **193**

BEHIND THE CURTAIN

Setting and Characters Remind students that although films often seem more realistic than plays presented on a stage, a theater stage puts living, breathing people in front of the audience. Spectators hear and see live action instead of action that is mediated by the camera. *Possible answer: A stage version uses a set that is less realistic than that in a film version. Furthermore, in a film, the audience sees only the world of the play; in a theater production, the audience sees the setting with the awareness that the stage itself is enclosed. In a stage version, the audience will see all the characters in the scene; in a film version, the camera can isolate characters—in this case, the girls—and present only their actions. Similarly, unlike a staged play, a film can show close-ups of the characters' expressions. Film also allows the actors to vary their vocal expressions to a much greater degree than is possible on stage; for example, stage actors cannot truly whisper, for no one in the audience would hear them.*

FOR ADVANCED LEARNERS/AP

Research and Contrast Productions Have students work in small groups to locate images from at least one stage production of *The Crucible*. Ask students to compare those representations to the text itself, as well as to photographs from the 1996 film version, which is represented in the student edition. Challenge students to contrast the strengths and weaknesses in the presentation of setting and characters in all three versions—print, stage, and film.

THE CRUCIBLE: ACT THREE **193**

REINFORCE *KEY IDEA:* HYSTERIA

Discuss What part does **hysteria** play in Mary's decision to turn against Proctor? *Possible answer: The hysteria manufactured by Abigail and the girls has made Mary completely irrational. She also realizes that she has a better chance of staying alive if she sides with Abigail, since Abigail seems to control Danforth and the court.*

SELECTION WRAP–UP

REFLECT Have students think about the danger of letting emotions run unchecked. What has happened to reason and logical thinking as the Salemites have begun to indulge pure emotional responses?

★ CRITIQUE

- Ask students whether Mary's decision to abandon Proctor was expected.

- After completing the After Reading questions on page 195, have students revisit their responses and tell whether they have changed their opinions.

Mary Warren. Don't touch me—don't touch me! (*At which the girls halt at the door.*)

Proctor (*astonished*). Mary!

Mary Warren (*pointing at* Proctor). You're the Devil's man! (*He is stopped in his tracks.*)

1110 **Parris.** Praise God!

Girls. Praise God!

Proctor (*numbed*). Mary, how—?

Mary Warren. I'll not hang with you! I love God, I love God.

Danforth (*to* Mary). He bid you do the Devil's work?

Mary Warren (*hysterically, indicating* Proctor). He come at me by night and every day to sign, to sign, to—

Danforth. Sign what?   **Targeted Passage** ⑥

Parris. The Devil's book? He come with a book?

1120 **Mary Warren** (*hysterically, pointing at* Proctor, *fearful of him*). My name, he want my name. "I'll murder you," he says, "if my wife hangs! We must go and overthrow the court," he says!

(*Danforth's head jerks toward* Proctor, *shock and horror in his face.*)

Proctor (*turning, appealing to* Hale). Mr. Hale!

Mary Warren (*her sobs beginning*). He wake me every night, his eyes were like coals and his fingers claw my neck, and I sign, I sign . . .

1130 **Hale.** Excellency, this child's gone wild!

Proctor (*as* Danforth's *wide eyes pour on him*). Mary, Mary!

Mary Warren (*screaming at him*). No, I love God; I go your way no more. I love God, I bless God. (*Sobbing, she rushes to* Abigail.) Abby, Abby, I'll never hurt you more! (*They all watch, as* Abigail, *out of her infinite charity, reaches out and draws the sobbing* Mary *to her, and then looks up to* Danforth.)

Danforth (*to* Proctor). What are you? (Proctor *is* 1140 *beyond speech in his anger.*) You are combined with anti-Christ,[17] are you not? I have seen your power; you will not deny it! What say you, Mister?

Hale. Excellency—

Danforth. I will have nothing from you, Mr. Hale! (*to* Proctor) Will you confess yourself befouled with Hell, or do you keep that black allegiance yet? What say you?

Proctor (*his mind wild, breathless*). I say—I say— God is dead!

1150 **Parris.** Hear it, hear it!

Proctor (*laughs insanely, then*). A fire, a fire is burning! I hear the boot of Lucifer, I see his filthy face! And it is my face, and yours, Danforth! For them that quail to bring men out of ignorance, as I have quailed, and as you quail now when you know in all your black hearts that this be fraud—God damns our kind especially, and we will burn, we will burn together!

Danforth. Marshal! Take him and Corey with him to the jail!

1160 **Hale** (*starting across to the door*). I denounce these proceedings!

Proctor. You are pulling Heaven down and raising up a whore!

Hale. I denounce these proceedings, I quit this court! (*He slams the door to the outside behind him.*)

Danforth (*calling to him in a fury*). Mr. Hale! Mr. Hale!

(*The curtain falls.*)

---

17. **combined with anti-Christ:** working with the Devil.

DIFFERENTIATED INSTRUCTION

FOR STRATEGIC READERS
⑥ **Targeted Passage [Lines 1151–1157]**

In this passage, Proctor passionately indicts both himself and the court.

- Whom does Proctor equate with the Devil (Lucifer) now?

- Why does Proctor think that God will judge him and the court harshly?

- What punishment does Proctor predict for himself and the judges?

Vocabulary Support As students reread the sentence beginning in line 1153, point out the word *quail*. Explain that although *quail* can refer to a small bird, in this context it is a verb meaning "to flinch" or "to draw back from because of fear." Help students paraphase these lines.

Comprehension

Comprehension

1. **Recall** Why does Mary Warren come to the court?

2. **Recall** What does John Proctor admit to the court?

3. **Clarify** Why is Proctor arrested at the end of the act?

Literary Analysis

4. **Make Inferences** What role do you suppose **hysteria** plays in the following situations? Cite specific evidence from Act Three.

   • Mary's inability to faint on command (lines 736–759)
   • Danforth's belief in the girls (lines 1030–1039)
   • the change in Mary's testimony (lines 1113–1138)

5. **Recognize Verbal Irony** Verbal irony occurs when someone states one thing and means another. According to the stage directions, Abigail draws the sobbing, repentant Mary to her side "out of her infinite charity" (lines 1136–1137). Why is this comment ironic?

6. **Draw Conclusions About Characters** Review the character traits you recorded in your chart for Danforth. How do these traits influence his relationship with the following?

   • John Proctor   • Reverend Hale
   • Abigail Williams   • Reverend Parris

7. **Make Judgments** What is your opinion of the way Danforth is conducting the court? Use details from the play to support your opinion.

8. **Analyze Character Motives** Why does Elizabeth lie to Danforth about her husband's relationship with Abigail?

9. **Analyze Conventions of Drama** Review the information on **types of characters** in the **Literary Analysis Workshop** on pages 128–129. Then determine the play's central character, or **protagonist,** its major **antagonists,** and **character foils.** List these characters in a chart like the one shown and take notes on their personalities and values. What effect does the interplay among these characters have on the play?

Character-Type	Personality	Values

Literary Criticism

10. **Different Perspectives** The real Abigail Williams was 11 years old in 1692 and had not had an illicit relationship with John Proctor. How would the play differ if Arthur Miller had not embellished the truth? What would be lost?

learn the truth initially leads him to listen to Hale; *Parris:* Danforth's sense of honor makes him despise Parris.

7. *Danforth is swayed by the girls and thus not conducting court well. He should know that Abigail is impious and a bully. He is acting according to the beliefs of the time. He thinks Abigail is a victim of the witches, which compels him to rely on her testimony.*

8. *Elizabeth wants to protect John's reputation and save him from being charged with adultery.*

9. ● **SKILLS FOCUS** Conventions of Drama
Protagonist: Proctor: rational, strong; truth, logic; Antagonist: Abigail: manipulative, vengeful; getting her way; Character Foils: Danforth, Hale, Mary, Elizabeth, Parris. The interplay heightens tension and further reveals their personalities and values.

10. *A completely factual presentation might eliminate much dramatic tension. Proctor's relationships with Abigail and Elizabeth would have been different, and Proctor's personal agony and guilt would not have been central.*

Practice and Apply

Practice and Apply

After Reading

Use these copy masters to check understanding and provide extra support:

R RESOURCE MANAGER—Copy Masters
Reading Check p. 281
Conventions of Drama p. 279
Question Support p. 282

Additional selection questions are provided for teachers on page 275.

ANSWERS

1. *to say that the girls are lying*

2. *that he had an intimate relationship with Abigail*

3. *because Mary says he is in league with the Devil and because he says God is dead*

Possible answers:

4. *Mary can faint only when she is influenced by the other girls' hysteria; Danforth believes the girls because he is convinced by their hysterical actions; Mary switches sides due to fear of condemnation by the court and pressure from the girls.*

5. *Abigail's action is insincere; she had just endangered Mary's life by lying. When Mary changes her testimony, Abigail feels victorious, not charitable.*

6. ■ **SKILLS FOCUS** Draw Conclusions About Characters
Proctor: Danforth's dedication to his cause makes him suspicious of Proctor; Abigail: His dedication also makes him believe Abigail; Hale: Danforth's determination to

Assess and Reteach

Assess

R RESOURCE MANAGER—Copy Masters
Selection Test A pp. 283–284
Selection Test B/C pp. 285–286

⊘ Test Generator CD

Reteach

S STANDARDS LESSON FILE
Literature Lessons 1–2: Characters
Literature Lesson 6: Conflict
Literature Lessons 23–24: Elements of Drama
Reading Lesson 9: Drawing Conclusions

Practice and Apply

Get Into the Act
SUMMARY

Act Four takes place in the Salem jail. Several "witches" have been executed; now Proctor and Rebecca are to hang, for they refuse to confess to crimes that they say they have not committed. Hale, Parris, and Elizabeth speak with Proctor. Proctor signs a false confession, to save his life for his family's sake, but then he tears it up to save his reputation. Elizabeth watches with pride and stoic grief as he is led to the gallows.

READING SKILL

■ DRAW CONCLUSIONS ABOUT CHARACTERS

As you read this page, what can you conclude about Sarah Good's state of mind? Explain. *Possible answer: Sarah's state of mind is fragile. She seems almost delirious: she responds to the Devil as an unseen master (lines 3–4, 38) and babbles about being transformed into a bluebird and flying off to Barbados with Tituba (lines 20–22).*

Extend the Discussion To what would you attribute Sarah's attitude in this scene?

Act *Four*

(*A cell in Salem jail, that fall.*

At the back is a high barred window; near it, a great, heavy door. Along the walls are two benches.

The place is in darkness but for the moonlight seeping through the bars. It appears empty. Presently footsteps are heard coming down a corridor beyond the wall, keys rattle, and the door swings open. Marshal Herrick enters with a lantern.

He is nearly drunk, and heavy-footed. He goes to a bench and nudges a bundle of rags lying on it.)

Herrick. Sarah, wake up! Sarah Good! (*He then crosses to the other bench.*)

Sarah Good (*rising in her rags*). Oh, Majesty! Comin', comin'! Tituba, he's here, His Majesty's come!

Herrick. Go to the north cell; this place is wanted now. (*He hangs his lantern on the wall.* Tituba *sits up.*)

Tituba. That don't look to me like His Majesty; look to me like the marshal.

Herrick (*taking out a flask*). Get along with you now,
10 clear this place. (*He drinks, and* Sarah Good *comes and peers up into his face.*)

Sarah Good. Oh, is it you, Marshal! I thought sure you be the devil comin' for us. Could I have a sip of cider for me goin'-away?

Herrick (*handing her the flask*). And where are you off to, Sarah?

Tituba (*as* Sarah *drinks*). We goin' to Barbados, soon the Devil gits here with the feathers and the wings.

Herrick. Oh? A happy voyage to you.

20 **Sarah Good.** A pair of bluebirds wingin' southerly, the two of us! Oh, it be a grand transformation, Marshal! (*She raises the flask to drink again.*)

Herrick (*taking the flask from her lips*). You'd best give me that or you'll never rise off the ground. Come along now.

Tituba. I'll speak to him for you, if you desires to come along, Marshal.

Herrick. I'd not refuse it, Tituba; it's the proper morning to fly into Hell.

30 **Tituba.** Oh, it be no Hell in Barbados. Devil, him be pleasure-man in Barbados, him be singin' and dancin' in Barbados. It's you folks—you riles him up 'round here; it be too cold 'round here for that Old Boy. He freeze his soul in Massachusetts, but in Barbados he just as sweet and—(*A bellowing cow is heard, and* Tituba *leaps up and calls to the window.*) Aye, sir! That's him, Sarah!

Sarah Good. I'm here, Majesty! (*They hurriedly pick up their rags as* Hopkins, *a guard, enters.*)

Resources for Act Four

 RESOURCE MANAGER UNIT 1

Plan and Teach pp. 287–292

Literary Analysis
Summary pp. 293†*, 294‡*
Conventions of Drama
    pp. 295, 296†*
Question Support p. 300*

Reading
Reading Check p. 299

Vocabulary
Practice p. 297
Strategy p. 298

Grammar and Style
Use Realistic Dialogue p. 301

Assessment
Selection Tests A, B/C
    pp. 303*, 305*
⊘ Test Generator CD

 BEST PRACTICES TOOLKIT

Differentiated Instruction
    pp. 31–38*

Scaffolding Instruction
    pp. 43–46*

Graphic Organizers/Strategies
Reporter's Questions • Y Chart
• New Word Analysis • Venn
Diagram

Reading Support
⊘ Audio Anthology CD*

Technology
ⓘ Literature, Vocabulary, and Writing Centers at
ClassZone.com

⊘ Write*Smart* CD

---

* Resources for Differentiation   † Also in Spanish   ‡ In Haitian Creole and Vietnamese

John Proctor going to the gallows

ANALYZE VISUALS

Activity Where are Proctor and the women probably being taken? What details in the photograph convey a sense of hopelessness? *Possible answer: Proctor and the women probably are being taken to a place of execution. In the text, Herrick comments that "it's the proper morning to fly into Hell" (lines 28–29), indicating that the day's events will be very grim. Hopelessness is conveyed through the jail-like appearance of the cart, whose pointed slats resemble prison bars. In addition, chains bind the characters, suggesting that there is no escape. The people seem hopeless, too: Proctor's vacant eyes give him the appearance of a caged animal; and the woman to his left stands with closed eyes, either trying to block out the scene or showing resignation.*

DIFFERENTIATED INSTRUCTION

For general guidelines on differentiating instruction, see

BEST PRACTICES TOOLKIT
Differentiated Instruction pp. 31–38

FOR STRATEGIC READERS

In combination with the *Audio Anthology CD*, use one or more Targeted Passages (pp. 198, 201, 202, 205, 208) to ensure that students focus on key story events and concepts. Targeted Passages are also good for English learners.

Preview Read the Summary aloud; then have students use a Reporter's Questions chart to isolate key information.

Who is featured in Act Four?	Proctor, Elizabeth, Hale, Parris
What is Proctor's dilemma?	whether to submit a false confession

 BEST PRACTICES TOOLKIT—Transparency
Reporter's Questions p. C9

FOR ALL STUDENTS

Preteach Vocabulary Students will encounter the following vocabulary words in Act Four. Supply them with these definitions as needed:

- line 246: **conciliatory** (kən-sĭl´ē-ə-tôr´ē) *adj.* showing goodwill to end an argument
- line 280: **adamant** (ăd´ə-mənt) *adj.* immovable, especially in opposing something

Center Column (Play Text)

Hopkins. The Deputy Governor's arrived.

Herrick (*grabbing* Tituba). Come along, come along.

Tituba (*resisting him*). No, he comin' for me. I goin' home!

Herrick (*pulling her to the door*). That's not Satan, just a poor old cow with a hatful of milk. Come along now, out with you!

Tituba (*calling to the window*). Take me home, Devil! Take me home!

Sarah Good (*following the shouting* Tituba *out*). Tell him I'm goin', Tituba! Now you tell him Sarah Good is goin' too!

(*In the corridor outside* Tituba *calls on—"Take me home, Devil; Devil take me home!" and* Hopkins' *voice orders her to move on.* Herrick *returns and begins to push old rags and straw into a corner. Hearing footsteps, he turns, and enter* Danforth *and* Judge Hathorne. *They are in greatcoats and wear hats against the bitter cold. They are followed in by* Cheever, *who carries a dispatch case[1] and a flat wooden box containing his writing materials.*)

Herrick. Good morning, Excellency.

Danforth. Where is Mr. Parris?

Herrick. I'll fetch him. (*He starts for the door.*)

Danforth. Marshal. (Herrick *stops.*) When did Reverend Hale arrive?

Herrick. It were toward midnight, I think.

Danforth (*suspiciously*). What is he about here?

Herrick. He goes among them that will hang, sir. And he prays with them. He sits with Goody Nurse now. And Mr. Parris with him.

Danforth. Indeed. That man have no authority to enter here, Marshal. Why have you let him in?

Herrick. Why, Mr. Parris command me, sir. I cannot deny him.

Danforth. Are you drunk, Marshal?

Targeted Passage ①

---

1. **dispatch case:** a case for carrying documents.
2. **Andover:** a town in Massachusetts northwest of Salem.

Right Column (Play Text continued)

Herrick. No, sir; it is a bitter night, and I have no fire here.

Danforth (*containing his anger*). Fetch Mr. Parris.

Herrick. Aye, sir.

Danforth. There is a prodigious stench in this place.

Herrick. I have only now cleared the people out for you.

Danforth. Beware hard drink, Marshal.

Herrick. Aye, sir. (*He waits an instant for further orders. But* Danforth, *in dissatisfaction, turns his back on him, and* Herrick *goes out. There is a pause.* Danforth *stands in thought.*)

Hathorne. Let you question Hale, Excellency; I should not be surprised he have been preaching in Andover[2] lately.

Danforth. We'll come to that; speak nothing of Andover. Parris prays with him. That's strange. (*He blows on his hands, moves toward the window, and looks out.*)

Hathorne. Excellency, I wonder if it be wise to let Mr. Parris so continuously with the prisoners. (Danforth *turns to him, interested.*) I think, sometimes, the man has a mad look these days.

Danforth. Mad?

Hathorne. I met him yesterday coming out of his house, and I bid him good morning—and he wept and went his way. I think it is not well the village sees him so unsteady.

Danforth. Perhaps he have some sorrow.

Cheever (*stamping his feet against the cold*). I think it be the cows, sir.

Danforth. Cows?

Cheever. There be so many cows wanderin' the highroads, now their masters are in the jails, and much disagreement who they will belong to now. I know Mr. Parris be arguin' with farmers all yesterday—

Left Column (Margin Notes)

LITERARY ANALYSIS

● **CONVENTIONS OF DRAMA**

In lines 52–80, stage directions and dialogue reveal the condition of the jail cell. What is it like? Cite evidence. **Possible answer:** *The cell is cold, because it is "bitter cold" outside (line 58) and there is no fire for warmth (lines 76–77). The only physical comfort is "old rags and straw" (line 55), and the smell is terrible (line 80).*

Extend the Discussion What does the condition of the jail indicate about the authorities' opinion of the prisoners?

READING SKILL

■ **DRAW CONCLUSIONS ABOUT CHARACTERS**

Why might Judge Danforth consider it "strange" for Parris to be praying with Hale (line 92)? **Possible answer:** *Meeting for prayer is "strange" because Hale and Parris have clashed over the witch trials. Parris has been ready to convict anyone charged with witchcraft, whereas Hale earlier quit the trials, decrying them as a sham.*

198   UNIT 1: EARLY AMERICAN WRITING

DIFFERENTIATED INSTRUCTION

FOR STRATEGIC READERS

① **Targeted Passage [Lines 95–111]**

This passage indicates that the trauma of the witchcraft scare can be seen as well as felt.

- Why is Hathorne worried about Parris? What does he think is affecting Parris?
- Why are cows roaming Salem's roads?
- Why are the wandering cows an additional source of stress in Salem?

Explore Settings Have students reread the stage directions that begin Act Three (page 176) and Act Four (page 196). Help them note key details about each set in the two "branches" of a Y Chart. Then discuss how the sets are similar and why Miller might have wanted a similarity between them. Record students' responses in the "trunk" of the Y Chart.

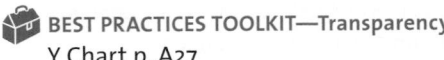 **BEST PRACTICES TOOLKIT—Transparency** Y Chart p. A27

FOR ADVANCED LEARNERS/AP

Research Andover [small-group option] Ask students to find and present a brief introduction to the town of Andover. (See lines 88–92.) The introduction might include a map showing the relative locations of Andover and Salem and a brief explanation of Andover's early history, including information about how the community responded to the witchcraft scare that began in Salem.

there is great contention, sir, about the cows. Contention make him weep, sir; it were always a man that weep for contention. (*He turns, as do* Hathorne *and* Danforth, *hearing someone coming up the corridor.* Danforth *raises his head as* Parris *enters. He is gaunt, frightened, and sweating in his greatcoat.*)

Parris (*to* Danforth, *instantly*). Oh, good morning, sir, thank you for coming, I beg your pardon wakin'

120 you so early. Good morning, Judge Hathorne.

Danforth. Reverend Hale have no right to enter this—

Parris. Excellency, a moment. (*He hurries back and shuts the door.*)

Hathorne. Do you leave him alone with the prisoners?

Danforth. What's his business here?

Parris (*prayerfully holding up his hands*). Excellency, hear me. It is a providence. Reverend Hale has returned to bring Rebecca Nurse to God.

Danforth (*surprised*). He bids her confess?

130 **Parris** (*sitting*). Hear me. Rebecca have not given me a word this three month since she came. Now she sits with him, and her sister and Martha Corey and two or three others, and he pleads with them, confess their crimes and save their lives.

Danforth. Why—this is indeed a providence. And they soften, they soften?

Parris. Not yet, not yet. But I thought to summon you, sir, that we might think on whether it be not wise, to—(*He dares not say it.*) I had thought to put

140 a question, sir, and I hope you will not—

Danforth. Mr. Parris, be plain, what troubles you?

Parris. There is news, sir, that the court—the court must reckon with. My niece, sir, my niece—I believe she has vanished.

Danforth. Vanished!

Parris. I had thought to advise you of it earlier in the week, but—

Danforth. Why? How long is she gone?

Parris. This be the third night. You see, sir, she told

150 me she would stay a night with Mercy Lewis. And next day, when she does not return, I send to Mr. Lewis to inquire. Mercy told him she would sleep in *my* house for a night.

Danforth. They are both gone?!

Parris (*in fear of him*). They are, sir.

Danforth (*alarmed*). I will send a party for them. Where may they be?

Parris. Excellency, I think they be aboard a ship. (Danforth *stands agape.*) My daughter tells me how

160 she heard them speaking of ships last week, and tonight I discover my—my strongbox is broke into. (*He presses his fingers against his eyes to keep back tears.*)

Hathorne (*astonished*). She have robbed you?

Parris. Thirty-one pound is gone. I am penniless. (*He covers his face and sobs.*)

Danforth. Mr. Parris, you are a brainless man! (*He walks in thought, deeply worried.*)

Parris. Excellency, it profit nothing you should blame me. I cannot think they would run off

170 except they fear to keep in Salem any more. (*He is pleading.*) Mark it, sir, Abigail had close knowledge of the town, and since the news of Andover has broken here—

Danforth. Andover is remedied.[3] The court returns there on Friday, and will resume examinations.

Parris. I am sure of it, sir. But the rumor here speaks rebellion in Andover, and it—

Danforth. There is no rebellion in Andover!

Parris. I tell you what is said here, sir. Andover have

180 thrown out the court, they say, and will have no part of witchcraft. There be a faction here, feeding on that news, and I tell you true, sir, I fear there will be riot here.

Hathorne. Riot! Why at every execution I have seen naught but high satisfaction in the town.

---

3. **remedied:** no longer a problem.

Lines 158–183
TIERED DISCUSSION PROMPTS

Use these prompts to help students explore the news about Abigail and Mercy Lewis:

Connect Have you ever known someone who felt so overwhelmed by a situation that he or she wanted to run away? Why does running away from stress sometimes seem like a good idea? *Accept all responses.*

Analyze Why would Abigail and Mercy Lewis "fear to keep in Salem" (line 170)? *Possible answer: Abigail and Mercy might fear a countermovement against the executions, for the people in nearby Andover have disbanded the witch trials there (lines 179–181). Because a faction in Salem is "feeding on that news" from Andover (lines 181–182), the girls who instigated the witch hunt are worried about their safety should public sentiment in Salem turn against the accusers.*

Synthesize Do you think that the girls' disappearance will affect Danforth's decision to carry out the remaining executions? Why or why not? *Possible answer: Danforth probably will not be affected by the girls' disappearance. He refuses to acknowledge any problems in Andover (lines 174–175, 178), and his stubbornness suggests that he will follow through with the planned executions. (Indeed, he later refuses to delay the executions that are about to take place [lines 246–248].)*

FOR STRATEGIC READERS

Make Inferences Point out that in lines 137–140, Parris cannot bring himself to ask Danforth a certain question. Explain that students must make an inference—a well-informed assumption—about the nature of that question. Help them review lines 126–136 and look ahead to lines 179–183 for information. Elicit or explain that Parris wants to ask Danforth to delay that day's executions. (He finally will make this request in lines 200–201.)

FOR ENGLISH LEARNERS

Vocabulary: Cognates Point out that the Spanish word *materiales* is spelled and pronounced almost like the English word *materials* (line 60). Help students understand these English words with Spanish cognates: *authority/autoridad* (line 71), *continuously/continuamente* (line 96), *providence/providencia* (line 127), *confess/confesar* (line 129), *discover/descubrir* (line 161), *innocence/inocencia* (line 208), *opinion/opinión* (lines 221–222), *pardon/perdón* (line 243), *pretense/pretensión* (line 479), *agony/agonía* (line 500), *physical/físico* (line 501), *mystical/místico* (line 534), *instruction/instrucción* (line 570), *urgently/urgentemente* (line 572).

◼ DRAW CONCLUSIONS ABOUT CHARACTERS

Reread lines 232–236. What does Parris mean when he refers to "this sort"? Why does he oppose the hanging of "this sort"? ***Possible answer:*** *Parris is referring to condemned prisoners, such as Proctor and Rebecca, who have good reputations in Salem and who are supported by much of the town. Because Parris was instrumental in condemning them, he fears that the town will harm him if Proctor and Rebecca die.*

Lines 203–210
REINFORCE *KEY IDEA:* HYSTERIA

Discuss Mob action that rises from **hysteria** feeds on excessive emotion from the crowd. Why does Parris want to curb the emotion that is being generated out of sympathy for those who have died? ***Possible answer:*** *Parris wants to curb the sympathizers' emotion because he is afraid that hysteria will be created in the opposite direction; in other words, he fears that a hysterical mob could form against the court if people decide that their friends and family have died unjustly. This mob would be dangerous for Parris, because he supported the executions.*

Parris. Judge Hathorne—it were another sort that hanged till now. Rebecca Nurse is no Bridget that lived three year with Bishop before she married him. John Proctor is not Isaac Ward that drank his family
190 to ruin. (*to* Danforth) I would to God it were not so, Excellency, but these people have great weight yet in the town. Let Rebecca stand upon the gibbet[4] and send up some righteous prayer, and I fear she'll wake a vengeance on you.

Hathorne. Excellency, she is condemned a witch. The court have—

Danforth (*in deep concern, raising a hand to* Hathorne). Pray you. (*to* Parris) How do you propose, then?

200 **Parris.** Excellency, I would postpone these hangin's for a time.

Danforth. There will be no postponement.

Parris. Now Mr. Hale's returned, there is hope, I think—for if he bring even one of these to God, that confession surely damns the others in the public eye, and none may doubt more that they are all linked to Hell. This way, unconfessed and claiming innocence, doubts are multiplied, many honest people will weep for them, and our good purpose is
210 lost in their tears.

Danforth (*after thinking a moment, then going to* Cheever). Give me the list.

(Cheever *opens the dispatch case, searches.*)

Parris. It cannot be forgot, sir, that when I summoned the congregation for John Proctor's excommunication[5] there were hardly thirty people come to hear it. That speak a discontent, I think, and—

Danforth (*studying the list*). There will be no postponement.

220 **Parris.** Excellency—

Danforth. Now, sir—which of these in your opinion may be brought to God? I will myself strive with him[6] till dawn. (*He hands the list to* Parris, *who merely glances at it.*)

Parris. There is not sufficient time till dawn.

Danforth. I shall do my utmost. Which of them do you have hope for?

Parris (*not even glancing at the list now, and in a quavering voice, quietly*). Excellency—a dagger—
230 (*He chokes up.*)

Danforth. What do you say?

Parris. Tonight, when I open my door to leave my house—a dagger clattered to the ground. (*Silence.* Danforth *absorbs this. Now* Parris *cries out.*) You cannot hang this sort. There is danger for me. I dare not step outside at night!

(Reverend Hale *enters. They look at him for an instant in silence. He is steeped in sorrow, exhausted, and more direct than he ever was.*)

240 **Danforth.** Accept my congratulations, Reverend Hale; we are gladdened to see you returned to your good work.

Hale (*coming to* Danforth *now*). You must pardon them. They will not budge.

(Herrick *enters, waits.*)

Danforth (**conciliatory**). You misunderstand, sir; I cannot pardon these when twelve are already hanged for the same crime. It is not just.

Parris (*with failing heart*). Rebecca will not confess?

250 **Hale.** The sun will rise in a few minutes. Excellency, I must have more time.

Danforth. Now hear me, and beguile yourselves no more. I will not receive a single plea for pardon or postponement. Them that will not confess will hang. Twelve are already executed; the names of

---

4. **gibbet** (jĭb′ĭt): gallows.

5. **excommunication:** banishment from a church. For the Puritans in New England, this punishment resulted in the loss of church privileges.

6. **strive with him:** struggle with him through prayer.

DIFFERENTIATED INSTRUCTION

FOR STRATEGIC READERS

Comprehension Support Make sure that students understand these points:

• Parris may not like Proctor, but he does not think that Proctor is evil (lines 186–190).

• There has been a threat against Parris's life (lines 232–236).

• Danforth considers it "not just" to offer pardon—not because the convicted may not be guilty but because other convicted people already have died (lines 246–248).

FOR ADVANCED LEARNERS/AP

Research Terminology [paired option] Point out the word *gibbet* in line 192 and its definition in the footnote. Have students find how the term originated and how it became part of the language of hanging. Invite students to report their findings to the class.

Targeted Passage ②

these seven are given out, and the village expects to see them die this morning. Postponement now speaks a floundering on my part; reprieve or pardon must cast doubt upon the guilt of them that died

260 till now. While I speak God's law, I will not crack its voice with whimpering. If retaliation is your fear, know this—I should hang ten thousand that dared to rise against the law, and an ocean of salt tears could not melt the resolution of the statutes. Now draw yourselves up like men and help me, as you are bound by Heaven to do. Have you spoken with them all, Mr. Hale?

Hale. All but Proctor. He is in the dungeon.

Danforth (*to* Herrick). What's Proctor's way now?

270 **Herrick.** He sits like some great bird; you'd not know he lived except he will take food from time to time.

Danforth (*after thinking a moment*). His wife—his wife must be well on with child now.

Herrick. She is, sir.

Danforth. What think you, Mr. Parris? You have closer knowledge of this man; might her presence soften him?

Parris. It is possible, sir. He have not laid eyes on her these three months. I should summon her.

280 **Danforth** (*to* Herrick). Is he yet **adamant**? Has he struck at you again?

Herrick. He cannot, sir, he is chained to the wall now.

Danforth (*after thinking on it*). Fetch Goody Proctor to me. Then let you bring him up.

Herrick. Aye, sir. (Herrick *goes. There is silence.*)

Hale. Excellency, if you postpone a week and publish to the town that you are striving for their confessions, that speak mercy on your part, not faltering.

Danforth. Mr. Hale, as God have not empowered me

290 like Joshua to stop this sun from rising,[7] so I cannot withhold from them the perfection of their punishment.

Hale (*harder now*). If you think God wills you to raise rebellion, Mr. Danforth, you are mistaken!

Danforth (*instantly*). You have heard rebellion spoken in the town?

Hale. Excellency, there are orphans wandering from house to house; abandoned cattle bellow on the highroads, the stink of rotting crops hangs every-

300 where, and no man knows when the harlots' cry will end his life—and you wonder yet if rebellion's spoke? Better you should marvel how they do not burn your province!

Danforth. Mr. Hale, have you preached in Andover this month?

Hale. Thank God they have no need of me in Andover.

Danforth. You baffle me, sir. Why have you returned here?

310 **Hale.** Why, it is all simple. I come to do the Devil's work. I come to counsel Christians they should belie themselves. (*His sarcasm collapses.*) There is blood on my head! Can you not see the blood on my head!!

Parris. Hush! (*For he has heard footsteps. They all face the door.* Herrick *enters with* Elizabeth. *Her wrists are linked by heavy chain, which* Herrick *now removes. Her clothes are dirty; her face is pale and gaunt.* Herrick *goes out.*)

Danforth (*very politely*). Goody Proctor. (*She is*

320 *silent.*) I hope you are hearty?

Elizabeth (*as a warning reminder*). I am yet six month before my time.

Danforth. Pray be at your ease, we come not for your life. We—(*uncertain how to plead, for he is not accustomed to it.*) Mr. Hale, will you speak with the woman?

Hale. Goody Proctor, your husband is marked to hang this morning.

(*pause*)

330 **Elizabeth** (*quietly*). I have heard it.

---

7. **like Joshua . . . rising:** According to the Bible, Joshua became leader of the Israelites after Moses died. He led the people to the Promised Land while the sun stood still.

Lines 295–303
TIERED DISCUSSION PROMPTS

Use these prompts to help students understand how grim things have become in Salem since the witch trials started:

Recall Why are there "orphans," "abandoned cattle," and "rotting crops" in Salem (lines 297–299)? *Possible answer: This situation has arisen because the men and women who are parents to the children and who tend to the cattle and crops have been jailed and even executed. (See also lines 108–110.)*

Interpret Why does Hale express surprise that an uprising has not yet occurred in Salem? *Possible answer: Hale expresses surprise because he thinks that the deadly miscarriage of justice is so bad and the circumstances so dire that people have legitimate reason to riot: Children whose parents have been taken have no home, cattle run loose because there is no one to care for them, and farms are in ruin because their owners are gone. People are fearful, for they know that they can lose their lives on the basis of a lie.*

Evaluate How effectively does Miller use descriptive language to provide information about conditions in Salem? Explain. *Possible answer: Miller effectively uses descriptive language by appealing to the audience's senses while providing information about Salem. For example, the orphans are "wandering" (line 297), a term that suggests a particular kind of movement. The cattle "bellow" (line 298) and the harlots "cry" (line 300). The rotting crops produce a "stink" (line 299).*

FOR STRATEGIC READERS

② **Targeted Passage [lines 257–267]**

This passage sheds light on Danforth's character and his role as a judge.

- What reasons does Danforth give for refusing to postpone the executions?

- What does he threaten to do in response to a possible rebellion from the Salemites?

- What does he say is not stronger than the law ("the statutes")?

- What does Danforth claim is his authority for making decisions of life and death?

Clarify Figurative Language Point out Hale's repeated "blood on my head" in lines 312–313. Explain that this is figurative, not literal, language; Miller means that Hale feels responsible for spilling the blood—that is, causing the deaths—of innocent people. Have students paraphrase lines 310–313, paying special attention to this phrase.

FOR ADVANCED LEARNERS/AP

Analyze Viewpoints By this point, several views about the fate of the convicted Salemites have been voiced. Ask students to identify the views of Danforth, Hale, and Parris. Then have students meet in three groups, each group discussing the strengths and weaknesses of one of the views. After group representatives have shared key discussion points with the class, discuss which view students think best reflects the attitude of the townspeople.

■ DRAW CONCLUSIONS ABOUT CHARACTERS

Reread lines 368–386. Why would Elizabeth show no emotion in response to Danforth's questions? Record character traits about Elizabeth in the prereading chart introduced on page 131. Include evidence. *Possible answer: Elizabeth would show no emotion because she is proud. She stands as silent and emotionless as a stone (line 373) because she refuses to be controlled by Danforth and his unjust court.*

Elizabeth	
Traits	proud, defiant
Evidence	"I promise nothing" (line 386)

Extend the Discussion Why would Elizabeth's silence and emotional restraint frustrate Danforth?

◆ GRAMMAR AND STYLE

Use Realistic Dialogue Reread lines 344–351. Hale is speaking of serious topics—his remorse and his beliefs about God—so his language is more poetic and less colloquial; still, it is realistic for that time. What inverted sentence can you find in these lines? *Answer: "... the very crowns of holy law I brought ..." (lines 347–348)* What unusual word appears in the final sentence of this passage, and what does it mean? *Answer:* cleave, *which means "to cling"*

Hale. You know, do you not, that I have no connection with the court? (*She seems to doubt it.*) I come of my own, Goody Proctor. I would save your husband's life, for if he is taken I count myself his murderer. Do you understand me?

Elizabeth. What do you want of me?

Hale. Goody Proctor, I have gone this three month like our Lord into the wilderness.[8] I have sought a Christian way, for damnation's doubled on a minis-
340 ter who counsels men to lie.

Hathorne. It is no lie, you cannot speak of lies.

Hale. It is a lie! They are innocent!

Danforth. I'll hear no more of that!

Hale (*continuing to* Elizabeth). Let you not mistake your duty as I mistook my own. I came into this village like a bridegroom to his beloved, bearing gifts of high religion; the very crowns of holy law I brought, and what I touched with my bright confidence, it died; and where I turned the eye of my
350 great faith, blood flowed up. Beware, Goody Proctor—cleave to no faith when faith brings blood. It is mistaken law that leads you to sacrifice. Life, woman, life is God's most precious gift; no principle, however glorious, may justify the taking of it. I beg you, woman, prevail upon your husband to confess. Let him give his lie. Quail not before God's judgment in this, for it may well be God damns a liar less than he that throws his life away for pride. Will you plead with him? I cannot think he will
360 listen to another.   ③

Elizabeth (*quietly*). I think that be the Devil's argument.   **Targeted Passage**

Hale (*with a climactic desperation*). Woman, before the laws of God we are as swine! We cannot read His will!

Elizabeth. I cannot dispute with you, sir; I lack learning for it.

Danforth (*going to her*). Goody Proctor, you are not summoned here for disputation. Be there no wifely
370 tenderness within you? He will die with the sunrise. Your husband. Do you understand it? (*She only looks at him.*) What say you? Will you contend with him? (*She is silent.*) Are you stone? I tell you true, woman, had I no other proof of your unnatural life, your dry eyes now would be sufficient evidence that you delivered up your soul to Hell! A very ape would weep at such calamity! Have the devil dried up any tear of pity in you? (*She is silent.*) Take her out. It profit nothing she should speak to him!

380 **Elizabeth** (*quietly*). Let me speak with him, Excellency.

Parris (*with hope*). You'll strive with him? (*She hesitates.*)

Danforth. Will you plead for his confession or will you not?

Elizabeth. I promise nothing. Let me speak with him. (*A sound—the sibilance of dragging feet on stone. They turn. A pause.* Herrick *enters with* John Proctor. *His wrists are chained. He is another man, bearded, filthy,*
390 *his eyes misty as though webs had overgrown them. He halts inside the doorway, his eye caught by the sight of* Elizabeth. *The emotion flowing between them prevents anyone from speaking for an instant. Now* Hale, *visibly affected, goes to* Danforth *and speaks quietly.*)

Hale. Pray, leave them, Excellency.

Danforth (*pressing* Hale *impatiently aside*). Mr. Proctor, you have been notified, have you not? (Proctor *is silent, staring at* Elizabeth.) I see light in the sky, Mister; let you counsel with your wife,
400 and may God help you turn your back on Hell. (Proctor *is silent, staring at* Elizabeth.)

Hale (*quietly*). Excellency, let—

(Danforth *brushes past* Hale *and walks out.* Hale *follows.* Cheever *stands and follows,* Hathorne *behind.* Herrick *goes.* Parris, *from a safe distance, offers.*)

---

8. **like our Lord . . . wilderness:** According to the New Testament, Jesus spent 40 days wandering in the desert.

DIFFERENTIATED INSTRUCTION

FOR STRATEGIC READERS

③ **Targeted Passage [Lines 344–360]**

In this passage, Hale admits that his initial views and zeal regarding the witch hunt were misdirected.

• What does Hale think happened as a result of his good intentions to defeat the Devil?

• According to Hale, what kind of faith should be abandoned?

• What is God's dearest gift to humanity?

• Which trait—dishonesty or pride—does Hale consider more harmful? Why?

FOR ADVANCED LEARNERS/AP

Analyze Tone [small-group option] Have students discuss Elizabeth Proctor's tone in Act Four, covering these moments:

• her interview with Danforth, Parris, and Hale (lines 319–386)

• her private conversation with her husband (lines 410–518)

• her words when he agrees to confess (lines 541–542, 552–554)

• her comments just before he is led off to be executed (lines 781–783)

Students should identify the tone in each passage, point out shifts in tone, and offer insights into Elizabeth's character. Invite students to share their observations with the class.

Parris. If you desire a cup of cider, Mr. Proctor, I am sure I—(Proctor *turns an icy stare at him, and he breaks off.* Parris *raises his palms toward* Proctor.) God lead you now. (Parris *goes out.*)

410 (*Alone.* Proctor *walks to her, halts. It is as though they stood in a spinning world. It is beyond sorrow, above it. He reaches out his hand as though toward an embodiment not quite real, and as he touches her, a strange soft sound, half laughter, half amazement, comes from his throat. He pats her hand. She covers his hand with hers. And then, weak, he sits. Then she sits, facing him.*)

Proctor. The child?

Elizabeth. It grows.

Proctor. There is no word of the boys?

420 **Elizabeth.** They're well. Rebecca's Samuel keeps them.

Proctor. You have not seen them?

Elizabeth. I have not. (*She catches a weakening in herself and downs it.*)

Proctor. You are a—marvel, Elizabeth.

Elizabeth. You—have been tortured?

Proctor. Aye. (*Pause. She will not let herself be drowned in the sea that threatens her.*) They come for my life now.

Elizabeth. I know it.

430 (*pause*)

Proctor. None—have yet confessed?

Elizabeth. There be many confessed.

Proctor. Who are they?

Elizabeth. There be a hundred or more, they say. Goody Ballard is one; Isaiah Goodkind is one. There be many.

Proctor. Rebecca?

Elizabeth. Not Rebecca. She is one foot in Heaven now; naught may hurt her more.

440 **Proctor.** And Giles?

Elizabeth. You have not heard of it?

Proctor. I hear nothin', where I am kept.

Elizabeth. Giles is dead.

(*He looks at her incredulously.*)

Proctor. When were he hanged?

Elizabeth (*quietly, factually*). He were not hanged. He would not answer aye or nay to his indictment; for if he denied the charge they'd hang him surely, and auction out his property. So he stand mute, and 450 died Christian under the law. And so his sons will have his farm. It is the law, for he could not be condemned a wizard without he answer the indictment, aye or nay.

Proctor. Then how does he die?

Elizabeth (*gently*). They press him, John.

Proctor. Press?

Elizabeth. Great stones they lay upon his chest until he plead aye or nay. (*with a tender smile for the old man*) They say he give them but two words. "More 460 weight," he says. And died.

Proctor (*numbed—a thread to weave into his agony*). "More weight."

Elizabeth. Aye. It were a fearsome[9] man, Giles Corey. (*pause*)

Proctor (*with great force of will, but not quite looking at her*). I have been thinking I would confess to them, Elizabeth. (*She shows nothing.*) What say you? If I give them that?

Elizabeth. I cannot judge you, John.

470 (*pause*)

Proctor (*simply—a pure question*). What would you have me do?

Elizabeth. As you will, I would have it. (*slight pause*) I want you living, John. That's sure.

Proctor (*pauses, then with a flailing of hope*). Giles' wife? Have she confessed?

Elizabeth. She will not.

---

9. **fearsome:** courageous.

Lines 410–428
REINFORCE *KEY IDEA:* HYSTERIA

Discuss How is the Proctor family a symbol of what **hysteria** has done to the people in and around Salem? *Possible answer: The family is a symbol because the reader sees the real-life effects of judgments driven by hysteria:*

- *A husband and wife are torn apart.*
- *A father will die unnecessarily.*
- *Children lose their parents (for Elizabeth has not seen her sons in months, and the baby that she is carrying never will know its father).*

The hysterical search for the Devil was supposed to protect people; instead, it is destroying them.

FOR STRATEGIC READERS
Concept Support Clarify the matter of property law that is addressed in the account of Giles Corey's death (lines 446–460).

- If Giles had acknowledged that charges had been made against him but had refused to confess, he would have been declared guilty of witchcraft and hanged. His family would have lost his land because it would have been sold at auction.

- Because Giles refused to acknowledge the charges against him, he avoided being condemned for witchcraft. He was still executed, but his silence meant that his family would keep his land.

Ask students to offer opinions about Giles's decision to remain silent and then to explain the effect that the account has upon Proctor.

FOR ENGLISH LEARNERS
Key Academic Vocabulary Use New Word Analysis to teach these words: *justify* (line 354), *physical* (line 501), *release* (line 553), *issue* (line 647), *document* (line 732), *final* (line 784).

 BEST PRACTICES TOOLKIT—Transparency New Word Analysis p. E8

■ DRAW CONCLUSIONS ABOUT CHARACTERS

In lines 481–487, why does Proctor say that it does not matter if he lies when confessing to acts that he did not commit? What conclusion can you draw about Proctor's opinion of himself? *Possible answer: Proctor says that it does not matter if he lies because that sin will be just one of many that he has committed; as he comments, "Nothing's spoiled . . . that were not rotten long before" (lines 483–485). Proctor seems to have a low opinion of himself, for he says, "I am no good man" (line 483).*

If students need help . . . Focus on Proctor's statement "My honesty is broke . . ." (lines 482–483). Ask:

- How has Proctor been dishonest in the past? *Possible answer: He has had and has tried to cover up a liaison with Abigail.*

- Why does he feel that his honesty has been broken and cannot be repaired? *Possible answer: His honesty has been irreparably broken because he has revealed his liaison to the court and because his relationship with Elizabeth has changed for the worse since then.*

Extend the Discussion How do Proctor and Elizabeth agree or disagree about Proctor's refusal to confess so far?

(*pause*)

Proctor. It is a pretense, Elizabeth.

480 **Elizabeth.** What is?

Proctor. I cannot mount the gibbet like a saint. It is a fraud. I am not that man. (*She is silent.*) My honesty is broke, Elizabeth; I am no good man. Nothing's spoiled by giving them this lie that were not rotten long before.

Elizabeth. And yet you've not confessed till now. That speak goodness in you.

Proctor. Spite only keeps me silent. It is hard to give a lie to dogs. (*Pause. For the first time he turns directly* 490 *to her.*) I would have your forgiveness, Elizabeth.

Elizabeth. It is not for me to give, John, I am—

Proctor. I'd have you see some honesty in it. Let them that never lied die now to keep their souls. It is pretense for me, a vanity that will not blind God nor keep my children out of the wind. (*pause*) What say you?

Elizabeth (*upon a heaving sob that always threatens*). John, it come to naught that I should forgive you, if you'll not forgive yourself. (*Now he turns away a little,* 500 *in great agony.*) It is not my soul, John, it is yours. (*He stands, as though in physical pain, slowly rising to his feet with a great immortal longing to find his answer. It is difficult to say, and she is on the verge of tears.*) Only be sure of this, for I know it now: Whatever you will do, it is a good man does it. (*He turns his doubting, searching gaze upon her.*) I have read my heart this three month, John. (*pause*) I have sins of my own to count. It needs a cold wife to prompt lechery.

Proctor (*in great pain*). Enough, enough—

510 **Elizabeth** (*now pouring out her heart*). Better you should know me!

Proctor. I will not hear it! I know you!

Elizabeth. You take my sins upon you, John—

Proctor (*in agony*). No, I take my own, my own!

Elizabeth. John, I counted myself so plain, so poorly made, no honest love could come to me! Suspicion kissed you when I did; I never knew how I should say my love. It were a cold house I kept! (*In fright, she swerves, as Hathorne enters.*)

520 **Hathorne.** What say you, Proctor? The sun is soon up.

(Proctor, *his chest heaving, stares, turns to* Elizabeth. *She comes to him as though to plead, her voice quaking.*)

Elizabeth. Do what you will. But let none be your judge. There be no higher judge under Heaven than Proctor is! Forgive me, forgive me, John—I never knew such goodness in the world! (*She covers her face, weeping.*)

(Proctor *turns from her to* Hathorne; *he is off the earth, his voice hollow.*)

530 **Proctor.** I want my life.

Hathorne (*electrified, surprised*). You'll confess yourself?

Proctor. I will have my life.

Hathorne (*with a mystical tone*). God be praised! It is a providence! (*He rushes out the door, and his voice is heard calling down the corridor.*) He will confess! Proctor will confess!

Proctor (*with a cry, as he strides to the door*). Why do you cry it? (*In great pain he turns back to her.*) It is 540 evil, is it not? It is evil.

Elizabeth (*in terror, weeping*). I cannot judge you, John, I cannot!

Proctor. Then who will judge me? (*suddenly clasping his hands*) God in Heaven, what is John Proctor, what is John Proctor? (*He moves as an animal, and a fury is riding in him, a tantalized search.*) I think it is honest, I think so; I am no saint. (*As though she had denied this he calls angrily at her.*) Let Rebecca go like a saint; for me it is fraud!

550 (*Voices are heard in the hall, speaking together in suppressed excitement.*)

DIFFERENTIATED INSTRUCTION

FOR ADVANCED LEARNERS/AP

Debate Proctor's Dilemma Have students reread lines 541–549 and think about Proctor's lament: "what is John Proctor?" (line 544) Then divide students into two groups and have them debate Proctor's dilemma: Should he submit to being hanged, or should he confess? Each group should argue for one of the options. Present these questions for students to consider:

- Would dying make Proctor a noble person, or a fraud?

- Would confessing make Proctor weak, or honest (honest about being a sinner—not honest about associating with the Devil)?

Conclude by discussing with all participants which option would better enable Arthur Miller, as the playwright, to highlight the ideas that he wanted to convey.

Elizabeth. I am not your judge, I cannot be. (*as though giving him release*) Do as you will, do as you will!

Proctor. Would you give them such a lie? Say it. Would you ever give them this? (*She cannot answer.*) You would not; if tongs of fire were singeing you you would not! It is evil. Good, then—it is evil, and I do it!

560 (Hathorne *enters with* Danforth, *and, with them,* Cheever, Parris, *and* Hale. *It is a businesslike, rapid entrance, as though the ice had been broken.*)

Targeted Passage

Danforth (*with great relief and gratitude*). Praise to God, man, praise to God; you shall be blessed in Heaven for this. (Cheever *has hurried to the bench with pen, ink, and paper.* Proctor *watches him.*) Now then, let us have it. Are you ready, Mr. Cheever?

Proctor (*with a cold, cold horror at their efficiency*). Why must it be written?

570 **Danforth.** Why, for the good instruction of the village, Mister; this we shall post upon the church door! (*to* Parris, *urgently*) Where is the marshal?

Parris (*runs to the door and calls down the corridor*). Marshal! Hurry!

John and Elizabeth Proctor before the marshal

THE CRUCIBLE: ACT FOUR **205**

Lines 560–574
TIERED DISCUSSION PROMPTS

Use these prompts to help students understand the chaos that results from Proctor's decision to confess:

Summarize How would a confession benefit Proctor? ***Possible answer:*** *A confession would save Proctor from execution.* How would it benefit the court? ***Possible answer:*** *It would prove the court right and represent a victory.*

Analyze Why is there such urgency in Danforth's and Parris's actions? ***Possible answer:*** *The stage directions note that Danforth speaks "with great relief and gratitude" (line 563); those positive emotions could speed up activity. In addition, both men act with haste because the hour of execution is upon them. Perhaps most important, they act with urgency because they want to record Proctor's confession as quickly as possible. They may fear that he will change his mind, thwarting their efforts.*

Synthesize Note Proctor's reaction to the chaos that follows his decision. Do you think that he will stick with his resolution to confess? Why or why not? ***Possible answer:*** *Proctor may change his mind and not confess, for he is filled with "a cold, cold horror" at seeing the court's haste. He asks suspiciously, "Why must it [the confession] be written?" (line 569)*

FOR STRATEGIC READERS

Targeted Passage [Lines 552–574]

In this passage, Proctor makes a decision that speeds the play's plot toward its climax.

- What advice does Elizabeth give Proctor? What does he think she would do if she were in his position?

- What announcement does Proctor make? How does Danforth respond?

- Why does Danforth insist on a written confession? How does Proctor seem to react?

Comprehension Support Point out that the scene in the photograph and the scene in this part of the play present the same action. The filmed scene is set outside, but the scene in the play occurs inside the jail. Briefly discuss these questions:

- Why might Miller have chosen to set the scene in the play indoors rather than outdoors?

- Why might the film director have chosen to create an outdoor setting for the scene?

Danforth. Now, then, Mister, will you speak slowly, and directly to the point, for Mr. Cheever's sake. (*He is on record now, and is really dictating to* Cheever, *who writes.*) Mr. Proctor, have you seen the Devil in your life? (Proctor's *jaws lock.*) Come, man, there
580 is light in the sky; the town waits at the scaffold; I would give out this news. Did you see the Devil?

Proctor. I did.

Parris. Praise God!

Danforth. And when he come to you, what were his demand? (Proctor *is silent.* Danforth *helps.*) Did he bid you to do his work upon the earth?

Proctor. He did.

Danforth. And you bound yourself to his service? (Danforth *turns, as* Rebecca Nurse *enters, with*
590 Herrick *helping to support her. She is barely able to walk.*) Come in, come in, woman!

Rebecca (*brightening as she sees* Proctor). Ah, John! You are well, then, eh?

(Proctor *turns his face to the wall.*)

Danforth. Courage, man, courage—let her witness your good example that she may come to God herself. Now hear it, Goody Nurse! Say on, Mr. Proctor. Did you bind yourself to the Devil's service?

Rebecca (*astonished*). Why, John!

600 **Proctor** (*through his teeth, his face turned from* Rebecca). I did.

Danforth. Now, woman, you surely see it profit nothin' to keep this conspiracy any further. Will you confess yourself with him?

Rebecca. Oh, John—God send his mercy on you!

Danforth. I say, will you confess yourself, Goody Nurse?

Rebecca. Why, it is a lie, it is a lie; how may I damn myself? I cannot, I cannot.

610 **Danforth.** Mr. Proctor. When the Devil came to you did you see Rebecca Nurse in his company? (Proctor *is silent.*) Come, man, take courage—did you ever see her with the Devil?

Proctor (*almost inaudibly*). No.

(Danforth, *now sensing trouble, glances at* John *and goes to the table, and picks up a sheet—the list of condemned.*)

Danforth. Did you ever see her sister, Mary Easty, with the Devil?

620 **Proctor.** No, I did not.

Danforth (*his eyes narrow on* Proctor). Did you ever see Martha Corey with the Devil?

Proctor. I did not.

Danforth (*realizing, slowly putting the sheet down*). Did you ever see anyone with the Devil?

Proctor. I did not.

Danforth. Proctor, you mistake me. I am not empowered to trade your life for a lie. You have most certainly seen some person with the Devil.
630 (Proctor *is silent.*) Mr. Proctor, a score of people have already testified they saw this woman with the Devil.

Proctor. Then it is proved. Why must I say it?

Danforth. Why "must" you say it! Why, you should rejoice to say it if your soul is truly purged of any love for Hell!

Proctor. They think to go like saints. I like not to spoil their names.

Danforth (*inquiring, incredulous*). Mr. Proctor, do
640 you think they go like saints?

Proctor (*evading*). This woman never thought she done the Devil's work.

Danforth. Look you, sir. I think you mistake your duty here. It matters nothing what she thought— she is convicted of the unnatural murder of children, and you for sending your spirit out upon Mary Warren. Your soul alone is the issue here, Mister, and you will prove its whiteness or you cannot live in a Christian country. Will you tell me now what
650 persons conspired with you in the Devil's company? (Proctor *is silent.*) To your knowledge was Rebecca Nurse ever—

LITERARY ANALYSIS

● CONVENTIONS OF DRAMA

How does the dialogue in lines 610–633 create suspense? *Possible answer: In this passage, Proctor is urged to testify against Rebecca as she stands in front of him. Suspense builds as Danforth asks Proctor a series of questions that are meant to push him into incriminating his neighbors. The reader or audience waits anxiously for each of Proctor's answers to discover whether he will join the long list of those who have lied about their neighbors.*

If students need help . . . Explain that Proctor continues to waver in his decision to lie and confess. Review the preceding exchange (lines 592–609); then elicit that Rebecca's presence weakens Proctor's resolve because (1) she challenges his decision and (2) she still refuses to confess, even though she is just minutes away from her own execution.

DIFFERENTIATED INSTRUCTION

FOR STRATEGIC READERS

Concept Support As you point out the stage directions in lines 592–602, help students interpret these terms:

- "brightening" (line 592): The sight of Proctor makes Rebecca happy.

- "turns his face to the wall" (line 594): Proctor is too ashamed of himself to look Rebecca in the face.

- "through his teeth" (line 600): Proctor forces himself to speak.

FOR ADVANCED LEARNERS/AP

Interpret Irony Have students reread lines 575–582 and then write a brief explanation of how Proctor's answer of "I did" to Danforth's question "Did you see the Devil?" can be interpreted as irony. (You might point out that in this case, irony would be the contrast between what Proctor says and what he means.) After students have shared their interpretations, have the class decide whether Proctor means to be ironic.

Proctor. I speak my own sins; I cannot judge another. (*crying out, with hatred*) I have no tongue for it.

Hale (*quickly to* Danforth). Excellency, it is enough he confess himself. Let him sign it, let him sign it.

Parris (*feverishly*). It is a great service, sir. It is a weighty name; it will strike the village that Proctor
660 confess. I beg you, let him sign it. The sun is up, Excellency!

Danforth (*considers; then with dissatisfaction*). Come, then, sign your testimony. (*to* Cheever) Give it to him. (Cheever *goes to* Proctor, *the confession and a pen in hand.* Proctor *does not look at it.*) Come, man, sign it.

Proctor (*after glancing at the confession*). You have all witnessed it—it is enough.

Danforth. You will not sign it?

670 **Proctor.** You have all witnessed it; what more is needed?

Danforth. Do you sport with me? You will sign your name or it is no confession, Mister! (*His breast heaving with agonized breathing,* Proctor *now lays the paper down and signs his name.*)

Parris. Praise be to the Lord!

(Proctor *has just finished signing when* Danforth *reaches for the paper. But* Proctor *snatches it up, and now a wild terror is rising in him, and a boundless anger.*)

680 **Danforth** (*perplexed, but politely extending his hand*). If you please, sir.

Proctor. No.

Danforth (*as though* Proctor *did not understand*). Mr. Proctor, I must have—

Proctor. No, no. I have signed it. You have seen me. It is done! You have no need for this.

Parris. Proctor, the village must have proof that—

Proctor. Damn the village! I confess to God, and God has seen my name on this! It is enough!

690 **Danforth.** No, sir, it is—

Proctor. You came to save my soul, did you not?

Here! I have confessed myself; it is enough!

Danforth. You have not con—

Proctor. I have confessed myself! Is there no good penitence but it be public? God does not need my name nailed upon the church! God sees my name; God knows how black my sins are! It is enough!

Danforth. Mr. Proctor—

Proctor. You will not use me! I am no Sarah Good or
700 Tituba, I am John Proctor! You will not use me! It is no part of salvation that you should use me!

Danforth. I do not wish to—

Proctor. I have three children—how may I teach them to walk like men in the world, and I sold my friends?

Danforth. You have not sold your friends—

Proctor. Beguile me not! I blacken all of them when this is nailed to the church the very day they hang for silence!

710 **Danforth.** Mr. Proctor, I must have good and legal proof that you—

Proctor. You are the high court, your word is good enough! Tell them I confessed myself; say Proctor broke his knees and wept like a woman; say what you will, but my name cannot—

Danforth (*with suspicion*). It is the same, is it not? If I report it or you sign to it?

Proctor (*He knows it is insane*). No, it is not the same! What others say and what I sign to is not the same!

720 **Danforth.** Why? Do you mean to deny this confession when you are free?

Proctor. I mean to deny nothing!

Danforth. Then explain to me, Mr. Proctor, why you will not let—

Proctor (*with a cry of his whole soul*). Because it is my name! Because I cannot have another in my life! Because I lie and sign myself to lies! Because I am not worth the dust on the feet of them that hang! How may I live without my name? I have given you
730 my soul; leave me my name!

Lines 716–730
TIERED DISCUSSION PROMPTS

Use these prompts to help students understand why Proctor is so upset at the prospect of having his signed confession made public:

Restate Paraphrase Proctor's lament in lines 725–730. *Possible answer: Because my name is my reputation and my honor! Because I have only one chance to have a good reputation! Because I lied when I confessed and when I signed that false confession! Because I am worth so much less than the people who have died rather than confess! How may I live without my honor? I have given you my soul; leave me my good reputation!*

Interpret What does Proctor mean when he exclaims, "What others say and what I sign to is not the same" (line 719)? *Possible answer: Proctor means that someone else's words about him, even if the words are true, do not have the moral authority of Proctor's own signature—literally, his "name," which is synonymous with his reputation.*

Synthesize What do you think will happen after this heated exchange, and why? *Possible answer: Danforth, whose resolve shows no sign of weakening, will probably continue to demand that Proctor turn over the signed confession. At this point, Proctor seems equally resolved; he probably will do whatever he feels necessary to keep the confession out of Danforth's hands, even if doing so sends him to the gibbet.*

FOR ENGLISH LEARNERS

Vocabulary: Prefixes and Suffixes [shared-language groups] Explain that the prefix *con-* in *confess* (line 606) means "together." *Confess* literally means "to admit together"—that is, to admit sins to someone. Direct students' attention also to *condemned* ("sentenced together," line 617). Then have shared-language groups use a dictionary and follow these steps to explore some common prefixes and suffixes:

- Find *conspired* on page 206. Discuss the use of *con-*. **Possible answer:** *Conspired (line 650) means "overpowered together."*

- The prefix *mis-* gives *mistake* (line 627) the literal meaning of "to take (understand) incorrectly." Think of and define two other words with the same prefix. **Possible answer:** *Misapply means "to apply incorrectly"; misfile means "to file incorrectly."*

- The suffix *-ion* identifies nouns and means "an act of" or "a state of"; it gives *confession* (line 664) the literal meaning of "an act of confessing." Find the words *dissatisfaction* and *suspicion* on page 207. Discuss the use of *-ion* in each word. **Possible answer:** *Dissatisfaction (line 662) means "a state of being dissatisfied"; suspicion (line 716) means "an act or state of being suspicious."*

Lines 731–740
REINFORCE *KEY IDEA:* HYSTERIA

Discuss Why is Danforth's pronouncement of "I will not deal in lies" (line 733) ironic? *Possible answer: The pronouncement is ironic because Danforth's court and its judgments are based on lies—the lies of Abigail, the other girls, and adults who are emotionally overwrought or who use the situation to take advantage of their neighbors.* How would you describe the connection between lies and hysteria as the play now reaches its climax? *Possible answer: The connection is that hysteria has placed Proctor in this life-and-death climactic moment; ironically, the only way that he can save himself is to lie by signing a false confession.*

SELECTION WRAP–UP

REFLECT Have students think about Proctor's decision to tear up his confession. What does this act mean to him? Why does Elizabeth decide to let him go?

⭐ CRITIQUE

- Have students identify the part of *The Crucible* that had the strongest impact on them and then explain why.
- After completing the After Reading questions on page 209, have students revisit their responses and tell whether they have changed their opinions.

Danforth (*pointing at the confession in Proctor's hand*). Is that document a lie? If it is a lie I will not accept it! What say you? I will not deal in lies, Mister! (*Proctor is motionless.*) You will give me your honest confession in my hand, or I cannot keep you from the rope. (*Proctor does not reply.*) Which way do you go, Mister?

(*His breast heaving, his eyes staring,* Proctor *tears the paper and crumples it, and he is weeping in fury, but* 740 *erect.*)

Danforth. Marshal!

Parris (*hysterically, as though the tearing paper were his life*). Proctor, Proctor!

Hale. Man, you will hang! You cannot!

Proctor (*his eyes full of tears*). I can. And there's your first marvel, that I can. You have made your magic now, for now I do think I see some shred of goodness in John Proctor. Not enough to weave a banner with, but white enough to keep it from such dogs. 750 (Elizabeth, *in a burst of terror, rushes to him and weeps against his hand.*) Give them no tear! Tears pleasure them! Show honor now, show a stony heart and sink them with it! (*He has lifted her, and kisses her now with great passion.*)

Rebecca. Let you fear nothing! Another judgment waits us all!

Danforth. Hang them high over the town! Who weeps for these, weeps for corruption! (*He sweeps out past them.* Herrick *starts to lead* Rebecca, *who almost* 760 *collapses, but* Proctor *catches her, and she glances up at him apologetically.*)

Rebecca. I've had no breakfast.

Herrick. Come, man.

(Herrick *escorts them out,* Hathorne *and* Cheever *behind them.* Elizabeth *stands staring at the empty doorway.*)

Parris (*in deadly fear, to* Elizabeth). Go to him, Goody Proctor! There is yet time!

(*From outside a drumroll strikes the air.* Parris *is star-* 770 *tled.* Elizabeth *jerks about toward the window.*)

Parris. Go to him! (*He rushes out the door, as though to hold back his fate.*) Proctor! Proctor!

(*again, a short burst of drums*)

Hale. Woman, plead with him! (*He starts to rush out the door, and then goes back to her.*) Woman! It is pride, it is vanity. (*She avoids his eyes, and moves to the window. He drops to his knees.*) Be his helper!— What profit him to bleed? Shall the dust praise him? Shall the worms declare his truth? Go to him, take 780 his shame away!

Elizabeth (*supporting herself against collapse, grips the bars of the window, and with a cry*). He have his goodness now. God forbid I take it from him!

(*The final drumroll crashes, then heightens violently.* Hale *weeps in frantic prayer, and the new sun is pouring in upon her face, and the drums rattle like bones in the morning air. The curtain falls.*)

⑤ **Targeted Passage**

DIFFERENTIATED INSTRUCTION

FOR STRATEGIC READERS

⑤ **Targeted Passage [Lines 745–756]**

This passage illustrates the idea that being true to oneself can be a source of strength.

- What is Proctor's "first marvel" (line 746)?
- What does Proctor think that he now has? How has it come to him?
- Why does Proctor urge Elizabeth not to cry?
- Why does Rebecca tell John not to fear?

FOR ENGLISH LEARNERS

Related Vocabulary The climax of *The Crucible* is filled with great drama and strong passions. Make sure students are aware that Miller's word choices help create and support this mood. Then review or teach these interrelated words from the final scene:

- *heaving* (line 738), "rising and falling forcefully"
- *fury* (line 739), "intense anger"

- *hysterically* (line 742), "done in a way that suggests irrational emotionalism"
- *burst* (line 750), "sudden release"
- *terror* (line 750), "overwhelming fear"
- *collapses* (line 760), "falls down"
- *deadly* (line 767), "absolute, extreme"
- *plead* (line 774), "to make a sincere request"
- *frantic* (line 785), "marked by strong emotion and disorder"

Comprehension

1. **Recall** Why has Reverend Hale returned to Salem?

2. **Clarify** Why does Danforth summon Elizabeth Proctor?

3. **Summarize** What does John Proctor do when asked to sign a confession?

Literary Analysis

4. **Infer Character Motives** Explain why each of the following characters wants John and the other prisoners to confess. Support your answer with evidence.

   • Danforth   • Parris   • Hale

5. **Examine Dialogue** Reread Elizabeth Proctor's dialogue at the end of Act Four (lines 782–783) when she says of her husband, "He have his goodness now." What do you think she means? Do you agree with her?

6. **Analyze Conventions of Drama** Much of the **plot** of *The Crucible* is built around the internal and external conflicts of John Proctor. An **internal conflict** is a struggle between opposing forces within a character. An **external conflict**

Conflict	Internal or External?	How Resolved

pits a character against nature, society, or another character. Use a chart like the one shown to show the internal and external conflicts of John Proctor. How is each resolved?

7. **Draw Conclusions About Characters** Refer to the chart of character traits you have created. Which characters have changed over the course of the play? How have they changed? Cite specific details from the play.

8. **Interpret Symbol** A crucible is a severe test or trial. It is also a vessel in which materials are melted at high temperatures to produce a more refined substance. What do you think a crucible might symbolize in this drama?

9. **Synthesize Themes** A theme is a central idea the writer wishes to share with the reader. This idea may be a lesson about life or about people and their actions. What do you think are some of the themes of *The Crucible*?

Literary Criticism

10. **Critical Interpretations** Many critics have observed that Miller's play goes beyond the historical events of 17th- and 20th-century America and explores universal conflicts. What universal conflicts does the play deal with?

7. ■ **SKILLS FOCUS Draw Conclusions About Characters** *Proctor has changed by accepting his faults and fighting for the integrity that he has left. Hale has changed by questioning himself and then taking a more compassionate stance and by siding with the prisoners instead of the court.*

8. *A crucible might symbolize the witch trials, which put stress upon the entire community. The trials refine some characters and destroy others.*

9. *One strong theme is that even a seemingly stable society can be shaken by irrational fear. Another is that society can imprison and persecute people, but it cannot take away their integrity.*

10. *The play addresses conflicts such as good versus evil, dissent versus authority, the individual versus society, and fear versus courage.*

Practice and Apply

After Reading

Use these copy masters to check understanding and provide extra support:

R RESOURCE MANAGER—Copy Masters
   Reading Check p. 299
   Conventions of Drama p. 295
   Question Support p. 300
   Additional selection questions are provided for teachers on page 291.

ANSWERS

1. *Hale has returned to persuade the condemned to confess.*

2. *Danforth hopes that Elizabeth can persuade her husband to confess.*

3. *First, Proctor refuses to sign the confession. Then he signs it but will not give it to Danforth. Finally, he tears it up.*

Possible answers:

4. *Danforth believes that the prisoners are guilty; he wants to save their souls (lines 221–223).*

   Parris no longer believes that they are guilty; he fears that he will be held accountable for executing innocent people (lines 203–210 and 232–236).

   Hale does not believe that they are guilty; he wants to save their lives (lines 131–134).

5. *Elizabeth means that Proctor has shown true courage and character by not lying to save his life. Most students will agree.*

6. ● **SKILLS FOCUS Conventions of Drama**

   Struggle over feelings for Abigail; Internal; Comes to despise her when he sees what she has done

   Struggle over feelings for Elizabeth; Internal; Rediscovers his love for her when he sees her strength

   Struggle over decision to confess; Internal; Recants confession to save his reputation

   Struggle with Parris; External; Wins the battle by not confessing

   Struggle with Elizabeth; External; Rediscovers his love for her

   Struggle with the court; External; Refuses to confess and so is hanged

ANSWERS

Vocabulary in Context

VOCABULARY PRACTICE

1. *synonyms*	9. *synonyms*
2. *antonyms*	10. *synonyms*
3. *synonyms*	11. *antonyms*
4. *antonyms*	12. *antonyms*
5. *antonyms*	13. *synonyms*
6. *antonyms*	14. *synonyms*
7. *synonyms*	15. *synonyms*
8. *antonyms*	

R RESOURCE MANAGER—Copy Master
Vocabulary Practice p. 297

VOCABULARY IN WRITING

Urge students to consider how Mary's character is revealed in what she says, what she does, how she responds to other characters, and how other characters treat her. For example, Mary lets herself be influenced by others, a trait implied in the example sentence and seen in the fact that she ultimately rejoins Abigail and the other girls.

VOCABULARY STRATEGY: CONTEXT CLUES
(also an EL language objective)

Tell students to look at both the words and the punctuation around the word in question to figure out its meaning, as in this example:

> The anarchy, or lawlessness, in Salem was frightening.

Explain that *anarchy* means "lawlessness." "Lawlessness," a restatement of the vocabulary word, is set off with commas.

Answers

1. *(c) lower in importance*
2. *(c) wickedness*
3. *(a) improve*
4. *(a) angry*
5. *(b) presumptuousness*

R RESOURCE MANAGER—Copy Master
Vocabulary Strategy p. 298

ℹ Vocabulary Center at **ClassZone.com**
Additional Vocabulary Activities

Vocabulary in Context

VOCABULARY PRACTICE

Decide whether the words in each pair are synonyms or antonyms.

1. dissembling/lying
2. iniquity/goodness
3. contentious/argumentative
4. adamant/unsure
5. immaculate/filthy
6. trepidation/bravery
7. deposition/statement
8. deference/impudence
9. conciliatory/appeasing
10. anarchy/disorder
11. ameliorate/worsen
12. effrontery/humility
13. corroborate/substantiate
14. imperceptible/unnoticeable
15. subservient/subordinate

WORD LIST

adamant
ameliorate
anarchy
conciliatory
contentious
corroborate
deference
deposition
dissembling
effrontery
immaculate
imperceptible
iniquity
subservient
trepidation

VOCABULARY IN WRITING

Write a brief character sketch of Mary Warren, using details from the text to flesh out your portrayal of her. Include at least four vocabulary words. Here is a sample opening sentence.

> **EXAMPLE**
>
> Mary was a **subservient** young girl who did not know how to handle the power and attention she suddenly received.

VOCABULARY STRATEGY: CONTEXT CLUES

The words, sentences, paragraphs, and even punctuation marks that surround a word make up its **context**. Often context can help you figure out the meaning of an unfamiliar word.

PRACTICE Locate each word below in its context in the play. Then write the letter of the correct definition for each.

1. **subservient** (page 143): (a) forceful, (b) vengeful, (c) lower in importance
2. **iniquity** (page 147): (a) forgetfulness, (b) act of not caring, (c) wickedness
3. **ameliorate** (page 164): (a) improve, (b) aggravate, (c) move farther along
4. **contentious** (page 178): (a) angry, (b) generous, (c) misguided
5. **effrontery** (page 184): (a) patience, (b) presumptuousness, (c) desire to talk a lot

VOCABULARY PRACTICE
For more practice, go to the **Vocabulary Center** at **ClassZone.com.**

DIFFERENTIATED INSTRUCTION

FOR ENGLISH LEARNERS

Task Support: Vocabulary Practice Have students work together in small mixed-language groups to find words in the Word List that have cognates in their home language or other languages they know. Help students identify these words with Spanish cognates: *anarchy, conciliatory, corroborate, deposition, immaculate, imperceptible, iniquity, subservient.*

FOR ADVANCED LEARNERS/AP

Vocabulary in Writing Have students use several vocabulary words in a paragraph that describes another character in *The Crucible* from Mary Warren's point of view. Ask students to share these paragraphs with other students who choose the same character or with the entire class. Do students agree with the character sketch as presented from Mary's perspective?

Reading-Writing Connection

 W2.2

WRITING PROMPT

ANALYZE MOTIVATIONS Why does John Proctor change his mind and tear up the confession? How does his concern for what others might think of him influence his decision? In **four or five paragraphs,** discuss Proctor's perception of a morally righteous person and how that perception affects his decision. Think about Rebecca Nurse's reaction to his confession and Elizabeth's assertion that "there be no higher judge under Heaven than Proctor is!"

SELF-CHECK

A strong analysis will . . .
- explain the choices Proctor must make to arrive at his decision
- discuss how Proctor's idea of morality differs from that of the judges
- use quotations and examples from the play to support key points

GRAMMAR AND STYLE

 LC1.1

USE REALISTIC DIALOGUE A play consists almost entirely of dialogue; therefore, to ensure authenticity, it is important that the characters' speech match the play's setting. In *The Crucible,* Arthur Miller's **word choice** and use of **inverted sentences** accurately reflect the speech of the time, contributing to the playwright's realistic depiction of life in 17th-century Salem. Here are some examples:

> **Parris.** . . . *Let him look to medicine and put out all thought of unnatural causes here. There be none.*
>
> **Susanna.** *Aye, sir.* . . . (Act One, lines 50–52)
>
> **Abigail.** *Now look you. All of you. We danced.* . . . (Act One, line 353)

In the first piece of dialogue, notice how Miller uses *be* rather than *are,* the verb form that currently would be used in this context. And instead of *yes,* Miller uses the word *aye,* a word that was commonplace in the 1600s but is rarely used today.

In the second piece of dialogue, Miller forms an inverted sentence, with the verb preceding the subject. This type of inverted word order was common in 17th-century speech.

PRACTICE Rewrite the following sentences so that they better reflect the 17th-century speech patterns that Miller employs.

> **EXAMPLE**
> You go to the house!
> *Go you to the house!*

1. Yes, it is true I saw the devil with Rebecca Nurse.
2. Are you sure of their guilt?
3. You confess to these sins!

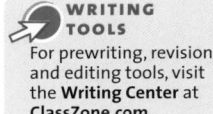 **WRITING TOOLS**
For prewriting, revision, and editing tools, visit the **Writing Center** at ClassZone.com.

FOR DEVELOPING WRITERS

Writing Support

- Have students reread Act Four, lines 677–749, and make some notes about the scene in question.
- Help students identify characters whose opinions Proctor would probably consider important (for example, Rebecca Nurse) or unimportant (for example, Reverend Parris).
- Use answers to some past After Reading questions to model the use of quotations and examples as support of key points.

- Suggest that students organize their analysis in this way:

Introduction: Explain what Proctor does (tears up his confession) and why he does it.

Body: Discuss his possible motivations (for example, he is worried about what others think of him, or he wants to be a moral person).

Conclusion: Review Proctor's action and make a statement about why Proctor seems to be at peace with his decision.

Reading-Writing Connection

WRITING PROMPT

Suggest that students complete a Venn Diagram to compare and contrast Proctor's concept of morality to that of the court (especially as represented by Judge Danforth). Have students incorporate their observations into their overall analysis of Proctor's motivation. Remind students to cite line references when they quote or give examples.

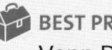 **BEST PRACTICES TOOLKIT—Transparency**
   Venn Diagram p. A26

For writing support, see

🛈 Writing Center at **ClassZone.com**

GRAMMAR AND STYLE

Tell students that if they pay attention to verbs as they read, they can quickly recognize an inverted sentence. Explain that inverted sentences contain a subject that follows the verb or that comes in the middle of a verb phrase. Inverted word order is often used to shift the emphasis in statements and exclamations. For more on inverted sentences, see page R71 in the **Grammar Handbook.**

Possible answers:

1. *Aye, true it be that I saw the Devil with Rebecca Nurse.*
2. *Be you sure of their guilt?*
3. *Confess you to these sins!*

📘 RESOURCE MANAGER—Copy Master
   Use Realistic Dialogue p. 301

Assess and Reteach

Assess

📘 RESOURCE MANAGER—Copy Masters
   Selection Test A pp. 303–304
   Selection Test B/C pp. 305–306

💿 Test Generator CD

Reteach

📄 STANDARDS LESSON FILE
   Literature Lessons 1–2, 6, 23–24
   Reading Lesson 9
   Writing Lessons 28, 44
   Vocabulary Lessons 11–16

Focus and Motivate

OBJECTIVES

Reading for Information

- understand and analyze literature in its historical context
- synthesize information
- read an online article
- read a newspaper article
- read a memoir

 R3.5, W2.2

SUMMARY

"*The Crucible* and McCarthyism" consists of three brief selections about Senator Joseph McCarthy's crusade against communists during the 1940s and 1950s: an online article that presents an overview of McCarthyism; a newspaper article in which Victor Navasky details Arthur Miller's comparison of Mc-Carthyism and the Salem witch trials; and an excerpt from Miller's memoir, in which he explains how he became interested in Salem's witch hunt.

Use Main Idea and Details notes to help students distinguish the three selections. Have them write the main idea of each selection in the first column of each chart. In the second column, have them write supporting details as they read, as well as any connections they see between details in the selection and details in *The Crucible*.

 BEST PRACTICES TOOLKIT—Transparency
Main Idea and Details p. B6

Teach

Skill Focus: Understand Historical Context

- Emphasize that the historical context of a literary work provides clues to the characters, plot, and themes of the work.

- Have students think about the perspective that they might encounter in each of these selections. For example, the excerpt from the memoir will offer Miller's explanation of the era in which he wrote.

R RESOURCE MANAGER—Copy Master
Understand Historical Context p. 315

Reading for Information

Use with *The Crucible*, page 132.

 R3.5, W2.2 (p. 217)

The Crucible and McCarthyism

- Online Article, page 213
- Newspaper Article, page 214
- Memoir, page 216

While Arthur Miller was writing *The Crucible,* a young senator named Joseph McCarthy was conducting a campaign to root out communists in American public life. In his memoir, *Timebends,* Miller reveals that he saw a connection between the Salem witch trials and McCarthy's campaign. The following selections will help you understand that connection by providing you with information about McCarthyism and its bearing on *The Crucible.* As you read, bear in mind that you will later be asked to explain how this information affects your sense of the play.

Skill Focus: Understand Historical Context

As you may recall, the **historical context** of a literary work is the social and political conditions of the times in which the writer lived. To varying degrees, most literature reflects this context, often through its portrayal of values and conflicts.

To better grasp the historical context of *The Crucible,* take notes as you read the selections. In particular, record the significant events, values, and issues that were of primary concern in American society while Miller was writing his play. Use a chart such as the one shown here.

Source	Relevant Historical Information
"McCarthyism"	. . .
"The Demons of Salem, With Us Still"	. . .
Timebends	. . .

Selection Resources

 R RESOURCE MANAGER UNIT 1

Plan and Teach pp. 307–311

Reading
Summary pp. 313†*, 314‡*
Understand Historical Context pp. 315, 316†*
Synthesize pp. 317, 318†*
Reading Check p. 319
Question Support p. 320

Assessment
Selection Tests A, B/C pp. 321*, 323*

 Test Generator CD

Reading Support
Audio Anthology CD*

 BEST PRACTICES TOOLKIT
Main Idea and Details • Two-Column Chart

* Resources for Differentiation   † Also in Spanish   ‡ In Haitian Creole and Vietnamese

BACK FORWARD STOP REFRESH HOME PRINT

McCARTHYISM

Throughout the 1940s and 1950s America was overwhelmed with concerns about the threat of communism growing in Eastern Europe and China. Capitalizing on those concerns, a young Senator named Joseph McCarthy made a public accusation that more than two hundred "card-carrying" communists had infiltrated the United States government. Though
10 eventually his accusations were proven to be untrue, and he was censured by the Senate for unbecoming conduct, his zealous campaigning ushered in one of the most repressive times in 20th-century American politics. **A**

Army counsel Joseph N. Welch, left, and Senator Joseph McCarthy

   While the House Un-American Activities Committee (HUAC) had been formed in 1938 as an anti-Communist organ, McCarthy's accusations heightened the political tensions of the times. Known as McCarthyism, the paranoid hunt for infiltrators was notoriously difficult on writers and entertainers, many of whom were labeled
20 communist sympathizers and were unable to continue working. Some had their passports taken away, while others were jailed for refusing to give the names of other communists. The trials, which were well publicized, could often destroy a career with a single unsubstantiated accusation. Among those well-known artists accused of communist sympathies or called before the committee were Paul Robeson, Arthur Miller, Aaron Copland, Leonard Bernstein, Charlie Chaplin and Elia Kazan. In all, three hundred and twenty artists were blacklisted, and for many of them this meant the end of exceptional and promising careers. **B**

30 During this time there were few in the press willing to stand up against McCarthy and the anti-Communist machine. Among those few were comedian Mort Sahl, and journalist Edward R. Murrow, whose strong criticisms of McCarthy are often cited as playing an important role in his eventual removal from power. By 1954, the fervor had died down and many actors and writers were able to return to work. Though relatively short, these proceedings remain one of the most shameful moments in modern U.S. history.

A HISTORICAL CONTEXT
What preoccupied Americans during the 1940s and 1950s? Record your answer on your chart.

B HISTORICAL CONTEXT
What does the term *McCarthyism* refer to? Identify the information in this paragraph that suggests a connection between McCarthyism and Miller's play.

INFORMATIONAL ANALYSIS

A HISTORICAL CONTEXT

Possible answer: Americans were preoccupied with the idea that communism could threaten the United States, for it had gained a foothold in Eastern Europe and China.

INFORMATIONAL ANALYSIS

B HISTORICAL CONTEXT

Possible answer: The term McCarthyism refers to the "paranoid hunt for [communist] infiltrators" (line 18). Connections to The Crucible include the facts that an "unsubstantiated accusation" (line 24) could destroy a person's reputation and that many of the accused were "jailed for refusing to give the names" of possible participants (lines 21–22).

If students need help . . . Use a Two-Column Chart like this to help students list points of McCarthyism that correspond to points from Miller's play.

McCarthyism	The Crucible
paranoid hunt for communists	paranoid hunt for witches
people jailed for not giving names	people jailed for not giving names
unsubstantiated accusations of communist sympathies	unsubstantiated accusations of witchcraft

 BEST PRACTICES TOOLKIT—Transparency Two-Column Chart p. A25

DIFFERENTIATED INSTRUCTION

FOR STRATEGIC READERS

Concept Support: Communism Note that communism is both a political philosophy and a form of government. Explain that many people think that communism is the opposite of democracy: communist governments have more control over citizens' lives and allow fewer personal freedoms than democratic governments do. Have students refer to this information as you discuss why the presence of communists in America was seen by many as a threat.

Options for Reading Read aloud the first sentence, whose many details make comprehension difficult. Model how students might break the sentence into shorter segments:

- "Throughout the 1940s and 1950s" = The selection is about something that happened during this time.
- "America was overwhelmed with concerns" = Americans were worried.
- "about the threat of communism" = People felt that communism was dangerous.

- "growing in Eastern Europe and China" = Communism was affecting people in other parts of the world.

As students continue to read, encourage them to break apart difficult sentences in the same way to understand their meaning.

Lines 1–18
TIERED DISCUSSION PROMPTS

Use these prompts to help students explore Navasky's perspective:

Recall According to the online article on page 213, how did Americans in the early 1950s feel about communism, and why? *Possible answer: Many Americans saw communism as a threat because it was growing in other parts of the world.*

Analyze What do "the so-called Red Menace" (line 4), "reckless charges" (lines 5–6), "'comsymps'" (line 6), and "center ring" (line 14) suggest about Navasky's view of McCarthyism? Explain. *Possible answer: The first term suggests that Navasky views McCarthyism as misguided; the second, as poorly handled; the third, as smug; and the fourth (a reference to a circus), as foolish.*

Synthesize If Navasky could have written during the McCarthy hearings, what do you think he would have urged people to do? *Possible answer: He would have urged people to require that those in charge of the investigation have a clear focus and conduct their work in an orderly, fair fashion.*

INFORMATIONAL ANALYSIS

C HISTORICAL CONTEXT

Possible answer: People were quick to ask about the connection because the hunt for communist subversives already had come to be called a "witch hunt." People wondered whether Miller meant to use the Salem witch trials as a metaphor for McCarthy's campaign.

Arthur Miller prepares to testify before the House Un-American Activities Commitee, 1956.

The Demons of Salem, With Us Still
by Victor Navasky

When Arthur Miller's drama *The Crucible* first opened on Broadway in 1953, the country was in a panic about the so-called Red Menace. Senator Joseph McCarthy, with his reckless charges of spies and "comsymps,"[1] occupied the front pages, while behind the scenes J. Edgar Hoover, the director of the F.B.I., presided over and 10 manipulated a vast internal security bureaucracy, issuing periodic bulletins intended to fan the flames of the domestic cold war.

In the center ring were the congressional inquisitor-investigators, asking "Are you now or have you ever been a member of the Communist Party?"

At the time, Mr. Miller and 20 Tennessee Williams were regarded as the world's two foremost playwrights. But that lofty status was an invitation rather than an obstacle to the red-hunters who wanted to talk to Mr. Miller. In fact, when he was finally summoned to appear, the committee chairman, Representative Francis Walters, let Mr. Miller know that things might go easier for him if he 30 persuaded his fiancee, Marilyn Monroe, to pose for a photograph with the chairman. Mr. Miller let that option lapse and was shortly indicted for contempt of Congress when he refused to answer the committee's questions about Communists he had known.

On the left, the hunt for subversives was routinely labeled a witch hunt, after the infamous Salem witch trials 40 of the late 17th century. And so when *The Crucible,* set in Salem in 1692 but written in the overheated atmosphere of the domestic cold war, appeared, two questions were quickly asked: Was Mr. Miller's depiction of the inhabitants and events of 1692 Salem faithful to the original? And was the original an appropriate metaphor for McCarthyism? **C**

C HISTORICAL CONTEXT
Reread lines 1–48. When *The Crucible* hit the stage, why were people so quick to ask about the connection between the play and McCarthy's campaign?

---

1. **"comsymps":** Communist sympathizers.

DIFFERENTIATED INSTRUCTION

FOR ENGLISH LEARNERS
Related Vocabulary Navasky uses a variety of terms to discuss the nation's interest in and fear of communists. Offer "Red Menace" (line 4) as an example, explaining that communism is associated with the color red and that a menace is something threatening. Then teach these related terms:

- *reckless* (line 5), "careless and unthinking"

- *inquisitor-investigators* (line 15), "questioners who are excessively harsh"

- *red-hunters* (lines 23–24), "people conducting searches for alleged communists"

- *indicted* (line 33), "formally accused of a crime"

- *subversives* (line 37), "people who want to overturn a government"

FOR ADVANCED READERS/AP
Research and Analyze Allusions [small-group option] Have students find out more about these people mentioned on this page:

- J. Edgar Hoover
- Tennessee Williams
- Marilyn Monroe

Call on volunteers to share a few fact-filled sentences about each person. Follow up with a discussion about what each allusion adds to the points that Navasky makes.

50 On the historical front it was generally conceded when the play was written that Mr. Miller's research was accurate. His principal changes involved fusing some characters and raising the age of John Proctor's accuser, Abigail Williams, from 11 to 17 (to accommodate Mr. Miller's story of how a liaison between Abigail and John was intertwined with the accusations of 60 witchcraft against Proctor's wife).

But even before the play was written, Mr. Miller was denounced for his metaphor. He had stopped off at the home of his friend and colleague Elia Kazan, who had directed Mr. Miller's two previous prize-winning hits, "All My Sons" and "Death of a Salesman," and who had been subpoenaed to appear before the House Committee on 70 Un-American Activities (where he ultimately named names).

They went for a walk in the Connecticut woods and discussed Mr. Kazan's dilemma. On the one hand to be an informer was unpalatable, but on the other, as Mr. Kazan put it at the time, "Secrecy serves the Communists." **D**

In his memoir *Timebends,* Mr. Miller 80 wrote that he was half inside his car when Molly, Kazan's wife, "came out and asked if I was staying at my house, half an hour away, and I said that I was on my way to Salem. She instantly understood what my destination meant, and her eyes widened in sudden apprehension and possible anger. 'You're not going to equate witches with this!'

Later, Mr. Kazan reported his wife's 90 views in his own memoir, *A Life.*

"What's going on here and now is not to be compared with the witch trials of that time," she said. "Those witches did not exist. Communists do. Here and everywhere in the world. It's a false parallel. Witch hunt! The phrase would indicate that there are no Communists

in government, none in the arts, none sending money from Hollywood to 100 12th Street." **E**

For me, the parallel worked. The term "Communist" had been so demonized that like the word "witch" it signified something that didn't really exist in its popular meaning. Certainly the entertainment community Communists like Mr. Kazan (and for a brief period, Mr. Miller himself, although he never fully joined the party) 110 were not conscious agents of an international monolithic conspiracy to overthrow the Government by force and violence; they were, for the most part, do-gooders, who thought—misguidedly, most of them later concluded—that the Communist Party was the best agency to do something about the depression and racism at home and fascism abroad.

As it turned out, despite mixed 120 notices for *The Crucible,* over the years it was to become Arthur Miller's most performed play, with productions in China, Poland, Britain, high schools and repertory theaters throughout the world. Now *The Crucible* is a $25 million motion picture, under the aegis of 20th Century Fox.

Although the playwright in Mr. Miller was originally drawn to think 130 about the political and moral pressures of the domestic cold war years, when I asked him about the applicability of the play to the here and now he said:

"I have had immense confidence in the applicability of the play to almost any time, the reason being it's dealing with a paranoid situation. But that situation doesn't depend on any particular political or sociological 140 development. I wrote it blind to the world. The enemy is within, and within stays within, and we can't get out of within. It's always on the edge of our minds that behind what we see is a nefarious plot." **F**

D HISTORICAL CONTEXT
Reread lines 11–77. In light of his comment, would you say that Elia Kazan took McCarthy's mission seriously? Explain.

E HISTORICAL CONTEXT
Given her husband's role in the McCarthy hearings, why do you think Molly Kazan might have objected to Miller's comparison between HUAC and Salem?

F HISTORICAL CONTEXT
Reread Miller's final comments in lines 133–144. In the end, how would you describe his feelings about the comparison between the Salem trials and the McCarthy hearings?

INFORMATIONAL ANALYSIS

D HISTORICAL CONTEXT

Possible answer: Yes, Kazan seems to have taken McCarthy's mission seriously; his comment, "Secrecy serves the Communists," indicates that he understood that McCarthy's goal was to discover information that generally had been kept secret to that point.

INFORMATIONAL ANALYSIS

E HISTORICAL CONTEXT

Possible answer: Molly Kazan might have objected to Miller's comparison because she feared the HUAC (lines 91–100). She might not have wanted her husband (who had directed two of Miller's earlier plays) to become involved in a play that could increase the HUAC's interest in him.

INFORMATIONAL ANALYSIS

F HISTORICAL CONTEXT

Possible answer: Miller feels that the comparison between the Salem trials and the McCarthy hearings is valid but that there are other "paranoid situation[s]" (line 137) that one might compare to events in Salem. Thus, the play can be applied "to almost any time" (lines 135–136).

FOR ENGLISH LEARNERS

Vocabulary: Cognates Point out that many Spanish cognates follow spelling patterns. For example, the Spanish word *pánico* ends in -*co* and is spelled almost exactly like the English word *panic* (line 3). Many English words that end in -*tion,* such as *invitation,* have Spanish cognates that end in -*ción* (*invitación*). Help students understand these English words with Spanish cognates:

• *domestic/doméstico* (line 13), *historical/ histórico* (line 50), *monolithic/monolítico* (line 111)

• *option/opción* (line 32), *accusations/acusaciones* (line 59), *international/internacional* (line 111), *productions/producciones* (line 122), *situation/situación* (line 137).

INFORMATIONAL ANALYSIS

G HISTORICAL CONTEXT

Possible answer: *Miller alludes to the significance of Starkey's book when he says that he received the book "As though it had been ordained" (lines 12–13); in other words, it was his destiny to read the book. Miller also says that eventually he felt "a living connection between [himself] and Salem" (line 21), a statement that reveals the powerful hold that the story had on him.*

INFORMATIONAL ANALYSIS

H HISTORICAL CONTEXT

Possible answer: *Miller identifies these parallels: Both were "profoundly and even avowedly ritualistic" (line 23); both wanted "the accused [to] make public confession, [and to] damn his confederates as well as his Devil master" (lines 28–29); and in both, the confessed would be "let loose to rejoin the society of extremely decent people" (line 30).*

TIMEBENDS

by Arthur Miller

I had known about the Salem witchcraft phenomenon since my American history class at Michigan, but it had remained in mind as one of those inexplicable mystifications of the long-dead past when people commonly believed that the spirit could leave the body, palpably and visibly. My mother might believe it still, if only in one corner of her mind, and I 10 suspected that there were a lot of other people who, like me, were secretly open to suggestion. As though it had been ordained, a copy of Marion Starkey's book *The Devil in Massachusetts* fell into my hands, and the bizarre story came back as I had recalled it, but this time in remarkably well-organized detail. **G**

Miller at his typewriter in 1959

At first I rejected the idea of a play on the subject. My own rationality was too strong, I thought, to really allow me to capture this wildly irrational outbreak. A 20 drama cannot merely describe an emotion, it has to become that emotion. But gradually, over weeks, a living connection between myself and Salem, and between Salem and Washington, was made in my mind—for whatever else they might be, I saw that the hearings in Washington were profoundly and even avowedly ritualistic. After all, in almost every case the Committee knew in advance what they wanted the witness to give them; the names of his comrades in the Party. The FBI had long since infiltrated the Party, and informers had long ago identified the participants in various meetings. The main point of the hearings, precisely as in seventeenth-century Salem, was that the accused make public confession, damn his confederates as well as his Devil master, and guarantee his sterling new allegiance by breaking disgusting old 30 vows—whereupon he was let loose to rejoin the society of extremely decent people. In other words, the same spiritual nugget lay folded within both procedures—an act of contrition done not in solemn privacy but out in the public air. The Salem prosecution was actually on more solid legal ground since the defendant, if guilty of familiarity with the Unclean One, had broken a law against the practice of witchcraft, a civil as well as a religious offense; whereas the offender against HUAC (House Un-American Activities Committee) could not be accused of any such violation but only of a spiritual crime, subservience to a political enemy's desires and ideology. He was summoned before the Committee to be called a bad name, but one that could destroy his career. **H**

G HISTORICAL CONTEXT
Reread lines 1–17. What details indicate the significance for him of finding Starkey's book?

H HISTORICAL CONTEXT
What parallels does Miller identify between the hearings in Washington and the Salem witch trials?

DIFFERENTIATED INSTRUCTION

FOR ENGLISH LEARNERS
Language: Verb Tenses Explain that Miller uses two past tenses: The past perfect tense (*had known* [line 1]) shows what already had happened before another event, also in the past, occurred; the simple past (*rejected* [line 18]) shows what happened at a particular time. Help students identify other uses of these tenses in these paragraphs (lines 12–17, for example); then elicit that this shift in tense indicates two different but related periods of time in Miller's past.

FOR ADVANCED LEARNERS/AP
Analyze Author's Perspective Have students write and share an analysis of lines 18–23, including responses to these questions:

- What does Miller mean when he says, "My own rationality was too strong . . . to really allow me to capture this wildly irrational outbreak" (lines 18–19)?
- How does Miller finally gain insight into the thinking that informed events long ago in Salem?

Comprehension

1. **Recall** What was Senator McCarthy's mission?

2. **Recall** What kinds of professionals were targeted by McCarthy's accusations?

3. **Recall** What was the catalyst for Miller's interest in the Salem witch trials?

Critical Analysis

4. **Evaluate Statements** Considering the historical context of *The Crucible* and Arthur Miller's own comments in *Timebends*, do you think Miller was really "blind to the world" when he wrote *The Crucible?* Support your opinion.

5. **Evaluate the Role of Historical Context** In your opinion, is knowing *The Crucible*'s historical context necessary to understand the playwright's message? Explain.

Read for Information: Synthesize

R3.5, W2.2

WRITING PROMPT

Think about the social and political conditions of the time during which Arthur Miller was writing *The Crucible.* In what ways has looking through this historical lens colored your understanding of the play? In developing your new analysis, support your thesis with information from the articles you have just read and details from the play.

To answer this prompt, follow these steps:

1. In a sentence or two, summarize how this historical information has added to or changed your understanding of the play. Consider using this summary as your thesis statement.

2. In your notes, identify elements of the play that you now view differently. How has your sense of these elements changed? For example, are there things you now see more clearly? Does the play seem more or less interesting? Note the historical details that caused you to think differently.

3. Using your thesis statement and notes, write a brief essay in which you explain how learning about the historical context of *The Crucible* affected your appreciation and understanding of the play.

READING FOR INFORMATION **217**

Practice and Apply

After Reading

Use these copy masters to check understanding and provide extra support:

R RESOURCE MANAGER—Copy Masters
Reading Check pp. 319
Question Support pp. 320
Synthesize pp. 317, 318

Additional selection questions are provided for teachers on page 310.

ANSWERS

1. *to identify communists in the United States and destroy their careers*

2. *writers and entertainers*

3. *Marion Starkey's* The Devil in Massachusetts, *a book that prompted Miller to think again about the Salem witch trials*

Possible answers:

4. *Miller was not really "blind to the world" when he wrote* The Crucible; *in fact, he says that thinking about the McCarthy hearings helped him connect to and write about the Salem trials (lines 20–23 and following).*

5. ■ SKILLS FOCUS **Historical Context** *Knowing the historical context adds an extra dimension to the play's theme, but it is not necessary for understanding the play's message, which is a warning against hysteria and intolerance.*

Read for Information: Synthesize

Writing Prompt *Responses will vary, but students should present a clear thesis statement that explains how knowing about McCarthyism has influenced their thinking about* The Crucible. *Students also should cite evidence from their reading to support their ideas.*

Assess and Reteach

Assess

R RESOURCE MANAGER—Copy Masters
Selection Test A pp. 321–322
Selection Test B/C pp. 323–324

Test Generator CD

Reteach

S STANDARDS LESSON FILE
Reading Lesson 14: Synthesize Information

FOR STRATEGIC READERS

Read for Information

- Direct students to write a brief summary of each of the three selections. Urge students to use these summaries as a guide for determining which historical facts made the greatest impact on their understanding of the play.

- Ask students to choose three elements of the play that have been affected by their knowledge of historical context. For each element, students should note a precise historical link that changed their thinking.

FOR ADVANCED LEARNERS/AP

Propose a New Play After students think about the message of *The Crucible* and the play's connection to Miller's historical context, have them write a proposal for a play that they might write, dealing with similar themes but reflecting their own political and social context. Encourage students to outline a plot and briefly develop characters that could tell a story with a modern message. Invite volunteers to share their proposals with the class.

READING FOR INFORMATION **217**

Focus and Motivate

OBJECTIVES

Media Literacy

- view a film clip from *The Crucible* to understand the challenges of adapting the original play for the big screen
- compare the differences in dialogue between the play and the film

 LS1.14

SUMMARY

In this film clip from *The Crucible,* John Proctor falsely confesses to witchcraft to escape hanging. He refuses, however, to accuse any fellow villagers of witchcraft. After signing, Proctor realizes he cannot let the lie be nailed to the church with his name on it. He tears up the paper, knowing that he will be hanged for his choice.

BACKGROUND

The photos that illustrate the play on pages 132–208 are stills from the movie *The Crucible.* In choosing Hog Island, Massachusetts, as the location for the film, the director and playwright were able to mirror the desperate themes of the play in the bleak, harsh, wintry landscape.

The Filmmakers' Challenge

Brainstorm ideas about how a movie is different from a play. Ask students to consider differences in dialogue, characterization, set, and scope of the story as they brainstorm.

ADDITIONAL TEACHING OPPORTUNITY

Write a Review After students watch the clip, have them write a review of the scene. Ask students to trade their reviews with their classmates, and then compare their responses to those of others. If time allows, have students find reviews of performances they have seen and books they have read to see how their responses compare with those of the reviewers.

Media Study

from The Crucible

Film Clip on MediaSmart DVD

 LS1.14

From Page to Screen

The Crucible is considered a modern classic of the American theater. Surprisingly, no one attempted a film version of the work in English until 1996, 43 years after the play's debut. In this lesson, view a scene from the film version to explore Arthur Miller's timeless tale in a different medium from the one originally intended.

The Filmmakers' Challenge

Translating a well-known play to the big screen poses a number of challenges for filmmakers. Writing the screenplay, perhaps the biggest hurdle, was made a little easier in the case of *The Crucible.* Arthur Miller adapted his own work and took an active role in the film's production. The playwright, consulting with the film's director, was able to take certain liberties. He could choose where a scene took place and weave in scenes not found in the original play. "I did some rewriting during production to take advantage of opportunities we had with this wonderful Hog Island [Massachusetts] location," Miller recalls.

On the set, Daniel Day-Lewis with Arthur Miller

Over the past five decades, *The Crucible*'s themes have reached far beyond the era and country in which the play was created. As Miller points out, the play's themes "find [their] relevance in every culture. I knew a woman imprisoned for six years under the [Chinese] Mao regime.... She told me that when she saw *The Crucible* in Shanghai she couldn't believe that a non-Chinese had written it, because the interrogations in *The Crucible* had been precisely the interrogations she had endured under the Cultural Revolution."

218

Media Study Resources

RESOURCE MANAGER UNIT 1

Plan and Teach pp. 325–328

Media Analysis
Summary pp. 329†*, 330‡*
Close Viewing p. 331

STANDARDS LESSON FILE

Literature Lesson 41: Dialogue and Dialect
Media Lesson 1: Active Viewing Strategies

Media Center at **ClassZone.com**

MEDIA VIEWING
Media*Smart* DVD

* Resources for Differentiation   † Also in Spanish   ‡ In Haitian Creole and Vietnamese

Comparing Texts: Dialogue

In taking his play from the page to the screen, Arthur Miller had to make certain decisions about how much of the original dialogue he would retain. During production, actors and directors will often make changes to the dialogue to fine-tune a scene.

Compare the dialogue from the play with the dialogue that appears in the film. Notice Miller's stage direction in the text and how actor Daniel Day-Lewis, in the role of John Proctor, interprets it.

> **Danforth** (*with suspicion*). It is the same, is it not? If I report it or you sign it?
>
> **Proctor** (*he knows it is insane*). No, it is not the same! What others say and what I sign is not the same!
>
> 5 **Danforth.** Why? Do you mean to deny this confession when you are free?
>
> **Proctor.** I mean to deny nothing!
>
> **Danforth.** Then explain to me, Mr. Proctor, why you will not let—
>
> **Proctor** (*with a cry of his whole soul*). Because it is my name! Because I cannot have another in my life! Because I lie and sign myself to lies! Because I am 10 not worth the dust on the feet of them that hang! How may I live without my name? I have given you my soul; leave me my name!

Viewing Guide

MediaSmart DVD

- **Film:** *The Crucible*
- **Director:** Nicholas Hytner
- **Genre:** Drama
- **Running Time:** 5 minutes

In the clip from *The Crucible*, the character John Proctor has finally agreed to sign a false confession that will save him from death.

Plan on viewing the clip several times. To help you analyze the dialogue and performance, refer to the questions.

NOW VIEW

CLOSE VIEWING: Media Analysis

1. **Analyze Setting** In the play, this scene is set in jail. How does moving the setting affect (or not affect) the scene?

2. **Compare Dialogue** Compare the dialogue from the play with the dialogue in the movie. Why do you think Miller changed some of his original dialogue for the movie?

3. **Evaluate Actor's Performance** Read the stage direction the playwright included for Proctor's speech. Do you think the actor playing Proctor succeeded in portraying "a cry of his whole soul"? Cite evidence from the scene to support your opinion.

MEDIA STUDY **219**

ANSWERS

CLOSE VIEWING: Media Analysis

1. *Changing the setting creates a contrast between the grim proceedings and the blue sky, beach, and woods, stressing Proctor's sacrifice in tearing up his confession.*

2. *Miller perhaps changed the dialogue to focus viewers' attention on Proctor's inner struggle. The dialogue explains Proctor's thoughts more fully. For example, the director replaces lines 3–4 with a more detailed*

version. Later, Proctor does not say the line "How may I live without my name?" (lines 10–11)

3. *Possible answer: Yes. Daniel Day-Lewis gives a powerful cry to the heavens. He quakes as he yells, and by the end of his speech he seems ready to collapse.*

Comparing Texts: Dialogue

Clarify that the text on page 219 is from the play. Explain that this text experienced two changes to reach the version in the film clip. First, the playwright reshaped it for the screen. Then the actor put his own mark on the screenplay, adding gesture, facial expression, and emphasis to convey his interpretation of the character and scene. Point out that lines 1–4 differ from play to film. Discuss possible reasons for the change. ***Possible answer:*** *The lines in the play are not entirely clear. More detail can help viewers understand Proctor's emotions and statement.*

Viewing Guide

1. As students prepare to view the film clip, explain that the clip includes visual cues that give information about each character.

   - Costuming and makeup give information about which characters hold power.

   - Facial expressions and body language reveal love, hopelessness, pride, and desperation.

2. Point out the characters that do not speak, such as the condemned women on the cart and Proctor's wife, who stands behind him. Remind students that these characters add impact and subtext to the scene.

R RESOURCE MANAGER—Copy Master
Close Viewing p. 331

Use this resource with the Viewing Guide:

MediaSmart DVD

MEDIA STUDY WRAP-UP

Have students summarize what they have learned about how dialogue changes from stage to film. Encourage students to consider what techniques a film uses to communicate intense emotions that are not possible for a stage production.

RETEACH

S STANDARDS LESSON FILE
Literature Lesson 41: Dialogue and Dialect
Media Lesson 1: Active Viewing Strategies

CONNECT

This selection provides additional information about the film clip that students have just viewed for the Media Study.

Reading for Information

Point out that "The Crucible" is a movie review. Have students preview it, noting the title, photograph, and caption. Then ask

- What information does the reader learn from the title and the photograph? *Possible answer: The reader learns that subject of the review is the movie version of* The Crucible; *the director and actors are probably featured in the discussion of the film.*

- Why would a movie review focus on the actors rather than on the characters? *Possible answer: The focus reflects the reviewer's desire to talk about the way in which the characters are represented rather than about the characters themselves.*

- What is the main purpose of this review? *Possible answer: The purpose is to evaluate components of the movie, such as the film's visual style and the actors' performances.*

TIERED DISCUSSION PROMPTS

Use these prompts to help students connect the movie review to the Media Study on pages 218–219:

Connect In what ways does this review help you respond to the information presented in the Media Study? *Possible answer: The review provides more detailed information about the film and helps the reader evaluate the success of acting and scene choices discussed in the Media Study.*

Interpret Reread the second paragraph. What does the reviewer think is the film's greatest strength? *Possible answer: The reviewer praises the film's "visual energy, passionate provocation and incendiary action"—that is, the power of the film.*

Synthesize From what you know about the movie version of the play, do you think that a playwright's involvement in a film adaptation is a help or hindrance? Explain. *Possible answer: It is a help. In this case,* The Crucible *is successful as a film; and according to the Media Study, Miller's involvement was crucial in preparing the play for film production.*

Reading for Information

MOVIE REVIEW *Rolling Stone* magazine reviewed Nicholas Hytner's film adaptation of *The Crucible* in 1996.

[**REVIEW**]

Director Nicholas Hytner with cast

The Crucible

Peter Travers

Arthur Miller is the first to admit that *The Crucible* must stand on its own. The playwright, now 81, sat near me at a screening of the film, unwittingly intimidating all around him. For the Pulitzer Prize–winning author of *Death of a Salesman,* attention must be paid. Miller asked for none of it. He talked with boyish zest of working with director Nicholas Hytner on re-crafting *The Crucible* as a $25 million film that would allow startling imagery to resonate with his language and burst the bounds of the stage.

Does it ever. *The Crucible,* despite some damaging cuts to the text, is a seductively exciting film that crackles with visual energy, passionate provocation and incendiary acting. . . .

The great Paul Scofield is triumphant, avoiding the easy caricature of Danforth as a fanatic. He brings the role something new: wit. We laugh with this judge, which heightens the horror later when he blinds himself to truth in the name of God and his own ambition. The scene in which he ignores Rev. Hale (Rob Campbell), who knows the girls are faking, and bullies the servant Mary Warren (Karron Graves) into delusion and madness chills the blood.

As the unforgiving wife whose "justice would freeze beer," in the words of her husband, Joan Allen is an absolute stunner in an award-caliber performance that is also a surprising source of warmth. By the seashore, where the pregnant Elizabeth has come to say goodbye to her condemned husband, she tells John, "I once counted myself so plain, so poorly made, that no honest love could come to me." Elizabeth's scene of tender reconciliation is the film's moral core. John need only sign a false confession of witchcraft to save himself from the gallows. Of course, he won't. "Because it is my name," he tells Danforth simply. "Because I cannot have another in my life."

In the film's most complex role, Daniel Day-Lewis performs with quiet power. Playing nobility can make actors insufferable, but Day-Lewis keeps John Proctor human even when saddled with smudgy makeup and fake brown teeth for his final scene. *The Crucible,* for all its timely denunciation of persecution masked as piety . . . comes down to individual resistance and how you search your heart to find it. The years haven't softened the rage against self-betrayal in *The Crucible.* This stirring film lets you feel the heat of Miller's argument and the urgent power of his kick.

ADDITIONAL TEACHING OPPORTUNITIES

Compare and Contrast Reviews Have students produce two reviews, which they will compare to other evaluations:

- Ask students to write their own review of the movie adaptation of *The Crucible,* based on the film clip that they have viewed. Students should comment on the actors' performances, as well as the visual imagery and atmosphere in the film. Then have students compare their opinions with the response presented in the review on page 220, noting similarities and differences.

- Now ask students to write a review of a movie, book, or music CD of their choice. Remind students that reviews discuss a variety of elements, such as the performers, the visual or auditory appeal, and the overall impression. Have students exchange and compare reviews.

The Puritan Legacy

In the minds of some, Puritanism is a thing of the past—an outmoded collection of beliefs from a dour and oddly-dressed group of people. Yet others insist that the spiritual, social, and cultural principles fostered by Puritanism are stubbornly present, in one way or another, in American society today. Somewhere in the middle of this debate are literary historians Richard Ruland and Malcolm Bradbury, who insist: "Puritans considered many of the literary questions we still ask today; they answered them differently."

Writing to Analyze

We can all agree that the Puritan style of dress is out of fashion, but are Puritan ideas also outmoded? Consider these "literary questions" discussed in the selections you have just read:

What is true love?

Why do bad things happen to good people?

How can faith sustain us?

How can people best serve God?

Are people worthy?

Are people basically good or bad?

In a brief essay, explain whether you think these questions are outmoded, still relevant today, or a mixture of the two. Give specific examples from current books, television programs, or movies to support your opinions.

Consider

- each of the above questions carefully. Can you think of a current book, movie, or TV show that explores that question?
- the general thrust of today's popular culture. As a whole, what types of themes and questions do today's authors and producers seem to focus on?

CALIFORNIA W2.2, W2.3

Extension

SPEAKING & LISTENING

Imagine you are a Puritan villager—a contemporary of the authors in this section—who is in charge of welcoming new settlers to your community. Using the selections you've just read as your resource, write and deliver an **informal speech** to your new neighbors, welcoming them and sharing a little about the values and beliefs held by those who live in your community.

The Puritan (1883–1886), Augustus Saint-Gaudens. Bronze figure. Private collection. © Art Resource, New York.

Wrap-Up: The Puritan Tradition

This Wrap-Up provides students with the opportunity to think about Puritan beliefs as they are characterized in these selections and to reflect on similarities and differences between Puritan culture and their own. Encourage students to consider which elements of Puritan culture they admire and which they find less appealing.

Writing to Analyze

- Remind students that to *analyze* is to break something down into parts or essential features in order to understand better how it works or what it means. Looking at different aspects of the Puritan experience sheds light on ways in which that culture continues to influence beliefs and behavior.

- To help students plan and write the essay, ask them to note a first impression for each question. Then have them work in groups to brainstorm examples of contemporary works (such as books, films, TV shows) that illustrate their opinions.

Extension

- Suggest that students work in groups and review the selections that they have read. Have them list the selection titles in the first column of a Two-Column Chart.

- As they revisit each selection, direct students to record notes about its most prominent Puritan values or beliefs in the second column of the chart.

- Students should choose the Puritan principles that appear frequently in the chart as the focus for their informal speech.

BEST PRACTICES TOOLKIT—Transparency Two-Column Chart p. A25

DIFFERENTIATED INSTRUCTION

FOR DEVELOPING WRITERS

Writing Support Help students get started by directing them to relevant passages in the selections. For example, students might draw on lines 488–501 in Act Two of *The Crucible* and lines 93–104 in "Sinners in the Hands of an Angry God" in response to the question "How can people best serve God?"

FOR ENGLISH LEARNERS

Write Topic Sentences Help students write topic sentences for their paragraphs by discussing sentence starters like these:

- One question that was important to the Puritans but that also resonates deeply in our culture today is _____.

- Although I do not think that it is an issue today, the Puritans were very concerned with the question of _____.

OBJECTIVES

- identify and analyze persuasive techniques
- identify and analyze rhetorical devices
- identify, analyze, and evaluate elements of an argument
- understand inductive and deductive development

CALIFORNIA R2.1, R2.6, LS1.5

A Cause for Argument

Deductively or Inductively? To help students distinguish deductive from inductive arguments, discuss how to form the two different kinds of argument for the proposition "The school day should be longer." Have students list arguments in a Two-Column Chart.

Proposition: The school day should be longer	
Deductive Reasoning	Inductive Reasoning
Generalization: More education is better than less.	Examples: Variety of activities possible in a longer day.
Examples: Variety of activities possible in a longer day.	Conclusion: A longer school day is worthwhile.

BEST PRACTICES TOOLKIT—Transparency
Two-Column Chart p. A25

Basics of an Argument Call students' attention to the sidebar on page 223. Ask whether the list gives more importance to logic or to emotion. (*logic*) Briefly discuss students' views on whether and why logic is more important to a sound argument.

Persuasive Rhetoric

How do you persuade someone to change his or her mind? **Persuasion** is built on the power of words—the types of words that grab your attention, keep you riveted, and finally influence what you think. **Persuasive rhetoric** is the art of using language to argue effectively for or against a set of beliefs or course of action, and to convince others to adopt a position or act in a certain way.

CALIFORNIA R2.1, R2.6, LS1.5

A Cause for Argument

America's history of persuasive rhetoric began with the impassioned pleas of statesmen, writers, and orators who held strong beliefs about the future direction of the colonized states. In the early days of the developing country, freedom—from tyranny, from taxes, and from censorship— was vigorously debated. Several writings, such as Thomas Jefferson's Declaration of Independence (page 236), were not only official state documents, but also well-crafted arguments that would set the foundation for democracy in the United States.

A 1792 British caricature of Thomas Paine, who was ridiculed in England for his appeal to overthrow the monarchy

In designing their arguments, statesmen like Jefferson, Thomas Paine, and Patrick Henry used the basic elements of an argument (see sidebar on page 223), framed them in a variety of structures, and dressed them with persuasive rhetoric to build strong, eloquent cases. The way ideas are organized in an **argument** can be key to its persuasive power. A writer can develop an argument **deductively,** by beginning with a generalization, or premise, and proceeding to marshal examples and facts that support it (as in the Declaration of Independence), or **inductively,** by beginning with examples or facts and proceeding to draw a conclusion from them.

The Power of Language

To be effective, a persuasive work should engage both the minds and the emotions of its audience. A writer may therefore use some words to arouse emotions and other words to develop sound reasoning. However, it is not the words alone that are persuasive, but how the words are put together that gives them power and strength. These **persuasive techniques** fall into three basic types.

- **Logical appeals** rely on logic and facts to support a claim. For example, "injuries and usurpations" committed by King George III are cited as evidence for the need for independence in the Declaration of Independence.

DIFFERENTIATED INSTRUCTION

For general guidelines on differentiating instruction, see

 BEST PRACTICES TOOLKIT
Differentiated Instruction pp. 31–38

FOR STRATEGIC READERS

Note Taking For students who need help with note taking, hand out the note-taking copy masters before discussing this spread. Explain that students will be learning many terms relating to persuasive rhetoric in

this workshop. Discuss the major terms on this spread (*deductively, inductively, logical appeals, claim, support, counterarguments, logic, conclusion, emotional appeals, ethical appeals, rhetorical question, antithesis, repetition, parallelism*) as students record notes on the copy masters.

 RESOURCE MANAGER—Copy Master
Note Taking p. 333

- **Emotional appeals** present ideas and images that elicit strong feelings. For example, Jefferson's statement that King George is attempting "to complete the works of death, desolation, and tyranny" would likely evoke a strong reaction from its audience.

- **Ethical appeals** use values or moral standards that are widely accepted as a way to persuade an audience. For example, to call forth his audience's sense of right, justice, and virtue, Jefferson reminded people that independence was a last resort, after the failure of other measures: "In every stage of these oppressions we have petitioned for redress, in the most humble terms; our repeated petitions have been answered only by repeated injury."

In addition to persuasive techniques, writers will often use **rhetorical devices** to enhance their arguments:

- A **rhetorical question** is a question that does not require a reply. Writers use rhetorical questions to suggest that the answer to the question is obvious or self-evident. In her letter to her husband, John Adams (page 258), Abigail Adams writes, "Shall we not be despised by foreign powers, for hesitating so long at a word?"

- **Antithesis** is a device in which contrasting ideas are expressed in a grammatically balanced statement. Notice the juxtaposition of ideas in this phrase from Thomas Paine's "The Crisis" (page 246): "I call not upon a few, but upon all."

- **Repetition** is the use of the same word or phrase more than once for emphasis. **Parallelism,** a form of repetition in which a grammatical pattern is repeated, is used effectively in this famous passage from the Declaration of Independence.

> We hold these truths to be self-evident:—That all men are created equal; that they are endowed by their Creator with certain unalienable rights; that among these are life, liberty, and the pursuit of happiness.
>
> **—Thomas Jefferson, the Declaration of Independence**

Rhetorical devices and persuasive techniques can be used to create arguments that are valid and sincere or artificial and insincere. It is up to the reader or listener to evaluate whether the argument is based on sound reasoning, and therefore credible and convincing, or whether the words and appeals are the sole strength of the argument.

BASICS OF AN ARGUMENT

To be effective, an argument should include

- a **claim,** or clear statement of a position on an issue
- **support** for the claim, which consists of reasons and evidence
- **counterarguments,** or statements that anticipate and refute opposing views
- sound **logic** and effective language
- a **conclusion** that sums up the reasons or the call for action

Close Read

In this passage, note the parallel clauses beginning with *that*. What is the effect of this **parallel structure?**

LITERARY ANALYSIS WORKSHOP **223**

The Power of Language

Persuasive Techniques Clarify these terms listed on pages 222–223:

- **Logical appeals:** Stress that in the Declaration of Independence the logical appeal consists of a list of injuries and usurpations. Ask what would be the purpose of a list of King George's unfair actions. ***Possible answer:*** *It would show evidence to support Jefferson's cause.*

- **Emotional appeals:** Ask students to describe likely reactions to the words "death, desolation, and tyranny." ***Possible answer:*** *They would create anger.*

- **Ethical appeals:** Ask students to read the quotation closely and decide how Jefferson portrayed himself. ***Possible answer:*** *He wanted to seem reasonable, moderate, fair, humble, and patient.*

Rhetorical Devices Discuss these different rhetorical devices:

- **Rhetorical questions:** Ask students for examples they might ask or hear in real life. ***Possible answer:*** *Is life always fair?*

- **Antithesis:** Write the word on the board and circle the prefix *anti-*. Ask what it means. *("against")* Emphasize that a sentence using antithesis contains a contrast between two opposing ideas or statements. Then read the quotation from Paine aloud and ask students to state its two opposing ideas. (*Paine speaks not to a few, but to all.*)

- **Parallelism:** Explain that parallelism can be repetition of any grammatical pattern, from an introductory word or phrase to an entire clause or sentence. Ask what the repeated pattern in the Jefferson quotation is. (*"That" followed by a clause.*)

Close Read

Possible answer: *The parallelism unifies the parts of the statement, which emphasizes the ideas expressed. Parallelism also adds rhythm.*

FOR ENGLISH LEARNERS

Language: Skill Words On the board, list the academic vocabulary shown in italics. Then share the definitions or examples and have students match them to the list.

- *logical:* appeals to reason, not emotion
- *emotional:* appeals to feelings
- *ethical:* consistent with moral values
- *rhetorical question:* "Isn't this great?"
- *antithesis:* "I'm not hungry, I'm thirsty."
- *parallelism:* "I see you, I hear you."

FOR ADVANCED LEARNERS/AP

Formulate an Argument [small-group option] Continue the argument for or against longer school days. Have students choose a position and brainstorm points to support it. Tell students to include at least one point each of logical, emotional, and ethical appeal, and then to classify each point by these categories. Finally, ask students whether they would choose to argue their case deductively or inductively, and why.

OBJECTIVES

Literary Analysis
- explore the key idea of a **decisive moment**
- analyze rhetorical devices
- read a speech

Reading
- understand techniques for reading aloud a persuasive speech

Vocabulary
- build vocabulary for reading and writing
- understand word origins from mythology *(also an EL language objective)*

Grammar and Writing
- use a variety of sentence types
- write a persuasive speech

 CALIFORNIA R2.1, R1.2, R2.4, W1.1, W1.3, W1.4, LC1.1

ABOUT THE AUTHOR

To clarify Henry's "loaded analogy," explain that Brutus and other Roman senators killed the dictator Julius Caesar for fear he had too much power, and Oliver Cromwell led the effort to execute King Charles I of Britain for treason. Ask what Henry meant by "George III may profit by their example."

USING THE *NOTABLE QUOTE*

Have students paraphrase this quote, in which **Patrick Henry** concludes his "loaded analogy" by daring his opponents to act on his "treason." ***Possible answer:*** *If you think my words are treasonous, then try to stop me.*

Speech in the Virginia Convention
by Patrick Henry

CALIFORNIA R2.1, R1.2 (p. 232), R2.4 (p. 231), W1.1 (p. 233), W1.3 (p. 233), W1.4 (p. 233), LC1.1 (p. 233)

NOTABLE QUOTE

"If this be treason, make the most of it."

FYI
Did you know that Patrick Henry . . .

- had 16 children—6 by his first wife, who died, and then 10 by his second wife?
- owned slaves?
- advocated the right to bear arms later guaranteed by the U.S. Constitution?
- strongly supported states' rights?

Author Online
For more on Patrick Henry, visit the **Literature Center** at ClassZone.com.

Virginia House of Burgesses

Patrick Henry
1736–1799

Known as "the Orator of Liberty," Patrick Henry made a name for himself with his speeches supporting American democracy. He was one of the earliest opponents of British rule in the American colonies. In 1765, after the British Parliament passed a tax bill called the Stamp Act, Henry was among the members of the Virginia legislature that challenged the legality of a British tax on the colonies. But he went farther than his colleagues by making a threat against the king. In his argument, so the story goes, he used a loaded analogy: "Caesar had his Brutus, Charles the First his Cromwell, and George III . . ."—at this point, shouts of "Treason!" erupted in the hall, but Henry continued—"may profit by their example." He ended his speech with the defiant words, "If this be treason, make the most of it." Henry did indeed make the most of his "treason," becoming a tireless and influential leader both before and after the Revolution.

Profitable Law Career Henry was born in Virginia to a prosperous landowner. His father, who had attended the University of Aberdeen in Scotland, gave him a classical education at home. His mother, Sarah Winston Syme, was from a wealthy family. Henry went out on his own at age 15. Although smart and industrious, he couldn't find success as a storekeeper or later as a tobacco planter. After marrying and starting a family, he decided to teach himself law, and in 1760, at the age of 24, he was admitted to the bar. Henry's eloquence, quick wit, and rhetorical gifts served him well, and his law practice grew increasingly profitable.

Popular Virginia Politician Henry is best known for his fervent "Speech in the Virginia Convention," which narrowly convinced the assembled leadership to prepare for war with Britain. In addition, he organized a Virginia militia that became part of the new Continental Army after independence was declared. He helped write the new state constitution and the Virginia Declaration of Rights, which was a major influence on the Bill of Rights added to the U.S. Constitution. He also served several terms as governor of Virginia and as a state legislator. Although President Washington offered him positions as secretary of state and Supreme Court justice, Henry declined and always remained suspicious of the federal government. In 1799, after being elected again to the state legislature, he died at his 700-acre plantation, Red Hill, before he could take office.

224

---

* Resources for Differentiation   † Also in Spanish   ‡ In Haitian Creole and Vietnamese

LITERARY ANALYSIS: RHETORICAL DEVICES

Rhetorical devices are structures within language that help communicate ideas.

- A **rhetorical question** is a question to which no answer is expected. (*But when shall we be stronger?*)
- **Antithesis** expresses contrasting ideas in parallel grammatical structures. (*Give me liberty, or give me death!*)
- **Repetition** is the recurrence of words, phrases, or lines. (*Let it come! I repeat it, sir, let it come!*)
- **Parallelism** is a kind of repetition in which words or phrases in the same grammatical form connect ideas. (*Is life so dear, or peace so sweet . . .*)

As you read Henry's speech, be on the lookout for rhetorical devices and how they might have affected his audience.

READING STRATEGY: READING A PERSUASIVE SPEECH

When reading a persuasive speech, imagine the techniques the speaker used to bring the speech to life, such as word emphasis, changes in pace, pauses, and changes in volume.
  As you read, use a chart like the one shown to record how you would emphasize certain passages if you were Patrick Henry.

Paragraph/Line Numbers	Technique
Paragraph 1 (lines 1–14)	

VOCABULARY IN CONTEXT

Use context clues to write a definition of each boldfaced word.

1. **Martial** Speech Sets Stage for War
2. **Subjugation** by Britain Called Unacceptable
3. British Claims Said Not to **Comport** with Facts
4. Colonists to **Remonstrate** with Governor Against Taxes
5. Never **Supinely** Accept Tyranny, Henry Says
6. **Invincible** Patriot Army Will Repel Attacks
7. **Insidious** Spies Reveal Patriots' Plans
8. Nothing Can **Extenuate** Tory Traitors
9. Citizens Told to Be **Vigilant**
10. America Must Remain **Inviolate**

When is it time to TAKE ACTION?

KEY IDEA Whether it's the winning shot in the final seconds of the game, the right moment to ask someone out, or the decision to accept a job offer—timing is everything. In the spring of 1775, Patrick Henry had had enough of compromise with the British; it was time for armed resistance. His address to the Virginia Convention turned out to be a **decisive moment** not only in his own life but in the life of the United States as well.

DISCUSS With a partner, think of examples from sports, politics, or everyday life when the time was right for decisive action. Then, for one example, analyze why it was the right action at the right time.

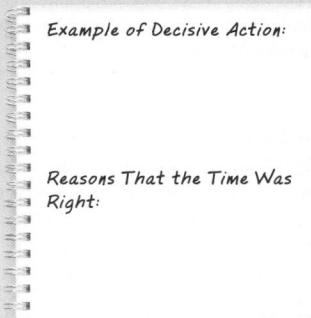

Example of Decisive Action:

Reasons That the Time Was Right:

When is it time to TAKE ACTION?

Lead into the **KEY IDEA** by asking the question. After pairs complete the **DISCUSS** activity, invite volunteers to share their examples. Then ask students to generalize how someone might recognize a **decisive moment** when it occurs.

SKILLS FOCUS

LITERARY ANALYSIS   R2.1

● RHETORICAL DEVICES

Remind students that they learned about rhetorical devices in the Literary Analysis Workshop on Persuasive Rhetoric (page 222). Ask volunteers to explain how each quote from Henry's speech uses the rhetorical device it exemplifies. ***Possible answer:*** *Rhetorical question: Henry does not expect an answer to his question. Antithesis: The quote presents two opposite choices in parallel grammatical form. Repetition: "Let it come!" is repeated. Parallelism: The grammatical form is parallel: noun + "so" + adjective.*

CHECK UNDERSTANDING Have students write a sentence that uses one of the rhetorical devices discussed on this page.

READING STRATEGY

■ READING A PERSUASIVE SPEECH

Explain to students that in their charts, they should list speaking techniques, not rhetorical devices. In addition to the oral techniques mentioned in the instruction, suggest that students consider other performance techniques, such as gestures and facial expressions. Also encourage students to consider how a speaker might use these techniques to reinforce the speech's written rhetorical devices.

> **R** RESOURCE MANAGER—Copy Master
>   Reading a Persuasive Speech p. 347
>   (for student use while reading the selection)

VOCABULARY

▲ VOCABULARY IN CONTEXT

DIAGNOSE WORD KNOWLEDGE To determine preteaching needs, have all students complete Vocabulary in Context. ***Possible answers:*** **1.** *warlike,* **2.** *total control,* **3.** *agree,* **4.** *protest,* **5.** *lying face up helplessly,* **6.** *undefeatable,* **7.** *treacherous,* **8.** *excuse,* **9.** *alert,* **10.** *untouched*

PRETEACH VOCABULARY Preteach vocabulary with this copy master. Read each item aloud.

> **R** RESOURCE MANAGER—Copy Master
>   Vocabulary Study p. 349

MORE VOCABULARY SUPPORT
For additional activities and guidelines, see

> **BEST PRACTICES TOOLKIT**
>   Scaffolding Vocabulary Instruction
>   pp. 43–46
> **i** Vocabulary Center at **ClassZone.com**

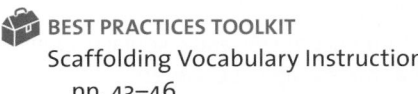

SUMMARY

Patrick Henry delivered this speech to an audience of Virginia delegates convened to decide whether to revolt against Britain. Henry begins by saying that he must speak out or consider himself guilty of treason. He argues that Britain is preparing for war against the colonies and that the colonists have tried peaceful arguments for a decade. Peace is no longer an option. If the colonists wish to be free, they must fight.

Lines 1–11
REINFORCE *KEY IDEA:* DECISIVE MOMENT

Discuss What details in this passage reveal that Henry believes he is speaking at a **decisive moment** for his country? Why does he feel that free debate is essential at such a moment?
Possible answer: Henry reveals his belief that he is speaking at a decisive moment for his country when he says, "This is no time for ceremony. The question before the House is one of awful moment to this country. For my own part I consider it as nothing less than a question of freedom or slavery . . ." (lines 6–8). He believes that free debate is essential at such a moment because the stakes are so high ("freedom or slavery"). The colonists won't be able to make the best decision for their country if they don't hear all points of view.

LITERARY ANALYSIS

Ⓐ RHETORICAL DEVICES

Possible answer: The phrases "same subject in different lights" (line 3) and "freedom or slavery" (line 8) are examples of antithesis. This rhetorical device emphasizes the stark contrast between the two points of view and the two choices facing the colonists.

If students need help . . . Tell them that writers and speakers often set off contrasting ideas with a conjunction such as *or* (as in the example in line 8) or *but* (as in the example on page 225).

SPEECH IN THE
Virginia Convention

Patrick Henry

ANALYZE VISUALS
This painting shows Patrick Henry speaking to the Virginia House of Burgesses. What different attitudes are reflected in the faces and postures of his audience members?

BACKGROUND In the spring of 1775, delegates from the state of Virginia could not agree whether to press for a peaceful solution with Britain or to prepare for war. Patrick Henry introduced resolutions calling for military preparedness. After politely listening to his colleagues' objections to armed rebellion, he rose to deliver this impassioned appeal.

March 23, 1775

Mr. President:[1] No man thinks more highly than I do of the patriotism, as well as abilities, of the very worthy gentlemen who have just addressed the House. But different men often see the same subject in different lights; and, therefore, I hope that it will not be thought disrespectful to those gentlemen, if, entertaining as I do opinions of a character very opposite to theirs, I shall speak forth my sentiments freely and without reserve. This is no time for ceremony. The question before the House is one of awful moment[2] to this country. For my own part I consider it as nothing less than a question of freedom or slavery; and in proportion to the magnitude of the subject ought to be the freedom of the debate. It is only in this
10 way that we can hope to arrive at truth, and fulfill the great responsibility which we hold to God and our country. Should I keep back my opinions at such a Ⓐ

① **Targeted Passage**

Ⓐ **RHETORICAL DEVICES**
Reread lines 1–11. What are some examples of **antithesis** and what kind of emphasis does it create?

---

1. **Mr. President:** the president of the Virginia Convention, Peyton Randolph.
2. **of awful moment:** of very grave importance.

Patrick Henry Before the Virginia House of Burgesses (1851), Peter F. Rothermel. Red Hill, The Patrick Henry National Memorial, Brookneal, Virginia.

DIFFERENTIATED INSTRUCTION

FOR ALL STUDENTS
Expert Groups Encourage students to become subject experts by selecting and researching one of these topics:

- the Virginia House of Burgesses
- British infringements of colonial rights in the 1760s and 1770s
- the Stamp Act of 1765 and colonial responses such as the Stamp Act Congress

FOR STRATEGIC READERS
In combination with the *Audio Anthology CD,* use one or more Targeted Passages (pp. 226, 228, 230) to ensure that students focus on key concepts in the selection. Targeted Passages are also good for English learners.

① **Targeted Passage [Lines 6–11]**
This passage conveys Henry's sense of urgency about the decision facing the Virginia Convention.

ANALYZE VISUALS

Possible answer: *Some of the audience members look troubled or suspicious. The man with his arm outstretched seems to be pleading with Henry to stop speaking.*

About the Art This painting by Peter Frederick Rothermel (1817–1895) shows the artist's skillful use of color to dramatize historical subjects. Henry's speech before the House of Burgesses, a decade before the Virginia Convention speech, includes the **NOTABLE QUOTE,** "If this be treason, make the most of it."

Lines 1–11
TIERED DISCUSSION PROMPTS

Use these prompts to help students understand Henry's introduction:

Connect If you were a delegate at the Virginia Convention, how would the beginning of Henry's speech affect you? *Accept all thoughtful responses.*

Interpret What is Henry's purpose for discussing the "freedom of the debate?" *Possible answer: Henry wants to get the delegates to listen to him with an open mind.*

Evaluate Is this an effective opening for a speech, or as a modern reader, do you think the speech begins too slowly? Explain your response. *Possible answer: The beginning of the speech was effective under the circumstances because it showed respect to the delegates and their opinions. However, for a modern audience, it might seem slow because it takes a while for Henry to make his point.*

- What does Henry mean when he says, "This is no time for ceremony"?

- What is the "question before the House"?

- What stark contrast does he present to convey the importance of this question?

- According to Henry, why is it so important to have "freedom of debate"?

- Why does he mention the delegates' responsibility to "God and our country?"

FOR ENGLISH LEARNERS

Key Academic Vocabulary Use Definition Mapping to teach these words: *debate* (line 9), *conduct* (line 24), *capable* (line 43), *abandon* (line 58), *acquire* (line 66).

 BEST PRACTICES TOOLKIT—Transparency Definition Mapping p. E6

Prereading For prereading instruction for English learners, see

 BEST PRACTICES TOOLKIT Scaffolding Reading Instruction pp. 43–46

FOR ADVANCED LEARNERS/AP

AP exercises in the bottom channel provide additional challenge for students. Use these suggestions for small groups or individuals.

ADDITIONAL GUIDELINES

For more help with differentiation and tips for classroom management, see

 BEST PRACTICES TOOLKIT Differentiated Instruction pp. 31–38

time, through fear of giving offense, I should consider myself as guilty of treason towards my country, and of an act of disloyalty towards the majesty of heaven, which I revere above all earthly kings. **B**

Mr. President, it is natural to man to indulge in the illusions of hope. We are apt to shut our eyes against a painful truth, and listen to the song of that siren, till she transforms us into beasts.[3] Is this the part of wise men, engaged in a great and arduous struggle for liberty? Are we disposed to be of the number of those who, having eyes, see not, and having ears, hear not,[4] the things which so nearly concern
20 their temporal salvation? For my part, whatever anguish of spirit it may cost, I am willing to know the whole truth—to know the worst and to provide for it. **C**

I have but one lamp by which my feet are guided; and that is the lamp of experience. I know of no way of judging of the future but by the past. And judging by the past, I wish to know what there has been in the conduct of the British ministry for the last ten years, to justify those hopes with which gentlemen have been pleased to solace themselves and the House? Is it that **insidious** smile with which our petition has been lately received? Trust it not, sir; it will prove a snare to your feet. Suffer not yourselves to be betrayed with a kiss.[5]

Ask yourselves how this gracious reception of our petition **comports** with these
30 warlike preparations which cover our waters and darken our land. Are fleets and armies necessary to a work of love and reconciliation? Have we shown ourselves so unwilling to be reconciled that force must be called in to win back our love? Let us not deceive ourselves, sir. These are the implements of war and **subjugation**— the last arguments to which kings resort. I ask gentlemen, sir, what means this **martial** array, if its purpose be not to force us to submission? Can gentlemen assign any other possible motives for it? Has Great Britain any enemy, in this quarter of the world, to call for all this accumulation of navies and armies? No, sir, she has none. They are meant for us; they can be meant for no other. They are sent over to bind and rivet upon us those chains which the British ministry
40 have been so long forging. **D**

And what have we to oppose to them? Shall we try argument? Sir, we have been trying that for the last ten years. Have we anything new to offer on the subject? Nothing. We have held the subject up in every light of which it is capable; but it has been all in vain. Shall we resort to entreaty and humble supplication? What terms shall we find which have not been already exhausted? Let us not, I beseech you, sir, deceive ourselves longer. **E**

---

3. **the illusions of hope . . . into beasts:** In the *Odyssey* of Homer, the goddess Circe lures men to her island and then magically transforms them into pigs. Henry suggests that the "illusions of hope" may transform people in a similar way.

4. **having eyes . . . hear not:** an allusion to Ezekiel 12:2 in the Bible, which speaks of "who have eyes to see, but see not, who have ears to hear, but hear not."

5. **betrayed with a kiss:** an allusion to Luke 22:47–48 in the Bible, wherein Judas betrayed Jesus to the Roman soldiers by kissing him and thus identifying him.

Side annotations

B PERSUASIVE SPEECH

Possible answer: The words "highly," "patriotism," "abilities," "worthy gentlemen," "disrespectful," "offense," and "revere" might be emphasized to show respect.

Extend the Discussion Do you think Henry's expressions of respect for his audience are sincere? Why or why not?

LITERARY ANALYSIS

C RHETORICAL DEVICES

Possible answer: The phrases "having eyes, see not, and having ears, hear not" (line 19) and "to know the whole truth—to know the worst" (line 21) are examples of parallelism. "Having eyes, see not, and having ears, hear not" is also an example of antithesis. Henry is making the point that those who do not want to fight are ignoring the obvious truth.

LITERARY ANALYSIS

D RHETORICAL DEVICES

Possible answer: The answer to each rhetorical question is "No," except for "what means this martial array . . . ?" Here the answer is to agree with Henry that "its purpose [is] . . . to force us to submission." A listener will likely respond by accepting Henry's analysis.

E GRAMMAR AND STYLE

Analyze Sentence Types Review the sentence types (see page 233), and make sure students recognize that "We have held the subject up . . ." is declarative because it expresses a statement; "Let us not, I beseech you . . ." is imperative because it expresses a request; and the other sentences in the passage are interrogative because they ask questions. Have students find one other example of each sentence type in lines 22–28.

B PERSUASIVE SPEECH
Henry speaks respectfully of those with whom he disagrees in lines 1–14. What words might be vocally emphasized to show respect?

C RHETORICAL DEVICES
What rhetorical device, besides a rhetorical question, is on display in lines 18–21? What point is he making about those who don't want to fight?

insidious (ĭn-sĭd'ē-əs) *adj.* treacherous

comport (kəm-pôrt') *v.* to agree

subjugation (sŭb'jə-gā'shən) *n.* control by conquering

martial (mär'shəl) *adj.* warlike

2 Targeted Passage

D RHETORICAL DEVICES
Reread lines 29–40, answering each of the **rhetorical questions.** How is a listener likely to respond to Henry's final statements in lines 37–40?

E GRAMMAR AND STYLE
Reread lines 43–46. Notice the use of **declarative, interrogative,** and **imperative** sentences.

DIFFERENTIATED INSTRUCTION

FOR STRATEGIC READERS

2 Targeted Passage [Lines 22–46]

In this passage, Henry summarizes previous failed efforts to negotiate with Britain.

- In lines 22–26, what point does Henry make about judging the future?

- What evidence does Henry cite to argue that the British are preparing for war?

- In lines 41–46, what is Henry's answer to those who favor talking to the British?

Comprehension Support Model how to break down Henry's long, complicated sentences into shorter, simpler ones. For example, divide sentences that contain semicolons into separate sentences. Point out that the sentence in line 38 can be simplified like this: "They are meant for us. They can be meant for no other." Then have students work in pairs to apply this strategy to the long sentences in lines 48–53.

The Bloody Massacre perpetrated in. . . Boston on March 5th, 1770 (1770), Paul Revere. Colored engraving. Private collection. /Art Resource, New York.

Sir, we have done everything that could be done to avert the storm which is now coming on. We have petitioned; we have **remonstrated;** we have supplicated; we have prostrated ourselves before the throne, and have implored
50 its interposition[6] to arrest the tyrannical hands of the ministry and Parliament. Our petitions have been slighted; our remonstrances have produced additional violence and insult; our supplications have been disregarded; and we have been spurned, with contempt, from the foot of the throne. In vain, after these things, may we indulge the fond hope of peace and reconciliation. There is no longer any room for hope.

remonstrate
(rĭ-mŏn'strāt') *v.* to object; to protest strongly

---

6. **we have prostrated . . . interposition:** We have thrown ourselves at the feet of the king and have begged for intervention.

Activity Ask students what viewpoint the engraving expresses. *Possible answer: It favors the colonists, showing the British attacking civilians.*

About the Art Paul Revere was known not only for his ride on April 18, 1775, but also as a silversmith, printer, and engraver. Revere made this engraving to illustrate the Boston Massacre, which occurred on March 5, 1770, five years before Patrick Henry's speech. Like that speech, the engraving helped turn American public opinion toward revolt.

Lines 47–55
REINFORCE *KEY IDEA:* DECISIVE MOMENT

Discuss Henry lists several actions the colonies have taken to protest their treatment by the British. How do these actions show that Henry is speaking at a **decisive moment** in American history? *Possible answer: Henry believes the colonies have exhausted peaceful avenues for settlement with the British. Thus, the moment has come for the colonists to resort to forceful means.*

FOR STRATEGIC READERS

Reading a Persuasive Speech To help students imagine delivering lines 47–55, have them return to the chart introduced on page 225 and fill it out for this page. Ask them to consider these questions:

- What words and phrases would they emphasize if they were giving the speech?
- Where would they pause for effect?
- Where would they speak loudly or softly?

Paragraph/ Line Numbers	Technique
Paragraph 6 (lines 47–55)	Emphasis: "everything," "petitioned," "remonstrated," "supplicated," "prostrated," "implored," "slighted," "violence," "spurned"
	pause: before last sentence

FOR ENGLISH LEARNERS

Vocabulary: Suffixes Write the word *painful* (line 16) on the board and put a slash between the base word and the suffix. Discuss what *-ful* means. Have students find words on pages 228–229 with suffixes such as *-tion*, *-ed*, and *-ous*. Work with students to construct word meanings by combining the meaning of the base word and the suffix.

 BEST PRACTICES TOOLKIT—Transparencies Suffixes and Base Words pp. E27, E28

F RHETORICAL DEVICES

Possible answer: The word sir *literally refers to the president of the Convention, but broadly it is intended to affect all the delegates by emphasizing Henry's respect for his audience. The repetition of "let it come!" shows his determination and courage in facing the conflict and is also designed to stir an emotional response.*

If students need help . . . Direct them to footnote 1 on page 226 for an explanation of the literal meaning of *sir.* Then, to help students understand Henry's rhetorical purpose, ask them why a speaker might use the word *sir* even though he is addressing a group. *Possible answer: Even though he is addressing a group, using the word* sir *makes it sound as if Henry is addressing each member of his audience individually.*

G PERSUASIVE SPEECH

Possible answer: He probably began quietly and calmly, with his words becoming increasingly loud, impassioned, and rapid. This change probably stirred the crowd to feel excitement, anger, and determination to take action.

SELECTION WRAP–UP

SUMMARIZE Have students sum up Henry's argument for urging the colonists to go to war against Britain.

⭐ CRITIQUE

- Have students choose the passages in Henry's speech that they find the most effective and then explain what makes them so powerful.

- After completing the After Reading questions on page 231, have students revisit their responses and tell whether they have changed their opinions.

If we wish to be free—if we mean to preserve **inviolate** those inestimable privileges for which we have been so long contending—if we mean not basely to abandon the noble struggle in which we have been so long engaged, and which we have pledged ourselves never to abandon until the glorious object of our contest 60 shall be obtained, we must fight! I repeat it, sir, we must fight! An appeal to arms and to the God of Hosts is all that is left us!

They tell us, sir, that we are weak—unable to cope with so formidable an adversary. But when shall we be stronger? Will it be the next week, or the next year? Will it be when we are totally disarmed, and when a British guard shall be stationed in every house? Shall we gather strength by irresolution and inaction? Shall we acquire the means of effectual resistance, by lying **supinely** on our backs, and hugging the delusive phantom of hope, until our enemies shall have bound us hand and foot?

Sir, we are not weak, if we make a proper use of those means which the God 70 of nature hath placed in our power. Three millions of people, armed in the holy cause of liberty, and in such a country as that which we possess, are **invincible** by any force which our enemy can send against us. Besides, sir, we shall not fight our battles alone. There is a just God who presides over the destinies of nations, and who will raise up friends to fight our battles for us. The battle, sir, is not to the strong alone;[7] it is to the **vigilant,** the active, the brave. Besides, sir, we have no election.[8] If we were base enough to desire it, it is now too late to retire from the contest. There is no retreat but in submission and slavery! Our chains are forged! Their clanking may be heard on the plains of Boston! The war is inevitable—and let it come! I repeat it, sir, let it come! **F**

80 It is in vain, sir, to **extenuate** the matter. Gentlemen may cry, "Peace! peace!"— but there is no peace. The war is actually begun! The next gale that sweeps from the north[9] will bring to our ears the clash of resounding arms! Our brethren are already in the field! Why stand we here idle? What is it that gentlemen wish? What would they have? Is life so dear, or peace so sweet, as to be purchased at the price of chains and slavery? Forbid it, Almighty God! I know not what course others may take; but as for me, give me liberty, or give me death! **G**

inviolate (ĭn-vī′ə-lĭt) *adj.* not violated; intact

supinely (soo-pīn′lē) *adv.* in a manner with the face upward

invincible (ĭn-vĭn′sə-bəl) *adj.* unbeatable

vigilant (vĭj′ə-lənt) *adj.* alert; watchful

F RHETORICAL DEVICES
Why do you think Henry repeats the word *sir* so often in this paragraph? Explain the likely effect of this **repetition** as well as that of the phrase "let it come!"

extenuate (ĭk-stĕn′yoo-āt′) *v.* to lessen the seriousness of, especially by providing partial excuses

③ Targeted Passage

G PERSUASIVE SPEECH
How might the speaker's **pace** and **emphasis** have changed over the course of the speech? How might his audience have responded to these changes? Explain.

---

7. **battle . . . strong alone:** an allusion to Ecclesiastes 9:11 in the Bible, "the race is not to the swift, nor the battle to the strong."

8. **election:** choice.

9. **the next gale . . . north:** Some colonists in Massachusetts had already shown open resistance to the British and were on the brink of war.

DIFFERENTIATED INSTRUCTION

FOR STRATEGIC READERS

③ Targeted Passage [Lines 80–86]

This passage brings Henry's rhetoric to its height of passion as the speech closes.

- What is Henry's tone in this paragraph?

- What mood might his speech have stirred in the audience?

- What does Henry mean when he says, "give me liberty, or give me death"?

- What does he hope to achieve by this cry?

FOR ADVANCED LEARNERS/AP

Synthesize [paired option] Have students write a news story for a colonial newspaper. Their stories should summarize Henry's key points—but because colonial newspapers were often not objective, students should slant their stories for or against Henry's position. Have students exchange news stories and analyze how each implies a bias.

💼 **BEST PRACTICES TOOLKIT—Transparency**
Writing Template: Eyewitness Report
pp. C16, C27

Comprehension

R2.1, R2.4
CALIFORNIA

1. **Recall** What does Patrick Henry urge the colonists to do?

2. **Paraphrase** Reread lines 22–28. What methods had the colonists already used to express their complaints against the British?

3. **Clarify** How did the British respond to those complaints?

Literary Analysis

4. **Analyze a Persuasive Speech** Look back at the chart you filled in as you read. Choose a section of Henry's speech to read aloud as he might have delivered it. How effective are the techniques you plan to use? Explain why you think so.

5. **Analyze Persuasive Strategy** Henry spends most of his speech arguing against hope, ordinarily not the best tactic when trying to inspire an audience. How does he manage to discredit hope? Why would he do this?

6. **Interpret Allusions** Review the following allusions to the *Odyssey* and the Bible that Henry uses in his speech. How does each allusion support the point Henry makes in the paragraph?

   - *Odyssey*, lines 15–17
   - Bible, lines 18–19
   - Bible, line 28
   - Bible, lines 74–75

7. **Evaluate Appeals** How does Henry convince his audience that the **decisive moment** to fight is at hand? In a chart, summarize his reasons. Then, beside each, note whether he appeals mainly to logic or emotion. Which reasons are strongest? Explain.

Reasons to Fight	Logical or Emotional
1. If we want to be free and keep the rights and privileges we have grown accustomed to, we have to fight. (lines 56–61)	logical
2.	

8. **Make Judgments About Rhetorical Devices** Review the rhetorical devices discussed on page 225. Which devices occur most frequently in Henry's speech? Do you think this is an effective way to communicate, or do you find it manipulative? Cite examples from the text to support your answer.

Literary Criticism

9. **Different Perspectives** Imagine that the following people heard Henry's speech from the visitor's gallery. How might each have reacted, and why?

   - the wife of one of the delegates
   - a farmer whose parents live in England
   - a member of the Virginia militia
   - a clergyman
   - an African enslaved in the colony

8. ● **SKILLS FOCUS Rhetorical Devices** Henry uses rhetorical questions and parallelism most often. Students may say that these devices are effective ways of presenting ideas. Others may say that the devices are manipulative because they stir emotions rather than present well-reasoned arguments.

9. *The wife might be concerned that her husband would have to fight the British. The farmer might worry that war would cut him off from his parents in England. The militiaman might be stirred by the call to action. The clergyman might respond favorably to Henry's biblical allusions. The slave might be encouraged by references to slavery to think that war would end his own bondage.*

Practice and Apply

After Reading

Use these copy masters to check understanding and provide extra support:

R RESOURCE MANAGER—Copy Masters
   Reading Check p. 352
   Rhetorical Devices p. 345
   Question Support p. 353

   Additional selection questions are provided for teachers on page 339.

ANSWERS

1. *to prepare to fight against the British*

2. *petitioning the government and asking the king to stop the tyranny*

3. *by spurning the colonists' complaints or responding violently*

Possible answers:

4. ■ **SKILLS FOCUS Reading a Persuasive Speech** *If students discover that the techniques they originally chose aren't effective, have them revise their plan.*

5. *Henry claims that hope is an illusion (line 15) and that British conduct over the last ten years gives no reason for hope (lines 24–26, 53–55). He wanted to persuade his audience to fight instead of hoping for peace.*

6. *Odyssey, lines 15–17: The hope for peace is a false lure. Bible, lines 18–19: Don't ignore clear evidence. Bible, line 28: Don't trust treacherous pretenses. Bible, lines 74–75: Our spirit can make up for our weaker force.*

7. *Reasons: 1. If we don't prepare now, we won't be able to resist (lines 56–60); emotional. 2. There are three million of us willing and able to fight (lines 70–72); logical. 3. God will help us win (lines 72–74); emotional. 4. It's too late to back down (lines 76–77); emotional. 5. The war has already begun (line 78); logical. 6. Give me liberty, or give me death (lines 84–86); emotional. Accept all reasonable ranking of reasons.*

ANSWERS

Vocabulary in Context

VOCABULARY PRACTICE

1. *false*
2. *true*
3. *false*
4. *false*
5. *false*
6. *true*
7. *true*
8. *false*
9. *false*
10. *true*

R RESOURCE MANAGER—Copy Master
Vocabulary Practice p. 350

VOCABULARY IN WRITING

Tell students to refer to the vocabulary definitions in the margin of the speech to find places where the words were used. Suggest that students discuss the same issues that prompted Henry to use these words.

VOCABULARY STRATEGY: WORDS FROM GODS AND MYTHOLOGY (also an EL language objective)

When students look up the words, tell them to notice the origin of each word as well as its meaning.

Possible answers:

1. *morose, gloomy; from Saturn, the gloomy ancestor of the gods*
2. *changeable; from Mercury, the fleet-footed, prankish messenger of the gods*
3. *merry; from Jove, the chief god, from the idea in astrology that people born under his sign will be merry*
4. *enemy; from Nemesis, the goddess of vengeance*
5. *greed; from Cupid, the god of desire*
6. *drunken, wildly carousing; from Bacchus, the god of wine*

R RESOURCE MANAGER—Copy Master
Vocabulary Strategy p. 351

ⓘ Vocabulary Center at **ClassZone.com**
Additional Vocabulary Activities

Vocabulary in Context

VOCABULARY PRACTICE

Decide whether these statements about the vocabulary words are true or false.

1. A good way to **remonstrate** with someone is to plan a picnic with that person.
2. An **invincible** chess champion is one who has not been beaten.
3. A statue that is lying **supinely** is lying face down.
4. A **vigilant** guard usually takes naps while on duty.
5. Circumstances that **extenuate** a bad decision are those that make it worse.
6. A country that is overrun by armies from another land is experiencing **subjugation.**
7. An **insidious** person is unlikely to express her opinions openly.
8. A vase that has broken into several pieces may be described as **inviolate.**
9. A **martial** gathering is one that is organized by peace demonstrators.
10. If two versions of a story **comport** with each other, they are in agreement.

WORD LIST
comport
extenuate
insidious
invincible
inviolate
martial
remonstrate
subjugation
supinely
vigilant

VOCABULARY IN WRITING

Imagine you were in the audience when Patrick Henry gave his speech. Using at least three vocabulary words, write a short explanation of why you agree or disagree with his views. Here is a sample beginning.

R1.2

> **EXAMPLE SENTENCE**
>
> I cannot agree with Mr. Henry that government by our mother country can be considered **subjugation**.

VOCABULARY STRATEGY: WORDS FROM GODS AND MYTHOLOGY

A number of English words are formed from the names of Greek and Roman gods and goddesses. Usually the meanings of these words are closely related to some characteristic the deity was known for. The vocabulary word *martial*, for example, is derived from Mars, the name of the Roman god of war.

PRACTICE For each numbered word, write a sentence that shows its meaning. Use a dictionary if you need help. Then write a short explanation connecting each word's meaning to the deity whose name it is derived from.

1. saturnine
2. mercurial
3. jovial
4. nemesis
5. cupidity
6. bacchanalian

VOCABULARY PRACTICE
For more practice, go to the **Vocabulary Center** at **ClassZone.com**.

DIFFERENTIATED INSTRUCTION

FOR ENGLISH LEARNERS

Task Support: Vocabulary in Writing Help students choose three vocabulary words. Review the word meanings orally, and invite clarifying questions. To prepare for writing, have students return to the speech and study the vocabulary words in context. Suggest that students write three sentences, using one vocabulary word per sentence.

FOR ADVANCED LEARNERS/AP

Words from Gods and Mythology Challenge students to find more English words derived from mythology. For example, *cereal* comes from Ceres, the Roman goddess of agriculture, and several words for days of the week come from Norse deities. The mythology need not be Greek or Roman; encourage students to look for words that come from other cultures.

Reading-Writing Connection

W1.1, W1.3, W1.4

WRITING PROMPT	SELF-CHECK

COMPOSE A PERSUASIVE SPEECH Patrick Henry's famous speech is a classic example of effective **oratory**, the art of public speaking. Using Henry's speech as a model, write a **three-to-five paragraph persuasive speech** on a topic you feel strongly about.

A persuasive speech will . . .
- present a clear argument
- cite reasons and other evidence
- use rhetorical devices
- close with a strong statement

GRAMMAR AND STYLE

LC1.1

VARY SENTENCE TYPES Review the **Grammar and Style** note on page 228. Part of Henry's style is to vary his sentences among the four basic types:

- **Declarative,** which expresses a statement of fact, desire, intent, or feeling and ends with a period. *This is no time for ceremony.* (line 6)

- **Interrogative,** which asks a question and ends with a question mark. *Shall we try argument?* (line 41)

- **Imperative,** which gives a command, request, or direction and ends usually with a period but sometimes for emphasis with an exclamation point. *Trust it not, sir; it will prove a snare to your feet.* (lines 27–28)

- **Exclamatory,** which expresses strong emotions and always ends with an exclamation point. *I repeat it, sir, we must fight!* (line 60)

Henry's skillful use of sentence variety is emotionally expressive and compelling. It not only creates an interesting melody, but also keeps the reader engaged by calling for frequent shifts in the reader's internal responses.

PRACTICE The following excerpt is taken from Henry's speech. For each sentence in the exercise, identify the type of sentence, and then compose your own sentence following the pattern in Henry's original. The example illustrates how.

> **EXAMPLE**
>
> The war is actually begun!
> *We won the game!*

(1) The next gale that sweeps from the north will bring to our ears the clash of resounding arms! (2) Our brethren are already in the field! (3) Why stand we here idle? (4) What is it that gentlemen wish? (5) What would they have? (6) Is life so dear, or peace so sweet, as to be purchased at the price of chains and slavery? (7) Forbid it, Almighty God!

WRITING TOOLS
For prewriting, revision, and editing tools, visit the **Writing Center** at ClassZone.com.

FOR DEVELOPING WRITERS
Writing Support

- Tell students to choose a topic quickly to avoid wasting time. Suggest that they pick an issue that they feel strongly about.

- Have students write a thesis statement and then brainstorm reasons, facts, and examples to support their views, using a cluster diagram or list.

- Have students include their thesis statement in their first paragraph and follow with two substantial body paragraphs.

- Remind students that they are writing a speech, not a paper to be read silently. Urge them to imagine an audience as they write, and to use conversational language, exclamatory sentences, and rhetorical questions.

- Suggest that students read their drafts aloud to themselves or partners.

Reading-Writing Connection

WRITING PROMPT

Suggest that students start with a quote or a catchy opening sentence. Recommend that they model their speech after Henry's by beginning with an introduction that flatters the audience and by ending with a rousing call to action. Use the Opening Lines strategy to help students compose beginnings for their speeches.

BEST PRACTICES TOOLKIT
   Opening Lines p. C1

For writing support, see

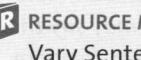 Writing Center at **ClassZone.com**

GRAMMAR AND STYLE

To familiarize students with the four types of sentences, return to lines 62–79 and ask students to find at least two examples of each type. Point out that both imperative and exclamatory sentences may end in exclamation points. (For more on sentence types, see **Grammar Handbook,** p. R64.) *Answers:*
1. *exclamatory,* **2.** *exclamatory,* **3.** *interrogative,* **4.** *interrogative,* **5.** *interrogative,* **6.** *interrogative,* **7.** *imperative*

Students' sentences should follow the pattern of Henry's original.

 RESOURCE MANAGER—Copy Master
   Vary Sentence Types p. 354

Assess and Reteach

Assess

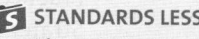 RESOURCE MANAGER—Copy Masters
   Selection Test A pp. 355–356
   Selection Test B/C pp. 357–358

Test Generator CD

Reteach

STANDARDS LESSON FILE
   Literature Lesson 35: Rhetorical Devices
   Writing Lesson 8: Creating Sentence
      Variety
   Vocabulary Lesson 25: Etymologies
   Speaking and Listening Lesson 8:
      Persuasive Speech

Focus and Motivate

OBJECTIVES

Literary Analysis
- explore the key idea of **rebellion**
- analyze a persuasive argument
- read a significant public legal document

Reading
- analyze text structure

Vocabulary
- build vocabulary for reading and writing
- understand specialized political vocabulary (also an EL language objective)

Grammar and Writing
- use complex and compound-complex sentences to vary sentence structure
- write a declaration

 R2.1, R2.2, R2.4, R2.6, R1.1, W1.1, W1.9

ABOUT THE AUTHOR

Refer students to "The Enlightenment" in the Historical Essay (page 18). Explain that Jefferson helped shape the American Enlightenment, drawing on European Enlightenment ideas about the contract between people and their rulers.

USING THE *NOTABLE QUOTE*

Ask students what **Thomas Jefferson** means by "the rights of men." *Students may say that he refers to basic civil rights, such as freedom of religion.* Then ask how the quote reflects Jefferson's times. *Possible answer: It reflects the Enlightenment focus on human rights.*

Selection Resources

The Declaration of Independence
Public Document by Thomas Jefferson

R2.1, R2.2, R2.4, R2.6, R1.1 (p. 242),
W1.1 (p. 243), **W1.9** (p. 243),
LC1.1 (p. 243)

NOTABLE QUOTE
"All eyes are opened, or opening, to the rights of men."

FYI
Did you know that Thomas Jefferson . . .
- played the violin?
- was an amateur inventor?
- developed the policy of the separation of church and state?
- favored the rights of the states over the federal government?
- died on July 4, the same day as his friend and political rival, John Adams?

Author Online
For more on Thomas Jefferson, visit the **Literature Center** at **ClassZone.com.**

Jefferson's home at Monticello

Thomas Jefferson
1743–1826

Thomas Jefferson was one of the most accomplished founding fathers. Active in the cause for independence, he was governor of Virginia during the Revolutionary War and U.S. minister to France afterward. He also served the new country as the first secretary of state, the second vice-president, and the third president. As president, he acquired the vast Louisiana Territory west of the Mississippi River to the Rocky Mountains, essentially doubling the size of the country. But more important than any political office he held was the lasting impact of Jefferson's ideals of liberty and self-government so eloquently expressed in the Declaration of Independence.

Brilliant Legal Mind The son of a surveyor and gentleman farmer, Jefferson was born into a life of privilege in rural Virginia. Educated at the College of William and Mary, he was tutored in the law and practiced successfully before entering politics at age 26. As a member of the colonial Virginia legislature, he fell in with a group of radicals, among them Patrick Henry. Lacking Henry's oratorical gifts, Jefferson distinguished himself by his legal writing. Significantly, Jefferson's indelible mark on American life came largely from the many legal documents and laws he wrote promoting democracy.

Passion for Learning Jefferson had an insatiable curiosity about the world and often indulged in what he called his "canine appetite for reading." In addition to devouring works on the classics, history, law, science, and philosophy, he taught himself architecture from books. He designed his elaborate estate at Monticello and the buildings of the University of Virginia, which he also founded as the embodiment of his principles of education and individual freedom.

The Issue of Slavery Charges of hypocrisy on the issue of slavery have tarnished Jefferson's image as the "apostle of liberty." In his early writings, he denounced slavery and tried unsuccessfully to include the issue in the Declaration. Yet Jefferson always owned slaves—as many as 600 over the course of his lifetime—and in later years, he remained undecided on this issue.

A Quintessential American Jefferson's problematic stand on slavery mirrored the nation's, which took a long time to rectify. In the end, Jefferson was a man of his time who had a noble vision for the country and the genius to articulate it, even though he did not always live up to his ideals.

RESOURCE MANAGER UNIT 1

Plan and Teach pp. 359–366

Literary Analysis
Summary pp. 367†*, 368‡*
Argument pp. 369, 370†*
Question Support p. 377*

Reading
Analyze Text Structure pp. 371, 372†*
Reading Check p. 376

Vocabulary
Study p. 373*
Practice p. 374
Strategy p. 375

Grammar and Writing
Vary Sentence Structure p. 378

Assessment
Selection Tests A, B/C pp. 379*, 381*
Test Generator CD

BEST PRACTICES TOOLKIT

Differentiated Instruction pp. 31–38*

Scaffolding Instruction pp. 43–46*

Graphic Organizers/Strategies
Word Questioning • Classification Chart • Problem and Solution Charts

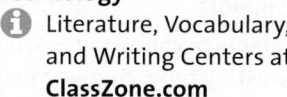 Reading Support
Audio Anthology CD*

Technology
Literature, Vocabulary, and Writing Centers at **ClassZone.com**

Write*Smart* CD

*** Resources for Differentiation**   **† Also in Spanish**   **‡ In Haitian Creole and Vietnamese**

LITERARY ANALYSIS: ARGUMENT

Jefferson's emphasis in the Declaration of Independence was on the logical argument to be made for independence. An **argument** expresses an opinion on an issue and supports it with reasons and evidence. Three important parts of an argument are

- **the claim:** the writer's position on an issue or problem
- **support:** reasons and evidence provided to prove a claim
- **counterargument:** arguments to answer opposing views

As you read, look for these elements of an argument.

READING SKILL: ANALYZE TEXT STRUCTURE

The Declaration of Independence has four main parts:

1. a **preamble,** or **foreword,** that announces the reason for the document
2. a **declaration** of people's natural rights and relationship to government
3. a long **list** of complaints against George III, the British king
4. a **conclusion** that formally states America's independence

As you read, use a chart such as the one shown to indicate the line numbers for each part, as well as a brief summary of each.

Part	Summary
1 Preamble lines 1–6	When one group of people have to form their own government, it is necessary to explain why.

▲ VOCABULARY IN CONTEXT

Match each vocabulary word in the first column with the word or phrase in the second column that is closest in meaning.

1. abdicate   a. correction
2. arbitrary   b. integrity
3. despotism   c. treachery
4. impel   d. abandon
5. mercenary   e. drive
6. perfidy   f. erratic
7. rectitude   g. a taking over
8. redress   h. hired soldier
9. unalienable   i. tyranny
10. usurpation   j. unchangeable

When is REBELLION *justified?*

KEY IDEA Many young people harbor a spirit of **rebellion**—against parents, teachers, bosses, rules, or any situation that "just isn't fair!" But how often do you attempt to explain your rebellion logically? In June of 1776, Thomas Jefferson and other colonial leaders had decided to rebel against British rule. But they needed to justify their dangerous action—to themselves, to the king, and to the world.

DISCUSS In a small group, think of several situations in which an individual or a group rebelled against a perceived injustice. The situations could be any of the following:

- local—an incident in your school or community, for example
- global—such as demonstrations against global trade policies
- historical—such as the American, French, or Russian revolutions

Then, as a group, evaluate the reasons for each rebellion and explain which ones you think are justified.

When is REBELLION *justified?*

After students read the question and **KEY IDEA**, note that Enlightenment thinker John Locke believed that **rebellion** against injustice was a basic right. Ask students whether they agree or disagree. Extend the debate during the *DISCUSS* activity.

SKILLS FOCUS

LITERARY ANALYSIS R2.4, R2.6

● ARGUMENT

Write this example of an argument on the board:

> Many people say that the loyal and friendly dog is man's (or woman's) best friend. However, I vote for the cat as our best friends. Cats are not only loyal and friendly, but also independent and undemanding. Best of all, cats make reliable foot warmers on cold nights, when dogs are snoring on the couch.

Have students identify the claim (*sentence 2*), the support (*sentences 3 and 4*), and the counterargument (*sentence 1*).

CHECK UNDERSTANDING Ask students to provide support and counterargument for this claim: "Nothing beats a climate with four seasons."

READING SKILL R2.1, R2.2

■ ANALYZE TEXT STRUCTURE

Point out that the four numbered parts listed on page 235 are elements included in most persuasive works, though with different labels. For example, a **declaration** and a **claim** are similar. Both present the writer's core position on an issue. Ask students to match the list of complaints to an element of argument (*support*).

CHECK UNDERSTANDING Ask students to suggest another common structural term for **preamble** or **foreword.**

 RESOURCE MANAGER—Copy Master
Analyze Text Structure p. 371 (for student use while reading the selection)

VOCABULARY

▲ VOCABULARY IN CONTEXT

DIAGNOSE WORD KNOWLEDGE To determine preteaching needs, have all students complete Vocabulary in Context. *Answers:* **1.** *d,* **2.** *f,* **3.** *i,* **4.** *e,* **5.** *h,* **6.** *c,* **7.** *b,* **8.** *a,* **9.** *j,* **10.** *g*

PRETEACH VOCABULARY Preteach vocabulary with this copy master. Read each item aloud.

RESOURCE MANAGER—Copy Master
Vocabulary Study p. 373

MORE VOCABULARY SUPPORT

For additional activities and guidelines, see

BEST PRACTICES TOOLKIT
Scaffolding Vocabulary Instruction pp. 43–46

ⓘ Vocabulary Center at **ClassZone.com**

SUMMARY

This public document by Thomas Jefferson asserts that the people have the right and duty to form a new government when the existing government abuses their "unalienable rights." Jefferson supports his assertion with a long list of grievances against British king George III. He then concludes with a declaration that the United Colonies are free and independent, and their connection with Great Britain dissolved.

LITERARY ANALYSIS

Ⓐ ARGUMENT

Possible answer: *Jefferson claims that the colonists owe the world an explanation for their need to sever ties with Great Britain. He says he will list the reasons that force the separation.*

If students need help . . . Refer them to the chart introduced on page 235, which provides a summary of lines 1–6. Then review this long sentence phrase by phrase, and explain the meaning of each phrase.

Part	Summary
Preamble lines 1–6	When one group of people have to form their own government, it is necessary to explain why.

The Declaration of *Independence*

Thomas Jefferson

BACKGROUND In September 1774, 56 delegates met in Philadelphia at the First Continental Congress to draw up a declaration of colonial rights. They agreed to reconvene in May 1775 if their demands weren't met. At this Second Continental Congress, Thomas Jefferson joined Benjamin Franklin and John Adams on the committee to draft the Declaration of Independence. The task of writing it fell to Jefferson. Although Congress made many changes to the list of grievances, Jefferson's declaration of rights remained untouched—an abiding testament to "self-evident" truths for the nation and the world.

ANALYZE VISUALS
This is an original copy of the Declaration. What might be some of the advantages of having the whole document appear on one large sheet of paper?

In Congress, July 4, 1776

When, in the course of human events, it becomes necessary for one people to dissolve the political bands which have connected them with another, and to assume, among the powers of the earth, the separate and equal station to which the laws of nature and of nature's God entitle them, a decent respect to the opinions of mankind requires that they should declare the causes which **impel** them to the separation. Ⓐ

We hold these truths to be self-evident:—That all men are created equal; that they are endowed by their Creator with certain **unalienable** rights; that among these are life, liberty, and the pursuit of happiness. That, to secure these
10 rights, governments are instituted among men, deriving their just powers from the consent of the governed; that, whenever any form of government becomes destructive of these ends, it is the right of the people to alter or to abolish it, and to institute a new government, laying its foundation on such principles, and organizing its powers in such form, as to them shall seem most likely to effect their safety and happiness. Prudence, indeed, will dictate that governments long established should not be changed for light and transient causes; and, accordingly,

impel (ĭm-pĕl′) v. to drive forward; force

Ⓐ ARGUMENT
What **claim** does Jefferson present in the preamble of the Declaration and what **support** does he say he will provide?

unalienable
(ŭn-āl′yə-nə-bəl) adj. not to be taken away (Today the usual form is *inalienable*.)

① Targeted Passage

DIFFERENTIATED INSTRUCTION

FOR ALL STUDENTS

Expert Groups Encourage students to become subject experts by selecting and researching one of these topics:

- John Locke and the impact of his ideas
- John Adams
- Second Continental Congress
- signers of the Declaration of Independence

FOR STRATEGIC READERS

In combination with the *Audio Anthology CD*, use one or more Targeted Passages (pp. 236, 239, 240) to ensure that students focus on key concepts in the selection. Targeted Passages are also good for English learners.

① Targeted Passage [Lines 7–15]

This passage establishes the right of the colonists to control their government.

The unanimous Declaration of the thirteen united States of America.

ANALYZE VISUALS

Possible answer: Having the document on one sheet meant that its parts could not be separated. Also, the document could be posted in one piece or easily held and read.

About the Art Copies of the newly printed Declaration of Independence went out immediately to the 13 colonies by horse and by boat. Crowds gathered to hear and cheer its reading. General George Washington read it to his troops in New York. A house painter read it to a crowd near the Massachusetts State House in Boston.

BACKGROUND

An Act of Courage On July 4, 1776, the Second Continental Congress officially approved the Declaration of Independence. Americans celebrate this event each year, perhaps without understanding the courage needed to sign this document. The 56 men who did so put their lives on the line, knowing that they would be hanged for treason if Great Britain prevailed. The odds were heavily against the colonists because of Great Britain's tremendous navy, wealth, and power. Yet those first representatives were willing to risk everything, as Thomas Jefferson so eloquently explained, for the "unalienable rights" of "life, liberty, and the pursuit of happiness."

- According to the document, what rights do people have that cannot be taken away?

- How do governments get their power?

- When do people have the right to form a new government?

FOR ENGLISH LEARNERS

Key Academic Vocabulary Use Word Questioning to teach these words: *secure* (line 9), *consent* (line 11), *commit* (line 64), *legislate* (line 76), *publish* (line 108).

 BEST PRACTICES TOOLKIT—Transparency
Word Questioning p. E9

Prereading For prereading instruction for English learners, see

BEST PRACTICES TOOLKIT
Scaffolding Reading Instruction pp. 43–46

FOR ADVANCED LEARNERS/AP

AP exercises in the bottom channel provide additional challenge for students. Use these suggestions for small groups or individuals.

ADDITIONAL GUIDELINES

For more help with differentiation and tips for classroom management, see

 BEST PRACTICES TOOLKIT
Differentiated Instruction pp. 31–38

B ARGUMENT

Possible answer: Jefferson anticipates the argument that it may be too dangerous to change a long-standing government. He claims that so many abuses have accrued that rebellion is justified (lines 19–22). He says that the British king has repeatedly injured the colonies and that he will provide facts to support his case (lines 24–27).

If students need help . . . Remind them that a counterargument responds to an opponent's views. Then read lines 15–16. Remind students that a claim is a writer's position on an issue. Then read lines 21–22.

C TEXT STRUCTURE

Possible answer: Jefferson wishes to show the overwhelming evidence that exists to support the case of the colonists. The long list makes it seem that there is virtually no end to the injuries inflicted on the colonies by an indifferent and tyrannical king.

If students need help . . . Point out the 18 separate complaints beginning with "He," each of which discusses one or more acts of the king opposed by the Colonies.

Lines 30–54
REINFORCE *KEY IDEA:* REBELLION

Discuss On the basis of Jefferson's evidence, were the Colonies justified in their **rebellion?** Explain. *Most students will say that Jefferson's long list is persuasive. Others may share the views of many colonists who believed rebellion to be an extreme measure.*

---

all experience hath shown that mankind are more disposed to suffer, while evils are sufferable, than to right themselves by abolishing the forms to which they are accustomed. But, when a long train of abuses and **usurpations,** pursuing
20 invariably the same object, evinces a design to reduce them under absolute **despotism,** it is their right, it is their duty, to throw off such government, and to provide new guards for their future security. Such has been the patient sufferance of these colonies; and such is now the necessity that constrains them to alter their former systems of government. The history of the present King of Great Britain[1] is a history of repeated injuries and usurpations, all having, in direct object, the establishment of an absolute tyranny over these States. To prove this, let facts be submitted to a candid world. **B**

He has refused his assent to laws[2] the most wholesome and necessary for the public good. **C**
30   He has forbidden his Governors to pass laws of immediate and pressing importance, unless suspended in their operation till his assent should be obtained; and, when so suspended, he has utterly neglected to attend to them.

He has refused to pass other laws for the accommodation of large districts of people, unless these people would relinquish the right of representation in the legislature—a right inestimable to them, and formidable to tyrants only.

He has called together legislative bodies at places unusual, uncomfortable, and distant from the depository of their public records, for the sole purpose of fatiguing them into compliance with his measure.

He has dissolved representative houses repeatedly, for opposing, with manly
40 firmness, his invasions on the rights of the people.

He has refused, for a long time after such dissolutions, to cause others to be elected; whereby the legislative powers, incapable of annihilation, have returned to the people at large for their exercise; the State remaining, in the meantime, exposed to all dangers of invasion from without, and convulsions within.

He has endeavored to prevent the population[3] of these States; for that purpose obstructing the laws for the naturalization of foreigners; refusing to pass others to encourage their migration hither, and raising the conditions of new appropriations of lands.

He has obstructed the administration of justice, by refusing his assent to laws
50 for establishing judiciary powers.

He has made judges dependent on his will alone for the tenure of their offices,[4] and the amount and payment of their salaries.

He has erected a multitude of new offices, and sent hither swarms of officers to harass our people and eat out their substance.[5]

---

1. **the present King of Great Britain:** George III, who reigned from 1760 to 1820.
2. **refused his assent to laws:** Laws passed in the colonies needed the king's approval; sometimes it took years for laws to be approved or rejected.
3. **to prevent the population:** to keep the population from growing.
4. **the tenure of their offices:** their job security.
5. **eat out their substance:** use up their resources.

---

usurpation (yōō′sər-pā′shən) *n.* the act of wrongfully taking over a right or power that belongs to someone else

despotism (dĕs′pə-tĭz′əm) *n.* government by a ruler with unlimited power

B ARGUMENT
What **counterargument** does Jefferson anticipate in lines 15–22? What **claim** does he make at the end of this paragraph and what does he say he is about to do?

C TEXT STRUCTURE
Why might the list of complaints make up the largest part of the four-part structure?

DIFFERENTIATED INSTRUCTION

FOR ADVANCED LEARNERS/AP

Analyze Grievances Ask students to identify categories of grievances, such as *legislative, judicial, military,* and *trade.* Then have them place specific grievances in each category. They might adapt a Classification Chart for this purpose.

 BEST PRACTICES TOOLKIT—Transparency
Classification Chart p. B17

Military grievances
Kept standing army
Quartered troops

Declaration of Independence in Congress, at the Independence Hall, Philadelphia, July 4, 1776 (1819), John Trumbull. Oil on canvas. The Granger Collection, New York.

He has kept among us, in times of peace, standing armies, without the consent of our legislatures.

He has affected to render the military independent of, and superior to, the civil power.

He has combined with others to subject us to a jurisdiction foreign to our
60 constitutions,[6] and unacknowledged by our laws; giving his assent to their acts of pretended legislation:

For quartering large bodies of armed troops among us;

For protecting them, by a mock trial, from punishment for any murders which they should commit on the inhabitants of these States;

For cutting off our trade with all parts of the world;

For imposing taxes on us without our consent;

For depriving us, in many cases, of the benefits of trial by jury;

For transporting us beyond the seas, to be tried for pretended offenses;

For abolishing the free system of English laws in a neighboring province,[7]
70 establishing there an **arbitrary** government, and enlarging its boundaries, so as to render it at once an example and fit instrument for introducing the same absolute rule into these colonies;

For taking away our charters, abolishing our most valuable laws, and altering, fundamentally, the forms of our governments;

For suspending our own legislatures, and declaring themselves invested with power to legislate for us in all cases whatsoever. **D**

---

6. **subject us . . . our constitutions:** Parliament had passed the Declaratory Act in 1766, stating that the king and Parliament could make laws for the colonies.

7. **a neighboring province:** the province of Quebec, which at the time extended south to the Ohio River and west to the Mississippi.

THE DECLARATION OF INDEPENDENCE   **239**

② Targeted Passage

arbitrary (är′bĭ-trěr′ē) *adj.* based on unpredictable decisions rather than law

D TEXT STRUCTURE
Reread lines 59–76. What is the significance of the itemized list of examples in lines 62–76?

ANALYZE VISUALS

Activity Ask students how the artist focuses viewers' attention on the document amidst so many figures. *Possible answer: In the painting, everyone's attention is directed toward the document. The glow of light on the document also draws attention to it.*

About the Art John Trumbull's oil painting measures about 30 inches wide and 20 inches high. Yet the artist fit 48 figures into this space. Jefferson stands in the middle. He is presenting the Declaration to John Hancock, president of the Second Continental Congress.

Lines 55–76
TIERED DISCUSSION PROMPTS

Use these prompts to help students understand the effect of the grievances list:

Recall What are Jefferson's purposes for listing the despotic acts of the king? *Possible answer: His purposes are to explain the need for a new government and to gain the sympathy of undecided colonists and nations.*

Interpret Reread lines 55–61. Why might each of these offenses of the king upset the colonists? *Possible answer: The colonists cannot govern themselves and make decisions that benefit them if they do not have control of the army or the government.*

Evaluate Which grievances in this passage are the most insufferable? *Students may point to the army kept on colonial soil without consent (line 55), to taxation without representation (line 66), and to the dissolution of colonial governments (lines 73–74).*

READING SKILL

D TEXT STRUCTURE
Possible answer: This list itemizes legislation of the British Parliament agreed to by the king but opposed by the Colonies.

FOR STRATEGIC READERS

② Targeted Passage [Lines 59–76]

This passage identifies legislation of the English Parliament that the Colonies oppose.

- Why do the Colonies oppose quartering the king's troops?

- Why do they oppose the king's taxes?

- Why do they oppose Parliament making laws for them?

FOR ADVANCED LEARNERS/AP

Analyze Acts [small-group option] Have students research online or in reference books acts of Parliament that drove the Colonies to rebellion, such as the Stamp Act, Townsend Acts, Tea Act, Intolerable Act, and Quartering Act. Ask small groups to share findings and create charts that show the provisions of each act. Invite groups to share and explain their charts to all students.

Discuss key concepts of self-government conveyed by the Declaration of Independence, such as the concept of sovereignty. Ask students how these concepts are reflected in America today. *Possible answer: The idea that sovereign states have the full power to "levy war, conclude peace, contract alliances, establish commerce" (lines 112–113) remains in force today.*

E GRAMMAR AND STYLE

Analyze Sentence Structure Jefferson suggests by his sentence structure that the colonists share the British public's "native justice" and "magnanimity" (lines 98–99) and therefore are entitled to British public support. Linking these ideas in one sentence is more effective than had Jefferson written two separate sentences.

LITERARY ANALYSIS

F ARGUMENT

Possible answer: Jefferson appears to be anticipating and refuting the claim that the British people were not aware of the intensity of Colonial dissatisfaction.

READING SKILL

G TEXT STRUCTURE

Possible answer: The conclusion provides a formal statement of independence.

SELECTION WRAP–UP

SUMMARIZE Have students summarize the main points of the Declaration of Independence.

⭐ CRITIQUE

- Ask students whether they think Jefferson succeeded in convincing any undecided colonists to support the rebellion.

- After completing the After Reading questions on page 241, have students revisit their responses and tell whether they have changed their opinions.

He has **abdicated** government here, by declaring us out of his protection, and waging war against us.

He has plundered our seas, ravaged our coasts, burnt our towns,[8] and destroyed
80 the lives of our people.

He is at this time transporting large armies of foreign **mercenaries** to complete the works of death, desolation, and tyranny, already begun with circumstances of cruelty and **perfidy** scarcely paralleled in the most barbarous ages, and totally unworthy the head of a civilized nation.

He has constrained our fellow citizens, taken captive on the high seas, to bear arms against their country, to become the executioners of their friends and brethren, or to fall themselves by their hands.

He has excited domestic insurrection amongst us,[9] and has endeavored to bring on the inhabitants of our frontiers the merciless Indian savages, whose known rule
90 of warfare is an undistinguished destruction of all ages, sexes, and conditions.

In every stage of these oppressions we have petitioned for **redress,** in the most humble terms; our repeated petitions have been answered only by repeated injury. A prince whose character is thus marked by every act which may define a tyrant is unfit to be the ruler of a free people.

Nor have we been wanting in our attentions to our British brethren. We have warned them, from time to time, of attempts by their legislature to extend an unwarrantable jurisdiction over us. We have reminded them of the circumstances of our emigration and settlement here. We have appealed to their native justice and magnanimity; and we have conjured them, by the ties of our common
100 kindred, to disavow these usurpations, which would inevitably interrupt our connections and correspondence. **E**

They, too, have been deaf to the voice of justice and of consanguinity.[10] We must, therefore, acquiesce in the necessity which denounces our separation; and hold them, as we hold the rest of mankind, enemies in war, in peace friends. **F**

WE, THEREFORE, THE REPRESENTATIVES OF THE UNITED STATES OF AMERICA, in General Congress assembled, appealing to the Supreme Judge of the world for the **rectitude** of our intentions, do, in the name and by the authority of the good people of these colonies, solemnly publish and declare, that these United Colonies are, and of right ought to be, Free and Independent States; that they are absolved
110 from all allegiance to the British crown, and that all political connection between them and the state of Great Britain is, and ought to be, totally dissolved; and that, as free and independent states, they have full power to levy war, conclude peace, contract alliances, establish commerce, and to do all other acts and things which independent states may of right do. And, for the support of this declaration, with a firm reliance on the protection of Divine Providence, we mutually pledge to each other our lives, our fortunes, and our sacred honor. ❧ **G**

---

8. **plundered . . . our towns:** American seaports such as Norfolk, Virginia, had already been shelled.

9. **excited . . . amongst us:** George III had encouraged slaves to rise up and rebel against their masters.

10. **deaf to . . . consanguinity:** The British have ignored pleas based on their common ancestry with the colonists.

abdicate (ăb′dĭ-kāt′) *v.* to give up responsibility for

mercenary (mûr′sə-nĕr′ē) *n.* a professional soldier hired to fight in a foreign army

perfidy (pûr′fĭ-dē) *n.* treachery

redress (rĭ-drĕs′) *n.* the correction of a wrong; compensation

E GRAMMAR AND STYLE
Reread lines 98–101. Notice how Jefferson uses a **compound-complex sentence,** which has two or more independent clauses and one or more subordinate clauses, in order to show the complex relationships between ideas.

F ARGUMENT
What objections does Jefferson appear to be anticipating and refuting with **counterarguments** in lines 102–104?

rectitude (rĕk′tĭ-tōōd′) *n.* morally correct behavior or thinking

❸ Targeted Passage

G TEXT STRUCTURE
What purpose does the final paragraph serve?

DIFFERENTIATED INSTRUCTION

FOR STRATEGIC READERS

❸ Targeted Passage [Lines 105–116]

This passage concludes the Declaration of Independence with a formal statement of the Colonies' right to be independent.

- What do the United Colonies declare to the world?

- What do they say about their ties to Great Britain?

- What powers of government do they claim for their independent state?

FOR ENGLISH LEARNERS

Comprehension: Text Structure Point out the problem-and-solution structure in the text, and have students record it in a Problem and Solution Chart. Direct them to the grievances against the king (lines 77–90), attempts to achieve justice (lines 91–101), and the action plan (lines 102–116).

 BEST PRACTICES TOOLKIT—Transparencies Problem and Solution Charts p. B20

Comprehension

R2.1, R2.2, R2.4, R2.6

1. **Recall** Name three complaints that the colonists had against the king.
2. **Recall** What rights are specified in the Declaration?
3. **Clarify** What does Jefferson say is the purpose of government?
4. **Clarify** According to the Declaration, who gives people their rights?

Literary Analysis

5. **Draw Conclusions** Which set of reasons for breaking away from British rule strikes you as most important, and why?
   - the colonists' philosophical ideals
   - the hardships colonists suffered as a result of British policies
   - the king's response to colonists' complaints

6. **Make Inferences** The Declaration clearly takes aim at the abuses of King George to justify the colonists' **rebellion.** But reread lines 102–104. To what extent does the document hold the British people responsible? What is the new relationship declared between Americans and their "British brethren," and how might it differ from the old?

7. **Analyze Diction** What is it about Jefferson's diction, or word choice and arrangement, that makes the declaration of rights so memorable? Explain the effects of the following words and phrases:
   - "We hold these truths to be self-evident" (line 7)
   - "endowed by their Creator" (line 8)
   - "unalienable rights" (line 8)
   - "secure these rights" (lines 9–10)

8. **Evaluate Text Structure** Review the chart you filled in. How effective is this four-part structure in stating the colonists' case? Would reordering the parts make any difference? Explain your answer.

9. **Evaluate Elements of an Argument** Identify the major claim and the support given in the Declaration. In your opinion, is the support sufficient for the claim? Does it have to be? Explain your answer.

10. **Compare Texts** Compare Jefferson's Declaration with Patrick Henry's speech in terms of the purpose of each.

Literary Criticism

11. **Historical Context** Jefferson's celebrated statement "All men are created equal" only applied to white men at the time. How has the meaning of Jefferson's statement changed over time? How has it stayed the same?

10. *Both men argue for rebellion on the basis of British abuses of power, but they use different rhetoric to suit different purposes. Henry uses strong emotional appeals while Jefferson is more thoughtful and deliberate, presenting a careful argument to justify forming an independent government.*

11. *Jefferson's statement has become more inclusive over the decades, expanding to apply to women and to people of color. Yet the basic concept that all people have sacred, natural rights remains a central precept of American government.*

Practice and Apply

After Reading

Use these copy masters to check understanding and provide extra support:

R RESOURCE MANAGER—Copy Masters
   Reading Check p. 376
   Argument p. 369
   Question Support p. 377

   Additional selection questions are provided for teachers on page 363.

ANSWERS

1. *Possible answers: kept a standing army, imposed taxes without consent, cut off trade*
2. *life, liberty, and the pursuit of happiness*
3. *to secure the rights, safety, and happiness of the people (lines 9–10)*
4. *God (line 8)*

Possible answers:

5. *Philosophical Ideas: Depriving them of basic rights is against natural law (lines 1–9). Hardships: Keeping an army, imposing taxes, and cutting off trade indicate disregard for their rights and their common ties (lines 28–101). King's Response: A despotic and indifferent attitude shows disregard and disrespect (lines 91–94).*

6. *The Declaration blames the British people for ignoring the colonists' appeals. It declares them no longer kin tied by blood and culture, but like any other nation: friends if at peace but enemies if at war.*

7. *Classifies human rights as a matter of reason and abiding truth; names God as the ultimate source of these sacred rights; stresses that unalienable rights are as natural as they are sacred; notes that protection of these rights is the only just purpose of government.*

8. ■ **SKILLS FOCUS Analyze Text Structure** *The four-part structure is effective in establishing the Colonies' case. Reordering it would destroy the logic and power of Jefferson's careful argument.*

9. ● **SKILLS FOCUS Argument** *The major claim is that the Colonies have the right and duty to separate from Great Britain and to form their own government. The long list of grievances supports this claim well. The Declaration needed strong evidence to win the support of undecided colonists and nations.*

242 UNIT 1: EARLY AMERICAN WRITING

ANSWERS

Vocabulary in Context

VOCABULARY PRACTICE

1. *(c) honesty*   6. *(b) model*
2. *(a) surrendering* 7. *(c) confiscate*
3. *(d) righteousness* 8. *(d) restrain*
4. *(c) mercenary*   9. *(a) tardy*
5. *(d) posture*   10. *(c) unalienable*

R RESOURCE MANAGER—Copy Master
Vocabulary Practice p. 374

VOCABULARY IN WRITING

Suggest that students start by reviewing the list of grievances in lines 28–90 and paraphrasing their meaning. As they work, have students jot down vocabulary words that might fit with each grievance.

VOCABULARY STRATEGY: POLITICAL WORDS
(also an EL language objective)

Help students to categorize the vocabulary words under types of rulers: *regency*; types of government: *oligarchy, republic*; government philosophies: *socialism, totalitarianism.*

Possible answers:

1. *oligarchy; etymology: Greek—*oligos, *"few, little"*
2. *regency; etymology: Latin—*regens, *present participle of* regere, *"to rule"*
3. *socialism; etymology: Latin—*socialis, *"of companionship"*
4. *totalitarianism; etymology:* total + *(author)*itarian
5. *republic; etymology: Latin—*respublica *(-*res, *"thing" +* publica, *"of the people")*

R RESOURCE MANAGER—Copy Master
Vocabulary Strategy p. 375

i Vocabulary Center at **ClassZone.com**
Additional Vocabulary Activities

Vocabulary in Context

VOCABULARY PRACTICE

Choose the word that is not related in meaning to the other words.

1. (a) disloyalty, (b) perfidy, (c) honesty, (d) treachery
2. (a) surrendering, (b) takeover, (c) commandeering, (d) usurpation
3. (a) despotism, (b) dictatorship, (c) tyranny, (d) righteousness
4. (a) monarch, (b) ruler, (c) mercenary, (d) king
5. (a) morality, (b) rectitude, (c) virtue, (d) posture
6. (a) redress, (b) model, (c) remedy, (d) compensation
7. (a) abandon, (b) renounce, (c) confiscate, (d) abdicate
8. (a) mobilize, (b) impel, (c) propel, (d) restrain
9. (a) tardy, (b) arbitrary, (c) unpredictable, (d) capricious
10. (a) vague, (b) unclear, (c) unalienable, (d) misleading

WORD LIST

abdicate
arbitrary
despotism
impel
mercenary
perfidy
rectitude
redress
unalienable
usurpation

VOCABULARY IN WRITING

Which grievances mentioned by Jefferson seem most serious and offensive? Write a paragraph or two explaining your ideas, using three or more vocabulary words. Here is a sample opening sentence.

> **EXAMPLE SENTENCE**
> The **usurpation** of colonists' rights to make their own laws strikes me as particularly serious.

VOCABULARY STRATEGY: POLITICAL WORDS

Many terms are used in speaking of governing systems. Some identify specific types of government; others, like the vocabulary word *despotism*, describe the practices of a government. It is useful to understand the meaning of such terms.

R1.1
CALIFORNIA

PRACTICE Choose the political word described by each numbered item. Then use a dictionary to trace the etymology of each word.

oligarchy   regency   republic   socialism   totalitarianism

1. a few people have the ruling power
2. a person rules in place of the regular ruler, who may be ill or too young
3. production of goods and services is under the control of government
4. one political group rules and suppresses all opposition, often with force
5. citizens elect representatives to manage the government

VOCABULARY PRACTICE
For more practice, go to the **Vocabulary Center** at **ClassZone.com**.

DIFFERENTIATED INSTRUCTION

FOR ENGLISH LEARNERS

Task Support: Vocabulary Practice In mixed-language groups, have students find cognates from their home languages for any of the answer choices in the activity. Ask each group to create a composite list, indicating the language of each cognate.

FOR ADVANCED LEARNERS/AP

Political Words Challenge students to identify additional words related to government, such as *democracy, monarchy, theocracy, monarch, president, premier, communism,* and *capitalism.* Have students create their own chart, using categories that they develop.

Reading-Writing Connection

 W1.1

WRITING PROMPT	SELF-CHECK
TAKE A STAND The Declaration of Independence has served as a model in several historical instances. Write a **declaration** for a group or individual of your choosing. Your declaration should have at least **three paragraphs** and be modeled on the Declaration of Independence. Feel free to be serious or lighthearted in your choice of topic.	**A good declaration will . . .** • include a brief declaration of rights • list at least ten complaints • conclude with a statement of independence or other resolution

GRAMMAR AND STYLE

 W1.9, LC1.1

VARY SENTENCE STRUCTURE Review the **Grammar and Style** note on page 240. Like most lawyers, who have to be precise as well as thorough, Jefferson uses **complex** and **compound-complex** sentences to pack in meaning.

• A **complex sentence** has one main clause (as in yellow), which can stand alone, and one or more subordinate clauses (as in green), which cannot.

A prince whose character is thus marked by every act which may define a tyrant is unfit to be the ruler of a free people. (lines 93–94)

• A **compound-complex sentence** has two or more independent clauses (as in yellow) and one or more subordinate clauses (as in green).

Such has been the patient sufferance of these colonies; and such is now the necessity that constrains them to alter their former systems of government. (lines 22–24)

PRACTICE Rewrite each pair of simple sentences as a complex or compound-complex sentence. Use the conjunction shown in parentheses. Use a comma to separate the two clauses.

> **EXAMPLE**
>
> The king exploits the people. The people move toward rebellion. (after)
> *After the king exploits the people, the people move toward rebellion.*

1. The people declare their grievances with British rule. The British king and parliament do not listen. (when)

2. The parliament learns of the dissatisfaction of the colonists. The parliament imposes even harsher laws. (as soon as)

3. The British ignore all appeals to reason. The American colonists had attempted to seek a peaceful solution. (while)

 WRITING TOOLS
For prewriting, revision, and editing tools, visit the **Writing Center** at ClassZone.com.

FOR DEVELOPING WRITERS
Writing Support

• Use the **KEY IDEA** exploration on page 235 to help students generate three ideas for a declaration.

• Have students work in small groups to brainstorm a list of complaints.

• Give students a sentence starter for a statement of independence, such as *We, therefore, being of sound mind and body, do declare that _____.*

Reading-Writing Connection

WRITING PROMPT
Suggest that students reread the **KEY IDEA** exploration on page 235 and recall situations they discussed as possible topics for their declaration. After choosing a situation, they might brainstorm complaints for their list.

For writing support, see

 Writing Center at **ClassZone.com**

GRAMMAR AND STYLE

• Have students read the examples of complex and compound-complex sentences and explain why each clause is independent or subordinate. Then ask them to complete the **PRACTICE.**

• For more on complex and compound-complex sentences, see **Grammar Handbook,** p. R68.

ANSWERS

1. *When the people declare their grievances with British rule, the king and parliament do not listen.*

2. *As soon as the parliament learns of the dissatisfaction of the colonists, it imposes even harsher laws.*

3. *The British ignored all appeals to reason, while the American colonists had attempted to seek a peaceful solution.*

R RESOURCE MANAGER—Copy Master
Vary Sentence Structure p. 378

Assess and Reteach

Assess

R RESOURCE MANAGER—Copy Masters
Selection Test A pp. 379–380
Selection Test B/C pp. 381–382

Test Generator CD

Reteach

S STANDARDS LESSON FILE
Informational Text Lesson 14: Elements of an Argument
Informational Text Lesson 20: Reading Public and Legal Documents
Writing Lesson 5: Combining Sentences and Sentence Parts

Focus and Motivate

OBJECTIVES

Literary Analysis
- explore the key idea of **loyalty**
- analyze persuasive techniques
- read a persuasive essay

Reading
- analyze main ideas and supporting details

Vocabulary
- build vocabulary for reading and writing
- use words from Middle English to build meaning *(also an EL language objective)*

CALIFORNIA R2.6

ABOUT THE AUTHOR

After students read about Thomas Paine, clarify that the January 1776 publication of *Common Sense* formed a backdrop for publication later that year of the selection, the first in a series of 16 "Crisis" papers. Explain further that Paine's call for independence in *Common Sense* was an act of high treason punishable by death. The pamphlet reached more people than any other political publication of that era. Challenge students to explain why Paine's raw, energetic language would be so important in calls for a popular revolution.

USING THE *NOTABLE QUOTE*

Ask students to consider what the quote reveals about **Thomas Paine's** character and political beliefs. *Students should recognize Paine's uncompromising opposition to all forms of oppression.*

---

from **The Crisis**

Essay by Thomas Paine

CALIFORNIA R2.6

NOTABLE QUOTE
"O! Ye that love mankind! Ye that dare oppose not only tyranny but the tyrant, stand forth!"

FYI
Did you know that Thomas Paine . . .
- failed out of school by age 12?
- was fired twice from a job as tax collector?
- didn't come to America until he was 37 years old?
- became involved in the French Revolution?

Author Online
For more on Thomas Paine, visit the **Literature Center** at **ClassZone.com**.

Thomas Paine
1737–1809

Brash, bold, and fearless—and at times angry and offensive—Thomas Paine was the firebrand of the American Revolution. In the fall of 1775, few American leaders dared to advocate openly for independence. Not only did they risk being accused of treason, they were uncertain how the common people would react to such a radical notion. They turned to Tom Paine to test the waters. Paine had arrived in Philadelphia from London only the year before but was already gaining a reputation as a revolutionary writer. He eagerly took up the task and in a few months wrote *Common Sense* (1776), a 50-page pamphlet that attacked the injustices of hereditary rule and urged the colonists to form their own independent country where "the law is king." Paine's pamphlet sold 120,000 copies in the first three months. Six months later, the colonies declared their independence.

New Voice for a New Political Audience Paine's political ideas in *Common Sense* were not particularly new or original. In the Age of Enlightenment, intellectual circles were buzzing with talk of natural rights and democracy. What was new was Paine's voice—raw, direct, full of energy. Unlike most political writers of the day, such as Thomas Jefferson, Paine addressed common men—farmers, craftsmen, and laborers—not the educated elite. His straightforward prose reinforced his democratic message that all men were capable of understanding and participating in government. People responded because Paine spoke their language. In his native England, he had worked as sailor, teacher, customs officer, grocer, and maker of ladies' corsets. He envisioned America as the place where working men like him could have political and economic power.

Limits of Success With American independence won, Paine left for Europe in 1787 to join the reform efforts brewing there. But his outspokenness got him into trouble in both conservative England and revolutionary France. His last major work, *The Age of Reason* (1794, 1795), attacked organized religion and alienated many of his supporters. By the time he returned to the United States in 1802, few politicians wanted to associate with him. He spent his last years in poverty and obscurity.

Legacy Despite Paine's later decline, his contribution to the intellectual and cultural life of Revolutionary America is indisputable. He was the radical the country needed, the spokesman for new American values and ideals.

Selection Resources

 RESOURCE MANAGER UNIT 1

Plan and Teach pp. 383–390

Literary Analysis
Summary pp. 391†*, 392‡*
Persuasive Techniques
  pp. 393, 394†*
Question Support p. 401*

Reading
Analyze Main Ideas and Support
  pp. 395, 396†*
Reading Check p. 400

Vocabulary
Study p. 397*
Practice p. 398
Strategy p. 399

Assessment
Selection Tests A, B/C
  pp. 403*, 405*
 Test Generator CD

 BEST PRACTICES TOOLKIT
Differentiated Instruction
  pp. 31–38*
Scaffolding Instruction
  pp. 43–46*
Graphic Organizers/Strategies
Word Squares

Reading Support
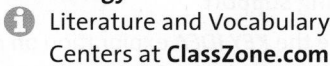 Audio Anthology CD*

Technology
Literature and Vocabulary Centers at **ClassZone.com**
WriteSmart CD

---

 * Resources for Differentiation   † Also in Spanish   ‡ In Haitian Creole and Vietnamese

LITERARY ANALYSIS: PERSUASIVE TECHNIQUES

Thomas Paine used a number of **persuasive techniques** in *The Crisis* to persuade Americans to join the cause.

- **Emotional appeals** are attempts to persuade by eliciting strong feelings, such as pity or fear.
- **Ethical appeals** call upon readers' sense of right and wrong.
- **Appeals to association** imply that one will gain acceptance or prestige by taking the writer's position.
- **Appeals to authority** call upon experts or others who warrant respect.

As you read, notice how Paine uses persuasive techniques in making various kinds of appeals to his audience.

READING SKILL: ANALYZE MAIN IDEAS AND SUPPORT

Paine supports his main ideas with reasons and evidence. As you read, use a chart such as the one shown to record main ideas and the reasons or evidence Paine uses to support those ideas.

Main Ideas	Reasons and Evidence
I see no real cause for fear.	made an orderly retreat; kept guns and ammunition

▲ VOCABULARY IN CONTEXT

Complete each phrase with the appropriate word from the list.

WORD LIST		
ardor	infidel	repulse
celestial	prudent	tyranny
dominion	relinquish	wrangling
esteem		

1. a wise ruler with _____ over a large kingdom
2. _____ brothers who never seemed to get along
3. able to _____ the enemy with our superior weapons
4. will fight _____ and other forms of oppression
5. a _____ decision in dangerous circumstances
6. should respect and _____ one's parents
7. would not _____ control of the property
8. music so sweet it seemed _____
9. expressed his _____ in mushy love poems
10. everyone welcome, believer or _____

Whose SIDE *are you on?*

KEY IDEA Loyalty is a value easily expressed but often difficult to uphold. Situations change, doubts creep in, and conflicts arise that can test the strongest bonds of loyalty. Paine's essay addresses the crisis of loyalty threatening the ranks of American soldiers during the dark days of the Revolutionary War.

QUICKWRITE Think about a time when your loyalty was tested and you were tempted to switch sides or give up. In a short paragraph, briefly describe the situation and explain what you decided. What was the most crucial factor in your decision?

245

Whose SIDE *are you on?*

Lead into the question and **KEY IDEA** by asking students for definitions of **loyalty.** Urge them to identify people and institutions that inspire loyalty, such as family, friends, or school. After students complete the **QUICK-WRITE,** have them revisit their definitions. Invite students to share and explain any revisions they would now make.

SKILLS FOCUS

LITERARY ANALYSIS R2.6

● PERSUASIVE TECHNIQUES

Share these examples of persuasive appeals:

- Basketball star Jo Hopper says Leaping Lizards shoes made all the difference in the world to her game.
- Join the parade of athletes and movie stars who wear Leaping Lizards.
- Do you want to be cool and hip? Then buy a pair of Leaping Lizards shoes today.

Ask students to identify the appeal in each example. **Answers:** *authority, association, emotional*

CHECK UNDERSTANDING Ask students what emotions the last example appeals to.

READING SKILL

■ ANALYZE MAIN IDEAS AND SUPPORT

Ask students which sentence states the main idea of **New Voice for a New Political Audience** in the author biography. **Answer:** *The third sentence states the main idea.* Have students identify one supporting detail. **Possible answer:** *Paine addresses common men, not the elite.*

 RESOURCE MANAGER—Copy Master Analyze Main Ideas and Support p. 395 (for student use while reading the selection)

VOCABULARY

▲ VOCABULARY IN CONTEXT

DIAGNOSE WORD KNOWLEDGE To determine preteaching needs, have all students complete Vocabulary in Context. **Answers:**
1. *dominion,* 2. *wrangling,* 3. *repulse,*
4. *tyranny,* 5. *prudent,* 6. *esteem,* 7. *relinquish,*
8. *celestial,* 9. *ardor,* 10. *infidel*

PRETEACH VOCABULARY Preteach vocabulary with this copy master. Read each item aloud.

 RESOURCE MANAGER—Copy Master Vocabulary Study p. 397

MORE VOCABULARY SUPPORT For additional activities and guidelines, see

BEST PRACTICES TOOLKIT Scaffolding Vocabulary Instruction pp. 43–46
ⓘ Vocabulary Center at **ClassZone.com**

SUMMARY

In this excerpt from his essay "The Crisis," Thomas Paine calls upon all colonists to stand firm and united despite recent military setbacks. There is no cause for fear, he argues. Their ranks and supplies are intact. God is on their side. With resolve and perseverance, they will win this war. He points out that the king's bids for peace are trickery, while independence is inevitable.

LITERARY ANALYSIS

Ⓐ PERSUASIVE TECHNIQUES

Possible answer: Loaded words include "shrink," "love," "Tyranny," "hell," "glorious," "triumph," "Heaven," "celestial," "slavery," "impious," and "God." Paraphrase of lines 1–12: These are difficult times. Some soldiers and citizens serve their country only in easy circumstances; those who stand up for their country in a time of crisis deserve credit and thanks. Overcoming a strong king is not easy. Accomplishing such a task makes the victory more meaningful. Winning freedom, in particular, has great value. Britain, with its powerful army, has asserted its authority not only to tax us, but also to make and enforce laws without our consent. No ruler on earth has the right to do this.

If students need help . . . Alternate reading aloud a sentence from "The Crisis" and a sentence of the paraphrase.

The CRISIS

Thomas Paine

ANALYZE VISUALS
A minuteman was pledged to be ready to fight on a minute's notice. What does this suggest about the preparedness of the colonists?

tyranny (tĭr'ə-nē) *n.* cruel and oppressive government or rule

esteem (ĭ-stēm') *v.* to set a high value on

celestial (sə-lĕs'chəl) *adj.* heavenly

BACKGROUND On the blustery Christmas Eve of 1776, the situation looked bleak for the Continental Army. General Washington's ragtag troops had retreated to the western banks of the Delaware River. Tom Paine was camped with them. The British were within striking distance of Philadelphia, and Washington knew he had to advance the next day or risk losing the war. To boost the morale of his ill-equipped and outnumbered soldiers, he ordered his officers to read aloud the following essay, which Paine had written the day before.

These are the times that try men's souls: The summer soldier and the sunshine patriot will, in this crisis, shrink from the service of his country; but he that stands it NOW, deserves the love and thanks of man and woman. **Tyranny,** like hell, is not easily conquered; yet we have this consolation with us, that the harder the conflict, the more glorious the triumph. What we obtain too cheap, we **esteem** too lightly:—' Tis dearness only that gives every thing its value. Heaven knows how to set a proper price upon its goods; and it would be strange indeed, if so **celestial** an article as FREEDOM should not be highly rated. Britain, with an army to enforce her tyranny, has declared, that she has a right (*not only to* TAX) but "to BIND us in
10 ALL CASES WHATSOEVER,"[1] and if *being bound in that manner* is not slavery, then there is not such a thing as slavery upon earth. Even the expression is impious, for so unlimited a power can only belong to God. Ⓐ

Ⓐ PERSUASIVE TECHNIQUES
Identify the **loaded language**—words with strong connotations—in lines 1–12. Then paraphrase the lines using neutral language.

① **Targeted Passage**

1. **"to BIND us in ALL CASES WHATSOEVER":** a reference to wording in the Declaratory Act of 1766, in which the British parliament asserted its "power and authority" to make and enforce laws over the American colonies.

Minute Man: Liberty or Death. Private collection.
© Scala/Art Resource, New York.

246 UNIT 1: EARLY AMERICAN WRITING

DIFFERENTIATED INSTRUCTION

FOR ALL STUDENTS

Expert Groups Encourage students to become subject experts by selecting and researching one of these topics:

- British campaign in the Middle states, 1776
- General William Howe
- Hessian mercenaries in the British army
- significance of the Battle of Trenton

FOR STRATEGIC READERS

In combination with the *Audio Anthology CD*, use one or more Targeted Passages (pp. 246, 248, 250) to ensure that students focus on key concepts in this selection. Targeted Passages are also good for English learners.

① **Targeted Passage [Lines 1–12]**

This passage defines a patriot, describes freedom as a worthy goal, and identifies the British as the patriots' enemy.

MINUTE MAN

LIBERTY
OR
DEATH

1774
-75

ANALYZE VISUALS

Possible answer: The name "minuteman" suggests that the colonists were ready, willing, and able to fight anytime, anyplace.

About the Art The minutemen fought the redcoats in the initial skirmishes at Lexington and Concord in April 1775. The colonists began calling for the formation of a "Grand American Army." On June 15, 1775, the Continental Congress elected George Washington as general. His job was to shape the ragtag colonial fighters, including the minutemen, into a disciplined, united Continental Army.

BACKGROUND

Surprise Attack By the late fall of 1776, British troops under General William Howe had pushed the Continental Army commanded by General George Washington across the Delaware River into Pennsylvania. Howe's troops, which included both British soldiers and paid Hessian mercenaries, settled in New Jersey and proceeded to loot, murder, and pillage. Meanwhile, the vast majority of Washington's troops had either deserted, been captured, or had expired enlistments, and fewer than 6,000 men remained under his command. On Christmas Eve of 1776, Washington prepared his men for an attack on Trenton, New Jersey, in part by having them listen to "The Crisis." The Continental Army surprised Howe's troops and won an easy victory. Washington's army took more than 900 prisoners and killed nearly 30. No colonists died, and only a few were wounded.

- Who does Paine thank in the opening?
- What does Paine say gives freedom its value?
- What words does Paine use to describe the actions of the British?

FOR ENGLISH LEARNERS

Key Academic Vocabulary Use Word Squares to teach these words: *enforce* (line 8), *principle* (line 42), *individual* (line 70), *link* (line 97), *credit* (line 104).

📦 BEST PRACTICES TOOLKIT—Transparency
Word Squares p. E10

Prereading For prereading instruction for English learners, see

📦 BEST PRACTICES TOOLKIT
Scaffolding Reading Instruction pp. 43–46

FOR ADVANCED LEARNERS/AP

AP exercises in the bottom channel provide additional challenge for students. Use these suggestions for small groups or individuals.

ADDITIONAL GUIDELINES

For more help with differentiation and tips for classroom management, see

📦 BEST PRACTICES TOOLKIT
Differentiated Instruction pp. 31–38

B MAIN IDEAS AND SUPPORT

Possible answer: *Paine says that, with time and resolve, the colonists will recover whatever they may have lost to the British under General Howe (lines 18–21). He also attributes Howe's recent victories to bad timing for the colonists (lines 13–17).*

If students need help . . . Show them how to record the main idea and support in a chart like the one introduced on page 245.

Main Ideas	Reasons and Evidence
All is not lost.	• Howe's ravage is not a real conquest. • With time and resolve, the colonists will recover their position.

C PERSUASIVE TECHNIQUES

Possible answer: *He says a parent should be more concerned about peace in his child's lifetime than in his own.*

If students need help . . . Read the italic text in lines 35–36 and clarify that Paine sees this as a selfish parent's statement. Then read the italic text in lines 37–38. Point out the word *generous* (line 37) and explain that it is a clue that Paine prefers the second statement from a parent to the first.

Extend the Discussion What is the emotional effect of this appeal?

Lines 47–51
REINFORCE *KEY IDEA:* LOYALTY

Discuss Paine calls for the continued support of the patriot cause with the "warm ardor of a friend." How might this particular appeal to **loyalty** affect Paine's audience? ***Possible answer:*** *By calling himself a friend, Paine suggests that he has the patriots' best interests at heart. This implies that his call for help from all citizens and States is a call for loyalty to friendship.*

Whether the Independence of the Continent was declared too soon, or delayed too long, I will not now enter into as an argument; my own simple opinion is, that had it been eight months earlier, it would have been much better. We did not make a proper use of last winter, neither could we, while we were in a dependant state. However, the fault, if it were one, was all our own; we have none to blame but ourselves. But no great deal is lost yet; all that Howe has been doing for this month past is rather a ravage than a conquest which the spirit of the Jersies a year
20 ago would have quickly repulsed, and which time and a little resolution will soon recover. **B**

   I have as little superstition in me as any man living, but my secret opinion has ever been, and still is, that God almighty will not give up a people to military destruction, or leave them unsupportedly to perish, who had so earnestly and so repeatedly sought to avoid the calamities of war, by every decent method which wisdom could invent. Neither have I so much of the **infidel** in me, as to suppose, that he has **relinquished** the government of the world, and given us up to the care of devils; and as I do not, I cannot see on what grounds the king of Britain can look up to heaven for help against us: A common murderer, a highwayman, or a
30 housebreaker, has as good a pretense as he. . . .

   I once felt all that kind of anger, which a man ought to feel, against the mean principles that are held by the Tories:[2] A noted one, who kept a tavern at Amboy,[3] was standing at his door, with as pretty a child in his hand, about eight or nine years old, as most I ever saw, and after speaking his mind as freely as he thought was **prudent,** finished with this unfatherly expression, *"Well! give me peace in my day."* Not a man lives on the Continent but fully believes that a separation must some time or other finally take place, and a generous parent would have said, *"If there must be trouble, let it be in my day, that my child may have peace;"* and this single reflection, well applied, is sufficient to awaken every man to duty. Not a
40 place upon earth might be so happy as America. Her situation is remote from all the **wrangling** world, and she has nothing to do but trade with them. A man may easily distinguish in himself between temper and principle, and I am as confident, as I am that God governs the world, that America will never be happy until she gets clear of foreign **dominion**. Wars, without ceasing, will break out until that period arrives, and the Continent must in the end be conqueror; for, though the flame of liberty may sometimes cease to shine, the coal never can expire. . . . **C**

   I turn with the warm **ardor** of a friend to those who have nobly stood, and are yet determined to stand the matter out: I call not upon a few, but upon all; not on this State or that State, but on every State; up and help us; lay your shoulders to
50 the wheel; better have too much force than too little, when so great an object is at stake. Let it be told to the future world, that in the depth of winter, when nothing but hope and virtue could survive, that the city and the country, alarmed at one

---

2. **the mean principles . . . Tories:** the small-minded beliefs of those colonists who remain loyal to Great Britain.
3. **Amboy:** probably Perth Amboy, a town in New Jersey.

How does Paine support his main idea that all is not lost for the colonists, despite their military defeats?

2 Targeted Passage

infidel (ĭn′fĭ-dəl) *n.* a person with no religious beliefs

relinquish (rĭ-lĭng′kwĭsh) *v.* to withdraw from; to give up

prudent (prōōd′nt) *adj.* showing caution or good judgment

wrangling (răng′glĭng) *adj.* arguing noisily **wrangle** *v.*

dominion (də-mĭn′yən) *n.* control; authority over

C PERSUASIVE TECHNIQUES
Notice that Paine makes an **ethical appeal** in lines 31–39. How does he say a parent should behave?

ardor (är′dər) *n.* intense enthusiasm; passion

DIFFERENTIATED INSTRUCTION

FOR STRATEGIC READERS

2 Targeted Passage [Lines 22–30]

In this passage, Paine asserts the justness of the patriots' cause.

• How does Paine answer those who say that the Colonies should have tried harder to avoid war?

• Why does Paine think that God would be on the side of the Colonies?

• To whom does he compare the king?

FOR ENGLISH LEARNERS

Language: Pronoun Referents Use the context to help students identify the antecedents of these difficult pronouns: *one* (line 17), fault (line 17); *who* (line 24), people (line 23); *he* (line 30), king (line 28); *her* (line 40) and *she* (line 41), America (line 40); *that* (line 61) and *he whose* (line 62), man (line 60); *those* (line 67), people in his house; *it* (line 68), [Paine's] house (line 66).

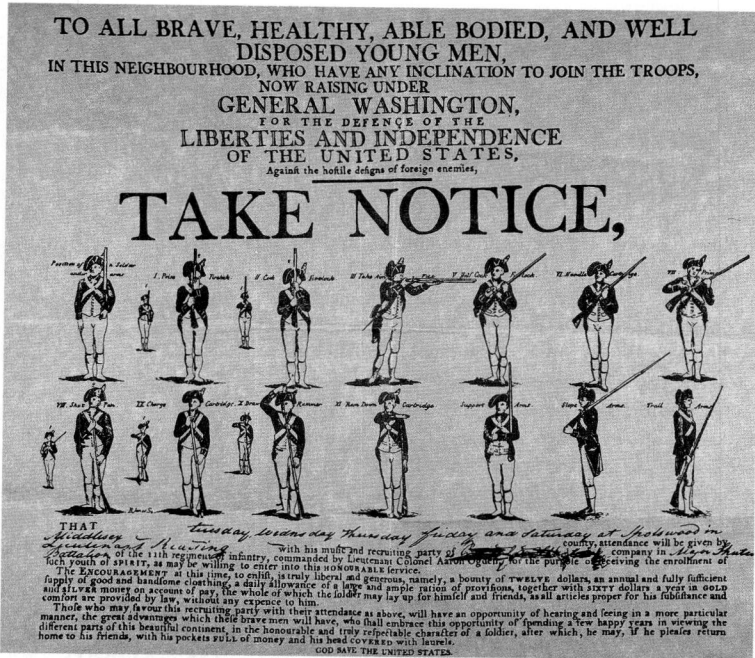

TO ALL BRAVE, HEALTHY, ABLE BODIED, AND WELL
DISPOSED YOUNG MEN,
IN THIS NEIGHBOURHOOD, WHO HAVE ANY INCLINATION TO JOIN THE TROOPS,
NOW RAISING UNDER
GENERAL WASHINGTON,
FOR THE DEFENCE OF THE
LIBERTIES AND INDEPENDENCE
OF THE UNITED STATES,
Against the hostile designs of foreign enemies,

TAKE NOTICE,

common danger, came forth to meet and to **repulse** it. Say not, that thousands are gone, turn out your tens of thousands; throw not the burden of the day upon Providence, but *"shew your faith by your works,"* that God may bless you. It matters not where you live, or what rank of life you hold, the evil or the blessing will reach you all. The far and the near, the home counties and the back, the rich and the poor, shall suffer or rejoice alike. The heart that feels not now, is dead: The blood of his children shall curse his cowardice, who shrinks back at a time

60 when a little might have saved the whole, and made *them* happy. I love the man that can smile in trouble, that can gather strength from distress, and grow brave by reflection. 'Tis the business of little minds to shrink; but he whose heart is firm, and whose conscience approves his conduct, will pursue his principles unto death. My own line of reasoning is to myself as strait and clear as a ray of light. **D** Not all the treasures of the world, so far as I believe, could have induced me to support an offensive war, for I think it murder; but if a thief break into my house, burn and destroy my property, and kill or threaten to kill me, or those that are in it, and to *"bind me in all cases whatsoever,"* to his absolute will, am I to suffer it?

repulse (rǐ-pŭls') *v.* to drive back by force

D PERSUASIVE TECHNIQUES
Reread lines 58–64. Identify some examples of loaded words and phrases in this passage. What point is Paine making about those who refuse to act?

THE CRISIS **249**

FOR ADVANCED LEARNERS/AP
Analyze Persuasive Arguments [small-group option] How strong is Paine's case, beyond his emotional appeals and his loaded words? Have small groups identify Paine's claims and supports and analyze their effectiveness. Ask each group to create an analysis chart of Paine's claims. Show this example for the claim made in paragraph one of the essay:

Claim: The harder the conflict, the greater the victory (lines 4–5)	Reason 1: People don't value success that comes too easily.	Analysis: This is an effective argument that appeals to people's desire to master difficult challenges.

Have groups share findings with the class.

ANALYZE VISUALS
Possible answer: The broadside appeals to the colonists' feelings of loyalty and justice and their desire to be brave, healthy, strong, and worthy.

LITERARY ANALYSIS

D PERSUASIVE TECHNIQUES

Possible answer: Loaded words and phrases include "The heart that feels not now is dead" (line 58), "The blood of his children shall curse his cowardice" (line 59), "'Tis the business of little minds to shrink" (line 62), and "will pursue his principles unto death" (line 63). Paine's point is that those who do not act are cowards, are failing their children, and have small minds.

If students need help . . . Remind them that loaded language carries strong emotional connotations that stir people's feelings.

Lines 53–68
TIERED DISCUSSION PROMPTS

Use these prompts to help students understand Paine's appeal for unity and support:

Connect Think about situations when people in your community or family joined together for a common cause. How does that experience help you understand Paine's appeal? *Accept all thoughtful responses.*

Interpret Paine says that nothing could have made him "support an offensive war." What does he mean? *Possible answer: Paine means that the colonies did not start the war; that they are only defending their homes and property. Therefore, their fighting is justified.*

Evaluate How effective is Paine's comment that "The blood of his children shall curse his cowardice, who shrinks back at a time when a little might have saved the whole, and made *them* happy"? *Students may say that Paine's appeal is overblown, but most will note the validity and strength of the argument that parents should stand up for their children's sake. They may also point out that this comment connects effectively with Paine's earlier example of the man from Amboy who thought of himself before his child (lines 31–40).*

THE CRISIS **249**

Lines 69–76
REINFORCE *KEY IDEA*: LOYALTY

Discuss Why does Paine say that he feels no **loyalty** to the King? *Possible answer: He says that the king is a "sottish, stupid, stubborn, worthless, brutish man" (lines 75–76) for his actions toward the Colonies, and therefore deserves no loyalty.*

LITERARY ANALYSIS

ⓔ PERSUASIVE TECHNIQUES

Possible answer: Paine states in line 79 that some situations cannot be overstated. This suggests that persuasive language such as "cunning of the fox" (line 84), "violence of the wolfe" (line 84), "threats" (line 85), "terrify or seduce" (line 86), "prey to the Indians" (line 91), "barbarous destruction" (line 99), and "rogues or fools" (line 99) does not overstate the reality and that Paine is using this language deliberately.

What signifies it to me, whether he who does it, is a king or a common man; my
70 countryman or not my countryman? whether it is done by an individual villain, or an army of them? If we reason to the root of things we shall find no difference; neither can any just cause be assigned why we should punish in the one case, and pardon in the other. Let them call me rebel, and welcome, I feel no concern from it; but I should suffer the misery of devils, were I to make a whore of my soul by swearing allegiance to one, whose character is that of a sottish, stupid, stubborn, worthless, brutish man. I conceive likewise a horrid idea in receiving mercy from a being, who at the last day shall be shrieking to the rocks and mountains to cover him, and fleeing with terror from the orphan, the widow and the slain of America.

There are cases which cannot be overdone by language, and this is one. There
80 are persons too who see not the full extent of the evil that threatens them; they solace themselves with hopes that the enemy, if they succeed, will be merciful. It is the madness of folly to expect mercy from those who have refused to do justice; and even mercy, where conquest is the object, is only a trick of war: The cunning of the fox is as murderous as the violence of the wolfe; and we ought to guard equally against both. Howe's first object is partly by threats and partly by promises, to terrify or seduce the people to deliver up their arms, and receive mercy. The ministry recommended the same plan to Gage, and this is what the Tories call making their peace; *"a peace which passeth all understanding"* indeed! A peace which would be the immediate forerunner of a worse ruin than any we
90 have yet thought of. Ye men of Pennsylvania, do reason upon those things! Were the back counties to give up their arms, they would fall easy prey to the Indians, who are all armed: This perhaps is what some Tories would not be sorry for. Were the home counties to deliver up their arms, they would be exposed to the resentment of the back counties, who would then have it at their power to chastise their defection at pleasure. And were any one State to give up its arms, that State must be garrisoned by all Howe's army of Britons and Hessians to preserve it from the anger of the rest. Mutual fear is a principal link in the chain of mutual love, and woe be the State that breaks the compact. Howe is mercifully inviting you to barbarous destruction, and men must be either rogues or fools that will not see it.
100 I dwell not upon the vapours of imagination; I bring reason to your ears; and in language, as plain as A, B, C, hold up truth to your eyes. ⓔ

I thank God that I fear not. I see no real cause for fear. I know our situation well, and can see the way out of it. While our army was collected, Howe dared not risk a battle, and it is no credit to him that he decamped from the White Plains, and waited a mean opportunity to ravage the defenceless Jersies; but it is great credit to us, that, with an handful of men, we sustained an orderly retreat for near an hundred miles, brought off our ammunition, all our field-pieces, the greatest part of our stores, and had four rivers to pass. None can say that our retreat was

❸ Targeted Passage

ⓔ PERSUASIVE TECHNIQUES
Reread lines 79–101. What statement does Paine make about the use of language at the beginning of this paragraph? What does this tell you about his use of **emotional appeals** and loaded language in this piece?

DIFFERENTIATED INSTRUCTION

FOR STRATEGIC READERS
❸ Targeted Passage [Lines 85–99]

In this passage, Paine warns that believing Howe's promises of peace is dangerous.

- What does Howe offer to get the colonists to accept his terms?
- What will happen to the back counties if they give up their arms?
- How will the other states react if one state gives up arms?

Washington Crossing the Delaware (1851), Eastman Johnson. Copy after the Emmanuel Leutze painting in the Metropolitan Museum, New York. Private collection. © Art Resource, New York.

precipitate, for we were near three weeks in performing it, and the country might
110 have time to come in. Twice we marched back to meet the enemy and remained
out till dark. The sign of fear was not seen in our camp, and had not some of the
cowardly and disaffected inhabitants spread false alarms through the country, the
Jersies had never been ravaged. Once more we are again collected and collecting;
our new army at both ends of the Continent is recruiting fast, and we shall be
able to open the next campaign with sixty thousand men, well armed and clothed.
This is our situation, and who will may know it. By perseverance and fortitude
we have the prospect of a glorious issue; by cowardice and submission, the sad
choice of a variety of evils—a ravaged country—a depopulated city—habitations
without safety, and slavery without hope—our homes turned into barracks and
120 bawdy-houses for Hessians, and a future race to provide for whose fathers we shall
doubt of. Look on this picture, and weep over it!—and if there yet remains one
thoughtless wretch who believes it not, let him suffer it unlamented. ◆ **F**

ANALYZE VISUALS
What figures and objects are emphasized by the **composition**, or the arrangement of shapes? Consider what this emphasis adds to the painting's meaning.

F MAIN IDEAS AND SUPPORT
The main idea is stated in the first line of this paragraph. What evidence does Paine give to support the idea that there is no cause for fear?

THE CRISIS **251**

ANALYZE VISUALS
Possible answer: The golden light makes Washington and the American flag the focal point of the painting and draws attention toward these figures. The light is like a halo. This visual metaphor underscores the superhuman task facing Washington and the divine quality of his undertaking.

About the Art Clarify that Eastman Johnson was a student of Emanuel Gottlieb Leutze, who first painted this scene. This heroic scene of Washington and his army at their most trying moment may be the most famous image of the Revolutionary War.

READING SKILL

F MAIN IDEAS AND SUPPORT
Possible answer: He says there is no cause for fear because the retreat was orderly (lines 106–107); the men saved their guns, ammunition, and supplies (lines 107–108); the men remain in good spirits (line 111); the army is gaining recruits (lines 111–115); and they will have over 60,000 men in the next campaign (line 115).

SELECTION WRAP–UP

SUMMARIZE Have students sum up Paine's message to Washington's soldiers.

★ CRITIQUE

- Ask students to evaluate the likely effect of Paine's message on the soldiers.
- After completing the After Reading questions on page 252, have students revisit their responses and tell whether they have changed their opinions.

FOR ENGLISH LEARNERS
Vocabulary Support: Outdated Forms Help students use context to define these forms no longer in common use: *who see not* (line 80), "who do not see"; *a peace which passeth* (line 88), "a peace which passes"; *near* (line 106), current usage would be *nearly* as an adverb; *an hundred* (line 107), in current usage would be *a* in front of a word beginning with *h*; *believes it not* (line 122), "does not believe it."

FOR ADVANCED LEARNERS/AP
Analyze Figurative Language [paired option] Thomas Paine uses imagery, metaphor, and simile throughout "The Crisis." For example, he writes that "The cunning of the fox is as murderous as the violence of the wolfe . . . (line 84) and "Mutual fear is a principal link in the chain of mutual love" (line 97). Have partners work together to identify and analyze examples of figurative language from "The Crisis."

Have students consider these questions: What function does figurative language serve in this essay? What is its emotional impact? How does it help Paine's audience to understand his themes? Allow time for students to share their findings and to discuss the effect of Paine's figurative language.

Practice and Apply

After Reading

Use these copy masters to check understanding and provide extra support:

R RESOURCE MANAGER—Copy Masters
Reading Check p. 400
Persuasive Techniques p. 393
Question Support p. 401

Additional selection questions are
provided for teachers on page 387.

ANSWERS

1. *perseverance and fortitude*

2. *They tried everything they could to avoid
war. God would not favor the cause of a
murderer such as the king.*

3. *Like fair-weather friends, they join in good
times and disappear in difficult times.*

Possible answers:

4. *He means that liberty can be temporarily suppressed but cannot die. The image
inspires loyalty by carrying the positive
connotation of home and hearth, and by
underscoring the idea that the fight is for
everything the soldiers hold dear.*

5. ■ **SKILLS FOCUS** Analyze Main Ideas and
Support *If we stand firm, we will triumph:
freedom is celestial (reason), impious enemy
goal (fact); We fought too late: troops could
have won last year (reason); God will not
allow our defeat: king is murderer (reason),
we tried to avoid war (fact); American independence inevitable: Tory wanted peace
for himself (testimony), wars will break out
until then (fact); Americans must be strong:
if not, our children will curse us (reason),
we didn't seek this war (fact); Don't be
fooled by false peace offers: Howe's timing
was lucky (fact), our preparation is secure
and improving (fact). Paine uses facts and
reasons, which he finds effective.*

6. ● **SKILLS FOCUS** Persuasive Techniques
*He favors appeals to logic, emotion, and
ethics: "Not a place . . . with them" (lines
39–41), logical to location, emotional to
happiness; "throw not . . . God may bless
you" (lines 54–55), appeal to authority of
Bible; "The blood of his children . . . made
them happy" (lines 59–60), emotional appeal of children, loaded language; "It is the
madness . . . trick of war" (lines 82–83), logical appeal to experience; "I dwell not . . . to*

After Reading

R2.6

Comprehension

1. **Recall** At the end of the essay, what two qualities does Paine say American
troops need to win the war?

2. **Summarize** In the third paragraph, what reasons does Paine give for assuring
the Americans that their cause is right?

3. **Clarify** What is implied by the terms "summer soldier" and "sunshine patriot"
in the first paragraph?

Literary Analysis

4. **Interpret Metaphor** A metaphor is a figure of speech that equates two unlike
things. Explain what Paine means by the metaphor in lines 45–46: "for,
though the flame of liberty may sometimes cease to shine, the coal can never
expire." How might this metaphor serve to inspire the troops' **loyalty?**

5. **Analyze Main Ideas and Support** Review the chart of main ideas and support
you completed as you read. What kind of support does Paine primarily use—
reasons, facts, or expert testimony? Explain why you think this is so.

6. **Analyze Persuasive Techniques** Review
the different persuasive techniques
explained on page 245. Then, go back
through the essay and find six examples
of Paine's strong persuasive appeals. In
a chart, record your examples and briefly
explain the type of appeal. What kinds of
techniques does Paine favor in his essay?

Example from "The Crisis"	Kind of Appeal
Those soldiers who stand firm in the "service of [their] country" deserve the "love and thanks of man and woman." (lines 2–3)	ethical appeal of "service to country" plus emotional appeal of love and gratitude
"God almighty will not give up a people to military destruction. . . ." (lines 23–24)	appeal to authority—in this case, the ultimate authority

7. **Evaluate Analogy** More detailed than
a metaphor, an **analogy** is a point-by-
point comparison in which an unfamiliar
subject is explained in terms of a familiar
one. Reread lines 65–68. Explain the
analogy of the thief in terms of the following four points. In your opinion,
does the analogy adequately justify the war? Explain why or why not.

- breaking and entering
- destroying property
- threatening to kill
- binding to his will

Literary Criticism

8. **Critical Interpretations** John Adams, second U.S. president and no fan of
Paine's, nonetheless acknowledged his crucial influence: "Without the pen
of Paine the sword of Washington would have been wielded in vain." Use
information from Paine's essay, as well as facts from his biography on page
244, to support Adams's assessment.

252 UNIT 1: EARLY AMERICAN WRITING

---

*your eyes" (lines 100–101), logical appeal to
reason; "by cowardice . . . unlamented" (lines
117–122), emotional appeal to fear.*

7. *The thief's actions of entering a house,
threatening those inside, and destroying
property are analogous to British actions
against the colonies. Students may say the
analogy supports the right to defend one's
property. Others may say it is overly simple.*

8. *Paine galvanized popular support for
independence among the common people
who would fight the war. Without a morale
boost, America's cause might have failed.*

---

252 UNIT 1: EARLY AMERICAN WRITING

Vocabulary in Context

VOCABULARY PRACTICE

Choose the letter of the phrase that defines or is related to the boldfaced word.

1. **celestial:** (a) an instrument, (b) a star in the sky, (c) a slogan
2. **tyranny:** (a) a country with no freedoms, (b) an old bicycle, (c) a relay race
3. **repulse:** (a) a long-winded speaker, (b) a resisted enemy, (c) a favorite shirt
4. **esteem:** (a) a temperature drop, (b) a cousin, (c) an honored guest
5. **ardor:** (a) a grove of trees, (b) a passion for justice, (c) an accounting mistake
6. **infidel:** (a) a religious skeptic, (b) a lieutenant, (c) a television game show
7. **dominion:** (a) a landlocked country, (b) a public garden, (c) a control freak
8. **relinquish:** (a) a building site, (b) a surrender of territory, (c) a bad argument
9. **prudent:** (a) a cautious investor, (b) a distant relative, (c) car insurance
10. **wrangling:** (a) a favor, (b) a rowing machine, (c) towns with border disputes

WORD LIST

ardor
celestial
dominion
esteem
infidel
prudent
relinquish
repulse
tyranny
wrangling

VOCABULARY IN WRITING

What emotions does Paine try to elicit from his readers in this essay? Using three or more vocabulary words, write a brief discussion of at least two emotions and the methods Paine uses to elicit them. You might start like this.

> **EXAMPLE SENTENCE**
> *Paine primarily wanted to stir up revolutionary **ardor** in his audience.*

VOCABULARY STRATEGY: WORDS FROM MIDDLE ENGLISH

Middle English was the language spoken in England roughly between A.D. 1100 and 1500. This form of English evolved after the Norman French, led by William the Conqueror, invaded and conquered England in 1066. Many modern words that first occurred in Middle English, such as the vocabulary word *ardor*, were derived from French. Others continued from Old English, the earliest recognized form of the language.

PRACTICE The boldfaced words in these sentences have their origins in Middle English. Use context clues to create a definition of each. Then check a dictionary etymology to find out the word's original meaning.

1. He demonstrated his athletic **prowess** by participating in the triathlon.
2. She has been a **recluse** ever since the death of her husband.
3. Her **fulsome** praise of his decision greatly embarrassed him.
4. He had the perfect **rejoinder** for every accusation of the committee.
5. The garden held a **plenitude** of rare plants and flowers.

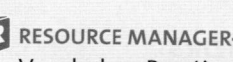 **VOCABULARY PRACTICE** For more practice, go to the **Vocabulary Center** at **ClassZone.com**.

DIFFERENTIATED INSTRUCTION

FOR ENGLISH LEARNERS

Task Support: Vocabulary Practice Have students work in mixed-language groups. Tell groups to review the words listed as choices for the *PRACTICE* items. Students can identify cognates from their home languages for these words, then work together to create a composite list of words and home-language cognates.

FOR ADVANCED LEARNERS/AP

Vocabulary in Writing Have students write a journal entry by a colonial soldier spending Christmas Eve on the banks of the Delaware River. Challenge them to convey the writer's emotions. Students should use at least three vocabulary words in their journal entry.

ANSWERS

Vocabulary in Context

VOCABULARY PRACTICE

1. *b*	6. *a*
2. *a*	7. *a*
3. *b*	8. *b*
4. *c*	9. *a*
5. *b*	10. *c*

R RESOURCE MANAGER—Copy Master
Vocabulary Practice p. 398

VOCABULARY IN WRITING

Help students brainstorm reasons why Paine wrote this essay and have them use this list in their writing.

VOCABULARY STRATEGY: WORDS FROM MIDDLE ENGLISH *(also an EL language objective)*

Remind students that knowing a word's etymology may help them to remember its current meaning. Point out differences between current usage and original meaning.

Possible answers:

1. *skill (original meaning: brave)*
2. *hermit (original meaning: to close up)*
3. *effusive (original meaning: loathsome)*
4. *answer (original meaning: to answer)*
5. *abundance (original meaning: full)*

R RESOURCE MANAGER—Copy Master
Vocabulary Strategy p. 399

i Vocabulary Center at **ClassZone.com**
Additional Vocabulary Activities

Assess and Reteach

Assess

R RESOURCE MANAGER—Copy Masters
Selection Test A pp. 403–404
Selection Test B/C pp. 405–406

⊚ Test Generator CD

Reteach

S STANDARDS LESSON FILE
Reading Lesson 4: Recognizing Main Idea and Details
Informational Text Lesson 15: Persuasive Techniques
Vocabulary Lesson 25: Etymologies

Focus and Motivate

OBJECTIVES

Literary Analysis
- explore the key idea of **authority**
- analyze diction and tone
- read a letter

Reading
- use strategies for reading primary sources

 R2.2

ABOUT THE AUTHORS

Phillis Wheatley Ask students to identify the details of Wheatley's life they find most surprising and notable. Explain that Wheatley's letter demonstrates her education and Biblical knowledge, as well as her interest in moral and religious issues.

Abigail Adams Have students restate Adams's beliefs about women. Explain that her letter reflects Adams's acceptance of her husband's political role and her belief that men should not have "absolute power" over their wives.

USING THE *NOTABLE QUOTES*

Clarify that Cain is a figure from the Old Testament of the Bible who murdered his brother but was still protected by God. Ask students what message **Phillis Wheatley's** comparison of Cain and African Americans gives to Christians. *(Even if Christians think of African Americans as unredeemable, God still believes in them.)* Ask students to speculate on what view of husbands **Abigail Adams** will advance in her letter. *(All men want to rule over their wives, but they should not be allowed to do so.)*

Selection Resources

CALIFORNIA R2.2

Letter to the Reverend Samson Occom
by Phillis Wheatley

Phillis Wheatley
c. 1753–1784

NOTABLE QUOTE
*"Some view our sable race with scornful eye . . .
Remember, Christians,
Negroes, black as Cain,
May be refin'd, and join th' angelic train."*

Phillis Wheatley became the first African-American poet to be published. Moreover, her unusual life is the stuff that movies are made of. Kidnapped at age seven in West Africa, she was sold to the prosperous Wheatley family at a Boston slave auction. Within 16 months, the precocious child had mastered English and could read the Bible. She then went on to learn Latin and Greek well enough to read the classics.

Startling Success Story With the encouragement of the Wheatley family, she started writing poetry as a teenager. She gained considerable fame both in the colonies and in England when newspapers began publishing her poems, most of

them on moral and religious subjects. While in London in 1773 to publish her book of poetry, Wheatley was the toast of society, which included many nobles and dignitaries and the visiting American patriot Ben Franklin.

Life as a Free Black Woman By 1778, Wheatley had gained her freedom and married a free black man. Their life together was a losing struggle against poverty, however, for in many respects living as a free black in a colonial city was as bad as being a slave. In late 1779, Wheatley tried to get a second book of her poems published, but war-torn, financially strapped Boston had lost interest in her.

Letter to John Adams
by Abigail Adams

Abigail Adams
1744–1818

NOTABLE QUOTE
"Remember all Men would be tyrants if they could."

Abigail Adams was the wife of the second U.S. president, John Adams, and mother of the sixth, John Quincy Adams. But she is equally well-known for her outspoken opinions as expressed in thousands of personal letters.

Intelligent and Competent The daughter of a wealthy minister, young Abigail read extensively in her father's well-stocked library. After marrying John Adams, she moved with him to a farm in Braintree, Massachusetts. As John became increasingly involved in colonial politics and the struggle for independence, Abigail took over management of the household and farm as well as John's business affairs.

An Early Feminist? Because of her support for women's education and her acute awareness of men's "absolute power," many have championed Abigail Adams as an early advocate of women's rights. However, although her thinking was clearly advanced for her time—she also favored the abolition of slavery—she held quite conventional views about a woman's subordinate role in society.

Author Online
For more on Wheatley and Adams, visit the **Literature Center** at ClassZone.com.

254

 RESOURCE MANAGER UNIT 1

Plan and Teach pp. 407–414

Literary Analysis
Summary pp. 415†*, 416‡*
Diction pp. 417, 418†*
Question Support p. 422*

Reading
Reading Primary Sources
   pp. 419, 420†*
Reading Check p. 421

Assessment
Selection Tests A, B/C
   pp. 423*, 425*
   Test Generator CD

 BEST PRACTICES TOOLKIT

Differentiated Instruction
   pp. 31–38*
Scaffolding Instruction
   pp. 43–46*

Graphic Organizers/Strategies
New Word Analysis

 Reading Support
   Audio Anthology CD*

Technology
   Literature Center at
   ClassZone.com
   WriteSmart CD

---

* Resources for Differentiation   † Also in Spanish   ‡ In Haitian Creole and Vietnamese

● LITERARY ANALYSIS: DICTION

Diction is a writer's choice of words. Diction includes both vocabulary (words) and syntax (arrangement of words). Diction can be formal or informal, common or technical, abstract or concrete. Note the formal diction in this excerpt from the letter written by Abigail Adams:

How many are the solitary hours I spend, ruminating upon the past, and anticipating the future, whilst you, overwhelmed with the cares of state, have but a few moments you can devote to any individual.

Writers often communicate **tone,** or attitude toward a subject, through their diction. As you read the letters, notice words and phrases that reveal each writer's attitude toward the issues of liberty and freedom.

■ READING STRATEGY: READING PRIMARY SOURCES

Primary sources are materials written or made by people who took part in or witnessed the events portrayed. These sources can provide unique insights on a subject. To get the most out of a primary source, consider the following:

- Who was the writer? The age, nationality, and social class of the writer can influence the point of view.
- What is the form of the document: letter, diary, speech? How might the form have affected the content?
- When and where was it written? The time and place of a primary source's writing can provide clues to the culture and history of the period.
- Who is the intended audience? In a private letter to a loved one, a writer might voice thoughts and feelings more freely than in an open letter to a public audience.

For help analyzing the letters of Wheatley and Adams, complete a chart such as the one shown here as you read each letter.

Writer:
Form:
When and Where Written:
Intended Purpose/Audience:

Explore the Key Idea

Who gets to make the RULES?

KEY IDEA Those in **authority** make the rules for others—whether it's in the halls of Congress or the classroom. The authors of these two letters, while agreeing wholeheartedly with the patriot cause, still felt left out of the process and the benefits of the American Revolution.

DISCUSS People today have not only more freedom than people did in colonial times but also more ways to change the laws. Think of at least three situations in which rules directly impact your life. Then for each situation, discuss ways that are available to change or modify those rules.

BALLOT BOX

Teach

Who gets to make the RULES?

Ask the question to introduce the **KEY IDEA**. As students complete the **DISCUSS** activity, have them identify the type of **authority** that made the rules under discussion. Encourage students to share their ideas for ways to change these rules.

SKILLS FOCUS

LITERARY ANALYSIS   R2.2

● DICTION

Write this excerpt from a letter on the board:

> I believe that you made the correct decision to acquire another company. Mr. Elvin, your decisions are always thoughtful, and I know that my project will benefit from this one.

Ask students to characterize the diction of this letter. *Possible answer: The diction is formal. The writer uses formal words and syntax—for example, the title "Mr. Elvin."*

CHECK UNDERSTANDING Ask students to identify the writer's attitude or tone regarding Mr. Elvin's decision.

READING STRATEGY

■ READING PRIMARY SOURCES

Have students reread the lines on the board, then answer the bulleted questions on page 255 about this text. Ask them to identify a likely intended purpose as well. *Possible answer: The writer is an employee in a large modern company, writing a letter to his or her boss. The audience is Mr. Elvin, the boss. The writer's intended purpose seems to be to support Mr. Elvin's decision.*

R RESOURCE MANAGER—Copy Master
   Reading Primary Sources p. 419
   (for student use while reading the selections)

DIFFERENTIATED INSTRUCTION

FOR STRATEGIC READERS

Vocabulary Support To support instruction, clarify the meaning of these words:

- *abstract,* "expressing something that can only be understood intellectually"
- *concrete,* "able to be seen or touched; existing in reality, not just an idea"
- *primary,* "something that is first in order; thus, the first person to see or experience an event"

Concept Support: Reading Primary Sources
To help students evaluate primary source letters, ask them to recall a letter they have written and identify its audience. Have them note information they would have omitted if the audience were different. As they read the selection letters, urge students to identify information each author might have omitted had she known the letter would be made public.

SUMMARY

Wheatley's letter applauds Occom's defense of the natural rights of African Americans, and points out that people cannot claim to love freedom yet oppress others.

LITERARY ANALYSIS

A **DICTION**

Possible answer: Wheatley's diction is formal. She uses long and difficult words, such as "obliging kind epistle" (line 1) and "glorious dispensation" (line 6). Her language is elevated and abstract (lines 4–5). White readers were probably surprised to encounter such writing from a black woman in a time when most black men and women were enslaved and illiterate. Wheatley's language might have caused white people to think differently about black people.

READING STRATEGY

B **PRIMARY SOURCES**

Possible answer: Wheatley's letter deals with the public issues of the natural right that African Americans have to freedom (line 3) and the contradiction in people fighting for freedom while supporting the oppression of black people (lines 17–19).

If students need help . . . Direct them to lines 2–3 and the words "natural rights." Then point out lines 17–19 and the phrases "cry for liberty" and "exercise of oppressive power over others."

Letter to the REVEREND SAMSON OCCOM

Phillis Wheatley

> **BACKGROUND** The Reverend Samson Occom was a Mohegan Indian who became a minister after converting to Christianity. In a letter to Phillis Wheatley, he had criticized some of his fellow ministers for owning slaves. Wheatley's response to her friend, dated February 11, 1774, was later published in colonial newspapers.

Reverend and honored sir,

I have this day received your obliging kind epistle, and am greatly satisfied with your reasons respecting the negroes, and think highly reasonable what you offer in vindication of their natural rights: Those that invade them cannot be insensible that the divine light is chasing away the thick darkness which broods over the land of Africa;[1] and the chaos which has reigned so long, is converting into beautiful order, and reveals more and more clearly the glorious dispensation of civil and religious liberty, which are so inseparably united, that there is little or no enjoyment of one without the other: Otherwise, perhaps, the Israelites had been less solicitous for their freedom from Egyptian slavery;[2] I do not say they would

10 have been contented without it, by no means; for in every human breast God has implanted a principle, which we call love of freedom; it is impatient **A** of oppression, and pants for deliverance; and by the leave of our modern Egyptians[3] I will assert, that the same principle lives in us. God grant deliverance in his own way and time, and get him honor upon all those whose avarice impels them to countenance and help forward the calamities of their fellow creatures. This I desire not for their hurt, but to convince them of the strange absurdity of their conduct, whose words and actions are so diametrically opposite. How well the cry for liberty, and the reverse disposition for the exercise of oppressive power over others agree—I humbly think it does not require the penetration[4] of a

20 philosopher to determine.— **B**

Phillis Wheatley

1. **insensible . . . the land of Africa:** unaware that Christianity is spreading throughout Africa.
2. **Israelites . . . Egyptian slavery:** a biblical allusion to the Israelites who were led out of Egypt by Moses.
3. **modern Egyptians:** the owners of African slaves.
4. **penetration:** understanding; insight.

ANALYZE VISUALS
This image shows a slave auction in New Amsterdam (New York). What does this tell you about slavery in colonial America?

① **Targeted Passage**

A **DICTION**
Describe Wheatley's **diction** in lines 1–11. How do you think her way of writing might have struck white readers at the time?

B **PRIMARY SOURCES**
Does Wheatley's letter deal with private or public issues? What are they?

*First Slave Auction in New Amsterdam, 1655.
The Granger Collection, New York.*

DIFFERENTIATED INSTRUCTION

FOR ALL STUDENTS

Provide these independent projects to extend the lesson:

- Create a chart to analyze figurative language.
- Create a political cartoon that conveys a message about government.

For further details on these projects, see

R **RESOURCE MANAGER**
Ideas for Extension pp. 412–413

FOR STRATEGIC READERS

In combination with the *Audio Anthology CD*, use one or more Targeted Passages (pp. 256, 258, 260) to ensure that students focus on key concepts in the selections. Targeted Passages are also good for English learners.

① Targeted Passage [Lines 1–13]

This passage clarifies Wheatley's view of the rights of African Americans and her acknowledgement of what they desire.

ANALYZE VISUALS

Possible answer: This image shows that slavery was a popular trade in colonial America. A white man is apparently attempting to sell a slave to one of the colonists. There are many colonists in the audience, which suggests that this was a common practice and that many colonists were interested in buying slaves.

Lines 10–19
REINFORCE *KEY IDEA:* AUTHORITY

Discuss Who does Wheatley think has the ultimate **authority** over people? What does she hope that authority will do? *Possible answer: Wheatley thinks that God has the ultimate authority over people. She believes God put the desire for freedom in every human heart and will deliver that freedom when ready (lines 13–14). She hopes that God will make those who support freedom while oppressing slaves realize the error of their thinking (line 14–15).*

- How does Wheatley feel about Reverend Occom's opinions about African Americans?
- What two rights does Wheatley believe cannot be separated?
- Who does Wheatley compare enslaved African Americans to? Why?

FOR ENGLISH LEARNERS

Key Academic Vocabulary Use New Word Analysis to teach these words: page 256: *convince* (line 16), *require* (line 19); page 260: *philosophy* (line 45).

 BEST PRACTICES TOOLKIT—Transparency
New Word Analysis p. E8

Prereading For prereading instruction for English learners, see

BEST PRACTICES TOOLKIT
Scaffolding Reading Instruction pp. 43–46

FOR ADVANCED LEARNERS/AP

AP exercises in the bottom channel provide additional challenge for students. Use these suggestions for small groups or individuals.

ADDITIONAL GUIDELINES

For more help with differentiation and tips for classroom management, see

 BEST PRACTICES TOOLKIT
Differentiated Instruction pp. 31–38

Abigail Adams begins her letter by expressing the value of her husband's work to found the nation over his family's needs. She then describes the chaos and lack of leadership in Boston. Adams urges the new government to declare sovereignty and points out that men's power over women contradicts their goal to liberate the nation.

READING STRATEGY

C PRIMARY SOURCES

Possible answer: *Adams is concerned with both public and private issues. She writes about personal issues, telling her husband that she misses him (lines 8–10). However, she also writes about the public issues of her husband's duties. She says that these public duties and the public issues of the time take precedence over their personal lives (lines 3–7). She believes that if a country falls, then the life of any individual will not matter (lines 7–8).*

Lines 13–18
REINFORCE *KEY IDEA:* AUTHORITY

Discuss How does Adams characterize the people who have **authority** over Boston and its colonists? *Possible answer: Adams does not think the rulers are doing a good job. She believes that they are being lazy and that they feel secure, when they should not (lines 13–15). She thinks they worry and focus on the wrong things (lines 15–16). She also believes they are not anticipating future danger, such as the need to protect Boston's harbor from attack (lines 16–18). She believes that they are not demonstrating good leadership qualities.*

Letter to JOHN ADAMS

Abigail Adams

> **BACKGROUND** In March of 1776, while John Adams was in Philadelphia with other delegates drafting a code of laws for the new independent country, Abigail wrote a letter asking him to "remember the ladies" in the new laws: "Be more generous and favorable to them than your ancestors. Do not put such unlimited power into the hands of husbands." John's response was to laugh and remark, "You are so saucy." The following is the next letter she sent to him.

Braintree, 7, May, 1776

How many are the solitary hours I spend, ruminating upon the past, and anticipating the future, whilst you, overwhelmed with the cares of state, have but a few moments you can devote to any individual. All domestic pleasures and enjoyments are absorbed in the great and important duty you owe your country, "for our country is, as it were, a secondary god, and the first and greatest parent. It is to be preferred to parents, wives, children, friends, and all things, the gods only excepted; for, if our country perishes, it is as impossible to save an individual, as to preserve one of the fingers of a mortified hand." Thus do I suppress every wish, and silence every murmur, acquiescing in a painful separation from the
10 companion of my youth, and the friend of my heart. **C**

I believe 't is near ten days since I wrote you a line. I have not felt in a humor to entertain you if I had taken up my pen. Perhaps some unbecoming invective[1] might have fallen from it. The eyes of our rulers have been closed, and a lethargy has seized almost every member. I fear a fatal security has taken possession of them. Whilst the building is in flames, they tremble at the expense of water to quench it. In short, two months have elapsed since the evacuation of Boston,[2] and very little has been done in that time to secure it, or the harbor, from future

ANALYZE VISUALS
These pastel portraits of Abigail and John Adams were done in 1766, about two years after their marriage. How do these portraits compare with those that might be done today of a young couple?

1 Targeted Passage

C PRIMARY SOURCES
Does Adams's letter concern itself with private or public issues in lines 1–10? What does she say about the relationship between the private and the public?

---

1. **unbecoming invective:** inappropriate abusive language.
2. **two months . . . Boston:** British troops under General William Howe and more than a thousand Loyalists evacuated Boston on March 17, 1776.

DIFFERENTIATED INSTRUCTION

FOR STRATEGIC READERS

1 Targeted Passage [Lines 3–14]

This passage shows Adams's view of the newly forming country and reveals aspects of her character and relationship with John.

- To what does Adams compare the new country? Why?
- What thoughts or feelings does Adams suppress?
- Why does Adams say that she hasn't written her husband for nearly ten days?

FOR ENGLISH LEARNERS

Vocabulary: Idioms Help students use context clues to determine the meanings of these idioms:

- *as it were* (line 5), "in a manner of speaking"
- *I wrote you a line* (line 11), "I wrote to you; I wrote you a letter"
- *In short* (line 16), "Briefly"
- *have turned out* (line 20), "have shown up"

ANALYZE VISUALS

Possible answer: These portraits are more formal than the portraits that most young couples would have done today. Most contemporary portraits would be photographs and would show the couple together. They might be posed informally in a familiar home or outdoor setting. They would probably be smiling and showing affection. The dress and hairstyles would also be more natural.

Lines 8–18
TIERED DISCUSSION PROMPTS

Use these prompts to have students consider Adams's evaluation of her nation's rulers:

Connect Have you or someone you know ever worried about small details at the expense of larger, more important issues? Explain. *Accept all thoughtful responses.*

Interpret Consider the time period in which Adams's letter is written, then reread lines 15–16. What does the "building in flames" represent? What does Adams mean when she writes, "they tremble . . . to quench it"? *Possible answer: The "building in flames" is the lingering fear in Boston of future invasion by the British. While British troops evacuated the city nearly two months before, nothing since has been done to secure it, because the "rulers" or Continental Congress in Philadelphia (to which her husband is a delegate) "tremble" and won't spend the money for troops and supplies.*

Evaluate What does Adams seem to think of the response of the citizens of Boston to the crisis? *Possible answer: Adams seems impressed by the sense of personal responsibility the citizens have taken to secure their city, an action that is in sharp contrast to the "lethargy" of Congress.*

FOR STRATEGIC READERS

Concept Support: Reading Primary Sources
As students read the letter, help them fill out the reading chart introduced on page 255. Direct their attention to the boldface date and location of writing. Have them read the **BACKGROUND** for help in identifying purpose and audience.

Writer:	*Abigail Adams*
Form:	*personal letter*
When and Where Written:	*at Adams's home in Braintree, on May 7, 1776*
Intended Purpose/Audience:	*letter to her husband, John, to inform him about colonial affairs and to remind him about being fair to women with the new laws*

Possible answer: The words that suggest a concern with political issues include "government," "stability," and "colony" (line 25); "Congress" (line 26); "maxims of state" (line 27); and "king" and "people" (line 28). Adams's diction shows that she uses sophisticated thinking and is comfortable discussing issues of public policy.

Possible answer: Adams points out that colonial men are interested in freeing themselves from Great Britain, but they continue to keep their wives and daughters enslaved (lines 32–34).

Possible answer: Relationships between husbands and wives were rather formal during colonial times. Even when talking about her children to her husband, Adams uses formal language and little emotion.

SELECTION WRAP–UP

SYNTHESIZE Ask students to explain how the message of Wheatley's and Adams's letters is similar.

★ CRITIQUE

• Have students evaluate whether both writers express their points clearly.

• After completing the After Reading questions on page 261, have students revisit their responses and tell whether they have changed their opinions.

---

invasion. The people are all in a flame, and no one among us, that I have heard of, even mentions expense. They think, universally, that there has been an amazing
20 neglect somewhere. Many have turned out as volunteers to work upon Noddle's Island, and many more would go upon Nantasket,[3] if the business was once set on foot. "'T is a maxim of state, that power and liberty are like heat and moisture. Where they are well mixed, every thing prospers; where they are single, they are destructive."

A government of more stability is much wanted in this colony, and they are ready to receive it from the hands of the Congress. And since I have begun with maxims of state,[4] I will add another, namely, that a people may let a king fall, yet still remain a people; but, if a king let his people slip from him, he is no longer a king.[5] And as this is most certainly our case, why not proclaim to the world, in
30 decisive terms, your own importance? **D**

Shall we not be despised by foreign powers, for hesitating so long at a word?

I cannot say that I think you are very generous to the ladies; for, whilst you are proclaiming peace and good-will to men, emancipating all nations, you insist upon retaining an absolute power over wives. But you must remember, that arbitrary power is like most other things which are very hard, very liable to be broken; and, notwithstanding all your wise laws and maxims, we have it in our power, not only to free ourselves, but to subdue our masters, and, without violence, throw both your natural and legal authority at our feet;—

"Charm by accepting, by submitting sway,
40   Yet have our humor most when we obey."[6] **E**

I thank you for several letters which I have received since I wrote last; they alleviate a tedious absence, and I long earnestly for a Saturday evening, and experience a similar pleasure to that which I used to find in the return of my friend upon that day after a week's absence. The idea of a year dissolves all my philosophy.

Our little ones, whom you so often recommend to my care and instruction, shall not be deficient in virtue or probity,[7] if the precepts of a mother have their desired effect; but they would be doubly enforced, could they be indulged with the example of a father alternately before them. I often point them to their sire,
50 "engaged in a corrupted state,
     Wrestling with vice and faction."[8] **F**

A. Adams

---

3. **Noddle's Island . . . Nantasket:** sites near the city of Boston. Noddle's Island is now called East Boston.

4. **maxims of state:** rules or short sayings related to government.

5. **king:** a reference to King George III, who ignored colonists' protests and put Massachusetts under military rule.

6. **"Charm . . . obey":** a couplet taken from Alexander Pope's poem *Moral Essays.*

7. **deficient . . . probity:** lacking in goodness or integrity.

8. **"engaged . . . faction":** lines taken from Joseph Addison's play *Cato.* Cato (234–149 B.C.) was a Roman politician who fought for high moral standards in the Roman Senate.

---

② Targeted Passage

DIFFERENTIATED INSTRUCTION

FOR STRATEGIC READERS

② Targeted Passage [Lines 32–51]

This passage reflects Adams's view of women's rights and duties.

• Why does Adams say that her husband and his colleagues aren't "very generous to the ladies"?

• Why does Adams appreciate her husband's letters?

• What qualities does Adams want to instill in her children?

FOR ADVANCED LEARNERS/AP

Analyze and Evaluate [small-group option] After students review lines 22–24, ask a volunteer to paraphrase this simile. *Example: Power and liberty, like heat and moisture, need to be balanced for things to grow well.* Organize students into small groups to discuss the statement. Ask them to list examples from current events or history that support or refute it. Invite students to share their views on the statement.

Comprehension

1. **Recall** What does Phillis Wheatley praise the Reverend Occom for doing?

2. **Clarify** In Wheatley's opinion, what is the cause of slavery?

3. **Recall** Why does Abigail Adams put her country before personal happiness?

4. **Clarify** What is the situation in Massachusetts that Adams complains to her husband about?

R2.2

Literary Analysis

5. **Compare and Contrast** In both letters, Wheatley and Adams reveal their powerlessness to change what they clearly see as wrong. How do they personally deal with this lack of **authority?** Discuss how they cope with the following situations:

   • slavery
   • lack of security due to inaction
   • absolute power of men

6. **Analyze Diction** For each letter, look for examples of diction that reveal the writer's **tone.** Then compare and contrast the tone of each, explaining possible reasons for any differences you find.

7. **Analyze Primary Sources** What are some of the advantages and disadvantages of these personal letters as historical documents? For example, what insights do they provide that more formal documents, such as the Declaration of Independence, do not? How are the letters useful or limited in their historical value? How does the identity of the writer influence the content? Draw upon your chart to cite examples from the letters to prove your points.

8. **Evaluate Argument** Each woman makes an argument in her letter: Wheatley against slavery, and Adams against the "arbitrary power" of men. In your opinion, who presents the stronger case? Cite evidence to support your opinion.

Literary Criticism

9. **Historical Context** Personal letters, even ones such as Wheatley's that were later published in newspapers, offer a rare opportunity to hear women's voices from the past. What distinguishes Wheatley's and Adams's writing from the rhetoric of Patrick Henry, Thomas Jefferson, and Tom Paine? What do their letters reveal about how women were expected to behave in early America?

details and insights about life of the times (Wheatley: lines 13–20; Adams: lines 13–24, 32–38). **Disadvantages:** *limited perspective: Adams's view is limited by personal vulnerability and fear. She expresses views atypical of women. Each writer is influenced by her specific situation as a former slave or the wife of a statesman.*

8. *Students might say that Wheatley's argument is stronger. Her facts are clear and she is unemotional. The personal details of Adams's letter can cloud her points. All answers should include support.*

9. *Henry, Jefferson, and Paine use forceful rhetoric. The women's writing is more accepting. The letters show that women were expected to accept their subordination with humility and contentment.*

Practice and Apply

After Reading

Use these copy masters to check understanding and provide extra support:

R RESOURCE MANAGER—Copy Masters
   Reading Check p. 421
   Diction p. 417
   Question Support p. 422

   Additional selection questions are provided for teachers on page 411.

ANSWERS

1. *supporting the "natural rights" of African Americans*

2. *greed*

3. *because if her country perishes, then saving individuals won't matter*

4. *The colony lacks security. Volunteers will help, but they need Congress's authority.*

Possible answers:

5. *Wheatley points out the hypocrisy of slaveholding ministers and trusts in God to stop slavery and its absolute power. Adams trusts in her husband for help with the colony's lack of security. She appears skeptical about men's absolute power changing. Both seem ultimately powerless.*

6. ● **SKILLS FOCUS** *Diction Lines 3–6 and 17–20 show Wheatley's formal, polite, controlled and impersonal tone. Lines 8–13, 25–30, 32–34, and 41–45 show Adams's informal, spontaneous, emotional, and personal tone. Adams's tone is more personally forceful than Wheatley's.*

7. ■ **SKILLS FOCUS** *Reading Primary Sources* **Advantages:** *The letters give useful personal*

Assess and Reteach

Assess

R RESOURCE MANAGER—Copy Masters
   Selection Test A pp. 423–424
   Selection Test B/C pp. 425–426

💿 Test Generator CD

Reteach

S STANDARDS LESSON FILE
   Literature Lesson 40: Word Choice and Diction
   Research Lesson 5: Using Primary Sources

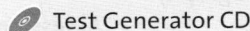

Focus and Motivate

OBJECTIVES

Literary Analysis
- explore the key idea of **self-improvement**
- analyze the characteristics of an auto-biography
- read an autobiography, aphorisms, and a magazine article

Reading
- make inferences about the author

Vocabulary
- build vocabulary for reading and writing
- use the Latin root *fic* to help unlock meaning *(also an EL language objective)*

 CALIFORNIA R2.5, R1.2

ABOUT THE AUTHOR

After students have read about Franklin's life, discuss with them why he might have decided to write an autobiography, and why people might have wanted to learn about his life. Explain to students that they are going to read an excerpt that demonstrates both his great mind and his ability to connect with people.

USING THE *NOTABLE QUOTE*

Ask students whether **Benjamin Franklin** took his own advice, based on what they learned in the biography. *Possible answer: Franklin wrote "things worth reading," such as satires and wise sayings, and did "things worth the writing," such as helping draft the Declaration of Independence. He took his own advice and was not forgotten.*

Selection Resources

---

from The Autobiography
by Benjamin Franklin

CALIFORNIA R2.5, R1.2 (p. 273)

NOTABLE QUOTE

*"If you would not be forgotten
As soon as you are dead and rotten,
Either write things worth reading,
Or do things worth the writing."*

FYI
Did you know that Benjamin Franklin . . .
- started the first public library and fire department in America?
- founded what became the University of Pennsylvania?
- invented bifocal eyeglasses?

Author Online

For more on Benjamin Franklin, visit the **Literature Center** at **ClassZone.com.**

Page from *Poor Richard's Almanack*

Benjamin Franklin
1706–1790

Printer, publisher, writer, scientist, inventor, businessman, philosopher, statesman—Benjamin Franklin's numerous roles only hint at the man's tremendous versatility and talent. As the oldest founding father, Franklin had already lived a full life when at the age of 70 he joined 40-year-old John Adams and 33-year-old Thomas Jefferson to draft the Declaration of Independence. Soon afterward, he loaned Congress a large sum of his own money and sailed on a leaky ship to France to arrange for more loans and a crucial alliance to fight the British. His masterly efforts abroad on behalf of the American cause earned him a reputation as one of the most successful American diplomats of all time. Only a few years before he died, his presence at the Constitutional Convention helped unify the delegates. So great was his influence that he is credited with convincing them to approve the final document by a vote of 39 to 3. A man of great integrity, intelligence, and charm, Ben Franklin embodied the best of the new nation and became its first celebrity.

Pulling Himself Up Born in Boston as the youngest of 15 children, Franklin did not want to follow in his father's footsteps to become a candle and soap maker. Instead, he joined his brother in the printing business as an apprentice. With only two years of formal education, Franklin taught himself to write by imitating the great essayists of his day. At the age of 16, he was contributing satirical pieces to his brother's newspaper. By his own account "too saucy and provoking" as a youth, he soon quarreled with his brother and struck out on his own for Philadelphia. Franklin did very well in Philadelphia, prospering in his own printing business, running the successful *Pennsylvania Gazette* newspaper, writing his popular *Poor Richard's Almanack* for 26 years, and being active in colonial politics.

Citizen of the World Franklin's writing—from humorous satires and wise sayings to serious political essays and scientific observations on electricity—as well as his diplomacy and charismatic personality made him an international celebrity. Although respected by the great minds of his age, he never lost his connection to the common people. In the words of John Adams: "His reputation is greater than that of Newton, Frederick the Great or Voltaire, his character more revered than all of them. There's scarcely a coachman or a footman or scullery maid who does not consider him a friend of all mankind."

FEBRUAR

e fmile at Florifts, we
d think their Hearts ei
t are thofe wifer, who
vey with Envy, and purfue with Fire?
at's he, who fights for Wealth, or Fame, or Power?
other *Florio*, doating on a Flower,
hort-liv'd Flower, and which has often fprung,

262

New ☽ 25 2 mo.
1 ♉ 9 Deg.
11 9

RESOURCE MANAGER UNIT 1

Plan and Teach pp. 427–434

Literary Analysis
Summary pp. 435†*, 436‡*
Characteristics of Autobiography pp. 437, 438†*
Question Support p. 445*

Reading
Make Inferences About the Author pp. 439, 440†*
Reading Check p. 444

Vocabulary
Study p. 441*
Practice p. 442
Strategy p. 443

Assessment
Selection Tests A, B/C pp. 447*, 449*
Test Generator CD

BEST PRACTICES TOOLKIT

Differentiated Instruction pp. 31–38*

Scaffolding Instruction pp. 43–46*

Graphic Organizers/Strategies
Definition Mapping • Venn Diagram • Analysis Frame: Literary Nonfiction • Three-Column Journal

Reading Support
Audio Anthology CD*

Technology
Literature and Vocabulary Centers at **ClassZone.com**
WriteSmart CD

---

* Resources for Differentiation   † Also in Spanish   ‡ In Haitian Creole and Vietnamese

- **LITERARY ANALYSIS: CHARACTERISTICS OF AUTOBIOGRAPHY**

An **autobiography** is the story of a person's life, written by that person. As you read this excerpt from Franklin's autobiography, notice the following characteristics of autobiography:

- **First person:** The author of an autobiography usually writes from the first-person point of view.

- **Dual perspective:** Often the author of an autobiography writes as an older person looking back on him- or herself as a younger person, providing opportunities for reflection.

- **Significant moments:** Autobiographies may vary from straightforward chronological accounts to impressionistic narratives. In either case, especially important events and people in the author's life are highlighted.

■ **READING SKILL: MAKE INFERENCES ABOUT THE AUTHOR**

Making inferences means "reading between the lines"—making logical guesses based on evidence in the text to figure out what is not directly stated. As you read the *Autobiography*, make inferences about the values and motives that seem characteristic of Franklin's personality. Use a chart like the one shown to record details from the text about the 13 virtues he hopes to acquire and how he goes about doing so. What inferences can you make about him?

Details or Evidence from Text	Inference

Review: **Connect**

▲ **VOCABULARY IN CONTEXT**

Franklin uses the following boldfaced words in describing his efforts to improve himself. Restate each phrase, using a different word or words for the boldfaced term.

1. **unremitting** storms that went on for weeks
2. **felicity** over her great good luck
3. a mansion as one symbol of **affluence**
4. dreamed up an **artifice** to avoid doing his job
5. **incorrigible** behavior that disgraced the family
6. a **trifling** problem, easily cleared up
7. would often **contrive** to secretly meet his friends
8. worked to **eradicate** smallpox around the world

Is PERFECTION *possible?*

KEY IDEA As a young man, Benjamin Franklin believed that human beings could actually achieve perfection in a given area. All you needed was a reasonable plan and a lot of self-discipline. Many people today also aim for perfection, although their quest may take a different path. Bookstores have whole sections devoted to **self-improvement** in a variety of areas, including diet, exercise, careers, and dating.

QUICKWRITE Do you think perfection is possible or at least worth striving for? If you think so, outline a self-improvement plan that shows how you might achieve your goal. If you don't think perfection is possible, write a paragraph in which you explain why you think it is unattainable.

THE AUTOBIOGRAPHY **263**

Is PERFECTION *possible?*

Read the question aloud, and ask students to read the **KEY IDEA**. Have students finish the **QUICKWRITE**, and then ask volunteers to share their **self-improvement** plans or to explain why perfection is impossible.

SKILLS FOCUS

● **CHARACTERISTICS OF AUTOBIOGRAPHY**

Have students read the first paragraph of the author biography on page 262. Ask them to identify significant moments in Franklin's life that they would expect to read about in his autobiography. ***Possible answer:*** *He helped draft the Declaration of Independence, he created an alliance with France, and he unified the nation's founders.*

CHECK UNDERSTANDING Ask students to identify a significant life moment for the person featured in an autobiography they have read or viewed on film.

■ **MAKE INFERENCES ABOUT THE AUTHOR**

Have students read **Pulling Himself Up.** Ask them to identify details about Franklin and make an inference about him based on these details. ***Possible answer:*** *He taught himself to write, and he started his own printing business. He must have been very intelligent and industrious.*

CHECK UNDERSTANDING Have students read *FYI* and make an inference about Franklin from these details.

 RESOURCE MANAGER—Copy Master
Make Inferences About the Author p. 439 (for student use while reading the selection)

▲ **VOCABULARY IN CONTEXT**

DIAGNOSE WORD KNOWLEDGE To determine preteaching needs, have all students complete Vocabulary in Context. ***Answers:*** 1. *nonstop,* 2. *cheerfulness,* 3. *wealth,* 4. *trick,* 5. *incurable,* 6. *unimportant,* 7. *plan,* 8. *eliminate*

PRETEACH VOCABULARY Preteach vocabulary with this copy master. Read each item aloud.

 RESOURCE MANAGER—Copy Master
Vocabulary Study p. 441

MORE VOCABULARY SUPPORT
For additional activities and guidelines, see

 BEST PRACTICES TOOLKIT
Scaffolding Vocabulary Instruction pp. 43–46
ⓘ Vocabulary Center at **ClassZone.com**

SUMMARY

This excerpt from Benjamin Franklin's *The Autobiography* details his attempt to reach moral perfection. He creates a list of 13 virtues that he decides he must possess in order to attain perfection. Next, he creates a book that lists the 13 virtues and helps him track his attempts to acquire one virtue each week. Although Franklin cannot attain moral perfection, struggling in particular to achieve Order, he feels the experiment made him a happier, better man.

LITERARY ANALYSIS

Ⓐ AUTOBIOGRAPHY

Possible answer: The characteristics of autobiography include Franklin's use of the pronoun I to tell about an important time in his life (lines 1–4) and his statement to the reader as to why this moment was significant (lines 9–12).

THE Autobiography

BENJAMIN FRANKLIN

BACKGROUND Franklin was a prolific writer, producing volumes of essays, travel journals, newspaper articles, satires, speeches, almanacs, letters, and even ballads. But his great masterpiece was his *Autobiography,* which is still very popular today. The following excerpt details Franklin's plan to achieve moral perfection. He was about 20 years old when he first conceived the idea on one of his long, trans-Atlantic voyages. The plan reveals his faith in reason, order, and human perfectibility, which was typical of 18th-century thought.

It was about this time I conceived the bold and arduous project of arriving at moral perfection. I wished to live without committing any fault at any time; I would conquer all that either natural inclination, custom, or company might lead me into. As I knew, or thought I knew, what was right and wrong, I did not see why I might not always do the one and avoid the other. But I soon found I had undertaken a task of more difficulty than I had imagined. While my care was employed in guarding against one fault, I was often surprised by another; habit took the advantage of inattention; inclination was sometimes too strong for reason. I concluded, at length, that the mere speculative conviction that it was our
10 interest to be completely virtuous, was not sufficient to prevent our slipping; and that the contrary habits must be broken, and good ones acquired and established, before we can have any dependence on a steady, uniform rectitude of conduct. For this purpose I therefore contrived the following method. Ⓐ

In the various enumerations of the moral virtues I had met with in my reading, I found the catalogue more or less numerous, as different writers included more or

ANALYZE VISUALS
What do the details of this famous painting suggest about Franklin?

❶ **Targeted Passage**

Ⓐ **AUTOBIOGRAPHY**
What characteristics of autobiography do you find in the first paragraph of this selection?

264 UNIT 1: EARLY AMERICAN WRITING

Benjamin Franklin (1767), David Martin. Oil on canvas.
© White House Historical Association, Washington, D.C.

DIFFERENTIATED INSTRUCTION

FOR ALL STUDENTS

Provide these independent projects to extend the lesson:

- Create a book of virtues.
- Analyze analogies and their meanings.

For further details on these projects, see

Ⓡ **RESOURCE MANAGER**
Ideas for Extension p. 432

FOR STRATEGIC READERS

In combination with the *Audio Anthology CD,* use one or more Targeted Passages (pp. 264, 266, 269, 270) to ensure that students focus on key concepts in the selection. Targeted Passages are also good for English learners.

❶ **Targeted Passage [Lines 1–13]**

This passage introduces students to the purpose of this part of Franklin's autobiography.

ANALYZE VISUALS

Possible answer: The details of this painting suggest that Benjamin Franklin was a thoughtful and literate man. He is reading and pondering, as denoted by his look of thoughtful contemplation. He wears a wig and is elegantly dressed, which suggests that he gained some wealth and status in his life.

Lines 5–9
REINFORCE *KEY IDEA:* SELF—IMPROVEMENT

Discuss Does Franklin find **self-improvement** easy? *Possible answer:* No. He realizes that when he focuses on fixing one fault, another one of his faults appears. He also finds that habit and temptation are both difficult to overcome.

- What goal does Franklin set for himself?
- Is Franklin easily able to control his faults? Explain.
- What does Franklin say must be done in order to maintain a "uniform rectitude of conduct"?

FOR ENGLISH LEARNERS

Key Academic Vocabulary Use Definition Mapping to teach these words: *task* (line 6), *mental* (line 18), *facilitate* (line 29), *constant* (line 31), *exceed* (line 75), *scheme* (line 82).

 BEST PRACTICES TOOLKIT—Transparency
Definition Mapping p. E6

Prereading For prereading instruction for English learners, see

 BEST PRACTICES TOOLKIT
Scaffolding Reading Instruction pp. 43–46

FOR ADVANCED LEARNERS/AP

AP exercises in the bottom channel provide additional challenge for students. Use these suggestions for small groups or individuals.

ADDITIONAL GUIDELINES

For more help with differentiation and tips for classroom management, see

 BEST PRACTICES TOOLKIT
Differentiated Instruction pp. 31–38

TIERED DISCUSSION PROMPTS

Use these prompts to have students reflect on Franklin's list of virtues:

Connect Think about a time when you set a goal to change an aspect of your behavior. How does that experience help you understand Franklin's goals? *Answers will vary but should show an understanding of the universality of Franklin's desire to improve.*

Interpret Read virtue #4: Resolution. How would achieving this virtue lead to moral perfection? ***Possible answer:*** *If people always do what they should and do what they promise to do, then they will be reliable and trustworthy—traits that a morally perfect person must have.*

Evaluate How do you respond to Franklin's list? Would you change the virtues on it, either by adding or removing virtues? Explain. *Answers should reflect a definition of moral perfection and how adding or removing specific virtues would help achieve such perfection.*

READING SKILL

B MAKE INFERENCES

Possible answer: *Franklin lists 13 areas in which he thinks he needs practice. This suggests that he feels the need for self-improvement in many areas and feels his moral character is far from perfect.*

---

fewer ideas under the same name. Temperance, for example, was by some confined to eating and drinking, while by others it was extended to mean the moderating every other pleasure, appetite, inclination, or passion, bodily or mental, even to our avarice and ambition. I proposed to myself, for the sake of clearness, to use
20 rather more names, with fewer ideas annexed to each, than a few names with more ideas; and I included under thirteen names of virtues all that at that time occurred to me as necessary or desirable, and annexed to each a short precept, which fully expressed the extent I gave to its meaning.

These names of virtues, with their precepts were:

1. **TEMPERANCE.** Eat not to dullness; drink not to elevation.

2. **SILENCE.** Speak not but what may benefit others or yourself; avoid **trifling** conversation.

3. **ORDER.** Let all your things have their places; let each part of your business have its time.

4. **RESOLUTION.** Resolve to perform what you ought; perform without fail what you resolve.

5. **FRUGALITY.** Make no expense but to do good to others or yourself; *i.e.,* waste nothing.

6. **INDUSTRY.** Lose no time; be always employed in something useful; cut off all unnecessary actions.

7. **SINCERITY.** Use no hurtful deceit; think innocently and justly; and, if you speak, speak accordingly.

8. **JUSTICE.** Wrong none by doing injuries, or omitting the benefits that are your duty.

9. **MODERATION.** Avoid extremes; forbear resenting injuries so much as you think they deserve.

10. **CLEANLINESS.** Tolerate no uncleanliness in body, clothes, or habitation.

11. **TRANQUILLITY.** Be not disturbed at trifles, or at accidents common or unavoidable.

12. **CHASTITY.** Rarely use venery but for health or offspring, never to dulness, weakness, or the injury of your own or another's peace or reputation.

13. **HUMILITY.** Imitate Jesus and Socrates.[1] **B**

My intention being to acquire the *habitude* of all these virtues, I judged it would be well not to distract my attention by attempting the whole at once, but to fix it on one of them at a time; and, when I should be master of that, then to proceed to another, and so on, till I should have gone through the thirteen; and, as the previous acquisition of some might facilitate the acquisition of certain others, I
30 arranged them with that view, as they stand above. Temperance first, as it tends to

---

1. **Socrates** (sŏk'rə-tēz'): Greek philosopher (470?–399 B.C.) who believed that true knowledge comes through dialogue and systematic questioning of ideas; he was executed for his beliefs.

trifling (trī'flǐng) *adj.* frivolous; inconsequential **trifle** *v.*

2 Targeted Passage

B MAKE INFERENCES Based on Franklin's list of virtues, what inference can you make about his view of his own moral character? Explain.

DIFFERENTIATED INSTRUCTION

FOR STRATEGIC READERS

2 Targeted Passage [Lines 24–30]

This passage presents Franklin's list of virtues and explains how he intends to follow it.

• What is the first virtue on the list? What is the last one?

• Does Franklin intend to focus on all virtues at the same time? Explain.

• How will acquiring each virtue help Franklin acquire the virtues that follow?

FOR ADVANCED LEARNERS/AP

Compare and Contrast [paired option] Have students review virtue #13: Humility. Ask pairs to briefly research the lives of Socrates and Jesus and list examples of how each man demonstrated humility. Have pairs use a Venn Diagram to compare and contrast the characters of Jesus and Socrates, then write a paragraph that explains how both men embody the virtue of humility. Have students conclude by suggesting why Franklin listed hu-

mility as the final virtue on his list. ***Example:*** *The preceding 12 virtues are necessary in order to achieve humility.* Encourage pairs to share their diagrams and paragraphs with the class.

BEST PRACTICES TOOLKIT—Transparency Venn Diagram p. A26

procure that coolness and clearness of head, which is so necessary where constant vigilance was to be kept up, and guard maintained against the **unremitting** attraction of ancient habits, and the force of perpetual temptations. This being acquired and established, Silence would be more easy; and my desire being to gain knowledge at the same time that I improved in virtue, and considering that in conversation it was obtained rather by the use of the ears than of the tongue, and therefore wishing to break a habit I was getting into of prattling, punning, and joking, which only made me acceptable to trifling company, I gave *Silence* the second place. This and the next, *Order,* I expected would allow me more time for

40 attending to my project and my studies. *Resolution,* once become habitual, would keep me firm in my endeavors to obtain all the subsequent virtues; *Frugality* and *Industry* freeing me from my remaining debt, and producing **affluence** and independence, would make more easy the practice of Sincerity and Justice, etc., etc. Conceiving then, that, agreeably to the advice of Pythagoras in his Golden Verses,[2] daily examination would be necessary, I **contrived** the following method for conducting that examination. **C**

I made a little book, in which I allotted a page for each of the virtues. I ruled each page with red ink, so as to have seven columns, one for each day of the week, marking each column with a letter for the day. I crossed these columns with

50 thirteen red lines, marking the beginning of each line with the first letter of one of the virtues, on which line, and in its proper column, I might mark, by a little black spot, every fault I found upon examination to have been committed respecting that virtue upon that day.

I determined to give a week's strict attention to each of the virtues successively. Thus, in the first week,

60 my great guard was to avoid every[3] the least offense against *Temperance,* leaving the other virtues to their ordinary chance, only marking every evening the faults of the day. Thus, if in the first week I could keep my first line, marked T, clear of spots, I supposed the habit of that virtue so much strengthened, and its opposite weakened, that I might venture

70 extending my attention to include the next, and for the following week keep both lines clear of spots. Proceeding

Form of the pages.

TEMPERANCE							
eat not to dullness; drink not to elevation.							
	S.	M.	T.	W.	T.	F.	S.
T.							
S.	•	•		•		•	
O.	••	•	•		•	•	•
R.			•			•	
F.		•			•		
I.			•	•			
S.							
J.							
M.							
C.							
T.							
C.							
H.							

---

2. **Pythagoras** (pĭ-thăg′ər-əs)...**Golden Verses:** Pythagoras was a Greek philosopher and mathematician (580?–500? B.C.).

3. **every:** even.

unremitting (ŭn′rĭ-mĭt′ĭng) *adj.* constant; never stopping

affluence (ăf′lōō-əns) *n.* wealth

contrive (kən-trīv′) *v.* to plan skillfully; to design

C MAKE INFERENCES What can you infer from lines 25–46 about Franklin's approach to problems?

READING SKILL

C MAKE INFERENCES

Possible answer: *Franklin is both methodical and disciplined when he attempts to solve a problem. He methodically determines a procedure for focusing on one virtue at a time (lines 25–30) and is able to explain why one virtue must be mastered before another (lines 30–44). He is disciplined enough to follow and maintain a "daily examination" of his conduct (line 45).*

If students need help. . . Refer them to lines 25–28, in which Franklin describes his methodology, and 30–44, in which he describes his reasons for that methodology. Then work with them to list details and inferences in the prereading chart introduced on page 263.

Details or Evidence from Text	Inference
He determines a method for focusing on one virtue at a time and puts the virtues in the order to be followed.	He is methodical.
He is willing to examine his daily conduct regarding the following of a virtue.	He is disciplined.

Lines 47–72
REINFORCE *KEY IDEA:* SELF–IMPROVEMENT

Discuss How does Franklin's chart help him in his quest for **self-improvement**? Do you think that a chart like this is useful? Explain.

Possible answer: *The chart helps Franklin to keep track of any faults he commits against the noted virtue and tells him when he can focus on the next virtue. It is useful because it gives physical evidence and therefore pushes Franklin to honestly recognize and evaluate his behavior.*

FOR STRATEGIC READERS

Summarize Reread lines 30–44 with students and ask them to explain in their own words why Franklin listed the first five virtues in the order that he did. For example, Franklin believed that temperance helped a person think clearly and avoid both old, damaging habits and temptations. This virtue, thus, would help him acquire the other 12 virtues.

FOR ENGLISH LEARNERS

Vocabulary: Multiple-Meaning Words [mixed-readiness groups] Explain that *confined* (line 16) means "restricted to" and also "shut or kept in." Help students use context clues to choose the first meaning. Have students work in groups to define these multiple-meaning words and select meanings that fit the context: *Order* (#3), *Wrong* (#8), *determined* (line 57), *guard* (line 60), *chance* (line 63), *clear* (line 66), *supposed* (line 67).

thus to the last, I could go through a course complete in thirteen weeks, and four courses in a year. And like him who, having a garden to weed, does not attempt to **eradicate** all the bad herbs at once, which would exceed his reach and his strength, but works on one of the beds at a time, and, having accomplished the first, proceeds to a second, so I should have, I hoped, the encouraging pleasure of seeing on my pages the progress I made in virtue, by clearing successively my lines of their spots, till in the end, by a number of courses, I should be happy in
80 viewing a clean book, after thirteen weeks' daily examination. . . . **D**

eradicate (ĭ-răd′ĭ-kāt′) v. to destroy completely

The precept of *Order* requiring that *every part of my business should have its allotted time*, one page in my little book contained the following scheme of employment for the twenty-four hours of a natural day.

D AUTOBIOGRAPHY
In what way do lines 47–80 provide an example of Franklin's **dual perspective**?

The Morning. *Question.* What good shall I do this day?	5 6 7	Rise, wash, and address *Powerful Goodness!* Contrive day's business, and take the resolution of the day; prosecute the present study, and breakfast.
	8 9 10 11	Work.
Noon.	12 1	Read, or overlook my accounts, and dine.
	2 3 4 5	Work.
Evening. *Question.* What good have I done today?	6 7 8 9	Put things in their places. Supper. Music or diversion, or conversation. Conversation. Examination of the day.
	10 11 12	
Night.	1 2 3 4	Sleep.

D AUTOBIOGRAPHY

Possible answer: These lines demonstrate Franklin's dual perspective because he writes as an older man and describes how as a young man he wished to lead a good and virtuous life. He writes about the plan he devised for achieving that goal (lines 47–74), and the analogy about the garden that he uses suggests a sense of humor about his youthful ambition to achieve perfection (lines 74–77).

DIFFERENTIATED INSTRUCTION

FOR STRATEGIC READERS

Characterization Read over the page of Franklin's book regarding Order and ask students these questions to help them characterize Franklin:

- What time does Franklin arise in the morning and what does he do? (5 A.M., *wash*)
- What does he do from 9 A.M. to 5 P.M.? (*work*)

- How does he spend his evenings? *Possible answer: He cleans up, eats, and listens to music or converses with others.*
- What words would you use to describe Franklin based on his daily schedule and activities? *Possible answer: serious, organized* Help students to recognize that Franklin is disciplined, serious, and industrious.

FOR ADVANCED LEARNERS/AP

Evaluate Have students create a daily log for a typical school day, using Franklin's format as a template. Challenge them to identify similarities in the basic structures of both typical days. Then ask them to evaluate the efficacy of fixed daily schedules in today's world. Are these useful in organizing school or work days or would a different structure be more effective? *Students may prefer a more flexible day.*

I entered upon the execution of this plan for self-examination, and continued it with occasional intermissions for some time. I was surprised to find myself so much fuller of faults than I had imagined; but I had the satisfaction of seeing them diminish. To avoid the trouble of renewing now and then my little book, which, by scraping out the marks on the paper of old faults to make room for new ones in a new course, became full of holes, I transferred my tables and precepts to the ivory
90 leaves of a memorandum book, on which the lines were drawn with red ink, that made a durable stain, and on those lines I marked my faults with a black-lead pencil, which marks I could easily wipe out with a wet sponge. After a while I went through one course only in a year, and afterward only one in several years, till at length I omitted them entirely, being employed in voyages and business abroad, with a multiplicity of affairs that interfered; but I always carried my little book with me. **E**

My scheme of *Order* gave me the most trouble; and I found that, though it might be practicable where a man's business was such as to leave him the disposition of his time, that of a journeyman printer, for instance, it was not possible to be exactly observed by a master, who must mix with the world, and
100 often receive people of business at their own hours. *Order,* too, with regard to places for things, papers, etc., I found extremely difficult to acquire. I had not been early accustomed to it, and, having an exceeding good memory, I was not so sensible of the inconvenience attending want of method. This article, therefore, cost me so much painful attention, and my faults in it vexed me so much, and I made so little progress in amendment, and had such frequent relapses, that I was almost ready to give up the attempt, and content myself with a faulty character in that respect, like the man who, in buying an ax of a smith, my neighbor, desired to have the whole of its surface as bright as the edge. The smith consented to grind it bright for him if he would turn the wheel; he turned, while the smith pressed
110 the broad face of the ax hard and heavily on the stone, which made the turning of it very fatiguing. The man came every now and then from the wheel to see how the work went on, and at length would take his ax as it was, without farther grinding. "No," said the smith, "turn on, turn on; we shall have it bright by-and-by; as yet, it is only speckled." "Yes," says the man, *"but I think I like a speckled ax best."* And I believe this may have been the case with many, who, having, for want of some such means as I employed, found the difficulty of obtaining good and breaking bad habits in other points of vice and virtue, have given up the struggle, and concluded that *"a speckled ax was best;"* for something, that pretended to be reason, was every now and then suggesting to me that such extreme nicety as I
120 exacted of myself might be a kind of foppery in morals,[4] which, if it were known, would make me ridiculous; that a perfect character might be attended with the inconvenience of being envied and hated; and that a benevolent man should allow a few faults in himself, to keep his friends in countenance. **F**

In truth, I found myself **incorrigible** with respect to Order; and now I am grown old, and my memory bad, I feel very sensibly the want of it. But, on the whole, though I never arrived at the perfection I had been so ambitious of

---

③ **Targeted Passage**

E MAKE INFERENCES
Reread lines 84–95. What can you infer about Franklin's persistence in pursuing his goals?

F CONNECT
What insight does Franklin come to about his quest for perfection? Consider what you have learned in your own life about perfection. Does his insight seem reasonable?

incorrigible
(ĭn-kôr′ĭ-jə-bəl) *adj.* incapable of being reformed or corrected

---

4. **foppery in morals:** excessive regard for and concern about one's moral appearance.

E MAKE INFERENCES

Possible answer: Franklin is persistent in pursuing his goals. He wears out the paper of the first book he started and has to replace it (lines 87–92). He uses phrases such as "for some time" (line 85), "in a year" (line 93), and "in several years" (line 93) to show that he continued his pursuit.

Lines 96–108
TIERED DISCUSSION PROMPTS

Use these prompts to help students understand Franklin's character:

Connect When have you struggled to accomplish something and wanted to give up trying? *Accept all reasonable responses.*

Analyze What causes Franklin to have such difficulty with Order? *Possible answer: Franklin had to deal with others and meet with people for business at hours convenient to them (lines 99–100). He also had a good memory and therefore never had to order things to find them (lines 101–103).*

Synthesize Based on what you know about Franklin's character, would you expect him to give up trying to acquire Order and the other virtues? *Possible answer: No. Franklin seems intelligent, disciplined, and determined. He seems clever enough to determine a way to overcome his bad habits, and seeing that he says he practiced his method over the years (line 93), he clearly does not stop trying.*

READING SKILL: *Review*

F CONNECT

Possible answer: Franklin decides that it might be better to accept and live with a few faults so that he won't be envied or seem too smug to his friends (lines 121–123). His insight seems reasonable, as people are imperfect and thus feel more comfortable with others who recognize this.

FOR STRATEGIC READERS

③ **Targeted Passage [Lines 84–107]**

This passage shows Franklin's diligence and describes his problems in seeking perfection.

- According to Franklin, how flawed is he? How does he respond to finding faults in himself?

- Does Franklin continue to work on perfecting these virtues after his first attempt?

- What virtue does Franklin struggle with most? How does he react to this struggle?

FOR ENGLISH LEARNERS

Vocabulary: Idioms Help students use context clues to determine the meanings of these idioms: *met with* (line 14), "found"; *gone through* (line 28), "completed"; *on the whole* (lines 125–126), "in summary"; *fell short of* (line 127), "failed"; *reap the benefit* (line 146), "gain or benefit."

ANALYZE VISUALS

Activity Ask students which virtue of Franklin's this picture best represents. *Possible answer: The picture suggests Franklin's success at Industry (lines 42–43, 138), as it shows him working hard at the Pennsylvania Gazette—the newspaper he ran.*

Lines 124–131
REINFORCE *KEY IDEA:* SELF–IMPROVEMENT

Discuss In what ways did Franklin succeed in his quest for **self-improvement?** In what ways did he fail? *Accept all thoughtful answers.*

LITERARY ANALYSIS

G AUTOBIOGRAPHY

Possible answer: *Franklin describes the significant moment when he realizes that he "fell short of" his goal of moral perfection (line 127), and yet he realizes that the attempt has still made him a better person (lines 127–128).*

SELECTION WRAP–UP

SUMMARIZE Have students sum up what Franklin learned about himself and people as he attempted to achieve moral perfection.

★ CRITIQUE

- Have students evaluate whether this part of Franklin's autobiography could inspire someone else to attempt moral perfection.

- After completing the After Reading questions on page 272, have students revisit their responses and tell whether they have changed their opinions.

obtaining, but fell short of it, yet I was, by the endeavor, a better and a happier man than I otherwise should have been if I had not attempted it; as those who aim at perfect writing by imitating the engraved copies, though they never reach
130 the wished-for excellence of those copies, their hand is mended by the endeavor, and is tolerable while it continues fair and legible. **G**

It may well be my posterity should be informed that to this little **artifice,** with the blessing of God, their ancestor owed the constant **felicity** of his life, down to his 79th year, in which this is written. What reverses may attend the reminder is in the hand of Providence; but, if they arrive, the reflection on past happiness enjoyed ought to help his bearing them with more resignation. To Temperance he ascribes his long-continued health, and what is still left to him of a good constitution; to Industry and Frugality, the early easiness of his circumstances and acquisition of his fortune, with all that knowledge that enabled him to be a useful
140 citizen, and obtained for him some degree of reputation among the learned; to Sincerity and Justice, the confidence of his country, and the honorable employs it conferred upon him; and to the joint influence of the whole mass of the virtues, even in the the imperfect state he was able to acquire them, all that evenness of temper, and that cheerfulness in conversation, which makes his company still sought for, and agreeable even to his younger acquaintance. I hope, therefore, that some of my descendants may follow the example and reap the benefit. ❧

G AUTOBIOGRAPHY
What **significant moment** or insight is described in this paragraph?

artifice (är′tə-fĭs) *n.* a clever means to an end

felicity (fĭ-lĭs′ĭ-tē) *n.* great happiness

④ **Targeted Passage**

DIFFERENTIATED INSTRUCTION

FOR STRATEGIC READERS

④ **Targeted Passage [Lines 132–146]**

This passage explains what Franklin gained from his quest for moral perfection.

- What virtues does Franklin name to show that he benefited from practicing?

- How does the imperfect practice of all of the virtues affect his life?

- What does Franklin want for his descendants?

FOR ADVANCED LEARNERS/AP

Analyze Literary Nonfiction [small-group option] Recall with students that they learn a lot about Franklin's character through both his topic choices and writing style. Organize students into small groups. Assign groups one or two topics from the Analysis Frame: Literary Nonfiction. Have groups discuss and then summarize their thoughts for the class.

 BEST PRACTICES TOOLKIT—Transparency Analysis Frame: Literary Nonfiction pp. D21, D48

from Poor Richard's Almanack

BENJAMIN FRANKLIN

He that cannot obey cannot command.

Don't count your chickens before they are hatched.

A mob's a monster; heads enough but no brains.

Well done is better than well said.

Lost time is never found again.

Early to bed, early to rise, makes a man healthy, wealthy and wise.

If you would know the worth of money, go and try to borrow some.

A friend in need is a friend indeed.

Fish and visitors smell in three days.

Love your neighbor; yet don't pull down your hedge.

God helps them that help themselves.

If you would keep your secret from an enemy, tell it not to a friend.

Be slow in choosing a friend, slower in changing.

Don't throw stones at your neighbors', if your own windows are glass.

Eat to live and not live to eat.

Love your enemies, for they tell you your faults.

Better slip with foot than tongue.

Three may keep a secret, if two of them are dead.

Never leave that till tomorrow, which you can do today.

A penny saved is a penny earned.

A rolling stone gathers no moss.

Make hay while the sun shines.

Beware of little expenses; a small leak will sink a great ship.

He that goes a borrowing goes a sorrowing.

Honesty is the best policy.

Little strokes fell big oaks.

He that lies down with dogs shall rise up with fleas.

TIERED DISCUSSION PROMPTS

Use these prompts to help students link Benjamin Franklin's sayings to the virtues he valued:

Connect What experiences do these sayings bring to mind? How do the sayings help you understand Franklin's character and search for moral perfection? *Possible answer: Accept all thoughtful answers. The sayings show that Franklin was witty, forthright, and honest, and that he valued productivity and relationships. Most of the sayings reflect at least one of his goals for moral perfection.*

Analyze Select five aphorisms. Under which of Franklin's 13 virtues would each of these aphorisms be listed? *Students' answers will vary but should reflect an understanding of the aphorism, the virtue, and a reasonable link between them. For example, the aphorism "Early to bed, early to rise, makes a man healthy, wealthy and wise" matches the virtue "Industry."*

Evaluate Focus on several aphorisms. Do you agree with the opinions Franklin expresses in them? Explain and defend your answer. *Students' answers will vary but should show an understanding of the sentiment expressed in each aphorism. For example, students may disagree with the idea of choosing friends slowly or agree with the idea of always being honest.*

Practice and Apply

After Reading

Use these copy masters to check understanding and provide extra support:

R RESOURCE MANAGER—Copy Masters
Reading Check p. 444
Characteristics of Autobiography p. 437
Question Support p. 445

Additional selection questions are provided for teachers on page 431.

ANSWERS

1. *Students can name any seven.*

2. *Jesus and Socrates*

3. *Franklin decides to attack one virtue at a time and believes that mastering some first would help him master the others later.*

4. *Franklin creates a 13-page book with pages for each virtue. He divides each page into seven columns for the days of the week and 13 rows for the virtues. Each day he marks the columns with a black spot for a lapse. Each week, he focuses on acquiring a different virtue (lines 47–72).*

Possible answers:

5. ■ **SKILLS FOCUS Make Inferences About the Author** *healthful living: temperance, moderation, cleanliness, tranquility; **succeeding in the world**: resolution, frugality, industry, order; **getting along with others**: silence, sincerity, justice, chastity, humility. Franklin's list of virtues reveal his belief in reason and his faith in humanity to improve and progress. He seems to value a life well lived.*

6. ● **SKILLS FOCUS Characteristics of Autobiography** *Young Franklin **Character Trait:** reasonable and methodical, funny, diligent; **Evidence in Text:** devises virtues list and orderly plan to achieve them (lines 14–30, 47–74), recognizes his habit of "prattling, punning, and joking" (lines 37–38), carries his little book with him (line 95); **Old Franklin Character Trait:** successful, trustworthy, cheerful, and even-tempered; **Evidence in Text:** acquired a fortune (line 139), gained his nation's confidence (line 141), became sought-after (lines 143–145). Students may conclude that Franklin portrays himself more favorably as an older man than as an inexperienced youth.*

Comprehension

1. **Recall** Name seven of Franklin's virtues.

2. **Recall** Who are Franklin's models for the virtue of humility?

3. **Clarify** Why does Franklin list the virtues in the order he does?

4. **Summarize** What is Franklin's method for acquiring the 13 virtues?

Literary Analysis

5. **Make Inferences About the Author** Look at the details and inferences you recorded in your chart. Now assign each of Franklin's 13 virtues to one of the following categories. What can you infer about Franklin's beliefs and values in general from his list of virtues?

   • healthful living   • succeeding in the world   • getting along with others

6. **Analyze Autobiography** Like most autobiographies, Franklin's has a dual perspective in which he is both main character and narrator. Go back through the excerpt to find characterizations of Franklin as a young man and as an older man looking back on his life. Record your answers in two charts as shown. What differences do you find?

Young Franklin	
Character Trait	Evidence in Text
1. Ambitious	1. "I conceived the bold and arduous project of arriving at moral perfection." (lines 1–2)
2.	

Old Franklin	
Character Trait	Evidence in Text
1. Honest	1. "In truth, I found myself incorrigible with respect to Order, and now I am grown old, . . . I feel very sensibly the want of it." (lines 124–125)
2.	

7. **Interpret Analogy** Reread lines 105–115. How does the analogy about the man buying an ax help explain Franklin's problems with order? How is Franklin like or different from the man with the ax?

8. **Evaluate Conclusions** Franklin ultimately fails to achieve moral perfection. What conclusions does he draw about his original plan? In terms of **self-improvement**, is it better to aim high and fall short or to set a lower goal?

Literary Criticism

9. **Critical Interpretations** Throughout history, Franklin has had his detractors as well as his admirers. Some consider him self-righteous and materialistic; others have ridiculed his plan for moral perfection as too regimented and superficial. Do you find any evidence for these charges in the excerpt? Explain.

---

7. *The analogy explains Franklin's temptation to give up on trying to achieve order. Like the man, he is tempted to make a virtue of giving up. Unlike the man, he rejects this argument and instead admits to honest failure (lines 114–123).*

8. *Franklin concludes that trying to achieve moral perfection makes him a "better and a happier man" (lines 127–128). Students' answers about self-improvement will vary but should reflect an understanding of the concept and comparisons to Franklin's experience.*

9. *Students may say that Franklin's virtues seem materialistic and regimented and leave no room for feelings. However, what some would see as smug or self-righteous can also appear as an honest assessment of the author's successes and failures (lines 136–146).*

Vocabulary in Context

VOCABULARY PRACTICE

Show your understanding of the vocabulary words by answering these questions.

WORD LIST
affluence
artifice
contrive
eradicate
felicity
incorrigible
trifling
unremitting

1. Which would cause **felicity,** doing well on a test or having trouble sleeping?
2. If someone created an **artifice,** would that person be shrewd or naïve?
3. If you want to **eradicate** the weeds in your yard, should you use a plant book or a garden tool?
4. To **contrive,** would you act impulsively or by plan?
5. Who is more likely **incorrigible,** a person with five parking tickets or one with five burglary convictions?
6. Is a **trifling** problem one you should ignore or act on immediately?
7. If you wanted to hide your **affluence,** would you probably drive an inexpensive car or take a trip around the world?
8. Is a person with **unremitting** joy constantly happy or never happy?

VOCABULARY IN WRITING

Choose a virtue from Franklin's list on page 266 that you have trouble with in your own life. Using at least two vocabulary words, write a brief plan explaining steps you could take to improve in this area. Here is a sample beginning.

> **EXAMPLE SENTENCE**
> Like Franklin, I need to **contrive** a plan to become more frugal.

VOCABULARY STRATEGY: THE LATIN ROOT *fic*

You are probably familiar with the Latin root *fac,* which means "make" or "do." Another common spelling of this root is *fic,* as in the vocabulary word *artifice.* Identifying a word's roots, as well as looking at context and at the other parts of the word, can often help you to figure out the word's meaning.

PRACTICE Choose the word from the word web that best completes each sentence. Use context clues to help you or consult a dictionary.

1. Who is the _____ on Grandma's life insurance policy?
2. A _____ in vitamin D can lead to rickets, a disease of the bones.
3. One_____ in the pipe was blocked, causing water to back up into it.
4. Due to the _____ of the Kelly family, the town has the money to build a new pool.
5. The speaker described the _____ of acupuncture as a treatment for several ailments.

R1.2
CALIFORNIA

word web: efficacy, artifice, orifice, **fic**, deficiency, beneficiary, munificence

VOCABULARY PRACTICE
For more practice, go to the **Vocabulary Center** at ClassZone.com.

ANSWERS

Vocabulary in Context

VOCABULARY PRACTICE

1. *doing well on a test*
2. *shrewd*
3. *garden tool*
4. *by plan*
5. *five burglary convictions*
6. *ignore*
7. *drive inexpensive car*
8. *constantly happy*

R RESOURCE MANAGER—Copy Master
Vocabulary Practice p. 442

VOCABULARY IN WRITING

Encourage students to model their plan on Franklin's methodical approach. They might freewrite to create the plan, then revise to include the selected vocabulary words.

VOCABULARY STRATEGY: THE LATIN ROOT

fic (also an EL language objective)

- For each item, help students use their knowledge of the root and context clues to determine word meaning.
- Have students consider the meanings of the common prefixes *de-* and *bene-* to help them define *deficiency* and *beneficiary.*

Answers:

1. *beneficiary*
2. *deficiency*
3. *orifice*
4. *munificence*
5. *efficacy*

R RESOURCE MANAGER—Copy Master
Vocabulary Strategy p. 443

i Vocabulary Center at **ClassZone.com**
Additional Vocabulary Activities

Assess and Reteach

Assess

Reteach

CONNECT

This selection connects with the pursuit of self-improvement that Franklin embarks on in his autobiography. You can also use it as a mini-lesson on reading for information.

Reading for Information

Point out that "50 Ways to Fix Your Life" is a magazine article. Then ask

- What does the title of a magazine article tell readers? What might the writer hope to accomplish with the title? *Possible answer: The title tells readers what an article's subject will be. The writer usually hopes to engage readers' interest.*

- What is the main idea of this article? *Possible answer: It is possible to transform your life if you are ready to do so.*

TIERED DISCUSSION PROMPTS

Use these prompts to help students connect modern approaches to self-improvement with Benjamin Franklin's ideas:

Connect How did reading this article affect your response to Franklin's goal of moral perfection? *Accept all reasonable answers.*

Interpret According to this article, why are Americans so attracted to the idea of self-improvement? *Possible answer: In America, people believe that they can change themselves and their lives. They are not restricted by their current situation or the class of their birth.*

Synthesize What do this writer and Franklin both say must happen for people to improve themselves? How are the two writers' views different? *Possible answer: Both Butler and Franklin say people must want to change, that they should record their progress, and that they will gain "lasting benefits" from making the effort, even if they experience setbacks along the way. Franklin does not mention the need for social support to help people improve.*

Reading for Information

MAGAZINE ARTICLE Benjamin Franklin's drive for self-improvement may seem a little excessive, but it remains a great American ideal. This article looks at the continuing American urge to change oneself for the better.

50 Ways to Fix Your Life

by Carolyn Kleiner Butler

Americans have long been captivated by the notion of self-improvement—none more so than Benjamin Franklin. An accomplished printer, author, postmaster, scientist, inventor, and diplomat who taught himself to speak five languages, this Founding Father "conceiv'd the bold and arduous project of arriving at moral perfection."

Today, self-help is not just a way of life—it's practically a national obsession. There are 7,500 books on the topic on amazon.com alone, covering just about every imaginable bad habit or dilemma.

Such offerings "appeal to the deeply felt American idea of 'before and after,'" says Robert Thompson, professor of media and popular culture at Syracuse University in New York, who points out the underlying similarities between Franklin and, say, Dr. Phil. "If you were born a peasant in a medieval village, you knew who you were and it was very hard to change that, but here there is fluidity of class, and entire industries pop up that reflect the ultimate optimism that really anybody can be a 'swan' and completely turn [his or her] life around."

Time to change. The hard truth is that lasting change doesn't usually happen in a single TV season. In reality, of the 40 to 45 percent of people who will make New Year's resolutions come January, fewer than half will succeed within six months, according to John Norcross, professor of psychology at the University of Scranton in Pennsylvania and coauthor of *Changing for Good*. But the fact is that when someone makes a serious commitment to transform his or her life, it is possible.

How can you cross that far-off finish line? First and foremost, you really have to be ready to do it and understand that the pros outweigh the cons. Also, research shows that keeping track of your development in a visible way—charting your weight loss, for one, or graphing your heart rate and stamina—is associated with sustainable lifestyle change, as is social support, whether in the form of friends, online discussion groups, or reliable, proven, self-help books.

Lastly, and most important, don't give up if you tumble off the wagon now and then. Triumphant changers often see a setback as a reason to recommit to their goal, and they get back on the horse immediately.

In the end, simply making a concerted effort to improve your lifestyle can have lasting benefits, no matter what the final result. Indeed, Franklin recounts, "On the whole, tho' I never arrived at . . . perfection . . . I was, by the endeavour, a better and happier man than I otherwise should have been if I had not attempted it."

Revolutionary Ideas

For colonists living in the 1770s, there was one topic around which most conversation and writing revolved: the Revolution. The writing of this period was political, and it was persuasive. It had a life-and-death purpose: to win over the hearts and minds of American colonists—and the rest of the world—to the belief that rebellion was necessary.

Writing to Persuade

Reflect briefly on each of the pieces you have just read, and select one or two you find particularly persuasive. Then, imagine you are a colonist of the time and write a letter to your local paper in which you voice your support for the ideas of the writer or writers chosen. Be sure to cite specific phrases or lines that you find convincing. Add your own thoughts and opinions to try to further persuade readers to support the rebellion.

Consider
- thought-provoking or incendiary sentences or passages
- your opinions on the issues discussed in the selections
- how to express your viewpoint clearly and convincingly

Extension

SPEAKING & LISTENING Imagine yourself on the village green, part of an impassioned gathering of colonists arguing both sides of independence from England. Recast your letter as a **speech** and deliver it to your friends, neighbors, and political opponents.

W2.2, LS2.3

Give Me Liberty or Give Me Death. Patrick Henry delivering his great speech on the *Rights of the Colonies* before the Virginia Assembly, Richmond, March 23, 1775. The Granger Collection, New York.

275

Wrap-Up: Writers of the Revolution

This Wrap-Up provides students with an opportunity to revisit ideas from the literature in this section about early America, including culture, customs, and commitment to change. Encourage students to examine their own views about early America in light of insights they gained from the selections.

Writing to Persuade

Review with students that *persuading* means using powerful words to influence others to agree with your way of thinking.

To help students write their letters, direct them to think about the selections they have read that most powerfully advanced colonial positions. Instruct them to choose a writer that they found interesting, or a position they identified with. Then, instruct them to go back to their selected piece and find excerpts that caught their attention. Have them write an outline of their letter before fleshing it out with supportive details and excerpts.

Extension

- Have students note the most passionate and persuasive comments in the selections from this section. Then ask students to consider how they might add appeals of this type to their letters. Review some of the persuasive techniques discussed in the Writing Workshop on pages 276–283.

- Direct students to organize their thoughts in a Three-Column Journal, using the headings *Author's Quotations, My Opinion,* and *Persuasive Appeals.* Remind students that their letters should include adequate support for any claims, as well as counterarguments.

 BEST PRACTICES TOOLKIT—Transparency
Three-Column Journal p. B10

DIFFERENTIATED INSTRUCTION

FOR DEVELOPING WRITERS
Writing Support Help students get started by directing them to relevant passages in the selections. For example, students might draw on lines 2–3 and 10–13 of "Letter to the Reverend Samson Occom" to write about natural rights and man's innate desire for freedom as arguments against slavery. Or they might draw on lines 13–31 of "Letter to John Adams" to write about what the colonists needed from their government, and why they needed to be free from England.

FOR ENGLISH LEARNERS
Persuasive Techniques Ask students which selections they found most convincing and why. Help them use their responses to this question as a starting point to developing their own viewpoint.

I found Thomas Jefferson's arguments for independence very convincing. I believe that the colonies should be independent because _____.

Focus and Motivate

OBJECTIVES

- analyze a student model that reflects the key traits of persuasive essays
- use the writing process to produce a persuasive essay
- revise and edit, using criteria for persuasive essays
- create and present a persuasive speech, considering audience and purpose

 W1.3, W1.4, W1.7, LC1.1, LS1.7, LS1.10

WRITER'S ROAD MAP

WRITING PROMPTS 1 AND 2

Point out the word *strongly* in both prompts. Emphasize that a topic to which students feel a strong personal connection will help them write an effective persuasive essay.

ADDITIONAL PROMPTS

Use these prompts for practice with business writing and writing in the humanities:

WRITING PROMPT 3

Writing in the Workplace Write a memo to an employer proposing that you be given more responsibilities, such as becoming the head of a new branch or department.

WRITING PROMPT 4

Writing About History Choose an event in world history that interests you. Write an essay persuading readers to share your opinion about the event. For example, did the event advance or restrict freedom? Did the people involved act justly or unjustly?

History That Might Inspire

- a crucial battle or election
- a technological advance
- a love affair that influenced global events

For additional writing prompts, see

- WriteSmart CD
- Writing Center at **ClassZone.com**

KEY TRAITS

Review the six **KEY TRAITS** with students, focusing on **ideas** and **word choice**. Compare the list of traits with the criteria on page 282.

Persuasive Essay

Here's an opportunity to think about what you believe in—and to persuade readers to agree with you and take action. Follow the **Writer's Road Map** to get started on a persuasive essay that will help you make your own mark on the world.

WRITER'S ROAD MAP
Persuasive Essay

WRITING PROMPT 1

Writing for the Real World Sometimes an issue affects you so strongly that you want to convince others to act in a certain way. Write a persuasive essay on an issue that is important to you.

Issues to Consider

- a local political issue, such as a curfew
- issues involving the environment or social justice
- freedoms and responsibilities of the media

WRITING PROMPT 2

Writing from Literature Choose an issue from Unit 1 that you feel strongly about. Write a persuasive essay that explains the issue and mentions the literary work in which you found it.

Literature to Consider

- Patrick Henry's speech to the Virginia Convention (What is liberty worth?)
- Benjamin Franklin's proverbs (Is honesty always the best policy?)
- *The Way to Rainy Mountain* (How can oppression be stopped?)
- The Declaration of Independence (When is it right to rebel?)

 WRITING TOOLS
For prewriting, revision, and editing tools, visit the **Writing Center** at ClassZone.com.

KEY TRAITS

1. IDEAS
- Clearly identifies the **issue**
- Presents a **thesis statement** that makes a clear, logical, and forceful **claim**
- Uses relevant and convincing **evidence** to **support** the position
- Anticipates and answers **opposing arguments** and counterclaims

2. ORGANIZATION
- **Introduces** the issue in an attention-getting way
- Connects ideas with **transitional words and phrases**
- **Concludes** with a summary or a call to action

3. VOICE
- Captures an appropriate **tone** for the subject matter

4. WORD CHOICE
- Addresses the **audience** directly, using appropriate language
- Uses **persuasive techniques** effectively

5. SENTENCE FLUENCY
- Employs **rhetorical devices** such as parallelism and repetition
- Varies **sentence types and lengths**

6. CONVENTIONS
- Employs **correct grammar and usage**

Writing Workshop Resources

 RESOURCE MANAGER UNIT 1

Plan and Teach pp. 451–454
Prewriting–Editing pp. 455–459
Writing Rubric p. 460
Speaking and Listening p. 461
Writing Support p. 462*

 STANDARDS LESSON FILE

Writing Lesson 8: Creating Sentence Variety
Writing Lesson 29: Persuasive Writing
Writing Lesson 9: Revising for Parallelism

 BEST PRACTICES TOOLKIT

Scaffolding Writing Instruction pp. 43–46*
Freewriting • Outline • Writing Template: Persuasive Essay • Logical Fallacies and Emotional Appeals • Making Generalizations

TECHNOLOGY
- Easy Planner DVD
- Writing Center at **ClassZone.com**
- WriteSmart CD

* Resources for Differentiation

Part 1: Analyze a Student Model

W1.3, W1.4 (pgs. 280, 281, 282), W1.7 (p. 279), LC1.1 (p. 282), LS1.7 (p. 283), LS1.10 (p. 283)

Online INTERACTIVE MODEL CLASSZONE.COM

Bruce Lomibao
Plainview High School

Cell Phone Use in Cars: Hang Up—Don't Bang Up!

Picture this: a man gets into a car, puts on a blindfold, starts the engine, puts his foot on the gas, and takes his hands off the wheel. That would never happen, you say? Maybe not, but something just as dangerous is happening all around you every day. Every time a motorist carries on a
5 cellular-phone conversation, that person is endangering not only his or her own life but also the lives of everyone else walking, bicycling, or driving nearby. Using cell phones while driving must be banned—now.

A new study by the Cellular Telecommunications & Internet Association found that more than 200 million Americans use cellular
10 telephones. People talk on the phone while watching a ballgame, walking the dog, washing the dishes, or driving to work. Although talking on a cell phone distracts people from what they are doing in each of these cases, this distraction can have serious—even fatal—consequences for drivers. I have just learned to drive myself, so I know how complicated it is and how much
15 concentration it takes. "It's absolutely clear from the research literature that talking on a cell phone while driving does elevate the risk of a crash," said Dr. Donald Reinfurt of the University of North Carolina's Highway Safety Research Center. "Using cell phones slows reaction times and degrades drivers' tracking abilities."

20 Do these slowed reflexes cause accidents? According to a study that Dr. Reinfurt conducted, about one of every 600 driving accidents involved the use of a cell phone. However, he believes that "cell phones are involved in many more crashes" because most drivers won't admit to police officers that they were on the phone at the time of the crash. According to a study of
25 drivers in Canada, "the risk of a collision when using a cellular telephone was four times higher than the risk when a cellular telephone was not being used."

KEY TRAITS IN ACTION

Memorable title identifies the **issue.** The parallelism and repetition of "Hang Up—Don't Bang Up!" is an effective **rhetorical device.**

Introduces the issue with a startling idea.

Strong words (*every time, endangering, must*) help to establish a serious **tone.** Thesis statement forcefully states a specific **claim.**

Relevant and convincing **evidence,** including an expert opinion and a statistic, add **support.**

Part 1: Analyze a Student Model

Have students read the student model and **KEY TRAITS IN ACTION.** Then discuss the model with the class, noting specific examples of each trait and building on what students have already noted. You may also wish to incorporate these activities:

- **Rhetorical Devices** Briefly review the definitions of parallelism and repetition, explaining that parallelism uses repeated grammatical patterns to express related ideas while repetition repeats words or phrases for emphasis. Then have students find examples of parallelism in the student model. ***Possible answers:*** *"walking, bicycling, or driving" (line 6); "watching a ballgame, walking the dog, washing the dishes, or driving to work" (lines 10–11).*

- **Introduction** Point out that the student model begins with a startling imaginary anecdote. Ask students to speculate on the writer's purpose for choosing this type of introduction. ***Possible answer:*** *Comparing driving while using the cell phone to an obviously absurd, dangerous style of driving, the writer makes driving while using a cell phone seem absurd and dangerous.*

- **Evidence** Review that different kinds of evidence provide different support for a writer's ideas. For example, expert opinions lend credibility to information, while statistics emphasize the raw facts. Ask students to identify the statistic in lines 20–22. ***Answer:*** *One in 600 driving accidents involved the use of a cell phone.*

DIFFERENTIATED INSTRUCTION

For general guidelines on differentiating writing instruction, see

 BEST PRACTICES TOOLKIT
Scaffolding Writing Instruction
pp. 43–46

FOR ENGLISH LEARNERS

Language: Skill Words Write these terms on the board and review them with students:

- *rhetorical devices:* techniques writers use to make their arguments more persuasive and memorable—for example, the rhyme of "Hang" and "Bang" and the repetition of "Up" in the title

- *commitment:* strong feelings about an issue—for example, Bruce Lomibao feels strongly that cell phones in cars are dangerous

- *claim:* a statement that the writer believes to be true—for example, that cell phone use in cars must be banned

- *thesis statement:* the sentence that states the main idea—for example, the highlighted sentence in line 7

- *evidence:* facts, statistics, examples, and expert opinions that support the writer's claim—for example, the statistic in line 21.

- **Opposing Arguments** Discuss possible risks to mentioning opposing arguments. Point out that presenting opposing arguments is a calculated risk that confident writers should take. If a persuasive case is strong, anticipating and rebutting opposition will enhance it. Ask why writers should always present opposition arguments fairly. ***Possible answer: Bias will throw readers' sympathy toward the opposing argument.***

- **Conclusion** Explain that a call to action usually asks readers to do something specific. Ask students to identify the call to action in the student model. ***Possible answer: The call to action asks readers to write their legislators requesting laws to ban cell phones in cars (lines 53—54).***

- **Audience** Ask students to identify the target audience for the student model. ***Possible answer: drivers, concerned citizens*** Point out that the model speaks to an American audience, unfavorably comparing American laws with those in other countries. Ask students to find other evidence for the model's American focus. ***Possible answer: "more than 200 million Americans" (line 9), "National Highway Traffic Safety Administration (line 39)*** Have students brainstorm how the model might be different if it were aimed at another audience, such as legislators or children.

For interactive student models, see

WriteSmart CD

Writing Center at **ClassZone.com**

Despite these frightening statistics, some people may say their time is so valuable that they absolutely need to talk while driving. What they fail to
30 consider is how much time they'd lose if they were injured—or worse—in a car accident. Others might argue that if lawmakers ban talking on a cell phone while driving, they will also have to ban other distractions such as eating, listening to music, and talking to passengers in the car. However, the Insurance Information Institute reports that "there is increasing
35 evidence that the dangers associated with cell-phone use outweigh those of other distractions." One reason may be that talking on a cell phone takes the driver's hands, mind, and even eyes away from the car and the road for extended periods. What about hands-free phones, then? In 2004, the National Highway Traffic Safety Administration found that drivers using
40 hands-free sets had to redial their calls more than twice as often as those using handheld phones. They also braked more slowly and were less aware of other drivers, pedestrians, and roadside landmarks.

Obviously, many people are already aware of this problem. But what are governments doing about it? Nearly 50 countries from Australia to
45 Zimbabwe have banned or restricted the use of cell phones while driving. In the United States, three states and the District of Columbia have forbidden motorists from driving while talking on the telephone, and four states have declared that only mature drivers may do so. More than two-thirds of the states and the federal government are considering legislation
50 related to cell phones and driving.

You could be the next victim of a driver distracted by a cell-phone conversation. So before that happens, remember: "Hang up—don't bang up!" Send letters or e-mails to your local, state, and federal legislators urging them to ban the use of these devices in cars. Do it today.

Transitional word (*Despite*) tells the reader that the writer is about to discuss and rebut **opposing arguments** and counterclaims.

Varied **sentence types and lengths** throughout the essay give the message maximum impact.

Strong **conclusion** addresses the **audience** directly. The appeal to fear (*You could be the next victim*) is a dramatic **persuasive technique.** The last two sentences are a call to action.

2

DIFFERENTIATED INSTRUCTION

FOR ENGLISH LEARNERS

Comprehension: Transitions List words and phrases from the student model that connect ideas, such as *although, but, so, maybe, and, however, despite, one reason, also,* and *according to*. Write these model sentences on the board:

- *Although* it is raining, we will still play.
- I called, *but* no one was home.
- It is late, *so* we must go.

- While some have moved away, *maybe* we should stay here.
- It was a good book because it was thrilling *and* well written.
- It was a tasty meal; *however,* there was no dessert.
- *Despite* how late it was, he wanted to stay up to watch the show.
- *One reason* I like swimming is that it is good exercise.

- Swimming *also* cools you off on a hot day.
- *According to* my mom, things were better in the old days.

Work with students to compose additional sentences using the listed transitional words and phrases.

To provide English learners with additional writing support, see

 RESOURCE MANAGER—Copy Master Writing Support p. 462

Part 2: Apply the Writing Process

PREWRITING

What Should I Do?

1. Make sure you understand the prompt.
Reread the prompt you chose on page 276.
<u>Underline</u> the type of writing you will do
and (circle) the purpose of that writing. Look
for information about your audience. If that
information is not given, you can assume that
your teacher and your classmates are your
audience.

2. Think of issues that you truly care about.
Use a graphic organizer to help you examine
your opinion—and opposing viewpoints—
about issues that concern you. Put an asterisk
by the issue you want to write about.

> **TIP** Be sure that there are two ways to
> look at your issue. There's no need to
> persuade people if everyone already agrees.

3. Write a working thesis statement.
Focus on your **claim**—the main idea that you
want to persuade readers about. Then express
that idea clearly in a sentence or two. You can
modify your statement as you gather evidence
and start drafting.

4. Collect support for your claim.
Search the Internet and talk to experts to
find facts, statistics, and other details that
strengthen and clarify your ideas.

See pages 1270–1273: Choosing the Right Research Tools

What Does It Look Like?

WRITING PROMPT Sometimes an issue affects you
so strongly that you want to convince others to act in a
certain way. Write a <u>persuasive essay</u> (to convince your
readers to agree with your point of view.)

> *I should write about something that really matters
> to me. But what?*

Issue	My View	Opposing Views
lower voting age to 16	many teens work, pay taxes	16-year-olds not mature enough
use of cell phones while driving*	extremely dangerous	necessary in this busy world
freedom of speech on the Internet	a right we should protect	should be limited—some ideas too dangerous

> *It would be a good idea to consider banning the use
> of cell phones while driving. If we don't, who knows
> how many innocent people will be injured or killed?*

> • *My own experience: Driving takes focus and
> concentration.*
> • *University study: Using cell phones slows drivers'
> reaction times.*
> • *Canadian study: Using a cell phone makes crash risk
> four times higher!*

FOR DEVELOPING WRITERS

Thesis Statement Help students use the
Freewriting strategy to develop ideas for
a thesis statement. Urge students to set a
time limit for their freewriting, but to write
continuously during that time. Point out that
even professional writers may develop key
ideas by choosing from many possibilities.

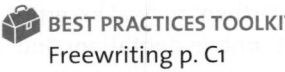 **BEST PRACTICES TOOLKIT**
Freewriting p. C1

FOR ENGLISH LEARNERS

Think of Issues As an alternative to the chart,
have students complete these statements:

• **Issue:** I am writing about _____
_____.

• **My View:** I think that _____ because
_____.

• **Opposing Views:** The other side thinks that
_____ because _____.

Practice and Apply

To support students during the writing process,
use these copy masters:

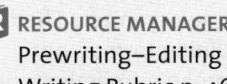 **RESOURCE MANAGER—Copy Masters**
Prewriting–Editing pp. 455–459
Writing Rubric p. 460
Writing Support p. 462 (for English
learners)

Part 2: Apply the Writing Process

PREWRITING

**1. Make sure you understand the
prompt.** Direct students' attention to the
circled phrase, "to convince your readers to
agree with your point of view." Point out
that matching the issue to the audience
is important to understanding a prompt.
Urge students to search for issues that they
and the defined audience will care about.

**2. Think of issues that you truly care
about.** As students work with the chart,
point out that they may list more than
three possible topics. After choosing a
topic, students should list as many statements as they can under **My View** and
Opposing Views. Direct students to the
TIP and tell them to be sure they can
think of at least one strong opposing
argument to their view.

3. Write a working thesis statement.
Ask whether the working thesis on this
page is the same as the thesis statement in
line 7 of the student model. (*No*) Ask why
the author revised the thesis statement.
Possible answer: *He wanted to make it
stronger and more concise.* Some students
may wish to write their thesis statements
after collecting support for their claims,
rather than before.

4. Collect support for your claim. Have
students brainstorm a list of key words
they might use in an Internet search on
their chosen prompt and a list of categories for possible experts, such as teachers,
scientists, and so on. Remind students to
take notes.

For interactive graphic organizers, see

⊘ Write*Smart* CD

ⓘ Writing Center at **ClassZone.com**

DRAFTING

1. **Put your ideas in a sensible order.** Refer students to the Outline organizer. Then review standard outlining format, noting that, typically, Roman numerals stand for major sections or ideas, capital letters stand for supporting ideas or reasons, and Arabic numerals stand for supporting details. Ask students to give an example of a detail to list with a capital letter. *Possible answer: Under II.A, one could list the number of people using cell phones.*

 BEST PRACTICES TOOLKIT—Transparency
   Outline p. B19

2. **Support your statements with reasons and evidence.** Discuss how to decide who is an expert. Emphasize that an individual's expertise in usually limited to a specific field. Thus, a scientist is only an expert in his or her specialty, not in other scientific areas, and a celebrity is usually not an expert on public issues. Ask students why Dr. Reinfurt qualifies as an expert on cell phones and driving. *Possible answer: Dr. Reinfurt is an expert because he works at the Highway Safety Research Center.*

3. **Use persuasive techniques.** Ask students what ethical appeal is made in the sample lines from the student model. *Possible answer: These lines appeal to people's ethics about not harming others with their behavior.*

For a persuasive essay writing template, see

BEST PRACTICES TOOLKIT—Transparency
   Writing Template: Persuasive Essay
   pp. C16, C31
WriteSmart CD
Writing Center at ClassZone.com

DRAFTING

What Should I Do?

1. **Put your ideas in a sensible order.**
   First, introduce the issue. Next, present your thesis statement. As you plan the rest of your essay, be sure to think of opposing arguments. Make sure that you think of at least one answer, or counterclaim, for every opposing argument. To be certain that you include all the points you want to make, you may want to create an outline before you start writing.

2. **Support your statements with reasons and evidence.**
   Include logical reasons for your point of view. Quote experts and share facts and statistics that make your position convincing. Explain how each piece of evidence backs up your claim.

3. **Use persuasive techniques.**
   Depending on your topic and your audience, you might appeal to readers' ethics or to their emotions. However, no one likes to feel bullied. Choose words that are strong but not overbearing.

   See page 245: Persuasive Techniques

What Does It Look Like?

> I. Introduction
> II. Evidence that the problem is widespread
>   A. Many people use cell phones. (How many?)
>   B. Driving takes concentration. I know from experience.
> III. Evidence that cell phone users cause accidents
>   A. Cite statistic from university study.
>   B. Cite statistic from Canadian study.
> IV. Opposing arguments (and counterclaims)
>   A. Time is valuable. (lose time in an accident)
>   B. Other distractions (phones even more distracting)
>   C. Hands-free phones (users brake slowly)
> V. Legislation passed or pending
>   A. In other countries
>   B. Within the United States
> VI. Conclusion

> This distraction can have serious—even fatal—consequences. — Main idea

> "It's absolutely clear from the research literature that talking on a cell phone while driving does elevate the risk of a crash," said Dr. Donald Reinfurt of the University of North Carolina's Highway Safety Research Center. — Support: expert opinion

> Every time a motorist carries on a cellular-phone conversation, that person is ~~dooming everyone who comes near~~ endangering not only his or her own life but also the lives of everyone else walking, bicycling, or driving nearby.

280   UNIT 1: EARLY AMERICAN WRITING

DIFFERENTIATED INSTRUCTION

FOR DEVELOPING WRITERS

Find a Sensible Order Model how to prepare an informal outline in which there is a number for each paragraph in the essay. Next to that number, the paragraph topic is summarized in a heading. Explain that this type of outline is flexible: for example, a heading can be a brief title or a longer description, and students can list supporting evidence along with a heading. Show students how the outline on page 280 could be written as an informal outline:

> 1. Cell Phone Use—Serious Problem:
> Many people use cell phones. Hard to concentrate on driving while talking.
>
> 2. Cell Phone Users Cause Accidents: statistics from studies for support

FOR ADVANCED LEARNERS/AP

Support Your Statements Remind students of the need to weave expert quotations smoothly into their essay. Quotations should be introduced or explained, and linked to the surrounding text. As students draft and revise, urge them to use transition words to help readers understand the importance of expert quotations. Ask them to read excerpts from their drafts that contain quotations and explain their use of transition words. Invite comments and questions.

REVISING AND EDITING

What Should I Do?

1. Energize your language.
- Read your draft aloud. [Bracket] words that sound vague or hesitant: *a good idea, fairly important, maybe, kind of,* and *possibly.*
- Replace these words with ones that appropriately express your strong feelings: imperatives such as *should* and *must,* adjectives such as *crucial,* and adverbs such as *immediately.*

2. Prop up any weak arguments.
- Reread your essay, underlining statements that have few or no supporting details or explanations.
- Think of clear, convincing reasons to strengthen your position. Add facts, statistics, or other evidence.

3. Watch for mistakes in logic.
- Ask a peer reader to circle any illogical statements in your essay. For example, have him or her look for words such as *all, every, no one,* and *never,* which often signal overgeneralizations.
- Instead, make accurate statements.

See page 282: Errors in Reasoning

4. Conclude concisely.
- Have a peer reader review your concluding paragraph. Does it sum up the issue? Does it spell out what you want him or her to do?
- Add information that summarizes the issue or makes a clear call for specific action.

See page 282: Ask a Peer Reader

What Does It Look Like?

▶ ~~It would be [a good idea] to [consider] banning the use of cell phones while driving.~~

Using cell phones while driving must be banned—now.

▶ *Others might argue that if lawmakers ban talking on a cell phone while driving, they will also have to ban other distractions such as eating, listening to music, and talking to passengers in the car.* ~~How ridiculous can you get?~~ *However, the Insurance Information Institute reports that "there is increasing evidence that the dangers associated with cell-phone use outweigh those of other distractions."*

▶ *Nearly 50 countries from*
Australia to Zimbabwe have
~~Every country outside of the United States has~~ *banned or restricted the use of cell phones while driving.*

▶ *You could be the next victim of a driver distracted by a cell-phone conversation. So before that happens, remember: "Hang up—don't bang up!" Send letters or e-mails to your local, state, and federal legislators urging them to ban the use of these devices in cars. Do it today.*

REVISING AND EDITING

1. Energize your language. Remind students to choose adjectives and adverbs that are specific and concrete. Have them list or use a thesaurus to find synonyms for general modifiers such as *great, good, nice,* and *really.* Also remind students to write in the active voice whenever possible, rather than in the passive voice.

2. Prop up any weak arguments. Urge students who find weak arguments in their drafts to reread their notes for additional supporting evidence. If the evidence is not in their notes, refer students to **Collect support for your claim** on page 279 for ideas.

3. Watch for mistakes in logic. Explain that a fallacy is an error in logic. Review the information on the referenced page to explain different errors in reasoning. Then have students use the Making Generalizations and the Logical Fallacies and Emotional Appeals organizers to make sure they have not overgeneralized or included logical fallacies.

🧰 BEST PRACTICES TOOLKIT—Transparencies
Logical Fallacies and Emotional Appeals
p. A67
Making Generalizations p. A31

4. Conclude concisely. Clarify that *concisely* means "in as few words as possible," but that students may still need to add to their conclusions rather than delete. For example, the student model writer added to his call for action. Emphasize that although the conclusion should be concise, it should not omit important parts.

For interactive revision tools, see

🔵 Write*Smart* CD

ℹ️ Writing Center at **ClassZone.com**

Review the GRAMMAR AND STYLE note on page 240. Remind students that using complex and compound-complex sentences helps vary the flow of their prose in order to keep readers interested.

FOR ENGLISH LEARNERS

Energize Your Language English learners may not be familiar with the connotations of synonyms, even if they know the definitions. For example, they may not know that *must* is stronger than *should,* or that *fairly* and *possibly* hint at doubt or equivocation. Have English learners work with native speakers to fine tune and energize language.

Suggest that partners focus on words and phrases that evaluate or call for action. Invite English speakers to identify words they consider weak and explain the connotations. Pairs can then use a thesaurus and dictionary to find energetic replacement words with the desired connotations.

Preparing to Publish

Support for meeting the goals in the writing criteria is supplied throughout the Writing Workshop on pages 279–281.

For Rubric Bank, see

 WriteSmart CD

ℹ️ Writing Center at ClassZone.com

Assess and Reteach

S STANDARDS LESSON FILE

Writing Lesson 8: Creating Sentence Variety

Writing Lesson 9: Revising for Parallelism

Writing Lesson 29: Persuasive Writing

Consider the Criteria

Use this checklist to make sure your persuasive essay is on track.

Ideas
☑ has a strong thesis statement
☑ persuasively supports the thesis with reasons, facts, or statistics
☑ addresses opposing arguments

Organization
☑ has a compelling introduction
☑ connects ideas clearly with transitional words and phrases
☑ concludes with a summary or a call to action

Voice
☑ maintains an appropriate tone

Word Choice
☑ uses language appropriate to the audience
☑ uses persuasive techniques

Sentence Fluency
☑ varies sentence types and lengths

Conventions
☑ uses correct grammar, spelling, and punctuation

Ask a Peer Reader
• Did my essay change your position? Why or why not?
• How could I strengthen the reasons and support in my essay?
• How could I improve my conclusion?

Errors in Reasoning

Circular reasoning: supporting an idea by simply restating it ("Cell phones are distracting because they divert drivers' attention.")

Overgeneralization: making a statement that is too broad or general to be proved ("Everyone has a cell phone nowadays.")

Either/or fallacy: ignoring possible alternate outcomes of an action ("Either you stop phoning while driving, or you'll have an accident.")

False cause: assuming that an event that follows another was the result of the first event ("Countries that have banned phone use in cars have experienced economic growth.")

See page R22: Identifying Faulty Reasoning

Check Your Grammar

Use parallel structure to express similar ideas.

Picture this: a man gets into a car, puts on a blindfold, starts the engine, ~~putting~~ *puts* his foot on the gas, and ~~his hands are off the wheel.~~ *takes*

See page R68: Parallel Structure

Writing Online

🔘 **PUBLISHING OPTIONS**
For publishing options, visit the **Writing Center** at **ClassZone.com.**

ASSESSMENT PREPARATION
For writing and grammar assessment practice, go to the **Assessment Center** at **ClassZone.com.**

LS1.7, LS1.10

Presenting a Persuasive Speech

You've spent time and effort crafting an outstanding persuasive essay. Now put your words into action by presenting a speech on the same topic.

Planning the Speech

1. **Remember your purpose and audience.** Review the reason you wrote your essay, and think about the readers you were originally addressing. Then consider what the audience for your speech might know about the issue. Will you speak to the audience as an authority or as a peer? If necessary, collect additional background information or consider eliminating specific points.

2. **Turn your essay into a script.** Mark up a copy of your essay indicating where to insert or delete information. Highlight statements you want to stress and indicate how you want to stress them—for example, by slowing down, raising your voice, or including gestures. Also think of helpful visuals to include, such as posters or video clips. Mark your script to indicate when you want to show them.

3. **Fine-tune your speech.** Practice in front of a mirror and with friends and family. Smoothly integrate the visuals with the speech. Ask for feedback and suggestions.

Delivering the Speech

1. **Look at your audience.** As you deliver your speech and display the visuals you have created, focus on different people throughout the room. This will show your audience that you are addressing everyone, even people who may not agree with your stance on the issue.

2. **Make your voice, facial expressions, and gestures work for you.** Vary your pace, tone of voice, and volume to hold your audience's attention and emphasize your points. Augment your message with appropriate facial expressions and gestures. For example, you might frown slightly when describing an opposing argument.

3. **Stay relaxed and responsive to audience reactions.** Remind yourself to stand naturally and speak slowly. Calmly respond to talking or fidgeting in the audience by picking up the pace or speaking more loudly and clearly.

See page R82: Evaluate a Persuasive Speech

SPEAKING AND LISTENING

Ask students to read this page to get an overview of how to plan, present, and deliver a persuasive speech. Students who choose this option should familiarize themselves with the features of a speech and with tools, such as a tape recorder, that might help them prepare.

Before students begin working, review these criteria with them so that they understand their goals:

Criteria A strong persuasive speech

- is written with a specific purpose and audience in mind

- adds or deletes information from the written version as appropriate for speaking and listening

- may include visuals such as posters or video clips

- gains strength from practice and feedback

- is delivered using eye contact with the audience, including focus on a number of specific audience members

- uses variation in pace, tone of voice, volume, facial expressions, and gestures to hold audience attention and emphasize points

- is delivered in a relaxed, natural way

- responds to audience cues such as fidgeting or talking

When students begin listening to the presentations, have them use the criteria to evaluate the effectiveness of their classmates' speeches.

R RESOURCE MANAGER—Copy Master
Speaking and Listening p. 461

S STANDARDS LESSON FILE
Speaking and Listening Lesson 8:
Persuasive Speech

CHECK READINESS

Read aloud the paragraph under **ASSESS** and stress to students that this is not the full Unit Test but a way for them to check their readiness for it. Then have students examine the skills listed under **REVIEW** and look back in the unit or in the **Student Resource Bank** for any skills they need to review.

READ THE SELECTION

Remind students to keep unit goals in mind as they read the passage, paying particular attention to these literary and reading skills:

- conflict
- setting
- mood
- make inferences
- chronological order

To help students focus on conflict and mood, encourage them to ask questions like these:

- What types of conflicts have you read about in stories? What other types of conflict have you heard about in the real world?
- What types of conflicts might a prolonged rainstorm cause?

ANSWER THE QUESTIONS

Direct students to pages R93–R101 of the **Handbook** to review test-taking strategies.

- Remind students to read directions carefully. In particular, they should focus on verbs because they tell the students what to *do*. Point out that many times, directions require that students do several different tasks. Remind students that terms such as *best*, *most*, and *two or three* are also very important. To be successful, students must do everything that is required.
- Remind students answering multiple-choice questions not to choose the first alternative that seems to fit. Instead, they should read through all the choices, eliminate any that are clearly wrong, and then choose the *best* answer—the one that is most accurate and complete.

ASSESS

The practice test items on the next few pages match skills listed on the Unit Goals page (page 14) and addressed throughout this unit. Taking this practice test will help you assess your knowledge of these skills and determine your readiness for the Unit Test.

REVIEW

After you take the practice test, your teacher can help you identify any skills you need to review.

- Elements of an Argument
- Persuasive Techniques
- Historical Context
- Descriptive Details
- Primary Source
- Multiple-Meaning Words
- Specialized Vocabulary: Political Words
- Adverb Clauses
- Complex and Compound-Complex Sentences
- Prepositional Phrases

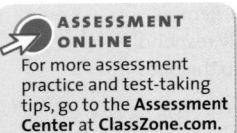

ASSESSMENT ONLINE
For more assessment practice and test-taking tips, go to the **Assessment Center** at ClassZone.com.

Reading Comprehension

DIRECTIONS *Read these selections and answer the questions that follow.*

from Defense of the Constitutions of Government in Massachusetts During the Revolution

John Adams

It is become a kind of fashion among writers, to admit, as a maxim, that if you could be always sure of a wise, active, and virtuous prince, monarchy would be the best of governments. But this is so far from being admissible, that it will forever remain true, that a free government has a great advantage over a simple monarchy. The best and wisest prince, by means of a freer communication with his people, and the greater opportunities to collect the best advice from the best of his subjects, would have an immense advantage in a free state over a monarchy. A senate consisting of all that is most noble, wealthy, and able in the nation, with a right to counsel the crown at all times, is a check to ministers, and a security
10 against abuses, such as a body of nobles who never meet, and have no such right, can never supply. Another assembly, composed of representatives chosen by the people in all parts, gives free access to the whole nation, and communicates all its wants, knowledge, projects, and wishes to government; it excites emulation among all classes, removes complaints, redresses grievances, affords opportunities of exertion to genius, though in obscurity, and gives full scope to all the faculties of man; it opens a passage for every speculation to the legislature, to administration, and to the public; it gives a universal energy to the human character, in every part of the state, such as never can be obtained in a monarchy.

There is a third particular which deserves attention both from governments
20 and people. In a simple monarchy, the ministers of state can never know their friends from their enemies; secret cabals undermine their influence, and blast their reputation. This occasions a jealousy ever anxious and irritated, which never thinks the government safe without an encouragement of informers and spies, throughout every part of the state, who interrupt the tranquillity of private life, destroy the confidence of families in their own domestics and in one another, and poison freedom in its sweetest retirements. In a free government, on the contrary, the ministers can have no enemies of consequence but among the members of the great or little council, where every man is obliged to take his side, and declare his opinion, upon every question. This circumstance alone, to every manly mind,
30 would be sufficient to decide the preference in favor of a free government.

DIFFERENTIATED INSTRUCTION

FOR ENGLISH LEARNERS
Assessment Practice: Work Backward
[mixed-readiness pairs] Prepare students by having them read the questions *before* reading the passages. Have pairs find unfamiliar words in test directions and questions, and follow these steps:

1. Write each word on an index card.
2. Look up the meaning in a dictionary and write it on the back of the card.
3. Use the cards to practice the words with your partner and to teach them to others.

Culture: Clarify Read aloud the title of the excerpt on page 285. Refer students to the Historical Essay, page 19, and read aloud the entry about the Boston Tea Party. Clarify that the Boston Tea Party was the name given to a colonial protest against the 1773 Tea Act. This act forced colonists to buy tea from British companies and their agents. Colonists dressed up as Native Americans and threw British tea into Boston Harbor.

from Boston Tea Party
George Hewes

It was now evening, and I immediately dressed myself in the costume of an Indian, equipped with a small hatchet, which I and my associates denominated the tomahawk, with which, and a club, after having painted my face and hands with coal dust in the shop of a blacksmith, I repaired to Griffin's wharf, where the ships lay that contained the tea. When I first appeared in the street after being thus disguised, I fell in with many who were dressed, equipped and painted as I was, and who fell in with me and marched in order to the place of our destination. . . .

We then were ordered by our commander to open the hatches and take out all the chests of tea and throw them overboard, and we immediately proceeded to
10 execute his orders, first cutting and splitting the chests with our tomahawks, so as thoroughly to expose them to the effects of the water.

In about three hours from the time we went on board, we had thus broken and thrown overboard every tea chest to be found in the ship, while those in the other ships were disposing of the tea in the same way, at the same time. We were surrounded by British armed ships, but no attempt was made to resist us.

We then quietly retired to our several places of residence, without having any conversation with each other, or taking any measures to discover who were our associates; nor do I recollect of our having had the knowledge of the name of a single individual concerned in that affair, except that of Leonard Pitt, the
20 commander of my division, whom I have mentioned. There appeared to be an understanding that each individual should volunteer his services, keep his own secret, and risk the consequence for himself. No disorder took place during that transaction, and it was observed at that time that the stillest night ensued that Boston had enjoyed for many months. . . .

Another attempt was made to save a little tea from the ruins of the cargo by a tall, aged man who wore a large cocked hat and white wig, which was fashionable at that time. He had sleightly slipped a little into his pocket, but being detected, they seized him and, taking his hat and wig from his head, threw them, together with the tea, of which they had emptied his pockets, into the water. In
30 consideration of his advanced age, he was permitted to escape, with now and then a slight kick.

The next morning, after we had cleared the ships of the tea, it was discovered that very considerable quantities of it were floating upon the surface of the water; and to prevent the possibility of any of its being saved for use, a number of small

GO ON

ITEM ANALYSIS

COMPREHENSION AND WRITTEN RESPONSE	ITEMS	UNIT PAGES
Elements of an Argument	1, 3, 15	223, 235
Persuasive Techniques	2, 4, 5	222–223, 245
Historical Context	6, 7, 10, 11	69, 212
Descriptive Details	7, 12, 14	79
Primary Source	8, 13, 14	66–67, 69

VOCABULARY	ITEMS	UNIT PAGES
Multiple-Meaning Words	4, 5, 6	97
Specialized Vocabulary	1, 2, 3	60

WRITING AND GRAMMAR	ITEMS	UNIT PAGES
Adverb Clauses	1	83, 87
Complex and Compound-Complex Sentences	2, 3	240, 243
Prepositional Phrases	4, 5	74, 77

FOR STRATEGIC READERS

Assessment Support Consider these options for completing the Assessment Practice:

- Have students "work backward" to review the test questions *before* reading the passage.

- Select random questions in the Assessment, and have students demonstrate *how* and *where* to look for the answers.

- Ask students to locate unfamiliar words in the Assessment. Elicit the words' meanings from the class.

- Have students record useful testing words and definitions in their journals for later reference.

- Read the selection or parts of it aloud to aid in student comprehension.

- Remind students to read beyond specified lines when searching for context clues and to consider the overall context of the text.

McDougal Littell
Assessment System

After checking student readiness with this Assessment Practice, you may administer the complete Unit 1 Test in order to more thoroughly evaluate student mastery of unit goals.

Comprehension

Model a thinking process for answering multiple-choice questions.

1. **C is correct.** *In lines 5–7 Adams says that a free society collects the best advice from the people. A is incorrect because Adams opposes the current monarchy. B is not a claim that Adams makes in the passage. D is incorrect because Adams says that even the best princes can gain from such freedom (lines 5–7).*

2. **B is correct.** *In context, Adams uses the words to raise fears about "simple monarchy." A, C, and D are incorrect because excitement, anger, and guilt are not appropriate to the context.*

3. **D is correct.** *A is incorrect because Adams does not make the claim in lines 26–29. B is incorrect because Adams does not mention tough-mindedness. C is incorrect because Adams does not mention the strength of the opinions.*

4. **A is correct.** *Adams assumes that his readers want to be among the "manly" minds. B is incorrect because the manly minds are not presented as authorities. C is incorrect because manliness is not presented as goodness. D is incorrect because "every manly mind" does not have the emotional connotations typical of loaded language.*

5. **D is correct.** *"Poison" is negatively loaded and "sweetest" is positively loaded. A, B, and C all use moderate language without strong emotional bias.*

6. **B is correct.** *The whole essay explores the idea of a new kind of government. A is incorrect because Adams does not prefer monarchy as a form of government. C is the opposite of the essay's message. D is incorrect because Adams's ideas are complex.*

7. **A is correct.** *Tomahawks, chests of tea, and coal dust all played specific roles in the Boston Tea Party. The items listed in B, C, and D, although present at the time, could also apply to other events and times.*

Comprehension

DIRECTIONS *Answer these questions about the excerpt from "Defense of the Constitutions of Government in Massachusetts During the Revolution."*

1. Which position on government does Adams favor?
   A Monarchies are the best form of government because they have wise and virtuous rulers.
   B Writers should be consulted when a country forms its government because they are well informed.
   C A free state is the best form of government because its ideas and opinions come from the people.
   D Only the best and wisest prince who communicates with his subjects should rule a nation.

2. The words *enemies, informers,* and *spies* in lines 20–26 appeal to the emotion of
   A excitement   C anger
   B fear   D guilt

3. Which claim does Adams make about a free government in lines 26–29?
   A The best way to run a free government is with a large assembly and a small one.
   B Members of a free government often take a tough-minded approach to governing.
   C People who serve in a free government often express strong opinions.
   D The leaders in a free government usually have few hidden enemies.

4. "Every manly mind" in line 29 is an example of which persuasive technique?
   A an appeal by association
   B an appeal to authority
   C an ethical appeal
   D loaded language

5. Which quote contains loaded language?
   A "monarchy would be the best of governments" (lines 2–3)
   B "such as a body of nobles who never meet" (line 10)
   C "gives free access to the whole nation" (line 12)
   D "poison freedom in its sweetest retirements" (line 26)

6. This excerpt reflects the view of colonists who
   A believed that political rivalries would destroy the British monarchy
   B questioned British rule and tried to form a new government
   C upheld the ideals of a monarchy
   D had simple ideas about government

DIRECTIONS *Answer these questions about the excerpt from "Boston Tea Party."*

7. Which descriptive details most clearly place this account in its historical context?
   A tomahawk, chests of tea, coal dust
   B armed ships, hatches, small boats
   C evening, three hours, next morning
   D sailors, citizens, aged man

286

---

8. **B is correct.** *A primary source is one written by someone who was present. A is incorrect because primary sources do not have to be political. C is incorrect because some primary sources may be inaccurate. D is incorrect because some primary sources are unpublished and many published documents are secondary sources.*

9. **D is correct.** *The question, which names Hewes as a shoemaker, confirms that he is of the common people. A is incorrect because Native Americans are not the subject of the document. B is incorrect because the participants were well led. C is incorrect because wealth is irrelevant to Hewes's account.*

8. This narrative is a primary source because it is

   A a political argument

   B a participant's report

   C an accurate history

   D a published document

9. This account by a colonial shoemaker calls attention to

   A an alliance between Native Americans and tradespeople

   B a lack of leadership during the Revolutionary War

   C the tension between wealthy and poor people in the colonies

   D the role of the common people in the Revolution

10. The colonists most likely dressed as Native Americans to

   A honor Native American traditions

   B forge an alliance against the British

   C protect themselves from the British

   D cause economic problems in the colonies

11. The descriptive anecdote in lines 25–31 suggests that

   A tea was a prized commodity among the colonists in Boston

   B the elderly were treated with disrespect in colonial times

   C many participants thought the Boston Tea Party was amusing

   D violent attacks were characteristic of the Boston Tea Party

12. The descriptive details in this account emphasize that the Boston Tea Party was

   A poorly planned

   B carried out in secret

   C led by Native Americans

   D authorized by the British

DIRECTIONS *Answer this question about both selections.*

13. Both primary sources give the reader insight into the

   A origins of the United States

   B benefits of a constitution

   C advantages of a monarchy

   D fashions of the period

Written Response

SHORT RESPONSE *Write three or four sentences to answer this question.*

14. Cite three details from George Hewes's account that identify it as a primary source.

EXTENDED RESPONSE *Write two or three paragraphs to answer this question.*

15. What argument does John Adams make in lines 11–18 in favor of an assembly of representatives? Cite three reasons he gives to support his argument.

GO ON

287

---

10. C *is correct.* *The colonists were "disguised" (line 6). A is incorrect because tossing tea overboard was not a Native American tradition. B is incorrect because the text never mentions alliances. D is incorrect because Native American dress did not cause economic problems.*

11. A *is correct.* *The old man wants to save some tea for his own use. B is incorrect because the old man's age gets him respect (line 30). C is incorrect because the text includes no sign of amusement. D is incorrect because the old man is not attacked violently.*

12. B *is correct.* *Lines 16–24 stress that the action was so secret, the participants did not know each other's identities. A is incorrect because the action clearly was planned in detail and went smoothly. C is incorrect because the participants were not Native Americans. D is incorrect because the British were the target.*

13. A *is correct.* *Both sources discuss issues of the American Revolution. B and C are incorrect because Hewes's document does not discuss political theory. D is incorrect because the disguises at the tea party were not a matter of fashion.*

Written Response

Possible short response:

14. *Details that identify Hewes's account as a primary source are: Hewes narrates his own role in the event (lines 1–7); Hewes relates what he saw, such as the other men's actions (lines 8–11); Hewes shows he has first-hand information, such as the commander's name (lines 18–20).*

Possible extended response:

15. *Adams argues that an assembly of representatives offers greater benefits than a monarchy. Three possible reasons are that elected representation "gives free access to the whole nation" (line 12), that it "redresses grievances" (line 14), and that it "gives full scope to all the faculties of man" (lines 15–16).*

Vocabulary

1. **A is correct.** *The context clue is "prince."* B *describes a republic.* C *describes an oligarchy.* D *describes a democracy.*

2. **C is correct.** *The context clues are "secret," "undermine their influence," and "blast their reputation," which all hint at conspiracy.* A, B, *and* D *refer to groups of people, but lack the negative connotations.*

3. **B is correct.** *The context clues are Adams's overall discussion of government and his description of ministers offering opinions to the "council" (lines 27–29).* A *uses* ministers *in a religious context.* C *is incorrect because Adams does not discuss foreign diplomacy.* D *is incorrect because it makes no sense in the context.*

4. **B is correct.** *By cutting and splitting the chests, the men were carrying out orders.* A *is incorrect because the men were following orders, not giving them.* C *is incorrect because it refers to* execution *in the context of killing people.* D *is incorrect because* validate *means "affirm something is true," which does not fit this context.*

5. **B is correct.** *The clues are in lines 17–18, which say that the participants didn't speak to one another or know each other's identities, thus went to different "places of residence."* A *is incorrect because the participants did not live in the same place.* C *and* D *are incorrect because they refer to the numerical meaning of* several.

6. **A is correct.** *Substituting* actions *for* measures *in the sentence verifies the meaning.* B *and* C *refer to physical measurements, which are not relevant in this context.* D *is incorrect because legislative bills are not relevant in the context and because bills do not "discover" information.*

Vocabulary

DIRECTIONS *Use context clues and your knowledge of specialized vocabulary to answer the following questions about political words in the excerpt from "Defense of the Constitutions of Government in Massachusetts During the Revolution."*

1. What is the most likely meaning of the word *monarchy* as it is used in line 2?

   "It is become a kind of fashion among writers, to admit, as a maxim, that if you could be always sure of a wise, active, and virtuous prince, <u>monarchy</u> would be the best of governments."

   A a state headed by a leader who usually rules by hereditary right

   B a body of elected officials who hold the supreme power in a nation

   C a small group of persons or a family who rule together

   D a government that shares power with the people

2. What is the most likely meaning of the word *cabals* as it is used in line 21?

   " . . . secret <u>cabals</u> undermine their influence, and blast their reputation."

   A social clubs

   B religious denominations

   C groups of conspirators

   D military organizations

3. What is the most likely meaning of the word *ministers* as it is used in line 27?

   "In a free government, on the contrary, the <u>ministers</u> can have no enemies of consequence. . . ."

   A church leaders   C foreign diplomats

   B public officials   D business tycoons

DIRECTIONS *Use context clues and your knowledge of multiple-meaning words to answer the following questions based on the excerpt from "Boston Tea Party."*

4. Which meaning of the word *execute* is used in line 10?

   " . . . and we immediately proceeded to <u>execute</u> his orders, first cutting and splitting the chests with our tomahawks, so as thoroughly to expose them to the effects of the water."

   A create

   B carry out

   C kill

   D validate

5. Which meaning of the word *several* is used in line 16?

   "We then quietly retired to our <u>several</u> places of residence. . . ."

   A same

   B separate

   C small number of

   D more than two or three

6. Which meaning of the word *measures* is used in line 17?

   " . . . without having any conversation with each other, or taking any <u>measures</u> to discover who were our associates . . ."

   A actions

   B dimensions

   C quantities

   D legislative bills

DIFFERENTIATED INSTRUCTION

FOR ENGLISH LEARNERS

Review Academic Vocabulary On the board, list the academic vocabulary shown in italics. Then give the examples in random order and have students classify them. Elicit additional examples from students.

- *claim:* In a free government, rulers get the benefit of advice from more people.

- *persuasive techniques:* Adams uses logical appeals and loaded language to show why a legislative government is best.

- *loaded language:* We don't want any cowards to infect our efforts.

- *historical context:* The Boston Tea Party took place in a time of sailing ships and of British control of the American colonies.

- *primary source:* George Hewes's description of his participation in the Boston Tea Party

- *argument:* A free government is best.

Writing & Grammar

DIRECTIONS *Read this passage and answer the questions that follow.*

> (1) George Washington hired engineer Pierre L'Enfant to plan a new capital city.
> (2) The new capital would be called Federal City and would be located in Maryland.
> (3) L'Enfant was later fired. (4) Surveyor Andrew Ellicott redrew the plans but upheld much of L'Enfant's vision. (5) By 1800, President John Adams had moved into the White House. (6) It was far from finished. (7) It was damp. (8) The city was later renamed. (9) Today, Washington, D.C., reflects L'Enfant's vision of a city of open space.

1. How might you rewrite sentence 1 by using an adverb clause?

   A George Washington hired engineer Pierre L'Enfant to plan a new capital city, which would be situated between two rivers.

   B In 1791, George Washington hired engineer Pierre L'Enfant to plan a new capital city.

   C When George Washington decided to establish a new capital city in 1791, he hired engineer Pierre L'Enfant to do the planning.

   D Excited about the prospect of a new capital city, George Washington hired engineer Pierre L'Enfant to plan it.

2. How might you combine sentences 3 and 4 to form a compound-complex sentence?

   A L'Enfant was later fired, but when surveyor Andrew Ellicott redrew the plans, he upheld much of L'Enfant's vision.

   B L'Enfant was later fired, and surveyor Andrew Ellicott redrew the plans but upheld much of L'Enfant's vision.

   C When redrawing the plans, surveyor Andrew Ellicott upheld much of L'Enfant's vision, even though L'Enfant was fired.

   D Much of L'Enfant's vision was upheld by surveyor Andrew Ellicott, who redrew the plans after L'Enfant was fired.

3. How might you combine sentences 5 and 6 to form a complex sentence?

   A By 1800, President John Adams had moved into the White House, even though it was far from finished.

   B By 1800, President John Adams had moved into the White House, but it was far from finished.

   C By 1800, President John Adams had moved into the White House; however, it was far from finished.

   D By 1800, President John Adams had moved into the White House; it was far from finished.

4. Identify a prepositional phrase that would add descriptive detail to the end of sentence 7.

   A and leaked incessantly

   B in many of the rooms

   C because the plaster was wet

   D and very musty

5. Identify a prepositional phrase that would add descriptive detail to the end of sentence 8.

   A even as it grew

   B to reflect Washington's involvement

   C Washington, D.C.

   D after Washington's death

289

ANSWERS
Writing & Grammar

1. **C *is correct.*** *"When George Washington decided to establish a new capital city in 1791" is a clause that modifies the verb* hired. *A is incorrect because "which would be situated between two rivers" is an adjective clause, modifying the noun* city. *B is incorrect because "In 1791" is an adverb phrase, not a clause. D is incorrect because "Excited about the prospect of a new capital city" is an adjective phrase modifying the noun* Washington.

2. **A *is correct.*** *A contains two independent clauses and the subordinate clause "when surveyor Andrew Ellicott redrew the plans." B is incorrect because it is a compound sentence containing two independent clauses, the second of which has a compound predicate. C is incorrect because it is a complex sentence with one independent and one subordinate clause. The adverb phrase "When redrawing the plan" is part of the independent clause. D is incorrect because it is a complex sentence containing one independent and one subordinate clause.*

3. **A *is correct.*** *The clause "even though it was far from finished" is subordinate because it cannot stand alone as a sentence. B, C, and D are all compound sentences consisting of two independent clauses.*

4. **B *is correct.*** *The words "in many of the rooms" are a prepositional phrase because they contain a phrase and related words but no subject or verb. A and C are noun clauses modifying* damp. *D is a subordinate clause preceded by the coordinating conjunction* and.

5. **D *is correct.*** *The preposition is "after." A is incorrect because it is a clause, not a phrase. B is incorrect because it is an infinitive phrase, not a prepositional phrase. C is incorrect because it is an adverb modifying* renamed.

INTRODUCE *GREAT READS*

In Unit 1, students have discussed a number of big questions. Invite students to tell which question they found most intriguing and why, and then focus attention on the four that appear on pages 290–291. Discuss the recommended books and their summaries, pointing out how each connects to the related question. Encourage students to choose one or more of these "great reads" to read independently.

ⓘ ClassZone.com

To find additional books that match students' interests and ability levels, visit the Literature Center at **ClassZone.com**.

Great Reads

UNIT 1

Ideas for Independent Reading

Continue exploring the Questions of the Times on pages 16–17 with these additional works.

Who owns the LAND?

The Narrative of the Captivity and Restoration of Mrs. Mary Rowlandson
by Mary Rowlandson

In February 1676, during a land dispute called King Philip's War, a minister's wife named Mary Rowlandson was taken hostage by Wampanoag warriors. Packed with violence, cruelty, piety, and anger, Rowlandson's account of her three-month captivity became one of the first bestsellers in colonial America.

The Portable North American Indian Reader
edited by Fredrick W. Turner

As an introduction to the verbal art of Native Americans, this anthology has few equals. It includes myths, tales, poetry, and speeches from the many diverse Native American cultures who thrived before, during, and after contact with European explorers and settlers. Modern selections show how traditional Indian kinship with the land continues to the present day.

Finding the Center: The Art of the Zuni Storyteller
translated by Dennis Tedlock

Thought to have descended from the Anasazi, a cliff-dwelling people of 1,000 years ago, the Zuni of present-day New Mexico enjoy a rich oral heritage handed down from long before the first Europeans arrived. The folklorist Dennis Tedlock has collected, translated, and transcribed many key Zuni stories in this volume, placing the words on the page in a manner that mimics their oral performance.

What makes an EXPLORER?

The Four Voyages
by Christopher Columbus

In these journals and eyewitness accounts, Christopher Columbus comes across as a complex, driven, yet entirely understandable person. In place of the confident adventurer of story, we see a man of mixed motives, influenced equally by greed, religious passion, and scientific curiosity. These journals shed light on the impulses that pushed Columbus to make the most significant journeys of his time.

Love and Hate in Jamestown
by David Price

In 1607, 105 Englishmen arrived in what would become the Virginia settlement of Jamestown. They came seeking gold, a route to the Orient, and survivors from the lost Roanoke Colony. What they found instead were Native American people—some friendly, some brutally hostile—and day after day of challenges, hardship, and misery.

Voyages and Discoveries
by Richard Hakluyt

Early English explorers were a fascinating breed. These sailors were willing—even eager—to face unknown dangers for the sake of their country and the glory and adventure it would bring. Using ships' records, charts, and logs, Richard Hakluyt pulls together the stories of such adventurers as Sir Francis Drake, whose yen for exploration enabled the European settlement of America.

290

Are people basically GOOD?

The Diary and Life of Samuel Sewall
edited by Mel Yazawa

Samuel Sewall served as one of the judges in the Salem witchcraft trials, voting to hang 19 people for wholly imaginary offenses. Yet in his diary, we see another side of this forbidding figure. He wrestles with lingering guilt over his role in that public hysteria, feels remorse over the unfair treatment of the Indians, recalls the pleasures of food and marriage, and grieves bitterly over the loss of friends and family.

A Short Account of the Destruction of the Indies
by Bartolomé de Las Casas

A Spanish priest and missionary, Las Casas was appalled by the abuse and enslavement of Native Americans. He dedicated himself to their emancipation, returning to Spain to plead their case before the king, then going back to the New World to serve as their official protector.

Letters from an American Farmer
by Michel Guillaume Jean de Crèvecœur

Crèvecœur's "letters," originally written as essays, paint a mesmerizing portrait of a fertile country populated with rough-mannered yet skilled and kindhearted people. Crèvecœur addresses such difficult topics as the hardships of the frontier, the plight of women, and the evils of slavery. Yet such problems fade before his faith in the righteousness of American individualism.

Who has the right to RULE?

1776
by David McCullough

How did a ragtag group of farmers manage to defeat the world's most powerful army? That is the question historian David McCullough explores in this fascinating look at one pivotal year in our nation's history. Persistence, optimism, ingenuity, leadership, luck, and weather are the elements to which McCullough attributes the colonists' success in the Revolutionary War.

The Puritan Dilemma: The Story of John Winthrop
by Edmund S. Morgan

As the leader of Massachusetts Bay Colony for nearly 20 years, John Winthrop spent his life combining religious devotion with power politics. This biography shines a spotlight upon issues that mattered most to Winthrop: the relationship between individual liberties and community harmony, and the legitimacy of political authority.

The Adams-Jefferson Letters
edited by Lester J. Cappon

Divided by political party and regional affiliation, Thomas Jefferson of Virginia and John Adams of Massachusetts were united in their love of country and their concern for the future of democracy. This collection of letters, including contributions by Abigail Adams (John Adams's gifted wife), touches upon virtually every major issue that faced the young republic.

291

Preview Unit Goals

This page presents an overview of the skills and strategies covered in this unit. Explain to students that they can get more from their reading by previewing. Then ask them to skim the page to preview the skills that they will learn. Note that each strand or category of skill is color-coded on this page and throughout the unit.

Model the strategy of copying the Academic Vocabulary and writing a preliminary definition for each term. Suggest that students use a journal or a notebook for this purpose. Encourage them to use the terms in discussions and in writing. Also urge students to revisit each term throughout the unit and to refine its meaning.

ADDITIONAL UNIT GOALS

These skills will be taught in this unit but are not the major focus of the unit:

Literary Analysis
- Understand similarities and differences among writers of romantic literature
- Analyze elements of a short story and of nonfiction
- Understand structure
- Evaluate aphorisms
- Examine author's perspective
- Identify cultural characteristics

Reading
- Develop strategies for reading traditional poetry
- Make inferences
- Analyze main ideas and details
- Understand structure
- Evaluate aphorisms
- Identify cultural characteristics

Writing and Grammar
- Write an analysis essay
- Add descriptive details
- Write an evaluation of a literary piece
- Use participles and participial phrases

Speaking, Listening, and Viewing
- Deliver an oral interpretation
- Participate in a group discussion

Vocabulary
- Research word origins as a way to understand spelling

UNIT 2

CALIFORNIA

Included in this unit: R1.2, R2.2, R2.5, R3.1, R3.3, R3.4, R3.5, R3.6, R3.7, W1.1, W1.2, W1.3, W1.4, W1.5, W1.9, W2.1, W2.2, W2.3, W2.4, LC1.1, LS1.3, LS1.10, LS2.5

Preview Unit Goals

LITERARY ANALYSIS
- Understand romanticism as a literary movement
- Identify elements of transcendentalism
- Identify and analyze blank verse
- Identify and examine stanza, rhyme scheme, and meter
- Analyze elements used to create mood
- Identify and evaluate sound devices and imagery
- Interpret symbol and allegory
- Identify and analyze satire and unity of effect
- Analyze elements of an essay

READING
- Paraphrase main ideas; summarize information; take notes
- Clarify meaning of archaic vocabulary; examine complex sentences

WRITING AND GRAMMAR
- Write a reflective essay
- Use rhetorical questions
- Identify and use parallelism and adjective clauses
- Use imperative sentences and dashes

SPEAKING, LISTENING, AND VIEWING
- Conduct an interview
- Analyze how meaning is conveyed in visual media

VOCABULARY
- Use knowledge of word roots and affixes to determine word meaning
- Research word origins

ACADEMIC VOCABULARY
- romanticism
- allegory
- blank verse
- symbol
- satire
- transcendentalism

Online LITERATURE CLASSZONE.COM

Literature and Reading Center
Writing Center
Vocabulary Center

292

DIFFERENTIATED INSTRUCTION

FOR ENGLISH LEARNERS

Academic Vocabulary Use the copy master to help students learn the Academic Vocabulary.

1. Read aloud each Academic Vocabulary term on page 292 and have students locate it on their copy masters.

2. Discuss the meaning or example shown on the copy master, and complete the chart as a class.

3. Have students work in small groups to complete the remaining activities on the copy master.

Additional Academic Vocabulary Use the copy master to help students learn academic words they will use in subsequent lessons and on the Assessment Practice. Follow the same procedure as for the Academic Vocabulary copy master.

 RESOURCE MANAGER—Copy Masters
Academic Vocabulary p. 11
Additional Academic Vocabulary p. 12

American Romanticism

Nathaniel Hawthorne

1800–1855
CELEBRATING THE INDIVIDUAL

- The Early Romantics
- The Fireside Poets
- The Transcendentalists
- American Gothic

293

For help in planning this unit, see

RESOURCE MANAGER UNIT 2
pp. 1–13

INTRODUCE THE UNIT

Call students' attention to the pictures on this page. Explain that the large picture, *A View of the Mountain Pass Called the Notch of the White Mountains,* is a painting by Thomas Cole, known for his grand natural scenes. Tell students that they will read about Cole on page 299, in the historical essay.

Ask students if they know of Nathaniel Hawthorne (1804–1864), the author shown in the smaller picture. Explain that in his writing, Hawthorne often examined the darker side of human nature and dealt with such themes as sin, hypocrisy, and tolerance. Tell students that in this unit they will read one of Hawthorne's short stories and an excerpt from his classic novel *The Scarlet Letter.* Also note that students can read more about Hawthorne on pages 454 and 456.

About the Art English-born American painter Thomas Cole (1801–1848), one of the best-known members of the Hudson River School, painted *A View of the Mountain Pass Called the Notch of the White Mountains* in 1839. Both the painting and the Hudson River School are discussed in **The Artists' Gallery** on page 299.

Unit Resources

PRINT RESOURCES

 RESOURCE MANAGER UNIT 2

 BEST PRACTICES TOOLKIT

 STANDARDS LESSON FILE

CALIFORNIA ASSESSMENT FILE

GRAMMAR FOR WRITING

TECH RESOURCES

- EasyPlanner DVD-ROM
- WriteSmart CD-ROM
- ClassZone.com
- Audio Anthology CD
- Multi-Language Academic Vocabulary Online
- eEdition DVD-ROM & Online
- McDougal Littell Assessment System
- Test Generator CD-ROM
- MediaSmart DVD-ROM
- Literature in Context DVD-ROM

UNIT 2
Standards

CALIFORNIA

SKILLS STRAND

SKILLS STRAND	Unit 2 Introduction pp. 294–309 • Questions of the Times • Historical Essay • Timeline • Legacy of Romanticism	Literary Analysis Workshop • The Art of the Essay pp. 358–359	The Devil and Tom Walker Short Story pp. 310–327 *Lexile: 1120* *Fry: 9* *Dale-Chall: 7.3*	Thanatopsis Poem pp. 328–332	A Psalm of Life/ The Tide Rises, The Tide Falls Poetry pp. 334–339
Literary Analysis	Historical and Cultural Context of American Romanticism pp. 296–307 R3.5 Similarities and Differences Among American Romantic Writers pp. 300–305 R3.5	Characteristics of an Essay pp. 358–359 R2.2, R3.3	Satire pp. 311, 314, 317, 320, 321, 322, 325 R3.1	Blank Verse pp. 329, 330, 331, 332 R3.3	Stanza and Rhyme Scheme pp. 335, 336, 338, 339 R3.3
Reading and Informational Texts	Build Context for Reading pp. 294–295 Use Prior Knowledge pp. 294–295 Connect pp. 294–295, 306–307, 308–309 Take Notes pp. 297–305 Identify Main Idea and Details p. 297 Read a Timeline pp. 306–307	Analyze the Literature p. 359 R2.2, R3.3	Interpret Imagery pp. 311, 312, 314, 320, 322, 324, 325 R3.3 Review: Make Inferences pp. 315, 317	Understand Poetic Structure pp. 329, 330, 331, 332 R3.3	Strategies for Reading Traditional Poetry pp. 335, 337, 338, 339
Vocabulary		Academic Vocabulary pp. 358–359	Word Acquisition pp. 311, T311, 326 Context Clues p. T311 Latin Roots (spec) p. 326 R1.2		
Writing, Grammar, and Style			Writing Prompt p. 327 R3.6, W1.2, W2.1 Parallelism pp. 319, 327 LC1.1		
Speaking, Listening, Viewing, and Media	Discuss pp. 294–295, T296–T309 Analyze Visuals pp. 299, 300, T305	Discuss pp. T358–T359	Discuss pp. T310, 311, T312–T324, 325 Analyze Visuals pp. 312, 316, T318, 323	Discuss pp. T328, 329, T330–T331, 332	Discuss pp. T334, 335, T336–T338, 339 Analyze Visuals p. 337

293A | Standards Designations R = Reading W = Writing LC = Language Conventions LS = Listening and Speaking T = Teacher's Edition page

The Chambered Nautilus/ Old Ironsides Poetry pp. 340–345	from Snowbound/ The First Snowfall Poetry pp. 346–356	from Self-Reliance/ from Nature Essays pp. 360–369	from Walden/from Civil Disobedience Themes Across Cultures: On Civil Disobedience Essays/Speech pp. 370–391, 392–393
		Lexile: 1010/980 Fry: 10/7 Dale-Chall: 7.0/6.8	Lexile: 1230/880 Fry: 12/10 Dale-Chall: 6.5/6.2
Meter pp. 341, 342, 344, 345 R3.3	Mood pp. 347, 348, 350, 351, 353, 354, 355, 356 R3.4	Transcendentalism pp. 361, 362, 364, 365, 366, 367 R2.5	Essay pp. 371, 372, 374, 375, 377, 378, 380, 388, 389 R3.3 Review: Transcendentalism pp. 377, 378, 380 R2.5
Make Inferences pp. 341, 343, 344, 345	Paraphrase pp. 347, 350, 352, 354, 356 Review: Make Inferences pp. 353, 355	Identify Aphorisms pp. 361, 364, 367 R2.5	Evaluate Ideas pp. 371, 374, 375, 376, 379, 380, 382, 384, 385, 387, 389 R2.5 Read a Magazine Article p. 381 Read a Speech pp. 392–393
		Word Acquisition pp. 361, T361, 368 Context Clues p. T361 Words with Multiple Affixes p. 368	Word Acquisition pp. 371, T371, 390 Context Clues p. T371 Prefixes (ab-, per-) p. 390 R1.2
		Writing Prompt p. 369 W1.1, W1.3 Adjective Clauses as Modifiers pp. 364, 369 LC1.1	Writing Prompt p. 391 W1.1, W1.3, W1.4, W2.2 Rhetorical Questions pp. 385, 391 W1.9
Discuss pp. T340, 341, T342–T344, 345 Analyze Visuals pp. 343, 344	Discuss pp. T346, 347, T348–T355, 356 Analyze Visuals pp. 348, 355	Discuss pp. T360, 361, T362–T366, 367 Analyze Visuals pp. 362, 366	Discuss pp. T370, 371, T372–T379, 380, T381, T382–T388, 389, 393 Analyze Visuals pp. 372, 382, T386

	from *Woman in the Nineteenth Century* Nonfiction pp. 394–400	*The Fall of the House of Usher* Short Story pp. 402–426	*The Masque of the Red Death* Short Story pp. 427–436	*The Raven* Poem pp. 437–445
	Lexile: 1170 Fry: 7 Dale-Chall: 7.0	Lexile: 1440 Fry: 9 Dale-Chall: 8.6	Lexile: 1240 Fry: 8 Dale-Chall: 8.0	
Literary Analysis	Author's Perspective pp. 395, 398, 400 **R2.5**	Unity of Effect pp. 403, 406, 409, 415, 421, 422, 424 **R3.3**	Allegory pp. 427, 430, 432, 434, 435 **R3.1**	Sound Devices pp. 437, 438, 440, 441, 443 **R3.4** Review: Stanza and Rhyme Scheme p. 440
Reading and Informational Texts	Paraphrase Main Ideas pp. 395, 396, 398, 399, 400	Understand Complex Sentences pp. 403, 407, 409, 410, 417, 424	Clarify Meaning pp. 427, 428, 432, 433, 435	Make Inferences pp. 437, 438, 441, 442, 443 Read a Parody p. 445
Vocabulary		Word Acquisition pp. 403, T403, 425 Context Clues p. 403 Greek Roots (*path*) p. 425 **R1.2**	Word Acquisition pp. 427, T427, 436 Context Clues p. T427 Affixes and Spelling Changes p. 436	
Writing, Grammar, and Style		Writing Prompt p. 426 **W1.1, W1.2** Participles and Participial Phrases as Modifiers pp. 407, 426 **LC1.1**		Writing Prompt p. 444 **W1.1, W1.2** Effective Writing with Imperative Sentences and Dashes p. 444 **W1.5, LC1.1**
Speaking, Listening, Viewing, and Media	Discuss pp. T394, 395, T396–T399, 400 Analyze Visuals p. 396	Discuss pp. T402, 403, T404–T423, 424 Analyze Visuals pp. 404, 410, 411, T416, T419, 422	Discuss pp. 427, T428–T434, 435 Analyze Visuals p. T431	Discuss pp. 437, T438–T442, 443, T445 Analyze Visuals p. 438

Media Study: Illustrations Inspired by Poe / Themes Across Time: from Danse Macabre — Image Collection/Essay pp. 446–449, 450–451	The Minister's Black Veil — Short Story pp. 456–472	Wrap-Ups	Writing Workshop: Reflective Essay pp. 474–481
	Lexile: 1260 / *Fry: 10* / *Dale-Chall: 7.8*	• The Early Romantics p. 333 / • The Fireside Poets p. 357 / • The Transcendentalists p. 401 / • American Gothic p. 473	
	Symbol pp. 457, 461, 463, 464, 465, 470, 471		
Read an Essay pp. 450–451	Identify Cultural Characteristics pp. 457, 458, 462, 465, 468, 471 R3.5		Analyze a Reflective Essay pp. 475–476, 480
Academic Vocabulary (Illustrations) p. 447	Word Acquisition pp. 457, T457, 472 / Context Clues p. T457 / Latin Roots (*ambi*) p. 472 R1.2		
		Write to Analyze p. 333 R2.5, W2.2 / Write to Evaluate p. 357 W2.2 / Write to Reflect p. 401 W2.3 / Write to Analyze p. 473 W2.2	Write a Reflective Essay pp. 474–480 W1.9, W2.1, W2.3 / Quotation Marks in Dialogue p. 480 / Consistency in Verb Tenses p. 480 LC1.1
Discuss pp. 446, 449 / Analyze Art Elements in Illustrations pp. 447–448 LS1.3 / Create Gothic Artwork p. 449 LS1.10	Discuss pp. T456, 457, T458–T470, 471 / Analyze Visuals pp. 458, T462, 467	Study a Romantic Painting p. 333 / Present an Oral Interpretation of a Poem p. 357 LS2.5 / Conduct Internet Research p. 401 / Discuss Fears p. 473	Discuss pp. 474–476 / Conduct an Interview p. 481 W2.4

Skills Assessed on the Unit 2 Test:

Literary Analysis
- Identify and examine elements of poetry (stanza, rhyme scheme, meter)
- Identify and evaluate sound devices
- Analyze elements used to create mood
- Interpret symbol
- Understand satire
- Identify elements of transcendentalism

Reading and Informational Texts
- Paraphrase main ideas

Vocabulary
- Use knowledge of Greek and Latin roots to understand the meanings of words
- Apply knowledge of prefixes to determine the meanings of words

Writing, Grammar, and Style
- Write a reflective essay
- Use rhetorical questions for emphasis
- Use parallelism to create emphasis or add rhythm
- Identify and use adjective clauses
- Use participles and participial phrases to add descriptive details
- Additional writing and grammar skills

For additional lesson planning help, see **Easy Planner DVD-ROM.**

CALIFORNIA	ASSESS PRIOR KNOWLEDGE Diagnostic	ONGOING ASSESSMENT Reteaching
BEGINNING OF UNIT		
Unit Opener	Preview Unit Goals, **TE** p. 292	
UNIT LESSONS		
Before every lesson	Big Question activity, **SE** Preteach vocabulary, **TE**	Check Understanding, **TE**
During every lesson		Annotations, **SE** Check Understanding, **TE** Tiered Discussion Prompts, **TE**
After every lesson		Post Reading pages, **SE** Assess and Reteach, **TE** Reading Check, **RM** Selection Tests A and B/C, **AF**
END OF UNIT		
Writing Workshop	Checklist, **SE** p. 480 Rubric for Evaluation, **RM** p. 296	Assess and Reteach, **TE** p. 480
Speaking & Listening	Criteria, **TE** p. 481	For reteaching options, see **TE** p. 481
Assessment	Assessment Practice, **SE** pp. 482–487	Unit Test, **AF** **MLAS**

For systematic instruction of grammar, use *Grammar for Writing*.

Key to Abbreviations:
SE = Student's Edition
TE = Teacher's Edition
RM = Resource Manager
AF = Assessment File
MLAS = McDougal Littell Assessment System

Universal Access

	Strategic Reader	Benchmark	Advanced Learner	English Learner	Students with Disabilities
SE STUDENT'S EDITION					
Vocabulary strategy instruction	✔	✔	✔	✔	✔
Instructional annotations	✔	✔	✔	✔	✔
English/Spanish glossary				✔	
TE TEACHER'S EDITION					
Skill annotation support	✔	✔	✔	✔	✔
Tiered discussion prompts	✔	✔	✔	✔	✔
Differentiated instruction	✔	✔	✔	✔	✔
R RESOURCE MANAGER					
Selection summaries in four languages	✔	✔	✔	✔	✔
Skill copy masters in English and Spanish	✔				
Vocabulary preteaching and support	✔				✔
Additional leveled selection questions	✔	✔	✔		✔
Question support	✔				✔
Writing support	✔	✔	✔		✔
Extension activities		✔	✔		
AF ASSESSMENT FILE					
Leveled selection and unit tests	✔	✔	✔	✔	✔
S STANDARDS LESSON FILE					
Leveled and reteaching copy masters	✔	✔	✔		✔
BEST PRACTICES TOOLKIT					
Strategy bank	✔	✔	✔	✔	✔
Graphic organizers	✔	✔	✔	✔	✔
TECHNOLOGY					
WriteSmart Rubrics and student models	✔	✔	✔	✔	✔
Audio Anthology CD	✔			✔	✔
CLASSZONE					
Instructional centers	✔	✔	✔	✔	✔
Audio summaries of selections	✔			✔	✔
Multilanguage glossary				✔	

Questions of the Times

Read aloud the questions on pages 294 and 295 and the paragraphs that follow them. Open the discussion of each idea by having students respond to the questions that conclude each paragraph. Use these notes to prompt further exploration of the ideas.

Is the price of progress ever TOO HIGH?

Challenge students to give specific examples (from history or personal knowledge) of instances in which the negative consequences of progress have outweighed the benefits. Encourage students to consider both short-term and long-term effects. Extend the discussion by having students speculate about how their lives today would be different if the changes described in the paragraph had not occurred.

Is it patriotic to protest one's GOVERNMENT?

Urge students to suggest why they might want to protest the problems mentioned in the paragraph. Then challenge students to suggest specific situations in which citizens should not be allowed to protest. Encourage debate, but stress that students must support their viewpoints with well-considered reasons and examples.

UNIT 2

Questions of the Times

DISCUSS In small groups or as a class, discuss the following questions. Then read on to learn how writers—and other Americans—grappled with these issues during the **American romantic** period.

Is the price of progress ever TOO HIGH?

During the romantic period, America seemed limitless— new frontiers were being explored every day, and inventions advanced both farming and industry. Yet to many people, life felt frantic and soulless. Is progress always worth its price?

Is it patriotic to protest one's GOVERNMENT?

Democracy was flourishing in the early 19th century and citizens felt optimistic about their country. Yet the problems of the age—slavery, women's disenfranchisement, the mistreatment of workers—were severe, and protestors agitated for change. What role do you think activism plays in a democracy? Under what circumstances, if any, should citizens lose their right to protest?

294

Does everyone have a "DARK SIDE"?

Although most romantic writers reflected the optimism of their times, some pondered the darker side of human nature. Edgar Allan Poe, for example, conjectured that in extreme situations people would reveal their true, evil natures. Do you think everyone has a dark side? What might make the dark side prevail?

Where do people look for TRUTH?

To escape the materialism and hectic pace of industrialization, many writers of the age turned to nature and to the self for simplicity, truth, and beauty. In earlier centuries, people had looked to reason or to God for answers. Where do you think people turn to make sense of their lives today?

295

Does everyone have a "DARK SIDE"?

Invite students to explain their concept of a "dark side" and to describe situations in which a person might have to struggle to keep his or her dark side under control. Urge students to draw upon their experiences reading and viewing TV or films as they cite examples in response to the questions.

Where do people look for TRUTH?

Discuss why some people—not just writers—might find nature a comfort and an inspiration. Challenge students to consider how people may continue to seek truth in nature, the self, or human reason—and where else they might turn to find ways to make sense of modern life. Extend the discussion by asking students how and why a person's search for truth might change as he or she grows older.

OBJECTIVES

- understand the historical and cultural context of American romanticism
- be introduced to major American romantic and transcendentalist writers
- take notes by charting main ideas and details

 R3.5

To provide a motivating introduction to this unit and give students a sense of time and place for the romantic period, see

 Literature in Context DVD

The following essay (pages 296–305) provides students with a historical context for the Unit 2 reading selections. It presents a brief overview of important events occurring during the time period 1800–1855 and discusses key people and concepts of that era.

To get started, read and discuss the opening paragraph on page 296. List these contradictory pairs of words on the board: *patriotic/individualistic, urban/untamed, wealthy/enslaved.* Elicit or explain the ways in which each pair expresses a contradiction. Then briefly discuss why living in a "complex, inconsistent society" might cause people to turn inward to find truth.

READING STRATEGY

■ PREVIEW

Have students preview the historical essay by reading the **KEY IDEAS** and by skimming the heads, boldfaced terms, and **Taking Notes** side-column features. Ask volunteers to summarize what the essay is about.

About the Art *Summer Afternoon on the Hudson* is an oil painting by Jasper Francis Cropsey (1823–1900). Such scenes on the Hudson River were a common sight for Cropsey, who was born in New York State. Cropsey was an early member of the Hudson River School (discussed on page 299). This example of his work demonstrates the romantic fascination with the majesty of the natural world.

Celebrating the *Individual*

Patriotic and individualistic, urban and untamed, wealthy and enslaved—Americans in the first half of the 19th century embodied a host of contradictions. Struggling to make sense of their complex, inconsistent society, writers of the period turned inward for a sense of truth. Their movement, known as romanticism, explored the glories of the individual spirit, the beauty of nature, and the possibilities of the imagination.

296

DIFFERENTIATED INSTRUCTION

FOR STRATEGIC READERS
Preteach Academic Vocabulary

- *individualistic,* "emphasizing the interests of the individual rather than a group or society; independent in thought or action"
- *relocate,* "to move to a new place"
- *annex,* "to add or incorporate"
- *immoral,* "not moral; contrary to what is right"
- *contiguous,* "touching; connected"

- *agrarian,* "having to do with land, farmers, or farming"
- *industrialization,* "becoming increasingly based upon mechanized production (rather than upon farming)"
- *commercialism,* "emphasis on doing business, making money, and being successful"

Use this copy master to help students take notes on the essay, pages 296–305:

 RESOURCE MANAGER—Copy Master
Note Taking p. 16

Romanticism: Historical Context

KEY IDEAS Historical forces clearly shaped the literature of the American romantic period. Writers responded—positively and negatively—to the country's astonishing growth and to the booming Industrial Revolution.

The Spirit of Exploration

WESTWARD EXPANSION Writers of the romantic period were witness to a period of great growth and opportunity for the young American nation. With that growth, however, came a price. In 1803, the Louisiana Purchase doubled the country's size. In the years that followed, explorers and settlers pushed farther and farther west. Settlers moved for largely practical reasons: to make money and to gain land. But each bit of land settled by white Americans was taken from Native American populations who had lived there for generations. The Indian Removal Act of 1830, for example, required Native Americans to relocate west. As whites invaded their homelands, many Native Americans saw no choice but to comply. And those who did not were simply—and often brutally—forced to leave.

Toward the middle of the century, Americans embraced the notion of **"manifest destiny"**—the idea that it was the destiny of the United States to expand to the Pacific Ocean and into Mexican territory. Mexicans disagreed, of course. When Texas was annexed from Mexico by the United States in 1845, it set off the Mexican-American War. Many Americans, including writer **Henry David Thoreau,** found the war to be immoral—a war fought mainly to expand slavery. "Can there not be a government," he wrote, "in which majorities do not virtually decide right and wrong, but conscience?" In the end, the United States defeated Mexico and, through treaties and subsequent land purchases from the Mexican government, established the current borders of the 48 contiguous United States.

Growth of Industry

The stories and essays of the romantic period reflect an enormous shift in the attitudes and working habits of many Americans. When the War of 1812 interrupted trade with the British, Americans were suddenly forced to produce many of the goods they had previously imported. The **Industrial Revolution** began, changing the country from a largely agrarian economy to an industrial powerhouse.

The factory system changed the way of life for many Americans, but not always for the better. People left their farms for the cities, working long hours for low wages in harsh conditions. In addition, Northeastern textile mills' demand for cotton played a role in the expansion of slavery in the South. Writers of this period reacted to the negative effects of industrialization—the commercialism, hectic pace, and lack of conscience—by turning to nature and to the self for simplicity, truth, and beauty.

Detail of *Summer Afternoon on the Hudson* (1852), Jasper Francis Cropsey. © Christie's Images/Corbis.

> ▶ **TAKING NOTES**
>
> **Outlining** As you read this introduction, use an outline to record the main ideas about the characteristics and the literature of the period. You can use article headings, boldfaced terms, and the information in these boxes as starting points. (See page R49 in the **Research Handbook** for more help with outlining.)
>
> **I. Historical Context**
>   A. Spirit of Exploration
>   1. Westward Expansion
>   2. Manifest Destiny
>   B. Growth of Industry

> ⚡ **ADDITIONAL BACKGROUND**
> For more on the American romantic period, visit the **Literature Center** at ClassZone.com.

Romanticism: Historical Context

KEY IDEAS This section of the essay (page 297) describes America's westward expansion during the first half of the 19th century and explains some negative aspects of that expansion. The text also describes the beginning of the Industrial Revolution and its impact upon Americans.

TIERED DISCUSSION PROMPTS

Use these prompts to help students understand the ideas in **The Spirit of Exploration** and **Growth of Industry:**

Interpret Reread the second sentence of **The Spirit of Exploration.** What was the "price" of the physical expansion of the United States? *Possible answer: Expansion cost Native Americans their land and often their lives. In addition, belief in the concept of "manifest destiny" led to the Mexican-American War, which cost soldiers' lives on both sides.*

Analyze What were the chief effects of the Industrial Revolution? *Possible answer: The Industrial Revolution changed the basis of the national economy from agriculture to industry and prompted the migration of people from farms to cities. It also encouraged the expansion of slavery in the South and prompted writers to seek answers to life in nature and the self.*

Synthesize Reread the final sentence of **Growth of Industry.** How does the earlier Thoreau quotation connect to that idea? *Possible answer: Thoreau's comment emphasizes the importance of conscience, an idea that reflects a belief in the ability to find "simplicity, truth, and beauty" in the self.*

FOR ENGLISH LEARNERS

Set a Purpose After introducing the *KEY IDEAS* on this page, ask students to look for cause-effect relationships between events as they read about westward expansion and the Industrial Revolution. Encourage students to use a graphic organizer to make the relationships clear, as in this example:

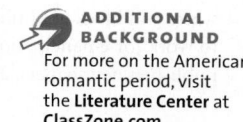

> Many Americans believed that the United States should expand (manifest destiny).
>
> ↓
>
> The U.S. annexed Texas and went to war with Mexico to keep it.

FOR ADVANCED LEARNERS/AP

Research and Analyze [small-group option] Have small groups of students gather more information about the concept of "manifest destiny": the origin of the term, ways in which the concept was debated in the United States and abroad, and its political impact. Have students present their findings to the class and explain why this doctrine was significant.

Cultural Influences

KEY IDEAS This section of the essay (pages 298–299) explains the growing split between North and South over the issue of slavery. The text also describes how an increasing number of Americans called for social reform, speaking out against slavery and supporting the rights of workers and women.

DISCUSSION PROMPT

Use this prompt to help students understand the ideas in **The Tragedy of Slavery:**

Synthesize Consider what you know about slavery from the account by Olaudah Equiano in Unit 1 or from any other account you have read or seen. What conclusion might you draw from this section, which describes slavery a generation after Equiano's account was published? *Possible answer: Because of increased cotton production, slavery had expanded in the American South, and its brutality affected more persons than ever. Enslaved families were broken up, and men, women, and children were subjected to cruel treatment. Southern plantation owners considered slavery essential for increasing their profits, increasing tension between pro-slavery Southerners and Northerners who considered slavery to be immoral.*

Cultural Influences

KEY IDEAS Many romantic writers were outspoken in their support for human rights. Their works created awareness of the injustice of slavery and called for reform in many other areas as well.

The Tragedy of Slavery

From 1793 to 1860, cotton production rose greatly, due to the invention of the cotton gin and other farming machinery. So did the number of enslaved workers. Plantation owners were the wealthiest and most powerful people in the South, yet they were relatively few in number. Most Southern farmers held few or no slaves, but they aspired to. They felt that slavery had become necessary for increasing profits.

For slaves, life was brutal. Field workers—men, women, and children—rose before dawn and worked in the fields until bedtime. Many were beaten or otherwise abused. And worst of all, family members were sold away from one another. Often family members attempted to escape to be with one another again. Unfortunately, escapes were rarely successful.

Tension over slavery increased between the North and the South. Many in the North saw slavery as immoral and worked to have it abolished. Others worried as the balance of power between free and slave states shifted with each new state entering the Union. Romantic poets **James Russell Lowell** and **John Greenleaf Whittier** wrote abolitionist journalism and poetry, and even **Henry Wadsworth Longfellow** published a volume of antislavery poems. Perhaps the greatest social achievement of the romantics was to create awareness of slavery's cruelty.

Call for Social Reform

By the mid-19th century, many Americans had joined together to fight slavery and the other social ills of the time. Many leading writers of the romantic movement were outspoken in their support for human rights. **William Cullen Bryant** and **James Russell Lowell,** for example, were prominent abolitionists who also supported workers' and women's rights.

The abolition movement began by advocating resettlement of blacks in Africa. But most enslaved African Americans had been born and raised in the United States and resented the idea of being forced to leave. Instead, white and black abolitionists (including women) began to join together to work for emancipation. They formed societies, spoke at conventions, published newspapers, and swamped Congress with petitions to end slavery.

This antislavery medal was created to help grow support for the abolition movement.

> **A Voice from the Times**
>
> *Men! Whose boast it is that ye*
> *Come of fathers brave and free,*
> *If there breathe on earth a slave,*
> *Are ye truly free and brave?*
> *If ye do not feel the chain,*
> *When it works a brother's pain,*
> *Are ye not base slaves indeed,*
> *Slaves unworthy to be freed?*
>
> **—James Russell Lowell**
> *from "Stanzas on Freedom"*

DIFFERENTIATED INSTRUCTION

FOR STRATEGIC READERS

Taking Notes Ask students to record the main ideas relating to **Cultural Influences** (pages 298–299) in outline form. Then have students exchange papers and evaluate each other's work. Instruct students to offer specific suggestions for improvement.

Sample notes:

I. *The Tragedy of Slavery*
  A. *Demand for cotton = increase in slavery*
  B. *Brutal treatment of enslaved workers*
  C. *Increase of North-South tension over the issue*
    1. *View of South: slavery as economically necessary*
    2. *View of North: slavery as immoral*
  D. *Involvement of writers*
II. *Call for Social Reform*
  A. *Rise in opposition to social ills*
    1. *End to slavery*
    2. *Improved conditions for workers*
    3. *Opportunities for women*
  B. *Involvement of writers*

In the 1830s and 1840s, workers began to agitate as well, protesting low wages and deteriorating working conditions. Many struck, but few were successful—a large pool of immigrants was always ready to take their places. Still, workers began forming unions, and slowly conditions improved.

Women in the early 19th century found much to protest. They could neither vote nor sit on juries. Their education rarely extended beyond elementary school. When they married, their property and money became their husband's. Many even lacked guardianship rights over their children. Throughout this period, women worked for change, gathering in 1848 at Seneca Falls, New York, to continue their long fight for women's rights.

Ideas of the Age

KEY IDEAS Reflecting the optimism of their growing country, American romantic writers forged a national literature for the very first time. Yet sectionalism threatened to tear the nation apart.

Nationalism vs. Sectionalism

In the early 1800s, many Supreme Court decisions strengthened the federal government's power over the states. At the same time, Secretary of State John Quincy Adams established a foreign policy guided by **nationalism**—the belief that national interests should be placed ahead of regional concerns or the interests of other countries. Reflecting the national pride and optimism of the American people, writers of this age forged a literature entirely the nation's own. For the first time, writers were not imitating their European counterparts, but were listening to their own voices and writing with a distinctly American accent.

However, this new spirit of nationalism was challenged by the question of slavery. Up until 1818, the United States had consisted of ten free and ten slave states. As new territories tried to enter the Union, the North and South wrangled over the balance of power between free and slave states. Economic interests also challenged nationalism. Tariffs on manufactured goods from Britain forced Southerners to buy more expensive, Northern-manufactured goods. From the South's point of view, the North was getting rich at the South's expense. Sectionalism, or the placing of the interests of one's own region ahead of the nation as a whole, began to take hold.

The Hudson River School

The paintings on pages 296 and 300 are excellent examples of the works of the Hudson River School artists. This group of landscape painters flourished between 1825 and 1870. The artists knew one another and used similar techniques for portraying nature scenes.

American Style Thomas Cole painted *A View of the Mountain Pass Called the Notch of the White Mountains* (1839), shown here and on page 293. He and the other Hudson River artists created passionate wilderness scenes that appealed to the imagination and made earlier American landscapes seem weak and unobserved. Like the American romantic writers of the time, the Hudson River School artists made a conscious effort to create an American style—one based on nature and the emotions.

Real-Life Inspiration The painting shown in detail here has an interesting history. Author Nathaniel Hawthorne wrote a short story about a real-life landslide at Crawford Notch that took the lives of nine people. The story may have piqued Cole's interest in the scene. In the painting Cole highlights the insignificance and vulnerability of the human figures in the face of the coming storm. One barely notices the settlers' homes or the rider, who seems oblivious to the ominous clouds gathering at the upper left—hinting of disaster to come.

THE ARTISTS' GALLERY

The Hudson River School, whose landscape paintings captured the natural grandeur of the Hudson River Valley, Niagara Falls, the White Mountains, and other parts of New England, was influenced by European romantic ideas about nature. *A View of the Mountain Pass Called the Notch of the White Mountains* is representative of the dramatic, colorful painting of Thomas Cole, a founder and leader of the Hudson River School. Point out that Cole's placement of gnarled trees (better seen in the larger illustration on page 293) alongside the stumps of trees that have been cut down reflects the romantic opposition to the destruction of America's forests.

Activity Ask students how Cole's use of color and contrast adds drama to the painting. ***Possible answer:*** *The vivid colors and contrast of light and dark (especially in the sky) give the painting emotional depth.*

CHECK UNDERSTANDING

Ask students to explain how protest was a part of the 1830s and '40s. Then ask students why they think most of this protest took place in the North rather than in the South.

Ideas of the Age

KEY IDEAS This section of the essay (page 299) describes how sectionalism, focused largely upon the issue of slavery, threatened a rising nationalistic spirit.

CHECK UNDERSTANDING

Ask students to define *nationalism* in their own words and to explain how slavery undermined feelings of nationalism.

FOR STRATEGIC READERS
Preteach Academic Vocabulary

- *abolitionist,* "person who advocated the end of slavery"
- *emancipation,* "freedom from bondage"
- *tariff,* "tax placed on imported goods"
- *free state,* "U.S. state in which slavery was prohibited before the Civil War"
- *slave state,* "U.S. state in which slavery was legal until the Civil War"

FOR ADVANCED LEARNERS/AP

Synthesize Point out that issues relating to nationalism and sectionalism are by no means limited to the nineteenth century. Have students write a brief essay explaining how conflicts over nationalism and sectionalism persist to this day. Encourage students to use their knowledge of current events and to do additional research as needed to support their ideas with specific examples.

Romantic Literature

KEY IDEAS This section of the essay (pages 300–305) focuses on the themes and writing of the American romantic movement. The text describes the work of the following groups:

- the early romantics, including William Cullen Bryant, Washington Irving, and James Fenimore Cooper
- the Fireside Poets, including Henry Wadsworth Longfellow, James Russell Lowell, Oliver Wendell Holmes, and John Greenleaf Whittier
- the transcendentalists, including Ralph Waldo Emerson and Henry David Thoreau
- the "brooding" romantics, including Edgar Allan Poe, Nathaniel Hawthorne, and Herman Melville

ANALYZE VISUALS

Possible answer: The paintings are similar in their depiction of nature's beauty. However, Cole used a striking combination of colors in his painting, while Durand's use of color is more limited and subdued.

About the Art American artist Asher Brown Durand (1796–1886) was a successful engraver when he developed a growing interest in oil painting, especially landscapes. (Indeed, the attention to fine detail in *Kindred Spirits* reflects an engraver's skill.) Durand and Thomas Cole are considered to be the founders of the Hudson River School (see page 299), and *Kindred Spirits* often is cited as the most famous painting to come from this group. Set in the Catskill Mountains, it shows the majesty of nature; and though the human beings in the scene look small by comparison to their surroundings, they fit "naturally" into the scene—an idea that early romantic writers would have embraced. Furthermore, the distance indicated in the background suggests the optimism of early romanticism.

Romantic Literature

KEY IDEAS Themes of individualism and nature unified the writing of the American romantic movement, despite dramatic differences in the writers' focus and style.

The Early Romantics

The early American romantic writers may have been influenced more by the literature of another continent than by that of their own. **Romanticism** had first emerged in Europe in the late 18th century, in reaction to the neoclassicism of the period that had preceded it. Where neoclassical writers admired and imitated classical forms, the romantics looked to nature for inspiration. Where neoclassicists valued reason, the romantics celebrated emotions and the imagination. The first American romantic writers grew

▶ *For Your Outline*

THE EARLY ROMANTICS

- were inspired by the beauty of nature
- emphasized emotions and the imagination over reason
- celebrated the individual spirit

Kindred Spirits (1849), Asher B. Durand. © Francis G. Mayer/Corbis.

ANALYZE VISUALS
This painting is a memorial to painter Asher B. Durand's friend and fellow Hudson River School artist Thomas Cole (here shown with romantic poet William Cullen Bryant).
    Although Durand was influenced by Cole, his works express stillness and a realistic imitation of nature, in contrast to Cole's more expressive rendering. Compare this painting with Cole's on the previous page. How are they similar? How are they different?

DIFFERENTIATED INSTRUCTION

FOR STRATEGIC READERS
Vocabulary Support The "classical forms" that neoclassical writers admired and imitated were the creative works of the ancient Greeks and Romans in literature, art, and architecture. These works were characterized as simple (that is, not artificially ornate), elegant, and (as might be expected in a movement that valued reason) symmetrical.

Preteach Academic Vocabulary

- *neoclassicism,* "revival of the artistic tastes and styles of ancient Greece and Rome"
- *rationality,* "reliance upon reason"
- *human nature,* "the qualities that all people share; what defines a being as human"
- *supernatural,* "that which exists or occurs beyond the natural world"

A collection of major works by early American romantics

out of this European tradition, shaping and molding it to fit their unique American identity. They too were reacting to what had come before—the rationality of the Age of Reason and the strict doctrines of Puritanism.

Indeed, much had changed since the Puritan era in America, and the writers of the early romantic period reflected the more modern sensibilities of their day. As the U.S. population exploded and the country's borders moved westward, American writers aimed to capture the energy and character of their growing country. They saw the limits of reason and instead celebrated the glories of the individual spirit, the emotions, and the imagination as basic elements of human nature. The splendors of nature inspired the romantics more than the fear of God, and some of them felt a fascination with the supernatural.

William Cullen Bryant's 1817 poem "Thanatopsis" went a long way toward establishing romanticism as the major force in the literature of mid-19th century America. Bryant followed the trend of the English romantics by celebrating nature in his work. Romanticism was not only a movement in poetry, however. **Washington Irving,** the first American writer esteemed abroad, pioneered the short story as a literary form. He put America on the literary map and also influenced other writers, particularly Nathaniel Hawthorne. **James Fenimore Cooper** is remembered for writing the first truly original American novel. He celebrated the American spirit in all his frontier novels, known as *The Leatherstocking Tales.* The early romantic writers were the pioneers of America's national literature, setting the course for those who would follow.

> ### A Voice from the Times
>
> *To him who in the love of Nature holds*
> *Communion with her visible forms, she speaks*
> *A various language; for his gayer hours*
> *She has a voice of gladness, and a smile*
> *And eloquence of beauty, and she glides*
> *Into his darker musings, with a mild*
> *And healing sympathy, that steals away*
> *Their sharpness, ere he is aware. . . .*
>
> **—William Cullen Bryant**
> *from* "Thanatopsis"

TIERED DISCUSSION PROMPTS
Use these prompts to help students understand the ideas in **The Early Romantics:**

Restate What did the romantics reject, and what did they admire? *Possible answer: The romantics rejected the neoclassical love of reason and classical forms; they admired nature, emotion, and imagination.*

Interpret What were "the more modern sensibilities" that the early romantics reflected? How did these writers respond? *Possible answer: These sensibilities were an awareness and appreciation of the country's dynamic growth. In response, the early romantics focused more upon individualism, emotion, and imagination than upon reason; they also found greater inspiration in nature than in the fear of God.*

Synthesize Given what you already know about American literature and culture, which writer of early romanticism—Bryant, Irving, or Cooper—do you think has had the greatest impact, and why? *Accept all reasonable responses.*

FOR ADVANCED LEARNERS/AP
Research Influences on Romanticism Explain that inspiration for the early American romantic writers came in part from the French writer and philosopher Jean Jacques Rousseau (1712–1778) and the German poet Johann Wolfgang von Goethe (1749–1832). Ask small groups of students to research Rousseau and Goethe. Then challenge each group to create a poster that presents this information:

- key facts about each writer's life, including major works and accomplishments
- a summary of each writer's ideas
- notes about each writer's impact upon other writers and thinkers of the time

Invite group representatives to present the posters to the class.

Use these prompts to help students understand the ideas in **The Fireside Poets:**

Restate Why were these poets called the Fireside Poets? *Possible answer: In the 19th century, a common form of family entertainment was reading poetry aloud beside the fire.*

Analyze In what sense did each member of the Fireside Poets attempt to improve the United States? *Possible answer: Lowell, Holmes, and Whittier were concerned about social issues, and they used their poetry to advocate for social reform in the United States. Longfellow may not have been as openly committed to social reform, but by frequently writing about America's past, he may have been trying to improve the United States by giving Americans a heritage of which they could be proud.*

The legendary Hiawatha, memorialized in Longfellow's poem "The Song of Hiawatha"

The Fireside Poets

Other writers influential in forging an American literature were the Fireside Poets, a group of New England poets whose work was morally uplifting and romantically engaging. The group's name came from the family custom of reading poetry aloud beside a fire, a common form of entertainment in the 19th century. With the Fireside Poets, the poetry of American writers was, for the first time, on equal footing with that of their British counterparts.

Henry Wadsworth Longfellow, the best-known member of the group, stressed individualism and an appreciation of nature in his work. His poems took for their subject matter the more colorful aspects of America's past. "Evangeline," for example, tells of lovers who are separated during the French and Indian War, while "The Song of Hiawatha" takes its themes from Native American folklore. Longfellow's fame was so great that after his death, he was honored with a plaque in Poets' Corner of Westminster Abbey in London—the only American poet ever to receive such an honor.

The other Fireside Poets, **James Russell Lowell, Oliver Wendell Holmes,** and **John Greenleaf Whittier,** were strongly committed to using poetry to bring about social reform. They were interested in such issues as abolition, women's rights, improvement of factory conditions, and temperance. They also championed the common person—perhaps as an outgrowth of the form of democracy that had been sweeping the land since President Jackson took office in 1829. Jackson had crusaded against control of the government by the wealthy and promised to look out for the interests of common people. One can see this regard for the common person in the work of Whittier, for example, who wrote of farmers, lumbermen, migrants, and the poor.

▶ *For Your Outline*

THE FIRESIDE POETS

- emphasized moral themes in work
- were viewed as equals of British poets of the day
- stressed individualism and an appreciation of nature
- were committed to social reform

302 UNIT 2: AMERICAN ROMANTICISM

DIFFERENTIATED INSTRUCTION

FOR STRATEGIC READERS

Vocabulary Support The word *temperance* means "the practice of abstaining from alcoholic beverages." The link between drunkenness and other social problems had long been noted, but the movement to improve public life by banning alcohol gained momentum in the first half of the 19th century. By the 1830s, thousands of temperance societies around the United States and in other countries were working to reduce the consumption of alcohol.

FOR ADVANCED LEARNERS/AP

Research Quakers such as John Greenleaf Whittier played a key role in the growth of the Abolitionist movement in the United States. Have students research the origins of the Society of Friends and their contributions to Abolitionism, such as their foundation of numerous Abolitionist societies, the "Underground Railroad," and schools for freed slaves. Have students report their findings to the class. Allow time for questions and discussion.

The Transcendentalists

By the mid-1800s, Americans were taking new pride in their emerging culture. **Ralph Waldo Emerson,** a New England writer, nurtured this pride. Emerson led a group practicing **transcendentalism**—a philosophical and literary movement that emphasized living a simple life and celebrating the truth found in nature and in personal emotion and imagination. Exalting the dignity of the individual, the transcendentalist stressed American ideas of optimism, freedom, and self-reliance.

The term transcendentalism came from Immanuel Kant, a German philosopher who wrote of "transcendent forms" of knowledge that exist beyond reason and experience. Emerson gave this philosophy a peculiarly American spin: he said that every individual is capable of discovering this higher truth on his or her own, through intuition. The transcendentalists believed that people are inherently good and should follow their own beliefs, however different these beliefs may be from the norm. Both Emerson's essay "Self-Reliance" and **Henry David Thoreau's** "Civil Disobedience" address this faith in the integrity of the individual.

Not surprisingly, a major target for the transcendentalists' criticism was their Puritan heritage, with its emphasis on material prosperity and rigid obedience to the laws of society. The transcendentalists disliked the commercial, financial side of American life and stressed instead spiritual well-being, achieved through intellectual activity and a close relationship to nature. Thoreau put his beliefs into practice by building a small cabin on Walden Pond and living there for two years, writing and studying nature.

Transcendental ideas lived on in American culture in the works of later poets such as Walt Whitman, Robert Frost, and Wallace Stevens and through the civil rights movement of the 20th century. In the short term, however, transcendentalists' optimism began to fade when confronted with the persistence of slavery and the difficulty in abolishing it.

> ▶ *For Your Outline*
>
> **THE TRANSCENDENTALISTS**
>
> - emphasized living a simple life
> - stressed a close relationship to nature
> - celebrated emotions and the imagination
> - stressed individualism and self-reliance
> - believed intuition can lead to knowledge
> - believed in the inherent goodness of people
> - encouraged spiritual well-being over financial well-being

A replica of Thoreau's 10-by-15-foot cabin on the shore of Walden Pond

> ### A Voice from the Times
>
> *Go confidently in the direction of your dreams! Live the life you've imagined. As you simplify your life, the laws of the universe will be simpler.*
>
> —Henry David Thoreau

TIERED DISCUSSION PROMPTS

Use these prompts to help students understand the ideas in **The Transcendentalists:**

Restate What did the transcendentalists reject, and what did they admire? *Possible answer: The transcendentalists rejected commercialism and Puritan attitudes; they admired individualism, intuition, intellectualism, and a spiritual relationship with nature.*

Interpret How was Emerson's adaptation of transcendentalism "peculiarly American"? *Possible answer: Emerson stressed the individual's role in finding "higher truth" through intuition. This emphasis on individualism was very much in keeping with the American values of the era.*

Evaluate Consider what you know of American life at this time. How would you respond to someone who called transcendentalism an impractical philosophy? *Encourage answers that demonstrate an awareness of these points:*

- *the transcendentalists' unorthodoxy vs. the nation's Puritan heritage*
- *the transcendentalists' belief in reflection and personal conscience vs. the sense of national pride, unity, and drive that marked the country as a whole in the early 1800s*

FOR STRATEGIC READERS
Preteach Academic Vocabulary

- *reform,* "change for the better; correction or removal of what is wrong"
- *nurture,* "to nourish and promote"
- *self-reliance,* "trust in or dependence upon one's own abilities and efforts"
- *intuition,* "insight gained through personal impression rather than logic"
- *integrity,* "personal honesty and honor"

FOR ADVANCED LEARNERS/AP

Analyze a Quotation Ask students to reflect upon Henry David Thoreau's quotation in **A Voice from the Times.** Have students discuss how the quotation relates to the ideas of the transcendentalists. Extend the discussion by asking students to write a paragraph explaining why they think Thoreau's words still are quoted today, more than a century after he wrote them. Then have them read their paragraphs aloud.

Use these prompts to help students understand the ideas in **American Gothic: The "Brooding" Romantics**:

Analyze How does the work of these writers compare and contrast with that of the early romantics? *Possible answer: Like the early romantics, these writers emphasized individuality, imagination, and emotion. However, these writers had a darker view of the world, humankind, and the imagination.*

Interpret Explain this statement from the essay: "For the dark romantics, the imagination led to the threshold of the unknown...." *Possible answer: The "brooding" romantics cast off the restrictions of reason and followed their imagination into the darker side of human experience. Writers such as Poe, Hawthorne, and Melville explored some of the negative forces at work in human psychology and their effect on human life.*

Synthesize Why would you expect a writer from this group to be reluctant about trusting personal intuition? *Possible answer: The "brooding" romantics focused on the dark mysteries of human psychology, so they probably would not trust intuition the way that optimists such as the transcendentalists did.*

American Gothic: The "Brooding" Romantics

Not all American romantics were optimistic or had faith in the innate goodness of humankind, however. Three other giants from this period, **Edgar Allan Poe, Nathaniel Hawthorne,** and **Herman Melville** are what have been called **"brooding" romantics** or **"anti-transcendentalists."** Theirs is a complex philosophy, filled with dark currents and a deep awareness of the human capacity for evil. While Irving had been satisfied if his work kept "mankind in good humor with one another," Hawthorne, Melville, and Poe were haunted by a darker vision of human existence. Their stories are characterized by a probing of the inner life of their characters, and examination of the complex and often mysterious forces that motivate human behavior. They are romantic, however, in their emphasis on emotion, nature, the individual, and the unusual.

EXPLORING THE DARKNESS Poe and Hawthorne, and to a lesser extent Melville, used **gothic** elements such as grotesque characters, bizarre situations, and violent events in their fiction. The gothic tradition had begun in Europe, perhaps inspired by the gothic architecture of the Middle Ages. European writers of the 19th century, such as Mary Shelley, author of *Frankenstein,* delighted readers with their deliciously creepy accounts of monsters, vampires, and humans with a large capacity for evil. The romantic movement itself also gave rise to gothic literature. Once the romantics freed the imagination from the restrictions of reason, they could follow it wherever it might go. For the dark romantics, the imagination led to the threshold of the unknown—that shadowy region where the fantastic, the demonic, and the insane reside.

Edgar Allan Poe, of course, was the master of the gothic form in the United States. He explored human psychology from the inside, using first-person narrators who were sometimes criminal or even insane. His plots involved extreme situations—not just murder, but live burials, physical and mental torture, and retribution from beyond the grave.

Nathaniel Hawthorne agreed with the romantic emphasis on emotion and the individual. However, he did not see these as completely positive forces. His works, such as *The Scarlet Letter* and "The Minister's Black Veil," examine the darker facets of the human soul—for example, the psychological effects sin and guilt may have on human life.

Herman Melville's early works were mostly adventure stories set in the South Pacific. *Moby Dick,* however, departed from that pattern. By concentrating on a ship's captain's obsessive quest for the whale that took his leg, Melville explores such issues as madness and the conflict of good and evil. Later, in "Bartleby the Scrivener," Melville

▶ *For Your Outline*

AMERICAN GOTHIC: THE "BROODING" ROMANTICS

- did not believe in the innate goodness of people
- explored the human capacity for evil
- probed the inner life of characters
- explored characters' motivations
- agreed with romantic emphasis on emotion, nature, and the individual
- included elements of fantasy and the supernatural in works

A Voice from the Times

I looked upon the scene before me—upon the mere house, and the simple landscape features of the domain—upon the bleak walls—upon the vacant eye-like windows—upon a few rank sedges—and upon a few white trunks of decayed trees—with an utter depression of soul which I can compare to no earthly sensation more properly than to the after-dream of the reveller upon opium—the bitter lapse into everyday life—the hideous dropping off of the veil.

—**Edgar Allan Poe**
from "The Fall of the House of Usher"

DIFFERENTIATED INSTRUCTION

FOR ADVANCED LEARNERS/AP

Research *Frankenstein* [small-group option] Mary Shelley's most famous book was published in 1818 (when she was only 20 years old) and has inspired a multitude of stories, novels, plays, and movies; indeed, Frankenstein's monster is a cultural icon. Have one or more small groups of students research Mary Shelley and write an essay about her life and work. Ask them also to explore the reasons for the lasting popularity of *Frankenstein* and to discuss how Shelley's novel reflects the gothic tradition. To extend the activity, encourage students to read portions of *Frankenstein* and to compare the actual text with their expectations about the story.

Like an Open-Doored Marble Tomb, George Klauba. Acrylic on panel, 18″ × 14.5″. Courtesy Ann Nathan Gallery, Chicago. © George Klamba.

reveals the dark side of material prosperity by exploring how the struggle for material gain affects the individual.

Perhaps the dark vision of Hawthorne, Melville, and Poe foreshadowed the tumult and tragedy that was soon to erupt in civil war in America. There is no question that these three writers profoundly affected the development of the American literary voice throughout the remainder of the 19th century.

ANALYZE VISUALS

Activity In what sense might the image in this painting symbolize the way that the "brooding" romantics thought about life and their writing? *Possible answer: In the image, Moby Dick is mostly hidden in the ocean depths, but he is approaching the boat, his intent of destruction clear. Similarly, the "brooding" romantics explored the mysterious, hidden aspects of human psychology and often seemed haunted by the threat of impending disaster.*

DISCUSSION PROMPT

Use this prompt to help students understand the ideas in **American Gothic: The "Brooding" Romantics:**

Synthesize What aspects of early gothic literature are apparent in modern-day works? *Possible answer: Such gothic elements as "grotesque characters, bizarre situations, and violent events" remain a mainstay of modern-day horror writers, such as Stephen King.*

CHECK UNDERSTANDING

Identify a few characteristics of each of these groups of writers:

- The Early Romantics
- The Fireside Poets
- The Transcendentalists
- The "Brooding" Romantics

FOR STRATEGIC READERS

Preteach Academic Vocabulary

- *brooding,* "absorbed in gloomy thoughts"
- *innate,* "inborn; natural"
- *material,* "relating to physical things, rather than to spiritual or intellectual concerns"
- *foreshadow,* "to indicate beforehand"

Connecting: Literature, History, and Culture

OBJECTIVES
- read a timeline
- make connections among the perspectives and events of literature, history, and culture

---

READING SKILL

■ READ A TIMELINE

Elicit or explain that each of the three horizontal sections of the timeline—*American Literary Milestones, Historical Context,* and *World Culture and Events*—displays a sequence of events that occurred between 1800 and 1855. By looking at the vertical columns on the timeline, students can see which events were taking place at about the same time.

Have students locate, for example, each of these events on the timeline in the 1820s column:

- **1823** Beethoven completes his Ninth Symphony. (See *World Culture and Events*.)
- **1824** Washington Irving's "The Devil and Tom Walker" is published. (See *American Literary Milestones*.)
- **1825** The Erie Canal is opened. (See *Historical Context*.)

Ask students to identify events that occurred between 1815 and 1817. **Answer:** *Levi Coffin established the Underground Railroad in 1815; Rossini wrote* The Barber of Seville *in 1816; Bryant's "Thanatopsis" was published in 1817.*

Connecting Literature, History, and Culture

Use this timeline and the questions on the next page to gain insight about how developments during the American romantic period reflected what was happening in the world as a whole.

AMERICAN LITERARY MILESTONES

1800	1810	1820
1806 Noah Webster's first dictionary is published. It includes 5,000 words related to American customs that have never before been collected.	**1817** "Thanatopsis," composed by William Cullen Bryant at age 18, is published in *The North American Review.* ▼	**1824** Irving's "The Devil and Tom Walker" is published.
1809 Washington Irving publishes *A History of New York,* satirizing the young nation.		**1826** James Fenimore Cooper writes *The Last of the Mohicans.*
		1827 *Freedom's Journal,* the first African-American newspaper, is founded. ▼

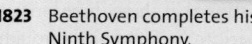

HISTORICAL CONTEXT

1800	1810	1820
		1820 Missouri Compromise prohibits slavery in western territories but allows slavery in Arkansas Territory and Louisiana.
		1823 The Monroe Doctrine bans European colonization in the Americas.
1803 Thomas Jefferson doubles ▲ the country's size by buying Louisiana Territory from France.	**1812** United States declares war ▲ on Great Britain. American industry booms.	**1825** The Erie Canal is opened, linking Lake Erie with the Hudson River.
1807 Robert Fulton launches *Clermont,* the first steamboat.	**1815** Quaker Levi Coffin establishes the Underground Railroad.	**1828** Construction begins on the first railroad in the United States.
1808 United States bans slave trade.		

WORLD CULTURE AND EVENTS

1800	1810	1820
1804 Napoleon is crowned emperor of France.	**1813** Jane Austen publishes *Pride and Prejudice.*	**1821** Venezuela and Mexico declare independence from Spain. ▶
1806 The Holy Roman Empire reaches its last days.	**1816** Rossini writes the comic opera *The Barber of Seville.*	**1823** Beethoven completes his Ninth Symphony.
1807 British slave trade is abolished.	**1819** Factory work is outlawed in England for children under nine years old.	**1829** Slavery is abolished in Mexico.

DIFFERENTIATED INSTRUCTION

FOR STRATEGIC READERS
Understanding a Timeline Explain that the timeline runs chronologically (in time order) from left to right across the page. Each of the six columns represents a ten-year period between 1800 and 1855 except for the last column, which covers only about five years. The three parallel rows of the timeline represent events occurring simultaneously. By comparing the three rows, readers can better understand what events in literature, history, and culture were taking place at about the same time.

MAKING CONNECTIONS

- Which European authors were contemporaries of American romantic writers?
- What evidence do you see that slavery was not only an American problem?
- What nations were battling for independence or dealing with its challenges?
- What inventions were moving the world into a more technological age?

1830

1835 Emerson, Thoreau, Margaret Fuller, and others form the Transcendental Club.

1838 Henry Wadsworth Longfellow's "A Psalm of Life" is published.

1839 Edgar Allan Poe's "The Fall of the House of Usher" is published.

1840

1845 Henry David Thoreau moves to Walden Pond.

1846 Herman Melville's first novel, *Typee*, is published. ▼

1850

1850 Nathaniel Hawthorne's *The Scarlet Letter* is published.

1851 Sojourner Truth delivers her "Ain't I a Woman?" speech to the Women's Rights Convention in Akron, Ohio. ▶

1852 Harriet Beecher Stowe publishes *Uncle Tom's Cabin.*

1830

1830 Indian Removal Act authorizes relocation of southeastern Native American tribes to territories west of Mississippi River.

1832 Samuel B. Morse invents the telegraph. ▼

1840

1845 Florida and Texas become the 27th and 28th states.

1848 Gold discoveries in California lead to first gold rush. ▼

1850

1850 Congress passes the Fugitive Slave Act, forcing officials in Northern states to return escaped slaves to their owners.

1851 Isaac Singer devises the sewing machine. ▼

1830

1838 Slaves mutiny aboard the ▲ Spanish ship *Amistad*.

1840

1843 Charles Dickens writes *A Christmas Carol.*

1847 Emily Brontë publishes *Wuthering Heights.*

1848 Karl Marx and Friedrich Engels publish *The Communist Manifesto.*

1850

1852 Dr. Livingston explores Zambesi.

1853 Verdi's opera *La Traviata* is first performed in Venice; Crimean War begins, involving Turkey, Russia, Britain, and France.

MAKING CONNECTIONS

Answers:

- *Jane Austen, Charles Dickens, Emily Brontë, Karl Marx, and Friedrich Engels were contemporaries of the American romantics.*

- *Slavery was not only an American problem, as evidenced by these facts: The British slave trade was abolished in 1807; slavery was abolished in Mexico in 1829; and slaves mutinied aboard the Spanish ship* Amistad *in 1838.*

- *Venezuela and Mexico were seeking independence; the United States was dealing with its challenges.*

- *The steamboat (1807), the telegraph (1832), and the sewing machine (1851) were technological inventions of the era.*

ADDITIONAL QUESTIONS

1. Which American author published his first novel 20 years after James Fenimore Cooper wrote *The Last of the Mohicans?* What was the title? ***Answer:** Herman Melville published* Typee *(1846).*

2. How many years after the United States banned the slave trade did Mexico abolish slavery? ***Answer:** Twenty-one years passed (1829).*

3. What innovations in transportation took place in the United States during this era? ***Answer:** the launching of the first steamboat (1807), the opening of the Erie Canal (1825), and the start of construction on the first railroad in the United States (1828).*

FOR ADVANCED LEARNERS/AP

Making Additional Connections Ask students to choose one of the six decades shown in the timeline and to research online, in encyclopedias, or in history texts other events that took place during that same ten-year time span. Challenge students to identify events for each category: *American Literary Milestones, Historical Context,* and *World Culture and Events.* Have students work individually, with partners, or in small groups to prepare and present brief oral reports. The students should summarize significant events and discuss their connection to events shown in the timeline or discussed in class.

OBJECTIVE

- to connect the legacy of romanticism to present times

Civil Rights

Have students read the paragraph. Elicit or explain that *civil disobedience* means refusing to obey the law as a nonviolent way of calling attention to injustice. People who practice civil disobedience hope to persuade the government to change or repeal unjust laws. Explain that civil disobedience usually takes the form of "passive resistance"—that is, opposition through noncooperation.

DISCUSS Work with students to explore examples of civil disobedience, discussing to what extent the actions taken were successful, and why. Connect the civil disobedience of Dr. Martin Luther King Jr. to the civil rights movement in the United States; also elicit or briefly explain the role that civil disobedience played in the work of Mohandas Gandhi in India. Then discuss Thoreau's statement, encouraging students to support their opinions with thoughtful reasons. Extend the discussion by asking students whether they think that penalties for breaking the law should be different in cases in which people are practicing civil disobedience rather than breaking the law for personal gain.

Civil Rights

When faced with unjust government actions, Henry David Thoreau called for Americans to practice civil disobedience in protest. This nonviolent form of protest attained full flower in the civil rights movement of the 1960s and remains an important tactic for activists today. In strikes, marches, and candlelight vigils, protestors across the United States use nonviolent means to make their voices heard.

DISCUSS As a class, think of recent examples of citizens using civil disobedience to protest government action. Were their protests successful? Was Thoreau right when he said, "If the alternative is to keep all just men in prison, or give up . . . , the State will not hesitate which to choose"?

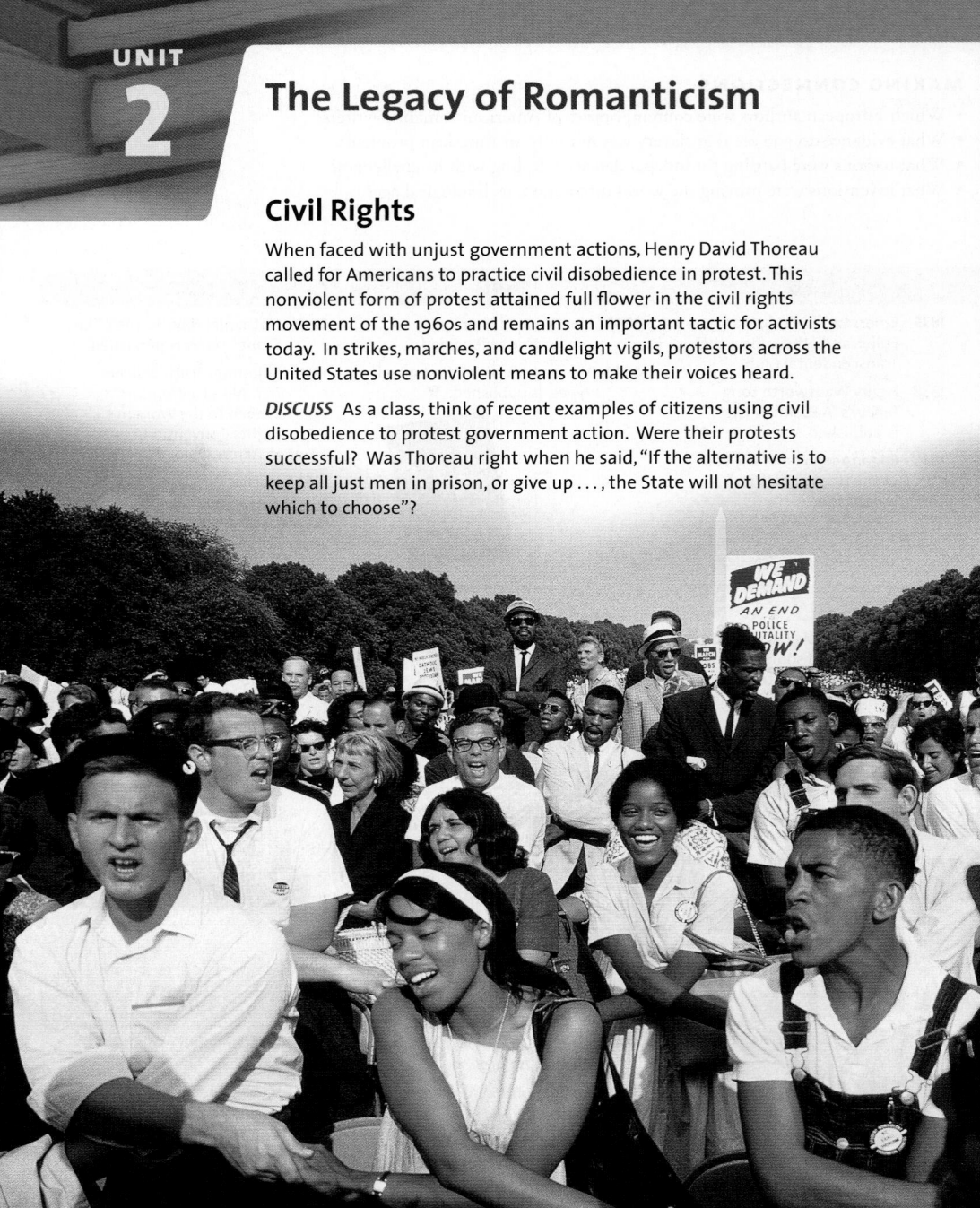

308

DIFFERENTIATED INSTRUCTION

FOR STRATEGIC READERS
Vocabulary Support

- *tactic,* "an action taken or method used to achieve a goal"

- *activist,* "a person who takes strong action to support or oppose a cause"

- *vigil,* "keeping watch for a particular purpose"

FOR ADVANCED LEARNERS/AP
Research Civil Disobedience Today [small-group option] Note the comment that civil disobedience "remains an important tactic for activists today." Then instruct small groups of students to find examples of civil disobedience within the past year or two. Have each group decide how to present its findings—for example, a bulletin-board display or a set of brief oral reports—always concluding with an evaluation of the effectiveness of civil disobedience.

Modern Gothic

The influence of Edgar Allan Poe is alive and well—make that undead and decaying—in the works of modern horror authors such as Stephen King and Anne Rice, and in many of the graphic novels lining today's bookstore shelves. Though their settings may be modern, these works share Poe's fascination with the dark side of humankind.

QUICKWRITE Why do you think people enjoy being frightened? Write a paragraph or two giving your reasons why so many people read gothic literature and enjoy films written in this same tradition.

The Romantic Hero

The romantic writers' focus on the individual led to the creation of a different kind of hero: unique, bold, sometimes brooding or eccentric. From the obsessed Captain Ahab, searching for his white whale in *Moby Dick,* to *The Last of the Mohicans'* noble Natty Bumppo, living on the fringes of society as both a white man and a Native American, romantic heroes were often larger than life, and always unforgettable. Their stories are still told today, and they have inspired a modern array of equally vivid characters.

CREATE With a small group, brainstorm a memorable hero for a new novel, TV show, or movie. Your hero should exemplify key aspects of the romantic spirit and must be utterly unique, a dynamic or mesmerizing individual who would capture people's imaginations.

Indiana Jones, from the movie *Raiders of the Lost Ark,* is a typical romantic hero.

Modern Gothic

After students have read the paragraph, invite comments about any of the literature mentioned with which they are familiar. Help students compile a list of elements of horror that they think most people would find frightening.

QUICKWRITE Ask volunteers to read their paragraphs to the class. Use students' responses to launch a discussion of the overall appeal of gothic literature. Expand the discussion by asking whether students think that this type of literature appeals to some groups more than others—for example, is it more popular with boys than girls, or with young people rather than older people?

The Romantic Hero

Have students read the paragraph. Ask for additional examples, drawn from novels, short stories, TV, and movies, of the "unique, bold, sometimes brooding or eccentric" romantic hero. Explore the common characteristics of the heroes that students name. Extend the discussion by asking whether students think that a romantic hero must be of a particular age or gender.

CREATE After students have finished brainstorming, challenge them to outline or summarize the plot for a story in which their hero is the main character. The plot should allow the hero to exhibit the representative characteristics of a romantic hero. Work with students to prepare a format for sharing their ideas.

FOR STRATEGIC READERS
Vocabulary Support

- *eccentric,* "odd; unusual"
- *obsessed,* "overly and unreasonably concerned about something"
- *array,* "group"
- *dynamic,* "forceful; energetic"
- *mesmerizing,* "fascinating"

FOR ADVANCED LEARNERS/AP

Write a Short Story [paired option] Have students write a short story based on the adventures of a romantic hero. They may use the hero that their group brainstormed or create a new hero of their own. Encourage students to develop the characters in their stories and to include dialogue and descriptive details.

Focus and Motivate

OBJECTIVES

Literary Analysis
- explore the key idea of **consequences**
- identify and analyze satire
- read a short story

Reading
- identify and analyze imagery

Vocabulary
- build vocabulary for reading and writing
- apply knowledge of the Latin root *spec* to help determine the meaning of words *(also an EL language objective)*

Grammar and Writing
- identify and use parallelism to create emphasis or add rhythm

 CALIFORNIA R3.1, R3.3, R1.2, R3.6, W1.2, W2.1, LC1.1

ABOUT THE AUTHOR

Call attention to Irving's comment that he always enjoyed "observing strange characters and manners." Point out that the selection demonstrates Irving's ability to translate his observations of human nature into fiction.

USING THE *NOTABLE QUOTE*

Ask students whether people's regard for "the almighty dollar" represents a particular time or place or if such "devotion" is indeed "universal." *Students should recognize that people's desire for money is not limited to any time or place. However, money serves as a stronger motivation for some individuals than for others.*

Selection Resources

The Devil and Tom Walker

Short Story by Washington Irving

 CALIFORNIA

R3.1, R3.3, R1.2 (p. 326), R3.6 (p. 327), W1.2 (p. 327), W2.1 (p. 327), LC1.1 (p. 327)

NOTABLE QUOTE
"The almighty dollar, that great object of universal devotion . . ."

FYI
Did you know that Washington Irving . . .
- was a spectator at the trial of Aaron Burr?
- served as a colonel in the War of 1812?
- inspired the name of the New York Knicks basketball team?
- lost the love of his life when she died at 17?

Author Online
For more on Washington Irving, visit the **Literature Center** at **ClassZone.com**.

Sleepy Hollow Cemetery

Washington Irving
1783–1859

The Headless Horseman has thundered through readers' nightmares for nearly 200 years. Rip Van Winkle has been inspiring laughter for just as long. These characters, along with scores of others that populate his writing, helped make Washington Irving the first American writer to achieve an international reputation.

A Reluctant Lawyer Born when the nation was new and patriotism at its fiercest, Washington Irving was named for the country's first president. He began studying law at 16 but never showed much enthusiasm for it. He did, however, have a passion for writing, a playful mind, and keen powers of observation. "I was always fond of visiting new scenes and observing strange characters and manners," he once wrote. In 1807, he began publishing light satirical pieces about New York politics, culture, and theater.

Also Known As . . . In 1809, Irving penned *A History of New York from the Beginning of Time Through the End of the Dutch Dynasty,* a satire of both historical texts and the local politics they chronicled. It was considered a comic masterpiece, but for a time no one knew who had written it—the manuscript was said to have been left at an inn by an old lodger named Diedrich Knickerbocker. Knickerbocker was one of many eccentric narrators created by Irving, who didn't sign his own name to his works until he was over 40.

American Abroad In 1815, Irving began traveling through Europe, remaining there for 17 years. With the encouragement of Sir Walter Scott—the author of *Ivanhoe* and a fan of Irving's *History*—he began writing a series of stories that blended the legends of Europe with the tales he had heard while wandering as a young man through New York's Catskill Mountains and Hudson Valley. The stories, including both "The Legend of Sleepy Hollow"and "Rip Van Winkle," appeared in 1820 as *The Sketch-Book of Geoffrey Crayon, Gent.* The collection was wildly successful. However, in 1824, Irving published *Tales of a Traveller* (which contained "The Devil and Tom Walker"), and the book was not well received. In fact, the criticism was so harsh that Irving stopped writing fiction altogether.

Irving returned to America in 1832 to live with his brother on the Sunnyside estate. He died at the age of 76 and was buried near the haunting ground of his famous horseman—in New York's Sleepy Hollow Cemetery.

Selection Resources

 RESOURCE MANAGER UNIT 2

Plan and Teach pp. 17–24

Literary Analysis
Summary pp. 25†*, 26‡*
Satire pp. 27, 28†*
Question Support p. 35*

Reading
Interpret Imagery pp. 29, 30†*
Reading Check p. 34

Vocabulary
Study p. 31*
Practice p. 32
Strategy p. 33

Grammar and Writing
Recognize Parallelism p. 36

Assessment
Selection Tests A, B/C pp. 37*, 39*
Test Generator CD

BEST PRACTICES TOOLKIT

Differentiated Instruction
pp. 31–38*

Scaffolding Instruction
pp. 43–46*

Graphic Organizers/Strategies
Word Questioning • Jigsaw
Reading • Writing Template:
Short Story • Sequence Chain

Reading Support
Audio Anthology CD*

Technology
Literature, Vocabulary, and Writing Centers at **ClassZone.com**
Write*Smart* CD

---

 * Resources for Differentiation   † Also in Spanish   ‡ In Haitian Creole and Vietnamese

● LITERARY ANALYSIS: SATIRE

Irving was a master of **satire**, a literary device in which people, customs, or institutions are ridiculed with the purpose of improving society. In this passage, Irving pokes fun at quarrelsome, complaining women:

. . . Though a female scold is generally considered to be a match for the devil, yet in this instance she appears to have had the worst of it.

Satire is often subtle, so as you read, watch for its indicators: humor, exaggeration, absurd situations, and irony.

● READING SKILL: INTERPRET IMAGERY

Through the creative use of **imagery**—words and phrases that appeal to the five senses—Irving develops his characters and establishes mood.

. . . There lived near this place a meager, miserly fellow, of the name of Tom Walker. He had a wife as miserly as himself. . . . They lived in a forlorn-looking house that stood alone and had an air of starvation.

As you read, use a chart like the one shown to record images that support the story's characterization and mood.

Images	Characterization	Mood
house with a look of starvation	Tom and his wife are miserly.	depressing

Review: **Make Inferences**

▲ VOCABULARY IN CONTEXT

The following words are critical to the story of a miser who would trade his soul for money. Check your understanding of each one by rewording the sentence in which it appears.

1. The **melancholy** sight of the graveyard chilled him.
2. The **persecution** of the Puritans went unchallenged.
3. The mention of gold awakened his **avarice.**
4. The corrupt **usurer** charged 20 percent interest.
5. **Speculating** in land deals held the promise of quick profits.
6. Hard economic times are **propitious** for moneylenders.
7. People who flaunt their wealth are guilty of **ostentation.**
8. He was a strict **censurer** of other people's vices.

Are you willing to PAY ANY PRICE?

KEY IDEA People who'll stop at nothing to achieve wealth, success, or fame are often said to have "sold their soul." In other words, they have sacrificed something important—moral beliefs, privacy, family—in order to get what they want. Consider this kind of trade-off. Do you think it might ever be worth the **consequences?**

DISCUSS Working with a partner, list several people—real or fictional—who fit this profile. Then pick one such person and list his or her gains and their consequences. Assign a value to each item and decide whether, overall, the prize was worth the price. Share your conclusions with the rest of the class.

311

Are you willing to PAY ANY PRICE?

Lead into the **KEY IDEA** by asking the question. Explore with students the concept of trade-offs and the idea that negative **consequences** can outweigh benefits. Tell students to keep these considerations in mind as they complete the *DISCUSS* activity.

SKILLS FOCUS

LITERARY ANALYSIS R3.1

● SATIRE

Write this passage on the board:

> Sam struggled to think of what could possibly mar his otherwise perfect self. He knew he had piercing blue eyes. He was impressed by his sculpted, golden hair. He was even amused by his own devilish laugh. "I know what's wrong," he said to himself one day. "For all of my perfect attributes, I'm just too humble!"

Ask students what the author is suggesting about people like Sam. *Possible answer: They are too vain to see their own vanity.*

CHECK UNDERSTANDING Ask students to give examples of satire they are familiar with, such as a television show, film, or Web site.

READING SKILL R3.3

▣ INTERPRET IMAGERY

Have students reread the passage on the board. Ask them to identify imagery that appeals to the five senses. *Possible answers: "piercing blue eyes," "sculpted, golden hair," "devilish laugh"*

CHECK UNDERSTANDING Elicit other examples of sensory imagery from stories or poems.

R RESOURCE MANAGER—Copy Master
Interpret Imagery p. 29 (for student use while reading the selection)

▲ VOCABULARY IN CONTEXT

DIAGNOSE WORD KNOWLEDGE To determine preteaching needs, have all students complete Vocabulary in Context. Students' sentences should reflect their understanding of the words as defined in the selection:
1. *melancholy* (p. 315), 2. *persecution* (p. 317), 3. *avarice* (p. 319), 4. *usurer* (p. 320), 5. *speculating* (p. 321), 6. *propitious* (p. 321), 7. *ostentation* (p. 322), 8. *censurer* (p. 322).

PRETEACH VOCABULARY Preteach vocabulary with this copy master. Read each item aloud.

R RESOURCE MANAGER—Copy Master
Vocabulary Study p. 31

MORE VOCABULARY SUPPORT
For additional activities and guidelines, see

BEST PRACTICES TOOLKIT
Scaffolding Vocabulary Instruction pp. 43–46

❶ Vocabulary Center at **ClassZone.com**

SUMMARY

In this short story, miserly Tom Walker takes a shortcut home through a swamp. There, he meets the devil, who offers Tom buried pirates' treasure on certain conditions. When Tom tells his greedy wife, she sets off to bargain for herself and is never seen again. Tom eventually accepts the devil's offer and becomes a usurer. After a life of cold-blooded financial success, Tom regrets the deal he's made and tries to escape his fate, but to no avail. The devil claims him and obliterates his ill-gotten fortune.

READING SKILL

A IMAGERY

Possible answer: Details that suggest this is an ill-fated place include: "thickly wooded swamp or morass" (line 3), "the devil presided at the hiding of the money and took it under his guardianship" (lines 11–12), and "treasure . . . has been ill-gotten" (line 13).

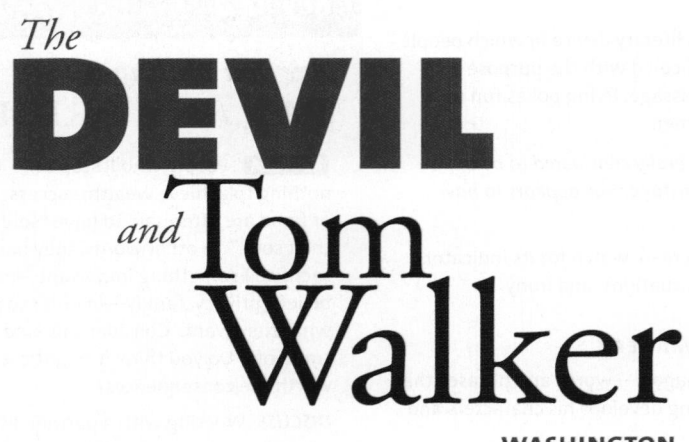

The DEVIL
and Tom Walker

WASHINGTON IRVING

> **BACKGROUND** The story of Tom Walker is a variation on the legend of Faust, a 16th-century magician and astrologer who was said to have sold his soul to the devil for wisdom, money, and power. Washington Irving reinvented the tale, setting it in the 1720s in an area of New England settled by Quakers and Puritans. In Irving's comic retelling of the legend, the writer satirizes people who present a pious public image as they "sell their soul" for money.

A few miles from Boston in Massachusetts, there is a deep inlet, winding several miles into the interior of the country from Charles Bay, and terminating in a thickly wooded swamp or morass. On one side of this inlet is a beautiful dark grove; on the opposite side the land rises abruptly from the water's edge into a high ridge, on which grow a few scattered oaks of great age and immense size. Under one of these gigantic trees, according to old stories, there was a great amount of treasure buried by Kidd the pirate. The inlet allowed a facility to bring the money in a boat secretly and at night to the very foot of the hill; the elevation of the place permitted a good lookout to be kept that no one was at hand; while
10 the remarkable trees formed good landmarks by which the place might easily be found again. The old stories add, moreover, that the devil presided at the hiding of the money and took it under his guardianship; but this, it is well-known, he always does with buried treasure, particularly when it has been ill-gotten. Be that as it may, Kidd never returned to recover his wealth; being shortly after seized at Boston, sent out to England, and there hanged for a pirate. **A**

312   UNIT 2: AMERICAN ROMANTICISM

ANALYZE VISUALS
Artist John Quidor is remembered today for his series of fantastic, grotesque paintings based on the writings of Washington Irving. In this detail from a Quidor painting, a man discovers a store of hidden gold. What aspects of the painting help create its emotional impact?

A IMAGERY
Reread lines 1–15. What details in the description suggest that this is an ill-fated place?

The Money Diggers (1832), John Quidor.
© Brooklyn Museum of Art/Corbis.

DIFFERENTIATED INSTRUCTION

FOR ALL STUDENTS

Provide these independent projects to extend the lesson:

- Prepare a visual representation of the story's setting and mood.
- Prepare and present an oral reading of a passage from the story.

For further details on these projects, see

R RESOURCE MANAGER
Ideas for Extension pp. 22–23

FOR STRATEGIC READERS

In combination with the *Audio Anthology CD,* use one or more Targeted Passages (pp. 314, 317, 320, 322, 324) to ensure that students focus on key story events and concepts. Targeted Passages are also good for English learners.

About the year 1727, just at the time that earthquakes were prevalent in New England, and shook many tall sinners down upon their knees, there lived near this place a meager, miserly fellow, of the name of Tom Walker. He had a wife as miserly as himself: they were so miserly that they even conspired to cheat each other.
20 Whatever the woman could lay hands on, she hid away; a hen could not cackle but she was on the alert to secure the new-laid egg. Her husband was continually prying about to detect her secret hoards, and many and fierce were the conflicts that took place about what ought to have been common property. They lived in a forlorn-looking house that stood alone and had an air of starvation. A few straggling savin trees, emblems of sterility, grew near it; no smoke ever curled from its chimney; no traveler stopped at its door. A miserable horse, whose ribs were as articulate as the bars of a gridiron,[1] stalked about a field, where a thin carpet of moss, scarcely covering the ragged beds of puddingstone,[2] tantalized and balked his hunger; and sometimes he would lean his head over the fence, look piteously
30 at the passerby and seem to petition deliverance from this land of famine. **B**

The house and its inmates had altogether a bad name. Tom's wife was a tall termagant,[3] fierce of temper, loud of tongue, and strong of arm. Her voice was often heard in wordy warfare with her husband; and his face sometimes showed signs that their conflicts were not confined to words. No one ventured, however, to interfere between them. The lonely wayfarer shrunk within himself at the horrid clamor and clapper-clawing;[4] eyed the den of discord askance;[5] and hurried on his way, rejoicing, if a bachelor, in his celibacy. **C**

One day that Tom Walker had been to a distant part of the neighborhood, he took what he considered a shortcut homeward, through the swamp. Like most
40 shortcuts, it was an ill-chosen route. The swamp was thickly grown with great gloomy pines and hemlocks, some of them ninety feet high, which made it dark at noonday, and a retreat for all the owls of the neighborhood. It was full of pits and quagmires, partly covered with weeds and mosses, where the green surface often betrayed the traveler into a gulf of black, smothering mud; there were also dark and stagnant pools, the abodes of the tadpole, the bullfrog, and the water snake; where the trunks of pines and hemlocks lay half-drowned, half-rotting, looking like alligators sleeping in the mire. **D**

Tom had long been picking his way cautiously through this treacherous forest; stepping from tuft to tuft of rushes and roots, which afforded precarious footholds
50 among deep sloughs; or pacing carefully, like a cat, along the prostrate trunks of trees; startled now and then by the sudden screaming of the bittern,[6] or the quacking of wild duck rising on the wind from some solitary pool. At length he arrived at a firm piece of ground, which ran out like a peninsula into the deep bosom of the swamp. It had been one of the strongholds of the Indians during their wars

1 Targeted Passage

B IMAGERY
Identify the images in lines 16–30 that help to characterize Tom and his wife. What **character traits** do these images reveal?

C SATIRE
In lines 31–37, Irving satirizes scolding women and the institution of marriage. What humorous details indicate this satire?

D IMAGERY
What kind of **mood** is established by the description of the swamp in lines 40–47?

---

1. **as articulate . . . gridiron:** as clearly separated as the bars of a grill.
2. **puddingstone:** a rock consisting of pebbles and gravel cemented together.
3. **termagant** (tûr´mə-gənt): a quarrelsome, scolding woman.
4. **clapper-clawing:** scratching or clawing with the fingernails.
5. **eyed . . . askance** (ə-skăns´): looked disapprovingly at the house filled with arguing.
6. **bittern:** a wading bird with mottled, brownish plumage and a deep, booming cry.

DIFFERENTIATED INSTRUCTION

FOR STRATEGIC READERS

1 Targeted Passage [Lines 16–39]

This passage establishes the setting of the story and introduces two of the main characters: Tom Walker and his wife.

- When does this story take place?
- What sort of person is Tom Walker?
- What is Tom Walker's wife like?
- How do Tom and his wife get along?
- As the story begins, where is Tom going?

FOR ADVANCED LEARNERS/AP

Analyze Style [paired/small-group option]
Ask students to reread the scenes described in lines 16–30 and 38–47. Then have them meet in pairs or in small groups and analyze Irving's style. Tell them to consider his use of imagery, tone, diction, and sentence length. Then have them work individually and write a one- or two-paragraph description, in the style of Irving, of one scene from the story. Invite students to share their analyses and paragraphs with the class.

with the first colonists. Here they had thrown up a kind of fort, which they had looked upon as almost impregnable, and had used as a place of refuge for their squaws and children.

Nothing remained of the old Indian fort but a few embankments, gradually sinking to the level of the surrounding earth, and already overgrown in part by
60 oaks and other forest trees, the foliage of which formed a contrast to the dark pines and hemlocks of the swamp.

It was late in the dusk of evening when Tom Walker reached the old fort, and he paused there awhile to rest himself. Anyone but he would have felt unwilling to linger in this lonely, **melancholy** place, for the common people had a bad opinion of it, from the stories handed down from the time of the Indian wars, when it was asserted that the savages held incantations[7] here, and made sacrifices to the evil spirit.

Tom Walker, however, was not a man to be troubled with any fears of the kind. He reposed himself for some time on the trunk of a fallen hemlock, listening to
70 the boding cry of the tree toad, and delving with his walking staff into a mound of black mold at his feet. As he turned up the soil unconsciously, his staff struck against something hard. He raked it out of the vegetable mold, and lo! a cloven skull, with an Indian tomahawk buried deep in it, lay before him. The rust on the weapon showed the time that had elapsed since this death-blow had been given. It was a dreary memento of the fierce struggle that had taken place in this last foothold of the Indian warriors.

"Humph!" said Tom Walker, as he gave it a kick to shake the dirt from it. **E**

"Let that skull alone!" said a gruff voice. Tom lifted up his eyes, and beheld a great black man seated directly opposite him, on the stump of a tree. He was ex-
80 ceedingly surprised, having neither heard nor seen anyone approach; and he was still more perplexed on observing, as well as the gathering gloom would permit, that the stranger was neither Negro nor Indian. It is true he was dressed in a rude half-Indian garb, and had a red belt or sash swathed round his body; but his face was neither black nor copper-color, but swarthy and dingy, and begrimed with soot, as if he had been accustomed to toil among fires and forges. He had a shock of coarse black hair, that stood out from his head in all directions, and bore an ax on his shoulder.

He scowled for a moment at Tom with a pair of great red eyes.

"What are you doing on my grounds?" said the black man, with a hoarse,
90 growling voice.

"Your grounds!" said Tom, with a sneer, "no more your grounds than mine; they belong to Deacon Peabody."

"Deacon Peabody be d—d," said the stranger, "as I flatter myself he will be, if he does not look more to his own sins and less to those of his neighbors. Look yonder, and see how Deacon Peabody is faring."

---

7. **incantations:** verbal charms or spells recited to produce a magic effect.

THE DEVIL AND TOM WALKER   **315**

---

melancholy
(mĕl′ən-kŏl′ē) *adj.*
gloomy; sad

E MAKE INFERENCES
Look again at lines 68 and 77. What can you infer about Tom Walker from his reaction to the swamp and to his grisly discovery of the skull?

Lines 78–92
TIERED DISCUSSION PROMPTS
Use these prompts to help students understand Irving's use of details to develop characters:

Connect When have you or someone you know unexpectedly encountered an intimidating stranger? What feelings did the encounter elicit? *Accept all responses.*

Analyze How does Washington Irving use descriptive details to create a frightening image of the man whom Tom meets in the forest? *Possible answer: Irving describes him as having a "gruff voice," "swarthy and dingy face" that was "begrimed with soot," "a shock of coarse black hair," and "great red eyes." The man, who seems to have appeared out of nowhere, is carrying an ax on his shoulder, and he scowls at Tom and challenges him in "a hoarse, growling voice."*

Evaluate Does Tom react to the stranger as one would expect? Explain your answer. *Possible answer: Some students may say that Tom should react with fear rather than defiance ("'Your grounds!' said Tom, with a sneer....") Others may feel that Tom has already shown himself to be a man who is not easily intimidated.*

READING SKILL: *Review*

E MAKE INFERENCES
Possible answer: From Tom Walker's untroubled reaction to the swamp and his careless treatment of the skull, readers can infer that he is a fearless and callous person.

FOR ENGLISH LEARNERS
Vocabulary: Multiple-Meaning Words
[mixed-readiness groups] Explain that *common* (line 23) means "belonging to or shared by two people." However, *common* can also mean "familiar," as in "Smith is a common name." Discuss how context clues can help students determine the appropriate meaning. Then have mixed-language-ability Jigsaw groups investigate these other multiple-meaning words and report their findings:

air (line 24), *grown* (line 40), *pits* (line 42), *trunks* (line 46), *bosom* (line 53), *shock* (line 85), *bore* (line 86).

BEST PRACTICES TOOLKIT
Jigsaw Reading p. A1

316 UNIT 2: AMERICAN ROMANTICISM

ANALYZE VISUALS

Possible answer: Quidor's choices of color and shading capture the murkiness of the swamp and the dark atmosphere of the story. The artist's depiction of Tom seems somewhat milder and more timid than the image readers might get from the story of a man undaunted by the devil.

The Devil and Tom Walker (1856), John Quidor. Oil on canvas, 68.8 cm × 86.6 cm.
© The Cleveland Museum of Art, Mr. and Mrs. William H. Marlatt Fund, 1967.18.

ANALYZE VISUALS
This Quidor painting illustrates the first meeting between Tom and the devil. In your opinion, how well do the artist's choices of color and shading and his depiction of Tom's **character** match the story? Explain.

DIFFERENTIATED INSTRUCTION

FOR ENGLISH LEARNERS

Vocabulary: Outdated Forms Tell students that this 19th-century text uses some word meanings that are not common today. Provide these definitions for students and then have them reread the lines, substituting the definitions for the outdated words.

- *beheld* (line 96), "saw"
- *without* (line 97), "outside"
- *sturdily* (line 119), "firmly"
- *credited* (line 123), "believed"
- *commencement* (line 127), "beginning"
- *propitiated* (line 131), "caused to gain the goodwill of"

Tom looked in the direction that the stranger pointed, and beheld one of the great trees, fair and flourishing without, but rotten at the core, and saw that it had been nearly hewn through, so that the first high wind was likely to blow it down. On the bark of the tree was scored the name of Deacon Peabody, an eminent man, who had
100 waxed wealthy by driving shrewd bargains with the Indians. He now looked around, and found most of the tall trees marked with the name of some great man of the colony, and all more or less scored by the ax. The one on which he had been seated, and which had evidently just been hewn down, bore the name of Crowninshield; and he recollected a mighty rich man of that name, who made a vulgar display of wealth, which it was whispered he had acquired by buccaneering.[8] **F**

"He's just ready for burning!" said the black man, with a growl of triumph. "You see, I am likely to have a good stock of firewood for winter."

"But what right have you," said Tom, "to cut down Deacon Peabody's timber?"

"The right of a prior claim," said the other. "This woodland belonged to me
110 long before one of your white-faced race put foot upon the soil."

"And pray, who are you, if I may be so bold?" said Tom.

"Oh, I go by various names. I am the wild huntsman in some countries; the black miner in others. In this neighborhood I am he to whom the red men consecrated this spot, and in honor of whom they now and then roasted a white man, by way of sweet-smelling sacrifice. Since the red men have been exterminated by you white savages, I amuse myself by presiding at the **persecutions** of Quakers and Anabaptists;[9] I am the great patron and prompter of slave dealers, and the grand master of the Salem witches." **G**

"The upshot of all which is that, if I mistake not," said Tom, sturdily, "you are
120 he commonly called Old Scratch."[10]

"The same, at your service!" replied the black man, with a half-civil nod.

Such was the opening of this interview, according to the old story; though it has almost too familiar an air to be credited. One would think that to meet with such a singular personage, in this wild, lonely place, would have shaken any man's nerves; but Tom was a hard-minded fellow, not easily daunted, and he had lived so long with a termagant wife that he did not even fear the devil.

It is said that after this commencement they had a long and earnest conversation together, as Tom returned homeward. The black man told him of great sums of money buried by Kidd the pirate, under the oak trees on the high ridge, not far
130 from the morass. All these were under his command, and protected by his power, so that none could find them but such as propitiated his favor. These he offered to place within Tom Walker's reach, having conceived an especial kindness for him; but they were to be had only on certain conditions. What these conditions were may be easily surmised, though Tom never disclosed them publicly. They must have been very hard, for he required time to think of them, and he was not a man

---

F MAKE INFERENCES
Reread lines 96–105. Why do you think the trees are marked with the men's names

persecution
(pûr´sĭ-kyoo´shən) *n.* the act or practice of oppressing or harassing with ill-treatment, especially because of race, religion, gender, or beliefs

G SATIRE
Reread lines 115–118. What do they tell you about the author's attitude toward the activities of the early settlers? What led you to make that inference?

2 Targeted Passage

---

8. **buccaneering:** robbing ships at sea; piracy.
9. **presiding . . . Anabaptists:** exercising authority over the oppression of Christian groups that the Puritans considered heretical.
10. **Old Scratch:** a nickname for the devil.

F MAKE INFERENCES

Possible answer: The trees are marked with the names of men who have made deals with the devil, selling their souls in exchange for wealth or power.

If students need help . . . Ask these questions to help them connect the men's names with the devil.

- Whose ax has scored the men's names into the trees?
- What is the likely connection between these rich and powerful men and the devil?

Extend the Discussion What message about Deacon Peabody does Irving convey symbolically by noting that the tree with his name on it was "fair and flourishing without, but rotten at the core"?

LITERARY ANALYSIS

G SATIRE

Possible answer: By indicating that the devil is behind the activities of the early settlers, the passage suggests that Irving condemns the settlers' activities as evil.

BACKGROUND

Persecuted Groups The man in black notes several groups persecuted by New England Puritans. Quakers and Anabaptists were radical followers of the Protestant Reformation who believed in pacifism and the separation of church and state. The "Salem witches" (line 118) refers to victims of the hysteria that spread in Salem, Massachusetts, in 1692.

FOR STRATEGIC READERS

2 Targeted Passage [Lines 111–134]

This passage reveals that the stranger is the devil and explains how he offers Tom the treasure buried by Kidd the pirate.

- Who is the stranger that Tom meets in the woods?
- According to the author, why does Tom show no fear?
- What offer does the stranger make to Tom?
- What were the devil's conditions for granting Tom the treasure?

Activity How is Durand's depiction of the forest on page 318 different from Quidor's vision on page 316? *Possible answer: Durand's painting focuses on the landscape itself, emphasizing its beauty. Quidor's painting focuses on the two individuals, and depicts a dreary forest as atmospheric background.*

About the Art Like other paintings by American artist Asher Brown Durand (1796–1886), *Forest Landscape* captures the beauty and grandeur of the Hudson River Valley. For more information about Durand and the Hudson River school of painters, see page 299.

Lines 144–149
REINFORCE *KEY IDEA:* CONSEQUENCES

Discuss What does Crowninshield's death suggest about the **consequences** of making a pact with the devil? *Possible answer: Crowninshield had become a "rich buccaneer" (line 145), but in the end, the devil had cut down his tree and taken his due. Crowninshield's fate is a reminder that bargaining with the devil has inescapable consequences.*

Forest Landscape (1800s), Asher Brown Durand. Oil on canvas, 76.2 cm × 66 cm. © Brooklyn Museum of Art/Bridgeman Art Library.

to stick at trifles when money was in view. When they had reached the edge of the swamp, the stranger paused. "What proof have I that all you have been telling me is true?" said Tom. "There's my signature," said the black man, pressing his finger on Tom's forehead. So saying, he turned off among the thickets of the swamp, and
140 seemed, as Tom said, to go down, down, down, into the earth, until nothing but his head and shoulders could be seen, and so on, until he totally disappeared.

When Tom reached home, he found the black print of a finger burnt, as it were, into his forehead, which nothing could obliterate.

The first news his wife had to tell him was the sudden death of Absalom Crowninshield, the rich buccaneer. It was announced in the papers with the usual flourish that "a great man had fallen in Israel."[11]

---

11. **a great man . . . Israel:** a biblical reference—"Know ye not that there is a prince and a great man fallen this day in Israel?" (2 Samuel 3:38)—used, with unconscious irony, by the papers to mean that an important member of God's people on earth had passed away.

DIFFERENTIATED INSTRUCTION

FOR ADVANCED LEARNERS/AP
Analyze and Evaluate Symbolism Have students reread lines 137–143 and discuss the symbolic significance of the two images described: the devil gradually disappearing into the earth and "the black print of a finger burnt" into Tom's forehead. Ask students whether they think these images are effective in the context of this story, and why or why not. Encourage students to give specific reasons to support their response.

Extend the discussion by asking students to recall other stories they may have read in which the devil was a character. Ask how Irving's portrayal of the devil compares to other writers' depictions.

Tom recollected the tree which his black friend had just hewn down and which was ready for burning. "Let the freebooter[12] roast," said Tom; "who cares!" He now felt convinced that all he had heard and seen was no illusion.

150   He was not prone to let his wife into his confidence; but as this was an uneasy secret, he willingly shared it with her. All her **avarice** was awakened at the mention of hidden gold, and she urged her husband to comply with the black man's terms, and secure what would make them wealthy for life. However Tom might have felt disposed to sell himself to the devil, he was determined not to do so to oblige his wife; so he flatly refused, out of the mere spirit of contradiction. Many and bitter were the quarrels they had on the subject; but the more she talked, the more resolute was Tom not to be damned to please her.

    At length she determined to drive the bargain on her own account, and if she succeeded, to keep all the gain to herself. Being of the same fearless temper as her
160 husband, she set off for the old Indian fort toward the close of a summer's day. She was many hours absent. When she came back, she was reserved and sullen in her replies. She spoke something of a black man, whom she met about twilight hewing at the root of a tall tree. He was sulky, however, and would not come to terms; she was to go again with a propitiatory offering, but what it was she forbore to say.

    The next evening she set off again for the swamp, with her apron heavily laden. Tom waited and waited for her, but in vain; midnight came, but she did not make her appearance; morning, noon, night returned, but still she did not come. Tom now grew uneasy for her safety, especially as he found she had carried off in her apron the silver teapot and spoons, and every portable article of value. Another night elapsed,
170 another morning came; but no wife. In a word, she was never heard of more.

    What was her real fate nobody knows, in consequence of so many pretending to know. It is one of those facts which have become confounded by a variety of historians. Some asserted that she lost her way among the tangled mazes of the swamp, and sank into some pit or slough; others, more uncharitable, hinted that she had eloped with the household booty and made off to some other province; while others surmised that the tempter had decoyed her into a dismal quagmire, on the top of which her hat was found lying. In confirmation of this, it was said a great black man, with an ax on his shoulder, was seen late that very evening coming out of the swamp, carrying a bundle tied in a check apron, with an air
180 of surly triumph. Ⓗ

    The most current and probable story, however, observes that Tom Walker grew so anxious about the fate of his wife and his property that he set out at length to seek them both at the Indian fort. During a long summer's afternoon he searched about the gloomy place, but no wife was to be seen. He called her name repeatedly, but she was nowhere to be heard. The bittern alone responded to his voice, as they flew screaming by; or the bullfrog croaked dolefully from a neighboring pool. At length, it is said, just in the brown hour of twilight, when the owls began to hoot, and the bats to flit about, his attention was attracted by the clamor of carrion crows[13] hovering about a cypress tree. He looked up, and beheld a bundle tied in a

---

12. **freebooter:** pirate.

13. **carrion crows:** crows that feed on dead or decaying flesh.

THE DEVIL AND TOM WALKER   **319**

avarice (ăvʹə-rĭs) *n.* immoderate desire for wealth; greed

Ⓗ **GRAMMAR AND STYLE**
Irving emphasizes ideas and creates lyricism through the use of **parallelism,** the repetition of grammatical structures. In lines 173–177, for example, the writer uses parallelism to present three possible fates of Tom's wife.

Lines 150–157
TIERED DISCUSSION PROMPTS
Use these prompts to help students understand Tom and his wife:

Summarize What does Tom's wife want him to do? Why doesn't Tom want to do it? *Possible answer: She wants him to agree to the devil's terms so that they can be rich. He spitefully doesn't want to do this because it would please his wife.*

Analyze What does Tom's reluctance "to sell himself to the devil" suggest about his character and his relationship with his wife? *Possible answer: Tom is as spiteful as he is greedy, and his relationship with his wife is thoroughly adversarial. He may be willing to make a pact with the devil to get rich, but not if it means pleasing his wife.*

Evaluate How effective is Irving in showing how Tom and his wife feel about each other? Explain. *Possible answer: Very effective: Irving shows that Tom's wife's only concern is for wealth (certainly not for her husband's welfare), while Tom's main concern is spiting his wife.*

Ⓗ **GRAMMAR AND STYLE**

Analyze Structure The use of parallelism in phrases or sentences adds to the rhythm and flow of words. For this reason, the use of parallel structure is common not only in written text but also in speeches and songs. Ask students to find other examples of parallelism in Irving's story, such as line 32 and lines 166–167.

FOR ENGLISH LEARNERS
Vocabulary: Idioms Help students use context clues to determine the meaning of these idioms in the story: *on her own account* (line 158), "by and for herself"; *in vain* (line 166), "without success"; *make her appearance* (lines 166–167), "come"; *made off* (line 175), "went away"; *nowhere to be heard* (line 185), "not present"; *At length* (lines 186–187), "finally."

FOR ADVANCED LEARNERS/AP
Analyze Technique Have students discuss how the author uses sensory imagery and descriptive words to create a particular mood in lines 183–191. Ask students to explain whether this mood heightens the satiric effect in the subsequent lines or detracts from it, and why.

THE DEVIL AND TOM WALKER   **319**

check apron, and hanging in the branches of the tree, with a great vulture perched hard by, as if keeping watch upon it. He leaped with joy; for he recognized his wife's apron and supposed it to contain the household valuables. ❶

"Let us get hold of the property," said he consolingly to himself, "and we will endeavor to do without the woman."

As he scrambled up the tree, the vulture spread its wide wings, and sailed off screaming into the deep shadows of the forest. Tom seized the checked apron, but, woeful sight! found nothing but a heart and liver tied up in it!

Such, according to this most authentic old story, was all that was to be found of Tom's wife. She had probably attempted to deal with the black man as she had
200 been accustomed to deal with her husband; but though a female scold is generally considered a match for the devil, yet in this instance she appears to have had the worst of it. She must have died game, however; for it is said Tom noticed many prints of cloven feet stamped upon the tree, and found handfuls of hair that looked as if they had been plucked from the coarse black shock of the woodman. Tom knew his wife's prowess by experience. He shrugged his shoulders, as he looked at the signs of a fierce clapper-clawing. "Egad," said he to himself, "Old Scratch must have had a tough time of it!" ❶

Tom consoled himself for the loss of his property with the loss of his wife, for he was a man of fortitude. He even felt something like gratitude towards the black
210 woodman, who, he considered, had done him a kindness. He sought, therefore, to cultivate a further acquaintance with him, but for some time without success; the old blacklegs played shy, for, whatever people may think, he is not always to be had for calling for: he knows how to play his cards when pretty sure of his game.

At length, it is said, when delay had whetted Tom's eagerness to the quick, and prepared him to agree to anything rather than not gain the promised treasure, he met the black man one evening in his usual woodsman's dress, with his ax on his shoulder, sauntering along the swamp, and humming a tune. He affected to receive Tom's advances with great indifference, made brief replies, and went on humming his tune.

By degrees, however, Tom brought him to business, and they began to haggle
220 about the terms on which the former was to have the pirate's treasure. There was one condition which need not be mentioned, being generally understood in all cases where the devil grants favors; but there were others about which, though of less importance, he was inflexibly obstinate. He insisted that the money found through his means should be employed in his service. He proposed, therefore, that Tom should employ it in the black traffic; that is to say, that he should fit out a slave ship. This, however, Tom resolutely refused: he was bad enough in all conscience; but the devil himself could not tempt him to turn slave trader.

Finding Tom so squeamish on this point, he did not insist upon it, but proposed, instead, that he should turn **usurer;** the devil being extremely anxious for
230 the increase of usurers, looking upon them as his peculiar people.

To this no objections were made, for it was just to Tom's taste.

"You shall open a broker's shop in Boston next month," said the black man.

"I'll do it tomorrow, if you wish," said Tom Walker.

"You shall lend money at two percent a month."

"Egad, I'll charge four!" replied Tom Walker.

Sidebar (right margin)

❶ IMAGERY
Which images in lines 189–192 suggest that Tom's discovery won't be a pleasant one?

❶ SATIRE
How does Irving use **humor** and **exaggeration** to satirize a "female scold" in lines 199–207?

❸ Targeted Passage

usurer (yoo´zhər-ər) *n.* one who lends money, at interest, especially at an unusually or unlawfully high rate of interest

---

❶ IMAGERY

Possible answer: Such images as "carrion crows hovering," "bundle tied in a check apron," and the "vulture perched . . . as if keeping watch" suggest that Tom's discovery will be unpleasant.

If students need help . . . Have them fill out a chart like the one introduced on page 311.

Images	Characterization	Mood
"carrion crows hovering" "bundle tied in a check apron" "vulture perched . . . as if keeping watch"		ominous

❶ SATIRE

Possible answer: Irving uses humor and exaggeration in relating details of the fight—for example, "handfuls of hair," "fierce clapper-clawing"—and explaining that "a female scold is generally considered a match for the devil" (lines 200–201). Irving also describes how Tom feels sympathy for the devil, not for his wife.

DIFFERENTIATED INSTRUCTION

FOR STRATEGIC READERS

❸ Targeted Passage [Lines 196–233]

This passage tells how Tom loses his wife and shows his reaction to her death. It also describes how Tom reaches an agreement with the devil.

• What happens to Tom's wife?

• How does Tom react to his wife's fate?

• Summarize the conversation between Tom and the devil.

• How does Tom feel about the idea of becoming a usurer?

Concept Support: Bargains with the Devil
After students read lines 220–222, discuss the "one condition which need not be mentioned, being generally understood in all cases where the devil grants favors." Elicit or explain that, traditionally, when a character makes a pact with the devil, the character agrees to give the devil his or her soul, thereby condemning himself or herself to hell.

"You shall extort bonds, foreclose mortgages, drive the merchants to bankruptcy—"

"I'll drive them to the d——l," cried Tom Walker.

"You are the usurer for my money!" said blacklegs with delight. "When will 240 you want the rhino?"[14]

"This very night."

"Done!" said the devil.

"Done!" said Tom Walker. So they shook hands and struck a bargain. **K**

A few days' time saw Tom Walker seated behind his desk in a countinghouse[15] in Boston.

His reputation for a ready-moneyed man, who would lend money out for a good consideration, soon spread abroad. Everybody remembers the time of Governor Belcher, when money was particularly scarce. It was a time of paper credit. The country had been deluged with government bills; the famous Land Bank[16] 250 had been established; there had been a rage for **speculating**; the people had run mad with schemes for new settlements; for building cities in the wilderness; land-jobbers[17] went about with maps of grants, and townships, and Eldorados[18] lying nobody knew where, but which everybody was ready to purchase. In a word, the great speculating fever, which breaks out every now and then in the country, had raged to an alarming degree, and everybody was dreaming of making sudden fortunes from nothing. As usual the fever had subsided; the dream had gone off, and the imaginary fortunes with it; the patients were left in doleful plight, and the whole country resounded with the consequent cry of "hard times."

At this **propitious** time of public distress did Tom Walker set up as usurer in 260 Boston. His door was soon thronged by customers. The needy and adventurous, the gambling speculator, the dreaming land-jobber, the thriftless tradesman, the merchant with cracked credit; in short, everyone driven to raise money by desperate means and desperate sacrifices hurried to Tom Walker.

Thus Tom was the universal friend of the needy and acted like a "friend in need"; that is to say, he always exacted good pay and good security. In proportion to the distress of the applicant was the hardness of his terms. He accumulated bonds and mortgages; gradually squeezed his customers closer and closer; and sent them at length, dry as a sponge, from his door.

In this way he made money hand over hand, became a rich and mighty man, 270 and exalted his cocked hat upon 'Change.[19] He built himself, as usual, a vast

---

14. **rhino:** a slang term for money.

15. **countinghouse:** an office in which a business firm conducts its bookkeeping, correspondence, and similar activities.

16. **Land Bank:** Boston merchants organized the Land Bank in 1739. Landowners could take out mortgages on their property and then repay the loans with cash or manufactured goods. When the Land Bank was outlawed in 1741, many colonists lost money.

17. **land-jobbers:** people who buy and sell land for profit.

18. **Eldorados:** places of fabulous wealth or great opportunity. Early Spanish explorers sought a legendary country named El Dorado, which was rumored to be rich with gold.

19. **exalted . . . 'Change:** proudly raised himself to a position of importance as a trader on the stock exchange.

K SATIRE
Reread lines 232–243. How does Tom compare with the devil in terms of his greed and mercilessness? Decide what comment Irving is making about usurers in general.

speculating
(spĕk′yə- lā′tĭng) n. engaging in risky business transactions on the chance of a quick or considerable profit

propitious
(prə-pĭsh′əs) adj. helpful or advantageous; favorable

BACKGROUND

The Devilish Work of Usurers A borrower pays interest to a lender in return for use of the lender's money. However, usurers charge exorbitant interest rates, often making it all but impossible for the borrower to repay the debt. When a borrower is unable to repay a loan with interest in the agreed-upon time, the lender may seize the borrower's pledged assets. For example, if a homeowner cannot repay a home mortgage loan, the lender can foreclose on, or take possession of, the home. This power of usurers to ruin people's lives helps to explain why the devil in Irving's tale views usurers as "his peculiar people" (line 230).

LITERARY ANALYSIS

K SATIRE

Possible answer: Tom is even greedier and more merciless than the devil. Irving is making clear that he considers usurers cold-blooded, ruthless creatures.

FOR ENGLISH LEARNERS

Vocabulary: Idioms Help students use context clues to determine the meaning of these idioms in the story: *play his cards* (line 213), "use strategy"; *to the quick* (line 214), "to the extreme"; *turn (slave trader)/turn (usurer)* (lines 227, 229), "become a"; *raise (money)* (line 262), "get for some purpose"; *squeezed . . . dry as a sponge* (lines 267–268), "deprived of assets"; *made money hand over hand* (line 269), "became wealthy."

FOR ADVANCED LEARNERS/AP

Analyze Tone and Language Have students reread lines 246–268 and reflect on the author's tone and choice of language as he recalls what happened during "the time of Governor Belcher." What is Irving's view of people who get caught up in "the great speculating fever"? Does he think they get what they deserve? To what extent does he feel that they are simply victims of usurers such as Tom Walker? Have students present and support their views in a discussion.

L IMAGERY

Possible answer: *The images show that Tom is greedy, cruel, and merciless and that even after he becomes rich, he is still a mean, miserly, and self-centered person.*

If students need help . . . Work with them to fill in the prereading chart introduced on page 311 and draw conclusions about Tom and his methods.

Images	Characterization	Mood
"universal friend of the needy . . . acted like a 'friend in need'"	pretends to be a friend	
"gradually squeezed his customers closer and closer . . . sent them . . . dry as a sponge, from his door"	takes everything his customers have	
builds huge house "out of ostentation" but leaves it unfinished "out of parsimony"	rich show-off, but miserly	
"nearly starved the horses"	wants to show off carriage but not feed horses	

M SATIRE

Possible answer: *Tom represents the most hypocritical of churchgoers: a person who regularly attends church and strenuously criticizes others for their sins, yet who is himself a vile, unrepentant sinner.*

---

house, out of **ostentation**; but left the greater part of it unfinished and unfurnished, out of parsimony. He even set up a carriage in the fullness of his vainglory,[20] though he nearly starved the horses which drew it; and as the ungreased wheels groaned and screeched on the axletrees, you would have thought you heard the souls of the poor debtors he was squeezing. **L**

As Tom waxed old, however, he grew thoughtful. Having secured the good things of this world, he began to feel anxious about those of the next. He thought with regret on the bargain he had made with his black friend, and set his wits to work to cheat him out of the conditions. He became, therefore, all of a sudden,
280 a violent churchgoer. He prayed loudly and strenuously, as if heaven were to be taken by force of lungs. Indeed, one might always tell when he had sinned most during the week, by the clamor of his Sunday devotion. The quiet Christians who had been modestly and steadfastly traveling Zionward[21] were struck with self-reproach at seeing themselves so suddenly outstripped in their career by this new-made convert. Tom was as rigid in religious as in money matters; he was a stern supervisor and **censurer** of his neighbors, and seemed to think every sin entered up to their account became a credit on his own side of the page. He even talked of the expediency of reviving the persecution of Quakers and Anabaptists. In a word, Tom's zeal became as notorious as his riches. **M**

290   Still, in spite of all this strenuous attention to forms, Tom had a lurking dread that the devil, after all, would have his due.[22] That he might not be taken unawares, therefore, it is said he always carried a small Bible in his coat pocket. He had also a great folio Bible on his countinghouse desk, and would frequently be found reading it when people called on business; on such occasions he would lay his green spectacles in the book, to mark the place, while he turned round to drive some usurious bargain.

Some say that Tom grew a little crackbrained in his old days, and that fancying his end approaching, he had his horse new shod, saddled and bridled, and buried with his feet uppermost; because he supposed that at the last day the world would
300 be turned upside down; in which case he should find his horse standing ready for mounting, and he was determined at the worst to give his old friend a run for it. This, however, is probably a mere old wives' fable. If he really did take such a precaution, it was totally superfluous; at least so says the authentic old legend, which closes his story in the following manner:

One hot summer afternoon in the dog days, just as a terrible black thundergust was coming up, Tom sat in his countinghouse, in his white linen cap and India silk morning gown. He was on the point of foreclosing a mortgage, by which he would complete the ruin of an unlucky land speculator for whom he had professed the greatest friendship. The poor land-jobber begged him to grant a few
310 months' indulgence. Tom had grown testy and irritated, and refused another day.

---

20. **vainglory:** boastful, undeserved pride in one's accomplishments or qualities.

21. **Zionward:** toward heaven.

22. **the devil . . . due:** a reference to the proverb "Give the devil his due," used to mean "Give even a disagreeable person the credit he or she deserves." Here, of course, the expression is used literally rather than figuratively.

Sidebar

ostentation
(ŏs´ tĕn-tā'shən) *n.* display meant to impress others; boastful showiness

L IMAGERY
Find the images in lines 264–275 that are used to describe both Tom and his clients. What do these images tell you about Tom and his methods?

censurer
(sĕn'shər-ər) *n.* one who expresses strong disapproval or harsh criticism

4 Targeted Passage

M SATIRE
What kind of churchgoer is represented by Tom in lines 276–289? Think about what Irving is suggesting about this kind of individual.

DIFFERENTIATED INSTRUCTION

FOR STRATEGIC READERS

4 Targeted Passage [Lines 276–296]

This passage describes Tom's regrets and explains how he hopes to escape his fate.

- As Tom grows old, what does he begin to worry about?

- Why does Tom begin to regret the bargain he has made?

- Describe the things that Tom does in hopes of "cheating" the devil.

FOR ADVANCED LEARNERS/AP

Quakers and Anabaptists In line 288, the author refers to "the persecution of Quakers and Anabaptists." This is the second such reference in the story, the first occurring in lines 116–117. Have students discuss the connection between the two references. Then have them write a paragraph that explains the significance of these references for Irving's characterization of Tom Walker.

"My family will be ruined and brought upon the parish," said the land-jobber. "Charity begins at home," replied Tom; "I must take care of myself in these hard times."

"You have made so much money out of me," said the speculator.

Tom lost his patience and his piety. "The devil take me," said he, "if I have made a farthing!"[23]

Just then there were three loud knocks at the street door. He stepped out to see who was there. A black man was holding a black horse, which neighed and stamped with impatience.

320 "Tom, you're come for," said the black fellow, gruffly. Tom shrank back, but too late. He had left his little Bible at the bottom of his coat pocket, and his big Bible on the desk buried under the mortgage he was about to foreclose; never was a sinner taken more unawares. The black man whisked him like a child into the saddle,

---

23. **farthing:** a coin worth one-fourth of a penny, formerly used throughout the British Empire.

Tom Walker's Flight (about 1856), John Quidor. Oil on canvas, 26¾″ × 33¼″. The Fine Arts Museums of San Francisco, Gift of Mr. and Mrs. John D. Rockefeller 3rd, 1979.7.84.

ANALYZE VISUALS
What elements in this painting by Quidor emphasize the human fear of the supernatural and the consequences of greed? Explain.

THE DEVIL AND TOM WALKER **323**

gave the horse the lash, and away he galloped, with Tom on his back, in the midst of the thunderstorm. The clerks stuck their pens behind their ears, and stared after him from the windows. Away went Tom Walker, dashing down the streets; his white cap bobbing up and down, his morning gown fluttering in the wind, and his steed striking fire out of the pavement at every bound. When the clerks turned to look for the black man, he had disappeared.

330   Tom Walker never returned to foreclose the mortgage. A countryman, who lived on the border of the swamp, reported that in the height of the thundergust he had heard a great clattering of hoofs and a howling along the road, and running to the window caught sight of a figure, such as I have described, on a horse that galloped like mad across the fields, over the hills, and down into the black hemlock swamp toward the old Indian fort; and that shortly after a thunderbolt falling in that direction seemed to set the whole forest in a blaze.

⑤ **Targeted Passage**

The good people of Boston shook their heads and shrugged their shoulders, but had been so much accustomed to witches and goblins, and tricks of the devil, in all kinds of shapes, from the first settlement of the colony, that they were not

340   so much horror-struck as might have been expected. Trustees were appointed to take charge of Tom's effects. There was nothing, however, to administer upon. On searching his coffers[24] all his bonds and mortgages were found reduced to cinders. In place of gold and silver, his iron chest was filled with chips and shavings; two skeletons lay in his stable instead of his half-starved horses, and the very next day his great house took fire and burnt to the ground. **N**

Such was the end of Tom Walker and his ill-gotten wealth. Let all griping money brokers lay this story to heart. The truth of it is not to be doubted. The very hole under the oak trees whence he dug Kidd's money is to be seen to this day; and the neighboring swamp and old Indian fort are often haunted in stormy nights

350   by a figure on horseback, in morning gown and white cap, which is doubtless the troubled spirit of the usurer. In fact the story has resolved itself into a proverb so prevalent throughout New England, of "The Devil and Tom Walker." ❧

N IMAGERY
Reread lines 341–345. What **message** do these images suggest about material possessions and those who seek them?

---

24. **coffers:** safes or strongboxes designed to hold money or other valuable items.

READING SKILL

N IMAGERY

Possible answer: The images suggest that wealth and material possessions are of no use to you when you are dead. People who are obsessed with acquiring riches are pursuing something that has no real meaning, but which puts them at risk of losing their souls to greed.

SELECTION WRAP–UP

REFLECT Have students think about Tom Walker's character. Does Tom have any redeeming qualities? Ask students if the story would be more or less effective if Tom were a more likable character.

⭐ CRITIQUE

- Have students evaluate the ending of the story and explain why they think it is or is not effective. Ask students whether they feel the final paragraph (lines 346–352) is really necessary or whether it detracts from the story.

- After completing the After Reading questions on page 325, have students revisit their responses and tell whether they have changed their opinions.

DIFFERENTIATED INSTRUCTION

FOR STRATEGIC READERS

⑤ **Targeted Passage [Lines 326–347]**

This passage describes the demise of Tom Walker and the disappearance of his riches.

- What happens to Tom Walker?
- What becomes of all the riches Tom has acquired?
- What does Washington Irving mean when he writes, "Let all griping money brokers lay this story to heart"?

FOR ENGLISH LEARNERS

Vocabulary: Idioms Help students use context clues to determine the meaning of these idioms in the story:

- *caught sight of* (line 333), "saw"
- *like mad* (line 334), "at top speed"
- *take charge of* (line 341), "manage"
- *In place of* (line 343), "instead of"

Comprehension

1. **Recall** What character traits do Tom Walker and his wife share?

2. **Recall** What bargain does Tom make with the stranger in the forest?

3. **Summarize** How does Tom try to avoid fulfilling his end of the bargain?

Literary Analysis

4. **Compare Character Traits** As Tom gets older, he begins to worry about his actions and becomes "a violent churchgoer." But does he really change? Support your opinion with examples from the story. Use a chart like the one shown to collect evidence.

	Before the Bargain	As He Ages
Attitude		
Statements		
Actions		

5. **Draw Conclusions** In your opinion, is there any way Tom could have escaped the **consequences** of his deal with the devil? Use evidence from the story and your own knowledge of human nature to support your answer.

6. **Interpret Imagery** Review the examples of images you recorded as you read the story. How does Irving use each of the following images to support characterization and mood?
   • the description of the trees and the swamp (lines 40–47)
   • the description of the hewn trees (lines 96–102)
   • the description of Tom's new house (lines 270–272)
   • the description of Tom as a churchgoer (lines 279–289)

7. **Analyze Satire** Through statements he makes about Tom Walker, his wife, and his community, what messages is Irving communicating about
   • women (lines 31–37)?
   • the Puritan attitude (lines 115–118)?
   • the slave trade (lines 224–227)?
   • moneylenders (lines 228–230)?

8. **Analyze Irony** Much of the humor in this tale is based on irony, where what happens or is said is the opposite of what one would expect. Look again at lines 290–296. What is ironic about Tom's mix of Bible study and business?

Literary Criticism

9. **Critical Interpretations** The story of Tom Walker engaged readers both here and in Europe for many different, and sometimes conflicting, reasons. Look at the story again through the eyes of each of the following people. What reasons would you give for recommending the story to others?
   • businessman
   • banker
   • English critic
   • revolutionary
   • Puritan
   • American politician

THE DEVIL AND TOM WALKER **325**

9. *Students may say that they would recommend the story for such reasons as these: businessman—as a cautionary tale to not lose sight of what's important in life; revolutionary—might enjoy seeing people in power face the consequences of their actions; banker—as a reminder to act with compassion when dealing with people in need; Puritan—would enjoy seeing a sinner pay for his sins; English critic—might be amused by this American version of the Faust legend; American politician—as a warning against hypocrisy.*

Practice and Apply

After Reading

Use these copy masters to check understanding and provide extra support:

RESOURCE MANAGER—Copy Masters
Reading Check p. 34
Satire p. 27
Question Support p. 35

Additional selection questions are provided for teachers on page 21.

ANSWERS

1. *Tom and his wife are both miserly, grasping, mean-spirited, and without conscience.*

2. *In exchange for the pirate's treasure, Tom becomes a usurer. It is also implied that the devil will have his soul (lines 220–222).*

3. *Tom becomes zealously religious and keeps one Bible in his coat pocket and another on his desk.*

Possible answers:

4. *Tom does not really change. He goes on sinning (lines 281–282) despite his fervent church attendance, and he continues his work as a usurer, as cold-bloodedly as ever (lines 308–313).*

5. *Answers may vary, but most students are likely to say that Tom could not have escaped. His only chance for doing so might have been to repent and become a truly good person—most unlikely considering his nature.*

6. ■ **SKILLS FOCUS Interpret Imagery**
   trees and swamp—dismal mood; hewn trees—ominous mood; new house—Tom likes to show off, but he is still miserly; Tom as churchgoer—hypocritical nature

7. ● **SKILLS FOCUS Satire** *women—a scolding woman makes life miserable for everyone; Puritan attitudes—the Puritans committed terrible acts in the name of God; slave trade—slavery is supremely evil; moneylenders—moneylenders do the devil's work.*

8. *Tom's Bible study is only for show; he sets the Bible aside to conduct his usurious business.*

ANSWERS
Vocabulary in Context
VOCABULARY PRACTICE

1. *censurer*   5. *persecution*
2. *melancholy*   6. *speculating*
3. *propitious*   7. *usurer*
4. *ostentation*   8. *avarice*

R RESOURCE MANAGER—Copy Master
Vocabulary Practice p. 32

VOCABULARY IN WRITING

Encourage students to include descriptive
words and phrases that have not previously
been used in the text or in class discussion.
For instance, point out that in the example
sentence the writer used the word *corrupt*
to characterize Tom. Remind students that
obituaries contain biographical information,
which they can draw from the story or from
their imagination.

VOCABULARY STRATEGY: THE LATIN ROOT
spec (also an EL language objective)

• Help students use their knowledge of the
root and other word parts to match the
definitions in the text.

• Explain how figuring out the part of speech
from the wording of the definition can help
them narrow their choices. You may want to
point out that three of the words are nouns,
and three are adjectives.

Answers:

1. *introspective*   4. *circumspect*
2. *spectator*   5. *perspective*
3. *specter*   6. *spectrum*

R RESOURCE MANAGER—Copy Master
Vocabulary Strategy p. 33

ⓘ Vocabulary Center at **ClassZone.com**
Additional Vocabulary Activities

Vocabulary in Context

VOCABULARY PRACTICE

Choose the vocabulary word that best matches each description below.

1. someone who loves to nag, criticize, and sneer
2. your mood if you suddenly lost your job, your best friend, or your dog
3. what a hot day is to lemonade vendors
4. a pretentious display that is meant to impress others
5. what the Bill of Rights was written to prevent
6. what someone who buys stock in a struggling company is doing
7. a person you don't want to have help you out of financial difficulties
8. a feeling that can make someone drool in a department store

WORD LIST
avarice
censurer
melancholy
ostentation
persecution
propitious
speculating
usurer

VOCABULARY IN WRITING

Using at least four vocabulary words, write an obituary that might have been
published after the death of Tom Walker. Remember as you write that he
was not a well-loved figure, so there is no need to be diplomatic. An example
beginning is shown below.

> **EXAMPLE SENTENCE**
>
> *Tom Walker, the corrupt **usurer** who has been the source of much misery
> in this town, disappeared last week and is presumed dead.*

CALIFORNIA R1.2

VOCABULARY STRATEGY: THE LATIN ROOT *spec*

When Tom Walker's neighbors speculated in land, they were
hoping to spot opportunities for a quick profit. The Latin root
spec in the word *speculating* actually means "to look at" or "to
see or behold." Words containing this root, or the related forms
spect and *spic*, usually have something to do with light, sight,
or clarity.

circumspect**
spectator
intro**spec**tive
**spec,
spect**
specter
perspect**ive
spectrum

PRACTICE Match each definition below with the appropriate
word from the word web, considering what you know about the
Latin root *spec* and the other word parts shown.

1. tending to look within, at one's own thoughts or feelings
2. an observer of an event
3. a ghostly sight or apparition
4. showing unwillingness to act rashly; prudent
5. a point of view
6. a range of colored light

**🔍 VOCABULARY
PRACTICE**
For more practice, go
to the **Vocabulary Center**
at **ClassZone.com**.

DIFFERENTIATED INSTRUCTION

FOR ENGLISH LEARNERS
Task Support: Vocabulary Strategy Help
students create a home-language word web
using words that contain the Latin root *spec*.
For example, Spanish-speaking students may
suggest such words as *espectáculo, espectador, inspector,* and *perspectiva.*

FOR ADVANCED LEARNERS/AP
Vocabulary in Writing Ask students to use
as many vocabulary words as they can in a
paragraph written in the first person from
the point of view of someone who borrowed
money from Tom Walker.

Reading-Writing Connection

R3.6, W1.2, W2.1

WRITE A STORY An archetypal plot is a basic storyline that serves as a frame for stories across time and cultures. Any Faust-like tale of a person who "sells his soul" for personal gain is based on an archetype. The story of Cinderella also has its origins in an archetype.

Choose a contemporary situation, such as a political race, or a well-known character type, such as a social climber. Write a **one-to-three-page story** around it that fits the Faustian archetype. Be sure to show the consequences of the main character's actions.

SELF-CHECK

A successful story will . . .

- have a well-developed main character
- clearly show the character's goals and choices
- effectively portray the consequences of the choices
- reflect the Faustian archetype

GRAMMAR AND STYLE

RECOGNIZE PARALLELISM Review the **Grammar and Style** note on page 319. One of the many delights of Irving's style is his use of parallelism—the repetition of grammatical structures—to create emphasis or to add rhythm. Here is an example from the story:

LC1.1

> *Tom's wife was a tall termagant, fierce of temper, loud of tongue, and strong of arm.* (lines 31–32)

Notice that each of the highlighted phrases contains an adjective (*fierce, loud,* and *strong*) followed by a prepositional phrase (*of temper, of tongue,* and *of arm*). Read the sentence aloud. How does it sound? How does the parallelism affect the description of Tom's wife?

PRACTICE Write down each of the following sentences from the selection. Then identify the parallel elements from each sentence as shown and write your own sentence with similar parallel elements.

EXAMPLE

. . . No smoke ever curled from its chimney; no traveler stopped at its door.

No frown ever crossed his face; no complaint crossed his lips.

---

1. "Oh, I go by various names. I am the wild huntsman in some countries; the black miner in others. . . . I am the great patron and prompter of slave dealers, and the grand master of the Salem witches."

2. . . . Midnight came, but she did not make her appearance; morning, noon, night returned, but still she did not come.

3. He built himself, as usual, a vast house, out of ostentation; but left the greater part of it unfinished and unfurnished, out of parsimony.

WRITING TOOLS
For prewriting, revision, and editing tools, visit the **Writing Center** at ClassZone.com.

FOR DEVELOPING WRITERS
Writing Support

- Help students brainstorm possible scenarios that reflect the Faustian archetype.
- Encourage students to explain the choices their main character has to make and to make clear in their story how these choices affect that character as well as other characters.

- Use modeling to show students how to include dialogue between characters.
- Suggest that students create a Sequence Chain of plot events to help them in planning their story.

BEST PRACTICES TOOLKIT—Transparency
Sequence Chain p. B21

Reading-Writing Connection

WRITING PROMPT

Encourage students to be imaginative in their adaptation of the Faustian archetype. Point out that the main character may be a male or female of any age and that the story may be serious or, like "The Devil and Tom Walker," satirical. Project the short story writing template transparency and review strategies for planning and organizing a short story.

 BEST PRACTICES TOOLKIT—Transparency
Writing Template: Short Story pp. C16, C39

For writing support, see

Writing Center at **ClassZone.com**

GRAMMAR AND STYLE

Explain that parallelism can make printed or spoken text dramatic. Share with students some notable examples, such as the opening paragraph of *A Tale of Two Cities* ("It was the best of times, it was the worst of times").

Possible answers:

Parallel elements: **1.** *"I am the wild . . . ," "I am the great . . .";* **2.** *"Midnight came, but she did not . . . ," "morning . . . returned, but still she did not . . .";* **3.** *"out of ostentation," "out of parsimony."* *Students' sentences should reflect similar parallel elements.*

RESOURCE MANAGER—Copy Master
Recognize Parallelism p. 36

For more on parallelism, see page R68 in the Grammar Handbook.

Assess and Reteach

Assess

RESOURCE MANAGER—Copy Masters
Selection Test A pp. 37–38
Selection Test B/C pp. 39–40

Test Generator CD

Reteach

STANDARDS LESSON FILE
Literature Lesson 26: Imagery
Literature Lesson 37: Parody and Satire
Writing Lesson 9: Revising for Parallelism
Writing Lesson 22: Short Story
Vocabulary Lesson 7: Latin Roots

OBJECTIVES

Literary Analysis
- explore the key idea of **lessons**
- identify characteristics of blank verse
- read poetry

Reading
- understand structure

 R3.3

ABOUT THE POET

Have students read page 328 and summarize important points of Bryant's biography. Call attention to Bryant's passion for the natural world, and point out that his love of nature is strongly reflected in "Thanatopsis."

USING THE *NOTABLE QUOTE*

Have students read the quotation and think about its meaning. Then ask whether students would associate the quotation with **William Cullen Bryant** the poet, Bryant the "committed political and social activist," or both. *Possible answer: Students should recognize that the idea of the enduring power of truth is probably part of a political or social statement. However, the vivid imagery of the statement suggests a poet's imagination.*

CALIFORNIA R3.3

Thanatopsis

Poem by William Cullen Bryant

NOTABLE QUOTE
"Truth, crushed to earth, shall rise again."

FYI
Did you know that William Cullen Bryant . . .
- could say the alphabet at 16 months of age?
- helped found the Republican Party?
- was an early abolitionist and staunch supporter of Abraham Lincoln?

Author On|ine

For more on William Cullen Bryant, visit the **Literature Center** at **ClassZone.com**.

William Cullen Bryant
1794–1878

In his own day, William Cullen Bryant was a literary superstar. Schoolchildren recited his poetry. Adults pored over his newspaper editorials. And other writers praised his genius. James Fenimore Cooper even went so far as to call Bryant "the author of America" for helping to create a distinctive American literature.

All-American Poet Born in 1794 in Cummington, Massachusetts, Bryant began his writing career at an early age. At 10, he translated poems written in Latin; at 13, he published "The Embargo," a poem satirizing the policies of President Thomas Jefferson.

But the young Bryant was most inspired to write poetry about the natural world. As a boy, he spent hours exploring the forests and hills near his home. His earliest efforts reflected the influence of the English romantic poets.

In time, however, Bryant discovered his American voice. At the ripe old age of 18, he wrote "Thanatopsis," a poem inspired by his wanderings in the countryside. The American editor who published the poem was so struck by its brilliance that he asserted, "No one on this side of the Atlantic is capable of writing such a verse."

Career Moves At his father's urging, Bryant attended law school and spent ten years as a lawyer in Plainsfield, Massachusetts. But he was destined for a career in literature and writing. Leaving behind the "disagreeable drudgery" of his law practice, Bryant moved to New York City in 1825 to become a journalist.

Eventually, he became the editor-in-chief of the *New York Evening Post,* a position he held until his death. A committed political and social activist, Bryant used the newspaper to advocate for human rights and the protection of the environment.

Lifelong Naturalist Unfortunately, Bryant's journalistic work took a toll on his poetry. Nonetheless, Bryant left his mark on American literature as one of the first poets to overthrow what he called the "servile habit of copying" English poets.

Above all, Bryant is celebrated for his power to portray the wild American landscape. Walking up to 40 miles a day, he developed a deep knowledge of America's forests, streams, mountains, and valleys. "Even as an old man," noted one critic, "Bryant was never content unless he knew the name of every tree, bush, and weed in sight."

328

Selection Resources

 RESOURCE MANAGER UNIT 2

Plan and Teach pp. 41–48

Literary Analysis
Blank Verse pp. 49, 50†*
Question Support p. 53*

Reading
Understand Structure pp. 51, 52†*

Assessment
Selection Tests A, B/C pp. 55*, 57*
 Test Generator CD

 BEST PRACTICES TOOLKIT

Differentiated Instruction pp. 31–38*

Reading Support
 Audio Anthology CD*

Technology
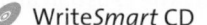 Literature Center at **ClassZone.com**
WriteSmart CD

---

* Resources for Differentiation **† Also in Spanish**

LITERARY ANALYSIS: BLANK VERSE

William Cullen Bryant wrote "Thanatopsis" in a verse form known as blank verse. **Blank verse** is unrhymed poetry written in **iambic pentameter**. In this meter, each line has five iambic feet, a pattern consisting of an unstressed syllable (˘) followed by a stressed syllable (′). Read the following lines from "Thanatopsis" aloud to hear the rhythm:

˘ ′ ˘ ′ ˘ ′ ˘ ′ ˘ ′
To him who in the love of Nature holds
˘ ′ ˘ ′ ˘ ′ ˘ ′ ˘ ′
Communion with her visible forms, she speaks

Notice that the lines do not have a singsong quality as some lines of rhymed poetry do. In fact, good blank verse imitates the natural rhythms of spoken English and so sounds very much like the way people talk. Bryant also achieves this effect through the use of **enjambment,** which means that one line ends without a pause and continues into the next line for its meaning. As you read "Thanatopsis," notice how the poem's rhythm imitates natural speech.

READING SKILL: UNDERSTAND STRUCTURE

In poetry, **structure** is the arrangement of words and lines to produce a desired effect. The structure of a poem usually emphasizes important aspects of content and can help a poet indicate shifts in mood. Use the following strategies to help you understand the structure and effects of Bryant's poem:

- Notice the indented line that indicates the beginning of each of the three verse sections in the poem.
- Summarize each section to understand the content and central ideas.
- Look for details and word choices that convey mood.

As you read "Thanatopsis," use a chart like the one shown to record the ideas and mood evoked in each section of the poem.

Section	Ideas	Mood
1st	Death comes to everyone.	bleak
2nd		
3rd		

Explore the Key Idea

What can DEATH *teach us about life?*

KEY IDEA Some people view death as the ultimate enemy. Others, however, consider it a natural part of life. Acceptance of that fact is a theme of William Cullen Bryant's "Thanatopsis." But death—and life—have other important **lessons** to teach us. One is recognizing that death, since it comes to us all, makes us all equal. What are some other important life lessons?

SURVEY With a partner, conduct a survey among your classmates, friends, and family and ask them to name the five greatest lessons that life—or death—has taught them. Compile the results and share them with the rest of the class.

329

DIFFERENTIATED INSTRUCTION

FOR STRATEGIC READERS
Vocabulary Support

Clarify the meaning of these words:

- *meter,* "measure that refers to the pattern of stressed and unstressed syllables in a line of poetry"
- *feet,* "units of meter consisting of combinations of syllables"; for example, one iambic foot consists of an unstressed syllable followed by a stressed syllable.

Concept Support: Blank Verse

Explain that unrhymed iambic pentameter, or blank verse, is one of the most common metrical patterns used for English poetry. Shakespeare used blank verse in his plays, and Milton used it in *Paradise Lost.* Point out that blank verse is *not* the same as *free verse,* which has no specific metrical pattern.

Teach

What can DEATH *teach us about life?*

Lead into the **KEY IDEA** by asking the question. Explore with students how life's experiences—both good and bad—can teach many different **lessons** if people are open to learning them. Then have students do the **SURVEY** activity.

SKILLS FOCUS

LITERARY ANALYSIS   R3.3

● BLANK VERSE

To help students understand blank verse, write these lines on the board:

> *Made strong by life and love and firm in will*

> *To crawl, to walk, to run, and not to pause.*

Ask students to explain the metric pattern of these lines. *Answer: The lines are written in iambic pentameter—five iambic feet (unstressed syllables followed by stressed syllables).*

CHECK UNDERSTANDING Ask students to explain how these lines exemplify enjambment.

READING SKILL   R3.3

■ UNDERSTAND STRUCTURE

Explain that in poetry, just as in other forms of literature, poets create a structure that helps to convey their intended meaning. For example, one stanza of a poem may present a problem while the next stanza presents a solution. Elicit other examples of structure that authors and poets use, such as chronological order or spatial order. Point out that because of the concentrated nature of poetry, poets have to narrow their focus to the arrangement of individual words and lines.

 RESOURCE MANAGER—Copy Master Understand Structure p. 51 (for student use while reading the selection)

SUMMARY

William Cullen Bryant's "Thanatopsis" is a poetic reflection on death. The poem begins with a statement of the consolation and "healing sympathy" that benign and beautiful Nature provides. The poet then suggests how to accept the mortality that all humans share and to face death without fear, "sustained and soothed by unfaltering trust . . . like one who . . . lies down to pleasant dreams."

LITERARY ANALYSIS

Ⓐ BLANK VERSE

Possible answer: Enjambment occurs in lines 1–2 ("holds / Communion"), 2–3 ("speaks / A various language"), 3–4 ("for his gayer hours / She has"), 4–5 ("a smile / And eloquence"), 5–6 ("glides / Into"), 6–7 ("a mild / And healing sympathy"), and 7–8 ("steals away / Their sharpness"). This enjambment makes the lines flow naturally, echoing the rhythms of conversation.

READING SKILL

Ⓑ STRUCTURE

Possible answer: The central idea of the poem's first section is that all people die and their remains return to earth to become part of the whole of nature.

If students need help . . .

• Have them read lines 17–22. Discuss the imagery Bryant uses to describe a person who is dying.

• Have students read lines 22–30. Discuss Bryant's description of how people are "resolved to earth again . . . to mix forever with the elements."

Thanatopsis

William Cullen Bryant

To him who in the love of Nature holds
Communion with her visible forms, she speaks
A various language; for his gayer hours
She has a voice of gladness, and a smile
5 And eloquence of beauty, and she glides
Into his darker musings, with a mild
And healing sympathy, that steals away
Their sharpness, ere he is aware. When thoughts Ⓐ
Of the last bitter hour come like a blight
10 Over thy spirit, and sad images
Of the stern agony, and shroud, and pall,
And breathless darkness, and the narrow house,
Make thee to shudder, and grow sick at heart;—
Go forth, under the open sky, and list
15 To Nature's teachings, while from all around—
Earth and her waters, and the depths of air—
Comes a still voice—Yet a few days, and thee
The all-beholding sun shall see no more
In all his course; nor yet in the cold ground,
20 Where thy pale form was laid, with many tears,
Nor in the embrace of ocean, shall exist
Thy image. Earth, that nourished thee, shall claim
Thy growth, to be resolved to earth again,
And, lost each human trace, surrendering up
25 Thine individual being, shalt thou go
To mix forever with the elements,
To be a brother to the insensible rock
And to the sluggish clod, which the rude swain
Turns with his share, and treads upon. The oak
30 Shall send his roots abroad, and pierce thy mold. Ⓑ

Yet not to thine eternal resting-place
Shalt thou retire alone—nor couldst thou wish
Couch more magnificent. Thou shalt lie down
With patriarchs of the infant world—with kings,
35 The powerful of the earth—the wise, the good,
Fair forms, and hoary seers of ages past,
All in one mighty sepulcher.—The hills
Rock-ribbed and ancient as the sun,—the vales

2 communion: a close relationship.

Ⓐ BLANK VERSE
Reread lines 1–8 aloud. Identify the places where a phrase begins at the end of a line and continues on the next line. How does this **enjambment** affect the flow of the lines?

11–12 shroud . . . the narrow house: A shroud is a burial garment, while a pall is a heavy garment draped over a coffin. The narrow house is the grave or coffin.

28–29 the sluggish clod . . . share: the heavy mass of earth, which the farmer loosens with his plow.

Ⓑ STRUCTURE
What is the central idea of the poem's first section, lines 1–30?

33 couch: bed.

36 hoary seers: ancient wise men.

37 sepulcher: grave.

DIFFERENTIATED INSTRUCTION

For general guidelines on differentiating instruction, see

 BEST PRACTICES TOOLKIT
Differentiated Instruction pp. 31–38

FOR STRATEGIC READERS

Options for Reading: Audio Recording

• Have students listen to "Thanatopsis" on the *Audio Anthology CD* (also recommended for English learners) while they read along in their texts. Ask students to notice the meter and rhythm of the poem.

• Call students' attention to the shift in content, focus, and mood that occurs as the poem proceeds from one section to the next. Also direct their attention to the way in which Bryant concludes the poem with lines 73–81, beginning with an imperative communicated in the speaker's voice: "So live. . . ."

Stretching in pensive quietness between;
40 The venerable woods—rivers that move
In majesty, and the complaining brooks
That make the meadows green; and, poured round all,
Old ocean's gray and melancholy waste,—
Are but the solemn decorations all
45 Of the great tomb of man. The golden sun, **C**
The planets, all the infinite host of heaven,
Are shining on the sad abodes of death,
Through the still lapse of ages. All that tread
The globe are but a handful to the tribes
50 That slumber in its bosom.—Take the wings
Of morning—and the Barcan desert pierce,
Or lose thyself in the continuous woods
Where rolls the Oregon, and hears no sound,
Save his own dashings—yet—the dead are there;
55 And millions in those solitudes, since first
The flight of years began, have laid them down
In their last sleep—the dead reign there alone.
So shalt thou rest—and what if thou withdraw
Unheeded by the living—and no friend
60 Take note of thy departure? All that breathe
Will share thy destiny. The gay will laugh
When thou art gone, the solemn brood of care
Plod on, and each one as before will chase
His favorite phantom; yet all these shall leave
65 Their mirth and their employments, and shall come
And make their bed with thee. As the long train **D**
Of ages glide away, the sons of men,
The youth in life's green spring, and he who goes
In the full strength of years, matron and maid,
70 The speechless babe, and the gray-headed man—
Shall one by one be gathered to thy side,
By those, who in their turn shall follow them.

So live, that when thy summons comes to join
The innumerable caravan, which moves
75 To that mysterious realm, where each shall take
His chamber in the silent halls of death,
Thou go not, like the quarry-slave at night,
Scourged to his dungeon, but, sustained and soothed
By unfaltering trust, approach thy grave,
80 Like one who wraps the drapery of his couch
About him, and lies down to pleasant dreams. **E**

40 **venerable:** impressive and worthy of respect because of age.

51 **Barcan desert:** a desert region in northern Africa.

53 **Oregon:** old name for the Columbia River, which flows between the states of Washington and Oregon.

C **STRUCTURE**
Identify the **mood** in lines 31–45. How does it contrast with the mood in the first section?

D **BLANK VERSE**
Tap your foot to the rhythm as you read lines 61–66. Note the motion described in these lines. How does the rhythm suggest this motion?

E **STRUCTURE**
Reread the last section of the poem, lines 73–81. How would you **summarize** these lines?

THANATOPSIS 331

READING SKILL

C **STRUCTURE**

Possible answer: *The mood in these lines is hopeful and joyous, in contrast with the gloomier mood of the first section.*

If students need help . . . Work with them to fill in the prereading chart introduced on page 329 and draw conclusions about the mood.

Section	Ideas	Mood
1st	Death comes to everyone.	bleak
2nd	When you die, you will not be alone. Nature will decorate your tomb.	hopeful, joyous, reassuring

LITERARY ANALYSIS

D **BLANK VERSE**

Possible answer: *The insistent rhythm suggests the relentless forward movement of time and the inevitability of death.*

READING SKILL

E **STRUCTURE**

Possible answer: *Live fully while you can, but when the time comes for you to join all those who have died before you, you can meet death serenely, like a person who is about to settle down to a peaceful sleep.*

SELECTION WRAP-UP

REFLECT The first version of "Thanatopsis" did not include lines 73–81. Ask students whether the added lines improve or detract from the poem.

FOR STRATEGIC READERS
Comprehension Support Call students' attention to lines 48–50. Explain that when Bryant wrote "Thanatopsis," fewer people were alive on earth than the total number who had previously died. This changed in the late 1900s as the world's population grew, and the number of people living came to exceed the number who had already lived and died.

FOR ADVANCED LEARNERS/AP
Comparison Bryant composed the original draft of "Thanatopsis" in 1815. In that same year, he composed another well-known poem, "To a Waterfowl." Have students read the poem and note comparisons and contrasts with "Thanatopsis," in terms of mood and tone, setting, and theme. Ask students to write one or two paragraphs on these comparisons and contrasts and read them aloud to the class.

Practice and Apply

After Reading

Use these copy masters to check understanding and provide extra support:

RESOURCE MANAGER—Copy Masters
Blank Verse p. 49
Question Support p. 53

Additional selection questions are provided for teachers on page 45.

ANSWERS

1. *Nature soothes and comforts people during times of sadness.*

2. *When people die, their bodies mix with the earth's elements.*

3. *People need not fear death because they will not be alone; rather, they will be joining all those who have died before.*

Possible answers:

4. *Death is viewed as a natural part of life (lines 22–30). It is not frightening or lonely (lines 31–37; 66–72), but rather welcoming and peaceful (lines 79–81).*

5. ■ **SKILLS FOCUS** Understand Structure
Central idea: section 1: Death comes to everyone; section 2: When you die, you won't be alone; section 3: Live fully so you can meet death serenely. The three-part structure helps develop the message that death should not be feared but accepted as natural and inevitable.

6. *Examples: "Earth, that nourished thee, shall claim / Thy growth" (lines 22–23)— thoughtful; "nor couldst thou wish / Couch more magnificent" (lines 32–33)—comforting; "So live . . . pleasant dreams" (lines 73–81)—encouraging. Tone: thoughtful, soothing, formal, gentle*

Assess and Reteach

Assess

RESOURCE MANAGER—Copy Masters
Selection Test A pp. 55–56
Selection Test B/C pp. 57–58

Test Generator CD

Reteach

STANDARDS LESSON FILE
Literature Lesson 17: Structure of Poetry
Literature Lesson 20: Rhythm and Meter

R3.3

Comprehension

1. **Recall** According to the speaker, how does nature help people cope during times of sadness?

2. **Recall** According to lines 22–30, what happens to people when they die?

3. **Clarify** Why, according to the speaker, should people greet death without fear?

Literary Analysis

4. **Analyze Title** The title of the poem combines the Greek words *thanatos* ("death") and *opsis* ("a vision"). Cite specific details from the poem to explain the vision of death presented in "Thanatopsis."

5. **Understand Structure** Review the notes you recorded in your chart on the ideas and mood in each section of "Thanatopsis." Identify the central idea in each section, and explain how the poem's structure helps develop an overall message.

6. **Draw Conclusions About Tone** A writer establishes his or her tone, or attitude toward a subject, through a variety of language choices. Use a chart to jot down important examples of Bryant's word choices, details, and direct statements. Then draw conclusions about the poem's tone.

Examples	Tone

7. **Interpret Ideas** Use details from the poem to determine what **lessons** Bryant conveys about

   • life   • nature   • religion

8. **Evaluate Blank Verse** How would the impact of Bryant's message differ if he had used a fixed meter and regular rhythm in his poem? Evaluate whether his use of blank verse is an effective or pleasing way to express his ideas. Give reasons for your opinion.

9. **Recognize Characteristics of Romanticism** How does "Thanatopsis" reflect Romantic notions of nature and democratic values?

Literary Criticism

10. **Different Perspectives** Bryant wrote "Thanatopsis" when he was a very young man. He was also greatly influenced by the English romantic poets. Given what you have learned about the Puritans and the romantic poets, how do you think the following people might have reacted to the poem?

    • Bryant at age 70   • a Puritan   • an English romantic poet

---

7. *Life should be lived to the fullest; nature teaches us about life and death and provides beauty and comfort; people should look forward to a peaceful afterlife without necessarily expecting the heaven promised in traditional religion.*

8. ● **SKILLS FOCUS** Blank Verse
Answers will vary. Students may note that blank verse is effective because it conveys the poem's message in a more natural manner that is also formal.

9. *Images of nature serve to inspire and comfort; all people are united in death, regardless of station or status.*

10. *Bryant at age 70 might have viewed death more fearfully and less optimistically; a Puritan would likely be offended by the lack of reference to God or heaven; a romantic poet probably would find the poem's view of nature inspirational.*

Elements of Romantic Style

On the surface, it seems as if William Cullen Bryant's "Thanatopsis" and Washington Irving's "The Devil and Tom Walker" could hardly be more different. One is an elegant nature poem written in formal language.

Go forth, under the open sky, and List / To Nature's teachings
from "Thanatopsis"

The other is a short story about strange, supernatural deeds and is written in a down-to-earth, casual style.

Tom's wife was a tall termagant, fierce of temper, loud of tongue, and strong of arm.
from "The Devil and Tom Walker"

But with a more careful reading, one can find elements of romanticism in each work.

Writing to Analyze

In general, America's romantic writers shared several characteristics. They looked to nature for inspiration, they celebrated individualism, they valued emotion and the imagination, and they sometimes explored the supernatural in their work. Which of these elements can you find in the two works you've just read? Create a chart like the one here, and use it to write a brief essay explaining why these two very different writers were each good examples of the romantic movement.

Element	Selection(s)	Example(s)
nature	"Thanatopsis"	"To him who in the love of Nature holds / Communion with her visible forms, she speaks / A various language"
	"The Devil and Tom Walker"	"On one side of this inlet is a beautiful dark grove; on the opposite side the land rises abruptly from the water's edge into a high ridge, on which grow a few scattered oaks of great age and immense size."
individualism		
emotion or passion		
imagination		
supernatural		

Extension

VIEWING & REPRESENTING

Romanticism was not only a literary movement; it was a movement of the other arts as well. Romantic artists shared many of the same concerns as writers of the day. Examine the painting shown here. (If you have trouble making out the painting's details, turn to page 318, where you can view it in a larger format.) With a partner, discuss what elements you think might indicate that the work is a good example of a romantic painting.

R2.5, W2.2

Wrap-Up: The Early Romantics

This Wrap-Up provides students with an opportunity to review elements of romanticism and reflect on how these elements were treated in different kinds of romantic writing.

Writing to Analyze

Review with students that *analyzing* means breaking down a subject into parts and then examining each part in order to gain a fuller understanding of the subject. Analyzing the works of romantic writers helps to make clear how their literary works shared certain characteristics.

To help students create their charts, suggest that they work together in pairs or small groups to identify examples of the various elements of romanticism in "The Devil and Tom Walker" and "Thanatopsis."

Extension

- Suggest that students first study the painting individually and draw their own conclusions. Then have them compare their observations with those of their partner.
- To help students get started, encourage them to refer back to the charts they created to help them write their essay about elements of romanticism.

DIFFERENTIATED INSTRUCTION

FOR DEVELOPING WRITERS

Writing Support Help students get started by directing them to relevant passages in the selections. For example, students might examine lines 78–88 of "The Devil and Tom Walker" to write about Irving's imaginative depiction of the devil. Or, they might draw on lines 37–48 of "Thanatopsis" to write about Bryant's passionate feelings for the splendors of nature.

FOR ENGLISH LEARNERS

Writing Topic Sentences To help students create topic sentences for their paragraphs, provide sentence starters such as these:

- Washington Irving's detailed and imaginative descriptions show _____.
- In "Thanatopsis," William Cullen Bryant demonstrates why _____.

Remind students to support their topic sentences with specific examples from the selections.

Focus and Motivate

OBJECTIVES

Literary Analysis
- explore the key idea of **purpose**
- identify and analyze stanza and rhyme scheme
- read poetry

Reading
- use strategies for reading traditional poetry

 R3.3

ABOUT THE POET

As students read the biography, note that although Longfellow came from a cultured family, was highly educated, and enjoyed early success, he suffered personal tragedies. Point out his statements about the value of nature and personal reflection in **Voice of America**. Then tell students that the poems in this lesson will show how Longfellow applied these values as he wrote about life and loss.

USING THE *NOTABLE QUOTE*

After a student reads the quote aloud, invite paraphrases. Ask students how **Henry Wadsworth Longfellow** here expresses an aspect of the American romantic view of life that they read about in the historical essay.
Possible answer: *The comment emphasizes the romantic ideals of self-reliance and the value of the individual rather than the group.*

The Fireside Poets

R3.3

A Psalm of Life
The Tide Rises, the Tide Falls

Poetry by Henry Wadsworth Longfellow

NOTABLE QUOTE

"We judge ourselves by what we feel capable of doing, while others judge us by what we have already done."

FYI

Did you know that Henry Wadsworth Longfellow . . .
- was a child prodigy?
- spoke 11 languages?
- read 18 languages?
- grew a beard to hide the scars of a fire that killed his wife?

Author Online

For more on Henry Wadsworth Longfellow, visit the **Literature Center** at ClassZone.com.

Westminster Abbey

Henry Wadsworth Longfellow
1807–1882

For nearly 150 years, Longfellow's "Paul Revere's Ride" has captivated readers. Its lines are as familiar as a nursery rhyme, and the image of Revere galloping into danger is imprinted on our minds. This poem, along with a number of others, made Henry Wadsworth Longfellow one of America's most popular poets.

Boy Genius Longfellow grew up in a literary household in Portland, Maine. His mother, Zilpah Wadsworth, often read aloud to him, while his father, Stephen, supplied him with numerous books. An exceptionally intelligent child, Longfellow entered school at the age of three and at six received this flattering report: "Master Henry Longfellow is one of the best boys we have in school. He spells and reads very well. He can also add and multiply numbers. His conduct is very correct and amiable."

Professor and Poet At age 13 Longfellow became a published poet, and at 15 he entered Bowdoin College in Maine where, like his classmate Nathaniel Hawthorne, he decided to devote his life to writing. While in college, he published poems in national magazines. Longfellow studied a number of foreign languages, including French, Spanish, and Italian. He was such a gifted translator that the college offered him upon graduation the first professorship in modern languages. Longfellow taught at Bowdoin until 1834, when he transferred to Harvard. He remained there until 1854.

Voice of America Although he worked hard to introduce European literature to an American audience, Longfellow wrote about American subjects. He sought inspiration in American history and lore, as well as in the country's landscape. A poet, argued Longfellow, should take his subjects from "nature and not from books" and should try to "fathom the recesses of his own mind, and bring up rich pearls from the secret depths of thought."

Literary Fame With the publication of his books *Evangeline, A Tale of Acadie* (1847) and *The Song of Hiawatha* (1855), Longfellow became a household name. Personal tragedy, however, cast a shadow over his achievement. His first wife died following a miscarriage and his second wife was fatally burned in a fire. Longfellow coped by immersing himself in his work. In his final years, Longfellow was showered with accolades. When he died, he became the first American writer to be honored with a bust in Poets' Corner of London's Westminster Abbey.

Selection Resources

 RESOURCE MANAGER UNIT 2

Plan and Teach pp. 59–66

Literary Analysis
Stanza and Rhyme Scheme
  pp. 67, 68†*
Question Support p. 71*

Reading
Reading Traditional Poetry
  pp. 69, 70†*

Assessment
Selection Tests A, B/C pp. 73*, 75*
 Test Generator CD

 BEST PRACTICES TOOLKIT

Differentiated Instruction
  pp. 31–38*

Graphic Organizers/Strategies
Two-Column Chart

Reading Support
 Audio Anthology CD*

Technology
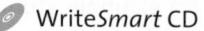 Literature Center at
  ClassZone.com
  WriteSmart CD

---

 * Resources for Differentiation   † Also in Spanish

LITERARY ANALYSIS: STANZA AND RHYME SCHEME

Poets often organize their ideas and images in compact units known as **stanzas**—groups of lines sometimes characterized by a repeated pattern of rhyme and number of lines. Each stanza generally develops a separate idea, image, or example of figurative language; recognizing stanzas will help you trace this development.

A **rhyme scheme** is the pattern of end rhyme in a stanza or an entire poem. Rhyme helps to make the words of a poem memorable and is often used to emphasize important words in the poem.

> *Life is real! Life is earnest!*
> *And the grave is not its goal;*
> *Dust thou art, to dust returnest,*
> *Was not spoken of the soul.*

Here the rhyme scheme is *abab*; that is, the first and third lines (*a* and *a*) rhyme, as do the second and fourth lines (*b* and *b*).

As you read, note how Longfellow makes use of these conventions to organize his thoughts about life and express them in a form that the reader will remember.

READING STRATEGY: READING TRADITIONAL POETRY

To appreciate the musical qualities of these Longfellow poems, try the following strategies:

- Read each poem silently to interpret the basic meaning.
- Then, read them aloud, listening for the end rhyme. Notice which words are emphasized by rhyme.

In a web diagram like the one shown, note some important words that are emphasized through rhyme. You will need a separate diagram for each poem.

What gives life PURPOSE?

KEY IDEA People who live with **purpose** may be more likely to feel a sense of satisfaction or accomplishment. What is it that gives life value or meaning? Is it self-expression, creativity, following one's dream, or serving humanity? In the poems that follow, Longfellow offers his thoughts about how to lead a purposeful life.

QUICKWRITE Think of a person you know or have read about who has led a life you truly admire. How has this person made a difference in the world? Describe his or her impact on family, community, or country in a short paragraph.

335

What gives life PURPOSE?

Ask the question and have students read the **KEY IDEA**. Invite comments about the **purposes** named or other purposes that students suggest. Call on volunteers to share responses to the **QUICKWRITE** activity and to identify the purposes that they think these people's lives represent.

SKILLS FOCUS

LITERARY ANALYSIS

● STANZA AND RHYME SCHEME

Write these lines of verse on the board:

> The fiery sun, a burning blaze,
> Struck my soul into a daze
> And, with its rage of blinding light,
> Turned daytime thoughts to darkest night.

Elicit that these lines form a stanza that develops a single idea (that the blazing sun confused the speaker) and that they have a rhyme scheme of *aabb*.

CHECK UNDERSTANDING Have students give examples of stanzas and rhyme schemes in poems they have read or songs they know.

READING STRATEGY

■ READING TRADITIONAL POETRY

Refer students to the stanza from the Literary Analysis activity. Discuss how rhyme emphasizes words that point to important ideas (*blaze/daze* and *light/night* emphasize the power of the sun on the speaker). Then, as students examine the web diagram, ask them why the rhyming words *dream* and *seem* might be important in a poem. ***Possible answer:*** *In a poem about life (as the title suggests), this rhyme might address the idea that things in life that seem real to us are only a dream.*

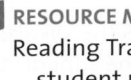 **RESOURCE MANAGER—Copy Master**
Reading Traditional Poetry p. 69 (for student use while reading the selection)

DIFFERENTIATED INSTRUCTION

FOR STRATEGIC READERS

Concept Support: Reading Traditional Poetry Explain that traditional poetry usually has a clear meter, or rhythm, and it often follows a predictable rhyme scheme. Traditional poetry also may include outdated terms, such as *o'er* and *thou*. Most traditional poetry was written prior to the 20th century, but the style continues to be used today; for example, many popular song lyrics use the meters and rhyme schemes

found in traditional poetry. Have students reread the Longfellow stanza on this page and identify the qualities that mark it as traditional poetry. ***Possible answer:*** *The stanza was written generations ago, it has a clear meter and rhyme scheme, and it includes the outdated terms* thou, art, *and* returnest.

Practice and Apply

SUMMARY

In this poem, the speaker refutes the idea that life is only "an empty dream." He declares that living a purposeful, "sublime" life, patiently but actively working toward a goal, can inspire others to do the same.

Lines 1–20
TIERED DISCUSSION PROMPTS

Use these prompts to help students explore the poetic speaker's main ideas:

Connect What thoughts have you sometimes had about the purpose of life? How similar is your view to the speaker's view? *Accept all responses.*

Interpret What do lines 5–6 mean? *Possible answer: Life has a serious purpose; we are not here only to live out our lifespan and then die meaninglessly.*

Evaluate How convincing is the speaker's argument? How well does he support the idea that life has a serious, heroic purpose? *Accept all reasonable responses.*

A Psalm of Life

Henry Wadsworth Longfellow

*What the Heart of the Young Man
Said to the Psalmist[1]*

Tell me not, in mournful numbers,[2]
    Life is but an empty dream!—
For the soul is dead that slumbers,
    And things are not what they seem.

5 Life is real! Life is earnest!
    And the grave is not its goal;
Dust thou art, to dust returnest,
    Was not spoken of the soul.

Not enjoyment, and not sorrow,
10   Is our destined end or way;
But to act, that each tomorrow
    Find us farther than today.

Art is long, and Time is fleeting,
    And our hearts, though stout[3] and brave,
15 Still, like muffled drums, are beating
    Funeral marches to the grave.

In the world's broad field of battle,
    In the bivouac[4] of Life,
Be not like dumb, driven cattle!
20   Be a hero in the strife!

A STANZA AND RHYME SCHEME
Review the rhyme scheme of the first two stanzas. How does the rhyme scheme contribute to the poem's **tone,** or attitude? Explain.

---

1. **Psalmist** (sä′mĭst): the author of the poems in the biblical Book of Psalms, many of which comment on the fleeting nature of life. King David of Israel is regarded as the author of most of the psalms.
2. **numbers:** metrical feet or lines; verses.
3. **stout:** strong.
4. **bivouac** (bĭv′ōō-ak′): a temporary encampment of troops.

DIFFERENTIATED INSTRUCTION

For general guidelines on differentiating instruction, see

📚 **BEST PRACTICES TOOLKIT**
Differentiated Instruction pp. 31–38

FOR STRATEGIC READERS
Options for Reading: Audio Recording

- Have students listen to the two poems on the *Audio Anthology CD*. Urge students to listen for each poem's rhyme and rhythm.

- Have students compare and contrast the tone and pace that the audio reader uses in each poem. Work with students to connect those elements to the meaning of each poem.

The Calm After the Storm (1866), Edward Moran. Oil on canvas. Private collection. © SuperStock, Inc./SuperStock.

Trust no Future, howe'er pleasant!
    Let the dead Past bury its dead!
Act,—act in the living Present!
    Heart within, and God o'erhead!

25 Lives of great men all remind us
    We can make our lives sublime,
And, departing, leave behind us
    Footprints on the sands of time; **B**

Footprints, that perhaps another,
30   Sailing o'er life's solemn main,[5]
A forlorn and shipwrecked brother,
    Seeing, shall take heart again.

Let us, then, be up and doing,
    With a heart for any fate;
35 Still achieving, still pursuing,
    Learn to labor and to wait.

---

5. **main:** open ocean.

ANALYZE VISUALS
How might the title of this painting (*The Calm After the Storm*) connect to the **theme** of this poem?

B **TRADITIONAL POETRY**
Note the word emphasized by the end rhyme in lines 25 and 27. What might be the significance of this word?

A PSALM OF LIFE   **337**

338   UNIT 2: AMERICAN ROMANTICISM

SUMMARY

The speaker of this poem describes a traveler coming to a town by way of the shore, while the tide rises and falls endlessly. The ceaselessness of the waves contrasts with the traveler's brief stay.

LITERARY ANALYSIS

C STANZA AND RHYME SCHEME

Possible answer: *Words that rhyme with* falls *occur in the first, second, and fifth lines of each stanza, emphasizing* falls. *The rhyme suggests a pattern of recurrence that imitates the rise and fall of the tide.*

READING STRATEGY

D TRADITIONAL POETRY

Possible answer: *The difference is that daylight returns each morning but the traveler never will return.*

If students need help . . . Have them paraphrase lines 13–14 by substituting a modern word for *nevermore* and modern word order for "returns the traveler to the shore." **Possible answer:** *The day returns, but the traveler never returns to the shore.*

SELECTION WRAP–UP

SYNTHESIZE Ask students to identify basic similarities and differences in the two poems.

⭐ CRITIQUE

- Ask students what, if anything, they find too simple in Longfellow's poems, and what, if anything, they find too difficult.

- After completing the discussion questions on page 339, have students revisit their responses and tell whether they have changed their opinions.

THE TIDE RISES,
The Tide Falls

Henry Wadsworth Longfellow

The tide rises, the tide falls,
The twilight darkens, the curlew[1] calls;
Along the sea sands damp and brown
The traveler hastens toward the town,
5   And the tide rises, the tide falls. **C**

Darkness settles on roofs and walls,
But the sea in the darkness calls and calls;
The little waves, with their soft white hands,
Efface[2] the footprints in the sands,
10   And the tide rises, the tide falls.

The morning breaks; the steeds in their stalls
Stamp and neigh, as the hostler[3] calls;
The day returns, but nevermore
Returns the traveler to the shore,
15   And the tide rises, the tide falls. **D**

---

1. **curlew:** a type of large bird often found along the shoreline.
2. **efface:** to wear away; wipe out.
3. **hostler:** person who takes care of horses.

C STANZA AND RHYME SCHEME
What rhyme occurs in three of the five lines of each stanza? What word is emphasized by this repeated rhyme? Consider the impact of this technique on the poem's meaning.

D TRADITIONAL POETRY
In terms of basic meaning, what is the difference between the day and the traveler in lines 13–14?

Singing Beach, Manchester (1863), Martin Johnson Heade. Oil on canvas, 50.8 cm × 91.4 cm. The Fine Arts Museums of San Francisco, Gift of Mr. and Mrs. John D. Rockefeller, 3rd, 1993.35.12.

DIFFERENTIATED INSTRUCTION

FOR STRATEGIC READERS

Explore Rhyme Have students use the web diagram introduced on page 335 to record the rhymes in "The Tide Rises, the Tide Falls" and to connect Longfellow's word choices to his ideas. Discuss the importance of the words *falls* and *calls;* lead students to see that, overall, the rhymes emphasize the idea that human life is short, compared to the ceaseless workings of nature.

FOR ADVANCED LEARNERS/AP

Analyze Tone Have students discuss these questions about the traveler:

- Who or what does the traveler represent?

- How does the absence of details about the traveler contribute to the tone and theme of the poem?

Then have students present their conclusions to the class.

Comprehension

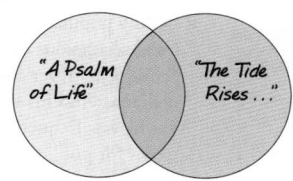
R3.3
CALIFORNIA

1. **Recall** What record does the traveler leave behind in "The Tide Rises, the Tide Falls"? What happens to this record and to the traveler?

2. **Recall** What, according to the speaker of "A Psalm of Life," is "our destined end" or purpose?

3. **Paraphrase** What does the speaker say about the value of the lives of great people in "A Psalm of Life"?

Literary Analysis

4. **Draw Conclusions About Traditional Poetry** Review the emphasized words you recorded in your web diagram for "A Psalm of Life." What can you conclude about the relationship between the poem's sound and its meaning?

5. **Analyze Metaphor** A metaphor compares two things that seem dissimilar. Think about the metaphor in lines 17–18 of "A Psalm of Life." What is Longfellow saying about the world and life by comparing them to a battlefield and a bivouac?

6. **Examine Stanza and Rhyme Scheme** Identify the rhyme scheme used in "The Tide Rises, the Tide Falls." How does this rhyme scheme reflect the poem's central image?

7. **Interpret Repetition** Longfellow repeats the line "the tide rises, the tide falls" throughout his poem. What idea is he trying to emphasize about the difference between nature and human life through this repetition?

8. **Compare and Contrast** Reread lines 8–10 in "The Tide Rises . . ." and 25–32 in "A Psalm of Life." Consider what happens to the footprints in each poem. Based on this and other images, how would you say Longfellow's outlook on life and death in each poem is similar? In what way is it different? Use a Venn diagram like the one shown to organize your thoughts.

"A Psalm of Life"   "The Tide Rises . . ."

9. **Evaluate the Author's Message** According to the speaker of "A Psalm of Life," what should people do to give their lives value, or **purpose?** Do you agree or disagree? Cite evidence to support your conclusions.

Literary Criticism

10. **Critical Interpretations** "Longfellow," writes critic Alan Trachtenberg, "remains one of the nation's abidingly popular poets; more poems of his are probably still taken to heart and committed to memory than those of any of his more luminous 19th century peers. . . ." Based on the two poems you've read, why do you think Longfellow was, and continues to be, so popular? Cite evidence to support your conclusions.

8. *The outlooks are similar in that both poems suggest that life is fleeting. There are several differences. For example, "The Tide Rises, the Tide Falls" is more somber than "A Psalm of Life." In "A Psalm of Life," individuals can have an enduring impact on the world (indicated by the footprints that remain)—a view that is denied in "The Tide Rises, the Tide Falls" (indicated by the footprints that the tide erases).*

9. *The speaker feels that people should strive to achieve a "sublime" life (line 26) and perhaps a better world and to inspire others to do the same (lines 27–32). Students' opinions and support will vary.*

10. *Longfellow's popularity may be due to the facts that his poems are accessible and that they deal with universal themes. His traditional use of rhyme and rhythm makes his poems memorable, as well.*

Practice and Apply

After Reading

Use these copy masters to check understanding and provide extra support:

R RESOURCE MANAGER—Copy Masters
Stanza and Rhyme Scheme p. 67
Question Support p. 71

Additional selection questions are provided for teachers on page 63.

ANSWERS

1. *The traveler leaves footprints in the sand. Waves efface the footprints (lines 8–9), and the traveler moves on (lines 13–14).*

2. *Our purpose is to act bravely and patiently to achieve our goals (lines 33–36).*

3. *Great people make their mark in the world and, through their example, inspire others to act (lines 25–32).*

Possible answers:

4. ■ **SKILLS FOCUS Reading Traditional Poetry** *The emphasized words convey the speaker's view of life as serious and purposeful.*

5. *Longfellow is saying that, like a battlefield, the world is full of strife, and that an individual's life in the world is only a temporary "encampment," like a bivouac.*

6. ● **SKILLS FOCUS Stanza and Rhyme Scheme** *The rhyme scheme is aabba/aacca/aadda. This pattern evokes the image of recurring waves and underscores the cyclical, ceaseless quality of nature.*

7. *He is emphasizing the difference between the sea, which seems eternal, and a human lifetime, which is momentary by comparison.*

Assess and Reteach

Assess

R RESOURCE MANAGER—Copy Masters
Selection Test A pp. 73–74
Selection Test B/C pp. 75–76

⊘ Test Generator CD

Reteach

S STANDARDS LESSON FILE
Literature Lesson 17: Structure of Poetry
Literature Lesson 19: Rhyme and Rhyme Scheme

Focus and Motivate

OBJECTIVES

Literary Analysis
- explore the key idea of **change**
- analyze meter
- read poetry

Reading
- make inferences

CALIFORNIA R3.3

ABOUT THE POET

As students read the biography, emphasize that Holmes had a range of interests. Point out that "The Chambered Nautilus" reflects his interest in nature and "Old Ironsides" shows his awareness and strong feelings about history and current events.

USING THE *NOTABLE QUOTE*

Read the comment aloud. Ask students to explain the figurative language that **Oliver Wendell Holmes** uses and then to express the literal meaning of the idea. *Possible answer: Holmes's metaphor compares the human mind to something physical that can be stretched out of shape. Holmes means that a new idea permanently reshapes one's thinking.* Invite students to supply examples of ideas that have affected them or society in such a way.

Selection Resources

R3.3
CALIFORNIA

The Chambered Nautilus
Old Ironsides

Poetry by Oliver Wendell Holmes

NOTABLE QUOTE
"Man's mind, once stretched by a new idea, never regains its original dimensions."

FYI
Did you know that Oliver Wendell Holmes ...
- dropped out of law school because it bored him?
- became dean of the Harvard Medical School?
- called the subconscious mind "the underground workshop of thought" 20 years before Freud published his study of the unconscious?

Author Online

For more on Oliver Wendell Holmes, visit the **Literature Center** at ClassZone.com.

Oliver Wendell Holmes
1809–1894

Many people climb the ladder of success, but few make their mark in two very different fields. Oliver Wendell Holmes was both a prize-winning physician and a wildly popular poet. His discovery of the contagious nature of puerperal ("childbed") fever changed the practice of medicine. And his verse was so beloved that he was frequently called upon to write poems for public occasions.

A Cultural Elite Holmes grew up in a family steeped in history and tradition. He was descended from prominent Boston families and early Dutch settlers. His father, a Calvinist minister in Cambridge, Massachusetts, nurtured his interests in books, religion, and nature. "I am very thankful," wrote Holmes, "that the first part of my life was not passed shut in between high walls and treading the unimpressible and unsympathetic pavement."

Literary Triumph At 15, Holmes enrolled at Phillips Andover Academy, where he impressed his teachers by translating the Roman poet Virgil's *Aeneid*. After receiving a bachelor's degree and a medical degree from Harvard University, he entered private practice in Boston. Holmes achieved literary stardom at the age of 21 with the appearance of his poem "Old Ironsides." Written to protest the planned destruction of a ship that fought in the War of 1812, the poem won Holmes instant fame. Following its publication, the USS *Constitution* was returned to active duty.

Talent for Talk After his first book of poems was published in 1836, Holmes joined the lecture circuit, where he entranced audiences with his ready wit. He was equally charming in the classroom, causing his students at Harvard Medical School to greet his lectures with "a mighty shout and stamp of applause." Holmes's eloquence was also on display at the Saturday Club, a group including Ralph Waldo Emerson and Nathaniel Hawthorne. The writers met regularly to share their latest works.

Renaissance Man In addition to poetry, Holmes wrote three novels, a biography of Emerson, and numerous essays. Many of the essays appeared in *The Atlantic Monthly,* a magazine edited by Holmes's friend James Russell Lowell. Printed under the title "The Autocrat of the Breakfast Table," these essays combined prose and poetry and explored the themes of human destiny and freedom.

340

RESOURCE MANAGER UNIT 2

Plan and Teach pp. 77–84

Literary Analysis
Meter pp. 85, 86†*
Question Support p. 89*

Reading
Make Inferences pp. 87, 88†*

Assessment
Selection Tests A, B/C pp. 91*, 93*
 Test Generator CD

 BEST PRACTICES TOOLKIT

Differentiated Instruction pp. 31–38*

Graphic Organizers/Strategies
Analysis Frame: Poetic Language and Style

Reading Support
 Audio Anthology CD*

Technology
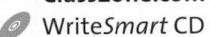 Literature Center at **ClassZone.com**
WriteSmart CD

---

* Resources for Differentiation   † Also in Spanish

LITERARY ANALYSIS: METER

Meter is one of the tools used by poets to make language memorable and pleasing to the ear. It is defined as the repetition of a regular rhythmic unit in a line of poetry. Each unit, known as a **foot,** has one stressed syllable (indicated by a ´) and either one or two unstressed syllables (indicated by a ˘). The two basic types of metrical feet used by Holmes in these poems are the **iamb,** in which an unstressed syllable is followed by a stressed syllable (˘´), and the **trochee,** in which a stressed syllable is followed by an unstressed syllable (´˘). Two words are used to describe the meter of a line. The first word identifies the type of metrical foot—iambic, trochaic— and the second word indicates the number of feet in a line: **monometer** (one), **dimeter** (two), **trimeter** (three), **tetrameter** (four), **pentameter** (five), **hexameter** (six), and so forth. Here is a line from "Old Ironsides" with the meter marked:

Her deck, once red with heroes' blood

As you read these two poems by Holmes, note the meter in each and consider what it contributes to the poem's meaning and aesthetic appeal.

READING SKILL: MAKE INFERENCES

Making inferences involves "reading between the lines"— making logical guesses based on evidence in the text to figure out what is not directly stated. As you read these two poems by Holmes, you will need to make inferences to get at the author's meaning. For each poem, create a chart like the one shown.

"The Chambered Nautilus"

Details or Evidence from Text	What I Know from Experience	Ideas Inferred
"Year after year beheld the silent toil / that spread his lustrous coil"	It takes a lot of practice to become good at a sport.	Change requires effort.

When is it time to MOVE ON?

KEY IDEA Sometimes people have to choose between cherishing the past and looking toward the future. For example, when you move out of your parents' house, will you expect them to keep your room exactly as it is or to convert it to a home office? **Change** can produce a renewed sense of well-being as well as a sense of loss.

DISCUSS Working with a partner, list situations or occasions in life when one must decide between holding on to the past and making a change. In each case, what are the benefits of either choice? After discussing this question with your partner, share your conclusions with others.

341

When is it time to MOVE ON?

Lead into the **KEY IDEA** by asking the question and having students share initial thoughts. Briefly discuss why people might be reluctant to make a **change** in their lives; urge students to keep that discussion in mind as they complete the **DISCUSS** activity.

SKILLS FOCUS

LITERARY ANALYSIS   R3.3

● METER

Tap the beat to help students distinguish an iamb from a trochee; also present the adjective forms *iambic* and *trochaic*. Note the prefixes in the names of the metrical feet and share a few other words that use the same prefixes (such as *triangular* and *pentagon*). Have students tap out the iambic tetrameter in the line from "Old Ironsides."

CHECK UNDERSTANDING Have students tap out examples of various meters, such as iambic pentameter (˘´ ˘´ ˘´ ˘´ ˘´) and trochaic trimeter (´˘ ´˘ ´˘).

READING SKILL

■ MAKE INFERENCES

To help students see how personal experience can aid understanding of a text, give this example: "Never did I expect the day / we all would sing his praise." Ask what students think the author means. *Possible answer: The person praised in the line is a person that no one had thought praiseworthy.*

CHECK UNDERSTANDING Call on volunteers to explain the use of the chart, focusing upon the application of personal experience to the detail from the poem.

R RESOURCE MANAGER—Copy Master
Make Inferences p. 87 (for student use while reading the selections)

DIFFERENTIATED INSTRUCTION

FOR STRATEGIC READERS

Concept Support: Make Inferences Students should find it easier to make inferences if they first "translate" figurative lines of verse into literal statements. Have them work in pairs or small groups to paraphrase passages. Suggest that they expand the first column of the chart presented on this page to show not only the detail or evidence from the text but also a modern paraphrase, as in this example:

"The Chambered Nautilus"

Details or Evidence from Text	What I Know from Experience	Ideas Inferred
"Year after year beheld the silent toil / That spread his lustrous coil" → **As time passed, the nautilus quietly worked to expand its shiny shell.**	It takes a lot of practice to become good at a sport.	Change requires effort.

SUMMARY

The speaker describes the process by which the chambered nautilus expands its spiral shell as it grows. He sees in that process a message about the importance of the soul's personal growth.

LITERARY ANALYSIS

Ⓐ METER

Possible answer: Many of the lines begin with a trochaic foot. This variation puts an emphasis on important words (such as the word Wrecked *in line 9) and thus helps convey the speaker's intellectual urgency.*

If students need help . . . Have them read lines 1, 2, and 9 aloud, listening to the accented first syllable of each line. If students need further examples of words that the beginning trochaic foot emphasizes, refer them to any or all of these lines: 15, 17, 19, 21, 22, 23, 24, 29, 31, 33, 35.

Lines 15–21
TIERED DISCUSSION PROMPTS

Use these prompts to help students grasp the process that this stanza describes:

Connect Have you or someone you know ever relocated to another school or place to live? How might that experience help someone identify with the chambered nautilus? *Accept all responses.*

Analyze What details suggest that the growth pattern of the chambered nautilus is a beautiful but natural phenomenon? *Possible answer: Details such as "lustrous coil" and "shining archway" suggest beauty. Details suggesting work over time—"Year after year beheld the silent toil," "as the spiral grew," "Built up"—point to a natural phenomenon.*

Synthesize On the basis of this stanza, predict what the speaker may say about the nature of change. *Possible answer: The speaker may say that change is a natural, and not a fearsome, phenomenon.*

The Chambered Nautilus

Oliver Wendell Holmes

This is the ship of pearl, which, poets feign,[1]
    Sails the unshadowed main,—
    The venturous bark that flings
On the sweet summer wind its purpled wings
5 In gulfs enchanted, where the Siren[2] sings,
    And coral reefs lie bare,
Where the cold sea-maids rise to sun their streaming hair.

Its webs of living gauze no more unfurl;
    Wrecked is the ship of pearl!
10   And every chambered cell,
Where its dim dreaming life was wont to dwell,
As the frail tenant shaped his growing shell,
    Before thee lies revealed,—
Its irised ceiling rent,[3] its sunless crypt unsealed! Ⓐ

15 Year after year beheld the silent toil
    That spread his lustrous coil;
    Still, as the spiral grew,
He left the past year's dwelling for the new,
Stole with soft step its shining archway through,
20   Built up its idle door,
Stretched in his last-found home, and knew the old no more.

Thanks for the heavenly message brought by thee,
    Child of the wandering sea,
    Cast from her lap, forlorn!
25 From thy dead lips a clearer note is born

Ⓐ **METER**
Although the basic meter of this poem is **iambic**, what kind of **foot** is substituted for the iamb at the beginning of many of the lines? How does this variation affect the feel of these lines?

---

1. **feign:** imagine.
2. **Siren:** a partly human female creature in Greek mythology that lured sailors to destruction with sweet, magical songs.
3. **its irised ceiling rent:** its rainbow-colored ceiling ripped apart.

DIFFERENTIATED INSTRUCTION

For general guidelines on differentiating instruction, see

 BEST PRACTICES TOOLKIT
Differentiated Instruction pp. 31–38

FOR STRATEGIC READERS
Options for Reading: Audio Anthology

- Have students listen to the poems on the *Audio Anthology CD* (also recommended for English learners) while they read along in their texts. Encourage students to listen for the meter in each poem.

- Urge students to compare and contrast the way in which each audio reader presents the poem. Invite comments about each reader's tone and the way in which it reflects the speaker's attitude in the text of the poem.

As the nautilus grows, it adds a new chamber to its spiral shell, abandoning the old chamber for the new one. What might this process of growth suggest about the role of change in life?

Than ever Triton blew from wreathèd horn![4]
    While on mine ear it rings,
Through the deep caves of thought I hear a voice that sings:—

Build thee more stately mansions, O my soul,
30   As the swift seasons roll!
    Leave thy low-vaulted past!
Let each new temple, nobler than the last,
Shut thee from heaven with a dome more vast,
    Till thou at length art free,
35 Leaving thine outgrown shell by life's unresting sea! **B**

B MAKE INFERENCES
Reread lines 29–35. What inference can you make about what it might mean for the soul to escape its shell?

---

4. **Triton . . . wreathèd horn:** Triton, a sea god in Greek mythology, is usually pictured blowing a wreathed, or coiled, conch-shell horn.

THE CHAMBERED NAUTILUS   **343**

ANALYZE VISUALS

Possible answer: This process of growth might suggest that change has a necessary role in life and that people should strive to achieve changes that enlarge them instead of just accepting the changes that come.

Activity Use the photograph to help students visualize the process that Holmes describes in the poem. Have students follow the spiral, beginning with its smallest, innermost segment and proceeding to the open end. Discuss the effectiveness of the nautilus as a metaphor for human life.

Lines 29–31
REINFORCE KEY IDEA: CHANGE

Discuss What kind of **change** is the speaker referring to when he talks of building "more stately mansions" (line 29)? How could people put that idea into practice? *Possible answer: The speaker is referring to a change to greater or nobler thoughts or endeavors. People could put that idea into practice by committing to improving themselves, experiencing new challenges, and becoming better human beings.*

FOR STRATEGIC READERS

Comprehension Support Have students work in pairs or small groups to solve problems of literal comprehension, using a dictionary if possible. Offer this advice:

- Look up difficult or old-fashioned words such as *wont* (line 11).

- Figure out which meaning is used in multiple-meaning words such as *bark* (line 3).

- Turn inverted word order (as in line 19) into standard word order.

FOR ADVANCED LEARNERS/AP

Analyze Poetic Language [paired option] Have students write and share an analysis of Holmes's language in this poem. Urge them to use a Poetic Language and Style Analysis Frame as they plan, making notes about Holmes's word choice and imagery and the effect that both would have upon readers of his time and ours.

    BEST PRACTICES TOOLKIT—Transparency
Analysis Frame: Poetic Language and Style
pp. D21, D38

SUMMARY

The ironic speaker first urges that the USS *Constitution*, which played a heroic role in American history, be destroyed as planned. He then recounts the ship's history and declares that it would be better for the ship to sink in a storm than to meet such a humiliating end.

ANALYZE VISUALS

Possible answer: The mood is one of somber awe and of respect for the noble ship.

LITERARY ANALYSIS

● METER

Possible answer: The basic meter is iambic. Odd-numbered lines are longer than even-numbered lines.

READING SKILL

● MAKE INFERENCES

Possible answer: The speaker is being ironic. He says that it would be better for the ship to be sunk than demolished, but he really wants it to be preserved as part of the nation's heritage.

Extend the Discussion What things or places today do you think should be declared parts of the nation's heritage? Explain your choices.

SELECTION WRAP–UP

SYNTHESIZE Both poems were extremely popular in their own time and remained so for many years. Ask students if each poem is meaningful in our time and if so, why.

OLD IRONSIDES
Oliver Wendell Holmes

Ay, tear her tattered ensign[1] down!
    Long has it waved on high,
And many an eye has danced to see
    That banner in the sky;
5 Beneath it rung the battle shout,
    And burst the cannon's roar;—
The meteor of the ocean air
    Shall sweep the clouds no more.

Her deck, once red with heroes' blood,
10   Where knelt the vanquished foe,
When winds were hurrying o'er the flood,
    And waves were white below,
No more shall feel the victor's tread,
    Or know the conquered knee;—
15 The harpies[2] of the shore shall pluck
    The eagle of the sea! ●

Oh, better that her shattered hulk
    Should sink beneath the wave;
Her thunders shook the mighty deep,
20   And there should be her grave;
Nail to the mast her holy flag,
    Set every threadbare sail,
And give her to the god of storms,
    The lightning and the gale! ●

---

1. **ensign:** flag.
2. **harpies:** evil monsters from Greek mythology that are half woman and half bird.

ANALYZE VISUALS
What **mood** is suggested by this image of the USS *Constitution* ("Old Ironsides") in the mist in Boston Harbor?

● METER
What is the basic meter of this poem? Notice which lines are longer and which are shorter.

● MAKE INFERENCES
Reread the third stanza. Based on what has been said in previous stanzas about the ship's gloried past, do you think the speaker is being sincere or **ironic** about the fate of Old Ironsides? Explain.

DIFFERENTIATED INSTRUCTION

FOR STRATEGIC READERS
Explore Allusion Point out the footnote that explains the allusion to "harpies" (line 15). Add to the explanation by telling students that harpies were terrible creatures that flew off with food, objects, and even people (thus, Holmes's "shall pluck / The eagle of the sea"). Elicit that the "harpies" to whom Holmes refers are those who might plan to have the USS *Constitution* destroyed.

FOR ADVANCED LEARNERS/AP
Compare and Contrast Poems Challenge students to compare and contrast Holmes's understanding of change in the two poems. Pose such questions as: What kind of change does Holmes view as natural and desirable? Why? What kind of change is unnatural and undesirable? Why? Have them write two paragraphs on their conclusions and share them with the class.

Comprehension

 R3.3

1. **Recall** What event involving Old Ironsides took place during the war?

2. **Recall** According to the speaker, what should be the ship's fate?

3. **Summarize** In lines 1–14 of "The Chambered Nautilus," what does the speaker imagine and notice about the nautilus?

Literary Analysis

4. **Analyze Symbol** What do you think the chambered nautilus **symbolizes**, or represents, for the speaker of the poem? Cite evidence to support your answer.

5. **Make Inferences** Look back at the inferences and evidence you recorded as you read. What ideas about **change** does Holmes convey in "The Chambered Nautilus"? How does Holmes use each of the following images to express his thoughts about change?

   • the shell's appearance in the speaker's hands (lines 8–14)
   • the growth of the shell (lines 15–21)
   • the message the shell conveys (lines 29–35)

6. **Identify Tone** The attitude that a writer takes toward a particular subject is called **tone**. How would you describe the tone of each poem? What words and figures of speech help establish this tone? Use a chart like the one shown to record your answers.

> "Old Ironsides"
> Tone: sardonic
> Words: "Oh, better that her shattered hulk / Should sink beneath the wave" (lines 17–18)
>
> "The Chambered Nautilus"
> Tone:
> Words:

7. **Interpret Meter** Review the metric pattern you identified in "Old Ironsides." Then read the poem aloud. How does this meter reflect the poem's subject matter? Explain.

Literary Criticism

8. **Author's Style** Recall from Holmes's biography on page 340 that the poem "Old Ironsides" was instrumental in saving the USS *Constitution*. What techniques and details used in the poem might have motivated readers to act? Cite evidence to support your answer.

Practice and Apply

After Reading

Use these copy masters to check understanding and provide extra support:

R RESOURCE MANAGER—Copy Masters
Meter p. 85
Question Support p. 89
Additional selection questions are provided for teachers on page 81.

ANSWERS

1. *The ship was victorious in battle.*

2. *The speaker says that it would be better for the ship to sink in a storm rather than be demolished.*

3. *The speaker imagines that the nautilus has sailed through the ocean realms where "Sirens" and mermaids live. He notices that the shell is now so damaged that he can see its chambers.*

Possible answers:

4. *It represents personal, spiritual growth, as Holmes explains in the final stanza.*

5. ■ **SKILLS FOCUS Make Inferences**
   Holmes indicates that change enables people to mature.

   • *Lines 8–14 convey that in life the nautilus saw many changes and that death also has changed it.*

   • *Lines 15–21 convey the process of change that the nautilus experienced as it grew.*

   • *Lines 29–35 convey the message that the speaker draws from the nautilus—namely, that it is important for people to undergo a change in which they embrace greater, nobler thoughts.*

6. *The tone of "Old Ironsides" is sardonic, angry, serious, and ironic; an example would be "Ay, tear her tattered ensign down!" (line 1). The tone of "The Chambered Nautilus" is romantic, as evidenced by such phrases as "ship of pearl" (line 1), "gulfs enchanted" (line 5), and "Child of the wandering sea" (line 23), and then inspirational in the entire final stanza.*

7. ● **SKILLS FOCUS Meter** *The odd-numbered lines of each stanza are in iambic tetrameter and the even-numbered lines in iambic trimeter, with variations when lines begin with a trochaic foot. The briskness of the meter reflects the speaker's urgency.*

8. *The poem's images, such as the tattered flag waving high and the deck red with heroes' blood, probably evoked readers' patriotism. The rhymes and meter create a stirringly oratorical rhythm.*

Assess and Reteach

Assess

R RESOURCE MANAGER—Copy Masters
Selection Test A pp. 91–92
Selection Test B/C pp. 93–94

Test Generator CD

Reteach

S STANDARDS LESSON FILE
Literature Lesson 20: Rhythm and Meter
Reading Lesson 8: Making Inferences

Focus and Motivate

OBJECTIVES

Literary Analysis
- explore the key idea of **nature**
- identify and analyze mood
- read poetry

Reading
- paraphrase

R3.4

ABOUT THE POETS

John Greenleaf Whittier Explain that the adjective *idyllic* often refers to writing that presents an idealized rural scene. (Students will see the noun *idyll* in the subtitle of "Snowbound.") Invite students to speculate about what Whittier might say in an idyllic poem about being snowbound—and where, given his background, he might set the poem.

James Russell Lowell After students have read about Lowell, point out the final sentence of the biography. Briefly discuss why someone's lasting fame might come from writing poetry instead of from other achievements.

USING THE *NOTABLE QUOTES*

Ask students what concept is the subject in the comments of both **Whittier** and **Lowell**. *Answer: beauty* Have students restate each comment and compare the poets' views on beauty. As students read the poems in this lesson, encourage them to consider possible links between the quotations and the poems.

R3.4

John Greenleaf Whittier
1807–1892

NOTABLE QUOTE
"Beauty seen is never lost."

from Snowbound
Poem by John Greenleaf Whittier

John Greenleaf Whittier embodied the idealism of his age, which combined social activism and literary activity. He devoted most of his waking hours to the abolition of slavery, even risking his own life for the cause. Yet he also managed to write hundreds of poems. Many express an idyllic view of rural life and a profound moral aversion to slavery.

Rural Childhood Whittier's social consciousness derived from his modest background. Born to devout Quakers, Whittier was taught to believe in the equality of all men and women, the immorality of war, and the importance of thrift. Working long days on his family's farm in Haverhill, Massachusetts, Whittier also learned about the cycles of nature.

Poet and Politician Unlike most of his literary contemporaries, Whittier received little formal schooling. He was, however, an avid reader, devouring books by John Milton, Robert Burns, and other poets. Burns's poems about rural life inspired Whittier to write his own. When he was 19, his poetry was discovered by the abolitionist and editor William Lloyd Garrison. In the years that followed, Whittier contributed poems to various newspapers. He was also a founding member of the Republican Party and of the American Anti-Slavery Society.

James Russell Lowell
1819–1891

NOTABLE QUOTE
"All the beautiful sentiments in the world weigh less than a single lovely action."

The First Snowfall
Poem by James Russell Lowell

To his contemporaries, James Russell Lowell was the quintessential New England man of letters. He wrote poetry that stirred the emotions, newspaper editorials that influenced public opinion, and literary criticism.

Rebel with a Cause Lowell was born into a prominent New England family. In 1834, he entered Harvard, where he exasperated his teachers with his spoiled, immature behavior. His flouting of school rules and his disregard for his studies eventually led to his suspension. In 1844, Lowell married Maria White, who set her husband on the path to more mature behavior. In later years, Lowell published several volumes of verse and numerous articles in support of the abolitionist movement. He opposed slavery, the Mexican War, and corruption in politics.

Poet and Diplomat Lowell's talents were not limited to writing. He served as editor of *The Atlantic Monthly,* as an American diplomat in Spain, and as ambassador to Great Britain. While he enjoyed much public success in these roles, Lowell is today best remembered for his poetry.

Author Online
For more on these poets, visit the **Literature Center** at ClassZone.com.

Selection Resources

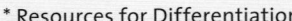

RESOURCE MANAGER UNIT 2

Plan and Teach pp. 95–102

Literary Analysis
Mood pp. 103, 104†*
Question Support p. 107*

Reading
Paraphrase pp. 105, 106†*

Assessment
Selection Tests A, B/C
pp. 109*, 111*
Test Generator CD

BEST PRACTICES TOOLKIT

Differentiated Instruction
pp. 31–38*

Graphic Organizers/Strategies
Cluster Diagram • What's Most Important • Showing, Not Telling, with Literature • Analysis Frame: Poetic Content • Jigsaw Reading

Reading Support
Audio Anthology CD*

Technology
Literature Center at
ClassZone.com
Write*Smart* CD

---

* Resources for Differentiation   *† Also in Spanish*

LITERARY ANALYSIS: MOOD

Mood is the feeling or atmosphere that a writer creates for the reader. Although it may seem that mood is simply inherent in a piece, it is actually achieved through the use of various devices, such as the following:

- **figurative language:** language that communicates ideas beyond the literal meaning of words
- **imagery:** descriptive words and phrases a writer uses to re-create sensory experiences
- **meter:** repetition of a regular rhythmic unit in a line of poetry
- **rhyme:** similarity of sound between two words

Notice, for example, how Lowell uses all four devices in the following stanza from "The First Snowfall":

> I stood and watched by the window
>   The noiseless work of the sky,
> And the sudden flurries of snowbirds,
>   Like brown leaves whirling by.

As you read the poems by Lowell and Whittier, look for the devices that help to create a different mood in each poem.

READING STRATEGY: PARAPHRASE

Sometimes, the surest way to get through a difficult passage is to **paraphrase** it, or restate the ideas in simpler words. To paraphrase a line or stanza in a poem, determine its main idea and replace difficult words with easier ones. In some cases, footnotes will help you clarify meaning. Consider the following lines from Lowell's poem "The First Snowfall":

> And the poorest twig on the elm-tree
>   Was ridged inch deep with pearl.

Here is a paraphrase of the same lines that restates the poet's idea in simpler language:

> An inch of snow covered the slender twig on the elm tree.

As you read, use a chart like the one shown to record difficult words or phrases and how you might paraphrase them.

Original Word(s)	My Paraphrase

Review: **Make Inferences**

What can NATURE teach us?

KEY IDEA What lessons about life have you learned from **nature**? Perhaps waiting out a thunderstorm taught you something about patience. Or maybe watching monkeys at the zoo helped you to understand group behavior. The selections that follow describe kernels of wisdom two poets gleaned from the natural world.

QUICKWRITE In your notebook, list some insights you have gained from nature. How could you apply these insights to your own life? Write down your thoughts and ideas in a short paragraph.

Scene or Event	Insights
thunderstorm	Nature puts things in perspective.

What can NATURE teach us?

Read the question aloud. Then have students read the **KEY IDEA**. Call on volunteers to suggest other lessons that might come from observing **nature** (for example, lessons about cleverness or cooperation). As students begin the **QUICKWRITE** activity, urge them to consider how the insights that they gained from nature challenged their thinking. Allow students to share their finished paragraphs in small groups.

SKILLS FOCUS

> **LITERARY ANALYSIS**
>
> ● **MOOD**
>
> Help students identify the four devices in the sample stanza: figurative language in the comparison of snowbirds to brown leaves; imagery in the "sudden flurries of snowbirds"; the meter, which mixes iambic and anapestic feet in a predictable pattern; and the *abcb* rhyme scheme. Elicit that the mood of the stanza is rather reflective and possibly sad.
>
> **CHECK UNDERSTANDING** Have students brainstorm a variety of possible moods that a poem could express.

> **READING STRATEGY**
>
> ■ **PARAPHRASE**
>
> To reinforce instruction, have students paraphrase the stanza from "The First Snowfall" in the Literary Analysis discussion. *Possible answer: I stood by the window and watched the busy but silent sky. The groups of snowbirds that flew by reminded me of swirls of brown leaves.*
>
> RESOURCE MANAGER—Copy Master
>   Paraphrase p. 105 (for student use
>   while reading the selection)

DIFFERENTIATED INSTRUCTION

FOR STRATEGIC READERS

Concept Support: Paraphrase [small-group option] Give small groups of students the same passage, five to eight sentences in length, from a piece of modern prose that is somewhat difficult but not as challenging as the poems in this lesson. A passage from a textbook on history or science might be a good choice. Instruct each group to make a chart similar to the one presented on this page and then to work together to para-phrase sentences, one by one. (Depending on the material, some sentences may not need much paraphrasing.) When the group arrives at a satisfactory paraphrase for a sentence, have a group secretary write the paraphrase on the chart. Post the original passage and the groups' paraphrase charts in the class-room for students to compare and contrast.

SUMMARY

The speaker recalls a childhood memory of the coming and aftermath of a snowstorm. He remembers wondering at the snow-transformed scene, digging a path through the snow to the barn, and spending a tranquil evening with his family by a blazing hearth fire.

LITERARY ANALYSIS

Ⓐ MOOD

Possible answer: *Imagery of a "cheerless" and "darkly circled" sun, gray hills, "sadder" light, and a "thickening sky" that hides the sun before sunset helps to set a mood of gloom and uncertainty.*

Lines 9–25
TIERED DISCUSSION PROMPTS

Use these prompts to help students explore the description of the gathering storm:

Connect How do you feel when a storm is approaching? Do your feelings vary according to the kind of storm? *Students may suggest excitement, worry, fear, and so on, especially if the approaching storm has potential for harm.*

Analyze In what way are some details like a weather report? ***Possible answer:*** *References to the bitter cold and the direction of the wind are similar to a weather report.* How does the speaker convey a sense of normalcy despite the gathering storm? ***Possible answer:*** *The speaker conveys normalcy by describing how he participated in the usual evening chores.*

Synthesize What does this passage suggest about the values of the speaker's family? Explain. ***Possible answer:*** *The details suggest that the family is alert to changing conditions but is practical enough to get work done while the conditions permit it.*

SNOWBOUND
A Winter Idyll

John Greenleaf Whittier

The sun that brief December day
Rose cheerless over hills of gray,
And, darkly circled, gave at noon
A sadder light than waning[1] moon.
5 Slow tracing down the thickening sky
Its mute and ominous prophecy,
A portent[2] seeming less than threat,
It sank from sight before it set. Ⓐ
A chill no coat, however stout,
10 Of homespun stuff could quite shut out,
A hard, dull bitterness of cold,
That checked, mid-vein, the circling race
Of lifeblood in the sharpened face,
The coming of the snowstorm told.
15 The wind blew east; we heard the roar
Of Ocean on his wintry shore,
And felt the strong pulse throbbing there
Beat with low rhythm our inland air.

Meanwhile we did our nightly chores,—
20 Brought in the wood from out of doors,
Littered the stalls, and from the mows
Raked down the herd's grass for the cows:
Heard the horse whinnying for his corn;
And, sharply clashing horn on horn,
25 Impatient down the stanchion rows[3]

---

1. **waning:** lessening in intensity.
2. **portent:** omen.
3. **stanchion** (stăn'chən) **rows:** lines of devices that fit loosely around the necks of animals such as cows in order to limit their motion.

Ⓐ MOOD
Think about the mood of these first eight lines. What **imagery** helps to set this mood?

ANALYZE VISUALS
To what senses does this photograph appeal, in addition to sight?

DIFFERENTIATED INSTRUCTION

For general guidelines on differentiating instruction, see

 BEST PRACTICES TOOLKIT
Differentiated Instruction pp. 31–38

FOR STRATEGIC READERS

Options for Reading: Audio Recording

- Have students listen to the two poems on the *Audio Anthology CD.* Encourage students to listen for ways in which the reader's voice sets a mood for each poem.

- Have students compare and contrast the poetic moods. Ask students to identify lines and phrases that the speaker has emphasized, or places where he has altered the pace, in order to signal mood.

ANALYZE VISUALS

Possible answer: The lack of human activity suggests silence, which appeals to the sense of hearing. The photograph also appeals to the sense of touch by suggesting the feel of tree bark, snowflakes, and coldness.

Lines 1–18
REINFORCE *KEY IDEA:* NATURE

Discuss What attitude toward **nature** does Whittier present in this first stanza—mainly positive, mainly negative, or a mix of both? *Possible answer: The view is mainly negative because the sky is an "ominous . . . portent" of the storm (lines 6–7), and images of cold and darkness prevail. However, there is also something exciting in feeling the "strong pulse" of the wind-stirred ocean (lines 15–18) and perhaps in seeing the fulfillment of the "prophecy" (line 6) of an approaching storm.*

CULTURAL CONNECTION

Storms Around the World Snowstorms are frequent in New England, where "Snowbound" is set. Other kinds of storms take place elsewhere in the United States and the world—tornadoes in the Midwest and Central Plains; hurricanes in the Atlantic Ocean, eastern Pacific Ocean, and the Caribbean; sandstorms in the Middle East and parts of Africa and China; and typhoons in Southeast Asia. Invite students to share information about and personal experiences with storms.

FOR STRATEGIC READERS

Explore Mood To help students sense the mood of the poem, have them imagine that they are members of the family portrayed. Have them work in pairs or small groups to fill out a Cluster Diagram, recording words and phrases that express what they might see, hear, and feel before, during, and after a snowstorm.

 BEST PRACTICES TOOLKIT—Transparency Cluster Diagram p. B18

FOR ADVANCED LEARNERS/AP

Analyze Poetic Balance In "Snowbound," Whittier balances a sense of danger, a sense of wonder, and a sense of quiet, ongoing daily life. Invite small groups of students to find evidence for each approach in the poem's text, to discuss how Whittier balances the approaches effectively, and to clarify how this balance contributes to the poem's mood. Invite group representatives to share key discussion points with the class.

Lines 31–54
REINFORCE *KEY IDEA*: NATURE

Discuss Identify some details of **nature** that Whittier presents in these lines. What do you think the speaker, as a young boy, learned from this experience with nature? *Possible answer: Natural details include the gray sky, night, whirling snowflakes, a blinding storm, snowdrifts, a sunless morning, geometric traces of snow, and a clear blue sky. The speaker might have learned that one's perception of the world can change suddenly and that nature can provide beauty and wonder in the midst of ordinary human life.*

LITERARY ANALYSIS

B MOOD

Possible answer: By comparing the clothes-line posts to ghosts, the poet presents a simile that creates a mood of eerie wonder.

READING STRATEGY

C PARAPHRASE

Possible answer: Familiar landmarks have been covered by snow, and the whole land-scape seems to consist of nothing but snow and sky.

If students need help . . . Remind them to use the chart introduced on page 347. Suggest that as students paraphrase, they should try to not be distracted by line breaks, for the meaning of a thought can run for several lines.

Original Word(s)	My Paraphrase
No cloud above, no earth below— / A universe of sky and snow!	All familiar features were erased. The landscape was made only of snow and sky.

The cattle shake their walnut bows;
While, peering from his early perch
Upon the scaffold's pole of birch,
The cock his crested helmet bent
30 And down his querulous[4] challenge sent.

Unwarmed by any sunset light
The gray day darkened into night,
A night made hoary with the swarm
And whirl-dance of the blinding storm,
35 As zigzag, wavering to and fro,
Crossed and recrossed the wingëd snow:
And ere the early bedtime came
The white drift piled the window frame,
And through the glass the clothesline posts
40 Looked in like tall and sheeted ghosts. **B**

So all night long the storm roared on:
The morning broke without a sun;
In tiny spherule[5] traced with lines
Of Nature's geometric signs,
45 In starry flake, and pellicle,[6]
All day the hoary meteor fell;
And, when the second morning shone,
We looked upon a world unknown,
On nothing we could call our own.
50 Around the glistening wonder bent
The blue walls of the firmament,
No cloud above, no earth below—
A universe of sky and snow! **C**
The old familiar sights of ours
55 Took marvelous shapes; strange domes and towers
Rose up where sty or corncrib stood,
Or garden wall, or belt of wood;
A smooth white mound the brush pile showed,
A fenceless drift what once was road;
60 The bridle post an old man sat
With loose-flung coat and high cocked hat;
The well curb[7] had a Chinese roof;

B MOOD
A **simile** is a figure of speech comparing two things using the words *like* or *as*. What mood does the poet create with the simile in lines 39–40?

C PARAPHRASE
How has the world been transformed by snow in lines 50–53?

---

4. **querulous** (kwĕr′ə-ləs): complaining.
5. **spherule** (sfîr′ōol): a little sphere.
6. **pellicle:** a thin film or skin.
7. **well curb:** framing around the neck of a well.

350 UNIT 2: AMERICAN ROMANTICISM

DIFFERENTIATED INSTRUCTION

FOR STRATEGIC READERS

Comprehension Support If students have trouble following the descriptions and events of the poem, point out that "Snowbound" is a narrative poem—that is, despite the abundance of descriptive details, the poem tells a story. Use the What's Most Important strategy to help students focus on the key events of the poetic narrative.

 BEST PRACTICES TOOLKIT
What's Most Important p. D4

FOR ENGLISH LEARNERS

Vocabulary: Outdated Forms Point out that much of the descriptive vocabulary of "Snow-bound" is old-fashioned or poetic. Have students work with English-fluent partners to paraphrase outdated words such as *hoary* (line 33), *firmament* (line 51), and *sage* (line 91) and poetic words such as *whirl-dance* (line 34), *wingëd* (line 36), and *ere* (line 37).

350 UNIT 2: AMERICAN ROMANTICISM

And even the long sweep,[8] high aloof,
In its slant splendor, seemed to tell
65 Of Pisa's leaning miracle.[9]

A prompt, decisive man, no breath
Our father wasted: "Boys, a path!"
Well pleased, (for when did farmer boy
Count such a summons less than joy?)
70 Our buskins[10] on our feet we drew;
With mittened hands, and caps drawn low,
To guard our necks and ears from snow,
We cut the solid whiteness through.
And, where the drift was deepest, made
75 A tunnel walled and overlaid
With dazzling crystal: we had read
Of rare Aladdin's wondrous cave,[11]
And to our own his name we gave,
With many a wish the luck were ours
80 To test his lamp's supernal[12] powers.
We reached the barn with merry din,
And roused the prisoned brutes within.
The old horse thrust his long head out,
And grave with wonder gazed about;
85 The cock his lusty greeting said,
And forth his speckled harem led;
The oxen lashed their tails, and hooked,
And mild reproach of hunger looked;
The hornèd patriarch of the sheep,
90 Like Egypt's Amun[13] roused from sleep,
Shook his sage head with gesture mute,
And emphasized with stamp of foot. **D**

All day the gusty north wind bore
The loosening drift its breath before;
95 Low circling round its southern zone,
The sun through dazzling snow-mist shone.
No church bell lent its Christian tone

D MOOD
Identify examples of **figurative language** and **imagery** in lines 66–92. What is the mood created by this language?

---

8. **sweep:** a long pole connected to a bucket, used for raising water from a well.

9. **Pisa's leaning miracle:** the Leaning Tower of Pisa, Italy.

10. **buskins:** high leather boots.

11. **Aladdin's wondrous cave:** In *The Thousand and One Nights*, the boy Aladdin used a magic lamp to discover a treasure in a cave.

12. **supernal:** heavenly; supernatural.

13. **Amun** (ä′mən): the supreme god of the ancient Egyptians, often represented as having a ram's head.

SNOWBOUND   **351**

Lines 66–92
TIERED DISCUSSION PROMPTS
Use these prompts to help students explore a practical aspect of the storm's aftermath:

Recall What do the tasks performed before the storm (lines 19–30) tell you about the family's daily life? *Possible answer: The tasks show that family members have daily chores, including taking care of the farm's animals.*

Interpret What is the main subject of this stanza? *Possible answer: The main subject is that the speaker and his family, while awe-struck by the scene, go to work to dig a path to the barn so that they can take care of their animals.* What does it add to the poem? *Possible answer: The stanza adds action to the narrative, brightens the tone, and widens the reader's view of the speaker's family.*

Evaluate Does Whittier succeed at making the chore that this stanza presents seem wondrous? Explain your answer. *Possible answer: Whittier succeeds because he describes the chore in exotic terms. For example, a tunnel through the snow is like Aladdin's cave (line 77). He also presents the animals in exotic, humorous terms—the grave old horse, the rooster and his harem of hens, the regal ram, and so on (lines 83–92).*

LITERARY ANALYSIS

D MOOD

Possible answer: Examples of figurative language include "his speckled harem" (line 86) and "Like Egypt's Amun roused from sleep" (line 90). Examples of imagery include "We cut the solid whiteness through" (line 73) and "A tunnel walled and overlaid / With dazzling crystal" (lines 75–76). The mood is one of enchantment, good humor, and youthful zeal.

FOR STRATEGIC READERS
Vocabulary Support Write these challenging terms on the board and have students find definitions. Urge students to substitute the definition for the term as they read the lines from the poem.

- *slant* (line 64), "slanting"
- *summons* (line 69), "a call to do something"
- *overlaid* (line 75), "covered"
- *din* (line 81), "loud noise"
- *prisoned* (line 82), "imprisoned," "trapped"
- *grave* (line 84), "very serious"
- *lusty* (line 85), "hearty"
- *forth* (line 86), "forward"
- *reproach* (line 88), "disapproval"
- *patriarch* (line 89), "male head of a family"
- *roused* (line 90), "awakened"
- *mute* (line 91), "silent"

REINFORCE *KEY IDEA:* NATURE

Discuss What overall impression of **nature** does the poet convey in this passage? What mood results from this description? Cite specific details that contribute to this effect.

Possible answer: *The overall impression is one of solitude, and the mood is rather melancholy. Details that create this effect include the lack of neighboring chimney smoke (lines 98–99), the shrieking and moaning of the wind in the trees (lines 102–103), the beating of sleet on glass windows (lines 104–105), and the absence of welcome sounds such as the brooklet (lines 110–111).*

READING STRATEGY

E PARAPHRASE

Possible answer: *The snowstorm makes the family feel isolated and enclosed within its home while the elements rage outside.*

If students need help . . . Use the Showing, Not Telling, with Literature strategy to guide them as they analyze the psychological effect that Whittier creates in the passage.

 BEST PRACTICES TOOLKIT
   Showing, Not Telling, with Literature
   p. D1

To the savage air, no social smoke
Curled over woods of snow-hung oak.
100 A solitude made more intense
By dreary-voicëd elements,
The shrieking of the mindless wind,
The moaning tree boughs swaying blind,
And on the glass the unmeaning beat
105 Of ghostly fingertips of sleet.
Beyond the circle of our hearth
No welcome sound of toil or mirth
Unbound the spell, and testified
Of human life and thought outside. **E**
110 We minded that the sharpest ear
The buried brooklet could not hear,
The music of whose liquid lip
Had been to us companionship,
And, in our lonely life, had grown
115 To have an almost human tone.

As night drew on, and, from the crest
Of wooded knolls that ridged the west,
The sun, a snow-blown traveler, sank
From sight beneath the smothering bank,
120 We piled, with care, our nightly stack
Of wood against the chimney back,—
The oaken log, green, huge, and thick,
And on its top the stout backstick;
The knotty forestick laid apart,
125 And filled between with curious art
The ragged brush; then, hovering near,
We watched the first red blaze appear,
Heard the sharp crackle, caught the gleam
On whitewashed wall and sagging beam,
130 Until the old, rude-furnished room
Burst, flowerlike, into rosy bloom;
While radiant with a mimic flame
Outside the sparkling drift became,
And through the bare-boughed lilac tree
135 Our own warm hearth seemed blazing free.
The crane and pendent trammels showed,
The Turks' heads on the andirons[14] glowed;

E PARAPHRASE
Reread lines 106–109. What effect does the snowstorm have on the family's sense of itself and the world outside?

---

14. **The crane . . . the andirons:** The crane was the movable arm on which the trammels, or adjustable pothooks, hung. The andirons, or metal supports holding the fireplace wood, were topped with turbanlike knots.

DIFFERENTIATED INSTRUCTION

FOR STRATEGIC READERS
Vocabulary Support

- *mirth* (line 107), "merriness"
- *testified* (line 108), "gave evidence"
- *minded* (line 110), "noticed"
- *knolls* (line 117), "small, rounded hills"
- *fancy* (line 138), "imagination"
- *prompt* (line 138), "quick"
- *Transfigured* (line 145), "Changed"
- *Dead* (line 147), "Completely"
- *save* (line 147), "except"
- *unwarming* (line 152), "not providing warmth"
- *baffled* (line 158), "frustrated"
- *rafter* (line 162), "beam that supports the roof"
- *draught* (line 163), "draft of air"
- *silhouette* (line 167), "shadow"
- *meet* (line 169), "fitting," "appropriate"

While childish fancy, prompt to tell
The meaning of the miracle,
140 Whispered the old rhyme: *"Under the tree,*
When fire outdoors burns merrily,
There the witches are making tea." **F**

The moon above the eastern wood
Shone at its full; the hill range stood
145 Transfigured in the silver flood,
Its blown snows flashing cold and keen,
Dead white, save where some sharp ravine
Took shadow, or the somber green
Of hemlocks turned to pitchy black
150 Against the whiteness at their back.
For such a world and such a night
Most fitting that unwarming light,
Which only seemed where'er it fell
To make the coldness visible.

155 Shut in from all the world without,
We sat the clean-winged hearth[15] about,
Content to let the north wind roar
In baffled rage at pane and door,
While the red logs before us beat
160 The frost line back with tropic heat; **G**
And ever, when a louder blast
Shook beam and rafter as it passed,
The merrier up its roaring draught
The great throat of the chimney laughed;
165 The house dog on his paws outspread
Laid to the fire his drowsy head,
The cat's dark silhouette on the wall
A couchant[16] tiger's seemed to fall;
And, for the winter fireside meet,
170 Between the andirons' straddling feet,
The mug of cider simmered slow,
The apples sputtered in a row,
And, close at hand, the basket stood
With nuts from brown October's wood.

---

15. **clean-winged hearth:** Hearths were commonly swept with a
turkey wing.

16. **couchant** (kou′chənt): lying down, but with head raised.

F MOOD
In lines 116–142, what techniques does the poet use to create a mood of security and warmth in the midst of nature's cold and snow?

G MAKE INFERENCES
Reread lines 155–160. Why is the north wind baffled?

LITERARY ANALYSIS

F MOOD

Possible answer: *The poet uses imagery, figurative language, allusion, and the connotations of carefully chosen words to create a mood of security and warmth. The imagery of firewood and a warm hearth runs throughout the passage, in descriptions such as "We watched the first red blaze appear, / Heard the sharp crackle, caught the gleam / On whitewashed wall . . . " (lines 127–129). Figurative language, such as "Burst, flowerlike, into rosy bloom" (line 131), enriches the scene. The allusion to an "old rhyme" (lines 140–142) creates a feeling of comfort in tradition. Words chosen for their positive connotation include* radiant *(line 132),* sparkling *(line 133),* warm hearth *(line 135),* glowed *(line 137), and* miracle *(line 139).*

Extend the Discussion Do you think that these techniques are effective, or do they make the mood overly sentimental? Defend your opinion.

READING STRATEGY: *Review*

G MAKE INFERENCES

Possible answer: *The north wind is baffled because it is blocked by the door and windowpane and by the heat of the fireplace.*

If students need help . . . Work with them to paraphrase these lines and to contrast the cold, windy outdoor scene with the interior scene by the cozy hearth.

FOR ADVANCED LEARNERS/AP

Analyze the Complete Text [small-group option] Explain to students that this excerpt of "Snowbound" is part of Whittier's much longer poem. Inform students that the remainder of the poem consists largely of character sketches and a description of the community digging itself out and reestablishing contact with the outside world—and that it reveals that the speaker and his brother are the only members of that family who are still alive. Have students locate and read the complete poem and then write an essay that responds to these questions:

- Whom does the speaker describe? Why are these people important to him?
- What mood or moods appear in the remainder of the poem?
- What conclusions does the speaker draw as he remembers these people and events?

Invite students to exchange and compare their finished essays.

Prereading for this poem is found on page 347.

SUMMARY

As the speaker watches the first snowfall of the year, he envisions the snow that is falling upon his dead daughter's grave. His living daughter enters and asks, "Father, who makes it snow?" He kisses her and tells her about God, but he does not tell her that his kiss is intended for her dead sister.

LITERARY ANALYSIS

H MOOD

Possible answer: The mood is quiet and dignified but observant. The simple rhymes, the abcb rhyme scheme, and the variances in meter keep the verse from being sing-songy and thus the mood from seeming contrived.

READING STRATEGY

I PARAPHRASE

Possible answer: Paraphrase: "I thought of a grave with a small headstone at Mount Auburn Cemetery; I imagined snow falling on it, gently protecting it, as a mother robin protects her young." The introduction of this image saddens the mood.

If students need help . . . Ask:

- What other place does the speaker think of as he watches the falling snow?
- What special detail comes to his mind?
- Why does he compare snowflakes to robins?
- How much of a change is this scene from the scene in lines 1–16?

THE FIRST SNOWFALL

James Russell Lowell

The snow had begun in the gloaming,[1]
    And busily all the night
Had been heaping field and highway
    With a silence deep and white.

5 Every pine and fir and hemlock
    Wore ermine[2] too dear for an earl,
And the poorest twig on the elmtree
    Was ridged inch deep with pearl.

From sheds new-roofed with Carrara[3]
10   Came Chanticleer's[4] muffled crow,
The stiff rails softened to swan's-down,
    And still fluttered down the snow.

I stood and watched by the window
    The noiseless work of the sky,
15 And the sudden flurries of snowbirds,
    Like brown leaves whirling by. **H**

I thought of a mound in sweet Auburn[5]
    Where a little headstone stood;
How the flakes were folding it gently,
20   As did robins the babes in the wood. **I**

Up spoke our own little Mabel,
    Saying, "Father, who makes it snow?"
And I told of the good All-father
    Who cares for us here below.

H MOOD
Reread lines 1–16. How would you describe the mood created by the poet's use of **rhyme** and **meter**? Explain your answer.

I PARAPHRASE
Paraphrase lines 17–20. How does the mood shift in these lines?

---

1. **gloaming:** twilight.
2. **ermine:** the expensive white fur of a type of weasel.
3. **Carrara:** Carrara marble, a white marble named after the Italian city where it is mined.
4. **Chanticleer's:** a rooster's.
5. **Auburn:** Mount Auburn Cemetery, located in Cambridge, Massachusetts.

DIFFERENTIATED INSTRUCTION

FOR STRATEGIC READERS

Comprehension Support Have groups of students read through "The First Snowfall" together, using the Analysis Frame: Poetic Content to grasp the core of the poem's subject, its speaker and other characters, its events, and its themes.

📋 BEST PRACTICES TOOLKIT—Transparency
Analysis Frame: Poetic Content
pp. D21, D36

FOR ENGLISH LEARNERS

Vocabulary: Multiple-Meaning Words Point out that, as in prose, words in poems can have more than one meaning. Direct students to the words *dear* (line 6), *poorest* (line 7), *folding/Folded* (lines 19 and 40), *cares* (line 24), *Alone* (line 36), and *close* (line 40). Have students work with English-fluent partners to look up each word and decide which meaning is meant in this context.

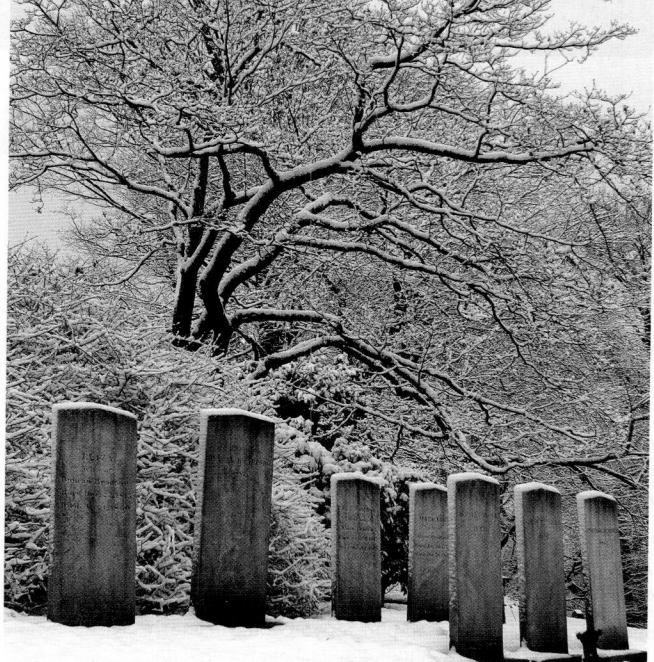

ANALYZE VISUALS
This photograph shows Mount Auburn Cemetery, which is mentioned in the poem. What **mood** is suggested by the photograph, what details support the mood, and how does the mood of the picture match that of the poem?

25   Again I looked at the snowfall,
        And thought of the leaden sky
    That arched o'er our first great sorrow,
        When that mound was heaped so high. **J**

    I remembered the gradual patience
30   That fell from that cloud like snow,
    Flake by flake, healing and hiding
        The scar that renewed our woe.

    And again to the child I whispered,
        "The snow that husheth all,
35 Darling, the merciful Father
        Alone can make it fall!" **K**

    Then, with eyes that saw not, I kissed her;
        And she, kissing back, could not know
    That *my* kiss was given to her sister,
40   Folded close under deepening snow.

J MAKE INFERENCES
In line 17, "mound" refers to the daughter's grave. What else does "mound" refer to in line 28?

K MOOD
What mood does the speaker create at the end of the poem by invoking the "merciful Father"?

THE FIRST SNOWFALL   **355**

ANALYZE VISUALS

Possible answer: The photograph suggests a reflective and somber or grieving mood. The details of the old gravestones, the snow, the bare tree, and the neutral color scheme support the mood. The mood of the photograph matches the mood of the poem in that both suggest sadness.

READING STRATEGY: *Review*

J MAKE INFERENCES

Possible answer: "Mound" also refers to a great sorrow that the speaker has felt.

If students need help . . . Explain that the word *mound* can be a figurative reference to a large amount of something.

LITERARY ANALYSIS

K MOOD

Possible answer: The reference to the "merciful Father" creates a spiritual mood—a sense of religious faith providing a means to deal with grief.

SELECTION WRAP-UP

SYNTHESIZE Ask students to comment on the meaning of snow in both poems. How is it similar? different?

⭐ CRITIQUE

- Ask students which poem presents the speaker's feelings more effectively.
- After completing the discussion questions on page 356, have students revisit their responses and tell whether they have changed their opinions.

FOR STRATEGIC READERS

Concept Support: Paraphrase The final four stanzas (lines 25–40) are crucial for understanding the speaker's grief and the family's history. Have students work in small groups to paraphrase these stanzas. You might use a Jigsaw strategy to have pairs or individual students specialize in paraphrasing different stanzas and then regroup to share their paraphrases.

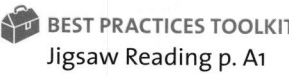
BEST PRACTICES TOOLKIT
Jigsaw Reading p. A1

FOR ADVANCED LEARNERS/AP

Compare Poetic Views [paired option] Ask students to present a brief comparison of William Cullen Bryant's "Thanatopsis," which appears earlier in this unit, with "The First Snowfall." Urge them to focus on these questions:

- How does each poem convey the idea that nature can soften thoughts of death?
- Are thoughts of nature sufficient comfort for each poem's speaker? How can you tell?

Practice and Apply

After Reading

Use these copy masters to check understanding and provide extra support:

 RESOURCE MANAGER—Copy Masters
Mood p. 103
Question Support p. 107

Additional selection questions are provided for teachers on page 99.

ANSWERS

1. *The family prepares by bringing in the wood from outside and feeding the animals. The family copes with the storm by staying indoors until the storm is over, by making a path through the snow when the sun appears, and by gathering around a fire when the wind blows hard.*

2. *The family seems to enjoy the adventure of being snowed in.*

3. *The snowfall transforms the landscape into something that is silent yet majestic.*

4. *The family has suffered the death of a daughter.*

Possible answers:

5. *At first they find the storm threatening, then dreary, and then a source of pleasure. Their responses suggest that they love each other and appreciate nature.*

6. *The simile of "gradual patience" falling "from that cloud like snow" suggests that the pain of sorrow eventually softens and that the family may find some solace in nature.*

7. ■ **SKILLS FOCUS** *Paraphrase Lowell believes in a God who controls the universe and loves humankind (lines 23–24 and 35). Believing that God ultimately is good helps the poet cope with his pain.*

Assess and Reteach

Assess

 RESOURCE MANAGER—Copy Masters
Selection Test A pp. 109–110
Selection Test B/C pp. 111–112

Test Generator CD

Reteach

S **STANDARDS LESSON FILE**
Literature Lesson 42: Mood

Comprehension

1. **Recall** In what ways does the family in "Snowbound" prepare for and cope with the storm?

2. **Clarify** How does the family in "Snowbound" feel about being snowed in?

3. **Summarize** How does the snowfall transform the landscape in lines 1–14 of "The First Snowfall"?

4. **Clarify** In "The First Snowfall," what has happened to the family?

Literary Analysis

5. **Make Inferences** How do the speaker and family in "Snowbound" respond to the storm? What do their responses suggest about their relationship to one another and to **nature?**

6. **Interpret Figurative Language** Reread lines 29–32 of "The First Snowfall." What does the figurative language in this stanza suggest about the family's grief and the relation of their sorrow to the natural world?

7. **Paraphrase to Draw Conclusions** Review the paraphrases you made in your chart as you read Lowell's poem. Describe Lowell's religious beliefs. How do they help the poet cope with his pain?

8. **Analyze Mood** Poets can use a variety of devices to establish mood, including **figurative language, imagery, rhyme,** and **meter.** In each of the poems, identify two devices used to create mood, giving examples. For each poem, which device would you say is the more important? Explain.

9. **Associate Ideas** In these poems and elsewhere, snow is often referred to as having a quieting effect. What are some common metaphors or images used to express our associations with these other kinds of weather?

- downpour
- torrid heat
- windstorm
- Indian summer

Literary Criticism

10. **Historical Context** Whittier and Lowell were two of a group known as the Fireside Poets. (See page 302.) This name refers to a popular family pastime of the period: reading poetry aloud in front of the fireplace after dinner. The poems of the group were very popular and read as entertainment not only in homes but also in schools. Why might the poetry of this group have played such an important role in people's lives? Support your opinion.

---

8. ● **SKILLS FOCUS** *Mood Each poem provides examples of all four techniques. In "The First Snowfall," for example, Lowell's personification of "The snow that husheth all" (line 34) helps establish a mood of quiet acceptance. In lines 66–92 of "Snowbound," Whittier's iambic tetrameter couplets convey an exuberant, cheerful mood. Answers will vary as to which technique is the most important in each poem.*

9. *Accept all reasonable answers.*

10. *Relatively little public entertainment was available during the time that the Fireside Poets wrote. Reading aloud made poetry a social rather than solitary pastime.*

Fireside Poets in Perspective

The Fireside Poets were extremely popular in their day. Indeed, they were so beloved that many families read their works aloud by the fire as a form of nightly entertainment. They were respected as well, becoming the first poets to be considered on equal footing with their British counterparts. Over the years, however, the group's works fell out of favor with critics, who began to look upon them with more affection than respect. Only in recent years have critics again begun to appreciate the craft of the Fireside Poets.

Writing to Evaluate

With a group of classmates, come up with several criteria for evaluating the poems on pages 336–355. Then use your criteria to write a brief evaluation of the work of the Fireside Poets as a whole.

Consider

- what elements (vivid imagery, precise word choice, or thought-provoking themes) you think distinguish "good" poetry from "bad"
- whether the poems contain those elements
- whether your opinion of the poems changed upon rereading

Extension

SPEAKING & LISTENING

Perform an **oral interpretation** of one poem from this group of Fireside Poets' work. Let your opinion of the Fireside Poets in general and of this work in particular inform your reading. For example, if you admire a particular poem, you may wish to read it in a lively and engaging voice. If, on the other hand, you found a poem too sentimental, let your reading reflect this judgment.

CALIFORNIA W2.2, LS2.5

357

This Wrap-Up provides students with the opportunity to consider the Fireside Poets' craft in light of changing literary tastes. Encourage students to think about their positive and negative responses to the poems of Longfellow, Holmes, Whittier, and Lowell and to give evaluations that express their views honestly while demonstrating an understanding of the tastes of the past.

Writing to Evaluate

- Review with students that *evaluating* means forming a reasoned judgment about value. Evaluating literature means expressing an opinion, but it is not a mere personal like or dislike; an effective evaluation must provide support for the opinion (in particular, citations from within the work).

- To help students write their evaluations, have groups begin by discussing criteria for poetry in general. Have them use an Evaluating a Poem form as they look for evidence for those criteria (or a lack thereof) in the work of the Fireside Poets. Point out that opinions of poetry are an individual matter, having much to do with how powerfully the poetry speaks to the reader.

BEST PRACTICES TOOLKIT—Transparency Evaluating a Poem p. D17

Extension

- A poem's mood will shape its oral interpretation, so have students review their notes from reading or class discussion about the mood of the chosen poem.

- Oral interpretations might include group or choral readings. Students who choose this option should spend time discussing the poem and should come to a consensus of opinion about it.

- Urge students to rehearse their oral interpretations several times in private before performing for the class.

DIFFERENTIATED INSTRUCTION

FOR ENGLISH LEARNERS

Writing Evaluative Sentences Provide students with a list of terms that signal evaluation, such as these:

- good/bad
- powerful/weak
- exceptional/dull
- in my opinion (view)
- I think (feel) that
- as I see it

Then discuss sentences such as these, which show some of these terms at work but which also set up some discussion of evidence for an opinion:

- In my view, "The Chambered Nautilus" is a powerful poem because it expresses ideas that people continue to care about today.
- As I see it, the simple rhymes in "A Psalm of Life" weaken the poem's message.

- identify characteristics of an essay

CALIFORNIA **R2.2, R3.3**

First Attempts

Essay Activate students' prior knowledge to compare and contrast the essay form with other short nonfiction forms, such as the news story, the feature article, the editorial, and the newspaper column. Display examples of these forms from a recent newspaper. Discuss whether some or all of these forms could be considered types of essays. ***Possible answer: The essay form is encompassing enough to include the column and the editorial; the news story and the feature article usually do not express the author's opinion and therefore are not essays.*** Provide examples of essays from various sources. Have volunteers read aloud the opening paragraphs of various essays to preview the form's diversity. Post the essays as a classroom library exhibit that students can examine to gain familiarity with this form.

Literary Analysis Workshop

The Art of the Essay

When you write an essay for class, you are taking part in a literary tradition that goes back hundreds of years. In classroom writing, the essay may have many rules governing its structure and topic, but in the literary world, essays come in all shapes and sizes, accommodate any topic, and can be found in books, magazines, and daily newspapers.

CALIFORNIA **R2.2, R3.3**

First Attempts

An **essay** is a short work of nonfiction that offers a writer's opinion on a particular subject. The length can vary greatly. Some are personal, while others are coldly factual. The essay originated with the 16th-century French philosopher Michel de Montaigne, who first introduced the form when he published a collection of writings entitled *Essais,* a French word meaning "attempts." English writers began using the form, and eventually it became commonplace.

Two masters of the American essay in the 19th century were Ralph Waldo Emerson and Henry David Thoreau. These writers used the form to express their philosophies and personal views on a variety of topics, from the ideal lifestyle to the beauty of nature. Using notes he recorded in his journals, Emerson created essays that gave his ideas structure and refined his concepts. In turn they became the cornerstone of **transcendentalism,**

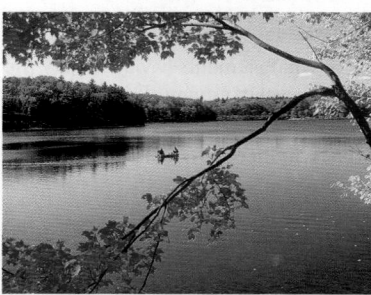

Thoreau's Walden Pond today, located just outside Concord, Massachusetts.

a literary and philosophical movement that emphasized individualism and intuition as a means to understanding reality. Among Thoreau's works is a series of essays, entitled *Walden,* in which he describes his experience of living out the ideals of individualism at Walden Pond (see page 372).

Emerson and Thoreau laid the groundwork for the American essay. Since then, numerous writers have gained reputations as respected authors of the form, including H. L. Mencken, Ernest Hemingway, E. B. White, Joan Didion, and Amy Tan.

The Craft of Expressing Ideas

Essays generally fall into one of two traditions. **Formal essays** explore topics in a serious and organized manner. **Informal essays** adopt a more casual tone and may include humor and unconventional topics. These essays are often more personal in nature. Emerson's "Self-Reliance" (see page 362) is a formal essay, whereas Thoreau's *Walden* essays are more informal.

DIFFERENTIATED INSTRUCTION

For general guidelines on differentiating instruction, see

 BEST PRACTICES TOOLKIT
Differentiated Instruction pp. 31–38

FOR STRATEGIC READERS

Note Taking For students who need help with note taking, hand out the note-taking copy master before discussing these pages.

Explain that students will be learning many terms relating to essays in this workshop. Discuss the major terms on this spread (*formal essay, informal essay, persuasive, expository, descriptive, narrative, organization, supporting details, diction, tone*) as students record notes on their copy masters.

 RESOURCE MANAGER—Copy Master
Note Taking p. 113

Whether the essay's purpose is to be **persuasive, expository, descriptive,** or **narrative,** essayists typically rely on these elements to express their ideas:

- **Organization** is the arrangement of the main ideas and supporting details. Some essays may be narratives that read like a story, while others may follow a strict pattern of organization, such as **cause-and-effect** or **compare-and-contrast.**

- **Supporting details** include facts, opinions, reasons, sensory details, anecdotes, and examples that support the **main idea,** the most important idea about a topic.

- **Diction** is the way a writer uses and arranges language. Some writers use simple and casual words and sentences that may create a personal voice. Others are more formal, using elevated language and complex sentence structures.

- **Tone** is the expression of a writer's attitude toward a subject and may be described as serious, humorous, sarcastic, and so on. The writer's diction and details will provide clues to his or her tone.

"Self-Reliance" is a carefully constructed argument in the form of an essay. Emerson organizes his ideas step by step, leading the reader to the conclusion he wants them to reach—an understanding of his philosophy of individualism. Note Emerson's **opinions,** abstract **language,** and formal **tone** in this passage from "Self-Reliance":

> There is a time in every man's education when he arrives at the conviction that envy is ignorance; that imitation is suicide; that he must take himself for better for worse as his portion . . . .
>
> —Ralph Waldo Emerson, "Self-Reliance"

Close Read

What ideas does Emerson introduce in this sentence? Paraphrase his ideas in your own words.

Thoreau, on the other hand, takes a more personal and informal approach in *Walden.* Even though his **sentence structure** is complicated and lengthy, the **language** is simple, and the **details** are concrete.

> When first I took up my abode in the woods, that is, began to spend my nights as well as days there, which, by accident, was on Independence day, or the fourth of July 1845, my house was not finished for winter, but was merely a defense against the rain, without plastering or chimney, the walls being of rough weather-stained boards, with wide chinks, which made it cool at night.
>
> —Henry David Thoreau, *Walden*

Close Read

Note the **diction** and **details** in this passage. What do they reveal about Thoreau's **tone?**

The Craft of Expressing Ideas

Formal and Informal Essays Tell students that modern essays tend to be personal and informal. Discuss each of the bulleted essay elements and invite students to suggest how these might appear in either a formal or an informal essay.

Possible answers:

- *Formal essays usually have clearly defined structures with few digressions, while informal essays may have loose and meandering structures.*

- *Supporting details in formal essays may emphasize facts, statistics, and expert opinions, while those in informal essays may emphasize anecdotes, examples, and sensory details.*

- *Diction in informal essays is likely to be conversational and may include colloquialisms, while formal essays will not contain colloquialisms.*

- *A humorous or sarcastic tone would usually not be found in formal essays, which typically have a more serious tone.*

Close Read

Possible answer: *Emerson introduces the idea that people should accept themselves rather than envy or imitate others. Paraphrase: There comes a time in everyone's life when he or she realizes that envying others is pointless; that imitating others is self-destructive; that you have to accept yourself as you are.*

Close Read

Possible answer: *The diction and details reveal that Thoreau's tone is conversational.*

If students need help . . . Direct their attention to the phrases "that is," "by accident," and "made it cool at night," which seem conversational within their historical context. Also point out the use of the first-person pronouns *I* and *my,* which suggest the writer is speaking to the reader, as if in a conversation.

FOR ENGLISH LEARNERS

Language: Skill Words To help students understand *tone,* suggest that they try to hear the author saying the words in their minds. As an example, say, "That's a nice haircut," first seriously and then sarcastically. To clarify *diction,* first say, "That's a nice haircut," and then, "That's a cool haircut." Ask which wording is more casual. *(the second wording)*

FOR ADVANCED LEARNERS/AP

Compare and Contrast Essays Have students find essays by writers such as Michel de Montaigne, Joseph Addison, Richard Steele, Charles Lamb, Robert Louis Stevenson, Virginia Woolf, George Orwell, Jorge Luis Borges, Natalia Ginzburg, Annie Dillard, and Lewis Thomas. Have students choose two writers, then compare and contrast their styles, tones, and topics. Invite students to share their thoughts orally.

Focus and Motivate

OBJECTIVES

Literary Analysis
- explore the key idea of **ideals**
- analyze transcendentalism
- read essays

Reading
- identify aphorisms

Vocabulary
- build vocabulary for reading and writing
- use structural analysis to define words with affixes *(also an EL language objective)*

Grammar and Writing
- use adjective clauses to add descriptive details
- write a speech

CALIFORNIA R2.5, W1.1, W1.3, LC1.1

ABOUT THE AUTHOR

Point out that after Emerson resigned as minister and before he settled in Concord, he traveled to Europe. There he met the English romantic writers William Wordsworth, Samuel Taylor Coleridge, and Thomas Carlyle, and German philosophers and writers whose ideas were a key influence on transcendentalism.

USING THE *NOTABLE QUOTE*

Ask students to explain what **Ralph Waldo Emerson** means when he advises people to "leave a trail." *Possible answer: Emerson thinks people should strive to express new ideas instead of repeating old ones.*

Selection Resources

The Transcendentalists

CALIFORNIA
R2.5, W1.1 (p. 369), W1.3 (p. 369), LC1.1 (p. 369)

from Self-Reliance
from Nature

Essays by Ralph Waldo Emerson

NOTABLE QUOTE

"Do not go where the path may lead, go instead where there is no path and leave a trail."

FYI

Did you know that Ralph Waldo Emerson . . .

- entered Harvard when he was only 14?
- was named class poet at Harvard—but only after seven other students had refused the honor?
- published *Nature*, one of his most famous works, anonymously?

Author Online

For more on Ralph Waldo Emerson, visit the **Literature Center** at **ClassZone.com.**

Old North Bridge, Concord, Massachusetts

Ralph Waldo Emerson
1803–1882

As the acknowledged leader of the transcendentalists, Ralph Waldo Emerson, poet, essayist, and lecturer, was a towering figure in the 19th-century literary world. He helped shape a new, uniquely American body of literature and is often cited as one of the most significant writers in American history. "All life is an experiment," the radical thinker and writer once said. "The more experiments you make, the better."

An Average Student Emerson was born in Boston, Massachusetts. His father, a prominent Unitarian minister, died when Emerson was eight, plunging the family into financial trouble. Although money was tight, funds were found to enroll Emerson at Harvard. When he graduated in 1821, ranked 30th out of a class of 59, there was little indication that Emerson would soon become one of the most celebrated literary figures of all time.

Spiritual Crisis In 1825, Emerson returned to Harvard to study for the Unitarian ministry and was ordained in 1829. Just over a year later, his beloved wife, Ellen, died of tuberculosis. Ellen's death threw Emerson into a state of spiritual crisis, causing him to question many aspects of the Christian tradition and his duties as a minister. In 1832, after much consideration, Emerson resigned his post.

The Voice of Transcendentalism Following his wife's death, Emerson settled in Concord, Massachusetts, and devoted himself to the study of philosophy, religion, and literature. In 1836 Emerson published *Nature,* in which he eloquently articulated his transcendental philosophy, an outgrowth of European romanticism. That same year, Emerson formed the Transcendental Club with a group of like-minded friends, including Henry David Thoreau and Margaret Fuller. *Nature,* with its emphasis on self-reliance and individuality, became the group's unofficial manifesto.

The Sage of Concord Those who met Emerson in person often thought him a rather stiff and formal person, dressed always in black. He reserved his passion for the page and the podium, where he elaborated upon his ideas in essays and a series of popular lectures. By the 1840s the Sage of Concord, as he was known, had become a major literary force whose influence is still evident in American culture today.

360

RESOURCE MANAGER UNIT 2

Plan and Teach pp. 115–122

Literary Analysis
Summary pp. 123†*, 124‡*
Transcendentalism pp. 125, 126†*
Question Support p. 133*

Reading
Identify Aphorisms pp. 127, 128†*
Reading Check p. 132

Vocabulary
Study p. 129*
Practice p. 130
Strategy p. 131

Grammar and Writing
Use Descriptive Details p. 134

Assessment
Selection Tests A, B/C pp. 135*, 137*
Test Generator CD

BEST PRACTICES TOOLKIT

Differentiated Instruction pp. 31–38*

Scaffolding Instruction pp. 43–46*

Graphic Organizers/Strategies
New Word Analysis • Freewriting • Spider Map

Reading Support
- Audio Anthology CD*

Technology
- Literature, Vocabulary, and Writing Centers at **ClassZone.com**
- Write*Smart* CD

---

* Resources for Differentiation   † Also in Spanish   ‡ In Haitian Creole and Vietnamese

LITERARY ANALYSIS: TRANSCENDENTALISM

Ralph Waldo Emerson's motto was "Trust thyself." This principle lies at the heart of **transcendentalism,** an intellectual movement that emphasized the dignity of the individual and advocated a simple, mindful life. The transcendentalists, led by Emerson himself, wanted to transcend—or go beyond—the limitations of the senses and everyday experience. Key tenets of transcendentalism include

- a theory that "transcendent forms" of truth exist beyond reason and experience; every individual is capable of discovering this truth on his or her own, through intuition
- a conviction that people are inherently good and should follow their own beliefs, however controversial they may be
- a belief that humankind, nature, and God are all interconnected

As you read, consider how Emerson's writing articulates his belief in the importance of the individual as well as his ideas about humankind's relationship to the natural world.

READING SKILL: IDENTIFY APHORISMS

An **aphorism** is a brief statement, usually one sentence long, that expresses a general principle or truth about life. Benjamin Franklin's famous declaration "Honesty is the best policy" is one example of an aphorism. As you read, use a chart to record aphorisms that stand out to you. Think about how these statements reflect Emerson's transcendentalist ideals.

"Self-Reliance"	Nature
"Trust thyself: every heart vibrates to that iron string."	

▲ VOCABULARY IN CONTEXT

Emerson uses these words to state his convictions. Test your knowledge by deciding which word is suggested by each phrase.

WORD LIST	aversion	exhilaration	nonconformist
	decorum	importune	occult

1. a food you can't stand
2. a race you have just won
3. a well-behaved crowd
4. a nagging younger sibling

Explore the Key Idea

What is your MOTTO?

KEY IDEA The ancient Roman poet Horace gravely advised, "Never despair." Modern comedian Woody Allen quipped that the secret to success in life is simple: "Eighty percent of success is showing up." Each of these mottos captures an individual's attitude toward life in one pithy phrase. Ralph Waldo Emerson's motto, "Trust thyself," distills the essence of the **ideals** he expressed in his essays and lectures.

QUICKWRITE Create your own personal motto. To get started, consider the traits or resources that helped you solve a difficult problem, or the best advice you've ever given a friend. Use your answers to develop a personal motto that is short and to the point.

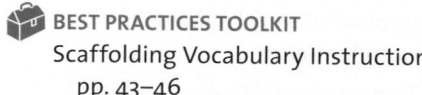

live the life you have imagined

361

Teach

What is your MOTTO?

Lead into the **KEY IDEA** by writing the United States' motto, *E Pluribus Unum* ("From Many, One"), on the board. Discuss why it is an appropriate motto to express our national **ideals.** Then suggest that students consider their own ideals and attitudes as they complete the *QUICKWRITE.*

SKILLS FOCUS

LITERARY ANALYSIS R2.5

● TRANSCENDENTALISM

For instructional support, ask students how the transcendentalists might have reacted to these statements:

1. Some people are just bad apples.
2. Go with your gut.

Possible answers: They would have disagreed with statement 1 because they believed that people are inherently good. They would have agreed with statement 2 because they believed that people should trust their intuition, or "gut."

CHECK UNDERSTANDING Ask students to come up with a statement that the transcendentalists would probably have agreed with, and to explain why.

READING SKILL R2.5

■ IDENTIFY APHORISMS

Point out to students that mottos (like the ones they discussed and created in the **KEY IDEA** activity) are often expressed as aphorisms. Then explain that an aphorism is similar to a proverb—a short, memorable folk saying that expresses a culture's beliefs and wisdom. For more examples, refer students to Benjamin Franklin's aphorisms (page 271), many of which he adapted from traditional proverbs.

R RESOURCE MANAGER—Copy Master
Identify Aphorisms p. 127 (for student use while reading the selections)

VOCABULARY

▲ VOCABULARY IN CONTEXT

DIAGNOSE WORD KNOWLEDGE To determine preteaching needs, have all students complete Vocabulary in Context. *Answers:*
1. *aversion,* 2. *exhilaration,* 3. *decorum,*
4. *importune*

PRETEACH VOCABULARY Preteach vocabulary with this copy master. Read each item aloud.

R RESOURCE MANAGER—Copy Master
Vocabulary Study p. 129

MORE VOCABULARY SUPPORT
For additional activities and guidelines, see

BEST PRACTICES TOOLKIT
Scaffolding Vocabulary Instruction pp. 43–46

ℹ Vocabulary Center at **ClassZone.com**

SUMMARY

In this excerpt from his essay, Emerson argues that people should trust their own judgment about what is right and wrong, rather than conform to other people's opinions. He insists that we should feel free to change our beliefs and concludes by offering historical examples to support his view that "[t]o be great is to be misunderstood."

LITERARY ANALYSIS

Ⓐ TRANSCENDENTALISM

Possible answer: *Summary: Since nothing good comes from envy or imitation, each of us must rely on ourselves and may profit only from our own work. Accept your place in the world, and be confident that God is working through you. "Self-reliance" is reliance on one's own capabilities and instincts.*

If students need help . . . Work through lines 1–11 with them, helping them paraphrase difficult phrases or clauses, such as "imitation is suicide." **Possible answer:** *Imitating others destroys a person's individuality.*

Self-Reliance

RALPH WALDO EMERSON

There is a time in every man's education when he arrives at the conviction that envy is ignorance; that imitation is suicide; that he must take himself for better for worse as his portion; that though the wide universe is full of good, no kernel of nourishing corn can come to him but through his toil bestowed on that plot of ground which is given to him to till. . . .

Trust thyself: every heart vibrates to that iron string. Accept the place the divine providence has found for you, the society of your contemporaries, the connection of events. Great men have always done so, and confided themselves childlike to the genius of their age, betraying their perception that the absolutely trustworthy[1]
10 was seated at their heart, working through their hands, predominating[2] in all their being. . . . Ⓐ

Whoso would be a man, must be a **nonconformist.** He who would gather immortal palms[3] must not be hindered by the name of goodness, but must explore if it be goodness. Nothing is at last sacred but the integrity of your own mind. Absolve you to yourself, and you shall have the suffrage[4] of the world. I remember an answer which when quite young I was prompted to make to a valued adviser

---

1. **the absolutely trustworthy:** God.
2. **predominating:** being predominant, or having controlling influence.
3. **immortal palms:** everlasting triumph and honor. In ancient times, people carried palm leaves as a symbol of victory, success, or joy.
4. **suffrage:** approval; support.

ANALYZE VISUALS
What elements of **transcendentalism** are reflected in the painting on page 363?

❶ Targeted Passage

Ⓐ TRANSCENDENTALISM
Summarize the ideas Emerson presents in lines 1–11. After reading these lines, how would you define self-reliance?

nonconformist
(nŏn′kən-fôr′mĭst) *n.* one who does not follow generally accepted beliefs, customs, or practices

Wanderer Above the Sea of Fog (1818), Caspar David Friedrich. Oil on canvas, 94.8 cm × 74.8 cm.

DIFFERENTIATED INSTRUCTION

FOR ALL STUDENTS

Expert Groups Encourage students to become subject experts by selecting and researching one of these topics:

- background of New England Transcendentalism
- the Transcendental Club
- *The Dial*

FOR STRATEGIC READERS

In combination with the *Audio Anthology CD*, use one or more Targeted Passages (pp. 362, 364, 366) to ensure that students focus on key concepts in these selections. Targeted passages are also good for English learners.

❶ Targeted Passage [Lines 1–11]

This passage introduces Emerson's crucial belief in the importance of relying on oneself.

ANALYZE VISUALS

Possible answers: *The solitary figure reflects the transcendentalist ideal of individualism. His contemplation of an awe-inspiring natural setting reflects the transcendentalist view that nature and humankind are interconnected.*

About the Art The landscapes of the German painter Caspar David Friedrich (1774–1840) capture romanticism's emphasis on the grandeur of nature. *Wanderer Above the Sea of Fog* shows a solitary figure with his back to the viewer, in a pose that recalls Emerson's famous description of himself in the presence of nature: "I become a transparent eye-ball; I am nothing; I see all" (page 365, lines 12–13).

BACKGROUND

Immanuel Kant The German philosopher Immanuel Kant (1724–1804) strongly influenced the transcendentalists. Kant argued that we impose certain structures (such as space, time, and causality) on what we perceive, and we can understand our perceptions only when they conform to this mental system. Kant also believed that there are some "unknowable" concepts (God, freedom, immortality) that exist independently of our mental rules and, therefore, can't be proved or disproved by reason. The transcendentalists reinterpreted Kant's philosophy of "transcendental idealism" to mean that there is knowledge that transcends reason that we can know only by intuition.

- How does Emerson feel about envy and imitation?
- What does Emerson believe that people must do to receive their share of the world's goodness—their "nourishing corn"?
- According to Emerson, why should people trust themselves?

FOR ENGLISH LEARNERS

Key Academic Vocabulary Use New Word Analysis to teach these words: from "Self-Reliance": *integrity* (line 14), *estimate* (line 32); from *Nature: period* (line 6), *reside* (line 26).

 BEST PRACTICES TOOLKIT—Transparency
New Word Analysis p. E8

Prereading For prereading instruction for English learners, see

 BEST PRACTICES TOOLKIT
Scaffolding Reading Instruction pp. 43–46

FOR ADVANCED LEARNERS/AP

AP exercises in the bottom channel provide additional challenge for students. Use these suggestions for small groups or individuals.

ADDITIONAL GUIDELINES

For more help with differentiation and tips for classroom management, see

 BEST PRACTICES TOOLKIT
Differentiated Instruction pp. 31–38

importune (ĭm'pôr-tōōn')
v. to ask urgently or
repeatedly; to annoy
or trouble

who was wont to **importune** me with the dear old doctrines of the church. On my
saying, "What have I to do with the sacredness of traditions, if I live wholly from
within?" my friend suggested—"But these impulses may be from below, not from
20 above." I replied, "They do not seem to me to be such; but if I am the Devil's child,
I will live then from the Devil." No law can be sacred to me but that of my nature.
Good and bad are but names very readily transferable to that or this; the only right
is what is after my constitution;[5] the only wrong what is against it. . . . **B**

What I must do is all that concerns me, not what the people think. This
rule, equally arduous in actual and in intellectual life, may serve for the whole
distinction between greatness and meanness.[6] It is the harder because you will
always find those who think they know what is your duty better than you know it.
It is easy in the world to live after the world's opinion; it is easy in solitude to live
after our own; but the great man is he who in the midst of the crowd keeps with
30 perfect sweetness the independence of solitude. . . . **C**

For nonconformity the world whips you with its displeasure. And therefore
a man must know how to estimate a sour face. The by-standers look askance on
him in the public street or in the friend's parlor. If this **aversion** had its origin
in contempt and resistance like his own he might well go home with a sad
countenance; but the sour faces of the multitude, like their sweet faces, have no
deep cause, but are put on and off as the wind blows and a newspaper directs. . . .

The other terror that scares us from self-trust is our consistency; a reverence for
our past act or word because the eyes of others have no other data for computing
our orbit than our past acts, and we are loth to disappoint them. . . .
40 A foolish consistency is the hobgoblin[7] of little minds, adored by little
statesmen and philosophers and divines.[8] With consistency a great soul has simply
nothing to do. He may as well concern himself with his shadow on the wall. Speak
what you think now in hard words and tomorrow speak what tomorrow thinks
in hard words again, though it contradict everything you said today.—"Ah, so
you shall be sure to be misunderstood."— Is it so bad then to be misunderstood?
Pythagoras was misunderstood, and Socrates, and Jesus, and Luther, and
Copernicus, and Galileo, and Newton,[9] and every pure and wise spirit that ever
took flesh. To be great is to be misunderstood. **D**

B TRANSCENDENTALISM
Transcendentalists
believed in disregarding
external authority in favor
of one's own experience
and intuition. What is
implied by the word
sacred in line 21?

C GRAMMAR AND STYLE
Emerson adds detail and
precision to his writing by
using **adjective clauses**,
which modify nouns
and pronouns. In line
27 and lines 29–30, he
uses adjective clauses
beginning with "who"
to describe specific types
of people.

aversion (ə-vûr'zhən) *n.* a
strong dislike

2 Targeted Passage

D IDENTIFY APHORISMS
Identify at least one
aphorism in lines 40–48.
How does that aphorism
reflect Emerson's
transcendentalist ideals?

---

5. **after my constitution:** consistent with my nature.
6. **meanness:** the state of being inferior in quality, character, or value.
7. **hobgoblin:** a source of fear or dread.
8. **divines:** religious leaders.
9. **Pythagoras** (pǐ-thăg'ər-əs) . . . **Newton:** great thinkers whose radical theories and viewpoints caused
    controversy.

LITERARY ANALYSIS

B TRANSCENDENTALISM

Possible answer: By using the word sacred, *Emerson implies that people should follow their own impulses because these impulses come from God.*

C GRAMMAR AND STYLE

Analyze Adjective Clauses Explain that adjective clauses help writers provide more specific information about a noun or pronoun by telling *which one, what kind,* or *how many.* Ask students to find two adjective clauses beginning with "that" in lines 37–48.

READING SKILL

D IDENTIFY APHORISMS

Possible answer: "To be great is to be mis-understood" (line 48) is an aphorism that reflects Emerson's transcendentalist ideal that people should trust their own intuition and ignore what others think.

Lines 24–31
REINFORCE *KEY IDEA:* IDEALS

Discuss According to Emerson, why is it so hard to follow his **ideal** of nonconformity?
Possible answer: It's hard because people think they know your duty better than you do, and "the world whips you with its displeasure" (line 31) when you ignore popular opinion.

DIFFERENTIATED INSTRUCTION

FOR STRATEGIC READERS

2 Targeted Passage [Lines 37–48]

In this passage, Emerson explains his belief that consistency is unimportant.

- According to Emerson, why are people afraid of being inconsistent?
- What kinds of people think that consistency is important?
- What kinds of people are not afraid to be inconsistent and misunderstood?

FOR ENGLISH LEARNERS

Vocabulary: Multiple-Meaning Words Help students understand Emerson's unusual use of the word *hobgoblin* in the famous sentence in lines 40–41. Clarify that "foolish consistency" is not the "hobgoblin" that "little minds" fear. Rather, the "foolish consistency" of "little minds" is the "hobgoblin" that we should fear. In other words, people with little minds foolishly believe they must be rigidly consistent in their ideas, when they should feel free to change their minds. Note that here, *little*

means "petty" or "narrow in thinking," not "small in size."

Next point out the sentence beginning with "Speak . . ." (lines 42–44). Explain that when Emerson refers to "hard words," *hard* means "strong" or "forceful," not "difficult." Also clarify his unusual use of *tomorrow.* First he uses the word in its conventional way as an adverb ("and tomorrow speak"), but then he uses it in an unconventional way as a noun ("what tomorrow thinks").

Nature

RALPH WALDO EMERSON

Nature is a setting that fits equally well a comic or a mourning piece. In good health, the air is a cordial of incredible virtue. Crossing a bare common, in snow puddles, at twilight, under a clouded sky, without having in my thoughts any occurrence of special good fortune, I have enjoyed a perfect **exhilaration.** I am glad to the brink of fear. In the woods too, a man casts off his years, as the snake his slough,[1] and at what period soever of life, is always a child. In the woods, is perpetual youth. Within these plantations of God, a **decorum** and sanctity reign, a perennial festival is dressed, and the guest sees not how he should tire of them in a thousand years. In the woods, we return to reason and faith. There I feel that
10 nothing can befall me in life,—no disgrace, no calamity, (leaving me my eyes,) which nature cannot repair. Standing on the bare ground,—my head bathed by the blithe air, and uplifted into infinite space,—all mean egotism vanishes. I become a transparent eye-ball; I am nothing; I see all; the currents of the Universal Being circulate through me; I am part or particle of God. The name of the nearest friend sounds then foreign and accidental: to be brothers, to be acquaintances,—master or servant, is then a trifle and a disturbance. I am the lover of uncontained and immortal beauty. In the wilderness, I find something more dear and connate[2] than in streets or villages. In the tranquil landscape, and especially in the distant line of the horizon, man beholds somewhat as beautiful as his own nature. **E**

---

1. **slough** (slŭf): the cast-off skin of a snake.
2. **connate**: agreeable; able to be related to.

exhilaration
(ĭg-zĭl´ə-rā´shən) *n.* a feeling of high spirits or lively joy

decorum (dĭ-kôr´əm) *n.* good taste in conduct or appearance

E TRANSCENDENTALISM
Review the elements of transcendentalism listed on page 361. Which aspect of transcendentalist thought is reflected in lines 12–19?

FOR STRATEGIC READERS

Comprehension Support Emerson's long, complicated sentences often contain a series of phrases or clauses. Model how to break down these sentences by reducing them to their basic components: subject, verb, and object. For example, the sentence in lines 2–4 begins with a series of five phrases, but can be reduced to these parts: *I* (subject) *have enjoyed* (verb) *exhilaration* (object). Have student pairs apply this strategy to the long sentences in lines 5–6, 7–9, and 11–12.

FOR ADVANCED LEARNERS/AP

Analyze Figures of Speech Emerson uses figures of speech to create vivid images and express complex ideas. For example, in line 7 he uses a metaphor when he describes the woods as "plantations of God." Have students analyze the figures of speech in *Nature* and "Self-Reliance." Tell them to pay close attention to implied metaphors—those that suggest a comparison without directly stating it. Have students present their analyses to the class, inviting questions and feedback.

SUMMARY

In this book excerpt, Emerson explores his powerful connection to nature. He says that in the presence of nature, he feels exhilarated, restored, and part of God. We delight in nature, he claims, because we behold in it something as beautiful as our own spiritual nature.

LITERARY ANALYSIS

E TRANSCENDENTALISM

Possible answer: *Lines 12–19 reflect the transcendentalist belief that humankind, nature, and God are all interconnected.*

Lines 1–14
TIERED DISCUSSION PROMPTS

Use these prompts to help students understand Emerson's intense connection to nature:

Connect Have you ever felt "perfect exhilaration" or any other strong emotion in a natural setting? Describe your experience. *Accept all thoughtful responses.*

Interpret What does Emerson mean when he says, "I become a transparent eye-ball" (lines 12–13)? ***Possible answer:*** *He means that in the presence of nature, he feels so connected to nature that he loses the awareness of his own self. Paradoxically, as he observes nature, he becomes part of what he is seeing.*

Synthesize According to Emerson, how are nature, God, and people interconnected? How does this connection reflect the philosophy of transcendentalism? ***Possible answer:*** *Emerson views nature and God as combined. He describes the woods as "plantations of God" (line 7) that inspire "faith" (line 9). He ascribes divine restorative power to nature, claiming that it can repair any misfortune (lines 10–11). He feels merged with nature (lines 11–13), that the "Universal Being circulate[s] through" him (lines 13–14), and that he is "part or particle of God" (line 14). This three-way connection reflects the transcendentalist belief that nature, God, and humankind are interconnected.*

The greatest delight which the fields and woods minister, is the suggestion of an **occult** relation between man and the vegetable. I am not alone and unacknowledged. They nod to me, and I to them. The waving of the boughs in the storm, is new to me and old. It takes me by surprise, and yet is not unknown. Its effect is like that of a higher thought or a better emotion coming over me, when I deemed I was thinking justly or doing right.

Yet it is certain that the power to produce this delight, does not reside in nature, but in man, or in a harmony of both. It is necessary to use these pleasures with great temperance. For, nature is not always tricked[3] in holiday attire, but the same scene which yesterday breathed perfume and glittered as for the frolic of the nymphs, is overspread with melancholy today. Nature always wears the colors of the spirit. To a man laboring under calamity, the heat of his own fire hath sadness in it. Then, there is a kind of contempt of the landscape felt by him who has just lost by death a dear friend. The sky is less grand as it shuts down over less worth in the population. 🔖 **F**

occult (ə-kŭlt') *adj.* secret or hidden from view

❸ Targeted Passage

F TRANSCENDENTALISM
Reread lines 30–34. What is Emerson saying about our perception of the natural world?

ANALYZE VISUALS
Emerson says that "nature always wears the colors of the spirit." What **mood** does this painting convey? Describe the elements of the painting that establish this mood.

---

3. **tricked:** dressed.

Ben Lomond (1829–1830), Thomas Doughty. Oil on canvas. © Christie's Images/SuperStock.

LITERARY ANALYSIS

❻ TRANSCENDENTALISM

Possible answer: *Emerson is saying that our perception of the natural world is colored by our mood.*

If students need help . . . Have them analyze the metaphor in lines 30–31. What are the "colors of the spirit," and how could nature "wear" them?

Extend the Discussion Does every person who feels a certain mood perceive nature in the same way? Explain.

ANALYZE VISUALS

Possible answer: *The painting conveys a tranquil mood. Elements such as the glowing sky and water, the fluffy clouds, and the feathery trees help establish this mood.*

About the Art Thomas Doughty (1793–1856) was an early member of the Hudson River School of landscape painters (see page 293). Like the transcendentalists of the same period, these artists wanted to depict the power and beauty of nature. Doughty is best known for his serene, pastoral landscapes of river valleys.

SELECTION WRAP–UP

SYNTHESIZE Ask students to explain at least one philosophical connection between "Self-Reliance" and *Nature*.

⭐ CRITIQUE

- Ask students whether they find Emerson's transcendentalist ideas persuasive, and why or why not.
- After completing the After Reading questions on page 367, have students revisit their responses and tell whether they have changed their opinions.

DIFFERENTIATED INSTRUCTION

FOR STRATEGIC READERS

❸ Targeted Passage [Lines 20–27]

In this passage, Emerson states his view of the connection between people and nature.

- According to Emerson, what is the "greatest delight" that nature provides?
- What does Emerson mean when he says that the fields and woods "nod" to him?
- What effect does nature have on Emerson?
- What causes our delight in nature?

FOR ADVANCED LEARNERS/AP

Interpret an Image The "transparent eyeball" (lines 12–13) is one of the most famous images in Emerson's writing. Have students write a journal entry interpreting this peculiar image. Tell them to begin by freewriting about what *transparent* means, both literally and figuratively. Encourage students to research how Emerson's idea of the "Over-Soul" connects to this image.

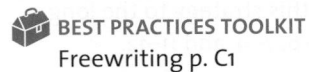 **BEST PRACTICES TOOLKIT**
Freewriting p. C1

Comprehension

R2.5

1. **Recall** According to "Self-Reliance," what is the only law that Emerson can hold sacred?

2. **Summarize** What are three ways the woods can transform a man, according to Emerson in *Nature*?

3. **Clarify** In *Nature*, Emerson discusses the "delight" the natural world often inspires. What does Emerson think this power to delight comes from?

Critical Analysis

4. **Draw Conclusions** Reread lines 37–48 of "Self-Reliance." What is Emerson speaking of when he mentions consistency, and why does he berate it as "the hobgoblin of little minds"? Consider the following examples of Emerson's statements as you formulate your response:

   • "Good and bad are but names very readily transferable to that or this...."
   • "...The sour faces of the multitude ... have no deep cause, but are put on and off as the wind blows...."

5. **Identify Elements of Transcendentalism** Review the elements of transcendentalism listed on page 361. Then reexamine "Self-Reliance" and *Nature*, identifying key ideas that reflect each tenet of transcendentalism. Record your answer in a chart like the one shown.

Element of Transcendentalism	Example from the Text
Every individual is capable of discovering higher truths on his or her own, through intuition.	"Nothing is at last sacred but the integrity of your own mind." ("Self-Reliance," line 14)

6. **Synthesize Ideas** Which **ideals** do the essays celebrate that reflect Emerson's motto, "Trust thyself"? Citing specific lines from both essays, explain how Emerson's main principles relate to his famous motto.

7. **Evaluate Aphorisms** Review the aphorisms you recorded as you read. Choose three or four that you found meaningful or evocative and explain whether or not they have stood the test of time.

Literary Criticism

8. **Critical Interpretation** Writer Henry James argued that Emerson had no concept of the evil that exists in the world. In James's words, it was "a side of life as to which Emerson's eyes were thickly bandaged.... He had no great sense of wrong ... no sense of the dark, the foul, the base." In your opinion, is this a valid criticism of Emerson? Citing evidence, explain why or why not.

SELF–RELIANCE / NATURE **367**

---

7. ■ **SKILLS FOCUS** Identify Aphorisms
Aphorisms such as "Trust thyself" and "Whoso would be a man, must be a nonconformist" are still relevant today, because it's still important to act on one's own principles. Some students will argue that "To be great is to be misunderstood" is still true, because modern society still devalues innovative thinkers.

8. *Students may say that Emerson himself would describe the term "evil" as just a name society ascribes to our actions rather than a definable concept. However, some students may support James's criticism by arguing that Emerson does not explain how his ideal of self-reliance applies to people who have committed terrible crimes.*

After Reading

Use these copy masters to check understanding and provide extra support:

R RESOURCE MANAGER—Copy Masters
Reading Check p. 132
Transcendentalism p. 125
Question Support p. 133

Additional selection questions are provided for teachers on page 119.

ANSWERS

1. *the law of his own intuition*

2. *The woods can make a man feel young again, restore his faith and reason, and create a sense of calm and tranquility.*

3. *The power to delight comes from man or from a harmony between man and nature.*

Possible answers:

4. *By "consistency," Emerson means not changing your beliefs. He berates it by arguing that consistency for its own sake can stifle personal discovery and growth.*

5. ● **SKILLS FOCUS** Transcendentalism
Element: Every individual is capable of discovering higher truths on his or her own, through intuition. Examples: "Nothing is at last sacred ... own mind" ("Self-Reliance," line 14); "No law can be sacred ... the only wrong what is against it" ("Self-Reliance," lines 21–23); "In the woods, we return to reason and faith" (Nature, line 9). Element: People are inherently good and should follow their own beliefs, however controversial these may be. Examples: "Whoso would be a man, must be a nonconformist" ("Self-Reliance," line 12); "What I must do ... the people think" ("Self-Reliance," line 24). Element: Humankind, nature, and God are all interconnected. Examples: "I become a transparent eye-ball ... I am part or particle of God" (Nature, lines 12–14); "The greatest delight ... not alone and unacknowledged" (Nature, lines 20–22); "Nature always ... the spirit" (Nature, lines 30–31).

6. *Students may cite these lines from "Self-Reliance" in support of the motto "Trust thyself": "Nothing is at last ... your own mind" (line 14), "No law can be ... my nature" (line 21), "Speak what you ... everything you said today" (lines 42–44).*

ANSWERS

Vocabulary in Context
VOCABULARY PRACTICE

1. *exhilaration*
2. *importune*
3. *decorum*
4. *occult*
5. *nonconformist*
6. *aversion*

R RESOURCE MANAGER—Copy Master
Vocabulary Practice p. 130

VOCABULARY IN WRITING

Guide students to explain their views to a partner before they begin writing. Have partners identify statements that might lend themselves to a vocabulary word. Tell students that they can incorporate additional vocabulary words as they draft and revise their writing.

VOCABULARY STRATEGY: WORDS WITH MULTIPLE AFFIXES (also an EL language objective)

- Model the practice using these examples: *unmentionable* and *irreplaceable*. Show students how to find the root by removing the prefix and suffix.

- Review spelling rules that apply to added suffixes: Keep the silent *e* if the base word ends in -*ge* or -*ce* and the suffix begins with *a* or *o*, as in *interchangeable* and *unnoticeable*. Keep the final silent *e* before adding a suffix that begins with a consonant, as in *hopefully*.

Possible answers:

1. *fabricate*
2. *diverse*
3. *repute*
4. *page*
5. *fatigue*
6. *negate*

R RESOURCE MANAGER—Copy Master
Vocabulary Strategy p. 131

ℹ Vocabulary Center at ClassZone.com
Additional Vocabulary Activities

Vocabulary in Context

VOCABULARY PRACTICE

Choose the vocabulary word that best completes each sentence.

1. An unexpected tragedy can quickly turn_____ into grief.
2. To constantly _____ a friend for favors can destroy the friendship.
3. One should act with _____ on serious or formal occasions.
4. It is not wise to pry into the _____ intrigues of others.
5. Certain values are held by every person, whether a traditionalist or a(n) _____.
6. It makes sense to avoid anything to which one has a(n) _____.

WORD LIST
aversion
decorum
exhilaration
importune
nonconformist
occult

VOCABULARY IN WRITING

Find a statement in these selections that you strongly agree or disagree with. Identify the statement and, using two or more vocabulary words, explain your views on it. Here is a sample beginning.

> **EXAMPLE SENTENCE**
> I share Emerson's **exhilaration** at walking in the woods, and I, too, see woods as a source of "reason and faith."

VOCABULARY STRATEGY: WORDS WITH MULTIPLE AFFIXES

You can decipher many long words if you are able to locate a recognizable base word within them. Removing the prefix and the suffix from the vocabulary word *nonconformist*, for example, reveals the base word *conform*. What meanings do the affixes add to the base word? Analyze similar words by separating them into a base word and affixes. Remember that many base words drop the final *e* before suffixes are added.

PRACTICE Write the base word and the affixes that make up each word listed. Then write a sentence that demonstrates the meaning of the longer word.

1. prefabricated
2. undiversified
3. disreputable
4. repagination
5. indefatigable
6. abnegation

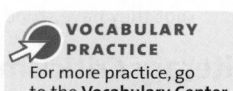

VOCABULARY PRACTICE
For more practice, go to the **Vocabulary Center** at **ClassZone.com**.

DIFFERENTIATED INSTRUCTION

FOR ENGLISH LEARNERS

Task Support: Vocabulary Practice Point out that the French cognate *conformer* is similar to the English word *conform*, which forms the base word in *nonconformist*. Encourage students who speak Latin-based languages to search for and explain vocabulary words similar to those in their home languages. Have students compare the similarities in their languages.

FOR ADVANCED LEARNERS/AP

Words with Multiple Affixes Use the word *transcendentalism* as the first entry on a list of words with multiple affixes. Have students add to the list by locating other multiple-affix words in the two Emerson pieces. Then challenge students to exchange word lists with a partner and try to create new forms for each of their partner's words by adding, removing, or replacing affixes.

Reading-Writing Connection

 W1.1, W1.3

WRITING PROMPT

UPDATE EMERSON'S MESSAGE Emerson's ideas about nonconformity were radical for their time—and they are still relevant today. Write a **three-to-five-paragraph speech** in which you present an updated version of Emerson's message for an audience of contemporary high school students. Recast his ideas about the importance of the individual, using up-to-date examples and descriptive details that will resonate with your audience.

SELF-CHECK

An effective speech will . . .

- have a clear thesis
- reflect the **ideals** and values Emerson presented in "Self-Reliance" and *Nature*
- engage the audience with relevant examples

GRAMMAR AND STYLE

USE DESCRIPTIVE DETAILS Review the **Grammar and Style** note on page 364. The power and precision of Emerson's prose owes a good deal to his skillful use of **adjective clauses**—subordinate clauses that, like adjectives, add important detail about nouns and pronouns. An adjective clause usually follows the word it modifies and is introduced by words such as *when, who, whom, whose, that,* and *which.* Here is an example from "Self-Reliance":

 LC1.1

> There is a time in every man's education when he arrives at the conviction that envy is ignorance; that imitation is suicide; that he must take himself for better for worse as his portion.... (lines 1–3)

Notice that each of the highlighted phrases offers information about the word it modifies. The first phrase tells you about the "time in every man's education" Emerson is discussing. The second, third, and fourth clauses explain what kind of convictions he embraces at this time.

PRACTICE Identify the adjective clause in each sentence from Emerson's work. Then write your own sentences, using adjective clauses as Emerson does.

EXAMPLE

He who would gather immortal palms must not be hindered by the name of goodness, but must explore if it be goodness.

Those who wish to make a true difference cannot worry what others might say behind their backs.

1. There is a kind of contempt of the landscape felt by him who has just lost by death a dear friend.
2. Nature is a setting that fits equally well a comic or a mourning piece.
3. There I feel that nothing can befall me in life,—no disgrace, no calamity, (leaving my eyes,) which nature cannot repair.

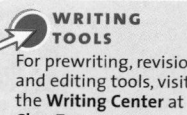 **WRITING TOOLS**
For prewriting, revision, and editing tools, visit the **Writing Center** at ClassZone.com.

FOR DEVELOPING WRITERS

Writing Support

- Limit the length of the speech to two or three paragraphs.
- Provide a sentence starter for students to use as they draft their thesis statements (such as *Emerson's ideas about self-reliance are still relevant today because* _____).
- Have students read their speeches aloud to a partner.

Reading-Writing Connection

WRITING PROMPT

Explain that the most convincing up-to-date examples of nonconformity would show how an individual's nontraditional thinking yielded a positive outcome. Have students use a Spider Map to list key ideals of Emerson's essays and contemporary examples that support each view.

BEST PRACTICES TOOLKIT—Transparency
Spider Map p. B22

For writing support, see

Writing Center at ClassZone.com

GRAMMAR AND STYLE

Tell students that they can improve their writing by using adjective clauses to combine short, choppy sentences. Have them reread their speeches, looking for ways to add adjective clauses. Before students complete the **PRACTICE,** explain that in the third sentence, Emerson uses *which* in an old-fashioned way; in modern usage, we begin an essential adjective clause with *that.* (For more on adjective clauses, see **Grammar Handbook,** page R67.)

Possible answers:

1. **Clause:** "who has just lost by death a dear friend." There is a kind of happiness felt by those who have just aced a test.
2. **Clause:** "that fits equally well a comic or a mourning piece." A library is a place that houses a wealth of knowledge.
3. **Clause:** "which nature cannot repair." There is no challenge that I can't overcome.

RESOURCE MANAGER—Copy Master
Use Descriptive Details p. 134

Assess and Reteach

Assess

RESOURCE MANAGER—Copy Masters
Selection Test A pp. 135–136
Selection Test B/C pp. 137–138

Test Generator CD

Reteach

STANDARDS LESSON FILE
Vocabulary Lesson 1
Speaking and Listening Lesson 1

Focus and Motivate

OBJECTIVES

Literary Analysis
- explore the key idea of **nonconformity**
- analyze essays
- read essays and a magazine article

Reading
- evaluate ideas

Vocabulary
- build vocabulary for reading and writing
- apply knowledge of the prefixes *ab-* and *per-* (also an EL language objective)

Grammar and Writing
- use interrogative sentences to ask rhetorical questions
- use writing to analyze literature

 R2.5, R3.3, R1.2, W1.1, W1.3, W1.4, W1.9, W2.2

ABOUT THE AUTHOR

Emphasize the importance of Thoreau's friendship with Emerson. Emerson urged Thoreau to keep a journal, and he published Thoreau's work in the transcendentalist magazine *The Dial*. Emerson also owned the land on which Thoreau built his cabin.

USING THE *NOTABLE QUOTE*

Discuss what students think **Henry David Thoreau** means by "lives of quiet desperation." *Possible answer: Thoreau means a way of life that people find hopelessly frustrating but suffer through instead of trying to improve.*

Selection Resources

---

from Walden
from Civil Disobedience

Essays by Henry David Thoreau

CALIFORNIA

R2.5, R3.3, R1.2 (p. 390), W1.1 (p. 391), W1.3 (p. 391), W1.4 (p. 391), W1.9 (p. 391), W2.2 (p. 391)

NOTABLE QUOTE

"The mass of men lead lives of quiet desperation."

FYI

Did you know that Henry David Thoreau . . .

- worked off and on as a pencil maker in his family's pencil factory?
- kept a journal that when published filled 20 volumes?
- pared down his expenses to 27 cents a week, which he earned by working only six weeks a year?

Author Online

For more on Henry David Thoreau, visit the **Literature Center** at ClassZone.com.

370

Henry David Thoreau
1817–1862

Henry David Thoreau (thə-rō′) advocated simple, mindful living and rejected a lifestyle dedicated to the pursuit of wealth. Thoreau spent much of his life writing and observing nature, devoting only a minimum of time to earning a wage. He published just two books, both of which sold very poorly in his own lifetime. Few of his contemporaries would have judged him much of a success. In the years since his death, however, his reputation has grown tremendously. Today, he is regarded as a writer of uncommon vision and remembered as one of the first environmentalists.

Independent Spirit Thoreau was born and raised in Concord, Massachusetts, and attended Harvard University. After graduating, he returned to Concord to teach school. Though some of Thoreau's neighbors viewed him as eccentric, he was a careful observer and a deep thinker. Taking to heart the ideas of his friend Ralph Waldo Emerson, Thoreau tried to live by his own values, often doing odd jobs that would earn him just enough money to meet his own modest needs.

Defiant Nonconformist Thoreau's life was full of examples of his nonconformity to society's norms. As a Harvard student, he was required to wear a black coat but sported a green one instead. In his first year of teaching, he refused to punish his students physically, a harsh but common practice of the time, and resigned his post. In 1845, he conducted his famous experiment, living simply and frugally in a small cabin on the shores of Walden Pond. In 1846, he was arrested and spent a night in jail for refusing to pay a poll tax, an act of protest against the U.S. government's war with Mexico and its support of slavery. This exercise of conscience over law later became known as civil disobedience.

Influential Thinker At the time of Thoreau's death from tuberculosis at age 44, he was viewed as an unsuccessful nature writer. Today, however, he is known as the father of American nature writing and an important political thinker. His observations about the natural world and the value of the simple life, as well as his promotion of nonviolent protest, have helped bring about great societal change. He has provided inspiration to many, including conservationist John Muir and civil rights leader Martin Luther King Jr.

 RESOURCE MANAGER UNIT 2

Plan and Teach pp. 139–146

Literary Analysis
Summary pp. 147†*, 148‡*, 149†*, 150‡*
Essay pp. 151, 152†*
Question Support pp. 159*, 160*

Reading
Evaluate Ideas pp. 153, 154†*
Reading Check p. 158

Vocabulary
Study p. 155*
Practice p. 156
Strategy p. 157

Grammar and Writing
Ask Rhetorical Questions p. 161

Assessment
Selection Tests A, B/C pp. 163*, 165*
Test Generator CD

 BEST PRACTICES TOOLKIT

Differentiated Instruction pp. 31–38*

Scaffolding Instruction pp. 43–46*

Graphic Organizers/Strategies
Definition Mapping • Open Mind • Word Questioning • Venn Diagram

Reading Support
- Audio Anthology CD*

Technology
- Literature, Vocabulary, and Writing Centers at ClassZone.com
- WriteSmart CD

 Resources for Differentiation † Also in Spanish ‡ In Haitian Creole and Vietnamese

● LITERARY ANALYSIS: ESSAY

An **essay** is a work of nonfiction that usually deals with a single main subject. Though essays can be formal or informal, they are often loosely structured and contain the personal views of the writer. To analyze an essay, pay careful attention to

- the writer's **tone,** or attitude toward his or her subject
- **figurative language** that makes abstract concepts more understandable and emphasizes ideas
- **anecdotes,** or short accounts of personal incidents
- **imagery** that creates vivid impressions for the reader

As you read, consider how these elements illuminate Thoreau's ideas and give readers a glimpse into his personality.

Review: Transcendentalism

■ READING SKILL: EVALUATE IDEAS

When you **evaluate** a writer's ideas, you examine them carefully and then make judgments about their value. Before you can judge a writer's ideas, however, you have to identify and understand them. **Summarizing** can help. As you read *Walden,* use a chart like the one shown to briefly restate Thoreau's philosophical ideas in your own words. As you tackle "Civil Disobedience," summarize the author's main political beliefs. After you summarize each idea, note your reaction to it.

	Thoreau's Ideas and Beliefs	My Reactions
Walden		
"Civil Disobedience"		

▲ VOCABULARY IN CONTEXT

Thoreau uses the following words to present his theories about simple, principled living. To see how many you know, choose the word that is closest in meaning to each numbered term.

WORD LIST	abject	impetuous	pervade
	congenial	misgiving	transgress
	deliberately	perturbation	

1. err
2. disturbance
3. doubt
4. wretched
5. friendly
6. permeate
7. impulsive
8. thoughtfully

Do you chart your own COURSE?

KEY IDEA "Cranks," "crackpots," "oddballs"—society is quick to apply a negative label to people outside the mainstream. Although Thoreau was probably never called an "oddball," he was certainly regarded as an eccentric. **Nonconformity** has never been an easy choice, as people often condemn nonconformists without bothering to find out why they embrace a different set of values. Nevertheless, history has shown that many nonconformists, like Thoreau, are often simply ahead of their time.

DISCUSS With a small group of classmates, create a list of famous nonconformists. How did the individuals you listed depart from the norms of their time? Were they punished for their actions? Were they able to win others to their point of view? Discuss these questions with your group.

Do you chart your own COURSE?

Ask the question, making sure that students understand the figure of speech. As students read the **KEY IDEA**, call on volunteers to suggest examples of **nonconformity** in tastes, opinions, and so on. Use responses to prompt the *DISCUSS* activity, and invite groups to share the lists that they create.

SKILLS FOCUS

LITERARY ANALYSIS   R3.3

● ESSAY

Share this example with students:

> The silvery pond was a mirror, reflecting the trees that leaned over the water, as if dipping their boughs into the sky.

Discuss the ideas that the figurative language in this image might evoke. **Possible answer:** *The figurative language might evoke the almost magical beauty of a natural scene and, therefore, a deep respect for nature.*

CHECK UNDERSTANDING Ask students how the imagery might change if the author wanted to convey an angry tone.

READING SKILL   R2.5

■ EVALUATE IDEAS

Have students summarize **Defiant Nonconformist** in the Thoreau biography and then express a reaction to it. **Possible answer:** *As a student and then a teacher, Thoreau refused to live by rules with which he disagreed. He lived simply at Walden Pond, and he briefly went to jail for refusing to pay a tax he felt was wrong. Reactions will vary.*

 RESOURCE MANAGER—Copy Master
Evaluate Ideas p. 153 (for student use while reading the selections)

VOCABULARY

▲ VOCABULARY IN CONTEXT

DIAGNOSE WORD KNOWLEDGE To determine preteaching needs, have all students complete Vocabulary in Context. **Answers:**
1. *transgress,* 2. *perturbation,* 3. *misgiving,*
4. *abject,* 5. *congenial,* 6. *pervade,*
7. *impetuous,* 8. *deliberately*

PRETEACH VOCABULARY Preteach vocabulary with this copy master. Read each item aloud.

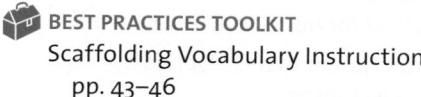 **RESOURCE MANAGER—Copy Master**
Vocabulary Study p. 155

MORE VOCABULARY SUPPORT
For additional activities and guidelines, see

BEST PRACTICES TOOLKIT
Scaffolding Vocabulary Instruction pp. 43–46
ℹ Vocabulary Center at **ClassZone.com**

Practice and Apply

SUMMARY

In these essay excerpts, Thoreau explains that he went to Walden Pond to experience the essentials of life. He describes feeling in tune with nature and being transformed by following his personal vision. Anecdotes such as the tale of a bug that hatches after a 60-year dormancy convey Thoreau's hope for human revival and transcendence.

LITERARY ANALYSIS

Ⓐ ESSAY

Possible answer: *Thoreau's tone is admiring (lines 6–9). The reader gets the sense that the essay will show the writer as someone who enjoys a simpler life and wants to share the benefits of simple, purposeful living.*

If students need help . . . Point out words and phrases with positive connotations, such as *abode, freshly planed, clean and airy,* and *saturated with dew,* to help students identify the tone as admiring.

Extend the Discussion On what day does Thoreau move into the house, full-time? What does that fact suggest about his views or personality, even though he calls the date an accident (line 2)?

WALDEN

Henry David Thoreau

> **BACKGROUND** Like Ralph Waldo Emerson and other transcendentalists, Thoreau felt a need to affirm his unity with nature. On July 4, 1845, he began an experiment in what he thought of as "essential living"—living simply, studying the natural world, and seeking truth within himself. On land owned by Emerson near Concord, Massachusetts, Thoreau built a small cabin by Walden Pond and lived there for more than two years, writing and studying nature. *Walden* is the record of his experiences.

from WHERE I LIVED, AND WHAT I LIVED FOR

When first I took up my abode in the woods, that is, began to spend my nights as well as days there, which, by accident, was on Independence day, or the fourth of July, 1845, my house was not finished for winter, but was merely a defense against the rain, without plastering or chimney, the walls being of rough weather-stained boards, with wide chinks, which made it cool at night. The upright white hewn studs and freshly planed door and window casings gave it a clean and airy look, especially in the morning, when its timbers were saturated with dew, so that I fancied that by noon some sweet gum would exude from them. . . . Ⓐ

10   I was seated by the shore of a small pond, about a mile and a half south of the village of Concord and somewhat higher than it, in the midst of an extensive wood between that town and Lincoln, and about two miles south of that our only field known to fame, Concord Battle Ground; but I was so low in the woods that the opposite shore, half a mile off, like the rest, covered with wood, was my most distant horizon. For the first week, whenever I looked out on the pond it impressed me like a tarn high up

ANALYZE VISUALS
Consider the tranquil scene depicted in the photograph on page 373. What aspect of the photograph is most responsible for conveying this sense of tranquility, and why?

❶ Targeted Passage

Ⓐ ESSAY
Think about Thoreau's **tone** as he describes his crude, unfinished house. What sense of the writer's views or personality do you get from these opening lines?

16 tarn: a small mountain lake or pool.

DIFFERENTIATED INSTRUCTION

FOR ALL STUDENTS

Provide these independent projects to extend the lesson:

- Prepare and conduct a mock trial of Thoreau for his refusal to pay taxes.
- Write a poem that is inspired by Thoreau's ideas.

For further details on these projects, see

Ⓡ RESOURCE MANAGER
Ideas for Extension pp. 144–145

FOR STRATEGIC READERS

In combination with the *Audio Anthology CD,* use one or more Targeted Passages (pp. 372, 376, 379, 382, 387, 388) to ensure that students focus on key concepts in these selections. Targeted passages are also good for English learners.

❶ Targeted Passage [Lines 1–15]

This passage introduces the setting outside Concord, Massachusetts where Thoreau's personal exploration will take place.

Possible answer: The sense of tranquility is conveyed mainly by the stillness of the pond. The gentle light on the pond and the leafy trees also add to the sense of peace. All of these features suggest a welcoming place where a visitor might rest and contemplate the scene.

BACKGROUND

The Walden Pond Cabin Thoreau's house was only 10 feet wide and 15 feet long—just large enough for a bed, a table, a desk, and three chairs. To save money on construction, Thoreau bought used windows, boards, and bricks from people whose houses were being torn down. His careful journal shows that the entire cabin cost him $28.12, an extremely low cost even by 1845 standards. The minimal price of construction, the small size of the cabin, and its setting in the woods allowed Thoreau to live up to his ideals of simplicity and appreciation of nature.

- At what time of year does Thoreau begin living in the house?
- How does Thoreau describe his house?
- What natural features surround Thoreau in his new home?

FOR ENGLISH LEARNERS

Prereading For prereading instruction for English learners, see

 BEST PRACTICES TOOLKIT
Scaffolding Reading Instruction pp. 43–46

FOR ADVANCED LEARNERS/AP

AP exercises in the bottom channel provide additional challenge for students. Use these suggestions for small groups or individuals.

ADDITIONAL GUIDELINES

For more help with differentiation and tips for classroom management, see

 BEST PRACTICES TOOLKIT
Differentiated Instruction pp. 31–38

B EVALUATE IDEAS

Possible answer: *Summary: Thoreau moved to the woods to live simply and deliberately and to experience the essence of life. Accept all thoughtful opinions.*

Extend the Discussion In lines 34–37, Thoreau refers to the first item in the *Westminster Larger Catechism,* a collection of questions and answers relating to the doctrine held by Puritans and some other Protestant groups. How does Thoreau—as an individual or as a transcendentalist—feel about that particular teaching? What would he say is "the chief end of man"?

C ESSAY

Possible answer: *The "clouds and storms and quicksands" might be the troubles that accompany a full, civilized life, such as problems with jobs, family, and finances. These demands might cause a person to "founder"—that is, to be so busy that he or she becomes incapable of discovering the real essence of life, which exists beyond everyday experience.*

If students need help . . . Explain that Thoreau uses the word *civilized* to refer to life in groups or communities. He is suggesting not that his life at Walden Pond is uncivilized, but that it is simple and uncomplicated.

---

on the side of a mountain, its bottom far above the surface of other lakes, and, as the sun arose, I saw it throwing off its nightly clothing of mist, and here and there, by degrees, its soft ripples or its smooth reflecting surface
20 was revealed, while the mists, like ghosts, were stealthily withdrawing in every direction into the woods, as at the breaking up of some nocturnal conventicle. The very dew seemed to hang upon the trees later into the day than usual, as on the sides of mountains. . . .

I went to the woods because I wished to live **deliberately,** to front only the essential facts of life, and see if I could not learn what it had to teach, and not, when I came to die, discover that I had not lived. I did not wish to live what was not life, living is so dear; nor did I wish to practice resignation, unless it was quite necessary. I wanted to live deep and suck out all the marrow of life, to live so sturdily and Spartan-like as to put to rout all that
30 was not life, to cut a broad swath and shave close, to drive life into a corner, and reduce it to its lowest terms, and, if it proved to be mean, why then to get the whole and genuine meanness of it, and publish its meanness to the world; or if it were sublime, to know it by experience, and be able to give a true account of it in my next excursion. For most men, it appears to me, are in a strange uncertainty about it, whether it is of the devil or of God, and have *somewhat hastily* concluded that it is the chief end of man here to "glorify God and enjoy him forever." **B**

Still we live meanly, like ants; though the fable tells us that we were long ago changed into men; like pygmies we fight with cranes; it is error
40 upon error, and clout upon clout, and our best virtue has for its occasion a superfluous and evitable wretchedness. Our life is frittered away by detail. An honest man has hardly need to count more than his ten fingers, or in extreme cases he may add his ten toes, and lump the rest. Simplicity, simplicity, simplicity! I say, let your affairs be as two or three, and not a hundred or a thousand; instead of a million count half a dozen, and keep your accounts on your thumbnail. In the midst of this chopping sea of civilized life, such are the clouds and storms and quicksands and thousand-and-one items to be allowed for, that a man has to live, if he would not founder and go to the bottom and not make his port at all, by dead
50 reckoning, and he must be a great calculator indeed who succeeds. Simplify, simplify. Instead of three meals a day, if it be necessary eat but one; instead of a hundred dishes, five; and reduce other things in proportion. . . . **C**

Why should we live with such hurry and waste of life? We are determined to be starved before we are hungry. Men say that a stitch in time saves nine, and so they take a thousand stitches today to save nine to-morrow. As for *work,* we haven't any of any consequence. We have the Saint Vitus' dance, and cannot possibly keep our heads still. If I should only give a few pulls at the parish bell-rope, as for a fire, that is, without setting the bell, there is hardly a man on his farm in the outskirts of Concord, notwithstanding that
60 press of engagements which was his excuse so many times this morning,

22 conventicle: a secret religious meeting.

deliberately (dĭ-lĭb'ər-ĭt-lē) *adv.* in an unhurried and thoughtful manner

29 Spartan-like: in a simple and disciplined way, like the inhabitants of the ancient city-state of Sparta.

B EVALUATE IDEAS
Reread lines 24–37. **Summarize** Thoreau's reasons for moving to the woods. What do you think of these reasons?

41 evitable: avoidable.

C ESSAY
In this essay, Thoreau often uses **figurative language** to present his observations. In lines 46–50, he likens civilized life to a rough sea. What might "the clouds and storms and quicksand" of life be? How might one "founder," or sink, in civilized life?

56 Saint Vitus' dance: a disorder of the nervous system, characterized by rapid, jerky, involuntary movements.

DIFFERENTIATED INSTRUCTION

FOR ENGLISH LEARNERS
Key Academic Vocabulary Use Definition Mapping to teach these words: *error* (line 39), *distinct* (line 168), *liberal* (line 180), *complex* (line 184), *mature* (line 192), *annual* (line 240).

 BEST PRACTICES TOOLKIT—Transparency Definition Mapping p. E6

FOR ADVANCED LEARNERS/AP
Make Judgments [small-group option] Ask students to reread and reflect upon lines 41–52, in which Thoreau criticizes overly complex lives. Then have students write an essay in which they respond to these questions:

• What does Thoreau mean when he says, "Our life is frittered away by detail" (line 41)?

• What are the advantages and disadvantages of living simply?

• What would it mean to simplify life to the barest necessities? Give examples.

• Do you agree with Thoreau's views on this topic? Why or why not?

Invite students to meet in small groups to compare their responses.

nor a boy, nor a woman, I might almost say, but would forsake all and follow that sound, not mainly to save property from the flames, but, if we will confess the truth, much more to see it burn, since burn it must, and we, be it known, did not set it on fire,—or to see it put out, and have a hand in it, if that is done as handsomely; yes, even if it were the parish church itself. Hardly a man takes a half hour's nap after dinner, but when he wakes he holds up his head and asks, "What's the news?" as if the rest of mankind had stood his sentinels. Some give directions to be waked every half hour, doubtless for no other purpose; and then, to pay for it, they tell
70 what they have dreamed. After a night's sleep the news is as indispensable as the breakfast. "Pray tell me any thing new that has happened to a man any where on this globe,"—and he reads it over his coffee and rolls, that a man has had his eyes gouged out this morning on the Wachito River; never dreaming the while that he lives in the dark unfathomed mammoth cave of this world, and has but the rudiment of an eye himself. **D**

For my part, I could easily do without the post-office. I think that there are very few important communications made through it. To speak critically, I never received more than one or two letters in my life—I wrote this some years ago—that were worth the postage. The penny-post is, commonly,
80 an institution through which you seriously offer a man that penny for his thoughts which is so often safely offered in jest. And I am sure that I never read any memorable news in a newspaper. If we read of one man robbed, or murdered, or killed by accident, or one house burned, or one vessel wrecked, or one steamboat blown up, or one cow run over on the Western Railroad, or one mad dog killed, or one lot of grasshoppers in the winter,—we never need read of another. One is enough. . . .

Let us spend one day as deliberately as Nature, and not be thrown off the track by every nutshell and mosquito's wing that falls on the rails. Let us rise early and fast, or break fast, gently and without **perturbation;** let
90 company come and let company go, let the bells ring and the children cry,— determined to make a day of it. . . .

Time is but the stream I go a-fishing in. I drink at it; but while I drink I see the sandy bottom and detect how shallow it is. Its thin current slides away, but eternity remains. I would drink deeper; fish in the sky, whose bottom is pebbly with stars. I cannot count one. I know not the first letter of the alphabet. I have always been regretting that I was not as wise as the day I was born. The intellect is a cleaver; it discerns and rifts its way into the secret of things. I do not wish to be any more busy with my hands than is necessary. My head is hands and feet. I feel all my best faculties concentrated
100 in it. My instinct tells me that my head is an organ for burrowing, as some creatures use their snout and fore-paws, and with it I would mine and burrow my way through these hills. I think that the richest vein is somewhere hereabouts; so by the divining rod and thin rising vapors I judge; and here I will begin to mine. **E**

D ESSAY
What situation does Thoreau exaggerate in lines 66–75? Would you respond differently to Thoreau's point if he simply stated his views on this subject?

79–81 penny-post . . . jest: Thoreau jokingly connects the postage rate at the time (a penny per letter) with the phrase "a penny for your thoughts."

perturbation (pûr′tər-bā′shən) *n.* disturbance of the emotions; agitation; uneasiness

E EVALUATE IDEAS
Summarize lines 87–104. What does Thoreau want to spend his time trying to understand, and how does he plan to achieve this understanding? Decide what you think about this desire.

WALDEN **375**

This is a delicious evening, when the whole body is one sense, and imbibes delight through every pore. I go and come with a strange liberty in Nature, a part of herself. As I walk along the stony shore of the pond in my shirt sleeves, though it is cool as well as cloudy and windy, and I see nothing special to attract me, all the elements are unusually **congenial** to me. The

110 bullfrogs trump to usher in the night, and the note of the whippoorwill is borne on the rippling wind from over the water. Sympathy with the fluttering alder and poplar leaves almost takes away my breath; yet, like the lake, my serenity is rippled but not ruffled. These small waves raised by the evening wind are as remote from storm as the smooth reflecting surface. Though it is now dark, the wind still blows and roars in the wood, the waves still dash, and some creatures lull the rest with their notes. The repose is never complete. The wildest animals do not repose, but seek their prey now; the fox, and skunk, and rabbit, now roam the fields and woods without fear. They are Nature's watchmen,—links which connect the days

120 of animated life. . . .

> Men frequently say to me, "I should think you would feel lonesome down there, and want to be nearer to folks, rainy and snowy days and nights especially." I am tempted to reply to such,—This whole earth which we inhabit is but a point in space. How far apart, think you, dwell the two most distant inhabitants of yonder star, the breadth of whose disk cannot be appreciated by our instruments? Why should I feel lonely? Is not our planet in the Milky Way? This which you put seems to me not to be the most important question. What sort of space is that which separates a man from his fellows and makes him solitary? I have found that no exertion of the legs
>
> 130 can bring two minds much nearer to one another. . . . **F**

congenial (kən-jēn'yəl) *adj.* suited to one's needs or nature; agreeable

② Targeted Passage

F EVALUATE IDEAS
Reread lines 121–130. **Summarize** Thoreau's ideas about loneliness. Do you agree with his assessment of this condition? Explain your answer.

from THE POND IN WINTER

Every winter the liquid and trembling surface of the pond, which was so sensitive to every breath, and reflected every light and shadow, becomes solid to the depth of a foot or a foot and a half, so that it will support the heaviest teams, and perchance the snow covers it to an equal depth, and it is not to be distinguished from any level field. Like the marmots in the surrounding hills, it closes its eye-lids and becomes dormant for three months or more. Standing on the snow-covered plain, as if in a pasture amid the hills, I cut my way first through a foot of snow, and then a foot of ice, and open a window under my feet, where, kneeling to drink, I look down into the quiet

140 parlor of the fishes, **pervaded** by a softened light as through a window of

135 **marmots:** burrowing rodents that hibernate in winter; also known as groundhogs or woodchucks.

pervade (pər-vād') *v.* to spread through every part of

F EVALUATE IDEAS

Possible answer: Summary: Loneliness is a result of spiritual distance between us, not physical distance. This is true because people can be physically close to others but feel lonely because they are spiritually disconnected. Students may say that they or others have felt lonely in a crowd because people don't always stop to understand an individual's emotions.

If students need help . . . Work with them to add to the chart introduced on page 371.

Essay	Thoreau's Ideas and Beliefs	My Reactions
Walden	Loneliness is a result of spiritual separation, not physical distance.	I feel distant from people if we don't understand each other, even if we are physically close.

DIFFERENTIATED INSTRUCTION

FOR STRATEGIC READERS

② Targeted Passage [Lines 121–130]

This passage illustrates Thoreau's views on solitude and loneliness.

- What does Thoreau frequently hear from other people?
- How does he respond to these comments?
- According to Thoreau, what truly makes people lonely?

FOR ADVANCED LEARNERS/AP

Analyze Tone [paired option] Remind students that word choice is one element that a writer uses to create tone. Have students analyze the tone of lines 105–120 and then create a diagram that identifies the tone and cites specific words and phrases that contribute to it. After students have presented their diagrams, invite the class to explore differences in interpretation.

ground glass, with its bright sanded floor the same as in summer; there a perennial waveless serenity reigns as in the amber twilight sky, corresponding to the cool and even temperament of the inhabitants. Heaven is under our feet as well as over our heads. . . . **G**

from SPRING

One attraction in coming to the woods to live was that I should have leisure and opportunity to see the spring come in. The ice in the pond at length begins to be honey-combed, and I can set my heel in it as I walk. Fogs and rains and warmer suns are gradually melting the snow; the days have grown sensibly longer; and I see how I shall get through the winter without adding
150 to my woodpile, for large fires are no longer necessary. I am on the alert for the first signs of spring, to hear the chance note of some arriving bird, or the striped squirrel's chirp, for his stores must be now nearly exhausted, or see the woodchuck venture out of his winter quarters. . . .

The change from storm and winter to serene and mild weather, from dark and sluggish hours to bright and elastic ones, is a memorable crisis which all things proclaim. It is seemingly instantaneous at last. Suddenly an influx of light filled my house, though the evening was at hand, and the clouds of winter still overhung it, and the eaves were dripping with sleety rain. I looked out the window, and lo! where yesterday was cold gray ice there lay
160 the transparent pond already calm and full of hope as in a summer evening, reflecting a summer evening sky in its bosom, though none was visible overhead, as if it had intelligence with some remote horizon. . . . **H**

from CONCLUSION

I left the woods for as good a reason as I went there. Perhaps it seemed to me that I had several more lives to live, and could not spare any more time for that one. It is remarkable how easily and insensibly we fall into a particular route, and make a beaten track for ourselves. I had not lived there a week before my feet wore a path from my door to the pond-side; and though it is five or six years since I trod it, it is still quite distinct. It is true, I fear that others may have fallen into it, and so helped to keep it open. The surface of
170 the earth is soft and impressible by the feet of men; and so with the paths which the mind travels. How worn and dusty, then, must be the highways of the world, how deep the ruts of tradition and conformity! I did not wish to take a cabin passage, but rather to go before the mast and on the deck of

G TRANSCENDENTALISM
What transcendentalist ideal is reflected in lines 143–144?

149 **sensibly:** noticeably.

H ESSAY
Imagery is a common feature of nature writing. Identify details in lines 145–162 that recreate sensory experiences for the reader. In what ways does this descriptive language enhance your mental picture of Walden Pond?

172–175 On a sailing ship, passengers stayed in private compartments, or cabins, near the middle of the ship, while the crew shared living quarters at the front, where more was visible.

WALDEN **377**

❶ ESSAY

Possible answer: Thoreau compares life to a voyage on a ship. The metaphor conveys Thoreau's reasons for leaving by explaining that he wants to be on "the deck of the world," participating in the voyage of life, not hidden away in a "cabin passage" (lines 173–174).

Lines 176–187
TIERED DISCUSSION PROMPTS

Use these prompts to explore what Thoreau has learned from his time at Walden Pond:

Recall What was the goal of Thoreau's experiment? *Possible answer: Thoreau wanted to see what he could learn by living simply and deliberately (lines 24–52).*

Interpret What does Thoreau mean by saying that castles should be built in the air? *Possible answer: Thoreau means that dreaming great goals is good for the spirit.* How has living at Walden Pond helped Thoreau build castles in the air? *Possible answer: Getting away from society's routines has made dreaming easier.*

Synthesize In what ways has Thoreau achieved his goals at Walden Pond? *Possible answer: Thoreau has learned to live life deliberately and simply. He has also realized that pursuing dreams is very important for personal growth.*

❶ TRANSCENDENTALISM

Possible answer: Thoreau embraces the transcendentalist value of following one's own beliefs—that is, living according to one's intuition rather than to society's expectations.

If students need help . . . Discuss the "different drummer" analogy. Elicit that Thoreau wants people to follow their personal beats, even if they fall out of step with others.

---

the world, for there I could best see the moonlight amid the mountains. I do not wish to go below now. ❶

I learned this, at least, by my experiment; that if one advances confidently in the direction of his dreams, and endeavors to live the life which he has imagined, he will meet with a success unexpected in common hours. He will put some things behind, will pass an invisible boundary; new, universal,
180 and more liberal laws will begin to establish themselves around and within him; or the old laws be expanded, and interpreted in his favor in a more liberal sense, and he will live with the license of a higher order of beings. In proportion as he simplifies his life, the laws of the universe will appear less complex, and solitude will not be solitude, nor poverty poverty, nor weakness weakness. If you have built castles in the air, your work need not be lost; that is where they should be. Now put the foundations under them. . . .

Why should we be in such desperate haste to succeed, and in such desperate enterprises? If a man does not keep pace with his companions,
190 perhaps it is because he hears a different drummer. Let him step to the music which he hears, however measured or far away. It is not important that he should mature as soon as an appletree or an oak. Shall he turn his spring into summer? If the condition of things which we were made for is not yet, what were any reality which we can substitute? We will not be shipwrecked on a vain reality. Shall we with pains erect a heaven of blue glass over ourselves, though when it is done we shall be sure to gaze still at the true ethereal heaven far above, as if the former were not? . . . ❶

However mean your life is, meet it and live it; do not shun it and call it hard names. It is not so bad as you are. It looks poorest when you are richest.
200 The fault-finder will find faults even in paradise. Love your life, poor as it is. You may perhaps have some pleasant, thrilling, glorious hours, even in a poorhouse. The setting sun is reflected from the windows of the almshouse as brightly as from the rich man's abode; the snow melts before its door as early in the spring. I do not see but a quiet mind may live as contentedly there, and have as cheering thoughts, as in a palace. The town's poor seem to me often to live the most independent lives of any. May be they are simply great enough to receive without **misgiving.** Most think that they are above being supported by the town; but it oftener happens that they are not above supporting themselves by dishonest means, which should be
210 more disreputable. Cultivate poverty like a garden herb, like sage. Do not trouble yourself much to get new things, whether clothes or friends. Turn the old; return to them. Things do not change; we change. Sell your clothes and keep your thoughts. God will see that you do not want society. If I were confined to a corner of a garret all my days, like a spider, the world would be just as large to me while I had my thoughts about me. The philosopher said: "From an army of three divisions one can take away its general, and put it in disorder; from the man the most **abject** and vulgar one cannot take away his thought." Do not seek so anxiously to be developed, to subject

---

❶ **ESSAY**
To what does Thoreau compare life in lines 172–175? Explain how this **metaphor** conveys Thoreau's reasons for leaving Walden.

189–191 If a man . . . away: This is one of Thoreau's most famous passages. The "different drummer" evolved from a journal entry describing how he fell asleep to the sound of someone beating a drum "alone in the silence and the dark." The phrase "marching to the beat of a different drummer" became popular during the 1960s and 1970s.

❶ **TRANSCENDENTALISM**
What key feature of transcendentalism does Thoreau embrace in lines 189–191?

misgiving (mĭs-gĭv′ĭng) *n.* a feeling of doubt, mistrust, or uncertainty

215 the philosopher: Confucius (551–479 B.C.), Chinese teacher of moral living, who had an influence on Thoreau's ideas.

abject (ăb′jĕkt′) *adj.* low; contemptible; wretched

DIFFERENTIATED INSTRUCTION

FOR ENGLISH LEARNERS

Comprehension: Text Structure Help students identify examples of the three main strands in "Conclusion": (1) why Thoreau left the woods, (2) life observations, and (3) aphorisms or life lessons. Read lines 198–199 aloud and paraphrase them to clarify: "If your life is difficult, make the best of it. Don't complain or avoid living fully." Urge students to paraphrase to better understand Thoreau's three idea strands.

FOR ADVANCED LEARNERS/AP

Research While Thoreau describes many of his experiences at Walden in minute detail, he omits other experiences entirely. Have students research what Thoreau's life was actually like during his *Walden* years and write one or two paragraphs on how experiences he does not recount in *Walden* might have influenced the personal growth he recounts in his book.

yourself to many influences to be played on; it is all dissipation. Humility
220 like darkness reveals the heavenly lights. The shadows of poverty and
meanness gather around us, "and lo! creation widens to our view." We are
often reminded that if there were bestowed on us the wealth of Croesus, our
aims must still be the same, and our means essentially the same. Moreover,
if you are restricted in your range by poverty, if you cannot buy books
and newspapers, for instance, you are but confined to the most significant
and vital experiences; you are compelled to deal with the material which
yields the most sugar and the most starch. It is life near the bone where it is
sweetest. You are defended from being a trifler. No man loses ever on a lower
level by magnanimity on a higher. Superfluous wealth can buy superfluities
230 only. Money is not required to buy one necessary of the soul. . . . **K**

The life in us is like the water in the river. It may rise this year higher than
man has ever known it, and flood the parched uplands; even this may be the
eventful year, which will drown out all our muskrats. It was not always dry
land where we dwell. I see far inland the banks which the stream anciently
washed, before science began to record its freshets. Every one has heard the
story which has gone the rounds of New England, of a strong and beautiful
bug which came out of the dry leaf of an old table of apple-tree wood,
which had stood in a farmer's kitchen for sixty years, first in Connecticut,
and afterward in Massachusetts,—from an egg deposited in the living tree
240 many years earlier still, as appeared by counting the annual layers beyond it;
which was heard gnawing out for several weeks, hatched perchance by the
heat of an urn. Who does not feel his faith in a resurrection and immortality
strengthened by hearing of this? Who knows what beautiful and winged
life, whose egg has been buried for ages under many concentric layers of
woodenness in the dead dry life of society, deposited at first in the alburnum
of the green and living tree, which has been gradually converted into the
semblance of its well-seasoned tomb,—heard perchance gnawing out now
for years by the astonished family of man, as they sat round the festive
board,—may unexpectedly come forth from amidst society's most trivial
250 and handselled furniture, to enjoy its perfect summer life at last!

I do not say that John or Jonathan will realize all this; but such is the
character of that morrow which mere lapse of time can never make to
dawn. The light which puts out our eyes is darkness to us. Only that day
dawns to which we are awake. There is more day to dawn. The sun is but a
morning star. ❧

222 Croesus (krē'səs): an ancient king legendary for his great wealth.

K EVALUATE IDEAS
Summarize Thoreau's ideas about poverty. Do you think his view of the poor and the lives they lead is realistic? Record your thoughts in your chart.

235 freshets: overflowings of a stream caused by heavy rain or melting snow.

3 Targeted Passage

245 alburnum (ăl-bûr'nəm): the part of a tree's trunk through which sap flows.

251 John or Jonathan: the common man (as in the more current expression "Tom, Dick, and Harry").

READING SKILL

K EVALUATE IDEAS

Possible answer: Thoreau believes that the poor and the rich can receive the same benefits from nature. He thinks that poverty gives people a certain independence, and he urges readers to "cultivate poverty" rather than be trapped in materialism (lines 210–213). Accept all thoughtful responses to Thoreau's ideas.

If students need help . . . Ask these questions to help students evaluate Thoreau's ideas about poverty:

- According to lines 223–227, what advantage is there in not having enough money to buy books and newspapers?
- What does *superfluities* (line 229) mean?
- How would you explain the image "life near the bone" (line 227)?

Lines 251–255
REINFORCE *KEY IDEA*: NONCONFORMITY

Discuss How does Thoreau's reference to "John or Jonathan" suggest that he recognizes his own **nonconformity**? *Possible answer: Thoreau knows that most people, represented by the common names John and Jonathan, will not appreciate his values. In this statement, he acknowledges that he is different from other people.*

FOR STRATEGIC READERS

3 Targeted Passage [Lines 235–250]

In this concluding passage, Thoreau explains how he draws inspiration from a frequently told anecdote.

- Where is the bug? What happens to it? What is unusual about its situation?
- How does this story restore faith?
- How does the story make Thoreau feel about life? about the future?

FOR ADVANCED LEARNERS/AP

Hypothesize Point out that many people's response to spending two years alone in the woods would have been much different from Thoreau's response. Challenge students to use Thoreau's "Conclusion" as a model for a journal entry in which someone with different values discusses leaving the woods and offers some observations and life lessons based on the experience. Invite volunteers to read their journal entries aloud for the class to compare and enjoy.

Practice and Apply

After Reading

Use these copy masters to check under-standing and provide extra support:

R RESOURCE MANAGER—Copy Masters

Reading Check p. 158
Essay p. 151
Question Support p. 159

Additional selection questions are provided for teachers on page 143.

ANSWERS

1. *to live simply and purposefully and to learn from nature*

2. *simplify, live deliberately, and ignore material gain*

3. *Most correspondence is worthless, the daily news contains no memorable or important information, and we place too much impor-tance on both forms of communication.*

Possible answers:

4. *The pond (lines 15–23), living deliberately (lines 24–34), living simply (lines 43–52), nature and solitude (lines 105–120), follow-ing one's own "drumbeat" (lines 189–191), and personal integrity (lines 207–210) were important to Thoreau.*

5. ● **SKILLS FOCUS** Essay *Metaphor: "The intellect is a cleaver" (line 97); Simile: "Still we live meanly, like ants" (line 38); Personification: "I look down into the quiet parlor of the fishes" (lines 139–140). The figurative language gives readers a vivid picture of Walden Pond and a deeper understanding of Thoreau's experiences.*

6. *Emerson's ideas about originality, non-conformity, and self-reliance inform the excerpts from* Walden. *Thoreau trusts himself, intending to live deliberately in the woods and to discover for himself, through his own instincts and observation, whether life is mean or sublime.*

7. ■ **SKILLS FOCUS** Evaluate Ideas *Answers should demonstrate a thorough understanding of Thoreau's ideas.*

8. *It would be more challenging for a modern American to live as Thoreau did because, as La Ferle suggests, we are used to more comfortable standards than were the norm in Thoreau's time. On the other hand, it would be as challenging today as it was then to live deliberately and to consider*

R2.5, R3.3

Comprehension

1. **Recall** What were Thoreau's reasons for moving to the woods?

2. **Recall** What does Thoreau advise people to do to ensure their lives are not "frittered away by detail"?

3. **Summarize** What are Thoreau's views on correspondence and the daily news?

Critical Analysis

4. **Make Inferences** Thoreau rejects many things as inessential or unimportant. List at least three things that *were* important to him, citing specific lines from the essay to support your answer.

5. **Analyze the Essay** Thoreau was a poet as well as an essayist, and in *Walden*, he uses **figurative language** to express abstract concepts. Complete the chart by finding examples of such language. Use your completed chart to describe what you think Thoreau's use of figurative language adds to this essay.

Type of Figurative Language	Examples from Walden
metaphor	"Time is but the stream I go a-fishing in."
simile	
personification	

6. **Analyze Transcendentalism** Thoreau practiced many of the transcendentalist ideals Emerson promoted. What connections do you see between the ideas Thoreau expresses in *Walden* and the ideas Ralph Waldo Emerson presents in "Self-Reliance" and *Nature*? Cite evidence to support your answer.

7. **Evaluate Ideas** Review the philosophical ideas you summarized as you read. Choose one idea—Thoreau's view of the poor, for example, or the way he feels about civilized life. Explain whether or not you think the idea you chose has merit, citing reasons for your opinion.

8. **Compare Texts** In "Thoreau Still Beckons, *if* I Can Take My Laptop" on page 381, Cynthia G. La Ferle argues that "making choices is so much more difficult in a culture fueled by sheer busyness and commercialism. There are few places . . . where one can escape." Do you agree that it would be more challenging for a modern American to live as Thoreau did? Explain why or why not, using details from both texts to support your opinion.

Literary Criticism

9. **Critical Interpretations** According to Frank Stewart, author of *A Natural History of Nature Writing*, nature writers are "moved by the joyous, wild, and dazzling beauty in the world." Do you think this comment applies to Thoreau? Cite examples from *Walden* to support your opinion.

---

every choice, avoiding blind conformity and mindless tradition, as Thoreau suggests.

9. *Yes, the comment applies. Thoreau of-ten shows his amazement at his natural surroundings, as in " . . . there a perennial waveless serenity reigns" (lines 141–142) and "I looked out the window, and lo! where yesterday was cold gray ice there lay the transparent pond . . . as if it had intelli-gence" (lines 158–162).*

THOREAU STILL BECKONS,
if I Can Take My Laptop

By Cynthia G. La Ferle

Thanks to the wonders of modern technology, I now have a mind-boggling array of options.

I can shop for birthday gifts on the Internet, watch a funeral in Britain on "live" television, and order a complete wardrobe from a computer catalog. . . .

Every day I have more choices than I can reasonably consider. And so, like other tired Americans, I carry the burden of complexity—a burden so overwhelming, in fact, that there are times when I imagine trading places with Henry David Thoreau.

It's only fitting that I rediscovered Thoreau the week I purged my home office with a dust rag and a vacuum cleaner. The autumn mornings felt ripe for pitching and sorting. "Walden," Thoreau's famous treatise on simple living, was jammed behind a pile of unread paperbacks. . . .

It occurred to me that things were vastly different for Thoreau. The "comforts of life" in the 1840s were not exactly cushy by today's standards. His concept of luxury might have been taking tea in his mother's bone china saucers. So what had he given up to commune with nature?

Even before he moved to Walden Pond, Thoreau hadn't accumulated three television sets or a closetful of designer clothes. He didn't own several pairs of expensive athletic shoes for all those philosophical walks he took. His cot in the cabin couldn't have been more lumpy than the straw-filled mattresses in most mid-19th-century homes. And Thoreau never had to trade a personal computer for a pencil.

With all due respect, I wonder, how tough was Thoreau's two-year sabbatical with simplicity? Is it true that he occasionally walked from Walden Pond back to Concord, where Emerson's wife had a home-cooked supper waiting for him? . . .

And yet, just as Thoreau did, I'd like to weed out, pare down, live deliberately, be a resident philosopher. . . .

Visiting the "real" Walden Pond this fall, I was amazed and disappointed to find the place overrun. Locals were strewn on its small beach. You couldn't walk the path around the pond without rubbing shoulders with other sightseers; there wasn't a spot left for solitary reflection.

If nothing else, my rendezvous with Thoreau got me thinking. What—and how much—do I really need? What price have I paid for modern technology and "convenience"? In which landfill will all my stuff end up? . . .

Could I survive in a one-room cabin with barely more than a chair, a wooden table, a bowlful of raw vegetables, and my laptop? Honestly, I wish I could.

Practice and Apply

SUMMARY

In these excerpts from "Civil Disobedience," Thoreau argues that citizens must follow their conscience and fight government injustice in a peaceful manner. For example, he refuses to pay taxes that fund causes that he opposes—an action that lands him in jail but frees him spiritually.

READING SKILL

Ⓐ EVALUATE IDEAS

Possible answer: By presenting an unusual interpretation of a common saying, these lines spark readers' interest and stir their emotions, encouraging them to continue reading. The lines establish that the essay will explore Thoreau's view of the proper role of government—a view that many readers may not share.

If students need help . . . Define the words *expedient* and *inexpedient* (lines 6–7), using these sentences to add clarification:

- The bridge was an **expedient** for getting across the river.
- It was **inexpedient** for us to travel over the mountain when we could have gone through the tunnel at its base.

Extend the Discussion Why might modern readers be less surprised by these comments than readers of Thoreau's time might have been?

Civil DISOBEDIENCE
Henry David Thoreau

ANALYZE VISUALS
The photographer who created the image on page 383 made a deliberate choice to focus not on the people in the crowd, but on their shadows. Why might she have made this choice?

BACKGROUND Thoreau put into practice the ideas expressed in Ralph Waldo Emerson's "Self-Reliance." In 1846, he spent a night in jail for refusing to pay a poll tax—a tax one had to pay in order to vote—as an act of protest against the U.S. government. Thoreau was enraged by the government's support of slavery and its war against Mexico, which he viewed as a case of a stronger country overpowering a weaker one simply to expand its own borders. Inspired by his experience in jail, Thoreau wrote this essay.

I heartily accept the motto, "That government is best which governs least;" and I should like to see it acted up to more rapidly and systematically. Carried out, it finally amounts to this, which also I believe,—"That government is best which governs not at all;" and when men are prepared for it, that will be the kind of government which they will have. Government is at best but an expedient; but most governments are usually, and all governments are sometimes, inexpedient. The objections which have been brought against a standing army, and they are many and weighty, and deserve to prevail, may also at last be brought against a standing
10 government. The standing army is only an arm of the standing government. The government itself, which is only the mode which the people have chosen to execute their will, is equally liable to be abused and perverted before the people can act through it. Witness the present Mexican war, the work of comparatively a few individuals using the standing government as their tool; for, in the outset, the people would not have consented to this measure. . . .

But, to speak practically and as a citizen, unlike those who call themselves no-government men, I ask for, not at once no government, but *at once a*

Ⓐ EVALUATE IDEAS
Reread lines 1–7. What effect might these lines have on Thoreau's readers?

① Targeted Passage

13 **the present Mexican war:** the 1846–1848 war between Mexico and the United States.

DIFFERENTIATED INSTRUCTION

FOR STRATEGIC READERS

① Targeted Passage [Lines 5–16]

In this passage, Thoreau explains that he is writing in response to perceived abuses by the government.

- To what does Thoreau compare a government? Why?
- What problems can government face?
- What war is going on when Thoreau is writing?

- How does Thoreau believe most people feel about the war?

FOR ENGLISH LEARNERS

Vocabulary: Suffixes Point out that sometimes more than one suffix is added to a root or base word. Have students identify the suffix or suffixes in each of these words:

- rapidly, systematically (line 2): *rapid + ly; system + atic + al + ly*
- government (line 5): *govern + ment*

- objections (line 7): *object + ions*
- weighty (line 8): *weight + y*
- comparatively (line 14): *compare + ative + ly*

Discuss how the word meanings change when suffixes are added.

BACKGROUND

The Mexican War As part of his 1844 reelection bid, President John Tyler pushed for the annexation of Texas, then an independent nation. Although Tyler lost the election, the issue consolidated opposing views: Southerners favored annexing Texas as a slave state, whereas Northerners feared that doing so would give slave states too much power in Congress. The annexation succeeded under Tyler's successor, James K. Polk, who inherited a boundary dispute with Mexico. Polk offered to buy the disputed area from Mexico, along with what is now New Mexico and California. When Mexico refused, war broke out. The hostilities lasted much longer than the quick series of battles that Polk had hoped for, but it finally ended with the Treaty of Guadalupe Hidalgo in 1848, in which the Rio Grande border was finalized and Mexico ceded New Mexico and California to the United States for $15 million.

B EVALUATE IDEAS

Possible answer: *Summary: Individual conscience should win out over majority rule. Doing what is right is more important than obeying the law. Accept all thoughtful reactions.*

Extend the Discussion How would a nation's government be affected if its leaders held Thoreau's position?

Lines 38–46
TIERED DISCUSSION PROMPTS

Use these prompts to help students explore Thoreau's challenging views about the military:

Restate What does Thoreau mean by an "undue respect for law"? **Possible answer:** *Thoreau refers to an unquestioning acceptance of a law, just because it is a law.*

Interpret How does Thoreau think that soldiers feel about going to war? **Possible answer:** *He thinks that soldiers go to war because they respect the law but that they usually don't wish to fight and often don't support the cause for which they fight.*

Synthesize How does Thoreau's view relate to his transcendentalist ideals? **Possible answer:** *Thoreau says that soldiers march "against their common sense and consciences" (line 41) and that they become "small movable forts and magazines" (lines 44–45). This view reflects the transcendentalist ideal of being an individual and following one's conscience, regardless of the majority view.*

---

better government. Let every man make known what kind of government
20 would command his respect, and that will be one step toward obtaining it.
    After all, the practical reason why, when the power is once in the hands of the people, a majority are permitted, and for a long period continue, to rule is not because they are most likely to be in the right, nor because this seems fairest to the minority, but because they are physically the strongest. But a government in which the majority rule in all cases cannot be based on justice, even as far as men understand it. Can there not be a government in which majorities do not virtually decide right and wrong, but conscience?—in which majorities decide only those questions to which the rule of expediency is applicable? Must the citizen ever for a moment,
30 or in the least degree, resign his conscience to the legislator? Why has every man a conscience, then? I think that we should be men first, and subjects afterward. It is not desirable to cultivate a respect for the law, so much as for the right. The only obligation which I have a right to assume is to do at any time what I think right. It is truly enough said, that a corporation has no conscience; but a corporation of conscientious men is a corporation *with* a conscience. Law never made men a whit more just; and, by means of their respect for it, even the well-disposed are daily made the agents of injustice. **B**
A common and natural result of an undue respect for law is, that you may see a file of soldiers, colonel, captain, corporal, privates, powder-monkeys,
40 and all, marching in admirable order over hill and dale to the wars, against their wills, ay, against their common sense and consciences, which makes it very steep marching indeed, and produces a palpitation of the heart. They have no doubt that it is a damnable business in which they are concerned; they are all peaceably inclined. Now, what are they? Men at all? or small movable forts and magazines, at the service of some unscrupulous man in power? Visit the Navy-Yard, and behold a marine, such a man as an American government can make, or such as it can make a man with its black arts—a mere shadow and reminiscence of humanity, a man laid out alive and standing, and already, as one may say, buried under arms with funeral
50 accompaniments, though it may be,—

> "Not a drum was heard, not a funeral note,
> As his corse to the rampart we hurried;
> Not a soldier discharged his farewell shot
> O'er the grave where our hero we buried."

    The mass of men serve the state thus, not as men mainly, but as machines, with their bodies. They are the standing army, and the militia, jailers, constables, *posse comitatus*, etc. In most cases there is no free exercise whatever of the judgment or of the moral sense; but they put themselves on a level with wood and earth and stones; and wooden men can perhaps
60 be manufactured that will serve the purpose as well. Such command no more respect than men of straw or a lump of dirt. They have the same sort of worth only as horses and dogs. Yet such as these even are commonly

---

B EVALUATE IDEAS

Reread lines 21–37. What position does Thoreau take on the conflict between majority rule and individual conscience? On your chart, **summarize** and react to his position.

39 powder-monkeys: boys with the job of carrying gunpowder to artillery crews.

45 magazines: places where ammunition is stored.

47–48 black arts: witchcraft.

51–54 "Not a drum . . . we buried": opening lines of "The Burial of Sir John Moore After Corunna" by the Irish poet Charles Wolfe (1791–1823).

57 *posse comitatus* (pŏs'ē kŏm-ə-tā'-təs): group of people that can be called on by the sheriff to help enforce the law [*Latin*, literally, the power of the county].

DIFFERENTIATED INSTRUCTION

FOR ENGLISH LEARNERS

Key Academic Vocabulary Use Word Questioning to teach these words: *assume* (line 33), *anticipate* (line 76), *alternative* (line 130), *enable* (line 134), *revolution* (line 135), *perceive* (line 179).

 BEST PRACTICES TOOLKIT—Transparency
Word Questioning p. E9

FOR ADVANCED LEARNERS/AP

Compare and Contrast Views [paired option] Pair students to study Thoreau's description of soldiers (lines 38–62). Have students use a Venn Diagram to compare Thoreau's interpretation of the soldiers' internal views with the government's view of them. Ask students to share their ideas.

 BEST PRACTICES TOOLKIT—Transparency
Venn Diagram p. A26

Internal Views
Don't want to fight but feel obligated.

Both
Recognize the obligation of soldiers.

Government Views
Men are machines for fighting.

esteemed good citizens. Others—as most legislators, politicians, lawyers, ministers, and office-holders—serve the state chiefly with their heads; and, as they rarely make any moral distinctions, they are as likely to serve the Devil, without *intending* it, as God. A very few—as heroes, patriots, martyrs, reformers in the great sense, and *men*—serve the state with their consciences also, and so necessarily resist it for the most part; and they are commonly treated as enemies by it. . . . **C**

70 Unjust laws exist: shall we be content to obey them, or shall we endeavor to amend them, and obey them until we have succeeded or shall we **transgress** them at once? Men generally, under such a government as this, think that they ought to wait until they have persuaded the majority to alter them. They think that, if they should resist, the remedy would be worse than the evil. But it is the fault of the government itself that the remedy *is* worse than the evil. *It* makes it worse. Why is it not more apt to anticipate and provide for reform? Why does it not cherish its wise minority? Why does it cry and resist before it is hurt? Why does it not encourage its citizens to be on the alert to point out its faults, and *do* better than it would have them? Why

80 does it always crucify Christ, and excommunicate Copernicus and Luther, and pronounce Washington and Franklin rebels? . . . **D**

If the injustice is part of the necessary friction of the machine of government, let it go, let it go: perchance it will wear smooth, certainly the machine will wear out. If the injustice has a spring, or a pulley, or a rope, or a crank, exclusively for itself, then perhaps you may consider whether the remedy will not be worse than the evil; but if it is of such a nature that it requires you to be the agent of injustice to another, then, I say, break the law. Let your life be a counter-friction to stop the machine. What I have to do is to see, at any rate, that I do not lend myself to the wrong which

90 I condemn. . . .

I meet this American government, or its representative, the state government, directly, and face to face, once a year—no more—in the person of its tax-gatherer; this is the only mode in which a man situated as I am necessarily meets it; and it then says distinctly, Recognize me; and the simplest, most effectual, and, in the present posture of affairs, the indispensablest mode of treating with it on this head, of expressing your little satisfaction with and love for it, is to deny it then. My civil neighbor, the tax-gatherer, is the very man I have to deal with,—for it is, after all, with men and not with parchment that I quarrel,—and he has voluntarily

100 chosen to be an agent of the government. How shall he ever know well what he is and does as an officer of the government, or as a man, until he is obliged to consider whether he shall treat me, his neighbor, for whom he has respect, as a neighbor and well-disposed man, or as a maniac and disturber of the peace, and see if he can get over this obstruction to his neighborliness without a ruder and more **impetuous** thought or speech corresponding with his action. I know this well, that if one thousand, if one hundred, if ten men

C EVALUATE IDEAS
Reread lines 55–69. Which way of serving the state does Thoreau approve of? Which ways does he condemn? Decide whether you agree with his assessment of soldiers and others who serve.

transgress (trăns-grĕs′) *v.* to violate a command or law

80 **Copernicus** (kō-pûr′nə-kəs) **and Luther:** Radicals in their time, Polish astronomer Nicolaus Copernicus theorized that the sun rather than the earth was the center of our planetary system; German theologian Martin Luther was a leader in the Protestant Reformation.

D GRAMMAR AND STYLE
In lines 70–81, Thoreau adds emphasis and emotion to his writing by asking **rhetorical questions**—questions that don't require a reply because the writer assumes the answers are obvious.

95 **posture of affairs:** situation.

impetuous (ĭm-pĕch′ōō-əs) *adj.* acting with sudden or rash energy; hasty

C EVALUATE IDEAS
Possible answer: Thoreau approves of those who serve the state as "heroes, patriots, martyrs, [and] reformers" (lines 66–67) because they serve with their consciences. He condemns those who serve with only their bodies (such as the militia) or only their heads (politicians, for example). Accept all thoughtful opinions about Thoreau's assessment.

D GRAMMAR AND STYLE
Ask Rhetorical Questions Point out that the tone of a question differs from that of a declarative sentence. Explain that **rhetorical questions** draw readers into the essay by seeming to require an opinion—that is, readers are thinking of an answer to the question, even if they never are asked to share it. Ask students to rewrite the paragraph, changing the rhetorical questions to declarative or exclamatory statements. Discuss whether the effect is more or less persuasive. Then have students find other examples of Thoreau's rhetorical questions. *Possible answers: lines 26–31, 44–46, 140–141, and 170–173*

Lines 91–106
REINFORCE *KEY IDEA:* NONCONFORMITY

Discuss In what way is Thoreau's **nonconformity** made more difficult because it must involve his neighbor, the tax-gatherer? *Possible answer: It is more difficult for Thoreau to be nonconformist because he likes his neighbor and feels respected by him. Thoreau does not want to destroy the neighborly relationship that he has.*

FOR STRATEGIC READERS
Comprehension Support Write these names from lines 80–81 on the board: Christ, Copernicus, Luther, Washington, Franklin. Explain that each of these people was judged harshly by his community but was exonerated later by history. Explain that by linking these people to his own unpopular resistance, Thoreau is suggesting that his behavior, too, will be validated eventually.

FOR ADVANCED LEARNERS/AP
Research and Analyze Have students do enough research to understand why each figure named in lines 80–81 faced condemnation. Ask students to compare and contrast Thoreau with the figures that he cites. Invite volunteers to form a panel discussion in which they share their observations and relate them to this comment in Emerson's "Self-Reliance": "For nonconformity the world whips you with its displeasure" (page 364, line 31).

Left: London police arresting a suffragist, 1914; *center:* Gandhi marching to the sea, in defiance of the British salt monopoly

ANALYZE VISUALS

Activity Invite comments about these historical images; then focus on the image of Mohandas K. Gandhi, whose writing students will sample on pages 392–393. Explain that in 1930, Indians were forbidden to take salt from the sea because of Britain's colonial monopoly on salt production. In protest, Gandhi led a 240-mile march to gather salt from the sea. He and his followers were arrested, but their act drew worldwide attention and condemnation of the British. Ask students which of Thoreau's ideas Gandhi would have agreed with. *Possible answer: Gandhi would have agreed with Thoreau's idea of a "peaceable revolution" (line 135).*

Lines 106–113
TIERED DISCUSSION PROMPTS

Use these prompts to help students grasp Thoreau's position on the use of civil disobedience to protest slavery:

Restate What is Thoreau's position on the value of being jailed for disobeying a law? *Possible answer: He believes that this method of protest is valuable.*

Interpret What does Thoreau mean by saying that the jailing of "one honest man" would bring "the abolition of slavery in America"? *Possible answer: Thoreau means that one man's action would inspire others to protest, beginning the process of change.*

Evaluate Do you agree with Thoreau's statement that "Reform keeps many scores of newspapers in its service, but not one man" (lines 112–113)? Why or why not? *Possible answers: Yes, because many people will read about problems but not do anything about them. No, because he himself has been arrested for his beliefs and thus disproves his point.*

---

whom I could name,—if ten *honest* men only,—ay, if *one* honest man, in this State of Massachusetts, *ceasing to hold slaves,* were actually to withdraw from this copartnership, and be locked up in the county jail therefor, it
110 would be the abolition of slavery in America. For it matters not how small the beginning may seem to be: what is once well done is done forever. But we love better to talk about it: that we say is our mission. Reform keeps many scores of newspapers in its service, but not one man. . . .

Under a government which imprisons any unjustly, the true place for a just man is also a prison. The proper place today, the only place which Massachusetts has provided for her freer and less desponding spirits, is in her prisons, to be put out and locked out of the State by her own act, as they have already put themselves out by their principles. It is there that the fugitive slave, and the Mexican prisoner on parole, and the Indian come to
120 plead the wrongs of his race should find them; on that separate, but more free and honorable ground, where the State places those who are not *with* her, but *against* her,—the only house in a slave State in which a free man can abide with honor. If any think that their influence would be lost there, and their voices no longer afflict the ear of the State, that they would not be as an enemy within its walls, they do not know by how much truth is stronger than error, nor how much more eloquently and effectively he can combat injustice who has experienced a little in his own person. Cast your whole vote, not a strip of paper merely, but your whole influence. A minority is powerless while it conforms to the majority; it is not even a minority then;
130 but it is irresistible when it clogs by its whole weight. If the alternative is to keep all just men in prison, or give up war and slavery, the State will not hesitate which to choose. If a thousand men were not to pay their tax bills

---

DIFFERENTIATED INSTRUCTION

FOR ENGLISH LEARNERS

Language: Pronoun Referents Explain that pronoun referents are the nouns or pronouns to which pronouns refer. Point out that sometimes a pronoun referent is unstated, making it difficult to tell what the author means. In addition, unusual pronouns may be used to replace nouns, such as *her* for the name of a state or ship. Help students identify the antecedent of these pronouns:

- *her* (line 116), "the state of Massachusetts"
- *any* (line 123), "protesters"
- *one* (line 136), "a tax-gatherer"
- *they* (line 153), "my townsmen"

Left: Dr. Martin Luther King Jr., jailed for civil disobedience; *center:* Vietnam war protester burns his military draft card; *right:* Beijing man stands in front of tanks during the 1989 Tiananmen Square uprising.

this year, that would not be a violent and bloody measure, as it would be to pay them, and enable the State to commit violence and shed innocent blood. This is, in fact, the definition of a peaceable revolution, if any such is possible. If the tax-gatherer, or any other public officer, asks me, as one has done, "But what shall I do?" my answer is, "If you really wish to do anything, resign your office." When the subject has refused allegiance, and the officer has resigned his office, then the revolution is accomplished. But
140 even suppose blood should flow. Is there not a sort of blood shed when the conscience is wounded? Through this wound a man's real manhood and immortality flow out, and he bleeds to an everlasting death. I see this blood flowing now. . . . **E**

I have paid no poll-tax for six years. I was put into a jail once on this account, for one night; and, as I stood considering the walls of solid stone, two or three feet thick, the door of wood and iron, a foot thick, and the iron grating which strained the light, I could not help being struck with the foolishness of that institution which treated me as if I were mere flesh and blood and bones, to be locked up. I wondered that it should have concluded
150 at length that this was the best use it could put me to, and had never thought to avail itself of my services in some way. I saw that, if there was a wall of stone between me and my townsmen, there was a still more difficult one to climb or break through before they could get to be as free as I was. I did not for a moment feel confined, and the walls seemed a great waste of stone and mortar. I felt as if I alone of all my townsmen had paid my tax. They plainly did not know how to treat me, but behaved like persons who are underbred. In every threat and in every compliment there was a blunder; for they thought that my chief desire was to stand the other side of

E EVALUATE IDEAS
Thoreau holds an **assumption**—an opinion or belief that is taken for granted—that civil disobedience is the only sensible and moral course to take. Reread lines 114–143. How convincing are the reasons Thoreau gives in support of his belief?

② **Targeted Passage**

157 **underbred:** ill-mannered.

CIVIL DISOBEDIENCE **387**

BACKGROUND
Poll Taxes The poll tax that Thoreau discusses was imposed upon every adult, usually as a requirement for voting. As a result, adults who could not afford to pay the tax—in Thoreau's time, poor white males—were unable to vote. Using the poll tax as a voting requirement was abolished nationwide by the 24th Amendment (1964) and by a Supreme Court ruling (1966), thus granting the vote to millions of Americans living in poverty.

READING SKILL

E EVALUATE IDEAS

Possible answer: Thoreau is convincing when he argues that truth holds power and that people should not fear to withhold support from an unjust government. He is less convincing when he argues that a thousand people should go to prison to protest the government, for this action is not practical for many.

Lines 144–156
REINFORCE *KEY IDEA:* NONCONFORMITY

Discuss Although Thoreau demonstrated his **nonconformity** by not paying his poll tax for six years, why does the night in jail make him feel as if he has been the only one to pay the tax? *Possible answer: By spending a night in jail, Thoreau feels that he has paid his tax by putting his ideas into practice. He has given the government what he has to give: his conviction to his ideals. Others have given their money but nothing of themselves.*

FOR STRATEGIC READERS
② Targeted Passage [Lines 144–153]

In this passage, Thoreau explains the result of his protest of the poll tax.

• For how long has Thoreau not paid his poll tax, and how long did he stay in jail?

• During that imprisonment, whom did he think was more free: himself, or the townspeople outside the jail?

• How did he feel about being confined?

FOR ADVANCED LEARNERS/AP
Research and Evaluate [small-group option] Remind students that the ideas in "Civil Disobedience" have inspired protests for more than 100 years. Draw attention to the photographs on these two pages. Have students choose two photographs, besides that of Gandhi, to research, using these search terms: *suffrage movement, Martin Luther King Jr.* or *civil rights movement, Vietnam draft resistance,* and *Tiananmen Square uprising.*

Instruct students to focus their research on answering this question: How is the protester using Thoreau's model to demonstrate his or her beliefs? Invite students to share their findings and conclusions with the class.

that stone wall. I could not but smile to see how industriously they locked
160 the door on my meditations, which followed them out again without let or
hindrance, and *they* were really all that was dangerous. As they could not
reach me, they had resolved to punish my body; just as boys, if they cannot
come at some person against whom they have a spite, will abuse his dog. I
saw that the State was half-witted, that it was timid as a lone woman with
her silver spoons, and that it did not know its friends from its foes, and
I lost all my remaining respect for it, and pitied it. **F**

160–161 without let or hindrance:
without encountering obstacles.

❸ Targeted Passage

Thus the State never intentionally confronts a man's sense, intellectual
or moral, but only his body, his senses. It is not armed with superior wit or
honesty, but with superior physical strength. I was not born to be forced.
170 I will breathe after my own fashion. Let us see who is the strongest. What
force has a multitude? They only can force me who obey a higher law than I.
They force me to become like themselves. I do not hear of *men* being *forced*
to live this way or that by masses of men. What sort of life were that to live?
When I meet a government which says to me, "Your money or your life,"
why should I be in haste to give it my money? It may be in a great strait, and
not know what to do: I cannot help that. It must help itself; do as I do. It is
not worth the while to snivel about it. I am not responsible for the successful
working of the machinery of society. I am not the son of the engineer. I
perceive that, when an acorn and a chestnut fall side by side, the one does
180 not remain inert to make way for the other, but both obey their own laws,
and spring and grow and flourish as best they can, till one, perchance,
overshadows and destroys the other. If a plant cannot live according to its
nature, it dies; and so a man. ꙮ **G**

F ESSAY
Why do you think Thoreau
includes this personal **anecdote**
about his night in jail? Consider
why he feels free as he stands in
his cell, contemplating his own
imprisonment.

G ESSAY
What **message** does Thoreau
convey through his example of
the acorn and the chestnut?

LITERARY ANALYSIS

F ESSAY

*Possible answer: Thoreau's anecdote illus-
trates how a jailed person with a clear conscience is freer than someone who blindly
serves an unjust system (lines 151–156).*

LITERARY ANALYSIS

G ESSAY

*Possible answer: Thoreau's example of
the acorn and the chestnut conveys the
message that he will not give in to the
government's demands. Instead, he will live
and die according to his own laws and his
own nature.*

If students need help . . . Ask them why
an acorn and a chestnut respond differently to their surroundings. Explain that
Thoreau believes that each person is as
different from the next as an acorn is from
a chestnut.

SELECTION WRAP–UP

SYNTHESIZE How did Thoreau's time at
Walden Pond reflect the ideas about living
according to conscience that he describes in
"Civil Disobedience"?

⭐ CRITIQUE

- What would society be like if everyone followed Thoreau's advice? Give examples.

- After completing the After Reading questions on page 389, have students revisit
their responses and tell whether they have
changed their opinions.

DIFFERENTIATED INSTRUCTION

FOR STRATEGIC READERS

❸ Targeted Passage [Lines 159–166]
In this passage, Thoreau explains his
attitude as a prisoner of conscience.

- What part of Thoreau did the locked
doors of the jail confine?

- To whom does Thoreau compare
the State?

- By the end of his stay in jail, what is
Thoreau's opinion of the State? Why?

FOR ENGLISH LEARNERS

Vocabulary Support Explain that Thoreau
contrasts his body and his mind to emphasize his sense of intellectual freedom in
jail. To help students grasp Thoreau's point,
clarify these contrasting elements:

- "me" vs. "my body" (line 162)

- "intellectual or moral" vs. "body"
(lines 167–168)

- "wit or honesty" vs. "physical strength"
(lines 168–169)

Comprehension

R2.5, R3.3

1. **Recall** According to Thoreau, what should be respected more than the law?

2. **Summarize** What should a citizen do about an unjust law?

3. **Clarify** List the three ways Thoreau says a citizen may serve the state. With which did Thoreau agree?

Critical Analysis

4. **Make Judgments** Consider the **historical context** of Thoreau's essays. Would it be easier or more difficult to practice his brand of **nonconformity** today? Consider the possible contemporary consequences of the following:

   • refusing to pay a tax ("Civil Disobedience," lines 144–166)

   • going to live alone in the woods (*Walden*, lines 1–37)

   • celebrating or "cultivating" poverty (*Walden*, lines 198–230)

5. **Analyze Essays** Even when they discuss serious or even lofty ideas, essays are often loosely structured and highly personal. **Skim** *Walden* and "Civil Disobedience," noting passages in which Thoreau refers to himself. Identify his personal feelings and instances when he shares his own experiences, such as the night he spent in jail. How do these passages influence your acceptance of his arguments? Explain, citing specific lines from both essays.

6. **Interpret Paradox** A paradox is a statement that seems to contradict itself but may nevertheless suggest an important truth. Reexamine both selections and record in a chart the examples of paradox you find. Then explain what truth or idea each paradox illustrates.

Paradox	Explanation
"I did not wish to live what was not life..." (<u>Walden</u>, lines 26–27)	

7. **Evaluate Ideas** Ralph Waldo Emerson said of Thoreau, "No truer American ever lived." Review the political ideas you summarized as you read "Civil Disobedience." Do you consider Thoreau's arguments to be those of a patriot or those of a traitor? In your response, consider Thoreau's points on

   • the necessity of government   • majority rule

   • how unjust laws may be changed

Literary Criticism

8. **Critical Interpretations** Critic Andrew Delbanco has asserted that Thoreau is, "despite all the barricades he erected around himself, an irresistible writer; to read him is to feel wrenched away from the customary world and delivered into a place we fear as much as we need." What does Delbanco mean when he says we both need and fear the world Thoreau creates? After you interpret the critic's statement, explain whether or not you agree with him.

that I was not as wise as the day I was born." (Walden, lines 96–97) **Explanation:** Sometimes it is better to know less about life than to be confused by too much information.

7. ■ **SKILLS FOCUS Evaluate Ideas**
Students' answers should demonstrate an understanding of Thoreau's positions: (1) that government should be smaller and less invasive; (2) that unjust laws will be changed if enough people protest them; and (3) that the majority is not always correct.

8. Delbanco means that we need Thoreau to remind us that a simple, unmaterialistic life is possible, as is a life dedicated to fighting for one's convictions; but that we fear Thoreau because we do not want to give up our possessions or go to jail. Accept all thoughtful responses to the critic's statement.

Practice and Apply

After Reading

Use these copy masters to check understanding and provide extra support:

R **RESOURCE MANAGER—Copy Masters**
Reading Check p. 158
Essay p. 151
Question Support p. 160

Additional selection questions are provided for teachers on page 143.

ANSWERS

1. *one's conscience or sense of right and wrong*

2. *disobey it*

3. *Citizens can serve with their bodies, as soldiers, jailers, and constables do; with their heads, as legislators and politicians do; or with their consciences, as heroes, patriots, and reformers do. Thoreau preferred serving with the conscience.*

Possible answers:

4. *Students' responses should consider each example and explain how they think Thoreau's actions would be received today.*

5. ● **SKILLS FOCUS Essay** *The excerpts from* Walden *are full of references to the author's life, such as when Thoreau gives his views of correspondence and the news (lines 76–86). Such references in "Civil Disobedience" include lines 91–106, where Thoreau describes his conflict between his respect for his tax-gatherer neighbor and his disrespect for the state; and lines 144–166, in which he describes how acting on his principles by protesting the poll tax landed him in jail. These personal experiences lend credibility to Thoreau's argument by revealing that he lives according to the philosophy that he preaches. However, the fact that he spent only one night in jail weakens his sacrifice and suggests an unpleasantly superior attitude.*

6. *Paradox: "'That government is best which governs least.'" ("Civil Disobedience," line 1) **Explanation:** A government that stays out of its citizens' personal actions is the strongest. **Paradox:** "We are determined to be starved before we are hungry." (Walden, lines 53–54) **Explanation:** People worry too much, even though they have plenty. **Paradox:** "I have always been regretting*

ANSWERS

Vocabulary in Context

VOCABULARY PRACTICE

1. *false*
2. *false*
3. *true*
4. *true*
5. *true*
6. *false*
7. *false*
8. *true*

R RESOURCE MANAGER—Copy Master
Vocabulary Practice p. 156

VOCABULARY IN WRITING

Begin with a brief brainstorming session of places to commune with nature, helping students to define *nature* as needed to incorporate your community setting. Have students choose an idea from the list and write freely as they draft a response. Urge them to use the revising stage to review their use of vocabulary words and to incorporate additional words, if possible.

VOCABULARY STRATEGY: THE PREFIXES *ab*- AND *per*- (also an EL language objective)

- Model the strategy, using these examples: *aboriginal, abnormal, abstain, peroxide, permissive, persistent.* Point out that the root word may not stand on its own, as a base word does.

- Encourage students to use a dictionary to define the Latin roots.

Possible answers:

1. *causing harm*
2. *to refrain from*
3. *decisive, absolute*
4. *careful, restrictive*
5. *indifferent, without concern; hidden (oneself) away*

R RESOURCE MANAGER—Copy Master
Vocabulary Strategy p. 157

i Vocabulary Center at **ClassZone.com**
Additional Vocabulary Activities

Vocabulary in Context

VOCABULARY PRACTICE

Decide whether each statement is true or false.

1. If an odor were to **pervade** a room, it would be escaping through a chimney.
2. A person who is experiencing **perturbation** usually feels relaxed and confident.
3. An **impetuous** act is one that you do on the spur of the moment.
4. If you have some **misgiving** about attending a party, you should consider not going.
5. A **congenial** person usually gets along with others.
6. If you act **deliberately,** you act with haste and lack of concern.
7. **Abject** sorrow is sadness that will pass quickly.
8. If you **transgress** a law, you break it.

VOCABULARY IN WRITING

Do you agree that the only place to experience nature is in a remote rural setting? Using two or more vocabulary words, write a short explanation of your opinion and what you base it on. You might start like this.

> **EXAMPLE SENTENCE**
>
> Peace and quiet may not **_pervade_** most urban settings, but there are still ways to commune with nature in the city.

VOCABULARY STRATEGY: THE PREFIXES *ab*- AND *per*-

Though the prefixes *ab*- and *per*- are sometimes combined with recognizable base words, often they are attached to Latin roots, as in the vocabulary words *abject* and *pervade*. When you think you recognize the prefix *ab*- or *per*- in a word, look for context clues that support your guess. Then use the meaning of the prefix—and of the root, if you know it—to decipher the word's definition.

PRACTICE The prefix *ab*- or *per*- occurs in each boldfaced word below. Use context clues and root and prefix meanings—or a dictionary, if necessary—to define each word.

1. That man's **pernicious** lies have totally destroyed his son's reputation.
2. To get out of debt, I have decided to **abjure** going to the mall for three months.
3. The recruits immediately obeyed the officer's **peremptory** command.
4. **Abstemious** eating habits can help a person lose weight.
5. His **perfunctory** effort to learn who had **absconded** with the money was unsuccessful.

Prefix	Meaning
ab-	"away"; "away from"
per-	"through"; "thoroughly, very"

VOCABULARY PRACTICE
For more practice, go to the **Vocabulary Center** at ClassZone.com.

DIFFERENTIATED INSTRUCTION

FOR ENGLISH LEARNERS

Task Support: Vocabulary Practice To increase understanding of the *Word List,* work through the **Vocabulary Practice** with students, pointing out context clues that suggest the actual meaning of each boldfaced word. Have students rewrite each false statement so that it uses the vocabulary word correctly.

FOR ADVANCED LEARNERS/AP

Vocabulary in Context To increase students' vocabulary and knowledge of affixes and word families, ask students to think of one additional form of each word in the *Word List,* such as *impetuosity* or *transgression.* Using the **Vocabulary Practice** as a model, have students write sentences for the new words. Ask pairs to exchange their sentences and decide if each new statement is true or false.

Reading-Writing Connection

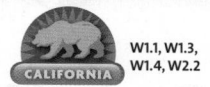
W1.1, W1.3, W1.4, W2.2

WRITING PROMPT

WRITE A LETTER TO THE EDITOR Thoreau proposed radical ideas in "Civil Disobedience." Some people found them thrilling; others found them threatening. Choose one of the ideas proposed in "Civil Disobedience." Write a **three-paragraph letter** to the editor of a local newspaper in which you explain the idea and argue for or against implementing it.

SELF-CHECK

A successful letter to the editor will ...

- state the issue and your position on the issue
- support your position with reasons and examples
- use rhetorical devices that will help reinforce your position

GRAMMAR AND STYLE

ASK RHETORICAL QUESTIONS Review the **Grammar and Style** note on page 385. Thoreau asks a number of thought-provoking questions in "Civil Disobedience." But he's not expecting any answers. The questions he asks are **rhetorical questions;** they don't require a reply, because the answers are considered obvious. Writers often use these types of **interrogative sentences** to drive home a point or evoke an emotional response. Here is an example from the text:

W1.9

> *But even suppose blood should flow.* Is there not a sort of blood shed when the conscience is wounded? (lines 139–141)

Read this passage aloud. Consider how it would sound if it lacked a rhetorical question—if the second sentence read, "A sort of blood flows when the conscience is wounded." Do you think the rhetorical question makes Thoreau's argument more compelling?

PRACTICE Rewrite the following paragraph, changing some sentences to rhetorical questions.

> Thoreau suggests that if citizens disagree with their government's actions, they should stop paying taxes. However, if a large number of Americans refused to pay their taxes this year, the results would be disastrous. Public schools would collapse, salaries for police officers and firefighters would go unpaid, and services from public transportation to public hospitals would crumble. I do not see how a good citizen could allow this to happen. I do not see the honor in such an act.

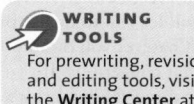
WRITING TOOLS
For prewriting, revision, and editing tools, visit the **Writing Center** at ClassZone.com.

FOR DEVELOPING WRITERS

Task Support Remind students that a letter to the editor is persuasive writing. Discuss these techniques, which can strengthen this type of persuasive appeal:

- Use direct, strong language—that is, language that is clear and vivid but that usually does not have over-emotional connotations.
- Consider omitting expressions such as "I think," "It seems to me," or "In my opinion";

readers assume that you are presenting and defending a viewpoint.

- Explain each point of your argument in a single paragraph. Carefully choose your support for each point; do not burden readers with unrelated details.
- Write a strong conclusion that restates your view and includes a call to action or other specific response from readers.

Reading-Writing Connection

WRITING PROMPT

Point out that letters to the editor are written in formal language, without slang or contractions. Convincing letters present a clear opinion, support it with a well-reasoned argument, and maintain a respectful tone. Urge students to follow standard business letter format.

For writing support, see

ℹ️ Writing Center at **ClassZone.com**

GRAMMAR AND STYLE

Explain that writers often use **rhetorical questions** to ask readers to consider an issue in depth. For example, in lines 30–31 of "Civil Disobedience," Thoreau asks, "Why has every man a conscience, then?" Thoreau does not answer the question, but he expects readers to answer it mentally. Urge students to use this technique in their letter to the editor.

Possible answer: Thoreau suggests that if citizens disagree with their government's actions, they should stop paying taxes. However, if a large number of Americans refused to pay their taxes this year, what would the results be? Public schools would collapse, salaries for police officers and firefighters would go unpaid, and services from public transportation to public hospitals would crumble. What good citizen would allow this to happen? Where is the honor in such an act?

R RESOURCE MANAGER—Copy Master
   Ask Rhetorical Questions p. 161

Assess and Reteach

Assess

R RESOURCE MANAGER—Copy Masters
   Selection Test A pp. 163–164
   Selection Test B/C pp. 165–166

💿 Test Generator CD

Reteach

S STANDARDS LESSON FILE
   Informational Text Lesson 17: Evaluating Argument
   Writing Lesson 29: Persuasive Writing
   Vocabulary Lesson 2: Prefixes

R2.5, R3.7

On *Civil Disobedience*

Mohandas K. Gandhi

> **BACKGROUND** Mohandas K. Gandhi (1869–1948), called Mahatma ("Great Soul"), helped free India of British rule. As a student, he greatly admired Thoreau's essay "Civil Disobedience." Thoreau's ideas helped shape Gandhi's key principle—*satyagraha* (sə-tyä′grə-hə), or "truth-force." In the following excerpt from a 1916 speech, Gandhi describes this powerful weapon for fighting oppression.

July 27, 1916

There are two ways of countering injustice. One way is to smash the head of the man who perpetrates injustice and to get your own head smashed in the process. All strong people in the world adopt this course. Everywhere wars are fought and millions of people are killed. The consequence is not the progress of a nation but its decline. . . . No country has ever become, or will ever become, happy through victory in war. A nation does not rise that way, it only falls further. In fact, what comes to it is defeat, not victory. And if, perchance, either our act or our purpose was ill-conceived, it brings disaster to both belligerents.[1]

10   But through the other method of combating injustice, we alone suffer the consequences of our mistakes, and the other side is wholly spared. This other method is *satyagraha*.[2] One who resorts to it does not have to break another's head; he may merely have his own head broken. He has to be prepared to die himself, suffering all the pain. In opposing the atrocious laws of the Government of South Africa,[3] it was this method that we adopted. We made it clear to the said Government that we would never bow to its outrageous laws. No clapping is possible without two hands to do it, and no quarrel without two persons to make it. Similarly, no State is possible without two entities, the rulers and the ruled. You are our sovereign, our Government, only so long as we consider ourselves your subjects. When we are not subjects, you are not the

20   sovereign either. So long as it is your endeavour to control us with justice and love, we will let you to do so. But if you wish to strike at us from behind, we cannot permit it. Whatever you do in other matters, you will have to ask our opinion about the laws that concern us. If you make laws to keep us suppressed in a wrongful manner and without taking us into confidence, these laws will merely adorn the statute-books. We will never obey them. Award us for it what punishment you like, we will put up with it. Send us to prison and we will live there as in a paradise. Ask us to mount the

---

1. **belligerents:** participants in a war.
2. **satyagraha** (sə-tyä′grə-hə) *Sanskrit:* insistence on truth. Gandhi used this term to describe his policy of seeking reform by means of nonviolent resistance.
3. **atrocious laws . . . South Africa:** Gandhi led the Indian community in opposition to racial discrimination in South Africa, where he lived for several years.

DIFFERENTIATED INSTRUCTION

FOR ENGLISH LEARNERS

Comprehension: Text Structure Explain that Gandhi sets up the contrast between two ideas in the first part of his speech. In doing so, he makes the first type of resistance seem undesirable and peaceful resistance seem desirable. Point out these text clues: "two ways" (line 2), "One way . . ." (line 2), and "the other method" (line 10). Then help students list the characteristics of each method Gandhi suggests.

Gandhi in 1948, after ending a six-day hunger strike for peace

scaffold[4] and we will do so laughing. Shower what sufferings you like upon us, we will calmly endure all and not hurt a hair of your body. We will gladly die and will not so much as touch you. But so long as there is yet life in these our bones, we will never

30 comply with your arbitrary laws. ∾

---

4. **mount the scaffold:** ascend the platform on which one is executed by hanging.

Literary Analysis

1. **Summarize** What two ways of countering injustice does Gandhi describe? Explain which approach Gandhi adopted.

2. **Interpret** Reread lines 16–20. What point is Gandhi making about the relationship between a government and its citizens?

3. **Compare Texts** Henry David Thoreau's ideas influenced many 20th-century reformers, including Gandhi. What connections do you see between the views Thoreau presents in *Walden* and "Civil Disobedience" and Gandhi's beliefs? Cite evidence from both texts to support your answer.

THEMES ACROSS CULTURES   **393**

ANSWERS

Possible answers:

1. *Gandhi describes countering injustice by smashing the heads of the men who perpetrate injustice or through satyagraha—what Ghandi called nonviolent resistance. Gandhi adopted satyagraha.*

2. *By the image of two hands clapping, Gandhi shows how a state is not possible if its two parts—the rulers and the ruled—do not exist in harmony. He further makes the point that a government in fact does not exist without people to govern.*

3. *Both Gandhi and Thoreau say that they are willing to suffer the consequences of their protest. In "Civil Disobedience," Thoreau says, "Let your life be a counter-friction to stop the machine" (line 88). Gandhi says, "He has to be prepared to die himself, suffering all the pain" (lines 13–14). Both argue that the government cannot rule without the consent of the governed. Thoreau writes, "When the subject has refused allegiance, and the officer has resigned his office, then the revolution is accomplished" ("Civil Disobedience," lines 138–139). Gandhi writes, "no State is possible without two entities, the rulers and the ruled" (lines 17–18).*

FOR ADVANCED LEARNERS/AP

Evaluate Ideas Tell students that Gandhi was educated as a lawyer and that he had spent many years in peaceful resistance of South Africa's government before returning to his homeland of India. He used hunger strikes, protest marches, and boycotts as methods of peaceful resistance.

Organize students into small groups to read the speech aloud and identify its elements of persuasive writing. Encourage students to consider the structure of Gandhi's speech, looking for such features as his use of facts, personal experience, explanation of theory, and call to action. Urge discussion of the speech's persuasiveness.

Focus and Motivate

from Woman in the Nineteenth Century

Nonfiction by Margaret Fuller

R2.5 CALIFORNIA

OBJECTIVES

Literary Analysis
- explore the key idea of **expectations**
- analyze author's perspective
- read nonfiction

Reading
- paraphrase main ideas

R2.5 CALIFORNIA

ABOUT THE AUTHOR

Margaret Fuller After students have read about Fuller, explain that although she had the privilege of a good education, her life was not without its problems. By the age of 20, she was plagued by migraine headaches nearly every day. Those who met her complimented her intelligence but not always her personality or behavior. In one account, Emerson expressed his annoyance at her nasal voice and habit of constantly blinking her eyes. Others complained that she was conceited, having too high an opinion of herself.

USING THE *NOTABLE QUOTE*

Explain to students that the "arbitrary barrier" **Margaret Fuller** refers to means laws or un-spoken rules based on preconceptions about, rather than actual differences between, men and women. Then have students list examples of such barriers. ***Possible answer: Examples include job taboos, wage inequality, and voting injustices.***

NOTABLE QUOTE

"We would have every arbitrary barrier thrown down. We would have every path laid open to woman as freely as to man."

FYI
Did you know that Margaret Fuller . . .

- learned to read when she was 3 years old?
- suffered from nightmares in which she dreamed horses were galloping across her head?
- inspired Edgar Allan Poe to quip, "There are three species: men, women, and Margaret Fuller"?

Author Online

For more on Margaret Fuller, visit the **Literature Center** at ClassZone.com.

Margaret Fuller
1810–1850

Margaret Fuller spent much of her life fighting to make women equal members of society. At a time when a woman's only place was thought to be the small sphere of the home, Fuller became a respected author, a commanding public speaker, a popular journalist, and a key figure in the transcendentalist movement. One literary historian observed that Fuller "transcended virtually every stereotype American women had to endure in the first half of the 19th century."

A Demanding Childhood Sarah Margaret Fuller was born in Cambridgeport, Massachusetts. Her father, a stern and formidable man, had high expectations for her. When she was only 10 years old, he counseled that excelling "in all things should be your constant aim." As a teenager, Fuller typically started her studies at five in the morning and sometimes did not finish until eleven at night.

Coming into Her Own Fuller's father died suddenly when she was 25, and she became a teacher to help support her family. Through a mutual acquaintance, she met Ralph Waldo Emerson, who was much impressed by her intelligence and wit. She began attending meetings of the Transcendental Club. In 1840, Fuller became the editor of *The Dial,* a short-lived but highly influential literary magazine. Fuller solicited poems, essays, and fiction from leading transcendentalists and wrote much of the content herself.

An Influential Voice In 1844, Fuller started writing the literary column for the *New York Tribune,* perhaps the most widely read newspaper of its day. In addition to reviewing literary works, she addressed social issues such as poverty and slavery. In 1845, Fuller published *Woman in the Nineteenth Century,* a revolutionary feminist work that paid tribute to women's intellectual and creative abilities and declared that women must be accepted as equal to men. The first edition sold out in two weeks.

Romance and Tragedy In 1846, the *New York Tribune* sent Fuller to cover civil unrest in Europe. She settled in Rome, where she fell in love with and married Italian aristocrat Giovanni Angelo Ossoli. When revolution broke out in Rome in 1848, Fuller supported the cause by volunteering at a hospital while her husband fought for the republic. The revolution failed, and Fuller, Ossoli, and their young son sailed to the United States in 1850. With New York City almost in sight, their ship hit a sandbar and sank. Fuller, Ossoli, and their son drowned.

Selection Resources

RESOURCE MANAGER UNIT 2

Plan and Teach pp. 167–174

Literary Analysis
Summary pp. 175†*, 176‡*
Author's Perspective pp. 177, 178†*
Question Support p. 182*

Reading
Paraphrase Main Ideas
pp. 179, 180†*
Reading Check p. 181

Assessment
Selection Tests A, B/C pp. 183*, 185*
Test Generator CD

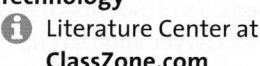 BEST PRACTICES TOOLKIT

Differentiated Instruction
pp. 31–38*

Scaffolding Instruction
pp. 43–46*

Graphic Organizers/Strategies
New Word Analysis • Open Mind

Reading Support
Audio Anthology CD*

Technology
Literature Center at
ClassZone.com
WriteSmart CD

---

* Resources for Differentiation   † Also in Spanish   ‡ In Haitian Creole and Vietnamese

LITERARY ANALYSIS: AUTHOR'S PERSPECTIVE

You know that people often look at a subject from different perspectives. For example, a Vietnam War veteran would bring a unique set of ideas and experiences to a discussion of that war. A person who spent the 1960s protesting that same war would approach the discussion with an entirely different set of beliefs. **Author's perspective** refers to the distinct combination of ideas, values, and beliefs that influence the way a writer looks at a topic. An author's perspective is rarely stated; instead, you have to look closely at details within the text. To determine an author's perspective, examine

- the writer's **tone,** or attitude toward the subject
- **details** the writer chooses to include or focus on
- how the writer portrays specific individuals

As you read the excerpt from *Woman in the Nineteenth Century*, use these elements to help you analyze Margaret Fuller's perspective.

READING STRATEGY: PARAPHRASE MAIN IDEAS

When you read challenging texts like this one, it is important to pay careful attention to the author's **main ideas.** One way to make sure you're understanding these key points is to **paraphrase** them, or restate the information in your own words. A good paraphrase is about the same length as the original text but is written in simpler language. As you read, paraphrase the annotated passages to achieve a better understanding of Fuller's main ideas. Record your work in a chart like the one shown.

Fuller's Main Ideas	My Paraphrases
"I was talking on this subject with Miranda, a woman, who, if any in the world could, might speak without heat or bitterness of the position of her sex."	I spoke about this with Miranda. If any woman can talk about gender issues calmly and rationally, Miranda can.

What does society **EXPECT** *of us?*

KEY IDEA In the 19th century, society expected women to be loving wives, adoring mothers, and expert housekeepers. Women were *not* expected to be great thinkers; they were to leave the thinking to men. Some women, including Margaret Fuller, rejected these limiting **expectations.**

SURVEY Does society still have different expectations for men and women? Complete the following survey, marking which jobs you think would most likely be held by men, which would mostly likely be held by women, and which would have roughly equal numbers of each. Then write a paragraph discussing what your results might indicate about how gender influences societal expectations.

Survey: **Gender and Jobs**

Occupation	Mostly Male	Mostly Female	Equal
1. Kindergarten teacher			
2. Carpenter			
3. Hairstylist			
4. Surgeon			
5. Firefighter			
6. College professor			
7. Personal shopper			
8. Architect			

What does society **EXPECT** *of us?*

Ask the question to lead into the **KEY IDEA**. Then point out that the **expectations** that women faced in Fuller's time were very different from those for women today. To help students explore this point, have them complete the **SURVEY** activity.

SKILLS FOCUS

LITERARY ANALYSIS
R2.5

● AUTHOR'S PERSPECTIVE

Write these lines on the board:

> The surgeon was kind in her relations with patients, expert in her understanding of illness, and intolerant of those who doubted her skill.

How do these lines reveal the author's perspective? *Possible answer: By portraying the individual with positive descriptions, the author shows belief in the woman's abilities.*

CHECK UNDERSTANDING Ask students how the passage would change if the author disapproved of the surgeon.

READING STRATEGY

■ PARAPHRASE MAIN IDEAS

Have students paraphrase the first paragraph of the author biography on page 394. *Possible answer: Margaret Fuller fought for equal rights for women. Though women's occupations were restricted, Fuller had a successful career as a speaker and writer. She did not fit the stereotypes of the early 19th century.*

 RESOURCE MANAGER—Copy Master Paraphrase Main Ideas p. 179 (for student use while reading the selection)

DIFFERENTIATED INSTRUCTION

FOR STRATEGIC READERS

Vocabulary Support To support instruction, clarify the meaning of these words:

- *perspective,* "a point of view"
- *annotated,* "marked with explanatory notes"
- *indicate,* "to signify or be a sign of"
- *societal,* "of or relating to society"

Concept Support: Paraphrase Main Ideas

Unlike a paraphrase, a summary restates only main ideas and thus will be shorter than the original. Explain that students may need to use dictionaries to find the meaning of new or unfamiliar words and thesauruses to find simpler alternative words. Urge students to list new words, meanings, and alternatives to reference when they paraphrase.

SUMMARY

This excerpt from Fuller's nonfiction writings begins with the fictional Miranda's childhood. An adoring father supports Miranda's education and quick mind. In time, Miranda's confidence impresses her friends and gains her the respect of both men and women. She explains, however, that many men see a smart woman as one with a "manly mind" and says that she wishes minds were not judged by their gender.

READING STRATEGY

Ⓐ PARAPHRASE MAIN IDEAS

Possible answer: *Miranda's father did not have idealized notions about women in general. He believed strongly in gender equality.*

If students need help . . . Work with them to organize their thoughts in the prereading chart introduced on page 395. To prompt students' thinking, discuss the main ideas that must be included in their paraphrase.

Fuller's Main Ideas	My Paraphrases
"Her father was a man who cherished no sentimental reverence for woman, but a firm belief in the equality of the sexes."	Miranda's father believed in the equality of men and women.

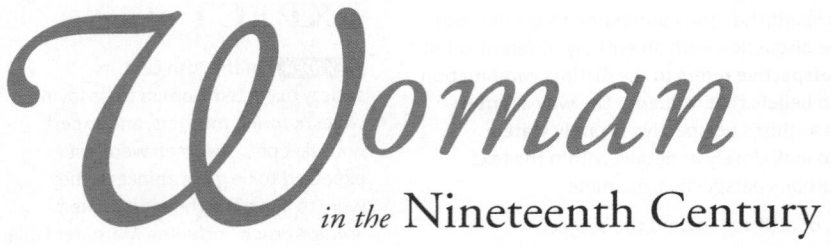

Woman
in the Nineteenth Century
MARGARET FULLER

> **BACKGROUND** From 1839 to 1844, Fuller led a series of seminars for women called "Conversations." She lectured on topics ranging from ethics to art and then asked her listeners to discuss each topic, thus helping the women to recognize their own intellectual abilities. The sessions led Fuller to write *Woman in the Nineteenth Century*, in which she insists society accept women and men as equals. Here, Fuller presents her views as a dialogue between herself and the fictional "Miranda," a woman who, like Fuller, had from childhood been encouraged to exercise her mind.

I was talking on this subject with Miranda, a woman, who, if any in the world could, might speak without heat and bitterness of the position of her sex. Her father was a man who cherished no sentimental reverence for woman, but a firm belief in the equality of the sexes. She was his eldest child, and came to him at an age when he needed a companion. From the time she could speak and go alone, he addressed her not as a plaything, but as a living mind. Among the few verses he ever wrote was a copy addressed to this child, when the first locks were cut from her head, and the reverence expressed on this occasion for that cherished head, he never belied. It was to him the temple of immortal intellect. He respected his child, however, too much
10 to be an indulgent parent. He called on her for clear judgment, for courage, for honor and fidelity; in short, for such virtues as he knew. In so far as he possessed the keys to the wonders of this universe, he allowed free use of them to her, and by the incentive of a high expectation, he forbade, as far as possible, that she should let the privilege lie idle. Ⓐ

Thus this child was early led to feel herself a child of the spirit. She took her place easily, not only in the world of organized being, but in the world of mind. A dignified sense of self-dependence was given as all her portion,[1] and she found it a

---

1. **all her portion:** something that she had a right to expect.

ANALYZE VISUALS
In your opinion, what **traits** does the subject of this portrait project? After you've read the selection, revisit your answer. Tell whether you think the woman in the portrait might share any of Miranda's qualities.

Ⓐ PARAPHRASE MAIN IDEAS
Paraphrase lines 2–4. What were Miranda's father's views on gender equality?

❶ Targeted Passage

Portrait of Ann Cochrells (1848), David Parr. Oil on canvas, 9″ × 11″. © Christie's Images Ltd.

DIFFERENTIATED INSTRUCTION

FOR ALL STUDENTS
Provide these independent projects to extend the lesson:

- Design a monument to Fuller.
- Conduct a conversation about society's expectations.
- Create an admirable character.

For further details on these projects, see

R RESOURCE MANAGER
Ideas for Extension pp. 172–173

FOR STRATEGIC READERS
In combination with the *Audio Anthology CD*, use one or more Targeted Passages (pp. 396, 399) to ensure that students focus on key events and concepts. Targeted passages are also good for English learners.

❶ **Targeted Passage [Lines 9–14]**

This passage shows that Miranda's father educated her and valued her mind.

ANALYZE VISUALS
Possible answer: The portrait's subject projects sensibility and modesty with her plain clothing and simple hairstyle. She seems to share Miranda's serious, no-nonsense approach to life.

BACKGROUND

Higher Education for Women In the early 19th century, women had few educational options after elementary school. However, opportunities were beginning to take shape. In 1837, Mount Holyoke College was established in South Hadley, Massachusetts. It was the first of what would be called the Seven Sisters: seven liberal arts colleges that admitted women only. The other six are Vassar (1861), Wellesley (1870), Smith (1871), Bryn Mawr (1885), Barnard (1889), and Radcliffe (1893).

Lines 1–14
TIERED DISCUSSION PROMPTS

Use these prompts to address Fuller's ideas about a parent's involvement in a child's education:

Connect How do you feel about Miranda's father? Explain. *Accept all thoughtful responses.*

Analyze What does the anecdote about Miranda's first haircut reveal? ***Possible answer: The poem shows the father's great love for his daughter.***

Synthesize How does Miranda's childhood reflect what you know about Fuller? ***Possible answer: Like Fuller, Miranda's father encouraged her studies and did not limit her because of her gender.***

- How did Miranda's father treat his daughter?
- What qualities did Miranda's father expect from her?
- How did Miranda's father help her learn about the world?

FOR ENGLISH LEARNERS

Key Academic Vocabulary Use New Word Analysis to teach these words: *sex* (line 2), *incentive* (line 13), *bias* (line 37), *attain* (line 40), *energy* (line 98).

 BEST PRACTICES TOOLKIT—Transparency New Word Analysis p. E8

Prereading For prereading instruction for English learners, see

 BEST PRACTICES TOOLKIT Scaffolding Reading Instruction pp. 43–46

FOR ADVANCED LEARNERS/AP

AP exercises in the bottom channel provide additional challenge for students. Use these suggestions for small groups or individuals.

ADDITIONAL GUIDELINES

For more help with differentiation and tips for classroom management, see

 BEST PRACTICES TOOLKIT Differentiated Instruction pp. 31–38

Ⓑ AUTHOR'S PERSPECTIVE

Possible answer: Fuller values Miranda's independence, self-sufficiency, originality, relationships with others, and self-respect.

Ⓒ PARAPHRASE MAIN IDEAS

Possible answer: Paraphrase: Only those people who think it is hopeless and those who try too hard are unable to overcome the restrictions placed on women. Fuller sees Miranda as an example of a woman capable of transcending society's limited view of women.

Ⓓ PARAPHRASE MAIN IDEAS

Possible answer: Paraphrase: This self-reliance, which I was praised for, is criticized in other women. They are taught to follow rules. I was taught to think of my own rules. Miranda is self-reliant and self-guided, while most women are not.

Ⓔ AUTHOR'S PERSPECTIVE

Possible answer: Details about being "over-loaded with precepts by guardians" (line 50) and how women's minds can be "impeded by doubts" (line 52) contrast Miranda's up-bringing with other women's. This contrast helps Fuller advocate an upbringing that encourages self-confidence and intellectual independence.

If students need help . . . Explain that Fuller expects the reader to make infer-ences about how women should be educated.

Extend the Discussion How did most par-ents raise their daughters in Fuller's era? What were the effects of such upbringing?

---

sure anchor. Herself securely anchored, her relations with others were established with equal security. She was fortunate in a total absence of those charms which
20 might have drawn to her bewildering flatteries, and in a strong electric nature, which repelled those who did not belong to her; and attracted those who did. With men and women her relations were noble,—affectionate without passion, intellectual without coldness. The world was free to her, and she lived freely in it. Outward adversity came, and inward conflict, but that faith and self-respect had early been awakened which must always lead at last, to an outward serenity and an inward peace. Ⓑ

Of Miranda I had always thought as an example, that the restraints upon the sex were insuperable[2] only to those who think them so, or who noisily strive to break them. She had taken a course of her own, and no man stood in her way.
30 Many of her acts had been unusual, but excited no uproar. Few helped, but none checked her, and the many men, who knew her mind and her life, showed to her confidence, as to a brother, gentleness as to a sister. And not only refined, but very coarse men approved and aided one in whom they saw resolution and clearness of design. Her mind was often the leading one, always effective. Ⓒ

When I talked with her upon these matters, and had said very much what I have written, she smilingly replied: "and yet we must admit that I have been fortunate, and this should not be. My good father's early trust gave the first bias, and the rest followed of course. It is true that I have had less outward aid, in after years, than most women, but that is of little consequence. Religion was early
40 awakened in my soul, a sense that what the soul is capable to ask it must attain, and that, though I might be aided and instructed by others, I must depend on myself as the only constant friend. This self dependence, which was honored in me, is deprecated as a fault in most women. They are taught to learn their rule from without, not to unfold it from within. Ⓓ

"This is the fault of man, who is still vain, and wishes to be more important to woman than, by right, he should be."

"Men have not shown this disposition toward you," I said.

"No! because the position I early was enabled to take was one of self-reliance. And were all women as sure of their wants as I was, the result would be the same.
50 But they are so overloaded with precepts by guardians, who think that nothing is so much to be dreaded for a woman as originality of thought or character, that their minds are impeded by doubts till they lose their chance of fair free proportions. The difficulty is to get them to the point from which they shall naturally develop self-respect, and learn self-help. Ⓔ

"Once I thought that men would help to forward this state of things more than I do now. I saw so many of them wretched in the connections they had formed in weakness and vanity. They seemed so glad to esteem women whenever they could.

"'The soft arms of affection,' said one of the most discerning spirits, 'will not suffice for me, unless on them I see the steel bracelets of strength.'"

---

2. **insuperable:** incapable of being overcome.

Ⓑ **AUTHOR'S PERSPECTIVE**
Consider Fuller's **tone** in lines 15–26. What can you **infer** about the traits Fuller found admirable?

Ⓒ **PARAPHRASE MAIN IDEAS**
Paraphrase the main idea Fuller states in lines 27–29. Of what does Fuller see Miranda as an "example"?

Ⓓ **PARAPHRASE MAIN IDEAS**
Paraphrase lines 42–44. How is Miranda different from most women of her time?

Ⓔ **AUTHOR'S PERSPECTIVE**
Consider the **details** Fuller chooses to focus on. By contrasting Miranda's upbringing with that of most 19th-century women, what type of upbringing is Fuller advocating?

DIFFERENTIATED INSTRUCTION

FOR ENGLISH LEARNERS

Language: Punctuation and Print Cues Point out the long sentences in lines 35–44, and help students use the punctuation cues to improve understanding. The comma in line 40 separates the explanation from the main idea, and the commas in lines 42–43 set off an adjective phrase from the rest of the sentence.

FOR ADVANCED LEARNERS/AP

Analyze [small-group option] Like Miranda, Fuller was blessed with a "total absence of those charms which might have drawn to her bewildering flatteries" (lines 19–20). Have small student groups analyze Fuller's sugges-tion that beauty or charm is a disadvantage for women who wish to be taken seriously. Does physical attractiveness have the same impact for men as it does for women? Invite groups to share their analysis with the class.

60　But early I perceived that men never, in any extreme of despair, wished to be women. On the contrary they were ever ready to taunt one another at any sign of weakness, with,

> *Art thou not like the women, who—*

The passage ends various ways, according to the occasion and rhetoric of the speaker. When they admired any woman they were inclined to speak of her as "above her sex." Silently I observed this, and feared it argued a rooted scepticism, which for ages had been fastening on the heart, and which only an age of miracles could eradicate. Ever I have been treated with great sincerity; and I look upon it as a signal instance of this, that an intimate friend of the other sex said, in a fervent

70　moment, that I "deserved in some star to be a man." He was much surprised when I disclosed my view of my position and hopes, when I declared my faith that the feminine side, the side of love, of beauty, of holiness, was now to have its full chance, and that, if either were better, it was better now to be a woman, for even the slightest achievement of good was furthering an especial work of our time. He smiled incredulously. "She makes the best she can of it," thought he. "Let Jews believe the pride of Jewry, but I am of the better sort, and know better."[3] **F**

Another used as highest praise, in speaking of a character in literature, the words "a manly woman."

"So in the noble passage of Ben Jonson:

80　　*'I meant the day-star should not brighter ride,*
　　　　Nor shed like influence from its lucent seat;
　　I meant she should be courteous, facile, sweet,
　　　　Free from that solemn vice of greatness, pride;
　　I meant each softest virtue there should meet,
　　　　Fit in that softer bosom to abide,
　　Only a learned and a manly *soul,*
　　　　I purposed her, that should with even powers,
　　The rock, the spindle, and the shears control
　　　　Of destiny, and spin her own free hours.'"[4]

②　Targeted Passage

90　"Methinks," said I, "you are too fastidious in objecting to this. Jonson in using the word 'manly' only meant to heighten the picture of this, the true, the intelligent fate, with one of the deeper colors."

"And yet," said she, "so invariable is the use of this word where a heroic quality is to be described, and I feel so sure that persistence and courage are the most womanly no less than the most manly qualities, that I would exchange these words for others of a larger sense at the risk of marring the fine tissue of the verse. Read 'A heavenward and instructed soul,' and I should be satisfied. Let it not be said, wherever there is energy or creative genius, 'She has a masculine mind.'" ꙮ

---

3. **'She makes . . . know better':** Miranda's male friend uses a religious slur to discount women.
4. **'I meant . . . free hours':** These lines are taken from the poem "On Lucy, Countess of Bedford." Their author, Ben Jonson (1573?–1637), was an English playwright and poet.

F　PARAPHRASE MAIN IDEAS

Paraphrase lines 65–68 in your chart. What way of thinking does Miranda describe, and how easy does she think it will be to reverse?

Lines 68–76
REINFORCE *KEY IDEA:* EXPECTATIONS

Discuss What **expectations** about men and women are revealed in the remark that Miranda "'deserved in some star to be a man'" (line 70)? What does Miranda's response convey about those expectations? ***Possible answer:*** *The remark suggests that women are not expected to think and act independently as men do. Miranda's response suggests that she rejects those expectations.*

READING STRATEGY

F　PARAPHRASE MAIN IDEAS

Possible answer: *Paraphrase: Men thought an admirable woman was not really a woman but was like a man. I worried that their view of women as by nature inferior to men could never be changed. Miranda suggests that this shows a deeply held belief about the inferiority of women, one that will be very hard to reverse.*

SELECTION WRAP-UP

SUMMARIZE Have students summarize Fuller's reactions to the adjectives *manly* and *masculine* for describing positive qualities.

FOR STRATEGIC READERS

②　Targeted Passage [Lines 79–98]

In this passage, Miranda explains her dislike of *manly* as a synonym for *heroic.*

- Which word in Jonson's poem does Miranda dislike?
- How does the speaker interpret Jonson's use of the word in his poem?
- How does Miranda think Jonson's poem should be worded?

FOR ADVANCED LEARNERS/AP

Evaluate Character　Distribute an Open Mind graphic organizer and have students explore the character of Miranda.

well educated
self-confident
independent
opinionated

Ask students to develop criteria for evaluating Miranda as a potential friend, teammate, or project partner. Challenge students to think about Miranda's intellectual characteristics and her personality. Invite students to share their organizers and responses with the class.

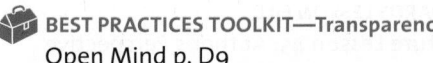

BEST PRACTICES TOOLKIT—Transparency Open Mind p. D9

Practice and Apply

After Reading

Use these copy masters to check understanding and provide extra support:

R RESOURCE MANAGER—Copy Masters
Reading Check p. 181
Author's Perspective p. 177
Question Support p. 182

Additional selection questions are provided for teachers on page 171.

ANSWERS

1. *Miranda's father believed that men and women were equal.*

2. *Miranda believes that her father's respect, high expectations, encouragement, and lack of condescension made her the self-reliant woman she is.*

3. *The men mean that Miranda possesses admirable qualities. They see the qualities of courage, confidence, and intelligence as male traits, and they view men as inherently better than women.*

Possible answers:

4. ■ **SKILLS FOCUS** **Paraphrase Main Ideas**
Fuller's main point is that persistence, courage, and other heroic qualities are not male qualities, but universal ones. She says they "are the most womanly no less than the most manly qualities" (lines 94–95). She no longer wants them to be labeled as male traits.

5. ● **SKILLS FOCUS** **Author's Perspective**
Fuller believes that self-reliance is crucial if a woman is to transcend society's expectations. She must have her own resources to overcome inward conflict and outward adversity.

Assess and Reteach

Assess

R RESOURCE MANAGER—Copy Masters
Selection Test A pp. 183–184
Selection Test B/C pp. 185–186
Test Generator CD

Reteach

S STANDARDS LESSON FILE
Literature Lesson 45: Author's Perspective
Research and Study Skills Lesson 12: Paraphrasing

R2.5

Comprehension

1. **Recall** What did Miranda's father believe in regard to the equality of the sexes?

2. **Summarize** According to Miranda, how did her relationship with her father shape her character?

3. **Clarify** What do the men Miranda describes mean when they comment that a woman they admire is "above her sex"?

Literary Analysis

4. **Analyze Main Ideas** Examine the main ideas you **paraphrased** as you read. Then reread the selection's last two paragraphs. What is Fuller's main point about "heroic" qualities such as persistence, confidence, and creativity? Use your own paraphrases as well as specific lines from the text to support your answer.

5. **Examine Author's Perspective** Recall that Fuller was in the Transcendental Club, and think about the ideals that this group embraced. Through her description of Miranda, what was Fuller saying about the traits a woman needed in order to transcend society's **expectations?** Restate Fuller's perspective in one or two sentences. Consider the following as you formulate your answer:

   • Miranda's statement that women "are taught to learn their rule without, not to unfold it from within." (lines 43–44)

   • The contrast between Miranda's upbringing and that of women "so overloaded with precepts by guardians . . . that their minds are impeded by doubts." (lines 50–52)

6. **Draw Conclusions About the Author's Technique** Why might Fuller have chosen to present her views as a dialogue between herself and the fictional Miranda, instead of simply stating her beliefs outright? Explain how the dialogue format helps the author achieve her **purpose.** Cite at least one example from the text to support your analysis.

7. **Compare Texts** Compare Fuller's main ideas with the beliefs Ralph Waldo Emerson sets forth in "Self-Reliance" (page 360). What common elements do the two texts share? In what ways does their focus differ? Cite examples.

Literary Criticism

8. **Historical Context** A friend of Fuller's once described her as possessing "what in woman is generally called a masculine mind; that is, its action was determined by ideas rather than sentiments." Was this just a 19th-century attitude, or is it still prevalent today? Do contemporary Americans still believe that men are governed by reason while women are driven by emotion? Explain your answer.

---

6. *This format allows Fuller to address and refute arguments more easily, as when she suggests Miranda's objections are too particular (lines 90–92).*

7. *Fuller's and Emerson's texts are similar because both present self-reliance as a crucial trait. They differ in focus because Fuller is concerned with how women gain or are prevented from gaining self-reliance and self-determination, whereas Emerson discusses nonconformity and consistency.*

8. *Answers will vary, but students should express and support opinions about emotional reactions as a womanly trait.*

The Transcendental Spirit

In the 19th century, transcendentalism emerged as a fresh intellectual framework for addressing social, economic, political, and cultural changes in America's increasingly complex society. Many of the issues writers of the day struggled with continue to be relevant today. Get into a "transcendental" frame of mind by taking the following quiz.

How TRANSCENDENTAL Are You?

* Do you ever take a walk with no destination in mind? ☐ yes ☐ no

* Do you express your opinions even when they aren't popular? ☐ yes ☐ no

* Would you accept very low pay for a job that you loved? ☐ yes ☐ no

* Do you think there are too many gadgets and gizmos in modern life and that we should all aim to simplify? ☐ yes ☐ no

* Would you go to jail rather than conform to a law that goes against your conscience? ☐ yes ☐ no

Writing to Reflect

Select one of the questions above and respond to it in a focused, well-developed paragraph. Give at least one example from your life to support your answer. Then write one more paragraph exploring how one of the transcendental writers whose work you've just read might have responded to the same question.

Consider

• which question resonated with you the most

• what example(s) from your life might best reveal your beliefs to your audience

• how particular sentences or passages in the readings relate to the question you chose

Extension Online

INQUIRY & RESEARCH Search the Internet for evidence of Henry David Thoreau's legacy. Use the key words *Thoreau* and *Walden* to find several different types of memorials for one of transcendentalism's greatest thinkers. You will find many nonprofit organizations, projects, schools, and centers dedicated to promoting or remembering Thoreau's ideas. Choose three of the most interesting to **report** back to the class on.

CALIFORNIA W2.3

Wrap-Up: The Transcendentalists

This Wrap-Up provides students with an opportunity to revisit the basic tenets of transcendentalism introduced in the literature of this section. How do students' personal beliefs coincide with these ideas? Encourage students to notice how the ideas of transcendentalism remain applicable today.

Writing to Reflect

• Remind students that to *reflect* is to think about an event or issue, then explore its meaning or importance. Reflecting helps readers internalize information they've read, such as about transcendentalism, and apply it to their own lives. In this way, they recall ideas longer and more vividly.

• To find material for the second paragraph, have students decide which author—Emerson, Thoreau, or Fuller—they think spoke most eloquently on transcendentalism. Suggest that students reread selections by that author looking for quotations or supporting ideas.

Extension Online

• As students research online, suggest that they open new windows for each new link. They might also save the URLs of each promising page to preserve them for ongoing reference.

• Instruct students to give a short presentation of their research findings. Presentations could include printed materials from the sites, quotations about the missions of the organizations, or other relevant artifacts that make the memorials interesting.

DIFFERENTIATED INSTRUCTION

FOR ENGLISH LEARNERS

Writing Topic Sentences To help students create a topic sentence, have them restate their chosen question as a sentence. Offer these suggestions:

• I often take a walk with no destination in mind.

• Sometimes I express my opinions even when they aren't popular.

• For a job I loved, I would accept very low pay.

• In modern life, there are too many gadgets and gizmos, and we should all aim to simplify.

• I would go to jail rather than follow a law that goes against my beliefs.

Focus and Motivate

OBJECTIVES

Literary Analysis
- explore the key ideas of things that are **terrifying, safety,** and **grief**
- analyze unity of effect, allegory, and sound devices
- read short stories and a poem

Reading
- understand complex sentences, clarify meaning, and make inferences

Vocabulary
- build vocabulary for reading and writing
- use the Greek root *path* and affixes to help determine meaning (*also an EL language objective*)

Grammar and Writing
- use participles and participial phrases to add descriptive details
- use imperative sentences effectively
- write a description and a monologue

 R3.1, R3.3, R3.4, R1.2, W1.1, W1.2, W1.5, LC1.1

ABOUT THE AUTHOR

After students read page 402, discuss how Poe's "unstable life" resembled a Gothic horror story, full of melodramatic gloom, psychological storms, and picturesque suffering.

USING THE *NOTABLE QUOTE*

Ask students how the quote expresses a Romantic point of view that applies to **Edgar Allan Poe's** work.

Selection Resources

CALIFORNIA

R3.3, R1.2 (p. 425), **W1.1** (p. 426), **W1.2** (p. 426), **LC1.1** (p. 426)

NOTABLE QUOTE
"All that we see or seem, is but a dream within a dream."

FYI
Did you know that Edgar Allan Poe . . .
- invented the modern detective story?
- inspired the name of the Baltimore Ravens football team?
- briefly wrote a literary gossip column?
- publicly denounced the work of Henry Wadsworth Longfellow?

Author Online
For more on Edgar Allan Poe, visit the **Literature Center at ClassZone.com.**

Baltimore, Maryland, scene of Poe's mysterious death

The Fall of the House of Usher
Short Story by Edgar Allan Poe

Edgar Allan Poe
c. 1809–1849

"The Raven" has been called the best-known poem in American literature; "The Fall of the House of Usher" is a masterpiece of Gothic horror. Both of these works were the creation of one feverish imagination, that of poet, critic, and fiction innovator Edgar Allan Poe.

Haunted by Death Once called one of literature's "most brilliant, but erratic, stars," Poe is as well-known for his unstable life as for his formidable talent. Abandoned by his father as an infant, Poe lost his mother to tuberculosis by the age of 3. He was taken in by John Allan, a wealthy Virginia businessman, but the two had a stormy relationship. At age 18, Poe got himself thrown out of college for gambling debts, beginning a lifelong pattern of self-sabotage. Estranged from Allan as a young man, Poe formed a new family with his aunt and his young cousin, Virginia Clemm. In 1836, he and Virginia married publicly, although they had probably married in secret the year before, when she was only 13. She died 11 years later, and the devastated Poe died 2 years after. Theories about the cause of his death range from alcohol poisoning to brain lesions to rabies.

Making Ends Meet For much of his adult life, Poe struggled to support his family. He landed promising positions at a series of literary magazines, spoiling one opportunity after another with his erratic behavior. At the same time, his scathing reviews made him a feared and respected critic, and his inventive short stories brought him acclaim. Although his life matched the Romantic ideal of the starving artist who suffered for the purity of his art, Poe's stories were designed to reach a wide audience. His successes with horror, science fiction, and detective stories proved his mastery of popular genres.

Tortured Soul Poe's distinctive themes included madness, untimely death, and obsession. Given his troubled life, many critics have interpreted Poe's deranged narrators as reflections of the author's own state of mind. But Poe was a brilliant and controlled stylist, whose theories of art championed rigorous structure, careful use of language, and the masterful creation of a single, calculated effect. His fascination with the macabre was equaled by his interest in logic; his supremely rational detective C. Auguste Dupin inspired Sir Arthur Conan Doyle's scientific sleuth Sherlock Holmes. Poe's life and work exemplify the deepest divisions of the self: the conflict of beautiful ideals and dark impulses.

402

 RESOURCE MANAGER UNIT 2
Plan and Teach pp. 187–194, 211–218, 235–242
Literary Analysis
Summary pp. 195†*, 196‡*, 219†*, 220‡*
Unity of Effect pp. 197, 198†*
Allegory pp. 221, 222†*
Sound Devices pp. 243, 244†*
Question Support pp. 205*, 229*, 247*
Reading
Complex Sentences pp. 199, 200†*

Clarify Meaning pp. 223, 224†*
Make Inferences pp. 245, 246†*
Reading Check pp. 204, 228
Vocabulary
Study pp. 201*, 225*
Practice pp. 202, 226
Strategy pp. 203, 227
Grammar and Writing pp. 206, 248
Assessment Selection Tests A, B/C pp. 207*, 209*, 231*, 233*, 249*, 251*
 Test Generator CD

📦 **BEST PRACTICES TOOLKIT**
Differentiated Instruction pp. 31–38*
Scaffolding Instruction pp. 43–46*
Graphic Organizers/Strategies
Definition Mapping • Jigsaw • Using a Dictionary or Thesaurus Effectively • Analysis Frames • Observation Chart • Making Inferences • Word Questioning • Freewriting

Reading Support
🔊 Audio Anthology CD*
Technology
ℹ️ Literature, Vocabulary, and Writing Centers at **ClassZone.com**
🔊 WriteSmart CD

---

* Resources for Differentiation   *† Also in Spanish*   *‡ In Haitian Creole and Vietnamese*

LITERARY ANALYSIS: UNITY OF EFFECT

Some writers insist that plot or character drives a story. Edgar Allan Poe wanted his stories to achieve a **unity of effect,** where every element—plot, character, setting, and imagery—helped create a single effect, or **mood,** as in this opening sentence from the selection:

During the whole of a dull, dark, and soundless day in the autumn of the year, when the clouds hung oppressively low ...

The ominous details set a scene of instant gloom. As you read, note the choices Poe makes to achieve his intended effect.

READING SKILL: UNDERSTAND COMPLEX SENTENCES

Poe's sentences have a nervous, excited quality: they pile on details and jump from one subject to another. Use these strategies to help you understand Poe's complex sentences:

- Focus on the main idea. Finding the main subject and verb of a sentence can help you identify its main idea.
- Break long sentences into shorter ones that focus on one idea. Group modifiers with the words they describe.
- Keep reading. Poe often restates ideas, and a confusing sentence might be followed by one easier to understand.

Apply these strategies as you read. Using a chart like the one shown, paraphrase five especially complex sentences.

Line Numbers for Poe's Sentence	My Paraphrase

VOCABULARY IN CONTEXT

Poe was fascinated with unusual language. Review the vocabulary words, noting any familiar roots, prefixes, or suffixes that might help you unlock the meanings of the words.

WORD LIST	affinity	demeanor	insipid
	alleviation	equivocal	pertinacity
	anomaly	inordinate	vagary
	apathy		

Where does TERROR *begin?*

KEY IDEA Fear can be a reasonable response to an immediate danger, like the instant alarm you would feel upon seeing a car racing toward you. But some of the things we find most **terrifying** don't present any real threat. A strange noise in the night, a creepy phone call, a creaking door slowly opening—what makes us afraid of things that can't really hurt us?

QUICKWRITE Recall times when you were frightened for no good reason: a walk in a familiar place that seemed strangely spooky or a sudden paranoia about being home alone. Describe what triggered your fear and why. How much of your terror was the result of your own imagination?

403

Where does TERROR *begin?*

Ask the question and then have a volunteer read the **KEY IDEA** aloud. Ask whether a **terrifying** feeling can sometimes be enjoyable, and if so, why. Have students complete the **QUICKWRITE.** Invite students who wish to read their quickwrites aloud to do so.

SKILLS FOCUS

LITERARY ANALYSIS

● UNITY OF EFFECT

To support instruction, share this example:

> The lone rider pulled his coat tightly around him to ward off the cold wind. Dark, threatening clouds rushed to fill the sky. He urged his nervous horse forward into the valley, where shadows obscured the path and unseen creatures screeched.

Have students describe the effect of the passage and cite details that contribute to it. *Possible answer: The effect is ominous; details include "lone rider," "cold wind," "dark, threatening clouds," "nervous horse," "shadows," and "unseen creatures."*

CHECK UNDERSTANDING Have students write sentences that add to the unity of effect of the passage.

READING SKILL

■ UNDERSTAND COMPLEX SENTENCES

Direct students' attention to the three bulleted strategies for understanding Poe's sentences. Guide them in applying these suggestions to the first sentence of "The Fall of the House of Usher" (p. 404, lines 1–5).

> **R** RESOURCE MANAGER—Copy Master
> Understand Complex Sentences p. 199 (for student use while reading the selection)

VOCABULARY

▲ VOCABULARY IN CONTEXT

DIAGNOSE WORD KNOWLEDGE To determine preteaching needs, have all students complete Vocabulary in Context. Definitions are provided on the pages indicated: *affinity* (p. 407), *alleviation* (p. 406), *anomaly* (p. 418), *apathy* (p. 410), *demeanor* (p. 418), *equivocal* (p. 407), *inordinate* (p. 408), *insipid* (p. 409), *pertinacity* (p. 414), *vagary* (p. 417).

PRETEACH VOCABULARY Preteach vocabulary with this copy master. Read each item aloud.

> **R** RESOURCE MANAGER—Copy Master
> Vocabulary Study p. 201

MORE VOCABULARY SUPPORT
For additional activities and guidelines, see

 BEST PRACTICES TOOLKIT
Scaffolding Vocabulary Instruction pp. 43–46
ⓘ Vocabulary Center at **ClassZone.com**

SUMMARY

This short story begins as the narrator arrives at the home of his boyhood friend, Roderick Usher. The narrator finds Usher greatly changed and depressed, and his home in decay. The narrator tries to raise his friend's spirits, but during his visit, Usher's ailing sister, Madeline, dies. After her burial, Usher and the narrator hear strange sounds. Then Madeline appears, dressed in her burial garments. Falling into each other's arms, brother and sister die together. As the narrator flees, the mansion splits apart and falls into the lake.

THE FALL OF THE
House of Usher

Edgar Allan Poe

Son coeur est un luth suspendu;
Sitôt qu'on le touche il résonne.
　　　　　　　　　　—De Béranger

"His heart is a hanging lute; / As soon as one touches it, it sounds" (lines from a poem by the 19th-century French poet Pierre Jean de Béranger).

ANALYZE VISUALS
What mood does this image convey? Identify specific elements, such as color, texture, and composition, that contribute to this mood.

(1) Targeted Passage

During the whole of a dull, dark, and soundless day in the autumn of the year, when the clouds hung oppressively low in the heavens, I had been passing alone, on horseback, through a singularly dreary tract of country, and at length found myself, as the shades of the evening drew on, within view of the melancholy House of Usher. I know not how it was—but, with the first glimpse of the building, a sense of insufferable gloom pervaded my spirit. I say insufferable; for the feeling was unrelieved by any of that half-pleasurable, because poetic, sentiment with which the mind usually receives even the sternest natural images of the desolate or terrible. I looked
10 upon the scene before me—upon the mere house, and the simple landscape features of the domain—upon the bleak walls—upon the vacant, eye-like windows—upon a few rank sedges—and upon a few white trunks of decayed trees—with an utter depression of soul which I can compare to no earthly sensation more properly than to the after-dream of the reveller

12 rank sedges: overgrown grassy plants.

Illustrations by Shane Rebenscheid.

DIFFERENTIATED INSTRUCTION

FOR ALL STUDENTS

Provide these independent projects to extend the lesson:

- Create music, drawings, or paintings to convey the spirit of Roderick Usher.

- Report on Poe's influence on succeeding generations of writers and artists.

For further details on these projects, see

R RESOURCE MANAGER
Ideas for Extension pp. 192–193

FOR STRATEGIC READERS

In combination with the *Audio Anthology CD,* use one or more Targeted Passages (pp. 404, 407, 409, 410, 415, 417, 420, 422) to ensure that students focus on key story events and concepts. Targeted Passages are also good for English learners.

(1) Targeted Passage [Lines 1–13]

This passage describes the narrator's journey to the House of Usher and establishes a unified effect of gloom.

ANALYZE VISUALS

Possible answer: The image conveys a mood of gloom, decay, melancholy, and foreboding. Specific elements that contribute to this mood include the dark colors, the bareness of the sky and earth, the bare branches in the foreground, the chilly white light on some of the branches, and the pattern of cracks that gives the effect of an old painting.

BACKGROUND

Poe and the Gothic Tale Emphasize to students that, as they read in the Unit 2 historical essay, Poe was a leading master of American gothic literature. As such, he sought to examine the emotional side of the human experience. When he describes the setting and characters of "The House of Usher" in minute detail, it is not for the primary purpose of creating a mental image for the reader, but rather to show the psychology of horror and madness through the perceptions of the narrator. This narrator not only witnesses madness and horror in the House of Usher, but participates in it as well.

- What is the narrator doing in this passage?
- What mood is the narrator in?
- What do the landscape and the house look like?

FOR ENGLISH LEARNERS

Related Vocabulary Teach these related words that help build mood: *dull, dark* (line 1); *oppressively* (line 2); *dreary* (line 3); *melancholy* (line 5); *gloom* (line 6); *desolate* (line 9); *bleak, vacant* (line 11); *decayed, depression* (line 13).

Prereading For prereading instruction for English learners, see

📙 **BEST PRACTICES TOOLKIT**
Scaffolding Reading Instruction pp. 43–46

FOR ADVANCED LEARNERS/AP

AP exercises in the bottom channel provide additional challenge for students. Use these suggestions for small groups or individuals.

ADDITIONAL GUIDELINES

For more help with differentiation and tips for classroom management, see

📙 **BEST PRACTICES TOOLKIT**
Differentiated Instruction pp. 31–38

Ⓐ UNITY OF EFFECT

Possible answer: The mood is one of gloom and dread. Details include "an iciness, a sinking, a sickening of the heart" (line 16); the narrator's unnerved feeling and "shadowy fancies" (lines 19–21); the "precipitous brink of a black and lurid tarn" (lines 28–29); and the narrator's "shudder" at the lake's "ghastly" reflections of the house (lines 30–31).

If students need help . . . Have them use the chart introduced on page 403 to paraphrase mood-creating details of the scene.

Line Numbers for Poe's Sentence	My Paraphrase
16–18	I felt a sinking, heartsick feeling, and I couldn't snap myself out of it.

Lines 33–46
TIERED DISCUSSION PROMPTS

Use these prompts to help students understand the characters and their background:

Recall What has been the narrator's relationship with Roderick Usher in the past? Why did Usher write to him? *Possible answer: Usher was one of the narrator's "boon companions in boyhood" (line 35), but the two have not seen each other in many years. Usher wrote to ask that the narrator visit him to alleviate a mysterious illness.*

Analyze What can you infer about Usher from the passage? *Possible answer: While Usher spoke of "acute bodily illness" (line 39), the letter showed signs of "nervous agitation" (line 39) and of a "mental disorder" (lines 39–40). The narrator also notices the "manner in which all this . . . was said" (line 43), which suggests that Usher is going through an emotional crisis.*

Synthesize How do these lines contribute to the story's unity of effect? *Possible answer: The description of Usher complements the setting's gloominess.*

---

upon opium—the bitter lapse into everyday life—the hideous dropping off of the veil. There was an iciness, a sinking, a sickening of the heart—an unredeemed dreariness of thought which no goading of the imagination could torture into aught of the sublime. What was it—I paused to think—what was it that so unnerved me in the contemplation of the House of
20 Usher? It was a mystery all insoluble; nor could I grapple with the shadowy fancies that crowded upon me as I pondered. I was forced to fall back upon the unsatisfactory conclusion, that while, beyond doubt, there *are* combinations of very simple natural objects which have the power of thus affecting us, still the analysis of this power lies among considerations beyond our depth. It was possible, I reflected, that a mere different arrangement of the particulars of the scene, of the details of the picture, would be sufficient to modify, or perhaps to annihilate its capacity for sorrowful impression; and, acting upon this idea, I reined my horse to the precipitous brink of a black and lurid tarn that lay in unruffled lustre by the dwelling, and gazed
30 down—but with a shudder even more thrilling than before—upon the remodelled and inverted images of the grey sedge, and the ghastly tree-stems, and the vacant and eye-like windows. Ⓐ

Nevertheless, in this mansion of gloom I now proposed to myself a sojourn of some weeks. Its proprietor, Roderick Usher, had been one of my boon companions in boyhood; but many years had elapsed since our last meeting. A letter, however, had lately reached me in a distant part of the country—a letter from him—which, in its wildly importunate nature, had admitted of no other than a personal reply. The MS. gave evidence of nervous agitation. The writer spoke of acute bodily illness—of a mental
40 disorder which oppressed him—and of an earnest desire to see me, as his best, and indeed his only personal friend, with a view of attempting, by the cheerfulness of my society, some **alleviation** of his malady. It was the manner in which all this, and much more, was said—it was the apparent *heart* that went with his request—which allowed me no room for hesitation; and I accordingly obeyed forthwith what I still considered a very singular summons.

Although, as boys, we had been even intimate associates, yet I really knew little of my friend. His reserve had been always excessive and habitual. I was aware, however, that his very ancient family had been noted, time
50 out of mind, for a peculiar sensibility of temperament, displaying itself, through long ages, in many works of exalted art, and manifested, of late, in repeated deeds of munificent yet unobtrusive charity, as well as in a passionate devotion to the intricacies, perhaps even more than to the orthodox and easily recognizable beauties, of musical science. I had learned, too, the very remarkable fact, that the stem of the Usher race, all time-honored as it was, had put forth, at no period, any enduring branch; in other words, that the entire family lay in the direct line of descent, and had always, with very trifling and very temporary variation, so lain. It was this

28–29 precipitous . . . tarn: steep bank of a small black, repulsive-looking mountain lake.

Ⓐ UNITY OF EFFECT
Reread lines 16–32. Describe the **mood** of the scene. What details of the narrator's reactions contribute to this effect?

38 had admitted of no other than: had required; **MS.:** an abbreviation of *manuscript.*

alleviation (ə-lē'vē-ā'shən) *n.* relief

52 munificent yet unobtrusive: generous yet inconspicuous.

DIFFERENTIATED INSTRUCTION

FOR ENGLISH LEARNERS

Key Academic Vocabulary Use Definition Mapping to teach these words: *temporary* (line 58), *estate* (line 65), *sole* (line 69), *volume* (line 354), *region* (line 389), *resolve* (line 414).

 BEST PRACTICES TOOLKIT—Transparency
Definition Mapping p. E6

deficiency, I considered, while running over in thought the perfect keeping
of the character of the premises with the accredited character of the people,
and while speculating upon the possible influence which the one, in the
long lapse of centuries, might have exercised upon the other—it was this
deficiency, perhaps, of collateral issue, and the consequent undeviating
transmission, from sire to son, of the patrimony with the name, which had, at
length, so identified the two as to merge the original title of the estate in the
quaint and **equivocal** appellation of the "House of Usher"—an appellation
which seemed to include, in the minds of the peasantry who used it, both
the family and the family mansion. **B**

I have said that the sole effect of my somewhat childish experiment—that
of looking down within the tarn—had been to deepen the first singular
impression. There can be no doubt that the consciousness of the rapid increase
of my superstition—for why should I not so term it?—served mainly to
accelerate the increase itself. Such, I have long known, is the paradoxical law of
all sentiments having terror as a basis. And it might have been for this reason
only, that, when I again uplifted my eyes to the house itself, from its image
in the pool, there grew in my mind a strange fancy—a fancy so ridiculous,
indeed, that I but mention it to show the vivid force of the sensations which
oppressed me. I had so worked upon my imagination as really to believe that
about the whole mansion and domain there hung an atmosphere peculiar
to themselves and their immediate vicinity—an atmosphere which had no
affinity with the air of heaven, but which had reeked up from the decayed
trees, and the gray wall, and the silent tarn—a pestilent and mystic vapor, dull,
sluggish, faintly discernible, and leaden-hued.

Shaking off from my spirit what *must* have been a dream, I scanned
more narrowly the real aspect of the building. Its principal feature seemed
to be that of an excessive antiquity. The discoloration of ages had been
great. Minute fungi overspread the whole exterior, hanging in a fine tangled
web-work from the eaves. Yet all this was apart from any extraordinary
dilapidation. No portion of the masonry had fallen; and there appeared to
be a wild inconsistency between its still perfect adaptation of parts, and the
crumbling condition of the individual stones. In this there was much that
reminded me of the specious totality of old wood-work which has rotted
for long years in some neglected vault, with no disturbance from the breath
of the external air. Beyond this indication of extensive decay, however,
the fabric gave little token of instability. Perhaps the eye of a scrutinizing
observer might have discovered a barely perceptible fissure, which, extending
from the roof of the building in front, made its way down the wall in a
zigzag direction, until it became lost in the sullen waters of the tarn. **C**

Noticing these things, I rode over a short causeway to the house. A
servant in waiting took my horse, and I entered the Gothic archway of the
hall. A valet, of stealthy step, thence conducted me, in silence, through
many dark and intricate passages in my progress to the *studio* of his master.

62–63 this deficiency . . . issue: for some reason, the Ushers have few descendants.

equivocal (ĭ-kwĭv′ə-kəl) *adj.* ambiguous

B COMPLEX SENTENCES
Identify the main idea of lines 62–68. What are the two meanings of the phrase "the House of Usher"?

affinity (ə-fĭn′ĭ-tē) *n.* a kinship or likeness

② Targeted Passage

92 specious totality: false appearance of soundness.

96 fissure: long narrow crack.

C GRAMMAR AND STYLE
Reread lines 95–98. Note how Poe uses the **participle** "scrutinizing" and the **participial phrase** "extending from the roof of the building in front" as modifiers.

THE FALL OF THE HOUSE OF USHER **407**

READING SKILL

B COMPLEX SENTENCES

Possible answer: *For some reason, the Ushers produce few descendants, so the only living members of the family are those who live in the mansion. The phrase "House of Usher" refers to the family members and to the house itself.*

If students need help . . .

- Have them look up difficult words such as *deficiency, collateral, consequent,* and *undeviating* (line 63).
- Point out that *collateral* and *issue* (line 63) are multiple-meaning words. Remind students to find the right meanings for the context.

Lines 71–74
REINFORCE *KEY IDEA*: TERRIFYING

Discuss According to the narrator, what is the "law" that rules all **terrifying** things? *Possible answer: The law is that when we become aware of being terrified, our awareness increases the terror.*

C GRAMMAR AND STYLE

Participles and Participial Phrases Remind students that a participle is a verb form that is used as an adjective. Participles ending in *-ing* are present participles; participles ending in *-ed* are past participles. A participial phrase is one that contains a participle and words that modify it. In lines 95–98, "scrutinizing" modifies "observer." The phrase "extending from the roof of the building in front" modifies "fissure." Invite students to find other examples of participles and participial phrases as they read.

FOR STRATEGIC READERS

② Targeted Passage [Lines 84–98]

This passage describes the house lived in by the Ushers.

- What is the main feature the narrator observes?
- In what condition is the house?
- What evidence of decay does the narrator describe?
- What is the "fissure"?

FOR ENGLISH LEARNERS

Comprehension: Text Structure Remind students that Poe often uses long, complex sentences with difficult constructions. Give the examples "It was possible . . . eye-like windows" (25–32) and "It was this deficiency . . . the family mansion" (58–68). Guide students in using one or more of the strategies for understanding complex sentences, outlined on page 403, to decipher these sentences.

THE FALL OF THE HOUSE OF USHER **407**

TIERED DISCUSSION PROMPTS

Use these prompts to help students understand Roderick Usher:

Summarize What are the principal qualities that mark Roderick Usher's appearance?
Possible answer: He has a striking, handsome face with a pale complexion, soft, fine hair, and a lack of energy. His complexion has become "ghastly."

Analyze What inner changes can you infer from the outer changes in Usher?
Possible answer: He is suffering from emotional distress.

Evaluate Do you think Poe overwrites in his description of Usher, or do you think the abundance of complex detail makes his description more effective? *Some students may say that Poe's style is antiquated and too ornate to convey a vivid picture; others will say that his rich descriptions draw the reader in.*

Much that I encountered on the way contributed, I know not how, to heighten the vague sentiments of which I have already spoken. While the objects around me—while the carvings of the ceilings, the sombre tapestries of the walls, the ebon blackness of the floors, and the phantasmagoric armorial trophies which rattled as I strode, were but matters to which, or to such as which, I had been accustomed from my infancy—while I hesitated not to acknowledge how familiar was all this—I still wondered to find how unfamiliar were the fancies which ordinary images were stirring up. On one of the staircases, I met the physician of the family. His countenance, I thought, wore a mingled expression of low cunning and perplexity. He accosted me with trepidation and passed on. The valet now threw open a door and ushered me through into the presence of his master.

The room in which I found myself was very large and lofty. The windows were long, narrow, and pointed, and at so vast a distance from the black oaken floor as to be altogether inaccessible from within. Feeble gleams of encrimsoned light made their way through the trellised panes, and served to render sufficiently distinct the more prominent objects around; the eye, however, struggled in vain to reach the remoter angles of the chamber, or the recesses of the vaulted and fretted ceiling. Dark draperies hung upon the walls. The general furniture was profuse, comfortless, antique, and tattered. Many books and musical instruments lay scattered about, but failed to give any vitality to the scene. I felt that I breathed an atmosphere of sorrow. An air of stern, deep, and irredeemable gloom hung over and pervaded all.

Upon my entrance, Usher arose from a sofa on which he had been lying at full length, and greeted me with a vivacious warmth which had much in it, I at first thought, of an overdone cordiality—of the constrained effort of the *ennuyé* man of the world. A glance, however, at his countenance convinced me of his perfect sincerity. We sat down; and for some moments, while he spoke not, I gazed upon him with a feeling of half pity, half of awe. Surely, man had never before so terribly altered, in so brief a period, as had Roderick Usher! It was with difficulty that I could bring myself to admit the identity of the wan being before me with the companion of my early boyhood. Yet the character of his face had been at all times remarkable. A cadaverousness of complexion; an eye large, liquid, and luminous beyond comparison; lips somewhat thin and very pallid, but of a surpassingly beautiful curve; a nose of a delicate Hebrew model, but with a breadth of nostril unusual in similar formations; a finely moulded chin, speaking, in its want of prominence, of a want of moral energy; hair of a more than web-like softness and tenuity; these features, with an **inordinate** expansion above the regions of the temple, made up altogether a countenance not easily to be forgotten. And now in the mere exaggeration of the prevailing character of these features, and of the expression they were wont to convey, lay so much of change that I doubted to whom I spoke. The now ghastly pallor of the skin, and the now miraculous lustre of the eye, above all things startled and

106–107 phantasmagoric armorial trophies (făn-tăz′mə-gôr′ĭk): fantastic wall decorations bearing coats of arms.

121 vaulted and fretted: arched and decorated with interlaced designs.

129 ennuyé (äṅ-nwē-yā′) *French:* bored.

136 cadaverousness of complexion: a corpselike appearance.

inordinate (ĭn-ôr′dn-ĭt) *adj.* exceeding reasonable limits; excessive

---

DIFFERENTIATED INSTRUCTION

FOR ENGLISH LEARNERS
Language: Punctuation and Print Cues Poe frequently uses dashes, as in lines 105, 108, 109, 128, 151, 153, 159, 160, 168, 182, 183, and 189. What effects do these print cues create?
Possible answer: They produce a spontaneous look and flow, as though the narrator is quickly jotting down his uncensored impressions.

FOR ADVANCED LEARNERS/AP
Critical Interpretation Many scholars point out the similarities between the instability of Usher's house and the physical and mental instability of Usher. At the very beginning of the story, we see the house in a state of decay, one that affects the narrator with "insufferable gloom" (line 6). When the narrator enters the house, he finds his friend in the same decaying condition. Ask students to identify and discuss other parallels between Usher and the house

and to provide an interpretation of the meaning of these connections.

even awed me. The silken hair, too, had been suffered to grow all unheeded, and as, in its wild gossamer texture, it floated rather than fell about the face, I could not, even with effort, connect its Arabesque expression with any idea
150 of simple humanity. **D**

In the manner of my friend I was at once struck with an incoherence—an inconsistency; and I soon found this to arise from a series of feeble and futile struggles to overcome an habitual trepidancy—an excessive nervous agitation. For something of this nature I had indeed been prepared, no less by his letter, than by reminiscences of certain boyish traits, and by conclusions deduced from his peculiar physical conformation and temperament. His action was alternately vivacious and sullen. His voice varied rapidly from a tremulous indecision (when the animal spirits seemed utterly in abeyance) to that species of energetic concision—that abrupt,
160 weighty, unhurried, and hollow-sounding enunciation—that leaden, self-balanced, and perfectly modulated guttural utterance, which may be observed in the lost drunkard, or the irreclaimable eater of opium, during the periods of his most intense excitement.

It was thus that he spoke of the object of my visit, of his earnest desire to see me, and of the solace he expected me to afford him. He entered, at some length, into what he conceived to be the nature of his malady. It was, he said, a constitutional and a family evil, and one for which he despaired to find a remedy—a mere nervous affection, he immediately added, which would undoubtedly soon pass off. It displayed itself in a host of unnatural
170 sensations. Some of these, as he detailed them, interested and bewildered me; although, perhaps, the terms and the general manner of their narration had their weight. He suffered much from a morbid acuteness of the senses; the most **insipid** food was alone endurable; he could wear only garments of certain texture; the odors of all flowers were oppressive; his eyes were tortured by even a faint light; and there were but peculiar sounds, and these from stringed instruments, which did not inspire him with horror.

To an anomalous species of terror I found him a bounden slave. "I shall perish," said he, "I *must* perish in this deplorable folly. Thus, thus, and not otherwise, shall I be lost. I dread the events of the future, not in themselves,
180 but in their results. I shudder at the thought of any, even the most trivial, incident, which may operate upon this intolerable agitation of soul. I have, indeed, no abhorrence of danger, except in its absolute effect—in terror. In this unnerved—in this pitiable, condition—I feel that the period will sooner or later arrive when I must abandon life and reason together, in some struggle with the grim phantasm, FEAR." **E**

I learned, moreover, at intervals, and through broken and equivocal hints, another singular feature of his mental condition. He was enchained by certain superstitious impressions in regard to the dwelling which he tenanted, and whence, for many years, he had never ventured forth—in
190 regard to an influence whose suppositious force was conveyed in terms too

149 Arabesque (ăr'a-běsk'): intricately interwoven, like the design of an Oriental rug.

D UNITY OF EFFECT
Reread lines 132–150. Poe often uses **exaggeration** to add drama to his descriptions. Which details of Roderick's appearance show this technique at work?

159 concision: terseness; brevity in use of words.

③ Targeted Passage

insipid (ĭn-sĭp'ĭd) *adj.* lacking in flavor; bland

175 but peculiar: only certain.

E COMPLEX SENTENCES
Reread the description of Roderick's state of mind in lines 177–185, and identify the idea that is repeatedly emphasized. What does Roderick seem to be afraid of?

190 suppositious: supposed.

D UNITY OF EFFECT

Possible answer: Details of Roderick's appearance that use exaggeration to add drama include his cadaverous complexion; his "eye large, liquid, and luminous beyond comparison" (lines 136–137); his thin and pale but beautiful lips; his unusual nostrils; the "inordinate expansion" above his temples (lines 141–142); the "ghastly pallor of the skin" (lines 145–146); his wild, floating hair; and the lack of connection between these features and "any idea of simple humanity" (lines 149–150).

E COMPLEX SENTENCES

Possible answer: Roderick believes his fear itself will kill him. He is as afraid of his own fear as he is of death.

FOR STRATEGIC READERS

③ Targeted Passage [Lines 164–185]

This passage describes Roderick's view of his own psychological state.

- What things has Roderick become sensitive to?

- What explanations does Roderick give for his current condition?

- What is Roderick afraid will happen to him?

FOR ADVANCED LEARNERS/AP

Epigraph Have students reread the epigraph at the beginning of the story on page 404. Ask them to discuss how this epigraph can be applied to the description of Roderick Usher on page 409. How do the description and the epigraph enhance each other's meaning?

shadowy here to be re-stated—an influence which some peculiarities in the mere form and substance of his family mansion had, by dint of long sufferance, he said, obtained over his spirit—an effect which the *physique* of the gray walls and turrets, and of the dim tarn into which they all looked down, had, at length, brought about upon the *morale* of his existence.

He admitted, however, although with hesitation, that much of the peculiar gloom which thus afflicted him could be traced to a more natural and far more palpable origin—to the severe and long-continued illness—indeed to the evidently approaching dissolution—of a tenderly beloved
200 sister—his sole companion for long years—his last and only relative on earth. "Her decease," he said, with a bitterness which I can never forget, "would leave him (him, the hopeless and the frail) the last of the ancient race of the Ushers." While he spoke, the lady Madeline (for so she was called) passed through a remote portion of the apartment, and, without having noticed my presence, disappeared. I regarded her with an utter astonishment not unmingled with dread—and yet I found it impossible to account for such feelings. A sensation of stupor oppressed me as my eyes followed her retreating steps. When a door, at length, closed upon her, my glance sought instinctively and eagerly the countenance of the brother—but he had buried
210 his face in his hands, and I could only perceive that a far more than ordinary wanness had overspread the emaciated fingers through which trickled many passionate tears.

The disease of the lady Madeline had long baffled the skill of her physicians. A settled **apathy,** a gradual wasting away of the person, and frequent although transient affections of a partially cataleptical character were the unusual diagnosis. Hitherto she had steadily borne up against the pressure of her malady, and had not betaken herself finally to bed; but on the closing in of the evening of my arrival at the house, she succumbed (as her brother told me at night with inexpressible agitation) to the prostrating
220 power of the destroyer; and I learned that the glimpse I had obtained of her person would thus probably be the last I should obtain—that the lady, at least while living, would be seen by me no more.

For several days ensuing, her name was unmentioned by either Usher or myself; and during this period I was busied in earnest endeavors to alleviate the melancholy of my friend. We painted and read together, or I listened, as if in a dream, to the wild improvisations of his speaking guitar. And thus, as a closer and still closer intimacy admitted me more unreservedly into the recesses of his spirit, the more bitterly did I perceive the futility of all attempt at cheering a mind from which darkness, as if an inherent positive
230 quality, poured forth upon all the objects of the moral and physical universe in one unceasing radiation of gloom. **F**

I shall ever bear about me a memory of the many solemn hours I thus spent alone with the master of the House of Usher. Yet I should fail in any attempt to convey an idea of the exact character of the studies, or of the

---

ANALYZE VISUALS
What techniques has the artist used to create contrast between Madeline and the two men?

④ Targeted Passage

apathy (ăp'ə-thē) *n.* lack of feeling or interest

215 transient . . . cataleptical (kăt'l-ĕp'tĭ-kəl) **character:** temporary episodes of a trancelike condition.

F COMPLEX SENTENCES
Reread lines 226–231. **Paraphrase** this sentence by breaking it into two shorter sentences, each beginning with the word *I*. What has changed in the narrator's relationship with Roderick?

READING SKILL

F COMPLEX SENTENCES

Possible answer: Paraphrase: I became closer to Roderick. I saw that it was useless to try to cheer him up. The narrator has learned more about Roderick but despairs of helping him in any way.

If students need help . . . Have students add to the chart introduced on page 403 by producing a written paraphrase.

Line Numbers for Poe's Sentence	My Paraphrase
226–231	I became closer to Roderick. I saw that it was useless to try to cheer him up.

DIFFERENTIATED INSTRUCTION

FOR STRATEGIC READERS

④ Targeted Passage [Lines 196–207]

This passage describes the appearance of Madeline Usher, Roderick's twin sister.

- What important event is described in this passage?
- What is wrong with Madeline?
- What would happen if Madeline died?
- How does the narrator react to Madeline's appearance?

FOR ENGLISH LEARNERS

Vocabulary: Outdated Forms Point out that Poe often uses words and phrases that are not used today. Provide the definitions and have students insert them in place of the older terms.

- *by dint of long sufferance* (lines 192–193), "over a long time"
- *not unmingled* (line 206), "mixed"
- *overspread* (line 211), "spread across"
- *borne up against* (line 216), "withstood"
- *betaken* (line 217), "committed"
- *her person* (lines 220–221), "her"
- *I shall ever bear* (line 232), "I will always carry"

ANALYZE VISUALS

Possible answer: The two men are seen only partially. One of them is in silhouette and mostly in shadow; the head of the other is outside the frame of the picture. Madeline, in contrast, is seen in detail and framed in a doorway to focus the viewer's eye. On the other hand, the men are in the foreground and Madeline in the background. This may imply that while Madeline is an intriguing figure, she is less important to the story than Roderick.

Activity Have students decide which of the male figures in the foreground is Roderick and which is the narrator. Have them explain their opinions.

FOR STRATEGIC READERS

Comprehension Support: Using the Illustration Have students compare the picture of Madeline on page 411 with the verbal portrait of her in lines 196–207 and 213–220. Have them find details in the illustration that convey traits described in the passage. ***Possible answer:** Her pallor and her frail, forlorn appearance confirm what the passages state about her illness.*

FOR ADVANCED LEARNERS/AP

Write: Interior Monologue Have students write brief interior monologues for Madeline, Roderick, and the narrator, expressing those characters' thoughts and feelings as Madeline walks through the house. Have students share their writings with the class. Discuss insights and interpretations that the writings provide.

Lines 239–275
REINFORCE *KEY IDEA:* TERRIFYING

Discuss Find words and phrases on page 412 that convey a mood of dread or that foreshadow **terrifying** things to come. *Possible answer: "I shuddered knowing not why" (lines 241–242), "an intensity of intolerable awe" (line 249), "phantasmagoric conceptions" (line 251), "ghastly" (line 259), "the tottering of his lofty reason" (line 275).*

Lines 261–275
TIERED DISCUSSION PROMPTS

Use these prompts to help students understand how Roderick's music signaled a collapse of his reason:

Recall What type of music is Roderick restricted to? Why? *Possible answer: Because of his nervous disorder, Roderick is restricted to music created by stringed instruments.*

Analyze Why does the narrator conclude from Roderick's music that his friend is losing control of his "lofty reason" (line 275)? *Possible answer: The narrator observes the "fervid facility" (line 265) of his playing, his intense concentration, his artificial excitement, and the "mystic current of its meaning" (line 273). He concludes from these qualities that his friend is losing his reason.*

Evaluate Do you agree with the narrator that artistic creations can give insight into a person's mental and emotional makeup? Explain. *Students may say that art is an expression of what its creator thinks and feels deeply, and as such gives a glimpse into the person's mind and emotional state.*

occupations, in which he involved me, or led me the way. An excited and highly distempered ideality threw a sulphureous lustre over all. His long improvised dirges will ring forever in my ears. Among other things, I hold painfully in mind a certain singular perversion and amplification of the wild air of the last waltz of Von Weber. From the paintings over which his
240 elaborate fancy brooded, and which grew, touch by touch, into vagueness at which I shuddered the more thrillingly, because I shuddered knowing not why,—from these paintings (vivid as their images now are before me) I would in vain endeavor to educe more than a small portion which should lie within the compass of merely written words. By the utter simplicity, by the nakedness of his designs, he arrested and over-awed attention. If ever mortal painted an ideal, that mortal was Roderick Usher. For me at least—in the circumstances then surrounding me—there arose out of the pure abstractions which the hypochondriac contrived to throw upon his canvas, an intensity of intolerable awe, no shadow of which felt I ever yet in the
250 contemplation of the certainly glowing yet too concrete reveries of Fuseli.

One of the phantasmagoric conceptions of my friend, partaking not so rigidly of the spirit of abstraction, may be shadowed forth, although feebly, in words. A small picture presented the interior of an immensely long and rectangular vault or tunnel, with low walls, smooth, white, and without interruption or device. Certain accessory points of the design served well to convey the idea that this excavation lay at an exceeding depth below the surface of the earth. No outlet was observed in any portion of its vast extent, and no torch or other artificial source of light was discernable; yet a flood of intense rays rolled throughout, and bathed the whole in a ghastly and
260 inappropriate splendor.

I have just spoken of that morbid condition of the auditory nerve which rendered all music intolerable to the sufferer, with the exception of certain effects of stringed instruments. It was, perhaps, the narrow limits to which he thus confined himself upon the guitar which gave birth, in great measure, to the fantastic character of his performances. But the fervid *facility* of his *impromptus* could not be so accounted for. They must have been, and were, in the notes, as well as in the words of his wild fantasias (for he not unfrequently accompanied himself with rhymed verbal improvisations), the result of that intense mental collectedness and concentration to which
270 I have previously alluded as observable only in particular moments of the highest artificial excitement. The words of one of these rhapsodies I have easily remembered. I was, perhaps, the more forcibly impressed with it as he gave it, because, in the under or mystic current of its meaning, I fancied that I perceived, and for the first time, a full consciousness on the part of Usher of the tottering of his lofty reason upon her throne. The verses, which were entitled "The Haunted Palace," ran very near, if not accurately, thus:—

236 distempered . . . sulphureous (sŭl-fər´ē-əs) **lustre:** diseased creativity gave a nightmarish quality.

239 Von Weber (vŏn vā´bər): the German romantic composer Karl Maria von Weber (1786–1826).

250 Fuseli (fyōō´zə-lē´): the Swiss-born British painter Henry Fuseli (1741–1825), many of whose works feature fantastic or gruesome elements.

266 impromptus (ăn-prôNp-tü´) *French:* musical pieces made up as they are played.

DIFFERENTIATED INSTRUCTION

FOR STRATEGIC READERS
Concept Support: Unity of Effect Remind students of Poe's belief that every detail in a story should contribute to building a single unified effect. Ask students to describe in one word the single effect, or mood, in "The Fall of the House of Usher." *Possible answer: terror.* Ask how the descriptions on this page help build that effect. *Possible answer: The descriptions of Roderick's paintings and music show him on the verge of a frightening mental breakdown.*

FOR ENGLISH LEARNERS
Vocabulary: Prefixes Help students identify the prefixes and clarify the meanings for these words: *distempered* (line 236), *improvised* (line 237), *endeavor* (line 243), *surrounding* (line 247), *hypochondriac* (line 248), *intolerable* and *exception* (line 262), *previously* (line 270), *impressed* (line 272), and *entitled* (line 276).

I

In the greenest of our valleys,
    By good angels tenanted,
Once a fair and stately palace—
    Radiant palace—reared its head.
In the monarch Thought's dominion—
    It stood there!
Never seraph spread a pinion
    Over fabric half so fair.

283–284 Never seraph (sĕr′əf) . . .
half so fair: No angel ever spread
its wing over half so beautiful a
structure.

II

Banners yellow, glorious, golden,
    On its roof did float and flow;
(This—all this—was in the olden
    Time long ago)
And every gentle air that dallied,
    In that sweet day,
Along the ramparts plumed and pallid,
    A winged odor went away.

III

Wanderers in that happy valley
    Through two luminous windows saw
Spirits moving musically
    To a lute's well-tunèd law,
Round about a throne, where sitting
    (Porphyrogene!)
In state his glory well befitting,
    The ruler of the realm was seen.

298 Porphyrogene (pōr-fîr′ə-jēn′):
a son born to a ruling king.

IV

And all with pearl and ruby glowing
    Was the fair palace door,
Through which came flowing, flowing, flowing
    And sparkling evermore,
A troop of Echoes whose sweet duty
    Was but to sing,
In voices of surpassing beauty,
    The wit and wisdom of their king.

Lines 277–308
REINFORCE *KEY IDEA:* TERRIFYING

Discuss Reread the first four stanzas of the poem. How does the palace in the poem underscore the **terrifying** nature of the House of Usher? *Possible answer: The palace is described as a "radiant" place, where banners fly and beautiful voices sing of "The wit and wisdom of their king" (line 308). The beauty of the palace starkly contrasts the dark, melancholy house of Usher.*

FOR STRATEGIC READERS

Paraphrase [small-group option] Have students use Jigsaw Reading to paraphrase the poem "The Haunted Palace." Divide the students into groups, with one group paraphrasing each stanza. Have students present their paraphrases aloud as well as in writing.

BEST PRACTICES TOOLKIT
Jigsaw Reading p. A1

FOR ADVANCED LEARNERS/AP

Discuss Have students compare and contrast the poem "The Haunted Palace" and the story in which it is inserted. Categories to discuss include style, imagery, theme, setting, plot, and characters. Have students discuss whether they find the poem effective in itself, and why or why not.

TIERED DISCUSSION PROMPTS

Use these prompts to help students comprehend and interpret the poem:

Recall What is the poem about? *Possible
answer: It is about a palace "in the olden /
Time long ago" (lines 287–288) that fell on
hard times.*

Interpret What do the haunted palace and
the House of Usher have in common? *Possible answer: They are both grand homes that
are haunted by the past and fall into ruin.*

Evaluate Does the poem contribute to the
story's unity of effect, or detract from it?
*Possible answers: It adds to the unity of ef-
fect by providing a comparison that parallels
the main story; it detracts from the unity
of effect by creating a digression that may
puzzle the reader.*

V

But evil things, in robes of sorrow,
    Assailed the monarch's high estate;
310 (Ah, let us mourn, for never morrow
    Shall dawn upon him, desolate!)
And, round about his home, the glory
    That blushed and bloomed
Is but a dim-remembered story
    Of the old time entombed.

VI

And travellers now within that valley,
    Through the red-litten windows see
Vast forms that move fantastically
320   To a discordant melody;
While, like a rapid ghastly river,
    Through the pale door,
A hideous throng rush out forever,
    And laugh—but smile no more.

I well remember that suggestions arising from this ballad led us into
a train of thought wherein there became manifest an opinion of Usher's
which I mention not so much on account of its novelty (for other men have
thought thus), as on account of the **pertinacity** with which he maintained
it. This opinion, in its general form, was that of the sentience of all vegetable
330 things. But, in his disordered fancy, the idea had assumed a more daring
character, and trespassed, under certain conditions, upon the kingdom of
inorganization. I lack words to express the full extent, of the earnest *abandon*
of his persuasion. The belief, however, was connected (as I have previously
hinted) with the gray stones of the home of his forefathers. The conditions
of the sentience had been here, he imagined, fulfilled in the method of
collocation of these stones—in the order of their arrangement, as well as
in that of the many *fungi* which overspread them, and of the decayed trees
which stood around—above all, in the long undisturbed endurance of
this arrangement, and in its reduplication in the still waters of the tarn. Its
340 evidence—the evidence of the sentience—was to be seen, he said (and I here
stared as he spoke), in the gradual yet certain condensation of an atmosphere
of their own about the waters and the walls. The result was discoverable,
he added, in that silent yet importunate and terrible influence which for
centuries had moulded the destinies of his family, and which made *him* what
I now saw him—what he was. Such opinions need no comment, and I will
make none.

Our books—the books which, for years, had formed no small portion of
the mental existence of the invalid—were, as might be supposed, in strict
keeping with this character of phantasm. We pored together over such works

pertinacity (pûr′tn-ăs′ĭ-tē) *n.*
stubbornness; persistence

329–330 sentience (sĕn′shəns) **of all
vegetable things:** consciousness of
all growing things.

DIFFERENTIATED INSTRUCTION

FOR STRATEGIC READERS

Vocabulary Support Work with students to
use context clues to understand words and
phrases important to the passage.

- *manifest* (line 326), "visible; understandable; clear"

- *abandon* (line 332), "wild freedom"

- *collocation* (line 336), "arrangement"

- *condensation* (line 341), "change of a gas
  into a liquid"

- *importunate* (line 343), "urgent"

- *invalid* (line 348), "someone inactive
  because of long illness"

- *phantasm* (line 349), "ghost; supernatural
  spirit"

350 as the *Ververt et Chartreuse* of Gresset; the *Belphegor* of Machiavelli; the
Heaven and Hell of Swedenborg; the *Subterranean Voyage of Nicholas
Klimm* by Holberg; the *Chiromancy* of Robert Flud, of Jean D'Indaginé,
and of De la Chambre; the *Journey into the Blue Distance* of Tieck; and
the *City of the Sun* of Campanella. Our favorite volume was a small octavo
edition of the *Directorium Inquisitorium*, by the Dominican Eymeric de
Gironne; and there were passages in Pomponius Mela, about the old African
Satyrs and Aegipans, over which Usher would sit dreaming for hours. His
chief delight, however, was found in the perusal of an exceedingly rare and
curious book in quarto Gothic—the manual of a forgotten church—the
360 *Vigiliae Mortuorum secundum Chorum Ecclesiae Maguntinae.*

I could not help thinking of the wild ritual of this work, and of its
probable influence upon the hypochondriac, when, one evening, having
informed me abruptly that the lady Madeline was no more, he stated his
intention of preserving her corpse for a fortnight (previously to its final
interment), in one of the numerous vaults within the main walls of the
building. The worldly reason, however, assigned for this singular proceeding,
was one which I did not feel at liberty to dispute. The brother had been led
to his resolution (so he told me) by consideration of the unusual character
of the malady of the deceased, of certain obtrusive and eager inquiries on
370 the part of her medical men, and of the remote and exposed situation of the
burial-ground of the family. I will not deny that when I called to mind the
sinister countenance of the person whom I met upon the staircase, on the
day of my arrival at the house, I had no desire to oppose what I regarded
as at best but a harmless, and by no means an unnatural, precaution.

At the request of Usher, I personally aided him in the arrangements for
the temporary entombment. The body having been encoffined, we two
alone bore it to its rest. The vault in which we placed it (and which had
been so long unopened that our torches, half smothered in its oppressive
atmosphere, gave us little opportunity for investigation) was small, damp,
380 and entirely without means of admission for light; lying, at great depth,
immediately beneath that portion of the building in which was my own
sleeping apartment. It had been used, apparently, in remote feudal times, for
the worst purposes of a donjonkeep, and, in later days, as a place of deposit
for powder, or some other highly combustible substance, as a portion of its
floor, and the whole interior of a long archway through which we reached
it, were carefully sheathed with copper. The door, of massive iron, had been,
also, similarly protected. Its immense weight caused an unusually sharp,
grating sound, as it moved upon its hinges.

Having deposited our mournful burden upon tressels within this region
390 of horror, we partially turned aside the yet unscrewed lid of the coffin,
and looked upon the face of the tenant. A striking similitude between the
brother and sister now first arrested my attention; and Usher, divining,
perhaps, my thoughts, murmured out some few words from which I learned

**350–356 Ververt et Chartreuse
...Pomponius Mela:** extravagantly
imaginative works of fiction,
theology, philosophy, and geography.

**360 *Vigiliae Mortuorum secundum
Chorum Ecclesiae Maguntinae* Latin:**
Wakes for the Dead, in the Manner
of the Choir of the Church of Mainz.

**364–365 for a fortnight...
interment:** for two weeks prior to its
final burial.

⑤ Targeted Passage

383 donjonkeep (dŏn′jən-kēp):
dungeon.

** UNITY OF EFFECT**
Reread lines 377–388. Why might
Poe have provided so much **detail**
about the structure of the vault?

THE FALL OF THE HOUSE OF USHER **415**

LITERARY ANALYSIS

ⓖ UNITY OF EFFECT

*Possible answer: Poe might have provided
so much detail in order to heighten the
reader's feeling of dread.*

If students need help . . . Ask these
questions:

• What words and phrases make the
description of Madeline's burial vault
especially vivid?

• What effect or mood do those details
create?

FOR STRATEGIC READERS

⑤ Targeted Passage [Lines 375–388]

This passage describes the burial of Madeline
Usher after her death.

• Where do Usher and the narrator bury
Madeline?

• What was the vault once used for?

• What is the atmosphere like in the vault?

FOR ENGLISH LEARNERS

Related Vocabulary [small-group option]
Several words on page 415 are related to the
subject of death: *interment* (line 365), *deceased*
(line 369), *entombment* (line 376), *vault* (line
377), *mournful* (line 389), and *coffin* (line 390).
Have students, working in groups, use a
dictionary or thesaurus to find the meanings
of the words. Tell students that some of the
words, such as *deceased, interment,* and *coffin,*
are commonly used, whereas other words are
less commonly used today.

🧰 **BEST PRACTICES TOOLKIT**
Using a Dictionary or Thesaurus
Effectively p. E2

ANALYZE VISUALS

Activity What aspects of the picture might be considered terrifying? *Possible answers: Aspects of the picture that might be considered terrifying include the open coffin and the lifelike pink flush and faint smile on the dead woman's face.*

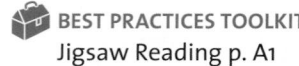

DIFFERENTIATED INSTRUCTION

FOR STRATEGIC READERS

Comprehension Support Have students find details in lines 395–403 that match the details of the illustration. *Possible answers: Madeline's "mockery of a faint blush upon . . . the face" and the "lingering smile upon the lip."*

FOR ENGLISH LEARNERS

Vocabulary: Idioms Have students work in Jigsaw groups and use context clues to figure out the meaning of these idioms on page 417:

- *gone out* (line 409), "disappeared"
- *to and fro* (lines 427–428), "one way and then the other way"
- *Shaking . . . off* (line 431), "Overcoming the feeling"

BEST PRACTICES TOOLKIT
Jigsaw Reading p. A1

that the deceased and himself had been twins, and that sympathies of a scarcely intelligible nature had always existed between them. Our glances, however, rested not long upon the dead—for we could not regard her unawed. The disease which had thus entombed the lady in the maturity of her youth, had left, as usual in all maladies of a strictly cataleptical character, the mockery of a faint blush upon the bosom and the face, and
400 that suspiciously lingering smile upon the lip which is so terrible in death. We replaced and screwed down the lid, and, having secured the door of iron, made our way, with toil, into the scarcely less gloomy apartments of the upper portion of the house.

And now, some days of bitter grief having elapsed, an observable change came over the features of the mental disorder of my friend. His ordinary manner had vanished. His ordinary occupations were neglected or forgotten. He roamed from chamber to chamber with hurried, unequal, and objectless step. The pallor of his countenance had assumed, if possible, a more ghastly hue—but the luminousness of his eye had utterly gone out. The
410 once occasional huskiness of his tone was heard no more; and a tremulous quaver, as if of extreme terror, habitually characterized his utterance. There were times, indeed, when I thought his unceasingly agitated mind was laboring with some oppressive secret, to divulge which he struggled for the necessary courage. At times, again, I was obliged to resolve all into the mere inexplicable **vagaries** of madness, for I beheld him gazing upon vacancy for long hours, in an attitude of the profoundest attention, as if listening to some imaginary sound. It was no wonder that his condition terrified—that it infected me. I felt creeping upon me, by slow yet certain degrees, the wild influences of his own fantastic yet impressive superstitions.

420 It was, especially, upon retiring to bed late in the night of the seventh or eighth day after the placing of the lady Madeline within the donjon, that I experienced the full power of such feelings. Sleep came not near my couch—while the hours waned and waned away. I struggled to reason off the nervousness which had dominion over me. I endeavored to believe that much, if not all of what I felt, was due to the bewildering influence of the gloomy furniture of the room—of the dark and tattered draperies, which, tortured into motion by the breath of a rising tempest, swayed fitfully to and fro upon the walls, and rustled uneasily about the decorations of the bed. But my efforts were fruitless. An irrepressible tremor gradually pervaded
430 my frame; and, at length, there sat upon my very heart an incubus of utterly causeless alarm. Shaking this off with a gasp and a struggle, I uplifted myself upon the pillows, and, peering earnestly within the intense darkness of the chamber, hearkened—I know not why, except that an instinctive spirit prompted me—to certain low and indefinite sounds which came, through the pauses of the storm, at long intervals, I knew not whence. Overpowered by an intense sentiment of horror, unaccountable yet unendurable, I threw on my clothes with haste (for I felt that I should sleep no more during the night), and endeavored to arouse myself from the pitiable condition into which I had fallen, by pacing rapidly to and fro through the apartment. **H**

G Targeted Passage

vagary (vă′gə-rē) n. strange idea

423 couch: bed.

430 incubus: something that burdens like a nightmare.

H COMPLEX SENTENCES
Reread lines 431–435. Identify the main subject and verb of the sentence. Which participial phrases modify this subject?

THE FALL OF THE HOUSE OF USHER 417

Lines 420–439
TIERED DISCUSSION PROMPTS
Use these prompts to help students comprehend and interpret the developing plot:

Connect What is the narrator feeling? Why? *Possible answer: He is feeling a sense of growing terror, due in part to his surroundings, but also due to his own inability to control his emotions.*

Analyze What evidence can you find that hints at the narrator's state of mind? *Possible answers: He cannot sleep; he tries to overcome his nervousness by rationalizing the situation; he becomes tremulous and stares intently into the darkness; he leaps out of bed and paces about the apartment to shake off his nervousness.*

Synthesize What kind of effect does Poe achieve in this passage? How? *Possible answer: Poe achieves a mood of building torment and terror by balancing the narrator's description of his surroundings—the "dark, tattered draperies" set in motion by "the breath of a rising tempest" (lines 426–427)—with the description of his inner struggles.*

READING SKILL

H COMPLEX SENTENCES

The main subject is *I*. There are two main verbs, since the sentence has a compound predicate: *uplifted* and *hearkened*. Participial phrases modifying the subject are *Shaking this off* and *peering earnestly*.

If students need help . . . Present this model:

Gazing out the window, she looked at the rain.

Ask students to identify the subject, verb, and participial phrase. *Answer: Subject: she; verb: looked; participial phrase: Gazing out the window.* Tell them to look for a similar pattern in the sentence in lines 431–435.

FOR STRATEGIC READERS
G Targeted Passage [Lines 404–419]

This passage describes Roderick Usher's advancing decline and the narrator's increasing terror.

- What changes come over Roderick after his sister's burial?

- How does the narrator change as he watches the alterations in Usher's looks and behavior?

REINFORCE *KEY IDEA:* TERRIFYING

Discuss How does the weather contribute to the **terrifying** atmosphere of this scene? *Possible answer: The whirlwind threatens to destroy the house. In addition, this weather is terrifying because of the unnatural—or supernatural—luminous gas that surrounds the mansion.*

---

440   I had taken but a few turns in this manner, when a light step on an adjoining staircase arrested my attention. I presently recognized it as that of Usher. In an instant afterward he rapped, with a gentle touch, at my door, and entered, bearing a lamp. His countenance was, as usual, cadaverously wan—but, moreover, there was a species of mad hilarity in his eyes—an evidently restrained *hysteria* in his whole **demeanor.** His air appalled me—but any thing was preferable to the solitude which I had so long endured, and I even welcomed his presence as a relief.

"And you have not seen it?" he said abruptly, after having stared about him for some moments in silence—"you have not then seen it?—but, stay! 450 you shall." Thus speaking, and having carefully shaded his lamp, he hurried to one of the casements, and threw it freely open to the storm.

The impetuous fury of the entering gust nearly lifted us from our feet. It was, indeed, a tempestuous yet sternly beautiful night, and one wildly singular in its terror and its beauty. A whirlwind had apparently collected its force in our vicinity; for there were frequent and violent alterations in the direction of the wind; and the exceeding density of the clouds (which hung so low as to press upon the turrets of the house) did not prevent our perceiving the lifelike velocity with which they flew careering from all points against each other, without passing away into the distance. I say that even 460 their exceeding density did not prevent our perceiving this—yet we had no glimpse of the moon or stars, nor was there any flashing forth of lightning. But the under surfaces of the huge masses of agitated vapor, as well as the terrestrial objects immediately around us, were glowing in the unnatural light of a faintly luminous and distinctly visible gaseous exhalation which hung about and enshrouded the mansion.

"You must not—you shall not behold this!" said I, shuddering, to Usher, as I led him, with a gentle violence, from the window to a seat. "These appearances, which bewilder you, are merely electrical phenomena not uncommon—or it may be that they have their ghastly origin in the rank 470 miasma of the tarn. Let us close this casement;—the air is chilling and dangerous to your frame. Here is one of your favorite romances. I will read, and you shall listen;—and so we will pass away this terrible night together."

The antique volume which I had taken up was the "Mad Trist" of Sir Launcelot Canning; but I had called it a favorite of Usher's more in sad jest than in earnest; for, in truth, there is little in its uncouth and unimaginative prolixity which could have had interest for the lofty and spiritual ideality of my friend. It was, however, the only book immediately at hand; and I indulged a vague hope that the excitement which now agitated the hypochondriac, might find relief (for the history of mental disorder is full of 480 similar **anomalies**) even in the extremeness of the folly which I should read. Could I have judged, indeed, by the wild overstrained air of vivacity with which he hearkened, or apparently hearkened, to the words of the tale, I might well have congratulated myself upon the success of my design.

demeanor (dĭ-mē′nər) *n.* behavior

458 careering: going at top speed.

462–463 huge masses . . . terrestrial objects: the huge, fast-moving clouds, as well as the objects on the ground.

470 miasma (mī-ăz′mə): poisonous vapors.

475–476 uncouth . . . prolixity (prō-lĭk′sĭ-tē): clumsy and unimaginative wordiness.

anomaly (ə-nŏm′ə-lē) *n.* departure from the normal rules

DIFFERENTIATED INSTRUCTION

FOR STRATEGIC READERS

Vocabulary Support Poe uses vivid but ornate vocabulary to describe the whirlwind and its effects. Help students find synonyms for the difficult words.

- *casements* (line 451), "windows"
- *impetuous* (line 452), "violent"
- *alterations* (line 455), "changes"
- *density* (line 456), "thickness"
- *velocity* (line 458), "speed"

- *careering* (line 458), "rushing"
- *perceiving* (lines 458, 460), "seeing"
- *terrestrial* (line 463), "earthly"
- *luminous* (line 464), "glowing"
- *enshrouded* (line 465), "covered"

FOR ENGLISH LEARNERS

Vocabulary: Multiple-Meaning Words [paired option] Have students work in pairs to look up these multiple-meaning words and decide which meaning applies: *arrested* (line 441), *species* (line 444), *air* (lines 445 and 481), *sternly* (line 453), *singular* (line 454), *rank* (line 469), *frame* (line 471), *design* (line 483). Challenge students to use the words in sentences.

ANALYZE VISUALS

Activity How does this image capture the narrator's description in lines 453–465 of the tempestuous night sky? *Possible answer: The image captures the eerie beauty of the night sky, one in which the "exceeding density of the clouds" (line 456) is broken by a "faintly luminous and distinctly visible gaseous exhalation" (line 464). The lone figure staring out from the half-open window could be either Roderick or the narrator.*

FOR ADVANCED LEARNERS/AP

Analyze Tone Have students analyze the tone of the passage in which the narrator helps Roderick confront the whirlwind (lines 440–472). Ask students to examine the diction of the descriptive passages and the two characters' dialogue in making their analyses. Point out that tone changes in the course of this passage; have them pinpoint places where the tone becomes more, or less, excited. Then invite students to rewrite passages to change the tone. They may wish to heighten the emotional intensity of the quieter passages such as lines 440–443, or they may wish to reduce the emotional intensity of the more frantic passages. Have students read their versions aloud. Discuss what impact these changes have on the effect of the tale.

Lines 497–527
TIERED DISCUSSION PROMPTS

Use these prompts to help students understand the story within the story and the connections between these two tales:

Recall What causes the narrator to pause in his reading of the story of the "Mad Trist"? *Possible answer: During his first pause, the narrator hears the sound of cracking and ripping similar to that described in the story. The second time he pauses, he hears a "harsh, protracted . . . screaming or grating sound" (lines 524–525), also like that in the story.*

Analyze How do events in the "Mad Trist" help build suspense? *Possible answer: The first sound described in the "Mad Trist" is replicated in the House of Usher. As a result, readers suspect that additional events described in the tale will also be echoed in events in the house. The reader anticipates these events and the anticipation builds suspense.*

Synthesize Based on events that have already occurred and on inferences you make from this description of events during the reading of the "Mad Trist," what do you predict will happen next? Explain. *Accept all thoughtful responses. Students should cite evidence and reasons for their predictions.*

I had arrived at that well-known portion of the story where Ethelred, the hero of the Trist, having sought in vain for peaceable admission into the dwelling of the hermit, proceeds to make good an entrance by force. Here, it will be remembered, the words of the narrative run thus:

"And Ethelred, who was by nature of a doughty heart, and who was now mighty withal, on account of the powerfulness of the wine which he
490 had drunken, waited no longer to hold parley with the hermit, who, in sooth, was of an obstinate and maliceful turn, but, feeling the rain upon his shoulders, and fearing the rising of the tempest, uplifted his mace outright, and, with blows, made quickly room in the plankings of the door for his gauntleted hand; and now pulling therewith sturdily, he so cracked, and ripped, and tore all asunder, that the noise of the dry and hollow-sounding wood alarumed and reverberated throughout the forest."

> At the termination of this sentence I started and, for a moment, paused; for it appeared to me (although I at once concluded that my excited fancy had deceived me)—it appeared to me that, from some very remote portion
> 500 of the mansion, there came, indistinctly, to my ears, what might have been, in its exact similarity of character, the echo (but a stifled and dull one certainly) of the very cracking and ripping sound which Sir Launcelot had so particularly described. It was, beyond doubt, the coincidence alone which had arrested my attention; for, amid the rattling of the sashes of the casements, and the ordinary commingled noises of the still increasing storm, the sound, in itself, had nothing, surely, which should have interested or disturbed me.

I continued the story:

"But the good champion Ethelred, now entering within the door, was sore enraged and amazed to perceive no signal of the maliceful hermit;
510 but, in the stead thereof, a dragon of scaly and prodigious demeanor, and of a fiery tongue, which sate in guard before a palace of gold, with a floor of silver; and upon the wall there hung a shield of shining brass with this legend enwritten—

> *Who entereth herein, a conqueror hath bin;*
> *Who slayeth the dragon, the shield he shall win;*

And Ethelred uplifted his mace, and struck upon the head of the dragon, which fell before him, and gave up his pesty breath, with a shriek so horrid and harsh, and withal so piercing, that Ethelred had fain to close his ears with his hands against the dreadful noise of it, the like whereof was never
520 before heard."

Here again I paused abruptly, and now with a feeling of wild amazement—for there could be no doubt whatever that, in this instance, I did actually hear (although from what direction it proceeded I found it impossible to say) a low and apparently distant, but harsh, protracted, and most unusual screaming or grating sound—the exact counterpart of what

492–494 uplifted his mace . . . gauntleted hand: raised his spiked club and cut a space in the door for his armored, gloved hand.

⑦ Targeted Passage

517 pesty: poisonous.

DIFFERENTIATED INSTRUCTION

FOR STRATEGIC READERS

⑦ Targeted Passage [Lines 497–507]

In this passage, the narrator reads from the "Mad Trist," a story that parallels events in the narrative.

- Why does the narrator pause in his reading?
- What does the narrator hear?
- How does he react?

FOR ENGLISH LEARNERS

Vocabulary: Outdated Forms Explain that Poe used many words and phrases that were seldom used in his time and are even more rarely used today. Have students substitute modern terms for the outdated ones.

- *hold parley* (line 490), "talk"
- *in sooth* (lines 490–491), "truly"
- *of an obstinate and maliceful turn* (line 491), "stubborn and mean"
- *therewith* (line 494), "with that"

- *sore enraged* (line 509), "very angry"
- *in the stead thereof* (line 510), "instead"
- *sate* (line 511), "sat"
- *slayeth* (line 515), "kills"
- *withal* (line 518), "also; besides"
- *had fain* (line 518), "was obliged"
- *whereof* (line 519), "of which"
- *tarried not* (line 548), "did not wait"
- *clangorous* (line 553), "loud"
- *Said I not* (line 565), "Didn't I say"

my fancy had conjured up for the dragon's unnatural shriek as described by the romancer. ❶

Oppressed, as I certainly was, upon the occurrence of this second and
most extraordinary coincidence, by a thousand conflicting sensations,
530 in which wonder and extreme terror were predominant, I still retained
sufficient presence of mind to avoid exciting, by any observation, the
sensitive nervousness of my companion. I was by no means certain that he
had noticed the sounds in question; although, assuredly, a strange alteration
had, during the last few minutes, taken place in his demeanor. From a
position fronting my own, he had gradually brought round his chair, so
as to sit with his face to the door of the chamber; and thus I could but
partially perceive his features, although I saw that his lips trembled as if he
were murmuring inaudibly. His head had dropped upon his breast—yet I
knew that he was not asleep, from the wide and rigid opening of the eye as I
540 caught a glance of it in profile. The motion of his body, too, was at variance
with this idea—for he rocked from side to side with a gentle yet constant
and uniform sway. Having rapidly taken notice of all this, I resumed the
narrative of Sir Launcelot, which thus proceeded:

"And now, the champion, having escaped from the terrible fury of the
dragon, bethinking himself of the brazen shield, and of the breaking up of
the enchantment which was upon it, removed the carcass from out of the
way before him, and approached valorously over the silver pavement of the
castle to where the shield was upon the wall; which in sooth tarried not for
his full coming, but fell down at his feet upon the silver floor, with a mighty
550 great and terrible ringing sound."

No sooner had these syllables passed my lips, than—as if a shield of brass
had indeed, at the moment, fallen heavily upon a floor of silver—I became
aware of a distinct, hollow, metallic, and clangorous, yet apparently muffled,
reverberation. Completely unnerved, I leaped to my feet; but the measured
rocking movement of Usher was undisturbed. I rushed to the chair in which
he sat. His eyes were bent fixedly before him, and throughout his whole
countenance there reigned a stony rigidity. But, as I placed my hand upon
his shoulder, there came a strong shudder over his whole person; a sickly
smile quivered about his lips; and I saw that he spoke in a low, hurried, and
560 gibbering murmur, as if unconscious of my presence. Bending closely over
him, I at length drank in the hideous import of his words.

"Not hear it?—yes, I hear it, and *have* heard it. Long—long—long—many
minutes, many hours, many days, have I heard it—yet I dared not—oh,
pity me, miserable wretch that I am!—I dared not—I *dared* not speak! *We
have put her living in the tomb!* Said I not that my senses were acute? I *now*
tell you that I heard her first feeble movements in the hollow coffin. I heard
them—many, many days ago—yet I dared not—*I dared not speak!* And
now—to-night—Ethelred—ha ha!—the breaking of the hermit's door, and
the death-cry of the dragon, and the clangor of the shield!—say, rather, the

❶ UNITY OF EFFECT
Reread lines 521–527. What
coincidence is repeated?

LITERARY ANALYSIS

❶ UNITY OF EFFECT

*Possible answer: The repeated coincidence
is that after reading about an eerie sound,
the narrator hears such a sound in the
house.*

Extend the Discussion Repetition is one
way Poe achieves unity of effect in this
story. What are some other ways?

FOR ADVANCED LEARNERS/AP

Synthesize The theme of burial alive was a
favorite of Poe's. He used it in several stories,
including "The Cask of Amontillado" and
"The Premature Burial." Why do you think
an author would turn to this same macabre
topic again and again? *Possible answers:
The topic is frightening, and so it helped Poe
achieve his intended effect on the reader; the
topic may have reflected an obsessive fear
in Poe.* Ask students to research Poe to find
evidence that either verifies or refutes their
responses. Have them discuss their findings
as a group and then share their conclusions
with the class.

J UNITY OF EFFECT

Possible answer: *The earlier description of the vault (lines 375–388) alerts the reader that there is something odd about the circumstances of the burial. The vault is "half smothered," which subtly foreshadows Madeline's condition. The "immense weight" of the door makes Madeline's later escape seem all the more horrible.*

ANALYZE VISUALS

Possible answers: *Yes, the artist's interpretation is effective, because the blood on Madeline's dress and the shadows on her face are frightening and ominous. No, the artist's interpretation is not as effective as the description, because it does not reproduce the sound and movement or capture the narrator's horror.*

570 rending of her coffin, and the grating of the iron hinges of her prison, and her struggles within the coppered archway of the vault! Oh! whither shall I fly? Will she not be here anon? Is she not hurrying to upbraid me for my haste? Have I not heard her footstep on the stair? Do I not distinguish that heavy and horrible beating of her heart? MADMAN!"—here he sprang furiously to his feet, and shrieked out his syllables, as if in the effort he were giving up his soul—"MADMAN! I TELL YOU THAT SHE NOW STANDS WITHOUT THE DOOR!" J

As if in the superhuman energy of his utterance there had been found the potency of a spell, the huge antique panels to which the speaker pointed threw slowly back, upon the instant, their ponderous and ebony jaws. It 580 was the work of the rushing gust—but then without those doors there did stand the lofty and enshrouded figure of the lady Madeline of Usher. There was blood upon her white robes, and the evidence of some bitter struggle upon every portion of her emaciated frame. For a moment she remained trembling and reeling to and fro upon the threshold—then, with a low moaning cry, fell heavily inward upon the person of her brother, and in her violent and now final death-agonies, bore him to the floor a corpse, and a victim to the terrors he had anticipated.

From the chamber, and from that mansion, I fled aghast. The storm was still abroad in all its wrath as I found myself crossing the old causeway. 590 Suddenly there shot along the path a wild light, and I turned to see whence a gleam so unusual could have issued; for the vast house and its shadows were alone behind me. The radiance was that of the full, setting, and blood-red moon, which now shone vividly through that once barely discernible fissure, of which I have before spoken as extending from the roof of the building, in a zigzag direction, to the base. While I gazed, the fissure rapidly widened—there came a fierce breath of the whirlwind—the entire orb of the satellite burst at once upon my sight—my brain reeled as I saw the mighty walls rushing asunder—there was a long tumultuous shouting sound like the voice of a thousand waters—and the deep and dank tarn at my feet closed 600 sullenly and silently over the fragments of the "HOUSE OF USHER."

J UNITY OF EFFECT

Reread lines 568–571. Recall the description of the vault you read earlier. In what way does that description help set up the situation of the story's **climax**?

⑧ Targeted Passage

ANALYZE VISUALS

Compare the image on page 423 with the description in lines 581–587. Is the artist's interpretation of the scene effective? Why or why not?

DIFFERENTIATED INSTRUCTION

FOR STRATEGIC READERS

⑧ **Targeted Passage** [Lines 573–587]

This passage highlights the story's height of horror.

- What does Roderick hear on the stair?
- Who stands outside the door?
- How does Roderick meet his end?

FOR ADVANCED LEARNERS/AP

Plot Devices [paired option] Have students work in pairs to use the Analysis Frame: Plot to analyze the plot devices Poe uses in "The Fall of the House of Usher" and to evaluate the effectiveness of those devices in the story.

🧰 **BEST PRACTICES TOOLKIT—Transparency**
Analysis Frame: Plot pp. D21, D28

REINFORCE *KEY IDEA:* TERRIFYING

Discuss How does the **terrifying** mood reach its most intense point in the story's concluding scene? *Possible answer: Madeline's appearance and the death of her and her brother bring all of the mysterious happenings to a culmination. Roderick's and the narrator's fears reach a breaking point that ends the story.*

SELECTION WRAP–UP

REFLECT Have students reflect on the experiences of the characters. Ask which experiences will be the most memorable for them, and why.

⭐ CRITIQUE

- Ask students to compare "The Fall of the House of Usher" to other terrifying stories or films. Have them explain their answers.

- After completing the After Reading questions on page 424, have students revisit their responses and tell whether they have changed their opinions.

FOR ADVANCED LEARNERS/AP

Critical Interpretation [small-group option] The story includes some interesting mirror images, including the image of the House of Usher mirrored in the tarn, the decay of the house mirrored in the decay of Roderick, and the twins, Roderick and Madeline, who mirror each other. Critics have offered many interpretations of the meaning of these double images. Invite students to work in groups to examine them further.

How many instances of mirror images can they find and how elaborate are they? Roderick and Madeline, for example, are twins and share a "striking similitude" (line 391), they share a family illness, and they die together. Have students develop their own interpretations of the purpose of these mirror images. How do they contribute to the theme and plot of the story? Ask groups to share their ideas with the class.

Practice and Apply

After Reading

Use these copy masters to check understanding and provide extra support:

 RESOURCE MANAGER—Copy Masters
Reading Check p. 204
Unity of Effect p. 197
Question Support p. 205

Additional selection questions are provided for teachers on page 191.

ANSWERS

1. *He has come to help his childhood friend Roderick Usher, who invited him to visit.*

2. *She takes to her bed and is expected to die soon.*

3. *He fears that her body may be stolen.*

Possible answers:

4. ■ **SKILLS FOCUS** Understand Complex Sentences *Students may say the mood is less terrifying when conveyed in simple, everyday language.*

5. *The first-person point of view shows how terror in the house overcomes a reasonable person.* **Narrator's response:** *The narrator is strangely afraid, but he believes his feeling is irrational.* **Opinion of Roderick:** *He feels that Roderick's ideas about the house are a product of mental distress.* **Roderick's influence:** *Roderick's attitude and actions disturb the narrator, changing his mood and heightening his uneasiness.* **Efforts to calm his fears:** *The narrator is so influenced by Roderick's ideas that he can no longer talk himself out of his own fear.*

6. *The title describes the decline and fall of both a family and a mansion. It anticipates both kinds of collapse.*

7. ● **SKILLS FOCUS** Unity of Effect *Setting: old, decaying house; windows inaccessible; feeble light; dark draperies, old furniture; gloomy atmosphere.* **Character traits:** *Roderick is distressed, distracted, and hypersensitive to light and sound.* **Plot developments:** *Madeline's illness, death, burial, and re-emergence parallel the intensity of Roderick's emotions and changes in the narrator.* **Imagery:** *images of darkness, dreariness, and decay throughout.*

Comprehension

1. **Recall** Why does the narrator come to the House of Usher?

2. **Recall** What change in Madeline's condition occurs shortly after the narrator's arrival?

3. **Clarify** What are Roderick's reasons for placing Madeline in the vault below the house?

Literary Analysis

4. **Examine Complex Sentences** Review the chart you created as you read. Compare your paraphrases with Poe's original sentences. Without Poe's elaborate language, does the story have the same **mood?** Explain.

5. **Draw Conclusions about Point of View** Explain what each of the following reveals about the narrator's changing response to the house and its inhabitants. How does Poe's use of the first-person point of view help communicate the experience of **terror?**

   • the narrator's response to the house (lines 63–83)
   • his opinion of Roderick (lines 186–195)
   • Roderick's influence on the narrator (lines 417–419)
   • his efforts to calm his own fears (lines 423–431)

6. **Interpret Title** Reread lines 58–68. Based on this passage, explain two possible meanings of the story's title. In what ways does the title help you anticipate the ending of the story?

7. **Analyze Unity of Effect** In what way does each of the following demonstrate Poe's principle of the single effect? Cite key details that show Poe's use of the specified story element to build **mood.**

   • setting (lines 115–125)
   • character traits (lines 172–176)
   • plot developments (lines 216–222)
   • imagery (lines 452–465)

8. **Evaluate Author's Technique** In your opinion, does Poe's technique of the unified effect accomplish its intended purpose? What, if any, are the disadvantages of his approach? Explain.

Literary Criticism

9. **Critical Interpretations** The literary critic Cleanth Brooks dismissed "The Fall of the House of Usher" as an "essentially meaningless" exercise in horror for its own sake. Considering your own reading of the story, do you agree or disagree with this opinion? Cite details to support your answer.

---

8. *Students may say yes because the mood is compelling and the elements of the story work together. Others may say that the mood overwhelms other aspects of the story.*

9. *Students may disagree by challenging the idea that a story must have deep meaning, or by saying that this story vividly portrays a sick mind. They may agree by citing story elements that seem chosen solely for sensationalistic effect.*

Vocabulary in Context

VOCABULARY PRACTICE

Choose the word that is not related in meaning to the other words.

1. (a) dull, (b) uninteresting, (c) insipid, (d) insecure
2. (a) demeanor, (b) antique, (c) manner, (d) interaction
3. (a) conception, (b) delusion, (c) vagary, (d) tome
4. (a) connection, (b) disturbance, (c) affinity, (d) relationship
5. (a) deviation, (b) oddity, (c) representative, (d) anomaly
6. (a) bureaucratic, (b) extravagant, (c) extreme, (d) inordinate
7. (a) apathy, (b) ecstasy, (c) indifference, (d) unconcern
8. (a) agony, (b) torment, (c) alleviation, (d) anguish
9. (a) persistence, (b) perseverance, (c) pretense, (d) pertinacity
10. (a) hazy, (b) ambiguous, (c) contentious, (d) equivocal

> **WORD LIST**
> affinity
> alleviation
> anomaly
> apathy
> demeanor
> equivocal
> inordinate
> insipid
> pertinacity
> vagary

VOCABULARY IN WRITING

The narrator describes Usher's instability, but how stable was the narrator himself? Write an explanation of your opinion, using evidence from the story. Include at least three vocabulary words. Here is a sample beginning.

> **EXAMPLE SENTENCE**
>
> The narrator's **inordinate** attention to the Ushers' quirks can be seen as one sign of his own instability.

VOCABULARY STRATEGY: THE GREEK ROOT *path*

The vocabulary word *apathy* contains the Greek root *path*, which means "feel" or "suffer." This root is found in a number of English words. To understand words with *path*, use context clues as well as your knowledge of the root's meaning.

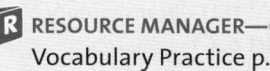
R1.2
CALIFORNIA

path: apathy, pathos, psychopathic, telepathy, empathize, antipathy

PRACTICE Choose the word from the word web that best completes each sentence. Consider what you know about the Greek root and the other word parts shown. If necessary, consult a dictionary.

1. Her brother's cruel actions caused her to feel a strong _____ for him.
2. The characters' tearful farewell evoked a sense of _____ in the audience.
3. Their thoughts were so aligned that it seemed they could communicate by _____.
4. Many criminals' behavior tends to be _____.
5. Parents are often able to _____ with their children's problems and frustrations.

> **VOCABULARY PRACTICE**
> For more practice, go to the **Vocabulary Center** at **ClassZone.com**.

ANSWERS

Vocabulary in Context

VOCABULARY PRACTICE

1. *(d) insecure*
2. *(b) antique*
3. *(d) tome*
4. *(b) disturbance*
5. *(c) extreme*
6. *(a) bureaucratic*
7. *(b) ecstasy*
8. *(c) alleviation*
9. *(c) pretense*
10. *(c) contentious*

R RESOURCE MANAGER—Copy Master
Vocabulary Practice p. 202

VOCABULARY IN WRITING

Tell students to determine their opinions about the narrator's stability first, and then search the vocabulary list for words expressing his stability or lack of it. Remind them that they can use the word *not* before a vocabulary word to reverse its meaning.

VOCABULARY STRATEGY: THE GREEK ROOT *path* *(also an EL language objective)*

In addition to context clues, tell students to use the other word parts in a *path* word in order to figure out its meaning. For example, *antipathy* contains the prefix *anti-* and the suffix *-y*. *Telepathy* has the prefix *tele-* and the suffix *-y*. *Apathy* has the prefix *a-* and the suffix *-y*. *Empathize* has the suffix *-ize*. The suffixes give clues to the words' parts of speech: *-y* for state-of-being nouns, and *-ize* for verbs.

Answers: 1. *antipathy*, **2.** *pathos*, **3.** *telepathy*, **4.** *psychopathic*, **5.** *empathize*

R RESOURCE MANAGER—Copy Master
Vocabulary Strategy p. 203

ℹ Vocabulary Center at **ClassZone.com**
Additional Vocabulary Activities

DIFFERENTIATED INSTRUCTION

FOR ENGLISH LEARNERS

Task Support: Vocabulary Practice Have students consult a dictionary to find the meanings of the words contained in the Word List. Then have them use those words in sentences to practice understanding.

FOR ADVANCED LEARNERS/AP

Vocabulary in Writing Tell students to write two paragraphs from Roderick Usher's point of view in which he describes the mental stability of his friend, the narrator. Have them use five of the vocabulary words.

Reading-Writing Connection

WRITING PROMPT

Have students use the Observation Chart to select details for their descriptions. Have them select an everyday location and write details on the chart as they visualize it. Tell them to refer to the chart as they write, adding modifiers to the details to make the description more eerie and terrifying.

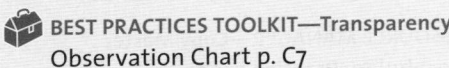 **BEST PRACTICES TOOLKIT—Transparency**
Observation Chart p. C7

For writing support, see

i Writing Center at **ClassZone.com**

GRAMMAR AND STYLE

Focus students' attention on the difference between participles ending in *-ed* or *-ing* and verbs with the same endings. Remind them that a participle modifies a noun or pronoun. An example is "the cooked food." In contrast, the word *cooked* could be a verb when it indicates an action, as in, "I cooked the food." (For more on participles and participial phrases, see page R66 in the **Grammar Handbook.**)

***Possible answers:* 1.** *The firefighters ran toward the burning building.* **2.** *Researching my report, I discovered many new facts.* **3.** *Snow fell thickly over the woods, creating an enchanted scene.*

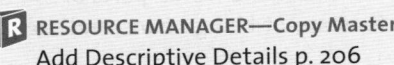 **RESOURCE MANAGER—Copy Master**
Add Descriptive Details p. 206

Assess and Reteach

Assess

R RESOURCE MANAGER—Copy Masters
Selection Test A pp. 207–208
Selection Test B/C pp. 209–210

⊘ Test Generator CD

Reteach

S STANDARDS LESSON FILE
Literature Lesson 42: Mood
Reading Lesson 4: Recognizing Main Idea and Details
Writing Lesson 21: Descriptive Writing
Vocabulary Lesson 6: Word Parts

Reading-Writing Connection

WRITING PROMPT	SELF-CHECK
WRITE A DESCRIPTION You don't need far-off locales and crumbling castles to inspire **terror.** Using a few well-chosen details, you can turn a familiar scene into an unsettling backdrop for eerie events. Write a **two-to-four paragraph description** that makes an everyday location seem terrifying. Choose descriptive details that suggest something strange or unsettling is at work.	**A successful description will . . .** • involve an appropriate setting • establish an unusual situation • contain evocative details that convey a strong sense of mood

GRAMMAR AND STYLE

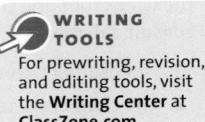

LC1.1

ADD DESCRIPTIVE DETAILS Review the **Grammar and Style** note on page 407. Poe is a master of elaborate, ornate descriptions that are packed with details. Some of his descriptive words are **participles,** verb forms that function as adjectives, as in this example:

> *His long improvised dirges will ring forever in my ears.* (lines 236–237)

Participles usually end in *-ing* or *-ed* and can be combined with modifiers and complements to make **participial phrases.**

PRACTICE Read each of the following sentences from Poe's story, noting the boldfaced participle or participial phrase. Then, write your own sentence, using a participle as instructed in parentheses. An example has been done for you.

> **EXAMPLE**
>
> His countenance, I thought, wore a **mingled** expression of low cunning and perplexity. (Use a past participle, one that ends with *-ed*.)
> *The cat, I noticed, carried a mangled mouse in her jaws.*

1. A sensation of stupor oppressed me as my eyes followed her **retreating** steps. (Use a present participle, one that ends with *-ing*.)

2. **Shaking off from my spirit what *must* have been a dream,** I scanned more narrowly the real aspect of the building. (Use a participial phrase to begin your sentence. Make sure your phrase modifies the subject.)

3. Minute fungi overspread the whole exterior, **hanging in a fine tangled web-work from the eaves.** (Use a participial phrase at the end of your sentence. Make sure the phrase modifies the subject.)

WRITING TOOLS
For prewriting, revision, and editing tools, visit the **Writing Center** at ClassZone.com.

DIFFERENTIATED INSTRUCTION

FOR DEVELOPING WRITERS
Writing Support

• Have students work in a group to brainstorm possible topics.

• Allow more than one student to use the same topic.

• Limit the description to two paragraphs.

• Have students' peers read the first drafts and provide feedback, especially concerning places where the writers could add more details and use more vivid words.

• If possible, allow students time for revision.

• Recommend that students use a thesaurus and a dictionary to find descriptive words.

The Masque of the Red Death

Short Story by
Edgar Allan Poe

CALIFORNIA R3.1

● LITERARY ANALYSIS: ALLEGORY

You can enjoy this story by Poe for its thrills, or you can read it as an **allegory,** a work of art with two levels of meaning. In an allegory, characters and objects stand for ideas outside the work, such as good and evil. Often meant to teach moral lessons, allegories typically feature simple characters and unnamed settings, somewhat like fairy tales.

The "Red Death" had long devastated the country.

In early allegories, ideas were **personified** as characters and given proper names (Good, Evil). As you read, note how Poe uses allegorical elements to suggest a moral lesson.

● READING STRATEGY: CLARIFY MEANING

Poe's unusual, archaic vocabulary reinforces this story's feeling of antiquity. The following strategies can help you clarify the meaning of difficult words and phrases:

- Consult the side notes for helpful information.
- Use **context clues** in surrounding phrases to figure out unfamiliar words.
- **Paraphrase** difficult passages, using simpler language.

As you read, pause to write summarizes of each paragraph. Note which parts of the story require further clarifying.

▲ VOCABULARY IN CONTEXT

Poe used the following words in his eerie tale. Complete each phrase with an appropriate word from the list.

WORD LIST	blasphemous	disapprobation	propriety
	cessation	impede	reverie

1. wandered the halls lost in a _____
2. a peace treaty following the _____ of hostilities
3. her friends' _____ after her unwise decision
4. tried not to _____ the flow of traffic
5. deeply offended by his _____ arguments
6. acted with decorum and _____

Is SAFETY *an illusion?*

KEY IDEA We like to feel that there are steps we can take to keep ourselves safe. To protect ourselves from theft, we can install an alarm or add high-security locks. To protect our health, we can exercise and eat healthy food. But do our precautions really keep danger away, or do they just give us an illusion of **safety?**

PRESENT Work with a small group to develop an argument for or against the question, *Is safety an illusion?* Choose at least two examples to support your argument. Then, taking turns with other groups, present your case to the class.

POSITION:

Safety is NOT an illusion.

ARGUMENT:

People can take steps to protect themselves from danger.

EXAMPLE:

A vaccine can provide nearly complete protection from a disease.

Is SAFETY *an illusion?*

Read the **KEY IDEA** question aloud and then read the first paragraph. Ask students to suggest present-day situations when **safety** might be an illusion. Then have students choose a side before working on the **PRESENT** activity.

SKILLS FOCUS

LITERARY ANALYSIS R3.1

● ALLEGORY

Write this allegory, based on the Greek myth of Sisyphus, on the board:

> The man pushed the rock uphill. He struggled for a long time and almost reached the top. As he gave a last heave, the rock slipped and rolled all the way down. He had to begin again. He had already begun a hundred times.

Help students hypothesize what the man, the rock, and the hill might stand for. *Possible answer: The man might stand for a person's life; the rock for work, knowledge, or other human endeavors; and the hill for the span of human life.*

READING STRATEGY

■ CLARIFY MEANING

Have students reread Literary Analysis: Allegory and choose words or phrases to clarify, using the bulleted strategies and the summarizing technique. Have students share their clarifications. *Possible answer: Allegories can be like fairy tales, with basic characters and nonspecific settings. They often teach a lesson.*

CHECK UNDERSTANDING Have students apply the methods of clarification to the Poe biography.

R RESOURCE MANAGER—Copy Master
Clarify Meaning p. 223 (for student use while reading the selection)

▲ VOCABULARY IN CONTEXT

DIAGNOSE WORD KNOWLEDGE To determine preteaching needs, have all students complete Vocabulary in Context. *Answers:*
1. *reverie,* 2. *cessation,* 3. *disapprobation,*
4. *impede,* 5. *blasphemous,* 6. *propriety*

PRETEACH VOCABULARY Preteach vocabulary with this copy master. Read each item aloud.

R RESOURCE MANAGER—Copy Master
Vocabulary Study p. 225

MORE VOCABULARY SUPPORT
For additional activities and guidelines, see

■ BEST PRACTICES TOOLKIT
Scaffolding Vocabulary Instruction
pp. 43–46

ℹ Vocabulary Center at **ClassZone.com**

SUMMARY

This short story tells the tale of Prince Prospero, whose country is plagued by a horrible epidemic of the Red Death. To escape the disease, the prince and his friends lock themselves away in the prince's abbey. Thinking themselves safe, the prince and his friends amuse themselves while the Red Death ravages the countryside. They hold a masked ball, where they discover an uninvited guest dressed as the Red Death. The guest turns out to be the plague itself, which brings death to all.

READING STRATEGY

Ⓐ CLARIFY MEANING

Possible answer: The Red Death had ravaged the country for a long time. Its symptoms were pain, dizziness, bleeding, and death. Once these appeared, the victim would be dead within half an hour. Possible inference: People are terrified.

If students need help . . . Have them use a Making Inferences Chart.

Details from Story		What I Know from Reading or Experience		My Inference
Pain, bleeding; disease killed in half an hour	+	Black Death killed about 1/4 of Europe.	=	People must have been terrified.

🧰 **BEST PRACTICES TOOLKIT—Transparency**
Making Inferences p. A13

THE
Masque
OF THE
RED DEATH

Edgar Allan Poe

BACKGROUND Around 1350, Europe was struck by an epidemic of bubonic plague (Black Death) that killed more than a quarter of its population. The plague killed its victims quickly—within three to five days—and there was no cure. Artwork from that time is full of haunting symbols like the Dance of Death, where Death, personified as a skeleton, whirls anonymous figures to their graves. These grisly allegorical images spoke to the deepest fears of their audience, for whom death was a nearby presence. Note how Poe borrows from this history in his own tale of death.

The "Red Death" had long devastated the country. No pestilence had ever been so fatal, or so hideous. Blood was its Avatar and its seal—the redness and horror of blood. There were sharp pains, and sudden dizziness, and then profuse bleeding at the pores, with dissolution. The scarlet stains upon the body, and especially upon the face of the victim, were the pest ban which shut him out from the aid and from the sympathy of his fellow men. And the whole seizure, progress, and termination of the disease were the incidents of half an hour. Ⓐ

But the Prince Prospero was happy and dauntless and sagacious. When his
10 dominions were half depopulated, he summoned to his presence a thousand hale and lighthearted friends from among the knights and dames of his court,

❶ Targeted Passage

2 Avatar (ăv'ə-tär'): the physical form of an unseen force.

5 pest ban: announcement of infection with the plague.

Ⓐ CLARIFY MEANING
Use the **side notes** to help you restate lines 1–8. What can you **infer** about the mood of the country from this description?

DIFFERENTIATED INSTRUCTION

FOR ALL STUDENTS

Expert Groups Encourage students to become subject experts by selecting and researching one of these topics relating to the illness and early death of three key figures in Poe's life:

- his mother, Eliza Poe
- his stepmother, Frances Allan
- his young wife, Virginia Clemm

FOR STRATEGIC READERS

In combination with the *Audio Anthology CD,* use one or more Targeted Passages (pp. 428, 433, 434) to ensure that students focus on key story events and concepts. Targeted Passages are also good for English learners.

❶ Targeted Passage [Lines 1–11]

This passage describes the Red Death and tells of Prince Prospero's response to it.

BACKGROUND

Black Death Poe's vision of the Red Death may have been influenced by the Black Death, which reached Europe from Asia in 1347. After fading in 1351, it recurred five more times in the 14th century. Towns had a higher death rate than the countryside, and monasteries had one of the highest rates. As in "The Masque of the Red Death," royalty did not escape the plague: Eleanor of Aragon and King Alfonso XI of Castile died, and Princess Joan of England died on the way to her wedding. Two successive Archbishops of Canterbury and one quarter of the papal court at Avignon, France, died. Social effects were many. Temporarily, wars ceased and trade slumped. More lastingly, a shortage of farm labor and of artisans enabled workers to demand higher wages, a change that resulted in greater spending power for those classes, and thus the rise of a new middle class and a weakening of the old feudal class distinctions.

Poe's vision of a plague may also have been affected by the frequent outbreaks of yellow fever and cholera that afflicted American cities in the early 1800s. In 1832, while Poe was living in Baltimore, a cholera epidemic killed 853 residents of that city.

- What is the Red Death?
- How does Prince Prospero feel? Is he concerned about it?
- When does he take action?
- Whom does he summon?

FOR ENGLISH LEARNERS

Prereading For prereading instruction for English learners, see

 BEST PRACTICES TOOLKIT
Scaffolding Reading Instruction pp. 43–46

FOR ADVANCED LEARNERS/AP

AP exercises in the bottom channel provide additional challenge for students. Use these suggestions for small groups or individuals.

ADDITIONAL GUIDELINES

For more help with differentiation and tips for classroom management, see

 BEST PRACTICES TOOLKIT
Differentiated Instruction pp. 31–38

B ALLEGORY

Possible answer: Details suggesting a mythical or fairy-tale setting include the abbey, knights, the prince, the ladies of court, the mention of a thousand friends, and the unrealistic idea of hiding in the abbey indefinitely.

Extend Discussion What details in the passage could be historical? Could any of the details be both historical and fairy-tale-like?

Lines 13–26
TIERED DISCUSSION PROMPTS

Use these prompts to help students understand how the prince and his friends reacted to the threat of the Red Death:

Connect Have you or someone you know ever tried to escape something that seemed unavoidable? How does that experience help you understand what Prospero was trying to do? *Accept all reasonable responses.*

Analyze Why did Prospero choose to hold the ball just as the "pestilence raged most furiously"? *Possible answer: After many months of living in confinement, the people probably needed a diversion to maintain their spirits and endure boredom. Also, Prospero refused to consider the threat outside the abbey.*

Predict Do you think the prince's precautions will protect those inside the abbey? Explain. *Possible answer: They didn't know how the Red Death spread. Closing doors might not keep it out.*

---

and with these retired to the deep seclusion of one of his castellated abbeys. This was an extensive and magnificent structure, the creation of the prince's own eccentric yet august taste. A strong and lofty wall girdled it in. This wall had gates of iron. The courtiers, having entered, brought furnaces and massy hammers and welded the bolts. They resolved to leave means neither of ingress or egress to the sudden impulses of despair or of frenzy from within. The abbey was amply provisioned. With such precautions the courtiers might bid defiance to contagion. The external world could take care of itself. In the meantime

20 it was folly to grieve, or to think. The prince had provided all the appliances of pleasure. There were buffoons, there were improvisatori, there were ballet-dancers, there were musicians, there was Beauty, there was wine. All these and security were within. Without was the "Red Death." **B**

It was toward the close of the fifth or sixth month of his seclusion, and while the pestilence raged most furiously abroad, that the Prince Prospero entertained his thousand friends at a masked ball of the most unusual magnificence.

It was a voluptuous scene, that masquerade. But first let me tell of the rooms in which it was held. There were seven—an imperial suite. In many palaces, however, such suites form a long and straight vista, while the folding

30 doors slide back nearly to the walls on either hand, so that the view of the whole extent is scarcely **impeded.** Here the case was very different; as might have been expected from the duke's love of the *bizarre.* The apartments were so irregularly disposed that the vision embraced but little more than one at a time. There was a sharp turn at every twenty or thirty yards, and at each turn a novel effect. To the right and left, in the middle of each wall, a tall and narrow Gothic window looked out upon a closed corridor which pursued the windings of the suite. These windows were of stained glass whose color varied in accordance with the prevailing hue of the decorations of the chamber into which it opened. That at the eastern extremity was

40 hung, for example, in blue—and vividly blue were its windows. The second chamber was purple in its ornaments and tapestries, and here the panes were purple. The third was green throughout, and so were the casements. The fourth was furnished and lighted with orange—the fifth with white—the sixth with violet. The seventh apartment was closely shrouded in black velvet tapestries that hung all over the ceiling and down the walls, falling in heavy folds upon a carpet of the same material and hue. But in this chamber only, the color of the windows failed to correspond with the decorations. The panes here were scarlet—a deep blood color. Now in no one of the seven apartments were there any lamp or candelabrum amid the profusion

50 of golden ornaments that lay scattered to and fro or depended from the roof. There was no light of any kind emanating from lamp or candle within the suite of chambers. But in the corridors that followed the suite, there stood, opposite to each window, a heavy tripod, bearing a brazier of fire that projected its rays through the tinted glass and so glaringly illumined the room. And thus were produced a multitude of gaudy and fantastic appearances. But in the western or black chamber the effect of the firelight that streamed upon the dark hangings through the blood-tinted panes, was

---

12 castellated abbeys (kăs′tə-lā′tĭd ăb′ēz): castle-like buildings once used as monasteries ("abbeys").

16–17 ingress (ĭn′grĕs′) or **egress** (ē′grĕs′): entry or exit.

18 provisioned: stocked with supplies.

21 improvisatori (ĭm-prŏv′ĭ-zə-tôr′ē): poets who compose verses aloud.

B ALLEGORY
Reread lines 9–23. Which details suggest a mythical or fairy-tale **setting?**

impede (ĭm-pēd′) *v.* to interfere with or slow the progress of

53 brazier (brā′zhər): metal pan for holding a fire.

DIFFERENTIATED INSTRUCTION

FOR STRATEGIC READERS

Concept Support To help students clarify the long description that covers all of page 430, use Jigsaw Reading so that students are responsible for smaller chunks of text and share their clarifications with others.

 BEST PRACTICES TOOLKIT
Jigsaw Reading p. A1

FOR ENGLISH LEARNERS

Key Academic Vocabulary Use Word Questioning to teach these words: *structure* (line 13), *external* (line 19), *correspond* (line 47), *emphasis* (line 66), *similar* (line 76), *role* (line 145).

 BEST PRACTICES TOOLKIT—Transparency
Word Questioning p. E9

Activity Ask students how the image on page 431 differs from yet captures the description of the setting and mood of Prince Prospero's apartment. *Possible answer: The clock in the image on page 431 does not match the description of the clock in the story, which is made of ebony (line 62). Moreover, the panes look out onto open scenery, while the "castellated" abbey in which the Prince and his courtiers have taken refuge is surrounded by a wall. However, like the masquerade, the image is fantastical and surreal. The clock dominates the image, superimposed upon blood red windows, making the barren landscape outside seem blighted and threatening.*

ghastly in the extreme, and produced so wild a look upon the countenances of those who entered, that there were few of the company bold enough to
60 set foot within its precincts at all.

It was in this apartment, also, that there stood against the western wall a gigantic clock of ebony. Its pendulum swung to and fro with a dull, heavy, monotonous clang; and when the minute hand made the circuit of the face, and the hour was to be stricken, there came from the brazen lungs of the clock a sound which was clear and loud and deep and exceedingly musical, but of so peculiar a note and emphasis that, at each lapse of an hour, the musicians of the orchestra were constrained to pause, momentarily, in their performance, to hearken to the sound; and thus the waltzers perforce ceased their evolutions; and there was a brief disconcert of the whole gay company;
70 and, while the chimes of the clock yet rang, it was observed that the giddiest turned pale, and the more aged and sedate passed their hands over their

58 **countenances** (koun′tə-nəns-əz): faces.

62 **ebony** (ĕb′ə-nē): a hard, very dark wood.

64 **brazen:** brass.

69 **evolutions:** intricate patterns of movement; **disconcert:** state of confusion.

FOR ADVANCED LEARNERS/AP

Compare and Contrast [small-group option] In his essay *Nature* (pages 365–366), Ralph Waldo Emerson praises contact with nature as a source of "perfect exhilaration." Have students work in groups to compare and contrast Emerson's view of nature with Poe's. Elicit an awareness that in "The Masque of the Red Death," nature is a source of disease. In "The Fall of the House of Usher," nature is a source of decay and destruction, represented by unhealthy vegetation and a bleak tarn.

Then point out that the contrast may not be as simple as that seems, for Emerson also sees a melancholy side of nature in lines 1 and 28–33 of his essay. To help students explore this viewpoint, have them consider these questions:

- What might Emerson say about Poe's view of nature?
- Would he necessarily disagree with it?
- If he did, with whom would you agree?

FOR ENGLISH LEARNERS

Vocabulary: Outdated Forms Provide these definitions for outdated terms. Have students reread the lines, substituting the definitions for the outdated words.

- *massy* (line 15), "heavy, bulky"
- *might bid defiance to contagion* (lines 18–19), "might disregard disease"
- *depended (from the roof)* (line 50), "hung"
- *hearken* (line 68), "listen carefully"

C ALLEGORY

Possible answer: The clock personifies the passage of time. The chime reminds the revelers of the passing of time—and their lives.

ADDITIONAL TEACHING OPPORTUNITY

Personification Tell students that allegories often personify abstract qualities, such as good or evil, as human characters. Personification can also be used to endow animals and objects with human traits, as in stories of talking animals.

- Which type of personification is used in "The Masque of the Red Death"?
- What ideas are personified in the story?

(To learn more about personification, see **Glossary of Literary Terms,** page R116.)

Lines 80–111
REINFORCE *KEY IDEA:* SAFETY

Discuss What details in lines 80–111 suggest that the partygoers feel an illusion of **safety?** What detail suggests that they may feel less safe than before? *Possible answer: Illusion of safety: Prospero's followers do not think him mad; the laughter when the peal of the clock fades. Less safe than before: the fact that no one goes into the seventh apartment.*

D CLARIFY MEANING

Possible answer: The light in that room becomes redder as the night wanes; the black decorations are unsettling; the clock is heard more loudly there than elsewhere.

If students need help . . . Have them continue working with the Making Inferences chart they began on page 428.

---

brows as if in confused <u>reverie</u> or meditation. But when the echoes had fully ceased, a light laughter at once pervaded the assembly; the musicians looked at each other and smiled as if at their own nervousness and folly, and made whispering vows, each to the other, that the next chiming of the clock should produce in them no similar emotion; and then, after the lapse of sixty minutes (which embrace three thousand and six hundred seconds of the Time that flies), there came yet another chiming of the clock, and then were the same disconcert and tremulousness and meditation as before. **C**

80   But, in spite of these things, it was a gay and magnificent revel. The tastes of the duke were peculiar. He had a fine eye for colors and effects. He disregarded the *decora* of mere fashion. His plans were bold and fiery, and his conceptions glowed with barbaric lustre. There are some who would have thought him mad. His followers felt that he was not. It was necessary to hear and see and touch him to be *sure* that he was not.

He had directed, in great part, the movable embellishments of the seven chambers, upon occasion of this great *fête;* and it was his own guiding taste which had given character to the masqueraders. Be sure they were grotesque. There were much glare and glitter and piquancy and phantasm—much of

90   what has been seen since in *Hernani.* There were arabesque figures with unsuited limbs and appointments. There were delirious fancies such as the madman fashions. There was much of the beautiful, much of the wanton, much of the *bizarre,* something of the terrible, and not a little of that which might have excited disgust. To and fro in the seven chambers there stalked, in fact, a multitude of dreams. And these—the dreams—writhed in and about, taking hue from the rooms, and causing the wild music of the orchestra to seem as the echo of their steps. And, anon, there strikes the ebony clock which stands in the hall of velvet. And then, for a moment, all is still, and all is silent save the voice of the clock. The dreams are stiff-

100   frozen as they stand. But the echoes of the chime die away—they have endured but an instant—and a light, half-subdued laughter floats after them as they depart. And now again the music swells, and the dreams live, and writhe to and fro more merrily than ever, taking hue from the many-tinted windows through which stream the rays of the tripods. But to the chamber which lies most westwardly of the seven, there are now none of the maskers who venture; for the night is waning away; and there flows a ruddier light through the blood-colored panes; and the blackness of the sable drapery appalls; and to him whose foot falls upon the sable carpet, there comes from the near clock of ebony a muffled peal more solemnly emphatic than

110   any which reaches *their* ears who indulge in the more remote gaieties of the other apartments. **D**

But these other apartments were densely crowded, and in them beat feverishly the heart of life. And the revel went whirlingly on, until at length there commenced the sounding of midnight upon the clock. And then the music ceased, as I have told; and the evolutions of the waltzes were quieted; and there was an uneasy <u>cessation</u> of all things as before. But now there were twelve strokes to be sounded by the bell of the clock; and thus

---

reverie (rĕv′ə-rē) *n.* daydream

C ALLEGORY
Identify the idea that is **personified** in lines 61–79. What object does Poe use to represent this concept?

82 *decora:* fine things.

90 *Hernani* (ĕr′nä-nē): a play by French writer Victor Hugo, first staged in 1830 and notable for its use of color and spectacle; **arabesque** (ăr′ə-bĕsk′): intricately designed.

D CLARIFY MEANING
Paraphrase lines 104–111. Why do none of the guests venture into the seventh room?

cessation (sĕ-sā′shən) *n.* a coming to an end; a stopping

DIFFERENTIATED INSTRUCTION

FOR ADVANCED LEARNERS/AP

Analyze Ask students to recall the three major types of irony: verbal, situational, and dramatic. Have them find examples of irony in the descriptions of the ball and identify the type of irony each example represents. Have students discuss the reasons for their choices. Students may find that some examples belong to more than one type.

it happened, perhaps, that more of thought crept, with more of time, into the meditations of the thoughtful among those who reveled. And thus, too, it happened, perhaps, that before the last echoes of the last chime had utterly sunk into silence, there were many individuals in the crowd who had found leisure to become aware of the presence of a masked figure which had arrested the attention of no single individual before. And the rumor of this new presence having spread itself whisperingly around, there arose at length from the whole company a buzz, or murmur, expressive of **disapprobation** and surprise—then, finally of terror, of horror, and of disgust.

In an assembly of phantasms such as I have painted, it may well be supposed that no ordinary appearance could have excited such sensation. In truth the masquerade license of the night was nearly unlimited; but the figure in question had out-Heroded Herod, and gone beyond the bounds of even the prince's indefinite decorum. There are chords in the hearts of the most reckless which cannot be touched without emotion. Even with the utterly lost, to whom life and death are equally jests, there are matters of which no jest can be made. The whole company, indeed, seemed now deeply to feel that in the costume and bearing of the stranger neither wit nor **propriety** existed. The figure was tall and gaunt, and shrouded from head to foot in the habiliments of the grave. The mask which concealed the visage was made so nearly to resemble the countenance of a stiffened corpse that the closest scrutiny must have had difficulty in detecting the cheat. And yet all this might have been endured, if not approved, by the mad revellers around. But the mummer had gone so far as to assume the type of the Red Death. His vesture was dabbled in *blood*—and his broad brow, with all the features of the face, was besprinkled with the scarlet horror. **E**

When the eyes of Prince Prospero fell upon this spectral image (which with a slow and solemn movement, as if more fully to sustain its *role*, stalked to and fro among the waltzers), he was seen to be convulsed, in the first moment with a strong shudder either of terror or distaste; but, in the next, his brow reddened with rage.

"Who dares?" he demanded hoarsely of the courtiers who stood near him—"who dares insult us with this **blasphemous** mockery? Seize him and unmask him—that we may know whom we have to hang at sunrise, from the battlements!"

It was in the eastern or blue chamber in which stood the Prince Prospero as he uttered these words. They rang throughout the seven rooms loudly and clearly—for the prince was a bold and robust man, and the music had become hushed at the waving of his hand.

It was in the blue room where stood the prince, with a group of pale courtiers by his side. At first, as he spoke, there was a slight rushing movement of this group in the direction of the intruder, who at the moment was also near at hand, and now, with deliberate and stately step, made closer approach to the speaker. But from a certain nameless awe with which the mad assumptions of the mummer had inspired the whole party, there

disapprobation (dĭs-ăp′rə-bā′shən) *n.* disapproval

130 **out-Heroded Herod:** been more extreme than the biblical King Herod, who ordered the deaths of all male babies in order to kill the infant Jesus. This expression is also used in Shakespeare's *Hamlet*.

propriety (prə-prī′ĭ-tē) *n.* the quality of being proper; appropriateness

137 **habiliments** (hə-bĭl′ə-mənts): clothing.

2 Targeted Passage

E CLARIFY MEANING
Reread lines 127–143. Use **context clues** to determine the meaning of the words *decorum, visage,* and *vesture.* What details help explain why the figure's appearance is so shocking?

blasphemous (blăs′fə-məs) *adj.* disrespectful or offensive

162 **mummer:** a person dressed for a masquerade.

Lines 134–152
TIERED DISCUSSION PROMPTS
Use these prompts to help students consider the significance of the unknown masked figure who appears at the ball:

Recall How do the partygoers respond to the stranger dressed as the Red Death? *Possible answer: They are frightened and disturbed.*

Interpret Why does Prince Prospero respond to the stranger's costume with "terror or distaste" and then with "rage"? *Possible answer: He is frightened of the plague and does not feel as secure in his abbey as he pretends to be.*

Synthesize What details in the description of the stranger suggest who he really is and what will happen to the prince and the guests? *Possible answer: The "habiliments of the grave," the realistic "countenance of a stiffened corpse," and the sprinkling of blood suggest the disease; the people's reaction of terror and the prince's "brow reddened with rage" suggest that they will succumb to it.*

READING STRATEGY

E CLARIFY MEANING

Possible answer: Decorum *means "polite behavior"; clues are "beyond the bounds" and "propriety."* Visage *means "face"; a clue is "mask which concealed."* Vesture *means "clothing"; a clue is "costume." The figure is shocking in costume and bearing: "neither wit nor propriety existed" (lines 135–136). The mask was so real that even close examination made it difficult to tell it from the real thing.*

FOR STRATEGIC READERS

2 Targeted Passage [Lines 134–152]

This passage describes the appearance of a masked figure dressed as the Red Death.

- What does the uninvited guest's costume look like?
- How does the prince respond to the guest?
- What does the prince order to be done to this masked figure?

FOR ENGLISH LEARNERS

Vocabulary Support Poe frequently uses words in close proximity that are opposites or show contrasts. Discuss the meanings and connotations of these examples:

- *beautiful, wanton* (line 92)
- *wild music* (line 96); *light, half-subdued laughter floats* (line 101); *again the music swells* (line 102); *music ceased* (line 115)
- *surprise, terror, horror, disgust* (line 126)

were found none who put forth hand to seize him; so that, unimpeded, he passed within a yard of the prince's person; and, while the vast assembly, as if with one impulse, shrank from the centers of the rooms to the walls, he made his way uninterruptedly, but with the same solemn and measured step which had distinguished him from the first, through the blue chamber to the purple—through the purple to the green—through the green to the orange—through this again to the white—and even thence to the violet,

170 ere a decided movement had been made to arrest him. It was then, however, that the Prince Prospero, maddening with rage and the shame of his own momentary cowardice, rushed hurriedly through the six chambers while none followed him on account of a deadly terror that had seized upon all. He bore aloft a drawn dagger, and had approached, in rapid impetuosity, to within three or four feet of the retreating figure, when the latter, having attained the extremity of the velvet apartment, turned suddenly and confronted his pursuer. There was a sharp cry—and the dagger dropped gleaming upon the sable carpet, upon which, instantly afterwards, fell prostrate in death the Prince Prospero. Then, summoning the wild courage

180 of despair, a throng of the revellers at once threw themselves into the black apartment, and seizing the mummer, whose tall figure stood erect and motionless within the shadow of the ebony clock, gasped in unutterable horror at finding the grave-cerements and corpselike mask, which they handled with so violent a rudeness, untenanted by any tangible form. **F**

And now was acknowledged the presence of the Red Death. He had come like a thief in the night. And one by one dropped the revellers in the blood-bedewed halls of their revel, and died each in the despairing posture of his fall. And the life of the ebony clock went out with that of the last of the gay. And the flames of the tripods expired. And Darkness and Decay and the Red

190 Death held illimitable dominion over all. ✺

LITERARY ANALYSIS

F ALLEGORY

Possible answer: The prince's fate is the opposite of his name: he does not prosper.

If students need help . . . Have a volunteer explain what irony is.

Lines 185–190
REINFORCE *KEY IDEA:* SAFETY

What happens to the prince's and the revelers' illusions of **safety** in the end? What meaning does this outcome have for life beyond the abbey walls? *Possible answer: Their illusions of safety are shattered. The larger meaning may be that all illusions of escaping death are foolish.*

SELECTION WRAP–UP

REFLECT Have students think about the character of the prince and his guests. How and why should these characters have behaved differently? Would it have changed the outcome?

⭐ CRITIQUE

- Ask students how well they feel the story holds up after more than 150 years. Have them explain their opinions.

- After completing the After Reading questions on page 435, have students revisit their responses and tell whether they have changed their opinions.

DIFFERENTIATED INSTRUCTION

FOR STRATEGIC READERS
❸ Targeted Passage [Lines 170–190]

This passage concludes the story by showing how fate catches up to the characters.

- What does Prince Prospero try to do, and what happens as a result?

- What do the guests find when they seize the stranger?

- What happens to the guests in the end?

FOR ADVANCED LEARNERS/AP

Analyze [paired option] Have students work in pairs to use the Analysis Frame: Setting to examine the influence that the time and place of the story have on its plot, themes, and other elements.

 BEST PRACTICES TOOLKIT—Transparency
Analysis Frame: Setting pp. D21, D30

Comprehension

1. **Recall** Why does Prince Prospero seal himself and his guests in the abbey?

2. **Recall** What effect does the striking of the clock have on the revellers?

3. **Summarize** What happens after the mysterious figure is unmasked?

Literary Analysis

4. **Make Inferences** What does each of the following reveal about Prince Prospero?
   - his response to the crisis in his country (lines 1–12)
   - his solution to the threat of disease (lines 15–23)
   - his plans for the masquerade (lines 86–94)
   - his response to the masked figure (lines 144–152)

5. **Clarify Meaning** Recall the summaries you wrote to help clarify each paragraph of the story. Which proved more difficult to understand, the events in the story or the descriptions that set the scene? Explain your answer.

6. **Analyze Descriptive Details** For each of the following examples, identify the contrast drawn between the seventh room and the rest of Prince Prospero's suite. Based on these contrasts, what might the seventh room represent?
   - its decorations (lines 44–48)
   - its location (lines 104–105)
   - its atmosphere (lines 56–60)
   - what occurs there (lines 174–179)

7. **Interpret Allegory** Using a chart like the one shown, identify a possible meaning for each character or object and list details from the text that support your interpretation. Based on your answers, what lesson is Poe's allegory intended to teach?

Main Story Elements	Possible Meaning	Supporting Details
Prince Prospero		
the abbey		
the series of seven rooms		
the clock		
the masked stranger		

8. **Evaluate Characters' Actions** Consider the desperate measures the characters take to achieve **safety**. In what ways, if any, do their behaviors reflect real-world responses to a deadly threat? Support your answer with details.

Literary Criticism

9. **Critical Interpretations** Some critics have argued that "The Masque of the Red Death" takes place in Prospero's mind. Cite details from the story that support this interpretation. How does this view change the story's meaning?

8. *Some students may say that many people run away from crises because of fear and try to forget their problems through reckless pleasures. Others may point out examples of people doing the opposite and facing problems courageously.*

9. *Details that support the interpretation include words like dreams, fancies, delirious, and phantasms; the comment that some thought Prospero mad; the unrealistic nature of the story; and the fact that Prospero is the only distinct character. In this interpretation the story might be less an allegory of life and death and more an illustration of madness.*

Practice and Apply

After Reading

Use these copy masters to check understanding and provide extra support:

RESOURCE MANAGER—Copy Masters
Reading Check p. 228
Allegory p. 221
Question Support p. 229

Additional selection questions are provided for teachers on page 215.

ANSWERS

1. *to escape the Red Death*

2. *It makes them pause fearfully.*

3. *The prince and all the guests die, the clock stops working, and the braziers go out.*

Possible answers:

4. *He is callous and self-centered (lines 1–12); he seeks pleasure and company (lines 15–23); he is a little odd, possibly insane, and enjoys garish spectacle (lines 86–95); he is arrogant and does not accept challenges to his authority (lines 144–152).*

5. ■ **SKILLS FOCUS Clarify Meaning** *Some students may say the descriptions were more difficult because of their length and difficult vocabulary.*

6. *The room is black with blood-red windows and is the only room in which the windows don't match the décor. It is the only room the guests are fearful of entering. It lies farthest west. Prospero is killed there. The room may represent death.*

7. ● **SKILLS FOCUS Allegory** *Prince Prospero: human arrogance; details: his name and position, his plan for the ball, his lack of fear of the room. The abbey: illusions of safety; details: the guests lock themselves in it and revel. The rooms: the stages of life; details: seven rooms going east to west; Prospero races through them; death comes at the end. The clock: time, warning of death; details: its effect on the guests; its location in the room of death. The masked stranger: death; details: his costume; he kills Prospero and the guests.*

ANSWERS

Vocabulary in Context

VOCABULARY PRACTICE

1. *slow down the process*
2. *controversial*
3. *detention*
4. *distracted*
5. *being polite*
6. *one participant walking away*

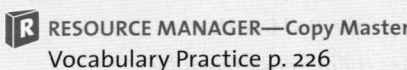 **RESOURCE MANAGER—Copy Master**
Vocabulary Practice p. 226

VOCABULARY IN WRITING

Students' proclamations should be two or more sentences long. Have students review the word list and ask brainstorming questions such as "What would I order the cessation of? What would a monarch consider blasphemous?"

VOCABULARY STRATEGY: AFFIXES AND SPELLING CHANGES

Point out that for some words, such as *cessation*, the word's etymology (Latin *cessare*, to stop) is helpful in determining the base word. *Students' sample sentences will vary.*

1. *deride; yes*   6. *revoke; yes*
2. *contend; yes*   7. *despise; yes*
3. *permeate; yes*   8. *cease; yes*
4. *pomp; yes*   9. *sober; no*
5. *acclaim; no*   10. *measure; no*

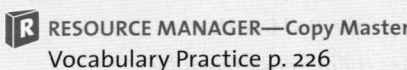 **RESOURCE MANAGER—Copy Master**
Vocabulary Strategy p. 227

ⓘ Vocabulary Center at **ClassZone.com**
Additional Vocabulary Activities

Assess and Reteach

Assess

 RESOURCE MANAGER—Copy Masters
Selection Tests A, B/C pp. 231–232, 233–234

🖎 Test Generator CD

Reteach

Ⓢ **STANDARDS LESSON FILE**
Literature Lesson 32
Reading Lesson 2
Vocabulary Lessons 1, 9

Vocabulary in Context

VOCABULARY PRACTICE

Show you understand the vocabulary words by answering these questions.

1. Will an attempt to **impede** the passage of a law speed up the process or slow it down?
2. Would a **blasphemous** comment be considered controversial or appeasing?
3. Which would more likely result in a parent's **disapprobation**—a detention or a school award?
4. Would someone's **reverie** make them attentive or distracted?
5. If I act with **propriety,** am I being polite or asking uncomfortable questions?
6. Which would cause the **cessation** of a conversation—one participant nodding in agreement or one participant walking away?

WORD LIST
blasphemous
cessation
disapprobation
impede
propriety
reverie

VOCABULARY IN WRITING

Poe's formal language echoes his story's setting in a royal court. Using at least two vocabulary words, write a royal declaration for your subjects to obey. You might start like this.

> **EXAMPLE SENTENCE**
> *I order the immediate **cessation** of this unlicensed and unauthorized behavior.*

VOCABULARY STRATEGY: AFFIXES AND SPELLING CHANGES

Some base words are hard to recognize because they are spelled differently when affixes are added. For example, the vocabulary word *cessation* includes the base word *cease* and the suffix *-ation*. Note how the spelling of the base word changes in the new word. These spelling changes may reflect the word's etymology (its history and origins), or they may simply reflect new pronunciation that made the word easier to say. To decipher words of this type, look for related base words and use context clues to unlock meaning.

PRACTICE Identify the appropriate base word for each of the following examples. Then write a sentence that demonstrates the meaning of each numbered word. Finally, use a dictionary to research the word's origins. Did the spelling change as a result of the word's history?

1. derisive   6. irrevocable
2. contentious   7. despicable
3. impermeable   8. incessant
4. pomposity   9. sobriety
5. acclamation   10. commensurate

↻ **VOCABULARY PRACTICE**
For more practice, go to the **Vocabulary Center** at **ClassZone.com**.

DIFFERENTIATED INSTRUCTION

FOR ENGLISH LEARNERS

Task Support: Vocabulary Practice Point out that several of the vocabulary words have suffixes that show their function as a part of speech. The *-ous* in *blasphemous* shows that the word is an adjective. The *-tion* in *cessation* and *disapprobation* and the *-ty* in *propriety* show that they are nouns. Have students say other words that have those endings. Remind students to consider the part of speech when figuring out the meaning of the vocabulary words.

FOR ADVANCED LEARNERS/AP

Connotations Have students explore the connotations of the vocabulary words by using each word in a paragraph about a subject of their choice. Then have them revise the paragraph, using more common synonyms for the vocabulary words. Have students assess the differences, in tone and meaning between the two versions. Students should find that the vocabulary words are more formal and old-fashioned than their synonyms.

The Raven

Poem by
Edgar Allan Poe

R3.4, W1.1 (p. 444),
W1.2 (p. 444), W1.5
(p. 444), LC1.1 (p. 444)

LITERARY ANALYSIS: SOUND DEVICES

First published in 1845, "The Raven" became an instant hit. Part of the poem's popularity was due to Poe's clever use of **sound devices**, patterns of word sounds used to create musical effects.

- **Rhyme,** the repetition of similar sounds, is one of the easiest sound devices to spot. Poe adds variety by using **internal rhyme,** rhyming words that fall inside a line.

    Ah, distinctly I <u>remember</u> it was in the bleak <u>December</u>;

- **Repetition,** of rhymes and of words and phrases, helps give "The Raven" its distinctive rhythm.

    As of someone gently <u>rapping</u>, <u>rapping</u> at my chamber door.

- **Alliteration,** the repetition of initial consonant sounds, is used to create rhythm or to stress key words.

    While I <u>nodded</u>, <u>nearly napping</u> . . .

- **Onomatopoeia** is the use of words that sound like their meaning, such as the word *rustling* in this example:

    And the silken, sad, uncertain rustling of each purple curtain

As you read, note how Poe combines these sound devices to form complex rhythmic patterns. Reading aloud will help you appreciate Poe's ingenious use of sound effects.

Review: **Stanza and Rhyme Scheme**

READING SKILL: MAKE INFERENCES

"The Raven" tells a story without directly stating all of the important details. You'll need to use clues in the poem to **make inferences** about the speaker's situation as the poem opens and about his state of mind during the events of the poem. As you read, use a chart like the one shown to record your inferences and the clues that helped you. By the end of the poem, you'll be able to **draw conclusions** about what the speaker experiences.

	Inferences About the Speaker	Clues
State of Mind		
Recent Experiences		

How do people handle LOSS?

KEY IDEA At some point in our lives, we all face loss—of someone we love, our favorite pet, or even a cherished dream. But even though the experience of loss is universal, people can choose many different ways to cope with the sadness and **grief** they feel. What do people need to do to face their grief and move on?

DISCUSS Working in small groups, think about some ways people respond to a serious loss. Discuss how they express their own feelings and what they do to adjust to the changes that the loss creates. What patterns can you identify?

437

How do people handle LOSS?

Read aloud the **KEY IDEA** question and then the paragraph. As students suggest ways in which people cope with **grief,** list their answers on the board. Encourage them to refer to the list as they complete the *DISCUSS* activity.

SKILLS FOCUS

LITERARY ANALYSIS R3.4

● SOUND DEVICES

Have students read these lines of verse:

> The clank of armor, the clank of steel
> Echoed all that dismal day.
> We in the crowd could keenly feel
> The gallant knights' strength slip away.

Have students find examples of rhyme, repetition, alliteration, and onomatopoeia in the lines. ***Possible answer:*** *rhyme: steel/feel, day/away; repetition: clank; alliteration: dismal/day, crowd/could/keenly, strength/slip; onomatopoeia: clank.*

CHECK UNDERSTANDING Ask students to find examples of the sound devices in other poems they know of.

READING SKILL

■ MAKE INFERENCES

To introduce the chart, have student fill out one or more inferences for the four-line verse in the Literary Analysis box. Then have students begin a chart for "The Raven" and complete it as they read.

R **RESOURCE MANAGER—Copy Master**
Make Inferences p. 245 (for student use while reading the selection)

DIFFERENTIATED INSTRUCTION

FOR STRATEGIC READERS

Concept Support: Make Inferences Remind students that the purpose of the chart on this page is to make inferences that are specifically about the speaker of the poem, not about other aspects of the poem. With the help of the chart, students should formulate an impression of the speaker. They should make guesses about what has happened in his life and how he has responded to it. They should seek clues to whether he is sane or mad, and whether he is believable or not.

SUMMARY

In this poem, the speaker is sitting at home grieving over the loss of his love, Lenore, when a raven enters through the window. The speaker asks the raven's name and the bird replies, "Nevermore." As the speaker asks the bird for relief from suffering, for assurance that he and Lenore will be reunited, and finally for the bird to leave, the bird repeats, "Nevermore."

LITERARY ANALYSIS

Ⓐ SOUND DEVICES

Answer: *There is a rhyming pair in the first line (dreary/weary) and one in the third line (napping/tapping), that repeats in the fourth and fifth lines (rapping, tapping). The pattern varies in subsequent stanzas.*

If students need help . . . Clarify that internal rhyme is rhyme that occurs within a single line of a poem, not at the ends of two different lines.

READING SKILL

Ⓑ MAKE INFERENCES

Possible answer: *Lenore is a woman the speaker loved, who has died. Clues: "sorrow for the lost Lenore," "angels."*

If students need help . . . Have them begin filling out the chart that was introduced on page 437.

	Inferences About the Speaker	Clues
State of Mind	grief	repetition of "sorrow"
Recent Experiences	lost his love, Lenore	"sorrow for the lost Lenore," "nameless here forevermore"

The
Raven
Edgar Allan Poe

Once upon a midnight dreary, while I pondered, weak and weary,
Over many a quaint and curious volume of forgotten lore—
While I nodded, nearly napping, suddenly there came a tapping,
As of someone gently rapping, rapping at my chamber door.
5 "'Tis some visitor," I muttered, "tapping at my chamber door—
    Only this and nothing more." Ⓐ

Ah, distinctly I remember it was in the bleak December;
And each separate dying ember wrought its ghost upon the floor.
Eagerly I wished the morrow;—vainly I had sought to borrow
10 From my books surcease[1] of sorrow—sorrow for the lost Lenore—
For the rare and radiant maiden whom the angels name Lenore—
    Nameless *here* forevermore. Ⓑ

And the silken, sad, uncertain rustling of each purple curtain
Thrilled me—filled me with fantastic terrors never felt before;
15 So that now, to still the beating of my heart, I stood repeating
"'Tis some visitor entreating entrance at my chamber door;—
Some late visitor entreating entrance at my chamber door;—
    That it is and nothing more."

ANALYZE VISUALS
What techniques has the photographer used that make the raven on page 439 seem mysterious?

Ⓐ SOUND DEVICES
Reread lines 1–6. What pattern of **internal rhyme** does Poe establish in the first stanza?

Ⓑ MAKE INFERENCES
Reread lines 9–12. What does this passage imply about Lenore's connection to the speaker and the reason for her absence? Give details to support your answer.

---

1. **surcease:** an end.

DIFFERENTIATED INSTRUCTION

FOR STRATEGIC READERS
Options for Reading: Audio Recording

- Have students listen to "The Raven" on the *Audio Anthology CD*. Encourage them to listen for how inflections in the reader's voice establish mood.

- Have students infer the state of mind of the poem's speaker from the tones and phrasing of the audio reader.

For general guidelines on differentiating instruction, see

 BEST PRACTICES TOOLKIT
Differentiated Instruction pp. 31–38

ANALYZE VISUALS

Possible answer: The photographer uses black and white with high contrast and blurred details, making the raven jump out at viewers while appearing slightly indistinct. The effect is one of uncertainty or mystery.

Lines 1–18
TIERED DISCUSSION PROMPTS

Use these prompts to help students understand the poem's emotions:

Connect Have you or anyone you know ever been startled by an unexpected visitor? How did it feel? *Accept all reasonable responses.*

Interpret What does the speaker's frequent repetition tell you about his emotional state? *Possible answer: He is agitated and obsessed.*

Evaluate Does Poe's use of repetition in the first three stanzas achieve its purpose? *Possible answer: It achieves its purpose by emphasizing the speaker's disturbed state.*

BACKGROUND

Ravens Ravens are large, loud, aggressive birds; they are keen-sighted, wary, and usually solitary. They are long-lived and, as pets, may learn to mimic several words. Ravens were a symbol of prophecy to many cultures who associated them with mystery, evil omens, death, and disease. Ravens' fearlessness and cleverness have earned them admiration. Poe's raven alights on a bust of the Greek goddess of wisdom, Pallas Athena, whose symbol was the owl. Poe first considered using an owl or parrot as his bird, but chose a raven because of its symbolic associations.

FOR STRATEGIC READERS

Comprehension Ask three volunteers to read each of the first three stanzas aloud. After all three stanzas have been read, ask students to predict who is tapping at the speaker's door and why.

FOR ENGLISH LEARNERS

Language: Punctuation and Print Cues
Students may be confused by Poe's frequent use of dashes. Point out that the dashes often introduce repetitions of word patterns or ideas, as in "perched above my chamber door— / Perched . . . just above my chamber door" (lines 40–41). These repetitions indicate the speaker's excited, distressed state of mind. Invite relatively fluent students to read such passages aloud in an appropriate dramatic tone.

C STANZA AND RHYME SCHEME

Answer: abcbbb. *The fourth and fifth lines repeat the same rhyming word, which is not true end rhyme.*

D SOUND DEVICES

Answer: *An example of onomatopoeia is "flutter."*

E SOUND DEVICES

Possible answer: shorn, shaven, sure, shore; ghastly, grim. *The alliterated words are emphasized.*

Extend the Discussion What mood or emotion is emphasized by the alliteration of these specific words?

Presently my soul grew stronger; hesitating then no longer,
20 "Sir," said I, "or Madam, truly your forgiveness I implore;
   But the fact is I was napping, and so gently you came rapping,
   And so faintly you came tapping, tapping at my chamber door,
   That I scarce was sure I heard you"—here I opened wide the door;—
      Darkness there and nothing more. **C**

25 Deep into that darkness peering, long I stood there wondering, fearing,
   Doubting, dreaming dreams no mortal ever dared to dream before;
   But the silence was unbroken, and the stillness gave no token,
   And the only word there spoken was the whispered word, "Lenore!"
   This I whispered, and an echo murmured back the word "Lenore!"
30   Merely this and nothing more.

Back into the chamber turning, all my soul within me burning,
   Soon again I heard a tapping somewhat louder than before.
   "Surely," said I, "surely that is something at my window lattice;
   Let me see, then, what thereat is, and this mystery explore—
35 Let my heart be still a moment and this mystery explore;—
      'Tis the wind and nothing more!"

Open here I flung the shutter, when, with many a flirt and flutter,
   In there stepped a stately Raven of the saintly days of yore.[2]
   Not the least obeisance[3] made he; not a minute stopped or stayed he;
40 But, with mien[4] of lord or lady, perched above my chamber door—
   Perched upon a bust of Pallas[5] just above my chamber door—
      Perched, and sat, and nothing more. **D**

Then this ebony bird beguiling my sad fancy into smiling,
   By the grave and stern decorum of the countenance it wore,
45 "Though thy crest be shorn and shaven, thou," I said, "art sure no craven,[6]
   Ghastly grim and ancient Raven wandering from the Nightly shore—
   Tell me what thy lordly name is on the Night's Plutonian[7] shore!"
      Quoth the Raven, "Nevermore." **E**

Much I marveled this ungainly fowl to hear discourse so plainly,
50 Though its answer little meaning—little relevancy bore;
   For we cannot help agreeing that no living human being

---

2. **days of yore:** days of long ago.
3. **obeisance** (ō-bā'səns): a gesture of respect.
4. **mien** (mēn): appearance.
5. **bust of Pallas:** statue of the head and shoulders of Pallas Athena, Greek goddess of wisdom.
6. **craven:** coward.
7. **Plutonian:** having to do with Pluto, Roman god of the dead and ruler of the underworld.

C STANZA AND RHYME SCHEME
Recall that a poem's rhyme scheme is its pattern of **end rhyme**. Describe the rhyme scheme of this poem. How does Poe use **repetition** as part of the rhyme scheme?

D SOUND DEVICES
Reread lines 37–38. What example of **onomatopoeia** can you find?

E SOUND DEVICES
Identify the **alliteration** in lines 45–46. What words are emphasized by using this technique?

DIFFERENTIATED INSTRUCTION

FOR STRATEGIC READERS
Vocabulary Support

- *implore* (line 20), "beg"
- *token* (line 27), "sign"
- *lattice* (line 33), "window frame"
- *beguiling* (line 43), "tricking"
- *decorum* (line 44), "formal behavior"
- *countenance* (line 44), "facial expression"
- *discourse* (line 49), "speech"

Ever yet was blessed with seeing bird above his chamber door—
Bird or beast upon the sculptured bust above his chamber door,
    With such name as "Nevermore."

55 But the Raven, sitting lonely on the placid bust, spoke only
That one word, as if his soul in that one word he did outpour.
Nothing farther then he uttered—not a feather then he fluttered—
Till I scarcely more than muttered "Other friends have flown before—
On the morrow *he* will leave me, as my hopes have flown before."
60   Then the bird said, "Nevermore." **F**

Startled at the stillness broken by reply so aptly spoken,
"Doubtless," said I, "what it utters is its only stock and store
Caught from some unhappy master whom unmerciful Disaster
Followed fast and followed faster till his songs one burden[8] bore—
65 Till the dirges[9] of his Hope that melancholy burden bore
    Of 'Never—nevermore.'"

But the Raven still beguiling all my fancy into smiling,
Straight I wheeled a cushioned seat in front of bird, and bust and door;
Then, upon the velvet sinking, I betook myself to linking
70 Fancy unto fancy, thinking what this ominous bird of yore—
What this grim, ungainly, ghastly, gaunt, and ominous bird of yore
    Meant in croaking, "Nevermore." **G**

This I sat engaged in guessing, but no syllable expressing
To the fowl whose fiery eyes now burned into my bosom's core;
75 This and more I sat divining,[10] with my head at ease reclining
On the cushion's velvet lining that the lamp-light gloated o'er,
But whose velvet violet lining with the lamp-light gloating o'er,
    She shall press, ah, nevermore!

Then, methought, the air grew denser, perfumed from an unseen censer
80 Swung by Seraphim[11] whose foot-falls tinkled on the tufted floor.
"Wretch," I cried, "thy God hath lent thee—by these angels he hath sent thee
Respite—respite and nepenthe[12] from thy memories of Lenore;
Quaff,[13] oh quaff this kind nepenthe and forget this lost Lenore!"
    Quoth the Raven, "Nevermore."

---

8. **burden:** the chorus or refrain of a song.
9. **dirges:** songs of mourning.
10. **divining:** guessing from incomplete evidence.
11. **censer / Swung by Seraphim** (sĕr'ə-fĭm): container of sweet burning incense swung by angels of the highest rank.
12. **respite . . . and nepenthe** (nĭ-pĕn'thē): temporary relief and a forgetfulness that eases grief.
13. **quaff:** drink deeply.

THE RAVEN **441**

F MAKE INFERENCES
Reread lines 58–59. What does this comment suggest about the speaker's past experiences and his current mood? Explain.

G SOUND DEVICES
Identify the sound device used in lines 71–72. What qualities of the raven are emphasized by the use of this device?

READING SKILL

F MAKE INFERENCES

Possible answer: *He has been abandoned, by Lenore and possibly by others; he is lonely and feels hopeless. The evidence is "'Other friends have flown before— / On the morrow* he *will leave me, as my hopes have flown before.'"*

If students need help . . . Have them continue working with the chart introduced on page 437.

LITERARY ANALYSIS

G SOUND DEVICES

Possible answer: *The use of alliteration (*grim, ungainly, ghastly, gaunt*) emphasizes the physically unpleasant and emotionally unsettling appearance of the raven.*

Lines 79–84
REINFORCE *KEY IDEA:* GRIEF
Discuss What **grief** does the speaker feel?
Possible answer: *He feels grief at the loss of his love, Lenore.*

FOR STRATEGIC READERS
Concept Support: Make Inferences To help students make inferences about the speaker's state of mind, suggest that they distinguish between the aspects of the poem that are fantasy and parts that could happen in real life. For instance, birds cannot really talk, but people really can grieve over loss. Have students focus on the realistic aspects in order to understand the speaker.

FOR ADVANCED LEARNERS/AP
Analyze [paired option] Have students work in pairs to use the Analysis Frame: Poetic Language and Style to deepen their understanding of Poe's use of sound devices in "The Raven."

 BEST PRACTICES TOOLKIT—Transparency
Analysis Frame: Poetic Language and Style pp. D21, D38

THE RAVEN **441**

REINFORCE *KEY IDEA*: GRIEF

Discuss With what words does the speaker express his hope for relief from **grief**? *Possible answer: "'Is there balm in Gilead?'" (line 89) is a request for relief from grief. "'Tell this soul with sorrow laden if . . . / It shall clasp a sainted maiden whom the angels name Lenore'" (lines 93–94) expresses the wish that he be united with Lenore in heaven.*

READING SKILL

H MAKE INFERENCES

Possible answer: The speaker is so desperate and grief-stricken that he clings to an irrational hope that the bird will say something comforting.

ADDITIONAL TEACHING OPPORTUNITY

Interpret Remind students that a work of literature may support more than one interpretation. In the case of a Poe poem or story, the question often arises, "How much of this is really happening, and how much takes place in the character's mind?" Ask students whether, in their opinion, the raven is a figment of the speaker's imagination. Have them find details in the text of the poem to support their view.

SELECTION WRAP–UP

REFLECT Have students think about the speaker's character. Ask them to describe him in a sentence or two.

⭐ CRITIQUE

• Ask students how convincing Poe makes this narrative.

• After completing the After Reading questions on page 443, have students revisit their responses and tell whether they have changed their opinions.

---

85 "Prophet!" said I, "thing of evil!—prophet still, if bird or devil!—
    Whether Tempter[14] sent, or whether tempest tossed thee here ashore,
    Desolate yet all undaunted, on this desert land enchanted—
    On this home by Horror haunted—tell me truly, I implore—
    Is there—*is* there balm in Gilead?[15]—tell me—tell me, I implore!"
90   Quoth the Raven, "Nevermore."

    "Prophet!" said I, "thing of evil!—prophet still, if bird or devil!
    By that Heaven that bends above us—by that God we both adore—
    Tell this soul with sorrow laden if, within the distant Aidenn,[16]
    It shall clasp a sainted maiden whom the angels name Lenore—
95 Clasp a rare and radiant maiden whom the angels name Lenore."
        Quoth the Raven, "Nevermore." H

    "Be that word our sign of parting, bird or fiend!" I shrieked, upstarting—
    "Get thee back into the tempest and the Night's Plutonian shore!
    Leave no black plume as a token of that lie thy soul hath spoken!
100 Leave my loneliness unbroken!—quit the bust above my door!
    Take thy beak from out my heart, and take thy form from off my door!"
        Quoth the Raven, "Nevermore."

    And the Raven, never flitting, still is sitting, *still* is sitting
    On the pallid bust of Pallas just above my chamber door;
105 And his eyes have all the seeming of a demon's that is dreaming,
    And the lamp-light o'er him streaming throws his shadow on the floor;
    And my soul from out that shadow that lies floating on the floor
        Shall be lifted—nevermore!

H MAKE INFERENCES
Given the bird's repeated response, what does the speaker's persistent questioning of the raven suggest about his state of mind? Explain your answer.

---

14. **Tempter:** the devil.
15. **balm** (bäm) **in Gilead** (gĭl'ē-əd): relief from suffering.
16. **Aidenn** (ād'n): heaven (from the Arabic form of the word *Eden*).

DIFFERENTIATED INSTRUCTION

FOR ADVANCED LEARNERS/AP

Evaluate Writing in 1893, naturalist and writer John Burroughs criticized Poe as a poet whose only skill was verbal acrobatics. He went on to say that Poe's writing showed a lack of literary thought and an absence of sympathy or love for anything. Ask students to write one or two paragraphs stating whether they agree with Burroughs and why. Remind them to use evidence from the poem, the two Poe stories they have read, and what they know about Poe's life. Allow time for students to read their paragraphs to the class. Encourage questions and discussion.

Comprehension

CALIFORNIA R3.4

1. **Recall** Where and when do the events of the poem take place?

2. **Recall** What is the raven's response to all of the speaker's questions?

3. **Clarify** What is the speaker's explanation of the raven's one response?

Literary Analysis

4. **Draw Conclusions** Review the **inferences** you made as you read. What conclusions did you draw about the speaker and his emotional state?

5. **Examine Tone** For each of the following passages, describe the speaker's tone, or attitude, toward the raven. What explains the speaker's changing responses to his mysterious visitor?

   • the raven's first appearance (lines 43–44)
   • the thoughts the raven inspires (lines 71–74)
   • the purpose the speaker attributes to the raven (lines 81–84)
   • the speaker's command to the raven (lines 97–98)

6. **Compare and Contrast Imagery** Poe uses imagery to create a stark contrast between Lenore and the raven. Using a chart like the one shown, list images used to describe each character. Based on these images, what main feeling or quality is each character used to communicate? Cite evidence.

Lenore	Raven

7. **Evaluate Sound Devices** Reread lines 79–84. Identify the sound devices used in this stanza, and give examples of each technique. Which of these devices do you find most compelling or effective? Explain your answer.

8. **Make Judgments** Consider the speaker's changing responses to the raven and the conclusions you drew about his state of mind. What does the speaker's **conflict** with the raven suggest about the behavior of people who are struggling with **grief**? Support your answer with details.

Literary Criticism

9. **Author's Style** In an essay about "The Raven," Poe claimed that he started with the word *nevermore* (he liked its vowel sounds), then added the death of a beautiful woman ("the most poetical topic in the world"). Only later did he invent the story and characters that readers have found so moving and memorable. Poe seems to have been more interested in form than content. Which do you find more important in this poem? Cite details in your answer.

THE RAVEN 443

Practice and Apply

After Reading

Use these copy masters to check understanding and provide extra support:

R RESOURCE MANAGER—Copy Masters
   Sound Devices p. 243
   Question Support p. 247

   Additional selection questions are provided for teachers on page 239.

ANSWERS

1. *The events take place at midnight on a stormy night in December in the speaker's chamber.*

2. *The raven's response is "Nevermore."*

3. *The speaker explains that the raven picked up the word from its master, who must have had exceptionally bad luck to have repeated the word often enough for the bird to learn it.*

Possible answers:

4. ■ SKILLS FOCUS **Make Inferences**
   Some students may say the speaker is mad with grief; others may say he is emotionally unstable, dreaming, or both.

5. *Lines 43–44: amused; lines 71–74: thoughtful, fascinated; lines 81–84: anguished; lines 97–98: enraged. The raven's unchanging response irritates and exasperates the speaker to madness.*

6. *Lenore: angels, radiant, sainted maiden; raven: black, stern, hellish, deathlike (Plutonian), ancient, grim, tempter. Based on these images, Lenore represents happiness, love, innocence; the raven represents torment and despair.*

7. ● SKILLS FOCUS **Sound Devices**
   Onomatopoeia: tinkled; alliteration: censer, swung, Seraphim, foot-falls, floor, tinkled, tufted; end-rhyme: floor, Lenore, Nevermore; internal rhyme: denser, censer, lent thee, sent thee, Nepenthe; repetition: words such as respite, quaff, and Lenore. Students' opinions of the devices will vary.

8. *Students may say that the speaker's true conflict is with himself, and the raven is a reflection of it. They may feel that people become obsessed with grief and can't see beyond it.*

9. *Accept all reasonable answers.*

Reading-Writing Connection

WRITING PROMPT

Have students use the Freewriting strategy to set their or their speaker's thoughts down spontaneously.

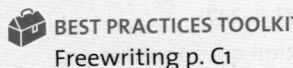 **BEST PRACTICES TOOLKIT**
Freewriting p. C1

For writing support, see

ℹ️ **Writing Center at ClassZone.com**

GRAMMAR AND STYLE

To further model the activity, ask volunteers to make up imperative sentences and say them aloud. Then have students add dashes to those sentences to give urgency. Since Poe often inserts dashes when adding repetitions of phrases or clauses, suggest that students use this technique in their sample sentences. (For more on imperative sentences, see Grammar Handbook, page R64.)

📋 **RESOURCE MANAGER—Copy Master**
Craft Effective Sentences p. 248

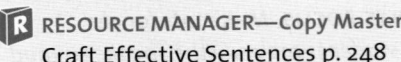
Assess and Reteach

Assess

📋 **RESOURCE MANAGER—Copy Masters**
Selection Test A pp. 249–250
Selection Test B/C pp. 251–252

💿 Test Generator CD

Reteach

📄 **STANDARDS LESSON FILE**
Literature Lesson 19: Rhyme and Rhyme Scheme
Literature Lesson 21: Alliteration, Assonance, and Consonance
Literature Lesson 22: Onomatopoeia
Reading Lesson 8: Making Inferences

Reading-Writing Connection

 W1.1, W1.2

WRITING PROMPT

WRITE A MONOLOGUE In a monologue, a character expresses thoughts in an uninterrupted flow, with no other character's words intervening. Monologues in literature often explore a character's feelings. They may be addressed to an absent or abstract listener, or they may be more random, following a person's train of thought.

Write a **one-page prose monologue**, in your own voice or that of a fictional character, that explores an emotion, such as grief, anger, or joy. Use your monologue to reveal details about your speaker's personality and the reasons for his or her emotional response.

SELF-CHECK

A successful monologue will...

- reflect the clearly defined voice of the speaker
- effectively convey the speaker's emotional state
- establish a convincing motivation for the speaker's feelings

GRAMMAR AND STYLE

 W1.5, LC1.1

CRAFT EFFECTIVE SENTENCES Poe uses **imperative sentences**—sentences that give orders or make requests—and **dashes** to convey his character's excitable state. The use of dashes and a tone of breathless urgency are distinctive features of Poe's style.

> *"Be that word our sign of parting, bird or fiend!" I shrieked, upstarting—*
> *"Get thee back into the tempest and the Night's Plutonian shore!"* (lines 97–98)

PRACTICE Using the following verse from "The Raven" as a model, compose your own stanza in the style of Poe, incorporating dashes and imperative sentences. Feel free to choose a different subject, but make sure to follow Poe's rhyme scheme and to echo his tone. A sample beginning is provided for you.

> **EXAMPLE**
>
> "Prophet!" said I, "thing of evil!—prophet still, if bird or devil!—
> *"You pest, begone!" I cried—near choking. "Take from me your wretched joking!*

"Prophet!" said I, "thing of evil!—prophet still, if bird or devil!—
Whether Tempter sent, or whether tempest tossed thee here ashore,
Desolate yet all undaunted, on this desert land enchanted—
On this home by Horror haunted—tell me truly, I implore—
Is there—*is* there balm in Gilead?—tell me—tell me, I implore!"
    Quoth the Raven, "Nevermore."

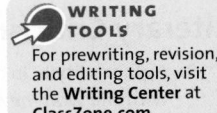
WRITING TOOLS
For prewriting, revision, and editing tools, visit the **Writing Center** at ClassZone.com.

DIFFERENTIATED INSTRUCTION

FOR DEVELOPING WRITERS
Writing Support

- Point out that a monologue may contain sentence fragments and run-on sentences in order to capture the feeling of real thought.

- Although students' freewriting may produce good first drafts by capturing a spontaneous flow of thought, urge students to revise their monologues carefully

to express the feelings and thoughts they want in exact language.

- Suggest that students choose a specific emotion first as a way of focusing their monologues.

- Remind students to include specific facts and details about the speaker's situation rather than merely expressions of feeling.

PARODY Like other well-known and well-loved works of literature, "The Raven" has inspired many a **parody**—a comic imitation of another work or type of literature. As you read the following parody, note the points of imitation in form or content. In what ways does the parodist turn Poe's ideas to comic effect?

What Troubled Poe's Raven

John Bennett

Could Poe walk again to-morrow, heavy with
   dyspeptic sorrow,
While the darkness seemed to borrow darkness
   from the night before,
From the hollow gloom abysmal, floating
   downward, grimly dismal,
Like a pagan curse baptismal from the bust above
   the door,
5 He would hear the Raven croaking from the dusk
   above the door,
     "Never, never, nevermore!"

And, too angry to be civil, "Raven," Poe would
   cry "or devil,
Tell me why you will persist in haunting Death's
   Plutonian shore?"
Then would croak the Raven gladly, "I will tell
   you why so sadly,
10 I so mournfully and madly, haunt you, taunt you,
   o'er and o'er,
Why eternally I haunt you, daunt you, taunt you,
   o'er and o'er —
     Only this, and nothing more.

"Forty-eight long years I've pondered, forty-eight
   long years I've wondered,
How a poet ever blundered into a mistake so sore.
15 How could lamp-light from your table ever in the
   world be able,
From *below*, to throw my sable shadow 'streaming
   on the floor,'
When I perched up here on Pallas, high above
   your chamber-door?
     Tell me that — if nothing more!"

Then, like some wan, weeping willow, Poe
   would bend above his pillow,
20 Seeking surcease in the billow where mad
   recollections drown,
And in tearful tones replying, he would groan
   "There's no denying
Either I was blindly lying, or the world was
   upside down—
Say, by Joe!—it was just midnight—so the
   world *was* upside down—
     Aye, the world was upside down!"

CONNECT: POEM **445**

Lines 1–24
TIERED DISCUSSION PROMPTS

Use these prompts to help students understand the connection between this parody and Poe's "The Raven":

Summarize What mistake in Poe's poem does the raven point out in "What Troubled Poe's Raven"? What two possible explanations does Bennett's Poe give in the last four lines? *Possible answer: The mistake is that Poe's poem describes the lamplight from below the table casting the raven's shadow onto the floor. This is optically impossible. The explanations are either that Poe was lying or that, in the context of the poem, the world was "upside down."*

Analyze What does the passage about the mistake (lines 13–24) show you about the personalities of Poe and of the raven? *Possible answer: Bennett's poem shows Poe as a shifty character who makes excuses for his errors, and the raven as highly perceptive and persistent but nitpicking.*

Evaluate How successful is Bennett's poem as a parody of "The Raven"? In what ways do you think it is most effective, and in what ways do you think it is least effective? *Possible answers: Accept reasonable answers, such as that the parody is effective in mimicking Poe's sound devices but that by concentrating on a trivial mistake, it fails to make any substantive points about Poe's poem.*

Focus and Motivate

OBJECTIVES

Media Literacy

- explore the key idea of **gothic spirit**
- view an image collection to identify and analyze visual elements and meaning of American gothic art
- create gothic artwork to apply knowledge of style through color, shape, and texture

LS1.3, LS1.10

SUMMARY

In this image collection, students view illustrations by Clive Barker, Gris Grimly, Edmund Dulac, Charles Addams, and others. They focus on two works by Arthur Rackham. In "The Fall of the House of Usher," a rider views a spooky, melancholy house that rises from a swampy lake and is framed by jagged, craggy trees. In the image "The Pit and the Pendulum," burning iron walls drive the prisoner to the edge of the deadly pit at the center of his cell.

What does GOTHIC *look like?*

To introduce the **KEY IDEA,** ask the question. Then, help students brainstorm elements that characterize the **gothic spirit,** such as frantic facial expressions, dramatic color schemes, and dark, foreboding scenes. Ask students why such a style is appropriate to Poe's work.

BACKGROUND

Arthur Rackham (1867–1939) is one of the foremost British children's illustrators of the early twentieth century. His work is characterized by magical fairies, fantastical gnomes, and ugly ogres. His illustrations of Poe's stories are less fantastical than most of his art, and reveal his understanding of human nature and its psychological depth.

Media Study

Illustrations Inspired by Poe

Image Collection on ⊙ **MediaSmart** DVD

CALIFORNIA LS1.3, LS1.10 (p. 449)

What does GOTHIC *look like?*

KEY IDEA Shadows and gargoyles and pervading gloom all evoke the **gothic spirit** that Edgar Allan Poe depicted so well in his stories and poems. Countless artists have been inspired by Poe's works—writers, musicians, architects, and certainly visual artists. British illustrator Arthur Rackham had a particular affinity for Poe's writing. In examining Rackham's illustrations in this lesson, you'll see how an artist influenced by Poe's gothic style expresses his own personal interpretation.

Background

American Gothic It's not simply the plots and characters Poe created that have mesmerized readers and artists over time. It's what his writing revealed of our dark side, of our capacity for decadence and even insanity, that has given him such lasting influence. Though the term *gothic* has been applied to other art forms such as architecture and music, it is in Poe's writing that the psychological elements of gothic are most sharply defined.

At the time Poe's work was first published, illustrators were regularly hired to create images to accompany his text. As Poe's reputation grew and more people read his often disturbing stories, painters and artists found great imaginative fodder in Poe's phantasmagorical tales. You can see his influence in the work of countless illustrators over the past 150 years, including Poe contemporary Gustave Doré, Arthur Rackham, Edward Gorey, Charles Addams (creator of "The Addams Family" cartoon), and even popular children's book illustrator Stephen Gammell. Many of today's graphic novelists are heavily influenced by Poe's sense of gothic.

446

Media Study Resources

---

* Resources for Differentiation   † Also in Spanish   ‡ In Haitian Creole and Vietnamese

Media Literacy: Art Elements in Illustrations

In Edgar Allan Poe's writing, he often expresses his style through imagery that re-creates certain sensory experiences. In "The Fall of the House of Usher," Poe's description of the house is one of decay and desolation. In order to translate such descriptions into a visual image, an illustrator relies on the art elements of **color, line, shape,** and **texture** to evoke similar feelings. Another aspect of visual art is **dominance,** which is created when one or more parts of an image are given more importance than the others.

Consider these elements when analyzing this 1935 Arthur Rackham illustration for "The Fall of the House of Usher." Think about the deliberate stylistic choices made by the illustrator to match the mood and tone of Poe's writing.

STRATEGIES FOR ANALYZING ILLUSTRATIONS

1 **Color** is used to highlight important aspects and create mood in an image. To analyze an illustrator's use of color, think about the overall mood of the image. Are the colors warm (red and orange) or cool (blue and green)? Do the muted colors in this image seem to reflect Poe's descriptions?

2 **Line** is a stroke or a mark. Vertical, horizontal, jagged, curved—lines have expressive qualities. Look at the style of lines an artist uses. Here, for example, the vertical lines are strong and varied and suggest the dreary atmosphere of Poe's setting.

3 **Shape** is the outline of an object in an image. Notice the tension created by the strong yet warped lines of the dead trees against the severe lines of the house.

4 **Texture** is the surface quality of an image. Examine how this artist manipulates visual elements to create different textures. Ask yourself: If I could touch this image, how would it feel?

5 Be aware of the primary object that draws your eye. Here the house of Usher is the dominant image.

MEDIA STUDY **447**

Teach

Media Literacy

Ask a volunteer to remind the class of the plot of "The Fall of the House of Usher." Review with students the mood and tone of Poe's writing. List descriptive words that students suggest, such as *ominous, eerie, psychological,* and *desolate.* Then discuss the illustration by Arthur Rackham and how it creates a similar mood.

- **Color** Point out that the image is drawn in a monochromatic color scheme. Ask students to describe the mood created by the gray, white, and black colors.

- **Line** Note that the line weights are stronger on the trees than on the house. The black lines of the trees further emphasize the emptiness inside them. Ask students how the lines help define the elements of the drawing that are most important.

- **Shape** Clarify that the illustrator emphasized the house's stiff, upright shape by framing it with twisted, curving trees.

- **Texture** Draw attention to the smudged, watercolor effect of the sky as it contrasts with the sharper pen-and-ink appearance of the road. Ask students what is different about these textures.

- **Dominance** Explain that dominance in a painting is created by color, size, line, and position. In this image, the house is the lightest part of the drawing, as well as the largest part. It is also framed by the lines of the trees on both sides and positioned close to the center of the illustration, making it the dominant image.

  MediaSmart DVD

MEDIA STUDY: TEACHING OPTIONS

Teaching Option 1: The Basics (1–2 Days)
1. Begin the Media Study using the material provided on pages 446–447.
2. Show the Introduction on Media*Smart.* Have students use the Viewing Guide on page 448, along with the corresponding copy master on page 259 of the Resource Manager. Discuss their responses.
3. Return to the pupil book for the extension activities on page 449.

Teaching Option 2: In-Depth Study (2–3 Days)
1. Begin the Media Study using pages 446–447.
2. Show the Introduction from Media*Smart.*
3. Continue on Media*Smart* with the Media Lessons, using the teacher notes available in the Resources section.
4. Show the Guided Analysis presentation. Have students record their observations on the Student Viewing Guide available in the Resources section of Media*Smart.*
5. Return to the pupil book, page 449.

MEDIA STUDY **447**

Practice and Apply

VIEWING GUIDE

1. As students prepare to view the images, tell them they will be asked to identify and analyze aspects of color, line, and dominance. Display each image one at a time, and then repeat the process. Encourage students to study all the images before answering the questions. Suggest that they pay attention to these points:

   - background details that convey information and set the mood of the illustration through **color, line,** and **shape**
   - the perspective from which the image is drawn and the position of the viewer in relation to the scene of the illustration
   - how ordinary items such as a staircase or a house are made to look frightening
   - how position and **dominance** of elements in the illustration support its mood

2. Encourage students to consider how each illustration reflects Poe's fascination with the macabre and creates a sense of terror. As they view the collection, help them make connections to related scenes from the Poe literature.

R RESOURCE MANAGER—Copy Masters
   Viewing Guide p. 259
   Close Viewing p. 260
   Media Activity p. 261

Use this resource with the Viewing Guide:

MediaSmart DVD

ANSWERS

FIRST VIEWING: Comprehension

1. *The narrator appears in the foreground across the moat from the house.*

2. *The man is standing at the edge of the pit.*

CLOSE VIEWING: Media Literacy

Possible answers:

3. *The colors are monochromatic, in shades of gray. They create a foreboding and frightening mood.*

4. *In "The Pit and the Pendulum," lines define the stone floor and suggest physical distress in the figure's legs and tunic. The shadowy vertical lines in the background hint at something evil or frightening. In "The Fall of the House of Usher," the primarily vertical lines define the twisted, craggy tree and the stoic, imposing house. Rackham uses lines most effectively in "The Fall of the House of*

MediaSmart DVD
- **Selection 1:** "The Fall of The House of Usher"
- **Selection 2:** "The Pit and the Pendulum"
- **Type:** Illustration
- **Illustrator:** Arthur Rackham

Viewing Guide for
Illustrations Inspired by Poe

Access the full-sized images on the DVD. Examine each image carefully, jotting down your initial impressions. Look for common elements, themes, and subjects in the images. To help you analyze each image in terms of color, shape, line, texture, and dominance, use the viewing strategies detailed on page 447. You can also refer to the Illustrations and Photographs section of the Media Handbook (pages R94–R95). Answer the questions to help you analyze the images.

NOW VIEW

FIRST VIEWING: Comprehension

1. **Describe** Where does the narrator of "The Fall of the House of Usher" appear in Rackham's illustration?

2. **Identify** Where is the man standing in "The Pit and the Pendulum" illustration?

CLOSE VIEWING: Media Literacy

3. **Analyze Color** What colors does Rackham use in the "House of Usher" illustration, and what mood do these create? Explain your answer.

4. **Compare Line** Look carefully at the way line is used in both illustrations. In which image is line used most effectively? Explain.

5. **Compare Dominance** Consider the images for "The Fall of the House of Usher" and "The Pit and the Pendulum." One part of each image is dominant. How does the illustrator achieve this effect? Think about
   - the use of shape in the images
   - how color is used to create dominance

448

Usher" because they are more severe and create a unified effect.

5. *In "The Fall of the House of Usher," the house is dominant. It is framed by the craggy trees, the glassy moat, and the dark grey sky. In "The Pit and the Pendulum," the man at the edge of the pit is dominant because of his central location and lighter color. The darker shapes behind him and at his feet help accent his dominance.*

Write or Discuss

LS1.3
CALIFORNIA

Describe Unity of Effect Poe believed in writing to achieve "unity of effect," in which every detail of a work contributes to a single overall feeling. This idea guided his word choices, sentence structures, and subject matter. Look at the two Rackham illustrations in this Media Study. How do you think Rackham's decisions as an artist create unity of effect? Write a brief description of what Rackham achieves with these gothic images. Consider these elements:

- Rackham's use of color, line, shape, and texture in the images
- the parts of Poe's stories that each work depicts
- the overall mood of each illustration

Produce Your Own Media

LS1.10
CALIFORNIA

Create Gothic Artwork How would you visually represent something in the gothic style? Use your understanding of the term to create a gothic piece of **artwork.** It can be a photograph, a painting, a computer-generated image, a drawing, even a collage of magazine clippings.

HERE'S HOW Here are a few suggestions for creating gothic visual art:

- No matter what type of gothic piece you will create, make notes on your intentions and how you plan to achieve them.
- Decide on the psychological mood you want to express.
- Keep in mind the visual art elements.
- Consider what colors you'll need to use. If creating a gothic photograph, consider the lighting effects you might employ, or whether to use color or black-and-white film.
- Try to establish a dominant element in your piece, something that the viewer will quickly focus on.

MEDIA TOOLS

For help creating gothic art, visit the **Media Center** at **ClassZone.com.**

Tech Tip

If available, use a design program to turn a photograph of a happy occasion into a gothic representation.

Further Exploration

Contrasting Styles Revisit the variety of additional Poe-inspired images on the DVD, or look for other examples on your own. Explore how these works are all influenced by Poe's writing in some way. What Poe-inspired similarities can you find between the images? Cite specific elements from the images. Think about

- line, shape, color, and texture
- how the images reflect a gothic sensibility
- how the images express the psychological

Find the Gothic in Your Life Think about other art forms—movies, music, live theater—where you find gothic elements. Describe a movie, song, or play in which you can identify these elements.

MEDIA STUDY **449**

MEDIA STUDY WRAP–UP

Have students summarize what they have learned about how illustrators convey mood through line, shape, color, and dominance. Encourage students to use their understanding as they evaluate illustrations throughout their reading.

RETEACH

 STANDARDS LESSON FILE

Media Lesson 1: Active Viewing Strategies
Media Lesson 2: Five Concepts of Media Literacy
Media Lesson 19: Analyzing Visuals

Assess and Reteach

Write or Discuss

Describe Unity of Effect In their descriptions, students should address the techniques Rackham uses to create the overall feeling of foreboding or horror in his illustrations, such as *line, color, shape,* and *texture.* For example, the textures in "The Pit and the Pendulum" image help unify it. The rough, wrinkled tunic emphasizes the desperation of the central figure. The shadowy skeleton and demons reveal a deep horror in the background. Remind students to discuss the moods in the illustrations and the related Poe literature and to support their ideas with examples.

Produce Your Own Media

Rubric: Create Gothic Artwork Strong artwork should have

- a unified mood that conveys gothic themes, such as psychological distress and deep emotion
- visual elements such as color, shape, and texture that support the mood
- effective lighting that creates a gothic effect
- a dominant figure or image created by color, line, and shape

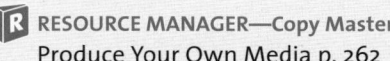 RESOURCE MANAGER—Copy Master
Produce Your Own Media p. 262

Further Exploration

Contrasting Styles Point out the bulleted text. Have students record these features for each work.

Find the Gothic in Your Life Recall the artists named in **Background** on page 446. Then, help students brainstorm additional examples of gothic work, such as Mary Shelley's *Frankenstein* or the film *Psycho.*

R2.5

from Danse Macabre

Essay by Stephen King

BACKGROUND Stephen King may well be the best-known writer of horror fiction since Edgar Allan Poe. In 1981, after writing a number of best-selling novels, King wrote *Stephen Kings's Danse Macabre*, a nonfiction work in which he discussed horror in literature and film and examined the psychology of terror. The book's title is a reference to the "Dance of Death," a symbolic representation of death, in the form of a skeleton, leading people to their graves. This dance was commonly depicted on cemetery walls and in the European art of the Middle Ages and the Renaissance.

I want to say something about imagination purely as a tool in the art and science of scaring people. The idea isn't original with me; I heard it expressed by William F. Nolan at the 1979 World Fantasy Convention. Nothing is so frightening as what's behind the closed door, Nolan said. You approach the door in the old, deserted house, and you hear something scratching at it. The audience holds its breath along with the protagonist as she or he (more often she) approaches that door. The protagonist throws it open, and there is a ten-foot-tall bug. The audience screams, but this particular scream has an oddly relieved sound to it. "A bug ten feet tall is pretty horrible," the audience thinks, "but I can deal with
10 a ten-foot-tall bug. I was afraid it might be a *hundred* feet tall.". . .

Bill Nolan was speaking as a screenwriter when he offered the example of the big bug behind the door, but the point applies to all media. What's behind the door or lurking at the top of the stairs is never as frightening as the door or the staircase itself. And because of this, comes the paradox: the artistic work of horror is almost always a disappointment. It is the classic no-win situation. You can scare people with the unknown for a long, long time (the classic example, as Bill Nolan also pointed out, is the Jacques Tourneur film with Dana Andrews, *Curse of the Demon*), but sooner or later, as in poker, you have to turn your down cards up. You have to open the door and show the audience what's behind it. And if what happens to be behind it is a bug,
20 not ten but a hundred feet tall, the audience heaves a sigh of relief (or utters a scream of relief) and thinks, "A bug a hundred feet tall is pretty horrible, but I can deal with that. I was afraid it might be a *thousand* feet tall." . . .

The danse macabre is a waltz with death. This is a truth we cannot afford to shy away from.

Like the rides in the amusement park which mimic violent death, the tale of horror is a chance to examine what's going on behind doors which we usually keep double-locked. Yet the human imagination is not content with locked doors.

450 UNIT 2: AMERICAN ROMANTICISM

BACKGROUND

Stephen King and Horror Fiction The term *horror fiction* refers to fiction that takes the reader into situations that produce powerful feelings of fear, anxiety, or the loss of courage. In King's novels, those situations are often everyday experiences—experiences with which most readers can identify—that twist in unexpected and terrifying ways. Edgar Allan Poe, who is considered a founder of modern literary horror, influenced Stephen King's writing, and many fans of the genre enjoy finding similarities between the two writers' works.

Dance of Death In the Middle Ages, widespread and deadly illnesses—most notably, the Black Death—were common, and people were very mindful of their mortality. It is not surprising, therefore, that Death was personified in popular culture and was shown as leading people from all walks of life, from poorest children to monarchs and popes, to the grave. The Danse Macabre, or "Dance of Death," found new popularity in 19th- and 20th-century literature, music, and even film (such as Ingmar Bergman's *The Seventh Seal*).

DIFFERENTIATED INSTRUCTION

FOR ENGLISH LEARNERS
Explore Allusions

- Point out to students that King's reference to Bluebeard (lines 33–35) comes from the fairy tale "Barbe Bleue," recorded by Charles Perrault more than 300 years ago. In that tale, Bluebeard warns his wife not to enter a certain room; still, she opens the door— and discovers the skeletons of Bluebeard's previous wives. (When Bluebeard learns what she has done, she escapes death only because her brothers arrive and rescue her.)

- Most students will recognize the name *Dracula,* the title character of Bram Stoker's 1897 novel. Explain that in lines 36–38, King alludes to Harker's encounter with three female vampires (an encounter from which Dracula rescues Harker).

- Invite students to comment about both stories and about King's possible reasons for not being specific about either outcome.

Somewhere there is another dancing partner, the imagination whispers in the night—a partner in a rotting ball gown, a partner with empty eyesockets, green
30 mold growing on her elbow-length gloves, maggots squirming in the thin remains of her hair. To hold such a creature in our arms? Who, you ask me, would be so mad? Well . . . ?

"You will not want to open this door," Bluebeard tells his wife in that most horrible of all horror stories, "because your husband has forbidden it." But this, of course, only makes her all the more curious . . . and at last, her curiosity is satisfied.

"You may go anywhere you wish in the castle," Count Dracula tells Jonathan Harker, "except where the doors are locked, where of course you will not wish to go." But Harker goes soon enough.

And so do we all. Perhaps we go to the forbidden door or window willingly
40 because we understand that a time comes when we must go whether we want to or not . . . and not just to look, but to be pushed through. Forever. ∿

Literary Analysis

1. **Summarize** According to King, what makes a closed door so frightening?

2. **Interpret Metaphor** Why does King compare the suspenseful experience of watching the forbidden door to a waltz with death?

3. **Compare Texts** What elements in "The Fall of the House of Usher" and "The Masque of the Red Death" might be considered analogous to King's metaphor of the closed, forbidden door? In these cases, do you agree with King's idea that the revelation of the unknown is a letdown? Explain, citing evidence.

Moby Dick
Herman Melville

ABOUT THE AUTHOR

Herman Melville In 1850, Melville and his wife bought a Massachusetts farm, called Arrowhead, near the home of Nathaniel Hawthorne. Melville and Hawthorne became friends, and Hawthorne proved to be a major influence upon Melville's decision to infuse *Moby Dick* with spiritual and allegorical elements. Ironically, those very elements contributed to the lack of critical praise for *Moby Dick* and to the book's poor sales (only 3,000 copies in Melville's lifetime). Today, however, *Moby Dick* is considered Melville's greatest achievement.

Chronology of Major Works These are the publication dates of Herman Melville's most important works:

1846	*Typee*
1847	*Omoo*
1851	*Moby Dick*
1853	"Bartleby the Scrivener"
1857	*The Confidence Man*
1924	*Billy Budd* (posthumously)

ABOUT THE NOVEL

Moby Dick Before students read the passage, explain these points:

- Moby Dick is a rare white sperm whale (a "parmacetty," Daggoo says). Hunted in the past, he has turned on his attackers and now is thought to be very dangerous.

- In a previous hunt, Ahab lost a leg to Moby Dick. He now has a peg leg made of whalebone—and an obsession with revenge.

- Tashtego, Daggoo, and Queequeg are harpooners aboard the *Pequod*. Starbuck, Stubb, and Flask are ship's officers.

American Masterpiece

Moby Dick

Herman Melville

Herman Melville
1819–1891

ABOUT THE AUTHOR Herman Melville was known during his lifetime as "the man who had lived among cannibals" because of his best-selling novels of the South Seas, *Typee* and *Omoo*. These novels fictionalized his experiences in the Marquesas Islands among the supposedly cannibalistic Typee people. But how did Melville come to be in such a place? The early death of his father and the loss of the family fortune had led Melville to try for a life at sea. He spent years as a young man working a variety of ships, including a whaling vessel. His experiences—jumping ship, living with the Typee people, taking part in a mutiny, and spending time in a Tahitian jail—provided vivid fodder for his later writing, and the reading public loved him for it. By the 1840s Melville was among the most celebrated of American authors.

Ironically, when Melville turned to more serious works, including the great American novel *Moby Dick,* his public deserted him. After a series of critical and financial failures, Melville saw his career in ruins, eventually abandoning the novel for poetry and a job as a customs inspector. Melville never regained his earlier popularity during his lifetime, but later critics and readers have embraced him as one of the greatest of American writers.

ABOUT THE NOVEL "Call me Ishmael," says the narrator of *Moby Dick* in the novel's famous opening words. Ishmael, the sole survivor of the lost whaling ship the *Pequod,* goes on to tell the story of his sea captain's obsessive hunting of the great white whale, Moby Dick. An adventure tale at its core, *Moby Dick* is also many other things—a discourse on whales and whaling, a critique of commercial expansion at sea, a tragedy of human obsession, and an examination of the conflicts between the individual and society, society and nature, and fate and free will. No wonder D. H. Lawrence once said of *Moby Dick:* "[It] commands a stillness in the soul, an awe. . . . [It is] one of the strangest and most wonderful books in the world." In the following passage, the ship's crew learns for the first time that their captain, Ahab, sees the voyage as his own personal quest for revenge.

"Whosoever of ye raises me a white-headed whale with a wrinkled brow and a crooked jaw; whosoever of ye raises me that white-headed whale, with three holes punctured in his starboard fluke—look ye, whosoever of ye raises me that same white whale, he shall have this gold ounce, my boys!"

"Huzza! huzza!" cried the seamen, as with swinging tarpaulins they hailed the act of nailing the gold to the mast.

"It's a white whale, I say," resumed Ahab, as he threw down the top-maul; "a white

452

DIFFERENTIATED INSTRUCTION

FOR STRATEGIC READERS

Character Remind students of the title of this novel and explain that the whale is much more than the object of a hunt: it is a character. As students read the passage, have them complete a Character Traits Web with details that describe the whale. Afterward, ask them what those details suggest about the whale. ***Possible answer:*** *The whale has battled with many hunters and is tough and dangerous.*

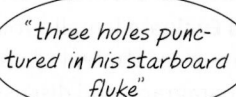 **BEST PRACTICES TOOLKIT—Transparency**
Character Traits Web p. D7

"three holes punctured in his starboard fluke"

THE WHITE WHALE

"that accursed white whale that razed me"

"harpoons lie all twisted and wrenched in him"

whale. Skin your eyes for him, men; look sharp for white water; if ye see but a bubble, sing out."

10   All this while Tashtego, Daggoo, and Queequeg had looked on with even more intense interest and surprise than the rest, and at the mention of the wrinkled brow and crooked jaw they had started as if each was separately touched by some specific recollection.

"Captain Ahab," said Tashtego, "that white whale must be the same that some call Moby Dick."

"Moby Dick?" shouted Ahab. "Do ye know the white whale then, Tash?"

"Does he fan-tail a little curious, sir, before he goes down?" said the Gay-Header deliberately.

"And has he a curious spout, too," said Daggoo, "very bushy, even for a
20 parmacetty, and mighty quick, Captain Ahab?"

"And he have one, two, tree-oh! good many iron in him hide, too, Captain," cried Queequeg disjointedly, "all twisketee be-twisk, like him—him—" faltering hard for a word, and screwing his hand round and round as though uncorking a bottle— "like him—him—"

"Corkscrew!" cried Ahab, "aye, Queequeg, the harpoons lie all twisted and wrenched in him; aye, Daggoo, his spout is a big one, like a whole shock of wheat, and white as a pile of our Nantucket wool after the great annual sheep-shearing; aye, Tashtego, and he fan-tails like a split jib in a squall. Death and devils! men, it is Moby Dick ye have seen—Moby Dick—Moby Dick!"

30   "Captain Ahab," said Starbuck, who with Stubb and Flask, had thus far been eyeing his superior with increasing surprise, but at last seemed struck with a thought which somewhat explained all the wonder. "Captain Ahab, I have heard of Moby Dick—but it was not Moby Dick that took off thy leg?"

"Who told thee that?" cried Ahab; then pausing, "Aye, Starbuck, aye, my hearties all round; it was Moby Dick that dismasted me; Moby Dick that brought me to this dead stump I stand on now. Aye, aye," he shouted with a terrific, loud, animal sob, like that of a heart-stricken moose; "Aye, aye! it was that accursed white whale that razed me; made a poor pegging lubber of me forever and a day!" Then tossing both arms, with measureless imprecations he shouted out: "Aye, aye! and I'll chase him
40 round Good Hope, and round the Horn, and round the Norway Maelstrom, and round perdition's flames before I give him up. And this is what ye have shipped for, men! to chase that white whale on both sides of land, and over all sides of earth, till he spouts black blood and rolls fin out. What say ye, men, will ye splice hands on it, now? I think ye do look brave."

"Aye, aye!" shouted the harpooneers and seamen, running closer to the excited old man: "A sharp eye for the White Whale; a sharp lance for Moby Dick!"

453

Use these prompts to help students consider Ahab's mindset:

Connect How have you or someone you know reacted when wronged or hurt in some way? How natural is a desire for revenge? *Accept all reasonable responses.*

Interpret How does Ahab introduce the true purpose of this voyage? *Possible answer: Ahab introduces the true purpose of the voyage—to find and kill Moby Dick—by offering an ounce of gold as a reward to the first person to see the white whale. As he speaks excitedly about Moby Dick, Starbuck makes the connection that Moby Dick is the whale responsible for Ahab's missing leg; and when he asks the question, Ahab confirms that this is to be a voyage of revenge.* What does Ahab want the crew to believe and to do? *Possible answer: Ahab wants the crew to believe that Moby Dick is evil and deserves to die. He wants the crew's help in hunting and killing the whale.*

Synthesize What evidence in this passage suggests that *Moby Dick* is "a tragedy of human obsession"? *Possible answer: Ahab's final speech in the passage clearly shows that he is obsessed with Moby Dick; for example, Ahab declares that he will chase the whale "round Good Hope, and round the Horn, and round the Norway Maelstrom, and round perdition's flames." This act of revenge has become Ahab's entire purpose for living.*

FOR STRATEGIC READERS
Vocabulary Support

- *starboard fluke* (line 3), "right-hand side of a whale's split tail"
- *tarpaulins* (line 5), "sheets of canvas, used as covers to keep things dry"
- *jib* (line 28), "a triangular sail"
- *squall* (line 28), "a sudden violent wind"
- *razed* (line 38), "demolished"
- *imprecations* (line 39), "curses"
- *perdition's* (line 41), "hell's"

FOR ADVANCED LEARNERS/AP
Analyze and Research Symbolism Remind students that Ahab obviously is obsessed with this white whale and that, to him, it appears to be far more than just an animal. Ask pairs of students to discuss what the whale might symbolize to Ahab; then have them check their ideas against one or more print or online sources. (Students can use keywords such as "white whale symbolism" or "symbolism in *Moby Dick*.") Encourage students to share their findings.

The Scarlet Letter

Nathaniel Hawthorne

ABOUT THE AUTHOR

Nathaniel Hawthorne The author's intense guilt over Judge Hathorne's role in the Salem witch trials caused him to change the spelling of his last name from "Hathorne" to "Hawthorne." His comment about removing "any curse incurred by them" is (at least, in part) a reference to the story that Sarah Good, one of Salem's convicted witches, had cursed Judge Hathorne before she died. In *The Scarlet Letter,* Hawthorne translates his personal experience with guilt into a literary theme that drives much of the story. It can be said that the novel exists because of Hawthorne's wife, Sophia. In 1848, Hawthorne lost his job at the Boston Custom House; Sophia, however, had saved enough money to support the family for a time, and she encouraged him to write the novel that became *The Scarlet Letter.*

ABOUT THE NOVEL

The Scarlet Letter Point out the universal themes that are mentioned; then explain that the novel also focuses on people's capacity for cruelty, as students will see in the upcoming passage. Elicit that the "punishing" letter *A* stands for *adultery* and that its scarlet color is meant to be noticed and to suggest the immorality of the act.

LEGACY OF A MASTERPIECE

Introduce the Passage Before students read the passage, point out that its dialogue (except for the final paragraph) occurs among the women of Salem. Explain that *goodwife* is a term of courtesy that generally was used before the name of a married woman. As students read, ask them to analyze the tone of the passage and to determine the consensus among the women regarding Hester Prynne.

American Masterpiece

The Scarlet Letter

Nathaniel Hawthorne

Nathaniel Hawthorne
1804–1864

ABOUT THE AUTHOR The descendant of a judge at the Salem witchcraft trials, Nathaniel Hawthorne was haunted by his Puritan ancestors' intolerance. He wrote *The Scarlet Letter* in part to absolve his guilt, saying in his introduction to the novel: "I take shame upon myself for their sakes and pray that any curse incurred by them . . . may be now and henceforth removed." Yet it seems Hawthorne bore no love for the people living in Salem in his day either, once commenting: "I detest this town so much that I hate to go into the streets, or to have the people see me. . . . I feel an infinite contempt for them, and probably have expressed more of it than I intended; for my preliminary chapter [of *The Scarlet Letter*] has caused the greatest uproar that ever happened here since witch-times." The novel, as well as most of Hawthorne's other writing, depicts human beings as imperfect and imperfectible, with a dark side to their natures—ironically, a view more in keeping with that of Hawthorne's detested Puritan ancestors than with the optimistic spirit of his times.

ABOUT THE NOVEL Published in 1850, *The Scarlet Letter* is a short historical novel set in Salem in the earliest days of the Massachusetts Bay colony. Vividly re-creating the world of Puritan New England, the novel explores universal themes of sin, retribution, and forgiveness. It traces the story of Hester Prynne, who commits the sin of adultery and is publicly punished for it, and the two men in her life—her one-time lover and her vengeful husband—who keep their own sins hidden from public view. Part of Hester's punishment is to wear, for all her life, a scarlet letter *A* sewn onto the bodice of her gown.

LEGACY OF A MASTERPIECE "The publication of *The Scarlet Letter* was in the United States a literary event of the first importance," wrote author and critic Henry James. The carefully crafted novel, with its serious themes and complex symbolism, showed that writers in the young nation could produce literature equal to that of Britain and could draw on America's history and heritage in producing it. In the following scene from the novel's opening, Hester Prynne is about to appear in public for the first time with the scarlet letter on her gown. Waiting for her appearance outside the jail door, members of the community heap their scorn on the sinner.

454

DIFFERENTIATED INSTRUCTION

FOR STRATEGIC READERS

Comprehension Support Work with students to complete a Two-Column Chart that contrasts the women's descriptions of themselves with their descriptions of Hester Prynne. Discuss what these descriptions suggest about the women's attitudes and whether such descriptions are fair.

Words Used to Describe Themselves	Words Used to Describe Hester Prynne
church members	hussy
good repute	naughty baggage

 BEST PRACTICES TOOLKIT—Transparency Two-Column Chart p. A25

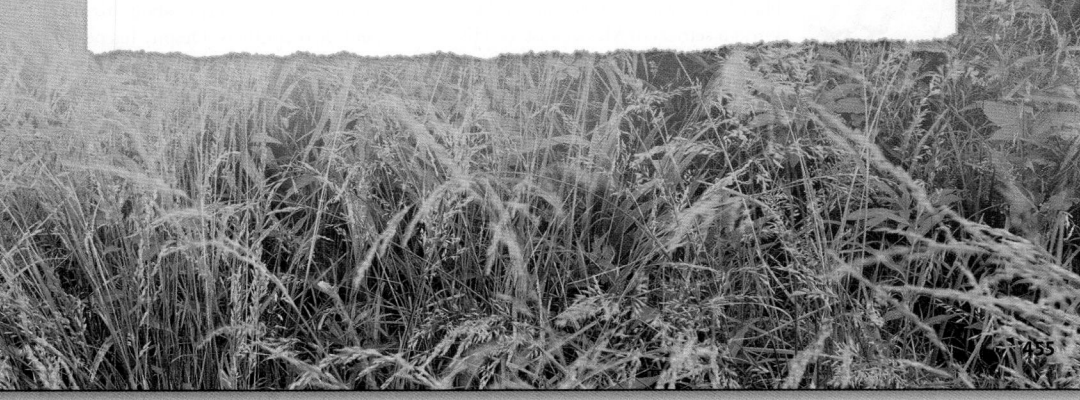

"Goodwives," said a hard-featured dame of fifty, "I'll tell ye a piece of my mind. It would be greatly for the public behoof, if we women, being of mature age and church-members in good repute, should have the handling of such malefactresses as this Hester Prynne. What think ye, gossips? If the hussy stood up for judgment before us five, that are now here in a knot together, would she come off with such a sentence as the worshipful magistrates have awarded? Marry, I trow not!"

"People say," said another, "that the Reverend Master Dimmesdale, her godly pastor, takes it very grievously to heart that such a scandal should have come upon
10 his congregation."

"The magistrates are God-fearing gentlemen, but merciful overmuch, — that is a truth," added a third autumnal matron. "At the very least, they should have put the brand of a hot iron on Hester Prynne's forehead. Madam Hester would have winced at that, I warrant me. But she, — the naughty baggage, — little will she care what they put upon the bodice of her gown! Why, look you, she may cover it with a brooch, or such like heathenish adornment, and so walk the streets as brave as ever!"

"Ah, but," interposed, more softly, a young wife, holding a child by the hand, "let her cover the mark as she will, the pang of it will be always in her heart."

"What do we talk of marks and brands, whether on the bodice of her gown,
20 or the flesh of her forehead?" cried another female, the ugliest as well as the most pitiless of these self-constituted judges. "This woman has brought shame upon us all, and ought to die. Is there not law for it? Truly there is, both in the Scripture and the statute-book. Then let the magistrates, who have made it of no effect, thank themselves if their own wives and daughters go astray!"

"Mercy on us, goodwife," exclaimed a man in the crowd, "is there no virtue in woman, save what springs from a wholesome fear of the gallows? That is the hardest word yet! Hush, now, gossips; for the lock is turning in the prison-door, and here comes Mistress Prynne herself."

455

TIERED DISCUSSION PROMPTS

Use these prompts to help students consider the themes in this passage:

Recall Why has Hester Prynne been jailed? **Answer:** *Hester Prynne has been jailed for having committed adultery.*

Interpret Reread the next-to-last paragraph. What does this woman think should happen to Hester Prynne? Why? **Possible answer:** *This woman thinks that Prynne should be executed for her adultery and that both the law and the Bible support her view. She believes that Prynne has given a bad name to women in general and that if she is not made an example of, then other women may stray.* Which characters come the closest to speaking up for Hester Prynne, and what do they say? What is the response to their words? **Possible answer:** *The young wife in the fourth paragraph expresses sympathy, and in the last paragraph, a man chastises the last woman to speak for the harshness of her words. The young wife is ignored; the excerpt does not reveal the reaction to the man's words.*

Synthesize How does this passage address themes mentioned in **ABOUT THE NOVEL?** **Possible answer:** *The passage addresses sin in the form of Hester Prynne's transgression and various responses to it; retribution, in the women's discussion of possible forms of punishment for that sin; and forgiveness, in the women's eagerness to talk about the sin and its punishment, without a thought of forgiveness.*

FOR STRATEGIC READERS
Vocabulary Support

- *behoof* (line 2), "benefit"
- *malefactresses* (line 4), "female criminals"
- *hussy* (line 5), "an immoral woman"
- *Marry* (line 7), "Well" (for emphasis)
- *trow* (line 7), "believe; think"
- *magistrates* (line 11), "officials who administer laws"
- *heathenish* (line 16), "irreligious; uncivilized"

FOR ADVANCED LEARNERS/AP

Evaluate [small-group option] Have small groups discuss these questions and then share their views:

- Do you agree with the woman who says, ". . . the pang of it will be always in her heart"? As you defend your answer, consider what a person must feel in order to experience "the pang of it."

- Would public shame be effective retribution today? Why or why not?

Focus and Motivate

OBJECTIVES

Literary Analysis
- explore the key idea of **estrangement**
- interpret a symbol
- read a short story

Reading
- identify cultural characteristics

Vocabulary
- build vocabulary for reading and writing
- understand and use the Latin root *ambi* (also an EL language objective)

 CALIFORNIA R3.5, R1.2

ABOUT THE AUTHOR

After students have read about Hawthorne's life, discuss why sin, hypocrisy, and guilt would be considered hidden character motivations—and why those themes might have appealed to a writer with Hawthorne's family history. As students read "The Minister's Black Veil," encourage them to watch for the appearance of these themes and to think about how they are connected to the "black veil" of the title.

USING THE *NOTABLE QUOTE*

Ask students to identify the tone in the comment and to connect it to the idea that **Nathaniel Hawthorne** was a groundbreaking writer. *Possible answer: The tone is rebellious and defiant. To reveal a hint of one's worst to the world—a chief trait of Hawthorne's writing—was a groundbreaking idea.*

R3.5, R1.2 (p. 472)
CALIFORNIA

NOTABLE QUOTE
"Show freely to the world, if not your worst, yet some trait whereby the worst may be inferred!"

FYI
Did you know that Nathaniel Hawthorne ...

- achieved his first literary success writing stories for children?
- was a mentor to Herman Melville, who dedicated *Moby Dick* to him?
- wrote a campaign biography for his college friend Franklin Pierce, who became the 14th U.S. president?

Author Online

For more on Nathaniel Hawthorne, visit the **Literature Center** at **ClassZone.com**.

456

The Minister's Black Veil
Short Story by Nathaniel Hawthorne

Nathaniel Hawthorne
c. 1804–1864

An intensely private man who allowed few to know him well, Nathaniel Hawthorne was fascinated by the dark secrets of human nature. In his greatest novels and short stories, including his masterpieces *The Scarlet Letter* and *The House of the Seven Gables*, he explored such themes as sin, hypocrisy, and guilt. One of the first American writers to explore his characters' hidden motivations, Hawthorne broke new ground in American literature with his morally complex characters.

Legacy of Guilt Born in Salem, Hawthorne was a descendant of the Puritan settlers of Massachusetts. His great-great-grandfather was a judge at the infamous Salem witch trials—the only one who refused to apologize for his role in sentencing innocent people to death. Though he tried to distance himself from his family's dark legacy, Hawthorne shared the Puritan belief that people are basically sinful. But where Puritans believed that society could be purified by the actions of a righteous few, Hawthorne was more pessimistic: he believed that perfection was impossible and remained skeptical of all attempts to reform or improve society.

Difficult Compromises Throughout his life, Hawthorne was torn between his literary calling and his desire for a stable, respectable profession. By the time he left for Bowdoin College in 1821, Hawthorne knew he wanted to write. After graduation, he lived alone for 12 years, dedicated to building his literary career. By 1842, he had achieved some success and had married his great love, Sophia Peabody. Their otherwise happy marriage was constantly shadowed by financial woes. When times were tough, Hawthorne had well-connected friends set him up with government jobs, whose dull routines choked his imagination and limited his time to write. Although he never stopped writing, work, illness, and family duties dominated Hawthorne's later years. He died in 1864 of a sudden illness.

Challenging Questions One of Hawthorne's great talents was his mastery of symbolism. He often chose symbols whose meaning was ambiguous, forcing readers to think deeply about his characters and their conflicts. Despite his pessimism, he found hope in the redeeming power of love, a theme he developed in his mature works. Hawthorne's efforts to come to terms with his own past inspired profound reflections on American identity that still resonate today.

Selection Resources

RESOURCE MANAGER UNIT 2

Plan and Teach pp. 263–270

Literary Analysis
Summary pp. 271†*, 272‡*
Symbol pp. 273, 274†*
Question Support p. 281*

Reading
Identify Cultural Characteristics pp. 275, 276†*
Reading Check p. 280

Vocabulary
Study p. 277*
Practice p. 278
Strategy p. 279

Assessment
Selection Tests A, B/C pp. 283*, 285*
Test Generator CD

BEST PRACTICES TOOLKIT

Differentiated Instruction pp. 31–38*

Scaffolding Instruction pp. 43–46*

Graphic Organizers/Strategies
Word Squares • Two-Column Chart • Character Traits and Textual Evidence • Analysis Frame: Theme

Reading Support
Audio Anthology CD*

Technology
Literature and Vocabulary Centers at **ClassZone.com**
Write*Smart* CD

---

* Resources for Differentiation   † Also in Spanish   ‡ In Haitian Creole and Vietnamese

LITERARY ANALYSIS: SYMBOL

A **symbol** is something concrete—a person, a place, an object, or an action—used to stand for an abstract idea or feeling. In some works, symbols may be subtle and hard to identify. In this story, Hawthorne identifies his main symbol outright:

Know, then, this veil is a type and a symbol...

The challenge, then, is to decide what the symbol means. A rich symbol has many possible interpretations rather than a single precise meaning. To interpret a symbol, pay close attention to its context in the work, including

• what ideas and feelings are associated with it

• its impact on characters and events

As you read, use a concept map to note details about the minister's black veil, the main symbol in this story.

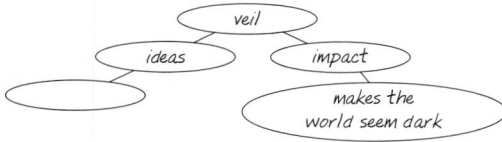

READING SKILL: IDENTIFY CULTURAL CHARACTERISTICS

The characters' reactions to the events of this story may not make sense to a modern reader. Keep in mind that the story is set in an 18th-century Puritan town. The parishioners' responses to their minister are meant to illustrate the traits that, in Hawthorne's eyes, define Puritan culture. As you read, think about the values, beliefs, and social constraints that are revealed by the parishioners' behavior.

VOCABULARY IN CONTEXT

The boldfaced words helped Hawthorne tell his tale of Puritan life. Use context clues to write a definition of each.

1. messages filled with confusion and **ambiguity**
2. a **zealous** speaker whose eyes blazed intensely
3. a tale of sin and **iniquity**
4. an event so unusual that it seemed **preternatural**
5. an **ostentatious** costume that made people stare
6. **imbued** with great hopes for the future
7. her **tremulous** voice that revealed her nervousness
8. a sign that might **portend** trouble ahead

How does someone become a STRANGER?

KEY IDEA Your best friend suddenly doesn't like the things she's always liked. Your brother comes home from college with a new haircut, listening to strange new music. What happens when someone you thought you knew changes the way they act or look? Can you still recognize the person you knew, or do his or her new behaviors lead to **estrangement?**

QUICKWRITE Recall a time when someone close to you changed in a way that made him or her seem like a different person. Write a paragraph to describe the change. Explain why it made you see the person so differently.

457

How does someone become a STRANGER?

Ask the question. As students read the **KEY IDEA**, explain that **estrangement** is the feeling of being alienated from others. After students have finished the **QUICKWRITE,** point out that this activity should help them understand how people could become estranged.

SKILLS FOCUS

LITERARY ANALYSIS

● SYMBOL

Read aloud this example:

Heidi's new hairstyle changed more than her appearance; everything about her now seemed different. Lisa no longer knew who Heidi was.

Have students explain what Heidi's new hairstyle symbolizes to Lisa. *Possible answer: an end to her friendship with Heidi.*

 RESOURCE MANAGER—Copy Master Symbol p. 273 (for student use while reading the selection)

READING SKILL R3.5

■ IDENTIFY CULTURAL CHARACTERISTICS

Have students reread **Legacy of Guilt** in the Hawthorne biography and identify some cultural characteristics of Puritans. *Possible answer: Puritans were concerned about sinfulness. They believed that people were essentially sinful, but they also believed that people who lived morally could improve society by their example.*

CHECK UNDERSTANDING Ask students to identify some cultural characteristics in another story that they have read or have seen on film or television.

VOCABULARY

VOCABULARY IN CONTEXT

DIAGNOSE WORD KNOWLEDGE To determine preteaching needs, have all students complete Vocabulary in Context. *Possible answers:* 1. *uncertainty,* 2. *very enthusiastic,* 3. *evil,* 4. *spooky,* 5. *showy,* 6. *filled,* 7. *unsteady,* 8. *foretell*

PRETEACH VOCABULARY Preteach vocabulary with this copy master. Read each item aloud.

RESOURCE MANAGER—Copy Master Vocabulary Study p. 277

MORE VOCABULARY SUPPORT For additional activities and guidelines, see

BEST PRACTICES TOOLKIT Scaffolding Vocabulary Instruction pp. 43–46

ℹ Vocabulary Center at **ClassZone.com**

SUMMARY

As Hawthorne's short story begins, the people of Milford are shocked to see that the Reverend Mr. Hooper has covered his face with a black veil. The veil makes people uncomfortable and alienates his fiancée, but Mr. Hooper will not clarify its meaning. Ironically, however, it makes him a more effective pastor, earning him the name "Father Hooper." He wears the veil for the rest of his life, even on his deathbed.

READING SKILL

A CULTURAL CHARACTERISTICS

Possible answer: The importance of Sunday worship is revealed by the fact that it is attended by a "throng" (line 6) of people of all ages. Furthermore, children are dressed in and understand the importance of "Sunday clothes" (lines 2–4), and bachelors feel that "Sabbath sunshine" (line 5) makes the young women more lovely.

THE MINISTER'S BLACK VEIL

Nathaniel Hawthorne

ANALYZE VISUALS
Simplicity was a central value of Puritan life. What elements of this painting help create its simple style? Consider the use of color, line, and texture, as well as the composition of the image, in your answer.

> **BACKGROUND** In the Puritan town of 18th-century Massachusetts, the meetinghouse was the center of the community life. Used for both religious and civil gatherings, meetinghouses were simple and plain, with no obviously religious decorations. Families did not sit together during religious services, which lasted most of the day on Sundays. Men and women sat on opposite sides, and worshipers were seated according to their age and social standing. The oldest and most distinguished citizens were rewarded with seats closest to the pulpit, the raised platform from which the pastor delivered his sermons. As services began, all eyes turned expectantly toward the pulpit, awaiting the pastor's entrance.

The sexton[1] stood in the porch of Milford meetinghouse, pulling lustily at the bell rope. The old people of the village came stooping along the street. Children, with bright faces, tripped merrily beside their parents, or mimicked a graver gait,[2] in the conscious dignity of their Sunday clothes. Spruce bachelors looked sidelong at the pretty maidens, and fancied that the Sabbath sunshine made them prettier than on weekdays. When the throng had mostly streamed into the porch, the sexton began to toll the bell, keeping his eye on the Reverend Mr. Hooper's door. The first glimpse of the clergyman's figure was the signal for the bell to cease its summons. **A**

A CULTURAL CHARACTERISTICS
Reread lines 1–9. What details reveal the importance of Sunday worship for the people of Milford?

---

1. **sexton:** church employee who takes care of church property and performs various other duties.
2. **mimicked a graver gait:** followed their parents' example and walked in a more dignified way.

458 UNIT 2: AMERICAN ROMANTICISM

Church at Head Tide #2 (1938–1940), Marsden Hartley. Oil on academy board, 37 $\frac{1}{4}$″ × 31 $\frac{1}{4}$″ × 2 $\frac{1}{4}$″. Gift of Mr. and Mrs. John Cowles. The Minneapolis Institute of Arts.

DIFFERENTIATED INSTRUCTION

FOR ALL STUDENTS

Provide these independent projects to extend the lesson:

- Conduct a discussion on the possibility of human improvement.
- Write an editorial about Mr. Hooper's life and ministry.

For further details on these projects, see

R RESOURCE MANAGER
Ideas for Extension pp. 268–269

FOR STRATEGIC READERS

In combination with the *Audio Anthology CD*, use one or more Targeted Passages (pp. 460, 461, 467, 469, 470) to ensure that students focus on key story events and concepts. Targeted Passages are also good for English learners.

ANALYZE VISUALS

Possible answer: *The simple style is achieved though the neutral colors of the painting, the plain lines of the church, and the relative lack of detail in both the church and the background. In addition, the texture of the painting is simple because the scene does not have much depth; the church almost blends into the background.*

About the Art Marsden Hartley (1877–1943), an American modernist painter, was born in Lewiston, Maine. Although they were not contemporaries, both Hartley and Hawthorne used their work to explore their New England roots. Furthermore, Hawthorne and Hartley were interested in religion: Hawthorne explored Puritan ideas in his writings, and many of Hartley's paintings present religious images. *Church at Head Tide #2* suggests the dominance of the Church, much as the meetinghouse is the focus of Puritan culture at the beginning of Hawthorne's story.

FOR ENGLISH LEARNERS

Vocabulary: Multiple-Meaning Words Point out that certain words have more than one meaning and that students must determine the appropriate definition in a given use. As students begin reading this story, help them use context clues to figure out the meaning of *lustily* (line 1), *bright* (line 3), *Spruce* (line 4), *toll* (line 7), and *figure* (line 8).

Prereading For prereading instruction for English learners, see

 BEST PRACTICES TOOLKIT
Scaffolding Reading Instruction pp. 43–46

FOR ADVANCED LEARNERS/AP

AP exercises in the bottom channel provide additional challenge for students. Use these suggestions for small groups or individuals.

ADDITIONAL GUIDELINES

For more help with differentiation and tips for classroom management, see

BEST PRACTICES TOOLKIT
Differentiated Instruction pp. 31–38

TIERED DISCUSSION PROMPTS

Use these prompts to help students explore Mr. Hooper's action and Hawthorne's purpose:

Connect Has someone ever done something out of the ordinary that caught your attention? How did you react? *Accept all responses.*

Interpret On first sight of the veil, how might the villagers interpret Mr. Hooper's appearance? Explain. *Possible answer: The villagers may think that Mr. Hooper has something to hide or be ashamed of. They may also think that he has gone insane.*

Synthesize Consider what you learned about Hawthorne on page 456. What might Hawthorne want readers to think about by presenting this odd event? *Possible answer: Hawthorne was interested in the "dark secrets" that people hide. He might want readers to think about what secrets they may be keeping—and how obvious their secrecy may be to others.*

Lines 34–39
REINFORCE *KEY IDEA:* ESTRANGEMENT

Discuss How do the comments in this passage show that people already feel some **estrangement** from their minister? *Possible answer: All three comments suggest alienation: The sexton cannot think of the person he sees as Mr. Hooper; the old woman says that the minister has become "something awful"; and Goodman Gray calls him "mad."*

---

10   "But what has good Parson Hooper got upon his face?" cried the sexton in astonishment.

    All within hearing immediately turned about, and beheld the semblance of Mr. Hooper, pacing slowly his meditative way towards the meetinghouse. With one accord they started, expressing more wonder than if some strange minister were coming to dust the cushions of Mr. Hooper's pulpit.

    "Are you sure it is our parson?" inquired Goodman[3] Gray of the sexton.

    "Of a certainty it is good Mr. Hooper," replied the sexton. "He was to have exchanged pulpits with Parson Shute of Westbury; but Parson Shute sent to excuse himself yesterday, being to preach a funeral sermon."

20   The cause of so much amazement may appear sufficiently slight. Mr. Hooper, a gentlemanly person about thirty, though still a bachelor, was dressed with due clerical neatness, as if a careful wife had starched his band, and brushed the weekly dust from his Sunday's garb. There was but one thing remarkable in his appearance. Swathed about his forehead, and hanging down over his face, so low as to be shaken by his breath, Mr. Hooper had on a black veil. On a nearer view, it seemed to consist of two folds of crape,[4] which entirely concealed his features, except the mouth and chin, but probably did not intercept his sight, farther than to give a darkened aspect to all living and inanimate things. With this gloomy shade before him, good Mr. Hooper walked onward, at a slow and quiet pace,

30 stooping somewhat and looking on the ground, as is customary with abstracted[5] men, yet nodding kindly to those of his parishioners who still waited on the meetinghouse steps. But so wonder-struck were they that his greeting hardly met with a return.

    "I can't really feel as if good Mr. Hooper's face was behind that piece of crape," said the sexton.

    "I don't like it," muttered an old woman, as she hobbled into the meetinghouse. "He has changed himself into something awful, only by hiding his face."

    "Our parson has gone mad!" cried Goodman Gray, following him across the threshold.

40   A rumor of some unaccountable phenomenon had preceded Mr. Hooper into the meetinghouse, and set all the congregation astir. Few could refrain from twisting their heads towards the door; many stood upright, and turned directly about; while several little boys clambered upon the seats, and came down again with a terrible racket. There was a general bustle, a rustling of the women's gowns and shuffling of the men's feet, greatly at variance with that hushed repose which should attend the entrance of the minister. But Mr. Hooper appeared not to notice the perturbation of his people. He entered with an almost noiseless step, bent his head mildly to the pews on each side, and bowed as he passed his oldest parishioner, a white-haired great-grandsire, who occupied an armchair in the

50 centre of the aisle. It was strange to observe how slowly this venerable man became conscious of something singular in the appearance of his pastor. He seemed not

① Targeted Passage

---

3. **Goodman:** the Puritan equivalent of Mr.

4. **crape** (krāp): a piece of dark material worn as a sign of mourning. Also called *crepe*.

5. **abstracted:** preoccupied, or lost in thought.

DIFFERENTIATED INSTRUCTION

FOR STRATEGIC READERS

① Targeted Passage [Lines 10–33]

This passage introduces Mr. Hooper's veil and the first reactions to it.

- Why are people initially unsure if the man walking toward them is Mr. Hooper?
- How does the veil affect the view of Mr. Hooper's face?
- Do the people of Milford quickly get used to the veil? How can you tell?

FOR ENGLISH LEARNERS

Vocabulary: Related Vocabulary Mr. Hooper's veil is mysterious, and Hawthorne describes it and its effects in several ways. Teach these terms that are related to the veil: *concealed* (line 26), *intercept* (line 27), *darkened aspect* (line 28), *gloomy shade* (lines 28–29), *prevailing wonder* (line 52), *mysterious emblem* (line 54), *obscurity* (line 55).

fully to partake of the prevailing wonder till Mr. Hooper had ascended the stairs, and showed himself in the pulpit, face-to-face with his congregation, except for the black veil. That mysterious emblem was never once withdrawn. It shook with his measured breath as he gave out the psalm; it threw its obscurity between him and the holy page, as he read the Scriptures; and while he prayed, the veil lay heavily on his uplifted countenance. Did he seek to hide from the dread Being[6] whom he was addressing?

60 Such was the effect of this simple piece of crape, that more than one woman of delicate nerves was forced to leave the meetinghouse. Yet perhaps the pale-faced congregation was almost as fearful a sight to the minister as his black veil to them.

Mr. Hooper had the reputation of a good preacher, but not an energetic one: he strove to win his people heavenward by mild persuasive influences, rather than to drive them thither by the thunders of the Word. The sermon which he now delivered was marked by the same characteristics of style and manner as the general series of his pulpit oratory. But there was something, either in the sentiment of the discourse itself, or in the imagination of the auditors, which made it greatly the most powerful effort that they had ever heard from their pastor's lips. It was tinged, rather more darkly than usual, with the gentle gloom
70 of Mr. Hooper's temperament. The subject had reference to secret sin, and those sad mysteries which we hide from our nearest and dearest, and would fain conceal from our own consciousness, even forgetting that the Omniscient[7] can detect them. A subtle power was breathed into his words. Each member of the congregation, the most innocent girl, and the man of hardened breast, felt as if the preacher had crept upon them, behind his awful veil, and discovered their hoarded **iniquity** of deed or thought. Many spread their clasped hands on their bosoms. There was nothing terrible in what Mr. Hooper said; at least, no violence; and yet, with every tremor of his melancholy voice, the hearers quaked. An unsought pathos came hand in hand with awe. So sensible were the audience of some
80 unwonted attribute in their minister, that they longed for a breath of wind to blow aside the veil, almost believing that a stranger's visage would be discovered, though the form, gesture and voice were those of Mr. Hooper. **B**

At the close of the services, the people hurried out with indecorous confusion, eager to communicate their pent-up amazement, and conscious of lighter spirits the moment they lost sight of the black veil. Some gathered in little circles, huddled closely together, with their mouths all whispering in the centre; some went homeward alone, wrapped in silent meditation; some talked loudly, and profaned the Sabbath day with **ostentatious** laughter. A few shook their sagacious heads, intimating that they could penetrate the mystery; while one or two affirmed that
90 there was no mystery at all, but only that Mr. Hooper's eyes were so weakened by the midnight lamp as to require a shade. After a brief interval, forth came good Mr. Hooper also, in the rear of his flock. Turning his veiled face from one group to another, he paid due reverence to the hoary heads, saluted the middle-aged with kind dignity, as their friend and spiritual guide, greeted the young with mingled

---

6. **the dread Being:** the awe-inspiring God.
7. **the Omniscient:** a title for God, signifying that he is all-knowing.

② **Targeted Passage**

iniquity (ĭ-nĭk′wĭ-tē) *n.* wickedness

B **SYMBOL**
Reread lines 62–82. Describe the change that occurs in Mr. Hooper's preaching. What seems to cause the listeners' unusual response?

ostentatious (ŏs′tĕn-tā′shəs) *adj.* loud; overdone

LITERARY ANALYSIS

B SYMBOL

Possible answer: *It seems as if the veil has given him a "subtle power" (line 73) to reach his audience and know their secrets (lines 74–78). The listeners' unusual response seems to rise from the topic of the sermon, combined with the audience's imagination (lines 66–67) and the minister's strange appearance.*

If students need help . . . Work with them to review these lines and to record some thoughts on the concept map introduced on page 457.

Extend the Discussion How might a modern audience react to the veil?

FOR STRATEGIC READERS
② Targeted Passage [Lines 62–82]

This passage shows how the veil actually enhances Mr. Hooper's abilities.

- What type of preacher has Mr. Hooper been in the past?
- What is the topic of Mr. Hooper's sermon this day? How is the sermon similar to and different from his previous sermons?
- How do members of the congregation react to the sermon?

FOR ENGLISH LEARNERS
Key Academic Vocabulary Use Word Squares to teach these words: *communicate* (line 84), *interval* (line 91), *topic* (line 168), *symbol* (line 193), *medium* (line 291), *apparent* (line 296).

🛄 **BEST PRACTICES TOOLKIT—Transparency** Word Squares p. E10

Vocabulary: Outdated Forms Ask students to record these outdated terms and their meanings in a Two-Column Chart. Then have them reread the lines, substituting the definitions for the terms.

- *thither* (line 64), "there"
- *would fain* (line 71), "would gladly"

Students can add to the chart as they read.

🛄 **BEST PRACTICES TOOLKIT—Transparency** Two-Column Chart p. A25

authority and love, and laid his hands on the little children's heads to bless them. Such was always his custom on the Sabbath day. Strange and bewildered looks repaid him for his courtesy. None, as on former occasions, aspired to the honor of walking by their pastor's side. Old Squire Saunders, doubtless by an accidental lapse of memory, neglected to invite Mr. Hooper to his table, where the good clergyman
100 had been wont to bless the food almost every Sunday since his settlement. He returned, therefore, to the parsonage, and at the moment of closing the door, was observed to look back upon the people, all of whom had their eyes fixed upon the minister. A sad smile gleamed faintly from beneath the black veil, and flickered about his mouth, glimmering as he disappeared. **C**

"How strange," said a lady, "that a simple black veil, such as any woman might wear on her bonnet, should become such a terrible thing on Mr. Hooper's face!"

"Something must surely be amiss with Mr. Hooper's intellects," observed her husband, the physician of the village. "But the strangest part of the affair is the effect of this vagary, even on a sober-minded man like myself. The black veil,

The Last Halt: Stop of Hooker's Band in East Hartford before Crossing River (1939), Alton S. Tobey. Study for East Hartford, Connecticut Postal Office. Oil on fiberboard, 26″ × 44 ¹/₈″. Transfer from General Services Administration. Smithsonian American Art Museum, Washington, D.C. © Smithsonian American Art Museum, Washington, D.C./ Art Resource, New York.

462 UNIT 2: AMERICAN ROMANTICISM

110 though it covers only our pastor's face, throws its influence over his whole person, and makes him ghost-like from head to foot. Do you not feel it so?"

"Truly do I," replied the lady; "and I would not be alone with him for the world. I wonder he is not afraid to be alone with himself!"

"Men sometimes are so," said her husband.

The afternoon service was attended with similar circumstances. At its conclusion, the bell tolled for the funeral of a young lady. The relatives and friends were assembled in the house, and the more distant acquaintances stood about the door, speaking of the good qualities of the deceased, when their talk was interrupted by the appearance of Mr. Hooper, still covered with his black veil. It was now an
120 appropriate emblem. The clergyman stepped into the room where the corpse was laid, and bent over the coffin, to take a last farewell of his deceased parishioner. As he stooped, the veil hung straight down from his forehead so that, if her eyelids had not been closed forever, the dead maiden might have seen his face. Could Mr. Hooper be fearful of her glance, that he so hastily caught back the black veil? A person, who watched the interview between the dead and the living, scrupled not to affirm that, at the instant when the clergyman's features were disclosed, the corpse had slightly shuddered, rustling the shroud[8] and muslin cap, though the countenance retained the composure of death. A superstitious old woman was the only witness of this prodigy. From the coffin, Mr. Hooper passed into the chamber
130 of the mourners, and thence to the head of the staircase, to make the funeral prayer. It was a tender and heart-dissolving prayer, full of sorrow, yet so **imbued** with celestial hopes, that the music of the heavenly harp, swept by the fingers of the dead, seemed faintly to be heard among the saddest accents of the minister. The people trembled, though they but darkly understood him, when he prayed that they, and himself, and all of mortal race might be ready, as he trusted this young maiden had been, for the dreadful hour that should snatch the veil from their faces. The bearers went heavily forth, and the mourners followed, saddening all the street, with the dead before them, and Mr. Hooper in his black veil behind. **D**

"Why do you look back?" said one in the procession to his partner.
140 "I had a fancy," replied she, "that the minister and the maiden's spirit were walking hand in hand."

"And so had I, at the same moment," said the other.

That night, the handsomest couple in Milford village were to be joined in wedlock. Though reckoned a melancholy man, Mr. Hooper had a placid cheerfulness for such occasions, which often excited a sympathetic smile, where livelier merriment would have been thrown away. There was no quality of his disposition which made him more beloved than this. The company at the wedding awaited his arrival with impatience, trusting that the strange awe, which had gathered over him throughout the day, would now be dispelled. But such was
150 not the result. When Mr. Hooper came, the first thing that their eyes rested on was the same horrible black veil, which had added deeper gloom to the funeral, and could **portend** nothing but evil to the wedding. Such was its immediate effect on the guests, that a cloud seemed to have rolled duskily from beneath the

---

8. **shroud:** burial garment.

imbued (ĭm-byōō'd) *adj.*
deeply influenced by
imbue *v.*

D SYMBOL
Paraphrase lines 133–138.
In this context, what
could Mr. Hooper mean
when he refers to "the
dreadful hour that should
snatch the veil from their
faces"?

portend (pôr-tĕnd') *v.* to
serve as an omen of; to
signify

Lines 105–114
REINFORCE *KEY IDEA:* ESTRANGEMENT

Discuss What does the conversation between husband and wife reveal about the villagers' **estrangement** from their pastor? ***Possible answer:*** *The villagers now fear Mr. Hooper and feel that he has brought his estrangement on himself.*

LITERARY ANALYSIS

D SYMBOL

Possible answer: *Paraphrase: "The people shook, even though they barely understood him, when Mr. Hooper prayed that everyone might be ready for the moment of death, as he hoped this young woman had been ready. Her body was carried out, and the grieving people followed, with Mr. Hooper following." Mr. Hooper's reference could mean death or Judgment Day, when all human secrets will be revealed.*

FOR ADVANCED LEARNERS/AP

Analyze Tone Invite students to respond to one or both of these prompts:

• Notice the narrator's comments in lines 98–100 and 128–129. How sympathetic is the narrator to Mr. Hooper?

• Review the funeral scene and the wedding scene. What words establish the tone of each scene? Are the tones identical, related, or sharply different?

Hypothesize [small-group option] Ask small groups to discuss this question: *Why do you think that Mr. Hooper wears this black veil everywhere he goes?* Have small groups write their answer in a paragraph and then share their paragraphs with one another. Be sure to have students review and perhaps amend their hypotheses once they finish reading the story.

black crape, and dimmed the light of the candles. The bridal pair stood up before the minister. But the bride's cold fingers quivered in the **tremulous** hand of the bridegroom, and her death-like paleness caused a whisper that the maiden who had been buried a few hours before was come from her grave to be married. If ever another wedding were so dismal, it was that famous one where they tolled the wedding knell.[9] After performing the ceremony, Mr. Hooper raised a glass

160 of wine to his lips, wishing happiness to the new-married couple, in a strain of mild pleasantry that ought to have brightened the features of the guests, like a cheerful gleam from the hearth. At that instant, catching a glimpse of his figure in the looking glass, the black veil involved his own spirit in the horror with which it overwhelmed all others. His frame shuddered—his lips grew white—he spilt the untasted wine upon the carpet—and rushed forth into the darkness. For the Earth, too, had on her Black Veil. **E**

The next day, the whole village of Milford talked of little else than Parson Hooper's black veil. That, and the mystery concealed behind it, supplied a topic for discussion between acquaintances meeting in the street, and good women

170 gossiping at their open windows. It was the first item of news that the tavern keeper told to his guests. The children babbled of it on their way to school. One imitative little imp covered his face with an old black handkerchief, thereby so affrighting his playmates that the panic seized himself, and he well-nigh lost his wits by his own waggery.[10]

It was remarkable that, of all the busybodies and impertinent people in the parish, not one ventured to put the plain question to Mr. Hooper, wherefore he did this thing. Hitherto, whenever there appeared the slightest call for such interference, he had never lacked advisers, nor shown himself averse to be guided by their judgment. If he erred at all, it was by so painful a degree of self-distrust

180 that even the mildest censure would lead him to consider an indifferent action as a crime. Yet, though so well acquainted with this amiable weakness, no individual among his parishioners chose to make the black veil a subject of friendly remonstrance. There was a feeling of dread, neither plainly confessed nor carefully concealed, which caused each to shift the responsibility upon another, till at length it was found expedient to send a deputation to the church, in order to deal with Mr. Hooper about the mystery, before it should grow into a scandal. Never did an embassy so ill discharge its duties. The minister received them with friendly courtesy, but became silent, after they were seated, leaving to his visitors the whole burden of introducing their important business. The topic, it might be supposed,

190 was obvious enough. There was the black veil, swathed round Mr. Hooper's forehead, and concealing every feature above his placid mouth, on which, at times, they could perceive the glimmering of a melancholy smile. But that piece of crape, to their imagination, seemed to hang down before his heart, the symbol of a fearful secret between him and them. Were the veil but cast aside, they might speak freely of it, but not till then. Thus they sat a considerable time, speechless,

---

9. **If . . . the wedding knell:** a reference to "The Wedding Knell," a story by Hawthorne in which a bell-tolling appropriate for a funeral is sounded at a wedding.

10. **waggery:** mischievous merriment.

UNIT 2: AMERICAN ROMANTICISM

---

tremulous (trĕm′yə-ləs) *adj.* trembling; quivering

E SYMBOL
Reread lines 162–166. Compare the references to veils in this passage with the earlier reference in lines 133–138. In what ways has the veil's meaning become more ambiguous, or unclear?

E SYMBOL

Possible answer: In this passage, the veil refers to night or darkness; earlier, it referred to death or Judgment Day. The comparison adds yet another meaning to the veil, making the symbolism unclear.

Lines 175–199
TIERED DISCUSSION PROMPTS

Use these prompts to help students grasp the changed relationship between Mr. Hooper and the people of Milford:

Summarize Thus far, what has been the general reaction to Mr. Hooper's altered appearance? *Possible answer: People seem confused by it and somewhat fearful of it.*

Analyze Why is it significant that "the busybodies and impertinent people in the parish" (lines 175–176) do not ask Mr. Hooper why he wears the veil? *Possible answer: The fact is significant because these are the people who have not hesitated to raise questions in the past (lines 177–179). Their silence now reflects their fear.*

Synthesize Why is it significant that the deputation from the church cannot raise the question about Mr. Hooper's veil? *Possible answer: The deputation probably consists of church leaders, the people in whom Mr. Hooper would most likely confide; their silence suggests that no one may be able to solve the mystery of the veil.*

DIFFERENTIATED INSTRUCTION

FOR STRATEGIC READERS

Characterization Have students reread lines 177–183; then discuss these questions to help them characterize Mr. Hooper:

- Does Mr. Hooper have a reputation for being unwilling to take advice?

- Does he take making mistakes lightly?

- Therefore, do you see him as the kind of person who would make a decision (such as wearing a black veil) easily or carelessly?

FOR ENGLISH LEARNERS

Vocabulary: Outdated Forms Have students continue to fill out their Two-Column Chart (see note on page 461) as they learn these outdated words:

- *affrighting* (line 173), "frightening"

- *ill* (line 187), "poorly"

- *suffer* (line 220), "allow"

- *do away* (line 232), "stop; end"

- *abroad* (line 234), "circulating"

---

464 UNIT 2: AMERICAN ROMANTICISM

confused, and shrinking uneasily from Mr. Hooper's eye, which they felt to be fixed upon them with an invisible glance. Finally, the deputies returned abashed to their constituents, pronouncing the matter too weighty to be handled, except by a council of the churches, if, indeed, it might not require a general synod.[11] **F**

200 But there was one person in the village unappalled by the awe with which the black veil had impressed all beside herself. When the deputies returned without an explanation, or even venturing to demand one, she, with the calm energy of her character, determined to chase away the strange cloud that appeared to be settling round Mr. Hooper, every moment more darkly than before. As his plighted wife,[12] it should be her privilege to know what the black veil concealed. At the minister's first visit, therefore, she entered upon the subject, with a direct simplicity, which made the task easier both for him and her. After he had seated himself, she fixed her eyes steadfastly upon the veil, but could discern nothing of the dreadful gloom that had so overawed the multitude: it was but a double fold of crape, hanging

210 down from his forehead to his mouth, and slightly stirring with his breath. **G**

"No," said she aloud, and smiling, "there is nothing terrible in this piece of crape except that it hides a face which I am always glad to look upon. Come, good sir, let the sun shine from behind the cloud. First lay aside your black veil: then tell me why you put it on."

Mr. Hooper's smile glimmered faintly.

"There is an hour to come," said he, "when all of us shall cast aside our veils. Take it not amiss, beloved friend, if I wear this piece of crape till then."

"Your words are a mystery too," returned the young lady. "Take away the veil from them, at least."

220 "Elizabeth, I will," said he, "so far as my vow may suffer me. Know, then, this veil is a type and a symbol, and I am bound to wear it ever, both in light and darkness, in solitude and before the gaze of multitudes, and as with strangers, so with my familiar friends. No mortal eye will see it withdrawn. This dismal shade must separate me from the world: even you, Elizabeth, can never come behind it!"

"What grievous affliction hath befallen you," she earnestly inquired, "that you should thus darken your eyes forever?"

"If it be a sign of mourning," replied Mr. Hooper, "I, perhaps, like most other mortals, have sorrows dark enough to be typified by a black veil."

"But what if the world will not believe that it is the type of an innocent

230 sorrow?" urged Elizabeth. "Beloved and respected as you are, there may be whispers that you hide your face under the consciousness of secret sin. For the sake of your holy office, do away this scandal!"

The color rose into her cheeks, as she intimated the nature of the rumors that were already abroad in the village. But Mr. Hooper's mildness did not forsake him. He even smiles again—that same sad smile, which always appeared like a faint glimmering of light proceeding from the obscurity beneath the veil.

"If I hide my face for sorrow, there is cause enough," he merely replied; "and if I cover it for secret sin, what mortal might not do the same?"

---

11. **a general synod:** a meeting of the governing body of the churches.

12. **plighted wife:** fiancée.

F CULTURAL CHARACTERISTICS
Paraphrase lines 175–186. Explain what motivates the parishioners to confront Mr. Hooper. What do their fears reveal about Puritan culture?

G SYMBOL
Reread lines 200–210. Contrast the response of the minister's fiancée to the veil with the responses of the other villagers. What might explain the difference in her response?

READING SKILL

F CULTURAL CHARACTERISTICS

Possible answer: Paraphrase: With all of these gossips around, it was surprising that no one bothered to ask Mr. Hooper why he wore the veil. People had never been shy about offering him advice before. He was so given to feelings of guilt that the slightest criticism could make him feel as if he'd done something terrible. Although everyone knew this about him, no one said anything. Finally, they sent a group to visit Mr. Hooper, lest his behavior grow into a scandal. Their fears suggest that features of Puritan culture include a discomfort about things that are different, a worry about scandal, and a superstitious nature.

LITERARY ANALYSIS

G SYMBOL

Possible answer: Elizabeth does not share the other villagers' fear of the veil (lines 208–209); she confronts Mr. Hooper directly about it (lines 206–207), unlike the parishioners, who never ask him. Elizabeth probably reacts differently because she loves him and because, as his fiancée, she knows him better than others do.

FOR STRATEGIC READERS

Comprehension Support Point out that in lines 218–221, Elizabeth is saying that both the veil and Mr. Hooper's words are mysterious. She asks him to "take away the veil" from his words—that is, to speak so that she can understand him. In response, Mr. Hooper says that the veil "is a type and a symbol"—it represents an idea that he wants to communicate visually, without verbal explanation.

FOR ADVANCED LEARNERS/AP

Analyze Character Mr. Hooper's conversation with Elizabeth is the first time that readers learn about Mr. Hooper from his own words instead of from the narrator's comments or the parishioners' dialogue. Readers also learn about Elizabeth in this conversation. Instruct students to reread the interaction between Elizabeth and Mr. Hooper (lines 200–259) and to fill out a Character Traits and Textual Evidence chart for each character as a

prewriting activity. Then have them use their notes to write a brief essay that addresses these questions:

- What insight into Mr. Hooper's character does his explanation of the veil provide?

- Does Hawthorne expect readers to agree with Elizabeth's final response to Mr. Hooper? Explain.

 BEST PRACTICES TOOLKIT—Transparency Character Traits and Textual Evidence p. D6

Portrait of Alice Irene Harvey (1912), Mark Gertler. Oil on canvas, 60.9 cm × 50.8 cm. © Leeds Museums and Galleries, Leeds, United Kingdom/Bridgeman Art Library.

DIFFERENTIATED INSTRUCTION

FOR ADVANCED LEARNERS/AP

Critical Interpretations [small-group option]
Critics disagree about the meaning of the black veil. Edgar Allan Poe once argued that the minister wears the veil out of remorse for a secret sin involving the young woman whose funeral he attends (lines 115–142). Other critics have interpreted the veil as a device that the minister uses to dramatize the universal idea that everyone has a secret sin and, therefore, we should not judge others.

A third interpretation is that the wearing of the veil is itself the minister's sin—Hooper's prideful obsession with an idea has warped his life and hurt others. Yet another interpretation is that Hawthorne does not intend readers to uncover the meaning of the veil. His story is about concealment, and the meaning of the veil is part of what is concealed. Have groups debate these interpretations, citing textual evidence for and against each view.

And with this gentle but unconquerable obstinacy did he resist all her
240 entreaties. At length Elizabeth sat silent. For a few moments she appeared lost in
thought, considering, probably, what new methods might be tried to withdraw
her lover from so dark a fantasy, which, if it had no other meaning, was perhaps a
symptom of mental disease. Though of a firmer character than his own, the tears
rolled down her cheeks. But, in an instant, as it were, a new feeling took the place
of sorrow: her eyes were fixed insensibly on the black veil, when, like a sudden
twilight in the air, its terrors fell around her. She arose, and stood trembling
before him.

"And do you feel it then at last?" said he mournfully.

She made no reply, but covered her eyes with her hand, and turned to leave
250 the room. He rushed forward and caught her arm.

"Have patience with me, Elizabeth!" cried he passionately. "Do not desert
me, though this veil must be between us here on earth. Be mine, and hereafter
there shall be no veil over my face, no darkness between our souls! It is but a
mortal veil—it is not for eternity! Oh! you know not how lonely I am, and how
frightened to be alone behind my black veil. Do not leave me in this miserable
obscurity forever!"

"Lift the veil but once, and look me in the face," said she.

"Never! It cannot be!" replied Mr. Hooper.

"Then, farewell!" said Elizabeth.

260 She withdrew her arm from his grasp and slowly departed, pausing at the door
to give one long, shuddering gaze that seemed almost to penetrate the mystery of
the black veil. But even amid his grief, Mr. Hooper smiled to think that only a
material emblem had separated him from happiness, though the horrors which
it shadowed forth must be drawn darkly between the fondest of lovers.

From that time no attempts were made to remove Mr. Hooper's black veil or,
by a direct appeal, to discover the secret which it was supposed to hide. By persons
who claimed a superiority to popular prejudice, it was reckoned merely an eccentric
whim, such as often mingles with the sober actions of men otherwise rational, and
tinges them all with its own semblance of insanity. But with the multitude, good
270 Mr. Hooper was irreparably a bugbear.[13] He could not walk the streets with any
peace of mind, so conscious was he that the gentle and timid would turn aside to
avoid him, and that others would make it a point of hardihood to throw themselves
in his way. The impertinence of the latter class compelled him to give up his
customary walk, at sunset, to the burial ground, for when he leaned pensively over
the gate, there would always be faces behind the gravestones, peeping at his black
veil. A fable went the rounds that the stare of the dead people drove him thence.
It grieved him to the very depth of his kind heart to observe how the children
fled from his approach, breaking up their merriest sports, while his melancholy
figure was yet afar off. Their instinctive dread caused him to feel, more strongly
280 than aught else, that a **preternatural** horror was interwoven with the threads of

13. **bugbear:** a source of dread or fear.

ANALYZE VISUALS
In what ways does the
woman depicted in the
painting on page 466
reflect the character of
Elizabeth as described
in lines 240–244? What
could the woman's white
dress **symbolize?**

③ Targeted Passage

preternatural
(prē′tər-năch′ər-əl) *adj.*
supernatural

ANALYZE VISUALS

*Possible answer: The woman in the painting
reflects the sadness and inner reflection that
Elizabeth experiences in the scene. Her white
dress could symbolize innocence or purity of
thought and action.*

Lines 248–258
REINFORCE KEY IDEA:
ESTRANGEMENT

Discuss What do Mr. Hooper's comments to
Elizabeth suggest about his willingness to experience **estrangement?** Explain your answer.
*Possible answer: His comments suggest that
his estrangement is a reluctant one. He is not
happy about how the veil makes him feel (line
248), and he begs Elizabeth not to abandon him
(lines 251–252). It is as if Mr. Hooper sincerely
regrets the estrangement that the veil causes,
yet he feels compelled to wear it, regardless of
the professional or personal cost.*

FOR STRATEGIC READERS

③ Targeted Passage [Lines 243–266]

This passage, a narrative turning point,
magnifies story conflicts.

- What does Mr. Hooper think that Elizabeth
  feels "at last" (line 248)?

- What does Mr. Hooper ask of Elizabeth?
  What does she ask of him?

- Why does Elizabeth leave? According to the
  narrator, why is her departure important?

Summarize Have students reread lines
266–270 and then summarize the two ways
in which the villagers now explain Mr. Hooper
and his black veil. Ask students to identify
the opinion that they agree with and to
defend their view.

FOR ENGLISH LEARNERS

Vocabulary: Cognates Point out that the
Spanish verb *resistir* and the French verb
résister are similar in form and meaning to
the English verb *resist* (line 239). Encourage
students who speak Latin-based languages to
search for and explain five words on page 467
that are similar to words in their home language. Have students compare the linguistic
similarities.

468

Lines 294–311
REINFORCE *KEY IDEA:* ESTRANGEMENT

Discuss How does Mr. Hooper's **estrangement**, caused by the veil, actually help others? Explain the irony in this situation. *Possible answer: The veil and the estrangement it causes make him a better minister; in particular, they seem to give him a power over people who are "in agony for sin" (line 297). The situation is ironic because the very estrangement that causes Mr. Hooper to suffer personally also enables him to help people, even people who are fearful of him (lines 301–304). The irony suggests that if Mr. Hooper had not experienced estrangement due to the black veil, he probably would not have become as effective a minister as he has.*

READING SKILL

H CULTURAL CHARACTERISTICS

Possible answer: Readers can conclude that Puritan worshipers are very concerned with recognizing and dealing with sin.

Extend the Discussion Why do you think that dying sinners want Mr. Hooper to come to them? What might they think that he can do for them?

---

the black crape. In truth, his own antipathy to the veil was known to be so great that he never willingly passed before a mirror, nor stooped to drink at a still fountain, lest, in its peaceful bosom, he should be affrighted by himself. This was what gave plausibility to the whispers that Mr. Hooper's conscience tortured him for some great crime too horrible to be entirely concealed, or otherwise than so obscurely intimated. Thus, from beneath the black veil there rolled a cloud into the sunshine, an **ambiguity** of sin or sorrow, which enveloped the poor minister, so that love or sympathy could never reach him. It was said that ghost and fiend consorted with him there. With self-shudderings and outward terrors, he walked

290 continually in its shadow, groping darkly within his own soul, or gazing through a medium that saddened the whole world. Even the lawless wind, it was believed, respected his dreadful secret, and never blew aside the veil. But still good Mr. Hooper sadly smiled at the pale visages of the worldly throng as he passed by.

Among all its bad influences, the black veil had the one desirable effect, of making its wearer a very efficient clergyman. By the aid of his mysterious emblem—for there was no other apparent cause—he became a man of awful power, over souls that were in agony for sin. His converts always regarded him with a dread peculiar to themselves, affirming, though but figuratively, that before he brought them to celestial light, they had been with him behind the

300 black veil. Its gloom, indeed, enabled him to sympathize with all dark affections. Dying sinners cried aloud for Mr. Hooper, and would not yield their breath till he appeared; though ever, as he stooped to whisper consolation, they shuddered at the veiled face so near their own. Such were the terrors of the black veil, even when Death had bared his visage! Strangers came long distances to attend service at his church, with the mere idle purpose of gazing at his figure, because it was forbidden them to behold his face. But many were made to quake ere they departed! Once, during Governor Belcher's[14] administration, Mr. Hooper was appointed to preach the election sermon. Covered with his black veil, he stood before the chief magistrate, the council, and the representatives, and wrought so

310 deep an impression that the legislative measures of that year were characterized by all the gloom and piety of our earliest ancestral sway. [15] H

In this manner Mr. Hooper spent a long life, irreproachable in outward act, yet shrouded in dismal suspicions; kind and loving, though unloved, and dimly feared; a man apart from men, shunned in their health and joy, but ever summoned to their aid in moral anguish. As years wore on, shedding their snows above his sable veil, he acquired a name throughout the New England churches, and they called him Father Hooper. Nearly all his parishioners, who were of a mature age when he was settled, had been borne away by many a funeral: he had one congregation in the church, and a more crowded one in the churchyard; and

320 having wrought so late into the evening, and done his work so well, it was now good Father Hooper's turn to rest.

---

14. **Governor Belcher's:** referring to Governor Jonathan Belcher (1682–1757), colonial governor of the Massachusetts Bay Colony from 1730 to 1741, and later of New Jersey.

15. **earliest ancestral sway:** the Puritans who held power in 17th-century America.

---

ambiguity
(ăm'bĭ-gyōō'ĭ-tē) *n.* unclearness; uncertainty

H **CULTURAL CHARACTERISTICS**
Once Mr. Hooper is perceived to have intimate knowledge of sin, he becomes a famous and respected clergyman. Based on this fact, what would you conclude is the main concern of Puritan worshipers?

DIFFERENTIATED INSTRUCTION

FOR STRATEGIC READERS

Paraphrase As students move into the final phase of the story, make sure they understand that Mr. Hooper continues to wear the veil in spite of his personal discomfort. Read aloud lines 281–283; then help students paraphrase it. *Possible answer: Truthfully, he disliked the veil so much that he never intentionally passed by a mirror or stopped to drink at a fountain, because he did not want to scare himself.*

FOR ADVANCED LEARNERS/AP

Hypothesize [small-group option] Point out the change from "Mr. Hooper" to "Father Hooper" (lines 315–317). Have students write a response to these questions and then compare their responses in small groups:

- When the story opens, Mr. Hooper already has the respect of his congregation. Why do you think that he does not receive the title of "Father" until late in his life?

- What might the change in title represent?

Several persons were visible by the shaded candlelight in the death chamber of the old clergyman. Natural connections[16] he had none. But there was the decorously grave, though unmoved physician, seeking only to mitigate the last pangs of the patient whom he could not save. There were the deacons, and other eminently pious members of his church. There, also, was the Reverend Mr. Clark, of Westbury, a young and **zealous** divine, who had ridden in haste to pray by the bedside of the expiring minister. There was the nurse, no hired handmaiden of death, but one whose calm affection had endured thus long, in secrecy, in solitude,
330 amid the chill of age, and would not perish, even at the dying hour. Who, but Elizabeth! And there lay the hoary head of good Father Hooper upon the death pillow, with the black veil still swathed about his brow and reaching down over his face, so that each more difficult gasp of his faint breath caused it to stir. All through life that piece of crape had hung between him and the world: it had separated him from cheerful brotherhood and woman's love, and kept him in that saddest of all prisons, his own heart; and still it lay upon his face, as if to deepen the gloom of his darksome chamber, and shade him from the sunshine of eternity.

For some time previous, his mind had been confused, wavering doubtfully between the past and the present, and hovering forward, as it were, at intervals,
340 into the indistinctness of the world to come. There had been feverish turns, which tossed him from side to side and wore away what little strength he had. But in the most convulsive struggles, and in the wildest vagaries of his intellect, when no other thought retained its sober influence, he still showed an awful solicitude lest the black veil should slip aside. Even if his bewildered soul could have forgotten, there was a faithful woman at his pillow, who, with averted eyes, would have covered that aged face, which she had last beheld in the comeliness of manhood. At length the death-stricken old man lay quietly in the torpor of mental and bodily exhaustion, with an imperceptible pulse, and breath that grew fainter and fainter, except when a long, deep, and irregular inspiration seemed to prelude the flight of his spirit.

350 The minister of Westbury approached the bedside.
"Venerable Father Hooper," said he, "the moment of your release is at hand. Are you ready for the lifting of the veil, that shuts in time from eternity?"

Father Hooper at first replied merely by a feeble motion of his head; then, apprehensive, perhaps, that his meaning might be doubtful, he exerted himself to speak.

"Yea," said he, in faint accents, "my soul hath a patient weariness until that veil be lifted."

"And is it fitting," resumed the Reverend Mr. Clark, "that a man so given to prayer, of such a blameless example, holy in deed and thought, so far as mortal
360 judgment may pronounce; is it fitting that a father in the church should leave a shadow on his memory that may seem to blacken a life so pure? I pray you, my venerable brother, let not this thing be! Suffer us to be gladdened by your

16. **natural connections:** relatives.

zealous (zĕl′əs) *adj.* eager and enthusiastic

④ **Targeted Passage**

Lines 333–357
TIERED DISCUSSION PROMPTS
Use these prompts to introduce students to the story's concluding deathbed scene:

Restate According to the narrator, what has wearing the black veil done to Mr. Hooper? *Possible answer: Wearing the veil has kept him from having friends and from being married; in short, it has made him lonely.*

Interpret What do you learn about Elizabeth from this passage? *Possible answer: Elizabeth is willing to let Mr. Hooper die as he wishes instead of lifting the veil for a last look at the man she once hoped to marry. In fact, she would cover his face if the veil slipped, because she knows that it is what he would want (lines 344–346).*

Evaluate How well does the narrator strike a balance in showing both Mr. Hooper's feebleness and his determination? Explain. *Possible answer: The narrator effectively strikes a balance. He tells readers that Mr. Hooper is suffering from confusion and from debilitating bouts with fever (lines 338–341); but he also makes it clear that the one thought that Mr. Hooper retains, despite his weakness and discomfort, is that his veil not be removed (lines 341–344).*

FOR STRATEGIC READERS
④ **Targeted Passage [Lines 350–362]**

In this passage, Mr. Hooper is presented with one final plea to remove his veil.

- Who speaks with the dying Mr. Hooper in these lines? What do we know about this person?

- What does Mr. Hooper tell him? To what "veil" is he referring?

- What reasons does Mr. Clark give Mr. Hooper for lifting the veil off his face?

Paraphrase Make sure students understand the loyalty and love that Elizabeth shows to Mr. Hooper in his last moments. Read aloud the full sentence that begins in line 344 and invite students to paraphrase it. *Possible answer: Even if he was too confused to know to keep the veil on, Elizabeth would have looked away and covered his lined and wrinkled face, the face that she had last seen when he was a handsome young man.*

FOR ADVANCED LEARNERS/AP
Analyze Theme [small-group option] Remind students that Hawthorne often explored the themes of sin, hypocrisy, and guilt. Organize students into small groups and have each group discuss the questions from the Core Analysis Frame: Theme. Encourage groups to compare their answers.

 BEST PRACTICES TOOLKIT—Transparency
Analysis Frame: Theme pp. D21, D32

REINFORCE *KEY IDEA:* ESTRANGEMENT

Discuss What does Mr. Clark's comment imply about the cause for Mr. Hooper's **estrangement?** What do you think is the cause? *Possible answer: Mr. Clark's comment suggests that Mr. Hooper wears the black veil to signify some terrible and secret sin—the implied cause for his estrangement. The real cause seems to be that the parishioners have judged him and have refused to examine themselves honestly.*

LITERARY ANALYSIS

❶ SYMBOL

Possible answer: Father Hooper reproaches the villagers for making him an object of fear (lines 379–383), when the true cause of their fear has been their unwillingness to be honest about themselves with one another and with God (lines 383–387). His comment that everyone wears a Black Veil (lines 386–387) suggests that the veil represents the part of a person's life that he or she tries to keep secret from others.

SELECTION WRAP-UP

REFLECT Ask students what wearing the black veil teaches Mr. Hooper about people and about himself.

★ CRITIQUE

- Ask students whether or not the black veil is an effective symbol. Have them back up their answer with textual evidence.

- After completing the After Reading questions on page 471, have students revisit their responses and tell whether they have changed their opinions.

---

triumphant aspect, as you go to your reward. Before the veil of eternity be lifted, let me cast aside this black veil from your face!"

And thus speaking, the Reverend Mr. Clark bent forward to reveal the mystery of so many years. But, exerting a sudden energy that made all the beholders stand aghast, Father Hooper snatched both his hands from beneath the bedclothes and pressed them strongly on the black veil, resolute to struggle, if the minister of Westbury would contend with a dying man.

370   "Never!" cried the veiled clergyman. "On earth, never!"

"Dark old man!" exclaimed the affrighted minister, "with what horrible crime upon your soul are you now passing to the judgment?"

Father Hooper's breath heaved; it rattled in his throat; but with a mighty effort, grasping forward with his hands, he caught hold of life, and held it back till he should speak. He even raised himself in bed; and there he sat shivering, with the arms of death around him, while the black veil hung down, awful, at that last moment, in the gathered terrors of a lifetime. And yet the faint, sad smile, so often there, now seemed to glimmer from its obscurity, and linger on Father Hooper's lips.

"Why do you tremble at me alone?" cried he, turning his veiled face round
380   the circle of pale spectators. "Tremble also at each other! Have men avoided me, and women shown no pity, and children screamed and fled, only for my black veil? What, but the mystery which it obscurely typifies, has made this piece of crape so awful? When the friend shows his inmost heart to his friend; the lover to his best beloved; when man does not vainly shrink from the eye of his Creator, loathsomely treasuring up the secret of his sin; then deem me a monster, for the symbol beneath which I have lived, and die! I look around me, and, lo! On every visage a Black Veil!" ❶

While his auditors shrank from one another, in mutual affright, Father Hooper fell back upon his pillow, a veiled corpse, with a faint smile lingering on his lips.
390   Still veiled, they laid him in his coffin, and a veiled corpse they bore him to the grave. The grass of many years has sprung up and withered on that grave, the burial stone is moss-grown, and good Mr. Hooper's face is dust; but awful is still the thought, that it mouldered beneath the Black Veil! ❧

❺ Targeted Passage

❶ SYMBOL
Explain Father Hooper's reproach in lines 380–387. What do his comments suggest about the meaning of the veil?

DIFFERENTIATED INSTRUCTION

FOR STRATEGIC READERS

❺ Targeted Passage [Lines 382–393]

This concluding passage suggests a meaning for the veil and presents the narrator's final commentary about it.

- What does Mr. Hooper say that people must do before they can call him a "monster"?

- What does he say that they hide? What does he say that they wear?

- What final image does the narrator present? How does he feel about that image?

FOR ENGLISH LEARNERS

Language: Punctuation and Print Cues
Point out the exclamation point in line 364 and explain that it indicates that Mr. Clark feels strongly about what he is asking Mr. Hooper to do. Have students discuss the use of exclamation points in lines 370, 371, 380, 386, and 387, and then in line 393. Discuss why exclamation points might be so prominent at the end of the story.

Comprehension

1. **Recall** What is the topic of the first sermon Mr. Hooper gives while wearing the veil?

2. **Recall** What reason does Mr. Hooper give Elizabeth for wearing the veil?

3. **Summarize** As time goes by, how do Mr. Hooper's relationships change?

Literary Analysis

4. **Identify Cultural Characteristics** What does the story reveal about Puritan religious beliefs, rules of behavior, and values and ideals?

5. **Interpret Symbol** Review the concept map you created as you read. Based on this information, what does the black veil represent? Explain your answer.

6. **Analyze Irony** To highlight his criticisms of Puritan society, Hawthorne uses verbal irony, where what is stated differs from what is really meant. In each of the following examples, explain what is ironic about the narrator's comments. What behavior, value, or belief is being criticized?

   • Squire Saunders's insult to Mr. Hooper (lines 98–100)
   • wild rumors (lines 125–129)
   • the deputation's visit to the minister (lines 195–199)
   • Mr. Hooper's new reputation (lines 295–297)

7. **Examine Character Ambiguity** The minister is an ambiguous character: he can be seen as an innocent victim of others' fears or as a man driven to isolate himself, convinced of his own moral superiority. Identify at least two details that support each perspective. Which interpretation do you find more compelling? Give reasons for your answer.

8. **Make Judgments About Character Motivations** Mr. Hooper's wearing of the black veil leads to his **estrangement** from his congregation. Based on the following passages, what argument would you make about the real causes of the villagers' discomfort in the minister's presence?

   • the first sighting of the minister (lines 34–39)
   • parishioners' comments after services (lines 105–113)
   • his arrival at the wedding (lines 147–152)
   • the attempt to confront him (lines 190–197)

Literary Criticism

9. **Biographical Context** Reread the biography of Hawthorne on page 456. Explain the personal motives that inspired Hawthorne's critical portrayal of Puritan culture. In what ways might Mr. Hooper represent Hawthorne's struggle with his own guilt?

efficient. **Criticism:** *Fear, not love or goodness, drives the Puritans' religious beliefs.*

7. *Innocent victim: He remains a good, kind person; he begs Elizabeth not to leave him (lines 251–256).* **Arrogant isolationist:** *He chooses to wear the veil (lines 220–224); he refuses to offer a clear explanation of it (lines 220–240).*

8. *The villagers' discomfort is caused by their own fears, which lead them to be intolerant of differences and to see sin and evil everywhere.*

9. *Hawthorne was critical because he felt guilty about having a Puritan ancestor who was an intolerant persecutor. Mr. Hooper might represent Hawthorne's struggle in that both are aware of flaws in Puritan culture but are unable to escape them.*

Practice and Apply

After Reading

Use these copy masters to check understanding and provide extra support:

R RESOURCE MANAGER—Copy Masters
Reading Check p. 280
Identify Cultural Characteristics p. 275
Question Support p. 281

Additional selection questions are provided for teachers on page 267.

ANSWERS

1. *The sermon topic is secret sin.*

2. *Mr. Hooper never gives a straight answer, but says that the veil is a symbol that he must always wear.*

3. *The first change is that Mr. Hooper goes from being respected and loved to being feared and avoided. Over time, however, people seek him out. They think that he is intimate with sin and therefore can help them deal with their own sins.*

Possible answers:

4. ■ **SKILLS FOCUS Identify Cultural Characteristics** *The story reveals the importance of Sunday worship (lines 1–9); the importance of rank (lines 92–98); the prevalence of gossip (lines 85–91 and 105–114) and superstition (lines 125–129 and 150–152); an obsession with sin (lines 73–78 and 230–232); and hypocrisy (lines 379–387). Students may suggest that some of these traits are not limited to Puritan culture.*

5. ● **SKILLS FOCUS Symbol** *The veil may be a symbol of sin. Mr. Hooper makes people feel that their wicked thoughts are known (lines 73–76 and 192–194). He implies such an interpretation in lines 227–228, 237–238, and 384–387.*

6. **Irony:** *Squire Saunders does not have an "accidental lapse of memory"; he does not want to invite Mr. Hooper.* **Criticism:** *social hypocrisy, concern with appearances, fear of public opinion.* **Irony:** *A "superstitious old woman" is not a reliable witness of an alleged supernatural event.* **Criticism:** *credulity, gossip, and superstition.* **Irony:** *The matter is not "too weighty"; the deputations fail because of their fear.* **Criticism:** *failures of leaders ruled by their own fear, which they can't admit.* **Irony:** *As Mr. Hooper becomes more distant and less human to his congregation, he becomes more*

ANSWERS
Vocabulary in Context
VOCABULARY PRACTICE

1. *antonyms*   5. *antonyms*

2. *antonyms*   6. *synonyms*

3. *synonyms*   7. *antonyms*

4. *synonyms*   8. *synonyms*

R RESOURCE MANAGER—Copy Master
Vocabulary Practice p. 278

VOCABULARY IN WRITING

Have students review the break-up scene (lines 200–264), making notes about the emotions that Elizabeth displays there. Encourage students to put themselves in her place and to consider whether time would affect her view of the break-up.

VOCABULARY STRATEGY: THE LATIN ROOT
ambi *(also an EL language objective)*

For each item, help students use their knowledge of the root, suffixes (which identify the part of speech needed), and context clues to choose the correct word.

Answers:

1. *ambidextrous*   4. *ambit*

2. *ambiance*   5. *ambient*

3. *ambivalent*

R RESOURCE MANAGER—Copy Master
Vocabulary Strategy p. 279

i Vocabulary Center at **ClassZone.com**
Additional Vocabulary Activities

Assess and Reteach

Assess

R RESOURCE MANAGER—Copy Masters
Selection Test A pp. 283–284
Selection Test B/C pp. 285–286

Test Generator CD

Reteach

S STANDARDS LESSON FILE
Literature Lesson 30: Symbol and Symbolism
Reading Lesson 8: Making Inferences
Vocabulary Lesson 7: Latin Roots

Vocabulary in Context

VOCABULARY PRACTICE

Decide whether the words in each pair are synonyms or antonyms.

1. ostentatious/discreet
2. ambiguity/clarity
3. portend/predict
4. iniquity/vice
5. zealous/halfhearted
6. imbued/infused
7. preternatural/ordinary
8. tremulous/quaking

VOCABULARY IN WRITING

Assume the role of the minister's fiancée, and write a journal entry to describe your feelings at some point after the breakup. Use at least two vocabulary words in your entry. You might begin like this.

> **EXAMPLE SENTENCE**
> *It has been eight months now, and I still am **tremulous** and weepy whenever I think of Mr. Hooper.*

VOCABULARY STRATEGY: THE LATIN ROOT *ambi*

The vocabulary word *ambiguity* contains the Latin root *ambi*. This root, which can mean either "both" or "around," can be found in many English words. When you encounter *ambi* in a word, you can often use context clues to determine which meaning of the root is involved.

R1.2
CALIFORNIA

ambit *ambiguity* *ambient* **ambi** *ambiance* *ambidextrous* *ambivalent*

PRACTICE Choose the word from the word web that best completes each sentence. Consider what you know about the Latin root and the other word parts shown. If necessary, consult a dictionary.

1. Because Peter was _____, he could write with either hand.
2. Their home had a pleasant and gracious _____.
3. Beth was _____ about joining the group and could not make up her mind.
4. The _____ of their property extends to that line of trees.
5. Too much _____ noise can interfere with the quality of a recording.

VOCABULARY PRACTICE
For more practice, go to the **Vocabulary Center** at **ClassZone.com**.

DIFFERENTIATED INSTRUCTION

FOR ENGLISH LEARNERS

Task Support: Vocabulary Strategy [small-group option] Have small groups work with a dictionary to locate the etymology of each word in the word web. Help them create a very literal definition for each word, based on the meaning of *ambi*. (For example, students might define *ambidextrous* as "both right-handed" and *ambiance* as "aroundness.")

FOR ADVANCED LEARNERS/AP

Vocabulary in Writing Ask students to assume the role of Mr. Hooper and write a journal entry that describes how he feels about his break-up with Elizabeth. Ask them to use at least four of the vocabulary words in their entry. Encourage students to share their journal entries and to compare them to the entries written from Elizabeth's perspective.

The Gothic Perspective

Although the romantic period was mostly characterized by a feeling of optimism, American gothic literature showed a fascination with the dark side of human nature. Sin, deception, hedonism, guilt, death—all are subjects upon which gothic writers based their dark tales, as illustrated beautifully in this excerpt from Edgar Allan Poe's "The Masque of the Red Death."

> *"The 'Red Death' had long devastated the country. No pestilence had ever been so fatal, or so hideous. Blood was its Avatar and its seal—the redness and horror of blood. There were sharp pains, and sudden dizziness, and then profuse bleeding at the pores, with dissolution. . . .*
>
> *But the Prince Prospero was happy and dauntless and sagacious. When his dominions were half depopulated, he summoned to his presence a thousand hale and lighthearted friends from among the knights and dames of his court, and with these retired to the deep seclusion of one of his castellated abbeys."*

Literary critic Paul Zweig has a few words to say about the importance of Poe's dark perspective.

> *"Poe's achievement . . . was to give literary expression to the dread that haunted America's dream of success in the 19th century. If anything was possible in this land of wealth and change, then personal failure, even simple unhappiness, was obscene, a skeleton in the cellar of democracy."*

© Gary Kelley, 1996.

Writing to Analyze

Nathaniel Hawthorne is also a master of the gothic genre. Do you think Zweig's comments about Poe can apply to Hawthorne's work as well? Write a brief response, citing evidence from "The Minister's Black Veil" to support your opinion.

Consider

- characters' personal failings
- characters' unhappiness or fears
- the message you take away from the story

Extension

SPEAKING & LISTENING

Although Poe and Hawthorne both wrote gothic literature, the nature of their work differs quite a bit. While Poe was the master of supernatural horror, Hawthorne focused on more everyday, realistic fears. With your classmates, **discuss** what frightens you more—the fantastic or the realistic?

W2.2

FOR DEVELOPING WRITERS

Writing Support Help students paraphrase Zweig's comments, making sure that they understand these words and phrases:

- *to give literary expression to,* "to write about"
- *dread,* "intense fear"
- *obscene,* "offensive; disgusting"
- *a skeleton in the cellar,* "something that is terrible and that should be kept hidden"

Elicit that Zweig is saying that Americans felt that their personal failures and unhappiness should be hidden as potential sources of shame in a society that valued success above all else. Also help students write a thesis statement, such as "Zweig's comments apply not only to Poe but also to Hawthorne. In 'The Minister's Black Veil,' the characters. . . ."

Wrap-Up: American Gothic

This Wrap-Up provides students with the opportunity to revisit the major ideas of gothic literature and to compare two gothic writers. Encourage students to examine their own views about the subjects that gothic writers frequently explored.

Writing to Analyze

- Remind students that *analyzing* involves examining complex things. In analytical writing, students discuss elements of a complex idea (noted in this feature by the bulleted list under **Consider**) as they support a general determination (a main idea) about the topic.

- To help students plan and write the essay, have them first paraphrase and discuss Zweig's statement. Then suggest that they focus on the words *dread* and *failure* in the statement and think about how both words reflect the "dark side" in gothic writing. Have students jot down their thoughts about each word in the context of "The Minister's Black Veil" and then relate each note to one of the three bulleted considerations in the prompt.

Extension

- Before students enter into discussion, have them summarize what they consider to be the most frightening but realistic parts of "The Minister's Black Veil" and the most frightening and supernatural elements of the Poe selections that they read.

- Ask students to discuss which selection frightened them the most and why. Then have them answer the discussion question.

Focus and Motivate

OBJECTIVES

- analyze a student model that shows the traits of reflective essays
- use the writing process to produce a reflective essay
- revise and edit, using criteria for reflective essays
- plan and conduct an interview, considering audience and purpose

 W2.1, W2.3, W1.9, W2.4, LC1.1

WRITER'S ROAD MAP

WRITING PROMPTS 1 AND 2

Remind students that *reflect* in this context implies thinking about a subject important to them and expressing their thoughts and feelings about it to the reader. Reflection often involves reviewing memories and finding meaning in them.

ADDITIONAL PROMPTS

Use these prompts for practice with writing for the real world and writing about art:

WRITING PROMPT 3

Writing for the Real World Recall an action you took at school, at a job, or in a community activity that made a difference, either positive or negative. Reflect on what you did and why it had the impact it had.

WRITING PROMPT 4

Writing Inspired by Fine Art In an art book or online source, find a work of art that moves you. Study the art and reflect on aspects of it that move you and why.

Art That Might Inspire

- self-portraits by painters such as Rembrandt, Van Gogh, or Dürer
- scenes that show people interacting
- landscapes, seascapes, or cityscapes

For additional writing prompts, see

WriteSmart CD

Writing Center at **ClassZone.com**

KEY TRAITS

Review the six **KEY TRAITS** with students, focusing on ideas and voice. Compare the list of traits with the criteria on page 480.

Writing Workshop

NARRATION

Reflective Essay

In this unit, you have read Ralph Waldo Emerson's and Henry David Thoreau's reflections about life, based on their own experiences. Now you will reflect on and write about an experience that changed you significantly.

WRITER'S ROAD MAP

Reflective Essay

WRITING PROMPT 1

Writing from Your Life Write an essay in which you reflect on an experience that taught you an important lesson. Include details that help your reader understand the people and events you are writing about. Explain how the experience changed you.

Experiences to Consider

- a victory or a defeat in a competition
- an incident that strongly affected you, such as a "random act of kindness" or a conflict

WRITING PROMPT 2

Writing from Literature Choose a quotation from a literary work in this unit. Write a reflective essay that relates the quotation to an event in your life. Your essay should tell why the event matters to you and explain whether you agree or disagree with the author.

Quotations to Consider

- "If a man does not keep pace with his companions, perhaps it is because he hears a different drummer." (*Walden*)
- "...though I might be aided and instructed by others, I must depend on myself as the only constant friend." (*Woman in the Nineteenth Century*)

 WRITING TOOLS
For prewriting, revision, and editing tools, visit the **Writing Center** at **ClassZone.com**.

KEY TRAITS

1. IDEAS
- Focuses on a single, well-defined **experience**
- Maintains a **balance** between describing the experience and explaining personal beliefs or ideas

2. ORGANIZATION
- Intrigues the reader with a fresh, original **introduction**
- Has a clear **sequence**
- **Concludes** by summarizing the **significance** of the experience

3. VOICE
- Has an individual **style** that shows the writer's beliefs and personality
- Maintains a **tone** that is appropriate for the audience, purpose, and subject matter

4. WORD CHOICE
- **Re-creates** the experience for the reader by using elements such as figurative language, sensory details, or dialogue

5. SENTENCE FLUENCY
- Structures sentences using the **active voice**

6. CONVENTIONS
- Employs **correct grammar and usage**

474 UNIT 2: AMERICAN ROMANTICISM

Writing Workshop Resources

 RESOURCE MANAGER UNIT 2
Plan and Teach pp. 287–290
Prewriting–Editing pp. 291–295
Writing Rubric p. 296
Speaking and Listening p. 297
Writing Support p. 298*

 STANDARDS LESSON FILE
Writing Lessons 1, 43
Grammar Lessons 16, 17

 BEST PRACTICES TOOLKIT
Scaffolding Writing Instruction pp. 43–46*
- Freewriting • Timeline • Opening Lines •
Writing Template: Reflective Essay • Cliché Array

TECHNOLOGY
Easy Planner DVD
Writing Center at **ClassZone.com**
WriteSmart CD

 * Resources for Differentiation

Part 1: Analyze a Student Model

Online INTERACTIVE MODEL CLASSZONE.COM

Ashley Jackson
Carlisle High School

Learning to Trust Myself

What has eight legs and only one head? The answer is a group of four girls in middle school. At least that was true of the group I formed four years ago with my so-called friends Annie, Selina, and Madison. Although I didn't realize it at the time, I understand now that from the moment we
5 banded together in seventh grade, it was a disaster in the making.

Looking back on that year, I see four girls who regarded being alone as a dreaded disease. We did everything together, including shopping, going to games and dances, and doing homework. Whenever one of us had to go somewhere or needed something, it meant that all of us did. "We're all in
10 this together," we would say.

Unfortunately, our togetherness extended into some dark corners. One night, Annie stole money from her mother's wallet, and we all went to LaRusso's Pizza and spent it. When Madison lost her math book, we chatted with Jason Villalta while she swiped his book, and he ended up
15 paying the fine for lost school property. We laughed about these events as if they were amusing or unimportant, but they bothered me. Still, we never visited the land of separate opinions. We were unanimous about our ideas, or we kept them to ourselves.

One night, Selina's mom dropped us off at Crosstown Mall. We spent
20 most Friday nights there, and this one was no different until Annie smirked at Selina and said, "I dare you to steal a pair of sunglasses off that cart in front of Bath & Bubble!"

Selina laughed and said, "Why should I do that?"

Annie answered, "Well, when you bring the glasses back, then you get
25 to dare someone else! We'll play a game and see who's chicken first."

Did Selina hesitate? When I reflect on that moment, I want to believe that she did. Nevertheless, she smiled and said, "No problem, Annie!" Then

KEY TRAITS IN ACTION

Surprising, unusual **introduction** helps to create a distinctive writing **style.**

The entire essay strikes a **balance** between retelling and reflecting. (The reflective parts of this paragraph are highlighted.)

Focuses on a single, well-defined **experience** (a conflict among friends) and relates it in the **active voice.**

Uses **dialogue** to **re-create** the experience.

Teach
CALIFORNIA

Part 1: Analyze a Student Model
Have students read the student model and **KEY TRAITS IN ACTION.** Then discuss the model with the class, noting specific examples of each trait and building on what students have already noted. You may also wish to incorporate these activities:

- **Style** Remind students that style refers to all the ways a writer uses words to create effects and achieve his or her intentions. Each writer has an individual style, and chooses words, types of sentences, and figures of speech that convey his or her meaning. Ask students to consider their own personal styles in life: Are they loud and active? quiet and thoughtful? trendy? traditional? Suggest that students develop writing styles that express their self-image.

- **Balance** Tell students that a reflective essay must focus on reflections that are important to the writer or it will not be interesting to readers. Narrative elements get the reader interested in the events the writer is reflecting on. To make reflections more interesting, writers often alternate passages of narrative with passages that respond to the narrative events.

DIFFERENTIATED INSTRUCTION

For general guidelines on differentiating writing instruction, see

 BEST PRACTICES TOOLKIT
Scaffolding Writing Instruction
pp. 43–46

FOR ENGLISH LEARNERS
Language: Skill Words Write these terms on the board and review them with students:

- *introduction:* the beginning of an essay—for example, the first paragraph of "Learning to Trust Myself"

- *active voice:* sentence structure in which the subject of the verb performs the action—for example, "Annie stole money" (line 12) instead of "the money was stolen by Annie"

- *dialogue:* a person's exact words, set off with quotation marks—for example, "We're all in this together" in lines 9–10

- *tone:* a writer's attitude toward the topic—for example, the model has a serious tone

- *sequence:* order—for example, first Annie stole money, then Selina stole sunglasses

- **Sequence** Write this sequence of events from the model on the board:

1. Ashley refuses to steal.
2. Selina steals sunglasses.
3. Selina dares Ashley to steal.
4. The girls swipe Jason's math book.
5. Annie takes money from her mother's wallet.

Ask students whether this is the order in which the events happen in the essay. (*No*) Have students state the correct order, and write it on the board. **Answer:** *1. Annie takes money from her mother's wallet. 2. The girls swipe Jason's math book. 3. Selina steals sunglasses. 4. Selina dares Ashley to steal. 5. Ashley refuses to steal.* Tell students that in most cases, writers present events in the order in which they happened. When reflecting, however, they may wish to write about events from different times that evoke similar thoughts and feelings. The important goal is to make sure readers can keep track of when each event happened.

- **Significance** Remind students that the topic of a reflective essay should hold significance to its writer. Ask students what significance the events Ashley describes held for her. *Possible answer: They presented a turning point at which Ashley discovered that her friends were dishonest and decided she would rather be alone than join that behavior.* Point out that to focus readers on the significance of her decision, Ashley avoids including events and reflections that are less important. For example, she does not describe what she and her friends were wearing.

For interactive student models, see

📀 Write*Smart* CD

ℹ Writing Center at **ClassZone.com**

---

the three of us stared dumbfounded as she shoplifted a pair of sunglasses. After showing them to us, she dropped them in the trash, clearly very
30 pleased with herself, and then she pointed triumphantly to me.

"Ashley, you are next, girl!" she grinned. "How 'bout you get me one of those little pink bears off the Cuddle Teddy cart?"

"I don't think so," I said, as shy as a mouse trying to please a cat.

"Oh, but you *do* think so," Selina crooned. "I can just *tell* you think so.
35 And, hey, we're all in this together," she added.

Quickly sizing up the cart, I noticed that the woman who ran it had only a limited view of all the goods she sold. With the throngs of kids and shoppers around, the woman wouldn't notice if I grabbed something small and inconsequential from the far edge. Almost as if I were hypnotized, I
40 turned and started walking toward the cart.

When I got there, however, I just kept going. I didn't want a pink teddy bear, I didn't want to play this juvenile game, and, most of all, I didn't want to steal. Knowing that I was leaving my so-called friends forever, I took out my cell phone and asked my dad to take me home.
45 In school the next Monday, Selina, Annie, and Madison taunted me. For a few days, they hissed "Chicken!" and made little "bawk, bawk, bawk" sounds when they saw me, but soon they acted as if I didn't exist. It was a long time before I made new friends or felt a sense of belonging. Eventually, however, I began to feel proud of being independent. Over
50 time, I met other people who weren't scared to be alone. I gradually realized that the friendships I formed with these people weren't mindless loyalty pacts; instead, they were built on mutual respect.

That day at the mall marked the beginning of my adult life. On that day, I had to make a decision that mattered, and I had to make it alone. I
55 trusted myself then to distinguish between my values and those that others wanted to impose on me, and I stayed true to myself. I still trust myself to know the difference between right and wrong.

2

Presents a clear **sequence** of events.

Uses a serious **tone** that is appropriate to the topic.

Explores the **significance** of the experience in the **conclusion**.

DIFFERENTIATED INSTRUCTION

FOR ENGLISH LEARNERS

Comprehension: Transitions List transitional words or phrases that are often used in reflective essays. Point out that some are transitions that show sequence, such as "four years ago," "at the time," "now," "one night," "when," "until," "after," "then," "next Monday," "soon," "eventually," "gradually," and "that day." Add the common sequence transitions *first, second, next, later, last, before,* and *finally.*

Other relevant transitions show reflection or evaluation; for example, "I understand that," "unfortunately," "but," "still," "when I reflect on that moment," "nevertheless," "I noticed, most of all," "however," "I realized," and "instead." Add common evaluative transitions such as *fortunately, because, most important, as a result, perhaps,* and *despite.*

Have students find the model examples. Help them use context to build meaning for the words. Then, ask them to demonstrate two of

the sequence terms, and write a sentence using one of the evaluative transitions.

To provide English learners with additional writing support, see

🅡 RESOURCE MANAGER—Copy Master Writing Support p. 298

Part 2: Apply the Writing Process

PREWRITING

What Should I Do?	What Does It Look Like?

1. Travel to your past to find a topic.
To go back in time, look through your old photographs, ticket stubs, Weblog entries, and souvenirs. Or use a chart like this one to trigger memories. Highlight the experience you want to write about.

TIP If you can't think of an event to write about, reread the bulleted lists under each prompt on page 474.

Types of Experiences	My Experiences
a victory or a defeat	won the camp diving contest
an incident that strongly affected me	volunteered at a soup kitchen
a conflict	realized I had to say no to my friends when they started shoplifting

2. Freewrite about the experience.
Your freewriting might include what you said, what others said, your feelings, and even the sounds, sights, and smells of the experience. To refresh your memory, consider interviewing a friend or family member who was present. See page ooo for interviewing tips.

TIP If your story is too personal to share with an audience, choose a different topic from the chart you created in step 1.

> It was a Friday night … the mall was really crowded … lots of kids running around, crabby shoppers … I can still hear the stupid tinkly music they used to play there … Selina walked up to one of those carts and grabbed a pair of sunglasses. Nobody even saw her … except us!!
> She looked so proud of herself.
> Then she dumped the glasses in the trash and pointed to me.

3. Reflect on why the experience matters to you.
Put your topic to the test before you start drafting. Ask yourself:
- Will this event interest my audience?
- Was it truly meaningful in my life?
- What did I learn?
- How did I change?

Try using a chart like this one.

What Happened?	Why Does It Matter?
I hung out with three friends.	I stopped being myself; I was scared to be on my own.
My friends dared me to shoplift.	I had to decide which was more important: honesty or popularity.
I refused to steal.	I learned to be independent. I started to grow up.

FOR DEVELOPING WRITERS

Reflect As an alternative to the chart in step 3, have students return to their freewriting as a way to understand the meaning of their chosen experience. Tell them to reread their freewrites and reflect on what they have written. Then have them add a final sentence to the freewrite, beginning with "This experience matters because …"

FOR ENGLISH LEARNERS

Freewrite Many English learners will feel more comfortable and more spontaneous freewriting in their home language. Allow them to do so in order to get their deepest thoughts and feelings down on paper. Then, have them translate their freewritings into English, either on their own or with more fluent partners.

Practice and Apply

To support students during the writing process, use these copy masters:

 RESOURCE MANAGER—Copy Masters
Prewriting–Editing pp. 291–295
Writing Rubric p. 296
Writing Support p. 298 (for English learners)

Part 2: Apply the Writing Process

PREWRITING

1. Travel to your past to find a topic. For students who respond, "Nothing interesting ever happens to me," have them revisit their earliest memories as well as turning points such as moves, family additions, or new interests or travels. For students who can't decide among their listed alternatives, suggest that they pick the memory that would best convey their personality to someone meeting them for the first time. Refer students to the **TIP** and page 476 for additional ideas.

2. Freewrite about the experience. Use the Freewriting strategy. For students who have trouble getting started, state a time limit such as five minutes and suggest that students try to fill half a page. After students read the **TIP**, point out that they may be able to recast a personal event in more general terms or omit certain details. The goal is to reflect on a meaningful event.

3. Reflect on why the experience matters to you. Draw students' attention to the four bulleted questions in the instruction, and point out that each can help students respond to the chart question, "Why does it matter?" Suggest that students answer the bulleted questions before completing their charts.

 BEST PRACTICES TOOLKIT
Freewriting p. C1

For interactive graphic organizers, see

📀 Write*Smart* CD

ℹ️ Writing Center at **ClassZone.com**

DRAFTING

1. **Outline your essay.** Refer students to the **TIP**. Suggest that they use a Timeline to set out the events of their experience in order. Above each entry on the timeline, students should note their reflections about the event. These notes will help them create balance between narrative and reflection.

    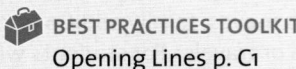 **BEST PRACTICES TOOLKIT—Transparency**
    Timeline p. B23

2. **Craft a stylish introduction.** Use the Opening Lines strategy to help students create introductions that grab the reader's attention.

    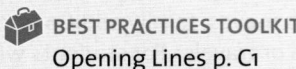 **BEST PRACTICES TOOLKIT**
    Opening Lines p. C1

3. **Include the thoughts and feelings you experienced at the time.** Recommend that students choosing the interior monologue approach review the monologues they wrote for the Reading-Writing Connection on page 444. Point out that interior monologue can be used at carefully chosen points in an essay to emphasize an idea or feeling, to help readers access an idea or feeling, and to build the connection between writer and reader. Discourage students, however, from embellishing every thought or feeling with a passage of interior monologue.

For a reflective-essay writing template, see

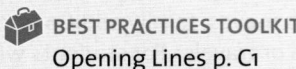 **BEST PRACTICES TOOLKIT—Transparency**
Writing Template: Reflective Essay
   pp. C16, C37

⊙ Write*Smart* CD

ⓘ Writing Center at **ClassZone.com**

DRAFTING

What Should I Do?	*What Does It Look Like?*
1. Outline your essay. You have two important goals in this essay: to retell an experience and to explain what you learned from it. Creating an outline can help you meet both requirements. Here is one basic plan for a reflective essay: • Introduce the issue, hinting at the lesson you learned. • Retell the experience. • Reflect on how you have changed. Notice how the writer of this outline balanced reflection and retelling. **TIP** Make sure your outline includes a clear sequence of events. Your reader shouldn't have to ask what happened or when events took place.	**Intro:** 1. Get audience attention. 2. *Reflect* on what I understand now: that group was not good for me. **Body:** 1. *Describe* who we were. 2. *Reflect* on what being together all the time meant, including doing sneaky things. 3. *Describe* the night at the mall. 　A. Annie suggests an "I dare you" game. 　B. Selina takes the dare, then dares me. 　C. I walk away. 4. *Describe* and *reflect* on what happened after. **Conclusion:** *Reflect* on how the experience changed me.
2. Craft a stylish introduction. Your introduction should grab your reader's attention and hint at your overall reflection about the experience. Consider including a surprising contrast, a memorable description, or a joke, a riddle, or some other bit of humor.	**Contrast** *Crosstown Mall is a brightly lit, busy place where dark deeds can occur.* **Humor** *What has eight legs and only one head? The answer is a group of four girls in middle school.*
3. Include the thoughts and feelings you experienced at the time. Avoid a bare-bones account: "First I did this, then I did that." Instead, describe what you thought and how you felt. Consider using **interior monologue**—presenting your thoughts as you might have said them to yourself.	**Writer's thoughts and feelings** *I noticed that the woman who ran the cart had only a limited view of what she sold. Almost as if I were hypnotized, I turned and started walking toward the cart.* **Interior monologue** *Could I really do this? I asked myself.*

DIFFERENTIATED INSTRUCTION

FOR DEVELOPING WRITERS

Include Thoughts and Feelings Use the Cliché Array strategy to help students avoid stale language. Remind them that their purpose is to express their own thoughts and feelings, and clichés create overly generalized and impersonal writing.

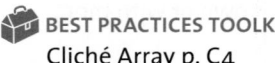 **BEST PRACTICES TOOLKIT**
Cliché Array p. C4

FOR ENGLISH LEARNERS

Vocabulary: Idioms To help students understand the task of writing a reflection, review the meanings of these idioms used in the instruction:

• *grab your reader's attention,* "get the reader interested in what you write"

• *bare-bones account,* "only the basic information about what happened, without descriptive details"

REVISING AND EDITING

What Should I Do?	What Does It Look Like?

1. Show, don't tell.
- Reread your draft, looking for vivid descriptions.
- If your writing seems boring, consider adding similes (comparisons that use *like* or *as*) or metaphors (comparisons that do not use *like* or *as*).

See page 111: Literary Analysis: Figurative Language

▶ Tells: "*I don't think so,*" *I said, scared.*
Shows with a simile: "*I don't think so,*" *I said, as shy as a mouse trying to please a cat.*

Tells: *We never disagreed.*
Shows with a metaphor: *We never visited the land of separate opinions.*

2. Use the active voice.
- (Circle) examples of the passive voice.
- To make your essay livelier, use the active voice whenever possible.

TIP Passive voice is acceptable when the doer of the action is not important (The house *was built* in 1920) or when the doer is unknown (The money *was stolen* last night).

▶ *They bothered me.*
~~*I was bothered by them.*~~

We kept our ideas to ourselves.
~~*Our ideas were kept to ourselves.*~~

3. Keep a consistent tone.
- Have a peer reader draw a [box] around passages that shift in tone. For example, parts of your essay may contain too much slang or jargon.
- Decide whether your overall tone is appropriate to your topic. For example, if you are writing about a tragic event, your tone should be serious.

See page 480: Ask a Peer Reader

▶ *When I got there, however, I just kept going.* ~~*Then it totally hit me: no way was I gonna do this! I was SO out of there.*~~ *I didn't want ...*

Quickly sizing up the cart, ~~*Hastily assessing the parameters of my hypothetical mission.*~~ *I noticed ...*

4. Make sure your conclusion specifies why the experience matters.
- Avoid vague or overused statements such as "It's hard to grow up" or "Honesty is the best policy."
- Make your conclusion forceful and specific.

▶ *That day at the mall marked the beginning of my adult life. On that day, I had to make a decision that mattered, and I had to make it alone. I trusted myself then to distinguish between my values and those that others wanted to impose on me, and I stayed true to myself. I still trust myself to know the difference between right and wrong.*

REVISING AND EDITING

1. **Show, don't tell.** Remind students also to add adjectives and adverbs. Tell them to choose specific, concrete modifiers over those that are vague and abstract. Reread lines 41–43 of the model. Ask students to identify modifiers and explain how they add to the sentence. *Possible answer: The words* pink *and* juvenile *are adjectives; most of all is an adverb phrase. These modifiers help readers visualize Ashley's experience and appreciate the depth of her feelings.* Stress that descriptive language should add vividness, not just extra words.

2. **Use the active voice.** To illustrate the value of the active voice, have students rewrite active-voice sentences from the model to make them passive. For example, "We laughed about these events" (line 15) might become "These events were laughed at by us." Read the **TIP** and clarify that in each case the doer is unstated.

3. **Keep a consistent tone.** Point out that a consistent tone does not mean having the same tone in every sentence. For example, some incidents in an essay may be amusing and some serious. Shifts in tone should be appropriate to the material. Tell students to avoid inappropriate shifts in tone, such as injecting sarcasm into a serious passage.

4. **Make sure your conclusion specifies why the experience matters.** Tell students to avoid sentence beginnings that obviously signal their conclusion, such as, "This experience mattered to me because ...." Point out how Ashley instead sums up what she learned, and assumes that this conveys to readers why the experience mattered.

For interactive revision tools, see

Write*Smart* CD

Writing Center at **ClassZone.com**

FOR ENGLISH LEARNERS

Use the Active Voice Reinforce the meaning of the term *active voice* by saying simple sentences using that voice, such as "I did the homework" and "She likes to draw." Write the sentences on the board. Then, underneath each sentence, rewrite it in the passive voice. Explain that active voice makes it easier to know who is doing what. Tell students that spoken English usually uses the active voice.

FOR ADVANCED LEARNERS/AP

Use Stylistic Devices Suggest that students examine the excerpts from Ralph Waldo Emerson's "Self-Reliance" and *Nature* (pages 362–366) to study and emulate the use of descriptive details in a reflective essay. Students might also reread writing on a reflective topic they have done for the Wrap-Up on transcendentalism (page 401).

Preparing to Publish

Support for meeting the goals in the writing criteria is supplied throughout the Workshop on pages 477–479.

For Rubric Bank, see

 WriteSmart CD

Writing Center at ClassZone.com

Assess and Reteach

S STANDARDS LESSON FILE

Writing Lesson 1: Finding a Writing Idea
Writing Lesson 43: Developing a Voice
Grammar Lesson 16: Basic Verb Tenses
Grammar Lesson 17: Mixing Verb Tenses

Consider the Criteria

Use this checklist to make sure your reflective essay is on track.

Ideas
☑ retells a single experience and reflects on why it was important
☑ keeps a balance between retelling and reflecting

Organization
☑ has a creative, attention-getting introduction
☑ presents a clear sequence
☑ ends with a summary of the event's significance

Voice
☑ has an appropriate tone
☑ has a fresh, individual style

Word Choice
☑ uses vivid dialogue, figurative language, and sensory details

Sentence Fluency
☑ uses the active voice

Conventions
☑ uses correct grammar, spelling, and punctuation

Ask a Peer Reader

• In your own words, why was this experience significant to me?
• How would you describe my tone?
• What could I do to make my writing more vivid?

Check Your Grammar

• When you write dialogue, enclose each speaker's words in quotation marks. Each time the speaker changes, begin a new paragraph.

> "I don't think so," I said, as shy as a mouse trying to please a cat.
> "Oh, but you *do* think so," Selina crooned.

• End punctuation goes inside the quotation marks.

> "Why should I do that?"

See page R54: Quick Reference: Punctuation

• For events from the past, maintain the past tense. For present-day reflections, however, you may need to use the present tense.

> Consistent Past:
> I noticed that the woman who ran the cart had only a limited view of all the goods she sold. I saw the throngs of kids and shoppers.
> Present:
> I still trust myself to know the difference between right and wrong.

See pages R59–R60: Verb Tense

Writing On|ine

 PUBLISHING OPTIONS
For publishing options, visit the **Writing Center** at ClassZone.com.

ASSESSMENT PREPARATION
For writing and grammar assessment practice, go to the **Assessment Center** at ClassZone.com.

W2.4
CALIFORNIA

Conducting an Interview

Conducting an interview can help you recall your own history. It can also allow you to discover another person's perspective of a past event.

Planning the Interview

1. **Choose someone to interview.** You might interview someone who experienced an important event with you or someone who lived through an exciting historical event or time.

2. **Seek permission.** Begin by explaining your purpose and the incident or topic you want to focus on. Then set up a time and place. You can interview someone by telephone, by e-mail, by fax, or in person. Choose a setting that has few distractions. If you want to make a video or audio recording of the interview, discuss that in advance with your interviewee.

3. **Plan ahead.** First, research or reflect on the topic so you know enough to ask interesting questions. Then write down some open-ended questions. Such questions cannot be answered with a simple yes or no. Instead, they ask why or say, "Tell me about when . . . ," and ideally they lead to full, rich answers.

Conducting the Interview

1. **Ask your planned questions, and follow up when necessary.** Ask about facts before asking about personal matters and opinions. Whenever you receive a particularly interesting answer, you can always add, "Could you tell me more about that?"

2. **Inquire about photographs and other items.** Ask if your interviewee has any photographs, newspaper clippings, awards, or other items related to the topic of your interview. These mementoes can improve your understanding of the topic and the person.

See pages R85–R86: Interviews

SPEAKING AND LISTENING

Ask students to read this page to get an overview of how to plan and conduct a speech. Students who choose this option should familiarize themselves with the features of an interview and with tools, such as a tape recorder, that might help them plan and conduct it. Before students begin working, review these criteria with them so that they understand their goals:

Criteria A strong interview

- has an interesting human subject
- focuses on a significant topic or incident the interviewer knows about
- obtains permission from the interviewee
- is conducted in a format the interviewee finds comfortable
- is researched or prepared in advance
- relies on a list of well-considered open-ended questions
- asks factual questions before personal questions
- uses follow-up questions to obtain in-depth answers
- may contain photographs or other items related to the human subject and the interview topic

When students present their interviews, have their peers use the criteria to evaluate the final product.

R RESOURCE MANAGER—Copy Master
Speaking and Listening p. 297

S STANDARDS LESSON FILE
Speaking and Listening Lesson 11:
Interview

Assessment Practice

CHECK READINESS

Read aloud the paragraph under **ASSESS** and stress to students that this is not the full Unit Test, but a way for them to check their readiness for it. Then have students examine the skills listed under **REVIEW** and look back in the unit or in the **Student Resource Bank** for any skills they need to review.

READ THE SELECTIONS

Remind students to keep unit goals in mind as they read the passages, paying particular attention to these literary and reading skills:

- stanza, rhyme scheme, and meter
- symbol
- mood
- sound devices
- paraphrase

To help students focus on sound devices while reading, encourage them to ask questions such as

- What important words does Poe repeat in "A Dream Within a Dream"?
- How does Longfellow use alliteration to help describe the town in the second stanza?

ANSWER THE QUESTIONS

Direct students to pages R96–R103 of the **Test-Taking Handbook** to review test-taking strategies.

- Remind students not to choose the first alternative that seems to fit when answering a multiple-choice question. Instead, they should read through all the choices, eliminate any that are clearly wrong, and then choose the *best* answer—the one that is most accurate and complete.

- Also remind students not to change an answer unless they are sure that their first answer is incorrect. First instincts are usually reliable unless the student has misunderstood either the directions or the question. Urge students to always read all directions carefully and to check these against a question to make sure they can apply the directions.

Reading Comprehension

ASSESS
The practice test items on the next few pages match skills listed on the Unit Goals page (page 292) and addressed throughout this unit. Taking this practice test will help you assess your knowledge of these skills and determine your readiness for the Unit Test.

REVIEW
After you take the practice test, your teacher can help you identify any skills you need to review.

- Stanza, Rhyme Scheme, and Meter
- Symbol
- Mood
- Sound Devices:
  - Internal Rhyme
  - Repetition
  - Alliteration
  - Onomatopoeia
- Paraphrase
- Participles and Participial Phrases
- Parallelism
- Adjective Clauses

ASSESSMENT ONLINE
For more assessment practice and test-taking tips, go to the **Assessment Center** at ClassZone.com.

DIRECTIONS *Read these poems and answer the questions that follow.*

A Dream Within a Dream
Edgar Allan Poe

Take this kiss upon the brow!
And, in parting from you now,
Thus much let me avow—
You are not wrong, who deem
5 That my days have been a dream;
Yet if Hope has flown away
In a night, or in a day,
In a vision, or in none,
Is it therefore the less *gone?*
10 *All* that we see or seem
Is but a dream within a dream.

I stand amid the roar
Of a surf-tormented shore,
And I hold within my hand
15 Grains of the golden sand—
How few! yet how they creep
Through my fingers to the deep,
While I weep—while I weep!
O God! can I not grasp
20 Them with a tighter clasp?
O God! can I not save
One from the pitiless wave?
Is *all* that we see or seem
But a dream within a dream?

The Fire of Driftwood
Henry Wadsworth Longfellow

Devereux Farm near Marblehead

We sat within the farmhouse old,
    Whose windows, looking o'er the bay,
Gave to the sea-breeze damp and cold,
    An easy entrance, night and day.

5 Not far away we saw the port,
    The strange, old-fashioned, silent town,
The lighthouse, the dismantled fort,
    The wooden houses, quaint and brown.

DIFFERENTIATED INSTRUCTION

FOR ENGLISH LEARNERS
Assessment Practice: Work Backward
Prepare students by having them read the questions *before* reading the passages. Have them work in pairs to find unfamiliar words in test directions and questions and follow these steps:

1. Write each word on an index card.

2. Look up the meaning in a dictionary and write it on the back of the card.

3. Use the cards to practice the words with your partner and to teach them to others.

We sat and talked until the night,
10   Descending, filled the little room;
Our faces faded from the sight,
    Our voices only broke the gloom.

We spake of many a vanished scene,
    Of what we once had thought and said,
15 Of what had been, and might have been,
    And who was changed, and who was dead;

And all that fills the hearts of friends,
    When first they feel, with secret pain,
Their lives thenceforth have separate ends,
20   And never can be one again;

The first slight swerving of the heart,
    That words are powerless to express,
And leave it still unsaid in part,
    Or say it in too great excess.

25 The very tones in which we spake
    Had something strange, I could but mark;
The leaves of memory seemed to make
    A mournful rustling in the dark.

Oft died the words upon our lips,
30   As suddenly, from out the fire
Built of the wreck of stranded ships,
    The flames would leap and then expire.

And, as their splendor flashed and failed,
    We thought of wrecks upon the main,
35 Of ships dismasted, that were hailed
    And sent no answer back again.

The windows, rattling in their frames,
    The ocean, roaring up the beach,
The gusty blast, the bickering flames,
40   All mingled vaguely in our speech;

GO ON

ITEM ANALYSIS

COMPREHENSION AND WRITTEN RESPONSE	ITEMS	UNIT PAGES
Stanza, Rhyme Scheme, and Meter	6, 7, 15	329, 335, 341
Symbol	4, 11, 17	457
Mood	5, 9, 14	347
Sound Devices	2, 3, 12, 16	437
Internal Rhyme	2	
Repetition	3, 16	
Alliteration	12	
Onomatopoeia	13	
Paraphrase	1, 8, 10	347

WRITING AND GRAMMAR	ITEMS	UNIT PAGES
Participles and Participial Phrases	1, 6, 8, 9	426
Parallelism	2, 4	327
Adjective Clauses	3, 5, 7	369

FOR STRATEGIC READERS

Assessment Support Consider these options for completing the Assessment Practice:

- Have students "work backward" to review the test questions *before* reading the passage.

- Select random questions in the Assessment, and have students demonstrate *how* and *where* to look for the answers.

- Ask students to locate unfamiliar words in the Assessment. Elicit the words' meanings from the class.

- Have students record useful testing words and definitions in their journals for later reference.

- Read the selection or parts of it aloud to aid in student comprehension.

McDougal Littell
Assessment System

After checking student readiness with this Assessment Practice, you may administer the complete Unit 2 Test in order to more thoroughly evaluate student mastery of unit goals.

Comprehension

Model a thinking process for answering multiple-choice questions.

1. D is correct. *The question "Is it therefore the less gone?" (line 9) sums up the idea. A is incorrect because the passage does not mention the future. B is incorrect because the poem refers to a universal condition. C is incorrect because in the passage, hope has already flown away.*

2. C is correct. *The internal rhyme is* seem/dream, *which is also the end-rhyme. The other choices are untrue.*

3. B is correct. *The repetition refers to the images of night and day, vision and lack of vision (lines 7–8), which are contrasting images. A is incorrect because the mood of hopelessness is constant. C is incorrect because the expressions are not childlike. D is incorrect because the images are of literal, not symbolic, elements.*

4. A is correct. *Lines 12–24 develop the metaphor of the ocean as representing time's passage. B is incorrect because it refers to a literal fact, not a symbol. C is incorrect because the ocean described is not stormy. D is incorrect because the speaker's thoughts are not linked to the wave.*

5. D is correct. *The repeated reference to weeping expresses melancholy. Choices A, B, and C contain intimations of melancholy, but not intensely or directly.*

6. C is correct. *"Having four feet per line" is the meaning of "tetrameter." A would be bimeter. B would be trimeter. D would be pentameter.*

7. B is correct. *The stanzas describe the farmhouse overlooking the bay (lines 1–2) and the port (lines 5–6). A is incorrect because symbolism is developed further in descriptions of the driftwood fire (lines 45–48). C is incorrect because the main theme develops in the fourth stanza. D is incorrect because the speaker's identity is never firmly established.*

8. C is correct. *The words "pain," "separate ends," and "never can be one again" express the idea. A and D are incorrect because*

Until they made themselves a part
    Of fancies floating through the brain,
The long-lost ventures of the heart,
    That send no answers back again.

45 O flames that glowed! O hearts that yearned!
    They were indeed too much akin,
The driftwood fire without that burned,
    The thoughts that burned and glowed within.

Comprehension

DIRECTIONS *Answer these questions about "A Dream Within a Dream."*

1. Which statement is the best paraphrase of lines 6–9?
- **A** There is no time left to hope for the future.
- **B** Some people have hope, while others have none.
- **C** If you are not careful, hope can disappear overnight.
- **D** Once hope has disappeared, it doesn't matter how it was lost.

2. Which lines contain internal rhyme?
- **A** lines 1–2
- **B** lines 4–5
- **C** lines 10–11
- **D** lines 21–22

3. In lines 7–8, the repetition of the words "in a" calls attention to
- **A** shifting moods
- **B** contrasting images
- **C** childlike expressions
- **D** symbolic meanings

4. The "pitiless wave" in line 22 most likely symbolizes the
- **A** passage of time
- **B** changing shoreline
- **C** force of a storm
- **D** speaker's thoughts

5. Which line best expresses the melancholy mood of the poem?
- **A** "Take this kiss upon the brow!" (line 1)
- **B** "In a night, or in a day" (line 7)
- **C** "Grains of the golden sand" (line 15)
- **D** "While I weep—while I weep!" (line 18)

DIRECTIONS *Answer these questions about "The Fire of Driftwood."*

6. Longfellow's poem is written in tetrameter lines. Each line contains how many feet?
- **A** two   **C** four
- **B** three   **D** five

7. The first two stanzas establish the
- **A** symbolism   **C** main theme
- **B** setting   **D** speaker's identity

---

their ideas are not expressed in the poem. B is incorrect because the separation is not based on grievances.

9. D is correct. *The words "long-lost" and "heart" convey the melancholy mood. A, B, and C are incorrect because they depict scenes that are not necessarily melancholy.*

10. D is correct. *The phrase "leaves of memory" refers figuratively to memories, not to literal leaves. A is incorrect because it focuses on a literal description of leaves, not on memory. B and C are incorrect because they do not include or emphasize the sadness of the memories.*

8. Which idea about friendship is expressed in lines 17–24?

   A Friends communicate best by sitting together quietly.

   B Grievances among friends are hard to resolve.

   C It is sad to realize that friends have grown apart.

   D People find comfort in talking with old friends.

9. Which line best conveys the melancholy mood of "The Fire of Driftwood"?

   A "An easy entrance, night and day" (line 4)

   B "The wooden houses, quaint and brown" (line 8)

   C "The ocean, roaring up the beach" (line 38)

   D "The long-lost ventures of the heart" (line 43)

10. Which statement most accurately paraphrases lines 27–28?

> "The leaves of memory seemed to make
> A mournful rustling in the dark."

   A Dried leaves made a sad sound.

   B Darkness brought on vivid memories.

   C The best memories were from long ago.

   D The friends were haunted by memories.

11. The "wreck of stranded ships" in line 31 most likely symbolizes

   A losses in life   **C** sinister forces

   B wasted lives   **D** desires for adventure

12. The alliteration of the phrase "fancies floating" in line 42 suggests the sound of a

   A pounding wave   **C** gentle breeze

   B gathering storm   **D** crackling fire

13. Which line contains an example of onomatopoeia?

   A "Our faces faded from the sight" (line 11)

   B "And who was changed, and who was dead" (line 16)

   C "The windows, rattling in their frames" (line 37)

   D "O flames that glowed! O hearts that yearned!" (line 45)

DIRECTIONS *Answer this question about both poems.*

14. Which setting do both poets use to create a mournful mood?

   A farmhouse   **C** campfire

   B seashore   **D** dream

Written Response

SHORT RESPONSE *Write three or four sentences to answer each question.*

15. Which of the two poems has a more varied rhyme scheme, stanza structure, and meter? Give an example of these devices from each poem to support your answer.

16. What effect does Poe achieve in "A Dream Within a Dream" by repeating the statement in lines 10–11 as a question at the end of the poem?

EXTENDED RESPONSE *Write two or three paragraphs to answer this question.*

17. What might the grains of sand and the driftwood symbolize in the two poems? Support your ideas with details from the poems.

GO ON

485

---

11. A *is correct.* *The speaker and his friends have been discussing past losses in the preceding passage. B is incorrect because "wasted lives" is too extreme a description of the losses implied. C is incorrect because the speaker implies that normal life, not sinister forces, is responsible for the losses. D is incorrect because desire for adventure may describe the ships' experiences, but not the people's.*

12. C *is correct.* *"Fancies" connotes mildness and "floating" suggests moving through air or water. A and B are incorrect because their connotations of violence are at odds with the image. D is incorrect because a crackling fire does not float.*

13. C *is correct.* *"Rattling" contains onomatopoeia. The other choices contain no onomatopoeic words.*

14. B *is correct.* *The seashore is in lines 12–24 of "A Dream Within a Dream" and throughout "The Fire of Driftwood." A and C are incorrect because "A Dream Within a Dream" does not describe a farmhouse or a campfire. D is incorrect because "The Fire of Driftwood" does not describe a dream.*

Written Response

Possible short responses:

15. *The rhyme scheme, stanza structure, and meter of "A Dream Within a Dream" vary. "The Fire of Driftwood" has a consistent abab rhyme scheme, iambic tetrameter, and four-line stanzas. Accept all accurate examples.*

16. *Some students will say that the repetition calls attention to the speaker's hopelessness and emphasizes the idea that life is a dream within a dream. Others may say that turning the statement into a question offers a ray of hope.*

Possible extended response:

17. *The grains of sand may symbolize hopes for the future. The speaker tries to grasp them, but cannot save even one (lines 21–22). The grains of sand may also symbolize the passage of time, which people are powerless to stop. The driftwood may symbolize wrecked friendships and the loss of old dreams. Driftwood comes from the wrecks of ships, and, like old friendships, is faded by time. The driftwood may also symbolize the possibility that past losses can be used productively in the present or future, much as driftwood is used to build fires.*

Writing & Grammar

1. **C is correct.** Complicated *is a participle. A is incorrect because* industrious *is an adjective that is not a aparticiple. B is incorrect because the adverb* often *is grammatically identical to* well. *D is incorrect because* sweet *is an adjective that is not a participle.*

2. **A is correct.** Exceptional memory *and* complex language system *are parallel constructions. B, C, and D are incorrect because in each case the two main sentence elements are grammatically different constructions.*

3. **B is correct.** *The clause* which scientists have studied in great detail *modifies the noun* memory. *A and D are simple sentences containing only one clause. C is incorrect because* To learn about the honeybee's short-term memory *is an infinitive phrase, not an adjective clause.*

4. **B is correct.** *The parallel construction is in* remembers where, knows when, *and* seeks out. *A is incorrect because* will seek out *is not parallel in tense to the other two verbs. C is incorrect because one of the three verbs is active and the other two are participial. D is incorrect because the participle* Remembering, *the present-tense verb* know, *and the future-tense verb* will seek *are not parallel.*

Writing & Grammar

DIRECTIONS *Read this passage and answer the questions that follow.*

> (1) The honeybee is well known for its production of honey and beeswax. (2) But it is also esteemed for its exceptional memory and its language system, which is complex. (3) The honeybee has an excellent short-term memory. (4) It remembers where the best food sources are, knows when their quality is best, and they will seek out these sources. (5) The honeybee locates these food sources by remembering the color and scent of the flowers. (6) The honeybee forms a short-term memory of the flower's color. (7) It converts this initial memory to a long-term memory through a biological process. (8) Even after winter hibernation, these foragers go right to the flowers they visited the summer before. (9) One group of honeybees was even able to fly through a maze!

1. How might you add a participle to sentence 1?

   A Change "The honeybee" to "The industrious honeybee."

   B Change "is well known" to "is often known."

   C Change "its production" to "its complicated production."

   D Change "honey and beeswax" to "sweet honey and beeswax."

2. How might you best rewrite sentence 2 to make its elements parallel?

   A But it is also renowned for its exceptional memory and complex language system.

   B But it is also renowned for its exceptional memory; also, its language system is complex.

   C But it is also renowned for its exceptional memory and has a language system that is complex.

   D But it is also renowned for its memory, which is exceptional, and it has a complex language system.

3. How might you add details to sentence 3 by using an adjective clause?

   A The small honeybee has an excellent short-term memory.

   B The honeybee has an excellent short-term memory, which scientists have studied in great detail.

   C To learn about the honeybee's short-term memory, scientists have studied it in great detail.

   D Scientists have carefully studied the honeybee's excellent short-term memory.

4. How might you best rewrite sentence 4 to make its elements parallel?

   A It remembers where the best food sources are and knows when their quality is best and will seek out these sources.

   B It remembers where the best food sources are, knows when their quality is best, and seeks out these sources.

   C It remembers the best food locations, knowing when their quality is best, seeking out these sources.

   D Remembering the best food sources, they know when their quality is best, and they will seek out these sources.

486

DIFFERENTIATED INSTRUCTION

FOR ENGLISH LEARNERS

Review Academic Vocabulary On the board, list the academic vocabulary terms shown in italics. Then give the examples in random order and have students classify them. Elicit additional examples from students.

- *repetition (sound devices):* "While I weep— while I weep!" (line 18, Poe)

- *symbol:* the driftwood in "The Fire of Driftwood" (symbol of life)

- *onomatopoeia (sound devices):* "rustling" (line 28, Longfellow)

- *alliteration (sound devices):* "Grains of the golden sand" (line 15, Poe)

- *meter:* iambic tetrameter, as in "The Fire of Driftwood"

5. How might you add details to sentence 5 by using an adjective clause?

  A The honeybee dutifully locates these food sources by remembering the color and scent of the flowers.

  B The honeybee locates these food sources by remembering the rich color and aromatic scent of the flowers.

  C The honeybee locates these food sources by remembering the color and scent of the flowers that provide the best pollen and nectar.

  D The honeybee locates these food sources by remembering the best pollen and nectar food sources and the color and scent of the flowers.

6. How might you change sentence 6 to include a participial phrase?

  A In its approach to the flower, the honeybee forms a short-term memory of its color.

  B As it approaches the flower, the honeybee forms a short-term memory of its color.

  C The honeybee approaches the flower and forms a short-term memory of its color.

  D Approaching the flower, the honeybee forms a short-term memory of its color.

7. How might you add details to sentence 7 by using an adjective clause?

  A It converts this initial memory to a long-term memory by cleverly using a biological process.

  B Like many mammals, it converts this initial memory to long-term memory through a biological process.

  C It converts this initial memory to long-term memory through a biological process that is similar to memory formation in higher mammals.

  D Through a biological process, it converts this initial memory to a long-term memory and uses it to navigate to various food sources.

8. How might you add a participle to sentence 8?

  A Change "winter hibernation" to "a long, cold hibernation."

  B Change "these foragers" to "these emerging foragers."

  C Change "go right to the flowers" to "go directly to the flowers."

  D Change "they visited the summer before" to "they remember from last summer."

9. How might you add a participial phrase to sentence 9?

  A One group of honeybees even followed a trail of dots and was able to fly through a maze!

  B Following a trail of dots, one group of honeybees was even able to fly through a maze!

  C A trail of dots was used by one group of honeybees to learn how to fly through a maze!

  D One large group of honeybees followed a trail of dots through a maze!

487

5. C *is correct.* *The clause* that provide the best pollen and nectar *modifies the noun* flowers. A *is incorrect because* dutifully *is an adverb.* B *is incorrect because* rich *and* aromatic *are individual adjectives, not an adjective clause.* D *is incorrect because it adds another direct object, not an adjective clause.*

6. D *is correct.* Approaching *is a participle and* approaching the flower *is a participial phrase.* A *is incorrect because* In its approach to the flower *is a prepositional, not participial, phrase.* B *is incorrect because* As it approaches the flower *is a subordinate clause.* C *is incorrect because* approaches the flower and *is part of a compound predicate, not a phrase.*

7. C *is correct.* *The clause* that is similar to memory formation in higher mammals *modifies the noun* process. *Choices* A, B, *and* D *are incorrect because their subordinate clauses are all adverb clauses that modify the verb* converts.

8. B *is correct.* Emerging *is a present participle.* A *is incorrect because* long, cold *is a non-participial adjective phrase.* C *is incorrect because* directly *is a non-participial adverb.* D *is incorrect because* remember *is a verb and* from last summer *is a prepositional phrase, not a participial phrase.*

9. B *is correct.* Following a trail of dots *is a participial phrase.* A *is incorrect because* followed a trail of dots *is not a phrase but part of a compound predicate.* C *is incorrect because* to learn how to fly through a maze *is an infinitive clause, not a participial phrase, and* was used by one group of honeybees *is the main predicate of the sentence, not a phrase.* D *is incorrect because no phrase has been added to the original sentence.*

FOR ENGLISH LEARNERS

Assessment Support: Participles and Parallelism

- Review with students that a participle is a verb form that is used as an adjective and ends with *-ed* or *-ing*. A participle modifies a noun or pronoun.

- Ask students to identify participles in lines 2 and 7 of "The Fire of Driftwood" (*looking* and *dismantled*).

- Review that parallelism is the repetition of words or phrases in the same grammatical form to link ideas; for example, "It's new, it's cool, it's here!"

- Have students find examples of parallelism in lines 19–22 of "A Dream Within a Dream." (*O God! can I not grasp / O God! can I not save; Them with a tighter clasp? / One from the piteous wave?*)

INTRODUCE *GREAT READS*

In Unit 2, students have discussed a number of big questions. Invite students to tell which question they found most intriguing and why, and then focus attention on the four that appear on pages 488–489. Discuss the recommended books and their summaries, pointing out how each connects to the related question. Encourage students to choose one or more of these "great reads" to read independently.

ℹ️ ClassZone.com

To find additional books that match students' interests and ability levels, visit the Literature Center at **ClassZone.com**.

Ideas for Independent Reading

Continue exploring the Questions of the Times with these additional works.

Is the price of progress ever TOO HIGH?

Rip Van Winkle and Other Stories
by Washington Irving

Behind the high jinks and folklore of the stories in this collection, there lurks a mingled sense of wonder and worry at the rapid changes taking place in America in the early 19th century. In the title tale, for example, Rip Van Winkle falls asleep in a British colony and wakes 20 years later in a new nation, his village's statue of King George replaced with one of George Washington. With insight and humor, Irving makes a profound social comment on the changes taking place in his time.

The Last of the Mohicans
by James Fenimore Cooper

The hero of this story, Natty Bumppo, lives on the borderline between two cultures—admired by both Indians and whites, but truly at home with neither. Here, Natty and his Indian friend Chingachgook escort two British maidens through hostile territory during the French and Indian War. Breathtaking chases and gun battles ensue. Yet through the course of the story a deeper theme emerges: that the United States, in its desire for wealth, may have forsaken the rewards of living in harmony with nature.

Is it patriotic to protest one's GOVERNMENT?

Uncle Tom's Cabin
by Harriet Beecher Stowe

Written toward the end of the romantic period, Stowe's novel changed history. Appalled by the institution of slavery, Stowe set out to make whites see slaves as human beings—mothers, fathers, children, *people* with hearts and souls like any other. Her work became immensely popular and did in fact influence opinions and garner support for the abolitionist movement. Indeed, the novel had so great an impact that it has often been cited as one of the causes of the Civil War.

The Night Thoreau Spent in Jail
by Jerome Lawrence and Robert E. Lee

Issues of moral and civic responsibility take center stage in this play dramatizing the risks Thoreau took to follow his conscience. As the curtain rises, Thoreau is behind bars—his punishment for committing an act of civil disobedience. When Ralph Waldo Emerson visits, Thoreau challenges him to defy a government that fosters injustice.

The Poetry of John Greenleaf Whittier: A Readers' Edition
by John Greenleaf Whittier

John Greenleaf Whittier was committed to using poetry to bring about social reform. This anthology includes several poems that explore the evils of slavery. One such poem, "Ichabod," savaged real-life senator Daniel Webster for his support of the Missouri Compromise and the Fugitive Slave Act.

488

Does everyone have a "DARK SIDE"?

The Fall of the House of Usher and Other Writings
by Edgar Allan Poe

Does everyone have a "dark side"? Over and over again, Poe answered that question with a resounding yes. In so doing, he helped establish the modes of horror and fantasy, which to this day dominate much of American culture. For an overview of the best of Poe's writing, this edition is the book to read. Murderous delusions, decadent appetites, and unspeakable cruelty pepper the stories and poems found here.

The House of the Seven Gables
by Nathaniel Hawthorne

This gothic romance tells of the Pyncheon family (owners of "the house of the seven gables"), whose ancestor Colonel Pyncheon has cursed them with his wicked deeds. In the book's preface, Hawthorne conveys its theme: "The wrong-doing of one generation lives into the successive ones, and … becomes a pure and uncontrollable mischief."

American Gothic Tales
edited by Joyce Carol Oates

Oates's anthology of haunting tales shows the far reaches of the gothic imagination in American literature. The collection includes short stories from over 40 of the best American horror writers of the past 200 years, ranging from Washington Irving to Stephen King.

Where do people look for TRUTH?

The Portable Thoreau
by Henry David Thoreau

An icon of individualism, Henry David Thoreau looked for the truth in two main places: nature and himself. Generations of readers have concluded not only that those are good places to search for the truth, but also that Thoreau—for all his peculiarities—did a fine job of finding it. This edition contains the full text of *Walden,* as well as poems, notebooks, journal entries, and essays such as "Civil Disobedience." These works allow readers to see past the confident sage of Walden to the prickly, affectionate, politically motivated man beneath.

The Essential Transcendentalists
edited by Richard G. Geldard

America's best transcendentalist thinkers and writers grappled with many questions of their day: What is woman's role in society? When and how should a person protest the government? How can we live ethical lives? Where can one find the truth? The works in this collection explore these and many other ideas as relevant today as they were nearly 200 years ago.

489

Preview Unit Goals

This page presents an overview of the skills and strategies covered in this unit. Explain to students that they can get more from their reading by previewing. Then ask them to skim the page to preview the skills that they will learn. Note that each strand or category of skill is color-coded on this page and throughout the unit.

Model the strategy of copying the Academic Vocabulary and writing a preliminary definition for each term. Suggest that students use a journal or a notebook for this purpose. Encourage them to use the terms in discussions and in writing. Also urge students to revisit each term throughout the unit and to refine its meaning.

ADDITIONAL UNIT GOALS

These skills will be taught in this unit but are not the major focus of the unit:

Literary Analysis
- Analyze characteristics of poetry (including free verse), a slave narrative, a short story, public documents, letters, and a diary
- Understand Whitman and Dickinson as transitional poets
- Read and understand a timeline
- Analyze point of view

Reading
- Develop strategies for reading poetry and a narrative
- Analyze main ideas and supporting details

Writing and Grammar
- Compare the works of Whitman and Dickinson
- Synthesize information about a historical period

Speaking, Listening, and Viewing
- Create a dialogue between Whitman and Dickinson
- Present an oral critique of a painting
- Use repetition as a rhetorical device

Vocabulary
- Use general context to understand word meaning

Included in this unit: R1.2, R2.1, R2.5, R3.2, R3.3, R3.4, R3.5, R3.7, W1.1, W1.2, W1.4, W1.5, W1.9, W2.1, W2.2, W2.3, W2.6, LC1.1, LS1.3, LS1.10, LS1.14

CALIFORNIA

Preview Unit Goals

LITERARY ANALYSIS	• Understand the historical and cultural contexts of romanticism and realism; understand realism as a literary movement
	• Analyze tone
	• Analyze and evaluate free verse
	• Analyze elements of style, including tone, sentence structure, figurative language, and dialogue
	• Analyze the styles of Whitman and Dickinson
	• Analyze narrative elements, including conflict and characterization
	• Analyze the relationship between audience and form and the ways in which form influences a message
READING	• Analyze primary sources
	• Analyze author's purpose and beliefs; analyze structure of a work
	• Take notes; synthesize information
WRITING AND GRAMMAR	• Make effective word choices; use vivid verbs
	• Use language that conveys tone
	• Write a biographical narrative
SPEAKING, LISTENING, AND VIEWING	• Compare and contrast print and film versions of a work
	• Produce a video documentary
VOCABULARY	• Use knowledge of Latin roots to understand word meaning
ACADEMIC VOCABULARY	• romanticism • free verse • primary source
	• realism • style

Literature and Reading Center
Writing Center
Vocabulary Center

490

DIFFERENTIATED INSTRUCTION

FOR ENGLISH LEARNERS

Academic Vocabulary Use the copy master to help students learn the Academic Vocabulary.

1. Read aloud each Academic Vocabulary term on page 490 and have students find it on their copy masters.

2. Discuss the meaning or example shown on the copy master.

3. Have students work in small groups to complete the remaining activities.

Additional Academic Vocabulary Use the copy master to help students learn academic words they will use in subsequent lessons and on the Assessment Practice. Follow the same procedure as for the Academic Vocabulary copy master.

 RESOURCE MANAGER—Copy Masters
Academic Vocabulary p. 11
Additional Academic Vocabulary p. 12

From Romanticism to Realism

Frederick Douglass

1855–1870
AN AGE OF TRANSITION

- Brilliant Mavericks: Whitman and Dickinson
- Literature of the Civil War

491

For help in planning this unit, see

R RESOURCE MANAGER UNIT 3
pp. 1–13

INTRODUCE THE UNIT

Call students' attention to the pictures on this page. Explain that the large picture, *Union Soldiers Fighting in the Field,* is a painting by Albert Bierstadt. Point out that it depicts the Civil War, a turning point in American life, and that students will be reading literature of the Civil War later in this unit.

Ask students if they know of Frederick Douglass (c. 1817–1895), the author shown in the smaller picture. Explain that Douglass was born into slavery but escaped to freedom as a young man. He became active in the antislavery cause as a writer, editor, and speaker. Tell students that they will read an excerpt from his autobiography later in this unit. Also note that students can read more about Douglass on page 536.

About the Art Artist Albert Bierstadt (1830–1902) was born in Germany but came to the United States with his family at the age of two. As an artist, he gained fame for his large, inspiring landscapes of the American West as well as for his Civil War scenes. *Union Soldiers Fighting in the Field* realistically portrays Union soldiers taking aim at Confederate cavalrymen on the far side of the field. The anonymity of the soldiers and the setting makes the viewer feel that these soldiers could be anyone, in any place. The landscape is idyllic and the cottage appears peaceful; in reality, however, the scene is one of destruction.

Unit Resources

PRINT RESOURCES

R RESOURCE MANAGER UNIT 3

T BEST PRACTICES TOOLKIT

S STANDARDS LESSON FILE

CALIFORNIA ASSESSMENT FILE

GRAMMAR FOR WRITING

TECH RESOURCES

⊘ EasyPlanner DVD-ROM

⊘ Write*Smart* CD-ROM

ⓘ ClassZone.com

⊘ Audio Anthology CD

ⓘ Multi-Language Academic Vocabulary Online

⊘ eEdition DVD-ROM & Online

ⓘ McDougal Littell Assessment System

⊘ Test Generator CD-ROM

⊘ Media*Smart* DVD-ROM

⊘ Literature in Context DVD-ROM

UNIT 3
Standards

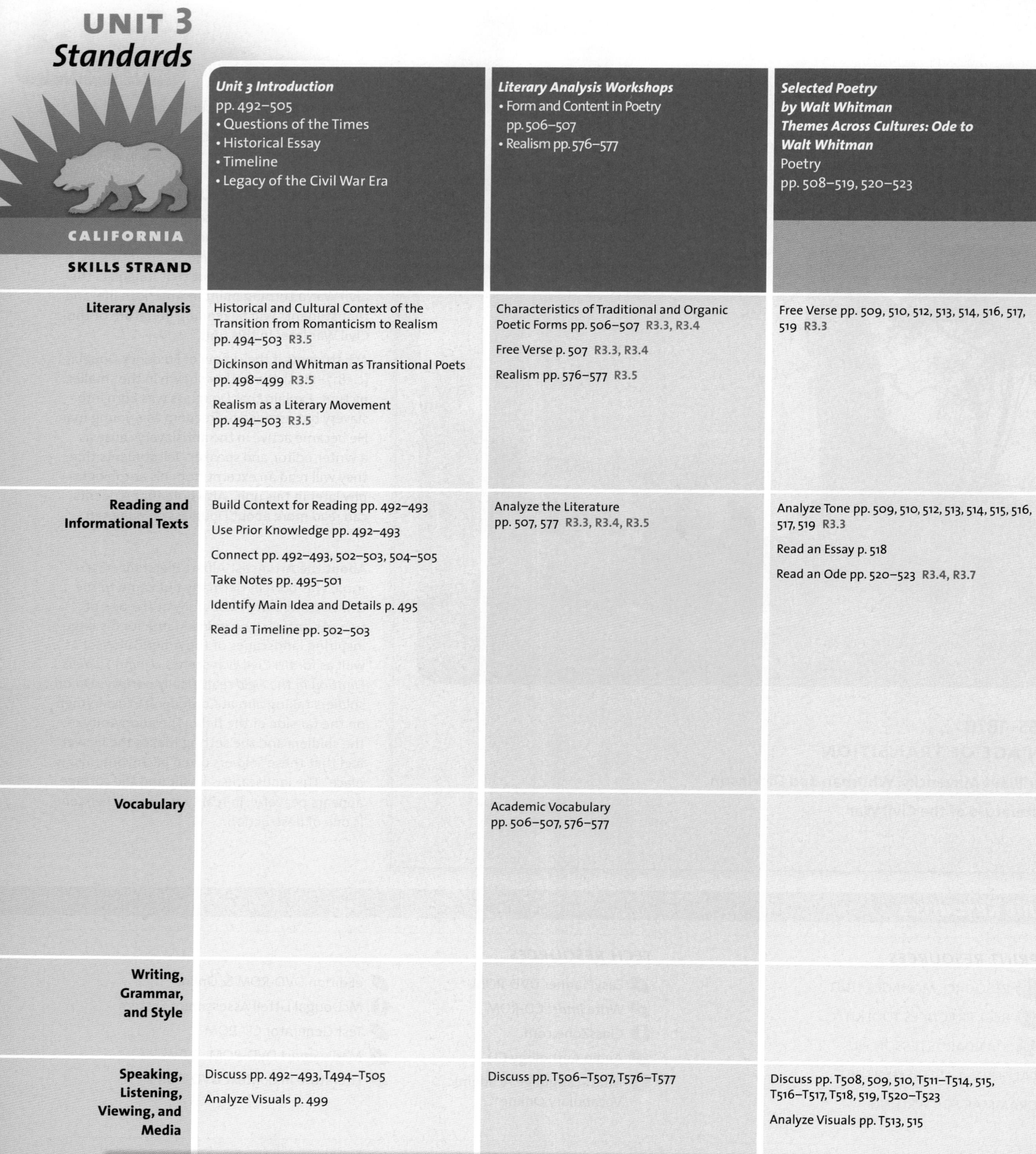

CALIFORNIA

SKILLS STRAND

	Unit 3 Introduction pp. 492–505 • Questions of the Times • Historical Essay • Timeline • Legacy of the Civil War Era	*Literary Analysis Workshops* • Form and Content in Poetry pp. 506–507 • Realism pp. 576–577	*Selected Poetry by Walt Whitman Themes Across Cultures: Ode to Walt Whitman* Poetry pp. 508–519, 520–523
Literary Analysis	Historical and Cultural Context of the Transition from Romanticism to Realism pp. 494–503 R3.5 Dickinson and Whitman as Transitional Poets pp. 498–499 R3.5 Realism as a Literary Movement pp. 494–503 R3.5	Characteristics of Traditional and Organic Poetic Forms pp. 506–507 R3.3, R3.4 Free Verse p. 507 R3.3, R3.4 Realism pp. 576–577 R3.5	Free Verse pp. 509, 510, 512, 513, 514, 516, 517, 519 R3.3
Reading and Informational Texts	Build Context for Reading pp. 492–493 Use Prior Knowledge pp. 492–493 Connect pp. 492–493, 502–503, 504–505 Take Notes pp. 495–501 Identify Main Idea and Details p. 495 Read a Timeline pp. 502–503	Analyze the Literature pp. 507, 577 R3.3, R3.4, R3.5	Analyze Tone pp. 509, 510, 512, 513, 514, 515, 516, 517, 519 R3.3 Read an Essay p. 518 Read an Ode pp. 520–523 R3.4, R3.7
Vocabulary		Academic Vocabulary pp. 506–507, 576–577	
Writing, Grammar, and Style			
Speaking, Listening, Viewing, and Media	Discuss pp. 492–493, T494–T505 Analyze Visuals p. 499	Discuss pp. T506–T507, T576–T577	Discuss pp. T508, 509, 510, T511–T514, 515, T516–T517, T518, 519, T520–T523 Analyze Visuals pp. T513, 515

491A

Standards Designations R = Reading W = Writing LC = Language Conventions LS = Listening and Speaking T = Teacher's Edition page

Selected Poetry by Emily Dickinson Poetry pp. 524–534	from **Narrative of the Life of Frederick Douglass, an American Slave** Slave Narrative pp. 536–549	from **Incidents in the Life of a Slave Girl** Slave Narrative pp. 550–561
	Lexile: 970 *Fry: 7* *Dale-Chall: 6.1*	*Lexile: 810* *Fry: 6* *Dale-Chall: 5.9*
Author's Style pp. 525, 526, 529, 530, 531, 532, 534 R3.3, R3.4	Style pp. 537, 538, 541, 542, 544, 548 R3.3	Narrative Elements pp. 551, 552, 554, 556, 557, 558 R3.5
Strategies for Reading Dickinson's Poetry pp. 525, 526, 528, 529, 530, 531, 532, 534 R3.3, R3.4 Read a Letter p. 533	Analyze Author's Purpose pp. 537, 541, 543, 547, 548	Strategies for Reading a Narrative pp. 551, 554, 557, 558 Read a Poem and a Traditional Spiritual pp. 560–561
	Writing Prompt p. 549 W2.3 Vivid Verbs pp. 541, 549 LC1.1	Writing Prompt p. 559 W1.2, W1.5 Adjectives That Establish Tone pp. 554, 559 W1.9
Discuss pp. T524, 525, T526–T527, 528, T529, 530, T531–T533, 534, T535 Analyze Visuals p. 526	Discuss pp. T536, 537, T538–T547, 548 Analyze Visuals pp. 538, 540, 544	Discuss pp. T550, 551, T552–T557, 558, T560–T561 Analyze Visuals p. 552

	Linked Selections		An Occurrence at Owl Creek Bridge
	The Gettysburg Address/The Emancipation Proclamation Speech/Proclamation pp. 562–569	*Voices from the Civil War* Letters, Diary Entry, Speech pp. 570–575	Short Story pp. 580–594
	Lexile: 1170/1990 Fry: 8/11 Dale-Chall: 7.0/9.4		Lexile: 1000 Fry: 9 Dale-Chall: 6.9
Literary Analysis	Audience and Form pp. 563, 564, 566, 568 R2.1		Point of View pp. 581, 582, 585, 586, 588, 592, 593
Reading and Informational Texts	Analyze an Author's Beliefs pp. 563, 564, 567, 568 R2.5	Analyze Primary Sources pp. 570, 571, 572, 573, 574, 575 R2.5 Synthesize p. 575 R2.5	Analyze Structure pp. 581, 585, 586, 593
Vocabulary			Word Acquisition pp. 581, T581, 594 Context Clues p. T581 Latin Roots (*lud*) p. 594 R1.2
Writing, Grammar, and Style	Writing Prompt p. 569 W1.1, W1.5, W2.2 Rhetorical Devices (Repetition) pp. 564, 569 W1.4, W1.9		
Speaking, Listening, Viewing, and Media	Discuss pp. T562, 563, T564–T567, 568 Analyze Visuals p. T565	Discuss pp. 570, T571–T574, 575	Discuss pp. T580, 581, T582–T592, 593, T595 Analyze Visuals pp. 582, 587, 591

Media Study: *from An Occurrence at Owl Creek Bridge* Film Clips pp. 596–597	**Wrap-Ups** • Brilliant Mavericks p. 535 • Literature of the Civil War p. 595	**Writing Workshop:** **Biographical Narrative** pp. 598–605	**Skills Assessed on the Unit 3 Test:**
			Literary Analysis • Analyze narrative elements • Analyze elements of an author's style, including free verse
		Analyze a Biographical Narrative pp. 599–600, 604	**Reading and Informational Texts** • Analyze tone • Analyze an author's beliefs
Academic Vocabulary (Film) p. 596			**Vocabulary** • Apply knowledge of Latin roots to help determine word meaning • Use general context to understand word meaning
	Write to Compare p. 535 R3.3, R3.4, W2.2 Write to Synthesize p. 595 W2.2, LS1.3	Write a Biographical Narrative pp. 598–605 W2.1 Clichés p. 604 W1.9 Verb Tense Shifts p. 604 LC1.1	**Writing, Grammar, and Style** • Write a biographical narrative • Establish tone • Use vivid verbs • Additional writing and grammar skills
Discuss pp. 596–597 Compare and Contrast Point of View in Film and Print Versions of a Story pp. 596–597 LS1.14 Understand the Filmmaker's Process p. 596 LS1.14	Present a Dialogue p. 535 Critique a Painting p. 595	Discuss pp. 598–600 Produce a Video Documentary p. 605 W2.6, LS1.10	

For additional lesson planning help, see **Easy Planner DVD-ROM.**

CALIFORNIA	ASSESS PRIOR KNOWLEDGE **Diagnostic**	ONGOING ASSESSMENT **Reteaching**
BEGINNING OF UNIT		
Unit Opener	Preview Unit Goals, **TE** p. 490	
UNIT LESSONS		
Before every lesson	Big Question activity, **SE** Preteach vocabulary, **TE**	Check Understanding, **TE**
During every lesson		Annotations, **SE** Check Understanding, **TE** Tiered Discussion Prompts, **TE**
After every lesson		Post Reading pages, **SE** Assess and Reteach, **TE** Reading Check, **RM** Selection Tests A and B/C, **AF**
END OF UNIT		
Writing Workshop	Checklist, **SE** p. 604 Rubric for Evaluation, **RM** p. 182	Assess and Reteach, **TE** p. 604
Publishing with Technology	Criteria, **TE** p. 605	For reteaching options, see **TE** p. 605
Assessment	Assessment Practice, **SE** pp. 606–611	Unit Test, **AF** **MLAS**

For systematic instruction of grammar, use *Grammar for Writing*.

Key to Abbreviations:
SE = Student's Edition
TE = Teacher's Edition
RM = Resource Manager
AF = Assessment File
MLAS = McDougal Littell Assessment System

Universal Access

	Strategic Reader	Benchmark	Advanced Learner	English Learner	Students with Disabilities
SE STUDENT'S EDITION					
Vocabulary strategy instruction	✔	✔	✔	✔	✔
Instructional annotations	✔	✔	✔	✔	✔
English/Spanish glossary				✔	
TE TEACHER'S EDITION					
Skill annotation support	✔	✔	✔	✔	✔
Tiered discussion prompts	✔	✔	✔	✔	✔
Differentiated instruction	✔	✔	✔	✔	✔
R RESOURCE MANAGER					
Selection summaries in four languages	✔	✔	✔	✔	✔
Skill copy masters in English and Spanish	✔				
Vocabulary preteaching and support	✔				✔
Additional leveled selection questions	✔	✔	✔	✔	✔
Question support	✔	✔	✔	✔	✔
Writing support	✔	✔	✔	✔	✔
Extension activities		✔	✔		
AF ASSESSMENT FILE					
Leveled selection and unit tests	✔	✔	✔	✔	✔
S STANDARDS LESSON FILE					
Leveled and reteaching copy masters	✔	✔	✔	✔	✔
BEST PRACTICES TOOLKIT					
Strategy bank	✔	✔	✔	✔	✔
Graphic organizers	✔	✔	✔	✔	✔
TECHNOLOGY					
WriteSmart Rubrics and student models	✔	✔	✔	✔	✔
Audio Anthology CD	✔			✔	✔
CLASSZONE					
Instructional centers	✔	✔	✔	✔	✔
Audio summaries of selections	✔			✔	✔
Multilanguage glossary				✔	

Questions of the Times

Read aloud the questions on pages 492 and 493 and the paragraphs that follow them. Open the discussion of each idea by having students respond to the questions that conclude each paragraph. Use these notes to prompt further discussion of the ideas.

What DIVIDES *a nation?*

Explain that students will learn more about the issues leading up to the Civil War when they read the Historical Essay (pages 494–501). For now, have students brainstorm a list of issues that divide Americans today and then rank their importance. Extend the discussion by asking

- What issues unite Americans today?
- Which are more powerful, the divisive issues or the uniting issues?

Is anything worth DYING FOR?

Invite students to identify causes for which they might risk their lives; have them explain their reasons. Challenge the class to create a master list of characteristics that make a cause great and a sacrifice worthwhile.

Questions of the Times

DISCUSS After reading these questions and talking about them with a partner, share your views with the class as a whole. Then read on to explore the ways in which writers of the Civil War era dealt with the same issues.

What DIVIDES *a nation?*

In the years leading up to the Civil War, the agrarian South, whose economy depended upon slave labor, and the industrialized North, which became increasingly opposed to slavery, began to see each other as enemies. Slavery was one of many issues that divided Americans of the day. What issues or beliefs typically cause conflict between citizens? What divides Americans today?

Is anything worth DYING FOR?

During the Civil War, boys and young men on both sides of the conflict marched off to war with visions of becoming heroes in the service of a great cause. Hundreds of thousands never returned home. Was their sacrifice worthwhile? Would you ever be willing to risk your life for a flag, a group, or an idea?

492

Why do people
BREAK RULES?

Poets Walt Whitman and Emily Dickinson broke well-established rules about poetic form and content, and today they are celebrated for their ingenuity. Yet, during their lives few readers recognized their genius because their work was radically different from the popular poetry of the day. Why do you think people break the rules if they will not be rewarded for it? Do artists, especially, tend to break the rules?

Is it important to
FACE REALITY?

After the horrors of the Civil War, romantic attitudes no longer captured the spirit of America. Instead, artists and writers turned to a new movement known as realism, which reflected a different view of life—unsentimental, honest, and often harsh or even ugly. Do you think writers and artists should deal with life's realities or take us away from them?

Why do people
BREAK RULES?

Ask students to give examples that distinguish between breaking rules for a constructive purpose and breaking rules for a destructive purpose. Then challenge students to cite cases in which people who are not artists—perhaps including the students themselves—break rules. Discuss positive and negative effects of such rule-breaking. Elicit that rewards are not always material things (such as money or trophies), nor is genius always recognized in a person's lifetime.

Is it important to
FACE REALITY?

Review key characteristics of romanticism, challenging students to name writers and works that they associate with that movement. Then ask students to define *face reality* in their own words. Focus on the question in the text by asking students to cite examples of realistic art and escapist art and to defend their preferences—realism versus escapism—in art and entertainment.

493

OBJECTIVES

- understand the historical context of the transition from romanticism to realism, the poetry of Whitman and Dickinson, and Civil War writings
- understand Whitman and Dickinson as transitional poets
- understand realism as a literary movement
- take notes by charting main ideas and details

 R3.5

To provide a motivating introduction to this unit and to give students a sense of time and place for the transition from romanticism to realism, see

💿 Literature in Context DVD

The following essay (pages 494–501) provides students with a historical context for the Unit 3 reading selections. It presents a brief overview of significant events occurring during the time period of 1855–1870 and introduces key people, places, and ideas of the times.

To get started, read and discuss the opening paragraph on page 494. Ask students how they would have answered the questions that appear early in the paragraph if they had been Northerners at that time and then if they had been Southerners.

READING STRATEGY

■ **PREVIEW**

Have students preview the historical essay by reading the **KEY IDEAS** and by skimming the heads, boldfaced terms, and **Taking Notes** side-column features. Ask volunteers to summarize what the essay is about.

About the Art This image is a detail from Mort Künstler's painting *Battle for the Shenandoah* (1982), which captures an 1864 campaign known for combat among soldiers on horseback.

From Romanticism to Realism
1855–1870

An Age of Transition

The Civil War was a violent clash, not just of armies, but of ideas. Who was right, and who was wrong? What did it mean to be an American? Was any price too high to pay to keep the nation whole? There was nothing theoretical about the conflict—real people died, hundreds of thousands of them: fathers, sons, and brothers. But the war began before a single shot was ever fired. Writers served as its first soldiers, and the battle lines were drawn in ink.

DIFFERENTIATED INSTRUCTION

FOR STRATEGIC READERS
Preteach Academic Vocabulary

- *regional,* "having to do with a particular part of the earth's surface"
- *financial,* "having to do with how money is managed"
- *economy,* "the production of goods and services in a nation or other group"
- *agricultural,* "having to do with farming"
- *export,* "the practice of sending things to be sold in a place where they are not made"

- *sidestep,* "to attempt to avoid"
- *confrontation,* "a clash or conflict"
- *ballots,* "votes"
- *abolitionist,* "one who works to bring an end to slavery"
- *sacking,* "the destructive stealing of things from a town"

Use this copy master to help students take notes on the essay, pages 494–501:

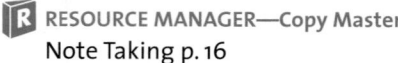 RESOURCE MANAGER—Copy Master
Note Taking p. 16

Emerging Realism: Historical Context

R3.5

KEY IDEAS The central influence on literature of this period was the conflict between North and South that ended in the Civil War. Although romantic attitudes helped push the nation into war, four years of bitter fighting led to a new realism.

A Cultural Divide

"A house divided against itself cannot stand," wrote **Abraham Lincoln** in 1858, referring to the bitterly divided United States. Since colonial times, the South and the North had shown strong regional differences. Most of the manufacturing and financial services of the nation were located in the North, whose economy was based primarily on trade and industry. In contrast, the South had developed an agricultural way of life—growing cotton, tobacco, and sugar cane for export to the North and Europe—that relied on the labor of nearly four million slaves. Most Southerners opposed any interference with slavery by the federal government because of the region's economic dependence on it, the widespread fear of slave unrest, and the belief that states should control their own affairs.

SLAVERY DIVIDES THE NATION Although national political leaders tried to sidestep the slavery issue, growing Northern opposition to slavery and its expansion into the West made confrontation inevitable. In the 1850s, several events moved the country to its breaking point. In Kansas, the vote over whether to join the Union as a free state or a slave state turned deadly when gun-toting mobs swarmed over the border from Missouri to cast illegal ballots in favor of slavery. Continuing violence between proslavery and antislavery settlers led people to begin calling the territory **Bleeding Kansas.** Abolitionist **John Brown** played a role in Bleeding Kansas in 1856, killing five proslavery men as revenge for the sacking of the antislavery town of Lawrence. Three years later, Brown again shocked the nation when he led a bloody raid on the federal arsenal at Harpers Ferry, hoping to spark a slave uprising. Writer **Henry David Thoreau** called Brown "an angel of light"; but fellow writer **Nathaniel Hawthorne** retorted, "No man was ever more justly hanged."

CONFLICT REACHES THE GOVERNMENT Even the floor of the U.S. Senate became a battleground. In 1856, Massachusetts senator Charles Sumner gave an impassioned speech against slavery, berating his colleagues for two days for their support of slavery. A few days later, Carolina congressman Preston S. Brooks retaliated by attacking Sumner with his cane, beating the Massachusetts senator unconscious. When writer **William Cullen Bryant** heard about the caning, he was outraged. "Has it come to this," he asked in the *New York Evening Post,* "that we must speak with bated breath in the presence of our Southern masters? . . . Are we, too, slaves, slaves for life, a

Battle for the Shenandoah © Mort Künstler, Inc.

> ▶ **TAKING NOTES**
>
> **Outlining** As you read this introduction, use an outline to record main ideas about the historical characteristics and literature of this period. You can use headings, boldfaced terms, and the information in boxes like this one as starting points. (See page R49 in the **Research Handbook** for more help with outlining.)
>
> I. Historical Context
> A. Cultural Divide
>   1. Northern economy based on trade and industry; Southern based on agriculture and slavery
>   2. slavery's expansion west provoked confrontation

ADDITIONAL BACKGROUND
For more on the Civil War era, visit **The Literature Center** at ClassZone.com.

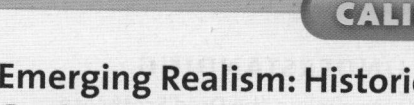
CALIFORNIA

Emerging Realism: Historical Context

KEY IDEAS This section of the essay (pages 495–497) summarizes the important events and political issues—chiefly, slavery and regional economic differences—that led to the Civil War. This section also describes the beginning of the war, whose early battles created a shocking reality for the nation's previously romantic mindset.

TIERED DISCUSSION PROMPTS

Use these prompts to help students understand the ideas in **A Cultural Divide:**

Interpret In what sense was the United States in 1858 "a house divided against itself?" **Possible answer:** *The United States was like a house because it was a large dwelling for many people and should have been unified; it was divided against itself because many people in that "house" upheld slavery at the same time that many other people wanted to see slavery end.*

Synthesize Compare and contrast the divisions in the United States during the pre–Civil War era with divisions that have occurred in later periods. **Possible answer:** *Political divisions in later periods sometimes have been sharp, but they have remained relatively peaceful in comparison to the divisions of the Civil War era.*

FOR ENGLISH LEARNERS

Set a Purpose After introducing the *KEY IDEAS* on this page, have students use the boldfaced terms to help locate important people and events that played roles in the conflict between North and South—that is, in the prelude to the Civil War. Encourage students to read the details to fully understand the boldfaced terms.

FOR ADVANCED LEARNERS/AP

Research and Analyze Present students with this question: "Given the state of the nation in the 1850s, was the Civil War inevitable?" Encourage students not only to reflect upon what they have read but also to do further research to form and support a view. Urge them, as well, to think beyond the simplistic "The South wanted slavery but the North did not," considering the economy of each part of the country and the importance of the

states' rights issue. Have students share their responses and reasoning in a class discussion. If you have students on both sides of the issue, work with them to present a brief debate.

Have students explain the **Dred Scott** case, focusing on (1) why it was harmful to African Americans and (2) how it reflected issues in the United States at that time.

TIERED DISCUSSION PROMPTS

Use these prompts to help students understand the ideas in **The Civil War:**

Restate Why did Lincoln's election cause the southern states to secede? ***Possible answer: The states seceded because of Lincoln's pledge to stop the spread of slavery into the West.***

Analyze How was the Civil War an expression of romanticism at first? How and why did that romantic attitude change? ***Possible answer: At first, people expected a quick, painless war. They had a romantic view of warfare and the people who fought it, and they welcomed the chance to earn glory in (or to be entertained by) battle. Later, when horrific battles such as Bull Run revealed the brutal reality of war, people began to abandon their romantic idealism.***

Synthesize Why would people idealize or romanticize a war in its early stages? ***Possible answer: At the beginning, a war would not have as many casualties as would mount up over time. If many years had passed since the previous war, the current generation would have little experience with war's horrors and therefore might idealize or romanticize what they had read or heard about war.***

---

target for their brutal blows, when we do not comport ourselves to please them?" Meanwhile, newspapers across the South applauded the attack, describing abolitionists as unruly dogs to be collared and disciplined. Such angry name-calling and accusations reflected—and added to—the growing sense on both sides that Northerners and Southerners were no longer simply Americans from different regions, but foreigners and enemies.

In 1857, the Supreme Court entered the fray by hearing the case of **Dred Scott,** a slave whose owner had taken him to spend several years in a free state. Scott argued that living in a free state made him free; the Supreme Court ruled against him. Worse, it went on to say that even free blacks "had no rights which a white man was bound to respect." The *Dred Scott* decision sent shock waves through the already divided nation. Northerners were outraged and alarmed. Was the South's "peculiar institution" of slavery to become the law of the whole land?

SOUTHERN CHIVALRY — ARGUMENT versus CLUB'S.

An 1856 cartoon of Congressman Preston S. Brooks attacking Senator Charles Sumner on the Senate floor.

The Civil War

Ironically, none of these acts led to the final break. Instead, the lawful election in 1860 of a politically moderate U.S. president, Abraham Lincoln ignited war. Enraged at Lincoln's pledge to stop the western spread of slavery, the Southern states seceded to form the **Confederate States of America.**

For a generation that had grown up on the literary ideal of the brave, dashing **Romantic hero,** the booming of Confederate cannons firing on Fort Sumter in the spring of 1861 was a call to glory. Boys and young men rushed off to join the Union or Confederate army. Southerners boasted that a single one of them could lick ten Yankees; Northerners were sure that "Johnny Reb" would turn and run at the first shot. For many, the biggest fear was that the war would end too soon and they would miss their chance to become heroes.

The mood was nearly festive on the sunny July day when fresh Union forces marched south into Virginia to confront the rebels at Bull Run. Soldiers wandered from their lines to pick blackberries and drink cool water from the creek, and the cream of Washington society drove down in carriages with bottles of champagne and picnic baskets to enjoy the spectacle.

REALITY STRIKES By late afternoon, thousands of dead and wounded soldiers lay near the banks of Bull Run. On the losing side, panic-stricken Union soldiers stumbled away from the battlefield, their feet tangling in shawls and parasols that had been dropped by terrified civilians as they fled. The party was over.

> **A Voice from the Times**
>
> *Future years will never know the seething hell and the black infernal background of countless minor scenes and interiors, (not the official surface courteousness of the Generals, not the few great battles) . . . the real war will never get in the books.*
>
> —Walt Whitman

DIFFERENTIATED INSTRUCTION

FOR STRATEGIC READERS

Main Ideas and Supporting Details [paired option] Ask pairs of students to summarize the main idea of the section **The Civil War** in one sentence. ***Possible answer:*** *At the beginning of the Civil War, some people did not take it seriously enough, but their view changed as the realities of battle became evident.* Then have the student pairs write details from the section that support the main idea. *Answers will vary but should address the idealization* *of the war at first, the way in which that view changed, and the great losses that the war ultimately produced.* Ask students to read their main idea sentences aloud; discuss differences among them. Remind students to use their main idea sentence in their outlines.

The blood-soaked **Battle of Bull Run** gave everyone (especially the losing Union side) a taste of the reality of war, but it was only the beginning. Four long years of fighting followed. Names of battle sites became synonymous with death: Shiloh, Antietam, Fredericksburg, Gettysburg, Vicksburg. When the war ended at last, in April 1865, with **General Robert E. Lee's** surrender to **General Ulysses S. Grant** at Appomattox Courthouse, approximately 618,000 men had died—nearly as many as have died in all other wars that the United States has ever fought. Much of the South lay in ruins, scarred by gutted plantation houses, burned bridges, and uprooted railroad lines.

Ideas of the Age

KEY IDEAS Americans in the postwar period embraced notions of freedom and unity. At the same time, they lost their taste for romanticism, having been confronted with the harsh realities of war.

Freedom and Unity

The United States was changed by the Civil War. It had suffered bitterly and was now a wiser, more somber nation. Yet the ideals of America's founders had survived the devastation of war. For the first time, the Declaration of Independence's notions of equality and liberty for all were brought closer to fruition. Slavery was dead—outlawed by Lincoln's bold **Emancipation Proclamation** and the **Thirteenth Amendment** to the Constitution. "We shout for joy that we live to record this righteous decree," said **Frederick Douglass**. "Free Forever!"

The Civil War had divided the country; its end brought the country back together. This time the country was united in a new way. Before the war, people were used to saying "The United States *are . . .* ," with the emphasis on the individual states more than on the united interests of all. After the war, people began saying "The United States *is . . .* ." A group of independent states had become one nation, indivisible, with the goal of liberty for all.

The Civil War changed not only American society but its literary culture as well. In the years following the war, American readers and writers found they had lost their taste for romanticism. Many had witnessed war's grim nature firsthand, and it shaped their view of life. Gallant heroism and adventure no longer suited America's tastes; nor did meditations on the beauty of nature or the worth of the individual. Writing became more honest, unsentimental, and ironic. A new style, **realism,** would predominate in the years to come.

> **A Voice from the Times**
>
> [W]e here highly resolve that these dead shall not have fought in vain—that this nation, under God, shall have a new birth of freedom—and that government of the people, by the people, for the people, shall not perish from the earth.
>
> —Abraham Lincoln

Abraham Lincoln Reading the Emancipation Proclamation Before His Cabinet Members, undated color illustration after painting by Francis Bicknell Carpenter. © Bettmann/Corbis.

Ideas of the Age

KEY IDEAS This section of the essay (page 497) explores the country's postwar focus on freedom, unity, and realism. The text also notes how the Civil War changed literary culture as well as societal tastes.

TIERED DISCUSSION PROMPTS

Use these prompts to help students understand the ideas in **Freedom and Unity:**

Analyze In what sense was the United States "a wiser, more somber nation" after the Civil War? *Possible answer: The United States was "wiser" and "more somber" after the war because Americans then understood more clearly the importance of being a unified nation. In addition, romantic idealizations of nature, adventure, and heroism no longer seemed as believable, and a more realistic view of life took hold.*

Synthesize How might one challenge the idea that the United States was wiser after the Civil War? *Possible answer: Refuters might point out that Reconstruction, the national process of reunification, generally is considered not to have been wisely conducted; in particular, it did not result in equality for African Americans, nor did it heal the bitterness of Southerners.*

About the Art This illustration, based on a painting by Francis Bicknell Carpenter (1830–1900), shows a meeting of Lincoln and his cabinet in September 1862. At that meeting they read the Emancipation Proclamation, which became effective on January 1, 1863.

FOR STRATEGIC READERS
Preteach Academic Vocabulary

- *comport,* "to behave in a certain way"
- *moderate,* "not taking extreme political positions"
- *seceded,* "broke away from membership [in the United States]"
- *festive,* "merry and partylike"
- *cream,* "the most refined people"
- *decree,* "a legal order"

- *independent,* "separate from each other"
- *indivisible,* "unable to be divided"
- *unsentimental,* "having little or no appeal to the emotions"
- *ironic,* "focusing on differences between what is expected and what actually happens"
- *predominate,* "to take and hold control"

FOR ADVANCED LEARNERS/AP

Analyze a Quotation Ask students to think about the quotation from Abraham Lincoln in **A Voice from the Times.** Have them discuss the tone of the comment and its connection to the Civil War. (You might explain that it comes from the Gettysburg Address, which students will read on page 564.) Extend the discussion by asking students why Americans consider Lincoln's words inspiring and relevant even today.

Literature of the Times

KEY IDEAS This section of the essay (pages 498–501) introduces the great American poets Walt Whitman and Emily Dickinson and their literary innovations. The section also surveys the literature of the Civil War, including these genres:

- slave narratives
- diaries and letters
- speeches

The section concludes by introducing the realism of the postwar period, exemplified by Stephen Crane and Ambrose Bierce.

TIERED DISCUSSION PROMPTS

Use these prompts to help students understand the ideas in **Brilliant Mavericks: Whitman and Dickinson:**

Interpret Reread the comment from Ralph Waldo Emerson. What did he want poetry to do? *Possible answer: Emerson wanted poetry to take life as its subject and to be deep without being ornate.*

Analyze How were Whitman and Dickinson alike? How were they unalike? *Possible answer: Whitman and Dickinson were alike in being individualists who broke with previous ideas about poetry. They both were ambitious, as well: Whitman wanted to cover the whole American experience, and Dickinson dealt with the deepest poetic themes. They were unalike in their lifestyles and their poetic styles. Whitman was an outgoing traveler; Dickinson, a shy recluse. Whitman wrote free verse in long lines; Dickinson wrote rhymed verse in short lines.*

Literature of the Times

KEY IDEAS The Civil War was a transitional period for writers of the day. Groundbreaking poets, former slaves, famous public figures and everyday people all contributed their ideas as the country and its literature moved from romanticism to realism.

Brilliant Mavericks: Whitman and Dickinson

In 1842, when the conflicts leading to the Civil War were just beginning to brew and the romantic movement was going strong, writer **Ralph Waldo Emerson** issued a challenge to America. The nation needed a poet worthy of itself—a truly fresh voice with limitless passion and originality. "I look in vain," lamented Emerson, "for the poet whom I describe. We do not with sufficient plainness, or sufficient profoundness, address ourselves to life. . . ." In the coming decades, two poets would answer Emerson's bold call: **Walt Whitman** and **Emily Dickinson.**

Outwardly, Whitman and Dickinson had little in common. Whitman, big, bearded, and outspoken, was always in the thick of things and wrote many poems about current issues and events, from the sad plight of the slave to the shocking assassination of President Lincoln. Dickinson, on the other hand, was shy and reclusive, living her whole life in her native New England, and finding inspiration for her poetry in her own thoughts.

RULE-BREAKERS The two, however, were not entirely unalike. Both felt hemmed in by conventional ideas of how poems ought to look and what poems ought to say. Both wrote poetry so radical in form and content that it took many years for readers to appreciate it. (In Dickinson's case, appreciation didn't come until after her death.) Together, they broke poetry wide open, creating the most remarkable work of the Civil War era.

In 1855, Whitman published at his own expense a book of poetry called *Leaves of Grass.* The book was small, but it contained a huge ambition. Whitman saw America as a great poem, the greatest in the world, and his job was to capture it on paper. A sprawling, rowdy, vigorous young nation, he believed, could not be squeezed into traditional poetic forms. Instead, he wrote in **free verse,** unconfined by formal patterns of rhyme and meter. His lines were loose and rambling, his language colorful and vigorous, and he refused to limit himself to "poetic" subjects. If it was a part of American life, it was his to write about, even if it was a topic others might consider common or vulgar.

Emily Dickinson also found traditional poetic forms inadequate. Yet, where Whitman's poems were expansive, hers were terse and compressed—a few brief lines packed with complex, original images. Her subject matter was intensely personal, and her themes

Emily Dickinson

Walt Whitman

▶ *For Your Outline*

BRILLIANT MAVERICKS

- Whitman and Dickinson answered Emerson's call for a national poet.
- Whitman was gregarious and outspoken; Dickinson, shy and reclusive.
- Both broke conventional rules of poetry.
- Whitman used free verse to write about everything American.
- Dickinson used compressed lines and complex imagery to explore personal themes.
- Both poets can be seen as transitional.

DIFFERENTIATED INSTRUCTION

FOR ENGLISH LEARNERS

Set a Purpose After introducing the *KEY IDEAS* on this page, ask students to look for information in this essay about each writer named. Encourage students to use a Character Traits Web to record key facts, as in this example:

 BEST PRACTICES TOOLKIT—Transparency Character Traits Web p. D7

shy, reclusive

almost unknown during her lifetime

Emily Dickinson

used short, compressed poetic lines and original imagery

wrote about cosmic themes

FOR ADVANCED LEARNERS/AP

Synthesize Why would a poet find the forms of his or her time inadequate? Why would a poet rebel against those forms and deliberately write in a way that readers would find unfamiliar? Have students discuss these questions and speculate about how poets today might innovate new forms. If time permits, have students write and share brief "manifestoes" that proclaim ideas for new poetic forms.

KNOCK KNOCK

OH DEAR

EMILY DICKINSON

VISITORS

I'LL JUST WAIT FOR THEM TO GO AWAY

KNOCK KNOCK

KNOCK KNOCK

OH COME ON. ISN'T IT OBVIOUS I'M NOT IN ?

KNOCK KNOCK

KNOCK KNOCK

PEACE AT LAST

© Tom Gauld/Heart USA Inc.

ANALYZE VISUALS
This cartoon is one artist's representation of Emily Dickinson's reclusive nature. What other personality traits does the artist suggest about Dickinson in these panels?

were the great themes of life: love, death, immortality, and nature. Although she wrote nearly 1,800 poems, only a handful appeared in print during her lifetime. In fact, she was virtually unknown in her time, living a reclusive life that belied the intense creative fervor of her inner world.

Neither Dickinson nor Whitman can be easily categorized. Although Whitman can be considered a romantic poet because of his emphasis on individualism, emotion, and nature, his exploration of topics others found vulgar was certainly not romantic. Dickinson, too, could be aggressively unromantic, with her images of ordinary household items and her abrupt, unemotional tone. Perhaps both poets can be seen as transitional, moving with Americans of the day from romanticism to realism.

ANALYZE VISUALS

Possible answer: The cartoon gives the impression that Dickinson was a quiet, shy person who may have been snobbish or fearful of the world—but who also may not have been entirely comfortable with her isolation.

TIERED DISCUSSION PROMPTS

Use these prompts to help students understand the ideas in **Brilliant Mavericks: Whitman and Dickinson:**

Analyze Reread Emerson's comment at the beginning of this section. How did Whitman and Dickinson fulfill Emerson's vision?
Possible answer: Emerson envisioned "plainness" in poetry, and both Whitman and Dickinson are very readable. Emerson also wanted "profoundness," and both poets presented original, important ideas. Finally, Emerson wanted poetry to address life; Whitman addressed the vital life of America, and Dickinson addressed her interior life.

Interpret What does the essay mean by calling these two writers "transitional" poets?
Possible answer: The essay means that Whitman and Dickinson do not fit easily into a category; rather, they create a link between one era (romanticism) and another (realism).

FOR STRATEGIC READERS
Preteach Academic Vocabulary

- *mavericks*, "people who do things their own way, not like everyone else"
- *conventional*, "accepted; traditional"
- *radical*, "extremely different"
- *rowdy*, "disorderly and rough"
- *expansive*, "covering a wide range of things"
- *terse*, "using few words"
- *compressed*, "short"

Concept Support Some students may not grasp how poetic form changes. Read aloud lines from a traditional poem that they have read, such as Holmes's "The Chambered Nautilus" (page 342). Then help students revise the lines experimentally, keeping the line breaks and imagery but removing meter and rhyme. Ask students to imagine what readers would think of the revision if the only poetry that they knew was the traditional kind; elicit that many readers would not even recognize the new style as poetry. (You might compare the

situation with people today who hear a new musical style and respond, "That's not music, it's noise!") Lead students to conclude that the first free-verse poets faced a challenge in persuading readers to accept a new kind of poetry.

Literature of the Civil War

Of all human actions, none speaks so dramatically nor so violently as war. Of all wars, civil war by its very nature divides a nation's voice into factions. Among the diverse literary voices heard during the Civil War, some of the most powerful were African American.

Often at the urging of abolitionists, former slaves who escaped to the North published **slave narratives** detailing their experiences. These tales of suffering were immensely important to the cause of antislavery. Not simply autobiography, they were testimony, giving lie to Southern claims that slaves were happy and well-treated, that slavery was a "positive good" for both master and slave, and that people of African descent were inferior to whites. More than that, the narratives made readers *care* by showing that slaves were real human beings who suffered and wept and longed for freedom.

Fugitive slaves flee a Southern plantation at night in an attempt to reach the North.

500

Personal experience was central to the literature of the time, because everyday life now had great historical significance. Writers—male and female, white and black, from the highest-ranking general down to the common foot soldier—shared "their" Civil War in **diaries** and **letters**.

Voices from the Times

Many times I sat down in the mud determined to go no further, and willing to die to end my misery. But soon a friend would pass and urge me to make another effort, and I would stagger a mile further.

—Union soldier Elisha Rhodes

I daily part with my raiment for food. We find no one who will exchange eatables for Confederate money. So we are devouring our clothes.

—Southern diarist Mary Chesnut

While these writers addressed their words to friends and family (or even to themselves), others, such as President **Abraham Lincoln,** wrote for a larger audience. Still, Lincoln underestimated the reach of his words. "The world will little note, nor long remember, what we say here," he proclaimed in his **Gettysburg Address,** which in fact proved to be one of the most enduring works of the Civil War era.

Lincoln's speech, with its inspiring message and elevated language, represents the highest ideals of the period. The fiction created after the war by realistic writers such as **Ambrose Bierce** and **Stephen Crane,** however, shows the period in a harsher light. Their stories focus on the human tragedy of a war that destroyed hundreds of thousands of American lives, even as it freed many more.

In the years to come, **realism** would grow and refine itself to include the work of writers countrywide, from the frozen arctic north of Jack London to the plains of Willa Cather's frontier. It would develop to include the work of naturalist writers who viewed human beings as passive victims of their environment. Brought on by the brutalities of the Civil War, realism would become the form that to some extent still dominates American literature today.

THE ARTISTS' GALLERY

Prisoners from the Front (1866), Winslow Homer. Oil on canvas, 24" × 38". The Metropolitan Museum of Art, Gift of Mrs. Frank B. Porter, 1922 (22.207). Photo © 1995 The Metropolitan Museum of Art, New York.

Winslow Homer

Known for his bold technique and unsentimental style, **Winslow Homer** was one of the most admired artists of the 19th century. He first rose to acclaim during the Civil War.

Behind Union Lines When war broke out, *Harper's Weekly* sent Homer south, to draw illustrations for the magazine. The young artist camped out with the Union army and shared the soldiers' hardships, from meager rations to the deadly threat of typhoid fever.

Homer rarely drew a battle scene, spurning the romantic elements of high drama and heroism. Instead, he recorded the reality of everyday life in camp—the boredom and sadness of men far from home. In 1863, a critic praised him as "the first of our artists who has endeavored to tell us any truth about the war."

Civil War Masterpiece At first glance, the painting shown here might seem like nothing special, just soldiers standing in an empty field. Yet *Prisoners from the Front,* painted just after the war ended, won acclaim as the most powerful painting of the war. Why?

For Americans, this work had a deep symbolic meaning. In the soldiers, Homer conveys two opposing worldviews: the romantic, long-haired Southern officer confronts his Northern counterpart, who eyes him coolly. Behind them, the devastated landscape of the South tells the story of how the Civil War ends.

THE ARTISTS' GALLERY

American artist Winslow Homer (1836–1910) painted *Prisoners from the Front* in 1866. After the war, Homer turned his attention to more peaceful scenes, especially everyday life, the countryside, and the sea. His depictions of those subjects are considered today to be among his finest work. An artist who worked in both watercolor and oil, Homer is known for his **realism** and his brilliant use of color. Tell students that they will see more of Homer's paintings accompanying the poems of Walt Whitman (pages 511 and 513).

Activity Ask students to interpret the thoughts and feelings of the characters in the painting. *Possible answer: The Union officer, on the right, looks smugly triumphant; the long-haired Confederate officer, in the center of the painting, seems to show a defiant sense of honor and pride at a time of loss; the Confederate enlisted man, with beard and folded hands, appears to be humbled.*

CHECK UNDERSTANDING

Have students identify a few names and characteristics for each of these literary groups:

- "mavericks" (Whitman, Dickinson)
- writers during the Civil War
- the early postwar realists

FOR STRATEGIC READERS

Main Ideas and Supporting Details Ask students why readers were so interested in the lives of ordinary people during the Civil War era. *Possible answer: Interest came from the fact that history can affect ordinary people in dramatic ways. Slaves, soldiers, people on the home front, and people recovering in the war's aftermath left written records; the whole country could identify with and learn from these accounts.*

FOR ADVANCED LEARNERS/AP

Analyze Quotations Ask students to reflect upon and compare the quotations by Elisha Rhodes and Mary Chesnut. Then discuss these questions:

- Why did Elisha Rhodes decide that he would rather die than keep going? Why did he go on? What lesson might readers learn from his account?
- Why was Mary Chesnut unable to use her Confederate money? What does her com-

ment that "we are devouring our clothes" mean? What lesson might readers learn from her account?

- If Elisha Rhodes and Mary Chesnut met, what might they say to each other?
- What do the two quotations, taken together, suggest about the experience of suffering during wartime?

Connecting Literature, History, and Culture

OBJECTIVES

- read a timeline
- make connections among the perspectives and events of literature, history, and culture

READING SKILL

■ READ A TIMELINE

Elicit or explain that each of the three horizontal sections of the timeline—*American Literary Milestones, Historical Context,* and *World Culture and Events*—displays a sequence of events that occurred between 1855 and 1870. By looking at the vertical columns on the timeline, students can see which events were taking place at about the same time. For example, have students locate these events, which occurred between 1863 and 1866:

- In 1863, Abraham Lincoln delivered the Gettysburg Address. (See *American Literary Milestones.*)
- In 1864, Louis Pasteur invented pasteurization. (See *World Culture and Events.*)
- In 1865, the Civil War ended. (See *Historical Context.*)

Ask students what events occurred in 1855. **Answer:** *Frederick Douglass published his autobiographical narrative,* My Bondage and My Freedom; *Walt Whitman published the first edition of* Leaves of Grass; *Florence Nightingale introduced hygienic standards into military hospitals.*

Connecting Literature, History, and Culture

As you read this timeline and answer the questions on the next page, think about the ways in which American literature was influenced by—and itself influenced—national and world events.

AMERICAN LITERARY MILESTONES

1855

1855 Frederick Douglass's autobiographical slave narrative, *My Bondage and My Freedom,* is published; Walt Whitman publishes the first edition of *Leaves of Grass* at his own expense.

1857 The *Atlantic Monthly,* a journal of literature and opinion, is founded. Over the years, Emerson, Longfellow, and other writers and editors will contribute to the magazine.

1859

1859 Henry David Thoreau writes "A Plea for Captain John Brown," in which he refers to the condemned abolitionist as "an angel of light."

1861 The first autobiography by a formerly enslaved woman, Harriet Jacobs's *Incidents in the Life of a Slave Girl,* is published. ▶

1862 Emily Dickinson writes 366 poems within the year.

HISTORICAL CONTEXT

1855

1856 Preston S. Brooks beats Massachusetts senator Charles Sumner with a cane on the floor of the Senate in retaliation for Sumner's antislavery speech.

1857 Supreme Court's *Dred Scott* decision declares that slaves and former slaves are not U.S. citizens and thus not entitled to basic rights. ▶

1859

1859 Abolitionist John Brown is hanged for treason after leading a raid on the federal arsenal at Harpers Ferry.

1860 Abraham Lincoln is elected president; in response, South Carolina secedes from the Union, followed eventually by ten other Southern states.

1861 Confederate guns fire on Fort Sumter, launching the Civil War. ▶

WORLD CULTURE AND EVENTS

1855

1855 British nurse Florence Nightingale introduces hygienic standards into military hospitals during the Crimean War. ▶

1856 Two states of Australia introduce the voting procedure known as the Australian, or secret, ballot.

1857 Indians rebel against British occupation of the subcontinent.

1859

1859 British naturalist Charles Darwin publishes *Origin of Species,* giving his theory of evolution.

1861 Czar Alexander II of Russia frees serfs; in England, Charles Dickens publishes *Great Expectations.*

1862 French physicist Jean Foucault calculates the speed of light; Victor Hugo publishes *Les Misérables.*

DIFFERENTIATED INSTRUCTION

FOR STRATEGIC READERS

Understanding a Timeline Explain that the timeline runs chronologically (in time order) from left to right across the page. Each of the four columns represents a four-year period between 1855 and 1870. The three parallel rows of the timeline represent events occurring simultaneously. By comparing the three rows, readers can better understand what events in literature, history, and culture were taking place at about the same time.

MAKING CONNECTIONS

- What examples do you see of American writers being influenced by political events?
- What evidence shows that the nation was sharply divided before the Civil War?
- How did African Americans contribute to the literary culture of America during this period?
- What important scientific theories and discoveries arose during this period?

1863

1863 Abraham Lincoln delivers Gettysburg Address. ▶

1864 The *New Orleans Tribune*, one of the first daily newspapers produced by African Americans, begins publication.

1865 Walt Whitman pens his classic ode to Abraham Lincoln, "When Lilacs Last in the Dooryard Bloom'd."

1863

1863 Lincoln signs Emancipation Proclamation; the 54th Massachusetts Volunteer Infantry, one of the first African-American regiments, is founded. ▶

1864 Union general William Tecumseh Sherman marches from Atlanta to the Atlantic Ocean.

1865 Civil War ends; Lincoln is assassinated; 13th Amendment abolishes slavery.

1863

1863 Leo Tolstoy publishes *War and Peace*.

1864 Louis Pasteur invents pasteurization.

1865 Telegraph cable is laid across the Atlantic Ocean. ▶

1866 Fyodor Dostoyevsky publishes *Crime and Punishment*.

1867

1867 Mark Twain publishes *The Celebrated Jumping Frog of Calaveras County, and Other Sketches*.

1868 Part 1 of *Little Women*, Louisa May Alcott's classic novel about four sisters, is published. ▶

1870 Bret Harte publishes story collection *The Luck of Roaring Camp and Other Sketches*.

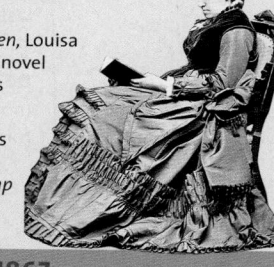

1867

1867 United States buys Alaska from Russia.

1868 Congress passes 14th Amendment, prohibiting discrimination against African Americans.

1869 The hammering of a golden spike at Promontory Point, Utah, marks completion of the transcontinental railroad. ▼

1870 The first African-American senator, Hiram R. Revels, takes his seat.

1867

1868 Remains of Cro-Magnon man discovered in Europe; Meiji era in Japan begins period of modernization.

1869 Suez Canal is completed in Egypt.

1870 After a troubled reign, Queen Isabella II of Spain abdicates throne in favor of her son, Alfonso XII.

FOR ADVANCED LEARNERS/AP

Making Additional Connections Ask students to choose one of the four time periods shown in the timeline and to do research online or in encyclopedias or history texts to learn about other events that took place during that same interval. Challenge students to identify events for each category: *American Literary Milestones, Historical Context,* and *World Culture and Events.* Have students work individually, with partners, or in small groups to prepare and present brief oral reports, summarizing significant events and discussing their connection to events shown in the timeline or discussed in class.

MAKING CONNECTIONS
Possible answers:

- *American writers who were influenced by political events include Frederick Douglass and Harriet Jacobs, who wrote about their experiences with slavery; Emerson and Longfellow, who contributed to a journal of opinion; Thoreau, who wrote an abolitionist essay; Lincoln, who wrote statesmanly rhetoric about major issues; and Whitman, who wrote an ode to Lincoln.*

- *Division is seen in these events: Preston Brooks beat Senator Charles Sumner with a cane on the floor of the Senate; the* Dred Scott *decision set back the cause of African-American freedom; John Brown was hanged for leading an anti-slavery raid; South Carolina seceded after Lincoln's election.*

- *African Americans contributed to literary culture by writing slave narratives and producing newspapers such as the* New Orleans Tribune.

- *Scientific theories and discoveries included the development of the theory of evolution; the calculation of the speed of light; the invention of pasteurization; and the discovery of prehistoric human remains.*

ADDITIONAL QUESTIONS

1. What advance in human rights occurred in Russia during the first year of the American Civil War? *Answer: Czar Alexander II advanced human rights by freeing the serfs (1861).*

2. What was significant about the railroad that was completed in 1869? *Answer: That railroad was significant because it spanned the North American continent.*

3. How many years passed between Whitman's publication of *Leaves of Grass* and his writing of "When Lilacs Last in the Dooryard Bloom'd"? *Answer: Ten years passed (from 1855 to 1865).*

OBJECTIVE

• to connect the legacy of the Civil War era's culture and writing to present times

War Stories

Have students read the paragraph. Discuss some aspects of the Civil War that led people to adopt a more realistic attitude toward war—for example, the war's high casualty rate (far higher than the total for all other American conflicts up to that time), the destruction of civilian property, and the way that the issues of the war split families. Also invite suggestions about why people sometimes romanticize war, even today.

DISCUSS Point out that Stephen Crane's Civil War novel *The Red Badge of Courage* (which students will read more about in the American Masterpieces feature on pages 578–579) began a tradition of realistic war fiction that later would include Ernest Hemingway's World War I novel *A Farewell to Arms,* World War II novels by Norman Mailer and James Jones, and Vietnam fiction by Tim O'Brien. Also note that movies such as Steven Spielberg's *Saving Private Ryan,* as well as television news reporting broadcasts right from the battlefield have greatly enhanced people's ability to visualize war. As students share their insights, challenge them to name factors that influence people's impressions of war.

The Legacy of the Era

War Stories

Before the Civil War, most American writers depicted war romantically, focusing on the glory of a battle, the justness of a cause, or the heroism of a leader. Later, writers such as Stephen Crane began to depict war in all its grim reality, uncovering the daily discomforts of military life, the horrors of the battlefield, and the lasting and unexpected consequences of war. Americans today are still drawn to war stories of all kinds.

DISCUSS As a class, discuss which elements in current war stories (novels, movies, TV shows, news reports) are realistic and which are romantic in nature. Give specific examples.

Steven Spielberg's 1998 movie *Saving Private Ryan* was noted for its realistic portrayal of battle.

DIFFERENTIATED INSTRUCTION

FOR ADVANCED LEARNERS/AP

Write a War Story Invite students to write brief stories set during a war that interests them. Urge students to strive for physical realism in their portrayal of war and for psychological realism in their depiction of characters' responses to the main event featured in each story's plot. In addition, encourage students to do enough research to keep their stories historically accurate, considering questions such as these:

• Why was the war being fought?

• What were the climate and terrain like?

• How did the characters dress? What arms were available to them?

• What kind of medical care did they have?

Have students who wish to do so present their work in an oral storytelling session. Afterward, invite the class to discuss aspects of the stories that they thought were especially realistic or otherwise powerful.

Artistic Innovators

Who are the blue men in this picture, and what do they have to do with Walt Whitman and Emily Dickinson? The Blue Man Group is just one example of many current artistic innovators who can tip their hats to the mavericks of an earlier era: Whitman and Dickinson. Since Whitman and Dickinson's bold experiments with poetic form and content in the 19th century, writers, musicians, and artists have increasingly pushed the limits of what is considered art, broadening Americans' tastes and imaginations in the process.

QUICKWRITE With your classmates, list as many artistic innovators as you can think of from the Civil War period to today. What do they have in common? What value do they bring to our society?

African-American Influence

One lasting legacy of the Civil War period has been the rise of African Americans to leadership positions and levels of prominence. Beginning with abolitionists such as Sojourner Truth and Frederick Douglass, African Americans have made their way into all spheres of American public life, from politics, education, and the sciences to the arts and entertainment.

CREATE With a partner, create a poster highlighting the achievements of three African American leaders today. Include photographs of three leaders who are working in different fields, and list their accomplishments along with quotations by or about each person.

From top, Scientist George Washington Carver, activist Rosa Parks, Senator Barack Obama, writer Maya Angelou, activist Martin Luther King Jr., media mogul Oprah Winfrey

Artistic Innovators

As students read the paragraph, explain that Blue Man Group combines music, comedy, and multimedia to create distinctive theatrical presentations. The group's name refers to the blue makeup that the performers wear. The group's unique instruments include the cimbalon and the Chapman Stick, which are stringed instruments; a two-story Drum Wall; airpoles, which are fiberglass tubes that make a swooshing sound in the air; and PVC tubes that are struck with paddles or sticks.

QUICKWRITE You might have students make their lists independently and then read them aloud to classmates; alternatively, have small groups work together on a list. Work with students to create master lists of common traits and values.

African-American Influence

Before students read the paragraph, review the meaning of *abolitionist* and the fact that the Civil War ultimately ensured freedom for African Americans. Invite students to share what they know of the people pictured and to name other African-American leaders.

CREATE Encourage students to use print and online resources for their research and to make the lists of accomplishments as up-to-date as possible. Have students organize and present a display of the finished posters for the class.

FOR STRATEGIC READERS

Vocabulary Support

- *justness,* "moral rightness"
- *consequences,* "results; outcomes"
- *innovators,* "people who do new things"
- *slew,* "large number"
- *prominence,* "importance; distinction"
- *spheres,* "areas"

FOR ADVANCED LEARNERS/AP

Research and Analyze [mixed-interest groups] Invite small groups of students to research one of the artistic innovators named in the *QUICKWRITE* activity on this page. Have each group create and give a multimedia presentation, teaching the class about the kind of art that the innovator created, why the art was innovative, and what influence it has had on other artists.

OBJECTIVES

- identify traditional and organic poetic forms
- analyze and evaluate free verse

CALIFORNIA R3.3, R3.4

Form and Function

Provide these brief explanations of the traditional fixed forms:

- A **sonnet** has 14 lines and a specific rhyme scheme and meter.
- A **ballad** tells a story and usually has meter, rhyme, and repeated passages.
- An **epic** is a long narrative about the adventures of a hero.
- An **elegy** is a long, thoughtful poem about a serious subject (especially death).
- An **ode** is a complex lyric poem (that is, a poem that expresses personal thoughts and feelings) on a serious, dignified theme.
- A **villanelle** has 19 lines arranged in a strict order, including repeated lines.
- **Blank verse** is unrhymed iambic pentameter.

Use a Two-Column Chart to discuss the differences between fixed and organic forms. Invite students to share thoughts about poems of either type that they have read or have written in the past.

Fixed Form	Organic Form
The form was invented before the poem was written.	Each poem has its own form, chosen by the poet.
Has regular rhythm; may have rhyme.	May or may not have regular rhythm and rhyme.

 BEST PRACTICES TOOLKIT—Transparency
  Two-Column Chart p. A25

Literary Analysis Workshop

Form and Content in Poetry

Do you think everything has already been said? Throughout American history, poets have prided themselves on finding new ways to say things, as well as inventing new poetic forms in which to say them.

Form and Function

CALIFORNIA R3.3, R3.4

All works of art have **form,** a particular organization of parts that makes a whole. In poetry, form is referred to as **poetic structure:** the way words are arranged in lines, lines are arranged in stanzas, and units of sound are organized to achieve rhythm and rhyme. In general, poetic forms fall into two categories, traditional and organic. Poems in **traditional form** follow certain fixed rules. For example, they can have a limited number of lines, a specified meter and rhyme scheme, and a definite structure. Such poems are also called **fixed form** poems and include the **sonnet,** the **ballad,** the **epic,** the **elegy,** the **ode,** the **villanelle,** and **blank verse.** Often, poets choose a form that fits the subject matter. For example, a sonnet was originally intended only for the subject of love. The great English poets, such as William Shakespeare and John Milton, used traditional poetic forms, as did many early American poets.

Engraving of Walt Whitman by Max Beerbohm, 1904

The **organic form** of poetry, also known as **irregular form,** developed in the early 19th century. The English romantic poets wanted more flexible verse forms to fit the new content of their poetry. Unlike traditional forms, which provide an ideal pattern for poems to follow, organic form takes its shape and pattern from the content of the poem itself. That is, the form of a poem "grows" naturally out of what the poem says. A poem in organic form may have meter and rhyme, but the poet may vary the rhythm and rhyme scheme in irregular and unexpected ways. In searching for ways to find new expression, several American poets, such as Walt Whitman and Emily Dickinson, began experimenting with organic form.

Poetic Form in Action

One way to understand the difference between traditional and organic forms is to compare the poetry of Henry Wadsworth Longfellow and Emily Dickinson. Longfellow was somewhat conventional in most of his poems, using a predictable alternating rhyme scheme and punctuation. The excerpted lines shown here from Longfellow's "Psalm of Life" have a regular meter (even the dash in the second line counts as an unstressed syllable).

DIFFERENTIATED INSTRUCTION

For general guidelines on differentiating instruction, see

 BEST PRACTICES TOOLKIT
  Differentiated Instruction pp. 31–38

FOR STRATEGIC READERS
Note Taking For students who are unfamiliar with poetry or need help with note taking, hand out the copy master before discussing this page. Explain that they will be learning many terms relating to poetic form in this

workshop. Discuss the major terms on this spread *(form/structure, traditional/fixed form, organic/irregular form, free verse)* as students record notes on their copy masters.

 RESOURCE MANAGER—Copy Master
  Note Taking p. 17

Tell me not, in mournful numbers,   *a*

Life is but an empty dream!—   *b*

For the soul is dead that slumbers,   *a*

And things are not what they seem.   *b*

—Henry Wadsworth Longfellow, "A Psalm of Life"

Now look at the first stanza of a poem by Dickinson. She also used meter and rhyme, but she added rhythmical variations, which characterize it as organic. The first line has four accents plus an unaccented dash, while the next three lines each has three accented syllables and is an **enjambed,** or **run-on,** line— a line that ends without a grammatical or normal speech pause.

My life closed twice before its close—   *a*

It yet remains to see   *b*

If Immortality unveil   *c*

A third event to me   *b*

—Emily Dickinson, "My life closed twice before its close"

Free verse is an organic form that lacks regular meter and rhyme. Although free verse still has rhythm and may include an occasional rhyme within a line, it does not follow any strict rules. Like all forms of poetry, however, it may include a variety of sound devices, such as repetition and alliteration, to achieve a musical quality.

The great master of free verse in American poetry was Walt Whitman. At a time when American poetry followed traditional forms, Whitman went his own way and created a form that grew purely out of the ideas expressed. In this passage from "I Hear America Singing," notice the language and sound devices that create a poetic effect in sentences that are almost like those in prose.

I hear America singing, the varied carols I hear,
Those of mechanics, each one singing his as it should be blithe and strong,
The carpenter singing his as he measures his plank or beam,
—Walt Whitman, "I Hear America Singing"

Close Read

Note that the metrical pattern of this passage is **trochaic tetrameter** (four stressed syllables in a line, with each accent followed by an unstressed syllable). Study the pattern of rhythm in the first two lines, and then sound out and note the stressed and unstressed syllables in lines 3 and 4.

Close Read

Notice the difference in rhythm between line 1 and lines 2–4. What effect does this shift have on the way the poem sounds? How might the change in rhythm emphasize the writer's meaning?

Close Read

Examine and compare the three examples on this page. How do they vary in content?

Poetic Form in Action

To help students understand enjambment, call their attention to the ends of lines in the Longfellow and Dickinson excerpts. Have students decide whether each line is meant to end with a normal speech pause. *Answer: All Longfellow's lines and the first line of Dickinson's poem end with a normal speech pause, but Dickinson's last three lines are enjambed.* Ask the same question after students have read the Whitman excerpt. *Answer: There is a normal speech pause after each of Whitman's lines, but his lines are much longer and have internal pauses as well.*

Close Read

Answer: *Lines 3 and 4 repeat the pattern of rhythm found in the first two lines.*

Close Read

Possible answer: *The shift makes the shorter lines seem quicker than the longer ones—more like a writer's spontaneous thought.*

If students need help . . . Point out that line 1 is a complete statement but that the next complete statement takes three lines to express. Discuss the link between breaking up the statement and changing the rhythm.

Close Read

Possible answer: *The Longfellow excerpt is energetic in rejecting the philosophy of life that some listeners may hold. The Dickinson excerpt also considers issues of life and death but expresses more uncertainty. Whitman's poem expresses exuberant optimism about life, with no mention of uncertainty or concerns about death.*

FOR ENGLISH LEARNERS

Language: Skill Words Help students understand the words *form* and *structure* by suggesting objects in the world that have a structure or form, such as a ball game or a building. Then discuss the difference between *fixed (traditional) form* and *organic (irregular) form:*

- Explain that if a form is *fixed,* the form doesn't change. Point out the other meaning of *fixed* and show the similarity; for example, if something broken is *fixed,* it becomes the same as before.

- Ask students if they have ever seen or eaten organic foods. Elicit or explain that organic foods are grown naturally. Similarly, *organic form* in poetry means that the form of a poem grows naturally from the poet's mind and that it is not based on a rule.

FOR ADVANCED LEARNERS/AP

Research and Analyze Form [small-group option] Ask students to research the history of the development of free verse and to write and share brief reports on the topic. Students should explore free verse that existed before Whitman, such as the biblical Psalms. They also should examine the tremendous variety of free verse that has been written since, by poets such as T. S. Eliot, William Carlos Williams, and Marianne Moore.

Focus and Motivate

OBJECTIVES

Poetic Form
- explore the key idea of **America**
- identify and analyze free verse
- read poetry

Reading
- analyze tone

 R3.3

ABOUT THE POET

After students have read the biography, point out these aspects of Whitman's life that give clues to the nature of his poetry:

- He grew up in a crowded American city, and he often described scenes of city life.
- He held many jobs, and he wrote about many occupations.
- He found inspiration in Emerson; like Emerson, he wrote in celebration of nature.
- He was independent, freewheeling, and optimistic—traits that appear in his poetry.

USING THE *NOTABLE QUOTE*

Read the comment by **Walt Whitman** aloud; then ask how the United States is like a poem. *Possible answer: The United States is inspiring, beautiful, and meaningful.* Discuss how the United States is a free-verse poem rather than a traditional poem. *Possible answers: The founding of the nation was an experiment in form; the United States is a place where people are free to decide their own ways of life.*

 R3.3

Selected Poetry
by Walt Whitman

Walt Whitman
1819–1892

When Walt Whitman's book of poems *Leaves of Grass* first appeared, many people were shocked by its controversial content and revolutionary form. Of the 800 copies printed, most were eventually thrown away. However, a few readers recognized the poet's genius. In a letter to Whitman, Ralph Waldo Emerson called *Leaves of Grass* "the most extraordinary piece of wit and wisdom that America has yet contributed."

The Making of a Poet Nothing Whitman wrote before *Leaves of Grass* contained any hint of what was to come. He burst onto the literary scene full-bodied and brash, like one of his poems.

His early years offered little in the way of preparation. Born in 1819, Whitman grew up in rural Long Island and crowded Brooklyn. He held a series of jobs including office boy, typesetter, printer, newspaper editor, school teacher, carpenter, and journalist.

In the 1840s, Whitman published a number of poems and short stories—and even a fairly successful novel—but these were conventional efforts.

Apparently, however, Whitman was just waiting for the proper inspiration. Upon reading Emerson, he realized that he could celebrate all aspects of nature and humanity by using spiritual language. "I was simmering, simmering, simmering," he once declared. "Emerson brought me to a boil."

An American Bard In the early 1850s, Whitman quit his job as a journalist and worked on *Leaves of Grass.* Declaring a kind of literary Independence Day, he printed his 12-poem book on July 4, 1855, at his own expense; he even set some of the type himself. Throughout his lifetime, Whitman would continue to rewrite, revise, and expand *Leaves of Grass.* The ninth and final edition, published in 1892, contained nearly 400 poems.

Unfettered by traditional poetic conventions and grammatical structures, Whitman captured the vitality, optimism, and voice of his native land. He celebrated all aspects of American life—the unique and the commonplace, the beautiful and the ugly.

Whitman once claimed that "the proof of a poet is that his country absorbs him as affectionately as he has absorbed it." By that measure and any other, Whitman is one of the most successful poets in history. Today *Leaves of Grass* is widely regarded as the most influential book of poetry in American literature.

508

Selection Resources

POETIC FORM: FREE VERSE

Walt Whitman is the great master of free verse in American poetry. **Free verse** is poetry that does not contain regular patterns of rhyme and meter. The lines in free verse often flow more naturally than do rhymed, metrical lines and so sound more like everyday speech. Note, however, that Whitman does use the following poetic devices to create rhythm:

- **cataloging:** frequent lists of people, things, and attributes

  The shoemaker singing as he sits on his bench, the hatter singing as he stands

- **repetition:** repeated words or phrases at the beginning of two or more lines

  Beat! beat! drums!—blow! bugles! blow!

- **parallelism:** related ideas phrased in similar ways

  Born here of parents born here from parents the same, and their parents the same

As you read the poems, notice how Whitman uses these devices to achieve rhythm, musical effects, and a style all his own.

READING SKILL: ANALYZE TONE

To help you understand Whitman's poems, pay attention to their tone. **Tone** is an expression of a writer's attitude toward his or her subject. For example, a writer's tone might be respectful, angry, or amused. Tone can be communicated through choice of words and details. Notice the triumphant tone in these lines from "Song of Myself":

I celebrate myself, and sing myself,
And what I assume you shall assume,
For every atom belonging to me as good belongs to you.

As you read Whitman's poems, jot down examples of words and details that communicate tone in a chart like the one shown.

	Examples	Tone
"I Hear America Singing"	"blithe and strong"	happy, confident
"Song of Myself"		
"A Noiseless Patient Spider"		
"Beat! Beat! Drums!"		

What does AMERICA look like?

KEY IDEA What images come to mind when you think about **America?** Maybe you see big cities or rolling farmland. Maybe you picture the mountains or the coasts. Or maybe you focus on the people rather than the land. Many of Walt Whitman's poems contain vivid images of America in the mid-1800s. What—and who—captures America's spirit and reality today?

DISCUSS Imagine that you have been asked to design a poster that will help introduce tourists and newcomers to America. Get together in a small group and discuss the images that represent the people and places of America. Be sure to include images that symbolize all aspects of the country.

What does AMERICA look like?

Ask the question. As students read the **KEY IDEA**, suggest that they visualize the scenes of **America** that it describes and add visualizations of other American scenes. Have them use their visualizations as a starting point for the **DISCUSS** activity; afterward, invite students to follow through and create a classroom display of posters.

SKILLS FOCUS

POETIC FORM R3.3

● FREE VERSE

Write these lines on the board:

> Going to school, I dress quickly, eat in a rush, run for the bus.

> Going to school, I read closely, listen, speak, write, rush to the next class.

Have students identify the use of catalog, repetition, and parallelism in the lines. *Possible answer: Catalog: the lists of actions; repetition: "Going to school"; parallelism: the grammatical structure "I + [verb] + [adverb]."*

CHECK UNDERSTANDING Have students write and share two lines of free verse on a topic of their choice.

READING SKILL R3.3

■ ANALYZE TONE

To help students identify tone in poetry, have them suggest words that describe the tone of the example of free verse in the previous activity. Then have them reread the free verse that they wrote for **CHECK UNDERSTANDING** and describe its tone.

 RESOURCE MANAGER—Copy Master Analyze Tone p. 29 (for student use while reading the selections)

DIFFERENTIATED INSTRUCTION

FOR STRATEGIC READERS

Concept Support: Tone To help students find tone in poetry, have them ask these questions as they reread the three lines from Whitman in the **READING SKILL** presentation:

- What is the speaker thinking?
- How does the speaker feel?
- What would his voice sound like if he were reading aloud?

Tell students to summarize their answers in single words or simple phrases.

FOR ADVANCED LEARNERS/AP

Contrast Free Verse and Prose [paired option] Ask pairs of students to discuss the differences between free verse and prose. Have them consider (1) whether some free verse is little more than prose broken into lines and (2) why that idea is not true of Whitman, whose free verse is clearly poetry. Invite students to share their insights with the class.

SUMMARY

The speaker catalogs the kinds of singing that he hears in the daily life and work of average Americans.

POETIC FORM

A **FREE VERSE**

Possible answer: The cataloging creates a rhythm that suggests movement and vitality.

READING SKILL

B **ANALYZE TONE**

Possible answer: Whitman expresses an admiring, grateful, fraternal attitude. Words and details that help convey this attitude include "robust," "friendly," "Singing with open mouths," "strong," and "melodious."

ANSWERS
Possible answers:

1. *Whitman celebrates men and women who work with their hands and keep the country going.*

2. *The singing represents the sound of people working in harmony and enjoying life, the hum of progress and the development of America.*

3. *Whitman may have omitted these Americans because he believes they are not the backbone of the country; they are in charge of others and don't perform the actual work themselves.*

I Hear America Singing

Walt Whitman

I hear America singing, the varied carols I hear,
Those of mechanics, each one singing his as it should be blithe
    and strong,
The carpenter singing his as he measures his plank or beam, **A**
The mason singing his as he makes ready for work, or leaves off
    work,
5 The boatman singing what belongs to him in his boat, the
    deckhand singing on the steamboat deck,
The shoemaker singing as he sits on his bench, the hatter singing
    as he stands,
The wood-cutter's song, the ploughboy's on his way in the
    morning, or at noon intermission or at sundown,
The delicious singing of the mother, or of the young wife at work,
    or of the girl sewing or washing,
Each singing what belongs to him or her and to none else,
10 The day what belongs to the day—at night the party of young
    fellows, robust, friendly,
Singing with open mouths their strong melodious songs. **B**

A **FREE VERSE**
Notice the use of **cataloging** throughout the poem. What rhythmic effect does the poet create with his list of the men and women at work in America?

B **ANALYZE TONE**
Reread lines 10–11. What attitude does the speaker express toward the young men? Note the words and details that help convey that attitude.

Literary Analysis

1. **Summarize** What types of workers does Whitman celebrate in this poem?

2. **Clarify** What do you think singing represents in the poem?

3. **Make Inferences** Why do you think Whitman does not mention wealthy entrepreneurs, prominent leaders, or powerful politicians?

The Reaper (1878), Winslow Homer. Watercolor. Private collection. Photo © Art Resource, New York.

510   UNIT 3: FROM ROMANTICISM TO REALISM

DIFFERENTIATED INSTRUCTION

For general guidelines on differentiating instruction, see

 BEST PRACTICES TOOLKIT
Differentiated Instruction pp. 31–38

FOR STATEGIC READERS
Options for Reading: Audio Recording

• Have students listen to the poems on the *Audio Anthology CD* (also recommended for English learners) while they read along in their texts. Ask students to listen for

and then describe the speaker's tone in each poem.

• Have a group of volunteers prepare and perform a choral reading of "I Hear America Singing." Remind them to review Whitman's intent and to discuss tone and pacing as they plan and rehearse their performance. Follow up by inviting participants to share any insights into the poem that they gained through the activity.

SUMMARY

The speaker rejoices in nature and in his own energetic, expansive spirit.

Lines 1–13
TIERED DISCUSSION PROMPTS

Use these prompts to help students understand the poem's ideas and tone:

Connect Do you identify with what the speaker says about himself? Why or why not? *Possible answers: Yes, because I like myself. No, because I think he is bragging.*

Interpret What impression of the speaker do these lines give you? *Possible answer: The speaker is confident, observant, at times reflective, at other times more enthusiastic.*

Synthesize Consider what you know about traditional poetic forms. How is the tone in this free-verse expression different from what it would be if the same ideas were expressed in a traditional poetic form? *Possible answer: Here the tone is freer, more expansive, more joyous.*

POETIC FORM

G FREE VERSE

Possible answer: The parallelism in "what I assume you shall assume" and in "belonging to me as good belongs to you" creates a bond between the speaker and the reader.

If students need help . . . Focus their attention on the details cited in the *Possible answer;* discuss the meaning of each.

READING SKILL

D ANALYZE TONE

Possible answer: The tone in lines 4–5 is quiet and contemplative; the tone in lines 12–13 is dynamic and energetic. The tone in both pairs of lines is self-affirming.

Song of Myself

Walt Whitman

1

I celebrate myself, and sing myself,
And what I assume you shall assume,
For every atom belonging to me as good belongs to you. **G**

I loaf and invite my soul,
5 I lean and loaf at my ease observing a spear of summer grass.

My tongue, every atom of my blood, form'd from this soil, this air,
Born here of parents born here from parents the same, and their
    parents the same,
I, now thirty-seven years old in perfect health begin,
Hoping to cease not till death.

10 Creeds and schools in abeyance,
Retiring back a while sufficed at[1] what they are, but never
    forgotten,
I harbor for good or bad, I permit to speak at every hazard,
Nature without check with original energy. **D**

6

A child said *What is the grass?* fetching it to me with full hands,
15 How could I answer the child? I do not know what it is any more
    than he.
I guess it must be the flag of my disposition, out of hopeful green
    stuff woven.

Or I guess it is the handkerchief of the Lord,
A scented gift and remembrancer designedly dropt,[2]

---

1. **sufficed at:** satisfied with.
2. **remembrancer designedly dropt:** a purposely dropped token of affection.

G FREE VERSE
Read lines 1–3 aloud and listen to the rhythm created by **parallelism.** In what ways does the use of this technique reflect the relationship between the speaker and the reader?

D ANALYZE TONE
Compare the tone in lines 4–5 with that in lines 12–13. How does the tone change? How is the tone in both pairs of lines similar?

DIFFERENTIATED INSTRUCTION

FOR STRATEGIC READERS

Concept Support: Paraphrase To help students with lines 10–13, have them use the Jigsaw Reading strategy, with each student or group paraphrasing one of the four lines. Point out words with multiple meanings: *schools, retiring, harbor, permit, hazard, check,* and *original.* Have students continue this process as they read, with each student or group specializing in a stanza.

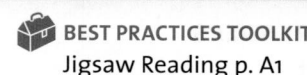
BEST PRACTICES TOOLKIT
Jigsaw Reading p. A1

Boys in Pasture, Winslow Homer. © Burstein Collection/Corbis.

Bearing the owner's name someway in the corners, that we may see
and remark, and say *Whose?*

20 Or I guess the grass is itself a child, the produced babe of the
vegetation.

Or I guess it is a uniform hieroglyphic,[3] **E**
And it means, Sprouting alike in broad zones and narrow zones,
Growing among black folks as among white,
Kanuck, Tuckahoe, Congressman, Cuff,[4] I give them the same, I
receive them the same.

25 And now it seems to me the beautiful uncut hair of graves.

Tenderly will I use you curling grass,
It may be you transpire[5] from the breasts of young men,
It may be if I had known them I would have loved them,
It may be you are from old people, or from offspring taken soon
out of their mothers' laps,
30 And here you are the mothers' laps. **F**

E **FREE VERSE**
Be aware of the **repetition**
in lines 16–21. What is the
relationship between the
repeated elements?

F **ANALYZE TONE**
What attitude does the
speaker express toward
the dead in lines 25–30?

3. **hieroglyphic:** a system of symbols that represent meanings or speech sounds.
4. **Kanuck, Tuckahoe, . . . Cuff:** slang terms for various groups of people. A Kanuck (now
   spelled Canuck) is a Canadian, especially a French Canadian; a Tuckahoe is someone
   from the coast of Virginia; a Cuff is an African American.
5. **transpire:** emerge; ooze out.

SONG OF MYSELF **513**

ANALYZE VISUALS

Activity Note that *Boys in Pasture* was painted
by Winslow Homer, the same artist who
painted *The Reaper* on page 511. Have students
examine both paintings and find resem-
blances that define Homer's subject matter
and style. Then have them complete a
Venn Diagram like this one to explore why
Homer's paintings make good illustrations
for Whitman's poems.

WHITMAN:
wrote
poems
about city
and country
poems
about
himself

BOTH:
showed
American
scenes
showed people
working
celebrated the
land and
people

HOMER:
painted
paintings
of country

BEST PRACTICES TOOLKIT—Transparency
Venn Diagram p. A26

POETIC FORM

E **FREE VERSE**

*Possible answer: The repeated element is
"I guess," which refers to possible metaphorical meanings of the grass.*

READING SKILL

F **ANALYZE TONE**

*Possible answer: The speaker expresses a
tender, loving attitude toward the dead.*

FOR ADVANCED LEARNERS/AP

Analyze Challenge students to extend their
analysis of these excerpts from "Song of
Myself" by responding briefly to one or more
of these writing prompts:

- Why does the speaker emphasize that his
  American heritage goes back for many
  generations (lines 6–7)?

- What does the speaker think of traditional
  institutions? What does he think is more

important? Cite evidence from Section 1 to
support your answers.

- What might the "child" (line 14) symbolize?

- In Section 6, how does Whitman keep his
  description of gravesites from becoming
  grotesque?

- How do the speaker's comments in Section
  52 recall Section 1? Do they bring the poem
  to a satisfying conclusion?

SONG OF MYSELF **513**

This grass is very dark to be from the white heads of old mothers,
Darker than the colorless beards of old men,
Dark to come from under the faint red roofs of mouths.

O I perceive after all so many uttering tongues,
35 And I perceive they do not come from the roofs of mouths for
    nothing.

I wish I could translate the hints about the dead young men and
    women,
And the hints about old men and mothers, and the offspring taken
    soon out of their laps.

What do you think has become of the young and old men?
And what do you think has become of the women and children?

40 They are alive and well somewhere,
The smallest sprout shows there is really no death,
And if ever there was it led forward life, and does not wait at the
    end to arrest it,
And ceas'd the moment life appear'd.

All goes onward and outward, nothing collapses,
45 And to die is different from what any one supposed, and luckier. **G**

52

The spotted hawk swoops by and accuses me, he complains of my
    gab and my loitering.

I too am not a bit tamed, I too am untranslatable,
I sound my barbaric yawp[6] over the roofs of the world. **H**

The last scud[7] of day holds back for me,
50 It flings my likeness after the rest and true as any on the shadow'd
    wilds,
It coaxes me to the vapor and the dusk.

I depart as air, I shake my white locks at the runaway sun,
I effuse my flesh in eddies,[8] and drift it in lacy jags.

---

6. **yawp:** loud, rough speech.
7. **scud:** wind-blown cloud.
8. **effuse ... eddies:** scatter my flesh in swirling currents.

G ANALYZE TONE
What words would you use to describe the tone in lines 38–45, where the speaker discusses life and death?

H FREE VERSE
Reread lines 47–48. What **poetic devices** in these lines emphasize the speaker's untamed nature?

CULTURAL CONNECTION

Afterlife In lines 38–45, the speaker presents a view of death and the afterlife. Many cultures have beliefs about the afterlife; for example, Hindus believe in reincarnation, based upon the good and bad actions of a person in earlier lives. Have students compare and contrast the view presented in these lines with beliefs in their culture and other beliefs with which they may be familiar.

READING SKILL

G ANALYZE TONE

Possible answer: The tone is hopeful, confident, optimistic, and fearless.

If students need help . . . Have them find words and phrases expressing the speaker's philosophy concerning death. Discuss how students might feel if they believed that "there is really no death" (line 41).

POETIC FORM

H FREE VERSE

Possible answers: The parallel structure of the defiant line 47, the repetition of "I" at the beginnings of lines, and the lines' strident rhythm emphasize an untamed nature.

Extend the Discussion What does the speaker mean by calling his poetry "my barbaric yawp" (line 48)? Do you like the idea of a poem being a "barbaric yawp"? Why or why not?

DIFFERENTIATED INSTRUCTION

FOR STRATEGIC READERS

Concept Support: Analyze Tone Have students continue working with the prereading chart from page 509. Because this excerpt from "Song of Myself" contains three distinct sections, instruct students to fill out at least one line for each section, analyzing the section's tone.

Examples	Tone
"Nature without check" (Section 1, line 13)	defiant
"mothers' laps" (Section 6, line 30)	nostalgic
"not a bit tamed" (Section 52, line 47)	proud

FOR ENGLISH LEARNERS

Language: Pronoun Referents [mixed-readiness groups] Point out the antecedent of *they* in line 35 (*tongues*) and make sure that students understand the grammatical relationship. Then have students work in groups of mixed fluency to identify pronoun referents for *their* in line 37 (*mothers*), for *They* in line 40 (*women and children*), for *it* in line 42 (*death*), and for *It* in lines 50 and 51 (*The last scud of day*).

I bequeath[9] myself to the dirt to grow from the grass I love,
55 If you want me again look for me under your boot-soles. **ⓘ**

You will hardly know who I am or what I mean,
But I shall be good health to you nevertheless,
And filter and fibre your blood.

Failing to fetch me at first keep encouraged,
60 Missing me one place search another,
I stop somewhere waiting for you.

_____

9. **bequeath:** hand over, as if in a will.

Literary Analysis

1. **Clarify** According to the speaker, in lines 40–43, why is there "really no death"?

2. **Summarize** To what does the speaker compare himself in section 52?

3. **Analyze Symbols** What do you think grass symbolizes in this poem?

Return from the Farm (1915–1920), Elliott Daingerfield. Smithsonian American Art Museum, Washington, D.C. Photo © Smithsonian American Art Museum/Art Resource, New York.

ⓘ ANALYZE TONE
What words and details does the poet use in lines 49–55 to create a defiant tone?

ANALYZE VISUALS
This painting by American artist Elliott Daingerfield shows a man returning home after working on his farm. What **images** in the painting are similar to those described in the poem?

SUMMARY

The speaker compares his soul's progress to a spider's web-building process.

About the Art Victor Hugo (1802–1885) was perhaps the greatest French romantic poet; he also wrote the classic novel *Les Misérables*, which inspired a hit musical that has played around the world. Hugo, however, also was a fine artist. He frequently drew and painted to explore ideas for his writing, much as Whitman here finds that observing the artistry of a spider has led him to a writing idea.

POETIC FORM

❶ FREE VERSE

Possible answer: The parallelism suggests a connection between spider and speaker: Both are alone and must launch themselves into the void in order to find an anchor.

If students need help . . . Ask:

• Whom is the speaker describing in line 5? in line 8?

• How are the two descriptions similar?

READING SKILL

❷ ANALYZE TONE

Possible answers: Overall, the tone is musing and thoughtful, suggesting a sense of aloneness. Details such as "isolated" (line 2), "vacant vast surrounding" (line 3), "detached" (line 7), and "measureless oceans of space" (line 7) communicate that tone.

Extend the Discussion How does the tone of this poem differ from the tone of the previous Whitman poems in this lesson?

Crossing the Spider Web, Victor Hugo. Watercolor. Maison Victor Hugo. Musée de la Ville de Paris. Photo © Giraudon/Art Resource, New York.

A Noiseless **Patient Spider**

Walt Whitman

A noiseless patient spider,
I mark'd where on a little promontory[1] it stood isolated,
Mark'd how to explore the vacant vast surrounding,
It launch'd forth filament, filament, filament, out of itself,
5 Ever unreeling them, ever tirelessly speeding them.

And you O my soul where you stand,
Surrounded, detached, in measureless oceans of space,
Ceaselessly musing, venturing, throwing, seeking the spheres to
     connect them, ❶
Till the bridge you will need be form'd, till the ductile[2] anchor
     hold,
10 Till the gossamer[3] thread you fling catch somewhere, O my soul. ❷

---

1. **promontory:** a high ridge of land or rock jutting out over water or land.
2. **ductile:** capable of being drawn or stretched out.
3. **gossamer:** extremely light or fine.

❶ **FREE VERSE**
Compare the use of **parallelism** in lines 5 and 8. What do these parallel elements suggest about the relationship between the spider and speaker?

❷ **ANALYZE TONE**
What is the overall tone of the poem? What details communicate that tone?

DIFFERENTIATED INSTRUCTION

FOR STRATEGIC READERS
Vocabulary Support

• *mark'd* (line 2), "noticed"

• *vast* (line 3), "vastness; huge space"

• *filament* (line 4), "a slender thread"

• *detached* (line 7), "not connected"

• *measureless* (line 7), "too big to measure"

• *musing* (line 8), "thinking"

FOR ADVANCED LEARNERS/AP
Compare and Contrast Poems Walt Whitman's musings about a spider (1868) are reminiscent of the musings that Oliver Wendell Holmes recorded (1858) in "The Chambered Nautilus" (page 342). Have students reread and reflect upon both poems. Then have them write an essay that compares the poems. Work with students to create a format for sharing their insights.

Beat! Beat! Drums!

Walt Whitman

Beat! beat! drums!—blow! bugles! blow!
Through the windows—through doors—burst like a ruthless force,
Into the solemn church, and scatter the congregation,
Into the school where the scholar is studying;
5 Leave not the bridegroom quiet—no happiness must he have now
     with his bride,
Nor the peaceful farmer any peace, ploughing his field or
     gathering his grain,
So fierce you whirr and pound you drums—so shrill you bugles
     blow. **L**

Beat! beat! drums!—blow! bugles! blow!
Over the traffic of cities—over the rumble of wheels in the streets;
10 Are beds prepared for sleepers at night in the houses? no sleepers
     must sleep in those beds,
No bargainers' bargains by day—no brokers or speculators—
     would they continue?
Would the talkers be talking? would the singer attempt to sing?
Would the lawyer rise in the court to state his case before the
     judge?
Then rattle quicker, heavier drums—you bugles wilder blow.

15 Beat! beat! drums!—blow! bugles! blow!
Make no parley—stop for no expostulation,[1]
Mind not the timid—mind not the weeper or prayer,
Mind not the old man beseeching the young man,
Let not the child's voice be heard, nor the mother's entreaties,
20 Make even the trestles[2] to shake the dead where they lie awaiting
     the hearses,
So strong you thump O terrible drums—so loud you bugles blow. **M**

---

1. **parley:** a discussion or conference; **expostulation:** argument.
2. **trestles:** tables, in this case, upon which coffins sit until the undertaker comes to take them away.

A NOISELESS PATIENT SPIDER / BEAT! BEAT! DRUMS!   **517**

L ANALYZE TONE
Describe the tone in lines 1–7. Why is this tone appropriate for the subject matter?

M FREE VERSE
Notice the **parallel structure** in the last line of each stanza. What impact does this device have on the poem's message?

Prereading for this poem is found on page 508.

SUMMARY
The speaker addresses the drums and bugles of war, urging them to call people to action.

BACKGROUND
Drummer Boys In the Civil War, drummers and buglers accompanied army troops. Many of the musicians were mere boys. The most famous Civil War drummer boy, Johnny Clem, who enlisted at age 11, lived to be 85 and may have been the subject of the song "When Johnny Comes Marching Home."

READING SKILL

L ANALYZE TONE
Possible answers: The tone is loud, forceful, and urgent. This tone is appropriate because war can be characterized in all those ways.

POETIC FORM

M FREE VERSE
Possible answer: The parallel structure makes the sounds of the drums and bugles seem more insistent and loud, thus making the poem's message more forceful.

SELECTION WRAP–UP

SYNTHESIZE Ask students, on the basis of these poems, to explain the meaning of the word *Whitmanesque.*

FOR STRATEGIC READERS
Concept Support: Analyze Tone Have groups of students share their completed versions of the prereading chart from page 509. Ask them to offer feedback on their peers' perceptions of tone in the poems. Also invite students to discuss whether they think that there is a "typical" tone found throughout these poems or whether each poem has its own unique tone.

FOR ADVANCED LEARNERS/AP
Evaluate Remind students that Whitman was considered a disturbing, revolutionary poet when *Leaves of Grass* first appeared: He was considered revolutionary in his style and form; he was seen as disturbing for his voice, his ideas, his subject matter, and his personal image. Have students discuss whether there is still something disturbing or unconventional about Whitman or whether time has completely tamed him.

CONNECT

This selection provides additional information on Whitman's sense of Americanism. You can also use it as a minilesson on reading for information.

Reading for Information

Point out that the Preface to *Leaves of Grass* is a brief prose introduction to a book of poems. In this case, the Preface was written by the poet himself. Then ask:

- What help does this Preface provide for previewing the book that it introduces? *Possible answer: It gives the reader an idea of the subject matter of the book and the poet's attitude toward that subject.*

- What is the main idea of this Preface? *Possible answer: The main idea is that the United States is a vast and diverse nation, comparable to a free-verse poem.*

TIERED DISCUSSION PROMPTS

Use these prompts to help students relate Whitman's personal statement to the poems that they have just read:

Connect As you read this Preface, did you find it inspiring? informative? vivid? Provide other adjectives of your own to describe your response. *Accept all reasonable answers.*

Interpret In Whitman's view, what is great about the United States? *Possible answer: The United States is great because of the multitude and variety of its common people.*

Synthesize Suppose that you were a reader in Whitman's era, reading *Leaves of Grass* for the first time. How good a preparation for the poems do you think this Preface would be, and why? *Possible answer: The Preface would be an excellent preparation because (1) it reflects the tone and subject matter of the poems and (2) the styles of Whitman's prose and verse are similar.*

ESSAY Among the most important themes of Walt Whitman's poetry is the magnificence of America as seen in the nation's common people. In his preface to *Leaves of Grass*, his great life work, he introduces this idea quite emphatically.

from the Preface to

Leaves of GRASS
Walt Whitman

The Americans of all nations at any time upon the earth have probably the fullest poetical nature. The United States themselves are essentially the greatest poem. In the history of the earth hitherto the largest and most stirring appear tame and orderly to their ampler largeness and stir. Here at last is something in the doings of man that corresponds with the broadcast doings of the day and night. Here is not merely a nation but a teeming nation of nations. Here is action untied from strings necessarily blind to particulars and details magnificently moving in vast masses. Here is the hospitality which forever indicates heroes. . . . Here are the roughs and beards and space and ruggedness and nonchalance that the soul loves. Here the performance disdaining the trivial unapproached in the tremendous audacity of its crowds and groupings and the push of its perspective spreads with crampless and flowing breadth and showers its prolific and splendid extravagance. One sees it must indeed own the riches of the summer and winter, and need never be bankrupt while corn grows from the ground or the orchards drop apples or the bays contain fish or men beget children upon women.

Other states indicate themselves in their deputies . . . but the genius of the United States is not best or most in its executives or legislatures, nor in its ambassadors or authors or colleges or churches or parlors, nor even in its newspapers or inventors . . . but always most in the common people. Their manners speech dress friendships—the freshness and candor of their physiognomy—the picturesque looseness of their carriage . . . their deathless attachment to freedom—their aversion to anything indecorous or soft or mean—the practical acknowledgment of the citizens of one state by the citizens of all other states—the fierceness of their roused resentment—their curiosity and welcome of novelty—their self-esteem and wonderful sympathy—their susceptibility to a slight—the air they have of persons who never knew how it felt to stand in the presence of superiors—the fluency of their speech—their delight in music, the sure symptom of manly tenderness and native elegance of soul . . . their good temper and openhandedness—the terrible significance of their elections—the President's taking off his hat to them not they to him—these too are unrhymed poetry. It awaits the gigantic and generous treatment worthy of it.

Comprehension

R3.3
CALIFORNIA

1. **Recall** What two things does Whitman compare in "A Noiseless Patient Spider"?

2. **Summarize** In "Beat! Beat! Drums!" whom do the drums and bugles call to action?

3. **Paraphrase** How would you paraphrase lines 16–19 of "Beat! Beat! Drums!"?

Literary Analysis

4. **Examine Imagery** Think about the images of mid-19th-century **America** that Whitman conveys in his poems. How do these images compare with what America looks like today? Cite specific details from the poems to support your comparisons.

5. **Analyze Tone** Review the examples of tone that you recorded as you read the poems. What can you conclude about Whitman's attitude toward the following?

   • manual labor   • the soul   • himself   • war

6. **Analyze Metaphor** Reread lines 16–25 of "Song of Myself." What metaphors does the speaker use to describe what grass means to him? What ideas does each metaphor suggest?

7. **Compare Poems** Use a chart like the one shown to compare the **images** and **mood** of "A Noiseless Patient Spider" and "Beat! Beat! Drums!" Based on your notes, what is the overall impact of each poem?

	Images	Mood
"A Noiseless Patient Spider"		
"Beat! Beat! Drums!"		

8. **Compare Texts** In what ways are the pronouncements made in Whitman's preface (page 518) reflected in his poems? Consider the content of what he says as well as the manner in which he states it. Provide details to support your ideas.

9. **Evaluate Free Verse** Why is free verse an appropriate form for Whitman's poems? Support your opinion.

Literary Criticism

10. **Author's Style** In another section of "Song of Myself," Whitman writes: "He most honors my style who learns under it to destroy the teacher." What does he mean? Do you think Whitman encourages this position in the poems you have read? Use evidence from the poems to support your opinion.

---

and "the beautiful uncut hair of graves" (line 25) suggests the cycle of life and death.

7. "A Noiseless Patient Spider": images: isolation, detachment, and striving; mood: somber. The overall impact is of quiet contemplation. "Beat! Beat! Drums!": images: drums, bugles, people leaving civilian life; mood: martial enthusiasm. The overall impact is of noise and activity.

8. The democratic ideals in Whitman's Preface reflect "I Hear America Singing." His reference to grass and earth reflects "Song of Myself." His use of cataloging and parallelism, his reference to unrhymed poetry,

and his equation of people with poetry reflect his poems in general.

9. ● **SKILLS FOCUS** Free Verse *Because free verse really has no rules, it is an appropriate form to capture Whitman's individualistic views on America and life.*

10. *He urges an individualistic, unconventional way of approaching life. He encourages the position in "I Hear America Singing," where he values working people over wealthy people; in "Song of Myself" he expects the reader to answer questions independently. On the other hand, he honors obedience in "Beat! Beat! Drums!"*

Practice and Apply

After Reading

Use these copy masters to check understanding and provide extra support:

R RESOURCE MANAGER—Copy Masters
   Free Verse p. 27
   Question Support p. 31

Additional selection questions are provided for teachers on page 23.

ANSWERS

1. *Whitman compares the speaker's soul to a spider that is building a web.*

2. *The drums and bugles call churchgoers, scholars, bridegrooms, farmers, city dwellers (sleepers, shoppers, talkers), singers, and lawyers to action.*

3. *Possible answer: Don't listen to antiwar or timid voices.*

Possible answers:

4. *In "I Hear America Singing," Whitman's America is dominated by manual workers; today, many people work in service industries. In "Song of Myself," America is mainly agricultural; today, cities and suburbs dominate the country. In "Beat! Beat! Drums!" Whitman assumes that war will rally the nation; today, war often divides the nation.*

5. ■ **SKILLS FOCUS** Analyze Tone *Manual labor is honorable, necessary, and valuable; the soul is individualistic but united with the cosmos; he is expansive and energetic; war is a noble common cause.*

6. *The metaphor "the flag of my disposition" (line 16) suggests a display of life and hope; "the handkerchief of the Lord" (line 17) suggests a gift of God's love; "a child" (line 20) suggests possibility, promise, and innocence; "a uniform hieroglyphic" (line 21) suggests equality and fraternity among all people;*

Assess and Reteach

Assess

R RESOURCE MANAGER—Copy Masters
   Selection Test A pp. 33–34
   Selection Test B/C pp. 35–36

🖉 Test Generator CD

Reteach

S STANDARDS LESSON FILE
   Literature Lesson 43: Tone

R3.4 (p. 523),
R3.7 (p. 523)

BACKGROUND

Neruda: Latin-American Classic Pablo Neruda is considered perhaps the greatest Latin-American poet of the 20th century. His birth name was Neftalí Ricardo Reyes Basoalto. Because his family disapproved of poetry as a profession, he took the name Pablo Neruda when he published his first book of poems (having sold everything he owned to pay for its publication), at the age of 19. One year later, his volume *Twenty Love Poems and a Song of Despair* made Neruda famous.

Neruda in Government Appointing poets to posts in the diplomatic service is something of a tradition. (Students have seen this tradition at work in the biography of James Russell Lowell, in Unit 2. Other Latin-American poet/diplomats have included Octavio Paz of Mexico and Miguel Asturias of Guatemala.) In 1927 Neruda began his diplomatic career in Burma (today Myanmar); he later served as Chilean consul in Argentina, Spain, and Mexico. In 1945 he was elected to the Chilean Senate; however, when a new government took power, Neruda was expelled from the Senate and fled the country. He returned in 1952 when the government lifted the ban. Later, he was named Chilean ambassador to France. Neruda continued to write poetry prolifically throughout his public career. In 1971 he received the Nobel Prize for Literature. He died of leukemia on September 23, 1973.

Ode to Walt Whitman

PABLO NERUDA

> **BACKGROUND** Pablo Neruda (1904–1973), a Nobel Prize–winning poet from Chile, was greatly inspired by Walt Whitman's poetry. In a speech delivered in 1972, he said, "I was barely 15 when I discovered Walt Whitman, my primary creditor. I stand among you today still owing this marvelous debt that has helped me live." In the following poem, Neruda echoes Whitman's joyful exuberance.

I do not remember
at what age
nor where:
in the great damp South
5 or on the fearsome
coast, beneath the brief
cry of the seagulls,
I touched a hand and it was
the hand of Walt Whitman.
10 I trod the ground
with bare feet,
I walked on the grass,
on the firm dew
of Walt Whitman.

15 During
my entire
youth
I had the company of that hand,
that dew,
20 its firmness of patriarchal pine, its
prairie-like expanse,
and its mission of circulatory peace.

DIFFERENTIATED INSTRUCTION

FOR STRATEGIC READERS
Vocabulary Support

- *creditor* (background), "a person to whom one owes something"
- *exuberance* (background), "enthusiasm"
- *patriarchal* (line 20), "like a father"
- *circulatory* (line 21), "traveling around freely"
- *disdaining* (line 23), "looking down on; thinking ill of"

- *copious* (line 26), "plentiful"
- *capital* (line 27), "the top part of a column"
- *tutelary* (line 44), "teaching; acting as a tutor"
- *subterranean* (line 45), "underground"
- *humiliated* (line 66), "made to feel worthless"
- *stature* (line 68), "height; level of importance"
- *fireman* (line 71), "a person who tends a fire, such as a fire in a furnace"

- *stoke-hole* (line 73), "the opening in a furnace through which fuel is inserted"
- *acacia* (line 85), "a kind of tree"

Not
disdaining
the gifts
25 of the earth,
    nor the copious
    curving of the column's capital,
    nor the purple
    initial
30 of wisdom,
    you taught me
    to be an American,
    you raised
    my eyes
35 to books,
    towards
    the treasure
    of the grains:
    broad,
40 in the clarity
    of the plains,
    you made me see
    the high
    tutelary
45 mountain. From subterranean
    echoes,
    you gathered
    for me
    everything;
50 everything that came forth
    was harvested by you,
    galloping in the alfalfa,
    picking poppies for me,
    visiting
55 the rivers,
    coming into the kitchens
    in the afternoon.

    But not only
    soil
60 was brought to light
    by your spade:
    you unearthed
    man,
    and the
65 slave
    who was humiliated
    with you, balancing
    the black dignity of his stature,
    walked on, conquering
70 happiness.

    To the fireman
    below,
    in the stoke-hole,
    you sent
75 a little basket
    of strawberries.
    To every corner of your town
    a verse
    of yours arrived for a visit,
80 and it was like a piece
    of clean body,
    the verse that arrived,
    like
    your own fisherman beard
85 or the solemn tread of your acacia
       legs.

ODE TO WALT WHITMAN **521**

Lines 22–70
TIERED DISCUSSION PROMPTS

Use these prompts to help students explore the first section of Neruda's ode:

Summarize According to the speaker, what did Whitman teach him? ***Possible answer:*** *Whitman taught him to be an American (lines 31–32); to love books and the land (lines 33–57); and to love humankind (lines 62–70).*

Interpret Explain the meaning of this metaphor: "you made me see / the high / tutelary / mountain" (lines 42–45). ***Possible answer:*** *The speaker means that Whitman's poetry made him aware of the beauty and importance of the earth, which taught the speaker much.*

Evaluate Why might Neruda have chosen to write such short lines in this poem? Are the short lines an effective device, or would the poem have worked better if Neruda had joined some lines to make them longer? ***Possible answer:*** *The short lines highlight key words and cause the reader to slow down and consider the poem's meanings; the short lines are an affectation that tries to make the poem seem longer and thus more important.*

FOR ADVANCED LEARNERS/AP

Explore and Interpret Neruda Ask students to explore the poetry of Neruda in more depth. Suggest that students browse through collections such as *Twenty Love Poems and a Song of Despair* or *The Essential Neruda* and find two poems that strike them as intellectually or emotionally powerful. In addition, ask students to locate interpretations of Neruda's work (and of their chosen poems, if possible) in critical studies or biographies. Instruct students to use their findings to write brief essays in which they convey critics' interpretations and add their own. Have students read their chosen poems aloud and comment about the interpretations. Gather students' essays and make the collection available to the class.

Lines 97–133
TIERED DISCUSSION PROMPTS

Use these prompts to help students explore the final section of Neruda's ode:

Interpret What does "Elder first cousin / of my roots" (lines 98–99) mean? Why might Neruda use the word *cousin* rather than *father* or *brother*? ***Possible answer:*** *In these lines, the speaker views Whitman as a model, an inspiration, and an older poet who has shown him the way. The use of* cousin *may refer to the fact that because Whitman and Neruda lived at different times and in different lands and wrote in different languages, Neruda knew Whitman only at a distance and so could not claim a closer relationship.*

Evaluate In lines 111–133, the speaker brings public issues such as Lincoln's assassination into the poem. He might also be alluding to the outcome of the Spanish Civil War, in which the side that Neruda had supported lost. Does the poem gain from the allusion? Why or why not? *Accept all reasonable opinions, such as that the poem gains because Whitman wrote about Lincoln and cared about justice for all people; or, that the allusion represents Neruda's personal political views and should not intrude into a poem that celebrates life and art.*

Your silhouette
passed among the soldiers:
the poet, the wound-dresser,
the night attendant
90 who knows
the sound
of breathing in mortal agony
and awaits with the dawn
the silent
95 return
of life.

Good baker!
Elder first cousin
of my roots,
100 araucaria's
cupola,
it is
now
a hundred
105 years
that over your grass
and its germinations,
the wind
passes
110 without wearing out your eyes

New
and cruel years in your Fatherland:
persecutions,
tears,
115 prisons,
poisoned weapons
and wrathful wars
have not crushed
the grass of your book;
120 the vital fountainhead
of its freshness.
And, alas!
those
who murdered
125 Lincoln
now
lie in his bed.
They felled
his seat of honor
130 made of fragrant wood,
and raised a throne
spattered
with misfortune and blood.

View from Neruda's house on Isla Negra, Chile, with antique sailboat figureheads hanging in the window

DIFFERENTIATED INSTRUCTION

FOR STRATEGIC READERS
Vocabulary Support

- *araucaria* (line 100), "a Chilean cone-bearing tree"
- *cupola* (line 101), "small dome on a roof"
- *germinations* (line 107), "[cycles of] growth from seed"
- *fountainhead* (line 120), "source, as of a stream"

- *felled* (line 128), "cut down, as a tree is brought down"
- *vespertine* (line 141), "happening in the evening"
- *congregate* (line 158), "to gather"
- *magnitude* (line 160), "large size; broadness"

FOR ENGLISH LEARNERS
Culture: Connect [mixed-readiness groups] Have students find a copy of this ode in Spanish, or do so yourself. Then ask Spanish-speaking students, and native English speakers studying Spanish, to read the poem in its original language. Encourage students to try to make their own translations of passages from the poem. Have students read their translations aloud and comment upon differences from the translation in the text.

But
135 your voice
sings
in the suburban
stations,
in
140 the
vespertine
wharfs,
your word
splashes
145 like
dark water.
Your people,
white
and black,
150 poor
people,
simple people
like
all

155 people
do not forget
your bell:
They congregate singing
beneath
160 the magnitude
of your spacious life.
They walk among the peoples with your
love
caressing
the pure development
165 of brotherhood on earth.

Literary Analysis

1. **Analyze Metaphor** Neruda uses various metaphors to characterize Whitman's poems. What does each of these metaphors suggest about Whitman's verse?

   - Whitman's hand (lines 8–9)
   - Whitman as harvester (lines 47–70)
   - a basket of strawberries (lines 71–76)
   - a bell (lines 147–157)

2. **Compare Texts** Neruda has acknowledged Whitman's influence on his own verse. What elements of "Ode to Walt Whitman" reveal this influence? Be specific, citing evidence from this poem as well as from the Whitman poems you read on pages 510–517.

ANSWERS

Possible answers:

1. *Whitman's hand: Whitman's verse is welcoming, friendly, loving. Whitman as harvester: Whitman unearthed everything that he saw and experienced, from many parts of America, and he made the fruits of his "harvest" useful to the world. A basket of strawberries: Whitman's poetry was a gift of goodness and beauty in the midst of hard times. A bell: Whitman's voice called to the people of the world.*

2. *Accept all reasonable answers, such as the fact that both poets wrote free verse; that both cataloged occupations and land-scapes; and that both displayed democratic attitudes, seeking universal brotherhood and celebrating ordinary working people of all ethnicities.*

FOR ADVANCED LEARNERS/AP

Emulate Poets Challenge students to write poems that emulate the style, subject matter, and themes of a poet whose work they enjoy. The poems may be serious or parodic. Form, word count, and line length are up to the student. After volunteers have read their poems aloud, invite discussion about how each poem resembles (1) Neruda's ode and (2) the work of the poet who inspired it. Assemble the poems into a chapbook and display it, perhaps alongside the collection that resulted from the **Explore and Interpret Neruda** activity on page 521. Students who wish to do so may illustrate their poems or their peers' poems, as well.

Focus and Motivate

OBJECTIVES

Literary Analysis
- explore the key idea of **essential truths**
- analyze author's style
- read poetry

Reading
- develop strategies for reading Emily Dickinson's poetry

 CALIFORNIA R3.3, R3.4

ABOUT THE POET

As students read the biography, invite them to imagine Dickinson's way of life. Point out that she wrote her poems in secret, making them known only to a handful of trusted people, and that she published very few during her lifetime. Dickinson's poetry was also private, concerned with events on a small scale. However, while she remained in one house almost all her life, her thoughts and imagination ranged widely. Urge students to look for both traits—the small scale and the wide range—when they read these selections.

USING THE *NOTABLE QUOTE*

Read the comment aloud and ask students what they think **Emily Dickinson** meant. *Possible answer: Dickinson meant that great poetry makes the reader think about new things or think in new ways.* Invite volunteers to share any such feeling they have had when reading poetry or experiencing other forms of art.

Brilliant Mavericks: Whitman and Dickinson

CALIFORNIA R3.3, R3.4

Selected Poetry
by Emily Dickinson

Emily Dickinson
1830–1886

NOTABLE QUOTE
"If I feel physically as if the top of my head were taken off, I know that is poetry."

FYI
Did you know that Emily Dickinson . . .
- sometimes signed her letters "Uncle Emily"?
- dressed only in white in the last 16 years of her life?
- had eye problems and feared that she might go blind?

Author Online
For more on Emily Dickinson, visit the **Literature Center** at **ClassZone.com.**

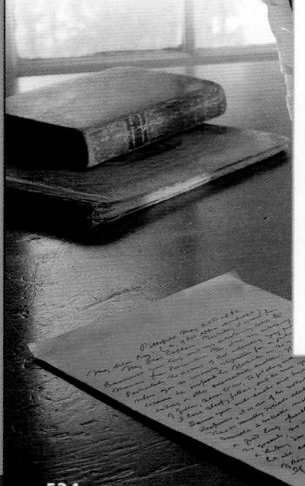

Emily Dickinson rarely ventured beyond the confines of her family home in Amherst, Massachusetts, but her restless mind and creativity knew no such boundaries. In her bedroom overlooking the village graveyard, Dickinson meditated on life and death and wrote about these subjects with startling originality. Today she and Walt Whitman are considered the greatest American poets of the 19th century.

Family Ties Dickinson was born in 1830 into a well-to-do family, which would become the center of her existence. She stood in awe of her father, a stern, imposing man committed to Puritan ideals, and felt estranged from her mother, who "did not," Dickinson once commented in a letter, "care for thought." However, she had a close relationship with her older brother, Austin, and her younger sister, Vinnie.

In 1847, Dickinson left home to attend Mount Holyoke Female Seminary in nearby South Hadley, but she left after just one year. She missed her family, but she also resented the intense pressure she felt there to join the church. All her life, Dickinson felt torn between her own convictions and the religious beliefs of those around her. This conflict is reflected in many of her poems.

A Writer's Life In the 1850s, Dickinson began to devote herself to poetry. Late at night, she wrote by candlelight. During the day, she jotted down her thoughts between household chores. Inspired by her own observations and experiences, Dickinson composed a remarkable number of profound, gemlike poems.

Perhaps because of this newfound focus on her writing, Dickinson gradually withdrew from the world. However, she did not become a total recluse. She entertained occasional visitors in her home and maintained contact with friends and family by means of a lively correspondence.

Poetic Legacy Early in 1886, Dickinson wrote a letter to her cousins that simply read "Called back." She seemed to have realized that she was dying. Following her death, her sister Vinnie discovered a box full of Dickinson's poems bound into neat booklets. As a result of Vinnie's perseverance, the first volume of Dickinson's poetry appeared four years after the poet's death. Her poems—1,775 in all—finally revealed to the world the passionate, witty woman who never flinched from the truth.

524

Selection Resources

 RESOURCE MANAGER UNIT 3

Plan and Teach pp. 37–44

Literary Analysis
Author's Style pp. 45, 46†*
Question Support p. 49*

Reading
Reading Dickinson's Poetry
  pp. 47, 48†*

Assessment
Selection Tests A, B/C pp. 51*, 53*
 Test Generator CD

 BEST PRACTICES TOOLKIT

Differentiated Instruction
  pp. 31–38*

Graphic Organizers/Strategies
Two-Column Chart • Visualizing
• Interactive Notes • Analysis
Frame: Poetic Content

Reading Support
 Audio Anthology CD*

Technology
Literature Center at **ClassZone.com**
WriteSmart CD

---

* Resources for Differentiation   † Also in Spanish

LITERARY ANALYSIS: AUTHOR'S STYLE

Emily Dickinson's style is as unique and personal as her observations about the world. Here are some of the distinctive stylistic elements you will find in Dickinson's poetry:

- dense **quatrains,** or four-line stanzas, that echo the simple rhythms of church hymns
- **slant rhymes,** or words that do not exactly rhyme ("chill"/ "Tulle")
- inventive punctuation and sentence structure, including the use of dashes to highlight important words and break up the rhythm of her poems
- irregular capitalization and inverted syntax to emphasize words
- surprisingly unconventional **figurative language,** including similes, metaphors, and personification

As you read, think about the effect of these style elements in Dickinson's poems.

READING STRATEGY: READING DICKINSON'S POETRY

To get the most out of Emily Dickinson's poetry, try reading each poem three times.

- The first time, read for an overall impression. Pause when you encounter dashes, and be aware of the poem's **rhythm.**
- The second time, note the use of **imagery** and **figurative language.** Pay attention to the words capitalized for emphasis.
- The third time, read the poem aloud. Think about what the imagery and figurative language convey about meaning.

Use a chart like the one shown for each poem. Jot down your thoughts and ideas after each reading.

"Because I could not stop for Death"		
1st Reading	2nd Reading	3rd Reading
Poem has a calm, reflective mood.	Images of death are not frightening.	Poem suggests that death and dying are not frightening.

Explore the Key Idea

CALIFORNIA

What are life's ESSENTIAL TRUTHS?

KEY IDEA Love, loss. Joy, death. When you focus on life's real meaning, you explore its **essential truths.** These truths, of course, are the natural focus of poets. For instance, in the poems that follow, Emily Dickinson has a great deal to say about death and dying. But does she—or any other poet—speak for you? What do you think about such weighty matters as death, success, and solitude? What is your truth?

QUICKWRITE Create your own top-five list of life's essential truths. Begin with number five and work your way up to number one. Feel free to express your truths in statements, phrases, questions, or any form you want.

525

Teach

CALIFORNIA

What are life's ESSENTIAL TRUTHS?

Ask the question and have students read and discuss the **KEY IDEA**. Emphasize that some **essential truths** may apply to a large number of people, whereas others may be highly individualistic. Have students complete the **QUICKWRITE;** then compare volunteers' lists in a brief, respectful discussion.

SKILLS FOCUS

LITERARY ANALYSIS   R3.3, R3.4

● AUTHOR'S STYLE

Write this quatrain from Dickinson's poem "My Life had stood—a Loaded Gun—" on the board:

> My Life had stood—a Loaded Gun—
> In Corners—till a Day—
> The Owner passed—identified—
> And carried Me away—

Have students find examples of the distinctive elements of Dickinson's style mentioned in the text. **Possible answer:** *inventive punctuation (dashes); inventive sentence structure; irregular capitalization of words within lines; figurative language in the speaker's comparison of her life to a loaded gun.*

READING STRATEGY   R3.3, R3.4

■ READING DICKINSON'S POETRY

Have students read the quatrain in the previous activity three times according to the directions in the text and then give their responses.

CHECK UNDERSTANDING Have students state their first impressions of what Dickinson's poetry is like.

R RESOURCE MANAGER—Copy Master Reading Dickinson's Poetry p. 47 (for student use while reading the selections)

DIFFERENTIATED INSTRUCTION

FOR STRATEGIC READERS

Concept Support: Style Ask students what the word *style* means to them. It might mean the way that someone wears his or her hair, or the kind of music the person likes. Elicit or explain that *style* in writing is similar: Just as each student has a personal way of wearing his or her hair or choosing music, each writer has a personal way of using words. Ask students to describe what they like in the styles of various writers.

FOR ADVANCED LEARNERS/AP

Analyze Authors' Styles Challenge students to think about the writing style of two or three authors whose work they have read in this text. Then ask students to write a description of each author's style, including a statement about what they like or dislike about that style. Invite students to share and compare their analyses.

SUMMARY

The speaker describes a ride in Death's carriage.

LITERARY ANALYSIS

Ⓐ AUTHOR'S STYLE

Possible answer: Death is personified as a kind gentleman who drives a carriage.

READING STRATEGY

Ⓑ DICKINSON'S POETRY

Possible answer: The house probably represents the speaker's grave.

If students need help . . . Urge them to visualize the quatrain. Ask:

- What is the purpose of a house?
- If the top of the house is "scarcely visible" and "in the Ground," where is the house?
- Why does this house resemble "A Swelling of the Ground"?

Lines 1–24
TIERED DISCUSSION PROMPTS

Use these prompts to help students explore the poem's ideas:

Restate What are Death and the speaker of the poem doing? *Possible answer: They are riding in a carriage.*

Analyze Which details indicate that the speaker is leaving her life behind? *Possible answer: She speaks of putting away both labor and leisure in lines 6–7; in lines 9–12 she passes schoolchildren at play, fields of grain, and even the setting sun.*

Synthesize How does the final quatrain change the reader's interpretation of the poem? *Possible answer: Up to the final quatrain, the reader assumes that the speaker has just died; in the final quatrain, the reader realizes that her "recent" memories are, in fact, centuries old.*

Because I could not stop for Death—

EMILY DICKINSON

Because I could not stop for Death—
He kindly stopped for me—
The Carriage held but just Ourselves—
And Immortality. Ⓐ

5 We slowly drove—He knew no haste
And I had put away
My labor and my leisure too,
For His Civility[1]—

We passed the School, where Children strove
10 At Recess—in the Ring—
We passed the Fields of Gazing Grain[2]—
We passed the Setting Sun—

Or rather—He passed Us—
The Dews drew quivering and chill—
15 For only Gossamer,[3] my Gown—
My Tippet—only Tulle[4]—

We paused before a House that seemed
A Swelling of the Ground—
The Roof was scarcely visible—
20 The Cornice[5]—in the Ground— Ⓑ

Since then—'tis Centuries—and yet
Feels shorter than the Day
I first surmised the Horses' Heads
Were toward Eternity—

---

1. **Civility:** politeness.
2. **Gazing Grain:** grain leaning toward the sun.
3. **Gossamer:** a thin, light cloth.
4. **My Tippet—only Tulle** (tōōl): My shawl was only a fine net cloth.
5. **Cornice** (kôr′nĭs): the molding around the top of a building.

Ⓐ AUTHOR'S STYLE
Reread lines 1–4 and notice the use of **personification,** a figure of speech in which an object, animal, or idea is given human characteristics. How is Death personified?

Ⓑ DICKINSON'S POETRY
Note the **imagery** used to describe the house in lines 17–20. What do you think the house represents?

ANALYZE VISUALS
Why might the artist have chosen to keep this photograph out of focus?

DIFFERENTIATED INSTRUCTION

For general guidelines on differentiating instruction, see

 BEST PRACTICES TOOLKIT
Differentiated Instruction pp. 31–38

FOR STRATEGIC READERS
Options for Reading: Audio Recording

- Have students listen to the poems on the *Audio Anthology CD* (also recommended for English learners) while they read along in their texts. Ask students to consider what makes each poem unusual.

- Invite volunteers to read the poems aloud. Encourage readers to strive for a tone that matches the meaning of the poem and to consider how they will convey Dickinson's unusual punctuation and capitalization. After each reading, discuss how the reader's oral interpretation affects the listeners' responses to the poem presented.

BACKGROUND

Dickinson's Amherst The town of Amherst, in west-central Massachusetts, was founded in 1703 and was a farming community in Dickinson's day. Today it is the home of two well-known institutions of higher learning: Amherst College and the University of Massachusetts. At various times, lexicographer Noah Webster (1758–1843) and poet Robert Frost (1874–1963) lived in Amherst. Dickinson's grandfather, Samuel Fowler Dickinson, helped establish Amherst College, which was founded to train Christian ministers and strove to reinforce the Puritan values of the early leaders of Massachusetts. Dickinson's father, Edward Dickinson, a strict Calvinist, served as the college's treasurer in addition to serving in the Massachusetts legislature and in Congress. Her brother, William Austin Dickinson, was a prominent attorney in town and lived next door to his parents and two sisters. The house in Amherst in which Emily Dickinson spent most of her life has been designated a National Historic Landmark.

FOR STRATEGIC READERS

Concept Support: Reading Dickinson's Poetry Have students reread the notes about this poem in the chart introduced on page 525. Work with students to find passages in the poem that might have prompted the notes. *Possible answer: Lines 5–8 might have prompted the first note; lines 9–12, the second note; and lines 1–4 and 21–24, in conjunction with the previous references, the third note.*

FOR ENGLISH LEARNERS

Language: Punctuation and Print Clues [mixed-readiness pairs] Early editions of Dickinson's poems regularized the poet's punctuation and capitalization. English learners will find reading Dickinson easier if they work with partners who are more fluent, turning the uppercase letters within lines to lowercase and substituting commas or periods for dashes. (If you use this activity, have students recall it when they answer Question 9 on page 534.)

SUMMARY

The speaker notes that people who fail appreciate success the most.

READING STRATEGY

C DICKINSON'S POETRY

Possible answer: The dashes in line 9, the dominant iambic meter, the assonance of long /e/ sounds, and the alliteration of /d/ and /s/ sounds create the rhythm.

ANSWERS

Possible answers:

1. The "purple Host" is the army that has achieved victory (symbolized by capturing the opponent's flag).

2. The dying soldier on the losing side, hearing the far-off sound of the winners' celebration, knows the meaning of victory better than the victors do.

3. Accept all reasonable responses.

Success is counted sweetest

EMILY DICKINSON

Success is counted sweetest
By those who ne'er succeed.
To comprehend a nectar[1]
Requires sorest need.

5 Not one of all the purple Host[2]
Who took the Flag[3] today
Can tell the definition
So clear of Victory

As he defeated—dying—
10 On whose forbidden ear
The distant strains of triumph
Burst agonized and clear! **C**

1. **To comprehend a nectar:** to fully appreciate a delicious beverage.
2. **Host:** army.
3. **took the Flag:** captured the enemy's flag as a token of victory.

C DICKINSON'S POETRY
Read lines 9–12 aloud. What elements create the **rhythm** in these lines?

Literary Analysis

1. **Clarify** Who is the "purple Host" in line 5?

2. **Paraphrase** Reread lines 9–12. How would you paraphrase these lines?

3. **Form Opinions** Do you agree that those who fail are better able to appreciate success than those who win? Explain your answer.

528

DIFFERENTIATED INSTRUCTION

FOR STRATEGIC READERS
Concept Support: Reading Dickinson's Poetry
Have students add to the chart introduced on page 525, as in this example:

"Success is counted sweetest"		
1st Reading	2nd Reading	3rd Reading
Idea seems contradictory, but makes sense.	Battle imagery makes the idea clearer.	Loss brings a sense of reality.

FOR ADVANCED LEARNERS/AP
Analyze Theme "Success is counted sweetest" evokes questions about success. Have students write and share an essay about success in which they address questions such as these:

• What is success? Does it mean something different to each person, or is there a meaning about which most people would agree?

• If success is appreciated more by people who lack it than by people who have it, how desirable is success?

• Is success a sham—that is, does success lose its allure once attained—or is there a kind of success that does not spoil, a kind that is more authentic and enduring than success in a competition? Is Dickinson an example of that kind of success?

• Would Dickinson have considered herself a success? Why or why not?

Much Madness is divinest Sense—

EMILY DICKINSON

Much Madness is divinest Sense—
To a discerning Eye—
Much Sense—the starkest Madness— **D**
'Tis the Majority
5 In this, as All, prevail—
Assent—and you are sane—
Demur[1]—you're straightway dangerous—
And handled with a Chain[2]—

---

1. **demur** (dĭ-mûr′): voice opposition; object.
2. **handled with a Chain:** In the 19th century, those who were considered insane were often kept chained in asylums.

D AUTHOR'S STYLE
Pay attention to the use of capitalization in lines 1–3. Which two words are twice capitalized? Why do you think Dickinson chose to capitalize those words?

My life closed twice before its close—

EMILY DICKINSON

My life closed twice before its close—
It yet remains to see
If Immortality unveil
A third event to me

5 So huge, so hopeless to conceive
As these that twice befell
Parting is all we know of heaven,
And all we need of hell. **E**

E DICKINSON'S POETRY
After your first reading of the poem, what is your overall impression of its subject?

SUMMARIES

Much Madness is divinest Sense—The speaker notes that standards of "madness" and "sense" are determined by the majority.

My life closed twice before its close—The speaker reflects upon the pain of parting.

LITERARY ANALYSIS

D AUTHOR'S STYLE

Possible answer: The words Madness *and* Sense *are repeatedly capitalized, perhaps to emphasize their importance.*

Lines 1–8
REINFORCE *KEY IDEA:* ESSENTIAL TRUTHS

Discuss What **essential truths** about one's place in society does Dickinson convey in "Much Madness is divinest Sense—"? *Possible answer: As Dickinson sees it, whatever group forms the majority in society determines what is "madness" and what is "sense." She also comments that a person who doesn't want to be considered "dangerous" needs to express agreement with the majority view.*

READING STRATEGY

E DICKINSON'S POETRY

Possible answer: The overall impression is that the poem's subject is loss, especially the pain of losing human relationships.

FOR STRATEGIC READERS

Comprehension Support Use a Two-Column Chart to help students distinguish the views in "Much Madness is divinest Sense—," as in this example:

Majority View	Speaker's View
Madness = "dangerous"	Madness = "divinest sense"
Sense = "assent" (agreement)	Sense = "starkest madness"

BEST PRACTICES TOOLKIT—Transparency
Two-Column Chart p. A25

FOR ADVANCED LEARNERS/AP

Analyze a Critical Interpretation [small-group option] Explain that Dickinson admired and reportedly was in love with a married minister, the Reverend Charles Wadsworth, who moved to California in 1862. That year, Dickinson wrote 366 poems. Dickinson's sister-in-law felt that Dickinson's separation from Wadsworth was partly responsible for her seclusion, but many scholars see that as an incomplete explanation. Ask small groups of students to reread "My life closed twice before its close—" in light of that theory, paying particular attention to lines 7–8. Instruct each group to research biographies and critical works. Then have groups decide (1) whether the poem is about a lost romance and (2) what role Wadsworth might have played in Dickinson's development as a poet. Have each group present its decisions.

SUMMARY

The speaker conveys the experience of choosing a friend.

F DICKINSON'S POETRY

Possible answer: *The dashes and the abbreviated use of words break up the rhythm; emphasize important words; and create an unusual rhythmic, musical effect.*

Extend the Discussion How do these stylistic techniques affect readers?

G AUTHOR'S STYLE

Possible answer: *The comparison suggests the emotional stoniness of the soul's decision to close off attention to all but one chosen person.*

If students need help . . . Ask these questions about the final word of the poem:

- What does it mean for a person to be like stone?
- How does stonily closing off attention fit in with the title of the poem?

ANSWERS

Possible answers:

1. *According to the quatrain, the Soul is not impressed by society's standards of greatness.*

2. *The Soul sometimes chooses to associate with one person out of all others.*

3. *"Society" means those with whom the Soul wishes to associate.*

The Soul selects her own Society—

EMILY DICKINSON

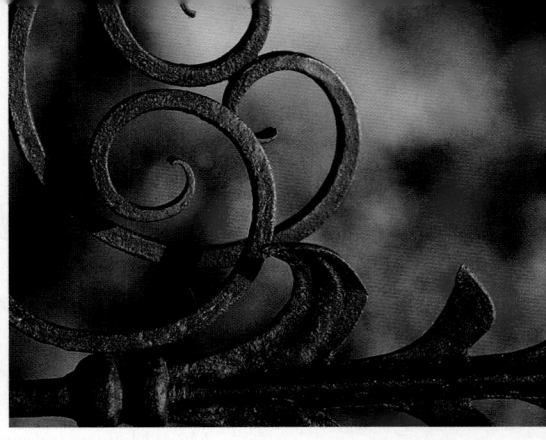

The Soul selects her own Society—
Then—shuts the Door—
To her divine Majority[1]—
Present no more—

5 Unmoved—she notes the Chariots[2]—pausing—
At her low Gate—
Unmoved—an Emperor be kneeling
Upon her Mat— **F**

I've known her—from an ample nation—
10 Choose One—
Then—close the Valves of her attention—
Like Stone— **G**

---

1. **divine Majority:** other souls.
2. **the Chariots:** the Emperor's chariots.

F DICKINSON'S POETRY
Reread lines 5–8. What are some of the effects of the dashes and the poet's abbreviated use of words?

G AUTHOR'S STYLE
A **simile** is a figure of speech that compares two things that have something in common, using *like* or *as*. What images does the comparison in the last quatrain suggest?

Literary Analysis

1. **Summarize** How would you summarize the second quatrain?

2. **Paraphrase** Reread lines 9–10. How would you paraphrase these lines?

3. **Draw Conclusions** What do you think the speaker means by "Society"?

DIFFERENTIATED INSTRUCTION

FOR STRATEGIC READERS
Vocabulary Support

- *Unmoved* (line 5), "not affected; remaining emotionally cold"
- *ample* (line 9), "large; having many people"
- *Valves* (line 11), "gates; devices that control by opening and shutting"

FOR ADVANCED LEARNERS/AP
Hypothesize Invite students to discuss how the theme of "The Soul selects her own Society—" may be an expression of Dickinson's decision to shut herself off from society. Extend the discussion by asking to what extent readers can infer elements of a poet's life from the poet's work; have students support their responses by referring to poets or other writers whose works they have read in this text.

I heard a *Fly buzz—* when I died—

EMILY DICKINSON

I heard a Fly buzz—when I died—
The Stillness in the Room
Was like the Stillness in the Air—
Between the Heaves[1] of Storm— **H**

5 The Eyes around—had wrung them dry—
And Breaths were gathering firm
For that last Onset—when the King[2]
Be witnessed—in the Room—

I willed my Keepsakes—Signed away
10 What portion of me be
Assignable—and then it was
There interposed[3] a Fly—

With Blue—uncertain stumbling Buzz—
Between the light—and me—
15 And then the Windows failed—and then
I could not see to see— **I**

---

1. **Heaves:** risings and fallings.
2. **the King:** God.
3. **interposed:** came between.

H AUTHOR'S STYLE
Notice the **simile** in the first quatrain. What is being compared? Why is this comparison appropriate?

I DICKINSON'S POETRY
Reread lines 13–16. What final images does the speaker describe? What is ironic about this **imagery**?

SELECTED POETRY BY EMILY DICKINSON **531**

SUMMARY

The speaker describes her final moments in life, the climax of which is interrupted by a buzzing fly.

H AUTHOR'S STYLE

Possible answer: The stillness in the room is being compared to the calm between storms. The comparison is appropriate because it describes the quiet before a death.

I DICKINSON'S POETRY

Possible answer: The speaker describes a fly that buzzes into her line of sight, blocking the dimming light from the windows as her eyes fail. The imagery is ironic because instead of describing something cosmic at a moment of supreme transition, the speaker describes something seemingly insignificant: a fly.

If students need help . . . Use these questions to focus on the poem's irony:

- Why were people quiet around the speaker? What were they expecting to happen?
- In what sense does the buzzing fly take the place of the Angel of Death?
- What does this irony suggest about the speaker's view of life and death?

FOR STRATEGIC READERS

Comprehension Support Use a Visualizing diagram to help students imagine and thus better understand the scene that the speaker of this poem describes.

 BEST PRACTICES TOOLKIT—Transparency Visualizing p. A11

FOR ADVANCED LEARNERS/AP

Compare and Contrast Texts "I heard a Fly buzz—when I died—" like "Because I could not stop for Death—" (found on page 526) describes the moment of death as an arrival of a visitor. Have students write a brief essay comparing and contrasting the two poems, focusing on how each visitor represents a different understanding of death.

As students prepare their essays, have them consider

- the language used to describe each visitor's arrival
- the speaker's experience after each arrival

Have students find opportunities to share their essays with the class.

SUMMARY
The speaker compares her life to a loaded gun.

LITERARY ANALYSIS

❿ AUTHOR'S STYLE

Possible answer: *The speaker's comparison of herself to a loaded gun (symbolizing the power to kill) is surprising because she is granting herself a power not usually associated with women (symbolic life-givers).*

READING STRATEGY

Ⓚ DICKINSON'S POETRY

Possible answers: *The lines suggest that their relationship is ambiguous; that the gun cannot die but also cannot live without the owner; that the gun is an essential part of the owner.*

Lines 1–24
REINFORCE *KEY IDEA:* ESSENTIAL TRUTHS

Discuss What **essential truths** about life does this poem express? **Possible answer:** *Every life needs a purpose; being aware of one's personal power is key to having a full life.*

SELECTION WRAP–UP

SYNTHESIZE Have students name the themes that are central to Dickinson's work.

My Life had stood— a Loaded Gun— EMILY DICKINSON

My Life had stood—a Loaded Gun—
In Corners—till a Day
The Owner passed—identified—
And carried Me away— ❿

5 And now We roam in Sovereign Woods[1]—
And now We hunt the Doe—
And every time I speak for Him—
The Mountains straight reply—

And do I smile, such cordial light
10 Upon the Valley glow—
It is as a Vesuvian[2] face
Had let its pleasure through—

And when at Night—Our good Day done—
I guard My Master's Head—
15 'Tis better than the Eider-Duck's
Deep Pillow—to have shared—

To foe of His—I'm deadly foe—
None stir the second time—
On whom I lay a Yellow Eye—
20 Or an emphatic Thumb—

Though I than He—may longer live
He longer must—than I—
For I have but the power to kill,
Without—the power to die— Ⓚ

❿ **AUTHOR'S STYLE**
Remember that a **metaphor** is a figure of speech that compares two things directly, without using *like* or *as*. What is surprising about the metaphor introduced in lines 1–4?

Ⓚ **DICKINSON'S POETRY**
Read the final quatrain aloud. What do the lines suggest about the relationship between the gun and its owner?

---

1. **Sovereign** (sŏv'ər-ĭn) **Woods:** God's woods.
2. **Vesuvian** (vĭ-sōō'vē-ən): marked by sudden or violent outbursts; after the volcano Mount Vesuvius, which erupted and destroyed Pompeii in A.D. 79.

532

DIFFERENTIATED INSTRUCTION

FOR STRATEGIC READERS
Concept Support: Reading Dickinson's Poetry Continue working with the chart introduced on page 525. Alternatively, model the use of Interactive Notes with the first quatrain of this poem; then have students continue on their own and draw upon their responses as you discuss the poem in class.

 BEST PRACTICES TOOLKIT—Transparency Interactive Notes p. B4

FOR ADVANCED LEARNERS/AP
Create a Learning Diagram [mixed learning profiles] Have analytical and visual learners work together to create a diagram that teaches this rather challenging poem. Suggest that students use an Analysis Frame: Poetic Content or create an original diagram to present the poem's themes and the techniques that Dickinson uses to convey the themes.

BEST PRACTICES TOOLKIT—Transparency Analysis Frame: Poetic Content pp. D21, D36

LETTER In April 1862, Thomas Wentworth Higginson wrote an essay offering advice to beginning writers, urging them, "Charge your style with life." Emily Dickinson, 32 years old at the time, responded to his essay, submitting four poems along with the following unsigned letter. In place of a signature, she enclosed a signed calling card.

Letter to Mr. T. W. Higginson

April 15, 1862

Mr Higginson,

Are you too deeply occupied to say if my Verse is alive?

The Mind is so near itself—it cannot see, distinctly—and I have none to ask—

Should you think it breathed—and had you the leisure to tell me, I should feel quick gratitude—

If I make the mistake—that you dared to tell me— would give me sincerer honor—toward you—

I enclose my name—asking you, if you please— Sir—to tell me what is true?

That you will not betray me—it is needless to ask— since Honor is it's own pawn—

Miss Emily E. Dickinson

READING FOR INFORMATION **533**

CONNECT

This selection provides additional information on Dickinson's sense of herself as a poet. You can also use it as a minilesson on reading for information.

Reading for Information

Point out that this selection is a letter written by Emily Dickinson to someone whom she had not met but whose essay of advice she had read. Then ask:

- What does the date on the letter indicate about the letter's historical context? ***Possible answer:*** *The date indicates that Dickinson wrote the letter during the Civil War.*

- Paraphrase the question that begins the letter. ***Possible answer:*** *If you are not too busy, could you tell me whether my poetry is any good?*

- What element of the typical letter is missing from this letter? ***Possible answer:*** *A signature is missing.*

TIERED DISCUSSION PROMPTS

Use these prompts to help students relate Dickinson's sense of herself to the poems that they have just read:

Connect Have you ever asked someone to evaluate your efforts? How did you feel about asking? *Accept all reasonable answers.*

Interpret What is the meaning of these lines: " . . . tell me what is true? That you will not betray me—it is needless to ask—since Honor is its own pawn—"? ***Possible answer:*** *Dickinson asks Higginson to be honest in evaluating her poems. She adds that she knows he will not tell others about her poems because he is an honorable person.*

Synthesize What inference might Higginson make about the writer of the letter? ***Possible answer:*** *Higginson might infer that she was shy, unworldly, and unsure of herself—or that she was secretly proud of her poetry while being outwardly modest.*

Practice and Apply

After Reading

Use these copy masters to check understanding and provide extra support:

R RESOURCE MANAGER—Copy Masters
Author's Style p. 45
Question Support p. 49

Additional selection questions are provided for teachers on page 41.

ANSWERS

1. *The speaker has died.*

2. *The speaker is disdainful of the Majority, fearful of its power, and wary of its misconceptions.*

3. *In these lines, the people in the room are preparing themselves for the moment of the speaker's death.*

Possible answers:

4. *"Because . . . ": Death is kindly, gentle, timeless; "My life . . . ": Parting from loved ones is a hellish experience; "I heard . . . ": Dying is mundane but also a prelude to something greater.*

5. ● **SKILLS FOCUS Author's Style**
"Success . . . ": Capitalization emphasizes symbols of success; "Much Madness . . . ": Capitalization emphasizes the dichotomy between madness and sense; "The Soul . . . ": Capitalization emphasizes the isolation of the soul.

6. ■ **SKILLS FOCUS Dickinson's Poetry**
The tone of Dickinson's poems is thoughtful, quirky, and often deceptively cheerful.

Assess and Reteach

Assess

R RESOURCE MANAGER—Copy Masters
Selection Test A pp. 51–52
Selection Test B/C pp. 53–54

📀 Test Generator CD

Reteach

S STANDARDS LESSON FILE
Literature Lesson 44: Style and Syntax
Literature Lesson 45: Author's Perspective

R3.3, R3.4

Comprehension

1. **Recall** What has happened to the speaker in "Because I could not stop for Death—"?

2. **Clarify** What do you think is the speaker's attitude toward the Majority in "Much Madness is divinest Sense"?

3. **Summarize** How would you summarize lines 5–8 of "I heard a Fly buzz—when I died—"?

Literary Analysis

4. **Make Inferences** What **essential truths** about death and dying does Dickinson convey in the following poems? Cite specific details.

   • "Because I could not stop for Death—"
   • "My life closed twice before its close—"
   • "I heard a Fly buzz—when I died—"

5. **Analyze Author's Style** What ideas are emphasized by the unusual use of capitalization in the following poems? Be specific.

   • "Success is counted sweetest"
   • "Much Madness is divinest Sense"
   • "The Soul selects her own Society—"

6. **Analyze Dickinson's Poetry** Review the thoughts and ideas you recorded as you read and reread the poems. Based on Dickinson's **imagery** and **figurative language,** how would you characterize the overall **tone** of her poems?

7. **Evaluate Paradox** A paradox is a statement that seems to contradict itself but may nevertheless suggest an important truth. Use a diagram like the one shown to identify the paradoxes in "Success is counted sweetest," "Much Madness is divinest Sense," and "My Life had stood—a Loaded Gun—." What truth does each paradox convey?

8. **Compare Texts** What style elements of the poet do you recognize in Emily Dickinson's letter to Thomas Wentworth Higginson (page 533)?

Literary Criticism

9. **Different Perspectives** Until 1955, editors published "corrected" versions of Dickinson's poems in which dashes had been deleted, rhyme and meter had been made regular, and metaphors replaced with more conventional figures of speech. Imagine what corrections might have been made. What would have been lost? Use details from the poems to support your ideas. Why do you think the editors might have decided to change the original versions?

---

7. *"Success . . . ": paradox—"Success is counted sweetest / By those who ne'er succeed"; truth—Failures value success more than successful people do. "Much Madness . . . ": paradox—"Much Madness is divinest Sense"; truth—It is hard to tell the difference between sanity and insanity. "My Life . . . ": paradox—"For I have but the power to kill, / Without—the power to die"; truth— Human beings, because they are mortal, have a sanctity that inanimate objects do not.*

8. *Common elements include the use of dashes, personification, metaphor, condensed words and syntax, unusual expressions, ambiguous meaning, and a primary focus upon impressions and feelings.*

9. *The "corrections" might have caused the poems to lose their power to surprise and disconcert; metaphors might have been changed, losing their startling originality; omitting dashes and regularizing rhyme and meter would have caused the poems to lose their unusual musicality. Students' choices of details will vary.*

The Innovations of Whitman and Dickinson

Although Emily Dickinson and Walt Whitman were both revolutionary in their approach to poetic form and content, their poems look quite different. Dickinson wrote short and concise lines; Whitman, long and sprawling ones.

> *Success is counted sweetest*
> *By those who ne'er succeed.*
> —**Emily Dickinson**
>
> *I wish I could translate the hints about the dead young men*
> *   and women,*
> *And the hints about old men and mothers, and the offspring taken*
> *   soon out of their laps.*
> —**Walt Whitman**

Dickinson concentrated on private and personal experiences; Whitman, on representative experiences of the American people.

> *I heard a Fly buzz—when I died—*
> —**Emily Dickinson**
>
> *I hear America singing, the varied carols I hear,*
> —**Walt Whitman**

© Mike Caplanis/Luminarygraphics.com.

Writing to Compare

Write an essay to further compare the work of Dickinson and Whitman. Cite specific lines from the poems on page 510 through 532 to support your comparison.

Consider

- each poet's style and form (that is, word choice, imagery, line length, stanzas, rhythm, rhyme)
- the poems' subject matter and general themes
- which words, lines, or stanzas will provide you with effective evidence and details

Extension

SPEAKING & LISTENING With a partner, imagine a dialogue that might have occurred between Whitman and Dickinson had they had a chance meeting. Create the dialogue of this momentous literary conversation, in which the poets discuss their topics, themes, and techniques. Then, **perform** your conversation for the class. Try to use speaking styles that you think are appropriate for the two poets.

R3.3, R3.4, W2.2

Wrap-Up: *Brilliant Mavericks*

This Wrap-Up provides students with an opportunity to compare and contrast the poetry of Walt Whitman and Emily Dickinson. After students have read the first pair of examples, briefly discuss how they can recognize the author of each example through the appearance of the lines. Then have students read the second pair of examples and describe the subject matter in a way that compares and contrasts.

Writing to Compare

- Remind students to consider similarities and differences in their essays, for the term *compare* can include both comparison and contrast. Students need not cite lines from every poem that they have read in this cluster, but urge them to cover at least two poems from each poet.
- Advise students not to choose poems at random. One way to choose is to select a quality or device, such as imagery, and then search for interesting examples in each poet's work. Another method is to choose poems that seem either especially different or especially alike.

Extension

- Suggest that students clarify their images of the two poets by recalling the poems and reading over any notes that they have taken.
- Suggest that partners review both poets and use Questioning the Author as they formulate questions and answers.
- Urge students to rehearse, refining their questions and answers as they do so.

 BEST PRACTICES TOOLKIT—Transparency
Questioning the Author p. D19

DIFFERENTIATED INSTRUCTION

FOR ENGLISH LEARNERS

Creating Dialogue For students who need practice with conversational English, use this dialogue to practice questions and answers. Start by modeling an exchange with an English-fluent volunteer. Pitch the conversation to the level that your English learners require. It may be as simple as "How are you, Walt?" / "I am fine, Emily." On the other hand, it may involve simple statements of poetic technique. Then have students try an exchange, using starter sentences such as these:

- "What kinds of poems do you write?"
- "Do you write free verse?"
- "I like using short lines in my poems. What kinds of lines do you write?"
- "I use rhyme and meter. Do you?"
- "I write about America. What do you write about?"

Focus and Motivate

OBJECTIVES

Literary Analysis
- explore the key idea of **self-determination**
- analyze style
- read a slave narrative

Reading
- analyze author's purpose

Grammar and Writing
- make effective word choices by using vivid verbs
- write a description

R3.3, W2.3, LC1.1

ABOUT THE AUTHOR

After students have read about Frederick Douglass, explain that the excerpt they are about to read takes place after he had left the Aulds' home (**Forbidden Education**) and before he had escaped to freedom (**From Slave to Abolitionist**). Also point out that in 1855, Douglass published an expanded version of his autobiography entitled *My Bondage and My Freedom,* which includes an account of his work as an abolitionist.

USING THE *NOTABLE QUOTE*

Ask students to speculate on what the quote reveals about **Frederick Douglass's** attitude toward human dignity. *Possible answer: The quote reveals that Douglass believed that even the degradation of slavery could not rob people of their essential humanity and self-worth.*

R3.3, W2.3 (p. 549), LC1.1 (p. 549)
CALIFORNIA

from Narrative of the Life of Frederick Douglass, an American Slave

Slave Narrative by Frederick Douglass

Frederick Douglass
c. 1817–1895

NOTABLE QUOTE
"The soul that is within me no man can degrade."

FYI
Did you know that Frederick Douglass . . .
- escaped to the North by disguising himself as a sailor?
- made his home a stop on the Underground Railroad?
- was an early defender of women's rights?

Author Online

For more on Frederick Douglass, visit the **Literature Center** at **ClassZone.com.**

Frederick Douglass endured 21 years of slavery before he escaped to freedom in the North, where he became an outspoken and influential abolitionist. In the years leading up to the Civil War, his powerful speeches spurred the nation to move against slavery and to extend equal rights to all its citizens.

Forbidden Education As a boy, Douglass worked as a slave in the home of Hugh and Sophia Auld of Baltimore, Maryland. Although it was against the law, Mrs. Auld taught Douglass how to read. After Mr. Auld commanded his wife to stop her lessons, Douglass educated himself in secret, studying from a textbook on public speaking titled *The Columbian Orator.*

From Slave to Abolitionist Douglass escaped and in 1838 settled in New Bedford, Massachusetts. Three years later, he spoke so eloquently to the Massachusetts Anti-Slavery Society that they hired him to lecture about his experiences. Proslavery hecklers frequently attacked him, hurling insults and even rotten eggs and vegetables, but Douglass continued, undeterred.

In 1845, with the publication of his autobiography, *Narrative of the Life of Frederick Douglass, an American Slave,* Douglass rose to international fame—dangerous attention for a runaway slave. To avoid being recaptured, Douglass left for a two-year speaking tour of Great Britain. During the trip, two friends raised the money to purchase his freedom.

Tireless Reformer Returning to the United States as a free man, Douglass settled in Rochester, New York, and founded an antislavery newspaper, the *North Star.* During the Civil War, he advised President Abraham Lincoln and helped recruit the first African-American soldiers for the Union army. For Douglass, the end of slavery was only a first step to achieving a greater goal: full and equal civil rights for African Americans.

In the years after the Civil War, Douglass was appointed to several government posts, including U.S. marshal for the District of Columbia and minister to Haiti. To the end of his life, he continued his fight for full citizenship for African Americans and his support for other causes, including women's rights, land reform, and public education.

Selection Resources

 RESOURCE MANAGER UNIT 3

Plan and Teach pp. 55–62

Literary Analysis
Summary pp. 63†*, 64‡*
Style pp. 65, 66†*
Question Support p. 70*

Reading
Analyze Author's Purpose pp. 67, 68†*
Reading Check p. 69

Grammar and Writing
Make Effective Word Choices p. 71

Assessment
Selection Tests A, B/C pp. 73*, 75*
Test Generator CD

 BEST PRACTICES TOOLKIT

Differentiated Instruction pp. 31–38*

Scaffolding Instruction pp. 43–46*

Graphic Organizers/Strategies
Word Questioning • Character Traits and Textual Evidence • Cluster Diagram • Timeline

Reading Support
 Audio Anthology CD*

Technology
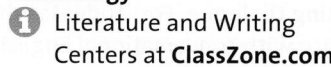 Literature and Writing Centers at **ClassZone.com**
WriteSmart CD

---

* Resources for Differentiation   † Also in Spanish   ‡ In Haitian Creole and Vietnamese

LITERARY ANALYSIS: STYLE

Style is a writer's distinctive way of expressing ideas—not what is said, but how it is said. Douglass uses a formal, elegant style that demonstrates his masterful command of language.

After running thus for a considerable distance, they finally upset the cart, dashing it with great force against a tree, and threw themselves into a dense thicket.

Elements that characterize style include

- **tone,** conveyed by choice of words and details
- **sentence patterns and structures**
- use of **figurative language**
- use of **dialogue**

Douglass combines crisp, factual narration with bursts of poetic language. As you read, note the choices Douglass makes that contribute to his sophisticated style.

READING SKILL: ANALYZE AUTHOR'S PURPOSE

An author creates a work to achieve a specific **purpose,** or goal. In general, an author writes to inform, to express thoughts or feelings, to persuade, or to entertain. However, a complex work will often have more than one purpose.

Frederick Douglass wrote his autobiography mainly to persuade readers that slavery should be abolished. To achieve his purpose, he describes the physical realities that slaves endure and his responses to his life as a slave.

We were often in the field from the first approach of day till its last lingering ray had left us . . .

As you read, use a chart like the one shown to take notes on Douglass's experiences. Notice when he provides factual details about the general conditions of slave life and when he describes his personal responses to his situation.

Physical Realities	Responses to Situation

Can you set yourself FREE?

KEY IDEA Separated from his parents, denied the right to an education, and moved from place to place at the convenience of his owners, Frederick Douglass learned that nothing in his life was under his control. Rejecting the injustice of slavery, he risked his life to escape. With his decision to set himself free, he claimed the right to **self-determination:** he would be a man and not a slave.

QUICKWRITE Without mentioning any names, contrast two people you know of—one who has self-determination and one who does not. Would you attribute the differences beween them more to circumstances or to attitude?

A—	M—
stands up to defend the rights of others	afraid to disagree with her boyfriend

537

Can you set yourself FREE?

Lead into the **KEY IDEA** by asking the question. Then invite students to suggest definitions for **self-determination,** such as "the freedom to make your own decisions" or "standing up for your beliefs." After students complete the **QUICKWRITE,** have them reevaluate their definitions. Invite volunteers to explain whether their definitions have changed.

SKILLS FOCUS

LITERARY ANALYSIS R3.3

● STYLE

Ask students to describe the style of the author biography on page 536. **Possible answer:** *Its style is straightforward and factual. The sentences are not extremely complex. The vocabulary is formal, not colloquial, but it is not poetic. There is no figurative language or dialogue.*

CHECK UNDERSTANDING Ask students to describe the style of an article in a newspaper or a popular magazine.

READING SKILL

■ ANALYZE AUTHOR'S PURPOSE

Ask students to identify the purpose of the biography about Frederick Douglass on page 536. **Possible answer:** *The purpose of the biography is to inform students about Frederick Douglass's life so that they are prepared to read the excerpt from his autobiography.*

CHECK UNDERSTANDING Have students identify the author's purpose or purposes in a newspaper editorial, a mystery novel, and a movie review.

 RESOURCE MANAGER—Copy Master
   Analyze Author's Purpose p. 67
      (for student use while reading
      the selection)

DIFFERENTIATED INSTRUCTION

FOR STRATEGIC READERS

Concept Support: Style To help students understand the concept of style, copy this chart on the board. Explain that the left column lists different elements of style, while the right column lists different ways to describe each stylistic element. Have students use the chart to analyze the style of one of the pieces of writing mentioned in the Check Understanding activities on this page.

Element	Description
words	long or short? formal or conversational? plain or fancy? specific or abstract?
sentences	long or short? simple or complex?
language	figurative language? (y/n) descriptive imagery? (y/n) dialogue? (y/n)

SUMMARY

In this excerpt from his slave narrative, Frederick Douglass describes a turning point in his life. When he is a teenager, his owner, Master Thomas, hires him out for a year to Mr. Covey to work as a field hand. Covey beats him mercilessly, but when Douglass turns to Master Thomas for protection, his owner orders him back to serve out his year. Determined never to take another beating, Douglass fights Covey, restoring his own self-respect and determination to be free.

Lines 1–11
REINFORCE *KEY IDEA:* SELF–DETERMINATION

Discuss How much **self-determination,** or control over his own life, does Douglass appear to have at the beginning of this excerpt? Explain. *Possible answer: Douglass appears to have no control over his own life. He cannot prevent his owner from hiring him out to a brutal man.*

LITERARY ANALYSIS

Ⓐ STYLE

Possible answer: "This affair" refers to his brutal whipping. The word choice is surprising because Douglass describes this act of violence in an offhand, neutral way.

If students need help . . . Reread lines 4–6, and then ask students what noun they would use to label the event Douglass describes. Contrast students' choices with the word *affair*.

Narrative
of the Life of Frederick Douglass

Frederick Douglass

BACKGROUND Douglass wrote his autobiography to convince skeptics that such an eloquent speaker had indeed once been a slave. His book became one of the most famous slave narratives ever published and played an enormous role in rallying support for the abolition of slavery. This excerpt recounts a period in Douglass's life during which his owner, Hugh Auld's brother, Thomas, had hired him out to a man with a reputation as a "slave breaker."

I left Master Thomas's house, and went to live with Mr. Covey, on the 1st of January, 1833. I was now, for the first time in my life, a field hand. In my new employment, I found myself even more awkward than a country boy appeared to be in a large city. I had been at my new home but one week before Mr. Covey gave me a very severe whipping, cutting my back, causing the blood to run, and raising ridges on my flesh as large as my little finger. The details of this affair are Ⓐ as follows: Mr. Covey sent me, very early in the morning of one of our coldest days in the month of January, to the woods, to get a load of wood. He gave me a team of unbroken oxen. He told me which was the in-hand ox, and which the off-
10 hand[1] one. He then tied the end of a large rope around the horns of the in-hand ox, and gave me the other end of it, and told me, if the oxen started to run, that

Ⓐ Targeted Passage
ANALYZE VISUALS
Describe the **style** of this painting. What impression of its subject does the painting convey?

Ⓐ STYLE
Explain what Douglass means by "this affair" in line 6. What is surprising about his **word choice?**

---

1. **in-hand . . . off-hand:** In a team of animals trained to pull loads, the in-hand animal is the one on the left; the animal on the right is the off-hand one.

Panel 30 from *The Frederick Douglass Series* (1938–1939), Jacob Lawrence. Hampton University Museum. © 2007 The Jacob and Gwendolyn Lawrence Foundation, Seattle/ Artists Rights Society (ARS), New York.

DIFFERENTIATED INSTRUCTION

FOR ALL STUDENTS
Expert Groups Encourage students to become subject experts by selecting and researching one of these topics:

- slave resistance and Nat Turner's rebellion
- fugitive slave laws
- Douglass's work as an abolitionist
- Douglass's work in the women's rights movement

FOR STRATEGIC READERS
In combination with the *Audio Anthology CD,* use one or more Targeted Passages (pp. 538, 541, 543, 544, 546, 547) to ensure that students focus on key events and concepts. Targeted Passages are also good for English learners.

Ⓐ Targeted Passage [Lines 1–10]

This passage introduces the setting and the conflict that Douglass faces in this excerpt from his narrative.

About the Art One of the most important American artists of the 20th century, Jacob Lawrence (1917–2000) created several series of paintings depicting important events and leaders in African-American history, such as Frederick Douglass and Harriet Tubman (see page 540). *The Frederick Douglass Series* comprises 32 paintings that present key moments in the abolitionist leader's life. The painting shown here celebrates his 1877 appointment as United States Marshal of the District of Columbia.

BACKGROUND

The Brutality of Slavery In 1830 (around the time period of this excerpt) there were 2.3 million African Americans in the United States. The vast majority were American-born slaves, like Frederick Douglass. White Southerners, even the two-thirds who owned no slaves, defended the institution of slavery. Slave owners wielded absolute authority over their "property." Slaves had no legal rights, and in addition to enduring grueling labor and appalling living conditions, many were regularly whipped. Perhaps even more frightening than the physical brutality was the emotional brutality of forced separation from their loved ones. Every year thousands of African-American families were torn apart when slaves were sold or, like Douglass, hired out to other owners.

- What kind of work does Douglass begin to do when he goes to live with Covey?
- Why is Douglass awkward in this work?
- What does Covey do to Douglass?
- Where does Covey send Douglass, and why is the trip so difficult?

FOR ENGLISH LEARNERS

Key Academic Vocabulary Use Word Questioning to teach these words: *team* (line 9), *considerable* (line 17), *pursue* (line 188), *stable* (line 210), *persist* (line 226).

 BEST PRACTICES TOOLKIT—Transparency Word Questioning p. E9

Prereading For prereading instruction for English learners, see

 BEST PRACTICES TOOLKIT Scaffolding Reading Instruction pp. 43–46

FOR ADVANCED LEARNERS/AP

AP exercises in the bottom channel provide additional challenge for students. Use these suggestions for small groups or individuals.

ADDITIONAL GUIDELINES

For more help with differentiation and tips for classroom management, see

 BEST PRACTICES TOOLKIT Differentiated Instruction pp. 31–38

ANALYZE VISUALS

Possible answer: Details that represent slavery include the leg irons and the harsh landscape. The shape and color of the feet blend into the shackles, suggesting that the slaves have lost their identity as anything other than slaves. Yet the colorful patterns on their clothes imply that they have not lost their individuality. By centering on the subjects' feet, Lawrence emphasizes their bondage.

About the Art In this painting from his *Life of Harriet Tubman* series, Jacob Lawrence (see page 539) portrays Tubman's enslavement symbolically. Other paintings in the series depict scenes from Tubman's life, including her work as a "conductor" on the Underground Railroad.

Lines 12–26
TIERED DISCUSSION PROMPTS

Use these prompts to help students understand the impossible demands Covey places on Douglass:

Connect Have you ever been asked to do a new and demanding task without instruction? Describe the experience. *Most students will say that the experience made them feel frustrated and even angry.*

Analyze What do you learn about Douglass's character from the way he faces the task of driving a team of oxen? *Possible answer: We learn that Douglass is hardworking, determined, resourceful, brave, and strong.*

Evaluate Do you think that Douglass has much chance of succeeding at the task? Do you think Covey expected him to succeed? Explain. *Possible answer: Douglass has little chance of success. He has never driven a team of oxen before, the task is hard, the terrain is rugged, and he has received no instruction. Covey seems to have set Douglass up for failure as part of his strategy to "break" him.*

The Life of Harriet Tubman, #9 (1940), Jacob Lawrence. Casein tempera on hardboard, 12″ × 17 7/8″. Hampton University Museum. Photo courtesy of Gwendolyn Knight Lawrence/Art Resource, New York © ARS, New York.

I must hold on upon the rope. I had never driven oxen before, and of course I was very awkward. I, however, succeeded in getting to the edge of the woods with little difficulty; but I had got a very few rods[2] into the woods, when the oxen took fright, and started full tilt, carrying the cart against trees, and over stumps, in the most frightful manner. I expected every moment that my brains would be dashed out against the trees. After running thus for a considerable distance, they finally upset the cart, dashing it with great force against a tree, and threw themselves into a dense thicket.

20   How I escaped death, I do not know. There I was, entirely alone, in a thick wood, in a place new to me. My cart was upset and shattered, my oxen were entangled among the young trees, and there was none to help me. After a long spell of effort, I succeeded in getting my cart righted, my oxen disentangled, and again yoked to the cart. I now proceeded with my team to the place where I had, the day before, been chopping wood, and loaded my cart pretty heavily, thinking in this way to tame my oxen. I then proceeded on my way home. I had now

ANALYZE VISUALS
Identify details in this painting that are used to represent the experience of slavery. What effects are achieved by centering the image of the figures' feet?

---

2. **rods:** units of length equal to 5 1/2 yards.

540   UNIT 3: FROM ROMANTICISM TO REALISM

DIFFERENTIATED INSTRUCTION

FOR STRATEGIC READERS

Comprehension Support Make sure students understand that up until now, Douglass has worked as a house slave rather than a field hand (lines 1–2). In addition, he has been sent to a new property, so he is unfamiliar with the surrounding countryside and the household's regular tasks. Help students identify details that show that Douglass responds to his situation with determination, resourcefulness, and courage.

FOR ENGLISH LEARNERS

Vocabulary: Outdated Forms Help students use context clues to figure out the meanings of these outdated forms: *spell* (line 23), "time"; *made him no answer* (line 38), "did not respond to him"; *Upon this* (line 40), "Because of this"; *scarce* (line 44), "hardly"; *taking our meals* (line 50), "eating our meals"; *being ever at hand* (line 67), "always being nearby."

consumed one half of the day. I got out of the woods safely, and now felt out of danger. I stopped my oxen to open the woods gate; and just as I did so, before I could get hold of my ox rope, the oxen again started, rushed through the gate,
30 catching it between the wheel and the body of the cart, tearing it to pieces, and coming within a few inches of crushing me against the gate-post. Thus twice, in one short day, I escaped death by the merest chance. On my return, I told Mr. Covey what had happened, and how it happened. He ordered me to return to the woods again immediately. I did so, and he followed on after me. Just as I got into the woods, he came up and told me to stop my cart, and that he would teach me how to trifle away my time, and break gates. He then went to a large gum-tree, and with his axe cut three large switches, and, after trimming them up neatly with his pocket-knife, he ordered me to take off my clothes. I made him no answer, but stood with my clothes on. He repeated his order. I still made him no answer,
40 nor did I move to strip myself. Upon this he rushed at me with the fierceness of a tiger, tore off my clothes, and lashed me till he had worn out his switches, cutting me so savagely as to leave the marks visible for a long time after. This whipping was the first of a number just like it, and for similar offenses. **B**

② Targeted Passage

I lived with Mr. Covey one year. During the first six months, of that year, scarce a week passed without his whipping me. I was seldom free from a sore back. My awkwardness was almost always his excuse for whipping me. We were worked fully up to the point of endurance. Long before day we were up, our horses fed, and by the first approach of day we were off to the field with our hoes and ploughing teams. Mr. Covey gave us enough to eat, but scarce time to eat it. We were often
50 less than five minutes taking our meals. We were often in the field from the first approach of day till its last lingering ray had left us; and at saving-fodder time, midnight often caught us in the field binding blades.³ **C**

Covey would be out with us. The way he used to stand it, was this. He would spend the most of his afternoons in bed. He would then come out fresh in the evening, ready to urge us on with his words, example, and frequently with the whip. Mr. Covey was one of the few slaveholders who could and did work with his hands. He was a hard-working man. He knew by himself just what a man or a boy could do. There was no deceiving him. His work went on in his absence almost as well as in his presence; and he had the faculty of making us feel that he was ever
60 present with us. This he did by surprising us. He seldom approached the spot where we were at work openly, if he could do it secretly. He always aimed at taking us by surprise. Such was his cunning, that we used to call him, among ourselves, "the snake." When we were at work in the cornfield, he would sometimes crawl on his hands and knees to avoid detection, and all at once he would rise nearly in our midst, and scream out, "Ha, ha! Come, come! Dash on, dash on!" This being **D** his mode of attack, it was never safe to stop a single minute. His comings were like a thief in the night. He appeared to us as being ever at hand. He was under every

---

3. **saving- fodder . . . binding blades:** They are gathering and bundling ("binding") corn-plant leaves ("blades") to use for livestock ("fodder").

B **STYLE**
Reread lines 31–43. What is the effect of Douglass's choice to use little imagery or figurative language in his narration?

C **AUTHOR'S PURPOSE**
Reread lines 46–52. What details does Douglass use to inform his readers about the working conditions of slaves?

D **GRAMMAR AND STYLE**
Reread lines 63–65. Note how Douglass uses the **vivid verbs** *crawl* and *scream* to characterize Covey's menacing behavior.

LITERARY ANALYSIS

B **STYLE**

Possible answer: By using minimal imagery and figurative language, Douglass creates a factual, understated tone. By offering a straightforward recitation of what happened, he lets the facts speak for themselves without embellishment.

READING SKILL

C **AUTHOR'S PURPOSE**

Possible answer: Douglass includes these details to inform readers about the slaves' working conditions: They worked "to the point of endurance" (line 47), were in the fields by daybreak (lines 47–49), had "less than five minutes" for meals (line 50), and worked from sunrise to well into the night (lines 50–52).

Extend the Discussion How does this catalog of information about working conditions serve Douglass's main purpose: to persuade readers that slavery should be abolished?

D **GRAMMAR AND STYLE**

Analyze Word Choice Ask students how the description of Covey would be different if Douglass had used the verbs *go* and *call* instead of *crawl* and *scream*. **Possible answer:** *The words* crawl *and* scream *have much stronger negative connotations. Crawl suggests that Covey behaved like a snake, while* scream *conveys brutal or savage anger.* Have students find other examples of vivid verbs in the excerpt.

FOR STRATEGIC READERS

② Targeted Passage [Lines 27–43]

This passage reveals Covey's character and the brutality of slavery.

- How do the oxen damage Covey's gate?
- Where does Covey send Douglass after he learns about the accident?
- What does Covey do to Douglass?
- How does Covey explain his actions?

FOR ADVANCED LEARNERS/AP

Analyze Character Development Have students use a Character Traits and Textual Evidence chart to analyze how Douglass develops Covey's character in this excerpt. As students discuss their analyses, encourage them to consider this irony: The slave is treated like an animal, but it is the slave owner who behaves like a brute.

🧰 BEST PRACTICES TOOLKIT—Transparency
Character Traits and Textual Evidence p. D6

tree, behind every stump, in every bush, and at every window, on the plantation.
He would sometimes mount his horse, as if bound to St. Michael's,[4] a distance of
70 seven miles, and in half an hour afterwards you would see him coiled up in the
corner of the wood-fence, watching every motion of the slaves. He would, for this
purpose, leave his horse tied up in the woods. Again, he would sometimes walk
up to us, and give us orders as though he was upon the point of starting on a long
journey, turn his back upon us, and make as though he was going to the house
to get ready; and, before he would get half way thither, he would turn short and
crawl into a fence-corner, or behind some tree, and there watch us till the going
down of the sun. . . .

If at any one time of my life more than another, I was made to drink the bitterest
dregs of slavery, that time was during the first six months of my stay with Mr.
80 Covey. We were worked in all weathers. It was never too hot or too cold; it could
never rain, blow, hail, or snow, too hard for us to work in the field. Work, work,
work, was scarcely more the order of the day than of the night. The longest days
were too short for him, and the shortest nights too long for him. I was somewhat
unmanageable when I first went there, but a few months of this discipline tamed
me. Mr. Covey succeeded in breaking me. I was broken in body, soul, and spirit.
My natural elasticity was crushed, my intellect languished, the disposition to read
departed, the cheerful spark that lingered about my eye died; the dark night of
slavery closed in upon me; and behold a man transformed into a brute! **E**
    Sunday was my only leisure time. I spent this in a sort of beast-like stupor,
90 between sleep and wake, under some large tree. At times I would rise up, a flash
of energetic freedom would dart through my soul, accompanied with a faint beam
of hope, that flickered for a moment, and then vanished. I sank down again,
mourning over my wretched condition. I was sometimes prompted to take my
life, and that of Covey, but was prevented by a combination of hope and fear. My
sufferings on this plantation seem now like a dream rather than a stern reality. . . .
    I have already intimated that my condition was much worse, during the first
six months of my stay at Mr. Covey's, than in the last six. The circumstances
leading to the change in Mr. Covey's course toward me form an epoch in my
humble history. You have seen how a man was made a slave; you shall see how a
100 slave was made a man. On one of the hottest days of the month of August, 1833,
Bill Smith, William Hughes,[5] a slave named Eli, and myself, were engaged in
fanning wheat.[6] Hughes was clearing the fanned wheat from before the fan. Eli
was turning, Smith was feeding, and I was carrying wheat to the fan. The work
was simple, requiring strength rather than intellect; yet, to one entirely unused to
such work, it came very hard. About three o'clock of that day, I broke down; my
strength failed me; I was seized with a violent aching of the head, attended with

E STYLE
Douglass uses **poetic devices** to enrich his prose. Reread lines 78–88. Identify examples of poetic devices including metaphor, repetition, and parallelism. What **tone** is created by this use of language?

LITERARY ANALYSIS

E STYLE

Possible answer: Metaphors: "bitterest dregs" (lines 78–79), "cheerful spark" (line 87), "dark night of slavery" (lines 87–88). Repetition: "worked/work" (lines 80–82), "breaking/broken" (line 85). Parallelism: "never too hot . . . never rain . . . too hard" (lines 80–81), "longest days . . . too short . . . shortest nights too long" (lines 82–83), "elasticity . . . crushed . . . intellect languished . . . disposition . . . departed . . . spark . . . died . . . dark night . . . closed" (lines 86–88). These poetic devices create an emotional, despairing tone that stresses the unending misery of Douglass's life.

Lines 78–95
TIERED DISCUSSION PROMPTS

Use these prompts to help students understand how Douglass uses his own experience to convey the effects of slavery:

Summarize How does Douglass change during his first six months with Covey? *Possible answer: He is completely "broken in body, soul, and spirit" (line 85). He loses his intellectual interest and sense of hope (lines 86 and 92). He feels that he has been "transformed into a brute" (line 88).*

Analyze Why is it significant that Douglass's transformation occurs in only six months? *Possible answer: Douglass is suggesting that slavery can dehumanize a person in a relatively short period of time.*

Synthesize Douglass is strong, intelligent, and resourceful. Consider how just six months of abuse affect him. What is Douglass suggesting about slavery's effects? *Possible answer: The brutality and degradation of slavery dehumanize a strong, lively, intelligent young man in just six months. Douglass is implying that slavery will destroy anyone, weak or strong.*

DIFFERENTIATED INSTRUCTION

FOR ENGLISH LEARNERS
Vocabulary: Idioms Help students use context clues to figure out the meanings of these idioms from the narrative: *make as though* (line 74), "pretend"; *breaking me* (line 85), "destroying my spirit"; *closed in upon* (line 88), "trapped; caught"; *broke down* (line 105), "got sick"; *it would never do* (line 108), "I could not; would not be allowed to"; *gaining my feet* (line 123), "standing up"; *made my way to* (line 139), "went to."

FOR ADVANCED LEARNERS/AP
Christianity and Slavery Point out line 89: "Sunday was my only leisure time." Clarify that slaves didn't work on Sunday because their Christian masters observed the Sabbath. Have students research and then discuss the role of Christianity in the lives of slaves, focusing on these questions: Why did slave owners initially resist efforts to convert slaves to Christianity? Why did they change their minds? How did slaves interpret Christianity differently from Southern whites?

extreme dizziness; I trembled in every limb. Finding what was coming, I nerved myself up, feeling it would never do to stop work. I stood as long as I could stagger to the hopper[7] with grain. When I could stand no longer, I fell, and felt as
110 if held down by an immense weight. The fan of course stopped; every one had his own work to do; and no one could do the work of the other, and have his own go on at the same time.

Mr. Covey was at the house, about one hundred yards from the treading-yard where we were fanning. On hearing the fan stop, he left immediately, and came to the spot where we were. He hastily inquired what the matter was. Bill answered that I was sick, and there was no one to bring wheat to the fan. I had by this time crawled away under the side of the post and rail-fence by which the yard was enclosed, hoping to find relief by getting out of the sun. He then asked where I was. He was told by one of the hands. He came to the spot, and, after looking at
120 me awhile, asked me what was the matter. I told him as well as I could, for I scarce had strength to speak. He then gave me a savage kick in the side, and told me to get up. I tried to do so, but fell back in the attempt. He gave me another kick, and again told me to rise. I again tried, and succeeded in gaining my feet; but, stooping to get the tub with which I was feeding the fan, I again staggered and fell. While down in this situation, Mr. Covey took up the hickory slat with which Hughes had been striking off the half-bushel measure, and with it gave me a heavy blow upon the head, making a large wound, and the blood ran freely; and with this again told me to get up. I made no effort to comply, having now made up my mind to let him do his worst. In a short time after receiving this blow, my head
130 grew better. Mr. Covey had now left me to my fate. At this moment I resolved, for the first time, to go to my master, enter a complaint, and ask his protection. In order to do this, I must that afternoon walk seven miles; and this, under the circumstances, was truly a severe undertaking. I was exceedingly feeble; made so as much by the kicks and blows which I received, as by the severe fit of sickness to which I had been subjected. I, however, watched my chance, while Covey was looking in an opposite direction, and started for St. Michael's. I succeeded in getting a considerable distance on my way to the woods, when Covey discovered me, and called after me to come back, threatening what he would do if I did not come. I disregarded both his calls and his threats, and made my way to the woods
140 as fast as my feeble state would allow; and thinking I might be overhauled by him if I kept the road,[8] I walked through the woods, keeping far enough from the road to avoid detection, and near enough to prevent losing my way. I had not gone far before my little strength again failed me. I could go no farther. I fell down, and lay for a considerable time. The blood was yet oozing from the wound on my head. For a time I thought I should bleed to death; and think now that I should have done so, but that the blood so matted my hair as to stop the wound. After lying there about three quarters of an hour, I nerved myself up again, and started on my

---

7. **hopper:** a funnel-shaped container for storing grain.
8. **kept the road:** stayed on the road.

③ Targeted Passage

F AUTHOR'S PURPOSE
Reread lines 121–128. Why might Douglass have chosen not to include details about his own reactions to the events he describes? Explain.

TIERED DISCUSSION PROMPTS

Use these prompts to help students understand slavery's dehumanizing effect:

Connect Have you ever asked for help
but been rejected? How did the experience make you feel? *Accept all thoughtful
responses.*

Analyze Why does Master Thomas refuse
to help Douglass? *Possible answer: He has
hired Douglass out to Covey for a year, so
if he allowed Douglass to leave Covey, he
would have to compensate Covey for his
financial loss. Master Thomas's financial
interest makes him unable to react humanely
to Douglass's situation. He is also probably
afraid of defying Covey—of supporting a
slave's complaint against a slave owner.*

Synthesize What do readers learn about
slavery from this scene? *Possible answer:
Treating a human being as property dehu-
manizes everyone, even those who might
otherwise have felt compassion for another
human being.*

LITERARY ANALYSIS

G STYLE

*Possible answer: The repetition of the
word* that *adds emphasis to each clause
and creates an insistent rhythm unlike the
conversational flow of quoted dialogue.
This repetition makes Thomas's responses
sound like a catalog of excuses and lies.*

If students need help . . . Reread the lines
aloud, emphasizing the word *that.*

---

way, through bogs and briers, barefooted and bareheaded, tearing my feet
sometimes at nearly every step; and after a journey of about seven miles,
150 occupying some five hours to perform it, I arrived at master's store. I then
presented an appearance enough to affect any but a heart of iron. From the crown
of my head to my feet, I was covered with blood. My hair was all clotted with dust
and blood; my shirt was stiff with blood. My legs and feet were torn in sundry
places with briers and thorns, and were also covered with blood. I suppose I
looked like a man who had escaped a den of wild beasts, and barely escaped them.
In this state I appeared before my master, humbly entreating him to interpose his
authority for my protection. I told him all the circumstances as well as I could,
and it seemed, as I spoke, at times to affect him. He would then walk the floor,
and seek to justify Covey by saying he expected I deserved it. He asked me what I
160 wanted. I told him, to let me get a new home; that as sure as I lived with Mr.
Covey again, I should live with but to die with him; that Covey would surely kill
me; he was in a fair way for it. Master Thomas ridiculed the idea that there was
any danger of Mr. Covey's killing me, and said that he knew Mr. Covey; that he
was a good man, and that he could not think of taking me from him; that, should
he do so, he would lose the whole year's wages; that I belonged to Mr. Covey for
one year, and that I must go back to him, come what might; and that I must not
trouble him with any more stories, or that he would himself *get hold of me.* After **G**
threatening me thus, he gave me a very large dose of salts,[9] telling me that I might
remain in St. Michael's that night, (it being quite late,) but that I must be off back
170 to Mr. Covey's early in the morning; and that if I did not, he would get *hold of me,*
which meant that he would whip me. I remained all night, and, according to his
orders, I started off to Covey's in the morning, (Saturday morning,) wearied in
body and broken in spirit. I got no supper that night, or breakfast that morning. I
reached Covey's about nine o'clock; and just as I was getting over the fence that
divided Mrs. Kemp's fields from ours, out ran Covey with his cowskin, to give me
another whipping. Before he could reach me, I succeeded in getting to the
cornfield; and as the corn was very high, it afforded me the means of hiding. He
seemed very angry, and searched for me a long time. My behavior was altogether
unaccountable. He finally gave up the chase, thinking, I suppose, that I must
180 come home for something to eat; he would give himself no further trouble in
looking for me. I spent that day mostly in the woods, having the alternative before
me,—to go home and be whipped to death, or stay in the woods and be starved to
death. That night, I fell in with Sandy Jenkins, a slave with whom I was somewhat
acquainted. Sandy had a free wife who lived about four miles from Mr. Covey's;
and it being Saturday, he was on his way to see her. I told him my circumstances,
and he very kindly invited me to go home with him. I went home with him, and
talked this whole matter over, and got his advice as to what course it was best for
me to pursue. I found Sandy an old adviser. He told me, with great solemnity, I

4 Targeted Passage

G STYLE
Reread lines 159–167.
Note that Douglass
chooses to convey this
dialogue without the
use of quotations. What
effect does he achieve
instead by repeating the
word *that?*

---

9. **salts:** mineral salts used to relieve faintness and headache or to reduce swelling.

DIFFERENTIATED INSTRUCTION

FOR STRATEGIC READERS

4 Targeted Passage [Lines 150–173]

This passage describes Douglass's encounter
with Master Thomas, his owner.

- How does Douglass look when he arrives
  at Master Thomas's store?

- What does he tell Master Thomas about
  what has happened to him and why he
  is there?

- What threat does Master Thomas make?

FOR ADVANCED LEARNERS/AP

Free African Americans Point out line 184:
"Sandy had a free wife. . . ." Have students
research the topic of free African Americans
in the South, focusing on these questions:
How had most free African Americans
achieved their freedom? Where did they
live? How did they support themselves?
What discrimination and restrictions did
they face? What churches and organizations
did they form? Have students present their
research in an oral report to the class.

Panel #10 from The Frederick Douglass Series of 1938-1940, *Jacob Lawrence. © 2007 The Jacob and Gwendolyn Lawrence Foundation, Seattle/Artists Rights Society (ARS), New York*

FOR STRATEGIC READERS

Comprehension Support Discuss why Master Thomas "would lose the whole year's wages" (line 165) if he allowed Douglass to return to him. Clarify that Master Thomas owns Douglass but has hired him out to Covey for a year, receiving payment in exchange for the value of Douglass's labor. If Douglass stopped working for Covey, Master Thomas would have to pay Covey the equivalent of Douglass's lost labor.

FOR ENGLISH LEARNERS

Language: Pronoun Referents Help students understand the long, complicated sentence in lines 162–167 by clarifying the different referents for the pronouns *he* and *him*. Explain that sometimes these pronouns refer to Master Thomas, while other times they refer to Mr. Covey. Write the first part of the sentence on the board, underlining the pronouns that refer to Master Thomas and double underlining those that refer to Mr. Covey: "Master Thomas ridiculed the idea that there was any danger of Mr. Covey's killing me, and said that <u>he</u> knew Mr. Covey; that <u>he</u> was a good man, and that <u>he</u> could not think of taking me from <u>him</u>; that, should <u>he</u> do so, <u>he</u> would lose the whole year's wages. . . ." Have students work in mixed-language groups to identify the referents for the pronouns *he* and *him* in the rest of the sentence, beginning with "that I belonged to Mr. Covey. . . ."

TIERED DISCUSSION PROMPTS

Use these prompts to help students understand how this encounter with Sandy affects Douglass:

Connect In your experience, how does kindness affect people who are experiencing problems in their lives? *Students will probably recognize that kindness can have a powerful, restorative effect on people, especially during desperate times.*

Analyze What does Sandy give Douglass, both literally and symbolically? ***Possible answer:*** *Literally, Sandy gives Douglass a root as a talisman that will supposedly protect him from being whipped. Symbolically, Sandy gives Douglass the gifts of self-confidence, courage, and hope. By showing Douglass kindness and providing him with a safe haven, Sandy empowers Douglass to move forward and face his problems.*

Synthesize In what ways might the root protect Douglass, even if it doesn't literally protect him against being whipped? ***Possible answer:*** *Douglass's belief in the power of the root might protect him against the worst degradation of slavery: losing his humanity. His restored self-confidence, the result of both his belief in the root and Sandy's kindness, might empower him to stand up for himself against Covey and thus turn him from a slave into a man (lines 99–100).*

---

must go back to Covey; but that before I went, I must go with him into another
190 part of the woods, where there was a certain *root,* which, if I would take some of it with me, carrying it *always on my right side,* would render it impossible for Mr. Covey, or any other white man, to whip me. He said he had carried it for years; and since he had done so, he had never received a blow, and never expected to while he carried it. I at first rejected the idea, that the simple carrying of a root in my pocket would have any such effect as he had said, and was not disposed to take it; but Sandy impressed the necessity with much earnestness, telling me it could do no harm, if it did no good. To please him, I at length took the root, and, according to his direction, carried it upon my right side. This was Sunday morning. I immediately started for home; and upon entering the yard gate, out
200 came Mr. Covey on his way to meeting.[10] He spoke to me very kindly, made me drive the pigs from a lot near by, and passed on towards the church. Now, this singular conduct of Mr. Covey really made me begin to think that there was something in the *root* which Sandy had given me; and had it been on any other day than Sunday, I could have attributed the conduct to no other cause than the influence of that root; and as it was, I was half inclined to think the *root* to be something more than I at first had taken it to be. All went well till Monday morning. On this morning, the virtue of the *root* was fully tested. Long before daylight, I was called to go and rub, curry, and feed, the horses. I obeyed, and was glad to obey. But whilst thus engaged, whilst in the act of throwing down some
210 blades from the loft, Mr. Covey entered the stable with a long rope; and just as I was half out of the loft, he caught hold of my legs, and was about tying me. As soon as I found what he was up to, I gave a sudden spring, and as I did so, he holding to my legs, I was brought sprawling on the stable floor. Mr. Covey seemed now to think he had me, and could do what he pleased; but at this moment— from whence came the spirit I don't know—I resolved to fight; and, suiting my action to the resolution, I seized Covey hard by the throat; and as I did so, I rose. He held on to me, and I to him. My resistance was so entirely unexpected, that Covey seemed taken all aback. He trembled like a leaf. This gave me assurance, and I held him uneasy, causing the blood to run where I touched him with the
220 ends of my fingers. Mr. Covey soon called out to Hughes for help. Hughes came, and, while Covey held me, attempted to tie my right hand. While he was in the act of doing so, I watched my chance, and gave him a heavy kick close under the ribs. This kick fairly sickened Hughes, so that he left me in the hands of Mr. Covey. This kick had the effect of not only weakening Hughes, but Covey also. When he saw Hughes bending over with pain, his courage quailed. He asked me if I meant to persist in my resistance. I told him I did, come what might; that he had used me like a brute for six months, and that I was determined to be used so no longer. With that, he strove to drag me to a stick that was lying just out of the stable door. He meant to knock me down. But just as he was leaning over to get

⑤ Targeted Passage

---

10. **meeting:** church service.

DIFFERENTIATED INSTRUCTION

FOR STRATEGIC READERS

⑤ Targeted Passage [Lines 209–228]

This passage describes the climax of Douglass's conflict with Covey.

- What does Covey try to do to Douglass in the stable?
- What is Douglass's response?
- What does Douglass do to Hughes when he tries to interfere? How does this affect Covey?
- Why won't Douglass stop resisting?

FOR ENGLISH LEARNERS

Vocabulary: Idioms Help students use context clues to figure out the meanings of these idioms from the narrative:

- *at length* (line 197), "eventually, finally"
- *what he was up to* (line 212), "what he was planning to do"
- *take hold of* (line 233), "grab"
- *getting . . . the worst end of the bargain* (line 238), "doing worse than [I] did"
- *never laid . . . his finger upon me* (line 240), "never hit me"
- *let it be known* (lines 253–254), "make it clear to everybody"

230 the stick, I seized him with both hands by his collar, and brought him by a sudden snatch to the ground. By this time, Bill came. Covey called upon him for assistance. Bill wanted to know what he could do. Covey said, "Take hold of him, take hold of him!" Bill said his master hired him out to work, and not to help to whip me; so he left Covey and myself to fight our own battle out. We were at it for nearly two hours. Covey at length let me go, puffing and blowing at a great rate, saying that if I had not resisted, he would not have whipped me half so much. The truth was, that he had not whipped me at all. I considered him as getting entirely the worst end of the bargain; for he had drawn no blood from me, but I had from him. The whole six months afterwards, that I spent
240 with Mr. Covey, he never laid the weight of his finger upon me in anger. He would occasionally say, he didn't want to get hold of me again. "No," thought I, "you need not; for you will come off worse than you did before."

This battle with Mr. Covey was the turning-point in my career as a slave. It rekindled the few expiring embers of freedom, and revived within me a sense of my own manhood. It recalled the departed self-confidence, and inspired me again with a determination to be free. The gratification afforded by the triumph was a full compensation[11] for whatever else might follow, even death itself. He only can understand the deep satisfaction which I experienced, who has himself repelled by force the bloody arm of slavery. I felt as I never felt before. It was
250 a glorious resurrection, from the tomb of slavery, to the heaven of freedom. My long-crushed spirit rose, cowardice departed, bold defiance took its place; and I now resolved that, however long I might remain a slave in form, the day had passed forever when I could be a slave in fact. I did not hesitate to let it be known of me, that the white man who expected to succeed in whipping, must also succeed in killing me.

From this time I was never again what might be called fairly whipped, though I remained a slave four years afterwards. I had several fights, but was never whipped. ∾

(6) **Targeted Passage**

(H) AUTHOR'S PURPOSE Reread lines 243–253. What effect might this description have had on Douglass's readers? **(H)**

---

11. **compensation:** payment; something of equivalent value.

Lines 243–250
REINFORCE *KEY IDEA:* SELF—DETERMINATION

Discuss How does Douglass's fight with Covey help him move toward **self-determination?**
Possible answer: His decision to fight back revives his sense of manhood and his "determination to be free" (line 246). It is the "turning-point" (line 243) that allows him to renounce the shackles of mental slavery, so that he is no longer "a slave in fact" (line 253).

READING SKILL

(H) AUTHOR'S PURPOSE

Possible answer: *Most readers would have been moved by his account of triumph over brutality and degradation.*

If students need help . . . Work with them to use the chart introduced on page 537 to analyze Douglass's responses to his fight with Covey. Then ask students to consider why Douglass might have chosen to express his feelings here, while elsewhere he lets the facts speak for themselves.

Physical Realities	Responses to Situation
"I resolved to fight ..." (line 215)	revived his sense of manhood and desire to be free (lines 243–246)

SELECTION WRAP–UP

SUMMARIZE Have students summarize the events that lead to Douglass's defiance and triumph over the bonds of slavery.

FOR STRATEGIC READERS

(6) **Targeted Passage [Lines 234–250]**

This passage presents the resolution of Frederick Douglass's conflict with Covey.

- Who wins the fight?
- How does Douglass feel afterward?
- What is he determined to do in the future?
- Why does Douglass describe his feelings after the fight as a "resurrection" (line 250)?

FOR ADVANCED LEARNERS/AP

Compare Philosophies Have students reread Douglass's reflections on his fight with Covey (lines 243–258) and compare his thoughts with Ralph Waldo Emerson's philosophy in "Self-Reliance" (see pages 362–364). Emerson's motto is "Trust thyself" (see page 362). Challenge students to come up with a motto that captures Douglass's ideals. Then have them use both mottos as the basis of a brief essay comparing and contrasting these writers' philosophies.

Practice and Apply

After Reading

Use these copy masters to check under-standing and provide extra support:

R RESOURCE MANAGER—Copy Masters
   Reading Check p. 69
   Style p. 65
   Question Support p. 70

Additional selection questions are provided for teachers on page 59.

ANSWERS

1. *Douglass had broken the gate and the oxcart (lines 29–30).*

2. *Master Thomas ridiculed Douglass's claim that Covey might kill him, saying that Covey was a good man. He told Douglass that he had to return to Covey because he belonged to him for a year. Master Thomas said that he would whip Douglass if he kept com-plaining (lines 162–167).*

3. *Douglass realized that he could defend himself and take control of his own life.*

Possible answers:

4. ■ SKILLS FOCUS **Analyze Author's Purpose** *Factual details inform readers about how brutally slaves were treated. Emotional details give readers insight into Douglass's personal experience. By using both kinds of details, Douglass can inform and persuade readers who respond to facts as well as those who respond to emotional appeals.*

5. ● SKILLS FOCUS **Style** *Tone: either de-tached and factual or emotional and poetic; Diction: complex sentences, strong verbs; Figurative language: occasional metaphor; Dialogue: indirect dialogue. Some students may link Douglass's credibility as a narra-tor to his detached tone and spare, objec-tive style. Others may argue that his more emotional passages establish his credibility because they show that he speaks from personal experience.*

6. *Inverted parallelism: "You have seen how a man was made a slave; you shall see how a slave was made a man." Douglass has described how his physical experiences crushed his spirit. Then he shows how, by standing up to Covey, he reasserts his humanity and regains his self-worth.*

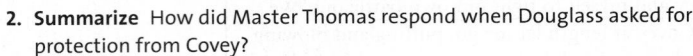

Comprehension

1. **Recall** What was Covey's first reason for beating Douglass?

2. **Summarize** How did Master Thomas respond when Douglass asked for protection from Covey?

3. **Clarify** How was the battle with Covey a turning point in Douglass's life as a slave?

Literary Analysis

4. **Analyze Author's Purpose** Review the chart you created as you read. Given his main purpose, why might Douglass have chosen to include both kinds of detail in his narrative? Explain your answer.

5. **Analyze Style** Describe the main elements of Douglass's style. Which elements, if any, help Douglass establish himself as a credible **narrator?** Support your answer with details.

6. **Examine Rhetorical Devices** Douglass was a great orator, and his style was influenced by his mastery of rhetorical devices. One of his signature techniques was his use of **inverted parallelism,** a reversal of ideas expressed in parallel phrases or clauses: "The longest days were too short for him, and the shortest nights too long for him." Identify the inverted parallelism in lines 99–100. In what ways does this reversal of ideas summarize Douglass's emotional experiences in this selection?

7. **Make Generalizations from Conflicts** What do the conflicts between Douglass and Covey reveal about slavery's effects on both slaves and masters? Use a chart like the one shown to make generalizations about slavery based on Douglass's experiences.

8. **Draw Conclusions** Consider how Douglass portrays his triumphant moment of **self-determination.** In what ways does his experience illustrate each of the following classic American ideas? Support your answers with details.

   • individual rights   • self-reliance   • resistance to tyranny

Literary Criticism

9. **Different Perspectives** In what ways might a slave narrative written by an enslaved woman differ from Douglass's account? Explain your answer.

7. *Effects on slaves: The abuse that masters like Covey inflicted on slaves robbed them of their humanity. Effects on masters: Slavery also turned masters into animals, whose brutality and insensitivity to suffering robbed them of their own humanity.*

8. *Individual rights: Douglass sees himself as a man who deserves full human rights. Self-reliance: Douglass decides to trust his own beliefs and take control of his own destiny. Resistance: Douglass asserts himself against injustice and brutality.*

9. *A woman's slave narrative would not identify freedom with manhood, as Doug-lass does, or focus on the kind of "manly" resistance at the heart of his narrative. A woman's narrative might describe differ-ent types of threats to her humanity and dignity.*

Reading-Writing Connection

W2.3

WRITING PROMPT

DESCRIBE A TURNING POINT Douglass viewed his fight with the cowardly overseer Covey as a turning point in his life. Think of an episode from your own life that you would describe as a turning point. Write a **three-paragraph description** of the episode. Make effective word choices to convey the significance of the event to your readers.

SELF-CHECK

A strong description will . . .
- have a clear focus
- use descriptive details and precise words to create a vivid image
- clearly demonstrate the significance of the event

GRAMMAR AND STYLE

LC1.1

MAKE EFFECTIVE WORD CHOICES Review the **Grammar and Style** note on page 541. To convey the brutal conditions he endured as a slave, Douglass used **vivid verbs,** ones that convey precise actions or emotions and draw readers into the reality of his experiences.

> *I was seized with a violent aching of the head, attended with extreme dizziness; I trembled in every limb. Finding what was coming, I nerved myself up, feeling it would never do to stop work. I stood as long as I could stagger to the hopper with grain.* (lines 106–109)

The verbs *seized, trembled, nerved,* and *stagger* help communicate the urgency of Douglass's situation.

PRACTICE Rewrite each sentence, replacing the boldfaced words with vivid verbs. An example has been done for you.

> **EXAMPLE**
> I **walked** into the room where the baby was **crying** and **helped** her back to sleep.
> *I crept into the room where the baby was whimpering and coaxed her back to sleep.*

1. The wind **blew** as he **walked** through the dark forest.
2. A sudden wave of illness made me **hold** my stomach.
3. The waves **moved** the ship back and forth as the storm **continued.**

WRITING TOOLS
For prewriting, revision, and editing tools, visit the **Writing Center** at ClassZone.com.

DIFFERENTIATED INSTRUCTION

FOR DEVELOPING WRITERS
Writing Support
- Limit the length of the assignment to two paragraphs.
- Provide a sentence starter for students to use as they draft their descriptions (such as *An event that had a great impact on me was _____*).
- Have students use a timeline to map out the sequence of events that occurred in the episode.

- As students draft their paragraphs, have them flesh out each event by adding descriptive details.
- Ask students to write a summary sentence that states what they learned from the episode.

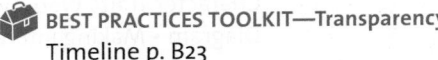
BEST PRACTICES TOOLKIT—Transparency
Timeline p. B23

Reading-Writing Connection

WRITING PROMPT
Give examples of possible turning points, such as confronting a strong-willed friend or older sibling, standing up for somebody else, speaking out for a cause, or choosing an independent path rather than going along with the crowd. Have students use a Cluster Diagram to brainstorm ideas and list elements of significance for each idea.

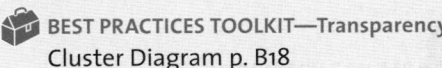
BEST PRACTICES TOOLKIT—Transparency
Cluster Diagram p. B18

For writing support, see

Writing Center at **ClassZone.com**

GRAMMAR AND STYLE
Suggest that students use a print or on-line thesaurus to find vivid verbs that they can substitute for weak ones. Remind students that vivid verbs are specific, rather than vague—but that they don't have to be elaborate or pretentious. (For more on using language effectively, see **Writing Handbook,** pp. R26–R38. For more on verbs, see **Grammar Handbook,** pp. R59–R61.)

Possible answers:
1. *blew:* raged, gusted; *walked:* staggered, strolled
2. *hold:* clutch, grasp
3. *moved:* rocked, pitched; *continued:* persisted, resumed

RESOURCE MANAGER—Copy Masters
Make Effective Word Choices p. 71

Assess and Reteach

Assess
RESOURCE MANAGER—Copy Masters
Selection Test A pp. 73–74
Selection Test B/C pp. 75–76

Test Generator CD

Reteach
STANDARDS LESSON FILE
Literature Lesson 44: Style and Syntax
Reading Lesson 3: Determining Author's Purpose
Writing Lesson 21: Descriptive Writing
Writing Lesson 39: Word Choice

Focus and Motivate

OBJECTIVES

Literary Analysis
- explore the key idea of **sacrifice**
- analyze narrative elements
- read a slave narrative

Reading
- use strategies for reading a narrative

Grammar and Writing
- use adjectives to establish tone
- write a response

 R3.5, W1.2, W1.5, W1.9

ABOUT THE AUTHOR

After students have read about Jacobs's life, ask them to point out several details that show her strong character. Explain that this excerpt from *Incidents in the Life of a Slave Girl* reveals Jacobs's character, explores her decision to leave her children, and describes some of her time in hiding.

USING THE *NOTABLE QUOTE*

Ask students to discuss how the meaning of **Harriet Jacobs's** quote might be demonstrated in her narrative and also applicable to all female slaves. *Students should recognize that Jacobs was a victim of unwanted sexual advances and as a result ultimately felt forced to give up her children.*

Literature of the Civil War

R3.5, W1.2 (p. 559), **W1.5** (p. 559), **W1.9** (p. 559)

NOTABLE QUOTE
"Slavery is terrible for men; but it is far more terrible for women."

FYI
Did you know that Harriet Jacobs . . .

- was described in a runaway slave notice as having run away "without any known cause or provocation"?
- used fictitious names in her autobiography because she "deemed it kind and considerate toward others"?
- was asked by the son of her former owner for help in getting a job after the Civil War?

Author Online

For more on Harriet Jacobs, visit the **Literature Center at ClassZone.com.**

from Incidents in the Life of a Slave Girl
Slave Narrative by Harriet Jacobs

Harriet Jacobs
1813–1897

Harriet Jacobs's *Incidents in the Life of a Slave Girl* is one of the few slave narratives to recount the anguish of slavery from a female point of view. The book ranks as one of the most powerful and important examples of the slave narrative genre.

Defying Her Owner Jacobs was born into slavery in Edenton, North Carolina. Her first owner was a relatively kind woman who taught her to read and sew. When Jacobs was 12, the woman died, and Jacobs was willed to the 3-year-old daughter of Dr. James Norcom—the man she calls "Dr. Flint" in her autobiography. Norcom began making sexual advances toward Jacobs when she was in her teens. Jacobs resisted him and instead started a relationship with Norcom's neighbor, a white lawyer named Samuel Sawyer ("Mr. Sands" in the narrative), hoping the relationship would put a stop to Norcom's unwanted attentions. Jacobs had two children with Sawyer, but Norcom continued harassing her. Infuriated by her refusals, he punished Jacobs by sending her and her young children to work for his son ("Mr. Flint"), who he hoped would be able to break her resistance.

Seven Years in Hiding Shortly after arriving at the son's plantation, Jacobs made the painful decision to run away and leave her children behind. She hoped that her leaving would make the Norcoms sell the children to their father, Sawyer. Unlike many runaways, Jacobs did not immediately flee north. She hid in a tiny attic space in her grandmother's house. She remained there for seven years, but was able to take comfort in the knowledge that her children had been bought by Sawyer and saved from plantation life. In 1842, friends arranged for Jacobs to escape to New York. Once there, she found work as a nanny for a white family. Even so, Jacobs was always in danger of losing her freedom. Fugitive slave laws allowed for slave catchers to capture slaves who had escaped to the North and return them to slavery in the South. Fortunately, in 1852, Jacobs's employer purchased Jacobs's freedom and that of her two children.

Abolitionist and Author In the North, Jacobs became involved in the abolitionist movement. Abolitionist friends encouraged her to write *Incidents in the Life of a Slave Girl,* which she published in 1861 under the pseudonym Linda Brent, the name she uses to refer to herself in the narrative.

550

Selection Resources

RESOURCE MANAGER UNIT 3

Plan and Teach pp. 77–84

Literary Analysis
Summary pp. 85†*, 86‡*
Narrative Elements pp. 87, 88†*
Question Support p. 92*

Reading
Reading a Narrative pp. 89, 90†*
Reading Check p. 91

Grammar and Writing
Establish Tone p. 93

Assessment
Selection Tests A, B/C pp. 95*, 97*
Test Generator CD

BEST PRACTICES TOOLKIT

Differentiated Instruction
pp. 31–38*

Scaffolding Instruction
pp. 43–46*

Graphic Organizers/Strategies
Analysis Frame: Theme •
Character Traits Web • Venn
Diagram • Making Inferences

Reading Support
Audio Anthology CD*

Technology
Literature and Writing
Centers at **ClassZone.com**
WriteSmart CD

---

* Resources for Differentiation   † Also in Spanish   ‡ In Haitian Creole and Vietnamese

LITERARY ANALYSIS: NARRATIVE ELEMENTS

The events in Jacobs's autobiography are true, not fictional, yet she selects and arranges them to tell a compelling story. Critics have noted, not always admiringly, how much her book resembles a novel. As you read, notice the following narrative characteristics:

- Linda, the main character, experiences internal and external **conflicts** resulting from slavery. An **internal conflict** is a struggle within a character; an **external conflict** is a struggle between a character and an outside force.
- These conflicts result in **suspense,** or excitement and tension, as readers wonder about the outcome of events.
- Direct comments and telling details build the strong **characterizations** of Linda and the slave owners, making their personalities clear yet complex.

READING STRATEGY: READING A NARRATIVE

Numerous characters are mentioned in this selection, and because the excerpt is from the middle of the book, it is not always clear who they are. Some are never given names. Study Jacobs's biography on page 550, then match characters in the narrative to the actual figures in Jacobs's life. Pay attention to the background paragraphs that precede each part of the selection. As you read, use a graphic organizer to keep track of the characters and their relation to the narrator. Note whether they support or oppose her.

Linda
(Harriet Jacobs)

narrator

Mr. Flint
(Mr. Norcom)

son of Linda's owner

What is the PRICE of freedom?

KEY IDEA Parents often put their children's welfare before their own. In Harriet Jacobs's case, the **sacrifice** she made for her children was tremendous. Running away put her at risk of being caught and severely beaten, jailed, or sold. In addition, she deprived herself of the opportunity to play a role in the raising of her own children.

DISCUSS Think about sacrifices people have made for their own or their children's freedom. Discuss examples from the past or the present with a group of classmates. Can the price of freedom ever be too high?

The Ride for Freedom, The Fugitive Slaves (1862), Eastman Johnson. Oil. The Granger Collection, New York.

551

What is the PRICE of freedom?

Explain that *price* in this context does not refer to the monetary expense of freedom. Instead, it means the personal cost or **sacrifice** required to gain freedom. Read the **KEY IDEA**, and have students generate examples for the **DISCUSS** activity. Then discuss the last question as a class.

SKILLS FOCUS

LITERARY ANALYSIS   R3.5

● NARRATIVE ELEMENTS

Read aloud this example from a narrative:

> Mrs. Bell wondered if her son would be happier at a different school. Mr. Evans said Stephen was the best football player on his team and hoped he would stay, but Mrs. Bell was not sure this was a good enough reason to keep Stephen at a school where he was unhappy.

Have students identify and define Mrs. Bell's conflict. *Possible answer: She has an internal conflict. She has to decide whether to keep Stephen at his current school or move him to a different school.*

CHECK UNDERSTANDING Ask students to identify the suspense in this passage. What do readers wonder?

READING STRATEGY

● READING A NARRATIVE

Read aloud the narrative example again. Ask students to identify how Mr. Evans is connected to Stephen and why he is important. *Possible answer: He is Stephen's football coach and probably cares about Stephen's happiness.*

 RESOURCE MANAGER—Copy Master
Reading a Narrative p. 89 (for student use while reading the selection)

DIFFERENTIATED INSTRUCTION

FOR STRATEGIC READERS

Concept Support: Narrative Elements To support instruction, clarify these narrative elements:

- *Internal conflict* happens inside a character's mind or emotions. Examples include a character's attempt to overcome a fear or need to make a difficult decision.
- *External conflict* can include a conflict between two characters or between one

character and a group of characters, as well as a conflict against a natural force such as a hurricane.

- *Characterization* includes direct comments and dialogue. Students can recognize dialogue in this narrative by its placement inside quotation marks. Harriet Jacobs also describes characters' actions to build her characterizations.

SUMMARY

This excerpt from the slave narrative *Incidents in the Life of a Slave Girl* begins with Linda's realization that the Flints will take control of her children to subdue her. To save her children, Linda decides to flee, hoping their father, a white man, will buy them. She hides at a friend's house while Mr. Flint searches for her and offers a reward for her capture. Linda's children, aunt, and brother are thrown in jail to pressure them for information about her.

LITERARY ANALYSIS

Ⓐ NARRATIVE ELEMENTS

Possible answer: The Flints are selfish and unfeeling people. Details that build this characterization include their lack of concern for the comfort or feelings of their servants (lines 6–8) and their singular focus on how their servants can serve them (lines 1–2).

Lines 9–13
REINFORCE *KEY IDEA:* SACRIFICE

Discuss What decision does Linda make that reflects her willingness to **sacrifice** for her children? Is this an easy decision for her? Explain. *Possible answer: She decides to leave her children so that they will not fall into the Flints' hands (lines 9–10). She sacrifices her safety and time with her children so that they will be safe. It is not an easy decision for her. She knows it will cause her grandmother worry and grief.*

Incidents in the Life of a Slave Girl

Harriet Jacobs

> **BACKGROUND** At this point in the narrative, Linda has spent six weeks at the plantation of old Dr. Flint's son, Mr. Flint, making the house ready for his new bride, who is now at the house. Mr. Flint has said openly that he plans to break Linda's willful spirit, as his father had not been able to do. In addition, Linda has learned that the next day, her children are to be brought from their grandmother's house, where they are loved, to the plantation, where they will be put to work and used to keep Linda in line. Be warned that this selection contains a racial slur.

The Flight

MR. FLINT was hard pushed for house servants, and rather than lose me he had restrained his malice. I did my work faithfully, though not, of course, with a willing mind. They were evidently afraid I should leave them. Mr. Flint wished that I should sleep in the great house instead of the servants' quarters. His wife agreed to the proposition, but said I mustn't bring my bed into the house, because it would scatter feathers on her carpet. I knew when I went there that they would never think of such a thing as furnishing a bed of any kind for me and my little one. I therefore carried my own bed, and now I was forbidden to use it. I did as I Ⓐ was ordered. But now that I was certain my children were to be put in their power, 10 in order to give them a stronger hold on me, I resolved to leave them that night. I remembered the grief this step would bring upon my dear old grandmother; and nothing less than the freedom of my children would have induced me to disregard her advice. I went about my evening work with trembling steps. Mr. Flint twice called from his chamber door to inquire why the house was not locked up. I replied that I had not done my work. "You have had time enough to do it," said he. "Take care how you answer me!"

ANALYZE VISUALS
What can you **infer** about the enslaved family pictured in this photograph from South Carolina?

❶ **Targeted Passage**

Ⓐ **NARRATIVE ELEMENTS**
Notice how the details in lines 1–8 build the **characterization** of the Flints. What kind of people are they?

DIFFERENTIATED INSTRUCTION

FOR ALL STUDENTS
Expert Groups Encourage students to become subject experts by selecting and researching one of these topics:

- slave literacy laws
- other slave narratives
- female African-American abolitionists, such as Harriet Tubman and Sojourner Truth
- procedures for buying a slave's freedom

FOR STRATEGIC READERS
In combination with the *Audio Anthology CD,* use one or more Targeted Passages (pp. 552, 554, 557) to ensure that students focus on key events and concepts. Targeted Passages are also good for English learners.

❶ **Targeted Passage [Lines 2–13]**

This passage introduces Linda's plight with the Flints, her reason for leaving her children, and the resulting conflicts.

BACKGROUND

Female Slave Narrative The female slave narrative was intended to influence white northern middle-class women. Many of the trials that Jacobs endures, such as separation from her children, resonated with white women who cared for their own children and saw themselves as the protectors of morality. This slave narrative's purpose was to make white women empathize with slave women and recognize that slavery was immoral.

Lines 1–16
TIERED DISCUSSION PROMPTS

Use these prompts to help students consider Linda's situation and agonizing decision:

Connect Have you or someone you know ever had to make a difficult decision? What made the situation difficult? *Accept all thoughtful responses.*

Interpret Why does Linda decide she must leave her children? *Possible answer: She believes that the Flints will take her children in order to subdue her (lines 9–10).*

Evaluate Does Linda's description of her circumstances justify her decision? Why or why not? *Possible answer: Yes. She explains how uncaring and thoughtless the Flints are (lines 4–9, 14–16). Her characterizations prove that leaving would save her children.*

ANALYZE VISUALS

Possible answer: The family members value one another. The women clasp the children, and the family has members of many ages. Everyone in the photo looks sad, as if perhaps they are fearful or unsure about whether they will be separated.

- Why do the Flints want Linda to stay in their house?
- How does Linda feel about her work?
- How do the Flints treat Linda?
- What do the Flints intend to do with Linda's children? How does that influence Linda's decision to leave her children?
- How does Linda hope her decision will help her children?
- What worry does she have about leaving?

FOR ENGLISH LEARNERS

Prereading For prereading instruction for English learners, see

 BEST PRACTICES TOOLKIT
   Scaffolding Reading Instruction pp. 43–46

FOR ADVANCED LEARNERS/AP

AP exercises in the bottom channel provide additional challenge for students. Use these suggestions for small groups or individuals.

ADDITIONAL GUIDELINES

For more help with differentiation and tips for classroom management, see

 BEST PRACTICES TOOLKIT
   Differentiated Instruction pp. 31–38

B NARRATIVE ELEMENTS

Possible answer: Linda has a conflict with the Flints, who plan to take her children (lines 9–10). She also has an internal conflict of worrying that running away will grieve her grandmother (line 11) or that she will fail and endanger her children (lines 19–21). Lines 17–21 build suspense as Linda waits to escape and fears being caught.

C READING A NARRATIVE

Possible answer: Sally is a friend who lives with Linda's grandmother. Mr. Sands is the father of Linda's children. Jacobs made up the name Mr. Sands to refer to Mr. Sawyer, who was the father of her real children.

If students need help . . . Model use of the graphic organizer introduced on page 551. Focus on lines 31–32 and the author's biography, and clarify that Jacobs used the name Linda to protect herself from discovery and capture.

```
Sally (friend of          Mr. Sands
Linda's grandmother)     (Samuel Sawyer)

            Linda
        (Harriot Jacobs)
```

D GRAMMAR AND STYLE

Establish Tone Jacobs's emotional writing style helps readers empathize with her horrid circumstances. Ask students to find charged adjectives in lines 50–54 and describe the resulting tone. *Possible answer: Adjectives include "fatherless and motherless" and "innocent little." The tone is desperate.*

I shut all the windows, locked all the doors, and went up to the third story, to wait till midnight. How long those hours seemed, and how fervently I prayed that God would not forsake me in this hour of utmost need! I was about to risk
20 everything on the throw of a die; and if I failed, O what would become of me and my poor children? They would be made to suffer for my fault. **B**

At half past twelve I stole softly down stairs. I stopped on the second floor, thinking I heard a noise. I felt my way down into the parlor, and looked out of the window. The night was so intensely dark that I could see nothing. I raised the window very softly and jumped out. Large drops of rain were falling, and the darkness bewildered me. I dropped on my knees, and breathed a short prayer to God for guidance and protection. I groped my way to the road, and rushed towards the town with almost lightning speed. I arrived at my grandmother's house, but dared not see her. She would say, "Linda, you are killing me;" and I
30 knew that would unnerve me. I tapped softly at the window of a room, occupied by a woman, who had lived in the house several years. I knew she was a faithful friend, and could be trusted with my secret. I tapped several times before she heard me. At last she raised the window, and I whispered, "Sally, I have run away. Let me in, quick." She opened the door softly, and said in low tones, "For God's sake, don't. Your grandmother is trying to buy you and de chillern. Mr. Sands was here last week. He tole her he was going away on business, but he wanted her to go ahead about buying you and de chillern, and he would help her all he could. Don't run away, Linda. Your grandmother is all bowed down wid trouble now." **C**

I replied, "Sally, they are going to carry my children to the plantation to-
40 morrow; and they will never sell them to any body so long as they have me in their power. Now, would you advise me to go back?"

"No, chile, no," answered she. "When dey finds you is gone, dey won't want de plague¹ ob de chillern; but where is you going to hide? Dey knows ebery inch ob dis house."

I told her I had a hiding-place, and that was all it was best for her to know. I asked her to go into my room as soon as it was light, and take all my clothes out of my trunk, and pack them in hers; for I knew Mr. Flint and the constable would be there early to search my room. I feared the sight of my children would be too much for my full heart; but I could not go out into the uncertain future without
50 one last look. I bent over the bed where lay my little Benny and baby Ellen. Poor little ones! fatherless and motherless! Memories of their father came over me. He wanted to be kind to them; but they were not all to him, as they were to my womanly heart. I knelt and prayed for the innocent little sleepers. I kissed them lightly, and turned away. **D**

As I was about to open the street door, Sally laid her hand on my shoulder, and said, "Linda, is you gwine all alone? Let me call your uncle. "

"No, Sally," I replied, "I want no one to be brought into trouble on my account."

---

1. **plague:** nuisance.

B NARRATIVE ELEMENTS Describe the **conflicts** presented in lines 9–21. Which lines build **suspense?**

2 Targeted Passage

C READING A NARRATIVE Reread lines 28–38. Who are Sally and Mr. Sands? Refer to Jacobs's biography on page 550 if necessary.

D GRAMMAR AND STYLE Examine lines 50–54. Notice how the writer uses emotionally charged **adjectives** to express the depth of her despair.

DIFFERENTIATED INSTRUCTION

FOR STRATEGIC READERS

2 Targeted Passage [Lines 22–45]

This passage describes the suspense of Linda's escape and reveals Mr. Sands's plans to buy freedom for Linda and the children.

- How does Linda get out of the Flints' house?
- Where does Linda first go when she escapes? Where does she go next?
- Does Sally agree with Linda's decision? What does Linda ask Sally to do?
- What does Mr. Sands plan to do?

FOR ENGLISH LEARNERS

Language: Conversational English Patterns Explain that Sally's dialect reflects the typical speech of many slaves. Read lines 42–44 aloud and help students decipher them. *Possible answer: "No, child, no. When they find that you are gone, they won't want the nuisance of the children; but where are you going to hide? They know every inch of this house."* Help pairs decipher Sally's other dialogue.

I went forth into the darkness and rain. I ran on till I came to the house of the friend who was to conceal me.

60   Early the next morning Mr. Flint was at my grandmother's inquiring for me. She told him she had not seen me, and supposed I was at the plantation. He watched her face narrowly, and said, "Don't you know any thing about her running off?" She assured him that she did not. He went on to say, "Last night she ran off without the least provocation. We had treated her very kindly. My wife liked her. She will soon be found and brought back. Are her children with you?" When told that they were, he said, "I am very glad to hear that. If they are here, she cannot be far off. If I find out that any of my niggers have had any thing to do with this damned business, I'll give 'em five hundred lashes." As he started to go to his father's, he turned round and added, persuasively, "Let her be brought back,
70   and she shall have her children to live with her."

The tidings made the old doctor rave and storm at a furious rate. It was a busy day for them. My grandmother's house was searched from top to bottom. As my trunk was empty, they concluded I had taken my clothes with me. Before

Lines 60–70
TIERED DISCUSSION PROMPTS

Use these prompts to help understand the tension and conflict between Mr. Flint and Linda's grandmother:

Connect Think about a time when someone has asked you for answers you could not supply. How did you feel? How did that person respond? *Accept all thoughtful responses.*

Interpret What does Mr. Flint's remark that Linda ran off "without the least provocation" tell you about him? How does he view Linda? *Possible answer: He can't imagine that the threat of putting her children to work would upset and provoke Linda. He doesn't view Linda as having a mother's normal feelings, but rather sees her as a disobedient possession.*

Synthesize On the basis of the selection and your own experiences, do you believe Mr. Flint's promise that Linda's children can live with her if she returns? Explain. *Possible answer: No; based on his character, he is probably lying to trick Linda's grandmother into giving up Linda.*

FOR ENGLISH LEARNERS
Vocabulary: Multiple-Meaning Words Point out the word *die* in line 20. Explain that in this context the word describes a small cube with dots on the sides, used in games of chance. The words *throw of a* are clues to the correct meaning. Explain further that Linda uses the phrase *throw of a die* as a metaphor for the gamble she is taking by fleeing. She realizes that she has little control over the situation's outcome.

FOR ADVANCED LEARNERS/AP
Analyze Theme [small-group option] Point out to students that although the selection is only an excerpt from Jacobs's narrative, some very powerful themes are established. Have students use textual evidence, make inferences, and consider their knowledge of slavery to determine some of the narrative's themes. Organize students into small groups, and have each group discuss the questions in the Analysis Frame: Theme. Encourage groups to share

their answers and decide whether the themes they identified are universal and still relevant today, or specifically pertinent to Jacobs's time.

 BEST PRACTICES TOOLKIT—Transparency
Analysis Frame: Theme p. D21, D32

Lines 76–79
REINFORCE *KEY IDEA*: SACRIFICE

Discuss Who makes a **sacrifice** for Linda? What does that sacrifice suggest about slave families? *Possible answer: Linda's grandmother makes a sacrifice for Linda by agreeing to take Linda's children. This shows that slave families were quite close and trusted and depended on one another. They banded together to help one another fight their oppressors.*

Ⓔ NARRATIVE ELEMENTS

Possible answer: Linda portrays herself as a "weak and oppressed" (line 97) victim who cunningly outwits a tyrant (lines 95–98). Readers are likely to feel sympathy for her and rejoice in her triumph.

If students need help . . . Urge them to visualize the scene Linda describes and identify how they feel about her. Then remind them that characterization is built from descriptions of a character's words, actions, and attitudes, and help them complete a Character Traits Web to identify information about Linda that created their response.

BEST PRACTICES TOOLKIT—Transparency
Character Traits Web p. D7

---

ten o'clock every vessel northward bound was thoroughly examined, and the law against harboring[2] fugitives was read to all on board. At night a watch was set over the town. Knowing how distressed my grandmother would be, I wanted to send her a message; but it could not be done. Every one who went in or out of her house was closely watched. The doctor said he would take my children, unless she became responsible for them; which of course she willingly did. The next day was
80 spent in searching. Before night, the following advertisement was posted at every corner, and in every public place for miles round:—

> $300 REWARD! Ran away from the subscriber,[3] an intelligent, bright, mulatto[4] girl, named Linda, 21 years of age. Five feet four inches high. Dark eyes, and black hair inclined to curl; but it can be made straight. Has a decayed spot on a front tooth. She can read and write, and in all probability will try to get to the Free States. All persons are forbidden, under penalty of the law, to harbor or employ said slave. $150 will be given to whoever takes her in the state, and $300 if taken out of the state and delivered to me, or lodged in jail. DR. FLINT.

For a week, Linda hides in the house of an unnamed friend. Her pursuers come so close to finding her that she rushes from the house into the bushes, where she is bitten by a poisonous snake or lizard. She suffers greatly until an old woman treats her with a folk remedy. Vowing "give me liberty or death," she refuses to return to the Flints. Then a sympathetic white woman, an old friend of her grandmother's, offers to conceal Linda in a small storage room in her house. The woman makes them promise never to tell, as she is the wife of a prominent slaveholder. The woman sends her cook, Linda's friend Betty, to meet Linda and take her to the house.

Months of Peril

90 I went to sleep that night with the feeling that I was for the present the most fortunate slave in town. Morning came and filled my little cell with light. I thanked the heavenly Father for this safe retreat. Opposite my window was a pile of feather beds. On the top of these I could lie perfectly concealed, and command a view of the street through which Dr. Flint passed to his office. Anxious as I was, I felt a gleam of satisfaction when I saw him. Thus far I had outwitted him, and I triumphed over it. Who can blame slaves for being cunning? They are constantly compelled to resort to it. It is the only weapon of the weak and oppressed against the strength of their tyrants. Ⓔ

Ⓔ **NARRATIVE ELEMENTS**
Consider the **characterization** of Linda in this paragraph. How are readers likely to feel toward her?

---

2. **harboring:** sheltering or protecting.
3. **the subscriber:** the person placing the notice, Dr. Flint.
4. **mulatto:** of mixed black and white ancestry.

DIFFERENTIATED INSTRUCTION

FOR ENGLISH LEARNERS
Language: Conversational English Patterns
Reread lines 128–130 and remind students that they reflect typical slave dialect. Clarify that *chile* means "child," and rephrase the lines for students. Explain that *chick'n hearted* means "weak and fearful like a chicken." Betty is telling Linda that she needs to be tougher if she is going to survive life's challenges.

FOR ADVANCED LEARNERS/AP
Synthesize Remind students that the law against harboring fugitives was read to every northbound ship (lines 74–75). Have students research to learn about fugitive slave laws. Ask students to write a short paragraph that might have been read aboard these ships. Encourage pairs to share their paragraphs with the class. Ask them to explain what would probably have happened to Linda had she been found.

I was daily hoping to hear that my master had sold my children; for I knew
100 who was on the watch to buy them. But Dr. Flint cared even more for revenge
than he did for money. My brother William, and the good aunt who had served
in his family twenty years, and my little Benny, and Ellen, who was a little over
two years old, were thrust into jail, as a means of compelling my relatives to give
some information about them. He swore my grandmother should never see one of
them again till I was brought back. They kept these facts from me for several days.
When I heard that my little ones were in a loathsome jail, my first impulse was to
go to them. I was encountering dangers for the sake of freeing them, and must I
be the cause of their death? The thought was agonizing. My benefactress[5] tried to
soothe me by telling me that my aunt would take good care of the children while
110 they remained in jail. But it added to my pain to think that the good old aunt,
who had always been so kind to her sister's orphan children, should be shut up in
prison for no other crime than loving them. I suppose my friends feared a reckless
movement on my part, knowing, as they did, that my life was bound up in my
children. I received a note from my brother William. It was scarcely legible, and
ran thus: "Wherever you are, dear sister, I beg of you not to come here. We are all
much better off than you are. If you come, you will ruin us all. They would force
you to tell where you had been, or they would kill you. Take the advice of your
friends; if not for the sake of me and your children, at least for the sake of those
you would ruin." **F**

120 Poor William! He also must suffer for being my brother. I took his advice and
kept quiet. My aunt was taken out of jail at the end of a month, because Mrs.
Flint could not spare her any longer. She was tired of being her own housekeeper.
It was quite too fatiguing to order her dinner and eat it too. My children remained
in jail, where brother William did all he could for their comfort. Betty went to see
them sometimes, and brought me tidings. She was not permitted to enter the jail;
but William would hold them up to the grated window while she chatted with
them. When she repeated their prattle, and told me how they wanted to see their
ma, my tears would flow. Old Betty would exclaim, "Lors, chile! what's you crying
'bout? Dem young uns vil kill you dead. Don't be so chick'n hearted! If you does,
130 you vil nebber git thro' dis world." **G**

3 Targeted Passage

F NARRATIVE ELEMENTS
What new **conflict**
is presented in this
paragraph?

G READING A NARRATIVE
Review the paragraph
that begins "For a
week . . ." on page 556.
Who is Betty, mentioned
in lines 124–130?

---

5. **benefactress:** a woman who gives aid.

INCIDENTS IN THE LIFE OF A SLAVE GIRL **557**

Lines 99–108
REINFORCE *KEY IDEA:* SACRIFICE

Discuss Linda has given up her children to
protect them. How does her family **sacrifice** to
help her meet that goal? *Possible answer: Her
children, her brother, and her aunt go to jail,
sacrificing their freedom in order to protect
Linda from discovery. They know that her
absence offers the best chance that Dr. Flint
will agree to sell the children to their father,
Mr. Sands.*

LITERARY ANALYSIS

F NARRATIVE ELEMENTS

*Possible answer: Linda has an internal
conflict with herself. Her brother, aunt,
and children are placed in jail, and she
wants to "go to them" (line 107). However,
Linda cannot risk going to them.*

READING STRATEGY

G READING A NARRATIVE

*Possible answer: Betty is Linda's friend,
who works for the white woman who is
hiding Linda.*

SELECTION WRAP–UP

SUMMARIZE Have students sum up what
Linda learns about the Flints and her own
family members after her escape.

FOR STRATEGIC READERS

3 Targeted Passage [Lines 101–121]

This passage shows some of the effects of
Linda's choice to flee.

- What happens to Linda's children, her aunt,
  and her brother? Who causes this to happen?

- How does Linda feel about what happens?

- What does William ask Linda to do? What
  does he mean by saying that her return will
  "ruin us all"?

- Does Linda honor her brother's request?

Recognize Tone Point out that Linda's tone is
sarcastic in the comment about Mrs. Flint that
it was "too fatiguing to order her dinner and
eat it too" (line 123). She characterizes Mrs.
Flint as unable to handle simple tasks and
completely selfish in her choices. Mrs. Flint
takes Linda's aunt out of jail because she does
not want to manage her own house or do any
work. She does not take her out of jail to be
fair or moral.

FOR ADVANCED LEARNERS/AP

Compare and Contrast Ask students to
complete a Venn Diagram that compares and
contrasts this excerpt with the excerpt from
Frederick Douglass's slave narrative. Then
have students write a brief essay in which
they explain the similarities and differences.
Encourage students to share their essays with
the class.

 BEST PRACTICES TOOLKIT—Transparency
Venn Diagram p. A26

INCIDENTS IN THE LIFE OF A SLAVE GIRL **557**

Practice and Apply

After Reading

Use these copy masters to check understanding and provide extra support:

RESOURCE MANAGER—Copy Masters

Reading Check p. 91
Narrative Elements p. 87
Question Support p. 92

Additional selection questions are provided for teachers on page 81.

ANSWERS

1. *She learns the Flints are going to take her children in order to control her.*

2. *They search her grandmother's house and northbound ships, offer a reward for her capture, and jail her relatives.*

3. *She wants Mr. Sands to buy them so they can be with their father and escape mistreatment by the Flints.*

Possible answers:

4. ■ **SKILLS FOCUS Reading a Narrative**
Opposing characters: The Flints and Linda's grandmother oppose her flight; Supportive characters: Linda's grandmother, Sally, Mr. Sands, William, Aunt Betty, and the white woman who hides her support her.

5. ● **SKILLS FOCUS Narrative Elements**
External conflicts: with Dr. Flint about sexual advances, with Mr. Flint about her children (lines 9–10), with her grandmother over running away (lines 10–13) Internal conflicts: love for children versus love for her grandmother (lines 11–13, 35–38), love for her children versus her safety (lines 19–21), wanting to convey her safety to her grandmother versus danger to herself and her grandmother (lines 76–78), wanting to rescue her children in jail versus dire consequence of this action (lines 106–119). The conflicts prove the injustice of slavery and highlight the painful sacrifices it required of slaves.

6. *She is hardworking (line 2). She loves her children deeply. She is considerate of others and takes responsibility for her own actions.*

7. *She characterizes the Flints as blind to their own cruelty, unfeeling, and selfish, and herself as a loving mother and oppressed victim.*

Comprehension

1. **Recall** What prompts Linda to make the decision to escape?

2. **Summarize** What actions do the Flints take after they find out Linda has left?

3. **Clarify** Why does Linda want the Flints to sell her children?

Literary Analysis

4. **Reading a Narrative** Review the web you made as you read. Which characters support Linda and which oppose her? Share questions you have about them.

5. **Examine Narrative Elements** Describe different **conflicts**—internal and external—that Linda faces in this excerpt. What do these conflicts reveal about the institution of slavery and the **sacrifices** forced by it?

6. **Analyze Characterization** How does the writer present herself? Discuss what you learn about her character and values from
   - her attitude toward her work (lines 2–3)
   - her thoughts as she visits her children (lines 48–54)
   - her insistence upon escaping alone (line 57)

7. **Contrast Characterizations** Contrast the writer's portrayal of herself with her portrayal of the Flints. What does she reveal about the Flints' character and values?

8. **Draw Conclusions** How might the writer's political purpose and the knowledge that she was writing for an audience of Northern white women have influenced her characterizations?

9. **Compare Texts** Read "Free Labor" and "Go Down, Moses" on pages 560 and 561. How do they compare with Harriet Jacobs's narrative in their **tone** and their messages about slavery?

Literary Criticism

10. **Author's Style** Jacobs's style was influenced by the literature popular in her time. Nineteenth-century women's novels were melodramatic, arousing readers' emotions with suspenseful plots that usually involved virtuous characters pitted against evil villains. *Uncle Tom's Cabin,* an immensely popular antislavery novel, included such elements as well. It also rendered the speech of slave characters in heavy dialect, a convention of the time. How do you, as a modern reader, respond to Jacobs's style? Evaluate the effects of her style on the power of her narrative.

8. *To convince Northern white women to act against slavery, she shows how her values as an enslaved woman and mother are similar to those of her audience. She wants to show Northern women how slavery subverts moral values in slaveholders and also how it victimizes women.*

9. *Both the poems and Jacobs's narrative speak of slavery in a somber tone. Both also express the similar message of slavery's inhumanity.*

10. *Students may say that Jacobs's emotional style contributes to the power of her work and enables readers to feel anger at the immorality of slavery. Others may argue that the use of slave dialect robs these characters of dignity.*

Reading-Writing Connection

W1.2, W1.5

WRITING PROMPT

EXPLORE POINT OF VIEW *Incidents in the Life of a Slave Girl* is told from the first-person point of view and thus focuses on the thoughts, words, and actions of the narrator, Linda (Harriet Jacobs). Choose one of the other people mentioned in the narrative—Sally, or Linda's grandmother, aunt, or brother. Write a **three-paragraph response**, told from that character's point of view, reacting to the news that Linda has run away. As a starting point, reread Linda's descriptions of how any of these characters did or would react.

SELF-CHECK

An effective response will...

- have a clear focus
- establish a consistent tone and point of view
- use precise words to convey the character's emotions
- establish a mood

GRAMMAR AND STYLE

W1.9

ESTABLISH TONE Review the **Grammar and Style** note on page 554. Tone is a writer's attitude toward a subject. In Jacobs's compelling narrative, she uses emotionally charged language to establish a tone of melancholy and desperation. In the following example, the **adjectives** *loathsome* and *agonizing* succinctly convey the turmoil and conflict the narrator is experiencing and help elicit empathy from her readers.

> *When I heard my little ones were in a loathsome jail, my first impulse was to go to them. I was encountering dangers for the sake of freeing them, and must I be the cause of their death? The thought was agonizing.* (lines 106–108)

PRACTICE Copy the sentences in the example. Then rewrite them, using adjectives, verbs, and additional phrases to effectively convey a tone of fear or sorrow. A sample answer has been done for you.

EXAMPLE

I fainted when I heard Linda had run off, leaving her children behind.

I collapsed to the floor when I heard poor Linda had run off, tearing herself away from the dear babies she cherished.

---

1. I'm an old woman, but I tried to be strong as Mr. Flint asked me questions about Linda.

2. The children cried when they heard their mother had left them behind.

3. It made me sad to see them feeling so bad. It is very hard for the little children.

WRITING TOOLS

For prewriting, revision, and editing tools, visit the **Writing Center** at **ClassZone.com.**

DIFFERENTIATED INSTRUCTION

FOR DEVELOPING WRITERS
Writing Support

- Help students to locate dialogue spoken by their character or comments by Linda about their character. Then help them make inferences and identify the character's point of view about Linda's flight.

- Ask students to describe the mood they think fits their character's feelings about Linda's flight. Encourage them to brainstorm a list of adjectives that will convey the character's emotions or the mood.

- Remind students that their response should be written in the first person and should include the pronoun *I*.

- Aid students in writing a point-of-view thesis statement in which they reveal their character's opinion of Linda's escape and set the mood for the response.

Reading-Writing Connection

WRITING PROMPT

Explain to students that they may have to make inferences about how their chosen character would react to Linda's escape. Review how to do this based on textual evidence and reader's experiences. Urge students to use a Making Inferences chart during prewriting to help them solidify the character's point of view.

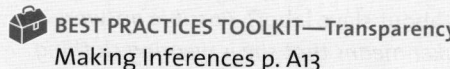

BEST PRACTICES TOOLKIT—Transparency
Making Inferences p. A13

For writing support, see

Writing Center at ClassZone.com

GRAMMAR AND STYLE

Encourage students to use a thesaurus to choose words with the desired meaning that also effectively convey fear or sorrow.

Possible answers:

1. *I'm just a feeble old woman, but I willed myself to be strong as Mr. Flint fired questions at me about Linda.*

2. *The children wept inconsolably on hearing their mother had abandoned them.*

3. *It broke my heart to see them so forlorn. What a burden for the innocent little ones to bear!*

RESOURCE MANAGER—Copy Master
Establish Tone p. 93

Assess and Reteach

Assess

RESOURCE MANAGER—Copy Masters
Selection Test A pp. 95–96
Selection Test B/C pp. 97–98

 Test Generator CD

Reteach

STANDARDS LESSON FILE
Literature Lesson 3: Characterization
Literature Lesson 6: Conflict and Suspense
Reading Lesson 2: Monitoring
Informational Text Lesson 2: Sequence and Chronological Order
Writing Lesson 42: Adapting a Tone

Free Labor

Frances Ellen Watkins Harper

I wear an easy garment,
   O'er it no toiling slave
Wept tears of hopeless anguish,
   In his passage to the grave.

5 And from its ample folds
   Shall rise no cry to God,
Upon its warp and woof shall be
   No stain of tears and blood.

Oh, lightly shall it press my form,
10   Unladened with a sigh,
I shall not 'mid its rustling hear,
   Some sad despairing cry.

This fabric is too light to bear
   The weight of bondsmen's tears,
15 I shall not in its texture trace
   The agony of years.

Too light to bear a smother'd sigh,
   From some lorn woman's heart,
Whose only wreath of household love
20   Is rudely torn apart.

Then lightly shall it press my form,
   Unburden'd by a sigh;
And from its seams and folds shall rise,
   No voice to pierce the sky,

25 And witness at the throne of God,
   In language deep and strong,
That I have nerv'd Oppression's hand,
   For deeds of guilt and wrong.

TIERED DISCUSSION PROMPTS

Use these prompts to help students compare how this poem's speaker and Linda view slavery:

Connect What response have you had when you or someone you know was unfairly treated? *Accept all thoughtful answers.*

Interpret What does the speaker mean in lines 1–8? How do these lines work with the poem's title to convey the speaker's feelings about slave labor? *Possible answer: The speaker means that she is wearing clothing that was not created by a slave. These lines, along with the poem's title, suggest that the speaker feels slave labor is unfair. Slaves are forced to work while they cry in "hopeless anguish" (line 3). The speaker does not want to support slave labor, and wants clothing made from paid, or freely given, labor.*

Synthesize What feelings does the poem's speaker share with Linda? Would Linda agree with the speaker's view of slave labor? *Possible answer: The speaker mentions the heart of a poor woman whose household is torn apart (lines 17–20), just as Linda's is. The speaker calls on God to recognize slavery's oppression (lines 25–28) as Linda cries to God for help (lines 18–19). Linda would agree with the speaker's view of slave labor, saying that it is unfair, and that the oppressors are wrong and guilty.*

Go Down, Moses

Traditional Spiritual

When Israel was in Egypt's land,
Let my people go!
Oppressed so hard they could not stand
Let my people go!

5 Go down, Moses
'Way down in Egypt's land,
Tell old Pharoah, "Let my people go!"

"Thus saith the Lord" bold Moses said,
Let my people go!
10 "If not I'll smite your first-born dead"
Let my people go!

Go down, Moses
'Way down in Egypt's land,
Tell old Pharoah, "Let my people go!"

15 No more in bondage shall they toil,
Let my people go!
Let them come out with Egypt's spoil
Let my people go!

Go down, Moses
20 'Way down in Egypt's land,
Tell old Pharoah, "Let my people go!"

561

TIERED DISCUSSION PROMPTS

Use these prompts to help students see how this traditional spiritual and Jacobs's narrative convey similar messages about slavery:

Connect Have you ever spoken out against something that is unfair to a group of people? What motivated you to do that? *Accept all thoughtful answers.*

Interpret This poem refers to the biblical story about the Pharaoh of Egypt, who unfairly enslaved the Israelites, and Moses' going to free them. Why would African-American slaves have sung this song? ***Possible answer:*** *Slaves saw a parallel between their situation and that of the enslaved Israelites.*

Synthesize What is the message of this poem? Would Harriet Jacobs agree with the message? ***Possible answer:*** *The message of this poem is that slavery places people in bondage (line 15) and is wrong. Jacobs would agree that slavery is wrong and that slaves should be released from bondage.*

Focus and Motivate

OBJECTIVES

Literary Analysis
- explore the key idea of **legacy**
- analyze audience and form
- read a speech
- read a proclamation

Reading
- analyze an author's beliefs

Grammar and Writing
- use repetition as an effective rhetorical device
- write a letter

CALIFORNIA R2.1, R2.5, W1.1, W1.4, W1.5, W1.9, W2.2

ABOUT THE AUTHOR

After students read about Lincoln, stress that his key political goal was to preserve the Union, not to abolish slavery. Then ask how Lincoln's political goals affected his decision to fight a civil war and to issue the Emancipation Proclamation. *Students should grasp that Lincoln fought the war to preserve the Union and supported emancipation to help the North win it.*

USING THE *NOTABLE QUOTE*

Explain that **Abraham Lincoln** said these famous words to begin his Senate race against Stephen Douglas. Ask students how the quote shows Lincoln's main political goals. *Possible answer: Lincoln's main goal was keeping the Union intact. He believed that division of the states would irreparably destroy the nation.*

Selection Resources

The Gettysburg Address

Speech by Abraham Lincoln

The Emancipation Proclamation

Proclamation by Abraham Lincoln

CALIFORNIA

R2.1, R2.5, W1.1 (p. 569), W1.4 (p. 569), W1.5 (p. 569), W1.9 (p. 569), W2.2 (p. 569)

NOTABLE QUOTE
"A house divided against itself cannot stand."

FYI
Did you know that Abraham Lincoln . . .
- loved the works of Edgar Allan Poe?
- was a talented mimic who enjoyed playing practical jokes?
- made Thanksgiving Day a national holiday?
- suffered from bouts of depression?

Author Online

For more on Abraham Lincoln, visit the **Literature Center** at **ClassZone.com.**

Abraham Lincoln
1809–1865

Abraham Lincoln led the United States during its greatest crisis—the Civil War. Dedicated to keeping the nation together, Lincoln guided the country toward a new national identity, that of a nation committed to the principle of union, in which slavery no longer had a place.

Humble Origins Born on the Kentucky frontier to illiterate parents, Lincoln rarely went to school and was largely self-educated. As a young man, he moved with his family to Illinois, where he worked as a shopkeeper, rail-splitter, and surveyor and studied law. He served in the state legislature from 1834 to 1841, becoming a lawyer in 1836.

Evolving Views Although Lincoln opposed slavery as "injustice and bad policy," he was not an abolitionist; he preferred to free slaves gradually. In 1854, he began a vigorous public campaign to block the expansion of slavery to the western territories. His eloquent speeches and famous debates with Senator Stephen A. Douglas raised his political profile and strengthened his opposition to slavery.

A House Divided In 1860, Lincoln was elected president on his antislavery platform, prompting seven Southern states to secede from the Union before he even took office. In 1861, two months after his inauguration, the Civil War began.

As the fighting wore on, Lincoln faced increasing pressure to move against slavery while he struggled to keep the loyalty of the Union states that permitted slavery within their borders. After nearly two years of fighting, Lincoln issued the Emancipation Proclamation, which freed slaves in the rebelling states.

Tragic Ending Throughout the war, Lincoln faced opposition and ridicule from the public, his generals, and his own cabinet. The prospect of a Union victory, however, earned him reelection, and the Confederate armies surrendered weeks into his second term. Just five days later, Lincoln was assassinated, the first such occurrence in American history. His shocking murder and the end of war made him an instant hero. Today, he is one of the country's most widely respected presidents.

View of Washington, D.C.

 RESOURCE MANAGER UNIT 3

Plan and Teach pp. 99–106

Literary Analysis
Summary pp. 107†*, 108‡*
Audience and Form pp. 109, 110†*
Question Support p. 114*

Reading
Analyze an Author's Beliefs
    pp. 111, 112†*
Reading Check p. 113

Grammar and Writing
Use Language Effectively p. 115

Assessment
Selection Tests A, B/C pp. 117*, 119*
Test Generator CD

 BEST PRACTICES TOOLKIT

Differentiated Instruction
    pp. 31–38*

Scaffolding Instruction
    pp. 43–46*

Graphic Organizers/Strategies
Definition Mapping • Two-Column Chart

Reading Support
Audio Anthology CD*

Technology
Literature and Writing Centers at **ClassZone.com**

WriteSmart CD

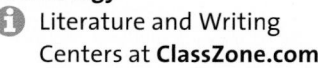

---

* Resources for Differentiation   † Also in Spanish   ‡ In Haitian Creole and Vietnamese

LITERARY ANALYSIS: AUDIENCE AND FORM

Lincoln was a master orator and an expert lawyer. He was keenly aware that the **form** a piece of writing takes affects what the writer can say to his or her **audience.**

- A **speech,** such as the Gettysburg Address, is often prepared for a specific audience. The speaker chooses details and language appropriate for the occasion so that the audience will be moved.

  We have come to dedicate a portion of that field as a final resting place for those who here gave their lives . . .

- A **proclamation,** such as the Emancipation Proclamation, is a legal document that announces official state business. As with any legal document, the writer is a person of authority and addresses the general public using precise language that can be clearly interpreted in a court of law.

  I, Abraham Lincoln, President of the United States, by virtue of the power in me vested as Commander-in-Chief . . .

As you read these two works of Lincoln's, note how the conventions of each form shape the way Lincoln expresses his message.

READING SKILL: ANALYZE AN AUTHOR'S BELIEFS

A thoughtful, principled man, Lincoln tried to act in accordance with his beliefs. To identify those beliefs in his writing, consider the ideals he invokes, the actions he takes, and the reasons he gives for his actions. As you read, note details that reveal

- the reason he felt the war was necessary
- his views on the responsibilities of the president
- the reasons he opposed slavery

Use a chart like the one shown to record your notes.

Beliefs About . . .	Gettysburg Address	Emancipation Proclamation
the necessity of war		
the duties of the president		
slavery		

What makes a great LEGACY?

KEY IDEA Washington, Jefferson, Lincoln—these legendary figures top most lists of greatest American presidents. In each case, the **legacy** is more complicated than the heroic myths suggest. What are the real reasons some leaders hold such a prominent place in history?

TEST YOURSELF What ideas come to mind when you think of Abraham Lincoln and the times in which he lived? Decide whether each statement is fact or myth.

Myth or History?

1. Hard-working Abe Lincoln was a poor country boy who rose to become president.
   ☐ TRUE ◯ FALSE

2. Lincoln led the fight to abolish slavery.
   ☐ TRUE ◯ FALSE

3. The Civil War was fought to free the slaves.
   ☐ TRUE ◯ FALSE

4. The Emancipation Proclamation ended slavery in the United States.
   ☐ TRUE ◯ FALSE

5. All of the Union states opposed slavery.
   ☐ TRUE ◯ FALSE

What makes a great LEGACY?

Read the question and **KEY IDEA**. Clarify that a **legacy** is how a figure from the past affects the present. After students suggest why some leaders have memorable legacies, have them consider their answers as they complete the *TEST YOURSELF* activity.

SKILLS FOCUS

LITERARY ANALYSIS R2.1

● AUDIENCE AND FORM

Ask students to identify the form and audience of the author biography on page 562. *Possible answer: It is a biographical sketch written as background for students who will study Lincoln's writings.*

CHECK UNDERSTANDING Ask how the convention of subheads serves the feature's form and helps its audience.

READING SKILL R2.5

■ ANALYZE AN AUTHOR'S BELIEFS

Share this example of a speech with students:

> My fellow students, Lisa Jones spoke out earlier today in favor of a school uniform. People booed and hissed so loudly, she couldn't finish. I'm speaking today because this behavior is wrong. Though I personally hate the idea of uniforms, we must hear each other out regardless of our personal beliefs.

Ask students to explain what this entry reveals about the speaker's beliefs about free speech. *Possible answer: The speaker's efforts on behalf of Lisa show he believes so strongly in free speech that he will even speak out for someone's right to express ideas different from his own.*

 RESOURCE MANAGER—Copy Master
Analyze an Author's Beliefs p. 111 (for student use while reading the selections)

DIFFERENTIATED INSTRUCTION

FOR STRATEGIC READERS

Concept Support: Audience and Form Use this chart to clarify the differences between a speech and a proclamation. Ask students to keep the listed differences in mind as they read each document, and to ask themselves the questions about each selection.

Form	Characteristics
speech	• specific **audience** • details, language fit the occasion • **question to ask**: Is the occasion serious?
proclamation	• general **audience** • legal document • precise, legal language • **question to ask**: What is the legal goal?

SUMMARY

In this speech, Lincoln recalls the principles upon which the Union was founded. He says that the purpose of the gathering is to consecrate a battlefield, but that the soldiers who fought and died have already sanctified it through their sacrifices. He exhorts the living to honor the fallen soldiers by continuing their struggle for freedom.

LITERARY ANALYSIS

Ⓐ AUDIENCE AND FORM

Possible answer: The tone is serious and elevated. Lincoln's mention of historic events, high ideals, and national purpose convey the occasion's importance.

If students need help . . . Point out specific references to the historic event of 1776 (line 1), to the high ideals of liberty and equality (lines 2–3), and the national purpose of passing the war's test of national unity (lines 4–5).

Ⓑ GRAMMAR AND STYLE

Use Language Effectively Ask students why Lincoln emphasizes the words *dedicate* and *consecrate*. *Possible answer: He is linking America's past with her present and future, connecting the founding fathers' dedication to the soldiers' dedication and, he hopes, his listeners' dedication to the principles of freedom. He is also linking the soldiers' honor in fighting for freedom with the goal of honoring them with equal dedication to the cause of freedom.*

READING SKILL

Ⓒ AUTHOR'S BELIEFS

Possible answer: The "great task" is making certain that the United States survives as a nation dedicated to the principles of freedom and liberty.

If students need help . . . Help them add to the chart introduced on page 563.

THE GETTYSBURG ADDRESS

Abraham Lincoln

> **BACKGROUND** The Battle of Gettysburg was fought July 1–3, 1863. The victory for Union forces marked a turning point in the Civil War, but the losses on both sides were staggering: 28,000 Confederate soldiers and 23,000 Union soldiers were killed or wounded. Lincoln delivered his Gettysburg Address on November 19, 1863, at a ceremony dedicating a national cemetery on the battle site.

Four score and seven years ago[1] our fathers brought forth on this continent a new nation, conceived in liberty, and dedicated to the proposition that all men are created equal.

Now we are engaged in a great civil war, testing whether that nation, or any nation so conceived and so dedicated, can long endure. We are met on a great battlefield of that war. We have come to dedicate a portion of that field as a final resting place for those who here gave their lives that that nation might live. It is altogether fitting and proper that we should do this. Ⓐ

But, in a larger sense, we cannot dedicate—we cannot consecrate—we cannot
10 hallow[2]—this ground. The brave men, living and dead, who struggled here have consecrated it far above our poor power to add or detract. The world will little note nor long remember what we say here, but it can never forget what they did Ⓑ here. It is for us, the living, rather, to be dedicated here to the unfinished work which they who fought here have thus far so nobly advanced. It is rather for us to be here dedicated to the great task remaining before us—that from these honored dead we take increased devotion to that cause for which they gave the last full measure of devotion; that we here highly resolve that these dead shall not have died in vain; that this nation, under God, shall have a new birth of freedom; and that government of the people, by the people, for the people, shall not perish from
20 the earth. ❧ Ⓒ

---

1. **four score . . . ago:** 87 years ago—that is, in 1776. (*Score* means "a group of 20.")
2. **hallow:** set apart as holy.

Ⓐ AUDIENCE AND FORM
Describe the **tone** of lines 1–8. What details help convey the importance of the occasion?

① Targeted Passage

Ⓑ GRAMMAR AND STYLE
Reread lines 9–13. Note how **repetition** emphasizes the verbs *dedicate and consecrate.*

Ⓒ AUTHOR'S BELIEFS
What is the "great task" Lincoln mentions in line 15?

DIFFERENTIATED INSTRUCTION

FOR ALL STUDENTS

Expert Groups Encourage students to become subject experts by selecting and researching one of these topics:

- causes of the Civil War
- the Battle of Gettysburg
- the writing of the Gettysburg Address
- African-American troops
- the Emancipation Proclamation

FOR STRATEGIC READERS

In combination with the *Audio Anthology CD*, use one or more Targeted Passages (pp. 564, 566) to ensure that students focus on key concepts in the selections. Targeted Passages are also good for English learners.

① Targeted Passage [Lines 6–14]

This passage explains the significance of the soldiers' sacrifices.

FOUR SCORE AND SEVEN YEAR
GO OUR FATHERS BROUGHT FORT
N THIS CONTINENT A NEW NATIO
ONCEIVED IN LIBERTY AND DEDICA
D TO THE PROPOSITION THAT AL
EN ARE CREATED EQUAL ·
NOW WE ARE ENGAGED IN A GREA
VIL WAR TESTING WHETHER THA
TION OR ANY NATION SO CON
EIVED AND SO DEDICATED CAN LON
DURE · WE ARE MET ON A GREA
TTLEFIELD OF THAT WAR · WE HAV
ME TO DEDICATE A PORTION O
HAT FIELD A FINAL RESTIN
FOR THE WHO HERE GAV
LIVES THAT NATIO

ANALYZE VISUALS

Activity Created by sculptor Daniel Chester French, the statue of Abraham Lincoln is the centerpiece of the Lincoln Memorial in Washington, D.C. The walls of the main chamber contain inscriptions of the Gettysburg Address and of Lincoln's second inaugural address. Ask students whether the Gettysburg Address is a fitting inscription for the Lincoln Memorial. Why or why not? *Students should recognize that the Gettysburg Address aptly honors Lincoln—his humanity, his devotion to the nation's ideals, and his recognition of the Civil War's importance to the nation.*

BACKGROUND

The Turning Tide In the summer of 1863, Confederate General Robert E. Lee led his troops into Pennsylvania. There, the Battle of Gettysburg began almost by chance. Out scouting for a supply of shoes, Southern soldiers ran into Union forces. The battle raged for three days and was a disaster for the Confederacy. It ended Lee's plans for attacking the North and left him entirely on the defensive. Vicksburg also fell, splitting the Confederacy in two and leaving the core of the South open to attack. The war's tide turned for the North.

Lines 10–14
REINFORCE *KEY IDEA:* LEGACY

Discuss What **legacy** does Lincoln say the fallen soldiers have "so nobly advanced"? *Possible answer: They have advanced the nation's legacies of liberty and equality.*

- According to Lincoln, why are he and others gathered at this battlefield?
- What were the soldiers fighting for?
- How can the living honor the dead?

FOR ENGLISH LEARNERS

Comprehension: Self-Monitor Help students paraphrase lines 14–20: *We should commit to the cause for which they died. We should make sure that their death serves a purpose. We should make sure our nation survives as a free and democratic land.*

Prereading For prereading instruction for English learners, see

 BEST PRACTICES TOOLKIT
Scaffolding Reading Instruction pp. 43–46

FOR ADVANCED LEARNERS/AP

AP exercises in the bottom channel provide additional challenge for students. Use these suggestions for small groups or individuals.

ADDITIONAL GUIDELINES

For more help with differentiation and tips for classroom management, see

 BEST PRACTICES TOOLKIT
Differentiated Instruction pp. 31–38

Practice and Apply

SUMMARY

In his proclamation, Lincoln declares that slaves residing in secessionist states are free.

BACKGROUND

A Moral Cause Although the Emancipation Proclamation applied only to slaves in areas outside Union control, it served important moral and political purposes. It heartened abolitionists and African Americans. For many Northerners, it highlighted abolition as the war's high moral cause. It drew outrage from Confederate President Jefferson Davis, who understood that the proclamation would settle the issue of slavery and quash Confederate hopes for recognition by pro-abolition European nations.

LITERARY ANALYSIS

D AUDIENCE AND FORM

Possible answer: The word choice is formal and legalistic; the sentence structure is phrase-heavy, convoluted, and complex. Lincoln uses the diction of a legal document, as befits a proclamation.

LITERARY ANALYSIS

E AUDIENCE AND FORM

Possible answer: Paraphrase: On January 1, 1863, the president will determine which states or parts of states are rebelling against the government. Those that participate in Congress will usually be seen as not rebelling. Lincoln's purpose is to establish clear, legal grounds for his actions.

Lines 1–11
REINFORCE *KEY IDEA*: LEGACY

Discuss The Emancipation Proclamation is considered a significant part of Lincoln's **legacy,** despite its limitations. Why? *Possible answer: The document advanced the legacy of the founding fathers—freedom, liberty, and equality—despite its limitations.*

THE EMANCIPATION PROCLAMATION

January 1, 1863

Abraham Lincoln

> **BACKGROUND** The Emancipation Proclamation was more of a symbolic gesture than an enforceable law. The document applied only to territory the Union did not control; it did not free slaves held by states that were loyal to the Union. Though the proclamation had little immediate legal impact, its promises inspired nearly 200,000 African Americans to join the Union army. Their efforts helped the North win the war.

A Transcription By the President of the United States of America: A Proclamation.

Whereas, on the twenty-second day of September, in the year of our Lord one thousand eight hundred and sixty-two, a proclamation was issued by the President of the United States, containing, among other things, the following, to wit: **D**

"That on the first day of January, in the year of our Lord one thousand eight hundred and sixty-three, all persons held as slaves within any State or designated part of a State, the people whereof shall then be in rebellion against the United States, shall be then, thenceforward, and forever free; and the Executive Government of the United States, including the military and naval authority thereof, will recognize and maintain the freedom of such persons, and will do no
10 act or acts to repress such persons, or any of them, in any efforts they may make for their actual freedom.

"That the Executive will, on the first day of January aforesaid,[1] by proclamation, designate the States and parts of States, if any, in which the people thereof, respectively, shall then be in rebellion against the United States; and the fact that any State, or the people thereof, shall on that day be, in good faith, represented in the Congress of the United States by members chosen thereto at elections wherein a majority of the qualified voters of such State shall have participated, shall, in the absence of strong countervailing[2] testimony, be deemed conclusive evidence that such State, and the people thereof, are not then in
20 rebellion against the United States." **E**

Now, therefore I, Abraham Lincoln, President of the United States, by virtue of the power in me vested as Commander-in-Chief, of the Army and Navy of

D AUDIENCE AND FORM
Describe the word choice and sentence structure of lines 1–3. In what ways does the form of the writing—namely, a presidential proclamation—affect Lincoln's **diction?**

1 Targeted Passage

E AUDIENCE AND FORM
Paraphrase lines 12–20. What is the **purpose** of the complicated and careful definitions in this paragraph?

---

1. **aforesaid:** mentioned earlier.
2. **countervailing:** contradicting.

DIFFERENTIATED INSTRUCTION

FOR STRATEGIC READERS

1 Targeted Passage [Lines 4–11]

In this passage, the president declares the freedom of slaves in rebellious states.

- When does the Emancipation Proclamation become law?
- Which states does it refer to?
- Which slaves does it free?
- What will the government do to help freed slaves?

FOR ENGLISH LEARNERS

Key Academic Vocabulary Use Definition Mapping to teach these words: *whereas* (line 1), *maintain* (line 9), *invoke* (line 52).

BEST PRACTICES TOOLKIT—Transparency Definition Mapping p. E6

---

the United States in time of actual armed rebellion against the authority and government of the United States, and as a fit and necessary war measure for suppressing said rebellion, do, on this first day of January, in the year of our Lord one thousand eight hundred and sixty-three, and in accordance with my purpose so to do publicly proclaimed for the full period of one hundred days, from the day first above mentioned, order and designate as the States and parts of States wherein the people thereof respectively, are this day in rebellion against the United

30 States, the following, to wit:

Arkansas, Texas, Louisiana, (except the Parishes of St. Bernard, Plaquemines, Jefferson, St. John, St. Charles, St. James Ascension, Assumption, Terrebonne, Lafourche, St. Mary, St. Martin, and Orleans, including the City of New Orleans)[3] Mississippi, Alabama, Florida, Georgia, South Carolina, North Carolina, and Virginia, (except the forty-eight counties designated as West Virginia,[4] and also the counties of Berkley, Accomac, Northampton, Elizabeth City, York, Princess Ann, and Norfolk, including the cities of Norfolk and Portsmouth), and which excepted parts, are for the present, left precisely as if this proclamation were not issued.

40 And by virtue of the power, and for the purpose aforesaid, I do order and declare that all persons held as slaves within said designated States, and parts of States, are, and henceforward shall be free; and that the Executive government of the United States, including the military and naval authorities thereof, will recognize and maintain the freedom of said persons.

And I hereby enjoin upon[5] the people so declared to be free to abstain from all violence, unless in necessary self-defence; and I recommend to them that, in all cases when allowed, they labor faithfully for reasonable wages.

And I further declare and make known, that such persons of suitable condition, will be received into the armed service of the United States to garrison[7] forts,

50 positions, stations, and other places, and to man vessels of all sorts in said service.

And upon this act, sincerely believed to be an act of justice, warranted by the Constitution, upon military necessity, I invoke the considerate judgment of mankind, and the gracious favor of Almighty God. **F**

In witness whereof, I have hereunto set my hand and caused the seal of the United States to be affixed.

Done at the City of Washington, this first day of January, in the year of our Lord one thousand eight hundred and sixty three, and of the Independence of the United States of America the eighty-seventh.

By the President: ABRAHAM LINCOLN
WILLIAM H. SEWARD, Secretary of State.

F AUTHOR'S BELIEFS
Reread lines 51–53. What reasons does Lincoln give for freeing the slaves?

---

3. **except the Parishes . . . New Orleans:** Parishes, or counties, occupied by Union forces.
4. **the forty-eight . . . Virginia:** the western counties of Virginia broke from the Confederacy to form a new state. West Virginia joined the Union as a slave state in 1863.
5. **enjoin upon:** to direct.
6. **garrison:** to occupy as troops.

FOR ENGLISH LEARNERS

Related Vocabulary Lincoln's document is filled with legal terminology, some of it outdated. Teach these interrelated words:

- *to wit* (line 3), "namely; that is to say"
- *whereof* (line 6), "of which"
- *by virtue of the power in me vested* (lines 21–22), "with my presidential power"
- *wherein* (line 29), "in which"
- *hereunto* (line 54), "on this document"

FOR ADVANCED LEARNERS/AP

Analyze Repetition Point out that the document declares the freedom of slaves in two places, lines 4–11 and lines 40–44. Invite students to analyze this repetition, considering its function in both locations. Challenge students to compare and contrast the two declarations and then to consider the legal, military, political, and ethical underpinnings of these two declarations.

Lines 40–53
TIERED DISCUSSION PROMPTS

Use these prompts to help students appreciate the many ramifications of the Emancipation Proclamation:

Connect How do you respond when an authority figure makes a rule that affects your life? *Accept all thoughtful responses.*

Analyze Why might some abolitionists and African Americans have felt betrayed by the proclamation? *Possible answer: The Emancipation Proclamation did not free all slaves. Its purpose was more political than ethical, and it left uncertainty around the issue of slavery.*

Synthesize The Emancipation Proclamation took effect six months before the Battle of Gettysburg. What effects of this document are apparent in the Gettysburg Address? *Possible answer: In the Gettysburg Address Lincoln focuses on freedom and equality as the causes for which his soldiers are fighting. His references to these causes are an allusion to emancipation.*

READING SKILL

F AUTHOR'S BELIEFS

Possible answer: Lincoln believes that emancipation is just, supported by the Constitution, and a military necessity.

SELECTION WRAP–UP

SUMMARIZE Have students sum up how Lincoln's two writings advance freedom.

⭐ CRITIQUE

- Do you think that Lincoln's views on slavery evolved between the writing of the Emancipation Proclamation and the writing of the Gettysburg Address?

- After completing the After Reading questions on page 568, have students revisit their responses and tell whether they have changed their opinions.

Practice and Apply

After Reading

Use these copy masters to check understanding and provide extra support:

R RESOURCE MANAGER—Copy Masters
Reading Check p. 113
Audience and Form p. 109
Question Support p. 114

Additional selection questions are provided for teachers on page 103.

ANSWERS

1. the dedication of a cemetery on the site of a major Civil War battle (lines 5–7)

2. The battle was fought to keep the nation alive and to defend its founding principles of freedom and democracy (lines 14–20).

3. He is the commander-in-chief in wartime (lines 51–53).

4. The proclamation applies only to areas in rebellion against the Union (lines 5–7).

Possible answers:

5. *Historical context, Address:* two years of war, a bloody battle leading to Union victory, after the Emancipation Proclamation; *Historical context, Proclamation:* Union needed soldiers, a way to weaken the South, a way to take the moral high ground. *Political pressures:* Some wanted more aggressive moves to end slavery, which would have further antagonized the South. Lincoln needed to inspire military victories to motivate and unite the public behind him.

6. ● **SKILLS FOCUS** Audience and Form
Address: Form: speech; *Audience:* mourners, union supporters; *Diction:* clear, rhetorical, poetic, straightforward *Tone:* solemn, reverent; *Proclamation: Form:* legal document; *Audience:* entire nation, southern slaves; *Diction:* legalistic, convoluted, complex, detailed *Tone:* official, serious; The form supports each message. In the address, simplicity, brevity, and straightforwardness underscore the point that the soldiers died for the freedom all Americans hold dear. The proclamation's complexity supports its legal and military message that slaves in rebellious states are free.

After Reading

Comprehension

R2.1, R2.5

1. **Recall** For what occasion did Lincoln deliver the Gettysburg Address?

2. **Clarify** According to Lincoln, for what cause or idea was the Battle of Gettysburg fought?

3. **Recall** What authority does Lincoln claim for issuing the Emancipation Proclamation?

4. **Summarize** What exceptions limit the effect of Lincoln's proclamation?

Literary Analysis

5. **Examine Historical Context** Using details from the author's biography on page 562 and from the background paragraphs on pages 564 and 566, describe the historical context of each document. What political pressures influenced Lincoln's public statements?

6. **Compare Audience and Form** Use a chart to compare and contrast Lincoln's two works. In what ways does the form used influence Lincoln's message?

	Gettysburg Address	Emancipation Proclamation
Form		
Audience		
Diction		
Tone		

7. **Draw Conclusions About Author's Beliefs** Review the chart you created as you read. Based on your answers, what would you consider to be Lincoln's fundamental values? Cite evidence to support your answer.

8. **Evaluate Form** Which of the two works better conveys each of the following ideas? Support your answers with details.

- a sense of presidential authority
- the value of freedom
- the urgency of the national crisis
- Lincoln's personal voice

9. **Synthesize Details** Review your answers to the quiz about Lincoln's life and times that you took before reading these works. Based on your reading and the historical information provided, explain which aspects of Lincoln's **legacy** are fact and which are myth. In your opinion, should Lincoln be considered a great leader? Give reasons for your answer.

Literary Criticism

10. **Critical Interpretations** Often critical of Lincoln's policies, Frederick Douglass also spoke warmly of his honesty and moral conviction. He stated, "The image of the man went out with his words, and those who read them knew him." Based on your own reading, what impressions do you have of Lincoln's character? Explain your answer.

---

7. ● **SKILLS FOCUS** Analyze an Author's Beliefs *Lincoln shows a fundamental belief in democracy, fairness, clear thinking, and responsibility.*

8. *Answers will vary, but should be supported with details from the relevant work.*

9. **1.** T, **2.** F, **3.** F, **4.** F, **5.** F *Opinions of Lincoln's achievements will vary but should note that Lincoln valued freedom but acted mostly for political and military reasons.*

10. *Students' responses should recognize that Lincoln was an honest man devoted to his country and its founding principles while also practical in pursuing his political aims.*

Reading-Writing Connection

W1.1, W1.5, W2.2

WRITING PROMPT

WRITE A LETTER Knowing he'd be speaking to an audience of people mourning the tremendous losses of the Civil War, Lincoln chose his words carefully. To show his respect for their heavy sacrifices, he used elevated language that conveyed a sense of their importance in history.

Imagine that you are a parent who lost a son at Gettysburg, fighting for either the Union or the Confederate army. Write a **three-paragraph letter** to Lincoln explaining your response to the Gettysburg Address.

SELF-CHECK

A successful letter will
- clearly state its purpose
- use precise words to express emotion
- convey a sense of historic importance
- use an appropriate tone

GRAMMAR AND STYLE

USE LANGUAGE EFFECTIVELY Review the **Grammar and Style** note on page 564. In the Gettysburg Address, Lincoln makes effective use of the rhetorical device of **repetition.** Here is an example:

W1.4, W1.9

> *It is for us, the living, rather, to be dedicated here to the unfinished work which they who fought here have thus far so nobly advanced. It is rather for us to be here dedicated to the great task remaining before us . . .* (lines 13–15)

To emphasize the purpose of the solemn occasion, Lincoln repeats the word *dedicate,* as well as other verbs and abstract nouns, throughout his address. As he repeats words, he sometimes introduces subtle shifts in their meaning, encouraging reflection among the mourners.

PRACTICE Rewrite the following paragraph, incorporating repetition to emphasize key points.

> I was among the mourners who heard your eloquent and inspiring speech at Gettysburg. It made me want to write to you, and it caused me to think about what we are fighting for. My son was 19 years old when he enlisted. He was 20 when he was killed. My family and I can hardly bear the loss, but we have no other choice. We can only hope that his death—and the loss of thousands of others—will not have been in vain. As a parent, it is my sincere hope this is true. Speaking as a citizen of the United States, I can only pray the soldiers have not died for nothing.

> **WRITING TOOLS**
> For prewriting, revision, and editing tools, visit the **Writing Center** at ClassZone.com.

DIFFERENTIATED INSTRUCTION

FOR DEVELOPING WRITERS

- Provide students with the *Possible answer* from Grammar and Style as an opening for their letters.
- Suggest that students focus a paragraph on each of these points: the loss of their son and the causes for the sacrifice. Talk with students about possible causes for the sacrifice, such as freedom, the nation's survival, and equality.

- Encourage them to add details to each paragraph. As a way to brainstorm such details, have students complete word webs for each point.

Reading-Writing Connection

WRITING PROMPT

Suggest that students begin by considering how parents might feel both *before* and *after* hearing Lincoln speak. Encourage them to use a Two-Column Chart to brainstorm their ideas about how the parent's perception of loss might have changed after hearing the speech.

Before	After
overwhelming sadness; desperation	pride
sense of waste	meaning in son's death

BEST PRACTICES TOOLKIT—Transparency
Two-Column Chart p. A25

For writing support, see

ℹ Writing Center at **ClassZone.com**

GRAMMAR AND STYLE

Point out to students other repeated words from the Gettysburg Address, such as *devotion* in lines 15 and 17.

Possible rewrite (first four sentences): *I was among the mourners who heard your eloquent and inspiring speech at Gettysburg. It inspired me to write to you, and it inspired me to think about what we are fighting for. My son was 19 years old when he enlisted. My son was 20 years old when he was killed.*

R RESOURCE MANAGER—Copy Master
Use Language Effectively p. 115

Assess and Reteach

Assess

R RESOURCE MANAGER—Copy Masters
Selection Test A pp. 117–118
Selection Test B/C pp. 119–120

Test Generator CD

Reteach

S STANDARDS LESSON FILE
Literature Lesson 35: Rhetorical Devices
Literature Lesson 45: Author's Perspective
Informational Text Lesson 20: Reading Public and Legal Documents

Focus and Motivate

OBJECTIVES

Reading for Information
- analyze primary sources
- synthesize information
- read letters, a diary, and a speech

 R2.5

SUMMARY

"Voices from the Civil War" consists of four primary sources: a letter from Robert E. Lee to his son, clarifying his ultimate allegiance to Virginia; a letter from Union officer Sullivan Ballou to his wife, expressing devotion to family and country; Southern socialite Mary Chesnut's wartime diary; Sojourner Truth's speech on extending civil rights to women.

Use the Directed Reading-Thinking Activity (DRTA) to prepare students for reading the selections. Have them quickly preview each primary source and make a prediction about its content. During reading, have them check each prediction and summarize main ideas.

 BEST PRACTICES TOOLKIT—Transparency
Directed Reading-Thinking Activity (DRTA) p. A20

Teach

Skill Focus: Analyze Primary Sources

- Remind students of other primary source selections they have read in Units 1 and 3, including Lincoln's writings on pages 562–569. Encourage them to list the genre of each and then brainstorm additional kinds of primary sources, such as newspaper articles, letters, photographs, or diary entries. Discuss what the examples have in common, and how they differ.

- For instructional support, have students use the chart on page 570 to analyze one of the primary sources they have read. *Answers will vary but should reflect students' understanding of the genre, their chosen selection, and the author.*

R **RESOURCE MANAGER—Copy Master**
Analyze Primary Sources p. 129

Reading for Information

Voices from the Civil War

- Letter, page 571
- Letter, page 572
- Diary Entry, page 573
- Speech, page 574

Use with the Gettysburg Address, page 564.

Abraham Lincoln delivered the Gettysburg Address to an audience gathered in honor of fallen Union soldiers. How do you think they reacted to it? Might the same speech have been received differently by a Southern audience? The following documents can give you some insight into differing perspectives on the Civil War. After reading each text, take a moment to imagine how each author might have responded to Lincoln's message; later, you'll be asked to write such a response.

 R2.5

Skill Focus: Analyze Primary Sources

As you know, **primary sources** are materials written or made by people who took part in or witnessed the events portrayed. As such, these sources give you something you would probably miss if you read a more removed account. Many primary sources describe individual, personal experiences expressed in the writers' own voices.

The letters, diary entry, and speech you are about to read are all primary sources of information on the Civil War. Read the background paragraph before each document as well as its title and date, noting

- the form of the document (letter, diary entry, or speech)
- when and where it was written or delivered
- whether it was intended for a public or private audience
- some of the details that shaped the author's perspective

Record what you learn on a chart such as the one shown here. Then, as you read the texts, consider how these factors may have influenced the content.

Author	Form of Writing	Time & Place Created	Intended Audience	Relevant Details About the Author
Robert E. Lee				
Sullivan Ballou				
Mary Chesnut				
Sojourner Truth				

570 UNIT 3: FROM ROMANTICISM TO REALISM

Selection Resources

 RESOURCE MANAGER UNIT 3

Plan and Teach pp. 121–125

Reading
Summary pp. 127†*, 128‡*
Analyze Primary Sources pp. 129, 131†*
Synthesize pp. 130, 132†*
Reading Check p. 133
Question Support p. 134*

Assessment
Selection Tests A, B/C pp. 135*, 137*

 Test Generator CD

Reading Support
Audio Anthology CD*

BEST PRACTICES TOOLKIT
DRTA • Jigsaw Reading • Reciprocal Questioning

* Resources for Differentiation   † Also in Spanish   ‡ In Haitian Creole and Vietnamese

Robert E. Lee had a distinguished career in the U.S. Army until his home state of Virginia seceded from the Union. At that point, his loyalty to Virginia compelled him to join the Confederate army, where he became a general and one of the Confederacy's greatest heroes.

Letter to His Son

January 23, 1861

. . . The South, in my opinion, has been aggrieved by the acts of the North, as you say. I feel the aggression, and am willing to take every proper step for redress. It is the principle I contend for, not individual or private gain. As an American citizen, I take pride in my country, her prosperity and institutions, and would defend any State if her rights were invaded. But I can anticipate no greater calamity for the country than a dissolution of the Union. It would be an accumulation of all the evils we complain of, and I am willing to sacrifice everything but honor for its preservation. I hope, therefore, that all constitutional means will be exhausted before there is a recourse to force. Secession is nothing but revolution. The framers of our
10 Constitution never exhausted so much labor, wisdom and forbearance in its **A** formation, and surrounded it with so many guards and securities, if it was intended to be broken by every member of the Confederacy at will. It was intended for 'perpetual union' so expressed in the preamble, and for the establishment of a government, not a compact, which can only be dissolved by revolution, or the consent of all the people in convention assembled. It is idle to talk of secession. Anarchy would have been established, and not a government by Washington, Hamilton, Jefferson, Madison, and the other patriots of the Revolution. . . . Still, a Union that can only be maintained by swords and bayonets, and in which strife and civil war are to take the place of brotherly love
20 and kindness, has no charm for me. I shall mourn for my country and for the welfare and progress of mankind. If the Union is dissolved, and the Government disrupted, I shall return to my native State and share the miseries of my people, and save in defence will draw my sword on none. **B**

A PRIMARY SOURCES
Reread lines 5–8. What does Lee want to preserve at any cost but his honor? What is his view of secession?

B PRIMARY SOURCES
Based on lines 18–21, how does Lee feel about maintaining the Union "by swords and bayonets"? Why?

571

Practice and Applly

INFORMATIONAL ANALYSIS

A PRIMARY SOURCES

Possible answer: *Lee wants to preserve the Union at all costs "but honor" (lines 5–8). He views secession as "revolution" (line 9).*

If students need help . . . Write lines 5–8 on the board. Use an arrow to clarify that the possessive pronoun "its" in line 7 refers back to the words "the Union" in line 6. Then read line 9 aloud, emphasizing the sentence "Secession is nothing but revolution."

INFORMATIONAL ANALYSIS

B PRIMARY SOURCES

Possible answer: *Lee says that maintaining the Union with "swords and bayonets" (lines 18–19) holds no charm for him, because it would make the Union a place where "strife and civil war" would "take the place of brotherly love and kindness" (lines 19–20).*

If students need help . . . Draw a chart like this one on the board and help students complete it as you reread lines 18–20.

Cause		Effect
Union maintained by swords and bayonets	→	Strife and war replace brotherly love
Cause		Effect
Lee has no interest in such a Union	→	

DIFFERENTIATED INSTRUCTION

FOR ENGLISH LEARNERS
Options for Reading Choose from these strategies to support student reading:
• Listen to the Audio Version—Have students listen to the audio version and follow along. Help them to paraphrase text they find difficult, such as lines 20–23 of Lee's speech.
Possible answer: *I would mourn the loss of the Union and its principals. If the Union dissolves, I will return home to stand with my fellow Virginians, but I will fight only in defense.*

• Reciprocal Questioning—Have students ask questions that lead to predictions, then work in pairs or groups to discuss and answer the questions.
• Jigsaw Reading—Have students read in groups, form expert groups for each entry date, then reconvene in home groups.

BEST PRACTICES TOOLKIT
Jigsaw Reading p. A1
Reciprocal Questioning p. A3

FOR STRATEGIC READERS
Comprehension Support Clarify that Robert E. Lee's career in the U.S. Army was so distinguished that Lincoln tried to enlist Lee as commander of the Union forces. Lee opposed secession but would not attack his own state of Virginia. Lee's letter was written a few weeks before seven Southern states formed the Confederate States of America on February 4, 1861. Virginia joined them on April 17, 1861.

READING FOR INFORMATION **571**

C PRIMARY SOURCES

Possible answer: Ballou is absolutely committed to the cause for which he is fighting and willing to die for it (lines 8–9). As justification for his feelings, he says that American Civilization depends on a Union victory (lines 5–6), and that he and his fellow citizens owe a great debt to those who fought in the Revolution to create the Union (lines 6–8).

Lines 14–31
TIERED DISCUSSION PROMPTS

Use these prompts to help students analyze the effect of Ballou's raw emotions:

Connect How do you feel about Ballou and the sentiments he expresses here? *Accept all thoughtful responses.*

Analyze Does your knowledge of Ballou's fate affect your reaction to this letter? Explain. *Possible answer: Knowing that Ballou did not survive to see his family again makes his letter all the more poignant.*

Synthesize How do Ballou's feelings about his cause compare with Abraham Lincoln's in the Gettysburg Address? *Possible answer: Ballou and Lincoln express similar sentiments about their devotion to the cause of the Founding Fathers and about their debt to the first Americans who fought the Revolutionary War.*

C PRIMARY SOURCES
How committed is Ballou to the cause for which he is fighting? What reasons does he give for this degree of commitment?

Major Sullivan Ballou of the Second Rhode Island Regiment wrote the following letter to his wife on July 14, 1861. He was killed about a week later, at the first battle of Bull Run.

Letter to Sarah Ballou

My very dear Sarah:

The indications are very strong that we shall move in a few days—perhaps tomorrow. Lest I should not be able to write again, I feel impelled to write a few lines that may fall under your eye when I shall be no more. . . .

I have no misgivings about, or lack of confidence in the cause in which I am engaged, and my courage does not halt or falter. I know how strongly American Civilization now leans on the triumph of the Government, and how great a debt we owe to those who went before us through the blood and sufferings of the Revolution. And I am willing—perfectly willing—to lay down all my joys in this life, to help maintain this Government, and to pay that debt. . . .

10 Sarah my love for you is deathless, it seems to bind me with mighty cables that nothing but Omnipotence could break; and yet my love of Country comes over me like a strong wind and bears me unresistibly on with all these chains to the battlefield. **C**

The memories of the blissful moments I have spent with you come creeping over me, and I feel most gratified to God and to you that I have enjoyed them so long. And hard it is for me to give them up and burn to ashes the hopes of future years, when, God willing, we might still have lived and loved together, and seen our sons grown up to honorable manhood, around us. I have, I know, but few and small claims upon Divine Providence, but something whispers to me—

20 perhaps it is the wafted prayer of my little Edgar, that I shall return to my loved ones unharmed. If I do not my dear Sarah, never forget how much I love you, and when my last breath escapes me on the battlefield, it will whisper your name. Forgive my many faults, and the many pains I have caused you. How thoughtless and foolish I have often times been! How gladly would I wash out with my tears every little spot upon your happiness. . . .

But, O Sarah! If the dead can come back to this earth and flit unseen around those they loved, I shall always be near you; in the gladdest days and in the darkest nights . . . always, always, and if there be a soft breeze upon your cheek, it shall be my breath, as the cool air fans your throbbing temple, it shall be my spirit

30 passing by. Sarah do not mourn me dead; think I am gone and wait for thee, for we shall meet again. . . .

DIFFERENTIATED INSTRUCTION

FOR STRATEGIC READERS

Comprehension Support Work with students to enter details about Sullivan Ballou's letter in the prereading chart introduced on page 570.

Form of Writing	Time & Place Created	Intended Audience	Relevant Details
letter	July 14, 1861, a week before his death at Bull Run	wife	White male, Union Army major, husband, father, Rhode Island resident

FOR ENGLISH LEARNERS

Vocabulary: Idioms Help students use context clues to define these idioms:

- *lay down* (line 8), "give up"
- *comes over me* (lines 11–12), "influences me, inspires me"
- *bears me . . . on* (line 12), "carries me along"
- *give them up* (line 16), "sacrifice them, lose them"

Wife of a former South Carolina senator, James Chesnut, and a member of the Southern gentility, Mary Chesnut socialized with many prominent Confederates. In her extensive diaries, she kept notes on the social and political conditions in the wartime South.

A Diary from Dixie

1864

September 1st — The battle is raging at Atlanta, our fate hanging in the balance.

September 2nd — Atlanta is gone. Well that agony is over. Like David, when the child was dead, I will get up from my knees, will wash my face and comb my hair. There is no hope, but we will try to have no fear. . . . **D**

September 21st — The President has gone West. He sent for Mr. Chesnut.
I went with Mrs. Rhett to hear Dr. Palmer. I did not know before how utterly hopeless was our situation. This man is so eloquent; it was hard to listen and not give way. Despair was his word, and martyrdom. He offered us nothing more in this world than the martyr's crown. He is not for slavery, he says; he is for freedom,
10 the freedom to govern our own country as we see fit. He is against foreign interference in our state matters. That is what Mr. Palmer went to war for, it appears. Every day shows that slavery is doomed the world over. For that he thanked God. He spoke of this time of our agony; and then came the cry: "Help us, Oh God! Vain is the help of man." So we came away shaken to the depths. . . .
The end has come, no doubt of the fact. Our Army has so moved as to uncover Macon and Augusta. We are going to be wiped off the face of the earth. Now what is there to prevent Sherman taking General Lee in the rear. We have but two armies, and Sherman is between them now. **E**

September 29th — These stories of our defeats in the Valley fall like blows upon
20 a dead body. Since Atlanta, I have felt as if all were dead within me, forever. Captain Ogden of General Chesnut's staff dined here today. Had ever a Brigadier with little or no brigade so magnificent a staff? The reserves, as somebody said, are gathered by robbing the cradle and the grave of men too old and boys too young. . . .
General Chesnut was away in Camden, but I could not wait. I gave the beautiful bride, Mrs. Darby, a dinner which was simply perfect. I was satisfied for once in my life with my own table, and I know pleasanter guests were never seated around any table whatsoever in the world. My house is always crowded. After all, what a number of pleasant people are thrown by war's catastrophes into Columbia. I call such society glorious. It is the wind-up, the Cassandra in me says; and the
30 old life means to die royally.

D PRIMARY SOURCES
What does Chesnut feel after the fall of Atlanta?

E PRIMARY SOURCES
According to Chesnut, why did Dr. Palmer go to war? What did he not fight for?

573

FOR ENGLISH LEARNERS
Culture: Clarify Explain Chesnut's references to Georgia's cities of Atlanta (line 1), Macon (line 16), and Augusta (line 16). Camden (line 24) is likely Chesnut's hometown in South Carolina, while Columbia (line 28) refers to that state's capital city. Also clarify that Cassandra (line 29) is a figure from Greek mythology. During the Trojan War, she predicted disasters, including the defeat of her native Troy, but nobody listened.

FOR ADVANCED LEARNERS/AP
Analyze Allusions Briefly explain the biblical allusion to David (lines 2–3): According to the Bible, David enraged the Lord by killing Uriah the Hittite and taking his wife. The prophet Nathan told David that, because of this sin, the Lord would take David's son. When the child became ill, David fasted and prayed for seven days but the child died. David cleaned himself, prayed, went home, and ate, the last of which puzzled his servants. David explained

that fasting would neither do his child good nor bring him back. Ask students to discuss how this allusion applies to the circumstances Mary Chesnut describes in her diary. Challenge students to continue their discussion by researching and explaining the allusion to Cassandra. Invite students to share their discussion and findings, and to analyze what Chesnut's references reveal about her.

Speech to the American Equal Rights Association

May 9, 1867

My friends, I am rejoiced that you are glad, but I don't know how you will feel when I get through. I come from another field—the country of the slave. They have got their liberty—so much good luck to have slavery partly destroyed; not entirely. I want it root and branch destroyed. Then we will all be free indeed. I feel that if I have to answer for the deeds done in my body just as much as a man, I have a right to have just as much as a man. There is a great stir about colored men getting their rights, but not a word about the colored women; and if colored men get their rights, and not colored women theirs, you see the colored men will be masters over the women, and it will be just as bad as it was before. So I am for keeping the thing going while things are stirring; because if we

10 wait till it is still, it will take a great while to get it going again. . . . I want women to have their rights. In the courts women have no right, no voice; nobody speaks for them. I wish woman to have her voice there among the pettifoggers. If it is not a fit place for women, it is unfit for men to be there. **F**

I am above eighty years old; it is about time for me to be going. I have been forty years a slave and forty years free, and would be here forty years more to have equal rights for all. I suppose I am kept here because something remains for me to do; I suppose I am yet to help to break the chain. I have done a great deal of work; as much as a man, but did not get so much pay. I used to work in the field and bind grain, keeping up with the cradler; but men doing no more, got twice as much pay; so with

20 the German women. They work in the field and do as much work, but do not get the pay. We do as much, we eat as much, we want as much. I suppose I am about the only colored woman that goes about to speak for the rights of the colored women. I want to keep the thing stirring, now that the ice is cracked. What we want is a little money. You men know that you get as much again as women when you write, or for what you do. When we get our rights we shall not have to come to you for money, for then we shall have money enough in our own pockets; and may be you will ask us for money. But help us now until we get it. It is a good consolation to know that when we have got this battle fought we shall not be coming to you any more. You have been having our rights so long, that you think, like a slaveholder, that you own us. I know that it is hard for

30 one who has held the reins for so long to give up; it cuts like a knife. It will feel all the better when it closes up again. I have been in Washington about three years, seeing about these colored people. Now colored men have the right to vote. There ought to be equal rights now more than ever, since colored people have got their freedom. **G**

F PRIMARY SOURCES
Is Sojourner Truth rejoicing over the outcome of the war? Why or why not?

G PRIMARY SOURCES
What is Sojourner Truth arguing for? What are two reasons she gives to support her claim?

INFORMATIONAL ANALYSIS

F PRIMARY SOURCES

Possible answer: No, she is rejoicing at the gladness of others who are pleased with the war's outcome (line 1), but she herself is still seriously focused on doing more work to destroy slavery "root and branch" (lines 3–4). She is also concerned that, until women get their rights, the Union will not be a fit place for anyone (lines 10–13).

INFORMATIONAL ANALYSIS

G PRIMARY SOURCES

Possible answer: She is arguing for full civil rights for women. Students should note at least two of these supporting reasons: 1) "If colored men get their rights . . . it will be just as bad as it was before" (lines 7–9). 2) "In the courts women have no right, no voice; nobody speaks for them" (lines 11–12). 3) "We [women] do as much [as men], we eat as much, we want as much" (line 21). Therefore, she argues, women should get paid as much. 4) If women get equal pay, then they won't have to come to men for money (lines 25–26). 5) "There ought to be equal rights now more than ever, since colored people have got their freedom" (lines 32–33).

DIFFERENTIATED INSTRUCTION

FOR STRATEGIC READERS

Check Predictions Have students complete the Directed Reading-Thinking Activity. Ask them to check their prereading predictions about the content of this letter, then summarize the letter's main points.

BEST PRACTICES TOOLKIT—Transparency DRTA p. A20

FOR ADVANCED LEARNERS/AP

Analyze Figurative Language Have students identify Sojourner Truth's use of figurative language. Ask students to classify each example as imagery, metaphor, or simile, and then to explain how each example serves Truth's writing goal: to advocate for the rights of African Americans and women. Invite students to create and share a chart showing their examples and explanations.

Comprehension

1. **Recall** How did Robert E. Lee plan to respond if the Union was dissolved?

2. **Recall** What did Sullivan Ballou think would be his fate in battle?

3. **Recall** How did Mary Chesnut spend her time during the month of September 1864?

4. **Summarize** In the primary sources you just read, Union and Confederate soldiers and civilians reveal some of the motives they had for engaging in the Civil War. Summarize these motives.

Critical Analysis

5. **Analyze Author's Purpose** Think about what Ballou shares with his wife, Sarah. For what purpose—or purposes—would you say he is writing to her? Explain.

6. **Analyze Primary Sources** For each document, speculate on how the private or public nature of its intended audience may have affected its content.

7. **Analyze Author's Perspective** An author's perspective is the combination of life experiences, culture, values, and beliefs that influences his or her view on a topic. Drawing upon the information you recorded on your chart, describe each author's perspective on the Civil War.

Read for Information: Synthesize

WRITING PROMPT

Choose one of the four writers whose documents you just read, and imagine how this person might have responded to Lincoln's Gettysburg Address. Then summarize the imagined response, and support your ideas with evidence from the text.

To answer this prompt, choose a writer whose perspective on the war you think you understand well. Then follow these steps:

1. Reread the Gettysburg Address to remind yourself of Lincoln's message.

2. Bearing in mind the personal experiences and loyalties of your chosen writer and the thoughts and feelings he or she expresses about the war, imagine how he or she might have reacted to Lincoln's speech. Summarize this imaginary response.

3. Support your notion of that person's response with evidence from your chart and from the primary source written by that individual.

letters and diary would have encouraged authors to be candid about their feelings, doubts, fears, and conflicts. By contrast, Sojourner Truth likely felt compelled to support her claims with a strong formal argument.

7. Students should recognize Ballou's belief in America's founding principles, Lee's and Chesnut's commitment to state rights, and Truth's devotion to civil rights for all.

Read for Information: Synthesize

Writing Prompt *Student responses should reflect an understanding of Lincoln's desire to preserve the Union and his belief in the principles of equality and freedom, and a response appropriate to the chosen writer's perspective as presented in the selection.*

Practice and Apply

After Reading

Use these copy masters to check understanding and provide extra support:

R RESOURCE MANAGER—Copy Masters
Reading Check p. 133
Question Support p. 134
Synthesize p. 130

Additional selection questions are provided for teachers on page 124.

ANSWERS

1. *He planned to return to Virginia to share the miseries of his people and, if necessary, to fight in defense.*

2. *Ballou hoped that he would return to his loved ones unharmed, but he knew that he might not.*

3. *She followed the news, attended a lecture by Dr. Palmer, had Captain Ogden to dinner, planned and threw a perfect dinner party for Mrs. Darby, and maintained an active social life and busy household.*

4. *Lee fought in self-defense, out of loyalty to families and neighbors. Sullivan Ballou fought to preserve the Union and from duty to the Founding Fathers. Dr. Palmer fought to preserve the right to self-government, while Sojourner Truth fought to gain rights for slaves and women.*

Possible answers:

5. *He is writing to explain his commitment to fighting, to express his love, to ask for forgiveness of his faults and of pain he may have caused, and to offer hope that he will return and consolation if he does not.*

6. ■ **SKILLS FOCUS** Analyze Primary Sources *In general, students should note that the private nature of the audiences for the two*

Assess and Reteach

Assess

R RESOURCE MANAGER—Copy Masters
Selection Tests A, B/C pp. 135, 137

💿 Test Generator CD

Reteach

S STANDARDS LESSON FILE
Reading Lesson 14: Synthesizing Information

Study Skills Lesson 5: Using Primary and Secondary Sources

OBJECTIVES

• identify realism

CALIFORNIA R3.5

The Rise of Realism

To help students understand the qualities of realism, draw attention to the photograph on page 576, and ask what makes the photograph realistic. **Possible answer:** *It is a photograph of real people in a real place. It shows ordinary people at their jobs. It does not glorify its subject.* Then show a copy of a recent issue of a major news or literary magazine such as *Time* or *The New Yorker,* and let students study both its editorial and advertising images. Ask students to classify photographs as either realistic or romantic, and to explain why.

Characteristics of Realism

COMPLEX CHARACTERS IN ORDINARY PLACES

Have students read the instructional passage and the three bulleted items under this heading. Then ask students to identify examples of realistic works of fiction, including films or television shows. *Students may suggest television crime or hospital dramas as examples of realism. They might also cite situation comedies as realistic if the settings, characters, and plots resemble reality.* Ask students to identify the specific ingredients that make each example realistic, listing these in a Three-Column Journal. For example, a show about detectives might present the detectives as hard-working ordinary people with personal problems, rather than as Sherlock-Holmes-type deductive geniuses. Such shows often portray urban settings realistically.

 BEST PRACTICES TOOLKIT—Transparency
Three-Column Journal p. B10

Literary Analysis Workshop

CALIFORNIA R3.5

Realism

Most modern readers expect stories to be like real life. In the mid-19th century, however, a "realistic" story was considered radical and was even criticized. Despite this outcry, several famous American writers persevered, and in doing so, they initiated one of the most enduring movements in literary history.

The Rise of Realism

Realism in literature refers to writing that offers an accurate and detailed portrayal of actual life. It also refers to a literary movement that first developed in France in the mid-19th century and then spread to England, Russia, and the United States. Realism was born as a reaction to **romanticism,** an artistic and literary movement that glorified the individual and celebrated the emotions and imagination; it dominated literature during the early 19th century. Unlike the romantics, realists did not want to glorify anything. They simply wanted to depict reality, no matter how ordinary the characters or their circumstances. In basing their literature on careful observations of commonplace events and people, the realists believed they could shed light on greater social issues and concerns.

New York City sweatshop, circa 1912

In the United States, realism was also the product of a rapidly changing society. By the end of the Civil War in 1865, America was changing from a predominantly rural society to an urban one and was experiencing the effects of the Industrial Revolution. Many writers were inspired to depict the effects of these dramatic social changes on the average citizen. The first American writers to experiment with realism—in the 1870s and 1880s—were Mark Twain, William Dean Howells, and Henry James. In the following decades, the realist movement spawned several related movements, such as **naturalism, regionalism,** and **local color** (see pages 632–633).

Characteristics of Realism

COMPLEX CHARACTERS IN ORDINARY PLACES

In realist fiction, character exploration and development became more important than plot. Often the characters were laborers, businessmen, or housewives from the lower and middle classes. Exploring details of a personality or a relationship could reveal important complexities, contradictions, and ironies, especially those related to social or economic issues.

576 UNIT 3: FROM ROMANTICISM TO REALISM

DIFFERENTIATED INSTRUCTION

For general guidelines on differentiating instruction, see

 BEST PRACTICES TOOLKIT
Differentiated Instruction pp. 31–38

FOR STRATEGIC READERS

Note Taking For students who are unfamiliar with realism or need help with note taking, hand out the copy master before discussing this page. Explain that they will be learning terms and concepts relating to

realism in this workshop. Discuss the difference between realism and romanticism as students record notes on the copy master.

 RESOURCE MANAGER—Copy Master
Note Taking p. 139

The realist writer might write long, involved descriptions of a character's inner thoughts, usually focused on personal concerns or the mundane events of his or her everyday life. Realist fiction would typically

- focus on **complex characters** who are ordinary people, not heroes or villains
- portray ordinary **settings,** especially those that allow for accurate depictions of society and culture
- depict true-to-life **dialogue** that captures the dialects and idioms of conversation

DETACHED NARRATION

Realist writers adopted the scientific method of detached observation. This allows the narrator of a story to sound unbiased and distant, as if simply recording the complete facts of the story. The reader is then allowed to draw his or her own conclusions. Notice the detached perspective of the narrator and the detailed **description** in this passage.

> A man stood upon a railroad bridge in northern Alabama, looking down into the swift water twenty feet below. The man's hands were behind his back, the wrists bound with a cord. A rope closely encircled his neck.
>
> —Ambrose Bierce, "An Occurrence at Owl Creek Bridge"

SOCIAL THEMES

The literature of realism sought to explore the key issues of the time: What are the implications of modern technology? What are the effects of urbanization? Realist **themes** are typically concerned with class conflicts, urbanization, marriage, and family life. In his novel *The Rise of Silas Lapham,* author William Dean Howells tells the story of a family coming to terms with new wealth, acquisition, and corruption. In the following passage, Howells relates the family's initial responses to their newfound wealth.

> Their first years there were given to careful getting on Lapham's part, and careful saving on his wife's. Suddenly the money began to come so abundantly that she need not save; and then they did not know what to do with it. A certain amount could be spent on horses, and Lapham spent it; his wife spent on rich and rather ugly clothes and a luxury of household appointments. Lapham had not yet reached the picture-buying stage of the rich man's development, but they decorated their house with the costliest and most abominable frescoes. . . .
>
> —William Dean Howells, *The Rise of Silas Lapham*

LITERARY ANALYSIS WORKSHOP **577**

ROMANTICISM VS. REALISM

To understand the different perspectives and subject matter of romanticism and realism, consider these two prose examples:

Romanticism
In that moment of the afternoon, the sun fell upon the snow drifts in an ethereal light, and all the heavens seemed to shine down upon the frozen fields, as if promising, one day, the ascent of spring.

Realism
At 4:00 each afternoon, the sunlight cast long shadows along the frozen landscape. The whistle of the clothing factory would blow, and the workers would stream out from the opened doors and squint into the last light of the day.

Close Read
What effect does the detached perspective in Bierce's passage have on the reader? From these few lines, what is your reaction to this character?

Close Read
What do you think might happen to the Laphams, given what you know about the typical **themes** in realism?

ROMANTICISM VS. REALISM

Have students read the examples and find words and phrases that exemplify romanticism and realism. ***Possible answers:*** *Romanticism: "ethereal light," "all the heavens seemed to shine"; Realism: "whistle of the clothing factory"*

DETACHED NARRATION

To reinforce comprehension, have students read the opening paragraphs of one or more news stories from a current issue of a newspaper. Make sure the articles are "hard news" rather than feature stories. Have students find similarities between the perspective of the articles and that of the Bierce paragraph.

Close Read
Some students will say the detached perspective makes them feel distant from the character. Others will say that objective details, such as the wrists bound with cord, make them see the scene more vividly. Students' reactions to the character may include sympathy for his fate, curiosity about why he is there and what has happened to him, and suspicion because he is apparently a criminal.

SOCIAL THEMES

Have students read the Howells paragraph. Discuss the social themes present in it (*money, upward mobility, marriage*). Brainstorm social themes that fiction today might deal with.

Close Read
Students may say that the Laphams will encounter marital conflict because of differences over money and spending, or that they will fall from wealth into poverty.

If students need help . . . Refer them to **Social Themes** and the themes of marriage and class conflict. Model a prediction that the Laphams will face conflicts in their marriage as their class status changes.

FOR ENGLISH LEARNERS

Language: Skill Words Clarify the word *detached* through contrast with the familiar word *attached.* Show and identify items, such as a decorative pin, as attached, then as detached. Explain that *perspective* describes how a person views objects, such as close up or far away, and contrast objects at each distance. In writing, a close perspective might show a character's thoughts, while a distant one would show only outward actions.

FOR ADVANCED LEARNERS/AP

Research Realism To broaden students' introduction to realism, suggest that they briefly research these 19th-century realists: Leo Tolstoy, Fyodor Dostoyevsky, Anton Chekhov, Gustave Flaubert, Honoré de Balzac, George Eliot, Henry James. Urge students to scan one work by any two authors and note similarities they find in character, setting, or dialogue.

The Red Badge of Courage
Stephen Crane

ABOUT THE AUTHOR

Stephen Crane The 14th child of a Methodist minister, Crane began writing stories when he was just 8 years old. By the time he was 16, Crane was writing articles for the *New York Tribune.* Although never a scholar, he did study at LaFayette College and Syracuse University. His years in the New York slums taught him the careful observation of psychological experience that informs *The Red Badge of Courage,* Crane's second novel, and makes it, to many, the first modern war novel.

ABOUT THE NOVEL

The Red Badge of Courage Clarify that this excerpt opens just before members of the Confederate army face Henry and his fellow Union soldiers. The passage describes the Union soldiers' reactions to the coming battle and actions during it. Point out that Henry uses a rifle that he loads and reloads quickly. Explain that rifles were new during the Civil War, and allowed soldiers to reload much more quickly than the muskets they replaced.

LEGACY OF A MASTERPIECE

Introduce the Passage As students begin to read, ask them to look for evidence of emotion in the soldiers' words and behavior. Urge them to note descriptive language, dialogue, and Henry's thoughts. Then ask students to discuss and describe the mood this passage creates. *Possible answer: The mood of this passage is frantic and terrifying.*

The Red Badge of Courage

Stephen Crane

Stephen Crane
1871–1900

ABOUT THE AUTHOR Stephen Crane had a knack for writing about his experiences—before he even had them! His first novel, *Maggie: A Girl of the Streets,* for example, exposed the brutal realities of New York slum life. Yet Crane wrote its first draft while still in college, *before* moving to the slums himself in search of work as a journalist. Similarly, Crane wrote *The Red Badge of Courage,* a Civil War novel acclaimed by soldiers and veterans for presenting combat realistically, having never seen battle himself. When asked how he knew so much about war, Crane once stated that he learned what it meant to fight while playing football as a boy. He also learned about war from his brother William, an expert on the battles of Chancellorsville and Gettysburg.

After *The Red Badge of Courage* became a hit, newspapers were eager to hire Crane. He was taken on as a war correspondent to cover the Greco-Turkish War and the Spanish-American War and was finally able to observe battle himself. However, Crane nearly drowned when his ship capsized on the way to Cuba to report on the insurrection there. The incident inspired his famous story "The Open Boat" (page 712); it also contributed to the poor health that claimed his life at the age of 28.

ABOUT THE NOVEL In *The Red Badge of Courage,* Crane focuses on a single, unnamed Civil War battle—the details suggest Chancellorsville—seen from the viewpoint of Henry Fleming, a young private who had recently enlisted in the Union army. Through Henry's eyes the reader experiences the long, tedious wait for battle; the utter chaos once the fighting begins; and the ironic twists of fate that determine who will survive and who will perish. Much of the "action" takes place in Henry's mind as he struggles to adapt to his environment, tries to comprehend his new experiences, and worries about whether he will prove courageous or cowardly.

LEGACY OF A MASTERPIECE "There was no real literature of our Civil War," Ernest Hemingway once observed, "until Stephen Crane wrote *The Red Badge of Courage.*" Crane's great novel is considered a pioneering work of realistic war fiction, breaking with tradition in a number of ways. First, it focuses not on kings or generals but on a lowly private caught up in the action. Second, it ignores the great sweep of history and deals instead with one character's impressions. Finally, the novel is almost completely devoid of heroics. "The idea of falling like heroes on ceremonial battlefields," remarked novelist and critic Ford Madox Ford, "was gone forever."

In the following passage, Henry Fleming (referred to as "the youth") gets his first real taste of battle.

DIFFERENTIATED INSTRUCTION

FOR STRATEGIC READERS

Identify Mood Help students identify the mood of this passage by asking them to fill out a Two-Column Chart that gives details from the text and the mood those details suggest. Point out details such as the colonel's stuttering, the rapid movements of the characters, and adjectives such as *wild* and *menacing.* Ask students how these details make them feel, and urge them to use their reactions as a guide to the mood.

Details	Mood Suggested
"smoke-infested fields"	death
"scold like a wet parrot"	fear

 BEST PRACTICES TOOLKIT—Transparency Two-Column Chart p. A25

"Here they come! Here they come!" Gun locks clicked.

Across the smoke-infested fields came a brown swarm of running men who were giving shrill yells. They came on, stooping and swinging their rifles at all angles. A flag, tilted forward, sped near the front.

As he caught sight of them the youth was momentarily startled by a thought that perhaps his gun was not loaded. He stood trying to rally his faltering intellect so that he might recollect the moment when he had loaded, but he could not.

A hatless general pulled his dripping horse to a stand near the colonel of the
10 304th. He shook his fist in the other's face. "You've got to hold 'em back!" he shouted, savagely; "you've got to hold 'em back!"

In his agitation the colonel began to stammer. "A-all r-right, General, all right, by Gawd! We-we'll do our—we-we'll d-d-do—do our best, General." The general made a passionate gesture and galloped away. The colonel, perchance to relieve his feelings, began to scold like a wet parrot. The youth, turning swiftly to make sure that the rear was unmolested, saw the commander regarding his men in a highly resentful manner, as if he regretted above everything his association with them.

The man at the youth's elbow was mumbling, as if to himself: "Oh, we're in for it now! oh, we're in for it now!"
20 The captain of the company had been pacing excitedly to and fro in the rear. He coaxed in schoolmistress fashion, as to a congregation of boys with primers. His talk was an endless repetition. "Reserve your fire, boys—don't shoot till I tell you—save your fire—wait till they get close up—don't be damned fools—"

Perspiration streamed down the youth's face, which was soiled like that of a weeping urchin. He frequently, with a nervous movement, wiped his eyes with his coat sleeve. His mouth was still a little way open.

He got the one glance at the foe-swarming field in front of him, and instantly ceased to debate the question of his piece being loaded. Before he was ready to begin—before he had announced to himself that he was about to fight—he threw
30 the obedient, well-balanced rifle into position and fired a first wild shot. Directly he was working at his weapon like an automatic affair.

He suddenly lost concern for himself, and forgot to look at a menacing fate. He became not a man, but a member. He felt that something of which he was a part— a regiment, an army, a cause, or a country—was in a crisis. He was welded into a common personality which was dominated by a single desire. For some moments he could not flee, no more than a little finger can commit a revolution from a hand.

TIERED DISCUSSION PROMPTS

Use these prompts to help students consider what Henry sees and feels:

Connect How have you or someone you know reacted when you were in a tense or dangerous situation? *Accept all thoughtful responses.*

Interpret Why do you think that Henry is "momentarily startled by a thought that perhaps his gun was not loaded"? Read the second to last paragraph. Why does he no longer question whether his gun is loaded at this point? ***Possible answer:*** *In the beginning of the passage, Henry sees the enemy approaching and is most likely nervous and scared, so he begins to doubt everything, including whether his gun is loaded. It is as if his brain is paralyzed by fear. By the end of the passage, Henry has overcome his fear and paralysis and is as ready as he can be for battle.*

Synthesize Reread **About the Novel.** Does Henry "adapt to his environment"? In this passage, does he prove "courageous" or "cowardly"? ***Possible answer:*** *Henry has adapted to his environment. He matures from being horribly nervous to being an effective fighter. He becomes courageous, as he no longer considers his "menacing fate" but instead thinks of himself as a member of a team who is helping his country.*

FOR ENGLISH LEARNERS

Vocabulary: Multiple-Meaning Words Point out that certain words have more than one meaning. Students must determine the appropriate definition for a given use. Help students use context clues to figure out the meaning of *rear* (line 16), *unmolested* (line 16), *regarding* (line 16), *fire* (line 22), *piece* (line 28), *directly* (line 30), *working at* (line 31), *automatic* (line 31), and *affair* (line 31).

FOR ADVANCED LEARNERS/AP

Analyze Similes [paired option] Have students identify several similes in the passage that Crane uses to enhance the feelings of the characters as well as to create the mood of the passage. Challenge pairs to write five similes that describe the feelings of the characters or that adequately portray the mood of the passage. Encourage pairs to share their similes.

Focus and Motivate

OBJECTIVES

Literary Analysis
- explore the key idea of **escape**
- analyze point of view
- read a short story

Reading
- analyze the structure of a literary work

Vocabulary
- build vocabulary for reading and writing
- use the Latin root *lud* to unlock meaning
  (also an EL language objective)

 R1.2, R3.2

ABOUT THE AUTHOR

After students have read about Bierce's life, have them discuss how his experiences in the Civil War may have changed his idealistic viewpoint. Explain that "An Occurrence at Owl Creek Bridge" describes the kind of "strange and horrible death" that fascinated Bierce, and it includes both idealistic and dark views of war and death.

USING THE *NOTABLE QUOTE*

Ask students how **Ambrose Bierce's** life experiences may have contributed to his belief in this statement. *Possible answer: Bierce fought in horrible Civil War battles. He "watched many of his comrades die and nearly died himself from a head wound." He most likely saw things that would seem improbable to civilians, and yet they were undeniably true.*

Selection Resources

R1.2 (p. 594), **R3.2** (p. 593)
CALIFORNIA

An Occurrence at Owl Creek Bridge

Short Story by Ambrose Bierce

NOTABLE QUOTE
"Nothing is so improbable as that which is true."

FYI
Did you know that Ambrose Bierce . . .
- was one of 13 children, whose names all began with the letter *A*?
- was awarded 15 commendations for bravery under fire?
- was nicknamed Bitter Bierce for his cynical humor and cruel wit?
- also wrote under the names Mrs. J. Milton Bowers and Dod Grile?

Author On|ine
For more on Ambrose Bierce, visit the **Literature Center** at **ClassZone.com**.

Ambrose Bierce
1842–c. 1914

As a Civil War soldier, Ambrose Bierce was an eyewitness to the harsh realities of war. The brutal contrast between soldiers' dreams of glory and the senselessness of warfare became a recurring theme in Bierce's postwar short stories, including his suspenseful tale "An Occurrence at Owl Creek Bridge."

In the Line of Fire Born into a poor, intensely religious family, Bierce spent his early years on an Indiana farm. At age 15, he left home for a job at a newspaper, where he set type. Three years later, the Civil War broke out, and the idealistic Bierce immediately volunteered for the Union army. Fighting in some of the war's bloodiest battles, Bierce watched many of his comrades die and nearly died himself from a head wound.

When the war was over, Bierce moved to San Francisco, which was then the literary center of the West. Determined to become a writer, Bierce took a job as a night watchman, which allowed him ample time for reading and for polishing his writing skills. He started writing a regular newspaper column and became infamous for exposing bigotry, hypocrisy, and corruption with razor-sharp satire. His cutting wit earned him the title "the Wickedest Man in San Francisco." Such a reputation delighted Bierce, who kept on his desk a human skull that he claimed belonged to one of his critics.

A Morbid Imagination Bierce began publishing short stories in the 1870s, when realism was becoming the dominant literary style in American fiction. Although Bierce's true-to-life war stories inspired realist writers like Stephen Crane, his fiction often included surreal or ghostly events. Like Edgar Allan Poe, to whom he was often compared, Bierce was fascinated with strange and horrible deaths, and he described them with his characteristic dark humor and a sense of irony. Bierce also went beyond realism in his experiments with narration, pioneering the use of multiple points of view in a single story.

Vanished At 71, Bierce revisited Civil War battle sites where he had fought and then went to Mexico to report on the Mexican Revolution as an observer with Pancho Villa's rebel army. He never returned to the United States, and no trace of him was found. Before he left, he wrote to a niece, "If you hear of my being stood up against a Mexican stone wall and shot to rags, please know that I think that a pretty good way to depart this life. It beats old age, disease or falling down the cellar stairs."

Union soldiers

580

---

* Resources for Differentiation   † Also in Spanish   ‡ In Haitian Creole and Vietnamese

● LITERARY ANALYSIS: POINT OF VIEW

Because the narrator is the voice that tells a story, the reader only knows what the narrator is able to tell. Therefore, the narrator's role in the story's events and his or her range of knowledge about the characters help reveal the story's point of view. Types of **point of view** include

- **first person:** told by a character in the work whose knowledge is limited to his or her own experiences
- **third-person omniscient:** told by a voice outside the story who reveals the thoughts and feelings of all the characters
- **third-person limited:** told by a voice outside the story who focuses on one character's thoughts and feelings

As you read, look for clues in the narration that help identify the point of view in Ambrose Bierce's story.

● READING SKILL: ANALYZE STRUCTURE

To analyze the **structure** of a literary work, you examine the relationship between its parts and its content. This story is divided into three numbered sections, each of which occurs at a different point in time. After you read each section, summarize the events that occur and note when they take place. Use a chart like the one shown to record your notes.

	What Happens	When
Section 1		

▲ VOCABULARY IN CONTEXT

Bierce used the words in Column A in his tale of a man facing death. Test your knowledge by matching each vocabulary word with its synonym in Column B.

Column A	Column B
1. interminable	a. swaying
2. poignant	b. painful
3. ineffable	c. predicting
4. summarily	d. unending
5. oscillation	e. indescribable
6. ludicrous	f. evil
7. presaging	g. immediately
8. malign	h. laughable

Explore the Key Idea

Can we escape the INEVITABLE?

KEY IDEA "An Occurrence at Owl Creek Bridge" opens with an execution about to take place. Standing on an isolated, heavily guarded bridge, with a noose around his neck, the protagonist is doomed. There is no **escape.** Or is there?

DISCUSS In a small group, list ways people respond when faced with a bad situation they cannot change. Classify each response as useful or destructive. When does it make sense to look for a way out, and when is it time to accept the inevitable?

581

Teach

Can we escape the INEVITABLE?

Lead into the **KEY IDEA** by asking the question. After the class speculates on the meaning of the question "Or is there?" have them complete the **DISCUSS** activity. Then, invite volunteers to explain when it is sensible to **escape** and when it is time to accept that there is no escape.

SKILLS FOCUS

LITERARY ANALYSIS

● POINT OF VIEW

To help students identify point of view, write this passage on the board:

> Harry knew that if the fire continued to spread, he would never escape. His fear paralyzed him. He knew little of fire, and had believed he had plenty of time to be rescued. Until he heard the stairs collapse.

Have students identify the point of view in this passage *(third person limited)*.

CHECK UNDERSTANDING Ask students to identify the point of view in a favorite story or novel.

READING SKILL

■ ANALYZE STRUCTURE

Explain to students that when a story's structure includes different time periods, readers must use textual evidence and context clues to put the parts together. For example, if a story begins with a character in crisis, readers will need clues that explain how the crisis arose. Ask students why authors might structure stories out of sequence. *Possible answer: Authors might structure stories out of sequence in order to generate interest and create suspense.*

📖 RESOURCE MANAGER—Copy Master
Analyze Structure p. 153 (for student use while reading the selection)

VOCABULARY

▲ VOCABULARY IN CONTEXT

DIAGNOSE WORD KNOWLEDGE To determine preteaching needs, have all students complete Vocabulary in Context. **Answers:**
1. *d*, 2. *b*, 3. *e*, 4. *g*, 5. *a*, 6. *h*, 7. *c*, 8. *f*

PRETEACH VOCABULARY Preteach vocabulary with this copy master. Read each item aloud.

📖 RESOURCE MANAGER—Copy Master
Vocabulary Study p. 155

MORE VOCABULARY SUPPORT
For additional activities and guidelines, see

💼 BEST PRACTICES TOOLKIT
Scaffolding Vocabulary Instruction pp. 43–46
ℹ️ Vocabulary Center at **ClassZone.com**

SUMMARY

Bierce's short story begins with Peyton Farquhar, a Southern planter, standing on a bridge in Alabama, about to be hanged by Union soldiers for attempting to set fire to Owl Creek Bridge. He falls through the bridge and hangs for a moment before the rope breaks and falls into the water. He unties his hands, dodges bullets, and swims ashore. He runs through the forest to his home, where he sees his wife. Then he feels a pain on his neck and hangs, dead. His escape was a fantasy.

LITERARY ANALYSIS

Ⓐ POINT OF VIEW

Possible answer: The point of view is third-person omniscient. The narrator describes a man who is about to be hung (lines 2–4) and the soldiers (lines 6–12) in a calm tone that suggests the narrator is detached and objective, able to report all aspects of the event factually.

If students need help . . . Point out to students the absence of the pronoun *I*, which would indicate first-person point of view.

An Occurrence at Owl Creek Bridge

Ambrose Bierce

I

A man stood upon a railroad bridge in northern Alabama, looking down into the swift water twenty feet below. The man's hands were behind his back, the wrists bound with a cord. A rope closely encircled his neck. It was attached to a stout cross-timber above his head and the slack fell to the level of his knees. Some loose boards laid upon the sleepers[1] supporting the metals of the railway supplied a footing for him and his executioners—two private soldiers of the Federal army, directed by a sergeant who in civil life may have been a deputy sheriff. At a short remove upon the same temporary platform was an officer in the uniform of his rank, armed. He was a captain. A sentinel at each end of the bridge stood with his
10 rifle in the position known as "support," that is to say, vertical in front of the left shoulder, the hammer resting on the forearm thrown straight across the chest—a formal and unnatural position, enforcing an erect carriage of the body. It did not appear to be the duty of these two men to know what was occurring at the center of the bridge; they merely blockaded the two ends of the foot planking that traversed it. Ⓐ

Beyond one of the sentinels nobody was in sight; the railroad ran straight away into a forest for a hundred yards, then, curving, was lost to view. Doubtless there was an outpost farther along. The other bank of the stream was open ground—a gentle acclivity[2] topped with a stockade of vertical tree trunks, loopholed for rifles,
20 with a single embrasure[3] through which protruded the muzzle of a brass cannon commanding the bridge. Midway of the slope between bridge and fort were the spectators—a single company of infantry in line, at "parade rest," the butts of the rifles on the ground, the barrels inclining slightly backward against the right

---

1. **sleepers:** railroad ties.
2. **acclivity:** an upward slope.
3. **embrasure:** a flared opening in a wall for a gun, with sides angled so that the inside opening is larger than that on the outside.

ANALYZE VISUALS
Based on this image, what do you predict will happen in the story?

❶ Targeted Passage

Ⓐ POINT OF VIEW
Identify the point of view used in lines 1–15. What does the **tone** of the description tell you about the narrator's perspective?

DIFFERENTIATED INSTRUCTION

FOR ALL STUDENTS

Provide these independent projects to extend the lesson:

- Create a portrait of Farquhar.
- Write a letter from Farquhar to his wife.
- Evaluate an ideological statement from the story.

R RESOURCE MANAGER
Ideas for Extension pp. 146–147

FOR STRATEGIC READERS

In combination with the *Audio Anthology CD*, use one or more Targeted Passages (pp. 582, 586, 588, 590, 592) to ensure that students focus on key story events and concepts. Targeted Passages are also good for English learners.

❶ Targeted Passage [Lines 1–15]

This passage introduces students to the story setting at Owl Creek Bridge as well as to the main character and his pending execution.

ANALYZE VISUALS

Possible answer: This image suggests that a man is going to hang from somewhere that drops him into water.

Lines 1–15
REINFORCE *KEY IDEA:* ESCAPE

Discuss Given what you know about the man's situation, does he have a chance of **escape?** Explain. *Possible answer: It does not seem that he has any chance at all of escape. He already is tied with a rope around his neck (lines 2–3). His executioners are already on the bridge (line 6), and soldiers guard both ends of the bridge (line 9).*

- Where and when does the story take place?
- What other people are with the man? What are they doing?
- What is happening to the man?

FOR ENGLISH LEARNERS

Key Academic Vocabulary Use Definition Mapping to teach these words: *Federal* (line 6), *code* (line 32), *undertake* (line 89), *reluctance* (line 140), *perspective* (line 255).

 BEST PRACTICES TOOLKIT—Transparency
Definition Mapping p. E6

Prereading For prereading instruction for English learners, see

 BEST PRACTICES TOOLKIT
Scaffolding Reading Instruction pp. 43–46

FOR ADVANCED LEARNERS/AP

AP exercises in the bottom channel provide additional challenge for students. Use these suggestions for small groups or individuals.

ADDITIONAL GUIDELINES

For more help with differentiation and tips for classroom management, see

 BEST PRACTICES TOOLKIT
Differentiated Instruction pp. 31–38

Lines 57–70
TIERED DISCUSSION PROMPTS

Use these prompts to help students envision the main character's situation:

Connect In your experience, how do people's senses change in an alarming situation? *Accept all thoughtful responses.*

Interpret Why does the man's ticking of his watch bother him so much? ***Possible answer:*** *The man appears to be in a state of heightened consciousness, perhaps from fear. He relates the regular ticking to "the tolling of a death knell" (line 65). The sounds of his watch do not really increase "in strength and sharpness" (line 68), but seem to as his fear increases. This fear also makes him experience the watch sounds more intensely, "like the thrust of a knife" (line 69).*

Evaluate Is it believable that a watch could become so loud? ***Possible answer:*** *Yes. For example, when a person gets really nervous, he may hear his heartbeat as if it is in his ear. Sounds and sensations become more pronounced in fearful situations, just as they have for the main character.*

shoulder, the hands crossed upon the stock.[4] A lieutenant stood at the right of the line, the point of his sword upon the ground, his left hand resting upon his right. Excepting the group of four at the center of the bridge, not a man moved. The company faced the bridge, staring stonily, motionless. The sentinels, facing the banks of the stream, might have been statues to adorn the bridge. The captain stood with folded arms, silent, observing the work of his subordinates, but making
30 no sign. Death is a dignitary who when he comes announced is to be received with formal manifestations of respect, even by those most familiar with him. In the code of military etiquette silence and fixity are forms of deference.

The man who was engaged in being hanged was apparently about thirty-five years of age. He was a civilian, if one might judge from his habit, which was that of a planter. His features were good—a straight nose, firm mouth, broad forehead, from which his long, dark hair was combed straight back, falling behind his ears to the collar of his well-fitting frock-coat. He wore a mustache and pointed beard, but no whiskers; his eyes were large and dark gray, and had a kindly expression which one would hardly have expected in one whose neck was in the hemp.
40 Evidently this was no vulgar assassin. The liberal military code makes provision for hanging many kinds of persons, and gentlemen are not excluded.

The preparations being complete, the two private soldiers stepped aside and each drew away the plank upon which he had been standing. The sergeant turned to the captain, saluted and placed himself immediately behind that officer, who in

---

4. **stock:** the wooden part of the rifle that serves as a handle.

DIFFERENTIATED INSTRUCTION

FOR STRATEGIC READERS

Characterization Point out lines 33–41 to students. Have students use a Character Traits Web to list everything they now know about the man. Clarify that line 40 means the man is a gentleman, not a common criminal. Urge students to add information to the Web as they read on.

 BEST PRACTICES TOOLKIT—Transparency
Character Traits Web p. D7

FOR ADVANCED LEARNERS/AP

Analyze Personification and Tone [paired option] Have students identify the figure of speech being used in lines 30–32 (*personification*) and paraphrase them for the class. Then have pairs write and exchange five sentences that personify fear and death. Finally, have small groups discuss these questions:

• How do these sentences explain the way soldiers are meant to react to death? How might that differ from civilian reactions?

• What do you think the "code of military etiquette" (line 32) means? What evidence have you seen so far in the story that displays military etiquette?

• What is the narrator's tone in lines 40–41? What is he suggesting in those lines about the military code?

turn moved apart one pace. These movements left the condemned man and the sergeant standing on the two ends of the same plank, which spanned three of the cross-ties of the bridge. The end upon which the civilian stood almost, but not quite, reached a fourth. This plank had been held in place by the weight of the captain; it was now held by that of the sergeant. At a signal from the former the

50 latter would step aside, the plank would tilt and the condemned man go down between two ties. The arrangement commended itself to his judgment as simple and effective. His face had not been covered nor his eyes bandaged. He looked a moment at his "unsteadfast footing," then let his gaze wander to the swirling water of the stream racing madly beneath his feet. A piece of dancing driftwood caught his attention and his eyes followed it down the current. How slowly it appeared to move! What a sluggish stream! **B**

He closed his eyes in order to fix his last thoughts upon his wife and children. The water, touched to gold by the early sun, the brooding mists under the banks at some distance down the stream, the fort, the soldiers, the piece of drift—all

60 had distracted him. And now he became conscious of a new disturbance. Striking through the thought of his dear ones was a sound which he could neither ignore nor understand, a sharp, distinct, metallic percussion like the stroke of a blacksmith's hammer upon the anvil; it had the same ringing quality. He wondered what it was, and whether immeasurably distant or near by—it seemed both. Its recurrence was regular, but as slow as the tolling of a death knell.[5] He awaited each stroke with impatience and—he knew not why—apprehension. The intervals of silence grew progressively longer; the delays became maddening. With their greater infrequency the sounds increased in strength and sharpness. They hurt his ear like the thrust of a knife; he feared he would shriek. What he heard

70 was the ticking of his watch.

He unclosed his eyes and saw again the water below him. "If I could free my hands," he thought, "I might throw off the noose and spring into the stream. By diving I could evade the bullets and, swimming vigorously, reach the bank, take to the woods and get away home. My home, thank God, is as yet outside their lines; my wife and little ones are still beyond the invader's farthest advance."

As these thoughts, which have here to be set down in words, were flashed into the doomed man's brain rather than evolved from it the captain nodded to the sergeant. The sergeant stepped aside. **C**

II

Peyton Farquhar was a well-to-do planter, of an old and highly respected Alabama

80 family. Being a slave owner and like other slave owners a politician he was naturally an original secessionist and ardently devoted to the Southern cause. Circumstances of an imperious nature, which it is unnecessary to relate here, had prevented him from taking service with the gallant army that had fought the disastrous campaigns ending with the fall of Corinth,[6] and he chafed under the

---

5. **the tolling of a death knell:** the slow, steady ringing of a bell at a funeral or to indicate death.

6. **Corinth:** a town in Mississippi that was the site of a Civil War battle in 1862.

B POINT OF VIEW
Note that the third-person point of view narrows from omniscient to limited. What **sensory details** alert you to this change in perspective?

C ANALYZE STRUCTURE
If the story were told in chronological order, what would you expect to happen next?

LITERARY ANALYSIS

B POINT OF VIEW

Possible answer: The sensory details that signify the change in point of view include the main character seeing the "swirling water of the stream" (lines 53–54) and the "piece of dancing driftwood" (line 54) that he thinks moves slowly. At this point, the narrator describes only the main character's sights and thoughts.

Lines 71–75
REINFORCE *KEY IDEA*: ESCAPE

Discuss How does the main character think he can **escape**? What does this suggest about human nature in general? *Possible answer: He thinks that he can untie his hands, take off his noose, swim in the water, and get to his home. This shows that even in the most desperate and hopeless situations, human beings continue to hope.*

READING SKILL

C ANALYZE STRUCTURE

Possible answer: At this point in the story, you would expect that the man would be hanged.

If students need help . . . Point them to lines 47–51 and explain that when the sergeant steps aside, the "plank would tilt," and the man would fall and thus hang. Have them note that in line 78, the sergeant steps aside.

FOR STRATEGIC READERS
Concept Support: Analyze Structure After students complete Section I, help them add to the prereading chart introduced on page 581. Have students use their charts to generate questions about Section I. Tell students to pause again after each remaining section to add to the chart and list more questions. Urge them to read on to answer their questions.

Clarify that in the prereading chart, the heading *When* refers to an event's place in the story sequence, not to its historical period.

What Happens	When
on a railroad bridge in northern Alabama, a man is about to be hanged	action takes place at beginning of story

FOR ENGLISH LEARNERS
Culture: Clarify Explain that the story is set during the American Civil War. Point out clues that explain Farquhar's allegiance to the Southern cause and therefore hint that he may be the man about to be hanged by Federal (Union) soldiers. Explain that he lives in the Southern state of Alabama and is a slave owner. He is a secessionist (line 81), which means that he supports the South's separating from the Union.

inglorious restraint, longing for the release of his energies, the larger life of the soldier, the opportunity for distinction. That opportunity, he felt, would come, as it comes to all in war time. Meanwhile he did what he could. No service was too humble for him to perform in aid of the South, no adventure too perilous for him to undertake if consistent with the character of a civilian who was at heart a
90 soldier, and who in good faith and without too much qualification assented to at least a part of the frankly villainous dictum that all is fair in love and war.

② **Targeted Passage**

One evening while Farquhar and his wife were sitting on a rustic bench near the entrance to his grounds, a gray-clad soldier rode up to the gate and asked for a drink of water. Mrs. Farquhar was only too happy to serve him with her own white hands. While she was fetching the water her husband approached the dusty horseman and inquired eagerly for news from the front.

"The Yanks are repairing the railroads," said the man, "and are getting ready for another advance. They have reached the Owl Creek bridge, put it in order and built a stockade on the north bank. The commandant has issued an order, which is
100 posted everywhere, declaring that any civilian caught interfering with the railroad, its bridges, tunnels or trains will be **summarily** hanged. I saw the order." **D**

"How far is it to the Owl Creek bridge?" Farquhar asked.

"About thirty miles."

"Is there no force on this side the creek?"

"Only a picket post[7] half a mile out, on the railroad, and a single sentinel at this end of the bridge."

"Suppose a man—a civilian and student of hanging—should elude the picket post and perhaps get the better of the sentinel," said Farquhar, smiling, "what could he accomplish?"

110 The soldier reflected. "I was there a month ago," he replied. "I observed that the flood of last winter had lodged a great quantity of driftwood against the wooden pier at this end of the bridge. It is now dry and would burn like tow."[8]

The lady had now brought the water, which the soldier drank. He thanked her ceremoniously, bowed to her husband and rode away. An hour later, after nightfall, he repassed the plantation, going northward in the direction from which he had come. He was a Federal scout. **E**

III

As Peyton Farquhar fell straight downward through the bridge he lost consciousness and was as one already dead. From this state he was awakened—ages later, it seemed to him—by the pain of a sharp pressure upon his throat,
120 followed by a sense of suffocation. Keen, **poignant** agonies seemed to shoot from his neck downward through every fiber of his body and limbs. These pains appeared to flash along well-defined lines of ramification[9] and to beat with an inconceivably rapid periodicity. They seemed like streams of pulsating fire heating

---

7. **picket post:** the camp of soldiers who are assigned to guard against a surprise attack.
8. **tow** (tō): coarse, dry fiber.
9. **flash . . . ramification:** spread out rapidly along branches from a central point.

summarily (sə-mĕr′ə-lē) *adv.* quickly and without ceremony

D ANALYZE STRUCTURE
Compare lines 97–101 with the description in lines 1–21. What details connect these two sections of the story?

E POINT OF VIEW
Reread lines 113–116. Explain what the reader knows that Peyton Farquhar does not. Which type of third-person point of view allows the author to give the reader details that are hidden from the characters?

poignant (poin′yənt) *adj.* physically or mentally painful

READING SKILL

D ANALYZE STRUCTURE

Possible answer: The details that connect these two sections of the story include the mention of the railroad bridge (lines 1 and 100–101), a hanging (lines 2–4 and 101), and the stockade (lines 19 and 99).

Extend the Discussion What do these details suggest about the man's situation at the beginning of the story?

LITERARY ANALYSIS

E POINT OF VIEW

Possible answer: The reader knows that the soldier who gives Farquhar the information about Owl Creek Bridge is actually a Federal spy (line 116). The third-person omniscient point of view gives readers details that the characters are unaware of.

If students need help . . . Clarify that a scout is a spy.

DIFFERENTIATED INSTRUCTION

FOR STRATEGIC READERS

Comprehension Support Point out that Bierce's long sentences can be difficult to understand. Help students use punctuation to break them into manageable chunks. Have students practice on lines 82–91. **Possible answer:** *Farquhar regrets that he did not fight in the war. He wants to find a way to help the Southern cause. He is willing to do anything he can, even if it is dangerous or dishonest.*

② Targeted Passage [Lines 92–116]

This passage sets up the actions that may later get Peyton Farquhar hanged.

- How do the Farquhars greet the visiting soldier? Do they view him as a friend?

- What does the soldier say about the Yanks? What order have they posted?

- What does Farquhar ask the soldier?

- What army is the soldier actually from?

FOR ENGLISH LEARNERS

Culture: Clarify Explain that Yanks (line 97) are Yankees or Northerners—those fighting against the South. Clarify that the soldier who approaches Farquhar is dressed in the gray uniform of the Southern army and appears as a comrade to him. In fact, line 116 reveals that he is a Federal, or Northern, scout in disguise. Farquhar takes information from a man he would consider an enemy.

him to an intolerable temperature. As to his head, he was conscious of nothing but a feeling of fullness—of congestion. These sensations were unaccompanied by thought. The intellectual part of his nature was already effaced; he had power only to feel, and feeling was torment. He was conscious of motion. Encompassed in a luminous cloud, of which he was now merely the fiery heart, without material substance, he swung through unthinkable arcs of **oscillation,** like a vast
130 pendulum. Then all at once, with terrible suddenness, the light about him shot upward with the noise of a loud plash; a frightful roaring was in his ears, and all was cold and dark. The power of thought was restored; he knew that the rope had broken and he had fallen into the stream. There was no additional strangulation; the noose about his neck was already suffocating him and kept the water from his lungs. To die of hanging at the bottom of a river!—the idea seemed to him **ludicrous.** He opened his eyes in the darkness and saw above him a gleam

oscillation (ŏs′ə-lā′shən) *n.* the action of swinging back and forth

ludicrous (lōō′dĭ-krəs) *adj.* laughably absurd; ridiculous

ANALYZE VISUALS
Whose point of view does the image reflect? What details can you not see when limited to this point of view?

Lines 85–112
TIERED DISCUSSION PROMPTS

Use these prompts to get students thinking about Farquhar's motivation and actions:

Recall What does Farquhar really wish to be? *Possible answer: He wishes to be a distinguished soldier for the Southern cause.*

Interpret What is Farquhar suggesting he might do? What are his motives? *Possible answer: Farquhar is suggesting that he will destroy the bridge. His motives are to help the Southern cause and become a hero.*

Synthesize Based on what you read about the Civil War in the historical essay (page 496), is it convincing that Farquhar would take such a risk with his life? Explain. *Possible answer: Yes. Farquhar likely grew up with the ideal of the romantic hero. He longs for glory and imagines himself an unrecognized hero (lines 85–91). He also does not know that he has been tricked by a Federal scout and so does not realize the danger he will face. He believes he can earn that hero's status with his actions while supporting the Southern cause.*

ANALYZE VISUALS

Possible answer: This image reflects Farquhar's point of view, as he stands on the plank and looks downward. This point of view does not allow one to see details about the scene, including the face of the person standing on the plank, where the rope is actually tied, and who else is standing nearby.

FOR STRATEGIC READERS

Concept Support: Analyze Structure Point out to students that Section III appears to continue where Section I left off. After students add Section II information to their prereading chart, suggest that they also plot the important story events on a Sequence Chain. Help students begin with the details from Section II.

 BEST PRACTICES TOOLKIT—Transparency Sequence Chain p. B21

FOR ENGLISH LEARNERS

Vocabulary Support Explain that Bierce uses opposites in his descriptive language to stress the intensity of Farquhar's experiences. Point out contrasts between light and dark, heat and cold: "pulsating fire . . . intolerable temperature" (lines 123–124), "fiery heart" (line 128), and "light . . . shot upward" (lines 130–131) versus "cold and dark" (line 132) and "in the darkness" (line 136).

FOR ADVANCED LEARNERS/AP

Analyze Realism Remind students that Bierce's writings frequently include surreal elements. As students read Section III, challenge them to determine whether this section is realistic or surreal and why. Have them identify important details of both types, then use these details to discuss why Bierce uses both realistic and surreal details in his short story.

🕞 POINT OF VIEW

Possible answer: *The point of view in the beginning of the story is third-person omniscient. In this part of the story, the point of view is third-person limited, which enables readers to see the events through Farquhar's eyes. Readers learn of Farquhar's feelings and inner thoughts, which draw them into the story as participants rather than as mere spectators.*

Lines 143–160
REINFORCE *KEY IDEA:* ESCAPE

Discuss Do you think Farquhar has been able to **escape**? Use details from the text to explain. *Possible answer: It is difficult to tell. Many of the details suggest that he hasn't really escaped but rather may be dreaming or having a near-death experience. For example, words such as "not conscious" (line 143) and "superhuman strength" (line 146), as well as Farquhar watching his "disobedient hands" (line 156) make the account seem dreamlike or like a near-death experience. However, there are also some details that describe a realistic escape, such as when he emerges from the water, finds the sunlight very bright, gulps air, and yells aloud (lines 158–160).*

---

of light, but how distant, how inaccessible! He was still sinking, for the light became fainter and fainter until it was a mere glimmer. Then it began to grow and brighten, and he knew that he was rising toward the surface—knew it with
140 reluctance, for he was now very comfortable. "To be hanged and drowned," he thought, "that is not so bad; but I do not wish to be shot. No; I will not be shot; that is not fair." 🕞

He was not conscious of an effort, but a sharp pain in his wrist apprised him that he was trying to free his hands. He gave the struggle his attention, as an idler might observe the feat of a juggler, without interest in the outcome. What splendid effort!—what magnificent, what superhuman strength! Ah, that was a fine endeavor! Bravo! The cord fell away; his arms parted and floated upward, the hands dimly seen on each side in the growing light. He watched them with a new interest as first one and then the other pounced upon the noose at his neck.
150 They tore it away and thrust it fiercely aside, its undulations resembling those of a water-snake. "Put it back, put it back!" He thought he shouted these words to his hands, for the undoing of the noose had been succeeded by the direst pang that he had yet experienced. His neck ached horribly; his brain was on fire; his heart, which had been fluttering faintly, gave a great leap, trying to force itself out at his mouth. His whole body was racked and wrenched with an insupportable anguish![10] But his disobedient hands gave no heed to the command. They beat the water vigorously with quick, downward strokes, forcing him to the surface. He felt his head emerge; his eyes were blinded by the sunlight; his chest expanded convulsively, and with a supreme and crowning agony his lungs engulfed a great
160 draught of air, which instantly he expelled in a shriek!

He was now in full possession of his physical senses. They were, indeed, preternaturally keen and alert. Something in the awful disturbance of his organic system had so exalted and refined them that they made record of things never before perceived. He felt the ripples upon his face and heard their separate sounds as they struck. He looked at the forest on the bank of the stream, saw the individual trees, the leaves and the veining of each leaf—saw the very insects upon them: the locusts, the brilliant-bodied flies, the gray spiders stretching their webs from twig to twig. He noted the prismatic colors in all the dewdrops upon a million blades of grass. The humming of the gnats that danced above the eddies of
170 the stream, the beating of the dragon-flies' wings, the strokes of the water-spiders' legs, like oars which had lifted their boat—all these made audible music. A fish slid along beneath his eyes and he heard the rush of its body parting the water.

He had come to the surface facing down the stream; in a moment the visible world seemed to wheel slowly round, himself the pivotal point, and he saw the bridge, the fort, the soldiers upon the bridge, the captain, the sergeant, the two privates, his executioners. They were in silhouette against the blue sky. They shouted and gesticulated, pointing at him. The captain had drawn his pistol, but did not fire; the others were unarmed. Their movements were grotesque and horrible, their forms gigantic.

🕞 **POINT OF VIEW**
Contrast the point of view used in lines 137–142 with that used in the opening of the story. What effect does this shift in perspective have on the reader's experience of the story?

🕒 **Targeted Passage**

---

10. **racked ... anguish:** stretched and twisted with unendurable physical pain.

DIFFERENTIATED INSTRUCTION

FOR STRATEGIC READERS

🕒 **Targeted Passage [Lines 147–164]**

This passage explains that Farquhar escapes and shows his heightened senses.

- How does Farquhar get rid of the noose?
- How does Farquhar feel while in the water? How does he get "full possession of his physical senses" (line 161)?
- What clues suggest that something strange is happening?

FOR ENGLISH LEARNERS

Related Vocabulary Explain to students that the narrator uses vivid sensory language to describe Farquhar's pain as he is under the water and swims to the surface. Help students to understand these physical descriptions of pain:

- *brain was on fire* (line 153), "head ached"
- *his heart ... gave a great leap* (lines 153–154), "his heart was beating hard"
- *body was racked and wrenched* (line 155), "body was twisted by the pain"
- *insupportable anguish* (lines 155–156), "unbearable pain"
- *his chest expanded convulsively* (lines 158–159), "he had difficulty catching his breath"
- *his lungs engulfed a great draught of air, which instantly he expelled in a shriek* (lines 159–160), "he took a great gulp, then yelled"

180 Suddenly he heard a sharp report and something struck the water smartly within a few inches of his head, spattering his face with spray. He heard a second report, and saw one of the sentinels with his rifle at his shoulder, a light cloud of blue smoke rising from the muzzle. The man in the water saw the eye of the man on the bridge gazing into his own through the sights of the rifle. He observed that it was a gray eye and remembered having read that gray eyes were keenest, and that all famous marksmen had them. Nevertheless, this one had missed.

A counter-swirl had caught Farquhar and turned him half round; he was again looking into the forest on the bank opposite the fort. The sound of a clear, high voice in a monotonous singsong now rang out behind him and came across the

190 water with a distinctness that pierced and subdued all other sounds, even the beating of the ripples in his ears. Although no soldier, he had frequented camps enough to know the dread significance of that deliberate, drawling, aspirated chant; the lieutenant on shore was taking a part in the morning's work. How coldly and pitilessly—with what an even, calm intonation, **presaging,** and enforcing tranquillity in the men—with what accurately measured intervals fell those cruel words:

"Attention, company! . . . Shoulder arms! . . . Ready! . . . Aim! . . . Fire!"

presaging (prĕs′ĭj-ĭng)
adj. predicting **presage** *v.*

Lines 173–186
TIERED DISCUSSION PROMPTS
Use these prompts to help students decide if details in this passage are real or fantastic:

Restate In lines 176–179, how does Farquhar describe the soldiers' reaction to his escape? *Possible answer: Farquhar describes the soldiers as shouting and gesturing, but not shooting. He says all but the captain were unarmed.*

Analyze Would you expect soldiers to respond this way to a prisoner's escape? Why or why not? *Possible answer: No, they would typically be armed, not unarmed (line 178), and they would shoot immediately at him, not wait (lines 177–178).*

Synthesize Use what you know about Farquhar's situation to decide if his descriptions here are realistic or fantastic. *Possible answer: The men seem to behave as Farquhar would want them to, which suggests that the descriptions are a fantasy. In addition, the words "grotesque and horrible, their forms gigantic" (lines 178–179) suggest fantastic images. Finally, Farquhar says that he could see the "gray eye" (line 185) of the shooter, which is unlikely, especially as the shooter misses Farquhar. All of these details suggest a scene that Farquhar hopes for or dreams.*

FOR STRATEGIC READERS
Visualize To aid comprehension, urge students to visualize Farquhar's situation as you describe it. Point out that Farquhar is in the water when he hears the dialogue in line 197. Farquhar hears the lieutenant speak these words as he orders the other soldiers to shoot at Farquhar. Direct students to line 198 and clarify that Farquhar dives into the water to evade the bullets.

FOR ENGLISH LEARNERS
Related Vocabulary Point out the vivid language the narrator uses to describe the ominous sounds Farquhar hears.

- *clear, high voice . . . that pierced and subdued* (lines 188–190), "a voice that was heard through and above any other voice"
- *dread significance . . . deliberate . . . aspirated chant* (lines 192–193), "importance of the careful, clearly stated orders "

Niagara Falls The "voice of Niagara" (line 199) refers to Niagara Falls, which is a massive waterfall on the border between New York State and Ontario, Canada. This reference means that the water was very loud in Farquhar's ears.

Lines 204–211
REINFORCE *KEY IDEA:* ESCAPE

Discuss Evaluate Farquhar's **escape.** Do you think he will succeed? Why or why not?
Possible answer: On the one hand, he seems to have made important progress toward escape. He is downstream away from the shooters (line 205), and feels energized by adrenaline (lines 209–210). On the other hand, his ability to think at lightning speed (line 211), and to swim while dodging bullets (lines 208–209) seems impossible. The escape seems less and less likely to succeed because it seems less and less believable. Instead, it seems more like a fantasy of events Farquhar wishes for.

Farquhar dived—dived as deeply as he could. The water roared in his ears like the voice of Niagara, yet he heard the dulled thunder of the volley and, rising
200 again toward the surface, met shining bits of metal, singularly flattened, oscillating slowly downward. Some of them touched him on the face and hands, then fell away, continuing their descent. One lodged between his collar and neck; it was uncomfortably warm and he snatched it out.

As he rose to the surface, gasping for breath, he saw that he had been a long time under water; he was perceptibly farther down stream—nearer to safety. The soldiers had almost finished reloading; the metal ramrods flashed all at once in the sunshine as they were drawn from the barrels, turned in the air, and thrust into their sockets. The two sentinels fired again, independently and ineffectually.

The hunted man saw all this over his shoulder; he was now swimming
210 vigorously with the current. His brain was as energetic as his arms and legs; he thought with the rapidity of lightning.

"The officer," he reasoned, "will not make that martinet's[11] error a second time. It is as easy to dodge a volley as a single shot. He has probably already given the command to fire at will. God help me, I cannot dodge them all!"

An appalling plash within two yards of him was followed by a loud, rushing sound, *diminuendo,*[12] which seemed to travel back through the air to the fort and died in an explosion which stirred the very river to its deeps! A rising sheet of water curved over him, fell down upon him, blinded him, strangled him! The cannon had taken a hand in the game. As he shook his head free from the
220 commotion of the smitten water he heard the deflected shot humming through the air ahead, and in an instant it was cracking and smashing the branches in the forest beyond.

"They will not do that again," he thought; "the next time they will use a charge of grape.[13] I must keep my eye upon the gun; the smoke will apprise me—the report arrives too late; it lags behind the missile. That is a good gun."

Suddenly he felt himself whirled round and round—spinning like a top. The water, the banks, the forests, the now distant bridge, fort and men—all were commingled and blurred. Objects were represented by their colors only; circular horizontal streaks of color—that was all he saw. He had been caught in a vortex
230 and was being whirled on with a velocity of advance and gyration that made him giddy and sick. In a few moments he was flung upon the gravel at the foot of the left bank of the stream—the southern bank—and behind a projecting point which concealed him from his enemies. The sudden arrest of his motion, the abrasion of one of his hands on the gravel, restored him, and he wept with delight. He dug his fingers into the sand, threw it over himself in handfuls and audibly blessed it.

④ **Targeted Passage**

It looked like diamonds, rubies, emeralds; he could think of nothing beautiful which it did not resemble. The trees upon the bank were giant garden plants; he

---

11. **martinet's:** alluding to a strict disciplinarian or person who demands that regulations be followed exactly.
12. *diminuendo* (dĭ-mĭn′yōō-ĕn′dō) *Italian:* gradually decreasing in loudness.
13. **grape:** short for grapeshot, a cluster of several small iron balls fired in one shot from a cannon.

DIFFERENTIATED INSTRUCTION

FOR STRATEGIC READERS

④ **Targeted Passage [Lines 226–235]**

This passage gives Farquhar's rationalized description of the landscape and shows readers that he is spinning in the water.

- How is Farquhar moving?
- What does he see as he moves? What happens to him after he stops moving?
- How does he feel while he is moving? How does he feel when he stops moving?

FOR ENGLISH LEARNERS

Related Vocabulary Review these movement words and help students build meaning for their use:

- Demonstrate the whirling motion Farquhar describes as *whirled round and round— spinning like a top* (line 226).
- Discuss how such movement affects people's vision and point out that Farquhar describes seeing everything as *commingled and blurred* (line 228), or blended together.

- Help students visualize a *vortex* (line 229) by explaining that it looks like water going down a drain.
- Explain that *velocity* (line 230) is speed.

noted a definite order in their arrangement, inhaled the fragrance of their blooms. A strange, roseate light shone through the spaces among their trunks and the wind
240 made in their branches the music of æolian harps.[14] He had no wish to perfect his escape—was content to remain in that enchanting spot until retaken.

A whiz and rattle of grapeshot among the branches high above his head roused him from his dream. The baffled cannoneer had fired him a random farewell. He sprang to his feet, rushed up the sloping bank, and plunged into the forest.

All that day he traveled, laying his course by the rounding sun. The forest seemed **interminable**; nowhere did he discover a break in it, not even a woodman's road. He had not known that he lived in so wild a region. There was something uncanny in the revelation.

ANALYZE VISUALS
Compare this image with the description given in lines 237–240. What associations does each scene call to mind?

interminable
(ĭn-tûr′mə-nə-bol)
adj. endless

14. **music of æolian** (ê-ō′lê-ən) **harps:** heavenly, or unearthly, music.

FOR STRATEGIC READERS
Foreshadowing Point out these references and help students recognize what these clues might foreshadow:

- *strange, roseate light shone through the spaces* (line 239)
- *æolian harps* (line 240)
- *enchanting spot* (line 241)
- *something uncanny in the revelation* (line 248)

Possible answer: *The light suggests a near-death experience and the heavenly harps reinforce this suggestion. These clues foreshadow Farquhar's death.*

FOR ADVANCED LEARNERS/AP
Analyze Character Behavior Challenge students to find textual evidence on pages 590–591 that Farquhar is actually aware that he is hanging (lines 219–222; 226–233). Ask them to write a brief essay outlining their findings and explaining why Farquhar might still be thinking positively instead of negatively at this point. Invite students to share their essays.

REINFORCE *KEY IDEA:* ESCAPE

Discuss How is Farquhar really going to **escape** his situation? What clues suggest his likely escape? *Possible answer: Farquhar is going to escape his present situation by dying. The pain he feels is actually the noose strangling him (lines 261–264). The road that he is walking down by himself is leading him to death, an experience everyone must go through alone (lines 250–252).*

LITERARY ANALYSIS

G POINT OF VIEW

Possible answer: The point of view changes from third-person limited, in which readers learn the details of thoughts inside Farquhar's own head, to third-person omniscient. This change in point of view allows readers to realize that much of the story has been Farquhar's hallucinations as he faces his imminent death.

SELECTION WRAP–UP

REFLECT Ask students to consider how they feel about Farquhar's story. Is he set up unfairly or do his actions merit punishment?

⭐ CRITIQUE

- Ask students if they enjoyed the uncertainty about whether Farquhar is really escaping.

- After completing the After Reading questions on page 593, have students revisit their responses and tell whether they have changed their opinions.

By night fall he was fatigued, footsore, famishing. The thought of his wife
250 and children urged him on. At last he found a road which led him in what he
knew to be the right direction. It was as wide and straight as a city street, yet it
seemed untraveled. No fields bordered it, no dwelling anywhere. Not so much as
the barking of a dog suggested human habitation. The black bodies of the trees
formed a straight wall on both sides, terminating on the horizon in a point, like
a diagram in a lesson in perspective. Overhead, as he looked up through this
rift in the wood, shone great golden stars looking unfamiliar and grouped in
strange constellations. He was sure they were arranged in some order which had
a secret and **malign** significance. The wood on either side was full of singular
noises, among which—once, twice, and again, he distinctly heard whispers in an
260 unknown tongue.

His neck was in pain and lifting his hand to it he found it horribly swollen.
He knew that it had a circle of black where the rope had bruised it. His eyes felt
congested; he could no longer close them. His tongue was swollen with thirst; he
relieved its fever by thrusting it forward from between his teeth into the cold air.
How softly the turf had carpeted the untraveled avenue—he could no longer feel
the roadway beneath his feet!

Doubtless, despite his suffering, he had fallen asleep while walking, for now he
sees another scene—perhaps he has merely recovered from a delirium. He stands
at the gate of his own home. All is as he left it, and all bright and beautiful in the
270 morning sunshine. He must have traveled the entire night. As he pushes open
the gate and passes up the wide white walk, he sees a flutter of female garments;
his wife, looking fresh and cool and sweet, steps down from the veranda to meet
him. At the bottom of the steps she stands waiting, with a smile of **ineffable** joy,
an attitude of matchless grace and dignity. Ah, how beautiful she is! He springs
forward with extended arms. As he is about to clasp her he feels a stunning blow
upon the back of the neck; a blinding white light blazes all about him with a
sound like the shock of a cannon—then all is darkness and silence!

Peyton Farquhar was dead; his body, with a broken neck, swung gently from
side to side beneath the timbers of the Owl Creek bridge. ❧ **G**

malign (mə-līn′) *adj.* evil; harmful

⑤ Targeted Passage

ineffable (ĭn-ĕf′ə-bəl) *adj.* beyond description; inexpressible

G POINT OF VIEW
Describe the change in point of view that occurs in lines 275–279. What impact does this change have on your understanding of the story?

DIFFERENTIATED INSTRUCTION

FOR STRATEGIC READERS
⑤ Targeted Passage [Lines 261–279]
This passage gives the final details of Farquhar strangling and lets readers know that he has been dying all along.

- What physical condition is Farquhar in?

- What is really happening to Farquhar now? What is he visualizing or thinking about?

- How and where does Farquhar die?

FOR ADVANCED LEARNERS/AP
Analyze Plot Remind students that this story has an atypical plot in many ways, largely because of its unconventional sequence. Organize students into small groups, and have each group discuss the questions in the Analysis Frame: Plot. Encourage groups to share their answers with one another.

 BEST PRACTICES TOOLKIT—Transparency
Analysis Frame: Plot p. D21, D28

Comprehension

1. **Summarize** What is Peyton Farquhar's background?

2. **Recall** How does Farquhar die?

3. **Clarify** Why did the soldier who visited Farquhar give him such detailed information about the bridge?

Literary Analysis

4. **Make Inferences** What is the Union soldiers' reason for hanging Farquhar? Cite evidence to support your inference.

5. **Analyze Structure** Review the chart you created as you read. How would the story be different if it were told in chronological order?

6. **Examine Point of View** Citing at least two examples from the story, explain how the shifts in point of view affect the level of **suspense**. What would be different about the story if it were told entirely from the **third-person omniscient** point of view?

7. **Make Judgments About Sensory Details** Bierce uses sensory details to provide clues to Farquhar's state of mind. In each of the following episodes, what sensory details suggest that Farquhar's perceptions may be unreliable?

   • on the bridge (lines 60–70)
   • in the river (lines 161–172)
   • reaching land (lines 231–240)
   • in the woods (lines 255–260)

8. **Interpret Themes** Reread lines 80–91. Based on the contrast between Farquhar's dreams of wartime glory and his ultimate fate, what point might Bierce be making about

   • heroism   • the realities of war   • the dangers of fantasy

9. **Evaluate Narrative Devices** In your opinion, did Bierce intend Farquhar's miraculous **escape** to seem believable? Cite evidence from the story to support your view.

Literary Criticism

10. **Author's Style** Compare Bierce's use of realistic and fantastic elements in this story. Which label—realistic or fantastic—best describes Bierce's style? Support your answer with details.

AN OCCURRENCE AT OWL CREEK BRIDGE **593**

7. *Farquhar's state of mind is suggested by his distorted perception of sounds and time while on the bridge, his absurdly acute senses while in the river, his odd perceptions of the surroundings and of heavenly harps when he reaches land, and the voices he hears and sinister perceptions he feels while in the woods.*

8. *Bierce suggests that heroism is a foolish dream; that war is treacherous and dangerous, not glorious or ideal; and that dreams can lead you into danger.*

9. *Answers may vary. Bierce uses many realistic details in Section I about the scene and Farquhar's hanging. The details get increasingly fantastic, which suggests by Section III that the escape is unlikely to be real.*

10. *Answers may vary. **Realistic:** military actions, conversation with Federal scout, description of scenes. **Fantasy:** hallucinatory imagery, escape details.*

Practice and Apply

After Reading
Use these copy masters to check understanding and provide extra support:

R RESOURCE MANAGER—Copy Masters
Reading Check p. 158
Point of View p. 151
Question Support p. 159

Additional selection questions are provided for teachers on page 145.

ANSWERS

1. *He is a wealthy Southern planter, slave owner, and Confederate sympathizer.*

2. *He is hanged at Owl Creek Bridge.*

3. *He was a Union spy. He was trying to trick Farquhar into committing a crime.*

Possible answers:

4. *They hang Farquhar because he was caught attempting to sabotage Owl Creek Bridge. Evidence includes the suggestive conversation between Farquhar and the Federal scout (lines 102–112), the fact that he wants to be a war hero (lines 85–87), and the opening scene of the hanging (lines 1–15).*

5. ■ **SKILLS FOCUS Analyze Structure** *Students may say there would be no suspense or surprise ending if readers knew why Farquhar is being hanged and that he does not escape.*

6. ● **SKILLS FOCUS Point of View** *The shifts in point of view increase the suspense in the story. When the point of view shifts from omniscient to limited in lines 42–56, readers know only how Farquhar feels. This draws them into Farquhar's experience. In Section III, the point of view again shifts from omniscient to limited. This allows readers to experience Farquhar's emotions and thoughts, creates suspense about his fate, and supports the fantasy. Without the departures into omniscient point of view, readers would not recognize the fantasy. Students may say that because much of the suspense comes from Farquhar's—and the reader's—ignorance of his fate, telling the story entirely in third-person omniscient would rob it of interest. They may also suggest that the fantasy passages would be less effective in third-person omniscient.*

ANSWERS
Vocabulary in Context

VOCABULARY PRACTICE

1. *false*   5. *false*

2. *false*   6. *false*

3. *true*   7. *true*

4. *true*   8. *true*

 RESOURCE MANAGER—Copy Master
Vocabulary Practice p. 156

VOCABULARY IN WRITING

Encourage students to reread lines 118–123, 226–241, and 261–266, then help them choose clues that they can describe.

VOCABULARY STRATEGY: THE LATIN ROOT
lud (also an EL language objective)

For each item, help students use their knowledge of the root and context clues to determine word meaning.

Answers:

1. *interlude*

2. *delusion*

3. *illusory*

4. *prelude*

5. *collusion*

 RESOURCE MANAGER—Copy Master
Vocabulary Strategy p. 157

ⓘ Vocabulary Center at **ClassZone.com**
Additional Vocabulary Activities

Assess and Reteach

Assess

 RESOURCE MANAGER—Copy Masters
Selection Test A pp. 161–162
Selection Test B/C pp. 163–164

🔘 Test Generator CD

Reteach

🅂 **STANDARDS LESSON FILE**
Literature Lesson 10: Types of Point of View
Reading Lesson 6: Recognizing Sequence and Chronological Order
Vocabulary Lesson 7: Latin Roots

Vocabulary in Context

VOCABULARY PRACTICE

Decide whether these statements using the vocabulary words are true or false.

1. A **ludicrous** TV show would probably make you cry.
2. A job that is performed **summarily** tends to take a long time.
3. An **ineffable** pleasure is likely to leave you speechless with joy.
4. A **malign** decision could cause others pain and suffering.
5. Climbing a very steep ladder is an example of **oscillation.**
6. You would typically describe a standup comic's performance as **poignant.**
7. Messages **presaging** happiness tend to make a fortuneteller popular.
8. If a school day seems **interminable,** it feels like it will never be over.

VOCABULARY IN WRITING

Looking back over this story, you might find several clues hinting at its ending. Using three or more vocabulary words, write a brief description of those clues. You might start like this.

> **EXAMPLE SENTENCE**
> *Both physical and psychological clues **presaging** Farquhar's fate are revealed through careful rereading of the story.*

VOCABULARY STRATEGY: THE LATIN ROOT *lud*

The vocabulary word *ludicrous* contains the Latin root *lud,* meaning "play." This root, which may also be spelled *lus,* can be found in a number of English words. To understand words with *lud* or *lus,* use context clues as well as your knowledge of the meaning of the root.

PRACTICE Choose the word from the word web that best completes each sentence. Consider what you know about the Latin root and the other word parts shown. If necessary, consult a dictionary.

1. In the _____ between the scenes, a violinist performed for the audience.
2. He suffers from the _____ that he is a good golfer.
3. Though she dresses expensively, her wealth is more _____ than real.
4. As a _____ to the main act, a young, inexperienced band played.
5. As a result of the two guards' _____, a prisoner was allowed to escape.

WORD LIST
ineffable
interminable
ludicrous
malign
oscillation
poignant
presaging
summarily

R1.2

illusory   ludicrous
interlude   **lud, lus**   prelude
delusion   collusion

➤ **VOCABULARY PRACTICE**
For more practice, go to the **Vocabulary Center** at **ClassZone.com.**

DIFFERENTIATED INSTRUCTION

FOR ENGLISH LEARNERS

Task Support: Vocabulary Practice Have home-language group students create word webs with cognates for four of the English words in the **WORD LIST.** If their home language has no cognates for these words, ask students to identify the common suffixes in the **WORD LIST** and provide a general meaning for each one.

FOR ADVANCED LEARNERS/AP

Vocabulary in Writing Have students use at least five of the words in the **WORD LIST** to write a short paragraph that summarizes the ending of the story. As an extension, students might write from the point of view of an observer to the hanging.

Voices of the Civil War

Near the outbreak of the Civil War, writer Ralph Waldo Emerson remarked, "All arts disappear in the one art of war." In other words, the necessities of warfare—military, political, economic, and social—act somehow to discourage or diminish the creation of what might be termed "serious literature." Yet fine nonfiction writing about searing national issues emerged in the years prior to, during, and immediately following the Civil War.

The selections beginning on page 538 include many forms of nonfiction: autobiography, speeches, documents, letters, and diaries. Perhaps these forms served as better vehicles than poems or short stories might have for the people of the day who wanted to explore their personal responses to the war. In any case, the nonfiction here is valuable for several reasons:

- It gives readers a glimpse into the events and culture of the writers' troubled time.
- It provides each writer's personal response to what was happening all around.
- It presents a good overview of the many different factions that made up the country at the time.

Writing to Synthesize

Write an essay describing both the historical and the personal insights you gained from reading the nonfiction in this unit.

Consider

- the historical facts you learned from the selections (important figures, dates, battles, and so forth)
- the personal concerns of the writers (their opinions, worries, pride, and so forth)
- what you can infer about the country as a whole from the many voices of its writers

CALIFORNIA

W2.2, LS1.3

Lincoln at Gettysburg II (1939–1942), William H. Johnson. Gouache and pen and ink on paper, 19 ³/₄" × 17 ¹/₁₆".

Extension

VIEWING & REPRESENTING

Perhaps the most important writer of this period was Abraham Lincoln. Presented with a divided nation, Lincoln took on the task of uniting all of its various factions. Examine the image of Lincoln shown here. Based upon your reading and your prior knowledge of President Lincoln, give a brief **oral critique** of how he is portrayed in this painting. Discuss the style of the work as a whole, Lincoln's placement in relation to other figures in the painting, the colors used, and any other aspects you consider important.

Wrap-Up: Literature of the Civil War

This Wrap-Up provides students with an opportunity to revisit ideas from the nonfiction literature in this section about the Civil War, and to reflect on how writers of that era responded to the major issues of their time. Urge students to reexamine their own views about the Civil War in light of insights gained from the selections.

Writing to Synthesize

Review with students that *synthesizing* means putting different parts together to make a whole. Students must combine their historical knowledge and the inferences they have made about this time period when writing their essays.

To help students write their essays, ask them to complete a Three-Column Journal with heads that correspond to the three bulleted items. Remind students that they should record as much as possible in their journals, but should plan to focus on only the best examples in their essays.

 BEST PRACTICES TOOLKIT—Transparency
Three-Column Journal p. B10

Extension

- Suggest that students first write a list of facts they know about Lincoln. Then have them consider these notes as they analyze the painting.
- Remind students to consider their knowledge of the time period as well as the title of the painting during their analysis. Explain that the critique should persuade listeners with a well-supported interpretation. Encourage students to write brief notes before giving their oral critiques.

FOR DEVELOPING WRITERS

Writing Support Have students circle some of the examples in their journals to write about and find textual evidence to support their statements and inferences. For example, in response to Harriet Jacobs's slave narrative, students might identify and support her personal concern that slavery was immoral and should be abolished. From this, they can infer that slavery was a "hot topic" during this time period.

FOR ENGLISH LEARNERS

Writing Topic Sentences Provide these topic sentence starters for essay support:

- One of the most important people during the Civil War period was _____.
- One popular opinion expressed by writers during the Civil War was _____.
- These writers' voices prove that the country was _____ during the Civil War.

Remind students to find details in the selections to support their topic sentences.

Focus and Motivate

OBJECTIVES

Media Literacy

- view film clips from *An Occurrence at Owl Creek Bridge* to understand the challenges of adapting a story for film
- compare and contrast point of view in film and print versions

 LS1.14

SUMMARY

In the first film clip from *An Occurrence at Owl Creek Bridge,* Peyton Farquhar is hanged by soldiers. When the rope breaks, he falls into the river, swims to shore, and charges off into the woods. The second clip shows his night walk and the visions he sees of his family. The third clip shows Farquhar reuniting with his wife; however, viewers are pulled back at the last moment by the sharp tightening of the noose. Farquhar's life has flashed before his eyes as he dies. The entire journey has taken place in his mind.

BACKGROUND

The actors cast as the soldiers in the film are not routine movie extras. Nearly 40 roles were cast from a pool of Civil War living history impressionists. Each actor had years of experience working to educate the public on Civil War history. They each gave careful attention to the accuracy of their appearance and deportment, giving the film an authentic feeling.

The Filmmakers' Challenge

Before students read the feature, ask them whether it is easier to express feelings, emotions, and thoughts in print than it is in film. Help students brainstorm devices that can be used to express thoughts or emotions in each genre. ***Possible answers:*** *In print, writers use point of view, internal monologue, dialogue, and description to express characters' thoughts and feelings. Filmmakers may use voice-overs, acting, shot selection, and dialogue.*

Media Study

from An Occurrence at Owl Creek Bridge

Film Clips on *MediaSmart* DVD

 LS1.14

From Page to Screen

Since 1932, the short story "An Occurrence at Owl Creek Bridge" has been adapted for the screen at least four times. Its Civil War setting, heart-pounding suspense, and surprise ending make it an ideal story to adapt to film. In this lesson, you'll view three clips from the 2005 version to explore one of the ways Ambrose Bierce's tale has been adapted for the big screen.

The Filmmaker's Challenge

The fact that the main action of the story takes place in the mind of the character Peyton Farquhar creates a challenge for a filmmaker. To reveal a character's thoughts, a filmmaker must rely on such devices as **voice-over narration,** in which the character speaks his or her thoughts, and **flashbacks,** which present a scene from the character's memory.

Brian James Egen directs an actor on location.

In his film, director Brian James Egen provided only subtle clues that what the audience sees is not what is actually happening. "I had to create a feeling," Egen says, "from the time the rope breaks to the end, as if it was real. I wanted the audience to be taken completely by surprise, so we created the scenes as realistically as possible."

Comparing Texts: Point of View

Point of view in film can be either objective or subjective. In the **objective point of view,** the camera acts as a neutral recorder of action. It is used to show scenes as they would occur in reality. In the **subjective point of view,** the camera becomes a participant in the scene and seems to get inside a character's head by showing the viewer exactly what the character sees.

596

Media Study Resources

R RESOURCE MANAGER UNIT 3	**S** STANDARDS LESSON FILE
Plan and Teach pp. 165–168	Media Lesson 4: Analyzing Visuals in Film and TV
Media Analysis Summary pp. 169†*, 170‡* Close Viewing p. 171	Media Lesson 7: Evaluating Films and TV Shows
	Media Center at **ClassZone.com**
	MEDIA VIEWING MediaSmart DVD

* Resources for Differentiation   † Also in Spanish   ‡ In Haitian Creole and Vietnamese

Read the following passage from the story and visualize the events. When you view the clips, pay special attention to this moment in the film. How close does the film come to the scene as you imagined it? Compare Bierce's use of the **third-person limited point of view** with the point of view used by the filmmaker. Notice the ways in which both the story and the film emphasize this moment.

> He felt his head emerge; his eyes were blinded by the sunlight; his chest expanded convulsively, and with a supreme and crowning agony his lungs engulfed a great draught of air, which instantly he expelled in a shriek!
>
> He was now in full possession of his physical senses. They were, indeed, pre-
> 5 ternaturally keen and alert. Something in the awful disturbance of his organic system had so exalted and refined them that they made record of things never before perceived. He felt the ripples upon his face and heard their separate sounds as they struck. He looked at the forest on the bank of the stream, saw the individual trees, the leaves and the veining of each leaf—saw the very
> 10 insects upon them: the locusts, the brilliant-bodied flies, the gray spiders stretching their webs from twig to twig. He noted the prismatic colors in all the dewdrops upon a million blades of grass.

Viewing Guide

◎ MediaSmart DVD
- **Film:** *An Occurrence at Owl Creek Bridge*
- **Director:** Brian James Egen
- **Genre:** Historical thriller
- **Running Time:** 14 minutes

The three clips you'll view from *An Occurrence at Owl Creek Bridge* include Farquhar's hanging and escape, his long walk through the night to reach his wife, and, of course, the sudden ending. You may want to watch the clips more than once in order to analyze them.

NOW VIEW

***CLOSE VIEWING:* Media Analysis**

1. **Compare Point of View** Think about the scene in the film that corresponds to the passage shown from the story. Did the filmmaker use the **objective** or **subjective point of view**? What is the effect of this point of view in comparison with Bierce's use of the **third-person limited**?

2. **Analyze Montage** A **montage** is a succession of shots, often short and without dialogue, intended to create a particular effect or suggest meaning. What do you think the filmmaker wanted to convey with the montage of Farquhar's family and home in the third clip?

3. **Evaluate the Adaptation** How effective do you think the filmmaker was in adapting Bierce's story to the big screen? Think about the following:
   - the rising suspense in the hanging scene
   - the voice-over narration
   - moments in the film that do not appear in the story

MEDIA STUDY **597**

ANSWERS

CLOSE VIEWING: Media Analysis
Possible answers:

1. *The filmmakers use the subjective point of view. Viewers see and hear Farquhar's experience directly as he escapes the noose and river. In contrast, Bierce's use of the third-person keeps the reader more distant.*

2. *The montage shows us what goes through Farquhar's mind in the moment before he dies. He sees the things he cares most about—his wife, children, home, and memories of good times from the past.*

3. *The adaptation is effective for the most part. Suspense is high in the moments before the hanging. The filmmaker uses story text as voice-over narration of Farquhar's thoughts. However, the elements of the film that do not appear in the story are unnecessary and take away from the effectiveness of the adaptation.*

Comparing Texts: Point of View

Replay the film clips several times. Have students point out the moments when the filmmaker uses an objective point of view (*when he shows the soldiers loading their guns*) and when he uses a subjective point of view (*when he films the grass and leaves, as seen through Farquhar's eyes*). Point out that the passage from Bierce's story does not shift its point of view.

Viewing Guide

1. To prepare students for the film clip, tell them that they will be asked to compare the points of view in the film and the story. Urge them to watch and listen for these elements:
   - lack of dialogue—the only audible words are the **voice-over narration** of Peyton Farquhar
   - the use of **flashbacks** that show Farquhar's visions of his family and how these change as the story progresses

2. Explain that the story takes place during the American Civil War.
   - Remind students that the northern soldiers wore blue uniforms.
   - Clarify that the main character is being hanged for attempting to burn Owl Creek Bridge.

℞ RESOURCE MANAGER—Copy Master
   Close Viewing p. 171

Use this resource with the Viewing Guide:
◎ Media*Smart* DVD

MEDIA STUDY WRAP–UP

Have students summarize what they have learned about how point of view differs in film and short story. Encourage students to use the terms *voice-over narration, flashbacks,* and *objective* and *subjective points of view* in their explanations.

RETEACH
Ⓢ STANDARDS LESSON FILE
   Media Lesson 4: Analyzing Visuals in Film and TV
   Media Lesson 7: Evaluating Films and TV Shows

Focus and Motivate

OBJECTIVES

- analyze a student model that shows the traits of biographical narratives
- use the writing process to produce a biographical narrative
- revise and edit, using criteria for biographical narratives
- create and present a video documentary

 CALIFORNIA W2.1, W1.9, W2.6, LC1.1, LS1.10

WRITER'S ROAD MAP

WRITING PROMPTS 1 AND 2

Stress that students should write about someone they consider important or influential, either personally or to the world. Someone personally influential could be a relative, friend, teacher, or author who has helped shape their identity. Clarify that world influence can be global, national, regional, or even in the student's own neighborhood.

ADDITIONAL PROMPTS

Use these prompts for more writing practice:

WRITING PROMPT 3

Writing for the Real World Choose a person you admire, such as a world leader, sports hero, inventor, or historical figure. Research your subject and then write a speech for an award ceremony, honoring the person for his or her contributions.

WRITING PROMPT 4

Writing Inspired by Art Look for portraits, past or present. The portraits may be photographs or paintings, known people or family members. Choose the person whose portrait most inspires you. Research and write a biographical narrative about the person.

For additional writing prompts, see

- *WriteSmart* CD
- Writing Center at **ClassZone.com**

KEY TRAITS

Review the six **KEY TRAITS** with students, focusing on ideas and organization. Compare the list of traits with the criteria on page 604.

Writing Workshop
NARRATION

Biographical Narrative

People and ideas like the ones you've read about in this unit are what change our world. To investigate how someone has influenced your life, write your own biographical narrative.

WRITER'S ROAD MAP

Biographical Narrative

WRITING PROMPT 1

Writing from Your Life Write a biographical narrative about a person who you believe is important or influential. Include anecdotes and details to help your reader visualize the person clearly. Make sure your reader understands why the person is important to you.

People to Write About
- a friend who taught you something important
- a teacher who made a difference to you
- a relative who helped you

WRITING PROMPT 2

Writing from Literature Writing about another person can give you insight into that person's life and his or her significance. Do some research and write a biographical narrative about one of the writers in this unit whose life inspires or intrigues you.

Writers to Consider
- Frederick Douglass
- Abraham Lincoln
- Sojourner Truth
- Mary Chesnut

 WRITING TOOLS
For prewriting, revision, and editing tools, visit the **Writing Center** at ClassZone.com.

KEY TRAITS

1. IDEAS
- Provides a **dominant impression** of a clearly identified person
- Includes **anecdotes** to describe the person
- Uses **dialogue** to show the subject's personality

2. ORGANIZATION
- Draws the reader in with an intriguing **introduction**
- Provides **background information** about the person as needed
- **Concludes** by showing the significance of the person

3. VOICE
- Uses a **tone** that clearly conveys the writer's attitude toward the person

4. WORD CHOICE
- Includes **sensory details** to help readers get a focused impression of the person
- Uses **precise words** to describe the person's physical appearance, personality traits, and actions

5. SENTENCE FLUENCY
- Varies **sentence beginnings and structures**

6. CONVENTIONS
- Employs **correct grammar and usage**

Writing Workshop Resources

 RESOURCE MANAGER UNIT 3

Plan and Teach pp. 173–176
Prewriting–Editing pp. 177–181
Writing Rubric p. 182
Publishing with Technology p. 183
Writing Support p. 184*

S STANDARDS LESSON FILE
Writing Lessons 16, 30, 33, 35
Grammar Lessons 16, 17
Media Lesson 20

 BEST PRACTICES TOOLKIT

Scaffolding Writing Instruction pp. 43–46*
Venn Diagram • Reporter's Questions •
Opening Lines • Cliché Array • Writing
Template: Biographical Narrative • Three-Column Journal • Color Coding

TECHNOLOGY
- Easy Planner DVD
- Writing Center at **ClassZone.com**
- *WriteSmart* CD

 * Resources for Differentiation

Part 1: Analyze a Student Model

W2.1, W1.9 (pgs. 603, 604), W2.6 (p. 605), LC1.1 (p. 604), LS1.10 (p. 605)

Travis Saelzler
Fayetteville High School

A Mentor to Remember

The first time I saw him, he was running down the hall with one end of his tie over his shoulder, his arms overflowing with books and notes, leaving papers fluttering to the floor behind him. He disappeared into Room 203, tie flapping. "That," I muttered to myself, "can only be Mr. Moore." A
5 school legend, Mr. Moore has become my most memorable teacher and mentor.

Mr. Moore was in a class by himself. That doesn't mean his classes were poorly attended. On the contrary, they were always filled to capacity. English, Russian, French, American history, world religions, Western
10 civilization—no matter what he taught, he made learning an exciting experience. That's because what mattered most to him wasn't the subject but the students. Mr. Moore respected and understood us and helped us understand ourselves.

One way we learned who we were was by just watching him be himself.
15 When the other teachers wore jeans and flannel shirts to class, he dressed in a suit and tie, "to be suitable," he punned. Because he was comfortable with who he was, it didn't matter to him that he looked somewhat out of place.

He was also endearingly absent-minded. I'll never forget the time the announcement came over the loudspeaker: "Anyone knowing about a car
20 abandoned by the side of the road a few blocks from the school should contact the office immediately."

"Oh! Well! I'll be back in just a moment!" Mr. Moore said as he scurried from the classroom.

"I bet that's Mr. Moore's car," I said, and several of my classmates
25 agreed. We just figured he had run out of gas and left the car where it had coughed to a stop. And that's exactly what had happened.

KEY TRAITS IN ACTION

Lively **introduction** uses **precise words** and strong **sensory details.**

The writer supplies helpful **background information** about Mr. Moore's classes and begins building a **dominant impression** of him: he is an unusual but talented teacher.

Reveals Mr. Moore's character by quoting **dialogue** and sharing an **anecdote.**

Teach

CALIFORNIA

Part 1: Analyze a Student Model

Have students read the student model and **KEY TRAITS IN ACTION.** Then discuss the model with the class, noting specific examples of each trait and building on what students have already noted. You may also wish to incorporate these activities:

- **Background Information** Tell students that background information should attract readers' interest while providing context for the biographical subject's experiences. Have students reread the second paragraph, and identify the items of background information. *Possible answers: Background includes that Mr. Moore's classes were always filled to capacity, and that he taught English, Russian, French, American history, world religions, and Western civilization.* Then have students think of background information that would fit in biographical narratives about themselves. Invite volunteers to share information.

- **Dominant Impression** Have students think about authors from this unit, such as Whitman, Dickinson, Douglass, and Jacobs. Ask them to write one-line descriptions of their dominant impressions of those authors. Ask volunteers to share their impressions, pointing out that these may differ. To reinforce, ask students to state dominant impressions of Mr. Moore that differ from the one in the model. Clarify that there is no single correct impression of a biographical subject. The goal instead is to convey one's impression clearly and vividly.

DIFFERENTIATED INSTRUCTION

For general guidelines on differentiating writing instruction, see

 BEST PRACTICES TOOLKIT
Scaffolding Writing Instruction
pp. 43–46

FOR ENGLISH LEARNERS
Language: Skill Words Write these terms on the board and review them with students:

- *precise words:* words that describe things specifically—for example, "overflowing," "books and notes," "fluttering" (lines 2–3)

- *sensory details:* details that describe what something looks, sounds, feels, smells, or tastes like—for example, "one end of his tie over his shoulder" (lines 1–2)

- *background information:* basic facts—for example, the classes Mr. Moore taught

- *dominant impression:* the main idea you associate with someone—for example, Mr. Moore was an unusual but excellent teacher

- *anecdote:* a brief story—for example, the story about Mr. Moore's car

- *tone:* a writer's attitude toward the person under discussion—for example, respect and admiration for Mr. Moore

- **Tone** Focus students' attention on the highlighted phrases in the first paragraph on page 600. Then ask students to revise the passages so that they convey a less admiring tone. Tell students to try to achieve the tonal changes without changing the meanings of the passages. For example, if students replace "cared deeply" with "didn't care," the change reverses the meaning. However, if students simply delete the word "deeply," the change creates a more neutral tone without reversing the meaning. Remind students that writers manipulate tone by carefully considering the connotations of words. For an example of how word connotations affect tone, have students reread Abraham Lincoln's Gettysburg Address and Emancipation Proclamation on pages 564–567.

- **Sentence Beginnings and Structures** For each sentence in lines 44–50, ask volunteers to analyze how the sentence begins. For example, the first sentence of the paragraph begins with the transitional word, "Then," connecting it to the previous paragraph. In contrast, the second sentence begins with an independent clause. After analyzing the sentence beginnings, have students notice the varied sentence lengths and structures. For example, the first sentence is a short, simple sentence, while the second sentence is a complex sentence and much longer.

For interactive student models, see

WriteSmart CD

Writing Center at **ClassZone.com**

Even though Mr. Moore seemed unaware of what others thought of him, he cared deeply about us and what we thought of ourselves. He knew exactly how to draw students out and encourage us to participate. The
30 way he listened carefully and found something valuable in every question made us feel important. When just learning the Russian alphabet gave me nightmares, Mr. Moore calmed me down, then found a student in his advanced class who agreed to tutor me in exchange for extra credit. When a student in our world religions class developed severe complications from
35 diabetes, Mr. Moore visited her in the hospital. He encouraged interaction, questions, debate, and different ways of looking at things, and his lessons addressed every possible learning style. In our Western civilization class, for example, we held a council of Greek gods and goddesses, made mobiles tracing the theme of guilt through history, and presented a song, poem,
40 dance, or pantomime depicting our visions of the future. After struggling with that last activity, I thought, "We're not just studying history, but learning to make it by figuring out what kind of world we want to help create."

Then there were Mr. Moore's tests. All his exams were open-book, and
45 we could bring along whatever additional materials we wanted. That's because he wasn't as interested in getting answers as he was in getting us to ask our own questions and come up with new ideas. For me, the only way to study for his tests was to freewrite about the material, letting my mind wander and make its own connections. His respect and trust meant more
50 than any grade I've ever gotten.

That gift will always be with Mr. Moore's students. Even if we forget who won the Trojan War or how to spell Thucydides, we will remember how Mr. Moore helped us get to know ourselves. He's already so much more than a teacher to me; I'm sure he will be a lifelong mentor. What
55 more can a teacher do for his or her students?

*Overall **tone** is respectful and admiring.*

Uses interior monologue to illustrate Mr. Moore's impact on the writer.

*A variety of **sentence beginnings and structures** hold the reader's interest.*

***Conclusion** shows Mr. Moore's lasting significance in the writer's life and leaves readers with a question to ponder.*

2

DIFFERENTIATED INSTRUCTION

FOR ENGLISH LEARNERS

Comprehension: Transitions List transitional words that can often be found in biographical narratives. Because a narrative is a story, many such transitions show time order. The student model begins with a time-order transition: *The first time.* List other common transitions showing time order, such as *when, then, before, after, next, finally,* and *last.* Time-order transitions can also use days or dates to orient readers, as with phrases such as *last*

Tuesday, yesterday, tomorrow, next week, and *2006.* Biographical narratives also use transitions that introduce anecdotes about their subjects. In the model, these include *When* (lines 31 and 33), *for example* (line 38), and *Then there were* (line 44).

Help students find transitions in the model. Then use the transitions as sentence starters, asking students to complete sentences about themselves or people they know.

To provide English learners with additional writing support, see

RESOURCE MANAGER—Copy Master
Writing Support p. 184

Part 2: Apply the Writing Process

PREWRITING

What Should I Do?

1. Analyze the prompt.
Choose one of the prompts on page 598 and read it at least twice. Circle the phrase that tells you the kind of writing you will be doing. Underline phrases that tell you what you must include. Also, think about your audience. Will you be writing just for your teacher or for your classmates as well?

2. Choose your subject.
Brainstorm a list of people who would be interesting to write about. Put an asterisk by the person you choose.

3. Describe the person.
How does (or did) he or she look, behave, speak, and interact with others? Which characteristics make the person so special? List those traits. Decide on a **dominant impression**—the main opinion or idea you want your reader to learn about this person.

TIP If you have selected Prompt 2, you will need to research the person you have chosen.

4. Gather typical anecdotes and incidents.
Think of stories about the person that support the dominant impression you want to convey. Use a graphic organizer to record specific sensory details.

TIP Choose stories and details that reveal something significant about your subject.

What Does It Look Like?

> **WRITING PROMPT** Write a (biographical) (narrative about a person who you believe is) (important or influential.) Include anecdotes and details to help your reader visualize the person clearly. Make sure your reader understands why the person is important to you.

Once I choose my subject, I should think about what my teacher and my classmates already know about him or her.

> *Grandma Freddi—taught me to be less judgmental*
> **Mr. Moore—respected me, made class fun*
> *Ed—my best friend for three years, helped me when I was in a car accident*

> *Mr. Moore's traits*
> - *absent-minded*
> - *does things his own way*
> - *really cares about students*
> - *helps us learn who we are*
>
> *Dominant impression: unusual but talented teacher*

WRITING WORKSHOP **601**

FOR DEVELOPING WRITERS

Describe the Person Tell students to list traits in these categories:

- how the person looks (including clothing)
- memorable comments the person said
- other people's thoughts about the person
- why the person is important or influential
- who or what the person influenced

FOR ENGLISH LEARNERS

Gather Anecdotes and Incidents Clarify the graphic organizer by pointing out that the center circle boldface text identifies the incident, and the outer circles describe details. Have students fill in their center circles in English if possible, but allowably in their home languages. Then ask students guiding questions to elicit details for the outer circles.

Practice and Apply

To support students during the writing process, use these copy masters:

R RESOURCE MANAGER—Copy Masters
  Prewriting–Editing pp. 177–181
  Writing Rubric p. 182
  Writing Support p. 184 (for English learners)

Part 2: Apply the Writing Process

PREWRITING

1. Analyze the prompt. To help students consider audience, have them use a Venn Diagram to examine the similarities and differences in knowledge and interests between teachers and classmates.

BEST PRACTICES TOOLKIT—Transparency
  Venn Diagram p. A26

2. Choose your subject. After students brainstorm, have them rank the names by importance or influence. Suggest that students choose subjects who rank high.

3. Describe the person. Have students read the **TIP** and Prompt 2. Discuss appropriate research sources. Then have students use the Reporter's Questions to gather facts about their chosen person. Have students use their responses to craft a dominant impression.

BEST PRACTICES TOOLKIT—Transparency
  Reporter's Questions p. C9

4. Gather typical anecdotes and incidents. Recommend that students use separate organizers for each anecdote. For example, the student writer might have also completed a second organizer labeled "Visit to Hospital." Students can then arrange their organizers in an appropriate order to begin to organize their narratives. Discuss the **TIP** and how each anecdote in the model adds to the portrait of Mr. Moore.

For interactive graphic organizers, see

  WriteSmart CD

  Writing Center at ClassZone.com

DRAFTING

1. **Plan your narrative.** Some students may find it helpful to draw sketches of their subjects in order to clarify and define their impressions. If students choose this technique, have them add written captions explaining details.

2. **Craft an intriguing introduction.** Have students use the Opening Lines strategy to help them plan introductory hooks. Suggest that students consider beginning with an anecdote about the person, or with a quotation that illustrates the person's character. Then have them read the **TIP** and use the Cliché Array strategy to avoid clichés in their writing. Suggest that they replace vague statements such as "She was the greatest athlete I've ever known" with specific, informative statements, such as "She was the captain of the softball, volleyball, and swim teams."

    BEST PRACTICES TOOLKIT
   Opening Lines p. C1
   Cliché Array p. C4

3. **End forcefully.** To help students understand the suggested strategies, ask why ending with a quotation or a thoughtful question creates forceful conclusions. *Possible answer: The strategies reinforce the dominant impression and give the reader something to think about.* Recommend that students write down their subject's single most memorable comment and the biggest question that he or she raises for the student.

For a biographical narrative writing template, see

 BEST PRACTICES TOOLKIT—Transparency
Writing Template: Biographical Narrative pp. C16, C19

⊘ Write*Smart* CD

ⓘ Writing Center at **ClassZone.com**

DRAFTING

What Should I Do?		What Does It Look Like?	

1. Plan your narrative.
Decide which points you want to make about your subject to convey a dominant impression of him or her. Make a chart of those points and the details or anecdotes that support them.

▶

Characteristic	Supporting Details
absent-mindedness	leaving car at side of road
being his own person	wearing suit and tie "to be suitable"
caring about students	arranging for tutoring, visiting student in hospital
helping us know ourselves	involving us in subject matter (visions-of-future assignment)

2. Craft an intriguing introduction.
Begin with a few well-chosen details or with an anecdote. Your goal is to "hook" your reader and give clues about your subject's values or personality.

TIP As you draft, avoid **clichés** (overused expressions). See page 604 for a list of clichés and suggestions for original alternatives.

▶

Intriguing details
The first time I saw him, he was running down the hall with one end of his tie over his shoulder, his arms overflowing with books and notes, leaving papers fluttering to the floor behind him.

A relevant anecdote
I'll never forget the time the announcement came over the loudspeaker: "Anyone knowing about a car abandoned by the side of the road a few blocks from the school should contact the office. . . ."

3. End forcefully.
Make sure your conclusion reinforces the dominant impression and leaves readers with something to think about. You might include a memorable quotation or question.

TIP Before revising, consult the **key traits** on page 598 and the **criteria** and **peer-reader questions** on page 604.

▶

A quotation
"The ability to learn is a gift," Mr. Moore used to tell us. That gift will always be with me.

A thoughtful question
He's already so much more than a teacher to me; I'm sure he will be a lifelong mentor. What more can a teacher do for his or her students?

DIFFERENTIATED INSTRUCTION

FOR ENGLISH LEARNERS
Craft an Introduction Write these sentence starters on the board to help students build an introduction:

- The first time I ever saw _____, he/she was _____.
- I remember _____ about _____.
- _____ was a person who _____.

FOR ADVANCED LEARNERS/AP
End Forcefully Challenge students to look past the commentary and analysis of their conclusion. Suggest these prompts:

- What factors contributed to the person's character or ability to influence?
- How could others benefit from these same factors?
- What would the world be like without this person?

REVISING AND EDITING

What Should I Do?

1. Include rich sensory details.
- Circle words that refer to sight, smell, touch, taste, or sound.
- If your draft doesn't have many circles, add fresh, inventive sensory details.

2. Delete irrelevant information.
- Underline details, anecdotes, descriptions, and dialogue that describe your subject.
- Review what you underlined, deleting material that doesn't support the dominant impression you want to get across.

3. Add background information.
- Ask a peer reader to point out statements that need more explanation.
- Weave in necessary background information.

See page 604: Ask a Peer Reader

4. Make the significance clear.
- Put [brackets] around passages that explain what makes this person interesting or significant.
- If you don't have many brackets, add details about your subject's importance to you.

What Does It Look Like?

I (watched) him close the door.
He disappeared into Room 203, tie flapping.

We just figured that he had run out of gas and left the car where it was, *had coughed to a stop.*

He knew exactly how to draw students out and encourage us to participate. ~~Once, when he pointed with a piece of chalk at someone who wanted to speak, it flew out of his hand and hit the window.~~ The way he listened carefully and found something valuable in every question made us feel important.

Peer reader's question: What subjects did Mr. Moore teach?
English, Russian, French, American history, world religions, Western civilization—no matter what he taught, He made learning an exciting experience.

[One way we learned who we were was by just watching him be himself.] When the other teachers wore jeans and flannel shirts to class, he dressed in a suit and tie, "to be suitable," he punned. Because he was comfortable with who he was, it didn't matter to him that he looked somewhat out of place.

All his exams were open-book, and we could bring along whatever additional materials we wanted. That's because he wasn't as interested in getting answers as he was in getting us to ask our own questions and come up with new ideas.

WRITING WORKSHOP **603**

REVISING AND EDITING

1. Include rich sensory details. Urge students to include details that appeal to at least three of the five senses. Suggest that they complete a chart listing possible details by sense. Not all five senses need be used. Sight is the sense most often described, with hearing second.

BEST PRACTICES TOOLKIT—Transparency
Three-Column Journal p. B10

2. Delete irrelevant information. Tell students that in addition to deleting passages that do not support the dominant impression, they should also delete passages that seem redundant, confusing, or slow.

3. Add background information. Remind students to keep their audience in mind in deciding how much and what type of background information to include. They should ask and answer the question, What does my audience already know about my subject? Reader knowledge may vary by age, interest, education, and occupation.

4. Make the significance clear. Have students scan the model for passages that make Mr. Moore's significance clear (lines 11–13, 27–31, 51–55). Guide students to see that the writer interweaves those passages with narrative or description that supports the significance.

For interactive revision tools, see

WriteSmart CD

Writing Center at **ClassZone.com**

FOR DEVELOPING WRITERS

Clarify Significance Explain that significance comes from the writer's commentary, not just from anecdotes and details. Have students use the Color Coding strategy to ensure a sufficient proportion of commentary in their narratives.

 BEST PRACTICES TOOLKIT—Transparency
Color Coding p. C12

FOR ENGLISH LEARNERS

Language: Skill Words Write these terms on the board and review them with students:

- *delete,* take out—for example, you should delete boring details
- *irrelevant,* not belonging—for example, details not about the subject are irrelevant
- *significance,* importance—for example, the significance of a person's work

Preparing to Publish

Support for meeting the goals in the writing criteria is supplied throughout the Writing Workshop on pages 601–603.

For Rubric Bank, see

 WriteSmart CD

ⓘ Writing Center at ClassZone.com

Assess and Reteach

Ⓢ STANDARDS LESSON FILE

Writing Lesson 16: Writing Conclusions
Writing Lesson 30: Personal Narrative
Writing Lesson 33: Elaborate with Sensory Details
Writing Lesson 35: Elaborate with Incidents, Examples, and Quotations
Grammar Lesson 16: Basic Verb Tenses
Grammar Lesson 17: Mixing Verb Tenses

 LC1.1

Preparing to Publish   Biographical Narrative

Consider the Criteria

Use this checklist to make sure your biographical narrative is on track.

Ideas
☑ clearly identifies the person
☑ creates a dominant impression of the person

Organization
☑ introduces the person so that readers want to know more
☑ adds background information for context and clarity
☑ concludes by summarizing the person's significance

Voice
☑ reveals the writer's attitude toward the person through an appropriate tone

Word Choice
☑ includes detailed descriptions and precise words

Sentence Fluency
☑ includes a variety of sentence beginnings and structures

Conventions
☑ uses correct grammar, spelling, and punctuation

Ask a Peer Reader

- How would you describe this person in your own words?
- What details, if any, do I need to add?
- Why is this person meaningful to me?

Avoid Clichés

Cliché	Creative Alternative
He had his head in the clouds.	He was endearingly absent-minded.
He was a people person.	What mattered most to him wasn't the subject but the students.
He was one in a million.	His respect and trust meant more than any grade I've ever gotten.
I am his number-one fan.	I'm sure he will be a lifelong mentor.

Check Your Grammar

Do not shift verb tenses needlessly. Inconsistent tenses can confuse your reader.

> All his exams were open-book, and we ~~can~~ could bring along whatever additional materials we ~~want~~ wanted.

See pages R59–R60: Verbs

Writing On|ine

 PUBLISHING OPTIONS
For publishing options, visit the **Writing Center** at **ClassZone.com.**

ASSESSMENT PREPARATION
For writing and grammar assessment practice, go to the **Assessment Center** at **ClassZone.com.**

W2.6, LS1.10

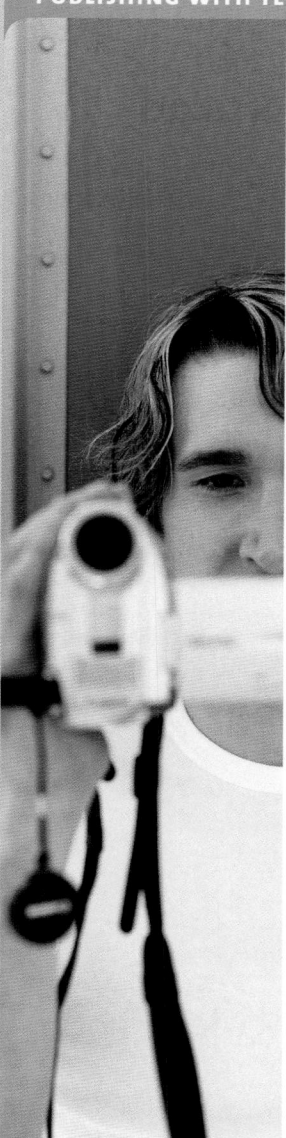

Producing a Video Documentary

Here's your chance to sit in the director's chair. Use your biographical narrative as the basis for a video documentary.

Planning the Documentary

1. **Look for audio and visual materials.** Can you interview the person on tape or video? Find out if he or she has photographs, newspaper clippings, or other visuals that you could use. If you wrote about a historical figure, you might look for an expert to interview about that person.

2. **Create a script.** Using your narrative as a starting point, create a **script** for your documentary. Think about where to use voice-over narration, interview footage, and music. Consider including opening and closing credits.

3. **Develop a storyboard.** Plan what your audience will see and hear shot by shot. Include several types of camera positions, such as **establishing shots** (wide-angle shots that set the scene), **medium shots,** and **close-ups.**

Voice-over A school legend, Mr. Moore has become my most memorable teacher and mentor.

Excerpt from interview "My job is to get students to come up with new ideas and learn to evaluate their own work."

Producing the Documentary

1. **Find out what equipment is available.** Your school may have a camcorder that you can borrow. If you have video editing software, you can record scenes in any order; if not, you will have to film each scene sequentially.

2. **Record the video and the voice-overs.** Follow your script and storyboard carefully.

3. **Pull it together.** Review your footage, reshooting as necessary. When you are satisfied, screen your documentary for neighbors or classmates. Ask for specific feedback so you can make your next documentary even better.

WRITING WORKSHOP **605**

PUBLISHING WITH TECHNOLOGY

Ask students to read this page to get an overview of how to plan and produce a documentary. Students who choose this option should familiarize themselves with the tasks of finding materials and creating a script and a storyboard, and should obtain and learn to operate video equipment.

Before students begin working, review these criteria with them so that they understand their goals:

Criteria A strong documentary

- begins with a clear narrative script
- reflects shot-by-shot planning on a storyboard
- uses techniques such as voice-over narration, interview footage, and music
- may include historical artifacts such as photographs or newspaper clippings
- varies camera positions for interest
- may have opening and closing credits
- is edited for maximum effect

When students show their documentaries, have the audience use the criteria to evaluate the final product.

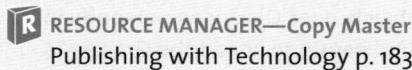 **RESOURCE MANAGER—Copy Master** Publishing with Technology p. 183

STANDARDS LESSON FILE **Media Lesson 20:** Producing a Video

Assessment Practice

CHECK READINESS

Read aloud the paragraph under **ASSESS** and stress to students that this is not the full Unit Test, but a way for them to check their readiness for it. Then have students examine the skills listed under **REVIEW** and look back in the unit or in the **Student Resource Bank** for any skills they need to review.

READ THE SELECTIONS

Remind students to keep unit goals in mind as they read the passages, paying particular attention to these literary and reading skills:

- author's style
  - figurative language
  - irregular capitalization
  - slant rhyme
  - inventive punctuation
  - cataloging
  - parallelism
  - repetition
  - free verse
- tone

To help students focus on author's style while reading, encourage them to ask questions such as:

- What objects does Dickinson personify in "The Wind begun to knead the Grass—"?
- Where does Whitman use repetition in "Patroling Barnegat"?

ANSWER THE QUESTIONS

Direct students to pages R96–R103 of the **Test-Taking Handbook** to review test-taking strategies.

- Remind students not to choose the first alternative that seems to fit when answering a multiple-choice question. Instead, they should read through all the choices, eliminate any that are clearly wrong, and then choose the *best* answer—the one that is most accurate and complete.

- Remind students to review the entire test for an overview of the question types and general focus. Students should then budget their time so as to be able to review the test completely after answering the questions.

ASSESS

The practice test items on the next few pages match skills listed on the Unit Goals page (page 490) and addressed throughout this unit. Taking this practice test will help you assess your knowledge of these skills and determine your readiness for the Unit Test.

REVIEW

After you take the practice test, your teacher can help you identify any skills you need to review.

- Author's Style
  - Figurative Language
  - Irregular Capitalization
  - Slant Rhyme
  - Inventive Punctuation
  - Cataloging
  - Parallelism
  - Repetition
  - Free Verse
- Tone
- Latin Roots and Words
- Context Clues
- Vivid Verbs
- Establish Tone

ASSESSMENT ONLINE
For more assessment practice and test-taking tips, go to the **Assessment Center** at **ClassZone.com.**

Reading Comprehension

DIRECTIONS *Read these poems and answer the questions that follow.*

The Wind begun to knead the Grass—

Emily Dickinson

The Wind begun to knead the Grass—
As Women do a Dough—
He flung a Hand full at the Plain—
A Hand full at the Sky—
5 The Leaves unhooked themselves from Trees—
And started all abroad—
The Dust did scoop itself like Hands—
And throw away the Road—

The Wagons quickened on the Street—
10 The Thunders gossiped low—
The Lightning showed a Yellow Head—
And then a livid Toe—
The Birds put up the Bars to Nests—
The Cattle flung to Barns—
15 Then came one drop of Giant Rain—
And then, as if the Hands
That held the Dams—had parted hold—
The Waters Wrecked the Sky—
But overlooked my Father's House—
20 Just Quartering a Tree—

DIFFERENTIATED INSTRUCTION

FOR ENGLISH LEARNERS
Assessment Practice: Work Backward
Prepare students by having them read the questions *before* reading the passages. Have pairs find unfamiliar words in test directions and questions and follow these steps:

1. Write each word on an index card.
2. Look up the meaning in a dictionary and write it on the back of the card.
3. Use the cards to practice the words with your partner and to teach them to others.

Patroling Barnegat

Walt Whitman

Wild, wild the storm, and the sea high running,
Steady the roar of the gale, with incessant undertone muttering,
Shouts of demoniac laughter fitfully piercing and pealing,
Waves, air, midnight, their savagest trinity lashing,
5 Out in the shadows there milk-white combs careering,
On beachy slush and sand spirts of snow fierce slanting,
Where through the murk the easterly death-wind breasting,
Through cutting swirl and spray watchful and firm advancing,
(That in the distance! is that a wreck? is the red signal flaring?)
10 Slush and sand of the beach tireless till daylight wending,
Steadily, slowly, through hoarse roar never remitting,
Along the midnight edge by those milk-white combs careering,
A group of dim, weird forms, struggling, the night confronting,
That savage trinity warily watching.

 GO ON

ITEM ANALYSIS

COMPREHENSION AND WRITTEN RESPONSE	ITEMS	UNIT PAGES
Author's Style	1, 2, 3, 4, 5, 7, 8, 9, 10, 11, 12, 13, 16, 17	525, 537
Figurative Language	2, 3, 4, 8	525
Irregular Capitalization	7	
Slant Rhyme	5	525
Inventive Punctuation	1	
Cataloging	12	509
Parallelism	10	509
Repetition	9, 13, 16	509, 569
Free Verse	11	509
Tone	6, 14, 15	509, 537

VOCABULARY	ITEMS	UNIT PAGES
Latin Roots and Words	1, 2, 3,	594
Context Clues	4, 5, 6	

WRITING AND GRAMMAR	ITEMS	UNIT PAGES
Vivid Verbs	2, 3, 5	549
Establish Tone	1, 4, 6	509

FOR STRATEGIC READERS

Assessment Support Consider these options for completing the Assessment Practice:

- Have students "work backward" to review the test questions *before* reading the passages.

- Select random questions in the Assessment, and have students demonstrate *how* and *where* to look for the answers.

- Ask students to locate unfamiliar vocabulary words in the Assessment. Elicit the words' meanings from the class.

- Have students record useful testing words and definitions in their journals for later reference.

- Read the selections or parts of them aloud to aid in student comprehension.

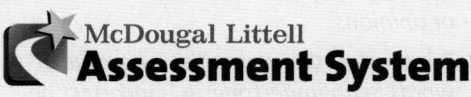

McDougal Littell
Assessment System

After checking student readiness with this Assessment Practice, you may administer the complete Unit 3 Test in order to more thoroughly evaluate student mastery of unit goals.

Comprehension

Model a thinking process for answering multiple-choice questions.

1. **C is correct.** *The dashes create pauses, which in turn affect the poem's rhythm. A is incorrect because the dashes do not de-emphasize any words. B is incorrect because dashes do not show figurative language. D is incorrect because the dashes do not end sentences or always precede rhyming words.*

2. **D is correct.** *Kneading dough requires strength. A is incorrect by implication as the opposite of D. B is incorrect because the poem's mention of baking is not literal. C is incorrect because kneading implies nothing about direction.*

3. **B is correct.** *All the comparisons are intended to help describe the storm. A, C, and D are all incorrect because they are part of the comparisons, not themselves the subjects of description.*

4. **C is correct.** *Flinging (line 3), unhooking (line 5), and scooping (line 7) are all powerful actions. A, B, and D all connote gentleness and thus are inappropriate for a storm.*

5. **B is correct.** *The slant rhyme of* abroad *and* road *suggests hasty, confused travel. A and C are incorrect because the wagons and travelers are only figurative, not literal. D is incorrect because the leaves and dust imply similar, not contrasting, images.*

6. **C is correct.** *The speaker enjoys the storm. A and B are incorrect by implication as opposite to C. D is incorrect because optimism and confidence do not suggest the excitement of a storm.*

7. **A is correct.** *Capitalization makes a word seem important. B is incorrect because rain plays a minor part in the description. C and D are incorrect because the capitalized words, mostly nouns, do not show emotions or opinions.*

8. **B is correct.** *Gossip implies a barrage of words in an undertone. A is incorrect because gossip is not usually openly displayed. C is incorrect because gossip is meaningful. D is incorrect because gossip may be mean, but isn't usually frightening.*

Comprehension

DIRECTIONS *Answer these questions about "The Wind begun to knead the Grass—."*

1. What effect do the dashes have on your reading and understanding of the poem?
   A They tell you to read some words without emphasis because they are less important to the poem's meaning.
   B They show where similes and metaphors occur and help convey their meaning.
   C They help establish the poem's rhythm and indicate a pause after each description.
   D They call attention to rhyming words and mark the end of sentences within the poem.

2. What does the simile in lines 1–2 suggest about the wind?
   A The wind is gently ruffling the grass.
   B A windy day is a good day for baking.
   C The direction of the wind is inconsistent.
   D The wind is strong as it pushes against the grass.

3. Dickinson uses similes and personification to describe different aspects of
   A someone's personality
   B a thunderstorm
   C a dam breaking
   D small-town life

4. The personification of the wind, the leaves, and the dust conveys a sense of
   A natural order
   B gentle guidance
   C unpredictable power
   D domestic happiness

5. The slant rhyme of *abroad* and *road* in lines 6 and 8 draws attention to the
   A wagons hurrying on the road
   B chaotic unruliness of the wind
   C travelers caught by the weather
   D contrast of the leaves against the dust

6. Which words best describe the speaker's tone in lines 1–18?
   A fearful and serious
   B gloomy and somber
   C exhilarated and playful
   D optimistic and confident

7. Dickinson most likely uses irregularly capitalized words in this poem to emphasize
   A key words that tell the story
   B the rhythm of the rain
   C her opinion of the events
   D emotions conveyed in the poem

8. Dickinson personifies the "Thunders" in line 10 as people who gossip to call attention to thunder's
   A dramatic display
   B sinister rumbling
   C meaningless noise
   D frightening power

DIRECTIONS *Answer these questions about "Patroling Barnegat."*

9. Which poetic devices does Whitman use in line 1 to make a dramatic exclamation?
   A cataloging and parallelism
   B simile and personification
   C repetition and inverted word order
   D slant rhymes and inventive punctuation

9. **C is correct.** *"Wild, wild" is repetition; "wild the storm" and "high running" are inverted word order. None of the devices listed in A, B, or D are present.*

10. By ending each line with a participle, Whitman is using

    A imagery to convey an idea

    B parallelism to create rhythm

    C details to communicate tone

    D personification to describe an object

11. Whitman uses the irregular meter of free verse to

    A convey the wildness of the storm

    B present a contrast with the subject

    C suggest daily life near the sea

    D establish movement in the poem

12. The effect of Whitman's catalog of sights and sounds on the beach is to

    A build tension

    B emphasize ideas

    C honor people

    D celebrate everyday diction

13. What effect does Whitman achieve by repeating the word *through* in lines 7–11?

    A He interrupts the chronological order of events.

    B He mimics the sound of the wind blowing across the beach.

    C He emphasizes the relentlessness of the darkness, the waves, and the wind.

    D He focuses attention on how a storm damages the surrounding area.

14. Which word best describes the tone Whitman creates in lines 1–8?

    A tragic   C triumphant

    B hysterical   D suspenseful

DIRECTIONS *Answer this question about both poems.*

15. Which statement best contrasts the tone at the end of the two poems?

    A The Dickinson poem is factual; the Whitman poem is reflective.

    B The Dickinson poem is sad; the Whitman poem is exuberant.

    C The Dickinson poem is peaceful; the Whitman poem is frantic.

    D The Dickinson poem is menacing; the Whitman poem is distant.

Written Response

SHORT RESPONSE *Write three or four sentences to answer this question.*

16. Whitman often repeats words and phrases in his poetry. What effect does he achieve in "Patroling Barnegat" by writing the phrases "savagest trinity" in line 4, "savage trinity" in line 14, and "milk-white combs careering" in lines 5 and 12?

EXTENDED RESPONSE *Write two or three paragraphs to answer this question.*

17. Compare Whitman's and Dickinson's writing styles. Which poetic devices does Dickinson use to describe a storm? Which poetic devices does Whitman use?

GO ON ➡

---

10. **B is correct.** Each line ends with the same grammatical structure, and the -ing ending links lines rhythmically. A, C, and D are incorrect because the participle ending does not convey imagery, detail, or personification.

11. **A is correct.** Free verse is untamed by form. B is incorrect because the freedom of the verse does not contrast with the subject. C is incorrect because the poem is not about daily life. D is incorrect because movement can be established in traditional verse, too.

12. **A is correct.** The list of images creates suspense about what will happen. B is incorrect because the images do not imply ideas. C is incorrect because the images are not about people. D is incorrect because the diction is not always everyday.

13. **C is correct.** Repeating *through* implies the storm's powerful force by showing what it can move through. A is incorrect because the lines do not address chronology. B is incorrect because while the sound of *through* may mimic wind, the repetition also addresses darkness and waves. D is incorrect because *through* does not describe damage.

14. **D is correct.** Lines 1–8 set up suspense and build the possibility of imminent danger. A is incorrect because no specific loss is shown. B is incorrect because Whitman does not show the storm as out of control. C is incorrect because the lines do not show triumph.

15. **A is correct.** Dickinson's poem ends with a simple description of the storm's limited damage. Whitman's poem ends by observing a watchful pause in the movement. In B, C, and D, none of the descriptions of tone are valid.

Written Response

Possible short answer:

16. Through repetitions Whitman achieves an effect of emphasizing the power and turbulence of the storm.

Possible extended answer:

17. The poets' styles contrast in many ways. Dickinson uses regular meter, slant rhyme, irregular capitalization, figurative language, concise diction, and inventive punctuation to describe the storm. Whitman creates drama with cataloging and repetition, and conveys images and meaning with sophisticated language.

DIFFERENTIATED INSTRUCTION

FOR ENGLISH LEARNERS

Assessment Vocabulary To help students understand the Comprehension questions, teach or review these key vocabulary words:

- Item 2: *suggest*, "to show without stating"
- Item 3: *aspects*, "sides; parts"
- Item 5: *draws attention to*, "points out"
- Item 7: *emphasize*, "to make important"
- Item 8: *personifies*, "gives human qualities"
- Item 15: *contrasts*, "shows differences"

ANSWERS

Vocabulary

1. **D is correct.** "Leaden colored" is the nearest of the choices to "blue." A, B, and C are incorrect because none describes a bluish color.

2. **A is correct.** Analysis of the word parts and the context shows that the sound does not stop. B and C are incorrect because they negate the meaning of the prefix in–. D is incorrect because the context describes sound that has not stopped.

3. **A is correct.** Of the choices, "letting up" is closest in meaning to "send back" and best describes an abating storm. B is incorrect because a storm, once begun, does not wait. C and D are incorrect because they describe human actions, not meteorological ones.

4. **C is correct.** In the context, the storm has split a tree. The other choices are incorrect because storms do not locate, measure, or make trees visible.

5. **B is correct.** Shouts of piercing laughter could be described as fiendish. A is incorrect because laugher that pierces and peals would not be considered thunderous. C is incorrect because the storm is described seriously, not comically. D is incorrect because sincerity is irrelevant to the sound of a storm.

6. **C is correct.** The waves move quickly. They rush. A is incorrect because the description emphasizes rapid motion, not sound. B is incorrect because growth is not relevant to the description of waves. D is incorrect because the waves are not described as falling.

Vocabulary

DIRECTIONS *Use context clues and the Latin word and root definitions to answer the following questions about words in the two poems.*

1. The Latin word *livere* means "to be bluish." The most likely meaning of the word *livid* as it is used line 12 of "The Wind begun to knead the Grass—" is
   A extremely furious
   B very pale
   C in a state of shock
   D leaden colored

2. The Latin prefix *in-* means "not" and the Latin word *cessare* means "to stop." The most likely meaning of the word *incessant* as it is used in line 2 of "Patroling Barnegat" is
   A continuing without interruption
   B concluding a recent action
   C pausing periodically
   D resuming activity

3. The word *remit* comes from the Latin prefix *re-*, which means "backward," and the Latin word *mittere*, which means "to send." The most likely meaning of the word *remitting* as it is used in line 11 of "Patroling Barnegat" is
   A letting up
   B waiting
   C forgiving
   D restoring

DIRECTIONS *Use context clues to answer the following questions about words in the two poems.*

4. The most likely meaning of the word *quartering* as it is used in line 20 of "The Wind begun to knead the Grass—" is
   A. locating
   B. measuring
   C. splitting into parts
   D. making visible

5. What is the most likely meaning of *demoniac* as it is used in line 3 of "Patroling Barnegat"?
   A. thunderous
   B. fiendish
   C comical
   D sincere

6. What is the most likely meaning of the word *careering* as it is used in lines 5 and 12 of "Patroling Barnegat"?
   A pounding
   B growing
   C rushing
   D falling

610

DIFFERENTIATED INSTRUCTION

FOR ENGLISH LEARNERS

Review Academic Vocabulary On the board, list the academic vocabulary shown in italics. Then give the examples and have students match each to the correct term. Elicit additional examples from students.

- *free verse:* "Patroling Barnegat" does not contain rhyme or meter.

- *style:* Dickinson uses personification throughout "The Wind begun to knead the Grass—".

Writing & Grammar

DIRECTIONS *Read this passage and answer the questions that follow.*

(1) With a weight of 13,632 tons and a length of 729 feet, the *Edmund Fitzgerald* was the largest carrier on the Great Lakes when it first sailed in 1958. (2) <u>Seventeen years later, the ship</u> would sink in Lake Superior. (3) At 2:20 P.M. on November 9th, 1975, the *Fitzgerald* departed Superior, Wisconsin, destined for Detroit. (4) Shortly afterwards, the National Weather Service issued gale warnings for the area. (5) The next day, winds gusting up to 70 knots and waves cresting as high as 30 feet <u>shook</u> the ship. (6) Water <u>came</u> onto the deck. (7) At approximately 7:15 that evening, the ship vanished from radar observation, and <u>all 29 crew members were lost.</u> (8) It was later discovered that the ship had <u>dropped</u> about 530 feet to the bottom of Lake Superior. (9) <u>That day</u> of November 10, 1975, will always be remembered.

1. Choose the best way to rewrite the underlined portion of sentence 2 to convey a more somber tone.
   A Seventeen years later, the hefty ship
   B Seventeen short years later, the ship
   C Seventeen productive years later, the ship
   D Seventeen years later, the doomed ship

2. Choose the best example of a vivid verb to replace the underlined word in sentence 5.
   A pushed   **C** propelled
   B stirred   **D** battered

3. Choose the best example of a vivid verb to replace the underlined word in sentence 6.
   A splashed   **C** crashed
   B washed   **D** seeped

4. Choose the best way to rewrite the underlined portion of sentence 7 to convey a more somber tone.
   A all 29 crew members were tragically lost.
   B all 29 crew members were unfortunately lost.
   C all 29 crew members were suddenly lost.
   D all 29 crew members were definitely lost.

5. Choose the best example of a vivid verb to replace the underlined word in sentence 8.
   A fallen   **C** sunk
   B plunged   **D** floated

6. Choose the best way to rewrite the underlined portion of sentence 9 to convey a more somber tone.
   A That unexpected day
   B That memorable day
   C That fateful day
   D That historic day

STOP

FOR STRATEGIC READERS
Assessment Support: Vivid Verbs and Establishing Tone

- Review with students that vivid verbs enhance reader interest by making descriptions clearer in the mind's eye.
- Ask students to find examples of vivid verbs in "The Wind begun to knead the Grass—" and "Patroling Barnegat."
- Remind students that writers establish tone through word choices. Use of adjectives and adverbs is often an important element of establishing tone, as shown in Questions 1, 4, and 6.
- Ask students to find words that help establish tone in "The Wind begun to knead the Grass—" and "Patroling Barnegat."

INTRODUCE *GREAT READS*

In Unit 3, students have discussed a number of big questions. Invite students to tell which question they found most intriguing and why, and then focus attention on the four that appear on pages 612–613. Discuss the recommended books and their summaries, pointing out how each connects to the related question. Encourage students to choose one or more of these "great reads" to read independently.

ⓘ ClassZone.com

To find additional books that match students' interests and ability levels, visit the Literature Center at **ClassZone.com**.

Ideas for Independent Reading

Continue exploring the Questions of the Times on pages 492–493 with these additional works.

What DIVIDES *a nation?*

Classic Slave Narratives
edited by Henry Louis Gates Jr.

This collection of classic slave narratives provides testimony to the horrors of bondage and sheds light on the American slave experience. The volume contains two of the best-known examples of "literature of escape"—the stories of Frederick Douglass and Olaudah Equiano—as well as two narratives by women—Harriet Jacobs and Mary Prince.

Battle Cry of Freedom
by James M. McPherson

This history of the Civil War brings all aspects of the conflict to vivid life, from the momentous episodes that preceded the war, to the battles, politics, and personalities of the war itself. James McPherson provides readers with the framework they need to understand the complex economic, political, and social forces that divided the nation and led the country to war.

Journal of a Residence on a Georgian Plantation in 1838–1839
by Frances Anne Kemble

After her marriage, Fanny Kemble discovered the source of her wealthy husband's income: rice plantations that depended upon the labor of more than 600 slaves. This journal, published after her divorce, describes the appalling conditions Fanny found on one of the plantations and her attempts to improve life for the slaves there.

Is anything worth DYING FOR?

The Personal Memoirs of Ulysses S. Grant
by Ulysses S. Grant

Dying of throat cancer, Ulysses S. Grant spent his last days looking back upon the most important years of his life—the years he spent as the commander of the Union army in the Civil War. Here, in what Mark Twain called "the best [memoirs] of any general's since Caesar," Grant recalls how he managed to defeat Robert E. Lee and the Confederate army.

Co. Aytch: A Confederate Memoir of the Civil War
by Sam R. Watkins

Sam Watkins was 21 years old when the Civil War broke out. A native of Columbia, Tennessee, he didn't want to miss out on the "big show." Volunteering as a private, he served in Company H of the Maury Grays, First Tennessee Regiment. From that lowly position, Watkins fought in almost every major clash, from the battle of Shiloh to the battle of Nashville.

Lincoln
by David Herbert Donald

Pulitzer Prize–winning author David Donald tells the story of Abraham Lincoln, the man who managed to hold together a nation of vastly differing regional interests during the turmoil and tragedy of the Civil War. Donald's Lincoln emerges as ambitious yet fallible, with a remarkable capacity for growth— a man who spent his whole life learning and growing to eventually become one of our nation's greatest presidents.

612

Why do people BREAK RULES?

Leaves of Grass
by Walt Whitman

Walt Whitman created a daring new kind of poetry that would become a major force in the world of literature. Whitman first published this volume himself, in 1855, with only 12 poems. He expanded and revised the book over the course of his life as his experiences and the nation's history changed and grew.

Letters of Emily Dickinson
by Emily Dickinson

Emily Dickinson's ingenuity, sensitivity, and wit course through her letters as well as her poetry. Compiled by a close friend, Dickinson's letters were first published in 1894, eight years after her death. Although she became increasingly reclusive and rarely saw her friends in her later years, this volume of letters shows that she thought of them often and affectionately.

Daisy Miller
by Henry James

In this short novel, a wealthy young woman named Daisy Miller takes the grand tour of Europe. In the 19th century, such a long trip was a rite of passage for well-to-do young Americans. In Rome, Daisy's friendship with an Italian man, though innocent, causes her to be shunned by her peers. Yet she refuses to change her carefree ways. By disregarding the social rules of her community, Daisy sets herself up for tragedy.

Is it important to FACE REALITY?

Shiloh: A Novel
by Shelby Foote

This modern novel gives readers an up-close impression of the battle of Shiloh from the perspectives of many different soldiers who fought in it. Each chapter consists of the first-person accounts of various narrators, Union and Confederate, telling of what transpires in their own little corner of the battle.

Ambrose Bierce's Civil War
by Ambrose Bierce, edited by William McCann

Ambrose Bierce is one of the few writers of his day who actually fought in the Civil War. As a result, his gritty depictions of battle and close observation of soldiers' daily lives have the ring of authenticity. This collection includes both personal memoirs and fictional accounts of the war.

Life in the Iron Mills
by Rebecca Harding Davis

Decades before most Americans took notice, Rebecca Harding Davis unveiled the human costs of industrialism in *Life in the Iron Mills*. She concentrated on the stunted lives of factory workers, showing the dirty hovels where they lived, their unwholesome food, their constant labor, and their lack of education. Her story was one of the first works of American fiction to acknowledge such realities. Yet Davis also looked beyond social conditions to explore her characters' hidden yearnings for artistic expression and lasting love.

613

Preview Unit Goals

This page presents an overview of the skills and strategies covered in this unit. Explain to students that they can get more from their reading by previewing. Then ask them to skim the page to preview the skills that they will learn. Note that each strand or category of skill is color-coded on this page and throughout the unit.

Model the strategy of copying the Academic Vocabulary and writing a preliminary definition for each term. Suggest that students use a journal or a notebook for this purpose. Encourage them to use the terms in discussions and in writing. Also urge students to revisit each term throughout the unit and to refine its meaning.

ADDITIONAL UNIT GOALS

These skills will be taught in this unit but are not the major focus of the unit:

Literary Analysis
- Analyze characteristics of an autobiography, a memoir, a short story, a tall tale, and a newspaper article
- Make judgments about a tall tale
- Evaluate the role of dialect in a story
- Analyze social context
- Analyze voice, including tone
- Analyze first-person narrator

Reading
- Predict
- Paraphrase
- Clarify meaning
- Outline text using text features

Writing and Grammar
- Create realistic characters
- Add descriptive details
- Use effective voice and verb tense
- Synthesize or compare information
- Use coordinating conjunctions
- Use personification
- Use present tense effectively

Speaking, Listening, and Viewing
- Role play a conversation

Vocabulary
- Identify homographs
- Use context clues
- Understand specialized vocabulary
- Research word origins

Included in this unit: R1.2, R2.5, R3.1, R3.2, R3.3, R3.5, R3.8, W1.1, W1.2, W1.3, W1.5, W1.9, W2.2, LC1.1, LS1.1, LS1.2, LS1.3, LS1.10, LS1.14, LS2.4

Preview Unit Goals

LITERARY ANALYSIS	• Analyze descriptive language, including imagery, figurative language, repetition, and diction • Understand regionalism and naturalism as literary movements • Analyze characteristics of regionalism and naturalism • Identify and analyze literary elements, including setting, plot, conflict, theme, and tone • Analyze irony
READING	• Make inferences and draw conclusions about characters • Analyze author's perspective • Analyze primary sources • Analyze how an author's choice of genre affects the expression of a theme or topic
WRITING AND GRAMMAR	• Write a literary analysis paper • Use gerunds and gerund phrases • Use passive and active voice effectively
SPEAKING, LISTENING, AND VIEWING	• Interpret and evaluate messages in photography and fine art • Create a visual representation • Create a power presentation
VOCABULARY	• Use knowledge of Latin roots to understand word meaning • Discriminate between connotative and denotative meanings of words • Read and understand analogies
ACADEMIC VOCABULARY	• regionalism • analogy • irony • naturalism • descriptive language • author's perspective

 Online LITERATURE CLASSZONE.COM

Literature and Reading Center
Writing Center
Vocabulary Center

614

DIFFERENTIATED INSTRUCTION

FOR ENGLISH LEARNERS

Academic Vocabulary Use the copy master to help students learn the Academic Vocabulary.

1. Read aloud each Academic Vocabulary term and have students locate it on their copy masters.

2. Discuss the meaning or example shown on the copy master, and complete the chart as a class.

3. Have students work in small groups to complete the remaining activities.

Additional Academic Vocabulary Use the copy master to help students learn academic words they will use in subsequent lessons and on the Assessment Practice. Follow the same procedure as for the Academic Vocabulary copy master.

 RESOURCE MANAGER—Copy Masters
Academic Vocabulary p. 11
Additional Academic Vocabulary p. 12

Regionalism and Naturalism

Willa Cather

1870–1910

CAPTURING THE AMERICAN LANDSCAPE

- Regionalism and Local Color Writing
- A New Role for Women
- The Rise of Naturalism

615

For help in planning this unit, see

R RESOURCE MANAGER UNIT 4
pp. 1–13

INTRODUCE THE UNIT

Call students' attention to the pictures on this page. Explain that the large picture, *The Jolly Flatboatmen*, is an oil painting by American artist George Caleb Bingham. Point out that it captures a distinctive way of life in one part of America—much as many of the writers in this unit have attempted to do in their writing.

Ask students if they have heard of Willa Cather (1873–1947), the author shown in the smaller picture. Explain that Cather was a novelist and short-story writer whose work was greatly influenced by her childhood on the Nebraska prairie. Tell students that they will read one of Cather's short stories in this unit. Also note that students can read more about Cather on page 692.

About the Art American artist George Caleb Bingham (1811–1879) painted *The Jolly Flatboatmen* in 1877–1878. Bingham's views of everyday life in the West often included scenes of the Missouri River. Explain to students that a *flatboat* is a boat with a flat bottom and square ends, used to transport freight. Ironically, by the time Bingham painted this work, steamboats and America's ever-growing railroad system had largely replaced flatboats, and the colorful flatboatmen quickly were becoming a memory.

Unit Resources

PRINT RESOURCES

R RESOURCE MANAGER UNIT 4

B BEST PRACTICES TOOLKIT

S STANDARDS LESSON FILE

CALIFORNIA ASSESSMENT FILE

GRAMMAR FOR WRITING

TECH RESOURCES

- EasyPlanner DVD-ROM
- Write*Smart* CD-ROM
- ClassZone.com
- Audio Anthology CD
- Multi-Language Academic Vocabulary Online

- eEdition DVD-ROM & Online
- McDougal Littell Assessment System
- Test Generator CD-ROM
- Media*Smart* DVD-ROM
- Literature in Context DVD-ROM

UNIT 4
Standards

	Unit 4 Introduction pp. 616–631 • Questions of the Times • Historical Essay • Timeline • Legacy of Regionalism and Naturalism	**Literary Analysis Workshops** • Setting in Regional Literature pp. 632–633 • Social Themes in Fiction pp. 756–757	from **The Autobiography of Mark Twain** Autobiography pp. 634–648	from **Life on the Mississippi** Memoir pp. 649–658
			Lexile: 1120 *Fry: College* *Dale-Chall: 7.1*	*Lexile: 1120* *Fry: 9* *Dale-Chall: 6.5*
Literary Analysis	Historical and Cultural Context of Regionalism and Naturalism pp. 618–629 R3.5	Regionalism as a Literary Movement p. 632 R3.5 — Characteristics of Regionalism pp. 632–633 R3.3, R3.5 — Setting in Regional Writing pp. 632–633 R3.3, R3.5 — Social Themes pp. 756–757 R3.2, R3.5	Irony pp. 635, 638, 641, 642, 645, 647 R3.3	Voice pp. 649, 652, 654, 656, 658 R3.3
Reading and Informational Texts	Build Context for Reading pp. 616–617 — Use Prior Knowledge pp. 616–617 — Connect pp. 616–617, 628–629, 630–631 — Take Notes pp. 619–627 — Read a Timeline pp. 628–629	Analyze the Literature pp. 633, 757	Predict pp. 635, 636, 640, 642, 644, 647 — Read Epigrams p. 646	Paraphrase pp. 649, 652, 653, 657, 658
Vocabulary		Academic Vocabulary pp. 632, 756	Word Acquisition pp. 635, T635, 648 — Context Clues p. T635 — Homographs p. 648	
Writing, Grammar, and Style				
Speaking, Listening, Viewing, and Media	Discuss pp. 616–627, T628–T629, 630–631 — Impressionism as a Style in Art p. 627 — Analyze Visuals p. 620	Discuss pp. T632–T633, T756–T757	Discuss pp. T634, 635, T636–T645, T646, 647 — Analyze Visuals p. 636	Discuss pp. T648, 649, T650–T657, 658 — Analyze Visuals pp. 650, T655

The Notorious Jumping Frog of Calaveras County Short Story pp. 659–669	The Outcasts of Poker Flat Themes Across Time: from Lake Wobegon Days Short Story/Novel pp. 672–687, 688–691	A Wagner Matinee Short Story pp. 692–704	Media Study: American Landscapes Image Collection pp. 706–709
Lexile: 1620 Fry: College Dale-Chall: 7.5	Lexile: 1170 Fry: 11 Dale-Chall: 7.8	Lexile: 1470 Fry: College Dale-Chall: 7.6	
Tall Tale pp. 659, 662, 664, 665 R3.1, R3.3	Regionalism pp. 673, 676, 677, 680, 682, 685 R3.5	Setting pp. 693, 694, 697, 699, 702, 703	
Understand Dialect pp. 659, 663, 664, 667 R3.3	Clarify Meaning pp. 673, 674, 676, 679, 680, 683, 684, 685 Read a Novel Excerpt pp. 688–691	Draw Conclusions pp. 693, 697, 698, 700, 701, 703	
Word Acquisition pp. 659, T659, 668 Context Clues p. T659 Words with Misleading Prefixes p. 668	Word Acquisition pp. 673, T673, 686 Context Clues p. T673 Latin Roots (equ) p. 686 R1.2	Word Acquisition pp. 693, T693, 704 Context Clues p. T693 Specialized Vocabulary (Music) p. 704	Academic Vocabulary (Photography and Painting) p. 707
Writing Prompt p. 669 W1.2 Coordinating Conjunctions and Punctuation in Dialogue pp. 666, 669 W1.9	Writing Prompt p. 687 W1.1, W1.2 Personification in Descriptions pp. 679, 687 W1.9		
Discuss pp. T658, 659, T660–T666, 667 Analyze Visuals p. 660	Discuss pp. T672, 673, T674–T684, 685 Analyze Visuals p. 674	Discuss pp. T692, 693, T694–T702, 703, T705 Analyze Visuals pp. 694, T701	Discuss pp. 706, 709 Analyze Composition, Perspective, Depth of Field, Texture, and Message in Photography pp. 706–709 LS1.3 Create a Personal Landscape p. 709

	Linked Selections		The Law of Life	The Story of an Hour
	The Open Boat Short Story pp. 710–737	**The Wreck of the Commodore** Newspaper Articles pp. 738–743	**The Law of Life** Short Story pp. 744–754	**The Story of an Hour** Short Story pp. 758–765
	Lexile: 980 Fry: 7 Dale-Chall: 6.3		Lexile: 910 Fry: 9 Dale-Chall: 6.5	Lexile: 970 Fry: 10 Dale-Chall: 6.2
Literary Analysis	Naturalism pp. 711, 714, 716, 717, 719, 721, 725, 727, 728, 730, 732, 733, 735 R3.3		Theme pp. 745, 746, 748, 750, 751, 752, 753 R3.2 Review: Naturalism pp. 749, 753	Plot and Conflict pp. 759, 762, 764
Reading and Informational Texts	Analyze Descriptive Language pp. 711, 712, 714, 715, 720, 725, 729, 730, 735 R3.3	Analyze Primary Sources pp. 738, 739, 740, 741, 742, 743 R3.3, LS1.1, LS1.14 Compare Forms p. 743 R3.3, LS1.1, LS1.14	Analyze Author's Perspective pp. 745, 748, 752, 753 R2.5	Predict pp. 759, 760, 762, 763, 764 R3.3
Vocabulary	Word Acquisition pp. 711, T711, 736 Context Clues p. T711 Greek Prefixes (epi-) p. 736 R1.2		Word Acquisition pp. 745, T745, 754 Context Clues p. T745 Denotation and Connotation p. 754	
Writing, Grammar, and Style	Writing Prompt p. 737 W1.2, W2.2 Gerunds and Gerund Phrases pp. 727, 737 LC1.1			Writing Prompt p. 765 W1.2, W1.5 Active and Passive Voice pp. 762, 765 LC1.1
Speaking, Listening, Viewing, and Media	Discuss pp. T710, 711, T712–T734, 735 Analyze Visuals pp. 712, T718, T724, 731	Discuss pp. 738, T739–T742, 743	Discuss pp. T744, 745, T746–T752, 753, T755 Analyze Visuals pp. 746, T751	Discuss pp. T758, 759, T760–T763, 764 Analyze Visuals p. 760

Standards Designations **R** = Reading **W** = Writing **LC** = Language Conventions **LS** = Listening and Speaking **T** = Teacher's Edition page

The Yellow Wallpaper
Short Story
pp. 766–787
	April Showers
	Short Story
	pp. 790–802
		Wrap-Ups
		• Regionalism & Local Color
		  Writing p. 705
		• The Rise of Naturalism p. 755
		• A New Role for Women
		  p. 803
			Writing Workshop:
			Literary Analysis
			pp. 804–811
				Skills Assessed on the Unit 4 Test:

Lexile: 930 *Fry: 7* *Dale-Chall: 5.8*	*Lexile: 1010* *Fry: 9* *Dale-Chall: 6.8*			**Literary Analysis** • Analyze setting • Analyze plot and conflict • Identify and interpret theme • Analyze tone (diction and repetition) • Identify and analyze characteristics of naturalism
First-Person Narrator pp. 767, 770, 773, 775, 778, 779, 780, 781, 782, 783, 785	Tone pp. 791, 792, 794, 796, 799, 800, 801 R3.3			**Reading and Informational Texts** • Make inferences about characters • Understand social context
Understand Social Context pp. 767, 768, 773, 774, 785 R3.5 Read a Journal Article p. 784	Make Inferences About Characters pp. 791, 794, 795, 801		Analyze a Literary Analysis Paper pp. 805–806, 810	**Vocabulary** • Use knowledge of Latin roots to help determine word meaning • Discriminate between connotative and denotative meanings of words
Word Acquisition pp. 667, T667, 786 Context Clues p. T767 Specialized Vocabulary (Temperament Words) p. 786	Word Acquisition pp. 791, T791, 802 Context Clues p. T791 Latin Roots (*rog*) p. 802 R1.2		Academic Vocabulary p. 810	**Writing, Grammar, and Style** • Write a literary analysis • Use verbs, gerunds, prepositional phrases, and gerund phrases to create effective descriptions
Writing Prompt p. 787 W2.2 Verb Tenses pp. 771, 787 LC1.1		Write to Synthesize p. 705 W2.2 Write to Evaluate p. 755 R2.5, W2.2 Write to Compare p. 803 R3.8, W2.2	Write a Literary Analysis Paper pp. 804–810 W1.9, W2.2 Correct Placement of Modifiers p. 810 LC1.1	• Use passive and active voice effectively • Use present tense verbs effectively • Additional writing and grammar skills
Discuss pp. T766, 767, T768–T784, 785 Analyze Visuals pp. 768, 772, 776, T780	Discuss pp. T790, 791, T792–T800, 801, T803 Analyze Visuals pp. 792, T798	Create a Cartoon to Represent a Region p. 705 Research and Discuss Online Newspaper Coverage p. 755 Role-Play a Conversation Between Characters p. 803	Discuss pp. 804–806 Produce a Power Presentation p. 811 LS2.4	

For additional lesson planning help, see **Easy Planner DVD-ROM.**

CALIFORNIA	ASSESS PRIOR KNOWLEDGE Diagnostic	ONGOING ASSESSMENT Reteaching
BEGINNING OF UNIT		
Unit Opener	Preview Unit Goals, **TE** p. 614	
UNIT LESSONS		
Before every lesson	Big Question activity, **SE** Preteach vocabulary, **TE**	Check Understanding, **TE**
During every lesson		Annotations, **SE** Check Understanding, **TE** Tiered Discussion Prompts, **TE**
After every lesson		Post Reading pages, **SE** Assess and Reteach, **TE** Reading Check, **RM** Selection Tests A and B/C, **AF**
END OF UNIT		
Writing Workshop	Checklist, **SE** p. 810 Rubric for Evaluation, **RM** p. 292	Assess and Reteach, **TE** p. 810
Publishing with Technology	Criteria, **TE** p. 811	For reteaching options, see **TE** p. 811
Assessment	Assessment Practice, **SE** pp. 812–817	Unit Test, **AF** **MLAS**

For systematic instruction of grammar, use *Grammar for Writing*.

Key to Abbreviations:
SE = Student's Edition
TE = Teacher's Edition
RM = Resource Manager
AF = Assessment File
MLAS = McDougal Littell Assessment System

Universal Access

	Strategic Reader	Benchmark	Advanced Learner	English Learner	Students with Disabilities
SE STUDENT'S EDITION					
Vocabulary strategy instruction	✔	✔	✔	✔	✔
Instructional annotations	✔	✔	✔	✔	✔
English/Spanish glossary				✔	
TE TEACHER'S EDITION					
Skill annotation support	✔	✔	✔	✔	✔
Tiered discussion prompts	✔	✔	✔	✔	✔
Differentiated instruction	✔	✔	✔	✔	✔
R RESOURCE MANAGER					
Selection summaries in four languages	✔	✔	✔		✔
Skill copy masters in English and Spanish	✔			✔	
Vocabulary preteaching and support	✔			✔	
Additional leveled selection questions	✔	✔	✔	✔	✔
Question support	✔	✔	✔	✔	✔
Writing support	✔	✔	✔	✔	✔
Extension activities		✔	✔		
AF ASSESSMENT FILE					
Leveled selection and unit tests	✔	✔	✔	✔	✔
S STANDARDS LESSON FILE					
Leveled and reteaching copy masters	✔	✔	✔	✔	✔
BEST PRACTICES TOOLKIT					
Strategy bank	✔	✔	✔	✔	✔
Graphic organizers	✔	✔	✔	✔	✔
TECHNOLOGY					
WriteSmart Rubrics and student models	✔	✔	✔	✔	✔
Audio Anthology CD	✔			✔	✔
CLASSZONE					
Instructional centers	✔	✔	✔		✔
Audio summaries of selections	✔			✔	✔
Multilanguage glossary				✔	

Questions of the Times

Read aloud the questions on pages 616 and 617 and the paragraphs that follow them. Open the discussion of each idea by having students respond to the questions that conclude each paragraph. Use these notes to prompt further exploration of the ideas.

What makes a place
UNIQUE?

Invite students to identify parts of the United States with regional identities today and to name characteristics of the region to which they feel the greatest connection. Urge students to be specific in their responses to the question, considering the concept of uniqueness in terms of geography, history, culture, and other regional characteristics.

Does the universe
CARE?

Challenge students to name some hardships that people faced during the post–Civil War era. Encourage opinions on both sides of the question, but urge students to support their views with thoughtful reasons and examples. Extend the discussion by asking students whether they consider this a universal, timeless question—and, if so, why.

UNIT
4

Questions of the Times

DISCUSS Consider the following questions with your classmates. Then read on to learn how these issues affected people living during this period and how the questions were reflected in the writing of the time.

What makes a place
UNIQUE?

In the post–Civil War years, the United States was growing and changing at such a rapid pace that many Americans felt they were losing their regional identities. People were proud of the things they felt made them unique, and writers responded to this impulse by attempting to record the character of the country's distinct regions. What is it exactly that makes a place unique?

Does the universe
CARE?

Life was quite difficult for many Americans during this period. Native Americans, African Americans, immigrants, factory workers, laborers, and farmers struggled daily against poverty and oppression. To many, it seemed that life was unfair—that despite their efforts, they could not escape their fate. Do you think people can control their destiny, or are they simply victims of circumstance?

616

How are women's ROLES CHANGING?

Women of this era were becoming more educated, politically aware, and ambitious. Yet they were not allowed to vote, and those who stepped outside their homes to become artists, writers, and reformers faced strong disapproval and warnings that such activities were "unnatural" for women. How have women's roles evolved over the years?

Why are there "haves" and "HAVE-NOTS"?

This period was a time of harsh extremes. Industry was controlled by a handful of businesses owned by a few people who became very wealthy. These businesses were supported by countless laborers who worked long hours for low wages in dangerous conditions. Why do some people reap huge benefits while others are locked into hardship? Should the government ensure opportunity for all?

617

How are women's ROLES CHANGING?

Have students explain the importance of being able to vote and comment on the fact that women of this era faced condemnation when they "stepped outside" traditional roles. Urge students to draw upon their knowledge of history and current events as they respond to the questions. Extend the discussion by asking how women's lives have become easier—and harder—since that time, and whether the term *women's roles* is relevant today.

Why are there "haves" and "HAVE-NOTS"?

Prompt students to explain the words *haves* and *have-nots,* both in terms of the discussion in the paragraph and in terms of society today. Encourage reasonable, well-supported comments as students debate the government's role in ensuring "opportunity for all."

Capturing the American Landscape

OBJECTIVES

- understand the historical and cultural context of regionalism and naturalism
- take notes by charting main ideas and details

R3.5

To provide a motivating introduction to this unit and to give students a sense of time and place for the regionalist and naturalist period, see

 Literature in Context DVD

The following essay (pages 618–627) provides students with a historical context for the Unit 4 reading selections. It presents a brief overview of important events occurring during the time period, 1870–1910, and introduces key people, places, and ideas of the times.

To get started, read and discuss the opening paragraph on page 618. Ask students to recall how the Civil War (1861–1865) affected the nation and its people. Discuss reasons why the postwar years were "filled with seemingly limitless possibility" but also were characterized by "hardship and even despair."

About the Art Massachusetts-born artist Childe Hassam (1859–1935), a relative of Nathaniel Hawthorne, captured the essence of a regional celebration in 1890 with *Country Fair, New England.* Adapting the style of French Impressionism, Hassam created vivid oil paintings, pastels, and watercolors of typically American scenes. He painted a variety of city scenes, rural landscapes, seascapes, and portraits, many of them noted for their use of color and light.

Vast, varied, filled with seemingly limitless possibility—that was the United States in the years following the Civil War. Yet, all around them in this land of hope and opportunity, writers saw fellow Americans living lives of hardship and even despair. Regionalism tried to capture the reality of ordinary people's lives; naturalism searched for explanations.

DIFFERENTIATED INSTRUCTION

FOR STRATEGIC READERS
Preteach Academic Vocabulary

- *primary,* "basic or most important"
- *transcontinental,* "extending across a continent"
- *diversity,* "variety, as of people and places"
- *local color,* "having to do with the atmosphere and features of a particular place and its people, as described in writing"
- *hub,* "center of activity; central point"

- *exponentially,* "rapidly and to a great degree"
- *prosperity,* "economic success or well-being"

Use this copy master to help students take notes on the essay, pages 618–627:

 RESOURCE MANAGER—Copy Master
Note Taking p. 16

Regionalism and Naturalism: Historical Context

KEY IDEAS The post–Civil War period saw the nation reunited and transformed. Writers responded by attempting to preserve in their writing the distinct character of America's regions and to come to terms with some of its harsh new realities.

Reconstruction's Failures and Successes

The Civil War left the South in ruins. Its primary labor system, slavery, had been abolished. Freed African Americans lacked money, property, education, and opportunity. Farms, factories, and plantations had been destroyed, and rail lines were unusable. The federal government had to come up with a plan to solve these problems and to readmit the Southern states to the union. That plan was **Reconstruction.**

Reconstruction did not go smoothly. The president and Congress clashed over how to best carry it out. Southern states resisted many of the protections granted to newly freed blacks, while blacks felt that too little was being done to ensure their civil rights and economic independence. However, Reconstruction did succeed in a few significant ways. African Americans gained citizenship and equal protection under the law as well as the right to vote, and all of the Confederate states returned to the Union.

Although Americans were glad to move past the divisiveness of the war years, they regretted losing their regional identities and were unsettled by the many changes taking place in the country. These circumstances influenced writers of the time to begin trying to capture the customs, character, and landscapes of the nation's distinct regions—a type of writing that would come to be called **regionalism.**

A Nation Transformed

In the decades following the Civil War, the country as a whole changed radically. In 1869, the first **transcontinental railroad** was completed. It was an event of huge importance. The railroad brought a flood of new settlers west—so many, in fact, that in 1890 the government announced the closing of the frontier. This westward expansion was yet another influence on writers of the time. It created an appreciation for America's diversity, which was celebrated by **local color writers** such as **Mark Twain** and **Bret Harte.**

The railroad also expanded industry. By 1885, four transcontinental lines had been completed, creating manufacturing hubs in Pittsburgh, Cleveland, Detroit, and Chicago. In turn, cities grew exponentially as more and more people came looking for work. In 1850, Chicago was a small town of 20,000; by 1910, the population was more than 2 million. Yet although new technologies and industrial modernization ensured the nation's prosperity, much of its wealth lay in the hands of only a few.

Country Fair, New England (1890), Childe Hassam. 24 ¼″ × 20 ⅛″.
© Manoogian Collection, Taylor, Michigan.

▶ **TAKING NOTES**

Outlining As you read this introduction, use an outline to record the main ideas about the characteristics and literature of the period. You can use headings, boldfaced terms, and the information in these boxes as starting points. (See page R49 in the **Research Handbook** for more help with outlining.)

I. Historical Context
  A. Reconstruction
    1. Failures
    2. Successes
    3. Effect on writers
  B. Transformed Nation

 **ADDITIONAL BACKGROUND** For more on this period, visit the **Literature Center** at ClassZone.com.

Regionalism and Naturalism: Historical Context

KEY IDEAS This section of the essay (page 619) summarizes the aftermath of the Civil War, focusing on the stress of Reconstruction and the loss of some regional identity. The text also describes the close of the American frontier and the growth of American cities, explaining how both led to new kinds of writing.

TIERED DISCUSSION PROMPTS

Use these prompts to help students understand the ideas in **Reconstruction's Failures and Successes** and **A Nation Transformed:**

Summarize In what ways was Reconstruction successful? *Possible answer: Reconstruction was successful in that during this era, African Americans gained citizenship, legal protection, and voting rights; in addition, all of the Confederate states rejoined the Union.*

Analyze How did the transcontinental railroad transform the United States? *Possible answer: The railroad transformed the United States by bringing many settlers to the West and by encouraging the expansion of industry. The expansion of industry caused cities to grow, as people came from rural areas in search of work.*

Synthesize Reread the final sentence of **A Nation Transformed.** Do you think the same might be said about America today? Why or why not? *Accept all answers that students can support.*

FOR ENGLISH LEARNERS

Set a Purpose After introducing the **KEY IDEAS** on this page, ask students to look for information in this essay about changes in American life. Encourage students to use a Two-Column Chart to make the relationships clear, as in this example:

Before the Civil War	After the Civil War
enslaved blacks throughout South	citizenship for African Americans
Population concentrated in the East and South	flood of new settlers in the West

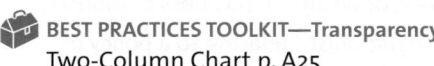 **BEST PRACTICES TOOLKIT—Transparency**
Two-Column Chart p. A25

FOR ADVANCED LEARNERS/AP

Analyze Historical Facts Ask students to use their prior knowledge of the era (from the end of the Civil War to the eve of World War I) to brainstorm a list of "harsh new realities" that Americans writing at the time might have wanted to address. Have students discuss which items on their list proved to be the most historically significant, and why.

Cultural Influences

KEY IDEAS This section of the essay (pages 620–622) emphasizes inequities of "the Gilded Age." At one end of the spectrum, a few men enjoyed wealth and power. At the other end, Native Americans were being forced off their land, African Americans were restricted by Jim Crow laws, immigrants labored in sweatshops, and farmers were losing their farms. The text also explains how naturalism reflected the helplessness that some Americans were feeling.

DISCUSSION PROMPT

Use this prompt to help students understand the ideas in **The Gilded Age:**

Analyze According to the text, why was this period called **The Gilded Age?** *Possible answer: The term captures the idea that the period was known for its "sparkle and glitter, luxury and excess," as evidenced by the mansions and jewels that industrial tycoons like the Rockefellers and Vanderbilts displayed. More money, innovations that encouraged spending, and more leisure time allowed many average Americans to enjoy a wealthier lifestyle than they once had known, as well.*

The Hatch Family (1871), Eastman Johnson. Oil on canvas, 48″ × 73 ⅜″. The Metropolitan Museum of Art, Gift of Frederic H. Hatch, 1926 (26.97. Photo © 1999 The Metropolitan Museum of Art.

ANALYZE VISUALS
What might have been the artist's purpose in rendering the scene in this painting? How would you describe the photographer's purpose for capturing the image on page 621?

Cultural Influences

KEY IDEAS Industry's success created a better life for many Americans. For a few, it brought great wealth, but others suffered poverty and hardship. Both regional and naturalist writers were influenced by these developments.

The Gilded Age

As the 1800s drew to an end, a very small group of men controlled the vast majority of industry, including the enormously profitable steel, railroad, oil, and meatpacking sectors. Captains of industry such as John D. Rockefeller, the oil tycoon, and Cornelius Vanderbilt, the railroad magnate, enjoyed showing off the vast fortunes they had made. They built palatial mansions, draped their wives and daughters in diamonds, and threw extravagant parties (at one, guests were handed silver shovels and invited to dig in a sandbox filled with jewels)—in short, they did everything but actually coat themselves in gold. When writers **Mark Twain** and **Charles Dudley Warner** dubbed this period "the Gilded Age," they did not exaggerate. It was a time of sparkle and glitter, luxury and excess.

Many ordinary people had more money too and all sorts of new things to spend it on. They could take the train to an amusement park and ride the Ferris wheel, then snack on soda and a candy bar. City dwellers could shop in the new department stores, while country folks pored over the mail-order catalog from Sears, Roebuck (known as "the wish book," it offered everything from skin lotion to bicycles, and even an entire house—assembly required).

> **A Voice from the Times**
> *The only way not to think about money is to have a great deal of it.*
>
> —Edith Wharton

DIFFERENTIATED INSTRUCTION

FOR STRATEGIC READERS
Preteach Academic Vocabulary

- *captain of industry,* "an important or powerful person in a particular type of manufacturing"

- *tycoon,* "a wealthy, powerful businessperson"

- *magnate,* "a person of great power, importance, or wealth in business or industry"

- *segregationist,* "relating to a policy of separating people of different races as a form of discrimination"

- *sharecropper,* "a farmer who works land owned by another person in return for a share of the value of the crops"

- *tenement,* "an apartment building that is poorly built or cared for"

- *sweatshop,* "a business that requires employees to work for long hours, at low wages, and under poor conditions"

There were telephones now, thanks to Alexander Graham Bell. In 1908 Henry Ford brought out the first Model T, a "horseless carriage" cheap enough for his own factory workers to buy. Thomas Edison alone patented more than 1,000 inventions, from the phonograph to the electric light bulb.

The Have-Nots

Unfortunately, the Gilded Age was not so shiny for many other Americans. The settling of the West forced Native Americans off their land and onto reservations. Although Native Americans fought back—among them **Chief Joseph** of the Nez Perce and the legendary Sioux warriors Crazy Horse and Sitting Bull—there was no stopping the tide.

Life was hard for freed African Americans as well. The failures of Reconstruction in the South left many poor and powerless, held down by segregationist Jim Crow laws and forced to work as sharecroppers under conditions much like slavery.

Others who found themselves facing hard times during this period were many immigrants who had come to America in search of freedom and opportunity. Russian, Italian, Scandinavian, German, Dutch, and Japanese immigrants—all were seeking a better life. Some joined the settlers heading west; others stayed in the cities, where they lived in crowded tenements and found work in factories. Unfortunately, many of these new city-dwelling Americans found themselves working 16-hour days in airless sweatshops for subsistence wages.

> **A Voice from the Times**
>
> *Hear me, my chiefs! I am tired; my heart is sick and sad. From where the sun now stands I will fight no more forever.*
>
> —**Chief Joseph of the Nez Perce,** from his 1877 surrender speech

Child Coal Mine Workers in Hughestown, Pennsylvania (1911). Lewis Wickes Hine/© Corbis.

FOR STRATEGIC READERS

Taking Notes Help students use a Main Idea and Details organizer to identify important ideas and supporting facts in **Cultural Influences** (pages 620–622).

 BEST PRACTICES TOOLKIT—Transparency
Main Idea and Details p. B6

Vocabulary Support Explain that Jim Crow laws were discriminatory laws, passed in Southern states after Reconstruction, that segregated African Americans and restricted their rights. For example, African Americans might be allowed to sit only in certain seats on railroad cars or to enter public establishments only through certain doors (if at all). The name "Jim Crow" came from an 1830s minstrel-show character and reflected negative stereotyping of African Americans.

TIERED DISCUSSION PROMPTS

Use these prompts to help students understand the ideas in **The Have-Nots:**

Analyze Generally speaking, which groups of people did not benefit from the advantages of the Gilded Age? Explain. *Possible answer: Groups that did not benefit included Native Americans, who were being driven from their land; African Americans, who were oppressed by Jim Crow laws; and recent immigrants, who were working long hours in sweatshops.*

Synthesize Think about the immigrants who had come to North America some 250 years earlier. How does their situation compare with that of the immigrants described here? *Possible answer: Both groups of immigrants were motivated by a desire for freedom and opportunity in a new land. The earlier immigrants had to build a new society, but they prospered; these later immigrants found a society ready to exploit them, and they struggled under unfair conditions.*

ANALYZE VISUALS

Possible answer: The purpose of the painting on page 620 is to portray the wealth, order, and stability of a prominent family. The purpose of the photograph on page 621 is to graphically expose the inhuman working conditions of child coal miners.

About the Art Eastman Johnson (1824–1906) painted scenes from everyday life as well as portraits of the wealthy and famous. The Hatch Family shows three generations of the family of Wall Street broker Alfrederick Hatch in the library of his mansion on Park Avenue in New York City. Lewis Wickes Hine (1874–1940) worked as an investigative reporter for the National Child Labor Committee. His photographs aroused public outrage over the hardships endured by child laborers.

CHECK UNDERSTANDING

Ask students to recall in what ways **The Gilded Age** was an era of both Haves and Have-Nots. *Possible answer: While the upper classes were enjoying a more luxurious lifestyle, many groups such as Native Americans, African Americans, and immigrants were fighting oppression, discrimination, and poverty.*

Ideas of the Age

KEY IDEAS This section of the essay (page 622) summarizes major scientific, political, and economic ideas of the era, including Darwin's theory of natural selection, laissez-faire economics, and the progressive movement.

DISCUSSION PROMPT

Use this prompt to help students understand the ideas in **Laissez Faire vs. Progressivism:**

Analyze Explain the connection between Darwin's theory of natural selection, the beliefs of the Social Darwinists, and progressivism. *Possible answer: Herbert Spencer called Darwin's theory of natural selection "survival of the fittest," and he applied the idea to people's success or lack of success in society. The Social Darwinists used Spencer's ideas to justify the gap between rich and poor people and to support a laissez-faire economic policy. Progressivism took issue with Social Darwinism, asserting that the government needed to protect people.*

Even independent farmers faced hard times. They borrowed money from the banks for new machinery that made them more productive than ever before; but high yields meant low prices, and when they couldn't pay back their loans they lost their farms.

People knew that they were missing out on the prosperity that others were enjoying, and it made them angry. Workers began to form **labor unions;** many farmers, white and black, joined the **Populist Party,** hoping to make the government more responsive to workers' needs. However, the opposition had money and power, and these early efforts often ended in bitter defeat.

More and more, the individual seemed helpless, at the mercy of forces beyond his or her understanding or control. Life became a constant struggle, and the world appeared to be a harsh, uncaring place. These feelings found their voice in a literary movement called **naturalism.** Naturalist writers, such as **Stephen Crane,** were concerned with the impact of social and natural forces on the individual. These writers tended to portray characters victimized by brutal forces and unable to control their lives.

Ideas of the Age

KEY IDEAS During this period, some Americans believed in "survival of the fittest," while others worked for social justice.

Laissez Faire vs. Progressivism

Many of the naturalists' ideas corresponded to new scientific, political, and economic theories emerging at the time. Various thinkers of the day felt that Charles Darwin's theory of natural selection could be applied to human society. An English philosopher named Herbert Spencer called this idea **survival of the fittest,** claiming that those who rose to the top of society were "fit," while those who suffered at the bottom were best left to die out. **Social Darwinists** used these ideas to justify the huge gap between rich and poor and to push a governmental policy of **laissez faire** (French for "allow to do"), meaning that business should not be regulated, because the law of nature would ensure success for the "fittest" and inevitable failure for everyone else.

This self-serving philosophy infuriated many Americans. A **progressive movement** emerged, which aimed to restore economic opportunities and correct injustices in American life. The progressives did not see inequality as the way of the world. They believed that social change was possible and necessary and that it was the job of the government to make laws to protect people.

Industrialist John D. Rockefeller is portrayed as a wealthy king, with the oil and railroad industries as the "jewels" in his crown.

A Voice from the Times

Let no one underestimate the need of pity. We live in a stony universe whose hard, brilliant forces rage fiercely.

—Theodore Dreiser

DIFFERENTIATED INSTRUCTION

FOR STRATEGIC READERS

Concept Support Charles Darwin's principle of *natural selection* described an evolutionary process in which those individuals or groups having traits best adapted to their environment tend to survive and pass those traits on to their offspring. Herbert Spencer's term *survival of the fittest* referred to a social order based on Darwin's theory.

FOR ADVANCED LEARNERS/AP

Research and Evaluate Challenge students to extend their knowledge by responding to one of these writing prompts:

- Gather information about the founding, goals, and achievements of the Populist Party. As you write, discuss how the Populist Party reflected concerns of the era and what value you think that it had in its short life.

- Find out more about Herbert Spencer: who he was, what his philosophical ideas were, and why these ideas were significant. As you write, clarify Spencer's connection with social Darwinism and comment about his continuing influence today.

- Do some research about the social causes with which the progressive movement was connected. As you write, identify some modern social causes that you think effectively carry on the progressive vision.

Regional and Naturalist Literature

KEY IDEAS The country's rapid growth and change was reflected in new literary movements and voices, including regionalism, naturalism, and women's writing.

Regionalism and Local Color Writing

The end of the Civil War, the country's rapid expansion, and the growth of industry all led to the birth of local color writing, a form of regionalism. Aware of the speed with which the nation was changing, regional writers sought to record for the future the unique character of their areas.

Prominent among the early local colorists were **Bret Harte** and **Mark Twain.** Their versions of life on the frontier captured the imagination of readers in the more settled communities of the East, Midwest, and South. For those who could not hop aboard the new transcontinental train and see the country for themselves, reading all about it was the next best thing. Americans were endlessly fascinated by tales of life in the mining camps, on the cattle ranches, and in the frontier towns. The new regionalist literature satisfied this curiosity with its honest portrayals of the people and their way of life in different areas of the country, especially the West. Writers carefully recorded how ordinary people spoke, dressed, acted, thought, and looked, from the knobby, roughened hands of a Nebraska farm woman to the dust-covered boots of a California gambler.

AN OUTGROWTH OF REALISM Regionalism, with its emphasis on everyday experience and accuracy, grew out of **realism.** Many regionalist writers, such as **Willa Cather,** shared the realist goal of showing ordinary lives as they

▶ *For Your Outline*

REGIONALISM AND LOCAL COLOR WRITING

- Writing was influenced by end of Civil war, country's expansion, and industry's growth.

- Regionalists sought to record for the future the unique character of a region.

- Regionalists captured life on the frontier and in other regions.

- Regionalsim was an outgrowth of realism.

- Native American oral literature was a form of regionalism.

- *Huckleberry Finn* is a masterpiece of regionalism.

Deadwood in 1876.

623

Regional and Naturalist Literature

KEY IDEAS This section of the essay (pages 623–627) focuses on the writing of the regionalist and naturalist movements. The text describes the work of these groups:

- regionalist writers, including Bret Harte, Mark Twain, and Willa Cather

- naturalist writers, including Theodore Dreiser, Frank Norris, Jack London, and Stephen Crane

- women writers, including Charlotte Perkins Gilman, Kate Chopin, Edith Wharton, and Mary Wilkins Freeman

DISCUSSION PROMPT

Use this discussion prompt to help students understand the ideas in **Regionalism and Local Color Writing:**

Summarize How did regionalist writing satisfy the curiosity of people who did not live on the frontier? *Possible answer: By sharing tales of life in mining camps, cattle ranches, and frontier towns, regionalist writing entertained distant readers and helped them learn about the West.*

FOR STRATEGIC READERS
Preteach Academic Vocabulary

- *labor union,* "an organization of workers formed to advance its members' interests, especially regarding wages and working conditions"

- *realism,* "a literary style that stresses a true and objective representation of life"

FOR ADVANCED LEARNERS/AP

Map a Movement [small-group option] Have one or more small groups of students create a map of the United States, c. 1880, showing states and territories. Use the finished map or maps as a springboard for a discussion in which students identify (1) some of the regions that probably were written about in the regionalist and local color movements and (2) a few likely distinct characteristics of each region.

Use these prompts to help students understand the ideas in **Native American Literature** and **An "American" Novel:**

Analyze How did the settlement of the West threaten the survival of Native American oral literature? *Possible answer: The settlement of the West caused Native American tribes to scatter, making it much more difficult to pass on oral literature. Children were separated from their parents and made to attend "Indian schools," where they were forced to disassociate themselves from their Native American heritage and to assimilate into the mainstream American society.*

Interpret In what sense did *The Adventures of Huckleberry Finn* mark a whole new level in regionalism and local color? *Possible answer: The Adventures of Huckleberry Finn was a landmark because it did more than just present regional characters and customs—it had a unique but consistent "American" voice, and it dealt with a widespread American issue in its handling of racism.*

---

were, without romance or sentimentality. Cather's story, "A Wagner Matinee," for example, gives a very unromantic view of life on the plains. Other writers tended to exaggerate a bit, either for comic effect—as in Twain's "The Notorious Jumping Frog of Calaveras County"—or to make their stories livelier. Our national legend of the Wild West, with its gunslingers, saloons, and sheriffs, had its origins in the picturesque settings and characters of writers like **Bret Harte.**

NATIVE AMERICAN LITERATURE While this kind of regional literature thrived, another was under siege. For generations, Native American tribes had passed down from one generation to the next folk tales, legends, and other **oral literature,** relying on the memories of traditional storytellers and their audiences. Now, the tribes found themselves scattered. Children were forcibly taken from their elders and sent away to "Indian schools," where teachers demanded they forget their language and heritage and assimilate into American society. Entire cultures were rapidly disappearing. However, through the efforts of Native Americans and sympathetic outsiders who helped them write their stories down, some of the literature was saved, thus giving another view of life in the West.

AN "AMERICAN" NOVEL With the publication in 1884 of Mark Twain's *The Adventures of Huckleberry Finn,* regionalism and local color writing reached a zenith. *Huckleberry Finn* was the first novel written entirely in "American"—that is, it was told in the colorful, colloquial, and often ungrammatical voice of its young narrator, Huck. Twain was known for using his gift of humor to make a serious point, and in this novel he used biting satire to tackle the issue of racism in America. Despite Twain's immense popularity with readers worldwide, critics of the time dismissed *Huckleberry Finn,* calling it vulgar and immoral, and libraries banned the book from their shelves as "the veriest trash." Today, many consider it not only Twain's finest work but possibly the best book ever written by an American author. The novel had a huge influence on later writers, among them Ernest Hemingway, who said, "All modern American literature comes from one book by Mark Twain called *Huckleberry Finn.* There was nothing before. There has been nothing as good since."

> **A Voice from the Times**
>
> *Authorship is not a trade, it is an inspiration; authorship does not keep an office, its habitation is all out under the sky, and everywhere the winds are blowing and the sun is shining and the creatures of God are free.*
>
> —Mark Twain

The Rise of Naturalism

As the 19th century came to a close, several factors led to the rise of a literary movement called **naturalism.** The final decades of the century were a time of rapid change and sharp contrasts—a time when "captains of industry" amassed vast fortunes by exploiting the cheap labor of immigrants and other workers who flooded the cities in search of work. By 1916, the majority of American workers were industrial laborers in factories.

DIFFERENTIATED INSTRUCTION

FOR STRATEGIC READERS
Preteach Academic Vocabulary

- *gunslinger,* "a person known for skill and speed in using a gun"
- *picturesque,* "memorably vivid"
- *oral literature,* "literature passed from one generation to the next through oral storytelling rather than writing"
- *assimilate,* "to absorb into the culture of a group of people"
- *veriest,* "most extreme"

FOR ADVANCED LEARNERS/AP
Research Critical Views This essay notes Ernest Hemingway's admiration for *The Adventures of Huckleberry Finn,* but he is not alone in that view. Ask students to locate another critical comment that summarizes the importance of Twain's novel. Have students share the comments in class, either now or when they read the American Masterpiece feature about *The Adventures of Huckleberry Finn* on pages 670–671.

WRITING REFLECTS REALITY The work of naturalist writers, such as Theodore Dreiser, reflected this harsh new reality. In the first pages of his novel *The Financier,* for example, a boy named Frank stares through the window of a fish shop at a lobster and a squid that have been placed together in a tank. Day after day, the two creatures battle it out, the sharp-clawed lobster attacking, the squid fighting for its life. At last, the lobster devours the squid. That's the way of the world, Frank thinks—one creature lives off another. When Frank grows up and becomes a banker, he applies this lesson to the ruthless world of business.

Why do people do the things they do? Are humans capable of choice, or do they act on instinct, like other animals? Is life a losing battle? Looking to the theories of Darwin and other scientists, naturalists such as **Dreiser, Frank Norris, Jack London,** and **Stephen Crane** saw human beings as helpless creatures moved by forces beyond their understanding or control.

Despite this grim attitude, many naturalist writers were quite popular. Some, like Frank Norris, gave a voice to ordinary people and portrayed the rich and influential in an unflattering light, as in his famous 1901 novel *The Octopus,* which attacked the railroad interests in his home state of California. Jack London, on the other hand, captured readers with his tales of an arctic world entirely outside their everyday experience. Riveted by the exotic setting and thrilling action of novels such as *White Fang* and *The Call of the Wild,* readers were willing to accept less-than-happy endings.

> ### A Voice from the Times
>
> *A man said to the universe:*
> *"Sir, I exist!"*
> *"However," replied the universe,*
> *"The fact has not created in me*
> *A sense of obligation."*
>
> —Stephen Crane

▶ *For Your Outline*

THE RISE OF NATURALISM

- Naturalism reflected time of rapid changes and sharp contrasts, when wealth was concentrated in few hands.
- Naturalists saw humans as helpless from forces beyond their control.

625

TIERED DISCUSSION PROMPTS
Use these prompts to help students understand the ideas in **The Rise of Naturalism:**

Analyze How did the work of naturalist writers reflect the harsh realities of the late 19th century? *Possible answer: While rich and powerful people continued to amass fortunes, the majority of workers were laboring in factories. Naturalist writers reflected the feelings of the many "have-nots"—people who felt trapped by forces beyond their control.*

Synthesize Review what the text says about naturalism in literature. Would you describe today's writing as "naturalistic"? Why or why not? *Encourage answers that demonstrate an awareness that naturalism views people as victims of forces they cannot understand or control.*

FOR STRATEGIC READERS

Taking Notes Have students record the key facts about the rise of naturalism (pages 624–625). Then ask students to exchange papers and evaluate each other's work, offering suggestions for possible improvement.

Sample notes:

- *The late 19th century was a time of changes and contrasts (for example, the very rich versus factory laborers).*

- *Naturalist writers reflected the harsh realities of that time.*

- *Influenced by the theories of Darwin and other scientists, naturalists saw human beings as helpless in the face of forces beyond their understanding or control.*

- *Important naturalists included Theodore Dreiser, Frank Norris, Jack London, and Stephen Crane.*

A New Role for Women

Women writing in this period in the United States tended to be realists. Some were regionalists and others embraced naturalist themes, but all were breaking barriers as women's roles slowly shifted. "The power of a woman is in her refinement, gentleness, and elegance; it is she who makes etiquette, and it is she who preserves the order and decency of society." So said a popular book of etiquette in 1880, voicing a widely held notion about women's place in society.

At the same time, however, the movement to give women the **right to vote** was reemerging after a period of inactivity in the years immediately following the Civil War, when male reformers argued that black and white women should wait until black men gained their rights. Women were growing impatient, not just for the vote, but to have a larger voice in every aspect of public life, from politics to literature.

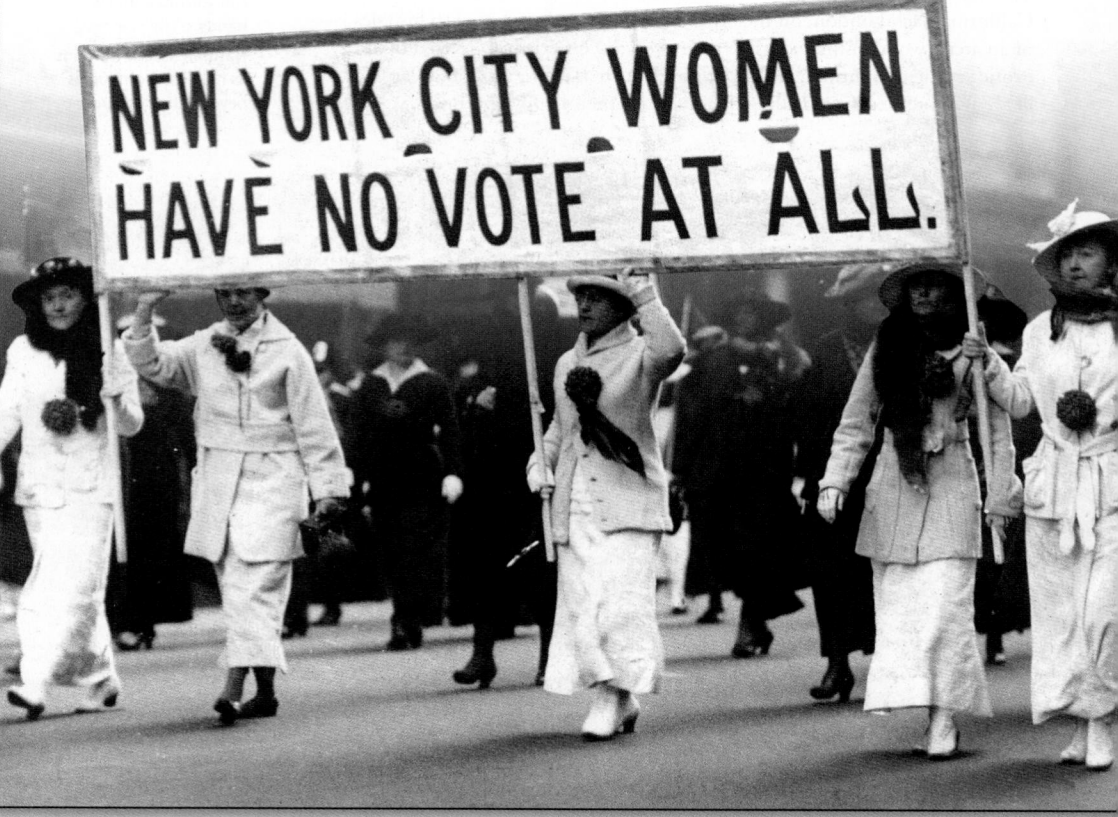

One important factor in the growth of the women's movement was the spread of **university education** among women of the era. Newspapers of the day trumpeted the dangers of this development. An 1896 *New York Journal* headline proclaimed: "Are We Destroying Woman's Beauty? The Startling Warning of a Great English Physician Against Higher Education of Women. How Intellectual Work Destroys Beauty." Despite such dire warnings, women continued to seek education. Then they found that the limited roles assigned them did not make full use of their abilities and knowledge.

BREAKTHROUGH WRITERS Charlotte Perkins Gilman— related on her father's side to a noted family of writers and social reformers that included Harriet Beecher Stowe, the author of *Uncle Tom's Cabin*—became one of the most well-known advocates for women. Fleeing a repressive marriage, **Gilman** moved from the East Coast to California, where she wrote and spoke out on behalf of women's rights and against male domination. One of her most famous stories is "The Yellow Wallpaper," about a woman writer who, as treatment for her "nervous condition," is forbidden to write.

Kate Chopin wrote fiction that articulates the frustrations of generations of women confined to a sort of extended childhood by the men in their lives. Her gentle stories depicting some of the most obvious of women's troubles were extremely popular in the 1890s. Her 1899 novel *The Awakening,* however, stepped over the line in its portrayal of a woman's hidden passion, arousing a public protest so vigorous that Chopin ceased writing completely.

Works by women of this period often end tragically, in madness, ruin, scandal, and death. In part, this was a reflection of their **naturalist** leanings; at the same time, though, it grew out of their own experiences in a culture that did not encourage women's artistic goals. **Edith Wharton,** who in novels such as *The Age of Innocence* and *The House of Mirth* decried the stifling small-mindedness of upper-class society, made her own escape by running off to Paris, only to have her marriage fall apart. Facing overwhelming obstacles, women writers fought with, in the words of New England's local color writer **Mary Wilkins Freeman**, "little female weapons." When the weapon was a pen, the impact could be revolutionary.

As the country moved farther into the 20th century, writers would begin to turn from regionalism and naturalism to the more experimental works that characterize modernism. Thankfully Twain, London, Chopin, and the other writers of their time captured for future generations the unique spirit of late 19th- and early 20th-century America.

American Impressionism

During this period, the revolutionary style pioneered by French painters such as Claude Monet and Auguste Renoir made its mark in the United States. American artists took the basic goal of **impressionism**—to capture reality as we actually see it in the moment, not as formal rules of art say we should see it—and adapted it to their own situation.

Style and Subject Like their European counterparts, American impressionists focused on the effects of light and color and liked to paint outdoors. Often they painted what a new American leisure class wanted to buy: idyllic landscapes that let them "get away" and portraits of themselves relaxing in their homes or picnicking at the seaside. Paintings like these were not only a pleasure to look at but a status symbol too—proof that the owner (perhaps the son or grandson of a penniless immigrant) had acquired taste and culture.

Progressive Woman One of the few women who exhibited with the impressionists in Paris was an American artist named **Mary Cassatt,** whose work *In the Garden* (1904) is shown here. At a time when no respectable woman traveled alone, lived alone, or pursued a career in art, Cassatt did all three. Known as "a painter of mothers and children," her works reflect a surprisingly modern sensibility. Though her paintings show women in conventional settings, she gives them a new sense of purpose. Cassatt's women do not exist just to be looked at; they are the heroes of their own lives.

THE ARTISTS' GALLERY

Freedom with the brush and the use of bright color are two characteristics of American impressionist art; they appear in Mary Cassatt's painting on this page and in Childe Hassam's painting on page 618. Information about Hassam appears on page 618 as well. American artist Mary Cassatt (1844–1926) was born in Pennsylvania but moved to Paris in 1874; she lived and worked in France for the rest of her life. Rather than paint commissioned portraits, Cassatt used family members as the subjects of her paintings. Her paintings reflect some influence of the French artist Edgar Degas, with whom she often worked. It was Degas, in fact, who introduced Cassatt to the French impressionists.

Activity Ask students to explain what Cassatt's painting may suggest about the artist's feelings about family. *Possible answer: The pleasant, upbeat feeling in this scene, which depicts a quietly shared mother-daughter moment, suggests that Cassatt placed high value on family closeness.*

CHECK UNDERSTANDING

Have students identify a few names and characteristics related to each of these topics:

- Regionalism and Local Color Writing
- The Rise of Naturalism
- A New Role for Women

FOR ADVANCED LEARNERS/AP

Research and Synthesize Review this comment from the first paragraph of page 627: "[women] found that the limited roles assigned them did not make full use of their abilities and knowledge." Invite students to gather information about some women of this era who refused to be bound by expectation. These are a few of the women that students might research:

- reformer Jane Addams
- journalist Nellie Bly
- attorney Belva Lockwood
- suffragist Elizabeth Cady Stanton

Have students present their findings in brief oral reports. To extend the activity, ask students whether or not this expectation persists to this day. Encourage them to support their responses with facts and examples drawn from their knowledge of modern society and current events.

Create an Impressionist Display [small-group option] Have a group of students collect and review a variety of impressionist paintings and share them with the class. Some paintings may come from the late 19th and early 20th centuries; others may be contemporary works that use impressionist techniques. Discuss why impressionism was so revolutionary and why it pleases many art lovers even today.

Connecting Literature, History, and Culture

OBJECTIVES
- read a timeline
- make connections among the perspectives and events of literature, history, and culture

Connecting Literature, History, and Culture

Use the timeline and the questions on the next page to gain insight about how developments in the United States during this period reflected those in the world as a whole.

AMERICAN LITERARY MILESTONES

1870

1870 Bret Harte publishes his story collection *The Luck of Roaring Camp and Other Sketches.* ▶

1876 Mark Twain completes *The Adventures of Tom Sawyer* and begins writing *The Adventures of Huckleberry Finn.*

1880

1881 Henry James publishes *The Portrait of a Lady.*

1883 Mark Twain's *Life on the Mississippi* is published. ▶

1885 Libraries across America ban Mark Twain's *The Adventures of Huckleberry Finn,* published the previous year; William Dean Howells publishes *The Rise of Silas Lapham.*

1887 Diary of Chief Seattle is published.

HISTORICAL CONTEXT

1870

1872 Susan B. Anthony is arrested and fined for leading a group of women to test their right to vote. ▶

1876 Alexander Graham Bell patents first telephone; at Battle of Little Bighorn, 1,500 Sioux and Cheyenne warriors defeat and kill about 200 U.S. Army troops, commanded by George A. Custer.

1877 Chief Joseph of the Nez Perce tribe surrenders to U.S. Army; Thomas Edison invents the phonograph.

1880

1880 John D. Rockefeller's Standard Oil Company of Ohio controls U.S. refining; George Eastman patents his rolled camera film.

1883 The first metal-framed skyscraper, ten stories high, is built in Chicago.

1886 The Statue of Liberty, a gift from France to the United States, is dedicated in New York Harbor. ▶

WORLD CULTURE AND EVENTS

1870

1871 Franco-Prussian War ends and Germany is unified; French naturalist writer Émile Zola publishes the first book in his 20-novel series *Les Rougon-Macquart.*

1872 Critics coin the term *impressionism* after viewing Claude Monet's painting *Impression: Sunrise.*

1879 The British defeat the Zulus in South Africa.

1880

1883 The Orient Express makes its first rail run from Paris to Istanbul.

1887 Fictional detective Sherlock Holmes makes his first appearance in *A Study in Scarlet,* by Sir Arthur Conan Doyle. ▶

1889 The Eiffel Tower is completed in Paris.

MAKING CONNECTIONS

- Who were some inventors at work in Europe and the United States?
- How did American women fare in gaining the right to vote as compared with New Zealand women?
- What evidence do you see that the United States was becoming an imperial power?
- Name two works of American literature from this period that describe real people or events.

1890	1900
1890 Charlotte Perkins Gilman describes the emotional and intellectual decline of a young wife and mother in "The Yellow Wallpaper."	**1900** Theodore Dreiser publishes *Sister Carrie*.
1893 Stephen Crane publishes *Maggie: A Girl of the Streets*; Paul Laurence Dunbar publishes his first volume of poetry, *Oak and Ivy*, while working as an elevator operator.	**1901** Booker T. Washington publishes *Up From Slavery: An Autobiography*.
1899 Kate Chopin publishes her novel *The Awakening*.	**1903** Jack London publishes *The Call of the Wild*; W. E. B. Du Bois publishes *The Souls of Black Folk*.
	1905 Edith Wharton publishes *The House of Mirth*.
	1906 Upton Sinclair's *The Jungle* ▶ exposes dangerous conditions in meatpacking factories.

1890	1900
1892 New York's Ellis Island becomes entry point for European immigrants.	**1901** William McKinley is assassinated; Theodore Roosevelt becomes president of the United States.
1896 Supreme Court upholds "separate but equal" doctrine of Jim Crow laws, widely used to discriminate against African Americans; the Klondike gold rush begins in Alaska and Canada.	
1898 The Spanish-American War results in United States gaining control of Guam, Puerto Rico, and the Philippines; U.S. also annexes Hawaii.	**1903** Near Kitty Hawk, North Carolina, Orville and Wilbur Wright make first flight in engine-powered airplane.
	1906 Earthquake and fire destroy much of San Francisco.
	1908 Ford Motor Company brings out the first Model T automobile.

1890	1900
1893 New Zealand becomes first country to grant women suffrage.	**1900** The Boxer Rebellion protests foreign influence in China.
1894 Rudyard Kipling publishes *The Jungle Book*.	**1901** After 64 years as ruler of Great Britain, Queen Victoria dies. ▶
1896 Italian physicist Guglielmo Marconi invents first radio; first modern Olympic games are held in Athens.	**1902** Joseph Conrad publishes *Heart of Darkness*.
1897 Edmond Rostand publishes *Cyrano de Bergerac*.	**1904** James Joyce begins *Dubliners*.
	1905 Albert Einstein formulates his theory of relativity.

MAKING CONNECTIONS

Possible answers:

- *Inventors Alexander Graham Bell, Thomas Edison, George Eastman, Orville and Wilbur Wright, and Guglielmo Marconi were at work during this time.*
- *Women in New Zealand gained the right to vote in 1893. At that time, American women were still fighting for that right.*
- *American imperialism is seen in two events from 1898: (1) the annexation of Hawaii and (2) the acquisition of Guam, Puerto Rico, and the Philippines as a result of the Spanish-American War.*
- *Answers will vary but may include any two:* Life on the Mississippi; *diary of Chief Seattle;* Up from Slavery: An Autobiography; The Souls of Black Folk; The Jungle.

ADDITIONAL QUESTIONS

1. Which English author published *The Jungle Book* 21 years after Mark Twain published *Life on the Mississippi*? **Answer:** *Rudyard Kipling published* The Jungle Book *in 1894.*

2. How long after the Orient Express made its first run from Paris to Istanbul did the Wright brothers make their first airplane flight? **Answer:** *The Wright Brothers made their flight 20 years later (in 1903).*

FOR ADVANCED LEARNERS/AP

Making Additional Connections Ask students to choose one of the four decades shown in the timeline and to do research online or in encyclopedias or history texts to learn about other events that took place during that ten-year time span. Challenge students to identify events for each category: *American Literary Milestones, Historical Context,* and *World Culture and Events*. Have students work individually, with partners, or in small groups to prepare and present brief oral reports, summarizing significant events and discussing their connection to events shown in the timeline or discussed in class.

The Legacy of the Era

OBJECTIVE

- to connect the legacy of regionalism and naturalism to present times

The Wild, Wild West

Have students read the paragraph. Explain that Western books, movies, and TV shows were especially popular from the 1940s through the 1960s. Ask students to name Western books, movies, TV shows, characters, and scenes (such as the depicted duel at high noon) with which they are familiar. Point out that some Western characters were fictional (for example, the Lone Ranger and Tonto) but that others were real people. Students may recall such Western characters—some heroes, some villains—as Wyatt Earp, Doc Holliday, Jesse James, Calamity Jane, and Annie Oakley, all of whom were real people in addition to being characters in books and on screen.

QUICKWRITE As students plan and write their paragraphs, encourage them to consider (1) why people generally enjoy reading about life in the past, and (2) why the Wild West seems appealing despite the real-life difficulties of living in such a time and place. After volunteers have shared their explanations, have the class reach a consensus opinion that completes this sentence: *The Wild West is an appealing image because* _____. Extend the discussion by asking whether students think that any other American setting—any region, at any time— holds the same kind of appeal.

The Wild, Wild West

It's high noon and two cowboys face off on a deserted street, spurs jingling, fingers twitching. Sound familiar? Although the real Wild West lasted just a few decades, it lives on today in Westerns—a genre of novels, television shows, and movies inspired originally by the stories of Bret Harte and other regionalist writers such as Zane Grey and Owen Wister.

QUICKWRITE What is it about the Wild West that makes it so appealing to Americans? Write a paragraph or two explaining why, in your opinion, the legend lives on.

630

DIFFERENTIATED INSTRUCTION

FOR STRATEGIC READERS
Vocabulary Support

- *spur,* "a pointed device attached to the heel of a rider's boot, used to urge the horse forward"

- *genre,* "a particular kind of literary or artistic work"

FOR ADVANCED LEARNERS/AP

Research Real Heroes [paired option] Have students do Internet research to identify popular TV Westerns of the 1950s and 1960s that were based on the lives of real people. Ask them to determine which people were truly heroes and which were simply glorified by Hollywood. As students share their findings, discuss how TV writers' portrayal of these characters influenced Americans' view of life in the old West.

The Labor Movement

In the post–Civil War period, many laborers, unhappy with the appalling working conditions of their day, began to join unions and strike for better wages and conditions. Business leaders feared the growth of unions and tried to break their power with lockouts, firings, and even violence. Slowly, however, unions increased their membership and their power, eventually changing the way many Americans worked.

ONLINE RESEARCH Today, workers consider 8 hours a full day. Contrast that with the 10 to 12 hours typically worked in the 19th century, and you will see one benefit won by early unions. What issues are today's unions focusing on? Visit the Web site of a modern labor union, and report to the class on its top concerns.

Regionalism Today

Local color writing is still very popular in America. Writers such as Garrison Keillor, Larry McMurtry, and Fannie Flagg capture regions as we know them today, from small-town Minnesota to the great spaces of Texas to sleepy towns of the South.

REPORT Do some research to find out if there are any writers working today who are capturing the flavor of the region in which you live. Report to the class on the writer or writers you discover. What have they written? Is their work well-known? Do they write in dialect, describe landscapes or towns, work in fiction or nonfiction? Explore these and any other questions that arise as you research.

Garrison Keillor

631

The Labor Movement

Review with students the definition of *labor union:* "an organization of workers formed to advance its members' interests." Then have students read and discuss the paragraph. In particular, discuss how the expression *There is strength in numbers* pertains to unions and why business leaders might be opposed to the formation of unions.

ONLINE RESEARCH Have students combine their findings by creating a chart of the largest labor unions in the United States. Charts should include such information as each union's total membership, its year of formation, and the union's goals and accomplishments.

Regionalism Today

Before students read the paragraph, review the fact that *local color* refers to writing that captures the atmosphere and features of a particular place, time, and people. As you discuss the paragraph, ask students whether they think that local color writing generally appeals only to people who live in the region described or whether it has a broad appeal.

REPORT Suggest that students begin by looking for writers who regularly contribute to local or regional newspapers and magazines. After students have done their research, invite volunteers to share passages that capture the flavor of your region. Discuss what makes each writer's approach to the material unique.

FOR STRATEGIC READERS

Vocabulary Support

- *appalling,* "awful; shocking"
- *lockout,* "an employer's closing of a workplace in order to prevent employees from working during a labor dispute"
- *dialect,* "a regional variety of a shared language"

FOR ADVANCED LEARNERS/AP

Write with Local Color Challenge students to try their hand at local color writing by writing a short story, essay, or article that captures the flavor of the region in which they live. Encourage students to consider such details as regional landmarks and events; also urge them to think about how people talk and the things about which they talk. Have volunteers share their finished work with the class.

OBJECTIVES

- understand regionalism as a literary movement
- identify and analyze characteristics of regionalism
- identify and analyze setting

 R3.3, R3.5

The Growth of Regional Literature

Regional Writing Explain that regional differences became increasingly evident as the United States grew in geographic size and in population. People's curiosity about these differences encouraged writers to capture the atmosphere and features of small-town and rural life, in particular, in the South, the West, New England, and other parts of the country. Such magazines as Boston's *Atlantic Monthly* and New York City's *Harper's New Monthly Magazine* brought local color to urban readers.

Ask students how today's readers satisfy their curiosity about various regions of the country, urban as well as rural. Elicit a range of local color sources, including regional and local newspapers and magazines, television and radio, the Internet, and movies.

The Importance of Setting

Setting Point out that setting is a key element in almost all literature but that it is especially important in regional literature. In regional literature, the setting is viewed not just as a contributing element; it is a subject that is interesting in itself. Furthermore, regional writers look to their settings for inspiration in creating characters, situations, and imagery. Point out, too, that even though regional writers might focus on a particular setting, their writing frequently deals with concerns that people everywhere find relevant.

Literary Analysis Workshop

Setting in Regional Literature

Many places in the world are fascinating, but some of the most ordinary places can be interesting, too, if you notice what is unique about them. In the last half of the 19th century, regional writers in the United States strove to depict in their stories the unique aspects of a specific place and of its people. These enduring tales give readers a glimpse into the past and inspire a tradition that continues to this day.

R3.3, R3.5

The Growth of Regional Literature

Regional literature arose from an effort to accurately represent the speech, manners, habits, history, folklore, and beliefs of people in specific geographical areas. Although regionalism is considered an offshoot of realism, it has been part of American literature from the beginning. Washington Irving's tales of Dutch New York and Nathaniel Hawthorne's stories of Puritan New England are just two examples. After the Civil War, however, when realism became the dominant literary movement, writers began to focus on the lives of ordinary people and to avoid the supernaturalism and sentimentality found in much of the work of Irving, Hawthorne, and Edgar Allan Poe.

Mark Twain relaxes on a ship's deck.

A factor that contributed to the growth of regional writing was the boom in publishing in the late 1800s. Popular magazines sprang up all over the United States to meet the demand for information about the rest of the country. Mark Twain's "The Notorious Jumping Frog of Calaveras County," for example, was first published in a New York magazine and became an immediate sensation.

The Importance of Setting

The effectiveness of regional writing depends to a large extent on the depiction of **setting,** the time and place in which a story's events occur. Key elements of setting in regional literature include the following:

- geographical location and physical features, such as a river, a camp, a house, or a mode of transportation
- the time in which the events take place—a season of the year or a historical period
- the jobs and daily activities of the characters
- the culture of the characters, including their religious and moral beliefs and the social and economic conditions in which they live

---

DIFFERENTIATED INSTRUCTION

For general guidelines on differentiating instruction, see

 BEST PRACTICES TOOLKIT
Differentiated Instruction pp. 31–38

FOR STRATEGIC READERS

Note Taking For students who are unfamiliar with setting in regional literature or need help with note taking, hand out the copy master before discussing these pages.

Explain to students that they will encounter several terms relating to setting in regional literature in this workshop. Discuss the major terms on this spread (*regional literature, setting, dialect, detailed description, local color writing*) as students record notes on the copy master.

 RESOURCE MANAGER—Copy Master
Note Taking p. 17

Two means of conveying setting that are commonly found in regional literature are the use of **dialects**—distinctive forms of language spoken in particular areas or by particular groups of people—and **detailed descriptions** of location. Take a look at the beginning of Simon Wheeler's rambling tale in Twain's "The Notorious Jumping Frog of Calaveras County" (page 660).

> "Rev. Leonidas W. H'm, Reverend Le— Well, there was a feller here once once by the name of Jim Smiley, in the winter of '49—or maybe it was the spring of '50—I don't recollect exactly, somehow, though what makes me think it was one or the other is because I remember the big flume warn't finished when he first come to the camp. . . ."
>
> **—Mark Twain, "The Notorious Jumping Frog of Calaveras County"**

The pronunciations indicated by the spellings *feller* and *warn't,* the expression "I don't recollect," and the use of *come* rather than *came* all contribute to the regional flavor of the piece.

Now look at this description from Willa Cather's "A Wagner Matinee" (page 694), in which the narrator recalls the Nebraska farm where he grew up. Notice the harshness and the lack of color in the setting described; both the landscape and the evidence of human habitation are black, pitted, and bare.

> I saw again the tall, naked house on the prairie, black and grim as a wooden fortress; the black pond where I had learned to swim, its margin pitted with sun-dried cattle tracks; the rain gullied clay banks about the naked house, the four dwarf ash seedlings where the dish-cloths were always hung to dry before the kitchen door.
>
> **—Willa Cather, "A Wagner Matinee"**

In regional literature, setting, characters, and plot are usually inseparable. As you read regional writing, notice the relationship between the characters and the setting. Ask yourself how the characters react to the setting. Then decide how this relationship is significant to the story's plot.

LOCAL COLOR REALISM

Prospectors pan for gold during the gold rush, 1889.

In 1868, a popular story about the California gold rush—Bret Harte's "The Luck of Roaring Camp"—launched a specific form of regional writing called **local color writing.** Mark Twain, with his memorable characters, was a master of this form. Other local color realists of the time include Joel Chandler Harris in the South and Sarah Orne Jewett and Mary Wilkins Freeman in New England. Later regional writers, such as Willa Cather, William Faulkner, and Flannery O'Connor, developed sophisticated ways of making universal statements about the human condition while focusing on the local and the particular.

Close Read

What feeling about life on the frontier do you get from the description? How could you rewrite the passage to change that feeling?

Dialects Explain that through well-written dialect, writers convey realism not only in setting but also in characterization. In addition to geographical origins, a particular dialect may suggest a character's educational background or social status. For example, an ungrammatical dialect may suggest that a character has had limited formal education. (Note that as the story unfolds, however, such a character may prove to be quite clever and may even be the story's hero.)

Detailed Descriptions Explain that writers convey setting through the use of sensory details—showing how things look, taste, smell, sound, and feel. Through such details, writers can give readers a clear impression of the setting and also create a mood or atmosphere, as Willa Cather does in the example on page 633.

LOCAL COLOR REALISM

Explain that local color realists tried to convey a realistic sense of specific towns or regions throughout the United States, such as villages in New England, the plains and cities of the Midwest and the towns, deserts, and mountains of the West.

Close Read

Possible answer: *The feeling is that life on the frontier was bleak, empty, and lonely. To change that feeling, a writer might add color to the description and use more upbeat and varied adjectives than* black *(used twice),* grim, *and* naked *(also used twice).*

FOR ENGLISH LEARNERS

Language: Skill Words

- *setting:* place and time in which the action of a literary work occurs—for example, San Francisco in 1889

- *dialect:* form of language of a particular region or group of people—for example, the New England and Coastal Southern dialects

- *description:* account that gives a vivid impression of an experience—for example, enjoying a home-cooked meal or seeing a new invention for the first time

FOR ADVANCED LEARNERS/AP

Consider Regional Differences Ask students to respond to these questions:

- What differences in perspective would you expect to find between a regional writer from the West and one from the East? What differences might there be between a writer who is a city dweller and a writer who lives in a rural town?

- How can reading the work of writers from various regions benefit a person?

Focus and Motivate

OBJECTIVES

Literary Analysis
- explore the key ideas of **deception, experience,** and **skepticism**
- analyze irony, voice, and the traits of a tall tale
- read an autobiography, a memoir, and a tall tale

Reading
- predict, paraphrase, evaluate dialect

Vocabulary
- build vocabulary for reading and writing
- identify homographs *(also an EL language objective)*
- use context clues to define words with *in-, non-,* and *un- (also an EL language objective)*

Grammar and Writing
- use coordinating conjunctions and dashes in realistic dialogue
- write a conversation

 CALIFORNIA R3.3, R3.1, W1.2, W1.9

ABOUT THE AUTHOR

Point out that Twain's *Autobiography* is a loose collection of character sketches, essays, diary entries, and letters.

USING THE *NOTABLE QUOTE*

Point out that **Mark Twain** was famous for his public "lectures"—humorous storytelling delivered deadpan. Ask students what kind of stories they would expect from a performer with this style. *Answers will vary.*

---

from **The Autobiography of Mark Twain**
by Mark Twain

CALIFORNIA R3.3

Mark Twain
1835–1910

NOTABLE QUOTE

"I like a story well told. That is the reason I am sometimes forced to tell them myself."

FYI
Did you know that Mark Twain . . .

- used multiple pen names, including S. L. C., Josh, and Thomas Jefferson Snodgrass?
- served briefly in the Confederate Army?
- took his name from a nautical term for water depth meaning "two fathoms deep"?

Author On*l*ine

For more on Mark Twain, visit the **Literature Center** at **ClassZone.com.**

Readers of all ages have followed the youthful adventures of Huck Finn and Tom Sawyer for more than 100 years. Many have also enjoyed the witty and sharp social commentary in Mark Twain's lectures and journalism. A man who found humor in a life filled with tragedy, Mark Twain remains one of America's greatest literary voices.

Life on the River Samuel Langhorne Clemens—as Twain was named at birth— grew up in the Mississippi River town of Hannibal, Missouri. The river and the town shaped young Clemens's early years. After his father's death, he began working at an early age to help support his family. Work for a printer and a newspaper began a lifelong connection to journalism and led to his first published writing—a humorous sketch. Planning to write travel sketches, Clemens signed on with a river pilot. He spent four years on the river, where he met many different kinds of people. After the Civil War, river travel was largely replaced by railroad travel, but Clemens remembered the river's lessons as he took the pen name by which his readers came to know him.

On the Move Twain kept traveling, first to the American West, where he panned for gold. He gained literary recognition with his tall tale "The Notorious Jumping Frog of Calaveras County," set in California. Twain also traveled the world, sharing his experiences in sketches, letters, and lectures. Travel writings such as *The Innocents Abroad* artfully combined wit and serious information and were vastly popular.

Twain's Great Legacy After his 1870 marriage, Twain based his growing family in Hartford, Connecticut, where he produced his most lasting works, *The Adventures of Tom Sawyer* and *The Adventures of Huckleberry Finn.* These books secured Twain's place as a great American novelist.

Tragedy Haunts the Later Years Despite literary success, Twain found himself in debt from unsuccessful business ventures. Facing bankruptcy in 1893, he traveled once again, delivering humorous lectures amidst the great personal sorrow of two daughters' deaths and his wife's fading health. Twain's last works reflect the sorrow and anger of this period, which lasted until his death.

Selection Resources

* Resources for Differentiation   † Also in Spanish   ‡ In Haitian Creole and Vietnamese

• LITERARY ANALYSIS: IRONY

One of the most distinctive elements of Twain's style is his use of **irony**—the contrast between appearance and actuality. In general, there are three types of irony:

- **situational irony**—a contrast between what is expected to happen and what actually does happen
- **dramatic irony**—when readers know more about a situation or character than the characters do
- **verbal irony**—a contrast between what is stated and what is meant

In this selection, Twain uses primarily two of the three types of irony. Watch for examples of them as you read and notice how they add tension and humor to the writing.

● READING SKILL: PREDICT

When you **predict,** you use text clues to make a reasonable guess about what will happen in a story. Sometimes a story will surprise you with a plot twist; sometimes your predictions will hit the mark. Either way, watching for text clues can help you find the situational irony in Twain's story. As you read, use a chart like the one shown to record your predictions and the clues from the text that that led you to make your educated guess.

Predictions	Text Clues
I predict he'll find a way to get involved.	Narrator says he can't resist the temptation to be a subject.

▲ VOCABULARY IN CONTEXT

Match each vocabulary word in the first column with the word in the second column that is closest in meaning.

1. unassailable   a. trust
2. multifariously   b. peeved
3. minutest   c. spellbound
4. implacable   d. overtrusting
5. credulity   e. tiniest
6. rapt   f. unquestionable
7. nettled   g. unyielding
8. gullible   h. variously

Explore the Key Idea

Have you ever put on an ACT?

KEY IDEA Occasionally we are tempted to try to fool others into thinking we are smarter, cooler, richer, or more popular than we really are. Sometimes it's as simple as putting on a new pair of sunglasses or pretending to know more about something than we really do. In his autobiography, Mark Twain recalls from his youth a more extreme version of this kind of **deception.**

DISCUSS With your classmates, come up with a list of ways in which people pretend to be something they're not. Examples can range from simple social posing to more outrageous, even criminal, forms of falsified identity. Then review these examples, considering people's motives for such deception.

635

Teach

Have you ever put on an ACT?

Lead into the **KEY IDEA** by asking the question. Extend the **DISCUSS** activity by asking students to explore the consequences of **deception.** Can fooling others ever lead to a positive outcome—and if so, for whom?

SKILLS FOCUS

LITERARY ANALYSIS   R3.3

● IRONY

Have students identify these examples of irony as situational, dramatic, or verbal:

1. Emily opens her lunch bag, pulls out a squashed baloney sandwich, and exclaims, "Another gourmet meal!" (*verbal irony*)

2. Jaime stays up until 2:00 a.m. studying for a math exam, only to fall asleep during the test. (*situational irony*)

3. Alex, a character in a movie, is worried that his girlfriend is spending a lot of time with his best friend, but the audience knows that they are planning Alex's surprise party. (*dramatic irony*)

CHECK UNDERSTANDING Have students offer examples of the three types of irony from literature, movies, television shows, or personal experience.

READING SKILL

■ PREDICT

Point out that even a story featuring situational irony includes text clues that help readers make predictions. The clues sometimes turn out to be false leads, tempting us to expect things that don't occur. Still, we can't enjoy these unexpected plot twists unless the writer has been careful to plant clues that set up our soon-to-be-toppled expectations.

> **RESOURCE MANAGER—Copy Master**
> Predict p. 31 (for student use while reading the selection)

VOCABULARY

▲ VOCABULARY IN CONTEXT

DIAGNOSE WORD KNOWLEDGE To determine preteaching needs, have all students complete Vocabulary in Context. *Answers:* **1.** *f,* **2.** *h,* **3.** *e,* **4.** *g,* **5.** *a,* **6.** *c,* **7.** *b,* **8.** *d*

PRETEACH VOCABULARY Preteach vocabulary with this copy master. Read each item aloud.

> **RESOURCE MANAGER—Copy Master**
> Vocabulary Study p. 33

MORE VOCABULARY SUPPORT
For additional activities and guidelines, see

> **BEST PRACTICES TOOLKIT**
> Scaffolding Vocabulary Instruction
> pp. 43–46
> **ⓘ** Vocabulary Center at **ClassZone.com**

SUMMARY

In this excerpt from his autobiography, Twain tells of a mesmerizer's visit to his hometown. Jealous of audience members who serve as the mesmerizer's subjects, the teenaged Twain fakes being hypnotized. He soon becomes the star of the show; in fact, he is so convincing that by the time the mesmerizer leaves town, Twain is the only person who doesn't believe in hypnotism. Years later, when he confesses the deception to his mother, she refuses to believe him. Twain concludes that a well-told lie has a long life.

READING SKILL

Ⓐ PREDICT

Possible answer: *Readers can predict that the young Twain might interact with the mesmerizer who has come to his village.*

Extend the Discussion What clues lead you to that prediction?

The Autobiography of Mark Twain

Mark Twain

BACKGROUND This excerpt from Mark Twain's autobiography focuses on a traveling show that visits Twain's small town around 1850. These entertainment shows were popular in a time before radio, television, or computers. They featured magic acts, ventriloquists, and mesmerizers (or hypnotists). Hypnotists placed people in suggestible, trancelike states and then ordered them to perform various antics.

An exciting event in our village was the arrival of the mesmerizer.[1] I think the year was 1850. As to that I am not sure but I know the month—it was May; that detail has survived the wear of fifty years. A pair of connected little incidents of that month have served to keep the memory of it green for me all this time; incidents of no consequence and not worth embalming,[2] yet my memory has preserved them carefully and flung away things of real value to give them space and make them comfortable. The truth is, a person's memory has no more sense than his conscience and no appreciation whatever of values and proportions. However, never mind those trifling incidents; my subject is the mesmerizer now. Ⓐ

10   He advertised his show and promised marvels. Admission as usual: 25 cents, children half price. The village had heard of mesmerism in a general way but had not encountered it yet. Not many people attended the first night but next day they had so many wonders to tell that everybody's curiosity was fired and after

---

1. **mesmerizer:** hypnotist; from the name of an Austrian physician, Franz Anton Mesmer, who popularized hypnotism in the 1770s.
2. **embalming:** preserving.

ANALYZE VISUALS
Look at the poster on page 637, especially at the image in the top circle. What can you **infer** about the mesmerizer depicted?

Ⓐ **PREDICT**
Based on the clues presented in this first paragraph, what can you predict about what might happen in the story?

DIFFERENTIATED INSTRUCTION

FOR ALL STUDENTS
Provide these independent projects to extend the lesson:

- Prepare an oral interpretation that captures Twain's style.

- Choose a dramatic scene from the *Autobiography*, decide how it could be staged, and write the stage directions for the actors who play Twain and the mesmerizer.

For further details on these projects, see

R RESOURCE MANAGER
Ideas for Extension pp. 24–25

FOR STRATEGIC READERS
In combination with the *Audio Anthology CD,* use one or more Targeted Passages (pp. 638, 640, 642, and 644) to ensure that students focus on key events and concepts. Targeted passages are also good for English learners.

THE MESMERIZER

ANALYZE VISUALS

Possible answer: The viewer can infer that the mesmerizer can control the behavior of other people—and can even defy the law of gravity—simply by using his hands.

BACKGROUND

Mesmerism Franz Anton Mesmer (1734–1815) was an Austrian doctor who gave his name to what he considered a system for curing illness. Mesmer believed that every part of the universe was connected by magnetic fluid and that illness occurred when the balance of fluid in a person's body was disturbed. According to Mesmer, magnetic passes of a doctor's hands over the patient's body could cure sickness by redirecting that fluid. After frenzied convulsions or hypnotic trances, Mesmer's patients reported themselves restored to health.

Mesmer experienced considerable success when he introduced his system of "animal magnetism" to Paris in 1778. King Louis XVI was skeptical, however, and he appointed a scientific commission to investigate Mesmer's claims. Benjamin Franklin and other commission members declared Mesmer a fraud, concluding that his cures were simply the product of people's imaginations.

Although Mesmer's theory of magnetism as a therapeutic technique was discredited, interest in the hypnotic trance state flourished during the 19th century. In the United States, mesmerism became a form of entertainment —the kind of traveling performance that young Mark Twain encounters in this account.

that for a fortnight[3] the magician had prosperous times. I was fourteen or fifteen years old, the age at which a boy is willing to endure all things, suffer all things short of death by fire, if thereby he may be conspicuous and show off before the public; and so, when I saw the "subjects" perform their foolish antics on the platform and make the people laugh and shout and admire I had a burning desire to be a subject myself.

20   Every night for three nights I sat in the row of candidates on the platform and held the magic disk[4] in the palm of my hand and gazed at it and tried to get sleepy, but it was a failure; I remained wide awake and had to retire defeated, like the majority. Also, I had to sit there and be gnawed with envy of Hicks, our journeyman;[5] I had to sit there and see him scamper and jump when Simmons the enchanter exclaimed, "See the snake! See the snake!" and hear him say, "My, how beautiful!" in response to the suggestion that he was observing a splendid sunset; and so on—the whole insane business. I couldn't laugh, I couldn't applaud; it filled me with bitterness to have others do it and to have people make a hero of Hicks and crowd around him when the show was over and ask him for more and 30 more particulars of the wonders he had seen in his visions and manifest in many ways that they were proud to be acquainted with him. Hicks—the idea! I couldn't stand it; I was getting boiled to death in my own bile.

On the fourth night temptation came and I was not strong enough to resist. When I had gazed at the disk a while I pretended to be sleepy and began to nod. Straightway came the professor and made passes over my head and down my body and legs and arms, finishing each pass with a snap of his fingers in the air to discharge the surplus electricity;[6] then he began to "draw" me with the disk, holding it in his fingers and telling me I could not take my eyes off it, try as I might; so I rose slowly, bent and gazing, and followed that disk all over the place, 40 just as I had seen the others do. Then I was put through the other paces. Upon suggestion I fled from snakes, passed buckets at a fire, became excited over hot steamboat-races, made love to imaginary girls and kissed them, fished from the platform and landed mud cats that outweighed me—and so on, all the customary marvels. But not in the customary way. I was cautious at first and watchful, being afraid the professor would discover that I was an impostor and drive me from the platform in disgrace; but as soon as I realized that I was not in danger, I set myself the task of terminating Hicks's usefulness as a subject and of usurping his place. **B**

It was a sufficiently easy task. Hicks was born honest, I without that incumbrance[7]—so some people said. Hicks saw what he saw and reported 50 accordingly, I saw more than was visible and added to it such details as could help. Hicks had no imagination; I had a double supply. He was born calm, I was

① Targeted Passage

B IRONY
Reread lines 33–47. Identify the **dramatic irony** in this paragraph. What sort of tension does this create?

---

3. **fortnight:** 14 days.
4. **magic disk:** the object used by the mesmerizer to focus a subject's attention, helping him or her to achieve a hypnotic state.
5. **journeyman:** a competent and experienced, but not brilliant, craftsman.
6. **discharge . . . electricity:** It was once erroneously believed that hypnosis was linked to electricity and magnetism.
7. **incumbrance:** earlier spelling of *encumbrance*, here meaning "burden; obligation."

Lines 20–47
TIERED DISCUSSION PROMPTS

Use these prompts to help students explore young Twain's motivation and character:

Recall Why does Twain pretend to be mesmerized? *Possible answer: Twain is jealous of the attention that Hicks is getting (lines 28–32) and wants to outdo him (lines 46–47). Since Twain seems resistant to mesmerism (lines 20–23), he decides to pretend.*

Analyze What does this passage reveal about young Twain's character? Cite evidence. *Possible answer: This passage shows that Twain cannot resist temptation. He is observant, able to imitate the other subjects by watching their actions. Twain is competitive, determined to replace Hicks; and he is dishonest, willing to deceive people to gain attention.*

Evaluate What do you think of Twain's character? Explain. *Even students who disapprove of Twain's dishonesty may find him amusing.*

LITERARY ANALYSIS

B IRONY

Possible answer: Although readers know that Twain is not really mesmerized, the audience believes that he is. The discrepancy between the readers' knowledge and the audience's knowledge heightens tension because it is not yet known if Twain will succeed.

If students need help . . . Work with them to trace the clues that Twain gives in the previous two paragraphs (lines 17–19, 22–23, 27–32, and 33) before actually stating his deception in line 34.

DIFFERENTIATED INSTRUCTION

FOR STRATEGIC READERS

① Targeted Passage [Lines 20–40]

This passage describes Twain's inner conflict as he watches the mesmerizer's show.

- How does Twain participate in the magician's attempts to hypnotize his subjects? What is the outcome?
- How do Simmons's mesmerized subjects behave on stage?
- How does Twain feel as he watches Hicks?

- How does Twain give in to temptation and resolve his frustration?

Comprehension Support Help students break down long, complicated sentences like the one in lines 14–19 by reducing them to one set or more of basic components: subject, verb, and object. Ask:

- Who or what is the sentence (clause) about?
- What action does the subject do?
- Who or what receives the action of the verb(s)?

FOR ENGLISH LEARNERS

Key Academic Vocabulary Use Word Questioning to teach these words: *thereby* (line 16), *tense* (line 74), *acknowledge* (line 142), *concentrate* (line 179), *trace* (line 187), *policy* (line 279).

📖 BEST PRACTICES TOOLKIT—Transparency Word Questioning p. E9

KELLAR

LEVITATION

born excited. No vision could start a rapture in him and he was constipated as to language, anyway; but if I saw a vision I emptied the dictionary onto it and lost the remnant of my mind into the bargain.

At the end of my first half-hour Hicks was a thing of the past, a fallen hero, a broken idol, and I knew it and was glad and said in my heart, "Success to crime!" Hicks could never have been mesmerized to the point where he could kiss an imaginary girl in public or a real one either, but I was competent. Whatever Hicks had failed in, I made it a point to succeed in, let the cost be what it might,
60 physically or morally. He had shown several bad defects and I had made a note of them. For instance, if the magician asked, "What do you see?" and left him to invent a vision for himself, Hicks was dumb and blind, he couldn't see a thing nor say a word, whereas the magician soon found out that when it came to seeing visions of a stunning and marketable sort I could get along better without his help than with it.

Then there was another thing: Hicks wasn't worth a tallow dip[8] on mute mental suggestion. Whenever Simmons stood behind him and gazed at the back of his skull and tried to drive a mental suggestion into it, Hicks sat with vacant face and never suspected. If he had been noticing he could have seen by
70 the **rapt** faces of the audience that something was going on behind his back that required a response. Inasmuch as I was an impostor I dreaded to have this test put upon me, for I knew the professor would be "willing" me to do something, and as

rapt (răpt) *adj.* deeply moved, delighted, or absorbed

---

8. **wasn't worth a tallow dip:** wasn't any good. A tallow dip was an inexpensive candle.

THE AUTOBIOGRAPHY OF MARK TWAIN **639**

Lines 55–65
REINFORCE *KEY IDEA:* DECEPTION

Discuss How effective is young Twain's **deception?** How can you tell? *Possible answer: Twain's deception is very effective: Within a half hour he replaces Hicks in the crowd's affections, and Simmons himself soon realizes that Twain is a better "subject" than Hicks.*

About the Art Harry Kellar (1849–1922), an entertainer who combined magic tricks with elaborate presentations, was known as the "Dean of American Magicians." His illusions, or misleading versions of reality, were accomplished by clever mechanical arrangements. This poster shows one of his most famous illusions: the levitation of a girl who rose from a couch and then disappeared into thin air.

FOR ENGLISH LEARNERS
Related Vocabulary Point out to students that Twain uses several words in addition to *mesmerizer* (line 1) to refer to Simmons: *magician* (lines 14, 61, 105, and 203), *enchanter* (line 25), and *professor* (lines 45, 72, 109, 113, 117, and 123). Have students look up the definitions of these words and discuss their similarities and differences.

FOR ADVANCED LEARNERS/AP
Research Hypnotism [small-group option] Have small groups of students find out more about hypnotism (mesmerism), focusing on topics such as these:

- the roots of hypnotism in the rites practiced by ancient Hindus and other early cultures
- the use of the power of suggestion in place of anesthesia for surgery
- the use of hypnotism in treating such conditions as stage fright or insomnia or such medical problems as high blood pressure, migraine headaches, or asthma
- reasons that the practice has been dismissed as a parlor trick practiced by charlatans

Give groups the option of presenting the results of their research in a symposium that supports or debunks the practice.

C PREDICT

Possible answer: *Given the character traits that Twain has exhibited and the state-ments that he has made about himself, readers can predict that he will rise to the challenge and invent a scenario that will both fool and entertain the audience.*

If students need help . . . Have them reread lines 48–81. Then work with students to record clues like these in the chart intro-duced on page 635:

Predictions	Text Clues
I predict that Twain will pretend to obey the "mental suggestion."	"...when it came to seeing visions of a stunning and marketable sort I could get along better without his help than with it" (lines 63–65)

Lines 74–98
REINFORCE *KEY IDEA:* DECEPTION

Discuss How does this part of Twain's account indicate that Twain isn't the only character with some skill at **deception?** In what sense is this turn of events an example of situational irony? *Possible answer: Twain is worried about being disgraced when his deception is revealed (lines 77–78), but he is not "exposed and denounced," because Simmons himself is an impostor who is happy to take advantage of Twain's deception (lines 93–98). Ironi-cally, Twain is not punished for his deception, because an even greater deception is going on—the mesmerizer's.*

I couldn't know what it was, I should be exposed and denounced. However, when my time came, I took my chance. I perceived by the tense and expectant faces of the people that Simmons was behind me willing me with all his might. I tried my best to imagine what he wanted but nothing suggested itself. I felt ashamed and miserable then. I believed that the hour of my disgrace was come and that in another moment I should go out of that place disgraced. I ought to be ashamed to confess it but my next thought was not how I could win the compassion of kindly
80 hearts by going out humbly and in sorrow for my misdoings, but how I could go out most sensationally and spectacularly. **C**

There was a rusty and empty old revolver lying on the table among the "properties" employed in the performances. On May Day two or three weeks before there had been a celebration by the schools and I had had a quarrel with a big boy who was the school bully and I had not come out of it with credit.[9] That boy was now seated in the middle of the house, halfway down the main aisle. I crept stealthily and impressively toward the table, with a dark and murderous scowl on my face, copied from a popular romance, seized the revolver suddenly, flourished it, shouted the bully's name, jumped off the platform and made a
90 rush for him and chased him out of the house before the paralyzed people could interfere to save him. There was a storm of applause, and the magician, addressing the house, said, most impressively—

"That you may know how really remarkable this is and how wonderfully developed a subject we have in this boy, I assure you that without a single spoken word to guide him he has carried out what I mentally commanded him to do, to the **minutest** detail. I could have stopped him at a moment in his vengeful career by a mere exertion of my will, therefore the poor fellow who has escaped was at no time in danger."

So I was not in disgrace. I returned to the platform a hero and happier than
100 I have ever been in this world since. As regards mental suggestion, my fears of it were gone. I judged that in case I failed to guess what the professor might be willing me to do, I could count on putting up something that would answer just as well. I was right, and exhibitions of unspoken suggestion became a favorite with the public. Whenever I perceived that I was being willed to do something I got up and did something—anything that occurred to me—and the magician, not being a fool, always ratified it. When people asked me, "How *can* you tell what he is willing you to do?" I said, "It's just as easy," and they always said admiringly, "Well, it beats *me* how you can do it."

Hicks was weak in another detail. When the professor made passes over him
110 and said "his whole body is without sensation now—come forward and test him, ladies and gentlemen," the ladies and gentlemen always complied eagerly and stuck pins into Hicks, and if they went deep Hicks was sure to wince, then that poor professor would have to explain that Hicks "wasn't sufficiently under the influence." But I didn't wince; I only suffered and shed tears on the inside. The miseries that a conceited boy will endure to keep up his "reputation"! And so

---

9. **credit:** honor or distinction.

C PREDICT
Reread lines 66–81. How do you predict Twain will respond to the challenge of "mute mental suggestion" from Simmons?

2 Targeted Passage

minutest (mī-nōō′tĭst) *adj.* smallest; most precise

DIFFERENTIATED INSTRUCTION

FOR STRATEGIC READERS

2 Targeted Passage [Lines 82–98]

In this passage, Twain continues his decep-tion through an inventive response to the mesmerizer's mental suggestion.

- How does Twain make use of his experi-ence with the school bully?
- How does the audience react?
- Why does the mesmerizer take credit for Twain's actions? How do his words keep Twain's secret safe?

FOR ENGLISH LEARNERS

Vocabulary: Idioms [mixed-readiness groups] Share or elicit the meanings of these expressions; then help students use them in original sentences:

- *count on* (line 102), "to be confident about"
- *putting up* (line 102), "creating"
- *it beats me* (line 108), "I don't understand"
- *was sure to* (line 112), "definitely would"
- *shed tears* (line 114), "cried"
- *air it* (line 134), "to speak about it in public"

will a conceited man; I know it in my own person and have seen it in a hundred thousand others. That professor ought to have protected me and I often hoped he would, when the tests were unusually severe, but he didn't. It may be that he was deceived as well as the others, though I did not believe it nor think it possible.

120 Those were dear good people but they must have carried simplicity and **credulity** to the limit. They would stick a pin in my arm and bear on it until they drove it a third of its length in, and then be lost in wonder that by a mere exercise of will power the professor could turn my arm to iron and make it insensible to pain. Whereas it was not insensible at all; I was suffering agonies of pain.

After that fourth night, that proud night, that triumphant night, I was the only subject. Simmons invited no more candidates to the platform. I performed alone every night the rest of the fortnight. Up to that time a dozen wise old heads, the intellectual aristocracy of the town, had held out as **implacable** unbelievers. I was as hurt by this as if I were engaged in some honest occupation. There is

130 nothing surprising about this. Human beings feel dishonor the most, sometimes, when they most deserve it. That handful of overwise old gentlemen kept on shaking their heads all the first week and saying they had seen no marvels there that could not have been produced by collusion; and they were pretty vain of their unbelief too and liked to show it and air it and be superior to the ignorant and the **gullible.** Particularly old Dr. Peake, who was the ringleader of the irreconcilables and very formidable; for he was an F.F.V.,[10] he was learned, white-haired and venerable, nobly and richly clad in the fashions of an earlier and a courtlier day, he was large and stately, and he not only seemed wise but was what he seemed in that regard. He had great influence and his opinion upon any matter was worth much

140 more than that of any other person in the community. When I conquered him at last, I knew I was undisputed master of the field; and now after more than fifty years I acknowledge with a few dry old tears that I rejoiced without shame. **D**

In 1847 we were living in a large white house on the corner of Hill and Main Streets—a house that still stands but isn't large now although it hasn't lost a plank; I saw it a year ago and noticed that shrinkage. My father died in it in March of the year mentioned but our family did not move out of it until some months afterward. Ours was not the only family in the house; there was another, Dr. Grant's. One day Dr. Grant and Dr. Reyburn argued a matter on the street with sword canes and Grant was brought home **multifariously** punctured. Old Dr.

150 Peake caulked the leaks and came every day for a while to look after him.

The Grants were Virginians, like Peake, and one day when Grant was getting well enough to be on his feet and sit around in the parlor and talk, the conversation fell upon Virginia and old times. I was present but the group were probably unconscious of me, I being only a lad and a negligible quantity. Two of

---

credulity (krĭ-dōō′lĭ-tē) *n.* an inclination to believe too readily

implacable (ĭm-plăk′ə-bəl) *adj.* impossible to satisfy

gullible (gŭl′ə-bəl) *adj.* easily deceived or tricked

D **IRONY**
Reread lines 125–131. Identify the **situational irony** in Twain's reaction to the skeptical wise old men in the crowd. What does this suggest about him?

multifariously (mŭl′tə-fâr′ē-əs-lē) *adv.* in many and various ways

---

10. **F.F.V.:** First Family of Virginia. Dr. Peake has high social status because his ancestors were among the first settlers of Virginia.

Lines 125–142
TIERED DISCUSSION PROMPTS

Use these prompts to help students understand that yet another conflict lies ahead for Twain:

Summarize So far, whom has Twain convinced of his ability to be mesmerized? *Possible answer: Twain seems to have convinced just about everyone in town.*

Interpret Twain looks ahead to the outcome of his story. Why does he need to deal with Dr. Peake? Why will conquering him be a great triumph? *Possible answer: Peake is respected as a wise man, but Twain needs to deal with him as a skeptic. If Twain can convince Peake that Twain was mesmerized, his triumph will lie in having defeated "the intellectual aristocracy of the town" (line 128).*

Evaluate Does Twain sharing his thoughts about the outcome of the story before actually telling the story ruin the outcome for readers? Why or why not? *Accept all reasonable answers.*

LITERARY ANALYSIS

D **IRONY**

Possible answer: The situational irony is that Twain's reaction to the wise old men's skepticism is the opposite of what readers would expect. Twain says that he was as hurt by their skepticism as if he were not trying to deceive them but were telling the truth (line 129). This ironic reaction suggests that he is fully engaged in the role that he has created—and, to some extent, has come to believe.

FOR STRATEGIC READERS
Draw Conclusions Call students' attention to lines 117–119. Ask students why they think that the mesmerizer does not try to protect Twain if, as Twain suspects, he is not fooled by Twain's performance. *Possible answers: The mesmerizer remains silent because he does not care about Twain's comfort; he is willing to let Twain suffer to gain more popularity for his show and, ultimately, more money for himself.*

Clarify Sequence Here, the adult Twain shares details out of chronological order. Help students understand these facts:

- The young Twain will overcome Dr. Peake's skepticism, but the adult Twain has not yet shared the details of that triumph (lines 140–142).
- The anecdotes that introduce Dr. Peake (lines 143–171) tell of events a few years before the mesmerizer comes to town.

FOR ADVANCED LEARNERS/AP
Analyze Figurative Language Twain uses metaphors to enliven ordinary language, encourage interpretation, and provide maximum meaning with a minimum of words. In lines 149–150, for example, he uses a plumbing metaphor to describe the nature of Dr. Grant's injuries and Dr. Peake's treatment. Challenge students to locate and explain other examples of Twain's use of metaphor, such as in lines 53, 189–191, and 278–279.

the group—Dr. Peake and Mrs. Crawford, Mrs. Grant's mother—had been of the audience when the Richmond theater burned down thirty-six years before, and they talked over the frightful details of that memorable tragedy. These were eyewitnesses, and with their eyes I saw it all with an intolerable vividness: I saw the black smoke rolling and tumbling toward the sky, I saw the flames burst
160 through it and turn red, I heard the shrieks of the despairing, I glimpsed their faces at the windows, caught fitfully through the veiling smoke, I saw them jump to their death or to mutilation worse than death. The picture is before me yet and can never fade.

In due course they talked of the colonial mansion of the Peakes, with its stately columns and its spacious grounds, and by odds and ends I picked up a clearly defined idea of the place. I was strongly interested, for I had not before heard of such palatial things from the lips of people who had seen them with their own eyes. One detail, casually dropped, hit my imagination hard. In the wall by the great front door there was a round hole as big as a saucer—a British cannon ball
170 had made it in the war of the Revolution. It was breathtaking; it made history real; history had never been real to me before.

Very well, three or four years later, as already mentioned, I was king bee and sole "subject" in the mesmeric show; it was the beginning of the second week; the performance was half over; just then the majestic Dr. Peake with his ruffled bosom and wrist-bands and his gold-headed cane entered, and a deferential citizen vacated his seat beside the Grants and made the great chief take it. This happened while I was trying to invent something fresh in the way of vision, in response to the professor's remark—

"Concentrate your powers. Look—look attentively. There—don't you see
180 something? Concentrate—concentrate! Now then—describe it." **E**

> Without suspecting it, Dr. Peake, by entering the place, had reminded me of the talk of three years before. He had also furnished me capital and was become my confederate, an accomplice in my frauds. I began on a vision, a vague and dim one (that was part of the game at the beginning of a vision; it isn't best to see it too clearly at first, it might look as if you had come loaded with it). The vision developed by degrees and gathered swing, momentum, energy. It was the Richmond fire. Dr. Peake was cold at first and his fine face had a trace of polite scorn in it; but when he began to recognize that fire, that expression changed and his eyes began to light up. As soon as I saw that, I threw the valves wide open and
> 190 turned on all the steam and gave those people a supper of fire and horrors that was calculated to last them one while! They couldn't gasp when I got through—they were petrified. Dr. Peake had risen and was standing—and breathing hard. He said, in a great voice:
> "My doubts are ended. No collusion could produce that miracle. It was totally impossible for him to know those details, yet he has described them with the clarity of an eyewitness —and with what **unassailable** truthfulness God knows I know!" **F**

I saved the colonial mansion for the last night and solidified and perpetuated

---

E PREDICT

Possible answer: Twain probably will succeed by thinking up some imaginative trick to convince the wise old men. He may describe a vision based on one or both of the accounts that he heard these men tell a few years earlier: the Richmond theater fire (lines 154–162) and the Peakes' colonial mansion (lines 164–171).

F IRONY

Possible answer: Readers know (as Dr. Peake does not) that Twain is not describing a mesmerism-induced vision but is retelling an overheard eyewitness account of the Richmond fire. The effect of this irony—the fact that Dr. Peake is taken in by Twain's deception—is to reinforce Twain's cunning (for Twain vividly remembers the details that he heard, and he realizes that Dr. Peake had not been aware of his presence during the conversation) and to suggest that the wise old men of the town may not be as wise as they seem.

E PREDICT
Predict how Twain will win over the wise old men of the town.

3 Targeted Passage

unassailable
(ŭn'ə-sā'lə-bəl) *adj.*
impossible to dispute or disprove

F IRONY
What do you know that Dr. Peake doesn't? Explain how this **dramatic irony** affects your impression of the characters involved, including young Twain.

DIFFERENTIATED INSTRUCTION

FOR STRATEGIC READERS

3 Targeted Passage [Lines 181–197]

In this passage, Twain converts his most notable skeptic to belief in mesmerism.

- What does Twain remember when Dr. Peake enters?

- Why does Dr. Peake's facial expression change as Twain describes his vision?

- Why does Twain refer to Dr. Peake as a "confederate" and an "accomplice"?

- Why is Dr. Peake convinced that he has experienced a miracle?

FOR ENGLISH LEARNERS

Language: Punctuation and Print Cues Have students reread lines 157–162. Note that each item in the series begins with "I saw," "I heard," or "I glimpsed," and the items are separated by commas. Note that Twain uses another comma within one of these items. Modern punctuation style usually mandates semicolons to separate items in a series if any of the items includes an internal comma.

FOR ADVANCED LEARNERS/AP

Analyze Local Color Urge students to review the section of the historical essay on regionalism and local color (pages 623–624) and the Literary Analysis Workshop on Setting in Regional Literature (pages 632–633). Then have them discuss these questions:

- How do Twain's comments in lines 164–171 highlight the local color?

- What do those comments indicate about his writing style?

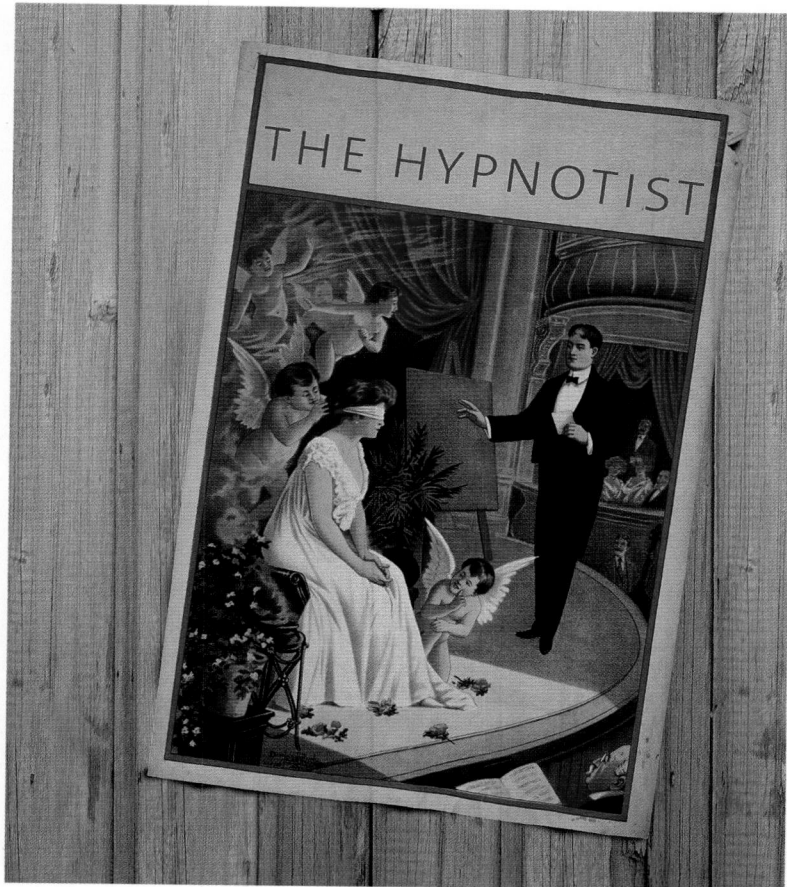

THE HYPNOTIST

Dr. Peake's conversion with the cannon-ball hole. He explained to the house that
200 I could never have heard of that small detail, which differentiated this mansion
from all other Virginian mansions and perfectly identified it, therefore the fact
stood proven that I had *seen* it in my vision. Lawks![11]

It is curious. When the magician's engagement closed there was but one person
in the village who did not believe in mesmerism and I was the one. All the others
were converted but I was to remain an implacable and unpersuadable disbeliever
in mesmerism and hypnotism for close upon fifty years. This was because I never
would examine them, in after life. I couldn't. The subject revolted me. Perhaps it
brought back to me a passage in my life which for pride's sake I wished to forget;

---

11. **Lawks!:** an expression of wonder or amusement, shortened from "Lord, have mercy!"

Lines 203–210
TIERED DISCUSSION PROMPTS

Use these prompts to help students explore Twain's reflection upon his experiences with the mesmerizer:

Restate How does Twain feel about his experience with the mesmerizer? *Possible answer: Twain is torn between feeling triumph for his achievement and regret for his deception.*

Analyze Why is it ironic that Twain became the "one person in the village who did not believe in mesmerism"? *Possible answer: It is ironic that Twain is the only doubter because it is his performance as a subject that has persuaded everyone else to believe in mesmerism.*

Evaluate Is Twain's cynical response to his experience believable? Defend your opinion. *Most students will find Twain's response believable, citing examples of cheaters who assume that the rest of the world is dishonest.*

FOR ADVANCED LEARNERS/AP

Analyze Tone Review with students the definition of *tone*: the author's attitude toward the subject, as conveyed through the choice of words and details. Have students contrast Twain's tone in lines 203–208 with the tone that he has previously used to describe his exploits, such as in lines 99–100 and 172–173. Ask students to write and share an essay in which they address these questions:

- What adjectives would you use to describe the tone in each of the three passages? In each case, what words and details help to convey Twain's tone?

- How does the tone change during the excerpt? What might cause the change?

- How does the tone influence your understanding of Twain's account?

Discuss What is Twain saying in this passage about the consequences of **deception,** at least for him? *Possible answer: Twain is saying that he was unable to enjoy the consequences of his deception because he became quite uncomfortable over repeated compliments about his fraudulent triumphs.* Is his experience typical, or do most liars and cheaters manage to enjoy the fruits of their deception—and even the glory of undeserved praise? Explain. *Accept all thoughtful responses.*

READING SKILL

Ⓖ PREDICT

Possible answer: Twain's mother may not believe him at first; he begins the paragraph by saying that it is hard to undo a lie (lines 227–228).

---

210 though I thought, or persuaded myself I thought, I should never come across a "proof" which wasn't thin and cheap and probably had a fraud like me behind it.

The truth is I did not have to wait long to get tired of my triumphs. Not thirty days, I think. The glory which is built upon a lie soon becomes a most unpleasant incumbrance. No doubt for a while I enjoyed having my exploits told and retold and told again in my presence and wondered over and exclaimed about, but I quite distinctly remember that there presently came a time when the subject was wearisome and odious to me and I could not endure the disgusting discomfort of it. I am well aware that the world-glorified doer of a deed of great and real splendor has just my experience; I know that he deliciously enjoys hearing about it for three or four weeks and that pretty soon after that he begins to dread the
220 mention of it and by and by wishes he had been with the damned before he ever thought of doing that deed. I remember how General Sherman[12] used to rage and swear over "While we were marching through Georgia," which was played at him and sung at him everywhere he went; still, I think I suffered a shade more than the legitimate hero does, he being privileged to soften his misery with the reflection that his glory was at any rate golden and reproachless in its origin, whereas I had no such privilege, there being no possible way to make mine respectable.

How easy it is to make people believe a lie and how hard it is to undo that work again! Thirty-five years after those evil exploits of mine I visited my old mother, whom I had not seen for ten years; and being moved by what seemed
230 to me a rather noble and perhaps heroic impulse, I thought I would humble myself and confess my ancient fault. It cost me a great effort to make up my mind; I dreaded the sorrow that would rise in her face and the shame that would look out of her eyes; but after long and troubled reflection, the sacrifice seemed due and right and I gathered my resolution together and made the confession. Ⓖ

To my astonishment there were no sentimentalities, no dramatics, no George Washington effects; she was not moved in the least degree; she simply did not believe me and said so! I was not merely disappointed, I was **nettled** to have my costly truthfulness flung out of the market in this placid and confident way when I was expecting to get a profit out of it. I asserted and reasserted, with rising heat,
240 my statement that every single thing I had done on those long-vanished nights was a lie and a swindle; and when she shook her head tranquilly and said she knew better, I put up my hand and *swore* to it—adding a triumphant, "*Now* what do you say?"

It did not affect her at all; it did not budge her the fraction of an inch from her position. If this was hard for me to endure, it did not begin with the blister she put upon the raw[13] when she began to put my sworn oath out of court with *arguments* to prove that I was under a delusion and did not know what I was talking about. Arguments! Arguments to show that a person on a man's outside can know better what is on his inside than he does himself. I had cherished some

---

Ⓖ PREDICT
Reread lines 227–234. How do you think Twain's mother will respond to his confession? Explain why you think this.

nettled (nĕt'əld) *adj.* irritated; annoyed **nettle** *v.*

④ Targeted Passage

---

12. **General Sherman:** William Tecumseh Sherman, Union commander who led a destructive march in 1864 from Atlanta, Georgia, to the Atlantic, cutting the Confederacy in two.

13. **the blister . . . raw:** a bad thing made even worse.

DIFFERENTIATED INSTRUCTION

FOR STRATEGIC READERS

④ Targeted Passage [Lines 228–249]

This passage explains what happens 35 years later, when Twain confesses the truth about his deception to his mother.

- How does Twain expect his mother to react to his confession? How does she actually react?
- How does Twain try to change his mother's mind, and what is her response?
- Why is he so bothered by her arguments?

FOR ENGLISH LEARNERS

Culture: Clarify Invite a volunteer to tell the story of George Washington and the cherry tree. Emphasize that Washington was praised for his honesty rather than reprimanded for his action. Then ask students to explain what Twain meant by his reference to "George Washington effects" (lines 235–236). *Possible answer: Twain might have been expecting praise for his honesty in confessing his deception, even 35 years after the event.*

FOR ADVANCED LEARNERS/AP

Comprehension: Text Structure Point out that in lines 217–226, Twain compares and contrasts his feelings with those of true heroes. Ask students in what way Twain sees himself as both similar to and different from the "hero who has attained real glory." *Possible answer: Both grow tired of hearing their praises sung. Twain, however, claims to suffer more than does the true hero, who at least knows that his heroic deed was real and respectable.*

contempt for arguments before, I have not enlarged my respect for them since.
She refused to believe that I had invented my visions myself; she said it was
folly: that I was only a child at the time and could not have done it. She cited
the Richmond fire and the colonial mansion and said they were quite beyond
my capacities. Then I saw my chance! I said she was right—I didn't invent those,
I got them from Dr. Peake. Even this great shot did not damage. She said Dr.
Peake's evidence was better than mine, and he had said in plain words that it was
impossible for me to have heard about those things. Dear, dear, what a grotesque
and unthinkable situation: a confessed swindler convicted of honesty and
condemned to acquittal by circumstantial evidence furnished by the swindled! **H**

I realized with shame and with impotent vexation that I was defeated all along
the line. I had but one card left but it was a formidable one. I played it and stood
from under. It seemed ignoble to demolish her fortress after she had defended it
so valiantly but the defeated know not mercy. I played that master card. It was the
pin-sticking. I said solemnly—

"I give you my honor, a pin was never stuck into me without causing me
cruel pain."

She only said—

"It is thirty-five years. I believe you do think that now but I was there and
I know better. You never winced."

She was so calm! and I was so far from it, so nearly frantic.

"Oh, my goodness!" I said, "let me *show* you that I am speaking the truth. Here
is my arm; drive a pin into it—drive it to the head—I shall not wince."

She only shook her gray head and said with simplicity and conviction—

"You are a man now and could dissemble the hurt; but you were only a child
then and could not have done it."

And so the lie which I played upon her in my youth remained with her as
an unchallengeable truth to the day of her death. Carlyle[14] said "a lie cannot
live." It shows that he did not know how to tell them. If I had taken out a life
policy on this one the premiums would have bankrupted me ages ago. ✑

H IRONY
Reread lines 244–259.
Identify the **situational
irony** that underlies
Twain's confession to his
mother. What statement
is Twain making about
honesty and deception?

---

14. **Carlyle:** Thomas Carlyle, a British historian and essayist.

THE AUTOBIOGRAPHY OF MARK TWAIN   **645**

LITERARY ANALYSIS

H IRONY

*Possible answer: The situational irony is
that when Twain finally tells his mother the
truth about his deception, she thinks that
he is lying (or, at least, failing to remember
the truth). Moreover, she offers as proof of
his past honesty the very proof that he used
to carry out his deception. Twain is making
the point that honesty and deception can
be hard to prove and that a lie can be
difficult to undo.*

SELECTION WRAP-UP

SUMMARIZE Have students summarize
what Twain might have learned from this
experience—and how and why it might
have changed him.

★ CRITIQUE

- Ask students how true to life they find
Twain's autobiographical account. To what
extent might Twain have elaborated on the
factual details of his experiences?

- After completing the After Reading questions on page 647, have students revisit
their responses and tell whether they have
changed their opinions.

FOR ENGLISH LEARNERS
Language: Conversational English Patterns
Help students use context clues to figure out
the meaning of these phrases. Point out that
the last expression is an idiom.

- *No doubt* (line 213), "probably"

- *there . . . came a time* (line 215), "then; later"

- *Dear, dear* (line 257), polite exclamation of
surprise or sympathy

- *played that master card* (line 263), "used a
key resource to gain an advantage"

FOR ADVANCED LEARNERS/AP
Analyze Point of View Ask students to analyze how Twain's first-person point of view
contributes to the excerpt's dramatic and
situational irony. Elicit that the first-person
point of view creates dramatic irony because
readers know the truth about Twain's actions
but other characters do not. The first-person
point of view also allows readers to appreciate
the excerpt's situational irony (and humor) by
highlighting the contrast between what

Twain expects to happen and what really does
happen.

To test this analysis, have students rewrite a
brief section of the excerpt from the point of
view of a minor character—for example, Hicks
or Dr. Peake. Then ask students to consider
this question: Is there a narrator whose first-
person point of view might create a completely different type of dramatic irony? If so, what
would this narrator and dramatic irony be like?

THE AUTOBIOGRAPHY OF MARK TWAIN   **645**

TIERED DISCUSSION PROMPTS

Use these prompts to help students appreciate Twain's wit and wisdom:

Restate Express one of Twain's epigrams in your own words. What twist does Twain add to an otherwise straightforward observation or piece of advice? *Possible answer: Restatements will vary. In general, Twain adds a skepticism to his observations and advice about life, especially when it comes to personal virtue and human interactions.*

Analyze Which epigram best fits the theme or message of the excerpt from Twain's *Autobiography*? Explain the connection. *Accept all well-reasoned responses; for example, students may choose the epigram about a lie's having more lives than a cat, because young Twain's experience with the mesmerizer was built on a lie.*

Evaluate Which epigram do you find the most relevant to your life or the lives of people you know? Explain why you consider this epigram particularly insightful or personally meaningful. *Accept all thoughtful responses.*

Connect: Epigrams

A popular writer and a sought-after public speaker, Mark Twain was full of witty remarks. What do these **epigrams**—short, clever, and sometimes paradoxical statements—reveal about Twain's view of human nature?

Epigrams
Mark Twain

Don't, like the cat, try to get more out of an experience than there is in it. The cat, having sat upon a hot stove lid, will not sit upon a hot stove lid again. Nor upon a cold stove lid.

. . . .

It is by the goodness of God that in our country we have those three unspeakably precious things: freedom of speech, freedom of conscience, and the prudence never to practice either of them.

. . . .

Man is the only animal that blushes. Or needs to.

. . . .

I am an old man and have known a great many troubles, but most of them have never happened.

. . . .

Nothing so needs reforming as other people's habits.

. . . .

When I was a boy of fourteen, my father was so ignorant I could hardly stand to have the old man around. But when I got to be twenty-one, I was astonished at how much the old man had learned in seven years.

. . . .

Put all your eggs in one basket, and—watch the basket.

There are several good protections against temptations, but the surest is cowardice.

. . . .

If you pick up a starving dog and make him prosperous, he will not bite you. This is the principal difference between a dog and a man.

. . . .

Good breeding consists in concealing how much we think of ourselves and how little we think of the other person.

. . . .

To promise not to do a thing is the surest way in the world to make a body want to go and do that very thing.

. . . .

Habit is habit, and not to be flung out of the window by any man, but coaxed downstairs a step at a time.

. . . .

One of the most striking differences between a cat and a lie is that a cat only has nine lives.

. . . .

Each person is born to one possession which outvalues all the others—his last breath.

. . . .

Everyone is a moon, and has a dark side which he never shows to anybody.

Comprehension

1. **Recall** What position or role does young Twain want to have? Why?

2. **Summarize** What weaknesses made Hicks a bad subject?

3. **Clarify** What does Twain do to get the mesmerizer to choose him?

R3.3
CALIFORNIA

Literary Analysis

4. **Examine Predictions** Review your list of predictions and clues. Were you able to correctly predict everything that happened? Or were you surprised by how some aspects of the story developed? Cite details from the story in your answer.

5. **Contrast Characters** To become the mesmerizer's subject, Twain must displace Hicks. Twain presents himself as very different from Hicks. Based on this contrast, what does Twain seem to value and admire in a person? Use a chart like the one shown to collect evidence.

Hicks	Twain

6. **Analyze Irony** By its very nature, irony presents a degree of tension wherever it appears—the tension between expectations and reality. In many cases, it also adds humor. Review Twain's use of irony in the following passages. What's funny about them?

   • "Hicks was born honest, I without that incumbrance [burden]—so some people said." (lines 48–49)

   • Young Twain is genuinely hurt by those who do not believe his performances. (lines 127–129)

   • Twain identifies with great heroes who tire of hearing their praises sung. (lines 213–223)

7. **Draw Conclusions About Changing Perspective** In writing this piece, the adult Twain had a different view of himself, his boyhood **deception**, and the people of his hometown than he had as a young boy. What does this dual perspective show you about his growth from boyhood to adulthood?

Literary Criticism

8. **Author's Perspective** Reread Twain's epigrams on page 646. What view of human nature do you find in these sayings? Explain how this view is played out in this episode of the *Autobiography*, giving evidence from both texts to support your answer.

THE AUTOBIOGRAPHY OF MARK TWAIN **647**

7. As a boy, Twain is impressed with his ability to fool people. He thinks that the people of his hometown are gullible and foolish, and he feels superior to them. As an adult, he is ashamed of his deception and his need for attention and glory; he also realizes that a lie has a long life, even if the liar wants to confess the truth. His dual perspective suggests that people are gullible and perhaps foolish—but that he is able to recognize his own foolishness, as well.

8. Students should point to the cynical, critical view of human nature that Twain expresses in his epigrams; then they should cite specific text details to show how this cynicism appears throughout the excerpt from the Autobiography.

Practice and Apply

After Reading
Use these copy masters to check understanding and provide extra support:

R RESOURCE MANAGER—Copy Masters
Reading Check p. 37
Irony p. 29
Question Support p. 36

Additional selection questions are provided for teachers on page 23.

ANSWERS

1. Twain wants to be the star subject in the mesmerizer's show because he wants to be the center of attention.

2. According to Twain, Hicks is a bad subject because he has no imagination, is too calm, can't use inventive language, and can describe only what he sees.

3. Twain gets the mesmerizer to choose him by pretending to be hypnotized.

Possible answers:

4. ■ SKILLS FOCUS **Predict** Students should cite specific events from the excerpt and explain why they were or were not able to predict these events based on text clues.

5. Young Twain values imagination, enthusiasm, verbal dexterity, craftiness, self-control, and the abilities to read people and think on one's feet. **Hicks:** Honest (line 48), unimaginative (lines 51 and 61–63); calm (line 51); describing only what he sees (lines 49–50); not good with words (lines 52–53); unable to take "mental suggestions" (lines 66–67); unable to ignore pain (lines 109–114). **Twain:** Dishonest (lines 48–49); embellishes everything (lines 50–51); imaginative (line 51); able to use language well (lines 53–54); able to figure out what is expected and fake it (lines 63–65 and 82–91); able to ignore pain (line 114).

6. ● SKILLS FOCUS **Irony** *Lines 48–49:* Honesty usually is regarded as a positive trait, but Twain regards it as a burden that he has been spared. *Lines 127–129:* Instead of being satisfied by the number of people whom he has deceived, Twain is hurt that "a dozen wise old heads" have not fallen for his tricks. *Lines 213–223:* Twain is far from being a great hero.

THE AUTOBIOGRAPHY OF MARK TWAIN **647**

ANSWERS
Vocabulary in Context

VOCABULARY PRACTICE

1. *true*   5. *false*
2. *true*   6. *true*
3. *false*   7. *false*
4. *true*   8. *true*

R RESOURCE MANAGER—Copy Master
Vocabulary Practice p. 34

VOCABULARY IN WRITING

Encourage students to select appropriate vocabulary words for the topic. Point out that they can use these words for any answer.

VOCABULARY STRATEGY: WORDS PRONOUNCED DIFFERENTLY *(also an EL language objective)*

Point out that students will not know how to pronounce a homograph until they see it in the context of a sentence. Also explain that when homographs are listed in a dictionary, students should read all the definitions to find the meaning that best fits.

Possible answers:

1. *b, garbage, H*
2. *b, musical instrument with low tones, H*
3. *a, mineral materials used in making concrete*
4. *b, to strike against forcefully, H*
5. *b, a concept, idea, or model*

R RESOURCE MANAGER—Copy Master
Vocabulary Strategy p. 35

i Vocabulary Center at **ClassZone.com**
Additional Vocabulary Activities

Assess and Reteach

Assess
R RESOURCE MANAGER—Copy Masters
Selection Tests A, B/C pp. 39–40, 41–42
Test Generator CD

Reteach
S STANDARDS LESSON FILE
Literature Lesson 36: Irony
Reading Lesson 1: Predicting
Vocabulary Lesson 20: Homonyms and Homographs

648 UNIT 4: REGIONALISM AND NATURALISM

Vocabulary in Context

VOCABULARY PRACTICE

Decide whether these statements about the vocabulary words are true or false.

1. Someone with many career changes can be said to have worked **multifariously.**
2. Believing everything a fortuneteller tells you is an example of **credulity.**
3. A person who pays **rapt** attention to a performance is probably bored with it.
4. You might feel **nettled** if it rains on your picnic.
5. If you are **gullible,** you have an enormous appetite for sweet foods.
6. A defendant with an **unassailable** alibi should feel confident testifying in court.
7. If you record the **minutest** facts about an event, you are noting how long it took.
8. A person with **implacable** demands is not likely to be easily satisfied.

WORD LIST
credulity
gullible
implacable
minutest
multifariously
nettled
rapt
unassailable

VOCABULARY IN WRITING

Would people today be taken in by Twain's performance? Use two or more vocabulary words in a paragraph telling your opinion. You could start this way.

> **EXAMPLE SENTENCE**
> *I think the average person is as **gullible** as ever.*

VOCABULARY STRATEGY: WORDS PRONOUNCED DIFFERENTLY

Some words are spelled the same but have different meanings and may have different pronunciations. An example is *minute* (mī-nōōt′), meaning "small," and *minute* (mĭn′ĭt), meaning "60 seconds." When these words also have different etymologies, they are called homographs, from the Latin root *graph* ("written") and prefix *homo-* ("the same"). Most dictionaries give homographs separate entries and mark them with superscripts: minute[1], minute[2].

Other words have multiple pronunciations depending on their part of speech. *Progress*, for example, is pronounced (prŏg′rĕs′) when used as a noun and (prə-grĕs′) when used as a verb.

PRACTICE Write the letter of the correct pronunciation for each boldfaced word; then define the word. Write *H* after the definition of any homograph.

1. take the household **refuse** to the dump   **a.** (rĭ-fyōōz′)   **b.** (rĕf′yōōs)
2. the band has a new upright **bass** player   **a.** (băs)   **b.** (bās)
3. crushed stone used in an **aggregate**   **a.** (ăg′rĭ-gĭt)   **b.** (ăg′rĭ-gāt)
4. allowed the wind to **buffet** the boat   **a.** (bə-fā′)   **b.** (bŭf′ĭt)
5. proposed a theoretical **construct**   **a.** (kən-strŭkt′)   **b.** (kŏn′strŭkt′)

VOCABULARY PRACTICE
For more practice, go to the **Vocabulary Center** at ClassZone.com.

DIFFERENTIATED INSTRUCTION

FOR ENGLISH LEARNERS

Task Support: Vocabulary in Writing Suggest that students use a Main Idea and Details organizer to plan their paragraph. For each detail that they list to support their opinion (the main idea), have them choose a vocabulary word that makes sense.

 BEST PRACTICES TOOLKIT—Transparency
Main Idea and Details p. B6

FOR ADVANCED LEARNERS/AP

Write with Homographs [paired option] Challenge pairs of students to compose and share sentences that use the feature's homograph pairs correctly. *Example: As partygoers lined up at the buffet, heavy winds began to buffet the tables.* To extend the activity, have partners brainstorm a list of additional homographs and then create and share similar sentences using them.

from Life on the Mississippi

Memoir by
Mark Twain

R3.3

● LITERARY ANALYSIS: VOICE

Voice is a writer's unique use of language. It allows a reader to "hear" the writer's personality in his or her writing. Mark Twain's distinctive voice is full of dry wit.

Here was something fresh—this thing of getting up in the middle of the night.... It was a detail ... that had never occurred to me at all. I knew that boats ran all night, but somehow I had never happened to reflect that somebody had to get up out of a warm bed to run them.

A writer's voice is established through **diction,** or word choice and order, and **tone,** or attitude toward the subject. As you read, look for Twain's ironic or humorous tone.

■ READING STRATEGY: PARAPHRASE

Twain's readers enjoy his deadpan humor and insights. However, it can take some digging through difficult sentences to figure out just what he's saying. **Paraphrasing** can help; if you can slow down and restate hard sentences in simpler language, you'll find it easier to follow him. And by recognizing his use of **understatement** (downplaying the importance of things) or his use of **hyperbole** (exaggeration) and other figures of speech, you can paraphrase better.

Within ten seconds more I was set aside in disgrace, and Mr. Bixby was ... flaying me alive with abuse of my cowardice.

With a dictionary, you can paraphrase this sentence.

1. **Paraphrase it literally:** "I was promptly disgraced, and Mr. Bixby was skinning me alive and calling me a coward."

2. **Notice where Twain is stretching the truth:** Bixby is not really skinning him alive, but abusing him verbally.

Your final paraphrase can read, "Soon I had gotten into trouble and Mr. Bixby was shouting at me, calling me a coward." Record your paraphrases in a chart like the one shown.

Difficult Passage	Literal Paraphrase	Final Paraphrase (when appropriate)

DIFFERENTIATED INSTRUCTION

FOR STRATEGIC READERS

Concept Support: Paraphrase Review these strategies for paraphrasing with students:

- Identify the main idea and supporting details, as if you were outlining the passage.

- Use a dictionary to check the meaning of old-fashioned or otherwise unfamiliar words; then replace those words with more familiar synonyms.

- If the writing uses inverted word order, rewrite it so that the order is more natural.

- Break long, complicated sentences into shorter, simpler sentences that you can paraphrase more easily.

In addition, remind students that a paraphrase is not a summary; rather, it is about the same length as the original, only in simpler language. (In other words, a summary does paraphrase, but a paraphrase does not summarize.)

Explore the Key Idea

Is IGNORANCE *really bliss?*

KEY IDEA People who don't pay attention to the news or world affairs are sometimes described as burying their heads in the sand. This is not a compliment. However, it's also acknowledged that these people are sometimes happier or less worried than those who **experience** more. Mark Twain discovers that his experiences on the Mississippi River come at a price.

PRESENT Consider people you know who seek varied experiences and others who prefer to remain sheltered. Then list the advantages and disadvantages of each approach. Decide which approach makes the most sense to you, and identify two reasons for your choice. Share your conclusions with the class.

649

Is IGNORANCE *really bliss?*

Ask the question; then lead into the **KEY IDEA** by pointing out that the question comes from a poem by Thomas Gray: "... where ignorance is bliss, / 'Tis folly to be wise." As students complete the **PRESENT** activity, have them think about ways in which the things that people **experience** bring happiness or unhappiness.

SKILLS FOCUS

LITERARY ANALYSIS
R3.3

● VOICE

Discuss these questions to help students grasp the humor and irony that mark Twain's tone:

- Twain refers to having to work in the middle of the night as "something fresh." How does that diction create humor? *Possible answer: The humor lies in the fact that the expression suggests something welcome, but Twain finds the call to get up unwelcome.*

- Irony arises when the expected and unexpected clash. How does this excerpt show such a clash? *Possible answer: Twain's expectation that the boat will run through the night clashes with the unexpected reality that he and others must work to make it run.*

READING STRATEGY

■ PARAPHRASE

Write this sentence on the board:

While the crisp night air proved salubrious, I'd have willingly traded it for a lengthier period of recuperation in my bunk.

Ask students to paraphrase the sentence. *Possible answer: The cool night air turned out to be good for my health, but I would rather have had a little more sleep.*

CHECK UNDERSTANDING Have students paraphrase the excerpt from Twain's memoir in the Literary Analysis discussion.

R RESOURCE MANAGER—Copy Master Paraphrase p. 55 (for student use while reading the selection)

SUMMARY

In this excerpt from his memoir *Life on the Mississippi*, Twain recalls his first lessons as an apprentice riverboat pilot. Naïve and inexperienced, he is shocked at first by the realities of the work. As Twain learns to read the river and pilot the boat, he laments that he has lost his appreciation for the beauty and romance of the Mississippi River.

Lines 1–10
REINFORCE *KEY IDEA:* EXPERIENCE

Discuss From the details in these lines, what can you infer about Twain's desire to **experience** life? *Possible answer: Twain's resolve to follow through on his fascination with "river life" and his plan to explore the Amazon imply that he desires to experience the adventures that life has to offer.*

Life on the Mississippi

Mark Twain

> **BACKGROUND** In this excerpt from his memoir, Mark Twain describes his first days as an apprentice riverboat pilot. Piloting a paddle steamboat was dangerous and tricky, because the Mississippi was constantly changing. The powerful current moved from one side to the other, especially in the windy parts of the river. Along this twisting course lurked hidden sandbars and submerged wrecks. Riverboat pilots gathered—and exchanged—precious information about the river's changing current.

A Cub-Pilot's Experience

What with lying on the rocks four days at Louisville, and some other delays, the poor old *Paul Jones* fooled away about two weeks in making the voyage from Cincinnati to New Orleans. This gave me a chance to get acquainted with one of the pilots, and he taught me how to steer the boat, and thus made the fascination of river life more potent than ever for me. . . .

❶ Targeted Passage

I soon discovered two things. One was that a vessel would not be likely to sail for the mouth of the Amazon under ten or twelve years; and the other was that the nine or ten dollars still left in my pocket would not suffice for so impossible an exploration[1] as I had planned, even if I could afford to wait for a ship. Therefore
10 it followed that I must contrive a new career. The *Paul Jones* was now bound for

ANALYZE VISUALS
What does this illustrated map tell you about the size of the Mississippi River compared with the town on its banks? What other impressions of the river do you glean?

---

1. **mouth of the Amazon . . . exploration:** Twain, having read that an American expedition had been unable to finish its exploration of the Amazon River, went to New Orleans with the idea that he would be able to travel to South America and complete the job.

DIFFERENTIATED INSTRUCTION

FOR ALL STUDENTS
Expert Groups Encourage students to become subject experts by selecting and researching one of these topics:

- the significance of Mississippi riverboats prior to the Civil War
- the training and function of a cub pilot on Mississippi riverboats
- Mark Twain's actual apprenticeship with Horace Bixby

FOR STRATEGIC READERS
In combination with the *Audio Anthology CD*, use one or more Targeted Passages (pp. 650, 652, 654, and 657) to ensure that students focus on key events and concepts. Targeted Passages are also good for English learners.

❶ Targeted Passage [Lines 1–10]
This introductory passage sets the scene and explains how Twain became interested in learning to pilot a steamboat.

ANALYZE VISUALS

Possible answers: The broad river makes the town look small and sparse by contrast. The river appears smooth and quiet, not full of hazards as Twain later describes it to be.

About the Art This map, with Twain's picture inset, is a bird's-eye view of the Mississippi River as it flows through Hannibal, Missouri, Twain's boyhood home. Mapmaker Albert Ruger (d. 1899) created panoramic views like this one for many U.S. towns. Point out the skewed dimensions of the map, explaining that panoramic maps such as this one presented a general overview of major streets and buildings rather than exact dimensions and correct perspective.

BACKGROUND

Apprenticeship An apprentice pays a fee to a master in the desired trade; then the master teaches the skills of that trade to the apprentice. Mr. Bixby required five hundred dollars, with one hundred dollars upfront before training, and Twain had to borrow the money from his brother-in-law. As Twain's skills increased, however, demand for his piloting services grew. Twain's salary soon enabled him to indulge in a few luxuries and send money home to his mother.

Cultural Connection Around the world, traditional apprenticeships continue to provide an alternative to college or trade school, especially for young people with limited finances. Invite students to share what they may know about apprenticeships.

- What is the *Paul Jones,* and where is it when the passage opens?

- Why is Twain aboard the *Paul Jones?*

- What two things does Twain discover during the first two weeks?

- Why does Twain decide that he needs to choose a new career?

FOR ENGLISH LEARNERS

Prereading For prereading instruction for English learners, see

 BEST PRACTICES TOOLKIT
   Scaffolding Reading Instruction pp. 43–46

FOR ADVANCED LEARNERS/AP

AP exercises in the bottom channel provide additional challenge for students. Use these suggestions for small groups or individuals.

ADDITIONAL GUIDELINES

For more help with differentiation and tips for classroom management, see

BEST PRACTICES TOOLKIT
   Differentiated Instruction pp. 31–38

I planned a siege against my pilot, and at the end of three hard days he surrendered. He agreed to teach me the Mississippi River from New Orleans to St. Louis for five hundred dollars, payable out of the first wages I should receive after graduating. I entered upon the small enterprise of "learning" twelve or thirteen hundred miles of the great Mississippi River with the easy confidence of my time of life. If I had really known what I was about to require of my faculties, I should not have had the courage to begin. I supposed that all a pilot had to do was to keep his boat in the river, and I did not consider that that could be much of a trick, since it was so wide. **A**

20   The boat backed out from New Orleans at four in the afternoon, and it was "our watch" until eight. Mr. Bixby, my chief, "straightened her up," plowed her along past the sterns of the other boats that lay at the Levee,[2] and then said, "Here, take her; shave those steamships as close as you'd peel an apple." I took the wheel, and my heartbeat fluttered up into the hundreds; for it seemed to me that we were about to scrape the side off every ship in the line, we were so close. I held my breath and began to claw the boat away from the danger; and I had my own opinion of the pilot who had known no better than to get us into such peril, but I was too wise to express it. In half a minute I had a wide margin of safety intervening between the *Paul Jones* and the ships; and within ten seconds more I
30   was set aside in disgrace, and Mr. Bixby was going into danger again and flaying me alive with abuse of my cowardice. I was stung, but I was obliged to admire the easy confidence with which my chief loafed from side to side of his wheel, and trimmed the ships so closely that disaster seemed ceaselessly imminent. When he had cooled a little he told me that the easy water was close ashore and the current outside, and therefore we must hug the bank, upstream, to get the benefit of the former, and stay well out, downstream, to take advantage of the latter. In my own mind I resolved to be a downstream pilot and leave the upstreaming to people dead to prudence.[3] **B**

      Now and then Mr. Bixby called my attention to certain things. Said he, "This
40   is Six-Mile Point." I assented. It was pleasant enough information, but I could not see the bearing of it. I was not conscious that it was a matter of any interest to me. Another time he said, "This is Nine-Mile Point." Later he said, "This is Twelve-Mile Point." They were all about level with the water's edge; they all looked about alike to me; they were monotonously unpicturesque. I hoped Mr. Bixby would change the subject. But no; he would crowd up around a point, hugging the shore with affection, and then say: "The slack water ends here, abreast this bunch of China trees; now we cross over." So he crossed over. He gave me the wheel once or twice, but I had no luck. I either came near chipping off the edge of a sugar plantation, or I yawed[4] too far from shore, and so dropped back into disgrace
50   again and got abused.

      The watch was ended at last, and we took supper and went to bed. At midnight the glare of a lantern shone in my eyes, and the night watchman said, "Come!

---

2. **Levee** (lĕv'ē): a landing place for boats on a river.
3. **dead to prudence:** lacking good judgment.
4. **yawed:** swerved.

652   UNIT 4: REGIONALISM AND NATURALISM

---

② Targeted Passage

A VOICE
Reread lines 6–19. What does Twain's **tone** suggest about his youthful confidence?

B PARAPHRASE
Reread and paraphrase lines 33–38. What does Twain learn about the upstream and downstream currents? What decision does he make about the future?

LITERARY ANALYSIS

A VOICE

Possible answer: Twain's tone suggests that his younger self is overconfident—that is, he believes that the pilot's job is easy to do and easily learned. The tone also suggests that Twain is highly confident about his intelligence and his ability to learn.

READING STRATEGY

B PARAPHRASE

Possible answer: Paraphrase: When Mr. Bixby had calmed down, he explained that the waters are calm closer to the shore of the river and that the current is strong in the center. Therefore, a pilot should stay close to the shore when going upstream, to take advantage of the calm water, and should stay farther out when going downstream, to take advantage of the stronger current. Twain learns how the two currents are different and why that information is important to a pilot. He decides that in the future, he will pilot ships that are going downstream only because then he will not need to steer so dangerously close to other boats when he encounters them.

If students need help . . . Have them use the chart introduced on page 649 to paraphrase the passage, one sentence at a time.

Difficult Passage	Literal Paraphrase	Final Paraphrase
Mr. Bixby "trimmed the ships so closely that disaster seemed ceaselessly imminent."	Mr. Bixby was so close to the other steamboats that it seemed at any moment he would cause disaster.	Mr. Bixby steered so close to the other steamboats that it seemed he would wreck the boat.

DIFFERENTIATED INSTRUCTION

FOR STRATEGIC READERS

② Targeted Passage [Lines 11–19]

In this passage, Twain recalls his new plan and the assumptions that lay behind it.

- What does young Twain pester the pilot to do for him? What terms does the pilot set when he agrees?
- What does Twain expect his training to be like? What does he not expect?
- Looking back, what does the older Twain think of his youthful decision?

FOR ENGLISH LEARNERS

Vocabulary: Idioms [mixed-readiness groups] Help students to use context clues to determine meaning of these words:

- *Now and then* (line 39), "At various times"
- *came near* (line 48), "almost succeeded in"
- *Turn out* (line 53), "Get out of bed"
- *as like as not* (line 57), "probably"
- *turning in* (line 59), "going to bed"
- *made for* (line 72), "went toward"
- *this beats anything* (line 84), "this is amazing"

Turn out!" And then he left. I could not understand this extraordinary procedure; so I presently gave up trying to, and dozed off to sleep. Pretty soon the watchman was back again, and this time he was gruff. I was annoyed. I said,

"What do you want to come bothering around here in the middle of the night for? Now, as like as not, I'll not get to sleep again to-night."

The watchman said, "Well, if this ain't good, I'm blessed."

60 The "offwatch"[5] was just turning in, and I heard some brutal laughter from them, and such remarks as "Hello, watchman! ain't the new cub turned out yet? He's delicate, likely. Give him some sugar in a rag, and send for the chambermaid to sing 'Rock-a-by Baby' to him." **C**

About this time Mr. Bixby appeared on the scene. Something like a minute later I was climbing the pilothouse steps with some of my clothes on and the rest in my arms. Mr. Bixby was close behind, commenting. Here was something fresh—this thing of getting up in the middle of the night to go to work. It was a detail in piloting that had never occurred to me at all. I knew that boats ran all night, but somehow I had never happened to reflect that somebody had to get up out of a warm bed to run them. I began to fear that piloting was not quite so 70 romantic as I had imagined it was; there was something very real and worklike about this new phase of it. . . .

Mr. Bixby made for the shore and soon was scraping it, just the same as if it had been daylight. And not only that, but singing:

Father in heaven, the day is declining, etc.

It seemed to me that I had put my life in the keeping of a peculiarly reckless outcast. Presently he turned on me and said, "What's the name of the first point above New Orleans?"

I was gratified to be able to answer promptly, and I did. I said I didn't know. "Don't *know?*"

80 This manner jolted me. I was down at the foot[6] again, in a moment. But I had to say just what I had said before.

"Well, you're a smart one!" said Mr. Bixby. "What's the name of the *next* point?" Once more I didn't know.

"Well, this beats anything. Tell me the name of *any* point or place I told you." I studied awhile and decided that I couldn't.

"Look here! What do you start out from, above Twelve-Mile Point, to cross over?"
"I—I—don't know."

"You—you—don't know?" mimicking my drawling manner of speech. "What *do* you know?"

90 "I—I—nothing, for certain."

"By the great Caesar's ghost, I believe you! You're the stupidest dunderhead I ever saw or ever heard of, so help me Moses! The idea of *you* being a pilot—*you!* Why, you don't know enough to pilot a cow down a lane."

---

5. **"offwatch"**: those sailors who had just completed their watch.

6. **down at the foot**: at the bottom of the class.

C PARAPHRASE
Twain's frequent use of **dialogue** and **dialect**, or regional speech, is one of the challenging qualities about his writing. Paraphrase the dialogue in lines 51–61. What are the other crew members saying about him?

READING STRATEGY

C PARAPHRASE

Possible answer: *Paraphrase: "Come on, get out of bed!" / "Why do you keep interrupting my sleep? Now I'll probably never get back to sleep!" / "Well, I can't believe this!" / "Hey, watchman! Isn't the new pilot out of bed yet? Maybe he's spoiled. Feed him something sweet, and call his nurse to sing him a lullaby." The other crew members are saying that Twain is too immature to become a pilot.*

Lines 72–93
TIERED DISCUSSION PROMPTS

Use these prompts to help students explore the relationship between Twain and Bixby:

Connect Have you ever learned a skill from a master? Describe the experience. *Accept all thoughtful responses.*

Analyze How does Twain reveal the tension between master and apprentice as the scene progresses? Cite examples. ***Possible answer:*** *Twain reveals the tension through Mr. Bixby's dialogue. He first questions Twain in a casual way (lines 76–77). When Twain cannot answer, the italics in Mr. Bixby's reply (line 79) suggest irritation. Tension grows with the sarcastic "Well, you're a smart one!" (line 82) and the frustrated "Well, this beats anything" (line 84). Finally, Mr. Bixby angrily mocks Twain's halting speech (line 88) and insults him (lines 91–93).*

Evaluate Is Mr. Bixby an effective teacher? Why or why not? ***Possible answers:*** *No. Mr. Bixby has failed to explain to his pupil the nature of their lessons. Yes. He has reinforced for Twain just how much he has to learn.*

FOR ENGLISH LEARNERS
Key Academic Vocabulary Use Word Squares to teach these words: *margin* (line 28), *benefit* (line 35), *phase* (line 71), *feature* (line 147), *channel* (line 175).

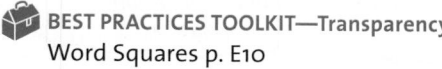 **BEST PRACTICES TOOLKIT—Transparency** Word Squares p. E10

FOR ADVANCED LEARNERS/AP
Analyze Dialogue [paired option] In lines 75–93, Twain often describes his replies rather than quoting them, yet he always uses dialogue to report Mr. Bixby's comments. Ask students to rewrite this scene, first by using dialogue for both speakers and then by describing their words without using dialogue. Have students read both versions aloud to a partner and then discuss how the decision to report or describe dialogue affects the scene's pace and focus.

D VOICE

Possible answer: Twain's choice of language makes the descriptions of Mr. Bixby much more lively and vivid; phrases such as "red-hot profanity" allow readers to hear what Mr. Bixby sounds like. Most of the paragraph is a lengthy description of Mr. Bixby's cursing and frenetic energy; the humor lies in the change of pace when he settles down to speak gently to young Twain, having emptied himself of curses.

Extend the Discussion Why does Mr. Bixby calm down? What might he now realize about his lesson on the river?

E VOICE

Possible answer: Twain's tone becomes more factual ("the information was to be found only in my notebook—none of it was in my head") but also a bit sad and nostalgic ("It made my heart ache to think I had only got half of the river set down....").

Lines 117–125
REINFORCE *KEY IDEA*: EXPERIENCE

Discuss What life lessons does young Twain learn as he **experiences** the river on the way to St. Louis? *Possible answer: Humbled by his experience, Twain learns to respect a profession that he had underestimated and to be a more realistic judge of his abilities, which he had overestimated.*

Oh, but his wrath was up! He was a nervous man, and he shuffled from one side of his wheel to the other as if the floor was hot. He would boil awhile to himself, and then overflow and scald me again.

"Look here! What do you suppose I told you the names of those points for?"

I tremblingly considered a moment, and then the devil of temptation provoked me to say, "Well to—to—be entertaining, I thought."

100 This was a red rag to the bull.[7] He raged and stormed so (he was crossing the river at the time) that I judged it made him blind, because he ran over the steering oar of a trading scow.[8] Of course the traders sent up a volley of red-hot profanity. Never was a man so grateful as Mr. Bixby was, because he was brimful, and here were subjects who could *talk back*. He threw open a window, thrust his head out, and such an irruption followed as I never had heard before. The fainter and farther away the scowmen's curses drifted, the higher Mr. Bixby lifted his voice and the weightier his adjectives grew. When he closed the window he was empty. You could have drawn a seine[9] through his system and not caught curses enough to disturb your mother with. Presently he said to me in the gentlest way, "My boy,
110 you must get a little memorandum book; and every time I tell you a thing, put it down right away. There's only one way to be a pilot, and that is to get this entire river by heart. You have to know it just like A B C." **D**

That was a dismal revelation to me, for my memory was never loaded with anything but blank cartridges. However, I did not feel discouraged long. I judged that it was best to make some allowances, for doubtless Mr. Bixby was "stretching." . . .[10]

By the time we had gone seven or eight hundred miles up the river, I had learned to be a tolerably plucky upstream steersman, in daylight; and before we reached St. Louis I had made a trifle of progress in night work, but only a trifle.
120 I had a notebook that fairly bristled with the names of towns, "points," bars, islands, bends, reaches, etc.; but the information was to be found only in the notebook—none of it was in my head. It made my heart ache to think I had only got half of the river set down; for as our watch was four hours off and four hours on, day and night, there was a long four-hour gap in my book for every time I had slept since the voyage began. . . . . **E**

The face of the water, in time, became a wonderful book—a book that was a dead language to the uneducated passenger, but which told its mind to me without reserve, delivering its most cherished secrets as clearly as if it uttered them with a voice. And it was not a book to be read once and thrown aside, for
130 it had a new story to tell every day. Throughout the long twelve hundred miles there was never a page that was void of interest, never one that you could leave unread without loss, never one that you would want to skip, thinking you could find higher enjoyment in some other thing. There never was so wonderful a book

---

7. **a red rag to the bull:** Bullfighters wave capes to both provoke and distract the bull.
8. **scow:** a flat-bottomed boat used chiefly to transport freight.
9. **seine** (sān): large fishing net.
10. **"stretching":** exaggerating.

---

3 Targeted Passage

D VOICE
Reread this paragraph, focusing on lines 104–112. Notice the elaborate **diction** Twain uses to describe Mr. Bixby's behavior, especially as Mr. Bixby finally quiets down. How does this choice of language affect the pacing and humor of this paragraph?

E VOICE
Reread lines 117–125. What **tone** does Twain take here in describing his own progress? Give details from the text to support your answer.

DIFFERENTIATED INSTRUCTION

FOR STRATEGIC READERS

3 Targeted Passage [Lines 109–125]

In this passage, Twain finally realizes the full extent of what he must learn before he can pilot the boat safely.

- What "homework" does Mr. Bixby assign Twain?
- Why is Twain worried about completing this assignment?

- Why isn't he discouraged for long?
- Why does Twain's heart "ache" when he considers his notebook?

FOR ENGLISH LEARNERS

Comprehension: Text Structure Point out that in lines 126–145, Twain develops an extended metaphor comparing the river with a book. To help students understand the comparison, have them complete a Two-Column Chart.

River	Book
Lines 126–130: The river is like . . .	a fascinating book that can be read repeatedly.
Lines 130–135: The river's surface is like . . .	a page packed with important information.

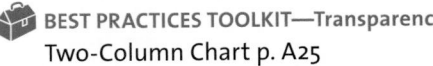

BEST PRACTICES TOOLKIT—Transparency
Two-Column Chart p. A25

Activity In this selection, Twain stresses the mental work of learning to be a pilot. Have students examine the image closely and then describe what it suggests about the physical work of piloting. *Possible answer: The image shows that the pilot is hard at work, straining his back as he grasps the wheel to steer. The pilot seems to be in good physical shape; he undoubtedly needs strength to do the job. Wind blows the pilot's shirt and neckerchief, indicating that exposure to the elements was part of the physical aspect of the job.*

written by man; never one whose interest was so absorbing, so unflagging, so sparklingly renewed with every reperusal.[11] The passenger who could not read it was charmed with a peculiar sort of faint dimple on its surface (on the rare occasions when he did not overlook it altogether); but to the pilot that was an *italicized* passage; indeed, it was more than that, it was a legend of the largest capitals,[12] with a string of shouting exclamation points at the end of it, for it

140 meant that a wreck or a rock was buried there that could tear the life out of the strongest vessel that ever floated. It is the faintest and simplest expression the water ever makes, and the most hideous to a pilot's eye. In truth, the passenger who could not read this book saw nothing but all manner of pretty pictures in it,

---

11. **reperusal** (rē'pə-rōō'zəl): rereading.

12. **a legend of the largest capitals:** an inscription in large capital letters.

FOR ADVANCED LEARNERS/AP

Analyze Style [paired option] Lines 126–141 are carefully crafted and organized. Challenge students to identify these three types of repetition and to explain how they strengthen the meaning of the passage:

- the repetition of the word *book,* which strengthens the extended metaphor that structures the passage

- the repetition of the word *never* in lines 131–134, which strengthens Twain's main point about the allure of the river to the pilot

- the repetition of the word *so* plus an adjective in lines 133–135, which piles expression upon expression to intensify meaning

Have students practice reading the passage in pairs, using their voices to emphasize Twain's repetition. Encourage students to discuss how the meaning or focus of the passage might change if Twain had not used repetition.

F VOICE

Possible answer: *Twain's descriptions change to become more vivid and more detailed, revealing close observation. Twain also uses figurative language, whereas before he presented simple, rather plain descriptions. His diction is more serious than before, reflecting his new maturity.*

If students need help . . . Have them contrast the tone and diction in these lines with that in lines 39–50.

Lines 146–164
TIERED DISCUSSION PROMPTS

Use these prompts to help students appreciate Twain's imagery:

Connect Have you ever witnessed a sunset or other scene of natural beauty? How did it affect you? *Accept all thoughtful responses.*

Analyze How does Twain appeal to the reader's sense of sight? *Possible answer: Twain recalls colors (for example, blood reds and golden reflections in lines 152–153) and contrasts (for example, the black log against the golden-red river in lines 153–154).*

Evaluate Does Twain's description convince readers of "the grace, the beauty, the poetry" of the river (lines 149–150)? Explain. *Students may suggest that Twain's respectful tone and vivid poetic language capture these aspects of the river.*

About the Art The firm of Nathaniel Currier (1813–1888) and James Merritt Ives (1824–1895) became famous for its popular lithographs, producing more than 7,000 images that chronicled scenes and events of the 19th century.

---

painted by the sun and shaded by the clouds, whereas to the trained eye these were not pictures at all, but the grimmest and most dead earnest of reading matter.

Now when I had mastered the language of this water, and had come to know every trifling feature that bordered the great river as familiarly as I knew the letters of the alphabet, I had made a valuable acquisition. But I had lost something, too. I had lost something which could never be restored to me while I lived. All the
150 grace, the beauty, the poetry, had gone out of the majestic river! I still keep in mind a certain wonderful sunset which I witnessed when steamboating was new to me. A broad expanse of the river was turned to blood; in the middle distance the red hue brightened into gold, through which a solitary log came floating, black and conspicuous; in one place a long, slanting mark lay sparkling upon the water; in another the surface was broken by boiling, tumbling rings, that were as many-tinted as an opal; where the ruddy flush was faintest, was a smooth spot that was covered with graceful circles and radiating lines, ever so delicately traced; the shore on our left was densely wooded, and the somber shadow that fell from this forest was broken in one place by a long, ruffled trail that shone like silver; and high
160 above the forest wall a clean-stemmed dead tree waved a single leafy bough that glowed like a flame in the unobstructed splendor that was flowing from the sun. There were graceful curves, reflected images, woody heights, soft distances; and over the whole scene, far and near, the dissolving lights drifted steadily, enriching it every passing moment with new marvels of coloring. **F**

Champions of the Mississippi, Currier and Ives. Lithograph. Museum of the City of New York, New York. © Scala/Art Resource, New York.

656 UNIT 4: REGIONALISM AND NATURALISM

DIFFERENTIATED INSTRUCTION

FOR STRATEGIC READERS

Explore Voice Guide students in a comparison of the professional, pragmatic language of lines 171–181 with the more poetic language of lines 146–164. Suggest that students use a Two-Column Chart, like the one shown, to match professional and poetic details in the passages. Discuss the results, helping students note how differences in tone and diction distinguish the passages in meaning and effect.

Professional Voice	Poetic Voice
Lines 171–172: The sunset means that wind is coming.	Lines 150–156: The sunset bathes the river in glorious colors.
Line 172: The floating log means that the river is rising.	Lines 153–154: The floating log provides a striking color contrast.

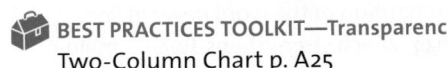 **BEST PRACTICES TOOLKIT—Transparency**
Two-Column Chart p. A25

I stood like one bewitched. I drank it in, in a speechless rapture. The world was new to me, and I had never seen anything like this at home. But as I have said, a day came when I began to cease from noting the glories and the charms which the moon and the sun and the twilight wrought upon the river's face; another day came when I ceased altogether to note them. Then, if that sunset scene had
170 been repeated, I should have looked upon it without rapture, and should have commented upon it, inwardly, after this fashion: "This sun means that we are going to have wind tomorrow; that floating log means that the river is rising, small thanks to it; that slanting mark on the water refers to a bluff reef[13] which is going to kill somebody's steamboat one of these nights, if it keeps on stretching out like that; those tumbling 'boils' show a dissolving bar and a changing channel there; the lines and circles in the slick water over yonder are a warning that that troublesome place is shoaling up[14] dangerously; that silver streak in the shadow of the forest is the 'break' from a new snag, and he has located himself in the very best place he could have found to fish for steamboats; that tall dead tree, with a single living
180 branch, is not going to last long, and then how is a body ever going to get through this blind place at night without the friendly old landmark?"

No, the romance and beauty were all gone from the river. All the value any feature of it had for me now was the amount of usefulness it could furnish toward compassing the safe piloting of a steamboat. Since those days, I have pitied doctors from my heart. What does the lovely flush in a beauty's cheek mean to a doctor but a "break" that ripples above some deadly disease? Are not all her visible charms sown thick with what are to him the signs and symbols of hidden decay? Does he ever see her beauty at all, or doesn't he simply view her professionally, and comment upon her unwholesome condition all to himself? And doesn't he sometimes wonder
190 whether he has gained most or lost most by learning his trade? ～ G

④ Targeted Passage

G PARAPHRASE
Reread lines 184–190 and paraphrase the comments about what a doctor sees. What parallel is Twain drawing between the doctor's plight and his own?

---

13. **bluff reef:** an underwater ridge of rock.

14. **shoaling up:** becoming too shallow for safe navigation because of a buildup of sand or silt in the riverbed.

REINFORCE *KEY IDEA:* EXPERIENCE

Discuss How do the young Twain's **experiences** change his thoughts about the river? *Possible answer: As he gains piloting experience, Twain thinks less about the river's "charms," until he finally loses all sense of wonder.*

READING STRATEGY

G PARAPHRASE

Possible answer: Paraphrase: Since then, I have sincerely pitied doctors. To a doctor, might not a beautiful woman have pink cheeks because she is deathly ill? Are not her lovely physical traits overshadowed by possible symptoms of illness? Can the doctor ever recognize her beauty, or does he see her only as a patient, and speak of her to himself as such? And doesn't he sometimes wonder whether learning his profession has been worth that cost? Twain's parallel makes the point that professional knowledge stifles one's sensitivity to beauty.

SELECTION WRAP–UP

SUMMARIZE Ask students to summarize what Twain learns during his apprenticeship.

★ CRITIQUE

- Ask students whether they are convinced of the young Twain's rapid maturation from careless cub pilot to confident veteran pilot.

- After completing the After Reading questions on page 658, have students revisit their responses and tell whether they have changed their opinions.

---

④ Targeted Passage [Lines 166–184]

In this passage, the mature Twain reflects on what he lost by gaining the experience needed to pilot a steamboat.

- According to Twain, what happened on a certain day?

- Before Twain became a pilot, the Mississippi River seemed enchanting and peaceful. How does it seem to him now?

- Does Twain regret having learned to pilot? Explain your answer.

FOR ADVANCED LEARNERS/AP

Synthesize In both the excerpt from *The Autobiography of Mark Twain* and the excerpt from *Life on the Mississippi*, a mature author reflects on his younger self. The episode from the *Autobiography* comes from Twain's adolescence; the period of apprenticeship to Mr. Bixby dates to Twain's early 20s. Have students develop and share profiles of the three versions of Twain they encounter in these selections, drawing evidence from both texts. Urge students to respond to these questions:

- What matters most to Twain at each time of his life?

- What mistakes are the boy and young man prone to make?

- How has Twain matured between his participation in the mesmerizer's act and his apprenticeship to Mr. Bixby?

- What characteristics have stayed with Twain from boyhood through maturity?

Practice and Apply

After Reading

Use these copy masters to check understanding and provide extra support:

R RESOURCE MANAGER—Copy Masters
Reading Check p. 57
Voice p. 53
Question Support p. 58

Additional selection questions are provided for teachers on page 47.

ANSWERS

1. *Twain begins the job of apprentice to a riverboat pilot.*

2. *Twain reacts by ignoring the instruction.*

3. *Twain learns to read and respect the river.*

Possible answers:

4. ■ **SKILLS FOCUS** Paraphrase *Students may mention regional dialect or technical terminology as difficult aspects of Twain's writing.*

5. *Lines 23–38: Twain's attitude is fear—he is afraid to steer the boat to open but less calm waters. Lines 51–71: Twain's attitude is amazement—he is ignorant about work obligations. Lines 75–112: Twain's attitude is frustration—he seems unable to learn the river. In each case, the humor relates to young Twain's overconfidence.*

6. ● **SKILLS FOCUS** Voice *To that point, readers hear the voice of an overconfident cub who cannot learn from Mr. Bixby because he thinks that he already knows it all. As Twain learns more about the river and what it takes to be a pilot, his diction becomes more sophisticated and his tone more respectful.*

Assess and Reteach

Assess

R RESOURCE MANAGER—Copy Masters
Selection Test A pp. 59–60
Selection Test B/C pp. 61–62

● Test Generator CD

Reteach

S STANDARDS LESSON FILE
Literature Lesson 40: Word Choice and Diction
Research and Study Skills Lesson 12: Paraphrasing

After Reading

Comprehension

1. **Recall** What new job does Mark Twain begin?

2. **Recall** How does Twain react to Mr. Bixby's initial instruction?

3. **Summarize** As Twain's training continues, what does he learn?

Literary Analysis

4. **Examine Paraphrases** Review the paraphrases you recorded as you read. In the end, what were the most difficult aspects of Twain's writing? Explain.

5. **Analyze Humor** In any piece of humorous writing, the humor usually springs from a general underlying attitude toward the subject. Review the following humorous passages from the selection and in each case identify the attitude expressed. What do the passages have in common?

   • Twain tries to steer the boat for the first time (lines 23–38)
   • Twain fails to show up for his first night watch (lines 51–71)
   • Twain learns that he has to learn the entire river by heart (lines 75–112)

6. **Analyze Voice** Twain's voice undergoes a distinct change at line 126. Describe his voice both up to and after this point in terms of its **diction** and **tone**. What change in attitude is reflected by this change in voice?

7. **Draw Conclusions** In this selection, Twain develops an **extended metaphor** comparing the river with a book. In a chart like this one, identify the points of this comparison. Through this metaphor, what is he saying about the river and his **experience** as a student pilot?

Line Numbers	Passage	What It Says About the River
126–127	"The face of the water ... became a wonderful book—a book that was a dead language to the uneducated passenger"	It's "wonderful" but cannot be understood by the uneducated.

8. **Compare Literary Works** How does the humorous attitude you described in answer to question 5 compare with that expressed in Twain's *Autobiography*? Which piece do you think is funnier? Cite details to support your answer.

Literary Criticism

9. **Author's Style** *Life on the Mississippi* first appeared serially in the *Atlantic Monthly* magazine in 1875. In 1874, Twain wrote the magazine's editor that he liked writing for the audience of the *Atlantic* "for the simple reason that it don't require a 'humorist' to paint himself stripèd and stand on his head every fifteen minutes." In other words, he liked an audience that appreciated subtle humor. Do you find this sensibility reflected in the selection you have just read? Explain.

---

7. *Lines 126–127: The river is like a book. Lines 130–135: Like a great book, the ever-changing river is endlessly fascinating. Lines 135–142: Passengers can see only the river's beauty, while the pilot sees each detail as important in "reading" the river. Lines 142–145: Passengers see "pictures," but pilots see the significance of every nuance. Twain uses the extended metaphor to say that the river is complex and that he has learned to understand it as the layman cannot.*

8. *In both pieces, the humor comes from the older Twain's poking fun at his egotistical younger self. Some students may think that the Autobiography is funnier because the story's premise is more humorous.*

9. *Most students will find that the selection reflects the sensibility: Its humor is subtle, based on voice rather than on situation.*

The Notorious Jumping Frog of Calaveras County

Short Story
by Mark Twain

CALIFORNIA

R3.1, R3.3, W1.2
(p. 669), W1.9
(p. 669)

● **LITERARY ANALYSIS: TALL TALE**

The **tall tale** is a distinctively American form of storytelling featuring outlandish characters and events, often with a comic effect. Based on oral tradition, the tall tale generally aims to fool or impress the listener or reader, using various devices. Look for these techniques and consider their impact:

• **Hyperbole**—a figure of speech exaggerating the truth

• **Understatement**—the technique of downplaying the significance of the outlandish, often to ironic or humorous effect

• **Local color**—writing that brings a region alive by portraying its dress, mannerisms, customs, character types, and speech

■ **READING SKILL: UNDERSTAND DIALECT**

Dialect is the distinct form of a language spoken in one geographic area or by a particular group. Writers use dialect to establish setting, provide local color, and develop characters. In this story, Twain uses a frontier dialect. Because of its unfamiliar idioms and strange spellings, dialect can be hard to read. These strategies will help:

• **Read slowly**—Try reading aloud to help you recognize words you may have heard but don't normally see in print.

• **Use context clues**—When Twain writes, "You'd see that frog whirling in the air like a doughnut—see him turn one summerset," context tells you that *summerset* must mean the same as *somersault*.

As you read, jot down unfamiliar words and what you think they mean.

▲ **VOCABULARY IN CONTEXT**

Which of the following words do you know? Write definitions for the words and then check the definitions as you read.

WORD LIST		
cavorting	enterprising	infamous
conjecture	garrulous	tranquil
dilapidated	indifferent	

Explore the Key Idea

Can you spot a
TALL TALE?

KEY IDEA You listen to a friend recount the events of the weekend and you're pretty sure the story is way too wild to be true. You hear a politician describe great accomplishments and you just know it's a stretch. These situations inspire the **skepticism** you need to read about a frog that turns somersaults.

DISCUSS Work with a small group to play the game "Two Truths and a Lie." Take a few minutes for each of you to come up with two truths and one lie. The statements can be about anything from personal experience to oddball facts. Take turns sharing statements. Can you guess which are the lies and which are the truths? Compare your answers and explain what made you believe or disbelieve each statement.

659

Teach

CALIFORNIA

Can you spot a
TALL TALE?

Ask the question. As students read the **KEY IDEA**, explain that **skepticism** means "doubt" or "disbelief." Invite students to tell about a time when they felt skeptical about a situation; then urge them to draw upon their experiences as they complete the activity.

SKILLS FOCUS

LITERARY ANALYSIS · R3.1, R3.3

● **TALL TALE**

Write this passage on the board:

> Sally Britches was taller than a redwood. Why, when she was born, her ma was sorter surprised-like to see that her baby gal was too big fer young'un clothes. "Oh, well," sighed her ma. "I guess you kin jist wear yer pa's ole britches fer the time bein'."

Ask students to identify the tall-tale devices in these lines. ***Possible answer: hyperbole:** "taller than a redwood"; **understatement:** "sorter surprised-like"; **local color:** regional speech (dialect)*

CHECK UNDERSTANDING Have students give examples of tall tales, such as stories about John Henry or Paul Bunyan.

READING SKILL · R3.3

■ **UNDERSTAND DIALECT**

Point out that dialect features slang, nonstandard grammar, and unconventional spellings. Read aloud the passage on the board. Then have students determine the meaning of these examples of dialect: *sorter, fer, young'un, kin, jist, yer, ole,* and *britches*. ***Answers:** "sort of," "for," "children's," "can," "just," "your," "old," "pants"*

R RESOURCE MANAGER—Copy Master
Understand Dialect p. 75 (for student use while reading the selection)

VOCABULARY

▲ VOCABULARY IN CONTEXT

DIAGNOSE WORD KNOWLEDGE To determine preteaching needs, have all students complete Vocabulary in Context. Check students' definitions against those on the selection pages: *cavorting* (p. 663), *conjecture* (p. 660), *dilapidated* (p.662), *enterprising* (p. 666), *garrulous* (p. 660), *indifferent* (p. 664), *infamous* (p. 660), *tranquil* (p. 662).

PRETEACH VOCABULARY Preteach vocabulary with this copy master. Read each item aloud.

R RESOURCE MANAGER—Copy Master
Vocabulary Study p. 77

MORE VOCABULARY SUPPORT
For additional activities and guidelines, see

BEST PRACTICES TOOLKIT
Scaffolding Vocabulary Instruction
pp. 43–46

i Vocabulary Center at **ClassZone.com**

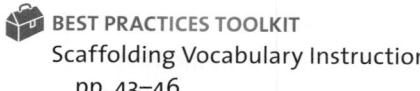

Practice and Apply

SUMMARY

At a friend's request, the narrator of this tall tale locates Simon Wheeler in a mining camp and asks if he knows Leonidas W. Smiley. Wheeler does not, but launches into a reminiscence about *Jim* Smiley, who would bet on anything. After recounting several stories about Smiley, Wheeler tells how Smiley once engaged a stranger in a frog jumping contest. The stranger tricked Smiley by making Smiley's frog swallow quail shot so that it was too heavy to jump. The narrator makes his escape just as Wheeler launches into another story.

Lines 1–9
TIERED DISCUSSION PROMPTS

Use these prompts to help students understand Twain's narrative technique:

Connect Have you ever had to listen to a long, boring story? Describe the experience. *Accept all responses.*

Analyze Why does Twain begin by having the narrator describe Wheeler's story as "exasperating," "long," "tedious," and "useless"? *Possible answer: The description establishes a conflict between the author, who thinks that Wheeler's tale is worth telling, and his narrator, who disagrees. This conflict calls to attention the relationship between the author and the narrator, the role of the narrator, the use of the framing device, and the use of dual narrators.*

Evaluate Is this introduction effective, or does the narrator undermine Wheeler's tale by describing it as boring? Explain. *Students may consider the opening effective because it makes readers realize that they can't accept the narrator's opinion as truth.*

The Notorious
JUMPING FROG
of Calaveras County

Mark Twain

BACKGROUND Twain got the idea for this story during his days panning for gold in California. Local storytellers told this tale without cracking a smile, teaching Twain two important lessons about humor: one, that the manner in which a person tells a story is what makes it funny, and two, that a humorist should always pretend to be dead serious.

ANALYZE VISUALS
What techniques in this illustration can be compared with the storytelling techniques of a tall tale? Explain.

In compliance with the request of a friend of mine who wrote me from the East, I called on good-natured, **garrulous** old Simon Wheeler and inquired after my friend's friend, Leonidas W. Smiley, as requested to do, and I hereunto append[1] the result. I have a lurking suspicion that *Leonidas W.* Smiley is a myth, that my friend never knew such a personage, and that he only **conjectured** that if I asked old Wheeler about him, it would remind him of his **infamous** *Jim* Smiley and he would go to work and bore me to death with some exasperating reminiscence of him as long and as tedious as it should be useless to me. If that was the design, it succeeded.

garrulous (găr′ə-ləs) *adj.* extremely talkative

conjecture (kən-jĕk′chər) *v.* to guess

infamous (ĭn′fə-məs) *adj.* having a very bad reputation; disgraceful

① Targeted Passage

---

1. **hereunto append:** add to this document.

DIFFERENTIATED INSTRUCTION

FOR ALL STUDENTS
Expert Groups Encourage students to become subject experts by selecting and researching one of these topics:

- the California gold rush
- life in a mining camp
- frontier humor
- the tradition of the frame story

FOR STRATEGIC READERS

In combination with the *Audio Anthology CD*, use one or more Targeted Passages (pp. 660, 664, 665, 666) to ensure that students focus on key story events and concepts. Targeted Passages are also good for English learners.

① Targeted Passage [Lines 1–9]

This passage sets up the narrative structure of the frame story, or story within a story, by introducing the narrator of the outer story and preparing readers to meet Simon Wheeler, the narrator of the inner story.

661

I found Simon Wheeler dozing comfortably by the barroom stove of the **dilapidated** tavern in the decayed mining camp of Angel's, and I noticed that he was fat and baldheaded and had an expression of winning gentleness and simplicity upon his **tranquil** countenance. He roused up and gave me good day. I told him that a friend of mine had commissioned me to make some inquiries about a cherished companion of his boyhood named *Leonidas W.* Smiley—*Rev. Leonidas W.* Smiley, a young minister of the Gospel, who he had heard was at one time a resident of Angel's Camp. I added that if Mr. Wheeler could tell me anything about this Rev. Leonidas W. Smiley, I would feel under many obligations to him.

20 Simon Wheeler backed me into a corner and blockaded me there with his chair, and then sat down and reeled off the monotonous narrative which follows this paragraph. He never smiled, he never frowned, he never changed his voice from the gentle-flowing key to which he tuned his initial sentence, he never betrayed the slightest suspicion of enthusiasm, but all through the interminable narrative there ran a vein of impressive earnestness and sincerity which showed me plainly that, so far from his imagining that there was anything ridiculous or funny about his story, he regarded it as a really important matter and admired its two heroes as men of transcendent genius in *finesse*.[2] I let him go on in his own way and never interrupted him once. **A**

"Rev. Leonidas W. H'm, Reverend Le—Well, there was a feller here once by
30 the name of *Jim* Smiley, in the winter of '49—or maybe it was the spring of '50—I don't recollect exactly, somehow, though what makes me think it was one or the other is because I remember the big flume[3] warn't finished when he first come to the camp; but anyway, he was the curiousest man about always betting on anything that turned up you ever see, if he could get anybody to bet on the other side, and if he couldn't he'd change sides. Any way that suited the other man would suit *him*—any way just so's he got a bet, *he* was satisfied. But still he was lucky, uncommon lucky; he most always come out winner. He was always ready and laying for a chance; there couldn't be no solit'ry thing mentioned but that feller'd offer to bet on it and take ary side you please, as I was just telling you. If
40 there was a horse race, you'd find him flush or you'd find him busted at the end of it; if there was a dogfight, he'd bet on it; if there was a cat fight, he'd bet on it; if there was a chicken fight, he'd bet on it; why, if there was two birds setting on a fence, he would bet you which one would fly first; or if there was a camp meeting, he would be there reg'lar to bet on Parson Walker, which he judged to be the best exhorter about here, and so he was too, and a good man. If he even see a straddlebug[4] start to go anywheres, he would bet you how long it would take him to get to—to wherever he was going to, and if you took him up, he would foller that straddlebug to Mexico but what he would find out where he was bound for and how long he was on the road. Lots of the boys here has seen that Smiley and
50 can tell you about him. Why, it never made no difference to *him*—he'd bet on

---

2. **men of . . . finesse:** exceptionally brilliant men.
3. **flume:** a wooden trough built as a channel for running water—used in gold mining for separating particles of gold.
4. **straddlebug:** a long-legged beetle.

---

dilapidated
(dĭ-lăp′ĭ-dā′tĭd) *adj.* in a state of disrepair; rundown **dilapidate** *v.*

tranquil (trăng′kwəl) *adj.* undisturbed; peaceful

A TALL TALE
Reread lines 19–28, and describe Simon Wheeler's manner of storytelling. What does the narrator suggest about the relationship between Wheeler's manner and the substance of his story?

LITERARY ANALYSIS

A TALL TALE

Possible answer: Simon Wheeler's manner of storytelling is monotonous, humorless, and interminable, yet earnest and sincere (though not enthusiastic). The narrator suggests that Wheeler's respect for the "heroes" of his tale is completely at odds with the ridiculous nature of the story.

Extend the Discussion What would a story told in this manner sound like? Read this paragraph aloud, trying to match Wheeler's storytelling style. Listen to classmates read it aloud, too, and decide which reading best matches Wheeler's style, as you imagine it.

Lines 29–56
REINFORCE *KEY IDEA:* SKEPTICISM

Discuss Which elements of Wheeler's story make you feel **skepticism**? *Possible answer: Wheeler's claim that Smiley would follow a straddlebug to Mexico to win a bet (lines 45–49) creates skepticism, as does Wheeler's account of Smiley's wanting to bet that Parson Walker's wife would not recover from her illness (lines 51–56).*

DIFFERENTIATED INSTRUCTION

FOR STRATEGIC READERS

Explore Narrators Make sure students understand that there are two narrators in Twain's story. The story begins with an unnamed narrator who provides the context for the tall tale told by Simon Wheeler, the second narrator. Explain that the first narrator is telling the outer story of a frame story, whereas Simon Wheeler is telling the inner story about Jim Smiley. Have students distinguish the narrators by recording details in this graphic organizer:

Narrator: formal language; irritated, skeptical, bored

Simon Wheeler: dialect; earnest, sincere, humorless, rambling, exaggerating

FOR ENGLISH LEARNERS

Language: Conversational English Patterns Explain that some contractions in the story are examples of dialect, reflecting regional pronunciation. Help students use context clues to figure out the meaning of these nonstandard contractions: *warn't* (line 32), "wasn't"; *solit'ry* (line 38), "solitary"; *feller'd* (line 39), "fellow would"; *reg'lar* (line 44), "regularly"; *inf'nite* (line 54), "infinite"; *'peared* (line 84), "appeared."

any thing—the dangdest feller. Parson Walker's wife laid very sick once for a good while, and it seemed as if they warn't going to save her; but one morning he come in and Smiley up and asked him how she was, and he said she was considerable better—thank the Lord for his inf'nite mercy—and coming on so smart that with the blessing of Prov'dence she'd get well yet; and Smiley, before he thought, says, 'Well, I'll resk two-and-a-half she don't anyway.' **B**

"Thish-yer Smiley had a mare—the boys called her the fifteen-minute nag but that was only in fun, you know, because of course she was faster than that—and he used to win money on that horse, for all she was so slow and always had the
60 asthma, or the distemper, or the consumption,[5] or something of that kind. They used to give her two or three hundred yards' start and then pass her under way, but always at the fag end[6] of the race she'd get excited and desperatelike, and come **cavorting** and straddling up and scattering her legs around limber, sometimes in the air and sometimes out to one side among the fences, and kicking up m-o-r-e dust and raising m-o-r-e racket with her coughing and sneezing and blowing her nose—and always fetch up at the stand just about a neck ahead, as near as you could cipher it down.[7]

"And he had a little small bull-pup, that to look at him you'd think he warn't worth a cent but to set around and look ornery and lay for a chance to steal
70 something. But as soon as money was up on him he was a different dog; his underjaw'd begin to stick out like the fo'castle[8] of a steamboat and his teeth would uncover and shine like the furnaces. And a dog might tackle him and bullyrag[9] him, and bite him and throw him over his shoulder two or three times, and Andrew Jackson—which was the name of the pup—Andrew Jackson would never let on but what *he* was satisfied and hadn't expected nothing else—and the bets being doubled and doubled on the other side all the time, till the money was all up; and then all of a sudden he would grab that other dog jest by the j'int of his hind leg and freeze to it—not chaw, you understand, but only just grip and hang on till they throwed up the sponge,[10] if it was a year. Smiley always come out winner on that pup till he
80 harnessed a dog once that didn't have no hind legs, because they'd been sawed off in a circular saw, and when the thing had gone along far enough and the money was all up and he come to make a snatch for his pet holt,[11] he see in a minute how he'd been imposed on and how the other dog had him in the door, so to speak, and he 'peared surprised, and then he looked sorter discouragedlike and didn't try no more to win the fight, and so he got shucked out bad. He give Smiley a look, as much as to say his heart was broke, and it was *his* fault for putting up a dog that hadn't no hind legs for him to take holt of, which was his main dependence in a fight, and

---

5. **distemper . . . consumption:** Distemper is a viral disease caught by dogs and other four-legged mammals. Consumption is an old-fashioned name for tuberculosis.

6. **fag end:** final part.

7. **cipher** (sī'fər) **it down:** calculate it; figure it.

8. **fo'castle** (fōk'səl): forecastle—here, the protruding front deck of a steamboat.

9. **bullyrag:** harass.

10. **throwed up the sponge:** gave up.

11. **pet holt:** favorite grip.

B DIALECT
Paraphrase the passage written in dialect in lines 29–56. What point is Simon Wheeler making about Smiley?

cavorting (kə-vôr'tĭng) *adj.* prancing about in a playful manner **cavort** *v.*

C TALL TALE

Possible answer: The main characteristic is hyperbole: Wheeler's assertion that Andrew Jackson wouldn't fight back until bets were doubled (lines 74–79), that the dog died of a broken heart after losing and feeling betrayed by Jim Smiley (lines 85–88), and that the dog was a "genius" (line 90).

READING SKILL

D DIALECT

Possible answer: The use of dialect in the characterization adds to the humor and makes the frog seem like the kind of colorful character that belongs in the frontier setting of the story. The frog is characterized as "modest," "straight-for'ard," and "gifted," human character traits that usually are not attributed to an animal.

BACKGROUND

Daniel Webster Daniel Webster (1782–1852), a lawyer who argued cases before the Supreme Court, was highly regarded as a politician and as a speaker. Twain creates a comic effect in naming the frog after such a prestigious figure. Daniel Webster the politician was a critic of Andrew Jackson and a supporter of business interests; Daniel Webster the frog supports Wheeler's "business interest" in betting.

---

then he limped off a piece and laid down and died. It was a good pup, was that Andrew Jackson, and would have made a name for hisself if he'd lived, for the stuff
90 was in him and he had genius—I know it, because he hadn't no opportunities to speak of, and it don't stand to reason that a dog could make such a fight as he could under them circumstances if he hadn't no talent. It always makes me feel sorry when I think of that last fight of his'n and the way it turned out. **C**

"Well, thish-yer Smiley had rat terriers, and chicken cocks, and tomcats and all them kind of things till you couldn't rest, and you couldn't fetch nothing for him to bet on but he'd match you. He ketched a frog one day and took him home, and said he cal'lated[12] to educate him; and so he never done nothing for three months but set in his back yard and learn that frog to jump. And you bet you he *did* learn him, too. He'd give him a little punch behind, and the next minute you'd see that
100 frog whirling in the air like a doughnut—see him turn one summerset, or maybe a couple if he got a good start, and come down flatfooted and all right, like a cat. He got him up so in the matter of ketching flies, and kep' him in practice so constant, that he'd nail a fly every time as fur as he could see him. Smiley said all a frog wanted was education and he could do 'most anything—and I believe him. Why, I've seen him set Dan'l Webster down here on this floor—Dan'l Webster was the name of the frog—and sing out, 'Flies, Dan'l, flies!' and quicker'n you could wink he'd spring straight up and snake a fly off'n the counter there, and flop down on the floor ag'in as solid as a gob of mud, and fall to scratching the side of his head with his hind foot as **indifferent** as if he hadn't no idea he'd been doin' any more'n
110 any frog might do. You never see a frog so modest and straight-for'ard as he was, for all he was so gifted. And when it come to fair and square jumping on a dead level, he could get over more ground at one straddle than any animal of his breed you ever see. Jumping on a dead level was his strong suit, you understand; and when it come to that, Smiley would ante up money on him as long as he had a red.[13] Smiley was monstrous proud of his frog, and well he might be for fellers that had traveled and been everywheres all said he laid over any frog that ever *they* see. **D**

"Well, Smiley kep' the beast in a little lattice box, and he used to fetch him downtown sometimes and lay for a bet. One day a feller—a stranger in the camp, he was—come acrost him with his box and says:
120 "'What might it be that you've got in the box?'

"And Smiley says, sorter indifferent-like, 'It might be a parrot, or it might be a canary, maybe, but it ain't—it's only just a frog.'

"And the feller took it and looked at it careful, and turned it round this way and that, and says, 'H'm—so 'tis. Well, what's *he* good for?'

"'Well,' Smiley says, easy and careless, 'he's good enough for *one* thing, I should judge—he can outjump any frog in Calaveras County.'

"The feller took the box again and took another long, particular look, and give it back to Smiley and says, very deliberate, 'Well,' he says, 'I don't see no p'ints[14] about that frog that's any better'n any other frog.'

---

12. **cal'lated:** calculated; intended.

13. **a red:** a red cent (slang for a penny).

14. **p'ints:** points.

C TALL TALE
Reread lines 68–93. What device characteristic of the tall tale is on display in this paragraph?

2 Targeted Passage

indifferent (ĭn-dĭf′ər-ənt) *adj.* having no particular interest

D DIALECT
Reread lines 110–111. How does the dialect in this sentence, and throughout the paragraph, help to characterize the frog?

DIFFERENTIATED INSTRUCTION

FOR STRATEGIC READERS

2 Targeted Passage [Lines 94–116]

This passage introduces the jumping frog of the story's title.

- What name did Smiley give to the frog?
- What kind of education did Smiley give the frog?
- What was the frog's "strong suit"?
- How did Smiley plan to use the frog?

FOR ADVANCED LEARNERS/AP

Research and Analyze [small-group option]
Tell students that Twain was so annoyed by the first French translation of this story that he "retranslated" it from French into English to point out its stupidity. He gave the tongue-in-cheek retranslation this subtitle: "In English, then in French, then clawed back into a civilized language once more by patient, unremunerated toil." Ask a small group of students to read Twain's retranslation. Have them prepare a group essay answering these questions:

- In addition to the comic plot of the story, what makes the retranslation humorous?
- What techniques does Twain use to show—directly or indirectly—that the French translation was a poor one? Give some examples.
- What humorous elements in the retranslation are similar to humorous elements in the original?

Frog of Calaveras County. The Granger Collection, New York.

130 "'Maybe you don't,' Smiley says. 'Maybe you understand frogs and maybe you don't understand 'em; maybe you've had experience and maybe you ain't only a amature, as it were. Anyways, I've got *my* opinion, and I'll resk forty dollars that he can outjump any frog in Calaveras County.'

"And the feller studied a minute and then says, kinder sad-like, 'Well, I'm only a stranger here and I ain't got no frog; but if I had a frog, I'd bet you.'

"And then Smiley says, 'That's all right—that's all right—if you'll hold my box a minute, I'll go and get you a frog.' And so the feller took the box and put up his forty dollars along with Smiley's, and set down to wait. **E**

"So he set there a good while thinking and thinking to himself, and then he got
140 the frog out and prized his mouth open and took a teaspoon and filled him full of quail shot[15]—filled him pretty near up to his chin—and set him on the floor. Smiley he went to the swamp and slopped around in the mud for a long time, and finally he ketched a frog and fetched him in and give him to this feller, and says:

"'Now, if you're ready, set him alongside of Dan'l, with his forepaws just even with Dan'l's, and I'll give the word.' Then he says, 'One—two—three—*git!*' and him and the feller touched up the frogs from behind, and the new frog hopped off

③ Targeted Passage

E TALL TALE
Reread the dialogue in lines 120–138. What does the straightfaced understatement reveal about the two characters?

---

15. **quail shot:** small lead pellets for firing from a shotgun.

E TALL TALE

Possible answer: The understatement reveals that both characters are good at gambling. Neither Smiley nor the stranger seems to reveal everything that he knows about the situation.

Lines 134–135
**REINFORCE *KEY IDEA:*
SKEPTICISM**

Discuss Explain whether Smiley should feel more **skepticism** when the stranger makes this statement. *Possible answer: Smiley should recognize that the stranger is pretending to be more innocent or gullible than he actually is. Smiley already has wondered if the stranger has experience with frogs (lines 130–132); but now he should be more skeptical, for the stranger's sadness about not having a frog seems too strong an emotion for the situation.*

FOR STRATEGIC READERS

③ Targeted Passage [Lines 130–141]

This passage shows how the stranger plans to beat Smiley at his own game.

• What does Smiley think of the stranger?

• How much money do Smiley and the stranger agree to bet?

• How does the stranger get time alone with Smiley's frog?

• What does the stranger do to the frog? How might he win the contest?

FOR ADVANCED LEARNERS/AP

Analyze Archetypal Characters Point out that the humorous characters in this story represent universal types: the outsider, the deadpan storyteller, the trickster, and the stranger (who may be a trickster, too). Have students identify these archetypal characters in the story and then brainstorm other examples of these character types from folk tales, fiction, movies, television, or cartoons.

F GRAMMAR AND STYLE

Analyze Dialogue Grammar and word choice are tools that authors use to convey how dialogue should be read. Remind students that coordinating conjunctions such as *and, but, or, nor, for,* and *yet* are used to join clauses that hold equal importance. Dashes are used to show sudden breaks or changes in speech. As Wheeler reaches the end of his tale, the coordinating conjunctions and dashes show that he is so excited that he cannot pause for breath and that he is hardly able to include all the details. Have students find other places in the story where Twain uses coordinating conjunctions or dashes in dialogue to convey the way that a character sounds when speaking.

SELECTION WRAP–UP

REFLECT Ask students what insight Twain offers readers about people and their interactions through this story. How accurate is this insight, based on students' experiences?

★ CRITIQUE

- Ask students to consider why Twain uses two narrators and to evaluate the effectiveness of this narrative technique.

- After completing the After Reading questions on page 667, have students revisit their responses and tell whether they have changed their opinions.

---

lively, but Dan'l give a heave and hysted up his shoulders—so—like a Frenchman, but it warn't no use—he couldn't budge; he was planted as solid as a church, and he couldn't no more stir than if he was anchored out. Smiley was a good deal

150 surprised, and he was disgusted too, but he didn't have no idea what the matter was, of course. **F**

"The feller took the money and started away, and when he was going out at the door, he sorter jerked his thumb over his shoulder—so—at Dan'l and says again, very deliberate, 'Well,' he says, '*I* don't see no p'ints about that frog that's any better'n any other frog.'

"Smiley he stood scratching his head and looking down at Dan'l a long time, and at last he says, 'I do wonder what in the nation that frog throw'd off for—I wonder if there ain't something the matter with him—he 'pears to look mighty baggy, somehow.' And he ketched Dan'l by the nap of the neck and hefted him,

160 and says, 'Why, blame my cats if he don't weigh five pound!' and turned him upside down and he belched out a double handful of shot. And then he see how it was, and he was the maddest man—he set the frog down and took out after that feller, but he never ketched him. And—"

[Here Simon Wheeler heard his name called from the front yard and got up to see what was wanted.] And turning to me as he moved away, he said: "Just set where you are, stranger, and rest easy—I ain't going to be gone a second."

But, by your leave, I did not think that a continuation of the history of the **enterprising** vagabond *Jim* Smiley would be likely to afford me much information concerning the Rev. *Leonidas W.* Smiley and so I started away.

170 At the door I met the sociable Wheeler returning, and he buttonholed me and recommenced:[16]

"Well, thish-yer Smiley had a yaller one-eyed cow that didn't have no tail, only just a short stump like a bannanner, and—"

However, lacking both time and inclination, I did not wait to hear about the afflicted cow but took my leave.

16. **buttonholed . . . recommenced:** detained me for conversation and began talking again.

666 UNIT 4: REGIONALISM AND NATURALISM

F GRAMMAR AND STYLE
Reread lines 144–151. Notice how Twain uses **coordinating conjunctions** and **dashes** to convey Simon's breathless retelling of the story.

④ Targeted Passage

enterprising (ĕn′tər-prī′zĭng) *adj.* possessing imagination and initiative

---

DIFFERENTIATED INSTRUCTION

FOR STRATEGIC READERS

④ Targeted Passage [Lines 149–163]

In this passage, Smiley solves the mystery of his loss, and Wheeler's tale ends.

- How does the stranger react to winning the contest? How does Smiley react to losing?

- How does Smiley figure out what happened to his frog?

- How does Smiley react after he realizes that he has been tricked?

FOR ADVANCED LEARNERS/AP

Analyze Style In addition to hyperbole, understatement, and local color, Twain uses other stylistic elements that contribute to the humor of his writing, such as dialect and idioms, humorous subject matter, irony, offbeat similes and metaphors, rambling, and indirect narrative. Have students use an Analysis Frame: Author's Craft to identify and analyze examples of these elements in Twain's writing. Include the excerpts from

the *Autobiography* and *Life on the Mississippi*. Invite students to meet in groups to share and compare their analyses.

BEST PRACTICES TOOLKIT—Transparency Analysis Frame: Author's Craft pp. D21, D24

Comprehension

1. **Recall** How does the narrator hear the story of the jumping frog?

2. **Recall** What is Smiley always willing to do?

3. **Summarize** What happens to Smiley's frog?

Literary Analysis

4. **Make Inferences About Characters** What can you infer about Jim Smiley based on each of the following examples?

   • Smiley betting on the health of the parson's wife

   • Smiley spending three months teaching a frog to jump

   • Smiley studying why the frog couldn't jump

5. **Understand Dialect** Review the dialect and translations you recorded as you read. In general, what does the use of dialect contribute to **characterization** and **setting** in this story? Cite specific examples.

6. **Analyze Hyperbole** Simon Wheeler makes liberal use of hyperbole in describing Jim Smiley; some of what he says is totally improbable, and some is simply a bit of a stretch. List five to ten examples of this hyperbole and rate each on a scale of one to five, with five being the most outrageous. At any point, did your **skepticism** prevent you from enjoying the story? Explain.

7. **Make Judgments About the Tall Tale** Twain sets this story in a **frame**—a story within a story—in which the first-person narrator asks about a man named Leonidas Smiley but gets a story about Jim Smiley instead. In the end, the narrator makes a show of going away disappointed. How does this device contribute to the impact of the tall tale? Explain how the story would be different if the original first-person narrator had simply told the story in his own voice, or if Wheeler himself were the first-person narrator. Do you think this is an effective technique? Why or why not?

Literary Criticism

8. **Critical Interpretations** According to one critic, Twain's organization of this tale "seems wholly directionless," yet "actually it is carefully molded for climax." Do you agree? Look back at the story and explain how the elaborate setup affects the impact of the story's punchline. Use examples from the story to support your ideas.

R3.1, R3.3
CALIFORNIA

---

not set in contrast to the narrator's dry voice and bored response. If the narrator had told the story himself, the tale would lack hyperbole, dialect, and local color. If Wheeler had narrated the story alone, readers would not understand the condescending perspective of the narrator or appreciate Twain's view that the story is not tedious.

8. *Despite the appearance of Wheeler's wandering narrative, every detail in the tale demonstrates both the character of Jim Smiley and his community. Because Wheeler appears to ramble, readers may be lulled into distraction, allowing the story's twist to come as a surprise.*

Practice and Apply

After Reading

Use these copy masters to check understanding and provide extra support:

R RESOURCE MANAGER—Copy Masters
   Reading Check p. 80
   Tall Tale p. 73
   Question Support p. 81

   Additional selection questions are provided for teachers on page 67.

ANSWERS

1. *The narrator visits Simon Wheeler to ask about a man named Leonidas W. Smiley. Wheeler's response is to tell the narrator stories about Jim Smiley instead.*

2. *Smiley is always willing to place a bet.*

3. *The frog wins many bets for Smiley but loses when a crafty stranger weighs the frog down with quail shot.*

Possible answers:

4. *The parson's wife: Smiley values gambling over sensitivity or kindness. Teaching the frog: Smiley is determined and patient. Studying the frog: Smiley is intelligent, thorough, and good at solving problems.*

5. ■ **SKILLS FOCUS Understand Dialect** *The dialect contributes to characterization by capturing Wheeler's talkative, colorful, folksy, and naïve personality and Smiley's shrewd frontier attitude. The dialect helps depict the setting by conveying the language spoken in the California mining camp, showing who is part of that community and who is an outsider. Examples of character-revealing dialect include the beginning of Simon Wheeler's story and the dialogue that he quotes between Smiley and the stranger.*

6. *Examples of hyperbole include "If he even see a straddlebug . . ." (lines 45–49); "But as soon as money was up on him he was a different dog" (line 70); "He gave Smiley . . . laid down and died" (lines 85–88); "he never done . . . jump" (lines 97–98); and "And when . . . you ever see" (lines 111–113). Most students will feel that their skepticism added to their enjoyment of the story.*

7. ● **SKILLS FOCUS Tall Tale** *The frame story structure allows readers to understand the techniques of the tall tale. Wheeler's tale would not be as outrageous if it were*

Vocabulary in Context

VOCABULARY PRACTICE

1. *(d) lonesome*   5. *(d) conjecture*
2. *(b) argumentative*   6. *(b) expensive*
3. *(c) unhappy*   7. *(d) unnoticeable*
4. *(a) unusual*   8. *(a) cavorting*

📖 **RESOURCE MANAGER—Copy Master**
Vocabulary Practice p. 78

VOCABULARY IN WRITING

Suggest that students begin by selecting the words that they will use in their descriptions. If necessary, have them review the definitions on the selection pages.

VOCABULARY STRATEGY: WORDS WITH MISLEADING PREFIXES *(also an EL language objective)*

- Explain the other meanings of the prefixes *in-* and *im-* ("in, within, toward, on").
- Model the use of a dictionary to determine the role of the prefix in the meaning of a word. For example, checking a dictionary shows that in *unnerve,* the prefix *un-* means "to reverse or remove," not "not" (its more common meaning, especially in adjectives). When the correct meaning of *un-* is added to *nerve* ("to give courage to"), the resulting definition is "to remove courage from."

Possible answers:

1. *to cause to lose one's courage or self-confidence*
2. *mildly ill*
3. *intolerable; unbearable*
4. *extending back beyond memory or record*
5. *made perplexed or unable to think*

📖 **RESOURCE MANAGER—Copy Master**
Vocabulary Strategy p. 79

ℹ️ Vocabulary Center at **ClassZone.com**
Additional Vocabulary Activities

Vocabulary in Context

VOCABULARY PRACTICE

Choose the word that is not related in meaning to the other words.

1. (a) dilapidated, (b) decaying, (c) neglected, (d) lonesome
2. (a) chatty, (b) argumentative, (c) garrulous, (d) verbose
3. (a) serene, (b) tranquil, (c) unhappy, (d) placid
4. (a) unusual, (b) infamous, (c) disreputable, (d) notorious
5. (a) comfort, (b) condolence, (c) consolation, (d) conjecture
6. (a) imaginative, (b) expensive, (c) enterprising, (d) resourceful
7. (a) unconcerned, (b) detached, (c) indifferent, (d) unnoticeable
8. (a) cavorting, (b) trembling, (c) shaking, (d) jarring

WORD LIST
cavorting
conjecture
dilapidated
enterprising
garrulous
indifferent
infamous
tranquil

VOCABULARY IN WRITING

If you had seen the jumping frog contest, would you have found it humorous or foolish? Write a short description of the event, making your attitude clear. Use two or more vocabulary words. Here is a sample opening.

> **EXAMPLE SENTENCE**
>
> *Enterprising* people can always find ways to cheat and win. But filling a frog with shot seems especially cruel.

VOCABULARY STRATEGY: WORDS WITH MISLEADING PREFIXES

The prefix *in-* (and its variant *im-*) generally has a negative meaning, as do the prefixes *un-* and *non-*. When you see these prefixes attached to a base word, it is usually easy to figure out the meaning of the new word. Sometimes, though, the process doesn't quite work: *infamous,* for example, doesn't mean "not famous." Using context clues is one way of understanding words that are not quite what they seem.

PRACTICE Use context clues, or if necessary a dictionary, to help you create a definition of each boldfaced word.

1. The bill collector tried to **unnerve** Mom with his threats.
2. Jason is **indisposed** with a chest cold.
3. Her letter described the **insufferable** heat of Texas in July.
4. The old building has been there since time **immemorial**.
5. Everyone was **nonplused** by the surprising turn of events.

🔎 **VOCABULARY PRACTICE**
For more practice, go to the **Vocabulary Center** at ClassZone.com.

DIFFERENTIATED INSTRUCTION

FOR ENGLISH LEARNERS

Task Support: Vocabulary Practice Point out that the Spanish cognate *tranquilo* and the French cognate *tranquille* are similar to the English word *tranquil.* Encourage students who speak Latin-based languages to find home-language cognates for at least two other vocabulary words.

FOR ADVANCED LEARNERS/AP

Vocabulary in Writing Challenge students to use as many vocabulary words as they can to write two paragraphs—one from the point of view of a casual onlooker (who may find the contest foolish) and one from the point of view of someone who knows about Smiley's love of wagering (and who may find the contest humorous). Invite students to compare their responses in small groups to see how they used the words and to discuss how the narrator's attitude determines word choice.

Reading-Writing Connection

W1.2

GRAMMAR AND STYLE

W1.9

CREATE REALISTIC CHARACTERS Review the **Grammar and Style** note on page 666. Mark Twain creates convincing dialogue to help establish the character of Simon Wheeler. Look at this example from the story:

> And a dog might tackle him and <u>bullyrag</u> him, and bite him and throw him over his shoulder two or three times, and Andrew Jackson—which was the name of the pup—Andrew Jackson would never let on but what he was satisfied and hadn't expected nothing else.... (lines 72–75)

Notice how Twain uses the highlighted **coordinating conjunctions** to construct long, rambling sentences that reflect Simon's chatty nature. He also uses **dashes** to show how Simon will interrupt himself. Finally, the underlined text demonstrates elements of dialect, which shows that Simon is rooted in his local culture.

PRACTICE Revise the dialogue you wrote in response to the writing prompt, this time writing it in dialect. You may wish to use the same Western dialect that Twain uses in his short story, or use another dialect that is familiar to you. Make use of coordinating conjunctions, dashes, and regional vocabulary, as well as any special spellings or contractions that will help your reader "hear" the rhythm and pronunciation of the dialect as it would be spoken aloud.

> **EXAMPLE**
>
> "My goodness! If I had known you felt that way about it, I never would have said anything in the first place."
>
> *"Well, shet my mouth! If I'd a known you felt that way 'bout it, I never woulda said nothin' in th' first place."*

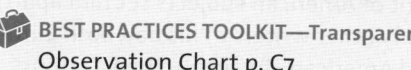

WRITING TOOLS
For prewriting, revision, and editing tools, visit the **Writing Center** at ClassZone.com.

Reading-Writing Connection

WRITING PROMPT

As part of the prewriting process, encourage students to watch a conversation on a television program that they enjoy. Suggest that students use an Observation Chart to record key points in the conversation as well as the characters' facial expressions, gestures, and body language. Students can use these notes as a starting point for their dialogues.

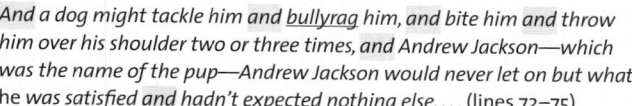 **BEST PRACTICES TOOLKIT**—Transparency
Observation Chart p. C7

For writing support, see

ℹ **Writing Center** at **ClassZone.com**

GRAMMAR AND STYLE

Encourage students to use the grammar and usage aspects of the dialect that they choose rather than simply producing random phonetic misspellings. Caution students against using dialect to ridicule particular social or ethnic groups.

R RESOURCE MANAGER—Copy Master
Create Realistic Characters p. 82

Assess and Reteach

Assess

R RESOURCE MANAGER—Copy Masters
Selection Test A pp. 83–84
Selection Test B/C pp. 85–86

Ⓐ Test Generator CD

Reteach

S STANDARDS LESSON FILE
Literature Lesson 41: Dialogue and Dialect
Literature Lesson 44: Style and Syntax
Writing Lesson 44: Writing Dialogue
Vocabulary Lesson 1: Base Words, Suffixes, and Roots
Vocabulary Lesson 2: Prefixes
Vocabulary Lesson 3: Prefixes with Multiple Meanings

FOR DEVELOPING WRITERS

Writing Support [paired option] As students review the draft of their dialogues, help them focus on the effectiveness of each comment in the conversation.

- Explain that dialogue serves two functions: characterization and plot advancement.

- Using their draft or a copy of it (on which students might reduce the text to provide a wide margin), have students highlight each line of dialogue with a colored marker, using a different color for each character.

- Provide these notations: **1.** Shows character trait: _____; **2.** Reveals attitude: _____; **3.** Reveals background information: _____.

- In the margins, have students write the correct notation for each line of dialogue by filling in the trait, attitude, or background information that they intend to convey.

- Then have students share their annotated dialogues with a partner. Ask partners to comment on whether each line conveys the writer's intent. If not, have partners offer specific suggestions for revising the dialogue.

The Adventures of Huckleberry Finn

Mark Twain

ABOUT THE AUTHOR

Mark Twain Emphasize that Twain's contribution to literature was more than just that of a humorist: His focus on American culture and his colloquial style and realistic, down-to-earth treatment of American subjects set him apart from many other writers of his day, both European and American. Twain also had a strong influence on subsequent masters of American literature, including Ernest Hemingway and William Faulkner.

ABOUT THE NOVEL

The Adventures of Huckleberry Finn Explain that Twain based the character of Huck Finn on an older childhood friend with whom young Sam Clemens shared various adventures in Hannibal. As students read the excerpt from *Huckleberry Finn,* ask them to think about ways in which Mark Twain's childhood experiences may have influenced his writing.

LEGACY OF A MASTERPIECE

Introduce the Passage As students prepare to read the excerpt, point out that because Huck Finn is the narrator, readers see everything from his perspective. Afterward, discuss how Huck's thoughts and actions reveal his character.

American Masterpiece

The Adventures of Huckleberry Finn

Mark Twain

Mark Twain
1835–1910

ABOUT THE AUTHOR "Half twain! Quarter twain! Mark twain!"—such were the cries of 19th-century Mississippi riverboatmen, indicating that the water was deep enough to cross. Samuel Clemens heard those cries as a boy growing up in Hannibal, Missouri, and as a young man working as a riverboat pilot. Later he chose the cry of "Mark twain!" for his pen name. Although Twain first won fame as a Western humorist writing about life in the California gold-mining camps, he drew on his Missouri childhood for many of his best-known works. These include *The Adventures of Tom Sawyer* (1876), his popular tale of a boy growing up in a town not unlike Hannibal; *Life on the Mississippi* (1883), his memoir of his days as a riverboat pilot; and *The Adventures of Huckleberry Finn* (1884), Tom Sawyer's more mature sequel.

ABOUT THE NOVEL *The Adventures of Huckleberry Finn* takes place in the years before the Civil War, when slavery was still legal in Missouri, where the novel opens. Huck Finn, a friend of Tom Sawyer's, is the son of an abusive, drunken lout and has been taken in by the kindly Widow Douglas and her sister, Miss Watson. Huck's neglectful father appears and steals Huck away, taking the boy to live with him in an isolated cabin. Huck escapes to Jackson's Island, where he meets Jim, Miss Watson's runaway slave. Fleeing together down the Mississippi River on a raft in an attempt to reach Ohio and freedom, the two outcasts form a close friendship and experience all sorts of strange adventures.

LEGACY OF A MASTERPIECE Regarded as the quintessential American coming-of-age novel, *The Adventures of Huckleberry Finn* is also a scathing satire of 19th-century social institutions and a pioneering work of American regionalism. In *Huck Finn,* Twain brilliantly captures the flavor of a particular time and place. During the journey down the Mississippi, for example, Huck meets a wide variety of characters whom Twain used to portray nearly every social class living on or along the river in that day. In addition, in Huck's speech, Twain manages to capture the dialect of an uneducated Missouri boy while still being able to humorously and vividly describe scenes and characters. In the end, though, it may be best to enjoy the novel—in the words of Huck's friend Tom Sawyer—for "the *adventure* of it."

In the following excerpt, Huck has just done what his society has taught him is the right thing to do: he has written a note to Miss Watson, reporting the whereabouts of her runaway slave, Jim. However, Huck has deep misgivings about this action.

670

DIFFERENTIATED INSTRUCTION

FOR STRATEGIC READERS

Taking Notes Ask students to record the main ideas of each section on page 670 in outline form. Then have students exchange papers, evaluate each other's work, and offer suggestions for possible improvement.

Possible beginning of outline:

I. About the author
 A. Before becoming a writer
  1. Sam Clemens's youth in Hannibal, Missouri

2. His work as a riverboat pilot
3. "Mark Twain" = Mississippi riverboat workers' shout
 B. As a writer
  1. Famous humorist
  2. Best-known works: The Adventures of Tom Sawyer *(1876);* Life on the Mississippi *(1883);* The Adventures of Huckleberry Finn *(1884)*

 BEST PRACTICES TOOLKIT—Transparency
Outline p. B19

I felt good and all washed clean of sin for the first time I had ever felt so in my life, and I knowed I could pray now. But I didn't do it straight off, but laid the paper down and set there thinking—thinking how good it was all this happened so, and how near I come to being lost and going to hell. And went on thinking. And got to thinking over our trip down the river; and I see Jim before me, all the time, in the day, and in the nighttime, sometimes moonlight, sometimes storms, and we a floating along, talking, and singing, and laughing. But somehow I couldn't seem to strike no places to harden him against him, but only

10 the other kind. I'd see him standing my watch on top of his'n, stead of calling me, so I could go on sleeping; and see him how glad he was when I come back out of the fog; and when I come to him again in the swamp, up there where the feud was; and such-like times; and would always call me honey, and pet me, and do everything he could think of for me, and how good he always was; and at last I struck the time I saved him by telling the men we had small-pox aboard, and he was so grateful, and said I was the best friend old Jim ever had in the world, and the only one he's got now; and then I happened to look around, and see that paper.

It was a close place. I took it up, and held it in my hand. I was a trembling, because I'd got to decide, forever, betwixt two things, and I knowed it. I studied

20 a minute, sort of holding my breath, and then says to myself:

"All right, then, I'll *go* to hell"—and tore it up.

It was awful thoughts, and awful words, but they was said. And I let them stay said; and never thought no more about reforming. I shoved the whole thing out of my head; and said I would take up wickedness again, which was in my line, being brung up to it, and the other warn't. And for a starter, I would go to work and steal Jim out of slavery again; and if I could think up anything worse, I would do that, too; because as long as I was in, and in for good, I might as well go the whole hog.

Then I set to thinking over how to get at it, and turned over considerable many ways in my mind; and at last fixed up a plan that suited me. So then I took the

30 bearings of a woody island that was down the river a piece, and as soon as it was fairly dark I crept out with my raft and went for it, and hid it there, and then turned in. I slept the night through, and got up before it was light, and had my breakfast, and put on my store clothes, and tied up some others and one thing or another in a bundle, and took the canoe and cleared for shore. I landed below where I judged was Phelps's place, and hid my bundle in the woods, and then filled up the canoe with water, and loaded rocks into her and sunk her where I could find her again when I wanted her, about a quarter mile below a little steam sawmill that was on the bank.

671

OBJECTIVES

Literary Analysis
- explore the key idea of **exile**
- analyze regionalism
- read a short story

Reading
- clarify meaning

Vocabulary
- build vocabulary for reading and writing
- use knowledge of the Latin root *equ-* to help determine word meaning *(also an EL language objective)*

Grammar and Writing
- use personification to enliven descriptions
- write a description

 CALIFORNIA R3.5, R1.2, W1.1, W1.2, W1.9

ABOUT THE AUTHOR

After students read Bret Harte's biography, explain that in "The Outcasts of Poker Flat" they will encounter several of the familiar Western characters mentioned in the first sentence.

USING THE *NOTABLE QUOTE*

Ask students how the information about the life of **Bret Harte** supports the meaning of the quotation. *Students should recognize that Harte's life had its share of ups and downs. For example, his "good luck" at being offered a lucrative contract with* Atlantic Monthly *gave way to "bad luck" when the contract was not renewed and his literary career declined.* Extend the discussion by asking students whether people can "make" their own luck.

CALIFORNIA

R3.5, R1.2 (p. 686), W1.1 (p. 687),
W1.2 (p. 687), W1.9 (p. 687)

NOTABLE QUOTE
"Luck is a mighty queer thing. All you know about it for certain is that it's bound to change."

FYI
Did you know that Bret Harte . . .

- was called "Dickens among the pines" for the vivid and recognizable characters he created?
- worked as a shotgun rider on a California stagecoach?
- worked as an abolitionist during the Civil War, often speaking out against the harsh treatment of minorities?

Author On|ine

For more on Bret Harte, visit the **Literature Center** at ClassZone.com.

The Outcasts of Poker Flat
Short Story by Bret Harte

Bret Harte
1836–1902

Many of the familiar characters in Western stories and films—saloon keepers, fallen ladies, hard-bitten gamblers, mining prospectors, and dewy-eyed youngsters—can be found in the stories of Bret Harte. Harte's colorful writing helped shape the Western genre. It also inspired emigration to the developing region of the American west. Harte's writing made him—for a short while—one of America's most popular and highly paid literary figures.

A Man of Many Hats Born into an educated but financially struggling family, Bret Harte moved often during his childhood. Although the frequent moves and his poor health kept him from formal schooling, he read widely on his own and published his first writing at age 11. After his father died, Harte began working—first for a pharmacist, then a lawyer, and later as a tutor, a miner, and finally a journalist for a newspaper in California, where the family had moved after his mother's remarriage. It was at this newspaper that Harte began to publish his stories and articles.

Good Times In the early 1860s, Harte moved to San Francisco and began to hone his literary craft. He wrote and edited stories, articles, humor, and literary criticism for two newspapers, the *Golden Era* and then the *Californian.* At the *Californian,* Harte helped along the career of a young, unknown Mark Twain. Becoming founding editor of the *Overland Monthly,* Harte soon wrote and published "The Luck of Roaring Camp" and "The Outcasts of Poker Flat," stories of outcasts with hearts of gold. These stories put him on the literary map. Suddenly, he was the talk of the town with his work much discussed, often imitated, and highly sought after. When the *Atlantic Monthly* in Boston offered Harte an annual contract with a big salary, he moved his family back east.

. . . And Bad Times Harte was careless about fulfilling his *Atlantic Monthly* contract, and it was not renewed. He tried lecturing, novel writing (*Gabriel Conroy*), and playwriting with Mark Twain (*Ah Sin*), but was left with a failing literary career. His marriage had also deteriorated. Finally, in 1877, friends helped Harte get an appointment as U.S. consul in Germany. By 1885 he had landed in London. Bret Harte, who played a key role in creating the popular portrait of the Old West, lived in London for the rest of his life, dying there in 1902.

 RESOURCE MANAGER UNIT 4

Plan and Teach pp. 87–94

Literary Analysis
Summary pp. 95†*, 96‡*
Regionalism pp. 97, 98†*
Question Support p. 105*

Reading
Clarify Meaning pp. 99, 100†*
Reading Check p. 104

Vocabulary
Study p. 101*
Practice p. 102
Strategy p. 103

Grammar and Writing
Personification p. 106

Assessment
Selection Tests A, B/C pp. 107*, 109*

 Test Generator CD

BEST PRACTICES TOOLKIT

Differentiated Instruction
pp. 31–38*

Scaffolding Instruction
pp. 43–46*

Graphic Organizers/Strategies
Definition Mapping • Jigsaw
Reading • Cluster Diagram

Reading Support
Audio Anthology CD*

Technology
Literature, Vocabulary, and Writing Centers at **ClassZone.com**

Write*Smart* CD

● LITERARY ANALYSIS: REGIONALISM

Regionalism was a literary movement of the 19th century that strove to accurately represent the speech, manners, habits, history, and beliefs of people in a specific geographic area. A natural outgrowth of realism, regionalism often focused on the lives of ordinary people. As you read Bret Harte's famous story, note his use of the following characteristics of regional literature:

- detailed description of the physical features of **setting**
- attention to the specific time in which events occur, for example, a season of the year or a historical period
- depiction of the social and economic conditions of the **characters,** as well as any religious or moral beliefs that become apparent
- the use of **dialect,** which reflects the unique speech of a region during a particular time

■ READING SKILL: CLARIFY MEANING

Harte's style of writing can pose challenges to any reader. As you read this story, make sure to **clarify** any portions of the story that seem unclear on first reading. Stop and ask yourself questions such as these:

- What just happened?
- What do the characters' words and actions reveal about them?
- What meaning can be extracted from the narrator's comments and expressions?

▲ VOCABULARY IN CONTEXT

Harte uses a rich and challenging vocabulary in this story of the Old West. Choose the word from the list that you would associate with or use to describe an individual who

1. can see into the future	6. is friendly to everyone
2. is constantly joking	7. is an exile
3. criticizes others	8. has a steady outlook
4. complains all the time	9. weeps in sad movies
5. utters a curse	10. is avoided by others

WORD LIST		
amicable	jocular	prescience
anathema	maudlin	querulous
equanimity	pariah	vituperative
expatriated		

What does it mean to be an OUTCAST?

KEY IDEA In ancient times, people were sent into **exile** as a form of punishment. They were cast out of society and set adrift, often in harsh and dangerous wilderness. In "The Outcasts of Poker Flat," the characters are exiled into the California mountains, where they face both psychological and physical challenges. Consider why exile might be such an effective and extreme punishment.

DEBATE In a small group, prepare arguments for or against the statement "We need society to live." In developing your argument, consider the various consequences of living outside of society. After the debate, discuss whether you would support exile as a form of modern punishment.

673

Teach

CALIFORNIA

What does it mean to be an OUTCAST?

Lead into the **KEY IDEA** by asking the question. After students share their ideas about why **exile** is both an effective and an extreme punishment, tell them to recall these ideas as they carry out the *DEBATE* activity.

SKILLS FOCUS

LITERARY ANALYSIS R3.5

● REGIONALISM

Write this passage on the board:

> The town of Bickforth in 1853 was as bleak, barren, and gray a place as any in the world. Dust and dirt seemed to cover the stores and people alike. Jethro Rank had lived in Bickforth for all 16 years of his life, and he was fed up.
>
> "Gonna get me a new horse and ride outta this-here town," Jethro told his friend Tully.
>
> Tully snickered. "You all a time talkin' like that, but you ain't never really gonna do it."

Ask students what characteristics of regional literature they see in this passage. *Possible answer: description of setting, use of dialect*

CHECK UNDERSTANDING Ask students to find a passage in present-day literature that similarly captures the flavor of time and place.

READING SKILL

■ CLARIFY MEANING

Have students reread the passage on the board. Ask them what the characters' words reveal about them. *Possible answer: They have known each other for some time; Tully does not take Jethro's words seriously.*

[R] RESOURCE MANAGER—Copy Master
Clarify Meaning p. 99 (for student use while reading the selection)

VOCABULARY

▲ VOCABULARY IN CONTEXT

DIAGNOSE WORD KNOWLEDGE To determine preteaching needs, have all students complete Vocabulary in Context. *Answers:*
1. *prescience,* **2.** *jocular,* **3.** *vituperative,*
4. *querulous,* **5.** *anathema,* **6.** *amicable,*
7. *expatriated,* **8.** *equanimity,* **9.** *maudlin,*
10. *pariah*

PRETEACH VOCABULARY Preteach vocabulary with this copy master. Read each item aloud.

[R] RESOURCE MANAGER—Copy Master
Vocabulary Study p. 101

MORE VOCABULARY SUPPORT
For additional activities and guidelines, see

🧰 BEST PRACTICES TOOLKIT
Scaffolding Vocabulary Instruction pp. 43–46
ⓘ Vocabulary Center at **ClassZone.com**

SUMMARY

The citizens of Poker Flat cast out of their town certain undesirable persons: the gambler John Oakhurst, "The Duchess," "Mother Shipton," and "Uncle Billy." While traveling to a neighboring town, the outcasts meet young Tom Simson and his fiancée Piney Woods. The group is snowed in as they cross the mountains, and Billy sneaks off with their mules. As the days pass, supplies dwindle and the outcasts remain trapped. They draw comfort from one another, but eventually perish. Oakhurst, "at once the strongest and yet the weakest," commits suicide.

READING SKILL

A CLARIFY MEANING

Possible answer: *The first paragraph suggests that Mr. John Oakhurst, a gambler, has violated the moral standards of Poker Flat (lines 2–3; lines 5–6) and earned the disapproval of its citizens (line 4).*

Extend the Discussion What does the author mean when he writes that the men "exchanged significant glances"? That the settlement was "unused to Sabbath influences"?

The Outcasts of Poker Flat

Bret Harte

> **BACKGROUND** Many of Bret Harte's stories highlighted both the lure of gold in California and the challenge of battling a harsh landscape of huge spaces and towering mountains. During the California Gold Rush, which began in 1848, thousands of people poured into the state, creating towns such as the one in this story. These towns, which developed from miners' camps, were often rough and featured the homemade style of justice that sets this story's events in motion.

As Mr. John Oakhurst, gambler, stepped into the main street of Poker Flat on the morning of the twenty-third of November, 1850, he was conscious of a change in its moral atmosphere since the preceding night. Two or three men, conversing earnestly together, ceased as he approached, and exchanged significant glances. There was a Sabbath lull in the air, which, in a settlement unused to Sabbath influences, looked ominous. **A**

Mr. Oakhurst's calm, handsome face betrayed small concern in these indications. Whether he was conscious of any predisposing cause, was another question. "I reckon they're after somebody," he reflected; "likely it's me." He
10 returned to his pocket the handkerchief with which he had been whipping away the red dust of Poker Flat from his neat boots, and quietly discharged his mind of any further conjecture.

In point of fact, Poker Flat was "after somebody." It had lately suffered the loss of several thousand dollars, two valuable horses, and a prominent citizen. It was experiencing a spasm of virtuous reaction, quite as lawless and ungovernable as any of the acts that had provoked it. A secret committee had determined to rid the town of all improper persons. This was done permanently in regard of two

ANALYZE VISUALS
Describe the sense of time and place conveyed in this image. What details give you this sense?

A CLARIFY MEANING
Reread the first paragraph. What has happened thus far?

① Targeted Passage

Deadwood, South Dakota, 1877. The Granger Collection, New York.

DIFFERENTIATED INSTRUCTION

FOR ALL STUDENTS

Provide these independent projects to extend the lesson:

- Write an essay interpreting the author's perspective.
- Prepare a visual presentation of the story's setting.

For further details on these projects, see

R RESOURCE MANAGER
Ideas for Extension pp. 92–93

FOR STRATEGIC READERS

In combination with the *Audio Anthology CD*, use one or more Targeted Passages (pp. 674, 676, 679, 684) to ensure that students focus on key story events and concepts. Targeted Passages are also good for English learners.

① Targeted Passage [Lines 1–12]

This passage establishes the setting of the story and introduces the main character, John Oakhurst.

Possible answer: *The photograph conveys the atmosphere of a rugged frontier town of the mid-19th century. The simple wooden buildings, cluttered street, horse and buggy, and old-time signs help to create this feeling.*

BACKGROUND

The American Frontier The concept of the frontier—a region at the edge of or just beyond settled land—has played a key role in American identity and popular culture. Because of its distance from Eastern political institutions, the frontier was a free-spirited place that beckoned many like the outcasts of Poker Flat. Frontier towns, much like those in the story, maintained their own standards of justice and means of law enforcement. By 1890, the frontier line had disappeared, but the frontier remained as a fabled time and place. In his famous if somewhat idealized essay of 1893, "The Significance of the Frontier in American History," the historian Frederick Jackson Turner memorialized those who braved the frontier when he declared "this expansion westward with its new opportunities, its continuous touch with the simplicity of primitive society, furnish the forces dominating American character."

- What character is introduced as the story begins?
- What does this character do for a living?
- What is the character's state of mind?
- When does this story take place?
- Where does the story take place?

FOR ENGLISH LEARNERS

Key Academic Vocabulary Use Definition Mapping to teach these words: *significant* (line 4), *professional* (line 21), *shift* (line 118), *prospect* (line 171), *theory* (line 230).

 BEST PRACTICES TOOLKIT—Transparency Definition Mapping p. E6

Prereading For prereading instruction for English learners, see

 BEST PRACTICES TOOLKIT Scaffolding Reading Instruction pp. 43–46

FOR ADVANCED LEARNERS/AP

AP exercises in the bottom channel provide additional challenge for students. Use these suggestions for small groups or individuals.

ADDITIONAL GUIDELINES

For more help with differentiation and tips for classroom management, see

 BEST PRACTICES TOOLKIT Differentiated Instruction pp. 31–38

men who were then hanging from the boughs of a sycamore in the gulch, and temporarily in the banishment of certain other objectionable characters. I regret
20 to say that some of these were ladies. It is but due to the sex, however, to state that their impropriety was professional, and it was only in such easily established standards of evil that Poker Flat ventured to sit in judgment. **B**

Mr. Oakhurst was right in supposing that he was included in this category. A few of the committee had urged hanging him as a possible example, and a sure method of reimbursing themselves from his pockets of the sums he had won from them. "It's agin justice," said Jim Wheeler, "to let this yer young man from Roaring Camp[1]—an entire stranger—carry away our money." But a crude sentiment of equity residing in the breasts of those who had been fortunate enough to win from Mr. Oakhurst overruled this narrower local prejudice. **C**
30 Mr. Oakhurst received his sentence with philosophic calmness, none the less coolly that he was aware of the hesitation of his judges. He was too much of a gambler not to accept Fate. With him life was at best an uncertain game, and he recognized the usual percentage in favor of the dealer.

A body of armed men accompanied the deported wickedness of Poker Flat to the outskirts of the settlement. Besides Mr. Oakhurst, who was known to be a coolly desperate man, and for whose intimidation the armed escort was intended, the **expatriated** party consisted of a young woman familiarly known as "The Duchess," another who had won the title of "Mother Shipton,"[2] and "Uncle Billy," a suspected sluice-robber[3] and confirmed drunkard. The cavalcade
40 provoked no comments from the spectators, nor was any word uttered by the escort. Only, when the gulch which marked the uttermost limit of Poker Flat was reached, the leader spoke briefly and to the point. The exiles were forbidden to return at the peril of their lives.

As the escort disappeared, their pent-up feelings found vent in a few hysterical tears from the Duchess, some bad language from Mother Shipton, and a Parthian volley of expletives[4] from Uncle Billy. The philosophic Oakhurst alone remained silent. He listened calmly to Mother Shipton's desire to cut somebody's heart out, to the repeated statements of the Duchess that she would die in the road, and to the alarming oaths that seemed to be bumped out of Uncle Billy as he
50 rode forward. With the easy good-humor characteristic of his class, he insisted upon exchanging his own riding-horse, "Five Spot," for the sorry mule which the Duchess rode. But even this act did not draw the party into any closer sympathy. The young woman readjusted her somewhat draggled plumes with a feeble, faded coquetry; Mother Shipton eyed the possessor of "Five Spot" with malevolence, and Uncle Billy included the whole party in one sweeping **anathema**. **D**

---

1. **Roaring Camp:** name applied to a wild California settlement that was established in the 1830s by Isaac Graham. Harte used the name in his story "The Luck of Roaring Camp."
2. **"Mother Shipton":** originally, a 16th-century English woman who was accused of being a witch.
3. **sluice-robber** (slōōs'rŏb-ər): a person who steals gold from sluices, or the water troughs used by miners to sift gold.
4. **Parthian volley of expletives:** crude or hostile remarks made when leaving. Soldiers from the ancient Asian land of Parthia typically shot at their enemies while pretending to retreat on horseback.

Margin notes (right column of textbook page)

B CLARIFY MEANING
Reread lines 13–22. What is the narrator's attitude toward the "virtuous reaction" of Poker Flat?

C REGIONALISM
What can you **infer** about life in Poker Flat?

expatriated
(ĕk-spā'trē-ā'tĭd) adj. sent out of a country or area; banished **expatriate** v.

2 Targeted Passage

anathema (ə-năth'ə-mə) n. a strong denunciation; a curse

D CLARIFY MEANING
Reread lines 44–55. What is your impression of Oakhurst at this point in the story? Compare him with the other outcasts.

Teacher margin (left column)

READING SKILL

B CLARIFY MEANING

Possible answer: The narrator is critical of the "virtuous reaction" because it is "quite as lawless and ungovernable as any of the acts that had provoked it" (lines 15–16).

LITERARY ANALYSIS

C REGIONALISM

Possible answer: It can be inferred that Poker Flat is governed by some narrow-minded people whose moral proclamations may be at times both self-serving and hypocritical.

Lines 23–50
REINFORCE *KEY IDEA*: EXILE

Discuss On what information do the citizens of Poker Flat base their decision to send these four people into **exile**? *Possible answer: The "spasm of virtuous reaction" (line 15) and secret committee suggest the decision was based on questionable information, hearsay, and rumors.*

READING SKILL

D CLARIFY MEANING

Possible answer: Oakhurst is calm and philosophical in his acceptance of events, in contrast to the other characters' more emotional responses.

If students need help . . .

- Have them read lines 30–33 and 50–52. Discuss Oakhurst's quiet resignation and the kindness he shows to the Duchess.
- Have them read lines 44–55. Discuss the emotional reactions of the Duchess, Mother Shipton, and Uncle Billy.

Extend the Discussion What does the author mean when he refers to "the easy good-humor characteristic of his [Oakhurst's] class" (line 50)?

DIFFERENTIATED INSTRUCTION

FOR STRATEGIC READERS

2 Targeted Passage [Lines 34–50]

This passage introduces "The Duchess," "Mother Shipton," and "Uncle Billy." It also explains the outcasts' situation and describes their reactions.

- Which characters are described here?
- Why have these characters been escorted out of town?
- How does each character react to the situation?

FOR ADVANCED LEARNERS/AP

Analyze Tone As students read the story, have them reflect on the author's tone. What are Bret Harte's apparent feelings toward each of the characters? What does he think about their situation? Are their circumstances simply a matter of luck? Ask students to write a few paragraphs summarizing their observations and supporting their conclusions. Then have them share their paragraphs with the class.

The road to Sandy Bar—a camp that, not having as yet experienced the regenerating influences of Poker Flat, consequently seemed to offer some invitation to the emigrants—lay over a steep mountain range. It was distant a day's severe travel. In that advanced season, the party soon passed out of the moist,
60 temperate regions of the foot-hills into the dry, cold, bracing air of the Sierras.[5] The trail was narrow and difficult. At noon the Duchess, rolling out of her saddle upon the ground, declared her intention of going no farther, and the party halted.

The spot was singularly wild and impressive. A wooded amphitheatre, surrounded on three sides by precipitous cliffs of naked granite, sloped gently toward the crest of another precipice that overlooked the valley. It was, undoubtedly, the most suitable spot for a camp, had camping been advisable. But Mr. Oakhurst knew that scarcely half the journey to Sandy Bar was accomplished, and the party were not equipped or provisioned for delay. This fact he pointed out to his companions curtly, with a philosophic commentary on the folly of
70 "throwing up their hand before the game was played out." But they were furnished with liquor, which in this emergency stood them in place of food, fuel, rest, and **prescience.** In spite of his remonstrances, it was not long before they were more or less under its influence. Uncle Billy passed rapidly from a bellicose state into one of stupor, the Duchess became **maudlin,** and Mother Shipton snored. Mr. Oakhurst alone remained erect, leaning against a rock, calmly surveying them.

Mr. Oakhurst did not drink. It interfered with a profession which required coolness, impassiveness, and presence of mind, and, in his own language, he "couldn't afford it." As he gazed at his recumbent fellow-exiles, the loneliness begotten of his **pariah**-trade, his habits of life, his very vices, for the first time
80 seriously oppressed him. He bestirred himself in dusting his black clothes, washing his hands and face, and other acts characteristic of his studiously neat habits, and for a moment forgot his annoyance. The thought of deserting his weaker and more pitiable companions never perhaps occurred to him. Yet he could not help feeling the want of that excitement which, singularly enough, was most conducive to that calm **equanimity** for which he was notorious. He looked at the gloomy walls that rose a thousand feet sheer above the circling pines around him; at the sky, ominously clouded; at the valley below, already deepening into shadow. And, doing so, suddenly he heard his own name called. **E**

A horseman slowly ascended the trail. In the fresh, open face of the new-comer
90 Mr. Oakhurst recognized Tom Simson, otherwise known as "The Innocent" of Sandy Bar. He had met him some months before over a "little game," and had, with perfect equanimity, won the entire fortune—amounting to some forty dollars—of that guileless youth. After the game was finished, Mr. Oakhurst drew the youthful speculator behind the door and thus addressed him: "Tommy, you're a good little man, but you can't gamble worth a cent. Don't try it over again." He then handed him his money back, pushed him gently from the room, and so made a devoted slave of Tom Simson.

---

5. **Sierras:** the Sierra Nevada range of mountains, in eastern California.

prescience (prĕsh′əns) *n.* knowledge of events before they occur

maudlin (môd′lĭn) *adj.* excessively sentimental

pariah (pə-rī′ə) *n.* an outcast, someone or something looked down on by others

equanimity (ē′kwə-nĭm′ĭ-tē) *n.* evenness of temper, especially under stress

E REGIONALISM
Reread lines 56–88. In what way is this passage typical of regionalist writing?

LITERARY ANALYSIS

E REGIONALISM

Possible answer: The passage is typical of regionalist writing in that it provides a vivid and detailed description of the setting—in this case, the physical features of the surrounding mountainous environment.

If students need help . . . Call attention to examples of Harte's description, such as these: "the dry, cold, bracing air of the Sierras" (line 60); the "precipitous cliffs of naked granite" (line 64); and "the gloomy walls that rose a thousand feet sheer above the circling pines" (lines 85–86).

FOR ADVANCED LEARNERS/AP

Recognizing Stock Characters Explain that Bret Harte's stories include characters who may seem somehow familiar. This is in part because they are *stock characters*—characters in fiction or drama who represent types of characters rather than unique individuals. Examples of stock characters in literature include the rakish hero, the fool, the scheming villain, the innocent youth, the wicked witch, and the fallen woman with a heart of gold. When reading fiction, it is useful to be familiar with stock characters in order to recognize the roles they are intended to play in a story. As students read about Mr. Oakhurst, the Duchess, Mother Shipton, Uncle Billy, Tom Simson, and Piney Woods, have them identify stock traits in each character and share their findings with the class.

TIERED DISCUSSION PROMPTS

Use these prompts to help students better understand the character of John Oakhurst:

Connect Have you ever felt the need to stand up for, or protect, someone younger than you? Why did you feel that way? *Accept all thoughtful responses.*

Analyze How does Harte use the relationship between Oakhurst and Tom Simson to further develop Oakhurst's character?
Possible answer: Oakhurst's attitude toward "The Innocent" is protective almost to the point of being paternal. Not only does Oakhurst return Tom's poker money, but he also tries to dissuade him from gambling again (lines 94–96). Oakhurst kicks Uncle Billy to keep him quiet (lines 110–111), and he tries to talk Tom out of remaining with their group (lines 112–114).

Evaluate Is it believable that a professional gambler like Oakhurst would be concerned about someone like Tom? Why or why not?
Possible answers: Yes, because Oakhurst recognizes young Tom's youthful innocence and perhaps recalls when he himself was Tom's age. No, because Oakhurst does not trouble himself with sentiment, and may really think of "Innocent" Tom only as a potential liability.

There was a remembrance of this in his boyish and enthusiastic greeting of Mr. Oakhurst. He had started, he said, to go to Poker Flat to seek his fortune. "Alone?"
100 No, not exactly alone; in fact (a giggle), he had run away with Piney Woods. Didn't Mr. Oakhurst remember Piney? She that used to wait on the table at the Temperance House?[6] They had been engaged a long time, but old Jake Woods had objected, and so they had run away, and were going to Poker Flat to be married, and here they were. And they were tired out, and how lucky it was they had found a place to camp and company. All this the Innocent delivered rapidly, while Piney, a stout, comely damsel of fifteen, emerged from behind the pine tree, where she had been blushing unseen, and rode to the side of her lover.

Mr. Oakhurst seldom troubled himself with sentiment, still less with propriety; but he had a vague idea that the situation was not fortunate. He retained,
110 however, his presence of mind sufficiently to kick Uncle Billy, who was about to say something, and Uncle Billy was sober enough to recognize in Mr. Oakhurst's kick a superior power that would not bear trifling. He then endeavored to dissuade Tom Simson from delaying further, but in vain. He even pointed out the fact that there was no provision, nor means of making a camp. But, unluckily, the Innocent met this objection by assuring the party that he was provided with an extra mule loaded with provisions, and by the discovery of a rude attempt at a log house near the trail. "Piney can stay with Mrs. Oakhurst," said the Innocent, pointing to the Duchess, "and I can shift for myself."

---

6. **Temperance House:** a place where customers could not drink.

DIFFERENTIATED INSTRUCTION

FOR ENGLISH LEARNERS

Vocabulary: Multiple-Meaning Words Explain that *hanging* (line 24) means "executing (someone) by suspending by the neck until dead." However, *hanging* can also mean "attaching without support from below," as in "hanging a picture." Discuss how context clues can help students determine the appropriate meaning of multiple-meaning words. Then have mixed-language-ability Jigsaw groups investigate these other multiple-meaning words and report their findings: *body* (line 34), *bracing* (line 60), *coolness* (line 77), *habits* (line 81), *want* (line 84), *wait* (line 101), *provision* (line 114).

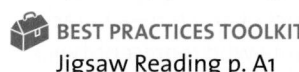 **BEST PRACTICES TOOLKIT**
Jigsaw Reading p. A1

Nothing but Mr. Oakhurst's admonishing foot saved Uncle Billy from bursting
120 into a roar of laughter. As it was, he felt compelled to retire up the canyon until
he could recover his gravity. There he confided the joke to the tall pine trees, with
many slaps of his leg, contortions of his face, and the usual profanity. But when
he returned to the party, he found them seated by a fire—for the air had grown
strangely chill and the sky overcast—in apparently **amicable** conversation. Piney
was actually talking in an impulsive, girlish fashion to the Duchess, who was
listening with an interest and animation she had not shown for many days. The
Innocent was holding forth, apparently with equal effect, to Mr. Oakhurst and
Mother Shipton, who was actually relaxing into amiability. "Is this yer a d—d
picnic?" said Uncle Billy, with inward scorn, as he surveyed the sylvan group, the
130 glancing firelight, and the tethered animals in the foreground. Suddenly an idea
mingled with the alcoholic fumes that disturbed his brain. It was apparently of
a **jocular** nature, for he felt impelled to slap his leg again and cram his fist into
his mouth. **F**

As the shadows crept slowly up the mountain, a slight breeze rocked the tops
of the pine trees, and moaned through their long and gloomy aisles. The ruined
cabin, patched and covered with pine boughs, was set apart for the ladies. As
the lovers parted, they unaffectedly exchanged a kiss, so honest and sincere
that it might have been heard above the swaying pines. The frail Duchess and
the malevolent Mother Shipton were probably too stunned to remark upon this
140 last evidence of simplicity, and so turned without a word to the hut. The fire was
replenished, the men lay down before the door, and in a few minutes were asleep. **G**

Mr. Oakhurst was a light sleeper. Toward morning he awoke benumbed and
cold. As he stirred the dying fire, the wind, which was now blowing strongly,
brought to his cheek that which caused the blood to leave it—snow!

He started to his feet with the intention of awakening the sleepers, for there
was no time to lose. But turning to where Uncle Billy had been lying, he found
him gone. A suspicion leaped to his brain and a curse to his lips. He ran to the
spot where the mules had been tethered; they were no longer there. The tracks
were already rapidly disappearing in the snow.

150 The momentary excitement brought Mr. Oakhurst back to the fire with his
usual calm. He did not waken the sleepers. The Innocent slumbered peacefully,
with a smile on his good-humored, freckled face; the virgin Piney slept beside her
frailer sisters as sweetly as though attended by celestial guardians, and Mr. Oakhurst,
drawing his blanket over his shoulders, stroked his mustaches and waited for the
dawn. It came slowly in a whirling mist of snowflakes, that dazzled and confused the
eye. What could be seen of the landscape appeared magically changed. He looked
over the valley, and summed up the present and future in two words—"snowed in!"

A careful inventory of the provisions, which, fortunately for the party, had
been stored within the hut, and so escaped the felonious fingers of Uncle Billy,
160 disclosed the fact that with care and prudence they might last ten days longer.

amicable (ăm'ĭ-kə-bəl)
adj. characterized by
friendly goodwill

jocular (jŏk'yə-lər) *adj.*
humorous

F CLARIFY MEANING
Reread lines 117–133.
What effect has the
arrival of Tom and Piney
had on the outcasts?

G GRAMMAR AND STYLE
Reread lines 134–135.
Note that the **verbs** *crept*
and *moaned* are used to
personify the shadows
and the breeze.

3 Targeted Passage

H CLARIFY MEANING

Possible answer: *Piney thinks that the Duchess is a woman of taste and refinement. She thinks that Poker Flat is something more than just a rough and dusty settlement.*

If students need help . . .

- Have them discuss the meaning of lines 175–177.
- Discuss how Piney, a "provincial maiden" (line 176), is far less worldly and experienced than the Duchess.

Extend the Discussion In what way is the relationship between the Duchess and Piney parallel to the relationship between Tom and Oakhurst?

LITERARY ANALYSIS

I REGIONALISM

Possible answer: *Despite the sinfulness of some and the innocence of others, the characters all seem to share a cultural background of traditional religious beliefs and practices.*

"That is," said Mr. Oakhurst, *sotto voce*[7] to the Innocent, "if you're willing to board us." If you ain't—and perhaps you'd better not—you can wait till Uncle Billy gets back with provisions." For some occult reason, Mr. Oakhurst could not bring himself to disclose Uncle Billy's rascality, and so offered the hypothesis that he had wandered from the camp and had accidentally stampeded the animals. He dropped a warning to the Duchess and Mother Shipton, who of course knew the facts of their associate's defection. "They'll find out the truth about us *all* when they find out anything," he added, significantly, "and there's no good frightening them now."

170 Tom Simson not only put all his worldly store at the disposal of Mr. Oakhurst, but seemed to enjoy the prospect of their enforced seclusion. "We'll have a good camp for a week, and then the snow'll melt, and we'll all go back together." The cheerful gaiety of the young man and Mr. Oakhurst's calm infected the others. The Innocent, with the aid of pine boughs, extemporized a thatch for the roofless cabin, and the Duchess directed Piney in the rearrangement of the interior with a taste and tact that opened the blue eyes of that provincial maiden to their fullest extent. "I reckon now you're used to fine things at Poker Flat," said Piney. The Duchess turned away sharply to conceal something that reddened her cheeks through its professional tint, and Mother Shipton requested Piney not to "chatter." But when Mr. Oakhurst returned
180 from a weary search for the trail, he heard the sound of happy laughter echoed from the rocks. He stopped in some alarm, and his thoughts first naturally reverted to the whiskey, which he had prudently cached.[8] "And yet it don't somehow sound like whiskey," said the gambler. It was not until he caught sight of the blazing fire through the still-blinding storm and the group around it that he settled to the conviction that it was "square fun." H

Whether Mr. Oakhurst had cached his cards with the whiskey as something debarred the free access of the community, I cannot say. It was certain that, in Mother Shipton's words, he "didn't say cards once" during the evening. Haply the time was beguiled by an accordion, produced somewhat ostentatiously by
190 Tom Simson from his pack. Notwithstanding some difficulties attending the manipulation of this instrument, Piney Woods managed to pluck several reluctant melodies from its keys, to an accompaniment by the Innocent on a pair of bone castanets. But the crowning festivity of the evening was reached in a rude camp-meeting hymn, which the lovers, joining hands, sang with great earnestness and vociferation. I fear that a certain defiant tone and Covenanter's swing[9] to its chorus, rather than any devotional quality, caused it speedily to infect the others, who at last joined the refrain:

"I'm proud to live in the service of the Lord,
And I'm bound to die in His army."[10] I

---

7. ***sotto voce*** (sŏt′ō vō′chĕ) *Italian*: in a low voice.

8. **prudently cached** (kă-shād′): wisely hidden away.

9. **Covenanter's swing:** the strong rhythms of songs sung by Scottish Presbyterians, who made covenants or agreements to oppose the Church of England.

10. **"I'm proud . . . army":** lines from the early American spiritual "Service of the Lord."

H CLARIFY MEANING
Reread lines 170–185. What is Piney's impression of the Duchess? of Poker Flat?

I REGIONALISM
Reread lines 186–199. From the information given, what can you **infer** about the characters and the culture to which they belong?

DIFFERENTIATED INSTRUCTION

FOR STRATEGIC READERS

Comprehension Support Call attention to the challenging word order and vocabulary in lines 186–187. Elicit or provide the meaning of *cached* ("hidden") and *debarred* ("excluded from"). Then help students paraphrase the sentence. **Possible answer:** *I don't know if Oakhurst had hidden his cards along with whiskey to keep everyone away from them.*

Vocabulary Support To support instruction, clarify the meaning of these words:

- *occult* (line 163), "secret or unknown"
- *defection* (line 167), "desertion"
- *extemporized* (line 174), "improvised"
- *thatch* (line 174), "a roof made from plant materials"
- *provincial* (line 176), "unsophisticated; simple"
- *vociferation* (line 195), "noisy shouting"

200   The pines rocked, the storm eddied and whirled above the miserable group, and the flames of their altar leaped heavenward, as if in token of the vow.

    At midnight the storm abated, the rolling clouds parted, and the stars glittered keenly above the sleeping camp. Mr. Oakhurst, whose professional habits had enabled him to live on the smallest possible amount of sleep, in dividing the watch with Tom Simson, somehow managed to take upon himself the greater part of that duty. He excused himself to the Innocent, by saying that he had "often been a week without sleep." "Doing what?" asked Tom. "Poker!" replied Oakhurst, sententiously; "when a man gets a streak of luck, he don't get tired. The luck gives in first. Luck," continued the gambler, reflectively, "is a mighty queer thing. All
210 you know about it for certain is that it's bound to change. And it's finding out when it's going to change that makes you. We've had a streak of bad luck since we left Poker Flat—you come along, and slap you get into it, too. If you can hold your cards right along you're all right. For," added the gambler, with cheerful irrelevance,

> "I'm proud to live in the service of the Lord,
> And I'm bound to die in His army."

    The third day came, and the sun, looking through the white-curtained valley, saw the outcasts divide their slowly decreasing store of provisions for the morning meal. It was one of the peculiarities of that mountain climate that its rays diffused
220 a kindly warmth over the wintry landscape, as if in regretful commiseration of the past. But it revealed drift on drift of snow piled high around the hut—a hopeless, uncharted, trackless sea of white lying below the rocky shores to which the castaways still clung. Through the marvelously clear air the smoke of the pastoral village of Poker Flat rose miles away. Mother Shipton saw it, and from a remote pinnacle of her rocky fastness, hurled in that direction a final malediction.[11] It was her last **vituperative** attempt, and perhaps for that reason was invested with a certain degree of sublimity. It did her good, she privately informed the Duchess. "Just you go out there and cuss, and see." She then set herself to the task of amusing "the child," as she and the Duchess were pleased to call Piney. Piney was
230 no chicken, but it was a soothing and original theory of the pair thus to account for the fact that she didn't swear and wasn't improper.

    When night crept up again through the gorges, the reedy notes of the accordion rose and fell in fitful spasms and long-drawn gasps by the flickering campfire. But music failed to fill entirely the aching void left by insufficient food, and a new diversion was proposed by Piney—storytelling. Neither Mr. Oakhurst nor his female companions caring to relate their personal experiences, this plan would have failed, too, but for the Innocent. Some months before he had chanced upon a stray copy of Mr. Pope's ingenious translation of the *Iliad*.[12] He now proposed

vituperative
(vī-tōō′pər-ə-tĭv) *adj.*
abusively critical

---

11. **malediction:** curse.

12. **Mr. Pope's . . . *Iliad*:** British poet Alexander Pope published his translation of Homer's *Iliad* in 1720.

FOR STRATEGIC READERS

Comprehension Support Call attention to the challenging style and outdated language of lines 224–227. Elicit or provide the meaning of *pinnacle* ("peak"), *fastness* ("a secure place"), and *sublimity* ("grandness"). Point out that the author is using imagery when he describes Mother Shipton hurling a curse "from a remote pinnacle of her rocky fastness." Then help students paraphrase the sentences. ***Possible answer:*** *Mother Shipton saw the smoke*

rise from Poker Flat and directed a heartfelt curse toward the village. Perhaps because it was her final outcry against the village, her words took on a certain grandness.

Lines 217–224
TIERED DISCUSSION PROMPTS
Use these prompts to help students understand the role that nature plays in the story:

Summarize What is the situation that threatens the outcasts? *Possible answer: Heavy snows have trapped them in the mountains, and Uncle Billy has run off with their mules. The outcasts have already consumed more than two days' worth of their provisions.*

Analyze Oakhurst, the Duchess, and Mother Shipton all seem to have both a rough side to their character and a gentler side. How does Harte reflect a similar contrast in his depiction of nature? *Possible answer: Harte describes how the sun's rays "diffused a kindly warmth over the wintry landscape, as if in regretful commiseration of the past." He also mentions "the marvelously clear air." However, at the same time, Harte also tells how the snow drifts have created "a hopeless, uncharted, trackless sea of white."*

Synthesize Predict what will happen to the outcasts. Will their "streak of bad luck" (line 211) change? Why or why not? *Accept all reasonable responses.*

❶ REGIONALISM

Possible answer: Words that seem especially descriptive of the characters' situation include "the sun again forsook them"; "from leaden skies, the snowflakes were sifted over the land"; and "they looked from their prison over drifted walls of dazzling white."

Lines 246–255
TIERED DISCUSSION PROMPTS

Use these prompts to help students understand the outcasts' situation:

Summarize How has the outcasts' predicament become worse? *Possible answer: They are almost out of food, it is still snowing, the drifts are far over their heads, and firewood is scarce.*

Analyze Consider the reactions of Tom and Piney, the Duchess, and Oakhurst to their situation. Do these characters behave as expected? Explain. *Possible answer: Tom and Piney are young lovers, and they take comfort in each other, which one might expect considering their age and innocence. The Duchess occupies herself with caring for young Piney, which perhaps suggests that the older woman is feeling maternal. Oakhurst, consistent with his character, "settled himself coolly to the losing game before him" (line 254).*

Evaluate Despite the outcasts' difficult situation, "no one complained" (line 252). Is this believable? Why or why not? *Possible answer: It seems they would complain about their lack of food, the extreme conditions, and dangers they are facing. Perhaps they are trying to be strong for each other by not complaining.*

to narrate the principal incidents of that poem—having thoroughly mastered the
240 argument and fairly forgotten the words—in the current vernacular of Sandy Bar.
And so for the rest of that night the Homeric demigods again walked the earth.
Trojan bully and wily Greek wrestled in the winds, and the great pines in the
canyon seemed to bow to the wrath of the son of Peleus.[13] Mr. Oakhurst listened
with quiet satisfaction. Most especially was he interested in the fate of "Ash-heels,"
as the Innocent persisted in denominating the "swift-footed Achilles."

So with small food and much of Homer and the accordion, a week passed over
the heads of the outcasts. The sun again forsook them, and again from leaden skies
the snowflakes were sifted over the land. Day by day closer around them drew
the snowy circle, until at last they looked from their prison over drifted walls of
250 dazzling white, that towered twenty feet above their heads. It became more and ❶
more difficult to replenish their fires, even from the fallen trees beside them, now
half hidden in the drifts. And yet no one complained. The lovers turned from the
dreary prospect and looked into each other's eyes, and were happy. Mr. Oakhurst
settled himself coolly to the losing game before him. The Duchess, more cheerful
than she had been, assumed the care of Piney. Only Mother Shipton—once the
strongest of the party—seemed to sicken and fade. At midnight on the tenth day
she called Oakhurst to her side. "I'm going," she said, in a voice of **querulous**
weakness, "but don't say anything about it. Don't waken the kids. Take the bundle
from under my head and open it." Mr. Oakhurst did so. It contained Mother
260 Shipton's rations for the last week, untouched. "Give 'em to the child," she said,
pointing to the sleeping Piney. "You've starved yourself," said the gambler. "That's

❶ REGIONALISM
Reread lines 246–250.
What words used to
describe the characters'
physical surroundings
seem especially
descriptive of their
situation?

querulous (kwĕr′ə-ləs)
adj. complaining

---

13. **son of Peleus** (pē′lē-əs): Achilles (ə-kĭl′ēz), the Greek hero in the *Iliad*. Tom Simson mispronounces his name as "Ash-heels."

DIFFERENTIATED INSTRUCTION

FOR ADVANCED LEARNERS/AP
Analyze Stylistic Technique Ask students to study lines 246–252. Then have them discuss the author's technique, especially his use of imagery, metaphor ("snowflakes were sifted over the land"; "they looked from their prison"), and descriptive details to create a mood. Also discuss the author's economy of style ("a week passed over the heads of the outcasts") in narrating the passage of time. Next, have students choose a scene of their own and

write a one- or two-paragraph description in the style of Bret Harte. Challenge students to use figurative language and descriptive details as Harte does to create a vivid scene and establish a mood. Have students share their descriptions with the class.

what they call it," said the woman, querulously, as she lay down again, and, turning her face to the wall, passed quietly away. **K**

The accordion and the bones were put aside that day, and Homer was forgotten. When the body of Mother Shipton had been committed to the snow, Mr. Oakhurst took the Innocent aside, and showed him a pair of snowshoes, which he had fashioned from the old pack saddle. "There's one chance in a hundred to save her yet," he said, pointing to Piney; "but it's there," he added, pointing toward Poker Flat. "If you can reach there in two days she's safe." "And
270 you?" asked Tom Simson. "I'll stay here," was the curt reply.

The lovers parted with a long embrace. "You are not going, too?" said the Duchess, as she saw Mr. Oakhurst apparently waiting to accompany him. "As far as the canyon," he replied. He turned suddenly, and kissed the Duchess, leaving her pallid face aflame, and her trembling limbs rigid with amazement.

Night came, but not Mr. Oakhurst. It brought the storm again and the whirling snow. Then the Duchess, feeding the fire, found that someone had quietly piled beside the hut enough fuel to last a few days longer. The tears rose to her eyes, but she hid them from Piney.

The women slept but little. In the morning, looking into each other's faces,
280 they read their fate. Neither spoke; but Piney, accepting the position of the stronger, drew near and placed her arm around the Duchess's waist. They kept this attitude for the rest of the day. That night the storm reached its greatest fury, and, rendering asunder[14] the protecting pines, invaded the very hut.

Toward morning they found themselves unable to feed the fire, which gradually died away. As the embers slowly blackened, the Duchess crept closer to Piney, and broke the silence of many hours: "Piney, can you pray?" "No, dear," said Piney,

---

14. **rending asunder:** forcefully ripping apart.

K CLARIFY MEANING
What happens to Mother Shipton? Explain whether or not you were surprised by this development, and why or why not.

K CLARIFY MEANING

Possible answer: Mother Shipton starves herself in order to save her food for Piney, so that the girl might survive. This is a surprising development, since Mother Shipton has been severe up until this point.

Extend the Discussion Why did Mother Shipton do what she did?

Lines 265–277
TIERED DISCUSSION PROMPTS

Use these prompts to help students understand the worsening circumstances:

Recall Why has the outcasts' situation now become dire? *Possible answer: They are out of food, nearly out of firewood, and still trapped by the snow with no sign of a break in the storm.*

Interpret What last-ditch efforts does Oakhurst make to save the outcasts? *Possible answer: He makes snowshoes for Tom, in hopes that Tom can reach Poker Flat and get help. Readers can also infer that it was Oakhurst who piled firewood beside the hut (lines 276–277).*

Synthesize How will the story end for Oakhurst, the Duchess, and Piney? Cite evidence for the prediction. *Accept all reasonable responses.*

FOR ENGLISH LEARNERS
Vocabulary: Idioms Help students use context clues to determine the meaning of these idioms in the story:

- *feeding the fire* (line 276), "supplying wood for the fire"
- *read their fate* (line 280), "realized what would happen"
- *broke the silence* (lines 286), "interrupted the silence by speaking"

FOR ADVANCED LEARNERS/AP
Evaluate Direct students' attention to lines 271–274. Ask why Oakhurst kisses the Duchess at this point. Have students write a paragraph explaining whether this action is or is not consistent with Oakhurst's character, and why. After students finish reading the story, have them review their paragraphs and decide whether they maintain their original answers.

Possible answer: *The Duchess and Piney froze to death, "locked in each other's arms" (line 299). The narrator seems to be making the point that black-and-white judgments of innocence and guilt are irrelevant in the face of death and perhaps were unfair to begin with.*

simply. The Duchess, without knowing exactly why, felt relieved, and, putting her head upon Piney's shoulder, spoke no more. And so reclining, the younger and purer pillowing the head of her soiled sister upon her virgin breast, they fell asleep.

290 The wind lulled as if it feared to waken them. Feathery drifts of snow, shaken from the long pine boughs, flew like white-winged birds, and settled about them as they slept. The moon through the rifted clouds looked down upon what had been the camp. But all human stain, all trace of earthly travail, was hidden beneath the spotless mantle mercifully flung from above.

They slept all that day and the next, nor did they waken when voices and footsteps broke the silence of the camp. And when pitying fingers brushed the snow from their wan faces, you could scarcely have told from the equal peace that dwelt upon them, which was she that had sinned. Even the law of Poker Flat recognized this, and turned away, leaving them still locked in each other's arms. **L**

300 But at the head of the gulch, on one of the largest pine trees, they found the deuce of clubs[15] pinned to the bark with a bowie-knife. It bore the following, written in pencil, in a firm hand:

L CLARIFY MEANING
Summarize what has happened to the Duchess and Piney. What point does the narrator seem to be making in lines 279–299?

2♣

BENEATH THIS TREE
LIES THE BODY
OF
JOHN OAKHURST
WHO STRUCK A STREAK OF BAD LUCK
ON THE 23ʳᵈ OF NOVEMBER, 1850,
AND
HANDED IN HIS CHECKS
ON THE 7ᵗʰ DECEMBER, 1850.

④ Targeted Passage

And pulseless and cold, with a Derringer[16] by his side and a bullet in his heart, though still calm as in life, beneath the snow lay he who was at once the strongest and yet the weakest of the outcasts of Poker Flat. **M**

M CLARIFY MEANING
Why has Oakhurst committed this final act?

---

15. **deuce of clubs:** the lowest card in a deck of playing cards—thus a loser's card.
16. **Derringer:** a short-barreled pistol invented by American gunsmith Henry Derringer.

Possible answer: *Perhaps Oakhurst, thinking as a gambler, coolly assessed the odds of his desperate situation, realized that he had no chance of surviving, and took his own life.*

SELECTION WRAP–UP

REFLECT Have students think about the ending of the story. Discuss possible reasons why Harte chose to conclude his story in such a somber fashion.

⭐ CRITIQUE

• Have students rate the story on a scale of 1 to 5. Ask students whether they would have rated the story higher if it had ended differently. Why or why not?

• After completing the After Reading questions on page 685, have students revisit their responses and tell whether they have changed their opinions.

DIFFERENTIATED INSTRUCTION

FOR STRATEGIC READERS

④ Targeted Passage [Lines 295–305]

This passage concludes the story with a character's final desperate act.

• What happens to the Duchess and Piney Woods at the end of the story?

• What happens to Oakhurst?

FOR ENGLISH LEARNERS

Vocabulary Support Discuss the meaning of these opposites:

• *purer, virgin/soiled* (line 289): Innocent Piney and the "soiled" Duchess die together.

• *human stain/spotless mantle* (lines 293–294): The "human stain" of the outcasts is covered by the "spotless mantle" of snow.

• *strongest/weakest* (lines 304–305): Oakhurst showed strength as a leader but weakness in committing suicide.

Comprehension

1. **Recall** Why do Mr. Oakhurst and the others leave Poker Flat?

2. **Recall** Who joins the traveling group at their camp?

3. **Summarize** What happens to the travelers at the camp?

Literary Analysis

4. **Clarify Meaning** Review the following quotations within the context of the story and summarize what they mean:

   • "There was a Sabbath lull in the air, which, in a settlement unused to Sabbath influences, looked ominous." (lines 5–6)

   • "Mr. Oakhurst seldom troubled himself with sentiment, still less with propriety; but he had a vague idea that the situation was not fortunate." (lines 108–109)

   • "...Beneath the snow lay he who was at once the strongest and yet the weakest of the outcasts of Poker Flat." (lines 304–305)

5. **Examine the Main Character** Bret Harte was known for portraying outcast characters with hearts of gold. How does John Oakhurst fit this formula of the character with contradictory traits? Use a chart to explore this question.

Outcast Traits	Virtuous Traits

6. **Interpret Author's Perspective** Personal experience and historical context influence the characters and conflicts that a writer chooses to depict. Based on events in this story and their outcome, how would you describe Harte's opinion of the following?

   • John Oakhurst
   • society in the Old West
   • human nature
   • the other outcasts
   • the young couple

7. **Analyze Theme** In your opinion, what message does this story convey?

8. **Evaluate Use of Regionalism** The goal of regionalists was to capture life at a particular time in history. In your opinion, how well did Harte convey the region, the people, and the times in "The Outcasts of Poker Flat"? Cite evidence to support your view.

Literary Criticism

9. **Critical Interpretations** Mark Twain said that it was Bret Harte who "trimmed and schooled me patiently until he changed me from an awkward utterer of coarse grotesqueness to a writer of paragraphs and chapters." Harte also influenced Ambrose Bierce and Rudyard Kipling. Why do you think Harte might have had a strong impact on so many writers?

THE OUTCASTS OF POKER FLAT **685**

8. ● **SKILLS FOCUS** Regionalism *Harte effectively captures the different types of people living in the rough settlement, contending with the moral code of the times and the merciless power of nature.*

9. *Harte created interesting and complex characters who have both positive and negative traits—just as real people do.*

Practice and Apply

After Reading

Use these copy masters to check understanding and provide extra support:

RESOURCE MANAGER—Copy Masters
Reading Check p. 104
Regionalism p. 97
Question Support p. 105

Additional selection questions are provided for teachers on page 91.

ANSWERS

1. *Oakhurst and the others are forced to leave when the town deems them to be undesirable influences.*

2. *Two innocent young people—Tom Simson and his fiancée, Piney Woods—join the group at the camp.*

3. *The travelers get snowed in and eventually perish.*

Possible answers:

4. ■ **SKILLS FOCUS** Clarify Meaning *"There was...": The silence suggested that something significant or worrisome was taking place; "Mr. Oakhurst...": Although Oakhurst is generally unconcerned with social conventions, he has a bad feeling about the Innocents joining their group; "...Beneath...": As strong a role as Oakhurst had played in the group, he weakly gave in to the situation and committed suicide.*

5. *Outcast Traits: gambler, loner, no emotional attachments; Virtuous Traits: kind, caring*

6. *Oakhurst: heroic, yet vulnerable, and not as strong as everyone thinks; other outcasts: more positive traits than outward appearance might suggest (except for Uncle Billy); society: perhaps too narrowly restrictive in its moral code; young couple: likeable but too naïve to survive; human nature: surprisingly good, for the most part, though positive traits may be hidden beneath rough exteriors.*

7. *There is kindness within most people, despite outward appearances; nature is unforgiving toward the innocent and the guilty alike.*

THE OUTCASTS OF POKER FLAT **685**

ANSWERS
Vocabulary in Context

VOCABULARY PRACTICE

1. *calm*
2. *a mushy love story*
3. *find fault*
4. *in exile*
5. *a party host*
6. *shunned*
7. *anger*
8. *a comedian*
9. *predict future events*
10. *scold them*

RESOURCE MANAGER—Copy Master
Vocabulary Practice p. 102

VOCABULARY IN WRITING

Encourage students to support their choice with specific reasons. To broaden the activity, have students rank all the main characters in order from most admirable to least admirable and explain their ranking, using as many vocabulary words as they can.

VOCABULARY STRATEGY: THE LATIN ROOT *equ* *(also an EL language objective)*

- Point out that students will recognize the prefix form of the root from such words as *equal, equator, equation,* and *equinox.*

- Explain how figuring out the part of speech from the sentence context can help students narrow their choices. You may want to point out that three of the words are nouns, two are adjectives, and one is a verb.

Answers:

1. *equivocate*
2. *equidistant*
3. *equilibrium*
4. *equivalency*

RESOURCE MANAGER—Copy Master
Vocabulary Strategy p. 103

Vocabulary Center at ClassZone.com
Additional Vocabulary Activities

Vocabulary in Context

VOCABULARY PRACTICE

Show you understand the vocabulary words by answering these questions.

1. If I handled a situation with **equanimity,** would I be upset about it or calm?
2. Which could be considered **maudlin,** a stern lecture or a mushy love story?
3. Would a **querulous** person be more likely to enjoy a party or find fault with it?
4. If I am **expatriated,** am I living in exile or returning to my own country?
5. Is a party host or a prosecuting lawyer more likely to be **amicable?**
6. Is a **pariah** shunned or welcomed into gatherings?
7. If a person utters an **anathema,** is he or she expressing anger or compassion?
8. Who is more likely to be **jocular,** a runner or a comedian?
9. Does someone with **prescience** predict future events or excel in chemistry?
10. Would a **vituperative** tutor encourage her students or scold them?

WORD LIST
amicable
anathema
equanimity
expatriated
jocular
maudlin
pariah
prescience
querulous
vituperative

VOCABULARY IN WRITING

In your opinion, which character in this story proves to be most admirable? Identify the character and defend your ideas, using events in the story. Include at least three vocabulary words. You might start this way.

> **EXAMPLE SENTENCE**
> *Though hard and **querulous**, Mother Shipton ultimately proved to have a better heart than any of the others.*

R1.2
CALIFORNIA

VOCABULARY STRATEGY: THE LATIN ROOT *equ*

The vocabulary word *equanimity* contains the Latin root *equ,* which means "even," "just," or "equal." This root, which is occasionally spelled *iqu,* is found in a number of English words. In its prefix form *equi,* it is sometimes combined with existing words to form new words, as in *equiprobable.* To understand words with *equ,* use context clues as well as your knowledge of the meaning of the root.

PRACTICE Apply what you know about *equ, equi,* and other word parts to help you understand the words in the web. Then choose the word that best completes each sentence. If necessary, consult a dictionary.

1. If you _____, it may be said that you are talking out of both sides of your mouth.
2. What town is _____ between Chicago and Milwaukee?
3. The accident affected her _____, and she often felt dizzy.
4. Passing a high school _____ test can take the place of actually graduating.

VOCABULARY PRACTICE
For more practice, go to the **Vocabulary Center** at **ClassZone.com.**

686   UNIT 4: REGIONALISM AND NATURALISM

DIFFERENTIATED INSTRUCTION

FOR ENGLISH LEARNERS

Task Support: Vocabulary Strategy Discuss words in home languages with the Latin root *equ/iqu* or the Latin prefix *equi-.* There are other forms of some of the words in the web on page 686 that may occur in home languages as well. For example, *equi,* meaning "wrong" or "incorrect," appears in Spanish *equívoco.*

FOR ADVANCED LEARNERS/AP

Vocabulary in Writing Ask students to use as many vocabulary words as they can in a brief dialogue between two of the characters from the story.

686   UNIT 4: REGIONALISM AND NATURALISM

Reading-Writing Connection

 W1.1, W1.2

WRITING PROMPT

WRITE A DESCRIPTION Choose a real or fictional society—one from history, for example, or one crafted entirely from imagination. Write a **three-or four-paragraph description** of the society that reflects the perspective of one who has been sent into **exile.**

SELF-CHECK

A successful description will describe . . .
- the society's institutions
- the interactions of people
- the society's buildings
- the society's holidays

GRAMMAR AND STYLE

 W1.9

ADD DESCRIPTIVE DETAILS Review the **Grammar and Style** note on page 679. Harte uses **personification**—the attribution of human qualities to objects or ideas—to enliven his descriptions of inanimate objects. Here is an example from the story:

> *The third day came, and the sun, looking through the white-curtained valley, saw the outcasts divide their slowly decreasing store of provisions for the morning meal.* (lines 217–219)

Harte's use of the highlighted **participial phrase** and **verb** creates an ethereal image of the sun "watching" the outcasts.

PRACTICE Rewrite each of the following sentences to include personification.

> **EXAMPLE**
>
> We could see the town at the top of the mountain but couldn't see most of its buildings.
>
> *The town seemed to turn its back on us, hiding its buildings from our view down in the valley.*

1. The mountain was solid rock, very steep, and very tall.

2. Lights were shining in some of the windows.

3. Snow began to fall, making it harder to see the town way above us.

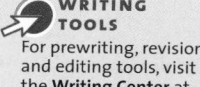 **WRITING TOOLS**
For prewriting, revision, and editing tools, visit the **Writing Center** at ClassZone.com.

FOR DEVELOPING WRITERS
Writing Support

- Help students brainstorm institutions, buildings, holidays, and other aspects of their society.

- Help students project themselves into their society and imagine how their fellow citizens from various socioeconomic backgrounds interact with one another.

- Offer students suggestions for beginning their description. For example, they might start with a broad overview and then focus on specific places or people. Or, they might first discuss people, then places, then customs and beliefs.

- Remind students to include specific details —especially sensory details that make their descriptions come alive.

Reading-Writing Connection

WRITING PROMPT

Suggest that students use a Cluster Diagram to help them brainstorm their society's institutions, buildings, and holidays. Encourage students to reflect on the interactions between people of various social and economic groups and people of different ages and genders.

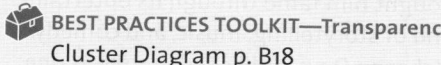 **BEST PRACTICES TOOLKIT**—Transparency
Cluster Diagram p. B18

For writing support, see

ⓘ Writing Center at **ClassZone.com**

GRAMMAR AND STYLE

Point out that personification may be based in a metaphor or simile. Help students compare these examples: *The clock radio told me to wake up* (metaphor); *The cat stood like an angry parent ready to scold us for forgetting to feed her* (simile).

Possible answers:

1. *The mountain stood before us like a muscular athlete challenging his opponents.*

2. *Lights greeted us happily from the windows.*

3. *The falling snow covered our eyes with wintry fingers.*

Ⓡ **RESOURCE MANAGER**—Copy Master
Personification p. 106

Assess and Reteach

Assess

Ⓡ **RESOURCE MANAGER**—Copy Masters
Selection Test A pp. 107–108
Selection Test B/C pp. 109–110

💿 Test Generator CD

Reteach

Ⓢ **STANDARDS LESSON FILE**
Writing Lesson 21: Descriptive Writing
Vocabulary Lesson 7: Latin Roots

BACKGROUND

Garrison Keillor, Storyteller Born in 1942 in Anoka, a town about 20 miles northwest of Minneapolis, Keillor began demonstrating his skills while involved with his college literary magazine and radio station. Those experiences set him on the path that eventually led to *A Prairie Home Companion,* the radio program that brought him fame through its entertaining blend of storytelling, music, and comedy. *Lake Wobegon Days,* published in 1985, is one of numerous books by Keillor, some with and some without Lake Wobegon connections.

Lines 1–7
TIERED DISCUSSION PROMPTS

Use these prompts to help students explore Keillor's description of Lake Wobegon:

Connect Have you ever visited a place like Lake Wobegon? If so, what was it like? If not, what might living in such a place be like? *Accept all thoughtful responses.*

Analyze In this opening paragraph, how does Keillor establish the location and spirit of Lake Wobegon? *Possible answer: Keillor creates a description that lets readers know that Lake Wobegon is an out-of-the-way place (lines 1–2) with a folksy charm (as seen in events such as Toast 'n Jelly Days) and perhaps a greater affection for its own people than for outsiders (lines 1–2). Keillor's conversational style makes Lake Wobegon seem like a place that readers would want to visit.*

Evaluate How effective is Keillor in creating a small-town atmosphere? Explain. *Accept all thoughtful responses.*

---

from Lake Wobegon Days

GARRISON KEILLOR

BACKGROUND Garrison Keillor has been classed with such great American humorists as Ring Lardner, James Thurber, and Mark Twain. A Minnesota native, he began his career in radio. He made a name for himself with his weekly radio variety show, *A Prairie Home Companion,* which began in 1974 and, after one six-year hiatus, continued to run into the 21st century. Among the show's most beloved features has been Keillor's weekly monologue in which he delivers the news from Lake Wobegon, a fictionalized version of his hometown in Minnesota. *Lake Wobegon Days* is a novel based on this small town in America's heartland and its earnest, hard-working inhabitants.

People who visit Lake Wobegon come to see somebody, otherwise they missed the turn on the highway and are lost. *Ausländers,* the Germans call them. They don't come for Toast 'n Jelly Days, or the Germans' quadrennial Gesuffa Days, or Krazy Daze, or the Feast Day of St. Francis, or the three-day Mist County Fair with its exciting Death Leap from the top of the grandstand to the arms of the haystack for only ten cents. What's special about here isn't special enough to draw a major crowd, though Flag Day—you could drive a long way on June 14 to find another like it.

Flag Day, as we know it, was the idea of Herman Hochstetter, Rollie's dad, who ran the dry goods store and ran Armistice Day, the Fourth of July, and Flag Day. For the
10 Fourth, he organized a double-loop parade around the block which allowed people to take turns marching and watching. On Armistice Day, everyone stepped outside at 11 A.M and stood in silence for two minutes as Our Lady's bell tolled eleven times.

DIFFERENTIATED INSTRUCTION

FOR STRATEGIC READERS
Vocabulary Support

- *quadrennial* (line 3), "occurring every four years"
- *feast day* (line 4), "a celebration that honors a religious figure [in this case, a Roman Catholic saint]"
- *grandstand* (line 5), "a seating structure for spectators at an outdoor event"

FOR ADVANCED LEARNERS/AP

Analyze Tone [small-group option] As students read the excerpt from *Lake Wobegon Days,* ask them to consider the author's tone and to determine how Garrison Keillor feels about the people and events that he describes and how he makes that tone clear. Have students write a paragraph that summarizes their observations and any conclusions they can draw and that supports both with specific details from the text. Invite students to share their thoughts in small groups.

TIERED DISCUSSION PROMPTS

Use these prompts to help students under-stand how Keillor creates an entertaining narrative:

Recall What problem does Herman en-counter in creating the Living Flag? *Possible answer: The people forming the flag want to break out of their positions to see what the flag looks like from overhead.*

Analyze How does Keillor integrate humor into his account of Herman Hochstetter's efforts? Be specific. *Possible answer: Keillor creates lively visual images that are amusing to picture. For example, he creates the image of the flag participants racing up to the roof in order see what their Living Flag looks like (lines 55–56). When too many participants leave, Keillor describes how the flag looked as though it had been "shot through by cannon fire" (lines 73–74). Finally, he creates the im-age of participants looking up into the mirror on the roof—which, of course, only causes the flag to disappear (lines 77–79).*

Evaluate Are Keillor's descriptions of people and events realistic? Defend your opinion. *Many students will say that the descriptions are realistic, for they arise from Keillor's good understanding of small-town life. Some may find the descriptions simplistic and idealized.*

Flag Day was his favorite. For a modest price, he would install a bracket on your house to hold a pole to hang your flag on, or he would drill a hole in the sidewalk in the front of your store with his drill gun powered by a .22 shell. *Bam!* And in went the flag. On patriotic days, flags flew all over; there were flags on the tall poles, flags on the short, flags in the brackets on the pillars and the porches, and if you were flagless you could expect to hear from Herman. His hairy arm around your shoulder, his poochlike face close to yours, he would say how proud he was

20 that so many people were proud of their country, leaving you to see the obvious, that you were a gap in the ranks.

In June 1944, the day after D-Day, a salesman from Fisher Hat called on Herman and offered a good deal on red and blue baseball caps. "Do you have white also?" Herman asked. The salesman thought that white caps could be had for the same wonderful price. Herman ordered two hundred red, two hundred white, and one hundred blue. By the end of the year, he still had four hundred and eighty-six caps. The inspiration of the Living Flag was born from that overstock.

On June 14, 1945, a month after V-E Day, a good crowd assembled in front of the Central Building in response to Herman's ad in the paper:

30   Honor "AMERICA" June 14 AT 4 p.m. Be proud
        of "Our Land & People". Be part of the "LIVING
        FLAG". Don't let it be said that Lake Wobegon was
        "Too Busy". Be on time. 4 p.m. "Sharp".

His wife Louise handed out the caps, and Herman stood on a stepladder and told people where to stand. He lined up the reds and whites into stripes, then got the blues into their square. Mr. Hanson climbed up on the roof of the Central Building and took a photograph, they sang the national anthem, and then the Living Flag dispersed. The photograph appeared in the paper the next week. Herman kept the caps.

40 In the flush of victory, people were happy to do as told and stand in place, but in 1946 and 1947, dissension cropped up in the ranks: people complained about the heat and about Herman—what gave *him* the idea he could order *them* around? "People! Please! I need your attention! You blue people, keep your hats on! Please! Stripe No. 4, you're sagging! You reds, you're up here! We got too many white people, we need more red ones! Let's do this without talking, people! I can't get you straight if you keep moving around! Some of you are not paying attention! Everybody shut up! Please!"

One cause of resentment was the fact that none of them got to see the Flag they were in; the picture in the paper was black and white. Only Herman and Mr. Hanson

50 got to see the real Flag, and some boys too short to be needed down below. People wanted a chance to go up to the roof and witness the spectacle for themselves.

"How can you go up there if you're supposed to be down here?" Herman said. "You go up there to look, you got nothing to look at. Isn't it enough that you're doing your part?"

On Flag Day, 1949, just as Herman said, "That's it! Hold it now!" one of the reds made a break for it—dashed up four flights of stairs to the roof and leaned over and had a long look. Even with the hole he left behind, it was a magnificent sight. The

DIFFERENTIATED INSTRUCTION

FOR ENGLISH LEARNERS

Culture: Clarify Explain the meaning of these terms:

- *D-Day* (line 22), June 6, 1944, the day on which Allied forces began invading France during World War II

- *V-E Day* (line 28), "Victory in Europe" Day: May 8, 1945, the day on which the surrender of Germany to the Allies was declared during World War II

FOR ADVANCED LEARNERS/AP

Rewrite a Scene Keillor's simple, breezy style makes his narrative come to life. Have students describe the same scene that Keillor does in lines 34–74, but in their own style. Encourage students to draw upon details from the text but also to use their imagina-tion to expand and develop those details as needed. Have volunteers share their work with the class; invite insights and construc-tive criticism.

Living Flag filled the street below. A perfect Flag! The reds so brilliant! He couldn't take his eyes off it. "Get down here! We need a picture!" Herman yelled up to him.
60 "How does it look?" people yelled up to him. "Unbelievable! I can't describe it!" he said.

So then everyone had to have a look. "No!" Herman said, but they took a vote and it was unanimous. One by one, members of the Living Flag went up to the roof and admired it. It *was* marvelous! It brought tears to the eyes, it made one reflect on this great country and on Lake Wobegon's place in it. One wanted to stand up there all afternoon and just drink it in. So, as the first hour passed, and only forty of the five hundred had been to the top, the others got more and more restless. "Hurry up! Quit dawdling! *You've* seen it! Get down here and give someone else a chance!" Herman sent people up in groups of four, and then ten, but after two hours, the Living Flag
70 became the Sitting Flag and then began to erode, as the members who had had a look thought about heading home to supper, which infuriated the ones who hadn't. "Ten more minutes!" Herman cried, but ten minutes became twenty and thirty, and people snuck off and the Flag that remained for the last viewer was a Flag shot through by cannon fire.

In 1950, the Sons of Knute took over Flag Day. Herman gave them the boxes of caps. Since then, the Knutes have achieved several good Flags, though most years the attendance was poor. You need at least four hundred to make a good one. Some years the Knutes made a "no-look" rule, other years they held a lottery. One year they experimented with a large mirror held by two men over the edge of the roof, but
80 when people leaned back and looked up, the Flag disappeared, of course. ❧

Literary Analysis

1. **Analyze Local Color** One of the primary characteristics of regional writing is **local color,** or writing that portrays the customs, character types, mannerisms, and speech of a region. What elements of local color do you find in this excerpt? Citing evidence from the text, characterize the residents of small-town Minnesota as portrayed by Keillor.

2. **Compare Texts** As Twain does in the excerpt from his *Autobiography* and in "The Notorious Jumping Frog of Calaveras County," Keillor depicts a community event in a small town. Which author takes a more mocking **tone,** and which is gentler? In either case, do you think that one of the authors is writing with a greater degree of affection for the people portrayed? Explain, citing evidence from the texts.

ANSWERS

Possible answers:

1. *The main element of local color is Keillor's depiction of residents who enjoy celebrating holidays, such as Flag Day and the Fourth of July, and taking part in such local activities as "Toast 'n Jelly Days" and the county fair. Keillor shows that they share activities as a close-knit community: everyone stepping outside for two minutes of silence on Armistice Day, for example, and people working together to create a Living Flag on Flag Day.*

2. *Students may decide that Twain has the more mocking tone and Keillor the gentler one. Twain's tale is about deception, and he tells it with wry wit; Keillor's tale is about sincere patriotic feelings, and he tells it with affection. Accept all answers, however, that are reasonable and that are supported with evidence from both narratives.*

FOR ADVANCED LEARNERS/AP

Analyze Style Have students write and share an essay in which they analyze Keillor's writing style. Ask students to discuss these stylistic elements, plus others that they discern:

- simple sentences (lines 57–61)
- parallelism (lines 64–65)
- exaggeration (lines 1–2)
- imaginative imagery (lines 18–19, 73–74)
- the integration of spoken words into the narrative (lines 40–47, 62–74)

Ask students to explain how the elements work, both individually and in combination, to create the overall "feel" of the piece.

Focus and Motivate

OBJECTIVES

Literary Analysis
- explore the key idea of **places**
- analyze setting
- read a short story

Reading
- draw conclusions about characters

Vocabulary
- build vocabulary for reading and writing
- understand specialized vocabulary
- research word origins as a way to understand spelling

R3.5

ABOUT THE AUTHOR

After students have read about Willa Cather, ask them to summarize key points of her biography. Point out that students will see Cather's application of her early experiences on the Nebraska prairie in the characters and settings of "A Wagner Matinee."

USING THE **NOTABLE QUOTE**

Ask students how the quotation expresses the path that **Willa Cather** chose for her life. *Possible answer: The fact that writing interested Cather "more than any other activity I've ever found" is evidenced by her moving to New York City to write full-time. The concluding comment about writing books and living the kind of life that makes such a career possible underscores Cather's devotion to her path.*

Selection Resources

R3.5 (p. 703)

A Wagner Matinee
Short Story by Willa Cather

NOTABLE QUOTE
"The only reason I write is because it interests me more than any other activity I've ever found."

FYI
Did you know that Willa Cather . . .

- had such a sharp memory for mannerisms and turns of speech that she never took notes?
- wrote six novels about her home town of Red Cloud, Nebraska, while living in New York's Greenwich Village?
- received the Pulitzer Prize in 1923?

Author On|ine
For more on Willa Cather, visit the **Literature Center** at ClassZone.com.

Willa Cather
1873–1947

Willa Cather believed that "the most basic material a writer works with is acquired before the age of 15." Indeed, it was the American West of Cather's early years that inspired the majority of her literary successes.

The Power of Place At age nine, Virginia-born Willa Cather moved to Nebraska with her family. The prairie challenged Cather—and almost all other settlers—with its "erasure of personality" and made her feel that she "would go under." But after a difficult transition, Cather grew to love the harsh prairie and to admire the immigrants—especially women—who struggled daily against an unforgiving climate. Though they lived by hard physical labor, many of these immigrants were educated people. They introduced Cather to French and German literature, also teaching her Latin and Greek. Nebraska and Cather's childhood neighbors —whose stories "went round and round in [her] head"— dramatically influenced her writing.

Seeing the World After college, where she did some writing, Cather went back east and worked as a journalist, teacher, and magazine editor. During this time, she met her best friend, Isabelle McClung, who sparked in her a lifelong interest in music, which can be seen in "A Wagner Matinee." She also formed lifelong relationships with her companion Edith Lewis and writer Sarah Orne Jewett. Cather also saw something of the world on several trips to France and then to the American Southwest.

Developing a Voice Around 1906, Cather moved to New York City and began a full-time writing career. Though she never lived in Nebraska again, the prairie was never far from her work. Many of her 12 novels and 58 stories had prairie settings or immigrant characters, showing Cather's respect for the grit needed to endure everyday life. Some of these characters were directly drawn from real people Cather had known, such as childhood friend Annie (Anna) who formed the basis of the main character in her novel *My Ántonia*.

Choices Willa Cather chose an artist's life rather than the everyday family life she so closely observed in her Nebraska neighbors. She once said to a friend that "nothing mattered to her but writing books, and living the kind of life that makes it possible to write them." Willa Cather lived that life until her death in 1947.

692

---

* Resources for Differentiation   † Also in Spanish   ‡ In Haitian Creole and Vietnamese

LITERARY ANALYSIS: SETTING

In Willa Cather's fiction, the development of the plot and characters is heavily influenced by the **setting,** or the time and place in which the story occurs. In "A Wagner Matinee," the narrator's aunt has moved from Boston to the Nebraska frontier; these places determine the kind of person she becomes. Setting can also serve as a **symbol.** As you read, note the details of each location and what they seem to represent.

READING SKILL: DRAW CONCLUSIONS ABOUT CHARACTER

Understanding a character in a story is like getting to know a real person. You **draw conclusions,** or make reasonable judgments, about the person by combining the impressions you have already formed with new facts you discover. To become better acquainted with Aunt Georgiana, the main character in "A Wagner Matinee," look closely at the details as you read the story. Create a chart like the one shown, using it to record details and **make inferences** about Aunt Georgiana. At the end of the story, you will use these specific inferences to draw larger conclusions about her character.

Observations About ...	What They Reveal
physical appearance: • •	
major decision: • •	
actions and reactions: • •	

▲ VOCABULARY IN CONTEXT

Cather uses the listed words to develop setting and character. Choose a word from the list to complete each phrase.

WORD LIST		
callow	overture	tentatively
excruciatingly	somnambulant	veritable
myriad	sordid	

1. _____ employees with more bravado than experience
2. _____ tasks to complete—almost too many to count
3. living in _____, disgusting conditions
4. agreed _____ to take on the additional work

Does it matter where we LIVE?

KEY IDEA Imagine life on an island with only a few dozen other people. How would it shape your social life? your work habits? your relationship to nature? Now think about life in a big city. How would these things be different? The **places** we live really shape our personality and values.

DISCUSS As a class, choose two very different places and discuss the lifestyles of the people who live there. Then consider how life in each place would shape the personalities of its inhabitants.

Does it matter where we LIVE?

Ask the question; then have students read the **KEY IDEA** and discuss the questions. As students address the **DISCUSS** activity, urge them to draw upon memories of **places** where they have actually lived rather than possibilities that they imagine or that they have seen portrayed on TV and in films.

SKILLS FOCUS

LITERARY ANALYSIS

● SETTING

Write this passage on the board:

> Jason wiped the sweat from his sun-burned brow, surveyed the half-plowed field, and groaned. As a boy, he'd planned to be living in a big city by June 14, 1891, his 18th birthday. But here he was, 22 years old and still breaking his back in tiny, dusty Greenville. He'd give anything to be gone, but he couldn't do that to his folks. Without his help, they'd never survive.

Ask students what they learn about setting from this passage. ***Possible answer: According to the passage, the setting is a family farm in "tiny, dusty Greenville" in 1895 or 1896.***

CHECK UNDERSTANDING Ask students to find and share a passage in another work that they feel effectively conveys the setting.

READING SKILL

▪ DRAW CONCLUSIONS ABOUT CHARACTER

Have students reread the passage on the board and draw a conclusion about Jason. ***Possible answers: Jason feels trapped and frustrated; he is loyal to his parents.***

> **R** RESOURCE MANAGER—Copy Master
> Draw Conclusions About Character
> p. 123 (for student use while reading the selection)

VOCABULARY

▲ VOCABULARY IN CONTEXT

DIAGNOSE WORD KNOWLEDGE To determine preteaching needs, have all students complete Vocabulary in Context. *Answers:* **1.** *callow,* **2.** *myriad,* **3.** *sordid,* **4.** *tentatively*

PRETEACH VOCABULARY Preteach vocabulary with this copy master. Read each item aloud.

> **R** RESOURCE MANAGER—Copy Master
> Vocabulary Study p. 125

MORE VOCABULARY SUPPORT
For additional activities and guidelines, see

> 🧰 BEST PRACTICES TOOLKIT
> Scaffolding Vocabulary Instruction
> pp. 43–46
> ℹ Vocabulary Center at **ClassZone.com**

SUMMARY

A visit from Aunt Georgiana causes Clark, the narrator of this story, to recall her caring for him when he was a boy on the Nebraska prairie. Aunt Georgiana had been a music teacher in Boston before eloping to Nebraska, where she and her husband have been homesteading for thirty years under harsh conditions. Clark, now living in Boston, takes his aunt to a concert. Though she has seemed distracted and aloof, she is profoundly affected by Wagner's music: When the concert ends, she cries out that she does not want to leave.

LITERARY ANALYSIS

Ⓐ SETTING

Possible answer: *The description shows that the letter probably comes from a place where such conveniences as post offices are not easily accessible. The narrator's observations show that he lives in a place where people are unaccustomed to seeing letters in such condition.*

If students need help . . .

- Call attention to the descriptive details in lines 3–4. Elicit that the letter comes from a place where transporting mail seems not to be a high priority.

- Ask students what they can infer from the narrator's reaction to the letter. Is he surprised by its condition, or is he used to seeing letters in such a state?

A Wagner Matinee

Willa Cather

BACKGROUND "A Wagner Matinee" takes place in Nebraska and Boston around 1900. At the time, Bostonians could attend concerts of works by European composers such as Richard Wagner (väg'nər). Americans who moved west, such as Willa Cather's family and Aunt Georgiana in this story, left such worldly pleasures behind. Instead, the settlers endured long hours of strenuous labor, and natural disasters such as drought, flood, and prairie fires.

ANALYZE VISUALS
Look at the painting on page 695. What might souvenirs like this signify to a settler who left the city for life on the prairie? Explain.

I received one morning a letter, written in pale ink on glassy, blue-lined note-paper, and bearing the postmark of a little Nebraska village. This communication, worn and rubbed, looking as though it had been carried for some days in a coat pocket that was none too clean, was from my Uncle Howard and informed me that his wife had been left a small legacy by a bachelor relative who had recently died, and that it would be necessary for her to go to Boston to attend to the settling of the estate. He requested me to meet her at the station and render her whatever services might be necessary. On examining the date indicated as that of her arrival, I found it no later than tomorrow. He had characteristically delayed
10 writing until, had I been away from home for a day, I must have missed the good woman altogether. Ⓐ

The name of my Aunt Georgiana called up not alone her own figure, at once pathetic and grotesque, but opened before my feet a gulf of recollection so wide and deep, that, as the letter dropped from my hand, I felt suddenly a stranger to all the present conditions of my existence, wholly ill at ease and out of place amid the familiar surroundings of my study. I became, in short, the gangling farmer-boy

❶ Targeted Passage

Ⓐ SETTING
What does the **description** of the letter tell you about the place from which it was sent? What does it suggest about the place it is sent to? Give details to support your answer.

694   UNIT 4: REGIONALISM AND NATURALISM

Old Souvenirs (about 1881–1901), John F. Peto. Bequest of Oliver Burr Jennings, 1968 (68.205.3). Metropolitan Museum of Art, New York.

DIFFERENTIATED INSTRUCTION

FOR ALL STUDENTS

Provide these independent projects to extend the lesson:

- Discuss and plan a scenario for a sequel to the story.

- Listen to Richard Wagner's music and share examples with the class.

For further details on these projects, see

R RESOURCE MANAGER
Ideas for Extension pp. 116–117

FOR STRATEGIC READERS

In combination with the *Audio Anthology CD*, use one or more Targeted Passages (pp. 694, 697, 699, 702) to ensure that students focus on key story events and concepts. Targeted Passages are also good for English learners.

❶ Targeted Passage [Lines 1–11]

This passage establishes the first-person narrator and the reason for his aunt's journey to Boston.

- From whom does the narrator receive a letter? Where does the letter come from?

- Why is the narrator's aunt coming to Boston?

- What does the letter ask?

- How does the narrator feel about the person who wrote the letter? How can you tell?

FOR ENGLISH LEARNERS

Key Academic Vocabulary Use Word Questioning to teach these words: *section* (line 45), *flexible* (line 62), *text-book* (line 70), *passive* (line 111), *theme* (line 151), *relax* (line 231).

 BEST PRACTICES TOOLKIT—Transparency Word Questioning p. E9

Prereading For prereading instruction for English learners, see

 BEST PRACTICES TOOLKIT Scaffolding Reading Instruction pp. 43–46

FOR ADVANCED LEARNERS/AP

AP exercises in the bottom channel provide additional challenge for students. Use these suggestions for small groups or individuals.

ADDITIONAL GUIDELINES

For more help with differentiation and tips for classroom management, see

 BEST PRACTICES TOOLKIT Differentiated Instruction pp. 31–38

TIERED DISCUSSION PROMPTS

Use these prompts to help students grasp the narrator's reaction to the letter:

Connect Have someone's words ever made you recall experiences from your childhood? Explain. *Accept all thoughtful responses.*

Analyze What effect does the letter's reference to Aunt Georgiana have upon the narrator? *Possible answer: The letter causes the narrator to recall in vivid detail his boyhood life on a Nebraska farm. The recollection is so strong that it disorients him (lines 14–16).*

Evaluate How effective is Cather's use of detail in describing the narrator's memories? Explain. *Possible answer: The use of detail is quite effective, for the description is vivid and appeals to the senses.*

Lines 30–33
REINFORCE *KEY IDEA:* PLACES

Discuss How does the narrator's comparison in these lines show that he is aware of the effect that **places** have upon people? *Possible answer: The comparison of haggard Aunt Georgiana to explorers who have faced the rigors of the Arctic and Africa shows that the narrator understands that a place can take a physical toll upon a person.*

my aunt had known, scourged with chilblains[1] and bashfulness, my hands cracked and sore from the corn husking. I felt the knuckles of my thumb **tentatively,** as though they were raw again. I sat again before her parlor organ, fumbling the
20 scales with my stiff, red hands, while she, beside me, made canvas mittens for the huskers.[2]

The next morning, after preparing my landlady somewhat, I set out for the station. When the train arrived I had some difficulty in finding my aunt. She was the last of the passengers to alight, and it was not until I got her into the carriage that she seemed really to recognize me. She had come all the way in a day coach; her linen duster[3] had become black with soot and her black bonnet grey with dust during the journey. When we arrived at my boarding-house the landlady put her to bed at once and I did not see her again until the next morning.

Whatever shock Mrs. Springer experienced at my aunt's appearance, she
30 considerably concealed. As for myself, I saw my aunt's misshapen figure with that feeling of awe and respect with which we behold explorers who have left their ears and fingers north of Franz-Josef-Land, or their health somewhere along the Upper Congo.[4] My Aunt Georgiana had been a music teacher at the Boston Conservatory, somewhere back in the latter sixties. One summer, while visiting in the little village among the Green Mountains[5] where her ancestors had dwelt

tentatively
(tĕn′tə-tĭv-lē) *adv.* in a hesitant or uncertain manner

---

1. **scourged with chilblains:** tormented with painful swelling or sores on the hands or feet caused by exposure to the cold.
2. **huskers:** farm workers who remove cornhusks by hand.
3. **duster:** a long, lightweight overgarment to protect clothing from dust
4. **Franz-Josef-Land . . . Upper Congo:** Franz-Josef-Land is a group of small, mostly ice-covered islands in the Arctic Ocean, north of Russia. The Upper Congo, in central Africa, is now called the Zaire River.
5. **Green Mountains:** a mountain range in Vermont.

Family and Their Dugout (1870s), Anonymous. Photo 11″ × 14″. Near McCook, Nebraska. © Nebraska State Historical Society, Lincoln, Nebraska.

DIFFERENTIATED INSTRUCTION

FOR ENGLISH LEARNERS
Related Vocabulary Discuss these sets of descriptive phrases, clarifying individual words as needed:

Aunt Georgiana's physical appearance:

- *linen duster . . . black with soot; black bonnet grey with dust* (line 26)
- *misshapen figure* (line 30)
- *soiled linen duster* (line 53)
- *sunken chest* (lines 58–59)
- *no stays* (line 59)
- *ill-fitting false teeth* (line 60)
- *skin . . . as yellow as a Mongolian's* (lines 60–61)

School studies:

- *Latin declensions and conjugations* (line 68)
- *irregular verbs* (line 69)
- *my first Shakespeare . . . mythology* (line 70)
- *scales and exercises* (lines 71–72)

for generations, she had kindled the **callow** fancy of the most idle and shiftless of all the village lads, and had conceived for this Howard Carpenter one of those extravagant passions which a handsome country boy of twenty-one sometimes inspires in an angular, spectacled woman of thirty. When she returned to her

40 duties in Boston, Howard followed her, and the upshot of this inexplicable infatuation was that she eloped with him, eluding the reproaches of her family and the criticisms of her friends by going with him to the Nebraska frontier. Carpenter, who, of course, had no money, had taken a homestead in Red Willow County,[6] fifty miles from the railroad. There they had measured off their quarter section themselves by driving across the prairie in a wagon, to the wheel of which they had tied a red cotton handkerchief, and counting off its revolutions. They built a dugout in the red hillside, one of those cave dwellings whose inmates so often reverted to primitive conditions. Their water they got from the lagoons where the buffalo drank, and their slender stock of provisions was always at the

50 mercy of bands of roving Indians. For thirty years my aunt had not been further than fifty miles from the homestead. **B**

But Mrs. Springer knew nothing of all this, and must have been considerably shocked at what was left of my kinswoman. Beneath the soiled linen duster which, on her arrival, was the most conspicuous feature of her costume, she wore a black stuff[7] dress, whose ornamentation showed that she had surrendered herself unquestioningly into the hands of a country dressmaker. My poor aunt's figure, however, would have presented astonishing difficulties to any dressmaker. Originally stooped, her shoulders were now almost bent together over her sunken chest. She wore no stays, and her gown, which trailed unevenly behind, rose in a sort

60 of peak over her abdomen. She wore ill-fitting false teeth, and her skin was as yellow as a Mongolian's from constant exposure to a pitiless wind and to the alkaline water which hardens the most transparent cuticle into a sort of flexible leather. **C**

I owed to this woman most of the good that ever came my way in my boyhood, and had a reverential affection for her. During the years when I was riding herd for my uncle, my aunt, after cooking the three meals—the first of which was ready at six o'clock in the morning—and putting the six children to bed, would often stand until midnight at her ironing-board, with me at the kitchen table beside her, hearing me recite Latin declensions and conjugations,[8] gently shaking me when my drowsy head sank down over a page of irregular verbs. It was to her, at her ironing

70 or mending, that I read my first Shakespeare, and her old text-book on mythology was the first that ever came into my empty hands. She taught me my scales and exercises, too—on the little parlor organ, which her husband had bought her after fifteen years, during which she had not so much as seen any instrument, but an accordion that belonged to one of the Norwegian farmhands. She would sit beside me by the hour, darning and counting while I struggled with the "Joyous Farmer,"[9] but she seldom talked to me about music, and I understood why. She was a pious

---

6. **Red Willow County:** county in southwestern Nebraska, bordering on Kansas.

7. **stuff:** a woolen material.

8. **Latin declensions and conjugations:** forms of Latin nouns and verbs representing different cases and tenses.

9. **"Joyous Farmer":** one of a series of musical pieces for children by German composer Robert Schumann.

callow (kăl′ō) *adj.* lacking adult experience; immature

② Targeted Passage

D DRAW CONCLUSIONS

Possible answer: Aunt Georgiana's treatment of her nephew suggests that she is a kind, loving person and a tireless worker. She regrets some of the sacrifices that she has made, but she takes comfort in religion.

If students need help . . .

- Discuss Clark's feelings for his aunt (lines 63–64).

- Note the effort that Aunt Georgiana puts into caring for her home and family (lines 64–76).

- Discuss the sacrifices that Aunt Georgiana has made and the strength that she finds in "the consolations of religion" (lines 76–82).

Lines 94–105
TIERED DISCUSSION PROMPTS

Use these prompts to help students explore Aunt Georgiana's state of mind:

Connect How do you feel about Aunt Georgiana so far? Why? *Accept all thoughtful responses.*

Interpret How has Aunt Georgiana's attitude toward city life changed over the past 30 years? Explain. *Possible answer: When she used to live and work in Boston, Aunt Georgiana was at ease in and seemed to enjoy life in the city. Now, however, she seems timid, out of place, distracted, and disoriented. She appears to be preoccupied with farm chores rather than focused on the city around her (lines 100–105).*

Synthesize Will Aunt Georgiana enjoy attending the concert? Why or why not? *Accept all thoughtful responses.*

---

woman; she had the consolations of religion and, to her at least, her martyrdom was not wholly **sordid.** Once when I had been doggedly beating out some easy passages from an old score of *Euryanthe*[10] I had found among her music books, she came up
80 to me and, putting her hands over my eyes, gently drew my head back upon her shoulder, saying tremulously, "Don't love it so well, Clark, or it may be taken from you. Oh! dear boy, pray that whatever your sacrifice may be, it be not that." **D**

When my aunt appeared on the morning after her arrival, she was still in a semi-**somnambulant** state. She seemed not to realize that she was in the city where she had spent her youth, the place longed for hungrily half a lifetime. She had been so wretchedly train-sick throughout the journey that she had no recollection of anything but her discomfort, and, to all intents and purposes, there were but a few hours of nightmare between the farm in Red Willow County and my study on Newbury Street. I had planned a little pleasure for her that
90 afternoon, to repay her for some of the glorious moments she had given me when we used to milk together in the straw-thatched cowshed and she, because I was more than usually tired, or because her husband had spoken sharply to me, would tell me of the splendid performance of the *Huguenots*[11] she had seen in Paris, in her youth. At two o'clock the Symphony Orchestra was to give a Wagner program, and I intended to take my aunt; though, as I conversed with her, I grew doubtful about her enjoyment of it. Indeed, for her own sake, I could only wish her taste for such things quite dead, and the long struggle mercifully ended at last. I suggested our visiting the Conservatory and the Common[12] before lunch, but she seemed altogether too timid to wish to venture out. She questioned me
100 absently about various changes in the city, but she was chiefly concerned that she had forgotten to leave instructions about feeding half-skimmed milk to a certain weakling calf, "old Maggie's calf, you know, Clark," she explained, evidently having forgotten how long I had been away. She was further troubled because she had neglected to tell her daughter about the freshly-opened kit of mackerel in the cellar, which would spoil if it were not used directly.

I asked her whether she had ever heard any of the Wagnerian operas,[13] and found that she had not, though she was perfectly familiar with their respective situations, and had once possessed the piano score of *The Flying Dutchman*. I began to think it would have been best to get her back to Red Willow County
110 without waking her, and regretted having suggested the concert.

From the time we entered the concert hall, however, she was a trifle less passive and inert, and for the first time seemed to perceive her surroundings. I had felt some trepidation lest she might become aware of the absurdities of her attire, or might experience some painful embarrassment at stepping suddenly into the world to which she had been dead for a quarter of a century. But, again, I found how superficially I

---

sordid (sôr'dĭd) *adj.* wretched; dirty; morally degraded

D DRAW CONCLUSIONS
Reread lines 63–82. What does Aunt Georgiana's treatment of her nephew reveal about her?

somnambulant (sŏm-năm'byə-lənt) *adj.* sleepwalking

---

10. *Euryanthe* (yŏŏr'ē-än'thē): an opera by German composer Carl Maria von Weber.

11. *Huguenots* (hyōō'gə-nŏts'): an opera by German composer Giacomo Meyerbeer.

12. **the Common:** Boston Common, a public park.

13. **Wagnerian operas:** The orchestra will play selections from several operas composed by Wagner, including *The Flying Dutchman, Tannhäuser, Tristan and Isolde*, and a cycle of four operas called *The Ring of the Nibelung*.

DIFFERENTIATED INSTRUCTION

FOR ADVANCED LEARNERS/AP
Analyze Tone and Characterization [small-group option] Encourage students to reflect upon Willa Cather's tone and characterization. What can students infer about her feelings toward Aunt Georgiana?

- Does Cather respect her? admire her? feel sorry for her?

- Does Cather imply an opinion as to whether Aunt Georgiana has made wise decisions in life or poor ones? How does Cather seem to feel about Clark?

- How does the story's narrator, or person who has had a relationship with Georgiana, affect tone and characterization in the story?

Ask students to write two paragraphs summarizing and supporting their conclusions. Then have students meet in small groups to compare their observations.

had judged her. She sat looking about her with eyes as impersonal, almost as stony, as those with which the granite Rameses[14] in a museum watches the froth and fret that ebbs and flows[15] about his pedestal—separated from it by the lonely stretch of centuries. I have seen this same aloofness in old miners who drift into the Brown
120 hotel at Denver, their pockets full of bullion,[16] their linen soiled, their haggard faces unshaven; standing in the thronged corridors as solitary as though they were still in a frozen camp on the Yukon, conscious that certain experiences have isolated them from their fellows by a gulf no haberdasher[17] could bridge.

We sat at the extreme left of the first balcony, facing the arc of our own and the balcony above us, **veritable** hanging gardens, brilliant as tulip beds. The matinée audience was made up chiefly of women. One lost the contour of faces and figures, indeed any effect of line whatever, and there was only the color of bodices past counting, the shimmer of fabrics soft and firm, silky and sheer; red, mauve, pink, blue, lilac, purple, ecru, rose, yellow, cream, and white, all the colors that an
130 impressionist[18] finds in a sunlit landscape, with here and there the dead shadow of a frock coat. My Aunt Georgiana regarded them as though they had been so many daubs of tube-paint on a palette.

When the musicians came out and took their places, she gave a little stir of anticipation and looked with quickening interest down over the rail at that invariable grouping, perhaps the first wholly familiar thing that had greeted her eye since she had left old Maggie and her weakling calf. I could feel how all those details sank into her soul, for I had not forgotten how they had sunk into mine when I came fresh from ploughing forever and forever between green aisles of corn, where, as in a treadmill, one might walk from daybreak to dusk without
140 perceiving a shadow of change. The clean profiles of the musicians, the gloss of their linen, the dull black of their coats, the beloved shapes of the instruments, the patches of yellow light thrown by the green shaded lamps on the smooth, varnished bellies of the 'cellos and the bass viols in the rear, the restless, wind-tossed forest of fiddle necks and bows—I recalled how, in the first orchestra I had ever heard, those long bow strokes seemed to draw the heart out of me, as a conjurer's stick reels out yards of paper ribbon from a hat. **E**

The first number was the *Tannhauser* **overture.** When the horns drew out the first strain of the Pilgrim's chorus, my Aunt Georgiana clutched my coat sleeve. Then it was I first realized that for her this broke a silence of thirty years; the
150 inconceivable silence of the plains. With the battle between the two motives, with the frenzy of the Venusberg theme and its ripping of strings, there came to me an overwhelming sense of the waste and wear we are so powerless to combat;

3 Targeted Passage

veritable (vĕr'ĭ-tə-bəl) *adj.* true; not unreal or imaginary

E SETTING
Reread lines 133–146. How does Aunt Georgiana respond to the setting of the Boston concert hall?

overture (ō'vər-chōōr') *n.* the orchestral introduction to a musical dramatic work

---

14. **Rameses** (răm'ĭ-sēz'): one of the ancient kings of Egypt of that name.
15. **froth . . . flows:** happiness and sadness that come and go.
16. **bullion:** gold.
17. **haberdasher:** a dealer in men's clothing and accessories.
18. **impressionist:** a follower of a movement in French painting that emphasized the play of light and color.

Lines 111–123
REINFORCE *KEY IDEA:* PLACES

Discuss Cather compares Aunt Georgiana's initial reaction to the concert hall to the "aloofness in old miners" who visit a Denver hotel. How are Aunt Georgiana and the miners alike? *Possible answer: They are alike in that both have been strongly affected by the places in which they have lived—harsh places, away from the mainstream of society—and the length of time that they have lived there. The miners, who have lived "in a frozen camp on the Yukon," now feel isolated from the people around them in the hotel. Aunt Georgiana, who has lived on the Nebraska frontier for thirty years, acts as though she feels similarly isolated in Boston.*

LITERARY ANALYSIS

E SETTING

Possible answer: At first, Aunt Georgiana seems rather detached and passive. When the musicians enter, however, she becomes increasingly interested.

Extend the Discussion What does Clark mean when he says that he "could feel how all those details sank into her soul, for I had not forgotten how they had sunk into mine . . ." (lines 136–137)? What inferences can you make about the ways in which Clark's life has changed since he left Nebraska?

FOR STRATEGIC READERS

3 Targeted Passage [Lines 116–132]

This passage contrasts the concert hall setting with Aunt Georgiana's attitude.

- Describe the appearance of the audience.
- How does Aunt Georgiana react to her surroundings in the concert hall?
- What does the narrator mean when he says that his aunt regarded the audience members "as though they had been so many daubs of tube-paint on a palette"?

FOR ENGLISH LEARNERS

Comprehension: Text Structure Help students identify the particular qualities that Cather is calling attention to by establishing these comparisons:

- Aunt Georgiana compared first to "the granite Rameses" (lines 116–119) and then to "old miners" (lines 119–123)
- the concert hall and audience compared first to flowers (lines 124–125) and then to impressionistic painting (lines 126–132)

TIERED DISCUSSION PROMPTS

Use these prompts to help students understand the barrenness of prairie life:

Summarize What impression does Clark give of the prairie? *Possible answer: Clark gives the impression that the prairie is a primitive, grim place that seems to go on forever.*

Analyze How does Clark's description underscore the contrast between Aunt Georgiana's life and the Boston concert hall? *Possible answer: Clark's description mentions "the inconceivable silence of the plains" and presents as a symbol of the bleak, empty, lonely feeling of prairie life a "tall, naked house . . . black and grim as a wooden fortress. . . . " This description contrasts sharply with the description of the music of the concert hall and the colorful details of lines 124–131.*

Evaluate How well does Cather's description capture the atmosphere of the narrator's early life on the prairie? Explain. *Accept all answers that students can support.*

READING SKILL

F DRAW CONCLUSIONS

Possible answer: The reader can infer that Aunt Georgiana has retained her love of music and that she acutely feels the low priority that it has had in her life as a Nebraska homesteader.

Extend the Discussion Is the narrator's comparison of the soul to "that strange moss which . . . grows green again" an effective analogy? Why or why not?

---

and I saw again the tall, naked house on the prairie, black and grim as a wooden fortress; the black pond where I had learned to swim, its margin pitted with sundried cattle tracks; the rain-gullied clay banks about the naked house, the four dwarf ash seedlings where the dish-cloths were always hung to dry before the kitchen door. The world there was the flat world of the ancients; to the east, a cornfield that stretched to daybreak; to the west, a corral that reached to sunset; between, the conquests of peace, dearer bought than those of war.

160   The overture closed, my aunt released my coat sleeve, but she said nothing. She sat staring at the orchestra through a dullness of thirty years, through the films made little by little by each of the three hundred and sixty-five days in every one of them. What, I wondered, did she get from it? She had been a good pianist in her day I knew, and her musical education had been broader than that of most music teachers of a quarter of a century ago. She had often told me of Mozart's operas and Meyerbeer's, and I could remember hearing her sing, years ago, certain melodies of Verdi's. When I had fallen ill with a fever in her house she used to sit by my cot in the evening—when the cool, night wind blew in through the faded mosquito netting tacked over the window and I lay watching a certain bright

170   star that burned red above the cornfield—and sing "Home to our mountains, O, let us return!" in a way fit to break the heart of a Vermont boy near dead of homesickness already.

I watched her closely through the prelude to *Tristan and Isolde,* trying vainly to conjecture what that seething turmoil of strings and winds might mean to her, but she sat mutely staring at the violin bows that drove obliquely downward, like the pelting streaks of rain in a summer shower. Had this music any message for her? Had she enough left to at all comprehend this power which had kindled the world since she had left it? I was in a fever of curiosity, but Aunt Georgiana sat silent upon her peak in Darien.[19] She preserved this utter immobility throughout

180   the number from *The Flying Dutchman,* though her fingers worked mechanically upon her black dress, as though, of themselves, they were recalling the piano score they had once played. Poor old hands! They had been stretched and twisted into mere tentacles to hold and lift and knead with; the palms unduly swollen, the fingers bent and knotted—on one of them a thin, worn band that had once been a wedding ring. As I pressed and gently quieted one of those groping hands, I remembered with quivering eyelids their services for me in other days.

Soon after the tenor began the "Prize Song," I heard a quick drawn breath and turned to my aunt. Her eyes were closed, but the tears were glistening on her cheeks, and I think, in a moment more, they were in my eyes as well. It never

190   really died, then—the soul that can suffer so **excruciatingly** and so interminably; it withers to the outward eye only; like that strange moss which can lie on a dusty shelf half a century and yet, if placed in water, grows green again. She wept so throughout the development and elaboration of the melody. **F**

---

19. **peak in Darien:** a mountain in what is now Panama, referred to in English poet John Keats's "On First Looking into Chapman's Homer" as a place where the Pacific was contemplated with silence and awe by Spanish explorers.

excruciatingly
(ĭk-skrōō′shē-ā′tĭng-lē) *adv.* in a way that causes great pain or distress

F DRAW CONCLUSIONS
Reread lines 187–193. What **inferences** can you make about Aunt Georgiana's feeling for music, based upon her reaction to it?

DIFFERENTIATED INSTRUCTION

FOR ENGLISH LEARNERS

Vocabulary: Multiple-Meaning Words [mixed-readiness groups] Explain that *bows* (line 175) refers here to the rod that a violinist draws across the strings of the instrument. However, *bow* also has several other meanings, such as "a weapon used to shoot arrows." Discuss how students can use context clues to figure out the appropriate meaning of multiple-meaning words. Then have mixed-readiness Jigsaw groups investigate these other multiple-meaning words (all of which have at least one meaning that relates to music) and share their findings: *strings, winds* (line 174); *number* (line 180); *band* (line 184); *drawn* (line 187); *concert* (line 194).

BEST PRACTICES TOOLKIT
Jigsaw Reading p. A1

FOR ADVANCED LEARNERS/AP

Analyze Choice of Narrator Cather chose to tell this story in the first-person words of Clark, a male narrator. Ask students why she might have used this approach. Discuss how the story might have differed in tone and content if Cather had chosen to narrate it in the third person, perhaps by a female narrator—perhaps even by Aunt Georgiana herself. Urge students to support their opinions with evidence from the story.

During the intermission before the second half of the concert, I questioned my aunt and found that the "Prize Song" was not new to her. Some years before there had drifted to the farm in Red Willow County a young German, a tramp cow puncher, who had sung the chorus at Bayreuth,[20] when he was a boy, along with the other peasant boys and girls. Of a Sunday morning he used to sit on his gingham-sheeted bed in the hands' bedroom which opened off the kitchen, cleaning the leather of his boots and saddle, singing the "Prize Song," while my aunt went about her work in the kitchen. She had hovered about him until she had prevailed upon him to join the country church, though his sole fitness for this step, in so far as I could gather, lay in his boyish face and his possession of this divine melody. Shortly afterward he had gone to town on the Fourth of July, been drunk for several days, lost his money at a faro table, ridden a saddled Texas steer on a bet, and disappeared with a fractured collar-bone. All this my aunt told me huskily, wanderingly, as though she were talking in the weak lapses of illness. **G**

200

G DRAW CONCLUSIONS
Reread lines 194–207. Explain Aunt Georgiana's poignant association with the "Prize Song." Why do you think it causes her to weep?

---

20. **Bayreuth** (bī-roit′): a town in the Bavarian region of Germany where annual Wagner music festivals are held.

Two on the Aisle (1927), Edward Hopper © Francis G. Mayer/Corbis. © Heirs of Josephine N. Hopper, licensed by the Whitney Museum of American Art.

ⓗ SETTING

Possible answer: The metaphor suggests that years of strenuous daily labor on the prairie, with the only musical outlet being the singing of hymns, might wear down a person's ability to comprehend or appreciate a wider "world" of music.

Lines 223–229
REINFORCE *KEY IDEA*: PLACES

Discuss How do the **places** that Aunt Georgiana visits—in her imagination—as the music plays compare to the place from which she has come? **Possible answer:** *The imagined places may be happy, even though they are compared to graveyards; at least, they are places of hope and rest—a contrast to the hopelessly bleak life of backbreaking work that Aunt Georgiana has known on the Nebraska prairie.*

SELECTION WRAP–UP

REFLECT Review the *KEY IDEA* question: "Does it matter where we live?" Ask students how Cather's story answers the question.

⭐ CRITIQUE

- Point out that Cather's story contains almost no dialogue. Ask students whether they think that the lack of dialogue detracts from the story. Why or why not?
- After completing the After Reading questions on page 703, have students revisit their responses and tell whether they have changed their opinions.

"Well, we have come to better things than the old *Trovatore*²¹ at any rate, Aunt Georgie?" I queried, with a well meant effort at jocularity.

210   Her lip quivered and she hastily put her handkerchief up to her mouth. From behind it she murmured, "And you have been hearing this ever since you left me, Clark?" Her question was the gentlest and saddest of reproaches.

The second half of the program consisted of four numbers from the *Ring*, and closed with Siegfried's funeral march. My aunt wept quietly, but almost continuously, as a shallow vessel overflows in a rainstorm. From time to time her dim eyes looked up at the lights which studded the ceiling, burning softly under their dull glass globes; doubtless they were stars in truth to her. I was still perplexed as to what measure of musical comprehension was left to her, she who had heard nothing but the singing of Gospel Hymns at Methodist services in the
220   square frame school-house on Section Thirteen for so many years. I was wholly unable to gauge how much of it had been dissolved in soapsuds, or worked into bread, or milked into the bottom of a pail. ⓗ

The deluge of sound poured on and on; I never knew what she found in the shining current of it; I never knew how far it bore her, or past what happy islands. From the trembling of her face I could well believe that before the last numbers she had been carried out where the **myriad** graves are, into the grey, nameless burying grounds of the sea; or into some world of death vaster yet, where, from the beginning of the world, hope has lain down with hope and dream with dream and, renouncing, slept.

230   The concert was over; the people filed out of the hall chattering and laughing, glad to relax and find the living level again, but my kinswoman made no effort to rise. The harpist slipped its green felt cover over his instrument; the flute-players shook the water from their mouthpieces; the men of the orchestra went out one by one, leaving the stage to the chairs and music stands, empty as a winter cornfield.

I spoke to my aunt. She burst into tears and sobbed pleadingly. "I don't want to go, Clark, I don't want to go!"

I understood. For her, just outside the door of the concert hall, lay the black pond with the cattle-tracked bluffs; the tall, unpainted house, with weather-curled boards;
240   naked as a tower, the crook-backed ash seedlings where the dish-cloths hung to dry; the gaunt, molting turkeys picking up refuse about the kitchen door. ༄

ⓗ SETTING
Reread lines 220–222. What does this **metaphor** suggest about how a place might affect one's appreciation of music?

myriad (mĭr′ē-əd) *adj.* exceedingly numerous

④ Targeted Passage

---

21. ***Trovatore*** (trō′vä-tôr′ĕ): *Il Trovatore* is an opera by the Italian composer Giuseppe Verdi.

DIFFERENTIATED INSTRUCTION

FOR STRATEGIC READERS
Explore Metaphor [small-group option]
Point out that in lines 223–227, Cather offers a detailed metaphor that compares the music in the concert hall to flowing water. Work with small groups of students to identify key words and phrases in the metaphor and the qualities that they convey: *deluge, poured* (line 223); *current, bore* (line 224); *carried out* (line 226); *grey, nameless burying grounds of the sea* (lines 226–227).

④ Targeted Passage [Lines 230–241]
In this concluding passage, Aunt Georgiana voices her thoughts about returning to her homestead.

- What does Aunt Georgiana do while everyone else is leaving the concert hall?
- How does she react when Clark speaks to her? What emotion or emotions is she showing?
- What place is Clark describing in the final paragraph?

Comprehension

R3.5
CALIFORNIA

1. **Recall** Why does Aunt Georgiana travel to Boston?

2. **Recall** Why does Clark take his aunt to the concert?

3. **Summarize** How do Clark and his aunt respond to the concert?

Literary Analysis

4. **Predict Events** In your opinion, will Aunt Georgiana return to Nebraska, or will she stay in Boston? Give evidence to support your answer.

5. **Make Inferences** Aunt Georgiana warns Clark, "Don't love it so well, Clark, or it may be taken from you." What does this suggest about the role of music in her own life?

6. **Draw Conclusions About Character** Look back at the **inferences** you recorded in your chart as you read. Judging from the choices that Aunt Georgiana has made in her life, what conclusions can you draw about her character? What emotions does she seem to experience, and how does she handle them?

7. **Contrast Settings** The two settings in this story—the Nebraska prairie and the Boston concert hall—are both significant for Aunt Georgiana. What do they **symbolize?** Support your answer with details from the story.

8. **Make Judgments** How might Aunt Georgiana be different if she had stayed in Boston? Use examples from the story and your views about the importance of **place** to support your answer.

Literary Criticism

9. **Biographical Context** "A Wagner Matinee" created a stir when it appeared in 1904. Cather's family objected to the fictional portrait of her real-life aunt Franc. One of her friends remarked: "The stranger to this state will associate Nebraska with the aunt's wretched figure, her ill-fitting false teeth, her skin yellowed by the weather." Do you agree? Examine the **imagery** and **figurative language** used to describe the people and scenes of Nebraska. Do you think Cather's Nebraska relatives were justified in taking offense? Cite evidence from the story to support your answer.

A WAGNER MATINEE **703**

8. *If Aunt Georgiana had stayed, she probably would have continued her career as a music teacher while partaking in the musical and other cultural offerings of Boston. Her elopement seemed an act of desperation; had she stayed in Boston, she might never have married. City life probably would not have taken such a physical and emotional toll on her as frontier life has done, and certainly her appearance would be not only healthier but also more stylish.*

9. *Students' answers and evidence will vary, but many students are likely to agree that Cather's portrayal of Aunt Georgiana and her life on the Nebraska prairie is harsh and unflattering.*

Practice and Apply

After Reading

Use these copy masters to check understanding and provide extra support:

R RESOURCE MANAGER—Copy Masters
Reading Check p. 128
Setting p. 121
Question Support p. 129

Additional selection questions are provided for teachers on page 115.

ANSWERS

1. *Aunt Georgiana travels to Boston to claim a small legacy left by a bachelor relative.*

2. *Clark takes his aunt to the concert because he knows that she loves music and because he wants to give something back to her for all that she did for him as a child.*

3. *Clark at first wonders whether his aunt can still appreciate music, but he then sees that she does retain deep feelings for it. Aunt Georgiana is emotionally overwhelmed by the music and doesn't want to leave.*

Possible answers:

4. *Aunt Georgiana's reaction at the end of the concert suggests that she may be tempted to remain in Boston. However, she has lived in Nebraska for thirty years, and her roots there are likely to draw her back.*

5. *The warning suggests that Aunt Georgiana loves music and has deep regrets about having sacrificed it in exchange for a harsh life on the prairie.*

6. ■ **SKILLS FOCUS Draw Conclusions About Character** *The reader can conclude that once Aunt Georgiana makes a commitment, she has the courage to stick with it, as evidenced by her thirty years on the frontier with her husband. Although she may feel loneliness, sadness, and regret, she does not let these feelings rule her life.*

7. ● **SKILLS FOCUS Setting** *The elegant, vibrant opera house represents culture and sophistication; the Nebraska prairie represents hard work and practicality. The main support comes from vivid description, which contrasts the lavishness of the opera house with the bleakness of the homestead.*

A WAGNER MATINEE **703**

ANSWERS
Vocabulary in Context

VOCABULARY PRACTICE

1. *tentatively*   5. *callow*
2. *somnambulant*   6. *veritable*
3. *sordid*   7. *overture*
4. *myriad*   8. *excruciatingly*

 RESOURCE MANAGER—Copy Master
Vocabulary Practice p. 126

VOCABULARY IN WRITING

Encourage students to imagine themselves as
Aunt Georgiana and to consider their senses
as well as their emotions. For example, what
do they see, hear, and smell as they walk
around the city? How does the experience
make them feel, and why?

**VOCABULARY STRATEGY: MUSIC
TERMINOLOGY** *(also an EL language objective)*

- Explain that musical terminology is an example of jargon. Invite examples of jargon from
  other fields, such as sports or computers.

- Model how to research word origin using the
  etymology of *concert,* which comes from the
  Italian *concerto.*

Answers:

1. *f*   4. *e*
2. *d*   5. *b*
3. *a*   6. *c*

 RESOURCE MANAGER—Copy Master
Vocabulary Strategy p. 127

 Vocabulary Center at **ClassZone.com**
Additional Vocabulary Activities

Assess and Reteach

Assess

 RESOURCE MANAGER—Copy Masters
Selection Test A pp. 131–132
Selection Test B/C pp. 133–134

Test Generator CD

Reteach

STANDARDS LESSON FILE
Literature Lesson 9: Setting and Its Roles
Reading Lesson 9: Drawing Conclusions
Vocabulary Lesson 25: Etymologies

Vocabulary in Context

VOCABULARY PRACTICE

Choose the word from the list that best completes each sentence.

WORD LIST
callow
excruciatingly
myriad
overture
somnambulant
sordid
tentatively
veritable

1. Though uncertain whether Aunt Georgiana would enjoy the concert, Clark
   _____ made plans to go.
2. Earlier, his aunt had seemed dazed, walking around in an almost _____ state.
3. Her life on the farm, while not _____, was certainly harsh and difficult.
4. She was worn down from the _____ jobs she performed from dawn to dusk.
5. But Aunt Georgiana was not a(n) _____ young girl with no experience or
   culture.
6. She was a(n) _____ treasure chest of musical knowledge.
7. When the _____ was played, she became a new woman.
8. Yet she found it _____ difficult to listen to the beautiful music.

VOCABULARY IN WRITING

Using two or more vocabulary words, assume the role of Aunt Georgiana and
describe your experience in Boston in a few paragraphs. Here is a sample beginning.

> **EXAMPLE SENTENCE**
>
> *It had been years since I'd been in Boston, and I was unprepared
> for its **myriad** sights and sounds.*

VOCABULARY STRATEGY: MUSIC TERMINOLOGY

The world of classical music employs its own specialized vocabulary to help
describe the people, the musical forms, and the expressive qualities it comprises.
The vocabulary word *overture,* for example, refers in music to the introductory
piece at the beginning of an opera or other musical drama. Becoming familiar with
musical terminology can not only enhance your vocabulary; it can also increase
both your understanding of classical music and your cultural literacy in general.

PRACTICE Match each term in the lefthand column with its definition in the
righthand column. Research the origin of each word to see which words, as
they are used today, have retained their Italian spelling.

1. concerto   **a.** an elaborate melody in an opera, sung by one person
2. contralto   **b.** a moderately slow tempo, or pace
3. aria   **c.** a man who sings with a higher voice
4. diva   **d.** a woman who sings with a lower voice
5. andante   **e.** a leading woman soloist in an opera company
6. tenor   **f.** a piece in which a soloist performs with an orchestra

VOCABULARY PRACTICE
For more practice, go
to the **Vocabulary Center**
at **ClassZone.com.**

FOR ENGLISH LEARNERS

Task Support: Vocabulary Strategy [paired
option] Some students may find that many
musical terms in English are similar or even
identical to the terms in their home language.
For example, such words as *tenor, soprano,* and
andante have the same spellings and meanings in both English and Spanish. Ask pairs of
students who speak the same home language
to identify other such cognates and then share
their findings with the class.

FOR ADVANCED LEARNERS/AP

Vocabulary in Writing Challenge students
to use as many vocabulary words as they can
in a paragraph written in the first person
from Clark's point of view but set after Aunt
Georgiana's return to Nebraska (or her decision to remain in Boston). Invite volunteer to
read the results to the class.

America's Literary Regions

Indiana author Edward Eggleston made this claim in 1892.

> "It used to be a matter of no little jealousy to us, I remember, that the manners, customs, thoughts and feelings of New England country people filled so large a place in books, while our life, not less interesting, not less romantic, and certainly not less filled with humorous and grotesque material, had no place in literature. It was as though we were shut out of good society."

By the end of the 19th century, however, virtually every region of the country—from the cities of the Northeast, to the mining camps of California, to the Southern bayou, to the northern plains—had its own local colorist capturing the region's distinctive features in writing. These local color writers portrayed the dialects, dress, mannerisms, customs, character types, and landscapes of their regions with an eye for accurate detail.

Writing to Synthesize

Make a chart like the one shown, listing each of the selections you've read in this section (pages 634–704). On your chart, note what you've learned about the way the people in each region speak, the way they dress, their customs, and their landscapes. Then use your chart to write a one-paragraph description of each region you've encountered in your reading.

	How People Speak	How People Dress	Local Customs	Local Landscape
The Autobiography of Mark Twain				

Extension

VIEWING & REPRESENTING
Create a **single-frame cartoon** to represent the region you live in. You may want to focus on the way people speak and dress, or you may prefer to characterize the landscape.

 W2.2
CALIFORNIA

A homesteader's dugout house in Pie Town, New Mexico

705

Wrap-Up: Regionalism and Local Color Writing

This Wrap-Up provides students with an opportunity to review elements of regionalism and local color writing and to reflect on how these elements capture the flavor of different parts of the United States. Have students read and comment on the statement from Edward Eggleston; elicit that he probably would want to read or write about life in the Midwest.

Writing to Synthesize

- Review with students the concept of *synthesizing*—combining ideas and facts with other information and prior knowledge in order to understand a subject better or to develop new ideas. In this activity, synthesizing will help students draw conclusions about various regions of the United States and the people who live there.

- As students create their charts, suggest that they work in pairs to list specific details relating to speech, dress, customs, and landscape for each selection. Urge students to note specific passages that they can refer to when writing their paragraphs.

Extension

- Point out that a cartoon, like a written work, has a purpose and a tone. For example, a cartoon might entertain through gentle humor and an affectionate tone. Encourage students to identify a tone and a purpose before sketching their cartoons.

- Invite students to be imaginative in combining text and visual images. Suggest that they look at single-frame cartoons in newspapers or magazines for ideas.

DIFFERENTIATED INSTRUCTION

FOR DEVELOPING WRITERS
Writing Support Help students get started by directing them to relevant passages in a few selections. For example, students might review lines 1–29 of "The Outcasts of Poker Flat" or lines 1–12 of *Lake Wobegon Days* to get a sense of people and customs; they might review lines 39–62 of "A Wagner Matinee" for information about landscape and dress.

FOR ENGLISH LEARNERS
Writing Topic Sentences To help students create topic sentences for their paragraphs, provide sentence starters such as these:

- Garrison Keillor's account of the people and events of Lake Wobegon suggests that
_____.

- In "A Wagner Matinee," Willa Cather makes clear that life on the frontier _____.

Remind students to support their topic sentences with specific details from the selections.

Focus and Motivate

OBJECTIVES

Media Literacy

- explore the key idea of **Western expansion**
- view an image collection to analyze how visual elements are used to convey naturalist images, and to interpret and evaluate messages in those images
- create a personal landscape to express an interpretation of a natural space

 LS1.3, LS1.2

SUMMARY

The four images in this collection present a contrast between photography and painted landscapes. The first pair of images depicts a canyon in Yellowstone National Park. Thomas Moran's painting reveals the grandeur of the waterfall and rock formations. William Henry Jackson's photograph captures the same scene in black and white. The second pair of images focuses on the Park's Castle Geyser. Both artists make artistic choices, Jackson to make the pool dominate and Moran to blend land and sky more fluidly.

Can pictures DEVELOP *new frontiers?*

Read the question aloud. Remind students that 19th-century **Western expansion** occurred in response to many economic and social factors, and point out examples of these on page 619 of the historical essay. Ask students to consider how photography would have been useful to anyone wishing to encourage the expansion.

BACKGROUND

Moran and Jackson traveled on the newly completed transcontinental railroad to Yellowstone, then by horse and into the wilderness. Moran created rough watercolor sketches as the basis for his finished art. Jackson's photography equipment was fragile and heavy. Each photograph had to be prepared and developed on site, taking up to an hour to complete.

 Media Study

American Landscapes

Image Collection on **MediaSmart** DVD

706

LS1.3, LS1.2 (p. 707)

Can pictures DEVELOP *new frontiers?*

KEY IDEA Paintings and photographs can have a profound effect on us. They can enlighten us, frighten us, elicit our sympathies, even inspire us. In this lesson, you'll examine the landscape work of two 19th-century artists and discover how paintings and photographs helped to spur **Western expansion.**

Background

Framing New Views In the late 1800s, at a time when writer Mark Twain portrayed a romanticized view of the West, the new medium of photography gained popularity for revealing American life as it really was. For many painters of the day, photography posed a new challenge. While some saw it as displacing traditional forms of representation, others embraced it as a liberating artistic force.

Photography was also having an impact on the mass media. Because people were increasingly interested in facts and in realistic portrayals of events, they turned to the burgeoning newspaper industry and the day's more "realistic" writers. With the portability of cameras, photographers could supply newspapers, magazines, and advertisers with images in a short period of time, exposing viewers to faraway locations.

At the same time, Western expansion was being promoted by the federal government and by land developers from the East and Midwest. Photographic images of the new frontier were frequently used by advertisers and marketers to entice Americans to go West and settle the sparsely populated territory. In 1871, painter Thomas Moran joined forces with photographer William Henry Jackson and embarked on a geological expedition to document Western lands. These two artists found inspiration in surroundings of astounding natural beauty. Examples of their work appear in this lesson.

Media Study Resources

 RESOURCE MANAGER UNIT 4

Plan and Teach pp. 135–138

Media Analysis
Summary pp. 139†*, 140‡*
Viewing Guide p. 141
Close Viewing p. 142
Media Activity p. 143
Produce Your Own Media p. 144

STANDARDS LESSON FILE
Media Lesson 3: Influence of Media on Society
Media Lesson 19: Analyzing Visuals

Media Center at ClassZone.com

MEDIA VIEWING
MediaSmart DVD

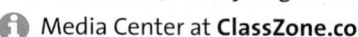
* Resources for Differentiation   † Also in Spanish   ‡ In Haitian Creole and Vietnamese

Media Literacy: Photographs and Paintings

The paintings of Thomas Moran and the photographs of William Henry Jackson were instrumental in convincing Congress to declare Yellowstone, in 1872, the country's first national park. Shown here are a painting by Moran and a photograph by Jackson of a canyon scene. Analyze these images by considering how each artist used certain elements to achieve compelling landscape art.

STRATEGIES FOR ANALYZING PHOTOGRAPHS AND PAINTINGS

Composition is the arrangement of subject elements within an image. Scan each image from top to bottom, side to side, and corner to corner, noting how each artist has arranged the elements in the frame. Ask yourself: Where is the **focal point,** or main focus, of the painting and of the photograph? What section of the image first catches my eye? In both of these images, the focal point is the waterfall.

For painters, **perspective** is a technique that creates the illusion of depth, making objects look three-dimensional. To determine the perspective of an image, try to identify the **horizon line,** the horizontal section that appears to your eye to be at the farthest distance in a landscape. In both of these images, the horizon line appears near the top, where the sky meets the uppermost part of the valley.

Depth of field is the area in front of and behind a focused subject in which the image appears sharp. Photographers achieved this effect by adjusting camera lenses. Notice in the photograph how depth of field creates an impression of distance.

Texture is the surface quality of an image—what the image would feel like if we could touch it. Ask yourself:
• What materials or techniques did the photographer use to create a sense of texture?
• With paintings, where does the paint seem to rise slightly from the canvas?
In these canyon images, your own knowledge of what is being depicted adds to your interpretation and appreciation of the textures conveyed.

MEDIA STUDY: TEACHING OPTIONS

Teaching Option 1: The Basics (1–2 Days)
1. Begin the Media Study using the material provided on pages 706–707.
2. Show the Introduction from Media*Smart*. Have students use the Viewing Guide on page 708, along with the corresponding copy master on page 139 of the Resource Manager. Discuss their responses.
3. Return to the pupil book for the extension activities on page 709.

Teaching Option 2: In-Depth Study (2–3 Days)
1. Begin the Media Study using pages 706–707.
2. Show the Introduction from Media*Smart*. Then continue on Media*Smart* with the Media Lessons, using the teacher notes available in the Resources section.
3. Show the Guided Analysis presentation. Have students record their observations on the Student Viewing Guide available in the Resources section of Media*Smart*.
4. Return to the pupil book, page 709.

Media Literacy

Help students analyze the images on page 707 by listing their similarities and differences on a Two-Column Chart. Discuss these points to help guide students' comparisons:

• **Composition** Point out that Moran's painting uses dark shadows to frame the light waterfall. Note that the waterfall appears in the center of both images, making a simple and striking composition.

• **Focal Point** Explain that although the focal point of the painting is the waterfall, Moran has included several figures in the foreground. Point out that these figures help show the great size of the canyon. They also invite viewers into the scene to visualize themselves in the setting.

• **Perspective** Offer an example of perspective in Jackson's photograph by pointing out the relative size of the trees. Those in the foreground are larger than those in the distance.

• **Horizon Line** Challenge students to imagine how the composition of Jackson's photograph would change if the horizon line did not appear in the photograph. How does the horizon line help the composition?

• **Depth of Field** Point out that the farthest hills in the photograph appear shrouded in haze. Explain that this adds depth to the image.

• **Texture** Encourage students to notice that in both the photograph and the painting, there are smooth and rough areas. The intricate textures add interest to the scene.

BEST PRACTICES TOOLKIT—Transparency Two-Column Chart p. A25

Media*Smart* DVD

Practice and Apply

VIEWING GUIDE

1. To prepare students for viewing the image collection, explain that the purpose of the exercise is not to determine which form of art is better or more effective, but rather to find the strengths of each form. Encourage them to consider these elements:

   - Point out that while all early photography was in black and white, both Jackson and Moran use color as elements of **composition.**

   - Jackson and Moran use **depth of field** to orient viewers in an image, a **focal point** to draw viewers' eyes to specific elements, and **perspective** to create realistic images. Together, these techniques convey the artists' reactions to Yellowstone's natural features.

   - The **textures** in the photographs and paintings show how the unfamiliar Yellowstone landscape would feel if viewers could touch it. This works with the visual images to help place viewers in the scene.

2. Remind students that one purpose of the art was to share the beauties of the natural setting with Americans who had never traveled west. For this reason, the artists were likely careful not to distort the scene.

R RESOURCE MANAGER—Copy Masters
   Viewing Guide p. 141
   Close Viewing p. 142
   Media Activity p. 143

Use this resource with the Viewing Guide:

MediaSmart DVD

ANSWERS

FIRST VIEWING: Comprehension

1. *The elements of nature in the images include the waterfall, trees, the canyon, the horizon, steep cliffs, and shadowy hills.*

2. *Moran's painting has people in it.*

CLOSE VIEWING: Media Literacy

Possible answers:

3. *The artists' composition sought to show the canyon's enormity, the great distance of the land, and the waterfall's power.*

4. *Moran's painting of the Grand Canyon has more texture than "Castle Geyser." The geysers appear smooth with a hazy sky and calm waters, whereas the canyon has*

MediaSmart DVD

Paintings by Thomas Moran
   - **Selection 1:** "Grand Canyon of the Yellowstone"
   - **Selection 4:** "Castle Geyser"

Paintings by William Henry Jackson
   - **Selection 2:** "The Grand Canyon of the Yellowstone"
   - **Selection 3:** "Castle Geyser"

708

Viewing Guide for

American Landscape Artists

Look at the full-sized images on the DVD. Examine each image carefully, jotting down your initial impressions. To help you analyze the paintings of Thomas Moran and the photographs of William Henry Jackson in terms of certain design elements, refer to the details on page 707. You can also refer to the Illustrations and Photographs section of the Media Handbook (pages R94–R95) to review the visual art elements of color, shape, line, and texture. Then consider these questions to help you analyze the images.

NOW VIEW

FIRST VIEWING: Comprehension

1. **Identify** In both Grand Canyon images, what elements of nature do you see?

2. **Clarify** Which Grand Canyon image has people in it?

CLOSE VIEWING: Media Literacy

3. **Analyze Composition** In each of the Grand Canyon images, the artist chose to depict the widest possible view. Through this composition, what effect do you think each artist was trying to achieve?

4. **Compare Texture** Consider both Moran paintings. Which appears to have more texture? Explain your choice.

5. **Analyze Perspective** In the color painting "Castle Geyser" by Thomas Moran, find the horizon line. Name whatever objects you can that rise up from this line.

6. **Compare Images** Both the painting and the photograph of the geyser on this page have an otherworldly look and feel. Which image looks more alien to you? Support your response in terms of your view of

   - in the painting, the stark color contrast between the deep blue of the pool and the lighter tone of the sky

   - in the photograph, the placement of the camera and the lens to make the pool seem as large as possible

---

ragged trees, jagged cliffs and solid rocky outcroppings that give textural contrast to the smooth plateau in the foreground.

5. *Two geysers, a rainbow, steam, and several trees rise from the horizon in Moran's "Castle Geyser."*

6. *In the painting, the stark color contrast between the dark pool and the light sky and earth show a formation that looks unnatural and invented. The wide pool in the photograph looks more realistic, since it includes such details such as trees, rocks, and steam—familiar, worldly features that can be seen in other places.*

LS1.3
CALIFORNIA

Write or Discuss

Judge an Image The landscape paintings and photographs of this lesson not only inspired thousands to journey to the West but also inspired the protection of one of America's most striking natural regions. Among these four images, pick one that you think is the most interesting. In a short evaluation, describe what elements it has that make it a fine example of landscape art. Base your criteria on these considerations

- the **composition** and **perspective** in the paintings or the effect of the **depth of field** in the photographs
- the aim of Thomas Moran and William Henry Jackson to capture stunning scenes of natural beauty
- the aspects of the painting or photograph that especially appeal to you (for example, the specific subject matter, use or absence of color, overall mood or feeling)

Produce Your Own Media

Create Your Personal Landscape Think of a favorite place. How would you represent it visually? Create a landscape image of your choice. It can be a photograph, a painting, a computer-generated image, or a drawing.

HERE'S HOW Decide what landscape you want to capture and which medium you want to use. Here are some things to keep in mind

- Be aware of composition. What you show and don't show in an image defines your vision of the landscape. Is there a dominant element you want to focus on?
- Try to provide some texture to your image regardless of the medium you've chosen.
- Give your work a horizontal landscape orientation. Experiment with giving your image an illusion of depth. For a drawing or painting, determine where to position the lines that will establish the perspective. For a photograph, determine the depth of field by adjusting lenses or camera position.
- No matter what type of image you create, make notes on what your intentions were and how you planned to create it.

 MEDIA TOOLS
For help with creating a landscape image, visit the **Media Center** at **ClassZone.com.**

Tech Tip

Use a software program to experiment with various effects.

Further Exploration

View More Photographs The equipment the early photographers used was quite unwieldy. Photographers had to carry their big box cameras and heavy film plates to their subjects, so you can imagine the rigors of filming a vast and remote landscape like the Grand Canyon.

Look at the early photographs housed on the DVD or find examples of early photography through your own research, and choose an image that most interests you.

Assess and Reteach

Write or Discuss

Judge an Image In their judgments, students should note the similarities between the works in terms of *composition, perspective, depth of field,* and *texture.* Students should also express an opinion about the piece of art, explaining why it is most interesting to them. For example, they may comment that the photography conveys less emotion but more visual accuracy, or that color intensifies the mood and feeling of the paintings in comparison to the photographs.

Produce Your Own Media

Rubric: Create Your Personal Landscape
A strong landscape should have

- a clear, dominant image shown by color, composition, or texture
- textural interest within the composition
- depth in the landscape created by lines or camera angle
- a clear, written explanation of the intention of the artwork and the methods that were used to create it

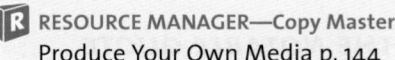 **RESOURCE MANAGER—Copy Master**
Produce Your Own Media p. 144

Further Exploration

View More Photographs Encourage students to use art and photography references from the library or the Internet to find examples of early photography. Suggest that students write captions that summarize the reasons for their choice. Post available photographs and captions in the classroom.

MEDIA STUDY WRAP-UP

Have students summarize what they have learned about analyzing photographs and paintings for technique and message. Urge students to use terms such as *composition, perspective, horizon line, depth of field,* and *texture.*

RETEACH

S STANDARDS LESSON FILE

Media Lesson 3: Influence of Media on Society
Media Lesson 19: Analyzing Visuals

Focus and Motivate

OBJECTIVES

Literary Analysis
- explore the key idea of **nature**
- analyze characteristics of naturalism
- read a short story

Reading
- analyze descriptive language

Vocabulary
- build vocabulary for reading and writing
- use the Greek prefix *epi-* to help determine word meaning *(also an EL language objective)*

Grammar and Writing
- use gerunds and gerund phrases to create effective description
- write a character sketch

 CALIFORNIA R3.3, R1.2, W1.2, W2.2, LC1.1

ABOUT THE AUTHOR

Point out that "The Open Boat" resulted from one of Crane's journeys as a war correspondent. Despite his status as a journalist, Crane also did the work of a crew member on the *Commodore*. His experiences on the journey contributed to his failing health.

USING THE *NOTABLE QUOTE*

Ask students on what naturalist teaching **Stephen Crane** bases his claim that a man "is not at all responsible for his vision." *Possible answer: Naturalists believe that instinct determines behavior. Thus, a man sees the world the way he is born to see it and has little control over his vision.*

Selection Resources

CALIFORNIA

R3.3, R1.2 (p. 736), W1.2 (p. 737),
W2.2 (p. 737), LC1.1 (p. 737)

NOTABLE QUOTE
"A man is born into the world with his own pair of eyes and he is not at all responsible for his vision. He is merely responsible for the quality of his personal honesty."

FYI
Did you know that Stephen Crane . . .
- spent most of his two semesters in college playing baseball?
- claimed that his understanding of combat in *The Red Badge of Courage* came from watching football games?
- wrote powerful poetry, including "Do Not Weep, Maiden, for War Is Kind"?

Author Online

For more on Stephen Crane, visit the **Literature Center** at **ClassZone.com**.

The Open Boat
Short Story by Stephen Crane

Stephen Crane
1871–1900

When Crane's novel *The Red Badge of Courage* was published in 1895, it caused a literary sensation. Critics hailed its unromanticized portrayal of a young soldier's struggles during one battle of the Civil War. As one reviewer exclaimed, "The style is as rough as it is direct. . . . But the original power of the book is great enough to set a new fashion in literature." War veterans, unimpressed by literary fashion, were struck by the graphic depiction of combat. So vivid was the battlefield experience in the novel that they assumed the story was a factual eyewitness account. But the author was only 23 years old at the time and had not yet seen war. Such was the power of Crane's imagination that he was able in his short life to create works of great integrity as well as artistic force.

Living on the Edge Born in Newark, New Jersey, the youngest of 14 children, Stephen Crane came from a family of writers. His father, a Methodist minister, and his mother both wrote religious articles, and two of his brothers were journalists. A stint in military school nourished the teenage Crane's interest in the Civil War, but college life bored him. "Not that I disliked books," he insisted, but that "humanity was a much more interesting study." And study it he did—first as a freelance journalist living in the slums of New York City's Bowery, then as a reporter traveling in Mexico and the American Wild West, and finally as a war correspondent shipping out to hot spots in Cuba and Greece. Twelve years of living on the edge gave Crane material not only for numerous news articles but also for three novels, several volumes of poetry, and some of the best-known short stories in American literature, including "The Open Boat," "The Blue Hotel," and "The Bride Comes to Yellow Sky."

The Cost of Adventure Adventure often comes at a price. Biographers cite the deprivations of Crane's years in the New York slums, the dangers of traveling to far-off places, and his own neglect of his health as contributing to his death from tuberculosis at age 28. But Crane had matured far beyond his years. True to his early intentions, he was a great student of humanity, and he developed a philosophy described by one critic as a "bold and robust humanism." As a naturalist writer, Crane believed that nature was a powerful force that shaped our lives. But as a humanist, he also had faith in his fellow humans' ability to act responsibly and honestly.

710

 RESOURCE MANAGER UNIT 4

Plan and Teach pp. 145–152

Literary Analysis
Summary pp. 153†*, 154‡*
Naturalism pp. 155, 156†*
Question Support p. 163*

Reading
Analyze Descriptive Language
  pp. 157, 158†*
Reading Check p. 162

Vocabulary
Study p. 159*
Practice p. 160
Strategy p. 161

Grammar and Writing
Use Effective Description p. 164

Assessment
Selection Tests A, B/C
  pp. 165*, 167*

 Test Generator CD

BEST PRACTICES TOOLKIT

Differentiated Instruction
  pp. 31–38*

Scaffolding Instruction
  pp. 43–46*

Graphic Organizers/Strategies
Making Inferences • Word Squares • Two-Column Chart • Freewriting • Personal Word List • Three-Column Journal • Sequence Chain • Character Traits and Textual Evidence

Reading Support
🔘 Audio Anthology CD*

Technology
ℹ️ Literature, Vocabulary, and Writing Centers at ClassZone.com
🔘 Write*Smart* CD

---

* Resources for Differentiation   † Also in Spanish   ‡ In Haitian Creole and Vietnamese

• LITERARY ANALYSIS: NATURALISM

Naturalism is an offshoot of **realism,** the 19th-century literary movement that featured detailed portrayals of life. Naturalist writers sought to describe the effect of natural and social forces on the individual. Naturalism typically

- renders common people and life accurately
- shows that environment and instinct determine behavior
- paints human destiny as beyond the control of the individual
- uses setting, theme, irony, and conflict to convey these ideas

As you read, look for characteristics of naturalism in the story and consider what they lend to the story's impact.

● READING SKILL: ANALYZE DESCRIPTIVE LANGUAGE

Naturalist writers made great use of **descriptive language,** lending vivid qualities to scenes, events, and characters. Effective description relies on various literary elements.

- **imagery**—descriptive words that create sensory experiences
- **figurative language**—language that goes beyond the literal
- **repetition**—recurrence of words, phrases, or lines
- **diction**—a writer's choice of words and word order
- **tone**—a writer's attitude toward the subject
- **mood**—the feeling the writer creates for the reader

As you read, record examples of Crane's use of these elements.

▲ VOCABULARY IN CONTEXT

Match each vocabulary word in the first column with the word or phrase in the second column that is closest in meaning.

1.	dearth	**a.**	comply
2.	ingenuously	**b.**	abnormality
3.	opprobrious	**c.**	raucous
4.	acquiesce	**d.**	compel
5.	motley	**e.**	insulting
6.	epithet	**f.**	relief
7.	respite	**g.**	insulting name
8.	obstreperous	**h.**	naively
9.	coerce	**i.**	assorted
10.	aberration	**j.**	shortage

Explore the Key Idea

CALIFORNIA

Does NATURE *play fair?*

KEY IDEA A lioness kills an antelope. An earthquake destroys one small town and leaves other nearby towns untouched. Diseases kill millions worldwide. Does this seem fair? Does **nature** stack the deck against certain creatures? As one of the leading writers in the naturalist movement, Stephen Crane addresses this issue in "The Open Boat."

DISCUSS With a small group, discuss how you explain the inequities found in nature. First, list some specific natural disasters or dangers that you know of. Then, discuss the reasons why each one may have happened the way it did.

711

Teach

CALIFORNIA

Does NATURE *play fair?*

Lead into the **KEY IDEA** by asking the question and challenging students to consider the ways in which people have learned to control, adapt to, or use **nature,** and the ways in which nature continues to be beyond human control. Ask students to keep this tenuous balance of control in mind as they complete the **DISCUSS** activity.

SKILLS FOCUS

LITERARY ANALYSIS   R3.3

● NATURALISM

Ask students how naturalists might have reacted to these statements:

1. Some people are kind to the core.
2. You can be whatever you want to be.

Possible answers: *They would have agreed with the first statement but doubted the second, because naturalists believed that heredity determines behavior and potential.*

CHECK UNDERSTANDING Ask students to create a statement that naturalists would likely support and to explain why.

READING SKILL   R3.3

■ ANALYZE DESCRIPTIVE LANGUAGE

Read aloud this example:

> The sluggish sun slouched over the glassy lake, its rays rippling across the ice like a spider flinging out strands of web.

Have students identify examples of imagery and figurative language. Ask them what tone is conveyed about nature. Is nature kind, neutral, graceful, or threatening? ***Possible answer:*** *Imagery includes "sluggish" and "glassy." Figurative language includes the simile comparing the sun to a spider. The tone is negative, casting nature as lazy and threatening.*

R **RESOURCE MANAGER—Copy Master**
Analyze Descriptive Language p. 157 (for student use while reading the selection)

VOCABULARY

▲ VOCABULARY IN CONTEXT

DIAGNOSE WORD KNOWLEDGE To determine preteaching needs, have all students complete Vocabulary in Context. ***Answers:*** **1.** *j,* **2.** *h,* **3.** *e,* **4.** *a,* **5.** *i,* **6.** *g,* **7.** *f,* **8.** *c,* **9.** *d,* **10.** *b*

PRETEACH VOCABULARY Preteach vocabulary with this copy master. Read each item aloud.

R **RESOURCE MANAGER—Copy Master**
Vocabulary Study p. 159

MORE VOCABULARY SUPPORT
For additional activities and guidelines, see

🧰 **BEST PRACTICES TOOLKIT**
Scaffolding Vocabulary Instruction pp. 43–46
ℹ Vocabulary Center at **ClassZone.com**

THE OPEN BOAT   **711**

SUMMARY

In this short story, Crane describes four men's experience escaping a shipwreck in a small boat. The ship's captain directs the men, who take turns rowing toward shore through a long day. Their troubles go unrecognized by those on land, and the men struggle to get to shore. After a long night contemplating eternity, they finally decide that they must chance it or die. They plunge shoreward, jumping from their capsizing boat to swim the final yards toward safety.

READING SKILL

A DESCRIPTIVE LANGUAGE

Possible answer: *Crane emphasizes the aspect of nature that endangers the men. The men are so focused on the threatening waves that they have no time to look at the sky (lines 3–4). The details that describe the waves—their color, size, shape, and motion—make it clear that the waves can kill the men, while the sky cannot (lines 4–8).*

If students need help . . . Work through lines 3–8 with students, highlighting the words "Their eyes glanced level." Ask students what is level with the men's eyes from their vantage point in the boat.

THE OPEN BOAT

STEPHEN CRANE

> **BACKGROUND** On New Year's Eve, 1896, Stephen Crane was traveling on the ship *Commodore* to Cuba to report on an impending revolution. Loaded with ammunition and Cuban rebels, the ship was damaged by a sandbar outside of Jacksonville, Florida, and two days later sank in the open sea. Most survivors filled the lifeboats, but Crane and four others ended up in a much smaller boat. This is the story he wrote about his harrowing ordeal. It has been called one of the world's great short stories.

A tale intended to be after the fact. Being the experience of four men from the sunk steamer *Commodore*.

I

None of them knew the color of the sky. Their eyes glanced level, and were fastened upon the waves that swept toward them. These waves were the hue of slate, save for the tops, which were of foaming white, and all of the men knew the colors of the sea. The horizon narrowed and widened, and dipped and rose, and at all times its edge was jagged with waves that seemed thrust up in points like rocks. **A**

Many a man ought to have a bathtub larger than the boat which here rode
10 upon the sea. These waves were most wrongfully and barbarously abrupt and tall, and each froth top was a problem in small boat navigation.

ANALYZE VISUALS
Look at the art on page 713. Apart from the men's appearance, what do the colors of the water and the sky suggest about their situation? Explain.

1 Targeted Passage

A DESCRIPTIVE LANGUAGE
The first paragraph is not really about the color of the sky. What does Crane emphasize by beginning the story this way?

German Shipwreck Survivors (image manipulated), Achille Beltrame. Engraving in Italian newspaper *La Domenica del Corriere*, February 1941. © Dagli Orti/The Art Archive.

DIFFERENTIATED INSTRUCTION

FOR ALL STUDENTS

Provide these independent projects to extend the lesson:

- Illustrate a graphic novel.
- Write a letter of recommendation for a crew member.
- Develop and dramatize a continuation of the story.

For further details on these projects, see

R RESOURCE MANAGER
Ideas for Extension pp. 150–151

FOR STRATEGIC READERS

In combination with the *Audio Anthology CD*, use one or more Targeted Passages (pp. 712, 714, 717, 721, 725, 730, 734) to ensure that students focus on key story events and concepts. Targeted Passages are also good for English learners.

1 Targeted Passage [Lines 3–11]

This passage introduces the conflict of men against nature and sets the scene at sea.

ANALYZE VISUALS

Possible answer: The shades of gray and the fade of the sea into the sky suggest that the men will soon add the threat of dangerous weather to the list of difficulties they face. The grays also suggest a sense of despair.

About the Art Achille Beltrame's original image showed World War II soldiers being rescued after their battleship sinks. A Red Cross rescue boat was visible in the original image. Without this rescue boat in the image, the men's situation appears to be very different and far more dire.

BACKGROUND

Cuban Rebellion Throughout the latter part of the 19th century, many Cubans sought to free themselves from the Spanish empire. Armed rebellion broke out between 1868 and 1878, and again in 1895. Some rebels were even based in the United States, and ships like the *Commodore* were used to run arms, ammunition, and expatriated Cuban soldiers to Cuba in support of the rebellion against Spain. Many Americans who had financial interests in Cuba read journalists' reports of events occurring there with interest. The United States finally intervened militarily in 1898 with the outbreak of the Spanish American War.

- Where are the men?
- What dangers does nature present to the men?
- What problem do they have?

FOR ENGLISH LEARNERS

Prereading For prereading instruction for English learners, see

 BEST PRACTICES TOOLKIT
  Scaffolding Reading Instruction pp. 43–46

FOR ADVANCED LEARNERS/AP

AP exercises in the bottom channel provide additional challenge for students. Use these suggestions for small groups or individuals.

ADDITIONAL GUIDELINES

For more help with differentiation and tips for classroom management, see

BEST PRACTICES TOOLKIT
  Differentiated Instruction pp. 31–38

B NATURALISM

Possible answer: Readers can infer that the "seven turned faces" were men who looked at the captain as the ship sank. The "stump of a topmast" was the captain's last view of the ship before it sank. These details tell readers that the captain watched his ship sink, and finds the memory traumatic.

If students need help . . . Discuss a captain's responsibility to his ship and crew. Then help students complete a Making Inferences chart to explore how a captain might react to failing at that responsibility:

Story Details	I Know	I Infer
captain sees ship sink	captains take care of ships	captain upset that ship sank

BEST PRACTICES TOOLKIT—Transparency Making Inferences p. A13

C DESCRIPTIVE LANGUAGE

Possible answer: The bronco metaphor emphasizes that the boat is hard to ride and moves unpredictably. The men may easily be unseated and tossed into the sea.

Lines 43–52
REINFORCE KEY IDEA: NATURE

Discuss How does **nature,** in the form of the waves, have an unfair advantage over the men? *Possible answer: The waves have no end and never tire, offering always "another . . . just as important" (lines 44–45). The men, by contrast, will tire soon.*

The cook squatted in the bottom and looked with both eyes at the six inches of gunwale[1] which separated him from the ocean. His sleeves were rolled over his fat forearms, and the two flaps of his unbuttoned vest dangled as he bent to bail out the boat. Often he said: "Gawd! That was a narrow clip." As he remarked it he invariably gazed eastward over the broken sea.

The oiler,[2] steering with one of the two oars in the boat, sometimes raised himself suddenly to keep clear of water that swirled in over the stern. It was a thin little oar and it seemed often ready to snap.

20 The correspondent, pulling at the other oar, watched the waves and wondered why he was there.

The injured captain, lying in the bow, was at this time buried in that profound dejection and indifference which comes, temporarily at least, to even the bravest and most enduring when, willy nilly, the firm fails, the army loses, the ship goes down. The mind of the master of a vessel is rooted deep in the timbers of her, though he command for a day or a decade, and this captain had on him the stern impression of a scene in the grays of dawn of seven turned faces, and later a stump of a topmast with a white ball on it that slashed to and fro at the waves, went low and lower, and down. Thereafter there was something strange in his voice.

30 Although steady, it was deep with mourning, and of a quality beyond oration or tears. **B**

"Keep 'er a little more south, Billie," said he.

"'A little more south,' sir," said the oiler in the stern.

A seat in this boat was not unlike a seat upon a bucking bronco, and, by the same token, a bronco is not much smaller. The craft pranced and reared, and plunged like an animal. As each wave came, and she rose for it, she seemed like a horse making at a fence outrageously high. The manner of her scramble over these walls of water is a mystic thing, and, moreover, at the top of them were ordinarily these problems in white water, the foam racing down from the summit

40 of each wave, requiring a new leap, and a leap from the air. Then, after scornfully bumping a crest, she would slide, and race, and splash down a long incline and arrive bobbing and nodding in front of the next menace. **C**

A singular disadvantage of the sea lies in the fact that after successfully surmounting one wave you discover that there is another behind it just as important and just as nervously anxious to do something effective in the way of swamping boats. In a ten-foot dinghy[3] one can get an idea of the resources of the sea in the line of waves that is not probable to the average experience, which is never at sea in a dinghy. As each slaty wall of water approached, it shut all else from the view of the men in the boat, and it was not difficult to imagine that

50 this particular wave was the final outburst of the ocean, the last effort of the grim water. There was a terrible grace in the move of the waves, and they came in silence, save for the snarling of the crests.

---

1. **gunwale** (gŭn'əl): the upper edge of a boat.
2. **oiler:** a worker who cares for the machinery in the engine room of a ship.
3. **dinghy** (dĭng'ē): a small open boat.

2 Targeted Passage

B NATURALISM
Reread lines 22–31. What can you **infer** about the "seven turned faces" and the "stump of a topmast"? Consider what these things tell you about the captain's recent experience.

C DESCRIPTIVE LANGUAGE
Notice the descriptive language in lines 34–42. What quality of the boat is emphasized by the bronco **metaphor**?

DIFFERENTIATED INSTRUCTION

FOR STRATEGIC READERS

 Targeted Passage [Lines 12–31]

This passage introduces the protagonists.

- Who are the stranded men?
- What was the relationship of these men while they were on the ship?
- How has that relationship changed now?
- Where is the captain? What has happened to him?

FOR ENGLISH LEARNERS

Key Academic Vocabulary Use Word Squares to teach these words: *decade* (line 26), *incline* (line 41), *occupy* (line 57), *occur* (line 190), *series* (line 286), *area* (line 307), *despite* (line 442).

BEST PRACTICES TOOLKIT—Transparency Word Squares p. E10

In the wan light, the faces of the men must have been gray. Their eyes must have glinted in strange ways as they gazed steadily astern. Viewed from a balcony, the whole thing would doubtlessly have been weirdly picturesque. But the men in the boat had no time to see it, and if they had had leisure there were other things to occupy their minds. The sun swung steadily up the sky, and they knew it was broad day because the color of the sea changed from slate to emerald green, streaked with amber lights, and the foam was like tumbling snow. The process of
60 the breaking day was unknown to them. They were aware only of this effect upon the color of the waves that rolled toward them. **D**

In disjointed sentences the cook and the correspondent argued as to the difference between a lifesaving station and a house of refuge. The cook had said: "There's a house of refuge just north of the Mosquito Inlet Light, and as soon as they see us, they'll come off in their boat and pick us up."

"As soon as who see us?" said the correspondent.

"The crew," said the cook.

"Houses of refuge don't have crews," said the correspondent. "As I understand them, they are only places where clothes and grub are stored for the benefit of
70 shipwrecked people. They don't carry crews."

"Oh, yes, they do," said the cook.

"No, they don't," said the correspondent.

"Well, we're not there yet, anyhow," said the oiler, in the stern.

"Well," said the cook, "perhaps it's not a house of refuge that I'm thinking of as being near Mosquito Inlet Light. Perhaps it's a lifesaving station."

"We're not there yet," said the oiler, in the stern.

II

As the boat bounced from the top of each wave, the wind tore through the hair of the hatless men, and as the craft plopped her stern down again the spray slashed past them. The crest of each of these waves was a hill, from the top of which the
80 men surveyed, for a moment, a broad tumultuous expanse, shining and wind-riven. It was probably splendid. It was probably glorious, this play of the free sea, wild with lights of emerald and white and amber.

"Bully good thing it's an on-shore wind,"[4] said the cook. "If not, where would we be? Wouldn't have a show."

"That's right," said the correspondent.

The busy oiler nodded his assent.

Then the captain, in the bow, chuckled in a way that expressed humor, contempt, tragedy, all in one. "Do you think we've got much of a show, now, boys?" said he.

90 Whereupon the three were silent, save for a trifle of hemming and hawing. To express any particular optimism at this time they felt to be childish and stupid, but they all doubtless possessed this sense of the situation in their mind. A young man thinks doggedly at such times. On the other hand, the ethics of their condition was decidedly against any open suggestion of hopelessness. So they were silent.

---

4. **on-shore wind:** wind that blows toward the shore.

THE OPEN BOAT **715**

D DESCRIPTIVE LANGUAGE
In lines 53–61, how does the author describe the dawn? Explain what this description tells you about the men and their state of mind.

READING SKILL

D DESCRIPTIVE LANGUAGE
Possible answer: The author describes the dawn only as it is reflected in the water (lines 57–59). This description stresses that the men are focused on and worried about the threatening waves.

Lines 62–76
TIERED DISCUSSION PROMPTS
Use these prompts to help students understand how the men's hopes and fears affect their conversation:

Connect Think about how hope and fear battle inside people during times of crisis. How does this help you understand the men's emotions? *Answers will vary but should show an understanding of the men's volatile emotions.*

Analyze Which dialogue indicates the men's hope that they will be saved? Which dialogue reveals their fears that they will drown? *Possible answers: The cook's claims of nearby help indicate hope (lines 64–65). The correspondent's doubt about houses of refuge is less hopeful (lines 68–70), and the oiler's repeated insistence that "we're not there yet" (lines 73, 76) hints at the fear that they won't get to shore at all.*

Evaluate In what way has Crane arranged the lines of dialogue to stress the push and pull between hope and fear among the men? Is this arrangement effective? Explain. *Possible answer: Crane arranges the dialogue to alternate between hope and fear. First, the cook is hopeful (lines 64–65), then the correspondent expresses doubt (lines 68–70). The two men debate the issue back and forth (lines 71–72). The oiler inserts reality (line 73) and tips the balance toward fear. The cook tries again to establish hope (lines 74–75), but the oiler has the last worrisome word (line 76). The arrangement is very effective as it pushes and pulls readers into the men's changing emotions.*

FOR ENGLISH LEARNERS
Vocabulary Support [mixed-readiness groups] Share or elicit definitions of these expressions, and then help students use them in original sentences:

- *bail out* (lines 14–15), "empty water from"
- *narrow clip* (line 15), "nearly tipped them over"
- *breaking day* (line 60), "dawn"
- *show* (line 84), "chance"

FOR STRATEGIC READERS
Comprehension Support Clarify Crane's meaning in lines 90–94. Explain that the men feel it would jeopardize their chances of rescue to speak their hopes aloud and also that as men they should not show such hope. They also feel that as men and sailors they should not speak their fear of dying aloud. Left unable to express either their hope or fear, they say nothing.

THE OPEN BOAT **715**

"Oh, well," said the captain, soothing his children, "we'll get ashore all right."

But there was that in his tone which made them think, so the oiler quoth: "Yes! If this wind holds!"

The cook was bailing. "Yes! If we don't catch hell in the surf."

100 Canton flannel gulls[5] flew near and far. Sometimes they sat down on the sea, near patches of brown seaweed that rolled over the waves with a movement like carpets on a line in a gale. The birds sat comfortably in groups, and they were envied by some in the dinghy, for the wrath of the sea was no more to them than it was to a covey of prairie chickens a thousand miles inland. Often they came very close and stared at the men with black bead-like eyes. At these times they were uncanny and sinister in their unblinking scrutiny, and the men hooted angrily at them, telling them to be gone. One came, and evidently decided to alight on the top of the captain's head. The bird flew parallel to the boat and did not circle, but made short sidelong jumps in the air in chicken fashion. His black eyes were wistfully fixed upon the captain's head. "Ugly brute," said the oiler to the bird.

110 "You look as if you were made with a jackknife." The cook and the correspondent swore darkly at the creature. The captain naturally wished to knock it away with the end of the heavy painter,[6] but he did not dare do it, because anything resembling an emphatic gesture would have capsized this freighted boat, and so with his open hand, the captain gently and carefully waved the gull away. After it had been discouraged from the pursuit the captain breathed easier on account of his hair, and others breathed easier because the bird struck their minds at this time as being somehow gruesome and ominous. **E**

In the meantime the oiler and the correspondent rowed. And also they rowed.

They sat together in the same seat, and each rowed an oar. Then the oiler

120 took both oars; then the correspondent took both oars; then the oiler; then the correspondent. They rowed and they rowed. The very ticklish part of the business was when the time came for the reclining one in the stern to take his turn at the oars. By the very last star of truth, it is easier to steal eggs from under a hen than it was to change seats in the dinghy. First the man in the stern slid his hand along the thwart[7] and moved with care, as if he were of Sèvres.[8] Then the man in the rowing seat slid his hand along the other thwart. It was all done with the most extraordinary care. As the two sidled past each other, the whole party kept watchful eyes on the coming wave, and the captain cried: "Look out now! Steady there!"

The brown mats of seaweed that appeared from time to time were like islands,

130 bits of earth. They were traveling, apparently, neither one way nor the other. They were, to all intents, stationary. They informed the men in the boat that it was making progress slowly toward the land.

The captain, rearing cautiously in the bow, after the dinghy soared on a great swell, said that he had seen the lighthouse at Mosquito Inlet. Presently the cook

---

5. **canton flannel gulls:** gulls looking as if they were made of canton flannel, a heavy type of cotton that is soft on one side and ribbed on the other.

6. **painter:** a line used for towing or securing a boat.

7. **thwart:** a seat that extends across a boat.

8. **Sèvres:** a type of fine china made in Sèvres, France.

---

remarked that he had seen it. The correspondent was at the oars, then, and for
some reason he too wished to look at the lighthouse, but his back was toward the
far shore and the waves were important, and for some time he could not seize an
opportunity to turn his head. But at last there came a wave more gentle than the
others, and when at the crest of it he swiftly scoured the western horizon.

140　　"See it?" said the captain.

"No," said the correspondent, slowly, "I didn't see anything."

"Look again," said the captain. He pointed. "It's exactly in that direction."

At the top of another wave, the correspondent did as he was bid, and this time
his eyes chanced on a small still thing on the edge of the swaying horizon. It was
precisely like the point of a pin. It took an anxious eye to find a lighthouse so tiny.

"Think we'll make it, Captain?"

"If this wind holds and the boat don't swamp, we can't do much else," said the
captain.

The little boat, lifted by each towering sea, and splashed viciously by the crests,
150　made progress that in the absence of seaweed was not apparent to those in her. She
seemed just a wee thing wallowing, miraculously, top up, at the mercy of five oceans.
Occasionally, a great spread of water, like white flames, swarmed into her. **F**

"Bail her, cook," said the captain, serenely.

"All right, Captain," said the cheerful cook.

III

It would be difficult to describe the subtle brotherhood of men that was here
established on the seas. No one said that it was so. No one mentioned it. But it
dwelt in the boat, and each man felt it warm him. They were a captain, an oiler,
a cook, and a correspondent, and they were friends, friends in a more curiously
ironbound degree than may be common. The hurt captain, lying against the
160　water jar in the bow, spoke always in a low voice and calmly, but he could never
command a more ready and swiftly obedient crew than the **motley** three of the
dinghy. It was more than a mere recognition of what was best for the common
safety. There was surely in it a quality that was personal and heartfelt. And after
this devotion to the commander of the boat there was this comradeship that the
correspondent, for instance, who had been taught to be cynical of men, knew
even at the time was the best experience of his life. But no one said that it was
so. No one mentioned it.

"I wish we had a sail," remarked the captain. "We might try my overcoat on
the end of an oar and give you two boys a chance to rest." So the cook and the
170　correspondent held the mast and spread wide the overcoat. The oiler steered, and
the little boat made good way with her new rig. Sometimes the oiler had to scull[9]
sharply to keep a sea from breaking into the boat, but otherwise sailing was a
success.

Meanwhile the lighthouse had been growing slowly larger. It had now almost
assumed color, and appeared like a little gray shadow on the sky. The man at the

---

9. **scull:** to propel a boat by rowing from side to side, reversing the oar at each turn.

❸ Targeted Passage

F NATURALISM
In lines 149–152, what
images, words, and
phrases suggest the
overwhelming power of
nature and the smallness
of humanity?

motley (mŏt′lē) *adj.*
composed of diverse,
often mismatched
elements

LITERARY ANALYSIS

F NATURALISM

Possible answer: *The power of nature is
suggested by the words "towering," "viciously," and "swarmed" and by the phrases
"at the mercy of five oceans" and "a great
spread of water, like white flames." The
smallness of humanity is represented by
the boat, which is "little" and "wee" and
survives the sea "miraculously."*

Extend the Discussion How are lines 153–
154, which include the modifiers *serenely*
and *cheerful*, a reaction to the description
of the sea and the boat?

FOR STRATEGIC READERS

❸ Targeted Passage [Lines 135–154]

This passage describes a key turning point in
the men's efforts to survive.

- What is the correspondent looking for?
  What does he see?

- What does the captain predict will happen
  to the men?

- What is the men's mood now?

FOR ADVANCED LEARNERS/AP

Analyze Theme Lines 155–167 interrupt the
plot to discuss the developing bonds among
the men. Have students examine the key idea
in the passage: ". . . there was this comradeship that the correspondent, for instance, who
had been taught to be cynical of men, knew
even at the time was the best experience of
his life" (lines 164–166).

Ask students to consider these questions:

- What circumstances led to the developing
  bonds?

- How can an ordeal at sea be "the best
  experience" of a life?

Have students explore their responses with
the Freewriting strategy, then write and share
a brief analysis of the passage's theme.

 BEST PRACTICES TOOLKIT
Freewriting p. C1

Lines 185–188
REINFORCE *KEY IDEA:* NATURE

Discuss In these lines, the wind dies down. How does this change in **nature** work against the men? How does it help them? *Possible answer: When the wind dies down, it no longer pushes the rigged sail, so the oiler and the correspondent must begin to row again (line 188). On the other hand, when the wind dies down, the cook and the correspondent are no longer "obliged to slave in order to hold high the oar" (line 186).*

ANALYZE VISUALS

Activity Ask students how the viewpoint of the painting and the meeting of sky and sea at the horizon help readers understand what the men see "at the top of each wave." *Possible answer: The viewpoint of the painting is from atop a wave. This gives viewers a better view of the horizon. Because the land in the story is so far away and so thinly spread on the horizon, the men can only see it from atop a wave.*

About the Art The son of immigrants, Thomas Moran (1837–1926) traveled the nation and frontier to sketch and paint wonders such as the Grand Canyon, Yellowstone, and the Rockies. Later, Moran became fascinated by seascapes as well as landscapes. He moved to Long Island, built a studio, and observed the moods of the sea. The location gave him many opportunities to observe and paint the shipwrecks along the coast, capturing the power of the sea.

The Much Resounding Sea (1884), Thomas Moran. 25″ × 62″.

oars could not be prevented from turning his head rather often to try for a glimpse of this little gray shadow.

At last, from the top of each wave the men in the tossing boat could see land. Even as the lighthouse was an upright shadow on the sky, this land seemed but a
180 long black shadow on the sea. It certainly was thinner than paper. "We must be about opposite New Smyrna,"[10] said the cook, who had coasted this shore often in schooners. "Captain, by the way, I believe they abandoned that lifesaving station there about a year ago."

"Did they?" said the captain.

The wind slowly died away. The cook and the correspondent were not now obliged to slave in order to hold high the oar. But the waves continued their old

---

10. **New Smyrna:** New Smyrna Beach, a city on the eastern coast of Florida, about 15 miles south of Daytona Beach.

DIFFERENTIATED INSTRUCTION

FOR STRATEGIC READERS

Concept Support: Tone After students read lines 180–184, discuss how tone can reveal meaning beyond a person's literal words. For example, here the men speak in a flat, emotionless tone that belies the damaging impact of their words. Help students understand that the men are probably trying to downplay their worry, both to each other and themselves.

FOR ENGLISH LEARNERS

Vocabulary: Outdated Forms Tell students that *woundily* (line 188) is not in use today. Students can build meaning, however, by linking the word to other familiar words. Have students make a cluster diagram, placing *woundily* in the center and more familiar words such as *wound* or *wounded* on the outside. Point out that *wound* can be both verb and noun.

impetuous swooping at the dinghy, and the little craft, no longer under way, struggled woundily over them. The oiler or the correspondent took the oars again.

Shipwrecks are *apropos* of nothing. If men could only train for them
190 and have them occur when the men had reached pink condition, there would be less drowning at sea. Of the four in the dinghy none had slept any time worth mentioning for two days and two nights previous to embarking in the dinghy, and in the excitement of clambering about the deck of a foundering[11] ship they had also forgotten to eat heartily. **G**

For these reasons, and for others, neither the oiler nor the correspondent was fond of rowing at this time. The correspondent wondered **ingenuously** how in the name of all that was sane could there be people who thought it amusing to row a boat. It was not an amusement; it was a diabolical punishment, and even

---

11. **foundering:** sinking.

G NATURALISM
In lines 189–194, the author uses **verbal irony**, suggesting something different from what is literally meant. In this paragraph, what is Crane suggesting about the timing of shipwrecks? Explain.

ingenuously
(ĭn-jĕn′yōō-əs-lē) *adv.* in a manner showing childlike innocence or simplicity

TIERED DISCUSSION PROMPTS

Use these prompts to help students understand the men's worsening situation:

Summarize What weather change has happened? *Possible answer: The wind that had been pushing the boat dies away.*

Analyze What information suggests that the men's chance of survival is dwindling? Give four details. *Possible answers: The men learn that the lifesaving station nearest them has been abandoned (lines 182–183). The wind dies down, and the boat no longer makes progress to shore (lines 185–187). The men get weaker and weaker (lines 191–194). The two men capable of rowing are wearing out (line 195–196).*

Synthesize How does the need for teamwork apply to the men as well as to other life-threatening situations? *Possible answer: Teamwork requires that individuals work together for the common good. The men must take turns rowing and must help each other stay focused and hopeful in order to survive. This is true in most life-threatening situations involving groups; all members must work together to achieve survival.*

LITERARY ANALYSIS

G NATURALISM

Possible answer: Crane is suggesting that the timing of shipwrecks is unpredictable and random. Here the wreck has happened at the worst possible time, when the men are already exhausted and weak. If people knew they would shortly be shipwrecked, Crane implies, they would eat well, get a good night's sleep, and be ready.

Extend the Discussion What grim humor does the verbal irony in lines 193–194 contain?

FOR ADVANCED LEARNERS/AP

Research Latin Terms [paired option] Crane uses the Latin term *apropos* (line 189). Have pairs of students define this term together. Then ask them to do research to identify four other Latin terms (such as *pro tem*) or abbreviations (such as *e.g.* and *i.e.*) still in common use, and write their definitions. Challenge students to determine if the use of Latin terms in English has changed since Crane's time.

Ask pairs to share and combine lists before adding the terms to their Personal Word Lists. Invite students to teach the terms and definitions to the class, using example sentences.

🧰 **BEST PRACTICES TOOLKIT**
Personal Word List p. E2

a genius of mental **aberrations** could never conclude that it was anything but a horror to the muscles and a crime against the back. He mentioned to the boat in general how the amusement of rowing struck him, and the weary-faced oiler smiled in full sympathy. Previously to the foundering, by the way, the oiler had worked double watch in the engine room of the ship.

"Take her easy, now, boys," said the captain. "Don't spend yourselves. If we have to run a surf[12] you'll need all your strength, because we'll sure have to swim for it. Take your time."

Slowly the land arose from the sea. From a black line it became a line of black and a line of white—trees and sand. Finally, the captain said that he could make out a house on the shore. "That's the house of refuge, sure," said the cook. "They'll see us before long, and come out after us."

The distant lighthouse reared high. "The keeper ought to be able to make us out now, if he's looking through a glass," said the captain. "He'll notify the lifesaving people."

"None of those other boats could have got ashore to give word of the wreck," said the oiler, in a low voice. "Else the lifeboat would be out hunting us."

Slowly and beautifully the land loomed out of the sea. The wind came again. It had veered from the northeast to the southeast. Finally, a new sound struck the ears of the men in the boat. It was the low thunder of the surf on the shore. "We'll never be able to make the lighthouse now," said the captain. "Swing her head a little more north, Billie."

"'A little more north' sir," said the oiler.

Whereupon the little boat turned her nose once more down the wind, and all but the oarsman watched the shore grow. Under the influence of this expansion doubt and direful apprehension was leaving the minds of the men. The management of the boat was still most absorbing, but it could not prevent a quiet cheerfulness. In an hour, perhaps, they would be ashore.

Their backbones had become thoroughly used to balancing in the boat and they now rode this wild colt of a dinghy like circus men. The correspondent thought that he had been drenched to the skin, but happening to feel in the top pocket of his coat, he found therein eight cigars. Four of them were soaked with seawater; four were perfectly scatheless. After a search, somebody produced three dry matches, and thereupon the four waifs rode impudently in their little boat, and with an assurance of an impending rescue shining in their eyes, puffed at the big cigars and judged well and ill of all men. Everybody took a drink of water. Ⓗ

IV

"Cook," remarked the captain, "there don't seem to be any signs of life about your house of refuge."

"No," replied the cook. "Funny they don't see us!"

A broad stretch of lowly coast lay before the eyes of the men. It was of dunes topped with dark vegetation. The roar of the surf was plain, and sometimes they

---

12. **run a surf:** row through the surf to get to shore.

aberration (ăb′ə-rā′shən) *n.* a disorder of the mind

Ⓗ DESCRIPTIVE LANGUAGE
Reread lines 227–234. Cite examples of the author's language that suggests the assurance of the men might be premature.

240 could see the white lip of a wave as it spun up the beach. A tiny house was blocked out black upon the sky. Southward, the slim lighthouse lifted its little gray length.

Tide, wind, and waves were swinging the dinghy northward. "Funny they don't see us," said the men.

The surf's roar here dulled, but its tone was, nevertheless, thunderous and mighty. As the boat swam over the great rollers, the men sat listening to this roar. "We'll swamp sure," said everybody.

It is fair to say here that there was not a lifesaving station within twenty miles in either direction, but the men did not know this fact and in consequence they made dark and **opprobrious** remarks concerning the eyesight of the nation's 250 lifesavers. Four scowling men sat in the dinghy and surpassed records in the invention of **epithets.**

"Funny they don't see us."

The lightheartedness of a former time had completely faded. To their sharpened minds it was easy to conjure pictures of all kinds of incompetency and blindness and, indeed, cowardice. There was the shore of the populous land, and it was bitter and bitter to them that from it came no sign. ❶

"Well," said the captain, ultimately, "I suppose we'll have to make a try for ourselves. If we stay out here too long, we'll none of us have strength left to swim after the boat swamps."

260 And so the oiler, who was at the oars, turned the boat straight for the shore. There was a sudden tightening of muscles. There was some thinking.

"If we don't all get ashore—" said the captain. "If we don't all get ashore, I suppose you fellows know where to send news of my finish?"

They then briefly exchanged some addresses and admonitions. As for the reflections of the men, there was a great deal of rage in them. Perchance they might be formulated thus: "If I am going to be drowned—if I am going to be drowned—if I am going to be drowned, why, in the name of the seven mad gods who rule the sea,[13] was I allowed to come thus far and contemplate sand and trees? Was I brought here merely to have my nose dragged away as I was about to nibble 270 the sacred cheese of life? It is preposterous. If this old ninny-woman, Fate, cannot do better than this, she should be deprived of the management of men's fortunes. She is an old hen who knows not her intention. If she has decided to drown me, why did she not do it in the beginning and save me all this trouble. The whole affair is absurd. . . . But, no, she cannot mean to drown me. She dare not drown me. She cannot drown me. Not after all this work." Afterward the man might have had an impulse to shake his fist at the clouds. "Just you drown me, now, and then hear what I call you!" ❶

The billows that came at this time were more formidable. They seemed always just about to break and roll over the little boat in a turmoil of foam. There was 280 a preparatory and long growl in the speech of them. No mind unused to the sea would have concluded that the dinghy could ascend these sheer heights in time.

---

13. **seven mad . . . the sea:** possibly a reference to the gods of the seven major seas of the world.

---

opprobrious (ə-prō′brē-əs) *adj.* scornful; derogatory

epithet (ĕp′ə-thĕt′) *n.* an abusive word or phrase

④ **Targeted Passage**

❶ **NATURALISM**
Dramatic irony is the technique of allowing the reader to know more than the characters do about their own situation. What does the author emphasize with his use of dramatic irony in lines 247–256?

❶ **NATURALISM**
Reread lines 264–277. What techniques does the author use here suggest the indifference or hostility of nature?

LITERARY ANALYSIS

❶ **NATURALISM**

Possible answer: Readers know that there is no lifesaving station nearby (lines 247–248). The author uses this dramatic irony to emphasize that the outcome of the men's situation is beyond their control.

If students need help . . . Refer them to the list of naturalist qualities on page 711. Discuss the third bullet and stress that the men had no control over ending up in an area without a lifesaving station. No one is to blame, despite the men's desire to fault someone.

LITERARY ANALYSIS

❶ **NATURALISM**

Possible answer: The author personifies nature as an "old-ninny woman, Fate" and suggests that this old woman is in charge of human affairs and managing them incompetently (lines 270–273). Crane also summarizes the men's thoughts about why they are again facing death (lines 272–275). This shows that the men view nature as indifferent or even hostile toward their survival (lines 275–277).

Extend the Discussion How does personifying nature give the men a focus for their rage?

FOR STRATEGIC READERS

④ **Targeted Passage [Lines 247–261]**

In this passage, the men realize that they may be responsible for their own rescue.

- What new problem do the men have?
- How do the men respond to the lack of response from shore?
- What is the alternative to rescue by boat?
- What causes the "sudden tightening of muscles" and "some thinking"?

FOR ADVANCED LEARNERS/AP

Analyze Style [small-group option] Have students look beyond their responses to ❶ to further analyze the author's style in lines 264–277. Ask them to discuss the effect of these stylistic devices:

- **Repetition** (lines 264–267): Why does the author repeat the first "if" statement three times, separated by dashes (lines 266–267)? Why does he repeat the phrase "She . . . drown me" but vary the language slightly (lines 274–275)?

- **Apostrophe** (lines 276–277): Why must the speaker use apostrophe, or direct speech to an absent and personified abstract entity, to express his anger?

Have students share their analysis with the class and respond to questions.

Lines 304–308

TIERED DISCUSSION PROMPTS

Use these prompts to help students relate to the physical struggles of the oarsmen:

Connect Have you or someone you know ever been so exhausted that you could sleep anywhere, no matter how uncomfortable the setting? *Accept all thoughtful responses.*

Interpret To what does Crane compare the physical pain of the oarsmen? How do these comparisons convey the depth of that pain and the author's opinion of the men? *Possible answers: First, Crane compares the men's back pains to all the pain that could be recorded in the medical history of a regiment of soldiers. Second, he compares the different muscle pains to conflicts played out on the battlefield or in the theatre of war. The author admires the oarsmen's willingness to suffer for their survival.*

Evaluate Is it believable that the men could sleep through their pain, the uncomfortable and moving boat, and the cold seawater drenching them? Explain. *Possible answer: Yes. The men are so exhausted and have worked so hard to overcome their pain, that they can sleep through anything.*

The shore was still afar. The oiler was a wily surfman. "Boys," he said, swiftly, "she won't live there minutes more and we're too far out to swim. Shall I take her to sea again, Captain?"

"Yes! Go ahead!" said the captain.

This oiler, by a series of quick miracles, and fast and steady oarsmanship, turned the boat in the middle of the surf and took her safely to sea again.

There was a considerable silence as the boat bumped over the furrowed sea to deeper water. Then somebody in gloom spoke. "Well, anyhow, they must have 290 seen us from the shore by now."

The gulls went in slanting flight up the wind toward the gray desolate east. A squall, marked by dingy clouds, and clouds brick-red, like smoke from a burning building, appeared from the southeast.

"What do you think of those lifesaving people? Ain't they peaches?"

"Funny they haven't seen us."

"Maybe they think we're out here for sport! Maybe they think we're fishin'. Maybe they think we're damned fools."

It was a long afternoon. A changed tide tried to force them southward, but wind and wave said northward. Far ahead, where coastline, sea, and sky formed 300 their mighty angle, there were little dots which seemed to indicate a city on the shore.

"St. Augustine?"[14]

The captain shook his head. "Too near Mosquito Inlet."

And the oiler rowed, and then the correspondent rowed. Then the oiler rowed. It was a weary business. The human back can become the seat of more aches and pains than are registered in books for the composite anatomy of a regiment. It is a limited area, but it can become the theatre of innumerable muscular conflicts, tangles, wrenches, knots, and other comforts.

"Did you ever like to row, Billie?" asked the correspondent.

310 "No," said the oiler. "Hang it."

When one exchanged the rowing seat for a place in the bottom of the boat, he suffered a bodily depression that caused him to be careless of everything save an obligation to wiggle one finger. There was cold seawater swashing to and fro in the boat, and he lay in it. His head, pillowed on a thwart, was within an inch of the swirl of a wave crest, and sometimes a particularly **obstreperous** sea came inboard and drenched him once more. But these matters did not annoy him. It is almost certain that if the boat had capsized he would have tumbled comfortably out upon the ocean as if he felt sure that it was a great soft mattress.

"Look! There's a man on the shore!"

320 "Where?"

"There! See 'im? See 'im?"

"Yes, sure! He's walking along."

"Now he's stopped. Look! He's facing us!"

"He's waving at us!"

obstreperous
(ŏb-strĕp′ər-əs) *adj.* very noisy and unruly

---

14. **St. Augustine:** a city about 65 miles north of New Smyrna Beach, along the northeastern coast of Florida.

DIFFERENTIATED INSTRUCTION

FOR STRATEGIC READERS

Read Dialogue [small-group option] Students sometimes read short lines of dialogue so quickly that they lose track of the events described. Organize students in groups of four to read the dialogue in lines 319–351 aloud. Allow students to choose which lines each will speak, since no dialogue tags identify the speakers, and then provide these instructions to guide students:

- Omit lines 329–333, which are not dialogue.

- Imagine the situation. Is rescue at hand or not? How would the men say each line under these terrible circumstances?

- Decide as a group where pauses and breaks in the dialogue would occur as the men watched the people on shore.

After groups finalize and practice their readings, have them present to the class.

FOR ENGLISH LEARNERS

Language: Conversational English Patterns [mixed-readiness groups] Share or elicit the meanings of these expressions, and then help students find similar expressions in their home languages: *Hang it* (line 310), "Darn"; *By thunder!* (line 325), "Amazing!"; *What the devil is that thing?* (line 345); "What could that be?"; *sure as fate* (line 356), "definitely"; *That ain't a flag, is it?* (line 362), "That isn't a flag"; *Oh, say . . .* (line 365), "Actually."

"So he is! By thunder!"

"Ah, now, we're all right! Now we're all right! There'll be a boat out here for us in half an hour."

"He's going on. He's running. He's going up to that house there."

330 The remote beach seemed lower than the sea, and it required a searching glance to discern the little black figure. The captain saw a floating stick and they rowed to it. A bath towel was by some weird chance in the boat, and, tying this on the stick, the captain waved it. The oarsman did not dare turn his head, so he was obliged to ask questions.

"What's he doing now?"

"He's standing still again. He's looking, I think. . . . There he goes again. Toward the house. . . . Now he's stopped again."

"Is he waving at us?"

"No, not now! He was, though."

"Look! There comes another man!"

340 "He's running."

"Look at him go, would you."

"Why, he's on a bicycle. Now he's met the other man. They're both waving at us. Look!"

"There comes something up the beach."

"What the devil is that thing?"

"Why, it looks like a boat."

"Why, certainly it's a boat."

"No, it's on wheels."

"Yes, so it is. Well, that must be the lifeboat. They drag them along shore on 350 a wagon."

"That's the lifeboat, sure."

"No, by——it's—it's an omnibus."[15]

"I tell you it's a lifeboat."

"It is not! It's an omnibus. I can see it plain. See? One of those big hotel omnibuses."

"By thunder, you're right. It's an omnibus, sure as fate. What do you suppose they are doing with an omnibus? Maybe they are going around collecting the lifecrew, hey?"

"That's it, likely. Look! There's a fellow waving a little black flag. He's standing 360 on the steps of the omnibus. There come those two other fellows. Now they're all talking together. Look at the fellow with the flag. Maybe he ain't waving it!"

"That ain't a flag, is it? That's his coat. Why, certainly, that's his coat."

"So it is. It's his coat. He's taken it off and is waving it around his head. But would you look at him swing it!"

"Oh, say, there isn't any lifesaving station there. That's just a winter resort hotel omnibus that has brought over some of the boarders to see us drown."

"What's that idiot with the coat mean? What's he signaling, anyhow?"

"It looks as if he were trying to tell us to go north. There must be a lifesaving

---

15. **omnibus:** bus. At this time, a bus would have been pulled by horses.

Lines 329–369
REINFORCE *KEY IDEA:* NATURE

Discuss In what way does **nature** make it hard for the men in the boat to see or hear the shore, and thus create obstacles that keep them from communicating with the people on the shore? How does nature help the men communicate? *Possible answer: Nature presents two main obstacles to communication. First, the beach is "remote" (line 329) because the men have been kept from the shore by the surf. Second, the sound of the sea is loud, so shouting across the distance is not possible. But nature helps the men by providing a stick they can tie the towel to.*

FOR ADVANCED LEARNERS/AP

Analyze Dialogue [paired option] Have students list examples of punctuation and style in lines 319–367 in a Three-Column Journal. Then, ask pairs to discuss:

- the frequent use of exclamation points
- the difference between dashes and ellipses and how each affects spoken language
- the increasing informality of the language

Exclamation Points	Dashes/ Ellipses	Informality
"Look!"	Ellipses: Lines 335–336	"ain't" (line 361)
"There!"		mild oath
"Yes, sure!"	Dashes: Line 352	"idiot" (line 367)

Have students also consider how the lack of dialogue tags affects readers' understanding. Invite pairs to share their charts and analysis with the class.

 BEST PRACTICES TOOLKIT—Transparency
Three-Column Journal p. B10

Activity Ask students to try, as the men in the boat repeatedly had to do, to discern what is on the horizon at the top of the painting. Have pairs compare their descriptions. Then discuss why it is difficult to determine what is on the horizon and ask students what skills they must use to guess what the brown form in the center top is. *Possible answers: There appears to be a boat on the horizon. It is difficult to discern the image because it is small and blends in to the horizon. Viewers must refer to mental images of what a boat looks like and contrast the brown image with the colors of the surrounding sky and water in forming a guess about the brown object.*

About the Art Like the men in the boat, impressionist painter Edouard Manet (1832–1883) was fascinated by the endless motion of the sea and attempted to capture it in the short, broken brushstrokes of the impressionist style. Impressionists tried to capture the way light illuminated and reflected off objects, and the naturally reflective surface of the water gave them opportunities to perfect this technique.

The Escape of Henri de Rochefort, March 20, 1874 (1880–1881), Edouard Manet. Oil on canvas, 80 cm × 73 cm. Musée d'Orsay, Paris. © Bridgeman Art Library.

station up there."

370   "No! He thinks we're fishing. Just giving us a merry hand. See? Ah, there, Willie."

"Well, I wish I could make something out of those signals. What do you suppose he means?"

"He don't mean anything. He's just playing."

"Well, if he'd just signal us to try the surf again, or to go to sea and wait, or go north, or go south, or go to hell—there would be some reason in it. But look at him. He just stands there and keeps his coat revolving like a wheel. The ass!"

"There come more people."

"Now there's quite a mob. Look! Isn't that a boat?"

FOR STRATEGIC READERS

Comprehension Support Use these questions to help students understand the men's confusion as they try to interpret the waving from shore:

- What do the men hope the waving means?
- What possible meanings for the waving do some of the men suggest?
- How do the men respond to the waving man's ineffective communication?

FOR ENGLISH LEARNERS

Comprehension: Self–Monitor [shared language groups] Note and clarify difficult elements in lines 396–397: *Holy smoke,* an idiom; *impious,* a challenging word; *monkeying,* animal metaphor; *flounder,* animal metaphor. Remind students to use fellow English learners as resources for understanding. Then have groups paraphrase the lines.

380   "Where? Oh, I see where you mean. No, that's no boat."

"That fellow is still waving his coat."

"He must think we like to see him do that. Why don't he quit it. It don't mean anything."

"I don't know. I think he is trying to make us go north. It must be that there's a lifesaving station there somewhere."

"Say, he ain't tired yet. Look at 'im wave."

"Wonder how long he can keep that up. He's been revolving his coat ever since he caught sight of us. He's an idiot. Why aren't they getting men to bring a boat out. A fishing boat—one of those big yawls[16]—could come out here all right.

390 Why don't he do something?"

"Oh, it's all right, now."

"They'll have a boat out here for us in less than no time, now that they've seen us."

A faint yellow tone came into the sky over the low land. The shadows on the sea slowly deepened. The wind bore coldness with it, and the men began to shiver.

"Holy smoke!" said one, allowing his voice to express his impious mood, "if we keep on monkeying out here! If we've got to flounder out here all night!"

"Oh, we'll never have to stay here all night! Don't you worry. They've seen us now, and it won't be long before they'll come chasing out after us."

400   The shore grew dusky. The man waving a coat blended gradually into this gloom, and it swallowed in the same manner the omnibus and the group of people. The spray, when it dashed uproariously over the side, made the voyagers shrink and swear like men who were being branded. **K**

"I'd like to catch the chump who waved the coat. I feel like soaking him one, just for luck."

"Why? What did he do?"

"Oh, nothing, but then he seemed so damn cheerful."

In the meantime the oiler rowed, and then the correspondent rowed, and then the oiler rowed. Gray-faced and bowed forward, they mechanically, turn by turn,

410 plied the leaden oars. The form of the lighthouse had vanished from the southern horizon, but finally a pale star appeared, just lifting from the sea. The streaked saffron in the west passed before the all-merging darkness, and the sea to the east was black. The land had vanished, and was expressed only by the low and drear thunder of the surf.

"If I am going to be drowned—if I am going to be drowned—if I am going to be drowned, why, in the name of the seven mad gods who rule the sea, was I allowed to come thus far and contemplate sand and trees? Was I brought here merely to have my nose dragged away as I was about to nibble the sacred cheese of life?" **L**

420   The patient captain, drooped over the water jar, was sometimes obliged to speak to the oarsman.

16. **yawls:** sailboats with two masts.

THE OPEN BOAT   **725**

5 Targeted Passage

K DESCRIPTIVE LANGUAGE
What mood is established by the **description** in lines 394–403?

L NATURALISM
Reread lines 416–419. There is something almost comical about the repeated image of a man "about to nibble the sacred cheese of life." Why do you think Crane might have chosen to strike such a **tone** in reference to such a serious topic? Explain.

Lines 394–414
REINFORCE *KEY IDEA:* NATURE

Discuss In this passage, the men complete their first day in the boat. What new threats will **nature** pose as night arrives? *Possible answer: Night brings colder temperatures to the soaked, exhausted men (line 395). Their already limited vision will be cut even further as the shore and waving man disappear (lines 400–402). The darkness means that the men cannot see the waves to prepare for them (lines 402–403). They are cut off from sight of shore and thus from possible help (lines 413–414).*

READING SKILL

K DESCRIPTIVE LANGUAGE

Possible answer: The description of the man on shore establishes a mood of growing frustration as what seems like a good sign—the men in the boat have been sighted—turns out to be nothing but a man waving to a passing boat. The men cannot at first believe that the man on shore does not react to their plight, and as they wonder what the man is up to, they become aware that the sun is setting (lines 400–402). The cold water, which before had not bothered them, lashes them cruelly as their hope dies (lines 402–403).

LITERARY ANALYSIS

L NATURALISM

Possible answer: The humorous tone is ironic, highlighting the indifference of nature to the fate of the individual by suggesting that people are no more important to nature than a mouse. Crane uses this tone perhaps to emphasize the men's sense of injustice in their predicament.

FOR STRATEGIC READERS

5 Targeted Passage [Lines 400–414]

In this passage, the men grow weary and realize that help is not coming soon.

- Does the waving man get help for the stranded men?
- Why is it getting cold and dark?
- What are the conditions on the boat as night falls?

FOR ADVANCED LEARNERS/AP

Compare and Contrast Have students examine lines 304–318 and 408–414. Ask them to compare and contrast the oarsmen in both passages, considering the men's physical actions and mental condition, as well as the imagery Crane uses to describe these elements. Have students write two journal entries, one for each story passage. The entries should clarify how the men have changed in the elapsed time, and why.

THE OPEN BOAT   **725**

TIERED DISCUSSION PROMPTS

Use these prompts to help students understand the conditions in the little boat:

Restate What are the men doing? *Answer: They are huddled in the bottom of the boat, sleeping in uncomfortable positions. Only the person rowing is awake.*

Analyze What details suggest that the men's physical condition is deteriorating? In contrast, what does the passage reveal about their mental state? *Possible answer: The men are now so tired that they can no longer fight off sleep. They are hardly roused even by large waves crashing into the boat (lines 442–445) and the oiler actually falls asleep while rowing (lines 450–451). Mentally, however, the men have maintained a sense of dignity and compassion for each other. They speak politely and even "meekly" to each other (line 453).*

Synthesize Identify the repeated references to sleep that mark this passage. Has sleep become a friend or a foe to the men? What will happen if the men all fall asleep? *Possible answer: The author refers to sleep in lines 445, 448, 450–451, and 455–456. Sleep has become both friend and foe to the men. They desperately need rest, but any time the oarsman falls asleep, they are in greater danger than ever. If the men all fall asleep, the boat may drift out to sea and the men will likely die.*

"Keep her head up! Keep her head up!"

"'Keep her head up,' sir." The voices were weary and low.

This was surely a quiet evening. All save the oarsman lay heavily and listlessly in the boat's bottom. As for him, his eyes were just capable of noting the tall black waves that swept forward in a most sinister silence, save for an occasional subdued growl of a crest.

The cook's head was on a thwart, and he looked without interest at the water under his nose. He was deep in other scenes. Finally he spoke. "Billie," he 430 murmured, dreamfully, "what kind of pie do you like best?"

V

"Pie," said the oiler and the correspondent, agitatedly. "Don't talk about those things, blast you!"

"Well," said the cook, "I was just thinking about ham sandwiches, and—"

A night on the sea in an open boat is a long night. As darkness settled finally, the shine of the light, lifting from the sea in the south, changed to full gold. On the northern horizon a new light appeared, a small bluish gleam on the edge of the waters. These two lights were the furniture of the world. Otherwise there was nothing but waves.

Two men huddled in the stern, and distances were so magnificent in the dinghy 440 that the rower was enabled to keep his feet partly warmed by thrusting them under his companions. Their legs indeed extended far under the rowing seat until they touched the feet of the captain forward. Sometimes, despite the efforts of the tired oarsman, a wave came piling into the boat, an icy wave of the night, and the chilling water waked them anew. They would twist their bodies for a moment and groan, and sleep the dead sleep once more, while the water in the boat gurgled about them as the craft rocked.

The plan of the oiler and the correspondent was for one to row until he lost the ability, and then arouse the other from his seawater couch in the bottom of the boat.

450 The oiler plied the oars until his head drooped forward, and the overpowering sleep blinded him. And he rowed yet afterward. Then he touched a man in the bottom of the boat, and called his name. "Will you spell me for a little while?" he said, meekly.

"Sure, Billie," said the correspondent, awakening and dragging himself to a sitting position. They exchanged places carefully, and the oiler, cuddling down in the seawater at the cook's side, seemed to go to sleep instantly.

The particular violence of the sea had ceased. The waves came without snarling. The obligation of the man at the oars was to keep the boat headed so that the tilt of the rollers would not capsize her, and to preserve her from filling when the 460 crests rushed past. The black waves were silent and hard to be seen in the darkness. Often one was almost upon the boat before the oarsman was aware.

In a low voice the correspondent addressed the captain. He was not sure

---

DIFFERENTIATED INSTRUCTION

FOR ENGLISH LEARNERS

Related Vocabulary Lines 484–501 use many words and phrases that describe light and how it reflects on the shark's movement through the water. Help students locate these words and phrases, define them, and organize them in a word web. Point out that some of the words, such as *blue* and *bluish*, describe the color of the light, while others, such as *gleaming* and *crystalline*, describe the quality of the light. Students should locate these words and phrases:

- *gleaming trail of phosphorescence* (lines 484–485)
- *blue flame* (line 485)
- *long flash of bluish light* (line 489)
- *crystalline spray* (line 492)
- *long glowing trail* (line 492)
- *long sparkling streak* (line 498)

movement words: flame, spray, trail, streak

light

color words: blue, bluish

quality words: gleaming, flash, glowing, sparkling

that the captain was awake, although this iron man seemed to be always awake. "Captain, shall I keep her making for that light north, sir?"

The same steady voice answered him. "Yes. Keep it about two points off the port bow."[17]

The cook had tied a life belt around himself in order to get even the warmth which this clumsy cork contrivance could donate, and he seemed almost stovelike when a rower, whose teeth invariably chattered wildly as soon as he ceased his
470 labor, dropped down to sleep.

The correspondent, as he rowed, looked down at the two men sleeping under foot. The cook's arm was around the oiler's shoulders, and, with their fragmentary clothing and haggard faces, they were the babes of the sea, a grotesque rendering of the old babes in the wood.[18]

Later he must have grown stupid at his work, for suddenly there was a growling of water, and a crest came with a roar and a swash into the boat, and it was a wonder that it did not set the cook afloat in his life belt. The cook continued to sleep, but the oiler sat up, blinking his eyes and shaking with the new cold. **M**

"Oh, I'm awfully sorry, Billie," said the correspondent, contritely.
480 "That's all right, old boy," said the oiler, and lay down again and was asleep.

Presently it seemed that even the captain dozed, and the correspondent thought that he was the one man afloat on all the oceans. The wind had a voice as it came over the waves, and it was sadder than the end.

There was a long, loud swishing astern of the boat, and a gleaming trail of phosphorescence, like blue flame, was furrowed on the black waters. It might have been made by a monstrous knife.

Then there came a stillness, while the correspondent breathed with the open mouth and looked at the sea.

Suddenly there was another swish and another long flash of bluish light, and
490 this time it was alongside the boat, and might almost have been reached with an oar. The correspondent saw an enormous fin speed like a shadow through the water, hurling the crystalline spray and leaving the long glowing trail.

The correspondent looked over his shoulder at the captain. His face was hidden, and he seemed to be asleep. He looked at the babes of the sea. They certainly were asleep. So, being bereft of sympathy, he leaned a little way to one side and swore softly into the sea.

But the thing did not then leave the vicinity of the boat. Ahead or astern, on one side or the other, at intervals long or short, fled the long sparkling streak, and there was to be heard the whiroo of the dark fin. The speed and power of
500 the thing was greatly to be admired. It cut the water like a gigantic and keen projectile. **N**

The presence of this biding thing did not affect the man with the same horror that it would if he had been a picnicker. He simply looked at the sea dully and swore in an undertone.

---

17. **two points off the port bow:** two compass points, or a total of 45 degrees, to the left.

18. **babes in the wood:** a reference to an old nursery rhyme in which two children are abandoned in the woods and die there in the night.

M GRAMMAR AND STYLE
Reread lines 475–478. With his unusual use of the **gerund phrase** "a growling of water," Crane characterizes the sea as a wild or angry animal, emphasizing its danger.

N NATURALISM
Reread lines 484–501. What might the shark symbolize? Consider what this symbol contributes to the development of the **theme.**

M GRAMMAR AND STYLE

Analyze Description Clarify that a gerund is when the -*ing* form of a verb functions as a noun, as in "<u>Walking</u> is good exercise." A gerund phrase adds modifying words to the gerund, as in "<u>Walking two miles briskly</u> is good exercise." Ask students how Crane's use of the gerund phrase helps him to foreshadow events ahead. ***Possible answer: Portraying the water as a wild or angry animal foreshadows the shark that appears soon thereafter.*** Have students read lines 592–595 and identify the gerund phrase and its effect. ***Possible answer: The phrase is "a fresh soaking." This phrase again personifies the water as persistent.***

LITERARY ANALYSIS

N NATURALISM

Possible answer: The shark symbolizes both the power of the sea and the vulnerability of the men. The shark moves easily in its element. Waves do not threaten it (lines 500–501) while the men are at the risk of capsizing in any wave. This suggests that nature prefers the shark to the men, developing the theme of nature's indifference or hostility toward human life.

If students need help . . . Recall the definition and function of a symbol. Lead students to list the shark's qualities and what these suggest about it as a symbol.

FOR ADVANCED LEARNERS/AP

Analyze Understatement [small-group option] Ask students to define literary *understatement* and then locate three examples of this technique on page 727 (lines 479–480, 495–496, and 502–503). In small groups, have students consider for each example

- what the author understates and why

- what the use of understatement reveals about the men involved in the event

- how the understatement affects the pacing of the plot

- how the author's understatement relates to the naturalist tenet that nature is indifferent to the most terrible human plight

◉ NATURALISM

Possible answer: The tone of the third repetition is more desperate than the earlier repetitions. It is shorter, with no hint of humor and no personification of Fate. The tone has shifted from philosophical and reflective to bitter and angry.

If students need help . . . Refer them to the first two repetitions in lines 264–277 and 415–419. Point out the difference in the passage lengths. Then ask students what is missing from the third repetition and what this absence suggests about the outcry.

℗ NATURALISM

Possible answer: The author says that nature regards the individual as no more important or necessary than any single thing—a wave, a shark, a sunset, a mouse. This is not a nature that people can worship and admire. It is a nature that people want to smash.

If students need help . . . Clarify the reference to throwing "bricks at the temple" (line 520). Ask students why people normally go to a temple, and what it would mean if they suddenly wanted to damage the temple rather than worship in it.

Nevertheless, it is true that he did not wish to be alone with the thing. He wished one of his companions to awaken by chance and keep him company with it. But the captain hung motionless over the water jar and the oiler and the cook in the bottom of the boat were plunged in slumber.

VI

"If I am going to be drowned—if I am going to be drowned—if I am going to be
510 drowned, why, in the name of the seven mad gods who rule the sea, was I allowed to come thus far and contemplate sand and trees?" ◉

During this dismal night, it may be remarked that a man would conclude that it was really the intention of the seven mad gods to drown him, despite the abominable injustice of it. For it was certainly an abominable injustice to drown a man who had worked so hard, so hard. The man felt it would be a crime most unnatural. Other people had drowned at sea since galleys[19] swarmed with painted sails, but still—

When it occurs to a man that nature does not regard him as important, and that she feels she would not maim the universe by disposing of him, he at first
520 wishes to throw bricks at the temple, and he hates deeply the fact that there are no bricks and no temples. Any visible expression of nature would surely be pelleted with his jeers. ℗

Then, if there be no tangible thing to hoot he feels, perhaps, the desire to confront a personification and indulge in pleas, bowed to one knee, and with hands supplicant, saying: "Yes, but I love myself."

A high cold star on a winter's night is the word he feels that she says to him. Thereafter he knows the pathos of his situation.

The men in the dinghy had not discussed these matters, but each had, no doubt, reflected upon them in silence and according to his mind. There was
530 seldom any expression upon their faces save the general one of complete weariness. Speech was devoted to the business of the boat.

To chime the notes of his emotion, a verse mysteriously entered the correspondent's head. He had even forgotten that he had forgotten this verse, but it suddenly was in his mind.

> *A soldier of the Legion lay dying in Algiers,*
> *There was lack of woman's nursing, there was **dearth** of woman's tears;*
> *But a comrade stood beside him, and he took that comrade's hand,*
> *And he said: "I never more shall see my own, my native land."*[20]

In his childhood, the correspondent had been made acquainted with the fact
540 that a soldier of the Legion lay dying in Algiers, but he had never regarded it as important. Myriads of his schoolfellows had informed him of the soldier's plight, but the dinning had naturally ended by making him perfectly indifferent. He had never considered it his affair that a soldier of the Legion lay dying in Algiers, nor

---

19. **galleys:** large medieval ships propelled by sails and oars.
20. **A soldier . . . native land:** condensed first stanza of Caroline E. S. Norton's poem "Bingen on the Rhine." The Legion is the French Foreign Legion; Algiers is the capital city of the African nation Algeria.

◉ NATURALISM
What is the tone of this third repetition of the men's outcry against fate?

℗ NATURALISM
What does the author say about nature's regard for the individual in lines 518–522?

dearth (dûrth) *n.* lack

DIFFERENTIATED INSTRUCTION

FOR STRATEGIC READERS

Clarify Meanings Point out the word *pathos* in line 527. Explain that *pathos* is an emotion of sympathetic pity. In this situation, nature makes the man feel alone and unimportant because it does not acknowledge his existence. He feels great pity, or pathos, for himself. Then focus on the poem the correspondent recalls in lines 535–538, clarifying it to ensure that students will recognize the parallels between it and the correspondent's

situation. Make sure students understand that the soldier misses the comfort that women bring to the injured, that the soldier is not alone as he dies, and that the pronoun "he" in line 538 refers to the soldier, not to his comrade.

FOR ENGLISH LEARNERS

Conversational English Patterns Point out these two elliptical speeches: *Pretty long night* (lines 567–568); *Wish I had known you were awake* (line 572). Explain that people sometimes converse in incomplete thoughts, leaving out words that make sentences clear. Readers must then infer the missing words to get the sentences' meanings. Help students complete the lines.

had it appeared to him as a matter for sorrow. It was less to him than the breaking of a pencil's point.

Now, however, it quaintly came to him as a human, living thing. It was no longer merely a picture of a few throes in the breast of a poet, meanwhile drinking tea and warming his feet at the grate; it was actuality—stern, mournful, and fine.

The correspondent plainly saw the soldier. He lay on the sand with his feet out
550 straight and still. While his pale left hand was upon his chest in an attempt to thwart the going of his life, the blood came between his fingers. In the far Algerian distance, a city of low square forms was set against a sky that was faint with the last sunset hues. The correspondent, plying the oars and dreaming of the slow and slower movements of the lips of the soldier, was moved by a profound and perfectly impersonal comprehension. He was sorry for the soldier of the Legion who lay dying in Algiers.

The thing which had followed the boat and waited had evidently grown bored at the delay. There was no longer to be heard the slash of the cutwater,[21] and there was no longer the flame of the long trail. The light in the north still glimmered,
560 but it was apparently no nearer to the boat. Sometimes the boom of the surf rang in the correspondent's ears, and he turned the craft seaward then and rowed harder. Southward, some one had evidently built a watch fire on the beach. It was too low and too far to be seen, but it made a shimmering, roseate reflection upon the bluff back of it, and this could be discerned from the boat. The wind came stronger, and sometimes a wave suddenly raged out like a mountain-cat and there was to be seen the sheen and sparkle of a broken crest.

The captain, in the bow, moved on his water jar and sat erect. "Pretty long night," he observed to the correspondent. He looked at the shore. "Those lifesaving people take their time."
570 "Did you see that shark playing around?"

"Yes, I saw him. He was a big fellow, all right."

"Wish I had known you were awake."

Later the correspondent spoke into the bottom of the boat.

"Billie!" There was a slow and gradual disentanglement. "Billie, will you spell me?"

"Sure," said the oiler.

As soon as the correspondent touched the cold comfortable seawater in the bottom of the boat, and had huddled close to the cook's life belt he was deep in sleep, despite the fact that his teeth played all the popular airs. This sleep was so
580 good to him that it was but a moment before he heard a voice call his name in a tone that demonstrated the last stages of exhaustion. "Will you spell me?"

"Sure, Billie."

The light in the north had mysteriously vanished, but the correspondent took his course from the wide-awake captain.

Later in the night they took the boat farther out to sea, and the captain directed the cook to take one oar at the stern and keep the boat facing the seas. He was to

---

21. **cutwater:** the front part of a ship.

Q DESCRIPTIVE LANGUAGE

The description in lines 549–556 paints the correspondent's mental picture of the soldier in the poem. What does this **imagery** suggest about the correspondent's own plight?

Q DESCRIPTIVE LANGUAGE

Possible answer: The imagery suggests the correspondent's own torturous situation. Like the soldier trying to hold back his blood, the correspondent tries to hold back each wave. Like the soldier aware of the city's distant light, the correspondent views the coast and rescue as just out of reach. Both men are weakening gradually and becoming more likely to die.

If students need help . . . Help them complete a Two-Column Chart with details about the soldier and the correspondent.

Soldier	Correspondent
attempts to stop blood flow	attempts to fend off waves
can see city on horizon	can see shoreline in distance

 BEST PRACTICES TOOLKIT—Transparency
Two-Column Chart p. A25

Lines 557–566
TIERED DISCUSSION PROMPTS

Use these prompts to help students analyze the author's imagery:

Recall To what earlier event does Crane refer in lines 557–559? *Crane refers to the arrival of the shark.*

Analyze How does Crane describe the "thing" of line 557, and why does he not name it? *Possible answers: The author describes the shark's effects on the water—the sound it makes swimming and the trail it leaves behind—rather than the shark itself. Crane does not name the shark because it is more threatening as a nameless but powerful menace.*

Evaluate How well does Crane use images of light to create mood? Explain. *Accept all thoughtful responses.*

FOR ENGLISH LEARNERS

Vocabulary: Multiple-Meaning Words Guide students in using context to choose the correct meaning for each of these words:

- *matters* (line 528), "issues"
- *save* (line 530), "except"
- *craft* (line 561), "boat"
- *spell* (line 575), "take a turn so I can rest"
- *airs* (line 579), "songs"
- *course* (line 584), "path or route"

FOR STRATEGIC READERS

Clarify Time [paired option] In lines 567–582, the author compresses the passage of time. Help students figure out the chronology by highlighting the time jump between lines 577 and 582. Have them estimate the likely amount of elapsed time and record events on a Sequence Chain.

BEST PRACTICES TOOLKIT—Transparency
Sequence Chain p. B21

call out if he should hear the thunder of the surf. This plan enabled the oiler and the correspondent to get **respite** together. "We'll give those boys a chance to get into shape again," said the captain. They curled down and, after a few preliminary
590 chatterings and trembles, slept once more the dead sleep. Neither knew they had bequeathed to the cook the company of another shark, or perhaps the same shark.

As the boat caroused on the waves, spray occasionally bumped over the side and gave them a fresh soaking, but this had no power to break their repose. The ominous slash of the wind and the water affected them as it would have affected mummies.

"Boys," said the cook, with the notes of every reluctance in his voice, "she's drifted in pretty close. I guess one of you had better take her to sea again." The correspondent, aroused, heard the crash of the toppled crests.

As he was rowing, the captain gave him some whiskey and water, and this
600 steadied the chills out of him. "If I ever get ashore and anybody shows me even a photograph of an oar—"

At last there was a short conversation.

"Billie. . . . Billie, will you spell me?"

"Sure," said the oiler.

VII

When the correspondent again opened his eyes, the sea and the sky were each of the gray hue of the dawning. Later, carmine and gold was painted upon the waters. The morning appeared finally, in its splendor, with a sky of pure blue, and the sunlight flamed on the tips of the waves. **R**

On the distant dunes were set many little black cottages, and a tall white
610 windmill reared above them. No man, nor dog, nor bicycle appeared on the beach. The cottages might have formed a deserted village.

The voyagers scanned the shore. A conference was held in the boat. "Well," said the captain, "if no help is coming, we might better try a run through the surf right away. If we stay out here much longer we will be too weak to do anything for ourselves at all." The others silently **acquiesced** in this reasoning. The boat was headed for the beach. The correspondent wondered if none ever ascended the tall wind tower, and if then they never looked seaward. This tower was a giant, standing with its back to the plight of the ants. It represented in a degree, to the correspondent, the serenity of nature amid the struggles of the individual—nature
620 in the wind, and nature in the vision of men. She did not seem cruel to him then, nor beneficent, nor treacherous, nor wise. But she was indifferent, flatly indifferent. It is, perhaps, plausible that a man in this situation, impressed with the unconcern of the universe, should see the innumerable flaws of his life and have them taste wickedly in his mind and wish for another chance. A distinction between right and wrong seems absurdly clear to him, then, in this new ignorance of the grave edge, and he understands that if he were given another opportunity he would mend his conduct and his words, and be better and brighter during an introduction, or at a tea. **S**

respite (rĕs'pĭt) *n.* a period of rest or relief

R DESCRIPTIVE LANGUAGE
Note the change in mood. What descriptive language has been used to achieve this?

acquiesce (ăk'wē-ĕs') *v.* to comply or give in

G Targeted Passage

S NATURALISM
Reread lines 612–628. Which sentence in this paragraph do you think most effectively expresses the indifference of nature to the struggles of the individual? Explain.

READING SKILL

R DESCRIPTIVE LANGUAGE

Possible answer: The mood shifts to one of greater hope. The author uses color imagery to achieve this change in mood, for example, describing the sky as "pure blue" and the waters as golden (lines 606–608). Also, the time of day is symbolically significant as dawn often symbolizes the hope that a new day offers. Because this is a dawn of "splendor," that hope is greater.

Extend the Discussion What does the mood change suggest might happen next?

LITERARY ANALYSIS

S NATURALISM

Accept all reasonable answers. Some students may cite the sentence in which the lighthouse tower is compared to a giant and humans to ants as best expressing nature's indifference (lines 617–618). Others may cite the sentence following, in which the correspondent links the tower to nature amidst individual struggles (lines 618–620).

DIFFERENTIATED INSTRUCTION

FOR STRATEGIC READERS

G Targeted Passage [Lines 612–628]

This passage explores the men's choices and regrets as they face the prospect of death.

- What have the men decided they must do? Why?

- To what does the correspondent compare nature? What does he think of nature?

- What regrets does the correspondent have about his life?

FOR ENGLISH LEARNERS

Comprehension: Text Structure Help students complete a Two-Column Chart to explore the contrast in lines 617–620 between the correspondent's view of nature and reality. Discuss how people read meaning into natural events that actually have no intrinsic meaning.

BEST PRACTICES TOOLKIT—Transparency
Two-Column Chart p. A25

Correspondent's View	Reality
"The tower was a giant, standing with its back to . . ."	The tower is a tall, man-made structure and cannot turn its back on anything.
". . . the plight of the ants."	The "ants" are people. Smaller than the tower, they are still not powerless.

730   UNIT 4: REGIONALISM AND NATURALISM

Moonlit Shipwreck at Sea (1901), Thomas Moran. 30″ × 40 ¼″. © Christie's Images Limited.

"Now, boys," said the captain, "she is going to swamp sure. All we can do is to
630 work her in as far as possible, and then when she swamps, pile out and scramble
for the beach. Keep cool now, and don't jump until she swamps sure."

The oiler took the oars. Over his shoulders he scanned the surf. "Captain,"
he said, "I think I'd better bring her about, and keep her head-on to the seas and
back her in."

"All right, Billie," said the captain. "Back her in." The oiler swung the boat then
and, seated in the stern, the cook and the correspondent were obliged to look over
their shoulders to contemplate the lonely and indifferent shore.

The monstrous inshore rollers[22] heaved the boat high until the men were
again enabled to see the white sheets of water scudding up the slanted beach.
640 "We won't get in very close," said the captain. Each time a man could wrest his

---

22. **inshore rollers:** long waves swelling close to the shore.

ANALYZE VISUALS
In your opinion, how well
does this painting reflect
the men's situation?
Reread the description of
the waves on this page
and compare them to the
waves as portrayed by
the artist.

ANALYZE VISUALS

*Accept all reasonable responses. Students may
say that the painting's waves are darker than
those described in the text (line 639) but that
their "monstrous" height (line 638) is similar.*

About the Art As Crane does with words,
Thomas Moran attempts with visual images to
capture and describe the sound of the sea.

FOR ADVANCED LEARNERS/AP

Make Judgments Ask students to study the
critical passage in lines 612–628 and reflect
on the correspondent's many musings about
nature. Challenge them to draw conclusions
about the correspondent's final word on the
matter, and decide whether they agree with
it. Have students convey their conclusions in
a short opinion essay. Offer these questions
as a guide:

- Where does the correspondent finally stake
his claim—on nature's kindness, its cruelty,
or its nonengagement with humanity?

- How does the correspondent's conclusion
lead to regrets about his life?

- Is the correspondent's mental leap between
nature's involvement in his life and how he
wished he had lived logical?

ⓣ NATURALISM

Possible answer: *It is ironic that the correspondent worries about his fingers getting wet after having been soaked by the waves for many hours (lines 660–662). The boat, by contrast, seems to want to sink after the men's long effort to save it (lines 663–664). These ironies heighten the mood of anticipation as readers wait to learn if the men survive or die.*

If students need help . . . Clarify the definition of irony by asking them to recall a moment when they reacted to something in contrast to what would be expected.

Lines 669–683
TIERED DISCUSSION PROMPTS

Use these prompts to help students comprehend the men's dire situation:

Connect Have you heard the phrase "Out of the frying pan, into the fire"? What does it mean? *Accept all thoughtful responses.*

Analyze When the men are swept from the boat, how does their situation worsen? How does it also change for the better? Explain. *Possible answer: The men's situation worsens because they no longer have the boat to keep them afloat and must fight through the rough surf to land. Also, they are now on their own, unable to support each other. However, the men have decided to seize control of their ordeal and so are no longer at the mercy of the sea.*

Synthesize How might the advantages and disadvantages of seizing control be reflected in an attempt to face a challenge or to escape a danger? *Possible answer: Many situations offer the advantage of gaining control over difficulty or danger, but there is the risk of harm as a result of that control. For example, to take control and escape a fire, one might need to climb out a window.*

---

attention from the rollers, he turned his glance toward the shore, and in the expression of the eyes during this contemplation there was a singular quality. The correspondent, observing the others, knew that they were not afraid, but the full meaning of their glances was shrouded.

As for himself, he was too tired to grapple fundamentally with the fact. He tried to **coerce** his mind into thinking of it, but the mind was dominated at this time by the muscles, and the muscles said they did not care. It merely occurred to him that if he should drown it would be a shame.

There were no hurried words, no pallor, no plain agitation. The men simply
650 looked at the shore. "Now, remember to get well clear of the boat when you jump," said the captain.

Seaward the crest of a roller suddenly fell with a thunderous crash, and the long white comber[23] came roaring down upon the boat.

"Steady now," said the captain. The men were silent. They turned their eyes from the shore to the comber and waited. The boat slid up the incline, leaped at the furious top, bounced over it, and swung down the long back of the wave. Some water had been shipped and the cook bailed it out.

But the next crest crashed also. The tumbling boiling flood of white water caught the boat and whirled it almost perpendicular. Water swarmed in from all
660 sides. The correspondent had his hands on the gunwale at this time, and when the water entered at that place he swiftly withdrew his fingers, as if he objected to wetting them.

The little boat, drunken with this weight of water, reeled and snuggled deeper into the sea. ⓣ

"Bail her out, cook! Bail her out," said the captain.

"All right, Captain," said the cook.

"Now, boys, the next one will do for us, sure," said the oiler. "Mind to jump clear of the boat."

The third wave moved forward, huge, furious, implacable. It fairly swallowed
670 the dinghy, and almost simultaneously the men tumbled into the sea. A piece of life belt had lain in the bottom of the boat, and as the correspondent went overboard he held this to his chest with his left hand.

The January water was icy, and he reflected immediately that it was colder than he had expected to find it off the coast of Florida. This appeared to his dazed mind as a fact important enough to be noted at the time. The coldness of the water was sad; it was tragic. This fact was somehow so mixed and confused with his opinion of his own situation that it seemed almost a proper reason for tears. The water was cold.

When he came to the surface he was conscious of little but the noisy water.
680 Afterward he saw his companions in the sea. The oiler was ahead in the race. He was swimming strongly and rapidly. Off to the correspondent's left, the cook's great white and corked back bulged out of the water, and in the rear the captain was hanging with his one good hand to the keel of the overturned dinghy.

---

23. **comber:** a large wave that breaks on a beach.

coerce (kō-ûrs′) *v.* to force

ⓣ NATURALISM
What is **ironic** about the description of the correspondent and then the boat in lines 660–664? Consider the impact of this tone on these paragraphs.

DIFFERENTIATED INSTRUCTION

FOR ENGLISH LEARNERS
Vocabulary: Prefixes [small-group option]
Have students work in small groups to define these words:

- *overboard* (line 672), over—across, board—side of a boat
- *overturned* (line 683), over—across, turned—flipped
- *immovable* (line 684), im—not, movable—able to be moved
- *extraordinary* (line 699), extra—beyond, ordinary—the usual
- *undressing* (line 720), un—to remove, dress—clothing

For each word listed, groups should identify and define the prefix and root, then check the definition of the word in context.

There is a certain immovable quality to a shore, and the correspondent wondered at it amid the confusion of the sea.

It seemed also very attractive, but the correspondent knew that it was a long journey, and he paddled leisurely. The piece of life preserver lay under him, and sometimes he whirled down the incline of a wave as if he were on a hand sled.

But finally he arrived at a place in the sea where travel was beset with difficulty.
690 He did not pause swimming to inquire what manner of current had caught him, but there his progress ceased. The shore was set before him like a bit of scenery on a stage, and he looked at it and understood with his eyes each detail of it.

As the cook passed, much farther to the left, the captain was calling to him, "Turn over on your back, cook! Turn over on your back and use the oar."

"All right, sir." The cook turned on his back, and, paddling with an oar, went ahead as if he were a canoe.

Presently the boat also passed to the left of the correspondent with the captain clinging with one hand to the keel. He would have appeared like a man raising himself to look over a board fence, if it were not for the extraordinary gymnastics
700 of the boat. The correspondent marveled that the captain could still hold to it.

They passed on, nearer to shore—the oiler, the cook, the captain—and following them went the water jar, bouncing gaily over the seas.

The correspondent remained in the grip of this strange new enemy—a current. The shore, with its white slope of sand and its green bluff, topped with little silent cottages, was spread like a picture before him. It was very near to him then, but he was impressed as one who in a gallery looks at a scene from Brittany[24] or Holland.

He thought: "I am going to drown? Can it be possible? Can it be possible? Can it be possible?" Perhaps an individual must consider his own death to be the final phenomenon of nature. ○

710 But later a wave perhaps whirled him out of this small deadly current, for he found suddenly that he could again make progress toward the shore. Later still, he was aware that the captain, clinging with one hand to the keel of the dinghy, had his face turned away from the shore and toward him, and was calling his name. "Come to the boat! Come to the boat!"

In his struggle to reach the captain and the boat, he reflected that when one gets properly wearied, drowning must really be a comfortable arrangement, a cessation of hostilities accompanied by a large degree of relief, and he was glad of it, for the main thing in his mind for some moments had been horror of the temporary agony. He did not wish to be hurt.

720 Presently he saw a man running along the shore. He was undressing with most remarkable speed. Coat, trousers, shirt, everything flew magically off him.

"Come to the boat," called the captain.

"All right, Captain." As the correspondent paddled, he saw the captain let himself down to bottom and leave the boat. Then the correspondent performed his one little marvel of the voyage. A large wave caught him and flung him with

○ **NATURALISM**
Reread lines 707–709. How does the correspondent come to view death as he is faced with the prospect of drowning?

---

24. **Brittany:** a region in northwestern France.

LITERARY ANALYSIS

○ **NATURALISM**

Some students may say that the correspondent becomes somewhat detached from the prospect of drowning, as if it is just another natural event to observe. Others may say that he comes to think death represents the final reconciliation of the individual and nature.

If students need help . . . Remind them that naturalists believed human destiny was beyond the individual's control.

Extend the Discussion Why might people feel resignation at the edge of death? How does death's approach affect the human desire for life?

FOR ADVANCED LEARNERS/AP

Synthesize Refer students to the *Notable Quote* on page 710. Ask students to decide if the correspondent in the story shares the views expressed in the quote. Have them discuss the quote in light of the selection's final pages, focusing on these questions:

• In what new ways has the correspondent's experience with nature changed his vision of the world, as he describes in lines 689–692 and 703–706?

• How does the correspondent's vision of the world fit with the personal qualities that led him to be a reporter or storyteller? How does it fit the "eyes he was born with"?

• How do lines 707–709 reveal the quality of the correspondent's personal honesty?

• How does the correspondent's realization of nature's indifference, expressed in lines 612–628, prepare him for this final crisis?

Lines 725–728
REINFORCE *KEY IDEA:* NATURE

Discuss After deciding the sea is indifferent to his fate, why does the correspondent now consider the wave "a true miracle of the sea"? How might this experience affect his views about **nature**? *Possible answer: He considers the wave a miracle because after nearly killing him, the sea has saved him. He may reconsider his assessment of nature as indifferent or he may see this as further evidence of nature's randomness.*

SELECTION WRAP-UP

REFLECT Refer students to the explanation of naturalism in the historical essay (pages 622, 624), and ask them whether "The Open Boat" is entirely a naturalist piece of writing.

⭐ CRITIQUE

- Ask students to evaluate the story's ending and tell if they think it is a fitting end to the saga. Ask students how they would feel if the captain or the correspondent had not survived.

- After completing the After Reading questions on page 735, have students revisit their responses and tell whether they have changed their opinions.

---

ease and supreme speed completely over the boat and far beyond it. It struck him even then as an event in gymnastics, and a true miracle of the sea. An overturned boat in the surf is not a plaything to a swimming man.

730 The correspondent arrived in water that reached only to his waist, but his condition did not enable him to stand for more than a moment. Each wave knocked him into a heap, and the undertow pulled at him.

Then he saw the man who had been running and undressing, and undressing and running, come bounding into the water. He dragged ashore the cook, and then waded toward the captain, but the captain waved him away, and sent him to the correspondent. He was naked, naked as a tree in winter, but a halo was about his head, and he shone like a saint. He gave a strong pull, and a long drag, and a bully heave at the correspondent's hand. The correspondent, schooled in the minor formulæ, said: "Thanks, old man." But suddenly the man cried: "What's that?" He pointed a swift finger. The correspondent said: "Go."

740 In the shallows, face downward, lay the oiler. His forehead touched sand that was periodically, between each wave, clear of the sea.

⑦ Targeted Passage

The correspondent did not know all that transpired afterward. When he achieved safe ground he fell, striking the sand with each particular part of his body. It was as if he had dropped from a roof, but the thud was grateful to him.

It seems that instantly the beach was populated with men with blankets, clothes, and flasks, and women with coffeepots and all the remedies sacred to their minds. The welcome of the land to the men from the sea was warm and generous, but a still and dripping shape was carried slowly up the beach, and the land's welcome for it could only be the different and sinister hospitality of the grave.

750 When it came night, the white waves paced to and fro in the moonlight, and the wind brought the sound of the great sea's voice to the men on shore, and they felt that they could then be interpreters. ∾

DIFFERENTIATED INSTRUCTION

FOR STRATEGIC READERS
⑦ Targeted Passage [Lines 729–741]

This passage resolves the plot by explaining what becomes of the men.

- Why is reaching the shore not enough to save the correspondent?
- How is the correspondent saved?
- What happens to the oiler?

FOR ENGLISH LEARNERS
Language: Pronoun Referents Clarify the nouns or pronouns referenced by each of these pronouns:

- *It* (line 726), the wave tossing him to safety
- *he* (line 732), the correspondent
- *He* (line 733), the man from the shore
- *It* (line 745), the correspondent's experience
- *it* (line 749), the oiler's dead body
- *they* (line 752), the men on shore

FOR ADVANCED LEARNERS/AP
Make Inferences Ask students to discuss why the only named character is also the only character that dies. Have them use these questions to make inferences: Why might the author have withheld the other characters' names? How does the correspondent's pity for the death of the fictional Legion soldier of Algiers prepare readers for the oiler's death?

 BEST PRACTICES TOOLKIT—Transparency Making Inferences p. A13

Comprehension

1. **Recall** Which character in the story doesn't survive?

2. **Clarify** Why don't the men row the boat directly onto the beach?

3. **Clarify** Why don't the people on shore rescue the men?

Literary Analysis

4. **Draw Conclusions About Conflict** The sea is the great **antagonist** in Crane's story. Are the men saved primarily by their own efforts or by chance? Think about the following dangers the men face in the open boat and what they do to combat the dangers:

   - distance from shore
   - size of waves
   - sharks
   - exposure to weather
   - exhaustion

5. **Examine Naturalism** Reread lines 509–522 at the beginning of section VI, where the correspondent rails against the "abominable injustice" of **nature.** Is nature really unjust in the story? What characteristics of nature are suggested in these lines and in other places in the story?

6. **Examine Dramatic Irony** Naturalistic writers generally apply heavy doses of irony to express their worldview. Find two instances in "The Open Boat" in which the characters' perceptions don't match the reality of the situation. Then, explain how the two examples of irony contribute to Crane's naturalistic theme.

7. **Analyze Tone** The narrative voice of this story is quite detached, relating highly dramatic events with a mild and even slightly humorous tone. Find examples of this detachment. How does this tone affect the story's message or overall impact? Explain.

8. **Evaluate Descriptive Language** Identify the section of the story (a page or more) that you find most compelling. Now review the examples of descriptive elements that you recorded as you read. What role does descriptive writing play in this passage? How do you think the description affects your feelings about it? Cite details from the text to support your answer.

Literary Criticism

9. **Author's Style** One writer described Stephen Crane's stories as "intensely realistic." He attributed this realism to Crane's training as a reporter, saying "his English flow[s] simple and pure." Do you agree? Explain why or why not, citing evidence from the story to support your answer.

THE OPEN BOAT 735

8. ● **SKILLS FOCUS** Analyze Descriptive Language *Accept all well-analyzed section choices. In lines 34–42, Crane describes the boat's motion by comparing it to riding a bronco. He also uses vivid language to describe that motion, from "a leap from the air" to "slide, and race, and splash." This description stresses nature's unpredictability and creates a vivid image that makes the passage compelling.*

9. *Students who agree that Crane's realism derives from his journalistic training may cite Crane's strictly chronological text structure as realistic and related to newspaper reporting. Students who disagree may cite Crane's use of figurative language, such as his description of the shark as "a monstrous knife" (line 486), which detracts from a journalist's typical straightforward tone.*

Practice and Apply

After Reading

Use these copy masters to check understanding and provide extra support:

R RESOURCE MANAGER—Copy Masters
Reading Check p. 162
Naturalism p. 155
Question Support p. 163

Additional selection questions are provided for teachers on page 149.

ANSWERS

1. *The oiler, Billie, does not survive.*

2. *The strong surf will capsize the boat.*

3. *These people are not trained lifesavers, or they do not realize the men are in danger.*

Possible answers:

4. *The men's efforts to keep the boat afloat and their sense of brotherhood save them. Chance also plays a role: the shipwreck happens close to shore, weather is fair, and a wave pulls one man out of a deadly current. Past events also matter: the oiler may have drowned because he was exhausted from working a double shift.*

5. ● **SKILLS FOCUS** Naturalism *Nature is not unjust, "cruel . . . nor wise" (lines 620–621). Instead, the sea is as unfeeling as a "high cold star on a winter's night" (line 526). The story shows nature to be ultimately "indifferent" (line 622).*

6. *Ironic misperception occurs when those in the boat and on shore misunderstand each other. The men think a lifesaving station is near and wonder why the people do not organize a rescue. An ironic reversal is the strong, calm oiler's death. These ironies show that nature's unpredictability limits human ability to shape fate.*

7. *Examples of detachment include: "A singular . . . swamping boats" (lines 43–46); "Shipwrecks . . . eat heartily" (lines 189–194); "But the thing . . . projectile" (lines 497–501). The detached, mildly humorous tone stresses the naturalist theme that humans' fate rests with forces beyond our control. Even grim events are just factual and inevitable.*

ANSWERS

Vocabulary in Context

VOCABULARY PRACTICE

1. *(a) someone being robbed*

2. *(c) a show of anger*

3. *(a) polka dots with plaid*

4. *(b) a noisy argument*

5. *(c) a shortage of good ideas*

6. *(a) halftime at a game*

7. *(c) the habits of an eccentric*

8. *(b) a believer in fairy tales*

9. *(b) a scornful laugh*

10. *(a) an army's surrender*

R RESOURCE MANAGER—Copy Master
   Vocabulary Practice p. 160

VOCABULARY IN WRITING

- Help students locate three story scenes in which the correspondent reveals his feelings about the situation.

- Ask students to choose a word or words from the word list to describe these feelings.

- Point out that students now have a word and a scene outline to use as they write.

VOCABULARY STRATEGY: THE GREEK PREFIX
epi- *(also an EL language objective)*

- Help students use their knowledge of the root words and context clues to determine word meaning.

- For Item 2, point out other words that tell about skin, such as *dermatologist,* as an aid to comprehension.

Answers:

1. *epicenter*

2. *epidermis*

3. *epidemic*

R RESOURCE MANAGER—Copy Master
   Vocabulary Strategy p. 161

ⓘ Vocabulary Center at **ClassZone.com**
   Additional Vocabulary Activities

Vocabulary in Context

VOCABULARY PRACTICE

Choose the letter of the phrase that defines or is related to the boldfaced word.

1. **coerce:** (a) someone being robbed, (b) someone singing, (c) someone writing

2. **epithet:** (a) a sincere apology, (b) a two-handed card game, (c) a show of anger

3. **motley:** (a) polka dots with plaid, (b) a portrait of twins, (c) a thunderstorm

4. **obstreperous:** (a) a severe cold, (b) a noisy argument, (c) a lazy summer day

5. **dearth:** (a) a large fireplace, (b) a song played at funerals, (c) a shortage of good ideas

6. **respite:** (a) halftime at a game, (b) jealous anger, (c) paying back a debt

7. **aberration:** (a) a pilot in training, (b) a small city park, (c) the habits of an eccentric

8. **ingenuously:** (a) a sudden change in weather, (b) a believer in fairy tales, (c) a clever invention

9. **opprobrious:** (a) a clever comedian, (b) a scornful laugh, (c) a wildlife refuge

10. **acquiesce:** (a) an army's surrender, (b) a child's naptime, (c) a bird's piercing call

VOCABULARY IN WRITING

How did the correspondent's attitude about his situation change through the story? Using three or more vocabulary words, describe the changes in his state of mind. You could start like this.

> **EXAMPLE SENTENCE**
> The correspondent experienced a fair range of emotions, but ultimately he seemed willing to **acquiesce** to the sea.

R1.2

VOCABULARY STRATEGY: THE GREEK PREFIX *epi-*

The vocabulary word *epithet* contains the Greek prefix *epi-,* which means "upon," "among," or "in addition." This prefix is found in a number of English words, both scientific and nonscientific. To understand words with *epi-,* look for context clues and also use your knowledge of the meaning of the prefix.

PRACTICE Choose the word from the word web that best completes each sentence. Consider what you know about the Greek prefix and the other word parts shown. If necessary, consult a dictionary.

1. The _____ of the earthquake was 200 miles from the city.

2. The top layer of skin in humans is called the _____.

3. The _____ spread illness and disease throughout the region.

➤ VOCABULARY PRACTICE
For more practice, go to the **Vocabulary Center** at **ClassZone.com.**

DIFFERENTIATED INSTRUCTION

FOR ENGLISH LEARNERS

Task Support: Vocabulary Practice Point out that although *epi-* is a Greek prefix, it was borrowed into Latin and appears in Romance languages such as Spanish. Students may know cognates for words beginning with *epi-* in their home languages, for example, *epithet/epíteto* and *epidemic/epidemia.*

FOR ADVANCED LEARNERS/AP

Vocabulary in Writing Have students write a definition of *naturalism* using appropriate vocabulary words. Suggest that they use their description of the correspondent's changing attitude toward his situation as a starting point.

Reading-Writing Connection

W1.2, W2.2

WRITING PROMPT

WRITE A CHARACTER SKETCH The sea in "The Open Boat" is the most compelling character in the story. It is more fully described than any of the four humans in the boat. Crane frequently uses **personification,** a figure of speech in which an object is given human characteristics, in order to describe the sea.

Write a **three-paragraph character sketch** of the sea in "The Open Boat." You might look through the story for examples of personification to form the basis of your character sketch.

SELF-CHECK

A successful character sketch will . . .

• characterize the sea as a human being

• describe how the sea is perceived by the human characters

• give examples, quotations, and other evidence from the story to support your interpretation

GRAMMAR AND STYLE

LC1.1

USE EFFECTIVE DESCRIPTION Review the **Grammar and Style** note on page 727. Crane uses gerunds and gerund phrases in some unusual ways, creating energetic phrases and sentences. A **gerund** is a verb form that ends in -*ing* and functions as a noun. A **gerund phrase** includes a gerund and its modifiers and complements. In this example from "The Open Boat," notice how "snarling of the crests" functions as a noun in the sentence:

> *There was a terrible grace in the move of the waves, and they came in silence, save for the snarling of the crests.* (lines 51–52)

The gerund emphasizes the action of the waves more than the simple noun *snarl* would. It's a subtle difference that, when used strategically in your writing, can have a cumulative impact.

PRACTICE Rewrite each of the following sentences so that it contains a gerund phrase. You may want to change an existing verb into a gerund or add an entirely new idea. (Remember that a participial phrase, which also uses the -*ing* form of a verb, is used as an adjective, whereas a gerund phrase is used as a noun.)

> **EXAMPLE**
>
> The sun sank gradually, and their hearts sank soon after.
> *The gradual sinking of the sun was followed by the sinking of their hearts.*

1. The surf roared, announcing the nearness of the shore.

2. The gulls cried and gave voice to their own despair.

3. The men looked warily at the shark fin as it coolly sliced the water.

WRITING TOOLS
For prewriting, revision, and editing tools, visit the **Writing Center** at ClassZone.com.

THE OPEN BOAT   **737**

FOR DEVELOPING WRITERS

Writing Support

• Limit the length of the sketch to one or two paragraphs.

• Provide sentences that model how to incorporate textual support with correct punctuation and citation format. Review the rules for quoting, paraphrasing, and summarizing text.

• Provide a starter sentence: In Stephen Crane's short story "The Open Boat," the sea is a _____ character and interacts with the human characters.

Reading-Writing Connection

WRITING PROMPT

Guide students to gather and organize information for their paragraphs by using a Character Traits and Textual Evidence chart. Students may skim the story for material or refer to their notes and to the marginal annotations to focus on likely passages.

📦 BEST PRACTICES TOOLKIT—Transparency
Character Traits and Textual Evidence p. D6

For writing support, see

ℹ️ Writing Center at **ClassZone.com**

GRAMMAR AND STYLE

Help students distinguish between gerund and participial -*ing* forms by asking them to write a pair of sentences for reference. Provide these sentences as models:

• *I enjoy playing guitar.* Here, *playing* is a gerund that is the object of the verb *enjoy*.

• *The playing puppy collapsed.* Here, *playing* is a participle that modifies *puppy*.

(For more on gerunds and gerund phrases, see **Grammar Handbook,** page R66.)

Possible answers:

1. *The roaring of the surf announced the nearness of the shore.*

2. *The gulls' crying gave voice to their own despair.*

3. *The men looked warily at the cool slicing of the shark's fin through the water.*

R RESOURCE MANAGER—Copy Master
Use Effective Description p. 164

Assess and Reteach

Assess

R RESOURCE MANAGER—Copy Masters
Selection Test A pp. 165–166
Selection Test B/C pp. 167–168

💿 Test Generator CD

Reteach

S STANDARDS LESSON FILE
Literature Lesson 26: Imagery
Literature Lesson 27: Simile and Metaphor
Literature Lesson 36: Irony
Writing Lesson 21: Descriptive Writing
Vocabulary Lesson 2: Prefixes

THE OPEN BOAT   **737**

Focus and Motivate

OBJECTIVES

Reading for Information
- analyze primary sources
- compare forms
- read newspaper articles

CALIFORNIA R3.3, LS1.1, LS1.14

SUMMARY

In these newspaper articles, reporters and survivors of the wreck of the *Commodore* inform the public of the details and losses of the accident and praise its heroes. The articles appear over a period of five days, during which more facts and stories come to light. The final article, by Crane himself, gives the fullest account of the accident.

Use a KWL (Know, Want to Know, Learned) chart to prepare students for reading. In the first column, have students recall what they already know about the wreck of the *Commodore* from "The Open Boat." In the second column, have them write questions about what they want to know. After reading, have students complete the chart with what they have learned about the wreck.

> **BEST PRACTICES TOOLKIT—Transparency**
> KWL p. A21

Teach

Skill Focus: Analyze Primary Sources

- Remind students that primary sources are materials created by people who were present at events, either as participants or observers. Such sources provide direct, first-hand knowledge about an event or person, which can help readers understand an event and its participants as close observers did.

- Ask students to consider to what extent they can assume that a primary source is accurate, and remind them that sometimes eyewitnesses to and even participants in the event may not remember or report details accurately.

> **RESOURCE MANAGER—Copy Master**
> Analyze Primary Sources p. 177

Reading for Information

The Wreck of the *Commodore*
Newspaper Articles

"The Open Boat" was based on Stephen Crane's experience with the wreck of the *Commodore*, a ship on a private mission to arm rebels fighting in the Cuban civil war. Crane had joined these filibusters, as these men were known, in search of adventure and a good story. When the ship went down, however, he acted as far more than a journalist. You'll now read news stories about this sensational event, including an account by Crane himself.

Use with "The Open Boat," page 712.

CALIFORNIA R3.3, LS1.1, LS1.14

Skill Focus: Analyze Primary Sources

The 1897 articles about the wreck of the *Commodore* are **primary sources** of information on that event. You can also look to them as evidence of the kind of writing that appeared in newspapers of the day. As you read each article, make notes about your impressions of it. Keep the following questions in mind:

- Who is the intended **audience**?
- What techniques are used to capture the readers' interest?
- What is the **tone** of the piece?
- What is its **scope** and **focus**? In other words, how much is covered, and what in the piece is most important?
- How much **imagery** or other colorful language does it contain?
- How does the piece differ from something you might find in a newspaper today?

Note your observations and impressions in a chart such as this one.

"The Commodore Sinks at Sea"	"More of the Filibusters Safe"	"Stephen Crane and His Work"	"Stephen Crane's Own Story"
lots of stacked headlines			

738 UNIT 4: REGIONALISM AND NATURALISM

Selection Resources

RESOURCE MANAGER UNIT 4

Plan and Teach pp. 169–173

Reading
Summary pp. 175†*, 176‡*
Analyze Primary Sources pp. 177, 179†*
Compare Forms pp. 178, 180†*
Reading Check p. 181
Question Support p. 182*

Assessment
Selection Tests A, B/C pp. 183*, 185*

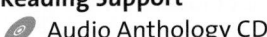 Test Generator CD

Reading Support
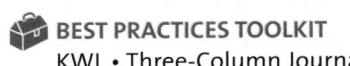 Audio Anthology CD*

> **BEST PRACTICES TOOLKIT**
> KWL • Three-Column Journal

---

* Resources for Differentiation   † Also in Spanish   ‡ In Haitian Creole and Vietnamese

THE FLORIDA TIMES-UNION

SUNDAY, JANUARY 3, 1897   PRICE 5 CENTS.

THE COMMODORE SINKS AT SEA

The Little Vessel Lost with Her Cargo of Arms and Ammunition

HER NUMEROUS COMPANY REACH LAND IN SAFETY

They are Compelled to Take to the Boats and Abandon the Sinking Vessel

An Overload of Coal the Probable Cause ⓐ

THE STEAMER COMMODORE, which left here Thursday night with an expedition for the Cuban insurgents, is now resting on the bottom of the sea, twenty fathoms below the surface, about eighteen miles northeast of Mosquito Inlet.

All of the men on the vessel, twenty-eight in number, reached the
10 shore in safety, and twelve of them arrived in Jacksonville last night over the Florida East Coast railway. The other sixteen are still down the coast, but are expected to arrive here on a special train this morning. . . .

DETAILS OF THE ACCIDENT

About 12 o'clock Friday night it was discovered that the boat was leaking badly. The swash of the water in the hold as the vessel rolled from side to side
20 soon alarmed everyone on board. A panic ensued, but Captain Murphy, Stephen Crane, R. A. Delgado and one or two others soon quieted the excitement and put everybody to work on the pumps and with buckets. The steam pump was started and for two hours the water was poured over the sides in streams.

At 2:30 A.M., it was seen that the
30 water was steadily gaining, and it was decided to abandon the vessel.

IN THE BOATS

Paul Rojo, R. A. Delgado, Franco Blanco, the old Cuban pilot, and nine other men took one of the boats and left the steamer. Captain Murphy, the first and second mate, the engineer and assistant, Stephen Crane and ten men took the large yawl boat, and at 3 o'clock they left the Commodore to
40 her fate. The night was dark and they could not see what became of her, but as she was rapidly filling with water, they are all confident that she is now resting on the bottom, and old Neptune has been supplied with enough arms and ammunition to blow up the island of Cuba. . . . ⓑ

ⓐ **PRIMARY SOURCES**
Compare these headlines with those in papers today. Why do you think there are so many?

ⓑ **PRIMARY SOURCES**
Reread lines 43–47. What does the writer mean by this comment?

READING FOR INFORMATION   **739**

INFORMATIONAL ANALYSIS

ⓐ PRIMARY SOURCES

Possible answer: Today's papers have at most a headline and a subhead. This article has a headline, three small subheads, and a subhead in capital letters. These heads serve as an outline of the most important details about the accident. Students may say that there were many headlines because the event was hugely interesting or because this was one way to sell newspapers.

If students need help . . . Bring in a current newspaper so that students have a model for comparison with the 1897 articles.

INFORMATIONAL ANALYSIS

ⓑ PRIMARY SOURCES

Possible answer: The writer means that the arms and ammunition meant for rebels in Cuba are now on the sea floor.

Extend the Discussion What is the effect of alluding to Neptune in these lines?

BACKGROUND

Neptune According to Roman mythology, Neptune was the god of the sea. Greek myths give the name Poseidon to the same figure. Neptune was the son of Saturn, and brother to Jupiter and Pluto.

DIFFERENTIATED INSTRUCTION

FOR STRATEGIC READERS
Vocabulary Support

- *fathoms* (line 5), "a unit of length used to measure depth of water"

- *swash* (line 18), "the motion of water splashing and the sound this makes"

- *hold* (line 19), "the area below the deck of a ship where cargo is carried"

- *ensued* (line 21), "happened next or as a result of"

- *gaining* (line 30), "rising"

FOR ENGLISH LEARNERS

Options for Reading Use a directed reading strategy to guide students' reading. Review with them that their reading purpose is to gather information that explains and expands on the events in "The Open Boat." Then have students read each article one subsection at a time. After they complete each subsection, confirm comprehension by asking students to summarize.

C PRIMARY SOURCES

Possible answer: The writer of this article chose to quote the cook at length as a way of assuring readers that he has not told any "awful woppers."

If students need help . . . Point out that direct quotation brings an exciting event to life for readers. Discuss what the cook's quotation tells readers that simple description would not.

Extend the Discussion Were you surprised to find the cook so talkative, given how many lines of dialogue he has in the story? Explain.

D PRIMARY SOURCES

Possible answer: The editors chose to emphasize Crane's publishing credits and foreign correspondence work because they are thrilled to be able to claim a fellow writer as a hero.

If students need help . . . Help them identify the article's tone as more speculative and boastful than straightforward and factual.

C PRIMARY SOURCES
Note that this article consists entirely of a quotation by the cook. Why do you think the writer of this article chose to quote him at such length?

D PRIMARY SOURCES
This paper portrays Crane as quite a hero, citing his bravery and pluck. In this article, why do you think the editors have chosen to make so much of his "Cuban letters," or his work as a foreign correspondent?

The New York Press

MONDAY, JANUARY 4, 1897   SECTION 1

MORE OF THE FILIBUSTERS SAFE

STEPHEN CRANE, NOVELIST, SWIMS ASHORE

DAYTONA, Fla., Jan. 3.—"That newspaper feller was a nervy man," said the cook of the ill-fated Commodore to-night in reference to Stephen Crane, the novelist, who is after material for stories. "He didn't seem to know what fear was. When we started out he insisted upon doing a seaman's work, and he did it well, too.

"When the boats were launched he was the last one, except Captain Murphy, to get in, and his nerve greatly encouraged all hands. In the small dingy he rowed as well as the others, notwithstanding he was so worn out that he could hardly hold his oar straight in the terrific seas.

SAVES A DROWNING MAN

"Both he and Captain Murphy were thrown out on the same side. Crane was partially thrown under the overturned boat and but for Captain Murphy's readiness in catching him by the collar he would have gone under. We all battled there in the water for hours, it seemed to us. Crane was a good swimmer, and he really saved one of the sailors, as the man could not swim a stroke, and Crane had to keep him up by the aid of an oar. These newspaper fellers have got spunk, if they do tell such awful woppers at times," concluded the cook, as he took another big swig of the "life preservative" provided by the good people here. . . . **C**

STEPHEN CRANE AND HIS WORK
How He Came to Be on the Unlucky Commodore
TO WRITE FOR THE PRESS
Brilliant Author Not of the Sort to Give Up His Cuban Letters Because of Shipwreck

STEPHEN CRANE, the writer, is safe and readers of The Press may expect in a short time a treat from his versatile pen. . . .

Mr. Crane was on the way to Cuba to write about the war there. He will get to Cuba as soon as he can. He is not of the sort who are frightened by an experience in a lifeboat. His letters will appear in The Press as soon as they arrive.

Mr. Crane has not intimated just what he is going to write; probably he does not know himself. But that his letters will be intensely interesting and true to life readers of his stories, "The Red Badge of Courage," "The Third Violet," "George's Mother" and "Maggie, a Girl of the Streets," feel assured. **D**

DIFFERENTIATED INSTRUCTION

FOR STRATEGIC READERS
Concept Support: Analyze Primary Sources
[small-group option] Have students add to the chart introduced on page 738, listing details of the wreck as the cook recalls them and answering the other bulleted questions on page 738.

"More of the Filibusters Safe"	"Stephen Crane and His Work"
Audience: readers of New York Press	**Audience**: readers of New York Press
Techniques: long quotation	**Techniques**: details about Crane's talent and fame
Imagery: Crane thrown overboard	**Imagery**: little

FOR ENGLISH LEARNERS
Language: Conversational English Patterns
[shared-language groups] Explain that *feller* (line 2) is slang for "fellow" or "man." Discuss what slang is and ask students to share appropriate examples from their home language. Then help them use context to define the cook's slang: *nervy* (line 2), "brave"; *spunk* (line 30), "spirit, liveliness"; *awful woppers* (line 31), "elaborate lies."

The New York Press

THURSDAY, JANUARY 7, 1897   SECTION 1

STEPHEN CRANE'S OWN STORY

JACKSONVILLE, FLA., Jan. 6.—It was the afternoon of New Year's. The *Commodore* lay at her dock in Jacksonville and negro stevedores processioned steadily toward her with box after box of ammunition and bundle after bundle of rifles. Her hatch, like the mouth of a monster, engulfed them. It might have been the feeding
10 time of some legendary creature of the sea. It was in broad daylight and the crowd of gleeful Cubans on the pier did not forbear to sing the strange patriotic ballads of their island. . . . The revenue cutter *Boutwell*, the old isosceles triangle that protects United States interests in the St. John's, lay at anchor, with no sign of excitement aboard her. **E**

SLEEP IMPOSSIBLE

As darkness came upon the waters,
20 the *Commodore* was a broad, flaming path of blue and silver phosphorescence, and as her stout bow lunged at the great black waves she threw flashing, roaring cascades to either side. And all that was to be heard was the rhythmical and mighty pounding of the engines.

THE COOK IS HOPEFUL

The cook was asleep on a bench in the galley. He woke as I entered the galley and delivered himself of some
30 dolorous sentiments: "I don't feel right about this ship, somehow. It strikes me that something is going to happen to us. I don't know what it is, but the old ship is going to get it in the neck, I think."

Author Stephen Crane

"Well, how about the men on board of her?" said I. "Are any of us going to get out, prophet?"

"Yes," said the cook. "Sometimes I have these damned feelings come over
40 me, and they are always right, and it seems to me, somehow, that you and I will both get [out] and meet again somewhere, down at Coney Island, perhaps, or some place like that."

Here I first came to know a certain young oiler named Billy Higgins. He was sloshing around this inferno filling buckets with water and passing them to a chain of men that extended up the
50 ship's side.

A WHISTLE OF DESPAIR

Now the whistle of the *Commodore* had been turned loose, and if there ever was a voice of despair and death, it was in the voice of this whistle. It had gained a new tone. It was as if its throat was already choked by the water, and this cry on the sea at night, with a wind blowing

continued

E PRIMARY SOURCES
Note that this article is written by Crane himself. How, if at all, has the style of writing changed from that in the previous articles? Explain.

Lines 1–26
TIERED DISCUSSION PROMPTS

Use these prompts to help students consider the language Crane uses to describe the *Commodore*:

Summarize What activities are described in these lines? *The* Commodore *is loaded with its cargo and departs on its trip.*

Analyze What descriptive techniques does Crane use to help readers visualize the ship? What senses does he emphasize? What visual associations does he draw? ***Possible answer:** Crane uses simile (lines 7–11) to characterize the ship as large and strong. He uses sensory details (lines 19–26) to help readers hear and see the ship move through the water. He emphasizes the sounds of the water being displaced by the bow and of the constantly running engines. Crane also associates the generally positive colors of blue and silver with the ship (line 21).*

Evaluate How well does Crane succeed in casting the ship as a heroic character in this adventure? ***Possible answer:** Although the image of the ship as a hungry monster is not attractive, the description of the ship in lines 19–26 is exciting and heroic.*

INFORMATIONAL ANALYSIS

E PRIMARY SOURCES

Possible answer: *Crane's style is more story-like than the more straightforward journalistic tone in the first two articles and less formal than the style of the third article. He uses descriptive and figurative language, as he does in "The Open Boat."*

FOR ADVANCED LEARNERS/AP

Analyze Figurative Language Have students write an essay analyzing how Crane uses figurative language to create mood and establish tone. Urge them to begin by completing a Three-Column Journal or other graphic organizer with examples of figurative language in the article. Ask students to share their organizers and analysis with the class.

Simile	Sensory Language	Metaphor
"like the mouth of a monster"	"blue and silver phosphorescence"	"a chain of men"

🧰 BEST PRACTICES TOOLKIT—Transparency
Three-Column Journal p. B10

F PRIMARY SOURCES

Possible answer: *In lines 19–26, Crane uses imagery of the boat as a moving light and a powerful force that carves through water. In lines 51–63, Crane uses the image of the boat as a living thing crying out in loss. The mood in the early lines is one of power and hope, while in the later lines the mood has shifted to loss and grief.*

G PRIMARY SOURCES

Possible answer: *According to lines 89–102, the men still aboard the ship drowned. The captain could not get the boat close enough to let the stranded men board without endangering the three men with him, and the extra weight probably would have swamped the boat as well had he tried to.*

If students need help . . . Students may be confused because the first article claims that all hands were rescued (lines 8–10). Clarify that the first article was written four days earlier, before all the information about the accident was available.

H PRIMARY SOURCES

Possible answer: *Crane adopts a tone of admiration for Kitchell, while entirely omitting his own bravery. Crane's tone likely makes readers believe his accounting as accurate because it does not flatter him.*

F **PRIMARY SOURCES**
Reread lines 51–63. Identify the **imagery** used to characterize the *Commodore*. What **mood** does Crane achieve with this language?

G **PRIMARY SOURCES**
Reread lines 81–102. What happened to the men still aboard the ship?

H **PRIMARY SOURCES**
What **tone** does Crane adopt in the last paragraph? Explain how this tone affects your perception of these events.

JANUARY 7, 1897   THE NEW YORK PRESS   SECTION 1

the spray over the ship, and the waves roaring over the bow, and swirling white
60 along the decks, was to each of us probably a song of man's end. The boat moved at last and swung down toward the water. **F**

IN THE TEN-FOOT DINGY

The captain was just about to swing over the rail when a dark form came forward and a voice said: "Captain, I go with you."

The captain answered: "Yes, Billy; get in."

HIGGINS LAST TO LEAVE SHIP

70 It was Billy Higgins, the oiler. Billy dropped into the boat and a moment later the captain followed, bringing with him an end of about forty yards of lead line. The other end was attached to the rail of the ship.

As we swung back to leeward the captain said: "Boys, we will stay right near the ship till she goes down."

This cheerful information, of course,
80 filled us all with glee.

When came the gray shade of dawn, the form of the Commodore grew slowly clear to us as our little ten-foot boat rose over each swell. She was floating with such an air of buoyancy that we laughed when we had time, and said "What a gag it would be on those other fellows if she didn't sink at all."

But later we saw men aboard of her,
90 and later still they began to hail us.

We rowed back to the ship, but did not approach too near, because we were four men in a ten-foot boat, and we knew that the touch of a hand on our gunwale would assuredly swamp us. . . .

THE COMMODORE SINKS

The cook let go of the line. We rowed around to see if we could not get a line from the chief engineer, and

all this time, mind, there were no
100 shrieks, no groans, but silence, silence and silence, and then the Commodore sank. **G**

She lurched to windward, then swung afar back, righted and dove into the sea, and rafts were suddenly swallowed by this frightful maw of the ocean. And then by the men of the ten-foot dingy were words said that were still not words—something far beyond
110 words.

The lighthouse of Mosquito Inlet stuck up above the horizon like the point of a pin. We turned our dingy toward the shore.

The history of life in an open boat for thirty hours would no doubt be instructive for the young, but none is to be told here and now. For my part I would prefer to tell the story at once,
120 because from it would shine the splendid manhood of Captain Edward Murphy and of William Higgins, the oiler, but let it suffice at this time to say that when we were swamped in the surf and making the best of our way toward the shore the captain gave orders amid the wildness of the breakers as clearly as if he had been on the quarter deck of a battleship.

130 John Kitchell of Daytona came running down the beach, and as he ran the air was filled with clothes. If he had pulled a single lever and undressed, even as the fire horses harness, he could not seem to me to have stripped with more speed. He dashed into the water and dragged the cook. Then he went after the captain, but the captain sent him to me, and then it was that he saw Billy
140 Higgins lying with his forehead on sand that was clear of the water, and he was dead. **H**

STEPHEN CRANE

DIFFERENTIATED INSTRUCTION

FOR STRATEGIC READERS

Clarify Meaning Point out and clarify the ironic statements that occasionally surface in Crane's narrative. In lines 79–80, for example, the men in the boat receive the "cheerful information" with anything but glee. In lines 107–110, the men speak words that are not words because there are no words sufficient to describe what they feel about the disaster.

FOR ENGLISH LEARNERS

Vocabulary: Multiple-Meaning Words Share or elicit the usual meanings of these words. Then help students use context to build appropriate meaning:

- *lead* (line 73), "a rope used to control something, like a leash"
- *shade* (line 81), "color"
- *air* (line 85), "spirit or mood"
- *gag* (line 87), "joke or trick"
- *dove* (line 104), "past tense of *dive*"

Comprehension

1. **Clarify** Over how many days did these articles appear in the newspapers?

2. **Summarize** What happened to the *Commodore* and her crew?

Critical Analysis

3. **Examine Text Features** Review the headlines of these articles. Consider their content and number. What **tone** do they convey? Explain.

4. **Analyze Primary Sources** Consider the headlines, contents, and tone of the articles. Based on these examples, what general statements might you make about 19th-century journalism? Cite evidence to support your generalization.

Read for Information: Compare Forms

 R3.3, LS1.1, LS1.14

WRITING PROMPT

In Stephen Crane's article about the wreck of the *Commodore*, he wrote:

The history of life in an open boat for thirty hours would no doubt be instructive for the young, but none is to be told here and now. . . . I would prefer to tell the story at once, because from it would shine the splendid manhood of Captain Edward Murphy and of William Higgins, the oiler.

Based on your reading of "The Open Boat" and "Stephen Crane's Own Story," why might Crane have reserved the tale of the open boat for a short story? What does he do with the short story that he can't or doesn't do in the article?

The following steps will help you answer the prompt:

1. Compare the short story and the article, considering the following elements:

	Article	Short Story
Audience and Purpose	to describe shipwreck for newspaper readers	
Character Development		
Coverage of Events		
Imagery and Figurative Language		
Theme and Main Idea		

2. Based on this comparison, consider why Crane may have made the choices he did in writing each piece.

3. Finally, try to explain Crane's decision to write "The Open Boat" by evaluating the strengths of the short story over the article. Support your ideas with details from each text.

FOR STRATEGIC READERS

Read for Information

- Direct students to complete the chart first for just the article, and then for just the short story alone, addressing one piece at a time.

- Urge them to consider the process in Step 2 piece by piece as well. This process will allow them to gain mastery of each piece before proceeding to the more complex task of comparing the two pieces.

FOR ADVANCED LEARNERS/AP

Analyze Author's Purpose After students have completed the writing exercise, challenge them to debate whether "The Open Boat" is in fact "instructive for the young," as Crane says it "would no doubt" be (last article, lines 115–117). After the debate, invite students to present the consensus of the group to the whole class.

Practice and Apply

After Reading

Use these copy masters to check understanding and provide extra support:

R RESOURCE MANAGER—Copy Masters
Reading Check p. 181
Question Support p. 182
Compare Forms p. 178

Additional selection questions are provided for teachers on page 172.

ANSWERS

1. *The articles appeared over five days, from January 3rd through January 7th.*

2. *The* Commodore *sank and many of her crew drowned. Crane and three other men escaped in a small dinghy. After 30 hours, they reached shore but one man died.*

Possible answers:

3. *There are many headlines because these allow readers to get the gist quickly and also pique readers' curiosity.*

4. ■ **SKILLS FOCUS** Analyze Primary Sources *General statements: 19th-century journalism was sensational (using zingy headlines), subjective (giving writers' feelings on topics), and colorful (calling liquor a "life preservative"). It used narrative elements such as foreshadowing, imagery, and mood.*

Read for Information: Compare Forms

Writing Prompt *Responses will vary, but students should explain Crane's writing choices and contrast the strengths of the two works, supporting their ideas with details.*

Assess and Reteach

Assess

R RESOURCE MANAGER—Copy Masters
Selection Test A pp. 183–184
Selection Test B/C pp. 185–186

🖸 Test Generator CD

Reteach

S STANDARDS LESSON FILE
Writing Lesson 23: Comparison-Contrast Essay

Research and Study Skills Lesson 5: Using Primary and Secondary Sources

OBJECTIVES

Literary Analysis
- explore the key idea of **death**
- analyze theme
- read a short story

Reading
- analyze author's perspective

Vocabulary
- build vocabulary for reading and writing
- use denotation and connotation to enhance word meaning (*also an EL language objective*)

 CALIFORNIA R2.5, R3.2

ABOUT THE AUTHOR

Jack London pursued writing as he did everything else, with enthusiasm and relentless energy. He studied magazine content, analyzed readers' desires, and composed at least 1,000 words a day on his way to fame and financial success.

USING THE *NOTABLE QUOTE*

This quote is taken from **Jack London's** "Credo," which was published by London's literary executor many years after the writer's death. While no direct written source has been discovered to authenticate these lines, critics have noted that their style, syntax, and sentiment seem pure Jack London. Ask students whether or not they agree with this assessment. *Accept all reasonable responses.*

 The Rise of Naturalism

 CALIFORNIA R2.5, R3.2

The Law of Life

Short Story by Jack London

NOTABLE QUOTE

The proper function of man is to live, not to exist. I shall not waste my days in trying to prolong them. I shall use my time."

FYI

Did you know that Jack London . . .

- was the first American author to become a millionaire from his writing?
- pioneered the field of sports writing?
- covered the Russo-Japanese War and the Mexican Revolution as a correspondent?

Author On|ine

For more on Jack London, visit the **Literature Center** at ClassZone.com.

Jack London
1876–1916

According to critic Alfred Kazin, The greatest story Jack London ever wrote was the story he lived." Before London had turned 21 he had had more adventures than a Hollywood action hero. Once he began publishing stories about his experiences, he became an international celebrity. His works, many set in the wilds of Alaska and the American West, brought before the reading public a fresh style and subject matter that proved popular and profitable.

The Call of Adventure Born in San Francisco, Jack London grew up in Oakland, California. Disowned by his biological father, he took the name of his stepfather, John London. Although a decent man, the stepfather couldn't make much of a living, so London spent much of his youth working. Periods of backbreaking manual labor—in factories, canneries, a power plant, and a laundry—alternated with high adventure. The 16-year-old Jack

became an oyster pirate in San Francisco Bay before switching sides to join the shore police. At age 17, he boarded a ship for a seal-hunting expedition to the Bering Sea. At 18, he quit work altogether to travel the country as a hobo. These escapades came to an abrupt halt when he was arrested for vagrancy in New York State and jailed for 30 days. Moved by the hard-luck stories of the men he had met on the road and in prison, London could see where his life was heading and decided to turn it around. I ran back to California and opened the books," he explained. By the time he was 20, he had enrolled at the University of California at Berkeley and become a writer

From Rags to Riches Although writing steadily, London could get nothing published. News of the Klondike Gold Rush in 1897 inspired him to head to Alaska in hopes of striking it rich. Instead of finding gold, however, he got a bad case of scurvy and returned home after less than a year. Still, London admitted, It was in the Klondike that I found myself." Equally important, he found a wealth of material and formulated the naturalistic philosophy that would make him a blockbuster writer. He shot to international fame with *The Call of the Wild* (1903), and within six years had produced most of his greatest works—*The Sea Wolf* (1904), *White Fang* (1906), *The Road* (1907), the autobiographical *Martin Eden* (1909), and several collections of short stories. London inspired many in the next generation of writers, including Ernest Hemingway, Jack Kerouac, and Norman Mailer.

744

 RESOURCE MANAGER UNIT 4

Plan and Teach pp. 187–194

Literary Analysis
Summary pp. 195†*, 196‡*
Theme pp. 197, 198†*
Question Support p. 205*

Reading
Analyze Author's Perspective pp. 199, 200†*
Reading Check p. 204

Vocabulary
Study p. 201*
Practice p. 202
Strategy p. 203

Assessment
Selection Tests A, B/C pp. 207*, 209*

 Test Generator CD

BEST PRACTICES TOOLKIT

Differentiated Instruction pp. 31–38*

Scaffolding Instruction pp. 43–46*

Graphic Organizers/Strategies
New Word Analysis • T Chart •
Making Inferences • Setting
Diagram • Personal Word List

Reading Support
Audio Anthology CD*

Technology
Literature and Vocabulary Centers at **ClassZone.com**

WriteSmart CD

---

* **Resources for Differentiation**   † **Also in Spanish**   ‡ **In Haitian Creole and Vietnamese**

LITERARY ANALYSIS: THEME

Theme is the central message communicated by a literary work. It may not be explicit but often emerges as a set of ideas expressed through literary elements. The answers to certain questions can help you identify a story's theme.

- What is the resolution of the primary **conflict?**
- What traits do the main **characters** display?
- What about the physical or cultural **setting** is significant?
- What **point of view** is used to describe the experiences of the main character?
- What objects or figures have **symbolic** meaning?
- What does the **title** refer to?

Ask yourself these questions as you read The Law of Life," recording the answers and other details in a chart.

Details Revealing Theme					
Conflict	Character	Setting	Point of View	Symbol	Title

Review: Naturalism

READING SKILL: ANALYZE AUTHOR'S PERSPECTIVE

An **author's perspective** is the unique combination of background, experiences, beliefs, and values that influences the way a writer looks at a topic. The Law of Life" contains echoes of of London's own life experiences in Alaska and the Klondike, where he had gone in hopes of striking it rich in the goldfields. Carefully read London's biography on page 744. As you read the story, draw on what you know of London's life to help you understand his perspective on such subjects as youth and old age, strength and weakness, survival and death.

▲ VOCABULARY IN CONTEXT

Restate each phrase, using a different word or words for the boldfaced term.

1. need to **replenish** the water supply
2. a **slovenly** fellow, with dirty hair and unshined shoes
3. the **inexorable** passage of time
4. willing to **attest** to his honesty
5. a cat attempting to **harry** the mouse it caught

How do people face DEATH?

KEY IDEA Death comes to all of us, but different cultures approach the inevitable end in various ways. The death described in London's story may seem cruel to you, but consider the cultural context of the community described in the story.

QUICKWRITE Think about how your own culture treats people who are dying. Are they treated with indifference or respect? In a more hostile environment, such as a natural disaster, do you think society could maintain the same customs? In your notebook, jot down your thoughts about these issues.

745

How do people face DEATH?

Lead into the **KEY IDEA** by asking the question and inviting students to share traditions their culture has for preparing for **death.** As students complete the **QUICKWRITE,** suggest that they consider how such traditions serve individuals, families, and friends who must face death.

SKILLS FOCUS

LITERARY ANALYSIS   R3.2

● THEME

Recall "The Open Boat" from pages 710–737 and suggest this possible theme: *Working together is the only way to survive adversity.* Ask students to recall films or stories they have read and propose themes. For several examples, have students answer the bulleted questions about theme and then work as a class to agree on theme statements for several examples.

CHECK UNDERSTANDING Ask students how a story's theme is like and unlike its subject.

 RESOURCE MANAGER—Copy Master
Theme p. 197 (for student use while reading the selection)

READING SKILL   R2.5

■ ANALYZE AUTHOR'S PERSPECTIVE

Direct students' attention to the *Notable Quote,* and ask them what it suggests about how London will view the characters and action in the story. Elicit students' ideas about the kinds of characters someone with London's perspective would admire, and the kinds of actions he would expect these characters to take.

CHECK UNDERSTANDING Have students cite examples from the author biography that support their ideas about London's perspective.

VOCABULARY

▲ VOCABULARY IN CONTEXT

DIAGNOSE WORD KNOWLEDGE To determine preteaching needs, have all students complete Vocabulary in Context. *Possible answers:* **1.** *refill,* **2.** *sloppy,* **3.** *relentless,* **4.** *confirm,* **5.** *pester*

PRETEACH VOCABULARY Preteach vocabulary with this copy master. Read each item aloud.

 RESOURCE MANAGER—Copy Master
Vocabulary Study p. 201

MORE VOCABULARY SUPPORT
For additional activities and guidelines, see

 BEST PRACTICES TOOLKIT
Scaffolding Vocabulary Instruction pp. 43–46
ⓘ Vocabulary Center at **ClassZone.com**

Practice and Apply

SUMMARY

This short story opens with the blind, aged former leader of an Alaskan tribe listening to the sounds of his tribe departing for new hunting grounds. The old man knows he will be left behind and bids his son a ritual but loving farewell. As he awaits death in the snow, he recalls moments from his youth and considers the inevitable end of all living things. Finally, his fire goes out and a ring of wolves prepares to attack.

Lines 1–12
REINFORCE *KEY IDEA*: DEATH

Discuss What details in the text alert readers that Koskoosh is nearing **death?** Why will he be left behind when the tribe leaves? *Possible answer: He is blind and wrinkled, and his hand is palsied. He will be left behind when the tribe leaves because he can no longer contribute and will slow the tribe's travel down.*

LITERARY ANALYSIS

A THEME

Possible answer: The setting is that of a camp in the snow being broken as the characters prepare for a long day's journey (lines 5–9). The mood created is wintry and bleak, which reflects the grandfather's forlorn and helpless state.

If students need help . . . Have them reread lines 5–9 and note setting and action words.

THE LAW OF LIFE

JACK LONDON

BACKGROUND Written when London was about 25 years old, this story was included in his second collection of short stories about Alaska, *Children of the Frost* (1902). The characters are members of a nomadic native tribe whose customs are shaped by the harsh conditions of the Arctic. The law they live by expresses London's naturalistic vision at its most brutal.

ANALYZE VISUALS
Look at the image on page 747. What elements of the man's clothing and facial expression give clues to the photo's **setting?** Explain.

Old Koskoosh listened greedily. Though his sight had long since faded, his hearing was still acute, and the slightest sound penetrated to the glimmering intelligence which yet abode behind his withered forehead, but which no longer gazed forth upon the things of the world. Ah! that was Sit-cum-to-ha, shrilly anathematizing the dogs as she cuffed and beat them into the harness. Sit-cum-to-ha was his daughter's daughter, but she was too busy to waste a thought upon her broken grandfather, sitting alone there in the snow, forlorn and helpless. Camp must be broken. The long trail waited while the short day refused to linger. Life called her, and the duties of life, not death. And he was very close to death now. **A**

① **Targeted Passage**

10 The thought made the old man panicky for the moment, and he stretched forth a palsied hand which wandered tremblingly over the small heap of dry wood beside him. Reassured that it was indeed there, his hand returned to the shelter of his mangy furs, and he again fell to listening. The sulky crackling of half-frozen hides told him that the chief's moose-skin lodge had been struck, and

A **THEME**
What is significant about the **setting** described in the first paragraph, and what **mood** does it create?

746   UNIT 4: REGIONALISM AND NATURALISM

DIFFERENTIATED INSTRUCTION

FOR ALL STUDENTS

Provide these independent projects to extend the lesson:

- Analyze other Jack London stories for elements of naturalism.
- Research the Athabascan culture.

For further details on these projects, see

R **RESOURCE MANAGER**
Ideas for Extension pp. 192–193

FOR STRATEGIC READERS

In combination with the *Audio Anthology CD,* use one or more Targeted Passages (pp. 746, 748, 752) to ensure that students focus on key story events and concepts. Targeted Passages are also good for English learners.

① Targeted Passage [Lines 1–9]

This passage introduces the main character, Koskoosh; the Arctic setting; and the presence of death in the story.

- Who is Koskoosh?
- What are the conditions like where he is?
- What activity is he listening to?
- Why doesn't he participate in the activity?

ANALYZE VISUALS

Possible answer: The man's fur hat suggests that he lives in a very cold setting. His facial expression suggests that he is bracing himself against something difficult, such as cold weather or a difficult physical task.

BACKGROUND

Nomadic Life Tribes living in Koskoosh's area of Alaska were part of a larger group of Native Americans called Athabascans. Some Athabascans fished for salmon for food, while others hunted large animals, especially caribou. Their way of life was to follow migrating herds in winter, setting up and then quickly striking camps as necessary to keep up with the herds. In summer many Athabascan peoples set up fishing camps on rivers and lakes and briefly lived a more settled life.

FOR ENGLISH LEARNERS

Key Academic Vocabulary Use New Word Analysis to teach this word: *intelligence* (line 2).

 BEST PRACTICES TOOLKIT—Transparency New Word Analysis p. E8

Prereading For prereading instruction for English learners, see

 BEST PRACTICES TOOLKIT Scaffolding Reading Instruction pp. 43–46

FOR ADVANCED LEARNERS/AP

AP exercises in the bottom channel provide additional challenge for students. Use these suggestions for small groups or individuals.

ADDITIONAL GUIDELINES

For more help with differentiation and tips for classroom management, see

 BEST PRACTICES TOOLKIT Differentiated Instruction pp. 31–38

B THEME

Possible answer: Readers see events from the third-person limited point of view of Koskoosh. He is thinking about the contrasting ideas of heat and cold (lines 11–12, 24), life and death (lines 15–20, 22–27), strength and weakness (lines 10–12, 16, 23), and youth and old age (lines 10–12, 15–16).

If students need help . . . Review different points of view and their characteristics.

Lines 45–47
REINFORCE *KEY IDEA:* DEATH

Discuss Why does Koskoosh feel that **death** is coming at the right time for him? *Possible answer: Koskoosh feels that it is the right time for him to die because his strength is gone. Also, it is hard for him to walk, he can't see, and he's tired and ready to give up the struggle of life.*

C AUTHOR'S PERSPECTIVE

Possible answer: London's experience with scurvy must have given him a keen sense of human frailty and an appreciation for the difficulties of surviving in this harsh environment. That appreciation is reflected in his description of the old man's losing battle with the deadly environment.

---

even then was being rammed and jammed into portable compass. The chief was his son, stalwart and strong, head man of the tribesmen, and a mighty hunter. As the women toiled with the camp luggage, his voice rose, chiding them for their slowness. Old Koskoosh strained his ears. It was the last time he would hear that voice. There went Geehow's lodge! And Tusken's! Seven, eight, nine; only
20 the shaman's[1] could be still standing. There! They were at work upon it now. He could hear the shaman grunt as he piled it on the sled. A child whimpered, and a woman soothed it with soft, crooning gutturals.[2] Little Koo-tee, the old man thought, a fretful child, and not overstrong. It would die soon, perhaps, and they would burn a hole through the frozen tundra and pile rocks above to keep the wolverines away. Well, what did it matter? A few years at best, and as many an empty belly as a full one. And in the end, Death waited, ever-hungry and hungriest of them all. B

   What was that? Oh, the men lashing the sleds and drawing tight the thongs. He listened, who would listen no more. The whip-lashes snarled and bit among
30 the dogs. Hear them whine! How they hated the work and the trail! They were off! Sled after sled churned slowly away into the silence. They were gone. They had passed out of his life, and he faced the last bitter hour alone. No. The snow crunched beneath a moccasin; a man stood beside him; upon his head a hand rested gently. His son was good to do this thing. He remembered other old men whose sons had not waited after the tribe. But his son had. He wandered away into the past, till the young man's voice brought him back.
   "Is it well with you?" he asked.
   And the old man answered, "It is well."
   "There be wood beside you," the younger man continued, "and the fire burns
40 bright. The morning is gray, and the cold has broken. It will snow presently. Even now it is snowing."
   "Ay, even now it is snowing."
   "The tribesmen hurry. Their bales are heavy, and their bellies flat with lack of feasting. The trail is long and they travel fast. I go now. It is well?"
   "It is well. I am as a last year's leaf, clinging lightly to the stem. The first breath that blows, and I fall. My voice is become like an old woman's. My eyes no longer show me the way of my feet, and my feet are heavy, and I am tired. It is well."
   He bowed his head in content till the last noise of the complaining snow had died away, and he knew his son was beyond recall. Then his hand crept out in
50 haste to the wood. It alone stood between him and the eternity that yawned in upon him. At last the measure of his life was a handful of fagots.[3] One by one they would go to feed the fire, and just so, step by step, death would creep upon him. When the last stick had surrendered up its heat, the frost would begin to gather strength. First his feet would yield, then his hands; and the numbness would travel, slowly, from the extremities to the body. His head would fall forward upon his knees, and he would rest. It was easy. All men must die. C

---

1. **shaman's:** belonging to a priest who uses magic to cure the sick or predict events.
2. **gutturals:** sounds that are made in the throat.
3. **fagots:** sticks of wood.

B THEME
Reread lines 10–27. From whose **point of view** are we experiencing the events described? What are some of the contrasting ideas running through this character's head?

2 Targeted Passage

C AUTHOR'S PERSPECTIVE
Reread the biography on page 744 and consider the experience that forced London to leave Alaska. How might this experience be reflected in lines 48–56? Explain.

DIFFERENTIATED INSTRUCTION

FOR STRATEGIC READERS

2 Targeted Passage [Lines 32–56]

This passage reveals the crucial story concept: death is inevitable and must be met honorably for the good of the tribe.

- Who comes to talk to Koskoosh? Why?
- What does Koskoosh say about his situation?
- What does Koskoosh think will happen to him?

FOR ENGLISH LEARNERS

Vocabulary Support Explain that London uses many contrasting words and phrases. For example, in line 53, he contrasts *heat* and *frost*. Help students locate and record these pairs in a T Chart. Then model how to use knowledge of one word in the pair to build meaning for the other. Point out that London may use many contrasts to highlight the extreme environment and situation.

London contrasts . . .	with . . .
heat (line 53)	frost (line 53)
individual (line 60)	species (line 61)
rise of the sap (lines 62–63)	fall of the yellow leaf (line 63)

BEST PRACTICES TOOLKIT—Transparency
T Chart p. A25

He did not complain. It was the way of life, and it was just. He had been born close to the earth, close to the earth had he lived, and the law thereof was not new to him. It was the law of all flesh. Nature was not kindly to the flesh. She had
60 no concern for that concrete thing called the individual. Her interest lay in the species, the race. This was the deepest abstraction old Koskoosh's barbaric mind was capable of, but he grasped it firmly. He saw it exemplified in all life. The rise of the sap, the bursting greenness of the willow bud, the fall of the yellow leaf—in this alone was told the whole history. But one task did Nature set the individual. Did he not perform it, he died. Did he perform it, it was all the same, he died. Nature did not care; there were plenty who were obedient, and it was only the obedience in this matter, not the obedient, which lived and lived always. The tribe of Koskoosh was very old. The old men he had known when a boy, had known old men before them. Therefore it was true that the tribe lived, that it stood for
70 the obedience of all its members, way down into the forgotten past, whose very resting-places were unremembered. They did not count; they were episodes. They had passed away like clouds from a summer sky. He also was an episode, and would pass away. Nature did not care. To life she set one task, gave one law. To perpetuate was the task of life, its law was death. A maiden was a good creature to look upon, full-breasted and strong, with spring to her step and light in her eyes. But her task was yet before her. The light in her eyes brightened, her step quickened, she was now bold with the young men, now timid, and she gave them of her own unrest. And ever she grew fairer and yet fairer to look upon, till some hunter, able no longer to withhold himself, took her to his lodge to cook and toil
80 for him and to become the mother of his children. And with the coming of her offspring her looks left her. Her limbs dragged and shuffled, her eyes dimmed and bleared, and only the little children found joy against the withered cheek of the old squaw by the fire. Her task was done. But a little while, on the first pinch of famine or the first long trail, and she would be left, even as he had been left, in the snow, with a little pile of wood. Such was the law. **D**

He placed a stick carefully upon the fire and resumed his meditations. It was the same everywhere, with all things. The mosquitoes vanished with the first frost. The little tree-squirrel crawled away to die. When age settled upon the rabbit it became slow and heavy, and could no longer outfoot its enemies. Even the
90 big bald-face grew clumsy and blind and quarrelsome, in the end to be dragged down by a handful of yelping huskies. He remembered how he had abandoned his own father on an upper reach of the Klondike one winter, the winter before the missionary came with his talk-books and his box of medicines. Many a time had Koskoosh smacked his lips over the recollection of that box, though now his mouth refused to moisten. The "painkiller" had been especially good. But the missionary was a bother after all, for he brought no meat into the camp, and he ate heartily, and the hunters grumbled. But he chilled his lungs on the divide by the Mayo,[4] and the dogs afterwards nosed the stones away and fought over his bones.

D NATURALISM
Reread lines 57–85. In one or two sentences, summarize the relationship between nature and the individual expressed in this paragraph.

---

4. **the Mayo:** a small river in the Yukon Territory in northwestern Canada.

THE LAW OF LIFE   **749**

Lines 57–74
TIERED DISCUSSION PROMPTS
Use these prompts to help students understand how Koskoosh and his people view Nature:

Connect Have you ever felt that Nature was indifferent to people's wishes and needs? Explain. *Accept all thoughtful responses.*

Interpret What is the one task Nature requires of people? Why is it important that they fulfill it? Is there a reward? *Possible answer: The one task is to reproduce (lines 62–64). If they fail in this task, their species will die out. Individuals get no reward, as even those who have children die, but there is a reward to the species (line 65).*

Evaluate Have Koskoosh and his people done well according to Nature's goals? Explain. *Possible answer: Yes, the tribe has succeeded in meeting Nature's goals. It is healthy, with a long history behind it (lines 68–69) and a promising future ahead of them. Koskoosh remembers old men and himself has a son, now chief, and at least one grandchild. The tribe is a success, even if he dies.*

LITERARY ANALYSIS: *Review*

D NATURALISM

Possible answer: Nature does not care about the individual, only about making sure that the species continues.

FOR ADVANCED LEARNERS/AP
Analyze Figures of Speech [small–group option] London personifies Nature in lines 57–74. Have students write a journal entry exploring the effect of this personification on Koskoosh's understanding of "the law." To prepare, have student groups discuss these questions:

• Why does London personify Nature as a woman rather than as a man?

• Do you view Nature as a single entity with desires, commands, and laws? Why or why not?

• Does thinking of Nature as a person change the way people think about it? Why?

Use these prompts to help students understand the connection Koskoosh makes between plenty and warfare:

Connect Are you more agreeable or more argumentative when things are going your way? *Accept all thoughtful responses.*

Interpret What can readers infer about why the tribe is more warlike when it is well-fed? *Possible answer: When the people are hungry, they are weaker and must spend their energy on finding food. They can't bother with war. But when they have food surpluses, they have time to do something other than hunt, fish, and gather. Then "ancient quarrels" (line 117) come to mind, and they decide to finish the conflict begun by men older than they.*

Evaluate London follows his description of famine's cruelty with a paragraph on abundance. Is this an effective way to highlight the impact of famine? Explain. *Possible answer: Yes. London's contrasts are effective in highlighting famine's devastation. He describes famine in which the "children wailed and died" (line 110), the dogs were "bundles of bones" (line 109), and many died. He then contrasts these images with those of abundance, in which children are everywhere, the dogs are "fat and worthless" (line 114), and the men are populous enough to think of war (lines 116–118). The images of the dogs and children, in particular, stress the contrast.*

LITERARY ANALYSIS

❺ THEME

Possible answer: Koskoosh's memory is ironic because at the time, the old man watched the death of the moose with excitement. Now, his situation is similar as he faces his own death.

If students need help . . . Clarify the meaning of *ironic* in this context.

---

100 Koskoosh placed another stick on the fire and harked back deeper into the past. There was the time of the Great Famine, when the old men crouched empty-bellied to the fire, and let fall from their lips dim traditions of the ancient day when the Yukon ran wide open for three winters, and then lay frozen for three summers. He had lost his mother in that famine. In the summer the salmon run had failed, and the tribe looked forward to the winter and the coming of the caribou. Then the winter came, but with it there were no caribou. Never had the like been known, not even in the lives of the old men. But the caribou did not come, and it was the seventh year, and the rabbits had not **replenished,** and the dogs were naught but bundles of bones. And through the long darkness the 110 children wailed and died, and the women, and the old men; and not one in ten of the tribe lived to meet the sun when it came back in the spring. That *was* a famine!

But he had seen times of plenty, too, when the meat spoiled on their hands, and the dogs were fat and worthless with overeating—times when they let the game go unkilled, and the women were fertile, and the lodges were cluttered with sprawling men-children and women-children. Then it was the men became high-stomached, and revived ancient quarrels, and crossed the divides to the south to kill the Pellys, and to the west that they might sit by the dead fires of the Tananas.[5] He remembered, when a boy, during a time of plenty, when he saw a moose pulled 120 down by the wolves. Zing-ha lay with him in the snow and watched—Zing-ha, who later became the craftiest of hunters, and who, in the end, fell through an air-hole on the Yukon. They found him, a month afterward, just as he had crawled halfway out and frozen stiff to the ice.

But the moose. Zing-ha and he had gone out that day to play at hunting after the manner of their fathers. On the bed of the creek they struck the fresh track of a moose, and with it the tracks of many wolves. "An old one," Zing-ha, who was quicker at reading the sign, said—"an old one who cannot keep up with the herd. The wolves have cut him out from his brothers, and they will never leave him." And it was so. It was their way. By day and by night, never resting, snarling on his 130 heels, snapping at his nose, they would stay by him to the end. How Zing-ha and he felt the blood-lust quicken! The finish would be a sight to see! ❺

Eager-footed, they took the trail, and even he, Koskoosh, slow of sight and an unversed tracker, could have followed it blind, it was so wide. Hot were they on the heels of the chase, reading the grim tragedy, fresh-written, at every step. Now they came to where the moose had made a stand. Thrice the length of a grown man's body, in every direction, had the snow been stamped about and uptossed. In the midst were the deep impressions of the splay-hoofed game, and all about, everywhere, were the lighter footmarks of the wolves. Some, while their brothers **harried** the kill, had lain to one side and rested. The full-stretched impress of their 140 bodies in the snow was as perfect as though made the moment before. One wolf had been caught in a wild lunge of the maddened victim and trampled to death. A few bones, well picked, bore witness.

---

5. **Pellys . . . Tananas:** *Pellys* probably refers to native peoples who lived near the Pelly River. The Tananas are native people who traditionally lived in areas of Alaska and the Yukon.

replenish (rǐ-plěn′ǐsh) *v.* to fill up again

❺ **THEME**
In lines 124–131, the third-person limited point of view reveals Koskoosh's memory of the old moose and his own reaction at the time. What is **ironic** about this recollection?

harry (hăr′ē) *v.* to torment, often by constant attack

DIFFERENTIATED INSTRUCTION

FOR STRATEGIC READERS

Make Inferences London often implies information rather than stating it directly. Readers must make inferences to dig out the implied information. Model for students the use of a Making Inferences chart.

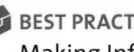 BEST PRACTICES TOOLKIT—Transparency
Making Inferences p. A13

Story Details +	What I Know =	Inference
The boys played at hunting in the "manner of their fathers" (lines 124–125).	Young people often play at grown-up jobs such as teaching or firefighting.	Zing-ha and Koskoosh were young men when they followed the moose.

Again, they ceased the uplift of their snowshoes at a second stand. Here the great animal had fought desperately. Twice had he been dragged down, as the snow **attested,** and twice had he shaken his assailants clear and gained footing once more. He had done his task long since, but none the less was life dear to him. Zing-ha said it was a strange thing, a moose once down to get free again; but this one certainly had. The shaman would see signs and wonders in this when they told him. **F**

150 And yet again, they came to where the moose had made to mount the bank and gain the timber. But his foes had laid on from behind, till he reared and fell back upon them, crushing two deep into the snow. It was plain the kill was at hand, for their brothers had left them untouched. Two more stands were hurried past, brief in time-length and very close together. The trail was red now, and the clean stride of the great beast had grown short and **slovenly.** Then they heard the first sounds of the battle—not the full-throated chorus of the chase, but the short, snappy bark which spoke of close quarters and teeth to flesh. Crawling up the wind, Zing-ha bellied it through the snow, and with him crept he, Koskoosh, who was to be chief of the tribesmen in the years to come. Together they shoved aside the under

160 branches of a young spruce and peered forth. It was the end they saw.

The picture, like all of youth's impressions, was still strong with him, and his dim eyes watched the end played out as vividly as in that far-off time. Koskoosh

attest (ə-tĕst′) *v.* to affirm to be true; to be proof of

F THEME
Reread lines 143–149. What is surprising about the moose's struggle with the wolves? Consider the significance of this **conflict.**

slovenly (slŭv′ən-lē) *adj.* untidy in personal appearance

ANALYZE VISUALS

Activity Have students describe how the composition of the photograph on page 751 particularly defines the wolf as a predator. *Possible answer: The focal point of the photograph is the wolf's open mouth and sharp teeth. The background of the wolf is blurred, emphasizing the focus of the wolf's predatory qualities.*

About the Art Larry Fanning worked as a minister, a radio talk show host, and a motivational speaker before he began a career in art at age fifty. A member of the Society of Animal Artists, Fanning has won numerous awards and is famous for his paintings of wolves and of his beloved Rocky Mountains.

LITERARY ANALYSIS

F THEME

Possible answer: The surprising element of the moose's struggle is that it actually manages to briefly get away from its stronger predators (lines 147–148). The moose's struggle can be seen to represent the determination of living things to resist even certain death.

FOR ENGLISH LEARNERS

Comprehension: Text Structure Koskoosh's reflections ramble and often jump among subjects or to contrasting views. Model how to locate and navigate these jumps, using transition phrases such as these:

- "But he had seen times" (line 113)
- "But the moose" (line 124)
- "but this one" (lines 147–148)
- "And yet again" (line 150)

FOR ADVANCED LEARNERS/AP

Analyze Perspective and Theme Ask students to consider how the author's perspective affects theme. First, have students retell the moose's struggle with an emphasis on the wolves. To help students retell the story with London's attention to detail, encourage them to use a Setting Diagram to develop and organize details. Then, have students read their retellings dramatically and discuss how shifting the perspective to focus on the wolves might

affect the story's theme. *Example: London's perspective stresses the theme and value of the universal struggle for survival. Focusing on the wolves shifts the perspective to survival of the group even at individual cost and thus becomes a metaphor for Koskoosh's situation.*

 BEST PRACTICES TOOLKIT—Transparency Setting Diagram p. D12

G AUTHOR'S PERSPECTIVE

Possible answer: This passage demonstrates a harsh means of settling differences (lines 164–166) and shows that people are accustomed to violence. London's travels among hard, tough people convey this image.

Lines 179–187
REINFORCE *KEY IDEA:* DEATH

Discuss How does Koskoosh's vision of his **death** change in these lines? *Possible answer: He realizes that it will not be an easy death after all (line 179), but a painful, violent death by "slavered fangs" (line 184).*

H THEME

Possible answer: The old bull moose stands for the aged chief, cut off from his herd and vulnerable. This symbol suggests a thematic message that we face death alone.

If students need help . . . Refer them to the prereading chart introduced on page 745. Have students examine their entries about the moose and Koskoosh. Point out traits the two have in common.

SELECTION WRAP–UP

REFLECT Have students think about the man Koskoosh was in his youth and adulthood and at his death. Is his death an event his tribe should mourn?

⭐ CRITIQUE

- Ask students to evaluate the story's ending and decide if the unexpected violence of Koskhoosh's death is effective in supporting London's theme.
- After completing the After Reading questions on page 753, have students revisits their responses and tell whether they have changed their opinions.

---

marvelled at this, for in the days which followed, when he was a leader of men and a head of councillors, he had done great deeds and made his name a curse in the mouths of the Pellys, to say naught of the strange white man he had killed, knife to knife, in open fight. **G**

For long he pondered on the days of his youth, till the fire died down and the frost bit deeper. He replenished it with two sticks this time, and gauged his grip on life by what remained. If Sit-cum-to-ha had only remembered her grandfather, 170 and gathered a larger armful, his hours would have been longer. It would have been easy. But she was ever a careless child, and honored not her ancestors from the time the Beaver, son of the son of Zing-ha, first cast eyes upon her. Well, what mattered it? Had he not done likewise in his own quick youth? For a while he listened to the silence. Perhaps the heart of his son might soften, and he would come back with the dogs to take his old father on with the tribe to where the caribou ran thick and the fat hung heavy upon them.

He strained his ears, his restless brain for the moment stilled. Not a stir, nothing. He alone took breath in the midst of the great silence. It was very lonely. Hark! What was that? A chill passed over his body. The familiar, long-drawn howl 180 broke the void, and it was close at hand. Then on his darkened eyes was projected the vision of the moose—the old bull moose—the torn flanks and bloody sides, the riddled mane, and the great branching horns, down low and tossing to the last. He saw the flashing forms of gray, the gleaming eyes, the lolling tongues, the slavered fangs. And he saw the **inexorable** circle close in till it became a dark point in the midst of the stamped snow. **H**

A cold muzzle thrust against his cheek, and at its touch his soul leaped back to the present. His hand shot into the fire and dragged out a burning fagot. Overcome for the nonce[6] by his hereditary fear of man, the brute retreated, raising a prolonged call to his brothers; and greedily they answered, till a ring of 190 crouching, jaw-slobbered gray was stretched round about. The old man listened to the drawing in of this circle. He waved his brand wildly, and sniffs turned to snarls; but the panting brutes refused to scatter. Now one wormed his chest forward, dragging his haunches after, now a second, now a third; but never a one drew back. Why should he cling to life? he asked, and dropped the blazing stick into the snow. It sizzled and went out. The circle grunted uneasily, but held its own. Again he saw the last stand of the old bull moose, and Koskoosh dropped his head wearily upon his knees. What did it matter after all? Was it not the law of life? ❧

---

6. **for the nonce:** for the time being.

G AUTHOR'S PERSPECTIVE

Reread lines 162–166. What sensibility about human relationships is revealed in the struggle described here? Consider how this sensibility might be rooted in London's life experience.

❸ Targeted Passage

inexorable
(ĭn-ĕk'sər-ə-bəl) *adj.*
relentless

H THEME

Reread lines 177–185. What does the old bull moose represent? Consider the thematic message suggested by this **symbol.**

DIFFERENTIATED INSTRUCTION

FOR STRATEGIC READERS

❸ **Targeted Passage [Lines 177–197]**

This passage concludes the story with Koskoosh's surprising final moments: He will die by wolf attack, not from cold.

- What emotions does Koskoosh feel?
- What are the wolves doing?
- What does Koskoosh do to stop the wolves? Why does he stop doing it?

FOR ENGLISH LEARNERS

Related Vocabulary Violence is central to the story's final scene. To insure students understand the violence, teach these inter-related words and have students group them in a Personal Word List: *torn flanks, bloody sides* (line 181); *gleaming eyes, slavered fangs* (lines 183–184); *ring of crouching, jaw-slobbered gray* (lines 189–190); *panting brutes* (line 192).

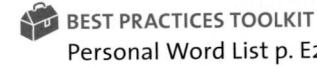 **BEST PRACTICES TOOLKIT**
Personal Word List p. E2

Comprehension

R2.5, R3.2

1. **Recall** How does Koskoosh die?

2. **Clarify** How has he expected to die?

3. **Summarize** Describe the conditions of life for the tribe.

Literary Analysis

4. **Interpret Theme** Look back at the details about narrative elements you recorded in your chart as you read. Taken together, what do these details suggest about the fate of Koskoosh and all humans?

5. **Analyze Cultural Context** Explain how each of the following factors might contribute to the tribe's attitude about **death:**

   • the tribe's connection "to the earth" (lines 57–67)
   • what the tribe sees as "the task of life" (lines 73–85)
   • the Arctic environment (lines 101–123)

6. **Analyze Point of View** Imagine that this story had been written without any insight into Koskoosh's thoughts. What information or ideas would be missing? With this in mind, explain whether or not you think the point of view plays a crucial role in expressing the story's **theme.** Cite evidence from the story to support your view.

7. **Examine Author's Perspective** In your opinion, has London created a credible portrayal of the native American tribe and their values? How do you think this portrayal reflects London's own life experiences? In developing your answer, give details from the story as well as from the biography on page 744.

8. **Compare Expressions of Naturalism** Compare and contrast London's portrayal of nature in this story with Crane's in "The Open Boat." Consider in particular the characters' fates and any differences in tone. Record your answers with evidence from the stories in a Venn diagram. In which version of nature would you prefer to live? Explain.

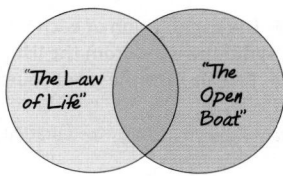

Literary Criticism

9. **Critical Interpretation** The writer E. L. Doctorow said, "It was Jack London's capacity for really living in the world, for taking it on in self-conscious and often reckless acts of courage, that made him our first writer-hero." Given what you have read in London's biography and your reading of "The Law of Life," do you agree with the notion of London as a hero? Explain.

8. *Difference: Crane's characters achieve brotherhood and stick together while London's main character is abandoned.* *Similarity: In both stories, nature is indifferent to human suffering.*

9. *Students may say that London lived heroically, seeking adventure from a young age and packing experience into every day. He also stood up to injustice.*

Practice and Apply

After Reading

Use these copy masters to check understanding and provide extra support:

R RESOURCE MANAGER—Copy Masters
Reading Check p. 204
Analyze Author's Perspective p. 199
Question Support p. 205

Additional selection questions are provided for teachers on page 191.

ANSWERS

1. *Wolves kill him.*

2. *He expected to freeze to death.*

3. *The tribe follows game that can be scarce.*

Possible answers:

4. ● **SKILLS FOCUS Theme** *The details suggest that death is the inevitable end of human life, and that nature does not wait for or care about individuals.*

5. *Tribe members are tied "to the earth" because they depend on nature for food and shelter and face death without rain and caribou. They see "the task of life" as having offspring to continue the tribe. As a result, those of childbearing age are most important, and people's value drops after these years. The harsh Arctic environment means that death is an ever-present threat. During famine those who contribute most to the tribe eat best.*

6. *Students may say that point of view is crucial to the story's theme because Koskoosh's memories are significant symbolic and expository elements of the story. Other students may say that the story of an aged man left to die alone is powerful as a thematic image no matter who tells it.*

7. ■ **SKILLS FOCUS Analyze Author's Perspective** *Students may say that London has romanticized the tribe and its values. Others may say that the portrayal is realistic. All students should cite London's hardscrabble experiences, in Alaska and beyond, as likely causes for his detached determinism.*

ANSWERS

Vocabulary in Context

VOCABULARY PRACTICE

1. *harry*
2. *inexorable*
3. *replenish*
4. *slovenly*
5. *attest*

R RESOURCE MANAGER—Copy Master
Vocabulary Practice p. 202

VOCABULARY IN WRITING

Guide students to explain their case to a partner before they begin writing. Have partners identify points of support that could incorporate a vocabulary word.

VOCABULARY STRATEGY: DENOTATION AND CONNOTATION *(also an EL language objective)*

- Preview the listed words by asking students if they have positive or negative associations with each.

- Model how to find a synonym that fits the connotation required by sentence context and match this to a list word.

1. *discriminating*   4. *subservient*
2. *charlatan*   5. *ostentatious*
3. *resolute*   6. *traditional*

R RESOURCE MANAGER—Copy Master
Vocabulary Strategy p. 203

i Vocabulary Center at **ClassZone.com**
Additional Vocabulary Activities

Assess and Reteach

Assess

R RESOURCE MANAGER—Copy Masters
Selection Test A pp. 207–208
Selection Test B/C pp. 209–210

🖉 Test Generator CD

Reteach

S STANDARDS LESSON FILE
Literature Lesson 11: Theme, Motif, and Epiphany
Literature Lesson 45: Author's Perspective
Vocabulary Lesson 17: Denotation and Connotation

Vocabulary in Context

VOCABULARY PRACTICE

Determine the relationship between the first pair of words in each analogy. Then choose the vocabulary word that best completes the second pair.

1. *Nurse* is to *care* as *pest* is to _____.
2. *Impressive* is to *splendid* as _____ is to *unyielding*.
3. *Agree* is to *contradict* as _____ is to *deplete*.
4. *Well-groomed* is to *dandy* as _____ is to *slob*.
5. *Refuse* is to *decline* as _____ is to *declare*.

WORD LIST
attest
harry
inexorable
replenish
slovenly

VOCABULARY IN WRITING

Make a case for or against leaving the elderly to die in a society such as the one in this story, and write a short defense of your opinion. Use one or two vocabulary words. Here is a sample beginning.

> **EXAMPLE SENTENCE**
> Death is certainly **inexorable**, but it should be delayed as long as possible.

VOCABULARY STRATEGY: DENOTATION AND CONNOTATION

Every word has a **denotation,** or basic dictionary meaning. Some words have certain **connotations,** or additional shades of meaning. For example, the word *slovenly* means "untidy," but it has a more strongly negative connotation. When you encounter a new word, be sure to consider whether its connotation fits the context.

PRACTICE The connotation of each boldfaced word makes it inappropriate in the context. Write the word from the list provided that would be more suitable in each case. Explain why the word you chose is a better match for the context.

> charlatan   discriminating   ostentatious   resolute   subservient   traditional

1. His **picky** taste was evident in his beautiful suits and well-chosen ties.
2. That **beguiler!** She convinced the children that she was their long-lost aunt.
3. I admire **inflexible** leaders who make hard decisions and then stick with them.
4. Her **humble** attitude impressed her employers, but behind their backs she belittled them constantly.
5. The **elegant** ballroom had more than its share of gold chandeliers, gaudy silk couches, and overly elaborate draperies.
6. The mayor espouses **reactionary** values such as hard work and love of family.

VOCABULARY PRACTICE
For more practice, go to the **Vocabulary Center** at **ClassZone.com**.

DIFFERENTIATED INSTRUCTION

FOR ENGLISH LEARNERS
Task Support: Vocabulary Strategy Tell students that all the listed words except one are adjectives. Review what adjectives are; then have students check each word to determine which is not an adjective (*charlatan*) and identify its part of speech (*noun*).

FOR ADVANCED LEARNERS/AP
Vocabulary in Writing Have students write a narrative describing the death of Zing-ha, alluded to in lines 120–123, using the five vocabulary words. Students may choose from what perspective they want to narrate the story.

Naturalistic Perspectives

As illustrated in the short stories by Stephen Crane and Jack London you have just read, the central assumption of naturalism is that human beings have very little control over their own lives, but instead are at the mercy of the natural world and the impersonal force of fate. The following quotations all explore a similarly naturalistic attitude.

> *"Nature, to be commanded, must be obeyed."*
> —**Sir Francis Bacon**
>
> *"It clearly matters very little to nature whether man has a mind or not."*
> —**Eugène Delacroix**
>
> *"At no time and in no place, will nature ever ask your permission."*
> —**Fyodor Dostoyevsky**
>
> *"Man and nature have such different views about the good of the world."*
> —**George Gissing**
>
> *"In nature there are neither rewards nor punishments—there are consequences."*
> —**R. G. Ingersoll**

Writing to Evaluate

Choose the quotation on this page that you think best represents the theme of "The Open Boat" or "The Law of Life." Write an essay defending your choice, using details from the story as support.

Consider

- the main message of each story
- the subtle and sometimes not-so-subtle differences between the quotations
- which details from the story support your choice of quotation

Extension Online

INQUIRY & RESEARCH A tornado demolishes a house yet skips its neighbor; a marathon runner dies of a heart attack; a woman loses her retirement fund after working loyally for a company for 25 years. Every day it seems there is another story in the newspaper about the randomness of nature or the inability of humans to control their own lives. **Search** three online newspapers for stories that seem to support the naturalistic viewpoint. Print out one story to share with your classmates.

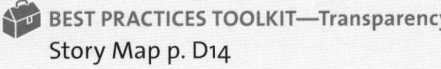

CALIFORNIA   R2.5, W2.2

755

Wrap-Up: The Rise of Naturalism

This wrap-up provides students with an opportunity to reconsider naturalism after having seen its tenets explored in stories. Encourage students to think carefully about the idea that humans lack control of their destinies, and remind them to use their own insights about human decision-making as they read the quotes.

Writing to Evaluate

Review with students that *evaluating* means making a judgment about something. Analysis often precedes evaluation because readers must understand thoroughly in order to evaluate effectively.

To help students write their essays, break down the process into these steps:

1. Choose a story and determine its main message.
2. Decide which quote best represents the story's main message.
3. Skim the story for details that support the quotation's ideas.
4. Outline and draft the essay.

Extension Online

- As students are researching online, suggest that they visit sites maintained by their local newspaper and by other well-known, reliable newspapers.
- Encourage students to complete a story map for the article they select in order to identify key story points for discussion.

BEST PRACTICES TOOLKIT—Transparency Story Map p. D14

FOR DEVELOPING WRITERS

Writing Support Urge students to write about "The Law of Life" because it is the shorter of the two stories. Success in analyzing a shorter piece will build confidence for future analysis of longer pieces. To make the tasks more manageable, encourage students to discuss main story ideas with a partner and skim for supporting details one page at a time.

FOR ENGLISH LEARNERS

Review Theme Remind students that the main message of a story is its theme. Then discuss these questions with them:

- What is the theme of the chosen story?
- What events, dialogue, or setting details from the story support this theme?
- How does the theme statement connect to the chosen quote?

OBJECTIVES

- identify and interpret theme
- analyze social context

 CALIFORNIA R3.2, R3.5

Dramatizing Social Issues

Social Themes Clarify that in the context of this workshop, the terms *theme* and *issue* are used interchangeably. Then, focus on the category of social issues and give students practice recognizing these themes. Have students identify the social issues among these examples and record them on a concept web:

- family connections
- racial prejudice *(social)*
- bonds of friendship
- religious intolerance *(social)*
- economic hardship *(social)*
- unfair working conditions *(social)*
- honesty
- homelessness *(social)*
- the power of the ocean

Explain that a theme typically requires a complete sentence to fully convey it. Urge students to write a theme statement about each social issue on their web. For example, for *racial prejudice,* they might write "Racial prejudice undermines hopes and dreams," while for *economic hardship,* they might write "Economic hardship wears down individuals."

 Literary Analysis Workshop

Social Themes in Fiction

People often talk about social issues—such as poverty, racism, or crime—in a general sense, but how do these issues affect individuals' lives in reality? In 19th-century America, writers began to explore these issues in fiction.

Dramatizing Social Issues

 R3.2, R3.5

Typical themes in literature deal with issues that are common to most people, such as the loss of innocence, difficult family relationships, or a new love. **Social themes,** however, deal with issues that concern a particular group of people, such as those in a certain neighborhood, geographical region, or religious community. These issues are usually specific to a time and place, but they may echo in other cultures and times as well. For example, the dynamics of Puritan society inspired a number of great literary works with social themes, from Nathaniel Hawthorne's *The Scarlet Letter* (1850) to Arthur Miller's *The Crucible* (1953). While Hawthorne explored the effects of Puritan morality on individual lives, Miller chose to expose the wrongs committed in the name of righteousness during the Salem witch trials as a way to explore parallel events of his own time.

Two suffragettes, circa 1905, stand on an American city street, promoting women's rights.

In the late 19th and early 20th centuries, novels and short stories with a contemporary social theme typically dealt with issues that generated strong public reaction and debate for that era. These issues included industrialism, urbanization, and the displacement of Native Americans. In this way, literature became a powerful tool for social change.

Identifying Social Themes

Novels and short stories of the period often portray characters struggling against poverty, prejudice, and other social obstacles. One social issue in particular that emerged in the second half of the 19th century was the role of women in society. This issue preoccupied writers of many nationalities during this time and inspired feminist writers in the 20th century. All of the stories in this part of Unit 4 address this issue in one way or another. To help you identify the social themes in these and other stories, consider the following:

- Look for **characters** who have little control over their fate, and ask yourself what **social factors** contribute to their situation.

DIFFERENTIATED INSTRUCTION

For general guidelines on differentiating instruction, see

 BEST PRACTICES TOOLKIT
Differentiated Instruction pp. 31–38

FOR STRATEGIC READERS

Note Taking For students who are unfamiliar with social themes in fiction or need help with note taking, hand out the copy master at the start of the workshop. Explain to students that they will be learning many

terms in this workshop related to social themes in fiction. Discuss the major terms on this spread (*themes, social themes, issues, characters, social factors, conflicts, character's or narrator's opinions*) as students record notes on the copy master.

 RESOURCE MANAGER—Copy Master
Note Taking p. 211

- Clarify the **conflicts** in the story and determine to what extent they are caused by forces beyond a character's control.

- Examine direct statements of a **character's or narrator's opinions** to see whether these provide clues to a theme.

- Think about the **author's reason** for writing the story. What was he or she trying to achieve?

Works that address social issues often focus on people who have few, if any, rights and privileges in society. The first-person narrator of "The Yellow Wallpaper" (page 768), although comfortably middle-class, has no control over her life. Early in the story, she explains her complete submission to her doctor and her husband.

> So I take phosphates . . . and tonics, and journeys, and air, and exercise, and am absolutely forbidden to "work" until I am well again.
> Personally, I disagree with their ideas.
> Personally, I believe that congenial work, with excitement and change, would do me good.
> But what is one to do?
>
> —**Charlotte Perkins Gilman, "The Yellow Wallpaper"**

Close Read

Based on the narrator's statements in this passage, how would you describe her relationship with the doctor and her husband?

In "The Story of an Hour" (page 760), the main character, after hearing that her husband is dead, reflects on the control he has exercised over her. Notice how her thoughts are a statement on the relationships between men and women in general.

> There would be no one to live for her during those coming years; she would live for herself. There would be no powerful will bending hers in that blind persistence with which men and women believe they have a right to impose a private will upon a fellow creature.
>
> —**Kate Chopin, "The Story of an Hour"**

Close Read

How is this character's attitude different from that expressed in "The Yellow Wallpaper"?

Identifying Social Themes

Suggest that students ask these questions to help them identify social themes:

- What do characters' comments—even those beyond directly stated opinions— suggest about a social message?
- What lessons do characters learn that reflect a social message?
- How do the time and place affect the characters?
- What part do social factors play in the story's conflict and resolution?
- Is the character struggling against poverty, prejudice, or injustice?

Review the excerpts on page 757 with students, clarifying the text as needed. Ask students to paraphrase each one.

Close Read

Possible answer: The narrator has strong opinions, but appears to fear conflict with others and also feels powerless to voice her opinions or to act on them.

If students need help . . . Ask these questions:

- How does the narrator feel about following the suggested regimens and giving up work?
- What does she believe would do her good?

Then read the final statement "But what is one to do?" and ask students what that statement suggests about the narrator's actions and feelings.

Close Read

Possible answer: Chopin's character seems more self-assured and able to act on her own views.

If students need help . . . Reread the first part of the second sentence: *There would be no powerful will bending hers.*

FOR ENGLISH LEARNERS
Language: Skill Words Help students use context to determine the meanings of the boldface words: *theme,* "big idea or message of a story"; *social themes,* "big ideas or messages that have to do with society or the general public"; *social factor,* "causes or reason having to do with society"; *conflicts,* "struggles, battles, disagreements."

FOR ADVANCED LEARNERS/AP
Analyze Social Themes Encourage students to identify social issues and themes in works they have read, such as *The Crucible,* "Common Sense," and Frederick Douglass's slave narrative. Encourage them to share their findings with the class.

Focus and Motivate

OBJECTIVES

Literary Analysis
- explore the key idea of **constraints**
- analyze plot and conflict
- read a short story

Reading
- predict

Grammar and Writing
- use effective voice

CALIFORNIA R3.3, W1.2, W1.5, LC1.1

ABOUT THE AUTHOR

Before students read the biography, remind them of the era in which Chopin lived: Women were making gains but had won the right to vote in only four Western States. Women who asserted and expressed themselves were told that their behavior was unnatural. After students read, discuss what the intense criticism of her novel suggests about this period in history. **Possible answer:** *The intense criticism shows that the turn-of-the-century public wasn't ready for Chopin's risqué subject matter.*

USING THE *NOTABLE QUOTE*

Invite students to speculate on what the quote suggests about **Kate Chopin** and her opinions about the traditional role of women. *Students should understand that Chopin recognized the need for women to overcome oppression and prejudice.*

Selection Resources

The Story of an Hour
Short Story by Kate Chopin

R3.3, W1.2 (p. 765), **W1.5** (p. 765), **LC1.1** (p. 765)

NOTABLE QUOTE
"The bird that would soar above the level plain of tradition and prejudice must have strong wings."

FYI
Did you know that Kate Chopin . . .

- had a story published in the very first issue of *Vogue* magazine?
- could write only one or two days a week while her children played around her?
- was paid about $15 to $30 for each short story she sold?

Author Online

For more on Kate Chopin, visit the **Literature Center** at ClassZone.com.

Kate Chopin
1850–1904

When her second volume of short stories was published in 1897, Kate Chopin's literary career was already thriving. Critics had praised her first collection, *Bayou Folk,* for its local-color realism, calling her tales "charming" and "quaint." Two years later came the bombshell: Chopin published *The Awakening,* a novel about a housewife's sexual and artistic awakening, complete with an adulterous affair and suicide as a last, desperate act of freedom. A chorus of outraged reviewers reviled the novel as immoral, drowning out the few brave enough to praise it. No publisher would touch her next collection, *A Vocation and a Voice,* which included "The Story of an Hour." Chopin died soon after, and *The Awakening* languished out of print for 50 years.

Faithful Wife and Mother Chopin was born Catherine O'Flaherty in St. Louis, Missouri, to a socially prominent family.

Esteemed for her beauty, intelligence, and ready wit, she fell in love with and married Oscar Chopin when she was 19. The Chopins settled in New Orleans, where their six children were born. Kate Chopin had no difficulty in reconciling the demands of her family with her strong independent streak. With the support of her husband, she smoked cigarettes and explored the city unescorted—scandalous behavior for an upper-class woman at the time.

A Budding Writer Chopin started writing at the age of 32. After her husband died, she returned to St. Louis, where her doctor suggested she write stories to work through her grief. Encouraged that her very first story was published, Chopin studied the work of French short story master Guy de Maupassant and honed her craft. She gradually developed an interest in complex issues such as the longing for freedom and self-fulfillment among women.

A Late-Blooming Classic Though *The Awakening* ended its author's career, it went on, after her death, to become a classic. Critics in the 1950s rediscovered the novel and, proclaiming Chopin "ahead of her time," sparked renewed interest in her modern sensibilities. Of *The Awakening*'s heroine, Edna Pontellier, Chopin once said, "I never dreamed of Mrs. Pontellier making such a mess of things. . . . If I had the slightest intimation of such a thing I would have excluded her from the company." The controversial heroine made Chopin a legend. Today, *The Awakening* is among the five most-read American novels in colleges and universities.

758

RESOURCE MANAGER UNIT 4

Plan and Teach pp. 213–220

Literary Analysis
Summary pp. 221†*, 222‡*
Plot and Conflict pp. 223, 224†*
Question Support p. 228*

Reading
Predict pp. 225, 226†*
Reading Check p. 227

Grammar and Writing
Use Effective Voice p. 229

Assessment
Selection Tests A, B/C
pp. 231*, 233*
Test Generator CD

 BEST PRACTICES TOOLKIT

Differentiated Instruction
pp. 31–38*

Scaffolding Instruction
pp. 43–46*

Graphic Organizers/Strategies
Definition Mapping • Three-Column Journal

Reading Support
Audio Anthology CD*

Technology
Literature and Writing Centers at **ClassZone.com**
Write*Smart* CD

LITERARY ANALYSIS: PLOT AND CONFLICT

What makes a great story? The power of a literary work comes partly from its **plot,** or sequence of actions and events. These events are often external—maybe one character rescues another, or the sky opens up with a ferocious downpour. They might also take place internally. These events invariably lead to both **internal** and **external conflict,** and it is this conflict that drives the plot to its **climax,** or turning point, and **resolution,** in which the conflict is settled one way or another.

The plot of "The Story of an Hour" begins with an external event that propels the main character into a dramatic inner conflict.

She was beginning to recognize this thing that was approaching to possess her, and she was striving to beat it back with her will. . . .

As you read this story, pay attention to the relationship between external and internal events and conflicts. In particular, look to see just how the conflict is resolved.

READING STRATEGY: PREDICT

Making accurate **predictions** as you read is not always easy—especially when certain elements in a story are not as straightforward as they initially seem. To create surprising plot twists, a writer often uses **situational irony,** a contrast between what readers expect to happen and what actually does happen. Other times, a writer lets the reader know more about a character or situation in the story than the characters themselves know. This is called **dramatic irony.**

As you read this story, note details that seem to reveal something important about a character or **foreshadow** an upcoming event, giving hints about what will take place. Use these clues to predict what will happen next. As events unfold, note whether your expectations were met or you were taken by surprise.

Clues from the Text	My Predictions	Actual Outcome
"Great care" is taken to delicately break the news of Mr. Mallard's death to his widow, who has a weak heart.		

Do all CAGES have bars?

KEY IDEA Prisons and detention centers, animal cages, even children's playpens—all have bars to keep their inhabitants from escaping. But are these the only kinds of **constraints** that restrict freedom? In "The Story of an Hour," Kate Chopin explores just how restrictive invisible bars can be.

PRESENT With a partner, brainstorm a list of different circumstances in which people can become trapped or otherwise kept from fulfilling themselves. Share your list with the class and explain which constraint you think is the biggest threat to an individual's freedom today.

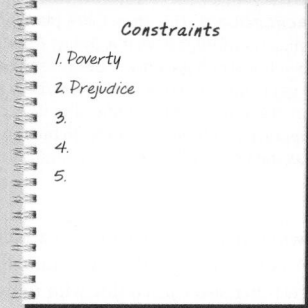

Constraints
1. Poverty
2. Prejudice
3.
4.
5.

Do all CAGES have bars?

Read the question and **KEY IDEA** paragraph with students. Make sure that they understand that a **constraint** is something that holds a person back. Then have partners do the **PRESENT** activity. After students share their lists, ask them what effect invisible constraints have on people.

SKILLS FOCUS

LITERARY ANALYSIS

● PLOT AND CONFLICT

Write this example on the board:

> Elizabeth wanted to study medicine. Her brothers criticized her for having un-natural ambitions. She lost confidence, but didn't give up on her goal. She found a university that accepted women and took a few courses. Ten years later she earned her medical degree.

Have students identify the plot, external and internal conflicts, and resolution. **Possible answer:** *Plot: Elizabeth wants an education; her brothers criticize her. She later earns an education. Conflicts: criticism, loss of confidence. Resolution: She finishes her medical degree.*

CHECK UNDERSTANDING Ask students for examples of internal and external conflicts from stories or movies.

READING STRATEGY R3.3

◼ PREDICT

Refer to the lines on the board. Ask students to predict what Elizabeth might do next and what clues from the text helped them make a prediction. **Possible answer:** *She will begin working as a doctor. Elizabeth is persistent.*

 RESOURCE MANAGER—Copy Master
Predict p. 225 (for student use while reading the selection)

DIFFERENTIATED INSTRUCTION

FOR STRATEGIC READERS

Concept Support: Conflict Review with students that an **external conflict** is a struggle between a character and an outside force, such as another character, society, or nature. An **internal conflict** is a struggle within the character's mind. It might involve a clash of feelings, a decision, or a choice. Ask students to identify each kind of conflict.

• Old Jake had never seen such enormous waves as those battering his ship. *(external)*

• *Should I say yes to his proposal?* Lucy whispered to herself. *(internal)*

• Jim gave Fred a nasty look before pushing his books off his desk. *(external)*

• Tom didn't know which job to accept: the vet's assistant or the high-paying sales position. *(internal)*

SUMMARY

This short story opens with a sensitive group of characters gathered around Mrs. Mallard. Because Mrs. Mallard suffers from heart trouble, her sister gently tells her the news of her husband's death. Mrs. Mallard weeps and then retreats to her room, where she gives in to joy over her new, free life. Coaxed from her room, she dies upon seeing her husband, who is not dead after all, as he enters their home.

READING STRATEGY

A PREDICT

Possible answer: She may collapse upon hearing the bad news; she may feel such grief that her heart gives out; or she may not wish to go on living without him.

If students need help . . . Rephrase the question, asking them why "great care" was taken to break the news to Mrs. Mallard. Then help students to fill in the second column of the prediction chart introduced on page 759.

Clues from the Text	My Predictions	Actual Outcome
"Great care" to break the news, "afflicted with a heart trouble"	She will collapse when she hears the news.	

The Story of an HOUR

KATE CHOPIN

BACKGROUND This story takes place around 1900, when the status of women was radically different than it is today. Because women could not vote, they had almost no political or legal power; because they could not own property and had few chances to gain education or employment, they had little or no financial independence. Few careers were open to middle- and upper-class women, who were expected to be supported by their husbands. In most American marriages of the time, the husband was the undisputed head of the household.

ANALYZE VISUALS
In the era in which this story is set, women were deemed fragile, sensitive, and submissive. What artistic elements help to convey these attributes in the painting?

Knowing that Mrs. Mallard was afflicted with a heart trouble, great care was taken to break to her as gently as possible the news of her husband's death. **A**

It was her sister Josephine who told her, in broken sentences; veiled hints that revealed in half concealing. Her husband's friend Richards was there, too, near her. It was he who had been in the newspaper office when intelligence of the railroad disaster was received, with Brently Mallard's name leading the list of "killed." He had only taken the time to assure himself of its truth by a second telegram, and had hastened to forestall any less careful, less tender friend in bearing the sad message.

① Targeted Passage

A PREDICT
What might this early mention of Mrs. Mallard's illness **foreshadow?** Use this clue to predict how she will react to the news of her husband's death. Record your prediction in your chart.

A Sketch of a Faraway Look, Herman Jean Joseph Richir. Bonhams, London. © Bridgeman Art Library/SuperStock.

DIFFERENTIATED INSTRUCTION

FOR ALL STUDENTS

Provide these independent projects to extend the lesson:

- Discuss what kind of marriage Chopin would advocate.
- Research activists for women's rights during Chopin's time.

For further details on these projects, see

R RESOURCE MANAGER
Ideas for Extension pp. 218–219

FOR STRATEGIC READERS

In combination with the *Audio Anthology CD,* use one or more Targeted Passages (pp. 760, 762, 763) to ensure that students focus on key story events and concepts. Targeted Passages are also good for English learners.

① Targeted Passage [Lines 1–6]

The opening passage establishes the main characters, the setting, and the major conflict.

BACKGROUND

Marriage at the Turn of the Century In 1900, around the time that Kate Chopin wrote "The Story of an Hour," most married women were homemakers. Nearly half of college-educated women chose not to marry at all. Only about five percent of college-educated women held jobs. However, the situation of women in the United States was changing. Divorce was rising: one of 12 marriages ended in divorce. Women who stayed at home to raise a family suddenly had more opportunities for self-fulfillment. Time-consuming tasks in the home were gradually being replaced by new technology (sewing and washing machines, vacuum cleaners)—allowing women to direct their attention to other endeavors. Professions in law, medicine, and journalism began to open up. The women's rights movement also led women to expect more about what roles they would play at home and in society.

- Where does the story take place?
- What is wrong with Mrs. Mallard?
- What news is she about to hear?
- Why is Mrs. Mallard's sister so worried about breaking this news?

She did not hear the story as many women have heard the same, with a
10 paralyzed inability to accept its significance. She wept at once, with sudden, wild
abandonment, in her sister's arms. When the storm of grief had spent itself she
went away to her room alone. She would have no one follow her.

There stood, facing the open window, a comfortable, roomy armchair. Into
this she sank, pressed down by a physical exhaustion that haunted her body and
seemed to reach into her soul.

She could see in the open square before her house the tops of trees that were
all aquiver with the new spring life. The delicious breath of rain was in the air. In
the street below a peddler was crying his wares. The notes of a distant song which
someone was singing reached her faintly, and countless sparrows were twittering
20 in the eaves.

There were patches of blue sky showing here and there through the clouds that
had met and piled one above the other in the west facing her window.

She sat with her head thrown back upon the cushion of the chair, quite
motionless, except when a sob came up into her throat and shook her, as a child
who has cried itself to sleep continues to sob in its dreams.

She was young, with a fair, calm face, whose lines bespoke repression and even
a certain strength. But now there was a dull stare in her eyes, whose gaze was
fixed away off yonder on one of those patches of blue sky. It was not a glance of
reflection, but rather indicated a suspension of intelligent thought.

30 There was something coming to her and she was waiting for it, fearfully. What
was it? She did not know; it was too subtle and elusive to name. But she felt it,
creeping out of the sky, reaching toward her through the sounds, the scents, the
color that filled the air. **B**

Now her bosom rose and fell tumultuously. She was beginning to recognize this
thing that was approaching to possess her, and she was striving to beat it back with
her will—as powerless as her two white slender hands would have been. **C**

When she abandoned herself a little whispered word escaped her slightly parted
lips. She said it over and over under her breath: "free, free, free!" The vacant stare
and the look of terror that had followed it went from her eyes. They stayed keen
40 and bright. Her pulses beat fast, and the coursing blood warmed and relaxed every
inch of her body. **D**

She did not stop to ask if it were or were not a monstrous joy that held her.
A clear and exalted perception enabled her to dismiss the suggestion as trivial.

She knew that she would weep again when she saw the kind, tender hands
folded in death; the face that had never looked save with love upon her, fixed and
gray and dead. But she saw beyond that bitter moment a long procession of years
to come that would belong to her absolutely. And she opened and spread her arms
out to them in welcome.

② Targeted Passage

B GRAMMAR AND STYLE
Reread lines 30–33.
Notice how Chopin uses
the **active voice,** with the
subjects performing the
action in the sentences.
Contrast this with her use
of the **passive voice** in the
first sentence of the story.

C PLOT AND CONFLICT
Reread lines 34–36. With
what is Mrs. Mallard
struggling? Explain
whether her conflict is
internal or **external.**

D PREDICT
Did Mrs. Mallard respond
to the revelation as you
predicted she would?
What is **ironic** about her
reaction?

B GRAMMAR AND STYLE

Possible answer: The active voice suggests the power of her feelings and emotions, in contrast to the delicacy and fragility implied with the use of the passive voice in the first sentence.

LITERARY ANALYSIS

C PLOT AND CONFLICT

Possible answer: Her conflict is internal: Mrs. Mallard is struggling to repress strong feelings that are bearing down on her; she fears that they will "possess" her (line 35), and she tries to "beat [them] back" (line 35).

If students need help . . . Remind them that an internal conflict is a struggle within a person. In this case, learning about her husband's death brings on Mrs. Mallard's inner turmoil.

READING STRATEGY

D PREDICT

Possible answer: Ironically, Mrs. Mallard feels joyous, strong, and free, instead of grief-stricken and lost, as most readers probably predicted.

Lines 44–48
**REINFORCE *KEY IDEA:*
CONSTRAINTS**

Discuss Mrs. Mallard is responding to the loosening of **constraints.** What are these constraints? What is her reaction to this change?
Possible answer: She believes that she will no longer be restrained by the wishes, needs, and demands of her husband and that the years ahead will "belong to her absolutely" (line 47). She joyously welcomes this change.

DIFFERENTIATED INSTRUCTION

FOR STRATEGIC READERS

② Targeted Passage [Lines 10–38]

In this passage, the rising action, climax, and resolution of the story occur.

- How does Mrs. Mallard react when her sister first breaks the news of her husband's death?

- In her room, what is she afraid of?

- Why does she say "free, free, free" over and over?

FOR ENGLISH LEARNERS

Vocabulary Support Have students list words related to life outside the house in lines 16–22. Provide an example, and then have partners identify additional examples: *open square, tops of trees* (line 16); *new spring life, rain* (line 17); *peddler, distant song* (line 18); *countless sparrows* (line 19); *patches of blue sky, clouds* (line 21).

There would be no one to live for her during those coming years; she would live for herself. There would be no powerful will bending hers in that blind persistence with which men and women believe they have a right to impose a private will upon a fellow creature. A kind intention or a cruel intention made the act seem no less a crime as she looked upon it in that brief moment of illumination.

And yet she had loved him—sometimes. Often she had not. What did it matter! What could love, the unsolved mystery, count for in face of this possession of self-assertion which she suddenly recognized as the strongest impulse of her being!

"Free! Body and soul free!" she kept whispering.

Josephine was kneeling before the closed door with her lips to the keyhole, imploring for admission. "Louise, open the door! I beg; open the door—you will make yourself ill. What are you doing, Louise? For heaven's sake open the door."

"Go away. I am not making myself ill." No; she was drinking in a very elixir of life[1] through that open window.

Her fancy was running riot along those days ahead of her. Spring days, and summer days, and all sorts of days that would be her own. She breathed a quick prayer that life might be long. It was only yesterday she had thought with a shudder that life might be long. **E**

She arose at length and opened the door to her sister's importunities. There was a feverish triumph in her eyes, and she carried herself unwittingly like a goddess of Victory. She clasped her sister's waist, and together they descended the stairs. Richards stood waiting for them at the bottom.

Someone was opening the front door with a latchkey. It was Brently Mallard who entered, a little travel-stained, composedly carrying his grip-sack[2] and umbrella. He had been far from the scene of accident, and did not even know there had been one. He stood amazed at Josephine's piercing cry; at Richards' quick motion to screen him from the view of his wife.

But Richards was too late.

When the doctors came they said she had died of heart disease—of joy that kills. ❧

E PLOT AND CONFLICT
Consider the feelings Mrs. Mallard struggles to repress when she first enters her room. How, in lines 42–67, is this conflict resolved?

3 Targeted Passage

---

1. **elixir of life:** a medicine that restores vigor or the essence of life.
2. **grip-sack:** a small traveling bag or satchel.

FOR STRATEGIC READERS

3 Targeted Passage [Lines 64–79]

This passage contains the story's surprise ending.

- How is Mrs. Mallard feeling when she leaves her room with her sister?
- Who comes through the front door?
- What happens to Louise when she sees that her husband is still alive?

FOR ADVANCED LEARNERS/AP

Oxymoron Remind students that an oxymoron is a figure of speech in which contradictory terms are connected. Have students discuss the final words of the story: "joy that kills." What is the literal and figurative meaning of this phrase? Compare this example with "monstrous joy" in line 42. How does each example contribute to the story's irony? Ask students to write two paragraphs about the use of oxymoron in the selection and share their findings with the class.

Lines 55–79
TIERED DISCUSSION PROMPTS

Use these prompts to help students understand the levels of irony at the end of the story:

Summarize What news has Louise just received? How does she react, publicly and privately? *Possible answer: Louise has just received news that her husband was killed. Publicly, she appears distraught; privately, she is elated.*

Analyze What does the reader know that Josephine does not? How does this dramatic irony work during the scene when Louise is alone in her room? *Possible answer: Josephine does not know that Louise is overjoyed with her anticipated freedom rather than devastated by her husband's death. It heightens the irony that Josephine is so worried about her sister's well-being.*

Evaluate How effective is the irony of the final scene, when Louise learns that her husband is alive and well? *Possible answer: Most students will recognize that the surprise ending is powerful and shocking.*

LITERARY ANALYSIS

E PLOT AND CONFLICT

Possible answer: She resolves her inner conflict by allowing the feelings that she has been repressing to freely enter her mind. She doesn't waste time or energy worrying that her thoughts are "monstrous" (line 42). She knows that she will cry at the "bitter moment" when she sees his dead face (lines 44–46), but she focuses on the freedom and joy she feels, drinking in the "elixir of life" (lines 62–63). She embraces her new life, hoping it will be long (lines 66–67).

SELECTION WRAP—UP

REFLECT What message does the surprise ending convey about Louise and other women like her?

Practice and Apply

After Reading

Use these copy masters to check understanding and provide extra support:

R RESOURCE MANAGER—Copy Masters
Reading Check p. 227
Plot and Conflict p. 223
Question Support p. 228

Additional selection questions are provided for teachers on page 217.

ANSWERS

1. *She is afflicted with heart disease.*

2. *She learns that her husband has died in a train accident; she feels more joy over her new freedom than grief over her loss.*

3. *Mrs. Mallard dies of a heart attack after her husband, who is very much alive, walks through the door.*

Possible answers:

4. ● **SKILLS FOCUS** Plot and Conflict *Mrs. Mallard struggles to repress the joy she feels over her husband's death. Eventually, she gives in to these feelings and anticipates with pleasure a long, free, happy life. This sets up the reader to be shocked when she dies upon seeing her husband walk into the house.*

5. ■ **SKILLS FOCUS** Predict *Chopin uses irony to deliver surprise twists by setting readers up to believe that Mrs. Mallard will be heartbroken, and then revealing that she is actually elated; making readers consider the long, free life ahead of Mrs. Mallard, then cutting it short with her sudden death; and letting readers in on the secret that Mrs. Mallard's death is caused not by joy that her husband is alive but by disappointment.*

6. *The sights and sounds from her window are images of life, hope, promise, and freedom; they support her yearning for freedom because these images are all outside and distant. These images suggest that freedom is a natural right, making her aspirations more sympathetic.*

7. **Mrs. Mallard:** *free only outside marriage; resents male power; not in control of own destiny until widowed; begins to dream of self-fulfillment only when she finds herself alone.*

Comprehension

1. **Recall** What illness afflicts Mrs. Mallard?

2. **Summarize** Describe the news Mrs. Mallard receives at the beginning of the story and explain how she reacts.

3. **Clarify** What happens at the end of the story?

Literary Analysis

4. **Analyze Plot and Conflict** The plot of "The Story of an Hour" is driven by Mrs. Mallard's **internal conflict.** Describe her conflict; then explain how this secret inner struggle sets up the story's **surprise ending.**

5. **Examine Predictions** Review the chart you filled in as you read. Were your predictions accurate? Consider how Chopin uses **irony** to play on readers' expectations and deliver surprise plot twists in each of the following cases. Does this manipulation increase or decrease your enjoyment of the story?

   • Mrs. Mallard's reaction to the news that her husband is dead (lines 34–58)
   • Mrs. Mallard's wish that "life might be long" (lines 64–67)
   • the doctor's explanation of the cause of Mrs. Mallard's death (lines 78–79)

6. **Interpret Imagery** Reread lines 16–22. How does Chopin's use of imagery contribute to your understanding of Mrs. Mallard's character and situation? Did the imagery make you more or less sympathetic toward her? Explain, citing specific lines from the story that influenced your response.

7. **Compare Characters** Both Mrs. Mallard and Aunt Georgiana in "A Wagner Matinee" by Willa Cather (page 694) face **constraints** that confine them to a specific way of life. In a Venn diagram like the one shown, compare and contrast these two characters' situations. Use your completed diagram to explain what message each author might be trying to convey through her main character.

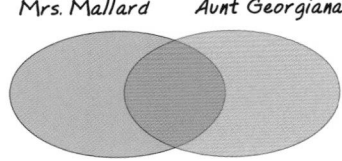

Mrs. Mallard   Aunt Georgiana

Literary Criticism

8. **Social Context** Women's roles have certainly changed since Chopin wrote this story, but has the institution of marriage? Reread lines 49–54 of "The Story of an Hour." Is the imposition of will by both men and women that Chopin describes still an issue in contemporary marriages? Explain your opinion.

Aunt Georgiana: *works within constraints of marriage; revolts only when opportunity arises and she's sure she's right; accepts husband's power; fights for her rightful domain (home and children); takes pride in her role as wife and mother.*

Both: *repress their desires; taste freedom and don't want to let it go*

8. *Students may say that with greater equality women are more likely to be happy in marriage. Others may say that women's freedom creates more conflict. Some may point out that divorces are on the rise and that conflicts are as problematic as ever.*

Reading-Writing Connection

 W1.2, W1.5

WRITING PROMPT

COMPOSE A JOURNAL ENTRY "The Story of an Hour" focuses on Mrs. Mallard's conflicted feelings about her husband's rumored death. Think about the moment her feelings suddenly shift from sorrow to joy. What are some of the possibilities she thinks her newfound "freedom" might offer her? How does she foresee her life changing? Imagine you are Mrs. Mallard. Write a **three-paragraph journal entry** in which you detail some of the thoughts that might have gone through her mind as she pondered a future free of **constraints**.

SELF-CHECK

A strong journal entry will . . .
- reflect Mrs. Mallard's initial struggle with her feelings
- give concrete examples of how she believes her life might change
- use language and sentence types that capture her emotions

GRAMMAR AND STYLE

USE EFFECTIVE VOICE Review the **Grammar and Style** note on page 762. The **active voice** indicates that the subject of a sentence is *performing* the action. It is the voice writers use most of the time. The **passive voice** indicates that the subject of a sentence is *receiving* the action. Though the passive voice is generally avoided in formal writing, writers will sometimes use it to create a particular effect or to indicate that the performer of an action is indefinite or unknown. Here are examples of each type of voice:

 LC1.1

Active: *Someone was opening the front door with a latchkey.* (line 72)

Passive: *It was he who had been in the newspaper office when intelligence of the railroad disaster was received. . . .* (lines 5–6)

Kate Chopin effectively uses the active and passive voices to mirror her character's emotional transition from repression to liberation. She begins the story in the passive voice, when Mrs. Mallard is still under constraint, but later switches to the active voice as Mrs. Mallard begins to acknowledge her own identity.

PRACTICE Change the voice of the following sentences as indicated in parentheses.

> **EXAMPLE**
> He gave me my freedom. (Change to the passive voice.)
> *Freedom was given to me.*

1. A life of adventure is desired by everyone. (Change to the active voice.)
2. I will spend my days as I wish. (Change to the passive voice.)
3. No one will be consulted about my plans. (Change to the active voice.)

 WRITING TOOLS
For prewriting, revision, and editing tools, visit the **Writing Center** at ClassZone.com.

DIFFERENTIATED INSTRUCTION

FOR DEVELOPING WRITERS
Writing Support

- Offer students a starter for their journal entry, such as: My first reaction upon hearing the terrible news of my husband's death was profound grief. My second reaction was _____.

- Suggest that they use two areas of concern from their Three-Column Journal as a basis for writing two paragraphs. Encourage them to add details to each paragraph, if they can.

Reading-Writing Connection

WRITING PROMPT
Suggest that students list Mrs. Mallard's feelings and inner conflicts about different parts of her life. Encourage them to use a Three-Column Journal to write their ideas about how she felt about each part of her life before and after she learned of her husband's death.

Feelings About	Before the news	After the news
child care	overburdened	will get more help
finances	dependent	independent
education; artistic pursuits	unfulfilled	will go to college; will write

 BEST PRACTICES TOOLKIT—Transparency
Three-Column Journal p. B10

For writing support, see

Writing Center at **ClassZone.com**

GRAMMAR AND STYLE
Ask students to identify the subject and verb in each example. Point out the location of the subjects in relation to the verbs. (For more on active and passive voice, see page R60 in the **Grammar Handbook**.)

Answers:

1. *Everyone desires a life of adventure.*
2. *My days will be spent according to my wishes.*
3. *I will consult no one about my plans.*

RESOURCE MANAGER—Copy Master
Use Effective Voice p. 229

Assess and Reteach

Assess

RESOURCE MANAGER—Copy Masters
Selection Test A pp. 231–232
Selection Test B/C pp. 233–234

Test Generator CD

Reteach

STANDARDS LESSON FILE
Literature Lesson 5: Elements of Plot
Literature Lesson 6: Conflict and Suspense
Reading Lesson 1: Predicting

Focus and Motivate

OBJECTIVES

Literary Analysis
- explore the key idea of being **powerless**
- analyze first-person narrator
- read a short story

Reading
- understand social context

Vocabulary
- build vocabulary for reading and writing
- analyze specialized temperament words
  (also an EL language objective)

Grammar and Writing
- choose verb tenses for greatest effect
- write a personal response

 CALIFORNIA R3.5, R3.8, W2.2, LC1.1

ABOUT THE AUTHOR

After students read Gilman's biography, ask how the Beechers might have affected her. **Possible answer:** *They fostered her interest in women's rights and social change.* Have students predict what might cause the narrator in "The Yellow Wallpaper" to go mad. *Students may suggest that unhappiness with inequality leads to the narrator's madness.*

USING THE *NOTABLE QUOTE*

Ask students what **Charlotte Perkins Gilman** means by "the first duty." **Possible answer:** *She emphasizes the importance of making a whole-hearted contribution to society.*

Selection Resources

The Yellow Wallpaper
Short Story by Charlotte Perkins Gilman

R3.5, R3.8 (p. 785), **W2.2** (p. 787), **LC1.1** (p. 787)

NOTABLE QUOTE
"The first duty of a human being is to assume the right relationship to society— more briefly, to find your real job, and do it."

FYI
Did you know that Charlotte Perkins Gilman ...

- moved 19 times in her first 18 years?
- produced eight novels, six nonfiction books, almost 200 short stories, hundreds of poems, and thousands of essays?
- founded and ran her own feminist magazine, the *Forerunner*?

Charlotte Perkins Gilman
1860–1935

As a feminist writer, social activist, public lecturer, editor, and publisher, Charlotte Perkins Gilman rode the wave of reform that washed over the United States in the late 19th and early 20th centuries. Her 1898 landmark study, *Women and Economics*—called "the Bible of the woman's movement" at the time—argued persuasively that women's economic dependence on men made them veritable slaves in U.S. society. To rectify the inequities, she advocated child-care centers and communal kitchens so that women could earn money outside the home. In addition, her startlingly original story "The Yellow Wallpaper," published in 1892, discredited a popular treatment for women's so-called "nervous disorders." Looking beyond suffrage, Gilman sought to free women from domestic servitude and foster their intellectual and emotional growth.

Formative Early Years Gilman got a rather shaky start in life. Her father abandoned the family shortly after her birth in Hartford, Connecticut. Her mother, possibly in reaction to her dire circumstances, adopted the odd child-rearing habits of withholding affection and forbidding her daughter to read fiction or form close friendships. Fortunately, financial hardship forced the family to live with relatives, the most prominent among them being Harriet Beecher Stowe, the abolitionist author of *Uncle Tom's Cabin,* and the feminists Catherine Beecher and Isabella Beecher Hooker. Guided by her strong, successful aunts, young Charlotte grew into a well-adjusted, independent woman.

Sweetening Reform with Humor Gilman's first published work was a volume of poetry, *In This Our World,* which attracted attention for the humorous way she ridiculed social injustice and inequality. *Women and Economics* garnered similar praise despite its frontal assault on conventional marriage. One reviewer praised the "wit and sarcasm" that made Gilman's "profound social philosophy" such an entertaining read. After publishing several more sociological studies, Gilman returned to writing fiction. *Herland* (1915) is a science-fiction satire about the comic misadventures of three men who stumble upon an all-female society. Still, Gilman's most popular work continues to be "The Yellow Wallpaper," the grim but fascinating portrait of a woman's descent into madness. The one-of-a-kind story has never gone out of print.

766

 RESOURCE MANAGER UNIT 4

Plan and Teach pp. 235–242

Literary Analysis
Summary pp. 243†*, 244‡*
First-Person Narrator
   pp. 245, 246†*
Question Support p. 253*

Reading
Understand Social Context
   pp. 247, 248†*
Reading Check p. 252

Vocabulary
Study p. 249*
Practice p. 250
Strategy p. 251

Grammar and Writing
Choose Effective Verb Tense
   p. 254

Assessment
Selection Tests A, B/C
   pp. 255*, 257*
   Test Generator CD

 BEST PRACTICES TOOLKIT

Differentiated Instruction
   pp. 31–38*

Scaffolding Instruction
   pp. 43–46*

Graphic Organizers/Strategies
T Chart • New Word Analysis • Comparison Matrix • Three-Column Journal • Two-Column Chart • Open Mind • Classification Chart

Reading Support
- Audio Anthology CD*

Technology
- Literature, Vocabulary, and Writing Centers at **ClassZone.com**
- Write*Smart* CD

---

* Resources for Differentiation   † Also in Spanish   ‡ In Haitian Creole and Vietnamese

LITERARY ANALYSIS: FIRST-PERSON NARRATOR

A story's narrator—the character or voice that relates events to the reader—can have a marked effect on how you perceive those events. A **first-person narrator** is a character in the story. "The Yellow Wallpaper" is narrated by an unnamed woman diagnosed with a "nervous condition"; readers get to know her through her journal entries. As you read, allow yourself to perceive things as she does. Occasionally, though, stand back to examine her perceptions and actions with a critical eye.

READING SKILL: UNDERSTAND SOCIAL CONTEXT

The **social context** of a work is the social conditions that inspired or influenced its creation. You know that in 1892, when this story was written, women held a drastically different place in society than they do today. Use your prior knowledge, as well as the background on page 768, to analyze the social context of this story as you read. Note what the annotated passages reveal about how women were treated and how they were expected to behave. Consider what Gilman may have thought about these conditions and how she responds to them in "The Yellow Wallpaper."

Story Passages	Notes on Social Context
"John laughs at me, of course, but one expects that in marriage."	The narrator does not expect that a husband would take his wife's ideas seriously. At this time, men wielded the power in most American households.

▲ VOCABULARY IN CONTEXT

Gilman uses these words in her harrowing story of stress and power. Determine the meaning of each word from its context.

1. doctor's orders **misconstrued** because of their complexity
2. a **recurrent** ailment, returning every few months
3. a delicate **temperament,** prone to worrying
4. disturbed by intense, **lurid** dreams
5. flashy, **flamboyant** drawings representing her state of mind
6. **undulating** patterns that made her feel seasick
7. a twisted **convolution** of nightmarish thoughts
8. feared the **derision** of cruel household help
9. a **patent** lie that fooled no one
10. ignorant remarks that demonstrated her **fatuity**

Explore the Key Idea

What if no one took you SERIOUSLY?

KEY IDEA A friend rolls his or her eyes in disbelief as you tell a story. Your parents don't believe that you really *are* sick, not just feigning illness to get out of a test. A teacher or coach refuses to listen to your perspective before launching into a lecture. On at least one occasion, you've probably felt the sting of someone dismissing your feelings or refusing to listen to you. An isolated instance is bad enough, but if everyone around you refused to take you seriously, you might feel utterly **powerless.**

QUICKWRITE Try to imagine a whole day during which, no matter what happened, no one took you seriously. Envision yourself in the middle of such a day; then write a journal entry describing your reaction.

767

Teach

What if no one took you SERIOUSLY?

Read the question and **KEY IDEA** paragraph with students. Invite them to offer definitions of **powerless.** After they complete the *QUICKWRITE* have them revisit their definitions and suggest possible revisions.

SKILLS FOCUS

LITERARY ANALYSIS

● FIRST–PERSON NARRATOR

Share this example with students:

> If only my son Jesse's math teacher saw his brilliance. Jesse's memory of baseball statistics is amazing for a high school student. The teacher should not worry that Jesse is failing math. One day Jesse will find a job he loves—then, look out!

Ask students to describe the narrator's attitude toward Jesse. *Possible answer: He puts a positive spin on Jesse's failure, and perhaps overestimates his strengths.*

CHECK UNDERSTANDING Ask students how Jesse's math teacher might respond to the narrator's attitude.

READING SKILL   R3.5

■ UNDERSTAND SOCIAL CONTEXT

Remind students that besides drawing on their prior knowledge, they can also research a story's historical context to better understand the social context of the work. Suggest that students fill out the Understand Social Context chart with any passage they think might relate to social context. They can discuss any passage they are uncertain of.

 RESOURCE MANAGER—Copy Master Understand Social Context p. 247 (for student use while reading the selection)

VOCABULARY

▲ VOCABULARY IN CONTEXT

Diagnose Word Knowledge To determine preteaching needs, have all students complete Vocabulary in Context. *Possible answers:* 1. *misinterpreted,* 2. *repeated,* 3. *personality,* 4. *shocking,* 5. *gaudy,* 6. *wavy,* 7. *jumble,* 8. *scorn,* 9. *obvious,* 10. *foolishness*

PRETEACH VOCABULARY Preteach vocabulary with this copy master. Read each item aloud.

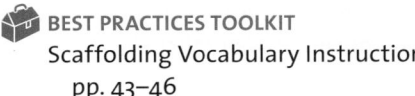 **RESOURCE MANAGER—Copy Master** Vocabulary Study p. 249

MORE VOCABULARY SUPPORT

For additional activities and guidelines, see

 BEST PRACTICES TOOLKIT Scaffolding Vocabulary Instruction pp. 43–46
ⓘ Vocabulary Center at **ClassZone.com**

THE YELLOW WALLPAPER   **767**

SUMMARY

In this short story, the narrator, whose doctor-husband has prescribed a "rest cure" for her depression, keeps a secret diary of a summer spent mostly in bed at a rented country home. She grows increasingly obsessed with the room's yellow wallpaper, imagining a woman trapped in it and wanting to free her by peeling off the paper. Finally, her husband finds her creeping around the room, certain she has freed *herself* from the torn-off wallpaper.

READING SKILL

Ⓐ SOCIAL CONTEXT

Possible answer: Gilman conveys the belief about women's instability through John. He dismisses his wife's feelings and intuitions as unscientific and superstitious, and he laughs and scoffs at her (lines 7–10). He does not believe she is ill (line 14).

If students need help . . . Review the chart introduced on page 767 and help students list additional examples.

Story Passages	Notes on Social Context
"John is practical . . . in figures." (lines 8–10)	Doctors at this time discounted emotional issues as unimportant.
"He does not believe I am sick!" (line 14)	Emotional illness was not taken seriously

Lines 11–15
REINFORCE *KEY IDEA:* POWERLESS

Discuss How does the narrator's passivity reinforce her sense that she is **powerless?**
Possible answer: After describing her husband's assessment of her condition, the narrator muses, "And what can one do?" (line 15). This comment suggests that she feels powerless and must acquiesce to her husband's and others' opinions, rather than trusting her own feelings, which might help her to heal.

The Yellow WALLPAPER

CHARLOTTE PERKINS GILMAN

BACKGROUND If a woman sought medical treatment for a disorder such as depression or anxiety in 1892, her ills were often diagnosed as trivial "nervous conditions," curable through isolation and prolonged rest. Today it is believed that some of these disorders were caused in part by the stress of living within the rigid social roles to which women were confined. Doctors of the time, however, typically felt that their patients' gender lay at the root of the problem. Many saw women as weak and emotionally unstable, and thus predisposed to illness.

ANALYZE VISUALS
Examine this painting. Describe the woman's size, position, and coloring relative to the flowers in the foreground. How does she look next to the flowers? Explain.

It is very seldom that mere ordinary people like John and myself secure ancestral halls for the summer.

A colonial mansion, a hereditary estate, I would say a haunted house, and reach the height of romantic felicity—but that would be asking too much of fate!

Still I will proudly declare that there is something queer about it.

Else, why should it be let so cheaply? And why have stood so long untenanted?

John laughs at me, of course, but one expects that in marriage.

John is practical in the extreme. He has no patience with faith, an intense horror of superstition, and he scoffs openly at any talk of things not to be felt and
10 seen and put down in figures.

John is a physician, and *perhaps*—(I would not say it to a living soul, of course, but this is dead paper and a great relief to my mind)—*perhaps* that is one reason I do not get well faster.

You see he does not believe I am sick!

And what can one do? Ⓐ

① **Targeted Passage**

Ⓐ **SOCIAL CONTEXT**
Consider what you learned from the background paragraph at the top of this page. How does Gilman convey the belief prevalent in her time that women were emotionally unstable and prone to illness?

Geraniums (1888), Childe Hassam. 18 1/4" × 12 7/8". The Hyde Collection, Glens Falls, New York. Photo © Michael Fredericks.

DIFFERENTIATED INSTRUCTION

FOR ALL STUDENTS

Expert Groups Encourage students to become subject experts by selecting and researching one of these topics:

• psychiatric hospitals and treatments for mental illness, circa 1900

• Gilman's own experience of the "rest cure" of Doctor Simon Weir Mitchell

FOR STRATEGIC READERS

In combination with the *Audio Anthology CD,* use one or more Targeted Passages (pp. 768, 771, 773, 776, 778, 780, 783) to ensure that students focus on key story events and concepts. Targeted Passages are also good for English learners.

① **Targeted Passage [Lines 1–15]**

This passage introduces the main characters of the narrator and her husband, the rented home setting, and the main conflict over the narrator's health.

ANALYZE VISUALS

Possible answer: The woman, sitting in the corner, perhaps doing needlework, seems small in relation to the flowers in the foreground. In coloring, her white dress contrasts with the colored flowers, while her dark hair and white dress blend into the background.

About the Art Childe Hassam (1859–1935), America's leading impressionist, painted country life in America as it was once lived in houses like the one the narrator and her husband have rented, using light and color to convey nostalgia for that lifestyle gone by.

Lines 8–13
TIERED DISCUSSION PROMPTS

Use these prompts to help students explore the conflict between the two main characters:

Connect What does the expression "opposites attract" mean? How does it help you understand the narrator's relationship with her husband? *Accept all thoughtful answers.*

Analyze In what way does the narrator imply that she and John are opposites? *Possible answer: She suggests that John is practical and rational, while she is emotional and intuitive.*

Synthesize How would you expect their differences to prove problematic for the narrator? *Possible answer: The narrator believes that she is sick. John's doubt of this and his dismissal of her instincts could cause problems if her condition persists or worsens.*

- Where does the story take place?
- Who is narrating the story?
- What does the narrator's husband do?
- About what do the narrator and her husband disagree?

FOR ENGLISH LEARNERS

Prereading For prereading instruction for English learners, see

 BEST PRACTICES TOOLKIT
Scaffolding Reading Instruction pp. 43–46

FOR ADVANCED LEARNERS/AP

AP exercises in the bottom channel provide additional challenge for students. Use these suggestions for small groups or individuals.

ADDITIONAL GUIDELINES

For more help with differentiation and tips for classroom management, see

 BEST PRACTICES TOOLKIT
Differentiated Instruction pp. 31–38

REINFORCE *KEY IDEA:* POWERLESS

Discuss How does the narrator's husband contribute to her sense of being **powerless?**
Possible answer: The narrator's husband insists that her only problem is a nervous depression (lines 17–18). He prescribes a cure that does not allow her to work (line 22), despite her belief that it would do her good (lines 24–25). The fact that he ignores her feelings, wishes, and needs makes her feel helpless and contributes to her illness.

LITERARY ANALYSIS

Ⓑ FIRST-PERSON NARRATOR

Possible answer: The narrator hides her feelings, desires, and unhappiness about her treatment from her husband. Unlike John, the narrator believes that "work, with excitement and change," would help cure her (lines 24–25).

If students need help . . . Help them complete a T Chart with details that contrast the narrator's opinion of the cure with that of her husband.

The Narrator's Opinion	John's Opinion
"... I believe that congenial work, with excitement and change, would do me good."	"... forbidden to 'work'"

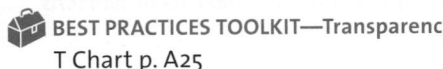 **BEST PRACTICES TOOLKIT—Transparency**
T Chart p. A25

If a physician of high standing, and one's own husband, assures friends and relatives that there is really nothing the matter with one but temporary nervous depression—a slight hysterical[1] tendency—what is one to do?

20 My brother is also a physician, and also of high standing, and he says the same thing.

So I take phosphates or phosphites—whichever it is, and tonics, and journeys, and air, and exercise, and am absolutely forbidden to "work" until I am well again.

Personally, I disagree with their ideas.

Personally, I believe that congenial work, with excitement and change, would do me good.

But what is one to do?

I did write for a while in spite of them; but it *does* exhaust me a good deal—having to be so sly about it, or else meet with heavy opposition.

I sometimes fancy that in my condition if I had less opposition and more 30 society and stimulus—but John says the very worst thing I can do is to think about my condition, and I confess it always makes me feel bad.

So I will let it alone and talk about the house.

The most beautiful place! It is quite alone, standing well back from the road, quite three miles from the village. It makes me think of English places that you read about, for there are hedges and walls and gates that lock, and lots of separate little houses for the gardeners and people.

There is a *delicious* garden! I never saw such a garden—large and shady, full of box-bordered paths, and lined with long grape-covered arbors with seats under them.

40 There were greenhouses, too, but they are all broken now.

There was some legal trouble, I believe, something about the heirs and coheirs; anyhow, the place has been empty for years.

That spoils my ghostliness, I am afraid, but I don't care—there is something strange about the house—I can feel it.

I even said so to John one moonlight evening, but he said what I felt was a *draft,* and shut the window.

I get unreasonably angry with John sometimes. I'm sure I never used to be so sensitive. I think it is due to this nervous condition.

But John says if I feel so, I shall neglect proper self-control; so I take pains to 50 control myself—before him, at least, and that makes me very tired. Ⓑ

I don't like our room a bit. I wanted one downstairs that opened on the piazza and had roses all over the window, and such pretty old-fashioned chintz hangings![2] but John would not hear of it.

He said there was only one window and not room for two beds, and no near room for him if he took another.

He is very careful and loving, and hardly lets me stir without special direction.

Ⓑ FIRST-PERSON NARRATOR
What, in addition to her writing, is the narrator hiding from her husband? Explain how her opinion of the cure for her disorder differs from his.

1. **hysterical:** Hysteria is the presence of a physical ailment with no underlying physical cause.
2. **chintz hangings:** curtains made out of chintz, a printed cotton fabric.

DIFFERENTIATED INSTRUCTION

FOR STRATEGIC READERS

Visualize Gilman uses strong visual images to create the story's setting. Ask students to try to picture these descriptions as you read aloud: the grounds (lines 33–40), the top-floor room (lines 63–70), and the wallpaper (lines 71–80). Challenge students to recall details after each description. As they read on, urge them to notice how the narrator's perception of each element changes as her mental health deteriorates.

FOR ENGLISH LEARNERS

Key Academic Vocabulary Use New Word Analysis to teach these words: *draft* (line 46), *schedule* (line 57), *sequence* (line 294), *hypothesis* (line 325).

 BEST PRACTICES TOOLKIT—Transparency
New Word Analysis p. E8

FOR ADVANCED LEARNERS/AP

Synthesize Author's Views [small-group option] Have students reread the author biography on page 766, then relate Gilman's thesis in *Women and Economics* to the views on self-control expressed in lines 49–50 of the story. Small groups might consider these questions: What does John mean by "self-control"? How does enslavement relate to control and self-control? Have students share their discussion results.

I have a schedule prescription for each hour in the day; he takes all care from me, and so I feel basely ungrateful not to value it more.

He said we came here solely on my account, that I was to have perfect rest and
60 all the air I could get. "Your exercise depends on your strength, my dear," said he, "and your food somewhat on your appetite; but air you can absorb all the time." So we took the nursery at the top of the house.

It is a big, airy room, the whole floor nearly, with windows that look all ways, and air and sunshine galore. It was nursery first and then playroom and gymnasium, I should judge; for the windows are barred for little children, and there are rings and things in the walls.

The paint and paper look as if a boys' school had used it. It is stripped off—the paper—in great patches all around the head of my bed, about as far as I can reach, and in a great place on the other side of the room low down. I never saw a worse
70 paper in my life.

One of those sprawling **flamboyant** patterns committing every artistic sin.

It is dull enough to confuse the eye in following, pronounced enough to constantly irritate and provoke study, and when you follow the lame uncertain curves for a little distance they suddenly commit suicide—plunge off at outrageous angles, destroy themselves in unheard of contradictions.

The color is repellent, almost revolting; a smouldering unclean yellow, strangely faded by the slow-turning sunlight.

It is a dull yet **lurid** orange in some places, a sickly sulphur tint in others.

No wonder the children hated it! I should hate it myself if I had to live in this
80 room long.

There comes John, and I must put this away, —he hates to have me write a word.

We have been here two weeks, and I haven't felt like writing before, since that first day.

I am sitting by the window now, up in this atrocious nursery, and there is nothing to hinder my writing as much as I please, save lack of strength. ◔

John is away all day, and even some nights when his cases are serious.

I am glad my case is not serious!

But these nervous troubles are dreadfully depressing.

John does not know how much I really suffer. He knows there is no *reason* to
90 suffer, and that satisfies him.

Of course it is only nervousness. It does weigh on me so not to do my duty in any way!

I meant to be such a help to John, such a real rest and comfort, and here I am a comparative burden already!

Nobody would believe what an effort it is to do what little I am able,—to dress and entertain, and order things.

flamboyant (flăm-boi′ənt) *adj.* marked by strikingly elaborate or colorful display

lurid (lŏŏr′ĭd) *adj.* shocking; gruesome

② **Targeted Passage**

◔ **GRAMMAR AND STYLE**
Notice that Gilman chose to tell this story in the **present tense.** This lends the narrative a sense of immediacy and allows readers to feel as though they're witnessing new developments in the narrator's condition as they unfold.

Lines 62–81
TIERED DISCUSSION PROMPTS
Use these prompts to help students understand the narrator's state of mind:

Connect What words and moods do you associate with the color yellow? *Most students will associate yellow with bright, cheerful moods, sunshine, and yellow flowers such as buttercups and sunflowers.*

Analyze What do the details of the room suggest about its function for the narrator? *Possible answer: The barred windows, rings in the wall, and patches of torn paper suggest a prison cell or asylum designed to keep the narrator under control.*

Synthesize How are the narrator's reactions to the yellow wallpaper and the room different from the way most people would respond to them? What does this suggest about her state of mind? *Possible answer: The narrator sees yellow as a repellent, unclean color, and the wallpaper as an attack on her senses. She finds the room intolerable and imagines other occupants have felt this way too. Her perceptions suggest that she is depressed and off-kilter.*

◔ **GRAMMAR AND STYLE**
Analyze Verb Tense Gilman's use of present tense enhances her first-person narrator by focusing on the character's immediate thoughts. Ask students how this changes the narrative. *Possible answer: Present tense makes the narrator's emotions seem more intense.*

FOR ENGLISH LEARNERS
Related Vocabulary The wallpaper is central to the narrator's experience and deteriorating mental condition. Help students list words related to the wallpaper in lines 72–77, then use context to determine meaning:

- *dull* (line 72), "boring"
- *confuse* (line 72), "puzzle"
- *irritate* (line 73), "annoy"
- *provoke* (line 73), "urge"
- *lame* (line 73), "weak"
- *uncertain* (line 73), "unsure"
- *commit suicide* (line 74), "disappear"
- *outrageous* (line 75), "bizarre"
- *unheard of contradictions* (line 75), "strange patterns"
- *repellent* (lines 76), "disgusting"
- *revolting* (line 76), "sickening"

FOR STRATEGIC READERS
② **Targeted Passage [Lines 82–96]**

This passage provides important information about the narrator's life and marriage.

- When does John work?
- Why has the narrator not been writing?
- How does the narrator feel about her duty to John?

It is fortunate Mary is so good with the baby. Such a dear baby!

And yet I *cannot* be with him, it makes me so nervous.

I suppose John never was nervous in his life. He laughs at me so about this
100 wallpaper!

At first he meant to repaper the room, but afterwards he said that I was letting
it get the better of me, and that nothing was worse for a nervous patient than to
give way to such fancies.

He said that after the wallpaper was changed it would be the heavy bedstead, and
then the barred windows, and then that gate at the head of the stairs, and so on.

"You know the place is doing you good," he said, "and really, dear, I don't care
to renovate the house just for a three months' rental."

"Then do let us go downstairs," I said, "there are such pretty rooms there."

Then he took me in his arms and called me a blessed little goose, and said he

A Woman Seated at a Table by a Window, Carl Holsoe. Oil on canvas. © SuperStock.

ANALYZE VISUALS
How would you describe the **mood** of this painting? In your opinion, is it similar to or different from the mood of the story? Explain, citing specific details from each that influenced your answer.

ANALYZE VISUALS

Possible answer: The painting, unlike the story, has a serene and calm mood. The woman sits meditatively gazing out the window. It is open, not barred. The room is simple but attractive, not decaying as in the story. The yellow light reinforces the calm, open feeling, while in the story it suggests decay. The woman's pose beside the door suggests that she may be waiting for someone's arrival, expectantly but without the desperation of the story narrator.

About the Art Carl Holsoe (1863–1935), a Danish contemporary of Gilman's, reproduced everyday objects and spaces in his paintings. Many of his paintings, like this one, focus on domestic interiors and celebrate the beautiful light of his country.

DIFFERENTIATED INSTRUCTION

FOR ADVANCED LEARNERS/AP

Compare and Contrast [small-group option] Point out the narrator's comment that "John never was nervous in his life" (line 99). Have small groups discuss similarities and differences between the narrator and her husband. Urge them to explore these questions:

• How do their differences drive the action of the story?

• What effect do their differences have on the narrator's illness?

• What do they have in common?

• What feelings do they seem to have for each other?

Ask them to create a graphic organizer, such as a Comparison Matrix, to illustrate their findings. Invite students to share their work.

 BEST PRACTICES TOOLKIT—Transparency
Comparison Matrix p. A24

110 would go down to the cellar, if I wished, and have it whitewashed into the bargain. **D**

But he is right enough about the beds and windows and things.

It is an airy and comfortable room as anyone need wish, and, of course, I would not be so silly as to make him uncomfortable just for a whim.

I'm really getting quite fond of the big room, all but that horrid paper.

Out of one window I can see the garden, those mysterious deepshaded arbors, the riotous old-fashioned flowers, and bushes and gnarly trees.

Out of another I get a lovely view of the bay and a little private wharf belonging to the estate. There is a beautiful shaded lane that runs down there from the house. I always fancy I see people walking in these numerous paths and arbors,
120 but John has cautioned me not to give way to fancy in the least. He says that with my imaginative power and habit of story-making, a nervous weakness like mine is sure to lead to all manner of excited fancies, and that I ought to use my will and good sense to check the tendency. So I try.

I think sometimes that if I were only well enough to write a little it would relieve the press of ideas and rest me.

But I find I get pretty tired when I try.

It is so discouraging not to have any advice and companionship about my work. When I get really well, John says we will ask Cousin Henry and Julia down for a long visit; but he says he would as soon put fireworks in my pillowcase as to
130 let me have those stimulating people about now.

I wish I could get well faster.

But I must not think about that. This paper looks to me as if it *knew* what a vicious influence it had!

There is a **recurrent** spot where the pattern lolls like a broken neck and two bulbous eyes stare at you upside down.

I get positively angry with the impertinence of it and the everlastingness. **E** Up and down and sideways they crawl, and those absurd, unblinking eyes are everywhere. There is one place where two breadths didn't match, and the eyes go all up and down the line, one a little higher than the other.
140 I never saw so much expression in an inanimate thing before, and we all know how much expression they have! I used to lie awake as a child and get more entertainment and terror out of blank walls and plain furniture than most children could find in a toy store.

I remember what a kindly wink the knobs of our big, old bureau used to have, and there was one chair that always seemed like a strong friend.

I used to feel that if any of the other things looked too fierce I could always hop into that chair and be safe.

The furniture in this room is no worse than inharmonious, however, for we had to bring it all from downstairs. I suppose when this was used as a playroom they
150 had to take the nursery things out, and no wonder! I never saw such ravages as the children have made here.

Targeted Passage

D SOCIAL CONTEXT
Reread lines 99–110 and describe the relationship between the narrator and her husband. What might Gilman be saying about how women were viewed in the late 1800s?

recurrent (rĭ-kûr′ənt) *adj.* occurring time after time

E FIRST-PERSON NARRATOR
How are the narrator's feelings about the wallpaper changing? Explain whether or not her response to the room's décor seems rational to you.

READING SKILL

D SOCIAL CONTEXT

Possible answer: The narrator is subservient to her husband. He treats her dismissively, like a child who is not capable of making serious decisions or thinking wisely for herself (lines 101–105). With this portrait of the marriage, Gilman illustrates how much husbands controlled and infantilized their wives in the late 1800s.

If students need help . . . Ask them how John responds to the narrator's wishes to change the wallpaper or live downstairs. Point out that the endearment "blessed little goose" (line 109) is more suited to addressing a young child than a wife.

LITERARY ANALYSIS

E FIRST–PERSON NARRATOR

Possible answer: The wallpaper is capturing more and more of the narrator's attention. It seems, in her mind, to be coming to life, as she attributes to it human qualities such as "impertinence" (line 136) and says that it seems to know what a "vicious influence" (line 133) it has.

Extend the Discussion How does the narrator connect her feelings about the wallpaper to those about her health?

FOR STRATEGIC READERS

Targeted Passage [Lines 134–143]

This passage shows the narrator's changing perception of the wallpaper.

- What does the narrator now see in the wallpaper?
- How does she feel about what she sees?
- What childhood "entertainment" does the narrator recall?

FOR ENGLISH LEARNERS

Related Vocabulary Provide this Three-Column Journal and model examples of each category from lines 115–133. Help students find and list additional examples.

garden	narrator's temperament	Wallpaper
• mysterious • deepshaded	• imaginative power	• vicious influence

BEST PRACTICES TOOLKIT—Transparency
Three-Column Journal p. B10

The wallpaper, as I said before, is torn off in spots, and it sticketh closer than a brother—they must have had perseverance as well as hatred.

Then the floor is scratched and gouged and splintered, the plaster itself is dug out here and there, and this great heavy bed which is all we found in the room, looks as if it had been through the wars.

But I don't mind it a bit—only the paper.

There comes John's sister. Such a dear girl as she is, and so careful of me! I must not let her find me writing.

160   She is a perfect and enthusiastic housekeeper, and hopes for no better profession. I verily believe she thinks it is the writing which made me sick!

But I can write when she is out, and see her a long way off from these windows. **F**

There is one that commands the road, a lovely shaded winding road, and one that just looks off over the country. A lovely country, too, full of great elms and velvet meadows.

This wallpaper has a kind of sub-pattern in a different shade, a particularly irritating one, for you can only see it in certain lights, and not clearly then.

But in the places where it isn't faded and where the sun is just so—I can see a strange, provoking, formless sort of figure, that seems to skulk about behind that
170   silly and conspicuous front design.

There's sister on the stairs!

Well, the Fourth of July is over! The people are all gone and I am tired out. John thought it might do me good to see a little company, so we just had mother and Nellie and the children down for a week.

Of course I didn't do a thing. Jennie sees to everything now.

But it tired me all the same.

John says if I don't pick up faster he shall send me to Weir Mitchell[3] in the fall.

But I don't want to go there at all. I had a friend who was in his hands once, and she says he is just like John and my brother, only more so! **G**

180   Besides, it is such an undertaking to go so far.

I don't feel as if it was worth while to turn my hand over for anything, and I'm getting dreadfully fretful and querulous.

I cry at nothing, and cry most of the time.

Of course I don't when John is here, or anybody else, but when I am alone.

And I am alone a good deal just now. John is kept in town very often by serious cases, and Jennie is good and lets me alone when I want her to.

So I walk a little in the garden or down that lovely lane, sit on the porch under the roses, and lie down up here a good deal.

I'm getting really fond of the room in spite of the wallpaper. Perhaps *because*
190   of the wallpaper.

It dwells in my mind so!

I lie here on this great immovable bed—it is nailed down, I believe—and

---

3. **Weir Mitchell:** Dr. Silas Weir Mitchell, a physician famous for his "rest cure" for nervous diseases, which is no longer considered effective.

774   UNIT 4: REGIONALISM AND NATURALISM

F SOCIAL CONTEXT
Consider the narrator's description of John's sister in lines 158–162. What information does her description offer about a woman's accepted roles in society?

G SOCIAL CONTEXT
Explain what the narrator means by this description of Dr. Mitchell. What is suggested or highlighted by the fact that all the male characters in the story share common opinions and **traits?**

READING SKILL

F SOCIAL CONTEXT

Possible answer: The narrator's description of John's sister suggests that society expects women to be "perfect and enthusiastic housekeeper[s]" (line 160), and to find happiness and fulfillment in domestic life.

Extend the Discussion What does the narrator's comment that John's sister "hopes for no better" (line 160) suggest about the narrator herself?

READING SKILL

G SOCIAL CONTEXT

Possible answer: The narrator means that Dr. Mitchell, too, will bully and dismiss her (lines 178–179). The fact that all male characters in the story share these traits suggests that the traits are widely found among men of the time period and underscores how stifling conditions were for women.

DIFFERENTIATED INSTRUCTION

FOR STRATEGIC READERS

Concept Support Clarify the allusion in lines 152–153. It refers to the words "and there is a friend that sticketh closer than a brother," which appear in the Book of Proverbs in the Hebrew Bible, or Old Testament. Ask students what the narrator means. *Possible answer: The narrator means that the wallpaper is glued tightly to the wall, and therefore, the children who tore it off must have been very determined to do so.*

FOR ADVANCED LEARNERS/AP

Analyze Character Foil [paired option] Remind students that a foil is a minor character that presents a striking contrast with a main character. This contrast sheds light on the traits and motivations of the main character. Ask students what purpose the contrast between John's sister and the narrator serves. What do readers learn about the narrator because of the sister's presence in the story? Have partners brainstorm responses to this question, then

write character descriptions of the narrator with and without the information provided by the foil of John's sister. Invite students to share their descriptions to prompt a class discussion of how the sister adds to the story.

774   UNIT 4: REGIONALISM AND NATURALISM

follow that pattern about by the hour. It is as good as gymnastics, I assure you. I start, we'll say, at the bottom, down in the corner over there where it has not been touched, and I determine for the thousandth time that I *will* follow that pointless pattern to some sort of a conclusion.

I know a little of the principle of design, and I know this thing was not arranged on any laws of radiation, or alternation, or repetition, or symmetry, or anything else that I ever heard of.

200 It is repeated, of course, by the breadths, but not otherwise.

Looked at in one way each breadth stands alone, the bloated curves and flourishes—a kind of "debased Romanesque" with *delirium tremens*[4]—go waddling up and down in isolated columns of **fatuity.**

fatuity (fə-tōō′ĭ-tē) *n.* something foolish or stupid

But, on the other hand, they connect diagonally, and the sprawling outlines run off in great slanting waves of optic horror, like a lot of wallowing seaweeds in full chase.

The whole thing goes horizontally, too, at least it seems so, and I exhaust myself in trying to distinguish the order of its going in that direction.

They have used a horizontal breadth for a frieze, and that adds wonderfully to 210 the confusion.

There is one end of the room where it is almost intact, and there, when the crosslights fade and the low sun shines directly upon it, I can almost fancy radiation after all,—the interminable grotesques seem to form around a common center and rush off in headlong plunges of equal distraction.

It makes me tired to follow it. I will take a nap I guess.

I don't know why I should write this.

I don't want to.

I don't feel able.

And I know John would think it absurd. But I *must* say what I feel and think 220 in some way—it is such a relief!

But the effort is getting to be greater than the relief.

Half the time now I am awfully lazy, and lie down ever so much.

John says I mustn't lose my strength, and has me take cod liver oil and lots of tonics and things, to say nothing of ale and wine and rare meat.

Dear John! He loves me very dearly, and hates to have me sick. I tried to have a real earnest reasonable talk with him the other day, and tell him how I wish he would let me go and make a visit to Cousin Henry and Julia.

But he said I wasn't able to go, nor able to stand it after I got there; and I did not make out a very good case for myself, for I was crying before I had finished. **H**

230 It is getting to be a great effort for me to think straight. Just this nervous weakness I suppose.

And dear John gathered me up in his arms, and just carried me upstairs and laid me on the bed, and sat by me and read to me till it tired my head.

---

4. **"debased Romanesque" with *delirium tremens*:** Romanesque is an artistic style characterized by simple ornamentation. *Delirium tremens* refers to violent trembling and hallucinations caused by excessive drinking.

Ⓗ FIRST-PERSON NARRATOR Imagine the "real earnest reasonable talk" the narrator describes. How might the account of this scene be different if John were the narrator?

Lines 152–171
TIERED DISCUSSION PROMPTS

Use these prompts to help students link the narrator's deteriorating state of mind to her obsession with the wallpaper:

Connect How would you respond if a friend said that he or she had seen a "formless figure" in the wallpaper? *Most students will express worry for the friend's mental state.*

Analyze Why doesn't the narrator mention the "formless figure" to her sister-in-law? *Possible answer: The narrator doesn't trust her and also may fear that she would be dismissive or would relate the narrator's report to John.*

Synthesize How would you characterize the narrator's changing perception of the wallpaper? *Possible answer: The narrator's perception has grown increasingly distorted. At first, the wallpaper repelled her; then she saw moving eyes in it. Now, she glimpses a formless figure there. Her hallucinations are becoming more distinct and animated as her mental health deteriorates.*

LITERARY ANALYSIS

Ⓗ FIRST–PERSON NARRATOR

Possible answer: Readers may doubt that the narrator is capable of a "real earnest reasonable talk," especially since she tells us that she started crying before she could finish. John would have focused on her emotional outburst and on his own view of her condition. He might have given a rational account of the situation, but ignored her feelings.

FOR ENGLISH LEARNERS

Vocabulary Support Point out and help students use context to define these expressions:

- *it had been through the wars* (line 156), "it had been used a lot"
- *tired out* (line 172), "exhausted"
- *had [people] down* (lines 173–174), "had [people] visit"
- *sees to everything* (line 175), "takes care of everything"
- *all the same* (line 176), "even so"
- *pick up* (line 177), "improve"
- *in his hands* (line 178), "under his care"
- *a good deal* (line 188), "often"
- *on the other hand* (line 204), "in contrast"
- *to say nothing of* (lines 224), "and also"
- *to think straight* (line 230), "concentrate"

ANALYZE VISUALS

Possible answer: The subject's expression conveys worry, concern, and even helplessness. Some students may say that the image of a concerned doctor makes them feel more sympathy, as it stresses John's good intentions. Others may say that John's good intentions do not compensate for his inability to empathize with his wife or to really listen to what she is telling him.

Lines 236–237
REINFORCE *KEY IDEA:* POWERLESS

Discuss John tells the narrator that she is not **powerless** over her situation. What power does he suggest she has? How useful or realistic is that power, especially in the situation John has placed the narrator? *Possible answer: John suggests that the narrator can affect her situation by using the power of her will and self-control to restrain her imagination. This power is not very useful or realistic because her imagination is central to her identity. Also, he has placed her in a situation where she has little to do but imagine.*

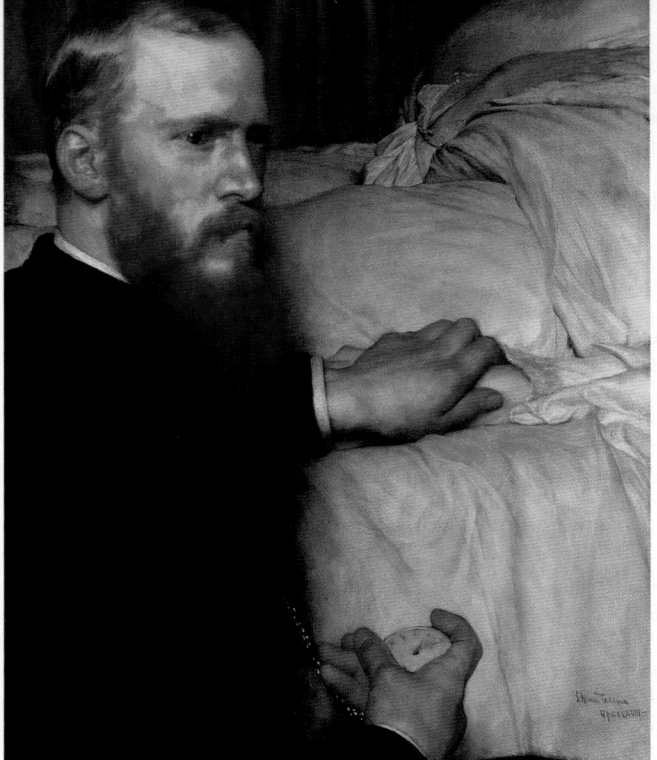

Portrait of Dr. Washington Epps, My Doctor (1885), Sir Lawrence Alma-Tadema. Oil on canvas, 64.2 cm × 51 cm. Private collection. © Bridgeman Art Library.

He said I was his darling and his comfort and all he had, and that I must take care of myself for his sake, and keep well.

He says no one but myself can help me out of it, that I must use my will and self-control and not let any silly fancies run away with me.

There's one comfort, the baby is well and happy, and does not have to occupy this nursery with the horrid wallpaper.

240   If we had not used it, that blessed child would have! What a fortunate escape! Why, I wouldn't have a child of mine, an impressionable little thing, live in such a room for worlds.

I never thought of it before, but it is lucky that John kept me here after all, I can stand it so much easier than a baby, you see.

Of course I never mention it to them any more—I am too wise,—but I keep watch of it all the same.

There are things in that paper that nobody knows but me, or ever will.

Behind that outside pattern the dim shapes get clearer every day.

It is always the same shape, only very numerous.

④ Targeted Passage

ANALYZE VISUALS
Study this painting, then describe the emotion conveyed by the subject's facial expression. Does this image make you feel more or less sympathetic toward John, the narrator's husband? Explain your answer.

776   UNIT 4: REGIONALISM AND NATURALISM

DIFFERENTIATED INSTRUCTION

FOR STRATEGIC READERS

④ Targeted Passage [Lines 236–249]

This passage shows the narrator's battle for sanity and her husband's misguided approach to helping her.

- How does John say that the narrator can get well?
- Why doesn't the narrator mention what she sees in the wallpaper?
- How has the wallpaper changed?

FOR ENGLISH LEARNERS

Vocabulary Support Clarify that Gilman is contrasting self-control with imagination. Work with students to complete a Two-Column Chart to list and define the vocabulary that establishes this contrast.

 BEST PRACTICES TOOLKIT—Transparency Two-Column Chart p. A25

Self-Control	Imagination
• *will* (line 236), "determination, strength of character"	• *silly fancies* (line 237), "foolish daydreams or fantasies"
• *self-control* (line 237), "discipline, restraint"	• *run away with* (line 237) "take control of"
• *stern* (line 285), "strict, harsh"	• *fancy* (line 289), "unwise impulse"

776   UNIT 4: REGIONALISM AND NATURALISM

250 And it is like a woman stooping down and creeping about behind that pattern. I don't like it a bit. I wonder—I begin to think—I wish John would take me away from here!

It is so hard to talk with John about my case, because he is so wise, and because he loves me so.

But I tried it last night.

It was moonlight. The moon shines in all around just as the sun does.

I hate to see it sometimes, it creeps so slowly, and always comes in by one window or another.

260 John was asleep and I hated to waken him, so I kept still and watched the moonlight on that **undulating** wallpaper till I felt creepy.

The faint figure behind seemed to shake the pattern, just as if she wanted to get out.

I got up softly and went to feel and see if the paper *did* move, and when I came back John was awake.

"What is it, little girl?" he said. "Don't go walking about like that—you'll get cold."

I thought it was a good time to talk, so I told him that I really was not gaining here, and that I wished he would take me away.

"Why darling!" said he, "our lease will be up in three weeks, and I can't see how 270 to leave before.

"The repairs are not done at home, and I cannot possibly leave town just now. Of course if you were in any danger, I could and would, but you really are better, dear, whether you can see it or not. I am a doctor, dear, and I know. You are gaining flesh and color, your appetite is better, I feel really much easier about you."

"I don't weigh a bit more," said I, "nor as much; and my appetite may be better in the evening when you are here, but it is worse in the morning when you are away!"

"Bless her little heart!" said he with a big hug, "she shall be as sick as she pleases! But now let's improve the shining hours[5] by going to sleep, and talk about it in the morning!"

280 "And you won't go away?" I asked gloomily.

"Why, how can I, dear? It is only three weeks more and then we will take a nice little trip of a few days while Jennie is getting the house ready. Really dear you are better!"

"Better in body perhaps—" I began, and stopped short, for he sat up straight and looked at me with such a stern, reproachful look that I could not say another word.

"My darling," said he, "I beg of you, for my sake and for our child's sake, as well as for your own, that you will never for one instant let that idea enter your mind! There is nothing so dangerous, so fascinating, to a **temperament** like yours. It is a false and foolish fancy. Can you not trust me as a physician when I tell you so?"

undulating (ŭn′jə-lā′tĭng) *adj.* appearing to move in waves **undulate** *v.*

temperament (tĕm′prə-mənt) *n.* a person's characteristic mode of emotional response

---

5. **improve the shining hours:** make good use of time—an allusion to the poem "Against Idleness and Mischief" by Isaac Watts.

Lines 267–289
TIERED DISCUSSION PROMPTS

Use these prompts to help students relate the narrator's frustration with her husband to her deteriorating mental health:

Connect In your experience, how hard is it to change somebody's mind when the person is convinced of an idea? *Students should recognize that it can be very difficult to overcome strong convictions.*

Analyze Why is John so convinced about the causes of and appropriate treatment for his wife's illness? Consider his training as a doctor and his expectations as a husband. *Possible answer: As a doctor, John has been trained to treat his wife's symptoms in a prescribed way. As a husband, he has been conditioned to value his views over his wife's. This training prevents him from seeing that the treatment isn't working, from really hearing his wife, and from trying a different approach.*

Evaluate In your opinion, could the narrator say or do anything to change John's mind? Why or why not? *Students should recognize that the narrator is in the frustrating position of being unable to communicate with her husband.*

FOR ADVANCED LEARNERS/AP

Contrast Character Types [small-group option]
Have students work in groups to explore whether John is a flat or round character. Ask groups to poll members and tally the results. Then, urge groups to discuss these questions:

• What character traits define John?

• What emotions does he display?

• How, if at all, is he stereotypical?

• How, if at all, does John change in the course of the story?

• How does his character development reflect his role in the story?

After the discussion, challenge groups to revisit the question of whether John is a round or flat character. Have them take a new poll and tally. Invite groups to share both tallies and explain any changes in their response.

❶ FIRST–PERSON NARRATOR

Possible answer: Her mind is beginning to seem anything but normal. She now sees a figure shaking the wallpaper, as if trying to escape.

If students need help . . . Reread lines 257–262 and 291–293 with them.

Lines 319–329
REINFORCE *KEY IDEA*: POWERLESS

Discuss The narrator follows John's orders to rest after every meal, despite her belief that this is a bad habit. How does this suggest that she feels **powerless?** How do the narrator's feelings toward John seem to be changing as a result? *Possible answer: She is beginning to fear John (line 323) and to suspect that the paper is influencing him (lines 325–326).*

---

290   So of course I said no more on that score, and we went to sleep before long. He thought I was asleep first, but I wasn't, and lay there for hours trying to decide whether that front pattern and the back pattern really did move together or separately.

On a pattern like this, by daylight, there is a lack of sequence, a defiance of law, that is a constant irritant to a normal mind. ❶

The color is hideous enough, and unreliable enough, and infuriating enough, but the pattern is torturing.

You think you have mastered it, but just as you get well underway in following, it turns a back-somersault and there you are. It slaps you in the face, knocks you

300   down, and tramples upon you. It is like a bad dream.

The outside pattern is a florid arabesque,[6] reminding one of a fungus. If you can imagine a toadstool in joints, an interminable string of toadstools, budding and sprouting in endless **convolutions**—why, that is something like it.

That is, sometimes!

There is one marked peculiarity about this paper, a thing nobody seems to notice but myself, and that is that it changes as the light changes.

When the sun shoots in through the east window—I always watch for that first long, straight ray—it changes so quickly that I never can quite believe it.

That is why I watch it always.

310   By moonlight—the moon shines in all night when there is a moon—I wouldn't know it was the same paper.

At night in any kind of light, in twilight, candle light, lamplight, and worst of all by moonlight, it becomes bars! The outside pattern I mean, and the woman behind it is as plain as can be.

I didn't realize for a long time what the thing was that showed behind, that dim sub-pattern, but now I am quite sure it is a woman.

By daylight she is subdued, quiet. I fancy it is the pattern that keeps her so still. It is so puzzling. It keeps me quiet by the hour.

I lie down ever so much now. John says it is good for me, and to sleep all I can.

320   Indeed he started the habit by making me lie down for an hour after each meal.

It is a very bad habit I am convinced, for you see I don't sleep.

And that cultivates deceit, for I don't tell them I'm awake—O no!

The fact is I am getting a little afraid of John.

He seems very queer sometimes, and even Jennie has an inexplicable look.

It strikes me occasionally, just as a scientific hypothesis,—that perhaps it is the paper!

I have watched John when he did not know I was looking, and come into the room suddenly on the most innocent excuses, and I've caught him several times *looking at the paper!* And Jennie too. I caught Jennie with her hand on it once.

330   She didn't know I was in the room, and when I asked her in a quiet, a very quiet voice, with the most restrained manner possible, what she was doing with

---

❶ FIRST-PERSON NARRATOR
Consider the narrator's statement in lines 294–295. Based on her description of the wallpaper, would you say she has "a normal mind"? Explain your answer.

convolution
(kŏn′və-lōō′shən) *n.* a form or shape that is folded into curved, complicated windings

⑤ Targeted Passage

---

6. **florid arabesque:** an elaborate interwoven pattern.

DIFFERENTIATED INSTRUCTION

FOR STRATEGIC READERS

⑤ Targeted Passage [Lines 305–318]

This passage reveals the narrator's hallucinations about the wallpaper.

- What does the narrator say happens to the wallpaper as the light changes? Why does she watch it?

- What does she see behind the wallpaper?

- Why does the narrator think the woman remains still?

Concept Support Point out to students that paranoia is an acute mental disorder in which the patient experiences extreme feelings of being victimized, imagining that others are trying to harm him or her. A paranoid person often feels suspicious and distrustful. Ask students whether they think the narrator is paranoid.

the paper—she turned around as if she had been caught stealing, and looked quite angry—asked me why I should frighten her so!

Then she said that the paper stained everything it touched, that she had found yellow smooches[7] on all my clothes and John's, and she wished we would be more careful!

Did not that sound innocent? But I know she was studying that pattern, and I am determined that nobody shall find it out but myself!

Life is very much more exciting now than it used to be. You see I have something
340 more to expect, to look forward to, to watch. I really do eat better, and am more quiet than I was.

John is so pleased to see me improve! He laughed a little the other day, and said I seemed to be flourishing in spite of my wallpaper.

I turned it off with a laugh. I had no intention of telling him it was *because* of the wallpaper—he would make fun of me. He might even want to take me away.

I don't want to leave now until I have found it out. There is a week more, and I think that will be enough.

I'm feeling ever so much better! I don't sleep much at night, for it is so interesting to watch developments; but I sleep a good deal in the daytime.
350 In the daytime it is tiresome and perplexing.

There are always new shoots on the fungus, and new shades of yellow all over it. I cannot keep count of them, though I have tried conscientiously.

It is the strangest yellow, that wallpaper! It makes me think of all the yellow things I ever saw—not beautiful ones like buttercups, but old foul, bad yellow things.

But there is something else about that paper—the smell! I noticed it the moment we came into the room, but with so much air and sun it was not bad. Now we have had a week of fog and rain, and whether the windows are open or not, the smell is here.

It creeps all over the house.
360 I find it hovering in the dining room, skulking in the parlor, hiding in the hall, lying in wait for me on the stairs.

It gets into my hair.

Even when I go to ride, if I turn my head suddenly and surprise it—there is that smell!

Such a peculiar odor, too! I have spent hours in trying to analyze it, to find what it smelled like.

It is not bad—at first, and very gentle, but quite the subtlest, most enduring odor I ever met.

In this damp weather it is awful, I wake up in the night and find it hanging
370 over me.

It used to disturb me at first. I thought seriously of burning the house—to reach the smell.

---

7. **smooches:** smudges.

J FIRST-PERSON NARRATOR
Reread lines 323–338. How has the narrator's attitude toward John and Jennie changed? What do you think they might say about her feelings if they were aware of them?

Activity Ask students to imagine they are viewing this painting at a museum. Ask students what response they would have to the subject of the painting and to the wallpaper within it. Challenge them to consider how their response differs from viewing the painting in the context of this story. ***Possible answer:*** *Viewed in a museum, the painting seems to show a peacefully idle and sensuous woman surrounded by merely decorative wallpaper. In the context of the story, the painting reflects some of the disturbed qualities of the narrator and her perception of the wallpaper, making the woman seem distressed and the wallpaper seem overdone.*

In Bed (1878), Federico Zandomeneghi. Oil on canvas, 60.5 cm × 73.5 cm. Galleria d'Arte Moderna, Florence. © Alinari/Art Resource, New York.

LITERARY ANALYSIS

Ⓚ FIRST–PERSON NARRATOR

Possible answer: *At this point, the woman's mind is becoming unhinged. She seriously considers burning her own house down "to reach the smell" (lines 371–372), and she has become obsessed with the wallpaper. She sees it as a living entity and spends hours analyzing it (lines 365–366). She is increasingly agitated, secretive, desperate, and irrational as her mental illness deepens.*

If students need help . . . Urge them to reread lines 348–374.

But now I am used to it. The only thing I can think of that it is like is the *color* of the paper! A yellow smell. Ⓚ

There is a very funny mark on this wall, low down, near the mopboard. A streak that runs round the room. It goes behind every piece of furniture, except the bed, a long, straight, even *smooch*, as if it had been rubbed over and over.

I wonder how it was done and who did it, and what they did it for. Round and round and round—round and round and round—it makes me dizzy!

380 I really have discovered something at last.

Through watching so much at night, when it changes so, I have finally found out. The front pattern *does* move—and no wonder! The woman behind shakes it!

Sometimes I think there are a great many women behind, and sometimes only one, and she crawls around fast, and her crawling shakes it all over.

Ⓖ **Targeted Passage**

Ⓚ **FIRST-PERSON NARRATOR**
Describe the woman's state of mind at this point as an impartial, **omniscient narrator** might describe it.

DIFFERENTIATED INSTRUCTION

FOR STRATEGIC READERS

Ⓖ **Targeted Passage [Lines 380–388]**

This passage shows the narrator's changing perception of the "woman" in the wallpaper.

- Why does the narrator think the front pattern moves?
- Whom does the narrator see behind the front pattern?
- What is the woman behind the pattern trying to do?

FOR ENGLISH LEARNERS

Vocabulary: Idioms and Phrasal Verbs Use context to clarify these idioms from pages 780–781:

- *used to it* (line 373), "accustomed to it"
- *found out* (line 381), "discovered"
- *keeps still* (line 385), "doesn't move"
- *takes hold* (line 386), "grabs"
- *half so bad* (line 391), "terrible"

- *away off* (line 409), "far away"
- *open country* (line 409), "distance"
- *It does not do* (line 413–414), "It is not advisable"
- *a good deal* (line 419), "a lot"
- *see through him* (line 423), "see his deception"

Then in the very bright spots she keeps still, and in the very shady spots she just takes hold of the bars and shakes them hard.

And she is all the time trying to climb through. But nobody could climb through that pattern—it strangles so; I think that is why it has so many heads.

⑥ **Targeted Passage**
continued

390 They get through, and then the pattern strangles them off and turns them upside down, and makes their eyes white!

If those heads were covered or taken off it would not be half so bad.

I think that woman gets out in the daytime!

And I'll tell you why—privately—I've seen her!

I can see her out of every one of my windows!

It is the same woman, I know, for she is always creeping, and most women do not creep by daylight.

I see her on that long road under the trees, creeping along, and when a carriage comes she hides under the blackberry vines.

I don't blame her a bit. It must be very humiliating to be caught creeping by
400 daylight!

I always lock the door when I creep by daylight. I can't do it at night, for I know John would suspect something at once.

And John is so queer now, that I don't want to irritate him. I wish he would take another room! Besides, I don't want anybody to get that woman out at night but myself.

I often wonder if I could see her out of all the windows at once.

But, turn as fast as I can, I can only see out of one at one time.

And though I always see her, she *may* be able to creep faster than I can turn!

I have watched her sometimes away off in the open country, creeping as fast
410 as a cloud shadow in a high wind.

If only that top pattern could be gotten off from the under one! I mean to try it, little by little.

I have found out another funny thing, but I shan't tell it this time! It does not do to trust people too much.

There are only two more days to get this paper off, and I believe John is beginning to notice. I don't like the look in his eyes.

And I heard him ask Jennie a lot of professional questions about me. She had a very good report to give.

She said I slept a good deal in the daytime.

420 John knows I don't sleep very well at night, for all I'm so quiet!

He asked me all sorts of questions, too, and pretended to be very loving and kind.

As if I couldn't see through him! ❶

❶ FIRST-PERSON NARRATOR
Consider the narrator's statements in lines 403–404 and line 423. Why is she turning against her husband? Explain what John's real concerns might be.

Lines 392–410
TIERED DISCUSSION PROMPTS
Use these prompts to help students understand the narrator's confusion and bizarre behavior:

Connect Have you ever known a small child who imagines people or animals or monsters? How does that experience help you understand the narrator's mental state? *Students should recognize that, like a small child, the narrator has lost the ability to differentiate fantasy and reality.*

Analyze Why does the narrator lock the door when she creeps by daylight? *Possible answer: The narrator does not wish to be seen by Jennie or John. She is now fearful and paranoid about their intentions. On some level she may also be aware that her behavior is odd.*

Evaluate How would you assess the effects of the "rest cure" on the narrator? *Most students will recognize that the rest cure is an abysmal failure that has contributed to the narrator's mental deterioration.*

LITERARY ANALYSIS

❶ FIRST-PERSON NARRATOR

Possible answer: The narrator is turning against her husband because she believes that John is not motivated by love, but by malevolent intentions (lines 413–414). She thinks that he wants to remove the woman from the wallpaper (lines 404–405). Students should recognize that the narrator's perceptions are paranoid and distorted. However, they should also appreciate that John's real concerns—his desire to help his wife and keep her safe—have backfired and harmed her.

Extend the Discussion In what ways does John deserve the narrator's antagonism? Explain.

FOR ADVANCED LEARNERS/AP

Symbolism Have students speculate on the meaning of the woman in the wallpaper. Who does she represent? Is she an aspect of the narrator's mind or a symbol of women in general? Does her situation reflect the narrator's plight or the plight of all women of Gilman's time? Encourage students to write a persuasive paragraph in response to these questions. Have the class consider the paragraphs and voice opinions.

Ⓜ FIRST–PERSON NARRATOR

Possible answer: The narrator interprets Jennie's comment (line 441) as a sly attempt to sound sympathetic while actually trying to keep the narrator from removing the paper. She suspects that Jennie wants to be the one to tear off the paper and free the woman behind it. Students should recognize that the narrator's assessment of Jennie's motives is distorted and inaccurate.

Lines 443–467
TIERED DISCUSSION PROMPTS

Use these prompts to help students trace the narrator's mental collapse:

Connect How do you feel about the narrator at this point in the story? What are your concerns for her? *Accept all thoughtful responses.*

Analyze How would you characterize the narrator's behavior? Give examples to support your characterization. *Possible answer: The narrator is behaving bizarrely. She has torn down the wallpaper (lines 443, 465), gnawed and chewed on the bedstead (lines 453, 463–464), locked the door and thrown the key out the window (line 455), brought up a rope to tie up the woman (lines 459–460), and tried pushing the nailed bed until she was lame (line 463).*

Synthesize How will John respond to the narrator's turn for the worse? *Some students will say that John will finally recognize that his treatment has failed. Others will say that he, like Jennie, will try in vain to pacify the narrator.*

Still, I don't wonder he acts so, sleeping under this paper for three months.

It only interests me, but I feel sure John and Jennie are secretly affected by it.

Hurrah! This is the last day, but it is enough. John to stay in town overnight, and won't be out until this evening.

Jennie wanted to sleep with me—the sly thing! but I told her I should undoubtedly rest better for a night all alone.

430   That was clever, for really I wasn't alone a bit! As soon as it was moonlight and that poor thing began to crawl and shake the pattern, I got up and ran to help her.

I pulled and she shook, I shook and she pulled, and before morning we had peeled off yards of that paper.

A strip about as high as my head and half around the room.

And then when the sun came and that awful pattern began to laugh at me, I declared I would finish it today!

We go away tomorrow, and they are moving all my furniture down again to leave things as they were before.

Jennie looked at the wall in amazement, but I told her merrily that I did it out
440   of pure spite at the vicious thing.

She laughed and said she wouldn't mind doing it herself, but I must not get tired. How she betrayed herself that time! Ⓜ

But I am here, and no person touches this paper but me,—not *alive!*

She tried to get me out of the room—it was too **patent!** But I said it was so quiet and empty and clean now that I believed I would lie down again and sleep all I could; and not to wake me even for dinner—I would call when I woke.

So now she is gone, and the servants are gone, and the things are gone, and there is nothing left but that great bedstead nailed down, with the canvas mattress we found on it.

450   We shall sleep downstairs tonight, and take the boat home tomorrow.

I quite enjoy the room, now it is bare again.

How those children did tear about here!

This bedstead is fairly gnawed!

But I must get to work.

I have locked the door and thrown the key down into the front path.

I don't want to go out, and I don't want to have anybody come in, till John comes.

I want to astonish him.

I've got a rope up here that even Jennie did not find. If that woman does get
460   out, and tries to get away, I can tie her!

But I forgot I could not reach far without anything to stand on!

This bed will *not* move!

I tried to lift and push it until I was lame, and then I got so angry I bit off a little piece at one corner—but it hurt my teeth.

Then I peeled off all the paper I could reach standing on the floor. It sticks horribly and the pattern just enjoys it! All those strangled heads and bulbous eyes and waddling fungus growths just shriek with **derision!**

Ⓜ **FIRST-PERSON NARRATOR**
Explain what the narrator means when she says that Jennie has "betrayed herself." Do you think her assessment of Jennie's **motives** is accurate?

patent (păt'nt) *adj.* obvious; apparent

derision (dĭ-rĭzh'ən) *n.* harsh ridicule or mockery; scorn

DIFFERENTIATED INSTRUCTION

FOR ADVANCED LEARNERS/AP

Analyze Word Choice Encourage students to study the dictionary definitions for the word *creep.* Have them work in pairs to discuss the word's various meanings and connotations, then to consider these questions: How does the word connect with the narrator's feelings about the colonial mansion, her husband, and her general predicament? Is Gilman's use of this word ironic? How does the word accumulate new meaning and connotation during the course of the narrative? How would the final scenes of the story be different if Gilman had used a different word, such as *sneak, slink,* or *skulk?* Invite partners to share their thoughts with the class.

I am getting angry enough to do something desperate. To jump out of the window would be admirable exercise, but the bars are too strong even to try.

470   Besides I wouldn't do it. Of course not. I know well enough that a step like that is improper and might be **misconstrued.**

I don't like to *look* out of the windows even—there are so many of those creeping women, and they creep so fast.

I wonder if they all come out of that wallpaper as I did? ⓝ

But I am securely fastened now by my well-hidden rope—you don't get *me* out in the road there!

I suppose I shall have to get back behind the pattern when it comes night, and that is hard!

It is so pleasant to be out in this great room and creep around as I please!

480   I don't want to go outside. I won't, even if Jennie asks me to.

For outside you have to creep on the ground, and everything is green instead of yellow.

But here I can creep smoothly on the floor, and my shoulder just fits in that long smooch around the wall, so I cannot lose my way.

Why there's John at the door!

It is no use, young man, you can't open it!

How he does call and pound!

Now he's crying for an axe.

It would be a shame to break down that beautiful door!

490   "John dear!" said I in the gentlest voice, "the key is down by the front steps, under a plantain leaf!"

That silenced him for a few moments.

Then he said—very quietly indeed, "Open the door, my darling!"

"I can't," said I. "The key is down by the front door under a plantain leaf!"

And then I said it again, several times, very gently and slowly, and said it so often that he had to go and see, and he got it of course, and came in. He stopped short by the door.

"What is the matter?" he cried. "What are you doing!"

I kept on creeping just the same, but I looked at him over my shoulder.

500   "I've got out at last," said I, "in spite of you and Jane.[8] And I've pulled off most of the paper, so you can't put me back!"

Now why should that man have fainted? But he did, and right across my path by the wall, so that I had to creep over him every time! ❧

⑦ **Targeted Passage**

---

8. **in spite of you and Jane:** As Jane is, previously unmentioned, the name may be a typographical error by the original printer of the story in place of the name of the housekeeper, Jennie, or Cousin Julia; or it may denote the narrator herself, freed from her commonplace, wifely, "Jane" persona.

---

misconstrued
(mĭs′kən-strōōd′)
adj. misunderstood; misinterpreted
misconstrue *v.*

ⓝ **FIRST-PERSON NARRATOR**
What does the narrator now believe about the wallpaper?

LITERARY ANALYSIS

ⓝ **FIRST–PERSON NARRATOR**

Possible answer: The narrator now believes that she has freed all the women in the wallpaper and that she herself has escaped from it.

If students need help . . . Reread lines 392–394 and 472–474.

Lines 477–484
REINFORCE *KEY IDEA:* POWERLESS

Discuss In your opinion, does the narrator feel **powerless** at this point in the story? Why or why not? *Possible answer: The narrator says that it is "pleasant" to be out and creeping about the room "as I please" (line 479). Her comments suggest that, ironically, she is contented. She has achieved a kind of freedom from her concerns about pleasing John and meeting the expectations of other people. Now she is doing what she chooses, however crazy it may be, and so feels less powerless.*

SELECTION WRAP–UP

REFLECT Ask students to think about the marital conflicts in this story and where they lead. How do they change the narrator? How do they change John?

⭐ **CRITIQUE**

• Ask students why they think this story has never gone out of print.

• After completing the After Reading questions on page 785, have students revisit their responses and tell whether they have changed their opinions.

FOR STRATEGIC READERS

⑦ **Targeted Passage [Lines 485–503]**

This passage shows the narrator's final descent into madness.

• How does John get into the room?

• What is the narrator doing?

• What is John's reaction?

FOR ENGLISH LEARNERS

Vocabulary Support Point out and teach these expressions on page 783, using context to help students build meaning:

• *well enough* (line 470), "of course"

• *as I please* (line 479), "as much as I want to"

• *lose my way* (line 484), "get lost, wander"

• *stopped short* (lines 496–497), "stopped suddenly"

• *kept on* (line 499), "continued"

• *just the same* (line 499), "as I was before"

CONNECT

This selection provides insight into Gilman's approach to writing "The Yellow Wallpaper." You can also use it as a minilesson on reading for information.

Reading for Information

Point out that "Why I Wrote 'The Yellow Wallpaper'" is an article that Charlotte Perkins Gilman wrote for her feminist magazine. Discuss the article's likely audience. Then ask

- Who is the likely audience of *Forerunner*?
- How might awareness of her audience affect Gilman's writing?

TIERED DISCUSSION PROMPTS

Use these prompts to help students link Gilman's personal experience with mental illness to her writing of "The Yellow Wallpaper":

Connect In what ways can it be helpful during a difficult time to hear how someone else survived a difficult experience? *Accept all thoughtful responses.*

Analyze Gilman's mental breakdown followed an unhappy and stifling marriage. Use this information and her article to explain why she wrote "The Yellow Wallpaper." *Possible answer: She wrote it to illustrate the dangers of "rest cures" for depression, to help others suffering from similar conditions, and perhaps to share the devastating effects of an unhappy marriage.*

Synthesize What traits and experiences do you think Gilman and the narrator of "The Yellow Wallpaper" have in common? *Possible answer: Both Gilman and the narrator have imaginative power and a habit of story-making, a tendency toward melancholia, and a strong desire to write and to work. Both felt powerless in their marriages and both wished to be more than just enthusiastic housekeepers.*

JOURNAL ARTICLE Charlotte Perkins Gilman herself suffered a profound depression and was prescribed a "rest cure" by a noted neurologist of the day. In this 1913 article from her feminist journal *Forerunner*, she says she wrote "The Yellow Wallpaper" to bear witness to the horrors of this "cure" and to attest to her recovery.

THE FORERUNNER
A MONTHLY MAGAZINE
CHARLOTTE PERKINS GILMAN

WHY I WROTE "THE YELLOW WALLPAPER"

Many and many a reader has asked that. When the story first came out, in the *New England Magazine* about 1891, a Boston physician made protest in *The Transcript.* Such a story ought not to be written, he said; it was enough to drive anyone mad to read it.

Another physician, in Kansas I think, wrote to say that it was the best description of incipient insanity he had ever seen, and—begging my pardon—had I been there?

Now the story of the story is this:

For many years I suffered from a severe and continuous nervous breakdown tending to melancholia—and beyond. During about the third year of this trouble I went, in devout faith and some faint stir of hope, to a noted specialist in nervous diseases, the best known in the country. This wise man put me to bed and applied the rest cure, to which a still good physique responded so promptly that he concluded there was nothing much the matter with me, and sent me home with solemn advice to "live as domestic a life as far as possible," to "have but two hours' intellectual life a day," and "never to touch pen, brush or pencil again as long as I lived." This was in 1887.

I went home and obeyed those directions for some three months, and came so near the border line of utter mental ruin that I could see over.

Then, using the remnants of intelligence that remained, and helped by a wise friend, I cast the noted specialist's advice to the winds and went to work again—work, the normal life of every human being; work, in which is joy and growth and service, without which one is a pauper and a parasite; ultimately recovering some measure of power.

Being naturally moved to rejoicing by this narrow escape, I wrote *The Yellow Wallpaper,* with its embellishments and additions to carry out the ideal (I never had hallucinations or objections to my mural decorations) and sent a copy to the physician who so nearly drove me mad. He never acknowledged it.

The little book is valued by alienists and as good a specimen of one kind of literature. It has to my knowledge saved one woman from a similar fate—so terrifying her family that they let her out into normal activity and she recovered.

But the best result is this. Many years later I was told that the great specialist had admitted to friends of his that he had altered his treatment of neurasthenia since reading *The Yellow Wallpaper.*

It was not intended to drive people crazy, but to save people from being driven crazy, and it worked.

Comprehension

1. **Summarize** Describe the "rest cure" treatment and explain why it is prescribed for the narrator.

2. **Recall** Why does the narrator hate the wallpaper at first?

3. **Clarify** Who does the narrator think she is at the end of the story?

Literary Analysis

4. **Examine Character Change** How does the narrator change once she "discovers" the woman in the wallpaper? At what point does she begin to lose her grip on reality? Citing examples from both the beginning and the end of the story, explain how the writing style reflects her psychological transformation.

5. **Analyze First-Person Narrator** The narrator of this story is **unreliable**—you can't always trust that what she says is true. What are the advantages and disadvantages of using a first-person narrator to tell this story, especially in light of her condition?

6. **Interpret Symbolism** Reread lines 380–391 and consider the narrator's **powerlessness.** What might the yellow wallpaper symbolize in the story? Consider the following as you formulate your answer:
   - the narrator's attitude toward both her "condition" and her marriage
   - what she sees in the "strangling" pattern of the paper
   - her exhilaration when she rips the wallpaper off the wall

7. **Understand Social Context** Examine the chart you filled in as you read. What conclusions can you draw about the social conditions that shaped Gilman's work? Citing evidence from both the short story and "Why I Wrote 'The Yellow Wallpaper'" on page 784, explain
   - how wives were expected to behave in the 1890s
   - how women seem to have been treated by the men—husbands, brothers, doctors—who cared for them
   - what Gilman thought about women being denied meaningful work and personal power, and how she addresses these issues in this story

Literary Criticism

8. **Different Perspectives** At the time it was published, most critics read "The Yellow Wallpaper" as a horror tale about madness or, after Gilman's explanation appeared in 1913, as an exposé of women's medical treatment. Only a few saw what feminists in the 1970s would interpret as Gilman's **political assumptions.** They viewed the story as a harsh criticism of marriage and the oppression of women. Explain which of these interpretations you favor, citing evidence from the text.

Women were dismissed, infantilized, controlled, scoffed at, told not to question (lines 7, 9, 14, 219, 267–279, 345; article paragraphs 4–5). Gilman thought that work generates meaning, power, and self-confidence (lines 24–25; article paragraph 6). Gilman wrote her story in response to experiencing this treatment of women in her own life.

8. **Gothic Horror Tale:** the setting; the "living" wallpaper; the trapped woman that drives the narrator insane; **Exposé:** treatment harmed both the narrator and Gilman; **Feminist Critique:** women's social and economic oppression leads to madness; "cure" makes them worse.

Practice and Apply

After Reading

Use these copy masters to check understanding and provide extra support:

RESOURCE MANAGER—Copy Masters
Reading Check p. 252
First-Person Narrator p. 245
Question Support p. 253

Additional selection questions are provided for teachers on page 239.

ANSWERS

1. *The rest cure calls for little activity or stimulation and long hours of sleep. It is prescribed for the narrator's depression.*

2. *Its sickly yellow color and gaudy, chaotic pattern offend her artistic sensibility.*

3. *She thinks she is one of the women released from the wallpaper.*

Possible answers:

4. *After discovering the woman in the wallpaper, the narrator becomes increasingly obsessed. She loses her grip on reality when she ascribes a "vicious influence" to the wallpaper (lines 132–133) or at her first sighting of a figure in the wallpaper (lines 168-170). As the story progresses, the paragraphs get shorter and more fragmentary. The choppy writing style reflects the narrator's increasingly agitated state.*

5. ● **SKILLS FOCUS First-Person Narrator** *Advantages: Readers experience a compelling account of madness in which it is unclear whether the narrator is sane. Disadvantages: The narrator is unreliable, so readers struggle to separate reality from hallucination and may find the end of the story unclear.*

6. *The wallpaper, with its elaborately changing patterns and trapped women, could represent the narrator's madness. It could also symbolize her marriage, which imprisons, then enrages, and finally drives her mad. Or it might represent society that imprisons women with expectations.*

7. ■ **SKILLS FOCUS Understand Social Context** *Women should avoid artistic pursuits, control emotions and imagination, limit intellectual activity, and find happiness in domesticity (lines 49–50, 81, 109, 121–123, 219, 236–237; article paragraph 4).*

ANSWERS

Vocabulary in Context

VOCABULARY PRACTICE

1. *(d) lowly*   6. *(c) refused*
2. *(a) undulating* 7. *(b) favor*
3. *(c) decision*   8. *(b) misconstrued*
4. *(a) consideration* 9. *(d) vapid*
5. *(b) reserved*   10. *(a) humidity*

R **RESOURCE MANAGER—Copy Master**
Vocabulary Practice p. 250

VOCABULARY IN WRITING

Suggest that students eliminate words from the list that do not belong in a discussion of character. They might also write several sentences about John, and then revise three of the sentences, inserting a vocabulary word into each one.

VOCABULARY STRATEGY: TEMPERAMENT WORDS *(also an EL language objective)*

Ask volunteers to offer synonyms of each temperament word, for example:

- *melancholic,* "sad; unhappy; depressed"
- *phlegmatic,* "placid; calm; unemotional"
- *sanguine,* "cheerful; confident; optimistic"
- *choleric,* "angry; sour; bitter"

Answers:

1. *choleric*   3. *sanguine*
2. *phlegmatic*   4. *melancholic*

R **RESOURCE MANAGER—Copy Master**
Vocabulary Strategy p. 251

i Vocabulary Center at **ClassZone.com**
Additional Vocabulary Activities

Vocabulary in Context

VOCABULARY PRACTICE

Choose the word that is not related in meaning to the other words.

1. (a) extravagant, (b) showy, (c) flamboyant, (d) lowly
2. (a) undulating, (b) flying, (c) soaring, (d) gliding
3. (a) mockery, (b) derision, (c) decision, (d) contempt
4. (a) consideration, (b) convolution, (c) intricacy, (d) complexity
5. (a) clear-cut, (b) reserved, (c) patent, (d) evident
6. (a) periodic, (b) repeated, (c) refused, (d) recurrent
7. (a) fatuity, (b) favor, (c) silliness, (d) folly
8. (a) miscellaneous, (b) misconstrued, (c) various, (d) diversified
9. (a) vivid, (b) lurid, (c) sensational, (d) vapid
10. (a) humidity, (b) personality, (c) disposition, (d) temperament

WORD LIST
convolution
derision
fatuity
flamboyant
lurid
misconstrued
patent
recurrent
temperament
undulating

VOCABULARY IN WRITING

How is John, the narrator's husband, portrayed in this story? Write a short description of his personality, using three or more vocabulary words.

> **EXAMPLE SENTENCE**
>
> *John seems to have a pleasant* **temperament***, but in many ways he treats his wife like a foolish child.*

VOCABULARY STRATEGY: TEMPERAMENT WORDS

The vocabulary word *temperament* can relate to personality study, which has fascinated people since ancient times. One theory popular into the Middle Ages classified people into four basic personality types—choleric, phlegmatic, sanguine, and melancholic—depending on how much of certain body fluids, such as blood and bile, they possessed. Modern medicine has debunked this theory, but the terms are still used to define certain temperament traits today.

PRACTICE Read each personality description and then choose the word from the list provided that identifies it. Use a dictionary to define the terms if you need to.

> melancholic   phlegmatic   sanguine   choleric

1. Mrs. Peabody flies into a rage every time someone disagrees with her.
2. Even a tornado tearing the roof off his house could not upset Dr. Lewis.
3. No matter how far behind schedule a project runs, Ms. Tenny is always optimistic that it will be finished on time.
4. The only movies Mr. Ioacca wants to watch are those with unhappy endings.

 VOCABULARY PRACTICE
For more practice, go to the **Vocabulary Center** at **ClassZone.com**.

DIFFERENTIATED INSTRUCTION

FOR ENGLISH LEARNERS

Task Support: Vocabulary Practice Ask students which words in the box are cognates from their home languages. Discuss whether students have heard or read the words in those languages. Urge them to use their knowledge of the cognate meanings to help construct meaning for the English word.

FOR ADVANCED LEARNERS/AP

Temperament Words Ask partners to brainstorm additional temperament words, then classify the words by the four categories in the **Practice** or other categories of their choosing. Urge students to use a Classification Chart or other appropriate graphic organizer to organize and analyze the frequency of words in the different categories. Which category has the most words? What range of words is available, from mild to extreme, in each category? Invite

students to speculate about the reasons for variations in frequency and range.

BEST PRACTICES TOOLKIT—Transparency
Classification Chart p. B17

Reading-Writing Connection

W2.2

WRITING PROMPT

WRITE A PERSONAL RESPONSE Although most contemporary readers respond positively to "The Yellow Wallpaper," the editor of the *Atlantic Monthly* in 1892 rejected it for publication. By way of explanation, he offered this candid reaction: "I could not forgive myself if I made others as miserable as I have made myself." How did the story affect you? Write a **three-to-five-paragraph personal response** explaining your own thoughts and feelings about the story.

SELF-CHECK

A strong personal response will . . .

- identify the story and clearly state your overall response to it in the introduction
- give specific reasons for your response or more detailed reactions to specific aspects of the story
- support your statements with details, examples, and quotations from the story

GRAMMAR AND STYLE

LC1.1

CHOOSE EFFECTIVE VERB TENSE Review the **Grammar and Style** note on page 771. The immediacy and power of "The Yellow Wallpaper" comes in part from Gilman's choice to have the narrator tell the story mostly in the **present tense** as though writing in a diary. In this way, the reader plunges directly into the narrator's mind and follows its dark descent. Notice the use of **present-tense verbs** in this chilling example from the end of the story:

> But I *am securely fastened* now by my well-hidden rope—you *don't get* me *out* in the road there! (lines 475–476)

PRACTICE The following paragraph is a sample from another short story. Notice how the past-tense verbs create a certain distance between the reader and the events. Revise the paragraph, writing it in the present tense to achieve a different effect.

> I threw another log on the fire, waiting for Ahmer to come home. Dinner sat on the table, growing cold. Ahmer had been gone for hours and I was sure he had left with hurt feelings. Why did we always argue this way on special occasions? It was as though we didn't really want to celebrate, or didn't know how.

 WRITING TOOLS
For prewriting, revision, and editing tools, visit the **Writing Center** at ClassZone.com.

FOR DEVELOPING WRITERS

Writing Support

- Offer this thesis sentence starter for students' personal response: My overall response to "The Yellow Wallpaper" was _____.

- Suggest that students use two literary features from the Two-Column Chart as a basis for writing two paragraphs after their thesis statement.

- Encourage students to add details that support their opinions.

Reading-Writing Connection

WRITING PROMPT

Have students begin by listing their response to story features—topic, character, setting, plot, and theme—in a Two-Column Chart.

Feature	My Response
topic	Mental illness is too grim.
character	The narrator was interesting, but John was too "flat."
setting	It was cool and spooky.

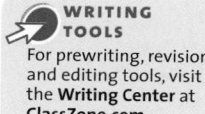 **BEST PRACTICES TOOLKIT—Transparency**
Two-Column Chart p. A25

For writing support, see

ⓘ Writing Center at **ClassZone.com**

GRAMMAR AND STYLE

Help students rewrite the first example in the past tense for comparison. ***Possible answer:*** *But I was securely fastened by my well-hidden rope—you could not have gotten me out in the road!* (For more on verb tenses, see page R59 of the **Grammar Handbook**.)

Possible answer: *I throw another log on the fire. Then I wait for Ahmer to come home. Dinner sits on the table. It grows cold. Ahmer has been gone for hours, and I am sure that his feelings are hurt. Why do we always argue this way on special occasions? It is as though we don't really want to celebrate, or don't know how.*

Ⓡ **RESOURCE MANAGER—Copy Master**
Choose Effective Verb Tense p. 254

Assess and Reteach

Assess

Ⓡ **RESOURCE MANAGER—Copy Masters**
Selection Test A pp. 255–256
Selection Test B/C pp. 257–258

💿 Test Generator CD

Reteach

Ⓢ **STANDARDS LESSON FILE**
Literature Lesson 10: Types of Point of View
Grammar Lesson 16: Basic Verb Tenses

Ethan Frome
Edith Wharton

ABOUT THE AUTHOR

Edith Wharton Before students read this feature, tell them that Edith Wharton was a prolific writer. Her writings include 25 novels and novellas, more than 80 short stories, an autobiography, a book on the theory of fiction, several collections of poetry and nonfiction, plus numerous translations, reviews, and articles, including accounts of her visits to the front line during World War I. Wharton received the Pulitzer Prize for her novel *The Age of Innocence* (1920).

ABOUT THE NOVEL

Ethan Frome Before students read this feature, tell them that Ethan Frome, like other Wharton protagonists, resists social expectations and taboos with tragic consequences. After reading the feature, invite students to identify differences between Ethan and Mattie, then speculate about character traits that Ethan Frome and Mattie Silver might have in common. ***Possible answer:*** *Ethan is older than Mattie. His life is in a small village, while she is from the city. Mattie is optimistic, while Ethan is worn out. Students may suggest that both characters are sensitive, curious, and longing for connection with others.*

LEGACY OF A MASTERPIECE

Introduce the Passage Remind students that Edith Wharton was part of the literary movement called naturalism. Naturalists believed that people were helpless in the wake of certain forces that determined the outcome of their lives. As they read, have students notice the kinds of economic, social, and natural/physical forces that play a role in the life of Ethan Frome.

American Masterpiece

Ethan Frome
Edith Wharton

Edith Wharton
1862–1937

ABOUT THE AUTHOR In the late 19th century, it was sometimes said that only 400 people really "mattered" in New York society—the number of people who could fit into millionaire socialite Caroline Astor's posh Fifth Avenue ballroom. Edith Wharton grew up in this rarefied society and wrote about it in most of her novels. Yet *Ethan Frome,* her best-known work, was not set in uppercrust New York society, but rather in a poor New England village. Wharton got her first taste of New England at the fashionable resort of Newport, Rhode Island, where families like hers and the Astors summered when she was a girl. However, Wharton also observed a different side of New England—its world of tiny villages and hardscrabble farms where poor families eked out a living from the bleak landscape. After she and her husband purchased an estate in the Berkshire Mountains of western Massachusetts, Wharton was inspired to write about that very different world in her novel *Ethan Frome.*

ABOUT THE NOVEL So short that it is sometimes called a novella, *Ethan Frome* is set in a Massachusetts village called Starkfield, the name clearly evoking the bleak lifestyle that Wharton wished to portray. The story is told by an engineer who visits Starkfield and grows interested in a "ruin of a man" he sees there named Ethan Frome. Frome himself, we learn, had always wanted to be an engineer and to live in cities, "where there were lectures and big libraries." Instead, poverty and tradition have restricted him to a barren farm and an equally barren marriage. A visit from his sickly wife Zeena's young cousin, Mattie Silver, brings a spark of joy into Frome's grim life. His tragic attempt to grasp that joy forms the central conflict of the tale.

LEGACY OF A MASTERPIECE *Ethan Frome* was not a huge success when it first appeared in 1911, but in time it became Wharton's best-known work. Told in prose as spare and lean as the New England farm on which it is set, its style is in sharp contrast to Wharton's lushly detailed portraits of Gilded Age Manhattan. Though different in style and setting, *Ethan Frome* is similar to Wharton's other books, however, in that its characters seem to have very little control over their own lives. In this resepct, Wharton was a naturalist writer exploring the power that environment holds over human beings.

The following passage describes Ethan Frome's changing relationship with Mattie Silver and the strong emotions that she has awakened in him.

DIFFERENTIATED INSTRUCTION

FOR STRATEGIC READERS

Note-Taking Ask students to identify the main ideas and important details of each section on page 788. Remind them that the main idea is what the section is mostly about. Details are facts and information that support the main idea. Use this example to model:

About the Author

Main Idea: Wharton's life in New York's wealthy society influenced her writing.

Detail 1: New York society is the subject of most Wharton novels.

Detail 2: Time spent at Newport and her Berkshire estate gave Wharton firsthand knowledge of farming villages.

Frome was in the habit of walking into Starkfield to fetch home his wife's cousin, Mattie Silver, on the rare evenings when some chance of amusement drew her to the village. It was his wife who had suggested, when the girl came to live with them, that such opportunities should be put in her way. Mattie Silver came from Stamford, and when she entered the Fromes' household to act as her cousin Zeena's aid it was thought best, as she came without pay, not to let her feel too sharp a contrast between the life she had left and the isolation of a Starkfield farm. But for this—as Frome sardonically reflected—it would hardly have occurred to Zeena to take any thought for the girl's amusement.

When his wife first proposed that they should give Mattie an occasional evening out he had inwardly demurred at having to do the extra two miles to the village and back after his hard day on the farm; but not long afterward he had reached the point of wishing that Starkfield might give all its nights to revelry.

Mattie Silver had lived under his roof for a year, and from early morning till they met at supper he had frequent chances of seeing her; but no moments in her company were comparable to those when, her arm in his, and her light step flying to keep time with his long stride, they walked back through the night to the farm. He had taken to the girl from the first day, when he had driven over to the Flats to meet her, and she had smiled and waved to him from the train, crying out, "You must be Ethan!" as she jumped down with her bundles, while he reflected, looking over her slight person: "She don't look much on housework, but she ain't a fretter, anyhow." But it was not only that the coming to his house of a bit of hopeful young life was like the lighting of a fire on a cold hearth. The girl was more than the bright serviceable creature he had thought her. She had an eye to see and an ear to hear: he could show her things and tell her things, and taste the bliss of feeling that all he imparted left long reverberations and echoes he could wake at will.

It was during their night walks back to the farm that he felt most intensely the sweetness of this communion. He had always been more sensitive than the people about him to the appeal of natural beauty. His unfinished studies had given form to this sensibility and even in his unhappiest moments field and sky spoke to him with a deep and powerful persuasion. But hitherto the emotion had remained in him as a silent ache, veiling with sadness the beauty that evoked it. He did not even know whether any one else in the world felt as he did, or whether he was the sole victim of this mournful privilege. Then he learned that one other spirit had trembled with the same touch of wonder: that at his side, living under his roof and eating his bread, was a creature to whom he could say: "That's Orion down yonder; the big fellow to the right is Aldebaran, and the bunch of little ones—like bees swarming— they're the Pleiades . . . ."

TIERED DISCUSSION PROMPTS

Use these prompts to help students understand the dynamic between Ethan Frome and Mattie Silver:

Connect Did you ever meet a new friend just when you were feeling terribly bored or miserable? How does that experience help you to understand Ethan Frome's reaction to Mattie? *Students should recognize that Mattie Silver provided Ethan Frome relief from his grim existence.*

Analyze What feelings does Mattie evoke in Ethan Frome? *Possible answer: She evokes feelings of happiness and connection to others. She makes him feel more effective, more alive, and less lonely than he had felt before her arrival.*

Synthesize What contrast does Wharton suggest between Ethan Frome's old life on a "barren farm" and in a "barren marriage" and his new relationship with Mattie? How do these contrasts affect readers? *Possible answer: Wharton shows that Ethan's relationship with Mattie contains wonder, excitement, and an interest in nature and beauty, all qualities that have been deadened by Ethan's barren marriage and barren farm life. These contrasts make the reader feel for and sympathize with Ethan Frome's budding hopes and desires.*

FOR STRATEGIC READERS

Characterization Help students create two Character Traits Webs, one for Ethan Frome and one for Mattie Silver. After they finish, have students circle any traits that the two characters have in common.

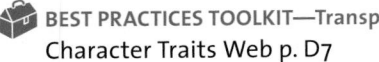 BEST PRACTICES TOOLKIT—Transparency Character Traits Web p. D7

FOR ADVANCED LEARNERS/AP

Hypothesize Ask students to suggest the forces at work on Ethan Frome and Mattie. Have them consider how these forces drive the characters together and keep them apart. Then challenge students to hypothesize on the remaining plot events in the novel. Urge them to read the novel to check their hypotheses, or if they know the novel, to explain whether they were surprised by its outcome.

Focus and Motivate

OBJECTIVES

Literary Analysis
- explore the key idea of **ambition**
- analyze tone
- read a short story

Reading
- make inferences about characters

Vocabulary
- build vocabulary for reading and writing
- use the Latin root *rog* to help unlock word meaning (also an EL language objective)

 CALIFORNIA R3.3, R1.2

ABOUT THE AUTHOR

Point out that although Wharton had an interest in women's roles in society, she was not specifically a feminist writer. Rather, she was interested in the way society's roles trap people, by gender or by other features. In "April Showers," Wharton uses light social satire to gently attack the roles confining a young woman with artistic aspirations.

USING THE *NOTABLE QUOTE*

Have a volunteer read **Edith Wharton's** quote. Then ask students what kinds of lives are suggested by *tight-rope* and *featherbed*. What can they infer about Wharton from her preference? *Possible answer:* Tight-rope *suggests a life that is uncertain but exciting.* Featherbed *suggests luxury and calm. Wharton would rather take risks than have an easy, boring life.*

 CALIFORNIA R3.3, R1.2 (p. 802)

April Showers
Short Story by Edith Wharton

NOTABLE QUOTE
"Life is either always a tight-rope or a featherbed. Give me a tight-rope."

FYI
Did you know that Edith Wharton . . .

- privately published her first book of poetry at age 16?
- published a book each year from 1902 until her death in 1937?
- entertained President Theodore Roosevelt at her home in France?
- had such a forceful personality that her friends pretended to cower in fear when they saw her coming?

Author On|ine
For more on Edith Wharton, visit the **Literature Center** at **ClassZone.com.**

Edith Wharton
1862–1937

To understand Edith Wharton is to know something about the insular upper-class society that produced her. Rich and fashionable "old New York" consisted of established families, like Wharton's own, descended from English and Dutch colonists and having inherited "old money" made in banking, shipping, and real estate. For Wharton, it was a restrictive world of narrow minds and rigid, arbitrary rules, where "'bad manners' were the supreme offense." It was a world already starting to disintegrate in the late 19th and early 20th century as new immigrants poured into New York and "new money" was being made in industry and manufacturing. But it was the world Wharton struggled with and wrote about with the satiric wit of an insider who had found a way to be free.

The Compensations of Wealth Wharton was educated at home by governesses and spent her youth as expected, traveling with her parents to Europe and dutifully attending the lavish balls and dinners during New York's social season. Her happiest times, however, were spent in her father's large library, reading and writing. Her cold, domineering mother thwarted the young Edith's literary ambitions by limiting her supply of paper and forcing her to marry a rich banker 12 years her senior. Depressed by her empty marriage and frivolous social life, Wharton used her characteristic moral strength and imaginative powers to break out. She had her own country estate built in Lenox, Massachusetts, where she could associate with people who shared her interests in art and literature. She also escaped to Europe each winter, where she cultivated friendships with famous artists and writers, such as her mentor, rival, and long-time friend, Henry James. Ultimately, she divorced her husband and moved permanently to France, living alternately outside Paris and on the Riviera.

Fame and Fulfillment? The novel that brought Wharton her first great success was *The House of Mirth* (1905), the story of a young woman crushed by the ranks of old New York when she tries to live by her own moral standards. Many of Wharton's other novels and stories sympathetically portray individuals who try but fail to find happiness in unconventional ways. *Ethan Frome* (1911), perhaps her best-known novel, depicts a doomed pair of lovers in a poor farming community. Wharton was the most celebrated American woman writer of her time but had a rather skeptical view of personal fulfillment. "If only we'd stop trying to be happy," she once said, "we could have a pretty good time."

790

Selection Resources

RESOURCE MANAGER UNIT 4

Plan and Teach pp. 259–266

Literary Analysis
Summary pp. 267†*, 268‡*
Tone pp. 269, 270†*
Question Support p. 277*

Reading
Make Inferences About Characters pp. 271, 272†*
Reading Check p. 276

Vocabulary
Study p. 273*
Practice p. 274
Strategy p. 275

Assessment
Selection Tests A, B/C pp. 279*, 281*
Test Generator CD

BEST PRACTICES TOOLKIT

Differentiated Instruction pp. 31–38*

Scaffolding Instruction pp. 43–46*

Graphic Organizers/Strategies
Word Questioning • Character Traits and Textual Evidence • Two-Column Chart

Reading Support
Audio Anthology CD*

Technology
Literature and Vocabulary Centers at **ClassZone.com**
WriteSmart CD

---

* Resources for Differentiation   † Also in Spanish   ‡ In Haitian Creole and Vietnamese

● LITERARY ANALYSIS: TONE

Occasionally, a writer's **tone,** or attitude toward a subject, is so recognizable that it leaps out from the first sentence. Usually, however, tone is more subtle. Readers must analyze the writer's choice of words and details to determine whether his or her tone is somber or playful, sarcastic or admiring. As you read this story, consider how Wharton describes different characters and their actions. Try to detect the writer's attitude toward her characters, particularly Theodora, a young woman who is attempting to become a writer herself.

■ READING SKILL: MAKE INFERENCES ABOUT CHARACTERS

You know that writers don't state everything about their characters directly. Instead, they often leave it up to the reader to **make inferences,** or logical assumptions, about characters based on how those characters think and behave. To be logical, inferences must be supported by evidence from the text. As you read, jot down telling actions and dialogue. Note what you can infer about each character from his or her behavior.

Evidence from the Text	My Inferences
"Lingeringly, tenderly she gathered up the pages of her novel . . . and tied them with the blue satin ribbon. . . . She had meant to wear the ribbon with her new dotted muslin on Sundays, but this was putting it to a nobler use. She bound it round her manuscript, tying the ends in a pretty bow."	Theodora cares more abut her novel than she does about her clothes. But she's also dressing up the novel like a doll, not just sending it out, as a serious, more experienced writer would do.

▲ VOCABULARY IN CONTEXT

Wharton uses these words in her story about a writer waiting for a lucky break. Choose the word that completes each phrase.

WORD LIST		
admonitory	harassing	predecessor
commiseration	impending	retrospective
dastardly	interrogation	

1. wrote stories of evil villains and their _____ deeds
2. ignored _____ advice that success doesn't come overnight
3. modeled herself after her famous _____
4. sent impatient letters _____ those reviewing her work
5. feared _____ failure when no one responded

Explore the Key Idea

What is your DREAM JOB?

KEY IDEA You've probably answered the question "What do you want to be when you grow up?" more than a few times. But take a minute to think about your ultimate **ambition.** What is it about your dream job that's so appealing? Money? Fame? The thrill of doing something you love? The main character in this story dreams of becoming a writer, but does she have what it takes?

QUICKWRITE Imagine you're filling out an application for your dream job (even if your chosen job—be it rock star or international soccer sensation—isn't one you'd typically fill out an application to get). What skills or traits make you the perfect candidate for the job? Why do you want it? What are you willing to do to get it?

791

Teach

What is your DREAM JOB?

Read the question and **KEY IDEA** paragraph with students. Ask them whether **ambition** is a good motivator. What negative impact can ambition have? After students identify appealing aspects of their dream job, have them complete the *QUICKWRITE.* Discuss trade-offs students are willing to make.

SKILLS FOCUS

> **LITERARY ANALYSIS** R3.3
>
> ### ● TONE
>
> Share this example with students:
>
> Dave devoted hours every day to working on his 1954 Chevy. He had rescued the car from a junkyard and diligently taught himself auto mechanics to fix it. Dave planned to use the car to drive seniors to doctors' appointments, knowing that its comfortable interior would relieve their anxiety.
>
> Ask students to identify the writer's tone toward Dave. ***Possible answer:*** *The writer admires Dave's goals and effort.*
>
> **CHECK UNDERSTANDING** Have students identify words that contribute to the tone.

> **READING SKILL**
>
> ### ■ MAKE INFERENCES ABOUT CHARACTERS
>
> Ask students what they can infer from the author biography on page 790 about why Wharton was interested in characters "who try but fail to find happiness in unconventional ways." ***Possible answer:*** *Wharton herself lived an unconventional life for her time. She became a writer despite her mother's disapproval. She left an unhappy, conventional marriage and moved to Paris. She likely sympathized with those who tried to live on their own terms.*
>
> **RESOURCE MANAGER—Copy Master** Make Inferences About Characters p. 271 (for student use while reading the selection)

VOCABULARY

▲ VOCABULARY IN CONTEXT

DIAGNOSE WORD KNOWLEDGE To determine preteaching needs, have all students complete Vocabulary in Context. *Answers:* **1.** *dastardly,* **2.** *admonitory,* **3.** *predecessor,* **4.** *harassing,* **5.** *impending*

PRETEACH VOCABULARY Preteach vocabulary with this copy master. Read each item aloud.

[R] **RESOURCE MANAGER—Copy Master** Vocabulary Study p. 273

MORE VOCABULARY SUPPORT For additional activities and guidelines, see

🧰 **BEST PRACTICES TOOLKIT** Scaffolding Vocabulary Instruction pp. 43–46

ⓘ Vocabulary Center at **ClassZone.com**

SUMMARY

In this short story, young Theodora sends her first novel to *Home Circle*, dreaming that it will bring her fame and fortune. An acceptance letter offers fleeting glory, until she discovers that the magazine had meant the letter for another writer. Her father's sympathy softens the blow, as Theodora learns of his failed literary efforts long ago.

LITERARY ANALYSIS

Ⓐ TONE

Possible answer: *Wharton's tone is not entirely serious. She seems to be gently mocking Theodora. The last sentence of the novel is unbelievably sappy, yet Theodora reads it aloud as though it shows unsurpassed loveliness. Wharton tells us that Theodora finds the ending "beautiful" (line 2) and "pathetic" (line 3). Her tone and the last line of Theodora's novel let the reader know that Theodora is vastly overrating her own work.*

If students need help . . . Reread the last line of Theodora's novel, and explain that it is a flowery way of saying that Guy never got over Muriel's death.

Lines 1–18
REINFORCE *KEY IDEA:* AMBITION

Discuss On the basis of the opening scene, what is Theodora's **ambition?** How is she working to achieve it? *Possible answer: Theodora hopes to become a famous writer. To achieve her ambition, she is working late into the night to finish her novel.*

April Showers

EDITH WHARTON

BACKGROUND By the turn of the 20th century, popular magazines—*Scribner's, Harper's, Century,* the *Atlantic Monthly,* and *Ladies' Home Journal*—paid good money to publish short stories, essays, and also longer works in serial form as, say, several chapters per issue. Edith Wharton first published her stories in magazines and serialized her Pulitzer Prize–winning novel, *The Age of Innocence,* as well as her autobiography. Such a publishing bonanza was great encouragement for writers of varying degrees of talent.

ANALYZE VISUALS
Describe the **mood** suggested in this painting. Which is more responsible for conveying the mood, the subject's pose and expression, or the artist's use of light and shadow? Explain your choice

"But Guy's heart slept under the violets on Muriel's grave."

It was a beautiful ending; Theodora had seen girls cry over last chapters that weren't half as pathetic. She laid her pen aside and read the words over, letting her voice linger on the fall of the sentence; then, drawing a deep breath, she wrote across the foot of the page the name by which she had decided to become known in literature—Gladys Glyn. Ⓐ

Downstairs the library clock struck two. Its muffled thump sounded like an **admonitory** knock against her bedroom floor. Two o' clock! and she had promised her mother to be up early enough to see that the buttons were sewn
10 on Johnny's reefer, and that Kate had her cod-liver oil[1] before starting for school!

Lingeringly, tenderly she gathered up the pages of her novel—there were five hundred of them—and tied them with the blue satin ribbon that her Aunt Julia had given her. She had meant to wear the ribbon with her new dotted muslin on Sundays, but this was putting it to a nobler use. She bound it round her manuscript, tying the ends in a pretty bow. Theodora was clever at making bows, and could have trimmed hats beautifully, had not all her spare moments been given to literature. Then, with a last look at the precious pages, she sealed and addressed the package. She meant to send it off next morning to the *Home Circle.*[2] She knew it would be hard to obtain access to a paper which numbered so many popular authors among
20 its contributors, but she had been encouraged to make the venture by something her Uncle James had said the last time he had come down from Boston.

Ⓐ TONE
Consider the literary merit of the last sentence of Theodora's novel, and think about the way in which she reads it out loud. Do you think Wharton's tone is entirely serious in these lines? Explain why or why not.

admonitory
(ăd-mŏn′ĭ-tôr′ē) *adj.* warning

❶ Targeted Passage

---

1. **cod-liver oil:** a foul-tasting liquid once commonly taken as a source of vitamins A and D.
2. ***Home Circle:*** a magazine popular in the late 19th and early 20th centuries.

Girl Reading (1909), Edmund Charles Tarbell. Oil on canvas, 32 ¼″ × 28 ½″. The Hayden Collection, Charles Henry Hayden Fund 09.209. © Museum of Fine Arts, Boston.

DIFFERENTIATED INSTRUCTION

FOR ALL STUDENTS

Provide these independent projects to extend the lesson:

- Create a cartoon to show satire.
- Dramatize a romantic ending.
- Debate security versus excitement.

For further details on these projects, see

R RESOURCE MANAGER
Ideas for Extension pp. 264–265

FOR STRATEGIC READERS

In combination with the *Audio Anthology CD,* use one or more Targeted Passages (pp. 792, 795, 797, 798, 800) to ensure that students focus on key story events and concepts. Targeted Passages are also good for English learners.

❶ Targeted Passage [Lines 7–18]

The opening passage establishes the setting; the main character, Theodora; and the story's central conflict.

ANALYZE VISUALS

Possible answer: The mood is intense and serious. Both the subject's solemn expression and deep concentration and the artist's use of dark shadows are responsible for conveying this mood.

About the Art Edmund Charles Tarbell (1862–1938) was born the same year as Wharton and died just one year later than she. Like Wharton, Tarbell moved to Paris, where he studied art. Three years later, he returned to his home in Boston. Tarbell painted many interiors such as this one, in which light filters onto young women involved in domestic activity.

Lines 8–13
TIERED DISCUSSION PROMPTS

Use these prompts to help students understand Theodora's circumstances:

Connect Have you ever worked long and hard on a creative product? How did you adjust your daily schedule during this time? How did you feel about the end result? *Accept all thoughtful responses.*

Analyze How does Theodora feel about her writing? How does writing affect her actions in everyday life? *Possible answer: She feels awed by it and passionately committed to it. It makes her forget everyday responsibilities.*

Evaluate Is it acceptable to forget everyday responsibilities in order to produce art? Explain. *Possible answer: Students today may say that producing art is an important personal goal that could take precedence over everyday chores. However, some may note that the trade-off only works if the art is great art, which Theodora's may not be.*

- Where is Theodora?
- What has she just finished?
- What does she think of her work?
- Where does she plan to send it?

FOR ENGLISH LEARNERS

Key Academic Vocabulary Use Word Questioning to teach these words: *obtain* (line 19), *contribute* (line 48), *publication* (line 158), *invest* (line 190).

 BEST PRACTICES TOOLKIT—Transparency
 Word Questioning p. E9

Prereading For prereading instruction for English learners, see

 BEST PRACTICES TOOLKIT
 Scaffolding Reading Instruction pp. 43–46

FOR ADVANCED LEARNERS/AP

AP exercises in the bottom channel provide additional challenge for students. Use these suggestions for small groups or individuals.

ADDITIONAL GUIDELINES

For more help with differentiation and tips for classroom management, see

 BEST PRACTICES TOOLKIT
 Differentiated Instruction pp. 31–38

B TONE

Possible answer: *Kathleen Kyd seems to be a writer of melodramatic romance novels for women. Wharton maintains her gently mocking tone, as Theodora reveals deep admiration for Kyd (lines 35–37).*

If students need help . . . Reread lines 35–37, showing the tone in your voice.

READING SKILL

C MAKE INFERENCES

Possible answer: *Uncle James distinguishes between "pleasant, social women" and "female writers" because he disapproves of the latter (line 40). He calls Kyd's writing "sentimental trash" and sternly warns that Theodora should not read it lest it "infect" her "system" (line 50). Uncle James seems both judgmental and sexist.*

If students need help . . . Continue the chart introduced on page 791.

Evidence from the Text	My Inferences
He says women writers are not "pleasant, sociable."	He makes unfair judgments.

Extend the Discussion Why is Kathleen Kyd's "rags to riches" life story so appealing to Theodora?

He had been telling his brother, Doctor Dace, about his new house out at Brookline.[3] Uncle James was prosperous, and was always moving into new houses with more "modern improvements." Hygiene was his passion, and he migrated in the wake of sanitary plumbing.

"The bathrooms alone are worth the money," he was saying, cheerfully, "although it *is* a big rent. But then, when a man's got no children to save up for—" he glanced compassionately round Doctor Dace's crowded table "—and it *is* something to be in a neighborhood where the drainage is A-one. That's what 30 I was telling our neighbor. Who do you suppose she is, by the way?" He smiled at Theodora. "I rather think that young lady knows all about her. Ever heard of Kathleen Kyd?"

Kathleen Kyd! The famous "society novelist," the creator of more "favorite heroines" than all her **predecessors** put together had ever turned out, the author of *Fashion and Passion, An American Duchess, Rhona's Revolt*. Was there any intelligent girl from Maine to California whose heart would not have beat faster at the mention of that name? B

"Why, yes," Uncle James was saying, "Kathleen Kyd lives next door. Frances G. Wollop is her real name, and her husband's a dentist. She's a very pleasant, sociable 40 kind of woman; you'd never think she was a writer. Ever hear how she began to write? She told me the whole story. It seems she was a saleswoman in a store, working on starvation wages, with a mother and a consumptive[4] sister to support. Well, she wrote a story one day, just for fun, and sent it to the *Home Circle*. They'd never heard of her, of course, and she never expected to hear from them. She did, though. They took the story and passed their plate for more. She became a regular contributor and eventually was known all over the country. Now she tells me her books bring her in about ten thousand a year. Rather more than you and I can boast of, eh, John? Well, I hope *this* household doesn't contribute to her support." He glanced sharply at Theodora. "I don't believe in feeding youngsters 50 on sentimental trash; it's like sewer gas—doesn't smell bad, and infects the system without your knowing it." C

Theodora listened breathlessly. Kathleen Kyd's first story had been accepted by the *Home Circle*, and they had asked for more! Why should Gladys Glyn be less fortunate? Theodora had done a great deal of novel reading—far more than her parents were aware of—and felt herself competent to pronounce upon the quality of her own work. She was almost sure that "April Showers" was a remarkable book. If it lacked Kathleen Kyd's lightness of touch, it had an emotional intensity never achieved by that brilliant writer. Theodora did not care to amuse her readers; she left that to more frivolous talents. Her aim was to stir the depths of human nature, 60 and she felt she had succeeded. It was a great thing for a girl to be able to feel that about her first novel. Theodora was only seventeen; and she remembered, with a touch of **retrospective** compassion, that George Eliot[5] had not become famous till she was nearly forty.

---

3. **Brookline:** a town in Massachusetts, just west of Boston.

4. **consumptive:** having consumption, or tuberculosis.

5. **George Eliot:** the pseudonym of the great 19th-century English novelist Mary Ann Evans.

predecessor (prĕd´ĭ-sĕs´ər) *n.* a person who precedes or comes before

B TONE
Judging from the stories' titles, describe the kind of writer you think Kathleen Kyd might be. What is Wharton's tone as she describes Theodora's reaction to the news about Kyd?

C MAKE INFERENCES
Why does Uncle James distinguish between "pleasant, sociable" women and female writers? Explain what you can infer about his character from these lines.

retrospective (rĕt´rə-spĕk´tĭv) *adj.* looking back into the past

---

DIFFERENTIATED INSTRUCTION

FOR STRATEGIC READERS

Flashback Make sure students understand that Uncle James's visit is a flashback, an event that occurred before the beginning of the story. Ask them how this flashback helps the reader understand Theodora better. **Possible answer:** *It helps to explain her motivation for sending out her first novel and her high hopes of success.*

FOR ENGLISH LEARNERS

Idioms and Phrasal Verbs [mixed-readiness groups] Share or elicit meanings for these expressions, and help students use them in original sentences:

• *for fun* (line 43), "for entertainment"

• *passed their plate for more* (line 45), "asked for more"

• *bring her in* (line 47), "earn for her"

• *write the book down* (line 67–68), "make the book easier to understand"

Vocabulary: Multiple-Meaning Words [paired option] Have partners use context to define these multiple-meaning words:

• *thrown* [into] (line 69), "engaged, occupied"

• *stooped to* (line 73), "lowered [themselves]"

No, there was no doubt about the merit of "April Showers." But would not an inferior work have had a better chance of success? Theodora recalled the early struggles of famous authors, the notorious antagonism of publishers and editors to any new writer of exceptional promise. Would it not be wiser to write the book down to the average reader's level, reserving for some later work the great "effects" into which she had thrown all the fever of her imagination? The

70 thought was sacrilege! Never would she lay hands on the sacred structure she had reared; never would she resort to the inartistic expedient of modifying her work to suit the popular taste. Better obscure failure than a vulgar triumph. The great authors never stooped to such concessions, and Theodora felt herself included in their ranks by the firmness with which she rejected all thought of conciliating an unappreciative public. The manuscript should be sent as it was. **D**

She woke with a start and a heavy sense of apprehension. The *Home Circle* had refused "April Showers"! No, that couldn't be it; there lay the precious manuscript, waiting to be posted. What was it, then? Ah, that ominous thump below stairs— nine o'clock striking! It was Johnny's buttons!

80 She sprang out of bed in dismay. She had been so determined not to disappoint her mother about Johnny's buttons! Mrs. Dace, helpless from chronic rheumatism, had to entrust the care of the household to her eldest daughter; and Theodora honestly meant to see that Johnny had his full complement of buttons, and that Kate and Bertha went to school tidy. Unfortunately, the writing of a great novel leaves little time or memory for the lesser obligations of life, and Theodora usually found that her good intentions matured too late for practical results.

Her contrition was softened by the thought that literary success would enable her to make up for all the little negligences of which she was guilty. She meant to spend all her money on her family; and already she had visions of a wheeled

90 chair for her mother, a fresh wallpaper for the doctor's shabby office, bicycles for the girls, and Johnny's establishment at a boarding school where sewing on his buttons would be included in the curriculum. If her parents could have guessed her intentions, they would not have found fault with her as they did; and Doctor Dace, on this particular morning, would not have looked up to say, with his fagged, ironical air:

"I suppose you didn't get home from the ball till morning?"

Theodora's sense of being in the right enabled her to take the thrust with a dignity that would have awed the unfeeling parent of fiction.

"I'm sorry to be late, father," she said.

100 Doctor Dace, who could never be counted on to behave like a father in a book, shrugged his shoulders impatiently.

"Your sentiments do you credit, but they haven't kept your mother's breakfast warm." **E**

"Hasn't mother's tray gone up yet?"

"Who was to take it, I should like to know? The girls came down so late that

MAKE INFERENCES
Consider Theodora's sympathy for George Eliot in lines 61–63 and her opinion of the "average reader." What inferences can you make about Theodora's character based on her thoughts about her own work?

② **Targeted Passage**

MAKE INFERENCES
Theodora muses repeatedly that Dr. Dace does not act as a father in a work of fiction would. What does she mean by this?

FOR STRATEGIC READERS

② Targeted Passage [Lines 76–86]

This passage shows the difficulty of Theodora's role in the family.

- Why does Theodora's mother need help?

- What was Theodora supposed to do for Mrs. Dace?

- On what does Theodora blame her forgetfulness?

FOR ADVANCED LEARNERS/AP

Analyze Satire Have students discuss the satire in Wharton's descriptions of Kathleen Kyd and her writing (lines 33–51) and of Theodora's literary aspirations (lines 52–75). What is Wharton's opinion of writers like Kyd? What is her opinion of Theodora's writing? Have students decide whom Wharton satirizes more sharply, Kyd or Theodora, and share their views with the class.

D **MAKE INFERENCES**

Possible answer: Theodora's sympathy for the great George Eliot is humorous and ironic. Readers can infer from her reaction that she can be pretentious and condescending, but also that she is naive. She is, after all, still a teenager, who has lived a relatively sheltered life, and who views herself as very special.

If students need help . . . Clarify that George Eliot is a famous and well-regarded novelist, while Theodora is a teenager trying to sell a mediocre first novel.

BACKGROUND

Rheumatism Much like arthritis, Mrs. Dace's chronic rheumatism would produce painful joints and muscles and make everyday chores such as sewing on a button very difficult.

Lines 87–96
REINFORCE *KEY IDEA*: AMBITION

Discuss What does this passage suggest about Theodora's **ambitions**? *Possible answer: Theodora dreams of fame for herself and fortune to help her family, which is struggling financially.* How do Theodora's dreams of helping her family soften readers' appraisal of her? *Possible answer: Her desire to help her family makes readers forgive her pretensions about her accomplishments and instead wish her well.*

READING SKILL

E **MAKE INFERENCES**

Possible answer: Theodora means that he doesn't act like the type of idealized, romanticized father that might be found in her book or in Kyd's book. Such a father would quickly understand, forgive, and forget Theodora's shortcomings. Dr. Dace doesn't act as Theodora wishes he would. Instead, he is reproachful and sarcastic.

TIERED DISCUSSION PROMPTS

Use these prompts to help students understand Theodora's state of mind, as she waits to hear from *Home Circle* magazine:

Connect Have you ever felt excited and nervous as you anticipated important news? How does that experience help you understand Theodora's reaction waiting for news from *Home Circle*? Explain. *Accept all reasonable responses.*

Analyze What effect is Theodora's nervous anticipation having on her family? *Possible answer: Theodora forgets to help her mother with the children and to do the mending.*

Synthesize Why is it so important for Theodora to sell her book? What will happen to her if she does not? *Possible answer: Theodora probably feels unhappy about her limited choices in life and the family responsibilities that she is expected to shoulder. If she does not sell her book, she will face "an obscure existence of mending and combing" (line 121).*

LITERARY ANALYSIS

F TONE

Possible answer: Miss Brill is the neighborhood busybody, a gossipy vulture whose visits make others feel terrible. Wharton's tone is satiric and ironic, as she notes that "It was very kind of her to come, for she was the busiest woman in Norton" (lines 134–135) and comments sarcastically that the town has the "benefit" of Miss Brill's "supervision" (lines 136–137).

If students need help . . . Work with them to complete a Character Traits and Textual Evidence chart like this one. Model how to use this evidence both to determine what kind of woman Miss Brill is and to identify the details Wharton uses to establish tone.

Quote (pg. 796):	Explanation:
"It was very kind of her to come, for she was the busiest woman in Norton."	Miss Brill is busy bothering people. Wharton's tone is sarcastic.

 BEST PRACTICES TOOLKIT—Transparency Character Traits and Textual Evidence p. D6

I had to hustle them off before they'd finished breakfast, and Johnny's hands were so dirty that I sent him back to his room to make himself decent. It's a pretty thing for the doctor's children to be the dirtiest little savages in Norton!"

110   Theodora had hastily prepared her mother's tray, leaving her own breakfast untouched. As she entered the room upstairs, Mrs. Dace's patient face turned to her with a smile much harder to bear than her father's reproaches.

"Mother, I'm *so* sorry—"

"No matter, dear. I suppose Johnny's buttons kept you. I can't think what that boy does to his clothes!"

Theodora sat the tray down without speaking. It was impossible to own to having forgotten Johnny's buttons without revealing the cause of her forgetfulness. For a few weeks longer she must bear to be misunderstood; then—ah, then if her novel were accepted, how gladly would she forget and forgive! But what if it were refused? She turned aside to hide the dismay that flushed her face. Well, then
120   she would admit the truth—she would ask her parents' pardon, and settle down without a murmur to an obscure existence of mending and combing.

She had said to herself that after the manuscript had been sent, she would have time to look after the children and catch up with the mending; but she had reckoned without the postman. He came three times a day; for an hour before each ring she was too excited to do anything but wonder if he would bring an answer this time, and for an hour afterward she moved about in a leaden stupor of disappointment. The children had never been so trying. They seemed to be always coming to pieces, like cheap furniture; one would have supposed they had been put together with bad glue. Mrs. Dace worried herself ill over Johnny's tatters,
130   Bertha's bad marks at school, and Kate's open abstention from cod-liver oil; and Doctor Dace, coming back late from a long round of visits to a fireless office with a smoky lamp, called out furiously to know if Theodora would kindly come down and remove the "East, West, home's best" that hung above the empty grate.

In the midst of it all, Miss Sophy Brill called. It was very kind of her to come, for she was the busiest woman in Norton. She made it her duty to look after other people's affairs, and there was not a house in town but had the benefit of her personal supervision. She generally came when things were going wrong, and the sight of her bonnet on the doorstep was a surer sign of calamity than a crepe bow on the bell.[6] After she left, Mrs. Dace looked very sad, and the doctor punished
140   Johnny for warbling down the entry:

> "Miss Sophy Brill
> Is a bitter pill!"

while Theodora, locking herself in her room, resolved with tears that she would never write another novel. **G**

The week was a long nightmare. Theodora could neither eat nor sleep. She was up early enough, but instead of looking after the children and seeing that breakfast

---

F TONE
What kind of person is Miss Brill? Describe Wharton's tone as she introduces this character, and point out the phrases and details that help establish this tone.

---

6. **crepe bow on the bell:** a signal that someone had died. Clothing made from black crepe (a silk material used to be worn by those in mourning).

DIFFERENTIATED INSTRUCTION

FOR STRATEGIC READERS

Concept Support Review with students that tone reflects the author's attitude toward the characters. One effective way to recognize tone is to read a work aloud in character. Often readers will naturally choose the correct tone of voice for the context. Work with students to read lines 134–150 aloud. As students find the correct tone, pause and ask them to describe the tone. Is it sarcastic, annoyed, amused, and so on?

FOR ADVANCED LEARNERS/AP

Compare and Contrast [small-group option] Have small groups analyze Theodora's role as the oldest daughter in her family. What do her parents expect of her? What is her daily routine like? What are her prospects for the future? Have groups compare and contrast Theodora's role with that of the eldest daughter in today's families. Then, ask students if they think the role of the eldest child has improved or not.

was ready, she wandered down the road to meet the postman, and came back wan and empty-handed, oblivious of her morning duties. She had no idea how long the suspense would last; but she didn't see how authors could live if they were kept
150 waiting more than a week.

Then suddenly, one afternoon—she never quite knew how or when it happened—she found herself with a *Home Circle* envelope in her hands, and her dazzled eyes flashing over a wild dance of words that wouldn't settle down and make sense.

"Dear Madam:" (They called her *Madam!* And then; yes, the words were beginning to fall into line now.) "Your novel, 'April Showers,' has been received, and we are glad to accept it on the usual terms. A serial on which we were counting for immediate publication has been delayed by the author's illness, and the first chapters of 'April Showers' will therefore appear in our midsummer number. Thanking you
160 for favoring us with your manuscript, we remain," and so forth.

❸ Targeted Passage

Theodora found herself in the wood beyond the schoolhouse. She was kneeling on the ground, brushing aside the dead leaves and pressing her lips to the little bursting green things that pushed up eager tips through last year's decay. It was spring—spring! Everything was crowding toward the light and in her own heart hundreds of germinating hopes had burst into sudden leaf. She wondered if the thrust of those little green fingers hurt the surface of the earth as her springing raptures hurt—yes, actually hurt!—her hot, constricted breast! She looked up through interlacing boughs at a tender, opaque blue sky full of the coming of a milky moon. She seemed enveloped in an atmosphere of loving comprehension.
170 The brown earth throbbed with her joy, the treetops trembled with it, and a sudden star broke through the branches like an audible "I know!"

Theodora, on the whole, behaved very well. Her mother cried, her father whistled and said he supposed he must put up with grounds in his coffee now, and be thankful if he ever got a hot meal again; while the children took the most deafening and **harassing** advantage of what seemed a sudden suspension of the laws of nature.

Within a week everybody in Norton knew that Theodora had written a novel, and that it was coming out in the *Home Circle*. On Sundays, when she walked up the aisle, her friends dropped their prayer books and the soprano sang false in
180 her excitement. Girls with more pin money than Theodora had ever dreamed of copied her hats and imitated her way of speaking. The local paper asked her for a poem; her old school teachers stopped to shake hands and grew shy over their congratulations; and Miss Sophy Brill came to call. She had put on her Sunday bonnet and her manner was almost abject. She ventured, very timidly, to ask her young friend how she wrote, whether it "just came to her," and if she had found that the kind of pen she used made any difference; and wound up by begging Theodora to write a sentiment in her album.

harassing (hə-răs′ĭng)
adj. persistently annoying
harass *v.*

Lines 155–171
REINFORCE *KEY IDEA*: AMBITION

Discuss How does Theodora react to the apparent realization of her **ambitions**? *Possible answer: Theodora is filled with joy and gratitude. Sitting outdoors, she feels a connection with the earth's blooming at the start of spring. It is as if the springtime is a reflection of her own hopes coming to life.*

FOR STRATEGIC READERS

❸ Targeted Passage [Lines 151–171]

This passage represents the climax to Theodora's conflict over whether or not her novel will be accepted.

- What envelope does Theodora hold?
- What news does her letter bring?
- How does she feel about the news?

FOR ENGLISH LEARNERS

Related Vocabulary [mixed-readiness groups] Help students list words from lines 161–171 that relate to nature in spring. Give an example, and then have groups identify additional examples:

- *ground, dead leaves* (line 162)
- *bursting green things, eager tips, last year's decay* (line 163)
- *little green fingers, surface of the earth* (line 166)
- *interlacing boughs, opaque blue sky* (line 168)
- *milky moon* (169)

Have groups work together to show meaning for the phrases, either by discussing them or by drawing them.

Activity Ask students to compare and contrast "In the Station Waiting Room, Boston" with "Girl Reading" on page 793, also painted by Edmund Charles Tarbell. Have them compare the use of light and shadow to convey mood and contrast the portrayal of women in each painting. *Possible answer: Both paintings create a pensive and serious mood and direct viewers' focus through the use of shadow and light. Both portray women at the turn of the 20th century. However, "In the Station Waiting Room, Boston," which is a later work, shows women out in the world, while "Girl Reading" shows a woman at home involved in domestic activity. The difference perhaps reflects the changing role of women, whose influence and spheres of activity were expanding. In addition, both works were painted in oil.*

Even Uncle James came down from Boston to talk the wonder over. He called Theodora a "sly baggage," and proposed that she should give him her earnings to 190 invest in a new patent grease-trap company. From what Kathleen Kyd had told him, he thought Theodora would probably get a thousand dollars for her story. He concluded by suggesting that she should base her next romance on the subject of sanitation, making the heroine nearly die of sewer gas poisoning because her parents won't listen to the handsome young doctor next door, when he warns them that their plumbing is out of order. That was a subject that would interest everybody, and do a lot more good than the sentimental trash most women wrote.

At last the great day came. Theodora had left an order with the bookseller for the midsummer number of the *Home Circle* and before the shop was open she was waiting on the sidewalk. She clutched the precious paper and ran home without 200 opening it. Her excitement was almost more than she could bear. Not heeding her father's call to breakfast, she rushed upstairs and locked herself in her room. Her hands trembled so that she could hardly turn the pages. At last—yes, there it was: "April Showers."

The paper dropped from her hands. What name had she read beneath the title? Had her emotion blinded her?

"April Showers, by *Kathleen Kyd*."

Kathleen Kyd! Oh, cruel misprint! Oh, **dastardly** typographer! Through tears of rage and disappointment Theodora looked again; yes, there was no mistaking the hateful name. Her glance ran on. She found herself reading a first paragraph

④ Targeted Passage

dastardly (dăs′tərd-lē) *adj.* characterized by underhandedness or treachery

In the Station Waiting Room, Boston (1915), Edmund Charles Tarbell. Oil on canvas, 24 ³/₈″ × 32″. Gift of Dr. Joseph R. Fazzano. © Crocker Art Museum, Sacramento, California.

DIFFERENTIATED INSTRUCTION

FOR STRATEGIC READERS

④ Targeted Passage [Lines 197–211]

This passage describes a surprising turn of events for Theodora's literary hopes.

- What does Theodora pick up at the bookseller's shop?
- What does she discover when she opens the magazine to "April Showers"?
- What does she realize when she reads the first paragraph?

FOR ENGLISH LEARNERS

Related Vocabulary [mixed-readiness groups] The mistake that *Home Circle* makes and Theodora's reaction to it convey important plot information. Make sure students understand that Theodora is disappointed and the magazine is regretful and embarrassed. Then teach these related words on pages 798–799:

- *cruel; dastardly* (line 207)
- *rage and disappointment* (line 208)
- *hateful* (line 209)
- *strange; horrible* (line 210)
- *bland apology; unfortunate accident* (line 235)
- *by mistake* (line 237)
- *should . . . have been; regrettable oversight* (line 238)
- *accidents . . . happen* (lines 238–239)
- *sure she understood* (line 239)

210 that she had never seen before. She read farther. All was strange. The horrible truth burst upon her: *It was not her story!*

④ **Targeted Passage**
continued

She never knew how she got back to the station. She struggled through the crowd on the platform, and a gold-banded arm pushed her into the train just starting for Norton. It would be dark when she reached home; but that didn't matter—nothing mattered now. She sank into her seat, closing her eyes in the vain attempt to shut out the vision of the last few hours; but minute by minute memory forced her to relive it; she felt like a rebellious school child dragged forth to repeat the same detested "piece."

Although she did not know Boston well, she had made her way easily enough
220 to the *Home Circle* building; at least, she supposed she had, since she remembered nothing till she found herself ascending the editorial stairs as easily as one does incredible things in dreams. She must have walked very fast, for her heart was beating furiously, and she had barely breath to whisper the editor's name to a young man who looked out at her from a glass case, like a zoological specimen. The young man led her past other glass cases containing similar specimens to an inner enclosure which seemed filled by an enormous presence. Theodora felt herself enveloped in the presence, submerged by it, gasping for air as she sank under its rising surges.

Gradually fragments of speech floated to the surface. "'April Showers?' Mrs.
230 Kyd's new serial? *Your* manuscript, you say? You have a letter from me? The name, please? Evidently some unfortunate misunderstanding. One moment." And then a bell ringing, a zoological specimen ordered to unlock a safe, her name asked for again, the manuscript, her own precious manuscript, tied with Aunt Julia's ribbon, laid on the table before her, and her outcries, her protests, her **interrogations**, drowned in a flood of bland apology: "An unfortunate accident—Mrs. Kyd's manuscript received the same day—extraordinary coincidence in the choice of a title—duplicate answers sent by mistake—Miss Dace's novel hardly suited to their purpose—should of course have been returned—regrettable oversight—accidents would happen—sure she understood."

240 The voice went on, like the steady pressure of a surgeon's hand on a shrieking nerve. When it stopped she was in the street. A cab nearly ran her down, and a car bell jangled furiously in her ears. She clutched her manuscript, carrying it tenderly through the crowd, like a live thing that had been hurt. She could not bear to look at its soiled edges and the ink stain on Aunt Julia's ribbon. **ⓖ**

The train stopped with a jerk and she opened her eyes. It was dark, and by the windy flare of gas on the platform she saw the Norton passengers getting out. She stood up stiffly and followed them. A warm wind blew into her face the fragrance of the summer woods, and she remembered how, two months earlier, she had knelt among the dead leaves, pressing her lips to the first shoots of green. Then
250 for the first time she thought of home. She had fled away in the morning without a word, and her heart sank at the thought of her mother's fears. And her father—how angry he would be! She bent her head under the coming storm of his derision.

interrogation
(ĭn-tĕr′ə-gā′shən) *n.* a questioning

ⓖ TONE
Compare Wharton's tone in earlier descriptions of Theodora with the tone she adopts in lines 240–244. How has Wharton's tone changed?

Lines 212–244
TIERED DISCUSSION PROMPTS
Use these prompts to help students understand Theodora's presence of mind as she deals with her great disappointment:

Connect How do many people react to terrible disappointment? *Responses should reflect an understanding that many people feel depressed and sad, and possibly angry.*

Analyze How would you characterize the way Theodora faces her disappointing situation? *Possible answer: She faces the situation bravely, taking a train into Boston and demanding to know what has happened.*

Evaluate Is Theodora's response admirable? Explain. *Possible answer: Theodora's response is admirable and hints at more depth of character than previously seen. She shows determination and strength. Though she cannot control what happened, she does not sit by passively without questioning the error.*

LITERARY ANALYSIS

ⓖ TONE

Possible answer: Wharton's tone is sympathetic. She has dropped the gently mocking tone she assumed in earlier passages in favor of compassion for her heroine's anguish.

If students need help . . . Reread lines 11–17 and 240–244. Then help students use a Two-Column Chart to compare the tone in each excerpt. Help students see that the first mocks Theodora with phrases such as *nobler use* (line 14) while the second sympathizes with her situation (*like a live . . . hurt* [line 243]).

Lines 11–17	Lines 240–244
"lingeringly, tenderly"	"surgeon's hand on a shrieking nerve"
"meant to wear the ribbon . . . nobler use"	"like a live thing that had been hurt"

 BEST PRACTICES TOOLKIT—Transparency
Two-Column Chart p. A25

FOR ADVANCED LEARNERS/AP
Analyze Realism Remind students that realism emphasizes everyday experience, depicting ordinary lives without romance or sentimentality. Encourage students to analyze Wharton's use of realism in this story. They might consider these questions:

• How would the story be different if Theodora's novel had been accepted by *Home Circle*?

• Is the turn of events a complete surprise?

• Is Wharton's realistic depiction of Theodora's rejection a commentary upon sentimental, romantic novelists in the mold of Kathleen Kyd?

• How does Wharton use realistic elements to ironic and satiric purposes?

Have students write brief essays responding to one or more of the questions; then launch a class discussion with their essays.

Lines 283–284
REINFORCE *KEY IDEA:* AMBITION

Discuss How were Dr. Dace's **ambitions** like Theodora's? *Possible answer: Both wanted to be novelists and to be viewed as special.*

LITERARY ANALYSIS

ⓗ TONE

Possible answer: Answers will vary, but most students will probably say that the change in Wharton's tone has made them more sympathetic to the characters. Theodora's concern for her mother, despite her disappointment (line 268) and her raw emotions (lines 266–267, 271, 274, 278, 285–287) elicit the reader's sympathy. So, too, Dr. Dace's kindness and empathy (lines 257–259, 277, 283–284) show that he is decent and caring, even if he can be, on occasion, sarcastic or overly demanding.

SELECTION WRAP–UP

REFLECT Ask students to consider Theodora's feelings about her writing. What does writing mean to her, and why?

★ CRITIQUE

- Ask students whether they think the main characters are flat (single trait) or round (many traits).

- After completing the After Reading questions on page 801, have students revisit their responses and tell whether they have changed their opinions.

800 UNIT 4: REGIONALISM AND NATURALISM

The night was cloudy, and as she stepped into the darkness beyond the station a hand was slipped in hers. She stood still, too weary to feel frightened, and a voice said, quietly:

"Don't walk so fast, child. You look tired."

"Father!" Her hand dropped from his, but he recaptured it and drew it through his arm. When she found voice, it was to whisper, "You were at the station?"

"It's such a good night I thought I'd stroll down and meet you."

260   Her arm trembled against his. She could not see his face in the dimness, but the light of his cigar looked down on her like a friendly eye, and she took courage to falter out: "Then you knew—"

"That you'd gone to Boston? Well, I rather thought you had."

They walked on slowly, and presently he added, "You see, you left the *Home Circle* lying in your room."

How she blessed the darkness and the muffled sky! She could not have borne the scrutiny of the tiniest star.

"Then mother wasn't very much frightened?"

"Why, no, she didn't appear to be. She's been busy all day over some toggery

270 of Bertha's."

Theodora choked. "Father, I'll—" She groped for words, but they eluded her. "I'll do things—differently; I haven't meant—" Suddenly she heard herself bursting out: "It was all a mistake, you know—about my story. They didn't want it; they won't have it!" and she shrank back involuntarily from his **impending** mirth.

She felt the pressure of his arm, but he didn't speak, and she figured his mute hilarity. They moved on in silence. Presently he said:

"It hurts a bit just at first, doesn't it?"

"O father!"

He stood still, and the gleam of his cigar showed a face of unexpected

280 participation.

"You see I've been through it myself."

"You, father? You?"

"Why, yes. Didn't I ever tell you? I wrote a novel once. I was just out of college, and didn't want to be a doctor. No; I wanted to be a genius, so I wrote a novel."

The doctor paused, and Theodora clung to him in a mute passion of **commiseration.** It was as if a drowning creature caught a live hand through the murderous fury of the waves.

"Father—O father!"

"It took me a year—a whole year's hard work; and when I'd finished it the

290 public wouldn't have it, either; not at any price and that's why I came down to meet you, because I remembered my walk home." ⟋ ⓗ

impending (ĭm-pĕn′dĭng) *adj.* to be about to occur
impend *v.*

---

⑤ Targeted Passage

commiseration (kə-mĭz′ə-rā′shən) *n.* a feeling of sympathy or pity

ⓗ TONE
Has the change in Wharton's tone affected how you feel about her characters? Explain whether you view Theodora or her father differently, and cite the lines that changed your opinion.

800 UNIT 4: REGIONALISM AND NATURALISM

DIFFERENTIATED INSTRUCTION

FOR STRATEGIC READERS

⑤ Targeted Passage [Lines 271–291]

This passage resolves the plot: Dr. Dace helps Theodora cope with disappointment.

- How does Theodora expect her father to react to her news? How does he react?

- What surprising information does Theodora learn about her father?

- How does Theodora feel about her father by the end of the story?

FOR ADVANCED LEARNERS/AP

Analyze Point of View Have students explore the story's limited third-person point of view, considering these questions: How does this point of view help Wharton convey Theodora's inner life? How would the story be different if Theodora had told it herself? What would have been lost or gained?

Challenge students to compare the choice of narrator to Wharton's own life experience of struggle to move beyond expected roles.

Comprehension

1. **Summarize** Describe Theodora's family situation and responsibilities.

2. **Recall** What does Theodora plan to do with the money she expects to earn?

3. **Clarify** How does the *Home Circle* editor explain the mix-up?

4. **Clarify** What does Theodora's father reveal to her at the end of the story?

Literary Analysis

5. **Draw Conclusions** Does this story have a happy ending? What kind of life does Theodora have to look forward to now that her **ambition** has been thwarted? Cite evidence from the story to support your conclusion.

6. **Analyze Tone** Reread lines 52–75. How does Wharton's tone in these lines let readers know that Theodora might not be the "great author" she thinks herself to be? Describe Wharton's tone, pointing out the words and details she employs to achieve it.

7. **Make Inferences About Characters** Review the inferences you recorded as you read, and recall Theodora's disappointment that her father does not act the way she thinks the parent in a novel would. How might their relationship change as a result of the disastrous "April Showers" incident?

8. **Interpret Satire** A satire ridicules ideas and behavior to expose human faults or weakness. Satire is sometimes hard to detect, but a writer's tone is often an indication—reading a satire can feel as though the author were winking at you while telling the story. Explain what characters and behavior Wharton satirizes in this story by filling out a chart like the one shown.

Character	Satirized for ...	Evidence in Story
Uncle James	being crude and materialistic	• talks obsessively about indoor plumbing and "sewer gas" at the dinner table (lines 24–51) • brags about his money and even asks Theodora to invest the money from her novel in one of his schemes (lines 26–29, 188–196)

Literary Criticism

9. **Historical Context** A contemporary critic commented, "When we look beneath the high surface gloss of Wharton's world, we see a marketplace, pure and simple. Hers is an almost purely economic conception of life." What insights does this story give you into the economic position of women at the turn of the 20th century? What kinds of work were available to them, and at what kinds of wages? Is it surprising that an educated young woman would try to make money by writing? Support your answer with evidence.

APRIL SHOWERS **801**

8. *Character:* Miss Brill, *Satirized for:* being a busybody, *Evidence:* lines 134– 137, 184–187; *Character:* Theodora, *Satirized for:* literary pretensions, *Evidence:* lines 11–18, 52–75,161–171; *Character:* Uncle James, *Satirized for:* small-mindedness and materialism, *Evidence:* lines 22–51, 188–196

9. Women in the story are stuck in lowly unpaid domestic work, like Theodora. They are ill, like Mrs. Dace and Kathleen Kyd's sister. They have low-paying, dull jobs, such as saleswomen, as Kyd was before selling her book, or hat trimmers (line 16). It makes sense that Theodora would want to be a writer, as this is the only attractive occupation for women in the story.

Practice and Apply

After Reading

Use these copy masters to check understanding and provide extra support:

RESOURCE MANAGER—Copy Masters
Reading Check p. 276
Tone p. 269
Question Support p. 277
Additional selection questions are provided for teachers on page 263.

ANSWERS

1. *Theodora's mother is ill and confined to bed, leaving Theodora the household chores and care of her three siblings.*

2. *Theodora plans to spend the money on her family.*

3. *Another author sent the magazine a manuscript with the same title. In error, the magazine sent two acceptance letters, though it only wished to use Kyd's piece.*

4. *Dr. Dace reveals that he once wrote a novel and received a painful rejection.*

Possible answers:

5. *Students may say that the ending is happy, given Theodora's brave confrontation with the magazine editors (219–239) and the sweet reconciliation between her and Dr. Dace (lines 256–291). Others may say it is bleak, remembering Theodora's resolve to accept "an obscure existence of mending and combing" (line 121) if the novel were not accepted.*

6. ● **SKILLS FOCUS Tone** *Wharton's mocking tone suggests that Theodora has delusions of grandeur. Young Theodora is certain she has written a "remarkable book" (line 56), comparing herself favorably to George Eliot (lines 62–63) and insisting that she will never "dumb down" her work (lines 70–72).*

7. ■ **SKILLS FOCUS Make Inferences About Characters** *Students may say that Theodora and her father will achieve new closeness and respect. Others may say that demands on Theodora will still fray their relationship. Students should cite text evidence and life experience to support their views.*

ANSWERS

Vocabulary in Context

VOCABULARY PRACTICE

1. *betraying a friend*   5. *take it seriously*
2. *about to happen*   6. *get information*
3. *late*   7. *sending flowers*
4. *to irritate*   8. *my grandmother*

R RESOURCE MANAGER—Copy Master
   Vocabulary Practice p. 274

VOCABULARY IN WRITING

Have students begin by freewriting about
Theodora's state of mind. When they edit and
revise, students can insert appropriate vocabulary words.

VOCABULARY STRATEGY: THE LATIN ROOT

rog *(also an EL language objective)*

Point out to students that knowing prefixes
such as *ab-*, *pre-*, and *inter-* can help them use
a word's root to build meaning. Roots often
do not provide an exact meaning, so students
must also use context clues.

Answers:

1. *prerogative*   4. *derogatory*
2. *surrogate*   5. *abrogate*
3. *arrogate*

R RESOURCE MANAGER—Copy Master
   Vocabulary Strategy p. 275

ℹ Vocabulary Center at **ClassZone.com**
   Additional Vocabulary Activities

Assess and Reteach

Assess

R RESOURCE MANAGER—Copy Masters
   Selection Test A pp. 279–280
   Selection Test B/C pp. 281–282

◎ Test Generator CD

Reteach

S STANDARDS LESSON FILE
   Literature Lesson 43: Tone
   Reading Lesson 8: Making Inferences
   Vocabulary Lessons 7–8: Latin Roots

Vocabulary in Context

VOCABULARY PRACTICE

Show you understand the vocabulary words by answering these questions.

WORD LIST
admonitory
commiseration
dastardly
harassing
impending
interrogation
predecessor
retrospective

1. Which is a **dastardly** deed, betraying a friend or voting in an election?
2. If an investigation is **impending**, is it over or about to happen?
3. Would an artist have a **retrospective** exhibit early or late in his or her career?
4. What is the intent of a **harassing** letter, to schedule an appointment or to irritate the recipient into action?
5. If I make an **admonitory** statement, do I expect you to laugh or take it seriously?
6. Is an **interrogation** intended to get information or rehearse a performance?
7. Which would be a gesture of **commiseration,** sending flowers or watching a lengthy movie?
8. Who would be your mother's **predecessor** in life, you or your grandmother?

VOCABULARY IN WRITING

What was Theodora's state of mind after she submitted her manuscript? Write
a short explanation of how she felt , including at least two vocabulary words.

> **EXAMPLE SENTENCE**
> Waiting for ***impending*** news of the fate of her manuscript almost drove
> Theodora crazy.

R1.2

VOCABULARY STRATEGY: THE LATIN ROOT *rog*

The vocabulary word *interrogation* contains the Latin root *rog*,
which means "ask," "ask for," or "propose." This root is found
in several English words. To understand words built around
rog, use your knowledge of the meaning of the root as well as
context clues.

interrogate   *abrogate*
arrogate   **rog**   *prerogative*
surrogate   *derogatory*

PRACTICE Apply what you know about the Latin root *rog* and
the other word parts to help you understand the words in the
web. Then choose the word that best completes each sentence.
If necessary, consult a dictionary.

1. It is the race winner's _____ to wear the yellow jersey.
2. The official could not attend the ceremony, so he sent a(n) _____.
3. They feared that the new judge would _____ to herself powers that belonged to the legislature.
4. Jake tends to make _____ remarks about people he does not like.
5. People _____ their responsibility when they do not care for their pets.

➚ VOCABULARY PRACTICE
For more practice, go
to the **Vocabulary Center**
at **ClassZone.com.**

DIFFERENTIATED INSTRUCTION

FOR ENGLISH LEARNERS

Task Support: Vocabulary Practice To help
students remember the words on the Word
List, define these prefixes:

- *ad-*, "to, toward"
- *com-*, "together, with"
- *im-*, "against"
- *inter-*, "between"
- *pre-*, "before"
- *retro-*, "back"

FOR ADVANCED LEARNERS/AP

The Latin Root *rog* Ask partners to do a word
search for synonyms of each word containing
the root *rog*. Have them create a graphic organizer for each *rog* word and its synonyms,
illustrating differences in meaning. Students
might focus on differences of degree, connotation, or another criterion of their choosing.

Women's Changing Roles

A woman's role in American society was rigidly defined in the late 19th and early 20th centuries. Women of this period could not vote, few owned businesses, and few gained a higher education. Yet women were increasingly agitating for change in both big and small ways. The writers in this section (pages 758–802) gave voice to the struggles of women attempting to fashion a new role for themselves and break free from restricting social expectations. As critic Richard Gray noted, "Humanity, if it is repressed, will always have its revenge."

Writing to Compare

Think about how women's roles have changed since the times of Kate Chopin and Edith Wharton. Using the stories you have just read and your knowledge of American society today, write a comparison of women's roles then and now.

Consider

- what each selection tells you about society's expectations for women at that time
- how things have or have not changed since the days these writers were working
- what details from the selections best illustrate women's roles in the past
- what examples from today best illustrate women's roles now

Extension

SPEAKING & LISTENING
With a partner, **role-play** a conversation between two of the main characters from this section of the book. Discuss your family life, your work, your frustrations, and so on. Alternatively, role-play two of the main characters' husbands or fathers discussing the women in their lives.

CALIFORNIA   R3.8, W2.2

803

Focus and Motivate

OBJECTIVES

- analyze a student model that shows the traits of literary analysis
- use the writing process to produce a literary analysis
- revise and edit, using criteria for literary analysis
- create and present a power presentation

 W2.2, W1.9, LC1.1, LS2.4

WRITER'S ROAD MAP

WRITING PROMPTS 1 AND 2

To help students choose a prompt, emphasize that they may write about any story that they find compelling. It could be a non-fiction story if the student finds meaning in it, or even a real-life experience recounted by a friend. Stress, however, that students should analyze the story in terms of literary elements.

ADDITIONAL PROMPTS

Use these prompts for practice with writing for the real world and writing about art:

WRITING PROMPT 3

Writing from the News Choose a hard news or feature story from a newspaper. Analyze it as a work of literature, exploring its characters, events, setting, and themes.

WRITING PROMPT 4

Writing Inspired by Art Many works of art relate to or hint at a story. They may portray events from myth, religion, or history, or suggest an original narrative in the image itself. Find a work of art in an art book, museum, or art gallery that portrays a story. Briefly describe the art and the story it shows. Then, analyze the meaning you find in the art.

For additional writing prompts, see

- WriteSmart CD
- Writing Center at **ClassZone.com**

KEY TRAITS

Review the six **KEY TRAITS** with students, focusing on ideas, organization, and voice. Compare the list of traits with the criteria on page 810.

Writing Workshop

EXPOSITION

Literary Analysis

As you have seen in this unit, literature often reflects what is happening in the world and in the author's imagination. Analyzing how authors use literary elements will give you a better understanding and appreciation of what you read. The **Writer's Road Map** will guide you as you write a literary analysis.

WRITER'S ROAD MAP

Literary Analysis

WRITING PROMPT 1

Writing from Literature Analyzing a literary work can help you understand it more deeply. Write an essay in which you focus on one or more literary elements, such as setting, characters, or plot details, in a work of fiction. Explain how the element or elements contribute to the meaning.

Literature to Consider
- theme in "The Open Boat"
- setting in "The Law of Life"
- humor in "The Outcasts of Poker Flat"

WRITING PROMPT 2

Writing from the Real World Choose a story you have viewed or read that you just can't stop thinking about. Write an essay that briefly summarizes the story and examines its meaning. Focus on specific elements that make the story meaningful and memorable.

Sources of Stories
- television shows that use suspense or conflict
- movies that have strong characters
- magazines that publish fictional or real-life adventure stories

 WRITING TOOLS For prewriting, revision, and editing tools, visit the **Writing Center** at **ClassZone.com**.

KEY TRAITS

1. **IDEAS**
   - Presents a **thesis statement** that clearly identifies the key points of the discussion
   - Uses **evidence** from the text to support each key point

2. **ORGANIZATION**
   - Attention-getting **introduction** identifies the title and author of the work
   - Consistent **organizational pattern** includes **transitions** to connect ideas
   - **Conclusion** summarizes ideas and discusses the overall meaning of the work

3. **VOICE**
   - **Tone** is appropriate for the audience and purpose

4. **WORD CHOICE**
   - Uses **precise language** to examine and explain the work

5. **SENTENCE FLUENCY**
   - Varies **sentence structures and lengths**

6. **CONVENTIONS**
   - Employs **correct grammar and usage**

Writing Workshop Resources

 RESOURCE MANAGER UNIT 4

Plan and Teach pp. 283–286
Prewriting–Editing pp. 287–291
Writing Rubric p. 292
Publishing with Technology p. 293
Writing Support p. 294*

 STANDARDS LESSON FILE

Writing Lessons 8, 14, 16, 28, 35
Grammar Lesson 20
Media Lesson 22

 BEST PRACTICES TOOLKIT

Scaffolding Writing Instruction pp. 43–46*
Analyzing Setting • Character Traits and Textual Evidence • Freewriting • Microtheme • Writing Template: Literary Analysis • Color Coding • Peer Response Guide

TECHNOLOGY
- Easy Planner DVD
- Writing Center at **ClassZone.com**
- WriteSmart CD

* Resources for Differentiation

Part 1: Analyze a Student Model

W2.2, W1.9 (p. 809), LC1.1 (p. 810), LS2.4 (p. 811)

Amanda Olivares
Jackson Regional High School

"The Story of an Hour": Shock and Self-Discovery

How would you react if a friend came to you with a shocking piece of news? The first sentence of "The Story of an Hour" reveals that the main character's husband has died. As this short story develops, we find out her complicated and conflicting reactions to this tragedy. Throughout the story,
5 author Kate Chopin uses symbolism and irony to tell the tale of a woman's short-lived self-discovery.

Chopin wastes no words. The first several paragraphs give almost no details about the main character. Although we know that she is "afflicted" with a mysterious "heart trouble," we aren't told what her personality is
10 like, where she lives, or what she looks like. We don't even know her first name; she is simply "Mrs. Mallard." This lack of detail symbolizes how little the main character knows about her feelings and her identity. It also shows how women of that time period (the late 19th century) were portrayed—as selfless, dependent wives and mothers, devoted to their
15 families. Based on the story's beginning, we assume that Mrs. Mallard is a stereotypical woman of the era. However, as we read further, our impression of her begins to change.

It is only when the main character is alone that Chopin begins to reveal rich and symbolic details. "Pressed down by a physical exhaustion," Mrs.
20 Mallard sinks into an armchair and looks out an open window. Chopin writes, "She could see in the open square before her house the tops of trees that were all aquiver with the new spring life. The delicious breath of rain was in the air. . . . The notes of a distant song which someone was singing reached her faintly. . . ." By describing this "new spring life" in exquisite
25 detail, Chopin changes the pace of the story and symbolizes the new beginning that is now available to the main character.

KEY TRAITS IN ACTION

Intriguing **introduction** identifies the literary work.

Presents the key points of the analysis in a clear **thesis statement.**

Varied **sentence structures and lengths** maintain the reader's interest.

Uses **evidence** (details and quotations from the story) to illustrate and support statements. The writer of this analysis carefully assesses how subtle details affect the story's meaning.

Teach

CALIFORNIA

Part 1: Analyze a Student Model

Have students read the student model and **KEY TRAITS IN ACTION.** Then discuss the model with the class, noting specific examples of each trait and building on what students have already noted. You may also wish to incorporate these activities:

- **Thesis Statement** Remind students that the thesis statement consists of one or two sentences that convey the main point of the literary analysis. The thesis statement is usually found in the introduction, often in the first or last sentence of the first paragraph. Have students look at the highlighted thesis statement in the model. Point out that it refers to two literary elements (*symbolism* and *irony*) and to the meaning the writer finds in the story (*a woman's short-lived self-discovery*). Urge students to refer to both these aspects in their thesis statements.

- **Evidence** Ask students to explain what evidence is in a literary analysis. ***Possible answer:*** *Evidence consists of details in the text that support the thesis of the analysis.* Have students reread the third paragraph of the student model and state the evidence referred to. ***Possible answers:*** *The evidence consists of the description of Mrs. Mallard's exhaustion and her perception of the "'new spring life'" around her (lines 19–22).* Then have students state what the evidence shows. ***Possible answer:*** *It shows that Mrs. Mallard is ready for a new beginning in her life.*

DIFFERENTIATED INSTRUCTION

For general guidelines on differentiating writing instruction, see

 BEST PRACTICES TOOLKIT
  Scaffolding Writing Instruction
    pp. 43–46

FOR ENGLISH LEARNERS
Language: Skill Words Write these terms on the board and review them with students:

- *thesis:* main idea—for example, an idea about the meaning of "The Story of an Hour"

- *sentence structure:* the form of a sentence—for example, a simple sentence or a complex sentence

- *evidence:* facts that support an idea—for example, evidence that Mrs. Mallard is tired

- *organizational pattern:* the connections between parts of an essay—for example, organization by the order of events in the story

- *tone:* expression of writer's attitude toward the subject, the reader, or both—for example, conversational, humorous, sarcastic, formal

- **Organizational Pattern** Have students reread lines 27–36 and find the sentences that follow the order of events in "The Story of an Hour." Then have them read on to lines 37–44 in order to discover that the chronological sequence is continued. Have students list the events in lines 27–44 in sequence. Point out that the student writer, Amanda Olivares, has summarized the plot of "The Story of an Hour." Tell students to include a plot summary in their literary analyses.

- **Precise Language** Have students reread the concluding paragraph of the model and cite words and phrases that are especially precise. **Possible answers:** *Precise language includes "woman's discovery," "loss," "identity," "surprising twists and turns," "shocks," "the hours of our own lives."* Then have student groups each examine one other paragraph of the essay and identify precise language there. Clarify that "precise language" in literary analysis means more than just specific sensory detail. Precise language refers to nouns, verbs, and modifiers that state specifically what the author means.

For interactive student models, see

 WriteSmart CD

Writing Center at **ClassZone.com**

As we learn more about Mrs. Mallard's thoughts and hopes, the story takes an ironic turn. At first the new widow is stunned and exhausted, with an increasing feeling of dread. Because her husband has just died and she
30 has "heart trouble," we can assume that she will be utterly miserable. She might even die of grief. Instead, however, she repeats a single word under her breath: "free, free, free!" Her husband was always kind and loving to her, but his death means that "there would be no one to live for her during those coming years; she would live for herself." Ironically, the event that
35 readers think will ruin her life actually brings her "a monstrous joy." Brently Mallard's death has given his wife a chance at freedom and independence.

Transformed by "self-assertion which she suddenly recognized as the strongest impulse of her being," Mrs. Mallard comes out of her room to rejoin the world "like a goddess of Victory." As she goes back downstairs,
40 she sees her husband coming in the door, as alive as ever. The resulting shock is too much for her to bear. Everyone assumes that Mrs. Mallard dies of the "joy that kills." Ironically, she actually dies because she cannot stand the idea of losing her independence, even though she experienced it for just one hour.

45 From the title of this short story to its last words, Kate Chopin uses irony and symbolism to describe a woman's discovery—and loss—of her own identity. As we follow the surprising twists and turns of "The Story of an Hour," we can't help thinking, what shocks and self-discoveries might the hours of our own lives have in store?

Logical **organizational pattern** follows order of events in the story. **Transitions** show how ideas are related.

Tone is formal without being stuffy.

Conclusion uses **precise language** to summarize the main points of the analysis and identify its effect on readers. Repetition of words from the essay title create a feeling of closure.

2

DIFFERENTIATED INSTRUCTION

FOR ENGLISH LEARNERS

Comprehension: Transitions List transitional words that can often be found in literary analyses. Some of these words show differences between ideas—for example, *although, however, instead, even though,* and *but.* Others introduce ideas, such as *also, because, in addition* and *as,* in the sense of *as we learn* or *as the story shows.*

Have the students find transitions in the model. Then, give students sentence starters

beginning with these transitions and others from the list provided. Ask students to complete the sentences to tell about events or people they know in life.

To provide English learners with additional writing support, see

R RESOURCE MANAGER—Copy Master
Writing Support p. 294

Part 2: Apply the Writing Process

PREWRITING

What Should I Do?	What Does It Look Like?

1. Revisit the work you're analyzing.
Reading or viewing the work several times will reveal details you may have missed the first time around. Note your thoughts about the characters, events, dialogue, or style in a learning log.

Details from the Story	My Thoughts
Mrs. Mallard's "heart trouble"	could have two meanings—physical or emotional (or both)
Husband's death makes her feel free.	We expect her to be unhappy.
He's really alive.	turns everything in the story upside down

2. Freewrite to explore your ideas.
As you freewrite, don't worry about spelling, grammar, or organization. Just let the comments and ideas flow freely.

See page 810: Review Literary Terms

> Lots of surprises in this story ... Mrs. M seems to care about her husband, but when she thinks he's dead, she's sort of glad because now she can be independent. But he's NOT really dead, and she's so shocked that <u>she</u> dies when she learns this. That's called irony, I think.

3. Develop a working thesis statement.
Review your learning log and your freewriting. Decide on the main idea you want to make about the work and condense it into a sentence or two. You can refine this statement as you draft your analysis.

> Working thesis statement:
> In "The Story of an Hour," Kate Chopin tells the tale of a woman's self-discovery. The author uses symbolism and irony to help explain what happens to the woman and why.

4. Find evidence to support your key points.
Carefully read through the work again. List quotations, details, and other examples that back up the main ideas in your working thesis statement.

> **TIP** Focus on how one or two elements help get the meaning of the work across. The writer of the student model focused on symbolism and irony.

Evidence	How It Conveys Meaning
The reader doesn't know Mrs. Mallard's first name until late in the story.	symbolizes her lack of identity
"the tops of trees that were all aquiver with the new spring life"	symbolizes Mrs. Mallard's self-discovery
She dies of "joy that kills."	ironic, since she really dies from grief for herself

FOR DEVELOPING WRITERS

Find Evidence To help students extract meaning from narratives, recommend that they imagine themselves as friends of the main character. They have observed what is happening in that character's life. Ask students to list thoughts they would have about what the character is doing and examples from the narrative that explain those thoughts.

FOR ENGLISH LEARNERS

Freewrite [mixed-readiness pairs] Review the Freewriting strategy. Allow English learners to freewrite in their home languages. Then, have them work with more fluent partners to translate the freewriting into English. As a challenge, ask students to add one sentence in English to their original freewriting.

 BEST PRACTICES TOOLKIT
Freewriting p. C1

Practice and Apply

To support students during the writing process, use these copy masters:

R RESOURCE MANAGER—Copy Masters
Prewriting–Editing pp. 287–291
Writing Rubric p. 292
Writing Support p. 294 (for English learners)

Part 2: Apply the Writing Process

PREWRITING

1. Revisit the work you're analyzing. Tell students also to revisit class notes, test essays, and homework assignments that might relate to their chosen work. Urge them to include setting as an element of their analysis by completing an Analyzing Setting diagram.

BEST PRACTICES TOOLKIT—Transparency
Analyzing Setting p. D13

2. Freewrite to explore your ideas. After students freewrite, have them underline any literary terms they have used. In addition, help them identify two literary elements, such as setting, character, plot, theme, symbolism, or irony, that reflect their freewriting. Direct students to page 844 for information about these terms and suggest that students focus on analyzing these features in their essays.

3. Develop a working thesis statement. Tell students to include the following in their thesis statements: the story title, the author's name, and one or two literary elements that convey the theme. If students have more than one thesis idea, advise them to choose the one for which there is most evidence in the text.

4. Find evidence to support your key points. Refer students to the **TIP** and remind them of the literary elements named in their thesis statements. Suggest that students look for at least one example each of dialogue, action by the main character, and descriptive text as evidence. To analyze character, have students use a Character Traits and Textual Evidence diagram.

BEST PRACTICES TOOLKIT—Transparency
Character Traits and Textual Evidence p. D6

For interactive graphic organizers, see

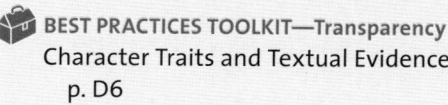

WriteSmart CD

Writing Center at **ClassZone.com**

DRAFTING

1. **Plan your organization.** Have students use a Microtheme diagram to organize their literary analyses into introduction, thesis statement, main body, and conclusion.

   📦 BEST PRACTICES TOOLKIT—Transparency
   Microtheme p. C13

2. **Back up your key points with evidence from the work.** Direct students to the **TIP**, and ask them why it is not appropriate to discuss every detail in a literary analysis. *Possible answers: The goal of a literary analysis is to make specific points about a work. Discussing every detail distracts readers from the main points of analysis and thus dilutes the impact of the analysis.*

3. **Create a strong, thoughtful conclusion.** If students have difficulty finding new ideas for their conclusions, suggest that they reread their story's ending. The outcome of a plot, which often shows how the main character has changed, may imply thematic ideas. Meaningful ironies are also found often in story outcomes. Such ideas and ironies can sometimes provide students with ways to connect stories to life.

   For a literary analysis writing template, see

   📦 BEST PRACTICES TOOLKIT—Transparency
   Writing Template: Literary Analysis
   pp. C16, C30

   💿 WriteSmart CD

   ⓘ Writing Center at **ClassZone.com**

DRAFTING

What Should I Do?	What Does It Look Like?
1. Plan your organization. Experiment with different ways of presenting your ideas. You might want to discuss your points in the order that they appear in the work, as Amanda Olivares did (Pattern 1). You could also discuss the end of the work first and then trace how that ending came about (Pattern 2).	**PATTERN 1** — *Introduction and thesis* 1. Beginning of story: lack of first name symbolizes character's lack of identity 2. Middle: "new spring life" symbolizes her new life 3. Middle: ironic that tragic event brings joy 4. End: ironic that she dies from lack of independence, not from joy — *Conclusion* **PATTERN 2** — *Introduction and thesis* A. Irony 1. The main character dies from lack of independence, not from "joy that kills." 2. Why would a tragic event bring joy? B. Symbolism 1. Lack of first name at beginning of story symbolizes lack of identity. 2. "New spring life" parallels her new life. — *Conclusion*
2. Back up your key points with evidence from the work. Choose examples, details, and quotations that clearly support your ideas. **TIP** Remember, you don't have to—and shouldn't—discuss every detail of the work.	His death means that "there would be no one to live for her during those coming years; she would live for herself." Ironically, the event that readers think will ruin her life actually brings her "a monstrous joy." — Explanations and quotations Brently Mallard's death has given his wife a chance at freedom and independence. — Key point
3. Create a strong, thoughtful conclusion. Summarize the ideas you've discussed and leave your reader with something more to think about—maybe a way to relate the overall message of the work to his or her own life. **TIP** Before revising, consult the key traits on page 804 and the criteria and peer-reader questions on page 810.	From the title of this short story to its last words, Kate Chopin uses irony and symbolism to describe a woman's discovery—and loss—of her own identity. — Summary As we follow the surprising twists and turns of "The Story of an Hour," we can't help thinking, what shocks and self-discoveries might the hours of our own lives have in store? — Relating the work to reader's life

808 UNIT 4: REGIONALISM AND NATURALISM

DIFFERENTIATED INSTRUCTION

FOR ENGLISH LEARNERS

Create a Conclusion Write these sentence starters on the board for use by English learners:

- [Author's name] is telling us that _____ _____.

- The lesson of the story for today's readers is _____ _____.

- From this story, we learn that _____ _____.

FOR ADVANCED LEARNERS/AP

Expand the Conclusion Advanced learners will be especially interested in writing conclusions that make readers think. Direct students to book or film reviews to note the kinds of ideas authors put in their conclusions. Urge students to emulate examples that fit their chosen stories and theses.

REVISING AND EDITING

What Should I Do?	What Does It Look Like?

1. Enliven your introduction.
- Read your introduction aloud. (Circle) statements that seem dull or unclear.
- Recast these sentences so they immediately capture the reader's attention.

How would you react if a friend came to you with a shocking piece of news? The first sentence of "The Story of an Hour" reveals ~~The Story of an Hour" is a short story by Kate Chopin~~ We learn in the first sentence that the main character's husband has died. As this short story develops, we find out her complicated and conflicting reactions to this tragedy.

2. Use exact, specific words.
- Have a peer reader <u>underline</u> words that are too general or that should be replaced with precise literary terms.
- Substitute lively language and specific terms.

main character
It is only when the <u>woman</u> is alone that Chopin <u>adds details</u>, begins to reveal rich and symbolic details.

Mrs. Mallard's thoughts and hopes,
As we learn more about <u>her</u>, the story ~~changes~~ takes an ironic turn.

3. Vary your sentence structures and lengths.
- Are many of your sentences short and choppy or long and droning? Draw a box around sentences that are of similar lengths or that have the same structure.
- Combine or separate some sentences to give your readers variety.

~~She goes downstairs. She sees her husband come in. He is alive! It is a terrible shock.~~

As she goes back downstairs, she sees her husband coming in the door, as alive as ever. The resulting shock is too much for her to bear.

4. Emphasize the meaning.
- Ask a peer reader to highlight sentences that explain the author's message.
- If your analysis has little or no highlighting, add information about the story's significance.

See page 810: Ask a Peer Reader

Although we know that she is "afflicted" with a mysterious "heart trouble," we aren't told what her personality is like, where she lives, or what she looks like. We don't even know her first name; she is simply "Mrs. Mallard." This lack of detail symbolizes how little the main character knows about her feelings and her identity. It also shows how women of that time period (the late 19th century) were portrayed—as selfless, dependent wives and mothers, devoted to their families.

REVISING AND EDITING

1. **Enliven your introduction.** Suggest that students delete or move introductory sentences that merely identify the story without describing its contents. As an option for introducing their literary analysis, students might describe a crucial story scene that clearly illustrates their thesis.

2. **Use exact, specific words.** Have paired writers and peer readers use a dictionary and a thesaurus to search for lively, specific synonyms to replace general terms. Remind students to look for words that are concrete rather than abstract.

3. **Vary your sentence structures and lengths.** Tell students to actually count the words in their sentences to accurately determine if they have sufficiently varied the length, and point out that they can do this electronically if word processing. Remind students that readable paragraphs usually contain a mix of long and short sentences. Advise students to read their work aloud to search for choppy or droning sentences.

4. **Emphasize the meaning.** Have students use Color Coding to find out whether their analyses contain healthy proportions of analysis and plot summary.

🧰 **BEST PRACTICES TOOLKIT—Transparency** Color Coding p. C12

For interactive revision tools, see

💿 Write*Smart* CD

ℹ️ Writing Center at **ClassZone.com**

FOR DEVELOPING WRITERS

Working with Peers As students move through the editing stage, have them use a Peer Response Guide to work effectively with partners. Also, help students clarify the questions on page 810.

 BEST PRACTICES TOOLKIT—Transparency Peer Response Guide p. C14

FOR ADVANCED LEARNERS/AP

Use Exact Words Remind students that effective writing usually uses the fewest words necessary to advance the writer's ideas clearly. After students think they are finished revising, have them reread their papers and revise one more time, for concision. Students may be surprised at how much better they write when they delete unnecessary words or sentences.

Preparing to Publish

Support for meeting the goals in the writing criteria is supplied throughout the Writing Workshop on pages 807–809.

For Rubric Bank, see

- WriteSmart CD
- Writing Center at ClassZone.com

Assess and Reteach

S STANDARDS LESSON FILE

Writing Lesson 8: Creating Sentence Variety

Writing Lesson 14: Writing a Thesis Statement

Writing Lesson 16: Writing Conclusions

Writing Lesson 28: Writing About Literature

Writing Lesson 35: Elaborate with Incidents, Examples, and Quotations

Grammar Lesson 20: Misplaced and Dangling Modifiers

Preparing to Publish — Literary Analysis

Consider the Criteria

Use this checklist to make sure your literary analysis is on track.

Ideas
- ☑ has a clear thesis statement
- ☑ supports statements with details and examples from the text

Organization
- ☑ identifies the author and the work in an interesting introduction
- ☑ organizes ideas sensibly, using appropriate transitions
- ☑ concludes with a summary of key points and work's overall meaning

Voice
- ☑ uses a tone suited to the purpose and audience

Word Choice
- ☑ uses precise language

Sentence Fluency
- ☑ varies sentence structure

Conventions
- ☑ uses correct grammar, spelling, and punctuation

Ask a Peer Reader

- What did you learn from my analysis?
- Do my statements need more explanation? If so, which ones?
- Are there places where I retell events without explaining their significance? If so, where?

Review Literary Terms

Irony: a contrast between appearance and actuality (In "The Story of an Hour," the husband's death brings the wife joy, not misery.)

Point of view: the perspective from which a story is told (Chopin's story has a third-person omniscient narrator. See "Point of view" on page R000 to learn more.)

Symbolism: the use of one idea or object to represent another (The buds on the trees symbolize Mrs. Mallard's new life.)

Theme: an underlying message about life or human nature that the writer wants readers to understand (Some critics say the theme of Chopin's story is "Women crave independence.")

Check Your Grammar

Make sure modifiers are placed as close as possible to the words they modify.

As she goes back downstairs, (as alive as ever,) she sees her husband coming in the door.

See page R63: Misplaced Modifiers

Writing Online

PUBLISHING OPTIONS
For publishing options, visit the **Writing Center** at **ClassZone.com**.

ASSESSMENT PREPARATION
For writing and grammar assessment practice, go to the **Assessment Center** at **ClassZone.com**.

LS2.4

CALIFORNIA

Producing a Power Presentation

Share your literary analysis by turning it into a power presentation—a series of slides that you create using computer software.

Planning the Presentation

1. **Focus on your main ideas.** Sketch out at least one slide apiece for your introduction, your conclusion, and every key point you made. Each sketch should include a headline and three to five short bullet points.

2. **Decide on a design.** Choose one of the templates available with the software program you are using. Or, if you prefer, choose your own fonts and colors. Your slides must be readable throughout the room, so use type that is 14 points or larger.

3. **Spice it up.** Create or find visuals that illustrate your points. Consider adding music or sound effects.

4. **Practice and fine-tune.** If possible, run through your presentation with the equipment and in the room you will be using. Otherwise, use a printed copy of the slides to present to friends and family. Make sure information is logical and in order, quotations are accurate, and spelling is correct.

Symbolism of View from Window

- Mrs. Mallard sees trees "aquiver with the new spring life"

- Changes the pace of the story

- Symbolizes her new beginning

Delivering the Presentation

1. **Make it a presentation, not a reading.** Maintain eye contact with your audience most of the time. Elaborate on each point with additional details and evidence from the work to strengthen your statements.

2. **Ask for feedback.** Create a simple questionnaire on the content and style of your presentation. Distribute copies of the questionnaire to audience members. Use the feedback to power up your next power presentation.

PUBLISHING WITH TECHNOLOGY

Ask students to read this page to get an overview of how to plan and produce a power presentation. Students who choose this option should familiarize themselves with the available software and with the tasks of sketching slides and choosing templates, fonts, or colors. Before students begin working, review these criteria with them so that they understand their goals:

Criteria A strong power presentation

- focuses on main ideas
- puts each key point on a separate slide
- uses a headline and short bulleted points to convey each key point
- appears in a readable, attractive design
- incorporates visuals and possibly music
- presents information logically and in order
- reflects accurate spelling and mechanics
- evidences preparation and rehearsal
- is presented effectively, using eye contact and additional details
- includes audience feedback, possibly in the form of a questionnaire

When students give their presentations, have the audience use the criteria to evaluate the final product.

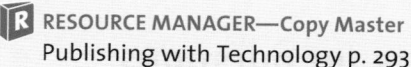 **RESOURCE MANAGER—Copy Master**
Publishing with Technology p. 293

STANDARDS LESSON FILE
Media Lesson 22: Creating a Power Presentation

Assessment Practice

CHECK READINESS

Read aloud the paragraph under **ASSESS** and stress to students that this is not the full Unit Test, but a way for them to check their readiness for it. Then have students examine the skills listed under **REVIEW** and look back in the unit or in the **Student Resource Bank** for any skills they need to review.

READ THE SELECTIONS

Remind students to keep unit goals in mind as they read the passage, paying particular attention to these literary and reading skills:

- Theme
- Setting
- Naturalism
  - Character
  - Plot and Conflict
- Tone
  - Diction
  - Repetition
- Make Inferences

To help students focus on setting and naturalism while reading, encourage them to ask questions such as:

- What grim details does "I Will Fight No More Forever" describe?
- What view does the excerpt from *Sister Carrie* take about the people's daily lives?

ANSWER THE QUESTIONS

Direct students to pages R96–R103 of the **Test-Taking Handbook** to review test-taking strategies.

- Remind students not to choose the first alternative that seems to fit when answering a multiple-choice question. Instead, they should read through all the choices, eliminate any that are clearly wrong, and then choose the *best* answer—the one that is most accurate and complete.
- Urge students to refer to the selections as needed for details. It is better to take an extra moment to find the correct answer than to hastily choose an incorrect answer.

Assessment Practice

ASSESS

The practice test items on the next few pages match skills listed on the Unit Goals page (page 614) and addressed throughout this unit. Taking this practice test will help you assess your knowledge of these skills and determine your readiness for the Unit Test.

REVIEW

After you take the practice test, your teacher can help you identify any skills you need to review.

- Theme
- Setting
- Naturalism
  - Character
  - Plot and Conflict
- Tone
  - Diction
  - Repetition
- Make Inferences
- Latin Words and Roots
- Denotation and Connotation
- Active and Passive Voice
- Gerunds and Gerund Phrases

ASSESSMENT ONLINE
For more assessment practice and test-taking tips, go to the **Assessment Center** at ClassZone.com.

Reading Comprehension

DIRECTIONS *Read these selections and answer the questions that follow.*

These two selections represent the end of one way of life and the beginning of another at the close of the 19th century. Chief Joseph delivered his surrender speech in 1877, as the Nez Perce were being relocated to a reservation. Dreiser's novel, set in 1889, recounts the experiences of Carrie Meeber, a fictional character based on the thousands of rural Americans who came to industrial cities (like Chicago) in search of new opportunities.

I Will Fight No More Forever
Chief Joseph

Tell General Howard I know his heart. What he told me before, I have in my heart. I am tired of fighting. Our chiefs are killed. Looking Glass is dead. Toohoolhoolzote is dead. The old men are all dead. It is the young men who say yes or no. He who led on the young men is dead. It is cold and we have no blankets. The little children are freezing to death. My people, some of them, have run away to the hills, and have no blankets, no food; no one knows where they are—perhaps freezing to death. I want to have time to look for my children and see how many of them I can find. Maybe I shall find them among the dead. Hear me, my chiefs! I am tired; my heart is sick and sad. From where the sun now
10 stands I will fight no more forever.

from Sister Carrie
Theodore Dreiser

With the wane of the afternoon went her hopes, her courage and her strength. She had been astonishingly persistent. So earnest an effort was well deserving of a better reward. On every hand, to her fatigued senses, the great business portion grew larger, harder, more stolid in its indifference. It seemed as if it was all closed to her, that the struggle was too fierce for her to hope to do anything at all. Men and women hurried by in long, shifting lines. She felt the flow of the tide of effort and interest, felt her own helplessness without quite realizing the wisp on the tide that she was. She cast about vainly for some possible place to apply but found no door which she had the courage to enter. It would be the same thing
10 all over. The old humiliation of her pleas rewarded by curt denial. Sick at heart and in body, she turned to the west, the direction of Minnie's flat, which she had now fixed in mind, and began that wearisome, baffled retreat which the seeker for

---

DIFFERENTIATED INSTRUCTION

FOR ENGLISH LEARNERS
Assessment Practice: Work Backward
Prepare students by having them read the questions *before* reading the passages. Have pairs find unfamiliar words in test directions and questions and follow these steps:

1. Write each word on an index card.
2. Look up the meaning in a dictionary and write it on the back of the card.

3. Use the cards to practice the words with your partner and to teach them to others.

employment at nightfall too often makes. In passing through Fifth Avenue, south
towards Van Buren Street, where she intended to take a car, she passed the door of
a large wholesale shoe house, through the plate glass window of which she could
see a middle-aged gentleman sitting at a small desk. One of those forlorn impulses
which often grow out of a fixed sense of defeat, the last sprouting of a baffled
and uprooted growth of ideas, seized upon her. She walked deliberately through
the door and up to the gentleman who looked at her weary face with partially
20 awakened interest.

"What is it?" he said.

"Can you give me something to do?" asked Carrie.

"Now I really don't know," he said kindly. "What kind of work is it you want—
you're not a typewriter, are you?"

"Oh, no," answered Carrie.

"Well, we only employ book keepers and typewriters here. You might go round
to the side and inquire upstairs. They did want some help upstairs a few days ago.
Ask for Mr. Brown."

She hastened around to the side entrance and was taken up by the elevator to
30 the fourth floor.

"Call Mr. Brown, Willie," said the elevator man to a boy near by.

Willie went off and presently returned with the information that Mr. Brown
said she should sit down and that he would be around in a little while.

It was a portion of a stock room which gave no idea of the general character of
the floor, and Carrie could form no opinion of the nature of the work.

"So you want something to do," said Mr. Brown, after he inquired concerning
the nature of her errand. "Have you ever been employed in a shoe factory before?"

"No sir," said Carrie.

"What is your name?" he inquired, and being informed, "Well, I don't know as
40 I have anything for you. Would you work for four and a half a week?"

Carrie was too worn by defeat not to feel that it was considerable. She had not
expected that he would offer her less than six. She acquiesced, however, and he
took her name and address.

"Well," he said finally—"you report here at eight o'clock Monday morning. I
think I can find something for you to do."

He left her revived by the possibilities, sure that she had found something to
do at last. Instantly the blood crept warmly over her body. Her nervous tension
relaxed. She walked out into the busy street and discovered a new atmosphere.
Behold, the throng was moving with a lightsome step. She noticed that men
50 and women were smiling. Scraps of conversation and notes of laughter floated

ITEM ANALYSIS

COMPREHENSION AND WRITTEN RESPONSE	ITEMS	UNIT PAGES
Theme	4, 6, 12, 17, 18	745
Setting	5, 9, 10, 16	673, 693
Naturalism	4, 6, 7, 8, 11	711, 745 745
Character	8, 11	745, 759
Plot and Conflict	6, 7	
Tone	1, 3, 14	649, 791
Diction	14, 15	649, 711,
Repetition	2	738
Make Inferences	10, 12, 13	693, 791

VOCABULARY	ITEMS	UNIT PAGES
Denotation and Connotation	1, 2, 3, 4	754
Latin Roots and Words	5, 6, 7	686, 802

WRITING AND GRAMMAR	ITEMS	UNIT PAGES
Active and Passive Verbs	1, 2, 3	765
Gerunds and Gerund Phrases	4, 5	737

FOR STRATEGIC READERS

Assessment Support Consider these options
for completing the Assessment Practice:

- Have students "work backward" to review
  the test questions *before* reading the
  passages.

- Select random questions in the Assessment, and have students demonstrate
  how and *where* to look for the answers.

- Ask students to locate unfamiliar vocabulary words in the Assessment. Elicit the
  words' meanings from the class.

- Have students record useful testing words
  and definitions in their journals for later
  reference.

- Read the selections or parts of them aloud
  to aid in student comprehension.

McDougal Littell
Assessment System

After checking student readiness with this
Assessment Practice, you may administer
the complete Unit 4 Test in order to more
thoroughly evaluate student mastery of
unit goals.

ANSWERS

Comprehension

Model a thinking process for answering multiple-choice questions.

1. **B is correct.** *"I am tired; my heart is sick and sad" (line 9), says Chief Joseph. A is incorrect because he obviously means everything he says. C is incorrect because he is not pleading for anything. D is incorrect because he does not direct his feelings at his enemies.*

2. **A is correct.** *Repeated mention of the dead makes the audience face facts. B is incorrect because the lines refer to deaths before relocation. C is incorrect because the topic is defeat, not honor. D is incorrect because the tone is factual, not ashamed.*

3. **C is correct.** *The sun marks the progress of the day, so the phrase means "from this time on." A and D are incorrect because Chief Joseph is not speaking about place. B is incorrect because the sun's position most commonly tells time of day, not the season.*

4. **B is correct.** *The crowd is described as a flowing tide (line 6); Carrie feels "indifference" (line 4) around her. A is incorrect because she feels threatened, not safe. C is incorrect because she feels despair. D is incorrect because she feels "fatigued" (line 3), not excited.*

5. **B is correct.** *Line 7 refers to her "helplessness." A is the opposite of what the passage describes. C is incorrect because home is not mentioned. D is incorrect because Carrie is uncomfortable.*

6. **B is correct.** *Carrie makes the decision impulsively. A is incorrect because her job search is deliberate, not impulsive. C is incorrect because the offer is not described as impulsive. D is incorrect because people leave work through habit, not impulse.*

7. **D is correct.** *Carrie seeks a job because she needs money. A is incorrect because she is frustrated and weary, not angry. B and C are incorrect because she does not face competition or corruption.*

---

to her. The air was light. People were already pouring out of the buildings, their labor ended for the day. She noticed that they were pleased, and thoughts of her sister's home, and the meal that would be awaiting her, quickened her steps. She hurried on, tired perhaps, but no longer weary of foot. What would not Minnie say! Ah, long the winter in Chicago—the lights, the crowd, the amusement. This was a great, pleasing metropolis after all. Her new firm was a goodly institution. Its windows were of huge plate glass. She could probably do well there. Thoughts of Drouet returned, of the things he had told her. She now felt that life was better. That it was livelier, sprightlier. She boarded a car in the best of spirits, feeling her
60 blood still flowing pleasantly. She would live in Chicago, her mind kept saying to itself. She would have a better time than she ever had before—she would be happy.

Comprehension

DIRECTIONS *Answer these questions about "I Will Fight No More Forever."*

1. Which words best describes Chief Joseph's tone?
   A brash and ironic
   B weary and heavy-hearted
   C self-pitying and imploring
   D suspicious and angry

2. Reread lines 2–4. The repetition in Chief Joseph's roll call of the dead emphasizes the
   A losses suffered in the conflict with U.S. troops
   B risks incurred in relocating to a reservation
   C honor bestowed on the Nez Perce warriors
   D shame associated with the Nez Perce's defeat

3. Chief Joseph's phrase "From where the sun now stands" emphasizes
   A a measured distance
   B the change of seasons
   C an exact point in time
   D his geographic location

DIRECTIONS *Answer these questions about the excerpt from* Sister Carrie.

4. Dreiser's description in lines 3–10 reflects the naturalist theme that the world is
   A safe and predictable
   B indifferent to the individual
   C filled with economic opportunities
   D fast-paced and exciting

5. Which word best describes how Carrie feels in the business district in lines 3–10?
   A energized   C homesick
   B powerless   D comfortable

6. Which event exemplifies the naturalist view that humans are controlled by impulses?
   A Carrie's long and fruitless search for a job
   B Carrie's decision to ask for work in the shoe house
   C Mr. Brown's offer of four and a half dollars a week
   D people leaving work at the end of the day

---

8. **B is correct.** *Carrie does not even know what kind of job she is seeking. A is incorrect because the realism appears in external description. C is incorrect because Carrie's thoughts are sincere. D is incorrect because she does not think about class conflict.*

9. **B is correct.** *After the job offer, Carrie's mood lifts. A is incorrect because she now perceives pleasantness in the crowd. C is incorrect because the lightness in the passage is of spirit. D is incorrect because the people leaving work move predictably.*

7. Which of these forces does Carrie struggle with in this excerpt?

   A inner anger

   B unfair competition

   C political corruption

   D economic need

8. By revealing Carrie's innermost thoughts and impressions the narrator

   A creates a realistic scenario

   B emphasizes her bewilderment

   C undermines her credibility

   D highlights class conflict

9. In lines 48–52, Carrie now perceives Chicago's business district as

   A stifling   C well lit

   B friendly   D chaotic

10. Why does Carrie see the business district differently at the end of the excerpt?

   A It is late in the day.

   B The air is clear.

   C The street is busy.

   D She just got a job.

11. The characters in this excerpt typify naturalism's focus on what kind of people?

   A common men and women

   B young job seekers

   C business professionals

   D strong individualists

12. Which image suggests that human destiny is shaped by forces beyond our control?

   A "fatigued senses" (line 3)

   B "wisp on the tide" (lines 7–8)

   C "baffled retreat" (line 12)

   D "great, pleasing metropolis" (line 56)

13. From Carrie's experience in this excerpt, you might infer that newcomers to cities in the late 19th century

   A received an enthusiastic welcome

   B caused problems for local officials

   C often had to accept low-paying jobs

   D were ridiculed for their behavior

DIRECTIONS *Answer this question about both selections.*

14. Which statement accurately compares the diction used in the two selections?

   A Both selections rely on nature imagery.

   B The speech uses comparisons; the excerpt does not.

   C The speech is spare and simple; the excerpt is formal and literary.

   D The speech uses abstract language; the excerpt uses colorful language.

Written Response

SHORT RESPONSE *Write three or four sentences to answer each question.*

15. What is unusual about Chef Joseph's diction in the statement "I will fight no more forever"? What effect does he achieve with that choice of words?

16. Dreiser depicts Chicago as what type of city? Cite three details to support your answer.

17. Identify one theme that emerges in the excerpt from *Sister Carrie*.

EXTENDED RESPONSE *Write two or three paragraphs to answer this question.*

18. Materialism is a recurring theme in Theodore Dreiser's works. Which details in this excerpt illustrate that theme?

GO ON ➡

---

10. **D is correct.** Carrie is "revived by the possibilities" the job offer creates (line 46). A is incorrect because the lateness could have made her feel worse. B is incorrect because her change of mood just makes the air seem different. C is incorrect because the street has been busy all along.

11. **A is correct.** The characters are ordinary workers. B is incorrect because Carrie is the only job seeker in the scene. C is incorrect because she is not a business professional. D is incorrect because the characters are part of a crowd.

12. **B is correct.** A wisp on a tide is a small thing borne away by something larger. A is incorrect because fatigued senses are not an outside force. C is incorrect because Carrie's retreat is an individual action. D is incorrect because its mood is positive.

13. **C is correct.** Carrie is given a low-paying job offer. A, B, and D describe experiences Carrie does not have.

14. **C is correct.** The sentence beginning "One of those forlorn impulses" (lines 16–18) uses literary diction. A is incorrect because the excerpt emphasizes city imagery. B is incorrect because the speech does not use comparisons. D is incorrect because the speech's diction is concrete.

Written Response

Possible short responses:

15. *Chief Joseph uses two absolute terms, "no more" and "forever," instead of simply saying, "I will fight no more." The effect is to emphasize the finality of his decision.*

16. *Dreiser describes Chicago as a busy, exciting metropolis. Possible examples include people pouring out of buildings (line 51), the description of wintertime in Chicago (line 55), and the phrase "great, pleasing metropolis" (line 56).*

17. *Themes in the excerpt include that people are guided by impulse, that they have little control over their destiny, and that the world can be cold and indifferent.*

Possible extended response:

18. *Carrie's view of reality is colored by how materially successful she feels. At the beginning, she is downcast because she can't find work. At the end, she is cheered up by the prospect of material security.*

DIFFERENTIATED INSTRUCTION

FOR ENGLISH LEARNERS

Assessment Vocabulary To help students understand the Comprehension questions, teach or review these key vocabulary words:

- Item 2: *emphasizes*, "gives importance to"
- Item 6: *exemplifies*, "is an example of"
- Item 11: *typify*, "are typical of"
- Item 16: *depicts*, "shows"
- Item 18: *recurring*, "repeated"

Vocabulary

1. **B is correct.** *Carrie keeps looking for a job. A is incorrect because she feels humbled. C is incorrect because she is still hopeful. D is incorrect because she has lost strength and shows no hostility.*

2. **D is correct.** *The word reflects Carrie's being small and tossed about. A is incorrect because she is shown as subject to society. B is incorrect because she feels separate. C is incorrect because she is uncertain.*

3. **C is correct.** *Her forlornness springs from "a fixed sense of defeat" (line 17). A is incorrect because she is like many other people. B is incorrect because she moves "deliberately" and is "weary" (lines 18–19). D is incorrect because the passage's emphasis is completely material.*

4. **B is correct.** *Carrie agrees to the low offer. A is incorrect because she shows no suspicion. C is incorrect because she is "worn by defeat" (line 41), not hostile. D conveys the opposite of her feelings.*

5. **B is correct.** *The denials were brief. A is incorrect because neither the passage nor the root suggest it. C is incorrect because its meaning is not as close to "shortened" as "brief" is. D is incorrect because it means "diluted," not "shortened."*

6. **C is correct.** *The passage refers to an unplanned action by a human being. A and B are incorrect because they refer to physics, not to human actions. D is incorrect because it does not include the lack of planning in Carrie's action.*

7. **A is correct.** *The passage states that life seems better and livelier. B is incorrect because it does not suit the content of the passage. C is incorrect because it refers to cleanness, not to vigor or breath. D is incorrect because it clashes with the meaning of the sentence in line 59.*

Vocabulary

DIRECTIONS *Use context clues and your knowledge of denotation and connotation to answer the following questions about words from* Sister Carrie.

1. What connotation does the word *persistent* have in line 2?
   A arrogance
   B determination
   C pessimism
   D ruthlessness

2. What connotation does the word *wisp* have in line 7?
   A freedom
   B openness
   C steadiness
   D insignificance

3. What connotation does the word *forlorn* have in line 16?
   A uniqueness
   B swiftness
   C abandonment
   D spirituality

4. What connotation does the word *acquiesced* have in line 42?
   A wariness
   B submissiveness
   C hostility
   D enthusiasm

DIRECTIONS *Use context clues and your knowledge of Latin words and roots to answer the following questions about words from* Sister Carrie.

5. The word *curt* derives from the Latin word *curtus*, which means "shortened." What is the most likely meaning of *curt* as it is used in line 10?
   A grammatically incorrect
   B rudely brief
   C unusually direct
   D watered down

6. The word *impulses* derives from the Latin prefix *in-*, which means "into," and the Latin root *pel*, which means "to push or drive." What is the most likely meaning of *impulses* as it is used in line 16?
   A changes in momentum produced by the force in a time interval
   B surges of electrical power in one direction
   C sudden urges that prompt unplanned acts
   D motion produced by strong forces

7. The word *sprightlier* derives from the Latin word *spiritus*, which means "vigor" or "breath." What is the most likely meaning of *sprightlier* as it is used in line 59?
   A more full of vitality
   B breathing more heavily
   C cleaner than in the past
   D in need of more fresh air

DIFFERENTIATED INSTRUCTION

FOR ENGLISH LEARNERS
Review Academic Vocabulary On the board, list the academic vocabulary shown in italics. Then give the examples in random order and have students classify them. Elicit additional examples from students.

- *naturalism:* Dreiser shows human beings as subject to powerful forces they cannot control.

- *descriptive language:* Chief Joseph uses simple words and short sentences to make his audience see the dead.

Writing & Grammar

DIRECTIONS *Read this passage and answer the questions that follow.*

> (1) In the 1770s, the first permanent settlement in Chicago was established by a Haitian trader named Jean Baptiste Point du Sable. (2) The community developed slowly at first. (3) The growth of Chicago was spurred by the construction of railroads in the mid-1800s. (4) Unfortunately, its progress came to a halt when <u>the city was destroyed by a fire in 1871</u>. (5) <u>Organizations immediately offered aid</u>, however. (6) Triumphantly, the city bounced back. (7) In 1893, Chicago hosted the World's Fair.

1. Choose the correct way to rewrite sentence 1 in the active voice.

   A In the 1770s, a Haitian trader named Jean Baptiste Point du Sable established the first permanent settlement in Chicago.

   B The first permanent settlement in Chicago was established in the 1770s by a Haitian trader named Jean Baptiste Point du Sable.

   C In Chicago in the 1770s, the first permanent settlement was established by a Haitian trader named Jean Baptiste Point du Sable.

   D The first permanent settlement in Chicago was established by a Haitian trader named Jean Baptiste Point du Sable in the 1770s.

2. Choose the correct way to rewrite sentence 3 in the active voice.

   A The growth of Chicago was spurred in the mid-1800s by railroads that were constructed.

   B The growth of Chicago was spurred by railroads that were constructed in the mid-1800s.

   C The construction of railroads in the mid-1800s spurred the growth of Chicago.

   D Railroads were constructed in the mid-1800s, spurring the growth of Chicago.

3. Choose the correct way to rewrite the underlined part of sentence 4 in the active voice.

   A in 1871, the destruction of the city was caused by a fire

   B in 1871, the city was destroyed by a fire

   C the city's ruin was caused by a fire in 1871

   D a fire destroyed the city in 1871

4. Choose the correct way to rewrite the underlined part of sentence 5 by using a gerund phrase.

   A Organizations immediately started forming relief and clean-up crews

   B Organizations immediately started to arrange cleaning crews to assist the city

   C Organizations immediately helped

   D Assisting organizations immediately helped

5. Choose the correct way to rewrite sentence 6 by using a gerund phrase.

   A Triumphantly, the city began reconstructing itself.

   B The city was hoping to triumph.

   C Triumphantly, the city was determining its future.

   D The city, a lightning force, was triumphant.

STOP

Writing & Grammar

1. **A is correct.** A *changes the passive "was established by" to the active "established."* B, C, *and* D *are incorrect because they all retain the passive "was established by."*

2. **C is correct.** C *changes the passive "was spurred by" to the active "spurred."* A *and* B *are incorrect because they retain the passive "was spurred by" and add the passive "that were constructed."* D *is incorrect because it adds the passive "were constructed," and the change from "was spurred by" to "spurring" is a change to a participle, not an active verb.*

3. **D is correct.** D *changes the passive "was destroyed by" to the active "destroyed."* A *and* C *are incorrect because "was caused by" is in the passive voice.* B *is incorrect because it retains the passive "was destroyed by."*

4. **A is correct.** *The word "forming" is a verbal used as a noun.* B *is incorrect because "cleaning" is used as an adjective, not a noun, and is therefore not a gerund.* C *is incorrect because it contains no -ing verbal.* D *is incorrect because "assisting," is used as an adjective, not a noun.*

5. **A is correct.** *The verbal "reconstructing" is used as a noun, the direct object of the verb "began."* B *and* C *are incorrect because their -ing verbals, "hoping" and "determining," are used as active verbs.* D *is incorrect because in "lightning" the -ing is a noun suffix, not a verbal ending.*

FOR STRATEGIC READERS

Assessment Support: Active Voice and Gerund Phrases

- Review with students that in the active voice, the verb performs the action rather than receiving the action.

- Ask students to find examples of the active and passive voices in the two selections.

- Review with students that a gerund is a verb form ending in *-ing* and functioning as a noun. A gerund phrase consists of a gerund and the words relating to it.

- Have students find gerund phrases in the excerpt from *Sister Carrie*.

INTRODUCE *GREAT READS*

In Unit 4, students have discussed a number of big questions. Invite students to tell which question they found most intriguing and why, and then focus attention on the four questions that appear on pages 616–617. Discuss the recommended books and their summaries, pointing out how each connects to the related question. Encourage students to choose one or more of these "great reads" to study independently.

ℹ ClassZone.com

To find additional books that match students' interests and ability levels, visit the Literature Center at **ClassZone.com**.

Ideas for Independent Reading

Continue exploring the Questions of the Times on pages 616–617 with these additional works.

What makes a place UNIQUE?

My Ántonia
by Willa Cather

This novel, recognized as Willa Cather's finest, depicts through the voice of the immigrant Ántonia Shimerda the hardships and rewards of pioneer life and the strength of America's frontier women. As Ántonia grows into womanhood, she overcomes poverty, disappointment, and family tragedy to become a mother and a successful farmer—a woman who "had not lost the fire of life."

American Indian Stories, Legends, and Other Writings
by Zitkala-Sa

This collection of works by Sioux writer and activist Zitkala-Sa (1876–1938) contains retellings of traditional Native American legends as well as stories, poems, essays, and speeches focused on the Native American experience.

The Virginian: A Horseman of the Plains
by Owen Wister

The strong-but-silent cowboy, the saintly schoolmarm, the climactic shootout—all have become standards of American Westerns but were brand-new ideas when Owen Wister penned *The Virginian* in 1902. His story of "the Virginian," a man torn between his love for a woman and his quest for justice, was the first true American Western.

Does the universe CARE?

Sister Carrie
by Theodore Dreiser

Carrie Meeber arrives in Chicago filled with vague hopes of fun and comfort. Meanwhile, across town, George Hurstwood, a well-to-do restaurant manager, is living the life of his dreams, respected by his peers and hobnobbing with famous actors. In *Sister Carrie*, Dreiser brings these two people together and lets us watch, amazed and appalled, as Carrie is taken to heights of glory while Hurstwood falls to the depths of despair.

The Best Short Stories of Jack London
by Jack London

No issue engaged writer Jack London more consistently than the clash between a seemingly uncaring natural world and the striving creatures who inhabit it. Intense, thrilling, and thought-provoking, the ten short stories in this collection show why London was so popular in his day and remains one of the most widely read of all American authors.

McTeague: A Story of San Francisco
by Frank Norris

Frank Norris set the literary establishment on its ear when he published *McTeague*, a naturalistic story of a San Francisco dentist. The title character, spurred by a strange force of self-destruction, makes one bad decision after another. Finally, he commits a murder and winds up fighting for his life in the harsh alkali deserts of California.

818

How are women's ROLES CHANGING?

The Awakening
by Kate Chopin

Causing a storm of controversy when published in 1899, *The Awakening* follows the daily life of an attractive, well-to-do New Orleans matron named Edna Pontellier. Married into a prominent family, Edna leads a very comfortable existence, with good friends, a fine house, and nothing very pressing to do. Yet Edna is assailed by a nameless discontent. Although she cannot articulate exactly what she wants, she knows that the options open to women in her society are slowly making her die inside.

The House of Mirth
by Edith Wharton

The daughter of a failed New York businessman, Lily Bart is pretty, independent-minded, and cultivated. She is also penniless. Living with her rich yet miserly aunt, she spends her time socializing with New York's aristocrats. In such a situation, Lily's course of action is obvious to everyone. If she wants to maintain her lifestyle, she must find a rich man and marry him. Yet selling her beauty to the highest bidder strikes Lily as savage. Unable to find a path that would bring her both self-respect and material comfort, Lily drifts from party to party, trying not to think about what is going to happen to her. Lily's ultimately tragic fate is clearly the blame of a society that values wealth and convention above all.

Why are there "haves" and "HAVE-NOTS"?

The Jungle
by Upton Sinclair

No other novel in American literature has had a more direct impact upon daily life than *The Jungle*. Based upon extensive research conducted in Chicago's slaughterhouses, Sinclair's novel was intended to turn a blinding light on unfair labor practices and rally readers to the cause of socialism. Instead, its descriptions of unclean meatpacking practices caused a steep decline in the sales of beef and pork and brought about federal laws to keep food healthy. "I aimed at the public's heart, and by accident hit it in the stomach," Sinclair ruefully remarked. Nevertheless, *The Jungle* remains jarring in its description of the appalling conditions laborers were forced to endure.

A Hazard of New Fortunes
by William Dean Howells

In this novel of class conflict, a mild-mannered editor moves to New York from Boston, looking to enhance his career. He takes charge of a magazine sponsored by a ruthless financier and comes into contact with his old German tutor, who has become a political radical. Torn between his sympathy for the working poor and his need to stay on good terms with his rich patron, the editor does not know what to do. When a violent streetcar strike breaks out, he can no longer remain a bystander. He has to decide whether to support what he knows is right or to play it safe and keep his job.

819

Preview Unit Goals

This page presents an overview of the skills and strategies covered in this unit. Explain to students that they can get more from their reading by previewing. Then ask them to skim the page to preview the skills that they will learn. Note that each strand or category of skill is color-coded on this page and throughout the unit.

Model the strategy of copying the Academic Vocabulary and writing a preliminary definition for each term. Suggest that students use a journal or a notebook for this purpose. Encourage them to use the terms in discussions and in writing. Also urge students to revisit each term throughout the unit and to refine its meaning.

ADDITIONAL UNIT GOALS

These skills will be taught in this unit but are not the major focus of the unit:

Literary Analysis
- Analyze characteristics of literary criticism and journalism

Reading
- Interpret analogies
- Analyze ambiguity and speaker's attitude
- Summarize stanzas
- Identify sequence of events, including flashback and foreshadowing
- Synthesize and analyze details
- Interpret author's message

Writing and Grammar
- Write to analyze and evaluate
- Write modern poetry
- Write with a variety of sentences
- Use sentence fragments for emphasis
- Establish voice, objective tone, and point of view, using varied grammatical structures
- Use imagery and descriptive details
- Conduct online research

Speaking, Listening, and Viewing
- Recite poetry
- Analyze characteristics of documentary

Vocabulary
- Use context clues

UNIT 5

Included in this unit: R1.1, R1.2, R2.4, R2.5, R3.1, R3.2, R3.3, R3.4, R3.5, R3.6, W1.1, W1.2, W1.3, W1.5, W1.9, W2.1, W2.2, W2.3, LC1.1, LC1.2, LS1.3, LS1.7, LS1.10, LS1.14, LS2.4, LS2.5

CALIFORNIA

Preview Unit Goals

LITERARY ANALYSIS	• Understand Harlem Renaissance and modernism as literary movements • Identify and analyze literary elements, including tone, theme, diction, voice, mood, irony, imagery, and character traits and motives • Identify and analyze form and meaning in poetry • Identify and analyze individual styles, including Frost's and Hemingway's • Analyze and interpret modern, narrative, and imagist poetry
READING	• Make inferences and draw conclusions • Identify and analyze author's purpose and position • Distinguish literal from figurative meaning • Identify explicit and implicit main ideas
WRITING AND GRAMMAR	• Write a comparison-contrast essay • Craft effective sentences by using vivid language, phrases, and coordinating conjunctions
SPEAKING, LISTENING, AND VIEWING	• Interpret and evaluate the way events and information are presented in media • Analyze and evaluate persuasive techniques in print advertising • Deliver an oral interpretation
VOCABULARY	• Use knowledge of Latin and Greek word roots to understand word meaning • Research word origins to understand historical influences in English
ACADEMIC VOCABULARY	• Harlem Renaissance • tone • form in poetry • modernism • irony • meaning in poetry • imagery

Online LITERATURE CLASSZONE.COM

Literature and Reading Center
Writing Center
Vocabulary Center

820

DIFFERENTIATED INSTRUCTION

FOR ENGLISH LEARNERS

Academic Vocabulary Use the copy master to help students learn the Academic Vocabulary.

1. Read aloud each Academic Vocabulary term and have students locate it on their copy masters.

2. Discuss the meaning or example shown on the copy master, and complete the chart as a class.

3. Have students work in small groups to complete the remaining activities on the copy master.

Additional Academic Vocabulary Use the copy master to help students learn academic words they will use in subsequent lessons and on the Assessment Practice. Follow the same procedure as for the Academic Vocabulary copy master.

 RESOURCE MANAGER—Copy Masters
Academic Vocabulary p. 11
Additional Academic Vocabulary p. 12

The Harlem Renaissance & Modernism

Langston Hughes

CALIFORNIA

1910–1940
A CHANGING AWARENESS

- The Harlem Renaissance
- The New Poetry
- The Modern Short Story
- Journalism as Literature

821

For help in planning this unit, see

 RESOURCE MANAGER UNIT 5
pp. 1–13

INTRODUCE THE UNIT

Call students' attention to the pictures on this page. Explain that the large picture, *The Bicycle Race* (1912), is a painting by Lyonel Feininger. Tell students that Feininger's work is influenced by such modern artistic movements as Cubism and Futurism. Students will read modern poetry and short stories later in this unit.

Ask students whether they know the writer, Langston Hughes, shown in the smaller picture on the page. Point out that Langston Hughes is recognized as a central figure of the Harlem Renaissance, a period of artistic flowering in the African-American community. Explain that Hughes was a writer of the people. He wrote works about ordinary people that were intended for ordinary people to read. Tell students that they will read some of his works in this unit. Also note that students can read more about Langston Hughes on page 838.

About the Art Although American artist Lyonel Feininger (1871–1956) was born in New York City, he lived and worked in Europe for most of his professional career. Dividing his time between Germany and France, Feininger began his career as a cartoonist, working for a number of magazines and newspapers both in America and abroad. While living in Paris in the early 1900s, Feininger fell under the artistic influence of Cubism and Futurism, which inspired his later work as a painter. Feininger's work attracted the scrutiny of the Nazi Party and was labeled as "degenerate art" in 1937, causing Feininger to flee Germany for the United States.

Unit Resources

PRINT RESOURCES

 RESOURCE MANAGER UNIT 5

BEST PRACTICES TOOLKIT

STANDARDS LESSON FILE

CALIFORNIA ASSESSMENT FILE

GRAMMAR FOR WRITING

TECH RESOURCES

- EasyPlanner DVD-ROM
- WriteSmart CD-ROM
- ClassZone.com
- Audio Anthology CD
- Multi-Language Academic Vocabulary Online

- eEdition DVD-ROM & Online
- McDougal Littell Assessment System
- Test Generator CD-ROM
- MediaSmart DVD-ROM
- Literature in Context DVD-ROM

	Unit 5 Introduction pp. 822–837 • Questions of the Times • Historical Essay • Timeline • Legacy	Literary Analysis Workshops • Modernism pp. 894–895 • Journalism as Literature pp. 1046–1047	Selected Poetry by Langston Hughes Poetry pp. 838–845	My City/If We Must Die Poetry pp. 846–851	Any Human to Another/Storm Ending/A Black Man Talks of Reaping Poetry pp. 852–857	How It Feels to Be Colored Me Essay pp. 858–867 Lexile: 920 Fry: 11 Dale-Chall: 6.4	Themes Across Time: Thoughts on the African-American Novel Literary Criticism pp. 868–874 Lexile: 1130 Fry: College Dale-Chall: 7.0
Literary Analysis	The Harlem Renaissance and Modernism pp. 822–837 R3.5 Historical and Cultural Context pp. 824–827 R3.5	Modernism as a Literary Movement pp. 894–895 R3.5 Characteristics of Journalism as Literature pp. 1046–1047 R3.3	Speaker pp. 839, 842, 843, 845	Sonnet pp. 847, 848, 850, 851 R3.4	Theme pp. 853, 854, 856, 857 R3.2	Tone pp. 859, 860, 862, 865 R3.3	Literary Criticism pp. 869, 872, 873, 874
Reading and Informational Texts	Build Context pp. 822–823 Use Prior Knowledge pp. 822–823 Connect pp. 822–823, 834–837 Take Notes pp. 825–832 Read a Timeline pp. 834–835	Analyze the Literature pp. 895, 1047	Analyze Rhythm and Repetition pp. 839, 840, 842, 844, 845 R3.4	Understand Form and Meaning pp. 847, 848, 850, 851	Distinguish Figurative from Literal Meaning pp. 853, 854, 855, 856, 857 R3.4	Identify Main Ideas pp. 859, 862, 864, 865	Identify Author's Position pp. 869, 872, 873, 874 R2.4
Vocabulary		Academic Vocabulary pp. 894–895				Word Acquisition pp. 859, T859, 866 Context Clues p. T859 Greek Roots (cosm) p. 866 R1.2	
Writing, Grammar, and Style						Writing Prompt p. 867 W1.2, W1.5, W2.3 Variety in Sentences pp. 864, 867 W1.9	
Speaking, Listening, Viewing, and Media	Discuss pp. 822–823, T824–T837	Discuss pp. T894–T895, T1046–T1047	Discuss pp. T838, 839, 840, 843, 845 Analyze Visuals p. 840	Discuss pp. T846, 847, T848–T850, 851 Analyze Visuals p. 848	Discuss pp. T852, 853, T854–T856, 857 Analyze Visuals p. 856	Discuss pp. T858, 859, T860–T864, 865 Analyze Visuals pp. 860, T863	Discuss pp. T868, 869, T870–T873, 874 Analyze Visuals p. 870

Standards Designations R = Reading W = Writing LC = Language Conventions LS = Listening and Speaking T = Teacher's Edition page

Media Study: Jump at the Sun Documentary pp. 876–879	Richard Cory/Miniver Cheevy/Lucinda Matlock Poetry pp. 880–887	Chicago/Grass Poetry pp. 888–893	Selected Poetry by Robert Frost Poetry pp. 896–902	The Death of the Hired Man Narrative Poem pp. 903–911	In a Station of the Metro/Helen/Spring and All/This Is Just to Say Poetry pp. 912–919	anyone lived in a pretty how town/Poetry/Recuerdo Poetry pp. 920–927
	Characterization in Narrative Poetry pp. 881, 882, 884, 886, 887 R3.4 Review: Meter pp. 884, 885	Tone and Diction pp. 889, 890, 892, 893 R3.3 Review: Personification pp. 892, 893	Frost's Style pp. 897, 898, 900, 901, 902 R3.3, R3.4	Narrative Poetry pp. 903, 904, 906, 907, 908, 909, 910 R3.1 Review: Blank Verse p. 906	Imagism pp. 913, 914, 916, 917, 918 R3.4	Form in Modern Poetry pp. 921, 922, 924, 926, 927 R3.3
	Analyze Speaker's Attitude pp. 881, 882, 885, 886, 887	Synthesize Details pp. 889, 890, 893	Recognize Ambiguity pp. 897, 898, 901, 902 R3.3	Understand Form in Poetry pp. 903, 904, 906, 908, 910	Make Inferences pp. 913, 914, 918	Strategies for Reading Modern Poetry pp. 921, 922, 924, 925, 926, 927
Academic Vocabulary (Film) p. 877						
				Writing Prompt p. 911 R3.2, W1.3, W2.2 Effective Use of Infinitive Phrases p. 911 LC1.1	Writing Prompt p. 919 W1.2, W1.5 Vivid Adjectives in Creating Imagery p. 919 W1.9	
Discuss pp. 876, 879 Analyze and Plan a Documentary pp. 877–879 LS1.3, LS1.10, LS2.4	Discuss pp. T880, 881, T882–T884, 885, T886, 887 Analyze Visuals p. 886	Discuss pp. T888, 889, T890–T892, 893 Analyze Visuals pp. 891, T892	Discuss pp. T896, 897, T898–T901, 900, 902 Analyze Visuals p. 898	Discuss pp. 903, T904–T909, 910 Analyze Visuals p. 904	Discuss pp. T912, 913, T914–T917, 918	Discuss pp. T920, 921, T922–T926, 927 Analyze Visuals pp. 922, 924

	The Love Song of J. Alfred Prufrock Poem pp. 928–934	Winter Dreams Short Story pp. 936–961	Media Study: Advertising in the Jazz Age Print Advertisements pp. 964–967	In Another Country Short Story pp. 968–977	Photo Essay: The Grapes of Wrath Photo Essay pp. 980–987	The Jilting of Granny Weatherall Short Story pp. 988–1001	A Worn Path Short Story pp. 1002–1017
		Lexile: 1100 Fry: College Dale-Chall: 6.6		Lexile: 1050 Fry: 6 Dale-Chall: 5.4	Lexile: 1200 Fry: College Dale-Chall: 7.6	Lexile: 820 Fry: 6 Dale-Chall: 5.4	Lexile: 770 Fry: 12 Dale-Chall: 5.1
Literary Analysis	Stream of Consciousness pp. 929, 931, 932, 933, 934 **R3.3**	Character Motivation and Traits pp. 937–959 Review: Theme pp. 951, 959		Style pp. 969, 970, 974, 975 **R3.3**		Stream of Consciousness pp. 989, 990, 992, 993, 995, 996, 998, 999 **R3.3**	Universal Theme pp. 1003–1015 **R3.2, R3.6**
Reading and Informational Texts	Summarize Stanzas pp. 929, 931, 934	Predict Story Development pp. 937, 940, 952, 955, 959		Make Inferences pp. 969, 972, 973, 975	Analyze Photographs pp. 980–987 **LS1.3** Compare Fiction and a Photo Essay p. 987 **LS1.3**	Clarify Sequence pp. 989, 993, 994, 999	Monitor pp. 1003, 1007, 1009, 1010, 1015 Read a Memoir p. 1014
Vocabulary		Word Acquisition pp. 937, T937, 960 Context Clues p. T937 Words from the Jazz Age p. 960 **R1.1**	Academic Vocabulary (Ads) p. 965	Word Acquisition pp. 969, T969, 976 Word Maps p. T969 Words from Italian p. 976		Word Acquisition pp. 989, T989, 1000 Context Clues p. T989 Nouns and Verbs p. 1000	Word Acquisition pp. 1003, T1003, 1016 Context Clues p. T1003 Latin Roots (med) p. 1016 **R1.2**
Writing, Grammar, and Style		Writing Prompt p. 961 **W1.3** Techniques for Establishing Voice pp. 951, 961 **LC1.1**		Writing Prompt p. 977 **W2.2** Objective Tone in Writing pp. 974, 977 **W1.9**		Writing Prompt p. 1001 **W1.2, W2.1** Repetition and Coordinating Conjunctions pp. 994, 1001 **W1.9**	Writing Prompt p. 1017 **W1.2, W2.1** Descriptive Details pp. 1007, 1017 **W1.9**
Speaking, Listening, Viewing, and Media	Discuss pp. T928, 929, T930–T933, 934	Discuss pp. T936, 937, T938–T958, 959 Analyze Visuals pp. 938, 942, T949, 953	Discuss pp. 964, 967 Analyze Persuasive Techniques Used in Ads pp. 965–967 **LS1.14** Create an Ad Poster p. 967 **LS1.10**	Discuss pp. T968, 969, T970–T974, 975 Analyze Visuals p. 970	Discuss pp. 980, T981–T986, 987	Discuss pp. T988, 989, T990–T998, 999 Analyze Visuals p. 990	Discuss pp. T1002, 1003, T1004–T1014, 1015 Analyze Visuals pp. 1004, T1008, 1010

A Rose for Emily Short Story pp. 1018–1031	The Life You Save May Be Your Own Short Story pp. 1032–1044	A New Kind of War News Dispatch pp. 1048–1057	A Book of Great Short Stories Book Review pp. 1058–1065	The Duty of Writers Essay pp. 1066–1070	Wrap-Ups • The Harlem Renaissance p. 875 • Poetry p. 935 • Short Story p. 1045 • Journalism p. 1071	Writing Workshop: Comparison-Contrast Essay pp. 1072–1079
Lexile: 1120 Fry: 11 Dale-Chall: 6.4	Lexile: 1000 Fry: 7 Dale-Chall: 5.6	Lexile: 990 Fry: 9 Dale-Chall: 5.7	Lexile: 1030 Fry: 9 Dale-Chall: 7.0	Lexile: 1210 Fry: College Dale-Chall: 7.7		
Mood pp. 1019, 1020, 1022, 1023, 1029 R3.3	Irony pp. 1033, 1037, 1038, 1039, 1042, 1043, 1044 R3.3	Subjectivity in Reporting pp. 1049–1056 R2.5, R3.3 Dialogue p. 1054	Voice pp. 1059, 1060, 1062, 1064 R2.5, R3.3	Style and Diction pp. 1067, 1069, 1070 R3.3		
Analyze Sequence pp. 1019, 1022, 1024, 1026, 1029 R3.3	Analyze Descriptive Details pp. 1033, 1034, 1037, 1039, 1041, 1044 R3.3	Analyze Descriptive Details pp. 1049, 1052, 1053, 1056 R3.3	Strategies for Reading a Book Review pp. 1059, 1063, 1064	Interpret Author's Message pp. 1067, 1069, 1070 R2.5		Analyze a Comparison-Contrast Essay pp. 1073–1074, 1078
Word Acquisition pp. 1019, T1019, 1030 Context Clues p. T1019 Etymologies p. 1030 R1.1						
Writing Prompt p. 1031 W1.3, W2.2 Point of View in Writing pp. 1024, 1031 LC1.1		Writing Prompt p. 1057 W1.2 Point of View in Writing pp. 1052, 1057 LC1.1	Writing Prompt p. 1065 W1.2, W1.3, W1.5 Techniques for Establishing Voice pp. 1063, 1065 W1.9		Write to Analyze p. 875 W2.2 Write to Synthesize p. 935 W1.1, W1.2, W1.5 Write to Evaluate pp. 1045, 1071 W1.2, W1.5	Write a Comparison-Contrast Essay pp. 1072–1078 W1.9, W2.2 Quotations, Prepositional Phrases p. 1078 LC1.2
Discuss pp. T1018, 1019, T1020–T1028, 1029 Analyze Visuals p. T1021	Discuss pp. T1032, 1033, T1034–T1043, 1044 Analyze Visuals pp. 1034, 1038	Discuss pp. T1048, 1049, T1050–T1055, 1056 Analyze Visuals p. 1050	Discuss pp. T1058, 1059, T1060–T1063, 1064 Analyze Visuals p. 1060	Discuss pp. T1066, 1067, T1068–T1069, 1070	Present Oral Readings of Internet Findings p. 875 Recite a Poem p. 935 LS2.5 Create an Image p. 1045 Create a Poster p. 1071	Discuss pp. 1075–1077 Deliver an Oral Interpretation p. 1079 LS1.7, LS2.5

Skills Assessed on the Unit 5 Test:

Literary Analysis
- Identify and analyze tone
- Identify imagery
- Identify and analyze character traits and motives
- Identify and interpret irony (dramatic and situational)
- Identify universal theme

Reading and Informational Texts
- Make inferences

Vocabulary
- Use knowledge of Latin roots to understand word meaning
- Research word origins as an aid to understand historical influence on the English language

Writing, Grammar, and Style
- Write a comparison-contrast essay
- Use infinitive phrases to create rhythm
- Use vivid adjectives effectively to create imagery
- Use diction to create an objective tone
- Additional writing and grammar skills

Speaking, Listening, Viewing, and Media
- Analyze persuasive techniques in print ads

For additional lesson planning help, see **Easy Planner DVD-ROM.**

CALIFORNIA	ASSESS PRIOR KNOWLEDGE Diagnostic	ONGOING ASSESSMENT Reteaching
BEGINNING OF UNIT		
Unit Opener	Preview Unit Goals, **TE** p. 820	
UNIT LESSONS		
Before every lesson	Big Question activity, **SE** Preteach vocabulary, **TE**	Check Understanding, **TE**
During every lesson		Annotations, **SE** Check Understanding, **TE** Tiered Discussion Prompts, **TE**
After every lesson		Post Reading pages, **SE** Assess and Reteach, **TE** Reading Check, **RM** Selection Tests A and B/C, **AF**
END OF UNIT		
Writing Workshop	Checklist, **SE** p. 1078 Rubric for Evaluation, **RM** p. 500	Assess and Reteach, **TE** p. 1078
Speaking & Listening	Criteria, **TE** p. 1079	For reteaching options, see **TE** p. 1079
Assessment	Assessment Practice, **SE** pp. 1080–1085	Unit Test, **AF** **MLAS**

For systematic instruction of grammar, use *Grammar for Writing*.

Key to Abbreviations:
SE = Student's Edition
TE = Teacher's Edition
RM = Resource Manager
AF = Assessment File
MLAS = McDougal Littell Assessment System

Universal Access

	Strategic Reader	Benchmark	Advanced Learner	English Learner	Students with Disabilities
SE STUDENT'S EDITION					
Vocabulary strategy instruction	✔	✔	✔	✔	✔
Instructional annotations	✔	✔	✔		✔
English/Spanish glossary				✔	
TE TEACHER'S EDITION					
Skill annotation support	✔	✔	✔	✔	✔
Tiered discussion prompts	✔	✔	✔	✔	✔
Differentiated instruction	✔	✔	✔	✔	✔
R RESOURCE MANAGER					
Selection summaries in four languages	✔	✔	✔	✔	✔
Skill copy masters in English and Spanish	✔			✔	
Vocabulary preteaching and support	✔			✔	✔
Additional leveled selection questions	✔	✔	✔	✔	✔
Question support	✔	✔	✔	✔	✔
Writing support	✔	✔	✔	✔	✔
Extension activities		✔	✔		
AF ASSESSMENT FILE					
Leveled selection and unit tests	✔	✔	✔	✔	✔
S STANDARDS LESSON FILE					
Leveled and reteaching copy masters	✔	✔	✔	✔	
BEST PRACTICES TOOLKIT					
Strategy bank	✔	✔	✔	✔	✔
Graphic organizers	✔	✔	✔	✔	✔
TECHNOLOGY					
WriteSmart Rubrics and student models	✔	✔	✔	✔	✔
Audio Anthology CD	✔			✔	✔
CLASSZONE					
Instructional centers	✔	✔	✔	✔	✔
Audio summaries of selections	✔			✔	✔
Multilanguage glossary				✔	

Questions of the Times

Read aloud the questions on pages 822 and 823 and the paragraphs that follow them. Open the discussion of each idea by having students respond to the questions that conclude each paragraph. Use these notes to prompt further exploration of the ideas.

What is MODERN?

Encourage students to consider what interests them about the traditions of their communities as well as what they enjoy about contemporary culture. Also, ask students to think about the importance of technology in their lives. Discuss why people so often want the latest and most up-to-date models of computers, cell phones, and music players.

Can ideals survive CATASTROPHE?

Invite students to brainstorm a list of dire events that have occurred in recent history. In light of these events, ask students to discuss their feelings regarding the future. Do they feel hopeful or cynical about the future? Why?

UNIT 5

Questions of the Times

DISCUSS Share your views about the following questions with a small group or in a whole-class discussion. As you read the selections in this unit, reflect on how the writing of the **Harlem Renaissance** and the **modernist period** was shaped by these questions.

What is MODERN?

Americans in the first half of the 20th century consciously moved away from the traditions of their past and embraced all things modern. From the shiny new automobiles rolling off Henry Ford's assembly line to the esoteric poetry of T. S. Eliot—Americans' love affair with modernism was in full swing. What does *modern* mean to you? Why do you think people like to be on the "cutting edge"?

Can ideals survive CATASTROPHE?

The years between 1910 and 1940 were scarred by two historical events: World War I and the Great Depression. Faced with a world at war followed by deep economic instability at home, many American writers began to see the world with a new cynicism. How can people hold on to their idealism in light of dire events? Is it even possible?

How can people honor their HERITAGE?

The writers of the Harlem Renaissance were quite diverse stylistically, yet they shared a pride in their heritage that shines through their work. Why do you think writing might be a good vehicle for honoring one's past? How else do people honor their heritage?

What drives HUMAN BEHAVIOR?

Newly familiar with Sigmund Freud's groundbreaking work in human psychology, American writers of this period began to examine the unconsious motivations that affect human behavior. Do you think people regulate their behavior through reason and understanding, or are they driven by unconscious desires?

How can people honor their HERITAGE?

Prompt students to think about their cultural and ethnic backgrounds. Ask students to share how they celebrate or honor these aspects of their identities.

What drives HUMAN BEHAVIOR?

Challenge students to think about times when they have acted without thinking. Have them contrast this behavior with a time when they carefully planned a particular action. Invite students to contrast what motivates their behavior during these different times.

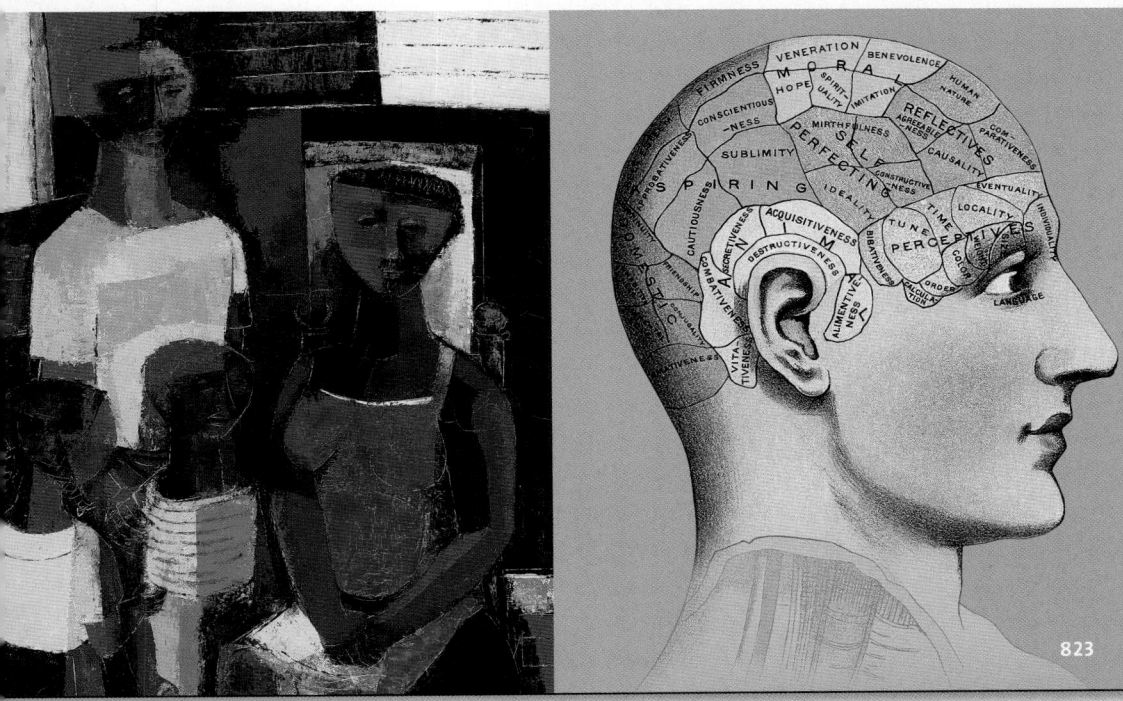

823

OBJECTIVES

- understand the Harlem Renaissance and modernism as literary movements
- understand the historical and cultural context of the Harlem Renaissance and modernism
- take notes by charting main ideas and details

 R3.5

To provide a motivating introduction to this unit and to give students a sense of time and place for modern American writing, see

 Literature in Context DVD

The following essay (pages 824–833) provides students with a historical context for the Unit 5 reading selections. It presents a brief overview of significant events occurring during the time period 1910–1940 and introduces key people, places, and ideas of the times.

To get started, read and discuss the opening paragraph on page 824. Call students' attention to key events: World War I, the economic boom of the Roaring Twenties, the passage of the 19th Amendment giving women the right to vote, the Great Depression. Ask students to speculate how each of these events helped create "a whole new world." Discuss the challenges that Americans of this era faced, and ask why writers of the time would have been motivated to search for new truths.

READING STRATEGY

■ PREVIEW

Have students preview the historical essay by reading the *KEY IDEAS* and by skimming the heads, boldfaced terms, and **Taking Notes** side-column features. Ask volunteers to summarize what the essay is about.

About the Art American artist John Sloan (1871–1951) painted scenes of New York life throughout his career. His art reflects real affection for the city, even its dirt and poverty. As *The City from Greenwich Village* shows, Sloan animated his paintings with a sense of movement and character.

The Harlem Renaissance and Modernism

1910–1940

A Changing Awareness

Change was the only constant for Americans in the early 20th century. In 30 short years, they faced a world war, an economic boom followed by the Great Depression, shifting attitudes toward women's place in society, and a mass culture that isolated and alienated the individual. In this swirl of uncertainty, traditional values seemed to slip out of reach or were actively discarded as Americans—writers and nonwriters alike—searched for truths in what felt like a whole new world.

824

DIFFERENTIATED INSTRUCTION

FOR STRATEGIC READERS
Preteach Academic Vocabulary

- *modernism,* "art or writing that reflects a loss of hope after World War I and believes individuals are threatened and isolated by society and mass culture"
- *influential,* "having or exerting power over another"
- *carnage,* "bloody, extended slaughter"
- *obscene,* "offensive to one's feelings or commonly held ideas of decency"
- *hedonism,* "the pursuit of pleasure as a way of life"
- *disillusioned,* "disappointed"
- *emancipated,* "freed from control or social expectations"

Use this copy master to help students take notes on the essay, pages 824–833:

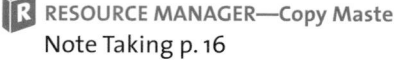 RESOURCE MANAGER—Copy Master
Note Taking p. 16

The Harlem Renaissance and Modernism: Historical Context

R3.5

KEY IDEAS Catastrophic historical events—including a devastating war and a deep economic depression—as well as rapid societal change profoundly affected the writing of this period.

A World at War

World War I—the **Great War**—was perhaps the most influential force on American writers of the early 20th century. The war broke out in Europe in 1914; before it ended in 1918, it involved 32 nations, including the United States, and took the lives of over 20 million people. It was a new kind of war, waged on a massive scale with terrible new weapons that reflected the technological advances of the time—machine guns, poison gases, airplane bombers, and submarines. Old ideals about the purposes and meaning of war were destroyed in the carnage. As Lieutenant Frederic Henry, a character in **Ernest Hemingway's** 1929 novel *A Farewell to Arms,* observed: "Words such as glory, honor, courage, or hallow were obscene." For many Americans, the war signaled an end to idealism and ushered in an era marked by hedonism, political corruption, and ruthless business practices.

The Jazz Age

Some Americans, disillusioned with the traditional values that had led to war, sought escape in the pleasures of entertainment and good times. The 1920s, with its booming economy, became known as the **Roaring Twenties.** Writer **F. Scott Fitzgerald** called this decade "the greatest, gaudiest spree in history." As incomes rose, people were able to spend more money on goods and leisure activities. In addition, many young people began, for the first time, to rebel as a group against the values of the past and the authority of their elders. They experimented with new fashions and new attitudes, actively seeking out fun and freedom.

A NEW ERA FOR WOMEN Women of the period saw their lives change in fundamental ways. In 1920, the passage of the **19th Amendment** finally gave women the right to vote. But the vote was just one facet of the changing nature of womanhood. The 1920s saw the emergence of the **flapper,** an emancipated young woman who embraced new fashions and the urban attitudes of the day. By 1930, ten million American women were earning wages in the workplace—another new frontier. In addition, family life was made increasingly easier by technological innovations, from ready-made clothes to sliced bread. Many women writers, such as **Edna St. Vincent Millay** and **Dorothy Parker,** were celebrated as much for their modern lifestyles as for their writing. In turn, they often wrote about the clash between traditional and modern values, celebrating youth, independence, and freedom from social constraints.

The City from Greenwich Village (1922), John Sloan. Gift of Helen Farr Sloan. © 2006 Board of Trustees, National Gallery of Art, Washington, D.C. 1970.1.1 Photo © Superstock.

> ▶ **TAKING NOTES**
>
> **Outlining** As you read each section of this introduction, add the information you learn to an outline like the one started for you here. You can use headings, boldfaced terms, and the information in these boxes as starting points. (See page R49 in the **Research Handbook** for more help with outlining.)
>
> I. *Historical Context*
>
>   A. *A World at War*
>   1. *influence on writers*
>   2. *affected millions*
>   3. *new kind of war*
>   4. *destroyed ideals*
>   B. *The Jazz Age*

> ⟳ **ADDITIONAL BACKGROUND**
> for more on the Harlem Renaissance and modernism, visit the **Literature Center** at **ClassZone.com.**

The Harlem Renaissance and Modernism: Historical Context

KEY IDEAS This section of the essay (pages 825–826) tells how modern American writers described the catastrophic historical events and rapid societal change that occurred in this period of American history. The text also explains the changing nature of war, of women's roles, and of the role government plays in American culture.

TIERED DISCUSSION PROMPTS

Use these prompts to help students understand the ideas in **A World at War:**

Summarize How was World War I different from previous wars? *Possible answer: World War I was waged on a massive scale, using terrible new technological weapons such as machine guns, poison gas, airplane bombers, and submarines.*

Analyze How does the quotation from *A Farewell to Arms* illustrate the effect new methods of warfare had on people's beliefs? Explain. *Possible answer: The quotation shows how new methods of warfare led people to realize that human ingenuity could bring about death on a massive scale. With this realization, people questioned whether they could believe in values such as courage, glory, and honor.*

FOR ENGLISH LEARNERS

Set a Purpose After introducing the *KEY IDEAS,* ask students to look for supporting details as they read about how historical catastrophe and societal change redefined American values.

FOR ADVANCED LEARNERS/AP

Brainstorm Ask students to use their prior knowledge of the historical period from 1910 to 1940. Then have them brainstorm a list of the catastrophic historical events and societal changes that writers would have been most likely to chronicle. Have students discuss which items on their list proved to have the greatest cultural significance, and why.

CHECK UNDERSTANDING

Have students describe the significance of these items:

- "Great War"
- Roaring Twenties
- 19th Amendment
- Prohibition
- Jazz Age
- Great Depression
- Dust Bowl
- New Deal

TIERED DISCUSSION PROMPTS

Use these prompts to help students understand the ideas in **The Great Depression:**

Summarize What were two main causes of the Great Depression? *Possible answer: The stock market crash of 1929 and a severe drought in the early 1930s were two main causes of the Great Depression.*

Analyze How was President Roosevelt's New Deal a different approach to solving the nation's economic problems? *Possible answer: Roosevelt's New Deal took the approach that government spending could help solve economic problems.*

About the Art *Migrant Mother* (1936) is a photograph by Dorothea Lange (1895–1965). During the Depression, the government hired Lange to photograph people affected by poverty in California. Lange would casually talk with people in the labor camps until she established a rapport and then she would photograph them. Because of these human connections, Lange's photographs reflect an understanding of her subjects. *Migrant Mother* is one of Lange's most famous works.

JAZZ CULTURE This period also saw the passage of **Prohibition** (1920–1933), in which alcohol was made illegal. In defiance of this restriction, many people drank in illegal nightclubs called speakeasies, as gangsters made fortunes running and supplying the clubs. At the fancy Cotton Club in New York's Harlem neighborhood, the guests—all whites—rubbed shoulders with celebrities and gangsters as they listened to the great jazz performers—all blacks—who helped give the era its name: the **Jazz Age.**

The Great Depression

The good times came to a dramatic end when the stock market crashed in October 1929, plunging the nation into economic depression. During the **Great Depression**, so called for its length and severity, many banks failed, businesses floundered, and workers lost their jobs. By 1933, the unemployment rate had grown to 25 percent. Unable to pay their bills, thousands of people lost their homes, and millions went hungry.

THE DUST BOWL A severe drought that began in the early 1930s added to the nation's pain. When the drought began, winds picked up dirt from the dry, exhausted fields of the Great Plains. Huge dust storms arose, damaging farms across a 150,000-square-mile region called the **Dust Bowl.**

Ruined farmers set off with their families to find work, many traveling west to California. Unfortunately, little work was to be found in California, for it, like the rest of the nation, was suffering through the Great Depression. Writers such as **John Steinbeck** captured the uncertainty and despair of the times: "Carloads, caravans, homeless and hungry; twenty thousand and fifty thousand and a hundred thousand and two hundred thousand. They streamed over the mountains, hungry and restless—restless as ants, scurrying to find work to do."

Migrant Mother by Dorothea Lange, 1936. This photograph of Florence Owens Thompson with her children came to symbolize the Great Depression for many Americans.

THE NEW DEAL The country was desperate for help. During his presidential campaign in 1932, Franklin Delano Roosevelt pledged to give the country a "new deal." When elected, he fulfilled his promise by enacting various **New Deal** programs—relief for the homeless and hungry, recovery for agriculture and business, and various economic reforms to prevent such a severe depression from occurring again. Yet in truth, it was the massive spending and production spurred by World War II that finally brought the economic crisis to an end.

DIFFERENTIATED INSTRUCTION

FOR STRATEGIC READERS
Preteach Academic Vocabulary

- *homogenization,* "made identical or similar"
- *conformity,* "following common rules, customs, or attitudes"
- *materialism,* "interest in material goods instead of spiritual or intellectual pursuits"
- *unconscious,* "not realized or intended"

FOR ENGLISH LEARNERS
Analyze Cultural Influences Have students paraphrase the **KEY IDEAS** on page 827. After they read the section, ask them to explain and give an example of the listed terms, then explain an idea linked to the listed names:

Terms	Names
• mass culture	• Albert Einstein
• mass media	• Sigmund Freud
• mass production	• Karl Marx

Cultural Influences

KEY IDEAS A developing mass culture and ideas that challenged traditional thought provided fodder for writers of the time.

New Directions

MASS CULTURE The 1920s was the first decade to be significantly shaped by **mass media.** New goods—from cars to toasters to beauty products—were flooding the market, and businesses relied on advertising to sell them. Thanks to advertising, items people had formerly considered luxuries were now deemed necessities. Mass media quickly became the ultimate source for this manufacturing of desire.

    Mass production quickly and efficiently produced Americans' newfound necessities, but efficiency came with a price. Henry Ford perfected the assembly-line system, but its repetitiveness and monotony reduced workers to nameless, faceless cogs in the production process. And its products, efficiently mass-produced, led to the homogenization of American culture. **Sinclair Lewis** and many other significant writers of the day were alienated by the new values and lifestyles of their peers and soon began to criticize what they saw as Americans' conformity and materialism.

NEW IDEAS The writers of this period were also influenced by exciting new ideas that were challenging Americans' traditional views. A literary technique called **stream of consciousness** developed from the psychoanalytic theories of **Sigmund Freud**, who proposed that unconscious forces drive human beings and that the key to understanding behavior lay in this deeper realm of the mind. **Karl Marx's** socioeconomic theories—that history is a constant struggle between classes, for example—found their way into some of the literature of the day, mainly that of Depression-era writers. And **Albert Einstein's** theory that everything is relative, that there are no absolutes, offered writers a fresh new way of looking at the world.

Print advertisements from the 1920s and 1930s

A Voice from the Times

It's the fellow with four to ten thousand a year . . . and an automobile and a nice little family in a bungalow . . . that makes the wheels of progress go round! That's the type of fellow that's ruling America today[!]

—Sinclair Lewis
from *Babbitt*

Cultural Influences

KEY IDEAS This section of the essay (page 827) explains the effect of mass media and mass production on American culture. The text also points out the effects of such thinkers as Freud, Marx, and Einstein on American writers.

TIERED DISCUSSION PROMPTS

Use these prompts to help students understand the ideas in **New Directions:**

Recall What effect did advertising have on Americans? ***Possible answer:*** *Items once viewed as luxuries became necessities.*

Interpret What does Lewis mean by the comment that it's "the fellow with . . . an automobile and a nice little family" who's ruling America? ***Possible answer:*** *Lewis suggests that because companies want to sell their products, real power to promote the progress of new ideas comes from the ordinary people who can buy those products rather than from officials and executives.*

Evaluate Is Marx correct in his theory that history is a constant struggle between classes? Explain. ***Possible answer:*** *Marx is correct that history often shows those in power trying to keep their power and those without power trying to get some power.*

CHECK UNDERSTANDING

Have students describe the significance of these ideas in American culture and writing:

- conformity
- materialism
- stream-of-consciousness

FOR STRATEGIC READERS

Main Ideas and Supporting Details Have students carefully examine the advertisements on page 827, noting composition, color, shape, and text. Point out that each advertisement bears the title of the product advertised, but very little copy to describe it. Instead, each advertisement relies upon associations with objects and colors to sell its product. Ask students which images draw their attention and what associations they make with the colors and shapes. Then point out the importance of the placement of objects to create certain suggestions in the viewer's mind, such as suggesting elegance by arranging the electric cord to resemble fancy script in the advertisement for vacuum cleaners. Link this discussion and the art images to the main ideas in **Cultural Influences** by pointing out how these advertisements "manufacture desire." Ask students to explain the role of advertising and to summarize how mass culture affected the writers of the 1920s.

FOR ADVANCED LEARNERS/AP

Research New Ideas Have students learn more about the theories of Freud, Marx, and Einstein. Invite students to make informal oral presentations to the class, sharing their findings and explaining how the theories of these men are reflected or refuted in contemporary American life.

KEY IDEAS This section of the essay (pages 828–833) focuses on modern American writing. The text describes

- new poetic literary movements, including modernism, imagism, and objectivism
- modern short stories
- the works of the Harlem Renaissance

TIERED DISCUSSION PROMPTS

Use these prompts to help students understand the ideas in **The New Poetry:**

Summarize What were the concerns of poets at the beginning of the 20th century? *Possible answer: Poets at that time were concerned with the effects of industrialization, war, threats to individualism, mass culture, and urbanization.*

Interpret What does Williams mean when he says that "there are no ideas but in things"? *Possible answer: Ideas must be concrete, as captured in actual objects, rather than abstract.*

Synthesize In what ways was modernist poetry a response to mass society of the time? Explain. *Possible answer: Modernist poets saw mass society as a threat to individualism. Therefore, their poetry emphasized experimentation and a rejection of past forms in favor of new modes of expression.*

Modern Literature and the Harlem Renaissance

KEY IDEAS The writers of this period, working in a variety of genres and focusing on discrete themes, were markedly influenced by the events and culture of the day. Many responded by embracing all things new, while others celebrated their heritage.

The New Poetry

At the beginnning of the century, rapid industrialization and urbanization caused many Americans to feel that the social order governing their lives was crumbling. Poets of the day began to explore in their work the impact of rapid change and uncertainty on the individual.

Edgar Lee Masters, in his famous collection *Spoon River Anthology,* used free verse to probe the discontent beneath the apparent stability of small-town life in the United States. *Spoon River Anthology* found a wide audience, in part because it voiced concerns shared by many Americans about the transformation from a rural to an industrialized society. Like Masters, **Edwin Arlington Robinson** also exposed the tensions underlying small-town life. His poems draw psychological portraits of characters isolated in the midst of American society. In portraying their isolation, Robinson was a forerunner of the modernist movement. These poets charted new territory by challenging conventional attitudes.

Others, such as **Carl Sandburg, Robert Frost,** and **Edna St. Vincent Millay,** seemed to be more connected to earlier traditions that focused on nature and common people. Yet they, too, revealed an awareness of the changes sweeping the American landscape. For this reason, Millay, Sandburg, and Frost can be called transitional poets, those who connect past traditions with modern thought.

MODERNISM Other poets of this period belong to the literary movement called **modernism** (see page 894). Modernism arose as a direct response to the social and intellectual forces shaping the 20th century. Modernist writers, many of whom were expatriates living in Europe, responded to the loss of idealism they felt in the wake of World War I. Living abroad, they experienced both the immediate and the long-term effects of World War I more acutely than did Americans at home. Most modernists also saw mass society as a threat to the individual, especially the artist. They felt that the standardization of culture resulted in alienation—a theme they captured in their work.

Experimentation was a distinguishing characteristic of these writers. "Make it new," extolled **Ezra Pound** as he urged fellow poets to abandon the artifice of past forms and search for their individual voices. **Harriet Monroe,** editor of *Poetry* magazine, wrote that the new poetry "has set before itself an ideal of absolute simplicity and sincerity—an ideal which implies an individual, unstereotyped diction; and an individual, unstereotyped rhythm." The lack of

Works by transitional poets Millay, Frost, and Sandburg

▶ *For Your Outline*

THE NEW POETRY

- Poets began to challenge conventional thought.
- Modernists responded to historical forces such as WWI and an increasing mass society.
- Experimentation characterized modernism.
- Imagists believed that poetry should be expressed through the "rendering of concrete objects."
- Imagists favored free verse.
- In objectivist poetry, objects speak for themselves.

DIFFERENTIATED INSTRUCTION

FOR STRATEGIC READERS

Concept Support Share the definitions; then direct students to examples:

- *free verse,* "poetry without any predictable patterns" (pages 914–924)
- *rhyme or metric scheme,* "predictable pattern of sound and rhythm" (pages 514–536)

Have students use the examples to show their understanding of the concepts.

FOR ENGLISH LEARNERS

Modern Literature Have students paraphrase the *KEY IDEAS.* Emphasize that one aspect of modern literature was experimentation. Writers, like chemists in a laboratory, experimented with language, grammar, tradition, and the work of other writers—mixing and rejecting these elements to discover varying effects.

"stereotypes," however, made any recognizable movement hard to sustain: as soon as a style became accepted, it also became a new standard against which to rebel. The result was that modernist poetry as a body of work is as fragmented as many of its individual poems.

IMAGISM Many of the so-called new poets did, however, share the belief that poetry is most profoundly expressed through the "rendering of concrete objects." Ezra Pound called this kind of poetry **imagism** because it sought to re-create an image—not comment on it, not interpret it, but just present it. Pound became the center of a circle of poets, including **H. D.** (Hilda Doolittle) and **Amy Lowell,** who cast off the sentimentality, formal structures, and rhyme schemes of their predecessors and exploded into **free verse** (poetry without a predictable rhyme or metric scheme). Ezra Pound was especially taken with the poetry of **T. S. Eliot,** whose *The Waste Land* is considered one of the most representative and influential of modernist poems.

OBJECTIVISM One modernist poet, **William Carlos Williams,** however, vehemently disliked *The Waste Land* for its intellectualism and its references to classical literature. In response to Eliot's complex ideas and academic references, Williams famously stated that there are "no ideas but in things." Williams became the center of a new movement in modernist poetry called **objectivism,** in which poets let the objects they rendered speak for themselves. These poets invited readers to experience the homely simplicity of an object for no other reason than to understand its "this-ness."

The modernist movement had an enormous impact on later poets. Many poets today prefer to communicate through images rather than direct statements. They believe in economy of words and continue to experiment with free verse. Poetry had been altered irrevocably.

> **A Voice from the Times**
>
> so much depends
> upon
>
> a red wheel
> barrow
>
> glazed with rain
> water
>
> beside the white
> chickens.
>
> —**William Carlos Williams**
> "The Red Wheelbarrow"

Sculpture inspired by William Carlos Williams's poem
The Red Wheelbarrow (1992), Frank Jensen. © Frank Jensen.

CHECK UNDERSTANDING

Have students describe the significance of these movements:

- modernism
- imagism
- objectivism

About the Art Franklin L. Jensen was born in 1933 and is based in Augusta, Kansas. Many of his sculptures, such as *The Red Wheelbarrow*, were inspired by works of literature. Point out to students that *The Red Wheelbarrow* was created from found pieces of junk. Ask them how this information could help them to view the sculpture in terms of modernist ideas. ***Possible answer:*** *Students might answer that Jensen's use of discarded material recalls Ezra Pound's dictum to "make it new," while the sculpture as a whole speaks to Williams's notion that "there are no ideas but in things."*

FOR STRATEGIC READERS

Preteach Academic Vocabulary

- *industrialization,* "growth of large industries, machine production, and the number of workers in cities"

- *idealism,* "seeing the world as it should be or as one would wish it to be"

- *standardization,* "without variations or differences"

- *alienation,* "feeling of being separate or unconnected"

FOR ADVANCED LEARNERS/AP

Analyze [paired option] Challenge students to respond to William Carlos Williams's poem "The Red Wheelbarrow" in the light of his statement that "there are no ideas but in things." Have pairs of students brainstorm a list of ideas that the poem conveys. Then have pairs share those ideas with the class.

The Modern Short Story

Poetry was not the only form popular during this period. In fact, the period from 1890 to 1930 has been called "the Age of the Short Story" in American literature. The great popularity of the short story has often been attributed to the American temperament. Americans living in the first half of the 20th century were too impatient and too much in a hurry to read longer works. They wanted "fast" literature, just as Americans today want fast food.

Other factors contributed to the popularity of the short story as well. New methods of advertising had brought about a boom in magazine publication. As the number of magazines grew, so did the demand for short stories. In turn, magazines paid their writers handsome fees. At one point, **F. Scott Fitzgerald** was receiving as much as $4,000 for a single story. **William Faulkner,** who complained that writing short stories interfered with his more serious, longer works, earned more from the sale of four short stories to the *Saturday Evening Post* than he did from his first four novels.

THEMES PULLED FROM LIFE The upheavals of this period in American history provided rich fodder for short story writers. World War I turned many Americans' idealism into uncertainty. Civilization as people had known it was being destroyed, and writers sought to capture in their work the resulting alienation and confusion. Indeed, World War I shook the ideological foundations of some young American writers so profoundly that **Gertrude Stein,** an American writer living in Paris, called them **"the lost generation."**

These alienated writers broke with the traditions of the past, turning to new methods and stylistic devices to carry their themes. **Ernest Hemingway** and other writers composed short, fragmentary stories without traditional beginnings or endings. They left out a narrative voice, leaving readers alone to figure out what might be going on or what a character might be feeling. "I always try to write on the principle of the iceberg," Hemingway said. "There is seven-eighths of it under water for every part that shows."

The boom years of the Roaring Twenties inspired its own literature. Writers such as **F. Scott Fitzgerald** revealed the negative side of the period's gaiety and freedom by portraying wealthy and attractive people leading empty lives in their gilded surroundings. Writer **John Steinbeck** is most closely identified with the bust years of the Great Depression. Declaring that a writer's duty is to "set down his time as nearly as he can understand it," Steinbeck managed to tell, perhaps better than anyone else, the stories of ordinary people caught up

An illustration of the Roaring Twenties high life, which served as inspiration for writers such as F. Scott Fitzgerald

▶ *For Your Outline*

MODERN SHORT STORY

- 1890–1930 called the "Age of the Short Story"
- stories' popularity due to American temperament and growth of magazines
- "lost generation" alienated by WWI
- wrote fragmentary stories without traditional beginning or ending

THE HARLEM RENAISSANCE

- a flowering of African-American arts
- expressions of what it meant to be black in a white-dominated world
- came to an end with the Great Depression

Use these prompts to help students discuss **The Modern Short Story:**

Recall Why did the short story become popular in the early 20th century? ***Possible answer:*** *The popularity of the short story in the early 20th century may relate to Americans' short attention span or to the boom in the publication of magazines needing short stories to fill their pages.*

Interpret What did Stein mean when she called young Americans a "lost generation?" ***Possible answer:*** *Stein called young Americans a "lost generation" because World War I had undermined the ideals on which they had grown up. They felt lost because they were no longer sure of what it meant to be an American.*

Evaluate Explain whether Hemingway's principle of writing is a good one. ***Possible answer:*** *Forcing readers to look below the surface of a story is a good way to involve readers in the creative process.*

DIFFERENTIATED INSTRUCTION

FOR STRATEGIC READERS
Preteach Academic Vocabulary

- *temperament,* "one's usual frame of mind or natural mood"
- *upheaval,* "sudden, violent change"
- *ideological,* "related to the views or opinions of an individual or group"
- *generation,* "all the people born in a certain time period"

FOR ADVANCED LEARNERS/AP
The Writer's Duty Have students locate literature by F. Scott Fitzgerald, William Faulkner, Gertrude Stein, John Steinbeck, Ernest Hemingway, or Eudora Welty. Note Steinbeck's view that it is each writer's duty to "set down his time as nearly as he can understand it," and ask students to use the literature to conclude what their writer understood about his or her time period. Invite students to share their conclusions.

in the Great Depression and lost from the devastation of the Dust Bowl.

Steinbeck, **Eudora Welty,** and many other writers of the time were beneficiaries of one of President Roosevelt's New Deal programs, the Works Progress Administration (WPA). The WPA was set up to create as many jobs as possible, as quickly as possible, including work for the nation's artists and writers. As the head of the WPA put it, "They've got to eat just like other people." Eudora Welty traveled around Mississippi for the WPA, writing articles about various projects under way in the state. She later said that these travels introduced her to the very different ways in which people lived, inspiring her later writing.

The Harlem Renaissance

Beginning in 1916 and continuing throughout the 1920s, in what came to be known as the **Great Migration,** millions of black farmers and sharecroppers moved to the urban North in search of opportunity and freedom from oppression and racial hostility. Thousands of these migrants settled in Harlem, a New York City neighborhood that quickly became the cultural center of African-American life.

Soon, the very air in Harlem seemed charged with creativity as black men and women drew on their own cultural resources—their folk traditions as well as a new urban awareness—to produce unique forms of expression. Harlem attracted worldly and race-conscious African Americans who nurtured each other's artistic, musical, and literary talents and created a flowering of African-American arts known as the **Harlem Renaissance.**

A LITERARY MOVEMENT The event that unofficially kicked off the Harlem Renaissance as a literary movement was a dinner given on March 21, 1924. Some of the nation's most celebrated writers and thinkers, black and white, gathered at New York City's Civic Club. The sponsors of the dinner— an older generation of African-American intellectuals that included **W. E. B. Du Bois, James Weldon Johnson,** and **Charles S. Johnson**—had begun organizations such as the National Urban League and the National Association for the Advancement of Colored People to promote equality for African Americans. These organizations published journals in which the writings of a younger generation were first published. **Countee Cullen, Zora Neale Hurston,** and **Langston Hughes** were among the young writers who received recognition and sometimes cash awards for

832   UNIT 5: THE HARLEM RENAISSANCE AND MODERNISM

TIERED DISCUSSION PROMPTS

Use these prompts to continue discussion of **The Harlem Renaissance:**

Recall Despite differences in their backgrounds, what did the writers of the Harlem Renaissance share? *Possible answer: The writers of the Harlem Renaissance shared a deep pride in their heritage and cultural identity.*

Interpret What did Langston Hughes mean when he said that "jazz is a heartbeat"? *Possible answer: Hughes used this metaphor to suggest that jazz music is a life force. It is not an art that someone practices. Jazz must be lived.*

Evaluate Is writing literature an effective means of creating a cultural identity? Explain. *Possible answer: Literature is an effective means of creating a cultural identity because members of a culture can read about those living similar lives or with similar values and concerns.*

their work in these journals, and many were present at this "coming-out party" for the writers of the Harlem Renaissance.

These young writers considered themselves the founders of a new era in literature. They looked inward and expressed what it meant to be black in a white-dominated world. They represented what came to be called "the New Negro," a sophisticated and well-educated African American with strong racial pride and self-awareness. In fact, connections made at that dinner led to a popular and enduring anthology of writing, published in 1925, titled *The New Negro.*

MANY VOICES Yet this new generation of writers did not speak with only one voice. Harvard-educated **Countee Cullen,** for example, used a classical style to explore the black struggle. Others cast off more formal language and styles and wrote with the pulse of jazz rhythms. "Jazz is a heartbeat," wrote Langston Hughes, "and its heartbeat is yours." Some, like Jamaican-born **Claude McKay,** were militant. McKay's poem "If We Must Die," written after race riots in 1919, ends with an image of African Americans "pressed to the wall, dying, but fighting back!" Others, such as **Jean Toomer,** were more interested in exploring their own identities than the concerns of a whole race. "I was inescapably myself," he wrote. Despite their varied perspectives, however, these writers shared a deep pride in their heritage and asserted their cultural identity through their work.

Zora Neale Hurston, Harlem Renaissance writer

The Harlem Renaissance was brought to a premature end by the economic collapse of the Great Depression. Many of the writers who had gathered in Harlem were forced to scatter and take other jobs to support themselves. Nevertheless, their work planted seeds that continue to generate important writing from the African-American perspective.

Journalism as Literature

In the early decades of the 20th century, journalism came into its own as an influential part of the literary scene (see page 1046). The sensationalism and reckless misinterpretation of facts that had characterized journalism in the last decades of the 19th century were being replaced by an interest in stylistic quality and the recognition that there was more to news than scandal. Many of the writers who were to become major figures in American literature learned their craft—and developed some of their most compelling subjects—writing for newspapers or magazines.

REPORTING THE ERA Fresh out of high school in 1917, **Ernest Hemingway** worked as a reporter for the *Kansas City Star.* The newspaper's strict rules of

> ▶ *For Your Outline*
>
> **JOURNALISM AS LITERATURE**
>
> - Journalism turned from sensationalism.
> - Writers honed their craft at newspapers and magazines.
> - Hemingway, Porter, and Steinbeck reported on the day's big news
> - White, Thurber, and Parker built their reputations at *New Yorker.*

DIFFERENTIATED INSTRUCTION

FOR ADVANCED LEARNERS/AP

Compare Fiction and Nonfiction [small-group option] Have students locate nonfiction articles by Ernest Hemingway, Katherine Anne Porter, and John Steinbeck. Then direct them to fiction by each of these authors, such as the samples collected for the activity on page 830 or showcased on pages 968, 978, or 988. After reading the samples, ask each group to focus on one writer. Have students compare the writer's fiction and nonfiction work.

Students should comment on these literary elements:

- subject
- style
- theme

Ask students to share their results with the class through short, informal oral presentations.

style helped him develop the clear, provocative prose that characterizes his work: "Use short sentences. Use short first paragraphs. Use vigorous English. Be positive, not negative." Hemingway was also a war correspondent who reported on the Spanish Civil War, and he was the first Allied journalist to enter Paris on August 25, 1944—the day it was liberated from Nazi control.

Some other writers who became well-known for their fiction produced fine journalism as well. **Katherine Anne Porter,** for example, worked for several newspapers and magazines. On assignment in 1920, she traveled to Mexico and arrived in the middle of a revolution. Her observations of this conflict later became the subject of several short stories in a collection called *Flowering Judas* (1930), which launched her literary career. **John Steinbeck** turned his hand to journalism as well, reporting in 1936 for the *San Francisco News* about the plight of California's migrant farm workers and working in 1943 as a war correspondent for the *New York Herald Tribune*.

MAGAZINES ON THE RISE In the first decades of the 20th century, the popular magazine came into its own as new magazines were created to satisfy every taste and interest. The *New Yorker,* which first appeared in 1925, was founded by one-time newspaperman **Harold Ross.** To staff his new magazine, Ross sought writers with newspaper experience, writers who could grind out "the gleams and sparkles of humor and satire from the grist of human nature and the news of the world." Among them were **E. B. White, James Thurber,** and **Dorothy Parker,** who went on to write poetry, short stories, and novels. Yet these writers' reputations as witty, satiric observers of contemporary society were built on the essays, commentary, and book and theater reviews (and in the case of Thurber, cartoons too) that they contributed to the *New Yorker.*

Like poetry and short stories, literary journalism continues to be popular. Today's writers can thank the innovators of the modernist movement, America's giants of the short story form, the groundbreaking writers of the Harlem Renaissance, and the literary journalists of this earlier era for many of the themes, styles, and forms currently in use.

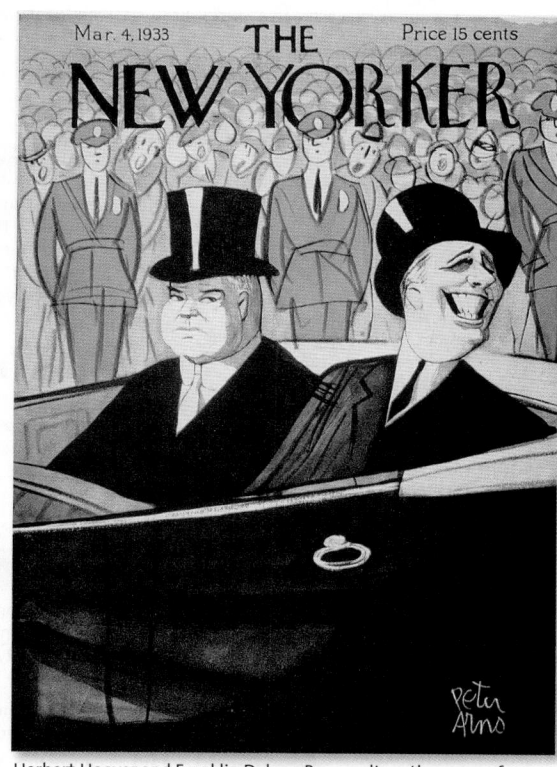

Herbert Hoover and Franklin Delano Roosevelt on the cover of the *New Yorker*, 1933

TIERED DISCUSSION PROMPTS

Use these prompts to help students understand the ideas in **Journalism as Literature:**

Recall How did many modern American writers develop their craft? *Possible answer: Many modern American writers developed their craft by writing for newspapers and magazines.*

Synthesize How might reporting on war or labor help writers develop their fiction? *Possible answer: Although fiction is imaginary, its primary focus is the human condition. Reporting on real instances of the human condition could help writers make their fiction more realistic and insightful.*

Evaluate Which is more valuable for humanity—literature or journalism? Explain. *Possible answer: Both literature and journalism have important value to humanity. Journalism chronicles current history, making people aware of their surroundings. Literature chronicles universal themes, forging connections among people.*

CHECK UNDERSTANDING

Have students describe the significance of these ideas, events, and terms:

- "lost generation"
- Great Migration
- Harlem Renaissance
- journalism

FOR STRATEGIC READERS
Preteach Academic Vocabulary

- *cultural identity,* "sense of self as it relates to one's culture"
- *sensationalism,* "use of very emotional material in order to shock or startle"
- *provocative,* "intending to provoke or invite action, thought, or feeling"
- *migrant,* "someone who moves from place to place"

FOR ADVANCED LEARNERS/AP

Synthesize Point out and have students discuss the idea that modern thinkers and writers embraced the new and, at the same time, celebrated the past through heritage. Ask students to discuss whether the same can be said of contemporary Americans. Challenge students to identify specific cultural examples to support this assessment or to provide an alternate characterization of contemporary American values.

Connecting Literature, History, and Culture

OBJECTIVES
- read a timeline
- make connections among the perspectives and events of literature, history, and culture

READING SKILL

■ READ A TIMELINE

Point out that each of the three horizontal sections of the timeline—*American Literary Milestones, Historical Context, World Culture and Events*—displays a sequence of events that occurred between 1910 and 1940. By looking at the vertical columns on the timeline, students can see which events were going on at approximately the same time.

Have students locate, for example, each of these events on the timeline between 1910 and 1914:

- **1911** Marie Curie won the Nobel Prize for chemistry. (See *World Culture and Events*.)

- **1912** *Titanic* sank, killing more than 1,500 people. (See *Historical Context*.)

- **1913** Ezra Pound formed an imagist group of poets in London. (See *American Literary Milestones*.)

Ask students to identify events that occurred between 1936 and 1940. ***Answer:*** *Margaret Mitchell published* Gone with the Wind. *Zora Neale Hurston's* Their Eyes Were Watching God *was published. Richard Wright's* Native Son *was published. The Fair Labor Standards Act set a minimum wage and limited the workweek to 40 hours. Judy Garland starred in* The Wizard of Oz. *The Spanish Civil War broke out. Japan invaded China. World War II began with the German invasion of Poland.*

Connecting Literature, History, and Culture

The literature and culture of the United States during this period reflect developments occurring elsewhere in the world. Use the timeline and the questions on the next page to find connections.

AMERICAN LITERARY MILESTONES

1910	1915	1920
1912 Harriet Monroe founds *Poetry: A Magazine of Verse*; Edna St. Vincent Millay publishes "Renascence."	**1915** Edgar Lee Masters examines small-town life in *Spoon River Anthology*.	**1920** Edith Wharton's *The Age of Innocence* is published.
1913 Ezra Pound forms a group of imagist poets in London.	**1916** Carl Sandburg publishes *Chicago Poems*.	**1921** Langston Hughes's poem "The Negro Speaks of Rivers" appears in *The Crisis* magazine.
	1919 Claude McKay publishes his militant "If We Must Die."	**1922** T. S. Eliot's *The Waste Land* captures modern sensibilities.
		1924 Robert Frost wins the first of his four Pulitzer Prizes.

HISTORICAL CONTEXT

1910	1915	1920
1911 The National Urban League is founded.	**1916** Jeannette Rankin of Montana becomes the first woman elected to the U.S. House of Representatives.	**1920** The 18th Amendment ushers in the era of Prohibition, and the 19th Amendment assures women of the right to vote.
1912 The *Titanic* sinks, killing more than 1,500 people.	**1917** The United States enters World War I.	**1921** Albert Einstein presents a lecture in New York City about his theory of relativity.
1913 The Armory Show in New York City introduces European modernist paintings and sculpture to shocked Americans.	**1919** Race riots break out in 25 U.S. cities. 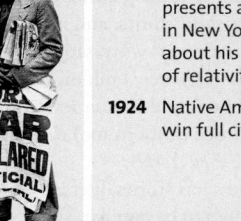	**1924** Native Americans win full citizenship.

WORLD CULTURE AND EVENTS

1910	1915	1920
1911 Marie Curie wins the Nobel Prize in chemistry.	**1915** The short story "Rashomon" by Japanese modernist writer Akutagawa Ryunosuke is published.	**1922** James Joyce publishes his masterpiece, *Ulysses*.
1914 World War I begins with the assassination of Archduke Francis Ferdinand of Austria.	**1918** A flu pandemic kills more than 20 million people worldwide.	**1923** Sigmund Freud publishes *The Ego and the Id*, examining the causes of human behavior.
	1919 The Treaty of Versailles spells out the peace terms for the end of World War I.	

DIFFERENTIATED INSTRUCTION

FOR STRATEGIC READERS

Understanding a Timeline Explain that the timeline runs chronologically (in time order) from left to right across the page. Each of the four columns represents a five-year period between 1910 and 1940. The three parallel rows of the timeline represent events occurring simultaneously. By comparing the three rows, readers can better understand what events in literature, history, and culture were taking place at about the same time.

MAKING CONNECTIONS

- Why was the year 1913 an important one for poetry and art?
- Violence stirred in the years between 1910 and 1940. Give an example from each of the three main sections of the timeline that support this observation.
- Name three women of this period who were gaining recognition or breaking barriers in literature, politics, and science.

1925	1930	1935
1925 F. Scott Fitzgerald's *The Great Gatsby* explores the American dream. **1926** Ernest Hemingway's novel *The Sun Also Rises* chronicles expatriates after WWI. **1929** William Faulkner's *The Sound and the Fury* experiments with stream of consciousness and multiple viewpoints.	**1930** *Flowering Judas* by Katherine Anne Porter is published. ▶ **1932** Pearl S. Buck wins a Pulitzer Prize for *The Good Earth*. **1933** William Faulkner's *A Green Bough* is published.	**1936** Margaret Mitchell publishes *Gone with the Wind*. **1937** Zora Neale Hurston's *Their Eyes Were Watching God* is published. **1940** Richard Wright's *Native Son* is published.

1925	1930	1935
1927 Charles Lindbergh makes his historic solo nonstop flight from New York to Paris; the first talking movie, *The Jazz Singer*, stars Al Jolson. **1929** The Wall Street stock market crashes and the Great Depression begins. ▼ 	**1931** The Empire State building is completed. ▶ **1932** Franklin Delano Roosevelt is elected president for the first of his four terms. **1933** Roosevelt's New Deal tries to put Americans back to work.	**1938** The Fair Labor Standards Act sets a minimum wage and limits the workweek to 40 hours. **1939** Judy Garland stars in *The Wizard of Oz*. ▼

1925	1930	1935
1925 Virginia Woolf's innovative novel *Mrs. Dalloway* is published in England. **1928** Joseph Stalin becomes dictator of Communist Russia. Chiang Kai-shek becomes head of the Nationalist government in China.	**1930** Mahatma Gandhi leads a nonviolent march to protest British taxes. **1932** Japan takes control of Manchuria. **1933** Adolf Hitler takes control of Germany.	**1936** The Spanish Civil War breaks out. **1937** Japan invades China. **1939** World War II begins with the German invasion of Poland.

MAKING CONNECTIONS
***Possible answers*:**

- *In 1913, Ezra Pound formed an imagist group of poets in London. In this same year, the Armory Show introduced European modernist paintings to a shocked America.*
- *These examples support the observation that violence stirred in the years between 1910 and 1940: Claude McKay published his militant "If We Must Die" (1919), the United States entered World War I (1917), and the Spanish Civil War broke out (1936).*
- *These women broke barriers or gained recognition: Zora Neale Hurston in literature, Jeanette Rankin in politics, and Marie Curie in science.*

ADDITIONAL QUESTIONS

1. The stream-of-consciousness technique employed by William Faulkner in *The Sound and the Fury,* published in 1929, may have been influenced by the publication of what work in 1923? ***Answer:** Sigmund Freud's* The Ego and the Id

2. The decadent American lifestyle chronicled in F. Scott Fitzgerald's *The Great Gatsby,* published in 1925, was undermined by what historic event in 1929? ***Answer:** the stock market crash*

FOR ADVANCED LEARNERS/AP

Making Additional Connections Ask students to choose one of the six time periods shown in the timeline and to research online, in encyclopedias, or in history texts other events that occurred during the five-year time span. Challenge students to identify events for each category: *American Literary Milestones, Historical Context,* and *World Culture and Events.* Have students prepare and present brief oral reports, summarizing significant events and discussing their connection to events shown in the timeline or discussed in class.

OBJECTIVE

- to connect the legacy of the Harlem Renaissance and modernism to present times

Mass Culture

Have students read the paragraph. (You may also want to ask students to review the section titled **New Directions** on page 827 of the historical essay.) Discuss the legacy of mass culture. Point out that it is nearly impossible for Americans to escape the effects—both positive and negative—of mass culture.

DISCUSS Have students suggest examples of mass culture. Make sure that students list examples from each of these categories:

- automobiles
- clothing
- electronics
- food
- media

Display students' examples on the board. Then have students agree on positive and negative effects to list in a two-column chart on the board. ***Possible answers: Positive effects:*** *speed, ease, efficiency;* ***negative effects:*** *materialism, conformity, intolerance.* Extend the discussion by asking students to suggest ways Americans could combat the negative effects of mass culture. Also, invite students to speculate on the future of American culture given the current trends in mass culture.

 BEST PRACTICES TOOLKIT—Transparency Two-Column Chart p. A25

The Legacy of the Era

Mass Culture

Many American writers of the early 20th century were reacting against a rising mass culture and the conformity and materialism they saw as its inevitable effects. These writers would likely be astounded to see the extent to which mass culture has overtaken the United States today. From the restaurant business, with nationwide chains replacing family-owned places, to a fashion scene in which only a very few styles (and sizes) are considered desirable—mass culture is everywhere you look.

DISCUSS In small groups, brainstorm ten examples of our current mass culture. Then discuss what you see as the effects—positive and negative—of mass culture on our society as a whole.

DIFFERENTIATED INSTRUCTION

FOR STRATEGIC READERS
Vocabulary Support

- *inevitable,* "cannot be avoided"
- *astounded,* "suddenly surprised"

FOR ADVANCED LEARNERS/AP

Track Mass Culture Have students create a timeline showing how an aspect of mass culture such as audio technology has evolved. For example, one could trace the journey from LP records to iPods. Have students annotate their timelines with dates, illustrations, descriptions, and the positive and negative effects of each incarnation. Invite students to draw conclusions about the effects of their topic on American culture and then to share their work.

Trends in Journalism

Many of the best writers of the early 20th century, such as Ernest Hemingway, E. B. White, and William Faulkner, sharpened their skills writing for newspapers and magazines. Today there is no shortage of talented journalists, yet the nature of the business has changed. Thousands of newspapers and magazines—one for nearly every conceivable interest—are printed every day. Twenty-four-hour news stations and Web sites give minute-by-minute accounts of current events, and blogs allow people to respond personally to the news.

QUICKWRITE With all of the venues available for today's writers to publish their ideas, how much of it is worthwhile literature? Is some simply a lot of hot air? Write several paragraphs sharing your opinions about today's journalists and the everyday people who, thanks to the Internet, can reach the masses with their words.

The New Deal Today

Several of President Roosevelt's New Deal programs remain in place today: Social Security (to pay out retirement pensions), the FDIC (to insure bank deposits), agricultural price supports (to protect farmers from price devaluation), and the SEC (to regulate the stock market). Yet some of these long-running programs have become politically controversial in today's world.

RESEARCH With a partner, research one of these programs. Summarize for your class why the program is politically controversial, what suggestions have been made to reform or eliminate it, and your opinion of its merit.

Trends in Journalism

Have students read the paragraph. Ask volunteers to summarize the text, explaining in their own words the prevalence of media in contemporary American culture.

QUICKWRITE Have students work in small groups to brainstorm the criteria for "worthwhile literature." Invite a spokesperson from each group to contribute ideas to a class rubric for "worthwhile literature." Then provide student groups with examples of media text from different sources, or have students contribute examples. Have students compare each example with the class rubric to determine its value. Encourage students to use these ideas and examples as they write their paragraphs.

The New Deal Today

Have students read the paragraph. Discuss what role the federal government should play in these areas: retirement, money and the economy, and agriculture. Extend the discussion by adding other topics to the list such as education and healthcare.

RESEARCH As students research their topics, recommend that they consult encyclopedias, Internet sites, and history texts. Suggest that students record their notes in a Three-Column Journal with these headings: *Controversy, Suggestions for Reform or Elimination,* and *Merit*. Remind students that their opinions regarding merit should be based on solid reasons, examples, and evidence.

 BEST PRACTICES TOOLKIT—Transparency
Three-Column Journal p. B10

FOR STRATEGIC READERS
Vocabulary Support

- *conceivable,* "that can be understood, imagined, or believed"

- *blogosphere,* "the environment, or 'world,' of Internet sites where people can post and exchange ideas"

- *venues,* "media outlets, such as the Internet, books, magazines, or newspapers"

- *controversial,* "likely to invite argument or disagreement"

FOR ADVANCED LEARNERS/AP
Write to Congress Have students use their research to write informed letters to their local Congressional members regarding the future of these continuing New Deal programs. Instruct students to express their opinions in business letter format and to use formal language. Encourage students to send their letters by mail or e-mail and to share any responses that they receive with the class.

Focus and Motivate

 R3.4

OBJECTIVES

Literary Analysis
- explore the key idea of **identity**
- analyze speaker
- read poetry

Reading
- analyze rhythm and repetition

 R3.4

ABOUT THE POET

After students read about Langston Hughes, recap main points, noting his focus on African-American experiences, his direct language, and his incorporation of musical structures and rhythms. Connect these points to the poems students will read. In "Harlem," Hughes captures the fragmented, clashing images of life in Harlem through the riffs and rhythms of bebop jazz. In "The Negro Speaks of Rivers," he forges a human connection among various world cultures. In "I, Too," Hughes addresses the evils of segregation. In "The Weary Blues," he fuses early blues with the conventions of formal poetry.

USING THE *NOTABLE QUOTE*

Ask students what **Langston Hughes** meant about the role humor can play in helping people face challenges. *Possible answer: Humor allows people to laugh at their circumstances, and thus maintain their humanity and their dignity when others would deny them these basic human rights.*

Selection Resources

The Harlem Renaissance

CALIFORNIA R3.4

Selected Poetry
by Langston Hughes

NOTABLE QUOTE
"Humor is laughing at what you haven't got when you ought to have it."

FYI
Did you know that Langston Hughes ...
- was one of the first African Americans to earn a living solely from writing?
- was dubbed the "poet low-rate" of Harlem by some African-American intellectuals?
- wrote radio jingles during World War II to promote the purchase of war bonds?

Author Online

For more on Langston Hughes, visit the **Literature Center** at **ClassZone.com.**

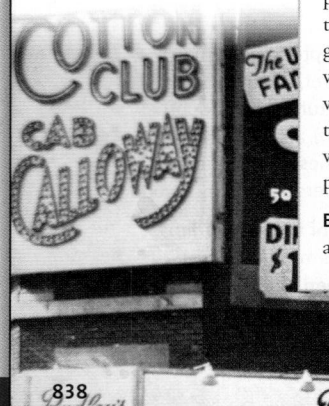

Langston Hughes
1902–1967

Langston Hughes was one of the leading poets of the Harlem Renaissance as well as an accomplished novelist, playwright, and essayist. His writings center on poor and working-class African Americans, a group whom literature had generally ignored.

Early Inspirations James Mercer Langston Hughes started writing poetry in seventh grade, when his classmates elected him class poet. He admired the work of Paul Laurence Dunbar and Carl Sandburg, two poets known for their efforts to capture the voices of everyday Americans. After graduating from high school, Hughes went to live with his father in Mexico, where he became fluent in Spanish. On the train journey south, he composed what would become one of his most famous poems, "The Negro Speaks of Rivers."

Busboy Poet In 1921, Hughes enrolled at Columbia University in New York City. He left after one year to travel the world as a cook's assistant aboard a ship. In 1925, Hughes settled in Washington, D.C., and took a job busing tables at a hotel restaurant. One day Vachel Lindsay, a well-known poet, came to the hotel. Hughes mustered the courage to slip three of his poems, including "The Weary Blues," beside Lindsay's plate. Lindsay liked the poems, and the next morning's newspapers reported Lindsay's discovery of the "busboy poet."

A year later, Hughes published his first poetry collection, *The Weary Blues.* His gritty depiction of "workers, roustabouts, and singers and job hunters" angered some African-American critics who felt that members of the race should always be portrayed in the best possible light. Hughes responded to these criticisms, saying, "I knew only the people I had grown up with, and they weren't people whose shoes were always shined. . . . But they seemed to me good people, too."

Poet Laureate of Harlem As a poet, Hughes kept his language direct; he made no attempt to be obscure or pretentious. He celebrated the lively nightlife and the everyday experiences of working-class African Americans, often re-creating the structures and rhythms of blues and jazz music in works such as *Montage of a Dream Deferred* (1951), a book-length suite of related poems. Hughes became informally known as the Poet Laureate of Harlem and today is universally recognized as the most influential voice of the Harlem Renaissance.

838

R RESOURCE MANAGER UNIT 5

Plan and Teach pp. 17–24

Literary Analysis
Speaker pp. 25, 26†*
Question Support p. 29*

Reading
Analyze Rhythm and Repetition
pp. 27, 28†*

Assessment
Selection Tests A, B/C pp. 31*, 33*
Test Generator CD

BEST PRACTICES TOOLKIT

Differentiated Instruction
pp. 31–38*

Graphic Organizers/Strategies
Read Aloud/Think Aloud •
Comparison Matrix • Writing
Template: Poem • T Chart

Reading Support
Audio Anthology CD*

Technology
Literature Center at
ClassZone.com
Write*Smart* CD

* Resources for Differentiation   † Also in Spanish

LITERARY ANALYSIS: SPEAKER

You know that the **speaker** of a poem, like the narrator of a story, is the voice that talks to the reader. In his poems, Langston Hughes created speakers who represented important aspects of African-American culture. Sometimes his speaker is the voice of the culture itself.

I've known rivers ancient as the world and older than the
flow of human blood in human veins.

Hughes also uses his speakers to portray the joys and struggles of working-class African Americans.

In a deep song voice with a melancholy tone
I heard that Negro sing, that old piano moan—

As you read each poem, try to identify the speaker of the poem and what aspects of African-American life the speaker describes.

READING SKILL: ANALYZE RHYTHM AND REPETITION

When Hughes began writing, most African-American poets tried to sound like the white poets they read in school. Instead, Hughes drew his inspiration from jazz and blues music, using the rhythm and repetition of these musical forms to structure his poetry. Musical elements found in Hughes's poetry include

- jazz-influenced **rhythm** (the pattern of stressed and unstressed syllables) that features strong accents, quick changes in rhythm, and irregular beats
- rhythmic **repetition** of words and phrases, like that used in blues lyrics
- the **refrain,** one or more repeated lines of poetry that function like the chorus of a song

As you read each poem, use a chart like the one shown to record examples of these musical patterns.

Rhythm	Repetition	Refrain

What shapes your IDENTITY?

KEY IDEA Hughes wrote poetry to honor his African-American heritage, but he didn't limit himself to great heroes and historical events. For Hughes, it was the vibrant culture of everyday people—their music, their slang, and their experiences of life in the city—that shaped his sense of **identity.**

DISCUSS What everyday experiences help shape your identity? List images and activities that characterize the way you live: the sounds and smells of your neighborhood, the places you go, the foods you eat, and so on. In a small group, compare your answers. Which experiences, if any, do group members have in common?

839

What shapes your IDENTITY?

Define **identity** as "the qualities that a person regards as essential and unique to his or her personality"; then ask the question. Have students consider their responses as they read the **KEY IDEA**. Invite students to list ethnic, cultural, or gender groups that help shape their identities. Urge them to draw on these associations as they complete the **DISCUSS** activity.

SKILLS FOCUS

LITERARY ANALYSIS

● **SPEAKER**

After students read the page, have them suggest aspects of African-American heritage, culture, or life that the speakers describe in the examples on page 839.
Possible answer: *The speaker in the first example suggests that African-American culture is as old as the oldest rivers and the earliest humans. The speaker in the second example refers to a pervasive sadness that may result from racism or oppression affecting African Americans.*

CHECK UNDERSTANDING Have students clarify how the speaker and poet are related.

READING SKILL R3.4

■ **ANALYZE RHYTHM AND REPETITION**

Emphasize that Hughes adopted the patterns of African-American speech and music in order to highlight the beauty of his culture. To detect rhythm, suggest that students read the poems aloud, listening for the rhythm. Students may also benefit from tapping the rhythm as they read. Model these practices for students.

 RESOURCE MANAGER—Copy Master
Analyze Rhythm and Repetition p. 27
(for student use while reading the selections)

DIFFERENTIATED INSTRUCTION

FOR STRATEGIC READERS
Concept Support: Analyze Rhythm and Repetition

Write these words on the board:

mu·́sic   to·mor·́row

Point out that the dots indicate syllable breaks and the accent marks indicate which syllable is stressed. Read the words aloud to show that in *music* the first syllable is stressed, and in *tomorrow* the second syllable

is stressed. Show students the dictionary entries for these words and explain that dictionaries are tools for determining syllable breaks and stress patterns. Using dictionaries, have students divide these words into syllables and mark the stressed syllables: *ancient, melancholy, piano,* and *older.* Then help students read and determine rhythm in the excerpts from Langston Hughes's poems that appear on page 839.

SUMMARY

Drawing on the rhythms of 1940s bebop jazz, this poem expresses the festering tension felt by African Americans unable to realize their dreams.

READING SKILL

A RHYTHM AND REPETITION

Answers: Stress pattern: *RAIsin / FESter / ROTten / SUgar / SYRupy;* ***words emphasized:*** *dry / raisin, sun / fester, sore / then run / does, stink, rotten, meat / crust, sugar / syrupy, sweet*

Extend the Discussion Describe the rhythm and the feelings it evokes. If you marked the lines differently, explain your variation. ***Possible answer:*** *The rhythm is disjointed as well as fast and abrupt. This rhythm evokes feelings of tension, dissatisfaction, anger, or anxiety. Students with different line markings should be able to explain what they hear.*

ANSWERS

1. ***Possible answer:*** *A dream deferred is one that remains unrealized. In this case, the speaker may mean the promise of social equality.*

2. ***Possible answer:*** *The poem's last line hints at an outbreak of violence.*

3. ***Possible answer: Similes:*** *"like a raisin in the sun" (line 3), "like a sore" (line 4), "like rotten meat" (line 6), "like a syrupy sweet" (line 8), "like a heavy load" (line 10). The similes may reveal the speaker's bitterness or disgust toward the current social situation and the endless delays in improving it.*

Harlem

Langston Hughes

What happens to a dream deferred?

    Does it dry up
    like a raisin in the sun?
    Or fester like a sore—
5   And then run?
    Does it stink like rotten meat?
    Or crust and sugar over—
    like a syrupy sweet?

    Maybe it just sags
10   like a heavy load.

Or does it explode?

ANALYZE VISUALS
What elements of this painting help capture the thriving street life in Harlem?

A RHYTHM AND REPETITION
Identify the pattern of stresses in lines 2–8. Which words are emphasized by this rhythm?

Literary Analysis

1. **Clarify** What does the speaker mean by "a dream deferred"?

2. **Make Inferences** What social or political consequences are hinted at in the poem's last line?

3. **Interpret Figurative Language** List the **similes** the speaker uses to describe the effect of a deferred dream. What do these comparisons reveal about the speaker's attitude?

Street Shadows (1959), Jacob Lawrence. Egg tempera on hardboard, 24″ × 30″. Private collection, New York. Photograph courtesy of Gwendolyn Knight Lawrence/Art Resource, New York. © 2007 The Jacob and Gwendolyn Lawrence Foundation, Seattle/ Artists Rights Society (ARS), New York.

DIFFERENTIATED INSTRUCTION

For general guidelines on differentiating instruction, see

 BEST PRACTICES TOOLKIT
Differentiated Instruction pp. 31–38

FOR STRATEGIC READERS

Options for Reading: Read Aloud

- Have students read along in their texts as you read the poem aloud. Ask students to notice rhythm and repetition in each poem.

- For "The Weary Blues," point out to students that the word *syncopated* in the first line concerns rhythm. Help students to notice that the poem contains long flowing lines, short emphatic lines, and repetition, all of which contribute to the poem's rhythm.

 BEST PRACTICES TOOLKIT—Transparency
Read Aloud/Think Aloud p. A34

Lines 1–11
TIERED DISCUSSION PROMPTS

Use these prompts to help students understand the effect of deferred dreams:

Connect Describe a dream or goal that you have that has not yet been realized. How do you feel about the situation and why? *Accept all thoughtful responses.*

Interpret What is the poem's main message or theme? ***Possible answer:*** *If dreams are denied, serious or even violent consequences can happen.*

Evaluate Do you agree or disagree with the speaker's opinion regarding the impact of deferred dreams? Explain. *Students may agree by citing examples regarding the destructive effects of dreams that are lost or postponed. Others may say that deferred dreams inspire people to work harder.*

ANALYZE VISUALS

Possible answer: *The thriving street life of Harlem is conveyed through Lawrence's use of color, shape, and composition. The warm reds, yellows, and oranges interact with the cool blues, suggesting motion and energy. Both the windows in the background and the street in the foreground are crowded, suggesting an active community life.*

About the Art American artist Jacob Lawrence (1917–2000) loved to paint the neighborhoods and streets of New York City. As Langston Hughes invites readers into the African-American experience with his words, Jacob Lawrence invites viewers to participate in its movement, sound, and liveliness.

FOR STRATEGIC READERS

Concept Support: Rhythm [paired option] Explain that "Harlem" draws on the rhythm of 1940s bebop jazz. Traditional jazz often includes syncopation, rhythm accents, and improvisation. Bebop jazz moves beyond these, speeding up the pace of rhythmic change and including more complex melodies. Play some examples of bebop jazz for students and have pairs take turns reading "Harlem" aloud as the music plays.

FOR ADVANCED LEARNERS/AP

Compare Literary Texts Refer students back to the events that Frederick Douglass recounts in his *Narrative,* found on pages 538–547. Ask them to discuss the ways in which Douglass's triumph over Covey, an event that "rekindled the few expiring embers of freedom" (line 244), describes Hughes's prediction of what happens to a dream deferred.

SUMMARY

In this poem, the speaker is the voice of African-American culture with its ancient connection to the earth and all of humanity.

LITERARY ANALYSIS

B SPEAKER

Possible answer: The speaker is old and wise, having knowledge of the beginning of the world and the beginning of humanity.

READING SKILL

C RHYTHM AND REPETITION

Answer: The refrain is "I've known rivers" (lines 1, 11).

REINFORCE *KEY IDEA:* IDENTITY

Discuss What do the poem's images convey about the speaker's sense of **identity?** *Possible answer: Images of ancient and modern rivers from around the world suggest that the speaker embraces an identity encompassing time and place.*

The Negro Speaks of Rivers

Langston Hughes

The Negro Speaks of Rivers (1998), Phoebe Beasley. Silkscreen. © Phoebe Beasley.

I've known rivers:
I've known rivers ancient as the world and older than the
    flow of human blood in human veins. **B**

My soul has grown deep like the rivers.

5 I bathed in the Euphrates[1] when dawns were young.
I built my hut near the Congo and it lulled me to sleep.
I looked upon the Nile and raised the pyramids above it.
I heard the singing of the Mississippi when Abe Lincoln
    went down to New Orleans,[2] and I've seen its muddy
10   bosom turn all golden in the sunset.

I've known rivers:
Ancient, dusky[3] rivers.

My soul has grown deep like the rivers. **C**

B SPEAKER
Reread lines 1–3. What traits of the speakers are emphasized by Hughes's word choice?

C RHYTHM AND REPETITION
Reread the poem. Which line serves as the poem's **refrain?**

---

1. **Euphrates** (yōō-frā'tēz): a river flowing through present-day Turkey, Syria, and Iraq. The valley between the Tigris and Euphrates rivers was the site of one of the world's earliest civilizations.
2. **when Abe Lincoln went down to New Orleans:** Lincoln's first glimpse of the horrors of slavery reportedly came on his trip to New Orleans as a young man.
3. **dusky:** dark; shadowy.

842   UNIT 5: THE HARLEM RENAISSANCE AND MODERNISM

DIFFERENTIATED INSTRUCTION

FOR STRATEGIC READERS

Comprehension Support Have students locate these rivers on world maps: the Euphrates, the Congo, the Nile, and the Mississippi. Clarify that the rivers are in places around the world. Then help students link the first-person speaker to each place and river in the poem. Lead them to identify the speaker as the voice of African-American culture.

FOR ADVANCED LEARNERS/AP

Compare and Contrast Point out that Phoebe Beasley's painting has the same title as Hughes's poem. Invite students to compare and contrast the two works: Is the artwork a literal illustration of the poem or an interpretation of its ideas? Have students use a Comparison Matrix to discuss features such as character, setting, theme, sensory details, and symbolism.

 BEST PRACTICES TOOLKIT—Transparency
Comparison Matrix p. A24

I, Too

Langston Hughes

I, too, sing America.

I am the darker brother.
They send me to eat in the kitchen
When company comes,
5 But I laugh,
And eat well,
And grow strong. **D**

Tomorrow,
I'll be at the table
10 When company comes.
Nobody'll dare
Say to me,
"Eat in the kitchen,"
Then.

15 Besides,
They'll see how beautiful I am
And be ashamed—

I, too, am America.

D SPEAKER
Reread lines 1–7. Identify the speaker of the poem. What aspects of the African-American experience does the speaker describe?

Literary Analysis

1. **Summarize** In "I, Too," what is the speaker's attitude toward America?

2. **Interpret Imagery** What is the significance of the four rivers mentioned in "The Negro Speaks of Rivers"?

3. **Compare and Contrast Speakers** What qualities do the speakers of both poems share? In what ways are they different?

SUMMARY

This poem is a protest that asserts the right of African Americans to sit equally at the metaphoric table of American society.

BACKGROUND

"I, Too" is Hughes's response to Walt Whitman's "I Hear America Singing." Hughes was a great admirer of Whitman, believing that Whitman's work reflected the real meaning of democracy—a democracy without the racial discrimination addressed in much of Hughes's work.

LITERARY ANALYSIS

D SPEAKER

Possible answer: The speaker is the voice of the African-American community and describes that community's common experience with discrimination, segregation, and social inequality.

ANSWERS

1. *Possible answer:* The speaker is critical of segregation and racism but considers himself to be a part of American culture.

2. *Possible answer:* The Euphrates signifies Mesopotamia, the cradle of civilization. The Congo signifies Africa, where the slaves were captured. The Nile signifies Egypt, where the mysterious pyramids were built. The Mississippi signifies the southern United States, the seat of slavery in the U.S.

   If students need help . . . Refer them to history books or encyclopedias for basic information about the four rivers.

3. *Possible answer:* Both speakers have an awareness of suffering, an outside perspective, and cultural pride. In "The Negro Speaks of Rivers," the speaker identifies with all of humanity. In "I, Too," the speaker defines himself as American.

FOR STRATEGIC READERS

Clarify Meaning: Figurative Language Point out that Hughes uses an extended metaphor in "I, Too." Remind students that a metaphor compares two unrelated objects without the words *like* or *as*. An extended metaphor maintains the comparison throughout a passage. Help students interpret the metaphors of the kitchen and the dining room table and recognize that these are symbols of segregation in American society.

FOR ADVANCED LEARNERS/AP

Write a Metaphor [small-group option] Have groups brainstorm a list of societal divisions within American society, past or present. Using Hughes's metaphor as a model, have each student then develop an original metaphor for one division on the list. Ask students to extend their metaphors into written passages of prose or poetry and then share their work with the class.

BEST PRACTICES TOOLKIT—Transparency
Writing Template: Poem pp. C16, C35

SUMMARY

This poem expresses the speaker's admiration for the blues and its musicians. Hughes's rhythm recalls the syncopation common in blues music, which traces its roots to African-American spirituals and call-and-response songs.

READING SKILL

E RHYTHM AND REPETITION

Possible answer: *Examples of repetition include "he did a lazy sway" (lines 6, 7), "Thump, thump, thump" (line 23), and "Blues!" (lines 11, 14, and 16). "Blues!" is also the poem's refrain.*

If students need help . . . Work with them to record examples of musical patterns in the prereading chart introduced on page 839.

Rhythm	Repetition	Refrain
free verse mixed with rhyme	"He did a lazy sway."	"O Blues!" "Sweet Blues!"

SELECTION WRAP–UP

SYNTHESIZE Ask students to list emotions suggested by the four poems.

The *Weary* Blues

Langston Hughes

Droning a drowsy syncopated[1] tune,
Rocking back and forth to a mellow croon,
  I heard a Negro play.
Down on Lenox Avenue[2] the other night
5 By the pale dull pallor[3] of an old gas light
  He did a lazy sway. . . .
  He did a lazy sway. . . .
To the tune o' those Weary Blues.
With his ebony hands on each ivory key
10 He made that poor piano moan with melody.
  O Blues!
Swaying to and fro on his rickety stool
He played that sad raggy tune like a musical fool.
  Sweet Blues!
15 Coming from a black man's soul.
  O Blues!
In a deep song voice with a melancholy tone
I heard that Negro sing, that old piano moan—
  "Ain't got nobody in all this world,
20 Ain't got nobody but ma self.
  I's gwine to quit ma frownin'
  And put ma troubles on the shelf."
Thump, thump, thump, went his foot on the floor.
He played a few chords then he sang some more— **E**
25 "I got the Weary Blues
  And I can't be satisfied.
  Got the Weary Blues
  And can't be satisfied—
  I ain't happy no mo'
30 And I wish that I had died."
And far into the night he crooned that tune.
The stars went out and so did the moon.
The singer stopped playing and went to bed
While the Weary Blues echoed through his head.
35 He slept like a rock or a man that's dead.

E RHYTHM AND REPETITION
Identify three examples of repetition in the poem thus far. Which line or phrase might be considered the poem's refrain?

---

1. **syncopated** (sĭng'kə-pā'tĭd): characterized by a shifting of stresses from normally strong to normally weak beats.
2. **Lenox Avenue:** a main north-south street in Harlem.
3. **pallor** (păl'ər): lack of color.

DIFFERENTIATED INSTRUCTION

FOR STRATEGIC READERS

Cause and Effect In three of the four poems, racial discrimination affects the speaker's sense of identity. Help students use T Charts to isolate this aspect of the works.

 BEST PRACTICES TOOLKIT—Transparency
T Chart p. A25

Poem	Effect on Speaker
Harlem	stifled dreams; could lead to violence
I, Too	strong; confident will end
The Weary Blues	empathy for musician and any oppressed

FOR ADVANCED LEARNERS/AP

Research and Analyze [mixed-interest groups] In "The Weary Blues," Hughes incorporates blues lyrics. Using print, online, and audio resources, have students learn more about the blues: What are the roots of blues music? Who are some well-known blues musicians? How has the blues influenced other forms of music? In short informal presentations that include musical samples, have students share their findings.

Comprehension

1. **Clarify** What hope does the speaker of "I, Too" express?

2. **Recall** Who are the individuals described in "The Weary Blues"?

3. **Summarize** What happens to the speaker of "The Weary Blues"?

R3.4
CALIFORNIA

Literary Analysis

4. **Identify Sensory Details** Many of Hughes's poems are rich in details that appeal to the five senses. Reread "Harlem" and "The Weary Blues." For each poem, use a chart like the one shown to record examples of each kind of sensory detail. Which example did you find especially vivid? Explain your answer.

5. **Analyze Rhythm and Repetition** Review the chart you created while you read the poems. Which poem seems most influenced by the rhythms of jazz music? Support your answer with details.

6. **Examine Style** Describe the differences between the two blues verses in "The Weary Blues" (lines 19–22 and 25–30) and the other lines of the poem. In your opinion, do the two styles work well together? Explain your answer.

7. **Draw Conclusions About Author's Perspective** Use the events, situations, and ideas presented in each of Hughes's poems to draw conclusions about his views on African-American **identity.** In Hughes's eyes, what characteristics define African-American culture?

8. **Evaluate Speakers** Consider the four poems you read. In your opinion, which speaker best achieves each of the following goals? Cite details from the poems in your answers.

   - captures Hughes's pride in African-American culture
   - reflects the everyday life of African Americans
   - conveys the sounds of African-American speech
   - represents the feelings of African Americans today

Literary Criticism

9. **Critical Interpretations** In a review of Hughes's poetry collection *The Weary Blues,* poet Countee Cullen criticized Hughes for "too much emphasis on strictly Negro themes" and questioned whether jazz poems belong to "that select and austere circle of high literary expression which we call poetry." Do you agree with Cullen's concerns? Why or why not?

Practice and Apply

After Reading

Use these copy masters to check understanding and provide extra support:

R RESOURCE MANAGER—Copy Masters
Speaker p. 25
Question Support p. 29

Additional selection questions are provided for teachers on page 21.

ANSWERS

1. *The speaker expresses the hope that he will one day be recognized as an equal member of American society.*

2. *The speaker describes an African-American piano player.*

3. *The speaker listens to the piano player sing the blues until the player goes home.*

Possible answers:

4. *"Harlem": hearing: "explode"; sight: "fester like a sore," "dry up like a raisin in the sun," "crust"; touch: "sags like a heavy load"; taste: "syrupy sweet"; smell: "stink like rotten meat." "The Weary Blues": hearing: "droning . . . syncopated tune," "mellow croon," "thump"; sight: "pale dull pallor," "ebony hands on ivory keys," "swaying on his rickety stool," "stars went out." Students should explain their choice of vivid detail.*

5. ■ **SKILLS FOCUS** Analyze Rhythm and Repetition *Like jazz music, "Harlem" has strong accents, quick changes in rhythm, and irregular beats.*

6. *The blues verses feature dialect and more regular rhythms than the other lines of the poem. Students may say that the two styles*

Assess and Reteach

Assess

R RESOURCE MANAGER—Copy Masters
Selection Test A pp. 31–32
Selection Test B/C pp. 33–34

💿 Test Generator CD

Reteach

S STANDARDS LESSON FILE
Literature Lesson 18: Speaker and Persona
Literature Lesson 20: Rhythm and Meter

---

work well together to invite readers to join the speaker's experience.

7. *Hughes defines African-American culture as including hardship, sorrow, injustice, ancient wisdom, strength, and a love of music.*

8. ● **SKILLS FOCUS** Speaker *"The Negro Speaks of Rivers" best captures Hughes's pride in African-American culture because it recognizes the connection among all of humanity. "I, Too" best reflects the everyday life of African Americans because it chronicles discrimination. "The Weary*

Blues" best conveys the sounds of African-American speech because it includes dialect. "Harlem" and "I, Too" capture the feelings of African Americans in that they convey anger about racial injustice, hope for a more just future, and unity in the common bond of being an American.

9. *Cullen's concerns are invalid, because they ignore the cultural aspect of all literature and the musical aspect of all poetry.*

Focus and Motivate

OBJECTIVES

Literary Analysis
- explore the key idea of **revival**
- analyze sonnets
- read poetry

Reading
- analyze form and meaning in poetry

 R3.4

ABOUT THE POETS

James Weldon Johnson After students read about Johnson, note the poet's restlessness and his work in New York. Then point out the title "My City." Ask what *My* suggests about New York's effect on the poet. *Possible answer: The city has captured Johnson's restless spirit.*

Claude McKay After students read about McKay, explain that the title "If We Must Die" suggests the need to commit fully to a cause. Link this idea to Churchill's interest in the poem, clarifying that Britain faced attack by the Nazis and needed people's full commitment to resistance.

USING THE *NOTABLE QUOTES*

Ask how **Johnson's** life showed the world his people's greatness. *Possible answer: Johnson's many vocations show the versatile talents of one African American.* Ask how **McKay's** priority of individuality compares with Johnson's notion of a group identity. *Possible answer: McKay feels that individuality comes first but, like Johnson, values his link to the group.*

My City

Poem by James Weldon Johnson

James Weldon Johnson
1871–1938

NOTABLE QUOTE
"The world does not know that a people is great until that people produces great literature and art."

A leading light of the Harlem Renaissance, James Weldon Johnson was also a lawyer, teacher, songwriter, diplomat, and civil rights activist. He dedicated his life to fighting prejudice and inspiring African Americans to new heights of social and literary achievement.

Unstoppable Talent After graduating from Atlanta University in 1894, Johnson worked as a school principal, founded a daily newspaper, and became the first African-American lawyer since Reconstruction to be admitted to the Florida bar. In 1901, the restless Johnson

traveled to New York, where he and his younger brother became successful Broadway songwriters. One of their early songs, "Lift Every Voice and Sing," eventually became known as the African-American national anthem.

Renaissance Man Johnson also published works in many genres of literature. Among his best-known works are his novel *The Autobiography of an Ex-Colored Man,* his poetry collection *God's Trombones,* and a cultural history, *Black Manhattan.* He also edited several groundbreaking collections of African-American poetry and spirituals.

If We Must Die

Poem by Claude McKay

Claude McKay
c. 1890–1948

NOTABLE QUOTE
"If a man is not faithful to his own individuality, he cannot be loyal to anything."

Hailed by James Weldon Johnson as "the poet of rebellion," Jamaican-born Festus Claudius McKay made his name as a fierce critic of racism in the United States. His poetry collection *Harlem Shadows,* published in 1922, is considered one of the founding works of the Harlem Renaissance.

Poet of Rebellion Already established as a poet, 23-year-old McKay arrived in the United States in 1912. In 1919, the country was torn apart by a wave of violent attacks against African Americans. Racial tensions erupted into 26 riots across the country during a period known as the Red Summer. "If We Must Die" was McKay's anguished response, which became instantly popular among African Americans.

Enduring Message During World War II, the poem took on new meaning when British Prime Minister Sir Winston Churchill quoted from it during a speech. The poem went on to become a battle cry for the Allies in their fight against the Nazis. McKay often complained that the fame of this one poem had overshadowed his other work, which included the novels *Home to Harlem* and *Banana Bottom.*

Author On|ine
For more on James Weldon Johnson and Claude McKay, visit the **Literature Center** at ClassZone.com.

Selection Resources

 RESOURCE MANAGER UNIT 5

Plan and Teach pp. 35–42

Literary Analysis
Sonnet pp. 43, 44†*
Question Support p. 47*

Reading
Understand Form and Meaning
  pp. 45, 46†*

Assessment
Selection Tests A, B/C pp. 49*, 51*
 Test Generator CD

 BEST PRACTICES TOOLKIT

Differentiated Instruction
pp. 31–38*

Graphic Organizers/Strategies
Two-Column Chart • Comparison Matrix

Reading Support
 Audio Anthology CD*

Technology
 Literature Center at **ClassZone.com**
 Write*Smart* CD

---

* Resources for Differentiation   † Also in Spanish

● LITERARY ANALYSIS: SONNET

New ideas help keep poetic traditions alive. The centuries-old **sonnet,** a 14-line lyric poem with specific patterns of rhythm and rhyme, has been reimagined by many poets. The poems in this lesson are based on two classic types of sonnets.

- The **Italian,** or **Petrarchan, sonnet** is divided into two parts: an **octave,** or eight-line grouping, and a **sestet,** or six-line grouping. The usual rhyme scheme for the octave is *abbaabba*. The rhyme scheme for the sestet varies but is often *cdccde* or *cdccdc*.
- The **English,** or **Shakespearean, sonnet** has a rhyme scheme of *abab cdcd efef gg*. This divides the poem into four distinct line groups: three **quatrains,** or four-line units, followed by a **couplet,** a pair of rhymed lines.

Sonnets are often written in **iambic pentameter.** In this meter, each line includes five pairs of syllables, the first unstressed, the second stressed. However, modern poets often break the rules when writing sonnets. As you read, note how each poet adapts this classic form to a modern message.

● READING SKILL: UNDERSTAND FORM AND MEANING

Understanding a sonnet's structure can help you interpret its meaning. Keep in mind the following:

- In many sonnets, quatrains, octaves, and other line groupings are not set apart by stanza breaks. Use the rhyme scheme to determine the poem's line groupings.
- Each line grouping usually expresses one main idea.
- The first line grouping of the sonnet describes the speaker's situation or problem. The last line grouping resolves, concludes, or reacts to that situation.

As you begin to read each sonnet, identify the line groupings, listing them in a chart like the one shown. Also record in your chart the main idea expressed in each line grouping.

Title:	
Line Grouping	Main Idea
1st quatrain	

Explore the Key Idea

When does old become NEW *again?*

KEY IDEA When CDs came on the market, vinyl records seemed doomed. Then, hip-hop artists made the scratching of a needle on vinyl the signature sound of a new style of music. Artists often bring back old ideas to give them new meaning. Poets James Weldon Johnson and Claude McKay did just that with their **revival** of the sonnet, breathing new life into a 700-year-old poetic form.

PRESENT Think of an artist, a musician, or a writer from the past whose work you admire. Create a plan to adapt this person's work to make a creation of your own, and present your plan to the class.

847

Teach

When does old become NEW *again?*

Ask the question. Before students read the **KEY IDEA**, explain that **revival** means "bringing or coming back into use, attention, or being, after a decline." Invite students to suggest music, fashions, or slang that were popular, fell from use, and have made recent reappearances in popular culture. Then urge students to draw upon these examples as they complete the **PRESENT** activity.

SKILLS FOCUS

LITERARY ANALYSIS   R3.4

● SONNET

Write this line on the board:

I rise and greet the shades of fading night

Ask students to identify the meter by identifying the syllable pairs and the pattern of stressed and unstressed syllables. ***Possible answer:*** *The meter is iambic pentameter, because there are five pairs of unstressed/ stressed syllables.* Ĭ rĭse / ănd gréet / thĕ shádes / ŏf fád / ĭng níght.

CHECK UNDERSTANDING Ask students to explain the difference between the Italian, or Petrarchan, sonnet, and the English, or Shakespearean, sonnet.

READING SKILL

■ UNDERSTAND FORM AND MEANING

Review with students how to determine the rhyme scheme of a poem, assigning the letter *a* to the first end word and any end word that rhymes with it. Students should assign the letter *b* to the next end word that does not rhyme with the first and so on. Refer students to another poem the class has read and have them identify the rhyme scheme in the poem.

 RESOURCE MANAGER—Copy Master Understand Form and Meaning p. 45 (for student use while reading the selections)

DIFFERENTIATED INSTRUCTION

FOR STRATEGIC READERS
Vocabulary Support

- *meter,* "measured, patterned arrangement of syllables"
- *rhyme,* "regular recurrence of corresponding end sounds"
- *rhyme scheme,* "pattern of rhymes"
- *rhythm,* "regular recurrence of grouped stressed and unstressed, long and short, or high-pitched and low-pitched syllables"

- *stanza,* "group of versed lines forming the divisions of poetry"
- *stressed,* "relative force or loudness with which a syllable is uttered"
- *syllable,* "word or word part pronounced with a single, uninterrupted sounding of voice"
- *unstressed,* "relative softness with which a syllable is uttered"

SUMMARY

In this poem, the speaker considers what he will miss when he dies and decides he will miss his home—Manhattan—most of all.

READING SKILL

Ⓐ FORM AND MEANING

Answer: *The stanza break divides the poem into two line groupings, an octave and a sestet. Lines 1–8 raise the question of what the speaker will miss most after death and provide several unsatisfying responses.*

LITERARY ANALYSIS

Ⓑ SONNET

Answer: *On the basis of the line groupings, this sonnet is Petrarchan.*

Extend the Discussion What relationship exists between the main ideas in the two line groupings?

Lines 1–14
REINFORCE *KEY IDEA:* REVIVAL

Discuss How does Johnson's **revival** of a form often associated with love poetry support the message of "My City"? ***Possible answer:*** *"My City" is a poem expressing the poet's love for his city. As a love poem of sorts, its subject is well suited to the form.*

My City

James Weldon Johnson

When I come down to sleep death's endless night,
The threshold of the unknown dark to cross,
What to me then will be the keenest loss,
When this bright world blurs on my fading sight?
5 Will it be that no more I shall see the trees
Or smell the flowers or hear the singing birds
Or watch the flashing streams or patient herds?
No, I am sure it will be none of these. Ⓐ

But, ah! Manhattan's sights and sounds, her smells,
10 Her crowds, her throbbing force, the thrill that comes
From being of her a part, her subtle spells,
Her shining towers, her avenues, her slums—
O God! the stark, unutterable pity,
To be dead, and never again behold my city! Ⓑ

ANALYZE VISUALS
What details in this photo correspond to the poet's vision of his city?

Ⓐ **FORM AND MEANING**
Use the **stanza break** to identify the line groupings of this poem. What is the main idea of lines 1–8?

Ⓑ **SONNET**
Judging from its line groupings, what type of sonnet is this?

View of Broadway near Times Square in Manhattan, 1920s

DIFFERENTIATED INSTRUCTION

For general guidelines on differentiating instruction, see

 BEST PRACTICES TOOLKIT
Differentiated Instruction pp. 31–38

FOR STRATEGIC READERS
Options for Reading: Audio Recording

• Have students listen to the poems on the *Audio Anthology CD* (also recommended for English learners) while they read along in

their texts. Ask students to notice the main ideas, rhyme, and line groupings in each poem.

• For "My City," students will need help with syntax and figurative language to unlock main ideas. Listen to line 2 several times; then help students unravel inverted syntax there and elsewhere. Then use line 11 to model using context clues to build meaning for figurative language.

Lines 1–14
TIERED DISCUSSION PROMPTS

Use these prompts to help students under-stand the urban vitality that characterized the Harlem Renaissance:

Connect Think about life in big cities. What is it like? *Accept all thoughtful responses.*

Analyze How does the speaker personify the city? ***Possible answer:*** *The speaker personifies the city as a vital, magical woman who possesses a shining exterior as well as a dark side.*

Evaluate Is the speaker's description of Manhattan appealing? Explain. ***Possible answer:*** *The speaker's description is ap-pealing because of its sensual quality and because it conveys a strong love of the city.*

ANALYZE VISUALS

Possible answer: The background of the pho-tograph shows the "shining towers" Johnson mentions in line 12, while the foreground shows two broad avenues that might be said to cast "subtle spells" through enticing advertisements and theatre marquees.

FOR STRATEGIC READERS

Concept Support: Form and Meaning To help students visualize the form of "My City," work with them to complete Two-Column Charts. Have students list lines from the poem in the appropriate category. When students are finished, help them determine and mark the poem's rhyme scheme.

BEST PRACTICES TOOLKIT—Transparency
Two-Column Chart p. A25

Question	Lines 1–4
Incorrect Answer	Lines 5–8
Correct Answer	Lines 9–14

FOR ADVANCED LEARNERS/AP

Analyze Point out to students that the "I" present in lines 1, 5, and 8 is absent from lines 9–14, the lines in which the speaker describes the city. How does the absence of the "I" emphasize the power that the poet ascribes to Manhattan? Have students discuss this ques-tion and present their conclusions to the class.

SUMMARY

This poem is a defiant call to protest. The speaker warns against passive acceptance of hostility and urges people to fight back. He suggests that death is inevitable but can be noble if it serves a cause. The final couplet states the speaker's resolve to die fighting.

LITERARY ANALYSIS

C SONNET

***Possible answer:** The rhyme scheme is abab, cdcd. On the basis of this rhyme scheme, the sonnet is Shakespearean.*

If students need help . . . Refer them to page 847 and the definitions of Petrarchan and Shakespearean sonnets.

READING SKILL

D FORM AND MEANING

***Possible answer:** The speaker decides that he will fight back even if he dies fighting.*

If students need help . . . Have them record line groupings and main ideas in the pre-reading chart introduced on page 847.

Line Grouping	Main Idea
First quatrain	We won't die like hogs hunted by dogs.
Second quatrain	If we must die, we will do it nobly.

SELECTION WRAP–UP

SYNTHESIZE Invite students to comment on what Johnson's and McKay's works contributed to the Harlem Renaissance.

If We Must Die

Claude McKay

If we must die, let it not be like hogs
Hunted and penned in an inglorious[1] spot,
While round us bark the mad and hungry dogs,
Making their mock at our accursed lot.
5 If we must die, O let us nobly die,
So that our precious blood may not be shed
In vain; then even the monsters we defy
Shall be constrained[2] to honor us though dead! **C**
O kinsmen! we must meet the common foe!
10 Though far outnumbered let us show us brave,
And for their thousand blows deal one deathblow!
What though before us lies the open grave?
Like men we'll face the murderous, cowardly pack,
Pressed to the wall, dying, but fighting back! **D**

1. **inglorious:** shameful; disgraceful.
2. **constrained:** forced.

C SONNET
State the **rhyme scheme** of lines 1–8. Considering the rhyme scheme, what type of sonnet is this?

D FORM AND MEANING
By the end of the poem, what resolution has the speaker reached?

DIFFERENTIATED INSTRUCTION

FOR STRATEGIC READERS

Comprehension Support [paired option]
Have student pairs work together to respond to these questions about "If We Must Die":

- Who is the speaker?

- What is the speaker's message?

Invite pairs to share their responses. Ask students to explain their thinking by providing examples from the poem.

FOR ADVANCED LEARNERS/AP

Research McKay wrote "If We Must Die" during the "Red Summer," a term coined by James Weldon Johnson to describe the racially violent summer and fall of 1919 during which African Americans were the victims of violent attacks. Have students research the causes of these events, noting in particular the significance of McKay's poem as a part of the response to them. Find opportunities for students to present their findings to the class.

Comprehension

1. **Recall** In "My City," what will the speaker most regret about death?

2. **Clarify** In "If We Must Die," what type of death does the speaker argue for?

3. **Paraphrase** In "If We Must Die," what is the meaning of the phrase "making their mock at our accursed lot"?

Literary Analysis

4. **Identify Form** McKay's poem closely follows the conventions of a traditional sonnet. Which kind of sonnet is it? Explain your answer.

5. **Make Inferences About Audience** Recall the events that inspired McKay to write "If We Must Die." What audience can you infer the speaker is addressing? Describe the speaker's relationship to this audience.

6. **Classify Sonnet** Johnson's poem includes features of both Shakespearean and Petrarchan sonnets. Using a chart like the one shown, decide whether each listed feature of the poem's structure is characteristic of Shakespearean sonnets, Petrarchan sonnets, or both. Based on your answers, which label is the better description of Johnson's sonnet?

	Shakespearean	Petrarchan
Structure		
Rhyme Scheme		
Meter		
Final Couplet		

7. **Analyze Form and Meaning** Review the chart you completed as you read. Notice Johnson's use of a stanza break, whereas McKay uses none. In your opinion, how does this choice contribute to each poem's meaning? Explain.

8. **Examine Author's Purpose** Consider the motives that might have inspired African-American poets to express themselves in European poetic forms. What artistic and social messages are suggested by the Harlem Renaissance **revival** of the sonnet?

9. **Evaluate Style** In your opinion, which poem more successfully updates the sonnet for a modern audience? Include details in your answer.

Literary Criticism

10. **Critical Interpretations** Claude McKay once stated that he hoped his poems could convey universal meaning. Reread the background on "If We Must Die" included in the author biography. Does the poem's history suggest McKay was successful in his goal? Explain your answer.

produce great literature through mastery of classical forms and a social message that African-American experiences are worthy of commemoration.

9. *Students may cite McKay's poem for its direct attack on racial discrimination.*

10. *The poem's history shows that many readers have identified with the speaker's message. This identification transcends race, social context, and geography, suggesting that the poem conveys universal meaning as McKay intended.*

Practice and Apply

After Reading

Use these copy masters to check understanding and provide extra support:

R RESOURCE MANAGER—Copy Masters
Sonnet p. 43
Question Support p. 47

Additional selection questions are provided for teachers on page 39.

ANSWERS

1. *The speaker will regret not being able to see his city.*

2. *The speaker argues for a noble death.*

3. *The line means "laughing at our poor condition."*

Possible answers:

4. ■ **SKILLS FOCUS** **Understand Form and Meaning** *On the basis of its rhyme scheme and its line groupings of three quatrains and a couplet, the sonnet is Shakespearean.*

5. *The speaker addresses an African-American audience, whose identity he shares, evidenced by the references to kinsmen and common foe (line 9).*

6. ● **SKILLS FOCUS** **Sonnet** *Shakespearean: meter, final couplet; Petrarchan: structure, rhyme scheme, meter. Students can argue for either form but should provide support.*

7. ■ **SKILLS FOCUS** **Understand Form and Meaning** *Johnson's sonnet poses a question and an answer, which the stanza breaks support. McKay's poem addresses a continuous message, so there is no need for stanza breaks.*

8. *Reviving the sonnet suggests an artistic message that African Americans can*

Assess and Reteach

Assess

R RESOURCE MANAGER—Copy Masters
Selection Test A pp. 49–50
Selection Test B/C pp. 51–52

◎ Test Generator CD

Reteach

S STANDARDS LESSON FILE
Literature Lesson 13: Sonnet

Focus and Motivate

OBJECTIVES

Literary Analysis
- explore the key idea of **outlook**
- analyze theme
- read poetry

Reading
- distinguish figurative from literal meaning

CALIFORNIA R3.2, R3.4

ABOUT THE POETS

Countee Cullen After students read about Countee Cullen, point out the quotation that closes the biography. Ask students to draw connections between the quotation and the title of the Cullen poem they will read. *Possible answer: In the quotation, Cullen expresses his wish to address all readers. His title "Any Human to Another" stresses that the poem speaks to all readers.*

Jean Toomer After students read, highlight the poet's interest in precise, striking images. Ask students to describe the image created by the precise language of Toomer's title "Storm Ending." *Possible answer: In just two words, Toomer creates a vivid image of a storm clearing.*

Arna Bontemps Focus students' attention on Bontemps's inspiration by Southern roots. Explain that the poem they will read uses rural imagery and metaphor to convey the poet's message.

Countee Cullen
1903–1946

Any Human to Another
Poem by Countee Cullen

In 1925, while still an undergraduate at New York University, Countee Cullen (kŭl′ən) published his first poetry collection, *Color,* which won immediate critical acclaim.

Cullen's greatest poetic influences were the English Romantic poets, especially John Keats. Although some of Cullen's poetry deals directly with experiences specific to African Americans, much of his work addresses universal concerns such as love and faith. Cullen adamantly believed that poetry could break down racial barriers and disliked being pigeonholed, once stating, "If I am going to be a poet at all, I am going to be a Poet and not a Negro Poet."

Jean Toomer
1894–1967

Storm Ending
Poem by Jean Toomer

Born in Washington, D.C., Nathan Eugene Toomer grew up in a prominent, racially mixed family. Toomer could pass for white, and as a young man, often changed his racial identification from white to black and back again. As an adult, he rejected the concept of race altogether and embraced an idealistic vision of himself as a founder of a "united human race."

Toomer was drawn to Eastern philosophy and Imagist poetry—poetry that conveys meaning through the use of precise, striking images. His reputation rests mainly on his novel *Cane* (1923), an experimental work exploring the African-American experience through fragments of poetry and prose.

Arna Bontemps
1902–1973

A Black Man Talks of Reaping
Poem by Arna Bontemps

After graduating from college in 1923, Arna Bontemps (bŏn-tän′) discovered a thriving literary scene in Harlem that he called a "foretaste of paradise." Despite his love for the bustle of the Northern cities, Bontemps was most deeply inspired by the Southern roots of African-American culture. Nearly all of his stories, novels, and plays are set in the South and provide vivid portrayals of rural life.

Bontemps, who earned his living as an educator, left Harlem in 1931 and spent most of his career in the South. His major works include the short story collection *The Old South* and the novel *God Sends Sunday,* which is often cited as the final work of the Harlem Renaissance.

Author Online
For more on these poets, visit the **Literature Center** at **ClassZone.com**.

852

Selection Resources

● LITERARY ANALYSIS: THEME

In poetry, the speaker's descriptions of the world will often help you identify a poem's **theme,** its underlying message about life or human nature. In most works, the theme is implied, rather than directly stated. Consider these lines:

Your grief and mine
Must intertwine

The speaker might be talking to a loved one or making a general point about sorrow. To uncover the message of a poem, use these strategies:

- Consider the title. What information does it reveal?
- Identify the speaker. Is the speaker the voice of an individual or of a group?
- Notice key images and think about their meaning.
- Consider the mood, or feeling, the speaker conveys.

Readers notice different details and often find different themes in the same work. As you read, try to draw your own conclusions about each poet's message.

■ READING SKILL: DISTINGUISH FIGURATIVE FROM LITERAL MEANING

You've learned that poets use **figurative language,** such as similes, metaphors, and personification, to go beyond the literal meaning of words. Use these steps to uncover this extra level of meaning:

- Read each poem once to grasp its overall meaning.
- Reread the poem, noting important words and phrases.
- Ask questions about comparisons you notice. What is being compared, and how are these things alike?
- Uncover hidden metaphors by noting descriptive details. What do these details remind you of?

As you read each poem, record examples of figurative language in a chart like the one shown. Then, jot down some of the impressions created by the words the poet chooses.

Example	Impressions
like an arrow	

How do you VIEW *the world?*

KEY IDEA You can see a glass as half empty or half full. You can see a pile of old newspapers as trash to be thrown away or as the makings of papier-mâché. The way you see things—your **outlook**—says a lot about who you are.

QUICKWRITE Many factors shape your outlook—your personality, your life experiences, your state of mind. Write one or two sentences describing your outlook. Then, explain the factors you think have most influenced the way you look at the world.

853

How do you VIEW *the world?*

Ask the question and have students read the **KEY IDEA** paragraph. Then group those who view the pictured glass as half-full and those who view it as half-empty. Urge groups to explore how this **outlook** applies elsewhere in their lives. Have students draw upon their discussion to complete the **QUICKWRITE.**

SKILLS FOCUS

LITERARY ANALYSIS R3.2

● THEME

Tell students that the excerpted lines are from "Any Human to Another." Ask students what the title suggests about the poem's theme and speaker. ***Possible answer:*** *The title suggests that the speaker is not a specific individual but rather any person. This suggests a general theme about the human condition.*

CHECK UNDERSTANDING Ask students what mood is suggested by the image of intertwined grief.

READING SKILL R3.4

■ DISTINGUISH FIGURATIVE FROM LITERAL MEANING

Have students identify figurative language in the **KEY IDEA**. Ask them to explain the comparisons that are suggested. ***Possible answer:*** *Attitudes of optimism or pessimism are compared to a half-full or half-empty glass of water and to a pile of trash or potential art source.*

CHECK UNDERSTANDING Ask students to describe the impressions created by the language *half-empty* and *half-full.*

R RESOURCE MANAGER—Copy Master
Distinguish Figurative from Literal Meaning p. 63 (for student use while reading the selections)

DIFFERENTIATED INSTRUCTION

FOR STRATEGIC READERS
Concept Support: Figurative Language
Review similes, metaphors, and personification with students by helping them identify the figurative language in these paraphrases from the poems:

- Thunder is a clapper, striking our ears. *(metaphor)*
- Grief is as sharp as a knife. *(simile)*

- The sun bites flowers in full bloom. *(personification)*
- My sorrow pierces my bone like an arrow. *(simile)*
- The flowers bleed rain. *(personification)*
- Your grief is a sea; mine is a river. *(metaphor)*

Practice and Apply

SUMMARY

In this poem, the speaker compares sorrow to an arrow's piercing and a knife cut and suggests that it is a universal emotion shared as river and sea share water.

LITERARY ANALYSIS

A THEME

Possible answer: *The sorrow of humanity runs deep and is a shared experience.*

If students need help . . . Point out language such as "not me alone," "intertwine," and "fused and mingle."

READING SKILL

B FIGURATIVE MEANING

Possible answer: *Joy and sorrow are personified. Joy reflects a quality of rareness while sorrow has a quality of universality.*

Lines 13–19
REINFORCE *KEY IDEA:* OUTLOOK

Discuss What **outlook** on life is expressed in these lines? **Possible answer:** *The speaker expresses the outlook that life's experiences will touch everyone equally.*

Any Human to Another

Countee Cullen

The ills I sorrow at
Not me alone
Like an arrow,
Pierce to the marrow,
5 Through the fat
And past the bone.

Your grief and mine
Must intertwine
Like sea and river,
10 Be fused and mingle,
Diverse yet single,
Forever and forever. **A**

Let no man be so proud
And confident,
15 To think he is allowed
A little tent
Pitched in a meadow
Of sun and shadow
All his little own.

20 Joy may be shy, unique,
Friendly to a few,
Sorrow never scorned to speak
To any who
Were false or true.

25 Your every grief
Like a blade
Shining and unsheathed¹
Must strike me down.
Of bitter aloes² wreathed,
30 My sorrow must be laid
On your head like a crown.

---

1. **unsheathed:** removed from its protective case.
2. **bitter aloes:** spiny-leafed plants whose juice is used to make a bad-tasting medicine.

A THEME
Reread lines 1–12. Consider the title of the poem. Based on the title, what message about sorrow is expressed in these lines?

B FIGURATIVE MEANING
Identify two examples of **personification** in lines 20–24. What qualities are indicated by these lines?

DIFFERENTIATED INSTRUCTION

For general guidelines on differentiating instruction, see

 BEST PRACTICES TOOLKIT
Differentiated Instruction pp. 31–38

FOR STRATEGIC READERS
Options for Reading: Read Aloud

- Have students echo your reading of the poems. Ask students to notice figurative language in each poem.

- With "Any Human to Another," model how to use punctuation to read the lines. For example, the simile that winds its way through lines 7–9 must be read continuously without pause.

BEST PRACTICES TOOLKIT—Transparency
Read Aloud/Think Aloud p. A34

Storm *Ending*

Jean Toomer

Thunder blossoms gorgeously above our heads,
Great, hollow, bell-like flowers,
Rumbling in the wind,
Stretching clappers to strike our ears . . **C**
5 Full-lipped flowers
Bitten by the sun
Bleeding rain
Dripping rain like golden honey—
And the sweet earth flying from the thunder.

C FIGURATIVE
MEANING
What is thunder
compared to in lines 1–4?
Explain what qualities
are emphasized by this
comparison.

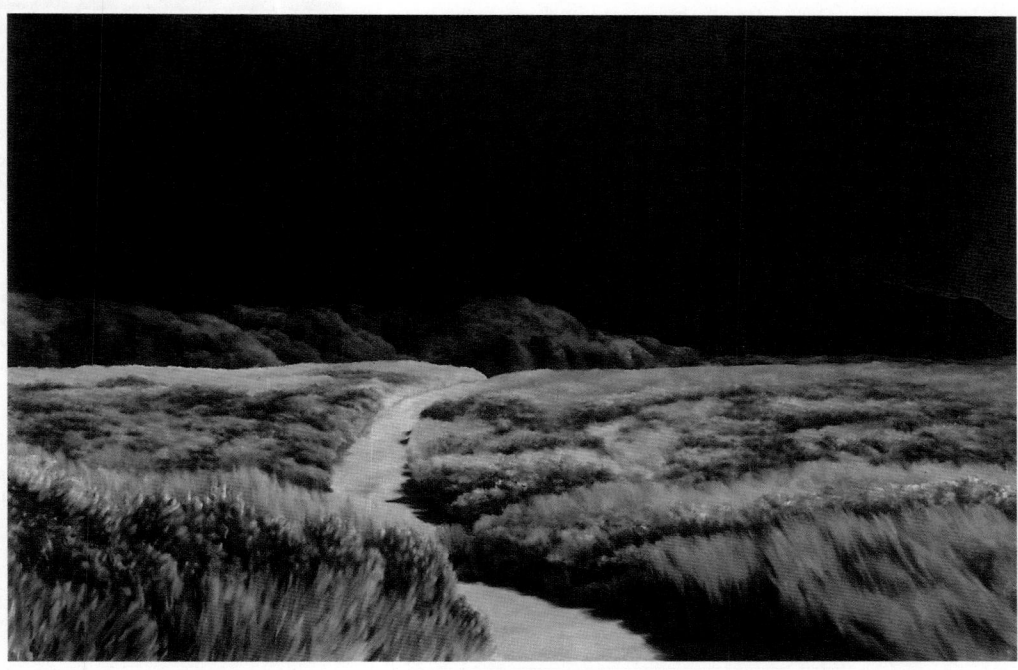

Field and Storm (2003), April Gornik. Oil on linen, 74″ × 95″. Courtesy of the artist and Danese Gallery, New York.

SUMMARY
In this poem, the speaker compares a thunderstorm to the blossoming of flowers.

READING SKILL

C FIGURATIVE MEANING

Answer: *Thunder is compared to flowers,
emphasizing beauty, shape, and movement.*

If students need help . . . Point out the
metaphor and help students add the
language and their impressions to the prereading chart introduced on page 853.

Example	Impressions
Thunder blossoms gorgeously above our heads.	The thunder grows like a flower. It is alive and beautiful.

Lines 1–9
TIERED DISCUSSION PROMPTS

Use these prompts to help students understand figurative language:

Connect Think about the sound of thunder. How would you describe it? *Accept all
thoughtful responses.*

Analyze How does the speaker personify
the sun, and to what effect? *Possible answer: The speaker says that the sun bites the
flowers. The effect is that nature is living and
violent.*

Evaluate Do you find the speaker's description of the storm effective? Explain.
*Possible answer: The description is effective
because its images are so vibrant and vivid
that the comparison comes alive.*

FOR STRATEGIC READERS
Concept Support: Sensory Images Help
students use Sensory Notes organizers to
categorize the images in "Storm Ending"
according to the five senses. Then lead
students in a discussion about the effect of
these sensory images. Point out that the
many sensory images complement the idea
that the storm is alive.

BEST PRACTICES TOOLKIT—Transparency
Sensory Notes p. B9

I See . . .	Most Important Image
huge blossoms	thunder clouds exploding

FOR ADVANCED LEARNERS/AP
Poetry Writing [paired option] Challenge
students to select one line from "Storm Ending"
and use it as a first line for a poem of their own
composition. Students may choose rhymed
or free verse, and may depart from Toomer's
subject of a storm. Invite students to share
their poems with a partner.

SUMMARY

This poem compares the struggles of African Americans in a racist society to the efforts of a tenant farmer. The farmer sows, but when it's harvest time, he discovers that someone else reaps the rewards and that his children must steal to survive.

ANALYZE VISUALS

Possible answer: The farmer in the painting appears grim and determined, much like the speaker of the poem. His clothes are worn, suggesting that he has led a life of hard work, but the poverty of the buildings in the background suggests that, like the speaker, the material rewards of his labor go elsewhere.

About the Art Painter, graphic designer, and illustrator Charly Palmer's (born 1960) subject matter is often concerned with historical subjects, including the African-American experience, Native Americans, and the Jewish Holocaust.

READING SKILL

D FIGURATIVE MEANING

Possible answer: The words "sown," "planted," and "grain" suggest farming.

LITERARY ANALYSIS

E THEME

Possible answer: The children's gleanings are bitter because the wealth of the father's work goes elsewhere—to the sons of the landowner.

SELECTION WRAP-UP

SYNTHESIZE Ask students what feature of the poems is most similar.

A Black Man Talks of Reaping

Arna Bontemps

Sunflowers, Charly Palmer. Mixed media collage on canvas, 48" × 24". © Charly Palmer.

I have sown beside all waters in my day.
I planted deep, within my heart the fear
That wind or fowl would take the grain away.
I planted safe against this stark, lean year. **D**

5 I scattered seed enough to plant the land
In rows from Canada to Mexico,
But for my reaping[1] only what the hand
Can hold at once is all that I can show.

Yet what I sowed and what the orchard yields
10 My brother's sons are gathering stalk and root,
Small wonder then my children glean[2] in fields
They have not sown, and feed on bitter fruit. **E**

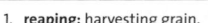

1. **reaping:** harvesting grain.
2. **glean:** gather grain left behind by reapers.

ANALYZE VISUALS
What elements of this painting reflect the theme of the poem?

D **FIGURATIVE MEANING**
Reread lines 1–4. What idea do the words *sown, planted,* and *grain* have in common?

E **THEME**
In lines 11–12, why are the children's gleanings described as "bitter fruit"?

DIFFERENTIATED INSTRUCTION

FOR STRATEGIC READERS
Concept Support: Extended Metaphor [paired option] Explain that metaphors may function on more than one level, suggesting a narrow and a broader comparison. Have pairs discuss possible meanings in the final stanza:

- *orchard,* "American society"
- *brother's sons,* "the white majority"
- *my children glean in fields,* "the status of African Americans forced to accept leftovers"
- *bitter fruit,* "racial resentment and strife"

FOR ADVANCED LEARNERS/AP
Research and Analyze [small-group option] Have groups research sharecropping in the American South to define and explain the system. Challenge students to analyze the balance of power in the system: Who held the social, political, and economic power? Could those without power gain it? Why did sharecroppers agree to participate? Ask students to find and share connections between this system and contemporary American social institutions.

Comprehension

1. **Summarize** In "Any Human to Another," what comparisons does the speaker use to describe grief?

2. **Clarify** In "Storm Ending," what event is described in the last line of the poem?

3. **Clarify** In "A Black Man Talks of Reaping," how much has the speaker reaped from all the seed he has scattered?

Literary Analysis

4. **Distinguish Figurative from Literal Meaning** Review the notes you took on Bontemps's poem. Bontemps uses an **extended metaphor,** a lengthy comparison of two things that have many points in common. Identify the extended metaphor Bontemps uses. What is this metaphor meant to suggest?

5. **Examine Imagery** "Storm Ending" includes several examples of **synesthesia,** imagery that uses one type of sensory experience to describe a different one—for example, a sound decribed as a smell. Identify two examples of synesthesia in the poem. Which two senses are combined in each image?

6. **Compare and Contrast Tone** Describe the tone, or attitude toward the subject, of Cullen's and Bontemps's poems. What **outlook** on the prospects for social equality does each poem suggest?

7. **Analyze Theme** Complete a chart like the one shown for each poem. What do you conclude is the theme of each poem?

Title Reveals:	Speaker's Identity:
Key Images:	Mood:

Literary Criticism

8. **Biographical Context** Reread the author biographies on page 852. In each case, what connections can you make between the poet's life story and the worldview expressed in his work? Be specific.

7. ● **SKILLS FOCUS** Theme *"Any Human to Another"*: **Title Reveals:** speaker's identity; **Key Images:** "pierce to the marrow," "solitary tent"; **Speaker's Identity:** human being; **Mood:** instructive or reflective; **Theme:** Sorrow is a shared experience. *"Storm Ending"*: **Title Reveals:** subject of poem; **Key Images:** "blossoming thunder," "bleeding rain"; **Speaker's Identity:** observer; **Mood:** intense natural beauty; **Theme:** What is fierce or dangerous is also beautiful. *"A Black Man Talks of Reaping"*: **Title Reveals:** speaker's identity; **Key Images:** "scattered seed," "bitter fruit"; **Speaker's Identity:** black sharecropper; **Mood:** bitter or sorrowful; **Theme:** Injustice has lasting consequences.

8. Cullen resisted defining himself by race. Similarly, his poem emphasizes connections among members of the human race. Toomer was influenced by imagist poetry. His poem focuses on images rather than social messages. Bontemps cherished his Southern roots. His poem features a black sharecropper in the South.

Practice and Apply

After Reading

Use these copy masters to check understanding and provide extra support:

R RESOURCE MANAGER—Copy Masters
Theme p. 61
Question Support p. 65

Additional selection questions are provided for teachers on page 57.

ANSWERS

1. *The speaker describes grief as an arrow (line 3), a river flowing into the sea (line 9), an unsheathed blade (lines 26–27), and a bitter aloe (line 29).*

2. *The last line of "Storm Ending" describes the wind blowing the storm clouds away.*

3. *The speaker of "A Black Man Talks . . . " reaps only what he can hold in his hand.*

Possible answers:

4. ■ **SKILLS FOCUS Distinguish Figurative from Literal Meaning** *Bontemps compares the African-American experience to farming. The metaphor suggests that African Americans have been deprived of the fruits of their labor, with harmful results.*

5. *Thunder blossoming combines sound and sight (line 1). Bitten by the sun combines touch and sight (line 6).*

6. *The tone of Cullen's poem is instructive. The tone of Bontemps's poem is despairing. Cullen's poem presents a more positive outlook on the prospect of social equality than does Bontemps's poem, suggesting that universal truths bind us more than our differences separate us.*

Assess and Reteach

Assess

R RESOURCE MANAGER—Copy Masters
Selection Test A pp. 67–68
Selection Test B/C pp. 69–70

Test Generator CD

Reteach

S STANDARDS LESSON FILE
Literature Lesson 11: Theme, Motif, and Epiphany
Writing Lesson 40: Imagery and Figurative Language

Focus and Motivate

OBJECTIVES

Literary Analysis
- explore the key idea of **personality**
- analyze tone
- read an essay

Reading
- identify explicit and implicit main ideas

Vocabulary
- build vocabulary for reading and writing
- use the Greek root *cosm/cosmo* to build meaning *(also an EL language objective)*

Grammar and Writing
- use sentence fragments for emphasis and to vary sentence structure
- write an autobiographical essay

 R3.3, R1.2, W1.2, W1.5, W1.9, W2.3

ABOUT THE AUTHOR

After students read the biography, ask them if they think Hurston followed her mother's advice, and why. *Possible answer: Yes, Hurston's life reflects the pursuit of seemingly impossible dreams. She finished school, went to college, became the first African American to graduate from Barnard, and published her works.*

USING THE *NOTABLE QUOTE*

Ask students what **Zora Neale Hurston** means by "it." *Possible answer: She means an energy that makes people special.* Point out that "it" was her strong sense of self-confidence, despite racial prejudice and discrimination.

Selection Resources

How It Feels to Be Colored Me
Essay by Zora Neale Hurston

CALIFORNIA

R3.3, R1.2 (p. 866), W1.2 (p. 867), W1.5 (p. 867), W1.9 (p. 867), W2.3 (p. 867)

NOTABLE QUOTE
"Those that don't got it, can't show it. Those that got it, can't hide it."

FYI
Did you know that Zora Neale Hurston . . .

- dressed so flamboyantly that one acquaintance referred to her as a "macaw of brilliant plumage"?
- shocked some people by wearing pants in public?
- became a fan of British poet John Milton after rescuing one of his books from the trash?

Author On|ine
For more on Zora Neale Hurston, visit the **Literature Center** at **ClassZone.com.**

Zora Neale Hurston
c. 1891–1960

Raised in the all-black town of Eatonville, Florida, Zora Neale Hurston followed her mother's advice to "jump at de sun"—to follow her dreams, no matter how impossible they seemed. In 1925, she arrived in New York with "$1.50, no job, no friends, and a lot of hope." Hurston's flair, talent, and sheer nerve soon made her one of the leading African-American novelists of the 1930s.

Early Days When Hurston was 13 years old, her family life fell apart. Her mother died, her father remarried, and by the age of 14, Hurston was on her own. Working an endless series of menial jobs, Hurston tried for years to earn enough money to send herself back to school. After 12 years of trials and adventures, she finally completed high school and scraped together a year's tuition for Howard University, "the Negro Harvard," where in 1921 she published her first story.

Collector of Stories By 1925, Hurston's efforts began to pay off. She won a scholarship to Barnard College, where she studied with the renowned anthropologists Franz Boas and Ruth Benedict. After graduating from Barnard in 1928—the first known African American to do so—Hurston returned to the South to collect African-American folklore. "I had to go back, dress as they did, talk as they did, live their life," she said, "so I could get into my stories the world I knew as a child." The lively, hilarious stories she collected soon became material for her own fiction. In the 1930s and '40s, she published a series of major works, including the folklore collection *Mules and Men* (1935), the novel *Their Eyes Were Watching God* (1937), and her autobiography, *Dust Tracks on a Road* (1942).

Down But Not Out Hurston often came under fire by African-American writers who felt she minimized the seriousness of racial prejudice. By the late 1940s, her books had fallen out of favor and out of print. During the last 20 years of her life, Hurston struggled to earn a living, once again working as a maid to pay her bills. In 1960, Hurston died in a welfare home, poor and nearly forgotten, and was buried in an unmarked grave in Fort Pierce, Florida. Thanks to the efforts of author Alice Walker, Hurston's work was rediscovered in the 1970s. Hurston is now acknowledged as an influential figure in the history of African-American literature.

858

RESOURCE MANAGER UNIT 5

Plan and Teach pp. 71–78

Literary Analysis
Summary pp. 79†*, 80‡*
Tone pp. 81, 82†*
Question Support p. 89*

Reading
Identify Main Ideas pp. 83, 84†*
Reading Check p. 88

Vocabulary
Study p. 85*
Practice p. 86
Strategy p. 87

Grammar and Writing
Vary Sentence Structure p. 90

Assessment
Selection Tests A, B/C pp. 91*, 93*
Test Generator CD

BEST PRACTICES TOOLKIT

Differentiated Instruction pp. 31–38*

Scaffolding Instruction pp. 43–46*

Graphic Organizers/Strategies
New Word Analysis • Cluster Diagram • Spider Map

Reading Support
Audio Anthology CD*

Technology
Literature, Vocabulary, and Writing Centers at **ClassZone.com**
Write*Smart* CD

---

* Resources for Differentiation   † Also in Spanish   ‡ In Haitian Creole and Vietnamese

LITERARY ANALYSIS: TONE

Famously outspoken, Zora Neale Hurston wasn't afraid to stand out from the crowd. In this essay, she writes about race with a distinctive **tone,** or attitude toward the topic, that sets her apart from other Harlem Renaissance writers.

I do not belong to that sobbing school of Negrohood who hold that nature somehow has given them a lowdown dirty deal....

A writer establishes tone through choice of words and details. Note Hurston's use of informal language (*lowdown*) and her flippant reference to other African-American writers (*sobbing school of Negrohood*). As you read the essay, think about her choice of words and details and the tone they create.

READING SKILL: IDENTIFY MAIN IDEAS

You know that the **main idea** of a paragraph is the basic point it makes. Sometimes, the main idea is **explicit,** or directly stated in the text. However, main ideas may also be only **implicit**—suggested or hinted at by the details in the text. In such cases, you'll need to analyze the details the author presents to discover the main idea.

As you read, use a chart like the one shown to record the main idea of each paragraph. If the main idea is implicit, note key details that helped you identify the main idea.

Paragraph	Main Idea	Key Details
1	I'm not ashamed to be colored.	offers no "extenuating circumstances"

◆ VOCABULARY IN CONTEXT

Hurston uses the following words to make her points about African-American identity. Restate each phrase, using a different word or words for the boldfaced term.

1. collected a **miscellany** of objects on her travels
2. did not use **pigmentation** to judge character
3. excused from penalties because of **extenuating** factors
4. dressed in colorful **raiment**
5. spoke **exultingly** of her triumphs
6. saw herself as **cosmic** rather than small and narrow

What makes you YOU?

KEY IDEA Think of the things that make you unique: your style, your sense of humor, the way you keep your head (or don't) when things get tense. Of all the qualities and behaviors that make you who you are, which ones do you think best define your **personality?**

SURVEY Of the things you do, what best expresses your personality? Create a snapshot of yourself by completing each statement in the following quiz.

The Insider's Guide to Me

1. To find me in a crowd, look/ listen for _____

2. The story my friends/family all tell about me is _____

3. Most people in school know me as _____

4. The thing I do that is most "me" is _____

What makes you YOU?

Lead into the **KEY IDEA** paragraph by asking the question. Invite students to use five words only to define their **personalities.** Urge them to draw upon these descriptions as they complete the *SURVEY* activity.

SKILLS FOCUS

LITERARY ANALYSIS   R3.3

● TONE

Write these lists on the board:

- "sobbing school of Negrohood"
- African-American writers
- brothers and sisters
- "low-down dirty deal"
- disadvantaged circumstance
- unfortunate situation

Ask students to brainstorm their associations with each phrase. **Possible answers: *sobbing school:* flippant, insulting; *African-American writers:* proper, politically correct; *brothers and sisters:* communal, inclusive; *low-down dirty deal:* slang, accusatory; *disadvantaged circumstance:* politically correct, distant; *unfortunate situation:* luck, chance**

CHECK UNDERSTANDING Have students discuss how replacing Hurston's phrases with the listed alternatives changes Hurston's tone and thus her meaning.

READING SKILL

■ IDENTIFY MAIN IDEAS

Direct students to **Early Days** on page 858. Point out that the text does not state the main idea directly. Ask students to use details to determine the main idea. ***Possible answer:** Hurston was determined and persistent in pursuing her goals, despite significant hardships.*

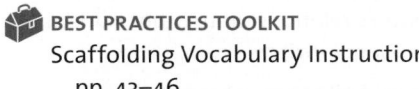 **RESOURCE MANAGER—Copy Master** Identify Main Ideas p. 83 (for student use while reading the selection)

VOCABULARY

◆ VOCABULARY IN CONTEXT

DIAGNOSE WORD KNOWLEDGE To determine preteaching needs, have all students complete Vocabulary in Context. ***Possible answers:** 1. variety, 2. skin color, 3. justifying, 4. clothing, 5. happily, 6. worldly*

PRETEACH VOCABULARY Preteach vocabulary with this copy master. Read each item aloud.

RESOURCE MANAGER—Copy Master Vocabulary Study p. 85

MORE VOCABULARY SUPPORT For additional activities and guidelines, see

BEST PRACTICES TOOLKIT Scaffolding Vocabulary Instruction pp. 43–46

ℹ Vocabulary Center at **ClassZone.com**

Practice and Apply

SUMMARY

Hurston describes herself as a little girl growing up in the all-African-American community of Eatonville, Florida, where she boldly interacts with white tourists, much to her family's chagrin. At the age of 13, Hurston goes to Jacksonville to attend school, where she discovers that she is a colored girl. Hurston discusses the impact of this lesson on her adult personality and her worldview, explaining that she finds race both important and irrelevant to her identity.

LITERARY ANALYSIS

Ⓐ TONE

Possible answer: *The tone reflects curiosity or novelty. Hurston reveals herself to be an acute observer of people and their behavior. Her tone suggests that she sees herself as equal to whites regardless of how others view her.*

How It Feels to Be Colored Me

Zora Neale Hurston

BACKGROUND Between 1865 and 1900, more than 100 independent towns were founded by African Americans trying to escape racial prejudice. Eatonville, Florida, a small town just north of Orlando, was the oldest of these self-governing black communities. Growing up in Eatonville, Zora Neale Hurston was sheltered from the experiences of exclusion and contempt that shaped the lives of many African Americans. As you read this essay, think about how these early experiences influenced Hurston's opinions on race.

ANALYZE VISUALS
What words would you use to describe the girl in the painting? Identify the techniques or elements that lend her these qualities.

I am colored but I offer nothing in the way of **extenuating** circumstances except the fact that I am the only Negro in the United States whose grandfather on the mother's side was *not* an Indian chief.

extenuating
(ĭk-stĕn′yōō-ā′tĭng) *adj.* lessening the severity of **extenuate** v.

I remember the very day that I became colored. Up to my thirteenth year I lived in the little Negro town of Eatonville, Florida. It is exclusively a colored town. The only white people I knew passed through the town going to or coming from Orlando. The native whites rode dusty horses, the Northern tourists chugged down the sandy village road in automobiles. The town knew the Southerners and never stopped cane chewing when they passed. But the Northerners were something
10 else again. They were peered at cautiously from behind curtains by the timid. The more venturesome would come out on the porch to watch them go past and got just as much pleasure out of the tourists as the tourists got out of the village. Ⓐ

Ⓘ **Targeted Passage**

Ⓐ **TONE**
Describe the tone of lines 1–12. What does Hurston's tone reveal about the way she sees herself?

The front porch might seem a daring place for the rest of the town, but it was a gallery seat to me. My favorite place was atop the gate-post. Proscenium box for a born first-nighter.[1] Not only did I enjoy the show, but I didn't mind the actors knowing that I liked it. I actually spoke to them in passing. I'd wave at them and when they returned my salute, I would say something like this: "Howdy-do-well-

---

1. **proscenium . . . first-nighter:** A proscenium box is a box seat near the stage. A first-nighter is a person who attends the opening night of a performance.

860   UNIT 5: THE HARLEM RENAISSANCE AND MODERNISM

Girl in a Red Dress (1934), Charles Alston. Oil on canvas, 71″ × 55.9″. © The Harmon and Harriet Kelley Collection of African American Art. Courtesy of Michael Rosenfeld Gallery, LLC, New York.

DIFFERENTIATED INSTRUCTION

FOR ALL STUDENTS
Expert Groups Encourage students to become subject experts by selecting and researching one of these topics:

- Hurston's relationship to other Harlem Renaissance writers
- Barnard College in the 1920s
- African-American towns such as Eatonville, Florida

FOR STRATEGIC READERS
In combination with the *Audio Anthology CD*, use one or more Targeted Passages (pp. 860, 862, 864) to ensure that students focus on key events and concepts. Targeted Passages are also good for English learners.

Ⓘ **Targeted Passage [Lines 4–12]**
This passage introduces Hurston and the setting of her childhood, the all-black community of Eatonville, Florida.

ANALYZE VISUALS

Possible answer: Students may respond that the girl appears tough, proud, or defiant (her straight posture, her fixed stare away from the viewer). They might also note that the girl is alone and set in sharp contrast with the background, suggesting she is isolated or lonely.

About the Art American artist Charles Alston (1907–1977) drew upon his study of African sculpture to paint human figures, using the canvas as a place to investigate color, space, and form.

Lines 13–23
REINFORCE *KEY IDEA:* PERSONALITY

Discuss How does Hurston's behavior define her **personality?** What role does Hurston see for herself in her life? *Possible answer: Hurston's behavior defines her personality as outgoing and dramatic, with a sense of humor. She sees herself as the star of her life's drama.*

- Where did Hurston live until she was 13 years old?
- What was unique about this place?
- How were Northern and Southern whites different?
- How did the townspeople respond to Northerners differently than they did to Southerners?

FOR ENGLISH LEARNERS

Key Academic Vocabulary Use New Word Analysis to teach these words: *register* (line 46), *potential* (line 48), *generation* (line 49), *achieve* (line 61), *contrast* (line 69).

 BEST PRACTICES TOOLKIT—Transparency New Word Analysis p. E8

Prereading For prereading instruction for English learners, see

 BEST PRACTICES TOOLKIT Scaffolding Reading Instruction pp. 43–46

FOR ADVANCED LEARNERS/AP

AP exercises in the bottom channel provide additional challenge for students. Use these suggestions for small groups or individuals.

ADDITIONAL GUIDELINES

For more help with differentiation and tips for classroom management, see

 BEST PRACTICES TOOLKIT Differentiated Instruction pp. 31–38

B MAIN IDEAS

Possible answer: Main Idea: One must be strong to succeed in life, regardless of color. Hurston implies that she is critical of those who make injustice and oppression the main features of black identity (lines 39–41).

If students need help . . . Determine the implied main idea by working together to add details about paragraph 6 to the pre-reading chart introduced on page 859.

Main Idea	Key Details
One must be strong to succeed in life, regardless of color.	"the world is to the strong . . . pigmentation"

LITERARY ANALYSIS

C TONE

Possible answer: It is unusual that Hurston is dismissive of slavery. This comment might offend African-American readers, while easing the guilt of white readers.

Extend the Discussion Should slavery be dismissed as an institution of the past, or is it important to recognize its ongoing effects for people of color?

I-thank-you-where-you-goin'?" Usually automobile or the horse paused at this, and after a queer exchange of compliments, I would probably "go a piece of the
20 way" with them, as we say in farthest Florida. If one of my family happened to come to the front in time to see me, of course negotiations would be rudely broken off. But even so, it is clear that I was the first "welcome-to-our-state" Floridian, and I hope the Miami Chamber of Commerce will please take notice.

During this period, white people differed from colored to me only in that they rode through town and never lived there. They liked to hear me "speak pieces" and sing and wanted to see me dance the parse-me-la,[2] and gave me generously of their small silver for doing these things, which seemed strange to me for I wanted to do them so much that I needed bribing to stop. Only they didn't know it. The colored people gave no dimes. They deplored any joyful tendencies in me, but
30 I was their Zora nevertheless. I belonged to them, to the nearby hotels, to the county—everybody's Zora.

But changes came in the family when I was thirteen, and I was sent to school in Jacksonville. I left Eatonville, the town of the oleanders,[3] as Zora. When I disembarked from the riverboat at Jacksonville, she was no more. It seemed that I had suffered a sea change.[4] I was not Zora of Orange County any more, I was now a little colored girl. I found it out in certain ways. In my heart as well as in the mirror, I became a fast brown—warranted not to rub nor run.

② **Targeted Passage**

But I am not tragically colored. There is no great sorrow dammed up in my soul, nor lurking behind my eyes. I do not mind at all. I do not belong to the
40 sobbing school of Negrohood who hold that nature somehow has given them a low-down dirty deal and whose feelings are all hurt about it. Even in the helter-skelter skirmish that is my life, I have seen that the world is to the strong regardless of a little **pigmentation** more or less. No, I do not weep at the world—I am too busy sharpening my oyster knife.[5] **B**

Someone is always at my elbow reminding me that I am the grand-daughter of slaves. It fails to register depression with me. Slavery is sixty years in the past. The operation was successful and the patient is doing well, thank you. The terrible struggle that made me an American out of a potential slave said "On the line!" The Reconstruction said "Get set!"; and the generation before said "Go!" I am
50 off to a flying start and I must not halt in the stretch to look behind and weep. Slavery is the price I paid for civilization, and the choice was not with me. It is a bully adventure and worth all that I have paid through my ancestors for it. No one on earth ever had a greater chance for glory. The world to be won and nothing to be lost. It is thrilling to think—to know that for any act of mine, I shall get twice as much praise or twice as much blame. It is quite exciting to hold the center of the national stage, with the spectators not knowing whether to laugh or to weep. **C**

---

2. **parse-me-la:** a dance movement popular with Southern African Americans of the period.

3. **oleanders** (ō′lē-ăn′dərz): evergreen shrubs with fragrant flowers.

4. **sea change:** complete transformation.

5. **oyster knife:** a reference to the saying "The world is my oyster," implying that the world contains treasure waiting to be taken, like the pearl in an oyster.

pigmentation
(pĭg′mən-tā′shən) *n.* coloring

B MAIN IDEAS
State the main idea of lines 38–44. What criticism is implied by the author's statement?

C TONE
Reread lines 51–52. Explain what is unusual about Hurston's tone. What effect might this comment have on an African-American reader? a white reader?

DIFFERENTIATED INSTRUCTION

FOR STRATEGIC READERS

② **Targeted Passage [Lines 32–37]**

This passage explains the change in color consciousness that Hurston experienced at age 13.

- Where did Hurston go when she turned 13?

- How was Hurston viewed differently in Jacksonville than in Eatonville?

- What effect did her move have on Hurston's sense of self?

FOR ENGLISH LEARNERS

Vocabulary: Idioms Clarify the reference to a race in lines 47–49. Explain that "on the line" calls racers to the race starting point, "get set" prepares them to start, and "go" tells them to begin racing.

Bal Jeunesse (about 1927), Palmer Hayden. Watercolor on paper, 14″ × 17″. Collection of Meredith and Gail Wright Sirmans.

The position of my white neighbor is much more difficult. No brown specter pulls up a chair beside me when I sit down to eat. No dark ghost thrusts its leg against mine in bed. The game of keeping what one has is never so exciting as the
60 game of getting.

I do not always feel colored. Even now I often achieve the unconscious Zora of Eatonville before the Hegira.[6] I feel most colored when I am thrown against a sharp white background.

For instance at Barnard. "Beside the waters of the Hudson"[7] I feel my race. Among the thousand white persons, I am a dark rock surged upon, overswept by a creamy sea. I am surged upon and overswept, but through it all, I remain myself. When covered by the waters, I am; and the ebb but reveals me again.

Sometimes it is the other way around. A white person is set down in our midst, but the contrast is just as sharp for me. For instance, when I sit in the
70 drafty basement that is The New World Cabaret with a white person, my color comes. We enter chatting about any little nothing that we have in common and are seated by the jazz waiters. In the abrupt way that jazz orchestras have, this one plunges into a number. It loses no time in circumlocutions, but gets right down to business. It constricts the thorax and splits the heart with its tempo and narcotic harmonies. This orchestra grows rambunctious, rears on its hind legs and attacks

---

6. **Hegira** (hĭ-jī'rə): journey (from the name given to Muhammad's journey from Mecca to Medina in 622).

7. **Barnard . . . Hudson":** Barnard is the college in New York City from which Hurston graduated in 1928. "Beside the waters . . ." is a reference to the first line of the college song.

FOR ADVANCED LEARNERS/AP

Research and Analyze Description [mixed-interest groups] Have students locate and listen to jazz music from the 1930s. Then ask students to analyze Hurston's description of jazz in lines 68–82. Students should pay attention to Hurston's word choice, sentence structure, sensory detail, and figurative language, listing examples of each in a Cluster Diagram. Have groups draw conclusions about how jazz affects Hurston and why.

Challenge students to use Hurston's prose as a model for their own descriptions of a favorite musical style or genre, conveying how the style or genre affects them emotionally.

🧰 BEST PRACTICES TOOLKIT—Transparency
Cluster Diagram p. B18

Activity Lead students to discuss how Hayden suggests movement in this painting. *Possible answer: The artist uses curving lines and shadow figures to suggest movement.*

About the Art American artist Palmer Hayden (c. 1890–1973) focused much of his work on depictions of African-American family and community life. While Hayden's time in Paris is likely reflected in this painting, the title of which roughly translates to *Youth Ball*, the image also evokes the jazz cabarets Zora Neale Hurston describes.

Lines 57–67
TIERED DISCUSSION PROMPTS

Use these prompts to help students understand Hurston's experience with color consciousness:

Connect Think about a situation in which you stood apart from the group for any reason—race, ethnicity, culture, age, gender, inexperience. How does that experience help you understand Hurston's feelings about her racial identity? *Accept all thoughtful responses.*

Interpret What does Hurston mean by "The game of keeping what one has is never so exciting as the game of getting"? *Possible answer: Hurston suggests that white people spend their time and energy trying to keep their status and are thus in a state of fear. Black people, on the other hand, spend their time and energy trying to gain equality and experience excitement through their efforts.*

Evaluate How effective is Hurston's use of imagery to explain her sense of color consciousness? *Possible answer: Hurston's imagery is very effective. She uses natural imagery (lines 65–67) and color imagery (lines 62–63) to describe moments when she feels most aware of her race.*

D MAIN IDEAS

Possible answer: *Hurston's response to the music is physical, while the man's response is merely auditory. This contrast implies that blacks experience life musically and emotionally, while whites observe it intellectually and from a distance.*

E GRAMMAR AND STYLE

Vary Sentence Structure Authors sometimes use sentence fragments to highlight details, add emphasis, or slow the pace or fluency of a passage. Ask students to identify the fragments in lines 108–111 and to explain their effect. ***Possible answer:*** *The entire sentence is composed of fragments. The effect is that of inviting readers to visualize this list of vivid details.* Then, have them find a sentence fragment in lines 99–101 and explain its effect.

SELECTION WRAP–UP

SUMMARIZE Have students sum up Hurston's views about the importance of race and color.

⭐ CRITIQUE

- Ask students to evaluate whether Hurston's view of race relations is valid in today's world. Why or why not?

- After completing the After Reading questions on page 865, have students revisit their responses and tell whether they have changed their opinions.

---

the tonal veil with primitive fury, rending it, clawing it until it breaks through to the jungle beyond. I follow those heathen—follow them **exultingly.** I dance wildly inside myself; I yell within, I whoop; I shake my assegai[8] above my head, I hurl it true to the mark *yeeeeooww!* I am in the jungle and living in the jungle way. My face is painted red and yellow, and my body is painted blue. My pulse is throbbing like a war drum. I want to slaughter something—give pain, give death to what, I do not know. But the piece ends. The men of the orchestra wipe their lips and rest their fingers. I creep back slowly to the veneer we call civilization with the last tone and find the white friend sitting motionless in his seat, smoking calmly.

"Good music they have here," he remarks, drumming the table with his fingertips.

Music! The great blobs of purple and red emotion have not touched him. He has only heard what I felt. He is far away and I see him but dimly across the ocean and the continent that have fallen between us. He is so pale with his whiteness then and I am *so* colored. **D**

At certain times I have no race, I am *me.* When I set my hat at a certain angle and saunter down Seventh Avenue, Harlem City, feeling as snooty as the lions in front of the Forty-Second Street Library, for instance. So far as my feelings are concerned, Peggy Hopkins Joyce on the Boule Mich[9] with her gorgeous **raiment,** stately carriage, knees knocking together in a most aristocratic manner, has nothing on me. The **cosmic** Zora emerges. I belong to no race nor time, I am the eternal feminine with its string of beads.

I have no separate feeling about being an American citizen and colored. I am merely a fragment of the Great Soul that surges within the boundaries. My country, right or wrong.

Sometimes, I feel discriminated against, but it does not make me angry. It merely astonishes me. How *can* any deny themselves the pleasure of my company! It's beyond me.

But in the main, I feel like a brown bag of **miscellany** propped against a wall. Against a wall in company with other bags, white, red, and yellow. Pour out the contents, and there is discovered a jumble of small things priceless and worthless. A first-water[10] diamond, an empty spool, bits of broken glass, lengths of string, a key to a door long since crumbled away, a rusty knife-blade, old shoes saved for a road that never was and never will be, a nail bent under the weight of things too heavy for any nail, a dried flower or two, still a little fragrant. In your hand is the brown bag. On the ground before you is the jumble it held—so much like the jumble in the bags, could they be emptied, that all might be dumped in a single heap and the bags refilled without altering the content of any greatly. A bit of colored glass more or less would not matter. Perhaps that is how the Great Stuffer of Bags filled them in the first place—who knows? ∾

8. **assegai** (ăs′ə-gī′): a type of light spear used in southern Africa.
9. **Peggy ... Boule Mich:** a wealthy woman of Hurston's day, walking along the Boulevard Saint-Michel in Paris.
10. **first-water:** of the highest quality or purity.

exultingly (ĭg-zŭlt′ĭng-lē) *adv.* joyfully

D MAIN IDEAS
Describe the two responses that are contrasted in lines 88–91. What does this contrast imply about the differences between whites and blacks?

raiment (rā′mənt) *n.* clothing; garments

cosmic (kŏz′mĭk) *adj.* of or relating to the universe

3 Targeted Passage

miscellany (mĭs′ə-lā′nē) *n.* a mixture of various things

E GRAMMAR AND STYLE
Reread lines 105–111. Note how Hurston uses **sentence fragments** to highlight specific details in her description.

DIFFERENTIATED INSTRUCTION

FOR STRATEGIC READERS
3 Targeted Passage [Lines 99–105]

This passage summarizes Hurston's views on racial identity and on her place in humanity.

- How does Hurston feel about being an American citizen?
- Of what is Hurston a "fragment"? (line 100)
- How does Hurston feel about being discriminated against?

- Why does Hurston call herself "a brown bag of miscellany" (line 105)?

FOR ENGLISH LEARNERS
Related Vocabulary The list of items in the colored bags includes both descriptive imagery and figurative language that stands for ideas beyond the text. Make sure students understand the meaning of these descriptions:

- *a key ... away* (line 109), "something from the past that is no longer useful"
- *old shoes ... will be* (lines 109–110), "memories or items related to a choice not made"
- *a nail ... any nail* (lines 110–111), "an experience that was an emotional burden"
- *a dried ... fragrant* (line 111), "an emotional, and probably happy, memory"

Comprehension

1. **Recall** In Hurston's description, what kind of community was Eatonville?

2. **Recall** What was the big change Hurston experienced at age 13?

3. **Paraphrase** What is Hurston's view on slavery?

Literary Analysis

4. **Identify Main Ideas** Review the chart you created as you read. What is the main idea of the essay? In what ways does race shape Hurston's sense of identity?

5. **Analyze Tone** Describe the tone of this essay. What point does Hurston make by choosing this tone to discuss the subject of race?

6. **Make Inferences** Judging from the anecdotes Hurston includes in her essay, what experiences and traits does she consider distinctively African-American? Support your answer with details.

7. **Interpret Analogy** An analogy is a point-by-point comparison that uses one thing or idea to make sense of another. Reread the analogy Hurston develops in lines 105–116. What message does this comparison convey? In your response, explain the meaning of each part of the analogy, including

   • the colored bags   • the "Great Stuffer of Bags"   • the bags' contents

8. **Compare and Contrast Author's Perspectives** Hurston's views set her apart from most of her Harlem Renaissance contemporaries. Choose one of the poets you have read in this unit, and use a chart like the one shown to contrast his perspectives with Hurston's. What similarities and differences do you find?

	Hurston's Views	_____'s Views
What Defines Black Identity		
Goals of Black Writers		
Opinions of Whites		

9. **Synthesize Details** Reread the author biography on page 858 and the background on page 860. What connections can you draw between Hurston's **personality**, her life experiences, and her unique perspective on race?

Literary Criticism

10. **Critical Interpretations** The author Alice Walker, one of Hurston's greatest admirers, finds Hurston's views sometimes "exasperating." She notes that this essay "presents two stereotypes: the 'happy darky' who sings and dances for white folks, for money and for joy; and the educated black person who is, underneath the thin veneer of civilization, still a 'heathen.'" Do you agree with Walker's views? Why or why not? Be specific in your response.

rather than as oppressors. Hurston was clearly a bold and independent thinker.

10. There is strong evidence in the essay to support Walker's position. Hurston's account of singing and dancing for whites (lines 25–28) complements the "happy darky" stereotype. Her physical reaction to jazz music and the primitive impulses it stirs complement the "heathen" stereotype (lines 77–82). The view of slavery as the "price I paid for civilization" (line 51) implies that blacks were uncivilized before enslavement. Although Hurston may intend her sentiments to be funny and liberating, many readers will take offense.

Practice and Apply

After Reading

Use these copy masters to check understanding and provide extra support:

📖 RESOURCE MANAGER—Copy Masters
   Reading Check p. 88
   Tone p. 81
   Question Support p. 89

   Additional selection questions are provided for teachers on page 75.

ANSWERS

1. Eatonville is an exclusively black and close-knit community.

2. Hurston's family situation changes, and she is sent to school in Jacksonville. Here, she is exposed to racial distinctions.

3. Hurston says that slavery is part of a closed past (lines 45–51).

Possible answers:

4. ■ **SKILLS FOCUS Identify Main Ideas**
   Main Idea: People of all colors are part of humanity, equal and beautiful. Race shapes Hurston's sense of identity when she is around white people, but she otherwise defines herself by personality.

5. ● **SKILLS FOCUS Tone** The essay is flippant, irreverent, and sometimes sarcastic. Hurston's point is that black identity isn't limited to the experience of oppression. She finds joy in who she is.

6. African-American experiences and traits include humor (lines 22–23), a strong sense of community (lines 13–22), and a passionate response to music (lines 68–85).

7. The bags represent different skin colors. The Great Stuffer of Bags is a higher being. The bags' contents are unique personalities. The analogy's message is that all people are made up of interchangeable traits and should be evaluated by traits, not by color.

8. Responses will vary depending on the poet chosen. **Hurston: Defining Black Identity:** community life, music, strong emotional responses. **Goals:** to write well. **Opinions of Whites:** amused sympathy.

9. Hurston's childhood in an all-black community shields her from humiliation and segregation during her formative years and gives her a strong sense of pride. She views whites as both similar to and different from herself

ANSWERS

Vocabulary in Context

VOCABULARY PRACTICE

1. *(c) regulation*   4. *(c) zoology*

2. *(c) weathering*   5. *(a) determinedly*

3. *(d) fictional*   6. *(d) exaggerating*

📘 **RESOURCE MANAGER—Copy Master**
Vocabulary Practice p. 86

VOCABULARY IN WRITING

Suggest that students begin by reviewing the definitions on the selection pages and the context of Hurston's use of each word. Then urge students to freewrite their ideas before inserting vocabulary words.

VOCABULARY STRATEGY: THE GREEK ROOT *COSM* OR *COSMO* (also an EL language objective)

- For each word in the web, help students use their knowledge of the root to determine word meaning.

- Review these Greek root meanings: *micro-*, "small"; *-graphy*, "writing"; *-naut*, "sailor"; *-logy*, "word"; *-polis*, "city." Clarify how these English words are built from the meanings of Greek roots.

Possible answers:

1. *cosmology*

2. *cosmonaut*

3. *cosmography*

4. *microcosm*

5. *cosmopolitan*

📘 **RESOURCE MANAGER—Copy Master**
Vocabulary Strategy p. 87

ℹ️ **Vocabulary Center at ClassZone.com**
Additional Vocabulary Activities

Vocabulary in Context

VOCABULARY PRACTICE

Choose the word that is not related in meaning to the other words.

1. (a) collection, (b) miscellany, (c) regulation, (d) assortment
2. (a) apparel, (b) clothing, (c) weathering, (d) raiment
3. (a) vast, (b) cosmic, (c) universal, (d) fictional
4. (a) shading, (b) pigmentation, (c) zoology, (d) coloration
5. (a) determinedly, (b) exultingly, (c) delightedly, (d) ecstatically
6. (a) extenuating, (b) moderating, (c) mitigating, (d) exaggerating

WORD LIST
cosmic
extenuating
exultingly
miscellany
pigmentation
raiment

VOCABULARY IN WRITING

What about Hurston's personality most impressed you? Using at least two vocabulary words, write a brief explanation of your opinion. Here is a sample beginning.

> **EXAMPLE SENTENCE**
> I was impressed that Hurston spoke **exultingly** of her good experiences and seemed to ignore any bad ones.

R1.2

VOCABULARY STRATEGY: THE GREEK ROOT *COSM* OR *COSMO*

The vocabulary word *cosmic* is derived from the Greek word *kosmos*, which means "world" or "universe." This root, which is spelled *cosm* or *cosmo* in English, is found in a number of words, both scientific and nonscientific. To understand words with *cosm* or *cosmo*, use your knowledge of the root as well as any context clues provided.

microcosm
cosmic
cosmopolitan
cosm, cosmo
cosmography
cosmology
cosmonaut

PRACTICE Apply what you know about the Greek root *cosm* or *cosmo* to the words in the web. Then, choose the word from the web that best completes each sentence. If you need to, consult a dictionary.

1. Many myths of creation also include a _____, or a theory of the universe.

2. A _____ is an explorer of outer space.

3. The science called _____ includes astronomy, geography, and geology.

4. A _____ can be any type of miniature community or world.

5. A _____ person tends to have a sophisticated view of the world.

VOCABULARY PRACTICE
For more practice, go to the **Vocabulary Center** at **ClassZone.com**.

DIFFERENTIATED INSTRUCTION

FOR ENGLISH LEARNERS

Task Support: Vocabulary Practice Point out the vocabulary words in the practice items. Have students identify familiar words among the remaining choices, and use dictionaries to define any unfamiliar words. Tell students to find any two word choices that are similar, and then to compare the remaining choices to this pair.

FOR ADVANCED LEARNERS/AP

Vocabulary in Writing Challenge students to consider the opinion other Harlem Renaissance poets might have about Hurston's ideas. Ask students to write a response to Hurston's essay from the view of one of the Harlem Renaissance poets, such as Langston Hughes, Claude McKay, or Countee Cullen. Urge them to use vocabulary words from the Word List in their writing.

Reading-Writing Connection

W1.2, W1.5, W2.3

WRITING PROMPT

WRITE AN AUTOBIOGRAPHICAL ESSAY Imagine that you have entered a writing contest sponsored by a heritage society. Draft a **three-to-five-paragraph autobiographical essay**, modeled after Hurston's essay, in which you share your feelings about your own heritage.

SELF-CHECK

An effective essay will . . .

- have a clear focus and sense of purpose
- use precise words and imagery to establish a mood or express emotion
- include relevant supporting details

GRAMMAR AND STYLE

VARY SENTENCE STRUCTURE Review the **Grammar and Style** note on page 864. Zora Neale Hurston's independent and unconventional personality shines through in her writing style. She wasn't afraid to bend the rules of formal writing, adding punch and emphasis through the use of **sentence fragments**. Here are two examples from the essay:

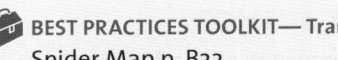

W1.9

> *I feel most colored when I am thrown against a sharp white background. For instance at Barnard.* (lines 62–64)

> *"Good music they have here," he remarks, drumming the table with his fingertips. Music! The great blobs of purple and red emotion have not touched him.* (lines 86–88)

The single-word fragment "Music" brings the reader to an abrupt halt, creating a dramatic pause before the exuberant description of the music's effects. The change in sentence rhythm helps emphasize the cultural gulf between Hurston and her white companion.

PRACTICE Rewrite the following paragraph in Zora Neale Hurston's style, incorporating one or two intentional sentence fragments. Add or delete any words as necessary.

> My parents were always finding opportunities to point out how much the world owed to China. We learned that our Chinese ancestors had invented paper, books, kites, gunpowder, compasses, fishing reels, and umbrellas. Was there anything that hadn't been invented by the Chinese? One day we went to eat at an Italian restaurant. As I dug into my plate of pasta, I told my mom, "Well, here's one thing the Chinese didn't invent." I was wrong! The Chinese invented pasta, she explained, and they invented restaurants, too!

WRITING TOOLS
For prewriting, revision, and editing tools, visit the **Writing Center** at ClassZone.com.

FOR DEVELOPING WRITERS
Writing Support

- Allow students to write a three-paragraph essay. The first paragraph should use an incident from early childhood, the second paragraph should relate an incident from school-age years, and the third should relate a more recent incident. In either the first or last paragraph, students should identify their heritage and state their feelings about it.

- To help them get started, ask students to decide on a particular feeling they want to convey about their heritage, such as proud, confused, or neutral. Urge students to choose three to five incidents from their life that reflect this feeling.

- For each incident they will discuss, have students list words that describe it. Work with students to replace general words with more specific and vivid language.

Reading-Writing Connection

WRITING PROMPT

Explain that students may define their heritage however they wish. Suggest that they begin by writing this definition in the center of a Spider Map. Tell students to fill the outer cells with features that support the definition, such as descriptions of family members, bits of dialogue, anecdotes, rituals or traditions, and so on.

🧰 **BEST PRACTICES TOOLKIT— Transparency** Spider Map p. B22

For writing support, see

ℹ️ Writing Center at **ClassZone.com**

GRAMMAR AND STYLE

Have students read the excerpts aloud to hear the change in rhythm created by sentence fragments. Urge students to continually compare their writing against the essay's style as they complete the **PRACTICE** activity. **Possible answer:** *My parents were always finding opportunities to point out how much the world owed to China. Paper. Books. Kites. Gunpowder. Compasses. Fishing reels. Umbrellas. One day while we were eating in an Italian restaurant, I slurped my pasta and said, "Well, here's one thing that the Chinese didn't invent!" Wrong again. Pasta.*

📘 **RESOURCE MANAGER—Copy Master** Vary Sentence Structure p. 90

Assess and Reteach

Assess

📘 **RESOURCE MANAGER—Copy Masters**
Selection Test A pp. 91–92
Selection Test B/C pp. 93–94

💿 Test Generator CD

Reteach

📄 **STANDARDS LESSON FILE**
Literature Lesson 43: Tone
Reading Lesson 4: Recognizing Main Idea and Details
Writing Lesson 8: Creating Sentence Variety
Vocabulary Lesson 6: Word Parts

Focus and Motivate

OBJECTIVES

Literary Analysis
- explore the key idea of **culture**
- analyze characteristics of literary criticism
- read literary criticism

Reading
- analyze author's position

CALIFORNIA R2.4

ABOUT THE AUTHOR

Clarify the reference to allegorical names in **A Major Literary Force,** explaining that an allegory is a work in which the characters are understood to represent something else, such as figures and ideas from religious texts. Point out that the selection also has religious references in it, although they are not allegorical. Ask students how Morrison's early upbringing sparked her interest in religion. *Possible answer: Morrison heard a lot of biblical references in her early years, which probably helped her view religious materials as both a part of daily life and a source for story ideas.*

USING THE *NOTABLE QUOTE*

Ask students why writers might want to familiarize the strange and mystify the familiar. What does this suggest about **Toni Morrison's** view of a writer's obligation? *Possible answer: Familiarizing the strange and mystifying the familiar invites readers to consider new perspectives. Morrison believes that it is a writer's job to provide readers with new perspectives.*

Selection Resources

Themes Across Time

CALIFORNIA R2.4

Thoughts on the African-American Novel
Literary Criticism by Toni Morrison

NOTABLE QUOTE
"The ability of writers to imagine what is not the self, to familiarize the strange and mystify the familiar, is the test of their power."

FYI
Did you know that Toni Morrison . . .

- was once a textbook editor?
- raised two sons as a single mother after her first marriage ended?
- changed her first name in college because "Chloe" was hard to pronounce?
- was the first African American to win the Nobel Prize in literature?

Author Online

For more on Toni Morrison, visit the **Literature Center** at ClassZone.com.

Toni Morrison
born 1931

Toni Morrison was born Chloe Anthony Wofford in Lorain, Ohio. This working-class town had a small, close-knit African-American community with a vibrant oral culture. In stories, songs, and everyday speech, Morrison heard an imaginative blend of biblical phrases, rhetorical devices, slang, and conventional English. This early awareness of the power of language and storytelling was a powerful influence on Morrison's work.

Accidental Novelist After earning a bachelor's degree from Howard University (1953) and a master's in English from Cornell University (1955), Morrison embarked on a teaching career. While teaching at Howard, she joined a writers' group for fun, showing up at meetings with what she called "old junk" that she'd written in high school. When she ran out of "junk" before one meeting, she quickly

scribbled down a story—a story that later inspired her first novel, *The Bluest Eye.* Published in 1969, the book recounts the story of a troubled African-American girl who, conditioned by white society's ideals of beauty, longs to have blue eyes. The novel's themes, such as the trauma of racism and the importance of community, set the stage for Morrison's later work.

A Major Literary Force The novels *Sula* (1973), *Song of Solomon* (1977), and *Tar Baby* (1981) established Morrison as a major author with a unique voice. Her novels typically have richly symbolic plots that include supernatural or fantastic elements. Within this imaginative context, Morrison provides a realistic treatment of social issues. Her characters, who often have allegorical or biblical names, confront the central struggles of African-American life: the impact of violence and injustice on their lives and the search for cultural identity.

Morrison has been nominated for every major literary honor; she has received, among others, the National Book Critics Circle Award, the Pulitzer Prize, and the Nobel Prize in Literature. She has written several novels and numerous works of commentary and cultural analysis. More recent novels include *Paradise* (1998) and *Love* (2003). Morrison lectures and teaches at various universities across the country. She is widely considered one of the most innovative stylists in contemporary American literature.

RESOURCE MANAGER UNIT 5

Plan and Teach pp. 95–102

Literary Analysis
Summary pp. 103†*, 104‡*
Literary Criticism pp. 105, 106†*
Question Support p. 110*

Reading
Identify Author's Position
    pp. 107, 108†*
Reading Check p. 109

Assessment
Selection Tests A, B/C pp. 111*, 113*
    Test Generator CD

BEST PRACTICES TOOLKIT

Differentiated Instruction
    pp. 31–38*
Scaffolding Instruction
    pp. 43–46*
Graphic Organizers/Strategies
Definition Mapping • Comparison Matrix

Reading Support
    Audio Anthology CD*

Technology
    Literature Center at
    ClassZone.com
    Write*Smart* CD

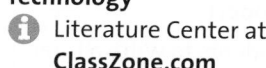

---

* Resources for Differentiation   † Also in Spanish   ‡ In Haitian Creole and Vietnamese

● LITERARY ANALYSIS: LITERARY CRITICISM

If you've ever read a book review, you're already familiar with **literary criticism,** writing that focuses on literary works, genres, and ideas. Works of literary criticism, which are most often essays or book reviews, are written to make readers more knowledgeable about, and appreciative of, the literature they read. Typically, these works

- describe a specific aspect—such as origins, characteristics, or impact—of a literary work, genre, or idea
- provide a historical or literary context for their subject
- describe standards for measuring the excellence of literary works

As you read, see what features of literary criticism you can identify in this essay.

■ READING SKILL: IDENTIFY AUTHOR'S POSITION

Works of literary criticism are written to communicate a position, or an opinion, on a topic. To identify an author's **position,** look for direct statements that express the author's viewpoint, such as the following:

I don't regard Black literature as simply books written by Black people, or simply as literature written about Black people . . .

You'll also want to look for the specific reasons and evidence the writer presents to support his or her opinion. As you read, identify Morrison's position on the importance of the novel to society and on the characteristics that define the African-American novel. In a chart like the one shown, record the reasons and evidence she uses to support her positions. Consider whether you find these positions persuasive.

	Position	Reasons and Evidence
Importance of the Novel		
What Defines the African-American Novel		

Can CULTURE *be captured in words?*

KEY IDEA You can think of **culture** as the things people make, such as food, books, music, and crafts. But culture is also the things people do: the way they talk, the relationships they build, the values they hold dear. In this essay, Toni Morrison talks about her struggle to capture the essence of African-American culture on the printed page.

QUICKWRITE Think about the cultures you belong to—your ethnicity, your religion, even your region or town. If you were writing about one of these cultures, what would you need to include? List three or more features you would use to capture the experience of that culture.

869

Can CULTURE *be captured in words?*

Lead into the **KEY IDEA** by asking the question. Discuss the definitions of **culture** and invite students to suggest additional examples. Have students use these ideas in completing the **QUICKWRITE.**

SKILLS FOCUS

LITERARY ANALYSIS

● LITERARY CRITICISM

Review with students that genre refers to the literary category in which a work belongs, such as novel or biography. Share an example of a book review with students. Work with them to find these elements of literary criticism:

- the work's genre
- the literary or historical context
- the review writer's standards for measuring excellence
- the key aspects of the work discussed

CHECK UNDERSTANDING Ask students if they ever choose books to read on the basis of reviews. Why or why not?

READING SKILL R2.4

■ IDENTIFY AUTHOR'S POSITION

Have students reread the **Notable Quote** on page 868. Ask them to identify Morrison's position on the qualities of a good writer. Have students identify supporting evidence for the stated position. ***Possible answer:*** *Morrison believes a good writer has strong imaginative powers. Evidence is the three tasks a good writer should be able to accomplish, because all three require imaginative powers.*

 RESOURCE MANAGER—Copy Master Identify Author's Position p. 107 (for student use while reading the selection)

DIFFERENTIATED INSTRUCTION

FOR STRATEGIC READERS
Vocabulary Support

- *context,* "background or overall situation related to a particular literary work"
- *criticism,* "analysis of qualities and opinion about relative worth"
- *evidence,* "information that helps prove an idea"
- *persuasive,* "having the power to change others' views"

- *position,* "one's attitude or opinion on a subject"
- *standards,* "something created as a basis of comparison to judge worth"
- *viewpoint,* "mental position from which things are judged"

Practice and Apply

SUMMARY

In this essay, Toni Morrison describes the novel as an art form that developed to help a rising middle class understand its world. She explains that novels enlighten, instruct, and identify problems and conflicts without offering recipes for solution. Morrison then focuses on the role of the novel for African Americans, and the need for black novels to function simultaneously as written and oral literature that requires readers to stand, speak, and act.

Lines 1–13
TIERED DISCUSSION PROMPTS

Use these prompts to help students think about the function of art:

Connect Name a song, movie, TV show, or book that taught you something about how to live your life. What message did it convey? *Accept all thoughtful responses.*

Interpret What does Morrison mean by "the novel always functioned for the class or the group that wrote it"? *Possible answer: Morrison means that the novel addresses issues of concern and interest to the group or class from which its writer emerges.*

Evaluate Do you agree or disagree with Morrison's claim that the purpose of art is to tell people something that they don't know? Explain. *Students will likely agree that art should offer people information or perspective beyond their current circumstances, and thereby teach and uplift. Others may disagree by noting that art should publicize and celebrate the insights that a culture has already arrived at.*

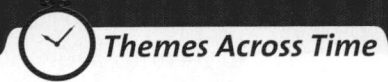
Themes Across Time

Thoughts
on the
African-American
Novel

Toni Morrison

The label "novel" is useful in technical terms because I write prose that is longer than a short story. My sense of the novel is that it has always functioned for the class or the group that wrote it. The history of the novel as a form began when there was a new class, a middle class, to read it, it was an art form that they needed. The lower classes didn't need novels at that time because they had an art form already: they had songs, and dances, and ceremony, and gossip, and celebrations. The aristocracy didn't need it because they had the art that they had patronized, they had their own pictures painted, their own houses built, and they made sure their art separated them from the rest of the world. But when the
10 industrial revolution began, there emerged a new class of people who were neither peasants nor aristocrats. In large measure they had no art form to tell them how to behave in this new situation. So they produced an art form: we call it the novel of manners, an art form designed to tell people something they didn't know. That is, how to behave in this new world, how to distinguish between the good guys and the bad guys. How to get married. What a good living was. What would happen

ANALYZE VISUALS
Read lines 1–15. How might the painting on page 871 be compared with the "novel of manners" referred to in lines 12–13? Explain.

① Targeted Passage

Family (1955), Charles H. Alston. Oil on canvas, 48¹/₄″ × 35³/₄″. Whitney Museum of American Art, New York. Purchase, with funds from the Artists and Students Assistance Fund 55.47. © Estate of Charles H. Alston.

DIFFERENTIATED INSTRUCTION

FOR ALL STUDENTS

Provide these independent projects to extend the lesson:

- Participate in a call-and-response format.
- Evaluate the purposes of a novel.
- Describe a character from one of Morrison's novels.

For further details on these projects, see

RESOURCE MANAGER
Ideas for Extension pp. 100–101

FOR STRATEGIC READERS

In combination with the *Audio Anthology CD*, use one or more Targeted Passages (pp. 870, 872) to ensure that students focus on key concepts in the selection. Targeted Passages are also good for English learners.

① Targeted Passage [Lines 9–15]

This passage explains Morrison's view of the novel's function for the middle class.

ANALYZE VISUALS

Possible answer: *Like the novel of manners, the painting seems to provide a model of family life for the viewer. In contrast, the painting is strikingly modern and uses an African-American family as the standard to follow.*

About the Art More abstract than his "Girl in a Red Dress" found on page 861, Charles Alston's (1907–1977) "Family" shows the diversity of his artistic style as well as his commitment to depicting African-American life.

BACKGROUND

Industrial Revolution Beginning in Britain in the 18th century, the Industrial Revolution marked a change from agricultural to industrial economies because physical labor was replaced by machines. This economic shift created large-scale social changes, such as the growth of cities and the challenges of living in them.

Lines 3–11
REINFORCE *KEY IDEA:* CULTURE

How is membership in an economic or social class part of one's **culture?** *Possible answer: One's economic or social class provides or limits opportunities for leisure, education, consumerism, and so on, which directly affect one's cultural affiliations.*

- What new group in society resulted from the Industrial Revolution?
- What did this new group lack?
- How did they respond to this situation?
- What is the novel of manners?

FOR ENGLISH LEARNERS

Key Academic Vocabulary Use Definition Mapping to teach these words: *technical* (line 1), *incorporate* (line 40), *expand* (line 48), *criteria* (line 84), *style* (line 91).

 BEST PRACTICES TOOLKIT—Transparency
    Definition Mapping p. E6

Prereading For prereading instruction for English learners, see

 BEST PRACTICES TOOLKIT
    Scaffolding Reading Instruction pp. 43–46

FOR ADVANCED LEARNERS/AP

AP exercises in the bottom channel provide additional challenge for students. Use these suggestions for small groups or individuals.

ADDITIONAL GUIDELINES

For more help with differentiation and tips for classroom management, see

 BEST PRACTICES TOOLKIT
    Differentiated Instruction pp. 31–38

if you strayed from the fold. So that early works such as *Pamela,* by Samuel Richardson, and the Jane Austen material¹ provided social rules and explained behavior, identified outlaws, identified the people, habits, and customs that one should approve of. They were didactic² in that sense. That, I think, is probably

20 why the novel was not missed among the so-called peasant cultures. They didn't need it, because they were clear about what their responsibilities were and who and where was evil, and where was good. Ⓐ

But when the peasant class, or lower class, or what have you, confronts the middle class, the city, or the upper classes, they are thrown a little bit into disarray. For a long time, the art form that was healing for Black people was music. That music is no longer *exclusively* ours, we don't have exclusive rights to it. Other people sing it and play it; it is the mode of contemporary music everywhere. So another form has to take that place, and it seems to me that the novel is needed by African-Americans now in a way that it was not needed before—and it is

30 following along the lines of the function of novels everywhere. We don't live in places where we can hear those stories anymore; parents don't sit around and tell their children those classical, mythological archetypal³ stories that we heard years ago. But new information has got to get out, and there are several ways to do it. One is in the novel. I regard it as a way to accomplish certain very strong functions—one being the one I just described. Ⓑ

It should be beautiful, and powerful, but it should also *work.* It should have something in it that enlightens; something in it that opens the door and points the way. Something in it that suggests what the conflicts are, what the problems are. But it need not solve those problems because it is not a case study,⁴ it is not a

40 recipe. There are things that I try to incorporate into my fiction that are directly and deliberately related to what I regard as the major characteristics of Black art, wherever it is. One of which is the ability to be both print and oral literature: to combine those two aspects so that the stories can be read in silence, of course, but one should be able to hear them as well. It should try deliberately to make you stand up and make you feel something profoundly in the same way that a Black preacher requires his congregation to speak, to join him in the sermon, to behave in a certain way, to stand up and to weep and to cry and to accede or to change and to modify—to expand on the sermon that is being delivered. In the same way that a musician's music is enhanced when there is a response from the audience.

50 Now in a book, which closes, after all—it's of some importance to me to try to make that connection—to try to make that happen also. And, having at my disposal only the letters of the alphabet and some punctuation, I have to provide the places and spaces so that the reader can participate. Because it is the affective

---

1. **the Jane Austen material:** Jane Austen (1775–1817) wrote several novels focused on middle-class life in her era.
2. **didactic** (dī-dăk′tĭk): intended to instruct.
3. **archetypal** (är′kĭ-tī′pəl): serving as a pattern for later examples.
4. **case study:** an intensive analysis of a group, individual or unit and its development.

DIFFERENTIATED INSTRUCTION

FOR STRATEGIC READERS

② **Targeted Passage [Lines 23–35]**

This passage explains why Morrison believes that the novel is important to African Americans.

- What art form has often been healing for African Americans?

- Why is this art form no longer healing?

- What art form do African Americans need now?

- What need does that art form meet?

FOR ADVANCED LEARNERS/AP

Discuss Point out to students that Edith Wharton is also considered to be a novelist of manners. Even though "April Showers" is a short story and not a novel, have students re-read it on pages 792 to 800. Then have them discuss whether or not the story is "didactic" in the sense that Morrison describes at the top of page 872.

and participatory relationship between the artist or the speaker and the audience that is of primary importance, as it is in these other art forms that I have described. **C**

To make the story appear oral, meandering, effortless, spoken—to have the reader *feel* the narrator without *identifying* that narrator, or hearing him or her knock about, and to have the reader work *with* the author in the construction
60 of the book—is what's important. What is left out is as important as what is there. To describe sexual scenes in such a way that they are not clinical, not even explicit[5]—so that the reader brings his own sexuality to the scene and thereby participates in it in a very personal way. And owns it. To construct the dialogue so that it is heard. So that there are no adverbs attached to them: "loudly," "softly," "he said menacingly." The menace should be in the sentence. To use, even formally, a chorus. The real presence of a chorus. Meaning the community or the reader at large, commenting on the action as it goes ahead.

In the books that I have written, the chorus has changed but there has always been a choral note, whether it is the "I" narrator of *Bluest Eye,* or the town
70 functioning as a character in *Sula,* or the neighborhood and the community that responds in the two parts of town in *Solomon.*[6] Or, as extreme as I've gotten, all of nature thinking and feeling and watching and responding to the action going on in *Tar Baby,* so that they are in the story: the trees hurt, fish are afraid, clouds report, and the bees are alarmed. Those are the ways in which I try to incorporate, into that traditional genre the novel, unorthodox novelistic characteristics—so that it is, in my view, Black, because it uses the characteristics of Black art. I am not suggesting that some of these devices have not been used before and elsewhere—only the reason why I do. I employ them as well as I can. And those are just some; I wish there were ways in which such things could be talked about
80 in the criticism. My general disappointment in some of the criticism that my work has received has nothing to do with approval. It has something to do with the vocabulary used in order to describe these things. I don't like to find my books condemned as bad or praised as good, when that condemnation or that praise is based on criteria from other paradigms.[7] I would much prefer that they were dismissed or embraced based on the success of their accomplishment within the culture out of which I write. **D**

I don't regard Black literature as simply books written *by* Black people, or simply as literature written *about* Black people, or simply as literature that uses a certain mode of language in which you just sort of drop *g*'s. There is something
90 very special and very identifiable about it and it is my struggle to *find* that elusive but identifiable style in the books. My joy is when I think that I have approached it; my misery is when I think I can't get there. ❧

---

5. **not clinical, not even explicit:** not coldly impersonal or even clearly detailed.

6. *Solomon:* Morrison's novel *Song of Solomon*.

7. **paradigms** (păr′ə-dīmz′): theoretical frameworks or patterns.

C LITERARY CRITICISM
What does Morrison regard as the main characteristic of African-American art?

D AUTHOR'S POSITION
Reread lines 68–86. What examples from her own work does Morrison cite as **evidence** for her position?

C LITERARY CRITICISM

Possible answer: African-American art demands audience participation (lines 53–56).

Extend the Discussion How can readers participate in a literary work?

READING SKILL

D AUTHOR'S POSITION

Possible answer: Morrison cites these examples to support her position: the "I" narrator as a chorus in The Bluest Eye *(line 69), the town as a character in* Sula *(lines 69–70), a responsive community in* Song of Solomon *(lines 70–71), and personified nature in* Tar Baby *(lines 71–74).*

If students need help . . . Work with them to complete the prereading chart introduced on page 869.

Position	Evidence
African-American literature requires reader participation.	• "I" narrator as a chorus in *The Bluest Eye* • town as a character in *Sula*

SELECTION WRAP-UP

SUMMARIZE Have students sum up Morrison's position on the importance and defining characteristics of the African-American novel.

⭐ **CRITIQUE**

• Have students evaluate Morrison's position (lines 82–86) that art is bound by the artist's culture and should be evaluated within the framework of that culture.

• After completing the After Reading questions on page 874, have students revisit their responses and tell whether they have changed their opinions.

FOR ENGLISH LEARNERS

Language: Conversational English Patterns
Point out dashes and sentence fragments in lines 57–67. Explain that the dashes are used to set text apart. Urge students to read the sentence without the text inside the dashes and then add it back. Use lines 61–63 to model how to restate the sentence fragments in complete sentences by adding implied text or attaching fragments to nearby complete sentences. Have students apply this strategy to lines 63–67.

FOR ADVANCED LEARNERS/AP

Write Dialogue [paired option] Have students reread lines 63–65 in which Morrison describes her goals for dialogue. Challenge students to develop a dialogue that reflects these goals, imbuing each sentence with the tone it should contain. Ask students to work in pairs to present a dramatic reading of each partner's dialogue.

Practice and Apply

After Reading

Use these copy masters to check understanding and provide extra support:

R **RESOURCE MANAGER—Copy Masters**
Reading Check p. 109
Literary Criticism p. 105
Question Support p. 110

Additional selection questions are provided for teachers on page 99.

ANSWERS

1. *Morrison associates the novel with the middle class.*

2. *The novel is especially important for African Americans because they have no other art forms that are exclusively theirs. They also need to be reconnected with classical, mythical, archetypal stories.*

3. *The chorus allows Morrison to provide an oral element to her written stories.*

Possible answers:

4. ■ **SKILLS FOCUS** Identify Author's Position
Students may feel that Morrison supports her positions well, with detailed examples and reasons. Others may feel that Morrison's arguments are vague and that her support focuses on literary qualities found in many cultures.

5. ● **SKILLS FOCUS** Literary Criticism
Morrison's essay focuses on a single genre and describes its origins. She also creates a literary context for her discussion and describes the standards for assessing black art.

Assess and Reteach

Assess

R **RESOURCE MANAGER—Copy Masters**
Selection Test A pp. 111–112
Selection Test B/C pp. 113–114

📀 Test Generator CD

Reteach

S **STANDARDS LESSON FILE**
Literature Lesson 25: Recognizing Critical Approaches
Reading Lessons 14–17: Persuasion and Argumentation

R2.4

Comprehension

1. **Recall** With what social class does Morrison associate the novel?

2. **Clarify** According to Morrison, why is the novel especially important for African Americans?

3. **Clarify** Why is it important to Morrison to include a chorus in her fiction?

Literary Analysis

4. **Examine Author's Position** Review the chart you created as you read. In your opinion, does Morrison provide compelling support for her positions? Explain your answer.

5. **Analyze Literary Criticism** Review the bulleted list on page 869. In what ways is Morrison's essay typical of a work of literary criticism? Support your answer with details.

6. **Analyze Details** Explain the comparison Morrison makes in lines 44–48. What does this comparison reveal about the way Morrison views her work?

7. **Compare and Contrast Authors' Perspectives** Consider the aspects of African-American culture Morrison tries to capture in her novels. What artistic goals does Morrison share with the writers of the Harlem Renaissance? How does her vision of black culture compare with theirs? Explain your answer.

8. **Evaluate Author's Purpose** Literary criticism has three main purposes: to inform readers, to express the writer's opinions, and to persuade readers to accept those opinions. Based on your reading, which of these purposes was Morrison trying to achieve with her essay? Which, if any, did she achieve? Support your answer with details.

Literary Criticism

9. **Critical Interpretations** Consider the qualities Morrison identifies as characteristic of African-American art forms. Which of the Harlem Renaissance works you read would meet Morrison's criteria for African-American art? Cite details in your answer.

---

6. *The comparison suggests that Morrison views her work as having a moral or didactic function to inspire understanding. Morrison also believes that readers should share in the work of creating the novel.*

7. *Morrison tries to capture the sense of community and interactive participation in African-American culture. She defines that culture in terms of oral tradition. Morrison borrows a European form to express her message but infuses it with elements that are distinctively black. She shares with Harlem Renaissance writers the goal of present-*

ing authentic visions of the black experience, a deference to the oral tradition, and the belief that art can affect society.

8. *Students will find evidence in Morrison's essay to support all three purposes. They should support their evaluations with details.*

9. *Students may suggest the work of Langston Hughes or Zora Neale Hurston.*

Perspectives on the Harlem Renaissance

Literary historian Richard Gray states the following about the writers of the Harlem Renaissance.

> "[W]hat is notable about them is how they explored different literary forms to express the condition of African Americans in their times. Facing a racial experience the determining feature of which was that it was mixed and conflicted, they were prepared individually to confront and collectively to debate the question of just how their experience should be turned into literature."

Because the experiences of the Harlem Renaissance writers were "mixed and conflicted," their works naturally examined different aspects of African-American life.

Writing to Analyze

Imagine that you are a publisher who is planning to print the works beginning on page 840 in a slim anthology called *The Harlem Renaissance*. You'd like to organize the works into thematic groupings to help your readers gain a sense of some of the issues and concerns that these writers, despite their varied experiences, collectively held in common. With a partner, work together to create a table of contents for your book, with the works grouped under thematic headings, such as "Social Protest" or "Reflections on Heritage." Then write a brief explanation of why you grouped the works as you did.

Consider

- which selections deal with similar topics or themes (some selections may explore several themes, giving you the option to group them in more than one way)
- what overarching phrases might best express those topics or themes
- what, specifically, from each selection led you to place it in its particular grouping

Writers Jessie Fauset, Langston Hughes, and Zora Neale Hurston

Extension Online

RESEARCH Go online to find two additional works by Harlem Renaissance writers to add to your anthology. You may choose works by writers already represented in your anthology, or works by other Harlem Renaissance writers, such as Paul Laurence Dunbar or Helene Johnson. Give an **oral reading** for the class, and explain where you would place the works in your anthology.

CALIFORNIA W2.2

DIFFERENTIATED INSTRUCTION

FOR DEVELOPING WRITERS

Writing Support Suggest that students work with the provided thematic headings "Social Protest" and "Reflections upon Heritage." Make sure that students understand the meanings of each of these phrases. Then tell students to place the works in the category where they best fit. Help students identify examples in each work that support their placement. Tell students to use these examples when writing their explanations.

FOR ENGLISH LEARNERS

Writing Explanatory Notes To help students write explanations of their literary placements, provide sentence starters:

- [Title] belongs in the "Social Protest" grouping because _____.
- [Title] belongs in the "Reflections upon Heritage" grouping because _____.

Tell students to find details in the selections to support each placement.

Wrap-Up: The Harlem Renaissance

This Wrap-Up provides students with an opportunity to revisit ideas from the literature in this section about writers of the Harlem Renaissance and to consider how these writers sought to express the African-American experience. Encourage students to examine their own understandings of African-American culture in light of insights gained from the selections.

Writing to Analyze

- Review with students that *analyzing* means examining the parts of a literary work so as to discover its nature, purpose, style, theme, and so on. This process helps readers better understand the work as a whole, as well as find relationships among works.
- To help students create their table of contents, suggest that they use colored self-stick tags or notes to mark the works for topics and themes. Urge students to make an index card summarizing the topics and themes identified for each work. Partners can then group and regroup the cards to experiment with different combinations.

Extension Online

- If students are researching online, suggest that they search by the writers' names. Some additional writers to consider include Waring Cuney, Nella Larsen, and Angelina W. Grimke. Students might also use key phrases such as *Harlem Renaissance, African-American literature,* or *literature of social protest*.
- Direct students to practice reading the identified additional works aloud before presenting them to the class. Remind students to read according to punctuation and with feeling. Also, suggest that students also write out and rehearse their explanations ahead of time.

 BEST PRACTICES TOOLKIT—Transparency Read Aloud/Think Aloud p. A34

Focus and Motivate

OBJECTIVES

Media Literacy

- explore the key idea of a **documentary**
- view a documentary to understand how visual and sound techniques are used to craft a biographical narrative
- research and plan a biographical documentary

 CALIFORNIA LS1.3, LS1.10, LS2.4

SUMMARY

In this documentary, African-American novelist Veronica Chambers narrates the life of Zora Neale Hurston, from Hurston's beginning in Eatonville, Florida, to her end in obscurity. Opening with Hurston's proud assertion, "I am not tragically colored," the film presents her adolescent discovery of literature, her 1925 arrival in New York City, her early literary success, and her anthropology study. The film also chronicles the historical contexts of the Harlem Renaissance and racial conflict after World War I.

How do you DOCUMENT *a life?*

Lead into the **KEY IDEA** by asking the question. Discuss students' ideas about what they would include in a **documentary** of their lives. Then ask what media forms they would include, such as video clips, still photographs, writings, interviews with themselves or others, and voice-over narration. Tell students to look for these forms of information as they view the film.

BACKGROUND

Veronica Chambers, who narrates this film, is an American writer whose writings reflect her African and Latin heritage. Chambers has written for many national magazines, including *Glamour, Seventeen,* and *Newsweek.* Her young adult novels include *Marisol and Magdalena* and *Quinceañera Means Sweet 15.* With film director John Singleton she co-wrote *Poetic Justice: Filmmaking South Central Style.* She is best known for her 1996 memoir, *Mama's Girl,* about growing up in the 1970s.

Media Study

Jump at the Sun

Documentary on **MediaSmart** DVD

CALIFORNIA LS1.3, LS1.10 (p. 879), LS2.4 (p. 879)

How do you DOCUMENT *a life?*

KEY IDEA Think about how you would tell the story of your life. What events would you include to help someone understand the essential you? What would you leave out? Filmmakers face similar questions when they make a biographical **documentary.** The many details of a person's life must be boiled down to the key events that influenced and shaped that person. As you view *Jump at the Sun,* notice the details chosen to tell Zora Neale Hurston's life story.

Background

A Vibrant Life Zora Neale Hurston lived her life fully by following her mother's advice. "Mama exhorted her children at every opportunity to 'jump at de sun,'" Hurston explained. "We might not land on the sun, but at least we would get off the ground."

Hurston was a passionate woman who celebrated her role as a black female writer at a time when that was not an easy role to play. She was confident and proud of her heritage, making no apologies for who she was or what she did.

Hurston's dazzling personality and the dynamic times she lived through made her an ideal subject for a documentary film. Thus, the idea for *Jump at the Sun* was born. The filmmakers faced a challenge, though—Hurston died nearly a half-century ago, and film footage of her was not available. The filmmakers, therefore, had to find a way to bring her strong personality to life for the viewer, relying primarily on photographs, paintings, music, and readings from Hurston's own work. The filmmakers' challenge was to shape this material into a coherent and interesting film that tells the story of her life and work.

Jump at the Sun imparts to the viewer both the facts—the actual events that made up Hurston's life—and the exuberance of her personality. As you study the film, you'll explore the techniques used to bring life to the Harlem Renaissance and one of its most spirited writers.

Zora Neale Hurston

876

Media Study Resources

 RESOURCE MANAGER UNIT 5

Plan and Teach pp. 115–118

Media Analysis
Summary pp. 119†*, 120‡*
Viewing Guide p. 121
Close Viewing p. 122
Media Activity p. 123
Produce Your Own Media p. 124

 STANDARDS LESSON FILE

Media Lesson 4: Analyzing Visuals
Media Lesson 5: Analyzing Sound
Media Lesson 7: Evaluating Films and TV Shows
Media Lesson 20: Producing a Video

 Media Center at **ClassZone.com**

MEDIA VIEWING
 Media*Smart* DVD

* Resources for Differentiation † Also in Spanish ‡ In Haitian Creole and Vietnamese

Media Literacy: Documentary

A **documentary** is a nonfiction film that often presents social, political, or historical subject matter. Prominent people make good subjects, as they allow the filmmaker to explore both an interesting life and its greater social context.

Feature filmmakers and other storytellers often repeat an old adage: "Show, don't tell." Many documentary filmmakers follow the same principle, presenting their material as a story that unfolds before the viewer's eyes. The use of **primary sources,** which include photographs, film clips, letters, and eyewitness accounts, helps to immerse the viewer in the subject's world.

DOCUMENTARY TOOLS AND TECHNIQUES

Visual
- **Footage** is recorded material used to reveal information about a subject. It includes film clips, news reports, photographs, interviews, and text. Footage can be used to create a visual and emotional impression of the times.
- **Camera movement**—such as zooming in from a long shot to a close-up, and tracking shots, which move the camera parallel to the object being filmed—can give a dynamic feel to a still picture.

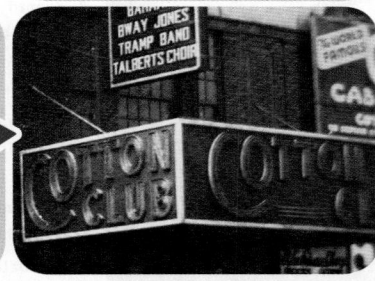

RACE RIOTERS FIRE
AND SHOOT OR HA
DEAD ESTIMATE

MANY BODIES IN THE RUINS | *More Sto*

Sound
- **Voice-over narration** is the voice of an unseen speaker that can be heard in a documentary.
- The style and tempo of the **music** will generally match the mood of the story and signal transitions to different settings or time periods.
- **Sound effects** are often used to help re-create a scene. For example, filmmakers may add crowd and traffic noise over a picture of a city.

STRATEGIES FOR VIEWING

As you view a documentary, consider the filmmakers' purpose in creating the film. Realize that documentaries reflect the point of view of the filmmaker. They do not always represent objective truth.
- Notice the different types of **footage** used in a documentary. Pay special attention to the use of **primary sources.** Note how they help to bring the story to life by using the "show, don't tell" principle.
- Listen to the different types of **voice-over narration.** In this documentary, the main narrator provides the facts of the subject's life story. The second narrator evokes Hurston's personality with a lively reading of her work.
- Consider how the **visual** and **sound techniques** work together. Think about why the particular footage was chosen to accompany each type of voice-over narration. Notice how the music changes with each major shift in the story.

MEDIA STUDY **877**

Media Literacy

Have students imagine that they are making a documentary about someone living in the 1920s. Specify that they would have no film or video clips showing the person. Have them suggest ways to make up for this lack, using the elements on the chart on page 877. Discuss each element as it is mentioned.

- **Visual** Have students brainstorm ways to use **footage** such as still photographs, newspaper articles, and other texts to add visual information to a documentary. Call attention to the news headline on page 877, and ask how **camera movement** emphasizes it on the page. ***Possible answer:*** *A close-up shot emphasizes the text.*

- **Sound** Tell students to assume that there are no sound recordings of their subject. Instead they will use **voice-over narration** that includes readings of the subject's words and other people's comments about the subject. Ask students how they differentiate the two for viewers. ***Possible answer:*** *The subject's words could be read in a voice similar to that person's, while other people's comments could be read in various voices.*

STRATEGIES FOR VIEWING

Call attention to the idea that documentaries reflect the filmmaker's perspective and do not always represent objective truth. Ask students how a documentary made up entirely of factual materials could reflect a subjective opinion. ***Possible answer:*** *The filmmaker's choice of what details to include and what to exclude reflects a point of view. Music, visuals, and the tone of voice-over can also convey a perspective.*

MediaSmart DVD

MEDIA STUDY: TEACHING OPTIONS

Teaching Option 1: The Basics (1–2 Days)
1. Begin the Media Study using the material provided on pages 876–877.
2. Show the Introduction on MediaSmart. Then show the First Viewing. As they watch, have students use the Viewing Guide on page 878, along with the corresponding copy master on page 121 of the Resource Manager. Discuss their responses.
3. Return to the pupil book for the extension activities on page 879.

Teaching Option 2: In-Depth Study (2–3 Days)
1. Begin the Media Study using pages 876–877.
2. Show the Introduction and First Viewing from MediaSmart. Then continue on MediaSmart with the Media Lessons, using the teacher notes available in the Resources section.
3. Show the Guided Analysis presentation. Have students record their observations on the Student Viewing Guide available in the Resources section from MediaSmart.
4. Return to the pupil book, page 879.

Practice and Apply

VIEWING GUIDE

1. Before viewing, inform students that the documentary presents Zora Neale Hurston's life in the context of her historical times, especially the 1920s. Ask students to briefly discuss their prior knowledge of American literature and society in the 1920s, including the Harlem Renaissance.

2. Point out that any given documentary may rely more on some tools and techniques than on others, depending on the available sources and on the director's stylistic choices. Suggest that students notice which tools and techniques "Jump at the Sun" relies on most, and think about why. Urge them in particular to watch and listen for these elements:

   - the **vocal qualities** of the narrator that convey her youth and her admiration for Hurston

   - **visuals** that capture the character and vibrancy of Hurston's hometown

   - **music** that captures the spirit of Hurston's time

R RESOURCE MANAGER—Copy Masters
   Viewing Guide p. 121
   Close Viewing p. 122
   Media Activity p. 123

Use this resource with the Viewing Guide:

⊘ Media*Smart* DVD

ANSWERS

FIRST VIEWING: Comprehension

1. *Samuel Taylor Coleridge*

2. *Hurston thought it was more important to write about the thoughts, feelings, and motivations of people in general than to write specifically about race.*

CLOSE VIEWING: Media Literacy

3. *They wanted to educate or inform. The film concentrates on facts about Hurston and quotations from her work. It is positive about her work without pushing an agenda.*

4. *Using a young writer to narrate Hurston's life story shows the influence her work continues to have today.*

⊙ **MediaSmart** *DVD*
- **Film:** *Jump at the Sun*
- **Genre:** Documentary
- **Voice-Over Narrator:** Veronica Chambers
- **Running Time:** 9 minutes

878

Viewing Guide for
Jump at the Sun

Filmmakers face a difficult challenge when they set out to tell a true story. They must carefully choose which details are necessary to bring the tale to life. Consider the documentary techniques you examined as you view the Zora Neale Hurston biography. Think about how each element contributes to the story being told. You may need to watch the documentary more than once in order to analyze it properly.

NOW VIEW

FIRST VIEWING: Comprehension

1. **Recall** What poet's work so influenced Hurston that she was moved to devote herself to literature?

2. **Clarify** What were Hurston's feelings about whether African-American writers have a duty to write about race relations?

CLOSE VIEWING: Media Literacy

3. **Identify Filmmakers' Purpose** Documentaries are made for a variety of purposes. For example, they can educate, inform, or influence opinion. What do you think the makers of *Jump at the Sun* wanted to achieve? Explain.

4. **Analyze the Voice-Over** The documentary is narrated by the writer Veronica Chambers. Why do you think the filmmakers chose a young writer to narrate the story of Hurston's life?

5. **Analyze Visuals** What types of images are shown to depict Hurston's hometown? Why do you think this type of footage was chosen?

6. **Evaluate Technique** In your opinion, which of the techniques in *Jump at the Sun* is the most effective in conveying Hurston's personality? Cite evidence from the film to support your opinion. Think about

   - the use of such **primary sources** as photographs, film clips, and the actual text read from Hurston's *Dust Tracks on a Road*

   - **music** that suggests the 1920s

   - the two types of **voice-over narration**

5. *Paintings of life in a small African-American town are shown. They were probably chosen because not many photographs of Eatonville exist from Hurston's time. Also, the paintings represent the town colorfully and well.*

6. *Some students will say that reading from Hurston's work is the most effective technique because the narrator's accent and enthusiasm capture Hurston's personality and bring her to life.*

Assess and Reteach

Write or Discuss

Compare the Texts Zora Neale Hurston was known for her unique personality. Think about the most memorable parts of Hurston's essay "How It Feels to Be Colored Me." Now consider the ways Hurston is depicted in the documentary. Write a paragraph that compares the Zora portrayed in the film with the Zora you know from the text. Think about

LS1.3

- the tone evident in the essay and in the documentary
- the quotes from Hurston's work that are included in the film, and the style in which they're read
- the selection of images and music in the film

Produce Your Own Media

Plan a Documentary Imagine you are making a documentary about someone you know well. Gather the materials you'll need to film your documentary and present them to the class. They should include **primary source material** from your subject's life, **interviews** with friends or family members, and a script for the **voice-over narration.**

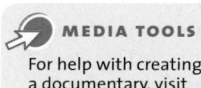
LS1.10, LS2.4

HERE'S HOW Write interview questions about your subject for two or three friends or family members to answer. Write a script for the voice-over narration that gives a brief overview of the life you're describing. Collect your primary source material. Consider these suggestions:

- Choose photographs or home video footage.
- Find out about the people or events that have had the greatest impact on your subject's life. Find ways to represent them visually.
- Decide what music might be appropriate. Match it to the events you'll cover.

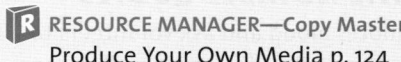
MEDIA TOOLS
For help with creating a documentary, visit the **Media Center** at **ClassZone.com.**

Tech Tip
If a video camera is available, film your documentary.

Further Exploration

Create a Shooting Plan Now that you've gathered the materials for your documentary, plan how you will shoot it. Decide on the best image to start your film. Plan where you'll use the interviews you conducted, and over what images the voice-over narration will play. Think about when you'll play the music you've chosen. Remember that your film should both inform the audience and keep them interested throughout. Write a description of your film that includes the order in which you'll present your footage, the sounds that will accompany each segment, and the types of shots you'll use.

Write or Discuss

Compare the Texts Students' paragraphs should compare *tone, quotations, images,* and *music* as appropriate in each text. Their responses should also show understanding of Hurston's personality as evoked in both media, and should compare the visual and written presentations. For example, students might say that Hurston's self-confidence and winning personality come to life more effectively in the documentary because her words are read aloud.

Produce Your Own Media

Rubric: Plan a Documentary A strong film plan should have

- materials gathered from primary sources, including interviews
- a script for voice-over narration
- description of footage, such as photographs or home video
- other visual representations, such as still photographs and important documents from the subject's life
- a description of appropriate music

R RESOURCE MANAGER—Copy Master
   Produce Your Own Media p. 124

Further Exploration

Create a Shooting Plan Suggest that students divide their plan into numbered scenes and divide each scene into shots. They might begin by dividing the voice-over narration into small chunks and choosing material to illustrate each chunk. Remind students to consider using camera movement to enliven still photos or other still shots.

MEDIA STUDY WRAP–UP

Have students summarize what they have learned about visual and sound tools and techniques that documentary filmmakers use to portray real people and events. Urge students to refer back to specific elements, such as *footage, camera movement, voice-over narration, music,* and *sound effects* when explaining.

RETEACH

S STANDARDS LESSON FILE

Media Lesson 4: Analyzing Visuals in Film and TV

Media Lesson 5: Analyzing Sound in Film and TV

Media Lesson 7: Evaluating Films and TV Shows

Media Lesson 20: Producing a Video

Focus and Motivate

OBJECTIVES

Literary Analysis
- explore the key idea of **contentment**
- analyze characterization in narrative poetry
- read poetry

Reading
- analyze speaker's attitude

R3.4

ABOUT THE POETS

Edward Arlington Robinson Have students cite aspects of Robinson's life that indicate failure or disappointment. *Possible answer: His family fortunes declined, which forced him to drop out of Harvard, and he struggled as a poet for many years.* Tell them that Robinson's characters often experience failure and disappointment as well.

Edgar Lee Masters Ask students to find evidence in the biography that Masters's view of his characters might be complex. *Possible answer: He both admired and despised rural people.*

USING THE *NOTABLE QUOTES*

Read the quotes aloud and ask volunteers to paraphrase them. *Possible answers: Robinson: He knows that people try to look better than they really are. Masters: What if a person's inner life is bigger than his outer life?* Point out that both quotations contrast reality and appearance and that the three poems students will read do as well.

Selection Resources

R3.4

Edwin Arlington Robinson
1869–1935

NOTABLE QUOTE
"He knows much of what men paint themselves would blister in the light of what they are."

Richard Cory
Miniver Cheevy

Poetry by Edwin Arlington Robinson

Failure is a familiar subject in the poetry of Edwin Arlington Robinson, and one the artist knew well. Robinson wrote poetry for years before achieving recognition, and he witnessed family members suffer one personal defeat after another.

A Difficult Youth His father's financial struggles forced Robinson to curtail his studies at Harvard University. The family's fortunes continued to decline and Robinson's mother died of diphtheria in 1896. In addition, he lost both of his brothers to fatal addictions.

Devotion to His Craft Despite his tragic past and his own struggles with alcoholism, Robinson devoted his life to his craft. Over time he gained a reputation as one of the country's most accomplished narrative poets.

Reflections of the Past Robinson's best known poems explore the inner lives of the citizens of Tilbury Town, a fictional community modeled on Robinson's hometown of Gardiner, Maine. Many poems grew out of the tragic experiences of his family and childhood acquaintances. Often, the poems focus on individuals who are brought low because of their own personal failings and the town's repressive, materialistic culture.

Edgar Lee Masters
1868–1950

NOTABLE QUOTE
"How shall the soul of man be larger than the life he has lived?"

Lucinda Matlock

Poetry by Edgar Lee Masters

When his brilliant portrait of rural life, *Spoon River Anthology,* first appeared in 1915, Edgar Lee Masters became a literary sensation. Both the general public and renowned critics embraced the book, making it an American classic.

The Making of a Poet The book grew out of Masters's memories of growing up in the central Illinois towns of Lewiston and Petersburg. Living on his grandparents' farm in Petersburg and in the semi-industrialized Lewiston, Masters acquired both an appreciation and a distaste for rural culture. While he admired the hard work and resilience of rural folk, he despised their small-mindedness and bigotry. Eventually Masters left rural Illinois for the big city, residing in Chicago and New York City.

Literary Masterpiece Masters remains most famous for his *Spoon River Anthology.* In this book, 244 deceased inhabitants of the fictional town of Spoon River deliver monologues in which they bare their souls. The cast of characters is varied, ranging from prostitutes and thieves to librarians and Masters's own grandmother Lucinda, the model for "Lucinda Matlock."

Author Online
For more on these poets, visit the **Literature Center** at ClassZone.com.

Selection Resources

R RESOURCE MANAGER UNIT 5

Plan and Teach pp. 125–132

Literary Analysis
Characterization in Narrative
  Poetry pp. 133, 134†*
Question Support p. 137*

Reading
Analyze Speaker's Attitude
  pp. 135, 136†*

Assessment
Selection Tests A, B/C pp. 139*, 141*
⊘ Test Generator CD

BEST PRACTICES TOOLKIT

Differentiated Instruction
  pp. 31–38*

Graphic Organizers/Strategies
Visualizing • Comparison Matrix

Reading Support
⊘ Audio Anthology CD*

Technology
ⓘ Literature Center at
  ClassZone.com
⊘ Write*Smart* CD

---

* Resources for Differentiation   † Also in Spanish

LITERARY ANALYSIS: CHARACTERIZATION IN NARRATIVE POETRY

While most modernist poets turned their efforts to lyric poetry, Edward Arlington Robinson and Edgar Lee Masters continued to develop the tradition of narrative poetry, often telling stories of interesting characters in the context of their communities. Like fiction, **narrative poetry** tells a story using elements of plot, character, and setting. To develop character, poets may adapt methods of **characterization** typically used in fiction.

- physical description of the character, including vivid **imagery**
- the character's own actions, words, thoughts, and feelings
- comments, thoughts, or actions of other characters
- direct comments about the character by the poem's speaker

As you read these poems, pay attention to the methods used by the poet to develop the characters.

***Review:* Meter**

READING SKILL: ANALYZE SPEAKER'S ATTITUDE

In many poems, the **speaker** has a persona that is distinct from the poet. It is the speaker's **attitude** that shapes our view of the poem's subject. In each of the following poems, a speaker delivers a character sketch; in one case, the speaker is describing herself. By noticing the details and phrases the speaker uses to describe the character, we can learn about his or her attitude not only toward the character but toward life.

To analyze the speaker's attitude toward the character in each poem, use a chart like the one shown. As you read, jot down the details and phrases from each poem that reflect that attitude. One example has been filled in for you.

Details and Phrases Reflecting Speaker's Attitude		
"Richard Cory"	"Miniver Cheevy"	"Lucinda Matlock"
"He was a gentleman from sole to crown"		

What makes for a FULL LIFE?

KEY IDEA Everyone wants to be happy, but happiness comes more easily to some people than to others. What is the secret? Some seek happiness in close, loving relationships. Others pursue their dreams and try to remain true to their inner voice. Still others strive for the comforts of material success and prosperity. The following poems portray characters who have met with varying degrees of success in their search for **contentment**.

DISCUSS With a partner, make a list of some different ways in which people seek happiness. Which are the most likely to succeed? Which are the least likely? After discussing these questions, present your conclusions to the class.

881

What makes for a FULL LIFE?

Lead into the **KEY IDEA** by asking the question and inviting students' answers. Note the routes to **contentment** mentioned in the paragraph and ask students to suggest examples of these routes. Have students bring their ideas to the ***DISCUSS*** activity.

SKILLS FOCUS

LITERARY ANALYSIS R3.4

● CHARACTERIZATION IN NARRATIVE POETRY

Invite students to characterize Robinson or Masters using the information on page 880. The photographs supply physical description. The ***NOTABLE QUOTES*** supply the characters' own words. The text supplies direct comments about the characters. Have students share their impressions of the poets' characters.

READING SKILL

■ ANALYZE SPEAKER'S ATTITUDE

Ask students to imagine two poems about a teacher. In one poem, the speaker is the teacher herself; in the other poem, the speaker is one of the teacher's students. How would the attitudes of those two speakers toward the teacher be different? *Students may say that the teacher's attitude would be highly personal and reflective while the student's attitude might focus on how the teacher affected him or her.*

CHECK UNDERSTANDING Ask students to name a famous person and state two or more attitudes that different people could have about the person.

 RESOURCE MANAGER—Copy Master Analyze Speaker's Attitude p. 135 (for student use while reading the selections)

DIFFERENTIATED INSTRUCTION

FOR STRATEGIC READERS

Concept Support: Analyze Speaker's Attitude Clarify that *attitude* describes how the speaker feels about the poem's subject, such as admiring or disappointed. Urge students to look for descriptive nouns, adjectives, and verbs that suggest such attitudes. For example, the excerpt on page 881 uses the word *gentleman,* which conveys a positive attitude. The word *crown* for "head" also suggests a positive attitude, conveying an image of a king or queen.

Practice and Apply

SUMMARY

The title character of this poem is the rich industrialist of a small town, envied by all until he commits suicide without warning.

LITERARY ANALYSIS

Ⓐ CHARACTERIZATION

Possible answer: Richard Cory is elegant, polished, and attractive. By saying "he fluttered pulses" (line 7) and "he glittered when he walked" (line 8), the speaker is saying that even when Cory attempts to be friendly, his wealth and status distance him from those he lives among.

If students need help . . . Discuss why someone's voice and appearance would cause pulses to flutter. Help students see that objects that glitter are usually valuable, which suggests Cory's wealth. Ask students how others often feel about those who are wealthy.

READING SKILL

Ⓑ SPEAKER'S ATTITUDE

Possible answer: Cory's wealth gives him apparent ease, while the townspeople seem beset by problems (lines 13–14). They regard him with envy (lines 11–12).

RICHARD CORY

Edwin Arlington Robinson

Whenever Richard Cory went down town,
We people on the pavement looked at him:
He was a gentleman from sole to crown,
Clean favored,[1] and imperially slim.

5 And he was always quietly arrayed,
And he was always human when he talked;
But still he fluttered pulses when he said,
"Good-morning," and he glittered when he walked. Ⓐ

And he was rich—yes, richer than a king—
10 And admirably schooled in every grace:[2]
In fine,[3] we thought that he was everything
To make us wish that we were in his place.

So on we worked, and waited for the light,
And went without the meat, and cursed the bread;
15 And Richard Cory, one calm summer night,
Went home and put a bullet through his head. Ⓑ

Ⓐ **CHARACTERIZATION**
Reread lines 1–8. Describe Richard Cory's appearance and manners. What do you think the speaker means by "he fluttered pulses" and "he glittered when he walked"?

Ⓑ **SPEAKER'S ATTITUDE**
Reread lines 11–14. What contrast does the speaker draw between Richard Cory and the townspeople? How do they seem to regard him?

---

1. **clean favored:** having a tidy appearance.
2. **schooled in every grace:** extremely well-mannered and cultured.
3. **in fine:** in short.

Sir Philip Sassoon (1923), John Singer Sargent. Oil on canvas, 95.2 cm x 57.8 cm. Tate Gallery, London. © Tate Gallery, London/Art Resource, New York.

DIFFERENTIATED INSTRUCTION

For general guidelines on differentiating instruction, see

 BEST PRACTICES TOOLKIT
Differentiated Instruction pp. 31–38

FOR STRATEGIC READERS
Options for Reading: Audio Recording

- Have students listen to the poems on the *Audio Anthology CD* (also recommended for English learners) while they read along in their books. Have students listen to the reader's tone and use it to infer the attitude of the poems' speakers.

- Note the absence of rhyme in "Lucinda Matlock." Urge students to read according to punctuation, not line breaks.

883

TIERED DISCUSSION PROMPTS

Use these prompts to help students understand Richard Cory's behavior:

Connect Think of a time you envied someone, then learned that he or she was actually very unhappy. How does that experience help you understand Richard Cory's behavior? *Students' responses should show an awareness of the possible contradiction between inner feelings and outward appearances.*

Analyze At what point do readers realize that Richard Cory is unhappy? Looking back, does the poem provide any clues to this outcome? Explain. *Possible answer: Readers realize Cory's unhappiness in the last line of the poem. The isolation hinted at in lines 7–12 is a clue to the ending.*

Evaluate Is the surprise ending effective? Why or why not? Explain. *Possible answer: Some students will say it is effective, because it mirrors the surprise of the events described. Others will say it is implausible because there is not enough evidence to explain Cory's unhappiness.*

FOR STRATEGIC READERS

Concept Support: Analyze Speaker's Attitude
Help students add to the prereading chart introduced on page 881, noting details that express the speaker's attitude toward Richard Cory. Point out that the comment "richer than a king" suggests the speaker's envy and even a little resentment.

Details and Phrases Reflecting Attitude
"Richard Cory"
"he was rich—yes, richer than a king"

FOR ADVANCED LEARNERS/AP

Speculate about Character Cory's suicide is a surprise to readers and to his fellow citizens. Have students speculate either orally or in writing about the reasons for Cory's suicide. Urge them to identify possible external reasons, such as scandal or business failure, as well as internal ones. Then ask students to create descriptions of Cory's life and character based on their inferences.

MINIVER CHEEVY

Edwin Arlington Robinson

Reading in a Study, Walt Louderback. Oil on plywood, 76.2 cm × 59.7 c⊓ collection. Photo ©Bridgeman Art Library.

Miniver Cheevy, child of scorn,
    Grew lean while he assailed[1] the seasons;
He wept that he was ever born,
    And he had reasons.

5 Miniver loved the days of old
    When swords were bright and steeds
      were prancing;
The vision of a warrior bold
    Would set him dancing. **C**

Miniver sighed for what was not,
10   And dreamed, and rested from his labors;
He dreamed of Thebes and Camelot,
    And Priam's neighbors.[2]

Miniver mourned the ripe renown
    That made so many a name so fragrant;
15 He mourned Romance, now on the town,
    And Art, a vagrant.

Miniver loved the Medici,[3]
    Albeit[4] he had never seen one;
He would have sinned incessantly
20   Could he have been one. **D**

---

1. **assailed:** attacked violently, in this case with words.
2. **Thebes** (thēbz) **...Camelot...Priam's** (prī′əmz) **neighbors:** Thebes was an ancient Greek city, the setting of many famous legends; Camelot was the site of King Arthur's legendary court; Priam's neighbors were participants in the Trojan War, during which Priam was king of Troy.
3. **Medici** (mĕd′ə-chē): a powerful Italian family that funded the arts and ruled Florence, sometimes with cruel and immoral leaders, during the Renaissance.
4. **albeit** (ôl-bē′ĭt): even though.

Miniver cursed the commonplace
     And eyed a khaki suit with loathing;
He missed the medieval grace
     Of iron clothing. **E**

25 Miniver scorned the gold he sought,
       But sore annoyed was he without it;
    Miniver thought, and thought, and thought,
       And thought about it.

    Miniver Cheevy, born too late,
30   Scratched his head and kept on thinking;
    Miniver coughed, and called it fate,
       And kept on drinking. **F**

E SPEAKER'S ATTITUDE
Identify the **irony** in lines 23–24. What does this irony suggest about the speaker's attitude toward Miniver's love of the medieval?

F METER
How does the last line of the poem change your understanding of Miniver? Recall your earlier analysis of the poem's meter, and explain its effect in this stanza.

Literary Analysis

1. **Recall** What is the townspeople's initial impression of Richard Cory?

2. **Recall** Why does Miniver Cheevy claim to be unhappy?

3. **Compare Texts** What is similar about the ways the two poems end? In each case, how do the last two lines change your view of the character?

REINFORCE *KEY IDEA*: CONTENTMENT
Discuss Is **contentment** possible for Miniver? Why or why not? What does he do about it?
Possible answer: *Contentment is possible for Miniver because his life is not bad, but he turns away from this possibility to brood and drink.*

READING SKILL

E SPEAKER'S ATTITUDE
Possible answer: *The notion that "iron clothing" could be graceful is ironic. The irony suggests that the speaker doesn't take Miniver's love of the medieval seriously.*

LITERARY ANALYSIS: *Review*

F METER
Possible answer: *The revelation that Miniver is a drinker tells readers that Miniver has deeper problems than a longing for the past. The change in meter underscores the seriousness of this sudden revelation.*

ANSWERS

1. *Initially, the townspeople are impressed by Richard Cory's wealth and gentility.*

2. *Miniver Cheevy claims to be unhappy because he was not born in the Middle Ages.*

3. *The two poems end by revealing something shocking about the characters. In each case, the last two lines show that the character is more deeply troubled than he appears on the surface.*

FOR STRATEGIC READERS
Compare and Contrast Characters To help students compare texts, suggest that they create a Comparison Matrix for Richard Cory and Miniver Cheevy. Categories might include wealth, happiness, self-destructive actions, tastes, and other categories that students devise.

	Richard Cory	Miniver Cheevy
Wealth	wealthy	poor

BEST PRACTICES TOOLKIT—Transparency
Comparison Matrix p. A24

Prereading for this poem is found on page 880.

SUMMARY

In this first-person poem, the speaker describes her 96 years of rural hard work, family life, tragedy, and joy, and expresses a view that life should be lived fully.

ANALYZE VISUALS

Possible answer: Qualities of quiet, homespun grace and dignity can be seen in the dancers and in Lucinda Matlock.

About the Art This 1941 oil painting by Jenne Magafan (1916–1952) is a study for a mural made for the Anson, Texas, post office. Its qualities of rustic simplicity and stately grace can also be found in Lucinda Matlock's poetic voice.

LITERARY ANALYSIS

G CHARACTERIZATION

Possible answer: The speaker's behavior reveals a healthy, life-affirming joy.

READING SKILL

H SPEAKER'S ATTITUDE

Possible answer: She might be addressing her sons and daughters or, figuratively, the younger generation that is angry, sad, or disappointed. She feels they are weak.

If students need help . . . Reread lines 18–22 aloud to emphasize the speaker's tone.

SELECTION WRAP-UP

SYNTHESIZE Have students describe the view of small-town or rural early 20th century America portrayed in these three poems.

LUCINDA MATLOCK

Edgar Lee Masters

Detail of *Cowboy Dance* (mural study, Anson, Texas, post office) (1941), Jenne Magafan. Oil on fiberboard. Photo © Smithsonian American Art Museum, Washington, D.C./Art Resource, New York.

I went to the dances at Chandlerville,
And played snap-out[1] at Winchester.
One time we changed partners,
Driving home in the moonlight of middle June,
5   And then I found Davis.
We were married and lived together for seventy years,
Enjoying, working, raising the twelve children,
Eight of whom we lost
Ere I had reached the age of sixty.
10 I spun, I wove, I kept the house, I nursed the sick,
I made the garden, and for holiday
Rambled over the fields where sang the larks,
And by Spoon River gathering many a shell,
And many a flower and medicinal weed—
15 Shouting to the wooded hills, singing to the green valleys. **G**
At ninety-six I had lived enough, that is all,
And passed to a sweet repose.[2]
What is this I hear of sorrow and weariness,
Anger, discontent and drooping hopes?
20 Degenerate[3] sons and daughters,
Life is too strong for you—
It takes life to love Life. **H**

ANALYZE VISUALS
What qualities do you sense in the dancers portrayed in this painting? Do you find them to have anything in common with Lucinda Matlock? Explain.

G CHARACTERIZATION
Reread lines 1–15. What does the speaker's behavior reveal about her?

H SPEAKER'S ATTITUDE
Whom do you think the speaker is addressing in lines 18–22? How does she seem to feel about them? Explain.

---

1. **snap-out:** a game in which players join hands in a line, then run about trying to shake off those at the end of the line.

2. **repose:** here, the peaceful sleep of death.

3. **degenerate** (dĭ-jĕn'ər-ĭt): showing a decline in vigor or moral strength.

DIFFERENTIATED INSTRUCTION

FOR ADVANCED LEARNERS/AP

Synthesize Remind students that both Edwin Arlington Robinson and Edgar Lee Masters created complex, realistic series of poems about characters drawn from the people of their hometowns. Robinson said that he was more interested in the people who were failures than in those who were successes, while Masters's poem "Lucinda Matlock" suggests an interest in people who get the job done. Ask students whether they agree that failure makes better literary subject matter than success. Encourage students to brainstorm reasons for both responses and to cite examples of works of literature featuring success or failure. Have students indicate which category they generally have preferred as reading matter and which they feel offers deeper, more meaningful ideas. Ask students to share and explain their responses.

Comprehension

1. **Recall** What pleasures and sorrows did Lucinda Matlock experience in her life?

2. **Clarify** Overall, was Lucinda content with the life she lived?

Literary Analysis

3. **Compare Characters** Richard Cory, Miniver Cheevy, and Lucinda Matlock have found widely varying degrees of **contentment.** In your view, what is the primary reason for each character's happiness or unhappiness? Give details to support your answer.

4. **Examine Characterization in Narrative Poetry** What details does Robinson use to reveal each of the following character traits of Richard Cory and Miniver Cheevy? What impact does this characterization have on your sympathy or distaste for the characters? Explain.

   - Richard's perfectionism
   - Miniver's laziness
   - Richard's self-restraint
   - Miniver's romanticism

5. **Analyze Speaker's Attitude** Review the chart you created as you read. What attitude does the speaker of each poem express toward the main character? Would you say that the speaker is sympathetic to or critical of the character described? In each case, what does this attitude tell you about the speaker's own personality and values? Give evidence to support your answer.

6. **Evaluate Author's Style** Robinson's poems use **rhyme, meter,** and **humor** in a playful way that is somewhat at odds with the grim revelations made in the last lines. How does this playfulness shape the impact of these final lines? Explain whether or not you find this an effective technique, and why.

Literary Criticism

7. **Critical Interpretations** Literary critic Bill Peschel has said that in Robinson's Tilbury Town poems, "the town's Puritan ethic, portrayed as repressive and critical, combined with the materialistic aspects of society, conspires to bring down its citizens." Do you find evidence of this repressive Puritan ethic in the attitudes of the speakers in the Robinson poems? Explain why or why not.

Practice and Apply

After Reading

Use these copy masters to check understanding and provide extra support:

R RESOURCE MANAGER—Copy Masters
Characterization in Narrative Poetry p. 133
Question Support p. 137
Additional selection questions are provided for teachers on page 129.

ANSWERS

1. **Pleasures:** *marriage, gardening, and nursing;* **Sorrows:** *loss of eight children*

2. *Yes, Lucinda was content overall.*

Possible answers:

3. *Cory appears depressed by a life made of wealth and solitude. Cheevy is unhappy because of alcoholism and the sense of being mismatched with his time. Matlock is happy because she has inner strength.*

4. ● **SKILLS FOCUS** *Characterization in Narrative Poetry* **Perfectionism:** *Richard is perfectly dressed (lines 3–4) and behaved (line 10).* **Self-restraint:** *His difficulties are entirely hidden.* **Laziness:** *Miniver takes time from working to daydream (line 10).* **Romanticism:** *Miniver longs for "days of old" (line 5). Students' responses to the characters will vary but should reflect the details they have chosen.*

5. ■ **SKILLS FOCUS** Analyze Speaker's Attitude **Richard Cory:** *The speaker first envies Richard Cory, but then grimly observes his death. The speaker does not*

value wealth much. **Miniver Cheevy:** *The speaker mocks Cheevy and finds little value in daydreaming.* **Lucinda Matlock:** *Lucinda states the facts of her life bluntly, then praises herself at the end of the poem. She values energy.*

6. *Students may appreciate the ironic twist of serious topics presented playfully and feel it gives the poems' endings greater impact. Others may feel the playfulness undercuts the poems' serious themes.*

7. *Students may feel that the judgmental attitude of the speakers toward Richard Cory and Miniver Cheevy stems from a Puritan ethic.*

Assess and Reteach

Assess

R RESOURCE MANAGER—Copy Masters
Selection Test A pp. 139–140
Selection Test B/C pp. 141–142

Test Generator CD

Reteach

S STANDARDS LESSON FILE
Literature Lesson 3: Characterization
Literature Lesson 16: Narrative vs. Lyric Poetry
Literature Lesson 18: Speaker and Persona
Literature Lesson 20: Rhythm and Meter
Literature Lesson 36: Irony

Focus and Motivate

OBJECTIVES

Literary Analysis
- explore the key idea of **place**
- analyze tone and diction
- read poetry

Reading
- synthesize details

CALIFORNIA R3.3

ABOUT THE POET

After students read the biography, have them identify details in Sandburg's life that allowed him to become "the voice of America." ***Possible answer:*** *Sandburg could speak for America because he experienced poverty and was self-made, he worked at many jobs, he traveled widely around the country, and he was active in politics.*

USING THE *NOTABLE QUOTE*

Read the quote aloud and ask a volunteer to interpret its meaning. ***Possible answer:*** *The first step toward achieving anything is to envision a goal.* Then ask students how following a dream might have helped **Carl Sandburg** rise from poverty to fame. ***Possible answer:*** *Sandburg needed a goal to keep him striving in the face of challenges such as poverty and incomplete schooling.*

The New Poetry

R3.3

CALIFORNIA

Chicago
Grass

Poetry by Carl Sandburg

NOTABLE QUOTE
"Nothing happens unless first a dream."

FYI
Did you know that Carl Sandburg . . .
- considered running for president of the United States?
- worked as a war correspondent during World War I?
- wrote books for children?
- spoke before Congress about Abraham Lincoln?

Author Online

For more on Carl Sandburg, visit the **Literature Center at ClassZone.com.**

Carl Sandburg
1878–1967

When Carl Sandburg died in 1967, President Lyndon Johnson was among the first to sing his praises. "Carl Sandburg," the president declared, "was more than the voice of America, more than the poet of its strength and genius. He was America." Johnson's feelings were not unique. Americans everywhere cherished Sandburg, believing his verse celebrated their spirit and speech as well as championed their cause.

A Hobo at Heart Sandburg grew up in America's heartland in Galesburg, Illinois. From his Swedish immigrant parents, August and Clara Sandburg, he learned to value hard work and education. His family's poverty, however, forced Sandburg to curtail his schooling at 13 in order to go to work. He labored at various jobs, ranging from shining shoes to delivering milk. When he turned 19, he left home to explore the American West, becoming one of the many hoboes who hopped freight trains in order to travel free.

Social Activist When the Spanish-American War erupted in 1898, Sandburg served for eight months in Puerto Rico. After his return, he studied at Lombard College but left without receiving a diploma. Overtaken once again by wanderlust, he rambled about the country, soaking up America's sights and songs. When he ran out of money, he returned to the Midwest, writing for journals in Chicago and joining the lecture circuit. His skill as an orator eventually earned him a job in Milwaukee as an organizer for the Wisconsin Social-Democratic Party. While living there, he married Lillian Steichen, who, like Sandburg, was committed to fighting social injustice.

Literary Celebrity In 1912, the couple moved to Chicago, where Sandburg became a reporter, editorial writer, and columnist for the *Chicago Daily News*. Two years later, his verse began to appear in *Poetry*, a prominent literary magazine. With the publication of his poetry collections *Chicago Poems, Cornhuskers,* and *Smoke and Steel,* Sandburg gained a reputation as the poet of the common people. The poetry readings he gave further heightened his popularity. Interspersing poetry with commentary and folk songs sung in his melodious baritone, Sandburg enthralled audiences wherever he went.

Sandburg won a number of awards and honors, including the 1951 Pulitzer Prize for poetry for *Complete Poems* and the 1939 Pulitzer Prize for history for *Abraham Lincoln: The War Years,* the last volume in a six-volume biography.

888

Selection Resources

RESOURCE MANAGER UNIT 5

Plan and Teach pp. 143–150

Literary Analysis
Tone and Diction pp. 151, 152†*
Question Support p. 155*

Reading
Synthesize Details pp. 153, 154†*

Assessment
Selection Tests A, B/C
pp. 157*, 159*

🖸 Test Generator CD

BEST PRACTICES TOOLKIT

Differentiated Instruction
pp. 31–38*

Graphic Organizers/Strategies
Two-Column Chart • Visualizing

Reading Support
🖸 Audio Anthology CD*

Technology
ⓘ Literature Center at
ClassZone.com
🖸 Write*Smart* CD

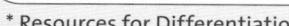

* Resources for Differentiation   † Also in Spanish

● **LITERARY ANALYSIS: TONE AND DICTION**

Some poems exhibit a subtle tone that is difficult to perceive and nearly impossible to describe. Others practically break forth with trumpets in the first stanza. Whether gently or boldly, poets generally convey tone, or attitude toward the subject, through **diction** (word choice and syntax) and choice of details. In the first lines of "Chicago," Carl Sandburg's diction creates a tone of admiration for a hard-working city:

Hog Butcher for the World,
Tool Maker, Stacker of Wheat,
Player with Railroads and the Nation's Freight Handler;
Stormy, husky, brawling,
City of the Big Shoulders....

Read these two poems by Sandburg aloud to help you identify the tone of each. If you read with emotion, your tone of voice may provide you with clues to the poem's tone.

Review: **Personification**

■ **READING SKILL: SYNTHESIZE DETAILS**

In "Chicago," Sandburg presents a long list, or catalog, of qualities, images, and statements about the city. It is the accumulation of these listed items that creates such a strong portrait of the city. As you read, pay attention to each item and allow yourself to absorb the ideas and images presented. After you read the poem, you'll be asked to **synthesize** numerous **details** into a single, coherent impression.

Would you rather live in the CITY or the COUNTRY?

KEY IDEA "If you would be known, and not know, vegetate in a village; if you would know, and not be known, live in a city," wrote the poet Reverend Charles Caleb Colton. What benefits and drawbacks do you associate with city living? with country living? What kind of **place** inspires you the most? In the poems that follow, Carl Sandburg explores different settings that have affected him.

QUICKWRITE Think about a city or a place in the country where you would like to live. What aspects of this setting particularly appeal to you? How might living there enrich your life? Spend a few minutes writing in response to these questions.

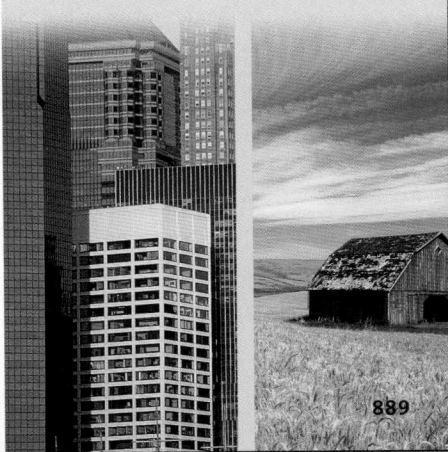
889

Would you rather live in the CITY or the COUNTRY?

Ask the question and elicit students' choices about the **place** they would like to live through a show of hands. Then read the **KEY IDEA**, pausing for discussion after the Colton quotation and to allow students to list benefits and drawbacks of city and country life. Have them refer to their lists as they complete the *QUICKWRITE.*

SKILLS FOCUS

● **TONE AND DICTION**

Ask students to compare and contrast the tone and diction of the "Chicago" excerpt on page 889 with these lines from "Grass":

What place is this?
Where are we now?

Possible answer: The lines from "Grass" are quieter in tone and simpler in diction.

CHECK UNDERSTANDING Have students cite examples of word choice, syntax, and detail choice that convey tone in the two examples.

READING SKILL

■ **SYNTHESIZE DETAILS**

Have students reread the excerpt from "Chicago" on page 889. Ask them to state the impression these lines make on them, and to cite details that helped create that impression. *Possible answer: The lines create an impression of a strong Chicago, capable of almost anything. Details that create this impression include vivid nouns such as "Butcher," "Maker," and "Handler," and descriptions such as "Stormy, husky, brawling," and "Big Shoulders."*

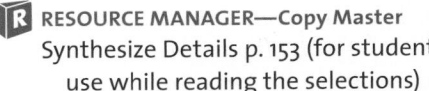 **RESOURCE MANAGER—Copy Master** Synthesize Details p. 153 (for student use while reading the selections)

DIFFERENTIATED INSTRUCTION

FOR STRATEGIC READERS
Concept Support: Synthesize Details Tell students that *synthesizing* means putting different parts together to form a new whole. Compare the process to putting ingredients together to cook a recipe, or putting pieces of a jigsaw puzzle together to make a picture appear. Similarly, when a reader synthesizes details in a poem, the reader looks at each detail individually, forms a mental picture of it, and then combines the separate details to

form a larger mental picture that unifies the whole poem and expresses its overall feeling or meaning. For practice, have students mention details in the words of "The Star-Spangled Banner" or another song of their choosing. Then have them describe the overall picture they synthesize from the details.

SUMMARY

This free verse poem describes the city of Chicago as Sandburg knew it in the early 1900s. The speaker personifies the city and praises its hard-working energy, while also noticing its crime, corruption, and poverty.

READING SKILL

A SYNTHESIZE DETAILS

Possible answer: The epithets convey that Chicago was a national railroad hub, the center of meatpacking and grain shipping. They convey that the city's economy and industry were booming.

If students need help . . . Help them jot notes on the meaning of each epithet in a Two-Column Chart like this one:

Epithet	What It Means
Hog Butcher for the World	Makes pork sold around the world

 BEST PRACTICES TOOLKIT—Transparency Two-Column Chart p. A25

Lines 10–11
REINFORCE *KEY IDEA*: PLACE

Discuss As described in the poem, is Chicago a **place** you would want to visit? Why or why not? *Possible answer: Students may be drawn to the city's energy; others may find its coarseness unappealing.*

LITERARY ANALYSIS

B TONE AND DICTION

Possible answer: The phrase "my city" (line 9) suggests the speaker's affection for Chicago. The image of Chicago "with lifted head singing so proud to be alive" (line 10) reveals his pride in it. He also dismisses critics who "sneer" at the city (line 9).

Chicago

Carl Sandburg

Hog Butcher for the World,
Tool Maker, Stacker of Wheat,
Player with Railroads and the Nation's Freight Handler;
Stormy, husky, brawling,
5   City of the Big Shoulders: **A**

They tell me you are wicked and I believe them, for I
    have seen your painted women under the gas lamps
    luring the farm boys.
And they tell me you are crooked and I answer: Yes, it
    is true I have seen the gunman kill and go free to
    kill again.
And they tell me you are brutal and my reply is: On the
    faces of women and children I have seen the marks
    of wanton[1] hunger.
And having answered so I turn once more to those who
    sneer at this my city, and I give them back the sneer
    and say to them:
10 Come and show me another city with lifted head singing
    so proud to be alive and coarse and strong and cunning. **B**
Flinging magnetic curses amid the toil of piling job on
    job, here is a tall bold slugger set vivid against the
    little soft cities;
Fierce as a dog with tongue lapping for action, cunning
    as a savage pitted against the wilderness,
        Bareheaded,
        Shoveling,

---

1. **wanton:** without limitation.

A SYNTHESIZE DETAILS
The brief descriptive phrases in lines 1–5, also known as **epithets,** are almost like nicknames; in fact, some of them have come into common use. What do they tell you about the city's economy and industry?

B TONE AND DICTION
Lines 6–8 contain harsh words such as *wicked* and *brutal.* Identify the language in lines 9–10 that counters this harshness. What does it reveal about Sandburg's feelings toward the city as well as its critics?

DIFFERENTIATED INSTRUCTION

For general guidelines on differentiating instruction, see

 BEST PRACTICES TOOLKIT Differentiated Instruction pp. 31–38

FOR STRATEGIC READERS
Options for Reading: Audio Recording

- Have students listen to the poems on the *Audio Anthology CD* (also recommended for English learners) while they read along in their books. Have students listen for the tones in which the two poems are read.

- Suggest that students note when the reader pauses or changes reading volume. Explain that pace, volume, and pauses can provide clues to the poem's tone.

South of the Loop (1936), Charles Turzak. Color woodcut, Image 10²/₃″ × 11³/₄″, sheet 11¹/₄″ × 15″. Mary and Leigh Block Museum of Art, Northwestern University, 1992.73 © Joan Turzak Van Hees.

15   Wrecking,
       Planning,
       Building, breaking, rebuilding,
  Under the smoke, dust all over his mouth, laughing with
     white teeth,
  Under the terrible burden of destiny laughing as a young
     man laughs,
20 Laughing even as an ignorant fighter laughs who has
     never lost a battle,
  Bragging and laughing that under his wrist is the pulse, and
     under his ribs the heart of the people,
            Laughing!
  Laughing the stormy, husky, brawling laughter of
     Youth, half-naked, sweating, proud to be Hog
     Butcher, Tool Maker, Stacker of Wheat, Player with
     Railroads and Freight Handler to the Nation.

ANALYZE VISUALS
What qualities of the city are emphasized by both the horizontal and the vertical lines in this woodcut? Refer to specific areas of the print when giving your answer.

CHICAGO   **891**

892 UNIT 5

SUMMARY

The grass growing over battlefields speaks of its role in healing the wounds of war.

LITERARY ANALYSIS: *Review*

PERSONIFICATION

Possible answer: *The speaker is the grass growing on the battlefields. Its role is to replace death and loss with new growth.*

If students need help . . . Have them use a Visualizing organizer to translate the poem's imagery into mental pictures.

> **BEST PRACTICES TOOLKIT—Transparency**
> Visualizing p. A11

LITERARY ANALYSIS

D TONE AND DICTION

Possible answer: *Examples of repetition include "Pile the bodies high," "I am the grass," and "Let me work." The repetition establishes a calm tone, reflecting the steady accumulation of bodies in battle and healing grass above.*

ANALYZE VISUALS

Activity Ask students what point of the process described by the poem this painting illustrates. ***Possible answer:*** *The painting shows the devastation of battle, before healing has begun, but without any bodies.*

About the Art Swiss painter Félix Vallotton (1865–1925) knew that this painting was visually uninspiring, but he wanted to portray the image that World War I soldiers saw— unending devastated earth.

SELECTION WRAP–UP

SYNTHESIZE Ask students to find places in both poems where they feel the diction is especially effective in establishing tone.

Grass

Carl Sandburg

Pile the bodies high at Austerlitz and Waterloo.[1]
Shovel them under and let me work—
   I am the grass; I cover all. **C**

And pile them high at Gettysburg
5 And pile them high at Ypres and Verdun.[2]
Shovel them under and let me work.
Two years, ten years, and passengers ask the conductor:
   What place is this?
   Where are we now?

10   I am the grass.
   Let me work. **D**

C PERSONIFICATION
Reread lines 1–3. Sandburg uses personification in establishing the speaker for this poem. Who is the speaker and what is its role in these scenes?

D TONE AND DICTION
Identify several examples of **repetition** in this poem. What **tone** is established by the repetition of these words and/or phrases?

---

1. **Austerlitz** (ô'stər-lĭts') **and Waterloo:** sites of significant battles during the Napoleonic Wars (1800–1815).
2. **Ypres** (ē'prə) **and Verdun** (vər-dŭn'): sites of significant battles during World War I.

Le Plateau de Bolante (1917), Félix Vallotton. Oil on canvas. Musée d'Histoire Contemporaine, Paris. © Musée d'Histoire Contemporaine-BDIC.

DIFFERENTIATED INSTRUCTION

FOR STRATEGIC READERS

Clarify Meaning Make sure that students understand lines 7–9. Restate line 7 this way: "In two years and in ten years, passengers will ask train conductors . . ." Clarify that the questions in lines 8–9 imply that the places will look so ordinary that passengers will ask the conductor what is special about these places.

FOR ADVANCED LEARNERS/AP

Analyze Author's Style and Theme Point out that "Chicago" and "Grass" are quite different in subject matter, tone, and diction. Ask students what makes both poems recognizable as works by Carl Sandburg. Invite them to consider both style and theme in their analyses. Have students share their ideas with the class.

Comprehension

1. **Recall** What negative aspects of Chicago are presented in lines 6–8?
2. **Clarify** What scenes are referred to in "Grass"?

Literary Analysis

3. **Synthesize Details** Think about the **litany,** or list, of images and ideas in "Chicago." Based on the accumulation of detail in this poem, what general statement can you make about the people who live and work in the city?

4. **Compare Tone and Diction** Identify the tone of each poem. Are the tones similar or different? Cite at least three examples of diction that reveal tone in each poem.

5. **Evaluate Personification** Sandburg uses personification in "Chicago" as well as in "Grass," giving human characteristics to objects, animals, or ideas. Describe the figure who personifies Chicago. What words and phrases capture his most important traits?

6. **Analyze Style** What poetic or other stylistic devices underscore Sandburg's characterization of Chicago as a brash, brawling, vibrant city? Consider such elements as line and stanza shape, rhythm, and other formal conventions. Be specific, citing examples from the text.

7. **Interpret Setting and Theme** Both "Chicago" and "Grass" depict a strong sense of place, each containing some contradiction. For each poem, identify this contradiction and use it to help you formulate a theme statement. Give evidence to support your answers.

8. **Compare and Contrast Writers** Carl Sandburg was greatly influenced by the poetry of Walt Whitman (see page 508). Compare and contrast the two poets in terms of the following points, citing specific lines from their work. Can you see Whitman's influence in Sandburg's poems? Explain why or why not.
   - use of **catalog** or **litany**
   - use of **repetition** and **parallelism**
   - **tone** and **diction**
   - ideas about America

Literary Criticism

9. **Critical Interpretations** Imagist poet William Carlos Williams once criticized Sandburg's poetry as "formless." Even some of Sandburg's supporters conceded that this was true. Do you agree or disagree? Cite evidence to support your response, also explaining whether you would count yourself among his supporters or his critics, and why.

7. **"Chicago":** The speaker loves the city despite its negative aspects, suggesting a theme that people can love flaws. **"Grass":** Death and life appear in the same place.

8. Whitman's influence is seen in Sandburg's use of cataloging, litany, repetition, and parallelism. Both poets use grandiose tones and the diction of their times. Both love American cities, the working class, and democracy. Students may observe that both poets revere an animated nature and could compare and contrast line 3 in "Grass" ("I am the grass, I cover all.") with line 41 in "Song of Myself" ("The smallest sprout shows there really is no death.").

9. Students may say that Sandburg's poetry has an organic form, such as the unifying effect of repetition and litany at the beginning and end of "Chicago."

Practice and Apply

After Reading

Use these copy masters to check understanding and provide extra support:

R RESOURCE MANAGER—Copy Masters
Tone and Diction p. 151
Question Support p. 155

Additional selection questions are provided for teachers on page 147.

ANSWERS

1. *Lines 6–8 present negative aspects of crime, corruption, and poverty.*

2. *"Grass" refers to battlefields of the Napoleonic Wars, the Civil War, and World War I.*

Possible answers:

3. ■ **SKILLS FOCUS** Synthesize Details
The people of Chicago are hardworking, optimistic laborers.

4. ● **SKILLS FOCUS** Tone and Diction
The tone of "Chicago" is loud, dramatic, and boisterous, with long lines and lists of epithets, while that of "Grass" is quiet, solemn, and elegiac, with shorter lines and calm repetition.

5. *The person who personifies Chicago is a young, pugnacious, optimistic laborer. His most important traits are described in lines 18–19 and 21, which show the city's vitality.*

6. *The long, flowing, rhythmic lines demonstrate Chicago's uncontainable energy. The fact that the poem also contains short lines shows the city's variety and unpredictability.*

Assess and Reteach

Assess

R RESOURCE MANAGER—Copy Masters
Selection Test A pp. 157–158
Selection Test B/C pp. 159–160

⊘ Test Generator CD

Reteach

S STANDARDS LESSON FILE
Literature Lesson 29: Personification
Literature Lesson 40: Word Choice and Diction
Literature Lesson 43: Tone
Reading Lesson 14: Synthesizing Information

OBJECTIVE

- understand modernism as a literary movement

Making It New

To help students understand the impact of styles that were new almost a century ago, ask them to brainstorm a list of new advances that have developed since they became teenagers: technologies, Web sites, activities, fashions, and forms of entertainment. Ask students to describe the impact of those developments on older people who were used to living without them. *Possible answer: People were surprised, unsettled, amazed, delighted.* Then direct attention to the photograph of Ezra Pound on this page. Ask how viewers used to realistic images might respond to this photograph. *Possible answer: Some would be confused or even angered. Others would be fascinated and inspired.* Inform students that this mix of reactions greeted the experimental art and literature of the early 20th century.

The Defining Features of Modernism

Have students speculate on the plots of Cather's "A Wagner Matinee" and Hemingway's "In Another Country," based on the passages on page 895. They will probably find it harder to predict the Hemingway story than the Cather story. Explain that because modernist writing does not give explanations, it requires readers to look beyond the text for meaning.

Modernism

R3.5

In 1860, most Americans lived their entire lives without using a powered machine of any sort. By 1940, nearly everyone used or owned radios, cars, telephones, or appliances. With the Industrial Revolution, the modern world had come into being. It was a world of contradictions: disillusion and hope, self-doubt and self-discovery, crumbling traditions and explosive creative energy. In response to these forces, there arose a literary and cultural movement known as **modernism.**

Making It New

Poet Ezra Pound is credited with bringing the techniques of literary modernism to the United States in the early 20th century. He urged his literary colleagues to "make it new": to experiment with literary forms, subjects, themes, and structure. The result of this experimentation was a diverse flowering of literary achievement, which became known as the modernist movement.

Experimental photograph of Ezra Pound, 1916

Though modernism as a literary movement had its seeds in the late 19th century, it did not flourish until the early decades of the 20th century and throughout World War II. Prose writers Ernest Hemingway, F. Scott Fitzgerald, William Faulkner, and Katherine Anne Porter and poets Ezra Pound, T. S. Eliot, H. D. (Hilda Doolittle), and William Carlos Williams were part of a generation of writers who created new ways of writing to respond to the post–World War I realities and the loss of stability felt so strongly between 1914 and 1945.

The Defining Features of Modernism

Modernism comprises a diversity of individual styles. Yet there are some common defining features of the literature that show a distinct break with the past.

- Modernists rejected traditional **subject matter** and **themes.** Instead of love, many modernists wrote of the inability to commit to, or even communicate with, others. For most modernists, nothing lasted, and therefore themes frequently focused on impermanence and change.

- Instead of "heroes" who stood for the values of society, modernists focused on alienated individuals. The **protagonist** of T. S. Eliot's poem "The Love Song of J. Alfred Prufrock" (page 930) is no heroic explorer but an insecure, lonely man who is consumed by self-doubt.

DIFFERENTIATED INSTRUCTION

For general guidelines on differentiating instruction, see

 BEST PRACTICES TOOLKIT
Differentiated Instruction pp. 31–38

FOR STRATEGIC READERS

Note Taking For students who are unfamiliar with modernism or need help with note taking, hand out the copy master before discussing these pages. Explain to students that they will be learning terms and concepts relating to modernism in this workshop. Discuss key features of modernism such as understatement, irony, symbols, and images as students record notes on their copy masters.

 RESOURCE MANAGER—Copy Master
Note Taking p. 161

- Modernists revealed important emotions and ideas with **understatement** and **irony**. They no longer felt confident directly stating universal truths in their works as the romantics and transcendentalists had before them.

- Rather than directly state meaning, modernists typically used **symbols** and **images** to suggest meaning. The speaker in Frost's "Acquainted with the Night" (page 898) never admits he's lonely or sad; the images, however, show this.

Although modernist writers often describe their characters' actions, feelings, and thoughts, they do not interpret them for the reader. A comparison of Ernest Hemingway's writing with Willa Cather's can help you see the difference between a modernist work and a more traditional one. Note how Cather's narrator in "A Wagner Matinee" (page 694) directly explains the significance of his relationship with his aunt.

> I owed to this woman most of the good that ever came my way in my boyhood, and had a reverential affection for her. During the years when I was riding herd for my uncle, my aunt, after cooking three meals . . . and putting the six children to bed, would often stand until midnight at her ironing-board with me at the kitchen table beside her, hearing me recite Latin declensions and conjugations, gently shaking me when my drowsy head sank down over a page of irregular verbs.
> —Willa Cather, "A Wagner Matinee"

In this excerpt from "In Another Country" (page 970), Hemingway's narrator, in contrast, does not explain the emotional significance of his relationships to the other characters, and the reader is left to infer how the characters feel about each other. Hemingway once explained such omissions this way: "I always try to write on the principle of the iceberg. There is seven-eighths of it under water for every part that shows."

> There were three boys who came each day who were about the same age I was. They were all three from Milan, and one of them was to be a lawyer, and one was to be a painter, and one had intended to be a soldier, and after we were finished with the machines, sometimes we walked back together to the Café Cova, which was next door to the Scala.
> —Ernest Hemingway, "In Another Country"

AMERICANS IN PARIS

French painter Henri Matisse was an inspiration to American writers in Paris.

At loose ends after World War I, many disillusioned Americans remained in Europe, often settling in the Left Bank district of Paris, where they were joined by numerous writers and artists. Ezra Pound, Ernest Hemingway, Gertrude Stein, F. Scott Fitzgerald, James Joyce, and George Orwell were just some of the many writers who lived for a time in Paris during the 1920s. Many of the expatriate community saw it as a place where they could be more open to life—in a way that was impossible in the United States. For others, it served for inspiration: The simplicity of both Ernest Hemingway's and Gertrude Stein's styles is said to have been inspired by the art of French painters Paul Cezanne and Henri Matisse. Ironically, Paris became known as the place where American literary style was cultivated and crafted.

Close Read

In Cather's passage, what details explain the aunt's character and the narrator's feelings about her? What do the details in Hemingway's passage reveal about his narrator?

LITERARY ANALYSIS WORKSHOP **895**

AMERICANS IN PARIS

Ask students where they would go today to attempt a career as an artist or writer, and why. *Students may mention New York, Hollywood, or a university. Such places are centers of artistic activity.* Point out that young American artists went to Paris in the 1920s because it was the art capital of the world, because they would meet other people with similar interests, and because it was inexpensive.

Close Read

Possible answer: In Cather's passage, the first sentence directly explains the narrator's feelings about his aunt. Her hard-working character is shown in the description of her domestic chores. Her nurturing nature is shown in the way she gently shakes the narrator. In Hemingway's passage, the phrase "three boys . . . who were about the same age as I was" shows that the narrator is young, but little else is revealed.

FOR ENGLISH LEARNERS
Language: Skill Words Define the academic vocabulary shown in italics.

- *protagonist:* the hero of a work of literature
- *understatement:* a way of stating ideas less dramatically than warranted
- *irony:* a contrast between expectation and reality
- *symbol:* a person, place, object, or activity that represents something else in addition to itself

- *image:* a word or group of words that appeals to the reader's senses

Then help students understand the word *modern* by eliciting the Spanish and French cognates *moderno* and *moderne* and their meanings. Define the suffix *-ism* as "a school of thought" and help students build a definition for *modernism* as "a school of thought that believes in making things new."

FOR ADVANCED LEARNERS/AP
Research Modernist Art To place modernist writing in context, have students look in art books for pictures of modernist painting and sculpture from the early 20th century by artists such as Pablo Picasso, Henri Matisse, Wassily Kandinsky, and Constantin Brancusi. Ask students to pick one artist from the era and briefly describe how the artist made his or her art form new.

LITERARY ANALYSIS WORKSHOP **895**

Focus and Motivate

OBJECTIVES

Literary Analysis
- explore the key ideas of **solitude** and **home**
- analyze Frost's style, including diction and mood
- analyze elements of narrative poetry
- interpret allusion
- read poetry

Reading
- analyze ambiguity
- analyze form and meaning in poetry

Grammar and Writing
- use infinitive phrases to create rhythm
- use writing to analyze literature

 CALIFORNIA R3.3, R3.4, R3.1, R3.2, W1.3, W2.2, LC1.1

ABOUT THE POET

Tell students that the *KEY IDEAS* for Frost's selections are **solitude** and **home.** Ask them to find clues in the biography about how these contrasting ideas are present in Frost's life and work. *Possible answer: As a farmer and as a poet, Frost worked mainly alone. His marriage to his high school sweetheart is a link to home.*

USING THE *NOTABLE QUOTE*

Read the quote aloud and ask students to paraphrase it. *Possible answer: Poetry is a way of focusing on the essentials in life.* Ask students to point out details in the biography that suggest **Robert Frost** took life by the throat. Students should begin to see Frost as a poet who explored serious themes concerning real life.

Selection Resources

CALIFORNIA R3.3, R3.4, W2.2 (p. 902)

Selected Poetry

by Robert Frost

NOTABLE QUOTE
"Poetry is a way of taking life by the throat."

FYI
Did you know that Robert Frost . . .

- was unable to read a poem at John F. Kennedy's inauguration because of bright sunlight and so recited one from memory?
- won 44 honorary degrees from prestigious universities but never earned a college degree himself?

Author Online
For more on Robert Frost, visit the **Literature Center at ClassZone.com.**

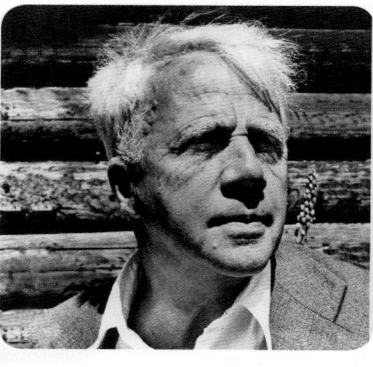

Robert Frost
1874–1963

Robert Frost once remarked that his life's goal was to write "a few poems it will be hard to get rid of." Undoubtedly, he succeeded. Frost's best poems lodge themselves in the reader's imagination and refuse to go away. As a result, Frost is one of the most beloved American poets.

Awakening to Poetry Although Frost is associated with rural New England, he spent his first 11 years in San Francisco. Following his father's death in 1885, Frost's mother brought her two children east, eventually settling in the industrial city of Lawrence, Massachusetts. As a boy, Frost developed a passion for baseball and poetry. By the time he graduated from high school, he knew he would be a poet.

Aimless Years Frost's early manhood was nonetheless filled with change. He enrolled at both Dartmouth College and Harvard University but did not remain at either place, tiring of the routine of college life. For several years he drifted working as a mill hand, a school teacher, and a reporter. One stabilizing event in his life was his marriage in 1895 to Elinor White, his high school sweetheart.

Voice of New England In 1900, Frost abandoned the indoor life of teaching for the outdoor life of farming. During the day Frost worked his poultry farm, and at night he wrote. The 11 years Frost spent farming were some of his most creative. Inspired by the rugged New Hampshire countryside and its plain-spoken inhabitants, Frost wrote poems that probed the mysteries of nature and the human heart.

Literary Acclaim At the age of 38, Frost moved his family to England, where he could "write and be poor." Less than two months later, a London publisher accepted the manuscript of *A Boy's Will* (1913) for publication. By the time Frost returned to the United States in 1915, he was hailed as a leading American poet.

In 1924, Frost's collection *New Hampshire* won a Pulitzer Prize, the first of four that he would receive. His public success, however, was overshadowed by personal tragedy. Between 1934 and 1940, Frost lost a daughter, his wife, and a son; another daughter was institutionalized for mental illness. As a result, his later poems often convey a bleak outlook on life.

 RESOURCE MANAGER UNIT 5

Plan and Teach pp. 163–170, 181–188

Literary Analysis
Summary pp. 189†*, 190‡*
Frost's Style pp. 171, 172†*
Narrative Poetry pp. 191, 192†*
Question Support pp. 175*, 195*

Reading
Recognize Ambiguity pp. 173, 174†*
Understand Form in Poetry pp. 193, 194†*

Grammar and Writing
Use Language Effectively p. 196

Assessment
Selection Tests A, B/C pp. 177*, 179*, 197*, 199*
 Test Generator CD

 BEST PRACTICES TOOLKIT

Differentiated Instruction pp. 31–38*

Graphic Organizers/Strategies
Connecting • Cluster Diagram • Jigsaw Reading • Three-Column Journal • Open Mind • What's Most Important • Analysis Frame: Poetic Content • Microtheme

Reading Support
 Audio Anthology CD*

Technology
Literature and Writing Centers at **ClassZone.com**
WriteSmart CD

---

 * Resources for Differentiation   † Also in Spanish   ‡ In Haitian Creole and Vietnamese

LITERARY ANALYSIS: FROST'S STYLE

Some of Robert Frost's poems seem so simple, yet they move people deeply. Why? It certainly has something to do with his powerful choice of theme and subject matter, but it's also a matter of his unique **style**—the distinctive way in which he uses words and poetic devices. For one thing, he makes skillful use of traditional rhyme, meter, and stanza form. He also uses other elements in a distinctive way.

- **Diction**—word choice and syntax, or word order
- **Imagery**—the descriptive phrases that appeal to the senses
- **Mood**—the overall feeling or atmosphere that a writer creates for the reader (often created with imagery)

Notice these elements in the opening lines of "'Out, Out—'":

The buzz saw snarled and rattled in the yard
And made dust and dropped stove-length sticks of wood,
Sweet-scented stuff when the breeze drew across it.

As you read these poems by Frost, pay close attention to his diction and his use of imagery and mood.

READING SKILL: RECOGNIZE AMBIGUITY

Many people approach poems like riddles; they are certain that the true meaning must lie in a single interpretation. This approach fails to take into account the **ambiguity** that lends richness and beauty to so many poems. Ambiguous works of literature contain more than one meaning; they are open to various, even opposing, interpretations, as in the opening lines of "Nothing Gold Can Stay."

Nature's first green is gold,
Her hardest hue to hold.

Are these lines referring to a golden hue of green, or are they making the point that nature's first green is precious, like gold? You don't have to choose between these meanings; skilled readers of poetry recognize ambiguity and live with it, even enjoy it, as they read and consider a poem. As you read, record different interpretations of lines from each poem.

"Acquainted with the Night"	"Nothing Gold Can Stay"	"'Out, Out—'"
	lines 1–2: • *golden shade of green* • *green is precious, like gold*	

Explore the Key Idea

What does it mean to be ALONE?

KEY IDEA Does **solitude** make you lonely? Or is it precious to you? It's a powerful idea, being alone. Some people can't get enough of it, and others have it in painful abundance. In any event, it offers opportunity for reflection. In "Acquainted with the Night," Robert Frost explores one person's emotional reaction to being alone.

QUICKWRITE What images and feelings does the word *solitude* evoke in you? Write a short poem describing a moment alone.

897

Teach

What does it mean to be ALONE?

Read the question as a lead-in to the **KEY IDEA**. Ask students to consider the questions about **solitude** and share ideas as they wish. Offer the *QUICKWRITE* as a way for them to explore reactions privately.

SKILLS FOCUS

LITERARY ANALYSIS   R3.3, R3.4

FROST'S STYLE

Write these lines from "'Out, Out—'" on the board and read them aloud:

> He saw all spoiled. "Don't let him cut my hand off—

> The doctor, when he comes. Don't let him, sister!" / So. But the hand was gone already.

Ask students to describe the imagery of the lines, to identify their mood, and to describe Frost's diction. ***Possible answer:*** *The imagery describes the aftermath of a serious accident, waiting for a doctor's arrival. The mood is tense and stark. The diction is straightforward.*

READING SKILL   R3.3

RECOGNIZE AMBIGUITY

In the lines from "'Out, Out—'" direct student attention to the sentence "He saw all spoiled." Challenge students to find two different meanings for the sentence. ***Possible answer:*** *It could mean "He saw his hand severely damaged," or "He saw his hopes for the future gone."*

CHECK UNDERSTANDING Have students explain the ambiguity in the phrase "starting off on the right foot."

 RESOURCE MANAGER—Copy Master
Recognize Ambiguity p. 173 (for student use while reading the selections)

DIFFERENTIATED INSTRUCTION

FOR STRATEGIC READERS
Concept Support: Recognize Ambiguity
Explain that *ambiguity* may reflect the poet's intention to convey multiple meanings or desire to have readers choose their own meaning as a way of interacting with the work. Point out also that the ambiguity may be among shades of meaning rather than the dramatically different meanings of the example on page 897. Explain that, as with this example, one meaning may be based on the

literal meaning of the words while the other is based on a figurative meaning. To search for ambiguity in meaning, students should consider both readings and match them to the context.

Practice and Apply

SUMMARY

In this poem, the speaker conveys his unhappy solitude by describing a lonely walk on a dark, rainy street.

LITERARY ANALYSIS

FROST'S STYLE

Possible answer: *Line 7 sets the stage by establishing a feeling of silence, against which the cry is particularly striking. The mood is one of loneliness and anguish.*

If students need help . . . Use a Connecting organizer to help students relate the passage to feelings it evokes.

🧰 BEST PRACTICES TOOLKIT—Transparency Connecting p. A8

READING SKILL

B RECOGNIZE AMBIGUITY

Possible answer: *Line 13 can mean "It is unclear whether the clock gives the right time or not" and "the speaker is unsure of whether the moment is right for some action he is contemplating." This proclamation suggests that the clock is an omen or a prophet, though a mysterious one.*

If students need help . . . Model how to note the ambiguity on the prereading chart introduced on page 897:

> "Acquainted with the Night"
>
> line no. 13:
> • clock may not give the right time
> • this may not be a good time for speaker's action

Acquainted
with the Night

Robert Frost

I have been one acquainted with the night.
I have walked out in rain—and back in rain.
I have outwalked the furthest city light.

I have looked down the saddest city lane.
5 I have passed by the watchman on his beat
And dropped my eyes, unwilling to explain.

I have stood still and stopped the sound of feet
When far away an interrupted cry
Came over houses from another street,

10 But not to call me back or say good-by;
And further still at an unearthly height
One luminary[1] clock against the sky

Proclaimed the time was neither wrong nor right.
I have been one acquainted with the night. B

ANALYZE VISUALS
Notice the shadowy human figures in relation to other objects in the photograph. What mood is established by the **composition,** or arrangement of shapes? How do the figures appear in relation to each other? Explain.

A **FROST'S STYLE**
Reread lines 7–10. In what way does line 7 set the stage for lines 8–10? Identify the **mood** evoked by the **image** of the interrupted cry.

B **RECOGNIZE AMBIGUITY**
Reread lines 11–14. Identify at least two possible meanings of "the time was neither wrong nor right." What does this proclamation suggest about the "luminary clock"? Explain.

---

1. **luminary:** giving off light.

DIFFERENTIATED INSTRUCTION

For general guidelines on differentiating instruction, see

🧰 BEST PRACTICES TOOLKIT
Differentiated Instruction pp. 31–38

FOR STRATEGIC READERS

Options for Reading: Audio Recording

• Have students listen to the poems on the *Audio Anthology CD* (also recommended for English learners) while they read along in their books. Urge students to visualize the poems' imagery as they listen, and to self-question about each poem's mood.

• Suggest that students write down words and phrases that confuse them as they listen. Invite volunteers to paraphrase and interpret.

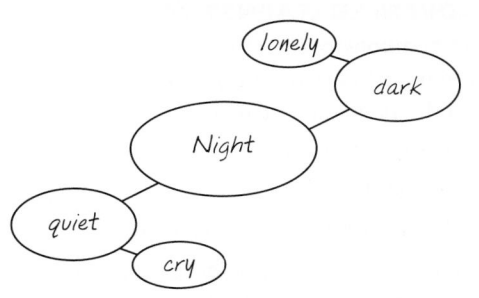

Lines 1–6
TIERED DISCUSSION PROMPTS

Use these prompts to help students understand the mood of the poem:

Connect Think about a time you spent alone. How does that experience help you understand the speaker's situation? *Responses should convey students' understanding of the speaker's solitude.*

Analyze Which image in these lines seems the gloomiest? Explain. *Possible answer: The image of standing alone in the rain, unwilling to talk even to the watchman, is extremely gloomy and suggests lack of hope.*

Synthesize The first five lines all begin with "I have" followed by a verb. What effect does this have on the mood of the poem? *Possible answer: The phrase emphasizes the speaker's aloneness and his self-absorption.*

Lines 1–14
REINFORCE *KEY IDEA:* SOLITUDE

Discuss What repeated word choices imply the speaker's **solitude?** *Possible answer: Repetition of "I" and "one" implies solitude.*

ANALYZE VISUALS

Possible answer: The composition of the photo emphasizes the solitude of the characters, who are outnumbered by the bare, lonely-looking trees and dwarfed by the large, impersonal buildings of the city. The figures seem somewhat distant from one another; they are certainly not engaged with each other. Rather, it seems each is going about his business in the dark, lonely night.

FOR STRATEGIC READERS

Imagery Have students fill in a Cluster Diagram to brainstorm words and phrases Frost's nighttime images evoke for them.

 BEST PRACTICES TOOLKIT—Transparency
Cluster Diagram p. B18

This eight-line poem uses the fate of a leaf as a metaphor for the transience and flawed nature of life.

About the Art George Bellows (1882–1925) was a famous American painter known mostly for urban scenes, paintings of boxing matches, and New England seascapes. This rural landscape, with its long shadows and dark colors, possesses a bleak beauty that matches Frost's poem.

LITERARY ANALYSIS

○ FROST'S STYLE

Possible answer: The mood is one of sadness, wistfulness, or grief at the impermanence of things. Diction and imagery include the terse, repetitive vocabulary, the simple rhymes, the end-stopped lines which create a blunt, sad tone, and the image of Eden sinking to grief (line 6) and dawn going "down to day" (line 7).

ANSWERS

1. *The speaker knows what the night is like because he has taken long walks in it often.*

2. *He sees the rain, the city streets and what is beyond them, the watchman, and the clock against the sky; he hears the sound of feet and the cry from another street.*

3. *Both Eden and the leaf experience a brief moment of perfection before succumbing to their fate.*

Nothing Gold Can Stay

Robert Frost

Haystacks and Barn (1909), George Wesley Bellows. Oil on canvas, 56.5 cm × 71.4 cm. © Museum of Fine Arts, Houston, Texas/Bridgeman Art Library.

Nature's first green is gold,
Her hardest hue to hold.
Her early leaf's a flower;
But only so an hour.
5 Then leaf subsides to leaf.
So Eden[1] sank to grief,
So dawn goes down to day.
Nothing gold can stay. ○

○ **FROST'S STYLE**
What is the **mood** of this poem? Identify the **diction** or **imagery** that most strongly establishes this mood for you.

---

1. **Eden:** the biblical Garden of Eden, from which Adam and Eve were expelled for disobeying God.

Literary Analysis

1. **Clarify** What does the speaker of the first poem mean when he says he's been "acquainted with the night"?

2. **Summarize** What does the speaker of "Acquainted with the Night" see and hear on his walk?

3. **Interpret Analogies** In "Nothing Gold Can Stay," how is the fate of a leaf similar to that of the Garden of Eden?

DIFFERENTIATED INSTRUCTION

FOR STRATEGIC READERS
Comprehension Support Have students work in Jigsaw groups to paraphrase the poem line by line. Give each group one line, if possible. If you have fewer groups, give each two lines. Then have groups reconvene to paraphrase the entire poem.

BEST PRACTICES TOOLKIT
Jigsaw Reading p. A1

FOR ADVANCED LEARNERS/AP
Analyze Symbolism Ask students to investigate and report back on the symbolic references in the poem. These include:

• the color green (line 1)

• the color gold (line 1)

• the biblical narrative of Eden (line 6)

Examples: Green is a symbol for youthful life. Gold can be a symbol of wealth or of excellence as in the Greek myth of the Golden Age. The

biblical narrative of Eden is a symbol of humanity's fall from perfection. Invite students to comment on the moods they associate with each symbol and to discuss how each serves Frost's stylistic goals.

"Out, Out—"

Robert Frost

The buzz saw snarled and rattled in the yard
And made dust and dropped stove-length sticks of wood,
Sweet-scented stuff when the breeze drew across it.
And from there those that lifted eyes could count
5 Five mountain ranges one behind the other
Under the sunset far into Vermont.
And the saw snarled and rattled, snarled and rattled, **D**
As it ran light, or had to bear a load.
And nothing happened: day was all but done.
10 Call it a day, I wish they might have said
To please the boy by giving him the half hour
That a boy counts so much when saved from work.
His sister stood beside them in her apron
To tell them "Supper." At the word, the saw,
15 As if to prove saws knew what supper meant,
Leaped out at the boy's hand, or seemed to leap—
He must have given the hand. However it was,
Neither refused the meeting. But the hand! **E**
The boy's first outcry was a rueful[1] laugh,
20 As he swung toward them holding up the hand
Half in appeal, but half as if to keep
The life from spilling. Then the boy saw all—
Since he was old enough to know, big boy
Doing a man's work, though a child at heart—
25 He saw all spoiled. "Don't let him cut my hand off—
The doctor, when he comes. Don't let him, sister!"
So. But the hand was gone already.
The doctor put him in the dark of ether.[2]
He lay and puffed his lips out with his breath.
30 And then—the watcher at his pulse took fright.
No one believed. They listened at his heart.
Little—less—nothing!—and that ended it.
No more to build on there. And they, since they
Were not the one dead, turned to their affairs. **F**

---

1. **rueful:** expressing sorrow or regret.
2. **ether:** a liquid used as an anesthetic. Its fumes cause unconsciousness when deeply inhaled.

D FROST'S STYLE
Reread lines 1 and 7. What sound is imitated by the repetition of words in these lines? Consider Frost's style here; how does this **imagery** contribute to the overall **mood?**

E FROST'S STYLE
Reread lines 13–18. What does the **diction** in these lines suggest about the accidental meeting of the saw and the hand? Explain the **irony** in these lines.

F RECOGNIZE AMBIGUITY
Identify the ambiguity in the last two lines of the poem. What does their **understatement** and lack of sentiment suggest about the survivors and their attitude toward the boy's death?

SUMMARY

In this poem, a boy cutting wood accidentally cuts his hand with the saw. He fears having his hand amputated, but soon dies of shock, as life goes on around him.

LITERARY ANALYSIS

D FROST'S STYLE

Possible answer: The repetition imitates the sound of the buzz saw. The image of the saw contributes to a mood of impending doom.

LITERARY ANALYSIS

E FROST'S STYLE

Possible answer: The diction personifies both hand and saw, presenting the meeting like a handshake both willingly embrace. This is ironic because, given the tragic results, the hand would surely have refused the saw.

READING SKILL

F RECOGNIZE AMBIGUITY

Possible answer: The lines suggest either a callous attitude or merely a realistic one. The understatement suggests that the survivors have little time or energy for grief and view death as a familiar part of life.

SELECTION WRAP-UP

SYNTHESIZE Ask students to explain why each of these poems has had such enduring appeal to readers over time.

⭐ CRITIQUE

- Ask students whether they think Frost's poems are too bleak, or does their bleakness add to their sense of realism.
- After completing the After Reading questions on page 902, have students revisit their responses and tell whether they have changed their opinions.

FOR ADVANCED LEARNERS/AP

Analyze Theme Invite students to discuss the themes that recur in these three Frost poems. *Examples: All life is transitory. Individuals are unimportant and are at the mercy of nature. We are all alone, no matter what is around us.* Have students write a one- or two-sentence description of each theme they find recurring in the poems. Ask students to justify their perception of theme by citing evidence from the texts. Students should then organize their evidence in a Three-Column Journal and refer to this as they present their ideas. Invite listeners to share similar theme interpretations in order to consolidate overlapping ideas.

💼 **BEST PRACTICES TOOLKIT—Transparency** Three-Column Journal p. B10

Practice and Apply

After Reading

Use these copy masters to check understanding and provide extra support:

R RESOURCE MANAGER—Copy Masters
Frost's Style p. 171
Question Support p. 175

Additional selection questions are provided for teachers on page 167.

ANSWERS

1. *Sunset on a farm in Vermont.*

2. *He cuts his hand badly on a saw and dies when the doctor puts him under ether.*

Possible answers:

3. *Rhymes: gold/hold, flower/hour, leaf/grief, and day/stay. Each pair links nature to a word evoking the passage of time, suggesting that beauty is fleeting.*

4. *Lines 33–34 especially emphasize solitude. The theme emerges that human relationships are limited and we are alone.*

5. *The quotation adds the sense that this tragedy in one family exemplifies the universal human condition of life's brevity.*

6. ● **SKILLS FOCUS** *Frost's Style Selections will vary, but students should identify elements of Frost's craft and show awareness of the qualities of bleakness and beauty present in the poems.*

7. ■ **SKILLS FOCUS** *Recognize Ambiguity Students may choose "So dawn goes down to day" ("Nothing Gold Can Stay," line 7) or "But the hand was gone already" ("'Out, Out—,'" line 27). The ambiguity in each allows that poem to have different meanings for each reader while still making an overall*

Assess and Reteach

Assess

R RESOURCE MANAGER—Copy Masters
Selection Test A pp. 177–178
Selection Test B/C pp. 179–180

● Test Generator CD

Reteach

S STANDARDS LESSON FILE
Literature Lesson 39: Ambiguity and Incongruity
Literature Lesson 44: Style and Syntax

After Reading

R3.3, R3.4, W2.2

Comprehension

1. **Clarify** What is the setting, including the time of day, of "'Out, Out—'"?

2. **Summarize** What happens to the boy?

Literary Analysis

3. **Identify Rhymes** Examine the pairs of rhyming words in "Nothing Gold Can Stay." What ideas do the rhymes help Frost convey about the nature of beauty?

4. **Examine Theme** "'Out, Out—'" provides a portrait of **solitude** even among family. Identify words and phrases in which Frost suggests the solitude of these characters in the face of tragedy. What theme emerges about human relationships?

5. **Interpret Allusion** The title of "'Out, Out—'" is an **allusion,** or indirect reference to a well-known person, place, or literary work—in this case, a famous speech in Shakespeare's *Macbeth* (Act Five, Scene 5). How does the following quotation from *Macbeth* color your sense of Frost's poem?

   . . . Out, out brief candle!
   Life's but a walking shadow, a poor player
   That struts and frets his hour upon the stage
   And then is heard no more.

6. **Analyze Frost's Style** Identify several lines in any one of the three poems where Frost's **diction,** his use of **imagery,** and/or **mood** is particularly striking. Explain why you find it noteworthy and how Frost's style helps deliver the poem's message.

7. **Evaluate Ambiguity** Consult the chart in which you recorded different interpretations as you read. Identify the ambiguity that you found the most puzzling, contradictory, or profound. In your opinion, what does the ambiguity add to each poem? Explain.

Literary Criticism

8. **Critical Interpretation** The literary critic and scholar Lionel Trilling hailed Frost for his "representation of the terrible actualities of life in a new way." Apply this comment to the three Frost poems you have just read. What are the "terrible actualities of life" in each poem? What might be considered "new" or unusual about Frost's portrayal of these realities? Explain.

---

point. It also provides a tension that adds richness to the poems.

8. *The terrible actuality in "Acquainted with the Night" is solitude. In "Nothing Gold Can Stay," that actuality is life's impermanence. The actuality in "'Out, Out—'" is death. Frost's portrayal of these actualities is unusual because he accepts them as everyday facts rather than as evidence for a moral viewpoint.*

The Death of the Hired Man

Poem by
Robert Frost

R3.1, R3.2 (p. 911), W1.3
(p. 911), W2.2 (p. 911),
LC1.1 (p. 911)

● LITERARY ANALYSIS: NARRATIVE POETRY

Though primarily a lyric poet, Robert Frost also wrote **narrative poetry.** In contrast to the shorter poems by Robinson and Masters on pages 882–886, "The Death of the Hired Man" tells a story with a more fully developed plot, setting, and characters.

- **Dialogue**—This poem consists almost entirely of a conversation between two people, so the dialogue plays a greater role than usual in developing the narrative elements.
- **Plot**—Although the "now-time" of the poem consists almost entirely of a single conversation, the dialogue itself indirectly relates events that have unfolded over years.
- **Characterization**—Frost uses very little direct description by the speaker; instead, he conveys the characters' traits through their own words and what others say about them.
- **Setting**—Again, Frost uses little direct description of time and place, conveying these things primarily through what the characters say about their work and their relationships.

Review: **Blank Verse**

■ READING SKILL: UNDERSTAND FORM IN POETRY

In poetry, **form** generally refers to the shape of text on the page. In a larger sense, however, it can refer to any technique used to convey meaning. The dialogue in this poem can be hard to follow; you won't find many *he said*'s or *she said*'s. However, Frost uses other devices to show who's speaking.

- **Quotation marks**—Double quotation marks indicate the beginning and end of each speech. Single quotation marks indicate dialogue within a speech.
- **Line breaks**—Frost leaves a blank line when the speaker changes; he never changes speaker in the middle of a line.
- **Point of view**—The poem's speaker uses only the third person; in dialogue, the characters speak in the first person.

Use a chart to keep track of who is speaking in the poem.

Elements of Form Used to Show Speakers		
Line Numbers	Who Is Speaking	How I Know

Explore the Key Idea

How do you know you're HOME?

KEY IDEA It's the moment when you close the door behind you, drop your bag on the floor, take off your coat, and kick off your shoes. Or maybe it's the greeting you get from a family member or even a pet. Walking up the driveway, seeing a familiar face, smelling a familiar food: we recognize **home** in various ways.

QUICKWRITE Identify the place where you feel the most at home. Then write a brief description of some moment or event that captures the features that make home different from other places.

903

Teach

How do you know you're HOME?

Ask the question and read the **KEY IDEA** aloud. Invite volunteers to share ideas prompted by the list of cues to **home.** Have students briefly visualize the place where they are most at home, then use these images to inform their **QUICKWRITE.**

SKILLS FOCUS

LITERARY ANALYSIS R3.1

● NARRATIVE POETRY

If they have not done so, have students read the Robinson poem "Richard Cory" on page 882. Ask students to cite the elements of narrative in this poem. *Possible answer: Dialogue: "Good-morning" (line 8). Plot: Wealthy and well-dressed Richard Cory keeps his distance from the hard-working citizens who envy him. Then he kills himself. Characterization: Robinson describes Cory through dress, style, actions, and reactions to him. Setting: small-town America.*

CHECK UNDERSTANDING Have students name a prose narrative and its parts.

READING SKILL

■ UNDERSTAND FORM IN POETRY

Write these lines from "The Death of a Hired Man" on the board:

"I wasn't looking for him—and he's changed.
Wait till you see."
"Where did you say he'd been?"
"He didn't say. . . . "

Ask students to find the quotation marks and line breaks and tell what they indicate. Ask them to identify the point of view in the lines. *Possible answer: Quotation marks show the beginning and end of each speaker's words; line breaks separate the speakers' words. The point of view is first person.*

R RESOURCE MANAGER—Copy Master Understand Form in Poetry p. 193 (for student use while reading the selection)

DIFFERENTIATED INSTRUCTION

FOR STRATEGIC READERS

Concept Support: Understand Form in Poetry Preview the beginning of the poem. Show students that the narrative begins in the third-person point of view. Point out the short passages of dialogue in lines 5 and 7, and the line break after line 10. Clarify that Warren begins to speak in line 11, whereas his wife Mary was speaking in the previous stanza. Have students look at line 22 and notice the single quotation marks. Explain that Warren, speaking to Mary, is reporting the conversation he previously had with Silas. The single quotation marks show a conversation within a conversation. Point out that Warren, when speaking, uses the first-person pronoun *I.*

SUMMARY

This narrative poem takes the form of a conversation between husband and wife on their farm on a winter night. Mary says that the elderly farmhand, Silas, has come to ask for work. Warren, finding Silas undependable and resenting that Silas has sometimes sought better pay elsewhere, argues against hiring him. Mary argues that they should provide Silas with shelter and a sense of usefulness in his old age. At Mary's urging, Warren rises to visit the old man, who has fallen asleep in a chair by the stove, but Warren finds Silas dead.

LITERARY ANALYSIS

Ⓐ NARRATIVE POETRY

Possible answer: The "lamp-flame" (line 1) tells readers that the era is pre-electricity, the table (line 1) suggests a kitchen, the reference to "market things" (line 8) suggests a rural community, and the wooden steps (line 10) and the name Silas (line 5) suggest an earlier time.

If students need help . . . Work with them to define "lamp-flame" and "market things."

READING SKILL

Ⓑ FORM IN POETRY

Possible answer: Summary: Warren expresses his frustration at the useless Silas, who comes looking for work when it suits him but leaves when he is most needed. In lines 22–24, Warren relates an exchange in which Silas threatens to go elsewhere for a higher wage, and Warren tells him to go ahead.

The DEATH of the HIRED MAN

Robert Frost

Mary sat musing on the lamp-flame[1] at the table,
Waiting for Warren. When she heard his step,
She ran on tiptoe down the darkened passage
To meet him in the doorway with the news
5 And put him on his guard. "Silas is back."
She pushed him outward with her through the door
And shut it after her. "Be kind," she said.
She took the market things from Warren's arms
And set them on the porch, then drew him down
10 To sit beside her on the wooden steps. Ⓐ

"When was I ever anything but kind to him?
But I'll not have the fellow back," he said.
"I told him so last haying,[2] didn't I?
If he left then, I said, that ended it.
15 What good is he? Who else will harbor him
At his age for the little he can do?
What help he is there's no depending on.
Off he goes always when I need him most.
He thinks he ought to earn a little pay,
20 Enough at least to buy tobacco with,
So he won't have to beg and be beholden.
'All right,' I say, 'I can't afford to pay
Any fixed wages, though I wish I could.'
'Someone else can.' 'Then someone else will have to.' Ⓑ
25 I shouldn't mind his bettering himself
If that was what it was. You can be certain,
When he begins like that, there's someone at him
Trying to coax him off with pocket money—
In haying time, when any help is scarce.
30 In winter he comes back to us. I'm done."

"Sh! not so loud: he'll hear you," Mary said.

---

1. **musing on the lamp-flame:** looking thoughtfully at the flame of an oil lamp.
2. **last haying:** the last time the hay was cut.

ANALYZE VISUALS

Notice the shapes of the landscape in this image. How do these shapes compare with the outlines of the human figures? What might this suggest about the relationship between humans and nature? Explain.

Ⓐ NARRATIVE POETRY

Reread lines 1–10. What clues do they contain about the poem's **setting?** Explain.

Ⓑ FORM IN POETRY

Reread lines 11–24. Summarize these lines. Who is speaking? What is happening in lines 22–24?

Detail of *Island Hay* (1945), Thomas Hart Benton. © T.H. Benton and R.P. Benton Testamentary Trusts/UMB Bank Trustee/Licensed by VAGA, New York, N.Y.

DIFFERENTIATED INSTRUCTION

For general guidelines on differentiating instruction, see

 BEST PRACTICES TOOLKIT
Differentiated Instruction pp. 31–38

FOR STRATEGIC READERS

Options for Reading: Audio Recording

- Have students listen to the poems on the *Audio Anthology CD* (also recommended for English learners) while they read along in their books. Students can use the audio accents and tones to visualize the speakers.

- Suggest that students also notice the pause when the speakers shift and stress that this reflects the line breaks in the printed poem.

906 UNIT 5

LITERARY ANALYSIS

C NARRATIVE POETRY

Possible answer: Silas's old age and rapid decline are revealed. Mary's compassion and concern are revealed.

READING SKILL

D FORM IN POETRY

Possible answer: Mary speaks in lines 38–39, Warren in the second half of 39, Mary in 40–43, Warren in 44, Mary in 45, Warren in the second half of 45 to 46, Mary in the first half of 47, Warren in the second half of 47, and Mary in 48. Line breaks and quotation marks show changes of speaker. The rapid changes of speaker emphasize the conflict between husband and wife.

If students need help . . . Work with them to add to the prereading chart introduced on page 903.

Lines	Speaker	Evidence
39 (end)	Warren	line break; new quotes

LITERARY ANALYSIS: *Review*

E BLANK VERSE

Possible answer: Students may say that the lack of rhyme and the simple diction resemble English speech, but that the regular rhythm of iambic pentameter is different from English speech.

"I want him to: he'll have to soon or late."

"He's worn out. He's asleep beside the stove.
When I came up from Rowe's I found him here,
35 Huddled against the barn door fast asleep,
A miserable sight, and frightening, too—
You needn't smile—I didn't recognize him—
I wasn't looking for him—and he's changed.
Wait till you see." **C**

"Where did you say he'd been?"

40 "He didn't say. I dragged him to the house,
And gave him tea and tried to make him smoke.
I tried to make him talk about his travels.
Nothing would do: he just kept nodding off."

"What did he say? Did he say anything?"

45 "But little."

"Anything? Mary, confess
He said he'd come to ditch[3] the meadow for me."

"Warren!"

"But did he? I just want to know."

"Of course he did. What would you have him say? **D**
Surely you wouldn't grudge the poor old man
50 Some humble way to save his self-respect.
He added, if you really care to know,
He meant to clear the upper pasture, too.
That sounds like something you have heard before?
Warren, I wish you could have heard the way
55 He jumbled everything. I stopped to look
Two or three times—he made me feel so queer—
To see if he was talking in his sleep.
He ran on[4] Harold Wilson—you remember—
The boy you had in haying four years since.
60 He's finished school, and teaching in his college.
Silas declares you'll have to get him back.
He says they two will make a team for work:
Between them they will lay this farm as smooth! **E**

---

3. **ditch:** plow.
4. **ran on:** talked about without stopping.

C NARRATIVE POETRY
Reread Mary's description of Silas in lines 31–39. What **character traits** are revealed about Silas in these lines? about Mary?

D FORM IN POETRY
Reread lines 38–48. Identify the speaker of each speech. What devices indicate this? Explain what the rapid change of speakers emphasizes about the tone of this discussion.

E BLANK VERSE
Poetry written in unrhymed **iambic pentameter,** or blank verse, is said to be the poetic form that most resembles English speech. Read aloud lines 58–63. Would you agree? Explain.

DIFFERENTIATED INSTRUCTION

FOR STRATEGIC READERS

Characterization Have students create Open Mind organizers for Mary and Warren. Students should use the organizers to describe each character's traits and feelings as the poem progresses.

 BEST PRACTICES TOOLKIT—Transparency
Open Mind p. D9

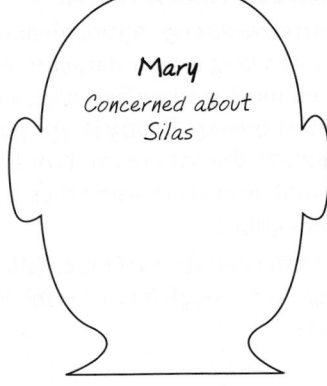

Mary
Concerned about Silas

The way he mixed that in with other things.
65 He thinks young Wilson a likely lad, though daft
On⁵ education—you know how they fought
All through July under the blazing sun,
Silas up on the cart to build the load,
Harold along beside to pitch it on."

70 "Yes, I took care to keep well out of earshot."

"Well, those days trouble Silas like a dream.
You wouldn't think they would. How some things linger!
Harold's young college-boy's assurance piqued⁶ him.
After so many years he still keeps finding
75 Good arguments he sees he might have used.
I sympathize. I know just how it feels
To think of the right thing to say too late.
Harold's associated in his mind with Latin.
He asked me what I thought of Harold's saying
80 He studied Latin, like the violin,
Because he liked it—that an argument!
He said he couldn't make the boy believe
He could find water with a hazel prong⁷—
Which showed how much good school had ever done him.
85 He wanted to go over that. But most of all
He thinks if he could have another chance
To teach him how to build a load of hay—" **F**

"I know, that's Silas' one accomplishment.
He bundles every forkful in its place,
90 And tags and numbers it for future reference,
So he can find and easily dislodge it
In the unloading. Silas does that well.
He takes it out in bunches like big birds' nests.
You never see him standing on the hay
95 He's trying to lift, straining to lift himself."

"He thinks if he could teach him that, he'd be
Some good perhaps to someone in the world.
He hates to see a boy the fool of books.
Poor Silas, so concerned for other folk,
100 And nothing to look backward to with pride,

---

5. **daft on:** crazy about; obsessed with.

6. **piqued** (pēkt): aroused resentment in.

7. **find . . . prong:** a reference to the practice of dowsing, in which a person uses a forked stick made of hazel wood to try to find underground water.

F NARRATIVE POETRY
Reread lines 79–87. How are Silas and Harold characterized in these lines?

G FORM IN POETRY

Possible answer: *The shift in point of view makes the poem's mood suddenly contemplative and delicately lyrical.*

If students need help . . . Point out that Mary and Warren are still seated on the porch talking. Help students describe the setting, emphasizing the images of the moon and of harp music.

Lines 118–120
TIERED DISCUSSION PROMPTS

Use these prompts to help students think about Frost's two definitions of home:

Restate Paraphrase the two definitions of home, and identify which character gives which definition. ***Possible answer:*** *Warren says that home is a place where people go when they have nowhere else to go, and where their family cannot refuse them. Mary says that home is a place where people can return even when they don't deserve to.*

Analyze Whose view of home is more optimistic, Mary's or Warren's? Explain. ***Possible answer:*** *Mary's view of home is more optimistic because it arises from a sense of forgiveness rather than duty.*

Evaluate Which view of home is closer to your view? Explain. *Accept all thoughtful answers that are well supported.*

H NARRATIVE POETRY

Possible answer: *The lines reveal that Silas is alienated from his family and that he is too proud to ask them for help or to discuss the matter with others.*

And nothing to look forward to with hope,
So now and never any different."

Part of a moon was falling down the west,
Dragging the whole sky with it to the hills.
105 Its light poured softly in her lap. She saw it
And spread her apron to it. She put out her hand
Among the harplike morning-glory strings,
Taut[8] with the dew from garden bed to eaves,
As if she played unheard some tenderness
110 That wrought on[9] him beside her in the night. **G**
"Warren," she said, "he has come home to die:
You needn't be afraid he'll leave you this time."

"Home," he mocked gently.
                                              "Yes, what else but home?
It all depends on what you mean by home.
115 Of course he's nothing to us, any more
Than was the hound that came a stranger to us
Out of the woods, worn out upon the trail."

"Home is the place where, when you have to go there,
They have to take you in."
                                              "I should have called it
120 Something you somehow haven't to deserve."

Warren leaned out and took a step or two,
Picked up a little stick, and brought it back
And broke it in his hand and tossed it by.
"Silas has better claim on us you think
125 Than on his brother? Thirteen little miles
As the road winds would bring him to his door.
Silas has walked that far no doubt today.
Why doesn't he go there? His brother's rich,
A somebody—director in the bank."

130 "He never told us that."
                                              "We know it, though." **H**

"I think his brother ought to help, of course.
I'll see to that if there is need. He ought of right
To take him in, and might be willing to—

G FORM IN POETRY
Reread lines 103–110. The poem's speaker has interrupted the dialogue between Mary and Warren. How does this shift in **point of view** affect the poem's **mood**?

H NARRATIVE POETRY
Reread lines 124–130. What do these lines add to your understanding of Silas?

---

8. **taut:** pulled tight; straight.
9. **wrought** (rôt) **on:** worked on.

DIFFERENTIATED INSTRUCTION

FOR STRATEGIC READERS

Comprehension Support Use the What's Most Important strategy to help students identify Mary's and Warren's differing views on family. Discuss how these contrasting views affect Mary's and Warren's reactions to Silas returning.

BEST PRACTICES TOOLKIT
What's Most Important p. D4

FOR ENGLISH LEARNERS

Vocabulary: Idioms Help students use context clues to determine the meanings of these idioms in the poem: *nodding off* (line 43), "falling asleep"; *well out of earshot* (line 70), "too far away to be heard"; *go over* (line 85), "repeat"; *as the road winds* (line 126), "distance traveled on the road"; *a somebody* (line 129), "an important person"; *what's between them* (line 139), "what their conflict is."

He may be better than appearances.[10]
135 But have some pity on Silas. Do you think
    If he had any pride in claiming kin
    Or anything he looked for from his brother,
    He'd keep so still about him all this time?"

    "I wonder what's between them."
                            "I can tell you.
140 Silas is what he is—we wouldn't mind him—
    But just the kind that kinsfolk can't abide.[11]
    He never did a thing so very bad.
    He don't know why he isn't quite as good
    As anybody. Worthless though he is,
145 He won't be made ashamed to please his brother."

    "I can't think Si ever hurt anyone."

    "No, but he hurt my heart the way he lay
    And rolled his old head on that sharp-edged chair-back.
    He wouldn't let me put him on the lounge.[12]
150 You must go in and see what you can do.
    I made the bed up for him there tonight.
    You'll be surprised at him—how much he's broken.
    His working days are done; I'm sure of it."

    "I'd not be in a hurry to say that."

155 "I haven't been. Go, look, see for yourself.
    But, Warren, please remember how it is:
    He's come to help you ditch the meadow.
    He has a plan. You mustn't laugh at him.
    He may not speak of it, and then he may.
160 I'll sit and see if that small sailing cloud
    Will hit or miss the moon." ❶
                            It hit the moon.
    Then there were three there, making a dim row,
    The moon, the little silver cloud, and she.

    Warren returned—too soon, it seemed to her—
165 Slipped to her side, caught up her hand and waited.

    "Warren?" she questioned.
                            "Dead," was all he answered.

----

10. **better than appearances:** better than he looks.

11. **abide:** put up with.

12. **lounge:** couch.

❶ **NARRATIVE POETRY**
In lines 150–161, the dialogue between Mary and Warren is coming to a head. What turn in the **plot** do you foresee?

Lines 147–153
REINFORCE *KEY IDEA:* HOME

Discuss In what way is Mary's and Warren's farm both a good **home** and a bad home for Silas? Explain. *Possible answer: The farm is a good home for Silas because Mary provides him with rest at the end of his life. It's a bad home because he isn't truly welcome, but merely has nowhere else to go.*

LITERARY ANALYSIS

❶ NARRATIVE POETRY

Possible answer: It seems that Warren and Silas are about to have a confrontation. Students may guess that Warren will kick Silas out, or that he will take pity on Silas. Some may foresee the ending.

If students need help . . . Ask them to recall the poem's title and to guess what it foreshadows.

SELECTION WRAP–UP

REFLECT Ask students to think about the effect Silas has had on Mary's and Warren's lives, and they on his. Which effects have been positive and which have been negative?

⭐ CRITIQUE

- Ask students to identify parts of the conversation they found difficult to follow, and to explain why.

- After completing the After Reading questions on page 910, have students revisit their responses and tell whether they have changed their opinions.

FOR ADVANCED LEARNERS/AP

Analyze Poetic Content [small-group option] Have students use the Analysis Frame: Poetic Content in order to explore the implications of "The Death of the Hired Man." Challenge groups to discuss the questions in the frame, then divide up the questions to briefly answer in written form. Have groups review their individual responses and choose three key points on which to focus. Ask students to generate a lesson presenting those key points about the poem to the class. Some options include

- larger meanings implied in the poem
- the speaker's attitude toward the people and situation
- the contribution of setting to the narrative
- contrasts in the poem
- how the ideas or values in the poem compare to one's own

💼 **BEST PRACTICES TOOLKIT—Copy Masters**
Analysis Frame: Poetic Content
pp. D21, D36, D37

Practice and Apply

After Reading

Use these copy masters to check understanding and provide extra support:

 RESOURCE MANAGER—Copy Masters
Narrative Poetry p. 191
Question Support p. 195

Additional selection questions are provided for teachers on page 185.

ANSWERS

1. *Silas is a farmhand who for years has been employed by Mary and Warren.*

2. *Silas looks worn out and miserable and keeps nodding off.*

3. *He thinks Silas is unreliable, because Silas demands fixed wages but then works for other farmers when Warren needs him.*

4. *Mary thinks Silas has returned to die.*

Possible answers:

5. *Silas's return: Mary is more sympathetic than Warren. She understands why Silas has returned and she perceives his ill health. Warren is still angry over his last disagreement with Silas. Silas's appearance and plans: Mary believes that Silas's plan comes from a desire to feel at home, while Warren thinks he is simply desperate. Silas's skills: Both spouses believe he is good at farm work. Silas's relationship to his brother: Warren thinks Silas should depend on his brother rather than on Mary and him. Mary understands that Silas is estranged from his brother. Personality traits: Mary is empathetic and generous. Warren is distant and pragmatic.*

6. *Silas has done more work on their farm than anywhere else. It is where he has felt most useful.*

7. ● **SKILLS FOCUS** *Narrative Poetry The poem's plot would be different in that the conflict between Mary and Warren about what to do with Silas might not be as clear. Their deliberation might have taken a different turn, which would have altered the development of the plot.*

8. ■ **SKILLS FOCUS** *Understand Form in Poetry Some students may feel confused by the changes of speaker. Some may feel that the rhythm of blank verse suited the speakers, while others may feel it limited their speech styles. Many will agree that*

Comprehension

 R3.1

1. **Recall** Who is Silas, and what is his relationship to Mary and Warren?

2. **Recall** How does Silas look and act when Mary finds him?

3. **Clarify** Why is Warren angry with Silas?

4. **Clarify** In Mary's mind, why has Silas returned to the farm?

Literary Analysis

5. **Analyze Characterization** What does the **dialogue** between Mary and Warren reveal about their differing attitudes toward the following subjects?

   • Silas's return (lines 5–30)
   • Silas's appearance and plans (lines 42–61)
   • Silas's skills (lines 88–102)
   • Silas's relationship to his brother (lines 124–145)

   Based on these attitudes, identify Mary's and Warren's chief personality traits.

6. **Draw Conclusions** Silas has a long history with Mary and Warren. Based on what they say about him and their past interactions with them, why do you think he has come to regard their farm as **home?**

7. **Examine Narrative Poetry** Compare the events that occur during the conversation between Mary and Warren with those events—revealed through **dialogue**—that have taken place over the entire time they have known Silas. How would the poem's **plot** be different if Mary and Warren had not talked at such length about these earlier events? Explain.

8. **Evaluate Form in Poetry** Review the chart in which you kept track of the changing speakers. In your opinion, what is gained or lost by Frost's style of writing dialogue in terms of the following elements? Overall, do you think his technique was effective? Explain.

   • clarity   • rhythm   • sense of drama

Literary Criticism

9. **Biographical Context** Robert Frost spent 11 years farming and drew tremendous inspiration from farm life. The poet Ezra Pound, reviewing Frost's second book of poetry, wrote, "I know more of farm life than I did before I had read his poems. That means I know more of 'Life.'" Think of the Frost poems you've read. In what ways can the themes of farm life as depicted by Frost be said to reflect life in general?

---

telling the story through dialogue heightened the drama.

9. *Farm life is an archetype of human life in general, reflecting the universal processes of aging and death, the relationships between husband and wife, and the problems that occur in relationships between employers and employees. As such, a farm setting can be seen as symbolic of the larger world.*

Reading-Writing Connection

R3.2, W1.3, W2.2

CALIFORNIA

WRITING PROMPT

ANALYZE THEME Write an **essay** in which you identify the central message or theme of "The Death of the Hired Man." First make a list of all the perceptions about life or people conveyed in the poem. Then determine which one is the most fully developed. Finally, describe the theme of the poem in **three or four paragraphs**. To support your interpretation, include details and quotations.

SELF-CHECK

A successful analysis will . . .

• include a sentence that states the theme

▶ • show how the details support the theme

• show attention to organization

GRAMMAR AND STYLE

USE LANGUAGE EFFECTIVELY Poets strive to use words and phrases that will give their poems a musical quality and convey emphasis. One kind of phrase Frost uses frequently is the **infinitive phrase,** consisting of an infinitive—a verb form that begins with *to*—plus its modifiers and complements. Infinitive phrases can function as nouns, adjectives, or adverbs. For instance, in the examples below, Frost uses parallel infinitive phrases, highlighted in yellow, as adverbs modifying the verbs highlighted in green.

LC1.1

CALIFORNIA

> She ran on tiptoe down the darkened passage
> *To meet him in the doorway with the news* (lines 3–4)

> She took the market things from Warren's arms
> And set them on the porch, then drew him down
> *To sit beside her on the wooden steps.* (lines 8–10)

Notice that the infinitive phrases help to give the poem a predictable rhythm and to call attention to Mary's actions.

PRACTICE Fill in the blank lines in the following poem with infinitive phrases that modify the boldfaced words.

He **ran** out to the garage

_____

A pair of bargain-hunters
Were fighting over a toaster.
He **tried** his best

_____

Offering a waffle iron,
But neither was satisfied.

WRITING TOOLS

For prewriting, revision, and editing tools, visit the **Writing Center** at ClassZone.com.

Reading-Writing Connection

WRITING PROMPT

To help students organize their analytical essays into an introduction, body, and conclusion, have them use a Microtheme chart. Students should begin by completing the top portion with context information and their theme ideas, then listing supporting details in the bottom of the organizer. Urge students to refer to the organizer as they draft.

🧰 **BEST PRACTICES TOOLKIT—Transparency** Microtheme p. C13

For writing support, see

ℹ️ Writing Center at **ClassZone.com**

GRAMMAR AND STYLE

To help students understand infinitives, write three or four common infinitive verbs on the board, such as *to write, to work,* and *to see.* Clarify also that while infinitive phrases can function as nouns, adjectives, or adverbs, both the examples and practice items on page 911 address the use of infinitives as adverbs. (For more about infinitives and infinitive phrases, see **Grammar Handbook,** page R65.)

Possible answers:

To watch the garage sale
To stop the fight

R RESOURCE MANAGER—Copy Master Use Language Effectively p. 196

Assess and Reteach

Assess

R RESOURCE MANAGER—Copy Masters
Selection Test A pp. 197–198
Selection Test B/C pp. 199–200

💿 Test Generator CD

Reteach

S STANDARDS LESSON FILE
Literature Lesson 16: Narrative vs. Lyric Poetry
Literature Lesson 17: Structure of Poetry
Writing Lesson 26: Analysis Essay

DIFFERENTIATED INSTRUCTION

FOR DEVELOPING WRITERS
Writing Support [small-group option]

• Remind students that a theme is a work's central message about life. Have student groups discuss and list the poem's perceptions about life or people.

• Have students work individually to develop theme statements. Then encourage peer response from their group.

• Tell students to state their theme as a thesis statement in their introduction.

• Limit the assignment to two or three paragraphs and one quotation. Remind students to identify the speaker and the lines and use correct quotation mark form. Urge them to paraphrase other passages of dialogue or text.

Focus and Motivate

OBJECTIVES

Literary Analysis
- explore the key idea of an **image**
- interpret imagist poetry
- read poetry

Reading
- make inferences

Grammar and Writing
- use vivid adjectives to create imagery
- write an imagist poem

 R3.4, W1.2, W1.5, W1.9

ABOUT THE POETS

Ezra Pound Read the biography aloud and then reread the second sentence, noting that it gives Pound's imagist theory in a nutshell. Tell students that Pound's poem in this selection is only two lines long. It describes an image meant to endure in readers' minds.

H. D. Read the biography aloud, pointing out the information that H. D.'s best poems retell Greek myths from the standpoint of women who suffer injustice. Explain that "Helen" is one such poem, and ask students what character named Helen appears in Greek mythology. *Answer: Helen of Troy*

William Carlos Williams Read the biography aloud and ask students how practicing medicine might inspire a poet. *Possible answer: Doctors touch the lives of many, use powers of observation also necessary for a poet, and witness moments of drama such as birth and death.*

The New Poetry

R3.4, W1.2 (p. 919), W1.5 (p. 919), W1.9 (p. 919)

Ezra Pound
1885–1972

In a Station of the Metro
Poetry by Ezra Pound

Ezra Pound may have been the most influential poet of the 20th century, promoting the careers of experimental writers and founding the literary movement known as imagism. Pound encouraged poets to use everyday language and to express emotions and ideas through precise, concrete images. In his own work, Pound drew upon the poetic traditions of numerous countries; his masterwork, *The Cantos,* features heroic figures from world history. In life, he was an inflammatory figure. During World War II, he made anti-American radio broadcasts from Rome. He was eventually arrested and confined to a mental hospital. Following his release, he lived a quiet, secluded life in Italy.

H. D. (Hilda Doolittle)
1886–1961

Helen
Poetry by H. D.

As a young woman, Hilda Doolittle coped with the pain of alienation by befriending other artists. At 15, she met the poet Ezra Pound, who became her close friend and, briefly, her fiancé. A few years later she met the poets Marianne Moore and William Carlos Williams, beginning lifelong nurturing friendships.

Although no longer romantically involved with Pound, Doolittle joined his circle of friends when she moved to London in 1911. Her first published poems appeared in *Poetry* magazine (1913) under the signature "H. D., *Imagiste,*" as suggested by Pound. That year she married Richard Aldington, another imagist, who shared her fascination with the classical world. H. D.'s best poems retell Greek myths from the perspective of women who have suffered injustice.

William Carlos Williams
1883–1963

Spring and All / This Is Just to Say
Poetry by William Carlos Williams

William Carlos Williams crammed two lives into one. He worked full time as a doctor in Rutherford, New Jersey, yet managed to publish more than 40 books of poetry, fiction, plays, and essays. Often, he found inspiration while caring for his patients.

Born to an English father and a Puerto Rican mother, Williams grew up in Rutherford and considered America his home. While his contemporaries fled to Europe, he decided to write poems about the world around him. Williams felt strongly that a poem should be rooted in everyday life and not abstract ideas.

Author Online
For more on these poets, visit the **Literature Center** at **ClassZone.com**.

912

● LITERARY ANALYSIS: IMAGISM

Early in the 20th century, a number of American and British poets undertook a collective effort to rejuvenate poetry in English, freeing it from standard conventions of form and subject matter. The **imagists,** influenced by Japanese haiku as well as ancient Greek lyric and French symbolist poetry, wrote according to strict principles.

- to use the language of **common speech;** yet also to choose words with extreme precision and economy
- to create new **rhythms** as a way of expressing new moods; this generally meant writing in **free verse**
- to have complete freedom in choice of **subject matter**
- to present a clear and highly concentrated **image**

The images in these poems do not generally carry a specific meaning; rather, they suggest a certain feeling or idea.

Ezra Pound and H. D. were among the most important founding members of imagism; William Carlos Williams emerged a few years later, making his own distinctive mark on the style. As you read their work, consider the principles outlined above. Be attuned to the images in these poems and think about what ideas or feelings they might suggest.

● READING SKILL: MAKE INFERENCES

Imagist poems are tightly compressed, leaving out details and explanations in favor of sharp, spare images. They can be seen as highly efficient, saying a lot with very few words. This economic use of language can occasionally leave room for confusion, often requiring you to **make inferences,** or logical guesses based on the text (or prior knowledge), about what is not directly stated. This is often referred to as "reading between the lines." As you read each poem, use a chart like the one shown to record your inferences and the evidence on which you base them.

"Helen"	
Inferences	Details from Text or Prior Knowledge
Helen is beautiful.	First stanza focuses on her white skin and its "lustre."

How do you capture a
MOMENT?

KEY IDEA "I'll never forget the sight of that wet scarf hanging out the car door." Many experiences leave us with a lingering mental **image,** which then becomes our means of remembering the experience. The gleaming surface of an empty swimming pool, a towering pile of unwashed dishes—something about such an image communicates the meaning or feeling of a moment. What is that meaning or feeling? How might you capture it?

QUICKWRITE Choose an image that stands out in your mind, whether it's from an important experience (your first day of school) or an ordinary moment (a walk to the store on a hot day). Then write a brief list of the sensory details that make the image so compelling for you.

913

How do you capture a
MOMENT?

Read the question aloud, and then discuss the **KEY IDEA** as a class. Ask students to visualize the wet scarf, the empty swimming pool, or the pile of dishes. Have students suggest meanings or feelings linked to the **image.** Urge them to use the discussion as a guide to completing the **QUICKWRITE.**

SKILLS FOCUS

● IMAGISM

Write these lines on the board:

Heavy pink petals:
The bent branch bobs.

Have students find elements of imagism in these lines. ***Possible answer:*** *The lines create a highly concentrated image with simple language written in free verse.*

CHECK UNDERSTANDING Ask students to state an image that comes into their minds when they visualize a tree.

READING SKILL

■ MAKE INFERENCES

Ask students to make inferences based on the poetry you wrote on the board. ***Possible answer:*** *It is spring in a place where trees or shrubs flower at that time. Wind or rain is making the heavy branch move.* Have students share their inferences and supporting evidence. Stress that imagist verse contains sparse clues, and readers must rely heavily on prior knowledge and the mental images that the words create.

R **RESOURCE MANAGER**—Copy Master Make Inferences p. 211 (for student use while reading the selections)

DIFFERENTIATED INSTRUCTION

FOR STRATEGIC READERS
Vocabulary Support

- *collective,* "as a group"
- *rejuvenate,* "to make young or new again"
- *haiku,* "poems of three lines, totaling seventeen syllables, focusing on one image"
- *lyric poetry,* "poetry with a musical quality that expresses personal emotions"
- *economy,* "avoidance of waste"
- *compressed,* "pushed into a small space"
- *spare,* "with little detail"

Concept Support: Imagism Students may be familiar with imagery from earlier reading. Connect their knowledge of language that creates mind pictures to the idea of imagism, but clarify that while imagery can be found in most poems, imagism was a specific style that aimed to exclude any content other than imagery. Readers looking for background information or philosophical commentary in an imagist poem must find it by inference.

Practice and Apply

SUMMARY
This two-line poem compares the crowd at a subway station to petals on a bough.

READING SKILL

Ⓐ MAKE INFERENCES

Possible answer: The word apparition *suggests that the faces in the crowd seem ghostly, fleeting, almost unreal.*

If students need help . . . Urge them to look up the word *apparition* in a dictionary.

SUMMARY
This poem describes Helen of Troy. Greece hates her, especially when she smiles or dreams of the past. Unmoved by her beauty, Greece would love Helen only if she were dead.

LITERARY ANALYSIS

Ⓑ IMAGISM

Possible answer: Helen's delicate beauty is depicted in these lines. Images that emphasize this quality include "lustre as of olives" (line 3) and "white hands" (line 5).

READING SKILL

Ⓒ MAKE INFERENCES

Possible answer: The Greeks hate Helen because she has been the occasion of "past enchantments and past ills" (lines 10–11), and perhaps also for her beauty.

Extend the Discussion Do people sometimes "revile" (line 6) those who are exceptional? Why?

IN A STATION OF THE METRO[1]

Ezra Pound

The apparition of these faces in the crowd;
Petals on a wet, black bough. Ⓐ

> Ⓐ **MAKE INFERENCES**
> Note the use of the word *apparition* to describe the faces in the crowd. What does this suggest about the people?

HELEN

H. D.

All Greece hates
the still eyes in the white face,
the lustre as of olives
where she stands,
5   and the white hands. Ⓑ

All Greece reviles[2]
the wan face when she smiles,
hating it deeper still
when it grows wan and white,
10 remembering past enchantments
and past ills.

Greece sees unmoved,
God's daughter[3], born of love,
the beauty of cool feet
15 and slenderest knees,
could love indeed the maid,
only if she were laid,
white ash amid funereal cypresses.[4] Ⓒ

> Ⓑ **IMAGISM**
> Reread the first stanza. What quality of Helen's is depicted in these lines? Identify the images that emphasize this quality.

> Ⓒ **MAKE INFERENCES**
> Based on information you find in the text, why do you think the Greeks hate Helen?

---

1. **the Metro:** the subway in Paris.
2. **reviles:** to attack with hateful language.
3. **God's daughter:** Helen was a daughter of Zeus, the king of the gods; and Leda, a mortal.
4. **funereal cypresses:** The cypress, a type of evergreen tree, has been associated with death and funeral services since ancient times.

914   UNIT 5: THE HARLEM RENAISSANCE AND MODERNISM

DIFFERENTIATED INSTRUCTION

For general guidelines on differentiating instruction, see

 BEST PRACTICES TOOLKIT
Differentiated Instruction pp. 31–38

FOR STRATEGIC READERS
Options for Reading: Audio Recording

- Have students listen to the poems on the *Audio Anthology CD* (also recommended for English learners) while they read along in their texts. Tell students to listen for words and phrases that evoke sensory details, and to visualize the images in the poems as if the words were photographs. Urge students to hold those images in mind throughout their study of the poems.

BACKGROUND

Helen of Troy In Greek mythology, the beautiful Helen was a cause of war. Taken to Troy by its prince, Paris, Helen's plight inspired her brother Agamemnon to invade Troy with a Greek army. The Greeks fought Troy for ten years, losing great warriors such as Achilles, before finally defeating the Trojans, burning Troy, and retrieving Helen. Some historians believe that Helen left for Troy willingly out of passion for Paris, perhaps inspiring her countrymen to hate her for the war that ensued.

Lines 12–18
TIERED DISCUSSION PROMPTS

Use these prompts to help students infer the situation and emotions in "Helen":

Connect How would you feel if you were standing alone in front of a crowd that hated you? *Student responses should include appropriate feelings such as sorrow, fear, and defiance.*

Analyze The speaker says that Greece is "unmoved" by Helen, but in fact the Greeks are moved to emotion. What emotion moves them when they see Helen? ***Possible answer:*** *The Greeks are moved to hatred.*

Evaluate Which images in the poem are most effective in conveying the feeling of the scene? Explain. ***Possible answer:*** *Images of whiteness are effective in conveying Helen's statuelike stillness and distance from the crowd, as if she is made of marble and they are judging her.*

FOR STRATEGIC READERS
Inverted Word Order Remind students that word order in poetry is sometimes different from word order in everyday usage. Ask students to paraphrase the phrases "Greece sees unmoved" (line 12) and "could love indeed the maid" (line 16). ***Possible answers:*** *Paraphrases: "Greece is unmoved when it sees," "could indeed love the maid."*

FOR ENGLISH LEARNERS
Language: Pronoun Referents [mixed-readiness pairs] Explain the referent for the pronoun *she* in line 4 of "Helen." The reference is to Helen, who has been named in the title but not yet in the poem. Then have students work with partners to find the pronoun referents for *it* in lines 8 and 9 and *she* in line 17. ***Possible answers:*** It *refers to* face *and* she *refers to* maid, *which in turn refers to Helen.*

FOR ADVANCED LEARNERS/AP
Synthesize [small-group option] Have students review the Literary Analysis Workshop on Modernism (pages 894–895) and pages 828–829 of the historical essay. Ask them to identify features of "Helen" that reflect the poet's participation in the overall modernist movement. Have students discuss their ideas in small groups.

916

SUMMARY

This poem describes a scene by a roadside on a cold, muddy, windy spring day. The poem describes budding plants entering the world uncertainly but then taking root firmly.

Ⓓ IMAGISM

Possible answer: The colors named are blue, brown, and "reddish purplish." These colors emphasize that spring arises from a deadened, dark winter, rather than emphasizing joy as other poets might.

If students need help . . . Work with them to complete a Cluster Diagram like this one, using color words and other words they associate with spring. Have them compare and contrast their words with Williams's to infer similarities and differences in feeling.

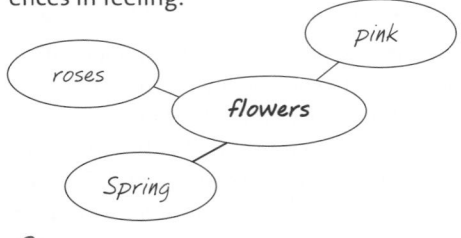

BEST PRACTICES TOOLKIT—Transparency
Cluster Diagram p. B18

SPRING AND ALL

William Carlos Williams

By the road to the contagious hospital[1]
under the surge of the blue
mottled clouds driven from the
northeast—a cold wind. Beyond, the
5 waste of broad, muddy fields
brown with dried weeds, standing and fallen

patches of standing water
the scattering of tall trees

All along the road the reddish
10 purplish, forked, upstanding, twiggy
stuff of bushes and small trees
with dead, brown leaves under them
leafless vines— Ⓓ

Lifeless in appearance, sluggish[2]
15 dazed spring approaches—

They enter the new world naked,
cold, uncertain of all
save that they enter. All about them
the cold, familiar wind— Ⓔ

20 Now the grass, tomorrow
the stiff curl of wildcarrot leaf

One by one objects are defined—
It quickens:[3] clarity, outline of leaf

But now the stark dignity of
25 entrance—Still, the profound change
has come upon them: rooted, they
grip down and begin to awaken

---

1. **contagious hospital:** place where people with contagious diseases are hospitalized.
2. **sluggish:** slow to respond.
3. **quickens:** comes alive; revives.

Ⓓ IMAGISM
Identify the colors named in lines 1–13. What aspect of spring is emphasized by these colors?

Ⓔ IMAGISM
Reread lines 16–19. What words and phrases does Williams use to characterize the newly growing plants in these lines? Then identify the language in lines 20–27 that describes the change that comes upon them.

Ⓔ IMAGISM

Possible answer: In lines 16–19 the phrase "naked, / cold, uncertain" emphasizes the newborn plants' vulnerability. In lines 20–27 words and phrases such as "stiff curl," "clarity, outline of leaf," "stark dignity," "rooted," "grip down," and "begin to awaken" describe the plants' growing strength and confidence.

DIFFERENTIATED INSTRUCTION

FOR STRATEGIC READERS
Concept Support: Make Inferences Have students work with the prereading chart introduced on page 913 to make inferences from the images in this poem.

"Spring and All"	
Inferences	Details
It's early spring.	cold wind, mud

FOR ADVANCED LEARNERS/AP
Analyze Figurative Language Ask students to explain the subtle personification in lines 16–18. *Example: The new roadside plants are described like newborn babies that "enter the new world naked, cold, uncertain . . . ."* Have students discuss the effects this figurative comparison has on reader response, and ask them to consider why the comparison is appropriate in a poem written by a doctor. Invite students to share their analysis and ideas with the class.

THIS IS JUST TO SAY

William Carlos Williams

I have eaten
the plums
that were in
the icebox

5 and which
you were probably
saving
for breakfast

Forgive me
10 they were delicious
so sweet
and so cold **F**

F IMAGISM
Williams has chosen to invoke only two senses in this poem. What are they? Explain how this choice affects your perception of those sensory details.

SUMMARY

The speaker apologizes to an unidentified "you" for eating plums that "you" was saving in the icebox for breakfast, but acknowledges that the plums were delicious.

LITERARY ANALYSIS

F IMAGISM

Possible answer: The two senses invoked in the poem are taste and touch. This choice concentrates and focuses the reader's attention on the sensory experience of eating the plums.

Lines 9–12
REINFORCE *KEY IDEA:* IMAGE

Discuss What feeling does an **image** of tasting and touching a plum create? What new sense is added to the image when readers visualize it? *Students may associate the image with feelings of joy, pleasure, or abandon. The sense of sight is added to the image through visualization.*

SELECTION WRAP–UP

SYNTHESIZE Ask students which of the four poems contains the strongest images. Have them explain their reasoning.

⭐ **CRITIQUE**

- Ask students whether imagist poems lose anything because of their strict focus on images, and if so, what.
- After completing the After Reading questions on page 918, have students revisit their responses and tell whether they have changed their opinions.

FOR STRATEGIC READERS

Concept Support: Make Inferences To help students find meaning underlying the images in the poems, use the Showing, Not Telling, with Literature strategy.

📦 **BEST PRACTICES TOOLKIT**
    Showing, Not Telling, with Literature
        p. D1

FOR ADVANCED LEARNERS/AP

Analyze Style Although William Carlos Williams's style of spare, imagistic free verse seemed innovative in its time, it may be hard for students to appreciate its experimentalism since so much similar verse has been written since. Ask students to read other poetry in Unit 5, such as by Robert Frost or Carl Sandburg, and explain to the class how Williams's poem would seem daring or experimental in comparison.

Practice and Apply

After Reading

Use these copy masters to check understanding and provide extra support:

 RESOURCE MANAGER—Copy Masters
Imagism p. 209
Question Support p. 213

Additional selection questions are provided for teachers on page 205.

ANSWERS

1. *In order for the Greeks to love Helen, she would have to be dead.*

2. *The speaker sees new plants poking up among the dead bushes, leaves, and vines.*

Possible answers:

3. ■ **SKILLS FOCUS Make Inferences** *On the basis of lines 10–11, "remembering past enchantments / and past ills," the Greeks once loved Helen but now hold her responsible for their misfortune.*

4. *The information makes the Greeks' hatred of Helen a matter of complex history rather than mere envy.*

5. *Comparing the faces in the crowd to "petals on a wet, black bough" suggests that the faces are delicate and vulnerable.*

6. ● **SKILLS FOCUS Imagism** *"In a Station of the Metro": loneliness in a crowd "Helen": tension from Helen's beauty and stillness, and the Greeks' hatred "Spring and All": determination and hope from the process of the dazed spring emerging from confusion "This Is Just to Say": happiness from the sweetness and coldness of the plums*

7. *Examples of Williams's ordinary diction from "Spring and All" include "By the road to the contagious hospital" (line 1); "Lifeless in appearance" (line 14); "They enter the new world naked" (line 16). Examples from "This is just to say" include "you were probably / saving / for breakfast" (lines 6–8). Most students may find Williams's work more approachable and interesting in its clarity, while others may be intrigued by the more formal diction of H.D. in lines such as "Greece sees unmoved / God's daughter, born of love" (lines 12–13).*

Comprehension

1. **Clarify** In "Helen," what would it take for the Greeks to love Helen?

2. **Summarize** What signs of new life does the speaker of "Spring and All" notice by the road?

Literary Analysis

3. **Make Inferences** Reread the chart you created as you read "Helen." On the basis of these notes, what can you say about Helen's past and present relationship with the Greeks?

4. **Analyze Allusion** H. D. wrote many poems alluding to Greek mythology. The title "Helen" is an allusion to Helen of Troy, a great beauty whose abduction by Paris, a Trojan prince, prompted the Greeks to take up arms against Troy in a war that lasted for ten long years. How does this information change or deepen your understanding of the poem? Explain, citing evidence from the text.

5. **Examine Metaphor** The juxtaposition of the two images in "In a Station of the Metro" has the effect of a metaphor. What does the image in line 2 suggest about the faces in line 1?

6. **Interpret Imagist Poetry** Choose one of the poems in this lesson and identify its most prominent image or images. What feeling or idea are you left with at the end of the poem? Citing evidence from the text, explain what it is about the imagery that suggests this feeling.

7. **Compare Diction** William Carlos Williams favored the use of everyday language over highly formal poetic diction. Identify several examples of his ordinary diction in "Spring and All" and "This Is Just to Say." Compare Williams's language with the language H. D. uses in "Helen." Which, in your opinion, is more approachable? Which is more interesting? Cite details from the texts to support your opinion.

Literary Criticism

8. **Author's Style** Like other modernist poets, the Imagists eschewed the use of traditional rhyme schemes, meters, and other formal elements. Yet form was important to them; you may recall from page 893 that Williams once criticized Carl Sandburg's poetry as "formless." Choose one of the three poets featured in this lesson and examine his or her use of the following poetic devices, when relevant:

   • rhythm   • rhyme   • line breaks   • stanza breaks

   In your opinion, does the use of these elements seem deliberate or random? Cite evidence from the poem or poems to support your answer.

8. *Students may note the short lines in Williams's "This Is Just to Say," the stanza breaks in "Spring and All," or the rhyme and rhythm in H. D.'s "Helen." They should recognize that the use of formal devices by distinguished poets is deliberate rather than random.*

Reading-Writing Connection

W1.2, W1.5

WRITING PROMPT

WRITE AN IMAGIST POEM Think of a place that has inspired powerful emotions in you. What images come to mind when you think about that place? What feelings do your memories evoke in you? Use your responses to these questions as the starting point for an **eight-to-ten-line poem.** As you write, try to include concrete images that convey both emotions and meaning.

SELF-CHECK

A strong Imagist poem will . . .

- present a distinct image with sensory language
- contain concise, precisely chosen language
- be written in free verse
- display a sense of rhythm

GRAMMAR AND STYLE

W1.9

CREATE IMAGERY Writers use fresh, **vivid adjectives** to create images that bring scenes to life. In the poem "Spring and All," for instance, Williams uses adjectives that lead readers to picture the way a landscape looks in the change from late winter to early spring. Carefully examine the adjectives Williams uses in the following lines. Notice how keenly they evoke the sight of a landscape in transition.

> *All along the road the reddish*
> *purplish, forked, upstanding, twiggy*
> *stuff of bushes and small trees* (lines 9–11)

> *Lifeless in appearance, sluggish*
> *dazed spring approaches—* (lines 14–15)

PRACTICE Write down each of the following sentences. Then try to enliven these sentences by inserting vivid adjectives. An example has been done for you.

> **EXAMPLE**
>
> The crowd stared at Helen's hands and face.
> *The angry crowd stared at Helen's delicate hands and ash-colored face.*

1. She noticed fields and weeds by the side of the road.

2. I saw faces looking out from the windows of the train.

3. Slowly, the girl ate the peaches that we had plucked from the tree.

WRITING TOOLS
For prewriting, revision, and editing tools, visit the **Writing Center** at ClassZone.com.

Reading-Writing Connection

WRITING PROMPT

Suggest that students look back at their **QUICKWRITE** to recall a place they strongly associate with. Have them use the Free-writing strategy to activate sensory and emotional details of their memories.

BEST PRACTICES TOOLKIT
Freewriting p. C1

For writing support, see

ⓘ Writing Center at **ClassZone.com**

GRAMMAR AND STYLE

Remind students that an adjective modifies a noun or pronoun. Tell them that vivid adjectives name specific sensory qualities that help readers visualize the object, place, or person described. As students read the example from Williams, have them pause and visualize each highlighted adjective.

Possible answers:

1. *She noticed pathetic, browning fields and dwarfed, straggling weeds by the side of the cracked old asphalt road.*

2. *I saw hopeful, weary faces looking out from the smeared windows of the puffing, whistling train.*

3. *Slowly, the girl ate the juicy yellow peaches that we had plucked from the fruit-laden tree.*

R RESOURCE MANAGER—Copy Master
Create Imagery p. 214

Assess and Reteach

Assess

R RESOURCE MANAGER—Copy Masters
Selection Test A pp. 215–216
Selection Test B/C pp. 217–218

💿 Test Generator CD

Reteach

S STANDARDS LESSON FILE
Literature Lesson 26: Imagery
Reading Lesson 8: Making Inferences
Writing Lesson 40: Imagery and Figurative Language

DIFFERENTIATED INSTRUCTION

FOR DEVELOPING WRITERS
Writing Support

- Allow students to write poems of only four to six lines.

- Suggest that students prewrite by imagining the place as clearly as possible and jotting down words and phrases they associate with it.

- Encourage students to emulate Williams's use of very short lines and everyday diction.

- Have students show their first drafts to peer editors. Ask peer editors to identify places where images need to be made more vivid.

- Remind students that not every noun needs to be modified by an adjective or more than one adjective. Urge them to strive for clarity, not quantity.

Focus and Motivate

OBJECTIVES

Literary Analysis
- explore the key idea of **rules**
- analyze form and meaning in modern poetry
- read poetry

Reading
- use strategies for reading modern poetry

CALIFORNIA   R3.3

ABOUT THE POETS

E. E. Cummings After students read the biography, have them find words in it that hint at traits of Cummings's poetry. *Students may mention "love," "free-thinking," and "playful, innovative."*

Marianne Moore Read the biography aloud and direct students to the word "innovative" and to the words and phrases describing Moore's poetry, such as "complex" and "intricately crafted." Tell students that Moore's innovations are very different from Cummings's.

Edna St. Vincent Millay Invite students to read the biography aloud and identify words and phrases that describe Millay vividly. *Possible answers: Vivid descriptions include "emotional extremes," "intensity," "revolt," "avant-garde," "bohemian."* Ask students what kind of poems they would expect Millay to write. Clarify that while Millay was experimental in her life, she was the least innovative poet in this group.

---

anyone lived in a pretty how town
Poetry by E. E. Cummings

E. E. Cummings
1894–1962

E. E. Cummings believed deeply in two things: love and human individuality. He felt that both being an individual and being in a loving relationship led to joy and personal growth. His poems honor love in all its variety and pay tribute to people who resist group conformity and conventional thought.

Cummings's faith in love grew out of his tender relationship with his parents.

His father encouraged Cummings's literary ambitions and secured his release when he was imprisoned in France during World War I. After the war, Cummings lived in New York's Greenwich Village, a community of free-thinking artists and intellectuals, where he spent his days painting and writing. By the 1950s, Cummings's playful, innovative style had made him enormously popular.

Poetry
Poetry by Marianne Moore

Marianne Moore
1887–1972

Marianne Moore was a true original. Her interests ranged from baseball to Muhammad Ali to exotic animals, which she scrutinized during her frequent trips to the zoo. Gifted with an eye for detail, she wrote precise, witty descriptions of these and other subjects. Moore also affected an eccentric public appearance, often sporting a three-cornered hat and a black cape.

When she was 31, Moore moved to New York City, where she hobnobbed with other writers, served as editor of the prestigious literary journal *The Dial,* and wrote poetry. A highly innovative poet, she mixed direct observation with quoted material and experimented with stanza forms and line lengths. Her complex, meticulously crafted poems earned her the esteem of other poets, as well as a Pulitzer Prize.

Recuerdo
Poetry by Edna St. Vincent Millay

Edna St. Vincent Millay
1892–1950

In both her life and her art, Edna St. Vincent Millay expressed emotional extremes. This intensity, coupled with Millay's revolt against cultural expectations for women, made her a symbol of the "new woman" of the 1920s.

Although Millay endured childhood poverty and deprivation, she nevertheless managed to excel in school and to win poetry awards. After graduating from Vassar College, she became a central figure among the avant-garde set in New York's Greenwich Village. There, she led a bohemian lifestyle, juggling relationships and living in poverty so that she had ample time to write.

Author Online
For more on these authors, visit the **Literature Center** at **ClassZone.com**.

920

Selection Resources

● LITERARY ANALYSIS: FORM IN MODERN POETRY

Like other modernists, modern poets are known for challenging and experimenting with literary **form.** The term *form* refers primarily to the arrangement of words on the page and to the use of rhyme and meter, but also to the standard conventions of written language (spelling, punctuation, etc.). E. E. Cummings is widely noted for his playful sense of experimentation. In "anyone lived in a pretty how town," he abandons many rules of punctuation, spelling, grammar, and capitalization, creating striking (and sometimes puzzling) effects. Millay's "Recuerdo" is more traditional, with regular rhyme, stanzas, and meter.

Moore's poem "Poetry" is somewhere between these two. It observes the standard conventions of written language, yet it lacks regular rhyme, meter, and line length, giving it a more prose like feel than the other two poems. As you read, note how each poet responds to traditional form, whether by letting go of convention or adapting it. Remember that all good poets use form to help deliver or emphasize meaning.

■ READING STRATEGY: READING MODERN POETRY

Many readers enjoy the playful, unpredictable quality of modern poetry; others find it confusing or meaningless. There are a number of strategies that can help any reader enjoy these poems.

- **Paraphrase**—If a word, phrase, or sentence seems difficult, try restating it in your own words.
- **Read aloud**—Reading a poem aloud can sometimes help you hear the flow of a line or stanza and clarify its meaning, as well as emphasizing its musical qualities.
- **Observe mechanics**—Note the punctuation, spelling, capitalization, and grammar. How does this affect the sound or sense of the poem?

Using a chart like the one shown, record paraphrases for difficult lines in each poem, lines you would read aloud to help clarify meaning, and examples of unusual mechanics.

"anyone lived in a pretty how town"	"Poetry"	"Recuerdo"
Paraphrase: A character named "anyone" lived in some kind of town, year round, singing and dancing.		

Explore the Key Idea

Do poems have to follow the RULES?

KEY IDEA If it doesn't rhyme, is it still a poem? What if it's only two lines long? Do the lines have to break in a regular place? What if some of the words are upside-down on the page? The modernist poets asked questions like this, breaking **rules** right and left. Their work changed the accepted ideas about what poetry is.

DISCUSS With a small group, brainstorm a list of all the qualities you might find in a poem. From that list, come up with a set of rules that all poems follow.

Poetry Rules
- has to sound rhythmic
- must contain images

921

Teach

Do poems have to follow the RULES?

Read the question aloud. Then read the **KEY IDEA** one sentence at a time, allowing students to briefly respond to each question about poetic **rules.** Have students contribute their responses to the *DISCUSS* activity.

SKILLS FOCUS

LITERARY ANALYSIS R3.3

● FORM IN MODERN POETRY

Write these lines on the board:

> when i consider all
> in life that might befall
> me STOP say no more
> say i about it

Have students describe the form of the lines. What poetic conventions do they follow? What conventions do they break? *Possible answer: The lines reflect the poetic form of a stanza. The first two lines rhyme. Besides this, the lines break conventions of capitalization, word order, and punctuation.*

CHECK UNDERSTANDING Ask students to describe the form of another poem from Unit 5.

READING STRATEGY

■ READING MODERN POETRY

Review with students the strategies for reading modern poetry. Ask them if they have used any of these strategies in the past. Discuss these experiences and have students recall which strategies were effective and explain why.

 RESOURCE MANAGER—Copy Master Reading Modern Poetry p. 229 (for student use while reading the selections)

DIFFERENTIATED INSTRUCTION

FOR STRATEGIC READERS
Concept Support: Form in Modern Poetry
Although modernist innovations in mechanics were considered daring and puzzling in their time, many students will be aware of similar experiments in today's popular media, especially hip-hop lyrics and text messaging. In those two forms, unconventional spelling and punctuation are considered an enjoyable way to display one's creativity and freedom from conventions. For example, the letter *s*

is often replaced by *z* in words such as *boyz.* Ask students to supply other examples from prior knowledge. Point out that poets such as E. E. Cummings were experimenting in similar ways almost a century ago.

Practice and Apply

SUMMARY

This poem tells the story of a man named "anyone" and a woman named "noone" who don't fit in to their small town community, but nonetheless live, love, and eventually die together.

LITERARY ANALYSIS

Ⓐ FORM IN MODERN POETRY

Possible answer: The character of anyone "lived," "sang," and "danced," while the women and men "cared not for anyone at all," "sowed," and "reaped." This implies that anyone lives a carefree, impulsive life while the women and men work hard and feel resentful.

READING STRATEGY

Ⓑ READING MODERN POETRY

Possible answer: noone loves anyone deeply.

If students need help. . . Have them paraphrase using the prereading chart introduced on page 921:

> "anyone's any was all to her"
>
> Paraphrase noone loved anything that anyone did

LITERARY ANALYSIS

Ⓒ FORM IN MODERN POETRY

Possible answer: Cummings uses no commas and only one period. This creates a sense of continuity, a breathless quality that makes the death seem part of the motion of anyone's and noone's love. The absence of capital letters points out that distinctions are often arbitrary. In using parentheses to set off noone's kiss, Cummings emphasizes the quiet intimacy of the gesture.

Extend the Discussion How important are punctuation and other mechanics to the meaning of a statement?

---

anyone lived in a pretty how town

E. E. Cummings

anyone lived in a pretty how town
(with up so floating many bells down)
spring summer autumn winter
he sang his didn't he danced his did.

5 Women and men(both little and small)
cared for anyone not at all
they sowed their isn't they reaped their same
sun moon stars rain Ⓐ

children guessed(but only a few
10 and down they forgot as up they grew
autumn winter spring summer)
that noone loved him more by more

when by now and tree by leaf
she laughed his joy she cried his grief
15 bird by snow and stir by still
anyone's any was all to her Ⓑ

someones married their everyones
laughed their cryings and did their dance
(sleep wake hope and then)they
20 said their nevers they slept their dream

stars rain sun moon
(and only the snow can begin to explain
how children are apt to forget to remember
with up so floating many bells down)

25 one day anyone died i guess
(and noone stooped to kiss his face)
busy folk buried them side by side
little by little and was by was

all by all and deep by deep
30 and more by more they dream their sleep
noone and anyone earth by april
wish by spirit and if by yes. Ⓒ

Women and men(both dong and ding)
summer autumn winter spring
35 reaped their sowing and went their came
sun moon stars rain

Couple Above St. Paul, Marc Chagall. Private collection. © Scala/Art Resource, New York. © 2007 Artists Rights Society (ARS), New York/ADAGP, Paris.

ANALYZE VISUALS

Painter Marc Chagall is known for his whimsical and dream like images. Identify some unrealistic elements in the painting on page 923. What do they suggest about the couple depicted? Explain.

Ⓐ FORM IN MODERN POETRY

Many words in these stanzas are used in strange ways, but the verbs are still pretty straight forward. In lines 1–8, which actions are attributed to "anyone" and which to the women and men? What does this suggest about the differences between them?

Ⓑ READING MODERN POETRY

Paraphrase lines 13–16. How does "noone" feel about "anyone"?

Ⓒ FORM IN MODERN POETRY

Reread lines 25–32. Identify some ways in which Cummings breaks with the conventions of **mechanics.** How does this affect your sense of the poem? Explain.

DIFFERENTIATED INSTRUCTION

For general guidelines on differentiating instruction, see

 BEST PRACTICES TOOLKIT
Differentiated Instruction pp. 31–38

FOR STRATEGIC READERS

Options for Reading: Audio Recording

- Have students listen to the poems on the *Audio Anthology CD* (also recommended for English learners) while they read along in their texts. Use the Jigsaw Reading strategy to help students decipher the poems one stanza at a time.

- For the Cummings poem, clarify that "anyone" and "noone" are specific people while "someones" and "everyones" refers to other people in the town as a group. Urge students to think about why Cummings uses pronouns instead of names.

 BEST PRACTICES TOOLKIT
Jigsaw Reading p. A1

ANALYZE VISUALS

Possible answer: Unrealistic elements in the painting include the elongated couple that seems to float in midair, the partial horse floating behind it, and the oversized bouquet. These suggest that the couple is involved in a private dream.

About the Art Marc Chagall (1887–1985), born in Belarus to a poor Jewish family, was one of the most popular painters of the 20th century. He is known for his vibrant colors and for painting fantastical floating objects such as cows, fish, and fiddlers. In this typical Chagall painting, the whimsical, life-loving joy and the subject of love match the mood of Cummings's poem.

Line 7
REINFORCE *KEY IDEA:* RULES

Discuss What is E.E. Cummings suggesting about people who follow **rules**? *Possible answer: Cummings is suggesting that people who follow rules focus on "isn't" or what is not allowed, and end up with lives filled with sameness.*

FOR ENGLISH LEARNERS

Language: Punctuation and Print Clues
[mixed-readiness pairs] Have pairs work together to conventionalize the poem's punctuation and other mechanics, such as capitalization. Students can then regularize these parts of speech and word order issues:

- *did* as a noun (line 4)
- *was* as a noun (line 28)
- inverted word order in "cared for anyone not at all" (line 6)

With these issues resolved, have more fluent partners describe the poem's playful mood and the basic situation of the love story involving anyone and noone. Finally, encourage students to state the gist of the poem in a couple of sentences.

READING SKILL

D READING MODERN POETRY

Possible answer: Paraphrase: The speaker, like the reader, sometimes dislikes poetry but can also discover the genuine in poetry. Poetry can sometimes capture in an image something profoundly true and useful. Moore's lines "Hands that can grasp, eyes / that can dilate," and "hair that can rise" are important because they express the emotional impact of poetry.

If students need help . . . Work with them to answer this question:

- How does the speaker's opinion of poetry change from line 1 to lines 2–3?

Lines 6–11
TIERED DISCUSSION PROMPTS

Use these prompts to help students comprehend Moore's view of poetry:

Connect Which do you value more, complex ideas or useful advice? Explain. *Students' responses should present reasons for valuing or not valuing both options.*

Interpret What does Moore mean by "so derivative as to become unintelligible"? *Possible answer: Moore means that ideas can be diluted down by endless interpretation until they are meaningless.*

Evaluate Is Moore right that we do not admire what we cannot understand? Give examples pro and con. *Accept thoughtful answers that include examples.*

LITERARY ANALYSIS

E FORM IN MODERN POETRY

Possible answer: The line breaks in lines 20 and 22 focus attention on the thematically important words distinction *and* poetry.

Poetry

Marianne Moore

I, too, dislike it: there are things that are important beyond all this fiddle.
   Reading it, however, with a perfect contempt for it, one discovers in
   it, after all, a place for the genuine.
       Hands that can grasp, eyes
5   that can dilate,[1] hair that can rise
       if it must, these things are important not because a

high-sounding interpretation can be put upon them but because they are
   useful. When they become so derivative[2] as to become unintelligible,
   the same thing may be said for all of us, that we
10   do not admire what
      we cannot understand: the bat **D**
        holding on upside down or in quest of something to

eat, elephants pushing, a wild horse taking a roll, a tireless wolf under
   a tree, the immovable critic twitching his skin like a horse that feels a flea,
15   the base-
    ball fan, the statistician—
      nor is it valid
        to discriminate against "business documents and

school-books"; all these phenomena are important. One must make a
20   distinction
   however: when dragged into prominence by half poets, the result is not
               poetry, **E**
   nor till the poets among us can be
     "literalists[3] of
25   the imagination"—above
       insolence and triviality and can present

D READING MODERN POETRY
Reread and **paraphrase** lines 1–11. What is important about "Hands that can grasp, eyes / that can dilate, hair that can rise"?

ANALYZE VISUALS
Consider what the speaker of this poem has to say about poetry. How do you think she might respond to this abstract painting?

E FORM IN MODERN POETRY
Note the extremely indented lines at lines 15, 20, and 22. What do these oddities of form contribute to the poem's meaning? Explain.

---

1. **dilate** (dī-lāt'): enlarge; open wide.
2. **derivative:** lacking originality.
3. **literalists:** people who interpret words in their usual or most basic sense.

DIFFERENTIATED INSTRUCTION

FOR ADVANCED LEARNERS/AP
Evaluate Form Explain that "Poetry" is written in syllabic verse. This form appears at first glance to be free verse, but in fact is not. To explore the form have students begin by counting the syllables in the first and last lines of each stanza. They will find 19 syllables in the first lines, counting line 20 as a continuation of line 19, and 13 syllables in the last lines. Moore plays with form by varying line lengths and syllable counts in the remaining lines. Tell students that critical opinion on syllabic verse is divided and invite them to contribute to the debate by responding to these questions: Is syllable count too arbitrary to hinge a poem upon? Can syllable count create rhythm—or does rhythm arise from other aspects of the poem? Invite students to explain the poem's syllabic structure and their conclusions with the class.

Rising Moon (1965), Hans Hofmann. Private collection. © 2007 Renate, Hans and Maria Hofmann Trust/
Artists Rights Society (ARS), New York/Art Resource, New York.

for inspection, "imaginary gardens with real toads in them," shall we have
   it. In the meantime, if you demand on the one hand,
   the raw material of poetry in
30   all its rawness and
    that which is on the other hand
       genuine, you are interested in poetry. **F**

F **READING MODERN POETRY**
Reread lines 28–32 aloud.
How, if at all, does this
change your sense of the
line breaks?

Lines 19–28
REINFORCE *KEY IDEA:* RULES

Discuss How does Marianne Moore use
rules to determine if text is poetry? *Possible*
answer: Moore uses rules to identify poetry by
determining if text is well written, if it uses lan-
guage in understandable ways, if it rises above
triviality, and if it addresses real objects in an
imaginative way.

ANALYZE VISUALS

Possible answers: Since Moore wrote, "we / do
not admire what we cannot understand," she
might not admire the painting. Since she saw
artists as "literalists of the imagination," she
might see the painting as too abstract and not
literal enough. On the other hand, she might
respect Hofmann's exploration of his medium
and its limits.

About the Art Abstract painter Hans Hofmann
(1880–1966) produced a new kind of landscape
in his paintings. These landscapes consisted of
colors and planes instead of trees and landforms
found in nature. Hofmann's aim in painting was
to create "pulsating, luminous, and open surfaces that emanate a mystic light." His companions in adulthood included Picasso and Matisse,
and Hofmann synthesized aspects of their style
as well as those of other painters of 20th-cen-
tury abstract works to create his own style.

READING STRATEGY

F READING MODERN POETRY

Possible answers: The line breaks seem to
disappear when the lines are read aloud.
However, these breaks also make readers
emphasize particular words or phrases.

FOR STRATEGIC READERS

Clarify Meaning Make sure that students
understand Moore's concluding statement
about poetry. Help them retrace and restate
the two elements she says reflect an interest
in poetry:

- *the raw material of poetry* (line 29), "ideas
and images that produce an emotional
response"

- *that which . . . genuine* (lines 31–32), "ideas
that are clearly stated and useful"

FOR ADVANCED LEARNERS/AP

Evaluate Theme Moore makes a number of
complex or even ambiguous statements about
poetry. She says that poetry is "a place for the
genuine" (line 3), but does not define genuine.
She says that a physical and emotional response to poetry, as in "hair that can rise" (line
5) is "useful," but does not say how. She praises real poets, or "literalists of the imagination"
(lines 24–25), as opposed to the work of "half
poets" who represent "insolence and triviality"
(lines 21–26), but does not tell readers how to

distinguish between the two. Have students
discuss the kind of poetry Moore would like,
and why. Ask them to find examples of poems
she would like or dislike, including poems in
this book, and to share them with the class.

Prereading for this poem is found on page 920.

SUMMARY

The speaker of this poem remembers when she and a lover rode a ferry all night, eating apples and pears and giving fruit and money to a poor woman.

READING STRATEGY

G READING MODERN POETRY

Possible answer: Unlike the other two poems, "Recuerdo" rhymes and has meter. The rhyme and meter reflect the speaker and her companion going regularly "back and forth all night on the ferry," and the poem's cadence captures the playful quality of their experience.

LITERARY ANALYSIS

H FORM IN MODERN POETRY

Possible answer: Each stanza begins with the same two lines. This device emphasizes the speaker's nostalgia for the memory.

About the Art Swiss painter Paul Klee (1879–1940) was an important artist of the 20th century, popular for his playful, sometimes childlike style. *Port Scene* is as merry as Millay's poem about a ferry.

SELECTION WRAP–UP

SYNTHESIZE Ask students to discuss ways the three poets are similar despite their differences in style and form.

⭐ CRITIQUE

- Ask students to discuss the pros and cons of having rules in poetry.
- After completing the After Reading questions on page 927, have students revisit their responses and tell whether they have changed their opinions.

Recuerdo

Edna St. Vincent Millay

We were very tired, we were very merry—
We had gone back and forth all night on the ferry.
It was bare and bright, and smelled like a stable—
But we looked into a fire, we leaned across a table,
5 We lay on a hill-top underneath the moon;
And the whistles kept blowing, and the dawn came soon.

We were very tired, we were very merry—
We had gone back and forth all night on the ferry;
And you ate an apple, and I ate a pear,
10 From a dozen of each we had bought somewhere;
And the sky went wan,[1] and the wind came cold,
And the sun rose dripping, a bucketful of gold. **G**

We were very tired, we were very merry,
We had gone back and forth all night on the ferry.
15 We hailed, "Good morrow, mother!" to a shawl-covered head,
And bought a morning paper, which neither of us read;
And she wept, "God bless you!" for the apples and pears,
And we gave her all our money but our subway fares. **H**

---

1. **wan:** pale.

G READING MODERN POETRY
Read aloud lines 1–12. How does this poem sound different from the other two? What aspect of the subject matter is reflected by the poem's **rhyme** and **meter?**

H FORM IN MODERN POETRY
Identify the **repetition** that helps to shape each stanza. What meaning is emphasized by this device?

Port Scene, Paul Klee. Atheneum Museum, Helsinki, Finland. © Giraudon/Art Resource, New York. © 2007 Artists Rights Society (ARS), New York/VG Bild-Kunst, Bonn.

DIFFERENTIATED INSTRUCTION

FOR STRATEGIC READERS

Visualize Work with students to help them imagine the scene of Millay's poem. Direct them in completing a Sensory Notes organizer like this partial one:

| I smell ... The ferry smells like a stable. |
| I taste ... an apple and a pear |

 BEST PRACTICES TOOLKIT—Transparency
Sensory Notes p. B9

FOR ENGLISH LEARNERS

Culture: Connect Ask Spanish speakers what *recuerdo* means in that language ("souvenir" or "remembrance"). Use that information to help students understand the context of the poem, which is a nostalgic memory of happy young love. Invite other English learners to share similar words from their home languages. Discuss the difference between words that merely define memory and words that capture the sense of longing in Millay's poem.

Comprehension

1. **Clarify** Who are the lovers described in "anyone lived in a pretty how town"?

2. **Clarify** What does the speaker of "Poetry" dislike about poetry? What does she value in it?

3. **Clarify** Where and when does "Recuerdo" take place?

Literary Analysis

4. **Analyze Modern Poetry** Review the chart you filled in as you read. In the Cummings poem, it is important not to try to read every line literally, but rather aim for the gist of these nonsense phrases. Choose one stanza from this poem and explain the general impression you get from the language in each line. Then paraphrase the entire stanza, making use of these impressions.

5. **Interpret Ideas** In "Poetry," what idea about poetry is represented by each of the following items? Explain.

   • "hands that can grasp" (line 4)
   • "elephants pushing" (line 13)
   • "business documents and school-books" (lines 18–19)
   • "'imaginary gardens with real toads in them'" (line 27)

6. **Evaluate Form in Modern Poetry** Each of these poems has a playful, irreverent quality, sometimes achieved by breaking **rules** of traditional poetry and sometimes by following them. Examine the poems in this lesson, identifying the most playful elements of each. In your opinion, which poem is the most radical? Cite evidence to support your answer.

Literary Criticism

7. **Critical Interpretations** In a review, the critic Edmund Wilson argued that "Behind [the] formidable barrier of punctuations for which Mr. Cummings seems unfortunately to have achieved most celebrity, his emotions are conventional and simple in the extreme." Do you agree or disagree with Wilson's argument? Whether or not you agree, do you view Wilson's statement as a positive or negative comment? Cite evidence to support your opinion.

---

6. ● **SKILLS FOCUS** Form in Modern Poetry
Playful elements include Cummings's use of punctuation, Moore's outlandish imagery, and Millay's use of refrain. Students may see Cummings as the most radical for his diction, or Moore for her unique form and difficult ideas.

7. *Students may find the story of anyone and noone to be simple and fablelike, a quality that some will enjoy and others find trite. Other students will argue that the love between anyone and noone is complex, as are their relationships with the townspeople and with the passage of time. Opinions may vary about the positive or negative nature of Wilson's comment, but student answers should not confuse "simple" with simplistic.*

Practice and Apply

After Reading
Use these copy masters to check understanding and provide extra support:

 RESOURCE MANAGER—Copy Masters
Form in Modern Poetry p. 227
Question Support p. 231

Additional selection questions are provided for teachers on page 223.

ANSWERS

1. *The lovers are anyone and noone.*

2. *She dislikes its pretentiousness and triviality but likes its authenticity.*

3. *The poem takes place on a ferry and a city street, during the night, at dawn, and just after sunrise.*

Possible answers:

4. ■ **SKILLS FOCUS** Reading Modern Poetry
Students' choices of stanzas and paraphrases will vary. Students choosing the first stanza may note that "up so floating many bells down" and the list of seasons indicate time passing.

5. *"Hands that can grasp" represents the emotional content in poetry. "Elephants pushing" refers to instinctive actions that humans cannot understand. "Business documents and school-books" represents texts that poets might unjustly scorn. "'Imaginary gardens with real toads in them'" suggests that imaginative poetry can have importance.*

Assess and Reteach

Assess

 RESOURCE MANAGER—Copy Masters
Selection Test A pp. 233–234
Selection Test B/C pp. 235–236
🔘 Test Generator CD

Reteach

S STANDARDS LESSON FILE
Literature Lesson 17: Structure of Poetry
Research and Study Skills Lesson 12: Paraphrasing

Focus and Motivate

OBJECTIVES

Literary Analysis
- explore the key idea of **alienation**
- analyze stream of consciousness in a dramatic monologue
- read poetry

Reading
- summarize stanzas

R3.3

ABOUT THE POET

After students have read the biography, focus their attention on Stravinsky's remark in the first paragraph. Lead students in discussing what it means to be "a great sorcerer of words" and "the very key keeper of the language." Tell students that when they read "The Love Song of J. Alfred Prufrock," they will see a demonstration of the sorcerer's powers.

USING THE *NOTABLE QUOTE*

Read the quote aloud and invite volunteers to interpret it. Then ask listeners whether they agree. Ask students to cite examples from experience and knowledge that either support or debunk the claim that people cannot bear much reality. Tell them that **T. S. Eliot's** poem raises the question of whether its main character can or cannot bear reality.

The Love Song of J. Alfred Prufrock
Poem by T. S. Eliot

NOTABLE QUOTE
"Human kind cannot bear very much reality."

FYI
Did you know that
T. S. Eliot . . .
- was also an acclaimed playwright?
- wrote the book that inspired the musical *Cats*?
- won the Nobel Prize in literature in 1948?

Author Online

For more on T. S. Eliot, visit the **Literature Center** at **ClassZone.com**.

T. S. Eliot
1888–1965

When he was alive, T. S. Eliot was one of the most influential poets in the English-speaking world. His invention of new poetic rhythms, forms, and themes had an enormous impact on other writers and helped usher in a new era in poetry. Eliot, remarked the composer Igor Stravinsky, was "not only a great sorcerer of words, but the very key keeper of the language."

A Lover of Philosophy Eliot grew up in St. Louis, Missouri, in a household steeped in culture and tradition. His mother, Charlotte Champe Stearns, was an amateur poet, and his father, Henry Ware Eliot, was a successful businessman with New England roots. Eliot received a broad education, studying at Milton Academy and Harvard University. After earning both bachelor's and master's degrees from Harvard, Eliot continued his studies in philosophy at the Sorbonne in Paris and then back at Harvard. However, he never completed those

studies. While on a traveling fellowship in Europe, he met the poet Ezra Pound, who encouraged Eliot's poetic ambitions.

Literary Success Pound helped Eliot gain entry into London's avant-garde circle of writers, and he introduced Eliot's poetry to Harriet Monroe of *Poetry* magazine. In 1915, Eliot's masterpiece "The Love Song of J. Alfred Prufrock" appeared in *Poetry*. That same year, Eliot married Vivien Haigh-Wood, an Englishwoman. Struggling to make a living as a writer, Eliot worked as a teacher, a bank clerk, and finally as an editor.

Breakthroughs in Poetry The 1917 publication of Eliot's first book, *Prufrock and Other Observations,* signaled a distinct break with the past. Using colloquial speech laced with slang, Eliot created a new, highly original poetic diction. He also explored new poetic themes, such as the splendors and horrors of modern life and the effects of alienation. With the appearance of *The Waste Land* in 1922, Eliot's reputation was solidified. In this poem, Eliot articulated the disgust and disillusionment felt by his generation in the wake of World War I, as well as its longing for meaning in a chaotic, sometimes frightening, world.

Inspired by Religion Though a pioneer in poetry, Eliot became increasingly conservative in his personal views. Struggling with anxiety over his domestic troubles, he joined the Church of England in 1927 and embraced its traditional pieties. In his later collections, *Ash Wednesday* (1930) and *Four Quartets* (1943), he used poetry to stress the significance of accepting

928

Selection Resources

 RESOURCE MANAGER UNIT 5

Plan and Teach pp. 237–244
Literary Analysis
Summary pp. 245†*, 246‡*
Stream of Consciousness
  pp. 247, 248†*
Question Support p. 251*
Reading
Summarize Stanzas pp. 249, 250†*

Assessment
Selection Tests A, B/C
  pp. 253*, 255*
Test Generator CD

 BEST PRACTICES TOOLKIT

Differentiated Instruction
  pp. 31–38*
Graphic Organizers/Strategies
Three-Column Journal •
Core Analysis Frame: Poetry •
Questioning the Author

Reading Support
Audio Anthology CD*

Technology
Literature Center at
ClassZone.com
WriteSmart CD

* Resources for Differentiation   † Also in Spanish   ‡ In Haitian Creole and Vietnamese

● **LITERARY ANALYSIS: STREAM OF CONSCIOUSNESS**

Modern poets explored many ways of breaking free from the standard conventions of poetic form and even content, changing the nature of both narrative and lyric poetry. One of the most dramatic breaks from convention in the modern era was the development of **stream of consciousness.** Used by both poets and fiction writers, this technique presents a sometimes chaotic flow of images and ideas, meant to represent the unfiltered thoughts of the speaker or protagonist. "The Love Song of J. Alfred Prufrock" is a **dramatic monologue** in which Prufrock, the speaker, addresses a silent listener with a tumble of associative thoughts, allusions, and daydreams.

And indeed there will be time
For the yellow smoke that slides along the street
Rubbing its back upon the window-panes

As you read the poem, try not to be put off by the nonsensical nature of the verse, but be alert to any feelings or ideas that the images seem to suggest.

● **READING SKILL: SUMMARIZE STANZAS**

The difficult thing about reading stream of consciousness is figuring out how to connect seemingly unrelated ideas. A writer will often jump from one thought to the next without any clear transition. Fortunately, Eliot has done us the favor of grouping his thoughts in **stanzas.** If you read the stanzas closely, you will notice that each one expresses a fairly coherent idea. Once you **summarize** and identify the central idea or image of each stanza, you will have an easier time tracing the arc, and the sense, of the entire poem.

As you read, record your summary of each stanza in a chart like the one shown. Some stanzas have only two or three lines; in these cases, don't worry about providing a summary as much as a brief description of the central idea or image.

Stanza	Summary/Central Idea
1	Speaker suggests that listener join him on an evening trip through the lonely city streets.

What is
ALIENATION?

KEY IDEA So many of us know the feeling of standing at the edge of a party, wanting to join but having no idea what to say or do. Everyone else is having more fun, making better jokes, or wearing nicer clothes. And it's all the worse if you are hoping to approach the object of your affections; do you even stand a chance? In this poem, J. Alfred Prufrock approaches a party with a similar sense of **alienation.** Full of dread and self-doubt and fearful of female rejection, he wonders whether he dares to step in and draw attention to himself.

QUICKWRITE Create a list of images that suggest alienation or isolation to you. They could be explicit, such as that of a person hesitating at the edge of a group, or implicit, such as the image of a lonely window lit in the darkness.

929

What is
ALIENATION?

Read the question and the **KEY IDEA** aloud. Ask students to explain what **alienation** means. Then ask students to brainstorm situations in which people might feel alienated. Have students complete the **QUICKWRITE** and share their image lists.

SKILLS FOCUS

LITERARY ANALYSIS R3.3

● **STREAM OF CONSCIOUSNESS**

Write this stanza on the board:

What's the matter with me?
A car horn honks and
The dishes are dirty but
When will she be here?

Ask students to read the stanza carefully. Have them identify the thoughts it contains, then describe feelings or ideas its images suggest. ***Possible answer:*** *The stanza contains the speaker's worry about himself and about where an absent female is. It also contains the speaker's awareness that a car horn honks and the dishes are dirty. These lines suggest feelings of anxiety and images of visual disorder and loud sounds.*

CHECK UNDERSTANDING Ask students to silently track their thoughts for a minute. Invite volunteers to share.

READING SKILL

■ **SUMMARIZE STANZAS**

Remind students that a summary expresses the main idea of a text and provides a few important details. Finding this idea in poetry may require some inference by readers. Have students summarize to identify the central idea or image of the stanza on the board. ***Possible answer:*** *The central idea or image is one of a distressed person waiting.*

R RESOURCE MANAGER—Copy Master Summarize Stanzas p. 249 (for student use while reading the selection)

DIFFERENTIATED INSTRUCTION

FOR STRATEGIC READERS

Vocabulary Support To support instruction, clarify the meaning of these words:

- *conventions,* "usual ways of doing things"
- *chaotic,* "messy, formless, disorganized"
- *unfiltered,* "with nothing removed"
- *protagonist,* "main character"
- *associative,* "connected with the association of ideas"

- *allusions,* "indirect references to persons, places, events, or literary works with which the writer believes the reader will be familiar"
- *coherent,* "holding together, making sense"
- *arc,* "a curving or bow-shaped path"

Practice and Apply

SUMMARY
In this poem, the title character is the speaker and protagonist. As he goes to an evening social gathering, Prufrock expresses his thoughts and feelings, and ponders whether to ask an "overwhelming question"—perhaps a marriage proposal. Preoccupied with his appearance, his aging, and his sense of insignificance and fear, he wonders whether his activities are worthwhile and what his life really means. He ends his monologue inconclusively, his question unasked and unanswered.

Lines 1–14
TIERED DISCUSSION PROMPTS
Use these prompts to help students understand the speaker of the poem:

Connect What are your first impressions of J. Alfred Prufrock? Explain. ***Possible answer: Accept all reasonable responses, but students should note that Prufrock seems discontented and somewhat depressed.***

Analyze What lines in the poem provide clues about the kind of gathering in which Prufrock finds himself? ***Possible answer: Lines 13–14 in which "women come and go / Talking of Michelangelo" suggest that it is a gathering of sophisticated people.***

Synthesize What can you infer about Prufrock's feelings about being at the party? How do those feelings provide a sense as to the kind of person he is? Cite evidence from the poem to explain your answer. ***Possible answer: Lines 1 and 4 repeat the phrase "Let us go," suggesting that Prufrock is unhappy about being at the gathering but is somehow stalled in carrying out his desire to leave.***

THE LOVE SONG OF
J. Alfred Prufrock

T. S. Eliot

*S'io credessi che mia risposta fosse
a persona che mai tornasse al mondo,
questa fiamma staria senza più scosse.
Ma per ciò che giammai di questo fondo
non tornò vivo alcun, s'i'odo il vero,
senza tema d'infamia ti rispondo.*

Let us go then, you and I,
When the evening is spread out against the sky
Like a patient etherised upon a table;
Let us go, through certain half-deserted streets,
5 The muttering retreats
Of restless nights in one-night cheap hotels
And sawdust restaurants with oyster-shells:
Streets that follow like a tedious argument
Of insidious intent
10 To lead you to an overwhelming question . . .
Oh, do not ask, "What is it?"
Let us go and make our visit.

In the room the women come and go
Talking of Michelangelo.

15 The yellow fog that rubs its back upon the window-panes,
The yellow smoke that rubs its muzzle on the window-panes,
Licked its tongue into the corners of the evening,
Lingered upon the pools that stand in drains,
Let fall upon its back the soot that falls from chimneys,

S'io credessi . . . ti rispondo: These lines are from the *Inferno*, written in the early 14th century by Italian poet Dante Alighieri. As Dante visits hell, one of the damned agrees to speak of his torment only because he believes that Dante cannot return to the living world to repeat the tale.

3 etherised: given ether, a liquid used as an anesthetic.

9 insidious (ĭn-sĭd'ē-əs): more dangerous than it seems.

DIFFERENTIATED INSTRUCTION

For general guidelines on differentiating instruction, see

 BEST PRACTICES TOOLKIT
Differentiated Instruction pp. 31–38

FOR STRATEGIC READERS
Options for Reading: Audio Recording
- Have students listen to the poems on the *Audio Anthology CD* (also recommended for English learners) while they read along in their texts. Urge students to imagine themselves in the role of Prufrock as he wanders through the streets and rooms, observing and thinking.

- Point out that some of the stanzas flow from one page to another. Remind students to use Eliot's punctuation as their guide to his intended stanza breaks. Clarify that all the stanzas end in a period or question mark.

20 Slipped by the terrace, made a sudden leap,
    And seeing that it was a soft October night,
    Curled once about the house, and fell asleep. **Ⓐ**

    And indeed there will be time
    For the yellow smoke that slides along the street
25 Rubbing its back upon the window-panes;
    There will be time, there will be time
    To prepare a face to meet the faces that you meet;
    There will be time to murder and create,
    And time for all the works and days of hands
30 That lift and drop a question on your plate;
    Time for you and time for me,
    And time yet for a hundred indecisions,
    And for a hundred visions and revisions,
    Before the taking of a toast and tea.

35 In the room the women come and go
    Talking of Michelangelo.

    And indeed there will be time
    To wonder, "Do I dare?" and, "Do I dare?"
    Time to turn back and descend the stair,
40 With a bald spot in the middle of my hair—
    (They will say: "How his hair is growing thin!")
    My morning coat, my collar mounting firmly to the chin,
    My necktie rich and modest, but asserted by a simple pin—
    (They will say: "But how his arms and legs are thin!")
45 Do I dare
    Disturb the universe?
    In a minute there is time
    For decisions and revisions which a minute will reverse. **Ⓑ**

    For I have known them all already, known them all—
50 Have known the evenings, mornings, afternoons,
    I have measured out my life with coffee spoons;
    I know the voices dying with a dying fall
    Beneath the music from a farther room.
        So how should I presume?

55 And I have known the eyes already, known them all—
    The eyes that fix you in a formulated phrase,
    And when I am formulated, sprawling on a pin,
    When I am pinned and wriggling on the wall,
    Then how should I begin

Ⓐ STREAM OF CONSCIOUSNESS
Reread lines 1–22. Identify the figures of speech used to characterize the evening sky and the night fog. What **mood** or sensation do these images establish?

42 morning coat: a type of formal suit jacket with coattails.

Ⓑ SUMMARIZE STANZAS
Summarize lines 37–48. What do Prufrock's repeated questioning and his preoccupation with his appearance indicate about his state of mind?

54 presume: act overconfidently; dare.
56 formulated: reduced to a formula.
55–58 And I have . . . on the wall: Prufrock recalls being scrutinized by women at other parties. He portrays himself as a live insect that has been classified, labeled, and mounted for display.

Ⓐ STREAM OF CONSCIOUSNESS

Possible answer: Eliot uses the simile of the patient upon the table (lines 2–3) to create a mood of bleak numbness. He uses metaphor and personification to describe the fog as a catlike creature (lines 15–22), extending the bleakness toward eerie discomfort or even menace.

If students need help . . . Review figures of speech such as simile, metaphor, and personification. Then help students list examples in an organizer like this:

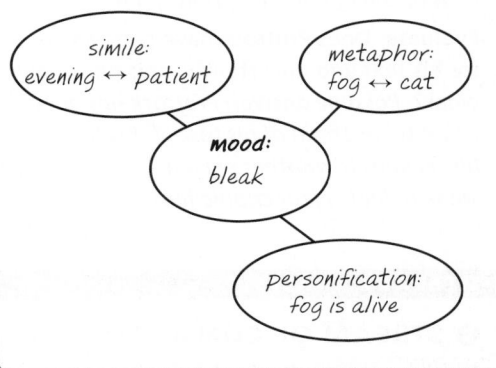

READING SKILL

Ⓑ SUMMARIZE STANZAS

Possible answer: Prufrock's repeated questioning and his preoccupation with his appearance indicate that he is deeply insecure and timid.

If students need help . . . Invite a volunteer to act out the scene described in the lines, using gesture and dialogue.

FOR STRATEGIC READERS

Clarify Meaning Work through lines 26–28 with students, helping them to paraphrase the text: "There will be time to reinvent myself to fit the people I will meet. There will be time to 'kill' my personality and replace it with another." Have students discuss why Prufrock might want to recreate himself for the people at the party. *Possible answer: Prufrock wants to reinvent himself because he does not think the partygoers will accept him as he is.*

FOR ENGLISH LEARNERS

Vocabulary: Prefixes [small-group option] Call student's attention to these words: *indecisions* (line 32), *visions* (line 33), *revisions* (lines 33, 48), and *decisions* (line 48). Have groups speculate about the words' meanings by combining the roots and prefixes. Explain that in this poem, *indecisions* means "hesitations," *visions* means "imaginings," and *revisions* means "changes."

FOR ADVANCED LEARNERS/AP

Analyze Metaphor Focus student attention on the famous metaphor, "I have measured out my life with coffee spoons." Ask students to interpret the metaphor and discuss what it shows about Prufrock's character. *Example: Like spoons of coffee, his days are doled out in small, almost identical units. His life is a matter of humdrum habits like that of drinking coffee. This suggests that his character is unadventurous and timid.*

TIERED DISCUSSION PROMPTS

Use these prompts to help students comprehend Prufrock's state of mind:

Restate Restate Prufrock's thoughts in this passage. *Possible answer: Prufrock wonders whether he is strong enough to face what he has to face. He recalls suffering and praying, but concludes that despite his efforts, he is afraid anyway.*

Interpret What is Prufrock afraid of in this moment? Overall? *Possible answer: In this moment, Prufrock is apparently afraid of revealing his feelings to a woman. Overall, he is afraid of engaging fully in life.*

Evaluate Does Prufrock have good cause for his fear and uncertainty, or is he simply weak? *Possible answer: Profrock has good cause to be afraid of his task, if it is to open his feelings to another person. However, he is weak to let his fear cripple him.*

LITERARY ANALYSIS

C STREAM OF CONSCIOUSNESS

Possible answer: Prufrock casts himself in the role of John the Baptist (line 82), in an image of entering the afterlife (line 85), and in the image of Lazarus (line 94). All three images relate to death and its aftermath.

---

60 To spit out all the butt-ends of my days and ways?
        And how should I presume?

    And I have known the arms already, known them all—
    Arms that are braceleted and white and bare
    (But in the lamplight, downed with light brown hair!)
65 Is it perfume from a dress
    That makes me so digress?
    Arms that lie along a table, or wrap about a shawl.
        And should I then presume?
        And how should I begin?
            • • • • •
70 Shall I say, I have gone at dusk through narrow streets
    And watched the smoke that rises from the pipes
    Of lonely men in shirt-sleeves, leaning out of windows? . . .

    I should have been a pair of ragged claws
    Scuttling across the floors of silent seas.
            • • • • •
75 And the afternoon, the evening, sleeps so peacefully!
    Smoothed by long fingers,
    Asleep . . . tired . . . or it malingers,
    Stretched on the floor, here beside you and me.
    Should I, after tea and cakes and ices,
80 Have the strength to force the moment to its crisis?
    But though I have wept and fasted, wept and prayed,
    Though I have seen my head (grown slightly bald) brought in
        upon a platter,
    I am no prophet—and here's no great matter;
    I have seen the moment of my greatness flicker,
85 And I have seen the eternal Footman hold my coat, and snicker,
    And in short, I was afraid.

    And would it have been worth it, after all,
    After the cups, the marmalade, the tea,
    Among the porcelain, among some talk of you and me,
90 Would it have been worth while,
    To have bitten off the matter with a smile,
    To have squeezed the universe into a ball
    To roll it towards some overwhelming question,
    To say: "I am Lazarus, come from the dead,
95 Come back to tell you all, I shall tell you all"—
    If one, settling a pillow by her head,
        Should say: "That is not what I meant at all.
        That is not it, at all." **C**

66 digress: wander away from the main topic; ramble.

73–74 I should . . . silent seas: Here Prufrock presents an image of himself as a crayfish.

77 malingers (mə-lǐng'ərz): pretends illness in order to avoid duty or work.

81–83 But though . . . prophet: an allusion to the biblical story of John the Baptist, who is imprisoned by King Herod (Matthew 14; Mark 6). At the request of his wife, Herod had the Baptist's head cut off and brought to him on a platter.

94 Lazarus: In the biblical story (John 11:17–44) Lazarus lay dead in his tomb for four days before Jesus brought him back to life.

C STREAM OF CONSCIOUSNESS
Reread lines 75–98. Prufrock casts himself in three different **images** in this stanza, two of which are biblical allusions. Identify these images and explain what they have in common.

DIFFERENTIATED INSTRUCTION

FOR ADVANCED LEARNERS/AP

Hypothesize In line 93, Prufrock refers again to an unstated "overwhelming question," first mentioned in line 10. What is that question? Invite students to frame as many hypotheses as possible. Tell them that some critics think the question is a marriage proposal (see page 934, Question 7). Have students evaluate this possibility, but urge them to look beyond it.

In addition, have students provide possible answers for the question. Suggest that students use a three-column journal like the one begun here to chart their questions, their answers, and Prufrock's possible answers.

Question	P's Answer	My Answer
What is life for?	To exist futilely	To pursue a dream

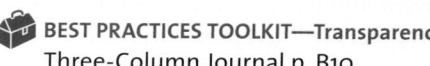
BEST PRACTICES TOOLKIT—Transparency
Three-Column Journal p. B10

And would it have been worth it, after all,
100   Would it have been worth while,
      After the sunsets and the dooryards and the sprinkled streets,
      After the novels, after the teacups, after the skirts that trail along
            the floor—
      And this, and so much more?—
      It is impossible to say just what I mean!
105   But as if a magic lantern threw the nerves in patterns on a
            screen:
      Would it have been worth while
      If one, settling a pillow or throwing off a shawl,
      And turning toward the window, should say:
            "That is not it at all,
110   That is not what I meant, at all."
            • • • • •
      No! I am not Prince Hamlet, nor was meant to be;
      Am an attendant lord, one that will do
      To swell a progress, start a scene or two,
      Advise the prince; no doubt, an easy tool,
115   Deferential, glad to be of use,
      Politic, cautious, and meticulous;
      Full of high sentence, but a bit obtuse;
      At times, indeed, almost ridiculous—
      Almost, at times, the Fool.

120   I grow old . . . I grow old . . .
      I shall wear the bottoms of my trousers rolled. **D**

      Shall I part my hair behind? Do I dare to eat a peach?
      I shall wear white flannel trousers, and walk upon the beach.
      I have heard the mermaids singing, each to each.

125   I do not think that they will sing to me.

      I have seen them riding seaward on the waves
      Combing the white hair of the waves blown back
      When the wind blows the water white and black.

      We have lingered in the chambers of the sea
130   By sea-girls wreathed with seaweed red and brown
      Till human voices wake us, and we drown.

105 magic lantern: a forerunner of the slide projector.

115 deferential: yielding to someone else's opinion.

116 meticulous: extremely careful and precise about details.

117 obtuse: slow to understand; dull.

D STREAM OF CONSCIOUSNESS
What similarities can you detect between the "attendant lord" described in lines 112–119 and Prufrock's image of himself in lines 120–121? Explain.

124–125 mermaids . . . to me: In mythology, mermaids attract mortal men by their beauty and their singing, sometimes allowing men to live with them in the sea.

THE LOVE SONG OF J. ALFRED PRUFROCK   **933**

Lines 109–110
REINFORCE *KEY IDEA:* ALIENATION

Discuss How does the statement in quotation marks express **alienation?** *Possible answer: Prufrock feels that no one understands what he is saying.*

LITERARY ANALYSIS

D STREAM OF CONSCIOUSNESS
Possible answer: The attendant lord is peripheral to the play Hamlet *and comically pretentious. Prufrock's image of an old man with "the bottoms of [his] trousers rolled" suggests similar traits.*

If students need help . . . Suggest that they summarize the stanza using the prereading chart introduced on page 929, as shown.

Stanza Number	Summary/Idea
14–15	P. sees himself as a foolish minor character in a play.

SELECTION WRAP–UP

REFLECT Have students consider Prufrock's anxiety. How has it affected Prufrock's life?

⭐ **CRITIQUE**

• Ask whether students feel the poem is too obscure or whether its complexity adds interest to its ideas.

• After completing the After Reading questions on page 934, have students revisit their responses and tell whether they have changed their opinions.

FOR STRATEGIC READERS
Comprehension Support Have students re-read the poem using the Core Analysis Frame: Poetry to get at the gist of the work. Urge them to work through the questions on the Analysis Frame one at a time, but to skip any that do not seem to apply to Eliot's poem.

 BEST PRACTICES TOOLKIT—Copy Masters
Core Analysis Frame: Poetry
pp. D21, D34, D35

FOR ADVANCED LEARNERS/AP
Evaluate Ideas The idea of alienation was fashionable at the time "Prufrock" was written. How appealing is it today? Have students explore this question by using a Questioning the Author chart to evaluate the poem and raise critical questions. Then ask them to compare and contrast Prufrock's view of life with their own. Invite students to share their charts and conclusions.

BEST PRACTICES TOOLKIT—Transparency
Questioning the Author p. D19

Practice and Apply

After Reading

Use these copy masters to check understanding and provide extra support:

R **RESOURCE MANAGER—Copy Masters**
Stream of Consciousness p. 247
Question Support p. 251

Additional selection questions are provided for teachers on page 241.

ANSWERS

1. *Prufrock reflects on going out for the evening with someone.*

2. *He is anxious and uncertain about the evening.*

3. *Prufrock feels self-hate or insecurity.*

Possible answers:

4. ■ **SKILLS FOCUS** *Summarize Stanzas Summaries should convey the poem's narrative arc from Prufrock fighting his insignificance and loneliness to becoming resigned to it.*

5. *They create a stalled feeling that reflects Prufrock's inaction and makes it comical.*

6. ● **SKILLS FOCUS** *Stream of Consciousness* **Lines 120–121:** *Prufrock feels distant from his youth.* **Lines 122–123:** *Despite timidity, he has made a small decision.* **Lines 124–125:** *He feels barred from happiness.* **Lines 126–131:** *Prufrock fantasizes about happiness but remains lost. At the end of the poem, readers are left with the idea that his longing remains unfulfilled.*

Assess and Reteach

Assess

R **RESOURCE MANAGER—Copy Masters**
Selection Test A pp. 253–254
Selection Test B/C pp. 255–256

💿 Test Generator CD

Reteach

S **STANDARDS LESSON FILE**
Literature Lesson 17: Structure of Poetry
Literature Lesson 19: Rhyme and Rhyme Scheme
Literature Lesson 26: Imagery
Literature Lesson 42: Mood
Research and Study Skills Lesson 13: Summarizing

After Reading

 R3.3

Comprehension

1. **Recall** What social situation does Prufrock reflect upon in this poem?

2. **Recall** How does he feel about this situation?

3. **Clarify** What is Prufrock's primary feeling about himself?

Literary Analysis

4. **Synthesize Summaries** Review the summaries and central ideas you recorded as you read. Now, viewing this series of ideas as a **narrative** with a conflict, a climax, and a resolution, write a summary of Prufrock's internal journey.

5. **Examine Poetic Devices** Review Eliot's use of **repetition** and **rhyme** in lines 23–34. Explain how these devices are used to convey Prufrock's sense of anxiety.

6. **Analyze Stream of Consciousness** In the final lines of the poem (lines 122–131), Prufrock offers his final reflection. For each of the following passages, offer an explication, or careful analysis. What does each group of lines suggest about Prufrock's sense of himself and his place in the world? What resonating idea are we left with at the poem's end?

   • lines 120–121 ("I grow old . . . trousers rolled.")
   • lines 122–123 ("Shall I part . . . walk upon the beach.")
   • lines 124–125 ("I have heard the mermaids . . . sing to me.")
   • lines 126–131 ("I have seen them riding seaward . . . and we drown.")

7. **Interpret Title** Some critics have contended that Prufrock's "overwhelming question" is actually a marriage proposal. True or not, it is clear that his relationships with women are a matter of concern to him. In what way can this poem be considered a love song? Consider the depictions of women and Prufrock's feelings of **alienation** from them. In your view, how does the poem's title color its meaning? Explain.

8. **Evaluate Form and Content** Consider the feelings and ideas that Eliot was trying to express; in what way can the stream of consciousness technique be said to reflect these ideas? Explain whether or not you think this technique is effective, citing evidence.

Literary Criticism

9. **Critical Interpretations** Literary critic Donald R. Fryxell wrote, "Prufrock is a trimmer . . . trimmers were those souls in Dante's *Inferno* who were condemned to the vestibule of hell because they had never really lived, although they were supposedly alive. . . . The Trimmers were lifeless, spiritless, mindless people." Do you agree or disagree with this statement? Give evidence from the text to support your answer.

---

7. *The poem is a love song expressing the best effort of an alienated character. The title prompts the reader to consider Prufrock's questions about love in light of a specific person rather than more generally.*

8. *The stream of consciousness shows the wavering, wandering, alienated, stuck quality of Prufrock's mind and thus reflects Eliot's ideas about alienation. Student's evaluative explanations should cite evidence from the text.*

9. *Many students will agree that Prufrock has not really lived and is weak-spirited. He never manages to ask his "overwhelming question," and instead daydreams about a happiness he feels unable to achieve. Others may say that Prufrock's intellectual and imaginative energy and romantic longings suggest a lively, if squelched, spirit.*

Modernist Style

While there is no one thing that makes a poem "modern," most modernist literature does share some defining features.

Features of Modernism:

• nontraditional subject matter and themes
• a focus on alienated individuals rather than heroes
• use of understatement and irony to reveal emotions and ideas
• use of symbols and images to suggest meaning
• experimentation with style and language

Writing to Synthesize

Review the poems beginnning on page 882 to get a feel for how they incorporate the features of modernism. Then write your own poem in the modernist style.

Consider

• what your poem will be about (remember that traditional themes, such as love, were rejected or reinterpreted by the modernists)
• whether your poem will feature a speaker, and what he or she will be like
• how to use understatement or irony to bring out emotions
• what symbols or images might best convey your meaning
• whether you wish to experiment with language or style

Extension

SPEAKING & LISTENING

Choose a more traditional poem from Units 1–4, such as Poe's "The Raven," and modernize it. **Rewrite** two stanzas of the poem as a modernist poet might, using the features of modernism as a guideline. Then **recite** your stanzas for your classmates, and discuss the techniques you used to "update" the poem. You may need to write out your stanzas on poster board to show how you manipulated line length, stanza form, capitalization and punctuation, or other elements of style.

W1.1, W1.2, W1.5, LS2.5

Wrap-Up: The New Poetry

This Wrap-Up provides students with an opportunity to revisit the modernist poetry in this section and write their own poems in modernist style. Encourage students to consider what *they* think makes a poem "modern."

Writing to Synthesize

Review with students that *synthesizing* means combining ideas and facts with other information and prior knowledge in order to better understand a subject or develop new ideas. Those new ideas can help students explore previously unfamiliar writing styles.

To help students write their poems, have them first discuss the traits of modernist literature listed on the pupil edition page. Ask students to cite examples of the traits in the poems in this section. Remind them that these examples reflect many different styles, some of which use traditional forms, as in the cases of Robert Frost, Edwin Arlington Robinson, and Edna St. Vincent Millay, and others of which use organic forms, such as Carl Sandburg, Ezra Pound, T. S. Eliot, E. E. Cummings, Marianne Moore, and William Carlos Williams.

Extension

• Encourage students to use free verse if updating a poem that is in traditional form.
• Suggest that students write their updates in a conversational, colloquial style.
• Urge students to consider creating an ironic or alienated view of the original poem.

DIFFERENTIATED INSTRUCTION

FOR DEVELOPING WRITERS

Writing Support [small-group option] Help students get started by organizing them in groups to brainstorm ideas, share insights into modernist poetry, and invent their own modernist styles. Suggest that students write about a single object, place, or image that they think symbolizes a modernist idea. Urge students to limit their experimentation to either theme or language and style, and to follow conventions in the remaining area.

FOR ENGLISH LEARNERS
Writing Support

• Allow students to write poems in their home languages and then translate the poems with more-fluent partners.
• Suggest that students write in the first-person voice of a speaker and begin each line with an identical word or phrase such as *I am, I saw, I think,* or *I know.*
• Invite volunteers to read the poems aloud in their first languages and then in English.

Focus and Motivate

OBJECTIVES

Literary Analysis
- explore the key idea of **status**
- analyze character motivation and traits
- read a short story

Reading
- predict story development

Vocabulary
- build vocabulary for reading and writing
- use context to determine meaning of words from the Jazz Age *(also an EL language objective)*

Grammar and Writing
- use coordinating conjunctions, dashes, and phrases to craft effective sentences
- write an advice letter

 R1.1, R3.2, W1.3, LC1.1

ABOUT THE AUTHOR

The publication of short stories such as "Winter Dreams" in top-market magazines built Fitzgerald's income and fame and allowed him to write novels. However, he regarded this aspect of his work as a creative burden.

USING THE *NOTABLE QUOTE*

Ask students what event **F. Scott Fitzgerald** is suggesting has caused people to give up on "all Gods" and "all faiths in man." *Possible answer: Fitzgerald likely is referring to World War I and its new killing technologies. The war left Fitzgerald's generation cynical.*

CALIFORNIA
R1.1 (p. 960), R3.2 (p. 959), W1.3 (p. 961), LC1.1 (p. 961)

NOTABLE QUOTE
"Here was a new generation . . . dedicated more than the last to the fear of poverty and the worship of success; grown up to find all Gods dead, all wars fought, all faiths in man shaken."

FYI
Did you know that F. Scott Fitzgerald . . .
- was named after his distant relative Francis Scott Key, who wrote the words to "The Star-Spangled Banner"?
- wrote his first novel while in the army, working on it solely on the weekends for just three months?

Winter Dreams
Short Story by F. Scott Fitzgerald

F. Scott Fitzgerald
1896–1940

F. Scott Fitzgerald experienced, and depicted in his fiction, both the material success and the crushing disillusionment that characterized the 1920s—a decade he dubbed the Jazz Age. He died young, famous for his flashy lifestyle, not his writing. But today, thanks to his dazzling prose style and piercing insight, Fitzgerald is heralded as the spokesperson of his era and as an American literary giant.

Midwest Boy Makes Good Born in St. Paul, Minnesota, Fitzgerald grew up in comfortable circumstances. His parents could afford to send him to prep school and then Princeton University, where he spent his time writing for the literary magazine and creating musical comedies. Low grades and the intervention of World War I kept him from graduating, but he left with a big dream. "I want to be one of the greatest writers who ever lived," he told a friend.

Jazz Age Romance In 1918, Fitzgerald fell madly in love with a flirtatious 18-year-old named Zelda Sayre. Zelda was as rich as she was beautiful and refused to marry him until he could support her financially. Two years later, Fitzgerald's first novel, *This Side of Paradise,* was finally published. Hailed as a daringly original story of the postwar generation's revolt against tradition, it more than doubled Fitzgerald's income, earned him widespread exposure as "the philosopher of the flapper," and won Zelda over. The two married and soon became the golden couple of the 1920s, partying at glamorous locations in the United States and Europe and living beyond the income Fitzgerald made from his writing.

Fall and Redemption Like the decade the Fitzgeralds epitomized, their high life came crashing down. In 1930, Zelda began the first of many hospital stays for mental illness, while Scott fell deeply into debt and alcoholism. *The Beautiful and Damned* (1922), a novel about the unraveling lives of a once-glamorous couple, was deemed "depressing" by reviewers, and Fitzgerald's masterpiece, *The Great Gatsby* (1925), was not the popular success he had hoped for. He died of a heart attack in 1940, at age 44, and it was years before he came to be regarded as anything more than a writer of showy period pieces. The reexamination of Fitzgerald's work was spurred not by critics, many of whom had always appreciated his talent, but by a new generation of readers who discovered the brilliance of his writing and told their friends. The year he died, his book sales—just 40 copies total—earned him $13.13 in royalties. Today, however, *The Great Gatsby* is a beloved American classic, and Fitzgerald's books sell about 500,000 copies annually.

936

Selection Resources

 RESOURCE MANAGER UNIT 5

Plan and Teach pp. 257–264

Literary Analysis
Summary pp. 265†*, 266‡*
Character Motivation and Traits
 pp. 267, 268†*
Question Support p. 275*

Reading
Predict Story Development
 pp. 269, 270†*
Reading Check p. 274

Vocabulary
Study p. 271*
Practice p. 272
Strategy p. 273

Grammar and Writing
Craft Effective Sentences p. 276

Assessment
Selection Tests A, B/C
 pp. 277*, 279*
 Test Generator CD

BEST PRACTICES TOOLKIT
Differentiated Instruction
 pp. 31–38*
Scaffolding Instruction
 pp. 43–46*

Graphic Organizers/Strategies
Personal Word List • Word Squares
• Venn Diagram • Sequence Chain
• Character Traits and Textual
Evidence • T Chart • Graphic Aids:
Line Plots • Cluster Diagram •
Problem and Solution Charts

Reading Support
Audio Anthology CD*

Technology
Literature, Vocabulary, and Writing Centers at **ClassZone.com**
WriteSmart CD

● LITERARY ANALYSIS: CHARACTER MOTIVATION AND TRAITS

Some characters are so vividly portrayed, they seem like real people. The characters' traits and motivations are often familiar to us; we see them in ourselves or in others we know. **Character traits** are those qualities shown by a character, as implied by his or her physical appearance and expressions of personality, such as boldness or gentleness. By recognizing a character's traits, you are able to better understand the **character's motivation**—the stated or implied reason(s) behind the character's actions. As you read, note the words, actions, thoughts, and appearance of the **protagonist,** or main character, as well as of the **antagonist,** the person against which the protagonist struggles. What do these descriptions indicate about the characters' traits and motivations?

Review: **Theme**

● READING SKILL: PREDICT STORY DEVELOPMENT

Predicting is the process of using text clues to make a reasonable guess about what will happen in a story. Sometimes your predictions will hit the mark, and other times the characters' actions and the story's events may surprise you. As you come to know the characters in "Winter Dreams," see if you can predict what will happen to them next, or how they will react or feel toward other characters and events. Record your predictions and the text clues that led you to make them.

Predictions	Text Clues

▲ VOCABULARY IN CONTEXT

Fitzgerald uses the boldfaced words in his story of love and status. Determine the definition of each word from its context.

1. a girl whose mere presence could **precipitate** a sudden crush
2. due to her **patrimony,** would inherit a **surfeit** of money
3. attended parties surrounded by her **retinue**
4. flirted **blatantly,** without a trace of self-consciousness
5. pouting and **petulance** that seemed to attract men
6. unfriendly to women—no **camaraderie** with them
7. turned her nose up at **mundane,** ordinary things
8. enjoyed the **flux** of life, its **precarious** nature

Will STATUS make you happy?

KEY IDEA It's easy to get caught up in the pursuit of wealth and **status**—and to imagine that obtaining them would guarantee a perfect life. But would it? Can money buy love, and does high status guarantee happiness?

QUICKWRITE Envision the life you hope to lead ten years from now. Wealth and status top the list of many people's "must-haves," but what else holds a prominent place in your dreams? Jot down some of your aspirations on a graph like the one shown. Then fill in the graph, rating on a scale of 1 to 10 the importance you attach to each goal. Use your completed graph to write a short paragraph explaining which goal holds the top spot on your list, and why.

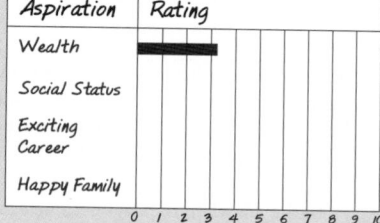

Aspiration	Rating
Wealth	
Social Status	
Exciting Career	
Happy Family	

0 1 2 3 4 5 6 7 8 9 10

Will STATUS make you happy?

Lead into the **KEY IDEA** paragraph by asking students to list achievements, possessions, and ranks that indicate people's **status.** As students consider whether status guarantees happiness, note that not all people define status by the same indicators. Urge students to choose status indicators they find meaningful as they complete the **QUICKWRITE** activity.

SKILLS FOCUS

LITERARY ANALYSIS

● CHARACTER MOTIVATION AND TRAITS

Read aloud this example:

Perched nervously on the chair, the boy watched the teacher pass out the graded exams. Ms. Reed smiled and tried to catch his eye as she handed him his exam, but he took it without looking up and placed it face down on his desk.

Ask students to identify traits and motivations of the two characters. *Possible answer: The boy is fearful and anxious. His unwillingness to look at the teacher or his exam suggests that he is worried about his exam results. The teacher recognizes his feelings and is motivated to reassure him.*

CHECK UNDERSTANDING Ask students to add two details to the example that further support the child's motivation.

READING SKILL

■ PREDICT STORY DEVELOPMENT

Read the example again. Ask students to predict what will happen next and to cite text clues that support their prediction. *Possible answer: The boy will discover after leaving the classroom that he has done well after all. The teacher's desire to reassure him supports this prediction.*

 RESOURCE MANAGER—Copy Master
   Predict Story Development p. 269
   (for student use while reading the selection)

VOCABULARY

▲ VOCABULARY IN CONTEXT

DIAGNOSE WORD KNOWLEDGE To determine preteaching needs, have all students complete Vocabulary in Context. *Possible answers:* 1. *lead to;* 2. *inheritance, surplus;* 3. *admirers;* 4. *openly and without shame;* 5. *irritability;* 6. *feelings of shared status;* 7. *common;* 8. *changeability, uncertain*

PRETEACH VOCABULARY Preteach vocabulary with this copy master. Read each item aloud.

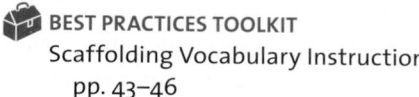 RESOURCE MANAGER—Copy Master
Vocabulary Study p. 271

MORE VOCABULARY SUPPORT
For additional activities and guidelines, see

BEST PRACTICES TOOLKIT
Scaffolding Vocabulary Instruction
   pp. 43–46
Vocabulary Center at **ClassZone.com**

SUMMARY

This short story opens when young Dexter Green quits his job as a golf caddy because he is asked to carry the clubs of a spoiled 11-year-old girl. After attending a prestigious university and gaining financial success, Dexter again meets the girl, Judy Jones. He pursues Judy, who treats him badly throughout their romance and then interferes with his engagement to another woman. Years later, Dexter feels lost when he learns that Judy, who was his idealized figure of an alluring woman, has lost her looks.

LITERARY ANALYSIS

Ⓐ MOTIVATION AND TRAITS

Possible answer: *The first paragraph provides socioeconomic information such as "poor as sin" (line 1), "wealthy people" (line 4), and "pocket-money" (line 4). Wealth and status matter greatly to Dexter, whose father's ownership of a grocery store makes him middle class but not wealthy enough to join the country club.*

Winter *Dreams*

F. Scott Fitzgerald

BACKGROUND Behind the glitz and glamour of the 1920s lay a profound loss of idealism. Though World War I gave rise to new opportunities and freedoms, especially for women, the shift to the modern age left a gap in values that the new generation struggled to fill. "Winter Dreams" mostly takes place before 1920, when a restless uncertainty was first being felt. The story appeared in the collection *All the Sad Young Men* (1926), a title that expresses Fitzgerald's deeper understanding of the decade.

ANALYZE VISUALS
How would you describe the subject of this portrait? Describe the **traits** you think he projects, citing details from the painting to support your answer.

I

Some of the caddies were poor as sin and lived in one-room houses with a neurasthenic[1] cow in the front yard, but Dexter Green's father owned the second best grocery-store in Black Bear—the best one was "The Hub," patronized by the wealthy people from Sherry Island—and Dexter caddied only for pocket-money. Ⓐ

In the fall when the days became crisp and gray, and the long Minnesota winter shut down like the white lid of a box, Dexter's skis moved over the snow that hid the fairways of the golf course. At these times the country gave him a feeling of profound melancholy—it offended him that the links should lie in enforced fallowness, haunted by ragged sparrows for the long season. It was dreary, too,
10 that on the tees where the gay colors fluttered in summer there were now only the desolate sand-boxes knee-deep in crusted ice. When he crossed the hills the wind blew cold as misery, and if the sun was out he tramped with his eyes squinted up against the hard dimensionless glare.

❶ **Targeted Passage**

Ⓐ **MOTIVATION AND TRAITS**
Consider the kind of information you receive in the story's very first paragraph. What do you learn about Dexter's family and social position?

---

1. **neurasthenic** (nō�ŏr′əs-thēn′ĭk): weak and lacking in vigor.

Homme au Chapeau (1900s), Jean Berque. Waterhouse and Dodd, London. © Bridgeman Art Library.

DIFFERENTIATED INSTRUCTION

FOR ALL STUDENTS

Expert Groups Encourage students to become subject experts by selecting and researching one of these topics:

- F. Scott Fitzgerald's experience of status during his boyhood, during his school years at the Newman School, and at Princeton

- his experience of status during the early 1920s, after his first success as a writer

FOR STRATEGIC READERS

In combination with the *Audio Anthology CD*, use one or more Targeted Passages (pp. 938, 940, 944, 947, 951, 955, 957) to ensure that students focus on key story events and concepts. Targeted Passages are also good for English learners.

❶ **Targeted Passage [Lines 1–13]**

This passage introduces the main character, Dexter Green, and the small-town setting, then hints at the conflict between wealthy and middle-class residents.

CULTURAL CONNECTION

Status In the United States today, wealth is the surest sign of status and the guaranteed path to power and influence. In Fitzgerald's time, as in many European countries, aristocratic lineage largely determined status and often brought with it wealth. Other cultures assign high status to military leaders, to priests and holy people, or to the elderly. Invite students to share status indicators from their home cultures and then to discuss why different cultures value different achievements and characteristics.

Lines 1–4
REINFORCE *KEY IDEA:* STATUS

Discuss Four levels of **status** are identified in these four short lines. What are these levels, and why might the story begin by introducing them? *Possible answer: The four levels of status are the caddies, who are "poor as sin" (line 1), Dexter's family, who owns the "second best grocery-store" (lines 2–3), the people who own the best grocery store, and, finally, "the wealthy people from Sherry Island" (lines 3–4). Status—who has it and who doesn't—will clearly be important in the story's conflict.*

- Where does the story take place?
- Why does Dexter work as a caddy? How is he different from the other caddies?
- What bothers Dexter about winter in Black Bear?

FOR ENGLISH LEARNERS

Prereading For prereading instruction for English learners, see

 BEST PRACTICES TOOLKIT
   Scaffolding Reading Instruction pp. 43–46

FOR ADVANCED LEARNERS/AP

AP exercises in the bottom channel provide additional challenge for students. Use these suggestions for small groups or individuals.

ADDITIONAL GUIDELINES

For more help with differentiation and tips for classroom management, see

 BEST PRACTICES TOOLKIT
   Differentiated Instruction pp. 31–38

In April the winter ceased abruptly. The snow ran down into Black Bear Lake scarcely tarrying for the early golfers to brave the season with red and black balls. Without elation, without an interval of moist glory, the cold was gone.

Dexter knew that there was something dismal about this Northern spring, just as he knew there was something gorgeous about the fall. Fall made him clinch his hands and tremble and repeat idiotic sentences to himself, and make brisk abrupt
20 gestures of command to imaginary audiences and armies. October filled him with hope which November raised to a sort of ecstatic triumph, and in this mood the fleeting brilliant impressions of the summer at Sherry Island were ready grist to his mill.[2] He became a golf champion and defeated Mr. T. A. Hedrick in a marvelous match played a hundred times over the fairways of his imagination, a match each detail of which he changed about untiringly—sometimes he won with almost laughable ease, sometimes he came up magnificently from behind. Again, stepping from a Pierce-Arrow automobile,[3] like Mr. Mortimer Jones, he strolled frigidly into the lounge of the Sherry Island Golf Club—or perhaps, surrounded by an admiring crowd, he gave an exhibition of fancy diving from the spring-board of
30 the club raft. . . . Among those who watched him in open-mouthed wonder was Mr. Mortimer Jones. **B**

And one day it came to pass that Mr. Jones—himself and not his ghost—came up to Dexter with tears in his eyes and said that Dexter was the — — best caddy in the club, and wouldn't he decide not to quit if Mr. Jones made it worth his while, because every other — — caddy in the club lost one ball a hole for him—regularly—

"No, sir," said Dexter decisively, "I don't want to caddy any more." Then, after a pause: "I'm too old."

"You're not more than fourteen. Why the devil did you decide just this
40 morning that you wanted to quit? You promised that next week you'd go over to the State tournament with me."

"I decided I was too old."

Dexter handed in his "A Class" badge, collected what money was due him from the caddy-master, and walked home to Black Bear Village.

"The best — — caddy I ever saw," shouted Mr. Mortimer Jones over a drink that afternoon. "Never lost a ball! Willing! Intelligent! Quiet! Honest! Grateful!"

The little girl who had done this was eleven—beautifully ugly as little girls are apt to be who are destined after a few years to be inexpressibly lovely and bring no end of misery to a great number of men. The spark, however, was perceptible.
50 There was a general ungodliness in the way her lips twisted down at the corners when she smiled, and in the—Heaven help us!—in the almost passionate quality of her eyes. Vitality is born early in such women. It was utterly in evidence now, shining through her thin frame in a sort of glow. **C**

---

2. **grist to his mill:** something that he could make good use of.

3. **Pierce-Arrow automobile:** a luxury car of the day.

B MOTIVATION AND TRAITS
Reread lines 17–31. What can you tell about Dexter's aspirations based on this glimpse into his thoughts?

2 Targeted Passage

C PREDICT
Consider what you've learned about both Dexter and the "beautifully ugly" girl. How might she cause him to quit his job? Give reasons for your prediction.

LITERARY ANALYSIS

B MOTIVATION AND TRAITS

Possible answer: Dexter longs for glory and adulation. He especially wants to impress and even outdo wealthy men such as those for whom he caddies.

If students need help . . . Use the phrases "imaginary audiences" (line 20) and "fairways of his imagination" (line 24) to clarify that Dexter is daydreaming events that are not really happening. Because it is a daydream, he can revise it so he has greater victory over the wealthy men.

READING SKILL

C PREDICT

Possible answer: Readers have learned that Dexter wants to impress those who are wealthier than he, and that the little girl is magnetic but hard to impress. Students may predict that Dexter is so taken with her that he would rather quit than feel humiliated by serving as her caddy.

If students need help . . . Encourage them to use the prereading chart introduced on page 937 to organize supporting clues.

Extend the Discussion Why would it be humiliating for Dexter to serve as Judy's caddy?

DIFFERENTIATED INSTRUCTION

FOR STRATEGIC READERS

2 Targeted Passage [Lines 37–53]

This passage sets up a key character motivator, Dexter's admiration for Judy, and suggests that it may lead him to make poor choices.

- What does Dexter decide to do? What reason does he give for his decision?
- How does Mr. Mortimer Jones respond?
- What is it about the girl that causes Dexter to make this decision?

FOR ENGLISH LEARNERS

Related Vocabulary Help students understand words related to the game of golf. Show them images of these words, or help them find such images themselves:

- *red and black balls* (line 15), "red and black golf balls that contrast with snow"
- *fairways* (line 24), "the area of a golf course between the tee and the green"
- *caddy* (line 33), "someone who carries a golfer's bag of clubs and helps the golfer"

- *hole* (line 35), "a small cavity or cup into which the golf ball is hit"

Have students add the words to a Personal Word List.

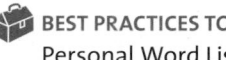 **BEST PRACTICES TOOLKIT**
Personal Word List p. E2

She had come eagerly out onto the course at nine o'clock with a white linen nurse and five small new golf-clubs in a white canvas bag which the nurse was carrying. When Dexter first saw her she was standing by the caddy house, rather ill at ease and trying to conceal the fact by engaging her nurse in an obviously unnatural conversation graced by startling and irrelevant grimaces from herself.

60 "Well, it's certainly a nice day, Hilda," Dexter heard her say. She drew down the corners of her mouth, smiled, and glanced furtively around, her eyes in transit falling for an instant on Dexter.

Then to the nurse:

"Well, I guess there aren't very many people out here this morning, are there?"

The smile again—radiant, **blatantly** artificial—convincing.

"I don't know what we're supposed to do now," said the nurse, looking nowhere in particular.

"Oh, that's all right. I'll fix it up."

Dexter stood perfectly still, his mouth slightly ajar. He knew that if he moved forward a step his stare would be in her line of vision—if he moved backward he 70 would lose his full view of her face. For a moment he had not realized how young she was. Now he remembered having seen her several times the year before—in bloomers.[4]

Suddenly, involuntarily, he laughed, a short abrupt laugh—then, startled by himself, he turned and began to walk quickly away.

"Boy!"

Dexter stopped.

"Boy—"

Beyond question he was addressed. Not only that, but he was treated to that absurd smile, that preposterous smile—the memory of which at least a dozen men 80 were to carry into middle age.

"Boy, do you know where the golf teacher is?"

"He's giving a lesson."

"Well, do you know where the caddy-master is?"

"He isn't here yet this morning."

"Oh." For a moment this baffled her. She stood alternately on her right and left foot.

"We'd like to get a caddy," said the nurse. "Mrs. Mortimer Jones sent us out to play golf, and we don't know how without we get a caddy."

Here she was stopped by an ominous glance from Miss Jones, followed 90 immediately by the smile.

"There aren't any caddies here except me," said Dexter to the nurse, "and I got to stay here in charge until the caddy-master gets here."

"Oh."

Miss Jones and her **retinue** now withdrew, and at a proper distance from Dexter became involved in a heated conversation, which was concluded by Miss Jones taking one of the clubs and hitting it on the ground with violence. For

---

4. **bloomers:** baggy pants that end just below the knee, formerly worn by girls.

blatantly (blāt'n-tlē) *adv.* in an extremely obvious way; conspicuously

retinue (rĕt'n-ōō') *n.* a group of attendants or followers

Lines 59–81
TIERED DISCUSSION PROMPTS
Use these prompts to help students explore Judy's character when Dexter meets her:

Connect Have you ever been around someone whom you wanted to impress? In what way does that experience help you understand Dexter? *Accept all thoughtful responses.*

Analyze What does Dexter particularly notice as he observes Judy, and what do these actions reveal about Judy? *Possible answer: Dexter notices her fake, calculated smile, which she uses not to express happiness but to get attention. He notices her glance, which betrays the uncertainty she tries hard to hide. These qualities reveal that she is manipulative but also scared.*

Evaluate How well has Fitzgerald used dialogue and narration to reveal Judy's opinion of herself and of others? Explain. *Possible answer: Fitzgerald uses Judy's dialogue brilliantly to show her desire to appear very important. She speaks impersonally to the nurse (line 63), brags arrogantly that she will fix the problem (line 67), and addresses Dexter impolitely as "Boy!" (line 75) as if he were younger than she and a servant. At the same time, the narration describes her furtive glance (line 60), which suggests that she isn't really sure of herself.*

FOR STRATEGIC READERS
Concept Support: Dashes Explain the use of dashes to suggest strong and potentially offensive language in Mr. Mortimer Jones's speech (lines 33, 35, 45). Distinguish these dashes (two in a row) from the single dashes that indicate interrupted speech patterns (lines 35–36, 51, 64, 77). Discuss ways that strong language is suggested or replaced today in writing, graphic novels, or on television.

FOR ENGLISH LEARNERS
Key Academic Vocabulary Use Word Squares to teach these words: *transit* (line 60), *overlap* (line 209), *survive* (line 321), *integral* (line 399), *notion* (line 444), *bulk* (line 559), *ultimate* (line 595).

 BEST PRACTICES TOOLKIT—Transparency Word Squares p. E10

FOR ADVANCED LEARNERS/AP
Analyze Relationships [small-group option] Have student groups analyze Dexter's response to Judy during their first meeting, using these questions:

- Who is in greater control of the situation at the golf club, Dexter or Judy?

- In what conflicting ways does Dexter react when Judy addresses him?

Have students find opportunities to share their insights with the class.

ANALYZE VISUALS
How does this painting
differ—in both content
and style—from the
portrait on page 939?
How might these
differences be said to
echo the changes in
Dexter Green?

further emphasis she raised it again and was about to bring it down smartly upon
the nurse's bosom, when the nurse seized the club and twisted it from her hands.

"You little mean old *thing!*" cried Miss Jones wildly.

100 Another argument ensued. Realizing that the elements of comedy were implied
in the scene, Dexter several times began to laugh, but each time restrained the
laugh before it reached audibility. He could not resist the monstrous conviction
that the little girl was justified in beating the nurse.

The situation was resolved by the fortuitous appearance of the caddy-master,
who was appealed to immediately by the nurse.

"Miss Jones is to have a little caddy, and this one says he can't go."

"Mr. McKenna said I was to wait here till you came," said Dexter quickly.

"Well, he's here now." Miss Jones smiled cheerfully at the caddy-master. Then
she dropped her bag and set off at a haughty mince[5] toward the first tee.

110 "Well?" The caddy-master turned to Dexter. "What you standing there like a
dummy for? Go pick up the young lady's clubs."

"I don't think I'll go out today," said Dexter.

"You don't—"

"I think I'll quit."

The enormity of his decision frightened him. He was a favorite caddy, and
the thirty dollars a month he earned through the summer were not to be made
elsewhere around the lake. But he had received a strong emotional shock, and his
perturbation required a violent and immediate outlet.

It is not so simple as that, either. As so frequently would be the case in the
120 future, Dexter was unconsciously dictated to by his winter dreams. **D**

D MOTIVATION AND
TRAITS
Why does Dexter quit
caddying? Explain what
his decision adds to your
understanding of him.

II

Now, of course, the quality and the seasonability of these winter dreams varied,
but the stuff of them remained. They persuaded Dexter several years later to pass
up a business course at the State university—his father, prospering now, would
have paid his way—for the **precarious** advantage of attending an older and more
famous university in the East, where he was bothered by his scanty funds. But
do not get the impression, because his winter dreams happened to be concerned
at first with musings on the rich, that there was anything merely snobbish in the
boy. He wanted not association with glittering things and glittering people—he
wanted the glittering things themselves. Often he reached out for the best without
130 knowing why he wanted it—and sometimes he ran up against the mysterious
denials and prohibitions in which life indulges. It is with one of those denials and
not with his career as a whole that this story deals.

He made money. It was rather amazing. After college he went to the city from
which Black Bear Lake draws its wealthy patrons. When he was only twenty-three
and had been there not quite two years, there were already people who liked to
say: "Now *there's* a boy—" All about him rich men's sons were peddling bonds
precariously, or investing **patrimonies** precariously, or plodding through the two
dozen volumes of the "George Washington Commercial Course," but Dexter

precarious (prĭ-kâr′ē-əs)
adj. risky; uncertain

patrimony (păt′rə-mō′nē)
n. estate or money
inherited from ancestors

5. **at a haughty mince:** taking short, dainty steps in an arrogant, snobbish way.

Lines 115–120
REINFORCE *KEY IDEA:* STATUS

Discuss In what ways does Dexter's decision
to quit affect his **status** in Black Bear? *Possible
answer:* He will no longer have $30 a month to
spend because such pay is unavailable elsewhere in town. In this regard, his decision lowers his status. On the other hand, he is pleased
with himself for quitting and sees it as a step
toward making his daydream of wealth a
reality. This raises his status in his own eyes.
Dexter has also protected his status in the eyes
of Judy and Mr. Jones.

LITERARY ANALYSIS

D MOTIVATION AND TRAITS

*Possible answer: Dexter quits in order to
rebel against the girl's arrogance, to maintain his dignity, and to uphold the self-
image his daydreams define. His decision
helps readers understand Dexter's sense of
image and independence.*

If students need help . . . Have them reread
lines 23–31 and 45–53. Point out that these
lines describe Dexter's fantasies and
suggest his goals.

DIFFERENTIATED INSTRUCTION

FOR STRATEGIC READERS

Compare and Contrast Section II compares
Dexter to the "rich men's sons" (line 136). Have
students use a Venn Diagram to identify and
organize the ways in which Dexter is like and
unlike these other young men. Encourage
them to refer and add to this diagram as they
read on, exploring whether Dexter becomes
more like the rich men's sons as time passes.

 BEST PRACTICES TOOLKIT—Transparency
Venn Diagram p. A26

FOR ENGLISH LEARNERS

Comprehension: Text Structure Clarify that
the text in lines 32–46 are a flashforward.
Chronologically, Dexter's discussion with Mr.
Jones comes after he tells the caddy-master
that he wants to quit. Section II then jumps
forward several years in time. Have students
use a Sequence Chain to record events in
chronological order.

 BEST PRACTICES TOOLKIT—Transparency
Sequence Chain p. B21

Portrait of Marquess Sommi (1925), Tamara De Lempicka. Oil on canvas, 100 cm × 73 cm. Albert and Victoria Benalloul.
© 2007 Artists Rights Society (ARS), New York/ADAGP, Paris.

ANALYZE VISUALS

Possible answer: Unlike the warm, soft tones in the portrait on page 939, this painting uses colder colors and sharper lines and geometry. The man's face and hand are distinct from the blackness of the painting. In addition, the man portrayed in this painting looks older, haughtier, and better-dressed than the young man on page 939. Like Dexter's transformation from small-town golf caddy to cosmopolitan business owner, the man in this painting appears much more well-off, self-important, and reserved than the more humble-looking young man in the other portrait. Both subjects, however, have a similarly determined-looking set of jaw.

About the Art Tamara De Lempicka (1898–1980) grew up in the Russian aristocracy and fled the country during the 1917 revolution. Her background led her to sophisticated and powerful circles of Paris, where she painted portraits of aristocrats and intellectuals. This portrait captures the subject's sense of authority and power, and suggests the kind of attitude that Dexter Green acquired as his wealth and status grew.

FOR ADVANCED LEARNERS/AP

Analyze Point of View In lines 125–128, the narrator addresses readers directly, using second-person point of view. Have students recall point-of-view options and then discuss these questions:

- In what point of view is "Winter Dreams" mostly written?
- How does the narrator's direct address alter the point of view?

- Why might Fitzgerald feel the need to caution or even scold his audience? What does this suggest about his view of them?

Ask students to use their answers to inform a broader discussion about the role of readers in this story and others. Have students identify different methods authors use to involve readers in a work and rate these, including Fitzgerald's use of second-person point of view, for effectiveness.

borrowed a thousand dollars on his college degree and his confident mouth, and
140 bought a partnership in a laundry.

> It was a small laundry when he went into it but Dexter made a specialty of
> learning how the English washed fine woolen golf-stockings without shrinking
> them, and within a year he was catering to the trade that wore knickerbockers.[6]
> Men were insisting that their Shetland hose and sweaters go to his laundry just as
> they had insisted on a caddy who could find golf-balls. A little later he was doing
> their wives' lingerie as well—and running five branches in different parts of the
> city. Before he was twenty-seven he owned the largest string of laundries in his
> section of the country. It was then that he sold out and went to New York. But the
> part of his story that concerns us goes back to the days when he was making his
150 first big success.

③ **Targeted Passage**

> When he was twenty-three Mr. Hart—one of the gray-haired men who liked
> to say "Now there's a boy"—gave him a guest card to the Sherry Island Golf Club
> for a weekend. So he signed his name one day on the register, and that afternoon
> played golf in a foursome with Mr. Hart and Mr. Sandwood and Mr. T. A.
> Hedrick. He did not consider it necessary to remark that he had once carried Mr.
> Hart's bag over this same links, and that he knew every trap and gully with his
> eyes shut—but he found himself glancing at the four caddies who trailed them,
> trying to catch a gleam or gesture that would remind him of himself, that would
> lessen the gap which lay between his present and his past.

160 It was a curious day, slashed abruptly with fleeting, familiar impressions. One
minute he had the sense of being a trespasser—in the next he was impressed by
the tremendous superiority he felt toward Mr. T. A. Hedrick, who was a bore and
not even a good golfer any more.

Then, because of a ball Mr. Hart lost near the fifteenth green, an enormous
thing happened. While they were searching the stiff grasses of the rough there
was a clear call of "Fore!" from behind a hill in their rear. And as they all turned
abruptly from their search a bright new ball sliced abruptly over the hill and
caught Mr. T. A. Hedrick in the abdomen.

"By Gad!" cried Mr. T. A. Hedrick, "they ought to put some of these crazy
170 women off the course. It's getting to be outrageous."

A head and a voice came up together over the hill:

"Do you mind if we go through?"

"You hit me in the stomach!" declared Mr. Hedrick wildly.

"Did I?" The girl approached the group of men. "I'm sorry. I yelled 'Fore!'"

Her glance fell casually on each of the men—then scanned the fairway for her
ball.

"Did I bounce into the rough?"

It was impossible to determine whether this question was ingenuous or
malicious. In a moment, however, she left no doubt, for as her partner came up
180 over the hill she called cheerfully:

"Here I am! I'd have gone on the green except that I hit something."

---

6. **knickerbockers:** loose pants that end in a gathering just below the knee and are worn with long socks. Formerly popular as golf wear.

Lines 151–163
TIERED DISCUSSION PROMPTS

Use these prompts to help students track the changes in Dexter's character as he enters the world of the wealthy:

Summarize What events lead to Dexter's first opportunity to play golf at the club? *Answer: A member, Mr. Hart, is impressed with Dexter's success and invites him as a guest at the club.*

Analyze How does Dexter feel when he first hits the fairway, and how do his feelings change during the day? *Possible answer: He feels at first like a "trespasser" (line 161). He wonders if he still has more in common with the caddies following him than with the other golfers (lines 157–159). His feelings quickly change as he sees himself as more worthy to be on the course than a long-time member (lines 161–163).*

Synthesize Given Dexter's upward mobility and his successful first game at the club, what will likely be his future relationship with the club? *Possible answer: Dexter will probably become a member of the club. He now has the money to be a member and has attracted the favor of influential members. In addition, he's developed a sense of belonging to the club, and he knows that rubbing shoulders with the members will support his plans for further success.*

DIFFERENTIATED INSTRUCTION

FOR STRATEGIC READERS
③ **Targeted Passage [Lines 141–159]**

This passage explains how Dexter makes his first fortune to enter the world of wealth.

- What business makes Dexter wealthy?
- What does Dexter do to ensure that his business will succeed?
- Who are Dexter's primary customers?
- How does his new wealth change Dexter's life?

FOR ENGLISH LEARNERS
Related Words Share the meanings of these additional golf terms, and guide students to add them to the Personal Word List begun on page 940:

- *links* (line 156), "holes on a golf course"
- *trap* (line 156), "obstacle or hazard"
- *rough* (line 165), "area where the grass is allowed to grow high"

- *Fore!* (line 166), "a word shouted to warn other golfers that a ball is headed their way"
- *sliced* (line 167), "hit such that it followed a curving path, perhaps by mistake"
- *go through* (line 172), "move ahead of the other group on the course"
- *green* (line 181), "closely mown area at the end of each hole, in which the hole for the ball is located"

As she took her stance for a short mashie[7] shot, Dexter looked at her closely. She wore a blue gingham dress, rimmed at throat and shoulders with a white edging that accentuated her tan. The quality of exaggeration, of thinness, which had made her passionate eyes and down-turning mouth absurd at eleven, was gone now. She was arrestingly beautiful. The color in her cheeks was centered like the color in a picture—it was not a "high" color, but a sort of fluctuating and feverish warmth, so shaded that it seemed at any moment it would recede and disappear. This color and the mobility of her mouth gave a continual impression of **flux**, of intense life, of
190 passionate vitality—balanced only partially by the sad luxury of her eyes.

She swung her mashie impatiently and without interest, pitching the ball into a sand-pit on the other side of the green. With a quick, insincere smile and a careless "Thank you!" she went on after it.

"That Judy Jones!" remarked Mr. Hedrick on the next tee, as they waited—some moments—for her to play on ahead. "All she needs is to be turned up and spanked for six months and then to be married off to an old-fashioned cavalry captain."

"My God, she's good-looking!" said Mr. Sandwood, who was just over thirty.

"Good-looking!" cried Mr. Hedrick contemptuously, "she always looks as if she
200 wanted to be kissed! Turning those big cow-eyes on every calf in town!"

It was doubtful if Mr. Hedrick intended a reference to the maternal instinct.

"She'd play pretty good golf if she'd try," said Mr. Sandwood.

"She has no form," said Mr. Hedrick solemnly.

"She has a nice figure," said Mr. Sandwood.

"Better thank the Lord she doesn't drive a swifter ball," said Mr. Hart, winking at Dexter.

Later in the afternoon the sun went down with a riotous swirl of gold and varying blues and scarlets, and left the dry, rustling night of Western summer. Dexter watched from the veranda of the Golf Club, watched the even overlap
210 of the waters in the little wind, silver molasses under the harvest-moon. Then the moon held a finger to her lips and the lake became a clear pool, pale and quiet. Dexter put on his bathing-suit and swam out to the farthest raft, where he stretched dripping on the wet canvas of the springboard.

There was a fish jumping and a star shining and the lights around the lake were gleaming. Over on a dark peninsula a piano was playing the songs of last summer and of summers before that—songs from "Chin-Chin" and "The Count of Luxemburg" and "The Chocolate Soldier"[8]—and because the sound of a piano over a stretch of water had always seemed beautiful to Dexter he lay perfectly quiet and listened.

220 The tune the piano was playing at that moment had been gay and new five years before when Dexter was a sophomore at college. They had played it at a prom once when he could not afford the luxury of proms, and he had stood

---

7. **mashie:** an old name for the golf club now known as a five iron.
8. **"Chin-Chin"..."The Chocolate Soldier":** three popular Broadway musicals, first performed in 1914, 1912, and 1909, respectively.

---

flux (flŭks): n. change

 MOTIVATION AND TRAITS
Reread lines 171–193. What character traits are revealed by the description of Judy and her actions?

LITERARY ANALYSIS

E MOTIVATION AND TRAITS

Possible answer: Judy is confident to the point of arrogance, self-absorbed, beautiful, animated, and insincere, willing to say anything to get what she wants.

If students need help . . . Help them complete a Character Traits and Textual Evidence organizer about Judy.

BEST PRACTICES TOOLKIT—Transparency Character Traits and Textual Evidence p. D6

Lines 207–219
REINFORCE *KEY IDEA*: STATUS

Discuss What images of luxury and **status** does Fitzgerald use to evoke the relaxed and pampered lifestyle of the club members? *Possible answer: Fitzgerald uses vivid color imagery, such as gold, blue, and scarlet, to describe the natural beauty that club members enjoy from their view on the veranda. In addition, he describes a private dock on a lake that is well lit and equipped for swimming and boating. Finally, he shows that the members are entertained by live music and have time to enjoy the club's amenities, as Dexter does during his swim.*

FOR ADVANCED LEARNERS/AP

Analyze Indirect Characterization [paired option] Fitzgerald characterizes Judy directly, by describing her, and indirectly, by showing the reactions of other characters. Have partners review lines 194–206 and then have each write a character sketch of Judy, one from Mr. Hendrick's reaction and one from Mr. Sandwood's reaction. Pairs should compare their sketches and work together to create a composite sketch that includes both views and Dexter's reaction to the adult Judy. Refer students to a Character Traits and Textual Evidence organizer as a helpful tool.

BEST PRACTICES TOOLKIT—Transparency Character Traits and Textual Evidence p. D6

TIERED DISCUSSION PROMPTS

Use these prompts to help students recognize Judy's expectations of Dexter:

Restate What does Judy ask Dexter to do? *Answer: She asks him to drive the motorboat to pull her on the surfboard behind it.*

Analyze In this meeting, what does Judy assume about Dexter and his usefulness to her? *Possible answer: Judy assumes that, even though she hardly knows him, Dexter will be at her service to get her whatever she needs. She is unconcerned with the possibility that she is invading his privacy or bothering him. She just smiles and expects to get what she wants.*

Evaluate How effective is Fitzgerald's language in showing that Judy has the upper hand in this new friendship? Explain. *Possible answer: Fitzgerald's language is very effective in demonstrating Judy's control. Before she knows Dexter's name, she wants him to tow her on the surfboard (lines 245–246). She gives her name, but does not bother to ask for his (line 246). She orders him to "'Go faster'" (line 261) and he responds "obediently" (line 262) and without question. The image of her standing regally on the surfboard (lines 263–264) communicates her queenly control of Dexter and of everything around her.*

LITERARY ANALYSIS

❺ MOTIVATION AND TRAITS

Possible answer: Judy has not changed. She neither notices nor cares about the results of her behavior; she attempts to cheat to impress her fellow golfers. She remains as spoiled and insincere as she was as a child.

If students need help . . . Refer them to lines 47–103, which describe young Judy.

---

outside the gymnasium and listened. The sound of the tune **precipitated** in him a sort of ecstasy and it was with that ecstasy he viewed what happened to him now. It was a mood of intense appreciation, a sense that, for once, he was magnificently attuned to life and that everything about him was radiating a brightness and a glamour he might never know again.

A low, pale oblong detached itself suddenly from the darkness of the Island, 230 spitting forth the reverberated sound of a racing motor-boat. Two white streamers of cleft water rolled themselves out behind it and almost immediately the boat was beside him, drowning out the hot tinkle of the piano in the drone of its spray. Dexter raising himself on his arms was aware of a figure standing at the wheel, of two dark eyes regarding him over the lengthening space of water—then the boat had gone by and was sweeping in an immense and purposeless circle of spray round and round in the middle of the lake. With equal eccentricity one of the circles flattened out and headed back toward the raft.

"Who's that?" she called, shutting off her motor. She was so near now that Dexter could see her bathing-suit, which consisted apparently of pink rompers.[9]

The nose of the boat bumped the raft, and as the latter tilted rakishly he was 240 precipitated toward her. With different degrees of interest they recognized each other.

"Aren't you one of those men we played through this afternoon?" she demanded.

He was.

"Well, do you know how to drive a motor-boat? Because if you do I wish you'd drive this one so I can ride on the surf-board behind. My name is Judy Jones"— she favored him with an absurd smirk—rather, what tried to be a smirk, for, twist her mouth as she might, it was not grotesque, it was merely beautiful—"and I live in a house over there on the Island, and in that house there is a man waiting for 250 me. When he drove up at the door I drove out of the dock because he says I'm his ideal." ❻

There was a fish jumping and a star shining and the lights around the lake were gleaming. Dexter sat beside Judy Jones and she explained how her boat was driven. Then she was in the water, swimming to the floating surf-board with a sinuous crawl. Watching her was without effort to the eye, watching a branch waving or a sea-gull flying. Her arms, burned to butternut, moved sinuously among the dull platinum ripples, elbow appearing first, casting the forearm back with a cadence of falling water, then reaching out and down, stabbing a path ahead.

They moved out into the lake; turning, Dexter saw that she was kneeling on 260 the low rear of the now uptilted surf-board.

"Go faster," she called, "fast as it'll go."

Obediently he jammed the level forward and the white spray mounted at the bow. When he looked around again the girl was standing up on the rushing board, her arms spread wide, her eyes lifted toward the moon.

"It's awful cold," she shouted. "What's your name?"

---

precipitate
(prĭ-sĭp'ĭ-tāt') v. to bring about, especially abruptly

❻ **MOTIVATION AND TRAITS**
Do you think Judy has changed since Dexter first encountered her on the golf course years before? Cite **details** and **dialogue** to support your conclusion.

---

9. **rompers:** a loose-fitting one-piece garment with bloomer like pants.

DIFFERENTIATED INSTRUCTION

FOR STRATEGIC READERS

Clarify Meaning Explain the meaning of lines 283–286 by clarifying that Dexter's mother is an immigrant who embarrassed him by never learning to speak English fluently. As a result, Dexter tries to follow customs carefully so he will not appear as an outsider like his mother. Work with students to help them recognize that Dexter believes his children will be able to behave "carelessly" because their father fits in so seamlessly. Then broaden the discussion by pointing out that Dexter could instead have taken pride in his mother's ability to speak two languages. Ask students to consider the challenge immigrants face in maintaining a home language in an English-speaking society. Invite English learners to participate.

He told her.

"Well, why don't you come to dinner tomorrow night?"

His heart turned over like the fly-wheel of the boat, and, for the second time, her casual whim gave a new direction to his life.

III

270 Next evening while he waited for her to come downstairs, Dexter peopled the soft deep summer room and the sun-porch that opened from it with the men who had already loved Judy Jones. He knew the sort of men they were—the men who when he first went to college had entered from the great prep schools with graceful clothes and the deep tan of healthy summers. He had seen that, in one sense, he was better than these men. He was newer and stronger. Yet in acknowledging to himself that he wished his children to be like them he was admitting that he was but the rough, strong stuff from which they eternally sprang.

When the time had come for him to wear good clothes, he had known who were the best tailors in America, and the best tailors in America had made him the
280 suit he wore this evening. He had acquired that particular reserve peculiar to his university, that set it off from other universities. He recognized the value to him of such a mannerism and he had adopted it; he knew that to be careless in dress and manner required more confidence than to be careful. But carelessness was for his children. His mother's name had been Krimslich. She was a Bohemian of the peasant class and she had talked broken English to the end of her days. Her son must keep to the set patterns.

At a little after seven Judy Jones came downstairs. She wore a blue silk afternoon dress, and he was disappointed at first that she had not put on something more elaborate. This feeling was accentuated when, after a brief
290 greeting, she went to the door of a butler's pantry and pushing it open called: "You can serve dinner, Martha." He had rather expected that a butler would announce dinner, that there would be a cocktail. Then he put these thoughts behind him as they sat down side by side on a lounge and looked at each other.

"Father and mother won't be here," she said thoughtfully.

He remembered the last time he had seen her father, and he was glad the parents were not to be here tonight—they might wonder who he was. He had been born in Keeble, a Minnesota village fifty miles farther north, and he always gave Keeble as his home instead of Black Bear Village. Country towns were well enough to come from if they weren't inconveniently in sight and used as footstools
300 by fashionable lakes. **G**

They talked of his university, which she had visited frequently during the past two years, and of the near-by city which supplied Sherry Island with its patrons, and whither Dexter would return next day to his prospering laundries.

During dinner she slipped into a moody depression which gave Dexter a feeling of uneasiness. Whatever **petulance** she uttered in her throaty voice worried him. Whatever she smiled at—at him, at a chicken liver, at nothing—it disturbed him

④ Targeted Passage

G MOTIVATION AND TRAITS
Reread lines 270–300. **Summarize** Dexter's ideas about social class and the status it confers. How does Dexter see himself? To what does he aspire?

petulance (pĕch'ə-ləns) *n.* ill temper; annoyance

Lines 287–293
REINFORCE *KEY IDEA:* STATUS

Discuss What indicators of **status** does Dexter expect to encounter at Judy's home? Are his expectations met? *Possible answer: Dexter expects Judy to be dressed elaborately, to have a butler announce dinner, and to be served cocktails. Instead, Judy is wearing merely "a blue silk afternoon dress" (lines 287–288), announces dinner herself, and does not serve cocktails. Dexter is, at least initially, "disappointed" (line 288) by the dinner.*

LITERARY ANALYSIS

G MOTIVATION AND TRAITS

Possible answer: Dexter believes that wealth and status are important, and that social class is affected by both factors. Dexter sees himself as "newer and stronger" (line 275) than Judy's old-money suitors, but he still aspires to be like them. He dresses like them (lines 278–280), imitates them, and wants his children to be like them (lines 275–276). He is ashamed of his parentage (lines 284–286) and usually lies about his hometown (lines 296–300).

If students need help . . . Urge them to reread lines 275–277 and recognize that they communicate Dexter's nervous sense that he is a trespasser among the wealthy.

FOR STRATEGIC READERS

④ Targeted Passage [Lines 287–300]

This passage relates Dexter and Judy's first date, which Dexter finds initially disappointing.

- What disappoints Dexter about his dinner with Judy?
- In what ways did Dexter expect this first date to be different?
- Why is Dexter relieved that Judy's parents are not present?

FOR ENGLISH LEARNERS

Vocabulary Support [mixed-readiness groups]
Review the definition of *connotation*. Then guide students to use context to classify the connotations of these words and phrases as reflecting positively or negatively on Judy:

- *sinuous*, line 254 (*negative*)
- *sea-gull flying*, line 256 (*positive*)
- *stabbing a path ahead*, line 258 (*negative*)

FOR ADVANCED LEARNERS/AP

Research and Analyze [small-group option]
Judy reflects a Jazz Age character type—the flapper. Ask students to research flappers to learn the origin of the term, the dress and behavior it describes, and the commonly held social views about flappers.

Challenge students to consider how recognizing Judy as a flapper helps readers understand, for example, why she is brazen enough to ask Dexter to dinner in a time when men typically did the asking.

TIERED DISCUSSION PROMPTS

Use these prompts to help students consider what motivates Judy as she dates men:

Connect How do you feel about Judy at this point in the story? What sort of behavior do you expect from her? *Students will likely say that they don't like Judy and that they expect her to behave badly.*

Interpret Is Judy being honest when she says that she could marry a poor man? Explain. *Possible answer: Judy is probably deceiving both Dexter and herself about her capacity to marry a poor man. She seems interested in poor men as novelties (lines 319–320) but is likely too accustomed to wealth to actually marry one. She is clearly very interested in her suitors' finances so her story about the poor suitor may be a play to learn about Dexter's finances. After all, when Dexter reports that he is wealthy, she smiles and kisses him as if this is what she wanted to hear (lines 330–331).*

Synthesize How has Fitzgerald hinted at Judy's fickleness earlier in the text? In what way does this technique shape readers' expectations about Dexter's interaction with Judy? *Possible answer: Fitzgerald has hinted at Judy's fickleness by foreshadowing her beauty and its effects on many men (lines 47–53, 78–80, 199–200). The technique shapes readers' expectations by suggesting that Judy cannot and will not be faithful to Dexter.*

---

that her smile could have no root in mirth, or even in amusement. When the scarlet corners of her lips curved down, it was less a smile than an invitation to a kiss.

310 Then, after dinner, she led him out on the dark sun-porch and deliberately changed the atmosphere.

"Do you mind if I weep a little?" she said.

"I'm afraid I'm boring you," he responded quickly.

"You're not. I like you. But I've just had a terrible afternoon. There was a man I cared about, and this afternoon he told me out of a clear sky that he was poor as a church-mouse. He'd never even hinted it before. Does this sound horribly **mundane?**"

"Perhaps he was afraid to tell you."

"Suppose he was," she answered. "He didn't start right. You see, if I'd thought
320 of him as poor—well, I've been mad about loads of poor men, and fully intended to marry them all. But in this case, I hadn't thought of him that way, and my interest in him wasn't strong enough to survive the shock. As if a girl calmly informed her fiancé that she was a widow. He might not object to widows, but—

"Let's start right," she interrupted herself suddenly. "Who are you, anyhow?"

For a moment Dexter hesitated. Then:

"I'm nobody," he announced. "My career is largely a matter of futures."

"Are you poor?"

"No," he said frankly, "I'm probably making more money than any man my age in the Northwest. I know that's an obnoxious remark, but you advised me to start right."

330 There was a pause. Then she smiled and the corners of her mouth drooped and an almost imperceptible sway brought her closer to him, looking up into his eyes. A lump rose in Dexter's throat, and he waited breathless for the experiment, facing the unpredictable compound that would form mysteriously from the elements of their lips. Then he saw—she communicated her excitement to him, lavishly, deeply, with kisses that were not a promise but a fulfillment. They aroused in him not hunger demanding renewal but **surfeit** that would demand more surfeit . . . kisses that were like charity, creating want by holding back nothing at all.

It did not take him many hours to decide that he had wanted Judy Jones ever since he was a proud, desirous little boy.

IV

340 It began like that—and continued, with varying shades of intensity, on such a note right up to the dénouement. Dexter surrendered a part of himself to the most direct and unprincipled personality with which he had ever come in contact. Whatever Judy wanted, she went after with the full pressure of her charm. There was no divergence of method, no jockeying for position or premeditation of effects—there was a very little mental side to any of her affairs. She simply made men conscious to the highest degree of her physical loveliness. Dexter had no desire to change her. Her deficiencies were knit up with a passionate energy that transcended and justified them.

mundane (mŭn-dān′) *adj.* characteristic of or concerned with the ordinary

surfeit (sûr′fĭt) *n.* a fullness beyond the point of satisfaction

---

DIFFERENTIATED INSTRUCTION

FOR STRATEGIC READERS

Clarify Meaning Help students navigate the rich figurative language Fitzgerald uses to describe the kisses Dexter and Judy share. Explain that the metaphor in lines 333–334 compares Judy and Dexter's kiss to the combination of chemical elements. When combined, the elements create a new and unpredictable product. The simile in line 337 compares the kisses to charity; because they are given without restraint, they make Dexter want more.

FOR ENGLISH LEARNERS

Vocabulary: Idioms [mixed-readiness groups] Share or elicit the meanings of these expressions, and then help students find similar expressions in their home languages:

- *out of a clear sky* (line 314), "unexpectedly"
- *poor as a church mouse* (lines 314–315), "very poor"
- *mad about* (line 319), "liked very much"
- *jockeying for position* (line 344), "careful planning"

When, as Judy's head lay against his shoulder that first night, she whispered, "I
350 don't know what's the matter with me. Last night I thought I was in love with a
man and tonight I think I'm in love with you—"—it seemed to him a beautiful
and romantic thing to say. It was the exquisite excitability that for the moment he
controlled and owned. But a week later he was compelled to view this same quality
in a different light. She took him in her roadster[10] to a picnic supper, and after
supper she disappeared, likewise in her roadster, with another man. Dexter became
enormously upset and was scarcely able to be decently civil to the other people
present. When she assured him that she had not kissed the other man, he knew she
was lying—yet he was glad that she had taken the trouble to lie to him. **H**

He was, as he found before the summer ended, one of a varying dozen who
360 circulated about her. Each of them had at one time been favored above all
others—about half of them still basked in the solace of occasional sentimental

---

10. **roadster:** a sporty, two-seat, open automobile.

H MOTIVATION AND TRAITS
Reread lines 340–358.
Dexter's thoughts
convey information
about Judy, but they
also reveal much about
Dexter himself. Explain
what you learn about
him from these lines.

Young Woman in Green (1927), Tamara de Lempicka. Musée National d'Art Moderne, Centre
Georges Pompidou, Paris. © CNAC/MNAM/Dist. Réunion des Musées Nationaux/Art Resource,
New York. © 2007 Artists Rights Society (ARS), New York/ADAGP, Paris.

LITERARY ANALYSIS

H MOTIVATION AND TRAITS

Possible answer: Dexter is so desperate to
have Judy's love that he interprets Judy's lie
as a sign of her affectionate wish to shield
him. He is willing to grasp at any hope, no
matter how flimsy, to continue believing
that Judy has a good nature.

Extend the Discussion What will probably
happen between Dexter and Judy as their
relationship progresses? Why?

ANALYZE VISUALS

Activity Ask students what elements of
Judy's character and appearance are reflected
in this artwork and how the work helps
them understand Judy's effect on Dexter.
Possible answers: Judy's scarlet lips, piercing
eyes, lithe figure, and style make her similar to
the woman in the portrait. The artwork helps
readers visualize vividly the charms and allure
for which Dexter "surrendered a part
of himself" (line 341).

About the Art Tamara de Lempicka's artworks
on pages 943, 949, and 953 all reflect the
groundbreaking Art Deco style, which arose
in Paris during the 1920s. Deco artists imbued
everything from fine art to home furnishings
with the clean, streamlined look of modern
machines. Like Dexter Green, they were
drawn to sleek images of wealth and fashion
and tried to introduce these to the masses.

FOR ADVANCED LEARNERS/AP

Analyze Theme [paired option] Have
students debate Dexter's claim that Judy's
"deficiencies were knit up with a passionate energy that transcended and justified
them" (lines 347–348), echoing his earlier
"monstrous conviction" that Judy's attack on
her nurse was "justified" (lines 102–103). As
students develop their arguments, urge them
to consider these factors:

- the grounds on which Dexter justifies
  Judy's actions
- Dexter's biases about Judy
- the idea that beauty, wealth, privilege,
  or "passionate energy" can justify bad
  behavior

After completing the debate, ask students to
use the activity to help them draw conclusions and generate a theme statement for
the story.

revals. Whenever one showed signs of dropping out through long neglect, she granted him a brief honeyed hour, which encouraged him to tag along for a year or so longer. Judy made these forays upon the helpless and defeated without malice, indeed half unconscious that there was anything mischievous in what she did.

When a new man came to town every one dropped out—dates were automatically canceled.

The helpless part of trying to do anything about it was that she did it all herself. She was not a girl who could be "won" in the kinetic sense—she was proof against
370 cleverness, she was proof against charm; if any of these assailed her too strongly she would immediately resolve the affair to a physical basis, and under the magic of her physical splendor the strong as well as the brilliant played her game and not their own. She was entertained only by the gratification of her desires and by the direct exercise of her own charm. Perhaps from so much youthful love, so many youthful lovers, she had come, in self-defense, to nourish herself wholly from within. **❶**

Succeeding Dexter's first exhilaration came restlessness and dissatisfaction. The helpless ecstasy of losing himself in her was opiate rather than tonic.[11] It was fortunate for his work during the winter that those moments of ecstasy came infrequently. Early in their acquaintance it had seemed for a while that there was
380 a deep and spontaneous mutual attraction—that first August, for example—three days of long evenings on her dusky veranda, of strange wan kisses through the late afternoon, in shadowy alcoves or behind the protecting trellises of the garden arbors, of mornings when she was fresh as a dream and almost shy at meeting him in the clarity of the rising day. There was all the ecstasy of an engagement about it, sharpened by his realization that there was no engagement. It was during those three days that, for the first time, he had asked her to marry him. She said "maybe some day," she said "kiss me," she said "I'd like to marry you," she said "I love you"—she said—nothing.

The three days were interrupted by the arrival of a New York man who visited
390 at her house for half September. To Dexter's agony, rumor engaged them. The man was the son of the president of a great trust company. But at the end of a month it was reported that Judy was yawning. At a dance one night she sat all evening in a motor-boat with a local beau, while the New Yorker searched the club for her frantically. She told the local beau that she was bored with her visitor, and two days later he left. She was seen with him at the station, and it was reported that he looked very mournful indeed.

On this note the summer ended. Dexter was twenty-four, and he found himself increasingly in a position to do as he wished. He joined two clubs in the city and lived at one of them. Though he was by no means an integral part of the stag-lines
400 at these clubs, he managed to be on hand at dances where Judy Jones was likely to appear. He could have gone out socially as much as he liked—he was an eligible young man, now, and popular with downtown fathers. His confessed devotion to Judy Jones had rather solidified his position. But he had no social aspirations and rather despised the dancing men who were always on tap for the Thursday

---

11. **opiate . . . tonic:** deadening rather than stimulating.

❶ MOTIVATION AND TRAITS
Consider characters or people you've encountered who are similar to Judy Jones. What might **motivate** Judy to act as she does? Cite details you used to draw this **conclusion**.

LITERARY ANALYSIS

❶ MOTIVATION AND TRAITS

Accept all thoughtful responses. Students should accurately characterize Judy and support their conclusions with textual evidence.

If students need help . . . Refer them to the Character Traits and Textual Evidence chart they began on page 945 and work with them to add to it and draw conclusions from the information listed.

 BEST PRACTICES TOOLKIT—Transparency Character Traits and Textual Evidence p. D6

Lines 389–396
REINFORCE *KEY IDEA:* **STATUS**

Discuss What about the **status** of the New York man makes him a greater threat to Dexter's hope than Judy's other beaus? What does Judy's reaction to this man suggest about her view of status? *Possible answers: The New York man has excellent credentials for wooing Judy. He is the son of "the president of a great trust company" (line 391), so he outranks Judy's other suitors. However, Judy is bored by this man (line 392), which suggests that despite her attachment to status and wealth, it is not enough on its own to hold her interest.*

DIFFERENTIATED INSTRUCTION

FOR ENGLISH LEARNERS

Vocabulary Support [paired option] Recall with students the many words Fitzgerald uses to describe Judy's character, and help students identify additional words from pages 950–951. Have student pairs list these words in a T Chart along with the words Fitzgerald uses to describe Irene in lines 413–414 and 442–443. Guide students to see that the two lists of words contrast sharply, as do the characters. Be sure that students can define any words they list.

Judy is . . .	Irene is . . .
haughty (line 109)	sweet (line 413)
arrestingly beautiful (line 186)	a little stout (line 414)
easily bored (lines 392–395)	knowledgeable about books and music (lines 442–443)

 BEST PRACTICES TOOLKIT—Transparency T Chart p. A25

or Saturday parties and who filled in at dinners with the younger married set. Already he was playing with the idea of going East to New York. He wanted to take Judy Jones with him. No disillusion as to the world in which she had grown up could cure his illusion as to her desirability.

Remember that—for only in the light of it can what he did for her be
410 understood.

Eighteen months after he first met Judy Jones he became engaged to another girl. Her name was Irene Scheerer, and her father was one of the men who had always believed in Dexter. Irene was light-haired and sweet and honorable, and a little stout, and she had two suitors whom she pleasantly relinquished when Dexter formally asked her to marry him.

Summer, fall, winter, spring, another summer, another fall—so much he had given of his active life to the incorrigible lips of Judy Jones. She had treated him with interest, with encouragement, with malice, with indifference, with contempt. She had inflicted on him the innumerable little slights and indignities possible
420 in such a case—as if in revenge for having ever cared for him at all. She had beckoned him and yawned at him and beckoned him again and he had responded often with bitterness and narrowed eyes. She had brought him ecstatic happiness and intolerable agony of spirit. She had caused him untold inconvenience and not a little trouble. She had insulted him, and she had ridden over him, and she had played his interest in her against his interest in his work—for fun. She had done everything to him except to criticize him—this she had not done—it seemed to him only because it might have sullied the utter indifference she manifested and sincerely felt toward him. **J**

> When autumn had come and gone again it occurred to him that he could not
> 430 have Judy Jones. He had to beat this into his mind but he convinced himself at last. He lay awake at night for a while and argued it over. He told himself the trouble and the pain she had caused him, he enumerated her glaring deficiencies as a wife. Then he said to himself that he loved her, and after a while he fell asleep. For a week, lest he imagine her husky voice over the telephone or her eyes opposite him at lunch, he worked hard and late, and at night he went to his office and plotted out his years.
>
> At the end of a week he went to a dance and cut in on her once. For almost the first time since they had met he did not ask her to sit out with him or tell her that she was lovely. It hurt him that she did not miss these things—that was all.
> 440 He was not jealous when he saw that there was a new man tonight. He had been hardened against jealousy long before. **K**
>
> He stayed late at the dance. He sat for an hour with Irene Scheerer and talked about books and about music. He knew very little about either. But he was

beginning to be master of his own time now, and he had a rather priggish notion that he—the young and already fabulously successful Dexter Green—should know more about such things.

That was in October, when he was twenty-five. In January, Dexter and Irene became engaged. It was to be announced in June, and they were to be married three months later.

J GRAMMAR AND STYLE
Reread lines 416–428. Fitzgerald's long sentences, held together by the **coordinating conjunction** *and* and broken up by **dashes,** convey Dexter's perplexed thoughts about Judy's behavior.

5 Targeted Passage

K THEME
How does Dexter's response to this autumn compare with his reactions to the season at the beginning of the story? What theme in the story is suggested by the change in Dexter?

J **GRAMMAR AND STYLE**

Craft Effective Sentences Point out that Fitzgerald's careful choice of punctuation in this paragraph reinforces the internal argument Dexter has over whether to give up Judy. Ask volunteers to read the paragraph aloud dramatically, using the coordinating conjunctions and dashes to set the pace and intensity. Help students hear the effect of what Fitzgerald has written into these lines. Have them discuss the impact of Fitzgerald's use of dashes (lines 505–508) and the use of the conjunction *and* (lines 679–683).

LITERARY ANALYSIS: Review

K **THEME**

Possible answer: *When he was a boy, he observed the subtleties of the season. Fall brought him hope that something good was coming and he invested the season with visions of his future (lines 17–31). Now, however, autumn has merely "come and gone again" (line 429) without his notice, he feels hopeless because he cannot secure Judy's love, and he now he feels the impossibility of those visions.* Accept all thoughtful statements of theme.

FOR STRATEGIC READERS

5 Targeted Passage [Lines 429–443]

This passage records Dexter's slow and reluctant change of heart about Judy.

- What does Dexter convince himself about Judy? How does he accomplish his goal?
- How does Dexter's decision affect Judy?
- What possibility for Dexter arises because of his decision about Judy?

FOR ADVANCED LEARNERS/AP

Analyze Style Have students analyze Judy's responses to Dexter's marriage proposals (lines 385–388). Students should rate each of Judy's responses on how encouraging or discouraging it is, then chart the five responses on a Line Plot. Have students use their completed graphs to lead a class discussion about Judy's motivation for her answers and how her evasions affect readers. For example, do readers expect Dexter to continue proposing

to Judy? Why or why not? In what ways do Judy's evasions develop her character?

 BEST PRACTICES TOOLKIT—Transparency Graphic Aids: Line Plots p. A64

450 The Minnesota winter prolonged itself interminably, and it was almost May when the winds came soft and the snow ran down into Black Bear Lake at last. For the first time in over a year Dexter was enjoying a certain tranquillity of spirit. Judy Jones had been in Florida, and afterward in Hot Springs,[12] and somewhere she had been engaged, and somewhere she had broken it off. At first, when Dexter had definitely given her up, it had made him sad that people still linked them together and asked for news of her, but when he began to be placed at dinner next to Irene Scheerer people didn't ask him about her any more—they told him about her. He ceased to be an authority on her.

May at last. Dexter walked the streets at night when the darkness was damp
460 as rain, wondering that so soon, with so little done, so much of ecstasy had gone from him. May one year back had been marked by Judy's poignant, unforgivable, yet forgiven turbulence—it had been one of those rare times when he fancied she had grown to care for him. That old penny's worth of happiness he had spent for this bushel of content. He knew that Irene would be no more than a curtain spread behind him, a hand moving among gleaming tea-cups, a voice calling to children . . . fire and loveliness were gone, the magic of nights and the wonder of the varying hours and seasons . . . slender lips, downturning, dropping to his lips and bearing him up into a heaven of eyes. . . . The thing was deep in him. He was too strong and alive for it to die lightly. **L**

470 In the middle of May when the weather balanced for a few days on the thin bridge that led to deep summer he turned in one night at Irene's house. Their engagement was to be announced in a week now—no one would be surprised at it. And tonight they would sit together on the lounge at the University Club and look on for an hour at the dancers. It gave him a sense of solidity to go with her—she was so sturdily popular, so intensely "great."

He mounted the steps of the brownstone house and stepped inside.

"Irene," he called.

Mrs. Scheerer came out of the living-room to meet him.

"Dexter," she said, "Irene's gone upstairs with a splitting headache. She wanted
480 to go with you but I made her go to bed."

"Nothing serious, I—"

"Oh, no. She's going to play golf with you in the morning. You can spare her for just one night, can't you, Dexter?"

Her smile was kind. She and Dexter liked each other. In the living-room he talked for a moment before he said good night.

Returning to the University Club, where he had rooms, he stood in the doorway for a moment and watched the dancers. He leaned against the door-post, nodded at a man or two—yawned.

"Hello, darling."

490 The familiar voice at his elbow startled him. Judy Jones had left a man and crossed the room to him—Judy Jones, a slender enameled doll in cloth of gold: gold in a band at her head, gold in two slipper points at her dress's hem. The fragile glow of her face seemed to blossom as she smiled at him. A breeze of

---

12. **Hot Springs:** a spa city in west-central Arkansas.

L PREDICT

Identify the **metaphors** that come to Dexter's mind with regard to Irene. What do they suggest about his feelings toward her? Predict how Dexter will treat Irene in the future. Cite text clues that helped you make this guess.

Lines 470–485
TIERED DISCUSSION PROMPTS

Use these prompts to help students explore the relationship between the Scheerers and Dexter:

Recall What did Irene's father think of Dexter before their engagement? *Answer: Irene's father supported and admired Dexter (lines 412–413).*

Analyze Is Fitzgerald's language when speaking of the Scheerers generally positive or negative? Explain. Why does this family seem a second-best choice for Dexter? *Possible answer: Fitzgerald's language is consistently positive in describing the Scheerers. The parents are encouraging and friendly. Irene is popular, stable, and gracious. Yet the family seems bland in contrast with the passion that Judy inspires.*

Synthesize What kind of relationship can Dexter and Irene expect to have, with each other and with her parents? Will this life satisfy Dexter? Explain. *Possible answer: Dexter and Irene can expect a pleasant, calm, rather uneventful family life. Dexter is friends with Irene and her parents. This quiet, comfortable life will not satisfy Dexter for long. His winter dreams of growth and change will resurface.*

DIFFERENTIATED INSTRUCTION

FOR STRATEGIC READERS

Comprehension Support Explain that Fitzgerald uses the seasons as symbols for Dexter's hopes and loves. Guide students to link the chilly, wet May with Dexter's affection for Irene and to note that the shift to "deep summer" (line 471) relates to Judy's return to Black Bear. Also point out the bridge imagery raised in line 471. The season will cross a fragile bridge, as will Dexter when Judy returns.

FOR ENGLISH LEARNERS

Vocabulary Support Fitzgerald's language contrasts Dexter's planned life with Irene and his dreamed-of life with Judy. Point out contrasts such as *tranquillity* (line 452) and *unforgivable* (line 461), or *solidity* (line 474) and *turbulence* (line 462). Help students identify others in lines 475 and 495–499. Guide students to list the words in a T Chart.

BEST PRACTICES TOOLKIT—Transparency T Chart p. A25

warmth and light blew through the room. His hands in the pockets of his dinner-jacket tightened spasmodically. He was filled with a sudden excitement.

"When did you get back?" he asked casually.

"Come here and I'll tell you about it."

She turned and he followed her. She had been away—he could have wept at the wonder of her return. She had passed through enchanted streets, doing things that were like provocative music. All mysterious happenings, all fresh and quickening hopes, had gone away with her, come back with her now.

500

She turned in the doorway.

"Have you a car here? If you haven't, I have."

"I have a coupé."

In then, with a rustle of golden cloth. He slammed the door. Into so many cars she had stepped—like this—like that—her back against the leather, so—her elbow resting on the door—waiting. She would have been soiled long since had there been anything to soil her—except herself—but this was her own self-outpouring.

Autoportrait (1925), Tamara De Lempicka. Oil on wood, 35 cm × 26 cm. Private collection. © 2007 Artists Rights Society (ARS), New York/ADAGP, Paris.

ANALYZE VISUALS
Tamara De Lempicka's posterlike oil paintings are often described as dramatic and aggressive. How does this description fit this particular painting? Explain, citing details.

WINTER DREAMS   **953**

REINFORCE *KEY IDEA:* STATUS

Discuss What details in the scene—in which the normally routine act of getting into a car becomes glamorous—demonstrate the high **status** of this enviable couple? *Possible answer: The car has expensive leather seats and is a stylish coupé. Dexter is dressed for an elegant dance, and Judy is "a rustle of gold" draped across the car's seats. They are a beautiful couple.*

ANALYZE VISUALS

Possible answer: The woman's aggressive side-long glance and unsmiling lips suggest disdain for viewers. Her stylish clothing suggests that she wants to be seen and admired, while her lax posture and careless hand on the wheel suggest dismissal of viewers' reactions. The contrast of wanting to be adored by all yet dismissing all is dramatic.

FOR ADVANCED LEARNERS/AP

Analyze Imagery [small-group option] Ask students to scan pages 952–953 for imagery linking Dexter to Judy and discuss its effect. Have students use a Cluster Diagram to categorize the imagery under these headings: color, emotion, seasons, times, weather, and sounds. Ask students to explain what plot events they expect to occur next and how Fitzgerald's profusion of imagery supports these likely events.

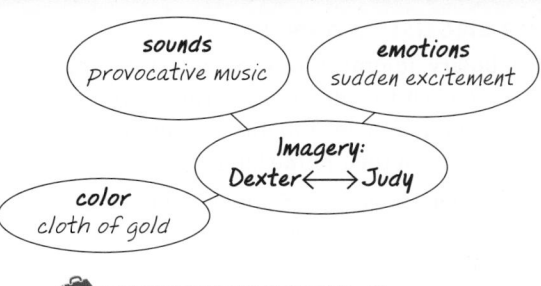

 BEST PRACTICES TOOLKIT—Transparency
Cluster Diagram p. B18

Lines 509–548
TIERED DISCUSSION PROMPTS

Use these prompts to help students track Dexter's weakening resistance to Judy:

Summarize What happens in these lines?
Possible answer: Dexter gives Judy a ride in his car, and she flirts with him and flatters him.

Analyze At what points in this awkward conversation does Dexter try to keep Judy's past behavior in mind, and to what effect?
Possible answer: In lines 509–511, Dexter assures himself that Judy's attentions are "nothing" and that he "had put her behind him." In lines 528–529 he recognizes her empty flattery but feels it nonetheless. In line 533 he becomes "confused" by Judy's words and can't respond rationally. In lines 547–548 he lets down his guard enough to wonder if Judy has changed.

Synthesize Why are lines 547–548, Dexter's last stated resistance, written as questions rather than statements? What prediction do these questions invite from readers?
Possible answer: Lines 547–548 are written as questions to show that Dexter's resistance to Judy is beginning to crumble. He no longer tells himself to stay out of danger, but now doubts the conclusions that he so painfully reached earlier. These questions invite readers to predict that Judy will achieve this latest conquest over Dexter, as she has achieved many times in the past.

With an effort he forced himself to start the car and back into the street. This 510 was nothing, he must remember. She had done this before, and he had put her behind him, as he would have crossed a bad account from his books.

He drove slowly downtown and, affecting abstraction,[13] traversed the deserted streets of the business section, peopled here and there where a movie was giving out its crowd or where consumptive or pugilistic[14] youth lounged in front of pool halls. The clink of glasses and the slap of hands on the bars issued from saloons, cloisters[15] of glazed glass and dirty yellow light.

She was watching him closely and the silence was embarrassing, yet in this crisis he could find no casual word with which to profane the hour. At a convenient turning he began to zigzag back toward the University Club.

520 "Have you missed me?" she asked suddenly.

"Everybody missed you."

He wondered if she knew of Irene Scheerer. She had been back only a day—her absence had been almost contemporaneous with his engagement.

"What a remark!" Judy laughed sadly—without sadness. She looked at him searchingly. He became absorbed in the dashboard.

"You're handsomer than you used to be," she said thoughtfully. "Dexter, you have the most rememberable eyes."

He could have laughed at this, but he did not laugh. It was the sort of thing that was said to sophomores. Yet it stabbed at him.

530 "I'm awfully tired of everything, darling." She called every one darling, endowing the endearment with careless, individual **camaraderie**. "I wish you'd marry me."

The directness of this confused him. He should have told her now that he was going to marry another girl, but he could not tell her. He could as easily have sworn that he had never loved her.

"I think we'd get along," she continued, on the same note, "unless probably you've forgotten me and fallen in love with another girl."

Her confidence was obviously enormous. She had said, in effect, that she found such a thing impossible to believe, that if it were true he had merely committed a 540 childish indiscretion—and probably to show off. She would forgive him, because it was not a matter of any moment but rather something to be brushed aside lightly.

"Of course you could never love anybody but me," she continued, "I like the way you love me. Oh, Dexter, have you forgotten last year?"

"No, I haven't forgotten."

"Neither have I!"

Was she sincerely moved—or was she carried along by the wave of her own acting?

"I wish we could be like that again," she said, and he forced himself to answer:

550 "I don't think we can."

camaraderie
(kä′mə-rä′də-rē) *n.* a spirit of friendly good-fellowship

---

13. **affecting abstraction:** pretending to be lost in thought.

14. **consumptive or pugilistic** (pyōō′jə-lĭs′-tĭc): sickly or aggressive.

15. **cloisters:** here, places to escape from life's problems.

DIFFERENTIATED INSTRUCTION

FOR ENGLISH LEARNERS
Vocabulary: Idioms [mixed-readiness groups]
Share or elicit the meanings of these expressions, and then help students find similar expressions in their home languages:

- *crossed a bad account from his books* (line 511), "cancelled a customer who didn't pay his bills"

- *to show off* (line 540), "to get attention"

- *to be brushed aside lightly* (lines 541–542), "not important"

- *hard-minded* (line 586), "unemotional"

- *popular opinion* (line 589), "widely held views"

"I suppose not. . . . I hear you're giving Irene Scheerer a violent rush."

There was not the faintest emphasis on the name, yet Dexter was suddenly ashamed.

"Oh, take me home," cried Judy suddenly; "I don't want to go back to that idiotic dance—with those children."

Then, as he turned up the street that led to the residence district, Judy began to cry quietly to herself. He had never seen her cry before.

The dark street lightened, the dwellings of the rich loomed up around them,
560 he stopped his coupé in front of the great white bulk of the Mortimer Joneses' house, somnolent, gorgeous, drenched with the splendor of the damp moonlight. Its solidity startled him. The strong walls, the steel of the girders, the breadth and beam and pomp of it were there only to bring out the contrast with the young beauty beside him. It was sturdy to accentuate her slightness—as if to show what a breeze could be generated by a butterfly's wing.

He sat perfectly quiet, his nerves in wild clamor, afraid that if he moved he would find her irresistibly in his arms. Two tears had rolled down her wet face and trembled on her upper lip.

"I'm more beautiful than anybody else," she said brokenly, "why can't I be happy?" Her moist eyes tore at his stability—her mouth turned slowly downward
570 with an exquisite sadness: "I'd like to marry you if you'll have me, Dexter. I suppose you think I'm not worth having, but I'll be so beautiful for you, Dexter."

A million phrases of anger, pride, passion, hatred, tenderness fought on his lips. Then a perfect wave of emotion washed over him, carrying off with it a sediment of wisdom, of convention, of doubt, of honor. This was his girl who was speaking, his own, his beautiful, his pride.

"Won't you come in?" He heard her draw in her breath sharply.

Waiting. **Ⓜ**

"All right," his voice was trembling, "I'll come in."

Ⓖ Targeted Passage

Ⓜ PREDICT
Do you think Judy has really changed? Will she really marry Dexter? Give reasons for your predictions.

V

It was strange that neither when it was over nor a long time afterward did he
580 regret that night. Looking at it from the perspective of ten years, the fact that Judy's flare for him endured just one month seemed of little importance. Nor did it matter that by his yielding he subjected himself to a deeper agony in the end and gave serious hurt to Irene Scheerer and to Irene's parents, who had befriended him. There was nothing sufficiently pictorial about Irene's grief to stamp itself on his mind.

Dexter was at bottom hard-minded. The attitude of the city on his action was of no importance to him, not because he was going to leave the city, but because any outside attitude on the situation seemed superficial. He was completely indifferent to popular opinion. Nor, when he had seen that it was no use, that he
590 did not possess in himself the power to move fundamentally or to hold Judy Jones, did he bear any malice toward her. He loved her, and he would love her until the

---

Lines 558–564
REINFORCE *KEY IDEA:* STATUS

Discuss What **status** does Dexter associate with the Mortimer Joneses' home? How is he affected by the home and its status? How does this affect his view of Judy? *Possible answer: Dexter associates the Mortimer Joneses' home with the wealth and success he has always sought. He feels overwhelmed by the mansion, which is "somnolent, gorgeous," ornamented by moonlight and reinforced by "strong walls" and "the steel of the girders" (lines 560–561). Next to the solid house, Judy seems to Dexter to be fragile, with a beauty that requires protection. Just as he believes status will protect him, he believes that with it he can protect Judy.*

READING SKILL

Ⓜ PREDICT

Possible answer: Judy has probably not really changed. Rather, she has probably found out that Dexter is engaged and is jealous—not of his love in particular, but of the idea that he could love anyone but her. She will not marry Dexter. When the novelty of having him back wears off, she will move on to the next conquest, because it is the conquest that thrills her.

Extend the Discussion Read the first two sentences of Section V. Do you still think your predictions will be accurate? Why or why not?

FOR STRATEGIC READERS

Ⓖ Targeted Passage [Lines 565–578]

This passage marks Dexter's next surrender to Judy's charms, this time against his body of experience with her.

- How does Dexter initially manage to resist Judy's charms?
- What does Judy do to break Dexter's resistance?
- Who is waiting in line 577, and for what?

FOR ADVANCED LEARNERS/AP

Analyze Characters' Actions [paired option] Challenge students to identify the persuasive tactics that Judy uses to wear down Dexter's emotional resistance and then to note Dexter's gradually failing resistance to the assault. Have students review logical and emotional appeals and rank the appeals in order of Judy's reliance on them. Invite students to share their ranking.

TIERED DISCUSSION PROMPTS

Use these prompts to help students understand Dexter's reaction to Judy's tempestuous
nature:

Summarize What strong emotions has Judy
produced in Dexter? *Possible answer: Judy
has produced passion, hope, shame, anger,
desperation, and other strong emotions
in Dexter. He has experienced everything
from "deep pain" to "deep happiness" (lines
592–594).*

Analyze When Judy leaves Dexter again,
how does he respond emotionally? Why?
*Possible answer: When Judy leaves Dex-
ter again, he seems incapable of further
emotional response. Judy appears to have
drained him of emotions. He is "beyond
any revulsion and any amusement" (lines
597–598) and eagerly seeks escape from the
"webs of tangled emotion" (line 604) she has
wrought.*

Synthesize Compared to Dexter's intense
emotions, how would you describe Judy's
emotions? *Possible answer: Judy's emotions,
other than her greed for adoration, seem pale
compared to Dexter's. She seems incapable
of love, or of real sorrow, or of regret. Her
emotional displays, as when she asks Dexter
on their first date if she may weep in his presence (line 311), are manipulative shams.*

---

day he was too old for loving—but he could not have her. So he tasted the deep
pain that is reserved only for the strong, just as he had tasted for a little while the
deep happiness.

Even the ultimate falsity of the grounds upon which Judy terminated the
engagement—that she did not want to "take him away" from Irene—Judy, who
had wanted nothing else—did not revolt him. He was beyond any revulsion or
any amusement.

600 He went East in February with the intention of selling out his laundries and
settling in New York—but the war came to America in March and changed his
plans. He returned to the West, handed over the management of the business to
his partner, and went into the first officers' training-camp in late April. He was
one of those young thousands who greeted the war with a certain amount of relief,
welcoming the liberation from webs of tangled emotion.

VI

This story is not his biography, remember, although things creep into it which
have nothing to do with those dreams he had when he was young. We are almost
done with them and with him now. There is only one more incident to be related
here, and it happens seven years farther on.

610 It took place in New York, where he had done well—so well that there were no
barriers too high for him. He was thirty-two years old, and, except for one flying
trip immediately after the war, he had not been West in seven years. A man named
Devlin from Detroit came into his office to see him in a business way, and then
and there this incident occurred, and closed out, so to speak, this particular side of
his life.

"So you're from the Middle West," said the man Devlin with careless curiosity.
"That's funny—I thought men like you were probably born and raised on Wall
Street. You know—wife of one of my best friends in Detroit came from your city.
I was an usher at the wedding."

Dexter waited with no apprehension of what was coming.

620 "Judy Simms," said Devlin with no particular interest; "Judy Jones she was
once."

"Yes, I knew her." A dull impatience spread over him. He had heard, of course,
that she was married—perhaps deliberately he had heard no more.

"Awfully nice girl," brooded Devlin meaninglessly, "I'm sort of sorry for her."

"Why?" Something in Dexter was alert, receptive, at once.

"Oh, Lud Simms has gone to pieces in a way. I don't mean he ill-uses her, but
he drinks and runs around—"

"Doesn't she run around?"

"No. Stays at home with her kids."

630 "Oh."

"She's a little too old for him," said Devlin.

"Too old!" cried Dexter. "Why, man, she's only twenty-seven."

DIFFERENTIATED INSTRUCTION

FOR ENGLISH LEARNERS

Language: Conversational English Patterns
[paired option] Explain that dialogue tags
are the words authors use to introduce or
follow quoted material. Write this example
on the board:

"Pass the pepper, please," she <u>said</u>.

Help students brainstorm a list of common
tags, such as *said* and *asked*. Note, however,
that more specific tags, such as *cried* or
shouted, add descriptive detail and variety.

Draw students' attention to the tags in lines
615–662: *said* (line 615), *brooded* (line 624),
apologized (line 635), and *agreed* (line 638).
Model each of the specific verbs and make
sure that students understand the speech
each indicates. Then ask student pairs to
read aloud the dialogue, matching their
voices to the tag used. Urge them to list
dialogue tags in a Personal Word List.

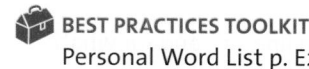 **BEST PRACTICES TOOLKIT**
Personal Word List p. E2

He was possessed with a wild notion of rushing out into the streets and taking a train to Detroit. He rose to his feet spasmodically.

"I guess you're busy," Devlin apologized quickly. "I didn't realize—"

"No, I'm not busy," said Dexter, steadying his voice. "I'm not busy at all. Not busy at all. Did you say she was—twenty-seven? No, I said she was twenty-seven."

"Yes, you did," agreed Devlin dryly.

"Go on, then. Go on."

640 "What do you mean?"

"About Judy Jones."

Devlin looked at him helplessly.

"Well, that's—I told you all there is to it. He treats her like the devil. Oh, they're not going to get divorced or anything. When he's particularly outrageous she forgives him. In fact, I'm inclined to think she loves him. She was a pretty girl when she first came to Detroit."

A pretty girl! The phrase struck Dexter as ludicrous.

"Isn't she—a pretty girl, any more?"

"Oh, she's all right."

650 "Look here," said Dexter, sitting down suddenly. "I don't understand. You say she was a 'pretty girl' and now you say she's 'all right.' I don't understand what you mean—Judy Jones wasn't a pretty girl, at all. She was a great beauty. Why, I knew her, I knew her. She was—"

Devlin laughed pleasantly.

"I'm not trying to start a row,[16]" he said. "I think Judy's a nice girl and I like her. I can't understand how a man like Lud Simms could fall madly in love with her, but he did." Then he added: "Most of the women like her." **(N)**

Dexter looked closely at Devlin, thinking wildly that there must be a reason for this, some insensitivity in the man or some private malice.

660 "Lots of women fade just like *that*," Devlin snapped his fingers. "You must have seen it happen. Perhaps I've forgotten how pretty she was at her wedding. I've seen her so much since then, you see. She has nice eyes."

A sort of dullness settled down upon Dexter. For the first time in his life he felt like getting very drunk. He knew that he was laughing loudly at something Devlin had said, but he did not know what it was or why it was funny. When, in a few minutes, Devlin went he lay down on his lounge and looked out the window at the New York sky-line into which the sun was sinking in dull lovely shades of pink and gold.

He had thought that having nothing else to lose he was invulnerable at last—
670 but he knew that he had just lost something more, as surely as if he had married Judy Jones and seen her fade away before his eyes.

The dream was gone. Something had been taken from him. In a sort of panic he pushed the palms of his hands into his eyes and tried to bring up a picture of the waters lapping on Sherry Island and the moonlit veranda, and gingham on

---

16. **row** (rou): a noisy argument or dispute.

(7) Targeted Passage

(N) MOTIVATION AND TRAITS
Based on Devlin's description of Judy, how would you say she has changed since Dexter knew her? What might have caused these changes?

Lines 624–634
REINFORCE *KEY IDEA*: STATUS

Discuss In what ways does Devlin's description of Judy undermine her role as a symbol of **status** in Dexter's life? How does Dexter respond to the idea that Judy has become ordinary? *Possible answer: Devlin's description undermines Judy as a symbol of status by showing her as just another unhappy wife. Judy had epitomized everything that Dexter wanted to be: graceful, stylish, elegant, worthy of pursuit. She had inspired him to better his own status. Devlin's description of her robs her of this power by making her ordinary. Dexter responds to this information with great distress and disbelief. He doesn't want to give up his unattainable status symbol.*

LITERARY ANALYSIS

(N) MOTIVATION AND TRAITS

Possible answer: Based on Devlin's description, Judy has changed in many ways since Dexter knew her. Devlin describes Judy as a rather drab, dutiful housewife who looks after her children and excuses her errant husband—quite the change from the Judy whom Dexter worshipped. These changes might result from time, from marrying someone who doesn't worship her, from the loss of beauty that comes with age, or from general sadness at how her life has turned out.

Extend the Discussion What is ironic about the way Judy's husband treats her?

FOR STRATEGIC READERS

(7) Targeted Passage [Lines 640–662]

In this passage Dexter faces the sad facts of how Judy has changed since he last saw her.

- What is Judy's marriage like?
- What has happened to her legendary beauty?
- How does Dexter react to Devlin's news?

FOR ADVANCED LEARNERS/AP

Hypothesize About Sources Tell students that Fitzgerald joined the army in 1917, the year that the United States entered World War I. Urge them to perform research to learn about his experiences in the service and then to consider how he translated these into fiction. For example, while in the service Dexter experiences "relief" (line 603) from emotional turbulence. Students should attempt to link this to biographical source material about Fitzgerald's army years. Have students use their research to inform a journal entry in which they consider how Dexter's service "liberated" him from the "webs of tangled emotion" (line 604) he felt caught up in.

About the Art American artist Georgia O'Keeffe (1887–1986) is best known for her paintings of natural settings, but, like many artists, O'Keeffe was drawn to New York City. This painting merges the fluid lines of natural features such as the clouds and sunlight with the stark lines of man-made structures. O'Keeffe's portrayal of the Shelton (a hotel in New York City) conveys a sense of the authority over nature that modernists applauded, and that Fitzgerald describes as the "gray beauty of steel that withstands all time" (line 683).

SELECTION WRAP–UP

REFLECT Have students decide if Dexter has realized his winter dreams and speculate on why he is not satisfied or pleased by his wealth and power.

⭐ CRITIQUE

- Ask students to evaluate the efficacy of Fitzgerald's central symbol—winter as a time of dreams, growth, and possibility—versus the traditional symbolism of spring.

- After completing the After Reading questions on page 959, have students revisit their responses and tell whether they have changed their opinions.

The Shelton with Sunspots (1926), Georgia O'Keeffe. Oil on canvas, 123.1 cm × 76.8 cm. The Art Institute of Chicago, gift of Leigh B. Block (1985.206) © 2007 The Georgia O'Keeffe Museum/Artists Rights Society (ARS), New York. Photo © 1994 The Art Institute of Chicago, all rights reserved.

the golf-links and the dry sun and the gold color of her neck's soft down. And her mouth damp to his kisses and her eyes plaintive with melancholy and her freshness like new fine linen in the morning. Why, these things were no longer in the world! They had existed and they existed no longer.

680 For the first time in years the tears were streaming down his face. But they were for himself now. He did not care about mouth and eyes and moving hands. He wanted to care, and he could not care. For he had gone away and he could never go back any more. The gates were closed, the sun was gone down, and there was no beauty but the gray beauty of steel that withstands all time. Even the grief he could have borne was left behind in the country of illusion, of youth, of the richness of life, where his winter dreams had flourished.

"Long ago," he said, "long ago, there was something in me, but now that thing is gone. Now that thing is gone, that thing is gone. I cannot cry. I cannot care. That thing will come back no more." ❧

958   UNIT 5: THE HARLEM RENAISSANCE AND MODERNISM

DIFFERENTIATED INSTRUCTION

FOR ADVANCED LEARNERS/AP

Synthesize [small-group option] Refer students to the *NOTABLE QUOTE* on page 936. Then have them discuss these questions:

- Does Dexter fit Fitzgerald's definition of the "new generation of people"? Explain.

- What faiths or gods did the boy Dexter have, and how were these faiths and gods tested and tried as he matured?

- What, if anything, could have saved Dexter's faith and fulfilled his winter dreams?

Invite students to share the results of their discussion with the class.

Comprehension

1. **Recall** How does Dexter's social **status** change in the story, and why?

2. **Clarify** Why doesn't Dexter marry either Judy Jones or Irene Scheerer?

3. **Summarize** What has happened to Judy Jones by the end of the story?

Literary Analysis

4. **Predict Story Development** Review your list of predictions and clues. Were you able to predict everything that happened? Or were you surprised by how some aspects of the story developed? Support your answer with evidence from the story.

5. **Analyze Character Motivation and Traits** What kind of man is Dexter Green? Consider his values and beliefs. Does he deserve sympathy, criticism, or both? Using examples from the text, describe Dexter's traits and the motivations for his actions and feelings.

6. **Examine Symbol** Reread lines 490–494. Consider how Dexter pursues and responds to Judy throughout "Winter Dreams," and think about the young man's feelings regarding **status**. What might Judy **symbolize** in this story? Explain, citing evidence to support your answer.

7. **Analyze Imagery** Fitzgerald is celebrated for his use of imagery, which infuses his fiction with the flush of highly tuned emotions. Locate four or five examples of imagery in "Winter Dreams" that successfully convey the emotional intensity of Dexter and Judy's entanglement. Then explain how each example achieves this purpose.

8. **Interpret Theme** Reread lines 669–688 and consider what exactly Dexter has lost. What theme, or message about the human condition, does Fitzgerald convey through this loss?

Literary Criticism

9. **Critical Interpretations** Critic Marius Bewley has argued that Fitzgerald's main subject is always "the American Dream, in which . . . his principal heroes are all trapped." How well does this statement apply to "Winter Dreams"? Use examples from the story to support your opinion.

WINTER DREAMS **959**

Practice and Apply

After Reading

Use these copy masters to check understanding and provide extra support:

RESOURCE MANAGER—Copy Masters
Reading Check p. 274
Character Motivation and Traits p. 267
Question Support p. 275

Additional selection questions are provided for teachers on page 261.

ANSWERS

1. *He rises from caddy to rich club member because he succeeds in the laundry business.*

2. *Dexter breaks his engagement with Irene to marry Judy; then Judy leaves him.*

3. *She has become the wife of an unfaithful drinking man. She's lost her looks but seems devoted to her children.*

Possible answers:

4. **SKILLS FOCUS Predict Story Development** *Accept all thoughtful answers based on completed lists of predictions and clues.*

5. **SKILLS FOCUS Character Motivation and Traits** *Dexter is an ambitious man and smart in many ways. He knows that he wants wealth and status. He pursues his goals with focus by attending a prestigious college and analyzing market needs. However, he deserves criticism because his obsession with Judy prompts him to behave badly toward Irene and her parents and to isolate himself from friends.*

6. *Judy symbolizes everything Dexter desires—wealth, high social status, effortless affluence—all wrapped up in a beautiful, charismatic package. She has the confidence he lacks. For example, she wears her elegant clothes with ease (lines 287–288), while Dexter has to take special care to dress well (lines 278–286).*

7. *Lines 214–219 use romantic imagery that primes Dexter to respond to Judy's beauty. Lines 256–258 describe Judy's animal grace. Lines 330–337 describe the first transcendent kiss. Lines 466–469 detail the effect of Judy's absence.*

8. *For Dexter, losing Judy's beauty means losing his romantic dream that there is more to life than everyday reality. The loss suggests a theme that we must all accept the limitations of adult life as romantic love settles into the compromises of marriage, and people stop expecting ecstasy. Without alternative ideals, as for Dexter, this transition is especially painful.*

9. *Dexter pursues the American Dream by hiding his humble beginnings and becoming a wealthy man so that he can attain a woman like Judy Jones. Dexter is trapped in this quest at the expense of everything else, including his own human decency.*

ANSWERS

Vocabulary in Context

VOCABULARY PRACTICE

1. *antonyms*	6. *synonyms*
2. *synonyms*	7. *antonyms*
3. *synonyms*	8. *antonyms*
4. *antonyms*	9. *synonyms*
5. *antonyms*	10. *antonyms*

R RESOURCE MANAGER—Copy Master
Vocabulary Practice p. 272

VOCABULARY IN WRITING

Guide students to locate three scenes in which Dexter encounters Judy. Then ask them to identify what Dexter finds most attractive about her in each scene, and to associate this attractive trait with a vocabulary word.

VOCABULARY STRATEGY: WORDS FROM THE JAZZ AGE *(also an EL language objective)*

Have students list unfamiliar words in the sentences; then help them identify Jazz Age terms. Urge students to define unfamiliar context words in a dictionary before using context to build meaning for Jazz Age terms.

Answers:

1. pushover, *"someone easily persuaded to change his or her mind"*

2. jalopy, *"old, beat-up automobile";* hovel, *"small, run-down home"*

3. gate-crashers, *"people trying to attend an event to which they were not invited"*

4. copasetic, *"okay, all right"*

5. gospel truth, *"reliable information";* baloney, *"nonsense"*

R RESOURCE MANAGER—Copy Master
Vocabulary Strategy p. 273

i Vocabulary Center at **ClassZone.com**
Additional Vocabulary Activities

Vocabulary in Context

VOCABULARY PRACTICE

Decide whether the words in each pair are synonyms or antonyms.

1. precipitate/prevent	6. patrimony/inheritance
2. flux/change	7. surfeit/shortage
3. retinue/troupe	8. blatantly/secretly
4. petulance/pleasure	9. camaraderie/friendship
5. mundane/extraordinary	10. precarious/secure

WORD LIST
blatantly
camaraderie
flux
mundane
patrimony
petulance
precarious
precipitate
retinue
surfeit

VOCABULARY IN WRITING

Do you think Dexter would have been as attracted to Judy if he had met her in less opulent surroundings, and if she herself had been less wealthy? Using three or more vocabulary words, write an explanation of your opinion. You might begin like this.

> **EXAMPLE SENTENCE**
> *If Judy had been less well-off, I think her egotism and* **petulance** *would have quickly disillusioned Dexter.*

VOCABULARY STRATEGY: WORDS FROM THE JAZZ AGE

A number of the terms in this story, such as *roadster,* came into English in the early decades of the 20th century. The 1920s and the years just prior to it gave the language a particularly large group of new words and expressions. Many of these phrases, such as *the cat's pajamas* to denote a remarkable person or thing, have diminished in usage. Others, however, are still commonly used. Most started out as slang but over time have gained acceptance as standard everyday English.

 R1.1

PRACTICE Identify the Jazz Age term or terms in each sentence. Use context clues to help understand and explain the meaning of each term. Refer to a dictionary if you need help.

1. Fred is no pushover; he sticks to what he believes in.
2. He drove an old jalopy and lived in a hovel.
3. A uniformed guard was placed at the entrance to head off gate-crashers.
4. Though not totally perfect, everything here is pretty copasetic.
5. She thinks the story is the gospel truth, but I know it is baloney.

VOCABULARY PRACTICE
For more practice, go to the **Vocabulary Center** at **ClassZone.com**.

DIFFERENTIATED INSTRUCTION

FOR ENGLISH LEARNERS

Task Support: Vocabulary Strategy Help students use these strategies for analysis:

- take words apart—*pushover,* "someone who can be pushed over, or moved easily"

- recognize allusions—*gospel truth,* "information as trustworthy as scripture"

- look for humor—*baloney,* "information that is as unreliable as the meats in baloney"

FOR ADVANCED LEARNERS/AP

Vocabulary in Writing Have students use appropriate vocabulary words in a definition of Jazz Age success and status. They should use Fitzgerald's descriptions of wealth and influence as a starting point. Then ask students to contrast their definitions with success and status as defined today.

Reading-Writing Connection

W1.3

WRITING PROMPT

COMPOSE A LETTER OF ADVICE If Dexter were your close friend, what advice would you give to him? In a **three-paragraph letter** (or email) to Dexter, explain what you think he should do to improve the quality of his life. Be sure to recommend something to fill the great void left by the loss of his youthful illusions.

SELF-CHECK

An effective letter will . . .
* identify the problem, using evidence from the story
* offer one or more reasonable solutions and explain how to put them into effect
* argue your points logically and persuasively

GRAMMAR AND STYLE

CRAFT EFFECTIVE SENTENCES Review the **Grammar and Style** note on page 951. Fitzgerald's rich, evocative style in "Winter Dreams" comes in part from long sentences held together by the **coordinating conjunction** *and*. He often breaks up those long descriptions with **dashes** and **phrases** in a series.

LC1.1

> *Early in their acquaintance it had seemed for a while that there was a deep and spontaneous mutual attraction—that first August, for example—three days of long evenings on her dusky veranda, of strange wan kisses through the late afternoon, in shadowy alcoves or behind the protecting trellises of the garden arbors, of mornings when she was fresh as a dream and almost shy at meeting him in the clarity of the rising day. There was all the ecstasy of an engagement about it, sharpened by his realization that there was no engagement.*
> (lines 379–385)

Notice that this description has no action verbs and consists almost entirely of prepositional phrases. In this way, Fitzgerald perfectly expresses Dexter's emotional surrender in both style and content.

PRACTICE Study the following paragraph from the story, noting

* coordinating conjunctions in the first sentence that connect multiple images
* participial phrases that add a sense of motion and emotional significance

Continue these stylistic elements by writing two or three additional sentences.

> *There was a fish jumping and a star shining and the lights around the lake were gleaming. Dexter sat beside Judy Jones and she explained how her boat was driven. Then she was in the water, swimming to the floating surf-board with a sinuous crawl. Watching her was without effort to the eye, watching a branch waving or a seagull flying. Her arms, burned to butternut, moved sinuously among the dull platinum ripples, elbow appearing first, casting the forearm back with a cadence of falling water, then reaching out and down, stabbing a path ahead.* (lines 252–258)

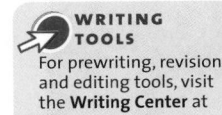
WRITING TOOLS
For prewriting, revision, and editing tools, visit the **Writing Center** at ClassZone.com.

WINTER DREAMS **961**

FOR DEVELOPING WRITERS
Writing Support

* Limit the scope of the letter to one problem and one solution. Guide students to address the problem in one paragraph and the solution in a second paragraph.

* Provide a model letter so that students can review greeting and closing.

* Discuss the informal tone of personal letters, stressing the use of first person and

familiar language suited to addressing someone the writer knows well.

* Provide this starter sentence: Dear Dexter, I've noticed recently that you seem to be unhappy, and I wonder if that's because you _____ .

Reading-Writing Connection

WRITING PROMPT

Suggest that students skim the story and their notes to identify at least two specific problems in Dexter's life. Have students list these on a Problem and Solution Chart. Urge them to work in pairs to brainstorm solutions before choosing the most helpful solutions to recommend in their letters.

 BEST PRACTICES TOOLKIT—Transparency
   Problem and Solution Charts p. B20

For writing support, see

Writing Center at **ClassZone.com**

GRAMMAR AND STYLE

Review with students the function of the coordinating conjunction *and*. Then review the form and function of participial phrases. Help students identify examples of each part of speech in the passage. Urge students to map out the information of their sentences, then craft the language.

Possible answer: Around her slim form, the waves rippled outward and spread towards the shore, diminishing as they flowed. The moonlight's reflection, shattered by the wavelets, shimmered and shook and cast uncertain light on Judy's face.

R RESOURCE MANAGER—Copy Master
   Craft Effective Sentences p. 276

Assess and Reteach

Assess

R RESOURCE MANAGER—Copy Masters
   Selection Test A pp. 277–278
   Selection Test B/C pp. 279–280

Test Generator CD

Reteach

S STANDARDS LESSON FILE
   Literature Lesson 1: Types of Characters and Character Traits
   Literature Lesson 2: Character Motivation
   Literature Lesson 11: Theme, Motif, and Epiphany
   Reading Lesson 1: Predicting
   Writing Lesson 8: Creating Sentence Variety

The Great Gatsby
F. Scott Fitzgerald

ABOUT THE AUTHOR

F. Scott Fitzgerald The desire to pursue his art and make a living often pulled Fitzgerald in different directions during his career. He considered his novels, such as *The Great Gatsby*, his masterpieces but felt that he had to write shorter works—screenplays and stories, articles, and reviews for magazines—to support the lifestyle he and his wife desired.

ABOUT THE NOVEL

The Great Gatsby Most critics consider Dexter Green, the protagonist of "Winter Dreams," a rough draft or prototype of Jay Gatsby. Both characters are young men whose financial success allows them to enter the world of the very wealthy. Both fall in love with beautiful women whose unavailability torments them. Both think—incorrectly—that money will help them secure their beloved. Point out to students that Fitzgerald cut substantial amounts of material from his early draft of *The Great Gatsby*. Among those cuts was a body of material that he reworked into another short story called "Absolution."

LEGACY OF A MASTERPIECE

Introduce the Passage Wolff's praise for *The Great Gatsby* honors Fitzgerald's willingness to record his characters' faults and vices as well as their positive traits. As Fitzgerald suggests in the *NOTABLE QUOTE* on page 936, many Americans had given up all beliefs except that wealth could shelter them from life's difficulties. These Americans pursued their own pleasure as a faith, seeking the best for pleasure's sake. In this excerpt, Nick responds positively to Gatsby because Gatsby seems to convey that something beyond wealth matters. As students read the excerpt, ask them to consider how Gatsby stands out from the crowd at this party.

The Great Gatsby

F. Scott Fitzgerald

F. Scott Fitzgerald
1896–1940

ABOUT THE AUTHOR F. Scott Fitzgerald's writing reflects the dreams and insecurities he experienced in his own life. Growing up comfortably among the country-club set of St. Paul, Minnesota, Fitzgerald was embarrassed by his father's career failures and his mother's immigrant background. At Princeton University, he excelled in writing but left without graduating. He joined the army and fell in love with Zelda Sayre, the pampered daughter of a distinguished judge. At first, Zelda would not marry Fitzgerald because he could not support her. They wed only after he sold his first novel, *This Side of Paradise*, in 1920, and for a time the handsome couple was the toast of New York and Paris. However, by 1930 their glittering lifestyle had burned itself out: Zelda suffered a mental collapse from which she never recovered, and her husband was drinking heavily. Fitzgerald was working in relative obscurity as a Hollywood screenwriter when he died of a heart attack at age 44.

ABOUT THE NOVEL Fitzgerald wrote *The Great Gatsby* in the early 1920s, when he and Zelda were living in Great Neck, Long Island. Fitzgerald modeled the setting of his novel (a neighborhood called West Egg) after his own fashionable New York suburb. The novel's narrator, a Midwesterner named Nick Carraway, moves to West Egg to a home that is next door to a rich, mysterious man who calls himself Jay Gatsby. Gatsby, who acquired his wealth in questionable ways, throws huge parties in the hope that his lost love, Daisy, will be one of the hundreds to attend. Daisy had spurned his attentions when he was young and poor, and she now lives just across the water in the even fancier suburb of East Egg with her rich husband, Tom Buchanan. When Nick helps Gatsby meet Daisy again, tragedy follows.

LEGACY OF A MASTERPIECE From the time it was published in 1925, *The Great Gatsby* was recognized as Fitzgerald's finest achievement. It "has interested and excited me more than any new novel I have seen," said poet T. S. Eliot; decades later, author Tobias Wolff said that Fitzgerald "saw our American world . . . with clearer eyes than any of his contemporaries." In the following excerpt, Nick gets a taste of the extravagant world Gatsby has created for himself.

> "This is an unusual party for me. I haven't even seen the host. I live over there—" I waved my hand at the invisible hedge in the distance, "and this man Gatsby sent over his chauffeur with an invitation."
>
> For a moment he looked at me as if he failed to understand.
>
> "I'm Gatsby," he said suddenly.
>
> "What!" I exclaimed. "Oh, I beg your pardon."

962

"I thought you knew, old sport. I'm afraid I'm not a very good host."

He smiled understandingly—much more than understandingly. It was one of those rare smiles with a quality of eternal reassurance in

10 it, that you may come across four or five times in life. It faced—or seemed to face—the whole external world for an instant, and then concentrated on *you* with an irresistible prejudice in your favor. It understood you just as far as you wanted to be understood, believed in you as you would like to believe in yourself, and assured you that it had precisely the impression of you that, at your best, you hoped to convey. Precisely at that point it vanished—and I was looking at an elegant young roughneck, a year or two over thirty, whose elaborate formality of speech just missed being absurd. Some time before he introduced himself I'd got a strong impression that he was picking his words with care.

20 Almost at the moment when Mr. Gatsby identified himself, a butler hurried toward him with the information that Chicago was calling him on the wire. He excused himself with a small bow that included each of us in turn.

"If you want anything just ask for it, old sport," he urged me. "Excuse me. I will rejoin you later."

When he was gone I turned immediately to Jordan—constrained to assure her of my surprise. I had expected that Mr. Gatsby would be a florid and corpulent person in his middle years.

"Who is he?" I demanded. "Do you know?"

"He's just a man named Gatsby."

30 "Where is he from, I mean? And what does he do?"

"Now *you're* started on the subject," she answered with a wan smile. "Well, he told me once he was an Oxford man."

A dim background started to take shape behind him, but at her next remark it faded away.

"However, I don't believe it."

"Why not?"

"I don't know," she insisted, "I just don't think he went there."

Something in her tone reminded me of the other girl's "I think he killed a man," and had the effect of stimulating my curiosity. I would have accepted without

40 question the information that Gatsby sprang from the swamps of Louisiana or from the lower East Side of New York. That was comprehensible. But young men didn't—at least in my provincial inexperience I believed they didn't—drift coolly out of nowhere and buy a palace on Long Island Sound.

"Anyhow, he gives large parties," said Jordan, changing the subject with an urban distaste for the concrete. "And I like large parties. They're so intimate. At small parties there isn't any privacy."

963

Use these questions to help students understand the narrator's experience at the party:

Summarize In what uncomfortable situation does the narrator find himself? *Possible answer: He is attending a party whose host he has not met.*

Analyze How does the narrator gather information about the party's host, and how does this information affect him? *Possible answer: The narrator gathers information about the host by asking different guests, one of whom turns out to be the host. He is surprised and a little embarrassed by his encounter with the host, but also positively impressed by the man. He is disturbed and confused when he recalls that another guest described the host as a murderer.*

Synthesize On the basis of what you read in **ABOUT THE NOVEL,** what can readers infer about Gatsby and his wealth, knowing that Dexter Green was an earlier and less-developed version of Gatsby? *Possible answer: Readers can infer that Gatsby, like Dexter Green, is a self-made man who has recently come into wealth from humbler beginnings and is proud of what he has accomplished. Readers may also infer that Gatsby, like Dexter, is still not comfortable with his newly exalted position in society. For example, Gatsby picks "his words with care" and is overly careful about social niceties such as bowing.*

FOR ENGLISH LEARNERS

Language: Conversational English Patterns
[mixed-readiness groups] Share or elicit the meanings of these expressions, and then help students find similar expressions in their home languages:

- *I beg your pardon* (line 6), "Excuse me"
- *old sport* (line 7), "good friend"
- *on the wire* (line 21), "by telephone"
- *I mean* (line 30), "What I mean is . . . ."

FOR ADVANCED LEARNERS/AP

Evaluate Title Point out to students that Fitzgerald considered many other titles for his novel other than *The Great Gatsby*. Based upon their reading of the excerpt, challenge students to evaluate Fitzgerald's choice in terms of the expectations that a title like *The Great Gatsby* raises for the central character as well as the irony that it hints at.

Focus and Motivate

OBJECTIVES

Media Literacy

- explore the key idea of the **American dream**
- view and evaluate print advertisements to understand how visual and print techniques are used to convey persuasive messages
- create an ad poster to demonstrate understanding of persuasive techniques

 LS1.14, LS1.10

SUMMARIES

"National Motor Car" This ad uses Jazz Age images of wealth, such as a well-dressed woman and elegant statuary, along with copy that describes high performance and luxury, in order to sell a car.

"Kodak" This ad uses an image of well-dressed people enjoying tennis and copy describing advanced technical abilities in order to sell a camera.

Whose DREAM *are you buying?*

Ask the question, then help students explore the *KEY IDEA* by inviting them to describe advertisements they have seen recently. Have students identify what the ads are selling and discuss how this product, service, or concept offers buyers a piece of the **American dream.**

BACKGROUND

National Motor Car and Vehicle Company was based in Indianapolis, Indiana, once a hub of early auto manufacturing. In 1909, its president, Arthur Newby, joined with other auto manufacturers to found the Indianapolis Motor Speedway as a testing ground for their vehicles. Eastman Kodak Company rose to prominence in the same era, when George Eastman developed a camera that could be used easily by ordinary people. In the early 20th century, Eastman's company continued to improve its camera, offering increasingly convenient features, such as the negative titling stressed in this ad.

Media Study

Advertising in the Jazz Age

Print Advertisements on ⊙ **MediaSmart** DVD

Whose DREAM *are you buying?*

 LS1.14, LS1.10 (p. 967)

KEY IDEA As a struggling writer, F. Scott Fitzgerald worked briefly for an advertising firm and became leery of the industry's emerging practices. In his writing, Fitzgerald expressed his views about materialism and the impact of advertising on the contemporary culture of his day. For him, advertising was part of the glittering surface of the **American dream,** a dream of success, whose cost was often underestimated. In this lesson, you'll study magazine ads of the 1920s to uncover persuasive techniques that took root during the Jazz Age and flourish to this day.

Background

Spending Spree The first years of the 1920s were a time of "more." Because of mass production, such innovations as the automobile and the radio were more available and affordable. Electrical power spread beyond big cities, enabling more Americans to use new, time-saving appliances. As modern-day conveniences took hold and salaries steadily rose, ordinary people reaped the benefits of more leisure time and more money to spend. "Buy now, pay later" installment plans made expensive items appear more obtainable by allowing consumers to pay bills over an extended period of time.

Because merchandise was now flooding the marketplace, a fundamental shift had to occur in how Americans spent money. Before, thriftiness had been the rule. To fuel consumer spending, advertising agencies enlisted the expertise of psychologists to find ways to motivate buyers. The result was advertising designed to appeal to the public's desire for convenience, youth, beauty, and, particularly, wealth and luxury.

With an emphasis on the visual, Jazz Age ads portrayed the lavish lifestyles of the rich. Over time, the print ads in the newspapers, magazines, and billboards contributed to the impression that it was now somehow possible for ordinary Americans to live a lifestyle similar to that of the "beautiful people." Due in part to the persuasive power of such ads, the United States became a nation of shoppers and thus a consumer society.

964

Media Study Resources

* Resources for Differentiation   † Also in Spanish   ‡ In Haitian Creole and Vietnamese

Media Literacy: Persuasion in 1920s Ads

The Jazz Age marks the period when the advertising industry developed. Numerous agencies were established on Madison Avenue in New York City, and ads began to appear in the new medium of mass-circulation magazines. As *Time*, the *New Yorker*, and the *Saturday Evening Post* became popular, the ads within them exposed a nationwide audience to a vast array of products and services.

Advertisers also devised more deliberate ways to persuade. In earlier decades, ads contained straightforward details about product features and prices. Magazine ads of the 1920s shifted away from the product to appeal more directly to the potential buyer. To explore some persuasive techniques commonly used in the 1920s, examine this automobile ad.

STRATEGIES FOR RECOGNIZING PERSUASIVE TECHNIQUES

- Understand the overall message. Behind the 1920s ads was the implication that purchases could bring higher social status and self-fulfillment.

- Look for **purr words,** words with positive connotations. For example, in the National car ad, the words *steady, flow, power, smoothly,* and *swiftly* suggest the car's ease of operation.

- Try to spot the **slogan,** the short phrase that, used in most ads, expresses something about the quality of the product or the company that makes it. Beginning in the 1920s, a slogan helped to make a product's name and purpose memorable to potential buyers.

- Recognize the technique of **transfer,** which refers to an advertiser's attempt to connect a product with someone or something that's pleasing or admired. Ask yourself: What might images of the rich at leisure have conveyed to working-class Americans of the 1920s?

MEDIA STUDY **965**

MEDIA STUDY: TEACHING OPTIONS

Teaching Option 1: The Basics (1–2 Days)
1. Begin the Media Study using the material provided on pages 964–965.
2. Show the Introduction on Media*Smart*. Have students use the Viewing Guide on page 966, along with the corresponding copy master on page 287 of the Resource Manager. Discuss their responses.
3. Return to the pupil book for the extension activities on page 967.

Teaching Option 2: In-Depth Study (2–3 Days)
1. Begin the Media Study using pages 964–965.
2. Show the Introduction from Media*Smart*. Then continue on Media*Smart* with the Media Lessons, using the teacher notes available in the Resources section.
3. Show the Guided Analysis presentation. Have students record their observations on the Student Viewing Guide available in the Resources section from Media*Smart*.
4. Return to the pupil book, page 967.

Teach

Media Literacy
Review with students the purpose of advertising and ask them to recall ads that have been effective in reaching them as consumers. Ask what made these ads effective, and list on the board answers that students generate, such as *message, images, slogans,* and *music.* Add the terms *purr words* and *transfer.* Then discuss the chart on page 965.

- **Overall Message** To help students analyze the overall message in ads, compare viewing an ad to choosing an outfit to wear. Ask students what an outfit can convey about the wearer, such as his or her body type, activity interests, color and fabric preferences, and even personality. Point out that an outfit conveys messages without stating them in words, but rather by associations such as a link between bold colors and bold personalities.

- **Purr Words** Have students think about the word *purr* and what a purr indicates in cats (*happiness*). Purr words are words that evoke pleasant ideas and feelings in viewers and speak to viewers' unspoken desires. Have students replace the purr words in the National ad with other, more neutral synonyms—for example, *quickly* in place of *swiftly*. Discuss how the ad's overall message changes if purr words are replaced.

- **Slogan** Explain that the word slogan once meant "battle cry"; then have students name some famous product slogans. Point out that, like a battle cry, an ad slogan must inspire all who hear it toward decisive action. Ask students what makes a slogan catchy, memorable, and effective.

- **Transfer** Have students name celebrities who endorse products. Ask them whether they are persuaded to buy products endorsed by celebrities, and why. Explain that endorsements create transfer by inviting viewers to link the advertised product or service with someone they admire.

 Media*Smart* DVD

MEDIA STUDY **965**

Practice and Apply

VIEWING GUIDE

1. As students prepare to view the ads, tell them that they will be asked to recognize the persuasive techniques that make each ad effective. Encourage them to look for these techniques:

   - each ad's **overall message** of a glamorous and desirable lifestyle, as presented by the clothing, the colors, the activity of tennis, or other elements of design

   - **purr words** that create positive associations between viewers' desires and a life including sports cars and tennis

   - **slogans,** such as at the bottom of the Kodak ad, that suggest connections between the product and the American dream of wealth and leisure

   - the technique of **transfer,** in which viewers' admiration for the lifestyle they associate with tennis or with well-dressed people is extended to admiration for Kodak cameras or National cars

2. Some students may have difficulty with the incomplete sentences used in both ads. Work through the text with students, adding implied words to clarify. Have students paraphrase the revised text to ensure their comprehension.

R RESOURCE MANAGER—Copy Masters
   Viewing Guide p. 287
   Close Viewing p. 288
   Media Activity p. 289

Use this resource with the Viewing Guide:

MediaSmart DVD

ANSWERS

FIRST VIEWING: Comprehension

1. *National Cars*
2. *The people are playing tennis.*

CLOSE VIEWING: Media Literacy

Possible answers:

3. *Words such as* grand, upscale, luxurious, successful, upper class, *or* refined *could describe these ads.*

4. *The message of the car ad is that this high-performance car is fit for a successful person who deserves and expects the best.*

MediaSmart DVD
- **Selection 1:** National Motor Car and Vehicle
- **Selection 2:** Eastman Kodak Company
- **Genre:** Print advertisements of the 1920s

For the out-of-doors days

KODAK

And not merely the alluring picture story, but on every negative at least a date; and a title, too, if you like. Titling is the work of but an instant with an Autographic Kodak; is as simple as making the picture itself—and there is no extra charge for Autographic film.

If it isn't an Eastman, it isn't a Kodak.

Viewing Guide for
Jazz Age Advertisements

To carefully examine the two advertisements, use the DVD. As you study them, keep in mind the high spirits and optimism of the Roaring Twenties. Use these questions as you examine the image and words of each ad.

NOW VIEW

FIRST VIEWING: Comprehension

1. **Recall** What product is advertised by a woman holding a bright orange parasol?
2. **Clarify** What leisure activity is depicted in the Kodak camera ad?

CLOSE VIEWING: Media Literacy

3. **Interpret Visuals** *Glamorous* and *elegant* are two words that would describe the images in these ads. What other words would you use to describe them?
4. **Analyze the Message** Note that in the National car ad, an expensive sports car is the dominant part of the visual presentation. Explain what message you think the 1920s advertisers specifically wanted to convey to average Americans through this image.
5. **Compare Advertisements** In what ways is the Kodak camera ad shown here similar to the ad for National cars?
6. **Evaluate an Advertisement** Choose the ad that appeals to you more. Evaluate it in terms of the effectiveness of its persuasive techniques. Think about
   - the ad's appeal to status, luxury, and style
   - the design of the visual and the choice and placement of text
   - how favorably you think 1920s Americans might have viewed the ad

966

5. *Both ads depict sophisticated people who have enough wealth to enjoy leisure time. The people are in relaxed postures, enjoying leisure, and the settings are private and estatelike, rather than public. Both ads use copy targeted at people who enjoy life's finer things.*

6. *National Car: Transfer is evident in the sophisticated image, with its placement of the car in the foreground and the elegantly dressed woman in the background. Purr words such as* lean *and* powerful *are used. Kodak: Transfer is evident in the presentation of well-to-do people enjoying leisure. Purr words such as* alluring *are used, and a slogan helps convey brand identity and superiority.*

Write or Discuss

Evaluate the Print Ads F. Scott Fitzgerald once wrote about the advertising profession: "Advertising is a racket.... You cannot be honest without admitting that its constructive contribution to humanity is exactly minus zero." In Fitzgerald's day, the advertising industry was taking root. Today, advertising is an integral part of everyday life. Think about the print ads in this lesson and how similar they might be to ads for similar products today. What persuasive techniques are still effective? Write a short evaluation of each ad. Keep the following points in mind:

LS1.14

- the deliberate appeals you saw that were embedded within the advertisements' visuals and text
- how potential buyers of the 1920s ads compare to today's buyers
- your own views about today's consumer society

Produce Your Own Media

Create a Contemporary Ad Poster Using one of the 1920s ads in this lesson as a model, create an advertisement as a modern-day counterpart. Individually or with a partner, decide on the product, target an audience of working-class buyers for the product, and determine the persuasive techniques you'll apply. Represent the ad in the form of a billboard poster.

LS1.10

HERE'S HOW As you design the ad, consider these suggestions:

- Put as much thought into the ad's visual design as into its wording. You might want to concentrate on designing the image of the ad while a partner focuses on devising the copy.
- Be sure to include appeals to status, wealth, and luxury through both the visual design and the text. Think about the leisure activities of today's wealthy people and what working people might find desirable about them.

MEDIA TOOLS
For help with creating a poster, visit the **Media Center** at **ClassZone.com.**

Tech Tip
If you create the ad on a computer, choose font styles and sizes with care.

Further Exploration

Explore Ads Across the 20th Century On the DVD, access examples of ads that exhibit the persuasive techniques of the 1920s in product advertisements from ensuing decades. What cleverly designed image or turn of phrase turns objects into necessities? What evidence do you see of such techniques as appeals to youth, beauty, wealth, and luxury? Examining these ads can offer insights into the evolving consumer culture of the United States.

MEDIA STUDY **967**

MEDIA STUDY WRAP-UP

Have students summarize what they have learned about the persuasive techniques used to market products to consumers. Encourage students to use terms such as *overall message, purr words, slogan,* and *transfer* in their explanations.

RETEACH

STANDARDS LESSON FILE

Media Lesson 13: Understanding the Basics of Advertising
Media Lesson 15: Analyzing Persuasive Techniques in Advertising
Media Lesson 16: Evaluating Ads

Assess and Reteach

Write or Discuss

Evaluate the Print Ads In their evaluations, students should address persuasive techniques used in the ads: communication of a clear *overall message,* effective use of *purr words,* a memorable *slogan,* and the *transfer* of admiration for the people and scene depicted in the ads to the products advertised. Make sure that students read the copy carefully for purr words designed to please and flatter viewers. For example, the Kodak ad uses the phrase "if you like" to imply that the product will give viewers just what they want and to assure viewers that they are in control. Students should determine whether such appeals would resonate with today's buyers and include their views about today's consumer society, citing evidence to support their responses.

Produce Your Own Media

Rubric: Create Contemporary Ad Posters
A strong contemporary ad poster should

- advertise a clearly identified product
- target a working-class audience
- include design and graphic elements that portray the product positively
- use copy that reinforces the positive associations between product and buyer
- appeal to status, wealth, and luxury in images and text
- use persuasive techniques such as purr words, a catchy slogan, and transfer

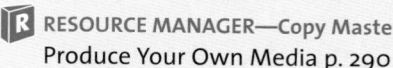
RESOURCE MANAGER—Copy Master
Produce Your Own Media p. 290

Further Exploration

Explore Ads Across the 20th Century Explain that the other ads on the DVD represent an advertising timeline from the Jazz Age to the present. Organize students in pairs and assign each pair one ad to analyze, using their understanding of persuasive techniques. Have student pairs respond to the questions on page 967 and then share their insights with other pairs.

Focus and Motivate

OBJECTIVES

Literary Analysis
- explore the key idea of **trauma**
- analyze style, including tone
- read a short story

Reading
- make inferences

Vocabulary
- build vocabulary for reading and writing
- understand words from Italian *(also an EL language objective)*

Grammar and Writing
- use declarative sentences and plain diction to establish tone
- write a character profile

 R3.3, W1.9, W2.2

ABOUT THE AUTHOR

Hemingway spent a month recovering in an Italian hospital after being wounded in World War I. He observed soldiers either being treated and released or dying from their wounds. War and its aftermath, he thought, provided ample opportunity to observe human nature.

USING THE *NOTABLE QUOTE*

Ask students how Hemingway's quote applies to journalism and to fiction. *Possible answer: In journalism, telling the truth means giving accurate facts about an event. In fiction, it means inventing characters, conflicts, and settings that are true to human nature.*

Selection Resources

In Another Country
Short Story by Ernest Hemingway

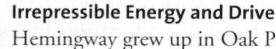 R3.3, W1.9 (p. 977), W2.2 (p. 977)

NOTABLE QUOTE
"A writer's job is to tell the truth."

FYI
Did you know that Ernest Hemingway . . .
- survived two car accidents, two plane crashes, and multiple wounds from two world wars?
- spoke five languages, including some Swahili?
- sold over 5 million copies of *The Old Man and the Sea* in two days?

Author Online
For more on Ernest Hemingway, visit the **Literature Center** at ClassZone.com.

Ernest Hemingway
1899–1961

The embodiment of rugged individualism, Ernest Hemingway's image looms large on the 20th-century American cultural landscape. Whether he was trout fishing in Michigan, skiing in Switzerland, cheering for bullfighters in Spain, big-game hunting in Africa, marlin fishing off the coast of Key West, or drinking wine in a Paris café, the world was his playground. But his world was also a battleground, ripped apart by wars and rife with violence, corruption, and despair. He experienced first hand the major events of his time—the Italian front in World War I, Paris in the 1920s, the Spanish Civil War, and D-day and the Battle of the Bulge during World War II. Behind the legendary persona, however, Hemingway was first and foremost a writer. His experiences provided the raw material for a distinguished body of work that captured the essence of modernity and left his indelible stamp on the century.

Irrepressible Energy and Drive
Hemingway grew up in Oak Park, Illinois, a suburb of Chicago. After high school he got a job as a reporter for the *Kansas City Star,* where he developed both his deceptively simple writing style and a devotion to the truth. During World War I, he volunteered as an ambulance driver for the American Red Cross and was severely wounded. After the war he made his way to Paris as a correspondent for the *Toronto Star.* Paris in the 1920s was a magnet for young artists and writers of the new modernist movement, and the vibrant, sociable Hemingway soon became a star. By the end of the decade, he had made his own contribution by publishing two collections of short stories, *In Our Time* (1925) and *Men Without Women* (1927), as well as two highly acclaimed novels, *The Sun Also Rises* (1926) and *A Farewell to Arms* (1929).

End of an Epic Life Hemingway was living in Cuba when he wrote what many consider his finest novel, *For Whom the Bell Tolls* (1940), based on his reporting of the Spanish Civil War. When World War II broke out, he served as a journalist, often putting himself in dangerous combat situations. His last major work published in his lifetime was the highly popular *The Old Man and the Sea* (1952). In his final years he suffered a variety of ills—including diabetes, liver problems, hypertension, and depression—that led to his suicide at age 62. He left behind five unpublished manuscripts and a towering literary legacy.

For more on Hemingway's days as a war

968

 RESOURCE MANAGER UNIT 5

Plan and Teach pp. 291–298

Literary Analysis
Summary pp. 299†*, 300‡*
Style pp. 301, 302†*
Question Support p. 309*

Reading
Make Inferences pp. 303, 304†*
Reading Check p. 308

Vocabulary
Study p. 305*
Practice p. 306
Strategy p. 307

Grammar and Writing
Establish Tone p. 310

Assessment
Selection Tests A, B/C pp. 311*, 313*
Test Generator CD

BEST PRACTICES TOOLKIT

Differentiated Instruction pp. 31–38*

Scaffolding Instruction pp. 43–46*

Graphic Organizers/Strategies
Definition Mapping • Personal Word List • Character Traits and Textual Evidence

Reading Support
Audio Anthology CD*

Technology
Literature, Vocabulary, and Writing Centers at **ClassZone.com**
Write*Smart* CD

---

 * Resources for Differentiation † Also in Spanish ‡ In Haitian Creole and Vietnamese

● **LITERARY ANALYSIS: STYLE**

The manner in which a writer chooses to tell a story can often be as arresting as the story itself. **Style** is the particular way a piece of literature is written; it is the writer's individual way of communicating ideas. Hemingway began his literary career as a reporter, and his spare, direct prose—even in his works of fiction—reflects those roots. Elements of Hemingway's journalistic prose style include

- short sentences
- few adverbs or adjectives
- an objective tone
- sharp, concrete images

As you read, consider how Hemingway's stylistic choices affect your response to the narrator—a young soldier—and your reactions to the events and people he describes.

■ **READING SKILL: MAKE INFERENCES**

One aspect of Hemingway's lean, journalistic style is that he is not explicit about the effect of important events on his characters. He relates the events and then leaves it up to his readers to **make inferences,** or logical assumptions. As you read, note revealing details about these events. Combine these clues with your own personal knowledge and experiences to infer how the characters are affected by their situation. Revise your inferences as you learn new information.

Details from the Text	How Characters Are Affected
"The people hated us because we were officers."	

▲ **VOCABULARY IN CONTEXT**

Hemingway uses these words to write about soldiers in a wartime hospital. Choose the word that you associate with each type of patient.

WORD LIST citation   detached   lurch   resign

1. a patient who remains aloof and uninterested
2. a decorated soldier
3. one who stoically tries to make the best of his situation
4. a soldier who has trouble walking due to injury

What are the COSTS *of war?*

KEY IDEA Some costs of war can be counted. World War I, the setting of Hemingway's story, claimed the lives of about 9 million soldiers and 13 million civilians. But what about the millions who survived the **trauma** of the bloodiest and most destructive war in history up to that time? What price did they pay?

DISCUSS Consider all the things that make a war and have to be paid for, in one way or another, by both soldiers and civilians. With a small group, list both the tangible and the intangible costs of war. Then get together with another group to compare and discuss your lists. In your opinion, which cost of war is the hardest to bear?

969

What are the COSTS *of war?*

Lead into the **KEY IDEA** by asking the question. Then define **trauma** as "an experience causing severe and long-lasting emotional distress" and ask what kinds of trauma people might suffer during war. Have students share their answers to begin the *DISCUSS* activity. Poll all groups for the cost of war deemed the hardest to bear.

SKILLS FOCUS

LITERARY ANALYSIS   R3.3

● **STYLE**

Ask students to describe the styles of the following statements:

1. It poured the weekend we camped.
2. The entire weekend was utterly ruined by a clammy, driving rain that gave no quarter to the bedraggled campers.

Possible answers: The first statement is short and objectively accurate. The second statement provides the same facts, but conveys an aggravated tone by describing the rain and the campers' reactions.

CHECK UNDERSTANDING Ask students to state the same information in a style that conveys a pleased tone.

READING SKILL

■ **MAKE INFERENCES**

Explain that students must complete an intermediate step to generate information for their charts. They must ask, "What similar situation have I been in or read about?" Have students answer this question about the quoted text on page 969. *Students may mention experiences when being in a position of authority drew resentment from others.* Point out that their answers will lead to inferences to list on the chart.

 RESOURCE MANAGER—**Copy Master**
    Make Inferences p. 303 (for student
        use while reading the selection)

▲ **VOCABULARY IN CONTEXT**

DIAGNOSE WORD KNOWLEDGE To determine preteaching needs, have all students complete Vocabulary in Context. *Answers:*
1. *detached,* **2.** *citation,* **3.** *resign,* **4.** *lurch*

PRETEACH VOCABULARY Preteach vocabulary with this copy master. Read each item aloud.

R RESOURCE MANAGER—**Copy Master**
    Vocabulary Study p. 305

MORE VOCABULARY SUPPORT
For additional activities and guidelines, see

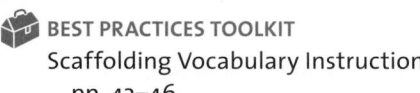 **BEST PRACTICES TOOLKIT**
    Scaffolding Vocabulary Instruction
        pp. 43–46
ⓘ Vocabulary Center at **ClassZone.com**

SUMMARY

In this short story, a young wounded American soldier tells of his treatment for a war wound in an Italian hospital. He recounts his interaction with an Italian major, who is struggling to recover from his wound and who teaches the narrator Italian grammar. When the major's wife dies unexpectedly, his grief adds to the hopelessness the narrator feels.

LITERARY ANALYSIS

▲ STYLE

Possible answer: Hemingway's short, terse clauses (line 5), vividly created images of "snow powdered in the fur of the foxes" (line 4), and objective, unsentimental tone all contribute to the paragraph's journalistic feel.

Lines 19–27
REINFORCE *KEY IDEA:* TRAUMA

Discuss What is the narrator's doctor's opinion of the **trauma** the narrator has suffered because of the war? *Possible answer: The doctor thinks the narrator should experience very little trauma because he will recover fully (lines 26–27).*

In ANOTHER Country
Ernest Hemingway

> **BACKGROUND** World War I was called the Great War and the War to End All Wars. It was the first large-scale modern war with the killing power of new technological weapons. Among the 21 million wounded was 18-year-old Ernest Hemingway, who later wrote this story about soldiers recuperating in Milan, Italy. "In the first war I was hurt very badly," he explained, "in the body, mind, and spirit, and also morally."

In the fall the war was always there, but we did not go to it any more. It was cold in the fall in Milan[1] and the dark came very early. Then the electric lights came on, and it was pleasant along the streets looking in the windows. There was much game hanging outside the shops, and the snow powdered in the fur of the foxes and the wind blew their tails. The deer hung stiff and heavy and empty, and small birds blew in the wind and the wind turned their feathers. It was a cold fall and the wind came down from the mountains. ▲

We were all at the hospital every afternoon, and there were different ways of walking across the town through the dusk to the hospital. Two of the ways were
10 alongside canals, but they were long. Always, though, you crossed a bridge across a canal to enter the hospital. There was a choice of three bridges. On one of them a woman sold roasted chestnuts. It was warm, standing in front of her charcoal fire, and the chestnuts were warm afterward in your pocket. The hospital was very old and very beautiful, and you entered through a gate and walked across a courtyard and out a gate on the other side. There were usually funerals starting from the courtyard. Beyond the old hospital were the new brick pavilions, and there we met every afternoon and were all very polite and interested in what was the matter, and sat in the machines that were to make so much difference.

The doctor came up to the machine where I was sitting and said: "What did
20 you like best to do before the war? Did you practise a sport?"

I said: "Yes, football."

"Good," he said. "You will be able to play football again better than ever."

My knee did not bend and the leg dropped straight from the knee to the ankle without a calf, and the machine was to bend the knee and make it move as in riding a tricycle. But it did not bend yet, and instead the machine **lurched** when it came to the bending part. The doctor said: "That will all pass. You are a fortunate young man. You will play football again like a champion."

In the next machine was a major who had a little hand like a baby's. He winked at me when the doctor examined his hand, which was between two leather straps
30 that bounced up and down and flapped the stiff fingers, and said: "And will I too

---

1. **Milan:** a city in northern Italy.

▲ STYLE
Reread lines 1–7. What style elements give this story's opening paragraph a journalistic feel? Explain, citing specific examples.

ANALYZE VISUALS
The photo on page 971 shows a young Ernest Hemingway at a Red Cross hospital in Milan in 1918. How does this photo, depicting real people in a real place, affect the way you read this work of fiction? Explain.

❶ Targeted Passage

lurch (lûrch) *v.* to lean or roll suddenly to one side; stagger

---

DIFFERENTIATED INSTRUCTION

FOR ALL STUDENTS

Provide these independent projects to extend the lesson:

- Create and present a war medal.
- Write an essay analyzing the major's body language.
- Discuss America's global military role.

For further details on these projects, see

R RESOURCE MANAGER
Ideas for Extension pp. 296–297

FOR STRATEGIC READERS

In combination with the *Audio Anthology CD*, use one or more Targeted Passages (pp. 970, 973, 974) to ensure that students focus on key story events and concepts. Targeted passages are also good for English learners.

❶ Targeted Passage [Lines 16–27]

This passage identifies the reason for the narrator's time at the hospital and describes his treatment.

BACKGROUND

Doughboys By 1918 Italian forces were exhausted from years of war, but they had a new ally to help them hold the front line: the Doughboys. Officially called the American Expeditionary Forces, these American soldiers began arriving in July 1918 at the request of Italy's government. They had two missions: to create fear in the enemy and to boost the morale of Italian soldiers who had been in the trenches for years. Before the AEF arrived, American pilots dropped leaflets over the line promising the Italian soldiers that the Dough-boys would arrive soon. Not only military units but medical and supply units reinforced the Italian front at this critical time. This is the force in which the young narrator of the story served.

B MAKE INFERENCES

Possible answer: The men's disillusionment can be inferred from their reactions. Even though the doctor displays a photograph of a hand improved by the machine, the major has no confidence that it will help him. The photograph does not show a convincing change in the injured hand.

If students need help . . . Urge them to reread lines 30–31 and 34–35 for clues to the major's views of the machine.

Lines 42–57
TIERED DISCUSSION PROMPTS

Use these prompts to help students understand how the war has interrupted the soldiers' lives:

Connect Have you ever had to delay plans for your future for an important reason? Explain. *Accept all thoughtful responses.*

Interpret What in the lives of the soldiers has the war postponed? How is the soldiers' ability to plan for the future affected? *Possible answer: The soldiers have had to postpone their careers to serve in the war. They cannot plan for the future because they have no idea how long the delay will be (lines 55–56).*

Synthesize On the basis of your reading in the historical essay (page 825) and the story, how might the soldiers' situation contribute to the loss of idealism common after World War I? *Possible answer: The new and serious injuries of World War I forced many soldiers to postpone life dreams and pursuits. Being in a state of limbo, without the ability to plan for and dream about the future, could lead to a loss of idealism, common after World War I.*

---

play football, captain-doctor?" He had been a very great fencer,[2] and before the war the greatest fencer in Italy.

The doctor went to his office in a back room and brought a photograph which showed a hand that had been withered almost as small as the major's, before it had taken a machine course, and after was a little larger. The major held the photograph with his good hand and looked at it very carefully. "A wound?" he asked.

"An industrial accident," the doctor said.

"Very interesting, very interesting," the major said, and handed it back to the doctor.

40   "You have confidence?"

"No," said the major. **B**

There were three boys who came each day who were about the same age I was. They were all three from Milan, and one of them was to be a lawyer, and one was to be a painter, and one had intended to be a soldier, and after we were finished with the machines, sometimes we walked back together to the Café Cova, which was next door to the Scala.[3] We walked the short way through the communist quarter because we were four together. The people hated us because we were officers, and from a wine-shop some one would call out, "A basso gli ufficiali!"[4] as we passed. Another boy who walked with us sometimes and made us five wore
50   a black silk handkerchief across his face because he had no nose then and his face was to be rebuilt. He had gone out to the front from the military academy and been wounded within an hour after he had gone into the front line for the first time. They rebuilt his face, but he came from a very old family and they could never get the nose exactly right. He went to South America and worked in a bank. But this was a long time ago, and then we did not any of us know how it was going to be afterward. We only knew then that there was always the war, but that we were not going to it any more.

We all had the same medals, except the boy with the black silk bandage across his face, and he had not been at the front long enough to get any medals. The tall
60   boy with a very pale face who was to be a lawyer had been a lieutenant of Arditi[5] and had three medals of the sort we each had only one of. He had lived a very long time with death and was a little **detached.** We were all a little detached, and there was nothing that held us together except that we met every afternoon at the hospital. Although, as we walked to the Cova through the tough part of town, walking in the dark, with light and singing coming out of the wine-shops, and sometimes having to walk into the street when the men and women would crowd together on the sidewalk so that we would have had to jostle them to get by, we felt held together by there being something that had happened that they, the people who disliked us, did not understand.

70   We ourselves all understood the Cova, where it was rich and warm and not too brightly lighted, and noisy and smoky at certain hours, and there were always girls

---

2. **fencer:** one who fences—that is, practices the art of attack and defense using blunted swords or sabers.

3. **the Scala:** La Scala, a famous opera house in Milan.

4. **"A basso gli ufficiali!"** (ä bä′sō lē ōō′fē-chä′lē) *Italian:* "Down with officers!"

5. **Arditi:** a carefully chosen group of volunteers who specialized in dangerous campaigns.

B MAKE INFERENCES

In lines 16–41, Hemingway doesn't directly state how the soldiers feel about the machines. What can you infer about their emotions from their statements and reactions? Explain, citing evidence.

detached (dǐ-tăcht′) *adj.* reserved; aloof **detach** *v.*

DIFFERENTIATED INSTRUCTION

FOR ENGLISH LEARNERS

Key Academic Vocabulary Use Definition Mapping to teach these words: *military* (line 51), *academy* (line 51), *uniform* (line 151).

 BEST PRACTICES TOOLKIT—Transparency Definition Mapping p. E6

FOR ADVANCED LEARNERS/AP

Analyze Repetition [paired option] Ask students to read lines 56–57 and identify where else in the story they have read this text (*line 1*). Have them analyze Hemingway's repetition and decide why he repeats this text. Ask partners to consider first what the soldiers mean and whether they are accurately describing the situation. Invite students to develop a cause-and-effect statement about how the tone of these repeated lines affects the story's theme.

at the tables and the illustrated papers on a rack on the wall. The girls at the Cova were very patriotic, and I found that the most patriotic people in Italy were the café girls—and I believe they are still patriotic.

The boys at first were very polite about my medals and asked me what I had done to get them. I showed them the papers, which were written in very beautiful language and full of *fratellanza* and *abnegazione*,[6] but which really said, with the adjectives removed, that I had been given the medals because I was an American. After that their manner changed a little toward me, although I was their friend
80 against outsiders. I was a friend, but I was never really one of them after they had read the **citations,** because it had been different with them and they had done very different things to get their medals. I had been wounded, it was true; but we all knew that being wounded, after all, was really an accident. I was never ashamed of the ribbons, though, and sometimes, after the cocktail hour, I would imagine myself having done all the things they had done to get their medals; but walking home at night through the empty streets with the cold wind and all the shops closed, trying to keep near the street lights, I knew that I would never have done such things, and I was very much afraid to die, and often lay in bed at night by myself, afraid to die and wondering how I would be when I went back to the front again. **C**

90 The three with the medals were like hunting-hawks; and I was not a hawk, although I might seem a hawk to those who had never hunted; they, the three, knew better and so we drifted apart. But I stayed good friends with the boy who had been wounded his first day at the front, because he would never know now how he would have turned out; so he could never be accepted either, and I liked him because I thought perhaps he would not have turned out to be a hawk either. **D**

The major, who had been the great fencer, did not believe in bravery, and spent much time while we sat in the machines correcting my grammar. He had complimented me on how I spoke Italian, and we talked together very easily. One day I had said that Italian seemed such an easy language to me that I could not
100 take a great interest in it; everything was so easy to say. "Ah, yes," the major said. "Why, then, do you not take up the use of grammar?" So we took up the use of grammar, and soon Italian was such a difficult language that I was afraid to talk to him until I had the grammar straight in my mind.

The major came very regularly to the hospital. I do not think he ever missed a day, although I am sure he did not believe in the machines. There was a time when none of us believed in the machines, and one day the major said it was all nonsense. The machines were new then and it was we who were to prove them. It was an idiotic idea, he said, "a theory, like another." I had not learned my grammar, and he said I was a stupid impossible disgrace, and he was a fool to have
110 bothered with me. He was a small man and he sat straight up in his chair with his right hand thrust into the machine and looked straight ahead at the wall while the straps thumped up and down with his fingers in them.

"What will you do when the war is over if it is over?" he asked me. "Speak grammatically!"

---

6. **fratellanza** and **abnegazione** (frä′tĕ-län′zä; äb-nĕ-gä-zē-o′nĕ) *Italian:* brotherhood and self-denial.

② Targeted Passage

citation (sī-tā′shən) *n.* a formal statement praising a soldier's achievements

C MAKE INFERENCES
Consider how the narrator describes his relationship with his fellow soldiers. How might such interactions affect him?

D MAKE INFERENCES
Reread lines 90–95. How does the **metaphor** about hawks further describe the difference between the narrator and the young Italian soldiers? What sense do you get of how the narrator feels about this difference?

Lines 87–89
REINFORCE *KEY IDEA*: TRAUMA

Discuss In what ways do the narrator's fears reflect the **trauma** he has experienced at the front? *Possible answer: He is afraid that he will die, though he is in no danger. This suggests that his experience at the front was profoundly frightening.*

READING SKILL

C MAKE INFERENCES

Possible answer: The narrator describes his relationship to the other soldiers by noting that they have been brave in combat, while he has not. Already in another country and shunned by its citizens (lines 47–49), he now also feels separated from his peers.

If students need help . . . Urge them to add to the chart begun on page 969.

READING SKILL

D MAKE INFERENCES

Possible answer: The metaphor heightens the difference between the narrator and the soldiers. They have a hawk's courage, instincts, or love of fighting, but he does not. Those who have not seen battle first-hand may not realize this, but the soldiers do, and this drives a wedge between the narrator and his peers. Despite his matter-of-fact description, the narrator's sense of isolation and alienation is clear.

If students need help . . . Review that metaphors compare unlike things and explain the comparison in lines 90–92.

FOR STRATEGIC READERS

② Targeted Passage [Lines 75–89]

This passage explains why the narrator has received a citation and why his feelings about it are mixed.

• How did the Italian soldiers earn their medals?

• How did the narrator earn his medal?

• What does he think about having been wounded?

• How does he feel about returning to the front?

FOR ENGLISH LEARNERS

Vocabulary: Multiple-Meaning Words Point out the word *papers* in lines 72 and 76, and explain that it refers to a different type of paper in each case. In line 72, *papers* refers to newspapers with pictures and news. In line 76, the word refers to the certificate honoring the narrator's service. Have students add these uses of the word *paper* to their Personal Word Lists.

 BEST PRACTICES TOOLKIT
Personal Word List p. E2

FOR ADVANCED LEARNERS/AP

Analyze Character Motivation [small-group option] Have students discuss this question as they make inferences about the major's character: Why, if the major does not "believe in the machines" (line 105), does he never miss a day at the hospital? Students should support their inferences with textual evidence and prior knowledge as they discuss the major's motivations.

Lines 116–139
TIERED DISCUSSION PROMPTS

Use these prompts to help students understand the major's impact on the narrator's war experience:

Summarize Describe the relationship between the major and the narrator. **Possible answer:** *The narrator admires the major (lines 96–98). The major teaches the narrator Italian grammar (lines 101–103).*

Analyze Why is it so important to the major to convince the narrator not to marry? **Possible answer:** *The major feels intensely sad. He thinks he would sacrifice marriage to escape the grief he feels now. Also, he wants to have control over something, as he had no control over his wife's death or his grief.*

Evaluate How effectively does Hemingway use the major's actions to communicate intense emotions? Explain. **Possible answer:** *Hemingway communicates the major's emotions very effectively through physical actions, such as the major jerking his hand out of the machine, hitting his thigh with it, and leaving the room to end the treatment session (lines 128–132).*

LITERARY ANALYSIS

E STYLE

Possible answer: *The harsh juxtaposition of the major's disciplined military bearing with his unstoppable tears is a vivid image that highlights the major's intense emotions.*

F GRAMMAR AND STYLE

Establish Tone Review that declarative sentences express a statement and that tone expresses the writer's attitude toward his topic. Plain diction uses short and mostly simple words. Have students describe how plain diction reinforces Hemingway's tone. **Possible answer:** *Hemingway's plain diction counterbalances the drama of the scene.*

SELECTION WRAP–UP

REFLECT Have students think about the major's role in the narrator's life. What does the narrator learn from him?

974 UNIT 5

"I will go to the States."

"Are you married?"

"No, but I hope to be."

"The more of a fool you are," he said. He seemed very angry. "A man must not marry."

120 "Why, Signor Maggiore?"[7]

"Don't call me 'Signor Maggiore.'"

"Why must not a man marry?"

"He cannot marry. He cannot marry," he said angrily. "If he is to lose everything, he should not place himself in a position to lose that. He should not place himself in a position to lose. He should find things he cannot lose."

He spoke very angrily and bitterly, and looked straight ahead while he talked.

"But why should he necessarily lose it?"

"He'll lose it," the major said. He was looking at the wall. Then he looked down at the machine and jerked his little hand out from between the straps and 130 slapped it hard against his thigh. "He'll lose it," he almost shouted. "Don't argue with me!" Then he called to the attendant who ran the machines. "Come and turn this thing off."

He went back into the other room for the light treatment and the massage. Then I heard him ask the doctor if he might use his telephone and he shut the door. When he came back into the room, I was sitting in another machine. He was wearing his cape and had his cap on, and he came directly toward my machine and put his arm on my shoulder.

"I am so sorry," he said, and patted me on the shoulder with his good hand. "I would not be rude. My wife has just died. You must forgive me."

140 "Oh—" I said, feeling sick for him. "I am *so* sorry."

He stood there biting his lower lip. "It is very difficult," he said. "I cannot **resign** myself."

He looked straight past me and out through the window. Then he began to cry. "I am utterly unable to resign myself," he said and choked. And then crying, his head up looking at nothing, carrying himself straight and soldierly, with tears on both his cheeks and biting his lips, he walked past the machines and out the door. **E**

The doctor told me that the major's wife, who was very young and whom he had not married until he was definitely invalided[8] out of the war, had died of pneumonia. She had been sick only a few days. No one expected her to die. The 150 major did not come to the hospital for three days. Then he came at the usual hour, wearing a black band on the sleeve of his uniform. When he came back, there were large framed photographs around the wall, of all sorts of wounds before and after they had been cured by the machines. In front of the machine the major used were three photographs of hands like his that were completely restored. I do not know where the doctor got them. I always understood we were the first to use the machines. The photographs did not make much difference to the major because he only looked out of the window. **F**

---

7. **Signor Maggiore** (sēn-yôr′ mäd-jō′rĕ) *Italian:* Mr. Major—a respectful way of addressing an officer.
8. **invalided:** removed from active service because of sickness or injury.

974 UNIT 5: THE HARLEM RENAISSANCE AND MODERNISM

---

resign (rĭ-zīn′) *v.* to submit or yield without complaint

E STYLE
Which **image** in lines 104–146 gives you the most vivid mental picture of the major? Explain why you found this image so evocative.

3 Targeted Passage

F GRAMMAR AND STYLE
Reread lines 149–157. Note that though Hemingway describes a highly emotional situation, his short, **declarative sentences** and **plain diction** keep his **tone** detached and objective.

DIFFERENTIATED INSTRUCTION

FOR STRATEGIC READERS

3 Targeted Passage [Lines 138–151]

This passage explains the major's behavior and shows the narrator's enduring sadness.

- What event provokes the major's angry words about marriage? How did it happen?
- How does the major view his outburst?
- Why does the doctor display pictures of cured hands?
- How does the narrator feel about the major's situation?

FOR ADVANCED LEARNERS/AP

Analyze Symbols Have students explore the symbolic value of machines in the story:

- What might machines symbolize?
- How does the narrator react to learning that others have used the machines before?
- How do the machines reflect modernist concerns?

Invite students to share their answers with the class.

Comprehension

1. **Recall** Why is the narrator in Milan?

2. **Recall** What did the major do before the war?

3. **Summarize** How is the narrator different from the other young soldiers?

Literary Analysis

4. **Make Inferences** Review the inferences you made as you read. The narrator of this story is literally "in another country"—he is far from home, in a foreign, war-torn nation. What other aspects of his situation serve to further isolate or alienate him? Describe the text clues and prior knowledge that allowed you to infer how the narrator's situation affects him. Be sure to address each of the following:

   • how the narrator differs from the young Italian officers
   • the Italian civilians' response to the soldiers
   • how the narrator's circumstances differ from the major's at the story's end

5. **Analyze Character** Review the story for details about what the major has lost, including information regarding what he does and does not believe in. What can you conclude is the damage wrought by the **trauma** of war?

6. **Analyze Style** Hemingway explained that he chose to focus on "what really happened in action; what the actual things were that produced the emotion you experienced." Reexamine the text, recording examples of each stylistic element listed on page 969. Then explain how Hemingway's style causes this story to be so emotionally charged despite the lack of direct commentary on the characters' emotions.

Stylistic Element	Examples
short sentences	

Literary Criticism

7. **Historical Context** Influential author and patron Gertrude Stein formed a community with Fitzgerald, Hemingway, and other modernist writers living as expatriates in Paris in the 1920s. Their particular disillusionment prompted her to characterize them as a "lost generation." In what way do the characters in both "Winter Dreams" on page 938 and "In Another Country" remain "lost" at the end of each story? What might this say about the era in which these stories were written? Explain, citing evidence from both stories.

They have aged out of youthful optimism before their time. The brutality of war isolates Hemingway's characters and makes them cynical. Dexter and possibly Judy lose the dream of ideal love. Dexter, especially, is alone in the end, like the major staring out the window, detached from the other soldiers by his traumatic loss. The stories chronicle the loss of optimism experienced by many in the years after World War I.

Practice and Apply

After Reading

Use these copy masters to check understanding and provide extra support:

R RESOURCE MANAGER—Copy Masters
Reading Check p. 308
Style p. 301
Question Support p. 309

Additional selection questions are provided for teachers on page 295.

ANSWERS

1. *The narrator is in Milan to receive physical therapy at the hospital.*

2. *He was an accomplished fencer.*

3. *He is an American. He did not receive his medal for a specific act of heroism.*

Possible answers:

4. ■ **SKILLS FOCUS Make Inferences** *In addition to his physical isolation, several factors further isolate the narrator. He received his medal for being American (lines 78–82), not brave like the Italian soldiers. He is not a "hawk" as he sees them (lines 90–92). The Italian civilians, who lack experience of war, "disliked" and "did not understand" the officers (line 69). The narrator cannot connect to the major's loss and thus loses his one friend and becomes even more alone.*

5. *The major loses his profession (lines 31–32). He loses his wife and his belief in marriage (line 123). The major loses his beliefs, deciding that bravery, unlike grammar, has no practical use, and that the machines won't work. Trauma has physically and emotionally crippled this once-strong man.*

6. ● **SKILLS FOCUS Style** *Stylistic Element: short sentences; objective tone; real-world modifiers; sharp, concrete images. Examples: "My wife has just died" (line 139); "No one . . . to die" (line 149); the café is "smoky" and "noisy" (line 71); "the wind . . . mountains" (line 7). His style is pared, forcing readers to dig for emotional clues. The contrast between the spare prose and the major's final wellspring of emotion is notable.*

7. *The soldiers in Hemingway's story, like Dexter at the end of "Winter Dreams," have lost their youthful illusions and remain detached, empty, and lonely as a result.*

ANSWERS
Vocabulary in Context

VOCABULARY PRACTICE

1. *citation* 3. *lurch*
2. *detached* 4. *resign*

 RESOURCE MANAGER—Copy Master
Vocabulary Practice p. 306

VOCABULARY IN WRITING

Guide partners to review the soldiers' situation before they begin writing. Have students identify attitudes and feelings that might lend themselves to a vocabulary word. Stress that people in such situations often experience many conflicting feelings.

VOCABULARY STRATEGY: WORDS FROM ITALIAN *(also an EL language objective)*

• Assist students with the pronunciation of the Italian words, especially those that are not pronounced as they appear.

• Guide students to identify cognates when possible: *rotunda*, for instance, is related to *rotund*, or *round*.

Answers:

1. *d* 5. *b*
2. *f* 6. *c*
3. *h* 7. *a*
4. *e* 8. *g*

RESOURCE MANAGER—Copy Master
Vocabulary Strategy p. 307

ⓘ Vocabulary Center at **ClassZone.com**
Additional Vocabulary Activities

Vocabulary in Context

VOCABULARY PRACTICE

Choose the word from the word list that best completes each sentence.

1. Though only a few soldiers had received a(n) _____ for bravery, many of the others had also performed commendably.
2. Some of the soldiers sought companionship, while others remained aloof and _____.
3. It was painful to see young men _____ around on unsteady legs.
4. Was it better to struggle or to _____ oneself to one's fate?

WORD LIST
citation
detached
lurch
resign

VOCABULARY IN WRITING

Imagine yourself in the place of one of the soldiers in this story. What kind of attitude might you take toward your situation? Use one or two vocabulary words in a short description of your feelings. You might start like this.

> **EXAMPLE SENTENCE**
>
> As a wounded soldier, I think remaining **detached** from others is the best way to keep my feelings under control.

VOCABULARY STRATEGY: WORDS FROM ITALIAN

As the narrator of this story would surely have noticed in his study of Italian, there are many English words derived from that language, especially in the areas of music, food, and architecture. Some Italian words have kept their original spelling, while others have changed somewhat. Many of these words trace their ultimate origins back to Latin.

PRACTICE Match each boldfaced term with its definition, consulting a dictionary if necessary. Then research the origin of each word to see which ones retain their Italian spelling.

1. **farfalle**   a. a circular part of a building, usually with a dome
2. **alfresco**   b. a slow movement in a piece of music
3. **vendetta**   c. a cave or cavern
4. **parapet**   d. butterfly-shaped pasta
5. **adagio**   e. a low wall at the edge of a balcony or roof
6. **grotto**   f. taking place in the open air
7. **rotunda**   g. potato dumplings
8. **gnocchi**   h. a bitter blood feud

VOCABULARY PRACTICE
For more practice, go to the **Vocabulary Center** at **ClassZone.com**.

DIFFERENTIATED INSTRUCTION

FOR ENGLISH LEARNERS

Task Support: Vocabulary Strategy Encourage students who speak Latin-based languages to search in their home language for words similar to those from Italian. Have students define the words for classmates and then compare the similarities in the various languages discussed.

FOR ADVANCED LEARNERS/AP

Words from Italian After students complete the exercise, refer them to the angry words that Italian citizens yell at the soldiers: *"A basso gli ufficiali!"* (line 48). Challenge students to locate and use two cognates in this cry to help them get its gist without the translation in the footnote. *Example:* *"Officers are low,"* which builds on a similarity between *"basso"* and base, *which means "low or bottom" and between "ufficiali" and* officers.

Reading-Writing Connection

 W2.2

WRITING PROMPT

WRITE A CHARACTER PROFILE Most of Hemingway's male protagonists share such strikingly similar traits that critics have named this type of character the "Hemingway hero." Using the examples of the narrator and the major in this story, create a **three-to-five-paragraph profile** of the Hemingway hero.

SELF-CHECK

A well-conceived character profile will . . .

▶
* explain the historical context of the Hemingway hero
* identify at least three of the hero's character traits
* cite examples of the narrator's and the major's behavior as evidence

GRAMMAR AND STYLE

 W1.9

ESTABLISH TONE Review the **Grammar and Style** note on page 974. **Tone** is the expression of a writer's attitude toward a subject. Hemingway's early training as a newspaper reporter heavily influenced the tone of his fiction, giving it the emotional detachment and objectivity of a news report. Such a tone is achieved partly through his use of short, **declarative sentences** and **plain diction,** a style he also picked up from newspapers. Notice the simple language and understated quality of the following sentences:

> *It was cold in the fall in Milan and the dark came very early. Then the electric lights came on, and it was pleasant along the streets looking in the windows. There was much game hanging outside the shops, and the snow powdered in the fur of the foxes and the wind blew their tails. The deer hung stiff and heavy and empty, and small birds blew in the wind and the wind turned their feathers. It was a cold fall and the wind came down from the mountains.* (lines 1–7)

PRACTICE Rewrite the following paragraph, adapting the language and sentence types to mimic Hemingway's objectivity.

> The horrible, fiery inferno had completely annihilated everything, like an angry, vengeful God. Only the charred foundation of the Harlington Hotel remained, with its lone chimney of chipped and blackened stone standing forlornly amid the devastation like a victim of survivor guilt. Never again would we see the thick forest in its green majestic splendor! Ugly black stumps studded the land like tombstones. It was the landscape of damnation! Gone were the songs of birds, the chirps of chipmunks, and the laughter of children! A deafening silence enveloped the area for miles around. Only black grasshoppers flitted about the soot, sending up tiny clouds of ash.

 WRITING TOOLS
For prewriting, revision, and editing tools, visit the **Writing Center** at ClassZone.com.

FOR DEVELOPING WRITERS

Writing Support

* Limit the character profile to two or three paragraphs.
* Refer students to the author biography on page 968 for historical context.
* Provide these sentence starters to help students draft their thesis statements: The Hemingway hero is characterized by three traits. These traits are _____, _____, and _____.

* Remind students to give examples from the story for each character trait they mention.
* Urge students to identify whether examples refer to the narrator or the major.

Reading-Writing Connection

WRITING PROMPT

To help students organize their ideas before writing, suggest that they complete a Character Traits and Textual Evidence chart for the narrator and the major. Have students scan the story for information, recording traits and the words, thoughts, and behaviors that reveal them.

 BEST PRACTICES TOOLKIT—Transparency Character Traits and Textual Evidence p. D6

For writing support, see

ℹ Writing Center at **ClassZone.com**

GRAMMAR AND STYLE

Provide news articles and have students read them aloud as if reporting the news for radio or television. Ask what is missing from such readings. *Possible response: Emotional reactions, opinions, and commentary are missing.* Explain that this is also Hemingway's style, which presents the facts in a straightforward manner. *Students' paragraphs should relate each event and detail from the model paragraph but in a sparse, journalistic style.*

R **RESOURCE MANAGER—Copy Master** Establish Tone p. 310

Assess and Reteach

Assess

R **RESOURCE MANAGER—Copy Masters** Selection Test A pp. 311–312 Selection Test B/C pp. 313–314

⊘ Test Generator CD

Reteach

S **STANDARDS LESSON FILE**
Literature Lesson 1: Types of Characters and Character Traits
Literature Lesson 27: Simile and Metaphor
Literature Lesson 40: Word Choice and Diction
Literature Lesson 43: Tone
Literature Lesson 44: Style and Syntax
Reading Lesson 8: Making Inferences
Writing Lesson 42: Adapting a Tone
Vocabulary Lesson 25: Etymologies

The Grapes of Wrath
John Steinbeck

ABOUT THE AUTHOR

John Steinbeck Journalist and novelist John Steinbeck was concerned throughout his writing career with human suffering. When he accepted the Nobel Prize in Literature in 1962, he spoke of the responsibility of writers to be in sympathy with the human condition and to tell stories both of people's weakness and failure and of people's courage and willingness to struggle towards better individual and community lives. Steinbeck covered social conditions in the United States, Mexico, Russia, and Vietnam during his career.

Chronology of Major Works These are the publication dates of John Steinbeck's most important works:

1929	*Cup of Gold*
1935	*Tortilla Flat*
1936	*In Dubious Battle*
1937	*Of Mice and Men*
1939	*The Grapes of Wrath*
1945	*Cannery Row*
1947	*The Pearl*
1952	*East of Eden*

ABOUT THE NOVEL

The Grapes of Wrath *The Grapes of Wrath* sold almost half a million copies in 1939 and earned Steinbeck the Pulitzer Prize, but it also brought criticism and suspicion. Because of his sympathies with the migrant farmers, Steinbeck was accused of communist beliefs at a time when such accusations could be ruinous. Critics claimed that he exaggerated the bad conditions in the migrant camps. First Lady Eleanor Roosevelt defended Steinbeck and his novel, however, and in time Congress investigated conditions in the migrant camps and changed labor laws to improve them.

American Masterpiece

The Grapes of Wrath
John Steinbeck

John Steinbeck
1902–1968

ABOUT THE AUTHOR John Steinbeck firmly followed the principle "Write about what you know." Much of his fiction is set in California's Salinas Valley, where he grew up, and other areas of California where he spent time. Often it deals with the problems of working men and women, which he knew first-hand from the string of odd jobs he held as a young man—fruit picker, ranch hand, and apprentice painter, to name just a few. Steinbeck published his first novel, *Cup of Gold,* just a few months before the stock market crash ushered in the Great Depression of the 1930s.

Many of his later works focus on the effects those hard times had on average Americans. Among those hit worst were farm families who left the drought-ravaged Dust Bowl for California, only to be packed into shantytowns and paid a pittance as farm laborers. In 1936, Steinbeck traveled from Oklahoma to California with a group of these migrants to report on their plight for the *San Francisco News;* it was this experience that inspired his greatest novel, *The Grapes of Wrath.*

ABOUT THE NOVEL The blockbuster novel of 1939, *The Grapes of Wrath* tells the story of the Joads, a family of Oklahoma migrant farmers, or "Okies," who leave their small farm in an old jalopy to make the long journey to California in search of work. Ma Joad holds the family together as they face untold hardships and disappointments. Despite their difficulties, the family never gives up their basic humanity and spirit of endurance. Interspersed between the chapters of their story are poetic chapters describing the situation in broader terms. The extract here, from one of those chapters, is a description of the temporary camps that the traveling farmers set up each night.

And the worlds were built in the evening. The people, moving in from the highways, made them with their tents and their hearts and their brains.

In the morning the tents came down, the canvas was folded, the tent poles tied along the running board, the beds put in place on the cars, the pots in their places. And as the families moved westward, the technique of building up a home in the evening and tearing it down with the morning light became fixed; so that the folded tent was packed in one place, the cooking pots counted in their box. And as the cars moved westward, each member of the family grew into his proper place, grew into

978

DIFFERENTIATED INSTRUCTION

FOR STRATEGIC READERS

Taking Notes Guide students to use Cornell Notes to help them track main ideas as they read the excerpt. For example, students can turn the topic sentences of paragraphs 2 and 3 into questions. As students read, have them answer the questions.

 BEST PRACTICES TOOLKIT—Transparency
Cornell Notes p. B3

Paragraph 2: What was life in the camps like?	*Camp life was orderly, with each person having a job to do and a sense of community arising quickly among the migrants.*
Paragraph 3: How did their lives change?	

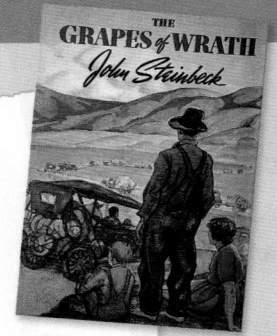

his duties; so that each member, old and young, had his place in the car;
10 so that in the weary, hot evenings, when the cars pulled into the camping
places, each member had his duty and went to it without instruction:
children to gather wood, to carry water; men to pitch the tents and
bring down the beds; women to cook the supper and to watch while the
family fed. And this was done without command. The families, which
had been units of which the boundaries were a house at night, a farm by
day, changed their boundaries. In the long hot light, they were silent in the cars moving
slowly westward; but at night they integrated with any group they found.

Thus they changed their social life—changed as in the whole universe only man
can change. They were not farm men any more, but migrant men. And the thought,
20 the planning, the long staring silence that had gone out to the fields, went now to the
roads, to the distance, to the West. That man whose mind had been bound with acres
lived with narrow concrete miles. And his thought and his worry were not any more
with rainfall, with wind and dust, with the thrust of the crops. Eyes watched the tires,
ears listened to the clattering motors, and minds struggled with oil, with gasoline,
with the thinning rubber between air and road. Then a broken gear was tragedy.
Then water in the evening was the yearning, and food over the fire. Then health to go
on was the need and strength to go on, and spirit to go on. The wills thrust westward
ahead of them, and fears that had once apprehended drought or flood now lingered
with anything that might stop the westward crawling.

30 The camps became fixed—each a short day's journey from the last.

And on the road the panic overcame some of the families, so that they drove night
and day, stopped to sleep in the cars, and drove on to the West, flying from the road,
flying from movement. And these lusted so greatly to be settled that they set their
faces into the West and drove toward it, forcing the clashing engines over the roads.

But most of the families changed and grew quickly into the new life. And when
the sun went down—

Time to look out for a place to stop.

And—there's some tents ahead.

The car pulled off the road and stopped, and because others were there first,
40 certain courtesies were necessary. And the man, the leader of the family, leaned from
the car.

Can we pull up here an' sleep?

Why, sure, be proud to have you.

TIERED DISCUSSION PROMPTS

Use these prompts to help students understand the migrants' experience and how it reflects John Steinbeck's views:

Summarize What great migration is described in this excerpt? ***Possible answer:*** *The excerpt describes a migration of many people from the ruined farms of Oklahoma to California in hope of finding work.*

Analyze Describe the daily travels and the nightly camp. Explain how the contrast of these elements affects the travelers. ***Possible answer:*** *During the day, the travelers face many risks. Cars may break down, tires may go flat, gas may run out, and therefore the ability to reach a new place to live and work is threatened. In contrast, orderly camps are set up at night, everyone knows his or her place, and a comforting regularity replaces the unpredictable hazards of the day. Each family is isolated on the road, but a community quickly forms in camp. Camp offers travelers a much-needed respite.*

Synthesize What details about the Okies does Steinbeck include that reveal his sympathetic feelings for working men and women? ***Possible answer:*** *Steinbeck's sympathy for working men and women is revealed in his admiring tone toward the Okies. He describes how civilly they behaved even under duress. They camped efficiently, every person independently carrying out assigned duties. They adapted quickly to harsh circumstances yet maintained dignity and politeness.*

FOR STRATEGIC READERS

Comprehension Support Work with students to explore the extreme change the drought has brought to the Okies' lives. Help students identify and discuss these contrasts described in paragraph 3:

- setting: contrast of acres and miles
- worries: contrast of crops and cars
- fears: drought or flood and obstacles to westward movement

FOR ENGLISH LEARNERS

Language: Punctuation and Print Cues [mixed-readiness groups] Work with students to review paragraphs 4–11. Point out the repeated use of dashes, explaining that these suggest either pauses or omitted text. Note as well that the final two lines are dialogue, but lack quotation marks. Clarify the dialect by helping students rewrite the sentences in standard English this way:

"Can we stop here to sleep?"

"Yes, we'd be happy to share our place."

FOR ADVANCED LEARNERS/AP

Analyze Allusion *The Grapes of Wrath* takes its title from the poem "The Battle Hymn of the Republic," written by Julia Ward Howe in 1861 after a visit to a Union Army camp. Ask students to locate and read the poem, then to write a paragraph explaining why this title may have appealed to Steinbeck. On the basis of what they know of the novel, have students argue whether Steinbeck's allusion is appropriate.

Focus and Motivate

OBJECTIVES

Reading for Information

- analyze photographs
- compare and evaluate
- read and view a photo essay

 LS1.3

SUMMARY

This photo essay appeared in *Life* magazine and includes a collection of Horace Bristol's photographs of Dust Bowl migrants in 1937–1938, captions by John Steinbeck, and a brief article that describes the migrants' plight. The three pieces combine to lend immediacy and poignancy to the plight of the migrant farmers in California.

Have students use a Three-Column Journal to organize information in the photo essay. Students should list main ideas for the photos, the captions, and the essay in each of the three columns. After reading, have students look for overlapping ideas among the three columns.

 BEST PRACTICES TOOLKIT—Transparency
Three-Column Journal p. B10

Teach

Skill Focus: Analyze Photographs

- Explain that analyzing something means considering separately the parts of a whole and understanding how they function together to make that whole.

- Encourage students to work slowly, responding to each part of a photograph—composition, focal point, vantage point, techniques, mood, and caption—then considering how it contributes to the whole.

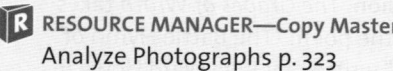 **RESOURCE MANAGER**—Copy Master
Analyze Photographs p. 323

Reading for Information

Photo Essay: The Grapes of Wrath

Before John Steinbeck wrote *The Grapes of Wrath*, he traveled through California's migrant labor camps with *Life* magazine photographer Horace Bristol. The following pictures were taken by Bristol at that time. The captions are Steinbeck's and the accompanying essay appeared along with the photos and captions. As you view "the worlds [that] were built in the evening" and the people who built and inhabited them, bear in mind that you will later be asked to decide which is more compelling, the photo essay or the excerpt from the novel.

Use with *The Grapes of Wrath*, page 978.

 LS1.3

Skill Focus: Analyze Photographs

The photographs on these next few pages can be analyzed and appreciated both as fine art and as a cultural record of how Depression-era migrant workers lived. Asking yourself the following questions as you view each photograph can help you do this:

- What shape or space is emphasized in the **composition?** What is the **focal point,** or spot that draws your attention? What else catches your eye?

- From what **vantage point,** or distance and position, did Bristol take the photograph? What impact does this have on your view of the subject?

- What **techniques** did Bristol use and why? For example, what sort of lighting did he choose, and what effect does it have?

- What is the **mood** created by the image?

- What information do you gather from the image and its **caption?**

For each image, note your observations on a chart like the one begun here.

Photograph #1: Ma Joad?	
Focal Point of Composition	Woman's face; I also notice her hands
Vantage Point and Its Impact	Next to woman at eye level; it makes me feel like I'm having a conversation with her, establishes a feeling of equality and intimacy
Techniques and Their Effects	Sunlight with shadow reveals wrinkles and dirt.
Mood	
Information from Image & Caption	

Selection Resources

 RESOURCE MANAGER UNIT 5

Plan and Teach pp. 315–319

Reading
Summary pp. 321†*, 322‡
Analyze Photographs pp. 323, 325†*
Compare and Evaluate pp. 324, 326†*
Reading Check p. 327
Question Support p. 328*

Assessment
Selection Tests A, B/C pp. 329*, 331*
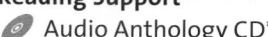 Test Generator CD

Reading Support
Audio Anthology CD*

 BEST PRACTICES TOOLKIT
Three-Column Journal • Analysis Frame: Informational Nonfiction • Personal Word List • Connecting

* Resources for Differentiation   † Also in Spanish   ‡ In Haitian Creole and Vietnamese

"I always kept 'em together and kept 'em fed. I planned for 'em. I can buy this house for ten dollars. I'll have a garden along there. Ducks can swim in the irrigation ditch. I got to get ten dollars."

The GRAPES of WRATH

Photographs by HORACE BRISTOL
Captions by JOHN STEINBECK

A ANALYZE PHOTOGRAPHS
What is emphasized in the photograph's **composition**? What does the **focal point** tell you about the woman? Explain.

In 1934, when the rest of the U.S. began to rise out of Depression, dust began to blow in Oklahoma and Montana, Arkansas and the Dakotas. Thousands of bewildered farmers and farm hands lost their holdings or their jobs and began to drift West. By the time the dust stopped blowing, the banks and the land companies found that mechanized farming over huge areas could make the land pay when individual farmers could not. The drift Westward continued and grew. Lured by assurances of green land and good money, the farmers sold their old tools and older houses, their livestock and furniture for anything they would bring. They used the money to buy shaky old cars, sawing off the bodies to
10 make sedans into flimsy trucks. Along Route 66, through the Texas Panhandle, New Mexico and Arizona, they squeaked and rattled by tens of thousands, a bedraggled leaderless horde, camping beside the creeks and prairie villages, headed for California as a promised land.

Practice and Apply

CALIFORNIA

INFORMATIONAL ANALYSIS

A ANALYZE PHOTOGRAPHS

Possible answer: The photo's composition is angular and draws attention to the lines in the woman's face, echoed by the geometric lines of the door behind her and in her hands. The focal point is the woman's face, which conveys worry that is emphasized by her clasped hands.

If students need help . . . Ask students where their eyes gravitate when they quickly look at this photograph. Clarify that this spot is the focal point.

ANALYZE VISUALS

About the Art Photographer Horace Bristol (1908–1997) started as a freelance photographer in California. Within two decades he was a sought-after documentary photographer whose work appeared in major magazines.

In 1937 Bristol conceived the idea of documenting the migrant camps in California's Central Valley for *Life* magazine. He asked writer John Steinbeck to accompany him to meet the people and write captions for the photographs. Bristol's photographs later supplied Hollywood with a template for sets and costumes for the movie version of *The Grapes of Wrath*.

DIFFERENTIATED INSTRUCTION

FOR STRATEGIC READERS
Vocabulary Support

- *Depression* (line 1), "the long period of slow economic activity or growth that began in the early 1930s"
- *holdings* (line 3), "land and buildings"
- *bring* (line 9), "sell for"
- *sedans* (line 10), "four-door passenger cars"
- *promised land* (line 13), "place where all needs will be met"

Options for Reading Have students listen to the text on the *Audio Anthology CD* as they view the photographs. Pause to allow students to view each photograph in the context of the caption and article text. Guide them in connecting the text with the images. Explain, for example, that the captions reflect Steinbeck's idea of what these people might be thinking at the moment they were photographed.

FOR ENGLISH LEARNERS
Language: Conversational English Patterns
Read the caption aloud, making sure to capture the sound of the dialect. Then explain that *'em* is a shortened version of *them*, and read the first two sentences aloud again, substituting the word *them* for the abbreviation *'em*. Explain that English speakers sometimes drop sounds. Supply other examples, such as *goin'* for *going*.

B ANALYZE PHOTOGRAPHS

Possible answer: The caption, by adding a narrative to the photograph, makes the plight of the couple, with their fiercely clasped hands, more tragic. The woman speaking thinks of her own death and the impact it will have on her husband. The narrative asks viewers to see this couple as suffering people, rather than as a statistic.

If students need help . . . Ask them to infer who speaks the lines by finding clues, such as the reference to the husband as "he."

C ANALYZE PHOTOGRAPHS

Possible answer: The men's attention is focused on the brightly lit papers on the desk, which draws viewers' eyes to them as well. The seated man looks stunned by the content of the papers. These details create a mood of tense anxiety.

If students need help . . . Work with them to complete the prereading chart introduced on page 980.

Photograph #3	
Focal Point of Composition	
Vantage Point and Its Impact	
Techniques and Their Effects	
Mood	anxiety and apprehension
Information from Image and Caption	

B ANALYZE PHOTOGRAPHS
Study the photograph and reread the **caption.** How does the text affect the impact of the photograph? Explain.

C ANALYZE PHOTOGRAPHS
What is the **focal point** of this photograph? What **mood** is established? Explain.

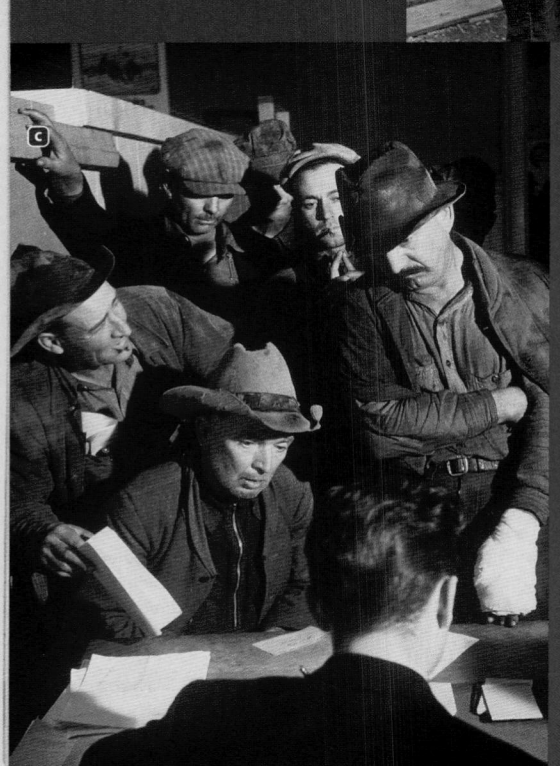

B

"Lettuce crate fell on my head. They give me fourteen dollars compensation. I'm the lucky one. I'm gonna die pretty soon now. I wish he didn't feel so bad about it."

"It's the kids. . . . A man can get hungry and it ain't so bad. A man gets sick when the kids are hungry."

982   UNIT 5: THE HARLEM RENAISSANCE AND MODERNISM

DIFFERENTIATED INSTRUCTION

FOR STRATEGIC READERS

Irony Discuss the caption of the top photo, clarifying the irony of the speaker's words. Ask students why the speaker considers herself "the lucky one" because she is about to die. Have students draw on what they have learned about the migrants' lives to explain the speaker's comment.

FOR ENGLISH LEARNERS

Language: Conversational English Patterns
Read aloud the captions on this page, then point out and clarify words that do not comply with grammatical English patterns:

- *give,* "gave"
- *gonna,* "going to"
- *ain't,* "isn't"

Read the captions again with the correct usage.

FOR ADVANCED LEARNERS/AP

Make Judgments Have students read the caption for the top photograph again. Then ask them to use the Internet to find an equation to convert the injured woman's $14 compensation to a rough equivalent in today's money. Ask students to share this amount with the class and to lead a brief discussion of the justness of this compensation.

In California the migrants found no promised land. Instead, they found that thousands of their own kind had already glutted the market for cheap itinerant labor. Furthermore, scrabbling about the State to look for work, fighting each other for jobs, they learned that California hated them because they were hungry and desperate. Because most of them came from Oklahoma, they were scornfully called "Okies," harried along between scarce jobs. Migrants are still in California,
20 squatting in hideous poverty and squalor on the thin margins of the world's richest land. Of the one-third of a nation which is ill-housed, ill-clad, ill-nourished these are the bitterest dregs.

The problem of the Okies, though grim, is not insoluble. Some hope of a solution is suggested by the fact that an American writer can not only write about the Okies but that the result can be hailed by U.S. critics as the book of the decade. In *The Grapes of Wrath* (The Viking Press, $2.75), John Steinbeck (*Of Mice and Men*) presents the Okies in all their stink and misery, their courage and confusion. His 600-page novel, which may become a 20th Century *Uncle Tom's Cabin,* is now a nationwide best-seller. Last week, Producer Darryl Zanuck paid
30 $75,000 for the right to make it into a movie.

"We just got in. Gonna work in the peas. Got a han'bill that says they's good wages pickin' peas."

D ANALYZE PHOTOGRAPHS
What details of Depression-era migrant worker life are recorded

READING FOR INFORMATION **983**

Lines 14–22
TIERED DISCUSSION PROMPTS
Use these prompts to help students understand why traveling to California did not solve all the migrants' problems:

Connect What is it like to arrive in a new place? Why are people sometimes rejected because of where they came from? *Accept all thoughtful responses.*

Analyze Why isn't California the "promised land" that migrants had hoped for? *Possible answer: So many migrants came that not enough work could be found for them all (lines 15–16). They had to keep moving, looking for jobs (lines 16–17). They began to see each other as competitors, and they were discriminated against by Californians (lines 18–19).*

Evaluate Is the contrast between the migrants' living conditions and the rich land of California (lines 20–21) effective? Explain. *Possible answer: This contrast is very effective, because it points out the irony and injustice of the situation. It shows that poverty and a land that produces wealth exist side by side, and implies that the poverty is therefore avoidable.*

INFORMATIONAL ANALYSIS

D ANALYZE PHOTOGRAPHS
Possible answer: This photo shows that migrant workers camped on the roadside in tents, ate meals informally, and learned to be at home in whatever conditions presented themselves. The cloth spread on the ground serves as a table, and a man tends the cooking fire. The migrants look as if they rarely have the chance to get clean or to wash or mend their clothes.

FOR STRATEGIC READERS
Vocabulary Support
- *glutted* (line 15), "overfilled"
- *itinerant* (line 15), "traveling from place to place"
- *harried* (line 19), "forced to move along"
- *ill-clad* (line 21), "inadequately clothed"

FOR ADVANCED LEARNERS/AP
Analyze Author's Purpose Ask students to discuss the likely purpose of the photo essay. Students may need to gather background from the Internet as they consider these questions:
- How widely read was *Life* magazine when the photo essay was published?
- What impact on the "problem of the Okies" does the article expect the publication of *The Grapes of Wrath* to have?

- Why is it important that Hollywood has optioned the novel?

When students have completed their research and discussion, have them respond to the questions about author's purpose in the Analysis Frame: Informational Nonfiction.

 BEST PRACTICES TOOLKIT—Copy Masters Analysis Frame: Informational Nonfiction pp. D21, D46, D47

E ANALYZE PHOTOGRAPHS

Possible answer: "The company" is run by people who are taking advantage of the migrant workers' plight. They don't charge for housing when the migrants work for them, but they do charge for housing when there is no cotton crop to pick—even when that housing is flooded and dangerous. Readers can infer that the company exploits workers as much as possible and views them as less than human, thus needing less than adequate housing.

If students need help . . . Remind them to make inferences by combining information from the text and photo with what they already know about people, housing, and work.

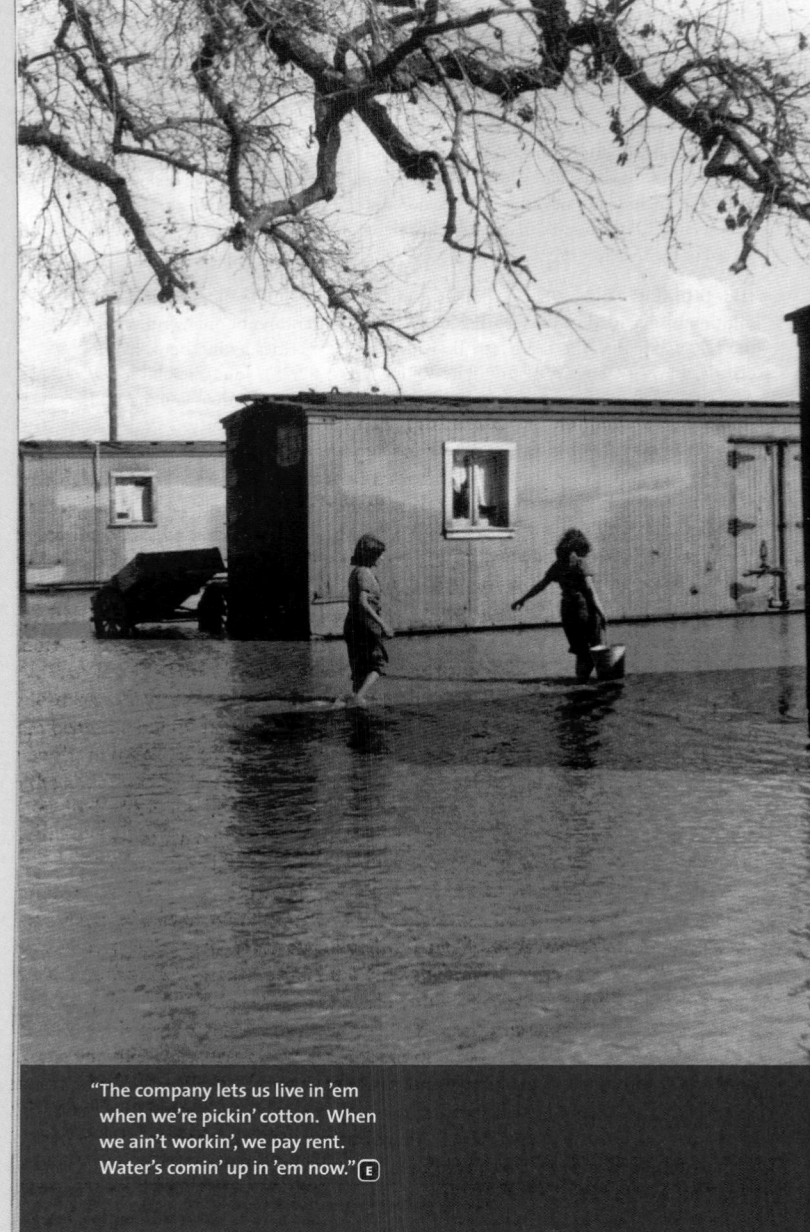

E ANALYZE PHOTOGRAPHS

Reread the caption. What information do you get about the company from this caption? Based on this information, what can you infer about the company?

"The company lets us live in 'em when we're pickin' cotton. When we ain't workin', we pay rent. Water's comin' up in 'em now." E

984   UNIT 5: THE HARLEM RENAISSANCE AND MODERNISM

DIFFERENTIATED INSTRUCTION

FOR ENGLISH LEARNERS

Language: Conversational English Patterns
[mixed-readiness group option] Help students translate the caption on page 984 into standard English. First, have students read it aloud and guess at the standard words behind the dialect: *them* for *'em, picking* for *pickin', isn't* for *ain't, working* for *workin', Water is* for *Water's, coming* for *comin',* and *them* for *'em.* Clarify the idiomatic usage in *coming up in them,* which means "rising." Then have students restate the full caption:

"The company lets us live in them when we're picking cotton. When we are not working, we pay rent. Water is coming up in them now."

Now ask students to rewrite the caption on page 985, substituting correct usage for the words that reflect dialect: *jus', so's, fellas, off'n,* and *groun'.* **Possible answer:** *"We have got to have a house when the rains come . . . just so as it has got a roof and a floor. Just to keep the little fellows off of the ground."*

"We got to have a house when the rains come . . . jus' so's it's got a roof and a floor. Just to keep the little fellas off'n the groun'."

The pictures on [these pages] are not simply types which resemble those described in *The Grapes of Wrath*. They are the people of whom Author Steinbeck wrote. Before starting his book, he lived in California's migratory labor camps. LIFE Photographer Horace Bristol accompanied him. The woman on [page 981] might well be Ma Joad, Author Steinbeck's heroine. The man with the double-edged ax [page 986] is a counterpart of his hero, Tom Joad. Captions for their pictures and all others on these pages were written by Steinbeck. Some are excerpts from his book. Others were written especially for LIFE's photographs.

F ANALYZE PHOTOGRAPHS
How would you contrast the **mood** of the photographs on pages 984 and 985?

G ANALYZE PHOTOGRAPHS
What do the shadows in this photograph serve to emphasize? Explain.

INFORMATIONAL ANALYSIS

F ANALYZE PHOTOGRAPHS

Possible answer: The mood of the photo on page 984 is serious because the flooded water creates hazards, and also the girls appear to be doing chores. The mood of the photo on page 985 is lighter because the young children are playing and seem to be having fun, even in the difficult conditions of their lives.

Extend the Discussion What can you conclude about children that these children find a way to play even though they have no toys or games and live in poverty?

INFORMATIONAL ANALYSIS

G ANALYZE PHOTOGRAPHS

Possible answer: The shadows emphasize the sun overhead and the lack of shade, suggesting how hot and dusty this camp is. The dust that the migrants tried to escape is still with them in this camp.

FOR ADVANCED LEARNERS/AP

Analyze Literary Terms Have students write definitions for these terms from page 985 and then provide the definitions to the whole class. If the definitions are new to listeners, have them add the words to their Personal Word Lists: *types, heroine, counterpart*.

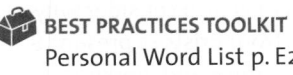 **BEST PRACTICES TOOLKIT**
Personal Word List p. E2

H ANALYZE PHOTOGRAPHS

Possible answer: Bristol probably chose not to crop out the man in the background because showing the man, standing idle, staring at the camera, while the other pauses from his hard work emphasizes the idea expressed in the caption: that the people who want work and the work that needs to be done "can't get together."

If students need help . . . Use your hands to model how to crop out the man standing in the background. Have students examine the resulting photo's composition and consider what is lost without the second man.

I ANALYZE PHOTOGRAPHS

Possible answer: The photo and its caption suggest that the workers made the best of their terrible situation, carrying on with their lives as best they could. The speaker looks at the positive, in this case, at a woman's beauty and abilities. He thinks of marriage, which implies that he is looking toward the future and hoping for a better life. He focuses on practical considerations also, noting that the woman has skills that could help him succeed.

H ANALYZE PHOTOGRAPHS
Horace Bristol could have **cropped,** or cut, the background figure out of this image without losing any part of the man and ax in the foreground. Reread the caption. What is the impact of having the second man in the background?

"The whole thing's nuts. There's work to do and people to do it, but them two can't get together. There's food to eat and people to eat it, and them two can't get together neither."

"She's awful pretty. An' she been to high school. She could help a man with figuring and stuff like that."

I ANALYZE PHOTOGRAPHS
From this last photograph and caption, what might you gather about people's attitudes toward their circumstances? How might the photographer's **vantage point** be said to contribute to this idea?

986 UNIT 5: THE HARLEM RENAISSANCE AND MODERNISM

DIFFERENTIATED INSTRUCTION

FOR STRATEGIC READERS

Concept Support: Analyze Photographs Have students review the chart they completed for each photograph. Students should make sure that each chart is complete and then record their reactions to the conditions that the migrants endured.

 BEST PRACTICES TOOLKIT—Transparency
Connecting p. A8

FOR ADVANCED LEARNERS/AP

Synthesize Have students view all or part of the film *The Grapes of Wrath.* Bristol's photographs served as a touchstone for the sets and costumes in the movie. Ask students to report on how closely the movie reflects the documentary evidence that Bristol's camera recorded. Students may also consider why the movie diverges from Bristol's presentation of the migrant camps and workers when it does.

Comprehension

1. **Recall** In the late 1930s, what combination of events and promises prompted many farmers in the plains states to travel westward?

2. **Recall** Who wrote the captions for the photographs in this photo essay? Are they fiction, nonfiction, or a mixture of both?

3. **Summarize** What typically happened to the Midwestern farmers who migrated to California? How were they regarded by Californians?

Critical Analysis

4. **Analyze Tone** How would you describe the attitude of the speaker in the caption for the image on page 984? How does the information conveyed by the photograph and caption on page 985 help you understand this attitude?

5. **Analyze Photographs** Based on this photo essay, what have you gathered about the living conditions and attitudes of Depression-era migrant workers?

6. **Evaluate** Reread lines 23–30 of the essay text. Do you agree or disagree with the writer's assertion? Explain.

Read for Information: Compare and Evaluate

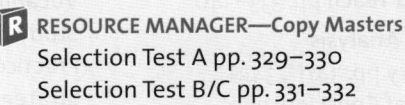

LS1.3

WRITING PROMPT

Reflect on the excerpt you read from *The Grapes of Wrath* and on the photo essay you just studied. In your opinion, which paints a more powerful portrait of the migrant farm workers? Why?

The following steps will help you answer the prompt:

1. Review the selections and decide based on your first reaction, which piece you find more powerful.

2. Now go back and analyze each piece, taking notes on the following elements:

   - the amount of information provided
   - the kinds of **details** and information conveyed
   - the ideas or **themes** emphasized
   - the **author's perspective** and the photographer's vantage point
   - the literary elements and the artistic techniques
   - the **mood** and thoughts evoked

3. Review your analysis. As you look at the relative strengths of each piece, do you still have the same opinion about which is more compelling? Why or why not?

4. Now state your opinion about which selection is more compelling, and give the reasons for your opinion, comparing the strengths and weaknesses of each piece.

FOR DEVELOPING WRITERS

Read for Information

- Direct students to narrow the essay's purpose to two points of comparison, such as the kinds of details and information conveyed and the mood these create.

- Encourage students to begin by writing their opinions in a topic sentence. Provide a starter sentence, such as *I think that _____ paints a more powerful portrait of the migrant farm workers because _____.*

Practice and Apply

After Reading

Use these copy masters to check understanding and provide extra support:

 RESOURCE MANAGER—Copy Masters
   Reading Check p. 327
   Question Support p. 328
   Compare and Evaluate p. 324

   Additional selection questions are provided for teachers on page 318.

ANSWERS

1. *Driven away by drought, farmers sought the promise of "green land" farther west.*

2. *John Steinbeck wrote the mix of fiction and nonfiction captions.*

3. *They didn't find enough work, lived in poverty, and were scorned by Californians.*

Possible answers:

4. *The speaker seems resigned. The caption and photo suggest that life could be worse.*

5. ■ **SKILLS FOCUS** **Analyze Photographs**
   People were poor and lived in shoddy housing or tents. They had few appliances for daily chores and had to haul water and make fires. Still, children played and adults carried on. Attitudes were dedicated, resigned, or even optimistic.

6. *Students may believe the novel's success means solutions are near, or that media attention does not always lead to solutions.*

Read for Information: Compare and Evaluate

Writing Prompt Students should state their opinions in a topic sentence and support them.

Assess and Reteach

Assess

 RESOURCE MANAGER—Copy Masters
   Selection Test A pp. 329–330
   Selection Test B/C pp. 331–332

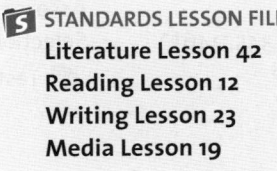 Test Generator CD

Reteach

STANDARDS LESSON FILE
   Literature Lesson 42
   Reading Lesson 12
   Writing Lesson 23
   Media Lesson 19

Focus and Motivate

OBJECTIVES

Literary Analysis
- explore the key idea of **memories**
- analyze stream of consciousness
- read a short story

Reading
- clarify sequence, including flashback

Vocabulary
- build vocabulary for reading and writing
- use context clues to understand figurative language (*also an EL language objective*)

Grammar and Writing
- use coordinating conjunctions and repetition to craft effective sentences
- write a stream-of-consciousness narrative

 CALIFORNIA R3.3, W1.2, W1.9, W2.1

ABOUT THE AUTHOR

Porter was just two when her mother died. Her father, bereft and directionless, relied on his own mother to lead the family. Porter's strong, resourceful grandmother became the model for her literary heroines. Her father provided a template for weak male characters.

USING THE *NOTABLE QUOTE*

Ask students how a writer might, as **Katherine Anne Porter** says, "take handfuls of confusion" and give them "shape and meaning." ***Possible answer:*** *A writer can choose particular events, actions, words, and traits to include in a story and others to omit. This selectivity helps readers focus on a single idea, character, or theme.*

Selection Resources

CALIFORNIA
R3.3, W1.2 (p. 1001), W1.9 (p. 1001), W2.1 (p. 1001)

NOTABLE QUOTE
"Human life itself may be almost pure chaos, but the work of the artist . . . is to take these handfuls of confusion and disparate things . . . and put them together in a frame to give them some kind of shape and meaning."

FYI
Did you know that Katherine Anne Porter . . .
- was a distant relative of the frontiersman Daniel Boone?
- taught singing and dancing as a teenager to help support her family?

Author Online
For more on Katherine Anne Porter, visit the **Literature Center** at **ClassZone.com.**

The Jilting of Granny Weatherall
Short Story by Katherine Anne Porter

Katherine Anne Porter
1890–1980

Katherine Anne Porter has been called a "writer's writer"; in her lifetime she was more popular with critics and her fellow writers than with the public. She wrote mostly short fiction, a form with which it was difficult to build a popular reputation. What's more, all of her 27 short stories, including those technically classified as novellas (short novels), could fit into a single book. Still, Porter's work is celebrated for its nearly flawless consistency and style. Each one of her stories is a polished gem reflecting a hard truth about human experience.

Survival and Resiliency She was born Callie Russell Porter on a scrappy dirt farm in central Texas, where she dreamed of becoming an actress. She had the good looks, the drive, and the talent for performing but lacked the stamina. A two-year bout with tuberculosis permanently dashed her dreams of acting. However, while recuperating at a sanitorium, Porter

befriended a journalist who helped her start writing for newspapers. Living in Denver in 1918, Porter was again stricken by illness, this time by the deadly flu epidemic that swept the globe after World War I, killing 550,000 people in the United States and at least 25 million worldwide. This second brush with death inspired an idea that was later to become part of her novella *Pale Horse, Pale Rider* (1939). After her recovery, convinced of her true calling, Porter left Denver for the New York literary scene and the wider world.

Deep in the Heart of Texas Like many writers of her generation, Porter traveled widely, living in Mexico, Bermuda, Germany, Switzerland, and France, as well as New York for much of the 1920s and 1930s. Some of these places inspired her fiction: her time in Mexico enriched her first published story, "Maria Concepción" (1922), and several others, while pre–World War II Berlin informed "The Leaning Tower" (1944). But for the most part, foreign travel provided what Porter called a "constant exercise of memory" and brought her closer to her native land. Some of her best fiction—notably, "Noon Wine" (1937), "Old Mortality" (1939), and a series called "The Old Order" (1955)—takes place in Texas. Many of these stories, and "The Jilting of Granny Weatherall" (1929) in particular, include a dynamic grandmother based on Porter's own who raised her until age 11 and exerted a strong influence. Porter even took her grandmother's name after she divorced her first husband and began life on her own.

988

RESOURCE MANAGER UNIT 5

Plan and Teach pp. 333–340

Literary Analysis
Summary pp. 341†*, 342‡*
Stream of Consciousness
   pp. 343, 344†*
Question Support p. 351*

Reading
Clarify Sequence pp. 345, 346†*
Reading Check p. 350

Vocabulary
Study p. 347*
Practice p. 348
Strategy p. 349

Grammar and Writing
Craft Effective Sentences p. 352

Assessment
Selection Tests A, B/C pp. 353*, 355*
   Test Generator CD

BEST PRACTICES TOOLKIT

Differentiated Instruction
   pp. 31–38*
Scaffolding Instruction
   pp. 43–46*

Graphic Organizers/Strategies
Visualizing • Word Squares •
Personal Word List • Freewriting •
Sequence Chain • Making
Inferences • Outline • Character
Traits Web • Plot Diagram

Reading Support
   Audio Anthology CD*

Technology
   Literature, Vocabulary, and Writing Centers at **ClassZone.com**
   Write*Smart* CD

---

* Resources for Differentiation   † Also in Spanish   ‡ In Haitian Creole and Vietnamese

LITERARY ANALYSIS: STREAM OF CONSCIOUSNESS

The very first paragraph of this story plunges readers directly into the thoughts of its protagonist. This literary technique, **stream of consciousness,** presents the flow of a character's seemingly unconnected thoughts, responses, and sensations. Rather than offering a logical account of events, it presents a series of associative connections, with one impression giving rise to another. This technique can be confusing to even the best readers; using these strategies will help:

- Remember that you are "inside" the main character's thoughts—the depictions of people and events you find there may not be completely reliable.
- Look for quotation marks to determine when Granny is speaking aloud and when she's not.
- Keep track of the twists and turns of Granny's thoughts to understand what she is reacting to.

READING SKILL: CLARIFY SEQUENCE

In this narrative, Porter shuffles together the past and the present to depict the distorted way Granny perceives the **sequence** of events. Porter achieves this effect in part through the use of **flashback,** in which she relates events that happened before the beginning of the story's "now" time. As you travel through Granny's memory, use a timeline to untangle the sequence of the main events in her life.

Jilting by George

Examination by Dr. Harry

▲ VOCABULARY IN CONTEXT

Porter uses these words to take readers into the mind of a woman on her deathbed. Complete each phrase with a word from the list.

WORD LIST	amethyst	dwindle	plague
	assign	embroidered	

1. kept an elaborately _____ blanket on the sickbed
2. had a valuable _____ ring to pass on to her daughter
3. felt her time _____ as she got weaker and weaker

Explore the Key Idea

CALIFORNIA

What makes a MEMORY *linger?*

KEY IDEA That perfect first date. The humiliating moment you realized you had failed your driving test. The elated, screaming crowd jumping to its feet as the last seconds of the big game ticked away. Whether pleasant or painful, there are some **memories** you just can't shake. In this story, as Granny Weatherall lies on her deathbed, she's haunted by an event that still affects her almost as powerfully as it did when she experienced it as a young woman.

QUICKWRITE Write a paragraph about a memory of your own that you can still recall in crisp detail. What images, feelings, sounds, or smells come to mind? Why do you think this moment lingers in your memory?

989

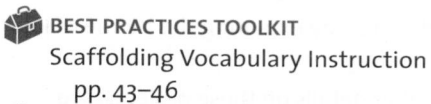

VOCABULARY

▲ VOCABULARY IN CONTEXT

DIAGNOSE WORD KNOWLEDGE To determine preteaching needs, have all students complete Vocabulary in Context. *Answers:* **1.** *embroidered,* **2.** *amethyst,* **3.** *dwindle*

PRETEACH VOCABULARY Preteach vocabulary with this copy master. Read each item aloud.

📓 **RESOURCE MANAGER**—Copy Master
Vocabulary Study p. 347

MORE VOCABULARY SUPPORT
For additional activities and guidelines, see

💼 **BEST PRACTICES TOOLKIT**
Scaffolding Vocabulary Instruction
pp. 43–46
ℹ️ Vocabulary Center at **ClassZone.com**

Teach

CALIFORNIA

What makes a MEMORY *linger?*

Lead into the **KEY IDEA** by asking students to identify **memories** that have affected their behavior, such as getting lost in a crowd as a child. Invite volunteers to share experiences; then urge all students to recall memories as they complete the **QUICKWRITE.**

SKILLS FOCUS

LITERARY ANALYSIS

● STREAM OF CONSCIOUSNESS

Ask students to consider a conversation among friends. One topic reminds speakers of another so the conversation changes topic again and again. Ask students why this happens and how the tendency is like stream-of-consciousness writing. ***Possible answers:*** *One topic reminds speakers of another and they jump to discuss this new idea. This free, undirected association also guides stream-of-consciousness writing as it follows the connections within a character's mind.*

CHECK UNDERSTANDING Have trios converse for five minutes, with one student recording when and how topics change. Ask students to trace how each new topic arose.

READING SKILL

◼ CLARIFY SEQUENCE

Recall that many films and TV shows present plots out of sequence. Point out that screen cues, such as a fade out or a sudden cut, alert viewers to such sequence breaks. Ask students what "cues" a writer might use to signal flashbacks and returns to sequence. ***Possible answer:*** *Writers might use time order words or hints that suggest the speaker's thinking is muddled or that refer to memory. Encourage students to look for such cues as they read.*

📓 **RESOURCE MANAGER**—Copy Master
Clarify Sequence p. 345 (for student use while reading the selection)

Practice and Apply

SUMMARY

This short story opens with 80-year-old Granny Weatherall nearing death. As her daughter Cornelia and Doctor Harry discuss her condition, Granny slips in and out of her memories. She recalls the challenges of managing the farm and four children after her husband's death. She thinks of her life's good moments but inevitably returns to a painful memory, her jilting by George. When death approaches, Granny hopes for a sign from God and feels again jilted that it does not arrive.

THE
Jilting
of
GRANNY WEATHERALL

Katherine Anne Porter

She flicked her wrist neatly out of Doctor Harry's pudgy careful fingers and pulled the sheet up to her chin. The brat ought to be in knee breeches.[1] Doctoring around the country with spectacles on his nose! "Get along now, take your schoolbooks and go. There's nothing wrong with me." Ⓐ

Doctor Harry spread a warm paw like a cushion on her forehead where the forked green vein danced and made her eyelids twitch. "Now, now, be a good girl, and we'll have you up in no time."

"That's no way to speak to a woman nearly eighty years old just because she's down. I'd have you respect your elders, young man."

10 "Well, Missy, excuse me." Doctor Harry patted her cheek. "But I've got to warn you, haven't I? You're a marvel, but you must be careful or you're going to be good and sorry."

"Don't tell me what I'm going to be. I'm on my feet now, morally speaking. It's Cornelia. I had to go to bed to get rid of her."

Her bones felt loose, and floated around in her skin, and Doctor Harry floated like a balloon around the foot of the bed. He floated and pulled down his waistcoat and swung his glasses on a cord. "Well, stay where you are, it certainly can't hurt you."

---

1. **knee breeches:** short pants formerly worn by young boys.

Ⓐ STREAM OF CONSCIOUSNESS
In lines 1–4, how does Porter create the effect that you, the reader, are "inside" Granny's mind? Explain how your intimacy with this character affects your impression of her.

① **Targeted Passage**

ANALYZE VISUALS
What does this unusual portrait suggest about its subject's thoughts or state of mind? Explain, citing details.

ANALYZE VISUALS

Possible answer: The head is open at the top, and there seem to be clouds floating out of it. The image suggests that the woman's thoughts are drifting away, like wispy clouds, instead of remaining contained in her head. In addition, the woman's face is pursed, as though she were trying to remember something that she cannot quite recall.

About the Art *Old Woman With Hair in the Clouds* by American artist Stephen F. Hayes (born 1955) captures the minute detail of an older woman's face. Bright white light on the woman's forehead and hair, as well as hair that merges with the clouds, suggests the mental deterioration that Granny Weatherall is experiencing.

Lines 2–4
REINFORCE *KEY IDEA:* **MEMORIES**

Discuss What do the comments about Doctor Harry in these lines reveal about Granny's **memories** of him? How do these memories affect her response to his treatment and advice? *Possible answer:* She is so much older than he that she can remember him as a little boy—or at least remember other little boys who resemble him. This memory makes her disdainful of him and leads to a lack of confidence in his treatment.

- Whose thoughts are revealed in lines 2–4? What do they reveal about the person who is having them?

- What is the physical condition of that person? How do you know?

- What do the person's continued thoughts reveal about her age and personality?

FOR ENGLISH LEARNERS

Prereading For prereading instruction for English learners, see

 BEST PRACTICES TOOLKIT
    Scaffolding Reading Instruction pp. 43–46

Culture: Clarify Clarify that Granny Weatherall's name is not "Missy." When Doctor Harry addresses her this way (line 10), he is using a diminutive for "young woman." Discuss why Doctor Harry calls Granny "Missy" and what she probably thinks of this form of address.

FOR ADVANCED LEARNERS/AP

AP exercises in the bottom channel provide additional challenge for students. Use these suggestions for small groups or individuals.

ADDITIONAL GUIDELINES

For more help with differentiation and tips for classroom management, see

BEST PRACTICES TOOLKIT
    Differentiated Instruction pp. 31–38

B STREAM OF CONSCIOUSNESS

Possible answer: Readers feel that they are listening in on Granny's thoughts because they know her thoughts, her feelings, her sensations—such as the way the pillow feels and the exact sounds she hears.

Lines 47–56
TIERED DISCUSSION PROMPTS

Use these prompts to help students understand Granny's character:

Connect How do you respond to the saying "A neat desk is the sign of an ordered mind"? *Accept all thoughtful responses.*

Interpret What kind of house has Granny always run, and why? *Possible answer: She has run an orderly, clean, disciplined house because order and cleanness give her great peace of mind (lines 50–56).*

Synthesize What details of housekeeping provide metaphors for how Granny approaches life? What predictions can you make about how she will approach death? *Possible answer: Making a bed neatly is a metaphor for leaving nothing that should be done undone and no necessary decisions unmade. The dust-free clock and carefully arranged rows of jars suggest Granny's need to control her life. She will probably try to organize her affairs carefully before death, and will likely try to control that process as much as she can.*

"Get along and doctor your sick," said Granny Weatherall. "Leave a well
20 woman alone. I'll call for you when I want you. . . . Where were you forty years
ago when I pulled through milk-leg[2] and double pneumonia? You weren't even
born. Don't let Cornelia lead you on," she shouted, because Doctor Harry
appeared to float up to the ceiling and out. "I pay my own bills, and I don't throw
my money away on nonsense!"

She meant to wave good-by, but it was too much trouble. Her eyes closed of
themselves, it was like a dark curtain drawn around the bed. The pillow rose and
floated under her, pleasant as a hammock in a light wind. She listened to the
leaves rustling outside the window. No, somebody was swishing newspapers: no,
Cornelia and Doctor Harry were whispering together. She leaped broad awake,
30 thinking they whispered in her ear. B

"She was never like this, *never* like this!" "Well, what can we expect?" "Yes,
eighty years old. . . ."

Well, and what if she was? She still had ears. It was like Cornelia to whisper
around doors. She always kept things secret in such a public way. She was always
being tactful and kind. Cornelia was dutiful; that was the trouble with her.
Dutiful and good: "So good and dutiful," said Granny, "that I'd like to spank her."
She saw herself spanking Cornelia and making a fine job of it.

"What'd you say, Mother?"

Granny felt her face tying up in hard knots.
40 "Can't a body think, I'd like to know?"

"I thought you might want something."

"I do. I want a lot of things. First off, go away and don't whisper."

She lay and drowsed, hoping in her sleep that the children would keep out and
let her rest a minute. It had been a long day. Not that she was tired. It was always
pleasant to snatch a minute now and then. There was always so much to be done,
let me see: tomorrow.

Tomorrow was far away and there was nothing to trouble about. Things were
finished somehow when the time came; thank God there was always a little
margin over for peace: then a person could spread out the plan of life and tuck in
50 the edges orderly. It was good to have everything clean and folded away, with the
hair brushes and tonic bottles sitting straight on the white **embroidered** linen: the
day started without fuss and the pantry shelves laid out with rows of jelly glasses
and brown jugs and white stone-china jars with blue whirligigs[3] and words painted
on them: coffee, tea, sugar, ginger, cinnamon, allspice: and the bronze clock with
the lion on top nicely dusted off. The dust that lion could collect in twenty-four
hours! The box in the attic with all those letters tied up, well, she'd have to go
through that tomorrow. All those letters—George's letters and John's letters and
her letters to them both—lying around for the children to find afterwards made
her uneasy. Yes, that would be tomorrow's business. No use to let them know how
60 silly she had been once.

992 UNIT 5: THE HARLEM RENAISSANCE AND MODERNISM

B STREAM OF CONSCIOUSNESS
How does the description in lines 25–30 reinforce the idea that you are listening in on Granny's thoughts?

embroidered
(ĕm'broi'dərd) *adj.* decorated with stitched designs **embroider** *v.*

DIFFERENTIATED INSTRUCTION

FOR STRATEGIC READERS

Visualize Encourage students to visualize the details of Granny's home described in lines 47–59. Explain that Granny's home reflects the person she is and the life she has lived. Ask students to suggest an adjective to describe Granny. *Possible answers: organized, neat, controlled*

 BEST PRACTICES TOOLKIT—Transparency
Visualizing p. A11

FOR ENGLISH LEARNERS

Key Academic Vocabulary Use Word Squares to teach these words: *job* (line 37), *appreciate* (line 240).

BEST PRACTICES TOOLKIT—Transparency
Word Squares p. E10

Culture: Connect Define these household items from Granny's, and stress that the item groups reflect homes in many cultures:

• comfort items: *pillow* (line 26), *hammock* (line 27)

• cooking items: *jelly glasses . . . allspice* (lines 52–54)

• hygiene items: *hair brushes and tonic bottles* (line 51)

• daily necessities: *clock* (line 54)

Ask students to match items to those from their home cultures. Students can record new words on their Personal Word List.

BEST PRACTICES TOOLKIT
Personal Word List p. E2

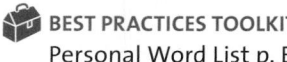

While she was rummaging around she found death in her mind and it felt clammy and unfamiliar. She had spent so much time preparing for death there was no need for bringing it up again. Let it take care of itself now. When she was sixty she had felt very old, finished, and went around making farewell trips to see her children and grandchildren, with a secret in her mind: This is the very last of your mother, children! Then she made her will and came down with a long fever. That was all just a notion like a lot of other things, but it was lucky too, for she had once for all got over the idea of dying for a long time. Now she couldn't be worried. She hoped she had better sense now. Her father had lived to be one
70 hundred and two years old and had drunk a noggin of strong hot toddy[4] on his last birthday. He told the reporters it was his daily habit, and he owed his long life to that. He had made quite a scandal and was very pleased about it. She believed she'd just **plague** Cornelia a little. **C**

"Cornelia! Cornelia!" No footsteps, but a sudden hand on her cheek. "Bless you, where have you been?"

"Here, Mother."

"Well, Cornelia, I want a noggin of hot toddy." **D**

"Are you cold, darling?"

"I'm chilly, Cornelia. Lying in bed stops the circulation. I must have told you
80 that a thousand times."

Well, she could just hear Cornelia telling her husband that Mother was getting a little childish and they'd have to humor her. The thing that most annoyed her was that Cornelia thought she was deaf, dumb, and blind. Little hasty glances and tiny gestures tossed around her and over her head saying, "Don't cross her, let her have her way, she's eighty years old," and she sitting there as if she lived in a thin glass cage. Sometimes Granny almost made up her mind to pack up and move back to her own house where nobody could remind her every minute that she was old. Wait, wait, Cornelia, till your own children whisper behind your back!

In her day she had kept a better house and had got more work done. She
90 wasn't too old yet for Lydia to be driving eighty miles for advice when one of the children jumped the track, and Jimmy still dropped in and talked things over: "Now, Mammy, you've a good business head, I want to know what you think of this? . . ." Old. Cornelia couldn't change the furniture around without asking. Little things, little things! They had been so sweet when they were little. Granny wished the old days were back again with the children young and everything to be done over. It had been a hard pull, but not too much for her. When she thought of all the food she had cooked, and all the clothes she had cut and sewed, and all the gardens she had made—well, the children showed it. There they were, made out of her, and they couldn't get away from that. Sometimes she wanted to see
100 John again and point to them and say, Well, I didn't do so badly, did I? But that would have to wait. That was for tomorrow. She used to think of him as a man, but now all the children were older than their father, and he would be a child beside her if she saw him now. It seemed strange and there was something wrong in the idea. Why, he couldn't possibly recognize her. She had fenced in a hundred

---

4. **noggin . . . toddy:** mug of a strong alcoholic drink.

---

plague (plāg) v. to annoy; harass

C **STREAM OF CONSCIOUSNESS**
Reread lines 47–73 and consider how Porter conveys the flow of Granny's thoughts. What idea triggers Granny's thoughts of death?

D **CLARIFY SEQUENCE**
Reread lines 61–77. Identify clues about the timing of Granny's father's "scandal" and subsequent death. What connection do you see between this memory and Granny's desire to "plague" Cornelia?

② **Targeted Passage**

Lines 61–73
REINFORCE *KEY IDEA*: MEMORIES

Discuss From what **memories** about death does Granny take comfort? *Possible answer: Granny takes comfort from her memory of preparing for death at age 60. Though ill, she did not die, and now she feels that she has already dealt with her death and can focus on more important matters. She also takes comfort from the memory of her father's aging, in which he lived a long time despite drinking and toyed with those who questioned his behavior.*

LITERARY ANALYSIS

C **STREAM OF CONSCIOUSNESS**

Possible answer: Porter traces Granny's thoughts as she skips from thinking about people looking through her letters in the attic to the idea of looking through her own attic of memories.

Extend the Discussion How is a mind like an attic? Why does Porter use the phrase "rummaging around" (line 61) to describe Granny's thought process?

READING SKILL

D **CLARIFY SEQUENCE**

Possible answer: Clues such as the use of the past perfect "had lived" (line 69) and reference to "his last birthday" (line 71) suggest that Granny's father died sometime in the past, before readers first encounter Granny on her own deathbed. Granny's memory of her father plaguing people with his elderly behavior leads her to consider plaguing Cornelia a bit.

If students need help . . . Remind them to add Granny's father's death to the timeline they began on page 989 and to place the event in relation to others already recorded.

FOR STRATEGIC READERS

② **Targeted Passage [Lines 89–99]**

In this passage, Granny reflects on her achievements with pride.

- What did Granny mostly do in the "old days"?

- How does she feel about those times and about her role in them?

- What does Granny wish could happen?

- How does Granny know that her adult children still value her?

FOR ADVANCED LEARNERS/AP

Analyze Character Have students read the brief dialogue between mother and daughter in lines 74–80 aloud. Then challenge them to draw conclusions about the two women's relationship. What does Cornelia think of Granny? What does Granny think of Cornelia? How do Porter's few lines of dialogue hint at years of such interchanges between the two? Invite students to share their ideas with the class.

Possible answer: Granny says that John would be a child compared to her because their children are now older than he was at his death.

If students need help . . . Point out clues to the sequence. For example, John lived long enough to father at least three children (lines 89–93). John's children are now old enough to have their own children (lines 90–91).

Lines 121–128
TIERED DISCUSSION PROMPTS

Use these prompts to help students understand the flashback to past nights:

Recall How does Granny feel about the days when the children were small? *Possible answer: She enjoyed them, though they were filled with hard work.*

Analyze In what way is Granny, as she prays, like her children as they waited for her to light the lamp? *Possible answer: Like her children, who were afraid of the dark and counted on their mother to light the lamp, Granny is afraid and turns to a more powerful being for help.*

Synthesize To what other lines on this page might Granny's prayers respond? *Possible answer: Granny's prayers might respond to her perception of the rising fog and the "army of ghosts" (lines 120–121).*

F GRAMMAR AND STYLE

Craft Effective Sentences Point out the repetition of "the day" (line 141), "hell" (lines 143, 144, 146), and "crept" (lines 141, 146). Direct students to the use of *and* as a coordinating conjunction in lines 144 and 145. Clarify that *and* functions as a coordinating conjunction when it joins two independent clauses. Ask students to find examples of this use in lines 181–183. *Possible answer: The sentence contains three independent clauses linked by and.*

---

acres once, digging the post holes herself and clamping the wires with just a negro boy to help. That changed a woman. John would be looking for a young woman with the peaked Spanish comb in her hair and the painted fan. Digging post holes changed a woman. Riding country roads in the winter when women had their babies was another thing: sitting up nights with sick horses and sick negroes and 110 sick children and hardly ever losing one. John, I hardly ever lost one of them! John would see that in a minute, that would be something he could understand, she wouldn't have to explain anything! **E**

It made her feel like rolling up her sleeves and putting the whole place to rights again. No matter if Cornelia was determined to be everywhere at once, there were a great many things left undone on this place. She would start tomorrow and do them. It was good to be strong enough for everything, even if all you made melted and changed and slipped under your hands, so that by the time you finished you almost forgot what you were working for. What was it I set out to do? she asked herself intently, but she could not remember. A fog rose over the valley, she saw it 120 marching across the creek swallowing the trees and moving up the hill like an army of ghosts. Soon it would be at the near edge of the orchard, and then it was time to go in and light the lamps. Come in, children, don't stay out in the night air.

Lighting the lamps had been beautiful. The children huddled up to her and breathed like little calves waiting at the bars in the twilight. Their eyes followed the match and watched the flame rise and settle in a blue curve, then they moved away from her. The lamp was lit, they didn't have to be scared and hang on to mother any more. Never, never, never more. God, for all my life I thank Thee. Without Thee, my God, I could never have done it. Hail, Mary, full of grace.[5]

I want you to pick all the fruit this year and see that nothing is wasted. There's 130 always someone who can use it. Don't let good things rot for want of using. You waste life when you waste good food. Don't let things get lost. It's bitter to lose things. Now, don't let me get to thinking, not when I am tired and taking a little nap before supper. . . .

The pillow rose about her shoulders and pressed against her heart and the memory was being squeezed out of it: oh, push down the pillow, somebody: it would smother her if she tried to hold it. Such a fresh breeze blowing and such a green day with no threats in it. But he had not come, just the same. What does a woman do when she has put on the white veil and set out the white cake for a man and he doesn't come? She tried to remember. No, I swear he never harmed 140 me but in that. He never harmed me but in that . . . and what if he did? There was the day, the day, but a whirl of dark smoke rose and covered it, crept up and over into the bright field where everything was planted so carefully in orderly rows. That was hell, she knew hell when she saw it. For sixty years she had prayed against remembering him and against losing her soul in the deep pit of hell, and now the two things were mingled in one and the thought of him was a smoky cloud from hell that moved and crept in her head when she had just got rid of Doctor Harry and was trying to rest a minute. Wounded vanity, Ellen, said a sharp voice in the top of her mind. Don't let your wounded vanity get the upper

---

5. **Hail . . . grace:** the beginning of a Roman Catholic prayer to the Virgin Mary.

E CLARIFY SEQUENCE
Why does Granny say that today, John would be a child compared to her? Record on your timeline the information you learn in this paragraph.

3 Targeted Passage

F GRAMMAR AND STYLE
Reread lines 143–147. Porter uses **repetition** as well as short clauses joined by the **coordinating conjunction** *and* to present the circular nature of Granny's thoughts.

DIFFERENTIATED INSTRUCTION

FOR STRATEGIC READERS

3 Targeted Passage [Lines 134–146]

This passage explains Granny's critical, and terrible, memory from youth—her fiancé did not show up at their wedding.

- What is Granny trying to do in lines 134–136?

- What memory does the fresh breeze that blows into the room trigger?

- Who is "he" in lines 137, 139, and 140?

- How long ago was it that Granny last explored this memory?

- What does Granny fear when this memory pushes its way into her consciousness?

hand of you. Plenty of girls get jilted. You were jilted, weren't you? Then stand up
to it. Her eyelids wavered and let in streamers of blue-gray light like tissue paper
over her eyes. She must get up and pull the shades down or she'd never sleep. She
was in bed again and the shades were not down. How could that happen? Better
turn over, hide from the light, sleeping in the light gave you nightmares. "Mother,
how do you feel now?" and a stinging wetness on her forehead. But I don't like
having my face washed in cold water! **G**

Hapsy? George? Lydia? Jimmy? No, Cornelia, and her features were swollen
and full of little puddles. "They're coming, darling, they'll all be here soon." Go
wash your face, child, you look funny.

Instead of obeying, Cornelia knelt down and put her head on the pillow. She
seemed to be talking but there was no sound. "Well, are you tongue-tied? Whose
birthday is it? Are you going to give a party?"

Cornelia's mouth moved urgently in strange shapes. "Don't do that, you bother
me, daughter."

"Oh, no, Mother. Oh, no. . . ."

Nonsense. It was strange about children. They disputed your every word. "No
what, Cornelia?"

"Here's Doctor Harry."

"I won't see that boy again. He just left five minutes ago."

"That was this morning, Mother. It's night now. Here's the nurse." **H**

"This is Doctor Harry, Mrs. Weatherall. I never saw you look so young and
happy!"

"Ah, I'll never be young again—but I'd be happy if they'd let me lie in peace
and get rested."

She thought she spoke up loudly, but no one answered. A warm weight on her
forehead, a warm bracelet on her wrist, and a breeze went on whispering, trying to
tell her something. A shuffle of leaves in the everlasting hand of God, He blew on
them and they danced and rattled. "Mother, don't mind, we're going to give you a
little hypodermic."[6] "Look here, daughter, how do ants get in this bed? I saw sugar
ants yesterday." Did you send for Hapsy too?

It was Hapsy she really wanted. She had to go a long way back through a great
many rooms to find Hapsy standing with a baby on her arm. She seemed to
herself to be Hapsy also, and the baby on Hapsy's arm was Hapsy and himself and
herself, all at once, and there was no surprise in the meeting. Then Hapsy melted
from within and turned flimsy as gray gauze and the baby was a gauzy shadow,
and Hapsy came up close and said, "I thought you'd never come," and looked at
her very searchingly and said, "You haven't changed a bit!" They leaned forward to
kiss, when Cornelia began whispering from a long way off, "Oh, is there anything
you want to tell me? Is there anything I can do for you?"

Yes, she had changed her mind after sixty years and she would like to see
George. I want you to find George. Find him and be sure to tell him I forgot
him. I want him to know I had my husband just the same and my children and
my house like any other woman. A good house too and a good husband that I

---

6. **hypodermic:** injection.

G STREAM OF CONSCIOUSNESS
Describe the major event revealed by Granny's thoughts in lines 134–155. What is the significance of the dark smoke Granny sees covering the green, orderly fields when she recalls this event?

H STREAM OF CONSCIOUSNESS
What clues in lines 156–169 reveal to readers how much Granny's condition is deteriorating?

Lines 147–150
REINFORCE *KEY IDEA:* MEMORIES
Discuss Who speaks to Granny, telling her to "stand up" to her painful **memories** about being jilted (line 149)? *Possible answer: Granny may be speaking to herself, calling herself by her name, Ellen, or she may be remembering someone who said these words to her after she was jilted—perhaps a mother, grandmother, aunt, or friend.*

LITERARY ANALYSIS

G STREAM OF CONSCIOUSNESS
Possible answer: Before she married John, Granny was jilted by another man. She has never gotten over the pain, and the memory still has the power to cast darkness over her life.

Extend the Discussion What emotions are common among memories that stay with people for life?

LITERARY ANALYSIS

H STREAM OF CONSCIOUSNESS
Possible answer: She can't hear properly (lines 159–160) and she is disoriented and can't keep track of time (lines 168–169). Also, Doctor Harry has come a second time in one day and brought a nurse with him.

FOR ENGLISH LEARNERS
Culture: Clarify Explain to students the literal and cultural meaning of *jilted,* clarifying the shame associated with being left at the altar. Ask students to describe the emotional pain a jilted woman might feel. *Possible answer: A jilted woman might feel humiliated, embarrassed, unattractive, tainted, and so on.* Invite students to describe how such an event would be received in their home cultures.

FOR ADVANCED LEARNERS/AP
Interpret Symbolism Challenge students to consider the significance of Granny's last name, Weatherall. In a journal entry, have students discuss what the name tells readers about Granny, and how it contributes to the developing theme of the story. To begin, have students freewrite about what *Weatherall* means, both literally and figuratively.

BEST PRACTICES TOOLKIT
Freewriting p. C1

loved and fine children out of him. Better than I hoped for even. Tell him I was given back everything he took away and more. Oh, no, oh, God, no, there was something else besides the house and the man and the children. Oh, surely they were not all? What was it? Something not given back. . . . Her breath crowded down under her ribs and grew into a monstrous frightening shape with cutting edges; it bored up into her head, and the agony was unbelievable: Yes, John, get the Doctor now, no more talk, my time has come.

④ Targeted Passage

200   When this one was born it should be the last. The last. It should have been born first, for it was the one she had truly wanted. Everything came in good time. Nothing left out, left over. She was strong, in three days she would be as well as ever. Better. A woman needed milk in her to have her full health. ❶

    "Mother, do you hear me?"

    "I've been telling you—"

    "Mother, Father Connolly's here."

    "I went to Holy Communion only last week. Tell him I'm not so sinful as all that."

    "Father just wants to speak to you."

    He could speak as much as he pleased. It was like him to drop in and inquire
210   about her soul as if it were a teething baby, and then stay on for a cup of tea and a round of cards and gossip. He always had a funny story of some sort, usually about an Irishman who made his little mistakes and confessed them, and the point lay in some absurd thing he would blurt out in the confessional showing his struggles between native piety and original sin. Granny felt easy about her soul. Cornelia, where are your manners? Give Father Connolly a chair. She had her secret comfortable understanding with a few favorite saints who cleared a straight road to God for her. All as surely signed and sealed as the papers for the new Forty Acres. Forever . . . heirs and **assigns** forever. Since the day the wedding cake was not cut, but thrown out and wasted. The whole bottom dropped out of the world,
220   and there she was blind and sweating with nothing under her feet and the walls falling away. His hand had caught her under the breast, she had not fallen, there was the freshly polished floor with the green rug on it, just as before. He had cursed like a sailor's parrot and said, "I'll kill him for you." Don't lay a hand on him, for my sake leave something to God. "Now, Ellen, you must believe what I tell you. . . ."

    So there was nothing, nothing to worry about any more, except sometimes in the night one of the children screamed in a nightmare, and they both hustled out shaking and hunting for the matches and calling, "There, wait a minute, here we are!" John, get the doctor now, Hapsy's time has come. But there was Hapsy
230   standing by the bed in a white cap. "Cornelia, tell Hapsy to take off her cap. I can't see her plain."

    Her eyes opened very wide and the room stood out like a picture she had seen somewhere. Dark colors with the shadows rising towards the ceiling in long angles. The tall black dresser gleamed with nothing on it but John's picture, enlarged from a little one, with John's eyes very black when they should have been blue. You never saw him, so how do you know how he looked? But the man insisted the copy was perfect, it was very rich and handsome. For a picture, yes, but it's not my husband. The table by the bed had a linen cover and a candle and

❶ STREAM OF CONSCIOUSNESS
Reread lines 189–203. What has Granny decided about George? Trace the path of her thoughts from this decision to the memory of the birth of her child.

assign (ə-sīn') n. a person to whom property is transferred in a will or other legal document

---

LITERARY ANALYSIS

❶ STREAM OF CONSCIOUSNESS

Possible answer: Granny has decided that she wants to see George again and show him what she's made of her life, the life that he rejected. She then wonders if a home, husband, and children are enough to satisfy her. This thought causes her pain, which brings to mind the memory of the pain of childbirth.

If students need help . . . Work with them to complete a Sequence Chain with ideas from the paragraph. Trace how each thought in Granny's mind leads to the next one.

 BEST PRACTICES TOOLKIT—Transparency Sequence Chain p. B21

Lines 218–225
TIERED DISCUSSION PROMPTS

Use these prompts to help students understand Granny's reaction to George's abandonment of her:

Recall What image has Granny already associated with the jilting? *Possible answer: She has associated the orderly fields being covered with black smoke with her jilting.*

Interpret What does Granny experience physically when George jilts her? How do her surroundings seem to change? Why does she respond this way? *Possible answer: When George jilts Granny, she feels "blind and sweating" (line 220) and cannot see or think clearly. She feels "nothing under her feet" (line 220) and that the walls are "falling away" (line 221). She thinks she has fallen down, though in fact she has not. Granny responds this way because George's behavior is so devastating to her that she expects the whole world to change forever.*

Evaluate Is it believable that George's actions could affect Granny so dramatically? *Possible answer: Yes. People who face an emotional shock often respond physically, become disoriented, or even collapse.*

DIFFERENTIATED INSTRUCTION

FOR STRATEGIC READERS

④ **Targeted Passage [Lines 193–196]**

In this passage Granny realizes that she lost something irretrievable when she was jilted.

• Who is the "him" that Granny wants to address?

• What was "given back"?

• Why did Granny get more than she hoped for? Who gave it to her?

• What was "not given back"?

FOR ENGLISH LEARNERS

Culture: Clarify Clarify these aspects of Granny's Catholic faith:

• Father Connolly, the priest, has come to give Granny extreme unction, a ritual of prayer and anointing that prepares her for death. He is not her biological father.

• The phrase "native piety" (line 214) refers to Father Connolly's desire for spiritual perfection, while "original sin" (line 214) means that all people, including Father Connolly, are born sinful.

a crucifix.[7] The light was blue from Cornelia's silk lampshades. No sort of light
240 at all, just frippery. You had to live forty years with kerosene lamps to appreciate
honest electricity. She felt very strong and she saw Doctor Harry with a rosy
nimbus[8] around him.

"You look like a saint, Doctor Harry, and I vow that's as near as you'll ever
come to it."

"She's saying something."

"I heard you, Cornelia. What's all this carrying-on?"

"Father Connolly's saying—"

Cornelia's voice staggered and bumped like a cart in a bad road. It rounded
corners and turned back again and arrived nowhere. Granny stepped up in the cart
250 very lightly and reached for the reins, but a man sat beside her and she knew him
by his hands, driving the cart. She did not look in his face, for she knew without
seeing, but looked instead down the road where the trees leaned over and bowed
to each other and a thousand birds were singing a Mass. She felt like singing too,
but she put her hand in the bosom of her dress and pulled out a rosary,[9] and
Father Connolly murmured Latin in a very solemn voice and tickled her feet. My
God, will you stop that nonsense? I'm a married woman. What if he did run away
and leave me to face the priest by myself? I found another a whole world better. I
wouldn't have exchanged my husband for anybody except St. Michael himself, and
you may tell him that for me with a thank you in the bargain.

260 Light flashed on her closed eyelids, and a deep roaring shook her. Cornelia, is
that lightning? I hear thunder. There's going to be a storm. Close all the windows.
Call the children in. . . . "Mother, here we are, all of us." "Is that you, Hapsy?"
"Oh, no, I'm Lydia. We drove as fast as we could." Their faces drifted above her,
drifted away. The rosary fell out of her hands and Lydia put it back. Jimmy tried
to help, their hands fumbled together, and Granny closed two fingers around
Jimmy's thumb. Beads wouldn't do, it must be something alive. She was so amazed
her thoughts ran round and round. So, my dear Lord, this is my death and I
wasn't even thinking about it. My children have come to see me die. But I can't,
it's not time. Oh, I always hated surprises. I wanted to give Cornelia the **amethyst**
270 set—Cornelia, you're to have the amethyst set, but Hapsy's to wear it when
she wants, and, Doctor Harry, do shut up. Nobody sent for you. Oh, my dear
Lord, do wait a minute. I meant to do something about the Forty Acres, Jimmy
doesn't need it and Lydia will later on, with that worthless husband of hers. I
meant to finish the altar cloth and send six bottles of wine to Sister Borgia for her
dyspepsia.[10] I want to send six bottles of wine to Sister Borgia, Father Connolly,
now don't let me forget.

Cornelia's voice made short turns and tilted over and crashed. "Oh, Mother, oh,
Mother, oh, Mother. . . ."

---

7. **crucifix** (krōō′sə-fĭks′): a cross bearing a sculptured representation of the crucified Christ.

8. **nimbus** (nĭm′bəs): halo of light.

9. **rosary** (rō′zə-rē): a string of beads used by Roman Catholics to count their prayers.

10. **dyspepsia** (dĭs-pĕp′shə): indigestion.

amethyst (ăm′ə-thĭst) n.
a purple form of quartz
used as a gemstone

Lines 268–276
REINFORCE *KEY IDEA:* MEMORIES

Discuss How do Granny's **memories** worry her after she realizes that her children "have come to see [her] die" (line 268)? *Possible answer: Now that it is too late to do anything more, she is flooded by memories of duties and tasks that she has left undone and overwhelmed by distaste at unfinished business and loose ends.*

FOR STRATEGIC READERS

Make Inferences Help students infer the double meaning of Granny's statement in line 229 that "Hapsy's time has come." On the one hand, Hapsy's "time" is the birth of her child, but it is also the moment of death for her and her baby. Recall line 180 when Hapsy fades to a ghostly "gray gauze" in Granny's memory and her baby turns into a "gauzy shadow."

BEST PRACTICES TOOLKIT—Transparency
Making Inferences p. A13

FOR ENGLISH LEARNERS

Vocabulary: Idioms [mixed-readiness pairs]
Have pairs use context to define these idioms:

- *cursed like a sailor's parrot* (line 223), "used profane and rude language as a parrot imitating a sailor might do"

- *Hapsy's time has come* (line 229), "Hapsy has gone into labor and will soon bear a child"

- *all this carrying-on* (line 246), "all this excitement over nothing"

FOR ADVANCED LEARNERS/AP

Synthesize Have students review the historical essay on page 827 for information about stream-of-consciousness writing and its origins. Challenge students to briefly research Sigmund Freud's theories. Ask them to decide if, and how, entering Granny Weatherall's stream-of-consciousness thought process provides a key to understanding her behavior. Invite students to share their ideas.

About the Art American artist Philip Hershberger (born ??) uses the ancient technique of encaustic painting in which hot wax, resin, and color are blended into a semi-liquid for painting. He describes his work as standing outside of any specific time and raising questions about whether an object is really present or not—qualities that vividly recall Granny Weatherall's experience.

LITERARY ANALYSIS

❶ STREAM OF CONSCIOUSNESS

Possible answer: *She is surprised, even though she knows it's coming and thinks that she has already calmly put the matter aside. For all her careful planning and putting things in order, she is not ready for death.*

If students need help . . . Have them review lines 61–69 and contrast how Granny expects to face death and how she actually faces it.

SELECTION WRAP–UP

REFLECT Have students think about Granny's heartbreak. In what ways did it cause her to approach life differently than she might have?

⭐ CRITIQUE

- Ask students whether they find Porter's description of death plausible and to explain why or why not.

- After completing the After Reading questions on page 999, have students revisit their responses and tell whether they have changed their opinions.

Blue House (2004), Philip Hershberger. Encaustic on panel, 78″ × 48″. © Philip Hersheberger

"I'm not going, Cornelia. I'm taken by surprise. I can't go." ❶

280 You'll see Hapsy again. What about her? "I thought you'd never come." Granny made a long journey outward, looking for Hapsy. What if I don't find her? What then? Her heart sank down and down, there was no bottom to death, she couldn't come to the end of it. The blue light from Cornelia's lampshade drew into a tiny point in the center of her brain, it flickered and winked like an eye, quietly it fluttered and **dwindled.** Granny lay curled down within herself, amazed and watchful, staring at the point of light that was herself; her body was now only a deeper mass of shadow in an endless darkness and this darkness would curl around the light and swallow it up. God, give a sign!

For the second time there was no sign. Again no bridegroom and the priest
290 in the house. She could not remember any other sorrow because this grief wiped them all away. Oh, no, there's nothing more cruel than this—I'll never forgive it. She stretched herself with a deep breath and blew out the light.

❶ **STREAM OF CONSCIOUSNESS**
Reread lines 266–279. What is **ironic** about Granny's response to the imminence of her death?

dwindle (dwĭn′dl) *v.* to become steadily less; to shrink

❺ **Targeted Passage**

998 UNIT 5: THE HARLEM RENAISSANCE AND MODERNISM

DIFFERENTIATED INSTRUCTION

FOR STRATEGIC READERS

❺ **Targeted Passage [Lines 280–291]**

This passage explains Granny's hopes about death and how she is disappointed again.

- For whom is Granny looking as she dies, and where does she look?

- What does Granny see as she dies?

- What disappointment does Granny say she will "never forgive" (line 291) as she dies?

FOR ADVANCED LEARNERS/AP

Hypothesize About Character Explain to students that some critics believe that Granny's jilting was so painful and shameful because she was pregnant with George's child, and that this child was the favored daughter, Hapsy. Have students discuss this interpretation, looking for text evidence to support or disprove it. Then ask them to produce an outline for an essay in which they explore the impact of this interpretation on Granny's character. Students should consider the societal attitudes towards unwed mothers during Granny's time as well as John's reaction to the jilting and to Granny's situation.

🧰 **BEST PRACTICES TOOLKIT—Transparency** Outline p. B19

998 UNIT 5: THE HARLEM RENAISSANCE AND MODERNISM

Comprehension

CALIFORNIA R3.3

1. **Recall** Which characters mentioned in the story belong exclusively to Granny Weatherall's past?

2. **Recall** Who is with Granny when she dies?

3. **Clarify** Who is Hapsy?

Literary Analysis

4. **Clarify Sequence** Using your timeline, retell the key events of Granny's life in chronological order. Which events mark the best and worst of Granny's life? Explain, citing Granny's own thoughts and feelings about each event.

5. **Make Inferences About Character** Go back through the story, noting thoughts and **memories** that linger in Granny's mind. What do they reveal about the kind of person she is? Record your answers in a chart like this one.

Granny's Thoughts	Character Traits Revealed
"It was good to have everything clean and put away ... nicely dusted off." (lines 50–55)	She likes putting things in order and having control in life.

6. **Analyze Stream of Consciousness** Porter uses stream of consciousness to dramatize Granny's interior life. What effect does this approach have on her readers? For example, how might your reaction to the story have been different if Porter had presented the same events in a more traditional narrative? Cite specific examples from the story in your response.

7. **Interpret Symbolism** Consider Granny's final act of blowing out the light. What might this symbolize? Given what you know about her character, do you see it as an act of resignation or one of defiance? Support your answer.

8. **Analyze Theme** Which of the following statements best expresses the theme Porter conveys in this story? Support your choice with evidence from the text.

   • There is no deed so wrong it can't be forgiven.
   • In youth we are all foolish; with age comes true wisdom.
   • Life does not provide the answers or reassurances that people want, even at the moment of death.

Literary Criticism

9. **Critical Interpretations** Novelist Reynolds Price asserts that Porter's stories are "lethal to the most widely cherished illusions of the species"—in other words, they destroy our sentimental notions about things like romance, self-regard, and parenthood. What "cherished illusions" does Porter destroy here? What truths does she portray instead? Support your answer.

THE JILTING OF GRANNY WEATHERALL **999**

8. The third bullet is the strongest statement of theme, but accept all thoughtful answers supported by textual evidence.

9. Students may discuss any of these illusions: romance, self-regard, gender roles, marriage, parentage. For example, students may say that the story destroys the sentimental illusion of romance because Granny's response to her jilting is one of shame and vanity, not love, and she then remembers her marriage to John as a partnership without romance or passion.

Practice and Apply

After Reading
Use these copy masters to check understanding and provide extra support:

RESOURCE MANAGER—Copy Masters
Reading Check p. 350
Stream of Consciousness p. 343
Question Support p. 351

Additional selection questions are provided for teachers on page 337.

ANSWERS

1. *George, John, and Hapsy belong to the past.*

2. *The doctor, a priest, and her surviving children—Cornelia, Lydia, and Jimmy—are with Granny when she dies.*

3. *Hapsy is her favorite daughter, who apparently died.*

Possible answers:

4. ■ **SKILLS FOCUS** Clarify Sequence *Events: father's death; jilting by George; marriage to John; raising her young children; death of Hapsy; death of John; hard work and community nursing; recovery at age 60 from long fever; illness again at almost age 80 and seeing doctor, priest, and death. The best events are raising young children and hard work and nursing. The worst events are being jilted by George, and Hapsy's death.*

5. *Accept all thoughtful inferences, for example: "Digging post holes ... changed a woman" (lines 105–106) and "It was good ... everything" (line 116) support the inference that Granny is proud of her competence and physical strength.*

6. ● **SKILLS FOCUS** Stream of Consciousness *Students may say that they felt more connected to Granny because of Porter's use of stream of consciousness, which made them privy to Granny's innermost thoughts. Had the story been told from an observer's point of view, this sense of intimacy would have been lost. For example, readers would not know the depth of Granny's sorrow over Hapsy's death or her pride in her life.*

7. *The light symbolizes Granny's life, and the gathering darkness symbolizes her death. Blowing out the light symbolizes the moment of death. Because she actively takes a deep breath to blow out the light, her act is one of defiance. She takes control of her death as she had always controlled her life.*

ANSWERS

Vocabulary in Context

VOCABULARY PRACTICE

1. *true*
2. *false*
3. *false*
4. *true*
5. *false*

R RESOURCE MANAGER—Copy Master
Vocabulary Practice p. 348

VOCABULARY IN WRITING

Have students explain their opinions to a partner before they begin writing. Partners should identify statements that might work with a vocabulary word. Tell students that they can incorporate additional vocabulary words as they draft and revise their writing.

VOCABULARY STRATEGY: NOUNS AND FIGURATIVE VERBS *(also an EL language objective)*

- Explain that a figurative verb is simply a verb used as figurative language, usually implying a comparison.
- Model the practice using the first item. Identify the noun *pepper* from the boldfaced verb; then define the noun and explain its figurative use in the sentence.

Possible answers:

1. *to toss in or over, as pepper is tossed or sprinkled over food; Ben sprinkles the expressions into his explanation.*

2. *to hold or keep secure, as a harbor is a secure place for ships; A person's mind can be a secure place to keep thoughts.*

3. *to design or build, as an engineer designs reliable items; The campaign managers designed a reliable plan for victory.*

4. *to tie firmly, as an anchor keeps a ship from floating away; The conclusions are securely attached to research.*

5. *to show off, to act to impress, as people in a grandstand can see and be seen; Someone showing off wants to be on display.*

R RESOURCE MANAGER—Copy Master
Vocabulary Strategy p. 349

ℹ Vocabulary Center at **ClassZone.com**
Additional Vocabulary Activities

Vocabulary in Context

VOCABULARY PRACTICE

Decide whether each statement is true or false.

1. If your supplies have begun to **dwindle,** you probably need to find a way to get more.
2. An **amethyst** is a special shawl worn for good luck.
3. A tablecloth that is **embroidered** has beautiful designs painted on it.
4. If I am an **assign** in your will, I should expect to inherit at least a portion of what you have.
5. People who **plague** others are transmitting symptoms of a serious disease.

WORD LIST
amethyst
assign
dwindle
embroidered
plague

VOCABULARY IN WRITING

Why do you think that Granny Weatherall remembered George for so many years? Write a paragraph or two stating your opinion, using two or more vocabulary words. You could start this way.

> **EXAMPLE SENTENCE**
>
> *I think that thoughts of George continued to **plague** Granny because of how he treated her.*

VOCABULARY STRATEGY: NOUNS AND FIGURATIVE VERBS

Many English words start out as nouns. Over time, however, they also take on meaning as verbs. For example, the noun form of the vocabulary word *plague* refers to an affliction or disaster. What connection can you see between this meaning and the meaning of the verb form of *plague,* as in the phrase "plagued by doubts"?

PRACTICE Use context clues to determine the meaning of each underlined verb. Then write a definition for each word and explain how the definition relates to the meaning of the original noun form.

1. Ben **peppered** his explanation with "Unbelievable!" and other expressions of surprise.
2. Despite their refusal to help her, Pauline **harbored** no ill will toward her brothers.
3. Through hard work and clever planning, they **engineered** an election victory for the underdog candidate.
4. These conclusions are **anchored** in several months of experimentation and solid research.
5. Adam is an excellent goalie who doesn't need to **grandstand** for the fans.

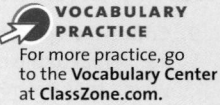

VOCABULARY PRACTICE
For more practice, go to the **Vocabulary Center** at **ClassZone.com.**

DIFFERENTIATED INSTRUCTION

FOR ENGLISH LEARNERS

Task Support: Vocabulary Strategy Ask students if their home languages also have figurative verbs that come from nouns, and invite them to share examples in translation. Then help them think of other examples in English. Have them use one example to create a sentence modeled on the practice exercises.

FOR ADVANCED LEARNERS/AP

Nouns and Figurative Verbs Challenge students to create a short glossary of recently created figurative verbs, especially those related to new technologies. For example, *access* and *google,* once a common and a proper noun, are now figurative verbs. Students can publish or post the glossary for class reference.

Reading-Writing Connection

W1.2, W2.1

WRITING PROMPT

USE STREAM OF CONSCIOUSNESS Katherine Anne Porter wasn't the only modernist to experiment with stream of consciousness; T. S. Eliot, James Joyce, and William Faulkner all used it to explore the intricacies of the human mind. Some writers use it today. Now you'll get a chance to try it for yourself. Write a **three- or four-paragraph narrative** in stream of consciousness, depicting the thoughts and impressions of a character having a particular experience. You can either write about yourself or create a fictional character.

SELF-CHECK

A compelling narrative will . . .

- give readers a clear sense of the character's traits
- indicate the situation that sparks the character's thoughts
- show meaningful connections among thoughts and emotions
- have a point—an overall reason for revealing the connections

GRAMMAR AND STYLE

W1.9

CRAFT EFFECTIVE SENTENCES Review the **Grammar and Style** note on page 994. Porter skillfully crafts her prose in "The Jilting of Granny Weatherall" to depict Granny's interior life—her secret longings, wishes, and memories. Through her use of **repetition** and the **coordinating conjunction** *and,* Porter reveals Granny's circular thoughts and hazy memories.

> *Then Hapsy melted from within and turned flimsy as gray gauze and the baby was a gauzy shadow, and Hapsy came up close and said, "I thought you'd never come," and looked at her very searchingly and said, "You haven't changed a bit!"* (lines 183–186)

Notice the dreamlike quality of the sentence, with its many *and*'s linking the images as well as its repetition of *gauze* and *gauzy* and related terms *flimsy* and *shadow.*

PRACTICE The following passage presents a character's thoughts as they might appear in a traditional third-person narrative. Rewrite the paragraph as a third-person stream of consciousness.

> Ron walked down the street whistling, his hands shoved deep into his pockets. He squinted up at the weak rays fighting to break through the winter cloud cover. When his gaze returned to street level, he almost tripped over his own feet. Abby was walking toward him.
> "I wonder if she'll even recognize me," Ron thought to himself, quickening his pace and trying to clear his face of emotion.

WRITING TOOLS
For prewriting, revision, and editing tools, visit the **Writing Center** at ClassZone.com.

THE JILTING OF GRANNY WEATHERALL **1001**

FOR DEVELOPING WRITERS

Writing Support

- Limit the length of the narrative to one or two paragraphs.
- Clarify the difference between stream-of-consciousness writing and the more typical first-person point of view. Have students write a draft from a purely first-person point of view and then adapt it as stream of consciousness.

- Have students read their stream-of-consciousness drafts to a partner, asking for new associations between thoughts and memories. Ask students to incorporate the feedback as they revise.

Reading-Writing Connection

WRITING PROMPT

Have students use organizers to identify character traits and plot events. Students can then explore possible connections among thoughts, feelings, and memories, perhaps using a Sequence Chain to track those connections.

 BEST PRACTICES TOOLKIT—Transparencies
   Character Traits Web p. D7
   Plot Diagram p. D10
   Sequence Chain p. B21

For writing support, see

 Writing Center at **ClassZone.com**

GRAMMAR AND STYLE

Tell students that in most writing situations, sentences composed of short phrases and clauses joined by *and* would be considered choppy and would invite revision. Stress that this style of writing has a specific function in Porter's story—to show Granny's feverish jumps from memory to memory. ***Possible answers:*** *Students' paragraphs should reflect a first-person stream of consciousness voice, as if they were simply recording Ron's thoughts.*

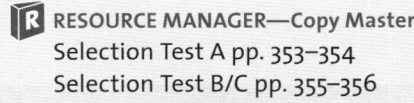 **RESOURCE MANAGER—Copy Master**
   Craft Effective Sentences p. 352

Assess and Reteach

Assess

 RESOURCE MANAGER—Copy Masters
   Selection Test A pp. 353–354
   Selection Test B/C pp. 355–356

 Test Generator CD

Reteach

STANDARDS LESSON FILE
   Literature Lesson 8: Foreshadowing and Flashback
   Literature Lesson 36: Irony
   Reading Lesson 6: Recognizing Sequence and Chronological Order

OBJECTIVES

Literary Analysis
- explore the key idea of **endurance**
- analyze universal theme
- read a short story

Reading
- monitor comprehension

Vocabulary
- build vocabulary for reading and writing
- use the root *med* to unlock meaning *(also an EL language objective)*

Grammar and Writing
- use action verbs and participial phrases to add descriptive details
- write a story

 CALIFORNIA R3.2, R3.6, R1.2, W1.2, W1.9, W2.1

ABOUT THE AUTHOR

Explain that Welty noted similarities between her work as a photographer and as a writer. To succeed at both, she had to gain enough distance from her subjects to understand their situations. This allowed her to slowly zoom in to learn more.

USING THE *NOTABLE QUOTE*

Ask students the reasons **Eudora Welty** might give for reading literature—and the limitation she would add. *Possible answer: Literature presents people, emotions, and settings for readers to get to know and enjoy, but it cannot tell readers how to live or think.*

The Modern Short Story

CALIFORNIA

R3.2, R3.6, R1.2 (p. 1016), W1.2 (p. 1017), W1.9 (p. 1017), W2.1 (p. 1017)

NOTABLE QUOTE
"There is absolutely everything in great fiction but a clear answer."

FYI
Did you know that Eudora Welty ...
- was voted "Best All-Round Girl" in high school?
- was awarded the Presidential Medal of Freedom in 1980?
- inspired the name of an e-mail program, "Eudora," so named by a Web designer who loved her stories?

Author Online

For more on Eudora Welty, visit the **Literature Center at ClassZone.com.**

One of Welty's WPA photographs from the 1930s

A Worn Path
Short Story by Eudora Welty

Eudora Welty
1909–2001

Mississippi born and bred, Eudora Welty wrote about her fellow Southerners at a crucial time in U.S. history. When she first began publishing her stories in the late 1930s, vestiges of the Old South still colored daily life. But Welty lived long enough to see the changes wrought by the civil rights movement in the 1960s and the rise of the New South on the eve of the new millennium. All the while, she recorded the lives of ordinary people, depicting the family life that sustained them and the small acts of heroism that dignified them. She was a modernist who believed in love, a Southerner who had faith in tolerance and change, and a successful, unmarried woman at a time when single women in Mississippi were not allowed to buy a house. At first dismissed as a regionalist and even a "feminine" writer, Welty lived long enough to see her fiction recognized for its artistic vision and universal appeal. Through it all, she accepted the changes with her characteristic sense of humor, modesty, and grace.

A Photographer's Eye Nourished by books and a close-knit community of family and friends, Welty lived most of her life in the house her father built in Jackson, Mississippi. Although she wrote stories even in childhood and attended college, her education as a writer didn't seriously begin until 1933, when she landed a job as a publicity agent with the federal government's Works Progress Administration (WPA). Interviewing and photographing all kinds of people throughout Mississippi during the Great Depression—one of the most impoverished regions during the poorest time in the nation's history—was an eye opener for Welty and gave her the first "real germ" of her writing. Her early stories, such as "Why I Live at the P.O." and "A Worn Path," are like photographs, capturing a specific moment that reveals something significant about a person and at the same time a greater truth about the human condition.

A Long, Productive Life Welty received numerous awards and honors for her works, including a Pulitzer Prize for her novel *The Optimist's Daughter* (1972) and an O. Henry Award for "A Worn Path." Her award-winning memoir, *One Writer's Beginnings* (1984), was a runaway bestseller. Despite being very articulate about her writing, sitting graciously through countless interviews, and receiving large numbers of young fans at her home, Welty remained a very private person who always maintained that "a fiction writer should let writing speak for

1002

RESOURCE MANAGER UNIT 5

Plan and Teach pp. 357–364

Literary Analysis
Summary pp. 365†*, 366‡*
Universal Theme pp. 367, 368†*
Question Support p. 375*

Reading
Monitor pp. 369, 370†*
Reading Check p. 374

Vocabulary
Study p. 371*
Practice p. 372
Strategy p. 373

Grammar and Writing
Add Descriptive Details p. 376

Assessment
Selection Test A, B/C pp. 377*, 379*
Test Generator CD

BEST PRACTICES TOOLKIT

Differentiated Instruction pp. 31–38*

Scaffolding Instruction pp. 43–46*

Graphic Organizers/Strategies
Word Questioning • Character Traits Web • Three-Column Journal • Comparison Matrix • Word Families • Story Frame • Character Sketch

Reading Support
Audio Anthology CD*

Technology
Literature, Vocabulary, and Writing Centers at **ClassZone.com**
Write*Smart* CD

---

* Resources for Differentiation   † Also in Spanish   ‡ In Haitian Creole and Vietnamese

LITERARY ANALYSIS: UNIVERSAL THEME

You know that theme is the underlying message a writer wants readers to understand. A **universal theme** is a message that can be found throughout literature of all times and places. Works that convey a universal theme often contain **archetypes**—basic patterns found in a variety of works from different cultures throughout history. The perilous journey is one such archetype; the main character in this story travels a long and uncertain path in search of something.

As you read, consider what this journey might symbolize. Think about the main character's traits and how she deals with obstacles on the path, as well as the story's title and its setting. Taken together, what universal theme do these elements suggest?

READING STRATEGY: MONITOR

This story has a dreamlike quality that can make it challenging to follow. **Monitoring** is the strategy of checking your comprehension as you are reading and using techniques such as **questioning** and **clarifying** to aid your understanding. As you read, stop every once in a while to consider how well you are comprehending the story. Jot down any questions that come to mind. Review what you do understand and use context clues and analysis of key words and details to clarify the meaning of anything you don't.

> Question:
> If Phoenix is alone on her journey, why does she keep speaking aloud?
> Clarification:

▲ VOCABULARY IN CONTEXT

Welty uses the boldfaced words in her story of one woman's pilgrimage. Replace each boldfaced word with a new word or phrase.

1. **Limber** branches swayed back and forth in the breeze.
2. She gazed at the **radiation** of ripples each raindrop created on the pond's surface.
3. He could not shake his **obstinate** cough.
4. The **meditative** hiker gazed at the sky.

Explore the Key Idea

What keeps us GOING?

KEY IDEA Endurance is crucial in any long-distance sport, and it's a necessity for surviving harsh conditions or extreme adventures. But what kind of endurance is required for daily life? And where does this type of endurance come from?

DISCUSS With a small group of classmates, discuss the preceding questions. Begin by talking about what you think motivates champion athletes or people facing extreme conditions. Then consider what motivates ordinary people to endure—to keep attending night school while working two day jobs, for example, or to sacrifice a favorite after school activity in order to drive younger siblings to theirs. In your opinion, is the motivation the same in both the extreme and the ordinary cases? If not, what's the difference?

1003

Teach

What keeps us GOING?

To lead into the **KEY IDEA** paragraph, ask students to list their weekly obligations and describe the kinds of **endurance** needed to complete the listed tasks. After they finish the **DISCUSS** activity, invite groups to share conclusions. Then, ask students to generate advice on the endurance needed for daily life.

SKILLS FOCUS

LITERARY ANALYSIS   R3.2, R3.6

● UNIVERSAL THEME

Ask students to list some plot structures from favorite TV shows, movies, or books. Note archetypal plots such as the quest for love, a precious object, or knowledge; the betrayal or proof of friendship; and the desire for vengeance. Discuss with students why the same stories are told again and again. Point out that these plots explore the greatest needs and desires in human life and thus generate universal themes.

CHECK UNDERSTANDING Ask students to identify a universal theme in one of the examples listed. Remind them that a theme is a message for readers, not a plot.

READING STRATEGY

■ MONITOR

Point out that students already use monitoring strategies to keep up with stories on serialized TV shows and to track current events among friends. Asking questions and clarifying are natural responses to confusion, as a friend might ask another "Why on earth did she do *that*?" Urge them to apply these life strategies to their reading.

CHECK UNDERSTANDING Have pairs dramatize a phone call in which friends ask questions to gain information and clarify.

> **R** RESOURCE MANAGER—Copy Master
> Monitor p. 369 (for student use while reading the selection)

VOCABULARY

▲ VOCABULARY IN CONTEXT

DIAGNOSE WORD KNOWLEDGE To determine preteaching needs, have all students complete Vocabulary in Context. *Answers:* **1.** *supple, bendable;* **2.** *motion from a central point outward in rings or rays;* **3.** *stubborn;* **4.** *thoughtful*

PRETEACH VOCABULARY Preteach vocabulary with this copy master. Read each item aloud.

> **R** RESOURCE MANAGER—Copy Master
> Vocabulary Study p. 371

MORE VOCABULARY SUPPORT
For additional activities and guidelines, see

> 🧰 BEST PRACTICES TOOLKIT
> Scaffolding Vocabulary Instruction pp. 43–46
> ⓘ Vocabulary Center at **ClassZone.com**

SUMMARY

In this story, Phoenix Jackson walks from her rural farm to the city of Natchez to get medicine for her injured grandson. The trip challenges the aging Phoenix's physical and mental strength, but she gets not only the medicine for her grandson but also a small toy that she knows will delight him. Then she begins the long walk home.

Lines 3–9
REINFORCE *KEY IDEA:* ENDURANCE

Discuss What words and descriptions in these lines hint at Phoenix's **endurance** as she begins this journey? *Possible answer: Words such as "kept tapping" (line 7) and "persistent noise" (line 8) hint at Phoenix's ability to endure, to keep going. The comparison of her gait to a clock's steady ticking also suggests endurance.*

LITERARY ANALYSIS

Ⓐ UNIVERSAL THEME

Possible answer: The journey's length is suggested by how early Phoenix begins the trip, by her slow, balanced gait, and by her need for the cane to help her see the path.

Extend the Discussion How does the season affect Phoenix's need to make the journey as quickly as possible?

A Worn Path

Eudora Welty

BACKGROUND This story takes place in rural Mississippi in the 1930s, an era in which segregation laws and racism, combined with the economic devastation of the Great Depression, restricted most Southern blacks to lives of rural poverty and hardship. Eudora Welty saw the need and inequality surrounding her. She based this story on an old woman she observed crossing a field: "I thought, she is bent on an errand. And I know it isn't for herself. It was just the look of her figure.... She was a black woman. But then I suppose it would be more likely to be a black woman who would be in such desperate need and live so remotely away from help and who would have so far to go."

It was December—a bright frozen day in the early morning. Far out in the country there was an old Negro woman with her head tied in a red rag, coming along a path through the pinewoods. Her name was Phoenix Jackson. She was very old and small and she walked slowly in the dark pine shadows, moving a little from side to side in her steps, with the balanced heaviness and lightness of a pendulum in a grandfather clock. She carried a thin, small cane made from an umbrella, and with this she kept tapping the frozen earth in front of her. This made a grave and persistent noise in the still air, that seemed **meditative** like the chirping of a solitary little bird. Ⓐ

ANALYZE VISUALS
What thematic ideas might you ascribe to this painting? Identify the elements of the painting that suggest these ideas.

meditative (mĕd′ĭ-tā′tĭv) *adj.* engaged in serious thought or reflection

Ⓐ UNIVERSAL THEME
What details in lines 1–9 suggest that Phoenix is in for a long journey? As you read, keep in mind other **archetypal** journeys you know of.

Brooding Silence (date unknown), John Fabian Carlson. Smithsonian American Art Museum, Washington, D.C. © Smithsonian American Art Museum, Washington, D.C./Art Resource, New York.

DIFFERENTIATED INSTRUCTION

FOR ALL STUDENTS
Provide these independent projects to extend the lesson:

- Explore endurance by brainstorming new uses for old items.
- Write an essay discussing Phoenix as an archetypical hero.
- Depict a rural Mississippi home.

For further details on these projects, see

Ⓡ **RESOURCE MANAGER**
Ideas for Extension pp. 362–363

FOR STRATEGIC READERS
In combination with the *Audio Anthology CD,* use one or more Targeted Passages (pp. 1006, 1009, 1010, and 1012) to ensure that students focus on key story events and concepts. Targeted passages are also good for English learners.

ANALYZE VISUALS

Possible answer: The painting suggests the theme of a journey, with the faint trace of a path visible amongst the trees. It also suggests loneliness, as there is snow on the ground and the few remaining leaves are brown.

About the Art The forest landscapes of painter John Fabian Carlson (1875–1945) are noted for their romantic, impressionistic depiction of nature. Precise detail in this landscape gives way to a strong sense of place. This forest may appear to viewers, in fact, somewhat as it appears to Phoenix, with her weak eyesight, as she walks through it.

BACKGROUND

Depression-Era Mississippi The economic devastation of the Great Depression hit a Mississippi already in distress. The state had not recovered from the Civil War, which damaged both the rich farm land and the people, or from reconstruction policies that created low-paying tenant-farming jobs. In addition, the great flood of the Mississippi River in 1927 caused further damage to farmlands. In these hard economic times, newly emancipated African Americans carried the dual burdens of practical disenfranchisement and lack of education.

FOR ENGLISH LEARNERS

Vocabulary: Multiple-Meaning Words Elicit or share the meanings of these words as used in context: *grave* (line 8), "solemn, serious"; *still* (line 8), "motionless." The first word may present a particular challenge to students familiar with its noun form. Have them use Word Questioning to further explore the words.

 BEST PRACTICES TOOLKIT—Transparency
Word Questioning p. E9

Prereading For prereading instruction for English learners, see

BEST PRACTICES TOOLKIT
Scaffolding Reading Instruction pp. 43–46

FOR ADVANCED LEARNERS/AP

AP exercises in the bottom channel provide additional challenge for students. Use these suggestions for small groups or individuals.

ADDITIONAL GUIDELINES

For more help with differentiation and tips for classroom management, see

 BEST PRACTICES TOOLKIT
Differentiated Instruction pp. 31–38

Lines 29–50
TIERED DISCUSSION PROMPTS

Use these prompts to help students understand Phoenix's character as her actions and words reveal it:

Recall What does the reader know about Phoenix? *Possible answer: She is old, small, uses a cane, and she has "a long way" to go (line 22) as she travels through the woods.*

Interpret What typically simple tasks does Phoenix struggle with, and why? *Possible answer: She struggles to walk up a hill, to see and avoid thorny brush, and to cross a creek on a log. These tasks are simple for people in good health, but Phoenix has poor eyesight, and is old and frail.*

Synthesize What do Phoenix's words and actions suggest about how she perceives the challenges she faces? *Possible answer: Phoenix seems to perceive the challenges as a conflict with herself as much as with nature. She notes that something inside her "pleads I should stay" (line 31) rather than climb the hill, but she climbs it. She fears crossing the log, but acts in faith as she closes her eyes and steps out.*

LITERARY ANALYSIS

B UNIVERSAL THEME

Possible answer: The thorny bush might symbolize any trial that Phoenix may face. Phoenix is philosophical about the trouble—the thorns are just doing what they are designed to do (lines 38–39). Her attitude suggests that she does not get upset about things she can't control.

---

10 She wore a dark striped dress reaching down to her shoe tops, and an equally long apron of bleached sugar sacks, with a full pocket: all neat and tidy, but every time she took a step she might have fallen over her shoelaces, which dragged from her unlaced shoes. She looked straight ahead. Her eyes were blue with age. Her skin had a pattern all its own of numberless branching wrinkles and as though a whole little tree stood in the middle of her forehead, but a golden color ran underneath, and the two knobs of her cheeks were illumined by a yellow burning under the dark. Under the red rag her hair came down on her neck in the frailest of ringlets, still black, and with an odor like copper.

① Targeted Passage

Now and then there was a quivering in the thicket. Old Phoenix said, "Out
20 of my way, all you foxes, owls, beetles, jack rabbits, coons and wild animals! . . . Keep out from under these feet, little bob-whites.[1] . . . Keep the big wild hogs out of my path. Don't let none of those come running my direction. I got a long way." Under her small black-freckled hand her cane, **limber** as a buggy whip, would switch at the brush as if to rouse up any hiding things.

limber (lĭm′bər) *adj.* bending or moving easily; supple

On she went. The woods were deep and still. The sun made the pine needles almost too bright to look at, up where the wind rocked. The cones dropped as light as feathers. Down in the hollow was the mourning dove—it was not too late for him.

The path ran up a hill. "Seem like there is chains about my feet, time I get this
30 far," she said, in the voice of argument old people keep to use with themselves. "Something always take a hold of me on this hill—pleads I should stay."

After she got to the top she turned and gave a full, severe look behind her where she had come. "Up through pines," she said at length. "Now down through oaks."

Her eyes opened their widest, and she started down gently. But before she got to the bottom of the hill a bush caught her dress.

Her fingers were busy and intent, but her skirts were full and long, so that before she could pull them free in one place they were caught in another. It was not possible to allow the dress to tear. "I in the thorny bush," she said. "Thorns, you doing your appointed work. Never want to let folks pass, no sir. Old eyes
40 thought you was a pretty little *green* bush."

Finally, trembling all over, she stood free, and after a moment dared to stoop for her cane.

"Sun so high!" she cried, leaning back and looking, while the thick tears went over her eyes. "The time getting all gone here." **B**

At the foot of this hill was a place where a log was laid across the creek.

"Now comes the trial," said Phoenix.

Putting her right foot out, she mounted the log and shut her eyes. Lifting her skirt, leveling her cane fiercely before her, like a festival figure in some parade, she began to march across. Then she opened her eyes and she was safe on the other side.
50 "I wasn't as old as I thought," she said.

B UNIVERSAL THEME
Reread lines 34–44, and explain what you think the thorny bush might **symbolize**. What does Phoenix's way of dealing with this obstacle suggest about her character?

---

1. **bob-whites:** game birds that are a type of quail.

1006 UNIT 5: THE HARLEM RENAISSANCE AND MODERNISM

DIFFERENTIATED INSTRUCTION

FOR STRATEGIC READERS

① Targeted Passage [Lines 10–18]

This passage uses vivid description to introduce the main character, Phoenix.

- Of what are Phoenix's clothes made?
- What is distinctive about her skin?
- How would you describe her gaze?
- What is potentially dangerous about her shoes?

FOR ENGLISH LEARNERS

Language: Conversational English Patterns
Point out and clarify nonstandard English such as *Don't let none* (line 22), which means "Don't let any." Read these examples, and help students restate them: *Seem like there is chains* (line 29), "I feel like there are chains"; *Thorns, you doing* (lines 38–39), "Thorns, you are doing"; *Old eyes thought you was* (lines 39–40), "Old eyes thought you were"; *The time getting all gone* (line 44), "The time is passing quickly."

FOR ADVANCED LEARNERS/AP

Interpret Symbolism [small-group option]
Have students reread lines 10–18, paying close attention to words that describe or suggest color. Then have them discuss:

- What colors are associated with Phoenix?
- What emotions and ideas do these colors connect to Phoenix?
- What predictions about Phoenix can readers base on this description?

Invite groups to share their conclusions.

But she sat down to rest. She spread her skirts on the bank around her and folded her hands over her knees. Up above her was a tree in a pearly cloud of mistletoe. She did not dare to close her eyes, and when a little boy brought her a plate with a slice of marble-cake on it she spoke to him. "That would be acceptable," she said. But when she went to take it there was just her own hand in the air. **C**

So she left that tree, and had to go through a barbed-wire fence. There she had to creep and crawl, spreading her knees and stretching her fingers like a baby trying to climb the steps. But she talked loudly to herself: she could not let her
60 dress be torn now, so late in the day, and she could not pay for having her arm or her leg sawed off if she got caught fast where she was.

At last she was safe through the fence and risen up out in the clearing. Big dead trees, like black men with one arm, were standing in the purple stalks of the withered cotton field. There sat a buzzard. **D**

"Who you watching?"

In the furrow she made her way along.

"Glad this not the season for bulls," she said, looking sideways, "and the good Lord made his snakes to curl up and sleep in the winter. A pleasure I don't see no two-headed snake coming around that tree, where it come once. It took a while to
70 get by him, back in the summer."

She passed through the old cotton and went into a field of dead corn. It whispered and shook and was taller than her head. "Through the maze now," she said, for there was no path. **E**

Then there was something tall, black, and skinny there, moving before her.

At first she took it for a man. It could have been a man dancing in the field. But she stood still and listened, and it did not make a sound. It was as silent as a ghost.

"Ghost," she said sharply, "who be you the ghost of? For I have heard of nary[2] death close by."
80 But there was no answer—only the ragged dancing in the wind.

She shut her eyes, reached out her hand, and touched a sleeve. She found a coat and inside that an emptiness, cold as ice.

"You scarecrow," she said. Her face lighted. "I ought to be shut up for good," she said with laughter. "My senses is gone. I too old. I the oldest people I ever know. Dance, old scarecrow," she said, "while I dancing with you."

She kicked her foot over the furrow, and with mouth drawn down, shook her head once or twice in a little strutting way. Some husks blew down and whirled in streamers about her skirts.

Then she went on, parting her way from side to side with the cane, through
90 the whispering field. At last she came to the end, to a wagon track where the silver grass blew between the red ruts. The quail were walking around like pullets,[3] seeming all dainty and unseen.

---

2. **nary:** not any.
3. **pullets:** young hens.

A WORN PATH **1007**

C MONITOR
Reread lines 51–56. What is happening in these lines? **Clarify** the meaning by considering the trials Phoenix has faced thus far, as well as how she feels at this point in her journey.

D UNIVERSAL THEME
Examine the images in lines 62–64. What **mood** do they help create? Explain.

E GRAMMAR AND STYLE
Welty uses a variety of sensory **details** to make Phoenix's journey riveting for readers. Reread lines 71–73, noting how the **verbs** *whispered* and *shook* conjure sights and sounds in your mind.

A WORN PATH **1007**

Snowy Woods at Dusk (date unknown), Dennis Sheehan. Oil, 20″ × 16″. Courtesy of Susan Powell Fine Art, Madison, Connecticut.

"Walk pretty," she said. "This the easy place. This the easy going." **F**

She followed the track, swaying through the quiet bare fields, through the little strings of trees silver in their dead leaves, past cabins silver from weather, with the doors and windows boarded shut, all like old women under a spell sitting there. "I walking in their sleep," she said, nodding her head vigorously.

In a ravine she went where a spring was silently flowing through a hollow log. Old Phoenix bent and drank. "Sweet-gum[4] makes the water sweet," she said, and

100 drank more. "Nobody know who made this well, for it was here when I was born."

The track crossed a swampy part where the moss hung as white as lace from every limb. "Sleep on, alligators, and blow your bubbles." Then the track went into the road.

Deep, deep the road went down between the high green-colored banks. Overhead the live-oaks[5] met, and it was as dark as a cave.

A black dog with a lolling tongue came up out of the weeds by the ditch. She was meditating, and not ready, and when he came at her she only hit him a little with her cane. Over she went in the ditch, like a little puff of milkweed.

---

4. **sweet-gum:** a tree of the witch hazel family.

5. **live-oaks:** oak trees of a type that has evergreen foliage.

1008 UNIT 5: THE HARLEM RENAISSANCE AND MODERNISM

1008 UNIT 5: THE HARLEM RENAISSANCE AND MODERNISM

Down there, her senses drifted away. A dream visited her, and she reached her
110 hand up, but nothing reached down and gave her a pull. So she lay there and
presently went to talking. "Old woman," she said to herself, "that black dog come
up out of the weeds to stall you off, and now there he sitting on his fine tail,
smiling at you."

A white man finally came along and found her—a hunter, a young man, with
his dog on a chain. **G**

"Well, Granny!" he laughed. "What are you doing there?"

"Lying on my back like a June-bug waiting to be turned over, mister," she said,
reaching up her hand.

He lifted her up, gave her a swing in the air, and set her down. "Anything
120 broken, Granny?"

"No sir, them old dead weeds is springy enough," said Phoenix, when she had
got her breath. "I thank you for your trouble."

"Where do you live, Granny?" he asked, while the two dogs were growling at
each other.

"Away back yonder, sir, behind the ridge. You can't even see it from here."

"On your way home?"

"No sir, I going to town."

"Why, that's too far! That's as far as I walk when I come out myself, and I get
something for my trouble." He patted the stuffed bag he carried, and there hung
130 down a little closed claw. It was one of the bob-whites, with its beak hooked
bitterly to show it was dead. "Now you go on home, Granny!"

"I bound to go to town, mister," said Phoenix. "The time come around."

He gave another laugh, filling the whole landscape. "I know you old colored
people! Wouldn't miss going to town to see Santa Claus!"

But something held old Phoenix very still. The deep lines in her face went into
a fierce and different **radiation**. Without warning, she had seen with her own eyes
a flashing nickel fall out of the man's pocket onto the ground.

"How old are you, Granny?" he was saying.

"There is no telling, mister," she said, "no telling."

140 Then she gave a little cry and clapped her hands and said, "Git on away from
here, dog! Look! Look at that dog!" She laughed as if in admiration. "He ain't
scared of nobody. He a big black dog." She whispered, "Sic him!"

"Watch me get rid of that cur," said the man. "Sic him, Pete! Sic him!"

Phoenix heard the dogs fighting, and heard the man running and throwing
sticks. She even heard a gunshot. But she was slowly bending forward by that
time, further and further forward, the lids stretched down over her eyes, as if she
were doing this in her sleep. Her chin was lowered almost to her knees. The yellow
palm of her hand came out from the fold of her apron. Her fingers slid down and
along the ground under the piece of money with the grace and care they would
150 have in lifting an egg from under a setting hen. Then she slowly straightened up,

G MONITOR
Reread lines 106–115. How can you tell when Phoenix is experiencing actual events or interacting with real people and when she has "drifted away" into her own imagination? Write two **questions** that help you understand what is real and what is not.

2 Targeted Passage

radiation (rā′dē-ā′shən) n. the movement of lines or rays from a center point

G MONITOR

Possible answer: Careful reading can help readers distinguish real events from Phoenix's drifting. Clarifying questions might include: Is the encounter fleeting or sustained? Do the details suggest that the encounter is real or imaginary?

Lines 123–143
TIERED DISCUSSION PROMPTS
Use these prompts to help students follow Phoenix's encounter with the hunter:

Recall Why does Phoenix, who has been self-reliant until this point, need help? *Possible answer: The dog knocked her into a ditch, and she is dazed and unable to get up on her own.*

Interpret What kind of man is the hunter? Explain. *Possible answer: The hunter is successful enough to have a gun and trained dog so he can hunt for food. He is proud of his ability, his dog, and the birds he has already bagged. He also thinks that he knows better than Phoenix what actions are right for her to take, and he underestimates her intelligence.*

Synthesize From what you know about people, why does Phoenix praise the black dog in front of the hunter? Why does he respond as he does? What does the interaction tell readers about Phoenix's intelligence? *Possible answer: Phoenix has seen a nickel fall out of the hunter's pocket. She praises the black dog to get the hunter's attention away from the nickel so that she can get it. He responds as he does to prove that his dog is stronger than the black dog. The interaction tells readers that Phoenix, despite her age and poverty, understands people and how to affect their behavior.*

FOR STRATEGIC READERS
2 Targeted Passage [Lines 114–134]

This passage uses Phoenix's interaction with a hunter to describe her character and show that she is determined to reach town.

• Who helps Phoenix up, and what is he doing there?

• What does the hunter advise Phoenix to do, and how does she respond?

• What reason for Phoenix's trip to town does the hunter assume?

FOR ENGLISH LEARNERS
Culture: Clarify Explain to students that a nickel, though not worth much today, had much greater purchasing power at the time of the story's setting. Phoenix feels that she has stolen something of value because she has a coin that could buy a good meal for her and her grandson.

H MONITOR

Possible answer: *The interaction indicates that it was acceptable, perhaps, for a young white man (or any white person) to treat an elderly black woman without respect, to threaten and patronize her.*

If students need help . . . Guide them to ask clarifying questions, such as these:

- How are younger people supposed to treat their elders?
- How are men expected to behave towards women?
- Does the hunter follow these social expectations?

Remind students to add these questions to the lists they began on page 1003.

I UNIVERSAL THEME

Possible answer: *Phoenix remains calm and collected (lines 157–160), but she is not above stealing the man's change. This resourcefulness has probably helped her during her long life, as it helps her on today's journey.*

Extend the Discussion What does Phoenix think of her own behavior? How might the hunter's claim that he has no money with him change readers' view of the theft?

---

she stood erect, and the nickel was in her apron pocket. A bird flew by. Her lips moved. "God watching me the whole time. I come to stealing."

The man came back, and his own dog panted about them. "Well, I scared him off that time," he said, and then he laughed and lifted his gun and pointed it at Phoenix.

She stood straight and faced him.

"Doesn't the gun scare you?" he said, still pointing it.

"No, sir, I seen plenty go off closer by, in my day, and for less than what I done," she said, holding utterly still.

160 He smiled, and shouldered the gun. "Well, Granny," he said, "you must be a hundred years old, and scared of nothing. I'd give you a dime if I had any money with me. But you take my advice and stay home, and nothing will happen to you." **H**

"I bound to go on my way, mister," said Phoenix. She inclined her head in the red rag. Then they went in different directions, but she could hear the gun shooting again and again over the hill. **I**

She walked on. The shadows hung from the oak trees to the road like curtains. Then she smelled wood-smoke, and smelled the river, and she saw a steeple and the cabins on their steep steps. Dozens of little black children whirled around her.

170 There ahead was Natchez shining. Bells were ringing. She walked on.

In the paved city it was Christmas time. There were red and green electric lights strung and criss-crossed everywhere, and all turned on in the daytime. Old Phoenix would have been lost if she had not distrusted her eyesight and depended on her feet to know where to take her.

She paused quietly on the sidewalk where people were passing by. A lady came along in the crowd, carrying an armful of red-, green- and silver-wrapped presents; she gave off perfume like the red roses in hot summer, and Phoenix stopped her.

"Please, missy, will you lace up my shoe?" She held up her foot.

"What do you want, Grandma?"

180 "See my shoe," said Phoenix. "Do all right for out in the country, but wouldn't look right to go in a big building." **3 Targeted Passage**

"Stand still then, Grandma," said the lady. She put her packages down on the sidewalk beside her and laced and tied both shoes tightly.

"Can't lace 'em with a cane," said Phoenix. "Thank you, missy. I doesn't mind asking a nice lady to tie up my shoe, when I gets out on the street."

Moving slowly and from side to side, she went into the big building, and into a tower of steps, where she walked up and around and around until her feet knew to stop.

She entered a door, and there she saw nailed up on the wall the document 190 that had been stamped with the gold seal and framed in the gold frame, which matched the dream that was hung up in her head.

H MONITOR
Keep the story's **setting** in mind as you contemplate the way the hunter treats Phoenix. What does their interaction tell you about this time and place in history?

I UNIVERSAL THEME
Reread lines 114–166, and describe the **character traits** Phoenix exhibits during this episode with the hunter. How do her traits help her overcome this particular obstacle in her journey?

ANALYZE VISUALS
What elements of this portrait give the woman a look of inner strength and determination? Be specific.

DIFFERENTIATED INSTRUCTION

FOR STRATEGIC READERS

3 Targeted Passage [Lines 175–185]

This passage reveals that it is important to Phoenix that she look her best in the city.

- Why does Phoenix ask for help with her shoelaces?
- Why can't she lace them herself?
- What kind of person does Phoenix ask for help?
- How does the lady respond?

FOR ENGLISH LEARNERS

Comprehension Support Ask students what the document described in lines 189–191 is. Explain that doctors often display certificates proving that they have completed necessary medical training. Show students photos of such certificates in books or online. Ask students how doctors' credentials are conveyed in their home countries.

FOR ADVANCED LEARNERS/AP

Compare and Contrast Have students analyze the contrasting settings in the story by completing a Comparison Matrix for the "worn path" that Phoenix walks so assuredly and the "paved city" of Natchez. Have students discuss the differing challenges of the two settings and decide which seems to pose the greater threat to Phoenix's success.

 BEST PRACTICES TOOLKIT—Transparency Comparison Matrix p. A24

Woman Peeling Apples (1924), Archibald J. Motley, Jr. Oil on canvas, 32¼″ × 28″. Art and Artifacts Division, Schomberg Center for Research in Black Culture, The New York Public Library, Astor, Lenox and Tilden Foundations.

ANALYZE VISUALS

Possible answer: The woman looks straight at the viewer, frankly and fearlessly. Her expression is serious but calm, and the lines of her face are strong. The organized pattern of her dress reinforces these lines. She holds her work in her lap, which suggests proficiency. All of these elements contribute to her look of strength and determination.

About the Art Archibald Motley (1891–1981) was the first African-American artist to receive the prestigious Guggenheim award, given annually to an artist or researcher whose past work is excellent, to support future work. While a young man, Motley worked for a time on the railroad, traveling and sketching the scenes and people that he saw. He is known for his portraits and narrative paintings, which capture the distinct personalities of each subject.

Lines 153–161
REINFORCE *KEY IDEA:* ENDURANCE

Discuss What does Phoenix's response to the hunter when he points his gun at her hint about her **endurance?** *Possible answer: Phoenix says she's seen guns "go off closer, in my day, and for less than what I done" (lines 158–159). This suggests that she has endured violence before, either as a freed slave or even during the era of slavery.*

FOR STRATEGIC READERS

Clarify Meaning Point out throughout the story, characters address each other by category labels rather than proper names. For example, the hunter calls Phoenix by the name "Granny" and the woman in Natchez calls her "Grandma," though neither person actually knows Phoenix to be a grandmother. They are using these terms of address as generic labels for an older woman. Phoenix calls the woman in Natchez "missy" as a label of respect, not as a specific name.

FOR ENGLISH LEARNERS

Culture: Clarify Make sure that students understand the description of the lights of Natchez in lines 171–172. Explain that at this time in America, many rural areas did not yet have electricity. Clarify that the lights are red and green because these colors are associated with Christmas. Then discuss why the lights might confuse Phoenix. *Possible answer: The lights confuse Phoenix by changing how familiar landmarks look.*

FOR ADVANCED LEARNERS/AP

Hypothesize Point out to students that the description of the lights, "and all turned on in the daytime" (line 172), is not something Phoenix says. Rather, the third person limited narrator inserts this comment. Ask students to use the Internet to find out about the Rural Electrification Act, to share their findings with the class, and to lead a discussion of why the narrator makes this comment.

The Old Natchez Trace The path that Phoenix walks, from "away back off the Old Natchez Trace" (line 204) is indeed an ancient path, part of a 444-mile long trail stretching from southern Mississippi to central Tennessee. Used for centuries by Native Americans, it later saw trade traffic and was also the site of Civil War conflict. The trail is now an American Byway; portions are accessible by car, but to see much of it, people must walk it just as Phoenix did.

Lines 213–228
TIERED DISCUSSION PROMPTS

Use these prompts to help students understand Phoenix's behavior upon arriving at her goal:

Connect What are some feelings you have had after a long journey? *Students' answers should reflect a range of emotions, such as anxiety, fear, relief, joy, or unhappiness.*

Analyze How do the attendant and the nurse react to Phoenix? Why? *Possible answer: The attendant is at first puzzled and then irritated by Phoenix's silence. The nurse recognizes Phoenix and knows why she's there, but she too becomes annoyed. Both women feel that Phoenix will "take up their time" (line 217). They are busy and want to get back to their work.*

Synthesize On the basis of what you know about Phoenix and about people, why does Phoenix apologize for her exhaustion and memory lapse? *Possible answer: Phoenix seems surprised and frightened by her memory lapse. Like most people, she probably doesn't want to admit to any weakness. Also, as an older black woman in the story's time and place, she has had years of experience showing deference to white people and may feel that she has, in fact, taken up too much of the nurse's time.*

"Here I be," she said. There was a fixed and ceremonial stiffness over her body.

"A charity case, I suppose," said an attendant who sat at the desk before her.

But Phoenix only looked above her head. There was sweat on her face, the wrinkles in her skin shone like a bright net.

"Speak up, Grandma," the woman said. "What's your name? We must have your history, you know. Have you been here before? What seems to be the trouble with you?"

Old Phoenix only gave a twitch to her face as if a fly were bothering her.

200 "Are you deaf?" cried the attendant.

But then the nurse came in.

"Oh, that's just old Aunt Phoenix," she said. "She doesn't come for herself—she has a little grandson. She makes these trips just as regular as clockwork. She lives away back off the Old Natchez Trace."[6] She bent down. "Well, Aunt Phoenix, why don't you just take a seat? We won't keep you standing after your long trip." She pointed.

The old woman sat down, bolt upright in the chair.

"Now, how is the boy?" asked the nurse.

Old Phoenix did not speak.

210 "I said, how is the boy?"

But Phoenix only waited and stared straight ahead, her face very solemn and withdrawn into rigidity.

"Is his throat any better?" asked the nurse. "Aunt Phoenix, don't you hear me? Is your grandson's throat any better since the last time you came for the medicine?"

With her hands on her knees, the old woman waited, silent, erect and motionless, just as if she were in armor.

"You mustn't take up our time this way, Aunt Phoenix," the nurse said. "Tell us quickly about your grandson, and get it over. He isn't dead, is he?"

At last there came a flicker and then a flame of comprehension across her face, 220 and she spoke.

"My grandson. It was my memory had left me. There I sat and forgot why I made my long trip."

"Forgot?" The nurse frowned. "After you came so far?"

Then Phoenix was like an old woman begging a dignified forgiveness for waking up frightened in the night. "I never did go to school, I was too old at the Surrender,"[7] she said in a soft voice. "I'm an old woman without an education. It was my memory fail me. My little grandson, he is just the same, and I forgot it in the coming."

"Throat never heals, does it?" said the nurse, speaking in a loud, sure voice to 230 old Phoenix. By now she had a card with something written on it, a little list. "Yes. Swallowed lye.[8] When was it?—January—two-three years ago—"

④ **Targeted Passage**

---

6. **Old Natchez Trace:** The Natchez Trace was an important wilderness road during the 18th and early 19th centuries, extending from Natchez, Mississippi, to Nashville, Tennessee.

7. **the Surrender:** the end of the Civil War, after which time slaves were free.

8. **lye:** a strong alkaline liquid used especially in making soap.

DIFFERENTIATED INSTRUCTION

FOR STRATEGIC READERS

④ **Targeted Passage [Lines 213–231]**

This passage reveals the reason for Phoenix's long journey and shows its effect on her.

- Why has Phoenix made the trip to Natchez?
- Why is the nurse irritated with Phoenix?
- Why does the nurse know Phoenix and know about her grandson?
- What is Phoenix's physical condition after her tiring journey?

FOR ENGLISH LEARNERS

Culture: Clarify Explain Phoenix's remark that she didn't go to school because she "was too old at the Surrender" (lines 225–226). Enslaved African Americans were not educated. After the Civil War, when free African Americans gained some access to education, Phoenix was too old to attend school. This detail clarifies how old Phoenix is and how much she has endured in her life.

Phoenix spoke unasked now. "No, missy, he not dead, he just the same. Every little while his throat begin to close up again, and he not able to swallow. He not get his breath. He not able to help himself. So the time come around, and I go on another trip for the soothing medicine." ❶

"All right. The doctor said as long as you came to get it, you could have it," said the nurse. "But it's an **obstinate** case."

"My little grandson, he sit up there in the house all wrapped up, waiting by himself," Phoenix went on. "We is the only two left in the world. He suffer and it
240 don't seem to put him back at all. He got a sweet look. He going to last. He wear a little patch quilt and peep out holding his mouth open like a little bird. I remembers so plain now. I not going to forget him again, no, the whole enduring time. I could tell him from all the others in creation."

"All right." The nurse was trying to hush her now. She brought her a bottle of medicine. "Charity," she said, making a check mark in a book.

Old Phoenix held the bottle close to her eyes, and then carefully put it into her pocket.

"I thank you," she said.

"It's Christmas time, Grandma," said the attendant. "Could I give you a few
250 pennies out of my purse?"

"Five pennies is a nickel," said Phoenix stiffly.

"Here's a nickel," said the attendant.

Phoenix rose carefully and held out her hand. She received the nickel and then fished the other nickel out of her pocket and laid it beside the new one. She stared at her palm closely, with her head on one side.

Then she gave a tap with her cane on the floor.

"This is what come to me to do," she said. "I going to the store and buy my child a little windmill they sells, made out of paper. He going to find it hard to believe there such a thing in the world. I'll march myself back where he waiting, holding it straight
260 up in this hand."

She lifted her free hand, gave a little nod, turned around, and walked out of the doctor's office. Then her slow step began on the stairs, going down. ❧

❶ **UNIVERSAL THEME**
What have you learned about Phoenix's **motivation** for making her perilous journey, and what can you **infer** about how often she makes it? Explain why Welty might have delayed revealing this information until the story's end.

obstinate (ŏb'stə-nĭt) *adj.* hard to control or treat

LITERARY ANALYSIS

❶ UNIVERSAL THEME

Possible answer: Phoenix makes this journey to get medicine to save her grandson. Readers can infer that she has made this journey many times, given the nurse's familiarity with her and the information on the card that the injury happened "two-three years ago" (line 231). Delaying this information until the end of the story lends the journey an air of mystery, increases its suspense, and allows it to stand as a symbol for all journeys of love.

Lines 238–243
REINFORCE *KEY IDEA:* ENDURANCE

Discuss How does the relationship between Phoenix and her grandson reflect **endurance**? *Possible answer: Phoenix says that her grandson will endure (line 240), but more importantly their love and devotion to each other will endure (line 239).*

SELECTION WRAP–UP

REFLECT Ask students what motivates Phoenix, or any person, to make great effort and even take risks to help another.

⭐ CRITIQUE

- Have students identify the leg of the journey that they believe most threatened Phoenix and explain their choice.
- After completing the After Reading questions on page 1015, have students revisit their responses and tell whether they have changed their opinions.

FOR STRATEGIC READERS

Comprehension Support Ask students to describe the "little windmill . . . made of paper" (line 258) that Phoenix plans to buy for her grandson. If necessary, explain the item and display or create one from paper, a pushpin, and a pencil. Have students discuss what it says about the grandson's experience that he will find it "hard to believe there such a thing in the world" (lines 258–259).

FOR ADVANCED LEARNERS/AP

Make Judgments [small-group option] Point out that Welty's story takes place at Christmastime. Prompt students to think of the stories they have read that are set at Christmastime, for example, O. Henry's "The Gift of the Magi" or Charles Dickens's *A Christmas Carol*. Have students discuss what unites "Christmas stories" and whether "A Worn Path" fits the criteria. Challenge them to explore how, if at all, this choice of time plays a role in Welty's theme.

MEMOIR Always shy of biographers, Eudora Welty published her own memoir at the age of 74. This account of growing up in the South pays special attention to her development as a writer.

CONNECT

This selection connects with Eudora Welty's story by providing information about the author's approach to character development. You may also use it as a minilesson on reading for information.

Reading for Information

Point out that this excerpt is part of a memoir. Then ask

- What is a memoir, and what does the title of this memoir suggest about its focus? *Possible answer: A memoir is an autobiographical account of its author's life. The title suggests that this memoir focuses on how events shaped the author as writer.*

- What is the main idea of this excerpt? *Possible answer: Welty's characters are entirely invented. She does not turn people she knows into characters.*

TIERED DISCUSSION PROMPTS

Use these prompts to help students connect Welty's comments on character creation with the characterization in "A Worn Path":

Connect In what ways do the characters in "A Worn Path" remind you of people that you know or have met? *Accept all thoughtful answers.*

Analyze Why doesn't Welty import into her stories characters from the real world? *Possible answer: Real people are too large to "yield to" (line 17) the narrow space of a story. Also, to use real people as characters invades their privacy (lines 11–13).*

Synthesize Does Phoenix "take on life" (line 25) as a "human being on the page" (lines 29–30)? Explain. *Students may say that Phoenix takes on life because of the personal and physical detail with which Welty endows her. Her character becomes more thoroughly developed by each detail, word, and action, from the red rag she wears to her decision to buy her grandson a Christmas gift rather then spend ten cents on necessities.*

One Writer's Beginnings
Eudora Welty

Eudora Welty, early in her career

The characters who go to make up my stories and novels are not portraits. Characters I invent along with the story that carries them. Attached to them are what I've borrowed, perhaps unconsciously, bit by bit, of persons I have seen or noticed or remembered in the flesh—a cast of countenance here, a manner of walking there, that jump to the visualizing mind when a story is underway. (Elizabeth
10 Bowen said, "Physical detail cannot be invented." It can only be chosen.) I don't write by invasion into the life of a real person: my own sense of privacy is too strong for that; and I also know instinctively that living people to whom you are close—those known to you in ways too deep, too overflowing, ever to be plumbed outside love—do not yield to, could never fit into, the demands of a story. On the other hand, what I do make my stories out of
20 is the *whole* fund of my feelings, my responses to the real experiences of my own life, to the relationships that formed and changed it, that I have given most of myself to, and so learned my way toward a dramatic counterpart. Characters take on life sometimes by luck, but I suspect it is when you can write most entirely out of yourself, inside the skin, heart, mind, and soul of a person who is not yourself, that a character becomes in his own right another human being
30 on the page.

Comprehension

R3.2, R3.6
CALIFORNIA

1. **Recall** Why does Phoenix Jackson travel to the city of Natchez?

2. **Recall** What does she intend to do with the ten cents she collects?

3. **Summarize** What physical problems does Phoenix seem to have, and how do they affect her on her journey?

Literary Analysis

4. **Monitor Reading** Look over the chart you filled in as you read. Identify at least one passage in the story that was challenging to understand. What clues in the text helped you **clarify** its meaning? Explain how they helped.

5. **Analyze Figurative Language** "A Worn Path" is rich with figurative language, especially **similes.** Skim the story, identifying examples of figurative language used to accomplish the following purposes. For each purpose, cite at least two examples.

   - give readers a clear mental picture of Phoenix's appearance
   - highlight Phoenix's main character traits
   - reveal the perilous nature of this journey
   - convey Phoenix's feelings about her grandson

6. **Understand Symbolism** In mythology, a phoenix is an immortal bird that represents renewal. It sets its nest on fire every 500 years; from the ashes, the phoenix is reborn. Why might Welty have bestowed this name upon her main character? In what way does the name fit the person who bears it?

7. **Interpret Universal Theme** Consider the trials and triumphs Phoenix faces on her journey, and think about what motivates her to **endure** her arduous trek. In what way does this **archetypal** journey mirror life itself? Use your answer to this question to formulate a sentence that states the theme of the story. Then explain what makes this theme universal.

Literary Criticism

8. **Critical Interpretations** This story's ambiguity has fascinated readers for over 65 years. Countless students have written Welty to ask if Phoenix's grandson is really alive at the story's end, or if Phoenix keeps making this journey though the boy is already gone. The author has replied, "It is the journey, the going of the errand, that is the story. . . . *Phoenix* is alive." In your opinion, does Welty bring this story to a satisfying conclusion? Explain why or why not, citing details from the text as well as your reaction to Welty's explanation.

A WORN PATH   **1015**

8. *Students may say that the ending is not satisfying. They, like many readers before them, will hunger to know what happens to the grandson and may question whether he is alive. Other students may agree with Welty that it is the fact that Phoenix is alive in the journey that matters most.*

Practice and Apply

After Reading

Use these copy masters to check understanding and provide extra support:

R **RESOURCE MANAGER—Copy Masters**
   Reading Check p. 374
   Universal Theme p. 367
   Question Support p. 375

   Additional selection questions are provided for teachers on page 361.

ANSWERS

1. *Phoenix travels to Natchez to get medicine for her grandson.*

2. *She plans to use the 10 cents to buy a present for her grandson.*

3. *Phoenix's problems—poor vision, fatigue, and forgetfulness—stem from her old age. They add risks to her important journey.*

Possible answers:

4. ■ **SKILLS FOCUS** **Monitor** *Accept all thoughtful responses. For example, the black dog seems to be a hallucination, but since the story says that the hunter also sees the dog, it must be real.*

5. *Students' examples may vary. The description of Phoenix's wrinkles, "as though a whole little tree stood in the middle of her head" (lines 14–15), creates a clear mental picture and highlights her wisdom. Phoenix's fall into the ditch "like a little puff of milkweed" (line 108) reveals the risks of the journey. Her likening of her grandson to "a little bird" reveals her protective love.*

6. *Phoenix embodies the endurance and resiliency of the mythic bird that is her namesake. Welty may have used the name to underscore Phoenix's ability to "rise up" after she falls, both physically and mentally.*

7. ● **SKILLS FOCUS** **Universal Theme** *Phoenix's journey has hazards, physical challenges, difficult interactions with others, and frightening moments, as well as moments of rest and pleasure—all things that people experience during the journey of life. Armed with deep determination born of love and an indomitable personality, Phoenix vanquishes the obstacles. Possible theme: Ordinary people are capable of rising to heroic levels and transcending the limitations imposed on their lives. This theme is universal because it applies to all people in any culture.*

A WORN PATH   **1015**

ANSWERS

Vocabulary in Context

VOCABULARY PRACTICE

1. *drag on for weeks*
2. *excel at stretching exercises*
3. *in a quiet garden*
4. *provides heat and light*

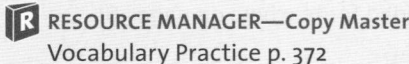 **RESOURCE MANAGER—Copy Master**
Vocabulary Practice p. 372

VOCABULARY IN WRITING

Have students begin by writing a brief character description of Phoenix using any words. Then have them look for places to substitute words from the word list, such as *meditative* for *thoughtful.*

VOCABULARY STRATEGY: THE ROOT *med* **AND ITS MEANINGS** *(also an EL language objective)*

Guide students to examine context first to decide which root meaning is appropriate. Point out that sentences such as item 5 that discuss medical issues will likely use the root meaning "heal," while those related to mathematic concepts, such as item 4, will likely use the root meaning "middle."

Possible answers:

1. *a go-between or mediator*
2. *a solution or answer to a problem*
3. *considered or planned before the event*
4. *average, middle*
5. *not treatable or responsive to medicines*

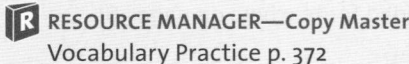 **RESOURCE MANAGER—Copy Master**
Vocabulary Strategy p. 373

Vocabulary Center at ClassZone.com
Additional Vocabulary Activities

Vocabulary in Context

VOCABULARY PRACTICE

Demonstrate your understanding of the vocabulary words by answering these questions.

1. Would an **obstinate** cold go away in a few days or drag on for weeks?
2. If your leg muscles are **limber,** would you be more likely to excel at stretching exercises or to cramp up while swimming?
3. Would you expect someone to be **meditative** in a pep rally or in a quiet garden?
4. Does **radiation** from the sun provide or absorb heat and light?

WORD LIST
limber
meditative
obstinate
radiation

VOCABULARY IN WRITING

What are Phoenix's most important qualities? Using at least two vocabulary words, write a brief character sketch about her. Here is a sample opening sentence.

> **EXAMPLE SENTENCE**
>
> *Phoenix is old and not particularly **limber**, but she has a single-mindedness that keeps her moving.*

VOCABULARY STRATEGY: THE ROOT *med* **AND ITS MEANINGS**

Sometimes roots can have several different meanings. The vocabulary word *meditative,* for example, is derived from the Latin root *med,* which can mean "think" or "ponder." In other words developed from this same root, however, *med* means "heal." There is another unrelated root, also spelled *med,* that means "middle." In dealing with words containing these roots, you will often have to rely on the context, and sometimes on affixes, to determine their correct meaning.

R1.2 CALIFORNIA

PRACTICE Using context clues and your knowledge of the root *med,* write a definition of each boldfaced word. Then check your definition against the one provided in a dictionary.

1. The two disputing groups had to call in an **intermediary** to resolve their differences.
2. The only **remedy** that the doctor could suggest was to get plenty of sleep.
3. Only a **premeditated** crime could be as carefully executed as this robbery was.
4. The **median** income in that city is considerably lower than the national average.
5. After considerable discussion, the workers on the case decided that her condition was **immedicable.**

VOCABULARY PRACTICE
For more practice, go to the **Vocabulary Center** at ClassZone.com.

DIFFERENTIATED INSTRUCTION

FOR ENGLISH LEARNERS

Task Support: Vocabulary Strategy Point out that because two of *med's* root meanings, "heal" and "think," are from Latin, languages derived from Latin may have cognates that use these roots (for example, Spanish *remedio*). Encourage students who speak Latin-based languages to search for and explain vocabulary words similar to those in their home languages.

FOR ADVANCED LEARNERS/AP

Etymology The vocabulary word *radiation* and its relatives *radiate, radiator, radio, radian,* and *radial* all form a word family important to science and mathematics. Ask students to explore the etymology of this word family. Have students complete and share a Word Families organizer to explain how the knowledge could be useful in various subject fields.

 BEST PRACTICES TOOLKIT—Transparency
Word Families p. E30

Reading-Writing Connection

 W1.2, W2.1

WRITING PROMPT

WRITE A STORY Eudora Welty wrote "A Worn Path" in the late 1930s, a time when being elderly, poor, and black in the South made life extremely difficult. Think of a similarly extreme situation today in which a contemporary "Phoenix" would have to make a perilous journey. What hazards might he or she face along the way? What values and strengths would he or she need in order to **endure**? Write a **one-to-three-page story** updating Welty's tale.

SELF-CHECK

A successful story will . . .
- feature a well-developed main character
- show how the time and place affect his or her journey
- give a compelling reason for the journey

GRAMMAR AND STYLE

 W1.9

ADD DESCRIPTIVE DETAILS Review the **Grammar and Style** note on page 1007. Welty's descriptions in the story give a wealth of sensory details that help readers get a clear picture of Phoenix and her actions. Welty makes particularly good use of **action verbs** (in yellow) and **participial phrases** (in green), as in this description of Phoenix crossing the precarious log bridge:

> *Putting her right foot out, she mounted the log and shut her eyes. Lifting her skirt, leveling her cane fiercely before her, like a festival figure in some parade, she began to march across.* (lines 47–49)

The highlighted participial phrases add key details to help readers visualize Phoenix. The first highlighted action verb, *mounted,* shows the physical exertion required for her to get on top of the log, while the third verb, *march,* works with the simile to suggest her regal bearing and sense of purpose.

PRACTICE The following sentences were written in response to the writing prompt above. Rewrite each sentence, adding more action verbs and participial phrases that help describe how things look, sound, smell, touch, or taste.

> **EXAMPLE**
> The sun was low on the horizon and made shadows between the bushes.
> *The sun crouched low on the horizon, casting long shadows between the scrubby bushes.*

1. Tashi, a refugee fleeing her war-torn village, was on the high bank above the river.
2. She knew she had to cross in the shallows where the sand bar was.
3. The baby was still asleep in her arms but would wake soon and be hungry.
4. Suddenly, a dog barked in the distance.

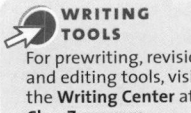 **WRITING TOOLS**
For prewriting, revision, and editing tools, visit the **Writing Center** at ClassZone.com.

Reading-Writing Connection

WRITING PROMPT

Suggest that students break the prewriting task into two sections, so that students first develop the main character using a Character Sketch and then imagine the journey that this character will take. Students should use a Story Frame to plan the plot before they begin writing.

 BEST PRACTICES TOOLKIT—Transparencies
Story Frame p. C10
Character Sketch p. C22

For writing support, see

Writing Center at ClassZone.com

GRAMMAR AND STYLE

To help students appreciate the impact of careful verb choice and precise modifiers, have them rewrite the sample sentence without these elements. Discuss the result. (For more on participles and participial phrases, see **Grammar Handbook,** p. R66.)

Possible answers:

1. *Pausing in flight from her war-torn village, Tashi surveyed the river from its high bank.*
2. *She had to find the higher ground of the sand bar to ford the river, swollen with spring rains.*
3. *The baby, sleeping trustingly in her arms, would wake soon, bawling his hunger.*
4. *A dog, barking in the distance, startled Tashi.*

RESOURCE MANAGER—Copy Master
Add Descriptive Details p. 376

Assess and Reteach

Assess

RESOURCE MANAGER—Copy Masters
Selection Test A pp. 377–378
Selection Test B/C pp. 379–380

Test Generator CD

Reteach

STANDARDS LESSON FILE
Literature Lessons 1, 2, 9, 11, 30, 31, 40
Reading Lessons 2, 8
Writing Lesson 22
Vocabulary Lesson 7

FOR DEVELOPING WRITERS
Writing Support

- Limit the length of the story to one page.
- Discuss with students, either in groups or one on one, what settings might qualify as an "extreme situation."
- Help students use the Character Sketch and Story Frame organizers to explore their character and to develop the time, place, problem, and probable solution appropriate to the assignment.

- Tell students that they may write from a third person or first person point of view. Students may be more comfortable, at least as they draft, writing in first person.
- Remind students that stories need a beginning, middle, and end.

BEST PRACTICES TOOLKIT—Transparencies
Stroy Frames p. C10
Character Sketch p. C22

Focus and Motivate

OBJECTIVES

Literary Analysis
- explore the key idea of **atmosphere**
- analyze mood
- read a short story

Reading
- analyze sequence

Vocabulary
- build vocabulary for reading and writing
- etymologies *(also an EL language objective)*

Grammar and Writing
- choose effective point of view
- write a persuasive argument

 R3.3, R1.1, W1.3, W2.2, LC1.1

ABOUT THE AUTHOR

Sense of place is crucial in Faulkner's fiction, as it was in his life. In 1930 he purchased a grand old house in Mississippi and named it Rowan Oak. Over the years he renovated the dilapidated house, adding plumbing, rebuilding walls, painting. Faulkner was, according to friends, never quite at home anywhere else.

USING THE *NOTABLE QUOTE*

Ask students what **William Faulkner** means when he says to "be better than yourself"—a seemingly impossible feat. ***Possible answer:*** *Faulkner means that people should challenge themselves beyond what they think they are capable of.*

Selection Resources

A Rose for Emily
Short Story by William Faulkner

CALIFORNIA R3.3, R1.1 (p. 1030), W1.3 (p. 1031), W2.2 (p. 1031), LC1.1 (p. 1031)

NOTABLE QUOTE

"Always dream and shoot higher than you know you can do. Don't bother just to be better than your contemporaries or predecessors. Try to be better than yourself."

FYI

Did you know that William Faulkner . . .

- dropped out of high school and took only a few college classes as a special student?
- worked almost three years at the post office, where he was considered lazy and inattentive, before he resigned?

Author Online

For more on William Faulkner, visit the **Literature Center** at **ClassZone.com.**

William Faulkner
1897–1962

Today, William Faulkner is considered one of the literary giants of the 20th century. This distinction didn't come easily, however. Faulkner took a while to find himself and his subject. Only after he decided to focus on his home state of Mississippi and his colorful family history was the full force of his creativity unleashed. Over an astonishing 13-year span, Faulkner churned out one masterpiece after another—among them, *The Sound and the Fury* (1929), *As I Lay Dying* (1930), *Sanctuary* (1931), *Absalom, Absalom!* (1936), and *Go Down, Moses* (1942). Of these artistic achievements, only *Sanctuary* was a bestseller—partly due to its scandalous subject matter—and none of the books earned Faulkner enough money to support his growing family. Although some critics raved about him, many others agreed with the *New York Times* that his South was "too often vicious, depraved, decadent, corrupt." By 1945, most of his books were out of print.

Yoknapa . . . What? Faulkner's initial unpopularity was directly related to his originality. Staking out new literary territory, he essentially broke all the rules—of chronology, of narrative structure, even of punctuation. Many of his short stories and 15 of his 19 novels take place in his imaginary world of Yoknapatawpha (yŏk′nə-pə-tô′fə) County, modeled on his own county in Mississippi and populated with an assortment of characters ranging from the bland to the bizarre. "I discovered," Faulkner explained, "that my own little postage stamp of native soil was worth writing about and that I would never live long enough to exhaust it." His themes often resonate with the thunder of the Old Testament, and his stream-of-consciousness narratives wander around the dark labyrinths of the heart and mind. To many readers, Faulkner's world was just too hard to understand and too weird to accept.

Resurgence In 1946, an enterprising editor named Malcolm Cowley published *The Portable Faulkner,* a collection of stories and novel excerpts that untangled Faulkner's elaborate saga. Cowley's blueprint plus a helpful introduction sparked new interest in Faulkner. With the anxieties of the Great Depression and World War II behind them, more readers were ready to accept Faulkner's challenge to revisit the crimes and passions of the South—and America itself—through a modern consciousness.

1018

RESOURCE MANAGER UNIT 5

Plan and Teach pp. 381–388

Literary Analysis
Summary pp. 389†*, 390‡
Mood pp. 391, 392†*
Question Support p. 399*

Reading
Analyze Sequence pp. 393, 394†*
Reading Check p. 398

Vocabulary
Study p. 395*
Practice p. 396
Strategy p. 397

Grammar and Writing
Choose Effective Point of View
p. 400

Assessment
Selection Tests A, B/C pp. 401*, 403*
Test Generator CD

BEST PRACTICES TOOLKIT

Differentiated Instruction
pp. 31–38*

Scaffolding Instruction
pp. 43–46*

Graphic Organizers/Strategies
Personal Word List • Definition Mapping • Comparison Matrix • Making Inferences • Word Squares • Greek and Latin Roots • Writing Template: Persuasive Essay

Reading Support
Audio Anthology CD*

Technology
Literature, Vocabulary, and Writing Centers at **ClassZone.com**
WriteSmart CD

---

* Resources for Differentiation   † Also in Spanish   ‡ In Haitian Creole and Vietnamese

LITERARY ANALYSIS: MOOD

A story's power to captivate us comes in part from its **mood**—the feeling or atmosphere that the writer creates for the reader. To analyze the mood Faulkner creates in "A Rose for Emily," pay close attention to his **diction,** or word choice and arrangement, as well as his use of **imagery** and **figurative language.** Think about how these elements work together to create a specific atmosphere in this description of Emily:

She looked bloated, like a body long submerged in motionless water, and of that pallid hue.

As you read, note passages that evoke a strong response from you. What part does the story's mood play in your reaction?

READING SKILL: ANALYZE SEQUENCE

Faulkner had an unorthodox way of treating a story's chronology. He often rearranged the **sequence** of events, using **flashbacks** to offer a window into a character's past or dropping hints that ominously **foreshadow** what is yet to come. As you read, use a chart like the one shown to analyze this story's sequence. In the left column, record the story's major events in the order in which you learn about them. In the right column, write the order in which these events actually happened.

Order in Which Narrator Reveals Events	Order in Which Events Occur
1. Miss Emily dies.	8
2. The aldermen visit about taxes.	7

▲ VOCABULARY IN CONTEXT

Faulkner uses these words to create a story rich with atmosphere. Try to define each, based on its context.

1. The sleepy little town faced an **inextricable** problem.
2. The **cabal** executed their shady plans in secret.
3. A conniving con artist, he **circumvented** the city's laws.
4. The swaggering boy approached him with **temerity.**
5. **Virulent** fumes wafted out of the polluted swamp.
6. The vines **encroached** on the garden, killing the flowers.
7. Moonlight made the rickety house into a terrifying **tableau.**
8. Her **imperviousness** made her impossible to frighten.

What makes your SKIN CRAWL?

KEY IDEA As the girl steps outside into the alley, the overpowering smell of rotting garbage assaults her nostrils. Her stomach turns as she tries not to stare at a mass of maggots eating a discarded hamburger, and she shies away from the dumpster, with its squeaking and squirming inhabitants. Certain scenes from books or movies are so evocative that they leave you shaky and nauseated. Part of what you're responding to is the creepy **atmosphere** the writers or directors have created to mesmerize and repulse you.

DISCUSS In a small group, talk about the one thing that really gives you the creeps. Spiders, rats, the sight of blood—do any of these make your skin crawl? What movies or books have used these things to create an atmosphere that makes you shudder? Which works top your "creepiness scale"? Record the responses of your group to share with others.

1019

What makes your SKIN CRAWL?

Introduce the question and ask students to read the **KEY IDEA** paragraph. Ask students to think of a scene from a horror story or movie and recall what details made the **atmosphere** creepy or scary. Then have them do the **DISCUSS** activity.

SKILLS FOCUS

LITERARY ANALYSIS R3.3

● MOOD

Write this list of rough synonyms on the board: *body, corpse, remains, carcass, cadaver.* Then ask students to consider the mood that each word supports. Ask them to think of the context in which they might read each word.

Possible answers: *Students may point out that* body *and* corpse *are associated with ominous, mysterious moods, while the word* remains *creates a more respectful mood,* carcass *a disrespectful mood, and* cadaver *a scientific or clinical mood.* Body *and* corpse *might appear in mysteries or police fiction;* remains *in an obituary or news report;* carcass *in a Western story; and* cadaver *in lab documents or medical texts.*

READING SKILL R3.3

■ ANALYZE SEQUENCE

Ask students to define *flashback* and *foreshadowing* and to explain the roles that these plot interruptions play in fiction. Ask how they keep track of the order of events when reading a book or watching a TV show that uses them.

CHECK UNDERSTANDING Ask students to identify the mood of a favorite movie or television program episode.

R **RESOURCE MANAGER—Copy Master**
Analyze Sequence p. 393 (for student use while reading the selection)

VOCABULARY

▲ VOCABULARY IN CONTEXT

DIAGNOSE WORD KNOWLEDGE To determine preteaching needs, have all students complete Vocabulary in Context. ***Answers:*** **1.** *unsolvable, inescapable;* **2.** *group that plots in secret;* **3.** *went around;* **4.** *boldness, audacity;* **5.** *intensely irritating;* **6.** *invaded, overran;* **7.** *scene;* **8.** *ability to withstand or ignore disturbance*

PRETEACH VOCABULARY Preteach vocabulary with this copy master. Read each item aloud.

R **RESOURCE MANAGER—Copy Master**
Vocabulary Study p. 395

MORE VOCABULARY SUPPORT
For additional activities and guidelines, see

 BEST PRACTICES TOOLKIT
Scaffolding Vocabulary Instruction pp. 43–46
ℹ Vocabulary Center at **ClassZone.com**

SUMMARY

In this story a townsperson recalls, through a series of flashbacks, Emily Grierson, whose father prevents her from marrying. Emily later is courted by a man the townspeople consider unacceptable; he appears to desert her. Forty years later, at Emily's death, the townspeople discover that she poisoned her suitor and has kept his corpse in a bedroom.

LITERARY ANALYSIS

Ⓐ MOOD

Possible answer: Faulkner immediately creates an eerie, creepy mood through his description of the Grierson house as an edifice of "stubborn and coquettish decay" (lines 9–10) and as "an eyesore among eyesores" (lines 10–11).

If students need help . . . Remind them of classic horror movies they have seen that feature a haunted house. The Grierson house evokes the same mood as a Hollywood haunted house, minus the lightning and hill-top venue.

A Rose for Emily

William Faulkner

BACKGROUND "A Rose for Emily," like the majority of Faulkner's stories, takes place in the fictional Yoknapatawpha County, Mississippi. Published in 1930, the story portrays social customs of the small-town South at the turn of the 20th century. Be warned that the narrator refers to African Americans with a term that is offensive to contemporary readers.

I

When Miss Emily Grierson died, our whole town went to her funeral: the men through a sort of respectful affection for a fallen monument, the women mostly out of curiosity to see the inside of her house, which no one save an old manservant—a combined gardener and cook—had seen in at least ten years.

It was a big, squarish frame house that had once been white, decorated with cupolas and spires and scrolled balconies in the heavily lightsome style of the seventies,[1] set on what had once been our most select street. But garages and cotton gins had **encroached** and obliterated even the august names of that neighborhood; only Miss Emily's house was left, lifting its stubborn and
10 coquettish decay above the cotton wagons and the gasoline pumps—an eyesore among eyesores. And now Miss Emily had gone to join the representatives of those august names where they lay in the cedar-bemused[2] cemetery among the ranked and anonymous graves of Union and Confederate soldiers who fell at the battle of Jefferson. Ⓐ

---

1. **the seventies:** the 1870s.
2. **cedar-bemused:** almost lost in cedar trees.

❶ **Targeted Passage**

encroach (ĕn-krōch') *v.* to take over the possessions or rights of another

Ⓐ **MOOD**
Reread lines 5–11. What mood does Faulkner establish with his initial description of the Grierson house? Identify the striking **phrases** and vivid **images** he uses to create this mood.

DIFFERENTIATED INSTRUCTION

FOR ALL STUDENTS

Expert Groups Encourage students to become subject experts by selecting and researching one of these topics:

- The history and geography of the fictional Yoknapatawpha County
- Faulkner's own family background in Mississippi

FOR STRATEGIC READERS

In combination with the *Audio Anthology CD,* use one or more Targeted Passages (pp. 1020, 1023, 1024, 1027, and 1028) to ensure that students focus on key story events and concepts. Targeted Passages are also good for English learners.

❶ Targeted Passage [Lines 1–7]

This passage introduces the main character and the home in which she has hidden for many years.

- What event begins the telling of the story?
- Why did everyone in town attend Miss Emily's funeral?
- What had been Miss Emily's social status when she was young and the house was new?

ANALYZE VISUALS

Activity Have students assume that the photograph is of the Grierson house, and ask them to write two more sentences describing this "eyesore among eyesores" (lines 10–11), keeping the mood of the paragraph and drawing on the photograph for details. *Accept all thoughtful and detailed responses, but students' sentences should draw attention to the contrast between gentility and decay, evident in such features as the delicate but chipped latticework on the porch or the white curtains visible behind the dilapidated window frame.*

BACKGROUND

Southern Gothic Faulkner is among a group of writers who wrote in a sub-genre called, mockingly at first, the Southern Gothic. Southern Gothic stories transferred the Gothic fascination with old European castles, with their secret passages, dark halls, and trapdoors, to the crumbling estates of the pre–Civil War South. The characters of Southern Gothics are often mysterious, their stories macabre and tinged with insanity. Yet Southern Gothics such as "A Rose for Emily" are also laments for a genteel way of life that, rather than dying gracefully away, lives on in stories of twisted honor and warped dreams.

FOR ENGLISH LEARNERS

Comprehension Support Help students visualize the Grierson house by explaining the architectural terms *cupolas, spires,* and *scrolled balconies* (line 6) and the modifiers *heavily lightsome* (line 6), *august* (line 8), and *coquettish* (line 10). Students can add the architectural terms to their Personal Word Lists.

 BEST PRACTICES TOOLKIT
Personal Word List p. E2

FOR ADVANCED LEARNERS/AP

AP exercises in the bottom channel provide additional challenge for students. Use these suggestions for small groups or individuals.

ADDITIONAL GUIDELINES

For more help with differentiation and tips for classroom management, see

BEST PRACTICES TOOLKIT
Differentiated Instruction pp. 31–38

Lines 32–41
REINFORCE *KEY IDEA:* ATMOSPHERE

Discuss How do the members of the deputation probably respond to the **atmosphere** of Miss Emily's parlor as they wait for her to meet them? *Possible answer: They probably respond by feeling ill at ease and perhaps disgusted by the dust, shadows, and "close, dank smell" of the room. They may feel trapped and wish they could flee.*

READING SKILL

B ANALYZE SEQUENCE

Possible answer: The events relayed in the opening paragraph (Emily's death and funeral) happen long after the business with the taxes. Faulkner announces the death at the outset because it piques readers' curiosity, creates suspense, and is a creepy way to begin the story.

If students need help . . . Refer them to the sequence chart they are completing, and guide them in listing these events in their chronologically correct order.

LITERARY ANALYSIS

C MOOD

Possible answer: Students may be repelled by Emily. They may point out the similes "like a body long submerged in motionless water" (line 46) and "like two small pieces of coal pressed into a lump of dough" (lines 47–48) and say that the feeling created is at once repulsive and fascinating.

Alive, Miss Emily had been a tradition, a duty, and a care; a sort of hereditary obligation upon the town, dating from that day in 1894 when Colonel Sartoris, the mayor—he who fathered the edict that no Negro woman should appear on the streets without an apron—remitted her taxes, the dispensation dating from the death of her father on into perpetuity.[3] Not that Miss Emily would have accepted
20 charity. Colonel Sartoris invented an involved tale to the effect that Miss Emily's father had loaned money to the town, which the town, as a matter of business, preferred this way of repaying. Only a man of Colonel Sartoris' generation and thought could have invented it, and only a woman could have believed it.

When the next generation, with its more modern ideas, became mayors and aldermen, this arrangement created some little dissatisfaction. On the first of the year they mailed her a tax notice. February came, and there was no reply. They wrote her a formal letter, asking her to call at the sheriff's office at her convenience. A week later the mayor wrote her himself, offering to call or to send his car for her, and received in reply a note on paper of an archaic shape, in a thin,
30 flowing calligraphy in faded ink, to the effect that she no longer went out at all. The tax notice was also enclosed, without comment.

They called a special meeting of the Board of Aldermen. A deputation waited upon her, knocked at the door through which no visitor had passed since she ceased giving china-painting lessons eight or ten years earlier. They were admitted by the old Negro into a dim hall from which a stairway mounted into still more shadow. It smelled of dust and disuse—a close, dank smell. The Negro led them into the parlor. It was furnished in heavy, leather-covered furniture. When the Negro opened the blinds of one window, they could see that the leather was cracked; and when they sat down, a faint dust rose sluggishly about their thighs,
40 spinning with slow motes in the single sun-ray. On a tarnished gilt easel before the fireplace stood a crayon portrait of Miss Emily's father.

They rose when she entered—a small, fat woman in black, with a thin gold chain descending to her waist and vanishing into her belt, leaning on an ebony cane with a tarnished gold head. Her skeleton was small and spare; perhaps that was why what would have been merely plumpness in another was obesity in her. She looked bloated, like a body long submerged in motionless water, and of that pallid hue. Her eyes, lost in the fatty ridges of her face, looked like two small pieces of coal pressed into a lump of dough as they moved from one face to another while the visitors stated their errand. **C**
50 She did not ask them to sit. She just stood in the door and listened quietly until the spokesman came to a stumbling halt. Then they could hear the invisible watch ticking at the end of the gold chain.

Her voice was dry and cold. "I have no taxes in Jefferson. Colonel Sartoris explained it to me. Perhaps one of you can gain access to the city records and satisfy yourselves."

"But we have. We are the city authorities, Miss Emily. Didn't you get a notice from the sheriff, signed by him?"

---

3. **remitted . . . perpetuity:** released her from paying taxes forever from the time of her father's death.

1022 UNIT 5: THE HARLEM RENAISSANCE AND MODERNISM

B ANALYZE SEQUENCE
Explain when the events of the story's first paragraph happen in relation to those described in lines 15–31. Why might Faulkner have chosen to immediately announce Emily's death before revealing more about her life? Explain.

C MOOD
What is your initial reaction to Emily? Cite two examples of **figurative language** in lines 42–49 and explain what feeling they create.

DIFFERENTIATED INSTRUCTION

FOR ENGLISH LEARNERS

Key Academic Vocabulary Use Definition Mapping to teach these words: *select* (line 7), *tradition* (line 15), *comment* (line 31), *dispose* (line 116), *attach* (line 225), *contemporary* (line 249).

 BEST PRACTICES TOOLKIT—Transparency
Definition Mapping p. E6

Prereading For prereading instruction for English learners, see

BEST PRACTICES TOOLKIT
Scaffolding Reading Instruction pp. 43–46

FOR ADVANCED LEARNERS/AP

Analyze Tell students that in Faulkner's stories and novels about the South, the extended Sartoris family stands for the Old South and represents the wealthy planter class that the Civil War destroyed. Then ask them to explain the last sentence in the paragraph (lines 22–23), with this knowledge in mind, in their journals. They may wish to finish reading Part I before they write.

"I received a paper, yes," Miss Emily said. "Perhaps he considers himself the sheriff . . . I have no taxes in Jefferson."

60   "But there is nothing on the books to show that, you see. We must go by the—"

"See Colonel Sartoris. I have no taxes in Jefferson."

"But, Miss Emily—"

"See Colonel Sartoris." (Colonel Sartoris had been dead almost ten years.) "I have no taxes in Jefferson. Tobe!" The Negro appeared. "Show these gentlemen out."

II

So she vanquished them, horse and foot, just as she had vanquished their fathers thirty years before about the smell. That was two years after her father's death and a short time after her sweetheart—the one we believed would marry her—had deserted her. After her father's death she went out very little; after her sweetheart went away, people hardly saw her at all. A few of the ladies had the **temerity** to 70 call, but were not received, and the only sign of life about the place was the Negro man—a young man then—going in and out with a market basket.

"Just as if a man—any man—could keep a kitchen properly," the ladies said; so they were not surprised when the smell developed. It was another link between the gross, teeming world and the high and mighty Griersons.

A neighbor, a woman, complained to the mayor, Judge Stevens, eighty years old.

"But what will you have me do about it, madam?" he said.

"Why, send her word to stop it," the woman said. "Isn't there a law?"

"I'm sure that won't be necessary," Judge Stevens said. "It's probably just a snake or a rat that nigger of hers killed in the yard. I'll speak to him about it."

80   The next day he received two more complaints, one from a man who came in diffident deprecation.[4] "We really must do something about it, Judge. I'd be the last one in the world to bother Miss Emily, but we've got to do something." That night the Board of Aldermen met—three graybeards and one younger man, a member of the rising generation.

"It's simple enough," he said. "Send her word to have her place cleaned up. Give her a certain time to do it in, and if she don't . . ."

"Dammit, sir," Judge Stevens said, "will you accuse a lady to her face of smelling bad?"

So the next night, after midnight, four men crossed Miss Emily's lawn and 90 slunk about the house like burglars, sniffing along the base of the brickwork and at the cellar openings while one of them performed a regular sowing motion with his hand out of a sack slung from his shoulder. They broke open the cellar door and sprinkled lime there, and in all the outbuildings. As they recrossed the lawn, a window that had been dark was lighted and Miss Emily sat in it, the light behind her, and her upright torso motionless as that of an idol. They crept quietly across the lawn and into the shadow of the locusts that lined the street. After a week or two the smell went away. **D**

temerity (tə-mĕr′ĭ-tē) *n.* foolish boldness

② **Targeted Passage**

D MOOD
What words and **images** help create an ominous mood in lines 89–97?

---

4. **diffident deprecation:** timid disapproval.

Lines 58–66
TIERED DISCUSSION PROMPTS
Use these prompts to help students understand Miss Emily's character and relation to the townspeople:

Connect For whom do you have respect in this scene? What compels your respect? *Accept all thoughtful responses.*

Interpret Whom does Miss Emily respect more, the sheriff or Colonel Sartoris? What does this say about her character? *Possible answer: Miss Emily respects the Colonel, "dead almost ten years" (line 63), much more than the man who "considers himself the sheriff" (lines 58–59). This tells readers that Miss Emily is possibly unaware of changes in the town. It also suggests that she demands to be treated as a wealthy town belle despite her current corpulence and poverty.*

Evaluate What does the narrator think of Miss Emily's refusal to pay her taxes? *Possible answer: The narrator seems almost proud of her for standing up to the deputation and not at all surprised; she "had vanquished their fathers" and just as easily "vanquished them" (line 65). The narrator doesn't judge her harshly or say that she did wrong.*

LITERARY ANALYSIS

D MOOD

Possible answer: Images of the eerie, putrid-smelling house and yard and the men "sniffing along" (line 90) with their mysterious sack, while Emily watches from her window, motionless "as an idol" (line 95), create an ominous mood.

FOR STRATEGIC READERS
② **Targeted Passage [Lines 80–97]**

This passage narrates an event that upsets the townspeople; it also sets up a later revelation.

- What is the problem with Miss Emily's house, according to her neighbors?
- Why doesn't Judge Stevens take the problem to Miss Emily herself?
- How do the townspeople solve the problem?

FOR ENGLISH LEARNERS
Comprehension Support Explain to students that *lime* (line 93) is a calcium compound that is widely used in many industries. In its hydrated form it is used to neutralize odors, especially from decaying matter or waste products, to inhibit bacterial growth, and to keep flies away from decaying matter. Faulkner includes the detail to increase the creepiness factor of the story—something has certainly died in or around Miss Emily's house, but what?

FOR ADVANCED LEARNERS/AP
Analyze Sequence Direct students' attention to the opening sentence of Part II, and ask them to identify the three time periods present in one sentence. Which event is part of the regular chronology? Which event constitutes a flashback? What phrase in the sentence foreshadows a mysterious event?

Have students add these subtle time shifts to the sequence chart they are creating.

That was when people had begun to feel really sorry for her. People in our town, remembering how old lady Wyatt, her great-aunt, had gone completely
100 crazy at last, believed that the Griersons held themselves a little too high for what they really were. None of the young men were quite good enough for Miss Emily and such. We had long thought of them as a **tableau,** Miss Emily a slender figure in white in the background, her father a spraddled silhouette in the foreground, his back to her and clutching a horsewhip, the two of them framed by the back-flung front door. So when she got to be thirty and was still single, we were not pleased exactly, but vindicated; even with insanity in the family she wouldn't have turned down all of her chances if they had really materialized. **E**

When her father died, it got about that the house was all that was left to her; and in a way, people were glad. At last they could pity Miss Emily. Being left
110 alone, and a pauper, she had become humanized. Now she too would know the old thrill and the old despair of a penny more or less.

The day after his death all the ladies prepared to call at the house and offer condolence and aid, as is our custom. Miss Emily met them at the door, dressed as usual and with no trace of grief on her face. She told them that her father was not dead. She did that for three days, with the ministers calling on her, and the doctors, trying to persuade her to let them dispose of the body. Just as they were about to resort to law and force, she broke down, and they buried her father quickly.

We did not say she was crazy then. We believed she had to do that. We
120 remembered all the young men her father had driven away, and we knew that with nothing left, she would have to cling to that which had robbed her, as people will. **F**

III

She was sick for a long time. When we saw her again, her hair was cut short, making her look like a girl, with a vague resemblance to those angels in colored church windows—sort of tragic and serene.

The town had just let the contracts for paving the sidewalks, and in the summer after her father's death they began the work. The construction company came with niggers and mules and machinery, and a foreman named Homer Barron, a Yankee—a big, dark, ready man, with a big voice and eyes lighter than his face. The little boys would follow in groups to hear him cuss the niggers,
130 and the niggers singing in time to the rise and fall of picks. Pretty soon he knew everybody in town. Whenever you heard a lot of laughing anywhere about the square, Homer Barron would be in the center of the group. Presently we began to see him and Miss Emily on Sunday afternoons driving in the yellow-wheeled buggy and the matched team of bays from the livery stable.

At first we were glad that Miss Emily would have an interest, because the ladies all said, "Of course a Grierson would not think seriously of a Northerner, a day laborer." But there were still others, older people, who said that even grief could not cause a real lady to forget *noblesse oblige*[5]—without calling it *noblesse oblige.*

---

5. ***noblesse oblige*** (nō-blĕs′ ō-blēzh′): the responsibility of people in a high social position to behave in a noble fashion.

1024 UNIT 5: THE HARLEM RENAISSANCE AND MODERNISM

---

tableau (tăb′lō′) *n.* a dramatic scene or picture

E GRAMMAR AND STYLE
Reread lines 98–107. The **pronouns** *we* and *our* indicate that this story is told from the **first-person plural point of view.** The narrator is not a single character, but the collective voice of the townspeople.

F ANALYZE SEQUENCE
Reread lines 108–121. Note Emily's reaction to her father's death, as well as the narrator's comments about her sanity. What might this **foreshadow?**

3 Targeted Passage

E GRAMMAR AND STYLE

Effective Point of View Ask students whether they get a sense of the town Miss Emily lives in—its size, its people—from Faulkner's use of the first person plural narrator. ***Possible answer:*** *Students may say that the town seems to be small and full of like-minded people. Only the occasional person takes umbrage against Miss Emily; most seem fond of her, perhaps as a representative of a former glorious time.*

READING SKILL

F ANALYZE SEQUENCE
Possible answer: *Her reaction foreshadows the possibility that she will become insane.*

Lines 127–134
REINFORCE KEY IDEA: ATMOSPHERE

Discuss How do the details describing the **atmosphere** of Miss Emily's town change when Homer Barron arrives? ***Possible answer:*** *Suddenly, details about action—cussing, singing, working—are part of the story; and color is introduced (the "yellow-wheeled buggy and the matched teams of bays" [lines 133–134] that Homer drives) to break up the shadows and sober hues of black.*

DIFFERENTIATED INSTRUCTION

FOR STRATEGIC READERS

3 Targeted Passage [Lines 125–134]

This passage introduces a character who has the power to change Miss Emily's life.

- Who is the "big, dark, ready man" (line 128), and why has he come to town?
- Where does the new man come from? What do the townspeople think of him?
- What seems to be the new man's relationship to Miss Emily?

FOR ENGLISH LEARNERS

Comprehension Support: Culture Familiarize students with these details specific to the story's historical setting:

- The horsewhip was a weapon for fathers chasing away unwelcome suitors.
- Yankees who grew rich by rebuilding the war-torn South were deeply resented.
- A matched set of horses and buggy was that day's version of an expensive sports car.

FOR ADVANCED LEARNERS/AP

Analyze Figurative Language [small-group option] Ask students to discuss the meaning of Miss Emily's fate as a pauper, to know, with the other townspeople, "the old thrill and the old despair of a penny more or less" (lines 110–111). Then ask them to explore in their journals why the townspeople are glad that her wealth is gone: Is this a case of misery loving company, or are other motives at work?

1024 UNIT 5: THE HARLEM RENAISSANCE AND MODERNISM

They just said, "Poor Emily. Her kinsfolk should come to her." She had some kin
140 in Alabama; but years ago her father had fallen out with them over the estate of
old lady Wyatt, the crazy woman, and there was no communication between the
two families. They had not even been represented at the funeral.

And as soon as the old people said, "Poor Emily," the whispering began. "Do
you suppose it's really so?" they said to one another. "Of course it is. What else
could . . ." This behind their hands; rustling of craned silk and satin behind
jalousies[6] closed upon the sun of Sunday afternoon as the thin, swift clop-clop-
clop of the matched team passed: "Poor Emily."

She carried her head high enough—even when we believed that she was
fallen. It was as if she demanded more than ever the recognition of her dignity
150 as the last Grierson; as if it had wanted that touch of earthiness to reaffirm her
imperviousness. Like when she bought the rat poison, the arsenic. That was over
a year after they had begun to say "Poor Emily," and while the two female cousins
were visiting her.

"I want some poison," she said to the druggist. She was over thirty then, still a
slight woman, though thinner than usual, with cold, haughty black eyes in a face
the flesh of which was strained across the temples and about the eye-sockets as you
imagine a lighthouse-keeper's face ought to look. "I want some poison," she said.

---

6. **jalousies** (jăl'ə-sēz): blinds or shutters containing overlapping slats that can be opened or closed.

imperviousness
(ĭm-pûr'vē-əs-nəs) *n.* an
inability to be affected
or disturbed

Lines 135–150
TIERED DISCUSSION PROMPTS
Use these prompts to help students understand the townspeople's reactions to the romance between Homer and Emily:

Recall What is Miss Emily's social standing in town? *Possible answer: She is the last of a grand and wealthy family who has fallen into financial hardship.*

Analyze Since the townspeople seem to like Homer, why do they disapprove of his courting Miss Emily? *Possible answer: First, Miss Emily's social standing is high; she shouldn't be interested in a working man. Second, Miss Emily embodies the ways of the old South, and Homer is a Yankee, from the part of the nation that defeated and laid waste to the old South. Finally, the public drives that Emily and Homer take (without a proper chaperone) scandalize the older townspeople.*

Evaluate What might Miss Emily see in Homer Barron that makes her defy social expectations? *Possible answer: Miss Emily may see in Homer a last chance. She is no longer young and wealthy. Her father kept her from marrying and left her nothing; marrying Homer is her chance to have the life she expected. Homer is lively and fun, and his ability to work makes him better off than Miss Emily, with only the house on which she can't even pay the taxes. And she may truly love him as well. These incentives would impel her to ignore the townspeople's disapproval and court Homer.*

FOR STRATEGIC READERS

Comprehension Support [paired option] Read lines 143–147 aloud to students. Then help them visualize the gossiping townspeople. Ask them

- Why do the townspeople talk "behind their hands" (line 145) rather than openly?

- Why do they peer at the couple through jalousies rather than openly confronting Miss Emily?

FOR ENGLISH LEARNERS

Culture: Clarify Explain to students that after the Civil War, many workers came from the Northern states to help rebuild the ravaged Southern states. These workers were referred to as Yankees; some were also called carpetbaggers because they came South with only the possessions they could stuff in a large bag. While many Northerners aided in the rebuilding of the Southern cities, some were exploitive. Many Southerners resented and despised these workers.

FOR ADVANCED LEARNERS/AP

Compare and Contrast Ask students to review lines 47–49 and 154–157. Both sections of text describe Emily's eyes. Have students write a short explanation of what each description reveals about Emily at these different points in her life; then ask them to evaluate each description for the effect it has on the story's mood and on characterization of Emily.

 BEST PRACTICES TOOLKIT—Transparency Comparison Matrix p. A24

"Yes, Miss Emily. What kind? For rats and such? I'd recom—"

"I want the best you have. I don't care what kind."

160 The druggist named several. "They'll kill anything up to an elephant. But what you want is—"

"Arsenic," Miss Emily said. "Is that a good one?"

"Is . . . arsenic? Yes, ma'am. But what you want—"

"I want arsenic."

The druggist looked down at her. She looked back at him, erect, her face like a strained flag. "Why, of course," the druggist said. "If that's what you want. But the law requires you to tell what you are going to use it for."

Miss Emily just stared at him, her head tilted back in order to look him eye for eye, until he looked away and went and got the arsenic and wrapped it up. The
170 Negro delivery boy brought her the package; the druggist didn't come back. When she opened the package at home there was written on the box, under the skull and bones: "For rats." **G**

IV

So the next day we all said, "She will kill herself"; and we said it would be the best thing. When she had first begun to be seen with Homer Barron, we had said, "She will marry him." Then we said, "She will persuade him yet," because Homer himself had remarked—he liked men, and it was known that he drank with the younger men in the Elks' Club—that he was not a marrying man. Later we said, "Poor Emily" behind the jalousies as they passed on Sunday afternoon in the glittering buggy, Miss Emily with her head high and Homer Barron with his hat
180 cocked and a cigar in his teeth, reins and whip in a yellow glove.

Then some of the ladies began to say that it was a disgrace to the town and a bad example to the young people. The men did not want to interfere, but at last the ladies forced the Baptist minister—Miss Emily's people were Episcopal—to call upon her. He would never divulge what happened during that interview, but he refused to go back again. The next Sunday they again drove about the streets, and the following day the minister's wife wrote to Miss Emily's relations in Alabama.

So she had blood-kin under her roof again and we sat back to watch developments. At first nothing happened. Then we were sure that they were to be married. We learned that Miss Emily had been to the jeweler's and ordered a man's
190 toilet set in silver, with the letters H. B. on each piece. Two days later we learned that she had bought a complete outfit of men's clothing, including a nightshirt, and we said, "They are married." We were really glad. We were glad because the two female cousins were even more Grierson than Miss Emily had ever been.

So we were not surprised when Homer Barron—the streets had been finished some time since—was gone. We were a little disappointed that there was not a public blowing-off,[7] but we believed that he had gone on to prepare for Miss Emily's coming, or to give her a chance to get rid of the cousins. (By that time it was a **cabal,** and we were all Miss Emily's allies to help **circumvent** the cousins.)

---

7. **blowing-off:** here, a celebration.

G ANALYZE SEQUENCE
Reread lines 154–172. What does this exchange indicate about Emily's character? What **foreshadowing** do you sense in her refusal to comply with the law?

cabal (kə-băl') *n.* a group united in a secret plot

circumvent (sûr'kəm-věnt') *v.* to avoid or get around by clever maneuvering

---

G ANALYZE SEQUENCE

Possible answer: *Miss Emily has steely courage, which is unnerving, given the story's ominous foreshadowing. She won't back down when challenged, and she doesn't seem quite sane.*

If students need help . . . Have two students act out the scene between the defiant Miss Emily and the meek druggist.

Extend the Discussion Ask students why the druggist doesn't return with the poison himself, but rather sends his delivery boy out with the package.

DIFFERENTIATED INSTRUCTION

FOR STRATEGIC READERS

Comprehension Support To fully understand "A Rose for Emily," students must draw many inferences. For instance, in lines 173–180, students must make several inferences about what the townspeople believe about Emily and Homer. Remind students that to make inferences, they connect what they learn from the story and what they know from experience.

Guide students to continue making inferences as they read on.

The story says	I know	I infer that
Emily looks "strained" and bought arsenic.	Arsenic is used to kill living things.	Emily will use the poison on a living thing.
Homer is "not a marrying man."	Emily wants to marry Homer.	

BEST PRACTICES TOOLKIT—Transparency
Making Inferences p. A13

FOR ENGLISH LEARNERS

Comprehension Support Explain to students that Miss Emily's purchases in lines 189–192 are purchases a bride might make for her groom or a wife for her husband. Emily purchases clothing and items for personal hygiene (the engraved toilet set). At the time of the story, a woman would not give such intimate items to a man unless they were engaged or married. This is why the townspeople assume, "They are married" (line 192).

Sure enough, after another week they departed. And, as we had expected all along,
200 within three days Homer Barron was back in town. A neighbor saw the Negro
man admit him at the kitchen door at dusk one evening.

And that was the last we saw of Homer Barron. And of Miss Emily for some
time. The Negro man went in and out with the market basket, but the front door
remained closed. Now and then we would see her at a window for a moment, as
the men did that night when they sprinkled the lime, but for almost six months
she did not appear on the streets. Then we knew that this was to be expected too;
as if that quality of her father which had thwarted her woman's life so many times
had been too **virulent** and too furious to die.

When we next saw Miss Emily, she had grown fat and her hair was turning
210 gray. During the next few years it grew grayer and grayer until it attained an even
pepper-and-salt iron-gray, when it ceased turning. Up to the day of her death at
seventy-four it was still that vigorous iron-gray, like the hair of an active man.

From that time on her front door remained closed, save for a period of six or
seven years, when she was about forty, during which she gave lessons in china-
painting. She fitted up a studio in one of the downstairs rooms, where the
daughters and granddaughters of Colonel Sartoris' contemporaries were sent to
her with the same regularity and in the same spirit that they were sent to church
on Sundays with a twenty-five-cent piece for the collection plate. Meanwhile her
taxes had been remitted.

220 Then the newer generation became the backbone and the spirit of the town,
and the painting pupils grew up and fell away and did not send their children
to her with boxes of color and tedious brushes and pictures cut from the ladies'
magazines. The front door closed upon the last one and remained closed for good.
When the town got free postal delivery, Miss Emily alone refused to let them
fasten the metal numbers above her door and attach a mailbox to it. She would
not listen to them.

Daily, monthly, yearly we watched the Negro grow grayer and more stooped,
going in and out with the market basket. Each December we sent her a tax notice,
which would be returned by the post office a week later, unclaimed. Now and
230 then we would see her in one of the downstairs windows—she had evidently shut
up the top floor of the house—like the carven torso of an idol in a niche, looking
or not looking at us, we could never tell which. Thus she passed from generation
to generation—dear, inescapable, impervious, tranquil, and perverse.

And so she died. Fell ill in the house filled with dust and shadows, with only a
doddering Negro man to wait on her. We did not even know she was sick; we had
long since given up trying to get any information from the Negro. He talked to
no one, probably not even to her, for his voice had grown harsh and rusty, as if
from disuse.

She died in one of the downstairs rooms, in a heavy walnut bed with a curtain,
240 her gray head propped on a pillow yellow and moldy with age and lack of sunlight.

4 **Targeted Passage**

virulent (vĭr'yə-lənt) *adj.*
extremely poisonous or
harmful

Lines 213–233
TIERED DISCUSSION PROMPTS

Use these prompts to help students understand how changing times fail to affect
Miss Emily:

Recall What is Miss Emily's financial situation, now that Homer is gone? *Possible answer: She has little money and will struggle
to get by.*

Analyze In what ways does Miss Emily
continue to be involved in town life? In
what ways does she isolate herself? *Possible
answer: Emily continues to be involved in
town life only for "six or seven years . . . during which she gave lessons in china painting"
(lines 213–215), probably because she needed
the money. For no other reason does she involve herself in town life, closing her door on
the town, ignoring her yearly tax notice, and
even refusing to receive mail. She isolates
herself from everyone but her servant, who
rarely speaks to others.*

Evaluate What does Faulkner accomplish
by having the narrator describe Emily as
"like the carven torso of an idol in a niche"
(line 231)? *Possible answer: Students may
say that this simile indicates that Miss Emily
is less a real person now to the townspeople
than a monument, perhaps to the past,
perhaps to the town's pride. She is no more
in touch with the people or the present than
an ancient statue in a museum niche, yet the
townspeople still respect her.*

FOR STRATEGIC READERS

4 **Targeted Passage [Lines 227–240]**

This passage relates Emily's death and brings
readers back to the story's first event.

- What do the townspeople know about
  Emily's later years?
- How do the townspeople continue to feel
  about Emily as she ages?
- Where does Emily die?
- Where does this event fall on the sequence
  chart?

FOR ENGLISH LEARNERS

Comprehension Support [mixed-readiness
groups] Help students comprehend the
narrator's final description of Emily's place in
the town in line 233 by using Word Squares to
develop definitions for each of the challenging
words in this line: *dear, inescapable, impervious, tranquil,* and *perverse.* Then ask students
to write a sentence or two in which they
explain what Emily meant to the town.

🧰 **BEST PRACTICES TOOLKIT—Transparency**
Word Squares p. E10

FOR ADVANCED LEARNERS/AP

Analyze Sequence A great amount of time
passes between the disappearance of Homer
and Emily's death, and Faulkner moves readers
through this long period in less than a page
of text. Have students analyze the strategies Faulkner uses to cover these decades; for
instance, he describes Miss Emily's servant,
"Daily, monthly, yearly . . . grow[ing] grayer and
more stooped" (line 227). Challenge students
to identify and discuss six such strategies on
this page.

The Negro met the first of the ladies at the front door and let them in, with their hushed, sibilant voices and their quick, curious glances, and then he disappeared. He walked right through the house and out the back and was not seen again.

The two female cousins came at once. They held the funeral on the second day, with the town coming to look at Miss Emily beneath a mass of bought flowers, with the crayon face of her father musing profoundly above the bier[8] and the ladies sibilant and macabre; and the very old men—some in their brushed Confederate uniforms—on the porch and the lawn, talking of Miss Emily as if she had been a contemporary of theirs, believing that they had danced with her and
250 courted her perhaps, confusing time with its mathematical progression, as the old do, to whom all the past is not a diminishing road but, instead, a huge meadow which no winter ever quite touches, divided from them now by the narrow bottle-neck of the most recent decade of years.

Already we knew that there was one room in that region above stairs which no one had seen in forty years, and which would have to be forced. They waited until Miss Emily was decently in the ground before they opened it.

The violence of breaking down the door seemed to fill this room with pervading dust. A thin, acrid pall[9] as of the tomb seemed to lie everywhere upon this room decked and furnished as for a bridal: upon the valance curtains of faded
260 rose color, upon the rose-shaded lights, upon the dressing table, upon the delicate array of crystal and the man's toilet things backed with tarnished silver, silver so tarnished that the monogram was obscured. Among them lay a collar and tie, as if they had just been removed, which, lifted, left upon the surface a pale crescent in the dust. Upon a chair hung the suit, carefully folded; beneath it the two mute shoes and the discarded socks.

The man himself lay in the bed.

For a long while we just stood there, looking down at the profound and fleshless grin. The body had apparently once lain in the attitude of an embrace, but now the long sleep that outlasts love, that conquers even the grimace of love, had cuckolded
270 him.[10] What was left of him, rotted beneath what was left of the nightshirt, had become **inextricable** from the bed in which he lay; and upon him and upon the pillow beside him lay that even coating of the patient and biding dust.

Then we noticed that in the second pillow was the indentation of a head. One of us lifted something from it, and leaning forward, that faint and invisible dust dry and acrid in the nostrils, we saw a long strand of iron-gray hair. ❧

⑤ Targeted Passage

inextricable
(ĭn-ĕk′strĭ-kə-bəl) *adj.*
incapable of being disentangled or untied

---

8. **bier:** coffin along with its stand.
9. **acrid pall:** bitter-smelling gloom.
10. **cuckolded him:** made his wife or lover unfaithful to him.

Lines 257–265
REINFORCE *KEY IDEA:* ATMOSPHERE

Discuss What **atmosphere** does Faulkner create in this paragraph, and how does it prepare readers for the discovery in the next paragraph? *Possible answer: The atmosphere is an eerie mix of bridal color (the faded curtains and shaded lights of rose color) and the dust and acrid air "as of the tomb" (line 258). The contrast of signifiers of the beginning of life together and those of death clash and create suspense; the empty suit, which readers remember Emily buying for Homer, is strangely ominous.*

SELECTION WRAP–UP

REFLECT Ask students at what point, if ever, they suspected that Emily had murdered Homer, and what led them to suspect foul play—or what led them astray so that they didn't suspect it.

⭐ CRITIQUE

- Have students identify elements that, now that they know how the story ends, hinted at Emily's crime.

- After completing the After Reading questions on page 1029, have students revisit their responses and tell whether they have changed their opinions.

DIFFERENTIATED INSTRUCTION

FOR STRATEGIC READERS

⑤ Targeted Passage [Lines 266–275]

This passage solves the mystery of where Homer Barron went when he disappeared.

- What happened to Homer Barron?

- How do the townspeople react to finding the body?

- Whose hair is on the second pillow?

- What have the townspeople discovered about Miss Emily?

FOR ENGLISH LEARNERS

Culture: Clarify Help students visualize the funeral scene by defining the words *sibilant* and *macabre* (line 247) and by explaining the presence of the "very old men . . . in their brushed Confederate uniforms" (lines 247–248). Ask them if they agree with the narrator that for the very old, the past is "a huge meadow which no winter ever quite touches" (lines 251–252).

FOR ADVANCED LEARNERS/AP

Analyze Craft Ask students to discuss and write about Faulkner's decisions about structure and paragraphing from line 257 to the end of the story: What does Faulkner gain by describing the room first, rather than its inhabitant? Why is the revelation of Homer's murder in a paragraph of a single line? What is the effect of beginning the final paragraph, with its horrid discovery, with the simple word "Then" (line 273)?

After Reading

Comprehension

1. **Recall** Why was it difficult for Emily to meet suitable men in her youth?

2. **Clarify** What happened to Homer Barron?

3. **Clarify** What does the appearance of the upstairs room in the Grierson house and the iron-gray hair on the pillow indicate?

Literary Analysis

4. **Make Inferences** Use clues in the story to infer Emily's **motivation** for murdering Homer. Why was the relationship considered a "disgrace" and a "bad example to the young people"? What were Homer's intentions?

5. **Examine Methods of Characterization** Emily is a character who leaves quite an impression. How does Faulkner characterize her so effectively? Citing evidence, explain what each of the following reveals about her character:
   - her conflict with the aldermen over her taxes
   - her gifts for Homer
   - her physical appearance at various stages in her life
   - what the townspeople say about the Griersons

6. **Analyze Mood** How would you describe the overall mood of "A Rose for Emily"? Skim the story, identifying at least three passages that create an especially strong **atmosphere** for the reader. Explain which literary elements contribute to each passage's mood.

7. **Interpret Point of View** This story is told in the first-person plural point of view, giving the impression that it is narrated collectively by the entire town. What is the town's attitude toward Emily? Why do they generally let her do whatever she wants but allow "the ladies" to interfere after she starts seeing Homer? Explain what you think Faulkner is saying about small-town life in the South with this story.

8. **Evaluate Sequence** Examine the chart you filled in as you read. How does the order in which the story's major events occur differ from the order in which the narrator presents them? Consider the effect created by Faulkner's manipulation of the story's sequence. What would the story lose if it were told in strict chronological order?

Literary Criticism

9. **Historical Context** Faulkner lived, as one critic put it, "with one foot deep in the traditions of the Old South and the other poised for the possibilities of a modern era." What are some of the indications that this story was written in another time? Citing evidence, describe how Faulkner's story reflects an American society different from our own.

A ROSE FOR EMILY **1029**

8. ■ **SKILLS FOCUS Analyze Sequence**
The flashbacks give the story a meandering quality like the telling of a family story recalled through associative memories, rather than a once-upon-a-time chronology. This quality enhances the mystery of Miss Emily and provides moments when readers sense that more is going on than is being told. Readers gradually accumulate Emily's history but can't see how the details fit together till the story's final shocking lines. If told chronologically, the story would lose the sense of eerie suspense and discovery.

9. *The derogatory words used to describe African Americans, the old-fashioned notion that a woman was "ruined" if she engaged in a premarital relationship, the horror the aldermen feel about telling a "lady" that her house smells bad—these are among the indicators that the story depicts an American society different from our own.*

Practice and Apply

After Reading
Use these copy masters to check understanding and provide extra support:

R RESOURCE MANAGER—Copy Masters
Reading Check p. 398
Mood p. 391
Question Support p. 399

Additional selection questions are provided for teachers on page 385.

ANSWERS
1. *No suitor met her father's high standards.*
2. *Emily poisoned him and kept his body.*
3. *The room is decorated for a wedding night; the hair on the pillow indicates that Emily had lain on the bed with the corpse.*

Possible answers:
4. *Students may infer that Homer wronged Emily by courting her without intending to marry her or that she would rather have him dead than be rejected, especially if, as the town suspects, they had premarital relations.*
5. *Her conflict over taxes reveals her presumption of special treatment. Her marriage gifts reveal her plan to make a gentleman out of Homer. Her appearance changes from slender maiden to corpulent matron, but her pale skin and elevated nose are constants. The town thinks the family holds themselves "a little too high" (line 100) and is glad when Emily becomes poor.*
6. ● **SKILLS FOCUS Mood** *Students may describe the mood as creepy or darkly comic and offer examples such as the description of bridal chamber with its contents, right down to "discarded socks" (line 265), or the portrait of Emily's father watching over her even in death.*
7. *The town's attitude is mixed: on the one hand, Emily is "a fallen monument" (line 2) they must look after; on the other, they resent her Grierson pride and enjoy pitying "Poor Emily" (line 143). Faulkner may be saying that a small town is a fishbowl where meddlesome ladies and ministers can interfere with people's choices. When Emily tries a different life, with Homer, the town ladies criticize her and try to push her back into expected behavior.*

A ROSE FOR EMILY **1029**

ANSWERS

Vocabulary in Context

VOCABULARY PRACTICE

1. *(b) control*
2. *(c) dismay*
3. *(a) enlist*
4. *(b) cabal*
5. *(c) decency*
6. *(d) reduced*
7. *(c) unwilling*
8. *(d) upland*

R RESOURCE MANAGER—Copy Master
Vocabulary Practice p. 396

VOCABULARY IN WRITING

Guide students to begin by writing two brief statements telling what the townspeople liked about the Griersons and what they didn't like. Students can then choose words from the word list that fit in each context.

VOCABULARY STRATEGY: ETYMOLOGIES

(also an EL language objective)

Walk students through a dictionary so that they know where to find etymologies and how to read the abbreviations used.

Possible answers:

1. *Latin, "three ways," a crossroads that leads many ways, so* common, unimportant
2. *Latin, "tenth," meaning to reduce by a tenth, thus* to reduce drastically
3. *Greek, "slab," a flat stone along which are grooves for mathematical calculations*
4. *Afrik, "earth pig," describes and names a mammal that digs in dirt for insects to eat*
5. *Latin, "forty," for the forty days ships could be kept at sea if illness was aboard; now* to isolate an ill person
6. *Italian, "bad air," from what people once thought caused the illness*
7. *Malay, "fish sauce," a condiment made from pureed tomatoes*
8. *Latin, "on the right," for the right hand which, in most people, is more able; meaning* skillful, competent with the hands, *or* mentally sharp and clever

R RESOURCE MANAGER—Copy Master
Vocabulary Strategy p. 397

ⓘ Vocabulary Center at **ClassZone.com**
Additional Vocabulary Activities

Vocabulary in Context

VOCABULARY PRACTICE

Chose the word that is not related in meaning to the other words.

1. (a) elude, (b) control, (c) circumvent, (d) sidestep
2. (a) overconfidence, (b) temerity, (c) dismay, (d) brashness
3. (a) enlist, (b) intrude, (c) infringe, (d) encroach
4. (a) contempt, (b) cabal, (c) disdain, (d) scorn
5. (a) endurance, (b) imperviousness, (c) decency, (d) resistance
6. (a) embroiled, (b) tangled, (c) inextricable, (d) reduced
7. (a) lethal, (b) virulent, (c) unwilling, (d) malignant
8. (a) tableau, (b) mesa, (c) plateau, (d) upland

WORD LIST
cabal
circumvent
encroach
imperviousness
inextricable
tableau
temerity
virulent

VOCABULARY IN WRITING

How did the Grierson family's position in the town affect the way Emily was treated? Write an explanation of your ideas, using three or more vocabulary words. You could start like this.

> **EXAMPLE SENTENCE**
> *The family's position in the town made it almost unthinkable that anyone would* **encroach** *on Miss Emily's privacy.*

VOCABULARY STRATEGY: ETYMOLOGIES

Many English words have intriguing **etymologies,** or word histories. The vocabulary word *cabal,* for instance, can be traced back to *kabbala,* the name of an ancient Jewish mystical belief system that at one time was followed by only an elite few. The sense of "secret group or society" came from this connotation. Other words also take their meaning from a reinterpretation of an older term. Though the etymologies of these words do not necessarily help in understanding their current meanings, they provide interesting examples of historical influence on English word meanings.

R1.1

PRACTICE Using an etymological dictionary or the Internet, explain the origins of the following words.

1. trivial
2. decimate
3. abacus
4. aardvark
5. quarantine
6. malaria
7. ketchup
8. dexterity

VOCABULARY PRACTICE
For more practice, go to the **Vocabulary Center** at **ClassZone.com.**

DIFFERENTIATED INSTRUCTION

FOR ENGLISH LEARNERS

Task Support: Vocabulary Practice Point out to students the words in the exercise that have Greek or Latin roots. Tell them that many English words have such roots. Knowing the roots can help readers guess the meaning of unfamiliar words. Guide students to keep lists of roots and add to their lists when they encounter new roots.

 BEST PRACTICES TOOLKIT—Transparencies
Greek and Latin Roots pp. E20, E21, E22

FOR ADVANCED LEARNERS/AP

Analyze Etymologies Direct students to the *Oxford English Dictionary,* found in most public and some school libraries. Assign each student a word from the exercise, and ask students to get the "whole story" from the OED's extended etymology of the word. Ask students to write a "life story" of the word and to post these stories on a class web site. Let students compare the brief etymologies contained in most dictionaries with the more complete information.

Reading-Writing Connection

 W1.3, W2.2

GRAMMAR AND STYLE

CHOOSE EFFECTIVE POINT OF VIEW Review the **Grammar and Style** note on page 1024. Part of what makes "A Rose for Emily" so interesting is the first-person plural point of view—using *we* and related **pronouns** to tell the story. Usually, the first-person point of view is singular, an *I* who acts as both narrator and character. Faulkner's use of the plural creates a curious mixture of intimacy and anonymity. That is, the voice behind the *we* sounds personal, but readers don't know exactly who the voice is:

 LC1.1

> *We learned that Miss Emily had been to the jeweler's and ordered a man's toilet set in silver, with the letters H. B. on each piece. Two days later we learned that she had bought a complete outfit of men's clothing, including a nightshirt, and we said, "They are married." We were really glad.* (lines 189–192)

This kind of narrator has the effect of making the town appear as a complete entity with a personality and opinions all its own.

PRACTICE Try using the first-person plural point of view to create a narrative of your own. Choose a group—a family, for example, or a sports team—and describe, in a paragraph, an event or experience from their point of view. Be sure to use the correct pronouns—*we, us, our, ours*—in your narrative.

WRITING TOOLS

For prewriting, revision, and editing tools, visit the **Writing Center** at ClassZone.com.

Reading-Writing Connection

WRITING PROMPT

Suggest that students discuss the "why" and "what if" questions in small groups before they begin drafting. Remind them to take notes during the discussion, as if they were brainstorming, so that they can choose the best ideas as they begin to draft their argument. Students may wish to use the Persuasive Essay writing template to organize this writing assignment.

 BEST PRACTICES TOOLKIT—Transparency
Writing Template: Persuasive Essay
pp. C16, C31

For writing support, see

ⓘ Writing Center at **ClassZone.com**

GRAMMAR AND STYLE

To help students appreciate the difference between first-person singular point of view and first-person plural point of view, have them rewrite lines 98–107 using first-person singular pronouns. Ask them to read and compare both versions of these lines, and then discuss how the use of singular pronouns changes the tone and intent of the lines. (For more on personal pronouns, see **Grammar Handbook,** p. R56.)

Students' narratives should use first-person plural pronouns to relate the events in first person plural point of view.

Ⓡ **RESOURCE MANAGER**—Copy Master
Choose Effective Point of View p. 400

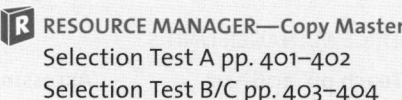

Assess and Reteach

Assess

Ⓡ **RESOURCE MANAGER**—Copy Masters
Selection Test A pp. 401–402
Selection Test B/C pp. 403–404

 Test Generator CD

Reteach

Ⓢ **STANDARDS LESSON FILE**
Literature Lesson 8: Foreshadowing and Flashback
Literature Lesson 10: Types of Point of View
Writing Lesson 29: Persuasive Writing
Vocabulary Lesson 25: Etymologies

FOR DEVELOPING WRITERS
Writing Support

- Limit the length of the argument to two or three paragraphs, and limit the prewriting discussion to one question: What might the townspeople have done to prevent Emily's insanity and thus Homer's murder?

- Explain to students what it means to address possible objections to their arguments.

- Help students draft a thesis statement to guide their writing. Students who think that the townspeople do bear responsibility for events might begin: *The townspeople in "A Rose for Emily" are partly responsible for what happens to Emily and Homer because* _____

- Allow students to draft in first person so that they will more naturally express their thoughts.

Focus and Motivate

OBJECTIVES

Literary Analysis
- explore the key idea of **deception**
- analyze irony
- read a short story

Reading
- analyze descriptive details

 R3.3

ABOUT THE AUTHOR

When Flannery O'Connor recognized the first symptoms of lupus in 1950, she believed, based on her father's experience, that she had only a few years to live. However, the disease, in which the body's immune system attacks and slowly destroys the organs, affects each patient differently. O'Connor moved to her mother's farm to pursue her writing in the time she had left, relying on grants and fellowships to support her. The stories she wrote during the next decade earned three O. Henry Awards and established her as a major American writer.

USING THE *NOTABLE QUOTE*

Ask students how **Flannery O'Connor** probably hoped other readers would respond to her stories. How can that response be a good response to literature? *Possible answer: O'Connor probably hoped other readers would also laugh when they read her stories. Laughter can be a good response to literature when human behavior is held up to criticism.*

The Modern Short Story

 R3.3 CALIFORNIA

The Life You Save May Be Your Own
Short Story by Flannery O'Connor

NOTABLE QUOTE
"The truth is I like [my stories] better than anybody and I read them over and laugh and laugh."

FYI
Did you know that Flannery O'Connor . . .
- began writing and illustrating stories at the age of 6?
- enrolled in college at age 16, graduating three years later?
- created cartoons for her high school newspaper?
- raised peacocks on her farm in Georgia?

Author Online
For more on Flannery O'Connor, visit the **Literature Center** at ClassZone.com.

Flannery O'Connor
1925–1964

As a child, Flannery O'Connor had a pet chicken that could walk backwards as well as forwards. News reporters—including a photographer all the way from New York City—were dispatched to her home in Savannah, Georgia, to take pictures of the unusual chicken. This experience, O'Connor later said, marked her for life. It began her preoccupation with the grotesque, a fascination she shares with other writers belonging to the literary tradition known as Southern Gothic. "Whenever I am asked why Southern writers particularly have a penchant for writing about freaks," O'Connor once commented, "I say it is because we are still able to recognize one."

Born to Write Always a bit shy but self-confident and spirited, O'Connor seemed born to be a writer. She wrote stories from an early age and described herself as a "pigeon-toed only child with a receding chin and a you-leave-me-alone-or-I'll-bite-you complex." In high school, she listed her hobby as "collecting rejection slips," as she was already sending out her stories to major literary journals. After graduating from college, she received a scholarship to attend the famed Writers' Workshop at the University of Iowa. In the late 1940s, she was twice invited to Yaddo, an exclusive artists' colony in upstate New York. In both places, she made lasting friends and developed the contacts she needed to succeed in the literary world.

A Life Cut Short At the age of 25, while writing her first novel, *Wise Blood* (1952), O'Connor was stricken with lupus, an autoimmune disease that had killed her father 9 years earlier. She moved with her mother to a farm outside of Milledgeville, Georgia, where she used her remaining 14 years to produce two highly acclaimed volumes of stories and another novel, *The Violent Bear It Away* (1960).

Defined by Region and Religion Being a Catholic in largely Protestant Georgia gave O'Connor a unique perspective. The South offered rich subject matter—sometimes violent, often humorous—and her Catholicism provided a unifying vision of the divine in everyday life. Her works, often difficult to categorize and to fully understand, weren't bestsellers and took some time to gain a following. Today, critics consider O'Connor one of the greatest short story writers of her time. Her novels and stories are more popular now than they've ever been.

1032

Selection Resources

R RESOURCE MANAGER UNIT 5

Plan and Teach pp. 406–412

Literary Analysis
Summary pp. 413†*, 414‡*
Irony pp. 415, 416†*
Question Support p. 420*

Reading
Analyze Descriptive Details
   pp. 417, 418†*
Reading Check p. 419

Assessment
Selection Tests A, B/C pp. 421*, 423*
Test Generator CD

BEST PRACTICES TOOLKIT

Differentiated Instruction
   pp. 31–38*

Scaffolding Instruction
   pp. 43–46*

Graphic Organizers/Strategies
Predicting • Definition Mapping • Timeline • Comparison Matrix

Reading Support
Audio Anthology CD*

Technology
Literature Center at ClassZone.com
WriteSmart CD

LITERARY ANALYSIS: IRONY

Irony is a contrast between appearance and actuality. You'll notice two kinds of irony at work in the story you're about to read.

- **Dramatic irony** occurs when readers know more about a situation than the characters themselves know —as though the writer is letting you in on a secret the characters aren't privy to.
- **Situational irony** is a contrast between what a character or reader expects to happen and what actually does happen. This kind of irony often takes the reader by surprise.

Irony is often indirect and subtle, making it difficult to detect. Recognizing it, however, can make a work infinitely more striking and memorable. As you read "The Life You Save May Be Your Own," look for examples of both situational and dramatic irony.

READING SKILL: ANALYZE DESCRIPTIVE DETAILS

O'Connor asserted that "distortion is the only way to make people see." To that end, she employed a wealth of **descriptive details** to flesh out her grotesque characters and their often perverse situations. As you read, use a chart like the one shown to note examples of these details. Record your personal reactions as well as your analysis of what these details reveal or highlight about the characters and their bizarre behavior.

Striking Details from the Story	My Reactions	Analysis
"He offered the old woman a piece [of gum] but she only raised her upper lip to indicate she had no teeth."	This old woman gives me the creeps. I can picture her hostile stance and her toothless gums.	The woman lives in a poor, isolated area and probably doesn't have access to dental or medical care. But she's not ashamed of her circumstances, and she doesn't waste words explaining herself.

Could you spot a CON ARTIST?

KEY IDEA We've all seen—or heard of or read about—an instance in which someone was duped by a con artist. If you've ever watched a schemer in action, you may have thought to yourself, "I never would have fallen for that one." But literature, movies, and even newspapers are full of stories of people being conned. Why? What makes a con artist's **deception** so hard to spot?

QUICKWRITE Write a quick description of a con you've seen—on the big screen or in real life—or read about. Why do you think the victim fell for the con artist's antics? What traits did the con artist possess? If you'd been in the victim's shoes, do you honestly think you could have seen through the con artist's scheme, or would you too have been duped?

1033

Could you spot a CON ARTIST?

Lead into the **KEY IDEA** by asking students if they have ever received an e-mail or letter "phishing" for important information or offering them a share in a multimillion-dollar windfall. Have students lay out the clues that helped them spot the **deception** in these scams. Before they complete their **QUICKWRITE,** ask them why some people don't spot the cons in this and other scams.

SKILLS FOCUS

LITERARY ANALYSIS R3.3

● IRONY

Tell students that the word *irony* comes from a Greek word meaning *dissembler*, someone who hides under a false appearance. Irony promises one thing out loud and does the opposite on the sly. Ask students how this etymology helps them make sense of irony in the story.

Possible answers: *Students may say that they must look beyond the words, actions, and events to find meanings buried beneath them. Words may mean the opposite of what they say; people may behave one way but have opposite intentions.*

CHECK UNDERSTANDING Have students recall other examples of dramatic and situational irony from stories and novels that they have read.

READING SKILL R3.3

■ ANALYZE DESCRIPTIVE DETAILS

Remind students that they learn a lot about how a person feels and what a person thinks by being aware of how that person looks, moves, and speaks. Observant people look for the reasons behind actions: Why is that person whispering? Why does he keep checking his watch? Readers must observe story characters as they do real people. Details reveal personality and motive.

R RESOURCE MANAGER—Copy Master Analyze Descriptive Details p. 417 (for student use while reading the selection)

DIFFERENTIATED INSTRUCTION

FOR STRATEGIC READERS

Concept Support: Irony Help students grasp the concepts of dramatic and situational irony by reviewing the simpler concept of verbal irony, in which a speaker says one thing but means the opposite. Write these sentences on the board:

- Of course I aced the geometry test.
- Hey—love that new 'do!
- Well, that was smart.

Ask students to think of situations in which these statements would mean just what they say. Then ask them to think of situations in which these statements' actual meaning is the opposite of what they say. Explain that all irony works by presenting one reality or meaning while intending another.

SUMMARY

In this story a tramp, Mr. Shiftlet, and an old widow, Mrs. Crater, attempt to con each other: Mr. Shiftlet wants to steal Mrs. Crater's car, while Mrs. Crater wants to marry off her mentally disabled daughter. Mr. Shiftlet does marry the daughter but then abandons her and takes the car. As the story ends, he offers a boy a ride and lectures him on right behavior, only to have the boy curse him and refuse his advice.

Lines 17–24
REINFORCE *KEY IDEA:* DECEPTION

Discuss What details about Mr. Shiftlet hint at his capacity for **deception?** *Possible answer: His facial features are sloped, his jaw is like a "steel-trap" (line 22), and he has a dissatisfied air. He looks untrustworthy and grasping.*

READING SKILL

A ANALYZE DETAILS

Possible answer: The old woman's careful assessment of the stranger might indicate shrewdness or caution; her refusal to rise indicates that she is not one to jump up for politeness' sake; her hand on her hip might suggest an in-charge or stubborn personality. The girl's obliviousness, followed by her agitation and "excited speechless sounds" (line 16) suggest that she is mentally disabled in some way.

Extend the Discussion Encourage students to add these details to the charts introduced on page 1033. Ask them to share what they write in the column labeled "My Reactions."

The Life You Save May Be Your Own

Flannery O'Connor

The old woman and her daughter were sitting on their porch when Mr. Shiftlet came up their road for the first time. The old woman slid to the edge of her chair and leaned forward, shading her eyes from the piercing sunset with her hand. The daughter could not see far in front of her and continued to play with her fingers. Although the old woman lived in this desolate spot with only her daughter and she had never seen Mr. Shiftlet before, she could tell, even from a distance, that he was a tramp and no one to be afraid of. His left coat sleeve was folded up to show there was only half an arm in it, and his gaunt figure listed slightly to the side as if the breeze were pushing him. He had on a black town suit and a brown felt hat
10 that was turned up in the front and down in the back and he carried a tin tool box by a handle. He came on, at an amble, up her road, his face turned toward the sun which appeared to be balancing itself on the peak of a small mountain.

The old woman didn't change her position until he was almost into her yard; then she rose with one hand fisted on her hip. The daughter, a large girl in a short blue organdy dress, saw him all at once and jumped up and began to stamp and point and make excited speechless sounds. **A**

Mr. Shiftlet stopped just inside the yard and set his box on the ground and tipped his hat at her as if she were not in the least afflicted; then he turned toward the old woman and swung the hat all the way off. He had long black slick hair
20 that hung flat from a part in the middle to beyond the tips of his ears on either side. His face descended in forehead for more than half its length and ended suddenly with his features just balanced over a jutting steel-trap jaw. He seemed to be a young man but he had a look of composed[1] dissatisfaction as if he understood life thoroughly.

"Good evening," the old woman said. She was about the size of a cedar fence post and she had a man's gray hat pulled down low over her head.

---

1. **composed:** calm; cool and collected.

ANALYZE VISUALS
What compositional elements lend this scene a sense of isolation? Cite specific examples in your answer.

1 Targeted Passage

A ANALYZE DETAILS
Reread lines 1–16, recording in your chart the descriptive details O'Connor includes about each character. What does the old woman's body language suggest about her character? What does the girl's behavior indicate?

Light of Lagrange (1997), Billy Morrow Jackson. Watercolor, 22″ × 29″. © Billy Morrow Jackson.

DIFFERENTIATED INSTRUCTION

FOR ALL STUDENTS
Provide these independent projects to extend the lesson:

- Explore and write about famous con artists.
- Research antisocial personality disorders and apply the information to the story.
- Interpret the description of Lucynell in an artistic medium.

For further details on these projects, see

R RESOURCE MANAGER
Ideas for Extension pp. 410–411

FOR STRATEGIC READERS
In combination with the *Audio Anthology CD,* use one or more Targeted Passages (pp. 1034, 1036, 1038, 1041, and 1042) to ensure that students focus on key story events and concepts. Targeted Passages are also good for English learners.

1 Targeted Passage [Lines 1–11]

This passage introduces the three characters whose actions and decisions shape the plot.

- What are the old woman and her daughter doing when they first see Mr. Shiftlet?
- What is the old woman's reaction to Mr. Shiftlet?
- What is distinctive about Mr. Shiftlet's appearance?

ANALYZE VISUALS

Possible answer: Students may say that the largeness of the sky, which dominates the picture, dwarfs the homestead, increasing the sense of isolation. There are no other buildings in sight, and the road stretches on, straight and empty, as far as the eye can see.

About the Art This landscape by American painter Billy Morrow Jackson (born 1926) combines a realistic view of the scene—the solitary farmstead, the details of texture and color—with a romantic use of inexact lines and play of light. As in many of his landscapes, the vast sky dominates and overwhelms both natural things (the trees) and manmade things (the buildings).

BACKGROUND

Disabilities in the Time of the Great Depression Today, people with mental or physical disabilities are protected by law. The Americans with Disabilities Act (1990) prohibits discrimination and assures accessibility to public places and services for all Americans. During the Great Depression, however, physical disability, though widespread, was a cause for work discrimination; this is perhaps why Mr. Shiftlet wanders, looking for work. People with mental disabilities, such as Lucynell, were often thought to be uneducable until the early 20th century. Now, the assumption is the opposite: people with mental disabilities can become productive and sometimes independent members of society.

FOR ENGLISH LEARNERS

Prereading For prereading instruction for English learners, see

 BEST PRACTICES TOOLKIT
Scaffolding Reading Instruction
pp. 43–46

FOR ADVANCED LEARNERS/AP

AP exercises in the bottom channel provide additional challenge for students. Use these suggestions for small groups or individuals.

ADDITIONAL GUIDELINES

For more help with differentiation and tips for classroom management, see

BEST PRACTICES TOOLKIT
Differentiated Instruction pp. 31–38

TIERED DISCUSSION PROMPTS

Use these prompts to help students interpret Mr. Shiftlet's enigmatic words and actions:

Connect Have you ever tried to converse with someone who dodges every question? What did you think about that person? *Accept all thoughtful responses.*

Analyze What questions does Mrs. Crater ask Mr. Shiftlet, and why does she want to know these things? ***Possible answer:*** *She asks where he's from and what he's doing out on the lonely road to her farm. She needs to know whether he is a threat.*

Evaluate What kind of person does Mr. Shiftlet make himself out to be, with his nonanswers and silences? ***Possible answer:*** *Accept all thoughtful answers. He doesn't say where he's from or why he's traveling; instead, he offers odd, almost philosophical replies about a world that "is almost rotten" (line 51) and the human heart. Either he is a thoughtful man, stricken by life's perplexities, or he wants to seem deeper than he really is, to avoid Mrs. Crater's questions and the truth about himself.*

The tramp stood looking at her and didn't answer. He turned his back and faced the sunset. He swung both his whole and his short arm up slowly so that they indicated an expanse of sky and his figure formed a crooked cross. The old
30 woman watched him with her arms folded across her chest as if she were the owner of the sun, and the daughter watched, her head thrust forward and her fat helpless hands hanging at the wrists. She had long pink-gold hair and eyes as blue as a peacock's neck.

He held the pose for almost fifty seconds and then he picked up his box and came on to the porch and dropped down on the bottom step. "Lady," he said in a firm nasal voice, "I'd give a fortune to live where I could see me a sun do that every evening."

"Does it every evening," the old woman said and sat back down. The daughter sat down too and watched him with a cautious sly look as if he were a bird that
40 had come up very close. He leaned to one side, rooting in his pants pocket, and in a second he brought out a package of chewing gum and offered her a piece. She took it and unpeeled it and began to chew without taking her eyes off him. He offered the old woman a piece but she only raised her upper lip to indicate she had no teeth.

Mr. Shiftlet's pale, sharp glance had already passed over everything in the yard—the pump near the corner of the house and the big fig tree that three or four chickens were preparing to roost in—and had moved to a shed where he saw the square rusted back of an automobile. "You ladies drive?" he asked.

"That car ain't run in fifteen year," the old woman said. "The day my husband
50 died, it quit running."

"Nothing is like it used to be, lady," he said. "The world is almost rotten."

"That's right," the old woman said. "You from around here?"

"Name Tom T. Shiftlet," he murmured, looking at the tires.

"I'm pleased to meet you," the old woman said. "Name Lucynell Crater and daughter Lucynell Crater. What you doing around here, Mr. Shiftlet?"

He judged the car to be about a 1928 or '29 Ford. "Lady," he said, and turned and gave her his full attention, "lemme tell you something. There's one of these doctors in Atlanta that's taken a knife and cut the human heart—the human heart," he repeated, leaning forward, "out of a man's chest and held it in his
60 hand," and he held his hand out, palm up, as if it were slightly weighted with the human heart, "and studied it like it was a day-old chicken, and lady," he said, allowing a long significant pause in which his head slid forward and his clay-colored eyes brightened, "he don't know no more about it than you or me."

"That's right," the old woman said.

"Why, if he was to take that knife and cut into every corner of it, he still wouldn't know no more than you or me. What you want to bet?"

"Nothing," the old woman said wisely. "Where you come from, Mr. Shiftlet?"

He didn't answer. He reached into his pocket and brought out a sack of tobacco and a package of cigarette papers and rolled himself a cigarette, expertly with one
70 hand, and attached it in a hanging position to his upper lip. Then he took a box of wooden matches from his pocket and struck one on his shoe. He held the burning match as if he were studying the mystery of flame while it traveled dangerously

2 Targeted Passage

DIFFERENTIATED INSTRUCTION

FOR STRATEGIC READERS

2 Targeted Passage [Lines 38–56]

This passage sets up the conflict between Mrs. Crater and Mr. Shiftlet.

- What small act of kindness does Mr. Shiftlet perform upon meeting the Craters?

- What does Mr. Shiftlet seem most interested in as he meets the Craters?

- What does Mrs. Crater want to know about Mr. Shiftlet? How does he respond?

FOR ENGLISH LEARNERS

Vocabulary: Dialect Point out to students the nonstandard use of language common to this story, especially the sentences from which verbs have been dropped (for example, lines 52, 53, 54, and 67). Guide students to insert meaningful verbs into such sentences to increase comprehension; for example, "You from around here?" (line 52) becomes "Are you from around here?"

FOR ADVANCED LEARNERS/AP

Name Symbolism [small-group option] Have students discuss Mr. Shiftlet's name and why O'Connor chooses it. Point out that this is not a common name, and ask students to consider whether it is a clue to his personality. Have them predict what kinds of behaviors and actions Mr. Shiftlet will engage in as the story proceeds.

 BEST PRACTICES TOOLKIT—Transparency Predicting p. A10

toward his skin. The daughter began to make loud noises and to point to his hand and shake her finger at him, but when the flame was just before touching him, he leaned down with his hand cupped over it as if he were going to set fire to his nose and lit the cigarette. **B**

He flipped away the dead match and blew a stream of gray into the evening. A sly look came over his face. "Lady," he said, "nowadays, people'll do anything anyways. I can tell you my name is Tom T. Shiftlet and I come from Tarwater, Tennessee, but
80 you never have seen me before: how you know I ain't lying? How you know my name ain't Aaron Sparks, lady, and I come from Singleberry, Georgia, or how you know it's not George Speeds and I come from Lucy, Alabama, or how you know I ain't Thompson Bright from Toolafalls, Mississippi?"

"I don't know nothing about you," the old woman muttered, irked.

"Lady," he said, "people don't care how they lie. Maybe the best I can tell you is, I'm a man; but listen lady," he said and paused and made his tone more ominous still, "what is a man?"

The old woman began to gum a seed. "What you carry in that tin box, Mr. Shiftlet?" she asked.
90 "Tools," he said, put back. "I'm a carpenter."

"Well, if you come out here to work, I'll be able to feed you and give you a place to sleep but I can't pay. I'll tell you that before you begin," she said.

There was no answer at once and no particular expression on his face. He leaned back against the two-by-four that helped support the porch roof. "Lady," he said slowly, "there's some men that some things mean more to them than money." The old woman rocked without comment and the daughter watched the trigger that moved up and down in his neck. He told the old woman then that all most people were interested in was money, but he asked what a man was made for. He asked her if a man was made for money, or what. He asked her
100 what she thought she was made for but she didn't answer, she only sat rocking and wondered if a one-armed man could put a new roof on her garden house. He asked a lot of questions that she didn't answer. He told her that he was twenty-eight years old and had lived a varied life. He had been a gospel singer, a foreman on the railroad, an assistant in an undertaking parlor, and he come over the radio for three months with Uncle Roy and his Red Creek Wranglers. He said he had fought and bled in the Arm Service of his country and visited every foreign land and that everywhere he had seen people that didn't care if they did a thing one way or another. He said he hadn't been raised thataway. **C**

A fat yellow moon appeared in the branches of the fig tree as if it were going to
110 roost there with the chickens. He said that a man had to escape to the country to see the world whole and that he wished he lived in a desolate place like this where he could see the sun go down every evening like God made it to do.

"Are you married or are you single?" the old woman asked.

There was a long silence. "Lady," he asked finally, "where would you find you an innocent woman today? I wouldn't have any of this trash I could just pick up."

The daughter was leaning very far down, hanging her head almost between her knees watching him through a triangular door she had made in her overturned

B ANALYZE DETAILS
Consider the wealth of details O'Connor offers about Tom Shiftlet in lines 45–76. Which details serve to reveal his important **traits**?

C IRONY
Reread lines 105–108. Explain the irony of Shiftlet's statement that he served in the "Arm Service."

THE LIFE YOU SAVE MAY BE YOUR OWN   **1037**

READING SKILL

B ANALYZE DETAILS

Possible answer: Mr. Shiftlet's "pale, sharp glance" (line 45) reveals his cunning, self-seeking nature; his theatrical cigarette-rolling performance reveals both his competence and his confidence—his desire to show off. Readers may suspect already that this man is less than genuine.

Lines 93–108
REINFORCE *KEY IDEA*: DECEPTION

Discuss What hints do students see that Mr. Shiftlet's résumé partakes of **deception**? *Possible answer:* Mr. Shiftlet seems to have been everywhere and done everything; perhaps he has done many of these things, but his claims seem flamboyant and exaggerated—can he really have visited "every foreign land" (line 106)? Also suspicious is the way he carries on with his autobiography even though Mrs. Crater does not respond to it in any way.

LITERARY ANALYSIS

C IRONY

Possible answer: Mr. Shiftlet's misuse of the term armed services *is ironic in light of the fact that he has lost his arm.*

If students need help . . . Provide context for students by reminding them that World War I had lately ended.

FOR STRATEGIC READERS

Comprehension Support Guide students to recognize the essential difference in the conversation topics that Mr. Shiftlet and Mrs. Crater introduce. Help them perceive that Mr. Shiftlet directs the conversation toward himself and his beliefs, while Mrs. Crater tries to bring the conversation back to practical matters: what kind of work he does, whether he's married, and so on.

FOR ENGLISH LEARNERS

Key Academic Vocabulary Use Definition Mapping to teach these words: *trigger* (line 97), *mechanism* (line 160).

 BEST PRACTICES TOOLKIT—Transparency Definition Mapping p. E6

FOR ADVANCED LEARNERS/AP

Analyze Ask students to use a dictionary to explore these questions about the term *con man:*

- From what word does *con* derive?
- What does this derivation imply about how a con man operates?
- What synonyms are there for con man, and what do these imply about this crime?

Then have students report their findings to the class.

hair; and she suddenly fell in a heap on the floor and began to whimper. Mr. Shiftlet straightened her out and helped her get back in the chair.

120 "Is she your baby girl?" he asked.

"My only," the old woman said, "and she's the sweetest girl in the world. I would give her up for nothing on earth. She's smart too. She can sweep the floor, cook, wash, feed the chickens, and hoe. I wouldn't give her up for a casket of jewels."

"No," he said kindly, "don't ever let any man take her away from you."

"Any man come after her," the old woman said, " 'll have to stay around the place."

Mr. Shiftlet's eye in the darkness was focused on a part of the automobile bumper that glittered in the distance. "Lady," he said, jerking his short arm up as 130 if he could point with it to her house and yard and pump, "there ain't a broken thing on this plantation that I couldn't fix for you, one-arm jackleg[2] or not. I'm a man," he said with a sullen dignity, "even if I ain't a whole one. I got," he said, tapping his knuckles on the floor to emphasize the immensity of what he was going to say, "a moral intelligence!" and his face pierced out of the darkness into a shaft of doorlight and he stared at her as if he were astonished himself at this impossible truth.

The old woman was not impressed with the phrase. "I told you you could hang around and work for food," she said, "if you don't mind sleeping in that car yonder."

"Why listen, Lady," he said with a grin of delight, "the monks of old slept in 140 their coffins!"

"They wasn't as advanced as we are," the old woman said.

> The next morning he began on the roof of the garden house while Lucynell, the daughter, sat on a rock and watched him work. He had not been around a week before the change he had made in the place was apparent. He had patched the front and back steps, built a new hog pen, restored a fence, and taught Lucynell, who was completely deaf and had never said a word in her life, to say the word "bird." The big rosy-faced girl followed him everywhere, saying "Burrttddt ddbirrrttdt," and clapping her hands. The old woman watched from a distance, secretly pleased. She was ravenous for a son-in-law.
>
> 150 Mr. Shiftlet slept on the hard narrow back seat of the car with his feet out the side window. He had his razor and a can of water on a crate that served him as a bedside table and he put up a piece of mirror against the back glass and kept his coat neatly on a hanger that he hung over one of the windows.

In the evenings he sat on the steps and talked while the old woman and Lucynell rocked violently in their chairs on either side of him. The old woman's three mountains were black against the dark blue sky and were visited off and on by various planets and by the moon after it had left the chickens. Mr. Shiftlet pointed out that the reason he had improved this plantation was because he had taken a personal interest in it. He said he was even going to make the automobile run.

---

2. **jackleg:** someone who does work he or she has not been trained to do.

DIFFERENTIATED INSTRUCTION

FOR STRATEGIC READERS

3 Targeted Passage [Lines 142–153]

This passage shows how Mr. Shiftlet begins to set up his con.

- What impact does Mr. Shiftlet have on the farm?
- What effect does he have on Lucynell?
- What kind of personal habits does he display?

FOR ENGLISH LEARNERS

Comprehension Support: Dialect Point out the use of the nonstandard word *ain't* in lines 130 and 132; elicit the standard verb for each sentence, and remind students to watch for other uses of the word and to make the needed substitution for comprehension. Help students with the challenging lines 126 and 127 by guiding them to perceive the if-then statement (*If* any man comes after her, *then* he'll have to stay).

FOR ADVANCED LEARNERS/AP

Analyze Strategy Ask students to create a chronology of the steps Mr. Shiftlet takes to perpetrate his con, and to add to the list as the story proceeds. Remind them to consider his actions, words, and subtle gestures and encourage them to evaluate each step for effectiveness. Students may organize the information on a timeline.

 BEST PRACTICES TOOLKIT—Transparency
Timeline p. B23

The Interloper (1958), Billy Morrow Jackson. Collection of Mrs. Virginia Penofsky.

160   He had raised the hood and studied the mechanism and he said he could tell that the car had been built in the days when cars were really built. You take now, he said, one man puts in one bolt and another man puts in another bolt and another man puts in another bolt so that it's a man for a bolt. That's why you have to pay so much for a car: you're paying all those men. Now if you didn't have to pay but one man, you could get you a cheaper car and one that had had a personal interest taken in it, and it would be a better car. The old woman agreed with him that this was so.

Mr. Shiftlet said that the trouble with the world was that nobody cared, or stopped and took any trouble. He said he never would have been able to teach
170   Lucynell to say a word if he hadn't cared and stopped long enough. **E**

"Teach her to say something else," the old woman said.

"What you want her to say next?" Mr. Shiftlet asked.

The old woman's smile was broad and toothless and suggestive. "Teach her to say 'sugarpie,'" she said.

Mr. Shiftlet already knew what was on her mind. **F**

The next day he began to tinker with the automobile, and that evening he told her that if she would buy a fan belt, he would be able to make the car run.

The old woman said she would give him the money. "You see that girl yonder?" she asked, pointing to Lucynell who was sitting on the floor a foot away, watching

E IRONY
A "1928 or '29 Ford" like this one would, in fact, have been made on an assembly line, a feature that greatly reduced the cost of automobiles. What does this knowledge, combined with Shiftlet's statements in lines 160–170, tell you about his character? Explain which type of irony O'Connor is using here.

F ANALYZE DETAILS
What are Mrs. Crater's **motives** for wanting Lucynell to learn to say "sugarpie"? What details in line 173 suggest this?

THE LIFE YOU SAVE MAY BE YOUR OWN   **1039**

LITERARY ANALYSIS

E IRONY

Possible answer: O'Connor uses dramatic irony: readers know that Shiftlet is talking nonsense, but Mrs. Crater is taken in. In this passage Shiftlet comes across as a pompous yet calculating liar.

READING SKILL

F ANALYZE DETAILS

Possible answer: Mrs. Carter is "ravenous for a son-in-law" (line 149). Her huge "suggestive" smile (line 173) gives her motive away.

FOR ENGLISH LEARNERS

Vocabulary: Idiom Elicit from students or provide meanings for these idioms:

- *took any trouble* (line 169), "spent the time needed to do something"

- *sugarpie* (line 174), "a nickname for someone sweet and beloved"

- *what was on her mind* (line 175), "what she was thinking about"

FOR ADVANCED LEARNERS/AP

Evaluate Argument Have students discuss Mr. Shiftlet's claims in lines 160–167: Is a car built one bolt by one man at a time more expensive than a car built by one man? Why? Does "personal interest" (lines 165–166) affect quality? Why would Mr. Shiftlet make such a claim? After students complete their discussion, have them present their conclusions to the class.

TIERED DISCUSSION PROMPTS

Use these prompts to help students understand Mrs. Crater's "business" (line 200):

Summarize How has Mr. Shiftlet changed the Craters' lives so far? *He has improved their farm, awakened understanding in Lucynell, and enlivened their nightly conversations.*

Analyze What qualities, in Mrs. Crater's opinion, would make Lucynell a good wife for Mr. Shiftlet? *Possible answer: Lucynell is "innocent" (line 201) in that she is too mentally impaired to have much will of her own. She would be entirely in her husband's control.*

Evaluate What do you think of Mrs. Crater's arguments for Lucynell? Whose interests does she have at heart? *Possible answer: Accept all thoughtful answers. Mrs. Crater may indeed think that Mr. Shiftlet would be a good husband to Lucynell and that she would suit him as a wife. However, it is more likely that Mrs. Crater sees Mr. Shiftlet as the best chance of free help for herself and her farm, and would say anything to convince Mr. Shiftlet.*

---

180 him, her eyes blue even in the dark. "If it was ever a man wanted to take her away, I would say, 'No man on earth is going to take that sweet girl of mine away from me!' but if he was to say, 'Lady, I don't want to take her away, I want her right here,' I would say, 'Mister, I don't blame you none. I wouldn't pass up a chance to live in a permanent place and get the sweetest girl in the world myself. You ain't no fool,' I would say."

"How old is she?" Mr. Shiftlet asked casually.

"Fifteen, sixteen," the old woman said. The girl was nearly thirty but because of her innocence it was impossible to guess.

"It would be a good idea to paint it too," Mr. Shiftlet remarked. "You don't
190 want it to rust out."

"We'll see about that later," the old woman said.

The next day he walked into town and returned with the parts he needed and a can of gasoline. Late in the afternoon, terrible noises issued from the shed and the old woman rushed out of the house, thinking Lucynell was somewhere having a fit. Lucynell was sitting on a chicken crate, stamping her feet and screaming, "Burrddttt! bddurrddtttt!" but her fuss was drowned out by the car. With a volley of blasts it emerged from the shed, moving in a fierce and stately way. Mr. Shiftlet was in the driver's seat, sitting very erect. He had an expression of serious modesty on his face as if he had just raised the dead.

200 That night, rocking on the porch, the old woman began her business at once. "You want you an innocent woman, don't you?" she asked sympathetically. "You don't want none of this trash."

"No'm, I don't," Mr. Shiftlet said.

"One that can't talk," she continued, "can't sass you back or use foul language. That's the kind for you to have. Right there," and she pointed to Lucynell sitting cross-legged in her chair, holding both feet in her hands.

"That's right," he admitted. "She wouldn't give me any trouble."

"Saturday," the old woman said, "you and her and me can drive into town and get married."

210 Mr. Shiftlet eased his position on the steps.

"I can't get married right now," he said. "Everything you want to do takes money and I ain't got any."

"What you need with money?" she asked.

"It takes money," he said. "Some people'll do anything anyhow these days, but the way I think, I wouldn't marry no woman that I couldn't take on a trip like she was somebody. I mean take her to a hotel and treat her. I wouldn't marry the Duchesser Windsor,"[3] he said firmly, "unless I could take her to a hotel and give her something good to eat.

"I was raised thataway and there ain't a thing I can do about it. My old mother
220 taught me how to do."

"Lucynell don't even know what a hotel is," the old woman muttered. "Listen here, Mr. Shiftlet," she said, sliding forward in her chair, "you'd be getting a

---

3. **Duchesser Windsor:** Duchess of Windsor. The title was given to the American divorcée Wallace Simpson upon her marriage to the former Edward VIII of England in 1937.

DIFFERENTIATED INSTRUCTION

FOR STRATEGIC READERS

Comprehension Support Help students follow and interpret the swift changes in the topic of conversation in lines 180–191. Ask two students to read just the dialogue, and ask students these questions: What does Mrs. Crater want to discuss? What does Mr. Shiftlet want to discuss? If this were an argument, who would have won?

FOR ENGLISH LEARNERS

Vocabulary: Idiom Elicit from students or provide meanings for these idioms:

- *drowned out* (line 196), "overcome by a louder sound"
- *trash* (line 202), "undesirable people"
- *sass you back* (line 204), "answer with scorn or disrespect"
- *thataway* (line 219), "in that way"

Help students understand Mr. Shiftlet's use of *No'm* (line 203) for "no, ma'am" and *Duchesser Windsor* (line 217) for "Duchess of Windsor."

FOR ADVANCED LEARNERS/AP

Evaluate Argument Ask students to add Mr. Shiftlet's explanation for needing money in lines 214–220 to their con chronologies and to discuss whether his argument is sound. Ask students to consider his appeal to his "old mother" (line 219) and Mrs. Crater's response to his argument.

permanent house and a deep well and the most innocent girl in the world. You don't need no money. Lemme tell you something: there ain't any place in the world for a poor disabled friendless drifting man."

The ugly words settled in Mr. Shiftlet's head like a group of buzzards in the top of a tree. He didn't answer at once. He rolled himself a cigarette and lit it and then he said in an even voice, "Lady, a man is divided into two parts, body and spirit."

The old woman clamped her gums together.

230 "A body and a spirit," he repeated. "The body, lady, is like a house: it don't go anywhere; but the spirit, lady, is like a automobile: always on the move, always . . ."

"Listen, Mr. Shiftlet," she said, "my well never goes dry and my house is always warm in the winter and there's no mortgage on a thing about this place. You can go to the courthouse and see for yourself. And yonder under that shed is a fine automobile." She laid the bait carefully. "You can have it painted by Saturday. I'll pay for the paint."

In the darkness, Mr. Shiftlet's smile stretched like a weary snake waking up by a fire. After a second he recalled himself and said, "I'm only saying a man's spirit means more to him than anything else. I would have to take my wife off for the week end

240 without no regards at all for cost. I got to follow where my spirit says to go."

"I'll give you fifteen dollars for a week end trip," the old woman said in a crabbed voice. "That's the best I can do."

"That wouldn't hardly pay for more than the gas and the hotel," he said. "It wouldn't feed her."

"Seventeen-fifty," the old woman said. "That's all I got so it isn't any use you trying to milk me. You can take a lunch."

Mr. Shiftlet was deeply hurt by the word "milk." He didn't doubt that she had more money sewed up in her mattress but he had already told her he was not interested in her money. "I'll make that do," he said and rose and walked off

250 without treating[4] with her further. **G**

On Saturday the three of them drove into town in the car that the paint had barely dried on and Mr. Shiftlet and Lucynell were married in the Ordinary's[5] office while the old woman witnessed. As they came out of the courthouse, Mr. Shiftlet began twisting his neck in his collar. He looked morose and bitter as if he had been insulted while someone held him. "That didn't satisfy me none," he said. "That was just something a woman in an office did, nothing but paper work and blood tests. What do they know about my blood? If they was to take my heart and cut it out," he said, "they wouldn't know a thing about me. It didn't satisfy me at all."

"It satisfied the law," the old woman said sharply.

260 "The law," Mr. Shiftlet said and spit. "It's the law that don't satisfy me."

He had painted the car dark green with a yellow band around it just under the windows. The three of them climbed in the front seat and the old woman said, "Don't Lucynell look pretty? Looks like a baby doll." Lucynell was dressed up in a white dress that her mother had uprooted from a trunk and there was a Panama

(4) Targeted Passage

G ANALYZE DETAILS
At this point in the story, what **conclusions** can you draw about each character? Cite details in lines 178–250 that influenced your judgments.

---

4. **treating:** discussing terms; negotiating.
5. **Ordinary's:** judge's.

Lines 153–161
REINFORCE *KEY IDEA:* DECEPTION

Discuss Are Mrs. Crater's "ugly words" (line 226) in lines 224–225 a **deception,** or is she telling the truth? *Possible answer: Accept all thoughtful answers. Students may say that the words are a deception, employed to get Mr. Shiftlet to stay. Mrs. Crater cannot know for certain whether Mr. Shiftlet is "friendless" (line 225), for example. Other students may counter, however, that Mrs. Crater sees Mr. Shiftlet for what he is and offers him, out of both pity and mutual need, a solution.*

READING SKILL

G ANALYZE DETAILS

Possible answer: Accept all thoughtful answers. Students may find Mrs. Crater sinister after she essentially sells her disabled daughter for a son-in-law to take care of the house. Her lies about the girl's age reveal her dishonesty, and her bargaining with Mr. Shiftlet reveals her stingy, calculating nature. Shiftlet is also callous and calculating, driven purely by self-interest.

If students need help . . . Refer them to the three-column chart they have been filling in as they read. Guide them to see how the details they have recorded gradually create a more complete picture of each character.

FOR STRATEGIC READERS

(4) Targeted Passage [Lines 232–250]

This passage relates an important agreement at which Mrs. Crater and Mr. Shiftlet arrive.

• What is Mrs. Crater's opening offer?

• What else does Mr. Shiftlet want? Why?

• Why does Mr. Shiftlet agree to Mrs. Crater's terms yet walk away "deeply hurt" (line 247)?

FOR ENGLISH LEARNERS

Vocabulary: Multiple-Meaning Words Make sure that students understand the different uses of the verb *treat* in this story: when Mr. Shiftlet says he wants to "treat" Lucynell at a hotel (line 216), he means that he wants to do something nice for her. When he refuses to "treat with" Mrs. Crater further on the matter of money (250), he means that he won't negotiate further. Remind students that *treat* can also be a noun meaning "a special pleasure."

FOR ADVANCED LEARNERS/AP

Compare and Contrast Have students explore the conflicting motives of Mrs. Crater and Mr. Shiftlet by completing a Comparison Matrix to answer these questions: What does each person value? What does each person consider unnecessary? What provides each person with a sense of well-being and security?

 BEST PRACTICES TOOLKIT—Transparency Comparison Matrix p. A24

TIERED DISCUSSION PROMPTS

Use these prompts to help students understand Lucynell's role in the events:

Recall How did Lucynell react during the parting from her mother? *Possible answer: She is distanced from the events, just as the "baby doll" (line 263) her mother describes her as would be.*

Analyze What causes Mr. Shiftlet to become alternately happy and dejected as he drives? *Possible answer: He is happy when he thinks of the car, but unhappy when he looks at Lucynell, who—oblivious—is entirely absorbed in destroying her hat. Mr. Shiftlet is wondering if he has made a good deal.*

Evaluate Why does O'Connor have the counter boy describes Lucynell as an "angel of Gawd" (line 299), and what does Mr. Shiftlet's one-word retort tell readers about how he sees Lucynell? *Possible answer: Accept all thoughtful answers. O'Connor may imply that Lucynell is an innocent who requires the protection of God and of people around her; she may imply that Lucynell offers Mr. Shiftlet a chance at redemption if he cares for her. His reply, "Hitch-hiker" (line 300), implies that he can discard her on the side of the road without compunction.*

LITERARY ANALYSIS

ⓗ IRONY

Possible answer: The name implies that the place is popular (or "hot"), but the Hot Spot is anything but hot. It is deserted except for the counter boy; Lucynell falls asleep on the counter.

---

hat on her head with a bunch of red wooden cherries on the brim. Every now and then her placid expression was changed by a sly isolated little thought like a shoot of green in the desert. "You got a prize!" the old woman said.

Mr. Shiftlet didn't even look at her.

They drove back to the house to let the old woman off and pick up the lunch. 270 When they were ready to leave, she stood staring in the window of the car, with her fingers clenched around the glass. Tears began to seep sideways out of her eyes and run along the dirty creases in her face. "I ain't ever been parted with her for two days before," she said.

Mr. Shiftlet started the motor.

"And I wouldn't let no man have her but you because I seen you would do right. Good bye, Sugarbaby," she said, clutching at the sleeve of the white dress. Lucynell looked straight at her and didn't seem to see her there at all. Mr. Shiftlet eased the car forward so that she had to move her hands.

The early afternoon was clear and open and surrounded by pale blue sky. 280 Although the car would go only thirty miles an hour, Mr. Shiftlet imagined a terrific climb and dip and swerve that went entirely to his head so that he forgot his morning bitterness. He had always wanted an automobile but he had never been able to afford one before. He drove very fast because he wanted to make Mobile[6] by nightfall.

> Occasionally he stopped his thoughts long enough to look at Lucynell in the seat beside him. She had eaten the lunch as soon as they were out of the yard and now she was pulling the cherries off the hat one by one and throwing them out the window. He became depressed in spite of the car. He had driven about a hundred miles when he decided that she must be hungry again and at the next 290 small town they came to, he stopped in front of an aluminum-painted eating place called The Hot Spot and took her in and ordered her a plate of ham and grits. The ride had made her sleepy and as soon as she got up on the stool, she rested her head on the counter and shut her eyes. There was no one in The Hot Spot but Mr. Shiftlet and the boy behind the counter, a pale youth with a greasy rag hung over his shoulder. Before he could dish up the food, she was snoring gently. ⓗ
>
> "Give it to her when she wakes up," Mr. Shiftlet said. "I'll pay for it now."
>
> The boy bent over her and stared at the long pink-gold hair and the half-shut sleeping eyes. Then he looked up and stared at Mr. Shiftlet. "She looks like an angel of Gawd," he murmured.
>
> 300 "Hitch-hiker," Mr. Shiftlet explained. "I can't wait. I got to make Tuscaloosa."[7]
>
> The boy bent over again and very carefully touched his finger to a strand of the golden hair, and Mr. Shiftlet left.

He was more depressed than ever as he drove on by himself. The late afternoon had grown hot and sultry and the country had flattened out. Deep in the sky a storm was preparing very slowly and without thunder as if it meant to drain every drop of air from the earth before it broke. There were times when Mr. Shiftlet

ⓢ Targeted Passage

ⓗ IRONY
Consider what most people would expect from an establishment called The Hot Spot. What is ironic about this restaurant's name?

---

6. **Mobile:** a city in southwestern Alabama, along the Gulf Coast.
7. **Tuscaloosa:** a city in west-central Alabama.

DIFFERENTIATED INSTRUCTION

FOR STRATEGIC READERS

ⓢ Targeted Passage [Lines 285–302]

This passage reveals Mr. Shiftlet's decision about his marriage to Lucynell.

- How does Lucynell behave as they drive?
- Why does Mr. Shiftlet stop at the Hot Spot?
- What relationship does Mr. Shiftlet claim to have with Lucynell, and why does he lie?
- What does Mr. Shiftlet mean by "I got to make Tuscaloosa" (line 300)?

FOR ENGLISH LEARNERS

Culture: Clarify When students reach line 300, explain that in the time that the story is set, few people had automobiles, and hitchhiking was not an unusual way to travel. Demonstrate, or have a student demonstrate, how a hitchhiker would thumb for a ride. Remind students that today, hitchhiking—or offering rides to hitchhikers, as Mr. Shiftlet does in the next scene—is not a safe thing to do.

FOR ADVANCED LEARNERS/AP

Interpret Figurative Language Read aloud, or have a student read aloud, the sentence that bridges lines 265–267. Ask students to discuss what this simile means. Have them consider the connotations of O'Connor's imagery and how those connotations add to the story's irony.

preferred not to be alone. He felt too that a man with a car had a responsibility to others, and he kept his eye out for a hitch-hiker. Occasionally he saw a sign that warned: "Drive carefully. The life you save may be your own." ❶

310 The narrow road dropped off on either side into dry fields and here and there a shack or a filling station stood in a clearing. The sun began to set directly in front of the automobile. It was a reddening ball that through his windshield was slightly flat on the bottom and top. He saw a boy in overalls and a gray hat standing on the edge of the road and he slowed the car down and stopped in front of him. The boy didn't have his hand raised to thumb the ride, he was only standing there, but he had a small cardboard suitcase and his hat was set on his head in a way to indicate that he had left somewhere for good. "Son," Mr. Shiftlet said, "I see you want a ride."

The boy didn't say he did or he didn't but he opened the door of the car and
320 got in, and Mr. Shiftlet started driving again. The child held the suitcase on his lap and folded his arms on top of it. He turned his head and looked out the window away from Mr. Shiftlet. Mr. Shiftlet felt oppressed. "Son," he said after a minute, "I got the best old mother in the world so I reckon you only got the second best."

The boy gave him a quick dark glance and then turned his face back out the window.

"It's nothing so sweet," Mr. Shiftlet continued, "as a boy's mother. She taught him his first prayers at her knee, she give him love when no one else would, she told him what was right and what wasn't, and she seen that he done the right thing. Son," he said, "I never rued a day in my life like the one I rued when I left that
330 old mother of mine."

The boy shifted in his seat but he didn't look at Mr. Shiftlet. He unfolded his arms and put one hand on the door handle.

"My mother was a angel of Gawd," Mr. Shiftlet said in a very strained voice. "He took her from heaven and giver to me and I left her." His eyes were instantly clouded over with a mist of tears. The car was barely moving.

The boy turned angrily in the seat. "You go to the devil!" he cried. "My old woman is a flea bag and yours is a stinking pole cat!" and with that he flung the door open and jumped out with his suitcase into the ditch.

Mr. Shiftlet was so shocked that for about a hundred feet he drove along slowly
340 with the door still open. A cloud, the exact color of the boy's hat and shaped like a turnip, had descended over the sun, and another, worse looking, crouched behind the car. Mr. Shiftlet felt that the rottenness of the world was about to engulf him. He raised his arm and let it fall again to his breast. "Oh Lord!" he prayed. "Break forth and wash the slime from this earth!"

The turnip continued slowly to descend. After a few minutes there was a guffawing peal of thunder from behind and fantastic raindrops, like tin-can tops, crashed over the rear of Mr. Shiftlet's car. Very quickly he stepped on the gas, and with his stump sticking out the window he raced the galloping shower into Mobile. ❧

THE LIFE YOU SAVE MAY BE YOUR OWN **1043**

❶ **IRONY**
What is the irony in Shiftlet's reasons for looking for a hitchhiker?

LITERARY ANALYSIS

❶ IRONY

Possible answer: Mr. Shiftlet tells himself that now that he owns a car, he has a responsibility to help others. However, to get the car, he callously abandoned his mentally disabled and helpless wife—an entirely irresponsible thing to do.

Lines 336–344
REINFORCE *KEY IDEA:* DECEPTION

Discuss Who is the intended victim of Mr. Shiftlet's **deception** in his prayer? *Possible answer: Accept all thoughtful answers. Students may say that the intended victim is the boy, but he escaped Mr. Shiftlet's deceptive moralizing by storming out of the car. Others may say that Mr. Shiftlet intends to deceive God in his prayer that "the slime" (line 344) of the earth be punished, though he himself is as morally "slimy" as a man can get.*

SELECTION WRAP–UP

REFLECT Ask students what causes Mr. Shiftlet, or any person, to behave selfishly, even when others are harmed.

★ CRITIQUE

- Have students identify and analyze the dramatic irony that closes the story.
- After completing the After Reading questions on page 1044, have students revisit their responses and tell whether they have changed their opinions.

FOR STRATEGIC READERS

Comprehension Support Help students understand the conclusions that the sharp-eyed Mr. Shiftlet makes about the boy, so that they will better understand why he lectures about mothers. The boy's youth, his suitcase, and his attitude all hint that he is running away from home after an argument, and the "quick dark glance" he gives Mr. Shiftlet upon hearing the topic of mothers confirms Mr. Shiftlet's suspicions.

FOR ADVANCED LEARNERS/AP

Analyze Plot Devices Ask students to look up the word *epiphany*, and tell them that O'Connor often includes, at the end of her stories, an epiphany or moment of grace in which a main character suddenly has a clear insight into the world and his or her place in it. Have students discuss whether Mr. Shiftlet has an epiphany or remains in the dark as to his own condition. Ask students to formalize their conclusions in writing in their journals.

Practice and Apply

After Reading

Use these copy masters to check understanding and provide extra support:

R RESOURCE MANAGER—Copy Masters
Reading Check p. 419
Irony p. 415
Question Support p. 420

Additional selection questions are provided for teachers on page 409.

ANSWERS

1. *mental impairment, deafness, poor eyesight, and inability to speak*

2. *He wants the car; she wants to trade room and board for work on the farm.*

3. *She'll buy paint and pay Shiftlet $17.50 if he'll marry Lucynell and run the farm.*

4. *He intended to con Mrs. Crater and exploit Lucynell's disabilities to get the car.*

Possible answers:

5. *Shiftlet is observant (he spots the car), shrewd (he spots Mrs. Crater's weakness), and patient (he works to build credibility). Mrs. Crater is the perfect victim because she's easily manipulated; she jeopardizes Lucynell to get help on the farm.*

6. ■ **SKILLS FOCUS** Analyze Descriptive **Details** *Details about Shiftlet's appearance are outward signs of his corrupt nature. His missing arm, "steel-trap jaw" (line 22), and crooked figure represent his fractured ethical sense and his desire to trap others. Details reveal Mrs. Crater's pride and greed; she acts "as if she were owner of the sun" (lines 30–31) and is "ravenous for a son-in-law" (line 149).*

Assess and Reteach

Assess

R RESOURCE MANAGER—Copy Masters
Selection Test A pp. 421–422
Selection Test B/C pp. 423–424

Test Generator CD

Reteach

S STANDARDS LESSON FILE
Literature Lesson 36: Irony

Comprehension

1. **Recall** What are Lucynell's disabilities?

2. **Recall** When they first meet, what do Mr. Shiftlet and Mrs. Crater want from each other?

3. **Summarize** What is the bargain struck between Mr. Shiftlet and Mrs. Crater over her daughter, Lucynell?

4. **Clarify** What does Mr. Shiftlet's treatment of Lucynell at the end reveal about his intentions all along?

Literary Analysis

5. **Analyze Character** Explain why Mr. Shiftlet is able to get what he wants from Mrs. Crater. What traits make him a good con artist? What makes Mrs. Crater the perfect victim for this kind of **deception?** Cite evidence to support your response.

6. **Analyze Descriptive Details** Review the chart you created as you read. Because Mr. Shiftlet and Mrs. Crater are both hiding something during much of the story, readers must mine the details given about each character for clues to their true selves. Since Mr. Shiftlet's words and thoughts can't be trusted, what can you learn about him from the descriptions of his physical appearance? What details reveal the flaws in Mrs. Crater's character and give her motives away? Support your analysis with evidence from the text.

7. **Interpret Irony** In this story, much of O'Connor's wry humor comes from **situational** and **dramatic irony.** Review the story to find at least two examples of each kind of irony. Also, see whether you can find one example that reveals both kinds at once. What do these multiple ironies suggest about O'Connor's view of her fellow human beings?

8. **Make Judgments** What is the significance of the story's title, taken from a road sign? Explain how you think O'Connor judges Tom T. Shiftlet, as well as how you yourself do. Be sure to address the following:

   • the way in which Mr. Shiftlet is a potential savior of his own life and the lives of others

   • how and why he fails in this role

   • whether you think he has any redeeming features or see him as hopelessly lost

Literary Criticism

9. **Author's Style** For Flannery O'Connor, a devout Catholic, evidence of divine grace was everywhere, and her stories are full of religious **imagery.** Find at least two examples of religious imagery in this story and explain what they contribute to its meaning and its message.

---

7. ● **SKILLS FOCUS** Irony *O'Connor uses irony to suggest that people don't understand themselves or others, and yet they self-righteously persist in their beliefs, often to the detriment of others.* **Situational irony:** *Mrs. Crater says she wouldn't trade Lucynell "for a casket of jewels" (lines 123–124) but pays Shiftlet $17.50 to marry her.* **Dramatic irony:** *Shiftlet complains about the rotten world; readers know that he is rotten. The storm is ironic, because Shiftlet doesn't expect the answer to his prayers to target him.*

8. *Students may say Shiftlet could have saved his life by honest work, or that by stealing the car he saved himself from the Craters. His deserting Lucynell may make him seem hopelessly lost, yet his capability for guilt may redeem him one day.*

9. *Students may note Shiftlet's posture, which forms the shape of "a crooked cross" (line 29) and his occupation as a carpenter; he could have saved the farm and the Craters. Lucynell's description as an "angel of Gawd" (line 299) suggests that she is an ironic messenger of Shiftlet's possible redemption at the end of the story.*

The Essence of a Short Story

Stories by modernist writers, such as Fitzgerald, Hemingway, and Faulkner, are often complex or ambiguous. These works demand much of readers, who must pay attention to details of character, setting, plot, dialogue, and language in order to decipher meaning.

Writing to Evaluate

After reflecting on each of the short stories you have just read, choose one and evaluate it in order to distill its essence—that which is utterly indispensable—in no more than 300 of the author's own words. You may use portions of sentences and combine them, if appropriate and necessary. In addition, you may create your own paragraphing structure in order to give your distillation a desirable "flow."

Consider

- introductions or important descriptions of characters
- plot events essential to the story, especially the climax
- descriptions of setting that reveal important information
- dialogue that reveals character, motivation, or theme
- particularly meaningful language

Extension

VIEWING & REPRESENTING

Working with a partner, **choose or create an image** that you feel captures the essence of the story you evaluated. You may look for an image from a magazine, Web site, book of art, or other source, or you may create your own. Share your image with the class, and explain why you feel it represents or illustrates the story's essence.

Ernest Hemingway, working as a war correspondent, 1944

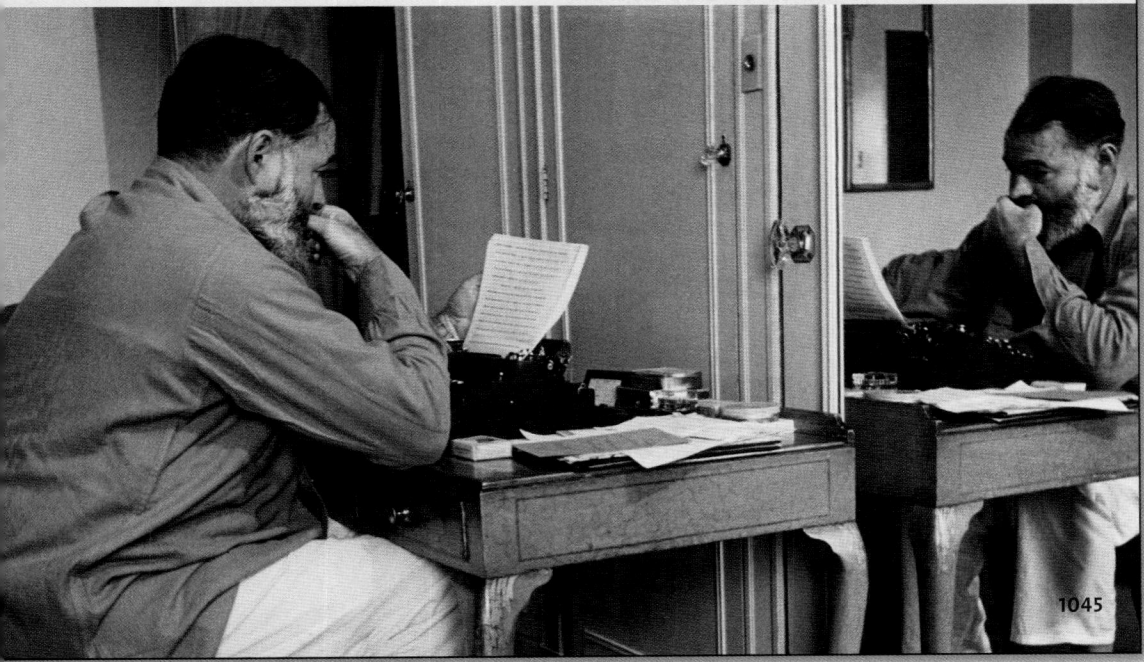

1045

Wrap-Up: The Modern Short Story

This Wrap-Up provides students with an opportunity to review the definition of modernist writing and to consider the elements that make the short stories they have read truly modern. Students can discuss the demands that modern short stories make on readers and the pleasures and surprises such stories provide.

Writing to Evaluate

- Review with students that *evaluating* a short story involves carefully considering the author's craft and use of literary elements, and then making a judgment about the impact of the author's choices. Evaluation leads readers to a fuller understanding of the essential elements in an author's work.

- To help students begin their evaluation, organize them in groups according to story choice. Tell groups to brainstorm for ideas and images that form the essence of the story. Have students work independently to search the story for representative text. Clarify that for this assignment, the evaluative step occurs when students distill the essential ideas of a story and choose text to reflect those ideas.

Extension

- Remind students that an image can be three dimensional, as a sculpture or a textural collage is.

- Provide materials—magazines, books of art prints, art media—and research suggestions—museum or gallery Web sites—to help students locate images.

- Before students present their images and explanations, have them organize their thoughts using a Venn Diagram to link the image to the story's essence.

BEST PRACTICES TOOLKIT—Transparency Venn Diagram p. A26

DIFFERENTIATED INSTRUCTION

FOR DEVELOPING WRITERS

Writing Support Help students get started by asking them to choose the short story they found easiest to read and most engaging. Then ask them these questions: What was engaging about the story? What part of the story was most suspenseful and engaging? Explain that the element that engaged students is probably the story's essence. The most engaging part of the story is a good place to look for representative words.

FOR ENGLISH LEARNERS

Narrowing the Topic To narrow the assignment's scope and simplify the search for representative words, ask students to consider only the story's characters and to search for text that describes and gives the words of the characters. Remind students that some stories in the unit do not use quotation marks to identify characters' words, and model how to find such words in the students' chosen stories.

OBJECTIVE

- analyze the characteristics of journalism as literature

The Fine Art of Journalism

Journalism and Literature Discuss the key distinctions between the two kinds of writing. Then have students use Two-Column Charts to classify these examples as journalism or literature, and ask volunteers to explain their answers:

- Today, an earthquake shook parts of Asia. (*journalism*)
- Her brunette hair hung in question marks around her face. (*literature*)
- The jury reported a guilty verdict in the case of Jones versus the state of Wyoming. (*journalism*)
- "Why are you smiling at me?" he questioned, his eyes sparkling with mischief. (*literature*)
- The green tapestry of vines hung from the tree branches. (*literature*)

 BEST PRACTICES TOOLKIT—Transparency
Two-Column Chart p. A25

Journalism as Literature

Some journalists are writers of literature in disguise. They put together a news story or an opinion piece that is so well written and riveting that the article is elevated to the realm of literature. Have you ever read a news report or editorial that seemed to stand out from anything else you'd read in the newspaper? If so, you may have read an emerging literary classic.

The Fine Art of Journalism

Traditionally, journalism and literature are considered to be very different forms. **Journalism** is known for being factual, informative, and written for the moment. **Literature,** on the other hand, is built from the imagination and meant to last. Its language is often figurative, its images are symbolic, and the setting and characters are representative of deeper meaning. When journalism becomes literature, it's not the imaginative use of facts that makes it so; rather, it's the imaginative use of language that transforms it from a standard news story into a piece of art.

Journalistic writing includes news reports, essays, editorials, feature articles, and critical reviews and has a long history in the United States. Many of the big issues of the day, since pre-Revolutionary times, have been debated in newspapers, magazines, and pamphlets. In the early 20th century, a number of serious literary writers began their writing careers as journalists, including Ernest Hemingway, E. B. White, and Dorothy Parker. The tradition of journalism as literature continued with writers such as Truman Capote, Tom Wolfe, and Joan Didion. In the 1960s, Wolfe coined the term "New Journalism" to describe the work of a journalist who sets out to create journalistic writing that uses literary techniques.

Tools of the Trade

Journalism that transcends the mundane and becomes literature is usually characterized by the use of certain literary techniques.

- **Imagery**—Traditionally, news writing contains only essential details, without any embellishment of description. In literary writing, the writer includes words and phrases that express sensory experiences in order to create a vivid picture or strong impression for the reader.

DIFFERENTIATED INSTRUCTION

For general guidelines on differentiating instruction, see

 BEST PRACTICES TOOLKIT
Differentiated Instruction pp. 31–38

FOR STRATEGIC READERS

Note Taking For students who are unfamiliar with journalism as literature or need help with note taking, hand out the copy master before discussing the spread. Explain that students will review many terms relating to

literature and journalism in this workshop. Discuss the major terms on this spread (*imagery, narrative elements, style, voice, perspective*) as students record notes on the copy masters.

R **RESOURCE MANAGER—Copy Master**
Note Taking p. 425

- **Narrative elements**—In the world of journalism, an article is figuratively called "a story." At times, this might be literally true, especially when a journalist relates an incident with all the elements of a good tale, including a suspenseful plot, detailed characterization and setting, and a well-defined point of view.

- **Style and voice**—Style is a writer's unique way of communicating ideas, and voice is the expression of his or her personality. Most news writing is made up of spare, plain prose, written for a mass audience. In literary writing, the writer may use figurative language, coin new words, or interject descriptive phrases. Each of these elements can add up to an original style and voice.

- **Writer's perspective**—In an editorial or literary review, you expect to find the writer's opinion, but in news reporting, the writer usually remains invisible. Hemingway and Jack London, however, were two journalists who wrote personal narratives of news events, including war experiences and unusual adventures, in which they interjected their own observations and opinions.

In the following passage from "A New Kind of War" (page 1050), notice how Hemingway included his observations instead of merely reporting the facts.

> In the war that I had known, men often lied about the manner of their wounding. Not at first; but later. I'd lied a little myself in my time. Especially late in the evening.
>
> —**Ernest Hemingway, "A New Kind of War"**

Close Read

What does Hemingway reveal about himself in this passage? Why wouldn't this be typical of journalism, which is known for being factual?

Dorothy Parker was always known for her acerbic wit. In the following excerpt from a literary review, notice the imagery and figurative language she uses in exaggerating the critics' reactions to Hemingway's first novel.

> Promptly upon its publication, Ernest Hemingway was discovered, the Stars and Stripes were reverentially raised over him, eight hundred and forty-seven book reviewers formed themselves into the word "welcome," and the band played "Hail to the Chief" in three concurrent keys.
>
> —**Dorothy Parker, "A Book of Great Short Stories"**

Close Read

In each of these examples, the writer's voice is well developed. How would you describe the personality of the writer in each?

Tools of the Trade

Literary Techniques Clarify these terms listed on pages 1046–1047:

- **Imagery** Tell students that imagery allows readers to use their senses to experience what the writer is describing. Ask students to give examples of sensory details. *Students should name details appealing to senses of sight, smell, touch, taste, or hearing.*

- **Narrative elements** Explain that narrative elements also involve readers in the plights of real-life characters. Ask students in what ways including real-life characters might affect readers. *Possible answer: Including real-life characters would probably draw readers into a news story.*

- **Style and voice** Tell students that a writer's word choice contributes to style and voice. Ask students to discuss the differences between these two sentences:
  - Over five hundred homes were destroyed by the hurricane.
  - The hurricane whipped through the community, destroying more than five hundred homes in its jagged path.

- **Writer's perspective** To identify a writer's perspective, suggest that students ask themselves these questions: What is the writer's opinion of these people or events, and why? What is the writer's connection to these people or events?

Close Read

Possible answer: Hemingway reveals that as circumstances dictate, he does not always tell the truth. This admission is unusual for a journalist who is expected to report the truth to his readers. It is also unusual to include the journalist in the story.

Close Read

Possible answer: Hemingway's personality is nostalgic and humorous. Parker is critical or sarcastic.

FOR ENGLISH LEARNERS

Culture: Clarify On the board, list these terms from the Hemingway and Parker excerpts. Share the explanations with students.

- *late in the evening:* time of day when people are prone to exaggerating stories for glorification or entertainment
- *Stars and Stripes:* the American flag
- *Hail to the Chief:* American patriotic song that plays when the president arrives at any official public occasion

FOR ADVANCED LEARNERS/AP

Compare Writers' Perspectives Have students further research the perspectives and works of Hemingway and Parker, focusing on their journalistic writings. With that research, have students create cartoon strips or storyboards that feature the two writers in conversation. Tell students to use factually accurate information to re-create the style and voice of each writer.

 BEST PRACTICES TOOLKIT—Transparency
Storyboard p. C11

Focus and Motivate

OBJECTIVES

Literary Analysis
- explore the key idea of **war**
- analyze subjectivity in reporting
- read a news dispatch

Reading
- analyze descriptive details

Grammar and Writing
- use the second-person pronoun to establish an effective point of view
- write a subjective news report

R2.5, R3.3, W1.2, LC1.1

ABOUT THE AUTHOR

Ask students how Hemingway's reporting of war's impact on ordinary people may have affected readers' views and attitudes. *Possible answer: His reporting probably led to a more intimate understanding of war and greater horror over war's damaging effects.*

USING THE *NOTABLE QUOTE*

Clarify that in this quotation, **Ernest Hemingway** insists war is a crime. Ask students: If war is a crime, who are the criminals, what is the crime, and who are the victims? *Possible answer: The criminals are the leaders of the warring nations. The crime is mental, spiritual, and physical murder. The victims include innocent civilians as well as soldiers who lose their humanity by committing the crime.*

Selection Resources

A New Kind of War

News Dispatch by Ernest Hemingway

CALIFORNIA

R2.5, R3.3, W1.2 (p. 1057),
LC1.1 (p. 1057)

NOTABLE QUOTE

"Never think that war, no matter how necessary, nor how justified, is not a crime."

FYI

Did you know that Ernest Hemingway ...

- began a romance in Spain with fellow war reporter Martha Gellhorn, who became his third wife?
- hunted Nazi submarines off the coast of Cuba in his private fishing boat?

Author Online

For more on Ernest Hemingway, visit the **Literature Center** at **ClassZone.com**.

Hemingway, center, among other correspondents covering the Spanish Civil War

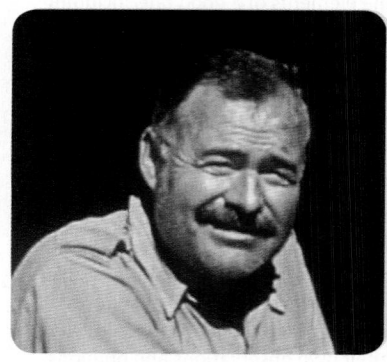

Ernest Hemingway

1899–1961

Ernest Hemingway never considered his journalism as important as his fiction, but his journalism was admired anyway, particularly his war correspondence. Before he published his first stories and novels in the 1920s, he reported on European affairs for the *Toronto Star*. He covered the Greco-Turkish War of 1922, describing 20 miles of Greek refugees trudging through the rain. He also interviewed the fascist Italian dictator Benito Mussolini, calling him the "biggest bluff in Europe."

Taking Sides in Spain By the 1930s, Hemingway had become a famous literary figure. He returned to war reporting in 1937 after civil war broke out in Spain, the country that he loved. Hemingway is perhaps most identified with this conflict, in which the right-wing army of General Francisco Franco (the Nationalists) fought against supporters of the left-wing elected government of Spain (the Loyalists or Republicans). This war was widely seen as a struggle against fascism, or dictatorial government. Many world writers, including Hemingway, were sympathetic to the Loyalist side. These writers were greatly disheartened by Franco's eventual victory in 1939.

Celebrity Journalist Hemingway covered the war for the North American Newspaper Alliance (NANA), receiving the highest fee ever paid a war correspondent. His NANA dispatches have been called "a new style of reporting that told the public about every facet of the war, especially . . . its effects on the common man, woman, and child." One of these dispatches, "A New Kind of War," is considered classic.

Writer or Fighter? After World War II broke out, Hemingway once again became a war reporter, this time for *Collier's* magazine. He memorably described the D-day landing at Normandy, the liberation of Paris, and the Allied movement into Germany in 1944. His command of a French guerrilla band and his storage of weapons in his hotel room led him to be investigated for violating the Geneva Convention, which forbids journalists to take up arms. He was cleared of misconduct and later awarded a Bronze Star for his service as a war correspondent.

See also the biography on page 968, which covers Hemingway's entire career.

1048

RESOURCE MANAGER UNIT 5

Plan and Teach pp. 427–434

Literary Analysis
Summary pp. 435†*, 436‡*
Subjectivity in Reporting
   pp. 437, 438†*
Question Support p. 442*

Reading
Analyze Descriptive Details
   pp. 439, 440†*
Reading Check p. 441

Grammar and Writing
Choose Effective Point of View
   p. 443

Assessment
Selection Tests A, B/C
   pp. 445*, 447*
Test Generator CD

BEST PRACTICES TOOLKIT

Differentiated Instruction
   pp. 31–38*

Scaffolding Instruction
   pp. 43–46*

Graphic Organizers/Strategies
Comparison Matrix • Venn
Diagram • Observation Chart •
Sensory Notes

Reading Support
Audio Anthology CD*

Technology
Literature and Writing Centers
   at **ClassZone.com**
Write*Smart* CD

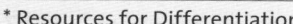

* Resources for Differentiation   † Also in Spanish   ‡ In Haitian Creole and Vietnamese

• LITERARY ANALYSIS: SUBJECTIVITY IN REPORTING

News reporters are trained to be **objective,** presenting facts without the intrusion of their own personal feelings or opinions. You will notice, however, that Hemingway does not strive for this ideal in his reporting on the Spanish Civil War. His writing is quite **subjective,** expressing his personal reactions to what he sees. He wants his readers to be in Madrid with him, experiencing exactly what he does. Toward this end he uses both the **second-person point of view** ("as you lie in bed, you hear the firing in the front line") and the **first-person point of view** ("I did not believe a word of it").

As you read, notice ways in which Hemingway reveals his feelings and opinions. Consider what his subjectivity offers that an objective news report could not.

Review: **Dialogue**

● READING SKILL: ANALYZE DESCRIPTIVE DETAILS

Hemingway makes powerful use of descriptive details. Many of these are **sensory details,** which appeal to the senses of sight, hearing, touch, smell, and taste. Notice the visual details in the following passage. What can you conclude from them?

On the corner, twenty yards away, is a heap of rubble, smashed cement and thrown up dirt, a single dead man, his torn clothes dusty, and a great hole in the sidewalk from which the gas from a broken main is rising. . . .

Other descriptive details are not sensory, but they still convey important ideas. What might it mean, for example, that the large rooms at the front of Hemingway's hotel only cost a dollar a day? As you read, jot down descriptive details about

- Madrid and the hotel
- Raven, the wounded soldier Hemingway meets
- Raven's commander, Jock Cunningham

React to these details and make inferences from them.

What can we learn from WAR?

KEY IDEA The Spanish Civil War did not have immediate consequences for most Americans, yet American newspapers thought it was important enough to cover. Consider our own times. Why do newspapers and broadcast networks send reporters to cover fighting in foreign countries? What do these reports usually show or tell an audience about **war?**

DISCUSS Think about war coverage you have read, seen on television, or heard on the radio. Working in a small group, list types of information you would expect to be included in such reporting—the number of people killed in an attack, for example. After completing your list, discuss insights about war that you have gained from journalists.

1049

What can we learn from WAR?

Lead into the **KEY IDEA** by asking the question. Invite feedback on why reporters are sent to cover **war** and what their reports convey. Urge students to share their ideas in the **DISCUSS** activity. Invite volunteers to share their lists and insights.

SKILLS FOCUS

LITERARY ANALYSIS R2.5, R3.3

● SUBJECTIVITY IN REPORTING

Highlight the use of first-person and second-person pronouns in the excerpt text. Explain that in first-person point of view, the pronouns *I* and *me* make the writer an active participant in the text. In second-person point of view, the pronoun *you* makes the reader a direct participant in the text. Ask students to describe specific ways in which each approach affects a text's subjectivity. ***Possible answer:*** *First-person point of view adds subjectivity by sharing the writer's feelings and thoughts. Second-person point of view creates subjectivity by inviting readers into a subjective experience.*

CHECK UNDERSTANDING Have students write and contrast sentences in first-person and second-person points of view.

READING SKILL R3.3

■ ANALYZE DESCRIPTIVE DETAILS

Point out that sensory details allow readers to fully experience the events described rather than simply read about them. Ask students to analyze the excerpt on page 1049 and to describe what reaction Hemingway wants to evoke from readers, and why. ***Possible answer:*** *The quote uses vivid sensory details about the objects in the rubble and the surrounding destruction. Hemingway may want to shock readers by reducing the dead man to an item in a pile.*

 RESOURCE MANAGER—Copy Master Analyze Descriptive Details p. 439 (for student use while reading the selection)

DIFFERENTIATED INSTRUCTION

FOR STRATEGIC READERS

Concept Support: Analyze Descriptive Details To help students analyze descriptive details, point out the strategy suggested on page 1049. Readers should note a detail, such as the cost of the hotel rooms, and then ask a question to understand that detail. Tell students to use this strategy as they read, formulating a question for each detail they note. Suggest these question ideas:

- What might this detail mean?
- Why does the writer include this detail?
- Why is this detail important?

Urge students to notice the conclusions they draw and the inferences they make as they answer their questions.

Practice and Apply

SUMMARY

This news dispatch begins with Hemingway lying in a hotel bed in Madrid, Spain, during the Spanish Civil War. Rifles and machine guns sound outside the open window and explosions awaken him. He goes downstairs to find destruction and death. Thankful for life, he eats breakfast and chats with other survivors. Hemingway then visits Raven, a badly wounded soldier, but doubts his graphic battle stories. When Hemingway meets Raven's commanding officer, who confirms the battle accounts, Hemingway is left to marvel over this "strange new war" in which ordinary people are so destroyed.

Lines 1–9
REINFORCE *KEY IDEA:* WAR

Discuss Which details of the description fit your expectation of **war?** Which details surprised you? *Students may say they expect the destruction, but not its proximity to people doing ordinary tasks such as lying in bed, falling asleep.*

LITERARY ANALYSIS

Ⓐ SUBJECTIVITY IN REPORTING

Possible answer: Hemingway hears rifle and machine gun fire through the open window of his hotel room (lines 1–5). He is grateful to be safe in bed rather than part of the violence. His feet are warming the cold foot of the bed, and he hears singing and arguing in the street before he falls asleep (lines 6–9).

A New Kind of War

ERNEST HEMINGWAY

> **BACKGROUND** Hemingway and other journalists covering the Spanish Civil War stayed at the Hotel Florida in Madrid, the Spanish capital, which was under siege by General Franco's Nationalist forces. Franco was aided by the fascist governments of Italy and Nazi Germany, which sent troops and weapons. The Loyalist forces of the Spanish government were aided by the Soviet Union and volunteer International Brigades from across Europe and the United States. The soldiers that Hemingway profiles in this article were part of the International Brigades.

NANA Dispatch · APRIL 14, 1937

MADRID—The window of the hotel is open and, as you lie in bed, you hear the firing in the front line seventeen blocks away. There is a rifle fire all night long. The rifles go tacrong, capong, craang, tacrong, and then a machine gun opens up. It has a bigger calibre and is much louder, rong, cararong, rong, rong. Then there is the incoming boom of a trench mortar shell and a burst of machine gun fire. You lie and listen to it and it is a great thing to be in bed with your feet stretched out gradually warming the cold foot of the bed and not out there in University City or Carabanchel.[1] A man is singing hard-voiced in the street below and three drunks are arguing when you fall asleep. Ⓐ

10   In the morning, before your call comes from the desk, the roaring burst of a high explosive shell wakes you and you go to the window and look out to see a man, his head down, his coat collar up, sprinting desperately across the paved

---

ANALYZE VISUALS
Examine the composition, or arrangement, of shapes in the photograph on page 1051. What does the angle of the photo contribute to its impact? Explain.

① Targeted Passage

Ⓐ SUBJECTIVITY IN REPORTING
What are Hemingway's thoughts and sensations in the first paragraph?

---

1. **University City or Carabanchel** (kär'-ə-bän-chel'): scenes of bloody battles in or on the outskirts of Madrid.

DIFFERENTIATED INSTRUCTION

FOR ALL STUDENTS

Expert Groups Encourage students to become subject experts by selecting and researching one of these topics:

- North American Newspaper Alliance
- Spanish Civil War
- General Francisco Franco
- fascism in 1930s Europe

FOR STRATEGIC READERS

In combination with the *Audio Anthology CD,* use one or more Targeted Passages (pp. 1050, 1052, 1054, 1055) to ensure that students focus on key events and concepts. Targeted Passages are also good for English learners.

① Targeted Passage [Lines 1–12]

This passage introduces Hemingway as the narrator and describes the setting in war-torn Madrid.

ANALYZE VISUALS

Possible answer: *Judging from the photograph, Madrid appears to be a war zone. The city has been bombed, resulting in fallen buildings and rubble that the people must factor into their daily comings and goings. Being in Madrid was probably terrifying, as well as difficult due to housing shortages and interrupted services. The crooked angle of the photograph is a literal representation of how the war has shaken the city.*

BACKGROUND

International Brigade By the 1930s Fascism was spreading throughout Europe. Fascist dictators Benito Mussolini and Adolph Hitler had assumed control of the governments of Italy and Germany respectively. In 1936, General Francisco Franco began the Spanish Civil War when he led Nationalist forces that ultimately overthrew the democratic republic of Spain in favor of a fascist style government. The spread of fascism in Spain alarmed people throughout the world. Despite their varying backgrounds and beliefs, some of these people joined the International Brigades and united in Spain to fight fascism. During the course of the war, the brigades made significant contributions to almost every important military campaign.

- Where is Hemingway?
- What is happening outside his window?
- What are his thoughts about where he is?
- What does he see out the window?

FOR ENGLISH LEARNERS

Prereading For prereading instruction for English learners, see

 BEST PRACTICES TOOLKIT
Scaffolding Reading Instruction pp. 43–46

Vocabulary: Onomatopoeia Point out and clarify words Hemingway uses to convey sounds: *tacrong, capong, craang* (line 3); *rong, carong* (line 4).

FOR ADVANCED LEARNERS/AP

AP exercises in the bottom channel provide additional challenge for students. Use these suggestions for small groups or individuals.

ADDITIONAL GUIDELINES

For more help with differentiation and tips for classroom management, see

 BEST PRACTICES TOOLKIT
Differentiated Instruction pp. 31–38

B DESCRIPTIVE DETAILS

Possible answer: Hearing: "roaring burst of a high explosive shell" (lines 10–11). Sight: man sprinting across street (line 12), blood spurting between woman's fingers (lines 17–18), heap of rubble (line 19), dead man with torn, dusty clothes (lines 19–20), hole in sidewalk with gas rising from broken main (lines 20–21). Smell: "acrid smell of high explosive" (line 13). Touch: cold morning air (line 21). The mood is one of terror and chaos.

C GRAMMAR AND STYLE

Choose Effective Point of View Tell students that second-person point of view is unusual. Emphasize that this rarity, and the view's awkwardness, demand readers' attention. Ask students to consider why Hemingway chooses to jar readers with this literary technique. *Possible answer: Hemingway may think that the only way to truly convey war's horror is to pull readers in and shock them with graphic details.*

D SUBJECTIVITY IN REPORTING

Possible answer: The feeling that characterizes war is a sense of relief that neither you nor your loved ones have been hurt or killed.

E SUBJECTIVITY IN REPORTING

Possible answer: Hemingway feels a connection to the Italian dead, he is contemptuous of the chauffeur, and he appreciates his beautiful, comfortable hotel room.

---

square. There is the acrid smell of high explosive you hoped you'd never smell again, and, in a bathrobe and bedroom slippers, you hurry down the marble stairs and almost into a middle-aged woman, wounded in the abdomen, who is being helped into the hotel entrance by two men in blue workmen's smocks. She has her two hands crossed below her big, old-style Spanish bosom and from between her fingers the blood is spurting in a thin stream. On the corner, twenty yards away, is a heap of rubble, smashed cement and thrown up dirt, a single dead man, his torn

20 clothes dusty, and a great hole in the sidewalk from which the gas from a broken main is rising, looking like a heat mirage in the cold morning air. **B**

"How many dead?" you ask a policeman.

"Only one," he says. "It went through the sidewalk and burst below. If it would have burst on the solid stone of the road there might have been fifty."

A policeman covers the top of the trunk,[2] from which the head is missing; they send for someone to repair the gas main and you go in to breakfast. A charwoman,[2] her eyes red, is scrubbing the blood off the marble floor of the corridor. The dead man wasn't you nor anyone you know and everyone is very hungry in the morning after a cold night and a long day the day before up at the

30 Guadalajara[3] front. **C**

"Did you see him?" asked someone else at breakfast.

"Sure," you say.

"That's where we pass a dozen times a day. Right on that corner." Someone makes a joke about missing teeth and someone else says not to make that joke. And everyone has the feeling that characterizes war. It wasn't me, see? It wasn't me. **D**

The Italian dead up on the Guadalajara front weren't you, although Italian dead, because of where you had spent your boyhood, always seemed, still, like our dead.[4] No. You went to the front early in the morning in a miserable little car with a more miserable little chauffeur who suffered visibly the closer he came to the

40 fighting. But at night, sometimes late, without lights, with the big trucks roaring past, you came on back to sleep in a bed with sheets in a good hotel, paying a dollar a day for the best rooms on the front. The smaller rooms in the back, on the side away from the shelling, were considerably more expensive. After the shell that lit on the sidewalk in front of the hotel you got a beautiful double corner room on that side, twice the size of the one you had had, for less than a dollar. It wasn't me they killed. See? No. Not me. It wasn't me anymore. **E**

Then, in a hospital given by the American Friends of Spanish Democracy, located out behind the Morata front along the road to Valencia,[5] they said, "Raven wants to see you."

50 "Do I know him?"

"I don't think so," they said, "but he wants to see you."

---

2. **charwoman:** a woman employed to clean houses or offices.

3. **Guadalajara:** a city in Spain to the northeast of Madrid, strategically important because of its nearness to the capital. Battle had raged there through most of March 1937, with the Loyalists finally winning.

4. **Italian dead ... our dead:** Italian forces fought on the side of the Nationalists; however, Hemingway had spent a long time in an Italian hospital as a young man during World War I.

5. **Morata ... Valencia:** Morata de Tejuña, a small town southeast of Madrid, was heavily damaged at this time. Valencia is on the eastern coast of Spain, about 240 miles southeast of Madrid.

B DESCRIPTIVE DETAILS
Identify **sensory details** in lines 10–21, and the senses they appeal to. What **mood** do they create?

② Targeted Passage

C GRAMMAR AND STYLE
Reread lines 28–30. Notice how the use of the **second-person pronoun** *you* places the reader in Hemingway's shoes.

D SUBJECTIVITY IN REPORTING
Interpret what Hemingway means by "the feeling that characterizes war."

E SUBJECTIVITY IN REPORTING
Reread lines 36–46. What is Hemingway's attitude toward the Italian dead? his chauffeur? his hotel room?

DIFFERENTIATED INSTRUCTION

FOR STRATEGIC READERS

② Targeted Passage [Lines 22–30]

This passage illustrates the ways in which people both participate in the war and detach themselves from it.

• What are the effects of the explosion?

• Describe the specific ways that each of these people respond to the scene: the policeman, the charwoman, and the narrator.

• For what is Hemingway grateful?

FOR ENGLISH LEARNERS

Vocabulary: Multiple-Meaning Words

Explain that the word *trunk* in line 25 is a multiple-meaning word. Help students use context clues, such as that the "head is missing," to determine the correct meaning. In this case, trunk means "torso" or "body" rather than "main stem of a tree," "chest," or "rear storage compartment of an automobile." The policeman covers the decapitated body.

"Where is he?"

"Upstairs."

In the room upstairs they are giving a blood transfusion to a man with a very gray face who lay on a cot with his arm out, looking away from the gurgling bottle and moaning in a very impersonal way. He moaned mechanically and at regular intervals and it did not seem to be him that made the sound. His lips did not move.

"Where's Raven?" I asked.

60 "I'm here," said Raven.

The voice came from a high mound covered by a shoddy gray blanket. There were two arms crossed on the top of the mound and at one end there was something that had been a face, but now was a yellow scabby area with a wide bandage cross where the eyes had been.

"Who is it?" asked Raven. He didn't have lips, but he talked pretty well without them and with a pleasant voice. **F**

"Hemingway," I said. "I came up to see how you were doing."

"My face was pretty bad," he said. "It got sort of burned from the grenade, but it's peeled a couple of times and it's doing better."

70 "It looks swell," I said. "It's doing fine."

I wasn't looking at it when I spoke.

"How are things in America?" he asked. "What do they think of us over there?"

"Sentiment's changed a lot," I said. "They're beginning to realize the government is going to win this war."

F DESCRIPTIVE DETAILS
What emotional reaction do you have to the description of Raven?

Members of the International Brigades near Madrid in late 1936

Lines 33–46
TIERED DISCUSSION PROMPTS
Use these prompts to help students understand the narrator's emotional reaction:

Connect Have you ever heard of someone making a joke or laughing during a time of sadness or tragedy? Why do you think the person did that? *Accept all thoughtful responses.*

Analyze What emotions does the narrator feel in response to the death and destruction around him? *Possible answer: He feels relief and even jubilation that others are dead while he has escaped.*

Evaluate Are the narrator's responses reasonable? Are they necessary? Explain. *Students may say that the narrator's responses are understandable and natural, but still upsetting. They may say that such responses are necessary to survive violence.*

READING SKILL

F DESCRIPTIVE DETAILS

Possible answer: Readers may be shocked or repulsed at Raven's description.

If students need help . . . Work with them to add details and responses to the organizer introduced on page 1049.

FOR ENGLISH LEARNERS

Language: Conversational English Patterns
Explain that in line 46, the narrator is speaking to himself, asking and answering his own questions. Work with students to paraphrase the text: Look, I'm alive. Do you understand? I was not the one who they killed. Clarify also that after line 47, the point of view switches. Hemingway now refers to himself as *I* rather than *you*.

FOR ADVANCED LEARNERS/AP

Compare and Contrast [small-group option]
Have student groups gather audio, video, or print examples of contemporary war correspondence by American reporters. Encourage students to use a Comparison Matrix to compare and contrast Hemingway's reporting style, content, and audience with these contemporary examples. Then ask students to draw conclusions about topics such as these: the role of the reporter, the purpose of

correspondence, and audience involvement in world affairs. Ask students to consider in what ways these issues have changed, if at all, over the years. Invite groups to share the results of their studies aloud with the class.

 BEST PRACTICES TOOLKIT—Transparency
Comparison Matrix p. A24

"Do you think so?"

"Sure," I said.

"I'm awfully glad," he said. "You know, I wouldn't mind any of this if I could just watch what was going on. I don't mind the pain, you know. It never seemed important really. But I was always awfully interested in things and I really wouldn't
80 mind the pain at all if I could just sort of follow things intelligently. I could even be some use. You know, I didn't mind the war at all. I did all right in the war. I got hit once before and I was back and rejoined the battalion in two weeks. I couldn't stand to be away. Then I got this." **G**

He had put his hand in mine. It was not a worker's hand. There were no calluses and the nails on the long, spatulate[6] fingers were smooth and rounded.

"How did you get it?" I asked.

"Well, there were some troops that were routed and we went over to sort of reform them and we did and then we had quite a fight with the fascists and we beat them. It was quite a bad fight, you know, but we beat them and then
90 someone threw this grenade at me."

Holding his hand and hearing him tell it, I did not believe a word of it. What was left of him did not sound like the wreckage of a soldier somehow. I did not know how he had been wounded, but the story did not sound right. It was the sort of way everyone would like to have been wounded. But I wanted him to think I believed it.

"Where did you come from?" I asked.

"From Pittsburgh. I went to the University there."

"What did you do before you joined up here?"

"I was a social worker," he said. Then I knew it couldn't be true and I wondered
100 how he had really been so frightfully wounded and I didn't care. In the war that I had known, men often lied about the manner of their wounding. Not at first; but later. I'd lied a little myself in my time. Especially late in the evening. But I was glad he thought I believed it, and we talked about books, he wanted to be a writer, and I told him about what happened north of Guadalajara and promised to bring some things from Madrid next time we got out that way. I hoped maybe I could get a radio. **H**

"They tell me Dos Passos and Sinclair Lewis[7] are coming over, too," he said.

"Yes," I said. "And when they come I'll bring them up to see you."

"Gee, that will be great," he said. "You don't know what that will mean to me."
110 "I'll bring them," I said.

"Will they be here pretty soon?"

"Just as soon as they come I'll bring them."

"Good boy, Ernest," he said. "You don't mind if I call you Ernest, do you?"

The voice came very clear and gentle from that face that looked like some hill that had been fought over in muddy weather and then baked in the sun.

"Hell, no," I said. "Please. Listen, old-timer, you're going to be fine. You'll be a lot of good, you know. You can talk on the radio."

---

6. **spatulate** (spăch′ə-lĭt): having a broad, rounded end.

7. **Dos Passos and Sinclair Lewis:** well-known American writers.

G DIALOGUE
What do Raven's words reveal about his character?

3 Targeted Passage

H SUBJECTIVITY IN REPORTING
Why doesn't Hemingway believe Raven? Do you believe Raven? Explain why or why not.

LITERARY ANALYSIS: *Review*

G DIALOGUE

Possible answer: *Raven's words reveal that he is brave and committed to the cause for which he is fighting (lines 77–83).*

LITERARY ANALYSIS

H SUBJECTIVITY IN REPORTING

Possible answer: *Hemingway doesn't believe Raven because he seems too refined to be a soldier and his story is too impressive. Additionally, Hemingway has known others—including himself—who lied about their exploits in battle. Because Hemingway doubts Raven, readers will be inclined to as well.*

BACKGROUND

John Dos Passos and Sinclair Lewis Writer and social critic John Dos Passos (1896–1970) is well-known for his experimental writing technique called "newsreel," where he juxtaposes lines from songs and news headlines into his text. Fellow writer and social critic Sinclair Lewis (1885–1951) penned *It Can't Happen Here* in 1935, a novel about a revolution that results in the fascist control of the United States.

DIFFERENTIATED INSTRUCTION

FOR STRATEGIC READERS

3 Targeted Passage [Lines 84–100]

This passage introduces Raven, a wounded soldier who asks to meet Hemingway.

- What is Raven's hand like? What does this mean to Hemingway?

- Why doesn't Raven sound "like the wreckage of a soldier"?

- What was Raven's job before the war?

- What details illustrate Hemingway's reaction to the story Raven tells about his wounding?

FOR ADVANCED LEARNERS/AP

Research and Analyze Have students research John Dos Passos and Sinclair Lewis, focusing on the authors' political and social beliefs. Students' research should include reading excerpts from or summaries of works by each writer, such as *Manhattan Transfer* and *It Can't Happen Here*. Then have students draw conclusions about why a meeting with these writers might be important to Raven. Challenge students to make inferences about whether in fact Hemingway has any knowledge about these writers' travel plans and whether he actually will bring them to meet Raven. If not, why does Hemingway confirm Raven's information and promise to arrange a meeting?

"Maybe," he said. "You'll be back?"

"Sure," I said. "Absolutely."

120 "Goodbye, Ernest," he said.

"Goodbye," I told him.

Downstairs they told me he'd lost both eyes as well as his face and was also badly wounded all through the legs and in the feet.

"He's lost some toes, too," the doctor said, "but he doesn't know that."

"I wonder if he'll ever know it."

"Oh, sure he will," the doctor said. "He's going to get well."

And it still isn't you that gets hit but it is your countryman now. Your countryman from Pennsylvania, where once we fought at Gettysburg.

Then, walking along the road, with his left arm in an airplane splint, walking
130 with the gamecock walk of the professional British soldier that neither ten years of militant party work nor the projecting metal wings of the splint could destroy, I met Raven's commanding officer, Jock Cunningham, who had three fresh rifle wounds through his upper left arm (I looked at them, one was septic[8]) and another rifle bullet under his shoulder blade that had entered his left chest, passed through, and lodged there. He told me, in military terms, the history of the attempt to rally retiring troops on his battalion's right flank, of his bombing raid down a trench which was held at one end by the fascists and at the other end by the government troops, of the taking of this trench and, with six men and a Lewis gun,[9] cutting off a group of some eighty fascists from their own lines, and of the
140 final desperate defense of their impossible position his six men put up until the government troops came up and, attacking, straightened out the line again. He told it clearly, completely convincingly, and with a strong Glasgow[10] accent. He had deep, piercing eyes sheltered like an eagle's, and, hearing him talk, you could tell the sort of soldier he was. For what he had done he would have had a V.C.[11] in the last war. In this war there are no decorations. Wounds are the only decorations and they do not award wound stripes. ❶

"Raven was in the same show," he said. "I didn't know he'd been hit. Ay, he's a good mon. He got his after I got mine. The fascists we'd cut off were very good troops. They never fired a useless shot when we were in that bad spot. They waited
150 in the dark there until they had us located and then opened with volley fire. That's how I got four in the same place."

We talked for a while and he told me many things. They were all important, but nothing was as important as what Jay Raven, the social worker from Pittsburgh with no military training, had told me was true. This is a strange new kind of war where you learn just as much as you are able to believe. ✍

4 Targeted Passage

❶ **SUBJECTIVITY IN REPORTING**
What is Hemingway's attitude toward Jock Cunningham? How can you tell?

---

8. **septic:** infected with bacteria.
9. **Lewis gun:** a lightweight machine gun.
10. **Glasgow:** a city in Scotland.
11. **V.C.:** the Victoria Cross, an award for valor "in the face of the enemy," given by Great Britain.

A NEW KIND OF WAR **1055**

Practice and Apply

After Reading

Use these copy masters to check understanding and provide extra support:

R RESOURCE MANAGER—Copy Masters
Reading Check p. 441
Subjectivity in Reporting p. 437
Question Support p. 442

Additional selection questions are provided for teachers on page 431.

ANSWERS

1. *A bomb bursts below the sidewalk, killing a man and wounding a woman.*

2. *Raven is a wounded soldier from Pennsylvania who is fighting for the Spanish Loyalists. He loses his eyes and face and sustains injuries in his legs and feet.*

3. *Raven and six other men are outnumbered by fascist soldiers when a grenade explodes in Raven's trench.*

Possible answers:

4. ■ **SKILLS FOCUS** **Analyze Descriptive Details** *Students should cite details about the Spanish woman trying to stanch her bleeding (lines 17–18), the moaning man's transfusion (lines 54–58), and the description of Raven (lines 61–64) to infer that war is destructive and cruel.*

5. ● **SKILLS FOCUS** **Subjectivity in Reporting** *Hemingway conveys people's alternating feelings of fear and relief, the tragic destruction of an idealistic young man, the bravery of the officers of the International Brigades, and the changing nature of war.*

6. *Hemingway includes dialogue perhaps to lend his dispatch a narrative quality that humanizes the characters.*

7. *This conflict is a new kind of war because the rules of combat are not as clear as they were in previous wars. Hemingway is surprised by the war's participants and by the lack of recognition that they receive for their sacrifices (lines 144–146, 152–155).*

8. *Hemingway's article is valuable because it teaches readers that war's consequences haven't changed since the Spanish Civil War. Normal life is disrupted, civilians get hurt, soldiers' lives and bodies are forever destroyed, people make unthinkable sacrifices, people commit unthinkable atrocities.*

R2.5, R3.3
CALIFORNIA

Comprehension

1. **Recall** What happens in front of Hemingway's hotel before breakfast?

2. **Recall** Who is Raven, and what are his injuries?

3. **Clarify** What is the truth about how Raven was wounded?

Literary Analysis

4. **Analyze Descriptive Details** Look back at the descriptive details you noted and circle the ones you found most vivid or affecting. What do you infer from any of these details that Hemingway doesn't tell you outright?

5. **Analyze Subjectivity in Reporting** Hemingway's article differs greatly from an objective news report. What is he able to convey about the war through each of the following?

   • his recurrent thought "It wasn't me" (lines 35 and 46)
   • his reaction to the sight of Raven and to the story Raven tells (lines 61–106)
   • his description of Jock Cunningham (lines 129–146)
   • his belief about the most important thing he was told (lines 152–155)

6. **Examine Dialogue** A written news report often contains quotations from sources, but rarely does it contain dialogue between two people. Why might Hemingway have chosen to include dialogue in his dispatch?

7. **Interpret Title** What makes this conflict "a new kind of war"? Note what seems to surprise Hemingway about it.

8. **Synthesize Themes** The Spanish Civil War ended more than 65 years ago. What value is there in reading Hemingway's article today? What insights about **war** does it provide?

9. **Compare Texts** What similarities in **style** and **theme** do you see in "A New Kind of War" and "In Another Country," the Hemingway short story on page 970?

Literary Criticism

10. **Critical Interpretations** When the New York University journalism department compiled its list of the 100 best works of 20th-century American journalism, Hemingway's Spanish Civil War reporting was ranked 33rd. Do you agree that it should be esteemed so highly? Support your answer.

---

9. *Both texts are written in the same understated style. Both show that warfare wounds people in irrevocable ways.*

10. *Some students may say that the ranking is deserved because this dispatch conveys the devastation of war through style. Others may think that the ranking is undeserved because this dispatch is not purely informative.*

Reading-Writing Connection

CALIFORNIA W1.2

GRAMMAR AND STYLE

CALIFORNIA LC1.1

CHOOSE EFFECTIVE POINT OF VIEW Review the **Grammar and Style** note on page 1052. At the beginning of his dispatch, Hemingway uses the **second-person pronoun** *you* to report his own experiences, where you would normally expect him to write in the first person. This has the effect of placing the reader ("you") at the point of the action. It also temporarily removes the narrator himself, creating a sense of detachment.

> *After the shell that lit on the sidewalk in front of the hotel you got a beautiful double corner room on that side, twice the size of the one you had had, for less than a dollar.* (lines 43–45)

Hemingway does periodically revert to the first person, as in the continuation of the preceding passage:

> *It wasn't me they killed. See? No. Not me. It wasn't me anymore.* (lines 45–46)

With this shifting point of view, Hemingway seems to step in and out of the narrative. The resulting detachment allows the reader to encounter the experience of war without added comment or sentiment.

PRACTICE Rewrite the following passage, inserting either first- or second-person pronouns to change the sense of immediacy or detachment.

> Hundreds of runners and spectators gather in Jonquil Park at dawn on Mother's Day. The air is crisp and the grass damp. The predominant color in the crowd is pink: pink ribbons, pink caps, pink shirts. Many people wear signs reading "In memory of . . ." There is an electric air of expectancy until the horn blasts. The runners are off!

WRITING TOOLS
For prewriting, revision, and editing tools, visit the **Writing Center** at ClassZone.com.

Reading-Writing Connection

WRITING PROMPT

Suggest that students prewrite by completing Observation Charts to list sensory details about their events. Urge students to record several details for each appropriate sense. Have students also brainstorm for comparisons such as creating similes or metaphors that can aid their descriptions.

🧰 **BEST PRACTICES TOOLKIT—Transparency**
Observation Chart p. C7

For writing support, see

ℹ **Writing Center at ClassZone.com**

GRAMMAR AND STYLE

Discuss with students the possible effects of first-person and second-person narrative, reviewing the instruction from page 1049. Ask students to determine how much immediacy or detachment they wish to create, then choose the point or points of view that best support their goal. (For more on personal pronouns, see **Grammar Handbook,** p. R56.)
Possible answer: *At dawn on Mother's Day, you join hundreds of runners and spectators in Jonquil Park. You feel the crisp air on your skin, and the damp grass tickles your ankles. You find yourself lost in a sea of pink ribbons, caps, and shirts, and signs reading "In memory of . . . ." The horn blasts, and your legs begin to move, joining the others who are running for life.*

📋 **RESOURCE MANAGER—Copy Master**
Choose Effective Point of View p. 443

Assess and Reteach

Assess

📋 **RESOURCE MANAGER—Copy Masters**
Selection Test A pp. 445–446
Selection Test B/C pp. 447–448

💿 **Test Generator CD**

Reteach

📄 **STANDARDS LESSON FILE**
Literature Lessons 10, 42, 45
Writing Lessons 21, 33, 44

DIFFERENTIATED INSTRUCTION

FOR DEVELOPING WRITERS
Writing Support

- Urge students to attend live events rather than writing from memory; help them find events to attend. Emphasize that events can be small, as long as they are vivid.

- Tell students to take notes during the events rather than waiting to record notes after the events have ended. Help students prepare Sensory Notes guides.

- Hold a writing conference with each student. Together, make prewriting decisions about points of view and dialogue.

- Help students determine the dominant impressions they want to convey through their reports. Then tell students to include only details that support these impressions.

🧰 **BEST PRACTICES TOOLKIT—Transparency**
Sensory Notes p. B9

Focus and Motivate

OBJECTIVES

Literary Analysis
- explore the key idea of **evaluation**
- analyze voice
- read a book review

Reading
- use strategies for reading a book review

Grammar and Writing
- use pronouns, dashes, and figurative language to establish voice
- write a book review

 R2.5, R3.3, W1.2, W1.3, W1.5, W1.9

ABOUT THE AUTHOR

Point out to students the descriptions of Parker as "sophisticated," "witty," "caustic," "smart-mouthed." Lead students to discuss how such character traits alternately led Parker to be revered as "one of the most quoted women of the 20th century" but also to be fired from *Vanity Fair* and summoned to the House Un-American Activities Committee.

USING THE *NOTABLE QUOTE*

Clarify that in this quotation, **Dorothy Parker** differentiates between wit and wisecracking, or joking. Have students explain the differences between truth and calisthenics. ***Possible answer:*** *Truth is universal and lasting, while calisthenics are merely physical and fleeting.*

CALIFORNIA

R2.5, R3.3, W1.2 (p. 1065),
W1.3 (p. 1065), W1.5 (p. 1065),
W1.9 (p. 1065)

NOTABLE QUOTE

"Wit has truth in it; wisecracking is simply calisthenics with words."

FYI
Did you know that Dorothy Parker . . .
- was expelled from convent school for making smart remarks?
- originated the saying "Men seldom make passes / At girls who wear glasses"?
- proposed "Excuse my dust" as her epitaph?

Author Online

For more on Dorothy Parker, visit the **Literature Center at ClassZone.com.**

A Book of Great Short Stories
Book Review by Dorothy Parker

Dorothy Parker
1893–1967

Dorothy Parker's sophisticated and witty voice made her one of the most quoted women of the 20th century. She belonged to the Algonquin Round Table, an informal group of writers who met daily at New York's Algonquin Hotel for lunch and clever conversation. Nicknamed the "Vicious Circle," they helped shape the literary tastes of the country.

Caustic Critic A well-read but smart-mouthed student, Parker left school at 14. When she was 19, her father died, and she was forced to find a job. After selling a poem to *Vanity Fair,* she was hired to write captions for its sister magazine, *Vogue.* She rose to become drama critic at *Vanity Fair* but was fired in 1920 for panning a play that starred the wife of one of the magazine's advertisers. She landed on her feet, becoming drama critic for another magazine, *Ainslee's.* She was also one of the founding editors of the *New Yorker* and served as its book reviewer for six years. Signing her reviews "Constant Reader," she championed writers she admired and demolished those she didn't. About one book she pronounced, "This is not a novel to be tossed aside lightly. It should be thrown with great force."

Popular Poet Parker's own books of poetry, *Enough Rope* and *Sunset Gun,* were bestsellers. They contained rueful verses, usually about failed love. One of her most quoted poems is "Résumé," which ends, "Guns aren't lawful; / Nooses give; / Gas smells awful; / You might as well live." Though often humorous, her poems grew out of great personal pain. She had an unhappy marriage to Edwin Parker, who returned from World War I with a drug addiction. Before divorcing him, she had disastrous love affairs that led her to several suicide attempts.

Screenwriter and Activist In 1933, Parker married Alan Campbell and moved with him to Hollywood, where they collaborated on screenplays. She also became more politically active, protesting racism, organizing the Screenwriters Guild, founding an anti-Nazi group, and going to Madrid to report on the Spanish Civil War. Her socialist sympathies caused her to be brought before the House Un-American Activities Committee in the 1950s. After she died of a heart attack in 1967, it was discovered that she had left her literary estate to Dr. Martin Luther King Jr. and the NAACP.

Selection Resources

 RESOURCE MANAGER UNIT 5

Plan and Teach pp. 449–456

Literary Analysis
Summary pp. 457†*, 458‡*
Voice pp. 459, 460†*
Question Support p. 464*

Reading
Reading a Book Review
    pp. 461, 462†*
Reading Check p. 463

Grammar and Writing
Establish Voice p. 465

Assessment
Selection Tests A, B/C
    pp. 467*, 469*
Test Generator CD

BEST PRACTICES TOOLKIT

Differentiated Instruction
    pp. 31–38*

Scaffolding Instruction
    pp. 43–46*

Graphic Organizers/Strategies
Common Prefixes • Venn Diagram • Two-Column Chart • Main Idea and Details • Writing Template: Critical Review

Reading Support
Audio Anthology CD*

Technology
Literature and Writing Centers at ClassZone.com
WriteSmart CD

---

* Resources for Differentiation   † Also in Spanish   ‡ In Haitian Creole and Vietnamese

LITERARY ANALYSIS: VOICE

Voice is that quality in writing that enables a reader to "hear" a personality behind the words. Style, tone, and level of language are some of the factors contributing to a writer's voice. Consider the voice in this passage:

After all the high screaming about The Sun Also Rises, I feared for Mr. Hemingway's next book. You know how it is—as soon as they all start acclaiming a writer, that writer is just about to slip downward.

What kind of person do you imagine is speaking? Male or female? Friendly or distant? Serious or playful? As you read, notice what makes Dorothy Parker's voice distinctive and entertaining. Use her comments to form an impression of her personality and attitude toward the literary world.

READING STRATEGY: READING A BOOK REVIEW

Most book reviews are published in newspapers and magazines. They usually

- describe a new or newly republished book
- give an evaluation of its literary worth
- offer reasons for this evaluation

As you read Dorothy Parker's review, look for the lines that fulfill these functions. She discusses three of Ernest Hemingway's books, not just one, and she mentions others' opinions as well as her own, so it may help to take notes on a chart like the one shown.

	Description	Parker's Evaluation	Reasons
The Sun Also Rises			
In Our Time			
Men Without Women			

What makes a GREAT short story?

KEY IDEA During your school years, you've read many classic stories described as "great," such as "The Necklace" by Guy de Maupassant and "The Tell-Tale Heart" by Edgar Allan Poe. But how can you learn about new stories that might be just as great? Would you trust a book reviewer's **evaluation?**

QUICKWRITE Think about the best short story you ever read, in school or on your own. With its qualities in mind, jot down the recipe for a great short story. What must one contain, in your opinion? In a small group, share your recipes. Do you all have similar tastes, or are your standards unique?

> Great Short Story
> • fascinating main character
> • fast-moving plot
> • surprise ending

What makes a GREAT short story?

Lead into the **KEY IDEA** by asking the question. Poll students on whether they would trust a reviewer's **evaluation** and discuss their reasons. Before students complete the **QUICKWRITE,** ask them to suggest favorite short stories and tell what they like about each story. Invite groups to share the conclusions drawn in the activity.

SKILLS FOCUS

LITERARY ANALYSIS   R2.5, R3.3

● VOICE

Review with students that style is a writer's word choice and syntax, tone is a writer's attitude toward his or her subject, and level of language describes how formally or informally the writer addresses readers. Have students describe the style, tone, and level of language of the passage on page 1059, and then describe Parker's voice. *Possible answer: Parker's style reflects both formal ("high screaming," "I feared," "acclaiming a writer") and informal ("you know how it is") word choice and level of language, as well as complex sentences. Her tone is condescending. Her voice is sophisticated, arrogant, and acerbic.*

CHECK UNDERSTANDING Have students imitate Parker's voice by writing several sentences about a literary work.

READING STRATEGY

■ READING A BOOK REVIEW

Note that Parker's review of Hemingway's works is buried within comments about literary critics, other writers, and a morning headache. Tell students that most of the information for their charts appears on the final page of the review.

> **R** RESOURCE MANAGER—Copy Master
> Reading a Book Review p. 461
> (for student use while reading the selection)

DIFFERENTIATED INSTRUCTION

FOR STRATEGIC READERS

Concept Support: Voice Point out to students that they can use their assessments of a writer's voice to draw conclusions about the writer's personality and attitude toward a subject. Suggest that students use an organizer such as this one to draw conclusions about Parker.

Parker's Voice: sophisticated, arrogant, acerbic	
↙	↘
Personality: outspoken, opinionated	**Attitude Toward Literary World:** superior

SUMMARY

In a witty and acerbic review of Ernest Hemingway's works *The Sun Also Rises*, *In Our Time*, and *Men Without Women*, Dorothy Parker takes issue with members of the literary community who herald Hemingway's novel but ignore his works of short fiction. Parker claims that Hemingway's stark, discerning, reportorial style makes him a master of short fiction.

LITERARY ANALYSIS

Ⓐ VOICE

Possible answer: *Parker exaggerates the response to Hemingway's publication, which helps to establish a voice that is irreverent and humorous.*

Extend the Discussion Will Parker's review of *The Sun Also Rises* be positive or negative? Why?

Lines 12–19
REINFORCE *KEY IDEA:* EVALUATION

Discuss What criteria does Parker think critics have used in their **evaluation** of Hemingway's work? Does she support those criteria? *Possible answer: Parker thinks that critics have rejected Hemingway's work because of the author's lifestyle. She does not support these criteria as a basis for literary criticism.*

A BOOK OF GREAT SHORT STORIES

Dorothy Parker

October 29, 1927

Ernest Hemingway wrote a novel called *The Sun Also Rises*. Promptly upon its publication, Ernest Hemingway was discovered, the Stars and Stripes were reverentially raised over him, eight hundred and forty-seven book reviewers formed themselves into the word "welcome," and the band played "Hail to the Chief" in three concurrent keys. All of which, I should think, might have made Ernest Hemingway pretty reasonably sick. Ⓐ

For, a year or so before *The Sun Also Rises,* he had published *In Our Time,* a collection of short pieces. The book caused about as much stir in literary circles as an incompleted dogfight on upper Riverside Drive. True, there were a few that
10 went about quick and stirred with admiration for this clean, exciting prose, but most of the reviewers dismissed the volume with a tolerant smile and the word "stark." It was Mr. Mencken[1] who slapped it down with "sketches in the bold, bad manner of the Café du Dôme," and the smaller boys, in their manner, took similar pokes at it. Well, you see, Ernest Hemingway was a young American living on the left bank of the Seine in Paris, France; he had been seen at the Dôme and the Rotonde and the Select and the Closerie des Lilas.[2] He knew Pound, Joyce, and Gertrude Stein. There is something a little—well, a little *you*-know—in all of those things. You wouldn't catch Bruce Barton or Mary Roberts Rinehart[3] doing them. No, sir.

---

1. **Mr. Mencken:** H. L. Mencken, an American journalist and literary critic.
2. **Dôme ... des Lilas:** cafés in Paris that were frequented by young American writers.
3. **Pound ... Rinehart:** Ezra Pound and Gertrude Stein were experimental American writers living in Paris; James Joyce was an experimental Irish writer. Bruce Barton and Mary Roberts Rinehart were more conventional American writers who lived in the United States.

1060 UNIT 5: THE HARLEM RENAISSANCE AND MODERNISM

ANALYZE VISUALS
What ideas are suggested by the cover designs of these books by Ernest Hemingway?

Ⓐ **VOICE**
Notice the **exaggeration** in the first paragraph. What voice does it help establish?

① **Targeted Passage**

DIFFERENTIATED INSTRUCTION

FOR ALL STUDENTS

Provide these independent projects to extend the lesson:

- Perform a dramatic reading using Parker's voice.
- Survey people's literary tastes.
- Write an essay comparing Hemingway and Parker.

For further details on these projects, see

R RESOURCE MANAGER
Ideas for Extension pp. 454–455

FOR STRATEGIC READERS

In combination with the *Audio Anthology CD*, use one or both Targeted Passages (pp. 1060, 1063) to ensure that students focus on key concepts in the selection. Targeted Passages are also good for English learners.

① **Targeted Passage [Lines 1–12]**

This passage introduces the topic of Parker's review, the works of Ernest Hemingway, and hints at her view of other literary critics.

THE SUN ALSO RISES

ERNEST HEMINGWAY
Author of
"IN OUR TIMES" and "THE TORRENTS OF SPRING"

MEN WITHOU[T]
WOMEN

BY
ERNEST HEMINGWAY
AUTHOR OF
THE SUN ALSO RISES

CHARLES SCRIBNER'S SONS

Possible answer: The cover of In Our Time *suggests ideas such as newspaper reporting and international affairs. The cover of* The Sun Also Rises *suggests ideas such as Greek mythology and female sensuality. The cover of* Men Without Women *suggests the idea of bullfighting.*

About the Art These three covers represent the original covers for the first edition publications of Hemingway's works. Like the critical response to these works, the cover of the novel is much showier than those of the short works collections.

BACKGROUND

Hemingway's Works *In Our Time* includes stories that are reminiscent of Hemingway's childhood in the forests of northern Michigan. Set in France and Spain, *The Sun Also Rises* is about a group of disenchanted Americans and Britons living in Europe at the end of World War I. *Men Without Women* includes "The Killers," a short story renowned for its account of imminent disaster.

---

is Dorothy Parker writing about?

t works will she consider?

was *The Sun Also Rises* received?

was *In Our Time* received?

t does Parker think of the different
tions these works inspired?

FOR ENGLISH LEARNERS
Key Academic Vocabulary Use Common Prefixes to teach this word: *concurrent* (line 5).

 BEST PRACTICES TOOLKIT—Transparency
Common Prefixes p. E14

Prereading For prereading instruction for English learners, see

 BEST PRACTICES TOOLKIT
Scaffolding Reading Instruction pp. 43–46

FOR ADVANCED LEARNERS/AP
AP exercises in the bottom channel provide additional challenge for students. Use these suggestions for small groups or individuals.

ADDITIONAL GUIDELINES
For more help with differentiation and tips for classroom management, see

 BEST PRACTICES TOOLKIT
Differentiated Instruction pp. 31–38

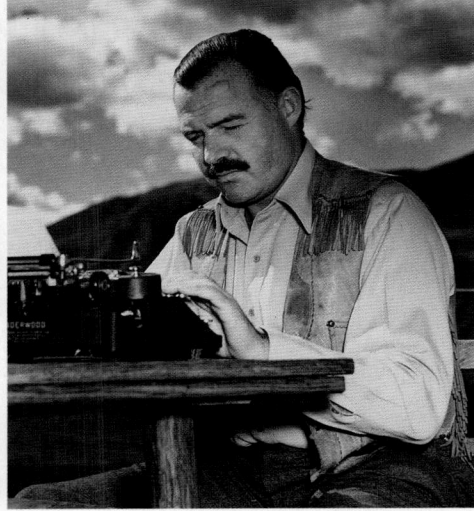

Dorothy Parker and Ernest Hemingway

20   And besides, *In Our Time* was a book of short stories. That's no way to start off. People don't like that; they feel cheated. Any bookseller will be glad to tell you, in his interesting *argot*,[4] that "short stories don't go." People take up a book of short stories and say, "Oh, what's this? Just a lot of those short things?" and put it right down again. Only yesterday afternoon at four o'clock sharp, I saw and heard a woman do that to Ernest Hemingway's new book, *Men Without Women*. She had been one of those most excited about his new novel. Ⓑ

Literature, it appears, is here measured by a yard-stick. As soon as *The Sun Also Rises* came out, Ernest Hemingway was the white-haired boy. He was praised, adored, analyzed, best-sold, argued about, and banned in Boston; all
30   the trimmings were accorded him. People got into feuds about whether or not his story was worth the telling. (You see this silver scar left by a bullet, right up here under my hair? I got that the night I said that any well-told story was worth the telling. An eighth of an inch nearer the temple, and I wouldn't be sitting here doing this sort of tripe.) They affirmed, and passionately, that the dissolute expatriates[5] in this novel of "a lost generation" were not worth bothering about; and then they devoted most of their time to discussing them. There was a time, and it went on for weeks, when you could go nowhere without hearing of *The Sun Also Rises*. Some thought it without excuse; and some, they of the cool, tall foreheads, called it the greatest American novel, tossing *Huckleberry Finn* and *The*
40   *Scarlet Letter*[6] lightly out the window. They hated it or they revered it. I may say, with due respect to Mr. Hemingway, that I was never so sick of a book in my life.

---

4. **argot** (är′gō) *French:* expressions and vocabulary that are used by a particular group.
5. **dissolute expatriates:** loose-living people—in this case, Americans—residing in a foreign land.
6. ***Huckleberry Finn* and *The Scarlet Letter*:** novels by Mark Twain and Nathaniel Hawthorne, respectively.

1062 UNIT 5: THE HARLEM RENAISSANCE AND MODERNISM

Now *The Sun Also Rises* was as "starkly" written as Mr. Hemingway's short stories; it dealt with subjects as "unpleasant." Why it should have been taken to the slightly damp bosom of the public while the (as it seems to me) superb *In Our Time* should have been disregarded will always be a puzzle to me. As I see it—I knew this conversation would get back to me sooner or later, preferably sooner—Mr. Hemingway's style, this prose stripped to its firm young bones, is far more effective, far more moving, in the short story than in the novel. He is, to me, the greatest living writer of short stories; he is, also to me, not the greatest living
50 novelist. **C**

After all the high screaming about *The Sun Also Rises,* I feared for Mr. Hemingway's next book. You know how it is—as soon as they all start acclaiming a writer, that writer is just about to slip downward. The littler critics circle like literary buzzards above only the sick lions. **D**

So it is a warm gratification to find the new Hemingway book, *Men Without Women,* a truly magnificent work. It is composed of thirteen short stories, most of which have been published before. They are sad and terrible stories; the author's enormous appetite for life seems to have been somehow appeased. You find here little of that peaceful ecstasy that marked the camping trip in *The Sun Also Rises*
60 and the lone fisherman's days in "Big Two-Hearted River" in *In Our Time*. The stories include "The Killers," which seems to me one of the four great American short stories. (All you have to do is drop the nearest hat, and I'll tell you what I think the others are. They are Wilbur Daniel Steele's "Blue Murder," Sherwood Anderson's "I'm a Fool," and Ring Lardner's "Some Like Them Cold," that story which seems to me as shrewd a picture of every woman at some time as is Chekhov's[7] "The Darling." Now what do *you* like best?) The book also includes "Fifty Grand," "In Another Country," and the delicate and tragic "Hills like White Elephants." I do not know where a greater collection of stories can be found.
70 Ford Madox Ford[8] has said of this author, "Hemingway writes like an angel." I take issue (there is nothing better for that morning headache than taking a little issue.) Hemingway writes like a human being. I think it is impossible for him to write of any event at which he has not been present; his is, then, a reportorial talent, just as Sinclair Lewis's[9] is. But, or so I think, Lewis remains a reporter and Hemingway stands a genius because Hemingway has an unerring sense of selection. He discards details with a magnificent lavishness; he keeps his words to their short path. His is, as any reader knows, a dangerous influence. The simple thing he does looks so easy to do. But look at the boys who try to do it. ✎ **E**

---

7. **Wilbur . . . Chekhov's:** Steele, Anderson, and Lardner were popular American writers of the era; Anton Chekhov was a 19th-century Russian short story writer and playwright.

8. **Ford Madox Ford:** an English writer, editor, and critic who lived for a time in Paris.

9. **Sinclair Lewis's:** Lewis was an American novelist and social critic who published articles in several popular magazines.

C BOOK REVIEW
Reread lines 42–50. Restate Parker's opinion of *In Our Time.* What does she say about Hemingway's **style?**

D GRAMMAR AND STYLE
In lines 51–54, notice how Parker uses the **first-person pronoun** *I* to refer to herself and addresses the reader with the **second-person pronoun** *you.* She also sets off her side remark with a **dash.** These choices establish an intimate conversational **voice.** Also notice her use of simile, comparing the critics to circling buzzards.

② Targeted Passage

E BOOK REVIEW
Reread lines 70–78. How highly does Parker rate Hemingway, and why?

C BOOK REVIEW

Possible answer: Parker finds In Our Time *to be superbly effective due to Hemingway's stripped-down, bare-bones style.*

If students need help . . . Direct them to lines 44–45 and 47–48 as they complete the chart introduced on page 1059.

D GRAMMAR AND STYLE

Establish Voice Point out that Parker's informal phrase "You know how it is" also contributes to her conversational voice. Discuss why Parker chooses such a voice for her book review, a work that would generally be viewed as scholarly, and have students find other examples of the voice.

E BOOK REVIEW

Possible answer: Parker rates Hemingway as a genius because he chooses details effectively (lines 75–76).

Lines 42–50
REINFORCE *KEY IDEA:* EVALUATION

Discuss On the basis of Parker's **evaluation,** which of Hemingway's works seems most interesting? Why? *Possible answer: Students may prefer Hemingway's short stories over the novels, citing Parker's labels of "effective" and "moving."*

SELECTION WRAP–UP

SUMMARIZE Have students explain Parker's definition of great literature.

FOR STRATEGIC READERS

② Targeted Passage [Lines 55–78]

This passage contains Parker's review of *Men Without Women* and minimal supporting evidence for that opinion.

• Describe *Men Without Women.*

• How does Parker view *Men Without Women?*

• On what criteria does Parker base her view? What evidence does she offer?

FOR ADVANCED LEARNERS/AP

Evaluate Stories Ask students if they are familiar with any of the stories Parker mentions. If not, ask students to consider other short stories they know and evaluate whether Parker might like the story. Encourage students to use their knowledge of Parker's literary criteria and give examples from this review as they share their opinions with the class.

Practice and Apply

After Reading

Use these copy masters to check under-standing and provide extra support:

 RESOURCE MANAGER—Copy Masters

Reading Check p. 463

Voice p. 459

Question Support p. 464

Additional selection questions are provided for teachers on page 453.

ANSWERS

1. *Hemingway's latest book at the time was* Men Without Women.

2. In Our Time *was virtually ignored, while* The Sun Also Rises *received both positive and negative attention.*

3. *Parker states that Lewis is merely a reporter, while Hemingway is a genius.*

Possible answers:

4. ■ **SKILLS FOCUS** **Reading a Book Review** *Parker believes that* The Sun Also Rises *is overrated, while* In Our Time *is superb and* Men Without Women *is magnificent. Her opinions are largely unsupported with the exception of a description of Hemingway's writing style as genius due to his selective use of detail.*

5. ● **SKILLS FOCUS** **Voice** *The use of* I *makes Parker's voice personal. Her exaggeration is humorous and reflects self-deprecation. The asides are also humorous. The figura-tive language is amusing and sophisticated. The informal diction is intimate.*

6. *Parker is not impressed with book critics. She refers to them irreverently as "Mr. Mencken" (line 12), "the smaller boys" (line 13), "they of the cool, tall foreheads" (lines 38–39), and "the littler critics circl[ing] like literary buzzards" (lines 53–54). She criticizes the reading public for dismissing short fiction (lines 22–26) and mocks them with the refer-ence to "the slightly damp bosom of the public" (line 44).*

7. *Students are likely to agree that* In Another Country *exhibits the characteristics that Parker names.*

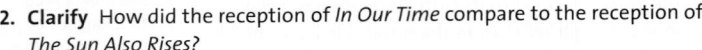

R2.5, R3.3

Comprehension

1. **Recall** What was Hemingway's latest book at the time Parker's review was written?

2. **Clarify** How did the reception of *In Our Time* compare to the reception of *The Sun Also Rises*?

3. **Paraphrase** What does Parker say is the difference between Hemingway and Sinclair Lewis?

Literary Analysis

4. **Reading a Book Review** Look back at the notes you took while reading, then summarize Parker's opinions of the three Hemingway books she discusses. With what evidence does she support her opinions?

5. **Analyze Voice** How would you describe Parker's voice in this book review? Discuss the effect of each of the following:

   • use of the first-person *I*
   • similes and metaphors
   • exaggeration
   • informal diction
   • parenthetical asides

6. **Interpret Tone** What is Parker's attitude toward book reviewers and the reading public? Support your answer with details.

7. **Evaluate Author's Work** Review Parker's statements about Hemingway's short stories (lines 42–50, 55–78). Then skim "In Another Country" (page 970). Do you agree with Parker's **evaluation** of Hemingway's short stories? Use a chart like the one shown to organize your thoughts.

"In Another Country"	Yes	No
Clean, Stripped-Down Prose		
Unpleasant Subject		
Sadness		
Reportorial Talent		
Effectiveness in Moving Readers		

Literary Criticism

8. **Critical Interpretations** One scholar wrote, "It is through Parker's refusal to claim authority . . . that her book reviews achieve it. She presents readers with an unpretentious, sometimes self-mocking voice that, while it expresses strong opinions, pretends no Olympian knowledge or status." Do you agree with this critic about the source of Parker's authority or trustworthiness? Explain your view.

---

8. *Students may agree that Parker seems trustworthy because she doesn't claim a su-perior status. Others will say that she quite authoritatively claims superiority but also conveys a deep knowledge of literature.*

Reading-Writing Connection

W1.2, W1.3, W1.5

WRITING PROMPT

WRITE A BOOK REVIEW Dorothy Parker wrote book reviews for many years, and to one critic, they are the best expression of her literary sensibility. Choose a great book, or an "ungreat book," and write a **three-to-five-paragraph** review in your own personal voice. You might be as funny as Dorothy Parker, but in a different way. Or you might inspire readers to discover a book that could transform their lives. Think about what your own voice sounds like—perhaps tape-record yourself talking about the book. Then try to reproduce that voice in writing.

SELF-CHECK

A successful book review will . . .

- describe the book
- offer a positive or negative evaluation
- give reasons for your evaluation
- express a distinctive voice

GRAMMAR AND STYLE

W1.9

ESTABLISH VOICE Review the **Grammar and Style** note on page 1063. Dorothy Parker's voice is intimate, enthusiastic, and humorously self-involved. Here is an example from her review:

> *As I see it—I knew this conversation would get back to me sooner or later, preferably sooner—Mr. Hemingway's style, this prose stripped to its firm young bones, is far more effective, far more moving, in the short story than in the novel.* (lines 45–48)

Notice Parker's use of the **first-person pronoun** *I* and her use of **dashes** to enclose a parenthetical comment about herself. It's as if Parker is having a conversation with the reader. Additionally, her use of **figurative language**—comparing Hemingway's prose to a fleshless body—creates a far more striking image than had she merely described it as "lean." You can use these and other elements to establish your own voice.

PRACTICE Rewrite each of the following sentences, using pronouns, figurative language, and punctuation, to achieve a voice that sounds like Dorothy Parker's. A sample answer has been done for you.

> **EXAMPLE**
>
> This book is not good.
>
> *This volume—in my view—is appallingly, criminally bad.*

1. Other reviewers have disliked this book.
2. Sales have been high.
3. Reviewing books can seem useless.

 WRITING TOOLS
For prewriting, revision, and editing tools, visit the **Writing Center** at ClassZone.com.

A BOOK OF GREAT SHORT STORIES **1065**

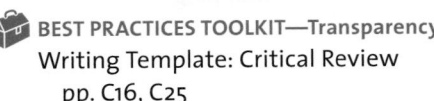
DIFFERENTIATED INSTRUCTION

FOR DEVELOPING WRITERS
Writing Support

- Encourage students to use the Writing Template: Critical Review.
- Urge students to begin their reviews with action, dialogue, or reaction that grabs the reader's attention. Then, help students state their overall view of the work and list three criteria for evaluation.
- In each body paragraph, have students explain one criterion for evaluation and

support it with examples from the work. Review with students how to incorporate, punctuate, and cite literary quotations.

- To conclude, have students summarize the main points of their evaluations and leave readers with a final, provocative thought.

 BEST PRACTICES TOOLKIT—Transparency
Writing Template: Critical Review
pp. C16, C25

Reading-Writing Connection

WRITING PROMPT

Suggest that students choose literary works about which they hold strong views, whether positive or negative. Then, have students use a Main Idea and Details organizer to list reasons for their views and examples to support those reasons. To help students to craft voice, suggest that they consider their peers as the intended audience. Encourage students to write about the literary works as if they are talking to those peers rather than writing academic essays for the teacher.

BEST PRACTICES TOOLKIT—Transparency
Main Idea and Details p. B6

For writing support, see

ⓘ Writing Center at **ClassZone.com**

GRAMMAR AND STYLE

Review with students that dashes show abrupt changes in thought or speech. Remind them that figurative language includes the similes that Parker uses as well as metaphors or personification.

Possible answers:

1. *Reviewers have given the book the admiration they would give a mound of pigeon droppings on Park Avenue.*

2. *I couldn't push my way into the bookstore for all the people lined up to buy it.*

3. *I sincerely think I should enter a more rewarding profession—I hear Ringling Brothers is looking for a lion tamer.*

RESOURCE MANAGER—Copy Master
Establish Voice p. 465

Assess and Reteach

Assess

RESOURCE MANAGER—Copy Masters
Selection Test A pp. 467–468
Selection Test B/C pp. 469–470

Test Generator CD

Reteach

STANDARDS LESSON FILE
Literature Lessons 25, 27, 43, 44
Reading Lessons 16, 17
Writing Lessons 28, 37, 43

A BOOK OF GREAT SHORT STORIES **1065**

Focus and Motivate

OBJECTIVES

Literary Analysis
- explore the key idea of **responsibility**
- analyze style and diction
- read an essay

Reading
- interpret author's message

 R2.5, R3.3

ABOUT THE AUTHOR

After students read about E. B. White, highlight the fact that the author published *Stuart Little* despite a librarian's comment that it was "unfit for children." Tell students that one of White's points in the essay they will read is that a writer has a duty to write about "what naturally absorbs his fancy." Ask students in what ways White's actions reflect his views.
Possible answer: *White's actions suggest that he wrote and published what interested him, even though others did not always like it.*

USING THE *NOTABLE QUOTE*

Have students explain what **E. B. White** means by "an audience of one." Ask them to contrast the writer-reader relationship resulting from White's approach with the relationship established when writing to a larger audience.
Possible answer: *White means that a writer should envision a specific audience, defined by a fully realized individual. This creates a more intimate relationship between writer and reader than writing to an anonymous crowd.*

Selection Resources

R2.5, R3.3 CALIFORNIA

The Duty of Writers
Essay by E. B. White

NOTABLE QUOTE
"The true writer always plays to an audience of one."

FYI
Did you know that E. B. White . . .

- hated his given name, Elwyn Brooks, and answered to his college nickname, Andy?
- preferred sailing to reading?
- was so afraid of public speaking that he made others deliver his acceptance speeches?

Author Online

For more on E. B. White, visit the **Literature Center at ClassZone.com.**

E. B. White
1899–1985

Admired for his graceful style and gentle humor, E. B. White has been called the best essayist of the 20th century. For years readers looked forward to his columns in the *New Yorker* and *Harper's* magazines. Midcareer, he became a beloved children's author, writing the classics *Stuart Little* and *Charlotte's Web.* Later, he gained more fame with his update of *The Elements of Style,* a handbook used by millions of student writers.

New York Wit White enjoyed writing even as a child and won his first award when he was nine, for a poem about a mouse. In 1925, following unsuccessful stints in reporting and advertising, he was hired by a new magazine, the *New Yorker.* Its editor wanted it to be light, witty, and satirical. White did much to give it that voice. He wrote its opening "Notes and Comment" page and composed newsbreaks, fillers between articles with

such headings as "Letters We Never Finished Reading" and "Neatest Trick of the Week." He did captions for cartoons and even once illustrated the magazine's cover. The *New Yorker* provided White with an outlet for his talent—and a wife: he married the fiction editor, Katharine, living happily with her for 48 years.

Up on the Farm Eventually White felt constrained by the brief length and sheer number of the pieces he had to write for the *New Yorker.* He took a leave from the magazine and moved to a farmhouse in Maine in 1938. There he raised chickens, geese, sheep, and a milk cow. He also began a monthly column for *Harper's* called "One Man's Meat" (an allusion to the saying "One man's meat is another man's poison.") Some of his most memorable essays were published in this column, including "Once More to the Lake," about revisiting the place where he vacationed as a child.

"Unfit for Children" In Maine, White wrote his first children's book, *Stuart Little,* about a family that has a mouse for a son. The head children's librarian at the New York Public Library called his manuscript "unfit for children," but he published it anyway in 1945. Young people loved it, and in 1952 he followed it up with *Charlotte's Web,* about a literate spider who saves a pig from slaughter.

White lived quietly until his death at 86 from Alzheimer's disease. Among his many awards were the Presidential Medal of Freedom and a special Pulitzer Prize for his entire body of work.

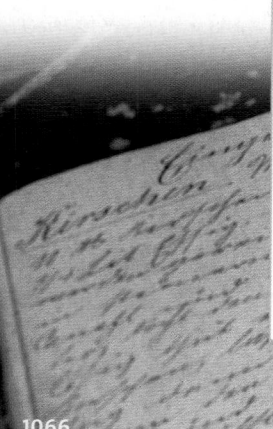

R RESOURCE MANAGER UNIT 5

Plan and Teach pp. 471–478

Literary Analysis
Summary pp. 479†*, 480‡*
Style and Diction pp. 481, 482†*
Question Support p. 486*

Reading
Interpret Author's Message
   pp. 483, 484†*
Reading Check p. 485

Assessment
Selection Tests A, B/C
   pp. 487*, 489*
  Test Generator CD

BEST PRACTICES TOOLKIT

Differentiated Instruction
   pp. 31–38*

Scaffolding Instruction
   pp. 43–46*

Graphic Organizers/Strategies
Two-Column Chart • Definition Mapping

Reading Support
  Audio Anthology CD*

Technology
  Literature Center at
   ClassZone.com
  Write*Smart* CD

* Resources for Differentiation   † Also in Spanish   ‡ In Haitian Creole and Vietnamese

LITERARY ANALYSIS: STYLE AND DICTION

Style is the particular way in which a piece of literature is written. It is not what is said, but how it is said. An essential element of style is **diction,** an author's choice of words and syntax. E. B. White's style is both casual and elegant. In the following passage, which particular words or phrases create casualness? elegance?

I was sorry to hear the other day that a certain writer, appalled by the cruel events of the world, had pledged himself never to write anything that wasn't constructive and significant and liberty-loving. I have an idea that this, in its own way, is bad news.

As you read this essay, notice what White's diction contributes to his style. Also, if an expression strikes you as humorous, think about what makes it so.

READING SKILL: INTERPRET AUTHOR'S MESSAGE

An **author's message** is the main idea of a particular work, or the point it makes. White's essay presents his personal opinions on a topic, the duty of writers. These opinions are signaled by such words and phrases as

- "I have an idea that"
- "I don't think"
- "should"
- "shouldn't"
- "This seems to me"

As you read, use such clues to identify what kind of writing White favors and what he opposes. Make notes on a chart like the one shown.

Favors	Opposes
	writing only what is constructive, significant, and liberty-loving

---

Explore the Key Idea

What do writers OWE *us?*

KEY IDEA People often debate what writers should write. Should writers uplift the community or constantly denounce wrongs? Should they report every detail about a war or protect national security? Can they be blasphemous? frivolous? Decide what you believe is the duty of writers. Do they have a special **responsibility** in troubled times?

EVALUATE AND DISCUSS Explore your own ideas about a writer's obligations by completing this sentence: "I hate it when a writer . . ." In a small group discuss your completed sentences. Is there any agreement about what writers should or should not do?

"Write about dogs!"

Teach

What do writers OWE *us?*

Lead into the **KEY IDEA** by asking the question. After students answer questions about writers' **responsibilities,** have them begin the **EVALUATE AND DISCUSS** activity by completing the sentence in several different ways. Urge students to offer their best sentences for discussion.

SKILLS FOCUS

LITERARY ANALYSIS R3.3

● STYLE AND DICTION

Have a volunteer read aloud the excerpt on page 1067. Ask students to share and explain their responses to the questions posed about it. *Possible answer: Use of the first person and colloquial phrases such as "the other day" and "bad news" create casualness. Phrases such as "had pledged himself" and "significant and liberty-loving" are elegant because they refer to high ideals.*

CHECK UNDERSTANDING Have students analyze the style and diction of the **KEY IDEA.**

READING SKILL R2.5

■ INTERPRET AUTHOR'S MESSAGE

Remind students that while opinions cannot be proven true, they must be supported by logical facts, reasoning, and evidence in order to be meaningful. As students use clue words to locate and record White's opinions, have them consider whether White's opinions are well-supported and convincing, and why or why not.

 RESOURCE MANAGER—Copy Master Interpret Author's Message p. 483 (for student use while reading the selection)

DIFFERENTIATED INSTRUCTION

FOR STRATEGIC READERS

Concept Support: Style and Diction Help students describe White's style and diction by isolating striking words or phrases and then applying descriptors to them. Students can list words or phrases that they find memorable or funny in one column of a Two-Column Chart and descriptors such as *elegant, casual,* or *funny* in the other column. Work with students to use their descriptors to describe White's style and diction in this essay.

Word or Phrase	Descriptor
"take up the sword"	patriotic, noble

 BEST PRACTICES TOOLKIT—Transparency Two-Column Chart p. A25

Prereading For prereading instruction for English learners, see

BEST PRACTICES TOOLKIT Scaffolding Reading Instruction pp. 43–46

SUMMARY

With humorous style and diction, White's essay challenges the patriotic notions of writers who feel it is their duty to give up lighthearted writing during times of world crises. White argues that humor and light-heartedness are more necessary during times of trouble than during any other time in history. He encourages writers to do their duty by writing about whatever subjects strike their fancies.

Line 35
REINFORCE *KEY IDEA:* RESPONSIBILITY

Discuss White essentially says that it is the **responsibility** of writers to ignore responsibility. Ask students to discuss White's meaning. *Possible answer: White suggests that the best and most important writing comes from writers' own interests rather than from any sense of duty to external ideas or standards.*

Lines 35–43
TIERED DISCUSSION PROMPTS

Use these prompts to help students understand White's view about the important and subversive nature of humor:

Connect Have you or someone you know ever told a joke or funny story during a tense or tragic time? What motivated the action, and what effect did it have? *Accept all thoughtful responses.*

Interpret What does White mean by his assertion that a humorist's duty is to ignore duty? *Possible answer: White means that humorists can contribute to free society by reminding people of the lighter side of events and by using humor to advance lively debate.*

Evaluate Is humor important during times of challenge? Explain. *Students may agree that comedy—and the resulting merriment or laughter—is important during times of challenge because it helps people to gain new perspectives on difficult situations.*

The Duty of Writers

E. B. White

> **BACKGROUND** This essay appeared in White's column for *Harper's* magazine in January 1939. It was a disturbing time, when it was clear that world war loomed. England and France had just appeased Hitler by allowing him to take over part of Czechoslovakia. The Nazis had looted and burned Jewish homes and businesses on a night that became known as Kristallnacht. Fascist forces were winning in the Spanish Civil War, and Japan had invaded China. In his State of the Union address, President Franklin D. Roosevelt warned that the freedoms Americans enjoyed were in danger.

I was sorry to hear the other day that a certain writer, appalled by the cruel events of the world, had pledged himself never to write anything that wasn't constructive and significant and liberty-loving. I have an idea that this, in its own way, is bad news.

All word-mongers,[1] at one time or another, have felt the divine necessity of using their talents, if any, on the side of right—but I didn't realize that they

---

1. **word-mongers:** those who deal in words for a living.

DIFFERENTIATED INSTRUCTION

FOR ALL STUDENTS

Expert Groups Encourage students to become subject experts by selecting and researching one of these topics:

- Adolf Hitler's rise to power
- Kristallnacht
- fascism and the Spanish Civil War
- Franklin D. Roosevelt's struggle with American isolationism

FOR STRATEGIC READERS

In combination with the *Audio Anthology CD*, use the Targeted Passage on page 1069 to ensure that students focus on key concepts in the selection. The Targeted Passage is also good for English learners.

① Targeted Passage [Lines 35–43]

This passage contains White's central explanation regarding the duty of writers.

were making any resolutions to that effect, and I don't think they should. When liberty's position is challenged, artists and writers are the ones who first take up the sword. They do so without persuasion, for the battle is peculiarly their own. In the nature of things, a person engaged in the flimsy business of expressing
10 himself on paper is dependent on the large general privilege of being heard. Any intimation that this privilege may be revoked throws a writer into a panic. **A** His is a double allegiance to freedom—an intellectual one springing from the conviction that pure thought has a right to function unimpeded, and a selfish one springing from his need, as a bread-winner, to be allowed to speak his piece. America is now liberty-conscious. In a single generation it has progressed from being toothbrush-conscious, to being air-minded, to being liberty-conscious. The transition has been disturbing, but it has been effected, and the last part has been accomplished largely by the good work of writers and artists, to whom liberty is a blessed condition that must be preserved on earth at all costs.

20   But to return to my man who has foresworn everything but what is good and significant. He worries me. I hope he isn't serious, but I'm afraid he is. Having resolved to be nothing but significant, he is in a fair way to lose his effectiveness. A writer must believe in something, obviously, but he shouldn't join a club. Letters flourish not when writers amalgamate,[2] but when they are contemptuous of one another. (Poets are the most contemptuous of all the writing breeds, and in the long run the most exalted and influential.) Even in evil times, a writer should cultivate only what naturally absorbs his fancy, whether it be freedom or cinch bugs, and should write in the way that comes easy. **B**

The movement is spreading. I know of one gifted crackpot who used to be
30 employed gainfully in the fields of humor and satire, who has taken a solemn pledge not to write anything funny or light-hearted or "insignificant" again till things get straightened around in the world. This seems to me distinctly deleterious[3] and a little silly. A literature composed of nothing but liberty-loving thoughts is little better than the propaganda which it seeks to defeat. **C**

In a free country it is the duty of writers to pay no attention to duty. Only under a dictatorship is literature expected to exhibit an harmonious design or an inspirational tone. A despot doesn't fear eloquent writers preaching freedom—he fears a drunken poet who may crack a joke that will take hold. His gravest concern is lest gaiety, or truth in sheep's clothing, somewhere gain a foothold, lest joy in
40 some unguarded moment be unconfined. I honestly don't believe that a humorist should take the veil[4] today; he should wear his bells night and day, and squeeze the uttermost jape,[5] even though he may feel more like writing a strong letter to the *Herald Tribune.* **D**

---

2. **Letters . . . amalgamate:** Writing and literature do not do well when writers form groups.

3. **deleterious:** harmful.

4. **take the veil:** become a nun or, here, a serious, religious person.

5. **wear his bells . . . jape:** consistently act like a jester (who wears a cap with bells) and see the humor in everything.

A STYLE AND DICTION
Paraphrase the passage beginning with "In the nature . . ." and ending with ". . . into a panic." How does changing the words affect the style?

B AUTHOR'S MESSAGE
In lines 26–28, what does White state that a writer should do?

C STYLE AND DICTION
What phrasings add humor to this paragraph?

 Targeted Passage

D AUTHOR'S MESSAGE
Reread lines 37–43. What value does White see in humor?

LITERARY ANALYSIS

A STYLE AND DICTION
Possible answer: Paraphrase: Writers, whose work is insubstantial, depend on others as readers. They get scared at the thought of having no readers. Changing White's words makes the style less elegant and less humorous.

READING SKILL

B AUTHOR'S MESSAGE
Possible answer: Writers should write about their interests in a manner that comes easily.

LITERARY ANALYSIS

C STYLE AND DICTION
Possible answer: Humor comes from juxtaposing the phrases "gifted crackpot" and "employed gainfully" (lines 29–30) and "distinctly deleterious" and "a little silly" (lines 32–33), as well as the idea of "literature composed of nothing but liberty-loving thoughts" (lines 33–34).

READING SKILL

D AUTHOR'S MESSAGE
Possible answer: White thinks that jokes and gaiety can weaken dictators.

SELECTION WRAP-UP

SUMMARIZE Have students explain White's definition of a writer's duty.

- What is a writer's duty?

- What kind of literature is expected under a dictatorship?

- What does a despot fear?

- What does White believe that humorists should do during difficult times?

ADDITIONAL GUIDELINES
For more help with differentiation and tips for classroom management, see

 BEST PRACTICES TOOLKIT
Differentiated Instruction pp. 31–38

FOR ENGLISH LEARNERS
Key Academic Vocabulary Use Definition Mapping to teach these words: *function* (line 13), *exhibit* (line 36).

BEST PRACTICES TOOLKIT—Transparency
Definition Mapping p. E6

Practice and Apply

After Reading

Use these copy masters to check under-standing and provide extra support:

R RESOURCE MANAGER—Copy Masters
Reading Check p. 485
Style and Diction p. 481
Question Support p. 486

Additional selection questions are provided for teachers on page 475.

ANSWERS

1. *White is sorry to hear that a certain writer has pledged not to write anything that isn't constructive, significant, and liberty-loving.*

2. *America has become conscious of liberty in a way that it wasn't previously.*

3. *If writers bind themselves to a single view-point or cause, no matter how important or serious, they risk losing their unique percep-tions and style and becoming redundant, inauthentic, and ultimately insignificant.*

Possible answers:

4. ■ **SKILLS FOCUS Interpret Author's Message** *White supports writers who write about what interests them in easy and humorous ways. He opposes writing that is intentionally serious and significant.*

5. *Students may agree that literature should not be rigid or narrowly focused in its themes; that, as artists, writers should write about topics of choice, even in evil times; that artists should not be bound by any sense of duty, and that despots should not fear direct messages but rather messages cloaked in seemingly harmless garb.*

Assess and Reteach

Assess

R RESOURCE MANAGER—Copy Masters
Selection Test A pp. 487–488
Selection Test B/C pp. 489–490

● Test Generator CD

Reteach

S STANDARDS LESSON FILE
Literature Lesson 43: Tone
Literature Lesson 44: Style and Syntax
Reading Lesson 4: Recognizing Main Idea and Details

Comprehension

R2.5, R3.3

1. **Recall** At the beginning of the essay, what is White "sorry to hear"?

2. **Clarify** How has America changed in a generation, according to White?

3. **Paraphrase** What does White mean when he says, "Having resolved to be nothing but significant, he is in a fair way to lose his effectiveness"?

Literary Analysis

4. **Interpret Author's Message** Look back at the chart you created as you read. What kind of writing does White favor, and what does he oppose? Summarize his main message.

5. **Evaluate Opinions** Do you agree with White's opinions about the **responsibility** of writers? React to each of the following statements:

   • "A literature composed of liberty-loving thoughts is little better than the propaganda which it seeks to defeat." (lines 33–34)

   • "Even in evil times, a writer should cultivate only what naturally absorbs his fancy...." (lines 26–27)

   • "In a free country it is the duty of writers to pay no attention to duty." (line 35)

   • "A despot doesn't fear eloquent writers preaching freedom—he fears a drunken poet who may crack a joke that will take hold." (lines 37–38)

6. **Analyze Style and Diction** Choose a sentence from the essay that you find particularly thought provoking. Does it contain expressions that are casual, elegant, humorous, or a combination? Explain your answer.

7. **Compare Texts** Both White and Dorothy Parker (page 1058) wrote for the *New Yorker* magazine. How is White's **voice** different from Parker's? What do both essays suggest about the magazine's **tone?**

Literary Criticism

8. **Historical Context** White was writing at a time when fascism was on the rise overseas but America had not yet become involved in World War II. Do you think his message would have been the same if he were writing later, say, after the horrors of the Holocaust had become known? Would it have been the same if America had been turning toward fascism?

---

6. ● **SKILLS FOCUS Style and Diction**
Answers will vary.

7. *White's and Parker's voices are both humor-ous, but White exhibits a gentler humor while Parker is more mocking and sarcastic. Both writers reflect that the magazine's tone is engaging and entertaining.*

8. *White might have had the same message, because he believed strongly in the ability of writers to serve as role models for freedom. However, he might have softened a bit in the face of genocide or American censorship.*

Journalism Beyond the Facts

Journalism is typically regarded as writing whose purpose is to convey to readers the facts as they are known—to answer the questions *who? what? when? where?* and *how?* Depending on their assignment and its purpose, journalists may strive for detached objectivity or may more subjectively shape the stories they report, the ideas they explore, and the claims they make.

Writing to Evaluate

Each of the selections beginning on page 1050 goes beyond "just the facts" and conveys the writer's perspective on a particular topic. This perspective largely determines the structure and flow of each piece. Skim each selection and look for words, phrases, or sentences that help you discern the writer's perspective. Then try your own hand at writing a news story that conveys more than just the facts. Choose an event, such as a school play, a varsity track meet, or even a typical lunch break in the cafeteria, and report it from your own perspective. Use the selections in this section as your inspiration.

Consider

- how the authors in this section revealed their personal perspectives and how their perspectives shaped their writing
- what basic facts you need to convey
- how best to reveal your thoughts about the event you witness

Extension

SPEAKING & LISTENING Much of journalism is distinguished by its tone. From factual, unemotional reporting to lurid mudslinging—today's journalism encompasses it all. Find three examples of current news stories that range widely in tone. You might search for stories in traditional newspapers, entertainment magazines, home decorating magazines, supermarket tabloids, or online news sources. Create a **poster** with copies of the stories and their headlines and **present** it to the class, explaining why you think—or do not think—the tone of each story is appropriate for its content.

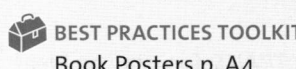 W1.2, W1.5

1071

Wrap-Up: Journalism as Literature

This Wrap-Up provides students with an opportunity to revisit ideas from the literature in this section about ways that journalists elevate reporting to a literary art form. What methods were discussed? What goals did writers identify for themselves as journalists? Urge students to examine their own views on the craft of journalism and impact in light of insights gained from the selections.

Writing to Evaluate

- Review with students that *evaluating* means judging or determining the worth or quality of something. This skill helps readers form their own opinions regarding events and ideas. Here, students will use evaluation to distill each writer's perspective from his or her writing, and then to select style elements that will convey their own perspective in a news story.

- To help students create their news stories, suggest that they first take objective notes about their events, noting both facts and sensory details. Then, have students write one sentence stating an overall impression of the event. Tell students to use these sentences as guides for their writing, selecting details and words that support this impression.

Extension

- Remind students that tone is the writer's attitude toward his or her subject as conveyed through style elements such as word choice and syntax.

- After students collect their news stories, have them list two to three words that could describe each writer's tone. Challenge them to identify supporting evidence from the article for their tone descriptions and then to choose a single descriptor for each article. Students can use these insights to plan their posters and presentations.

BEST PRACTICES TOOLKIT
Book Posters p. A4

DIFFERENTIATED INSTRUCTION

FOR DEVELOPING WRITERS

Writing Support Help students list strategies, such as sarcasm or humor, that each of the selection writers uses to reveal their personal perspectives. Discuss with students each technique's effect on the writer's message and on readers. Then, urge students to choose three of these strategies to use in their news stories. Help students choose strategies that support the dominant impressions they wish to convey.

FOR ENGLISH LEARNERS

Writing with Personal Perspective To help students state their personal impression of an event, provide these sentence starters:

- The school play made me think about _____.

- The track meet made me feel _____.

- Lunchtime in the cafeteria sounds like _____.

Urge students to use facts to support their personal impressions.

Focus and Motivate

OBJECTIVES

- analyze a student model that reflects the key traits of comparison-contrast essays
- use the writing process to produce a comparison-contrast essay
- revise and edit, using criteria for comparison-contrast essays
- plan and deliver an oral interpretation, considering effects of speed and volume

 W2.2, W1.9, LC1.1, LC1.2, LS1.7, LS2.5

WRITER'S ROAD MAP

WRITING PROMPTS 1 AND 2

To help students choose a prompt, clarify these points of comparison: *theme,* the real-life message of the work; *style,* the writer's word choices and syntax; *visual style,* the media maker's choices about composition, color, camera angles, wide or narrow shots, and so on; *characters,* static or dynamic, flat or round; and *time period,* setting and its influence on other narrative elements.

ADDITIONAL PROMPTS

Use these prompts for more writing practice:

WRITING PROMPT 3

Writing from Media Write an essay comparing and contrasting two works of journalism from this unit or the current media. Focus on aspects such as subject matter, objectivity or subjectivity, style, and tone, and offer readers new insight into the works.

WRITING PROMPT 4

Writing for the Real World Write a report for an employer comparing and contrasting two options, such as music to play in a store or the best online software. Include pros and cons of each option, but don't state opinions.

For additional writing prompts, see

 WriteSmart CD

Writing Center at ClassZone.com

KEY TRAITS

Review the six *KEY TRAITS,* focusing on ideas and organization. Compare the traits with the criteria on page 1078.

Writing Workshop
EXPOSITION

Comparison-Contrast Essay

In this unit, you read about hope and despair, wealthy people and poor people, enormous cities and small rural towns. Noticing similarities and differences helps you to develop a fuller, richer understanding of whatever you are studying. To present comparisons and contrasts effectively, follow the **Writer's Road Map.**

WRITER'S ROAD MAP
Comparison-Contrast Essay

WRITING PROMPT 1

Writing from Literature Write an essay comparing and contrasting two poems. Your essay should concentrate on key aspects of the poems, such as theme, style, or word choice, and should give readers new insight into the works.

Poems to Compare

- "The Negro Speaks of Rivers" and "I, Too"
- "Any Human to Another" and "A Black Man Talks of Reaping"
- "Richard Cory" and "Lucinda Matlock"

WRITING PROMPT 2

Writing from the Real World Compare and contrast two creative works that strongly interest you. Choose key aspects of the works as the basis of your comparison. For instance, you might focus on visual style, characters, theme, or time period. Your essay should give new insight into the works.

Sources to Consider

- two detective shows on television
- two paintings or two pieces of sculpture
- two action-adventure movies

 WRITING TOOLS
For prewriting, revision, and editing tools, visit the **Writing Center** at **ClassZone.com.**

KEY TRAITS

1. IDEAS
- Clearly **identifies the works** being compared and contrasted
- Includes a **thesis statement** that identifies similarities and/or differences
- Uses **specific examples** to support key ideas

2. ORGANIZATION
- Includes an attention-getting **introduction** and a thoughtful **conclusion**
- Follows a consistent **organizational pattern**
- Links ideas with **transitions**

3. VOICE
- Maintains an appropriate **tone** for the audience and purpose

4. WORD CHOICE
- Uses **precise words** to explain similarities and differences

5. SENTENCE FLUENCY
- Varies **sentence beginnings**

6. CONVENTIONS
- Employs **correct grammar and usage**

Writing Workshop Resources

 RESOURCE MANAGER UNIT 5

Plan and Teach pp. 491–494
Prewriting–Editing pp. 495–499
Writing Rubric p. 500
Speaking and Listening p. 501
Writing Support p. 502*

 STANDARDS LESSON FILE

Writing Lessons 8, 14, 20, 23, 35, 39, 42
Speaking and Listening Lesson 9

 BEST PRACTICES TOOLKIT

Scaffolding Writing Instruction pp. 43–46*
Mapping Main Ideas and Details •
Microtheme • Writing Templates: Compare and Contrast • Opening Lines

TECHNOLOGY
Easy Planner DVD
Writing Center at **ClassZone.com**
WriteSmart CD

* Resources for Differentiation

Part 1: Analyze a Student Model

W2.2, W1.9 (p. 1077), LC1.1 (p. 1078), LC1.2 (p. 1078), LS1.7 (p. 1079), LS2.5 (p. 1079)

 INTERACTIVE MODEL CLASSZONE.COM

Dan Brantingham
Columbus Technical High School

Pride of Place

When you think of a city, do you picture crowds of people and beautiful, tall buildings? Or do you think of crime, poverty, and overcrowding? According to the speakers in "Chicago" by Carl Sandburg and "My City" by James Weldon Johnson, both of these views are accurate.
5   The poems share a dramatic tone and present the same theme: that despite its drawbacks, the city is a living, thrilling place that is worthy of admiration.

The dramatic tone of "Chicago" is clear from the first line. Proudly, the speaker shouts "Hog Butcher for the World" and then calls out other active,
10 living qualities of the "City of the Big Shoulders." The speaker celebrates a vibrant city that makes tools, stacks wheat, and is "Stormy, husky, brawling." The high energy of the city is clearest near the end of the poem, when the speaker can't seem to stop "bragging and laughing" about "this / my city."

15 Although both poems have a dramatic tone, Johnson's piece is quieter and more serious. "My City" also praises big-city life, but it celebrates Manhattan instead of Chicago. Statements such as "threshold of the unknown dark to cross" create a formal tone because they use some uncommon words in an unusual order. The speaker doesn't shout or brag
20 as the speaker in "Chicago" does. Even so, the first lines of "My City" are full of emotional power: "When I come down to sleep death's endless night, / . . . What to me then will be the keenest loss . . . ?" The drama builds throughout the poem as the speaker compares the beauties of nature with the sights, sounds, and smells of Manhattan. "My City" ends with a
25 startling exclamation: "O God! the stark, unutterable pity, / To be dead, and never again behold my city!"

KEY TRAITS IN ACTION

Introduction "hooks" the reader and **identifies the works** being compared and contrasted. **Thesis statement** identifies two similarities (tone and theme).

Has a sensible **organizational pattern**, discussing tone in both poems before moving on to a discussion of theme in both poems. The writer quotes and describes **specific examples** from the poems to support key points.

Teach

CALIFORNIA

Part 1: Analyze a Student Model

Have students read the student model and **KEY TRAITS IN ACTION.** Then discuss the model with the class, noting specific examples of each trait and building on what students have already noted. You may also wish to incorporate these activities:

- **Thesis Statement** Point out to students that the thesis statement conveys the writer's main idea about the essay topic. That idea must then be supported by evidence in the body of the essay. Have students note the model's thesis statement appears at the end of the introductory paragraph. Although a thesis statement may appear anywhere in an essay, discuss with students why this placement is effective. **Possible answer: Placing the thesis statement early allows writers to orient readers to their ideas. The thesis then logically flows into supporting evidence.**

- **Organizational Pattern** To help them understand Dan's organizational pattern, ask students to identify the statements he makes about tone in both poems. **Possible answer: Dan states that "Chicago" has a dramatic tone, while "My City" has a quieter and more serious tone.**

- **Specific Examples** Point out to students how the writer interweaves paraphrases with actual quotations from the poems and discuss the value of each type of evidence. **Possible answer: Quotations have the power of the writer's original words, while paraphrases allow essay writers to smoothly summarize ideas.**

DIFFERENTIATED INSTRUCTION

For general guidelines on differentiating writing instruction, see

 BEST PRACTICES TOOLKIT
Scaffolding Writing Instruction
pp. 43–46

FOR ENGLISH LEARNERS

Language: Skill Words Write these terms on the board and review them with students:

- *hooks:* invites interest in—for example, by anecdote, dialogue, or reaction

- *thesis statement:* statement of the writer's main idea about the essay's topic—for example, lines 5–7 of student model

- *organizational pattern:* manner in which the writer orders his or her ideas—for example, point by point or subject by subject

- *tone:* writer's attitude toward his or her subject—for example, formal, scholarly, or conversational

- *theme:* the main message about how a work applies to real life—for example, lines 6–7 of student model

- *transitions:* words that show the relationship between ideas—for example, *similarly, like, however,* and *instead* in lines 37–43 of the student model.

- **Sentence Beginnings** Write the sentences in lines 37 to 44 separately on the board. To illustrate varied sentence beginnings, help students locate the subject in each sentence. *Answer: The sentence subjects are "'My City,'" "speaker," "speaker," "Revealing a flaw," and "slums."* Then, ask students how the writer varies the beginning of each sentence. *Possible answer: In the first and fifth sentences, the writer opens with an introductory transition word. The second sentence opens with the subject. The third sentence opens with an introductory phrase. The fourth sentence opens with a gerund phrase that serves as the sentence's subject.*

- **Conclusion** Point out to students that while a conclusion should summarize main points, it should also offer readers a final, insightful thought. Writers should ask themselves, What do I want my readers to be thinking about as they finish my essay? In this case, the writer suggests that the two poems about cities are really love poems. Point out that although this insight is supported by the preceding discussion, the writer saves it to surprise readers at the end.

For interactive student models, see

Write*Smart* CD

Writing Center at **ClassZone.com**

The dramatic tone of both poems matches their theme: that city life is wondrous and sometimes tragic. To the speaker of "Chicago," almost everything about that city is worth praising, from its smoke and dust to its

30 pulse and "the heart of the people." The speaker admits that the city can be a harsh, violent place where "the gunman [can] kill and go free to kill again" and where there is "wanton hunger." However, the speaker offers this challenge: "Come and show me another city with lifted head singing so proud to be alive and coarse and strong and cunning." This is an assertion

35 of Chicago's greatness despite its crime and hunger, a celebration of a city that is "alive" and "strong."

Similarly, "My City" praises "Manhattan's sights and sounds, her smells, / Her crowds, her throbbing force." The speaker is part of a living, breathing city that contains "shining towers." Like the speaker in

40 "Chicago," the speaker in "My City" admits that the city can be a harsh place by mentioning "her slums," a jarring note in a poem that is otherwise full of admiration. Revealing a flaw in the city does not change the speaker's overall opinion, however. Instead, the slums are just one part of the speaker's beloved city.

45 "My City" and "Chicago" use a dramatic tone and a common theme to describe two dynamic cities. The bold speaker of "Chicago" laughs and brags, while the speaker of "My City" is more formal, even somber. Both poems are full of emotion and conviction. Each poet has written a love letter to his city.

The writer of the student model uses a formal, straightforward **tone** that makes sense for the audience (teacher and classmates) and purpose (to give new insight into two poems).

Highlighted **transitions** help show comparison and contrast. **Precise words** and varied **sentence beginnings** add polish.

Concludes effectively by summarizing the main ideas and adding an appropriate final thought.

2

DIFFERENTIATED INSTRUCTION

FOR ENGLISH LEARNERS

Comprehension: Transitions Explain that transitions help readers connect one idea to the next. Start and share a word bank of comparison-contrast transitions, including *although, but, in the same way, meanwhile, nevertheless, nonetheless, on the other hand, still, when, while,* and *yet.*

1. Place a series of objects to be compared on a central table.

2. Using transitions from the word bank, model how to form comparison or contrast statements. For example, *The ruler is long, but the eraser is short.*

3. Have partners continue the activity.

To provide English learners with additional writing support, see

R RESOURCE MANAGER—Copy Master Writing Support p. 502

Part 2: Apply the Writing Process

PREWRITING

What Should I Do?	What Does It Look Like?
1. Decide which works you will compare. List pairs of works that you understand well or find appealing. Examine your list for pairs that have important similarities and distinct differences. Highlight the pair you choose.	**Ideas for Prompt 1: Pairs of Poems** • *"I, Too" and "Harlem" (both by Langston Hughes, both about social issues)* • *"Chicago" and "My City" (both about cities)* • *"Lucinda Matlock" and "Richard Cory" (one contented person, one discontented person)*
2. Analyze similarities and differences. Use a Venn diagram to analyze your two subjects. List all the points you can think of—you do not have to use them all in your paper. **TIP** If you can't list at least two or three major points in each section of the diagram, go back to your list and choose different works.	*"Chicago"* * *praises Chicago* * *busy, active city* * *brags, shouts, laughs* *Both* * *dramatic tone* * *theme: great city* *"My City"* * *praises Manhattan* * *contrasts nature and the city* * *formal words and tone*
3. Write your thesis. Your thesis statement can state similarities, differences, or both. Remember, your thesis is an overview of what your entire essay will explain. **TIP** The order of the points in your paper should follow the order of your thesis.	*Working Thesis:* *The poems both have a dramatic tone, and they have the same theme—that their city is a great place.*
4. Collect evidence for each key point. Use a chart or another graphic organizer to list evidence for each point you will make. Search for quotations and details in both works.	*Key Point: City Is a Great Place* <table><tr><td>*"Chicago"*</td><td>*"My City"*</td></tr><tr><td>• *"lifted head"* • *"so proud to be alive"* • *"strong"* • *a great city despite corruption and hunger*</td><td>• *living, breathing city* • *"shining towers"* • *mentions one flaw of Manhattan: "her slums"*</td></tr></table>

FOR DEVELOPING WRITERS

Collect Evidence Offer students the Microtheme organizer as an option for planning their essay. They can write their working thesis under Introduction, then list the key points they wish to make. Discuss the listed key points and help students find one item of evidence for each work for each key point. Remind students that they can choose the sequence of points as they draft.

BEST PRACTICES TOOLKIT—Transparency Microtheme p. C13

FOR ENGLISH LEARNERS

Write Your Thesis Provide students with these sentence starters to help them develop their thesis statements:

• (Title) and (Title) are similar in that they _____.

• (Title) and (Title) are different in that they _____.

Remind students that each key point and item of evidence should support the thesis statement.

Practice and Apply

To support students during the writing process, use these copy masters:

R **RESOURCE MANAGER—Copy Masters**
Prewriting–Editing pp. 495–499
Writing Rubric p. 500
Writing Support p. 502 (for English learners)

Part 2: Apply the Writing Process

PREWRITING

1. **Decide which works you will compare.** Pair students by chosen writing prompt in order to brainstorm possible subjects for comparison. Partners should then list topics, such as speaker, author, or theme that will yield similarities or differences among the subjects. Ask pairs to share their topic ideas with other pairs addressing the same prompt. Instruct groups to help each student select a topic that will interest readers.

2. **Analyze similarities and differences.** Urge students to try to list in their Venn Diagrams corresponding points in the outer circles for each subject. For example, the model diagram shows that both poems "praise" a city. Organizing ideas this way will make comparing and contrasting easier.

3. **Write your thesis.** To craft thesis statements, have students respond to these questions: How are (Title) and (Title) similar? How are they different? Remind students that they can revise their statements as they write.

4. **Collect evidence for each key point.** Have students identify three to five key supporting points. Remind them that each point should apply in some way to both works. Offer the Mapping Main Ideas and Details organizer as a way to gather evidence for each key point.

BEST PRACTICES TOOLKIT—Transparency Mapping Main Ideas and Details p. C6

For interactive graphic organizers, see

Write*Smart* CD

Writing Center at **ClassZone.com**

DRAFTING

1. **Choose an organizational pattern.** Ask students to name pluses and minuses for each organizational pattern. ***Possible answers:*** *One plus in a point-by-point pattern is that it directly highlights the comparison between two items. One minus is that it challenges writers to focus on two topics simultaneously, switching between them. A subject-by-subject pattern is appealing because it allows writers to focus attention on one work, then the other. One minus is that writers must work harder in discussing the second work to make the comparison clear.*

2. **Provide evidence for each key point.** Stress that a quotation by itself does not support a thesis statement. Writers must interpret the language and explain how it supports the thesis statement. Ask students to identify the interpretive and explanatory language in the student model excerpt. ***Possible answer:*** *Language such as "Proudly," "calls out other active, living qualities" and "The speaker celebrates a vibrant city that . . ." conveys the essay writer's interpretation of the examples or quotations that follow.* Tell students that the bulk of each body paragraph should be original writing rather than long quotations.

3. **Show how ideas are connected.** Remind students that their essays should include both similarities and differences. To ensure balance, have students highlight transition words, marking comparison words in one color and contrast words in another color.

For a comparison-contrast essay writing template, see

📦 **BEST PRACTICES TOOLKIT—Transparencies**
Writing Template: Compare-Contrast (by points) pp. C16, C23
Writing Template: Compare-Contrast (by subject) pp. C16, C24

💿 Write*Smart* CD

ℹ️ Writing Center at **ClassZone.com**

DRAFTING

What Should I Do?

1. **Choose an organizational pattern.**
Here are two ways to organize a comparison-contrast essay. The writer of the student model chose the point-by-point approach.

- **Point by Point**
Compares and contrasts both subjects, one point at a time

- **Subject by Subject**
Discusses all the points relating to the first subject, then moves on to the second subject

2. **Provide evidence for each key point.**
Whatever you claim, you must explain. Use details, examples, and quotations from both works. See page 1078 to learn how to punctuate quotations correctly.

TIP Be sure that each key point you make relates to your thesis.

See page 1078: Ask a Peer Reader

3. **Show how ideas are connected.**
To show how things are alike, you could use a transitional word, such as *both, like, similarly,* or *also.* To show how things are different, you could use *in contrast, instead, on the other hand,* or *however.*

What Does It Look Like?

POINT BY POINT

Point 1: Dramatic tone
Subject A ("Chicago"): includes laughing, bragging, and shouting
Subject B ("My City"): quiet, somber, formal

Point 2: Theme (love of the city)
Subject A ("Chicago"): speaker admires city but admits that tragedies occur there
Subject B ("My City"): speaker loves the city, even its slums

SUBJECT BY SUBJECT

Subject A: "Chicago"
Point 1: Tone (dramatic: shouts, brags, laughs)
Point 2: Theme (love of the city, despite some problems)

Subject B: "My City"
Point 1: Tone (dramatic, but more formal, with uncommon words)
Point 2: Theme (love of the city, even its slums)

The dramatic tone of "Chicago" is clear from the first line. — Point 1: dramatic tone

Proudly, the speaker shouts "Hog Butcher for the World" and then calls out other active, living qualities of the "City of the Big Shoulders." The speaker celebrates a vibrant city that makes tools, stacks wheat, and is "Stormy, husky, brawling." — Supporting evidence for Point 1

Similarly, "My City" praises "Manhattan's sights and sounds, her smells, / Her crowds, her throbbing force." The speaker is part of a living, breathing city that contains "shining towers." Like the speaker in "Chicago," the speaker in "My City" admits that the city can be a harsh place by mentioning "her slums," a jarring note in a poem that is otherwise full of admiration.

DIFFERENTIATED INSTRUCTION

FOR ENGLISH LEARNERS

Provide Evidence Work with students to review the grammar rules on page 1078, noting the differences between shorter and longer quotations. Clarify when and how to use such punctuation as colons and ellipses. Also, point out that students should not begin paragraphs with quotations. Suggest instead that they explain their key points, offer supporting quotations, and then provide further interpretation or explanation.

FOR ADVANCED LEARNERS/AP

Weave in Evidence As students revise their essays, suggest that they look for places to provide context for their supporting evidence. For example, they might include appropriate biographical or historical information as a way of leading up to a quotation or detail. Remind students to correctly cite any factual information they include.

REVISING AND EDITING

What Should I Do?	What Does It Look Like?

1. Begin with a "hook."
- A hook makes your reader want to keep reading. It should also help to show the direction your paper will take. Circle the first sentence or two in your draft.
- If your first few lines seem dull, consider adding a question, a quotation, or some other kind of attention grabber.

▶ ~~Some people don't like the city, but others think it's a great place to live.~~

When you think of a city, do you picture crowds of people and beautiful, tall buildings? Or do you think of crime, poverty, and overcrowding? According to the speakers in "Chicago" by Carl Sandburg and "My City" by James Weldon Johnson, both of these views are accurate.

2. Weave in supporting evidence.
- Underline supporting evidence—details, examples, and quotations.
- Ask yourself: Did I lead smoothly up to and out of the evidence? Or did I drop quotations and details into the essay without any context for them? Include explanations where they are needed.

▶ The speaker admits that the city can be a harsh, violent place where

~~The city is a place where~~ "the gunman [can] kill and go free to kill again" and where there is "wanton hunger."

However, the speaker offers this challenge:

~~The speaker says:~~ "Come and show me another city with lifted head singing so proud to be alive and coarse and strong and cunning." This is an assertion of Chicago's greatness despite its crime and hunger, a celebration of a city that is "alive" and "strong."

3. Double-check your transitions.
- Draw a box around each transition you used. Do you have enough transitions? Did you use the same one several times?
- Change or add transitions as necessary to make your essay clear and sophisticated.

▶ Although both poems have a dramatic tone, Johnson's piece is quieter and more serious. also ~~Although~~ "My City" praises big-city life, it but celebrates Manhattan instead of Chicago.

4. Improve your conclusion.
- Ask a peer reader to tell you whether your conclusion is clear and whether it gives your reader something to think about.
- Consider adding a summary, important details, or a new but related idea.

See page 1078: Ask a Peer Reader

▶ "My City" and "Chicago" use a dramatic tone and a common theme to describe two great cities. The bold speaker of "Chicago" laughs and brags, while the speaker of "My City" is more formal. Both poems are full of emotion and conviction. Each poet has written a love letter to his city.

WRITING WORKSHOP **1077**

REVISING AND EDITING

1. Begin with a "hook." Point out that the revised example is a reaction lead—it asks readers for a reaction. Use the Opening Lines strategy to familiarize students with other hooks, such as anecdotes or action descriptions. Then suggest that students write two or three different leads for their essays. Then, have students work with partners to select the most effective "hook."

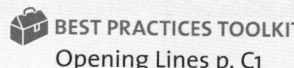 **BEST PRACTICES TOOLKIT**
Opening Lines p. C1

2. Weave in supporting evidence. Point out the improvement from the draft to the revision. Stress that each addition tells readers why the quotation is included. The final addition links the supporting evidence to one of the writer's key points—cities are thrilling but sometimes tragic places.

3. Double-check your transitions. Remind students that transitions signal to readers that the writer views two ideas as connected—in this essay because they are complimentary or contrasting. To stress the value of transitions, ask two volunteers to write a short paragraph from their essays on the board. Eliminate the transitions. Lead students to compare the effectiveness of both versions.

4. Improve your conclusion. Have peer readers describe their thoughts after reading partners' essays. Urge writers to consider the descriptions. Does the peer reader's reaction fulfill the writer's intention? If there is a gap between intention and execution, have writers explain their intentions to their peer readers. Ask students to work together to revise the conclusion.

For interactive revision tools, see

🖭 WriteSmart CD

ⓘ Writing Center at **ClassZone.com**

FOR ENGLISH LEARNERS

Ask a Peer Reader Point out that each of the Ask a Peer Reader questions on page 1078 includes several questions within it. For clarity, provide these sentence starters for students to use when answering these questions as peer readers:

- Question 1: The writer's thesis statement is _____. The writer compares _____ with _____. The writer uses a _____ organizational pattern.

- Question 2: The writer's key points are _____. The writer needs more evidence for the key point _____ because _____. One point that confuses me is _____ because _____.

- Question 3: At the end of the essay, I am thinking about _____. At the end of the essay, the writer might add _____.

Preparing to Publish

Support for meeting the goals in the writing criteria is supplied throughout the Writing Workshop on pages 1075–1077.

For Rubric Bank, see

 WriteSmart CD

 Writing Center at ClassZone.com

Assess and Reteach

S STANDARDS LESSON FILE

Writing Lesson 8: Creating Sentence Variety

Writing Lesson 14: Writing a Thesis Statement

Writing Lesson 20: Integrating Quotations

Writing Lesson 23: Comparison-Contrast Essay

Writing Lesson 35: Elaborate with Incidents, Examples, and Quotations

Writing Lesson 39: Word Choice

Writing Lesson 42: Adapting a Tone

 LC1.1, LC1.2

Preparing to Publish Comparison-Contrast Essay

Consider the Criteria

Use this checklist to make sure your essay is on track.

Ideas

☑ has a thesis identifying what is being compared and contrasted

☑ supports key ideas with evidence from both works

Organization

☑ begins with a "hook" and ends with a thoughtful summary

☑ is logically organized

☑ connects ideas with transitions

Voice

☑ uses an appropriate tone

Word Choice

☑ uses exact, specific words

Sentence Fluency

☑ varies sentence beginnings

Conventions

☑ employs correct grammar, spelling, and punctuation

Ask a Peer Reader

- What does my thesis statement tell you about the content and organization of my essay?

- Does any part of my essay need more evidence or explanation? If so, where?

- What, if anything, should I do to make my conclusion clearer or more polished?

Check Your Grammar

- When quoting from a work, enclose the exact words in quotation marks. The period goes inside the quotation marks.

> The city is "alive" and "strong."

- Use an ellipsis [...] to show the omission of quoted words. Use a slash mark [/] to show a line break in a poem. If a question mark is part of the quoted material, place it inside the quotation marks.

> "When I come down to sleep death's endless night, / ...What to me then will be the keenest loss ...?"

See pages R54: Quick Reference: Punctuation

- Use prepositional phrases to add important details.

> The dramatic tone of "Chicago" is clear from the first line.
>
> Each poet has written a love letter to his city.

See page R65: Prepositional Phrases

Writing Online

 PUBLISHING OPTIONS
For publishing options, visit the **Writing Center** at **ClassZone.com**.

ASSESSMENT PREPARATION
For writing and grammar assessment practice, go to the **Assessment Center** at **ClassZone.com**.

LS1.7, LS2.5

Delivering an Oral Interpretation

When you perform the poems you wrote about, listeners are able to experience the comparisons and contrasts.

Planning the Interpretation

1. **Develop a plan for presenting the poems together.** Will you read each poem in its entirety, or will you compare and contrast line by line, stanza by stanza, or part by part?
2. **Vary your pacing and your tone.** Find the right speed and volume for the individual words and phrases.
3. **Mark up copies of the poems.** Decide how you will use your voice to show meaning. For example, you might underline what you will stress and draw a box around words you will play down. In places where you plan to pick up the pace, you might link words with hyphens. Consider adding slash marks to places where you plan to slow the poem down. If you wish, add gestures, such as a wave or a nod.

> But, <u>ah!</u> / Manhattan's sights / and sounds, / her smells,
> Her crowds, her <u>throbbing force</u>, the <u>thrill</u> that comes
> From being of her a part . . .   [put fist on chest]

> <u>Building,-breaking,-rebuilding,</u> [nod slightly on each emphasized syllable]

4. **Practice your presentation several times.** Adjust the notes on your copy of the poem as needed. Have a partner listen and give you advice.

Performing the Interpretation

1. **Be confident.** Speak up! Don't rush. Make eye contact with audience members.
2. **Ask for constructive criticism.** After your performance, invite a few listeners to comment on it. Could they hear aspects of the poems that were alike and different? Were the pace, volume, and gestures appropriate? Think about what you might do differently the next time.

See page R85: Evaluate an Oral Interpretation

SPEAKING AND LISTENING

Students who responded to Writing Prompt 1 should read this page to get an overview of how to plan and deliver an oral interpretation. Encourage them to familiarize themselves with the features of an oral interpretation and with tools, such as marked copies of text or tape recorders, that might help them prepare.

Before students begin working on the oral interpretation, review these criteria with them so that they understand their goals.

Criteria A strong oral interpretation

- juxtaposes two works to show similarities and differences
- has effective pacing and tone
- uses voice to emphasize meaning
- reflects adequate rehearsal
- includes accurately stated quotations from the poems
- incorporates appropriate gestures
- demonstrates eye contact

For students who responded to Writing Prompt 2, suggest a multimedia presentation or oral report in place of the oral interpretation. Refer students to the relevant questions on page R84 of the **Speaking and Listening Handbook.**

When students begin listening to the presentations, have them use an appropriate set of criteria to evaluate the effectiveness of their classmates' presentations.

R RESOURCE MANAGER—Copy Master
Speaking and Listening p. 501

S STANDARDS LESSON FILE
Speaking and Listening Lesson 9: Oral Interpretation

Assessment Practice

CHECK READINESS

Read aloud the paragraph under **ASSESS** and stress to students that this is not the full Unit Test, but a way for them to check their readiness for it. Then have students examine the skills listed under **REVIEW** and look back in the unit or in the **Student Resource Bank** for any skills they need to review.

READ THE SELECTIONS

Remind students to keep unit goals in mind as they read the selections, paying particular attention to these literary and reading skills:

- character motivation and traits
- irony
- tone
- imagery
- make inferences
- media: persuasive techniques

To help students focus on irony while reading, encourage them to ask questions such as:

- What is ironic about the phrase "few enough eggs" in *Death in the Woods* (line 2)?
- What is ironic about the fact that a plum gives solace in "To a Poor Old Woman"?

ANSWER THE QUESTIONS

Direct students to pages R96–R103 of the **Test-Taking Handbook** to review test-taking strategies.

- Remind students not to choose the first alternative that seems to fit when answering a multiple-choice question. Instead, they should read through all the choices, eliminate any that are clearly wrong, and then choose the *best* answer—the one that is most accurate and complete.

- Remind students to avoid the pitfall of looking for patterns in the answer choices. Students should evaluate each set of answer choices without regard to letter, focusing only on the content of each choice.

ASSESS
The practice test items on the next few pages match skills listed on the Unit Goals page (page 820) and addressed throughout this unit. Taking this practice test will help you assess your knowledge of these skills and determine your readiness for the Unit Test.

REVIEW
After you take the practice test, your teacher can help you identify any skills you need to review.

- Character Motivation and Traits
- Irony
- Tone
- Imagery
- Make Inferences
- Media: Persuasive Techniques
- Etymology
- Latin Roots and Words
- Infinitive Phrases
- Vivid Adjectives

ASSESSMENT ONLINE
For more assessment practice and test-taking tips, go to the **Assessment Center** at ClassZone.com.

Reading Comprehension

DIRECTIONS *Read these selections and answer the questions that follow.*

from Death in the Woods
Sherwood Anderson

The stock in the barn cried to her hungrily, the dogs followed her about. In the winter the hens laid few enough eggs. They huddled in the corners of the barn and she kept watching them. If a hen lays an egg in the barn in the winter and you do not find it, it freezes and breaks.

One day in winter the old woman went off to town with a few eggs and the dogs followed her. She did not get started until nearly three o'clock and the snow was heavy. She hadn't been feeling very well for several days and so she went muttering along, scantily clad, her shoulders stooped. She had an old grain bag in which she carried her eggs, tucked away down in the bottom. There weren't 10 many of them, but in winter the price of eggs is up. She would get a little meat in exchange for the eggs, some salt pork, a little sugar, and some coffee perhaps. It might be the butcher would give her a piece of liver.

When she had got to town and was trading in her eggs, the dogs lay by the door outside. She did pretty well, got the things she needed, more than she had hoped. Then she went to the butcher and he gave her some liver and some dog-meat.

It was the first time anyone had spoken to her in a friendly way for a long time. The butcher was alone in his shop when she came in and was annoyed by the thought of such a sick-looking old woman out on such a day. It was bitter cold and the snow, that had let up during the afternoon, was falling again. The 20 butcher said something about her husband and her son, swore at them, and the old woman stared at him, a look of mild surprise in her eyes as he talked. He said that if either the husband or the son were going to get any of the liver or the heavy bones with scraps of meat hanging to them that he had put into the grain bag, he'd see him starve first.

Starve, eh? Well, things had to be fed. Men had to be fed, and the horses that weren't any good but maybe could be traded off, and the poor thin cow that hadn't given any milk for three months.

Horses, cows, pigs, dogs, men.

DIFFERENTIATED INSTRUCTION

FOR ENGLISH LEARNERS
Assessment Practice: Work Backward
Prepare students by having them read the questions *before* reading the passages. Have pairs find unfamiliar words in test directions and questions and follow these steps:

1. Write each word on an index card.
2. Look up the meaning in a dictionary and write it on the back of the card.

3. Use the cards to practice the words with your partner and to teach them to others.

Culture: Clarify Point out the poster on page 1081. Explain that during World War II, the U.S. government asked citizens to grow as much of their own food as possible. These "Victory Gardens," as they were known, allowed citizens to be as self-reliant as possible and also freed up manufacturing efforts to create food and supplies for the armed forces.

To a Poor Old Woman

William Carlos Williams

munching a plum on
the street a paper bag
of them in her hand

They taste good to her
5 They taste good
to her. They taste
good to her

You can see it by
the way she gives herself
10 to the one half
sucked out in her hand

Comforted
a solace of ripe plums
seeming to fill the air
15 They taste good to her

World War II Poster

PLANT A VICTORY GARDEN

OUR FOOD IS FIGHTING

A GARDEN WILL MAKE YOUR RATIONS GO FURTHER

Public service poster from the
United States Office of War
Information, 1943

GO ON →

COMPREHENSION AND WRITTEN RESPONSE	ITEMS	UNIT PAGES
Character Motivation and Traits	3, 6, 17	937
Irony	7, 10, 15	1033
Tone	1, 2, 16	859, 889
Imagery	5, 8, 11	881, 913
Make Inferences	4, 6, 9, 12, 17	913, 969
Media: Persuasion	13, 14	965

VOCABULARY	ITEMS	UNIT PAGES
Etymology	1, 2, 3, 4, 5	1030
Latin Roots and Words	6, 7, 8, 9	1016

WRITING AND GRAMMAR	ITEMS	UNIT PAGES
Infinitive Phrases	1, 4, 5	911
Vivid Adjectives	2, 3	919

FOR STRATEGIC READERS

Assessment Support Consider these options for completing the Assessment Practice:

- Have students "work backward" to review the test questions *before* reading the passage.

- Select random questions in the Assessment, and have students demonstrate *how* and *where* to look for the answers.

- Ask students to locate unfamiliar words in the Assessment. Elicit the words' meanings from the class.

- Have students record useful testing words and definitions in their journals for later reference.

- Read the selection or parts of it aloud to aid in student comprehension.

McDougal Littell **Assessment System**

After checking student readiness with this Assessment Practice, you may administer the complete Unit 5 Test in order to more thoroughly evaluate student mastery of unit goals.

ANSWERS

Comprehension

Model a thinking process for answering multiple-choice questions.

1. **A is correct.** The narrative is factual and objective. B is incorrect because the tone is not menacing despite the woman's situation. C is incorrect because the story is realistic. D is incorrect because the story is serious.

2. **A is correct.** The excerpt does not directly state the woman's condition. B is incorrect because the language is objective. C is incorrect because the situation described is clear. D is incorrect because the diction is conversational.

3. **C is correct.** The butcher seems angry that the woman is sick and outside on a cold day. A is never suggested in the excerpt. B is incorrect because he willingly gives to her. D is incorrect because he is friendly.

4. **A is correct.** The butcher implies that the husband and son neglect the woman. B is incorrect because he mentions no enemies. C is never suggested in the text. D is incorrect because he does speak to her.

5. **C is correct.** Images of few eggs and a dried-up cow convey poverty and hunger. A is unjustifiable. B is incorrect because the woman is busy. D is incorrect because her activities have a point, which is to survive.

6. **B is correct.** She goes to town to sell eggs and buy provisions. A is incorrect because she does not try to escape. C is incorrect because socializing is not her intent. D is incorrect because no doctor is mentioned.

7. **C is correct.** "Men" appears in the same list as the animals. A is incorrect because she does not show resentment. B and D are true of the story but irrelevant to the irony.

8. **D is correct.** The lines evoke the street and the woman eating plums. A is incorrect because the image does not dictate the form. B is incorrect because the speaker's attitude is unclear. C is incorrect because her appearance is not described.

9. **D is correct.** The woman experiences momentary pleasure eating plums. A is incorrect because the poem does not describe variety. B is incorrect because she does not seek freedom. C is a weaker choice because it is not about the plums.

Comprehension

DIRECTIONS *Answer these questions about the excerpt from "Death in the Woods."*

1. Which word best describes the tone in this excerpt?
   A matter-of-fact
   B menacing
   C fanciful
   D witty

2. The tone is conveyed through language that is
   A understated
   B emotional
   C ambiguous
   D formal

3. The butcher's reaction to the woman in lines 17–18 suggests that he
   A would like to marry her
   B resents her begging
   C feels sorry for her
   D finds her repulsive

4. From the butcher's remarks in lines 20–24 you can infer that the woman's family
   A treats her badly
   B has many enemies
   C is related to the butcher
   D does not communicate with her

5. The images of winter in the excerpt emphasize that the woman's life is
   A peaceful and fulfilling
   B boring and idle
   C cold and bitter
   D pointless and tragic

6. The woman goes into town because she
   A wants to escape from her cruel husband and son
   B thinks it is her duty to feed the people and animals on the farm
   C is looking for someone friendly to talk to
   D needs to find a doctor to treat her illness

7. You can tell that line 28 is ironic because
   A the animals need to eat, but the woman resents their hunger
   B the author doesn't explain why the woman is the only person living on the farm who cares for the animals
   C the reader expects men and animals to be thought of differently, but the woman does not distinguish between them
   D the woman is hungry, too, but she does not admit it

DIRECTIONS *Answer these questions about the poem "To a Poor Old Woman."*

8. The vivid image in lines 1–3 establishes the
   A form of the poem
   B speaker's attitude
   C old woman's appearance
   D poem's setting and subject

9. Which inference is most clearly supported by the poem?
   A Variety is the essence of life.
   B Freedom is worth any sacrifice.
   C Old age often brings loneliness and poverty.
   D Pleasure can be found in a momentary experience.

1082

10. **B is correct.** The contrast between poverty and the joy of eating is unexpected. A, C, and D are incorrect because although they make valid statements about the poem, those statements are not related to irony.

11. **C is correct.** Plums that "fill the air" implies scent. A, B, and D are incorrect because "fill the air" does not evoke those senses.

12. **A is correct.** Plums are simple things. The woman in the story works hard to get and sell eggs. B is incorrect because the poem does not say that the woman lives on the street. C is incorrect because family is not mentioned in the poem. D is incorrect because neither woman seems especially curious or sensitive.

10. Which statement explains the irony in the poem?

    A Images in the poem focus on an everyday activity.

    B The title suggests hardship, but the poem expresses enjoyment.

    C The reader never learns what the poet thinks of his subject.

    D The theme of the poem is implied, but it is never directly stated.

11. The image of "a solace of ripe plums / seeming to fill the air" (lines 13–14) appeals to the reader's sense of

    A sight

    B taste

    C smell

    D touch

DIRECTIONS *Answer this question about both selections.*

12. Which statement best describes the women?

    A The woman in the poem enjoys simple things; the woman in the story works hard.

    B The woman in the poem lives on the street; the woman in the story owns a farm.

    C The woman in the poem is a grandmother; the woman in the story is a beggar.

    D The woman in the poem is curious; the woman in the story is sensitive.

DIRECTIONS *Answer these questions about the poster.*

13. The words and images in the poster work together to

    A contrast each generation's wartime work

    B connect family gardens and military victory

    C illustrate the backbreaking nature of farming

    D emphasize the importance of financial prosperity

14. The slogan "Our Food Is Fighting" suggests that

    A fresh food builds a soldier's health and strength

    B in wartime, food is more important than fighting

    C those who don't fight will not have food to eat

    D people can help the war effort by growing food at home

Written Response

SHORT RESPONSE *Write three or four sentences to answer each question.*

15. In what way do the authors of "Death in the Woods" and "To a Poor Old Woman" use irony to help convey their ideas?

16. Describe the tone in "To a Poor Old Woman." Support your answer with details from the poem.

EXTENDED RESPONSE *Write two or three paragraphs to answer this question.*

17. What can you infer about the character of the woman in "Death in the Woods"? Cite two qualities that she exhibits and support your answer with details from the story.

GO ON

13. B is correct. *The poster implies that growing a garden helps the war effort. A is incorrect because no contrast is made between generations. C is incorrect because the poster encourages gardening. D is incorrect because prosperity is irrelevant.*

14. D is correct. *The slogan implies that efforts on the home front aid the military. A is incorrect because the poster does not invoke soldiers' health and strength. B is incorrect because the poster does not imply that fighting is less important. C is incorrect because the poster does not imply that fighting affects gardening.*

Written Response

Possible short responses:

15. *Irony in the story comes from the woman seeing people as equivalent to animals, from the fact that she works so hard for so little, and the fact that she works dutifully for whose who take advantage of her. Irony in the poem comes from the disjunction between the woman's poverty and the deep pleasure she takes in the momentary experiences of life.*

16. *The tone might be described as informal, detached, curious, and sympathetic. Details will vary but might include the simple, repetitive language, nonjudgmental tone, and evident enjoyment of the woman's pleasure in eating.*

Possible extended response:

17. *Qualities she exhibits might include stoicism, responsibility, hard-working nature, and submissiveness. Details will vary but might include the fact that she performs her work uncomplainingly while cold and ill. Students may also note that the woman is passive and timid, responding with surprise to the butcher's suggestion that her husband and son treat her ill.*

DIFFERENTIATED INSTRUCTION

FOR ENGLISH LEARNERS

Assessment Vocabulary To help students understand the Comprehension questions, teach or review these key vocabulary words:

- Item 1: *excerpt*—"part of a longer work"
- Item 2: *conveyed*—"shown"
- Item 5: *emphasize*—"highlight," "stress"
- Item 8: *establishes*—"shows"
- Item 14: *slogan*—"short, memorable phrase"

Vocabulary

1. **C is correct.** Scantily and skant are very close in sound. A bears no phonic relationship to skant. B begins similarly to skant but is not as close as scantily is. D is more phonically distant than B.

2. **B is correct.** Huddled is very close in sound to hudeln. A and D bear no phonic relation to hoderen or hudeln. C begins with the same letter as those words but is not as close as huddled.

3. **D is correct.** The sounds of boc and butcher are similar and the meaning "male goat" evokes a connection to butchering. A has no phonic connection to boc. B and C share only the /b/ sound with boc.

4. **A is correct.** Biter and bitter are close in sound and meaning. B and D are close in meaning but not in sound. C shares only an initial /b/ sound with biter.

5. **C is correct.** Winter and wintruz are close in sound, and winter can be wet. A and B are close in meaning to "wet" but are phonically unrelated to wintruz. D is not as phonically close to wintruz as winter is.

6. **A is correct.** Victory is a conquering of the opponent. B and C have /v/ sounds but are unrelated in meaning to victory. D is not equivalent to victory in meaning.

7. **D is correct.** Paper and papyrus are very close in sound. A, B, and C also begin with p but are more distant in sound.

8. **D is correct.** Exchange and barter are similar concepts and the /ch/ and /k/ sounds are related. A and C are unrelated in sound to cambire. B is remote in meaning.

9. **C is correct.** Both the sounds and meanings of pretium and price are related. A and D are unrelated in both aspects. B is phonically more distant from pretium.

Vocabulary

DIRECTIONS *Use the underlined etymology clues to help you choose the correct word that is missing from each of the following sentences.*

1. The ground was (Middle English *skant,* "insufficient," from Old Norse *skammr,* "short") covered by thatches of parched grass.
   - **A** barely
   - **B** scarcely
   - **C** scantily
   - **D** starkly

2. The campers (Middle English *hoderen,* "to crowd together," probably from Low German *hudeln*) around the fire to warm themselves.
   - **A** danced
   - **B** huddled
   - **C** herded
   - **D** came

3. The (Middle English, from Old French *boc,* "male goat") had a physically demanding job.
   - **A** son
   - **B** barber
   - **C** husband
   - **D** butcher

4. People turned up their collars against the (Middle English, from Old English *biter,* "biting") north wind.
   - **A** bitter
   - **B** heavy
   - **C** blustery
   - **D** raw

5. The cold (Middle English, from Old English, from Germanic *wintruz,* from Proto-Indo-European *wed,* "wet") kept people indoors for three months each year.
   - **A** showers
   - **B** snow
   - **C** winter
   - **D** weather

DIRECTIONS *Use context clues and your knowledge of Latin words and roots to answer the following questions.*

6. The word *victory* in the headline of the World War II poster comes from the Latin word *vincere.* What is the meaning of *vincere*?
   - **A** conquer
   - **B** avoid
   - **C** vacate
   - **D** fight

7. Which word from the selections most likely comes from the Latin word *papyrus*?
   - **A** plums
   - **B** poor
   - **C** piece
   - **D** paper

8. The Latin word *cambire* means "to barter." Which word in "Death in the Woods" most likely comes from the word *cambire*?
   - **A** starve
   - **B** carried
   - **C** followed
   - **D** exchange

9. The Latin word *pretium* means "reward, prize, or worth." Which word in "Death in the Woods" most likely comes from the word *pretium*?
   - **A** grain
   - **B** piece
   - **C** price
   - **D** eggs

1084

DIFFERENTIATED INSTRUCTION

FOR ENGLISH LEARNERS

Review Academic Vocabulary On the board, list the academic vocabulary shown in italics below. Then give the corresponding examples in random order and have students classify them. Elicit additional examples from students.

- *image:* In the excerpt from *Death in the Woods,* the butcher's gift to the woman is described as "heavy bones with scraps of meat hanging to them."

- *tone:* The narrator of *Death in the Woods* seems to pity the old woman.

- *irony:* In "To a Poor Old Woman," the woman is poor but she enjoys life richly.

Writing & Grammar

DIRECTIONS *Read this passage and answer the questions that follow.*

(1) In second grade, my teacher took our class on a special "trip." (2) We decorated our room with posters and Japanese paper, and we ate sushi with chopsticks. (3) One poster showed <u>a garden soaked in rainwater</u>. (4) I remember thinking how beautiful it was. (5) There was something exotic in those garden trees that I just had to experience for myself. (6) Years later, I <u>finally did</u>.

1. Choose the correct way to rewrite sentence 1 by using an infinitive phrase.
   A In second grade, my teacher took our class on a special "trip" for a day.
   B In second grade, my teacher took our class on a special "trip" to visit the island country of Japan.
   C In second grade, my teacher took our class on a special "trip" that I'll never forget.
   D In second grade, my teacher took our class on a special "trip of a lifetime."

2. Choose the best way to rewrite sentence 2 by adding vivid adjectives.
   A We eagerly decorated our room with posters and Japanese paper, and we ate cold sushi with chopsticks.
   B We decorated our room with vibrant posters and silky Japanese paper, and we ate spicy sushi with chopsticks.
   C We decorated our plain room with nice posters and Japanese paper, and we ate sushi with our chopsticks.
   D We decorated our classroom with posters and Japanese paper, and we even ate great sushi with chopsticks.

3. Choose the best way to add vivid adjectives to the underlined part of sentence 3.
   A a lush, sculpted garden soaked in glistening rainwater
   B a large, green garden soaked in rainwater
   C a pretty garden soaked in cold rainwater
   D a tranquil garden soaked in some rainwater

4. Choose the revision of sentence 4 that contains an infinitive phrase.
   A I remember thinking how beautiful the trees looked draping over the pond.
   B I remember thinking how beautiful it was and how I'd never seen anything like it before.
   C I remember thinking how beautiful and unusual it was.
   D I remember thinking how beautiful it was and how much I'd like to visit it someday.

5. Choose the correct way to replace the underlined part of sentence 6 with an infinitive phrase.
   A went to Japan
   B saw them for myself
   C got to see them in person
   D visited Japan

STOP

1085

ANSWERS

Writing & Grammar

1. **B is correct.** *The infinitive phrase is "to visit the island country of Japan." A is incorrect because "for a day" is a prepositional, not an infinitive, phrase. C is incorrect because "that I'll never forget" is a clause, not a phrase, and contains no infinitive. D is incorrect because "of a lifetime" is a prepositional phrase.*

2. **B is correct.** *Vibrant, silky, and spicy are vivid adjectives. A is incorrect because eagerly is an adverb, not an adjective. C and D are incorrect because nice and great are not vivid adjectives.*

3. **A is correct.** *Lush, sculpted, and glistening are vivid adjectives. B is incorrect because no adjective is added to rainwater and large is not vivid. C and D are incorrect because pretty and some are not vivid.*

4. **D is correct.** *The infinitive phrase is "to visit it someday." A is incorrect because "draping over the pond" is a verbal, not an infinitive, phrase. B is incorrect because "I'd never seen anything like it before" is a clause, not a phrase, and contains no infinitive. C is incorrect because the addition of "and unusual" does not add a phrase or an infinitive.*

5. **C is correct.** *The infinitive phrase is "to see them in person." A is incorrect because "to Japan" is not an infinitive form of a verb but instead includes the word to as a preposition preceding a noun. B and D contain no infinitives.*

FOR STRATEGIC READERS

Assessment Support: Vivid Adjectives and Infinitive Phrases

- Review with students that vivid phrases provide clear, concrete images that help the reader visualize specific things.

- Ask students to find vivid adjectives in the excerpt from *Death in the Woods* and "The Poor Old Woman."

- Review with students that the infinitive of a verb is the form beginning with *to,* and an infinitive phrase consists of the infinitive of a verb followed by words related to the action.

- Ask students to find an infinitive phrase in the excerpt from "To a Poor Old Woman." Point out that while the word *to* appears many times in the poem, it is used as a preposition except in the phrase "to fill the air" (line 14).

INTRODUCE *GREAT READS*

In Unit 5, students have discussed a number of big questions. Invite students to tell which question they found most intriguing and why, and then focus attention on the four questions that appear on pages 1086–1087. Discuss the recommended books and their summaries, pointing out how each connects to the related question. Encourage students to choose one or more of these "great reads" to study independently.

ℹ️ ClassZone.com

To find additional books that match students' interests and ability levels, visit the Literature Center at **ClassZone.com**.

Ideas for Independent Reading

Continue exploring the Questions of the Times on pages 822–823 by reading these additional works.

What is MODERN?

Prufrock and Other Observations
by T. S. Eliot

This volume contains 12 early poems by T.S. Eliot, including "The Love Song of J. Alfred Prufrock," regarded by some as the first modernist poem. The collection also includes "Portrait of a Lady," "Preludes," and "Rhapsody on a Windy Night,"three other great poems about loneliness and alienation. Ezra Pound praised the book for "its fine tone, its humanity, and its realism."

Spoon River Anthology
by Edgar Lee Masters

This is Edgar Lee Masters's best-known work, a collection of free-verse monologues written in the voices of inhabitants of a small-town cemetery. The interconnected poems reveal the hidden loves, thwarted longings, and bitterness of people who lived and died in the confines of a small town.

The Autobiography of Alice B. Toklas
by Gertrude Stein

Gertrude Stein was at the center of a sparkling community of American writers who lived in Europe following World War I. She knew Picasso, Matisse, Joyce, Hemingway, and other important modernist figures. This book is her memoir of those heady days in Paris, playfully written in the voice of her lifelong companion, Alice B. Toklas.

Can ideals survive CATASTROPHE?

The Sun Also Rises
by Ernest Hemingway

After the end of World War I, a group of American expatriates in Europe try to wrest pleasure from a life that has lost meaning. They meet in Paris bistros, fish in the trout streams of Spain, and watch bullfights in Pamplona. Can such pleasures compensate them for their lost illusions? *The Sun Also Rises* leaves this question unanswered.

Blood on the Forge
by William Attaway

Following World War I, three African-American brothers—Big Mat, Chinatown, and Melody—flee the rural South for jobs in the steel mills of Pittsburgh. In search of a better life, they instead find dangerous work, terrible living conditions, and ethnic conflict. Each of the three brothers copes with his new life in a different way.

Waiting for Lefty
by Clifford Odets

During the time of reexamination that followed the Great Depression, the plays of Clifford Odets were a jolt of working-class lightning. Their affirmation of hope energized theatergoers from coast to coast. *Waiting for Lefty* dramatizes the courage and doubts of a group of cabdrivers who are debating whether to strike for a living wage.

1086

How can people honor their HERITAGE?

The Souls of Black Folk
by W. E. B. Du Bois

This collection of essays, published in 1903, is unified by the idea of African-Americans' "double consciousness." As Americans, they are heirs to the nation's ideals of liberty and equality. But as a despised minority, they are barred from full participation in these ideals. W.E.B. Du Bois describes the struggles African Americans face and the gifts they offer the nation.

Their Eyes Were Watching God
by Zora Neale Hurston

Zora Neale Hurston brings an all-black Florida town to life in this moving love story. Janie Crawford has been taught by a fearful grandmother to value economic security over love. She marries an ambitious businessman who views her as a trophy rather than as a partner. When he dies, Janie finds fulfillment with the younger, free-spirited Tea Cake.

Cane
by Jean Toomer

Cane is a groundbreaking work of the Harlem Renaissance by a writer of mixed ancestry. It is composed of stories, poems, vignettes, and a short play. Part I, set in rural Georgia, presents the beauty of the land and the violence residents inflict on one another. Part II, set in the urban North, portrays a world of spiritual deadness. In Part III, a figure resembling Jean Toomer returns to the South to seek his identity.

What drives HUMAN BEHAVIOR?

As I Lay Dying
by William Faulkner

The dying wish of Addie Bundren, the wife of a Mississippi farmer, is to be buried in the county seat with the rest of her family. Her husband and children place her coffin in a wagon and undertake a dangerous odyssey. In a series of interior monologues, the characters—even the dead Addie—reveal the complex motivations that spur them forward.

Babbitt
by Sinclair Lewis

This satirical novel added a new word to American speech—*babbitt,* meaning "a smugly conventional person." When George Babbitt, a successful Midwestern businessman of the 1920s, rebels against his empty, conformist life, his friends reject him. Eventually he realizes that he is too old to rebel but that he can support his son's unconventional dreams.

Native Son
by Richard Wright

In this classic American novel, Wright questions whether people who are born poor, without any real opportunities, can ever be "free." Bigger Thomas is an impoverished African-American youth who resents the world of white power around him. Hired as a chauffeur by a white millionaire, he commits a shocking crime that seems oddly predestined. Who is responsible for Bigger's tragic life?

1087

Preview Unit Goals

This page presents an overview of the skills and strategies covered in this unit. Explain to students that they can get more from their reading by previewing. Then ask them to skim the page to preview the skills that they will learn. Note that each strand or category of skill is color-coded on this page and throughout the unit.

Model the strategy of copying the Academic Vocabulary and writing a preliminary definition for each term. Suggest that students use a journal or a notebook for this purpose. Encourage them to use the terms in discussions and in writing. Also urge students to revisit each term throughout the unit and to refine its meaning.

ADDITIONAL UNIT GOALS

These skills will be taught in this unit but are not the major focus of the unit:

Literary Analysis
- Identify characteristics of essays, poems, short stories, personal essays, letters, and autobiographies

Reading
- Identify and analyze methods of characterization
- Identify and analyze internal and external conflict
- Analyze and evaluate structure (flashback, frame story)
- Analyze and evaluate an eyewitness account
- Analyze and interpret author's message
- Analyze a personal essay
- Draw conclusions from a primary source

Writing and Grammar
- Use rhetorical devices, including parallelism
- Use informal language to create a conversational style
- Support an opinion
- Write a persuasive editorial
- Create mood
- Write to synthesize ideas into a poem
- Use the Internet to research topics
- Write to reflect on a writer's contributions

Speaking, Listening, and Viewing
- Present an oral reading of a poem
- Create a collage representing the diversity of contemporary American literature

Vocabulary
- Determine the meaning of analogies by analyzing comparisons and relationships

---

UNIT 6

CALIFORNIA

Included in this unit: R1.2, R1.3, R2.1, R2.2, R2.4, R2.5, R2.6, R3.1, R3.2, R3.3, R3.4, R3.5, R3.7, R3.8, R3.9, W1.1, W1.2, W1.3, W1.4, W1.6, W1.9, W2.1, W2.2, W2.3, W2.6, LC1.1, LS1.1, LS1.2, LS1.3, LS1.10, LS2.4, LS2.5

Preview Unit Goals

LITERARY ANALYSIS
- Understand and analyze historical and cultural context of contemporary literature
- Identify and interpret allusions
- Identify and interpret rhetorical devices, including paradox and repetition
- Identify and analyze tone, imagery, voice, personification, and sound devices

READING
- Identify and evaluate key ideas
- Identify main ideas and supporting details
- Analyze and trace elements of an argument, including claim, reasons, evidence, and counterargument
- Identify the general principle or assumption in an argument

WRITING AND GRAMMAR
- Write a problem-solution essay
- Use word choice, sentence structure, and tone to establish voice
- Use word choice, imagery, and tone to create mood

SPEAKING, LISTENING, AND VIEWING
- Create a Web site
- Analyze the impact of media on audience perceptions
- Compare and contrast perspectives in news reports

VOCABULARY
- Understand and use Greek prefixes to determine word meaning
- Use context clues to determine the meaning of idioms

ACADEMIC VOCABULARY
- historical context
- cultural context
- general principle
- allusion
- rhetorical devices
- elements of an argument
- contemporary literature

Online **LITERATURE** CLASSZONE.COM

Literature and Reading Center
Writing Center
Vocabulary Center

1088

DIFFERENTIATED INSTRUCTION

FOR ENGLISH LEARNERS

Academic Vocabulary Use the copy master to help students learn the Academic Vocabulary.

1. Read aloud each Academic Vocabulary term on page 1088 and have students locate it on their copy masters.

2. Discuss the meaning or example shown on the copy master, and complete the chart as a class.

3. Have students work in small groups to complete the remaining activities.

Additional Academic Vocabulary Use the copy master to help students learn academic words they will use in subsequent lessons and on the Assessment Practice. Follow the same procedure as for the Academic Vocabulary copy master.

 RESOURCE MANAGER—Copy Masters
Academic Vocabulary p. 11
Additional Academic Vocabulary p. 12

Contemporary Literature

Sandra Cisneros

1940–PRESENT
NEW PERSPECTIVES

- Modern American Drama
- Responses to War

- Civil Rights and Protest Literature
- A Mosaic of American Voices

1089

For help in planning this unit, see

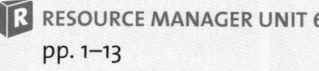 **RESOURCE MANAGER UNIT 6**
pp. 1–13

INTRODUCE THE UNIT

Call students' attention to the pictures on this page. Explain that the large picture, *Man in Red* (2003), was created by Diana Ong. Its medium is computer graphics and it reflects the diversity in both artistic media and subject matter that students will encounter in the selections in Unit 6.

Ask students if they are familiar with the writer Sandra Cisneros, shown in the smaller picture on the page. Explain that Cisneros (born 1954) is an award-winning author of fiction, essays, and poetry. Drawing on her background as the daughter of a Mexican father and a Chicana mother, Cisneros's works made her one of the first commercially successful Hispanic American writers. Tell students that they will read one of her essays, "Straw into Gold: The Metamorphosis of the Everyday," in this unit. Also note that students can read more about Cisneros on page 1222.

About the Art Diana Ong (born 1940) is a Chinese-American artist.

Unit Resources

PRINT RESOURCES

 RESOURCE MANAGER UNIT 6

BEST PRACTICES TOOLKIT

STANDARDS LESSON FILE

CALIFORNIA ASSESSMENT FILE

GRAMMAR FOR WRITING

TECH RESOURCES

EasyPlanner DVD-ROM

WriteSmart CD-ROM

ClassZone.com

Audio Anthology CD

Multi-Language Academic Vocabulary Online

eEdition DVD-ROM & Online

McDougal Littell Assessment System

Test Generator CD-ROM

MediaSmart DVD-ROM

Literature in Context DVD-ROM

	Unit 6 Introduction pp. 1090–1105 • Questions of the Times • Historical Essay • Timeline • Legacy of the Era from 1940 to the Present	Literary Analysis Workshop • Voice in Contemporary Literature pp. 1202–1203	Why Soldiers Won't Talk/The Death of the Ball Turret Gunner Essay/Poem pp. 1114–1121	Adam Themes Across Cultures: *from* Survival in Auschwitz Short Story/ Autobiography pp. 1122–1131 , 1132–1135	Ambush Short Story pp. 1136–1142
			Lexile: 940 Fry: 9 Dale-Chall: 6.4	Lexile: 740 Fry: 8 Dale-Chall: 6.2	Lexile: 940 Fry: 9 Dale-Chall: 5.6
Literary Analysis	Historical and Cultural Context of Contemporary Literature pp. 1090–1105 R3.5 Perspectives that Make Up Contemporary Literature pp. 1097–1101 R3.5	Contemporary Literature pp. 1202–1203 R3.5 Tone p. 1203 R3.3 Voice pp. 1202–1203 R3.3	Tone and Imagery pp. 1115, 1118, 1119, 1120 R3.3, R3.4	Characterization pp. 1123, 1124, 1126, 1128, 1129, 1131	Conflict pp. 1137, 1138, 1141, 1142
Reading and Informational Texts	Build Context for Reading pp. 1090–1091 Use Prior Knowledge pp. 1090–1091 Connect pp. 1090–1091, 1102–1103, 1104–1105 Take Notes pp. 1093–1100 Read a Timeline pp. 1102–1103	Analyze the Literature p. 1203 R3.3, R3.5	Adjust Reading Strategies pp. 1115, 1116, 1118, 1120 R3.4	Analyze Historical Context pp. 1123, 1126, 1127, 1128, 1129, 1131 R3.5 Read an Excerpt from an Autobiography pp. 1132–1135	Analyze Structure pp. 1137, 1138, 1140, 1142
Vocabulary		Academic Vocabulary pp. 1202–1203			
Writing, Grammar, and Style			Writing Prompt p. 1121 W1.1, W1.3 Methods for Establishing Voice pp. 1118, 1121 W1.9		
Speaking, Listening, Viewing, and Media	Discuss pp. 1090–1091, T1092–T1105	Discuss pp. T1202–T1203	Discuss pp. T1114, 1115, T1116–T1119, 1120 Analyze Visuals pp. 1116, T1119	Discuss pp. T1122, 1123, T1124–T1130, 1131, T1132–T1135 Analyze Visuals pp. 1124, 1130	Discuss pp. T1136, 1137, T1138–T1141, 1142 Analyze Visuals pp. 1138, T1141

Standards Designations R = Reading W = Writing LC = Language Conventions LS = Listening and Speaking T = Teacher's Edition page

from *Letter from Birmingham Jail* Letter pp. 1144–1159	*Linked Selections* from *Stride Toward Freedom/Necessary to Protect Ourselves* Nonfiction/Interview pp. 1160–1171	*Martin Luther King Jr.: He Showed Us the Way* Essay pp. 1172–1175	*Media Study: Perspectives in the News* TV Newscast Clip, Magazine Article pp. 1176–1179	from *Coming of Age in Mississippi* Autobiography pp. 1180–1191
Lexile: 1250 Fry: 12 Dale-Chall: 8.3	Lexile: 1060/1320 Fry: College/8 Dale-Chall: 8.8/7.3			Lexile: 880 Fry: 10 Dale-Chall: 5.9
Allusion pp. 1145, 1148, 1152, 1155, 1157	Historical Context pp. 1161, 1164, 1165, 1166, 1169, 1170			Eyewitness Account pp. 1181, 1184, 1186, 1187, 1190 R3.1
Trace the Elements of an Argument pp. 1145, 1146, 1148, 1151, 1157 R2.4, R2.6, R3.9 Read a Poem p. 1156	Compare and Contrast Authors' Beliefs pp. 1161, 1162, 1164, 1165, 1168, 1169, 1170 R2.5, R3.8	Analyze an Argument pp. 1172, 1173, 1174, 1175 R2.4, R3.8 Support an Opinion p. 1175 W1.3		Read a Primary Source pp. 1181, 1184, 1188, 1190 Read a Poem p. 1189
Word Acquisition pp. 1145, T1145, 1158 Context Clues p. T1145 Analogies p. 1158 R1.3	Word Acquisition pp. 1161, T1161, 1171 Context Clues p. T1161 Greek Prefixes (*syn-*) p. 1171 R1.2		Academic Vocabulary (TV News Reports) p. 1177 Academic Vocabulary (Magazine Article) p. 1177	
Writing Prompt p. 1159 W1.1, W1.3, W1.4 Rhetorical Devices (Parallelism) pp. 1150, 1159 LC1.1				Writing Prompt p. 1191 W1.1, W2.1 Methods for Creating Mood pp. 1186, 1191 W1.9
Discuss pp. T1144, 1145, T1146–T1155, 1156, 1157 Analyze Visuals pp. 1146, T1152	Discuss pp. T1160, 1161, T1162–T1169, 1170 Analyze Visuals pp. 1162, 1166	Discuss pp. 1172, T1173–T1174, 1175	Discuss pp. 1176, 1179 Compare and Contrast Perspectives in a News Report and a Magazine Article pp. 1177–1178 LS1.1, LS1.2, LS1.3 Create a News Feature p. 1179 W1.6, LS1.10, LS2.4	Discuss pp. T1180, 1181, T1182–T1188, 1189, 1190 Analyze Visuals p. 1182

	My Dungeon Shook: Letter to My Nephew Open Letter pp. 1192–1200	*Mother Tongue* Essay pp. 1204–1213	*from In Search of Our Mothers' Gardens* Essay pp. 1214–1221	*Straw into Gold: The Metamorphosis of the Everyday* Essay pp. 1222–1229	*Life for My Child Is Simple/Primer for Blacks* Poetry pp. 1230–1235
	Lexile: 1040 Fry: 12 Dale-Chall: 6.1	Lexile: 1120 Fry: 10 Dale-Chall: 6.7	Lexile: 1140 Fry: 8 Dale-Chall: 6.4	Lexile: 920 Fry: College Dale-Chall: 6.5	
Literary Analysis	Rhetorical Devices pp. 1193, 1196, 1197, 1199 R2.1	Personal Essay pp. 1205, 1206, 1209, 1210, 1212 R3.1	Author's Message pp. 1215, 1218, 1219, 1220, 1221 R2.5	Voice pp. 1223, 1224, 1227, 1228, 1229 R3.3	Repetition pp. 1231, 1232, 1234, 1235 R3.3
Reading and Informational Texts	Identify Ideas pp. 1193, 1197, 1198, 1199	Identify Main Ideas pp. 1205, 1208, 1211, 1212	Understand Cultural Context pp. 1215, 1216, 1218, 1221	Analyze Structure pp. 1123, 1226, 1227, 1228, 1229 R2.2	Compare and Contrast Poems pp. 1231, 1233, 1235 R3.2, R3.3
Vocabulary	Word Acquisition pp. 1193, T1193, 1200 Context Clues p. T1193 Idioms p. 1200				
Writing, Grammar, and Style		Writing Prompt p. 1213 W1.1, W1.2, W2.3 Levels of Language pp. 1208, 1213 W1.9			
Speaking, Listening, Viewing, and Media	Discuss pp. T1192, 1193, T1194–T1198, 1199 Analyze Visuals pp. 1194, T1198	Discuss pp. T1204, 1205, T1206–T1211, 1212 Analyze Visuals p. 1206	Discuss pp. T1214, 1215, T1216–T1220, 1221 Analyze Visuals p. 1216	Discuss pp. T1222, 1223, T1224–T1228, 1229 Analyze Visuals p. 1224	Discuss pp. T1230, 1231, T1232–T1234, 1235

Adolescence—III/ Testimonial Poetry pp. 1236–1241	The Man in the Moon/ Forgetfulness Poetry pp. 1242–1246	Wrap-Ups • Responses to War p. 1143 • Civil Rights & Protest Literature p. 1201 • A Mosaic of American Voices p. 1247	Writing Workshop: Problem-Solution Essay pp. 1248–1255
Sound Devices pp. 1237, 1238, 1240, 1241 R3.4	Imagery pp. 1243, 1244, 1246 R3.4		
Make Inferences About Speakers pp. 1237, 1238, 1240, 1241	Trace the Development of an Idea pp. 1243, 1244, 1245, 1246 R3.3		Analyze a Problem-Solution Essay pp. 1249–1250, 1254
		Write to Synthesize p. 1143 LS1.10 Write to Persuade p. 1201 W1.1, W1.3 Write to Reflect p. 1247 R2.5, R3.5, W2.2	Write a Problem-Solution Essay pp. 1248–1254 W1.1, W1.3 Transitions p. 1254 Active and Passive Voice p. 1254 W1.9 , LC1.1
Discuss pp. T1236, 1237, T1238–T1240, 1241 Analyze Visuals p. 1238	Discuss pp. T1242, 1243, T1244–T1245, 1246	Present an Oral Reading of a Poem p. 1143 LS2.5 Research Online and Present Findings p. 1201 Create a Collage p. 1247	Discuss pp. 1248–1250 Create a Web Site p. 1255 W2.6

Skills Assessed on the Unit 6 Test:

Literary Analysis
- Analyze historical context
- Identify and interpret allusions
- Analyze the use of repetition
- Identify author's message
- Analyze imagery

Reading and Informational Texts
- Understand the cultural context of a contemporary selection
- Identify and evaluate key ideas
- Identify main idea and supporting details

Vocabulary
- Use prefixes to help determine the meanings of words
- Use context clues and idioms to help determine the meanings of words
- Use analogies to understand the meanings of words

Writing, Grammar, and Style
- Write a problem-solution essay
- Use word choice, sentence structure, and tone to establish voice
- Use word choice, imagery, and tone to create mood
- Use parallelism for effect
- Use appropriate levels of language
- Additional writing and grammar skills

For additional lesson planning help, see **Easy Planner DVD-ROM.**

CALIFORNIA

	ASSESS PRIOR KNOWLEDGE Diagnostic	ONGOING ASSESSMENT Reteaching
BEGINNING OF UNIT		
Unit Opener	Preview Unit Goals, **TE** p. 1088	
UNIT LESSONS		
Before every lesson	Big Question activity, **SE** Preteach vocabulary, **TE**	Check Understanding, **TE**
During every lesson		Annotations, **SE** Check Understanding, **TE** Tiered Discussion Prompts, **TE**
After every lesson		Post Reading pages, **SE** Assess and Reteach, **TE** Reading Check, **RM** Selection Tests A and B/C, **AF**
END OF UNIT		
Writing Workshop	Checklist, **SE** p. 1254 Rubric for Evaluation, **RM** p. 328	Assess and Reteach, **TE** p. 1254
Publishing with Technology	Criteria, **TE** p. 1255	For reteaching options, see **TE** p. 1255
Assessment	Assessment Practice, **SE** pp. 1256–1261	Unit Test, **AF** **MLAS**

For systematic instruction of grammar, use *Grammar for Writing*.

Key to Abbreviations:
SE = Student's Edition
TE = Teacher's Edition
RM = Resource Manager
AF = Assessment File
MLAS = McDougal Littell Assessment System

Universal Access

	Strategic Reader	Benchmark	Advanced Learner	English Learner	Students with Disabilities
SE STUDENT'S EDITION					
Vocabulary strategy instruction	✔	✔	✔	✔	✔
Instructional annotations	✔	✔	✔	✔	✔
English/Spanish glossary				✔	
TE TEACHER'S EDITION					
Skill annotation support	✔	✔	✔	✔	✔
Tiered discussion prompts	✔	✔	✔	✔	✔
Differentiated instruction	✔	✔	✔	✔	✔
R RESOURCE MANAGER					
Selection summaries in four languages	✔	✔	✔	✔	✔
Skill copy masters in English and Spanish	✔			✔	
Vocabulary preteaching and support	✔			✔	✔
Additional leveled selection questions	✔		✔	✔	✔
Question support	✔	✔	✔	✔	✔
Writing support	✔	✔	✔	✔	✔
Extension activities		✔	✔		
AF ASSESSMENT FILE					
Leveled selection and unit tests		✔	✔	✔	✔
S STANDARDS LESSON FILE					
Leveled and reteaching copy masters	✔	✔	✔	✔	✔
BEST PRACTICES TOOLKIT					
Strategy bank	✔	✔	✔	✔	✔
Graphic organizers	✔	✔	✔	✔	✔
TECHNOLOGY					
WriteSmart Rubrics and student models	✔	✔	✔	✔	✔
Audio Anthology CD	✔			✔	✔
CLASSZONE					
Instructional centers	✔	✔	✔	✔	✔
Audio summaries of selections	✔			✔	✔
Multilanguage glossary				✔	

Questions of the Times

Read aloud the questions on pages 1090 and 1091 and the paragraph that follows them. Open the discussion of each idea by having students respond to the questions that conclude each paragraph. Use these notes to prompt further exploration of the ideas.

Are we responsible for the WHOLE WORLD?

Invite students to give reasons why America should or should not get involved in conflicts within, or among, other nations. Encourage students to discuss specific circumstances in which American involvement may be justified—or even mandatory.

Can America achieve EQUAL RIGHTS?

Challenge students to discuss both obvious and subtle ways in which racism and injustice continue. Prompt them to suggest how society as a whole can fight racism and prejudice. Extend the discussion by asking students to explain why Americans will—or will not—eventually become equal in one another's eyes.

UNIT 6

Questions of the Times

DISCUSS After reading these questions and talking about them with a partner, share with the class as a whole. Then read on to explore the ways in which writers of the contemporary era have dealt with the same issues.

Are we responsible for the WHOLE WORLD?

World War II brought the United States into a new role of increased power and involvement in the world, a role that expanded even further with the Cold War, Vietnam, and the "War on Terror." Do you believe America has a responsibility to intervene in other nations' conflicts? Does it have the right?

Can America achieve EQUAL RIGHTS?

In 1963, one hundred years after emancipation, African Americans still found themselves treated as second-class citizens, denied equal education, jobs, even the right to vote. The civil rights movement secured the legal right to equality, but in reality racism and injustice linger on. Do you believe America will ever achieve true equality?

What makes an
AMERICAN?

American writers of the 21st century reflect the diversity of the country itself. The United States has become a multicultural society whose citizens' experiences are endlessly varied. With no single "American experience" to bond citizens together, it seems logical to ask: What makes an American? Patriotism? Independence? Mere citizenship? Or something else?

What is the
AMERICAN
DREAM?

The Pilgrims and the Puritans dreamed of a new world where they would be free to practice their religion. Later immigrants dreamed of a country where any child could grow up to be the president. In the postwar era of the 1950s, the dream focused on consumer goods—"a car in every garage." How do you define the American dream?

What makes an
AMERICAN?

Encourage students to discuss what traits make Americans unique. Extend the discussion by comparing Americans' self-image with their image in the eyes of people in other parts of the world. Explore the reasons why Americans may see themselves differently from the way others see them.

What is the
AMERICAN
DREAM?

Prompt students to explain their concept of the American dream, encouraging them to be as specific as they can. Ask whether or not their concept is the same as that of the adults in their family, and why or why not. Extend the discussion by asking how the American dream may change in the future.

1091

- understand the historical and cultural context of contemporary literature
- understand various perspectives that make up contemporary literature, including modernism and postmodernism
- take notes by charting main ideas and details

 R3.5

To provide a motivating introduction to this unit and to give students a sense of time and place for contemporary American literature, see

 Literature in Context DVD

The following essay (pages 1092–1101) provides students with a historical context for the Unit 6 reading selections. It presents a brief overview of significant events occurring during the time period, 1940–present, and discusses key people and ideas of the times.

To get started, read and discuss the opening paragraph on page 1092. Ask students how the view of the "blue marble" adrift in the blackness of space provides a different perspective not just of the planet but also of its inhabitants. Students should recognize that the vastness of space that became so apparent during the Space Age encouraged people to see Earth in a new way: as one small part of an immense universe.

■ PREVIEW

Have students preview the historical essay by reading the **KEY IDEAS** and by skimming the heads, boldfaced terms, and **Taking Notes** side-column features. Ask volunteers to summarize what the essay is about.

Contemporary Literature
1940–PRESENT
New Perspectives

In the 1950s, America entered the Space Age—a beginning foray into our modern technological times. Looking down from space, the country's first astronauts marveled at the blue marble that was Earth floating in the blackness. From space, Earth looked peaceful and whole, with no divisions between nations, no conflict between races. It was a new way of looking at the world—just one of many new perspectives on modern life.

1092

DIFFERENTIATED INSTRUCTION

FOR STRATEGIC READERS

Preteach Academic Vocabulary

- *perspective,* "way of thinking about things, viewpoint"
- *expansionist,* "inclined to expand into new territories"
- *isolationism,* "a policy of avoiding international political alliances and economic relations"

- *atomic bomb,* "a bomb in which the release of energy from the splitting of atomic nuclei produces a tremendously powerful explosion"
- *superpower,* "an extremely powerful nation"
- *communism,* "a system in which all property is owned by the community as a whole"

Use this copy master to help students take notes on the essay, pages 1092–1101:

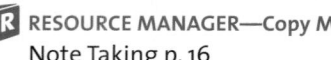 RESOURCE MANAGER—Copy Master
Note Taking p. 16

Contemporary Literature: Historical Context

R3.5
CALIFORNIA

KEY IDEAS Literature of the modern age reflects the uncertainty and anxiety brought on by the realities of war.

Modern Warfare

WORLD WAR II "Not a place on earth might be so happy as America," wrote Thomas Paine in the winter of 1776. "Her situation is remote from all the wrangling world." More than a century and a half later, as the Nazi army surged across Europe and Japan's expansionist government seized territories in Asia, many Americans still clung to the dream of isolationism—until **Pearl Harbor** woke them from their illusions.

On December 7, 1941, Japanese bombers struck the American naval base at Pearl Harbor, Hawaii, sinking ships, destroying planes, and killing over two thousand people. Though it lasted less than two hours, this surprise attack changed the course of history, bringing a reluctant United States into World War II.

The U.S. entry into the war turned the tide in favor of the Allies— England, France, and the Soviet Union—but it was a long, hard fight. By the time Germany and Japan surrendered to the Allied forces in 1945, more than 78 million people had been killed or wounded, including around six million Jews systematically murdered by the Nazis in what became known as the **Holocaust.** World War II was a catastrophe of epic dimensions, the first war in history in which more civilians than soldiers died. Never before had so many soldiers fought. Never before had such wholesale slaughter occurred. Writers such as **Randall Jarrell,** who had personal experience with the war, struggled to both document and examine the meaning of war on such a grand scale. Others, such as **Kurt Vonnegut** and **Bernard Malamud,** examined the rampant anti-Semitism that fueled the Holocaust. Malamud once remarked, "People say I write so much about misery, but you write about what you write best. As you are grooved, so you are grieved."

THE COLD WAR America came out of World War II a world power, wielding a new weapon of unparalleled destructive force: the atomic bomb. But along with strength and influence came deep uneasiness. The Soviet Union, once an ally, emerged as a rival superpower with equally large ambitions and a political system—communism—which many saw as a threat to the American way of life. Knowing any direct confrontation could end in nuclear annihilation, the two nations fought a "Cold War," each side racing to develop more and more devastating weapons while they jostled for strategic influence around the globe. As the arms race spiraled upward, ordinary citizens felt less and less secure. In literature, this pervasive fear of known and unknown dangers prompted a boom in **science fiction** writing, as writers pondered what might arise if the current trends continued.

▶ **TAKING NOTES**

Outlining As you read this introduction, use an outline to record the main ideas about the characteristics and literature of the period. You can use article headings, boldfaced terms, and the information in these boxes as starting points. (See page R49 in the **Research Handbook** for more help with outlining.)

I. *Historical Context*
  A. *World War II*
    1. isolationism
    2. Pearl Harbor
    3. Holocaust
  B. *Cold War*

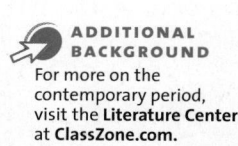
ADDITIONAL BACKGROUND
For more on the contemporary period, visit the **Literature Center** at ClassZone.com.

UNIT INTRODUCTION **1093**

CALIFORNIA

Contemporary Literature: Historical Context

KEY IDEAS This section of the essay (pages 1093–1094) summarizes the succession of conflicts that affected America and other nations of the world, including World War II, the Cold War between the United States and the Soviet Union, wars in Korea and Vietnam, and the Persian Gulf War. The text also mentions the breakup of the Soviet Union, the attack on the World Trade Center, and the U.S. invasions of Afghanistan and Iraq.

TIERED DISCUSSION PROMPTS

Use these prompts to help students understand the ideas in **Modern Warfare:**

Interpret The opening paragraph concludes with " . . . many Americans still clung to the dream of isolationism—until Pearl Harbor woke them from their illusions." What does the writer mean? *Possible answer: Americans thought they could keep from getting directly involved in events affecting Europe and Asia. However, their dream of remaining isolated proved to be an illusion when Japan attacked Pearl Harbor, Hawaii, which forced the United States to enter World War II.*

Analyze In what ways was World War II "a catastrophe of epic dimensions"? *Possible answer: It was a war of unprecedented slaughter—78 million people killed or wounded—and the first war in history in which more civilians died than soldiers. Anti-Semitism fueled the Holocaust, the Nazi murder of six million Jews and others.*

Synthesize In what sense did the Cold War directly affect even more people than previous "hot" wars? *Possible answer: The Cold War created a climate of pervasive fear in which ordinary citizens lived under the threat of nuclear annihilation.*

FOR STRATEGIC READERS

Science Fiction Explain that science fiction is fiction that deals mainly with the effects of actual or imagined science on the world and its people. These effects can be positive, as in stories describing miraculous new inventions, or negative, as in tales of robots or computers running amok. Point out that Cold War–era fears gave rise to numerous science fiction stories, novels, television shows, and movies about the dangers and consequences of nuclear war.

FOR ENGLISH LEARNERS

Set a Purpose After introducing the *KEY IDEAS,* ask students to look for details as they read about the effects of modern warfare on people and nations.

TIERED DISCUSSION PROMPTS

Use these prompts to continue the discussion of **Modern Warfare:**

Evaluate You read on page 1093 that Thomas Paine wrote: "Not a place on earth might be so happy as America. Her situation is remote from all the wrangling world." In light of subsequent events, do his words ring true? Why or why not? *Possible answers: No, his words do not ring true at all. In fact, since World War II, America has again and again become involved in conflicts and warfare with other nations of the world. Yes, he is right—the United States has not fought a war on its own soil in decades, though it did suffer terrorist attacks in 1995 and 2001.*

Synthesize John Updike wrote, "At all times an old world is collapsing and a new world arising." How does this statement reflect the global situation from 1940 to the present? *Possible answer: Violence and open warfare in various places around the globe create an unstable and ever-changing world. The spread of nuclear weapons has given rise to a world that seems to grow more precarious every year.*

CHECK UNDERSTANDING

Ask students what the Cold War was and how and when it finally ended.

MODERN CONFLICTS Meanwhile, in an effort to contain the spread of communism, the U.S. military became deeply involved in civil wars first in Korea, then in Vietnam. The longest war in American history, the **Vietnam War** lasted over 20 years and bred a degree of domestic conflict unseen since the Civil War. As the death toll among U.S. soldiers rose—reaching about 58,000 in all—many Americans questioned the wisdom of our intervention and took to the streets in protest. The literature of the time reflects the conflicts within the country. Writer **Tim O'Brien** once remarked that "It's not really Vietnam that I was concerned about . . . ; rather, it was to have readers care about what's right and wrong and about the difficulty of doing right, the difficulty of saying no to a war."

The Cold War finally came to an end with the breakup of the Soviet Union in 1991, but America was not finished with warfare. That same year, U.S. troops were sent to counter the Iraqi invasion of Kuwait in the first Persian Gulf War. A longer struggle began on September 11, 2001, when hijackers flew commercial airplanes into the Pentagon and the World Trade Center, killing thousands and leading to U.S. invasions of Afghanistan and Iraq. At the same time, violence raged around the globe, and with nuclear weapons no longer limited to two superpowers, possibilities for worldwide disaster loomed. Writers of the last several generations have been profoundly affected by the sense of instability that has been brought on by near-constant war. "At all times," wrote novelist **John Updike,** "an old world is collapsing and a new world arising."

U. S. Marines training for Operation Desert Shield, 1990

1094

DIFFERENTIATED INSTRUCTION

FOR STRATEGIC READERS
Preteach Academic Vocabulary

- *intervention,* "interference in the affairs of another nation"
- *segregation,* "forced separation of groups of people on the basis of their race"
- *protest marches,* "large groups walking together to promote an idea or cause"
- *boycott,* "refusal to deal with a business or organization as a way to force change"

FOR ADVANCED LEARNERS/AP
Research Vietnam War Protests Have students learn more about the Vietnam War and why this controversial war drew increasingly strong protest from Americans. Have students make oral presentations to the class, explaining their findings and, if possible, sharing pictures and actual news stories from the Vietnam War era. Students should include information about the draft and how it energized mass protests among young people.

Segregated drinking fountains, North Carolina

Cultural Influences

KEY IDEAS Writers have both recorded and reflected upon the civil rights movement of the 1950s and 1960s—perhaps the most important social change in modern time.

The Civil Rights Movement

The civil rights movement had its roots in protests and legal actions of the 1950s. In 1954, the Supreme Court's ***Brown v. Board of Education*** ruling struck down school segregation as unconstitutional. Other civil rights advances followed, pushed along by black and white activists who organized protest marches, boycotts, voter registration drives, and sit-ins. **Dr. Martin Luther King Jr.** emerged as a leader during these times. King advocated nonviolent civil disobedience based on the philosophies of Henry David Thoreau and Indian social reformer Mohandas Gandhi.

Sadly, many of the peaceful demonstrations of the civil rights movement were met with mob violence and police brutality. While the nation watched on television, protestors were beaten, attacked by police dogs, and sprayed with fire hoses. King himself endured repeated imprisonment for his efforts. But the violence did not stop the movement.

During the famous March on Washington in 1963, which drew 200,000 participants, demonstrators demanded civil rights legislation at the national level, backed strongly by federal enforcement. Largely as a result of King's efforts, Congress passed the 1964 **Civil Rights Act** outlawing segregation in public places and guaranteeing legal equality to black citizens. In the years since, America has still not achieved true equality and opportunity for all, yet the civil rights movement has brought it much closer to King's dream of a land where people would "not be judged by the color of their skin, but by the content of their character."

> **A Voice from the Times**
>
> *I have a dream that one day this nation will rise up and live out the true meaning of its creed: "We hold these truths to be self-evident, that all men are created equal."*
>
> —**Martin Luther King Jr.**

Cultural Influences

KEY IDEAS This section of the essay (page 1095) focuses on the civil rights movement of the 1950s and 1960s. The text highlights the important *Brown v. Board of Education* Supreme Court decision, explains the contribution of Dr. Martin Luther King Jr., and discusses the 1964 Civil Rights Act.

TIERED DISCUSSION PROMPTS

Use these prompts to help students understand the ideas in **The Civil Rights Movement:**

Summarize What important role did Dr. Martin Luther King Jr. play in the civil rights movement? ***Possible answer:*** *King was a leader of the movement and an advocate of civil disobedience as a way for African Americans to gain equality. King's work was instrumental in the passage of the 1964 Civil Rights Act, which guaranteed legal equality and outlawed racial segregation.*

Evaluate The essay writer states that "America has still not achieved true equality and opportunity for all," although the nation is much closer to King's vision of a time when people will be judged by their character rather than their skin color. Do you agree with the writer's assessment? Why or why not? ***Possible answer:*** *America has made significant progress toward equality, but there is still a long way to go. Citizens of all races have equal legal rights and equal opportunities, but far too many people still discriminate against others on the basis of personal prejudice.*

FOR STRATEGIC READERS

Civil Disobedience Explain that *civil disobedience* means refusing to obey laws as a nonviolent way of calling attention to injustice. Inspired by such leaders as Martin Luther King Jr. and Mohandas Gandhi, people in America and other parts of the world adopted the methods of civil disobedience as a means of compelling the government to change unfair laws or eliminate unjust practices.

FOR ENGLISH LEARNERS

Analyze Civil Disobedience Have students paraphrase the **KEY IDEAS.** After they read the section, ask them to list what the civil rights movement achieved and has yet to achieve.

Has Achieved	Has Yet to Achieve
African-American legal equality	true equality
racial segregation illegal	equal opportunity

FOR ADVANCED LEARNERS/AP

Research and Evaluate ***Brown v. Board of Education*** Invite students to learn more about the *Brown v. Board of Education* decision by researching the case and its impact. Have students prepare a brief report explaining how the case reversed the "separate but equal" policy of *Plessy v. Ferguson* and challenged Jim Crow laws. Students should also evaluate to what extent the *Brown v. Board of Education* decision has actually been implemented.

Ideas of the Age

KEY IDEAS This section of the essay (page 1096) discusses how the American dream has evolved over time. The text also discusses how several writers have addressed the idea of the American dream.

TIERED DISCUSSION PROMPTS

Use these prompts to help students understand the ideas in **The American Dream:**

Summarize How has the American dream changed over the years? *Possible answer: Before the 20th century, the American dream had been associated with such ideas as political and religious freedom, economic opportunity, and the chance to succeed through talent, education, and hard work. After the many challenges of the first half of the 20th century, however, many Americans narrowed the focus of the dream to the simple idea of owning a home in a safe and stable neighborhood. Before long, though, this idea expanded, as Americans placed increasing importance on material possessions.*

Synthesize If Jack Kerouac and Allan Ginsberg were alive and writing today, do you think they would they still find "shallowness and conformity" to protest in American society? Explain. *Possible answer: Probably, because people continue to overemphasize the importance of money and material things and, in general, they still strive to "keep up with the Joneses."*

Seattle-area neighborhood, 1955

Ideas of the Age

KEY IDEAS Modern writers have responded in a variety of ways to a peculiarly American philosophy: that of the American dream.

The American Dream

For earlier generations, the **American dream** had meant many things—political and religious freedom, economic opportunity, the chance to achieve a better life through talent, education, and hard work. After living through the Great Depression and two World Wars, however, many Americans in the 1950s whittled that dream down to something much simpler: the chance to own a home in a stable neighborhood.

For millions of mainly white Americans, life in the suburbs became the American dream. Families sought out communities with affordable single-family homes, good schools, shopping malls, and parking that was free and easy to find. People didn't care if their houses looked alike; they just wanted a safe place to raise their children.

As the years passed and the economy boomed, however, Americans began to add to their once-simple dream. *Things* became more important: a new television, car, or washing machine came to be seen as symbols of success. Soon the dream seemed to narrow to a vision of a consumer society in which conformity and "keeping up with the Joneses" was valued above all.

Writers from the mid-century to today have wrangled with the idea of the American dream. In the mid-'50s, **"beatniks"** such as **Jack Kerouac** and **Allen Ginsberg** protested the shallowness and conformity of American society. Dramatists such as **Arthur Miller** examined the strivings of ordinary Americans reaching for that American dream. Poets, novelists, short story writers—all have explored the many facets of the American dream.

DIFFERENTIATED INSTRUCTION

FOR STRATEGIC READERS

Taking Notes Have students record the main ideas about the American dream (page 1096) in outline form. Then ask them to trade papers, evaluate each other's work, and offer suggestions for improvement. Sample notes:

American Dream

- Earlier generations: freedom, opportunity, chance for better life

- 1950s: home in stable neighborhood

- Material things became most important

FOR ENGLISH LEARNERS

The American Dream Have students paraphrase the *KEY IDEAS*. Clarify that the **beatniks** were members of the Beat movement of the 1950s, which was characterized by certain political, social, and literary views. For example, they generally rejected the values, conventions, and conformity associated with the middle class.

Literature of the Times

KEY IDEAS The years between World War II and the present brought dramatic changes in the subjects and forms of literature, as well as a wider variety of authors represented.

Modern American Drama

In the years following World War II, some of the best and most influential writing was occurring within the community of American theater. Dramatists in the post-war years began to experiment stylistically and create works of social relevance that would prompt a revival in theater not only in America, but in Europe as well. Dramatists such as Arthur Miller and **Tennessee Williams** served as models of the liberated playwright—experimenting with stagecraft as well as modern themes often deemed provocative.

One of the most common themes explored by these playwrights was that of the American dream. "The American dream is the largely unacknowledged screen in front of which all American writing plays itself out," Arthur Miller once said. Indeed, Miller's Willy Loman, the main character in his *Death of a Salesman,* became the trademark figure of postwar American theater. A lowly salesman who has been discarded by the system to which he has mistakenly devoted his life, Willy Loman proved how the American dream could become twisted and broken.

A general disillusionment paired with an experimental style characterized many of the works of this period. While a play such as **Thornton Wilder's** *Our Town,* first produced in 1938, experimented with stagecraft by showing life literally "behind the scenes" on a stage bare of scenery, it still took a gentle view of small-town America. Works written in the 1940s and 1950s, however, were far less sympathetic. In *The Glass Menagerie* and *A Streetcar Named Desire,* for example, Southerner Tennessee Williams portrayed characters who, unsuited to modern life, retreat into the fantasy world of an earlier era. And Miller's critique of modern values in *Death of a Salesman* was found to be so threatening that Hollywood executives wanted to release the movie version along with a short film depicting the life of a salesman as blissful and carefree. Miller, however, protested.

Lorraine Hansberry's *A Raisin in the Sun,* written in 1957, looked at the American dream from the perspective of those who had been excluded. The first major Broadway play by an African-American writer, *A Raisin in the Sun* was hailed by critics as "universal," while also capturing unique aspects of the African-

Vivien Leigh and Marlon Brando in *A Streetcar Named Desire*

▶ *For Your Outline*

MODERN AMERICAN DRAMA

- postwar revival in theater
- common theme was American dream
- characterized by disillusionment and experimental style
- broke boundaries and opened doors

Literature of the Times

KEY IDEAS This section of the essay (pages 1097–1101) focuses on the mosaic of contemporary American literature since World War II:

- modern drama, including the plays of Arthur Miller, Tennessee Williams, Thornton Wilder, and Lorraine Hansberry
- literature responding to war, including that of John Hersey, John Steinbeck, Elie Wiesel, Joseph Heller, Kurt Vonnegut, and Tim O'Brien
- civil rights and protest literature, including that of Ann Petry, Richard Wright, Gwendolyn Brooks, Ralph Ellison, James Baldwin, Anne Moody, and Dudley Randall
- contrasting views expressed by Malcolm X and Martin Luther King Jr.

TIERED DISCUSSION PROMPTS

Use these prompts to help students understand the ideas in **Modern American Drama:**

Summarize What were some of the defining characteristics of post–World War II American drama? *Possible answer: Dramatists began to experiment stylistically and create socially relevant works. Dramas often addressed the American dream and expressed a general dis-illusionment.*

Analyze In what ways was Arthur Miller's *Death of a Salesman* representative of post–World War II American drama? *Possible answer: In* Death of a Salesman, *Miller focused on the American dream, one of the most common themes of the postwar years. Like many other dramatists of the time, Miller explored disillusionment through a thought-provoking work of social relevance.*

FOR STRATEGIC READERS
Preteach Academic Vocabulary

- *suburbs,* "residential neighborhoods on the edge of cities or large towns"
- *boomed,* "grew or expanded dramatically"
- *conformity,* "acting or thinking in accordance with a certain standard"
- *disillusionment,* "disappointment; dissatisfaction"

FOR ENGLISH LEARNERS

Clarify Cause and Effect Have students paraphrase the *KEY IDEAS.* Explain that changes in who was writing in America and what they were writing about can be directly linked to the historical and cultural changes discussed on pages 1093–1095. Encourage students to reread those pages for clarification.

FOR ADVANCED LEARNERS/AP

Synthesize Theme Disillusionment remains a theme in modern writing today, not just plays, but also works by novelists, poets, and filmmakers. Challenge students to identify contemporary works that address the theme of disillusionment and share their findings with the class. Discuss the kinds of disillusionment that each work addresses, and have students look for common threads.

Have students explain the significance of Lorraine Hansberry's *A Raisin in the Sun*.

TIERED DISCUSSION PROMPTS

Use these prompts to help students understand the ideas in **Responses to War:**

Analyze How have world events shaped literature in the 20th and 21st centuries? *Possible answer: Conflicts between nations frequently have erupted into war, especially World War II and the Vietnam War. Writers have struggled to come to terms with the horrors and absurdities associated with these wars. For example, some writers have addressed the subject with realistic accounts, while others have approached it with ironic humor.*

Synthesize During the Vietnam War, young men were subject to a draft, or conscription into military service. How might this fact help to explain the popularity of such writers as Heller and Vonnegut? *Possible answer: The draft drastically changed the lives of young men—or threatened to—regardless of their political views or feelings toward warfare in general. Anyone who received a draft notice was caught in circumstances beyond his control. The "cynicism toward authority and sense of helplessness in the face of huge, inhuman forces" that characterized the work of Heller and Vonnegut resonated with young people of the time because they shared the authors' feelings of cynicism and helplessness.*

American experience. Writer **James Baldwin** said of the play, "[I]n order for a person to bear his life, he needs a valid re-creation of that life, which is why, as Ray Charles might put it, blacks chose to sing the blues. This is why *Raisin in the Sun* meant so much to black people . . . . In the theater, a current flowed back and forth between the audience and the actors, flesh and blood corroborating flesh and blood—as we say, testifying. . . ." In addition, the play opened the door to writers from outside the mainstream, who would revitalize American theater in the decades to follow.

Responses to War

War, with all its moral complexities and attendant brutality, has had a strong influence on writers throughout the 20th and 21st centuries. World War II brought with it previously unimaginable horrors: millions of casualties, the genocide of the Holocaust, the use of nuclear weapons. Struggling to come to terms with such destruction, some writers worked in the **modernist** style—giving detailed, realistic, and somewhat detached accounts of the war, as if told by an outside observer such as a journalist.

In fact, much of the most powerful literature of World War II was straight nonfiction, such as war correspondent **John Hersey's** *Hiroshima,* an unforgettable account of the first hours and days after the United States dropped atomic bombs on two Japanese cities, bringing massive destruction and an end to the war. **John Steinbeck,** better known for his Depression-era literature, worked as a war correspondent as well, spending time with troops in North Africa and England. His essay "Why Soldiers Won't Talk" explores how soldiers cope with the things they have witnessed.

Many writers of this period wrote of their own experiences—including the horrors of the Holocaust. **Elie Wiesel,** who was born in Europe and became an American citizen much later in life, was taken as a 15-year-old boy to a Nazi concentration camp in Poland. His memoir, *Night,* describes his nightmarish experiences in the camp, where he was beaten, starved, and nearly worked to death. Most members of his family did not survive.

In the 1960s, **Joseph Heller's** *Catch-22* and **Kurt Vonnegut's** *Slaughterhouse-Five* introduced a new style of war literature. Both writers had seen combat in World War II, and their novels shared a dark, ironic humor that focused on the absurdity of war. One such absurdity is the "catch" in Catch-22. It refers to a mysterious Air Force regulation which asserts that any person willing to go into battle should be considered insane, yet the very act of asking to be excused would prove one's sanity—and send a pilot back into battle. With their cynicism toward authority and sense of helplessness in the face of huge, inhuman forces, Heller and Vonnegut spoke to a younger generation caught up in a very different war: Vietnam.

Where World War II had united Americans in moral certainty against a common enemy, Vietnam drove them apart. Protesters—among them

A Voice from the Times

One of the most sound ideas in dramatic writing is that, in order to create the universal, you must pay very great attention to the specific.

—Lorraine Hansberry

▶ *For Your Outline*
RESPONSES TO WAR

- war influenced 20th- and 21st-century writers
- some worked in modernist style
- others wrote powerful nonfiction
- later focus is on absurdity of war
- postmodern style questioned conventions
- some blurred line between fiction and nonfiction

DIFFERENTIATED INSTRUCTION

FOR STRATEGIC READERS

Modernist Style Clarify for students that the use of *modernist* on page 1098 refers to a style of writing that began in the early 20th century and continues through the present day. Point out early modernist writers found in Unit 5, particularly Ernest Hemingway. Emphasize that Hemingway's style in both "In Another Country" (pages 970–974) and "A New Kind of War" (pages 1050–1055) is both observant and detached. Connect this observation with the description of modernist writing on page 1098.

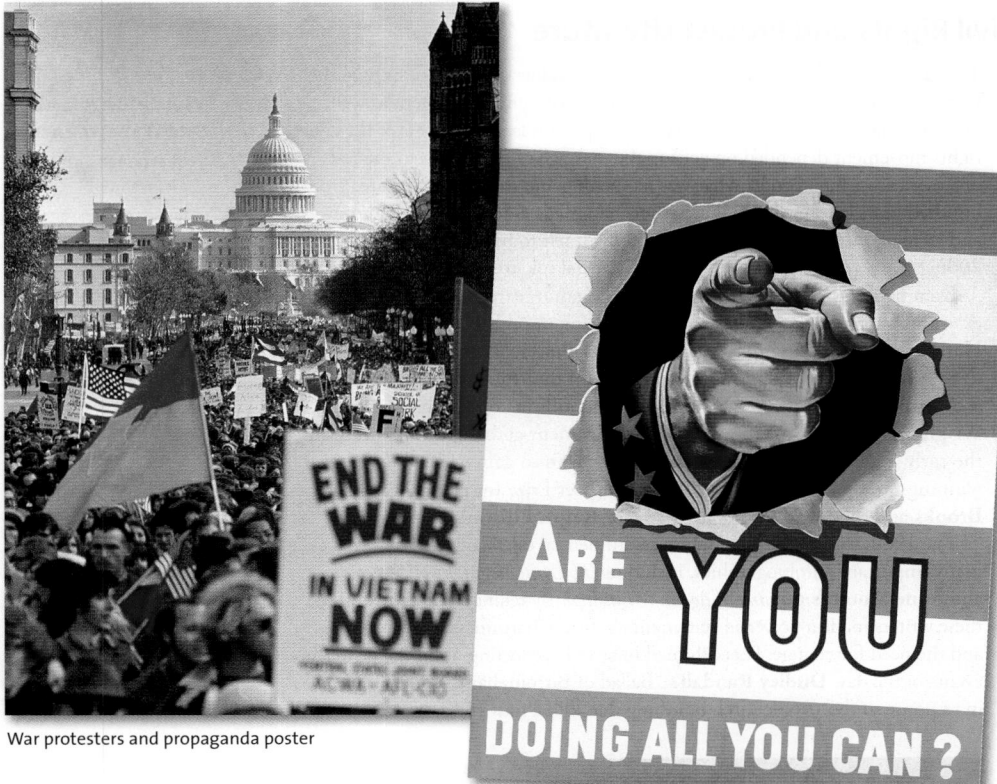

War protesters and propaganda poster

students, pacifists, and some returning veterans—marched in the streets, calling for an end to the war.

Writers of this time questioned authority, conventional values, and even the nature of reality. Some experimented with a "postmodern" style of fiction that drew attention to its own artificiality, pointing out the presence of the author by displaying its inner workings like a clock without a face. Others, like Vietnam veteran Tim O'Brien, wrote stories that blurred the lines between fiction and nonfiction. In *The Things They Carried*, O'Brien writes about telling his daughter how he killed a man in Vietnam—but this Tim O'Brien is a character, and the real O'Brien neither killed a man nor has a daughter. Can something that "didn't really happen" still be true? Postmodernism asks, What is fiction? What is truth?

ANALYZE VISUALS
The World War II propaganda poster shown here was meant to inspire support for the war. In your opinion, is it persuasive? How might the Vietnam War protesters shown in the other image have answered the question posed? How might they have responded to the intent of the poster?

ANALYZE VISUALS

Possible answer: The poster is persuasive in its use of direct address and a pointed finger, both of which arrest the viewer's attention. Protesters such as those in the photograph might have responded that they, too, were doing everything they could to end American involvement in a war that was against the country's best interests. The protesters might have objected to the poster's suggestion that patriotism can be only expressed through the unquestioning support of a war effort.

About the Art The poster represents World War II propaganda designed to increase support for the war effort. It reflects a time in America when public support for the nation's involvement in war was strong. As the photograph of Vietnam War protesters shows, many people opposed the war with a similar strength.

CHECK UNDERSTANDING
Identify ways that each writer or pair of writers responded to war:

- John Hersey and John Steinbeck
- Elie Wiesel
- Joseph Heller and Kurt Vonnegut
- Tim O'Brien

FOR STRATEGIC READERS
Preteach Academic Vocabulary

- *genocide*, "the deliberate and systematic annihilation of a racial or political group"
- *concentration camp*, "a prison camp run by Nazi Germany where prisoners endured horrible conditions and were put to death"
- *cynicism*, "contemptuous distrust of human nature, motives, and actions"
- *pacifist*, "a person opposed to war"
- *veteran*, "a person who has served in the armed forces"

FOR ADVANCED LEARNERS/AP

Research Photojournalism In addition to print responses, photography has been a crucial medium used to report the horror of war. Have students research the importance of photojournalism during World War II and Vietnam. Students might concentrate particularly on the work of:

- Joe Rosenthal
- Dickey Chapelle
- Eddie Adams
- John Filo

If possible, have students locate key photographs taken by each of these photojournalists and present them to the class. Students might then consider the relationship between the work of these photojournalists and the writers discussed on pages 1098 and 1099.

Use these prompts to help students understand the ideas in **Civil Rights and Protest Literature:**

Summarize How did African-American writers use personal experience to convey their message? Give examples. ***Possible answer:*** *African-American writers translated their personal experiences into novels, such as Ann Petry's* The Street, *Richard Wright's* Native Son, *and Ralph Ellison's* Invisible Man. *They also wrote essays and autobiographies, such as* The Autobiography of Malcolm X.

Interpret The essay writer explains, "The success of the civil rights movement depended on getting the message of justice out to the rest of America . . . ." How does this statement show the importance of writers during this period? ***Possible answer:*** *The statement acknowledges that in order for people in general—and government officials in particular—to be motivated to take action to end discrimination against African Americans, they first had to be made aware of the injustices to which minorities were being subjected. Writers played a key role in awakening the public to widespread racism and inequality and persuading people to share their concern.*

Analyze How did the viewpoints of Malcolm X and Martin Luther King Jr. differ regarding the issues affecting black people? ***Possible answer:*** *King believed in nonviolent resistance as a way to bring about change and end injustice, while Malcolm X advocated the use of militant armed resistance to fight against discrimination.*

Civil Rights and Protest Literature

The questioning of authority and conventional values applied not only to the writers of the Vietnam era but to those of the civil rights movement as well. To change laws, first it was necessary to change minds. The success of the civil rights movement depended on getting the message of justice out to the rest of America—telling people what was happening and making them care. One hundred years before, abolitionist writers had made a deep impact with novels and slave narratives that showed readers how it felt to live in bondage. In the 20th century, the written word still had a crucial role to play.

Even before the civil rights movement began in earnest, writers were examining issues of race and equality. Building upon the work of earlier Harlem Renaissance writers, black writers of the 1940s explored the dynamics of race relations and the injustice of discrimination in novels such as **Ann Petry's** *The Street,* which sold over a million copies, and **Richard Wright's** *Native Son.* As the civil rights movement gathered momentum in the early 1950s, African-American writers began to gain wider recognition, winning prestigious awards such as the Pulitzer Prize for poet **Gwendolyn Brooks** and the National Book Award for **Ralph Ellison's** *Invisible Man.*

The 1960s brought **James Baldwin's** influential essay collections as well as many important autobiographies, including *The Autobiography of Malcolm X* and **Anne Moody's** *Coming of Age in Mississippi.* By telling their own stories, these writers made a powerful statement about the harmful effects of racism and the need for change. Poets chimed in as well, reflecting upon the powerful events of the day. **Dudley Randall's** "Ballad of Birmingham," for example, was in response to the 1963 church bombing that killed four young girls.

▶ *For Your Outline*

CIVIL RIGHTS AND PROTEST LITERATURE

- questioned authority and tradition
- delivered message of justice
- examined race and equality
- reflected African-American experience
- showed varying viewpoints

A MOSAIC OF AMERICAN VOICES

- current outpouring from writers of various ethnicities
- new appreciation for diversity
- universal themes, yet rooted in culture

A Voice from the Times
We are not fighting for integration, nor are we fighting for separation. We are fighting for recognition as human beings.

—Malcolm X

Martin Luther King Jr. and Malcolm X

DIFFERENTIATED INSTRUCTION

FOR STRATEGIC READERS
Preteach Academic Vocabulary

- *abolitionist,* "advocating the abolition, or official ending, of slavery"
- *bondage,* "slavery, captivity"
- *militant,* "aggressive, warlike"
- *faction,* "a group within a larger group"
- *diversity,* "the inclusion of people of various races, cultures, and backgrounds"

The Harlem Renaissance Recall with students that the Harlem Renaissance, which occurred in the 1920s, was a period of exceptional literary productivity by African-American writers. Originating in Harlem, a part of New York City, the movement featured notable African-American writers of the time, such as Langston Hughes and Zora Neale Hurston.

Malcolm X and Martin Luther King Jr., two leaders of the civil rights movement, held opposing viewpoints on the use of violence as a means for change. Inspired by Thoreau and Gandhi, as well as the Bible, King's speeches and writings combined a steadfast belief in nonviolent resistance with a bold determination to bring an end to injustice. In his 1963 "I Have a Dream" speech, King argued, "Let us not seek to satisfy our thirst for freedom by drinking from the cup of bitterness and hatred. We must forever conduct our struggle on the high plane of dignity and discipline. We must not allow our creative protest to degenerate into physical violence." Malcolm X, on the other hand, advocated the use of militant armed resistance as a response to discrimination. "I *am* for violence," he said, "if nonviolence means we continue postponing a solution to the black man's problem—just to *avoid* violence." Their writings give readers insight into the various, and sometimes opposing, factions that made up the civil rights movement.

A Mosaic of American Voices

The last 30 years have seen an outpouring of talent from American writers of many different ethnic backgrounds, along with an increasingly widespread appreciation of diversity. Just a few decades ago, the literary scene was still dominated almost exclusively by men of European descent. Now, they have been joined by Native American writers such as **N. Scott Momaday** and **Louise Erdrich,** Asian-American writers such as **Maxine Hong Kingston** and **Amy Tan,** Hispanic writers such as **Rudolfo Anaya** and **Sandra Cisneros,** and African-American writers such as **Alice Walker, Rita Dove, Toni Morrison,** and **Maya Angelou,** to name just a few. Many of the most exciting contemporary writers are women; many, too, such as **Bharati Mukherjee** and **Edwidge Danticat,** were born outside the United States and bring a global perspective to American literature.

While earlier writers of color often focused on the experience of discrimination, writers today draw on different aspects of life in America, positive and negative, from family memories and relationships to contemporary politics. With such a broad array of published voices, no longer is any one author assumed to speak for all people of a given group. Instead, the most compelling work of today's literary marketplace is both expressive of the individual and rooted in culture and place, while still managing to speak to universal human concerns. American literature has changed, again, and will continue to evolve as long as writers continue to write.

Modern American Art

The power shift from Europe to the United States in the years after World War II had a parallel in the world of art. For the first time, international attention focused not on Paris's salon or London's Royal Academy but on the studios and galleries of New York City.

Abstract Expressionism During the 1940s and 1950s, a group of artists including **Mark Rothko** and **Jackson Pollock** dominated the New York art scene. Their style was abstract, intensely emotional, and focused as much on the process of painting as on the work itself. Jackson Pollock, who was famous for laying a giant canvas on the floor and throwing paint on it, described his art as "energy and motion made visible." Mark Rothko's signature style— floating rectangles of color aligned vertically against a colored background—is illustrated beautifully in his work *White Cloud Over Purple* (1957), shown here.

Pop Art In the early 1960s, a very different kind of art burst into public view. Pop art used familiar images from consumer culture to ask the question *What is art?* From **Andy Warhol,** with his silkscreened movie stars and soup cans, to **Roy Lichtenstein's** enormous blow-ups of comic strip panels, pop art celebrated modern methods of production while it subtly undermined the barrage of messages shaping Americans' attitudes and everyday lives.

THE ARTISTS' GALLERY

American artist Mark Rothko (1903–1970) was born in Russia and moved to the United States at the age of ten. Although Rothko is often considered an abstract expressionist, he insisted that he was not an abstract painter and was not interested in the relationship between color and form. Rather, he said he was concerned with expressing basic human emotions through his art.

Activity Ask students to reflect on Rothko's painting and describe the emotions it seems to convey. *Answers will vary.*

TIERED DISCUSSION PROMPTS

Use these prompts to help students understand the ideas in **A Mosaic of American Voices:**

Summarize Explain how diversity has increased among American writers. ***Possible answer:*** *There are many more women and people of color among contemporary American writers than in earlier historical periods.*

Analyze How has the increase in diversity changed the impact of each writer's voice? ***Possible answer:*** *Each writer's voice more specifically reflects his or her individual views and perspective rather than representing the voice of a group.*

FOR ADVANCED LEARNERS/AP

Synthesize [small-group option] Challenge students to use print and online resources to research some of the accomplishments of the civil rights movement. Students should consider in particular:

- the Civil Rights Act of 1968
- an increase in the number of African Americans holding elected office
- changes in sports, academia, and the entertainment industry

Have students present their findings to the class. The entire class should consider what work of the civil rights movement should continue in the present day. Encourage students to include in their discussion thoughts about the role of writers and journalists in keeping the movement alive.

Connecting Literature, History, and Culture

OBJECTIVES
- read a timeline
- make connections among the perspectives and events of literature, history, and culture

READING SKILL

◼ READ A TIMELINE

Point out that each of the three horizontal sections of the timeline—*American Literary Milestones, Historical Context,* and *World Culture and Events*—displays a sequence of events that occurred between 1940 and the present. By looking at the vertical columns on the timeline, students can see which events were occurring at approximately the same time.

Have students locate, for example, each of these events on the timeline between 1945 and 1948:

- **1945** The war in the Pacific ends after the United States drops atomic bombs on Japan. (See *Historical Context.*)

- **1947** *A Streetcar Named Desire* by Tennessee Williams is produced. (See *American Literary Milestones.*)

- **1948** The state of Israel is founded. (See *World Culture and Events.*)

Ask students what events occurred between 1974 and 1977. **Answer:** *President Richard M. Nixon resigned in 1974. South Vietnam surrendered in 1975. The first practical home computer reached the market in 1977.*

Connecting Literature, History, and Culture

Use this timeline and the questions on the next page to gain insight about how American developments during this period reflected those in the world as a whole.

AMERICAN LITERARY MILESTONES

1940	1950	1960
1945 Richard Wright details coming of age in *Black Boy*; Randall Jarrell publishes World War II poem "The Death of the Ball Turret Gunner."	**1951** J. D. Salinger's novel *The Catcher in the Rye* is published.	**1961** Joseph Heller's satirical war novel, *Catch-22*, is published.
1947 Tennessee Williams's *A Streetcar Named Desire* is first produced.	**1952** Bernard Malamud publishes his baseball novel, *The Natural*.	**1969** Kurt Vonnegut publishes *Slaughterhouse-Five*; N. Scott Momaday's *House Made of Dawn* wins Pulitzer Prize. ▶
	1953 Arthur Miller's *The Crucible* reflects contemporary "witch hunt" of McCarthyism.	

HISTORICAL CONTEXT

1940	1950	1960
1941 Japanese bomb Pearl Harbor, ▲ bringing United States into World War II.	**1954** In *Brown v. Board of Education*, the Supreme Court declares segregated schools unconstitutional. ▼	**1963** Martin Luther King gives "I Have a Dream" speech in Washington, D.C.; President John F. Kennedy is assassinated in Dallas.
1945 United States drops two atomic bombs on Japan, ending the war in the Pacific.	**1959** Alaska and Hawaii join the Union as the 49th and 50th states.	**1965** Malcolm X is assassinated.
		1967 Thurgood Marshall becomes the first African-American justice on the Supreme Court.
		1968 Assassinations of Martin Luther King Jr., and Robert F. Kennedy shock the nation.

WORLD CULTURE AND EVENTS

1940	1950	1960
1940 German forces conquer much of Europe.	**1953** Korean War ends.	**1965** First U.S. combat forces land in Vietnam.
1945 Germany surrenders to Allies.	**1957** Soviet Union launches first space satellite, *Sputnik*.	**1966** Mao Zedong launches Cultural Revolution in China (to 1976). ▶
1948 State of Israel is founded; South African policy of apartheid begins.	**1959** Fidel Castro takes control of Cuba after ouster of dictator.	**1969** U.S. astronauts land on moon.

DIFFERENTIATED INSTRUCTION

FOR STRATEGIC READERS

Understanding a Timeline Explain that the timeline runs chronologically (in time order) from left to right across the page. Each of the six columns represents a period of years between 1940 and the present. The three parallel rows of the timeline represent events occurring simultaneously. By comparing the three rows, readers can better understand what events in literature, history, and culture were taking place at about the same time.

- What important roles have new technologies played in this era?
- What evidence do you see that "American" and "world" events have become harder to separate?
- Which political and cultural trends have influenced American literature?

1970	1985	2000
1970 Maya Angelou publishes autobiographical *I Know Why the Caged Bird Sings.* **1983** Sandra Cisneros publishes *The House on Mango Street.* ▶ 	**1985** Anne Tyler publishes *The Accidental Tourist.* **1989** Amy Tan's *The Joy Luck Club* is published. **1993** Rita Dove becomes first African-American poet laureate; Toni Morrison wins Nobel Prize for literature. ▶	**2000** Lucille Clifton's poetry collection, *Blessing the Boats,* wins National Book Award. **2002** Diane McWhorter's history of Birmingham during the Civil Rights Movement, *Carry Me Home,* wins the Pulitzer Prize for Nonfiction. **2004** Ted Kooser is named U.S. poet laureate.

1970	1985	2000
1974 President Richard M. Nixon resigns to avoid impeachment over Watergate scandal. **1977** First practical home computer, Apple II, hits market. **1981** The space shuttle *Columbia* launches; Sandra Day O'Connor becomes the first woman to be appointed to the U.S. Supreme Court.	 **1989** The oil tanker *Exxon Valdez* ▲ runs aground, creating a huge oil spill along Alaskan coast. **1991** The Persian Gulf War begins; the United States leads allied coalition against Iraq.	**2000** Fears of massive breakdown caused by "Y2K" computer problem prove unfounded. **2001** Hijackers fly commercial planes into World Trade Center and Pentagon, killing thousands. **2005** Hurricane Katrina hits New Orleans and surrounding area, causing massive destruction. ▼

1970	1985	2000
1975 South Vietnam surrenders as North Vietnamese troops occupy Saigon. **1979** Egypt's Anwar Sadat and Israel's Menachem Begin sign treaty ending war between Egypt and Israel.	**1989** The Berlin Wall comes down; ▶ student protesters in China are killed in Tiananmen Square. **1991** Soviet Union breaks up into 15 republics.	**2003** U.S. troops invade Iraq, deposing leader Saddam Hussein. **2004** Poland joins European Union; Indian Ocean earthquake causes deadly tsunamis, killing hundreds of thousands.

MAKING CONNECTIONS

Possible answers:

- *Atomic bombs brought World War II to an end. The first practical home computer became available in 1977. Various space-related developments occurred, such as the launching of the first satellite in 1957, the first landing of astronauts on the moon in 1969, and the launching of the space shuttle* Columbia *in 1981.*
- *America was involved in a number of international conflicts, including World War II, the Korean War, the Vietnam War, the Persian Gulf War, and the invasion of Iraq. The United States competed with the Soviet Union in the space race.*
- *American literature shows the influence of the civil rights movement, McCarthyism, and international warfare.*

ADDITIONAL QUESTIONS

1. What satirical war novel was published 16 years after the end of World War II? ***Answer:*** *Joseph Heller's* Catch-22

2. In 1967, Thurgood Marshall became the first African-American Supreme Court Justice. Twenty-six years later, two African-American women had memorable accomplishments. Who were they, and what did they accomplish? ***Answer:*** *In 1993, Toni Morrison won the Nobel Prize for literature, and Rita Dove became the first African-American poet laureate.*

FOR ADVANCED LEARNERS/AP

Make Additional Connections Have students choose one of the six time periods shown in the timeline and research using conventional or electronic resources to learn about other events that occurred during the time span. Challenge students to identify events for each category: *American Literary Milestones, Historical Context,* and *World Culture and Events.* Have students prepare and present brief oral reports, summarizing important events and discussing their connection to events shown in the timeline or discussed in class.

OBJECTIVE

- to explore the legacy of contemporary American culture and literature

A New American Dream?

Have students read and discuss the paragraph. (You may also want to ask students to review the section on the American dream on page 1096 of the historical essay.) Elicit or provide examples of the kinds of societal changes that have raised "concerns about education, social mobility, family and community, the environment, and the hectic pace of modern life." For example, discuss such changes as the increasing number of families in which both parents work outside the home; the growing gap between rich and poor; and the effects of cell phones, wireless technology, and other such advancements on people's quality of life.

CREATE Explore with students how the American dream is both similar and different for various groups of people. For example, all groups may desire economic success, but new immigrants may dream first of political or religious freedom, while United States–born citizens may take such freedoms for granted. As students plan for the ***CREATE*** activity, ask them to think specifically about the point of view of each group. Suggest that students divide their artwork into panels, with each panel representing the vision of a different group.

UNIT 6

The Legacy of the Era

A New American Dream?

As rapid changes in society have given rise to fresh concerns about education, social mobility, family and community, the environment, and the hectic pace of modern life, it may be time to redefine the American dream for a new generation.

CREATE What might be the American dream for students and young adults today? For new immigrants? Working-class people? Others? As a class, share your thoughts. Then break into groups of four and create posters or collages that depict different aspects of today's American dream.

1104

DIFFERENTIATED INSTRUCTION

FOR STRATEGIC READERS
Vocabulary Support

- *social mobility*, "the capacity for moving to a higher social class or position"
- *hectic*, "characterized by activity, haste, or excitement"
- *collage*, "an artistic work composed of various materials (such as paper and cloth) pasted together on a surface"

FOR ADVANCED LEARNERS/AP

Reflect on the American Dream Ask students to consider whether, in general, the American dream places too much emphasis on money and material possessions. Should people be placing greater emphasis on other values, and if so, what values? Ask students to write an essay exploring these questions and expressing their views. Then have volunteers share their essays with the class as the basis for a group discussion.

The Future of Literature

Technology has affected both the form and content of literature, offering new possibilities from hypertext to hand-held e-books to online publishing—though the predicted death of the printed book (and of narrative as we know it) has not come to pass. What do you think literature will be like in 20 years?

QUICKWRITE Taking the role of a future critic, write a "book review" discussing one new form of literature. Include your opinions about the limitations and possibilities this form presents.

Living in the Global Village

America's isolationism ended abruptly with the attack on Pearl Harbor in World War II. In the postwar years, international trade and travel greatly expanded. Today, huge improvements in communications and transportation have made globalism possible on many levels: political, economic, and cultural. Day by day, Americans are becoming more aware of their ties with the rest of the world.

DISCUSS How does globalization affect your everyday life? Brainstorm ideas with a small group, then report back to the class. If you're stuck, try thinking about what you wear, what you eat, and how you earn and spend money.

The Future of Literature

Have students read the paragraph. Be sure everyone understands the meaning of the phrases "hypertext," "hand-held eBooks," and "online publishing." Ask students whether they think the printed book will ever really disappear, and why or why not. Discuss the future of literature, encouraging students to use their imagination. Then have them complete the **QUICKWRITE.**

QUICKWRITE As students evaluate the limitations and possibilities of the new form of literature, suggest that they consider various age groups. For example, would electronic media appeal equally to older and younger readers? Also have them think about practicality. For instance, would readers want to take a hand-held viewer to the beach? Encourage students to support their opinions with specific reasons and examples.

Living in the Global Village

After students read the paragraph, discuss how the Internet in particular has made Americans "more aware of their ties with the rest of the world." Ask how other forms of communication and media, such as movies and television, encourage globalism.

DISCUSS After students complete their brainstorming, extend the discussion by asking the class to list benefits of globalization and also to identify any disadvantages they see.

FOR STRATEGIC READERS
Vocabulary Support

- *hypertext,* "information stored in a computer system to link related items and allow them to be readily accessed"

- *global village,* "the world viewed as being a single community"

- *isolationism,* "policy of avoiding involvement in international alliances and relations"

- *globalism,* "belief that political decisions should reflect global concerns"

FOR ADVANCED LEARNERS/AP

Research Blogs Call students' attention to the picture at the top of page 1105. Have students find out more about "blogs," or Weblogs. What are they? Who writes them and who reads them? Why have they become so popular? Ask students to share their findings with the class. Then discuss how blogs are representative of our times and of the role of technology within the global village.

Our Town
Thornton Wilder

ABOUT THE AUTHOR

Thornton Wilder Some writers have popular appeal, but earn few, if any, literary prizes; others win prestigious prizes but never gain widespread readership. Thornton Wilder was one of those rare writers who achieved both. In addition, his enjoyable writing style brought him success as both a novelist and a play-wright. He won the Pulitzer Prize in 1928 for *The Bridge of San Luis Rey* and a National Book Award in 1968 for his later novel *The Eighth Day.* He also won two Pulitzer Prizes in drama: one for *Our Town,* in 1938, and another for *The Skin of Our Teeth,* in 1943.

ABOUT THE PLAY

Our Town Explain that the play's popularity stems in large part from Wilder's ability to create universally recognizable and believable characters set against the familiar backdrop of small-town America. The unusual bare staging also invites audience members to focus their attention on Wilder's words and themes and become actively involved in the play's characters and events.

Our Town, one of the most frequently pro-duced of all American plays, was produced once again to great acclaim in 2002. Well-known actor Paul Newman starred as the Stage Manager, a role for which he received a 2003 Tony Award nomination.

LEGACY OF A MASTERPIECE

Introduce the Excerpt Before students read the excerpt, remind them that *Our Town* dates back to 1938. Ask them to consider as they read in what ways the play still rings true today and in what ways it does not. In addition, urge them to think about the ways in which Wilder makes the conversation between George and Emily realistic and what character traits of George and Emily they can relate to. After students finish reading, ask what conclusions they can draw about the kind of people George and Emily are and the kind of relation-ship they are likely to have in their future.

American Masterpiece

Our Town

Thornton Wilder

Thornton Wilder
1897–1975

ABOUT THE AUTHOR Thornton Wilder spent several years of his childhood in China, where his father was a high-ranking American diplomat. He attended Oberlin, Yale, and Princeton universities; studied archaeology in Rome; and taught literature at the University of Chicago. A world traveler, he hobnobbed with the most talented minds of his day—Sigmund Freud, Gertrude Stein, and T. S. Eliot, to name just a few. You might expect someone with this background to produce complex, sophisticated writings aimed at an intellectual elite—but you would be wrong. From his best-selling novel *The Bridge of San Luis Rey* to his charming comedy *The Matchmaker* (adapted into the hit musical *Hello Dolly!*), most of Wilder's writings have enjoyed broad popular appeal. *Our Town* is no exception. Since it first appeared on Broadway in 1938, not a day has gone by when it has not been staged somewhere in the world.

ABOUT THE PLAY Set in the small town of Grover's Corners, New Hampshire, *Our Town* traces the everyday experiences of two neighboring families, the Gibbses and the Webbs. In Act I, which depicts a single day in 1901, a friendship blooms between the Gibbses' son George and the Webbs' daughter Emily. Act II takes place three years later on their wedding day; and Act III opens with a funeral nine years after that. The play has several unusual touches: it is performed on a stage bare of all scenery; it depicts some characters from beyond the grave; and it employs a folksy but eerily omniscient narrator called the Stage Manager, who reveals characters' futures as well as their pasts and even fills us in on the geology of the region and the history and sociology of the town.

LEGACY OF A MASTERPIECE "*Our Town*," Thornton Wilder once explained, "is an attempt to find value above all price for the smallest events in our daily life." Most critics consider Wilder's attempt a successful one. The play's power, one critic observes, is in its duality: the events are "simple, modest, easy, plain," but the Stage Manager's commentary weights them with "birth and marriage and death, with aging and with change," so that "simultaneously we are made aware of what is momentary and what is eternal." The following scene is from Act II and is a flashback to the beginning of George and Emily's courtship.

DIFFERENTIATED INSTRUCTION

FOR STRATEGIC READERS

Comprehension Support Help students complete a Three-Column Journal to draw conclusions about Emily and George based on their dialogue. Discuss each character's traits and explore ways in which the characters are alike and different.

 BEST PRACTICES TOOLKIT—Transparency Three-Column Journal p. B10

Character	Quotation	Conclusion
Emily	"I'm sorry if it hurts your feelings ..."	She is honest but considerate.
Emily	"...you've got awful conceited ..."	Emily knows him well enough to say this.
George	"I'm glad you said it ..."	George respects her opinion.

George. Emily, why are you mad at me?

Emily. I'm not mad at you.

George. You've been treating me so funny lately.

Emily. Well, since you ask me, I might as well say it right out, George,—— (*She catches sight of a teacher passing.*) Good-by, Miss Corcoran.

George. Good-by, Miss Corcoran. —Wha—what is it?

Emily (*not scoldingly; finding it difficult to say*). I don't like the whole change that's come over you in the last year. I'm sorry if that hurts your feelings, but I've got to—tell the truth and shame the devil.

10 **George.** A *change?* —Wha—what do you mean?

Emily. Well, up to a year ago, I used to like you a lot. And I used to watch you as you did everything . . . because we'd been friends so long . . . and then you began spending all your time at *baseball* . . . and you never stopped to speak to anybody any more. Not even to your own family you didn't . . . and, George, it's a fact, you've got awful conceited and stuck-up, and all the girls say so. They may not say so to your face, but that's what they say about you behind your back, and it hurts me to hear them say it, but I've got to agree with them a little. I'm sorry if it hurts your feelings . . . but I can't be sorry I said it.

George. I . . . I'm glad you said it, Emily. I never thought that such a thing was hap-
20 pening to me. I guess it's hard for a fella not to have faults creep into his character.

(*They take a step or two in silence, then stand still in misery.*)

Emily. I always expect a man to be perfect and I think he should be.

George. Oh . . . I don't think it's possible to be perfect, Emily.

Emily. Well, my *father* is, and as far as I can see *your* father is. There's no reason on earth why you shouldn't be, too.

George. Well, I feel it's the other way round. That men aren't naturally good; but girls are.

Emily. Well, you might as well know right now that I'm not perfect. It's not as easy for a girl to be perfect as a man, because we girls are more—more—nervous.—Now
30 I'm sorry I said all that about you. I don't know what made me say it.

George. Emily,—.

Emily. Now I can see it's not the truth at all. And I suddenly feel that it isn't important, anyway.

George. Emily . . . would you like an ice-cream soda, or something, before you go home?

Emily. Well, thank you. . . . I would.

Use these prompts to help students consider the relationship between George and Emily:

Restate What does Emily tell George? *Possible answer: She tells him he has changed in the past year in ways that are not attractive.*

Analyze In what ways does the interaction between George and Emily reveal their feelings toward each other? What are those feelings? *Possible answer: Both George and Emily speak to each other honestly and respectfully. Emily explains to George that she "used to like [him] a lot" but that he's changed—"got awful conceited and stuck-up." Rather than react defensively, George expresses gratitude and admits his faults. Their interaction shows that Emily cares enough to speak frankly to George and that George respects Emily's opinion and feels bad that she perceives imperfections in him.*

Synthesize In what ways does the conversation between George and Emily reflect an "everyday experience"? *Possible answer: Like young people everywhere, George and Emily are having a typical, everyday conversation about getting to know one another. As with so many such conversations, it reflects typical misconceptions people can form when they care about each other but feel awkward and ill at ease expressing their feelings.*

FOR STRATEGIC READERS

Vocabulary Support

- *hobnobbed,* "associated; was friendly"
- *elite,* "superior group of people"
- *folksy,* "having an informal, friendly manner"
- *eerily,* "weirdly; strangely"
- *omniscient,* "all-knowing"
- *duality,* "double nature"

FOR ENGLISH LEARNERS

Vocabulary: Idioms and Phrasal Verbs Share the meaning of these expressions, and then help students use them in sentences:

- *right out* (line 4), "directly"
- *hurts your feelings* (lines 8–9), "makes you feel sad or hurt"
- *stuck-up* (line 15), "conceited, snobbish"
- *to your face* (line 16), "in your presence"
- *behind your back* (line 16), "secretly"
- *other way round* (line 25), "opposite"

The Glass Menagerie
Tennessee Williams

ABOUT THE AUTHOR

Tennessee Williams Born in Columbus, Mississippi, Williams largely grew up in St. Louis, Missouri. Nevertheless, he set almost all of his plays in the South, and his work had a lasting impact on Southern literature. Williams wrote more than 70 plays, nine of which were made into movies. His plays are known for their dramatic scenes, lyrical dialogue, and original characters, many of which are based on Williams's family and friends. The author's best plays captivated audiences and critics alike by exploring the frustrations and passions of characters trying to survive a brutal world.

Chronology of Major Works These are the publication dates of Tennessee Williams's most important works:

1945 *The Glass Menagerie*

1947 *A Streetcar Named Desire*

1948 *Summer and Smoke*

1951 *The Rose Tattoo*

1955 *Cat on a Hot Tin Roof*

1958 *Suddenly Last Summer*

1959 *Sweet Bird of Youth*

1961 *Night of the Iguana*

ABOUT THE PLAY

The Glass Menagerie Explain that in creating the play, Williams drew on his family's past in Mississippi and his early life in Missouri. Appearing on Broadway in 1945, *The Glass Menagerie* received the New York Drama Critics' Circle award for best play of the season, a great achievement for its 34-year-old playwright. Five years later, the play was made into a movie, earning Williams many more admirers and adding to his fame.

In 1995, the play was staged in London with actresses Zoë Wanamaker as Amanda and Claire Skinner as Laura. The two women were praised for their performances. Skinner received a Best Actress Award from the London Critics Circle Theater Awards, while Wanamaker was nominated for a Laurence Olivier Theatre Award.

The Glass Menagerie

Tennessee Williams

**Tennessee Williams
1911–1983**

ABOUT THE AUTHOR The themes and characters in *The Glass Menagerie* were drawn from Tennessee Williams's own experiences. Williams suffered through a difficult childhood with an abusive, frequently absent father; a much-loved sister who suffered from mental illness; and a strong mother who desperately tried to hold the family together while longing for the happier days of her Southern girlhood. Williams showed early promise as a writer, but family problems often interrupted his education, and for a time his father forced him to work at the St. Louis shoe factory where he himself was employed. Eventually Williams returned to college and earned a degree from the University of Iowa, where his first full-length plays were performed. Moving to New York City, he began winning drama prizes. Financial success came in 1945, when *The Glass Menagerie* first appeared on Broadway.

ABOUT THE PLAY *The Glass Menagerie* tells the story of the Wingfield family, who live in a cramped apartment across the alley from the Paradise Dance Hall. The father is absent; Tom, the son, supports his mother and sister by working in a shoe factory—a job he hates. Laura, the sister, is lame from disease and painfully shy; she spends most of her time with her collection of old phonograph records and her "menagerie" of tiny glass animals—as fragile as she is. Amanda, the mother, is deeply concerned about her daughter's future. She wistfully recalls her youth as a Southern belle, when she once entertained 17 gentlemen callers at once, and wishes that Laura had a suitor who might offer the security of marriage. As the following scene opens, Amanda has been pressuring Tom to bring a friend home to meet Laura.

> **Tom.** Mother, you mustn't expect too much of Laura.
>
> **Amanda.** What do you mean?
>
> **Tom.** Laura seems all those things to you and me because she's ours and we love her. We don't even notice she's crippled any more.
>
> **Amanda.** Don't say crippled! You know that I never allow that word to be used!
>
> **Tom.** But face facts, Mother. She is and—that's not all—
>
> **Amanda.** What do you mean "not all"?

1108

DIFFERENTIATED INSTRUCTION

FOR STRATEGIC READERS

Comprehension Support Ask students to record the main ideas of About the Author and About the Play in Outline organizers. Then have students exchange papers, evaluate each other's work, and offer suggestions for possible improvement.

A. About the Author

  1. Tennessee Williams drew play's themes and characters from personal experience.

2. Williams had a difficult childhood.

  a. abusive, often absent father

  b. mentally ill sister

  c. education interrupted by family problems

3. Williams moved to New York City and began winning drama prizes.

4. *The Glass Menagerie* appeared on Broadway and led to financial success.

 BEST PRACTICES TOOLKIT—Transparency Outline p. B19

Tom. Laura is very different from other girls.

Amanda. I think the difference is all to her advantage.

10 **Tom.** Not quite all—in the eyes of others—strangers—she's terribly shy and lives in a world of her own and those things make her seem a little peculiar to people outside the house.

Amanda. Don't say peculiar.

Tom. Face the facts. She is.

(*The dance-hall music changes to a tango that has a minor and somewhat ominous tone.*)

Amanda. In what way is she peculiar—may I ask?

Tom (*gently*). She lives in a world of her own—a world of little glass ornaments, Mother. . . . (*He gets up.* Amanda *remains holding the brush, looking at him, troubled.*) She plays old phonograph records and—that's about all—

20 (*He glances at himself in the mirror and crosses to the door.*)

Amanda (*sharply*). Where are you going?

Tom. I'm going to the movies. (*He goes out the screen door.*)

Amanda. Not to the movies, every night to the movies! (*She follows quickly to the screen door.*) I don't believe you always go to the movies! (*He is gone.* Amanda *looks worriedly after him for a moment. Then vitality and optimism return and she turns from the door, crossing to portieres.*) Laura! Laura! (Laura *answers from kitchenette.*)

Laura. Yes, Mother.

Amanda. Let those dishes go and come in front! (Laura *appears with a dish towel.* Amanda *speaks to her gaily.*) Laura, come here and make a wish on the moon!

30 (*screen image: the moon*)

Laura (*entering*). Moon—moon?

Amanda. A little silver slipper of a moon. Look over your left shoulder, Laura, and make a wish! (Laura *looks faintly puzzled as if called out of sleep.* Amanda *seizes her shoulders and turns her at an angle by the door.*) Now! Now, darling, *wish!*

Laura. What shall I wish for, Mother?

Amanda (*her voice trembling and her eyes suddenly filling with tears*). Happiness! Good fortune!

(*The sound of the violin rises and the stage dims out.*)

FOR STRATEGIC READERS
Vocabulary Support

- *menagerie,* "a collection of animals kept for exhibition"
- *wistfully,* "longingly"
- *belle,* "an attractive woman or girl "
- *suitor,* "a man who courts a woman"
- *ominous* (line 15), "threatening, menacing"
- *vitality* (line 25), "energy, liveliness"
- *portieres* (line 26), "curtains hung in a doorway"

FOR ADVANCED LEARNERS/AP
Discuss Characterization [small-group option] Have small groups discuss these questions and then share their views:

- How do the contrasting views of Laura presented by Tom and Amanda convey Laura's character to audiences?

- What conclusions can you draw about Tom on the basis of this passage? What conclusions can you draw about Amanda? about Laura?

TIERED DISCUSSION PROMPTS
Use these prompts to help students consider the relationship between the members of the Wingfield family:

Connect Have you or someone you know ever misjudged another person's abilities? How does that experience help you understand Tom's feelings? *Accept all thoughtful responses.*

Interpret What does Tom mean when he says, "Mother, you mustn't expect too much of Laura"? *Possible answer: Tom feels that Laura's options are limited because she is lame and "terribly shy and lives in a world of her own." Does Amanda agree with Tom? Explain. Possible answer: Amanda appears to disagree with Tom, because she is either unwilling or unable to admit Laura's limitations.*

Synthesize If the character of Tom is based on Williams himself, and the character of Laura is based on Williams's sister, what does this suggest about Williams's early family life? *Possible answer: Williams may have felt caught in the middle between the mentally ill sister he loved and a mother who lived in denial of the difficulties their family was facing.*

Death of a Salesman

Arthur Miller

ABOUT THE AUTHOR

Arthur Miller The author's first play to be produced on Broadway was *The Man Who Had All the Luck,* which appeared in 1944. The play was a failure, closing after only four performances. Three years later, *All My Sons* earned Miller the New York Drama Critics' Circle award as the year's best play and also won two Tony awards. It was *Death of a Salesman,* however, that brought Miller international fame. The play has been acclaimed as one of the finest works of contemporary American theater.

ABOUT THE PLAY

Death of a Salesman Explain that, like many of Miller's plays, *Death of a Salesman* explores themes of morality and personal and social responsibility and presents the author's view of an ordinary man as a tragic hero. As students read the excerpt, have them pay attention to the author's parenthetical stage directions. Ask how these directions contribute to the reader's understanding of Willy's emotional state and Howard's response.

In 1998, successful film actor Brian Dennehy wowed critics and audiences alike with his interpretation of Willy Loman. Dennehy won both the 1999 Tony Award and Drama Desk Award.

LEGACY OF A MASTERPIECE

Introduce the Excerpt Point out that Willy does nearly all the talking in this scene, while Howard, Willy's boss, says very little. As students read, ask them how this imbalance contributes to their understanding of the relationship between the two men. Also have students consider how Miller wants readers to perceive Howard and Willy.

Death of a Salesman

Arthur Miller

Arthur Miller
1915–2005

ABOUT THE AUTHOR "Success is the great man-eater," Arthur Miller once observed; "surviving it is as hard as attaining it." Miller knew a great deal about success and failure from his own experiences. As a young man during the Great Depression, he witnessed the collapse of his father's successful coat-manufacturing business. To scrape together the money for college, Miller put $13 of every $15 he earned into a college fund. After graduating from the University of Michigan, he returned to New York with dreams of Broadway glory but instead was forced into a variety of odd jobs—even living for a time on welfare. Then, after finally achieving success with plays such as *All My Sons, Death of a Salesman,* and *The Crucible,* Miller had the humiliating experience of being called to testify before the House Un-American Activities Committee during the "red scare" of the 1950s. He was found in contempt of Congress for refusing to name names and was blacklisted in Hollywood. Fortunately, he was able to continue working in New York, where producers and theater owners ignored the pressure to blacklist, and went on to have a long career in theater.

ABOUT THE PLAY Willy Loman, the lead character in Miller's *Death of a Salesman,* would like to see himself as successful in his business and family life. Yet in both areas, Willy seems headed for failure. In his longtime job as a traveling salesman for the Wagner Company, he has been reduced from a regular salary to a mere commission, and now his position is further threatened by his poor performance on the road. In his family life, his son Biff—once the star of the high-school football team—now cannot seem to find his footing in the world, and the pressures that Willy puts on Biff only widen the painful rift between the two men.

LEGACY OF A MASTERPIECE Miller's story of Willy Loman's shattered hopes and dreams won him the Pulitzer Prize in 1949 and is widely regarded as his finest work. Some critics see it as a brilliant dissection of the American dream; others commend its perceptive portrayal of family tensions and personal failings. A few debate whether a character as average and everyday as Willy Loman actually qualifies as a tragic hero. Yet most agree that the combination of realism and sympathy with which Miller traces Willy's downfall makes for an emotional theater experience.

In this excerpt, Willy meets with Howard Wagner, who has become head of the Wagner Company after his father's death. Howard is disappointed with Willy's sales performance and wants to let him go.

1110

DIFFERENTIATED INSTRUCTION

FOR STRATEGIC READERS

Comprehension Support As students read the excerpt, work with them to complete a Two-Column Chart to help them make inferences and draw conclusions about Willy's words and feelings.

 BEST PRACTICES TOOLKIT—Transparency
Two-Column Chart p. A25

Quote	Significance
"...just listen for a minute. You don't understand this."	Willy feels Howard isn't giving him a chance to explain.
"...what could be more satisfying than to be ... remembered and loved ... by so many ... people?"	Willy loves being a salesman because he can connect with people.

Willy (*angrily*). Business is definitely business, but just listen for a minute. You don't understand this. When I was a boy—eighteen, nineteen—I was already on the road. And there was a question in my mind as to whether selling had a future for me. Because in those days I had a yearning to go to Alaska. See, there were three gold strikes in one month in Alaska, and I felt like going out. Just for the ride, you might say.

Howard (*barely interested*). Don't say.

Willy. Oh, yeah, my father lived many years in Alaska. He was an adventurous man. We've got quite a little streak of self-reliance in our family. I thought I'd go out
10   with my older brother and try to locate him, and maybe settle in the North with the old man. And I was almost decided to go, when I met a salesman in the Parker House. His name was Dave Singleman. And he was eighty-four years old, and he'd drummed merchandise in thirty-one states. And old Dave, he'd go up to his room, y'understand, put on his green velvet slippers—I'll never forget—and pick up his phone and call the buyers, and without ever leaving his room, at the age of eighty-four, he made his living. And when I saw that, I realized that selling was the greatest career a man could want. 'Cause what could be more satisfying than to be able to go, at the age of eighty-four, into twenty or thirty different cities, and pick up a phone, and be remembered and loved and helped by so many different people?
20   Do you know? when he died—and by the way he died the death of a salesman, in his green velvet slippers in the smoker of the New York, New Haven and Hartford, going into Boston—when he died, hundreds of salesmen and buyers were at his funeral. Things were sad on a lotta trains for months after that. (*He stands up. Howard has not looked at him.*) In those days there was personality in it, Howard. There was respect, and comradeship, and gratitude in it. Today, it's all cut and dried, and there's no chance for bringing friendship to bear—or personality. You see what I mean? They don't know me any more.

Howard (*moving away, to the right*). That's just the thing, Willy.

Willy. If I had forty dollars a week—that's all I'd need. Forty dollars, Howard.

30   **Howard.** Kid, I can't take blood from a stone, I—

Willy (*desperation is on him now*). Howard, the year Al Smith was nominated, your father came to me and—

Howard (*starting to go off*). I've got to see some people, kid.

Willy (*stopping him*). I'm talking about your father! There were promises made across this desk! You mustn't tell me you've got people to see—I put thirty-four years into this firm, Howard, and now I can't pay my insurance! You can't eat the orange and throw the peel away—a man is not a piece of fruit!

TIERED DISCUSSION PROMPTS

Use these prompts to help students understand how Willy Loman feels:

Connect Think about a time when you felt unappreciated or unfairly treated. How does that experience help you understand Willy's feelings? *Accept all thoughtful responses.*

Interpret What is it that Willy thinks Howard does not understand? Explain. ***Possible answer:*** *Willy thinks that Howard does not understand the essence of being a traveling salesman or how the profession has changed over the years. In Willy's view, being a salesman means having close personal relationships with buyers. However, the personal touch seems to have lost its importance. As Willy says, "Today, it's all cut and dried, and there's no chance for bringing friendship to bear—or personality."*

Synthesize Willy tells Howard, "You can't eat the orange and throw the peel away— a man is not a piece of fruit!" What does Willy mean? How does his statement function as a "dissection of the American dream"? ***Possible answer:*** *Willy means that it's not moral to use up a man's best efforts and then toss him aside when these are spent. His statement criticizes the company's behavior toward an employee of 34 years, suggesting that it is immoral to coldly discard a person who has contributed so much. Willy's words dissect the American dream by suggesting that those who follow it will be used up by it and tossed to the side by the next generation of seekers.*

FOR STRATEGIC READERS
Vocabulary Support

- *humiliating,* "causing embarrassment"
- *in contempt of,* "acting with willful disobedience or disrespect toward"
- *blacklisted,* "listed as someone not to be hired"
- *rift,* "a serious disagreement"
- *dissection,* "close analysis"

FOR ADVANCED LEARNERS/AP

Research House Un-American Activities Committee Arthur Miller was one of many well-known people called before the House Un-American Activities Committee. Ask students to research the purpose of this committee and find out why its tactics were so controversial. Also ask students to find out how the activities of the committee were reflected in Miller's award-winning play *The Crucible.* Have students share their findings with the class.

A Raisin in the Sun

Lorraine Hansberry

ABOUT THE AUTHOR

Lorraine Hansberry The youngest of four children, Hansberry was the daughter of a former school teacher and a successful realtor. Both parents fought actively against segregation laws and sent Lorraine to public schools, rather than private, in protest. Her father's role in a key antisegregation case heard by the Illinois Supreme Court helped to inspire the events in *A Raisin in the Sun*. The play's success enhanced Hansberry's role as an impassioned activist for equal rights for African Americans.

ABOUT THE PLAY

A Raisin in the Sun Point out that *A Raisin in the Sun* was the first play by an African-American woman to be produced on Broadway, and its director was the first African American in more than 50 years to direct a Broadway play. Explain that Hansberry was praised for her warm and funny style as well as her insightful portrayal of working-class people facing prejudice and economic hardship. Also note that a 1961 movie version of the play (starring many of the same actors) won a special award at the Cannes Film Festival. The critical and popular success of *A Raisin in the Sun* inspired and influenced many other African-American playwrights. It also inspired the play's 2004 Broadway revival, starring Phylicia Rashad as Lena Younger and Audra McDonald as Ruth Younger. Both women received awards for their portrayals.

LEGACY OF A MASTERPIECE

Introduce the Excerpt Before students read the excerpt, explain that it reflects the casual conversational English that is consistent with the particular characters and setting. Ask students how this use of language adds to the tone and emotional impact of the scene. Discuss whether the dialogue would be as effective if written in standard English.

Lorraine Hansberry
1930–1965

American Masterpiece

A Raisin in the Sun

Lorraine Hansberry

ABOUT THE AUTHOR "I was born black and female," Lorraine Hansberry reflected, but she triumphed over the limits society placed on her race and gender. She was born in Chicago in 1930 and raised in a respected, middle-class family. Both her parents were political and social activists. African-American leaders, including Langston Hughes, W. E. B. DuBois, and Paul Robeson frequently visited Hansberry's home. When she was a young girl, her family bought a house in an all-white Chicago neighborhood. The racism they encountered would inspire *A Raisin in the Sun*. Hansberry developed an interest in writing at an early age and largely focused her talent on the theater. Tragically, her career was cut short when she died of cancer at 34.

ABOUT THE PLAY "What happens to a dream deferred? / Does it dry up / like a raisin in the sun?" These lines from Langston Hughes's poem "Harlem" provided Hansberry with both a theme and a title for *A Raisin in the Sun*. Written in 1957, the play tells the story of the Youngers, an African-American family whose long-cherished dreams are almost realized when Mama, the family's matriarch, comes into some money. But Mama's plans to buy a house in a white neighborhood nearly destroy the family.

Hansberry had difficulty finding backers to fund her play. With its all-black cast and racial themes, *A Raisin in the Sun* was very daring for its time. But once it finally opened, it received the New York Drama Critics' Circle Award for the best American play of 1959. Hansberry was the youngest person and the first African American to win the award.

LEGACY OF A MASTERPIECE The *New York Times* called *A Raisin in the Sun* the play that "changed American theater forever." It inspired a generation of young black writers and actors and brought a whole new audience to the theater. A glimpse into the private lives of African Americans was also a revelation for Broadway's white audiences. As Hansberry once observed, "The intimacy of knowledge which the Negro may culturally have of white Americans does not exist in the reverse." In the following scene, Mama teaches her daughter, Beneatha, about love and forgiveness after her son, Walter, loses their money and is in danger of losing his soul.

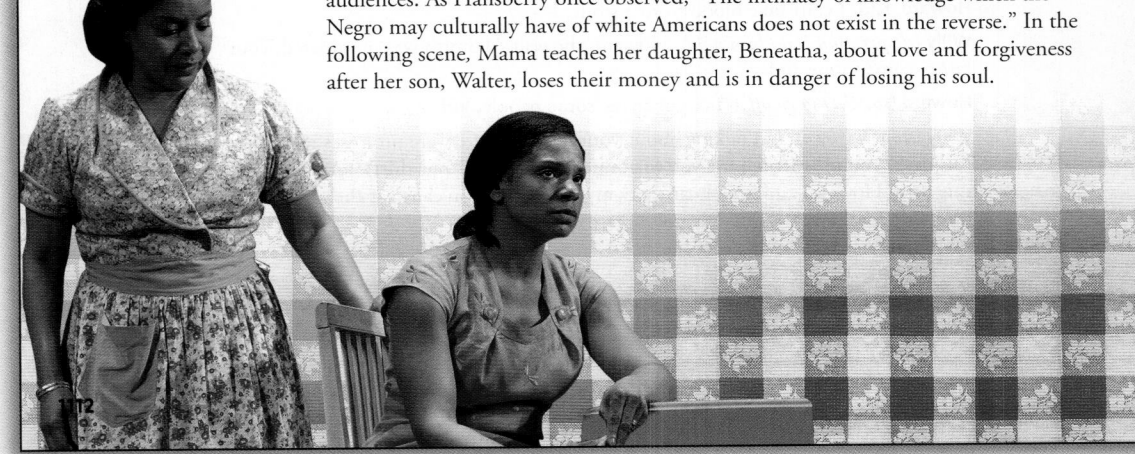

DIFFERENTIATED INSTRUCTION

FOR STRATEGIC READERS

Comprehension Support Use an Open Mind diagram to help students reflect on Mama's feelings as she talks with her daughter. Have students list thoughts that might be going through Mama's mind.

 BEST PRACTICES TOOLKIT—Transparency
Open Mind p. D9

> You shouldn't give up on people—especially not on your own family.
> Look for the good in people.
> To understand a person, you have to try to see the world through that person's eyes.

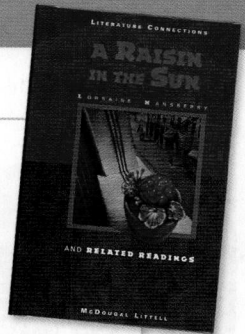

Beneatha. That is not a man. That is nothing but a toothless rat.

Mama. Yes—death done come in this here house. (*She is nodding, slowly, reflectively.*) Done come walking in my house on the lips of my children. You what supposed to be my beginning again. You—what supposed to be my harvest. (*to* Beneatha) You—you mourning your brother?

Beneatha. He's no brother of mine.

Mama. What you say?

Beneatha. I said that that individual in that room is no brother of mine.

Mama. That's what I thought you said. You feeling like you better than he is today?
10 (Beneatha *does not answer.*) Yes? What you tell him a minute ago? That he wasn't a man? Yes? You give him up for me? You done wrote his epitaph too—like the rest of the world? Well, who give you the privilege?

Beneatha. Be on my side for once! You saw what he just did, Mama! You saw him—down on his knees. Wasn't it you who taught me to despise any man who would do that? Do what he's going to do?

Mama. Yes—I taught you that. Me and your daddy. But I thought I taught you something else too . . . I thought I taught you to love him.

Beneatha. Love him? There is nothing left to love.

Mama. There is *always* something left to love. And if you ain't learned that, you
20 ain't learned nothing. (*looking at her*) Have you cried for that boy today? I don't mean for yourself and for the family 'cause we lost the money. I mean for him: what he been through and what it done to him. Child, when do you think is the time to love somebody the most? When they done good and made things easy for everybody? Well then, you ain't through learning—because that ain't the time at all. It's when he's at his lowest and can't believe in hisself 'cause the world done whipped him so! When you starts measuring somebody, measure him right, child, measure him right. Make sure you done taken into account what hills and valleys he come through before he got to wherever he is.

TIERED DISCUSSION PROMPTS

Use these prompts to help students understand the themes in this excerpt:

Restate What is Mama's advice to Beneatha? *Possible answer: Mama tells Beneatha to love and forgive her brother, not to judge him.*

Interpret What does Mama mean when she tells Beneatha: "When you starts measuring somebody, measure him right . . ."? *Possible answer: Mama means that it's not fair to judge someone without taking into account what the person may have experienced. In other words, a person's actions should be considered within the context of his or her life experiences.*

Synthesize What dream, discussed in **ABOUT THE PLAY,** has Walter's behavior destroyed? How did Hansberry's own life experiences prepare her to write about this dream? *Possible answer: Because of Walter's behavior, the Youngers lose their dream of owning a home along with Mama's hope to do so in a white neighborhood. Hansberry's experience of moving with her family into an all-white neighborhood likely gave her insight into the power of such a dream.*

FOR STRATEGIC READERS

Comprehension Support Call attention to Hansberry's use of questions in the dialogue between Mama and Beneatha, especially in Mama's last paragraph. Discuss how these questions add impact and drama to the interaction between mother and daughter. Point out that rhetorical questions, such as the ones that Mama asks, are intended for effect, not with the expectation of a reply.

FOR ENGLISH LEARNERS

Language: Conversational English Patterns Work with students to paraphrase the dialect and speech patterns in the excerpt. Help them translate idioms such as "toothless rat" (line 1) and rephrase dialect such as "done come in this here house" (line 2). Have student pairs read the excerpt aloud as the group works to restate the meaning of each line.

FOR ADVANCED LEARNERS/AP

Synthesize Before Hansberry chose the title inspired by Langston Hughes's poem, her play had the working title *The Crystal Stair,* which was also based on a line from a Hughes poem, "Mother to Son." Have students read these two poems and discuss how their themes relate to *A Raisin in the Sun* and to Hansberry's political activism.

Focus and Motivate

OBJECTIVES

Literary Analysis
- explore the key idea of **silence**
- analyze tone and imagery
- read an essay
- read a poem

Reading
- adjust and evaluate reading strategies

Grammar and Writing
- use word choice, sentence structure, and tone to establish voice
- write a persuasive essay

 R3.3, R3.4, W1.1, W1.3, W1.9

ABOUT THE AUTHORS

John Steinbeck After students read about Steinbeck, ask whether they find it surprising that an author acclaimed for his works of fiction also could be praised for his realistic writings. Why or why not?

Randall Jarrell Call students' attention to Jarrell's experience in the military. Discuss how this experience might affect a young poet.

USING THE *NOTABLE QUOTES*

Discuss the meaning of the quotations. Ask students how each quotation expresses the author's views on his craft. *Possible answers: Steinbeck points out that it is a writer's responsibility to help improve human nature. Jarrell focuses on the difficulty that poets have in finding readers.*

John Steinbeck
1902–1968

NOTABLE QUOTE
"[The writer] is charged with exposing our many grievous faults and failures, with dredging up to the light our dark and dangerous dreams for the purpose of improvement."

Why Soldiers Won't Talk
Essay by John Steinbeck

John Steinbeck created many memorable characters, from the downtrodden but dogged Joads in *The Grapes of Wrath* to George and Lennie in *Of Mice and Men*. Many of Steinbeck's characters convey his belief that people must fit into their surroundings—especially their natural surroundings—in order to find peace.

Childhood on the Land John Steinbeck grew up in the agricultural community of Salinas, California. The land profoundly influenced Steinbeck, who set many of his best works in these childhood scenes. He began to write early, encouraged by a high school teacher's praise.

Blending Life and Art While studying at Stanford University, Steinbeck worked in a factory and on road crews. Portraying people who lived by their hands became another key focus of Steinbeck's life and work. *The Grapes of Wrath* (1939) received a Pulitzer Prize for portraying down-and-out Oklahoma farmers during the Great Depression. Exhausted from writing the novel, Steinbeck moved in new directions. In 1943 he spent six months as a World War II correspondent, producing such writings as the following essay about the response of soldiers to combat. In 1962, he received the Nobel Prize in Literature "for his realistic as well as his imaginative writings."

Randall Jarrell
1914–1965

NOTABLE QUOTE
"If we were in the habit of reading poets, their obscurity would not matter; and, once we are out of the habit, their clarity does not help."

The Death of the Ball Turret Gunner
Poem by Randall Jarrell

Respected as a literary critic, Randall Jarrell is nonetheless best known for his searing poetry about World War II, notably a "stark five-line lyric . . . the ultimate poem of war." That poem is "The Death of the Ball Turret Gunner."

On the Road Again Born in Nashville, Tennessee, Jarrell moved often during his childhood. One important move took the family to a ranch in California. Later, Jarrell returned to California to live with his grandparents during his parents' divorce. Memories of this time filtered into one of Jarrell's best poems, "The Lost World," and childhood is a frequent, haunting topic throughout his work.

Making a Name With the help of a wealthy uncle, Jarrell went to college and began a lifelong career teaching literature in universities. At the same time, he worked at his own poetry. In 1942, he enlisted in the service, where he trained pilots and wrote poems capturing the horror and dreariness of military life.

Author Online
For more on John Steinbeck and Randall Jarrell, visit the **Literature Center** at **ClassZone.com**.

1114

Selection Resources

 RESOURCE MANAGER UNIT 6

Plan and Teach pp. 17–24

Literary Analysis
Summary pp. 25†*, 26‡*
Tone and Imagery pp. 27, 28†*
Question Support p. 32*

Reading
Adjust Reading Strategies
 pp. 29, 30†*
Reading Check p. 31

Grammar and Writing
Establish Voice p. 33

Assessment
Selection Tests A, B/C pp. 35*, 37*
Test Generator CD

 BEST PRACTICES TOOLKIT

Differentiated Instruction
 pp. 31–38*

Scaffolding Instruction
 pp. 43–46*

Graphic Organizers/Strategies
Definition Mapping • Sensory Notes • Cluster Diagram • Outline

Reading Support
Audio Anthology CD*

Technology
Literature and Writing Centers at **ClassZone.com**
WriteSmart CD

---

* Resources for Differentiation   † Also in Spanish   ‡ In Haitian Creole and Vietnamese

LITERARY ANALYSIS: TONE AND IMAGERY

A writer sometimes conveys **tone,** his or her attitude toward a subject, through imagery. **Imagery** consists of the descriptive words and phrases used to re-create sensory experiences. One of the interesting aspects of Steinbeck's essay is the contrast between his clinical, detached, almost scientific tone and his use of sensory-rich imagery. Jarrell's poem also uses vivid imagery to convey an attitude about its subject. As you read each selection, think about the relationship between tone and imagery. Decide what each of these elements adds to the experience of reading.

READING STRATEGY: ADJUST READING STRATEGIES

When you read literary works from different genres, you need to make adjustments in your reading strategies. For example, when you read an essay, follow these strategies:

- Identify the essay's **main ideas.**
- Look for **facts** and possibly **imagery** that support or reinforce the main ideas.
- Determine your own position on the ideas conveyed.

When reading a poem, try these strategies:

- Read the poem two or three times.
- Gather as much information as you can about the **speaker.**
- Try to picture the poem's **images** and think about what they convey.

As you read the two selections, make use of these strategies and any others that work for you. Take notes about the essay's main ideas and the poem's imagery and meaning.

When is SILENCE *louder than words?*

KEY IDEA People who have suffered greatly—fighting in a war, losing a loved one, witnessing tragedy— sometimes find it hard to communicate with others. Perhaps they cannot put their experiences and emotions into words. Perhaps they believe no one will understand. Others find silence and watchfulness more comfortable than talk and social engagement. Consider what silence can signify in a person's behavior, especially a soldier's in wartime.

QUICKWRITE Think of friends, family, peers, or even a character in a film or book. Identify someone you think of as more silent than talkative. Write a brief character description of this person. Read your description aloud, then share your ideas about why your subject is silent.

1115

When is SILENCE *louder than words?*

Introduce the question, and ask students to read the **KEY IDEA** paragraph. Have students reflect on the various reasons why a person might retreat into **silence.** Then have them complete the **QUICKWRITE.** Poll students for common reasons people are silent.

SKILLS FOCUS

LITERARY ANALYSIS   R3.3, R3.4

● TONE AND IMAGERY

Write this passage on the board:

> The sun cut through the wispy clouds like a laser, searing the ground. The exhausted soldiers dragged themselves on, muscles aching, throats parched, every man knowing that two days of torturous travel remained, but only one day of water.

Ask students in what way the imagery of this passage helps to convey the writer's tone. ***Possible answer:*** *The imagery conveys the sense of bone-weary men "dragging" themselves on, despite overwhelming obstacles. The writer's tone suggests admiration for the men's courage.*

CHECK UNDERSTANDING Elicit other examples of imagery that convey a writer's tone.

READING STRATEGY   R3.4

▣ ADJUST READING STRATEGIES

Have students reread the passage on the board. Ask them to identify the main ideas, both stated and implied. ***Possible answer:*** *The stated main idea is that a group of exhausted soldiers is struggling against great obstacles to get somewhere, despite intense heat. The implied main ideas are that the soldiers are courageous and that they will probably not survive their journey.*

R **RESOURCE MANAGER—Copy Master**
    Adjust Reading Strategies p. 29
      (for student use while reading
      the selections)

DIFFERENTIATED INSTRUCTION

FOR STRATEGIC READERS
Vocabulary Support

- *sensory,* "relating to the senses of sight, hearing, smell, taste, and touch"
- *genre,* "a particular category or kind of literary or artistic work"
- *main idea,* "the most important idea about a topic that a particular text conveys"
- *speaker,* "the voice that a poet creates to speak in a poem; not the poet"
- *image,* "a mental picture or visual idea"

Concept Support: Adjust Reading Strategies
Remind students that they are not limited to the strategies listed here. They should always choose the particular strategies that will be most helpful for the text they are reading. For example, when reading a nonfiction article, they might begin by skimming and scanning the text. When reading poetry, they might find their visualizing skills more helpful in creating a mental picture from text details.

1115

SUMMARY

In this essay, John Steinbeck suggests that ex-soldiers are unwilling to talk about their combat experiences because in fact they do not remember them very well. While under constant fire, soldiers experience a range of sensory and emotional effects that distort their perceptions and alter their behavior. When the battle ends, details of the experience become dreamlike, and the soldiers' memory of combat fades rapidly.

Lines 1–11
REINFORCE *KEY IDEA:* SILENCE

Discuss Does Steinbeck's explanation for the **silence** of ex-soldiers seem reasonable? Why or why not? Is the alternative explanation reasonable? Explain. *Possible answers: Yes: A soldier's mind may repress terrible memories. No: It would be impossible to forget such experiences. The first explanation Steinbeck gives—that soldiers simply do not want to relive their experiences by talking about them—is also reasonable.*

READING STRATEGY

A ADJUST READING STRATEGIES

Possible answer: Steinbeck is puzzled by his observation that ex-soldiers do not discuss their battle experiences. The main idea he provides to solve that mystery is that soldiers cannot remember their experiences.

Why Soldiers Won't Talk

JOHN STEINBECK

BACKGROUND Randall Jarrell's experience training pilots for the U.S. Army Air Force gained him firsthand knowledge of planes and gunners, including the view from the ball turret of a bomber. From this plexiglas bubble on the underside of the plane, gunners—totally exposed from below—fired at the enemy. During Steinbeck's time as a war correspondent, he too learned about bomber crews, as well as soldiers in the infantry.

During the years between the last war and this one, I was always puzzled by the reticence of ex-soldiers about their experiences in battle. If they had been reticent men it would have been different, but some of them were talkers and some were even boasters. They would discuss their experiences right up to the time of battle and then suddenly they wouldn't talk any more. This was considered heroic in them. It was thought that what they had seen or done was so horrible that they didn't want to bring it back to haunt them or their listeners. But many of these men had no such consideration in any other field.

Only recently have I found what seems to be a reasonable explanation, and the answer is simple. They did not and do not remember—and the worse the battle was, the less they remember. **A**

In all kinds of combat the whole body is battered by emotion. The ductless glands[1] pour their fluids into the system to make it able to stand up to the great demand on it. Fear and ferocity are products of the same fluid. Fatigue toxins[2] poison the system. Hunger followed by wolfed food distorts the metabolic pattern already distorted by the adrenaline[3] and fatigue. The body and the mind so disturbed are really ill and fevered. But in addition to these ills, which come from the inside of a man and are given him so that he can temporarily withstand pressures beyond his ordinary ability, there is the further stress of explosion.

Under extended bombardment or bombing the nerve ends are literally beaten. The eardrums are tortured by blast and the eyes ache from the constant hammering.

This is how you feel after a few days of constant firing. Your skin feels thick and insensitive. There is a salty taste in your mouth. A hard, painful knot is in your stomach where the food is undigested. Your eyes do not pick up much detail and the sharp outlines of objects are slightly blurred. Everything looks a little unreal. When

① Targeted Passage

A ADJUST READING STRATEGIES
Reread lines 1–11. What puzzles Steinbeck about soldiers, and what **main idea** provides the solution to his puzzlement?

ANALYZE VISUALS
How would you describe the look on this soldier's face? Explain what features convey this look.

---

1. **ductless glands:** glands, such as the thyroid or the pituitary gland, that secrete directly into the bloodstream.
2. **toxins:** poisons produced by the body that are capable of causing disease.
3. **adrenaline** (ə-drĕn′ə-lĭn): a substance secreted by the adrenal gland in response to stress.

DIFFERENTIATED INSTRUCTION

FOR ALL STUDENTS

Provide these independent projects to extend the lesson:

- Debate reasons that soldiers hesitate to discuss combat.
- Write a poem about war.
- Compare political climates during wartime.

For further details on these projects, see

R RESOURCE MANAGER
Ideas for Extension pp. 22–23

FOR STRATEGIC READERS

In combination with the *Audio Anthology CD*, use one or both Targeted Passages (pp. 1116 and 1118) to ensure that students focus on key concepts in the essay. Targeted Passages are also good for English learners.

① Targeted Passage [Lines 1–11]

This passage introduces the main theme of the essay.

ANALYZE VISUALS

Possible answer: *The soldier looks grim and exhausted. This look is conveyed by the soldier's unsmiling expression, partly open mouth, and dull, lifeless eyes.*

Lines 12–21
TIERED DISCUSSION PROMPTS

Use these prompts to help students trace Steinbeck's point that people respond physically to moments of great stress:

Connect Have you ever felt a physical response to an emotional situation? In what ways does that experience help you understand Steinbeck's description of combat? *Accept all thoughtful responses.*

Analyze How does Steinbeck use verbs to reinforce the ideas he presents? Give examples. *Possible answer: Steinbeck chooses strong verbs to convey the feeling of the body being assaulted in various ways. For example, he talks about food that is "wolfed" (line 15), "beaten" nerve ends (line 20), eardrums "tortured by blast" (line 21), and eyes that "ache from the constant hammering" (line 21).*

Synthesize In what ways does Steinbeck's description of combat's effects on the human body expand the reader's understanding of the selection? *Possible answer: Steinbeck's detailed description helps readers physically experience the vivid ways in which combat affects the senses and damages the body.*

- What does Steinbeck observe about ex-soldiers?
- Why does this observation surprise him?
- What is the "reasonable explanation" that Steinbeck has found?

FOR ENGLISH LEARNERS

Key Academic Vocabulary Use Definition Mapping to teach this word: *stress* (line 19).

 BEST PRACTICES TOOLKIT—Transparency Definition Mapping p. E6

Prereading For prereading instruction for English learners, see

 BEST PRACTICES TOOLKIT Scaffolding Reading Instruction pp. 43–46

FOR ADVANCED LEARNERS/AP

AP exercises in the bottom channel provide additional challenge for students. Use these suggestions for small groups or individuals.

ADDITIONAL GUIDELINES

For more help with differentiation and tips for classroom management, see

 BEST PRACTICES TOOLKIT Differentiated Instruction pp. 31–38

B TONE AND IMAGERY

Possible answer: Steinbeck uses sensory details to describe skin (lines 22–23), stomach pain (lines 23–24), and vision (lines 24–25). The scene reveals that soldiers under constant fire experience various sensory distortions and feel somewhat removed from reality.

If students need help . . . Work with them to complete a Sensory Notes organizer about lines 22–30, pointing out specific descriptive details that appeal to each sense.

 BEST PRACTICES TOOLKIT—Transparency Sensory Notes p. B9

C GRAMMAR AND STYLE

Establish Voice Point out that word choice is a key component in a writer's distinct voice. Review that sensory verbs evoke sensory reactions while describing actions. Steinbeck uses many sensory adjectives and verbs in this essay because he wants the reader to imagine and feel what soldiers feel. Ask students to find other such adjectives and verbs in the essay, such as *thick* (line 22), *salty* (line 23), *blurred* (line 25), *floaty* (line 26), *beaten* (line 31), and *deadened* (line 43).

D ADJUST READING STRATEGIES

Possible answer: Steinbeck uses the analogies of a woman experiencing the pain of childbirth and a person with a fever to convey the main idea of the paragraph: the body protects itself against an "experience which is beyond bearing" (line 61) by clouding and then removing the memory of it. Steinbeck's analogies suggest he may have had some firsthand experience with extremely painful situations.

---

you walk, your feet hardly seem to touch the ground and there is a floaty feeling all over your body. Even the time sense seems to be changed. Men who are really moving at a normal pace seem to take forever to pass a given point. And when you move it seems to you that you are very much slowed down, although actually you 30 are probably moving more quickly than you normally do. **B**

Under the blast your eyeballs are so beaten that the earth and the air seem to shudder. At first your ears hurt, but then they become dull and all your other senses become dull, too. There are exceptions, of course. Some men cannot protect themselves this way and they break, and they are probably the ones we call shell-shock cases.[4]

In the dullness all kinds of emphases change. Even the instinct for self-preservation is dulled so that a man may do things which are called heroic when actually his whole fabric of reaction is changed. The whole world becomes unreal. You laugh at things which are not ordinarily funny and you become enraged at trifles. During this time 40 a kind man is capable of great cruelties and a timid man of great bravery, and nearly all men have resistance to stresses beyond their ordinary ability.

Then sleep can come without warning and like a drug. Gradually your whole body seems to be packed in cotton. All the main nerve trunks are deadened, and out of the battered cortex[5] curious dreamlike thoughts emerge. It is at this time that many men see visions. The eyes fasten on a cloud and the tired brain makes a face of it, or an angel or a demon. And out of the hammered brain strange memories are jolted loose, scenes and words and people forgotten, but stored in the back of the brain. These may not be important things, but they come back with startling clarity into the awareness that is turning away from reality. And these memories are almost visions. **C**

50 And then it is over. You can't hear, but there is a rushing sound in your ears. And you want sleep more than anything, but when you do sleep you are dream-ridden, your mind is uneasy and crowded with figures. The anesthesia your body has given you to protect you is beginning to wear off, and, as with most anesthesia, it is a little painful.

And when you wake up and think back to the things that happened they are already becoming dreamlike. Then it is not unusual that you are frightened and ill. You try to remember what it was like, and you can't quite manage it. The outlines in your memory are vague. The next day the memory slips farther, until very little is left at all. A woman is said to feel the same way when she tries to remember what 60 childbirth was like. And fever leaves this same kind of vagueness on the mind. Perhaps all experience which is beyond bearing is that way. The system provides the shield and then removes the memory, so that a woman can have another child and a man can go into combat again. **D**

It slips away so fast. Unless you made notes on the spot you could not remember how you felt or the way things looked. Men in prolonged battle are not normal men. And when afterward they seem to be reticent—perhaps they don't remember very well. ❧

---

4. **shell-shock cases:** soldiers with a psychological disturbance as a result of prolonged exposure to active warfare.

5. **cortex:** part of the brain that plays an active role in consciousness.

B TONE AND IMAGERY
Reread lines 22–30, and note Steinbeck's use of **sensory detail.** What does this scene reveal about the soldier's mental state?

C GRAMMAR AND STYLE
Reread lines 42–47. Notice how Steinbeck establishes his voice partly by using descriptions that contain realistic sensory **adjectives** and **verbs,** such as *battered, hammered,* and *jolted.*

② **Targeted Passage**

D ADJUST READING STRATEGIES
Reread lines 55–63. What analogies does Steinbeck use to convey the **main idea** of this paragraph? What insight into experience does this suggest?

DIFFERENTIATED INSTRUCTION

FOR STRATEGIC READERS

② **Targeted Passage [Lines 42–63]**

This passage describes the body's mechanism for self-protection.

- According to Steinbeck, how does the body's "anesthesia" protect the soldier against the stresses of combat?
- What happens after this anesthesia wears off?
- How is the soldier's experience like that of a woman in childbirth?

FOR ENGLISH LEARNERS

Vocabulary: Idioms and Phrasal Verbs
[mixed-readiness groups] Share or elicit the meaning of these expressions, and then help students use them in original sentences:

- *slowed down* (line 29), "decreased in speed"
- *fasten on* (line 45), "become drawn to"
- *wear off* (line 53), "lessen in effect"
- *think back to* (line 55), "remember, recall"
- *slips away* (line 64), "fades, diminishes"

The Death of the Ball Turret Gunner

RANDALL JARRELL

From my mother's sleep I fell into the State,
And I hunched in its belly till my wet fur froze.
Six miles from earth, loosed from its dream of life,
I woke to black flak[1] and the nightmare fighters.
5 When I died they washed me out of the turret with a hose. **E**

---

1. **flak:** the fire of anti-aircraft guns.

E TONE AND IMAGERY
What does the imagery of the last line suggest about the speaker's attitude toward death?

SUMMARY

With vivid imagery evoking a fetus in its mother's womb, this poem conveys the nightmarish perspective of a gunner killed in aerial combat.

LITERARY ANALYSIS

E TONE AND IMAGERY

Possible answer: The imagery, which is horrifying, is described in a clinical manner, suggesting an unemotional, almost matter-of-fact attitude toward death.

ANALYZE VISUALS

Activity Ask students how the photograph reflects images in the poem. *Possible answer: The photograph shows the tiny space in which the gunner "hunched" and how that space is round like a "belly."*

About the Art This photograph was taken by well-known photojournalist Margaret Bourke-White (1906–1971). *Life* magazine sent Bourke-White to cover World War II. This photo captures a personal view of war.

SELECTION WRAP-UP

SYNTHESIZE Ask students to identify similarities and differences between Steinbeck's essay and Jarrell's poem.

★ CRITIQUE

- Have students identify the aspects of each selection that they found most meaningful, and explain why.

- After completing the After Reading questions on page 1120, have students revisit their responses and tell whether they have changed their opinions.

FOR ENGLISH LEARNERS

Comprehension: Self-Monitor Urge students to use the photograph on page 1119 to understand better the experience described in the poem, finding images in the photo that explain aspects of the poem. For example, the photograph clarifies the reference to the plane as a "mother" with a "belly" and helps readers visualize the gunner's total separation from the rest of the crew.

FOR ADVANCED LEARNERS/AP

Analyze Meaning [small-group option] In just five lines, Randall Jarrell conveys volumes about war and what it means to be a soldier in combat. Challenge students to write a paragraph or two interpreting and analyzing Jarrell's ideas. Encourage students to be specific in summarizing the message they find in the poem. Have them share their ideas in small groups, and then discuss and compare the various interpretations presented.

Practice and Apply

After Reading

Use these copy masters to check understanding and provide extra support.

R RESOURCE MANAGER—Copy Masters
Reading Check p. 31
Tone and Imagery p. 27
Question Support p. 32

Additional selection questions are provided for teachers on page 21.

ANSWERS

1. *Soldiers do not talk about combat because they do not remember it.*

2. *Soldiers experience a mixture of fear, adrenaline flow, and fatigue. Both body and mind are "ill and fevered" (lines 16–17). The skin feels "thick and insensitive" (lines 22–23). Objects appear slightly blurred. The senses deaden.*

3. *The speaker is killed during aerial combat.*

Possible answers:

4. *Steinbeck uses second person in order to place the reader in the soldier's shoes. This device makes the combat experience more vivid and immediate for readers.*

5. *Similar to a fetus awaiting birth, the gunner is crammed into a small space. Like a newborn violently thrust into the world, he is abruptly awakened to his surroundings.*

6. ● **SKILLS FOCUS Tone and Imagery**
Notable poem images: "hunched in its belly till my wet fur froze" (line 2), "the nightmare fighters" (line 4), "they washed me out of the turret with a hose" (line 5). Notable essay images: "eyeballs . . . so beaten that the earth and the air seem to shudder" (lines 31–32), "your whole body seems to be packed in cotton" (lines 42–43). Jarrell's attitude is one of bitterness regarding the gunner's expendability. Steinbeck's tone suggests sympathetic understanding of the horrors that soldiers must endure.

7. *Both authors convey the horror of war through grim detail, but Jarrell's horrifying last line suggests a more negative and less understanding viewpoint than Steinbeck's.*

8. ■ **SKILLS FOCUS Adjust Reading Strategies** *Answers will vary but should be specific.*

After Reading

Comprehension

R3.3, R3.4

1. **Recall** According to Steinbeck, why don't soldiers talk about combat?

2. **Summarize** What physical changes does Steinbeck say happen during combat?

3. **Summarize** In Jarrell's poem, what happens to the speaker?

Literary Analysis

4. **Examine Author's Purpose** Steinbeck uses the second-person *you* in his recounting of the physical effects of combat. Why do you think he chose this **stylistic device?**

5. **Interpret the Poem** In reference to his poem, Jarrell wrote that the gunner, who sat hunched up and revolved with the turret, looked like a fetus in the womb. Based on this information, how would you interpret the first four lines of the poem?

6. **Analyze Tone and Imagery** Skim the two selections, and make a list of notable images found in each work. Based on these images, what would you say is Jarrell's attitude toward the ball turret gunner and his predicament? What is Steinbeck's attitude toward combat and its effect on soldiers? Decribe the overall tone of each work.

7. **Compare Texts** Jarrell and Steinbeck address the topic of war from different angles and through different genres. Do you think the two authors offer consistent or conflicting accounts of what combat feels like? Support your opinion with details.

8. **Evaluate Reading Strategies** Look back at the notes you took as you read the essay and poem. For each work, which strategy was most useful in helping you understand the ideas and images presented?

Literary Criticism

9. **Critical Interpretations** In discussing "The Death of the Ball Turret Gunner," one critic stated, "In the combination of death and consciousness is the awakening and final recognition on the part of the gunner that he exists only to be a victim." Based on your own reading of the poem, do you agree with this interpretation? Support your response.

---

9. *Some students may agree with the interpretation, noting that it captures the poem's message about the destructiveness of war; other students may disagree with the interpretation, because the gunner must see himself as serving a purpose in combat beyond simply being a victim.*

Reading-Writing Connection

W1.1, W1.3

WRITING PROMPT

PERSUASIVE ESSAY Think about the adjustments veterans must make when they return from combat. What does society do to help ease their transition back into civilian life? What else do you think could be done? Write a **three-to-five-paragraph essay** on the importance of supporting veterans during this time of transition. Include specific suggestions of ways this might be effectively achieved.

SELF-CHECK

A convincing essay will . . .

- include information about current practices for helping veterans

- give reasons why your suggestions will make a difference

- establish a tone that helps persuade your readers

GRAMMAR AND STYLE

W1.9

ESTABLISH VOICE Review the **Grammar and Style** note on page 1118. Voice is the unique way a writer uses **word choice, sentence structure,** and **tone** to express his or her personality or vision. John Steinbeck's voice reflects his personal experience with war. It flows from his short sentences, straightforward tone, and sensory language suited to the somber nature of his subject.

> *The eardrums are tortured by blast and the eyes ache from the constant hammering.* (line 21)

> *This is how you feel after a few days of constant firing. Your skin feels thick and insensitive. There is a salty taste in your mouth. A hard, painful knot is in your stomach where the food is undigested.* (lines 22–24)

Notice that the examples include percussive-sounding words that reflect the pain of combat. The short sentences give the impression that all information provided is essential and honest.

PRACTICE In the following sentences, revise the sentence structure and word choice to match Steinbeck's voice. Note how the revisions made to the example help to capture Steinbeck's voice.

> **EXAMPLE**
>
> Like a jackhammer pounding at solid concrete, the TV announcer gabs on and on, creating perpetual background noise that pollutes our homes.
> *The TV announcer talks on, creating a persistent, polluting noise.*

1. The announcer chooses a topic, pushing it and pushing it as if it were bread dough, then kneading it into yet a new shape.

2. Must we sit there like zombies and put up with this endless chatter as though there were no alternative?

WRITING TOOLS

For prewriting, revision, and editing tools, visit the **Writing Center** at ClassZone.com.

DIFFERENTIATED INSTRUCTION

FOR DEVELOPING WRITERS
Writing Support

- Help students identify likely research resources, such as Web sites for the Veterans' Administration and veterans' advocacy groups.

- Suggest that students begin with a strong thesis statement clearly expressing their views about society's need to help veterans.

- Urge students to use outlines to plan their essays.

- Have students support their opening statement with specific reasons and facts.

- Ask students to write at least two body paragraphs giving concrete suggestions for assistance to veterans. Have them explain why each suggestion will make a difference.

- Suggest that students read their drafts aloud to a small group and ask for feedback.

BEST PRACTICES TOOLKIT—Transparency
Outline p. B19

Reading-Writing Connection

WRITING PROMPT

Suggest that student pairs use a Cluster Diagram to help them brainstorm effective ways that society can ease veterans' return to civilian life. Urge students to consider occupational, educational, financial, and other forms of assistance. To help students get started, have them conduct brief research into current practices for helping veterans.

BEST PRACTICES TOOLKIT—Transparency
Cluster Diagram p. B18

For writing support, see

Writing Center at ClassZone.com

GRAMMAR AND STYLE

Point out that the concepts of voice and tone are similar in many ways for writing and speaking. To illustrate this, suggest that students compare the tone of their oral response to a teacher's question with their response to the same question posed by a peer. How might their choice of language differ? How might they vary the length and structure of their sentences?

Possible answers:

1. *The announcer picks a topic. Then he jabs and jabs at it as if he were kneading dough, pounding it into a new shape.*

2. *We don't have to sit and listen like lifeless zombies. We don't have to put up with this machine-gun fire chatter. We have a choice.*

RESOURCE MANAGER—Copy Master
Establish Voice p. 33

Assess and Reteach

Assess

RESOURCE MANAGER—Copy Masters
Selection Test A pp. 35–36
Selection Test B/C pp. 37–38

Test Generator CD

Reteach

STANDARDS LESSON FILE
Literature Lessons 26, 40, 43
Reading Lesson 4
Writing Lessons 29, 39, 42, 43

Focus and Motivate

OBJECTIVES

Literary Analysis
- explore the key idea of **resilience**
- analyze methods of characterization
- read a short story

Reading
- analyze historical context

R3.5

ABOUT THE AUTHOR

Have students read about Vonnegut and summarize key points about his life and writing. Discuss how World War II directly affected him. Ask students how the author's experiences as a young soldier may have influenced his outlook and his work. *Students should recognize that a traumatic experience, such as being held prisoner of war and then narrowly escaping the total destruction of Dresden, would dramatically affect Vonnegut and thus his work.*

USING THE *NOTABLE QUOTE*

Ask students how the quotation exemplifies the writing of **Kurt Vonnegut Jr.,** as described in the first paragraph of the author biography. *Possible answer: The quotation is "deceptively simple" in style, but it makes readers stop and think.*

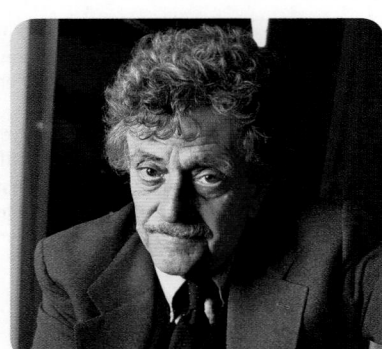

R3.5 CALIFORNIA

Adam
Short Story by Kurt Vonnegut Jr.

NOTABLE QUOTE
"People should be changed by world wars . . . else what are world wars for?"

FYI
Did you know that Kurt Vonnegut . . .
- hates computers, writing instead on an old typewriter?
- has a second creative career as an artist?

Author Online
For more on Kurt Vonnegut Jr., visit the **Literature Center** at **ClassZone.com.**

Kurt Vonnegut Jr.
born 1922

The writing of Kurt Vonnegut Jr. defies simple classification. When his stories examine the moral implications of technology, they are called science fiction. When they make comedy out of the horrors and absurdities of the human condition, they are called black humor. With his deceptively simple style, he entertains yet at the same time forces his readers to think deeply about society and the world at large.

A Scientific Bent The son and grandson of architects, Vonnegut was born in Indianapolis, Indiana, the youngest of three children. He has said that he owes his scientific bent to his father, a true believer in technology who insisted that his sons study "something useful." As a result, after high school, where he edited the daily paper, Vonnegut went to Cornell University to study biochemistry. But war interceded, and during his third year Vonnegut decided to quit college and join the army.

Art from Life As an infantry combat scout in World War II, Vonnegut was captured by German soldiers during the Battle of the Bulge in 1944. Held as a prisoner of war in Dresden, Germany, he survived the 1945 Allied bombing of Dresden because the American prisoners took shelter in a meat locker three stories below the ground. Protected from the firestorm that destroyed much of the city, the prisoners emerged to discover that thousands had been killed. Years later, Vonnegut came to terms with that experience in his novel *Slaughterhouse-Five.*

Writer on Contemporary Issues Despite the somewhat pessimistic philosophy conveyed in many of his works, in which human beings are victims of circumstance in an indifferent universe, Vonnegut believes strongly in the value of kindness and is preoccupied with moral issues. Throughout his writing career, this man of contrasts has maintained a reputation as a bit of an outsider while at the same time enjoying a wide public following.

In addition to *Slaughterhouse-Five,* Vonnegut's novels include *The Sirens of Titan* (1959), *Mother Night* (1961), *Cat's Cradle* (1963), *God Bless You, Mr. Rosewater* (1965), and *Breakfast of Champions* (1973).

1122

Selection Resources

 RESOURCE MANAGER UNIT 6

Plan and Teach pp. 39–46

Literary Analysis
Summary pp. 47†*, 48‡*
Characterization pp. 49, 50†*
Question Support p. 54*

Reading
Analyze Historical Context
   pp. 51, 52†*
Reading Check p. 53

Assessment
Selection Tests A, B/C pp. 55*, 57*
   Test Generator CD

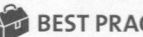 **BEST PRACTICES TOOLKIT**

Differentiated Instruction
   pp. 31–38*

Scaffolding Instruction
   pp. 43–46*

Graphic Organizers/Strategies
Timeline • Word Questioning •
Jigsaw Reading

Reading Support
- Audio Anthology CD*

Technology
- Literature Center at **ClassZone.com**
- WriteSmart CD

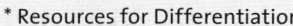 **Resources for Differentiation** † **Also in Spanish** ‡ **In Haitian Creole and Vietnamese**

LITERARY ANALYSIS: CHARACTERIZATION

In fiction, a writer sometimes describes a character's personality directly, leaving little to the reader's imagination. However, it is more often the case—especially in modern fiction—that a writer develops his or her characters in an indirect manner, revealing personality traits quite subtly and allowing the reader to interpret characters' motivations more thoroughly. Kurt Vonnegut and many other writers achieve this through the use of the following four basic methods of **characterization:**

- description of the character's physical appearance
- presentation of the character's own speech, thoughts, or feelings
- the speech, thoughts, or feelings of other characters in response to the character
- the narrator's own comments about the character

As you read this story, record what you learn about the main character, Heinz Knechtmann, through these methods of characterization.

Physical Appearance	Character's Speech, Thoughts, Feelings	Other Characters' Speech, Thoughts, Feelings	Narrator's Comments

READING SKILL: ANALYZE HISTORICAL CONTEXT

When you read a literary work set at a particular time and place in history, it is important to focus on the **historical context**—the conditions and events that inspired or influenced its creation. In the case of this story, that context is the aftermath of the Holocaust. During World War II, millions of people died from executions, beatings, disease, and malnutrition in the Nazi concentration camps. As you read "Adam," use this information and the background information on page 1124, in addition to other facts you might know about World War II and the concentration camps, to help you gain a better understanding of Vonnegut's purpose in writing "Adam."

How do you AFFIRM LIFE?

KEY IDEA In the aftermath of tragedy or heartbreak, people are often counseled that "time heals all wounds." Some are able to bounce back, whether from grave illness, a traumatic car accident, or even the horrors of war and genocide. Others cannot find this **resilience** and instead struggle to carry on.

DISCUSS Work with a small group to brainstorm the characteristics people need to affirm life after surviving a horrible experience. Share examples from history, literature, or personal knowledge of people who have found the strength and will to start again. As a group, list the characteristics common to these people. Then compare your group's list with that of other groups and create a final class list.

> What you need to affirm life:
> • forgiveness

How do you AFFIRM LIFE?

Read the question aloud, and ask students to read the **KEY IDEA** paragraph. Elicit or explain that **resilience** means "the ability to recover from or adjust to misfortune." Then carry out the **DISCUSS** activity, encouraging students to consider a wide range of examples. Ask students to generalize about the qualities that appear on the final class list.

SKILLS FOCUS

LITERARY ANALYSIS

● CHARACTERIZATION

Write this passage on the board:

> Samuel was a tall man, though his stooped shoulders and sullen expression made him appear much smaller, as if life's burdens had both reduced his size and darkened his outlook. He spoke little, and when someone wished him "good morning," he would only shrug, implying that there was nothing good about it.

Ask students in what ways the writer conveys a sense of Samuel. **Possible answer:** *The writer describes Samuel's appearance, feelings, and general demeanor.*

CHECK UNDERSTANDING Elicit ideas for another character's response to Samuel.

 RESOURCE MANAGER—Copy Master
Characterization p. 49 (for student use while reading the selection)

READING SKILL R3.5

■ ANALYZE HISTORICAL CONTEXT

Have students reread the passage on the board. Explore how different historical contexts would alter the nature of the passage. For example, ask students how their interpretation would change if they knew that Samuel had been freed from slavery after the Civil War or had been drafted for armed service during World War II.

DIFFERENTIATED INSTRUCTION

FOR STRATEGIC READERS
Vocabulary Support

- *motivations,* "reasons for behaving in a certain way; the desires or needs that cause a person to act"
- *Holocaust,* "the mass slaughter of more than six million Jews and millions of others by the Nazis during World War II"
- *malnutrition,* "poor nutrition as a result of insufficient intake of nutrients"

- *concentration camp,* "Nazi prison camp where large number of people were killed"
- *affirm,* "declare or adopt a positive attitude toward"
- *aftermath,* "the period of time following an event"
- *traumatic,* "causing severe emotional shock"
- *genocide,* "systematic killing of people from a national, ethnic, or other group"

Practice and Apply

SUMMARY

Heinz Knechtmann is in a hospital waiting for his wife, Avchen, to give birth. Both are German Holocaust survivors who have come to America. Heinz was the only member of his family not killed by the Nazis. When his son is born, Heinz is ecstatic. However, he feels isolated from people around him, because no one exhibits much excitement regarding the miracle of birth. His disappointment fades when he joins Avchen at her bedside, and together they share their poignant appreciation of the new life that has emerged despite their horrible experience.

LITERARY ANALYSIS

Ⓐ CHARACTERIZATION

Possible answer: A person so described might have a pleasing but rather shy demeanor. He might be reluctant to make or hold eye contact and might act deferentially toward others.

Lines 19–23
REINFORCE *KEY IDEA:* RESILIENCE

Discuss What does the fact that Knechtmann survived such horrific childhood experiences and continued on with his life suggest about the **resilience** of his character? *Possible answer: It suggests that Knechtmann is fundamentally a strong person with the skills needed to cope with life's grimmest challenges.*

Adam

KURT VONNEGUT JR.

> **BACKGROUND** In the short story "Adam," set during the early 1950s, the main character, Heinz Knechtmann (knĕκнт'män), has survived the atrocities of the Holocaust and, like many Jewish survivors, has come to the United States seeking a better life. As the story begins, he and another expectant father, Mr. Sousa, are in the waiting room of a maternity hospital.

It was midnight in a Chicago lying-in hospital.

"Mr. Sousa," said the nurse, "your wife had a girl. You can see the baby in about twenty minutes."

"I know, I know, I know," said Mr. Sousa, a sullen gorilla, plainly impatient with having a tiresome and familiar routine explained to him. He snapped his fingers. "Girl! Seven, now. Seven girls I got now. A houseful of women. I can beat the stuffings out of ten men my own size. But, what do I get? Girls."

"Mr. Knechtmann," said the nurse to the other man in the room. She pronounced the name, as almost all Americans did, a colorless Netman. "I'm
10 sorry. Still no word on your wife. She is keeping us waiting, isn't she?" She grinned glassily and left.

Sousa turned on Knechtmann. "Some little son of a gun like you, Netman, you want a boy, bing! You got one. Want a football team, bing, bing, bing, eleven, you got it." He stomped out of the room.

The man he left behind, all alone now, was Heinz Knechtmann, a presser in a dry-cleaning plant, a small man with thin wrists and a bad spine that kept him slightly hunched, as though forever weary. His face was long and big-nosed and thin-lipped, but was so overcast with good-humored humility as to be beautiful. Ⓐ His eyes were large and brown, and deep-set and longlashed. He was only twenty-
20 two, but seemed and felt much older. He had died a little as each member of his family had been led away and killed by the Nazis, until only in him, at the age of ten, had life and the name of Knechtmann shared a soul. He and his wife, Avchen, had grown up behind barbed wire.

ANALYZING VISUALS
What ideas are suggested by the images in the collage on page 1125? What is the cumulative impact of these images taken together? Explain.

Ⓐ CHARACTERIZATION
Reread lines 15–18. Here Vonnegut combines his physical description of Heinz Knechtmann with a reflection on his personality. What might it look like to see a person "so overcast with good-humored humility as to be beautiful"?

❶ Targeted Passage

Fatherhood (1990s). Ed Roskowski.
© Ed Roskowski/Corbis.

1124 UNIT 6: CONTEMPORARY LITERATURE

DIFFERENTIATED INSTRUCTION

FOR ALL STUDENTS
Provide these independent projects to extend the lesson:

- Write an essay exploring Vonnegut's view of the American Dream.
- Write a poem about resilience.
- Create a character web for Heinz.
- Brainstorm a story sequel.

For further details on these projects, see

Ⓡ RESOURCE MANAGER
Ideas for Extension pp. 44–45

FOR STRATEGIC READERS
In combination with the *Audio Anthology CD,* use one or more Targeted Passages (pp. 1124, 1128, and 1130) to ensure that students focus on key story events and concepts. Targeted Passages are also good for English learners.

❶ Targeted Passage [Lines 15–23]

This passage introduces the main character and provides key background information.

ANALYZE VISUALS

Possible answer: The collage suggests a traditional male figure of about 50 or 60 years ago. He is a father as the title of the collage indicates and clad in typical business attire and smoking a pipe. The other images, such as the baby and the old-fashioned Venetian blinds, highlight the paternal and familial aspects of his life. The cumulative impact of the juxtaposed images is that of a businessman/new father who has added a whole new dimension to his life.

BACKGROUND

German Names The narrator says that the nurse pronounces Knechtmann's name "as almost all Americans did, a colorless Netman" (lines 8–9). The name *Knechtmann* would have a guttural pronunciation in its native German. However, English speakers unfamiliar with the true pronunciation would simplify the sound to "Netman." This idea appears again on page 1126, lines 45–50.

- Describe Heinz Knechtmann's physical appearance.
- What happened to the members of Heinz's family?
- How old was Heinz when this happened?
- Who is Avchen?
- What terrible experience do Heinz and Avchen have in common?

FOR ENGLISH LEARNERS

Prereading For prereading instruction for English learners, see

BEST PRACTICES TOOLKIT
   Scaffolding Reading Instruction pp. 43–46

Culture: Clarify Explain these references:

- *lying-in hospital* (line 1), "maternity hospital"
- *had grown up behind barbed wire* (line 23), "the two were children together in a Nazi concentration camp"

FOR ADVANCED LEARNERS/AP

AP exercises in the bottom channel provide additional challenge for students. Use these suggestions for small groups or individuals.

ADDITIONAL GUIDELINES

For more help with differentiation and tips for classroom management, see

BEST PRACTICES TOOLKIT
   Differentiated Instruction pp. 31–38

He had been staring at the walls of the waiting room for twelve hours now, since noon, when his wife's labor pains had become regular, the surges of slow rollers coming in from the sea a mile apart, from far, far away. This would be his second child. The last time he had waited, he had waited on a straw tick in a displaced-persons camp in Germany. The child, Karl Knechtmann, named after Heinz's father, had died, and with it, once more, had died the name of one of the finest cellists ever to have lived. **B**

He had been staring at the walls of the waiting room for twelve hours now, since noon, when his wife's labor pains had become regular, the surges of slow rollers coming in from the sea a mile apart, from far, far away. This would be his second child. The last time he had waited, he had waited on a straw tick in a displaced-persons camp in Germany. The child, Karl Knechtmann, named after Heinz's father, had died, and with it, once more, had died the name of one of the
30 finest cellists ever to have lived. **B**

When the numbness of weary wishing lifted momentarily during this second vigil, Heinz's mind was a medley of proud family names, gone, all gone, that could be brought to life again in this new being—if it lived. Peter Knechtmann, the surgeon; Kroll Knechtmann, the botanist; Friederich Knechtmann, the playwright. Dimly recalled uncles. Or if it was a girl, and if it lived, it would be Helga Knechtmann, Heinz's mother, and she would learn to play the harp as Heinz's mother had, and for all Heinz's ugliness, she would be beautiful. The Knechtmann men were all ugly, the Knechtmann women were all lovely as angels, though not all angels. It had always been so—for hundreds and hundreds of years.

40 "Mr. Netman," said the nurse, "it's a boy, and your wife is fine. She's resting now. You can see her in the morning. You can see the baby in twenty minutes."

Heinz looked up dumbly.

"It weighs five pounds nine ounces." She was gone again, with the same prim smile and officious, squeaking footsteps.

"Knechtmann," murmured Heinz, standing and bowing slightly to the wall. "The name is Knechtmann." He bowed again and gave a smile that was courtly and triumphant. He spoke the name with an exaggerated Old World pronunciation, like a foppish footman announcing the arrival of nobility, a guttural drum roll, unsoftened for American ears. "KhhhhhhhhhhhhhhhNECHT!
50 mannnnnnnnnnnn." **C**

"Mr. Netman?" A very young doctor with a pink face and close cropped red hair stood in the waiting-room door. There were circles under his eyes, and he spoke through a yawn.

"Dr. Powers!" cried Heinz, clasping the man's right hand between both of his. "Thank God, thank God, thank God, and thank you."

"Um," said Dr. Powers, and he managed to smile wanly.

"There isn't anything wrong, is there?"

"Wrong?" said Powers. "No, no. Everything's fine. If I look down in the mouth, it's because I've been up for thirty-six hours straight." He closed his eyes,
60 and leaned against the doorframe. "No, no trouble with your wife," he said in a faraway voice. "She's made for having babies. Regular pop-up toaster. Like rolling off a log. Schnip-schnap."

"She is?" said Heinz incredulously.

Dr. Powers shook his head, bringing himself back to consciousness. "My mind—conked out completely. Sousa—I got your wife confused with Mrs. Sousa. They finished in a dead heat. Netman, you're Netman. Sorry. Your wife's the one with pelvis trouble."

B HISTORICAL CONTEXT
Reread lines 19–30. With the help of the historical information on page 1123 and the Background on page 1124, explain the various events that happened to Heinz and his family.

C CHARACTERIZATION
Reread lines 45–50. How does Heinz's pride in the birth of his son express itself in his words and actions?

READING SKILL

B HISTORICAL CONTEXT

Possible answer: Heinz and his family were German Jews who were imprisoned in Nazi concentration camps when Heinz was a child. The Nazis killed everyone in the family except Heinz. Before eventually coming to America, Heinz and his wife Avchen lived in a displaced-persons camp in Germany. Their first child died there. He is now—in the early 1950s—awaiting the birth of their second child.

If students need help . . . Work with them to infer and approximate the sequence of events in Heinz's life and plot them on a timeline spanning 1930–1955:

- Heinz born in Germany: early 1930s
- Heinz, age 10, family in concentration camp: early 1940s
- Heinz in displaced-persons camp: after World War II/post-1945
- Heinz, age 22, living in America: early 1950s

 BEST PRACTICES TOOLKIT—Transparency
Timeline p. B23

LITERARY ANALYSIS

C CHARACTERIZATION

Possible answer: Heinz's pride in the birth of his son is evident in his standing and bowing and in his "courtly and triumphant" smile. Heinz also expresses his feelings when he proudly proclaims the family name, sounding "like a foppish footman announcing the arrival of nobility" (line 48).

Extend the Discussion Why does Vonnegut choose the adjectives "courtly" and "triumphant" to characterize Heinz's smile?

DIFFERENTIATED INSTRUCTION

FOR ADVANCED LEARNERS/AP

Evaluate Author's Choices Vonnegut includes few details about the "atrocities of the Holocaust" that Heinz has survived. Readers are left to make inferences from such lines as 20–23. Ask whether students think Vonnegut should have provided more background to explain Heinz or whether such detail is unnecessary. Point out as well that Vonnegut chose to tell the story through a third-person omniscient narrator.

Ask students to evaluate the author's choice. Discuss how the narrative might differ in tone and content if narrated in the first person, either by Heinz or perhaps by Avchen. After discussing both issues, challenge students to write one to two paragraphs about one of the two, expressing their evaluation and supporting it with thoughtful reasons and textual evidence.

"Malnutrition as a child," said Heinz. **D**

"Yeah. Well, the baby came normally, but, if you're going to have another one,
70 it'd better be a Caesarean. Just to be on the safe side."

"I can't thank you enough," said Heinz passionately.

Dr. Powers licked his lips, and fought to keep his eyes open. "Uh huh. 'S
O.K.," he said thickly. "'Night. Luck." He shambled out into the corridor.

The nurse stuck her head into the waiting room. "You can see your baby,
Mr. Netman."

"Doctor—" said Heinz, hurrying out into the corridor, wanting to shake
Powers' hand again so that Powers would know what a magnificent thing he'd
done. "It's the most wonderful thing that ever happened." The elevator doors
slithered shut between them before Dr. Powers could show a glimmer of response.

80 "This way," said the nurse. "Turn left at the end of the hall, and you'll find the
nursery window there. Write your name on a piece of paper and hold
it against the glass."

Heinz made the trip by himself, without seeing another human being until he
reached the end. There, on the other side of a large glass panel, he saw a hundred
of them cupped in shallow canvas buckets and arranged in a square block of
straight ranks and files.

Heinz wrote his name on the back of a laundry slip and pressed it to the
window. A fat and placid nurse looked at the paper, not at Heinz's face, and
missed seeing his wide smile, missed an urgent invitation to share for a moment
90 his ecstasy.

She grasped one of the buckets and wheeled it before the window. She turned
away again, once more missing the smile.

"Hello, hello, hello, little Knechtmann," said Heinz to the red prune on the
other side of the glass. His voice echoed down the hard, bare corridor, and came
back to him with embarrassing loudness. He blushed and lowered his voice.
"Little Peter, little Kroll," he said softly, "little Friederich—and there's Helga in
you, too. Little spark of Knechtmann, you little treasure house. Everything is
saved in you."

"I'm afraid you'll have to be more quiet," said a nurse, sticking her head out
100 from one of the rooms.

"Sorry," said Heinz. "I'm very sorry." He fell silent, and contented himself with
tapping lightly on the window with a fingernail, trying to get the child to look at
him. Young Knechtmann would not look, wouldn't share the moment, and after
a few minutes the nurse took him away again.

Heinz beamed as he rode on the elevator and as he crossed the hospital lobby,
but no one gave him more than a cursory glance. He passed a row of telephone
booths and there, in one of the booths with the door open, he saw a soldier with
whom he'd shared the waiting room an hour before.

"Yeah, Ma—seven pounds six ounces. Got hair like Buffalo Bill. No, we
110 haven't had time to make up a name for her yet . . . That you, Pa? Yup, mother
and daughter doin' fine, just fine. Seven pounds six ounces. Nope, no name. . . ."

D HISTORICAL CONTEXT
Consider why Heinz's
wife might have suffered
malnutrition as a child.
What does this suggest
about the impact of
history on the present?

D HISTORICAL CONTEXT

*Possible answer: As children, both Heinz
and his wife were prisoners in a Nazi
concentration camp. No doubt, they were
severely deprived of nutritious foods. The
impact of his wife's childhood malnutrition
on her present-day "pelvis trouble" (line 67)
demonstrates how past events can seriously
affect the present.*

If students need help . . . Have them reread
lines 22–23 and discuss their meaning.
Clarify living conditions in the Nazi concentration camps, referring to the historical background on page 1123 or urging
students to pursue their own research.

Lines 87–98
TIERED DISCUSSION PROMPTS
Use these prompts to help students under-
stand Heinz's reaction to his son's birth:

Connect Have you ever spent time with or
seen a brand new parent? Describe the
person's emotional state. *Accept all
thoughtful responses.*

Interpret What does Heinz mean when he
says, "Little spark of Knechtmann, you little
treasure house. Everything is saved in you"?
*Possible answer: Heinz is expressing his grati-
tude that the newborn baby will continue
the family line. The Nazis killed the other
members of the Knechtmann family, but
the baby has preserved the "spark of Knechtmann" and qualities of all the murdered
Knechtmanns.*

Evaluate Is Heinz's response to his new
son believable? Explain. *Possible answer:
Heinz's response is quite believable because
his experience has been so devastating
that the birth of a child would seem truly
miraculous.*

FOR ENGLISH LEARNERS

Key Academic Vocabulary Use Word
Questioning to teach these words: *panel*
(line 84), *odd* (line 179).

 BEST PRACTICES TOOLKIT—Transparency
Word Questioning p. E9

Language: Conversational English Patterns
Clarify that when people speak, they often
omit letters or words. Explain that authors
try to represent this speech to make dialogue
sound realistic. Highlight the abbreviated
form *"'S O.K."* in lines 72–73, and ask students
what is missing (*It*). Then elicit or provide the
missing elements in *"'Night. Luck."* (line 73)
and *"Got hair like Buffalo Bill"* (line 109).
Encourage students to identify other examples in the story.

E CHARACTERIZATION

Possible answer: *Vonnegut emphasizes Heinz's isolation through the character's thoughts and feelings, the speech of other characters, and the narrator's comments.*

If students need help . . . Work with them to add to the chart introduced on page 1123, focusing on these three columns:

Character's Speech, Thoughts, Feelings	Other Characters' Speech, Thoughts, Feelings	Narrator's Comments
"Heinz longed to . . . tell the marvelous news."	The soldier is sharing similar news with his parents and sister.	"But there was no one to call, no one waiting for the news."

READING SKILL

F HISTORICAL CONTEXT

Possible answer: *By focusing attention on naming the baby, Vonnegut underscores the importance of the newborn to Heinz. The baby represents the miracle of life for Heinz, but perhaps even more than that, the baby is a link to Heinz's past and to the family members whom Heinz loved and so tragically lost.*

Extend the Discussion Why does Vonnegut present Sousa's attitude in such sharp contrast to Heinz's excitement?

That you, Sis? Pretty late for you to be up, ain't it? Doesn't look like anybody yet. Let me talk to Ma again. . . . That you, Ma? Well, I guess that's all the news from Chicago. Now, Mom, Mom, take it easy—don't worry. It's a swell-looking baby, Mom. Just the hair looks like Buffalo Bill, and I said it as a joke, Mom. That's right, seven pounds six ounces. . . ."

There were five other booths, all empty, all open for calls to anyplace on earth. Heinz longed to hurry into one of them breathlessly, and tell the marvelous news. But there was no one to call, no one waiting for the news. **E**

120   **B**ut Heinz still beamed, and he strode across the street and into a quiet tavern there. In the dank twilight there were only two men, tête-à-tête, the bartender and Mr. Sousa.

"Yes sir, what'll it be?"

"I'd like to buy you and Mr. Sousa a drink," said Heinz with a heartiness strange to him. "I'd like the best brandy you've got. My wife just had a baby!"

"That so?" said the bartender with polite interest.

"Five pounds nine ounces," said Heinz.

"Huh," said the bartender. "What do you know."

"Netman," said Sousa, "Wha'dja get?"

130   "Boy," said Heinz proudly.

"Never knew it to fail," said Sousa bitterly. "It's the little guys, all the time the little guys."

"Boy, girl," said Heinz, "it's all the same, just as long as it lives. Over there in the hospital, they're too close to it to see the wonder of it. A miracle over and over again—the world made new."

"Wait'll you've racked up seven, Netman," said Sousa. "Then you come back and tell me about the miracle."

"You got seven?" said the bartender. "I'm one up on you. I got eight." He poured three drinks.

140   "Far as I'm concerned," said Sousa, "you can have the championship."

Heinz lifted his glass. "Here's long life and great skill and much happiness to— to Peter Karl Knechtmann." He breathed quickly, excited by the decision.

"There's a handle to take ahold of," said Sousa. "You'd think the kid weighed two hundred pounds."

"Peter is the name of a famous surgeon," said Heinz, "the boy's great-uncle, dead now. Karl was my father's name." **F**

"Here's to Pete K. Netman," said Sousa, with a cursory salute.

"Pete," said the bartender, drinking.

"And here's to your little girl—the new one," said Heinz.

150   Sousa sighed and smiled wearily. "Here's to her. God bless her."

"And now, I'll propose a toast," said the bartender, hammering on the bar with his fist. "On your feet, gentlemen. Up, up, everybody up."

Heinz stood, and held his glass high, ready for the next step in camaraderie, a toast to the whole human race, of which the Knechtmanns were still a part.

"Here's to the White Sox!" roared the bartender.

"Minoso, Fox, Mele," said Sousa.

E CHARACTERIZATION
Reread lines 105–119. What main method of characterization does Vonnegut employ to emphasize Heinz's isolation?

2 Targeted Passage

F HISTORICAL CONTEXT
Reread lines 141–146. Why do you think Vonnegut focuses so much attention on the naming of the baby?

DIFFERENTIATED INSTRUCTION

FOR STRATEGIC READERS

2 Targeted Passage [Lines 124–150]

This passage contrasts Heinz's excitement with the jaded weariness of those nearby.

- Why does Heinz want to buy drinks for Sousa and the bartender?

- Why don't Sousa and the bartender share Heinz's excitement?

- What does Heinz mean that the people in the hospital are "too close to it to see the wonder of it"?

FOR ADVANCED LEARNERS/AP

Write a Journal Entry Have students reflect on the events of the story and make inferences based on textual evidence about Heinz's demeanor and personality before the birth of his son. Then ask them to imagine that Heinz is a close friend of theirs. Have students write and share a journal entry about the day Heinz's son is born and how he responds to the birth. Encourage them to include their own feelings about Heinz and Avchen.

"Fain, Lollar, Rivera!" said the bartender. He turned to Heinz. "Drink up, boy! The White Sox! Don't tell me you're a Cub fan."

"No," said Heinz, disappointed. "No—I don't follow baseball, I'm afraid." The
160 other two men seemed to be sinking away from him. "I haven't been able to think about much but the baby."

The bartender at once turned his full attention to Sousa. "Look," he said intensely, "they take Fain off of first, and put him at third, and give Pierce first. Then move Minoso in from left field to shortstop. See what I'm doing?"

"Yep, yep," said Sousa eagerly.

"And then we take that no-good Carrasquel and . . ."

Heinz was all alone again, with twenty feet of bar between him and the other two men. It might as well have been a continent.

He finished his drink without pleasure, and left quietly.

170 At the railroad station, where he waited for a local train to take him home to the South Side, Heinz's glow returned again as he saw a co-worker at the dry-cleaning plant walk in with a girl. They were laughing and had their arms around each other's waist.

"Harry," said Heinz, hurrying toward them. "Guess what, Harry. Guess what just happened." He grinned broadly.

Harry, a tall, dapper, snub-nosed young man, looked down at Heinz with mild surprise. "Oh—hello, Heinz. What's up, boy?"

The girl looked on in perplexity, as though asking why they should be accosted at such an odd hour by such an odd person. Heinz avoided her slightly
180 derisive eyes.

"A baby, Harry. My wife just had a boy."

"Oh," said Harry. He extended his hand. "Well, congratulations." The hand was limp. "I think that's swell, Heinz, perfectly swell." He withdrew his hand and waited for Heinz to say something else.

"Yes, yes—just about an hour ago," said Heinz. "Five pounds nine ounces. I've never been happier in my life."

"Well, I think it's perfectly swell, Heinz. You should be happy."

"Yes, indeed," said the girl.

There was a long silence, with all three shifting from one foot to the other.

190 "Really good news," said Harry at last.

"Yes, well," said Heinz quickly, "Well, that's all I had to tell you."

"Thanks," said Harry. "Glad to hear about it."

There was another uneasy silence.

"See you at work," said Heinz, and strode jauntily back to his bench, but with his reddened neck betraying how foolish he felt.

The girl giggled.

Back home in his small apartment, at two in the morning, Heinz talked to himself, to the empty bassinet, and to the bed. He talked in German, a language he had sworn never to use again.

200 "They don't care," said Heinz. "They're all too busy, busy, busy to notice life, to feel anything about it. A baby is born." He shrugged. "What could be duller?"

CHARACTERIZATION
What character trait of Heinz's does Vonnegut reveal through the sentence "Heinz avoided her slightly derisive eyes"?

HISTORICAL CONTEXT
Reread lines 197–199. What is Vonnegut's purpose in including this description of Heinz's use of and feelings about speaking German? Explain.

ADAM **1129**

Lines 151–169
TIERED DISCUSSION PROMPTS
Use these prompts to help students understand Heinz's feelings of isolation:

Interpret Why does Vonnegut include the dialogue about baseball? *Possible answer: The dialogue shows how little importance others give to the birth of Heinz's baby. At the same time, the dialogue shows how isolated Heinz is from those around him.*

Evaluate Is Heinz's expectation that others will share his excitement unrealistic? Why or why not? *Possible answer: Given Vonnegut's description of Sousa's and the bartender's personalities, Heinz's expectation does seem unrealistic.*

LITERARY ANALYSIS

CHARACTERIZATION

Possible answer: Through this sentence Vonnegut suggests Heinz's shy and self-effacing nature.

READING SKILL

HISTORICAL CONTEXT

Possible answer: Vonnegut's purpose is to show how Heinz is part of two worlds but feels at home in neither. On one hand, he finds his German childhood rising to the surface in this emotional moment. On the other hand, he identifies Germany with the hated Nazis and what they did to his family.

FOR ENGLISH LEARNERS
Language: Conversational English Patterns
[mixed-readiness groups] Point out that the story contains clipped forms, elliptical writing, and a number of dated or slang words and expressions. Have Jigsaw groups study the following examples and explain their examples to the class:

• *Sis* (line 112)

• *swell-looking baby* (line 114)

• *Wha'dja* (line 129)

• *racked up* (line 136)

• *Far as I'm concerned* (line 140)

• *take ahold of* (line 143)

• *Here's to* (line 147)

• *What's up, boy?* (line 177)

• *See you* (line 194)

Urge students to identify other examples in the story.

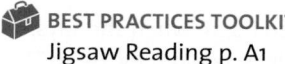 **BEST PRACTICES TOOLKIT**
Jigsaw Reading p. A1

FOR ADVANCED LEARNERS/AP
Compare Views Have students reread lines 211–243 and summarize the view Heinz and Avchen have about the value of life. Then ask students to compare that view with the one expressed in Randall Jarrell's poem (see page 1119). If the speaker in Jarrell's poem sees life as dispensable and expendable, how do Heinz and Avchen see it? Have students write a brief essay comparing and contrasting the two views.

ADAM **1129**

Possible answer: *The collage expresses the permanence of the marriage bond, through which two people in love can help each other overcome life's obstacles. In the story, the bond between Heinz and Avchen helps them survive the terrible experiences they have had in Germany.*

Lines 220–243
REINFORCE *KEY IDEA:* RESILIENCE

Discuss In what way does the story's conclusion underscore the **resilience** of Heinz and Avchen? *Possible answer: The conclusion shows that Heinz and Avchen not only have survived but have been able to create new life despite the hardships they have endured.*

SELECTION WRAP–UP

REFLECT Ask students whether they think Vonnegut's view of human nature in this story is mostly positive or negative. Why?

⭐ CRITIQUE

- Have students identify the passages in the story that they found most moving and then explain what makes these passages so meaningful. Urge students to be specific.

- After completing the After Reading questions on page 1131, have students revisit their responses and tell whether they have changed their opinions.

Who would be so stupid as to talk about it, to think there was anything important or interesting about it?"

He opened a window on the summer night, and looked out at the moonlit canyon of gray wooden porches and garbage cans. "There are too many of us, and we are all too far apart," said Heinz. "Another Knechtmann is born, another O'Leary, another Sousa. Who cares? Why should anyone care? What difference does it make? None."

He lay down in his clothes on the unmade bed, and, with a rattling sigh, went
210 to sleep.

He awoke at six, as always. He drank a cup of coffee, and with a wry sense of anonymity, he jostled and was jostled aboard the downtown train. His face showed no emotion. It was like all the other faces, seemingly incapable of surprise or wonder, joy or anger.

He walked across town to the hospital with the same detachment, a gray, uninteresting man, a part of the city.

In the hospital, he was as purposeful and calm as the doctors and nurses bustling about him.

220 When he was led into the ward where Avchen slept behind white screens, he felt only what he had always felt in her presence—love and aching awe and gratitude for her.

"You go ahead and wake her gently, Mr. Netman," said the nurse.

"Avchen—" He touched her on her white-gowned shoulder. "Avchen. Are you all right, Avchen?"

"Mmmmmmmmmm?" murmured Avchen.
230 Her eyes opened to narrow slits. "Heinz. Hello, Heinz."

"Sweetheart, are you all right?"

"Yes, yes," she whispered. "I'm fine. How is the baby, Heinz?"

"Perfect. Perfect, Avchen."

"They couldn't kill us, could they, Heinz?"

"No."

"And here we are, alive as we can be."

"Yes."
240 "The baby, Heinz—" She opened her dark eyes wide. "It's the most wonderful thing that ever happened, isn't it?"

"Yes," said Heinz.

③ **Targeted Passage**

Life Decisions (1995), Ed Roskowski. © Ed Roskowski/Corbis.

DIFFERENTIATED INSTRUCTION

FOR STRATEGIC READERS

③ **Targeted Passage [Lines 220–243]**

This final passage shows the strong bond between Heinz and Avchen and stresses their joy at survival and the miracle of life.

- Describe Heinz's feelings about Avchen.

- Describe Avchen's feelings about Heinz.

- What is the couple's reaction to having a new baby?

- What does Avchen mean when she says, "They couldn't kill us, could they, Heinz"?

FOR ENGLISH LEARNERS

Vocabulary: Cognates Point out that the Spanish word *cañón* is similar in spelling and pronunciation to the English word *canyon* (line 205). Call attention to these cognates:

- *anonymity* (line 212), anonimidad

- *incapable* (line 213), incapaz

- *surprise* (line 213), sorpresa

- *presence* (line 222), presencia

- *gratitude* (line 223), gratitud

- *murmured* (line 229), murmurar

Comprehension

R3.5

1. **Recall** From what country and historical events is Heinz Knechtmann a refugee?

2. **Recall** Why is he at the hospital?

3. **Summarize** Why is he so amazed that he and his wife have had a child?

Literary Analysis

4. **Make Inferences** In Jewish families, it is customary to name babies after family members who have died. Given this knowledge, what can you infer about Heinz from the following quotation: "Heinz's mind was a medley of proud family names, gone, all gone, that could be brought to life again in this new being—if it lived." (lines 32–33)

5. **Draw Conclusions** In your opinion, what gives Heinz and his wife the **resilience** to move forward with their lives after losing so much and seeing so much horror? Use evidence from the story and your own experience to support your answer.

6. **Examine Characterization** Look back at the chart you created as you read. Which method of characterization does Vonnegut depend on most heavily in his development of Heinz Knechtmann? Cite evidence.

7. **Analyze Historical Context** Vonnegut did not experience the Holocaust firsthand, yet this event in history inspired the creation of this story. In your opinion, what was Vonnegut's purpose in writing the story? Do you think that his purpose might have been better achieved in a historical essay, or was there an advantage in depicting historical events through a fictional lens? Support your opinions.

8. **Interpret Imagery** Each of the following images helps support an important **theme** in this story. Interpret each one.

   • "Heinz was all alone again, with twenty feet of bar between him and the other two men. It might as well have been a continent." (lines 167–168)

   • "They couldn't kill us, could they, Heinz?" (line 236)

9. **Evaluate the Title** Think about why Vonnegut might have chosen the title "Adam" for this story. In your opinion, is it an appropriate title? Explain.

Literary Criticism

10. **Social Context** Explain whether you agree with Heinz's conclusion that people in this country are "too busy," "too many," and "too far apart" to care about one another. Give reasons for your response.

---

7. ● **SKILLS FOCUS** Analyze Historical Context *Vonnegut's purpose appears to be to show that the human spirit can triumph over extreme adversity as Heinz and Avchen survive the death camps and create new life. This purpose is effectively achieved through a fictional lens because the story invites readers to identify with the characters.*

8. *Lines 167–168 support the theme that some life experiences isolate people forever, as Heinz is isolated from the other men by a past that has given him a greater*

appreciation for life. Line 236 supports the theme that the human spirit, and perhaps two people's love for each other, can triumph over adversity.

9. *Vonnegut probably chose his title because the name "Adam" represents the first man and the beginning of life in the biblical story of Adam and Eve. Views on the title's appropriateness will vary.*

10. *Accept all well-supported responses.*

Practice and Apply

After Reading

Use these copy masters to check understanding and provide extra support:

Ⓡ RESOURCE MANAGER—Copy Masters
   Reading Check p. 53
   Analyze Historical Context p. 51
   Question Support p. 54

   Additional selection questions are provided for teachers on page 43.

ANSWERS

1. *Heinz is a refugee from Germany and the Holocaust.*

2. *His wife is having a baby.*

3. *He and his wife were prisoners in a Nazi concentration camp and have managed to survive and bring new life into the world.*

Possible answers:

4. *Readers can infer than many members of Heinz's family have died, and thus he has a wide range of choices for baby names.*

5. *Students should recognize how mutual love and support give strength to Heinz and Avchen, as shown clearly in lines 220–243.*

6. ● **SKILLS FOCUS** Characterization *Vonnegut depends most heavily on presenting the character's own speech, thoughts, and feelings. For example, readers share Heinz's happiness about the baby's birth, his disappointment with the others' reactions to it, his feelings of isolation, and his love for Avchen.*

Assess and Reteach

Assess

Ⓡ RESOURCE MANAGER—Copy Masters
   Selection Test A pp. 55–56
   Selection Test B/C pp. 57–58

💿 Test Generator CD

Reteach

Ⓢ STANDARDS LESSON FILE
   Literature Lesson 3: Characterization
   Literature Lesson 11: Theme, Motif, and Epiphany
   Reading Lesson 14: Synthesizing Information

R3.2 (p. 1135),
R3.7 (p. 1135)

from SURVIVAL *in* Auschwitz

Primo Levi

> **BACKGROUND** Primo Levi (1919–1987) was an Italian chemist. In 1944, he was deported to Auschwitz, a Nazi concentration camp in Poland, where he remained for one year. Levi wrote about his nightmarish experiences in objective, scientific detail, believing that subjective commentary was unnecessary and that the events would speak for themselves. The following excerpt from his memoir describes the ritual in which prisoners were selected for condemnation.

Today is working Sunday, *Arbeitssonntag:* we work until 1 P.M., then we return to camp for the shower, shave and general control for skin diseases and lice. And in the yards, everyone knew mysteriously that the selection would be today.

The news arrived, as always, surrounded by a halo of contradictory or suspect details: the selection in the infirmary took place this morning; the percentage was seven per cent of the whole camp, thirty, fifty per cent of the patients. At Birkenau,[1] the crematorium chimney has been smoking for ten days. Room has to be made for an enormous convoy arriving from the Poznan ghetto.[2] The young tell the young that all the old ones will be chosen. The healthy tell the healthy that only the ill will
10 be chosen. Specialists will be excluded. German Jews will be excluded. Low Numbers[3] will be excluded. You will be chosen. I will be excluded.

At 1 P.M. exactly the yard empties in orderly fashion, and for two hours the gray unending army files past the two control stations where, as on every day, we are counted and recounted, and past the military band which for two hours without interruption plays, as on every day, those marches to which we must synchronize our steps at our entrance and our exit.

---

1. **Birkenau** (bûr′kən-ou): Also known as Auschwitz II, this camp stood about two miles from an older camp, called Auschwitz I. Between 1 million and 4 million people were murdered at Auschwitz-Birkenau during the years 1942–1945.
2. **Poznan** (pōz′năn′) **ghetto:** the area of the Polish city of Poznan in which Jews were forced to live.
3. **Low Numbers:** prisoners with low identification numbers.

Lines 4–11
TIERED DISCUSSION PROMPTS

Use these prompts to help students understand the anxiety and frustration that the prisoners suffered:

Connect Have you or someone you know had to wait for important news, while hearing only rumors? Describe how such a situation feels. *Accept all thoughtful responses.*

Interpret What does Primo Levi mean by "The news arrived, as always, surrounded by a halo of contradictory or suspect details . . ."? *Possible answer: Because no one knows for certain what the Nazis plan to do, information is impossible to verify, and rumors abound.*

Evaluate Does Levi effectively convey the uncertainty that the prisoners were forced to endure? Explain. *Students should recognize that Levi describes the way in which each individual group tries to believe that it will be spared. This description very effectively conveys the prisoners' uncertainty.*

DIFFERENTIATED INSTRUCTION

FOR STRATEGIC READERS
Vocabulary Support

- *contradictory* (line 4), "inconsistent; containing opposite views or information"
- *crematorium* (line 7), "a place where bodies are cremated or reduced to ashes by burning"
- *convoy* (line 8), "a group of vehicles or train cars traveling together"
- *synchronize* (line 15), "operate together at the same rate; coordinate"

FOR ADVANCED LEARNERS/AP
Research Primo Levi Have students conduct research to learn about the life and work of Primo Levi. Students should address such questions as: How did Levi manage to survive Auschwitz? What did he do after being liberated? What other books did he write? Ask students to summarize their research in an oral presentation.

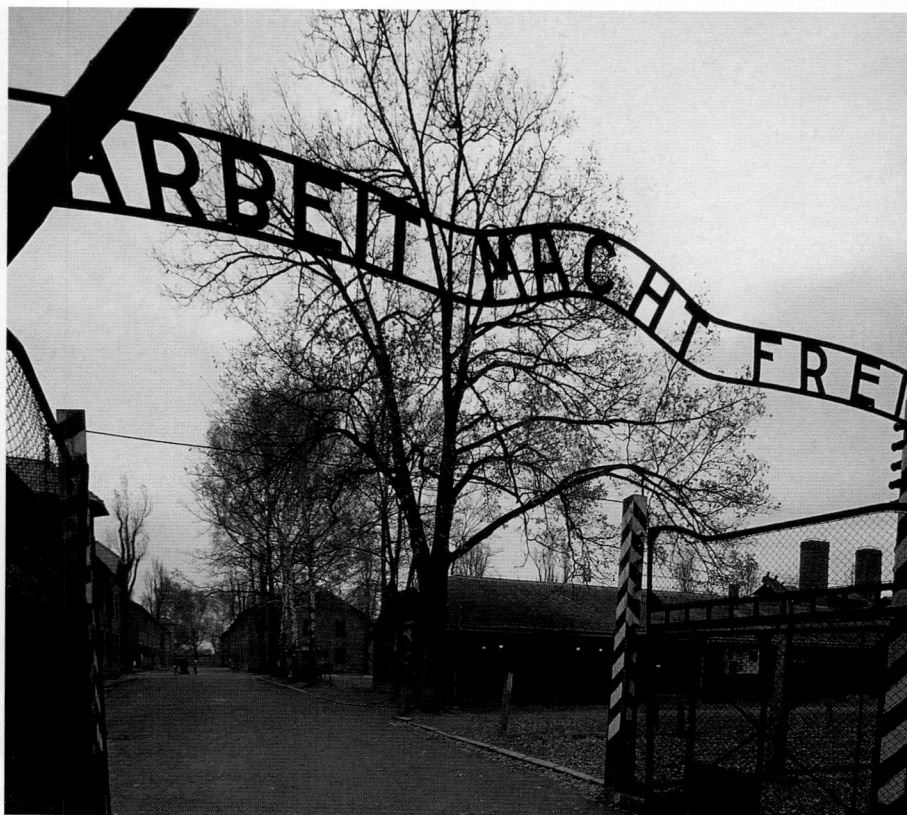

The German slogan *Arbeit macht frei* was posted above the gate to Auschwitz. It means "Work will make you free."

It seems like every day, the kitchen chimney smokes as usual, the distribution of the soup is already beginning. But then the bell is heard, and at that moment we realize that we have arrived.

20   Because this bell always sounds at dawn, when it means the reveille;[4] but if it sounds during the day, it means "*Blocksperre,*" enclosure in huts, and this happens when there is a selection to prevent anyone avoiding it, or when those selected leave for the gas, to prevent anyone seeing them leave.

  Our *Blockältester*[5] knows his business. He has made sure that we have all entered, he has made the door locked, he has given everyone his card with his number, name, profession, age and nationality and he has ordered everyone to undress completely, except for shoes. We wait like this, naked, with the card in our hands, for the commission to reach our hut. We are hut 48, but one can never tell if they are going to begin at hut 1

---

4. **reveille** (rĕv′ə-lē): a signal used to awaken people.
5. ***Blockältester*** (blŏ′käl-tĕs′tər) *German*: block elder—a prisoner cooperating with the German guards by serving as the head of a block, or barracks.

BACKGROUND

The Horror of Auschwitz Auschwitz comprised the largest of the Nazi concentration and extermination camps. Between 1.1 million and 1.5 million people, mostly Jews, are estimated to have died there. Every day, prisoners were transported to Auschwitz by train from all over Nazi-occupied Europe. Some were killed in gas chambers almost at once. Others were used as slave labor in factories, but most of these laborers were also eventually killed by the Nazis or else died as a result of mistreatment, illness, or starvation. Some Auschwitz prisoners were subjected to ghastly medical experimentation. Soviet soldiers finally liberated the camp in January 1945, finding fewer than 8,000 survivors. Today there is a museum at the Auschwitz site, to help the world remember the horrors that occurred there.

FOR ENGLISH LEARNERS

Vocabulary: Cognates Point out that the Spanish word *misteriosamente* is similar in spelling and pronunciation to the English word *mysteriously* (line 3). Then call attention to these other Spanish cognates:

- *contradictory* (line 4), contradictorio
- *suspect* (line 4), sospechoso
- *crematorium* (line 7), crematorio
- *counted* (line 14), contado
- *interruption* (line 15), interrupción
- *selection* (line 22), selección
- *pressure* (line 37), presión
- *condemned* (line 59), condenado
- *myope* (line 63), miope
- *examination* (line 65), examinación
- *eliminated* (line 67), eliminado
- *percentage* (line 68), porcentaje

Ask students to think of cognates in their home languages.

TIERED DISCUSSION PROMPTS

Use these prompts to help students understand the experiences of Levi and his fellow prisoners:

Summarize What is happening in this passage? *Possible answer: The Nazis are doing a cursory inspection of the prisoners to determine who will live and who will die.*

Analyze In what ways does Levi convey to readers what it felt like to be in the situation? Use examples to explain. *Possible answer: Levi conveys the feelings of the situation through vivid images and sensory detail. For example, he describes how the "crowd of frightened, naked people" (line 33) is driven along and becomes "a warm and compact human mass" (lines 35–36) crammed into the Quartermaster's office, "exercising such a pressure on the wooden walls as to make them creak" (lines 36–37). Then he describes how he crosses in front of the SS man, "trying to hold my head high, my chest forward and my muscles contracted . . . " (lines 51–52).*

Synthesize The background on page 1132 explains Levi's belief that "subjective commentary was unnecessary and that the events would speak for themselves." In what ways does Levi's description of events support that belief? Explain. *Possible answer: Levi's detached but detailed description provides a heightened sense of realism and immediacy, qualities that any further commentary might compromise.*

The shoes of victims, on display at the Auschwitz Museum

or hut 60. At any rate, we can rest quietly at least for an hour, and there is no reason
30 why we should not get under the blankets on the bunk and keep warm.

   Many are already drowsing when a barrage of orders, oaths and blows proclaims the imminent arrival of the commission. The *Blockältester* and his helpers, starting at the end of the dormitory, drive the crowd of frightened, naked people in front of them and cram them in the *Tagesraum* which is the Quartermaster's office.[6] The *Tagesraum* is a room seven yards by four: when the drive is over, a warm and compact human mass is jammed into the *Tagesraum,* perfectly filling all the corners, exercising such a pressure on the wooden walls as to make them creak. . . .

   The *Blockältester* has closed the connecting-door and has opened the other two which lead from the dormitory and the *Tagesraum* outside. Here, in front of the two
40 doors, stands the arbiter[7] of our fate, an SS subaltern.[8] On his right is the *Blockältester,* on his left, the quartermaster of the hut. Each one of us, as he comes naked out of the *Tagesraum* into the cold October air, has to run the few steps between the two

---

6. **Quartermaster's office:** the office of the person who distributes food and clothing to the prisoners.

7. **arbiter** (är′bĭ-tər): judge; decider.

8. **SS subaltern:** a low-ranking officer in the Nazi special security force.

DIFFERENTIATED INSTRUCTION

FOR STRATEGIC READERS
Vocabulary Support

- *barrage* (line 31), "an outpouring; shower"

- *imminent* (lines 32), "about to happen"

- *commission* (line 32), "a group of people with authority to carry out a task"

- *slacken* (line 50), "become less; decrease"

- *brisk* (line 51), "quick, energetic"

- *scruples* (line 57), "moral or ethical concerns that constrain behavior" doors, give the card to the SS man and enter the dormitory door. The SS man, in the fraction of a second between two successive crossings, with a glance at one's back and front, judges everyone's fate, and in turn gives the card to the man on his right or his left, and this is the life or death of each of us. In three or four minutes a hut of two hundred men is "done," as is the whole camp of twelve thousand men in the course of the afternoon.

50 Jammed in the charnel-house[9] of the *Tagesraum,* I gradually felt the human pressure around me slacken, and in a short time it was my turn. Like everyone, I passed by with a brisk and elastic step, trying to hold my head high, my chest forward and my muscles contracted and conspicuous. With the corner of my eye I tried to look behind my shoulders, and my card seemed to end on the right.

As we gradually come back into the dormitory we are allowed to dress ourselves. Nobody yet knows with certainty his own fate, it has first of all to be established whether the condemned cards were those on the right or the left. By now there is no longer any point in sparing each other's feelings with superstitious scruples. Everybody crowds around the oldest, the most wasted-away, and most "muselmann";[10] if their cards went to the left, the left is certainly the side of the condemned.

60 Even before the selection is over, everybody knows that the left was effectively the "*schlechte Seite,*" the bad side. There have naturally been some irregularities: René, for example, so young and robust, ended on the left; perhaps it was because he has glasses, perhaps because he walks a little stooped like a myope,[11] but more probably because of a simple mistake. . . .

There is nothing surprising about these mistakes: the examination is too quick and summary, and in any case, the important thing for the Lager[12] is not that the most useless prisoners be eliminated, but that free posts be quickly created, according to a certain percentage previously fixed. ॐ

---

9. **charnel-house:** vault for the bones of the dead (used here figuratively).

10. **"muselmann"** (mōō′zəl-män): concentration-camp slang for a person near death from starvation.

11. **myope** (mī′ōp′): nearsighted person.

12. **Lager** (lä′gər) *German:* camp.

Literary Analysis

1. **Clarify** What was the purpose of the "selection" taking place?

2. **Examine Tone** Reread lines 60–64. What is **ironic** about Levi's reference to the "simple mistake" of René's selection?

3. **Compare Texts** Both Kurt Vonnegut's "Adam" and *Survival in Auschwitz* make a comment about the value of human life in the shadow of World War II. How would you compare or contrast the statement made by each piece? Explain, citing evidence from both texts to support your answer.

ANSWERS

Possible answers:

1. *The purpose of the "selection" was to determine which prisoners would be put to death that day.*

2. *The irony is that this "simple mistake," which Levi describes in an almost offhand manner, will cost the unfortunate René his life.*

3. *Through Heinz Knechtmann, Vonnegut's "Adam" conveys a deep and sincere appreciation for the value of human life. Heinz makes clear through his words and actions just how precious he considers the miracle of life to be. By contrast, the Nazis in* Survival in Auschwitz *place no value at all on the lives of their prisoners. These innocent victims are, to the Nazis, inconsequential and utterly expendable.*

FOR ENGLISH LEARNERS

Comprehension: Text Structure Explain that Levi organizes his description spatially. He uses words to carefully paint a picture of exactly who is where. Work with students to review their knowledge of English spatial terms such as *at the end* (line 33), *in front of* (lines 33–34), *yards* (line 35), *between* (line 42), *back and front* (lines 44–45), and *on his right or his left* (line 45–46). Urge students to draw a map of the scene, using the many spatial clues to place objects and people.

FOR ADVANCED LEARNERS/AP

Hypothesize Levi's tone in this excerpt is understated and unemotional, perhaps surprisingly so. Have students discuss how Levi could possibly write about such horrifying experiences with such apparent objectivity. Is he suppressing his feelings in order to write a measured, reportorial account, or does he truly believe that the events are such that "subjective commentary was unnecessary"? Ask students to present their views to the class, inviting feedback and discussion.

Extend the discussion by asking students to consider whether, under the same circumstances, they could write an account as dispassionate as Levi's.

Focus and Motivate

OBJECTIVES

Literary Analysis
- explore the key idea of the **past**
- analyze internal and external conflict
- read a short story

Reading
- analyze structure, including flashback and frame story

 R3.2

ABOUT THE AUTHOR

Have students read about O'Brien and summarize key points about his life. Ask students in what ways O'Brien, as a young man, was directly affected by the Vietnam War. *Possible answer: He was drafted, had to choose whether to serve, and spent two years in combat in Vietnam.* Then discuss the ways his experiences in Vietnam have had a lasting impact on his life and writing.

USING THE *NOTABLE QUOTE*

Ask students how **Tim O'Brien's** remark summarizes the challenges and rewards of fiction writing. *Possible answer: Creating lifelike, believable characters is a huge challenge. However, it is also an enjoyable task, because authors have the opportunity to bring to life people who exist only in their imagination.*

Responses to War

R3.2 (p. 1142)

Ambush
Short Story by Tim O'Brien

NOTABLE QUOTE

"It's daunting to . . . invent fully realized characters. Having said all that, it's also fun to do it."

FYI
Did you know that Tim O'Brien . . .

- described his own experiences fighting in Vietnam in the memoir *If I Die in a Combat Zone?*

- wrote stories about a fictional character, also named Tim O'Brien, in *The Things They Carried?*

- does not actually have a daughter, as the fictional Tim O'Brien does?

Author Online

For more on Tim O'Brien, visit the **Literature Center** at ClassZone.com.

Tim O'Brien
born 1946

Over and over again, Tim O'Brien has presented characters who are marked by the Vietnam War. From an infantryman on his first tour of duty, to a veteran struggling to readjust to his hometown, to an antiwar radical obsessed with death, his protagonists bring to life the complex issues raised by the war.

Opening New Doors O'Brien's writing career began at an early age. One day he fled from humiliation in the Little League to the Worthington, Minnesota, library. There he found the book *Larry of the Little League,* and soothed himself by writing an imitation of it. The library's other books became an escape from "loneliness and frustration" and an outlet for O'Brien's fertile imagination. O'Brien realized that fiction would let him experience "what could have been or should have been."

A Critical Choice As a young man, O'Brien faced another new door. He returned from four years at Macalaster College, where the Vietnam War was on students' minds, to find a draft notice waiting for him. O'Brien, who opposed the war, struggled mightily with his conscience and even considered fleeing the country to avoid service. In the end, he could not bring himself to run, and he reported for duty.

What Can You Teach? O'Brien was an army infantryman from 1968 to 1970, seeing combat in Vietnam's Quang Nai province and receiving a Purple Heart. After the war, he studied at Harvard University, worked as a reporter for the *Washington Post,* and began writing novels. He asked himself, "What can you teach people, just for having been in a war?" He concluded that he could offer insight into the "complexity and ambiguity of a set of moral issues—but without preaching a moral lesson." O'Brien's nine books have all been connected to Vietnam and have vividly explored "its aftermath and effect on the human heart and mind."

Higher Ambitions Even after great success—a National Book Award and a Pulitzer Prize nomination—O'Brien still hopes to achieve more. He'd like to write a bestseller, and he works at it every day, no matter what. "You shape your own universe," he has said. "You practice all the time, then practice some more."

1136

Selection Resources

 RESOURCE MANAGER UNIT 6

Plan and Teach pp. 59–66

Literary Analysis
Summary pp. 67†*, 68‡*
Conflict pp. 69, 70†*
Question Support p. 74*

Reading
Analyze Structure pp. 71, 72†*
Reading Check p. 73

Assessment
Selection Tests A, B/C pp. 75*, 77*
 Test Generator CD

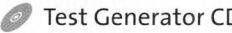 **BEST PRACTICES TOOLKIT**

Differentiated Instruction pp. 31–38*

Scaffolding Instruction pp. 43–46*

Graphic Organizers/Strategies
New Word Analysis • Sequence Chain

Reading Support
 Audio Anthology CD*

Technology
ⓘ Literature Center at **ClassZone.com**
 Write*Smart* CD

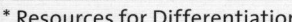 * Resources for Differentiation   † Also in Spanish   ‡ In Haitian Creole and Vietnamese

LITERARY ANALYSIS: CONFLICT

A story's **conflict** is the struggle between opposing forces that is the basis of the story's plot. **External conflict**—a struggle between a character and some outside force—is usually easy to identify in a work of fiction. **Internal conflict**—a struggle within a character—may be more subtle and complex. For example, an internal conflict may revolve around a decision a character has to make, or it may be reflected in behavior that is contradictory. As you read this story, watch for the development of internal conflicts in the main character.

READING SKILL: ANALYZE STRUCTURE

The **structure** of a literary work is the way in which it is put together—the arrangement of its parts. Tim O'Brien's story "Ambush" includes a **frame story,** or a story within a story. The first paragraph provides a frame—the narrator recalls answering a question his daughter once asked him. In the second paragraph, he begins to recount in a **flashback** an experience he had earlier, during the war. As you read, use a chart to summarize what happens within the outer story and the inner story.

> Beginning of Story 1:
>
> > Beginning of Story 2:
> >
> > Middle of Story 2:
> >
> > End of Story 2:
>
> End of Story 1:

How does the PAST affect the present?

KEY IDEA Perhaps more than any group in society, war veterans carry a difficult **past.** Some remember combat experiences vividly, some block them out entirely. The lucky ones find a way to reconcile their past with the present, to use the lessons of battle to inform their present perceptions and choices.

QUICKWRITE Think about war veterans you know or have heard about. They might have served in Vietnam, in the Persian Gulf, or in an international peacekeeping mission. Imagine one specific way in which a veteran's past experiences might affect his or her present life. How might they affect a father's relationship with his children, for example? Write down your thoughts and discuss them in a group.

1137

How does the PAST affect the present?

Introduce the question, and ask students to read the **KEY IDEA** paragraph. Have students reflect on the particular physical, psychological, and emotional **past** that combat veterans carry. After they complete the **QUICKWRITE,** ask groups to share their conclusions.

SKILLS FOCUS

LITERARY ANALYSIS

● CONFLICT

Write this passage on the board:

> Carl could still remember the exact moment, nearly 40 years ago, as though it had occurred only yesterday. His best friend, Greg Loomis, was less than 70 yards behind him on the road when Carl saw the flash. It happened so fast, though it seemed like slow motion at the time. One second Greg was there, the next, he was gone. Forever. "Nothing you could've done," the sergeant insisted. But the voice inside Carl's head disagreed. *You should have spotted that sniper,* the voice told him again and again and again.

Ask students what internal conflict Carl is experiencing. ***Possible answer:*** *Carl feels responsible for the death of his friend, because he failed to spot the sniper.*

CHECK UNDERSTANDING Ask students for other examples of internal conflicts from fiction or real life.

READING SKILL

■ ANALYZE STRUCTURE

Have students reread the posted passage and explain its structure. ***Possible answer:*** *The passage is set in the present, but built around Carl's flashback to the past.*

 RESOURCE MANAGER—Copy Master
Analyze Structure p. 71 (for student use while reading the selection)

DIFFERENTIATED INSTRUCTION

FOR STRATEGIC READERS
Vocabulary Support

- *subtle,* "slight and thus difficult to recognize"

- *contradictory,* "seeming to go in opposite directions; inconsistent"

- *flashback,* "a break in the typical time order sequence of a story, during which a scene showing past events is inserted"

- *international peacekeeping mission,* "soldiers from many nations sent into an area of conflict by an international organization such as the United Nations to keep peace but often not authorized to fight"

SUMMARY

In this short story, the narrator's young daughter, knowing that her father writes war stories, asks him if he has ever killed anyone. He says no, but resolves to tell her the truth one day. He then recalls that he did kill someone in Vietnam. While he was standing guard in the jungle, a young Vietnamese soldier approached. Instinctively, the narrator threw a grenade, killing the soldier. The narrator realizes that he could have let the man pass unharmed. Years later, the incident still haunts him.

LITERARY ANALYSIS

Ⓐ CONFLICT

Possible answer: The conflict that the narrator faces is deciding what answer to give his daughter. That is, he doesn't want to tell her that he killed someone, but at the same time he is reluctant to lie to her.

READING SKILL

Ⓑ ANALYZE STRUCTURE

Possible answer: The setting shifts from the narrator's home in the present to a trail in Vietnam in the past.

If students need help . . . Point out the colon at the end of line 8, which indicates that what follows is an explanation or example. Have students record the frame story in the chart from page 1137.

Ambush

Tim O'Brien

ANALYZE VISUALS
What **tone** is conveyed by this image?

> **BACKGROUND** "Ambush" is a short story based upon the writer's combat experiences in Vietnam. The Vietnam War lasted nine years, left 58,000 Americans dead, and left another 365,000 Americans wounded. Although they were better equipped and trained than the enemy, American troops fought in an unfamiliar landscape for a cause that many of them did not support or understand. Vietnamese Communists were skilled guerilla fighters whose tactics created a climate of frustration, confusion, and fear. American soldiers never knew when an attack might come and were haunted by their memories long after the war.

When she was nine, my daughter Kathleen asked if I had ever killed anyone. She knew about the war; she knew I'd been a soldier. "You keep writing these war stories," she said, "so I guess you must've killed somebody." It was a difficult moment, but I did what seemed right, which was to say, "Of course not," and then to take her onto my lap and hold her for a while. Someday, I hope, she'll ask again. But here I want to pretend she's a grown-up. I want to tell her exactly what happened, or what I remember happening, and then I want to say to her that as a little girl she was absolutely right. This is why I keep writing war stories: Ⓐ

He was a short, slender young man of about twenty. I was afraid of him—afraid
10 of something—and as he passed me on the trail I threw a grenade that exploded at his feet and killed him. Ⓑ

Ⓐ **CONFLICT**
Reread lines 1–8. What **internal conflict** does the narrator face in the first paragraph?

Ⓑ **ANALYZE STRUCTURE**
Reread lines 9–11. How does the **setting** of the story shift in the second paragraph?

① **Targeted Passage**

The Green Machine (1977), Frank Dahmer. Screenprint on paper, 13¹/₂″ × 17¹/₄″. © National Vietnam Veterans Art Museum.

1138 UNIT 6: CONTEMPORARY LITERATURE

DIFFERENTIATED INSTRUCTION

FOR ALL STUDENTS

Expert Groups Encourage students to become subject experts by selecting and researching one of these topics relating to the Vietnam War:

- the combatants of the Vietnam War
- key events of the war
- Vietcong guerilla warfare
- the aftermath of the war

FOR STRATEGIC READERS

In combination with the *Audio Anthology CD*, use one or both Targeted Passages (pp. 1138, 1141) to ensure that students focus on key story events and concepts. Targeted Passages are also good for English learners.

① **Targeted Passage [Lines 1–11]**

This passage introduces the narrator, identifies the key event, and establishes the frame story.

ANALYZE VISUALS

Possible answer: The image conveys a serious, alert, ready-for-action feeling.

About the Art Like Tim O'Brien, Frank Dahmer (born 1938) served in Vietnam, though as a commander. This screenprint shows the face of a combat soldier in the jungle, a soldier who could easily be Tim O'Brien's narrator.

BACKGROUND

Grenades A *grenade* is a small bomb that can be thrown by hand or projected by a special launcher. Soldiers in Vietnam often carried grenades, even though doing so could be dangerous. The pin that detonated a grenade could accidentally get caught on jungle shrubs, causing an unintentional explosion.

Lines 6–11
REINFORCE *KEY IDEA:* PAST

Discuss The narrator says, "This is why I keep writing war stories." What does this comment say about the impact of the **past?** Explain.
Possible answer: The comment suggests that the past has a profound impact. The narrator is still struggling to come to terms with events in his past.

- Who is the narrator of the story?
- Why does Kathleen think he "must've killed somebody"?
- Who does the narrator tell his story to?
- What happened to the "short, slender young man of about twenty"?
- When did this happen?

FOR ENGLISH LEARNERS

Prereading For prereading instruction for English learners, see

 BEST PRACTICES TOOLKIT
Scaffolding Reading Instruction pp. 43–46

FOR ADVANCED LEARNERS/AP

AP exercises in the bottom channel provide additional challenge for students. Use these suggestions for small groups or individuals.

ADDITIONAL GUIDELINES

For more help with differentiation and tips for classroom management, see

BEST PRACTICES TOOLKIT
Differentiated Instruction pp. 31–38

Or to go back:

Shortly after midnight we moved into the ambush site outside My Khe. The whole platoon was there, spread out in the dense brush along the trail, and for five hours nothing at all happened. We were working in two-man teams—one man on guard while the other slept, switching off every two hours—and I remember it was still dark when Kiowa shook me awake for the final watch. The night was foggy and hot. For the first few moments I felt lost, not sure about directions, groping for my helmet and weapon. I reached out and found three grenades and

20 lined them up in front of me; the pins had already been straightened for quick throwing. And then for maybe half an hour I knelt there and waited. Very gradually, in tiny slivers, dawn began to break through the fog, and from my position in the brush I could see ten or fifteen meters up the trail. The mosquitoes were fierce. I remember slapping at them, wondering if I should wake up Kiowa and ask for some repellent, then thinking it was a bad idea, then looking up and seeing the young man come out of the fog. He wore black clothing and rubber sandals and a gray ammunition belt. His shoulders were slightly stooped, his head cocked to the side as if listening for something. He seemed at ease. He carried his weapon in one hand, muzzle down, moving without any hurry up the center

30 of the trail. There was no sound at all—none that I can remember. In a way, it seemed, he was part of the morning fog, or my own imagination, but there was also the reality of what was happening in my stomach. I had already pulled the pin on a grenade. I had come up to a crouch. It was entirely automatic. I did not hate the young man; I did not see him as the enemy; I did not ponder issues of morality or politics or military duty. I crouched and kept my head low. I tried to swallow whatever was rising from my stomach, which tasted like lemonade, something fruity and sour. I was terrified. There were no thoughts about killing. The grenade was to make him go away—just evaporate—and I leaned back and felt my mind go empty and then felt it fill up again. I had already thrown the

40 grenade before telling myself to throw it. The brush was thick and I had to lob it high, not aiming, and I remember the grenade seeming to freeze above me for an instant, as if a camera had clicked, and I remember ducking down and holding my breath and seeing little wisps of fog rise from the earth. The grenade bounced once and rolled across the trail. I did not hear it, but there must've been a sound, because the young man dropped his weapon and began to run, just two or three quick steps, then he hesitated, swiveling to his right, and he glanced down at the grenade and tried to cover his head but never did. It occurred to me then that he was about to die. I wanted to warn him. The grenade made a popping noise—not soft but not loud either—not what I'd expected—and there was a puff of dust

50 and smoke—a small white puff—and the young man seemed to jerk upward as if pulled by invisible wires. He fell on his back. His rubber sandals had been blown off. There was no wind. He lay at the center of the trail, his right leg bent beneath him, his one eye shut, his other eye a huge star-shaped hole.

C ANALYZE STRUCTURE
In terms of the structure of this story, what does this line signal?

D ANALYZE STRUCTURE
Summarize what happens in lines 13–53. How do these lines relate to the first paragraph of the story?

READING SKILL

C ANALYZE STRUCTURE

Possible answer: Line 12 signals a further transition from the present to the past. The narrator is indicating that he will now use a detailed flashback to explain in greater detail the event described in lines 9–11.

If students need help . . . Have them reread lines 1–11. Clarify that "to go back" (line 12) means to go back in time to recall exactly what happened on the trail that day.

READING SKILL

D ANALYZE STRUCTURE

Possible answer: In lines 13–53, the narrator recalls being on guard in the jungle when a young Vietnamese soldier walked down the trail. Acting reflexively, the narrator threw a grenade at the soldier, killing him. These lines relate to lines 1–11 by describing the narrator's memory in response to his daughter's question.

Lines 25–53
TIERED DISCUSSION PROMPTS

Use these prompts to help students understand the narrator's actions:

Restate What does the narrator do when he sees the man? *Possible answer: He throws a grenade at him.*

Analyze Why does the narrator throw the grenade? *Possible answer: The narrator throws the grenade instinctively in a moment of terror. He is not trying to kill the soldier but just wants him to "go away" (line 38).*

Evaluate In what ways is O'Brien effective in describing the narrator's situation? Explain. *Possible answer: O'Brien is particularly effective through his use of one long paragraph packed with detail. The density of the paragraph parallels the compressed series of events that the narrator struggles to come to terms with, as well as the dense jungle setting where those events occur.*

DIFFERENTIATED INSTRUCTION

FOR ENGLISH LEARNERS

Key Academic Vocabulary Use New Word Analysis to teach this word: *site* (line 13).

🧰 BEST PRACTICES TOOLKIT—Transparency
   New Word Analysis p. E8

Related Vocabulary Use a Sequence Chain to help students define language related to the grenade and to track the narrator's use of it: *grenades* (line 19), "small explosives"; *pins* (line 20), "triggers"; *pulled the pin* (lines 32–33), "triggered the grenade"; *lob* (line 40), "throw gently"; *bounced* (line 43), "hit the ground and came up again"; *popping noise* (line 48), "sound like a gunshot"; *puff of dust and smoke* (lines 49–50), "short, sudden burst of dust and smoke"

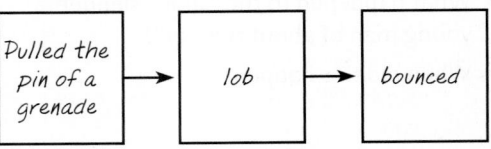

🧰 BEST PRACTICES TOOLKIT—Transparency
   Sequence Chain p. B21

Come a Little Closer (1997), Michael Brostowitz. Oil on board, 15¼″ × 19¾″. © National Vietnam Veterans Art Museum.

It was not a matter of live or die. There was no real peril. Almost certainly the young man would have passed by. And it will always be that way.

Later, I remember, Kiowa tried to tell me that the man would've died anyway. He told me that it was a good kill, that I was a soldier and this was a war, that I should shape up and stop staring and ask myself what the dead man would've done if things were reversed.

60   None of it mattered. The words seemed far too complicated. All I could do was gape at the fact of the young man's body. **E**

Even now I haven't finished sorting it out. Sometimes I forgive myself, other times I don't. In the ordinary hours of life I try not to dwell on it, but now and then, when I'm reading a newspaper or just sitting alone in a room, I'll look up and see the young man coming out of the morning fog. I'll watch him walk toward me, his shoulders slightly stooped, his head cocked to the side, and he'll pass within a few yards of me and suddenly smile at some secret thought and then continue up the trail to where it bends back into the fog. ⟋ **F**

E CONFLICT
Reread lines 54–61. What **internal conflict** does the narrator express?

② Targeted Passage

F CONFLICT
How does the vision the narrator imagines in lines 63–68 help resolve his conflict?

AMBUSH   **1141**

ANALYZE VISUALS

Activity Discuss ways in which the color and light in the painting, which are similar to that of the narrator's jungle surroundings, might affect the narrator's emotional state. *Possible answer: Such surroundings might add to the narrator's fear by limiting vision.*

About the Art Michael Brostowitz (born 1950) served in Vietnam and, like the story narrator, struggles with his memories.

LITERARY ANALYSIS

E CONFLICT

Possible answer: The narrator feels deep ambivalence over killing the Vietnamese soldier. On one hand, he reacted reflexively and, as Kiowa assured him, made "a good kill," one the Vietnamese soldier would likely also have made in the reverse situation. On the other hand, there was no immediate danger, and the soldier might have walked past without incident.

LITERARY ANALYSIS

F CONFLICT

Possible answer: The narrator's vision allows him to imagine that he did not throw the grenade, and the Vietnamese soldier continued up the trail unharmed, smiling "at some secret thought."

SELECTION WRAP-UP

REFLECT Have students reread line 62. Ask them what evidence they can find in the story to suggest that it is true.

★ CRITIQUE

- Ask students whether the narrator's claim that throwing the grenade was "entirely automatic" is believable. Why or why not?

- After completing the After Reading questions on page 1142, have students revisit their responses and tell whether they have changed their opinions.

FOR STRATEGIC READERS

② Targeted Passage [Lines 56–68]

This concluding passage shows clearly that the narrator's wartime act continues to trouble him in the present.

- In what ways does Kiowa respond to the narrator's actions?

- What does the narrator feel about what he did?

- What image lingers in the narrator's mind?

FOR ADVANCED LEARNERS/AP

Analyze Author's Tone Have students work in small groups to discuss the author's tone in the story. Ask whether the author appears to approve or disapprove of the narrator's actions, or whether he remains neutral. Extend the discussion by asking students if they think that author and narrator share one mind. If not, in what ways do they differ? Have groups share and compare their conclusions.

Practice and Apply

After Reading

Use these copy masters to check understanding and provide extra support:

R **RESOURCE MANAGER—Copy Masters**
Reading Check p. 73
Conflict p. 69
Question Support p. 74

Additional selection questions are provided for teachers on page 63.

ANSWERS

1. *The narrator tells his daughter, "Of course not."*

2. *He was on guard in the jungle when a Vietnamese soldier approached. The narrator threw a grenade at the soldier, killing him.*

3. *He sees the soldier walking toward him, passing by, smiling, and walking on up the trail.*

Possible answers:

4. ● **SKILLS FOCUS Conflict** *The narrator feels conflicted about whether or not to tell his young daughter he killed someone. He tells her no, but hopes to tell her the truth "someday" (line 5). The narrator also feels conflicted about whether his war killing was acceptable and if he can forgive himself for it. He writes war stories to try to resolve his several internal conflicts.*

5. ■ **SKILLS FOCUS Analyze Structure** *The frame shows the ways the wartime incident affected the narrator and continues to affect him.*

6. *The title refers to the narrator's fear of attack and to his surprise attack on the*

Assess and Reteach

Assess

R **RESOURCE MANAGER—Copy Masters**
Selection Test A pp. 75–76
Selection Test B/C pp. 77–78

🖉 Test Generator CD

Reteach

S **STANDARDS LESSON FILE**
Literature Lesson 6: Conflict and Suspense
Literature Lesson 8: Foreshadowing and Flashback

After Reading

 R3.2

Comprehension

1. **Recall** What does the narrator tell his daughter when she asks if he ever killed someone?

2. **Summarize** What happened to the narrator outside My Khe?

3. **Clarify** What vision does the narrator sometimes see in his mind?

Literary Analysis

4. **Examine Conflicts** Identify the **internal conflicts** the narrator experiences in this story. How would you describe the way he resolves or tries to resolve them? Explain your answer.

5. **Analyze Structure** What does the **frame** contribute to the impact of this story? Consider what would be lost without the first and last paragraphs.

6. **Interpret Title** In what ways does the title "Ambush" relate to the events of the story? Think about the frame as well as the inner story.

7. **Evaluate a Character's Actions** Kiowa tells the narrator that this "was a good kill." Do you agree? In your opinion, can there be a "good kill"?

8. **Apply Theme** What does this story suggest about the effects of the **past** on the present?

9. **Compare Texts** Compare "Ambush" and "Why Soldiers Won't Talk" (page 1116) as portrayals of a soldier's experience. On a chart, note what each presents as the physical sensations and emotional aftereffects of war. Which piece—the story or the essay—had more impact on you? Why?

	Physical Sensations	Emotional Aftereffects
"Ambush"		
"Why Soldiers Won't Talk"		

Literary Criticism

10. **Author's Style** "Ambush" is a work of fiction, but the story reads like a nonfiction account of a true event. To readers who wonder how much of his work is actually true, O'Brien responds, "The literal truth is . . . irrelevant." Do you agree? Does it matter that O'Brien the writer does not have a daughter and does not know whether he ever killed anyone?

---

soldier. It also refers to the way his memory affects him unexpectedly in the present.

7. *Answers will vary. Students should support their opinions with clear reasons.*

8. *The story suggests that past experiences never stop impacting people in the present.*

9. *"Ambush": Physical: feeling of fear in stomach, "fruity and sour" taste in mouth (lines 32, 35–37). Emotional: continued inner conflict over actions (lines 62–63). "Why Soldiers Won't Talk": Physical: "skin feels thick and insensitive"; "salty taste"; "hard,*

painful knot" in stomach; "objects are slightly blurred" (lines 22–25). Emotional: details of combat become dreamlike, and soldiers' memory fades (lines 10–11). Students should support their choice of which piece had more impact.

10. *Accept all thoughtful responses that also recognize that fiction writers create events and characters with a basis in truth, despite the writer's actual life experiences.*

The Literary Legacy of War

Modernist writer Gertrude Stein once said, "War is never fatal but always lost. Always lost." One after another, the wars of the 20th century forced Americans to reconcile their sense of patriotism with the disillusionment that naturally comes from facing the realities of modern warfare. If it is an artist's job to find meaning, what meaning can be discerned from the act of war?

Writing to Synthesize

Each of the selections you have just read presents a variety of ideas and images in response to World War II and the Vietnam War. What do these pieces have in common? Reread the selections, pulling words or phrases from each that you find especially compelling—whether beautiful, ugly, moving, or surprising. When you have gathered 15–30 phrases, combine them artfully to create a poem that delivers a coherent impression about war. Your poem might tell a story, describe an image, or deliver a set of thoughts or pronouncements. It can take place on the battlefield or on the home front.

Consider

- what primary thought or feeling you were left with after reading all of the selections
- which parts of each selection had the strongest impact on you
- how to arrange the phrases in a way that communicates your own response to the literature

Extension

SPEAKING & LISTENING Give an **oral reading** of your poem, using your voice, posture, and gestures to emphasize its meaning. If you think it would be effective, consider performing a choral reading with some of your classmates or setting your poem to music.

 CALIFORNIA LS1.10, LS2.5

American soldiers in Vietnam

1143

Wrap-Up: Responses to War

This Wrap-Up provides students with an opportunity to revisit ideas and reactions relating to the wars of the 20th century and to reflect on the expression of these ideas and feelings through literature. Encourage students to consider ways in which the selections affected their views.

Writing to Synthesize

- Review with students that *synthesizing* means combining ideas and facts with other information and prior knowledge in order to better understand a subject or develop new ideas. Through synthesis, students can draw conclusions about common themes in the selections they have read and gain deeper insight into the writers of the time.

- To help students choose their words and phrases from the selections, suggest that they look for vivid images and sensory details as well as sentences that made them stop and think or affected them emotionally. Urge students to sort through the chosen text, highlighting text that best fits the particular impression they wish to make.

Extension

- Encourage students to prepare for their oral reading by identifying words and phrases to emphasize and places to pause for effect or to adjust speaking volume.

- Suggest that students consider working with a partner, either alternating lines or reading lines together.

- Caution students setting their poems to music to select music that complements their presentation rather than distracts from it.

DIFFERENTIATED INSTRUCTION

FOR DEVELOPING WRITERS

Writing Support Remind students that fiction, nonfiction, and poetry all can be a source of memorable words and phrases. Offer such examples as these: "eyeballs . . . so beaten that the earth and the air seem to shudder" (lines 31–32 of "Why Soldiers Won't Talk"), "they washed me out of the turret with a hose" (line 5 of "The Death of the Ball Turret Gunner"), and "Sometimes I forgive myself, other times I don't" (lines 62–63 of "Ambush").

FOR ENGLISH LEARNERS

Gathering Words and Phrases Suggest students list their words and phrases in a Three-Column Journal such as this:

Vivid Images	Sensory Details	Memorable Sentences
" . . . his other eye a huge star-shaped hole"	"skin feels thick and insensitive"; "salty taste"	" . . . they washed me out of the turret with a hose."

 BEST PRACTICES TOOLKIT—Transparency
Three-Column Journal p. B10

Focus and Motivate

OBJECTIVES

Literary Analysis
- explore the key idea of **action**
- interpret allusion
- read a letter and a poem

Reading
- trace the elements of an argument

Vocabulary
- build vocabulary for reading and writing
- analyze analogies to build meaning (also an EL language objective)

Grammar and Writing
- use parallelism as a rhetorical device
- write a persuasive argument

CALIFORNIA R2.4, R2.6, R3.9, R1.3, W1.1, W1.3, W1.4, LC1.1

ABOUT THE AUTHOR

Point out words that describe King, such as *eloquent, shrewd,* and *visionary.* Discuss the role of leaders like King in the history of social justice. Ask students if charismatic leaders are an essential element of social change, and why. ***Possible answer:*** *Yes; charismatic leaders galvanize people's emotions and efforts.*

USING THE *NOTABLE QUOTE*

Clarify the figurative language in **Martin Luther King Jr.'s** quotation: *measure of a man,* "the depth of a man's character"; *where he stands,* "a man's moral position." Have students explain King's meaning. ***Possible answer:*** *Character is defined by the way a person faces challenges.*

Selection Resources

Civil Rights and Protest Literature

R2.4, R2.6, R3.9, R1.3 (p. 1158), W1.1 (p. 1159), W1.3 (p. 1159), W1.4 (p. 1159), LC1.1 (p. 1159)

NOTABLE QUOTE

"The ultimate measure of a man is not where he stands in moments of comfort and convenience, but where he stands at times of challenge and controversy."

FYI

Did you know that Martin Luther King Jr. . . .

- enrolled in college when he was 15 years old?
- was the first African American to be named *Time* magazine's "Man of the Year"?
- won the Nobel Peace Prize in 1964?
- was arrested 30 times for his activism?

Author Online

For more on Martin Luther King Jr., visit the **Literature Center** at **ClassZone.com.**

---

from Letter from Birmingham Jail

Letter by Martin Luther King Jr.

Martin Luther King Jr.
1929–1968

An eloquent orator, a shrewd tactician, and a visionary leader, Martin Luther King Jr. became the catalyst for some of the most far-reaching social changes in U.S. history. Under his skillful leadership, the civil rights movement spurred passage of the Civil Rights Act of 1964 and the Voting Rights Act of 1965, laws that legally abolished racial segregation and voting discrimination. A tireless advocate for justice, King wrote five books, delivered about 2,500 speeches, and traveled more than 6 million miles in an effort to make his dream of equality a reality.

Boycott in Montgomery It was in Alabama that King first emerged as a civil rights leader to be reckoned with. In 1955, when Rosa Parks was arrested for breaking Montgomery's bus segregation laws, local civil rights advocates banded together to form a protest organization. They chose King, then pastor of the Dexter Avenue Baptist Church, to lead the new group. King mobilized African Americans to boycott city buses. The 381-day boycott tested the endurance of the entire black community, especially King, who was subjected to threats and bomb attacks. The steadfast boycotters ultimately triumphed, and the U.S. Supreme Court struck down the city's bus segregation laws. The success of the boycott launched the charismatic young leader onto the national stage, where he promoted his bold strategy: using nonviolent, direct action to achieve social change.

Expanding Influence King cautiously expanded the civil rights struggle throughout the South. He was particularly effective at organizing interracial coalitions to put pressure on lawmakers. One shining moment came at the 1963 March on Washington, a gathering of about 250,000 peaceful demonstrators supporting civil rights legislation. King's impassioned "I Have a Dream" speech, delivered on the steps of the Lincoln Memorial, is considered one of the greatest speeches in U.S. history.

Warrior for Peace King never wavered in his commitment to nonviolence and tried to extend his campaign to fight poverty and end the Vietnam War. Ultimately, he was unable to stem the surge of violence that overtook the country in the mid-1960s. In 1968, King was assassinated in Memphis, where he had gone to support a sanitation workers' strike. In the 12 years between the Montgomery boycott and his death, he had helped achieve the greatest advance in racial justice since the abolition of slavery.

1144

---

* Resources for Differentiation   † Also in Spanish   ‡ In Haitian Creole and Vietnamese

LITERARY ANALYSIS: ALLUSION

An **allusion** is a reference within a work to historical, literary, or cultural details from outside the work. Writers choose allusions that are familiar to their target audience. In this case, because King is writing to fellow clergymen, he uses references to the Bible and to religious scholars to make his points.

I would agree with St. Augustine that "an unjust law is no law at all."

King's allusions help connect current events with respected historical and religious figures. As you read, use the footnotes to help you understand King's allusions.

READING SKILL: TRACE THE ELEMENTS OF AN ARGUMENT

King's letter is a beautifully written **argument** defending his activism. He organizes his letter as a series of counterarguments responding to public criticisms of his actions. He introduces each counterargument by partly restating these opposing positions. As you read, use King's restatements to infer what these positions are and record them in a chart like the one shown. Then, record King's own positions and the reasons and evidence he uses to support them.

Position of Opponents	King's Counterclaim	Reasons and Evidence
King doesn't belong in Birmingham.	"I am here because I have organizational ties here."	• leads the SCLC • invited by affiliated organization

▲ VOCABULARY IN CONTEXT

King uses the following words to argue his views. Test yourself by replacing each boldfaced term with one vocabulary word.

WORD LIST		
affiliated	moratorium	scintillating
cognizant	paradoxical	substantive
estrangement	rabid	
latent	retaliating	

1. **aware** of the difficulties involved
2. **hidden** emotions called up by the encounter
3. **contradictory** views seemed to say two things at once
4. **temporary stoppage** on further discussions

When does ACTION speak louder than words?

KEY IDEA When you're trying to confront a difficult issue, words are your first option. But once you've explained your position, presented your demands, and tried unsuccessfully to convince others to make a change, you're at the point when words give way to **action.** Martin Luther King Jr. explains how civil rights activists in Birmingham, Alabama, faced their own decisive moment in 1963.

DISCUSS When do you respond with words and when do you turn to action? Working with a small group, brainstorm situations that call for each type of response. What guidelines did you use to classify your examples?

1145

When does ACTION speak louder than words?

Lead into the **KEY IDEA** by asking the question. After groups complete the **DISCUSS** activity, invite volunteers to share their guidelines. Have students combine these into class guidelines on when to take **action** for change.

SKILLS FOCUS

LITERARY ANALYSIS

● ALLUSION

Explain that allusions lend credibility to a writer's argument by suggesting that recognized sources on the topic support that argument. Clarify that St. Augustine is regarded as one of Christianity's greatest theologians. Ask students why King might use this allusion in writing to Christian clergymen. ***Possible answer:*** *St. Augustine is a figure the clergymen would recognize and respect.*

CHECK UNDERSTANDING Identify topics and audiences; then have students suggest historical, literary, or cultural figures as useful allusions in each context.

READING SKILL R2.4, R2.6, R3.9

■ TRACE THE ELEMENTS OF AN ARGUMENT

Point out to students that citing and responding to critics is an effective persuasive technique because it anticipates and neutralizes criticism. As students complete their charts, urge them to evaluate the effectiveness of each of King's counterclaims.

R RESOURCE MANAGER—Copy Master
Trace the Elements of an Argument p. 91 (for student use while reading the selection)

VOCABULARY

▲ VOCABULARY IN CONTEXT

DIAGNOSE WORD KNOWLEDGE To determine preteaching needs, have all students complete Vocabulary in Context. ***Possible answers:*** **1.** *cognizant,* **2.** *latent,* **3.** *paradoxical,* **4.** *moratorium*

PRETEACH VOCABULARY Preteach vocabulary with this copy master. Read each item aloud.

R RESOURCE MANAGER—Copy Master
Vocabulary Study p. 93

MORE VOCABULARY SUPPORT
For additional activities and guidelines, see

BEST PRACTICES TOOLKIT
Scaffolding Vocabulary Instruction pp. 43–46
ℹ Vocabulary Center at **ClassZone.com**

SUMMARY

In this excerpt from his letter responding to the criticism of white clergymen, Martin Luther King Jr. justifies his direct-action approach to ending segregation in the South. He alludes to religious and philosophical leaders and events to legitimize the campaign's methods and goals. Recalling the deplorable conditions that led to the direct-action campaigns, King stresses that the goal is to force negotiation. He argues, relying on the ideas of St. Thomas Aquinas and others for support, that people have a moral obligation to disobey unjust laws, and he invites the clergymen to support his efforts.

READING SKILL

A ELEMENTS OF AN ARGUMENT

Possible answer: *Lines 10–11 contain the sentence that restates the position against which King argues. That position is that outsiders should not get involved in the racial strife in Birmingham.*

Letter from Birmingham Jail

Martin Luther King Jr.

BACKGROUND In the spring of 1963, Martin Luther King Jr. and his organization, the Southern Christian Leadership Conference (SCLC), targeted Birmingham, Alabama, with a series of peaceful demonstrations aimed at ending segregation. The police reacted violently with attack dogs and high-pressure fire hoses. Hundreds of protesters, including King, were jailed. At first, King was criticized for taking on Birmingham; eight white clergymen published a letter calling his actions "unwise and untimely." But he responded with his own letter citing philosophers, religious scholars, and biblical figures to justify his actions.

April 16, 1963

My Dear Fellow Clergymen:

While confined here in the Birmingham city jail, I came across your recent statement calling my present activities "unwise and untimely." Seldom do I pause to answer criticism of my work and ideas. If I sought to answer all the criticisms that cross my desk, my secretaries would have little time for anything other than such correspondence in the course of the day, and I would have no time for constructive work. But since I feel that you are men of genuine good will and that your criticisms are sincerely set forth, I want to try to answer your statement in what I hope will be patient and reasonable terms.

10   I think I should indicate why I am here in Birmingham, since you have been influenced by the view which argues against "outsiders coming in." I have the honor of serving as president of the Southern Christian Leadership Conference, an organization operating in every Southern state, with headquarters in Atlanta, Georgia. We have some eighty-five **affiliated** organizations across the South, and one of them is the Alabama Christian Movement for Human Rights. Frequently we share staff, educational, and financial resources with our affiliates. Several months ago the affiliate here in Birmingham asked us to be on call to engage in a nonviolent direct-action program if such were deemed necessary. We readily consented, and when the hour came, we lived up to our promise. So I, along with
20   several members of my staff, am here because I was invited here. I am here because I have organizational ties here. **A**

But more basically, I am in Birmingham because injustice is here. Just as the prophets of the eighth century B.C. left their villages and carried their "thus saith the Lord" far beyond the boundaries of their home towns, and just as the Apostle Paul left his village of Tarsus and carried the gospel of Jesus Christ to the

ANALYZE VISUALS
Look at this photograph of King in his jail cell in Birmingham. Based on the photo, what impressions do you have of his state of mind while in jail?

1 Targeted Passage

affiliated (ə-fĭl′ē-ā′tĭd) *adj.* joined in close association **affiliate** *v.*

A ELEMENTS OF AN ARGUMENT
Reread lines 10–21. Which sentence refers to the position that King is arguing against?

King in his jail cell in Birmingham

DIFFERENTIATED INSTRUCTION

FOR ALL STUDENTS

Expert Groups Encourage students to become subject experts by selecting and researching one of these topics:

- 1955–1956 Montgomery bus boycott
- 1963 March on Washington
- Civil Rights Act of 1964 and Voting Rights Act of 1965
- 1968 Memphis sanitation workers' strike
- Martin Luther King Jr.'s assassination

FOR STRATEGIC READERS

In combination with the *Audio Anthology CD*, use one or more Targeted Passages (pp. 1146, 1148, 1151, 1154) to ensure that students focus on key concepts in the selection. Targeted Passages are also good for English learners.

1 Targeted Passage [Lines 1–9]

This passage advances King's purpose for writing—to explain his actions in Birmingham to clergy who criticize them.

BACKGROUND

Southern Christian Leadership Conference (SCLC) In 1957, African-American church leaders and ministers formed the SCLC. The success of the Montgomery bus boycott led African-American leaders to believe that nonviolent social protest had the potential to end segregation and achieve social equality for African Americans. They believed that an organization was needed to coordinate non-violent protests throughout the South. These leaders encouraged other African Americans to seek justice and reject injustice while dedicating themselves to the principal of nonviolence. During the 1950s and early 1960s, the SCLC spearheaded the civil rights movement in America through a succession of protest campaigns that garnered national attention.

- Where is King when he writes this letter?
- To whom does King address his letter?
- Why does King usually not respond to criticism of his work and ideas?
- Why does King answer this criticism in particular?

FOR ENGLISH LEARNERS

Key Academic Vocabulary Use Definition Mapping to teach these words: *indicate* (line 10), *create* (line 86), *distort* (line 134), *positive* (line 223), *environment* (line 290).

 BEST PRACTICES TOOLKIT—Transparency Definition Mapping p. E6

Prereading For prereading instruction for English learners, see

 BEST PRACTICES TOOLKIT Scaffolding Reading Instruction pp. 43–46

FOR ADVANCED LEARNERS/AP

AP exercises in the bottom channel provide additional challenge for students. Use these suggestions for small groups or individuals.

ADDITIONAL GUIDELINES

For more help with differentiation and tips for classroom management, see

 BEST PRACTICES TOOLKIT Differentiated Instruction pp. 31–38

B ALLUSION

Possible answer: King uses religious allusions that are meaningful to his audience of clergymen, appealing to their senses of moral obligation and brotherhood.

C ELEMENTS OF AN ARGUMENT

Possible answer: To support his claim of racial injustice in Birmingham, King states that the people of Birmingham are guilty of segregation (lines 47–48), brutality (lines 48–49), biased courts (line 49), and unsolved bombings (lines 50–51).

If students need help . . . Work with them to list supporting evidence in the chart introduced on page 1145.

---

far corners of the Greco-Roman world, so am I compelled to carry the gospel of freedom beyond my own hometown. Like Paul, I must constantly respond to the Macedonian call for aid.[1] **B**

30   Moreover, I am **cognizant** of the interrelatedness of all communities and states. I cannot sit idly by in Atlanta and not be concerned about what happens in Birmingham. Injustice anywhere is a threat to justice everywhere. We are caught in an inescapable network of mutuality, tied in a single garment of destiny. Whatever affects one directly, affects all indirectly. Never again can we afford to live with the narrow, provincial "outside agitator" idea. Anyone who lives inside the United States can never be considered an outsider anywhere within its bounds.

    You deplore the demonstrations taking place in Birmingham. But your statement, I am sorry to say, fails to express a similar concern for the conditions that brought about the demonstrations. I am sure that none of you would want to rest content with the superficial kind of social analysis that deals merely

40 with effects and does not grapple with underlying causes. It is unfortunate that demonstrations are taking place in Birmingham, but it is even more unfortunate that the city's white power structure left the Negro community with no alternative.

    In any nonviolent campaign there are four basic steps: collection of the facts to determine whether injustices exist; negotiation; self-purification; and direct action. We have gone through all these steps in Birmingham. There can be no gainsaying the fact that racial injustice engulfs this community. Birmingham is probably the most thoroughly segregated city in the United States. Its ugly record of brutality is widely known. Negroes have experienced grossly unjust treatment in the courts.

50 There have been more unsolved bombings of Negro homes and churches in Birmingham than in any other city in the nation. These are the hard, brutal facts of the case. On the basis of these conditions, Negro leaders sought to negotiate with the city fathers. But the latter consistently refused to engage in good-faith negotiations. **C**

    Then, last September, came the opportunity to talk with leaders of Birmingham's economic community. In the course of the negotiations, certain promises were made by the merchants— for example, to remove the stores' humiliating racial signs.[2] On the basis of these promises, the Reverend Fred Shuttlesworth and the leaders of the Alabama Christian Movement for Human

60 Rights agreed to a **moratorium** on all demonstrations. As the weeks and months went by, we realized that we were the victims of a broken promise. A few signs, briefly removed, returned; the others remained.

    As in so many past experiences, our hopes had been blasted, and the shadow of deep disappointment settled upon us. We had no alternative except to prepare for direct action, whereby we would present our very bodies as a means of laying our case before the conscience of the local and the national community. Mindful of the difficulties involved, we decided to undertake a process of self-purification.

---

1. **Macedonian** (măs′ĭ-dō′nē-ən) **call for aid:** According to the Bible (Acts 16), the apostle Paul received a vision calling him to preach in Macedonia, an area north of Greece.
2. **racial signs:** signs marking segregated buildings and other facilities.

B ALLUSION
Explain why King's allusions in lines 22–28 are appropriate for his audience. What shared beliefs does King appeal to?

cognizant (kŏg′nĭ-zənt) *adj.* aware

2 Targeted Passage

C ELEMENTS OF AN ARGUMENT
Reread lines 46–54. What **reasons** and **evidence** does King use to support his **claim** that there is racial injustice in Birmingham?

moratorium (môr′ə-tôr′ē-əm) *n.* a temporary stoppage or waiting period

---

DIFFERENTIATED INSTRUCTION

FOR STRATEGIC READERS

2 Targeted Passage [Lines 44–54]

This passage identifies the four basic steps for a nonviolent campaign and justifies such a campaign in Birmingham.

- What are the four basic steps for a nonviolent campaign?

- Which steps have been completed in Birmingham, and to what result?

- What circumstances justify a nonviolent campaign in Birmingham?

FOR ENGLISH LEARNERS

Related Vocabulary Ask students to find words on pages 1146–1155 that fit into each of these categories: *Organizational Terms, Civil Rights Movement,* and *Reactions to Oppression.* Have students record the words in a Three-Column Journal, with each category serving as a column head.

 BEST PRACTICES TOOLKIT—Transparency Three-Column Journal p. B10

We began a series of workshops on nonviolence, and we repeatedly asked ourselves: "Are you able to accept blows without **retaliating?**" "Are you able to endure the ordeal of jail?" We decided to schedule our direct-action program for the Easter season, realizing that except for Christmas, this is the main shopping period of the year. Knowing that a strong economic-withdrawal program[3] would be the by-product of direct action, we felt that this would be the best time to bring pressure to bear on the merchants for the needed change.

Then it occurred to us that Birmingham's mayoral election was coming up in March, and we speedily decided to postpone action until after election day. When we discovered that the Commissioner of Public Safety, Eugene "Bull" Connor, had piled up enough votes to be in the runoff, we decided again to postpone action until the day after the runoff so that the demonstrations could not be used to cloud the issues. Like many others, we waited to see Mr. Connor defeated, and to this end we endured postponement after postponement. Having aided in this community need, we felt that our direct-action program could be delayed no longer.

You may well ask: "Why direct action? Why sit-ins, marches, and so forth? Isn't negotiation a better path?" You are quite right in calling for negotiation. Indeed, this is the very purpose of direct action. Nonviolent direct action seeks to create such a crisis and foster such a tension that a community which has constantly refused to negotiate is forced to confront the issue. It seeks so to dramatize the issue that it can no longer be ignored. My citing the creation of tension as part of the work of the nonviolent-resister may sound rather shocking. But I must confess that I am not afraid of the word "tension." I have earnestly opposed violent tension, but there is a type of constructive, nonviolent tension which is necessary for growth. Just as Socrates[4] felt that it was necessary to create a tension in the mind so that individuals could rise from the bondage of myths and half-truths to the unfettered realm of creative analysis and objective appraisal, so must we see the need for nonviolent gadflies to create the kind of tension in society that will help men rise from the dark depths of prejudice and racism to the majestic heights of understanding and brotherhood.

The purpose of our direct-action program is to create a situation so crisis-packed that it will inevitably open the door to negotiation. I therefore concur with you in your call for negotiation. Too long has our beloved Southland been bogged down in a tragic effort to live in monologue rather than dialogue.

One of the basic points in your statement is that the action that I and my associates have taken in Birmingham is untimely. Some have asked: "Why didn't you give the new city administration time to act?" The only answer that I can give to this query is that the new Birmingham administration must be prodded about as much as the outgoing one, before it will act. . . . My friends, I must say to you that we have not made a single gain in civil rights without determined legal and nonviolent pressure. Lamentably, it is a historical fact that privileged groups

retaliating (rĭ-tăl′ē-ā′tĭng) n. taking revenge **retaliate** v.

---

3. **economic-withdrawal program:** boycott.
4. **Socrates** (sŏk′rə-tēz′): Greek philosopher (470–399 B.C.) who was a major influence in the development of Western thought.

LETTER FROM BIRMINGHAM JAIL **1149**

Lines 84–98
REINFORCE *KEY IDEA:* ACTION

Discuss What is the relationship between verbal negotiation and **action?** *Possible answer: A breakdown in verbal negotiation breeds action. Action restores or repairs the breakdown.*

BACKGROUND

Nonviolent Action King was inspired in his beliefs about nonviolent protest (lines 84–88) by the life and work of Mohandas Gandhi. Gandhi successfully worked for Indian civil rights in South Africa and India through a principle he developed called *satyagraha,* which is Sanskrit for *truth* and *force.* Gandhi based his approach on the nonviolent teachings of the Christian Bible, Leo Tolstoy, and Henry David Thoreau. King studied Gandhi while attending theological seminary and later traveled to India to learn more about Gandhi's methods. These methods of nonviolent protest became central to the American civil rights movement.

Lines 84–100
TIERED DISCUSSION PROMPTS

Use these prompts to help students understand King's philosophy of direct action as a means for social change:

Summarize According to King, what is the purpose of direct action? *Possible answer: Direct action serves to force negotiation with those who refuse to negotiate.*

Interpret What is the meaning and purpose of King's allusion to Socrates in lines 93–95? *Possible answer: King's allusion to Socrates points out that tension is necessary for growth in thought. Alluding to a great philosopher lends credibility to King's ideas about growth in the negotiation process.*

Evaluate Does King effectively support his argument for direct action here? Explain. *Possible answer: King's argument is effective. He points out ways that direct action will be effective, supporting his argument by citing great thinkers who share his basic philosophy.*

FOR ENGLISH LEARNERS

Culture: Clarify Explain that in many American cities, the mayor is the head of the city government. On election day, cities are very busy as people travel to the polls, or voting places. When the first election day does not yield a clear winner, a *runoff* (line 78), or second election, is held, usually between the two leaders. Clarify that King's organization postponed action beyond the various elections to avoid interrupting the democratic process.

FOR ADVANCED LEARNERS/AP

Write a Dialogue [paired option] Invite students to use text from King's letter to construct a dialogue between the clergymen and King, editing as needed to create a meaningful flow. Suggest that students use the dialogues to develop live oral interpretations for the class. Remind students to use voice, tone, and pace to add emphasis and meaning.

TIERED DISCUSSION PROMPTS

Use these prompts to help students understand King's views on the link between morality and oppression:

Connect Think about a time when you or someone you know stood up to a bully. In what way does that experience help you understand King's views on oppression? *Accept all thoughtful responses.*

Interpret What does King mean when he says that groups are more immoral than individuals? ***Possible answer:*** *Groups provide people with anonymity. It is easier to act immorally if there is no individual accountability for one's actions or inactions.*

Evaluate Agree or disagree with King's assessment that freedom must be demanded by the oppressed. Explain. *Students are likely to agree with King because those who value power over others are not likely to abdicate this power willingly.*

▶ GRAMMAR AND STYLE

Analyze Parallelism Parallelism—the use of the same grammatical forms to express equivalent thoughts—helps King emphasize growing tension in his list of wrongs. He then introduces his dramatic and emphatic point by varying the parallel structure from *when you* to *then you*. Have students locate other examples of parallel structure in the letter and explain their effects.

---

110 seldom give up their privileges voluntarily. Individuals may see the moral light and voluntarily give up their unjust posture; but, as Reinhold Niebuhr[5] has reminded us, groups tend to be more immoral than individuals.

We know through painful experience that freedom is never voluntarily given by the oppressor; it must be demanded by the oppressed. Frankly, I have yet to engage in a direct-action campaign that was "well-timed" in the view of those who have not suffered unduly from the disease of segregation. For years now I have heard the word "Wait!" It rings in the ear of every Negro with piercing familiarity. This "Wait" has almost always meant "Never." We must come to see, with one of our distinguished jurists, that "justice too long delayed is justice denied."

120 We have waited for more than 340 years for our constitutional and God-given rights. The nations of Asia and Africa are moving with jetlike speed toward gaining political independence, but we still creep at horse-and-buggy pace toward gaining a cup of coffee at a lunch counter. Perhaps it is easy for those who have never felt the stinging darts of segregation to say, "Wait." But when you have seen vicious mobs lynch your mothers and fathers at will and drown your sisters and brothers at whim; when you have seen hate-filled policemen curse, kick, and even kill your black brothers and sisters; when you see the vast majority of your twenty million Negro brothers smothering in an airtight cage of poverty in the midst of an affluent society; when you suddenly find your tongue twisted and your speech

130 stammering as you seek to explain to your six-year-old daughter why she can't go to the public amusement park that has just been advertised on television, and see tears welling up in her eyes when she is told that Funtown is closed to colored children, and see ominous clouds of inferiority beginning to form in her little mental sky, and see her beginning to distort her personality by developing an unconscious bitterness toward white people; when you have to concoct an answer for a five-year-old son who is asking: "Daddy, why do white people treat colored people so mean?"; when you take a cross-country drive and find it necessary to sleep night after night in the uncomfortable corners of your automobile because no motel will accept you; when you are humiliated day in and day out by nagging

140 signs reading "white" and "colored"; when your first name becomes "nigger," your middle name becomes "boy" (however old you are) and your last name becomes "John," and your wife and mother are never given the respected title "Mrs."; when you are harried by day and haunted by night by the fact that you are a Negro, living constantly at tiptoe stance, never quite knowing what to expect next, and are plagued with inner fears and outer resentments; when you are forever fighting a degenerating sense of "nobodiness"—then you will understand why we find it difficult to wait. There comes a time when the cup of endurance runs over, and men are no longer willing to be plunged into the abyss of despair. I hope, sirs, you can understand our legitimate and unavoidable impatience. ▶

150 You express a great deal of anxiety over our willingness to break laws. This is certainly a legitimate concern. Since we so diligently urge people to obey the

▶ GRAMMAR AND STYLE
Reread lines 124–146. Note how King establishes **parallelism** by starting each subordinate clause with the words *when you*.

---

5. **Reinhold Niebuhr** (nēʹbŏŏrʹ): American theologian (1892–1971) whose writings deal mainly with moral and social problems.

DIFFERENTIATED INSTRUCTION

FOR ADVANCED LEARNERS/AP

Research King's letter was part of a series of events that occurred in Birmingham, Alabama, that drew national attention to the civil rights movement. Have students research those events, particularly:

- racial violence in Birmingham in the early 1960s
- the organization of "Project C" by the SCLC to address civil rights issues in Birmingham, April 1963

- King's arrest and release, April 12–April 20, 1963
- the "children's crusade," May 1963
- the bombing of the Sixteenth Street Baptist Church by white supremacists, killing four African-American girls, September 1963 (commemorated in "Ballad of Birmingham" on page 1156)

Allow time for students to present their findings to the class.

Supreme Court's decision of 1954 outlawing segregation in the public schools,[6] at first glance it may seem rather **paradoxical** for us consciously to break laws. One may well ask: "How can you advocate breaking some laws and obeying others?" The answer lies in the fact that there are two types of laws: just and unjust. I would be the first to advocate obeying just laws. One has not only a legal but a moral responsibility to obey just laws. Conversely, one has a moral responsibility to disobey unjust laws. I would agree with St. Augustine[7] that "an unjust law is no law at all."

160   Now, what is the difference between the two? How does one determine whether a law is just or unjust? A just law is a man-made code that squares with the moral law or the law of God. An unjust law is a code that is out of harmony with the moral law. To put it in the terms of St. Thomas Aquinas:[8] An unjust law is a human law that is not rooted in eternal law and natural law. Any law that uplifts human personality is just. Any law that degrades human personality is unjust. All segregation statutes are unjust because segregation distorts the soul and damages the personality. It gives the segregator a false sense of superiority and the segregated a false sense of inferiority. Segregation, to use the terminology of the Jewish philosopher Martin Buber,[9] substitutes an "I-it" relationship for an "I-thou" relationship and ends up relegating persons to the status of things. Hence 170 segregation is not only politically, economically, and sociologically unsound, it is morally wrong and sinful. Paul Tillich[10] has said that sin is separation. Is not segregation an existential expression of man's tragic separation, his awful **estrangement,** his terrible sinfulness? Thus it is that I can urge men to obey the 1954 decision of the Supreme Court, for it is morally right; and I can urge them to disobey segregation ordinances, for they are morally wrong.

Let us consider a more concrete example of just and unjust laws. An unjust law is a code that a numerical or power majority group compels a minority group to obey but does not make binding on itself. This is *difference* made legal. By the 180 same token, a just law is a code that a majority compels a minority to follow and that it is willing to follow itself. This is *sameness* made legal.

Let me give another explanation. A law is unjust if it is inflicted on a minority that, as a result of being denied the right to vote, had no part in enacting or devising the law. Who can say that the legislature of Alabama which set up that state's segregation laws was democratically elected? Throughout Alabama all sorts of devious methods are used to prevent Negroes from becoming registered voters, and there are some counties in which, even though Negroes constitute a majority of the population, not a single Negro is registered. Can any law enacted under such circumstances be considered democratically structured?

---

6. **Supreme Court decision . . . public schools:** the United States Supreme Court's decision in the case *Brown v. Board of Education of Topeka, Kansas.*

7. **St. Augustine** (ô′gə-stēn′): North African bishop (A.D. 354–430) regarded as a founding father of Christianity.

8. **St. Thomas Aquinas** (ə-kwī′nəs): noted philosopher and theologian (1225–1274).

9. **Martin Buber** (bōō′bər): influential philosopher (1878–1965) with great impact on Jewish and Christian theology.

10. **Paul Tillich** (tĭl′ĭk): German-born American theologian (1886–1965).

LETTER FROM BIRMINGHAM JAIL   **1151**

---

paradoxical
(păr′ə-dŏk′sĭ-kəl) *adj.* self-contradictory

❸ Targeted Passage

E ELEMENTS OF AN ARGUMENT
Reread lines 150–159. How does King's distinction between just and unjust laws help support his claim that it is sometimes appropriate to break the law?

estrangement
(ĭ-strānj′mənt) *n.* separation; alienation

E ELEMENTS OF AN ARGUMENT

Possible answer: *King's distinction between just and unjust laws supports his claim that it is sometimes appropriate to break the law because citizens should obey only laws that are morally correct.*

Extend the Discussion Are morals universal, such that everyone will agree on which laws are moral and which are immoral? Is King's standard for distinguishing which laws to obey and to disobey practical for a society based on laws? Explain.

**Lines 157–158
REINFORCE *KEY IDEA*: ACTION**

Discuss Is King correct that one has a moral responsibility to take **action** against unjust laws? Why or why not? *Students may agree with King in principle, but will likely note how difficult it is to accept the consequences of disobeying the law.*

FOR STRATEGIC READERS

❸ Targeted Passage [Lines 154–176]

This passage explains King's philosophy about just and unjust laws and the ways people should react to either.

• What types of laws does King define?

• In what ways should people react to just laws? unjust laws?

• In what ways should people distinguish these two types of laws?

FOR ENGLISH LEARNERS

Comprehension: Self-Monitor Urge students to pause and use paraphrasing to self-monitor understanding of the challenging philosophical language and concepts in lines 166–174.
Possible answer: *The laws that separate people on the basis of race are wrong because this separation hurts people. These laws incorrectly make some people think they are better than others. Separation between people objectifies one group. The separation of the races is bad for politics and the economy, and it is morally wrong. To separate is to sin. Hence, the separation between the races is a terrible sin.*

LETTER FROM BIRMINGHAM JAIL   **1151**

Activity Ask students to describe ways that the teens in the photograph reflect King's attitudes about nonviolent direct action. *Possible answer: The students in the photograph are seated calmly. They convey no threat in their posture or behavior, nor do they carry tools of aggression.*

About the Photograph The photograph shows high school students who were arrested during the Birmingham protests. So many students were arrested that the city jails were filled. The students shown are being held in the Birmingham stadium. On May 2, 1963, more than 1,000 young people demonstrated; 900 of them were arrested. The following day, more than 1,000 students arrived to protest. The sight of children being arrested, sprayed with firehoses, and attacked by police dogs shocked many Americans and boosted support for the civil rights movement.

LITERARY ANALYSIS

F ALLUSION

Possible answer: With these allusions, King sends the message that civil disobedience is part of a long and distinguished tradition. It is the central element of Christianity, Western civilization, and American democracy.

If students need help . . . Direct them to the footnotes on page 1152 for explanation of King's allusions.

High school students jailed in Birmingham protests of 1963

190   Sometimes a law is just on its face and unjust in its application. For instance, I have been arrested on a charge of parading without a permit. Now, there is nothing wrong in having an ordinance which requires a permit for a parade. But such an ordinance becomes unjust when it is used to maintain segregation and to deny citizens the First Amendment privilege of peaceful assembly and protest.

I hope you are able to see the distinction I am trying to point out. In no sense do I advocate evading or defying the law, as would the **rabid** segregationist. That would lead to anarchy. One who breaks an unjust law must do so openly, lovingly, and with a willingness to accept the penalty. I submit that an individual who breaks a law that conscience tells him is unjust, and who willingly accepts the 200 penalty of imprisonment in order to arouse the conscience of the community over its injustice, is in reality expressing the highest respect for law.

Of course, there is nothing new about this kind of civil disobedience. It was evidenced sublimely in the refusal of Shadrach, Meshach, and Abednego to obey the laws of Nebuchadnezzar,[11] on the ground that a higher moral law was at stake. It was practiced superbly by the early Christians, who were willing to face hungry lions and the excruciating pain of chopping blocks rather than submit to certain unjust laws of the Roman Empire. To a degree, academic freedom is a reality today because Socrates practiced civil disobedience. In our own nation, the Boston Tea Party[12] represented a massive act of civil disobedience. F

rabid (răb'ĭd) *adj.* unreasonably extreme; fanatical

F ALLUSION
Reread lines 202–209. What message about civil disobedience does King send with his choice of allusions?

---

11. **the refusal . . . Nebuchadnezzar** (nĕb'ə-kəd-nĕz'ər): In the Bible (Daniel 3), Shadrach (shăd'răk), Meshach (mē'shăch), and Abednego (ə-bĕd'nĭ-gō') are three Hebrews condemned to death for refusing to worship an idol set up by Nebuchadnezzar, king of Babylon. However, they were miraculously protected from the flames in the furnace into which they were thrown.

12. **Boston Tea Party:** In 1773, American rebels dumped 15,000 pounds of tea into Boston Harbor to protest the British Tea Act.

1152   UNIT 6: CONTEMPORARY LITERATURE

DIFFERENTIATED INSTRUCTION

FOR STRATEGIC READERS

Clarify Allusions [small-group option] Organize groups of three students. Ask each student to read an encyclopedia entry on one of these three people: Socrates (lines 93–95, 207–208), the Apostle Paul (lines 279–280), and Adolf Hitler (lines 210–214). Tell each student to write a paragraph explaining who the person is and why King includes this person in his argument. Have students combine their paragraphs to share aloud with other groups.

FOR ADVANCED LEARNERS/AP

Evaluate Literary Letters Have students consider whether King's letter qualifies as literature. First, students will need to develop a list of literary criteria that can be applied both to fiction and nonfiction. Explain to students that many works of fiction are written in epistolary form in which characters exchange letters, write in diaries or journals, or provide newspaper accounts of events. Students may benefit by skimming and scanning epistolary

works, if possible, such as *Dracula* or *Flowers for Algernon*, in developing their list of criteria. In evaluating King's letter, ask students to consider whether the clergymen appear to be King's only intended audience and why or why not.

We should never forget that everything Adolf Hitler did in Germany was
"legal" and everything the Hungarian freedom fighters[13] did in Hungary was
"illegal." It was "illegal" to aid and comfort a Jew in Hitler's Germany. Even
so, I am sure that, had I lived in Germany at the time, I would have aided and
comforted my Jewish brothers. If today I lived in a Communist country where
certain principles dear to the Christian faith are suppressed, I would openly
advocate disobeying that country's antireligious laws.

I must make two honest confessions to you, my Christian and Jewish brothers.
First, I must confess that over the past few years I have been gravely disappointed
with the white moderate. I have almost reached the regrettable conclusion that
the Negro's great stumbling block in his stride toward freedom is not the White
Citizen's Counciler or the Ku Klux Klanner,[14] but the white moderate, who is
more devoted to "order" than to justice; who prefers a negative peace which is
the absence of tension to a positive peace which is the presence of justice; who
constantly says: "I agree with you in the goal you seek, but I cannot agree with
your methods of direct action"; who paternalistically believes he can set the
timetable for another man's freedom; who lives by a mythical concept of time
and who constantly advises the Negro to wait for a "more convenient season."
Shallow understanding from people of goodwill is more frustrating than absolute
misunderstanding from people of ill will. Lukewarm acceptance is much more
bewildering than outright rejection.

I had hoped that the white moderate would understand that law and order exist
for the purpose of establishing justice and that when they fail in this purpose, they
become the dangerously structured dams that block the flow of social progress.
I had hoped that the white moderate would understand that the present tension
in the South is a necessary phase of the transition from an obnoxious negative
peace, in which the Negro passively accepted his unjust plight, to a **substantive**
and positive peace, in which all men will respect the dignity and worth of human
personality. Actually, we who engage in nonviolent direct action are not the
creators of tension. We merely bring to the surface the hidden tension that is
already alive. We bring it out in the open, where it can be seen and dealt with.
Like a boil that can never be cured so long as it is covered up but must be opened
with all its ugliness to the natural medicines of air and light, injustice must be
exposed, with all the tension its exposure creates, to the light of human conscience
and the air of national opinion before it can be cured.

In your statement you assert that our actions, even though peaceful, must be
condemned because they precipitate violence. But is this a logical assertion? Isn't
this like condemning a robbed man because his possession of money precipitated
the evil act of robbery? Isn't this like condemning Socrates because his unswerving
commitment to truth and his philosophical inquiries precipitated the act by
the misguided populace in which they made him drink hemlock? Isn't this like

substantive (sŭb'stən-tĭv)
adj. significant; with a
strong basis

---

13. **Hungarian freedom fighters:** Hungarians who participated in an unsuccessful 1956 rebellion against the
Communist government of their homeland. The rebellion was crushed by Soviet troops.

14. **the White . . . Klanner:** members of white supremacist groups.

Lines 238–244
TIERED DISCUSSION PROMPTS

Use these prompts to help students understand King's explanation of the value of tension to social change:

Restate What is King saying in these lines? *Possible answer: He and his followers did not cause the tension but simply took action as a response to the tension.*

Interpret What does King mean when he says that protesters do not create tension, they merely bring it to the surface? *Possible answer: Tension precedes the need for social change. Protesters do not create a problem; they react to and call attention to an existing problem.*

Evaluate Explain whether you agree with King that tension must erupt in order to be cured. *Students may note that if tension is allowed to fester, it becomes internally destructive. If tension is allowed to erupt, it may dissipate and ultimately heal.*

FOR ENGLISH LEARNERS

Vocabulary Support Help students use a Two-Column Chart and context to list and then decipher these opposing meanings:

- *negative peace/positive peace* (lines 222–223)
- *shallow understanding/absolute misunderstanding* (lines 228–229)
- *lukewarm acceptance/outright rejection* (lines 229–230)

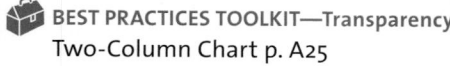 **BEST PRACTICES TOOLKIT—Transparency**
Two-Column Chart p. A25

Clarify Allusion Point out the allusion to Socrates in line 248, and the footnote 4 on page 1149, that identifies him. Explain that Socrates was executed when the Athenian city-state accused him of corrupting the city's young people by encouraging them to question tradition. Then help students explain King's allusion, which he uses to assert that the clergymen's logic in lines 245–246 is faulty. Have students decide if they agree with King's assertion.

FOR ADVANCED LEARNERS/AP

Make Judgments Have students summarize King's criticisms of the white moderates in lines 217–230. Then have them discuss why King includes details of such sentiments in this response to his "Christian and Jewish brothers." *Possible answer: Summary: The white moderates are African Americans' biggest obstacle because they value order over justice. Therefore, they argue to wait patiently for change. King wants to tell his accusers that they are part of the problem.*

REINFORCE *KEY IDEA:* ACTION

Discuss Is **action** in support of a moral ideal a form of extremism? If so, is it acceptable? Explain. *Possible answer: If action in support of a moral ideal goes against the commonly accepted social norms, then yes, it is extremism. If the ideal is truly moral, this extremism is acceptable.*

condemning Jesus because his unique God-consciousness and never-ceasing devotion to God's will precipitated the evil act of crucifixion? We must come to see that, as the federal courts have consistently affirmed, it is wrong to urge an individual to cease his efforts to gain his basic constitutional rights because the quest may precipitate violence. Society must protect the robbed and punish the robber. . . .

Oppressed people cannot remain oppressed forever. The yearning for freedom eventually manifests itself, and that is what has happened to the American Negro. Something within has reminded him of his birthright of freedom, and something without has reminded him that it can be gained. Consciously or unconsciously,
260 he has been caught up by the *Zeitgeist*,[15] and with his black brothers of Africa and his brown and yellow brothers of Asia, South America, and the Caribbean, the United States Negro is moving with a sense of great urgency toward the promised land of racial justice. If one recognizes this vital urge that has engulfed the Negro community, one should readily understand why public demonstrations are taking place. The Negro has many pent-up resentments and **latent** frustrations, and he must release them. So let him march; let him make prayer pilgrimages to the city hall; let him go on freedom rides—and try to understand why he must do so. If his repressed emotions are not released in nonviolent ways, they will seek expression through violence; this is not a threat but a fact of history. So I have not
270 said to my people: "Get rid of your discontent." Rather, I have tried to say that this normal and healthy discontent can be channeled into the creative outlet of nonviolent direct action. And now this approach is being termed extremist.

But though I was initially disappointed at being categorized as an extremist, as I continued to think about the matter, I gradually gained a measure of satisfaction from the label. Was not Jesus an extremist for love: "Love your enemies, bless them that curse you, do good to them that hate you, and pray for them which despitefully use you, and persecute you." Was not Amos[16] an extremist for justice: "Let justice roll down like waters and righteousness like an ever-flowing stream." Was not Paul an extremist for the Christian gospel: "I bear in my body the marks
280 of the Lord Jesus." Was not Martin Luther[17] an extremist: "Here I stand; I cannot do otherwise, so help me God." And John Bunyan:[18] "I will stay in jail to the end of my days before I make a butchery of my conscience." And Abraham Lincoln: "This nation cannot survive half slave and half free." And Thomas Jefferson: "We hold these truths to be self-evident, that all men are created equal. . . ." So the question is not whether we will be extremists, but what kind of extremists we will be. Will we be extremists for hate or for love? Will we be extremists for the preservation of injustice or for the extension of justice? In that dramatic scene on Calvary's hill[19] three men were crucified. We must never forget that all

4 Targeted Passage

latent (lāt'nt) *adj.* existing in a hidden form

---

15. ***Zeitgeist*** (tsīt'gīst') *German*: the spirit of the time; that is, the beliefs and attitudes shared by most people living in a particular period.

16. **Amos:** Hebrew prophet whose words are recorded in the Old Testament book bearing his name.

17. **Martin Luther:** German monk (1483–1546) who launched the Protestant Reformation.

18. **John Bunyan:** English preacher and author (1628–1688) who was twice imprisoned for unlicensed preaching.

19. **Calvary's hill:** the site of Jesus' crucifixion.

DIFFERENTIATED INSTRUCTION

FOR STRATEGIC READERS

4 Targeted Passage [Lines 256–272]

In this passage, King explains the inevitable results of oppression.

- What do oppressed people want?
- In what ways might this need reveal itself?
- What will happen to oppressed people if they cannot express their feelings?
- What label has been assigned to civil rights activism such as King describes?

FOR ENGLISH LEARNERS

Related Vocabulary Have students add to the Three-Column Journal they began on page 1148. On pages 1154–1155, they will find these and other words related to *Reactions to Oppression: oppressed, yearning* (line 256); *pent-up resentments, latent frustrations* (line 265); *repressed emotions, seek expression* (lines 268–269); *discontent* (line 270); *channeled, creative outlet* (line 271); *direct action, extremist* (line 272).

FOR ADVANCED LEARNERS/AP

Outline an Argument Point out that King cites history but no specific supporting evidence for his claim (lines 268–269) that repressed emotions will result in violence unless released in nonviolent ways. Challenge students to supply King with supporting historical examples. Invite volunteers to share their findings with the class.

three were crucified for the same crime—the crime of extremism. Two were
290 extremists for immorality, and thus fell below their environment. The other,
Jesus Christ, was an extremist for love, truth, and goodness, and thereby rose
above his environment. Perhaps the South, the nation and the world are in dire
need of creative extremists. . . . **G**

I wish you had commended the Negro sit-inners and demonstrators of
Birmingham for their sublime courage, their willingness to suffer, and their
amazing discipline in the midst of great provocation. One day the South will
recognize its real heroes. They will be the James Merediths,[20] with the noble
sense of purpose that enables them to face jeering and hostile mobs, and with
the agonizing loneliness that characterizes the life of the pioneer. They will be
300 old, oppressed, battered Negro women, symbolized in a seventy-two-year-old
woman in Montgomery, Alabama, who rose up with a sense of dignity and
with her people decided not to ride segregated buses, and who responded with
ungrammatical profundity to one who inquired about her weariness: "My feets
is tired, but my soul is at rest." They will be the young high school and college
students, the young ministers of the gospel and a host of their elders, courageously
and nonviolently sitting in at lunch counters and willingly going to jail for
conscience' sake. One day the South will know that when these disinherited
children of God sat down at lunch counters, they were in reality standing up
for what is best in the American dream and for the most sacred values in our
310 Judaeo-Christian heritage, thereby bringing our nation back to those great wells
of democracy which were dug deep by the founding fathers in their formulation
of the Constitution and the Declaration of Independence.

Never before have I written so long a letter. I'm afraid it is much too long to
take your precious time. I can assure you that it would have been much shorter if
I had been writing from a comfortable desk, but what else can one do when he is
alone in a narrow jail cell, other than write long letters, think long thoughts, and
pray long prayers?

If I have said anything in this letter that overstates the truth and indicates an
unreasonable impatience, I beg you to forgive me. If I have said anything that
320 understates the truth and indicates my having a patience that allows me to settle
for anything less than brotherhood, I beg God to forgive me.

I hope this letter finds you strong in the faith. I also hope that circumstances
will soon make it possible for me to meet each of you, not as an integrationist or
a civil-rights leader but as a fellow clergyman and a Christian brother. Let us all
hope that the dark clouds of racial prejudice will soon pass away and the deep
fog of misunderstanding will be lifted from our fear-drenched communities, and
in some not too distant tomorrow the radiant stars of love and brotherhood will
shine over our great nation with all their **scintillating** beauty.

Yours for the cause of Peace and Brotherhood,
330 **Martin Luther King Jr.**

---

20. **James Merediths:** people like James Meredith, who endured violent opposition from whites to become
the first African American to attend the University of Mississippi.

scintillating (sĭn'tl-ā'tĭng)
adj. sparkling **scintillate** *v.*

G ALLUSION
Reread lines 275–293.
Consider the usual
connotations of the word
extremist. How do King's
allusions prompt the
reader to think differently
about this idea?

LITERARY ANALYSIS

G ALLUSION

Possible answer: The term extremist *usually refers to one whose views undermine the existing structure and stability of society, or whose actions are destructive. King redefines the term as "heightened moral clarity." In support of his claim, he cites prophets and other widely respected visionary figures who changed global ideas.*

If students need help . . . Work with them to identify the people to whom King alludes and to interpret the allusions.

Lines 256–272
TIERED DISCUSSION PROMPTS
Use these prompts to help students understand King's views about the ways that people respond to oppression:

Connect Have you ever felt frustrated or angry because an authority imposed rules that were difficult for you to follow? Explain. *Accept all thoughtful responses.*

Interpret What does it mean to be oppressed? *Students should recognize that oppression is an unequal distribution of political, economic, and social power.*

Evaluate Will oppressed people ultimately rebel violently or nonviolently against their oppressors, as King says they will? *Students are likely to agree with King that people will strive to achieve freedom at any cost.*

SELECTION WRAP-UP

SUMMARIZE Have students explain King's views on oppression and social change.

FOR STRATEGIC READERS

Comprehension Support In lines 296–297, King says, "One day the South will recognize its real heroes." Clarify that King means that those who work for social change are often unrecognized in their own time but later admired. Ask students who King believes are the South's "real heroes," and why he views these people as heroes. *Possible answer: King believes that the real heroes are those who have stood up for their civil rights through actions such as* sitting in the whites' section of a segregated lunch counter. *He views these people as heroes because they have the courage to continue despite angry and even violent responses.*

FOR ADVANCED LEARNERS/AP

Analyze Conclusion Point out that in King's conclusion (lines 313–328), he offers several disclaimers or apologies about the length and content of his letter. Writing instructors would typically advise against disclaimers or apologies as they undermine a writer's argument and credibility. Have students discuss the effect of the disclaimers on readers as well as King's possible motivations for ending his letter this way.

TIERED DISCUSSION PROMPTS

Use these prompts to help students understand the sacrifices of civil rights activists such as Martin Luther King Jr.:

Summarize What happens to the child in this poem? *Possible answer: The child wants to join the protest in Birmingham. Her mother refuses because she thinks the protests will be dangerous, but she allows her daughter to go to a church function instead. The church is bombed and the daughter is killed.*

Analyze What is the mother's primary interest or motivation? What is the child's primary interest or motivation? *Possible answer: The mother cares more about protecting her child than fighting for racial equality. The child wants to join the fight for racial equality by marching through the streets of Birmingham.*

Synthesize On the basis of King's definition in lines 294–312 of his letter, is the child in the poem one of the South's heroes? Explain. *Students are likely to agree that the child is a hero because she sacrifices her life in the fight for racial justice.*

Ballad
of Birmingham
Dudley Randall

"Mother dear, may I go downtown
instead of out to play,
and march the streets of Birmingham
in a freedom march today?"

5 "No, baby, no, you may not go,
for the dogs are fierce and wild,
and clubs and hoses, guns and jails
ain't good for a little child."

"But, mother, I won't be alone.
10 Other children will go with me,
and march the streets of Birmingham
to make our country free."

"No, baby, no, you may not go,
for I fear those guns will fire.
15 But you may go to church instead,
and sing in the children's choir."

She has combed and brushed her nightdark hair,
and bathed rose petal sweet,
and drawn white gloves on her small brown hands,
20 and white shoes on her feet.

The mother smiled to know her child
was in the sacred place,
but that smile was the last smile
to come upon her face.

25 For when she heard the explosion,
her eyes grew wet and wild.
She raced through the streets of Birmingham
calling for her child.

She clawed through bits of glass and brick,
30 then lifted out a shoe.
"O, here's the shoe my baby wore,
but, baby, where are you?"

Comprehension

R2.4, R2.6, R3.9

1. **Summarize** What led to the decision to start the protests in Birmingham?

2. **Recall** What are the four steps involved in King's nonviolent campaigns?

3. **Clarify** What exactly does King mean by "nonviolent direct action"?

4. **Summarize** In King's view, what is the difference between defying the law and breaking an "unjust" law?

Literary Analysis

5. **Examine Elements of an Argument** Review the chart you created as you read. Which of King's **counterarguments** did you find most persuasive? Consider both his position, or claim, and his reasons and evidence in your answer.

6. **Understand Analogy** An analogy is an extended, point-by-point comparison of two different things, often using a familiar example to explain a difficult or abstract idea. In lines 241–244, King uses an analogy to explain his thoughts on injustice. Reread the analogy. What two things are compared, and in what ways are they similar?

7. **Interpret Allusions** Allusions can refer to people, places, events, or literary works. Choose at least four of King's allusions. Using the footnotes to help you, interpret the meaning of King's references and tell why you think King included each allusion. Record your answers in a chart like the one shown.

Allusion	Possible Meaning	Why Included

8. **Analyze Persuasive Techniques** King's writings and speeches are filled with allusions that reveal his rhetorical mastery and breadth of knowledge. In what ways, if any, do his allusions also help him achieve the following possible purposes? Cite specific allusions that support your answers.

   • appealing to his readers' sense of right and wrong
   • establishing his credibility
   • invoking democratic ideals
   • making his ideas accessible to a wider audience

9. **Compare Texts** Compare the message of "Ballad of Birmingham" (page 1156) with that of King's letter. In what ways is Randall's poem also an argument for taking **action** against injustice?

Literary Criticism

10. **Author's Style** King is a master of the **aphorism,** a short, expressive statement of principle or truth. Here's a memorable one: "Injustice anywhere is a threat to justice everywhere" (line 31). Find two or three more aphorisms in King's letter and explain their effects.

10. *Other aphorisms can be found in lines 113–114, 119, 228–229, 229–230, and 255. Students should recognize that aphorisms contain universal truths that resonate with readers of all backgrounds. The overall effect of King's aphorisms is to present his point of view as a commonsense truth.*

Practice and Apply

After Reading

Use these copy masters to check understanding and provide extra support:

R RESOURCE MANAGER—Copy Masters
Reading Check p. 96
Allusion p. 89
Question Support p. 97

Additional selection questions are provided for teachers on page 83.

ANSWERS

1. *Negotiations between local activists and government officials failed.*

2. *King uses these four steps: collection of facts, negotiation, self-purification, and direct action.*

3. *Nonviolent direct action encompasses confrontational and highly visible actions of civil disobedience, such as sit-ins or picket lines. Protesters do not retaliate if attacked.*

4. *Defying laws is a disregard for morally good laws. Breaking unjust laws expresses deep respect for morality by aligning human laws with those of a higher moral order.*

Possible answers:

5. ■ **SKILLS FOCUS** **Trace the Elements of an Argument** *Answers will vary. Students should cite reasons for their choices and provide supporting quotations or examples.*

6. *King compares injustice to a boil that must be cured. Exposure cures both; exposure creates discomfort for both; cures for both include the medicines of air (national opinion) and light (human conscience).*

7. ● **SKILLS FOCUS** **Allusion** *Answers will vary but students should explain in what way each allusion relates to King's message, to his audience, or both.*

8. *Answers will vary, but students should explain the relationship between each allusion and the listed purpose.*

9. *In the poem, the mother is fearful about allowing her child to participate in a racial protest. The mother feels that it is safer for her child to attend church. Sadly, the child is killed in the church as a result of racist violence, sending the message that there is no safe place when social injustice prospers. This message echoes King's arguments that no one may sit idly by while injustice reigns, and thus we must all take action.*

ANSWERS

Vocabulary in Context

VOCABULARY PRACTICE

1. *cognizant: I know about the plans.*

2. *paradoxical: difficult to make sense of*

3. *substantive: significant*

4. *rabid: involves shouting furiously*

5. *affiliated: partners*

6. *moratorium: a bad storm*

7. *scintillating: could describe a diamond*

8. *latent: a toothache*

9. *estrangement: could result from an argument*

10. *retaliating: could result from losing a game*

R RESOURCE MANAGER—Copy Master
Vocabulary Practice p. 94

VOCABULARY IN WRITING

Suggest that students review the definitions from the margins of King's letter. Urge them to respond to the ideas or claims that prompted King to use each word.

VOCABULARY STRATEGY: ANALOGIES *(also an EL language objective)*

Review the process for using context clues to determine meanings of unfamiliar words.

Possible answers:

1. *Birds migrating south are an indicator of seasonal change. The blooming of crocuses is also an indicator of seasonal change. Readers can infer that* harbinger *means "indicator."*

2. *Smoking is bad for one's health. High cholesterol is also bad for one's health. Readers can infer that* deleterious *means "harmful."*

3. *Physical violence is not tolerated by schools; neither is cheating. Readers can infer that* execration *means "violation."*

R RESOURCE MANAGER—Copy Master
Vocabulary Strategy p. 95

ⓘ Vocabulary Center at **ClassZone.com**
Additional Vocabulary Activities

Vocabulary in Context

VOCABULARY PRACTICE

Show your understanding of the vocabulary words by answering these questions.

1. If I am **cognizant** of your plans, do I know about them or have I forgotten them?
2. Would a **paradoxical** statement be easy or difficult to make sense of?
3. Would a **substantive** contribution be minimal or significant?
4. Would a **rabid** response involve shouting furiously or agreeing silently?
5. If my company is **affiliated** with yours, are they competitors or partners?
6. Which might cause a **moratorium** in road building, a bad storm or potholes?
7. Is a diamond or gold more accurately described as **scintillating?**
8. Which is a **latent** ailment, a toothache or a broken arm?
9. Would an argument cause **estrangement** or a meeting with a stranger?
10. Which might be a cause for **retaliating,** losing a game or taking a taxi?

VOCABULARY IN WRITING

What do you think of nonviolent protest? Explain your ideas in a short paragraph, using three or more vocabulary words. Here is a sample beginning.

> **EXAMPLE SENTENCE**
> By not **retaliating**, the protesters made their points effectively and powerfully.

VOCABULARY STRATEGY: ANALOGIES

An analogy compares two items that may have many points of similarity or may be alike in only one way. Analyzing an analogy is one way of determining the meaning of unfamiliar words in context, such as the word *boil* in this passage:

> *Like a boil that can never be cured so long as it is covered up but must be opened with all its ugliness to the natural medicines of air and light, injustice must be exposed, with all the tension its exposure creates, to the light of human conscience and the air of national opinion before it can be cured.* (lines 241–244)

Seeing that a boil is like an injustice to be cured only by exposure, we can infer that it is a sore that can be healed by exposure to air.

PRACTICE Use the comparison in each sentence as a context clue to help you define the boldfaced word. Then discuss the meaning of each analogy, including any inferences you draw based on the comparison and word choice.

1. Like birds migrating south, crocuses are a **harbinger** of seasonal change.
2. High cholesterol is thought to be as **deleterious** to health as smoking.
3. Our school considers cheating as much an **execration** as physical violence.

 R1.3

VOCABULARY PRACTICE
For more practice, go to the **Vocabulary Center** at **ClassZone.com**.

DIFFERENTIATED INSTRUCTION

FOR ENGLISH LEARNERS

Task Support: Vocabulary in Writing Provide these sentence starters to students:

• Nonviolent protest is *affiliated* with

_____.

• Protesters are *cognizant* of _____.

• There is *estrangement* between protesters and _____ because _____.

• Nonviolent protest is a result of *latent*

_____.

• *Substantive* change results from _____.

FOR ADVANCED LEARNERS/AP

Analogies Using King's comparison of a boil and injustice as a model, challenge students to write their own analogies for injustice or another social problem. First, have students choose the two ideas they will compare. Then have students brainstorm lists of associated words from which to draw as they write. Invite volunteers to share their analogies aloud with the class.

Reading-Writing Connection

W1.1, W1.3, W1.4

WRITE A PERSUASIVE ARGUMENT Civil disobedience has been controversial ever since Henry David Thoreau first advocated it in 1847. Opposition to Martin Luther King's brand of nonviolent resistance came from some black activists as well as white segregationists. People still argue over the issue today.

Write a **four-to-six-paragraph persuasive argument** explaining your position on the issue of nonviolent civil disobedience. Model your argument on King's, using counterarguments to anticipate objections to your view.

SELF-CHECK

An effective persuasive argument will . . .

- clearly state a position in the first paragraph
- support the position with facts, examples, quotations, or other forms of evidence
- address possible objections
- use logical reasoning
- conclude with a summary or a call to action

GRAMMAR AND STYLE

USE RHETORICAL DEVICES Review the **Grammar and Style** note on page 1150. In his letter, King uses **parallelism**—the repetition of grammatical structures—to create emphasis and to show comparisons, as in the following example:

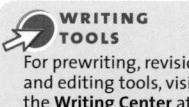
LC1.1

Just as the prophets of the eighth century B.C. left their villages and carried their "thus saith the Lord" far beyond the boundaries of their hometowns, and just as the Apostle Paul left his village of Tarsus and carried the gospel of Jesus Christ to the far corners of the Greco-Roman world, so am I compelled to carry the gospel of freedom beyond my own hometown. (lines 22–27)

Notice how King uses parallel adverb clauses beginning with "just as" to set up a comparison between himself and the biblical figures he cites. What is the impact of this comparison?

PRACTICE Identify the parallel adjective clauses in the following passage from King. Then write a paragraph of your own using similar parallel elements.

[T]he Negro's great stumbling block in his stride toward freedom is not the White Citizen's Counciler or the Ku Klux Klanner, but the white moderate, who is more devoted to "order" than to justice; who prefers a negative peace which is the absence of tension to a positive peace which is the presence of justice; who constantly says: "I agree with you in the goal you seek, but I cannot agree with your methods of direct action"; who paternalistically believes he can set the timetable for another man's freedom; who lives by a mythical concept of time and who constantly advises the Negro to wait for a "more convenient season."

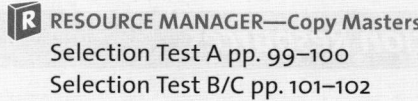

WRITING TOOLS

For prewriting, revision, and editing tools, visit the **Writing Center** at ClassZone.com.

FOR DEVELOPING WRITERS
Writing Support

- Provide students with this thesis statement: Nonviolent civil disobedience is an effective (or ineffective) means for social change.

- Then have students list three reasons that their thesis statements are true, such as 1) it forces public action, 2) it seeks to eliminate violence, and 3) it seeks to establish dialogue.

- For each reason that students list, have them write ways that critics might respond. For example, 1) it forces public reaction rather than action, 2) it breeds violence, and 3) it diverts attention from dialogue to public order.

- Tell students to write at least one paragraph for each of their three points. Remind students to acknowledge and address each of the critics' arguments in their explanations.

Reading-Writing Connection

WRITING PROMPT

Remind students that the first paragraph of their arguments should include a thesis statement expressing support or opposition to nonviolent civil disobedience. Students should then develop one supporting point in each body paragraph, including supporting facts, examples, quotations, allusions, and so on. Students should conclude by restating their main points and offering a final insight. Urge students to prepare outlines before they begin drafting.

 BEST PRACTICES TOOLKIT—Transparency
Outline p. B19

For writing support, see

 Writing Center at **ClassZone.com**

GRAMMAR AND STYLE

Suggest that students choose a topic from King's letters for their paragraphs. Have them draft their paragraphs for content first, then work on parallelism during the revision process. (For more on parallel structure, see **Grammar Handbook,** page R68.) *Possible answer: King establishes parallelism with the repetition of the word* who. *Paragraphs will vary.*

RESOURCE MANAGER—Copy Master
Use Rhetorical Devices p. 98

Assess and Reteach

Assess

RESOURCE MANAGER—Copy Masters
Selection Test A pp. 99–100
Selection Test B/C pp. 101–102

Test Generator CD

Reteach

STANDARDS LESSON FILE
Literature Lessons 34, 35
Informational Test Lessons 13–17
Writing Lessons 9, 29, 34, 35
Vocabulary Lesson 23

Focus and Motivate

OBJECTIVES

Literary Analysis
- explore the key idea of **injustice**
- analyze historical context
- read nonfiction and an interview

Reading
- compare and contrast authors' beliefs

Vocabulary
- build vocabulary for reading and writing
- use the Greek prefix *syn-* to help unlock meaning *(also an EL language objective)*

 CALIFORNIA R2.5, R3.8, R1.2

ABOUT THE AUTHOR

After students read about Malcolm X, have them discuss integration and separatism as responses to racial prejudice. What are the pros and cons of each? *Possible answer: Integration offers equal opportunity but is hard to achieve and may dilute cultural identity. Separatism offers control but may create hostility and tension.*

USING THE NOTABLE QUOTE

Help students define the American dream as the idea that equal opportunity permits any American to aspire to material success. Ask students to list reasons for **Malcolm X** to believe he has no access to that dream. *Possible answer: Malcolm X may see poverty, poor educational opportunities, social racism and prejudice, and discriminatory laws as obstacles to his pursuing the American dream.*

CALIFORNIA R2.5, R3.8, R1.2 (p. 1171)

from Stride Toward Freedom
Nonfiction by Martin Luther King Jr.

For a biography of Martin Luther King Jr., see page 1144.

Malcolm X
1925–1965

NOTABLE QUOTE
"I see America through the eyes of the victim. I don't see any American dream; I see an American nightmare."

Necessary to Protect Ourselves
Interview with Malcolm X by Les Crane

In 1944, while Martin Luther King Jr. was attending college classes in Atlanta, 19-year-old Malcolm Little was hustling on the streets of Harlem. By 1952, a jailhouse conversion transformed Little into the political firebrand we know as Malcolm X, whose separatist views posed a serious challenge to King's integrationist vision.

Bitter Legacy Where King grew up comfortably middle-class, Little's childhood was scarred by poverty and racial violence. His outspoken father, Earl Little, was an early advocate of black separatism who was murdered by white supremacists. His mother, left alone to raise eight children in dire poverty, suffered a mental breakdown. Her children, including Malcolm, were sent to separate foster homes.

By the time he was sent to prison in 1946, Little had been brutally disillusioned about his prospects in white-dominated society. While reading in the prison library, he discovered the teachings of a small religious sect called the Nation of Islam, or the Black Muslims, who called white people "a race of devils" and promoted a vision of black pride. They advocated a radical solution to the race problem: the establishment of a separate, self-reliant black nation.

Change of Heart Inspired by the Black Muslim vision, Malcolm Little converted to Islam and changed his last name to X, symbolizing his lost African name. Once released from prison, he became an influential spokesman for the Nation of Islam and was named their first national minister. Over time, however, he became critical of the organization. In 1964, Malcolm X experienced a second spiritual conversion while making a pilgrimage to Mecca. The sight of Muslims of many races worshipping together caused him to renounce all forms of racial hatred. On his return home, Malcolm X broke with the Nation of Islam and formed the Organization of Afro-American Unity, dedicated to promoting unity among black people all over the world.

Marked Man This new direction angered many Black Muslims, including the young Louis Farrakhan, who labeled Malcolm X a traitor. In February 1965, as Malcolm X was speaking to a crowd of 400 in Harlem, he was gunned down by three assassins, two of whom were Black Muslims.

Author Online
For more on the authors, visit the **Literature Center** at **ClassZone.com**.

1160

Selection Resources

 RESOURCE MANAGER UNIT 6

Plan and Teach pp. 103–110

Literary Analysis
Summary pp. 111†*, 112‡*
Historical Context pp. 113, 114†*
Question Support p. 121*

Reading
Compare and Contrast Authors'
   Beliefs pp. 115, 116†*
Reading Check p. 120

Vocabulary
Study p. 117*
Practice p. 118
Strategy p. 119

Assessment
Selection Tests A, B/C pp. 123*, 125*
Test Generator CD

BEST PRACTICES TOOLKIT

Differentiated Instruction
   pp. 31–38*
Scaffolding Instruction
   pp. 43–46*

Graphic Organizers/Strategies
Word Squares • Main Idea and
Details • Cause-and-Effect Chain
• New Word Analysis

Reading Support
Audio Anthology CD*

Technology
Literature and Vocabulary
   Centers at **ClassZone.com**
Write*Smart* CD

---

* Resources for Differentiation   † Also in Spanish   ‡ In Haitian Creole and Vietnamese

● LITERARY ANALYSIS: HISTORICAL CONTEXT

When you look at a literary work in its **historical context,** you consider how events of the author's time influenced the creation of the text. Martin Luther King Jr. and Malcolm X were political leaders responding to unfolding events. Whereas the meaning of phrases like "the present crisis in race relations" would have been clear to audiences of that time, today's readers may need additional information to fully appreciate the authors' points. Before you read each selection, study the background information provided. Then, as you read each work, consider how the author's views were influenced by events of his time.

● READING SKILL: COMPARE AND CONTRAST AUTHORS' BELIEFS

King and Malcolm X had very different **beliefs** about how to confront racism. As you read each work, note how the author explains his beliefs. Use the authors' direct statements and your own inferences to determine their beliefs about

- the most effective response to injustice
- what justifies the actions they recommend
- winning the support of whites

Use a chart like the one shown to organize your notes.

Issues	King	Malcolm X
response to injustice		
justification of actions		
support from whites		

▲ VOCABULARY IN CONTEXT

King and Malcolm X use the boldfaced words to express their opposing views. Restate each phrase, using a different word or words for the boldfaced term.

1. need to **repudiate** those who oppress us
2. by not speaking out, **tacitly** accepting bad situations
3. cannot **succumb** to defeatist attitudes
4. must take **militant** stands against repression
5. refuse to accept **glib** promises that really mean nothing
6. realize that prejudice is applied **indiscriminately**
7. success through a **synthesis** of ideas and approaches
8. rioting and **anarchy** in the streets

How do we fight INJUSTICE?

KEY IDEA Most people would agree that it's important to stand up for your rights if you're being treated unfairly. However, there are many different opinions about the best way to fight back against **injustice.** In this lesson, Martin Luther King Jr. and Malcolm X argue two very different perspectives on this issue.

PRESENT What considerations do you think are important when choosing how to respond to injustice? Working in a small group, make a list of relevant concerns, such as obeying the law or achieving quick results. Then, rank them in order of importance. Share your opinions with the class.

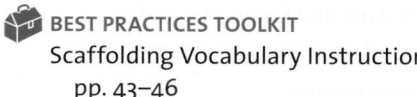
1161

How do we fight INJUSTICE?

Lead into the **KEY IDEA** paragraph by asking the question. After groups complete the **PRESENT** activity, invite volunteers to share their concerns about methods for fighting **injustice.** Discuss whether each concern supports an integrationist or a separatist approach to protest, and why.

SKILLS FOCUS

● HISTORICAL CONTEXT

Explain that historical context includes both immediate events and the history that shapes them. Thus, King and Malcolm X wrote in the context not just of "the present crisis" but all the circumstances that preceded it. Have students describe that context. *Students should describe racial tensions and events from the historical essay (page 1095) and "Letter from Birmingham Jail" (page 1144) or from other prior knowledge.*

■ COMPARE AND CONTRAST AUTHORS' BELIEFS

Write these two statements on the board:

"Violence as a way of achieving racial justice is both impractical and immoral." —Martin Luther King Jr.

" . . . we should get whatever is necessary to protect ourselves . . . where the governmental ability to protect us has broken down." —Malcolm X

Have students contrast these views of violence as a means for fighting racism. *Possible answer: King sees violence as ineffective and morally wrong. Malcolm X sees it as sometimes justified and necessary.*

CHECK UNDERSTANDING Have partners write, then compare and contrast, opposing statements about any topic.

> **R** RESOURCE MANAGER—Copy Master
> Compare and Contrast Authors' Beliefs p. 115 (for student use while reading the selections)

VOCABULARY

▲ VOCABULARY IN CONTEXT

DIAGNOSE WORD KNOWLEDGE To determine preteaching needs, have all students complete Vocabulary in Context. *Possible answers:* **1.** *need to reject those . . . ,* **2.** *silently accepting bad . . . ,* **3.** *cannot give in to defeatist . . . ,* **4.** *must take aggressive stands . . . ,* **5.** *refuse to accept casual promises . . . ,* **6.** *realize that prejudice is applied randomly,* **7.** *success through a coming together of ideas and approaches,* **8.** *rioting and lawlessness in the streets*

PRETEACH VOCABULARY Preteach vocabulary with this copy master. Read each item aloud.

> **R** RESOURCE MANAGER—Copy Master
> Vocabulary Study p. 117

MORE VOCABULARY SUPPORT

For additional activities and guidelines, see

> **▣** BEST PRACTICES TOOLKIT
> Scaffolding Vocabulary Instruction pp. 43–46
> **ℹ** Vocabulary Center at **ClassZone.com**

SUMMARY

In this excerpt from his nonfiction book, Dr. Martin Luther King Jr. reasserts nonviolent resistance as the best path to equality and civil rights for African Americans. Rejecting passive acceptance and physical violence as ineffective and immoral responses to oppression, he argues for a militant but nonviolent mass movement.

READING SKILL

A AUTHOR'S BELIEFS

Possible answer: *King alludes to biblical events and conflicts and to Shakespeare's play* Hamlet. *He is inspired by his religious faith, using Judeo-Christian references to justify his actions.*

If students need help . . . Assist them in using the footnotes to clarify King's allusions. Then work with students to add information to the chart introduced on page 1161:

Beliefs	King
Justification of actions	Biblical events show King that action is sometimes necessary to resist oppression.

STRIDE TOWARD FREEDOM

Martin Luther King Jr.

BACKGROUND In the 1950s, the civil rights movement focused its efforts on overturning the so-called Jim Crow laws, the segregation laws that kept African Americans from equal participation in public life. In 1954, the Supreme Court issued its decision in the landmark case *Brown v. Board of Education*. In this decision, the court declared that "separate but equal" education, a central provision of segregationist policy, was inherently discriminatory. Buoyed by this win, civil rights activists began to challenge Jim Crow through other forms of peaceful protest, such as the year-long mass boycott of segregated buses in Montgomery, Alabama, beginning in 1955. In *Stride Toward Freedom*, published in 1958, a confident and optimistic King describes the philosophy behind the successful boycott.

ANALYZE VISUALS
What does this photo reveal about the risks of nonviolent protest?

Oppressed people deal with their oppression in three characteristic ways. One way is acquiescence: the oppressed resign themselves to their doom. They **tacitly** adjust themselves to oppression, and thereby become conditioned to it. In every movement toward freedom some of the oppressed prefer to remain oppressed. Almost 2,800 years ago Moses set out to lead the children of Israel from the slavery of Egypt to the freedom of the promised land.[1] He soon discovered that slaves do not always welcome their deliverers. They become accustomed to being slaves. They would rather bear those ills they have, as Shakespeare pointed out, than flee to others that they know not of.[2] They prefer the "fleshpots of Egypt"[3]
10 to the ordeals of emancipation. A

① Targeted Passage

tacitly (tăs′ĭt-lē) *adj.* silently

A AUTHOR'S BELIEFS
Consider King's **allusions** in lines 5–10. What do these allusions reveal about King's beliefs and the principles he uses to justify his actions?

---

1. **promised land:** the land of Canaan, promised by God in the Bible (Genesis 12:1–3, 7) to Abraham's descendants.
2. **bear those ills . . . know not of:** an allusion to a line in Act 3, Scene 1, of *Hamlet* by William Shakespeare.
3. **prefer the "fleshpots of Egypt":** an allusion to a line in the book of Exodus in the Bible. As Moses was leading the Israelites out of Egypt, some of them grumbled and wished they had stayed there.

Civil rights protestors being sprayed with high-pressure hoses

---

DIFFERENTIATED INSTRUCTION

FOR ALL STUDENTS

Expert Groups Encourage students to become subject experts by selecting and researching one of these topics:

- Jewish-Christian Scriptures, particularly the books of Genesis and Exodus
- Roy Wilkins and Ralph Abernathy
- Nation of Islam
- Freedom Summer

FOR STRATEGIC READERS

In combination with the *Audio Anthology CD*, use the Targeted Passages (pp. 1162, 1165, 1166, 1169) to ensure that students focus on key concepts in the selections. The Targeted Passages are also good for English learners.

① Targeted Passage [Lines 1–10]

This passage identifies King's topic—the ways in which people respond to oppression—and discusses the first response, acquiescence.

ANALYZE VISUALS

Possible answer: This photo shows that non-violent protesters are still at risk for violent responses from their oppressors.

About the Art *The protesters in this photograph discovered that they could resist the fire hoses by holding on to one other. Uniting in this way eventually caused the firefighters to turn off their hoses, proving Dr. King's commitment to the impact of mass nonviolent protest.*

Lines 1–10
TIERED DISCUSSION PROMPTS

Use these prompts to help students understand King's image of oppression:

Recall What is one way that oppressed people resign themselves to oppression? *Possible answer: People may adjust and condition themselves to oppression.*

Analyze Why might some consider oppression to be more desirable than an unknown future? *Possible answer: Despite difficulties, the oppressed know that they can survive present conditions. The unknown future calls into question issues such as adaptation, change, and survival.*

Synthesize On the basis of your knowledge of King's philosophies and of the history of social revolution, what might be the two other ways that people "deal with their oppression"? *On the basis of the "Letter from Birmingham Jail," students may suggest nonviolent protest. On the basis of history, they may also suggest violent protest.*

- In how many ways does King believe that people respond to oppression?
- What is the first way in which people respond to oppression?
- Why do people sometimes respond to oppression in this way?
- What are "'the fleshpots of Egypt'" and "the ordeals of emancipation"?

FOR ENGLISH LEARNERS

Key Academic Vocabulary Use Word Squares to teach these words from *Stride Toward Freedom*: *adjust* (line 3), *goal* (line 76), *generate* (line 82).

 BEST PRACTICES TOOLKIT—Transparency
Word Squares p. E10

Prereading For prereading instruction for English learners, see

 BEST PRACTICES TOOLKIT
Scaffolding Reading Instruction pp. 43–46

FOR ADVANCED LEARNERS/AP

AP exercises in the bottom channel provide additional challenge for students. Use these suggestions for small groups or individuals.

ADDITIONAL GUIDELINES

For more help with differentiation and tips for classroom management, see

 BEST PRACTICES TOOLKIT
Differentiated Instruction pp. 31–38

There is such a thing as the freedom of exhaustion. Some people are so worn down by the yoke of oppression that they give up. A few years ago in the slum areas of Atlanta, a Negro guitarist used to sing almost daily: "Been down so long that down don't bother me." This is the type of negative freedom and resignation that often engulfs the life of the oppressed.

But this is not the way out. To accept passively an unjust system is to cooperate with that system; thereby the oppressed become as evil as the oppressor. Noncooperation with evil is as much a moral obligation as is cooperation with good. The oppressed must never allow the conscience of the oppressor to slumber.
20 Religion reminds every man that he is his brother's keeper.[4] To accept injustice or segregation passively is to say to the oppressor that his actions are morally right. It is a way of allowing his conscience to fall asleep. At this moment the oppressed fails to be his brother's keeper. So acquiescence—while often the easier way—is not the moral way. It is the way of the coward. The Negro cannot win the respect of his oppressor by acquiescing; he merely increases the oppressor's arrogance and contempt. Acquiescence is interpreted as proof of the Negro's inferiority. The Negro cannot win the respect of the white people of the South or the peoples of the world if he is willing to sell the future of his children for his personal and immediate comfort and safety. **B**

A second way that oppressed people sometimes deal with oppression is to
30 resort to physical violence and corroding hatred. Violence often brings about momentary results. Nations have frequently won their independence in battle. But in spite of temporary victories, violence never brings permanent peace. It solves no social problem; it merely creates new and more complicated ones.

Violence as a way of achieving racial justice is both impractical and immoral. It is impractical because it is a descending spiral ending in destruction for all. The old law of an eye for an eye[5] leaves everybody blind. It is immoral because it seeks to humiliate the opponent rather than win his understanding; it seeks to annihilate rather than to convert. Violence is immoral because it thrives on hatred rather than love. It destroys community and makes brotherhood impossible. It
40 leaves society in monologue rather than dialogue. Violence ends by defeating itself. It creates bitterness in the survivors and brutality in the destroyers. A voice echoes through time saying to every potential Peter, "Put up your sword."[6] History is cluttered with the wreckage of nations that failed to follow this command. **C**

If the American Negro and other victims of oppression **succumb** to the temptation of using violence in the struggle for freedom, future generations will be the recipients of a desolate night of bitterness, and our chief legacy to them will be an endless reign of meaningless chaos. Violence is not the way.

---

4. **his brother's keeper:** In the book of Genesis, after Cain killed his brother Abel, he denied knowing Abel's whereabouts by asking, "Am I my brother's keeper?" In general, the saying refers to a reluctance to accept responsibility for others.

5. **an eye for an eye:** an allusion to Exodus 21:23–25: "You shall give life for life, eye for eye. . . ."

6. **Peter . . . sword":** When Jesus' disciple Peter drew his sword to try to protect Jesus, Jesus condemned his use of violence.

LITERARY ANALYSIS

B HISTORICAL CONTEXT

Possible answer: Words or phrases such as "segregation," "Negro," and "white people of the South" reveal historical events that have shaped King's thinking.

READING SKILL

C AUTHOR'S BELIEFS

Possible answer: An effective response to injustice should achieve community and brotherhood.

Extend the Discussion By what means might these goals be achieved, and why might these means work?

B HISTORICAL CONTEXT
In lines 19–28, King states his position on how the oppressed should respond to oppression. What words and phrases reveal the specific historical example that has shaped his thinking?

C AUTHOR'S BELIEFS
Reread King's criticisms of violence in lines 34–43. In light of these criticisms, what does King believe an effective response to injustice should achieve?

succumb (sə-kŭm') *v.* to give in, especially to overpowering force or strength

---

DIFFERENTIATED INSTRUCTION

FOR ENGLISH LEARNERS

Comprehension: Text Structure Point out that King organizes his text as a list. He begins by stating that there are three ways people respond to oppression: acquiescence (line 2), physical violence (lines 29–30), and nonviolent resistance (lines 48–49). Have students use a Main Idea and Details chart to organize King's arguments.

 BEST PRACTICES TOOLKIT—Transparency
Main Idea and Details p. B6

FOR ADVANCED LEARNERS/AP

Debate In lines 18–19, King states, "Noncooperation with evil is as much a moral obligation as is cooperation with good." Although King does not condone violence under any circumstances, he believes that people should actively resist injustice. Have students form two groups to debate this statement: Cooperating with unjust policies is just as evil as committing violent acts. Invite students to develop debate arguments supported by

historical examples and personal anecdotes. If at any point during the debate students are convinced to change their original thinking, allow them to switch teams after stating why they are doing so. Invite listeners to join the dialogue.

The third way open to oppressed people in their quest for freedom is the way of nonviolent resistance. Like the **synthesis** in Hegelian philosophy,[7] the
50 principle of nonviolent resistance seeks to reconcile the truths of two opposites—acquiescence and violence—while avoiding the extremes and immoralities of both. The nonviolent resister agrees with the person who acquiesces that one should not be physically aggressive toward his opponent but he balances the equation by agreeing with the person of violence that evil must be resisted. He avoids the nonresistance of the former and the violent resistance of the latter. With nonviolent resistance, no individual or group need submit to any wrong, nor need anyone resort to violence in order to right a wrong.

It seems to me that this is the method that must guide the actions of the Negro in the present crisis in race relations. Through nonviolent resistance the Negro will
60 be able to rise to the noble height of opposing the unjust system while loving the perpetrators of the system. The Negro must work passionately and unrelentingly for full stature as a citizen, but he must not use inferior methods to gain it. He must never come to terms with falsehood, malice, hate, or destruction.

Nonviolent resistance makes it possible for the Negro to remain in the South and struggle for his rights. The Negro's problem will not be solved by running away. He cannot listen to the **glib** suggestion of those who would urge him to migrate en masse to other sections of the country. By grasping his great opportunity in the South he can make a lasting contribution to the moral strength of the nation and set a sublime example of courage for generations yet unborn. **D**
70 By nonviolent resistance, the Negro can also enlist all men of good will in his struggle for equality. The problem is not a purely racial one, with Negroes set against whites. In the end, it is not a struggle between people at all, but a tension between justice and injustice. Nonviolent resistance is not aimed against oppressors but against oppression. Under its banner consciences, not racial groups, are enlisted. **E**

If the Negro is to achieve the goal of integration, he must organize himself into a **militant** and nonviolent mass movement. All three elements are indispensable. The movement for equality and justice can only be a success if it has both a mass and militant character; the barriers to be overcome require both. Nonviolence is
80 an imperative in order to bring about ultimate community.

A mass movement of a militant quality that is not at the same time committed to nonviolence tends to generate conflict, which in turn breeds anarchy. The support of the participants and the sympathy of the uncommitted are both inhibited by the threat that bloodshed will engulf the community. This reaction in turn encourages the opposition to threaten and resort to force. When, however, the mass movement **repudiates** violence while moving resolutely toward its goal, its opponents are revealed as the instigators and practitioners of violence if it occurs. Then public support is magnetically attracted to the advocates of nonviolence, while those who employ violence are literally disarmed by
90 overwhelming sentiment against their stand. ❧

---

7. **Hegelian** (hă-gā'lē-ən) **philosophy:** the philosophy of Georg Hegel (1770–1831), which proposed that each situation has an opposite and that both extremes will eventually be reconciled.

---

synthesis (sĭn'thĭ-sĭs) *n.* the union of parts or elements into a whole

② **Targeted Passage**

glib (glĭb) *adj.* showing little thought, preparation, or concern

D HISTORICAL CONTEXT
Reread lines 65–69. What is the "great opportunity in the South" that King refers to?

E AUTHOR'S BELIEFS
Reread lines 70–75. What assumptions does King make about the value of gaining white support?

militant (mĭl'ĭ-tənt) *adj.* aggressively active, especially for a cause

repudiate (rĭ-pyōō'dē-āt') *v.* to reject or renounce

Lines 59–61
REINFORCE *KEY IDEA*: INJUSTICE
Discuss Is loving the perpetrators of an unjust system a necessary component of ending **injustice?** Explain. *Possible answers: Some students may agree that love or forgiveness is an essential element in healing the wounds of injustice. Others may say that love is a reciprocal emotion and cannot be present where injustice reigns.*

LITERARY ANALYSIS

D HISTORICAL CONTEXT
Possible answer: The great opportunity is the chance to help desegregate the South.

READING SKILL

E AUTHOR'S BELIEFS
Possible answer: King assumes that not all whites are racist and that whites of good conscience will support his cause. This white support works toward King's ultimate goal of ending oppression.

FOR STRATEGIC READERS

② **Targeted Passage [Lines 58–75]**

This passage explains King's philosophy of nonviolent resistance as a means for social change.

- What does King view as the best method to resolve the crisis in race relations?

- What advantages does nonviolent resistance offer?

- In what ways can nonviolent resistance involve people of all races?

FOR ADVANCED LEARNERS/AP

Cause and Effect [paired option] Ask partners to use King's explanation of militant, nonviolent, mass protest (lines 81–90) to develop a Cause-and-Effect Chain that explains his theory. Then invite student pairs to discuss whether they find King's argument persuasive and why. Ask students to consider whether history supports King's theory. Invite partners to share their ideas with the class.

💼 **BEST PRACTICES TOOLKIT**—Transparency
Cause-and-Effect Chain pp. B16, B39

SUMMARY

In this interview, Malcolm X argues that despite his belief in law and order, African Americans are entitled to protect their lives and property when the government does not. He recalls that the U.S. founders were oppressed people who revolted, arguing that African Americans are entitled to claim their heritage in the same way.

LITERARY ANALYSIS

ⓕ HISTORICAL CONTEXT

Possible answer: *Readers can identify the interview's moment in history because the interviewer cites civil rights leaders who were prominent during the 1950s and 1960s.*

If students need help . . . Direct them to footnote 1 for information on "Roy Wilkins" and "Abernathy."

NECESSARY *to* PROTECT OURSELVES

Interview with Malcolm X by Les Crane

ANALYZE VISUALS
Based on this photo, what impressions do you have of Malcom X as a leader?

BACKGROUND Malcolm X gave the following TV interview in 1964, at a time when violence against civil rights workers had escalated. Shocking images of protestors being beaten, clubbed, and tear-gassed had become staples of daily news coverage. Across the South, white supremacists tried to squelch the growing movement with murder, rifle attacks, bombings, and arson, crimes that frequently went unpunished. As attacks increased, many African Americans grew impatient with King's nonviolent tactics, expressing anger that chilled white listeners.

Events came to a head in 1964, with the Freedom Summer in Mississippi. Thousands of idealistic college students joined local civil rights activists in a massive voter registration drive, and violence exploded. Three young civil rights workers were murdered by local Klansmen with the help of the police. Despite increased FBI presence in the state, by summer's end 4 workers were dead, 80 had been beaten, and scores of black churches and businesses had been torched or bombed.

Crane: You've been a critic of some of the Negro leadership in this country—Martin Luther King, Roy Wilkins, Abernathy,[1] and others—have you changed in your feelings toward them of late? ⓕ

Malcolm X: I think all of us should be critics of each other. Whenever you can't stand criticism you can never grow. I don't think that it serves any purpose for the leaders of our people to waste their time fighting each other needlessly. I think that we accomplish more when we sit down in private and iron out

❶ Targeted Passage

ⓕ HISTORICAL CONTEXT
What details in the interviewer's question help you identify the point in history when this interview occurred?

Malcolm X at a Black Muslim rally

1. **Roy Wilkins, Abernathy:** Roy Wilkins (1901–1981) was executive secretary of the National Association for the Advancement of Colored People (NAACP) from 1955 to 1977. Ralph Abernathy (1926–1990) helped Martin Luther King Jr. found the Southern Christian Leadership Conference to combat racism.

DIFFERENTIATED INSTRUCTION

FOR STRATEGIC READERS

❶ **Targeted Passage [Lines 1–5]**

This passage creates the interview's context that Malcolm X has criticized his fellow African-American leaders and has emphasized his belief that such criticism is necessary.

• Who are Martin Luther King, Roy Wilkins, and Abernathy?

• What are Malcolm X's feelings toward the African-American leaders?

• What does Malcolm X believe about the role of criticism?

FOR ENGLISH LEARNERS

Vocabulary: Idioms and Phrasal Verbs Note that oral speech often includes idioms and phrasal verbs. Clarify these expressions:

• *of late* (line 3), "recently"

• *can't stand* (lines 4–5), "can't tolerate"

• *serves any purpose* (line 5), "achieves anything"

• *waste their time* (line 6), "don't achieve enough in"

• *iron out* (line 7), "resolve"

• *on the other hand* (line 9), "another view is that"

• *brotherhood* (line 29), "the bond between all African Americans"

• *at stake* (line 42), "threatened"

BACKGROUND

Black Muslims The photo on page 1167 shows Malcolm X at a Black Muslim rally. *Black Muslim* is a term used to describe—but is not exclusively limited to—members of the Nation of Islam. This group began in 1930 when leader Wallace D. Fard established a Detroit mosque. After Fard's disappearance in 1934, Elijah Muhammad, Fard's disciple, took over the Nation of Islam's leadership. Although the group numbered only about 8,000 when Muhammed assumed its leadership, it grew significantly during the 1950s and 60s, due to the preaching of one of its most famous converts, Malcolm X. Elijah Muhammad and Malcolm X disagreed over Muhammad's leadership. Black Muslims were blamed for the 1965 assassination of Malcolm X.

FOR STRATEGIC READERS

Concept Support: Authors' Beliefs Clarify that this text is a transcript of an interview. Discuss ways that the oral nature of the text might affect Malcolm X's message. Point out, for example, that Malcolm X must respond to the interviewer's questions without preparation, so his arguments may not appear as logical or well organized as King's. Students must make inferences to determine Malcolm X's main points.

FOR ADVANCED LEARNERS/AP

Analyze Media Impact Challenge students to locate other photos of Malcolm X that show him in various settings. Ask students to compare and contrast these images to analyze the ways that media images shape public perceptions of political leaders. Encourage students to use questions such as these to guide their analyses:

- What do objects or possessions in the image reveal or emphasize about Malcolm X?

- In what way does the image's setting suggest a context for Malcolm X's life?

- Why might the setting be obscured in the photo on page 1167? In what way does this emphasis shape viewers' perceptions of Malcolm X?

Ⓖ AUTHOR'S BELIEFS

Possible answer: Malcolm X invokes the principles of fairness, common sense, and the right to self-protection. Unlike King, Malcolm X cites largely practical rather than moral principles.

Lines 16–23
TIERED DISCUSSION PROMPTS

Use these prompts to help students understand Malcolm X's views about violence:

Connect What do you know about the situation in Mississippi that helps you understand Malcolm X's description of it? *Possible answer: Racial tension in Mississippi had left four civil rights workers dead and another 80 beaten, and yielded destruction of black churches and businesses.*

Interpret What does Malcolm X mean when he says the government has "proven its inability to protect us"? *Possible answer: Malcolm X means that the police and other government officials have not restrained or limited the violence against African Americans.*

Evaluate Malcolm X suggests that people may sometimes need to resort to aggressive measures to protect themselves from attack. Do you agree or disagree? Explain. *Students may agree with Malcolm X that violence is sometimes justified. Others may cite King in disagreeing and in insisting that violence is always immoral.*

Nation of Islam members at a community event in Harlem

whatever differences that may exist and try and then do something constructive for the benefit of our people. But on the other hand, I don't think that we should
10 be above criticism. I don't think that anyone should be above criticism.

Crane: Violence or the threat of violence has always surrounded you. Speeches that you've made have been interpreted as being threats. You have made statements reported in the press about how the Negroes should go out and arm themselves, form militias of their own. I read a thing once, a statement I believe you made that every Negro should belong to the National Rifle Association—

Malcolm X: No, I said this: That in areas of this country where the government has proven its—either its inability or its unwillingness to protect the lives and property of our people, then it's only fair to expect us to do whatever is necessary to protect ourselves. And in situations like Mississippi, places like Mississippi where the Ⓖ
20 government actually has proven its inability to protect us—and it has been proven that ofttimes the police officers and sheriffs themselves are involved in the murder that takes place against our people—then I feel, and I say that anywhere, that our people should start doing what is necessary to protect ourselves. This doesn't mean

Ⓖ AUTHOR'S BELIEFS
Reread lines 16–19. What principles does Malcolm X invoke to justify his position? How do his justifications differ from King's?

DIFFERENTIATED INSTRUCTION

FOR STRATEGIC READERS

Comprehension Support Model ways to break down Malcolm X's long, rambling sentences into shorter ones. For example, students can take sections separated by dashes or commas and restate them individually before rejoining them into one sentence. Point out that the sentence in lines 16–19 can be simplified like this: "Some areas of this country prove something about the government. The government is sometimes unable or unwilling to protect

the lives and property of African Americans. In these places, it is fair for African Americans to protect themselves any way they can." Have students work in small groups to apply this strategy to the long sentence in lines 19–23.

FOR ENGLISH LEARNERS

Related Vocabulary The concept of oppression and its damaging effects is central to Malcolm X's views. Clarify that oppression limits people's access to equal opportunity. Then teach these related words:

- *tyranny* (line 48), "cruel and unjust power over others"
- *exploitation* (line 48), "unfair treatment"
- *brutality* (line 48), "cruel treatment"
- *inflicted* (line 49), "imposed on"

that we should buy rifles and go out and initiate attacks **indiscriminately** against whites. But it does mean that we should get whatever is necessary to protect ourselves in a country or in an area where the governmental ability to protect us has broken down—

Crane: Therefore you do not agree with Dr. King's Gandhian philosophy[2]—

Malcolm X: My belief in brotherhood would never restrain me in any way from
30 protecting myself in a society from a people whose disrespect for brotherhood makes them feel inclined to put my neck on a tree at the end of a rope.[3] [*Applause*] **H**

Crane: Well, it sounds as though you could be preaching a sort of an **anarchy**—

Malcolm X: No, no. I respect government and respect law. But does the government and the law respect us? If the FBI, which is what people depend upon on a national scale to protect the morale and the property and the lives of the people, can't do so when the property and lives of Negroes and whites who try and help Negroes are concerned, then I think that it's only fair to expect elements to do whatever is necessary to protect themselves. **I**

And this is no departure from normal procedure. Because right here in New
40 York City you have vigilante committees[4] that have been set up by groups who see where their neighborhood community is endangered and the law can't do anything about it. So—and even their lives aren't at stake. So—but the fear, Les, seems to come into existence only when someone says Negroes should form vigilante committees to protect their lives and their property.

I'm not advocating the breaking of any laws. But I say that our people will never be respected as human beings until we react as other normal, intelligent human beings do. And this country came into existence by people who were tired of tyranny and oppression and exploitation and the brutality that was being inflicted upon them by powers higher than they, and I think that it is only fair
50 to expect us, sooner or later, to do likewise. ❧

---

indiscriminately
(ĭn´dĭ-skrĭm´ə-nĭt-lē) *adv.*
randomly

H AUTHOR'S BELIEFS
Reread lines 29–31. On the basis of this comment, how important is winning white support to Malcolm X? Explain.

anarchy (ăn´ər-kē) *n.*
an absence of political authority

I HISTORICAL CONTEXT
Reread lines 34–38. To what events is Malcolm X alluding? Review the background information and the footnotes for details.

② **Targeted Passage**

---

2. **Gandhian** (gän´dē-ən) **philosophy:** Mohandas Gandhi (1869–1948) was an Indian nationalist and spiritual leader. His use of nonviolent civil disobedience forced the British to grant India its independence in 1947.

3. **put my neck . . . rope:** an allusion to lynching, the practice of putting someone to death without due process of law. Many African Americans were lynched, usually by hanging.

4. **vigilante** (vĭj´ə-lăn´tē) **committees:** volunteer citizen groups that unlawfully assume powers such as pursuing and punishing suspected criminals or offenders.

READING SKILL

H AUTHOR'S BELIEFS

Possible answer: White support is not important to Malcolm X, because he views oppression as a conflict between the races and thus views whites as a threat.

If students need help . . . Refer them to the footnote that explains the practice of lynching, and clarify that the "people" Malcolm X holds responsible for lynching are whites.

LITERARY ANALYSIS

I HISTORICAL CONTEXT

Possible answer: Malcolm X is referring to the murders of black and white civil rights workers in Mississippi and the FBI's failure to provide protection for those workers.

SELECTION WRAP-UP

SYNTHESIZE Ask students to describe ways that reading King's description of violent response to oppression helped them understand Malcolm X's views.

⭐ CRITIQUE

- Have students choose the passages in King's letter and Malcolm X's interview that they find most compelling, and then analyze the passages' effects on readers.

- After completing the After Reading questions on page 1170, have students revisit their responses and tell whether they have changed their opinions.

FOR STRATEGIC READERS

② Targeted Passage [Lines 33–50]

In this passage, Malcolm X explains his position on anarchy and revolution.

- What does Malcolm X feel toward government and the law?

- In what ways does Malcolm X think that government and the law have failed African Americans?

- What is Malcolm X's historical justification for violent revolution?

FOR ENGLISH LEARNERS

Key Academic Vocabulary Use New Word Analysis to teach this word from "Necessary to Protect Ourselves": *react* (line 46).

📦 BEST PRACTICES TOOLKIT—Transparency
New Word Analysis p. E8

FOR ADVANCED LEARNERS/AP

Synthesize [small-group option] Recall that Patrick Henry, Thomas Jefferson, Abigail Adams, and others passionately voiced ideas regarding equality and natural rights at the country's inception. Have students review the work of these writers in Unit 1. Then have groups discuss ways that these early revolutionary writers might have responded to the views of King and Malcolm X, and why. Ask groups to share their thoughts with the class.

Practice and Apply

After Reading

Use these copy masters to check understanding and provide extra support:

R RESOURCE MANAGER—Copy Masters
Reading Check p. 120
Historical Context p. 113
Question Support p. 121

Additional selection questions are provided for teachers on page 107.

ANSWERS

1. *King identifies acquiescence, violence, and nonviolent resistance.*

2. *A movement must be militant, nonviolent, and massive to achieve integration.*

3. *Malcolm X says that criticism is a necessary element of growth.*

Possible answers:

4. *Malcolm X refers to the American Revolution to make the point that revolution against tyranny is an American value.*

5. ■ **SKILLS FOCUS Compare and Contrast Authors' Beliefs** *The main differences between the two leaders are views on violence as a means for achieving racial equality, a value for morality above practical logic, and the desirability of white support. Both leaders believe that racism is unjust and reflects a serious flaw in American society.*

6. ● **SKILLS FOCUS Historical Context** *King responds to "the present crisis in race relations" by saying that African Americans must work for full stature as citizens, remain in the South to struggle for their rights, and take part in this "great opportunity." Malcolm X responds to "situations like Mississippi" by referring to corrupt police officers, lynchings, and vigilante committees in New York, as well as by criticizing the FBI.*

7. *Response 1: Acquiescence. Problems: makes the oppressed as evil as the oppressor, is cowardly. Response 2: Violence. Problems: is immoral, defeats itself by creating bitterness. Response 3: Nonviolent resistance. Advantages: allows the oppressed to oppose injustice without creating bitterness and hatred.*

After Reading

Comprehension

R2.5, R3.8

1. **Recall** What three ways of dealing with oppression does Martin Luther King identify?

2. **Clarify** In King's view, what three qualities must a movement have in order to achieve the goal of integration?

3. **Summarize** How does Malcolm X justify his criticisms of other civil rights leaders?

Literary Analysis

4. **Identify Allusion** Reread lines 47–50 of "Necessary to Protect Ourselves." Identify the historical event that Malcolm X is alluding to. What point does he make by invoking this event?

5. **Compare and Contrast Authors' Beliefs** Review the chart you created as you read both texts. Based on your reading, what are the main differences between the two leaders? What beliefs, if any, do they have in common? Be specific in your answers.

6. **Examine Historical Context** Reread the background information on pages 1162 and 1166. In what ways does each author respond directly to the events of his time? Identify at least two examples for each work.

7. **Analyze Structure** The structure of King's argument follows the formal logic of Hegelian philosophy, in which two opposing ideas are merged into a unified concept, or synthesis. To analyze this structure, complete a diagram like the one shown. In what way does the third response resolve the problems of the first two?

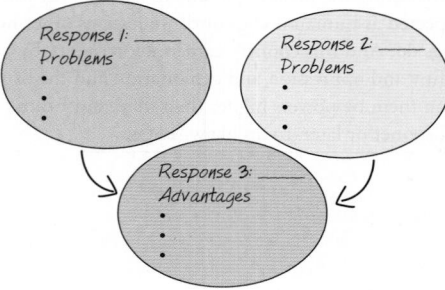

Response 1: _____ Problems
•
•
•

Response 2: _____ Problems
•
•
•

Response 3: _____ Advantages
•
•
•

8. **Make Judgments** Many commentators criticized Martin Luther King Jr. for using radical and provocative tactics. In what ways might perceptions of King's philosophy have changed after Malcolm X gained public prominence?

Literary Criticism

9. **Biographical Context** Reread the author biographies of King (page 1144) and Malcolm X (page 1160). What aspects of their personal histories may have influenced their different approaches to fighting racial **injustice**? Cite details in your answer.

1170 UNIT 6: CONTEMPORARY LITERATURE

8. *In comparison to Malcolm X, King probably began to seem less threatening to the status quo of American society.*

9. *King was well educated and an ordained minister. He achieved early success fighting segregation through nonviolent means. Malcolm X had a difficult childhood, and his family life was destroyed by racial violence. He educated himself in prison. Malcolm X's experiences may have caused him to view nonviolence as unrealistic or naive.*

1170 UNIT 6: CONTEMPORARY LITERATURE

Vocabulary in Context

VOCABULARY PRACTICE

Choose the letter of the phrase that defines or is related to the boldfaced word.

1. **succumb:** (a) a golfer practicing, (b) an army surrendering, (c) a teenager voting
2. **synthesis:** (a) a proposal combining several views, (b) a detailed analysis of a plan, (c) a group of protestors
3. **anarchy:** (a) an art auction, (b) an angry mob, (c) hereditary rule
4. **glib:** (a) a changing weather pattern, (b) a surprising viewpoint, (c) an insincere speaker
5. **indiscriminately:** (a) a decision based on evidence, (b) a choice made without thought, (c) unfair hiring practices
6. **militant:** (a) a pilot flying low, (b) a soldier asleep in the barracks, (c) a forceful march
7. **repudiate:** (a) retype a report, (b) vote someone out of office, (c) renew a promise
8. **tacitly:** (a) agree by nodding, (b) disagree by shouting, (c) celebrate by singing

> **WORD LIST**
> anarchy
> glib
> indiscriminately
> militant
> repudiate
> succumb
> synthesis
> tacitly

VOCABULARY IN WRITING

Choose King or Malcolm X, and write a paragraph explaining that leader's philosophy. Use at least three vocabulary words. You could start this way.

> **EXAMPLE SENTENCE**
> Malcolm X was known for his **militant** stance on the right to use violence.

CALIFORNIA R1.2

VOCABULARY STRATEGY: THE GREEK PREFIX *syn-*

The vocabulary word *synthesis* contains the Greek prefix *syn-*, which means "together" or "at the same time." This prefix, which may also be spelled *sym-* or in some cases *syl-*, is found in a number of English words, both scientific and nonscientific. To understand words with *syn-*, look for context clues and also use your knowledge of the meaning of the prefix. If these strategies do not work, consult a dictionary.

synthesis · synchronize · synopsis · symbiotic · syndicate · symmetrical · **syn-, sym-**

PRACTICE Choose the word from the word web that best completes each sentence. Use context clues to help you or, if necessary, check a dictionary.

1. They were able to _____ their watches and meet promptly at noon.
2. Though the halves of people's faces aren't exactly _____, they are fairly close.
3. Some animals have a _____ relationship and depend on each other for survival.
4. Groups or individuals in a _____ work together for some common interest.
5. A _____ can provide a quick overview of a story, play, or report.

> **VOCABULARY PRACTICE**
> For more practice, go to the **Vocabulary Center** at ClassZone.com.

DIFFERENTIATED INSTRUCTION

FOR ENGLISH LEARNERS

Task Support: Vocabulary in Writing Provide these possible sentence starters:

- King has no tolerance for *glib* _____.
- King advocates a *militant* approach to _____.
- King does not want African Americans to *succumb* to _____.
- Malcolm X *repudiates* _____.
- Malcolm X does not advocate *anarchy*; rather, he _____.

FOR ADVANCED LEARNERS/AP

Greek Prefixes Suggest that students choose another Greek prefix such as *amphi-, peri-,* or *tele-* to study. Have students create word webs listing examples of words containing the chosen prefix. Then have students write cloze sentences for each listed word, making sure to include context clues. Invite partners to trade word webs and sentences, then to complete each other's sentences.

ANSWERS

Vocabulary in Context

VOCABULARY PRACTICE

1. *(b) an army surrendering*
2. *(a) a proposal combining several views*
3. *(b) an angry mob*
4. *(c) an insincere speaker*
5. *(b) a choice made without thought*
6. *(c) a forceful march*
7. *(b) vote someone out of office*
8. *(a) agree by nodding*

R RESOURCE MANAGER—Copy Master
Vocabulary Practice p. 118

VOCABULARY IN WRITING

Urge students to write summaries in their own words, then add vocabulary words when revising. Suggest that students review the word definitions that appear in the text margins as well as the way each writer uses the words in sentences.

VOCABULARY STRATEGY: THE GREEK PREFIX *syn-* (also an EL language objective)

Review with students ways to use context clues and prefixes to determine the meanings of unfamiliar words.

1. *synchronize*
2. *symmetrical*
3. *symbiotic*
4. *syndicate*
5. *synopsis*

R RESOURCE MANAGER—Copy Master
Vocabulary Strategy p. 119

ℹ Vocabulary Center at **ClassZone.com**
Additional Vocabulary Activities

Assess and Reteach

Assess

R RESOURCE MANAGER—Copy Masters
Selection Test A pp. 123–124
Selection Test B pp. 125–126

⊘ Test Generator CD

Reteach

S STANDARDS LESSON FILE
Literature Lesson 34
Reading Lessons 8, 12, 14
Vocabulary Lessons 2, 6

Focus and Motivate

OBJECTIVES

Reading for Information

- analyze an argument
- support an opinion
- read an essay

 CALIFORNIA R2.4, R3.8, W1.3

SUMMARY

In memory of Dr. Martin Luther King Jr., César Chávez argues in support of nonviolent, militant protest as the only means for achieving fair treatment for migrant farm workers. Chávez reiterates King's points that violence undermines the protesters and their cause by destroying a regard for humanity.

Use a Y Chart to help students compare King's arguments with Chávez's arguments. Have students list Chávez's reasons for supporting nonviolent protest on the left and King's reasons on the right. Then have students identify similarities and differences between the two men's philosophies.

 BEST PRACTICES TOOLKIT—Transparency
Y Chart p. A27

Teach

Skill Focus: Analyze an Argument

- Explain that analyzing an argument means breaking the entire argument down into its smallest parts in order to understand its elements and evaluate the writer's logic.

- Point out that writers sometimes make generalizations based on too few examples. At other times, writers draw false comparisons or make inaccurate assumptions. Such errors in argumentation undermine a writer's position.

- Encourage students to assess the logic of Chávez's argument as they analyze its elements.

R RESOURCE MANAGER—Copy Master
Analyze an Argument p. 135

Martin Luther King Jr.: He Showed Us the Way
Essay

Use with "Stride Toward Freedom" and "Necessary to Protect Ourselves," beginning on pages 1162 and 1166.

 CALIFORNIA R2.4, R3.8 (p. 1175), W1.3 (p. 1175)

You have just read two civil rights leaders' positions on the use of force in political resistance. Now you will learn why César Chávez, a leader in the crusade for the fair treatment of migrant farm workers, advocated nonviolence to achieve his goals. As you read his argument, bear in mind that later you will be asked to support your own opinion on this weapon for social change.

Skill Focus: Analyze an Argument

Every day, political and social leaders, manufacturers and retailers, and even family and friends try to influence your beliefs and actions. You can begin to evaluate any argument by analyzing it, or breaking it down into its parts.

A well-formed argument typically contains

- a **claim**, or the writer or speaker's position on a problem or issue
- **support**, which consists of reasons and evidence that help to justify the claim
- **counterarguments**, or brief arguments that refute or answer objections to any claim that the opposition is likely to raise

A strong argument is usually based on a **general principle** or assumption that links the support to the claim. For example, someone arguing that a particular act is in violation of free speech is resting on the principle that free speech is a thing worth protecting. If you can't accept the general principle as a truth, then the entire argument falls apart.

To analyze the argument made by Chávez, as you read his speech complete a chart such as the one started here.

	Notes
Claim	Nonviolence is the "only weapon that Christians who struggle for social change can claim as their own."
General Principle	
Support	
Counterargument(s)	

Selection Resources

 RESOURCE MANAGER UNIT 6

Plan and Teach pp. 127–131

Reading
Summary pp. 133†*, 134‡*
Analyze an Argument pp. 135, 136†*
Support an Opinion pp. 137, 138†*
Reading Check p. 139
Question Support p. 140*

Assessment
Selection Tests A, B/C pp. 141*, 143*

⊘ Test Generator CD

Reading Support
⊘ Audio Anthology CD*

 BEST PRACTICES TOOLKIT
Y Chart • Jigsaw Reading • Cluster Diagram

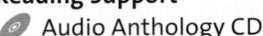

* Resources for Differentiation   † Also in Spanish   ‡ In Haitian Creole and Vietnamese

MARTIN LUTHER KING JR.:

He Showed Us the Way

César Chávez

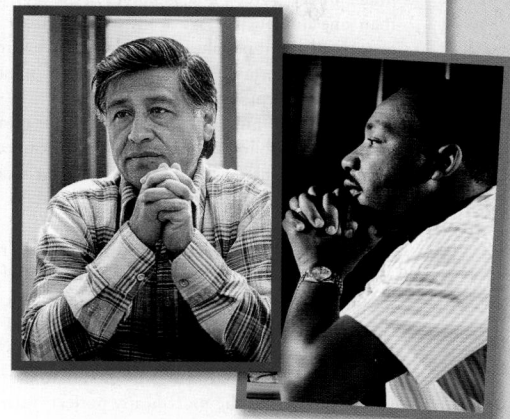

In honoring Martin Luther King Jr.'s memory we also acknowledge nonviolence as a truly powerful weapon to achieve equality and liberation—in fact, the only weapon that Christians who struggle for social change can claim as their own.

Dr. King's entire life was an example of power that nonviolence brings to bear in the real world. It is an example that inspired much of the philosophy and strategy of the farm workers' movement. This observance of Dr. King's death gives us the best possible opportunity to recall the principles with which our struggle has grown and matured. **A**

Our conviction is that human life is a very special possession given by God to man and that no one has the right to take it for any reason or for any cause, however just it may be.

We are also convinced that nonviolence is more powerful than violence. Nonviolence supports you if you have a just and moral cause. Nonviolence provides the opportunity to stay on the offensive, and that is of crucial importance to win any contest.

If we resort to violence then one of two things will happen: either the violence will be escalated and there will be many injuries and perhaps deaths on both sides, or there will be total demoralization of the workers. **B**

Nonviolence has exactly the opposite effect. If, for every violent act committed against us, we respond with nonviolence, we attract people's support. We can gather the support of millions who have a conscience and would rather see a nonviolent resolution to problems. We are convinced that when people are faced with a direct appeal from the poor struggling nonviolently against great odds, they will react positively. The American people and people everywhere still yearn for justice. It is to that yearning that we appeal.

A ANALYZE AN ARGUMENT
Notice that Chávez states his **claim** in his opening sentence. Now reread lines 4–7 to identify his first piece of **support** for this claim. Note this on your chart.

B ANALYZE AN ARGUMENT
Reread lines 11–16. What reasons does Chávez give to support his conviction that "nonviolence is more powerful than violence"? Note these reasons as "support" in your chart.

READING FOR INFORMATION **1173**

Practice and Apply CALIFORNIA

INFORMATIONAL ANALYSIS

A ANALYZE AN ARGUMENT

Possible answer: Chávez's first piece of support for his claim is King's entire life.

If students need help . . . Work with them to restate the claim Chávez makes in lines 1–3, then direct students to line 4 as the clearest statement of support for Chávez's claim. Help students list their notes in the chart begun on page 1172.

	Notes
Claim	Nonviolence is the only acceptable strategy for Christians who work for social change.
Support	King's life

INFORMATIONAL ANALYSIS

B ANALYZE AN ARGUMENT

Possible answer: Support for the power of nonviolence over violence includes that nonviolence supports just and moral causes and provides protesters with the opportunity to stay on the offensive.

DIFFERENTIATED INSTRUCTION

FOR STRATEGIC READERS
Vocabulary Support Have students work in small groups to define difficult words in the argument, such as *liberation* (line 2), *demoralization* (line 16), *insurmountable* (line 31), *seethe* (line 33), *self-determination* (line 39), *leverage* (line 50), and *espouse* (line 55). Help students paraphrase difficult sentences.

FOR ENGLISH LEARNERS
Vocabulary: Cognates Help students recognize and define these cognates: *honoring/honrado, memory/memoria* (line 1); *powerful/poderoso, equality/igualdad, liberation/liberación* (line 2); *possible/posible* (line 6); *possession/posesión* (line 8); *violence/violencia* (line 11); *cause/causa,* (line 12); *offensive/ofensiva* (line 13); *respond/responder* (line 18); *conscience/conciencia* (line 19); *problems/problemas,* (line 20); *justice/justicia* (line 22).

Options for Reading Have students use Jigsaw Reading with Chávez's argument. Form "home" groups, giving each student a number that corresponds to a portion of the text. Then have students move into their numbered groups to read and discuss the assigned text. Have students return to their home groups to share summaries of their assigned passages.

 BEST PRACTICES TOOLKIT
Jigsaw Reading p. A1

C ANALYZE AN ARGUMENT
In this paragraph, Chávez anticipates objection to his claim about the advantages of nonviolence. Identify these objections.

D ANALYZE AN ARGUMENT
What counterarguments does Chávez provide to refute the objections he just anticipated? Note these in your chart.

E ANALYZE AN ARGUMENT
What does Chávez say about those who espouse violence?

But if we are committed to nonviolence only as a strategy or tactic, then if it fails our only alternative is to turn to violence. So we must balance the strategy with a clear understanding of what we are doing. However important the struggle is and however much misery, poverty and exploitation exist, we know that it cannot be more important than one human life. We work on the theory that men and women who are truly concerned about people are nonviolent by nature. These people become violent when
30 the deep concern they have for people is frustrated and when they are faced with seemingly insurmountable odds.

We advocate militant nonviolence as our means of achieving justice for our people, but we are not blind to the feelings of frustration, impatience and anger which seethe inside every farm worker. The burdens of generations of poverty and powerlessness lie heavy in the fields of America. If we fail, there are those who will see violence as the shortcut to change. **C**

It is precisely to overcome these frustrations that we have involved masses of people in their own struggle throughout the movement. Freedom is best experienced through participation and self-determination, and free men and women instinctively prefer
40 democratic change to any other means. Thus, demonstrations and marches, strikes and boycotts are not only weapons against the growers, but our way of avoiding the senseless violence that brings no honor to any class or community. The boycott, as Gandhi taught, is the most nearly perfect instrument of nonviolent change, allowing masses of people to participate actively in a cause.

When victory comes through violence, it is a victory with strings attached. If we beat the growers at the expense of violence, victory would come at the expense of injury and perhaps death. Such a thing would have a tremendous impact on us. We would lose regard for human beings. Then the struggle would become a mechanical thing. When you lose your sense of life and justice, you lose your strength. **D**
50 The greater the oppression, the more leverage nonviolence holds. Violence does not work in the long run and if it is temporarily successful, it replaces one violent form of power with another just as violent. People suffer from violence. Examine history. Who gets killed in the case of violent revolution? The poor, the workers. The people of the land are the ones who give their bodies and don't really gain that much for it. We believe it is too big a price to pay for not getting anything. Those who espouse violence exploit people. To call men to arms with many promises, to ask them to give up their lives for a cause and then not produce for them afterwards, is the most vicious type of oppression. **E**

We know that most likely we are not going to do anything else the rest of our lives
60 except build our union. For us there is nowhere else to go. Although we would like to see victory come soon, we are willing to wait. In this sense time is our ally. We learned many years ago that the rich may have money, but the poor have time.

It has been our experience that few men or women ever have the opportunity to know the true satisfaction that comes with giving one's life totally in the nonviolent struggle for justice. Martin Luther King Jr., was one of these unique servants and from him we learned many of the lessons that have guided us. For these lessons and for his sacrifice for the poor and oppressed, Dr. King's memory will be cherished in the hearts of the farm workers forever.

DIFFERENTIATED INSTRUCTION

FOR ENGLISH LEARNERS

Language: Pronoun Referents Help students use paraphrasing to clarify these confusing pronoun referents:

- *there are <u>those</u> who* (line 35), "people who will see violence as a shortcut"
- *<u>such</u> a thing* (line 47), "violent victory"
- *it* (line 55), "violence"
- *Those who* (line 55), "people who espouse violence"
- *It* (line 63), "our experience"

FOR ADVANCED LEARNERS/AP

Research Migrant Farm Workers [small-group option] Challenge small groups to research the plight of migrant farm workers in California. Have groups create Cluster Diagrams to organize their information by main idea and details. Invite students to share their findings and diagrams with the class.

BEST PRACTICES TOOLKIT—Transparency
Cluster Diagram p. B18

Comprehension

1. **Clarify** In addition to serving as weapons against growers, how do boycotts benefit the masses of people who participate in them?

Critical Analysis

2. **Examine General Principle** What is Chávez's basic assumption about social change and just people? Might someone disagree with him? Explain.

3. **Analyze Argument** Chávez acknowledges that nonviolent resistance has certain limitations. How does he answer each of the following objections?

   • People who have been oppressed may feel legitimately frustrated or impatient and turn to violence as a shortcut to change.

   • Violence does sometimes bring about victory.

Read for Information: Support an Opinion

 R2.4, R3.8, W1.3 CALIFORNIA

WRITING PROMPT

What is your opinion of nonviolent resistance as a weapon of social change? State your position and support it with reasons and evidence from the three selections you have just read and, if you wish, with examples from history or your own experience.

The following steps will help you answer the prompt:

1. Carefully read the pieces by Chávez, King, and Malcolm X and determine your own opinion of nonviolent resistance. Write this opinion as a claim.

2. Gather support for your claim from the three selections, as well as from history or your own life experience.

3. Consider how an opponent might object to your claim. Insert one or more objections at the points in your essay where they would most naturally be raised. After anticipating each objection, write a counterargument to it.

4. Write a conclusion in which you restate your claim and summarize the most important elements of support.

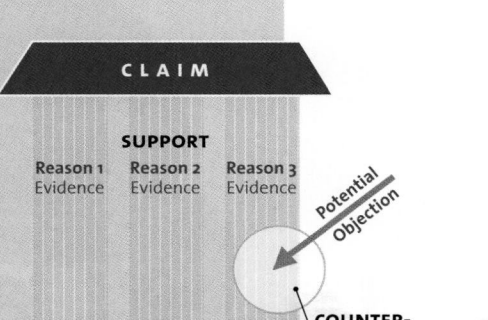

CLAIM

SUPPORT

Reason 1 — Evidence
Reason 2 — Evidence
Reason 3 — Evidence

Potential Objection

COUNTER-ARGUMENT

Practice and Apply

After Reading

Use these copy masters to check understanding and provide extra support:

R RESOURCE MANAGER—Copy Masters
Reading Check p. 139
Support an Opinion p. 137
Question Support p. 140

Additional selection questions are provided for teachers on page 130.

ANSWERS

1. *Boycotts help participants vent their frustrations in a positive and honorable way.*

Possible answers:

2. *Chávez's basic assumption is that social change is a moral pursuit that all just people will support. People who support the status quo and are suspicious of change might disagree with Chávez's assumption.*

3. ■ **SKILLS FOCUS** Analyze an Argument *Violence fails as a shortcut to change in that it squanders lives in the short term and causes people to devalue human life and justice, which undermines strength and victory. A victory reached by violence has strings attached, namely the loss of life and moral strength.*

Read for Information: Support an Opinion

Writing Prompt *Answers will vary, but should include a clearly stated opinion on the topic, adequate supporting reasons and evidence, response to potential criticisms, counterarguments for each criticism, logical organization, and a valid general principle.*

Assess and Reteach

Assess

R RESOURCE MANAGER—Copy Masters
Selection Test A pp.141–142
Selection Test B pp. 143–144

Test Generator CD

Reteach

S STANDARDS LESSON FILE
Reading Lesson 14: Synthesizing Information
Writing Lesson 29: Persuasive Writing
Writing Lesson 34: Elaborate with Facts and Statistics

FOR DEVELOPING WRITERS
Read for Information

• Provide students with this sentence to help them develop thesis statements: Nonviolent resistance is an effective (ineffective) weapon for social change. Tell students that they may revise this sentence as necessary to better suit their writing styles.

• Provide photocopies of the articles by King, Malcolm X, and Chávez. Encourage students to highlight text that supports their thesis statements.

FOR ADVANCED LEARNERS/AP

Tone Challenge students to convey their personal attitudes toward violence and nonviolence through careful word choice and allusion. Encourage students to analyze ways that King, Malcolm X, and Chávez use word choice and allusion to convey tone. Urge students to use these writers' works as models for their essays.

Focus and Motivate

OBJECTIVES

Media Literacy

- explore the key idea of **impressions**
- view a media clip and read a magazine article to analyze the impact of news on people's perceptions of political and social leaders
- compare and contrast perspectives in news reports
- create a news feature to celebrate the life of an important person

LS1.1, LS1.2, LS1.3, W1.6, LS1.10, LS2.4

SUMMARIES

TV News Report In this newscast clip, the death of César Chávez at age 66 serves as the basis for a retrospective look at his work for social justice.

"¡Sí se Puede!" In this magazine article, the life and work of César Chávez are remembered as his family opens the National Chávez Center at Nuestra Señora Reina de la Paz in California.

Does the news SHAPE history?

To help students explore the **KEY IDEA,** have them view a current news report on a public figure such as a political leader. Ask students to describe the report's contents and identify ways in which it impacts viewers' **impressions** of the person. Discuss the impact of news coverage on a person's legacy; for example, students might consider whether this figure will likely become part of history or gain only momentary attention.

BACKGROUND

The news report appeared on April 23, 1993. Its lead reporter, John Blackstone, is a veteran correspondent with CBS. Blackstone has often reported on events in the West and in California, where he lives. The magazine article was published to mark the 2004 opening of the National Chávez Center.

Media Study

Perspectives in the News

TV Newscast Clip / Magazine Article on ⊙ **MediaSmart** DVD

CALIFORNIA

LS1.1, LS1.2, LS1.3, W1.6 (p. 1179),
LS1.10 (p. 1179), LS2.4 (p. 1179)

Does the news SHAPE history?

KEY IDEA Recall the last time the news reported the death of someone who had played a pivotal role in history. Did the report provide new insights or change your opinion of the individual? Or did it reinforce your prior perceptions? In this lesson, you'll examine the way two different news forms covered a national figure and analyze the ways news reports can shape your **impressions** of that figure.

Background

Cultivating Activism As a teenager, César Chávez worked the fields of California with his family. After serving in the U.S. Navy in World War II, he returned to the fields but grew more politically active.

Inspired by the life and nonviolent teachings of Mohandas Gandhi and the activism of Martin Luther King Jr., Chávez helped found the National Farm Workers Association (NFWA) in 1962. "Nonviolence in action is a very potent force and it can't be stopped," said Chávez of the NFWA's founding principle. By staging peaceful strikes, marches, and boycotts, as well as fasting (as Gandhi had) in protest, Chávez garnered a wide swath of support for *La Causa* (the cause). Followers rallied to the call "*¡Si Se Puede!*" which, translated to English, means "Yes, we can!"

Another force contributing to Chávez's cause, as well as to the larger American civil rights movement of the 1950s and 60s, was mass media. Print and network TV news coverage of marches, boycotts, and other acts of protest helped to fuel a spirit of activism nationwide. Millions were stirred by coverage that spotlighted both extraordinary leaders like Chávez and ordinary people.

César Chávez died in 1993. In following the peaceful legacy of Gandhi and King, Chávez created one of his own.

Media Study Resources

R RESOURCE MANAGER UNIT 6

Plan and Teach pp. 145–148

Media Analysis
Summary pp. 149†*, 150‡*
Viewing Guide p. 151
Close Viewing p. 152
Media Activity p. 153
Produce Your Own Media p. 154

S STANDARDS LESSON FILE

Reading Lessons 12, 14
Informational Text Lesson 11
Media Lessons 3, 8–12

ⓘ Media Center at **ClassZone.com**

MEDIA VIEWING
⊘ Media*Smart* DVD

* Resources for Differentiation   † Also in Spanish   ‡ In Haitian Creole and Vietnamese

Media Literacy: Historical Perspectives in the News

The news media uses images and words to depict the work of political figures who, in time, become history makers. Just as writers of literature present their perspectives through the use of tone and diction, journalists convey certain ideas, values, and beliefs through those elements and others that are unique to news reports. In addition, journalists can shape an audience's perceptions by reporting on the individual from a particular perspective.

News reports can appear in both electronic and print forms. To help you analyze the perspective of a news report, examine the images and statements to determine the overall purpose of the report. Then think about how the report affects your perceptions of the person depicted.

STRATEGIES FOR ANALYZING NEWS REPORTS

TV News Reports
A typical TV news report is quite brief. To convey a strong impression of the report's subject, journalists choose the visual and verbal elements carefully.

- Focus on the **footage**—the film, videotape, and photographs that are edited into a report. The footage compiled on a historical figure can an be edited to portray the individual in different ways.
- Notice what the **anchorperson** says in the **lead-in,** the introduction. The emphasis journalists put on certain words can suggest a figure's historical significance.
- Pay attention to descriptive words used in a reporter's **voice-over,** the narration that plays as images are shown. Also, listen for **sound bites,** statements excerpted from interviews or speeches that are edited into the report. Sound bites can be selected to create a certain impression of subject.

Magazine Article
The typical magazine feature article might cover a subject in more than one page, providing in-depth coverage.

- Consider how the **headline** and **subhead** frame the content of the article for a reader.
- Preview the **opening paragraph,** which often sets the tone for the article and is intended to draw in the reader.
- Make inferences about the **images.** Think about why certain photographs were chosen for an article.
- Scrutinize **quotes,** which might be made by the subject of the article or by others. Determine what the quotes reveal about the subject.

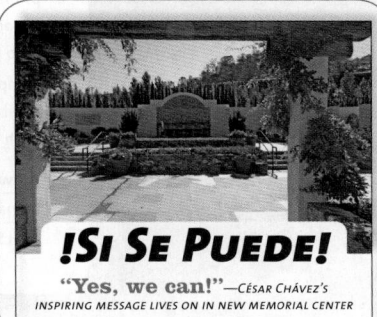

!SI SE PUEDE!
"Yes, we can!"—CÉSAR CHÁVEZ'S
INSPIRING MESSAGE LIVES ON IN NEW MEMORIAL CENTER

MEDIA STUDY 1177

MEDIA STUDY: TEACHING OPTIONS

Teaching Option 1: The Basics (1–2 days)

1. Begin the Media Study using the material provided on pages 1176–1177.
2. Show the Introduction on Media*Smart*. Then show the First Viewing. As they watch, have students use the Viewing Guide on page 1178, along with the corresponding copy master on page 151 of the Resource Manager. Discuss their responses.
3. Return to the pupil book for the extension activities on page 1179.

Teaching Option 2: In-Depth Study (2–3 days)

1. Begin the Media Study using pages 1176–1177.
2. Show the Introduction and First Viewing from Media*Smart*. Then continue on Media*Smart* with the Media Lessons, using the teacher notes available in the Resources section.
3. Show the Guided Analysis presentation. Have students record their observations on the Student Viewing Guide available in the Resources section from Media*Smart*.
4. Return to the pupil book, page 1179.

Media Literacy

Review with students the terms *tone* and *diction* and the way these elements help writers convey particular perspectives to readers. Tone is the writer's attitude toward his or her subject. Tone is revealed through word choice, or diction. Write these two lists of nouns on the board: *activist, hero, visionary; agitator, dissenter, troublemaker.* Lead students to discuss ways that each of these word lists reveals something about the writer's or speaker's attitude toward Chávez. Then discuss the chart on page 1177.

- **Footage vs. Images** Point out that like the images on page 1177, the full news report primarily features footage of people—from Chávez himself to migrant workers—while the article features images of the National Chávez Center. Ask students to suggest the impression such images likely create in each report. *Possible answer: Images of people, especially Chávez and those affected by him, create a personal impression of the man. Images of buildings create an impression of Chávez's wider impact on society.*

- **Lead-in vs. Opening Paragraph** Tell students that in the lead-in to the TV news report, the anchor calls Chávez a "fighter." In the opening paragraph of the magazine article, the writer calls Chávez a "national icon." Ask students to compare and contrast what each of these words suggests about Chávez's historical significance. *Possible answer: "Fighter" suggests that Chávez will be remembered for his tenacity and commitment. "National icon" suggests that he will be remembered for the way he inspired people.*

- **Sound Bites vs. Quotes** In the TV news report, the UFW's vice president says that Chávez's legacy is to "give one's life to help other people." In the magazine article, Chávez's granddaughter says, "People look at him like a saint or a mythical figure. . . . But I tell them he was my grandfather." Ask students to discuss what each of these quotations reveals about Chávez. *Possible answer: The quote in the news report reveals that Chávez was a great leader. The quote from the article suggests that he was a humble family man.*

Media*Smart* DVD

Practice and Apply

VIEWING GUIDE

1. As students prepare to view the clip and read the magazine article, tell them that they will be asked to describe ways that images and words contribute to their impressions of César Chávez. Encourage them to listen and watch for these elements:

   - **footage** and **images** that highlight particular aspects or qualities of Chávez
   - what the **lead-in** and **opening paragraph** suggest about Chávez's historical significance
   - ways that the **sound bites** and **quotes** create impressions of Chávez

2. Some students may have difficulty focusing simultaneously on images and words. Allow students to experience the news report once without words and once with closed eyes. Allow students to cover the images and words alternately as they review the magazine article.

RESOURCE MANAGER—Copy Masters
Viewing Guide p. 151
Close Viewing p. 152
Media Activity p. 153

Use this resource with the Viewing Guide:

MediaSmart DVD

ANSWERS

FIRST VIEWING: Comprehension

1. *Chávez says that his greatest accomplishment was to reduce workers' fears of their employers.*

2. *In addition to the National Center, César Chávez Day is an official holiday. Many public places have been named in his honor, including parks, schools, libraries, and other public facilities.*

CLOSE VIEWING: Media Literacy

Possible answers:

3. *News anchor Dan Rather describes Chávez as a "fighter." The news reporter says that Chávez was a man who fought for those no one else would fight for.*

4. *This sound bite provides an assessment of Chávez's impact on people from someone who either knew him or worked closely for his cause.*

MediaSmart DVD
- **Selection 1:** "Chávez" from the CBS Nightly News
- **Type:** Newscast clip
- **Anchor:** Dan Rather
- **Reporter:** John Blackstone
- **Running time:** 2.5 minutes
- **Selection 2:** "¡Si Se Puede!"
- **Type:** Magazine article

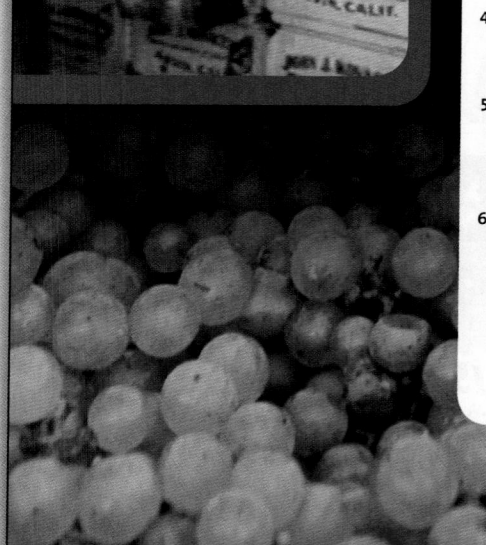

1178

Viewing Guide for
News Perspectives

View the news clip and access the full text of the magazine article on the DVD. As you watch the TV news report, focus on the images that are used to tell César Chávez's story and listen for any descriptive words about Chávez's life and work. As you read the magazine article, look for the ways in which the writer describes Chávez and his legacy. To help you analyze these pieces, refer to these questions.

NOW VIEW

FIRST VIEWING: Comprehension

1. **Recall** In the TV news report, what does Chávez say he regards as his "biggest single accomplishment"?

2. **Summarize** Based on your review of the headline, subhead, and opening paragraph of the magazine article, summarize the ways Chávez has been honored since his death.

CLOSE VIEWING: Media Literacy

3. **Analyze Statements** What **descriptions** did you notice in the news anchor's **lead-in,** or introduction to the Chávez piece, or in the reporter's **voice-over** that reveal respect for the historical figure's accomplishments?

4. **Analyze Sound Bites** The clip includes a **sound bite** in which an individual states about Chávez, "His biggest legacy was to give his life for other people." Why do you think the news report includes this sound bite?

5. **Make Judgments** Briefly review the magazine article to choose a word or phrase that you think was carefully chosen to comment on the legacy of César Chávez. Describe what meaning this choice would have for viewers who had not been old enough to be aware of the leader in his lifetime.

6. **Compare Purposes** When and why do you think the TV news report was created? When and why was the magazine article published? Examine each news format and use a comparison chart to compare the purposes.

News Report	When First Reported	Purpose for Report
"Chávez"		
"¡Si Se Puede!"		

---

5. *The phrases "national icon" and "committed person of vision" suggest that Chávez's work had as much significance in American life as the work of some of America's great military leaders.*

6. ***News Report:*** *It was delivered on the day of Chávez's death in 1993. Its purpose was to commemorate Chávez's life and work.*
Magazine Article: *It was written in 2004. Its purpose was to mark the opening of the National Chávez Center and to preserve Chávez's legacy.*

Write or Discuss

Determine Perspectives In two brief statements, describe the perspective of both the newscast clip and the magazine article. Review the reports closely, jotting down any descriptive words or phrases about César Chávez that give you a sense of him as a person and as a leader. In addition, refer to the chart you devised to compare the purposes of the news forms. Think about

 LS1.1, LS1.3

- the overall tone each news report conveys
- the details each piece presents about Chávez's life and times
- the visual elements
- the use of sources who provide sound bites and quotes

Produce Your Own Media

Create a News Feature Celebrate the life of someone who has made a positive impact on your community by creating a news feature. The subject could be a friend, a family member, or anyone else you admire. The feature can be a visual piece, in the form of video, or a written piece with photographs that illustrate it in the style of a magazine.

 W1.6, LS1.10, LS2.4

HERE'S HOW Here are some suggestions for creating your news feature:

- Decide on your perspective for the feature. The basis for your perspective might be the subject's achievements or personal qualities.
- Research your subject: do interviews, gather facts and any visual images you may want to use. If possible, interview the people who know the subject.
- For a TV news story, write a script that plots out which visuals you will use with your voice-over narration. Allow plenty of time for actually putting your scrapbook, video, or presentation piece together.
- For a magazine article based on your research, write a first draft that covers as much of the material as you see fit. Then edit your article with an eye on where you might be able to use an image or two of the person in the layout.

MEDIA TOOLS
For help creating your news feature, visit the **Media Center** at ClassZone.com.

Tech Tip
You can use digital pictures with a presentation software program and provide the voice-over in real time.

Further Exploration

Analyze Words With a partner or in a small group, find two different types of media that cover the same subject or event. For example, the report could be a TV newscast and a weekly newsmagazine about a development in the U.S. space program, or a hometown newspaper and a national sports magazine reporting on steroid use in baseball, and so on. Look closely at each news source and jot down the adjectives and adverbs used to describe the event or people involved. What perspective do you think these words convey? Consider

- who created the news piece and what their opinion of the subject might be
- what audience the news piece is written for

Cite specific examples from the media sources to support your impressions.

Assess and Reteach

Write or Discuss

Determine Perspectives In their statements, students should discuss tone, details, visuals, and quotations to support their assessments of the reporters' perspectives. Make sure that students understand that both pieces eulogize Chávez. In such writing, it would be unusual for reporters to include negative commentary.

Produce Your Own Media

Rubric: Create a News Feature A strong news feature should

- convey perspective through tone and choice of detail
- feature credible research, interviews, and source material
- contain visuals that support a dominant impression of the subject
- include well-written text that clearly expresses factual information and creates a meaningful portrait
- show evidence of revision and editing
- appear as a polished, finished final product

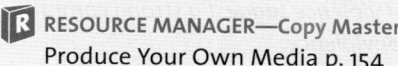 RESOURCE MANAGER—Copy Master
Produce Your Own Media p. 154

Further Exploration

Analyze Words Have students use word webs to collect descriptive adjectives and adverbs. Then students can use their webs to draw conclusions regarding tone, perspective, and audience.

MEDIA STUDY WRAP–UP

Have students summarize what they have learned about ways that introductions, visuals, and quotations in media create impressions of social and political figures. Urge students to use terms such as *footage, lead-in,* and *sound bites* in their summaries.

RETEACH

 STANDARDS LESSON FILE
Reading Lessons 12, 14
Informational Text Lesson 11
Media Lessons 3, 8–12

Focus and Motivate

OBJECTIVES

Literary Analysis
- explore the key idea of the ways people make **history**
- analyze and evaluate an eyewitness account
- read an autobiography and a poem

Reading
- draw conclusions from a primary source

Grammar and Writing
- use word choice, imagery, and tone to create mood
- write an eyewitness report

R3.1, W1.1, W1.9, W2.1

ABOUT THE AUTHOR

After students read about Moody's life, have them discuss the way the violent murders of her neighbors may have affected her as a young adult. *Possible answer: Her neighbors' murders may have made Moody angry and more likely to protest.* Ask students what her nonviolent response suggests about Moody. *Possible answer: Moody's actions in the face of personal violence suggest a strong commitment to nonviolence.*

USING THE *NOTABLE QUOTE*

Ask students what this quote tells them about **Anne Moody's** character. *Possible answer: Moody is humble and cared more for the cause than her own fame or personal fulfillment. She did not recount her actions to gain personal publicity but to record events for history.*

Selection Resources

---

from **Coming of Age in Mississippi**
Autobiography by Anne Moody

R3.1, W1.1 (p. 1191), **W1.9** (p. 1191), **W2.1** (p. 1191)

NOTABLE QUOTE
"I never really saw myself as a writer. I was first and foremost an activist in the civil rights movement in Mississippi."

FYI
Did you know that Anne Moody . . .
- went to college on a basketball scholarship?
- left the civil rights movement over concerns about black nationalism?
- rarely gives interviews or makes public appearances?

Author Online
For more on Anne Moody, visit the **Literature Center** at **ClassZone.com**.

Anne Moody
born 1940

Anne Moody was one of many dedicated college students who were on the frontlines in the battle for civil rights. In her award-winning autobiography, she details the dangers she and other young activists faced as they challenged segregation laws across the South. Her unflinching descriptions of taunts, beatings, and intimidation reveal the violent realities of nonviolent protest. They also call to mind the words of Martin Luther King Jr., who commended these brave young men and women for "their sublime courage, their willingness to suffer, and their amazing discipline in the midst of great provocation."

Climate of Fear Moody was the oldest of nine children born to desperately poor African-American farmers in rural Mississippi. When she was just nine years old, Moody began working after school as a maid to help her family pay for food and clothing. Periodic acts of racist violence effectively intimidated the black community in Moody's hometown. When local white supremacists set fire to her neighbor's shack, killing the family inside, her mother advised her, "Just act like you don't know nothing." But Moody was part of a new generation that would no longer be silenced.

Dedicated Activist Moody first attended Natchez Junior College and later transferred to Tougaloo College, graduating in 1964. As a college student, she worked with major civil rights organizations such as the Congress for Racial Equality (CORE) and the National Association for the Advancement of Colored People (NAACP). Later, she became civil rights coordinator at Cornell University. Throughout her time in the movement, Moody faced constant threats to her life and worked to the point of exhaustion to integrate public facilities, extend voting rights, and promote literacy. Commenting on King's famous speech "I Have a Dream," she once quipped, "We never have time to sleep, much less dream." Often frustrated and discouraged at the slow pace of social change, Moody came to see the civil rights struggle as part of a larger fight for universal human rights. As she explained, "It's the fight of every ethnic and racial minority, every suppressed and exploited person, every one of the millions who daily suffer one or another of the indignities of the powerless and voiceless masses." Her autobiography is a moving testament to the dedication and courage that inspired hundreds of thousands of people to take action for social justice.

Negro Sitdowns Stir Fear Of Wider Unrest in South

 RESOURCE MANAGER UNIT 6

Plan and Teach pp. 155–162

Literary Analysis
Summary pp. 163†*, 164‡*
Eyewitness Account pp. 165, 166†*
Question Support p. 170*

Reading
Reading a Primary Source pp. 167, 168†*
Reading Check p. 169

Grammar and Writing
Create Mood p. 171

Assessment
Selection Tests A, B/C pp. 173*, 175*
Test Generator CD

 BEST PRACTICES TOOLKIT

Differentiated Instruction pp. 31–38*

Scaffolding Instruction pp. 43–46*

Graphic Organizers/Strategies
Timeline • Word Questioning • Words with Multiple Meanings • Making Inferences • Two-Column Chart • Sequence Chain

Reading Support
Audio Anthology CD*

Technology
Literature and Writing Centers at **ClassZone.com**
WriteSmart CD

---

* Resources for Differentiation   † Also in Spanish   ‡ In Haitian Creole and Vietnamese

● LITERARY ANALYSIS: EYEWITNESS ACCOUNT

Anne Moody wrote this **eyewitness account** to document the violence she faced as a civil rights worker in Mississippi. Like a camera, Moody records events from her vantage point on the scene, using precise, factual descriptions to capture what she sees.

At exactly 11 A.M., Pearlena, Memphis, and I entered Woolworth's from the rear entrance.

Moody is not a journalist. The events she describes are part of her personal story. Her objective descriptions are interwoven with subjective details about her thoughts, feelings, and private life.

But something happened to me as I got more and more involved in the Movement. It no longer seemed important to prove anything.

As you read Moody's account, think about how her personal experiences influence the way she perceives events.

● READING STRATEGY: READING A PRIMARY SOURCE

Because Anne Moody had firsthand knowledge of the events she describes, her account is considered a **primary source.** From her recollections, you can learn practical details about the workings of the civil rights movement that you won't find in philosophical works on nonviolence. Note what Moody's account reveals about

- individuals and groups involved in the movement
- types of activities movement workers organized
- risks and obstacles faced by activists

As you read, use a chart like the one shown to take notes.

Individuals and Groups	Types of Activities	Risks and Obstacles

---

Explore the Key Idea

Who makes HISTORY?

KEY IDEA Most people assume that **history** is made by great leaders, the ones who get their pictures in textbooks. But those leaders don't make history by themselves. Their achievements depend on the combined efforts of people like your parents, your teachers, and you.

DISCUSS Working in a small group, think of three or four historical events. In what ways did these events depend on the efforts of ordinary people? Make a list for each event.

Rosa Parks Highway

COMING OF AGE IN MISSISSIPPI **1181**

Teach

Who makes HISTORY?

Lead into the **KEY IDEA** paragraph by asking the question. After small groups complete the **DISCUSS** activity, invite them to share their historical events and lists. Then ask them to generalize about ways that ordinary people affect **history.**

SKILLS FOCUS

> **LITERARY ANALYSIS** R3.1
>
> ### ● EYEWITNESS ACCOUNT
>
> Have students reread the author's biography on page 1180 and then predict subjective details they may find in Moody's autobiography. ***Possible answer:*** *Moody will most likely reveal her inner thoughts about her protest choices, along with the frustration, anger, and discouragement that she felt during this time. She may also reveal hopelessness, fear, and courage.*

> **READING STRATEGY**
>
> ### ■ READING A PRIMARY SOURCE
>
> Have students reread **Dedicated Activist** on page 1180 and identify some of the major groups and individuals that were involved in the civil rights movement. ***Possible answer:*** *The Congress for Racial Equality (CORE) and the National Association for the Advancement of Colored People (NAACP) were both involved in civil rights, as was Martin Luther King Jr.*
>
> **CHECK UNDERSTANDING** Ask students to discuss some of the risks and obstacles that the activists faced.
>
> RESOURCE MANAGER—Copy Master Reading a Primary Source p. 167 (for student use while reading the selection)

DIFFERENTIATED INSTRUCTION

FOR STRATEGIC READERS

Concept Support: Eyewitness Account Point out to students that an eyewitness account is written from the first-person point of view, so will use the pronouns *I, me,* and *we.* Discuss with students the ways that an eyewitness account of a civil rights activist might differ from an account written by someone who only experienced the event through media reports.

Concept Support: Primary Source Explain to students that primary sources are original accounts created by people with firsthand experience of historical events. Primary sources include journals, diaries, letters, memoirs, and autobiographies. Explain that Anne Moody's autobiography is a primary source that conveys firsthand knowledge of the civil rights movement.

SUMMARY

This excerpt from Moody's autobiography details the time when, as a college student in 1963, she participated in a sit-in at a Woolworth's lunch counter in Jackson, Mississippi. Moody and her two classmates ask to be served at a whites-only counter. Despite being denied service, they remain seated. The press soon arrives to question everyone present. Hecklers get involved and Moody and her companions are violently assaulted. They go back to their seats, but finally agree to leave after several hours. Moody later participates in a rally attended by Medgar Evans.

Background–Line 7
REINFORCE *KEY IDEA:* HISTORY

Discuss What do Moody's personal history and actions prove about people affecting **history?** *Possible answer: Moody was a struggling college student (lines 5–7) who believed so strongly in the movement seeking African-American rights that she participated in a sit-in. Her sit-in encouraged other sit-ins and the publicity of equal rights. Moody proves that a regular person can affect the history of a people.*

Coming of Age in Mississippi

ANNE MOODY

> **BACKGROUND** On February 1, 1960, four African-American college freshmen seated themselves at a whites-only lunch counter in Greensboro, North Carolina, refusing to leave until they were served. Within a week, 300 people had joined the sit-in; within two months, sit-ins were being held in 54 cities across the South, most of them organized by college and high school students. By August 1961, more than 70,000 protesters, black and white, had participated in sit-ins. Students, impatient with the slow pace of change, had decided to confront segregation head-on. As you'll read in Anne Moody's account, those confrontations made the ugliness of racism impossible to ignore. Be warned that in relating the confrontations, Moody repeats certain offensive racial epithets.

I had counted on graduating in the spring of 1963, but as it turned out, I couldn't because some of my credits still had to be cleared with Natchez College. A year before, this would have seemed like a terrible disaster, but now I hardly even felt disappointed. I had a good excuse to stay on campus for the summer and work with the Movement, and this was what I really wanted to do. I couldn't go home again anyway, and I couldn't go to New Orleans—I didn't have money enough for bus fare.

During my senior year at Tougaloo,[1] my family hadn't sent me one penny. I had only the small amount of money I had earned at Maple Hill.[2] I couldn't
10 afford to eat at school or live in the dorms, so I had gotten permission to move off campus. I had to prove that I could finish school, even if I had to go hungry every

ANALYZE VISUALS
What details in the photo help convey the tension of the scene at the protest?

Left to right: John Salter, Joan Trumpauer, and Anne Moody, seated at the Woolworth's lunch counter

---

1. **Tougaloo:** Tougaloo College, a traditionally African-American college on the northern edge of Jackson, Mississippi.

2. **Maple Hill:** a restaurant in New Orleans where Moody had worked in the summer.

DIFFERENTIATED INSTRUCTION

FOR ALL STUDENTS

Provide these independent projects to extend the lesson:

- Design a monument for participants in the sit-in.
- Dramatize a conversation between Moody and a social justice leader.
- Write letters exchanged by Moody and her mother.

For further details on these projects, see

 RESOURCE MANAGER
Ideas for Extension pp. 160–161

FOR STRATEGIC READERS

In combination with the *Audio Anthology CD,* use one or more Targeted Passages (pp. 1184, 1186, 1188) to ensure that students focus on key events and concepts. Targeted Passages are also good for English learners.

BACKGROUND

Segregation Laws and Sit-ins The segregation laws, or "Jim Crow" laws, that Anne Moody and other African Americans were fighting were laws in many Southern states that discriminated against African Americans. These laws denied African Americans the right to vote, the right to attend state universities, and the right to use public facilities, such as restrooms and lunch counters. The sit-in was one way that African Americans such as Moody protested these laws. A sit-in was a nonviolent form of protest that people used to integrate a public place. The people entered a facility, sat down, and refused to leave until they received service or attention. These protests led up to the Civil Rights Act of 1964, which finally put an end to the segregation laws that Moody helped fight.

ANALYZE VISUALS

Possible answer: Photo details that convey the tension of this protest scene include the hostile expressions on the faces of the white onlookers, and the large number of white males in the crowd relative to the two women, one of whom is African American, sitting at the counter waiting to be served. The three protesters at the counter appear to be trying to ignore the crowd and talk to one another, but are clearly in an uncomfortable position. Moreover, the clothing of the young man on the left appears to be stained, possibly from assaults by the onlookers.

FOR ENGLISH LEARNERS

Prereading For prereading instruction for English learners, see

 BEST PRACTICES TOOLKIT
Scaffolding Reading Instruction pp. 43–46

Culture: Clarify Explain that the phrase *coming of age* in the title refers to the process a person goes through to gain a deeper understanding of the world while becoming an adult. As students read this excerpt, have them consider what Moody might have learned about the world and people that contributed to her coming of age. Explain that Moody uses *Movement* (line 5) to refer to the civil rights movement.

FOR ADVANCED LEARNERS/AP

AP exercises in the bottom channel provide additional challenge for students. Use these suggestions for small groups or individuals.

ADDITIONAL GUIDELINES

For more help with differentiation and tips for classroom management, see

BEST PRACTICES TOOLKIT
Differentiated Instruction pp. 31–38

COMING OF AGE IN MISSISSIPPI **1183**

A EYEWITNESS ACCOUNT

Possible answer: Moody's personal challenges include loneliness and lack of money and family support. She is fighting just to get through school (lines 9–12). These personal challenges motivate her to get involved in the Movement, which gives her a sense of purpose and meaning (lines 14–15).

Extend the Discussion In what ways could personal reactions make a person both more and less effective as a civil rights worker?

B PRIMARY SOURCE

Possible answer: Summary: The picketing begins at 11 A.M. outside J.C. Penney's while protesters enter Woolworth's from the back (lines 31–32). During this time, Pearlena, Memphis, and Moody enter Woolworth's from the rear entrance (line 34). At 11:14 A.M., Pearlena and Moody join Memphis at the lunch counter (lines 36–37). At 11:15 A.M., they sit down (line 38). The protest planners most likely expected problems or opposition, and they planned carefully to assure that nothing actually went wrong.

If students need help . . . Suggest they use a Timeline to record the events that lead up to the actual sit-in. Point out to students why it was important that the participants followed the planned timing exactly.

 BEST PRACTICES TOOLKIT—Transparency Timeline p. B23

---

day. I knew Raymond and Miss Pearl[3] were just waiting to see me drop out. But something happened to me as I got more and more involved in the Movement. It no longer seemed important to prove anything. I had found something outside myself that gave meaning to my life. **A**

I had become very friendly with my social science professor, John Salter, who was in charge of NAACP[4] activities on campus. All during the year, while the NAACP conducted a boycott of the downtown stores in Jackson, I had been one of Salter's most faithful canvassers[5] and church speakers. During the last week
20 of school, he told me that sit-in demonstrations were about to start in Jackson and that he wanted me to be the spokesman for a team that would sit-in at Woolworth's lunch counter. The two other demonstrators would be classmates of mine, Memphis and Pearlena. Pearlena was a dedicated NAACP worker, but Memphis had not been very involved in the Movement on campus. It seemed that the organization had had a rough time finding students who were in a position to go to jail. I had nothing to lose one way or the other. Around ten o'clock the morning of the demonstrations, NAACP headquarters alerted the news services. As a result, the police department was also informed, but neither the policemen nor the newsmen knew exactly where or when the demonstrations would start.
30 They stationed themselves along Capitol Street and waited.

To divert attention from the sit-in at Woolworth's, the picketing started at J. C. Penney's a good fifteen minutes before. The pickets were allowed to walk up and down in front of the store three or four times before they were arrested. At exactly 11 A.M., Pearlena, Memphis, and I entered Woolworth's from the rear entrance. We separated as soon as we stepped into the store, and made small purchases from various counters. Pearlena had given Memphis her watch. He was to let us know when it was 11:14. At 11:14 we were to join him near the lunch counter and at exactly 11:15 we were to take seats at it. **B**

Seconds before 11:15 we were occupying three seats at the previously segregated
40 Woolworth's lunch counter. In the beginning the waitresses seemed to ignore us, as if they really didn't know what was going on. Our waitress walked past us a couple of times before she noticed we had started to write our own orders down and realized we wanted service. She asked us what we wanted. We began to read to her from our order slips. She told us that we would be served at the back counter, which was for Negroes.

"We would like to be served here," I said.

The waitress started to repeat what she had said, then stopped in the middle of the sentence. She turned the lights out behind the counter, and she and the other waitresses almost ran to the back of the store, deserting all their white customers.
50 I guess they thought that violence would start immediately after the whites at the counter realized what was going on. There were five or six other people at the counter. A couple of them just got up and walked away. A girl sitting next to me

---

3. **Raymond and Miss Pearl:** Moody's stepfather and step-grandmother.
4. **NAACP:** National Association for the Advancement of Colored People, an organization that works to end discrimination against African Americans and other minorities.
5. **canvassers:** people who go from door to door to get support for a cause or gather opinions on an issue.

A EYEWITNESS ACCOUNT
Reread lines 1–15. In what ways do Moody's personal challenges motivate her to get involved in the civil rights movement?

① Targeted Passage

B PRIMARY SOURCE
Reread lines 26–38. Summarize the timeline of the sit-in. Why might this protest have been so carefully planned?

DIFFERENTIATED INSTRUCTION

FOR STRATEGIC READERS

① Targeted Passage [Lines 16–26]

This passage shows Moody's character and her dedication to the Movement.

- How does Moody help the NAACP? What does this suggest about her character?
- What role does Salter want Moody to take at the Woolworth's sit-in?
- Why did the NAACP struggle to find sit-in volunteers? Why is Moody willing?

FOR ENGLISH LEARNERS

Culture: Clarify [mixed-readiness pairs] Explain that *picketing* (line 31) occurs when a group of people stand outside of an institution or business to express a grievance or to discourage people from entering. Picketers generally hold signs that express their grievances. Ask students to share impressions of any picketing they have seen. Then have pairs suggest and share statements that would have been suitable for the picketers in the passage to display.

FOR ADVANCED LEARNERS/AP

Hypothesize Point of View [small-group option] Remind students that Moody's first-person account describes the events from her perspective. Have groups explore the perspectives of others at the sit-in, such as the waitress, a reporter, or a member of the crowd. Urge students to use historical context to infer reactions, but not to assume stereotypical beliefs. For example, the supportive white customer is a native of Mississippi, but supports the protesters.

finished her banana split before leaving. A middle-aged white woman who had not yet been served rose from her seat and came over to us. "I'd like to stay here with you," she said, "but my husband is waiting."

The newsmen came in just as she was leaving. They must have discovered what was going on shortly after some of the people began to leave the store. One of the newsmen ran behind the woman who spoke to us and asked her to identify herself. She refused to give her name, but said she was a native of Vicksburg[6] and
60 a former resident of California. When asked why she had said what she had said to us, she replied, "I am in sympathy with the Negro movement." By this time a crowd of cameramen and reporters had gathered around us taking pictures and asking questions, such as Where were we from? Why did we sit-in? What organization sponsored it? Were we students? From what school? How were we classified?

I told them that we were all students at Tougaloo College, that we were represented by no particular organization, and that we planned to stay there even after the store closed. "All we want is service," was my reply to one of them. After they had finished probing for about twenty minutes, they were almost ready
70 to leave.

At noon, students from a nearby white high school started pouring in to Woolworth's. When they first saw us they were sort of surprised. They didn't know how to react. A few started to heckle and the newsmen became interested again. Then the white students started chanting all kinds of anti-Negro slogans. We were called a little bit of everything. The rest of the seats except the three we were occupying had been roped off to prevent others from sitting down. A couple of the boys took one end of the rope and made it into a hangman's noose. Several attempts were made to put it around our necks. The crowds grew as more students and adults came in for lunch.
80 We kept our eyes straight forward and did not look at the crowd except for occasional glances to see what was going on. All of a sudden I saw a face I remembered—the drunkard from the bus station sit-in. My eyes lingered on him just long enough for us to recognize each other. Today he was drunk too, so I don't think he remembered where he had seen me before. He took out a knife, opened it, put it in his pocket, and then began to pace the floor. At this point, I told Memphis and Pearlena what was going on. Memphis suggested that we pray. We bowed our heads, and all hell broke loose. A man rushed forward, threw Memphis from his seat, and slapped my face. Then another man who worked in the store threw me against an adjoining counter.
90 Down on my knees on the floor, I saw Memphis lying near the lunch counter with blood running out of the corners of his mouth. As he tried to protect his face, the man who'd thrown him down kept kicking him against the head. If he had worn hard-soled shoes instead of sneakers, the first kick probably would have

---

6. **Vicksburg:** a city in Mississippi, west of Jackson.

Lines 56–79
TIERED DISCUSSION PROMPTS
Use these prompts to help students consider Moody's character in a dangerous situation:

Connect Have you or someone you know ever participated in or supported an important, but controversial, effort? In what ways were you and others affected? *Accept all thoughtful responses.*

Interpret What do the reporters' questions suggest about their interest in the sit-in? What does Moody's response reveal about her motivation? What does the newsmen's renewed interest in the hecklers suggest about their motivations? ***Possible answer:*** *The reporters ask mostly factual questions, which suggests that they are not hugely interested in why the protesters are sitting-in (lines 61–65). Moody's response of just wanting service (line 68) simplifies her motivation and makes her reasoning powerful. The newsmen's renewed interest in the hecklers suggests that they are interested in sensationalism, controversy, and violence rather than civil rights.*

Evaluate How effective is Moody's initial description of the response to the sit-in? What details support her description? ***Possible answer:*** *Her description is powerful. She uses facts, not emotionalism, to portray the danger. She describes one white woman who empathizes with their cause, but is too fearful to identify herself (lines 53–61). She also reveals the true danger by detailing the boys' use of the rope as a hangman's noose (lines 77–78).*

FOR STRATEGIC READERS

Reading a Primary Source To help students keep track of important information related to the Movement, have them return to the chart introduced on page 1181 and complete it for pages 1184–1185. Direct students to record names of the individual protesters and groups such as NAACP, list what the protesters are doing, and identify the risks they face.

Individuals and Groups	Types of Activities	Risks and Obstacles

FOR ENGLISH LEARNERS

Key Academic Vocabulary Use Word Questioning to teach this word: *identify* (line 58).

🧰 BEST PRACTICES TOOLKIT—Transparency
Word Questioning p. E9

Prereading For prereading instruction for English learners, see

🧰 BEST PRACTICES TOOLKIT
Scaffolding Reading Instruction pp. 43–46

FOR ADVANCED LEARNERS/AP

Analyze Gesture Point out that the crowd and the protesters communicate continually but say almost nothing to one another. Ask students to read lines 47–95 carefully to identify body language and gestures that convey the conversation. Have students write a brief essay analyzing ways that Moody's use of these details affects the mood of her account. Invite students to share their essays with the class.

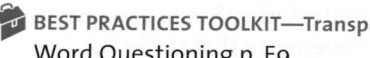

C EYEWITNESS ACCOUNT

Possible answer: Details that convey the danger of the protesters' situation include Moody being down on her knees (line 90), and Memphis bleeding (line 91) and being repeatedly kicked in the head (line 92). Moody's tone is surprisingly neutral and unemotional, considering the danger and injustice the protesters face.

Lines 96–118
REINFORCE *KEY IDEA*: HISTORY

Discuss What does the treatment that Moody and her fellow protesters undergo suggest about the qualities needed by people who try to make **history**? In what way do the protesters affect history here? *Possible answer: People who try to make history must be willing to undergo hardship and be misunderstood and ill-treated. They must also be brave and single-minded, willing to do whatever it takes to further their cause. Moody and her fellow protesters were willing to be hurt (lines 96, 106–10, 116), insulted (lines 101–102), and humiliated in order to prove their point. However, because they are willing to endure these hardships, the protesters made a public statement and also elicited empathy and support from white people (lines 97–99, 100–101, 110–113), thereby affecting the outcome of history.*

D GRAMMAR AND STYLE

Analyze Mood Help students understand the effect of Moody's strong choice of verbs and verbals by rereading lines 113–117, replacing *smearing* with "covering" and *gushed* with "came." Discuss ways that Moody's strong verbs and verbals better recreate the violence of the scene. Ask them to find examples of other strong verbs and verbals. *Possible answer: Strong verbs and verbals appear in lines 73–74, 82, 85, 87–89.*

---

killed Memphis. Finally a man dressed in plain clothes identified himself as a police officer and arrested Memphis and his attacker. **C**

Pearlena had been thrown to the floor. She and I got back on our stools after Memphis was arrested. There were some white Tougaloo teachers in the crowd. They asked Pearlena and me if we wanted to leave. They said that things were getting too rough. We didn't know what to do. While we were trying to make
100 up our minds, we were joined by Joan Trumpauer.[7] Now there were three of us and we were integrated. The crowd began to chant, "Communists, Communists, Communists." Some old man in the crowd ordered the students to take us off the stools.

"Which one should I get first?" a big husky boy said.

"That white nigger," the old man said.

The boy lifted Joan from the counter by her waist and carried her out of the store. Simultaneously, I was snatched from my stool by two high school students. I was dragged about thirty feet toward the door by my hair when someone made them turn me loose. As I was getting up off the floor, I saw Joan coming back
110 inside. We started back to the center of the counter to join Pearlena. Lois Chaffee, a white Tougaloo faculty member, was now sitting next to her. So Joan and I just climbed across the rope at the front end of the counter and sat down. There were now four of us, two whites and two Negroes, all women. The mob started smearing us with ketchup, mustard, sugar, pies, and everything on the counter. Soon Joan and I were joined by John Salter, but the moment he sat down he was hit on the jaw with what appeared to be brass knuckles. Blood gushed from his face and someone threw salt into the open wound. Ed King, Tougaloo's chaplain, rushed to him. **D**

At the other end of the counter, Lois and Pearlena were joined by George
120 Raymond, a CORE[8] field worker and a student from Jackson State College. Then a Negro high school boy sat down next to me. The mob took spray paint from the counter and sprayed it on the new demonstrators. The high school student had on a white shirt; the word "nigger" was written on his back with red spray paint.

We sat there for three hours taking a beating when the manager decided to close the store because the mob had begun to go wild with stuff from other counters. He begged and begged everyone to leave. But even after fifteen minutes of begging, no one budged. They would not leave until we did. Then Dr. Beittel, the president of Tougaloo College, came running in. He said he had just heard what was happening.
130 About ninety policemen were standing outside the store; they had been watching the whole thing through the windows, but had not come in to stop the mob or do anything. President Beittel went outside and asked Captain Ray to come and escort us out. The captain refused, stating the manager had to invite him in before he could enter the premises, so Dr. Beittel himself brought us out.

---

7. **Joan Trumpauer:** a white classmate of Moody's from Tougaloo College, who had been active in voter registration.

8. **CORE:** Congress of Racial Equality, a civil rights organization that coordinated marches and demonstrations in the 1960s.

C EYEWITNESS ACCOUNT
Reread lines 90–95. Identify details that convey the danger of the protesters' situation. What is surprising about Moody's **tone** in this passage?

D GRAMMAR AND STYLE
Reread lines 113–117. Note how Moody uses a serious tone and strong **verbs** and **verbals** like *smearing* and *gushed* to recreate the mood of the violent scene.

2 Targeted Passage

DIFFERENTIATED INSTRUCTION

FOR STRATEGIC READERS

2 Targeted Passage [Lines 119–134]

This passage shows the injustices Moody and the other protesters suffered and reveals police indifference to that suffering.

- In what ways are the protesters treated? Who treats them this way?

- Why does the manager decide to close the store?

- Who helps the protesters leave the store? Who doesn't help them?

FOR ENGLISH LEARNERS

Culture: Clarify Explain the chant of "Communists, Communists, Communists" in lines 101–102. At the time of the protest, the United States and the communist Soviet Union were at odds politically, so a label of *Communist* was an insult. The mob is denouncing the protesters as traitors because they support equal rights for African Americans, a view that was outside mainstream public opinion at the time.

Anne Moody and other protesters leaving the sit-in

He had told the police that they had better protect us after we were outside the store. When we got outside, the policemen formed a single line that blocked the mob from us. However, they were allowed to throw at us everything they had collected. Within ten minutes, we were picked up by Reverend King in his station wagon and taken to the NAACP headquarters on Lynch Street.

140   After the sit-in, all I could think of was how sick Mississippi whites were. They believed so much in the segregated Southern way of life, they would kill to preserve it. I sat there in the NAACP office and thought of how many times they had killed when this way of life was threatened. I knew that the killing had just begun. "Many more will die before it is over with," I thought. Before the sit-in, I had always hated the whites in Mississippi. Now I knew it was impossible for me to hate sickness. The whites had a disease, an incurable disease in its final stage. What were our chances against such a disease? I thought of the students, the young Negroes who had just begun to protest, as young interns. When these young interns got older, I thought, they would be the best doctors in the world 150 for social problems. **E**

      Before we were taken back to campus, I wanted to get my hair washed. It was stiff with dried mustard, ketchup and sugar. I stopped in at a beauty shop across the street from the NAACP office. I didn't have on any shoes because I had lost

E EYEWITNESS ACCOUNT
Reread lines 140–150. In what ways have Moody's attitudes and beliefs changed due to her experience at the sit-in?

Lines 135–144
TIERED DISCUSSION PROMPTS
Use these prompts to help students understand the hostile environment that Moody and the protesters face:

Recall What did Dr. Beittel tell the police? *Possible answer: He told them they had better protect the protesters.*

Analyze Do the police in fact protect the protesters? What does this suggest about them? *Possible answer: No, the police do the minimum they have to by blocking the mob (lines 136–137), but they allow the people to throw objects at the protesters (lines 137–138). Their behavior suggests that they oppose the protesters' actions and have let their personal beliefs and fears, rather then a commitment to justice, rule their actions.*

Synthesize Given her remarks before the sit-in, is it surprising that Moody continues her involvement in the Movement after realizing that the killing had just begun? Explain. *Possible answer: No, Moody's commitment is not surprising. She knew that her involvement in the Movement might involve danger and punishment, but before the sit-in acknowledged that the Movement gave her life purpose (lines 14–15) and that she had nothing to lose (line 26). Her actions agree with her self-portrait.*

LITERARY ANALYSIS

E EYEWITNESS ACCOUNT

Possible answer: Moody's hatred for whites (line 145) has changed into a hatred for the sickness of racism (lines 145–147). She is overwhelmed by the sickness of the racists' brutal behavior, and she knows that the killing has just begun (lines 143–144). She actually wonders whether the protesters can really succeed (line 147).

FOR ENGLISH LEARNERS

Vocabulary: Multiple-Meaning Words [paired option] Help pairs use context clues and an organizer to determine the meaning of these words: *plain clothes* (line 94), "civilian clothes"; *husky* (line 104), "gruff"; *smearing* (line 114), "covering"; *wound* (line 117), "cut"; *wild* (line 125), "unruly"; *line* (line 136), "row"; *sick* (line 140), "morally corrupt."

BEST PRACTICES TOOLKIT—Transparency Words with Multiple Meanings p. E31

FOR ADVANCED LEARNERS/AP

Analyze Racism [small-group option] Have groups discuss Moody's characterization of racism as a disease (lines 146–147). Ask students to list criteria that define a disease, such as having known signs and a cause. Then challenge students to debate whether racism meets the criteria. Finally, have groups share their conclusions with the class, linking Moody's disease metaphor to her description of protesters as interns training as doctors for social problems.

PRIMARY SOURCE

Possible answer: *The paragraph shows that the rally was crowded (line 163), and that people were inspired by the sit-in (lines 165–166). Rallies like this one would be important to the success of the Movement because these rallies promoted a strong sense of unity and commitment to the cause of civil rights.*

If students need help . . . Explain that they need to make inferences from text details in order to answer this question. Work with them to complete a Making Inferences chart with details from the paragraph.

🧰 **BEST PRACTICES TOOLKIT—Transparency** Making Inferences p. A13

Lines 173–184
REINFORCE *KEY IDEA:* HISTORY

Discuss In what way does Moody prove that she understands the dangers of changing history in a hostile environment? ***Possible answer:*** *Moody proves that she understands the dangers of changing history by acknowledging that her family might be killed for her deeds.*

SELECTION WRAP–UP

SUMMARIZE Have students sum up what happened to the protesters at the sit-in, then tell why sit-ins are important.

---

them when I was dragged across the floor at Woolworth's. My stockings were sticking to my legs from the mustard that had dried on them. The hairdresser took one look at me and said, "My land, you were in the sit-in, huh?"

"Yes," I answered. "Do you have time to wash my hair and style it?"

"Right away," she said, and she meant right away. There were three other ladies already waiting, but they seemed glad to let me go ahead of them. The hairdresser
160 was real nice. She even took my stockings off and washed my legs while my hair was drying.

There was a mass rally that night at the Pearl Street Church in Jackson, and the place was packed. People were standing two abreast in the aisles. Before the speakers began, all the sit-inners walked out on the stage and were introduced by Medgar Evers.[9] People stood and applauded for what seemed like thirty minutes or more. Medgar told the audience that this was just the beginning of such demonstrations. He asked them to pledge themselves to unite in a massive offensive against segregation in Jackson, and throughout the state. The rally ended with "We Shall Overcome" and sent home hundreds of determined people. It
170 seemed as though Mississippi Negroes were about to get together at last. **F**

> Before I demonstrated, I had written Mama. She wrote me back a letter, begging me not to take part in the sit-in. She even sent ten dollars for bus fare to New Orleans. I didn't have one penny, so I kept the money. Mama's letter made me mad. I had to live my life as I saw fit. I had made that decision when I left home. But it hurt to have my family prove to me how scared they were. It hurt me more than anything else—I knew the whites had already started the threats and intimidations. I was the first Negro from my hometown who had openly demonstrated, worked with the NAACP, or anything. When Negroes threatened to do anything in Centreville, they were either shot like Samuel O'Quinn or run
> 180 out of town, like Reverend Dupree.[10]

I didn't answer Mama's letter. Even if I had written one, she wouldn't have received it before she saw the news on TV or heard it on the radio. I waited to hear from her again. And I waited to hear in the news that someone in Centreville had been murdered. If so, I knew it would be a member of my family. ∾

F **PRIMARY SOURCE**
Reread lines 162–170. What does this paragraph tell you about the rally? Why would rallies like the one described be important to the success of the movement?

③ Targeted Passage

---

9. **Medgar Evers:** civil rights leader and organizer for the NAACP in Mississippi from 1954 until 1963, when he was killed by a sniper.

10. **Centreville . . . Samuel O'Quinn . . . Reverend Dupree:** In Centreville, the Mississippi town where Moody grew up, Samuel O'Quinn had been suspected of being associated with the NAACP. The Reverend Dupree had mentioned the NAACP in a sermon he preached.

DIFFERENTIATED INSTRUCTION

FOR STRATEGIC READERS

③ Targeted Passage [Lines 171–180]

This passage shows Moody's strained relationship with her family and the fear African Americans felt about protesting.

- What does Moody's mother ask of her?
- Why does Moody's mother's letter hurt Moody? What does Moody know has started?
- What happened to Samuel O'Quinn and Reverend Dupree?

FOR ADVANCED LEARNERS/AP

Analyze Protest Music Have students research the lyrics to "We Shall Overcome" and discuss why they think the rally ended with that song (line 169). Ask them to write several paragraphs that explain why the lyrics to that song would be important to the people at the rally. Paragraphs should include an explanation of what the African Americans hoped to overcome, and a deeper explanation of the song's lyrics. Have students begin by creating a Two-Column Chart to interpret the song's meaning:

Lyric	Meaning to Protesters
"We shall overcome"	We can withstand anger and work to end racism.

Have students share their interpretations and charts with the class. Invite the class to discuss why this song has become such a powerful symbol of the civil rights movement.

 BEST PRACTICES TOOLKIT—Transparency Two-Column Chart p. A25

Revolutionary Dreams

Nikki Giovanni

Love Letter I (1971), Charles Wilbert White. Color lithograph, 30" x 22 1/2". Gift of June Wayne. Image © 2007 Board of Trustees, National Gallery of Art, Washington, D.C. 1974.99.158.(B-27792)/PR.

i used to dream militant
dreams of taking
over america to show
these white folks how it should be
5 done
i used to dream radical dreams
of blowing everyone away with my perceptive powers
of correct analysis
i even used to think i'd be the one
10 to stop the riot and negotiate the peace
then i awoke and dug
that if i dreamed natural
dreams of being a natural
woman doing what a woman
15 does when she's natural
i would have a revolution

TIERED DISCUSSION PROMPTS

Use these prompts to help students compare and contrast the views expressed by the speaker of this poem and Anne Moody:

Connect What does the title "Revolutionary Dreams" mean to you? What are Anne Moody's revolutionary dreams? ***Possible answer:*** *Accept all thoughtful answers. Anne Moody's revolutionary dreams are equal rights for African Americans.*

Interpret What were the old dreams of the speaker of this poem? What are her new dreams? What does she think these will accomplish? ***Possible answers:*** *The speaker's old dreams were of taking over America from the white people (lines 2–5) and of using her mind to show people the right way to behave (lines 6–8). Her new dreams are that if she instead acts like a natural woman (lines 13–14), which likely includes emotions ranging from compassion to rage, there will then be a real revolution.*

Synthesize Would Moody agree with the views expressed in "Revolutionary Dreams"? Why or why not? ***Possible answer:*** *Moody would most likely agree with the speaker of this poem. The speaker seems to recognize the complexity in attempts at change, noting that the old dreams were simple but unattainable. She realizes that she needs to follow her instincts and seek small, natural, changes. Moody has a similar revelation in lines 140–151, when she realizes that racism, not white people, is the problem. She notes that it will take social doctors time to fix it, and that she cannot hate individuals. In other words, she must follow her instincts.*

Practice and Apply

After Reading

Use these copy masters to check under-standing and provide extra support:

RESOURCE MANAGER—Copy Masters
Reading Check p. 169
Eyewitness Account p. 165
Question Support p. 170

Additional selection questions are provided for teachers on page 159.

ANSWERS

1. *name-calling, physical violence, intimidation*

2. *The police watched but did not intervene.*

3. *The protesters believed in nonviolence.*

Possible answers:

4. *Moody knew that whites had been threat-ening people (lines 176–177). She thought the local racists might punish her family for her involvement in the protests.*

5. ■ **SKILLS FOCUS Reading a Primary Source** *Teachers such as Lois Chaffee, a white woman, supported the protesters (lines 110–111). Dr. Beittel brought the pro-testers to safety (lines 132–134). The people at the rally supported the protesters (lines 162–163). The movement needed the com-bined efforts of the community to complete the protests.*

6. *Students were critical to the success of the movement because they started and organized most of the sit-ins (Background, lines 100, 119–121). Students were more ag-gressive about civil rights than were adults (Background).*

7. *Moody was motivated to become part of history by anger over racism in her town (lines 175–180), the stress of her isolated life, the sense of purpose from the Movement (lines 8–15), and the desire to live her own life (line 174).*

8. ● **SKILLS FOCUS Eyewitness Account** *Moody is a credible reporter because she maintains a neutral tone, focuses on narra-ting facts, is honest about her own opin-ions, and seems to be a clear-sighted, strong individual.*

9. *Both writers seem to think a revolution is needed. Giovanni's speaker (lines 4–5) and Moody (line 140) think they know what is wrong with whites and both remain com-*

Comprehension

R3.1

1. **Recall** What kinds of abuses were directed at the protesters during the sit-in?

2. **Recall** What role did the police play in the sit-in?

3. **Clarify** Why didn't the protesters fight back?

Literary Analysis

4. **Make Inferences** After the sit-in, why was Anne Moody worried that a member of her family would be killed?

5. **Draw Conclusions from a Primary Source** Review the chart you created as you read. Identify three ways ordinary people contributed to the success of civil rights protest. Could the movement have succeeded without community support? Why or why not?

6. **Synthesize Details** In what ways were students critical to the success of the movement? Use details from the background and the selection in your answer.

7. **Analyze Author's Perspective** Consider what you learn about Moody's character and private life from the account. What factors contributed to her decision to take action and become part of **history?** Be specific in your answers.

8. **Evaluate an Eyewitness Account** In your opinion, is Moody a credible reporter of events? In your answer, consider each of the following aspects of her account:

   • presentation of facts (lines 31–38)
   • tone (lines 106–118)
   • opinions expressed (lines 140–147)
   • character traits (lines 171–180)

9. **Compare Texts** Reread the poem on page 1189. In what ways are Nikki Giovanni's thoughts about social change similar to Moody's? Cite details in your answer.

Literary Criticism

10. **Different Perspectives** Anne Moody and Martin Luther King Jr. provide different views of the struggle for civil rights: that of a rank-and-file activist and that of a movement leader. In what ways do their accounts reflect their different roles within the movement? Support your answer with details.

---

mitted to their beliefs about ways to change society. Each thinks she knows ways to do that (Giovanni, lines 11–16; Moody, lines 143–144, 174).

10. *Moody narrates day-to-day details of ways protests were organized, the dangers protesters faced, and the real-life stresses of social justice work. She includes details about her personal and family life. King talks about big ideas, uses lots of inspiring slogans and persuasive rhetoric. He doesn't reveal personal information.*

Reading-Writing Connection

 W1.1, W2.1

WRITING PROMPT

WRITE AN EYEWITNESS REPORT An effective eyewitness report puts the reader in the midst of the action while providing the context needed to understand the events described. Write a **three-to-five-paragraph eyewitness report** on an event of your choosing, such as a sporting event or a community gathering. Use precise details and a clear, logical structure to make the event accessible to your audience.

SELF-CHECK

A successful report will ...

• answer the five *W*'s: *who, what, when, where,* and *why*

• use precise language and sensory images

• relate the event in a logical order

GRAMMAR AND STYLE

 W1.9

CREATE MOOD Review the **Grammar and Style** note on page 1186. Mood is the feeling that a writer creates for the reader through such elements as **word choice, imagery,** and **tone.** Moody's account has a tense, serious mood that is appropriate to the scene she describes. She uses plain but powerful language, avoiding sensationalism to let the mob's actions speak for themselves.

> *Simultaneously, I was snatched from my stool by two high school students. I was dragged about thirty feet toward the door by my hair when someone made them turn me loose.* (lines 107–109)

The author's choice of strong **verbs** like *snatched* and *dragged* allows her to convey the violence of the scene while maintaining a calm, controlled tone. Note that Moody uses straightforward **declarative sentences** to describe her experiences, without adding details about her own responses to what occurs.

PRACTICE The following paragraph is written to create a tense, dramatic mood. Rewrite the paragraph, adjusting word choice, imagery, and tone to create a lighter, more comic mood. A sample beginning is provided for you.

> We all sat quietly, waiting for news. My palms began to sweat and I had trouble swallowing. I looked over at my friend, seated two rows away, but I couldn't catch her eye. She looked like she was about to cry. I was hoping the news wouldn't be as bad as we feared, but everyone else seemed to have accepted the worst. Then, the door opened and he walked in, scanning the room with a frown. I couldn't believe it. All the rumors were true: we'd been assigned the toughest teacher in the entire school for homeroom. It was going to be a long, long year.

WRITING TOOLS
For prewriting, revision, and editing tools, visit the **Writing Center** at ClassZone.com.

EXAMPLE

"Hi, everybody!" our new teacher said, holding a bunch of balloons. "Welcome to homeroom!"

DIFFERENTIATED INSTRUCTION

FOR DEVELOPING WRITERS
Task Support: Writing Prompt

• Tell students to choose an event that is uncomplicated and thus fairly easy to describe.

• Ask students to record sensory language associated with each action listed in their Sequence Chain. For example, students might record sounds of victory for an action such as scoring the winning point.

• Remind students that an eyewitness report is written from the first-person point of view, using the pronouns *I* and *me*. Students must still find a balance between personal feeling and factual recording.

• Ask students to identify the mood they intend to convey and the tone they will use before they begin writing. Encourage students to use strong verbs, too.

Reading-Writing Connection

WRITING PROMPT

Remind students that it is Moody's precise and vivid description of the events that makes her account so gripping. Suggest students use a Sequence Chain to record the most important actions and details of their chosen event before writing. This will help students write about the events in a logical order.

 BEST PRACTICES TOOLKIT—Transparency
Sequence Chain p. B21

For writing support, see

 Writing Center at **ClassZone.com**

GRAMMAR AND STYLE

Review that imagery is writing that creates mental pictures by appealing to the senses, that tone is a writer's attitude toward the subject, and that declarative sentences are statements that end in periods. ***Possible answer:*** *"Hi, everybody!" our new teacher said, holding a bunch of balloons. "Welcome to homeroom!" When I looked over at my best friend, she was actually crying with joy. We had both expected to get the toughest teacher in the school this year, and envisioned suffering through a miserable year. Instead, we were delighted to find the best-loved teacher in the school walk through our door. We knew we would have one of the best years yet!*

 RESOURCE MANAGER—Copy Master
Create Mood p. 171

Assess and Reteach

Assess

RESOURCE MANAGER—Copy Masters
Selection Test A pp. 173–174
Selection Test B/C pp. 175–176

Test Generator CD

Reteach

STANDARDS LESSON FILE
Literature Lesson 42: Mood
Literature Lesson 43: Tone
Writing Lesson 39: Word Choice
Research Lesson 5: Using Primary and Secondary Sources

OBJECTIVES

Literary Analysis
- explore the key idea of **self-worth**
- analyze and interpret rhetorical devices
- read an open letter

Reading
- identify and evaluate key ideas

Vocabulary
- build vocabulary for reading and writing
- use context clues to determine the meanings of idioms (also an EL language objective)

CALIFORNIA R2.1

ABOUT THE AUTHOR

After students read about Baldwin's life, have them draw conclusions about his character —for example, that he was intelligent and responsible. Ask them to speculate on ways that racial strife might have contributed to his "crisis of faith." Discuss ways in which the perspective of distance might help a writer bear witness to the place from which he came.

USING THE *NOTABLE QUOTE*

Ask students what this quote suggests about **James Baldwin** and his view of American history. *Possible answer: Baldwin believes that American history is complex, filled with contradictions, and often misunderstood. Despite Baldwin's frustration with aspects of that history, he recognizes its positive qualities, too.*

CALIFORNIA R2.1

My Dungeon Shook: Letter to My Nephew

Open Letter by James Baldwin

James Baldwin
1924–1987

NOTABLE QUOTE
"American history is longer, larger, more various, more beautiful, and more terrible than anything anyone has ever said about it."

FYI
Did you know that James Baldwin . . .
- was mentored by poet Countee Cullen in high school?
- moved to Paris at age 24 and only returned to the United States for visits?
- was working on a biography of Martin Luther King Jr. when he died?

Harlem in 1937

In the turbulent 1960s, James Baldwin became one of the country's most sought-after commentators on racial politics. But Baldwin never considered himself a spokesperson. Rather, he saw his role as bearing witness "to whence I came, where I am . . . to what I've seen and the possibilities that I think I see." This autobiographical vantage point is the hallmark of Baldwin's greatest works, from his moving first novel, *Go Tell It on the Mountain* (1953), to the provocative essays collected in *Notes of a Native Son* (1955), *Nobody Knows My Name* (1961), and *The Fire Next Time* (1963).

Early Struggles Born and raised in Harlem, Baldwin never knew his biological father and had a strained relationship with his stepfather, a domineering, bitter man who preached at a storefront evangelical church on weekends. A star pupil and voracious reader, the young James also helped his overworked mother raise his eight brothers and sisters. After a dramatic religious conversion at age 14, he gained local acclaim as a "boy-preacher." Then, at 18, a crisis of faith drove Baldwin to break with the church and leave home.

Emerging Artist Working to establish his literary career, Baldwin supported himself by writing book reviews and waiting tables. Baldwin achieved some success but felt increasingly stifled by the racist climate of the United States. In a life-changing decision in 1948, he bought a one-way plane ticket to Paris. "Once I found myself on the other side of the ocean," he later explained, "I could see where I came from very clearly, and I could see that I carried myself, which is my home, with me. You can never escape that."

Long-Distance Outrage With their penetrating insight and apocalyptic tone, Baldwin's essay collections were bestsellers. By the mid-1960s, he was an international celebrity, popular on the lecture circuit and in public debates, interviews, and panel discussions in the United States and Europe. In writing about his perceptions and personal torments, Baldwin made white Americans deeply, painfully aware of the realities of African-American life. As black leaders in the 1950s and 1960s looked outward to break down barriers, Baldwin looked inward to examine the psychological damage of racism and the search for black identity and self-realization. In the words of playwright Amiri Baraka, "Jimmy's voice, as much as Dr. King's or Malcolm X's, helped shepherd and guide us toward black liberation."

1192

 RESOURCE MANAGER UNIT 6

Plan and Teach pp. 177–184

Literary Analysis
Summary pp. 185†*, 186‡*
Rhetorical Devices pp. 187, 188†*
Question Support p. 195*

Reading
Identify Ideas pp. 189, 190†*
Reading Check p. 194

Vocabulary
Study p. 191*
Practice p. 192
Strategy p. 193

Assessment
Selection Tests A, B/C
pp. 197*, 199*
 Test Generator CD

BEST PRACTICES TOOLKIT

Differentiated Instruction
pp. 31–38*

Scaffolding Instruction
pp. 43–46*

Reading Support
🔊 Audio Anthology CD*

Technology
ⓘ Literature and Vocabulary Centers at **ClassZone.com**

🔊 Write*Smart* CD

---

* Resources for Differentiation   † Also in Spanish   ‡ In Haitian Creole and Vietnamese

LITERARY ANALYSIS: RHETORICAL DEVICES

Baldwin is known for his passionate and poetic style, which is based on his skillful use of **rhetorical devices.** These techniques are used to drive home a writer's points and to create rhythmic effects that echo spoken language.

- A **paradox** is a statement that seems contradictory but really points to an important truth. Baldwin uses this device to push his readers to think more deeply about familiar ideas.

    It is the innocence which constitutes the crime.

- **Repetition** is the use of the same word, phrase, or sentence more than once for emphasis. Baldwin uses repetition expressively, to convey deep emotions.

    You must accept them and accept them with love....

As you read, note the rhetorical devices Baldwin uses, and consider their effects.

■ READING STRATEGY: IDENTIFY IDEAS

Baldwin's sentences do more than simply explain his points; they stir powerful emotional responses in the reader. Often, the meaning of his statements becomes apparent only after careful thought and reflection. As you read this letter, use your own emotional responses to identify Baldwin's **ideas.** In a chart like the one shown, note five sentences that hit home for you. After you have finished the essay, review the sentences you chose and try to explain the key idea behind each one.

Baldwin's Sentence	Idea

▲ VOCABULARY IN CONTEXT

Baldwin uses the following words in his eloquent appeal. Complete each sentence with one of the words.

WORD LIST	constitute	mediocrity	unassailable
	impertinent	truculent	

1. You conceal your fears with a(n) _____ attitude.
2. Don't settle for _____; strive for excellence.
3. It is never _____ to speak honestly.
4. Know exactly what tasks and obligations _____ your duty.
5. Let your convictions be strong and your truth _____.

Explore the Key Idea

What protects your sense of SELF?

KEY IDEA Part of growing up is deciding who you want to be and how to make your vision a reality. But how do you keep your sense of self strong when others tell you who you can and cannot be? James Baldwin offers his nephew some advice on protecting his **self-worth** from the crushing forces of racism.

QUICKWRITE Think about the messages you get about yourself from family, friends, media, and other sources. Which ones support you and which ones seem to hold you back? List at least two examples in each category. Based on your list, what in your life most helps you protect your self-worth?

Support	Hold Back
1. With hard work you can achieve your dreams (my mom).	1. College is too expensive and not worth it (my friend George).
2.	2.

Teach

What protects your sense of SELF?

Lead into the **KEY IDEA** paragraph by asking the question. Have students suggest ways to protect one's sense of self from pressure. After students complete the **QUICKWRITE,** invite volunteers to share their examples. Then ask them to generalize ways in which people can protect their **self-worth.**

SKILLS FOCUS

LITERARY ANALYSIS   R2.1

● RHETORICAL DEVICES

Point out that writers often use rhetorical devices to persuade their readers, and remind students that Baldwin is trying to persuade his nephew to believe in himself. Ask students what is contradictory about Baldwin's first statement. ***Possible answer:*** *The words "innocence" and "crime" seem contradictory.* Explain that a full reading of context is critical for determining the meaning of a paradox.

CHECK UNDERSTANDING Have students write two sentences that use each of the rhetorical devices discussed here.

READING STRATEGY

■ IDENTIFY IDEAS

Have students reread **Emerging Artist** on page 1192 and focus on the quote by Baldwin. Ask them what emotional responses this quote might stir in readers and what idea his quote expresses. ***Possible answer:*** *This quote might inspire readers to wonder about their own lives and the way that their homes have affected them. The quote expresses the idea that everyone has a personal history that one cannot escape.*

📕 **RESOURCE MANAGER—Copy Master**
Identify Ideas p. 189 (for student use while reading the selection)

VOCABULARY IN CONTEXT

Diagnose Word Knowledge To determine preteaching needs, have all students complete Vocabulary in Context. ***Answers:***
1. *truculent,* **2.** *mediocrity,* **3.** *impertinent,*
4. *constitute,* **5.** *unassailable*

PRETEACH VOCABULARY Preteach vocabulary with this copy master. Read each item aloud.

📕 **RESOURCE MANAGER—Copy Master**
Vocabulary Study p. 191

MORE VOCABULARY SUPPORT
For additional activities and guidelines, see

🧰 **BEST PRACTICES TOOLKIT**
Scaffolding Vocabulary Instruction pp. 43–46
ⓘ Vocabulary Center at **ClassZone.com**

SUMMARY

Baldwin's letter to his nephew and namesake urges him to define himself in his own terms and not in the white world's terms. Baldwin writes that white people need to make African Americans believe they are inferior to whites, and that until white people understand the cruelty in their own history, they cannot be freed from it. He extols his nephew for not succumbing to the white man's definition of him. He encourages him to help whites see their true selves, because until they do, African Americans will never be free.

Lines 7–9
REINFORCE *KEY IDEA:*
SELF–WORTH

Discuss In what way does Baldwin characterize the grandfather's **self-worth?** What mistake did the grandfather make? What does that suggest about the grandfather's character? *Possible answer: Baldwin characterizes the grandfather's **self-worth** as essentially non-existent. He mistakenly believed what whites told him about himself (lines 8–9), and he therefore didn't believe himself worth anything. This suggests that the grandfather was not strong enough to ignore what others said about him. Instead, he let others' comments define him.*

My Dungeon Shook

Letter to My Nephew on the One Hundredth Anniversary of the Emancipation

James Baldwin

BACKGROUND In 1963, as the nation's perspective on the race problem grew more pessimistic, James Baldwin published his essay collection *The Fire Next Time*. Expressing the pain and anger that African Americans had concealed for so long, Baldwin addressed his provocative essays to a sympathetic white audience that had failed to grasp the full magnitude of racial injustice. His searing attack fit the national mood, and the collection soared up the bestseller lists. Its success made Baldwin an icon of black rage and a widely televised commentator on racial issues throughout the 1960s. The following letter, taken from *The Fire Next Time*, captures the extremes of Baldwin's style: the righteous anger that made him famous and his fervent belief in the redeeming power of love.

ANALYZE VISUALS
Describe the story that this painting seems to tell. Which elements help the artist connect the two figures in the foreground with the main story of the painting?

Dear James:
I have begun this letter five times and torn it up five times. I keep seeing your face, which is also the face of your father and my brother. Like him, you are tough, dark, vulnerable, moody—with a very definite tendency to sound **truculent** because you want no one to think you are soft. You may be like your grandfather in this, I don't know, but certainly both you and your father resemble him very much physically. Well, he is dead, he never saw you, and he had a terrible life; he was defeated long before he died because, at the bottom of his heart, he really believed what white people said about him. This is one of the reasons that he
10 became so holy.[1] I am sure that your father has told you something about all that. Neither you nor your father exhibit any tendency towards holiness: you really *are*

❶ Targeted Passage
truculent (trŭk′yə-lənt) *adj.* eager for a fight; fierce

---

1. **so holy:** Baldwin's stepfather was a minister who raised his children in a strict, conservative, religious environment.

Father, Charly Palmer. Mixed media collage on wood. 18″ × 12″. © Charly Palmer.

DIFFERENTIATED INSTRUCTION

FOR ALL STUDENTS

Provide these independent projects to extend the lesson:

- Create protest art.
- Write an open letter using rhetorical devices.
- Survey others about the concept of self-worth.

For further details on these projects, see

R RESOURCE MANAGER
Ideas for Extension pp. 182–183

FOR STRATEGIC READERS

In combination with the *Audio Anthology CD,* use one or more Targeted Passages (pp. 1194, 1196, 1198) to ensure that students focus on key concepts. Targeted Passages are also good for English learners.

❶ Targeted Passage [Lines 1–7]

This passage begins the letter by describing Baldwin's nephew James, and how he is like his father, Baldwin's brother.

BACKGROUND

The Emancipation Proclamation In 1863, Abraham Lincoln's Emancipation Proclamation freed all slaves in the Confederate States of America. This is the One Hundredth Anniversary to which Baldwin refers. He is writing this letter to his nephew approximately one hundred years after the proclamation, explaining that he thinks African Americans are celebrating freedom one hundred years too soon. He does not think that they are really free yet.

ANALYZE VISUALS

Possible answer: The story that the painting seems to be telling is the ongoing struggle of African Americans for dignity and human rights. The tall man at the center of the painting is dressed in a simple but dignified manner. He is linked to the silhouetted protesters behind him by the protest sign that he carries, asserting his humanity. The small boy in the forefront has his hand outstretched, linking him to the other figures in the painting in a plea for recognition.

About the Art Like James Baldwin's writings, many of Charly Palmer's (born 1960) paintings focus on aspects of African-American history.

- To whom is Baldwin writing?
- What is the relationship between Baldwin and James?
- In what ways does Baldwin say that James is like his father (Baldwin's brother)?
- Why does Baldwin say that his nephew behaves the way he does?
- In what ways does Baldwin say that James is like his grandfather (Baldwin's stepfather)?

FOR ENGLISH LEARNERS

Prereading For prereading instruction for English learners, see

 BEST PRACTICES TOOLKIT
Scaffolding Reading Instruction pp. 43–46

FOR ADVANCED LEARNERS/AP

AP exercises in the bottom channel provide additional challenge for students. Use these suggestions for small groups or individuals.

ADDITIONAL GUIDELINES

For more help with differentiation and tips for classroom management, see

BEST PRACTICES TOOLKIT
Differentiated Instruction pp. 31–38

TIERED DISCUSSION PROMPTS

Use these prompts to have students consider Baldwin's accusations and thoughts:

Connect Think of someone you have known for a long time. What can you know about this person from the story of his or her life? *Accept all thoughtful responses.*

Interpret What does Baldwin accuse mankind of doing? In what way does his accusation relate to his brother? ***Possible answer:*** *Baldwin accuses mankind of being capable of destruction and death without feeling any notable remorse (lines 34–35). Baldwin has seen his brother grow up and be slowly destroyed by the whites' perceptions of and limitations on African Americans (lines 26–29). His brother has narrowly escaped the death of his own self-definition.*

Evaluate Does Baldwin effectively prove his point about mankind? Explain. ***Possible answer:*** *Yes, Baldwin proves his point effectively. He gives examples to show how well he knows his brother (lines 16–26), which qualifies him to note the near destruction his brother has faced due to the whites. He justifies well his inability to forgive mankind by describing the many other African-American lives that have been destroyed, without anybody recognizing it (lines 29–33). His points about a brutal mankind seem both poignant and true.*

LITERARY ANALYSIS

Ⓐ RHETORICAL DEVICES

Possible answer: *Baldwin is saying that it is unfair for the people (whites) who are doing the destroying to be innocent or unaware of what they are doing. The fact that people are ignorant about the consequences of racism is unforgivable, or a crime.*

---

of another era, part of what happened when the Negro left the land and came into what the late E. Franklin Frazier[2] called "the cities of destruction." You can only be destroyed by believing that you really are what the white world calls a *nigger.* I tell you this because I love you, and please don't you ever forget it.

I have known both of you all your lives, have carried your Daddy in my arms and on my shoulders, kissed and spanked him and watched him learn to walk. I don't know if you've known anybody from that far back; if you've loved anybody that long, first as an infant, then as a child, then as a man, you gain a strange
20 perspective on time and human pain and effort. Other people cannot see what I see whenever I look into your father's face, for behind your father's face as it is today are all those other faces which were his. Let him laugh and I see a cellar your father does not remember and a house he does not remember and I hear in his present laughter his laughter as a child. Let him curse and I remember him falling down the cellar steps, and howling, and I remember, with pain, his tears, which my hand or your grandmother's so easily wiped away. But no one's hand can wipe away those tears he sheds invisibly today, which one hears in his laughter and in his speech and in his songs. I know what the world has done to my brother and how narrowly he has survived it. And I know, which is much worse, and this is
30 the crime of which I accuse my country and my countrymen, and for which neither I nor time nor history will ever forgive them, that they have destroyed and are destroying hundreds of thousands of lives and do not know it and do not want to know it. One can be, indeed one must strive to become, tough and philosophical concerning destruction and death, for this is what most of mankind has been best at since we have heard of man. (But remember: *most* of mankind is not all of mankind.) But it is not permissible that the authors of devastation should also be innocent. It is the innocence which **constitutes** the crime. Ⓐ

Now, my dear namesake, these innocent and well-meaning people, your countrymen, have caused you to be born under conditions not very far removed
40 from those described for us by Charles Dickens[3] in the London of more than a hundred years ago. (I hear the chorus of the innocents screaming, "No! This is not true! How *bitter* you are!"—but I am writing this letter to *you,* to try to tell you something about how to handle *them,* for most of them do not yet really know that you exist. I *know* the conditions under which you were born, for I was there. Your countrymen were *not* there, and haven't made it yet. Your grandmother was also there, and no one has ever accused her of being bitter. I suggest that the innocents check with her. She isn't hard to find. Your countrymen don't know that *she* exists, either, though she has been working for them all their lives.)

Well, you were born, here you came, something like fifteen years ago; and
50 though your father and mother and grandmother, looking about the streets through which they were carrying you, staring at the walls into which they brought you, had every reason to be heavyhearted, yet they were not. For here

constitute (kŏn'stĭ-tōōt') *v.* to amount to; equal

Ⓐ **RHETORICAL DEVICES**
Consider the **paradox** in lines 36–37. What point is Baldwin making?

② **Targeted Passage**

---

2. **E. Franklin Frazier:** African-American sociologist (1894–1962) who studied the structure of black communities.

3. **described . . . by Charles Dickens:** Dickens (1812–1870) was a British novelist whose works frequently described the hardships suffered by the poor in London.

DIFFERENTIATED INSTRUCTION

FOR STRATEGIC READERS

② Targeted Passage [Lines 38–52]

This passage conveys Baldwin's view of whites and the purpose of his letter.

- Who are the "countrymen" Baldwin names? Of what does he accuse them?

- What does Baldwin say is the purpose of this letter to his nephew?

- How old is Baldwin's nephew? What feelings does he say young James' parents should have felt at his birth?

FOR ENGLISH LEARNERS

Comprehension: Self-Monitor After students read lines 20–22, have them pause to self-monitor by explaining what Baldwin means. If necessary, tell students to imagine looking at photos of themselves at all ages since early childhood. Each early picture is included in the face of the later pictures. Clarify that because Baldwin is older than his brother, he can remember more about his brother's early life and can intimately see the ways that life has affected his brother.

you were, Big James, named for me—you were a big baby, I was not—here you were: to be loved. To be loved, baby, hard, at once, and forever, to strengthen you against the loveless world. Remember that: I know how black it looks today, for you. It looked bad that day, too, yes, we were trembling. We have not stopped trembling yet, but if we had not loved each other none of us would have survived. And now you must survive because we love you, and for the sake of your children and your children's children. **B**

60   This innocent country set you down in a ghetto in which, in fact, it intended that you should perish. Let me spell out precisely what I mean by that, for the heart of the matter is here, and the root of my dispute with my country. You were born where you were born and faced the future that you faced because you were black and *for no other reason*. The limits of your ambition were, thus, expected to be set forever. You were born into a society which spelled out with brutal clarity, and in as many ways as possible, that you were a worthless human being. You were not expected to aspire to excellence: you were expected to make peace with **mediocrity**. Wherever you have turned, James, in your short time on this earth, you have been told where you could go and what you could do (and *how* you could do it) and where you could live and whom you could marry. I know your countrymen do not agree with me about this, and I hear them saying, "You exaggerate." They do not know Harlem, and I do. So do you. Take no one's word for anything, including mine—but trust your experience. **C**

    Know whence you came. If you know whence you came, there is really no limit to where you can go. The details and symbols of your life have been deliberately constructed to make you believe what white people say about you. Please try to remember that what they believe, as well as what they do and cause you to endure, does not testify to your inferiority but to their inhumanity and fear. Please try to be clear, dear James, through the storm which rages about your youthful head

80 today, about the reality which lies behind the words *acceptance* and *integration*. There is no reason for you to try to become like white people and there is no basis whatever for their **impertinent** assumption that *they* must accept *you*. The really terrible thing, old buddy, is that *you* must accept *them*. And I mean that very seriously. You must accept them and accept them with love. For these innocent people have no other hope. They are, in effect, still trapped in a history which they do not understand; and until they understand it, they cannot be released from it. They have had to believe for many years, and for innumerable reasons, that black men are inferior to white men. Many of them, indeed, know better, but, as you will discover, people find it very difficult to act on what they know.

90 To act is to be committed, and to be committed is to be in danger. In this case, the danger, in the minds of most white Americans, is the loss of their identity. Try to imagine how you would feel if you woke up one morning to find the sun shining and all the stars aflame. You would be frightened because it is out of the order of nature. Any upheaval in the universe is terrifying because it so profoundly attacks one's sense of one's own reality. Well, the black man has functioned in the white man's world as a fixed star, as an immovable pillar: and as he moves out of his place, heaven and earth are shaken to their foundations. You, don't be afraid. I said that it was intended that you should perish in the ghetto, perish by never

---

B RHETORICAL DEVICES
Identify words and phrases that are repeated in lines 52–59. What does this **repetition** contribute to the paragraph's impact?

mediocrity
(mē′dē-ŏk′rĭ-tē) *n.* lack of quality or excellence

C IDENTIFY IDEAS
Reread lines 60–73. In your opinion, which sentence best expresses the basis for Baldwin's anger? Explain your answer.

impertinent
(ĭm-pûr′tn-ənt) *adj.* rude; ill-mannered

LITERARY ANALYSIS

B RHETORICAL DEVICES

Possible answer: Repeated words and phrases include "here you came/were" (lines 49, 52–54), "to be loved" (line 54), "trembling" (lines 56–57), "survive(d)" (lines 57–58), and "children" (lines 58–59). *The repetition creates a rhythmic flow, and makes the ideas in the paragraph easier to remember and more poignant.*

READING STRATEGY

C IDENTIFY IDEAS

Possible answer: This sentence best expresses the basis for Baldwin's anger: "You were born into a society which spelled out with brutal clarity, and in as many ways as possible, that you were a worthless human being" (lines 65–66). *With this sentence, Baldwin explains that society has been wrongly tearing down African Americans' self-worth for a long time, which has caused them to feel worthless.*

FOR STRATEGIC READERS

Concept Support: Identify Ideas Discuss with students ideas from pages 1196–1197 that evoked emotional responses. Have students record their ideas in the prereading chart introduced on page 1193.

Baldwin's Sentence	Idea
"If you know . . ." (lines 74–75)	Once you understand your history, you can achieve any goal.

FOR ENGLISH LEARNERS

Comprehension: Text Structure Urge students to use Baldwin's repetition as a guide to the text structure. In lines 60–68, the repeated phrase *You were* appears at the beginning of several key ideas. In lines 76–80, students can use the phrase *Please try to* in the same way. Have students paraphrase each sentence or clause that begins with the repeated phrases.

FOR ADVANCED LEARNERS/AP

Evaluate [small-group option] Ask students to reread lines 89–90, and have small groups discuss these questions:

- Do people find it difficult to act on what they know? Why? Give some examples to support your opinion.

- Why can being committed to something lead to danger? What examples from history or from your previous reading demonstrate this point?

Activity In what way does this boy evoke Baldwin's nephew? *Possible answer: He is a young African-American boy who seems to be pondering serious issues.*

About the Art *Thinking* reflects the impressionistic influences felt by Barbados-born Carlton Murrell. Short strokes and vibrant color convey an image of the self-awareness Baldwin hopes his nephew will achieve.

Lines 99–105
REINFORCE *KEY IDEA:* SELF—WORTH

Discuss In what way does Baldwin describe his nephew's **self-worth?** In what way does he describe the self-worth of whites? *Possible answer: Baldwin describes his nephew's self-worth as healthy because so far, he has defeated the whites' intention for him (line 100). He suggests that whites are losing their sense of self-worth, "their grasp of reality" (line 102), as they observe African Americans defy low expectations.*

READING STRATEGY

D IDENTIFY IDEAS

Possible answer: Baldwin's explanation includes helping his white brothers to overcome their fears and ignorance. He redefines the term to make it an act of superior tolerance on the part of black people, rather than white people.

SELECTION WRAP—UP

SUMMARIZE Have students sum up the advice Baldwin gives to his nephew.

Thinking (1990), Carlton Murrell. Oil on board. Private collection. © Bridgeman Art Library.

being allowed to go behind the white man's definitions, by never being allowed to
100 spell your proper name. You have, and many of us have, defeated this intention; and, by a terrible law, a terrible paradox, those innocents who believed that your imprisonment made them safe are losing their grasp of reality. But these men are your brothers —your lost, younger brothers. And if the word *integration* means anything, this is what it means: that we, with love, shall force our brothers to see themselves as they are, to cease fleeing from reality and begin to change it. For this is your home, my friend, do not be driven from it; great men have done great things here, and will again, and we can make America what America must become. It will be hard, James, but you come from sturdy, peasant stock, men who picked cotton and dammed rivers and built railroads, and, in the teeth of[4]
110 the most terrifying odds, achieved an **unassailable** and monumental dignity. You come from a long line of great poets, some of the greatest poets since Homer. One of them said, *The very time I thought I was lost, My dungeon shook and my chains fell off.*[5] **D**

You know, and I know, that the country is celebrating one hundred years of freedom one hundred years too soon. We cannot be free until they are free. God bless you, James, and Godspeed.

Your uncle,
James

3 Targeted Passage

unassailable
(ŭn′ə-sā′lə-bəl) *adj.* undeniable

D IDENTIFY IDEAS
Reread Baldwin's definition of *integration* in lines 103–105. In what ways does his explanation differ from the usual meaning of this word?

---

4. **in the teeth of:** in spite of.
5. *The very time ... fell off:* a quotation from the traditional spiritual "My Dungeon Shook." It alludes to the Biblical story of Paul and Silas (Acts 16), who were freed from an unjust imprisonment by the action of an earthquake.

DIFFERENTIATED INSTRUCTION

FOR STRATEGIC READERS

3 Targeted Passage [Lines 103–115]

This passage shows Baldwin's hopes for his nephew, the way he encourages him, and his view of America.

- What does Baldwin ask his nephew to do?
- With what reasons does Baldwin encourage his nephew?
- How does Baldwin feel about America celebrating one hundred years of freedom?

FOR ENGLISH LEARNERS

Vocabulary: Multiple-Meaning Words Help students use context to clarify the meaning of these words and phrases as used in the selection:

- *stock* (line 108), "ancestry"
- *dammed* (line 109), "blocked by a dam"
- *monumental* (line 110), "great and lasting"
- *line* (line 111), "family history"

FOR ADVANCED LEARNERS/AP

Analyze Tone Ask students to analyze the tone of this letter. Have students first record examples from the letter that convey tone, and then identify that tone. *Possible answer: The tone is angry and bitter yet also optimistic.* Have students discuss whether they think Baldwin's chosen tone fits the message, and the ways in which a different tone would change his message. Invite students to share their conclusions with the class.

Comprehension

1. **Recall** In Baldwin's view, why was the boy's grandfather defeated?

2. **Recall** What does Baldwin say *acceptance* means?

3. **Clarify** What crime does Baldwin accuse his country of committing?

Literary Analysis

4. **Identify Ideas** Review the five sentences that you selected and your interpretations of them. Which one best expresses the message of this letter? Explain your answer.

5. **Examine Rhetorical Devices** Baldwin sums up the themes of his letter with two concluding **paradoxes.** Reread lines 114–115. What insight about the problem of race in America do these two statements convey?

6. **Analyze Audience** Baldwin addressed this **open letter** to his 15-year-old nephew but published it in his book *The Fire Next Time.* In each of the following passages, identify details that seem directed to the nephew and those directed to a wider audience. Based on your analysis, who do you think is the primary audience of this work? Support your answer with details.
   - Baldwin's memories of his brother (lines 20–33)
   - criticisms of his readers (lines 38–44)
   - his advice to his nephew (lines 78–84)
   - his description of whites' fears (lines 90–97)

7. **Compare Style** Baldwin shared many of Martin Luther King's values, goals, and religious influences. What is similar and different about the authors' styles? In your answer, consider each author's tone as well as his use of logical arguments, allusions, and rhetorical devices.

8. **Make Judgments** Consider Baldwin's solution to the problem of racism. In your opinion, does Baldwin's letter contain useful advice for protecting his nephew's **self-worth?** Explain your opinions.

9. **Evaluate Impact** Reread the background information on page 1194. In your opinion, why did Baldwin's criticisms hit home for so many? In your answer, consider the author's style, themes, and the historical context of his work.

Literary Criticism

10. **Critical Interpretations** In *Soul on Ice* (1968), black activist Eldridge Cleaver criticized James Baldwin for his "grueling, agonizing, total hatred of the blacks, particularly of himself" and his "shameful, fanatical, fawning, sycophantic love of the whites." Do you see any evidence to support these accusations? Explain your answer, citing details from Baldwin's letter.

Baldwin doesn't suggest ways to change whites' perceptions is not useful.

9. Baldwin's criticisms hit home for many because the anger they conveyed matched the national perspective on race issues during the 1960s. His emotional style and ability to evoke readers' emotions, using his own knowledge to convey racism's horror, also resonated.

10. This letter does not support Cleaver's criticism. Baldwin blames whites for destroying African-American lives (lines 31–33), explains that whites are inhuman and fearful (line 78), and says that whites must be forced to change (lines 104–105).

Practice and Apply

After Reading

Use these copy masters to check understanding and provide extra support:

R RESOURCE MANAGER—Copy Masters
Reading Check p. 194
Rhetorical Devices p. 187
Question Support p. 195

Additional selection questions are provided for teachers on page 181.

ANSWERS

1. *He internalized racist views of himself.*

2. *African Americans must accept the limitations of whites' understanding.*

3. *Baldwin accuses his country of destroying lives and not wanting to know about it.*

Possible answers:

4. ■ **SKILLS FOCUS Identify Ideas**
   This sentence expresses the letter's message: "We cannot be free . . . are free" (line 115). Answers should reflect the idea that whites have destroyed African-American lives, and that no Americans will be free until whites recognize this.

5. ● **SKILLS FOCUS Rhetorical Devices**
   Baldwin uses his concluding paradoxes to convey the insight that racism remains a problem in America because all Americans remain trapped by narrow views on race.

6. *Memories: Nephew: personal memories of his brother, Wider Audience: accuses countrymen of destroying African-American lives. Reader Criticisms: Nephew: "dear namesake," Wider Audience: reference to Dickens and "chorus of innocents." Advice: Nephew: don't become like whites, accept whites with love, Wider Audience: whites' "impertinent assumption." Whites' Fears: Nephew: don't feel inferior because whites are afraid. Wider Audience: most white Americans fear losing their identity. The primary audience for this letter is whites; the letter is a vehicle for the message.*

7. *Baldwin's tone is more confrontational and bitter than King's, and his arguments are more emotional than King's. Both use a range of allusions and rhetorical devices.*

8. *Advice to defy whites' definition (line 100) and to change the way whites view blacks (lines 103–105) is useful. The fact that*

ANSWERS

Vocabulary in Context

VOCABULARY PRACTICE

1. *(a) insolent*
2. *(a) ordinariness*
3. *(c) indisputable*
4. *(b) ferocious*
5. *(b) compose*

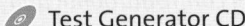 **RESOURCE MANAGER—Copy Master**
Vocabulary Practice p. 191

VOCABULARY IN WRITING

Suggest that students build on the sample sentence by discussing ways to handle various difficult situations.

VOCABULARY STRATEGY: IDIOMS *(also an EL language objective)*

Help students identify the main context clues in each sentence. In item 1, the main context clues are *pity* and *lost child.*

Possible answers:

1. *under his protection*
2. *out of trouble*
3. *made us laugh a lot*
4. *embarrassed*
5. *be critical*
6. *disdained*
7. *get right to the point*
8. *say something inappropriate*
9. *spoke directly without fear of the consequences*
10. *apologize and accept embarrassment*

RESOURCE MANAGER—Copy Master
Vocabulary Strategy p. 193

ⓘ Vocabulary Center at **ClassZone.com**
Additional Vocabulary Activities

Assess and Reteach

Assess

RESOURCE MANAGER—Copy Masters
Selection Test A pp. 197–198
Selection Test B/C pp. 199–200

💿 Test Generator CD

Reteach

STANDARDS LESSON FILE
Literature Lesson 35: Rhetorical Devices
Reading Lesson 4: Recognizing Main Idea
Vocabulary Lesson 22: Idioms

Vocabulary in Context

VOCABULARY PRACTICE

Choose the word that is closest in meaning to the boldfaced vocabulary word.

1. **impertinent:** (a) insolent, (b) impossible, (c) unfriendly
2. **mediocrity:** (a) ordinariness, (b) indifference, (c) complexity
3. **unassailable:** (a) landlocked, (b) unknown, (c) indisputable
4. **truculent:** (a) uncivilized, (b) ferocious, (c) boorish
5. **constitute:** (a) connect, (b) compose, (c) conclude

WORD LIST
constitute
impertinent
mediocrity
truculent
unassailable

VOCABULARY IN WRITING

What life advice might an older relative offer you? Write five sentences of advice, using each of the vocabulary words. Here is a sample sentence.

> **EXAMPLE SENTENCE**
> *Only rarely will you need to be **impertinent**; choose those situations carefully.*

VOCABULARY STRATEGY: IDIOMS

An **idiom** is an expression whose overall meaning is different from the meaning of the individual words that it includes. For example, in "My Dungeon Shook" Baldwin uses the expression *in the teeth of* to describe overcoming difficult odds.

If you encounter an unfamiliar idiom, use context clues to figure out its meaning or consult a dictionary. In many dictionaries, idioms are listed under the main word of the idiom, at the end of the entry. For example, *in the teeth of* would likely be found under *tooth,* as part of a list like this:

> **fight tooth and nail** fight fiercely; **put teeth into** make effective or forceful

PRACTICE Use context clues to write a definition for each boldfaced idiom. Use a dictionary if you need help.

1. Out of pity, he took the lost child **under his wing.**
2. No matter what trouble she's in, she always gets herself **off the hook.**
3. The puppy's playful antics **cracked us up.**
4. The meeting was a disaster, leaving us with **egg on our faces.**
5. You needn't **jump down my throat** for every little mistake.
6. Defiant to the end, he **thumbed his nose at** their offer of amnesty.
7. We don't have much time, so I'll **cut to the chase.**
8. Nervous and awkward, he always seemed to **put his foot in his mouth.**
9. She was a harsh critic who **pulled no punches.**
10. Once I discovered my mistake, all I could do was **eat crow.**

🔊 **VOCABULARY PRACTICE**
For more practice, go to the **Vocabulary Center** at **ClassZone.com.**

DIFFERENTIATED INSTRUCTION

FOR ENGLISH LEARNERS

Task Support: Vocabulary Practice [paired option] Point out the common suffixes *-ity* in *mediocrity* and *-able* in *unassailable.* Have pairs look up the meanings of the suffixes and discuss ways to use the definitions to build meaning for the words. Challenge pairs to identify words they know with these suffixes and then to use them in sentences.

FOR ADVANCED LEARNERS/AP

Idioms Challenge students to imagine they are Baldwin writing to his nephew, and have them use five of the idioms in sentences for a letter to young James. *Example: The whites cannot get off the hook so easily by simply celebrating our freedom.*

The March Toward Equality

In 1963, psychology professor Dr. Kenneth Clark conducted a series of interviews with Dr. Martin Luther King Jr., Malcolm X, and James Baldwin. Aired during a time of intense racial conflict, these interviews explored the differences in the ideals and world views of these three leading activists and thinkers. In his introduction to the interviews, Dr. Clark made this statement.

> "We have now come to the point where there are only two ways that America can avoid continued racial explosions. One would be total oppression. The other, total equality. There is no compromise. I believe, I hope, that we are on the threshold of a truly democratic America. It is not going to be easy to cross that threshold. But the achievement of the goals of justice, equality, and democracy for all American citizens involves the very destiny of our nation."

Writing to Persuade

Consider the state of civil rights in America today, in light of the goals and visions of the writers you have just read. In your opinion, have we reached total equality? Or would you say that we have arrived somewhere in between total equality and total oppression? Review the literature in this section and write a retrospective editorial in which you support a claim about whether or not the goals and visions of these writers have been realized.

Consider

- which ideas and details from the selections will help you articulate the vision of the civil rights leaders
- what stories, examples, or other details will help you support your view of civil rights in America today
- who your audience will be and what you want them to think or do
- how to express your viewpoint clearly and respectfully

Extension Online

INQUIRY & RESEARCH Use the Internet to **research** contemporary topics in civil rights. Look for news and commentary in mainstream and lesser-known publications, including private weblogs. Also look for Web sites of organizations devoted to advancing civil rights. Choose three issues that seem the most important or surprising to you and share them with your class.

 W1.1, W1.3

CALIFORNIA

Wrap-Up: Civil Rights & Protest Literature

This Wrap-Up provides students with an opportunity to revisit ideas from this section about the ways that civil rights activists created and defended their philosophies. What beliefs did activists hold? What strides were taken toward equality? What risks and sacrifices were necessary? Urge students to examine their own thinking in light of insights gained from the selections.

Writing to Persuade

- Review with students that *persuading* means convincing readers to adopt a viewpoint or to act. This skill helps writers share opinions and supporting evidence that can lead to social change.
- To help students create their editorials, suggest that they review contemporary media coverage of race relations in America. Students might also conduct interviews with people of varying cultural backgrounds, ages, and genders, in order to gather insights on the issue. Urge students to use their primary and secondary research to draw conclusions about the state of race relations in America. Then, help them compare their evidence and conclusions with the goals of such activists as King and Malcolm X.

Extension Online

- Remind students that civil rights is a global issue, not just an American issue. Encourage students to broaden their understanding by searching for international as well as domestic topics. To this end, direct students to Web sites such as www.hrweb.org/resource.htm/, which lists human rights organizations worldwide.
- Encourage students to use KWL charts to guide their studies. Before students share their findings with the class, encourage them to include why each issue is important or surprising in the *L* column of their charts.

 BEST PRACTICES TOOLKIT—Transparency
KWL: Know, Want to Know, Learned p. A21

FOR DEVELOPING WRITERS

Writing Support To help students organize their writing, suggest that they use the RAFT technique. Clarify students' role for this assignment as interpreters of history. Then, meet with students individually or in small groups to determine the best format for their discussions.

 BEST PRACTICES TOOLKIT—Transparency
RAFT: Role, Audience, Format, Topic p. C8

FOR ENGLISH LEARNERS

Writing Thesis Statements Provide the following models of thesis statements:

- Race relations in America have finally reached a state of total equality.
- Race relations in America teeter between total equality and total oppression.
- Race relations in America _____.

Point out language from the prompt in the first two samples. Recall that a thesis states an opinion that must be supported.

- analyze tone
- analyze and compare voice
- understand contemporary literature

 R3.3, R3.5

From Modern to Contemporary

Modern vs. Contemporary To help students understand this section, begin by asking volunteers to explain the difference between *modern* and *contemporary*. Use dictionary definitions to help students see that *contemporary* means "occurring at the present time or within a short span that includes the present." An event that happened more than a lifetime ago is not contemporary. *Modern* can refer to the present time, but it can also refer to a time period defined in various ways. For example, modern civilization defines a lengthy era that contrasts with ancient or medieval civilization. In literature, *modern* refers to a specific movement that had its heyday in the first half of the 20th century.

Ask students to name aspects of their lives that are contemporary, such as those that distinguish their lives and attitudes from those of previous generations.

Literary Analysis Workshop

R3.3, R3.5

Voice in Contemporary Literature

If you go into a bookstore and browse the "New Fiction" section, what types of books do you find? How are they different from literature of the past? Throughout this textbook, you have witnessed the evolution of American literature. Each period has been characterized by literary movements that determined the styles and themes in writing. What do you think the trends have been in your generation?

From Modern to Contemporary

The era of contemporary literature began around 1946, immediately after World War II. War has a way of changing a nation's literature because of its effects on an entire generation. Realism had risen from the ashes of the Civil War, while modernism had defined its vision through the ruins of World War I. After World War II, the development of the Cold War, the Vietnam War, and the civil violence of the 1960s, American literature changed again. Literature began to focus on personal experience as seen in the context of society. Writers began to address the emotional effects of wars, for example, as well as other issues of social, political, and cultural relevance.

Amy Tan

One of the most significant changes in American literature has been its increasing diversity—not only in forms and techniques, but in voices. With its history as the great "melting pot," the United States has been in a unique position to cultivate a literary community of authors from a wide variety of races, ethnicities, and religions. Increased publishing opportunities have given a public voice to more and more writers of African, Asian, Latino, and Native American descent, who often provide a new perspective on living in two cultures at once. Authors who have addressed such issues include Amy Tan, Sandra Cisneros, Rita Dove, Gwendolyn Brooks, Alice Walker, and N. Scott Momaday.

Rita Dove

N. Scott Momaday

Diverse Works, Common Ground

Several defining features set contemporary literature apart from the previous era of modernist literature.

Voice in literature is the expression of the writer's or narrator's personality. With its emphasis on personal experience, contemporary literature is often told from the first-person point of view, through a persona that represents the writer or main character. This persona has a distinctive personality that shapes a reader's experience with the text.

DIFFERENTIATED INSTRUCTION

For general guidelines on differentiating instruction, see

 BEST PRACTICES TOOLKIT
Differentiated Literature Instruction
pp. 31–38

FOR STRATEGIC READERS

Note Taking For students who are unfamiliar with voice in contemporary literature or need help with note taking, hand out the copy master before discussing these pages.

Explain that students will be learning terms and concepts related to contemporary literature in this workshop. Discuss these terms and concepts (*contemporary, voice, persona, tone, irony, humor, social context, social criticism*) as students record notes on the copy master.

 RESOURCE MANAGER—Copy Master
Note Taking p. 201

Tone is the attitude that a writer takes toward a subject. For the modernists, the numbing effects of the early 20th century led to a detached, unemotional tone. For example, Prufrock's failure at the end of T. S. Eliot's poem (page 930) is conveyed in a matter-of-fact tone that is sympathetic but distant. Compare this modernist aloofness to Tim O'Brien's Vietnam story "Ambush" (page 1138). The tone of this contemporary story is one of engagement rather than detachment.

> I did not hate the young man; I did not see him as the enemy; I did not ponder issues of morality or politics or military duty. I crouched and kept my head low. I tried to swallow whatever was rising from my stomach, which tasted like lemonade, something fruity and sour. I was terrified.
>
> —Tim O'Brien, "Ambush"

Close Read

How would you characterize the narrator of this passage? Do you think he would be personable? distant? intimidating?

As a rule, modernist writers did not view the irony of life as humorous; instead, they often expressed defeat in the face of life's irony. Contemporary writers, however, look at the absurdity of such situations as a cause for humor, which may then be expressed through an **ironic** presentation of characters and events.

Modernist writers typically viewed the individual in isolation, whereas contemporary writers present the individual in relation to the larger social context. Often contemporary writers hint at **social criticism.** They present a situation with only a suggestion of the social obstacles, and the reader must infer the writer's opinion. In her poem "Primer for Blacks" (page 1233), Gwendolyn Brooks encourages African Americans to appreciate their heritage. Note the unspoken message about social barriers for African Americans that Brooks conveys in this passage.

> Blackness
> is a title,
> is a preoccupation,
> is a commitment Blacks
> are to comprehend—
> and in which you are
> to perceive your Glory.
>
> —Gwendolyn Brooks, "Primer for Blacks"

Close Read

What is the social barrier for African Americans that Brooks wants her reader to infer?

Brooks is making an argument for self-respect and self-esteem among African Americans. However, she does not state what she is arguing against; she leaves it up to the reader to infer the social barriers she is addressing.

LITERARY ANALYSIS WORKSHOP **1203**

Diverse Works, Common Ground

Ironic Humor To emphasize the ironic humor prominent in contemporary culture, ask students to name movies or television shows that make fun of authorities such as political leaders, parents, or police. Point out that since the Vietnam War there has been a marked increase in cynicism about authority in American society. Those who doubt the wisdom of authority often use ironic humor to question or criticize its views. Thus, humor becomes a form of social criticism. This approach to social criticism appears in antiwar novels such as Joseph Heller's *Catch-22* and Kurt Vonnegut's *Slaughterhouse Five,* which students read about on page 1098 of the historical essay.

Close Read

Possible answer: The narrator is personable because he is honest and descriptive about his feelings. On the other hand, the fact that the narrator is a combat soldier makes him intimidating.

Close Read

Possible answer: The implied social barrier consists of negative stereotypes or attitudes concerning race and color.

If students need help ... Point out words such as "title" and "preoccupation" that suggest definitions or stereotypes, and words such as "comprehend" and "perceive" that suggest the attitudes that create stereotypes.

FOR ENGLISH LEARNERS

Language: Skill Words Help students understand the meanings of these terms:

- *generation,* "all the people born within a few years of each other"
- *relevance,* "importance to the topic that is being discussed"
- *diversity,* "variety"
- *personality,* "a person's individual character"

- *isolation,* "separation from others"
- *self-esteem,* "liking oneself, having a good opinion of oneself"

FOR ADVANCED LEARNERS/AP

Literature of Social Criticism Literary social criticism has made a significant contribution to social awareness throughout American history. Have students research and report on socially critical authors such as John Steinbeck, Clifford Odets, Sinclair Lewis, Upton Sinclair, and Frank Norris. Ask them to identify similarities and differences in the issues and styles these authors' works reflect.

Focus and Motivate

OBJECTIVES

Literary Analysis
- explore the key idea of **languages**
- analyze a personal essay
- read an essay

Reading
- identify main idea and supporting details

Grammar and Writing
- use informal language to create an appropriate conversational style
- write a personal essay

CALIFORNIA R3.1, W1.1, W1.2, W1.9, W2.3

ABOUT THE AUTHOR

Clarify that both of Amy Tan's parents were Chinese-born immigrants. Ask students to identify details in Tan's life that reflect her ethnic heritage. *Possible answer: She has written authentic and insightful portrayals of Chinese history and Chinese-American culture.* Tell students that the essay they are about to read expresses Tan's view of the ways language reflects cultural identity.

USING THE *NOTABLE QUOTE*

Read **Amy Tan's** quote aloud. Have students explain its meaning and how the quote relates to Tan's work. *Possible answer: Our memories are the raw material for the stories or fantasies that we imagine. Tan has written about her own cultural heritage and used her family experiences as the starting point for fiction.*

Selection Resources

CALIFORNIA

R3.1, W1.1 (p. 1213), W1.2 (p. 1213), W1.9 (p. 1213), W2.3 (p. 1213)

NOTABLE QUOTE
"Memory feeds imagination."

FYI
Did you know that Amy Tan . . .

- plays in a band called the Rock Bottom Remainders with Stephen King and other literary celebrities?
- has visited the White House five times?
- has had her works translated into more than 20 languages?

Author On|ine

For more on Amy Tan, visit the **Literature Center** at **ClassZone.com**.

Mother Tongue

Essay by Amy Tan

Amy Tan
born 1952

In 1989, Amy Tan's first book, *The Joy Luck Club*, spent 40 weeks on the *New York Times* bestseller list. Praised for its authentic dialogue and its rich portrayal of Chinese history, the book established Tan as an insightful chronicler of the Chinese-American experience and of the fierce and conflicted love between mothers and daughters.

Troubled Times Born in Oakland, California in 1952, Tan spent her early childhood in the San Francisco Bay area. She enjoyed her first literary success at the age of eight, winning first prize in an elementary school contest for her essay "What My Library Means to Me." Six years later, Tan's life took a tragic turn when both her father and her brother died from brain tumors. Her grief-stricken mother moved teenaged Amy and her surviving brother to Europe, settling in Montreux, Switzerland, where Tan graduated from high school in 1969.

Although her mother had pushed her to become a neurosurgeon, the rebellious Tan defied her mother's wishes and studied literature and linguistics in college. In 1974, she enrolled in a doctoral program in linguistics, but she abandoned her studies after a close friend was murdered. Tan then put her expertise to work as a language development consultant for programs serving disabled children. Five years later, she adopted a new career as a freelance technical writer.

Confronting the Past Tan took up writing fiction as a form of therapy, hoping to curb her workaholic tendencies. Her first short story, "End Game," appeared in *Seventeen* magazine, bringing her to the attention of prominent literary agent Sandra Dijkstra. With Dijkstra's encouragement, Tan began writing a series of stories that evolved into *The Joy Luck Club*. For this tightly woven collection of short stories, Tan drew upon her personal story, exploring the generational and cultural gap between Chinese mothers and their American-born daughters.

Two years later, Tan published her second book, *The Kitchen God's Wife,* a novel inspired by her mother's life in China. Though she switched her focus from mother-daughter love to sisterhood in her third novel, *The Hundred Secret Senses,* she once again drew on her mother's life story in her fourth, *The Bonesetter's Daughter.* As Tan explains, "My books have amounted to taking her stories—a gift to me—and giving them back to her. To me, it was the ultimate thing I ever could have done for myself and my mother."

1204

 RESOURCE MANAGER UNIT 6

Plan and Teach pp. 203–210

Literary Analysis
Summary pp. 211†*, 212‡*
Personal Essay pp. 213, 214†*
Question Support p. 218*

Reading
Identify Main Ideas pp. 215, 216†*
Reading Check p. 217

Grammar and Writing
Use Appropriate Language p. 219

Assessment
Selection Tests A, B/C
   pp. 221*, 223*
Test Generator CD

 BEST PRACTICES TOOLKIT

Differentiated Instruction
   pp. 31–38*

Scaffolding Instruction
   pp. 43–46*

Graphic Organizers/Strategies
New Word Analysis • Two-Column Chart • Freewriting

Reading Support
Audio Anthology CD*

Technology
Literature and Writing Centers at **ClassZone.com**
WriteSmart CD

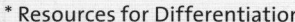 * Resources for Differentiation   † Also in Spanish   ‡ In Haitian Creole and Vietnamese

● LITERARY ANALYSIS: PERSONAL ESSAY

Amy Tan could have written a research paper to get across her points about language and cultural identity. Instead, she chose to write a **personal essay,** where she combines her insights on the topic with details from her own life.

Just last week, as I was walking down the street with [my mother], I again found myself conscious of the English I was using, the English I do use with her.

Unlike a scholarly paper or a newspaper article, a personal essay gives you a snapshot of the writer's life or personality as well as his or her thoughts on a specific topic. As you read this essay, note how Tan connects her ideas about the power of language with her own experiences.

■ READING SKILL: IDENTIFY MAIN IDEAS

Amy Tan's essay is organized into a series of paragraphs, most of which develop one **main idea,** or central point. Facts, descriptions, or examples that are related to the main idea are called **supporting details.** When a main idea is not directly stated, you can figure it out by asking yourself how these supporting details fit together.

Amy Tan uses vivid supporting details to make her points. As you read, use a diagram like the one shown to record the main idea of each paragraph and list its supporting details.

What LANGUAGES *do you speak?*

KEY IDEA Think about how you change the way you speak based on where you are and whom you're with. You might use slang when talking with friends but polite, formal language with adults. You might speak English at school and another language at home. In "Mother Tongue," you will read one writer's thoughts on her own different **languages.**

QUICKWRITE Make a list of places and situations where you use a different language or way of speaking. Then, for each situation, write a brief quotation that captures the sound of the language you use in that context.

1205

What LANGUAGES *do you speak?*

Read the question aloud and list students' answers. Read the **KEY IDEA** to introduce the concept that people who only speak one language may, through varied usage, in fact speak many different **languages.** After students complete the **QUICKWRITE,** invite them to share their examples.

SKILLS FOCUS

LITERARY ANALYSIS R3.1

● PERSONAL ESSAY

Clarify that in a personal essay, details and insights are often blended almost seamlessly. Ask students to identify the personal details and insights in the excerpt from Amy Tan's essay. *Possible answer: Personal details include Tan walking down the street with her mother and Tan speaking differently with her mother than elsewhere. Her insight is that she uses different kinds of English in different situations.*

CHECK UNDERSTANDING Have students write a sentence that combines an insight with details from their own lives.

READING SKILL

■ IDENTIFY MAIN IDEAS

Ask students to identify the main idea of the first paragraph under **Confronting the Past** on page 1204. *Possible answer: Tan began to write as an emotional outlet and in response to her personal experience as a Chinese American.*

CHECK UNDERSTANDING Ask students what steps they used to determine the main idea of the paragraph.

 RESOURCE MANAGER—Copy Master
Identify Main Ideas p. 215 (for student use while reading the selection)

DIFFERENTIATED INSTRUCTION

FOR STRATEGIC READERS
Vocabulary Support

- *research,* "finding information by looking it up in books or other sources"

- *identity,* "who a person is, as an individual or a member of a group"

- *insights,* "ideas that make a topic clearer"

Concept Support: Personal Essay Differentiate personal essays from other kinds of essays people write. In a personal essay, writers usually address their own experiences, thoughts, and feelings, often using the first-person voice and informal language. In other kinds of essays, such as persuasive essays, writers try to convince readers to adopt a certain view. In critical essays, writers analyze a topic and argue a particular understanding of it.

SUMMARY

In this essay, Amy Tan reflects on the different "Englishes" she uses in different contexts, focusing largely on the English she speaks with her mother. Tan's mother, articulate in Chinese, speaks a kind of English that limits her interactions with authorities such as her stockbroker and doctors reviewing her medical tests. Tan, although viewing her mother's English as clear and direct, sees the need to use standard English to succeed in American society. She extends her discussion to the linguistic problems the children of immigrants may have in school and concludes with appreciation for all the "Englishes" she speaks.

LITERARY ANALYSIS

Ⓐ PERSONAL ESSAY

Possible answer: *In the essay's opening lines, readers learn that the author is a writer who is fascinated by the many uses of language.*

If students need help . . . Point out the many sentences that begin with "I" or "I am . . . ." Help students list the qualities that Amy Tan ascribes to herself.

Lines 11–15
REINFORCE *KEY IDEA:* LANGUAGES

Discuss In what way does Tan's reaction as she gives her talk reflect her experience of speaking many **languages?** Explain. *Possible answer: When Tan realizes that her mother is at the talk, she feels strange because she is speaking a different English than the one she usually speaks with her mother.*

Mother Tongue

Amy Tan

I am not a scholar of English or literature. I cannot give you much more than personal opinions on the English language and its variations in this country or others.

I am a writer. And by that definition, I am someone who has always loved language. I am fascinated by language in daily life. I spend a great deal of my time thinking about the power of language—the way it can evoke an emotion, a visual image, a complex idea, or a simple truth. Language is the tool of my trade. And I use them all—all the Englishes I grew up with. Ⓐ

Recently, I was made keenly aware of the different Englishes I do use. I was
10 giving a talk to a large group of people, the same talk I had already given to half a dozen other groups. The talk was about my writing, my life, and my book, *The Joy Luck Club,* and it was going along well enough, until I remembered one major difference that made the whole talk sound wrong. My mother was in the room. And it was perhaps the first time she had heard me give a lengthy speech, using the kind of English I have never used with her. I was saying things like "the intersection of memory and imagination" and "There is an aspect of my fiction that relates to thus-and-thus"—a speech filled with carefully wrought grammatical phrases, burdened, it suddenly seemed to me, with nominalized[1] forms, past perfect tenses, conditional phrases, forms of standard English that I had learned
20 in school and through books, the forms of English I did not use at home with my mother.

---

1. **nominalized** (nŏm′ə-nəl-īz′d) **forms:** nouns formed from other parts of speech.

ANALYZE VISUALS
In this painting, the artist represents an apple in three different ways. What point about language might the artist be making?

Ⓐ PERSONAL ESSAY
Reread lines 1–8. What do you learn about the author in these opening lines?

 Targeted Passage

Apple (1983), Andy Warhol. Synthetic polymer paint and silkscreen ink on canvas, 14″ × 11″. © 2007 The Andy Warhol Foundation for the Visual Arts/Artists Rights Society (ARS), New York. © The Andy Warhol Foundation, Inc./Art Resource, New York.

DIFFERENTIATED INSTRUCTION

FOR ALL STUDENTS
Provide these independent projects to extend the lesson:

- Dramatize interaction between different "Englishes."

- Debate views on standard English.

- Write an essay evaluating Tan's theme and style.

For further details on these projects, see

Ｒ RESOURCE MANAGER
  Ideas for Extension pp. 208–209

FOR STRATEGIC READERS
In combination with the *Audio Anthology CD,* use one or more Targeted Passages (pp. 1206, 1209, 1210, 1211) to ensure that students focus on key events and concepts in the selection. Targeted Passages are also good for English learners.

ANALYZE VISUALS

Possible answer: The artist might be making the point that the same essential meaning can be expressed in many linguistic and nonlinguistic ways.

About the Art Andy Warhol (1928–1987) was the most famous Pop artist of the 1960s. Pop artists used images from mass media in their work and tried to blur the difference between fine art and commercial images such as book covers or ads. This silkscreen painting shows different ways to signify *apple*. Similarly, Tan's essay shows that there are many ways of expressing an idea.

BACKGROUND

Immigration Patterns In the past century, patterns of immigration to the United States have changed. Until the early 1900s, most immigrants came from Europe. Since the 1960s, however, over 80 percent of immigrants have come from non-European homelands, with 25 percent from Asia alone. This new pattern of immigration has changed the ethnic composition of the nation, with nonwhite ethnic groups forming a majority of the population in Tan's childhood state of California.

---

① Targeted Passage [Lines 9–15]

This passage describes how Tan became aware that she uses different "Englishes."

- Where was Amy Tan when she became aware of using different "Englishes"? What was she doing?

- In what way did Tan's mother contribute to Tan's moment of awareness?

- What does the phrase "different Englishes" mean?

FOR ENGLISH LEARNERS

Key Academic Vocabulary Use New Word Analysis to teach these words: *visual* (line 6), *aspect* (line 16), *quote* (line 32), *grade* (line 113), *challenge* (line 157).

 BEST PRACTICES TOOLKIT—Transparency New Word Analysis p. E8

Prereading For prereading instruction for English learners, see

 BEST PRACTICES TOOLKIT Scaffolding Reading Instruction pp. 43–46

FOR ADVANCED LEARNERS/AP

AP exercises in the bottom channel provide additional challenge for students. Use these suggestions for small groups or individuals.

ADDITIONAL GUIDELINES

For more help with differentiation and tips for classroom management, see

 BEST PRACTICES TOOLKIT Differentiated Instruction pp. 31–38

Just last week, as I was walking down the street with her, I again found myself conscious of the English I was using, the English I do use with her. We were talking about the price of new and used furniture, and I heard myself saying this: "Not waste money that way." My husband was with us as well, and he didn't notice any switch in my English. And then I realized why. It's because over the twenty years we've been together I've often used that same kind of English with him, and sometimes he even uses it with me. It has become our language of intimacy, a different sort of English that relates to family talk, the language I grew 30 up with.

So that you'll have some idea of what this family talk sounds like, I'll quote what my mother said during a conversation that I videotaped and then transcribed. During this conversation, she was talking about a political gangster in Shanghai who had the same last name as her family's, Du, and how in his early years the gangster wanted to be adopted by her family, who were rich by comparison. Later, the gangster became more powerful, far richer than my mother's family, and he showed up at my mother's wedding to pay his respects. Here's what she said in part: **B**

"Du Yusong having business like fruit stand. Like off-the-street kind. He is Du 40 like Du Zong—but not Tsung-ming Island[2] people. The local people call *putong.* The river east side, he belong to that side local people. That man want to ask Du Zong father take him in like become own family. Du Zong father wasn't look down on him, but didn't take seriously, until that man big like become a mafia. Now important person, very hard to inviting him. Chinese way, came only to show respect, don't stay for dinner. Respect for making big celebration, he shows up. Mean gives lots of respect. Chinese custom. Chinese social life that way. If too important won't have to stay too long. He come to my wedding. I didn't see, I heard it. I gone to boy's side, they have YMCA dinner. Chinese age I was nineteen."

You should know that my mother's expressive command of English belies how 50 much she actually understands. She reads the *Forbes*[3] report, listens to *Wall Street Week,* converses daily with her stockbroker, reads Shirley MacLaine's books[4] with ease—all kinds of things I can't begin to understand. Yet some of my friends tell me they understand fifty percent of what my mother says. Some say they understand eighty to ninety percent. Some say they understand none of it, as if she were speaking pure Chinese. But to me, my mother's English is perfectly clear, perfectly natural. It's my mother tongue. Her language, as I hear it, is vivid, direct, full of observation and imagery. That was the language that helped shape the way I saw things, expressed things, made sense of the world. **C**

Lately I've been giving more thought to the kind of English my mother speaks. 60 Like others, I have described it to people as "broken" or "fractured" English. But I wince when I say that. It has always bothered me that I can think of no way to describe it other than "broken," as if it were damaged and needed to be fixed, as if

---

2. **Tsung-ming** (tsŏŏng-mĭng) **Island:** an island near the mouth of the Yangtze River, near Shanghai, in eastern China.

3. *Forbes:* a financial magazine.

4. **Shirley MacLaine's books:** works by the American actress Shirley MacLaine (born 1934), many of which deal with reincarnation.

DIFFERENTIATED INSTRUCTION

FOR ENGLISH LEARNERS

Vocabulary: Cognates [mixed-readiness groups] Point out that the Spanish cognate *conversación* is similar to the English word *conversation* (line 32). Organize students who speak Latin-based languages in groups. Challenge groups to find at least five other words in the essay that are similar to words in their languages. Invite groups to merge their lists into a master list for class use.

FOR ADVANCED LEARNERS/AP

Compare and Contrast Have students obtain a copy of Tan's novel *The Joy Luck Club.* Assign individual students or small groups to read those chapters narrated by the fictional daughters. Then as a single group, have students compare and contrast the mother-daughter relationship depicted in the novel with the one depicted in Tan's essay. Have students report their conclusions to the class and note how reading Tan's essay affected their reading or rereading of *The Joy Luck Club.*

it lacked a certain wholeness and soundness. I've heard other terms used, "limited English," for example. But they seem just as bad, as if everything is limited, including people's perceptions of the limited-English speaker.

I know this for a fact, because when I was growing up, my mother's "limited" English limited my perception of her. I was ashamed of her English. I believed that her English reflected the quality of what she had to say. That is, because she expressed them imperfectly, her thoughts were imperfect. And I had plenty of
70 empirical evidence[5] to support me: the fact that people in department stores, at banks, and in restaurants did not take her seriously, did not give her good service, pretended not to understand her, or even acted as if they did not hear her. **D**

My mother has long realized the limitations of her English as well. When I was a teenager, she used to have me call people on the phone and pretend I was she. In this guise, I was forced to ask for information or even to complain and yell at people who had been rude to her. One time it was a call to her stockbroker in New York. She had cashed out her small portfolio, and it just so happened we were going to New York the next week, our first trip outside California. I had to get on the phone and say in an adolescent voice that was not very convincing, "This is Mrs. Tan."

80 My mother was standing in the back whispering loudly, "Why he don't send me check, already two weeks late. So mad he lie to me, losing me money."

And then I said in perfect English on the phone, "Yes, I'm getting rather concerned. You had agreed to send the check two weeks ago, but it hasn't arrived."

Then she began to talk more loudly. "What he want, I come to New York tell him front of his boss, you cheating me?" And I was trying to calm her down, make her be quiet, while telling the stockbroker, "I can't tolerate any more excuses. If I don't receive the check immediately, I am going to have to speak to your manager when I'm in New York next week." And sure enough, the following week, there we were in front of this astonished stockbroker, and I was sitting there
90 red-faced and quiet, and my mother, the real Mrs. Tan, was shouting at his boss in her impeccable broken English.

We used a similar routine more recently, for a situation that was far less humorous. My mother had gone to the hospital for an appointment to find out about a CAT scan[6] she had had a month earlier. She said she had spoken very good English, her best English, no mistakes. Still, she said, the hospital did not apologize when they informed her they had lost the CAT scan and she had come for nothing. She said they did not seem to have any sympathy when she told them she was anxious to know the exact diagnosis, since her husband and her son had died of brain tumors. She said they would not give her any more information
100 until the next time and she would have to make another appointment for that. So she said she would not leave until the doctor called her daughter. She wouldn't budge. And when the doctor finally called her daughter, me, who spoke in perfect English—lo and behold—we had assurances the CAT scan would be found, promises that a conference call on Monday would be held, and apologies for any suffering my mother had gone through for a most regrettable mistake.

---

5. **empirical evidence:** evidence derived from observation.
6. **CAT scan:** a three-dimensional image of structures inside the human body.

---

② **Targeted Passage**

D PERSONAL ESSAY
Reread lines 59–72. Explain Tan's point about the term "broken English." What personal experiences does she draw on to make her point?

D PERSONAL ESSAY

Possible answer: For Tan, the term "broken" implies there is something flawed or lacking about the speaker. She believes this term shapes the way people perceive those who are not fluent in English. She draws on her childhood perceptions of her mother to make this point.

Lines 92–105
TIERED DISCUSSION PROMPTS
Use these prompts to help students understand Mrs. Tan's problem at the hospital:

Summarize In what way did language cause a problem over Mrs. Tan's CAT scan? How was the problem resolved? *Possible answers: When Mrs. Tan tried to get her results using her own kind of English, she was treated disrespectfully. She resolved the problem by having Amy ask for her in standard English.*

Interpret What general point is Tan making through this anecdote? *Possible answer: Tan is saying that people's use of language affects the way others treat them.*

Synthesize How might the problem Tan highlights be affected by the increasing number of immigrants in American cities? *Possible answer: The problem will likely get worse as the number of immigrants increases. At the same time, as native English speakers meet more English learners, they may adjust their assumptions.*

FOR STRATEGIC READERS

② **Targeted Passage [Lines 66–79]**

This passage describes Tan's youthful responses to her mother's limited English.

- As a child, what did Tan feel about her mother's English?
- Why did she feel this way?
- In what ways did people treat Mrs. Tan because of her English?
- What did Tan do to help her mother communicate with people on the phone?

FOR ADVANCED LEARNERS/AP

Compare and Contrast Characters Have students use a Two-Column Chart like the one begun here to compare and contrast Amy Tan's and Mrs. Tan's experiences. Have students share their charts and describe the difference they think language made in the two women's lives.

Amy Tan	Mrs. Tan
Is treated respect-fully by people in offices	Is treated disrespect-fully by people in offices

 BEST PRACTICES TOOLKIT—Transparency
Two-Column Chart p. A25

E PERSONAL ESSAY

Possible answer: Tan believes that her mother's limited English affected her own linguistic development, making her English skills weaker than some of her peers'. Also, her mother encouraged Tan to think creatively and find many ways of looking at things, whereas tests demanded one answer that was usually not creative.

Extend the Discussion Should immigrant parents require their children to speak English at home? Why or why not?

Lines 130–144
TIERED DISCUSSION PROMPTS

Use these prompts to help students understand Tan's point about testing:

Connect Are there kinds of tests that you find easier than others? Which ones, and why? *Students' responses should show familiarity with and critical thinking about the topic of testing.*

Analyze What kept Tan from doing well on analogy test questions? *Possible answer: She was imaginative and therefore she thought of unexpected answers.*

Evaluate Are the traits Tan reveals about herself positive or negative? Explain.
Possible answer: Tan's traits are positive in that she shows her imaginative style of intelligence and her individuality. They are negative in that they diminish her ability to succeed on certain kinds of tests.

I think my mother's English almost had an effect on limiting my possibilities in life as well. Sociologists and linguists probably will tell you that a person's developing language skills are more influenced by peers than by family. But I do think that the language spoken in the family, especially in immigrant families
110 which are more insular,[7] plays a large role in shaping the language of the child. And I believe that it affected my results on achievement tests, IQ tests, and the SAT. While my English skills were never judged poor, compared with math, English could not be considered my strong suit. In grade school I did moderately well, getting perhaps B's, sometimes B-pluses, in English and scoring perhaps in the sixtieth or seventieth percentile on achievement tests. But those scores were not good enough to override the opinion that my true abilities lay in math and science, because in those areas I achieved A's and scored in the ninetieth percentile or higher.

This was understandable. Math is precise; there is only one correct answer. Whereas, for me at least, the answers on English tests were always a judgment call,
120 a matter of opinion and personal experience. Those tests were constructed around items like fill-in-the-blank sentence completion, such as, "Even though Tom was _____, Mary thought he was_____." And the correct answer always seemed to be the most bland combinations, for example, "Even though Tom was shy, Mary thought he was charming," with the grammatical structure "even though" limiting the correct answer to some sort of semantic opposites,[8] so you wouldn't get answers like, "Even though Tom was foolish, Mary thought he was ridiculous." Well, according to my mother, there were very few limitations as to what Tom could have been and what Mary might have thought of him. So I never did well on tests like that. **E**

130 The same was true with word analogies, pairs of words for which you were supposed to find some sort of logical semantic relationship, for instance, "Sunset is to nightfall as _____ is to_____." And here you would be presented with a list of four possible pairs, one of which showed the same kind of relationship: *red* is to *stoplight, bus* is to *arrival, chills* is to *fever, yawn* is to *boring*. Well, I could never think that way. I knew what the tests were asking, but I could not block out of my mind the images already created by the first pair, *sunset* is to *nightfall*—and I would see a burst of colors against a darkening sky, the moon rising, the lowering of a curtain of stars. And all the other pairs of words—*red, bus, stoplight, boring*— just threw up a mass of confusing images, making it impossible for me to see
140 that saying "A sunset precedes nightfall" was as logical as saying "A chill precedes a fever." The only way I would have gotten that answer right was to imagine an associative situation,[9] such as my being disobedient and staying out past sunset, catching a chill at night, which turned into feverish pneumonia as punishment— which indeed did happen to me.

I have been thinking about all this lately, about my mother's English, about achievement tests. Because lately I've been asked, as a writer, why there are not more Asian-Americans represented in American literature. Why are

③ Targeted Passage

E PERSONAL ESSAY
Reread lines 107–129. According to Tan, in what ways did her mother's use of English influence her own performance on standardized tests?

---

7. **insular:** isolated.
8. **semantic opposites:** words opposite in meaning.
9. **associative situation:** a circumstance or story based on mental connections.

DIFFERENTIATED INSTRUCTION

FOR STRATEGIC READERS
③ Targeted Passage [Lines 106–120]

This passage describes the ways Tan believes her mother's use of English affected Tan's school performance.

- In what ways does Tan think immigrant parents affect their children's English?
- Which subjects was Tan good at in school, and at which was she weak?
- What explains the discrepancy?

FOR ENGLISH LEARNERS
Culture: Clarify Explain that *achievement tests* (line 111), now known as SAT Subject Tests, examine accumulated knowledge in areas such as English, history, and math. Results include a ranking by percentile to show how an individual student performed relative to others taking the test. Tan's scores in the "ninetieth percentile" mean that she scored higher than 90 percent of those taking the test. *Analogies* (line 130), once a very common item on standardized tests, present a relationship between

two ideas, then ask students to choose the answer option that reflects the same relationship. In Tan's example, that relationship is sequence, but analogies can also reflect relationships such as opposites or parts of a whole. The IQ and the SAT (line 111) are both aptitude tests that suggest a person's intelligence and potential for critical thinking.

there few Asian-Americans enrolled in creative writing programs? Why do so many Chinese students go into engineering? Well, these are broad sociological

150 questions I can't begin to answer. But I have noticed in surveys—in fact, just last week—that Asian-American students, as a whole, do significantly better on math achievement tests than on English tests. And this makes me think that there are other Asian-American students whose English spoken in the home might also be described as "broken" or "limited." And perhaps they also have teachers who are steering them away from writing and into math and science, which is what happened to me.

Fortunately, I happen to be rebellious and enjoy the challenge of disproving assumptions made about me. I became an English major my first year in college, after being enrolled as pre-med. I started writing nonfiction as a freelancer the

160 week after I was told by my boss at the time that writing was my worst skill and I should hone my talents toward account management. **F**

But it wasn't until 1985 that I began to write fiction. At first I wrote using what I thought to be wittily crafted sentences, sentences that would finally prove I had mastery over the English language. Here's an example from the first draft of a story that later made its way into *The Joy Luck Club,* but without this line: "That was my mental quandary in its nascent state."[10] A terrible line, which I can barely pronounce.

Fortunately, for reasons I won't get into here, I later decided I should envision a reader for the stories I would write. And the reader I decided on was my mother,

170 because these were stories about mothers. So with this reader in mind—and in fact she did read my early drafts—I began to write stories using all the Englishes I grew up with: the English I spoke to my mother, which for lack of a better term might be described as "simple"; the English she used with me, which for lack of a better term might be described as "broken"; my translation of her Chinese, which could certainly be described as "watered down"; and what I imagined to be her translation of her Chinese if she could speak in perfect English, her internal language, and for that I sought to preserve the essence, but neither an English nor a Chinese structure. I wanted to capture what language ability tests can never reveal: her intent, her passion, her imagery, the rhythms of her speech and the

180 nature of her thoughts.

Apart from what any critic had to say about my writing, I knew I had succeeded where it counted when my mother finished reading my book and gave me her verdict: "So easy to read." ☙

❹ Targeted Passage

F MAIN IDEAS
Identify the main idea of lines 157–161. What details support this main idea?

---

10. **my mental quandary . . . state:** my mental predicament in its earliest form.

F MAIN IDEAS

Possible answer: Main idea: Tan is rebellious. Supporting details: She enrolled in college as pre-med but then became an English major; she started writing seriously after her boss told her that she was a bad writer.

If students need help . . . Remind students that main ideas are often stated in the first sentence of a paragraph.

Lines 162–167
REINFORCE *KEY IDEA:* LANGUAGES

Discuss Which of Tan's **languages** does the line she quotes represent? What does she feel about that language? What broader lesson does her response contain about writing? *Possible answer: The quoted line reflects Tan's early attempt to impress readers with her language ability. She now finds that language pretentious. The lesson is to write simply, clearly, and naturally.*

SELECTION WRAP-UP

SUMMARIZE Ask students to state Tan's ideas about the value of different levels of language.

★ CRITIQUE

- Ask students which of Tan's arguments they found most, or least, compelling.

- After completing the After Reading questions on page 1212, have students revisit their responses and tell whether they have changed their opinions.

FOR STRATEGIC READERS

❹ Targeted Passage [Lines 168–183]

This passage reflects Tan's view that accepting her mother's English helped her as a writer.

- What kinds of English did Tan use in her stories? Who was her imagined audience?

- What did Tan try to do when translating her mother's Chinese into English?

- What did her mother say about her stories? What did Tan feel in response?

FOR ENGLISH LEARNERS

Vocabulary: Idioms and Phrasal Verbs Help students use context clues to determine the meanings of these expressions: *lo and behold* (line 103), "that's unexpected"; *strong suit* (line 113), "activity someone is good at"; *judgment call* (line 119), "a close decision that rests on the individual's viewpoint"; *get into* (line 168), "talk much about"; *where it counted* (line 182), "when it mattered."

FOR ADVANCED LEARNERS/AP

Synthesize Urge students to learn about current testing practices and controversies in their community. Ask students to discuss ways that test-taking skills have helped or hindered them. Invite students to use their research and personal experiences to write one-page essays that analyze flaws and genuine uses for testing. Encourage students to propose alternatives to current practices.

Practice and Apply

After Reading

Use these copy masters to check understanding and provide extra support:

 RESOURCE MANAGER—Copy Masters
Reading Check p. 217
Personal Essay p. 213
Question Support p. 218

Additional selection questions are provided for teachers on page 207.

ANSWERS

1. *Tan uses "broken," "limited," "fractured" to describe her mother's English.*

2. *The reaction to her English was that people did not respond to Mrs. Tan's requests for help or information, they failed to understand her, and at times they ignored her.*

3. *Achievement tests fail to reveal the creative intelligence underlying the student's limited English proficiency.*

Possible answers:

4. ■ SKILLS FOCUS **Identify Main Ideas**
Language shapes the way people perceive others, as shown by the way people exclude, limit, or stereotype those who speak nonstandard English.

5. *In these situations, Tan takes on an adult role, representing her mother to authorities because of her mother's limited English. In a typical mother-daughter relationship, the mother would be the person in charge in such situations. Tan's mother's dependence on her imposes unusual responsibilities and expectations on the daughter and may reduce Mrs. Tan in her daughter's eyes.*

6. *Accept all thoughtful, well-supported responses.*

7. ● SKILLS FOCUS **Personal Essay**
When Tan was young, she was ashamed of the way her mother spoke (lines 66–69). As an adult, she came to admire qualities of her mother's English that others overlooked (lines 178–180). At first, Tan internalized the negative attitudes others held toward her mother. Later, she realized that those attitudes were prejudiced. Tan's struggle with those negative attitudes helped her understand how powerful language, and people's perceptions of it, can be.

After Reading

Comprehension

1. **Recall** What words does Tan typically use to describe her mother's English?

2. **Summarize** In general, how did people react to Mrs. Tan's use of English?

3. **Recall** According to Tan, what aspects of language do achievement tests fail to reveal?

Literary Analysis

4. **Identify the Main Idea** Review the diagram you created as you read. Based on your notes, what is the main idea of the entire essay? Explain your answer.

5. **Compare Roles** Tan describes situations in which she was forced to act as a go-between for her mother, as in the anecdote in lines 80–91. Describe the roles of Tan and her mother in these situations. In what ways do these interactions differ from the typical mother-daughter relationship? Be specific in your answer.

6. **Make Judgments** Tan describes her mother's English as "vivid, direct, full of observation and imagery." Reread the story Tan's mother tells in lines 39–48. Do you agree with Tan's opinion of her mother's speech? Why or why not?

7. **Analyze a Personal Essay** Describe Tan's changing perceptions of her mother's use of English. In what way did her changing views toward her mother influence her observations about the power of language? Include details from the essay in your answer.

8. **Interpret Title** Tan uses the expression "mother tongue" as the title of her essay. State the usual meaning of this expression. Then, use each of the following examples to develop a different or expanded meaning for this term:

   • the idea of family talk (lines 28–30)
   • Tan's description of her mother's speech (lines 55–58)
   • Tan's thoughts on language development (lines 107–110)

9. **Evaluate Author's Position** Tan claims that the **language** spoken within the family does more to shape the way a child speaks than the language spoken by his or her peers. Recall your answers to the opening activity on page 1205. Do you agree with Tan's opinion? Why or why not?

Literary Criticism

10. **Different Perspectives** Look at the essay again through the eyes of the following individuals. What important lessons about life and the uses of language might each draw from this essay?

    • an immigrant   • the child of an immigrant
    • a doctor   • a teacher

1212   UNIT 6: CONTEMPORARY LITERATURE

---

8. *"Mother tongue" refers to one's home language. The idea of family talk ties this concept to intimate or private language spoken to those closest to you. In the context of Mrs. Tan's speech, the phrase relates to how her English shaped Tan's development. In the context of language development, the phrase refers to the special challenges the children of immigrants face.*

9. *Accept all thoughtful, well-supported responses.*

10. *Immigrant: Practice standard English.*
Doctor: Be understanding with patients who speak limited English.
Child of immigrant: Respect your parents' English.
Teacher: Understand the challenges students face.

Reading-Writing Connection

 W1.1, W1.2, W2.3

WRITING PROMPT

WRITE AN ESSAY Choose a topic that lets you draw on your personal experiences—a longtime hobby, a trip you took, your family history. Write an **one-page essay** that communicates your unique perspective on this subject. Be sure to include relevant details from your own experiences in the essay.

SELF-CHECK

A successful essay will . . .
- open in a way that captures the reader's attention
- include appropriate and effective personal details
- create a compelling voice that conveys your personality

GRAMMAR AND STYLE

USE APPROPRIATE LANGUAGE Review the **Grammar and Style** note on page 1208. For this essay, Tan chooses a casual, conversational style that lets her establish a strong connection with her readers. One strategy that helps Tan create this distinctive style is her use of **informal language** that contains **contractions** and idiosyncratic terms like *Englishes*. She also addresses her readers in a personal voice, using the **pronoun** *you*, as in the following excerpt:

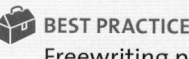 W1.9

> You should know that my mother's expressive command of English belies how much she actually understands. She reads the Forbes report, listens to Wall Street Week, converses daily with her stockbroker, reads Shirley MacLaine's books with ease—all kinds of things I can't begin to understand. (lines 49–52)

Whenever you write, consider the audience you are addressing and choose the appropriate level of formality.

PRACTICE Rewrite each of the following sentences using the kind of informal language Tan might have used.

> **EXAMPLE**
>
> It is often difficult to make sense of the rules of effective language.
> *Sometimes it's hard to understand what makes language work well.*

1. A lack of education caused my mother to speak a damaged, limited kind of English.

2. To demonstrate my use of these techniques, I have included some excerpts from my recent work.

3. A substantial portion of my fiction relates to my background and personal experiences.

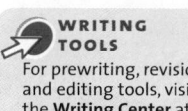
WRITING TOOLS
For prewriting, revision, and editing tools, visit the **Writing Center** at ClassZone.com.

MOTHER TONGUE **1213**

Reading-Writing Connection

WRITING PROMPT

Have students use Freewriting to find relevant details from their experiences. Then urge students to exchange ideas with a peer as they work to define their perspective on the topic.

BEST PRACTICES TOOLKIT
Freewriting p. C1

For writing support, see

Writing Center at ClassZone.com

GRAMMAR AND STYLE

To help students perceive elements of informal language, ask them to search the excerpt for contractions, idiosyncratic terms, and the pronoun *you* addressing the reader. Also invite students to suggest other strategies of informal language that Tan uses in her essay, such as dashes and sentences beginning with *and* or *but*.

Possible answers:

1. *Mom's lack of education caused her to speak a damaged, limited kind of English.*

2. *To show you how I use these techniques, I've included some excerpts from my recent work.*

3. *A lot of my fiction comes from my background and personal experiences.*

RESOURCE MANAGER—Copy Master
Use Appropriate Language p. 219

Assess and Reteach

Assess

RESOURCE MANAGER—Copy Masters
Selection Test A pp. 221–222
Selection Test B/C pp. 223–224

Test Generator CD

Reteach

STANDARDS LESSON FILE
Reading Lesson 4: Recognizing Main Idea and Details
Writing Lesson 30: Personal Narrative
Writing Lesson 38: Levels of Language

DIFFERENTIATED INSTRUCTION

FOR DEVELOPING WRITERS
Writing Support

- Recommend that students reread Tan's essay to see how she blends personal reflections with narrative.

- Urge visual learners to draw memories of the experience they will discuss.

- Remind students to write in informal language that reflects their own voice.

- Suggest that students read their first drafts aloud to peers and consider reader response.

- Encourage students to add sensory details when revising.

- Remind students to include their thoughts, feelings, and observations about the experience.

Focus and Motivate

OBJECTIVES

Literary Analysis
- explore the key idea of **creative outlet**
- analyze and interpret author's message
- read an essay

Reading
- analyze cultural content

 R2.5

ABOUT THE AUTHOR

Before students read the author biography, tell them that Alice Walker's essay expresses appreciation for her mother's influence on her life. As students read the author biography, ask them to find passages in it that hint at the essay's message. ***Possible answer:*** *The biography says that Walker's mother supported Alice's creativity and gave her gifts to help her get started.*

USING THE *NOTABLE QUOTE*

Ask students whether they agree with **Alice Walker** that creativity is "a very human need." Discuss the ways in which the creative urge might differ for people whose life work is a creative art and those in other fields. Encourage students to keep Walker's comment in mind as they respond to the *KEY IDEA* on page 1215.

Selection Resources

CALIFORNIA **R2.5**

***from* In Search of Our Mothers' Gardens**
Essay by Alice Walker

NOTABLE QUOTE
"It's a very human need, to make things, to create."

FYI
Did you know that Alice Walker ...
- became the first black woman to win the Pulitzer Prize for fiction?
- helped rediscover the writer Zora Neale Hurston?
- is an active environmentalist?

Author Online
For more on Alice Walker, visit the **Literature Center** at **ClassZone.com**.

Alice Walker
born 1944

Best known for her novels, author and activist Alice Walker also writes poems, short stories, and essays. Often inspired by her personal experiences, Walker portrays the struggles of African-American women to transcend the limits imposed on their lives by racism and sexism. Though her characters typically face violence and great hardships, Walker emphasizes the power of hope and the strength of the human will to survive.

Early Influences The daughter of a sharecropper, Walker grew up poor in Eatonton, Georgia. When she was eight, an accident left her permanently blind in her right eye. A shy and self-conscious Walker withdrew from the world and turned to poetry to soothe her feelings of isolation.

Although uneducated herself, Walker's mother supported her daughter's creative ambitions. Walker was an exceptional student who became class valedictorian

and won a scholarship to Spelman College, a historically black women's college in Atlanta, Georgia. When she left for college, her mother gave her three gifts: a typewriter, a sewing machine, and a suitcase. For Walker, these gifts represented creativity, domesticity, and freedom—a legacy of hopes, dreams, and unfulfilled longings passed from mother to daughter.

Fighting for Equality In 1965, after graduating from college, Walker received a travel fellowship to Senegal. Instead, she went to Mississippi to help fight for racial justice. "That summer," explains Walker, "marked the beginning of a realization that I could never live happily in Africa— or anywhere else—until I could live freely in Mississippi." In 1967, she defied state law to marry white civil rights lawyer Melvyn Leventhal. In retaliation for their interracial marriage, the couple was subjected to constant harassment and even death threats.

Speaking for the Oppressed During the 1970s, Walker published two novels and volumes of poetry and short stories. Her breakthrough came with the publication of her third novel, *The Color Purple* (1982), which was later made into a successful film. Many critics attacked this novel for its unflattering portrayals of African-American men. In response, Walker insisted her work reflected the painful realities of many black women's lives: "The black woman," she explained, "is one of America's greatest heroes. . . . Not enough credit has been given to the black woman who has been oppressed beyond recognition."

1214

 RESOURCE MANAGER UNIT 6

Plan and Teach pp. 225–232

Literary Analysis
Summary pp. 233†*, 234‡*
Author's Message pp. 235, 236†*
Question Support p. 240*

Reading
Understand Cultural Context, pp. 237, 238†*
Reading Check p. 239

Assessment
Selection Tests A, B/C pp. 241*, 243*
 Test Generator CD

 BEST PRACTICES TOOLKIT

Differentiated Instruction pp. 31–38*
Scaffolding Instruction pp. 43–46*

Graphic Organizers/Strategies
Main Idea and Details •
Definition Mapping

Reading Support
 Audio Anthology CD*

Technology
ⓘ Literature Center at **ClassZone.com**
WriteSmart CD

---

* Resources for Differentiation   † Also in Spanish   ‡ In Haitian Creole and Vietnamese

LITERARY ANALYSIS: AUTHOR'S MESSAGE

Authors write for a reason: they have a point to get across. In most nonfiction, you can find direct statements that reveal the **author's message,** as in this example:

And so our mothers and grandmothers have, more often than not anonymously, handed on the creative spark, the seed of the flower they themselves never hoped to see....

Statements like these, and the examples used to support them, will help you identify the lesson Walker wants to teach.

Walker also includes one of her poems in the essay. In the poem, her message is expressed indirectly, through elements such as **mood, imagery,** and **figurative language.** As you read the essay, notice the different techniques Walker uses to reveal her message.

READING SKILL: UNDERSTAND CULTURAL CONTEXT

When you analyze the **cultural context** of a literary work, you consider the social and cultural conditions that influenced how and why the work was written. Alice Walker's work reflects two key influences: her childhood experiences as a poor African-American female in the South and her adult commitment to feminist ideals. To fully appreciate Walker's points, use the following strategies:

- Before reading, study the details about cultural context provided in the background information on page 1216.
- Consult the footnotes as you read to clarify Walker's references to cultural details.
- Apply what you know about the social conditions that shaped the lives of African Americans in the South.

As you read, note details that reveal how Walker's social and cultural influences have shaped her views.

When does **LIFE** become art?

KEY IDEA Some people have an irresistible urge to create. Maybe they express it by sewing stylish clothes or cooking elaborate meals, by singing as they work, or by telling hilarious stories. For these people, even everyday chores can provide the **creative outlet** they need to release their artistic impulses.

DISCUSS In a small group, think of several ways that people express their creativity in everyday life. What do you think drives people to be creative? Record your responses and compare them with those of other groups.

1215

When does **LIFE** become art?

Read the question and then the **KEY IDEA** aloud. Invite students to think about what their **creative outlet** is, or what they would like it to be. Lead into the **DISCUSS** activity by asking students if they agree that everyday chores can be a creative outlet.

SKILLS FOCUS

LITERARY ANALYSIS R2.5

● AUTHOR'S MESSAGE

Have students reread the biography and identify a directly stated message in it. **Possible answer:** *"'The black woman . . . is one of America's greatest heroes.'"* Then ask them to find an indirectly expressed message in the biography. **Possible answer:** *"Although uneducated herself, Walker's mother supported her daughter's creative ambitions" indirectly expresses the message that Walker and her mother valued creativity.*

CHECK UNDERSTANDING Have students state the message of a favorite song or poem.

READING SKILL

■ UNDERSTAND CULTURAL CONTEXT

Have students find details in the author biography that suggest the cultural context of Walker's life and career. **Possible answer:** *Walker worked for civil rights in Mississippi in 1965.*

CHECK UNDERSTANDING Have students identify the cultural context of their chosen song and highlight lyrics that suggest that context.

R RESOURCE MANAGER—Copy Master
Understand Cultural Context p. 237
(for student use while reading the selection)

DIFFERENTIATED INSTRUCTION

FOR STRATEGIC READERS
Vocabulary Support

- *anonymously,* "without their names being known"
- *indirectly,* "without being stated in those words"
- *social,* "having to do with a community"
- *cultural,* "having to do with a people's way of life"

- *influences,* "factors that affect someone"
- *commitment,* "strong belief in or work toward a goal"
- *feminist,* "someone who believes in the need to secure rights and opportunities for women equal to those of men"
- *ideals,* "ideas about the way things should be"

SUMMARY

In this essay, Alice Walker describes the hard life of her mother, a sharecropper with a large family and much housework. Despite working all day in the fields and making her children's clothes and meals, Walker's mother found the energy for a creative activity: planting and tending gardens that were the talk of three counties. Her mother's creativity, and that of other unsung black women, inspires Walker to express her own creativity.

READING SKILL

Ⓐ CULTURAL CONTEXT

Possible answer: Details conveying the social conditions of African-American women in the early 20th century include the age of marriage, the number of children, and the list of chores.

If students need help . . . Work with them to begin a Main Idea and Details chart:

Main Idea	Details
Life was hard.	Her day began before sunup and ended late.

 BEST PRACTICES TOOLKIT—Transparency
Main Idea and Details p. B6

In Search of Our Mothers' Gardens

Alice Walker

BACKGROUND Alice Walker wrote this essay in 1974, after decades of civil rights activism had broken down many barriers for African Americans. At the same time, the women's movement had begun to raise awareness of the social constraints imposed on women's lives. Women of Walker's generation were poised to claim personal and social freedoms that earlier generations of women could never have dreamed of. As these women looked back into history to find role models for their own lives, they began to appreciate the extraordinary sacrifices these earlier generations had made. In this essay, Walker examines her mother's life to uncover a hidden legacy of resilience, strength, and overlooked talent passed on to the women of her own time.

ANALYZE VISUALS
Describe the style of this painting. In what ways does the artist's use of color, line, and texture contrast with the activity depicted?

In the late 1920s my mother ran away from home to marry my father. Marriage, if not running away, was expected of seventeen-year-old girls. By the time she was twenty, she had two children and was pregnant with a third. Five children later, I was born. And this is how I came to know my mother: she seemed a large, soft, loving-eyed woman who was rarely impatient in our home. Her quick, violent temper was on view only a few times a year, when she battled with the white landlord who had the misfortune to suggest to her that her children did not need to go to school.

She made all the clothes we wore, even my brothers' overalls. She made all
10 towels and sheets we used. She spent the summers canning vegetables and fruits. She spent the winter evenings making quilts enough to cover all our beds. Ⓐ

During the "working" day, she labored beside—not behind—my father in the fields. Her day began before sunup, and did not end until late at night. There was never a moment for her to sit down, undisturbed, to unravel her own private thoughts; never a time free from interruption—by work or the noisy inquiries of her many children. And yet, it is to my mother—and all our mothers who were not famous—that I went in search of the secret of what has fed that muzzled and often mutilated,[1] but vibrant, creative spirit that the black woman has inherited, and that pops out in wild and unlikely places to this day.

Ⓐ **CULTURAL CONTEXT**
What details in lines 1–11 convey the social conditions of African-American women in the early 20th century?

❶ **Targeted Passage**

---

1. **mutilated** (myōōt'l-ā'tĭd): irreparably damaged.

Washerwoman, James Amos Porter. Oil on canvas, 18″ × 13″. Private collection. Reproduction rights given by the Dorothy Porter Wesley Research Center, Fort Lauderdale, Florida.

DIFFERENTIATED INSTRUCTION

FOR ALL STUDENTS

Provide these independent projects to extend the lesson:

- Survey people's creative outlets.
- Design a garden from the essay.
- Write a poem honoring people of the past.

For further details on these projects, see

📁 **RESOURCE MANAGER**
Ideas for Extension pp. 230–231

FOR STRATEGIC READERS

In combination with the *Audio Anthology CD*, use one or more Targeted Passages (pp. 1216, 1219, 1220) to ensure that students focus on key concepts in the selection. Targeted Passages are also good for English learners.

❶ **Targeted Passage [Lines 9–19]**

This passage describes the work Alice Walker's mother did and expresses the questions it raised for Walker.

REINFORCE *KEY IDEA:* CREATIVE OUTLET

Discuss Why is the quilt "obviously" a work of great imagination and spirituality? In what ways does it reflect a **creative outlet** rather than a practical need for a warm quilt?
Possible answer: *The quilt's detail and reference to a biblical story suggest the quilter's imagination and spirituality. Choosing to adorn a quilt with a detailed and meaningful story suggests that the quilting process was a creative outlet; a warm quilt could be made without decoration.*

LITERARY ANALYSIS

Ⓑ AUTHOR'S MESSAGE

Possible answer: *The sentence that best states the message is, "If we could locate . . . allowed her to use."*

Extend the Discussion What might the anonymous quilter have been like?

READING SKILL

Ⓒ CULTURAL CONTEXT

Possible answer: *Walker changes the cultural references to equivalent African-American cultural ones, placing her version in brackets. She might have chosen to quote Virginia Woolf because Woolf was a prominent feminist writer, and Walker wants to address women's concerns within African-American culture.*

---

20   But when, you will ask, did my overworked mother have time to know or care about feeding the creative spirit?

The answer is so simple that many of us have spent years discovering it. We have constantly looked high, when we should have looked high—and low.

For example: in the Smithsonian Institution in Washington, D.C., there hangs a quilt unlike any other in the world. In fanciful, inspired, and yet simple and identifiable figures, it portrays the story of the Crucifixion.[2] It is considered rare, beyond price. Though it follows no known pattern of quilt-making, and though it is made of bits and pieces of worthless rags, it is obviously the work of a person of powerful imagination and deep spiritual feeling. Below this quilt I saw a note that
30   says it was made by "an anonymous Black woman in Alabama, a hundred years ago."

If we could locate this "anonymous" black woman from Alabama, she would turn out to be one of our grandmothers—an artist who left her mark in the only materials she could afford, and in the only medium her position in society allowed her to use. Ⓑ

As Virginia Woolf[3] wrote further, in *A Room of One's Own:*

Yet genius of a sort must have existed among women as it must have existed among the working class. [Change this to "slaves" and "the wives and daughters of sharecroppers."] Now and again an Emily Brontë or a Robert Burns [change this to "a Zora Hurston or a Richard Wright"[4]] blazes out and proves its presence. But
40   *certainly it never got itself on to paper. When, however, one reads of a witch being ducked, of a woman possessed by devils [or "Sainthood"[5]], of a wise woman selling herbs [our root workers], or even a very remarkable man who had a mother, then I think we are on the track of a lost novelist, a suppressed poet, of some mute and inglorious Jane Austen[6]. . . . Indeed, I would venture to guess that Anon, who wrote so many poems without signing them, was often a woman. . . .* Ⓒ

And so our mothers and grandmothers have, more often than not anonymously, handed on the creative spark, the seed of the flower they themselves never hoped to see: or like a sealed letter they could not plainly read.

And so it is, certainly, with my own mother. Unlike "Ma" Rainey's songs,
50   which retained their creator's name even while blasting forth from Bessie Smith's[7] mouth, no song or poem will bear my mother's name. Yet so many of the stories that I write, that we all write, are my mother's stories. Only recently did I fully

Ⓑ **AUTHOR'S MESSAGE**
Reread Walker's description of the quilt in lines 24–34. Which sentence best states the message behind Walker's observations?

Ⓒ **CULTURAL CONTEXT**
Reread lines 36–45. Consulting the footnotes as needed, explain how Walker adapts the Virginia Woolf quotation to her own cultural context. Why might Walker have chosen to quote this particular author?

---

2. **Crucifixion:** the death of Jesus Christ, who was nailed to a cross.
3. **Virginia Woolf:** English novelist, critic, and pioneering feminist (1882–1941). Her works frequently explore the inner lives of women living under severe social constraints.
4. **Emily Brontë . . . Richard Wright:** Brontë (1818–1848) was an English novelist and poet, and Burns (1759–1796) was a Scottish poet. Hurston (1891–1960) and Wright (1908–1960) were African-American writers.
5. **"Sainthood":** a reference to certain black women in the South called Saints. They were intensely spiritual women who were driven to madness by their unfulfilled creativity.
6. **Jane Austen:** British novelist (1775–1817), best known for *Pride and Prejudice.*
7. **"Ma" Rainey's . . . Bessie Smith's:** Ma Rainey was the nickname of Gertrude Malissa Nix Pridgett Rainey (1886–1939), a blues singer considered to be the mother of the blues. Bessie Smith (1894–1937), another blues singer, was mentored by Ma Rainey.

DIFFERENTIATED INSTRUCTION

FOR ENGLISH LEARNERS
Key Academic Vocabulary Use Definition Mapping to teach this word: *locate* (line 31).

 BEST PRACTICES TOOLKIT—Transparency
Definition Mapping p. E6

Culture: Clarify Work through the footnotes with students, confirming their understandings of the cultural references Walker makes.

FOR ADVANCED LEARNERS/AP
Evaluate In lines 44–45, Walker quotes a famous remark by Virginia Woolf. Invite students to explain this remark and then evaluate its likely validity. Have students brainstorm reasons for accepting the idea that most anonymous poets (and, by implication, other anonymous artists) were women, and reasons for rejecting the same notion. Have students share their explanations and reasons with the class.

realize this: that through years of listening to my mother's stories of her life, I have absorbed not only the stories themselves, but something of the manner in which she spoke, something of the urgency that involves the knowledge that her stories—like her life—must be recorded. It is probably for this reason that so much of what I have written is about characters whose counterparts in real life are so much older than I am.

But the telling of these stories, which came from my mother's lips as naturally
60 as breathing, was not the only way my mother showed herself as an artist. For stories, too, were subject to being distracted, to dying without conclusion. Dinners must be started, and cotton must be gathered before the big rains. The artist that was and is my mother showed itself to me only after many years. This is what I finally noticed:

Like Mem, a character in *The Third Life of Grange Copeland*,[8] my mother adorned with flowers whatever shabby house we were forced to live in. And not just your typical straggly country stand of zinnias, either. She planted ambitious gardens—and still does—with over fifty different varieties of plants that bloom profusely from early March until late November. Before she left home for the
70 fields, she watered her flowers, chopped up the grass, and laid out new beds. When she returned from the fields she might divide clumps of bulbs, dig a cold pit,[9] uproot and replant roses, or prune branches from her taller bushes or trees—until night came and it was too dark to see.

Whatever she planted grew as if by magic, and her fame as a grower of flowers spread over three counties. Because of her creativity with her flowers, even my memories of poverty are seen through a screen of blooms—sunflowers, petunias, roses, dahlias, forsythia, spirea, delphiniums, verbena . . . and on and on.

And I remember people coming to my mother's yard to be given cuttings from her flowers; I hear again the praise showered on her because whatever rocky
80 soil she landed on, she turned into a garden. A garden so brilliant with colors, so original in its design, so magnificent with life and creativity, that to this day people drive by our house in Georgia—perfect strangers and imperfect strangers—and ask to stand or walk among my mother's art.

I notice that it is only when my mother is working in her flowers that she is radiant, almost to the point of being invisible—except as Creator: hand and eye. She is involved in work her soul must have. Ordering the universe in the image of her personal conception of Beauty.

② **Targeted Passage**

Her face, as she prepares the Art that is her gift, is a legacy of respect she leaves to me, for all that illuminates and cherishes life. She has handed down respect for
90 the possibilities—and the will to grasp them.

For her, so hindered and intruded upon in so many ways, being an artist has still been a daily part of her life. This ability to hold on, even in very simple ways, is work black women have done for a very long time. **D**

D **AUTHOR'S MESSAGE**
Reread lines 88–93. What lessons does Walker take from her mother's life?

---

8. *The Third Life of Grange Copeland:* Alice Walker's first novel, published in 1970.

9. **cold pit:** shallow pit, usually covered with glass, used for rooting or sheltering young plants from temperature variations in the spring.

Lines 65–77
TIERED DISCUSSION PROMPTS
Use these prompts to help students understand the significance of the author's mother's garden:

Connect Have you ever been to or seen an elaborate garden or public park? What feelings do such places inspire in viewers? in their creators? *Students' responses should convey understanding of the pride and joy of creating or viewing beauty.*

Analyze What language does Walker use to help readers see the garden and feel her emotions? *Possible answers: Walker uses the names of flowers, descriptions of garden activities, and words that reflect the garden's impact in order to portray the garden and convey its emotional effect.*

Evaluate Does Walker succeed in making the reader share her emotions about her mother's garden? Explain. *Accept all thoughtful responses.*

LITERARY ANALYSIS

D **AUTHOR'S MESSAGE**

Possible answer: Walker takes from her mother's life the lesson that although her mother left behind no work imprinted with her name, she did the important work of keeping the artistic tradition of African-American women alive.

FOR STRATEGIC READERS

② **Targeted Passage [Lines 74–87]**

This passage clarifies that Walker is inspired by the creativity in her mother's gardening.

- For what was Walker's mother known?
- In what ways does the garden affect Walker's childhood memories?
- When Walker's mother works in the garden, what does Walker see in her?
- Why is gardening the work Walker's mother's "soul must have"?

FOR ENGLISH LEARNERS

Comprehension: Self-Monitor Clarify the meaning of these lines; then urge students to paraphrase them to monitor understanding:

- Lines 60–61 include personification of *stories* as beings that can be distracted or die.
- Lines 88–89 contain a metaphor comparing the expression on Walker's mother's face to a gift that can be given by one person to another.

FOR ADVANCED LEARNERS/AP

Synthesize Walker's description of her mother's garden highlights the many kinds of anonymous art, such as gardens or graffiti, that people see every day. Challenge students to consider the importance of knowing a work's creator. In what ways is it important for the artist? for the audience? What do audiences gain by knowing or imagining the life of the artist, whether named or not? Invite students to explore these questions in journal entries.

E AUTHOR'S MESSAGE

Possible answer: In her poem, Walker describes the women with images such as "Husky of voice," "Stout of / Step," "fists," "battered down / Doors," "led / Armies," and "Headragged Generals." Her images emphasize strength, determination, and militancy.

Lines 122–133
REINFORCE *KEY IDEA:* CREATIVE OUTLET

Discuss In what ways did other people's creativity help Walker find her own **creative outlet?** *Possible answer: The creativity of her mother and other African-American women and the creative literary ideas of Virginia Woolf played a role in inspiring Walker's writing.*

SELECTION WRAP–UP

SUMMARIZE Have students summarize ways that Walker's mother expressed her creativity.

⭐ CRITIQUE

- Ask students to identify ways that Walker effectively presents her message, both directly and indirectly.

- After completing the After Reading questions on page 1221, have students revisit their responses and tell whether they have changed their opinions.

This poem is not enough, but it is something, for the woman who literally covered the holes in our walls with sunflowers:

> They were women then
> My mama's generation
> Husky of voice—Stout of
> Step
> 100 With fists as well as
> Hands
> How they battered down
> Doors
> And ironed
> Starched white
> Shirts
> How they led
> Armies
> Headragged Generals
> 110 Across mined
> Fields
> Booby-trapped
> Kitchens
> To discover books
> Desks
> A place for us
> How they knew what we
> *Must* know
> Without knowing a page
> 120 Of it
> Themselves. **E**

 ❸ Targeted Passage

Guided by my heritage of a love of beauty and a respect for strength—in search of my mother's garden, I found my own.

And perhaps in Africa over two hundred years ago, there was just such a mother; perhaps she painted vivid and daring decorations in oranges and yellows and greens on the walls of her hut; perhaps she sang—in a voice like Roberta Flack's[10]—*sweetly* over the compounds of her village; perhaps she wove the most stunning mats or told the most ingenious stories of all the village storytellers. Perhaps she was herself a poet—though only her daughter's name is signed to the 130 poems that we know.

Perhaps Phillis Wheatley's mother was also an artist.

Perhaps in more than Phillis Wheatley's[11] biological life is her mother's signature made clear. ❧

---

10. **Roberta Flack's:** Flack is a popular African-American singer-songwriter.

11. **Phillis Wheatley's:** American poet Phillis Wheatley (1753?–1783), was born in Africa and brought to America in slavery. She is often referred to as the first African-American poet.

E AUTHOR'S MESSAGE
Reread the poem in lines 96–121. Identify images Walker uses to describe these women. What qualities are emphasized by these images?

DIFFERENTIATED INSTRUCTION

FOR STRATEGIC READERS

❸ Targeted Passage [Lines 96–121]

This passage uses a poem to convey Walker's pride in African-American women of her mother's generation.

- Who is the poem about?
- When did the women live?
- What did the women do?
- In what ways did the women help their children?

FOR ENGLISH LEARNERS

Language: Punctuation and Print Clues
Call attention to the long, complex sentence in lines 124–128, and to its two semicolons. Have students replace the semicolons with periods and paraphrase the resulting short sentences. *Possible answer: Perhaps long ago in Africa there was a mother who painted the walls of her hut beautifully. Perhaps she sang like Roberta Flack for the people of her village. Perhaps she wove the most creative mats or told the best stories.*

FOR ADVANCED LEARNERS/AP

Write Images Have students discuss their responses to the Literary Analysis question about author's message on page 1220. Challenge them to envision images Walker might have used if she had wanted to emphasize different qualities of the same women, such as love or patience or faith. Ask students to choose a quality Walker might have chosen to emphasize, and to write images that emphasize this quality. Invite students to share their work.

After Reading

Comprehension

R2.5

CALIFORNIA

1. **Recall** On what occasions did Walker's mother lose her temper?

2. **Summarize** What did Walker's mother do in a typical day?

3. **Recall** According to Walker, what change occurred in her mother as she worked in her garden?

Literary Analysis

4. **Make Inferences** Recall that a **paradox** is a statement that may appear contradictory but in fact communicates an important truth. Identify the paradox in Walker's poem in lines 117–121. What point is Walker making?

5. **Analyze Author's Message** Reread the conclusion of Walker's essay in lines 124–133. Explain what Walker means by her reference to Phillis Wheatley's mother. In what way does this passage express the message of Walker's essay?

6. **Examine Cultural Context** Consider the conditions that constrained Walker's mother's life. Within this context, what is so remarkable about what she achieved? Support your answer with details.

7. **Make Generalizations** Consider Walker's descriptions of the following works of art by African-American women. What does each of these examples tell you about this artistic tradition?

   • the description of the quilt (lines 24–34)
   • Walker's comments on her mother's stories (lines 49–56)
   • the garden Walker's mother plants (lines 65–77)

8. **Draw Conclusions** Think back to your discussion about the **creative outlets** people use to express their artistic impulses. Consider the creative outlets described in question 7. In your opinion, what inspires these women to make art despite the obstacles they face?

Literary Criticism

9. **Critical Interpretations** "Walker's optimism," writes critic Donna Haisty Winchell, "is ultimately born of her belief that something of the divine exists in every human and nonhuman participant in the universe. The inhabitants of her fictional world search . . . for that divine spark that makes them uniquely who they are." In what ways might this quote also apply to the women in this nonfiction essay? Cite evidence from the text to support your conclusions.

IN SEARCH OF OUR MOTHERS' GARDENS   **1221**

7. *The quilt suggests that beauty can be improvised from "worthless" materials. The stories suggest that a heritage lives on through generations. The garden suggests that artists can overcome severe obstacles.*

8. *The women are inspired by inner need or their hopes for the future.*

9. *The drive to create could be seen as a search for the divine in the restricted lives of those women.*

Practice and Apply

After Reading

Use these copy masters to check understanding and provide extra support:

R RESOURCE MANAGER—Copy Masters
   Reading Check p. 239
   Author's Message p. 235
   Question Support p. 240

   Additional selection questions are provided for teachers on page 229.

ANSWERS

1. *Walker's mother lost her temper when the landlord suggested that her children did not need to attend school.*

2. *She worked in the fields, made clothes, cooked, cared for her children, gardened.*

3. *Walker's mother became radiant when she worked in the garden.*

Possible answers:

4. *The women knew things they could not know and intuited that their children would know or achieve things the mothers could not.*

5. ● SKILLS FOCUS **Author's Message** *History knows nothing about Wheatley's mother, but Wheatley's success suggests that her mother was exceptional. The message is that successful people rise from the efforts of those who came before them.*

6. ■ SKILLS FOCUS **Understand Cultural Context** *It is remarkable that Walker's mother found a way to keep her creative self alive and changed her family's experience of poverty by surrounding them with beauty.*

Assess and Reteach

Assess

R RESOURCE MANAGER—Copy Masters
   Selection Test A pp. 241–242
   Selection Test B/C pp. 243–244

◉ Test Generator CD

Reteach

S STANDARDS LESSON FILE
   Literature Lesson 45: Author's Perspective
   Reading Lesson 4: Recognizing Main Idea and Details

IN SEARCH OF OUR MOTHERS' GARDENS   **1221**

Focus and Motivate

OBJECTIVES

Literary Analysis
- explore the key idea of **ideas**
- identify and interpret allusions
- analyze and compare voice
- read a personal essay

Reading
- analyze structure

 R2.2, R3.3

ABOUT THE AUTHOR

Before students read the author biography, tell them that Cisneros's essay is about the way a writer creates the material of literature from childhood experiences. Ask students to find details in the biography that they think could become literature.

USING THE *NOTABLE QUOTE*

Clarify that the phrase "doubly rich" is meant figuratively and suggests a richness of culture. Then have students suggest what the quote means about being bilingual. ***Possible answer: The quote means that speaking two languages gives people access to the thinking of two cultures and the descriptive and analytical power of two languages.*** Ask students if they agree with **Sandra Cisneros,** given what they know about bilingualism from personal experience or observation. *Students will likely agree and should gain an appreciation of bilingualism from the quote.*

 R2.2, R3.3

Straw into Gold: The Metamorphosis of the Everyday
Essay by Sandra Cisneros

NOTABLE QUOTE
"If you're bilingual you're doubly rich. You have two ways of looking at the world."

FYI
Did you know that Sandra Cisneros . . .

- wrote in secret as a child because she knew her family would disapprove?
- won a MacArthur "genius grant," a large monetary award given to honor "exceptional creativity and originality"?
- has had poems on display on Chicago subways and buses?

Author On|ine

For more on Sandra Cisneros, visit the **Literature Center** at ClassZone.com.

Sandra Cisneros
born 1954

"I'm trying to write the stories that haven't been written," Sandra Cisneros has proclaimed. With her rich, intimate portraits of Mexicans and Mexican Americans, Cisneros hopes to make readers of all races aware of the complexities of straddling two cultures. As a female minority writer, she sees herself as a voice for the voiceless. "I'm determined," she explains, "to fill a literary void."

Fighting Tradition Born to a Mexican father and a Mexican-American mother, Cisneros grew up on Chicago's South Side. The only girl among seven children, she felt as if she had "seven fathers" because her brothers tried to control her behavior. Like their father, they thought Sandra should adopt a quiet, traditional lifestyle. Fortunately, she was blessed with a mother "brave enough to raise her daughter in a nontraditional way." "My mother didn't force me to learn how to cook," says Cisneros. "And she always told me, 'Make sure you can take care of yourself.'"

Growing Up Lonely Cisneros formed few lasting friendships in early childhood, because her family moved frequently between Chicago and Mexico. "The moving back and forth, the new school, were very upsetting to me as a child," she once said. Retreating into herself, Cisneros became a keen observer of others and a secret writer of poetry. After years of clandestine composition, she encountered a teacher in high school who appreciated her experiences and her writing. With the teacher's encouragement, Cisneros began to share her work with her classmates.

The Value of Heritage In 1976, Cisneros entered the University of Iowa's prestigious Writers' Workshop. Surrounded by people from more privileged backgrounds, Cisneros felt intimidated. Soon, however, she came to realize that she could write about something her classmates could not. "It was not until this moment," Cisneros recalls, "when I separated myself, when I considered myself truly distinct, that my writing acquired a voice." Cisneros's realization gave rise to the acclaimed *The House on Mango Street* (1984), a series of interlocking prose poems about a poor Mexican-American family. Her reputation was cemented with the publication in 1991 of *Woman Hollering Creek,* a collection of stories. "In everything I've done in my life," she maintains, "including all the choices I've made as a writer, I've followed my gut and my heart. It's taken me where I've needed to go so far."

1222

Selection Resources

---

* Resources for Differentiation   † Also in Spanish   ‡ In Haitian Creole and Vietnamese

LITERARY ANALYSIS: VOICE

A writer's **voice** is his or her unique style of expression. This unique use of language is what allows you to "hear" a human personality behind the words you read. In "Straw into Gold," Sandra Cisneros writes:

I'd never seen anybody make corn tortillas. Ever.

The informal tone, the use of a contraction, the everyday words, the short sentence followed by a fragment, and the pauses before and after the word *ever*—all help create Cisneros's voice in this essay—one that is personal, relaxed, and almost conversational in its natural sound. As you read, look for instances when you "hear" Cisneros behind her words. Note the stylistic elements that help create this unique effect.

READING SKILL: ANALYZE STRUCTURE

The **structure** of a literary work, or how its different parts are organized, is directly tied to the author's purpose. Cisneros's purpose in this personal essay is twofold. She shares with readers some of her formative experiences—moments that helped shape her life as a writer. She also aims to convey a message about life.

Personal essays are often loosely structured, and "Straw into Gold" is no exception. Cisneros begins the essay with an **anecdote**—a brief story that makes a point. After you read it, summarize it in a chart like the one shown. As you continue to read, summarize Cisneros's other recollections.

Anecdote or Recollection	Summary
introductory anecdote (lines 1–30)	

Where do writers get their MATERIAL?

KEY IDEA Writers harvest **ideas** for their work in a variety of places. Some writers find inspiration in controversies ripped from the headlines. Others are intrigued by a particular moment in history. Literature can be inspired by a writer's travels around the world, but just as often, powerful stories start closer to home. In "Straw into Gold," you will meet a writer who has unearthed a wealth of ideas in her own experiences and heritage.

QUICKWRITE Think of a work of literature you're familiar with. Where do you think the writer came by his or her ideas? Whether it's a lyric poem about lost love or a novel about a historical event, try to imagine the writer's source of material. Explain your thoughts in a short paragraph.

 1223

Where do writers get their MATERIAL?

Read the question aloud and ask students what a writer's material is. Discuss that it is the life experience from which a writer gets **ideas.** Read the **KEY IDEA** and the **QUICK-WRITE.** After students write their paragraphs, invite them to share their work and identify common idea sources.

SKILLS FOCUS

LITERARY ANALYSIS R3.3

● VOICE

Write this passage on the board:

> Zap! Pow! That was childhood. A roaring, rollicking whirl of running games and fantasy heroes. It seemed to last forever—and now it's gone forever.

Ask students to describe the voice of the writer. Then have them cite details that create the voice. ***Possible answer: The voice in this passage is contemporary and fast-paced. Words such as "Zap!" and "whirl" convey this voice.***

CHECK UNDERSTANDING Have students contrast the way they speak with the way familiar adults speak.

READING SKILL R2.2

◼ ANALYZE STRUCTURE

Explain that the author biography on page 1222 includes several anecdotes and quotations. These convey aspects of Cisneros's life and character. Have students reread the author biography and record its structure using a chart like the one introduced on page 1223. Tell students to list quotations as well as anecdotes.

R RESOURCE MANAGER—Copy Master
Analyze Structure p. 257 (for student use while reading the selection)

DIFFERENTIATED INSTRUCTION

FOR STRATEGIC READERS
Vocabulary Support

- *unique,* "one-of-a-kind"
- *contraction,* "a word containing an apostrophe in place of a missing letter or letters"
- *instances,* "examples"
- *two-fold,* "having two parts"
- *formative,* "shaping"
- *recollections,* "memories"

Concept Support: Analyze Structure Spatial learners can easily imagine the structure of a building or a bridge, while mathematical learners can visualize the structure of a software code or an equation. Ask students to describe an accessible structure in their own terms, such as in a diagram or in words. Then invite them to think of text structure in the same way—as a collection of parts combined in a particular way to work together as a whole.

SUMMARY

In this personal essay, Sandra Cisneros shares the events and influences that helped shape her as a writer. Beginning with an anecdote about the daunting task of making tortillas by hand, she reflects on ways that her achievements have surpassed her expectations. She describes ways that her relationships to her parents and brothers affected her life and work. She has traveled far both literally and figuratively, turning the straw of everyday life into the gold of art.

LITERARY ANALYSIS

Ⓐ VOICE

Possible answer: The informal tone, everyday words such as "I guess" (line 8), contractions such as "didn't" and "I'd" (lines 7, 10), and mixture of short and long sentences (lines 5–6) allow Cisneros's conversational voice to emerge.

Straw into Gold:
The Metamorphosis of the Everyday
Sandra Cisneros

ANALYZE VISUALS
What does the image on page 1225 suggest about women's roles in traditional Mexican culture? Read the essay, then revisit your answer, citing details from the text.

BACKGROUND Cisneros originally delivered the text of "Straw into Gold" as a speech. The essay still retains some characteristics of an oral work—for example, the voice has a distinctly conversational character. The phrase "Straw into Gold" refers to the challenge faced by the heroine in "Rumplestiltskin." In this fairy tale, as you may recall, a miller's daughter will be put to death unless she can do the seemingly impossible— namely, spin gold out of mere straw. The word *metamorphosis* in the subtitle means "transformation."

When I was living in an artists' colony in the south of France, some fellow Latin-Americans who taught at the university in Aix-en-Provence[1] invited me to share a homecooked meal with them. I had been living abroad almost a year then on an NEA[2] grant, subsisting mainly on French bread and lentils so that my money could last longer. So when the invitation to dinner arrived, I accepted without hesitation. Especially since they had promised Mexican food.

What I didn't realize when they made this invitation was that I was supposed to be involved in preparing the meal. I guess they assumed I knew how to cook Mexican food because I am Mexican. They wanted specifically tortillas, though

10 I'd never made a tortilla in my life. Ⓐ

Ⓐ VOICE
Reread lines 1–10. What stylistic elements allow Cisneros's informal, conversational voice to emerge? Cite specific examples.

---

1. **Aix-en-Provence** (āk´sän-prō-väns´): French city about ten miles north of the Mediterranean Sea.
2. **NEA:** the National Endowment for the Arts, a federal agency that funds artistic projects of organizations and individuals.

1224 UNIT 6: CONTEMPORARY LITERATURE

Making Tortillas (1926), Diego Rivera. University of California, San Francisco. © Bridgeman Art Library.

DIFFERENTIATED INSTRUCTION

FOR ALL STUDENTS
Provide these independent projects to extend the lesson:

- Write in any genre about an interaction between Cisneros and Emerson.
- Discuss student literary voices in a workshop format.
- Write a critical essay comparing the role of structure in Cisneros's essay and another work.

- Create a two-column list of life experiences and possible writing topics.
- Develop and deliver a speech about inspirational experiences.

For further details about these projects, see

Ⓡ RESOURCE MANAGER
Ideas for Extension pp. 250–251

ANALYZE VISUALS

Possible answer: Students may first say that the image suggests that women's roles are limited to household work. On revisiting, they may say that Sandra Cisneros and her mother provide examples of expanded and nontraditional roles for women of Mexican descent.

About the Art Diego Rivera (1886–1957) was an important Mexican painter, perhaps best known for his murals. His work portrays the people and history of Mexico in a realistic, socially conscious style. *Making Tortillas* shows the process Sandra Cisneros felt nervous about performing, that of making tortillas by hand. The painting shows the women skillfully yet peacefully fulfilling the traditional roles of their culture—roles Cisneros transcended.

CULTURAL CONNECTION

Food Preparation In the opening anecdote Cisneros acknowledges that she misses Mexican food while abroad, partly because, despite being a Mexican American, she can't cook Mexican food. In many cultures, food and food preparation create important emotional associations and are linked to memories of growing up. For instance, Korean students might feel affection for *kimchi,* a spicy pickle, or *bulgoki,* barbecued marinated meat. Moroccan students might feel just as strongly about *couscous,* a dish of grain mixed with meat and vegetables in a sauce, or *kefta,* seasoned ground meat. Ask students to share information about the foods of their cultures.

FOR STRATEGIC READERS

In combination with the *Audio Anthology CD,* use one or more Targeted Passages (pp. 1226, 1228) to ensure that students focus on key events and concepts in the selection. Targeted Passages are also good for English learners.

FOR ADVANCED LEARNERS/AP

AP exercises in the bottom channel provide additional challenge for students. Use these suggestions for small groups or individuals.

ADDITIONAL GUIDELINES

For more help with differentiation and tips for classroom management, see

BEST PRACTICES TOOLKIT
Differentiated Instruction pp. 31–38

TIERED DISCUSSION PROMPTS

Use these prompts to help students grasp the meaning of Cisneros's anecdote:

Connect Think of a time when you had to complete a totally unfamiliar task. What does the experience tell you about the author's feelings? *Students should recognize the anxiety of the situation.*

Analyze Why does Cisneros feel she isn't up to the task of making corn tortillas? *Possible answer: Her mother's family made only flour tortillas. Her father's family ate store-bought corn tortillas. She has never seen corn tortillas being made.*

Synthesize Use prior knowledge of Latino culture to suggest why Cisneros's hosts expect her to cook well, and information from the author biography (page 1224) and the Rivera painting (page 1225) to suggest why the author is an exception to this expectation. *Students should recognize that in Latino culture women traditionally cook. Cisneros is unusual because her mother did not make her learn to cook.*

READING SKILL

B ANALYZE STRUCTURE

Possible answer: Cisneros considers both tasks to be seemingly impossible, just like the fairy tale task of making gold from straw.

If students need help . . . Have them add to the chart introduced on page 1223:

Recollection	Summary
making tortillas and writing MFA exam	tackles tough tasks and succeeds

---

It's true I had witnessed my mother rolling the little armies of dough into perfect circles, but my mother's family is from Guanajuato;[3] they are *provincianos*, country folk. They only know how to make flour tortillas. My father's family, on the other hand, is *chilango*[4] from Mexico City. We ate corn tortillas but we didn't make them. Someone was sent to the corner tortilleria to buy some. I'd never seen anybody make corn tortillas. Ever.

Somehow my Latino hosts had gotten a hold of a packet of corn flour, and this is what they tossed my way with orders to produce tortillas. *Así como sea.* Any ol' way, they said and went back to their cooking.

20 Why did I feel like the woman in the fairy tale who was locked in a room and ordered to spin straw into gold? I had the same sick feeling when I was required to write my critical essay for the MFA[5] exam—the only piece of noncreative writing necessary in order to get my graduate degree. How was I to start? There were rules involved here, unlike writing a poem or story, which I did intuitively. There was a step by step process needed and I had better know it. I felt as if making tortillas—or writing a critical paper, for that matter—were tasks so impossible I wanted to break down into tears.

Somehow though, I managed to make tortillas—crooked and burnt, but edible nonetheless. My hosts were absolutely ignorant when it came to Mexican
30 food; they thought my tortillas were delicious. (I'm glad my mama wasn't there.)

Thinking back and looking at an old photograph documenting the three of us consuming those lopsided circles I am amazed. Just as I am amazed I could finish my MFA exam. I've managed to do a lot of things in my life I didn't think I was capable of and which many others didn't think I was capable of either. Especially because I am a woman, a Latina, an only daughter in a family of six men. My father would've liked to have seen me married long ago. In our culture men and women don't leave their father's house except by way of marriage. I crossed my father's threshold with nothing carrying me but my own two feet. A woman whom no one came for and no one chased away. **B**

40 To make matters worse, I left before any of my six brothers had ventured away from home. I broke a terrible taboo. Somehow, looking back at photos of myself as a child, I wonder if I was aware of having begun already my own quiet war.

I like to think that somehow my family, my Mexicanness, my poverty, all had something to do with shaping me into a writer. I like to think my parents were preparing me all along for my life as an artist even though they didn't know it. From my father I inherited a love of wandering. He was born in Mexico City but as a young man he traveled into the U.S. vagabonding. He eventually was drafted and thus became a citizen. Some of the stories he has told about his first months in the U.S. with little or no English surface in my stories in *The House on Mango*
50 *Street*[6] as well as others I have in mind to write in the future. From him I inherited

1 Targeted Passage

B ANALYZE STRUCTURE
What does Cisneros's completion of her MFA exam have in common with the experience recounted in the tortilla anecdote? Explain how these experiences make Cisneros feel like "the woman in the fairy tale" she alludes to in lines 20–21.

---

3. **Guanajuato** (gwä'nä-hwä'tō): state in central Mexico.
4. *chilango* (chē-läng'gō) *Mexican slang:* native to Mexico City.
5. **MFA:** Master of Fine Arts, an academic degree.
6. *The House on Mango Street:* Cisneros's first book of fiction, published in 1983.

DIFFERENTIATED INSTRUCTION

FOR STRATEGIC READERS

1 Targeted Passage [Lines 31–45]

This passage summarizes the personal meaning of Cisneros's achievements.

- What is Cisneros's reaction to succeeding at tasks she didn't think herself capable of?
- In her culture, what is the usual way for young people to leave their parents' homes?
- What three factors helped Cisneros become a writer?

FOR ENGLISH LEARNERS

Key Academic Vocabulary Use Word Questioning to teach these words: *process* (line 25), *ignorant* (line 29), *chapter* (line 114).

 BEST PRACTICES TOOLKIT—Transparency Word Questioning p. E9

Prereading For prereading instruction for English learners, see

 BEST PRACTICES TOOLKIT Scaffolding Reading Instruction pp. 43–46

Vocabulary: Idioms and Phrasal Verbs Help students use context to determine meaning for these expressions:

- *break down into tears* (line 27), "start crying"
- *make matters worse* (line 40), "make the situation worse"
- *have in mind to write* (line 50), "plan to write one day"
- *a smart cookie* (line 55), "very smart"
- *odd woman out* (line 67), "a person who is left out of a group"

a sappy heart. (He still cries when he watches Mexican soaps—especially if they deal with children who have forsaken their parents.)

My mother was born like me—in Chicago but of Mexican descent. It would be her tough streetwise voice that would haunt all my stories and poems. An amazing woman who loves to draw and read books and can sing an opera. A smart cookie. **C**

When I was a little girl we traveled to Mexico City so much I thought my grandparents' house on La Fortuna, number 12, was home. It was the only constant in our nomadic ramblings from one Chicago flat to another. The house on Destiny Street, number 12, in the colonia Tepeyac would be perhaps the only
60 home I knew, and that nostalgia for a home would be a theme that would obsess me.

My brothers also figured greatly in my art. Especially the older two; I grew up in their shadows. Henry, the second oldest and my favorite, appears often in poems I have written and in stories which at times only borrow his nickname, Kiki. He played a major role in my childhood. We were bunk-bed mates. We were co-conspirators. We were pals. Until my oldest brother came back from studying in Mexico and left me odd woman out for always.

What would my teachers say if they knew I was a writer now? Who would've guessed it? I wasn't a very bright student. I didn't much like school because we
70 moved so much and I was always new and funny looking. In my fifth-grade report card I have nothing but an avalanche of C's and D's, but I don't remember being that stupid. I was good at art and I read plenty of library books and Kiki laughed at all my jokes. At home I was fine, but at school I never opened my mouth except when the teacher called on me.

When I think of how I see myself it would have to be at age eleven. I know I'm thirty-two on the outside, but inside I'm eleven. I'm the girl in the picture with skinny arms and a crumpled skirt and crooked hair. I didn't like school because all they saw was the outside me. School was lots of rules and sitting with your hands folded and being very afraid all the time. I liked looking out the window
80 and thinking. I liked staring at the girl across the way writing her name over and over again in red ink. I wondered why the boy with the dirty collar in front of me didn't have a mama who took better care of him.

I think my mama and papa did the best they could to keep us warm and clean and never hungry. We had birthday and graduation parties and things like that, but there was another hunger that had to be fed. There was a hunger I didn't even have a name for. Was this when I began writing? **D**

In 1966 we moved into a house, a real one, our first real home. This meant we didn't have to change schools and be the new kids on the block every couple of years. We could make friends and not be afraid we'd have to say goodbye to them
90 and start all over. My brothers and the flock of boys they brought home would become important characters eventually for my stories—Louie and his cousins, Meme Ortiz and his dog with two names, one in English and one in Spanish.

My mother flourished in her own home. She took books out of the library and taught herself to garden—to grow flowers so envied we had to put a lock

---

C VOICE
Reread Cisneros's description of her parents in lines 43–55. Identify the informal words, as well as the short sentences and fragments, that establish Cisneros's voice here.

D ANALYZE STRUCTURE
Identify the six recollections Cisneros presents in lines 43–86. What do they have in common? Explain why Cisneros might have chosen to include these particular memories.

E ANALYZE STRUCTURE

Possible answer: As in making corn tortillas by hand, Cisneros has done many things she did not think she would be able to do.

LITERARY ANALYSIS

F VOICE

Possible answer: Other examples include "provincianos" (line 12), "chilango" (line 14), and "Así como sea" (line 18). She includes these because her "Mexicanness" is part of her identity as a person and a writer.

Lines 114–116
REINFORCE *KEY IDEA*: IDEAS

Discuss In what way might a six-month residency on a 265-acre ranch help a writer find **ideas**? *Possible answer: The availability of time to think could help generate ideas, and the landscape could be inspiring.*

SELECTION WRAP–UP

SUMMARIZE Have students sum up the way that Cisneros's cultural heritage plays a role in her work.

⭐ CRITIQUE

- Ask students to state whether they find the essay inspiring, and why or why not.

- After completing the After Reading questions on page 1229, have students revisit their responses and tell whether they have changed their opinions.

---

on the gate to keep out the midnight flower thieves. My mother has never quit gardening.

This was the period in my life, that slippery age when you are both child and woman and neither, I was to record in *The House on Mango Street*. I was still shy. I was a girl who couldn't come out of her shell.

100   How was I to know I would be recording and documenting the women who sat their sadness on an elbow and stared out a window? It would be the city streets of Chicago I would later record, as seen through a child's eyes.

I've done all kinds of things I didn't think I could do since then. I've gone to a prestigious university, studied with famous writers, and taken an MFA degree. I've taught poetry in schools in Illinois and Texas. I've gotten an NEA grant and run away with it as far as my courage would take me. I've seen the bleached and bitter mountains of the Peloponnesus.[7] I've lived on an island. I've been to Venice twice. I've lived in Yugoslavia. I've been to the famous Nice[8] flower market behind the opera house. I've lived in a village in the pre-Alps and witnessed the daily parade

110   of promenaders. **E**

I've moved since Europe to the strange and wonderful country of Texas, land of polaroid-blue skies and big bugs. I met a mayor with my last name. I met famous Chicana and Chicano artists and writers and *políticos*.[9] **F**

Texas is another chapter in my life. It brought with it the Dobie-Paisano Fellowship,[10] a six-month residency on a 265-acre ranch. But most important, Texas brought Mexico back to me.

In the days when I would sit at my favorite people-watching spot, the snakey Woolworth's counter across the street from the Alamo[11] (the Woolworth's which has since been torn down to make way for progress), I couldn't think of anything

120   else I'd rather be than a writer. I've traveled and lectured from Cape Cod to San Francisco, to Spain, Yugoslavia, Greece, Mexico, France, Italy, and now today to Texas. Along the way there has been straw for the taking. With a little imagination, it can be spun into gold. ❧

2 Targeted Passage

E ANALYZE STRUCTURE
Reread lines 103–110. How does this list of accomplishments relate back to Cisneros's opening anecdote?

F VOICE
Cisneros's use of the word *políticos* in line 113 is one example of her technique of incorporating Spanish words and phrases in her writing. Find two other examples of this technique in the selection. What is her purpose for including these words?

---

7. **Peloponnesus** (pĕl'ə-pə-nē'-səs): peninsula forming the southern part of mainland Greece.

8. **Nice** (nēs): port city in southern France.

9. *políticos* (pō-lē'tē-kōs) *Spanish:* politicians.

10. **Dobie-Paisano** (dō'bē pī-zä'nō) **Fellowship:** a prestigious award offered to authors who are from or write about Texas. It includes cash as well as the use of living quarters.

11. **Alamo:** a mission chapel in San Antonio, Texas, site of a famous battle in Texas's war of independence from Mexico.

DIFFERENTIATED INSTRUCTION

FOR STRATEGIC READERS

2 Targeted Passage [Lines 103–123]

In this passage Cisneros concludes by noting that life provides plenty of writing material.

- Where has Cisneros traveled and lived? What has she done? What does she think about these experiences?

- What are Cisneros's feelings about being a writer? In what ways have her experiences helped her write?

FOR ENGLISH LEARNERS

Culture: Clarify Explain these references: *mayor with my last name* (line 112), "Henry Cisneros, the former mayor of San Antonio, Texas"; *Chicana and Chicano* (line 113) "a North American girl or boy of Mexican descent"; *Woolworth's* (line 118), "a store that sells inexpensive items such as sewing supplies and often has a coffee shop in it." Clarify that *Latina* (line 35) means "a female of Latin American descent."

FOR ADVANCED LEARNERS/AP

Synthesize Remind students that the essay was originally delivered as a speech. Ask them to imagine that they are in the audience hearing the speech the first time it was presented. Ask students to cite passages and rhetorical elements in the essay that would have made it an effective speech. Then ask students to share ways they might have responded to the speech.

Comprehension

R2.2, R3.3
CALIFORNIA

1. **Recall** What misunderstanding does Cisneros recount at the beginning of the essay?

2. **Recall** What traits do Cisneros and her father have in common?

3. **Summarize** As a child, how did Cisneros feel at school?

Literary Analysis

4. **Make Inferences** What childhood events and circumstances inspired Cisneros to become a writer? Cite evidence from the selection to support your inferences.

5. **Interpret Allusion** An allusion is an indirect reference to a person, a place, an event, or a literary work with which the writer believes the reader will be familiar. Reread lines 120–123 and consider the essay's title. By incorporating allusions to the fairy tale "Rumplestiltskin," what point is Cisneros making about ordinary experiences? What is she saying about the imagination?

6. **Draw Conclusions** From statements Cisneros makes in this essay, what can you conclude about her feelings regarding

   • traditional female roles in Latino culture (lines 33–42)?
   • home ownership (lines 56–61 and 87–90)?
   • racial or ethnic stereotypes (lines 7–16)?

7. **Analyze Structure** Review the chart you created. What idea does Cisneros return to throughout the essay? What is the function of this recurring idea in developing her message? Support your answer with evidence from the text.

8. **Compare Voice** In a chart, record examples of the stylistic elements that create Cisneros's unique voice. Then choose another prose selection from this unit, and analyze the voice of its author as well. Use your completed chart to explain how Cisneros's voice differs from that of the other writer's.

	Sentence Type/Length	Word Choice	Tone
Cisneros			
Other Writer			

Literary Criticism

9. **Critical Interpretations** Cisneros's candid recollections prompted one critic to say, "The memories that Cisneros offers . . . sometimes wrinkle the nose and scorch the palate." He went on to praise her talent for "evoking the sensations of the past in their full complexity." Why do you think Cisneros shares her insecurities and painful experiences as well as her triumphs? How might failing to do this have altered the essay's message? Explain, citing evidence.

---

7. ■ **SKILLS FOCUS Analyze Structure**
Throughout the essay, Cisneros returns to the "Rumplestiltskin" idea of turning straw into gold, and of having accomplished things she didn't think she could do. The idea helps her to develop themes about determination, experience, and imagination. Student evidence will vary.

8. ● **SKILLS FOCUS Voice** *Charts will vary based on the authors chosen, but should contain multiple examples of each writer's unique voice.*

9. *If she had shared only her triumphant moments, Cisneros would not seem as sympathetic or as easy to relate to, nor would her triumphs seem as impressive. It would be impossible to communicate her "Rumplestiltskin" theme if she did not admit that she felt daunted by her tasks.*

Practice and Apply

After Reading

Use these copy masters to check understanding and provide extra support:

R RESOURCE MANAGER—Copy Masters
   Reading Check p. 259
   Voice p. 255
   Question Support p. 260

Additional selection questions are provided for teachers on page 249.

ANSWERS

1. *Cisneros describes being asked to make tortillas by friends who assumed she knew how because she was Mexican American.*

2. *Cisneros and her father share a love of travel and a "sappy heart."*

3. *She felt alienated and uncomfortable.*

Possible answers:

4. *Cisneros was inspired by living in a patriarchal household in a patriarchal culture, hearing her father's stories and her mother's streetwise voice, being shy, being the only daughter among seven children.*

5. *Cisneros believes ordinary experiences are sources of ideas and inspiration, and that imagination is the magic that can turn this raw material into the gold of art.*

6. *Cisneros dislikes traditional female roles in Latino culture, believing they prevent women from reaching their potential. She venerates home ownership. She feels that stereotypes are oversimplified images that can't capture people's complex qualities.*

Assess and Reteach

Assess

R RESOURCE MANAGER—Copy Masters
   Selection Test A pp. 261–262
   Selection Test B/C pp. 263–264

💿 Test Generator CD

Reteach

S STANDARDS LESSON FILE
   Literature Lesson 34: Allusion
   Literature Lesson 44: Style and Syntax
   Writing Lesson 43: Developing a Voice

OBJECTIVES

Literary Analysis
- explore the key idea of what is worth **striving** for
- analyze repetition and anaphora and their impact on meaning
- read poems

Reading
- compare and contrast poems

CALIFORNIA **R3.2, R3.3**

ABOUT THE AUTHOR

After students read the author biography, ask them to point out the turning point when Brooks's approach to poetry changed. *Possible answer: In 1967, Brooks attended a conference of young black writers.* Tell students they will read poems in both of Brooks's styles. Invite them to predict ways that the two poems will be different. *Possible answer: One poem will focus on daily life for African Americans and the other will focus on political or societal issues affecting African Americans.*

USING THE *NOTABLE QUOTE*

Read the quote aloud and then focus attention on the first sentence: "Art hurts." Ask students what **Gwendolyn Brooks** means and have them give examples of art that "hurts." *Possible answer: Art pushes people to think and see and feel in ways they wouldn't otherwise. Examples include art that shows viewers difficult situations or evokes strong emotions.*

CALIFORNIA **R3.2, R3.3**

Life for My Child Is Simple
Primer for Blacks

Poetry by Gwendolyn Brooks

NOTABLE QUOTE

"Art hurts. Art urges voyages—and it is easier to stay at home."

FYI
Did you know that Gwendolyn Brooks . . .

- published her first poem at age 13?
- was the first African American to win a Pulitzer Prize?
- paid for prizes for student literary contests out of her own pocket?

Author Online

For more on Gwendolyn Brooks, visit the **Literature Center** at **ClassZone.com.**

Brooks at home on Chicago's South Side, 1960

1230

Gwendolyn Brooks

1917–2000

Decades before urban musicians introduced Americans to rap and hip hop, Gwendolyn Brooks captured some of these same rhythms in her writing. In verse celebrated for its lyrical beauty, Brooks portrays the thoughts, feelings, and, often, extraordinary heroism of African Americans living amidst poverty and segregation.

An Early Start Though born in Topeka, Kansas, Brooks spent almost her entire life in Chicago. Even as a young girl, she loved to write. When she was 7, Brooks began filling composition books with "careful rhymes," prompting her mother to exclaim, "You are going to be the lady Paul Laurence Dunbar." By the age of 16, Brooks was a frequent contributor to *The Defender,* a prominent black newspaper in Chicago. During her teenage years, leading African-American poets James Weldon Johnson and Langston Hughes also recognized her immense talent.

Literary Triumph At 28, Brooks published *A Street in Bronzeville,* named for the bustling black enclave on Chicago's South Side. Written in a range of traditional forms, the poems explored the difficult lives of those around her. "I wrote about what I saw and heard in the street," Brooks said. "I lived in a small second-floor apartment at the corner, and I could look first on one side and then the other. There was my material." In 1949, Brooks published *Annie Allen,* a series of poems that trace the life of a Bronzeville girl. The book achieved literary acclaim and propelled its author into the spotlight. In 1950, Brooks became the first African-American writer to receive the Pulitzer Prize. The award brought her worldwide fame. "Sometimes," she quipped, "I feel that my name is Gwendolyn Pulitzer Brooks."

A Fateful Encounter Brooks experienced another turning point in 1967, when she attended a conference of black writers, meeting young African-American poets. Impressed by their commitment to a black aesthetic and issues of racial justice, Brooks became interested in writing a new kind of poetry. "If it hadn't been for these young people," she later remarked, "I wouldn't know what I know about this society. By associating with them I know who I am." Brooks began to experiment with free verse and to focus on the problems of color and justice. She started a poetry workshop for members of a Chicago street gang and became a lifelong advocate for the next generation. "My greatest interest," Brooks once said, "is being involved with young people."

R RESOURCE MANAGER UNIT 6

Plan and Teach pp. 265–272

Literary Analysis
Repetition pp. 273, 274†*
Question Support p. 277*

Reading
Compare and Contrast Poems
pp. 275, 276†*

Assessment
Selection Tests A, B/C
pp. 279*, 281*

Test Generator CD

BEST PRACTICES TOOLKIT

Differentiated Instruction
pp. 31–38*

Graphic Organizers/Strategies
Evaluating a Poem • Two-Column
Chart

Reading Support

Audio Anthology CD*

Technology
Literature Center at
ClassZone.com
Write*Smart* CD

---

* Resources for Differentiation   † Also in Spanish

LITERARY ANALYSIS: REPETITION

What keeps a song or a poem stuck in your mind long after you've heard it on the radio or read it in the classroom? Often, the answer lies in the writer's use of **repetition**, a technique in which a sound, word, phrase, or line is repeated for emphasis or to create rhythm. A related technique is **anaphora**, in which the same word or phrase is repeated at the beginning of two or more lines. Consider this example from "Primer for Blacks":

Blackness
is a title,
is a preoccupation,
is a commitment . . .

As you read, pay close attention to Brooks's use of repetition and especially of anaphora. Consider what these techniques emphasize in each poem, and note the rhythm they help build.

READING SKILL: COMPARE AND CONTRAST POEMS

Brooks's poetry career spanned six decades. She wrote "Life for My Child Is Simple" early in her career; it comes from *Annie Allen,* which traces the life of a fictional character but draws much of its inspiration from Brooks's own experiences. "Primer for Blacks" was written many years later, when Brooks was developing a deeper commitment to political and social issues. As you read, **compare and contrast** these two poems in a chart as shown. The following tips can help you:

- Ask yourself about the **subject** of each poem. Is it personal or political? Does it focus on a group or an individual?
- Describe the **tone.**
- Consider **stylistic elements** such as diction, punctuation, and capitalization.
- Identify the **theme** of each poem. What message does each suggest about life?

	"Life for My Child Is Simple"	"Primer for Blacks"
Subject		
Tone		
Speaker		
Style		
Theme		

DIFFERENTIATED INSTRUCTION

FOR STRATEGIC READERS
Vocabulary Support

- *preoccupation,* "a constant thought or persistent interest in something"
- *commitment,* "a strong involvement in an interest or cause"
- *primer,* "a book for beginners"
- *diction,* "word choice, including both vocabulary (individual words) and syntax (the order or arrangement of words)"

Explore the Key Idea

CALIFORNIA

What should we REACH *for?*

KEY IDEA Gwendolyn Brooks advised her readers to "exhaust the little moment"—to live richly and **strive** higher in each moment of their lives. What, in your opinion, is worth striving for?

QUICKWRITE Brainstorm a list of things that are worth reaching for. Start by listing personal goals. Then move on to more global issues: if you had unlimited resources, what would you fix or change? Come up with a top-ten list of the things most worth striving for.

> 1. An end to world hunger
> 2. A cure for cancer

1231

Teach

CALIFORNIA

What should we REACH *for?*

Read the question and the **KEY IDEA** aloud. Ask students to discuss what it means to them to **strive** higher. After students complete the **QUICKWRITE,** invite volunteers to share and combine their top-ten lists.

SKILLS FOCUS

LITERARY ANALYSIS R3.3

● REPETITION

Write this passage on the board:

> How many stars are in the sky, and
> How many fish in the sea?
> How many years can my love be gone
> Before he comes back to me?

Have students identify the anaphora and discuss ways that it affects the rhythm and mood of the poem. ***Possible answer:** The anaphora is the repetition of "How many." It creates a demanding rhythm that echoes the poem's sorrowful mood and message.*

CHECK UNDERSTANDING Have students write a few lines containing anaphora.

READING SKILL R3.2, R3.3

■ COMPARE AND CONTRAST POEMS

Review that comparing shows similarities and contrasting shows differences. Ask volunteers to define the terms briefly in the chart on page 1231 and then to identify those traits in the passage on the board. ***Possible answer:** Subject is the topic of a work. Poem: romantic longing. Tone is the poet's attitude toward the work. Poem: serious. Speaker is the voice in a poem. Poem: abandoned lover. Style is the way a poet writes. Poem: rhythmically. Theme is a message about life. Poem: Love is hard.*

R RESOURCE MANAGER—Copy Master
Compare and Contrast Poems p. 275 (for student use while reading the selections)

Practice and Apply

SUMMARY

The speaker in this poem describes the boisterous activities of a young child, such as kicking over a chair and throwing blocks out a window. The speaker shares the child's adventurous glee and praises his fearless reaching-out.

Lines 15–18
REINFORCE *KEY IDEA*: STRIVE

Discuss In what way do these lines suggest that the speaker wants her child to **strive?**
Possible answer: *The speaker celebrates that her child has "never been afraid to reach" and that "reaching is his rule." This suggests that she wants him to strive.*

LITERARY ANALYSIS

 REPETITION

Possible answer: *The poem's pace accelerates as the repetition builds. The rhythm creates a feeling of urgency.*

If students need help . . . Use an Evaluating a Poem organizer to help them focus on ways that style and word choice affect the emotional power of the lines.

🧰 **BEST PRACTICES TOOLKIT—Transparency**
Evaluating a Poem p. D17

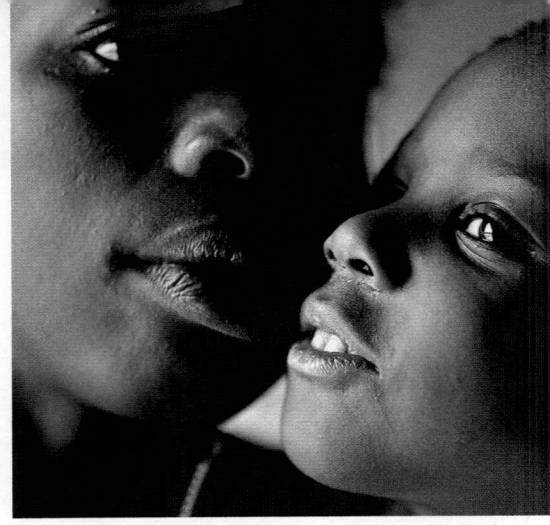

Life for My Child Is Simple

GWENDOLYN BROOKS

Life for my child is simple, and is good.
He knows his wish. Yes, but that is not all.
Because I know mine too.
And we both want joy of undeep and unabiding[1] things,
5 Like kicking over a chair or throwing blocks out of a window
Or tipping over an ice box pan[2]
Or snatching down curtains or fingering an electric outlet
Or a journey or a friend or an illegal kiss.
No. There is more to it than that. **Ⓐ**
10 It is that he has never been afraid.
Rather, he reaches out and lo the chair falls with a beautiful crash,
And the blocks fall, down on the people's heads,
And the water comes slooshing sloppily out across the floor.
And so forth.
15 Not that success, for him, is sure, infallible.[3]
But never has he been afraid to reach.
His lesions are legion.[4]
But reaching is his rule.

Ⓐ REPETITION
Reread lines 4–9 aloud. What happens to the poem's pace as the repetition builds? Describe the feeling created by the **rhythm** in these lines.

---

1. **unabiding:** not lasting; continually changing.
2. **ice box pan:** a pan for collecting melted ice in an old-fashioned refrigerator.
3. **infallible:** foolproof.
4. **His lesions are legion:** His injuries are many.

1232 UNIT 6: CONTEMPORARY LITERATURE

DIFFERENTIATED INSTRUCTION

For general guidelines on differentiating instruction, see

 BEST PRACTICES TOOLKIT
Differentiated Instruction pp. 31–38

FOR STRATEGIC READERS
Options for Reading: Audio Recording

- Have students listen to the poems on the *Audio Anthology CD* (also recommended for English learners) while they read along in their texts. Have students pay particular attention to repetition in the poems.

- When they listen to "A Primer for Blacks," tell students to notice the speaker's tone and emphasis on reading words that start with capital letters, as in "It's Great to be white" (lines 10 and 13) or that are entirely capitalized, such as "YOU" (line 50). The After Reading question 7 on page 1235 deals with this stylistic element in more depth.

Primer for Blacks

GWENDOLYN BROOKS

Blackness
is a title,
is a preoccupation,[1]
is a commitment Blacks
5 are to comprehend—
and in which you are
to perceive your Glory.

The conscious shout
of all that is white is
10 "It's Great to be white."
The conscious shout
of the slack[2] in Black is
"It's Great to be white."
Thus all that is white
15 has white strength and yours. **B**

The word Black
has geographic power,
pulls everybody in:
Blacks here—
20 Blacks there—
Blacks wherever they may be.
And remember, you Blacks, what they told you—
remember your Education:
"one Drop—one Drop[3]
25 maketh a brand new Black."

Oh mighty Drop.
And because they have given us kindly
so many more of our people

Everyman, Brenda Joysmith. 345″ × 58 1/4″. © Brenda Joysmith. Courtesy of Joysmith Gallery.

B COMPARE AND CONTRAST POEMS
So far, how does this poem differ from "Life for My Child Is Simple" in both **content** and **style?** Cite examples from both poems to support your answer.

1. **preoccupation:** something requiring full attention.
2. **slack:** lack of force.
3. **"one Drop":** At times in U.S. history, a person with only "one drop" of African blood has been considered black.

SUMMARY

This poem encourages African Americans to understand and take pride in their heritage and to live out their pride as a commitment in daily life.

About the Art African-American artist Brenda Joysmith (born 1952) grew up in Memphis, Tennessee, and studied at the University of Chicago. Her art typically celebrates the day-to-day experiences of African Americans. The sense of unity and pride depicted in *Everyman* mirrors the philosophy of Brooks's poem.

CULTURAL CONNECTION

Cultural Pride The Black Pride movement of the 1960s brought about major changes in the attitudes of both African Americans and other Americans. Similarly, Native Americans asserted their pride in protest actions during the same era. Ask students to share their knowledge of ways that ethnic or cultural groups have asserted pride.

READING SKILL

B COMPARE AND CONTRAST POEMS

Possible answer: This poem is more political, less personal, in content. It is more vehement, less musing, in tone. It uses many stanzas rather than one, as well as shorter lines and unconventional capitalization.

If students need help . . . Have them add to the chart begun on page 1231:

"Primer for Blacks"	
Subject	group pride
Tone	angry, proud
Style	multiple stanzas; short lines; unusual capitalization

FOR ENGLISH LEARNERS

Vocabulary: Cognates Point out that the Spanish word *preocupación* is similar to the word *preoccupation* in line 3. Ask Spanish-speaking students to find five other words in "Primer for Blacks" that are similar to Spanish words. Have them share their findings with the class. *Possible answer: Cognates include comprehend/comprender* (line 5); *perceive/ percibir, Glory/Gloria* (line 7); *conscious/consciente* (line 8); *geographic/geografico* (line 17).

FOR ADVANCED LEARNERS/AP

Analyze Connotations Have students use a Two-Column Chart like this one to compare and contrast the connotations of the words *white* and *black* in the poem.

White	Black
"white strength"	"geographic power"

 BEST PRACTICES TOOLKIT—Transparency
Two-Column Chart p. A25

C REPETITION

Possible answer: The anaphora emphasizes the equality of different shades of African-American skin. The point is to celebrate racial pride and to create a feeling of unity.

If students need help . . . Ask these questions and help students answer them:

- In what way are all these colors united?
- What feelings does the speaker have about the unity of these colors?

Lines 40–47
TIERED DISCUSSION PROMPTS

Use these prompts to help students comprehend the poem's message:

Connect With what groups do you feel connected? What feelings do you have about those groups? *Accept all thoughtful responses.*

Interpret In line 41, what does the word *Comprehend* tell African Americans to do? *Possible answer: It tells them to understand their heritage.*

Evaluate Is Brooks's statement that racial pride is the "lone ground" for success an overstatement? Why or why not? *Accept all thoughtful responses.*

SELECTION WRAP–UP

SYNTHESIZE Have students explain why Brooks's poems express the vision of a single author who grew and changed.

★ CRITIQUE

- Ask students to agree or disagree with the messages of the poems.
- After completing the After Reading questions on page 1235, have students revisit their responses and tell whether they have changed their opinions.

Blackness
30 stretches over the land.
Blackness—
the Black of it,
the rust-red of it,
the milk and cream of it,
35 the tan and yellow-tan of it,
the deep-brown middle-brown high-brown of it,
the "olive" and ochre[4] of it—
Blackness
marches on. C

40 The huge, the pungent[5] object of our prime out-ride
is to Comprehend,
to salute and to Love the fact that we are Black,
which *is* our "ultimate Reality,"[6]
which is the lone ground
45 from which our meaningful metamorphosis,
from which our prosperous staccato,[7]
group or individual, can rise.

Self-shriveled Blacks.
Begin with gaunt and marvelous concession:
50 YOU are our costume and our fundamental bone.

All of you—
you COLORED ones,
you NEGRO ones,
those of you who proudly cry
55 "I'm half INDian"—
those of you who proudly screech
"I'VE got the blood of George WASHington in MY veins"—
ALL of you—
you proper Blacks,
60 you half-Blacks,
you wish-I-weren't Blacks,
Niggeroes and Niggerenes.

You.

---

4. **ochre** (ō'kər): brownish orange-yellow.
5. **pungent** (pŭn'jənt): sharp and intense, like a powerful odor.
6. **the fact . . . "ultimate Reality":** a rewording of a quotation from black activist Ron Karenga.
7. **staccato** (stə-kä'tō): the playing of musical notes in a crisp, disconnected way.

C REPETITION
Reread lines 31–39. What does Brooks's use of **anaphora** emphasize about the many shades of blackness she lists? What point is she making here?

DIFFERENTIATED INSTRUCTION

FOR ENGLISH LEARNERS
Related Vocabulary Make sure students understand that the poem uses related words to describe variations in African-American skin colors. Use a dictionary and, if possible, a color wheel or other illustration to help students understand these color words: *rust-red* (line 33); *tan, yellow-tan* (line 35); *olive, ochre* (line 37).

FOR ADVANCED LEARNERS/AP
Evaluate Impact "Primer for Blacks" was written during and for the Black Pride movement. Ask students to think about whether the poem retains its original force several decades later. Is its message as vital as ever? Is its style as powerful as ever? Have students write brief evaluations expressing a contemporary response to the poem. After students share their responses with the class, invite the group to decide if Brooks's poem has retained its power.

Comprehension

R3.2, R3.3

1. **Recall** In "Life for My Child Is Simple," what things does the child enjoy doing?

2. **Clarify** How do the child's feelings differ from his mother's?

3. **Clarify** Reread lines 16–30 of "Primer for Blacks." Why does "the word Black" have "geographic power"?

4. **Clarify** What, according to Brooks, is the object of blacks' "prime out-ride," or most important undertaking?

Literary Analysis

5. **Interpret** Reread lines 10–18 of "Life for My Child Is Simple." Why has the speaker's son never been afraid of **striving** for what he wants? Why, in contrast, might the speaker have felt fearful?

6. **Examine Author's Purpose** Determine Brooks's intended audience for "Primer for Blacks." What do you think she wants her audience to feel? What action does she want her audience to take? Cite specific lines from the poem to support your answers.

7. **Analyze Style** Review "Primer for Blacks," noting Brooks's use of nonstandard capitalization. Why do you think she does this? How does this unorthodox capitalization affect the poem's meaning and contribute to the voice of the speaker?

8. **Analyze Repetition** Reconsider the annotated examples of repetition in Brooks's poems. Then find at least one other example in each work. Do your examples qualify as **anaphora?** In each case, what is the impact of repetition on the meaning?

9. **Compare and Contrast Poems** Using the chart you filled in as you read, summarize the similarities and the differences you found in the two poems. In your opinion, do the poems suggest similar or different ways of approaching life? Explain, citing evidence.

10. **Draw Conclusions About Theme** In these poems, what overall messages does Brooks communicate about

    • fulfilling one's potential?   • confidence and self-regard?

    • black identity?   • beauty?

Literary Criticism

11. **Author's Style** In the late 1960s, Brooks began experimenting with **free verse,** believing she was no longer living in "a sonnet kind of time." Why do you think Brooks chose free verse for these two poems? In your opinion, is free verse an appropriate poetic form for these works? Explain your opinions.

8. ● **SKILLS FOCUS Repetition** *Students' choices will vary, but anaphora appears in lines 12–14 of the earlier poem and lines 50–63 of the later poem. In general, repetition emphasizes ideas and drives the rhythm of the poems.*

9. ■ **SKILLS FOCUS Compare and Contrast Poems** *Charts should address each component listed. Differences include those identified in the response to annotation B, while both poems stress the importance of striving to fulfill one's potential.*

10. *Brooks may have felt that free verse liberated her from poetic forms developed by whites. If so, the form is appropriate to her message, which celebrates self-determination, fearlessness, and liberty.*

11. *Accept all reasonable answers.*

Practice and Apply

After Reading

Use these copy masters to check understanding and provide extra support:

R RESOURCE MANAGER—Copy Masters
Repetition p. 273
Question Support p. 277

Additional selection questions are provided for teachers on page 269.

ANSWERS

1. *The boy enjoys kicking over a chair, throwing blocks out a window, tipping over an ice box pan, snatching down curtains, fingering an electric outlet.*

2. *The child has never known fear.*

3. *"The word Black" has geographic power because the description unites people of African descent wherever they are and regardless of what portion of their heritage is African.*

4. *Blacks' most important undertaking is to "Comprehend, / to salute and to Love the fact that we are Black" (lines 41–42).*

Possible answers:

5. *The child has never had fear because he is young and protected. His mother has perhaps known fear because of discrimination.*

6. *Brooks's audience is African Americans who have not found identity. She wants them to discover and act with racial pride.*

7. *Brooks uses capitalization to emphasize key points, such as her call to rejoice in racial identity. The words in all capitals allow the reader to hear the speaker's strident, persuasive tone.*

Assess and Reteach

Assess

R RESOURCE MANAGER—Copy Masters
Selection Test A pp. 279–280
Selection Test B/C pp. 281–282

⊘ Test Generator CD

Reteach

S STANDARDS LESSON FILE
Literature Lessons 20, 35, 43, 44
Reading Lesson 12

OBJECTIVES

Literary Analysis
- explore the key idea of **perspective**
- analyze sound devices
- read poetry

Reading
- make inferences and draw conclusions about speakers

 R3.4

ABOUT THE AUTHOR

After students read the author biography, call attention to the quotations from Dove in **Illuminating the Everyday.** Ask students what she means by "all the moments that make up a human being." *Possible answer: Dove means that a person is affected and shaped by many different experiences.* Ask what students expect to find in poems that express that philosophy. *Possible answer: The poems will likely touch on many kinds of experiences.*

USING THE *NOTABLE QUOTE*

Point out that in this quote, **Rita Dove** again stresses her interest in particular moments. Ask students to give examples of "the smaller crystallized details we all hinge our lives on." *Possible answer: These details could be the experience of looking in the mirror, the trip to school each day, a friend's glance, and so on.* The discussion should prepare students to discover poetry that is both personal and universal.

Selection Resources

R3.4

Adolescence—III
Testimonial

Poetry by Rita Dove

NOTABLE QUOTE

"I prefer to explore the most intimate moments, the smaller crystallized details we all hinge our lives on."

FYI

Did you know that Rita Dove ...

- was the youngest person and first African American named poet laureate?
- produced her own TV show?
- is a classically trained singer and musician, as well as a ballroom dancer?

Author Online

For more on Rita Dove, visit the **Literature Center** at ClassZone.com.

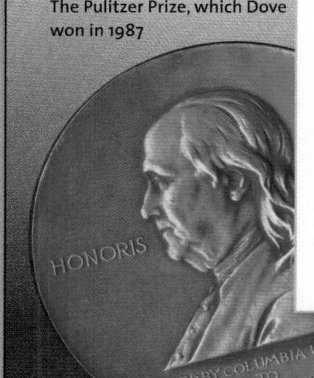

The Pulitzer Prize, which Dove won in 1987

Rita Dove
born 1952

For Rita Dove, the personal and the historical are equally important. "I've been fascinated," she says, "by what I've called before 'the underside of history,' the dramas of ordinary people." In her poetry, Dove often interweaves historical events with personal narratives, producing lyric images of everyday life.

High Achiever The daughter of a research chemist who broke the color barrier in the tire industry, Dove was always encouraged, she says, "to go as far as [she] could." Her parents drove Dove to excel in school and counseled her to never give up. Their guidance served her well. As a teenager, she was one of only 100 high school seniors named Presidential Scholar. She also distinguished herself in college, graduating Phi Beta Kappa from Miami University in 1973.

A Passion for Words Dove first became aware of the power of storytelling as a young girl. Listening to local storytellers in her hometown of Akron, Ohio, Dove discovered "the delight of shaping life with words." She also began a lifelong love affair with poetry, sparked by her discovery of an anthology in the local library. Though Dove began writing as a child, she did not fully embrace literary pursuits until college. Determining then that she wanted to be a writer, she applied and was accepted to the prestigious Iowa Writers' Workshop.

National Acclaim Publication in magazines had already earned Dove widespread praise when her first poetry collection, *The Yellow House on the Corner,* came out in 1980. Over the next few years, she published several more books, including *Thomas and Beulah,* hailed as her masterpiece. The book, which drew its inspiration from the quiet heroism of Dove's grandparents' lives, won a Pulitzer Prize in 1987. Since then, Dove has gone on to collect numerous literary honors.

Illuminating the Everyday Though she touches on issues of race, her poems, Dove asserts, "are about humanity." They attempt to convey something about the gamut of human experiences, not just the positive moments. "All the moments that make up a human being," Dove says, "have to be written about, talked about, painted, danced, in order to really talk about life."

1236

 RESOURCE MANAGER UNIT 6

Plan and Teach pp. 283–290

Literary Analysis
Sound Devices pp. 291, 292†*
Question Support p. 295*

Reading
Make Inferences About Speakers
pp. 293, 294†*

Assessment
Selection Tests A, B/C
pp. 297*, 299*
Test Generator CD

 BEST PRACTICES TOOLKIT

Differentiated Instruction
pp. 31–38*

Graphic Organizers/Strategies
Open Mind • Word Sorts

Reading Support
Audio Anthology CD*

Technology
Literature Center at **ClassZone.com**
Write*Smart* CD

---

* Resources for Differentiation † Also in Spanish

LITERARY ANALYSIS: SOUND DEVICES

A musician as well as a poet, Rita Dove believes a poem's sound is paramount. "If a poem doesn't have a sense of music," she explains, "then that poem probably won't move me very much." To infuse her poems with this quality, Dove employs **sound devices**—patterns of word sounds that create musical or rhythmic effects. As you read Dove's poems, listen for the following sound devices:

- **alliteration**—the repetition of initial consonant sounds
- **assonance**—the repetition of vowel sounds within words
- **consonance**—the repetition of consonant sounds within and at the ends of words

Think about how these sound devices impart a musical quality to the poems. Also consider what words, images, and feelings these devices serve to highlight.

READING SKILL: MAKE INFERENCES ABOUT SPEAKERS

The language in Dove's poems is often restrained and concise. She characterizes the **speaker** in each poem with a few well-chosen details but does not offer much explicit description or commentary. It is up to you to read between the lines, or **make inferences,** about each speaker's situation and state of mind. As you read, collect clues that tell you about each speaker's age, situation, and mindset. After you read, you'll use this information to **draw conclusions** about each speaker's experiences.

Clues from the Text	My Inferences and Reactions
"... Mom and I worked/ The dusky rows of tomatoes." (lines 1–2)	The speaker and her mother probably live in a rural area, not the city. They work hard in the fields.

Explore the Key Idea

How does your PERSPECTIVE change?

KEY IDEA As you get older, the way you think and feel about important events in your life changes. And your **perspective** on something that looms in your future—graduation, for instance—will probably change once that event has actually happened.

QUICKWRITE Think of a big event or an important moment from your recent past; write a paragraph describing your feelings about it. Then imagine how you will feel about this same event ten years from now. How might your perspective have changed? Pretending to be your future self, write a second paragraph describing the event from this later perspective.

Teach

How does your PERSPECTIVE change?

Read the question and the **KEY IDEA** aloud. Ask students to list situations about which a person's **perspective** might change over time. Encourage students to use their ideas as they complete the **QUICKWRITE** activity.

SKILLS FOCUS

R3.4

● SOUND DEVICES

Write this passage on the board:
Along the autumn paths
We strolled hand in hand,
Hopeful hearts upleaping—
And returning empty-handed.

Ask students to find alliteration, assonance, and consonance in the lines. ***Possible answer: Alliteration:*** "along" and "autumn," "hand in hand, / Hopeful hearts." ***Assonance:*** "strolled" and "hopeful," "hand in hand." ***Consonance:*** "Hopeful," "upleaping," "empty."

CHECK UNDERSTANDING Ask students to compose phrases containing the different sound devices.

READING SKILL

◼ MAKE INFERENCES ABOUT SPEAKERS

Ask students to make an inference about the speaker of the lines on the board. Point out that many inferences are possible. One inference that seems probable is that the speaker was disappointed in love.

 RESOURCE MANAGER—Copy Master
Make Inferences about Speakers p. 293 (for student use while reading the selections)

FOR STRATEGIC READERS
Vocabulary Support

- *paramount,* "most important"
- *infuse,* "fill with something"
- *impart,* "give"
- *restrained,* "quiet, not showy"
- *concise,* "brief, using few words"
- *explicit,* "stated directly"
- *mindset,* "an individual's way of thinking about situations, events, or ideas"

Concept Support: Make Inferences about Speakers To prepare students for making inferences about speakers, organize them in pairs for this practice exercise. Have one partner describe an object, speaking in that object's first-person point of view. For example, a cup of coffee might say, "I am liquid, hot, and brown." Have the listening partner make inferences about the speaker to guess what object is speaking.

SUMMARY

This poem's speaker is a fatherless teenage girl who works as a farm laborer and wears hand-me-down dresses. Her knees are scarred and the view from her window is of clay soil and chicken manure. She fantasizes about two men approaching her: an ideal lover, and her father.

READING SKILL

Ⓐ MAKE INFERENCES

Possible answer: The reader can infer that the speaker is an adolescent. It seems that she lives in the country with her single mother in circumstances of relative poverty.

If students need help . . . Have them add details to the chart introduced on page 1237:

Clues	Inferences
"scarred knees"	from working on her knees on the ground

LITERARY ANALYSIS

Ⓑ SOUND DEVICES

Possible answer: Alliteration includes "texture / twilight." The alliteration emphasizes a dreamy, melancholy time of day. Assonance includes "window-sill" / "lipstick" / "Glittered in." The repeated short i sound reinforces the image of the lipstick stubs, which reflect a poor girl's effort to become glamorous. Assonance also unifies the two lines.

Adolescence — III

Rita Dove

ANALYZE VISUALS
What words would you use to describe the girl in the painting? What details support your impressions?

BACKGROUND Dove wrote "Adolescence—III" early in her career, for her first published collection of poems. She composed "Testimonial" many years later and read it in the spring of 2001 at Howard University's commencement. "Whenever you think back," Dove told the graduating seniors, "and wonder where the future is going to lead you, remember that others have stood at this position and wondered, too. What you should do is take a step, one step at a time."

With Dad gone, Mom and I worked
The dusky rows of tomatoes.
As they glowed orange in sunlight
And rotted in shadow, I too
5 Grew orange and softer, swelling out
Starched cotton slips. Ⓐ

The texture of twilight made me think of
Lengths of Dotted Swiss.[1] In my room
I wrapped scarred knees in dresses
10 That once went to big-band dances;
I baptized my earlobes with rosewater.
Along the window-sill, the lipstick stubs
Glittered in their steel shells. Ⓑ

Looking out at the rows of clay
15 And chicken manure, I dreamed how it would happen:
He would meet me by the blue spruce,
A carnation over his heart, saying,
"I have come for you, Madam;
I have loved you in my dreams."
20 At his touch, the scabs would fall away.
Over his shoulder, I see my father coming toward us:
He carries his tears in a bowl,
And blood hangs in the pine-soaked air.

---

1. **Dotted Swiss:** crisp, sheer cotton fabric decorated with raised dots.

Ⓐ **MAKE INFERENCES**
What inferences can you make about the **speaker's** age from lines 1–6 and the poem's title? Do you get a sense of her family's situation in life? Explain.

Ⓑ **SOUND DEVICES**
Reread lines 7–13. Find one example of **alliteration** and one of **assonance** in these lines. What words or images are emphasized by these devices?

Evening Thoughts, Ernest Crichlow.
Lithograph, 25″ × 18″. Arisca Fine Art.

DIFFERENTIATED INSTRUCTION

For general guidelines on differentiating instruction, see

 BEST PRACTICES TOOLKIT
Differentiated Instruction pp. 31–38

FOR STRATEGIC READERS
Options for Reading: Audio Recording

Have students listen to the poems on the *Audio Anthology CD* (also recommended for English learners) while they read along in their texts. Have students pay particular attention to the sounds of both poems. You may want to play the CD more than once in order for students to hear the use of alliteration, assonance, and consonance.

ANALYZE VISUALS

Possible answer: *The girl in the painting appears to be timid and self-conscious. She is peering shyly toward the people in the background, who blend in more with the night than she does in her bright clothing. Her hand is lifted up to her mouth, perhaps as a nervous gesture. Like the speaker in Dove's poem, she seems more preoccupied with her own thoughts than with working.*

About the Art Known for his social realist style of art, Ernest Crichlow (1914–2005) first became famous during the Harlem Renaissance.

Lines 16–23
TIERED DISCUSSION PROMPTS

Use these prompts to help students understand the speaker's hopes:

Connect Think about times when you daydream. In what ways do fantasies usually compare to reality? *Students should recognize that people often fantasize about situations that are better than reality.*

Interpret Why does the speaker daydream? *Possible answer: She daydreams to take refuge from her unpleasant reality.*

Evaluate Is the image of an imaginary lover effective? Why or why not? *Students may find this image too obvious or too saccharine to be effective.* Does the image of the speaker's father effectively convey her views about him? Why or why not? *Students may find this image very effective in conveying the view of a father who regrets leaving his child.*

Lines 16–23
REINFORCE *KEY IDEA:*
PERSPECTIVE

Discuss In what way might the speaker's **perspective** change? *Possible answer: She might realize that her dreams are unrealistic.*

FOR STRATEGIC READERS

Concept Support: Make Inferences About a Speaker Have students complete an Open Mind diagram to record their impressions of the speaker's character and situation. Suggest starting entries such as: *She wants to be beautiful, She wants her father back,* or *She wants to be loved.*

BEST PRACTICES TOOLKIT—Transparency Open Mind p. D9

FOR ENGLISH LEARNERS

Vocabulary: Multiple-Meaning Words
Help students use context to determine the correct specific meaning for these words:

- *slips* (line 6), "garments worn under dresses or skirts"
- *lengths* (line 8), "measured cloth for sewing"
- *stubs* (line 12), "short, leftover parts"
- *shells* (line 13), "hard cases that protect"
- *hangs* (line 23), "seems present in"

SUMMARY

The speaker of this poem remembers a younger time when "the world called, and I answered," when luck was with her and promises were fulfilled.

About the Art German-born Alfred Gockel (born 1952) is known for his pop art and action paintings. *Discovery I* expresses youthful joy mixed with reflection similar to that in the poem.

READING SKILL

❻ MAKE INFERENCES

Possible answer: From the past-tense verbs and the imagery of a new earth, readers can infer that the speaker is an older person recalling youth and feeling thoughtful and perhaps wistful.

LITERARY ANALYSIS

❼ SOUND DEVICES

Possible answer: "Luck leaked" uses both alliteration and consonance. The musicality adds to the poem's musing tone.

SELECTION WRAP-UP

SYNTHESIZE Ask students to compare and contrast the age and situation of the two poems' speakers.

Testimonial
Rita Dove

Discovery I, Alfred Gockel. 39¼″ × 39¼″. © Alfred Gockel.

Back when the earth was new
and heaven just a whisper,
back when the names of things
hadn't had time to stick;

5 back when the smallest breezes
melted summer into autumn,
when all the poplars quivered
sweetly in rank and file . . .

the world called, and I answered.
10 Each glance ignited to a gaze.
I caught my breath and called that life,
swooned between spoonfuls of lemon sorbet. ❻

I was pirouette¹ and flourish,
I was filigree² and flame.
15 How could I count my blessings
when I didn't know their names?

Back when everything was still to come,
luck leaked out everywhere. ❼
I gave my promise to the world,
20 and the world followed me here.

---

1. **pirouette** (pĭr′ōō-ĕt′): in ballet, a full turn of the body on one foot.
2. **filigree:** delicate ornamentation, often made of wire.

❻ MAKE INFERENCES
Reread the poem's first three stanzas, noting the verb tense and the imagery. What can you infer about the **speaker's** age and state of mind?

❼ SOUND DEVICES
Identify the sound device used in line 18. What does this sense of musicality contribute to the poem's **tone?**

DIFFERENTIATED INSTRUCTION

FOR ENGLISH LEARNERS

Related Vocabulary Have students use Word Sorts to organize this language related to air and fire: **Air:** *whisper* (line 2), "speech that uses only air so it sounds soft"; *breezes* (line 5), "gentle winds." **Fire:** *melted* (line 6), "changed slowly"; *ignited* (line 10), "caught fire or attention suddenly"; *flame* (line 14), "intense feeling, like fire."

 BEST PRACTICES TOOLKIT—Transparency
Word Sorts p. E5

FOR ADVANCED LEARNERS/AP

Compare and Contrast Refer students back to the Notable Quote on page 1236. Ask them to think about ways that the Rita Dove poems they have just read "explore the most intimate moments" and "the smaller crystallized details we all hinge our lives on." Have students write one- to three-paragraph responses, using these questions as a guide:

- What "intimate" aspects of life do both poems explore?
- What sensory details in the poems add to the feeling of "crystallized" detail?
- Do both poems present "crystallized detail" equally well? Why or why not?
- What are the strengths and limitations of poetry that is about small moments?

LITERARY ANALYSIS: IMAGERY

When you read a poem, you enter a world filled with sights, sounds, smells, and textures all its own. Poets draw you into this world using **imagery,** words and images that re-create sensory experiences for the reader. Billy Collins owes some of his enormous popularity to the world he creates for his readers—a world that is often intensely familiar. Collins writes about everyday topics, presenting images from the natural world and the domestic sphere that are as recognizable as they are memorable. Note the words that appeal to your senses of sight and touch in these lines from "The Man in the Moon":

He used to frighten me in the nights of childhood,
the wide adult face, enormous, stern, aloft.
I could not imagine such loneliness, such coldness.

As you read, look for language that appeals to your senses, especially your sense of sight. Consider whether the images seem familiar to you and what ideas they serve to emphasize in each poem.

READING SKILL: TRACE THE DEVELOPMENT OF AN IDEA

Appreciating the sensory experience that a poem creates as you read it is one crucial aspect of analyzing poetry. Also important, however, is examining the **ideas** the poet presents. As you read, use the following strategies to trace the development of the ideas Collins puts forth in "The Man in the Moon" and "Forgetfulness." Use a chart like the one shown to organize your notes.

- Consider each poem's **title.** What idea does it suggest?
- Note the concept introduced or elaborated upon in each **stanza.** Consider how each stanza builds upon the one preceding it.
- Analyze Collins's **tone.** What attitude is expressed in each group of lines? Does the tone remain consistent throughout the poem, or does it change?

"The Man in the Moon"		
	Ideas Suggested	Tone
Title	The title makes me think of a children's story.	playful
Stanza 1		
Stanza 2		

What do the YEARS take with them?

KEY IDEA As we **age,** we gain some things, such as maturity and wisdom. Other things—energy, for example, or idealism—seem to slip from us. In your opinion, do the years take more than they give?

ROLE-PLAY With a partner, improvise a scene in which two characters talk about growing older. First, discuss what the characters might say to each other about the joys and ordeals of aging—maybe they miss letting their imaginations run wild, or perhaps they appreciate the wisdom they've developed over the years. Decide whether your scene will be a comic or a serious one. Then write a dialogue between the characters and act it out for the class.

1243

DIFFERENTIATED INSTRUCTION

FOR STRATEGIC READERS
Vocabulary Support

- *textures,* "the ways things feel to the touch"
- *sensory,* "appealing to the senses"
- *domestic sphere,* "related to home life"
- *aloft,* "high up"
- *elaborated,* "made fuller or more complex"
- *consistent,* "agreeing with what came before"

Concept Support: Imagery Provide students with Spider Maps in which to list sensory images as they read. Use the Collins excerpt and the lines on the board to model the use of the organizer.

BEST PRACTICES TOOLKIT—Transparency Spider Map p. B22

What do the YEARS take with them?

Lead into the **KEY IDEA** by asking the question. Discuss what the years take and give as people **age.** Then organize pairs for the **ROLE-PLAY** activity. Have volunteers present their dialogues, then help the class generalize about the pros and cons of aging.

SKILLS FOCUS

LITERARY ANALYSIS　　R3.4

● IMAGERY

Write this passage on the board:

The stars wink at each other across the
　dimly lit room of the sky,
Longing to meet, to escape this silent
　party
And laugh in the cool fresh air.

Ask students to find sensory images in the lines and to discuss ideas that the images emphasize. ***Possible answer:*** *Sensory images include "stars wink," "dimly lit," "rooms of the sky," "silent party," "cool fresh air." The images emphasize the ideas of distance and longing.*

CHECK UNDERSTANDING Have students use two or more sensory images to describe an everyday object.

READING SKILL　　R3.3

■ TRACE THE DEVELOPMENT OF AN IDEA

Have students reread the biography of Billy Collins and trace the development of its ideas about Collins, paragraph by paragraph. ***Possible answer:*** *Each paragraph's ideas reflect its subheading.* Explain that in poetry, ideas may be less clearly identified but that each stanza contributes to the overall idea in the same way that a paragraph contributes in an essay.

R RESOURCE MANAGER—Copy Master
Trace the Development of an Idea
　p. 311 (for student use while reading
　the selections)

Practice and Apply

SUMMARY

In this poem, the speaker recalls being scared by the man in the moon as a child. As an adult, the speaker compares the man in the moon to a bachelor in love.

READING SKILL

A TRACE IDEAS

Possible answer: Readers know that Collins is referring to the man in the moon because of the poem's title. In the first stanza, the speaker describes his childhood fear of the man in the moon; in the second, he explains the way his view has changed.

If students need help . . . Point out the words "But tonight" in line 4 as a clue to the shift in description. Have students add to the chart introduced on page 1243.

Ideas Suggested	Tone
He saw the moon as a cold, stern adult.	Nostalgic; eerie

LITERARY ANALYSIS

B IMAGERY

Possible answer: Students may cite any visual detail from the poem. The images underscore the speaker's changing attitudes toward the moon. Youth's fear describes the moon as stern and cold. Adult's comfort describes the moon as sympathetic.

Lines 1–12
TIERED DISCUSSION PROMPTS

Use these prompts to help students interpret the poem's images.

Connect In what ways can observing nature affect people's feelings? *Accept all thoughtful responses.*

Analyze Which words and phrases use images to express the speaker's feelings? *Possible answer: "I could not imagine such loneliness, such coldness" (line 3).*

Evaluate How engaging are the speaker's images about the man in the moon? Explain. *Students will likely find the speaker's images quite engaging. They will be able to imagine finding the moon scary and then finding it familiar.*

The Man in the **Moon**
Billy Collins

He used to frighten me in the nights of childhood,
the wide adult face, enormous, stern, aloft.
I could not imagine such loneliness, such coldness.

But tonight as I drive home over these hilly roads
5 I see him sinking behind stands of winter trees
and rising again to show his familiar face. **A**

And when he comes into full view over open fields
he looks like a young man who has fallen in love
with the dark earth,

10 a pale bachelor, well-groomed and full of melancholy,
his round mouth open
as if he had just broken into song. **B**

A TRACE IDEAS
Reread lines 1–6. How do you know what Collins is referring to when he says *He*? Explain how Collins's description of his subject changes from one stanza to the next. Record your answer in your chart.

B IMAGERY
Identify details that allow you to **visualize** the sight Collins describes. How does this description underscore the changing attitude of the speaker?

DIFFERENTIATED INSTRUCTION

For general guidelines on differentiating instruction, see

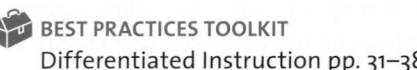 BEST PRACTICES TOOLKIT
Differentiated Instruction pp. 31–38

FOR STRATEGIC READERS
Options for Reading: Audio Recording

- Have students listen to the poems on the *Audio Anthology CD* (also recommended for English learners) while they read along in their texts. Encourage students to visualize the images and to connect them with the speaker's tone.

- For "The Man in the Moon," point out the shift that occurs in line 4, when the speaker begins to discuss the moon as an adult.

Forgetfulness

Billy Collins

The name of the author is the first to go
followed obediently by the title, the plot,
the heartbreaking conclusion, the entire novel
which suddenly becomes one you have never read, never
5   even heard of,

as if, one by one, the memories you used to harbor
decided to retire to the southern hemisphere of the brain,
to a little fishing village where there are no phones. **C**

Long ago you kissed the names of the nine Muses[1] goodbye
10 and watched the quadratic equation[2] pack its bag,
and even now as you memorize the order of the planets,

something else is slipping away, a state flower perhaps,
the address of an uncle, the capital of Paraguay.

Whatever it is you are struggling to remember
15 it is not poised on the tip of your tongue,
not even lurking in some obscure corner of your spleen.

It has floated away down a dark mythological river
whose name begins with an L[3] as far as you can recall,
well on your own way to oblivion where you will join those
20 who have even forgotten how to swim and how to ride a
    bicycle.

No wonder you rise in the middle of the night
to look up the date of a famous battle in a book on war.
No wonder the moon in the window seems to have drifted
25 out of a love poem that you used to know by heart.

---

1. **nine Muses:** in Greek mythology, goddesses of various fine arts and sciences.
2. **quadratic equation:** equation involving squaring of an unknown quantity or quantities, such as x^2.
3. **dark . . . an L:** the river Lethe, located in Hades, according to Greek mythology. Drinking its water caused one to forget the past.

C TRACE IDEAS
Reread lines 1–8. Describe Collins's **tone** as he introduces the idea of forgetfulness. What words and phrases help him achieve this tone? Note any changes in tone as you continue to read.

SUMMARY

In this poem, the speaker uses amusing imagery to give examples of ways that age brings forgetfulness.

READING SKILL

C TRACE IDEAS

Possible answer: *The tone is whimsical and rueful. Phrases such as "decided to retire" and "where there are no phones" help achieve the tone.*

Lines 22–25
REINFORCE *KEY IDEA:* AGE

Discuss What thoughts and feelings about **age** do these lines evoke? Explain. ***Possible answer:*** *Lines 22–25 evoke sad feelings and worried thoughts about age. The stanza shows age as frightening and lonely.*

SELECTION WRAP–UP

SYNTHESIZE Have students compare and contrast the speakers of the two poems.

⭐ CRITIQUE

- Ask students whether they understand why Collins's books are bestsellers.

- After completing the After Reading questions on page 1246, have students revisit their responses and tell whether they have changed their opinions.

FOR STRATEGIC READERS

Comprehension Support [small-group option]
Organize students in groups to discuss the poems, using the Core Analysis Frame: Poetry to cement their understanding of each poem.

 BEST PRACTICES TOOLKIT—Copy Master
    Core Analysis Frame: Poetry pp. D21, D34

FOR ADVANCED LEARNERS/AP

Analyze Poetic Form Point out that Collins's poems are written in free verse. Even the stanza lengths are irregular in "Forgetfulness," as if the speaker had forgotten how many lines to include in each. Challenge students to find poetic devices that Collins uses to unify each poem and distinguish it from prose. Encourage students to present their analysis of the poems to the class and to invite comments. ***Examples:*** *"The Man in the*

Moon": assonance such as "frighten/nights/childhood" (line 1), "round/mouth" (line 11), "open/broken" (lines 11–12); alliteration such as "sinking/stands" (line 5), "familiar/face/full/fields/fallen (lines 6–8); consonance such as "full/melancholy" (line 10); ***"Forgetfulness"*** *lines 22–24: anaphora such as "No wonder";* ***Both:*** *figurative language, and about four or five stressed syllables in most lines.*

Practice and Apply

After Reading

Use these copy masters to check understanding and provide extra support:

RESOURCE MANAGER—Copy Masters
Imagery p. 309
Question Support p. 313

Additional questions for teachers are provided on page 305.

ANSWERS

1. *The speaker no longer sees the moon as frightening and stern, but rather sees it in a fond, romantic light.*

2. *The speaker has forgotten novels once read, the names of the Muses, an uncle's address, the quadratic equation, and the name of the river Lethe.*

3. *The speaker is troubled by his inability to remember the date of a battle.*

Possible answers:

4. *As the years pass, the speaker becomes more knowledgeable about life and love and gains a more mature outlook. The years take away fear and replace it with ease.*

5. *Forgetting the Muses suggests that the speaker has forgotten something important about the arts themselves. Forgetting the name of the river of forgetfulness is humorous, but the connection with darkness makes the allusion ominous as well.*

6. *The "memories" in line 5 and the "quadratic equation" in line 9 are given human qualities. The personification helps Collins bring a humorous tone to an unnerving topic.*

Assess and Reteach

Assess

RESOURCE MANAGER—Copy Masters
Selection Test A pp. 315–316
Selection Test B/C pp. 317–318

Test Generator CD

Reteach

STANDARDS LESSON FILE
Literature Lesson 26: Imagery
Literature Lesson 43: Tone
Reading Lesson 4: Recognizing Main Idea and Details

Comprehension

 R3.3, R3.4

1. **Summarize** In "The Man in the Moon," how does the speaker's attitude toward the moon change as he gets older?

2. **Recall** List three things that the speaker of "Forgetfulness" has forgotten.

3. **Clarify** In "Forgetfulness," what troubles the speaker in the middle of the night?

Literary Analysis

4. **Interpret** What happens to the speaker of "The Man in The Moon" as the years pass? How does the speaker's outlook on life change? Citing evidence from the poem, describe what the years seem to take with them.

5. **Examine Allusions** In "Forgetfulness," what ideas are developed or underscored by each of the following allusions?
   - the Muses, the Greek goddesses who preside over the arts and sciences (line 9)
   - Lethe, the river of forgetfulness (lines 17–18)

6. **Analyze Personification** The giving of human qualities to an object, animal, or idea is called personification. Find at least two examples of personification in "Forgetfulness." What does Collins's use of this technique contribute to the poem's **tone?**

7. **Analyze Imagery** Reread lines 22–25 of "Forgetfulness." Compare the concrete image of the moon—the only real image that appears in the poem—with the fleeting, intangible nature of the things the speaker has forgotten. What does this contrast emphasize about the poem's meaning? Explain, citing lines that support your answer.

8. **Trace the Development of an Idea** Collins is known for writing poems that begin with humor and end in mystery and seriousness. Review the graphic organizer you filled in as you read. How, if at all, does the **tone** change over the course of each poem? Do the two poems present similar or different ideas about **aging?** Explain your answers, citing evidence from both poems.

Literary Criticism

9. **Critical Interpretations** Collins is beloved by readers for his fresh and often funny poems; he even won the Mark Twain Poetry Award, given for the "contribution of humor" to American verse. However, some critics argue that Collins's humor is hollow, weakened by clichés and lacking in originality and insight. On the basis of your reading of these poems, do you agree or disagree with this criticism? Explain your answer.

---

7. ● **SKILLS FOCUS Imagery** *The contrast emphasizes the fleeting nature of the facts that the speaker has forgotten and the way that memories slip through the cracks of an aging mind.*

8. ■ **SKILLS FOCUS Trace the Development of an Idea** *"The Man in the Moon" has a largely consistent tone, lyrical and melancholy, although the speaker's ideas about the moon change. This poem may be saying that as we age we become increasingly fond of the world, even of things that once scared us. "Forgetfulness" begins on a light tone,* *but becomes laced with sadness and wistfulness by the last stanza. This poem humorously reminds readers of frightening truths about decline and mortality.*

9. *Answers will vary, but should use text evidence to support stated opinions.*

A New Diversity

Late in the 20th century, it grew increasingly apparent that there was no single "American experience" and therefore no typical American voice. Once primarily the province of white men, the American literary canon—the body of works considered representative—exploded into a diverse chorus of ethnic voices. The number and range of voices continues to grow today.

Writing to Reflect

Every writer of any significance brings something new to a literary tradition, whether in subject matter, style, or way of looking at the world. As you reflect on the selections you have just read, consider what unique contributions might be attributed to each writer. Choose one author and write an essay about how his or her writing, as shown in this unit, can be said to do something different from writers of previous generations.

Consider

- the author's choice of subject matter
- his or her use of language, including style and tone
- any cultural or philosophical lens through which the author views the subject matter

Extension

VIEWING & REPRESENTING

Gather clippings of articles and literary texts from print media, photographs and other images of writers, and quotations from the selections in this section. Use these items to create a **collage**—your own "Mosaic of American Voices" representing the vibrancy and diversity of contemporary American literature.

R2.5, R3.5, W2.2
CALIFORNIA

Increibles Las Cosas Q'se Ven, 2001. Mural at Ashland Avenue and 19th Street in Chicago. © Jeffrey Zimmermann.

Wrap-Up: A Mosaic of American Voices

This Wrap-Up provides students with an opportunity to revisit the writings of the ethnically and artistically diverse group of authors and poets in this section. Begin by having students recall selections from this section and briefly recap the authors' ethnicities and the works' topics and ideas.

Writing to Reflect

- Review with students that *reflecting* means thinking about, exploring connections with, and finding meaning in. Such reflection can help students to appreciate the exploding mosaic of voices they have read.

- Guide students in choosing authors about whom to write. Suggest these guiding questions:
  - Which selection did I understand best?
  - Which author would I most like to learn more about?
  - Which selection has a subject that I can relate to especially well?

Extension

- Suggest sources from which to gather articles about and images of writers, such as the *New York Times Book Review* and the book review sections of other major newspapers and magazines, online encyclopedias, and the Web site of the Academy of American Poets, http://www.poets.org.

- Encourage students to use cross-references to find additional relevant writers for their collages. For example, an article on Gwendolyn Brooks might refer to Langston Hughes or Nikki Giovanni.

- Allow students to work in pairs. One student might design the collage and the partner might do research and select text.

- Tell students to add a meaningful title to their collages and to provide informational captions where appropriate.

DIFFERENTIATED INSTRUCTION

FOR ENGLISH LEARNERS

Writing Support [mixed-readiness groups]

- Review the writing prompt to clarify the gist of the assignment and the three bulleted points to consider. Explain that a *cultural or philosophical lens* reflects the perspective or viewpoint an author brings to writing. This usually reflects the specific community in which the author writes or was raised. Have more-fluent partners help students understand the meanings of other unfamiliar terms such as *subject matter, style*, and *tone*.

- Allow students to focus on the work of a chosen writer without comparing it to previous generations. Students may reflect on ways that the writer's work brings new insight or experience to them.

- Suggest that students compare their cultural lenses with the writer's.

- Suggest that students reflect on ways that the writer's texts helped increase their command of English.

Focus and Motivate

OBJECTIVES

- analyze a student model that reflects the key traits of a problem-solution essay
- use the writing process to produce a problem-solution essay
- revise and edit, using criteria for problem-solution essays
- plan and create a Web site, considering audience and choosing appropriate visuals

 W1.1, W1.3, W1.6, W1.9, W2.6, LC1.1

WRITER'S ROAD MAP

WRITING PROMPTS 1 AND 2

To help students choose a prompt, suggest that they brainstorm lists of five important global, community, and school problems. For Writing Prompt 2, clarify that the essay should not be a literary analysis. It should propose the student's solution to a problem suggested by a work of literature.

ADDITIONAL PROMPTS

Use these prompts for more writing practice:

WRITING PROMPT 3

Writing from the Real World Find a news article about a problem that interests you. Present your solution to the problem.

WRITING PROMPT 4

Writing from Images Find a photograph or work of fine art that portrays a problem. Identify the problem and give your solution.

Where to Find Images

- newspapers or newsmagazines
- photography or fine arts magazines
- museums and photograph galleries
- photography or fine arts books

For additional writing prompts, see

- WriteSmart CD
- Writing Center at **ClassZone.com**

KEY TRAITS

Review the six **KEY TRAITS** with students, focusing on ideas and organization. Compare the traits with the criteria on page 1254.

Writing Workshop

EXPOSITION

Problem-Solution Essay

Much of the literature in this unit deals with life-changing problems, such as war, racial inequality, and cultural isolation. All of us face problems in our lives and in our communities. For help in sharing your thoughts about an important problem and its possible solutions, follow the **Writer's Road Map.**

WRITER'S ROAD MAP

Problem-Solution Essay

WRITING PROMPT 1

Writing for the Real World Problems at school, in your community, and in the wider world are inescapable. Choose a problem that deeply interests you and write an essay in which you define the problem, examine its causes, and explore possible solutions.

Problems to Explore

- social issues, such as homelessness or prejudice
- environmental issues, such as energy use or wetlands destruction
- school policies, such as locker searches or rules about athletic participation

WRITING PROMPT 2

Writing from Literature Perhaps something you read in this unit made you think about a problem in a new way. Choose a problem you found in a literary work. Write an essay in which you describe the problem and identify a possible solution.

Selections to Explore

- "My Dungeon Shook: Letter to My Nephew" (racial discrimination)
- "Mother Tongue" (cultural conflicts)
- "Adolescence—III" (growing up)

 WRITING TOOLS
For prewriting, revision, and editing tools, visit the **Writing Center** at **ClassZone.com.**

KEY TRAITS

1. IDEAS
- States the **problem** in a clearly worded thesis statement
- Explores the **causes and effects** of the problem
- Uses relevant **details** to support the proposed solution
- Addresses **opposing viewpoints** and counterclaims

2. ORGANIZATION
- Shows the **significance** of the problem in the introduction
- Uses **transitions** to connect ideas
- Concludes by **summarizing** the proposed **solution**

3. VOICE
- **Tone** is suited to subject matter, audience, and purpose

4. WORD CHOICE
- Uses **precise words** to express the problem and solution

5. SENTENCE FLUENCY
- Uses a variety of **sentence types**

6. CONVENTIONS
- Employs **correct grammar and usage**

1248 UNIT 6: CONTEMPORARY LITERATURE

Writing Workshop Resources

 RESOURCE MANAGER UNIT 6

Plan and Teach pp. 319–322
Prewriting–Editing pp. 323–327
Writing Rubric p. 328
Publishing with Technology p. 329
Writing Support p. 330*

 STANDARDS LESSON FILE

Writing Lessons 8, 24, 25, 39, 42
Media Lesson 21

 BEST PRACTICES TOOLKIT

Scaffolding Writing Instruction pp. 43–46*
KWL • Mindstreaming • Three-Column Journal • Cause-and-Effect Graphics • Writing Template: Problem and Solution • Guiding Peer Review

TECHNOLOGY
- Easy Planner DVD
- Writing Center at **ClassZone.com**
- WriteSmart CD

Part 1: Analyze a Student Model

W1.1, W1.3, W1.6 (p. 1251), W1.9 (pgs. 1253, 1254), W2.6 (p. 1255), LC1.1 (p. 1254)

Online INTERACTIVE MODEL
CLASSZONE.COM

Jordan Turner
Kingston Academy

Parking-Lot Lottery

It happened again yesterday morning. Two cars collided in the mad rush to snag one of the few parking spaces in the school lot. Luckily, no one was hurt, but who can say what might happen next time? Inadequate parking at our school is a real—and dangerous—problem.

5   Since last fall, eight accidents have occurred in or at the entrance to the student parking lot. Most of these involved two cars moving at relatively slow speeds, so there were no injuries. Students walking or riding bikes in the area are at risk, however, and something needs to be done about it now. Because there are too many cars and not enough parking spaces, drivers
10 race to get into the lot, often ignoring the rules of the road and common courtesy. Even when this early-morning derby doesn't result in dents, scratched paint, or injuries, it leaves students stressed and jittery before the school day has even begun.

Should we extend the lot and create more parking spaces? That's what
15 the student council suggests. Our school is surrounded by privately owned land, though, so this solution is just not possible right now. Also, it is unreasonable to expect that fewer students will drive to school as time goes on. Enrollment has increased with redistricting, and many students must travel from areas where there is no public transportation. Based on these
20 realities, the problem can only get worse.

A cheap, fair, and easy-to-implement solution to this problem is just waiting to be set in motion—a parking-lot lottery run by the administration. Each fall and spring, juniors and seniors who drive to school would fill out a card and submit it to the principal. An administrator
25 would draw cards and assign each winner a numbered parking space. All juniors and seniors, including those with parking assignments, would be eligible to submit their names for the next lottery.

KEY TRAITS IN ACTION

Introductory paragraph shows the **significance** of the issue (students may be injured). Highlighted thesis statement clearly describes the **problem**.

Describes the **causes and effects** of the problem. Highlighted **transitions** help to show how ideas are related.

Examines an **opposing viewpoint** (in this case, another proposed solution) and explains why it is not workable. Varying **sentence types** by including a question keeps the essay fresh.

Proposes a **solution** and provides **details** about it.

Teach

CALIFORNIA

Part 1: Analyze a Student Model

Have students read the student model and **KEY TRAITS IN ACTION.** Then discuss the model with the class, noting specific examples of each trait and building on what students have already noted. You may also wish to incorporate these activities:

- **Significance** To trace the way the student model establishes the significance of the problem, ask these questions: What problem does the student model discuss? **Answer:** *The model discusses the lack of adequate parking space in the school lot.* Why is this problem important? **Answer:** *Competition for parking spaces causes many accidents.* What details in lines 1–6 reinforce the idea that the problem is important? **Possible answer:** *Anecdotes and statistics about accidents at the school lot reinforce the idea.* Clarify that Jordan uses both statements and supporting evidence to establish the importance of the problems presented.

- **Causes and Effects** Have students reread the second paragraph of the student model and list all the effects of the lack of adequate parking space in the school lot. **Possible answer:** *Drivers race for parking spaces, causing accidents, risk to pedestrians and cyclists, and stress for students.* Emphasize that in presenting the problem, Jordan specifies the undesirable results of the problem in order to convince readers of its significance.

DIFFERENTIATED INSTRUCTION

For general guidelines on differentiating writing instruction, see

 BEST PRACTICES TOOLKIT
Scaffolding Writing Instruction
pp. 43–46

FOR ENGLISH LEARNERS
Language: Skill Words Write these terms on the board and review them with students:

- *significance:* importance—for example, lack of parking space leads to accidents

- *cause:* an event or action that directly results in another action—for example, the race for parking spaces leads to stress

- *effect:* the direct or logical outcome of an event or action—for example, when cars race for parking spaces, accidents happen

- *opposing viewpoint:* the "other side" to the writer's argument—for example, the student council suggests creating more parking spaces

- *details:* words, phrases, and sentences that tell more about the main idea—for example, procedures for the parking-lot lottery

- *tone:* the expression of the writer's attitude toward a subject—for example, this writer is seriously concerned about accidents

- **Tone** To highlight the essay's straightforward, serious tone, invite students to suggest alternative tones that an essay on the same subject might have—for instance, sarcastic or panicky. Challenge students to write one or more sentences in an alternate tone, then compare their sentences with the model.

- **Precise Words** Write these imprecise words and phrases on the board: *said yes, plan, messy, open, sure, okay.* Ask students to compare these words with the highlighted words and phrases in lines 25–43. *Possible answer: The imprecise words don't help readers understand the specific situation, because they don't reflect the tone of the community's response or describe the lottery process in sufficient detail.*

- **Solution** Ask students to identify words and phrases in the conclusion that refer to driving. *Possible answer: Words related to driving include "traffic jam," "U-turn," and "direction."* Then have students explain the way that each of those driving terms is applied to the essay's proposed solution. *Possible answer: "Traffic jam" refers to the situation in the school parking lot. "U-turn" refers to changing the way the parking situation is handled. "Direction" refers to the path toward a solution to the parking problem.* Discuss other ways to conclude, such as asking a rhetorical question, or stating an afterthought that leaves readers thinking.

For interactive student models, see

Write*Smart* CD

Writing Center at **ClassZone.com**

This solution has several advantages. First, the only expense it would involve is paint and a few hours of labor to number the parking spaces. 30 Second, everyone would have an equal chance to get a space, since names would be drawn at random. Third, it would encourage students to carpool. This decrease in traffic would help protect student safety and the environment. Drivers who didn't abide by the system and parked in other students' spaces would be banned from the next lottery.

35 Students and administrators have responded positively to this idea. Almost everyone I asked agreed with the vice-principal that "It certainly would be worth a try." Although some students worried about having to carpool for months at a time, they said they preferred a lottery system to the current disorganized situation. A few students who didn't like the idea 40 said they wouldn't enter the lottery—which is fine, since participation would be voluntary. I'm confident that this system would work because a similar one has been running smoothly at my cousin's school for almost two years.

The student lot does not have to be a perpetual traffic jam. Let's agree 45 to make a U-turn and support a parking lottery. That way we can take this situation in a positive direction.

> Straightforward, serious **tone** and highlighted **precise words** help to make the essay smooth and convincing.

> Concludes with a summary of the proposed **solution.** By using words related to driving, the writer ends the essay in a clever and upbeat manner.

2

FOR ENGLISH LEARNERS

Comprehension: Transitions Direct student attention to the list of transitions on page 1254, and read the list aloud. Using the parking problem from the student model, write sample sentences on the board with transitions underlined, such as:

- <u>Despite</u> warnings, drivers keep having accidents.

- <u>First</u>, let's stop the accidents.

- <u>Although</u> a bigger parking lot would be nice, we can't build one.

- <u>If</u> we have a lottery, <u>then</u> parking spaces will be assigned fairly.

Finally, ask students to fill in the blanks with appropriate transitions in these sample sentences:

- Joe was careless, _____ he dented his car. (*so*)

- I have never had an accident. _____, I have seen one. (*However*)

- Accidents happen _____ of bad driving. (*as a result; because*)

To provide English learners with additional writing support, see

RESOURCE MANAGER—Copy Master Writing Support p. 330

Part 2: Apply the Writing Process

PREWRITING

What Should I Do?	What Does It Look Like?

1. Analyze the prompt.
Choose one of the prompts on page 1248. <u>Underline</u> the part of the prompt that tells you the general topic and format of your writing. Note any questions or comments that come to mind.

▶ **WRITING PROMPT** Problems at school, in your community, and in the wider world are inescapable. <u>Choose a problem that deeply interests you and write an essay in which you define the problem, examine its causes, and explore possible solutions.</u>

What issues really matter to me? Can I think of a topic that affects my life?

2. List problems that concern you.
Think of problems that you might like to write about. Categorize them in a chart to help you sort out your ideas. (Circle) the idea that you think would make the best essay.

▶
Environment	Community	School
• Turtle Creek • Lyme disease • oz-one layer	• creating a skate park • ending curfews	• (student parking) • phys ed cutbacks

3. Brainstorm possible solutions.
Use a cluster diagram or other graphic organizer to help you explore possible solutions.

TIP Make sure the problem is solvable. If it isn't, go back to step 2, and choose a different problem to write about.

▶
bigger parking lot? — *carpooling?* — *more bike racks?* — **Student Parking** — *lottery like at my cousin's school?*

4. Compile evidence about each possible solution.
Look for facts, statistics, and expert opinions that support—or discredit—each solution. Also note what kinds of evidence you still need to research.

▶
I Already Know	I Need to Find Out
• There's no room for more parking. • Lottery is working in cousin Ari's school. • Some kids already carpool.	• How would a lottery work? • What are student/administrator reactions? • Are more students willing to bike or carpool?

WRITING WORKSHOP **1251**

FOR DEVELOPING WRITERS

List Problems To help students list problems, provide a recent national newspaper or magazine. After students browse through the materials, tell them to list in their charts problems they identified in articles or images. Repeat the process with local and school publications. For students writing about literary problems, urge them to list the main conflicts of books they've read recently and then choose those they find interesting as problems to solve.

FOR ENGLISH LEARNERS

Analyze the Prompt Allow English learners to work with more fluent partners to analyze the prompt. Urge pairs to paraphrase the prompt orally to build comprehension. Partners should then discuss any questions the English learner has about the nature of the assignment.

Practice and Apply

To support students during the writing process, use these copy masters:

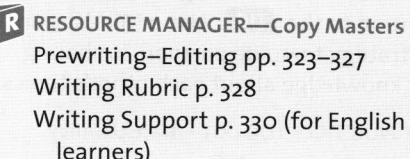 **RESOURCE MANAGER—Copy Masters**
Prewriting–Editing pp. 323–327
Writing Rubric p. 328
Writing Support p. 330 (for English learners)

Part 2: Apply the Writing Process

PREWRITING

1. Analyze the prompt. Remind students to read the prompt more than once. To find the important elements, students should look for a sentence that begins with an imperative verb, such as "Choose" in this workshop's prompts. Clarify that if students regret their first prompt choices, they may choose different ones—but they should not use too much time doing so.

2. List problems that concern you. Clarify that the chart's three column headings reflect the three major problem categories listed in the Writing Prompt 1 section of the Writer's Road Map on page 1248. If students use a different writing prompt, they will need to use different column headings for their charts.

3. Brainstorm possible solutions. Allow students to brainstorm in pairs. Partners need not choose the same problem, but should be working with similar types of problems. After students read the **TIP**, urge them to ask a third partner for solution ideas before abandoning their chosen problem.

4. Compile evidence about each possible solution. Suggest that students expand the graphic organizer shown into a KWL chart in order to add what they have learned.

 BEST PRACTICES TOOLKIT—Transparency KWL p. A21

For interactive graphic organizers, see

🖉 Write*Smart* CD

ℹ️ Writing Center at **ClassZone.com**

DRAFTING

1. **State the problem clearly.** Call students' attention to the **TIP**. Use a Mindstreaming strategy to guide partners in sharing prior knowledge about each other's topics.

🧰 **BEST PRACTICES TOOLKIT—Transparency**
   Mindstreaming p. A16

2. **Trace the causes and effects.** Remind students that a cause can also be an effect and vice versa, and that a problem can have multiple causes and effects. For example, the model, "Drivers have to hurry to get into the lot, and they act rude," is both a cause of stress and a result of inadequate parking space.

3. **Address possible concerns or objections.** Suggest that students use a Three-Column Journal with columns headed "My Solution," "Possible Objections," and "Answers to Objections."

🧰 **BEST PRACTICES TOOLKIT—Transparency**
   Three-Column Journal p. B10

4. **Organize your ideas.** Briefly discuss pros and cons of different placements for the writer's solution. Placing the writer's solution last works well if other solutions are well known or popular and need to be disputed. Placing the writer's solution first works well if other solutions are relatively easy to rebut.

For a problem-solution writing template, see

🧰 **BEST PRACTICES TOOLKIT—Transparency**
   Persuasive Writing: Problem and Solution
   pp. C16, C33

💿 Write*Smart* CD

ⓘ Writing Center at **ClassZone.com**

DRAFTING

What Should I Do?	What Does It Look Like?
1. **State the problem clearly.** In your introduction, explain exactly what problem you are writing about and why you feel strongly about it. ▶ **TIP** Include background information that will help your audience fully understand the problem.	*The parking situation at our school is a real problem. There was an accident there just yesterday. Luckily, there were no injuries. Students walking or riding their bikes in the area are at risk, though, so something needs to be done now.*
2. **Trace the causes and effects.** Include details that give insight into the problem's origins and its possible consequences. Depending on your topic, you might include facts, statistics, examples, quotations, or expert opinions. **See page 1254:** Use Transitions ▶	*There are too many cars and not enough parking spaces. Drivers have to hurry to get into the lot, and they act rude.* ⎤—Cause *Even when this situation doesn't end in dents, scratched paint, or injuries, it leaves students angry and jittery before school has even begun.* ⎤—Effects
3. **Address possible concerns or objections.** Anticipate, describe, and answer objections others might have to your solution. Also, discuss other solutions and indicate why they are inferior. ▶	*Should we make the lot bigger and create more parking spaces? That's what the student council wants.* —Alternate solution *Our school is surrounded by homes, though, so this solution is just impossible.* —Why it won't work
4. **Organize your ideas.** Present your ideas in a logical sequence. Begin with the problem. Then either discuss other solutions and end with your solution (as the writer of the student model did), or state your solution first and then discuss other possibilities. ▶ **TIP** Before revising, consult the **key traits** on page 1248 and the **criteria** and **peer-reader questions** on page 1254.	I. *Problem: lack of student parking* II. *Cause: too many cars/too little space; effects: accidents, jitters* III. *Some solutions: expand lot, have fewer students drive to school* IV. *Best solution: parking-lot lottery* V. *Conclusion*

DIFFERENTIATED INSTRUCTION

FOR DEVELOPING WRITERS
Trace Causes and Effects Urge students to use an appropriate organizer from Cause-and-Effect Graphics to chart the relationships they observe. For example, they might use a Cause-and-Effect Chain to show effects that are also causes. Students working with multiple causes or effects should use either a multiple causes or a multiple effects organizer.

🧰 **BEST PRACTICES TOOLKIT—Transparencies**
   Cause-and-Effect Graphics pp. B16,
   B37–39

FOR ADVANCED LEARNERS/AP
Address Concerns or Objections [paired option] Suggest that students write a one-paragraph response to their position from an opponent's point of view. The paragraph should concisely summarize the opponent's objections. Partners may work together, writing opposing paragraphs for each other's positions.

REVISING AND EDITING

What Should I Do?	What Does It Look Like?

1. Strengthen supporting details.
- Have a peer reader draw a box around examples or explanations that are vague or unrelated.
- Replace these examples with specific support for your ideas.

See page 1254: Ask a Peer Reader

▶ ~~We could have two lotteries per year.~~ Each fall and spring, juniors and seniors who drive to school would fill out a card and submit it to the principal. An administrator would draw cards and assign each winner a numbered parking space.

▶ This solution has several advantages. First, ~~it's cheap~~ the only expense it would involve is paint and a few hours of labor to number the parking spaces.

2. Vitalize your verbs.
- Circle weak verbs, such as forms of *be*, *have*, and *do*.
- Choose the best places to substitute stronger, more precise verbs.

▶ Two cars collided in their mad rush to snag one of the few parking spaces
~~There (was) an accident~~ in the school lot.

▶ race
Drivers (have to) ~~hurry~~ to get into the lot.

3. Check that you have answered opposing viewpoints fully.
- Underline your answers to opposing viewpoints or alternate solutions.
- If the underlined statements seem vague or unconvincing, add details that show audience members why you disagree.

▶ Also, it is unreasonable to expect that fewer students will drive to school as time goes on ~~since there are more and more cars on the road every day.~~ Enrollment has increased with redistricting, and many students must travel from areas where there is no public transportation.

4. Fine-tune your conclusion.
- Reread your conclusion. Does it summarize the problem and your proposed solution? If appropriate, include a direct call for action (such as "support a parking lottery").
- If necessary, add information or revise your writing to make your conclusion meaningful and memorable.

▶ The student lot does not have to be a perpetual traffic jam. Let's agree to make a U-turn and support a parking lottery. That way we can take this situation in a positive direction.

REVISING AND EDITING

1. **Strengthen supporting details.** Pair students for peer reading. Before they analyze their own drafts, have partners discuss the details deleted and added in the example, to make sure they understand the reasons for the changes.

2. **Vitalize your verbs.** Point out that substituting a vivid verb for a weaker one may involve changing nearby words as well and even changing the structure of a sentence. In the first example sentence, the noun *accident* is deleted because the verb *collided* implies the idea of an accident more vividly than the noun does. In the second example sentence, two verbs are deleted to make room for one more precise: the auxiliary *have to* and the main verb *hurry*.

3. **Check that you have answered opposing viewpoints fully.** Have students work with peer readers to make sure they have answered opposing viewpoints fully. Consult the Guiding Peer Review strategy for pointers.

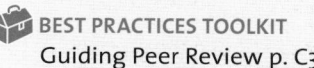 **BEST PRACTICES TOOLKIT**
Guiding Peer Review p. C3

4. **Fine-tune your conclusion.** Invite volunteers to name their topics. Work as a class to determine which topics require a call to action and which do not. The criteria in most cases depends on whether readers can realistically have an effect on the problem through a particular action.

For interactive revision tools, see

⊘ Write*Smart* CD

ⓘ Writing Center at **ClassZone.com**

FOR ENGLISH LEARNERS

Vitalize Verbs Allow less-fluent students considerable latitude in using basic verbs such as *be*, *have*, and *do* in their essays. Encourage more-fluent students to work with native English speakers, using a thesaurus and a dictionary, to find replacements for weak verbs.

FOR ADVANCED LEARNERS/AP

Answer Opposing Viewpoints Because the opposition can always find something to dispute even in a well-formed argument, encourage students to take the opposition's position. Challenge students to find and answer objections they had not addressed before. Invite them to share these opposing arguments and answers with the class as a model for other students.

Preparing to Publish

Support for meeting the goals in the writing criteria is supplied throughout the Workshop on pages 1251–1253.

For Rubric Bank, see

 WriteSmart CD

ℹ Writing Center at **ClassZone.com**

Assess and Reteach

Ⓢ STANDARDS LESSON FILE

Writing Lesson 8: Creating Sentence Variety

Writing Lesson 24: Cause-and-Effect Essay

Writing Lesson 25: Problem-Solution Essay

Writing Lesson 39: Word Choice

Writing Lesson 42: Adapting a Tone

Consider the Criteria

Use this checklist to make sure your problem-solution essay is on track.

Ideas

☑ includes an accurate thesis

☑ traces the causes and effects of the problem

☑ suggests a possible solution and gives relevant supporting details

☑ addresses opposing views

Organization

☑ introduces the problem and shows its significance

☑ links ideas with transitions

☑ has an effective conclusion

Voice

☑ maintains a tone suited to the audience and purpose

Word Choice

☑ uses precise words

Sentence Fluency

☑ varies sentence types

Conventions

☑ uses correct grammar, spelling, and punctuation

Ask a Peer Reader

• Why do you think I chose to write about this problem?

• Are any supporting details weak or confusing? If so, which ones?

• How could I make my proposed solution more convincing?

Use Transitions

accordingly	first
after	for this reason
although	however
as a result	if . . . then
because	next
before	on the contrary
consequently	since
despite	so
finally	therefore

Check Your Grammar

Use the active voice rather than the passive voice whenever possible.

> ~~Cards would be drawn by an administrator.~~ An administrator would draw cards.

> ~~An equal chance to get a space would be had by everyone.~~ Everyone would have an equal chance to get a space.

See page R60: Active and Passive Voice

 Writing On**l**ine

➔ **PUBLISHING OPTIONS**
For publishing options, visit the **Writing Center** at **ClassZone.com.**

ASSESSMENT PREPARATION
For writing and grammar assessment practice, go to the **Assessment Center** at **ClassZone.com.**

Creating a Web Site

You can continue exploring the problem you wrote about by creating a Web site dedicated to the issue.

Planning the Web Site

1. **Think about your audience.** Are you trying to reach people who know a great deal on your topic, people who know little about it, or both?

2. **Brainstorm elements to include and make a flow chart to organize them.** You'll need a home page describing the problem, with hyperlinks to other pages for relevant research, your solution, and other possible solutions. Consider including an e-mail address so users can send feedback. (For safety reasons, do not post your name, address, or telephone number.)

3. **Decide on visuals.** Create your own or search the Internet, books, magazines, newspapers, or other sources. Your visuals should powerfully convey your main ideas.

    TIP If you did not create the visual, include a source line telling where it came from. Some materials require permission from their creators. Check online sources for terms-and-conditions statements that may specify whether students can use the media elements in school projects.

4. **Make a storyboard showing the design of each page.** Draw rough sketches showing the placement of titles, explanatory text, visuals, and navigation buttons.

Producing the Web Site

1. **Write the text.** Express ideas clearly and concisely. Use charts or bulleted lists whenever possible. Define unfamiliar terms.

2. **Build your site.** Ask your school's computer specialist which authoring program to use. An authoring program allows you to combine media elements into a Web document.

3. **Test the site and make necessary revisions.** Proofread the text, check the visuals for correct positioning, and try out all links and navigation buttons. Ask teachers or classmates to review your site. Create a short survey or questionnaire so you can analyze their responses. Make revisions as needed.

4. **Upload your site.** Ask the computer specialist for permission to make your site available on your school's internal server or on the Web.

PUBLISHING WITH TECHNOLOGY

Ask students to read this page to get an overview of the process of planning and producing a Web site. Students who choose this option should familiarize themselves with the tasks of making a flow chart and a storyboard, and with tools, such as authoring programs, that might help them build and test a Web site. Before students begin working, review these criteria with them so that they understand their goals:

Criteria A strong Web site

- is aimed at a specific audience
- reflects a storyboard that shows the design of each page
- includes a home page describing the topic
- includes relevant hyperlinks
- offers contact information, such as an e-mail address, for user feedback
- contains appropriate visuals, with a source line as required
- uses clear, concise text and graphics
- appears in an appropriate authoring program

When students upload their Web sites, have the class use the criteria to evaluate each final product.

R RESOURCE MANAGER—Copy Master
Publishing with Technology p. 329

S STANDARDS LESSON FILE
Media Lesson 21: Creating a Web Site

Assessment Practice

CHECK READINESS

Read aloud the paragraph under **ASSESS** and stress to students that this is not the full Unit Test, but a way for them to check their readiness for it. Then have students examine the skills listed under **REVIEW** and look back in the unit or in the **Student Resource Bank** for any skills they need to review.

READ THE SELECTIONS

Remind students to keep unit goals in mind as they read the passages, paying particular attention to these literary and reading skills:

- Main Ideas
- Historical Context
- Rhetorical Devices
- Repetition
- Allusions

To help students focus on historical context while reading, encourage them to ask questions such as:

- What is the chronological relationship between the Birmingham demonstrations and Kennedy's speech?
- What is Kennedy saying about the status of African Americans in 1963?

ANSWER THE QUESTIONS

Direct students to pages R96–R103 of the **Test-Taking Handbook** to review test-taking strategies.

- Remind students not just to choose the first alternative that seems to fit when answering a multiple-choice question. Instead, they should read through all the choices, eliminate any that are clearly wrong, and then choose the *best* answer—the one that is most accurate and complete.

- Remind students to check their answers if there is time. Tell them that even people who know the answers may make careless mistakes. Going over test papers again can help students catch such errors and earn students the grade they truly deserve.

Assessment Practice

ASSESSMENT ONLINE
For more assessment practice and test-taking tips, go to the **Assessment Center** at ClassZone.com.

Reading Comprehension

DIRECTIONS *Read these selections and answer the questions that follow.*

from Police Dogs in Alabama Spur North Carolina Unrest

Cliff MacKay

GREENSBORO, N.C., June 1, 1963—"When a police dog bites us in Birmingham, people of color bleed all over America."

That was the terse explanation given Saturday by Jesse Jackson, 21-year-old A. and T. College student president, for the social upheaval which is sweeping this state and the South.

There have been no biting police dogs used in North Carolina, but that memorable picture from Birmingham has served to launch a tidal wave of racial unrest that thus far has overwhelmed ten cities and still shows no signs of abating.

On one thing all of North Carolina's freedom fighters are in agreement: there
10 will be no turning back; the status quo is gone forever.

The state's largest city, Charlotte, under Mayor Stan Brookshire has already fallen in line with an announcement that "all public facilities will be integrated immediately." The Chamber of Commerce backed his statement.

Businessmen of Thomasville have assured NAACP[1] President, the Rev. W. E. Banks, that all downtown establishments will no longer discriminate.

A Durham bi-racial committee has launched a series of meetings designed to end discriminatory practices in all places licensed to serve the public.

Greensboro's Mayor David Schenk has appointed a special committee headed by Dr. G. W. Evans and empowered it to seek a solution "to our pressing racial
20 problems."

Fifteen hundred arrests afterward, it has finally dawned on Greensboro officials that fear of jail would not halt the protests.

A word from liberal Gov. Terry Sanford, and the Bennett and A. and T. College students were released from makeshift lockups here, sorely disappointing some 3,000 others who had been eagerly waiting to experience "the thrills" of going to jail.

The demonstrations only gained momentum. From Greensboro, they have spread to nearby High Point and Winston-Salem; to Raleigh and Durham, to Fayetteville, Thomasville, Edenton, Wilmington and Charlotte.

Their point proved by overflowing the jails, the youthful freedom fighters,
30 sponsored by CORE[2], immediately developed a new strategy—the silent march.

---

1. **NAACP:** National Association for the Advancement of Colored People.
2. **CORE:** Congress of Racial Equality, founded in 1942 as the Committee of Racial Equality.

DIFFERENTIATED INSTRUCTION

FOR ENGLISH LEARNERS

Assessment Practice: Work Backward
Prepare students by having them read the questions *before* reading the passages. Have pairs find unfamiliar words in test directions and questions and follow these steps:

1. Write each word on an index card.
2. Look up the meaning in a dictionary and write it on the back of the card.
3. Use the cards to practice the words with your partner and to teach them to others.

Culture: Clarify Read aloud the first paragraph on page 1256. Recall the Birmingham unrest that led to the jailing of Dr. Martin Luther King Jr. Explain that during this period of unrest, Birmingham's police chief, Theophilus Eugene "Bull" Connor, ordered the use of police dogs in an attempt to control protesters. Officers used the dogs against a march of children and teenagers, and three teens were badly bitten and required hospital attention.

A dignified, highly disciplined line of as high as 4,000 marchers nightly walks silently, almost prayerfully, through the downtown area. Grim faces show no smiles. There is no conversation, not a cigarette glows. Just the slap-slap-slap of hundreds of marching feet.

from Radio and Television Report to the American People on Civil Rights, June 11, 1963

John F. Kennedy

We are confronted primarily with a moral issue. It is as old as the scriptures and is as clear as the American Constitution.

The heart of the question is whether all Americans are to be afforded equal rights and equal opportunities, whether we are going to treat our fellow Americans as we want to be treated. If an American, because his skin is dark, cannot eat lunch in a restaurant open to the public, if he cannot send his children to the best public school available, if he cannot vote for the public officials who represent him, if, in short, he cannot enjoy the full and free life which all of us want, then who among us would be content to have the color of his skin changed and stand in his place?

10 Who among us would then be content with the counsels of patience and delay?

One hundred years of delay have passed since President Lincoln freed the slaves, yet their heirs, their grandsons, are not fully free. They are not yet freed from the bonds of injustice. They are not yet freed from social and economic oppression. And this nation, for all its hopes and all its boasts, will not be fully free until all its citizens are free.

We preach freedom around the world, and we mean it, and we cherish our freedom here at home, but are we to say to the world and, much more importantly, to each other that this is a land of the free except for the Negroes; that we have no second-class citizens except Negroes; that we have no class or

20 caste system, no ghettoes, no master race except with respect to Negroes?

Now the time has come for this nation to fulfill its promise. The events in Birmingham and elsewhere have so increased the cries for equality that no city or state or legislative body can prudently choose to ignore them.

The fires of frustration and discord are burning in every city, North and South, where legal remedies are not at hand. Redress is sought in the streets, in

---

ITEM ANALYSIS

COMPREHENSION AND WRITTEN RESPONSE	ITEMS	UNIT PAGES
Main Ideas	1, 2, 3, 5, 11, 14	1205
Historical Context	4, 12, 13	1123, 1161
Rhetorical Devices	7, 10, 11	1193
Repetition	7, 10, 11	1231
Allusions	6, 8, 9	1145

VOCABULARY	ITEMS	UNIT PAGES
Idioms	1, 2, 3, 4	1200
Prefixes	5, 6, 7, 8	1171

WRITING AND GRAMMAR	ITEMS	UNIT PAGES
Create Mood	1, 2, 3	1191
Establish Voice	4, 5	1121

FOR STRATEGIC READERS

Assessment Support Consider these options for completing the Assessment Practice:

- Have students "work backward" to review the test questions *before* reading the passages.
- Select random questions in the assessment, and have students demonstrate *how* and *where* to look for the answers.

- Ask students to locate unfamiliar words in the assessment. Elicit the words' meanings from the class.
- Have students record useful testing words and definitions in their journals for later reference.
- Read the selections or parts of them aloud to aid in student comprehension.

McDougal Littell Assessment System

After checking student readiness with this Assessment Practice, you may administer the complete Unit 6 Test in order to more thoroughly evaluate student mastery of unit goals.

ANSWERS

Comprehension

Model a thinking process for answering multiple-choice questions.

1. **C is correct.** *The list appears in lines 11–20. A is incorrect because there were "no biting police dogs used in North Carolina." B and D are incorrect because the silent marches and the account of college students appear later in the article.*

2. **C is correct.** *It conveys the main action and its main effect. A is incorrect because it does not mention the effects of the action. B is incorrect because it is not an idea about the protesters' actions. D is incorrect because it does not mention the causes or effects of the release.*

3. **D is correct.** *This choice summarizes the content of the lines. A and B are incorrect because they deal with secondary aspects of the protest. C is incorrect because it does not describe the demonstrations.*

4. **B is correct.** *The organizations were formed to fight against racial injustice in the era of segregation. The other choices refer to events occurring during the period when the organizations were already active.*

5. **A is correct.** *It is the only choice that covers the overall historical impact of the events in the article. B, C, and D all deal with secondary points of the article.*

6. **D is correct.** *The allusion connects moral issues in the modern age and in older and ancient times. A is incorrect because the speech assumes people respect the documents. B is incorrect because the speech does not address differences in ideas. C is incorrect because the speech does not discuss Constitutional specifics.*

7. **A is correct.** *The passage lists many restrictions African Americans faced. B is incorrect because the passage emphasizes African-American experience, not governmental action. C is incorrect because the speech expresses understanding of impatience. D is incorrect because lack of support is not mentioned in the passage.*

---

demonstrations, parades, and protests which create tensions and threaten violence and threaten lives.

We face, therefore, a moral crisis as a country and as a people. It cannot be met by repressive police action. It cannot be left to increased demonstrations in the streets. 30 It cannot be quieted by token moves or talk. It is a time to act in the Congress, in your state and local legislative body and, above all, in all of our daily lives.

Comprehension

DIRECTIONS *Answer these questions about the excerpt from "Police Dogs in Alabama Spur North Carolina Unrest."*

1. To illustrate the idea in line 10 that "the status quo is gone forever," MacKay presents
   - **A** an image of dogs attacking protesters
   - **B** a description of the silent marches
   - **C** a factual list of changes made in four North Carolina cities
   - **D** an account of college students who participate in protests

2. Which statement conveys the main idea of lines 21–25?
   - **A** Many people were jailed in Greensboro.
   - **B** The local jails were too small to hold all of the arrested protesters.
   - **C** The arrest of 1,500 people did not stop the protesters.
   - **D** The governor released the protesters from jail.

3. What is the main idea of lines 29–34?
   - **A** Many of the protesters were young people.
   - **B** A civil rights group sponsored the freedom fighters.
   - **C** Civil rights workers staged their demonstrations in large cities.
   - **D** Thousands of people participated in silent nighttime marches for equality.

4. Which historical events most likely led African Americans to form the NAACP and CORE (lines 14 and 30)?
   - **A** proposed civil rights legislation
   - **B** Jim Crow laws and voting restrictions
   - **C** the integration of public facilities
   - **D** college students' civil rights activities

5. What is the main idea of this excerpt?
   - **A** Police actions in Alabama fueled civil rights protests in North Carolina and across the South.
   - **B** A. and T. College students took the lead in the struggle for racial equality.
   - **C** Police in Birmingham used harsh tactics in their attempts to end protests.
   - **D** People in North Carolina were willing to go to jail to protest racial injustice.

DIRECTIONS *Answer these questions about the excerpt from "Radio and Television Report to the American People on Civil Rights."*

6. Kennedy alludes to scriptures and the American Constitution in lines 1–2 to
   - **A** educate citizens about U.S. history
   - **B** point out that everyone has different ideas about equal rights
   - **C** clarify the distinction between religious and secular ideas
   - **D** remind his audience that there is moral and legal support for equality

1258

---

8. **B is correct.** *The sentence refers to "One hundred years of delay." A is incorrect because Kennedy does not mention Lincoln's eloquence. C is incorrect because Kennedy's statement does not require special knowledge. D is incorrect because the speech is not about the Civil War.*

9. **B is correct.** *Kennedy wishes to persuade listeners that racial justice is patriotic. A is incorrect because the national anthem would not stir sympathy. C is incorrect because militarism is irrelevant to the issue of civil rights. D is incorrect because indignity is not relevant to the allusion.*

7. The repetition of the phrase "if he cannot" in lines 5–9 highlights the
   A restrictions that African Americans have lived with in the United States
   B government's refusal to legally end racial inequality
   C importance of patience and mutual understanding in resolving inequality
   D lack of support for African-American small businesses at the local level

8. By alluding to President Lincoln in line 11, Kennedy calls particular attention to
   A his and Lincoln's reputations as eloquent speakers and debaters
   B the fact that African Americans were still denied freedoms guaranteed 100 years before
   C his knowledge of the history of race relations in the North and the South
   D the national discord that resulted from the Civil War

9. The phrase "land of the free" (line 18) appears in each stanza of "The Star Spangled Banner." Kennedy's allusion to the national anthem most likely invokes feelings of
   A sympathy   C militarism
   B patriotism   D indignity

10. What is the effect of Kennedy's repetition of "except" in lines 18–20?
    A It reveals how Kennedy would like to change the world's perception of the United States.
    B It shows that Americans are proud of their history of equality for all citizens.
    C It emphasizes the exclusion of African Americans from the freedoms experienced by most Americans.
    D It highlights Kennedy's view that the United States should spread freedom around the world.

11. In lines 28–30, the repetition of the phrase "it cannot be" emphasizes that
    A demonstrations are spreading rapidly throughout the country
    B social change can be brought about in many ways
    C protestors must engage in a dialogue with public officials
    D nothing less than a commitment to equality will end discrimination

DIRECTIONS *Answer this question about both selections.*

12. Which historical event of 1963 do MacKay and Kennedy both respond to in these excerpts?
    A integration of public facilities in Durham
    B repressive police action in Birmingham
    C passage of equal pay laws by Congress
    D silent marches in North Carolina

Written Response

SHORT RESPONSE *Write three or four sentences to answer this question.*

13. What historical change was occurring in North Carolina when "Police Dogs in Alabama Spur North Carolina Unrest" was written? Support your answer with two examples from the excerpt.

EXTENDED RESPONSE *Write two or three paragraphs to answer this question.*

14. What is Kennedy calling on people to do to end racial inequality? Identify two of his ideas and support your answer with quotations from the text.

10. **C is correct.** *The passage lists aspects of American freedom from which African Americans were excluded. A is incorrect because Kennedy wished to change realities, not just perceptions. B is incorrect because it states ways in which equality was not given to all. D is incorrect because the speech is mainly about domestic, not international, issues.*

11. **D is correct.** *By ruling out other methods, Kennedy leaves only a commitment to equality left as valid. A is incorrect because demonstrations are only one of several issues discussed. B is incorrect because Kennedy's emphasis is on ways that will not work. C is incorrect because it is not mentioned in the passage.*

12. **B is correct.** *MacKay's article reports on repressive police actions, and Kennedy's speech criticizes them. A and D are mentioned specifically by MacKay but not by Kennedy. C is not specifically mentioned by either.*

Written Response

Possible short response:

13. *At the time MacKay's article was written, public facilities were being desegregated. Integration of public facilities in Charlotte, the ending of discrimination in downtown Thomasville, biracial meetings to end discrimination in Durham, and a search for a solution in Greensboro support the answer.*

Possible extended response:

14. *To end racial inequality, Kennedy is calling on people to end discrimination in the way they think and in their daily lives, and to support state, local, and federal laws that end discrimination. Students' examples and citations will vary.*

DIFFERENTIATED INSTRUCTION

FOR ENGLISH LEARNERS
Assessment Vocabulary To help students understand the Comprehension questions, teach or review these key vocabulary words:

- Item 1: *status quo,* "the way things have been"
- Item 6: *alludes to,* "indirectly refers to"
- Item 6: *scriptures,* "sacred writings"
- Item 9: *stanza,* "a group of lines in a poem"
- Item 11: *emphasizes,* "treats as important"
- Item 13: *excerpt,* "portion of a longer text"
- Item 14: *inequality,* "difference in treatment"

Vocabulary

1. **D is correct.** *To fall in line is to join a group's action.* A is incorrect because the city's action is not a retreat. B is incorrect because the city acts in accordance with the announcement. C is incorrect because an announcement is not a law.

2. **C is correct.** *When something dawns upon a person, its truth becomes clear to that person.* A is incorrect because the context is not related to brightness. B is incorrect because the definition does not fit the context. D is incorrect because the context does not involve making an example.

3. **A is correct.** *Second-class is below first class in a society divided into classes.* B is incorrect because the phrase does not refer specifically to jobs. C is incorrect because the context is not school classes. D is incorrect because the context does not mention roles in government.

4. **B is correct.** *At hand means "nearby for convenient use."* A, C, and D are incorrect because the speech discusses availability of legal rights for African Americans, not acceptability, trustworthiness, practicality.

5. **D is correct.** *The events described were a sudden social change.* A, B, and C are incorrect because they are irrelevant to the context of the news story.

6. **A is correct.** *The country is faced with a moral issue.* B is incorrect because a moral issue does not attack. C is incorrect because the nation has not been defeated. D is incorrect because the nation is not bound. B, C, and D also do not belong with "with."

7. **B is correct.** *Racial unrest is tension from lack of agreement.* A is incorrect because the context is about sound. C is incorrect because a bond is not a discord. D is incorrect because it is irrelevant.

8. **A is correct.** *The speech addresses the context of injustice.* B and C are incorrect because they refer to irrelevant contexts. D is incorrect because redress is not protection.

Vocabulary

DIRECTIONS *Use context clues and your knowledge of idioms to answer the following questions.*

1. In line 12 of his news article, Cliff MacKay notes that the city of Charlotte has "fallen in line with an announcement" by the mayor. The idiom *fallen in line* means
   - **A** retreated from
   - **B** relied upon
   - **C** enacted into law
   - **D** conformed to

2. In line 21 of his news article, Cliff MacKay writes that it "dawned on Greensboro officials" that the threat of jail would not end the protests. The idiom *dawned on* means
   - **A** brightened up
   - **B** agreed with
   - **C** became evident to
   - **D** made an example of

3. In line 19 of his address, President Kennedy refers to "second-class citizens." This idiom describes people who
   - **A** are treated as inferior to others
   - **B** need help in finding a job
   - **C** have not finished high school
   - **D** play a minor role in government

4. In line 25 of his address, President Kennedy notes that discord is heightened "where legal remedies are not at hand." The idiom *at hand* means
   - **A** accepted
   - **B** available
   - **C** trusted
   - **D** practical

DIRECTIONS *Use context clues and your knowledge of prefixes to answer the following questions.*

5. The prefix *up-* means "upward," and the Old English word *hebban* means "to lift." What does the word *upheaval* mean in line 4 of the news story?
   - **A** a command given to sailors
   - **B** a raising of the earth's crust
   - **C** the act of gagging
   - **D** a sudden, violent disruption

6. The prefix *con-* means "with," and the Latin word *frons* means "front." What does the word *confronted* mean in line 1 of the president's address?
   - **A** faced
   - **B** attacked
   - **C** defeated
   - **D** bound

7. The prefix *dis-* means "apart," and the Latin stem *cor* means "heart." What does the word *discord* mean in line 24 of the president's address?
   - **A** harsh or unpleasant sounds from the mingling of tones
   - **B** tension or strife from the lack of agreement
   - **C** emotional or cultural bonds formed from birth
   - **D** lingering or chronic illness from damage to the aorta

8. The prefix *re-* means "again," and the Old French word *drecier* means "to arrange." What does the word *redress* mean in line 25 of the president's address?
   - **A** correction of a wrong
   - **B** correction of a factual error
   - **C** payment of a financial debt
   - **D** protection from enemies

DIFFERENTIATED INSTRUCTION

FOR ENGLISH LEARNERS

Review Academic Vocabulary On the board, list the academic vocabulary shown in italics. Then give the examples in random order and have students classify them. Elicit additional examples from students.

- *historical context:* Kennedy gave his speech at a time of civil rights protests.
- *allusion:* Kennedy used a phrase from "The Star Spangled Banner" in his speech.
- *rhetorical devices:* Kennedy repeats the phrase "if he cannot" in the second paragraph of his speech.

Writing & Grammar

DIRECTIONS *Read each passage and answer the questions that follow.*

> (1) They paddle the canoe swiftly through the darkness. (2) An owl hoots in the distance. (3) Mary gasps, not daring to speak. (4) Instead, she chomps down on a peanut butter sandwich. (5) The faint crackle of dry leaves comes from the shore. (6) Sam almost drops the paddle as a fish leaps from the water, startling both of them. (7) He stifles a warning as a large rock suddenly looms ahead. (8) The two strain to hear the sound of their pursuers, now closing in on them.

1. The verbs *gasps, stifles,* and *looms* help create a mood that is

  A sad   **C** suspenseful

  B humorous   **D** somber

2. Which sentence does not reflect the mood of the rest of the passage?

  A sentence 1   **C** sentence 5

  B sentence 4   **D** sentence 8

3. Which element does the writer use to help create mood in the passage?

  A a critical tone

  B figurative language

  C imperative sentences

  D sensory details

> (1) Although we had seen the TV footage and read the newspapers, no one was prepared for the mud-caked debris we found when we returned. (2) Where had our pristine home gone? (3) Louise covered her face as if, by blocking this sight, she could erase the devastation before us. (4) Despondently, we joined our neighbors, who had found an heirloom that had somehow survived the ferocious winds, endless rains, and raging floods. (5) It reminded us that we had once lived happily in this now beleaguered city. (6) As I held the heirloom in my hand, I wondered: where would we go from here?

4. Which of the following are characteristics of the writer's voice?

  A a sad tone and complex vocabulary

  B simple sentence structures and basic vocabulary

  C a lighthearted tone and sensory details

  D figurative language and short sentences

5. Choose the best way to rewrite the following sentence, using the same voice as the passage.

> The storm was over, but it had been bad.

  A The unpleasant storm was finally over.

  B What a storm it had been!

  C Although the fury of the storm had subsided, it left misery in its wake.

  D Though now over, the storm caused a lot of damage.

ANSWERS

Writing & Grammar

1. C is correct. *The verbs create an impression of fearful quiet and of sudden appearances. A and D are incorrect because the context is one of tense action, not the quiet of sadness or somberness. B is incorrect because the passage is intended seriously.*

2. B is correct. *Sentence 4 injects sudden incongruous humor into the passage. The other three sentences all maintain the mood of suspense.*

3. D is correct. *Details appealing to sight or sound include the owl hooting, Mary gasping, leaves crackling, the rock looming, and the faint sound of pursuers. A is incorrect because the tone is sympathetic to the characters, not critical of them. B is incorrect because the passage contains no figures of speech. C is incorrect because the passage contains no imperative sentences.*

4. A is correct. *Examples of sad tone include "Louise covered her face" and "despondently"; examples of complex vocabulary include "debris," "pristine," and "beleaguered." B is incorrect because several sentences are complex, and the vocabulary is sometimes difficult. C is incorrect because the subject matter and the narrator's response contradict a lighthearted tone. D is incorrect because the passage lacks figurative language, and most of its sentences are long.*

5. C is correct. *This choice contains complex vocabulary such as "subsided," a sad tone, and complex sentence structure. A and B are incorrect because their diction and sentence structure are simple. D is incorrect because its vocabulary is simple and its tone is unemotional.*

FOR STRATEGIC READERS

Assessment Support: Create Mood and Establish Voice

- Review with students that *mood* is the feeling or atmosphere in a work. The writer's use of connotation, imagery, figurative language, sound and rhythm, and other elements help create mood.

- Have students find examples of words and phrases that create mood in the passages, and identify those moods.

- Review with students that *voice* is the writer's or narrator's unique style of expression.

- Ask students to describe the voices of MacKay and Kennedy in these excerpts, and to cite words and phrases that express those voices.

Ideas for Independent Reading

Continue exploring the Questions of the Times on pages 1090–1091 with these additional works.

Are we responsible for the WHOLE WORLD?

Catch-22
by Joseph Heller

This hilarious, heartbreaking novel brilliantly satirizes the "logic" of warfare. In the words of WWII airman Yossarian: "The enemy . . . is anybody who's going to get you killed, no matter which side he's on." Unfortunately for Yossarian, each time he completes the number of missions required for his discharge, that number is raised by his commanders.

Hiroshima
by John Hersey

In 1945, faced with a war that seemed as if it might never end, President Truman made the decision to drop an atomic bomb on the Japanese city of Hiroshima, killing between 70,000 and 80,000 people. John Hersey recorded the stories of Hiroshima survivors shortly after the explosion, bringing home for Americans the magnitude of the devastation and loss.

The Things They Carried
by Tim O'Brien

This collection of short stories focuses on a platoon of American soldiers in Vietnam. The things they carry—letters, photographs, Bibles, hand grenades—hint at the confused inner landscape of each young man. In this masterpiece of war literature, O'Brien makes clear that the burdens of war continue to weigh on the troops long after they lay down their arms.

Can America achieve EQUAL RIGHTS?

At Canaan's Edge: America in the King Years, 1965–68
by Taylor Branch

Third in a series on civil rights leader Martin Luther King Jr., *At Canaan's Edge* discusses the final years of King's life. The book begins with King's last great success: the marches in Selma, Alabama, that led to the passage of the Voting Rights Act. It then moves through the Vietnam years to the national tragedy of King's untimely death.

Vintage Baldwin
by James Baldwin

Author James Baldwin was extremely influential in exposing America's racial divide. Much of his writing focuses on the civil rights movement and the experience of African Americans living in white-controlled America. This collection includes short stories, essays, an excerpt from a novel, and a play.

A Gathering of Old Men
by Ernest Gaines

This quiet novel of race relations begins with the killing of a white bully by the only African-American man who has the courage to stand up for his rights. Eighteen elderly African-American men arrive at the scene of the crime, each carrying a shotgun with discharged shells. When the sheriff arrives, all 18 claim to be the murderer, forcing the community to reconsider how they treat one another.

1262

What makes an
AMERICAN?

The Woman Warrior
by Maxine Hong Kingston

In this classic memoir, Maxine Hong Kingston encapsulates the confusion, anger, pleasure, and wonder of growing up Chinese American in California, the daughter of immigrants. Haunted by her mother's tales of the magical if sometimes brutal world she left behind, the young narrator is equally unsure about where she fits in among the "ghosts," her parents' term for the non-Chinese people they live among.

Arranged Marriage
by Chitra Banerjee Divakaruni

In this collection of short stories, Chitra Divakaruni focuses on the experiences of women living in India and of Indian women who have moved to America. The contrast between their two worlds, coupled with their inherent roles and expectations, is a common theme running throughout the stories.

Unsettling America
Edited by Maria Mazziotti Gillian and Jennifer Gillian

A diverse chorus of voices comment on ethnic pride and heritage, personal identity, and cultural stereotypes in this anthology of contemporary multicultural poetry. Pat Mora, Lucille Clifton, Li-Young Lee, Louise Erdrich, and Lawrence Ferlinghetti are among the notable poets included in this collection.

What is the
AMERICAN DREAM?

The Portable Arthur Miller
by Arthur Miller, edited by Christopher Bigsby

Playwright Arthur Miller once said, "Whoever is writing in the United States is using the American Dream as an ironical pole of his story. People elsewhere tend to accept, to a far greater degree anyway, that the conditions of life are hostile to man's pretensions." Miller's best work examines the average American's pursuit of the American dream and how that dream can become twisted or unattainable. This collection includes complete texts of his masterpieces *The Death of a Salesman* and *The Crucible,* as well as several later plays and excerpts from his memoir *Timebends.*

The Stories of John Cheever
by John Cheever

These stories describe a world that could be considered the epitome of the American dream—a place of leafy suburbs, summer homes, and cocktail parties. But beneath the surface lurks a darkness. Cheever's characters face a myriad of problems—aging, financial blunders, embarrassment, death. Cheever's graceful prose illuminates this world and makes readers care about the imperfect people who inhabit it.

1263

Preview Unit Goals

This page presents an overview of the skills and strategies covered in this unit. Remind students that they can get more from their reading by previewing; then encourage them to skim the page to preview the Unit Goals and to set some personal goals as they prepare for the unit. Also point out that as in previous units, each strand or category of skill is color-coded on this page and throughout the unit.

Model the strategy of copying the Academic Vocabulary and writing a preliminary definition for each term. Suggest that students use a journal or a notebook for this purpose. Encourage them to use the terms in discussions and in writing. In addition, urge students to revisit each term throughout the unit and to refine its meaning.

ADDITIONAL UNIT GOALS

These skills will be taught in this unit but are not the major focus of the unit:

Developing Research Skills

- Formulate research questions
- Distinguish between primary and secondary sources and their purposes
- Use search engines and databases to research a topic

Writing

- Analyze a research paper
- Create an outline
- Draft and develop a thesis statement
- Use transitional words and phrases to create flow
- Support ideas with evidence and eliminate unnecessary details

Speaking, Listening, and Viewing

- Create a multimedia presentation

UNIT 7

Included in this unit: R2.3, W1.3, W1.6, W1.7, W1.8, W2.4, W2.6, LC1.3, LS1.7, LS2.2, LS2.4

Preview Unit Goals

DEVELOPING RESEARCH SKILLS
- Select and shape a topic
- Plan research
- Choose the best research tools, including primary and secondary sources and online resources
- Evaluate information and sources, including nonfiction books, newspapers, periodicals, and Web sites
- Make source cards and take notes
- Paraphrase and summarize information
- Avoid plagiarism by quoting directly and crediting sources
- Verify information, detect bias, and develop own perspective

WRITING
- Write a research paper
- Document sources
- Prepare Works Cited list
- Format your paper

SPEAKING, LISTENING, AND VIEWING
- Present results of investigation

ACADEMIC VOCABULARY
- research topic
- research paper
- documentation
- resources
- sources
- Works Cited
- source cards
- plagiarism

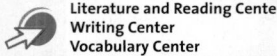

Literature and Reading Center
Writing Center
Vocabulary Center

1264

DIFFERENTIATED INSTRUCTION

FOR ENGLISH LEARNERS

Academic Vocabulary Use the copy master to help students learn the Academic Vocabulary listed on this page.

1. Read aloud each Academic Vocabulary term, and have students locate it on their copy masters.

2. Discuss the meaning or example shown on the copy master, and complete the chart as a class.

3. Have students work in small groups to complete the remaining activities.

Additional Academic Vocabulary Use the copy master to help students learn some of the Academic Vocabulary terms listed on pages 1270 and 1271. Follow the same procedure as for the Academic Vocabulary copy master.

 RESOURCE MANAGER—Copy Masters
Academic Vocabulary p. 6
Additional Academic Vocabulary p. 7

The Power of Research

SCOTCH SOAP

For help in planning this unit, see

RESOURCE MANAGER UNIT 7
pp. 1–13

INTRODUCE THE UNIT

This unit consists of two interactive workshops that guide students through the research and writing process.

The **Research Strategies Workshop,** pages 1268–1283, offers strategies for organizing, selecting, and evaluating information to answer both academic and real-world questions. Students practice accessing and navigating Web-based, electronic, audio-visual, and print resources. A wide range of activities allows students to practice their research skills in concrete situations.

The **Writing Workshop,** pages 1284–1303, provides a systematic approach for students to apply the strategies they have learned. Students will plan and write a research paper, adapting the strategies to their own projects and achieving mastery of research skills through practice and reflection.

RESEARCH WORKSHOPS

- **Research Strategies**
- **Writing Research Papers**

1265

Unit Resources

PRINT RESOURCES

R RESOURCE MANAGER UNIT 7

BEST PRACTICES TOOLKIT

S STANDARDS LESSON FILE

CALIFORNIA ASSESSMENT FILE

GRAMMAR FOR WRITING

TECH RESOURCES

- EasyPlanner DVD-ROM
- Write*Smart* CD-ROM
- ClassZone.com
- Audio Anthology CD
- Multi-Language Academic Vocabulary Online

- eEdition DVD-ROM & Online
- McDougal Littell Assessment System

UNIT 7
Standards

CALIFORNIA

SKILLS STRAND

SKILLS STRAND	Unit 7 Introduction: What Is the Power of Research? pp. 1266–1267	Research Strategies Workshop: Beginning Your Investigation pp. 1268–1283
Reading and Informational Texts	Build Context for Reading pp. 1266–1267 Use Prior Knowledge pp. 1266–1267 Connect pp. 1266–1267	
Research and Study Skills		Select and Shape a Research Topic p. 1268 Formulate Research Questions p. 1269 W1.6 Identify Relevant Sources p. 1269 R2.3 Distinguish Between Primary and Secondary Sources and Their Purposes p. 1270 Use Search Engines and Databases to Research a Topic pp. 1271–1273 W1.6 Evaluate Print and Nonprint Information and Sources for Relevance and Reliability pp. 1274–1277 R2.3 Take Notes p. 1278 W1.7 Paraphrase and Summarize Information p. 1279 W1.7 Avoid Plagiarism p. 1280 W1.7 Verify Information and Detect Bias pp. 1281–1283 R2.3 Draft a Thesis p. 1283
Vocabulary		Academic Vocabulary pp. 1270, 1271
Speaking, Listening, Viewing, and Media	Discuss pp. 1266–1267	Discuss pp. T1268–T1283

Writing Workshop: Research Paper
pp. 1284–1303

Reading and Informational Texts

Analyze a Research Paper pp. 1285–1290, 1301

Writing, Grammar, and Style

Write a Research Paper pp. 1284–1301 W1.3, W1.6, W2.4

Find and Focus a Research Topic pp. 1284, 1291 W1.6

Locate and Evaluate Sources p. 1292 W1.6

Make Source Cards p. 1292 W1.7

Take Notes and Create an Outline p. 1293 W1.7

Develop a Thesis Statement pp. 1291, 1293

Blend Information from Multiple Sources p. 1294 W1.3

Document Sources p. 1295 W1.7

Prepare a Works Cited List pp. 1296, 1299–1300 W1.7

Use Transitional Words and Phrases to Create Flow p. 1297

Support Ideas with Evidence and Revise for Unity and Conciseness pp. 1297–1298 W1.3

Format a Research Paper p. 1301 LC1.3

Speaking, Listening, Viewing, and Media

Discuss pp. T1284–T1290, 1301

Create a Multimedia Presentation pp. 1302–1303 W1.8, W2.6, LS1.7, LS2.2, LS2.4

Skills Assessed on the Unit 7 Test:

Reading and Informational Texts
- Analyze and evaluate parts of a research paper

Research and Study Skills
- Find and focus a research topic
- Distinguish between primary and secondary sources and their purposes
- Use search engines and databases to research a topic
- Evaluate print and nonprint sources of information for relevancy and reliability
- Verify information and detect bias
- Take notes and organize information
- Create source cards
- Summarize and paraphrase information
- Avoid plagiarism

Writing, Grammar, and Style
- Develop and focus a research topic
- Organize and outline information for a research paper
- Develop a thesis statement
- Determine facts to include in a research paper
- Use transitional words and phrases to connect ideas and create flow
- Support ideas with reasons and evidence and eliminate unnecessary details
- Draft a Works Cited list
- Additional writing and grammar skills

For additional lesson planning help, see **Easy Planner DVD-ROM.**

1265B

CALIFORNIA	ASSESS PRIOR KNOWLEDGE Diagnostic	ONGOING ASSESSMENT Reteaching
BEGINNING OF UNIT		
Unit Opener	Preview Unit Goals, **TE** p. 1264	
Research Strategies Workshop		Try It Out, **SE** Assess and Reteach, **SLF**
END OF UNIT		
Writing Workshop	Checklist, **SE** p. 1301	Assess and Reteach, **TE** p. 1301
Speaking & Listening	Criteria, **TE** p. 1302	For reteaching options, see **TE** p. 1302
Assessment		Unit Test, **AF** **MLAS**

For systematic instruction of grammar, use *Grammar for Writing*.

Key to Abbreviations:
SE = Student's Edition
TE = Teacher's Edition
SLF = Standards Lesson File
AF = Assessment File
MLAS = McDougal Littell Assessment System

Universal Access

	Strategic Reader	Benchmark	Advanced Learner	English Learner	Students with Disabilities
SE STUDENT'S EDITION					
Research Strategies Workshop	✔	✔	✔	✔	✔
Instructional annotations	✔	✔	✔	✔	✔
TE TEACHER'S EDITION					
Skill annotation support	✔	✔	✔	✔	✔
Differentiated instruction	✔	✔	✔	✔	✔
R RESOURCE MANAGER					
Skill copy masters	✔	✔		✔	✔
Writing support	✔	✔	✔		✔
AF ASSESSMENT FILE					
Leveled unit tests	✔	✔	✔	✔	✔
S STANDARDS LESSON FILE					
Leveled and reteaching copy masters	✔	✔	✔	✔	✔
BEST PRACTICES TOOLKIT					
Strategy bank	✔	✔	✔	✔	✔
Graphic organizers	✔	✔	✔	✔	✔
TECHNOLOGY					
WriteSmart Rubrics and student models	✔	✔	✔	✔	✔
CLASSZONE					
Instructional centers	✔	✔	✔	✔	✔
Multilanguage glossary				✔	

What Is the Power of Research?

Read aloud the questions on pages 1266 and 1267 and the paragraphs that follow them. Use these notes to prompt further exploration of the questions, ideas for research, and research papers.

What is it like to be AT WAR?

Invite students to discuss what they know about the experience of being at war and how they learned about the subject—for example, from movies, fiction, history books, or conversations with veterans. Point out that war, like most experiences, can be investigated from more than one perspective. To illustrate, ask how a historian's description of a battle might differ from a soldier's description; then discuss ways in which a soldier's personal report could help a historian.

How does SCIENCE affect you?

Encourage students to suggest ways of collecting data to answer the questions about acid rain, the importance of breakfast, and local earthquakes. Challenge students to name ways in which they would use the findings of other scientists to answer the questions, as well as methods for gathering original data. Discuss whether collecting original data would be equally appropriate for all three topics, and why or why not.

What Is the Power of Research?

Throughout this book, you have explored the "big questions" of literature, history, and life. You can take these questions to a new, more challenging level through formal research.

What is it like to be AT WAR?

You might investigate this question by writing a **historical research paper** that explores why some 18- and 19-year-olds enlisted to fight in Vietnam. Or you might create a **personal research paper** that describes how a particular war or conflict affected you or someone you know. How did that personal experience relate to the conflict as a whole?

How does SCIENCE affect you?

Is acid rain present in your community? Do high school students improve their academic performance if they eat breakfast each day? When and where was the last earthquake in your state? When you write a **scientific research paper,** you present data that you have collected yourself as well as the findings of others.

1266

How does LIFE influence literature?

Novels, stories, and poems reflect how authors see the world. They can also shape our view of places and events. One way to explore a work of literature is to write a **literary research paper** that traces how history influenced a particular literary work or vice versa. For instance, you could learn more about the real people who inspired John Steinbeck to write *The Grapes of Wrath*.

Are we ready for the next natural DISASTER?

The question that captivates you may touch on several fields of study. A **multidisciplinary research paper** allows you to ask questions related to science, government, history, and many other subject areas and investigate how those subjects relate to each other.

How does LIFE influence literature?

Invite students to list literary or artistic works that may have been inspired by historical events—for example, specific protest songs, war posters, plays, or movies. Then have students list works of literature or art that may have affected history. (One example might be Thomas Paine's pamphlet *Common Sense*.) Choose examples from both lists; then work with students to generate questions that explore connections between the work and historical events.

Are we ready for the next natural DISASTER?

Have students suggest natural disasters that might affect your community and then choose the one that seems most likely. On the board, create three columns labeled *Science*, *Government*, and *History*. For each category, have students suggest questions that they could use to determine the community's readiness for a particular disaster, as in these examples:

- **Science** What is the probability of a hurricane of Level 3 or higher striking this area?

- **Government** What agencies are responsible for preparing for and responding to such a disaster?

- **History** What damage has been done by past hurricanes?

Point out that a multidisciplinary paper would address many such questions and would answer them in the context of the overall question.

Teach

OBJECTIVES
- use research strategies
- use the Internet, library, and media center
- evaluate print and online sources
- take and document notes
- use various sources to develop a personal perspective on a topic

 R2.3, W1.7

Beginning Your Investigation

Explain that the Research Strategies Workshop introduces techniques and resources for finding information. Tell students that these skills will help them to use their time more efficiently and to succeed academically, as well as to make better decisions as workers, consumers, and citizens.

Selecting and Shaping a Topic

Ask students to name possible paper topics. Have them suggest one way to broaden each topic and one way to narrow it.

TRY OUT DIFFERENT "LENSES"

Divide the class into four groups, one for each "lens" in the diagram. Have each group develop and share two other questions about the Dust Bowl for that "lens."

 RESOURCE MANAGER—Copy Master
Selecting and Shaping a Topic p. 15

Research Workshop Resources

R2.3 (pgs. 1269, 1281), **W1.7** (pgs. 1278–1280)

Beginning Your Investigation

When you create a top-quality research paper, you go beyond merely finding and assembling information. Instead, you investigate, analyze, develop new perspectives, and perhaps do original research to reach your own conclusions.

Selecting and Shaping a Topic

In the past, your teacher probably assigned you a topic or had you choose from a list of topics. Now you may be asked to generate your own topic or put your own spin on an assigned topic. For instance, perhaps you need to write a paper for your American literature or American history class. Reading *The Grapes of Wrath* has heightened your interest in the historical events of that period, but you know that a topic like "the Dust Bowl" is too broad. Because you will spend hours researching and writing, you want to find a topic that will hold your interest over time. How can you shape a general idea into the right research topic for you?

TRY OUT DIFFERENT "LENSES"

To discover a unique approach to a particular topic, view it through different "lenses," or perspectives. A historian, an economist, a scientist, and an artist would look at the topic of the Dust Bowl in different ways. This cluster diagram illustrates questions you might develop when considering different aspects of a topic.

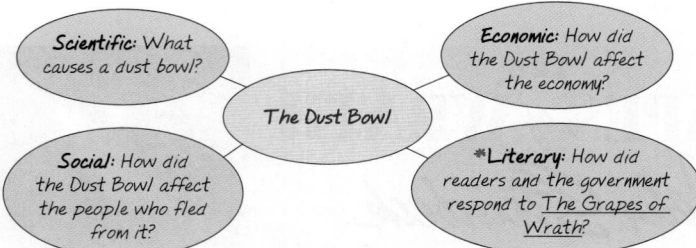

Scientific: What causes a dust bowl?

Economic: How did the Dust Bowl affect the economy?

The Dust Bowl

Social: How did the Dust Bowl affect the people who fled from it?

*Literary: How did readers and the government respond to <u>The Grapes of Wrath</u>?

Choose the question that intrigues you the most and write a goal statement to focus your thinking and guide your research. You are likely to change or refine this statement as you do your research, but write the clearest, most focused statement that you can right now.

> **GOAL:** to write a research paper that investigates how <u>The Grapes of Wrath</u> affected government response to Dust Bowl evacuees

Your goal statement will develop into your thesis after you have read, interpreted, and drawn conclusions from a variety of sources.

 RESOURCE MANAGER UNIT 7

Plan and Teach pp. 9–11, 14
Selecting and Shaping a Topic p. 15
Formulate Research Questions p. 16
Consult Search Engines p. 17
Explore Databases p. 18
Evaluate Web Sites p. 19
Evaluating Newspapers and Periodicals p. 20
Choosing Reliable Nonfiction Books p. 21
Finding the Right Sources p. 22

Note Taking and Plagiarism p. 23
Paraphrases and Summaries p. 24
Quote Information Accurately p. 25
Verifying Information p. 26
Detecting Bias p. 27
Drawing Conclusions from Your Research p. 28

 STANDARDS LESSON FILE
Reading Lessons 8–9, 17
Research and Study Skills Lessons 1, 3–9, 12–13
Media Lessons 12, 17–18

BEST PRACTICES TOOLKIT
Differentiated Instruction pp. 31–38*

Graphic Organizers/Strategies
Venn Diagram • Sequence Chain • Learning Log • Main Idea and Details • Open Mind

Technology
Easy Planner DVD
Write*Smart* CD

* Resources for Differentiation

Planning Your Research

To make your search efficient and effective, develop specific research questions and then choose the sources that are right for you.

FORMULATE RESEARCH QUESTIONS

List some questions that will help you investigate your topic. Highlight **keywords**—terms, names, and phrases that are specific to your topic. Later on, you might search for these keywords within a book's index, on a search engine, or in a database.

> How did the Dust Bowl affect the United States?
> Why did Steinbeck write *The Grapes of Wrath*? How did he do the research?
> What did the government do to help migrant workers like the Joad family?

IDENTIFY THE MOST RELEVANT SOURCES

The sources you choose depend on what your topic is and how much you already know about it. Take a few minutes to consider which sources make the most sense for the early stages of your research.

- **Encyclopedia articles** can provide a helpful overview of your topic as you begin researching.

- For the specific details you need, try **specialized reference works.** Visual dictionaries have diagrams and cross-sections, almanacs have facts and statistics, and biographical references have information on famous people. See page R44 to learn more about reference works.

- **Documentaries** often include valuable interviews , speeches, and "you are there" footage that help you understand historical, literary, and scientific topics.

- **Magazines and newspapers** can give insights into a topic's perceived importance. Has your topic ever been front-page news, or is it rarely covered? How has coverage of your topic changed over time? For topics related to economics, popular culture, or history, take a look at related **advertisements.**

- **Interviews and oral histories** are firsthand testimony about history and culture. Look for them on audio, on video, in books, or on Web sites.

- **Original research** is information you discover yourself. For example, you might interview an expert, listen to a speech or lecture, create a questionnaire, perform an experiment, or conduct field research. To learn more about original research, see page R47.

- Be creative as you search. You might find valuable information in song lyrics, illustrations, maps, photographs, obituaries, statistical data, government publications, or museum exhibits.

Share your research questions with a librarian. He or she can suggest print and electronic resources that you may not have considered.

> **RESEARCH TOOLS**
> For research tools and strategies, visit the **Research Center** at ClassZone.com.

RESEARCH STRATEGIES WORKSHOP **1269**

Planning Your Research

FORMULATE RESEARCH QUESTIONS

Work with students to list additional questions about the Dust Bowl. Have them identify words or phrases in the questions that could be used as keywords in a search.

IDENTIFY THE MOST RELEVANT SOURCES

- Invite students to connect the four "lenses" from page 1268 to possible sources on this list. Discuss which sources would be best for the early stages of research through each "lens," and why. For example, original research might be most appropriate for scientific questions, and oral histories might be most appropriate for social questions.

- Ask students to select one source and explain how it might be useful in researching the Dust Bowl. Point out that most of the sources can be applied to almost any topic.

S STANDARDS LESSON FILE
Research and Study Skills Lesson 1: Research Questions and Topic

R RESOURCE MANAGER—Copy Master
Formulate Research Questions p. 16

DIFFERENTIATED INSTRUCTION

FOR ALL STUDENTS

Use the following suggestions to help students with their research:

- Encourage students to find auditory sources of information, such as taped speeches, audio books, musical recordings, and taped interviews.

- Have pairs of students brainstorm prior knowledge of their topics that can help guide them toward sources.

- Have students use charts and maps to record and organize information.

FOR STRATEGIC READERS

Concept Support [small-group option]
Present groups of students with two different sources about the same topic—for example, a newspaper article about a current event and an interview with a participant in the event. Have each group use a Venn Diagram to compare and contrast the information that the two sources provide.

🧰 BEST PRACTICES TOOLKIT—Transparency
Venn Diagram p. A26

RESEARCH STRATEGIES WORKSHOP **1269**

Choosing the Right Research Tools

ACADEMIC VOCABULARY FOR THE LIBRARY

Read the terms aloud; then call on volunteers to share situations in which they have found these resources helpful when using school or community libraries. Elicit preliminary definitions of the terms. As students read and discuss this section, have them refine their definitions.

Primary and Secondary Sources

As students read the chart, have them compare and contrast the two types of sources. Ask them to discuss specific ways in which (1) either type of source might show bias, and (2) a researcher might use a primary source to correct the bias of a secondary source and vice versa.

- **Primary Sources** Emphasize that primary sources need not be in the first person; for instance, a newspaper article from November 22, 1963, on the assassination of President John F. Kennedy would be written in the third person. Primary sources can be found in a wide range of media aside from text; for example, a family portrait can be a primary source, as can an antique toy or map.

- **Secondary Sources** Emphasize that secondary sources can offer information and interpretations from a wide variety of viewpoints. Secondary source writers are sometimes assumed to be more objective than primary source writers; in reality, however, they are not always so.

 STANDARDS LESSON FILE

Research and Study Skills Lesson 5: Using Primary and Secondary Sources

---

Choosing the Right Research Tools

As you delve into your research, you will learn more about what types of sources are available and where you can find them.

Primary and Secondary Sources

Most research papers include both primary and secondary sources. As this chart shows, the two types have distinct differences, advantages, and disadvantages.

PRIMARY SOURCE	SECONDARY SOURCE
Definition: materials written or created by people who took part in events or observed them	**Definition:** records created after events occurred by people who were not directly involved
▼	▼
Examples: letters, diaries, speeches, photographs, autobiographies, e-mails, Weblogs, first-person newspaper and magazine articles, public documents such as birth certificates	**Examples:** biographies, textbooks, encyclopedias, third-person newspaper and magazine articles, most documentaries
▼	▼
Advantages: firsthand information; can give insight into attitudes and beliefs of the times; may contain very specific details	**Advantages:** sometimes include excerpts from many primary sources; often have a broad perspective and consider many viewpoints; useful for getting an overview of a topic
▼	▼
Disadvantages: limited perspective; may need interpretation; may be biased	**Disadvantages:** only as reliable as the sources on which they are based; may be biased

ACADEMIC VOCABULARY FOR THE LIBRARY

You will use these terms when doing research in the library or media center:
- primary source
- secondary source
- database
- catalog
- abstract
- bibliography
- index
- appendix
- preface

DIFFERENTIATED INSTRUCTION

FOR ENGLISH LEARNERS
Vocabulary Support

- *Weblogs,* "(also known as *blogs*) Web sites in which writers can make daily entries and readers can post comments"

- *first-person,* "written from the point of view of a single person, using the pronoun *I*"

- *firsthand,* "coming from direct personal knowledge or experience"

- *perspective,* "the way in which a writer looks at a topic"

- *biased,* "favoring one side of an issue instead of being impartial; prejudiced"

- *documentaries,* "works (especially films or TV programs) that provide information about historical, political, or social topics, often through a mix of news footage, interviews, and narration"

- *third-person,* "written from the point of view of someone outside the events, without using the pronoun *I*"

Online Resources

When you use online resources, can you locate exactly what you need? The next pages will show you how to improve your online search skills.

CONSULT SEARCH ENGINES

Many search engines are available to you, and each returns different results. For best results, click on the search engine's "advanced search" or "search tips" link. Follow these general rules for effective Internet searches.

- **Be specific.** Try combining two or three keywords. If you want to find out about labor camps in California, be sure *California* is one of your search terms.
- **Use search limiters.** Enclose phrases in quotation marks—for example, a search for *"The Grapes of Wrath"* will result in pages that have those words in that order. Some search engines allow you to add AND or a plus sign to be sure that certain results are included: *Depression AND California;* or *+Depression +California.* To exclude certain terms, use the word NOT or a minus sign: *evacuees NOT Katrina;* or *+evacuees -Katrina.* To learn more, see page R46.
- **Choose the most relevant pages.** Scan the first 10 to 15 descriptions the search engine provides. Which sites could help you answer your research questions? Consider adding, deleting, or changing keywords to improve your results.

TRY IT OUT! *Examine Search Engine Results*

Which of these results do you think would yield the most useful information?

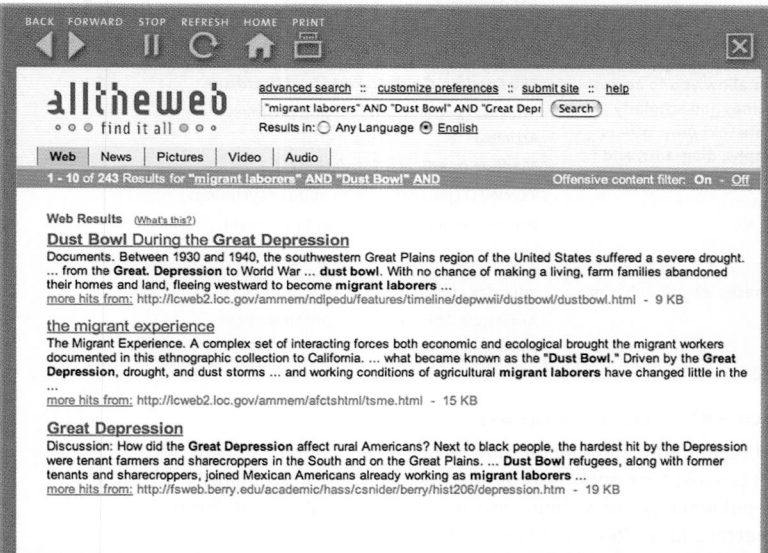

ACADEMIC VOCABULARY FOR THE INTERNET

Here are terms you will use when discussing the Internet:

- Web page
- Web site
- URL (uniform resource locator, also called Web address)
- search engine
- keyword search
- hyperlink
- menu

Close Read

1. This researcher did a search that combined three terms: "migrant laborers," "Dust Bowl," and "Great Depression." What are the advantages and disadvantages of doing such a specific search?

2. How might the search results change if the search was for "migrant laborers," "Dust Bowl," and "Oklahoma"?

3. What other search terms can you think of that might yield answers to the research questions on page 1269?

Online Resources

ACADEMIC VOCABULARY FOR THE INTERNET

Ask students which terms they find familiar. Discuss possible definitions; then urge students to refine those definitions as they encounter the terms in their reading.

CONSULT SEARCH ENGINES

Ask students to suggest the names of several search engines—for example, Google, Yahoo!, Alta Vista, and Ask.com—and conduct searches on those engines for keywords suggested by the instruction. Ask students to compare and contrast the results from different search engines.

Close Read

Possible answers:

1. *Advantages: Such a search may be quick to locate specific information on a topic.* ***Disadvantages:*** *If the terms are too specific, the search may not find any useful results; it also will not find relevant information that does not contain all of the keywords.*

2. *The search would locate state-specific information.*

If students need help . . . Have them identify the search term that has changed.

3. *Steinbeck;* Grapes of Wrath; *Okies; 1930s; New Deal.*

S STANDARDS LESSON FILE
Media Lesson 17: Understanding the Basics of Web Sites

R RESOURCE MANAGER—Copy Master
Consult Search Engines p. 17

FOR STRATEGIC READERS

Concept Support Inform students that many Web browsers include access to one or more search engines through their navigation toolbars. Call on a volunteer to show the feature to students. Have students use a search engine available through a browser on your school's computers to find the Web addresses of other major search engines. Show students how to bookmark those addresses.

FOR ADVANCED LEARNERS/AP

Advanced Search [small-group option] Have groups of students use the search engine Alltheweb (http://www.alltheweb.com) to conduct their own searches for the keywords *migrant laborers, Dust Bowl,* and *Great Depression.* Instruct groups to locate the three sites shown in the **Try It Out!** feature. Have them visit those sites and at least one other of the top ten sites produced by the search. Then have them report on the similarities and

differences among the sites, drawing conclusions about the sites' relative relevance.

To extend the activity, have groups locate the Advanced Search function on Alltheweb and repeat the same search using that function, with search limiters that they have chosen, such as word filters or domain filters. Have them compare and contrast the results of the basic and advanced searches.

EXPLORE DATABASES

- Emphasize that some databases are accessible to the general public for free; whereas others, such as InfoTrac, require a paid subscription. Point out, however, that since many public libraries subscribe to paid databases, library patrons can use those databases without charge—sometimes even accessing them from a home computer, using their library card numbers.

- Have students read the descriptions and examples of the five types of databases. Then challenge students to describe how they might use each type to locate information relevant to the Dust Bowl experiences portrayed in *The Grapes of Wrath*. For example, a researcher might use the *Readers' Guide to Periodical Literature* to find magazine articles from the 1930s about the Dust Bowl or about Steinbeck's novel. Students with family members who lived through the Dust Bowl might use a genealogy site to trace their ancestry back to that time and place.

- Have students investigate several of the databases mentioned and report their observations to the class.

S STANDARDS LESSON FILE

Research and Study Skills Lesson 3: Using Reference and Search Tools

R RESOURCE MANAGER—Copy Master
Explore Databases p. 18

EXPLORE DATABASES

A **database** is any organized collection of data, whether print or electronic. Some of the databases in this chart are free to all; others may be available for free through your library or media center's Web site.

TYPES OF DATABASES	EXAMPLES
Internet search engines let you create customized databases of Web pages that include your keywords. Search engines examine literally billions of Web pages.	google.com altavista.com search.ask.com alltheweb.com dogpile.com Reproduced with permission of Yahoo! Inc. © 2007 by Yahoo! Inc. YAHOO! and the YAHOO! logo are trademarks of Yahoo! Inc.
Library catalogs let you create a customized database of materials related to your keywords—not only books but also magazine and journal articles, e-books, audio books, and DVDs.	www.imcpl.org suncat.co.sarasota.fl.us libweb.ci.albany.or.us
Newspaper databases contain articles from one newspaper or from many. You can access recent articles or ones that are decades old.	America's Newspapers The *New York Times Index* *Los Angeles Times Index*
Article databases allow you to access text from magazines and scholarly journals. Some are text only; others include photographs, diagrams, and other graphics.	*The Readers' Guide to Periodical Literature* InfoTrac (general-interest and business articles) Medline (medical information) PsycINFO (journal articles about psychology) Noticias or Informe (articles in Spanish)
Genealogy databases let you delve into family histories.	ancestry.com America's Obituaries and Death Notices HeritageQuest Online

ADVANTAGES OF SPECIALIZED DATABASES

"Why should I spend time figuring out how to use these databases?" you might ask. "I can just type my keywords into my favorite search engine." That's true—but when you're writing a research paper, specialized databases are often a better choice. Read on to find out why.

DIFFERENTIATED INSTRUCTION

FOR ENGLISH LEARNERS

Oral Language Direct students' attention to the abbreviations and domain names in the chart's examples of online database addresses. Model the pronunciations, or have one or more volunteers do so. For example, explain that *alltheweb.com* is pronounced "all the web dot com," that *PsychINFO* is pronounced "sike info," and that the more complex Web addresses, such as *libweb.ci.albany.or.us*, would be spelled out orally, with the word *dot* spoken for each period. Have students take turns pronouncing the examples in the list.

FOR ADVANCED LEARNERS/AP

Create a Database [paired option] Challenge pairs of students to collaborate on creating a personal database for a topic of mutual interest. Remind students that a database can be in the form of print and that it can include bibliographical listings and abstracts rather than full articles. Have students tell the class what kind of database they created, what its features are, and ways in which it would be useful.

- **Specificity**—Some databases, such as the Internet Movie Database, cover only certain topics. Others cover only one type of material, such as articles from medical journals. Because these databases are targeted, you don't have to sift through pages of search results that have little or no relation to your topic.
- **No advertisements**—Unlike many search engines, most specialized databases do not have distracting pop-up windows or sidebar advertisements. No advertiser has paid to have a page show up first or in the top ten.
- **Access to the "invisible Web"**—Librarians call pages that are accessible through the Internet, but not through search engines, the "invisible Web." Many millions of Web pages are available through subscription-only databases—but if your library or media center subscribes to such databases, all you may need to access them is the bar code number on your library card.
- **Abstracts**—Many databases include an abstract—a short summary of an article's content—for each article. By reading abstracts, you can quickly decide whether the entire article is worth reading.

To find the most relevant results on a targeted database, read the article titles and notice the names of the publications the articles came from. Click on the most promising titles and read the abstracts or skim the first few paragraphs of each.

TRY IT OUT! *Examine Database Results*

These results are from a database called InfoTrac. Examine them and think about whether this search is effective.

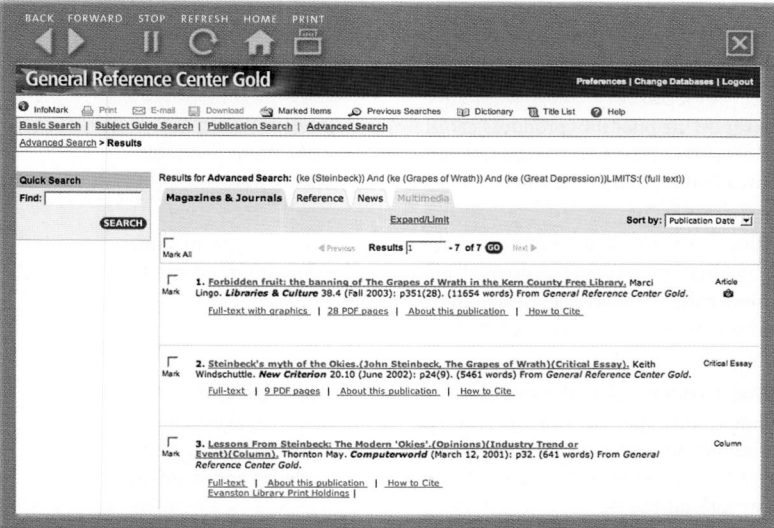

Close Read

1. Which three keyword phrases did this researcher use? On this database, the abbreviation "ke" means keyword.

2. Which result includes graphics? How do you know?

3. Of the three results shown here, which one is not likely to be useful? How do you know?

4. What other information does this database provide that the search engine on page 1271 does not? Give three examples.

ADVANTAGES OF SPECIALIZED DATABASES

- Have students preview the four advantages of databases by reading the boldfaced heads in the bulleted list. Then ask them to read each bulleted paragraph, pausing to discuss questions if necessary before moving on.
- Challenge students to think of possible disadvantages to using databases; then discuss. The overall point should be that databases offer more advantages than disadvantages and are worth exploring, especially for in-depth projects such as research papers.

Close Read

Possible answers:

1. *The keywords were* Steinbeck, Grapes of Wrath, *and* Great Depression.

2. *The first result includes graphics; it contains a link for "Full-text with graphics" and has a camera icon.*

3. *The third result is not likely to be useful; it is from a computer magazine and apparently focuses on today's computer industry.*

4. *Any three: The database offers citation guidelines, information about each publication, a link to holdings within a particular library, a description of the type of source, a way for the user to access previous searches, a dictionary, a list of titles, a way to search by subject rather than by keyword, and a way to search by publication.*

If students need help . . . Tell them to look closely at every hyperlink on the page. Pairs of students may work together to discuss the meaning of each hyperlink.

STANDARDS LESSON FILE
Research and Study Skills Lesson 4: Using a Web Site for Research

FOR STRATEGIC READERS

Task Support Guide students to a popular nonsubscription database, such as the Internet Movie Database (http://www. imdb.com). Work with them to locate the database's features, such as menus, icons, and hyperlinks. Then have students perform a sample search, record their search paths on a Sequence Chain, and share the results with the class.

BEST PRACTICES TOOLKIT—Transparency
Sequence Chain p. B21

FOR ADVANCED LEARNERS/AP

Accessing the "Invisible Web" Have students ask a school librarian or community librarian what subscription-only databases are available through their facilities. Instruct students to go online to access two or more such databases; then have them report to the class on (1) the kinds of information that they found on the "invisible Web" and (2) ways in which the databases might be useful in research.

Evaluating Sources

- Have students preview the guidelines by reading the italicized heads; then have them read each explanatory paragraph in turn. Pause after each paragraph to have students check their comprehension by paraphrasing the information.

- Consider including these comments and activities:

Relevance Have pairs of students compose lists of criteria for determining a source's relevance.

Timeliness Ask students to suggest at least two topics for which a ten-year-old source *would not* be useful and at least two for which such a source *would* be useful.

Accuracy Remind students that awareness of accuracy and bias is an especially important factor in online research since anyone can post a Web site. Emphasize that distinguishing between fact and opinion is a key research skill in relation to both online and print sources. Remind students that they can enter the term "bogus sites" into a search engine to find out which sites are fake, deliberately putting out inaccurate information.

Author's Credentials Suggest that students perform a search for the author's name in order to check his or her credentials.

Publisher's Credentials As examples of reputable publishers, give students the names of publishers of books found in your classroom or school library.

Author's Purpose Discuss the distinction between an author's credentials and an author's purpose; for example, an eminent scientist might write a persuasive essay about an important issue that is not related to his or her field.

Breadth and Depth of Information Suggest that students ask themselves whether the information is appropriate for their audience.

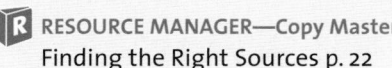 STANDARDS LESSON FILE
Reading Lesson 17: Author's Credibility

RESOURCE MANAGER—Copy Master
Finding the Right Sources p. 22

Evaluating Sources

In this section, you will learn how to select the most trustworthy and reliable sources, whether in print or online.

GUIDELINES FOR EVALUATING SOURCES

Relevance	Is the source related to the goal statement and research questions you wrote on pages 1268–1269? Your goals and questions may change as you write; however, don't allow interesting but irrelevant sources to distract you.
Timeliness	Topics in science, medicine, and sports often require recently updated information. Older sources can be valuable for historical or literary topics. For a print source, check the copyright page. For a documentary, look for a copyright notice on the label. For online materials, look for a "last updated" notice.
Accuracy	Most encyclopedias, dictionaries, and almanacs are considered accurate because they are updated regularly and go through a rigorous review process. Online sources can have information that is even more accurate because of frequent updates. However, some online sources may not go through the same rigorous review process. Whenever possible, verify and clarify facts in more than one source.
Author's Credentials	Look for an author who has written on the same topic before or who has a position or job title that qualifies him or her as an expert.
Publisher's Credentials	A reputable publisher produces carefully researched materials. University presses tend to be reputable. Most publications and Web sites that focus on celebrities, fad diets, and gossip are not.
Author's Purpose	Why was the source created—to inform, entertain, persuade, or some combination of these? In general, informative pieces are researched more carefully than ones designed to entertain or to sell. For information on bias, see page 1282.
Breadth and Depth of Information	Match your needs to the source. Examine the table of contents, index, and appendix if this information is available. They will help you find an overview of a topic or just one detailed aspect of it. Also, think about whether the source is too basic or too dense and scholarly for your purposes.

DIFFERENTIATED INSTRUCTION

FOR STRATEGIC READERS
Vocabulary Support

- *irrelevant,* "not related to the topic under consideration"
- *timeliness,* "relevance to current considerations"
- *rigorous,* "thorough"
- *verify,* "to test something's accuracy"
- *credentials,* "proof that one has the right to be believed or trusted"
- *reputable,* "deserving respect; honorable"

FOR ADVANCED LEARNERS/AP
Evaluate Accuracy Ask students to read an article in a current newspaper or magazine and then analyze, either orally or in writing, the extent to which it contains fact and opinion. Suggest that they accompany their presentation with a copy of the article in which facts are highlighted in one color and opinions in another. Have students wrap up their presentation by stating any biases that they found in the article and by giving the author a grade for accuracy.

Finding Trustworthy Web Sites

Anyone can create a Web site, so it is important to evaluate sites thoroughly.

QUESTIONS TO ASK ABOUT A WEB SITE

- **What does the address tell me?** Most sites with *.com* or *.net* in their addresses are personal or commercial sites. A personal site might be the work of just one person, so its information may not have been carefully checked. A commercial site exists to make a profit, so negative information about a product or service might be left out. Sites with the abbreviations *.edu* (educational), *.org* (nonprofit organization), or *.gov* (U.S. government) are more likely to be accurate because they are the work of many people.

- **Who created this site?** Look for sections labeled "About Us" or "Contact Us." How can you tell if an individual rather than an organization created a site? The lack of an institution name or logo is one clue. Other clues are the lack of an author biography, the absence of documentation for sources, or hyperlinks that lead nowhere or only to the author's own sites. You can also consult a domain lookup site, such as *easywhois.com*.

TIP Some *.org* and *.edu* sites are personal sites that are not reviewed by the sponsoring institution. A personal *.edu* address includes a forward slash and a tilde (/~) followed by a name or initials, as in *okies.utc.edu/~haylee*.

TRY IT OUT! *Evaluate a Web Site*

Would this site be useful for researching the goal statement from page 1268?

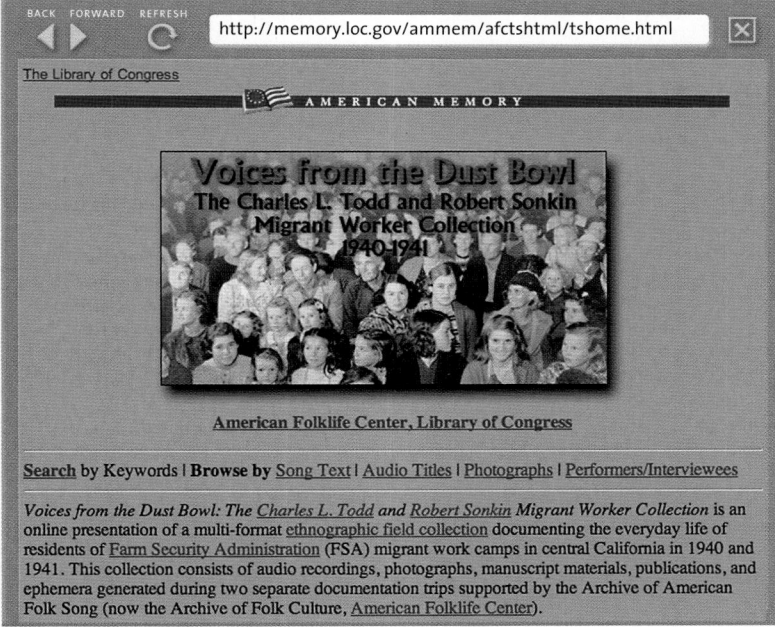

Close Read

1. What organization maintains this site? How do you know?

2. Why was the site created?

3. What clues do you have to the accuracy of the information on this site?

FOR ADVANCED LEARNERS/AP

Create Questions Have advanced learners create questions to help less-proficient readers practice evaluating Web sites. Explain that the questions should relate to using the Web page and links shown in the **Try It Out!** feature on this page, as in these examples:

- What link would you click to find the lyrics to songs about the Dust Bowl? ("Song Text")

- Where can you find two separate hyperlinks to the American Folklife Center? *(in the middle of the Web page, just below the photograph, and in the last line of the text on the page)*

Have advanced learners serve as tutors for less-proficient readers in a one-on-one setting.

Finding Trustworthy Web Sites

QUESTIONS TO ASK ABOUT A WEB SITE

- Point out that sites with the domain names *.edu, .org,* and *.gov* are likely to be trustworthy not only because they are group products but because they are the products of well-regarded institutions such as universities, charities, or governments.

- Call attention to the *TIP* and clarify that, for example, an individual university student may be allowed to set up a Web page to share his or her work with the public. Such Web pages should be evaluated as if they were individually owned sites, not institutional sites. Author's credentials are especially important in such cases.

- To get to a site's home page, delete the part of the Web address that appears after the domain name and then press Enter. The domain is the part of the address that identifies the site's owner, such as *loc.gov* for the Library of Congress.

Close Read

Possible answers:

1. *The Library of Congress maintains the site; the link is at the top of the Web page.*

If students need help . . . Direct their attention to the hyperlink in the upper left-hand corner of the Web page.

2. *The site was created to make the library's collection on an important historical topic available online to the general public.*

If students need help . . . Ask

- Who would want to use this site? Why?

- What would such users have to do if the site were not available?

3. *The identity of the source, one of the world's great libraries, makes it probable that the information is accurate. The .gov domain name also suggests accuracy.*

 STANDARDS LESSON FILE
Research and Study Skills Lesson 7: Evaluating Electronic Sources

Media Lesson 18: Evaluating Web Sites

R RESOURCE MANAGER—Copy Master
Evaluate Web Sites p. 19

Evaluating Newspapers and Periodicals

QUESTIONS TO ASK ABOUT NEWSPAPERS AND PERIODICALS

- Call on volunteers to name some newspapers and periodicals with which they are familiar. Have students briefly describe each publication's subject matter and target audience. Discuss whether students consider each publication reliable or not, and why.

- Distribute a variety of newspapers and periodicals, emphasizing well-known ones such as the *New York Times, Wall Street Journal, National Geographic,* and *Scientific American,* along with a local newspaper. Instruct students to skim through several top stories to find each writer's byline, the publication date, and (if applicable) any outside source from which the article came, such as the Associated Press (AP). Also have students turn to the masthead and the contributors' page if available. Ask students to evaluate the reliability of each article, stating the reasons for their evaluations.

Close Read

Possible answers:

1. *Shortly after* The Grapes of Wrath *became a controversial bestseller, John Steinbeck secluded himself in a remote area. He told the* Los Angeles Times *that his novel was accurate and that it was "moneyed people," not migrant workers, who objected to it.*

2. *Yes; large-circulation newspapers generally are reliable.*

3. *No; the article is a valuable source for someone who wants to know about how people initially reacted to* The Grapes of Wrath.

S STANDARDS LESSON FILE
Media Lesson 12: Evaluating News Reports

R RESOURCE MANAGER—Copy Master
Evaluating Newspapers and Periodicals
p. 20

Evaluating Newspapers and Periodicals

Magazines, newspapers, and scholarly journals can be tricky to evaluate because you need to assess the publication itself, the author of the article, and the article's content.

QUESTIONS TO ASK ABOUT NEWSPAPERS AND PERIODICALS

- **Is the publication well-known and well-respected?** Most large-circulation newspapers and national magazines are reliable sources. Beware of supermarket tabloids and other sensationalist publications.

- **Who is the author?** Look for the writer's credentials. Generally, staff writers are as reliable as the publication in which they appear.

- **How old is the information?** Depending on your topic, you may need up-to-the-minute information, or you might look for information from a specific era.

- **Did the article originally appear in another source?** If so, make sure the original source is reliable. News services such as AP (Associated Press) and the New York Times News Service are the original sources of many reprinted articles.

- **Can the information be verified?** The best way to tell if a particular piece of information is accurate is to check it against other sources.

TRY IT OUT! **Evaluate a Newspaper Article**
Read and evaluate this newspaper article.

---

from the Los Angeles Times, July 9, 1939
Dust Bowl Book Brings Trouble

BY TOM CAMERON, TIMES STAFF REPRESENTATIVE

LOS GATOS, July 8. (Exclusive)— John Steinbeck, author of the best-selling novel, "Grapes of Wrath," has betaken himself to Moody Gulch, a secluded canyon three miles from here, and padlocked himself against the world.

For the first time in his career, Steinbeck is inaccessible to friend and enemy alike. . . .

There have been reports of threats against the author which induced him to retreat to an almost inaccessible citadel—a refuge from the very economic refugees he sought to befriend. . . .

"It isn't the refugees who have taken exception to what I wrote,"

he asserted. "It's the moneyed people back there in Oklahoma—the big oil men and outfits like the Oklahoma City Chamber of Commerce. If anybody's sore at me for the book it's that kind of people." . . .

Regarding the report that Ruth Comfort Mitchell planned to write a refutation of some of the statements in his book, Steinbeck laughed in scorn.

"I know what I was talking about. I lived, off and on, with those Okies for the last three years. Anyone who tries to refute me will just become ridiculous."

Close Read

1. Briefly summarize this article.

2. The *Los Angeles Times* is California's most widely read newspaper, so would you expect this article to be reliable? Give reasons for your answer.

3. Is this article useless because it is so old? Explain.

DIFFERENTIATED INSTRUCTION

FOR ADVANCED LEARNERS/AP

Evaluate Information Explain the importance of fact-checking before a publication goes to press: Ideally, any fact that is not common knowledge should be checked for accuracy before being included for publication. (Some periodicals are more fastidious about fact-checking than others; the *New Yorker* is famously attentive to the checking of all facts.) Have students select an article from a periodical of their choice and check its facts, using tools such as encyclopedias, specialized reference books, and the Internet. In the case of news stories, tell students to make sure that every statement about an event is corroborated by a witness or by the reporter's direct observation. Have students report on any incorrect or unsupported facts that they discover; then have them give the article a grade for reliability.

Choosing Reliable Books

Just as you write for different purposes and audiences, publishers put books on the market for different reasons. Some books are rushed to market and aimed at making money fast. Others are the result of years of work, including multiple edits and rewrites.

QUESTIONS TO ASK ABOUT NONFICTION BOOKS

- **Is the author an expert on this subject?** Check for information about the author on the book jacket, at the beginning of the book, and at the end.
- **Is the book based on research?** Check the back of the book for a bibliography. Look for footnotes, in which the author credits his or her sources and provides additional insights or information. Check for an appendix, which might add other information, such as maps, statistical tables, or family trees.
- **What is the author's or publisher's purpose?** This may be stated in a **preface**, a short introductory essay. The preface may also tell you more about the writer's background and research.
- **What is the copyright date?** A series of updates and printings is often a sign that the source has been highly regarded for years and is probably reliable.

TRY IT OUT! *Evaluate a Nonfiction Book*

Decide whether this book, *Dust Bowl Migration*, would be useful to someone focusing on government response to Dust Bowl evacuees.

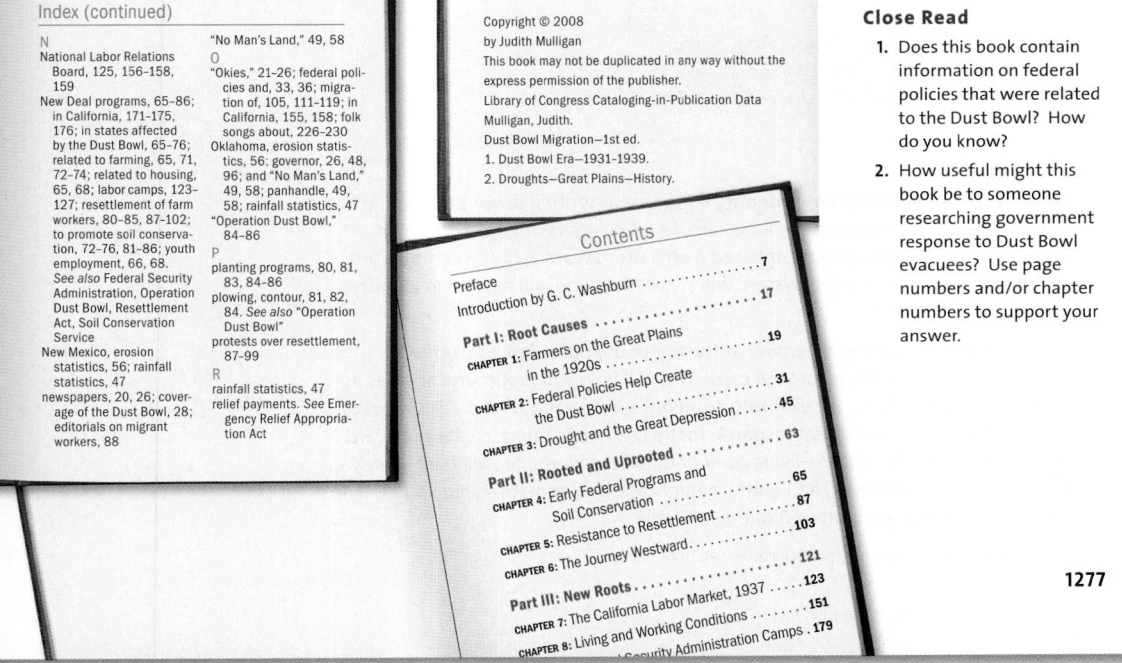

Close Read

1. Does this book contain information on federal policies that were related to the Dust Bowl? How do you know?

2. How useful might this book be to someone researching government response to Dust Bowl evacuees? Use page numbers and/or chapter numbers to support your answer.

1277

Choosing Reliable Books

QUESTIONS TO ASK ABOUT NONFICTION BOOKS

- Ask students to name a nonfiction book that they have read or consulted, either for a school report or for other reasons. Ask how each student decided that the book was reliable.
- Enhance students' understanding of specific parts of nonfiction books:

  —**Bibliography** Explain that a bibliography reflects the thoroughness of an author's research; it also gives readers guideposts for further study.

  —**Footnotes** Point out that endnotes often are used instead of footnotes.

  —**Appendix** Note that an appendix often gives statistical support for an author's ideas.

  —**Preface** Explain that a preface allows an author to discuss the book in a less formal voice. A preface may preview the book, for example, explain the author's purpose, or sketch the author's background.

  —**Copyright** Show students where to find a book's copyright notice.

Close Read

Possible answers:

1. *Yes; both the contents page and the index mention federal programs.*
2. *The book might be very useful. Chapters 2, 4, and 9 contain information on the subject; and the index lists the National Labor Relations Board, New Deal programs, planting programs, and the Emergency Relief Appropriations Act.*

If students need help . . . Advise them to look for key words that indicate governmental action, such as *act* and *administration*.

S STANDARDS LESSON FILE
Research and Study Skills Lesson 6: Evaluating Print Sources

R RESOURCE MANAGER—Copy Master
Choosing Reliable Nonfiction Books p. 21

FOR STRATEGIC READERS

Comprehension Support [paired option] Have pairs of students select three nonfiction books from the class or school library and create a checklist noting each book's copyright date, reprintings or revised editions, author's credentials, bibliography, footnotes or endnotes, preface, appendix, and additional features such as maps or glossaries. Have students write and share a statement about these elements.

FOR ADVANCED LEARNERS/AP

Evaluate Reliability Challenge students to locate a nonfiction book that they consider to be of dubious or imperfect reliability. They may add criteria of their own to the list on page 1277. Have students write a paragraph explaining why they have concluded that the book is not completely reliable. Invite students to display the book and read their evaluations to the class.

Note Taking and Plagiarism
Recording Information

SOURCE CARDS

- Direct students' attention to the sample source card. Have them identify all elements of the card: the author's name, the title of the article and the encyclopedia, the editor's name, the number of volumes in the encyclopedia, the name and location of the publisher, the date of publication, the page numbers on which the article appears, and the project's source number.

- Direct attention to the **TIP**. Elicit that cutting and pasting from the Web without crediting the source is plagiarism because it gives readers the impression that another writer's words are the researcher's own.

NOTE CARDS

Use these questions to evaluate students' comprehension of note taking:

- What is the difference between a source card and a note card? **Possible answer:** *A source card records where information was found; a note card records the information itself.*

- How does a researcher keep track of the source of the information on a note card? **Possible answer:** *On the note card, the researcher writes the number of the source card for the source of the information.*

- What is the purpose of writing a header or subtopic on a note card? **Possible answer:** *Doing so helps the researcher group facts on a given subtopic from separate sources.*

S STANDARDS LESSON FILE
   Research and Study Skills Lesson 8: Source Cards and Notecards

R RESOURCE MANAGER—Copy Master
   Note Taking and Plagiarism p. 23

Note Taking and Plagiarism

As you read and take notes from many sources, do not use the ideas of others without giving them credit. Plagiarism is dishonest and may result in your failing a class or being expelled.

TIP Cutting and pasting phrases, sentences, or paragraphs from a Web page or other electronic file into your research paper is plagiarism—unless you credit the source.

Recording Information

By taking careful notes, you will gather information and guard against plagiarism. One of the best ways of taking notes is by using index cards.

SOURCE CARDS

Begin by making one source card for every source. Assign each source a number, and write that number in the top right-hand corner. Then record the author and/or editor (if given), the title of the publication or Web page, and the date of publication. Also record the following for these sources:

- **Web source**—date created or posted, date accessed, Web address
- **Book**—publisher and publisher's location, library call number, relevant page numbers
- **Encyclopedia**—name and year of encyclopedia, publisher, publisher's location
- **Periodical article**—name of periodical, page numbers of article

Source Card: Encyclopedia Article

> ②
>
> Kite, Steven. "Dust Bowl." *Encyclopedia of the Great Depression and New Deal.* Ed. James Ciment. 2 vols. Armonk, NY: Sharpe, 2001. 107–111.

NOTE CARDS

Before you take your first note, identify its source by writing down the number you assigned to the source card. For example, if you are taking notes from an encyclopedia article that you numbered 6 on a source card, begin your note card with that number. Using this system will ensure that you will be able to identify the source of the note.

In addition to putting a number at the top of the note card, also write a specific header or subtopic for your card. This will help you group similar ideas as you prepare more cards. For example, someone writing about how *The Grapes of Wrath* influenced government response to the Dust Bowl might create note card headings such as *Dust Bowl—living conditions, Bank failures,* or *Steinbeck—early writings about Dust Bowl*. Then quote, paraphrase, or summarize your source. End each card with a page number, if one is available.

See page R48 for examples of source cards and note cards.

DIFFERENTIATED INSTRUCTION

FOR STRATEGIC READERS

Practice Note-Taking Methods [paired option] Have students work with more-proficient partners to practice making note cards, using this page's instruction as the information to be noted. Also have pairs review additional note-taking methods, such as a Learning Log or Main Idea and Details chart. Have them practice more than one method to note the same information, as in this example of a partial Main Idea and Details chart:

Main Ideas	Details
1. Use source cards.	A. Use a separate card for each source.
	B. Give each source a number

BEST PRACTICES TOOLKIT—Transparencies
   Learning Log p. B5
   Main Idea and Details p. B6

PARAPHRASES AND SUMMARIES

A **paraphrase** is a restatement of an author's ideas in your own words. It includes all the ideas in the original statement and is about the same length as the original text. A **summary** is also a restatement, but it includes only key ideas and is therefore shorter than the original text. As these examples show, paraphrasing and summarizing carefully will help you avoid plagiarism.

Original Source

> With the introduction of the Soil Conservation Service (SCS) in 1935, the federal government began educating farmers in environmentally friendly farming techniques, such as shelterbelts, crop rotation, and introduction of soil-stabilizing grasses, terracing, and contour plowing.
>
> *Kite, Steven. "Dust Bowl." Encyclopedia of the Great Depression and New Deal*

Responsible Paraphrase

Government response to dust storms ②

The government also established the Soil Conservation Service in 1935. This program taught farmers to terrace their crops, plow along naturally occuring contours in the land, rotate crops, and practice other farming techniques that would protect the topsoil (110).

Carefully restates information; provides source number and page number

Responsible Summary

Government response to dust storms ②

The government also established the Soil Conservation Service in 1935, which taught farmers techniques to protect the topsoil (110).

Skillfully condenses original passage; includes source number and page number

The following examples show how sloppy paraphrasing and careless summarizing can lead to plagiarism.

Plagarized Paraphrase

Government response to dust storms

The government introduced the Soil Conservation Service in 1935 to educate farmers in environmentally friendly farming techniques, including crop rotation, terracing, and contour plowing.

Reproduces several phrases from the original without explaining where words and ideas came from

Plagarized Summary

Government response to dust storms

In 1935 the federal government introduced the Soil Conservation Service to teach farmers environmentally friendly farming techniques.

Takes a key phrase—"environmentally friendly farming techniques"—from the source without credit

---

PARAPHRASES AND SUMMARIES

Focus students' attention on the examples of responsible paraphrase and summary. To check understanding, ask

- Why is the example on the left a paraphrase while the example on the right is a summary? ***Possible answer:*** *The paraphrase does not omit any of the source's ideas, and it is the same length as the source. The summary omits minor ideas and is shorter than the source.*

- How can you tell that these examples use the source material responsibly? ***Possible answer:*** *They alter the wording and sentence structure of the source.*

- Identify the page number and source number. ***Answer:*** *The page number is 110; the source number is 2.*

Then focus students' attention on the examples of plagiarized paraphrase and summary. Ask

- Which phrases in the paraphrase either come directly from the original or are similar to the original except for slight changes such as a different part of speech? ***Possible answer:*** *The phrases are* Introduced the Soil Conservation Service in 1935; to educate farmers; in environmentally friendly farming techniques; *and* crop rotation, . . . terracing, and contour plowing.

- How could the summary be rewritten to make it responsible? ***Possible answer:*** *" . . . Service, whose goal was to show farmers how to use methods that would not harm the environment."*

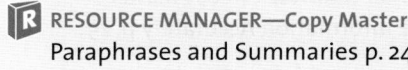 STANDARDS LESSON FILE

Research and Study Skills Lesson 12: Paraphrasing

Research and Study Skills Lesson 13: Summarizing

RESOURCE MANAGER—Copy Master Paraphrases and Summaries p. 24

FOR ADVANCED LEARNERS/AP

Practice Responsible Paraphrasing and Summarizing [paired option] Have advanced learners work with less-proficient partners to guide the latter in the skill of responsible paraphrasing and summarizing. Instruct students to select a paragraph in a nonfiction book. Have the advanced learner write a paraphrase and a summary of the paragraph, deliberately making one of them responsible and the other plagiaristic. Challenge the less-proficient partner to determine which is which and to explain why. Then have the partners switch roles so that the less-proficient partner composes the paraphrase and the summary and the advanced learner determines which is responsible and which is plagiaristic. Have the advanced learner suggest revisions if necessary.

Avoiding Plagiarism

QUOTE INFORMATION ACCURATELY

- Have students find the quoted phrase in the correctly quoted example and then in the original source. Ask why the writer chose to quote that phrase directly. **Possible answer:** *The phrase is vivid, enabling the reader to visualize the human aspect of the Dust Bowl.*

- Challenge students to paraphrase the phrase a *gritty nightmare* responsibly so that quoting would be unnecessary. They probably will conclude that the paraphrases do not work as well. Offer that conclusion as a criterion for deciding to quote directly.

CREDIT INFORMATION AND IDEAS FROM OTHERS

- Students may wonder where to draw the line between common knowledge and facts requiring citation. Offer this rule of thumb: If students find the same fact in three or more sources, they may consider it common knowledge. Remind them that when writing the fact in their own words, they should not use the wording of any of their sources.

- Advise students to check the accuracy of facts that they feel are common knowledge. Sometimes, a "fact" that one has believed to be true turns out not to be a fact at all. For example, a student who "knows" that Plymouth was the first English settlement in what is now the United States might be surprised to find that, in fact, the first permanent English settlement was at Jamestown.

 STANDARDS LESSON FILE
Research and Study Skills Lesson 9:
Avoiding Plagiarism

R RESOURCE MANAGER—Copy Master
Quote Information Accurately p. 25

Avoiding Plagiarism

By quoting and crediting information properly, you can include important ideas in your paper without plagiarizing them.

QUOTE INFORMATION ACCURATELY

Sometimes an idea is so significant or original that you want to reproduce it exactly as it was originally expressed. Place quotation marks around every word or phrase you take verbatim, or word for word, from a source. If you change the whole sentence except for one key phrase, that phrase still belongs to its author.

Original Source

> Life in what the newspapers call the Dust Bowl is becoming a gritty nightmare.
>
> Low, Ann Marie. <u>Dust Bowl Diary</u>. Qtd. in McElvaine, Robert S. <u>The Depression and New Deal: A History in Documents</u>

Plagiarized

> Dust Bowl—Impact on farm families   ⑦
>
> In human terms, the Dust Bowl was a time of terrible suffering. Day by day, it was a gritty nightmare.

Does a good job of creating a new context, but the words "gritty nightmare" are not enclosed in quotation marks

Correctly Quoted

> Dust Bowl—Impact on farm families   ⑦
>
> In human terms, the Dust Bowl was a time of terrible suffering. Day by day, it was "a gritty nightmare," a young North Dakotan named Ann Marie Low wrote in her diary (135).

Quotation marks and attribution show that the phrase "gritty nightmare" came from a source

CREDIT INFORMATION AND IDEAS FROM OTHERS

Sometimes it is difficult to know what needs to be credited and what does not. These tips can help you decide:

- **You must credit others' ideas.** Authors don't just compile facts and quotations; they give opinions and draw conclusions as well. If your paper includes a theory, explanation, or suggestion that you did not develop yourself, be sure to cite its source. For example, if one of your sources states that the Dust Bowl was more devastating than the stock-market crash, you must tell your reader where you found that assertion.

- **You do not need to credit facts that are considered common knowledge.** For instance, well-known historical information such as "Abraham Lincoln was president of the United States" does not need documentation. Neither do well-known sayings such as "Beauty is only skin deep" or general information such as "The sun rises in the east" and "Governments collect taxes from citizens and businesses." However, when in doubt, cite your source or sources.

DIFFERENTIATED INSTRUCTION

FOR STRATEGIC READERS
Vocabulary Support

- *significant,* "important"
- *gritty,* "rough"
- *attribution,* "credit for being the source of something"
- *devastating,* "destructive"
- *common knowledge,* "things that the average person knows"

FOR ADVANCED LEARNERS/AP

Practice Avoiding Plagiarism Ask students to write an abstract of an article in a current issue of a newspaper that deals with a topic of interest to them. Instruct students to include one correctly quoted phrase or sentence from the article and one plagiarized phrase or sentence. Have students label or highlight these elements in distinctive ways, such as with different colors or different symbols. Check their work informally.

Becoming a Critical Researcher

A critical researcher is one who carefully considers information from different sources and then uses that information to develop his or her own view of a topic.

Verifying Information

As you examine multiple sources, you may find information that appears to be incorrect. Here's how to review and evaluate sources that contradict each other.

RECONCILE DIFFERENCES

Even reliable experts can disagree. For example, historians disagree on exactly when the Dust Bowl started and on how many people abandoned their homes because of it. When you encounter varying sources, use the criteria listed on page 1274 to determine which sources are credible. If they all appear to be reliable, you could state in your paper that opinions vary and then describe the range that the different sources present.

Where can you check facts? Consult reputable print and online sources, such as encyclopedias, almanacs, and library databases. Here are some examples of reputable online sources.

FOR MORE INFORMATION . . .	TRY THIS ONLINE SOURCE
U.S. population statistics	www.census.gov (U.S. Bureau of the Census)
Primary sources, maps, audio, and video related to American history	www.loc.gov (Library of Congress)
Facts about the U.S. government	www.firstgov.gov (official U.S. government Web portal)
Facts about your state's history	your state's official Web site (visit www.firstgov.gov and click on "State Government")
International data	www.un.org (United Nations)
Information on technology	www.computerhistory.org (Computer History Museum) www.cnn.com/tech (CNN Technology News)
Data and resources on the environment	www.epa.gov (Environmental Protection Agency) www.webdirectory.com (The Environment Directory)
Information on space science	www.nasa.gov (NASA)

Becoming a Critical Researcher
Verifying Information

RECONCILE DIFFERENCES

- Ask students to suggest content areas in which they are likely to find varying expert opinions about the same topic. ***Possible answer:*** *critics' interpretations of literary or artistic works; historians' or social scientists' views on the causes and effects of events or social structures; scientists' theories on the origins of phenomena such as life and the universe. Even mathematicians may disagree about whether a given conjecture can be proven true.*

- Have pairs of students develop questions to pose that could be answered by one or more of the online sources listed. Challenge students to find the answers online and to report their findings to the class.

R RESOURCE MANAGER—Copy Master
Verifying Information p. 26

FOR ENGLISH LEARNERS

Oral Language The list in **Try This Online Source** gives students a further opportunity to practice pronouncing Web addresses. (See the **For English Learners** note on page 1272.) Point out that the *un* in *www.un.org* is pronounced as in "U.N.," not as in the prefix *un.* Similarly, the *loc* in *www.loc.gov* and the *epa* in *www.epa.gov* would be pronounced as if spelled out, using long vowels.

FOR ADVANCED LEARNERS/AP

Compare and Contrast Sources Use the example of the Dust Bowl to give students practice in finding disagreements among reputable sources. Have students check three or more sources to find out when the Dust Bowl started and how many people were displaced by it. Have students report their findings, including discrepancies and/or disagreements, and discuss how they would describe their findings in a research paper.

Detecting Bias

QUESTIONS TO HELP YOU DETECT BIAS

Have students practice detecting bias in a published work of nonfiction. Ask students to select articles about current events or personalities, making their choices from reputable general-interest magazines. Instruct them to read the articles and then to use the questions on the list to test them for bias. Have them report their findings orally to the class, showing the articles and reading examples of bias aloud; then invite discussion about the validity of these analyses. Students should find that subtle bias can be found even in works that seem objective.

Developing Your Own Perspective

MAKE INFERENCES AND DRAW CONCLUSIONS

- Remind students that an inference may be reasonable or unreasonable (justified or unjustified; supported or unsupported; weak or strong), depending upon whether the evidence supports or contradicts the inference.
- Clarify that making an inference, or a logical guess, is a step toward drawing a conclusion. Inferences often are based upon incomplete evidence; conclusions are formed after one has weighed all the relevant facts and inferences.

S STANDARDS LESSON FILE
Reading Lesson 8: Making Inferences
Reading Lesson 9: Drawing Conclusions

R RESOURCE MANAGER—Copy Masters
Detecting Bias p. 27
Drawing Conclusions from Your Research
p. 28

Detecting Bias

Bias is a preference or an attitude that can prevent a person from presenting information clearly and truthfully. Personal preferences and beliefs can sometimes be presented as facts. Sometimes bias is obvious; at other times it is very subtle.

QUESTIONS TO HELP YOU DETECT BIAS

- Who is the author, and what is his or her **background?** Does this person have ethical beliefs or personal experiences that might influence the writing?
- Why did the author write this piece? Did the **intent** influence his or her point of view? A person wishing to persuade readers may not fully present opposing viewpoints. For example, someone who contends that John Steinbeck single-handedly changed the government's response to migrant workers might leave out information about early government programs, private charities' efforts, and other artists' and writers' coverage of the problem.
- Are the writer's statements based on **verifiable evidence,** or are they speculation?
- Are **enough facts** presented to give a solid basis for the conclusions?
- Is the evidence **balanced,** or does one side get more support?
- How has the **time period** influenced the author's view of events or issues being discussed? For instance, a person writing during the Depression might be affected by the anxiety and despair of the time.
- Does the writer use **loaded language** that has extremely positive or extremely negative connotations, such as "Greedy bankers grew rich while despairing farmers starved"?

Developing Your Own Perspective

Each time you take notes, make connections by mentally attaching that note to something else you have read or discovered. As you synthesize more information, you will begin to develop your own viewpoint on your topic.

MAKE INFERENCES AND DRAW CONCLUSIONS

As you research, read between the lines of the author's words to find implied meanings and attitudes. An **inference** is a logical assumption that is based on observations or information in a text and one's own knowledge and experience. This chart shows the inference that one student made.

What the Source Says	What I Already Know	My Inference
Between 1929 and 1932, farm prices fell 55 percent.	The Great Depression started in 1929. The Dust Bowl started in the early 1930s.	Farmers were in serious trouble even before the Dust Bowl started.

DIFFERENTIATED INSTRUCTION

FOR STRATEGIC READERS
Concept Support [small-group option] Have students use an Open Mind diagram to record words and phrases that they might use to detect signs of bias in an author's work, using the questions and boldfaced terms on this page as sources. Ask students to share their diagrams in small groups, explaining the terms in their own words.

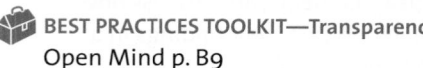 **BEST PRACTICES TOOLKIT—Transparency**
Open Mind p. B9

FOR ADVANCED LEARNERS/AP
Experiment with Loaded Language [paired option] Challenge pairs of students to create a three-column chart about loaded language. In the center column, have them list several statements in neutral, objective language. In the left-hand column, have them restate the same thoughts in language with negative connotations; in the right-hand column, have them use language with positive connotations. Encourage students to share their charts with the class.

If making an inference is "reading between the lines," then drawing a conclusion is "reading beyond the lines." A **conclusion** is a judgment or statement of belief based on evidence, experience, and reasoning. Making inferences is one of the necessary steps in drawing a conclusion, as you can see in this example.

What Sources Say	My Inferences	My Conclusion
John Steinbeck lived with migrant workers for about three years before he published <u>The Grapes of Wrath</u>.	Steinbeck's portrayal of the migrants was probably accurate.	<u>The Grapes of Wrath</u> was accurate, but not everyone wanted to believe its message.
Some growers in California got <u>The Grapes of Wrath</u> banned from several public libraries.	The book was controversial.	

DRAFT YOUR THESIS

As you read and take notes, think about what you are learning. Your thesis should be taking shape in your mind. That is, you will synthesize all that you have learned and thought about during your research. You will draw a larger conclusion about the topic you named in your goal statement.

This chart demonstrates the process of drafting a thesis based on your research.

Facts from My Research	My Conclusions	My Thesis
<u>The Grapes of Wrath</u> was published in 1939 and immediately became a best seller.	<u>The Grapes of Wrath</u> was one of the most important and influential novels of its era.	<u>The Grapes of Wrath</u> did not significantly affect the government's response to those who suffered from the effects of the Dust Bowl.
The President and the First Lady publicly discussed the book.		
As early as 1935, there were government programs to help Dust Bowl victims.	John Steinbeck was just one of many politicians, artists, and activists who were deeply concerned about the migrants.	
Many other writers and photographers chronicled the problems of the migrant laborers.		

Now it's time to put all your research and thinking to good use. In the next section, you will learn how to draft, revise, and perfect a research paper.—

DRAFT YOUR THESIS

- Remind students that a thesis is a statement of the main idea of a piece of writing.

- Explain that synthesizing information means combining pieces of information with other pieces of information and/or prior knowledge or experience, to gain a better understanding of a subject or to create a new idea. The writer of a research paper synthesizes information from a variety of sources to present a topic through a personal perspective, in a new way. The process begins with the note-taking phase of research and the cross-referencing of information from several sources. Summaries and paraphrases may synthesize information from multiple sources. These steps prepare the way for synthesizing information in the draft of a research paper.

- Direct students' attention to the chart. Discuss the three columns; elicit that there are fewer conclusions than facts and fewer theses—only one thesis, in fact—than conclusions. Ask students why the notes narrow in this way. ***Possible answer:*** *To be valid, a conclusion needs to be based on multiple facts. A research paper should be unified around a single thesis, but its details may involve specific conclusions that support the thesis.*

FOR STRATEGIC READERS

Comprehension Support Use this opportunity to wrap up and re-examine the Research Strategies Workshop. Invite students to ask questions about any parts of the workshop for which they still need clarification. Allow volunteers to answer the questions whenever possible. Advise students to consult the Research Strategies Workshop frequently as they go on to write a research paper in the Writing Workshop.

FOR ADVANCED LEARNERS/AP

Synthesize Invite students to discuss how they expect to use this workshop as a resource when writing their research paper. Have them share their ideas with the class to enrich all students' planning for this project. You might recommend additional works on the research process, such as *A Manual for Writers of Research Papers, Theses, and Dissertations,* by Kate L. Turabian et al., or Joseph Gibaldi's *MLA Handbook for Writers of Research Papers.*

Focus and Motivate

OBJECTIVES

- analyze a student model that illustrates the key traits of an effective research paper
- use the writing process to produce a research paper
- revise and edit, using criteria for research papers
- plan and deliver a presentation

 W1.3, W1.6, W2.4, W1.7, W1.8, W2.6, LS1.3, LS1.7, LS2.2, LS2.4

WRITER'S ROAD MAP

WRITING PROMPTS 1 AND 2

Suggest that students select the prompt in the academic subject—literature or history—that they prefer. Point out that the two prompts are likely to require an equal amount of work.

ADDITIONAL PROMPTS

Use these prompts for practice with business writing and writing in the humanities:

WRITING PROMPT 3

Writing About the Working World Write a research paper that outlines the kind of training that would help ensure success in a career of your choice. Include information gathered from online sources and from interviews with professionals now working in that career.

WRITING PROMPT 4

Writing About Fine Art Choose a notable work of art; then use research to draw a conclusion about its significance. Consider the artist's biography as well as the particular elements of the work and its position in art history.

For additional writing prompts, see

- WriteSmart CD
- Writing Center at **ClassZone.com**

KEY TRAITS

Review the six *KEY TRAITS* with students, focusing on ideas and organization. Compare the list of traits with the criteria on page 1301.

Writing Workshop
EXPOSITION

Research Paper

The true goal of most reading and research isn't repeating what you've read. Instead, it is putting together different sources of information to draw your own conclusions. The **Writer's Road Map** explains how to focus, synthesize, and interpret information in a carefully documented research paper.

WRITER'S ROAD MAP
Research Paper

WRITING PROMPT 1

Writing from Literature Develop a question about a piece of literature you have read. Write a research paper supporting a conclusion you reach about your topic. Present information from at least six sources as well as your own ideas and interpretations. Follow approved guidelines for format and documentation.

Literature to Consider

- *The Crucible*
- *The Scarlet Letter*
- *The Red Badge of Courage*
- *The Great Gatsby*

WRITING PROMPT 2

Historical Investigation Write a research paper that investigates an event or an idea from history. Your paper should present your own interpretations as well as information from at least six sources. Follow approved guidelines for format and documentation.

Questions to Investigate

- Was Reconstruction a success or a failure?
- Did propaganda lead the United States into World War I?
- Is my community typical of urban or suburban growth during the last 20 years?

 RESEARCH TOOLS
For research tools and citation guidelines, go to the **Research Center at ClassZone.com.**

KEY TRAITS

1. IDEAS
- Presents a **thesis statement** that identifies the controlling idea of the paper
- **Supports** the thesis with relevant and convincing evidence
- Synthesizes information from **multiple sources,** correctly **quoting** or **paraphrasing** those sources
- Includes the **writer's own ideas and interpretations**

2. ORGANIZATION
- Follows a clear **organizational pattern,** using transitions to connect ideas

3. VOICE
- Uses a **tone** that is suited to the audience, purpose, and subject
- Reflects the **writer's enthusiasm** for the topic

4. WORD CHOICE
- Uses **precise language** to convey ideas clearly

5. SENTENCE FLUENCY
- Varies **sentence lengths and structures**

6. CONVENTIONS
- Employs **correct grammar and usage**
- **Credits sources** properly
- Uses **correct formats and style**

Writing Workshop Resources

 RESOURCE MANAGER UNIT 7

Plan and Teach pp. 9, 12–14
Ask a Peer Reader p. 29
Presenting the Results of Your Investigation p. 30
Writing Support p. 31*

 STANDARDS LESSON FILE

Writing Lessons 1–2, 13–16, 19–20, 34–35
Research and Study Skills Lessons 1, 6–10, 16
Media Lessons 20–22

 BEST PRACTICES TOOLKIT

Scaffolding Writing Instruction pp. 43–46*
Monitoring • Comparison Matrix • Outline • Opening Lines • Writing Template: Informative Essay • Main Idea and Details • Guiding Peer Review • Cliché Array • Storyboard

TECHNOLOGY
- Easy Planner DVD
- Writing Center at **ClassZone.com**
- WriteSmart CD

* Resources for Differentiation

Part 1: Analyze a Student Model

W1.3, W1.6, W2.4, W1.7 (pgs. 1292–1293),
W1.8 (pgs. 1302–1303), W2.6 (pgs. 1302–1303),
LC1.3 (p. 1301), LS1.7 (pgs. 1302–1303),
LS2.2 (pgs. 1302–1303), LS2.4 (pgs. 1302–1303)

Barron 1

Chris Barron
Mrs. Machado
English III
29 April 2008

The Grapes of Wrath: A Reflection of Real Life

John Steinbeck's <u>The Grapes of Wrath</u>, now considered an American masterpiece, tells the gripping story of a family that abandons its Oklahoma farm during the Dust Bowl of the 1930s. Many people believe that the controversial novel raised public awareness about the suffering of "Okies"
5 who moved to California in search of a better life but found only poverty. Some experts also contend that Steinbeck's novel was the key factor in motivating the government to help these migrant workers. However, a close look at the evidence shows that although The Grapes of Wrath raised awareness of the Okies' plight, it did not significantly change how the
10 government responded to the crisis.

The Dust Bowl and Worsening Hard Times

To determine how much of an impact Steinbeck's novel had, it is important to have a clear understanding of what the Dust Bowl was and how it affected people. The Dust Bowl was a severe drought combined with
15 high heat and high winds. It occurred mainly in Oklahoma, Nebraska, Kansas, Texas, New Mexico, and Colorado, and it had its center at the Oklahoma panhandle. These conditions lasted about eight years, long enough to carry off tons of topsoil from the over-plowed fields in the region (Egan xi, 5). When Steinbeck wrote "the dawn came, but no day," he was
20 referring to the black clouds that swirled over the Great Plains during these desperate years (Steinbeck 5).

KEY TRAITS IN ACTION

A focused introduction leads up to a clear, original **thesis statement** (highlighted).

Has a clear **organizational pattern,** using headings to identify main parts.

Precise language makes the paper vivid and compelling.

WRITING WORKSHOP **1285**

Teach

CALIFORNIA

Part 1: Analyze a Student Model

Tell students that the format of the student model—margins, line spacing, and so on—has been modified to fit the textbook page. For formatting guidelines, students should consult the *MLA Handbook for Writers of Research Papers* or the "Format Your Paper" feature on page 1301. You also may wish to incorporate these activities as students examine the model:

- **Thesis Statement** Remind students that the thesis statement conveys the researcher's main conclusion and that it usually appears near the beginning or end of the introductory paragraph. Have students note the highlighted lines in the introductory paragraph of the model and explain why that statement, rather than the statement that begins the paragraph, is the thesis statement of the paper. *Possible answer: The highlighted sentence states the writer's main idea, having to do with the impact of* The Grapes of Wrath. *The first sentence merely summarizes the plot of* The Grapes of Wrath.

- **Organizational Pattern** Have students read the subhead on this page and preview the three subheads to come. Ask them to describe the paper's organization, using the subheads as evidence. *Possible answer: After the introductory paragraph, three three-paragraph body sections follow: (1) the Dust Bowl and its effect upon people; (2) public reactions to* The Grapes of Wrath; *and (3) the novel's historical impact. A concluding paragraph sums up the writer's evaluation of the historical importance of* The Grapes of Wrath.

DIFFERENTIATED INSTRUCTION

For general guidelines on differentiating writing instruction, see

 BEST PRACTICES TOOLKIT
Scaffolding Writing Instruction
pp. 43–46

FOR ENGLISH LEARNERS

Language: Skill Words Review these terms:

- *thesis:* the main idea of a paper—for example, an idea about how *The Grapes of Wrath* affected the thinking of people during the Great Depression

- *organizational pattern:* the way in which information and ideas are arranged in a paper—for example, from earliest event to most recent event, or from least important idea to most important idea

WRITING WORKSHOP **1285**

- **Transitions** Point out that transitions clarify the relationship between ideas and also between details, sentences, and paragraphs. Have students identify additional transitions in lines 22–33. *Possible answers: but (line 22), before (line 26), when (line 27), By the time (line 30).*

- **Multiple Sources** Point out that the writer follows each reference to a research source (whether the source is quoted, paraphrased, or summarized) with an abbreviated citation in parentheses. Have students locate the three examples of abbreviated citations in lines 34–44 and explain where the reader can find full citations of those sources. *Answer: The abbreviated citations appear in lines 37, 39, and 43. Full citations appear in the Works Cited list on page 1290.* Explain that students will learn how to "translate" all the information in the citations when they study the Works Cited list in depth.

Not all sources agree on when the Dust Bowl started, but some say that the first devastating storms hit in 1931 and suggest that the full-blown condition now called the Dust Bowl actually developed between 1933
25 and 1935 (Kite 107; "Timeline"). However, hard times were widespread in the area before the drought occurred. The Great Depression began in 1929 when the stock market crashed. The following year, people all across the country lost their jobs, and many banks could not pay their depositors (Egan 95). Farm prices fell sharply, too: between 1929 and 1932, they
30 dove 55 percent (Himmelberg 9). By the time the Dust Bowl started, Midwestern farm families had endured years of low prices and bank failures, and high unemployment rates meant that family members could not find work in nearby cities.

In human terms, the Dust Bowl was a time of terrible suffering. Each
35 day was "a gritty nightmare," a young North Dakotan named Ann Marie Low wrote in her diary. Sometimes dirt "lay inches deep on everything. Every towel and curtain was just black" (McElvaine 134, 135). Homes had to be shoveled out; nothing could be used before it was washed. The dust also choked and killed cattle—and even some children (Egan 5-6).
40 Unable to grow anything on the land, many farm families had to leave the Dust Bowl or die there. The estimate of just how many left varies widely. Depending on how one defines the Dust Bowl area and its dates, the number ranges from 16,000 to 315,000 (Windschuttle). Many families traveled to California in search of work, as Steinbeck describes in his novel.

45 **Reactions to The Grapes of Wrath**

Before Steinbeck began The Grapes of Wrath, he wrote newspaper articles about living conditions in the California labor camps (Windschuttle). He used this knowledge in his novel. "I know what I was talking about," he

> Uses **transitions** to show the reader how ideas are related.

> Synthesizes facts and details from **multiple sources, quoting** the most memorable and **paraphrasing** or **summarizing** the others.

DIFFERENTIATED INSTRUCTION

FOR DEVELOPING WRITERS

Concept Support As you discuss multiple sources, ask students to state what kind of information each of the three sources provides—in other words, what each source adds to the modeled research paper. *Possible answer: McElvaine provides an eyewitness account of the Dust Bowl; Egan provides examples of the Dust Bowl's effects; Windschuttle provides statistics about the Dust Bowl's impact.*

FOR ENGLISH LEARNERS

Comprehension: Text Structure [paired option] On the board, list several transitions that are useful in research papers, such as *however, yet, but, when, then, before, now, at the time, although, because, also, too, for example,* and *therefore.* Have pairs of students find examples of some of the listed transitions in the student model, such as in lines 7, 19, 46, and 78. Have the same pairs then compose sentences (or pairs of sentences) on any topic,

using transitions from the list. As students read their sentences aloud, correct composition and pronunciation as necessary. Ideally, ask students to compose at least two sentences, each using a different transition.

To provide English learners with additional writing support, see

R RESOURCE MANAGER—Copy Master
Writing Support p. 31

Barron 3

told a reporter in July 1939. "I lived, on and off, with those Okies for
50 the last three years" (Cameron A2). The way the migrants were treated
angered and disturbed Steinbeck. In one of the most haunting passages
in <u>The Grapes of Wrath</u>, he wrote, "[I]n the eyes of the hungry there is a
growing wrath. In the souls of the people the grapes of wrath are filling and
growing heavy, growing heavy for the vintage" (Steinbeck 477). Because
55 Steinbeck knew his topic so well and presented it with such emotional
power, the novel was a huge success. Just two weeks after its publication, it
topped bestseller lists in New York, Philadelphia, Washington, Atlanta, San
Francisco, and Los Angeles ("Best Sellers").

However, the book was not without controversy. Many people
60 disliked the novel; growers in California got it banned from several public
libraries there (Palos 22-23). When the <u>Los Angeles Times</u> reported that
some of the migrant workers had sent Steinbeck threatening letters, he
responded, "It isn't the refugees who have taken exception to what I wrote.
It's the moneyed people back there in Oklahoma—the big oil men and
65 outfits like the Oklahoma City Chamber of Commerce. If anybody's sore
at me for the book it's that kind of people" (Cameron A1-2). Steinbeck's
shocking novel brought him some influential enemies.

Steinbeck did have important supporters, though. In December 1939,
First Lady Eleanor Roosevelt responded publicly to the book. She said that,
70 although she had read and heard others' criticisms about the novel, she
knew from her own travels and investigations that the living conditions
depicted in the book were at least "partly true" ("First Lady"). Then, in a
January 1940 radio address, President Franklin Roosevelt said, "I have read
a book recently; it is called <u>Grapes of Wrath</u>. There are 500,000 Americans
75 that live in the covers of that book" (McElvaine 148).

> Serious **tone** is appropriate to the subject matter, purpose, and audience.

> **Varied sentence lengths and structures** help to create a smooth flow of ideas.

- **Tone** Remind students that tone refers to the writer's attitude toward his or her subject. Point out that using an appropriate tone for the subject is an important part of effective writing; then ask students what kind of tone is appropriate for most research papers. ***Possible answer:*** *A formal, serious, objective, impartial tone is appropriate.* Invite students to identify passages in the student model that exemplify such a tone; as they do so, explain that the writer of a research paper may quote a source that exhibits a different tone in order to make a point but that the writer's own tone should remain consistent throughout. (To explore this point in greater depth, see the For Advanced Learners note on this page.)

- **Varied Sentence Lengths and Structures** Have students find examples of short, long, and medium-length sentences on pages 1286–1287. Invite students also to find examples of simple sentences (as in line 34), compound sentences (as in lines 59–61), complex sentences (as in lines 54–56), and compound-complex sentences (as in lines 22–25). You may wish to have one or more volunteers read paragraphs from the model aloud in order to let students hear the flow of varied sentences.

FOR ADVANCED LEARNERS/AP

Evaluate Tone Point out that page 1287 of the student model includes passages of prose by three individuals: John Steinbeck, President Franklin Roosevelt, and student model author Chris Barron. In addition, the Steinbeck quotations come from two sources: the novel *The Grapes of Wrath,* and a newspaper interview in the *Los Angeles Times.* Ask students to describe Roosevelt's tone and the two distinct tones of Steinbeck's passages. ***Possible answer:*** *Roosevelt's tone is earnest and personal;* *the Steinbeck passage from the novel is sad and ominous; the Steinbeck passage from the interview is somewhat angry and defensive.* Discuss whether the mixing of tones adds to or detracts from the effectiveness of the research paper. Point out that just as varied sentence lengths and structures help create a smooth, interesting flow of ideas, so varied tones, within the overall context of seriousness, also maintain reader interest.

- **Writer's Ideas and Interpretations** Ask students to find one of writer Chris Barron's own ideas or interpretations in lines 77–80. *Possible answer: "... it is not easy to establish any cause-and-effect relationship between The Grapes of Wrath and improvements in the lives of Dust Bowl evacuees."* Then have students work in pairs to discover at least two other interpretive statements in the student model. Examples will vary but may include "It is also a mistake to assume that Steinbeck's novel was the sole reason that Americans focused their attention on victims of the Dust Bowl" (lines 94–95).

- **Support** Remind students of this model research paper's thesis by having them return briefly to the highlighted passage in the first paragraph on page 1285. Have them explain how the evidence in lines 81–95 supports that thesis. *Possible answer: The thesis is that The Grapes of Wrath raised public awareness of the plight of Dust Bowl migrants but did not significantly change the government's response. The evidence presented here shows that the federal government was taking important steps to alleviate the problem well before The Grapes of Wrath was published.*

Barron 4

Assessing the Novel's Impact

It is clear that Steinbeck's novel made a tremendous impression on some of the most powerful and influential people in the country. Yet it is not easy to establish any cause-and-effect relationship between The Grapes
80 of Wrath and improvements in the lives of Dust Bowl evacuees. The government had begun to respond to the problems of the Dust Bowl long before the book's publication. In 1935, four years before anyone read The Grapes of Wrath, the Emergency Relief Appropriation Act created jobs for unemployed farmers, set aside money for ranchers to feed their livestock
85 and farmers to buy seeds, and funded the construction of work camps for youths. In 1935, the Resettlement Administration began relocating farmers to better farming areas (Kite 107; "FSA Camp"). The government also established the Soil Conservation Service in 1935. This program taught farmers techniques to protect the topsoil (Kite 110). One of the most
90 important soil-saving programs was the Shelterbelt Project. This anti-erosion measure called for planting trees across the entire Great Plains. The program was already reducing blowing dirt by 1938, a year before The Grapes of Wrath appeared ("Timeline").

It is also a mistake to assume that Steinbeck's novel was the sole reason
95 that Americans focused their attention on victims of the Dust Bowl. For one thing, Steinbeck's wasn't the only voice crying out for justice. Woody Guthrie had long been writing social protest songs about the Okies. Bibliographies and library catalogs show several other books that could also be read as protests. For example, in 1939, Carey McWilliams
100 published Factories in the Field, an account of exploited migrants.

> The **writer's own ideas and interpretations** appear throughout the paper.

> Detailed evidence **supports** the thesis. The writer **credits sources** properly using **correct formats and style.**

DIFFERENTIATED INSTRUCTION

FOR DEVELOPING WRITERS

Comprehension Support To help students decode citations, ask these questions about the citations in lines 81–93:

- Look at the Works Cited list on page 1290. What does parenthetical "Kite 110" (line 89) mean? *Answer: The reference means that the information immediately preceding the citation was obtained from page 110 of Steven Kite's article, entitled "Dust Bowl," in The Encyclopedia of the Great Depression and the New Deal.*

- Why does the citation in line 87 refer to "Kite 107" while the citation in line 89 refers to "Kite 110?" *Answer: The citation in line 87 refers to information on page 107 of Kite's article; the citation in line 89 refers to page 110 of the same article.*

- Why is the citation "Kite 107" followed by a semicolon and "FSA Camp?" *Answer: The student writer used two sources for the information: Kite's article and a document entitled "FSA Migrant Labor Camp."*

- Why does the citation "Timeline" not give an author's name? *Answer: No author is named in the original source.*

Barron 5

It is also clear to anyone looking at Dorothea Lange's "Migrant Mother" and her other photographs that she was deeply concerned with the problems of poor people in California (McElvaine 105, 126, 175).

105   Steinbeck's novel and many other works raised awareness of the grim lives of the Okies. However, history makes it clear that what really changed Americans' lives in the years after the publication of <u>The Grapes of Wrath</u> was the buildup to World War II. By 1940, many new jobs had become available in factories—and in the military. The Great Depression ended; coincidentally, the drought in the Midwest also ended in 1939
110 ("Timeline"). These large forces are what truly put American workers back on the road to prosperity.

A Great Novel, but Only One Factor Among Many

    <u>The Grapes of Wrath</u> is one of the most important novels of the 20th century. At the time of its publication it captivated thousands of readers,
115 including the president of the United States, and it helped to make the suffering of California migrant workers an issue of national importance. However, it is overstating the case to claim that the book motivated the government to help these workers. Many government programs were already in place at the time of the book's publication, and many other
120 writers and activists helped bring the problem to public attention. Other, larger factors—the end of the drought, an improved economy, and the looming possibility of another world war—also had important effects on the migrant workers' situation. Although Steinbeck's novel was factually accurate and artistically important, a thorough evaluation of the evidence
125 shows that it did not change the course of history.

> Reflects the writer's interest in and **enthusiasm** for the subject matter.

> Concludes with a summary and a statement of the **writer's own ideas.**

- **Enthusiasm** Authorial enthusiasm is intangible and thus may be difficult for students to discern in a research paper. Point out that vivid diction often is a sign of enthusiasm. Reading aloud and listening for exciting sentence rhythms can provide another clue. Invite students to point out words, phrases, and sentences throughout the model paper, as well as in lines 104–116, that they feel convey the writer's enthusiasm. ***Possible answer:** Vivid diction—for example, "grim lives" (line 105), "truly put American workers back on the road to prosperity" (lines 110–111), "captivated thousands of readers" (line 114), and "helped to make the suffering of California migrant workers an issue of national importance" (lines 115–116)—suggests the writer's enthusiasm for the subject matter.* Ask students why it is a good idea for the writer of a research paper to express enthusiasm for his or her subject. ***Possible answer:** Authorial enthusiasm encourages the reader to become interested as well.*

- **Conclusion** To help students see that the concluding paragraph summarizes the research paper, have pairs of students work together to find specific passages earlier in the paper that are echoed in lines 112–125. ***Possible answer:** The subhead "A Great Novel, but Only One Factor Among Many" echoes the main idea of lines 94–103.*

FOR ADVANCED LEARNERS/AP

Synthesize Questions Remind students that a conclusion often leaves readers with something to think about, perhaps leading readers to ask research questions of their own. Have students reread the concluding paragraph of the student model and write one or more ideas that the passage prompts in their minds. Then have students rephrase those ideas as possible research questions and share both with the class. ***Samples:** What was the greatest single factor in ending the Great Depression? How were conditions for migrant laborers different after World War II than before it? What works of literature have changed the course of history? How can one prove that a work of literature has changed history?* Students should come away from this activity with the insight that research is not a closed process in which every question is answered for all time; rather, any given research question is likely to open up others.

Elicit that the Works Cited list in the student model contains a variety of kinds of sources: newspaper and magazine articles, an encyclopedia entry, online documents, primary-source and secondary-source nonfiction books, and a novel. Then discuss these questions:

- What ordering principle was used to organize this Works Cited list? *Answer: The list is organized according to alphabetical order by the author's name or, if the author's name is unavailable, by the title of the work.*

- How many different newspapers and magazines does the writer cite, and what are they? *Answer: The writer cites two newspapers, the* New York Times *and the* Los Angeles Times, *and two magazines,* California Historian *and* New Criterion.

- Why would you classify Robert S. McElvaine's book as a primary source, even though it was published many years after the Dust Bowl took place? *Answer: The book is a primary source because it is a collection of documents from the Great Depression.*

- Why is the list called Works Cited instead of Bibliography? *Answer: The list contains only the works that the writer actually cited (referred to by name) in the paper. A bibliography also would include works that the writer consulted but to which he did not directly refer.*

For interactive student models, see

Write*Smart* CD

Writing Center at **ClassZone.com**

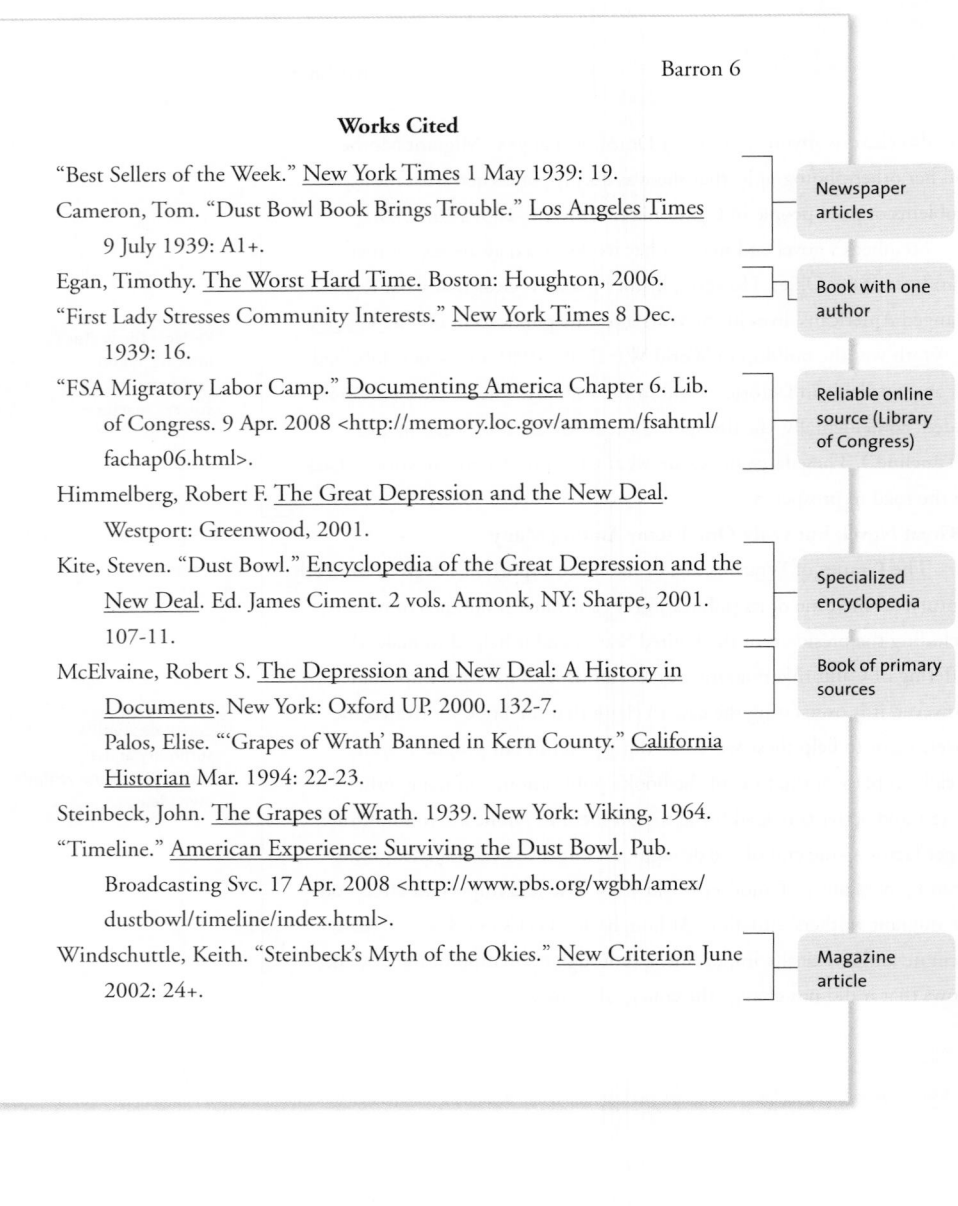

Barron 6

Works Cited

"Best Sellers of the Week." <u>New York Times</u> 1 May 1939: 19.

Cameron, Tom. "Dust Bowl Book Brings Trouble." <u>Los Angeles Times</u>
 9 July 1939: A1+.

Egan, Timothy. <u>The Worst Hard Time.</u> Boston: Houghton, 2006.

"First Lady Stresses Community Interests." <u>New York Times</u> 8 Dec.
 1939: 16.

"FSA Migratory Labor Camp." <u>Documenting America</u> Chapter 6. Lib.
 of Congress. 9 Apr. 2008 <http://memory.loc.gov/ammem/fsahtml/
 fachap06.html>.

Himmelberg, Robert F. <u>The Great Depression and the New Deal</u>.
 Westport: Greenwood, 2001.

Kite, Steven. "Dust Bowl." <u>Encyclopedia of the Great Depression and the</u>
 <u>New Deal</u>. Ed. James Ciment. 2 vols. Armonk, NY: Sharpe, 2001.
 107-11.

McElvaine, Robert S. <u>The Depression and New Deal: A History in</u>
 <u>Documents</u>. New York: Oxford UP, 2000. 132-7.

 Palos, Elise. "'Grapes of Wrath' Banned in Kern County." <u>California</u>
 <u>Historian</u> Mar. 1994: 22-23.

Steinbeck, John. <u>The Grapes of Wrath</u>. 1939. New York: Viking, 1964.

"Timeline." <u>American Experience: Surviving the Dust Bowl</u>. Pub.
 Broadcasting Svc. 17 Apr. 2008 <http://www.pbs.org/wgbh/amex/
 dustbowl/timeline/index.html>.

Windschuttle, Keith. "Steinbeck's Myth of the Okies." <u>New Criterion</u> June
 2002: 24+.

Labels (right margin): Newspaper articles · Book with one author · Reliable online source (Library of Congress) · Specialized encyclopedia · Book of primary sources · Magazine article

---

DIFFERENTIATED INSTRUCTION

FOR DEVELOPING WRITERS

Comprehension Support To check students' comprehension, ask

1. In the citation for "Timeline," what does *Pub. Broadcasting Svc.* stand for? *Answer: The term is an abbreviation for* Public Broadcasting Service.

2. Which book on the list was published most recently? *Answer: The most recent book is* The Worst Hard Time, *in 2006.*

3. Why are two dates given for *The Grapes of Wrath? Answer: The 1939 date is the book's first publication; 1964 is the date of the edition that the researcher consulted.*

4. Why does James Ciment's name appear in the citation for the article "Dust Bowl" by Steven Kite? *Answer: Ciment's name appears because he edited the encyclopedia in which the article appears.*

FOR ADVANCED LEARNERS/AP

Analyze Citation Form Ask students:

1. If another researcher referred to the same sources and to Chris Barron's essay, where should Barron's essay appear on that researcher's Works Cited list? *Answer: The essay should appear alphabetically.*

2. What additional information would you need in order to create a citation for Barron's essay? *Answer: A writer would need the name of the school.*

Part 2: Apply the Writing Process

PREWRITING

| **What Should I Do?** | **What Does It Look Like?** |

1. Analyze the prompt.
(Circle) words or phrases that tell you what you have to produce. Underline important details about the assignment. Take a few minutes to think about what you have to do and how you will do it. If you have questions about acceptable topics, format, paper length, or anything else, now is the time to ask your teacher.

WRITING PROMPT Develop a question about a piece of literature you have read. Write a research paper supporting a conclusion you reach about your topic. Present information from at least six sources as well as your own ideas and interpretations. Follow approved guidelines for format and documentation.

I have to ask my own question. I have to present and support my own ideas and conclusions. I have to use at least six sources. Also, I should try to find a subject that really interests me.

2. Find your topic.
Because you are going to be doing more than putting together other people's ideas, you need both a subject and an original approach to it. Explore a subject that interests you by looking at it through different "lenses" (see page 1268), by creating fresh new comparisons, by asking original questions, or by freewriting. One student's freewriting is shown here.

The Grapes of Wrath is such a vivid picture of what one family went through, in Oklahoma, on the road, and in California. Maybe Steinbeck was just writing a good story, or maybe he was trying to be a political activist and cause change. I wonder what the state of California or the federal government did after this book was published. Did Steinbeck's novel really make a difference?

3. Develop an original focus and a working thesis.
Find some general encyclopedia articles, some Web sites, or a video about your topic. Don't take notes yet; just read or view to develop background knowledge. Then list questions you still have. Choose one of them as your focus and (circle) it. Develop this question into a working thesis statement.

See page 1269: Formulate Research Questions

My Remaining Questions
How true to life was The Grapes of Wrath?
How did people at the time respond to the book? Was that different from readers' responses today?
(Did the book cause a government response?)
Working thesis statement: *The Grapes of Wrath changed the government's response to migrant workers.*

Practice and Apply

To support students during the writing process, use these copy masters:

R RESOURCE MANAGER—Copy Masters
Drawing Conclusions from Your Research p. 28
Ask a Peer Reader p. 29
Writing Support p. 31 (for English learners)

Part 2: Apply the Writing Process

PREWRITING

1. **Analyze the prompt.** After students have copied their writing prompt and have marked its key words and important details, have them restate the prompt as a list of writing requirements. Invite questions about the prompt before having students continue.

2. **Find your topic.** Point out that the nature of students' "lenses" may differ depending upon the prompt chosen. Invite small groups to develop "lenses" (on page 1268) for each prompt.

3. **Develop an original focus and a working thesis.** As students examine **My Remaining Questions,** emphasize that the questions that the writer did not choose also could have supplied good research topics. Have students speculate about why the writer chose the question about a government response to Steinbeck's novel. ***Possible answers:*** *The question seemed the most original; the writer was interested in government.*

For interactive graphic organizers, see
📀 Write*Smart* CD
ℹ️ Writing Center at **ClassZone.com**

FOR DEVELOPING WRITERS

Explore a Writing Focus To help students find a focus for their research paper, have them create a web of words and phrases that they associate with their topic. Instruct students to circle the most interesting entries and then to brainstorm for questions that relate to those entries.

RESEARCHING

1. **Investigate possible sources.** Review the wide range of sources available to students, as discussed in the Research Strategies Workshop. Remind students that the first step in finding online sources is to choose search terms—terms that are neither so broad that they bring in a host of irrelevant sources nor so narrow that they leave out relevant sources.

2. **Evaluate your sources.** Suggest that students use a Monitoring chart to evaluate how well they understand their sources—an important step in evaluating the overall usefulness of a source.

   BEST PRACTICES TOOLKIT—Transparency
   Monitoring p. A12

3. **Make source cards.** Point out that it is normal to consult more sources than one ultimately includes in a research paper; thus, it is normal to make more source cards at the outset than one ultimately will use. Emphasize that it is better to begin with too many sources than too few. Have students examine the sample source card and verify that all the information on it is used in the source's entry on the Works Cited list on page 1290.

RESEARCHING

What Should I Do?	**What Does It Look Like?**

1. Investigate possible sources.
Once you narrow your topic, you can begin searching for sources. Places to look include the Internet, your school's media center, and your public library. As you search, make a list of sources that appear to have relevant information. Include the title, the author's name (if available), and where you found it. Then comment on what you think the source offers.

See page 1269: Identify the Most Relevant Sources

Sources	Comments
World Wide Web	
"Timeline," _American Experience: Surviving the Dust Bowl_	lists several government responses to Dust Bowl
"Grapes of Wrath Banned in Kern County" by Elise Palos	article won an award from the California Historical Association
"Dust Bowl Days," www.athens.edu/~johanna	great graphics: sights and sounds of Dust Bowl
Public Library	
The Worst Hard Time by Timothy Egan (978.032 Egan)	terrific source: lots of facts, illustrations, explanation
"On the Cause of the 1930s Dust Bowl," _Science_ magazine	all about the weather patterns that created the Dust Bowl; excellent graphics

2. Evaluate your sources.
Use the criteria on pages 1274–1277 to evaluate your sources. By choosing only relevant and reliable sources, you will save yourself time and frustration.

Reasons for Rejecting a Source

"Dust Bowl Days": This site doesn't name the author or list the author's credentials. It has no footnotes or bibliography.

"On the Cause...": This is a well-documented article, but it isn't really on my topic.

3. Make source cards.
When you have decided which sources to keep, create a numbered card for each source. Your source cards will provide the information for your Works Cited list—titles, authors, locations, publishers, and other important information. See page R48 to learn how to make source cards for different types of sources.

"Timeline." _American Experience: Surviving the Dust Bowl._ Pub. Broadcasting Svc. 17 Apr. 2008 <http://www.pbs.org/wgbh/amex/dustbowl/timeline/index.html>.

DIFFERENTIATED INSTRUCTION

FOR ENGLISH LEARNERS

Investigate Possible Sources [mixed-readiness pairs] Have pairs of students undertake a close reading of the handwritten chart in **What Does It Look Like?** Have the more fluent student in each pair make sure that the less-proficient student understands (1) what kinds of sources the various notes refer to, (2) what the student writer says about each source, and (3) how each comment relates to the source's value.

FOR ADVANCED LEARNERS/AP

Evaluate Sources Point out that in addition to choosing among different categories of sources (such as Web sites, magazine articles, and books), researchers also must compare and contrast sources within a type. For example, a researcher might need to decide which of three biographies of an author will be the best source of information about the author's political views. Urge students to look for two or more sources per category for their topic.

Suggest that they create a Comparison Matrix chart to aid in evaluating those sources, using criteria of their choice.

BEST PRACTICES TOOLKIT—Transparency
Comparison Matrix p. A24

RESEARCHING

What Should I Do?	What Does It Look Like?

4. Start taking notes.
As you read your sources, look for information that supports or contradicts your working thesis statement. Record each piece of information on a separate index card. That way you can try different ways of organizing your ideas as you draft. On each card, include the main idea, the number of the source (from its source card), and a way of locating the information, such as a page number or section name.

> **TIP** Record information honestly, giving credit where it is due. See pages 1278–1280 to learn about note taking and plagiarism.

▶

> **Federal aid programs before Grapes of Wrath**
>
> The Shelterbelt program started in 1937. The government paid farmers to plant trees so that less topsoil would blow away. By 1938, the tree planting and other methods had reduced blowing soil by 65 percent (4).

5. Create an outline.
Group your note cards by subtopic. Then put those groups in a logical order. For example, you might begin with background information. Use your note cards to write an outline of your paper. A partial example is shown here.

▶

> **The Grapes of Wrath and the Dust Bowl**
>
> I. Background information: The Dust Bowl
>   A. What and where it was
>   B. When it took place
>   C. What people's lives were like
>   1. "A gritty nightmare" (Low's diary)
>   2. Dust killed children, animals
> II. Background information: The Grapes of Wrath
>   A. Based on Steinbeck's own research
>   B. Reaction to the book

6. Revise your working thesis.
Now that your research paper is taking shape, it's time to revisit your working thesis statement. Think about what you have learned about your topic. Does your thesis need only minor revisions, or should you make significant changes?

▶

> **Working thesis statement:** The Grapes of Wrath changed the government's response to migrant workers.
>
> **Revised thesis statement:** Although The Grapes of Wrath raised awareness of the Okies' plight, it did not significantly change how the government responded to the crisis.

4. Start taking notes. Remind students to keep their set of note cards separate from their set of source cards and to cross-reference the note cards with the numbers of the source cards in order to remember which sources provided which pieces of information. Discuss the **TIP**, asking why it is necessary to record source credit on note cards if the note cards are meant for the researcher's private use. *Possible answer: Recording source credit on note cards helps the researcher/writer to remember to supply credit in the finished paper.*

5. Create an outline. Use an Outline transparency to help students review the process of outlining and set up their own outlines.

> **BEST PRACTICES TOOLKIT—Transparency**
> Outline p. B19

6. Revise your working thesis. Point out that revising the working thesis is not always necessary—that it is possible that the working thesis statement can become the final thesis statement without alteration. Explain that because the writing process is recursive, students will have other chances to revise their thesis statements later, in the drafting and revising phases.

> **RESOURCE MANAGER—Copy Master**
> Drawing Conclusions from Your Research p. 28

FOR DEVELOPING WRITERS

Create an Outline [paired option] Have students work with partners to group their note cards by subtopic and to put the groups into logical order. Suggest that students use different fasteners for different levels of headings in their outlines; for instance, they might use large binder clips for headings represented by Roman numerals and paper clips for subheadings represented by capital letters.

1. **Draft your introduction.** Point out that the sentences that begin the sample introduction provide information that is not only interesting but essential. Elicit that the thesis statement would be confusing if it were not preceded by information that identified *The Grapes of Wrath* and explained the term *Okies*. Then use the Opening Lines strategy to help students draft captivating beginnings for their research papers.

   📋 **BEST PRACTICES TOOLKIT**
   Opening Lines p. C1

2. **Incorporate information from your note cards.** Have students examine the sample note cards and corresponding draft passage, making sure that students understand the relationship between them. Call on a volunteer to clarify the differing citation forms in the two samples. ***Possible answer: The circled number 5 in the upper right-hand corner of the note card corresponds to the parenthetical citation in the draft text. The former is for the researcher's own use; the latter is for the reader's benefit.***

3. **Blend material from multiple sources.** Point out that a researcher sometimes may cite more than one source to document the same statement, as shown in line 87 of the student model on page 1288. As students read the **TIP**, explain that introductory phrases in quotations in research papers do the same job as dialogue tags (such as "he said" or "she replied") in fiction; that is, they help the reader keep track of the source of the quotation, and they help create a smooth, readable flow of language.

For a writing template that can be adapted to a research paper, see

📋 **BEST PRACTICES TOOLKIT—Transparency**
Writing Template: Informative Essay
pp. C16, C29

💿 Write*Smart* CD

ℹ️ Writing Center at **ClassZone.com**

What Should I Do?	*What Does It Look Like?*
1. Draft your introduction. Many research papers begin by providing interesting background information that leads up to the thesis statement, which is often the final sentence of the introductory paragraph.	John Steinbeck's <u>The Grapes of Wrath</u>, now considered an American masterpiece, tells the gripping story of a family that leaves Oklahoma because of the Dust Bowl. Many people believe that the controversial novel raised public awareness about the suffering of "Okies." However, a close look at the evidence shows that although <u>The Grapes of Wrath</u> raised awareness of the Okies' plight, it did not significantly change how the government responded to the crisis.
2. Incorporate information from your note cards. Using your outline as a guide, incorporate facts, ideas, and quotations from your note cards into your rough draft. Be sure to include the name of each source as you add it, plus a page number if one is available. To learn how to do this, see "Document your sources" on the next page.	<u>Negative reaction to Grapes of Wrath</u> ⑤ Most of the novel takes place in Kern County, California. Steinbeck's version of events offended some landowners there. In August 1939 the county board of supervisors banned the novel from schools and libraries in the county (22-23). However, the book was not without controversy. Many people disliked the novel; growers in California got it banned from several public libraries there (Palos 22-23).
3. Blend material from multiple sources. If appropriate, compare and contrast ideas from different sources, or show how one source complements, enlarges, or expands on another. **TIP** Instead of dropping a quotation into the middle of your paper, weave it in with an introduction (*As Palos explains, . . .*) or by inserting phrases or words into a sentence (*Each day was "a gritty nightmare," . . .*).	In human terms, the Dust Bowl was a time of terrible suffering. — Topic sentence Each day was "a gritty nightmare," a young North Dakotan named Ann Marie Low wrote in her diary (McElvaine 135). — Quoted source The dust also choked and killed cattle—and even some children (Egan 5-6). — Paraphrased source

---

DIFFERENTIATED INSTRUCTION

FOR ADVANCED LEARNERS/AP

Create a Drafting Guide [small-group option] Invite groups of students to draw upon the information on pages 1294–1296, possibly other research-skills resources, and their past writing experiences to prepare a clear, engaging "how-to" guide for students who might need additional help in turning research notes into the draft of a research paper. The guide should include guidance (instructions and examples) in developing effective introductions and conclusions, blending material, and incorporating one's own interpretation of ideas. Invite groups to present their guide; then add it to the classroom library as a permanent reference.

DRAFTING

What Should I Do?	What Does It Look Like?
4. Share your own ideas and interpretations. Analyze others' ideas and make your own interpretations of them. Use facts, examples, and other evidence to support your ideas. **See pages 1282–1283:** Developing Your Own Perspective	▶ *It is a mistake to assume that Steinbeck's novel was the sole reason that people focused their attention on victims of the Dust Bowl. For one thing, Steinbeck's wasn't the only voice crying out for justice. Woody Guthrie had long been writing social protest songs about the Okies. Bibliographies and library catalogs show several other books that could also be read as protests. For example, in 1939, Carey McWilliams published <u>Factories in the Field</u>, an account of exploited migrants. It is also clear to anyone looking at Dorothea Lange's "Migrant Mother" and her other photographs that she was deeply concerned with the problems of poor people in California.* (McElvaine 105, 126, 175).

5. Document your sources.
Each time you quote, paraphrase, or summarize information from a source, include a parenthetical reference at the end of the sentence or sentences. In general, a parenthetical reference includes the author's **last name** and the **page number:** (Himmelberg 9). There are, however, many variations.

- **Author already mentioned in sentence**—give only the page number (110)
- **Author not known**—use a shortened form of the title of the work ("First Lady")
- **More than one author**—include last names for up to three authors (Lange and Taylor 409). For more than three authors, use the first author's last name and *et al.* (Zielonka et al. 138-145).
- **More than one source**—separate the information for each source with a semicolon (Kite 107; "Timeline")
- **More than one work by the same author**—include a shortened form of the work's title (Steinbeck, <u>Dubious</u> 61)

▶ *In 1935, the Resettlement Administration began relocating farmers to better farming areas (Kite 107).*] Basic documentation: author and page number

Not all sources agree on when the Dust Bowl started (Kite 107; "Timeline").] Evidence from two sources

The Great Depression ended; coincidentally, the drought in the Midwest also ended in 1939 ("Timeline").] Author and page number unknown

4. Share your own ideas and interpretations. Ask students to point out the student writer's interpretation in the sample passage. ***Possible answer:*** *"It is a mistake to assume that Steinbeck's novel was the sole reason that people focused their attention on victims of the Dust Bowl."* Discuss how the writer came up with the interpretation; then offer these ways of developing ideas and interpretations about a research topic:

- Find the traditional view of the subject and react to it with an alternative view.
- Connect the topic to other topics in order to provide a nontraditional approach.
- Suggest an interpretation that is unexpected but that still makes sense.
- Do in-depth research, synthesize the author's views, and respond with your own thoughts. (The writer of the model research paper probably used this method.)

5. Document your sources. Recommend that students use a highlighter to mark each parenthetical citation in their drafts. Doing so will help them compile their Works Cited list and proofread their citations.

FOR DEVELOPING WRITERS

Explore Interpretations [small-group option]
One common form of writing in which a writer presents evidence to support a personal interpretation is the editorial. Have a group of students examine an editorial from a local newspaper or national magazine, identifying the facts that the writer presents and discussing the ways in which he or she uses those facts to present a personal interpretation. Invite group representatives to share key discussion points with the class.

6. **Develop your concluding paragraph.** Point out that a strong concluding paragraph often includes a statement or restatement of the writer's individual interpretation, thus helping to fulfill point 4 of **Share Your Ideas and Interpretations** on page 1295. Ask students to identify statements of the writer's interpretations in the model passage. *Possible answer: "However, it is overstating the case to claim that the book motivated the government to help these workers."*

7. **Create a Works Cited list.** After you have called students' attention to the **TIP**, have them return to the model research paper on pages 1285–1290 and locate the parenthetical references. Elicit that there are more highlighted references within the paper than there are sources on the Works Cited list; then ask students to make an inference on the basis of this fact. *Possible answers: Some of the sources were used for multiple pieces of information; the sources cited most often may have been the ones that the writer found most valuable.*

DRAFTING

What Should I Do?	What Does It Look Like?
6. **Develop your concluding paragraph.** A thoughtful conclusion does more than just restate the facts you presented. It leaves your reader with something compelling to think about. The writer of the student model reflected on the overall significance of his topic. Other approaches include asking a thought-provoking question or including a compelling quotation.	<u>The Grapes of Wrath</u> is one of the most important novels of the 20th century. At the time of its publication it captivated thousands of readers, including the president of the United States, and it helped to make the suffering of California migrant workers an issue of national importance. However, it is overstating the case to claim that the book motivated the government to help these workers. Many government programs were already in place at the time of the book's publication, and many other writers and activists helped bring the problem to public attention. Other, larger factors—the end of the drought, an improved economy, and the looming possibility of another world war—also had important effects on the migrant workers' situation.
7. **Create a Works Cited list.** After you have written your draft, check that you have given proper credit in parentheses to each quotation or bit of information that you got from a source. Then go through your paper and find the source card for each parenthetical reference. Alphabetize the cards by the author's last name, if available, or by the title of the work. Then create a Works Cited list like the one shown. **TIP** To make sure that you include all your sources in the Works Cited list, go through your rough draft and highlight each parenthetical reference. **See pages 1299–1300:** MLA Citation Guidelines	**Works Cited** "Best Sellers of the Week." <u>New York Times</u> 1 May 1939: 19. Cameron, Tom. "Dust Bowl Book Brings Trouble." <u>Los Angeles Times</u> 9 July 1939: A1+. Egan, Timothy. <u>The Worst Hard Time</u>. Boston: Houghton, 2006. "First Lady Stresses Community Interests." <u>New York Times</u> 8 Dec. 1939: 16.

DIFFERENTIATED INSTRUCTION

FOR DEVELOPING WRITERS

Interpret Abbreviations Point out that the Works Cited list on page 1290 and the MLA Citation Guidelines on pages 1299–1300 include several abbreviations that students may need to look up in a dictionary or a book of research guidelines. Help students interpret these abbreviations:

- *1 May 1939: 19,* "May 1, 1939, page 19"
- *24+:* "page 24 and later pages of the periodical"

- *A1+:* "Section A of the newspaper, page 1 and later pages"
- *2 vols.:* "The work cited consists of two volumes."
- *Ed. James Ciment:* "James Ciment edited the book."
- *Rutkowski, J., et al:* "The book has several authors: J. Rutkowski and others."

FOR ADVANCED LEARNERS/AP

Analyze Conclusions Have students read the concluding paragraph of each source (or selected sources) that they are using in their own research. Then challenge them to write a brief description of the strategies that each author has used. Work with students to prepare a format for sharing the results; also suggest that students keep this list available as a source of ideas when they write their own concluding paragraphs.

REVISING AND EDITING

What Should I Do?	What Does It Look Like?

1. Improve your introduction.
- Reread your first paragraph. Does your first sentence surprise, challenge, or otherwise interest your reader? Did you explain terms your reader might not understand, such as *Okies*? Is your thesis clear?
- Add information or explanations to create a smooth flow of ideas leading up to your thesis.

> John Steinbeck's <u>The Grapes of Wrath</u>, now considered an American masterpiece, tells the gripping story of a family that ~~leaves Oklahoma because of the Dust Bowl~~ abandons its Oklahoma farm during the Dust Bowl of the 1930s.
>
> Many people believe that the controversial novel raised public awareness about the suffering of "Okies," who moved to California in search of a better life but found only poverty. Some experts also contend that Steinbeck's novel was the key factor in motivating the government to help these migrant workers.
>
> However, a close look at the evidence shows that...

2. Check the flow of your ideas.
- Ask a peer reader to draw a box around any places where ideas do not flow smoothly.
- Add transitional words and phrases where needed to link ideas.

See page 1301: Ask a Peer Reader

> It is clear that Steinbeck's novel made a tremendous impression on some of the most powerful and influential people in the country. It is not easy to establish a cause-and-effect relationship between <u>The Grapes of Wrath</u> and improvements in the lives of Dust Bowl evacuees.
> └Yet

3. Make sure that each idea has support.
- Examine each paragraph you wrote. Ask yourself, "Do I include enough explanation and evidence to support this point?"
- If needed, add more explanation, including correctly cited facts. Where appropriate, add your own insights and interpretations, too.

> The government had begun to respond to the problems of the Dust Bowl long before the book's publication. In 1935, four years before anyone read <u>The Grapes of Wrath</u>, the Emergency Relief Appropriation Act created jobs for unemployed farmers, set aside money for ranchers to feed their livestock and farmers to buy seeds, and funded the construction of work camps for youths (Kite 107). One of the most important soil-saving programs was the Shelterbelt Project. This anti-erosion measure called for planting trees across the entire Great Plains ("Timeline").

REVISING AND EDITING

1. Improve your introduction. Have students explain the revisions in the sample passages. **Possible answer:** *The first passage was revised to provide additional informative detail and vivid words (*abandons *instead of* leaves*). The second passage was revised to provide an explanation of the term* Okies *and add a challenging perspective ("Some experts also contend. . . . ").*

2. Check the flow of your ideas. Have students suggest alternate revisions that the writer could have made instead of adding *Yet* to the beginning of the second sentence in the sample. **Possible answers:** *Using* But, However, *or* Nevertheless *instead of* Yet; *adding* Although *to the first sentence and combining the two sentences into one; changing* It is not easy to. . . . *to* It is not easy, though, to. . . .

3. Make sure that each idea has support. Review with students some types of support that a research writer might provide. **Possible answer:** *Types of support include facts, statistics, examples, anecdotes, and quotations from experts.* Have students identify the types of support used in the sample. **Possible answer:** *The sample uses facts and examples.*

FOR DEVELOPING WRITERS

Make Sure That Each Idea Has Support
[small-group option] Have small groups return to the section on reactions to *The Grapes of Wrath* in the student model (pages 1286–1287). Instruct them to use a Main Idea and Details chart to identify the controlling idea of each paragraph in the section and the evidence that supports it.

🗂 **BEST PRACTICES TOOLKIT—Transparency**
Main Idea and Details p. B6

FOR ENGLISH LEARNERS

Language: Skill Words Review these terms:
- *compelling*, "forceful; requiring thought and perhaps agreement"
- *challenge*, "to require (someone) to do something difficult"
- *flow of ideas*, "the way in which ideas lead from one to the next in a way that makes sense and that interests the reader"
- *transitional*, "connecting one thing to another, such as one idea to another"
- *support*, "information that helps show that an idea is true"

Have students check their understanding by using each term in an original sentence about the writing process.

4. Eliminate unnecessary details. Use the Guiding Peer Review strategy to help students review the use of details in classmates' drafts.

🧰 **BEST PRACTICES TOOLKIT**
Guiding Peer Review p. C3

5. Refine your conclusion. As you call attention to the expression "fresh, new phrasing" in the instruction, point out that writers sometimes use tired phrases such as *In conclusion* or *To sum up* to signal a conclusion. Use the sample conclusion to illustrate the fact that such phrases often can be deleted without harming the flow of ideas. In addition, you might have students work with the Cliché Array strategy to help them eliminate stale language.

🧰 **BEST PRACTICES TOOLKIT**
Cliché Array p. C4

6. Proofread parenthetical documentation. Point out that if students highlighted their parenthetical documentation as suggested in the **TIP** on page 1296, this task will be easier. Also have students note the uses of punctuation in the Works Cited List on page 1290 and in the list of MLA Citation Guidelines on pages 1299–1300.

For interactive revision tools, see

💿 Write*Smart* CD

ℹ️ Writing Center at **ClassZone.com**

Ⓡ RESOURCE MANAGER—Copy Master
Ask a Peer Reader p. 29

REVISING AND EDITING

What Should I Do?	*What Does It Look Like?*
4. Eliminate unnecessary details. • Ask a peer reader to [bracket] any parts of your paper that are wordy or off topic. • Revise as needed until each paragraph is concise. **See page 1301: Ask a Peer Reader**	▶ Just two weeks after its publication, it topped bestseller lists in [the major American cities of] New York, Philadelphia, Washington, Atlanta, San Francisco, and Los Angeles. [That kind of success is very impressive!]
5. Refine your conclusion. • Reread your concluding paragraph. Be sure that you have used fresh, new phrasing for anything you have repeated for emphasis. • End with a final insight, a memorable phrase, or a question.	▶ It is overstating the case to claim that the book motivated the government to help these workers. Many government programs were already in place at the time of the book's publication, and many other writers and activists helped bring the problem to public attention. Other, larger factors—the end of the drought, an improved economy, and the looming possibility of another world war—also had important effects on the migrant workers' situation. Although Steinbeck's novel was factually accurate and artistically important, a thorough evaluation of the evidence shows that it did not change the course of history.
6. Proofread parenthetical documentation. • <u>Underline</u> any facts, key words, or other information that you haven't documented. • Add parenthetical references to show where you found the information. Check each citation throughout the paper for correct content, punctuation, and order.	▶ When Steinbeck wrote "the dawn came, but no day," he was referring to the black clouds that swirled over the Great Plains during these desperate years. (Steinbeck 5). Depending on how one defines the Dust Bowl and its dates, the number ranges from 16,000 to 315,000. (Windschuttle). She said that, although she had read and heard others' criticisms about the novel, she knew from her own travels and investigations that the living conditions depicted in the book were at least "partly true." ("First Lady").

DIFFERENTIATED INSTRUCTION

FOR DEVELOPING WRITERS
Proofread Parenthetical Documentation
[paired option] Remind students that every word and punctuation mark in every paper should be proofread; in research papers, however, it is especially important to proofread the documentation of sources. Have students take turns proofreading in pairs, with the writer reading aloud (including capitalization and punctuation marks) as the partner checks another copy of the draft.

FOR ADVANCED LEARNERS/AP
Peer Editing [paired option] Invite advanced learners to serve as peer editors for other students. Have pairs of mixed proficiency meet for conferences in which the advanced learner offers constructive suggestions. Emphasize that students should evaluate the suggestions that they receive and that they are free to decide whether to incorporate any of them.

REVIEW MLA GUIDELINES

MLA Citation Guidelines

The MLA (Modern Language Association) has developed guidelines for documenting research. Follow these examples to create the Works Cited list for your source cards and your research paper.

BOOKS

One author
Steinbeck, John. The Grapes of Wrath. 1939. New York: Viking, 1964.

Two authors or editors
Lange, Dorothea, and Paul Schuster Taylor. An American Exodus: A Record of Human Erosion.
    New York: Reynal & Hitchcock, 1939.

Three authors or editors
Scheibel, Jeremy, Anne Chatsworth, and Ridley Davis, eds. Stories from the Great Depression.
    Princeton: Princeton UP, 2008.

Four or more authors or editors
List the first author only. Then use the abbreviation et al., *which means "and others."*
Rutkowski, J., et al. American Immigration and Migration in the 1930s. Topeka: Sanders-Ellis, 2007.

No author given
American Literature: 1865 to the Present. Chicago: Omni, 2007.

PARTS OF BOOKS

An introduction, a preface, a foreword, or an afterword written by someone other than the author(s) of a work
Gorton, Terry. Foreword. John Steinbeck: A Centennial Tribute. Ed. Stephen K. George.
    Westport: Praeger, 2002. xvii-xviii.

A poem, a short story, an essay, or a chapter in a collection of works
Steinbeck, John. "The Leader of the People." The Portable Steinbeck. Ed. Pascal Covici, Jr.
    New York: Penguin, 1978. 397-415.

A poem, a short story, an essay, or a chapter in an anthology of works by several authors
Steinbeck, John. "The Red Pony." The American Short Story: A Collection of the Best Known
    and Most Memorable Short Stories by the Great American Authors. Ed. Thomas K.
    Parkes. New York: Galahad, 1994. 886-948.

A novel or a play in a collection
Steinbeck, John. The Grapes of Wrath. The Grapes of Wrath and Other Writings, 1936–1941.
    New York: Library of America, 1996.

REVIEW MLA GUIDELINES

As students examine the examples, discuss these questions:

- What is the correct format for citing the publisher of a book and the publisher's location? ***Answer:*** *Cite the location first, followed by a colon and the name of the publishing house.*

- When should you use a period instead of a comma? ***Answer:*** *Use a period after each separate category of information, such as the author's name, the title of the book, and the publication date.*

- When a book has two or three authors, what difference is there in the way in which their names are listed? ***Answer:*** *The first author's name is listed with the last name first; each of the other authors is listed with the first name first.*

- How many authors must a book have before *et al* is used? ***Answer:*** *There must be at least four authors.*

- In a collection of writings, what difference is there between the way in which a novel or play is listed and the way in which a poem, story, essay, or chapter title is listed? ***Answer:*** *For the former, underline the title of the shorter work. For the latter, place the title of the shorter work within quotation marks.*

- In the citation to a work by Terry Gorton, in the **PARTS OF BOOKS** category, why are the page numbers in Roman numerals? ***Answer:*** *The page numbers are Roman numerals in the foreword to the book.* What task did Terry Gorton perform in creating *John Steinbeck: A Centennial Tribute,* and what roles did other people play? ***Answer:*** *Terry Gorton wrote the foreword; the book was edited by Stephen K. George; and other authors contributed writings to it.*

FOR DEVELOPING WRITERS

Practice MLA Guidelines Have students create citations for fictitious reference works, using their own names as first author; classmates' names as other authors or editors; *How To Write a Research Paper* as the title of a book; "Getting Started" as the title of a chapter or article; "Research Book Co." as the name of a publisher to be located in your town; this year as the publication date; and page numbers of students' choice. Review their responses for accuracy.

FOR ADVANCED LEARNERS/AP

Research the MLA [small-group option] As this page suggests, the Modern Language Association speaks with authority about certain matters of writing style. Invite a group of students to find out more about the history and activities of this influential organization and to share their findings with the class.

REVIEW MLA GUIDELINES (CONTINUED)

Discuss these questions as students examine the additional examples:

- As shown here, are there any differences in the citation formats of an article from a newspaper and an article from a magazine? Explain. ***Answer: There are no differences.***

- In the citation of a video recording or film, what does *Perf.* mean? ***Answer: It means "Performers."***

- What does *Assoc.* stand for in the title *Film Preservation Assoc.?* ***Answer: The term is an abbreviation for "Association."***

- What is the difference between the two dates in an Internet site citation? ***Answer: One date is the date on which the site was launched (and, in this case, revised); the other is the date on which the researcher found the information at that site.***

- What does *UP Colorado* stand for in the citation for the online book *Americans View Their Dust Bowl Experience?* ***Answer: University Press of Colorado***

- In the citation for the *Encyclopaedia Britannica* CD-ROM, what does *ed* stand for in the date *2004 ed? **Answer: edition***

MAGAZINES, NEWSPAPERS, AND ENCYCLOPEDIAS

An article in a newspaper
Patel, Vikram. "Recalling the Days of Wrath." <u>Los Angeles Times</u> 8 Jan. 2008: 9.

An article in a magazine
Schubert, Siegfried D., et al. "On the Cause of the 1930s Dust Bowl." <u>Science</u> 19 Mar. 2004: 1855-60.

An article in an encyclopedia
Kite, Steven. "Dust Bowl." <u>Encyclopedia of the Great Depression and New Deal</u>. Ed. James Ciment. 2 vols. Armonk, NY: Sharpe, 2001. 107-11.

MISCELLANEOUS NONPRINT SOURCES

An interview
Sorenson, Elvina. Personal interview. 3 Feb. 2008.

A video recording or film
<u>Our Daily Bread</u>. Dir. King Vidor. Perf. Karen Morley, Tom Keene, Barbara Pepper, John Qualen. 1934. DVD. Film Preservation Assoc., 1999.

A sound recording
Guthrie, Woody. <u>Library of Congress Recordings/Woody Guthrie</u>. CD. Rounder, 1988.

ELECTRONIC PUBLICATIONS

A document from an Internet site
Include as much of the following information as available in the order given.

Author or compiler   Title or description of document   Title of Internet site
| Neary, Walter. | "Steinbeck & Salinas." | About John Steinbeck. |

Date of Internet site   Site sponsor   Date of access
| 5 June 1990. Rev. June 1995. | National Steinbeck Center. | 2 Apr. 2008 |

Complete URL enclosed in angle brackets. Break only after a slash.
| <http://www.steinbeck.org/MainFrame.html>. |

An online book or e-book
Wunder, John R., Frances Kaye, and Vernon Carstensen, eds. <u>Americans View Their Dust Bowl Experience</u>. Niwot: UP Colorado, 1999. NetLibrary. <http://library.minlib.net>.

A CD-ROM
"Dust Bowl." <u>Britannica Student Encyclopedia</u>. 2004 ed. CD-ROM. Chicago: Encyclopaedia Britannica, 2004.

DIFFERENTIATED INSTRUCTION

FOR DEVELOPING WRITERS

Concept Support Clarify that the guidelines on pages 1299–1300 are separated into categories for ease of instruction. In their Works Cited lists, however, students will not separate sources into categories; instead, they will use alphabetical order to list all of the sources, regardless of category, in a master list. To illustrate, refer students to the Works Cited list on page 1290.

FOR ADVANCED LEARNERS/AP

Compare and Contrast Citation Styles Point out that some writers prefer citation styles found in other manuals, such as *The Chicago Manual of Style* (University of Chicago Press, updated frequently). Have students look up the Chicago style equivalents for the citation formats listed on pages 1299–1300 and note any differences. You may wish to allow students to use either format, or you may prefer to specify one for them to use.

Preparing to Publish

Research Paper

LC1.3

Consider the Criteria

Use this checklist to make sure your research paper is on track.

Ideas

☑ presents a clear, original thesis statement

☑ supports the thesis with evidence from multiple sources

☑ includes the writer's own interpretations and conclusions

Organization

☑ has a focused introduction and an effective conclusion

☑ is logically organized

Voice

☑ maintains an appropriate tone

☑ reflects the writer's interest in the subject matter

Word Choice

☑ uses precise words

Sentence Fluency

☑ varies sentence structure

Conventions

☑ uses correct grammar, spelling, and punctuation

☑ correctly credits all sources

Ask a Peer Reader

- Do my ideas flow smoothly? If not, where should I add transitions?

- Did I include unnecessary details? If so, where?

Format Your Paper

Use these guidelines to prepare the final copy of your research paper:

- Double-space everything.

- Leave a one-inch margin at the left, right, top, and bottom of each page (except for page numbers).

- At the top left of the first page, type your name, your teacher's name, the class, and the date. Use a separate line for each item. On the rest of the pages, type your last name and the page number in the upper right corner, half an inch from the top.

- Indent all paragraphs one-half inch (or five spaces) and indent quotations of four or more lines one inch (or ten spaces) from the left margin.

- Start a new page for your Works Cited list. Begin each entry at the left margin, indenting any aditional lines one-half inch (or five spaces). End each entry with a period.

See the *MLA Handbook for Writers of Research Papers* for additional formatting guidelines.

Writing Online

PUBLISHING OPTIONS
For publishing options, visit the **Writing Center** at **ClassZone.com**.

ASSESSMENT PREPARATION
For writing and grammar assessment practice, go to the **Assessment Center** at **ClassZone.com**.

Preparing to Publish

Support for meeting the goals in the writing criteria is supplied throughout the Workshop on pages 1284–1300.

For Rubric Bank, see

🖸 Write*Smart* CD

ℹ️ Writing Center at **ClassZone.com**

Assess and Reteach

🆂 STANDARDS LESSON FILE

SPEAKING AND LISTENING

Have students read pages 1302–1303 for an overview of the steps in creating a presentation. If students choose this option for sharing their research and ideas, review these criteria with them to clarify their goals:

Criteria A strong presentation

- brings the subject matter to life
- is planned with the audience in mind
- uses technology effectively
- presents accurate, properly credited details from a variety of sources
- takes the form of explanation and discussion, not of reading aloud

Planning the Presentation

- Suggest that students make heavy use of photographs, since photos are visual primary sources that can be used for any of the suggested presentation options.

- Allow pairs or small groups to work together on the same presentation. They may wish to join groups on the basis of a chosen technology rather than a topic.

- Have students discuss the purposes of the model research paper (pages 1285–1290). Then have them consider possible purposes for their topics and choose a main purpose.

- Suggest that students use a Storyboard if they want to create a script in that form.

BEST PRACTICES TOOLKIT—Transparency
Storyboard p. C11

RESOURCE MANAGER—Copy Master
Presenting the Results of Your Investigation p. 30

STANDARDS LESSON FILE
Media Lesson 20: Producing a Video
Media Lesson 21: Creating a Web Site
Media Lesson 22: Creating a Power Presentation

Presenting the Results of Your Investigation

You can create a presentation to showcase what you have learned.

Planning the Presentation

1. **Consider the sights and sounds of your subject matter.** Review your research paper with a focus on how to bring the subject matter to life for an audience. If your research paper is on the Dust Bowl, you might present any or all of these materials:
   - newsreel footage (now available on video)
   - excerpts from *The Grapes of Wrath*
   - maps showing the migrants' travels
   - folk songs about the Okies
   - photographs of migrant families

   Think about which primary and secondary sources would make your subject accessible and compelling. Use your research paper as a guide, but consider incorporating other sources as well.

2. **Make technology work for you.** Think about the best way to present the materials you want to share. Consider these options:
   - Create a power presentation—slides that you create and display on a computer.
   - Develop a Web site that has one or more pages for each major point you make in your paper. Your site might include databases, spreadsheets, or other graphics.
   - Design a series of posters and charts for display in your classroom, elsewhere at your school, or at a local community center.
   - Produce a video or audio documentary.

   Ask your teacher which presentation options might work best. See page 605 for information on producing a documentary. See page 811 for details on creating power presentations. Information on creating a Web site is on page 1255.

3. **Decide on your purpose.** Are you providing audience members with information? Are you trying to persuade them to hold a particular point of view? Do you want to describe a process or explain a complex historical event? You may have more than one purpose.

4. **Develop your script.** Find out how long you will speak and how many people will be present. Consider how much audience members are likely to know about your topic. Your script may be as simple as a stack of index cards or as complicated as a storyboard with notations for visuals, narration, music, and effects.

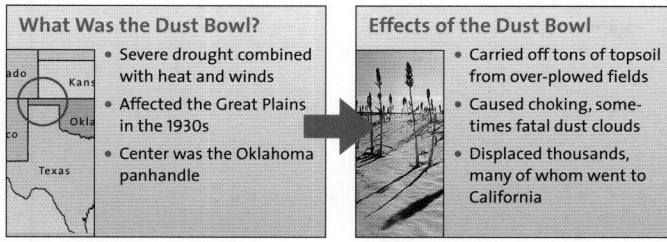

What Was the Dust Bowl?	Effects of the Dust Bowl

What Was the Dust Bowl?
- Severe drought combined with heat and winds
- Affected the Great Plains in the 1930s
- Center was the Oklahoma panhandle

Effects of the Dust Bowl
- Carried off tons of topsoil from over-plowed fields
- Caused choking, sometimes fatal dust clouds
- Displaced thousands, many of whom went to California

5. **Smoothly integrate materials from a variety of sources.** Visuals, audio or video clips, music, and other effects should all help audience members understand your topic. Avoid visuals and effects that are flashy but bring little new information.

6. **Get the details right.** Make sure that your information is accurate and properly credited. Any display text should be large enough to be read from the back of the room—and it should all be spelled correctly, too. If you are creating a Web site as part of your presentation, check that all links are working.

7. **Practice your presentation.** Practice will improve your delivery and soothe your nerves. Ideally, you should practice in the room where you will make your presentation and with the equipment you will use. Ask friends and family members to listen to your presentation. Invite them to give constructive criticism of your performance.

Making the Presentation

1. **Present, explain, elaborate.** Don't read to your audience. Discuss each point you make, providing details and examples from your sources. If certain sources disagree, point that out. Explain why some sources' perspectives may differ and what evidence you have for the sources' reliability.

2. **Invite audience members to ask questions.** Be sure to repeat any questions that audience members ask. That way you can confirm that you understand the question and make certain that the rest of the audience has heard it.

3. **Find out how you did.** Create a simple survey or questionnaire and ask audience members to complete it. Use what you learn to improve your next presentation's content and style.

- Have students brainstorm for video and audio effects that might enhance a spoken presentation of the model research paper. Point out that similar effects probably could be used in a wide range of research topics from literature and history. In addition, ask students to discuss components that might be especially effective in research papers about art (such as reproductions of works of art) and science (such as diagrams, charts, and models).

- Students who prepare a power presentation should include a Works Cited slide at the end of the presentation. Students who prepare a video documentary should create credits footage, including end notes and Works Cited, to place at the end. In an audio documentary, credits are spoken at the end, sometimes to the accompaniment of appropriate background music; when possible, documentation should be incorporated smoothly into the voice-over narrative. On posters and charts, room should be left for credits across the bottom or in a corner.

- Recommend that students videotape or audiotape and then review their practice presentations.

Making the Presentation

- Suggest that students give their presentations to listeners whom they trust. Encourage students to practice explaining, elaborating, and taking questions from the audience.

- Remind students to include all the items from the criteria on their survey or questionnaire, in addition to more specific questions that reflect their particular topics.

Student Resource Bank

R1

Reading any text—short story, poem, magazine article, newspaper, Web page—requires the use of special strategies. For example, you might plot events in a short story on a diagram, while you might use text features to spot main ideas in a magazine article. You also need to identify patterns of organization in the text. Using such strategies can help you read different texts with ease and also help you understand what you're reading.

Included in this handbook as indicated: R2.1 (p. R16), **R2.2** (pgs. R8–R12), **R2.3** (pgs. R15, R16, R17), **R2.4** (pgs. R19–R24), **LS1.5** (pgs. R20–R21), **LS1.12** (pgs. R20, R22–R23)

1 Reading Literary Texts

Literary texts include short stories, novels, poems, and dramas. Literary texts can also be biographies, autobiographies, and essays. To appreciate and analyze literary texts, you will need to understand the characteristics of each type of text.

1.1 READING A SHORT STORY
Strategies for Reading

- Read the title. As you read the story, you may notice that the title has a special meaning.

- Keep track of events as they happen. Plot the events on a diagram like this one.

- Using the details the writer provides, **visualize** the characters. **Predict** what they might do next.

- Look for specific adjectives that help you visualize the **setting**—the time and place in which events occur.

- Note **cause-and-effect relationships** and how these affect the **conflict.**

1.2 READING A POEM
Strategies for Reading

- Notice the **form** of the poem, or the arrangement of its lines and stanzas on the page.

- Read the poem aloud a few times. Listen for and note the **rhymes** and **rhythms.**

- **Visualize** the images and comparisons.

- **Connect** with the poem by asking yourself what message the poet is trying to send.

- Create a word web or another **graphic organizer** to record your reactions and questions.

1.3 READING A PLAY
Strategies for Reading

- Read the stage directions to help you **visualize** the setting and characters.

- **Question** what the title means and why the playwright chose it.

- Identify the main conflict (struggle or problem) in the play. To **clarify** the conflict, make a chart that shows what the conflict is and how it is resolved.

- **Evaluate** the characters. What do they want? How do they change during the play? You may want to make a chart that lists each character's name, appearance, and traits.

1.4 READING LITERARY NONFICTION
Strategies for Reading

- If you are reading a biography, an autobiography, or another type of biographical writing, such as a diary or memoir, use a family tree to keep track of the people mentioned.

- When reading an essay, **analyze** and **evaluate** the writer's ideas and reasoning. Does the writer present a thesis statement? use sound logic? adequately support opinions with facts and other evidence?

- For all types of nonfiction, be aware of the **author's purpose,** and note any personal **bias** of the writer's that might influence the presentation of information.

2 Reading Informational Texts: Text Features

An **informational text** is writing that provides factual information. Informational materials, such as chapters in textbooks and articles in magazines, encyclopedias, and newspapers, usually contain elements that help the reader recognize their purposes, organization, and key ideas. These elements are known as **text features.**

2.1 UNDERSTANDING TEXT FEATURES

Text features are design elements of a text that indicate its organizational structure or otherwise make its key ideas and information understandable. Text features include titles, headings, subheadings, boldface type, bulleted and numbered lists, and graphic aids, such as charts, graphs, illustrations, and photographs. Notice how the text features help you find key information on the textbook page shown.

Ⓐ The **title** identifies the topic.

Ⓑ A **subheading** indicates the start of a new topic or section and identifies the focus of that section.

Ⓒ **Boldface type** is used to make key terms obvious.

Ⓓ A **bulleted list** shows items of equal importance.

Ⓔ **Graphic aids,** such as illustrations, photographs, charts, graphs, diagrams, maps, and timelines, often clarify ideas in the text.

PRACTICE AND APPLY

1. What are the subheadings on the textbook page shown?

2. What are the key terms on the page? How do you know?

3. How do the bulleted list and the photograph help you understand the information on this page?

Ⓐ New Deal Programs:
Helping the American People

While working on banking and financial matters, the Roosevelt administration also implemented programs to provide relief to farmers, perhaps the hardest hit by the depression. It also aided other workers and attempted to stimulate economic recovery.

Ⓑ RURAL ASSISTANCE The **Ⓒ Agricultural Adjustment Act (AAA)** sought to raise crop prices by lowering production, which the government achieved by paying farmers to leave a certain amount of every acre of land unseeded. The theory was that reduced supply would boost prices. In some cases, crops were too far advanced for the acreage reduction to take effect. As a result, the government paid cotton growers $200 million to plow under 10 million acres of their crop. It also paid hog farmers to slaughter 6 million pigs. This policy upset many Americans, who protested the destruction of food when many people were going hungry. It did, however, help raise farm prices and put more money in farmers' pockets.

Background See *supply and demand* on page R46 in the Economics Handbook.

An especially ambitious program of regional development was the Tennessee Valley Authority (TVA), established on May 18, 1933. (See Geography Spotlight on page 520.) Focusing on the badly depressed Tennessee River Valley, the TVA renovated five existing dams and constructed 20 new ones, created thousands of jobs, and provided flood control, hydroelectric power, and other benefits to an impoverished region.

PROVIDING WORK PROJECTS The administration also established programs to provide relief through work projects and cash payments. One important program, the **Civilian Conservation Corps (CCC),** put young men aged 18 to 25 to work building roads, developing parks, planting trees, and helping in soil-erosion and flood-control projects. By the time the program ended in 1942, almost 3 million young men had passed through the CCC. The CCC paid a small wage, $30 a month, of which $25 was automatically sent home to the worker's family. It also supplied free food and uniforms and lodging in work camps. Many of the camps were located on the Great Plains, where, within a period of eight years, the men of the CCC planted more than 200 million trees. This tremendous reforestation program was aimed at preventing another Dust Bowl.

The Public Works Administration (PWA), created in June 1933 as part of the **National Industrial Recovery Act (NIRA),** provided money to states to create jobs chiefly in the construction of schools and other community buildings. When these programs failed to make a sufficient dent in unemployment, President Roosevelt established the Civil Works Administration in November 1933. It provided 4 million immediate jobs during the winter of 1933–1934. Although some critics of the CWA claimed that the programs were "make-work" projects and a waste of money, the CWA built 40,000 schools and paid the salaries of more than 50,000 schoolteachers in America's rural areas. It also built more than half a million miles of roads.

Ⓓ Civilian Conservation Corps

- The CCC provided almost 3 million men aged 18–25 with work and wages between 1933 and 1942.

- The men lived in work camps under a strict regime. The majority of the camps were racially segregated.

- By 1938, the CCC had an 11 percent African-American enrollment.

- Accomplishments of the CCC include planting over 3 billion trees, developing over 800 state parks, and building more than 46,000 bridges.

MAIN IDEA
Analyzing Effects
Ⓒ How did New Deal programs affect various regions of the United States?

The New Deal **491**

PRACTICE AND APPLY

ANSWERS

1. *Rural Assistance; Providing Work Projects*

2. *Agricultural Adjustment Act (AAA), Civilian Conservation Corps (CCC), National Industrial Recovery Act (NIRA); key terms are in boldface.*

3. *Bulleted list gives additional information about a key term; photograph offers visual support of key information.*

2.2 USING TEXT FEATURES

You can use text features to locate information, to help you understand it, and to categorize it. Just use the following strategies when you encounter informational text.

Strategies for Reading

- Scan the title, headings, and subheadings to get an idea of the main concepts and the way the text is organized.

- Before you begin reading the text more thoroughly, read any questions that appear at the end of a lesson or chapter. Doing this will help you set a purpose for your reading.

- Turn subheadings into questions. Then use the text below the subheadings to answer the questions. Your answers will be a summary of the text.

- Take notes by turning headings and subheadings into main ideas. You might enter them in a chart like the following.

New Deal Programs: Helping the American People		Main Heading
Rural Assistance	Notes: 1. Agricultural Adjustment Act was enacted to raise crop prices by lowering production. 2. In some cases, crops were too advanced for the program to be effective.	Subheading

2.3 TURNING TEXT HEADINGS INTO OUTLINE ENTRIES

You can also use text features to take notes in outline form. The following outline shows how one student used text headings from the sample page on page R3. Study the outline and use the strategies that follow to create an outline based on text features.

I. New Deal Programs: Helping the American People — **Main Heading** Roman numeral entry

A. Rural Assistance — **Subheading** capital letter entry

1. Agricultural Adjustment Act was enacted to raise crop prices by lowering production. — **Detail** number entry

2. In some cases, crops were too advanced for the program to be effective.

Strategies for Using Text Headings

- Preview the headings and subheadings in the text to get an idea of what different kinds there are and what their positions might be in an outline.

- Be consistent. Note that subheadings that are the same size and color should be used consistently in Roman-numeral or capital-letter entries in the outline. If you decide that a chapter heading should appear with a Roman numeral, then that's the level at which all other chapter headings should appear.

- Write the headings and subheadings that you will use as your Roman-numeral and capital-letter entries first. As you read, fill in numbered details from the text under the headings and subheadings in your outline.

PRACTICE AND APPLY

Find a suitable chapter in one of your textbooks and, using its text features, take notes on the chapter in outline form.

Preview the subheadings in the text to get an idea of the different kinds. Write the headings and subheadings you are using as your Roman-numeral and capital-letter entries first. Then fill in the details.

PRACTICE AND APPLY

ANSWERS

Students' work should resemble models shown in text.

2.4 GRAPHIC AIDS

Information is communicated not only with words but also with graphic aids. **Graphic aids** are visual representations of verbal statements. They can be charts, webs, diagrams, graphs, photographs, or other visual representations of information. Graphic aids usually make complex information easier to understand. For that reason, graphic aids are often used to organize, simplify, and summarize information for easy reference.

Graphs

Graphs are used to illustrate statistical information. A **graph** is a drawing that shows the relative values of numerical quantities. Different kinds of graphs are used to show different numerical relationships.

Strategies for Reading

Ⓐ Read the title.

Ⓑ Find out what is being represented or measured.

Ⓒ In a circle graph, compare the sizes of the parts.

Ⓓ In a line graph, study the slant of the line. The steeper the line, the faster the rate of change.

Ⓔ In a bar graph, compare the lengths of the bars.

A **circle graph,** or **pie graph,** shows the relationships of parts to a whole. The entire circle equals 100 percent. The parts of the circle represent percentages of the whole.

MODEL: CIRCLE GRAPH

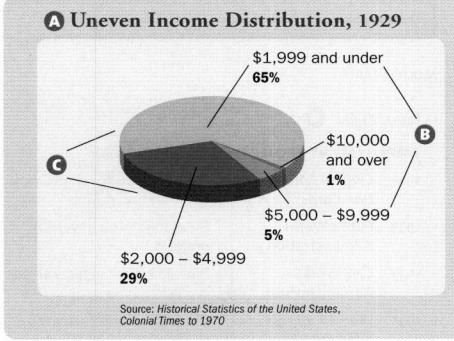

Ⓐ Uneven Income Distribution, 1929

$1,999 and under
65%

Ⓑ $10,000 and over
1%

$5,000 – $9,999
5%

$2,000 – $4,999
29%

Source: *Historical Statistics of the United States, Colonial Times to 1970*

Line graphs show changes in numerical quantities over time and are effective in presenting trends, such as unemployment rates. A line graph is made on a grid. Here, the vertical axis indicates the percentage of the work force that is unemployed, and the horizontal axis shows years. Points on the graph indicate data. The lines that connect the points indicate the trends or patterns.

MODEL: LINE GRAPH

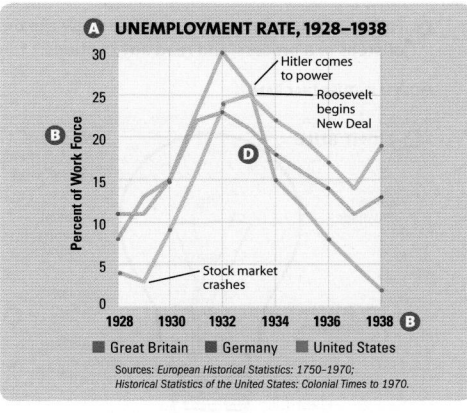

Ⓐ **UNEMPLOYMENT RATE, 1928–1938**

Hitler comes to power

Roosevelt begins New Deal

Ⓓ

Stock market crashes

■ Great Britain   ■ Germany   ■ United States

Sources: *European Historical Statistics: 1750–1970;*
Historical Statistics of the United States: Colonial Times to 1970.

In a **bar graph,** vertical or horizontal bars are used to show or compare categories of information, such as average annual income during wartime. The lengths of the bars typically indicate quantities.

MODEL: BAR GRAPH

Ⓐ The War Economy, 1914–1920

Year	Average Annual Income
1914	$627
1915	$633
1916	$706
1917	$830
1918	$1,047 Ⓔ
1919	$1,201
1920	$1,407

Source: *Historical Statistics of the United States*

WATCH OUT! Evaluate carefully the information presented in graphs. For example, circle graphs show major factors and differences well but tend to minimize smaller factors and differences.

Diagrams

A **diagram** is a drawing that shows how something works or how its parts relate to one another.

A **picture diagram** is a picture or drawing of the subject being discussed.

Strategies for Reading

Ⓐ Read the title.

Ⓑ Read each label and look at the part it identifies.

Ⓒ Follow any arrows or numbers that show the order of steps in a process, and read any captions.

MODEL: PICTURE DIAGRAM

Ⓐ LIGHT BULB

Mixture of inert gases at low pressure

Glass envelope

Coiled tungsten filament

Support wires Ⓑ

Glass fuse enclosure

Connecting wires

Electrical contact

Screw cap

In a **schematic diagram,** lines, symbols, and words are used to help readers visualize processes or objects they wouldn't normally be able to see.

MODEL: SCHEMATIC DIAGRAM

Ⓐ Panama Canal

1 — A ship enters a lock when the lower gates are open.

Ⓑ

2 — When all gates are shut, water is let into the lock through a sluice (small channel).

Ⓒ 3 — When the water has risen, the upper gates are opened, and the ship passes through the lock to the next level.

Charts and Tables

A **chart** presents information, shows a process, or makes comparisons, usually in rows or columns. A **table** is a specific type of chart that presents a collection of facts in rows and columns and shows how the facts relate to one another.

Strategies for Reading

Ⓐ Read the title to learn what information the chart or table covers.

Ⓑ Study column headings and row labels to determine the categories of information presented.

Ⓒ Look down columns and across rows to find specific information.

MODEL: CHART

Geographic Distribution of U.S. Population, 1930–1970 Ⓐ

Year	Central Cities	Suburbs	Ⓑ Rural Areas and Small Towns
1930	31.8%	18.0%	50.2%
1940	31.6%	19.5%	48.9%
1950	32.3%	23.8%	43.9%
1960	32.6%	30.7%	36.7%
1970	31.4%	37.6%	31.0%

Source: Adapted from U.S. Bureau of the Census, *Decennial Censuses, 1930–1970*

MODEL: TABLE

New Deal Ⓐ

EMPLOYMENT PROJECTS	PURPOSE Ⓑ
1933 Civilian Conservation Corps	Provided jobs for single males on conservation projects
1933 Public Works Administration	Created jobs on government projects
1933 Civil Works Administration	Provided work in federal jobs
1935 Works Progress Administration	Quickly created as many jobs as possible—from construction jobs to positions in symphony orchestras
1935 National Youth Administration	Provided job training for unemployed young people and part-time jobs for needy students

Maps

A **map** visually represents a geographic region, such as a state or country. It provides information about areas through lines, colors, shapes, and symbols. There are different kinds of maps.

- **Political maps** show political features, such as national borders, states and capitols, and population demographics.
- **Physical maps** show the landforms in areas.
- **Road or travel maps** show streets, roads, and highways.
- **Thematic maps** show information on a specific topic, such as climate, weather, or natural resources.

Strategies for Reading

A Read the title to find out what kind of map it is.

B Read the labels to get an overall sense of what the map shows.

C Look at the **key** or **legend** to find out what the symbols and colors on the map stand for.

MODEL: THEMATIC MAP

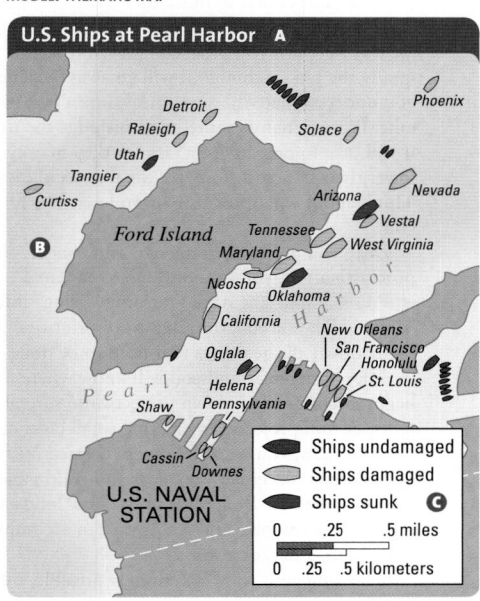

U.S. Ships at Pearl Harbor **A**

MODEL: ROAD MAP

HARLEM IN THE 1920s **A**

PRACTICE AND APPLY

Use the graphic aids on pages R5–R7 to answer the following questions.

1. According to the circle graph, what percentage of the population in the 1920s earned $10,000 or over?

2. According to the line graph, which country had the highest unemployment rate in 1936?

3. According to the bar graph, by how much did the average annual income increase between 1914 and 1920?

4. What is used to contain the inert gases in a light bulb, according to the picture diagram?

5. Using the schematic diagram of the Panama Canal, describe the function of a sluice in the lock system.

6. According to the chart, in which type of area did the population steadily decrease between 1930 and 1970?

7. Use the table to determine the types of jobs found through the Public Works Administration.

8. On the thematic map, identify three ships that were sunk.

9. Use the 1920s map of Harlem to give directions from the Apollo Theatre to the Savoy Theatre.

PRACTICE AND APPLY

ANSWERS

1. *one percent*

2. *United States*

3. *Income rose $780.*

4. *glass envelope*

5. ***Possible answer:*** *Once a ship is in the lock, a sluice lets water into the lock, causing the ship to rise.*

6. *rural areas and small towns*

7. *government projects*

8. *Answers should include three of the following: Arizona, Oglala, Oklahoma, and Utah.*

9. ***Possible answer:*** *125th to Seventh, turn left, Seventh to 140th, turn right, one block to Savoy*

3 Reading Informational Texts: Patterns of Organization

Reading any type of writing is easier once you recognize how it is organized. Writers usually arrange ideas and information in ways that best reveal how they are related. Here are the most common patterns of organization:

- order of importance
- chronological order
- cause-effect organization
- compare-and-contrast organization

3.1 ORDER OF IMPORTANCE

Order of importance is a pattern of organization in which information is arranged by its degree of importance. The information is often arranged in one of two ways: from **most important to least important** or from **least important to most important.** In the first way, the most important quality, characteristic, or fact is presented at the beginning of the text, and the remaining details are presented in an order ending with the least significant. The second pattern is the reverse: the text builds from the less important elements to the most important one. Order of importance is frequently used in persuasive writing.

Strategies for Reading

- To identify order of importance in a piece of writing, skim the text to see if it moves from items of greater importance to items of lesser importance, or the reverse.

- Next, read the text carefully. Look for words and phrases such as *first, second, mainly, more important, less important, least important* and *most important* to indicate the relative importance of the ideas and information.

- Identify the topic of the text and what aspect of the topic is being discussed—its complexity, size, effectiveness, varieties, or some other aspect. Note what the most important fact or idea seems to be.

- If you are having difficulty understanding the topic, try asking *who, what, when, where, why,* and *how* about the ideas or events.

Notice the degrees of importance of the ideas in the following model.

Subject	Words showing order of importance

MODEL

Why are some of us tempted to put off tasks when they could easily be done right away? In a word: procrastination. It affects all areas of life and can have some hefty consequences. By putting off tasks, we can cause unnecessary stress for ourselves and those around us. Many procrastinators say, "I work well under pressure," and this might be true. But better planning would lead to better grades, a more impressive report, and even career advancement. What can you do to curb your tendencies to delay the inevitable?

First, determine the cause of your procrastination. If you're honest with yourself, you might find that you set unrealistic goals, that you have a fear of failure or criticism, or that you feel guilty for delaying. Any of these reasons can paralyze your efforts to move forward.

The next important thing is to identify *the way in which* you procrastinate. Maybe you ignore the task as though it will go away. Maybe you underestimate the amount of time a task will take. Procrastinators sometimes misjudge the time it will take to prepare for a task, or they may even lower their standards to make the task seem easier. Think about what procrastination looks like for you.

Once you understand the *why* and *how* of procrastination, you can move on to the final and most important stage—turning "being" into "doing." First, keep a running list of priorities. Write down all the things that need to be done in order of urgency, and you will know where to begin. Second, break down projects into several tasks, or miniprojects. By creating small tasks out of larger ones, you won't feel overwhelmed by a single large task. Finally, set clear and reasonable goals for yourself. Be specific about how long each miniproject will take and what you can accomplish in an hour, a day, or a week.

Changing your ways is definitely possible, but it will take some honest evaluation. Hopefully, after the process of examining the *why* and *how* of procrastination, you will be ready to change your ways. Why not start right now?

Read each paragraph, and then do the following:

1. Identify whether the order is from most important to least important or from least important to most important.

2. Identify key words and phrases that helped you figure out the order.

3. What is the order of importance indicated in the paragraph beginning, "Once you understand … "? What are the key words?

3.2 CHRONOLOGICAL ORDER

Chronological order is the arrangement of events in their order of occurrence. This type of organization is used in fictional narratives, historical writing, biographies, and autobiographies. To indicate the order of events, writers use words such as *before, after, next,* and *later* and words and phrases that identify specific times of day, days of the week, and dates, such as *the next morning, Tuesday,* and *on July 4, 1776.*

Strategies for Reading

- Look in the text for headings and subheadings that may indicate a chronological pattern of organization.

- Look for words and phrases that identify times, such as *in a year, three hours earlier, in 1871,* and *the next day.*

- Look for words that signal order, such as *first, afterward, then, during,* and *finally,* to see how events or steps are related.

- Note that a paragraph or passage in which ideas and information are arranged chronologically will have several words or phrases that indicate time order, not just one.

- Ask yourself: Are the events in the paragraph or passage presented in time order?

Notice the words and phrases that signal time order in the first three paragraphs of the following model.

MODEL

History of the National Weather Service

Today, the U.S. National Weather Service is one of the best-known federal agencies. It was not always so popular, especially in its early years.

The first incarnation of the National Weather Service was founded in the wake of the Civil War, as an agency in the Army Signal Service Corps. Its mission was to "take observations at military stations and to warn of storms on the Great Lakes and on the Atlantic and Gulf Coasts." Very early in its existence the agency earned a reputation for the corruption of its personnel and the unreliability of its forecasting. In 1881, William Howgate, the chief financial manager of the agency, was arrested for embezzling a quarter million dollars. . . . During this time the U.S. military budget was about 40 million dollars. Howgate was tried and convicted, only to escape a year later. Other servicemen in stations around the country were investigated throughout the 1880s and fired in large numbers for reckless neglect. . . . Moreover, the agency's weather predictions were frequently and dangerously wrong. On March 12, 1888, the New York station's forecast called for "fair weather"; instead of fair weather, New York got the Blizzard of '88, which dumped 21 inches of snow on the city and killed 400 people throughout the Northeast. . . .

In 1891, the Army Signal Service Corps's weather service was honorably discharged from the Department of War and given a new home in the civilian Department of Agriculture. It was named the Weather Bureau: it would not be called the National Weather Service until 1970. During the years leading up to 1900, the Weather Bureau's servicemen took regular measurement of such atmospheric conditions as temperature, wind speed, air pressure, rainfall, and cloud conditions. They transmitted their findings to one another via wireless telegraphy.

> **Time words and phrases**

> **Order words and phrases**

> **Events**

PRACTICE AND APPLY

ANSWERS

1. *from least to most*

2. ***Possible answer:*** *"first," "next important," "final," "most important"*

3. *least to most important: "first," "second," "finally"*

PRACTICE AND APPLY

ANSWERS

1. Answers should include five of the following: "early in its existence," "during this time," "On March 12, 1888," "In 1891," "until 1970," "During the years leading up to 1900."

2. Timeline should include the following dates and events:

    1881: William Howgate is arrested for embezzlement.

    1880s: Servicemen in stations around the country are investigated and fired for reckless neglect.

    1888: The New York station forecasts fair weather and a blizzard hits.

    1891: Army Signal Service Corps's weather service is discharged from the Department of War, given a new home in the Department of Agriculture, and renamed the Weather Bureau.

    1890s: Weather Bureau's servicemen take regular measurement of atmospheric conditions and report them via telegraph.

    1970: Weather Bureau is renamed National Weather Service.

3. Cause: Chief financial manager embezzles money

    Cause: Many servicemen fired for reckless neglect

    Cause: Weather predictions dangerously wrong

    Effect: Army Signal Service Corps gains reputation for being corrupt and unreliable

---

Refer to the preceding model to do the following:

1. List at least five words or phrases from the model that indicate time order. Do not use words that are already highlighted.

2. Draw a timeline beginning in 1881 and ending with "today." On the timeline chart major events in the formation of the National Weather Service as described in the model.

3. Sometimes more than one pattern of organization is used to help organize a text. Reread paragraph two, and find at least three causes for the Army Signal Service Corps's reputation as a corrupt and unreliable agency. Use the "multiple causes with a single effect" form shown on this page to chart this information.

3.3 CAUSE-EFFECT ORGANIZATION

Cause-effect organization is a pattern of organization that establishes causal relationships between events, ideas, and trends. Cause-effect relationships may be directly stated or merely implied by the order in which the information is presented. Writers often use the cause-effect pattern in historical and scientific writing. Cause-effect relationships may take several forms.

One cause with one effect

One cause with multiple effects

Multiple causes with a single effect

A chain of causes and effects

Strategies for Reading

- Look for headings and subheadings that indicate a cause-effect pattern of organization, such as "The Effects of Improved Weather Forecasting."
- To find the effect or effects, read to answer the question, What happened?
- To find the cause or causes, read to answer the question, Why did it happen?
- Look for words and phrases that help you identify specific relationships between events, such as *because, since, so, had the effect of, led to, as a result, resulted in, for that reason, due to, therefore, if . . . then,* and *consequently.*
- Evaluate each cause-effect relationship. Do not assume that because one event happened before another, the first event caused the second event.
- Use graphic organizers like the diagrams shown to record cause-effect relationships as you read.

Notice the words that signal causes and effects in the following model.

MODEL

The Formation of a Hurricane: What Does It Take?

Hurricanes have waged war on U.S. cities like no other enemy. Each year, up to ten tropical storms may form in the Atlantic Ocean and make their way west. Typically, three to five have the potential to become a full-blown hurricane. These high-speed monsters are fueled by the simplest of natural elements: water, wind, and air. Given the right conditions, these essential elements for life can become lethal.

The first condition for the   **Causes**
formation of a hurricane involves warming ocean water in a relatively tranquil and tropical region of the Atlantic. By late summer, the surface water becomes thoroughly heated and begins to evaporate, or rise into the air. This process creates warm, moist air, which then   **Effect that in**
rises and eventually condenses to   **turn becomes**
form clouds and rain. During this   **a cause**
process, energy is released, warming the air further.

The second condition, ironically, is the lack of wind. In the tropical regions of the Atlantic, the air may be relatively stagnant in places, which causes the warm, moist air to remain in one spot. Because the air is continuing to warm and gain energy, it needs to move, and so it does: upward. This column of upward-moving warm air creates an area of low pressure over the water, which in turn draws even more air from the surrounding area toward the center of the column. In addition, the inward-moving air causes the warm air to rise even faster, which then draws even more air and increases its wind speed. Thus, the transfer of energy from ocean to air begins to fuel itself with ever-increasing speed.

> **Signal words and phrases**

As the air moves toward the column's center, it does not move in a straight line, but moves in a circular motion as a result of the earth's rotation. As the air moves up the column, it continues swirling.

A storm that continues in this cycle may grow up to 500 miles in diameter. Its westward movement ensures that it will eventually hit land if it doesn't dissipate, and what began as a simple combination of water, wind, and air could turn into a catastrophic storm.

PRACTICE AND APPLY

Refer to the preceding model to do the following:

1. Use the pattern of multiple causes with a single effect illustrated on page R10 to make a graphic organizer showing the causes described in the text and the effect of those causes.

2. List any words and phrases the writer uses to signal cause and effect in the third paragraph.

3.4 COMPARE-AND-CONTRAST ORGANIZATION

Compare-and-contrast organization is a pattern of organization that serves as a framework for examining similarities and differences in two or more subjects. A writer may use this pattern of organization to analyze two or more subjects, such as characters or movies, in terms of their important points or characteristics. These points or characteristics are called points of comparison. The compare-and-contrast pattern of organization may be developed in either of two ways.

Point-by-point organization—The writer discusses one point of comparison for both subjects, then goes on to the next point.

Subject-by-subject organization—The writer covers all points of comparison for one subject and then all points of comparison for the next subject.

Strategies for Reading

- Look in the text for headings, subheadings, and sentences that may suggest a compare-and-contrast pattern of organization, such as "East Coast and West Coast Living: More than a Continent Apart." These will help you identify where similarities and differences are addressed.

- To find similarities, look for words and phrases such as *like, similarly, both, also,* and *in the same way.*

- To find differences, look for words and phrases such as *unlike, but, on the other hand, in contrast,* and *however.*

- Use a graphic organizer, such as a Venn diagram or a compare-and-contrast chart, to record points of comparison and similarities and differences.

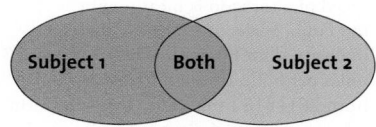

	Subject 1	Subject 2
Point 1		
Point 2		
Point 3		

PRACTICE AND APPLY

ANSWERS

1. *Responses will vary; should include three causes and the effect of a hurricane.*

   One possible answer may include:

   > *Cause: warm ocean water in a tranquil and tropical region of the Atlantic*

   > *Cause: water becomes heated and begins to evaporate*

   > *Effect: creates warm, moist air, which then rises and forms clouds and rain*

   OR

   > *Cause: warm ocean water in a tranquil and tropical region of the Atlantic*

   > *Cause: lack of wind*

   > *Cause: earth's rotation*

   > *Effect: storm that grows into a hurricane*

2. "causes," "Because," "in turn," "causes," "Thus"

Read the following models. As you read, use the signal words and phrases to identify the similarities and differences between the subjects and how the details are organized in each text.

MODEL 1

A Tale of Two Furies: Hurricane vs. Tornado

Two of the deadliest types of storms are hurricanes and tornadoes. [**Subjects**] While both are ferocious wind storms and require similar elements to form, each varies in speed and duration.

Hurricanes, like tornadoes, require the meeting of cool and warm air and begin as rain or thunderstorms. However, [**Contrast words and phrases**] one major difference between the two is that a hurricane forms at sea and moves toward land, while a tornado forms over, and remains on, land. Hurricanes require large amounts of warmth and moisture from ocean water to form, while tornadoes rely on the moisture already in the air. The duration of a hurricane is one week, on average. A few rare hurricanes have been known to last between 17 and 27 days. The average tornado, however, lasts 10 to 30 minutes, and may "touch down" on land for up to a minute.

Both [**Comparison words**] tornadoes and hurricanes can be measured. The difference is in *how* and *when.* The wind speed of a tornado is measured by the Fujita Scale, or F-Scale, which rates intensity from F0, with winds less than 73 miles per hour, through F5, with winds from 261–318 mph. Since tornados form very quickly and cannot be accurately predicted, the F-Scale can only measure the strength of a tornado *after* it has occurred. In contrast, the intensity of hurricanes can be measured *while* they are forming. This is because unlike tornados, hurricanes form slowly and can be photographed using satellite imagery. The satellite pictures are then studied, and the results applied to a scale of measure called the Saffir-Simpson Hurricane Scale. This scale rates intensity from Category One through the most intense Category 5 storm.

MODEL 2

Same Goal, Different Methods

Booker T. Washington and W. E. B. Du Bois were alike in many [**Subjects**] ways. Both were devoted to helping [**Comparison words**] their fellow African Americans attain equal rights. Both were educated black men with university teaching positions. Both also worked passionately toward their goal at the beginning of the 20th century. Nevertheless, they were not allies. Why? They had very different [**Contrast words and phrases**] ideas about how blacks should go about attaining equal rights.

Washington believed that for black people to achieve equal status and power as citizens they needed to focus on learning crafts, farming, and industrial skills. He argued that by gaining vocational skills and economic security, black people would naturally earn the respect and acceptance of the white community. To achieve these goals, however, Washington believed black people would need to let go temporarily of the fight for civil rights and political power.

In contrast to Washington, W. E. B. Du Bois believed that black people could not afford to stop fighting for civil rights and political power. In his opinion, only agitation and protest would achieve social change. According to Du Bois, in the climate of extreme racism that existed in America at the time, Washington's approach would merely cause blacks to suffer even more oppression.

So although these two African-American contemporaries had the same goal, their different approaches to achieving this goal made them adversaries rather than allies.

PRACTICE AND APPLY

Refer to the preceding models to do the following:

For each model, create a compare-and-contrast chart. In your chart, list the points of comparison in each model, and identify the similarities and differences between each model's subjects.

PRACTICE AND APPLY

ANSWERS

"Tale of Two Furies":

Similarities of hurricanes and tornadoes: deadliest storms, require similar elements, strength can be measured

Differences: Speed and duration; hurricane forms over sea and moves toward land, tornado forms over land and remains there; hurricanes require large amounts of moisture from ocean water, while tornadoes rely on moisture already in the air. Hurricane strength can be measured while the storm is forming, whereas a tornado's strength can only be measured after the storm has occurred.

"Same Goal, Different Methods":

Similarities between Booker T. Washington and W.E.B. DuBois: devoted to helping African Americans attain equal rights; educated; held teaching positions; worked passionately toward their goals

Differences: ideas about how African Americans should attain equal rights

4 Reading Informational Texts: Forms

Magazines, newspapers, Web pages, and consumer, public, and workplace documents are all examples of informational materials. To understand and analyze informational texts, pay attention to text features and patterns of organization.

4.1 READING A MAGAZINE ARTICLE

Because people often skim magazines for topics of interest, magazine publishers use devices to attract attention to articles and to highlight key information.

Strategies for Reading

A Read the **title** and other **headings** to find out more about the article's topic and organization.

B Notice whether or not the article has a **byline**, a line naming the author, and make note of the date and source.

C Examine **illustrations, photos,** or other **graphic aids** that visually convey or illustrate additional information, or information from the text.

D Notice **pull quotes,** or quotations that a publisher has pulled out of the text and displayed to get your attention.

PRACTICE AND APPLY

Refer to the article to answer the following questions:

1. What does the title indicate the topic will be?

2. Why is this particular pull quote significant? What information does it convey?

3. Considering the information in the text and the visual image in the photo, what can you conclude about the severity of the hurricane mentioned in the article?

Katrina's South American Sister

A Was Catarina an omen of things to come?

C

For people along the Gulf Coast, Hurricane Katrina was an unimaginable disaster. In meteorological terms, however, she was not unusual—a major storm for sure, but not atypical of what comes across the North Atlantic at that time of year. The one thing experts did note was that ocean temperatures in the Gulf of Mexico are especially warm these days.

D "The real shocker had come 18 months earlier . . . And her name was Catarina."

For hurricane watchers, however, the real shocker had come 18 months earlier. And her name was Catarina.

Catarina came ashore in Brazil on March 28, 2004—a category-one hurricane that damaged 30,000 homes. Scientists were baffled. Brazilian meteorologists didn't even use the term "hurricane" at first—not until they looked closely at the satellite images. Why? Very simply, no hurricanes had ever been recorded before in the South Atlantic. Conventional wisdom was that cool ocean temperatures and atmospheric differences made it impossible for hurricanes to form there.

But here was Hurricane Catarina, and, indeed, a couple of months earlier, on January 19th, a smaller tropical storm had also developed off the coast of Brazil.

The entire phenomenon was unprecedented. . . . Is it another indicator of global warming? Researchers say that any such analysis is, at this stage, speculative. Regardless, it might make sense to plan for the worst, rather than continually hoping for the best.

PRACTICE AND APPLY

ANSWERS

1. *Hurricanes; specifically, Hurricanes Katrina and Catarina*

2. *In some ways, Hurricane Catarina was more shocking than Hurricane Katrina.*

3. *It was devastating and resulted in massive destruction.*

4.2 READING A TEXTBOOK

Each textbook that you use has its own system of organization, based on the content in the book. Often an introductory unit will explain the book's organization and special features. If your textbook has such a unit, read it first.

Strategies for Reading

Ⓐ Before you begin reading the lesson or chapter, read any **questions** that appear at the end of it. Then use the questions to set your purpose for reading.

Ⓑ **Read slowly and carefully** to better understand and remember the ideas presented in the text. When you come to an unfamiliar word, first try to figure out its meaning from **context clues.** If necessary, find the meaning of the word in a **sidenote** on the page, in a **glossary** at the back of the book, or in a dictionary. Avoid interrupting your reading by constantly looking up words in a dictionary.

Ⓒ Use the book's **graphic aids,** such as illustrations, diagrams, and photos, to clarify your understanding of the text.

Ⓓ Take notes as you read. Use text features such as **subheadings** and **boldfaced terms** to help you organize your notes. Use graphic organizers, such as cause-effect charts, to help you clarify relationships among ideas.

PRACTICE AND APPLY

1. What is the definition of *nationalization?*

2. Where on the page do you find the combined private and public debt owed during this time? What was the total amount?

3. Use the text on this page and on R3 to answer the second question in the Section Review of the textbook page.

The New Deal Comes Under Attack

Ⓓ **THREE FIERY CRITICS** In 1934, some of the strongest conservative opponents of the New Deal banded together to form an organization called the American Liberty League. The American Liberty League opposed New Deal measures that it believed violated respect for the rights of individuals and property. Three of the toughest critics the president faced, however, were three men who expressed views that appealed to poor Americans: Charles Coughlin, Dr. Francis Townsend, and Huey Long.

Every Sunday, Father Charles Coughlin, a Roman Catholic priest from a suburb of Detroit, broadcast radio sermons that combined economic, political, and religious ideas. Initially a supporter of the New Deal, Coughlin soon turned against Roosevelt. He favored a guaranteed annual income and the **nationalization** of banks. At the height of his popularity, Father Coughlin claimed a radio audience of as many as 40–45 million people, but his increasingly anti-Semitic (anti-Jewish) views eventually cost him support.

Ⓑ **Vocabulary** **nationalization:** conversion from private to governmental ownership

Another critic of New Deal policies was Dr. Francis Townsend, a physician and health officer in Long Beach, California. He believed that Roosevelt wasn't doing enough to help the poor and elderly, so he devised a pension plan that would provide monthly benefits to the aged. The plan found strong backing among the elderly, thus undermining their support for Roosevelt.

Ⓓ Perhaps the most serious challenge to the New Deal came from Senator **Huey Long** of Louisiana. Like Coughlin, Long was an early supporter of the New Deal, but he, too, turned against Roosevelt. Eager to win the presidency for himself, Long proposed a nationwide social program called Share-Our-Wealth. Under the banner "Every Man a King," he promised something for everyone.

Ⓒ

A PERSONAL VOICE HUEY LONG

" We owe debts in America today, public and private, amounting to $252 billion. That means that every child is born with a $2,000 debt tied around his neck. . . . We propose that children shall be born in a land of opportunity, guaranteed a home, food, clothes, and the other things that make for living, including the right to education. "

—*Record,* 74 Congress, Session 1

Huey Long

Long's program was so popular that by 1935 he boasted of having perhaps as many as 27,000 Share-Our-Wealth clubs and 7.5 million members. That same year, however, at the height of his popularity, Long was assassinated by a lone gunman.

As the initial impetus of the New Deal began to wane, President Roosevelt started to look ahead. He knew that much more needed to be done to help the people and to solve the nation's economic problems.

Ⓐ ASSESSMENT

SECTION REVIEW

· Name the three outspoken critics of Roosevelt's New Deal.
· Describe one New Deal program, and explain one opponent's view of the New Deal.

· **Critical Thinking** Of the New Deal programs discussed, which do you consider the most important? Consider scope, impact, and type of assistance offered by each.

The New Deal **493**

PRACTICE AND APPLY

ANSWERS

1. *conversion from private to governmental ownership*

2. *Huey Long's quote; $252 billion*

3. *Responses will vary. Students may respond that the New Deal program provided economic aid to the American population suffering from the effects of the Great Depression. One opponent was Dr. Francis Townsend, who believed the New Deal program didn't do enough to help the poor.*

4.3 READING A CONSUMER DOCUMENT

Consumer documents are materials that accompany products and services. They usually provide information about the use, care, operation, or assembly of the products they accompany. Some common consumer documents are contracts, warranties, manuals, instructions, schedules, and Web pages.

Strategies for Reading

A Read the **title** to identify the purpose of the document.

B Read the **general directions** to get started.

C Look for **numbers** or **letters** that indicate the steps to be followed. Note whether the steps must be done in order and whether there are signal words such as *first, next, then,* and *finally* that indicate the order in which the steps should be followed. Follow the steps in order.

D Refer to any **illustrations, diagrams,** or other **graphic aids** that accompany the numbered instructions. Use the graphic aids to help you understand each step.

E Look for **verbs that describe actions you should take,** such as *press, use,* and *hold.*

PRACTICE AND APPLY

1. Explain the function of key number 10.

2. Identify the number of the key that allows you to engage the phone's locking function.

INSTRUCTIONS FOR USING A CELL PHONE

A PHONE OVERVIEW

B Use this guide to get a quick overview of your phone's functions.

C 1. **Earpiece** **E**
2. **Flip** Flip open the case to answer incoming calls and close to end calls.
3. **LCD Screen** Displays messages and icons.
4. **Left Soft Key** Use to display the function-setting menu.
5. **Headset Jack**
6. **END/POWER Key** Use to turn the power on or off and to end a call.
7. **Side Keys** Use to adjust the ringer volume in standby mode and the earpiece volume during a call.
8. **CLEAR Key** Press to delete a single space or character. Press and hold to delete entire words. Press this key once in a menu to go back one level.
9. **Navigation Key** Use for quick access to messages or Web.
10. **Speaker Key** Use to set Speaker on or off.
11. **Right Soft Key** Use to select an action in a menu.
12. **SEND Key** Use to place or answer calls.
13. **Message Key** Use to retrieve or send voice and text messages.
14. **Alphanumeric Keypad** Use the keys to enter numbers and characters and to select menu items.
15. **Lock Mode Key** Use in standby mode to set the lock function by pressing and holding the key for about 3 seconds.

PRACTICE AND APPLY

ANSWERS

1. *It turns the speaker phone on and off.*
2. *number 15*

PRACTICE AND APPLY

ANSWERS

1. *Knives are not allowed as carry-on items unless they are plastic or round-bladed butter knives. Knives are allowed as a checked item.*

2. *plastic with blunt tips, metal with blunt tips, ostomy scissors*

3. *to ensure prohibited items are not concealed*

4. *Responses will vary.*

4.4 READING A PUBLIC DOCUMENT

Public documents are documents that are written for the public to provide information that is of public interest or concern. These documents are often free. They can be federal, state, or local government documents. They can be speeches or historical documents. They may even be laws, posted warnings, signs, or rules and regulations. The following is a public document that has been posted on a U.S. government Web site and can be printed as a document.

Strategies for Reading

A Look at the **title** on the page to discover what the text is about.

B Note the **source** of the document.

C Carefully read **column headings** in the table. Items in a table are usually essential pieces of information.

D Be sure to read **parenthetical text** if there is any. This information may help clarify meaning, provide examples, or further explain an entry.

E Pay attention to **notes** and **asterisks** (*) and their accompanying footnotes. These will help clarify exceptions or exemptions to the rules, or add additional detail.

PRACTICE AND APPLY

Reread the TSA page and then answer the following questions:

1. Are knives allowed as a carry-on item? as a checked item?

2. Name the three types of scissors that are allowed as carry-on items.

3. Walking canes are allowed as a carry-on and as a checked item. Why do they need to be inspected?

4. Guidelines for acceptable carry-on and checked items on flights are revised periodically. Verify that the items listed here are up-to-date by checking the Transportation Security Administration Web site: www.tsa.gov. Search the site for a list of permitted and prohibited items. Key words to look for are *Travelers* and *Prohibited Items*.

RULES AND REGULATIONS FOR CARRY-ON ITEMS IN AIR TRAVEL

U.S. Department of Homeland Security
Transportation Security Administration
Arlington, VA 22202

A Permitted and Prohibited Items

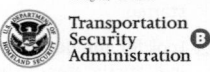 **B** Transportation Security Administration

C Can I take it?	Carry-on	Checked
Personal Items		
Cigar Cutters	Yes	Yes
Corkscrews	Yes	Yes
Cuticle Cutters	Yes	Yes
Eyeglass Repair Tools (including screwdrivers) **D**	Yes	Yes
Eyelash Curlers	Yes	Yes
Knitting and Crochet Needles	Yes	Yes
Knives - prohibited as carry-on except for plastic or round bladed butter knives.	No	Yes
Nail Clippers	Yes	Yes
Nail Files	Yes	Yes
Personal care or toiletries with aerosols, in limited quantities (such as hairsprays, deodorants)	Yes	Yes
Safety Razors (including disposable razors)	Yes	Yes
Scissors - plastic or metal with blunt tips	Yes	Yes
Scissors - metal with pointed tips and blades longer than four inches in length	No	Yes
Toy Transformer Robots	Yes	Yes
Toy Weapons (if not realistic replicas)	Yes	Yes
Tweezers	Yes	Yes
Umbrellas (allowed in carry-on baggage once they have been inspected to ensure that prohibited items are not concealed)	Yes	Yes
Walking Canes (allowed in carry-on baggage once they have been inspected to ensure that prohibited items are not concealed)	Yes	Yes

E Note Some personal care items containing aerosol are regulated as hazardous materials. The FAA regulates hazardous materials. This information is summarized at www.faa.gov, click on *Passengers*, then *Preparing to Fly*.

Medication and Special Needs Devices		
Braille Note-Taker, Slate and Stylus, Augmentation Devices	Yes	Yes
Diabetes-Related Supplies/Equipment, (once inspected to ensure prohibited items are not concealed) including: insulin and insulin loaded dispensing products; vials or box of individual vials; jet injectors; pens; infusers; and preloaded syringes; and an unlimited number of unused syringes, when accompanied by insulin; lancets; blood glucose meters; blood glucose meter test strips; insulin pumps; and insulin pump supplies. Insulin in any form or dispenser must be properly marked with a professionally printed label identifying the medication or manufacturer's name or pharmaceutical label.	Yes	Yes
Nitroglycerine pills or spray for medical use (if properly marked with a professionally printed label identifying the medication or manufacturer's name or pharmaceutical label)	Yes	Yes
Ostomy Scissors All scissors with blades four inches or less	Yes	Yes
Prosthetic Device Tools and Appliances, including drill, allen wrenches, pullsleeves used to put on or remove prosthetic devices, if carried by the individual with the prosthetic device or his or her companion	Yes	Yes

U.S. Department of Homeland Security
TSA- Rev. 12-1-2005

Page 3 of 5

4.5 READING A WORKPLACE DOCUMENT

Workplace documents are materials that are produced or used within a workplace, usually to aid in the functioning of a business. These documents include meeting minutes, sales reports, statements of company policy or organizational structure, and explanations of operating procedures. Workplace documents also include memos, business letters, job applications, and résumés.

Strategies for Reading

A Use **headings** and **subheadings** to help you locate information that is relevant or important to you.

B Read a workplace document slowly and carefully, as it may contain **details** that should not be overlooked.

C Notice how to contact the creator of the document. You will need this information to clear up anything that you don't understand.

PRACTICE AND APPLY

Refer to the company policy statement to answer the following questions:

1. How long does an employee need to work at HBA before he or she is eligible for three weeks of paid vacation?

2. Under which section(s) would you look if you traveled extensively for work and were interested in insurance that specifically covered accidents while traveling?

3. Does the company offer supplemental life insurance? Does the company or the employee pay for it?

4. How much short-term disability coverage does the company provide free of charge to an employee?

COMPANY POLICY STATEMENT

HBA Company
Employee Benefits Policy

Medical Benefits

HBA offers four medical choices, which include two options that are at no cost to our employees. We also offer dental, vision, and an Employee Assistance Program at no cost to employees.

Retirement and Savings Plan

HBA's contributions to your retirement plan are guaranteed at 5% of your annual earnings, plus up to an additional 10% variable contribution (based on company performance).

Life Insurance

At no cost to the employee, life insurance is provided for three times his or her annual base salary, not to exceed $500,000. Employees may also elect to purchase supplemental life insurance for themselves, their spouse, and eligible dependent children.

Disability Programs

Accidental Death and Dismemberment Insurance—Eligible employees are covered for up to three times their annual base salary, not to exceed $500,000, depending on the extent of injury.

Short-Term Disability—Eligible employees receive a short-term disability benefit of 60% of their salary and may elect to "buy-up" additional coverage to a maximum 70% benefit.

Long-Term Disability—Eligible employees are provided coverage at a benefit amount of 50% of their salary and may elect to "buy-up" additional coverage to a total benefit level of 67%.

Travel Accident Insurance—Eligible employees are covered for $35,000 to $500,000, depending on their annual base salary.

Time Off Benefits

Vacation—Employees earn time off at the rate of two weeks per year for the first five years of employment, three weeks per year after five years of employment, and four weeks per year after ten years of employment.

Sick Leave—Employees earn at a rate of one week per year.

Holidays—Employees are paid for eight calendar holidays. Employees also receive three floating holidays per calendar year after six months of employment.

If you have any questions, contact the HBA Human Resources Department.

PRACTICE AND APPLY

ANSWERS

1. *five years*

2. *Travel Accident Insurance*

3. *The company provides supplemental life insurance, which the employee purchases.*

4. *60% of the employee's salary*

4.6 READING ELECTRONIC TEXT

Electronic text is any text that is in a form that a computer can store and display on a screen. Electronic text can be part of Web pages, CD-ROMs, search engines, and documents that you create with your computer software. Like books, Web pages often provide aids to finding information. However, each Web page is designed differently, and information is not in the same location on each page. It is important to know the functions of different parts of a Web page so that you can easily find the information you want.

Strategies for Reading

A Look at the **title** of a page to determine what topics it covers.

B For an online source, such as a Web page or a search engine, note the **Web address,** known as a **URL** (uniform resource locator), in case you need to return to the page later or cite it as a source.

C Look for the **menu options,** or navigation options that allow you to navigate through the site's main categories and pages. These options are **links** to other pages providing more in-depth information on the topic listed.

D Read **introductory text** to get a sense of the site's subject matter and purpose.

E Use **hyperlinks** to get to other pages on the site. Hyperlinks may lead to pages listed in the menu options or to other Web sites related in subject matter.

F Look for **graphic aids,** such as photos, illustrations, or animation, that will provide you with more information about the site's topic(s).

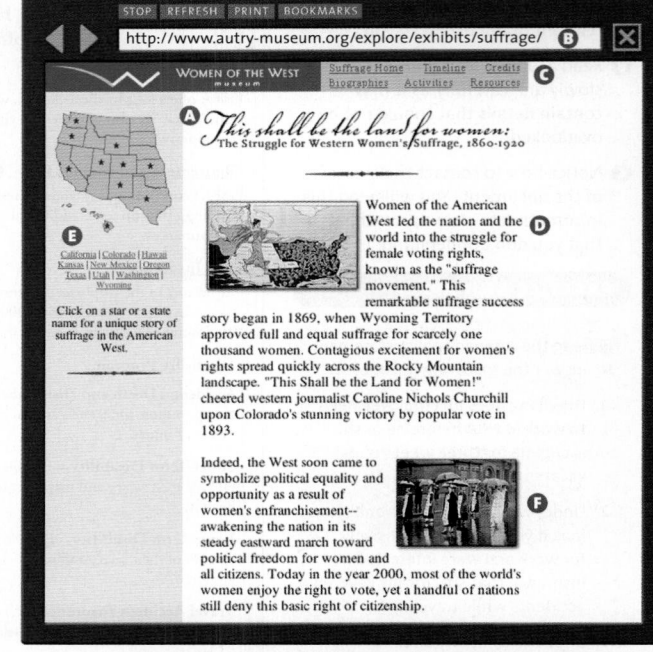

PRACTICE AND APPLY

1. What is the topic of this site?

2. If you were searching for information on suffrage in New Mexico, which links or hyperlinks would you use?

3. Who has produced this Web site?

4. Verify the information on women's suffrage in the Wyoming Territory presented on this Web page by consulting a reference source, such as an encyclopedia, or a government document.

PRACTICE AND APPLY

ANSWERS

1. *The topic is the struggle for Western women's suffrage between 1860 and 1920.*

2. *"New Mexico" or the star on the state of New Mexico*

3. *Women of the West museum*

4. *Students should consult government or encyclopedic sources to determine whether or not the site's information is accurate. Have students create a report comparing the information on the Web site with that in the other reference sources.*

5 Reading Persuasive Texts

5.1 ANALYZING AN ARGUMENT

An **argument** expresses a position on an issue or problem and supports it with reasons and evidence. Being able to analyze and evaluate arguments will help you distinguish between claims you should accept and those you should not. A sound argument should appeal strictly to reason. However, arguments are often used in texts that also contain other types of persuasive devices. An argument includes the following elements:

- A **claim** is the writer's position on an issue or problem.

- **Support** is any material that serves to prove a claim. In an argument, support usually consists of reasons and evidence.

- **Reasons** are declarations made to justify an action, a decision, or a belief—for example, "You should sleep on a good mattress *in order to avoid spinal problems.*"

- **Evidence** consists of the specific references, quotations, facts, examples, and opinions that support a claim. Evidence may also consist of statistics, reports of personal experience, or the views of experts.

- A **counterargument** is an argument made to oppose another argument. A good argument anticipates the opposition's objections and provides counterarguments to disprove or answer them.

Claim	Walt Whitman is one of the most important figures in American poetry.
Reason	He experimented with poetic form and content and created a quintessentially American voice in literature.
Evidence	His poetry influenced generations of poets. His poems celebrated the diversity and spirit of American culture.
Counterargument	No American poet before Whitman broke with tradition in the ways he did.

In the early 1900s, Elinore Pruitt Stewart (formerly Rupert), was living in Burnt Fork, Wyoming, as a homesteader, a person who received public land free of charge under the Homestead Act of 1862. In the following letter to a friend, she makes an argument for homestead living over an impoverished city existence. Use a chart like the one shown to identify the claim, reason, evidence, and counterargument in her letter.

> January 23, 1913
>
> Dear Mrs. Coney,—
> . . . When I read of the hard times among the Denver poor, I feel like urging them every one to get out and file on land. I am very enthusiastic about women homesteading. It really requires less strength and labor to raise plenty to satisfy a large family than it does to go out to wash, with the added satisfaction of knowing that their job will not be lost to them if they care to keep it. Even if improving the place does go slowly, it is that much done to stay done. Whatever is raised is the homesteader's own, and there is no house-rent to pay. This year Jerrine cut and dropped enough potatoes to raise a ton of fine potatoes. She wanted to try, so we let her, and you will remember that she is but six years old. We had a man to break the ground and cover the potatoes for her and the man irrigated them once. That was all that was done until digging time, when they were ploughed out and Jerrine picked them up. Any woman strong enough to go out by the day could have done every bit of the work and put in two or three times that much, and it would have been so much more pleasant than to work so hard in the city and then be on starvation rations in the winter.
> To me, homesteading is the solution of all poverty's problems, but I realize that temperament has much to do with success in any undertaking, and persons afraid of coyotes and work and loneliness had better let ranching alone. At the same time, any woman who can stand her own company, can see the beauty of the sunset, loves growing things, and is willing to put in as much time at careful labor as she does over the washtub, will certainly succeed; will have independence, plenty to eat all the time, and a home of her own in the end.

PRACTICE AND APPLY

ANSWERS

Claim
Women homesteading is the solution to poverty's problems.

Reason
Homesteading means job security and a home.

Evidence
It is possible to plant, grow, and harvest enough food for a family to eat through the winter.

Counterargument
It is not for those afraid of coyotes and hard work and loneliness, but for those who can do it, it will result in independence, plenty of food, and a home of one's own.

PRACTICE AND APPLY

ANSWERS

Answers could include the following:

"feel so splendid": transfer

"local celebrities . . . join them": testimonial, snob appeal

"necessities to less fortunate . . . least we can do": appeal to pity

---

5.2 RECOGNIZING PERSUASIVE TECHNIQUES

Persuasive texts typically rely on more than just the logical appeal of an argument to be convincing. They also rely on ethical and emotional appeals, as well as other **persuasive techniques**—devices that can sway you to adopt a position or take an action.

The chart shown here explains several of these techniques. Learn to recognize them, and you will be less likely to be influenced by them.

Persuasive Technique	Example
Appeals by Association	
Bandwagon appeal Suggests that a person should believe or do something because "everyone else" does	Join the millions who've contributed to The Cause: buy your 'Be Well' bracelet today.
Testimonial Relies on endorsements from well-known people or satisfied customers	DJ Super Dawg keeps songs spinning all day long with his new CompactM3 disc player. Give it a whirl!
Snob appeal Taps into people's desire to be special or part of an elite group	In Smart and Sassy cosmetics, you'll look and feel like the princess you are.
Transfer Connnects a product, candidate, or cause with a positive emotion or idea	Rediscover peace and tranquility with Back in Balance aromatherapy candles.
Appeal to loyalty Relies on people's affiliation with a particular group	Only Substantial Bank offers long-term customers better rates.
Emotional Appeals	
Appeals to pity, fear, or vanity Use strong feelings, rather than facts, to persuade	The cost of one candy bar can help buy a whole meal for a starving family.
Word Choice	
Glittering generality Makes a generalization that includes a word or phrase with positive connotations, such as *freedom* and *honor,* to promote a product or idea.	Improve your children's future: plant a tree on World Tree Day.

PRACTICE AND APPLY

Identify the persuasive techniques used in the model.

The Real Scoop

On my last trip to the Splendid Dan's Ice Cream Shoppe to get a Swirling Fantasia Double Dip Delight, I was thrilled to find yet another reason that makes buying dessert at Dan's feel so splendid. During the next 30 days at the downtown location, a whopping 40 percent of Dan's proceeds will go toward helping the homeless in our city. Forty percent! No wonder so many local celebrities, like news anchor Tandy Marquez and Mayor Donald Townsend, have been spotted at Dan's. They know that with each purchase, they are also providing food, clothing, and shelter for those in need. If you join them, you'll have not only the most amazing ice cream on the planet, but also the added joy of providing life's basic necessities to the less fortunate. It's the least we can do to better our city, so stop by Splendid Dan's—he's got the "real scoop."

5.3 ANALYZING LOGIC AND REASONING

When you evaluate an argument, you need to look closely at the writer's logic and reasoning. In doing this, it is helpful to identify the type of reasoning the writer is using.

The Inductive Mode of Reasoning

When a writer leads from specific evidence to a general principle or generalization, that writer is using **inductive reasoning.** Here is an example of inductive reasoning.

SPECIFIC FACTS

Fact 1 Harriet Beecher Stowe's *Uncle Tom's Cabin* helped alert Americans to the horrors of slavery.

Fact 2 Rachel Carson's *Silent Spring* helped make the public aware of the dangers of overuse of pesticides.

Fact 3 Betty Friedan's *The Feminine Mystique* prompted women to seek equal rights.

GENERALIZATION

Literature can sometimes help to shape public opinion.

Strategies for Determining the Soundness of Inductive Arguments

Ask yourself the following questions to evaluate an inductive argument:

- **Is the evidence valid and sufficient support for the conclusion?** Inaccurate facts lead to inaccurate conclusions. Make sure all facts are accurate.

- **Does the conclusion follow logically from the evidence?** Make sure the writer has used sound reasons—those that can be proved—as the basis for the conclusion and has avoided logical fallacies, such as circular reasoning and oversimplification.

- **Is the evidence drawn from a large enough sample?** The three facts listed in the example are enough to support the claim. By qualifying the generalization with words such as *sometimes, some,* or *many,* the writer indicates the generalization is limited to a specific group.

The Deductive Mode of Reasoning

When a writer arrives at a conclusion by applying a general principle to a specific situation, the writer is using **deductive reasoning.** Here's an example.

People have the right to revolt when oppressed.	General principle or premise

▼

| The American colonies are oppressed by British rule. | Specific situation |

▼

| The American colonies are justified in fighting for freedom from British rule. | Specific conclusion |

Strategies for Determining the Soundness of Deductive Arguments

Ask yourself the following questions to evaluate a deductive argument:

- **Is the general principle stated, or is it implied?** Note that writers often use deductive reasoning in an argument without stating the general principle. They assume readers will understand the principle. You may want to identify the general principle for yourself.

- **Is the general principle sound?** Don't assume the general principle is sound. Determine whether it is proven.

- **Is the conclusion valid?** To be valid, a conclusion in a deductive argument must follow logically from the general principle and the specific situation.

The following chart shows two conclusions drawn from the same general principle.

General Principle: All government offices were closed last Monday.	
Accurate Deduction	**Inaccurate Deduction**
West Post Office is a government office; therefore, West Post Office was closed last Monday.	Soon-Lin's Spa was closed last Monday; therefore, Soon-Lin's Spa is a government office.

The conclusion that Soon-Lin's Spa is a government office does not make logical sense because other factors determine whether or not it is a government office.

PRACTICE AND APPLY

Identify the mode of reasoning used in the following:

Detailed research shows that using a cell phone while driving is a key cause of traffic accidents. Many states have already passed laws making "hands free" devices mandatory for cell phone users while driving. However, ear pieces or speaker phones provide very few true safety benefits. The problem is not the way in which a driver is distracted, but the distraction itself. Looking up a phone number, dialing, and concentrating on the conversation can all take a driver's focus, and eyes, off the road.

Betsie Edens, a 19-year-old college student, says she uses her cell phone to get in touch with family, old friends, and fellow college students while making the three-hour drive from her parent's house to Denton State University. "I talk on the phone or send text messages at least two and a half of the three hours it takes to get there," she says.

Betsie is one of millions of teenagers world-wide who do more talking on a cell phone than safe driving. It is time these unsafe drivers focus more on the road and less on their friends' gossip. For the sake of everybody's safety, cell phones must be turned off while on the road.

PRACTICE AND APPLY

ANSWERS

Deductive reasoning is used.

> *General principle: Distractions while driving are unsafe.*
>
> *Specific situation: Using cell phones while driving is a distraction.*
>
> *Specific conclusion: Cell phones must be turned off while driving.*

Identifying Faulty Reasoning

Sometimes an argument at first appears to make sense but isn't valid because it is based on a fallacy. A **fallacy** is an error in logic. Learn to recognize these common fallacies.

TYPE OF FALLACY	DEFINITION	EXAMPLE
Circular reasoning	Supporting a statement by simply repeating it in different words	Sport utility vehicles are popular **because more people buy them than any other category of new cars.**
Either/or fallacy	A statement that suggests that there are only two choices available in a situation that really offers more than two options	**Either** we raise the legal driving age **or** accidents caused by teenage drivers will continue to happen.
Oversimplification	An explanation of a complex situation or problem as if it were much more simple than it is	If we would only be more tolerant of people's differences, there would be **no more wars.**
Overgeneralization	A generalization that is too broad. You can often recognize overgeneralizations by the use of words such as *all, everyone, every time, anything, no one,* and *none.*	**Every time** I want to do something my way, my parents say no.
Stereotyping	A dangerous type of overgeneralization. Stereotypes are broad statements about people on the basis of their gender, ethnicity, race, or political, social, professional, or religious group.	**People who work for large corporations** are followers, not leaders.
Attacking the person or name-calling	An attempt to discredit an idea by attacking the person or group associated with it. Candidates often engage in name-calling during political campaigns.	The governor wants to eliminate candy machines in school cafeterias, but **he doesn't know what he's talking about.**
Evading the issue	Refuting an objection with arguments and evidence that do not address its central point	I know I wasn't supposed to use the car last night, **but I did fill up the tank and check the tire pressure.**
Non sequitur	A conclusion that does not follow logically from the "proof" offered to support it. A non sequitur is sometimes used to win an argument by diverting the reader's attention to proof that can't be challenged.	Mr. Crandall is my guidance counselor. **I will definitely get accepted to a private college.**
False cause	The mistake of assuming that because one event occurred after another event in time, the first event caused the second one to occur	The cheerleading squad did the Super Slam Dance, **and because of that, Donny slam-dunked the basketball, and we won the game.**
False analogy	A comparison that doesn't hold up because of a critical difference between the two subjects	Jenny didn't do well in Spanish, **so she'll probably fail German as well.**
Hasty generalization	A conclusion drawn from too little evidence or from evidence that is biased	Two jet planes crashed this year. **Air travel is extremely unsafe.**

Look for examples of logical fallacies in the following argument. Identify each one and explain why you identified it as such.

> Elephants should be banned from circuses. Leaders of circus companies claim that healthy living environments are provided for the animals, but they, like most business owners, are liars. Sharp bullhooks are used for training, and the elephants are beaten severely everyday. Abuse makes animals more aggressive, everyone knows that. In the last 15 years, captive elephants have killed 65 people and injured 130, so it is clear the elephants are abused by their trainers. Legislation to stop this cruelty should be passed immediately!

5.4 EVALUATING PERSUASIVE TEXTS

Learning how to evaluate persuasive texts and identify bias will help you become more selective when doing research and also help you improve your own reasoning and arguing skills. **Bias** is an inclination for or against a particular opinion or viewpoint. A writer may reveal a strongly positive or negative opinion on an issue by presenting only one way of looking at it or by heavily weighting the evidence on one side of the argument. Additionally, the presence of either of the following is often a sign of bias:

Loaded language consists of words with strongly positive or negative connotations that are intended to influence a reader's attitude.

EXAMPLE: *The superior All-Star Road Warrior offers unparalleled excellence in all-wheel-drive capability and can outperform any car on the road.* (*Superior, unparalleled, excellence,* and *outperform* have positive connotations.)

Propaganda is any form of communication that is so distorted that it conveys false or misleading information. Many logical fallacies—such as name-calling, the either/or fallacy, and false causes—are often used in propaganda. The following example shows an oversimplification. The writer uses one fact to support a particular point of view but does not reveal another fact that does not support that viewpoint.

EXAMPLE: *Since the new administration took office, unemployment rates have been cut in half.* (The writer does not include information about legislation, passed by the previous administration, that created thousands of jobs.)

*For more information, see **Identifying Faulty Reasoning,** page R22.*

Strategies for Evaluating Evidence

It is important to have a set of standards by which you can evaluate persuasive texts. Use the questions below to help you critically assess facts and opinions that are presented as evidence.

- **Are the facts presented verifiable?** Facts can be proved by eyewitness accounts, authoritative sources such as encyclopedias and almanacs, experts, or research.

- **Are the opinions presented credible?** Any opinions offered should be supported by facts, research, eyewitness accounts, or the opinions of experts on the topic.

- **Is the evidence thorough?** Thorough evidence leaves no reasonable questions unanswered. If a choice is offered, background for making the choice should be provided. If taking a side is called for, all sides of the issue should be presented.

- **Is the evidence biased?** Be alert to evidence that contains loaded language or other signs of bias.

- **Is the evidence authoritative?** The people, groups, or organizations that provided the evidence should have credentials that verify their credibility.

- **Is it important that the evidence be current?** Where timeliness is crucial, as in the areas of medicine and technology, the evidence should reflect the latest developments in the areas.

PRACTICE AND APPLY

ANSWERS

Stereotyping, name-calling: "Leaders of circus companies claim that healthy living environments are provided for the animals, but they, like most business owners, are liars."

Overgeneralization: "Abuse makes animals more aggressive, everyone knows that."

Hasty generalization: "In the last 15 years, captive elephants have killed 65 people and injured 130, so it is clear the elephants are abused by their trainers."

PRACTICE AND APPLY

ANSWERS

Facts: *speed bumps being built, cars park bumper to bumper, cars stop in the middle of the street*

Opinions: *Speed bumps are "unnecessary"; no one will be killed if there aren't any speed bumps.*

Bias: *"[N]o-good politicians spend a lot of tax-payer money on a ridiculous irritation"; "they must figure wrongly"; "it is impossible to drive fast on these streets anyway!"*

PRACTICE AND APPLY

ANSWERS

Students' responses will vary but should evaluate the strength of the claim, the evidence supporting the claim, and the counterarguments.

Possible answer may include: *The claim is that the town needs to build an ice skating rink. Some of the evidence is adequate, but includes logical fallacies. The writer does not adequately address the counterargument presented.*

Read the argument below. Identify the facts, opinions, and elements of bias.

> In our city neighborhood, unnecessary speed bumps are being built on residential streets. Cars park bumper to bumper along both sides of the street, day and night. There is no place to pull over, causing cars to stop in the middle of the street to pick up and drop off passengers. My point is that it is impossible to drive fast on these streets anyway! Why do no-good politicians spend a lot of taxpayer money on a ridiculous irritation for drivers? They must figure wrongly that either they build speed bumps, or some little kid will get killed. That's never happened and it never will.

Strategies for Evaluating an Argument

Make sure that all or most of the following statements are true:

- The argument presents a claim or thesis.
- The claim is connected to its support by a general principle that most readers would readily agree with. Valid general principle: *It is the job of a corporation to provide adequate health benefits to full-time employees.* Invalid general principle: *It is the job of a corporation to ensure its employees are healthy and physically fit.*
- The reasons make sense.
- The reasons are presented in a logical and effective order.
- The claim and all reasons are adequately supported by sound evidence.
- The evidence is adequate, accurate, and appropriate.
- The logic is sound. There are no instances of faulty reasoning.
- The argument adequately anticipates and addresses reader concerns and counterclaims with counterarguments.

Use the preceding criteria to evaluate the strength of the following editorial:

> This town needs an ice skating rink. Everybody knows that ice skating is the only real way to learn balance and coordination, while also exercising. It is, after all, an Olympic event. That is why I believe it is the responsibility of the town council to put aside funding for a year-round ice skating rink.
>
> Our town has always believed that our children's future relies on good development. For intellectual stimulation, the council has provided the public library and the Nature Museum. For creativity, the council has funded the Community Art Center, where kids can learn to make pottery, paint, dance, and sing. But when it comes to a place where youth can go to develop physical skills of balance, rhythm, and strength, we have absolutely nothing.
>
> We also need a rink because ice skating is fun! The town council members are themselves boring individuals and don't think kids should have fun. As one member put it, "There are many places in this town built especially with youth in mind. Ice skating is not a top priority on our list of community needs this year." They obviously feel this way because our football team came in fifth in the conference last year.
>
> But the biggest reason we need an ice skating rink is so that kids can have a place to ice skate. And let's not forget, adults like ice skating, too. Most of the people who make it to the Olympics are over 18.
>
> Either the town council will help our children develop by putting up the rink, or they prove themselves stingy politicians who do not have the town's best interest at heart.

6 Adjusting Reading Rate to Purpose

You may need to change the way you read certain texts in order to understand what you read. To properly adjust the way you read, you need to be aware of what you want to get out of the text you are reading. Once you know your purpose for reading, you can adjust the speed at which you read in response to your purpose and the difficulty of the material.

Determine Your Purpose for Reading

You read different types of materials for different purposes. You may read a novel for enjoyment. You may read a textbook unit to learn a new concept or to master the content for a test. When you read for enjoyment, you naturally read at a pace that is comfortable for you. When you read for information, you need to read material more slowly and thoroughly. When you are being tested on material, you may think you have to read fast, especially if the test is being timed. However, you can actually increase your understanding of the material if you slow down.

Determine Your Reading Rate

The rate at which you read most comfortably is called your **independent reading level.** It is the rate that you use to read materials that you enjoy. To learn to adjust your reading rate to read materials for other purposes, you need to be aware of your independent reading level. You can figure out your reading level by following these steps:

1. Select a passage from a book or story you enjoy.
2. Have a friend or classmate time you as you begin reading the passage silently.
3. Read at the rate that is most comfortable for you.
4. Stop when your friend or classmate tells you one minute has passed.
5. Determine the number of words you read in that minute and write down the number.
6. Repeat the process at least two more times, using different passages.
7. Add the numbers and divide the sum by the number of times your friend timed you. The number you end up with is the average number of words you read per minute—your independent reading rate.

Reading Techniques for Informational Material

Use the following techniques to adapt your reading for informational texts, to prepare for tests, and to better understand what you read:

- **Skimming** is reading quickly to get the general idea of a text. To skim, read only the title, headings, graphic aids, and highlighted words of the text, as well as the first sentence of each paragraph. In addition, read any introduction, conclusion, or summary. Skimming can be especially useful when taking a test. Before reading a passage, you can skim questions that follow it in order to find out what is expected and to better focus on the important ideas in the text.

  When researching a topic, skimming can help you determine whether a source has information that is pertinent to your topic.

- **Scanning** is reading quickly to find a specific piece of information, such as a fact or a definition. When you scan, your eyes sweep across a page, looking for key words that may lead you to the information you want. Use scanning to review for tests and to find answers to questions.

- **Changing pace** is speeding up or slowing down the rate at which you read parts of a particular text. When you come across familiar concepts, you might be able to speed up without misunderstanding them. When you encounter unfamiliar concepts or material presented in an unpredictable way, however, you may need to slow down to process and absorb the information better.

WATCH OUT! Reading too slowly can diminish your ability to comprehend what you read. Make sure you aren't just reading one word at a time.

PRACTICE AND APPLY

Find an article in a magazine or textbook. Skim the article. Then answer the following questions:

1. What did you notice about the organization of the article?

2. What is the main idea of the article?

PRACTICE AND APPLY

ANSWERS

Accept answers that provide an accurate description of the organization of the article and its main ideas.

Writing is a process, a journey of discovery in which you can explore your thoughts, experiment with ideas, and search for connections. Through writing, you can explore and record your thoughts, feelings, and ideas for yourself alone, or you can communicate them to an audience.

Included in this handbook as indicated: **W1.1** (p. R26), **W1.9** (pgs. R26–R27), **W2.1a** (pgs. R34–R35), **W2.1b** (p. R34), **W2.1c** (p. R34), **W2.1d** (p. R34), **W2.1e** (p. R34), **W2.5a** (pgs. R40, R42), **W2.5b** (pgs. R40, R42), **W2.5c** (pgs. R40–R41), **W2.5d** (pgs. R40–R42), **LC1.3** (pgs. R40–R43)

WRITING TOOLS
Go to the **Writing Center** at **ClassZone.com** for interactive models, publishing ideas, and other support.

1 The Writing Process

The writing process consists of the following stages: prewriting, drafting, revising and editing, proofreading, and publishing. These are not stages that you must complete in a set order. Rather, you may return to an earlier stage at any time to improve your writing.

1.1 PREWRITING

In the prewriting stage, you explore what you want to write about, what your purpose for writing is, whom you are writing for, and what form you will use to express your ideas. Ask yourself the following questions to get started.

Topic	• Is my topic assigned, or can I choose it?
	• What am I interested in writing about?
Purpose	• Am I writing to entertain, to inform, or to persuade—or some combination of these?
	• What effect do I want to have on my readers?
Audience	• Who is the audience?
	• What might the audience members already know about my topic?
	• What about the topic might interest them?
Format	• Which format will work best: essay, poem, speech, short story, article, or research paper?

Find Ideas for Writing

Here are some methods for generating topics:

- Browse through magazines, newspapers, and Web sites.

- Start a file of articles to save for future reference.

- With a group, brainstorm as many ideas as you can. Compile your ideas into a list.

- Interview an expert on a particular topic.

- Write down anything that comes into your head.

- Use a cluster map to explore subordinate ideas that relate to a general topic.

Organize Ideas

Once you've chosen a topic, you will need to compile and organize your ideas. If you are writing a description, you may need to gather sensory details. Or you may need to record information from different sources for an essay or a research paper. To record notes from sources you read or view, use any or all of these methods:

- **Summarize:** Briefly retell the main ideas of a piece of writing in your own words.

- **Paraphrase:** Restate all or almost all of the information in your own words.

- **Quote:** Record the author's exact words.

Depending on what form your writing takes, you may also need to arrange your ideas in a certain pattern.

*For more information, see the **Writing Handbook**, pages R32–R39.*

1.2 DRAFTING

In the drafting stage, you put your ideas on paper and allow them to develop and change as you write. You don't need to worry about correct grammar and spelling at this stage. There are two ways that you can write a draft:

Discovery drafting is a good approach when you are not quite sure what you think about your subject. You just start writing and let your feelings and ideas lead you in developing the topic.

Planned drafting may work better if you know that your ideas have to be arranged in a certain way, as in a research paper. Try making a writing plan or an informal outline before you begin drafting.

1.3 REVISING AND EDITING

The revising and editing stage allows you to polish your draft and make changes in its content, organization, and style. Use the questions that follow to assess problems and determine what changes would improve your work.

- Does my writing have a **main idea** or central focus? Is my thesis clear?

- Have I used **precise** nouns, verbs, and modifiers?

- Have I incorporated **adequate detail** and **evidence?** Where might I include a telling detail, a revealing statistic, or a vivid example?

- Is my writing **unified?** Do all ideas and supporting details pertain to my main idea or advance my thesis?

- Is my writing clear and **coherent?** Is the flow of sentences and paragraphs smooth and logical?

- Have I used a consistent **point of view?**

- Do I need to add **transitional words, phrases,** or **sentences** to clarify relationships among ideas?

- Have I used a **variety of sentence types?** Are they well constructed? What sentences might I combine to improve the rhythm of my writing?

- Have I used a **tone** appropriate for my audience and purpose?

1.4 PROOFREADING

When you are satisfied with your revision, proofread your paper for mistakes in grammar, usage, and mechanics. You may want to do this several times, looking for a different type of mistake each time. Use the following questions to help you correct errors:

- Have I corrected any errors in **subject-verb agreement** and **pronoun-antecedent agreement?**

- Have I double-checked for errors in **confusing word pairs,** such as *it's/its, than/then,* and *too/to?*

- Have I corrected any **run-on sentences** and **sentence fragments?**

- Have I followed rules for **correct capitalization?**

- Have I used **punctuation marks** correctly?

- Have I checked the **spellings of all unfamiliar words** in the dictionary?

TIP If possible, don't begin proofreading just after you've finished writing. Put your work away for at least a few hours. When you return to it, it will be easier for you to identify and correct mistakes.

*For more information, see the **Grammar Handbook** and the **Vocabulary and Spelling Handbook,** pages R50–R79.*

Use the proofreading symbols in the chart to mark changes on your draft.

Proofreading Symbols	
∧ Add letters or words.	/ Make a capital letter lowercase.
⊙ Add a period.	¶ Begin a new paragraph.
≡ Capitalize a letter.	﹈ Delete letters or words.
⊃ Close up space.	∩ Switch the positions of letters or words.
∧ Add a comma.	

1.5 PUBLISHING AND REFLECTING

Always consider sharing your finished writing with a wider audience. Reflecting on your writing is another good way to finish a project.

Publishing Ideas

- Post your writing on a Weblog.

- Create a multimedia presentation and share it with classmates.

- Publish your writing in a school newspaper, local newspaper, or literary magazine.

- Present your work orally in a report, speech, reading, or dramatic performance.

Reflecting on Your Writing

Think about your writing process and whether you would like to add what you have written to your writing portfolio. You might attach a note in which you answer questions like these:

- Which parts of the process did I find easiest? Which parts were more difficult?

- What was the biggest problem I faced during the writing process? How did I solve the problem?

- What changes have occurred in my writing style?

- Have I noticed any features in the writing of published authors or my peers that I can apply to my own work?

1.6 PEER RESPONSE

Peer response consists of the suggestions and comments you make about the writing of your peers and also the comments and suggestions they make about your writing. You can ask a peer reader for help at any time in the writing process.

Using Peer Response as a Writer

- Indicate whether you are more interested in feedback about your ideas or about your presentation of them.

- Ask open-ended questions that will help you get specific information about your writing. Avoid questions that require yes-or-no answers.

- Encourage your readers to be honest.

Being a Peer Reader

- Respect the writer's feelings.

- Offer positive reactions first.

- Make sure you understand what kind of feedback the writer is looking for, and then respond accordingly.

For more information on the writing process , see the **Introductory Unit,** *pages 11–13.*

2 Building Blocks of Good Writing

Whatever your purpose in writing, you need to capture your reader's interest and organize your thoughts clearly.

2.1 INTRODUCTIONS

An introduction should capture your reader's attention and present a thesis statement.

Kinds of Introductions

There are a number of ways to begin an introduction. The one you choose depends on who the audience is and on your purpose for writing.

Make a Surprising Statement Beginning with a startling statement or an interesting fact can arouse your reader's curiosity about a subject, as in the following model.

> **MODEL**
>
> Although she wrote nearly 1,800 poems, Emily Dickinson probably did not want to publish any of them. Most of her poems were first published almost 100 years after they were written.

Provide a Description A vivid description sets a mood and brings a scene to life for your reader. In the following model, details about a horse's actions set the tone for an essay about horse training.

> **MODEL**
>
> Dust flew as the horse stomped the ground. The puffs of moisture blowing from his nostrils and the laid-back ears let the spectators know the stomping was not some clever performance. As the trainer approached cautiously, she could see the wild look in the horse's eyes.

Pose a Question Beginning with a question can make your reader want to read on to find out the answer. The following introduction asks questions about the fate of a well-known and respected writer.

> **MODEL**
>
> Zora Neale Hurston was one of the most successful writers of the Harlem Renaissance period. She wrote plays, novels, and essays that were enthusiastically received. How did it happen that such a talented and popular author died in poverty?

Relate an Anecdote Beginning with an anecdote, or brief story, can hook your reader and help you make a point in a dramatic way. The following anecdote introduces an interview with a retired school teacher.

> **MODEL**
>
> "Down in the valley
> Where the green grass grows. . . ."
> The words and rhythm of the chanting children on the playground brought tears to Clara Jones's eyes. Though she could barely see the forms of the youngsters, she knew exactly the structure of the old jump-rope game they played.
> I began softly to ask her about her 45 years of teaching at Pleasant Hills Elementary School.

Address the Reader Speaking directly to your reader establishes a friendly, informal tone and involves the reader in your topic.

MODEL

Do you know how many trees will be cut down for the new shopping mall to be built? Do you know how many families will have to give up their homes so that some shoppers can have yet another department store that sells the same things as five others in our area?

Begin with a Thesis Statement A thesis statement expressing a main idea may be woven into both the beginning and the end of a piece of nonfiction writing. The following is a thesis statement that introduces a literary analysis.

MODEL

In "The Death of the Hired Man," Robert Frost uses the hushed conversation of a husband and wife to explore the meaning of a lonely person's life. The whole poem seems to take place in whispers, though the message is strong.

TIP To write a strong introduction, you may want to try more than one of the methods and then decide which is the most effective for your purpose and audience.

2.2 PARAGRAPHS

A paragraph is made up of sentences that work together to develop an idea or accomplish a purpose. Whether or not it contains a topic sentence stating the main idea, a good paragraph must have unity and coherence.

Unity

A paragraph has unity when all the sentences support and develop one stated or implied idea. Use the following techniques to create unity in your paragraphs:

Write a Topic Sentence A topic sentence states the main idea of the paragraph; all other sentences in the paragraph provide supporting details. A topic sentence is often the first sentence in a paragraph. However, it may also appear later in a paragraph or at the end, to summarize or reinforce the main idea, as shown in the model that follows.

MODEL

Cats purr when they are being stroked by humans. Cats purr when they cuddle up with other cats. Many cats purr when they are in the veterinarian's office. Some cats purr when they are frightened. Since cats seem to purr in situations of both joy and stress, the cause of purring is still a mystery to humans.

Relate All Sentences to an Implied Main Idea A paragraph can be unified without a topic sentence as long as every sentence supports an implied, or unstated, main idea. In the example, all the sentences work together to create a unified impression of a frustrated writer trying to begin writing.

MODEL

He picked up his pencil at 9:27 and set it down purposefully on the tablet. A minute or so passed. Well, maybe he should sharpen the pencil. That took 30 seconds—now 9:29. He set his pencil down again. He readjusted his chair. He raked his left hand through his thick hair. Was there a spot of thinning hair? He got up to go look in the mirror. No, not yet. At 9:31 he sat down again and took up the pencil. This time he moved the tablet a little to the right.

Coherence

A paragraph is coherent when all its sentences are related to one another and each flows logically to the next. The following techniques will help you achieve coherence in paragraphs:

- Present your ideas in the most logical order.
- Use pronouns, synonyms, and repeated words to connect ideas.
- Use transitional devices to show relationships among ideas.

In the model shown here, the writer used some of these techniques to create a unified paragraph.

MODEL

After you figure out how big to make the model ship for your film of a shipwreck, you will need to take some other factors into account as well. You will have to figure out how much to stir the water and what speed to set the film. Perhaps even more important is to be sure no real objects at full size can be seen by the camera. In other words, don't let your towels and soap dish sneak into the picture and be sure the cat is locked out of the bathroom.

2.3 TRANSITIONS

Transitions are words and phrases that show connections among details. Clear transitions help show how your ideas relate to one another.

Kinds of Transitions

The types of transitions you choose depend on the ideas you want to convey.

Time or Sequence Some transitions help to clarify the sequence of events over time. When you are telling a story or describing a process, you can connect ideas with such transitional words as *first, second, always, then, next, later, soon, before, finally, after, earlier, afterward,* and *tomorrow.*

MODEL

Before a blood donation can be used, it must be processed carefully. First, a sample is tested for infectious diseases and identified by blood type. Next, preservatives are added. Finally, a blood cell separator breaks up the blood into its parts, such as red blood cells, platelets, and plasma.

Spatial Relationships Transitional words and phrases such as *in front, behind, next to, along, nearest, lowest, above, below, underneath, on the left,* and *in the middle* can help your reader visualize a scene.

MODEL

Two rows of corn grew along the south side of the garden. In front of them stood the tomatoes climbing on wire enclosures and a couple of okra plants. In the middle rows were medium-height plants—bush beans, peas, potatoes, and a few peppers. Low-growing plants filled the front of the garden—radishes on the right, then rows of lettuce, spinach, and onions. On the left, squash and cucumber vines spread over the ground.

Degree of Importance Transitional words and phrases such as *mainly, strongest, weakest, first, second, most important, least important, worst,* and *best* may be used to rank ideas or to show degrees of importance.

MODEL

There are several reasons to eat plenty of fresh fruits and vegetables. The most important reason is that they help to fortify your immune system!

Compare and Contrast Words and phrases such as *similarly, likewise, also, like, as, neither . . . nor,* and *either . . . or* show similarity between details. *However, by contrast, yet, but, unlike, instead, whereas,* and *while* show difference. Note the use of both types of transitions in the model.

MODEL

Although I like to shop in the big stores in the mall, when I'm really serious about buying something I go to a small store. Like big stores, many small stores carry a good selection of merchandise. Whereas the big stores may have lower prices, the small stores have more personal service and clerks who know about the products they sell.

TIP Both *but* and *however* can be used to join two independent clauses. When *but* is used as a coordinating conjunction, it is preceded by a comma. When *however* is used as a conjunctive adverb, it is preceded by a semicolon and followed by a comma.

Cause and Effect When you are writing about a cause-effect relationship, use transitional words and phrases such as *since, because, thus, therefore, so, due to, for this reason,* and *as a result* to help clarify that relationship and make your writing coherent.

> **MODEL**
>
> Due to the unusual amount of rain this summer, the grass is still lush and green in August.

2.4 CONCLUSIONS

A conclusion should leave readers with a strong final impression.

Kinds of Conclusions

Good conclusions sum up ideas in a variety of ways. Here are some techniques you might try:

Restate Your Thesis A good way to conclude an essay is by restating your thesis, or main idea, in different words. The following conclusion restates the thesis introduced on page R29.

> **MODEL**
>
> In Robert Frost's "The Death of the Hired Man," a sad human life unfolds in the whispered conversations between Mary and Warren. Quiet compassion is also evident and is the point of the poem.

Ask a Question Try asking a question that sums up what you have said and gives your reader something new to think about. The following question concludes an appeal for preventing unwanted cats and dogs.

> **MODEL**
>
> Considering how many kittens, puppies, cats, and dogs are put to sleep or die on the streets, don't you think it makes sense that all household pets be spayed or neutered?

Make a Recommendation When you are persuading your audience to take a position on an issue, you can conclude by recommending a specific course of action.

> **MODEL**
>
> Help protect animals from careless humans. Volunteer at an animal shelter. Distribute literature around your neighborhood.

Make a Prediction Readers are concerned about matters that may affect them and therefore are moved by a conclusion that predicts the future.

> **MODEL**
>
> If the city council approves the new shopping mall, we will lose the woodlands that help make our neighborhood quiet and attractive. In their place, we will have traffic congestion, exhaust fumes, bright lights long into the night, and a source of danger to our children.

Summarize Your Information Summarizing reinforces your main idea, leaving a strong, lasting impression. The model concludes with a statement that summarizes a book review.

> **MODEL**
>
> Patricia McKissack's biography gives a strong picture of W. E. B. Du Bois, who was a link between Frederick Douglass, whom he knew early in life, and Martin Luther King Jr., whom he knew late in life.

2.5 ELABORATION

Elaboration is the process of developing an idea by providing specific supporting details that are relevant and appropriate to the purpose and form of your writing. In some cases, you may want to present support with a visual aid.

Facts and Statistics A fact is a statement that can be verified, and a statistic is a fact expressed as a number. Make sure the facts and statistics you supply are from reliable, up-to-date sources, and support your statements, as in the following model.

A student who has an eye for beautiful gardens might consider a career in landscape architecture. The American Society of Landscape Architects has over 12,000 members, up 20 percent in the last five years. The average income of landscape architects is $74,644, which is higher than that of building architects.

Sensory Details Details that show how something looks, sounds, tastes, smells, or feels can enliven a description, making readers feel they are actually experiencing what you are describing.

MODEL

Sliding along on her cross-country skis, Sasha felt she was truly on top of the world. The action of the snow, skis, and sturdy boots massaged her feet. She opened her mouth to taste the sprinkles of snow. The view was a rainbow of color as snowflakes made tiny speckled prisms on her goggles.

Incidents From our earliest years, we are interested in "stories." One way to illustrate a point is to relate an incident or tell a story, as shown in the example.

MODEL

The East India Company had a monopoly on supplying tea to the American Colonies. Tea shipments took on the symbolism of the increasing tyranny of the English government. On December 16, 1773, a group of about 150 colonists put burnt cork on their faces, dressed as Mohawk warriors, boarded the tea-carrying ships, and proceeded to dump the entire tea cargoes into Boston Harbor.

Examples An example can help make an abstract idea concrete or can serve to clarify a complex point.

MODEL

Many of the stars and galaxies we see at night are showing us light from ancient times. Who knows where they really are today? For example, the light from the galaxy Andromeda has taken over 2 million years to get here.

Quotations Choose quotations that clearly support your points, and be sure that you copy each quotation word for word. Remember always to credit the source.

MODEL

Do you know anyone who says "you all" to mean "the group of you"? "Have you all seen this movie?" McCrum, Cran, and MacNeil explain in *The Story of English* that this famous Southern expression comes from a Scots-Irish translation of the plural for *you*. They say the expression "is typical both of Ulster and of the (largely southern) states of America." Did you all know that?

3 Descriptive Writing

Descriptive writing allows you to paint word pictures about anything, from events of global importance to the most personal feelings. It is an essential part of almost every piece of writing.

> **RUBRIC: Standards for Writing**
>
> **Successful descriptive writing should**
> - have a clear focus and sense of purpose
> - use sensory details and precise words to create a vivid image, establish a mood, or express emotion
> - present details in a logical order

3.1 KEY TECHNIQUES

Consider Your Goals What do you want to accomplish with your description? Do you want to show why something is important to you? Do you want to make a person or scene more memorable? Do you want to explain an event?

Identify Your Audience Who will read your description? How familiar are they with your subject? What background information will they need? Which details will they find most interesting?

Think Figuratively What figures of speech might help make your description vivid and interesting? What simile or metaphor comes to mind? What imaginative comparisons can you make? What living thing does an inanimate object remind you of?

Gather Sensory Details Which sights, smells, tastes, sounds, and textures make your subject come alive? Which details stick in your mind when you observe or recall your subject? Which senses does it most strongly affect?

You might want to use a chart like the one shown here to collect sensory details about your subject.

Sights	Sounds	Textures	Smells	Tastes

Create a Mood What feelings do you want to evoke in your readers? Do you want to soothe them with comforting images? Do you want to build tension with ominous details? Do you want to evoke sadness or joy?

3.2 OPTIONS FOR ORGANIZATION

Option 1: Spatial Order Choose one of these options to show the spatial order of elements in a scene you are describing.

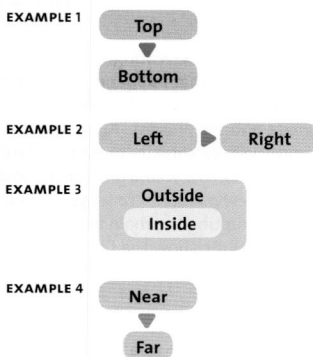

EXAMPLE 1 Top → Bottom

EXAMPLE 2 Left → Right

EXAMPLE 3 Outside / Inside

EXAMPLE 4 Near → Far

MODEL

Peering through the goggles, the diver surveyed the reef. To the left, a school of silvery fish swam near the surface. Below them, the reef was a rainbow of color. In the middle of the scene, bright, tiny fish nosed along the reef. Below them on the sand, a crab looked for food. Further right, a cluster of fan coral waved its purple fronds in the gentle current. Beyond it lay the barnacle-encrusted shape of a ship's propeller.

Option 2: Order of Impression Order of impression is the order in which you notice details.

What first catches your attention ▼ What you notice next ▼ What you see after that ▼ What you focus on last

MODEL

Rain pelted against the windshield. Robbie narrowed his eyes to try to see the road in the brief clearing spasms between swipes of wiper blades. He could barely see that there was a little clearing far off in the horizon. Dark clouds made distinct shapes. Suddenly he noticed that against a small patch of lighter color was a swirling black cloud beginning to take the shape of a funnel.

TIP Use transitions that help readers understand the order of the impressions you are describing. Some useful transitions are *after, next, during, first, before, finally,* and *then.*

Option 3: Order of Importance You can use order of importance as the organizing structure for a description.

Least important ▼ More important ▼ Most important

MODEL

I checked my backpack for the comforting essentials. Book? Yes. Journal and pencil? Yes. Water bottle? Yes. Tissues? Yes. Then I checked for the required essentials. Passport? Yes. Airline ticket? Yes. Map? Yes. Last of all, I checked the most important possession for this trip—a light heart and a sense of adventure. I was beginning my first real vacation in two years!

For more information, see **Transitions***, page R30.*

4 Narrative Writing

Narrative writing tells a story. If you write a story from your imagination, it is a fictional narrative. A true story about actual events is a nonfictional narrative. Narrative writing can be found in short stories, novels, news articles, personal narratives, and biographies.

RUBRIC: Standards for Writing

A successful narrative should

- hook the reader's attention with a strong introduction
- include descriptive details and dialogue to develop the characters, setting, and plot
- have a clear beginning, middle, and end
- have a logical organization, with clues and transitions that help the reader understand the order of events
- maintain a consistent tone and point of view
- use language that is appropriate to the audience
- demonstrate the significance of events or ideas

*For more information, see **Writing Workshop: Biographical Narrative**, pages 598–605.*

4.1 KEY TECHNIQUES

Identify the Main Events What are the most important events in your narrative? Is each event needed to tell the story?

Describe the Setting When do the events occur? Where do they take place? How can you use setting to create mood and to set the stage for the characters and their actions?

Depict Characters Vividly What do your characters look like? What do they think and say? How do they act? What details can show what they are like?

TIP Dialogue is an effective means of developing characters in a narrative. As you write dialogue, choose words that express your characters' personalities and that show how the characters feel about one another and about the events in the plot.

4.2 OPTIONS FOR ORGANIZATION

Option 1: Chronological Order One way to organize a piece of narrative writing is to arrange the events in chronological order, as shown in the following example.

EXAMPLE

A contemporary Navajo boy in New Mexico is nearing adulthood. His father wants him to learn the lore of his ancestors. His mother wants him to prepare for school instead.	**Introduction** *Characters and setting* ▼
The boy wants to please both his parents. He goes into the mountains to seek wisdom.	**Event 1** ▼
Animals visit the boy, representing both the old ways and the new.	**Event 2** ▼
The boy finds that he does not have to disappoint either parent. He finds that he must work hardest on learning what he himself is best suited for.	**End** *Perhaps showing the significance of the events*

Option 2: Flashback In narrative writing, it is also possible to introduce events that happened before the beginning of the story. You can use a flashback to show how past events led up to the present situation or to provide background about a character or event. Use clue words such as *last summer, as a young girl, the previous school year,* and *his earliest memories* to let your reader know that you are interrupting the main action to describe earlier events. Notice how the flashback interrupts the action in the model.

MODEL

Mr. Robbins picked up the small, white ball that had just smashed his kitchen window and felt angry that the boys playing across the street could be so careless. Then he remembered a summer day over 50 years ago, when he himself had hit a home run – right into the Nelsons' living room. How frightened he had been when Mrs. Nelson walked out of her front door, holding the baseball! But she had simply laughed as she gave it back to him and said, "Boys will be boys." Mr. Robbins shook his head at the memory and looked back at his broken pane of glass.

Option 3: Focus on Conflict When a fictional narrative focuses on a central conflict, the story's plot may be organized as shown in the following example.

EXAMPLE

The day after their high school graduation, Angela and her twin brother, Alex, decided to take their canoe out on the river that ran past their family home. They had done it many times since childhood, and the river was familiar to both of them.

> **Describe main characters and setting.**

For two hours they traversed the river under a calm, clear sky, but by noon, rather ominous clouds had rolled in. Meanwhile, they had floated far downstream, and had taken a winding inlet off the river. Soon, they heard thunder in the distance, and Angela looked off to the southwest where she had noticed lightning. She alerted Alex and insisted they turn back immediately. Alex did not seem concerned, however, and refused to go back.

> **Present conflict.**

As the storm began to get nearer, Angela again insisted they turn around, but Alex, who was steering the boat, said the storm was too far away to hurt them. As the rain began to fall on them, Angela began to plead with her brother that they either pull over to the shore or turn back immediately. To prove her point, she stopped paddling.

> **Relate events that make conflict complex and cause characters to change.**

Alex ignored his sister and continued to paddle himself and steer them further downstream. Finally a bolt of lightning hit close by, and the rain started to pour. "Now do you believe me?!" shouted Angela through the driving rain. Alex turned the boat toward shore and didn't say a word.

> **Present resolution or outcome of conflict.**

5 Expository Writing

Expository writing informs and explains. You can use it to evaluate the effects of a new law, to compare two movies, to analyze a piece of literature, or to examine the problem of greenhouse gases in the atmosphere. There are many types of expository writing. Think about your topic and select the type that presents the information most clearly.

5.1 COMPARISON AND CONTRAST

Compare-and-contrast writing examines the similarities and differences between two or more subjects. You might, for example, compare and contrast two short stories, the main characters in a novel, or two movies.

> **RUBRIC: Standards for Writing**
>
> **Successful compare-and-contrast writing should**
>
> - hook the reader's attention with a strong introduction
> - clearly identify the subjects that are being compared and contrasted
> - include specific, relevant details
> - follow a clear plan of organization
> - use language and details appropriate to the audience
> - use transitional words and phrases to clarify similarities and differences

Options for Organization

Compare-and-contrast writing can be organized in different ways. The examples that follow demonstrate point-by-point organization and subject-by-subject organization.

Option 1: Point-by-Point Organization

EXAMPLE

I. Different beliefs about burial practices.　　**Point 1**

　　Subject A. Leon: traditional Laguna way.

　　Subject B. Father Paul: last rites and a funeral mass.

II. Both want a proper burial.　　**Point 2**

　　Subject A. Leon: painted face, feather in hair, body to graveyard, cornmeal and pollen.

　　Subject B. Father Paul: decide whether to sprinkle holy water without full Catholic rites.

Option 2: Subject-by-Subject Organization

> **EXAMPLE**
>
> I. Leon: **Subject A**
>
>   Point 1. Believes in traditional
>   Laguna burial.
>
>   Point 2. Proper burial: painted face,
>   feather in hair, body to graveyard,
>   corn meal and pollen.
>
> II. Father Paul: **Subject B**
>
>   Point 1. Believes burial requires
>   last rites and a funeral mass.
>
>   Point 2. Must decide whether to
>   sprinkle holy water without full
>   Catholic rites.

*For more information, see **Writing Workshop: Reflective Essay,** pages 474–481; **Writing Workshop: Literary Analysis,** pages 804–811; **Writing Workshop: Comparison-Contrast Essay,** pages 1072–1079; **Research Paper,** pages 1284–1299.*

5.2 CAUSE AND EFFECT

Cause-effect writing explains why something happened, why certain conditions exist, or what resulted from an action or a condition. You might use cause-effect writing to explain a character's actions, the progress of a disease, or the outcome of a war.

> ### RUBRIC: Standards for Writing
>
> **Successful cause-effect writing should**
>
> - hook the reader's attention with a strong introduction
> - clearly state the cause-and-effect relationship
> - show clear connections between causes and effects
> - present causes and effects in a logical order and use transitions effectively
> - use facts, examples, and other details to illustrate each cause and effect
> - use language and details appropriate to the audience

Options for Organization

Your organization will depend on your topic and your purpose for writing.

Option 1: Effect-to-Cause Organization If you want to explain the causes of an event, such as the closing of a factory, you might first state the effect and then examine its causes.

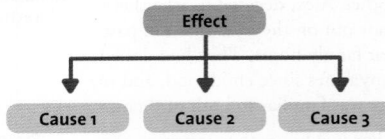

Option 2: Cause-to-Effect Organization If your focus is on explaining the effects of an event, such as the passage of a law, you might first state the cause and then explain the effects.

Option 3: Cause-Effect Chain Organization Sometimes you'll want to describe a chain of cause-effect relationships to explore a topic, such as the disappearance of tropical rain forests or the development of the Internet.

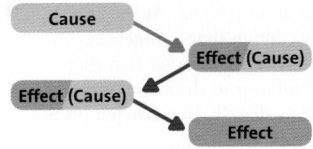

TIP Don't assume that a cause-effect relationship exists just because one event follows another. Look for evidence that the later event could not have happened if the first event had not caused it.

5.3 PROBLEM-SOLUTION

Problem-solution writing clearly states a problem, analyzes the problem, and proposes a solution to the problem. It can be used to identify and solve a conflict between characters, investigate global warming, or tell why the home team keeps losing.

RUBRIC: Standards for Writing

Successful problem-solution writing should

- hook the reader's attention with a strong introduction
- identify the problem and help the reader understand the issues involved
- analyze the causes and effects of the problem
- include quotations, facts, and statistics
- explore possible solutions to the problem and recommend the best one(s)
- use language, details, and a tone appropriate to the audience

Options for Organization

Your organization will depend on the goal of your problem-solution piece, your intended audience, and the specific problem you have chosen to address. The organizational methods that follow are effective for different kinds of problem-solution writing.

Option 1: Simple Problem-Solution

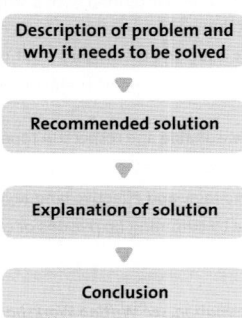

Option 2: Deciding Between Solutions

*For more information, see **Writing Workshop: Problem and Solution,** pages 1248–1255.*

5.4 ANALYSIS

In writing an analysis, you explain how something works, how it is defined, or what its parts are.

RUBRIC: Standards for Writing

A successful analysis should

- hook the reader's attention with a strong introduction
- clearly define the subject and its parts
- use a specific organizing structure to provide a logical flow of information
- show connections among facts and ideas through transitional words and phrases
- use language and details appropriate for the audience

Options for Organization

Organize your details in a logical order appropriate to the kind of analysis you're writing. Use one of the following options:

Option 1: Process Analysis A process analysis is usually organized chronologically, with steps or stages in the order in which they occur.

> **EXAMPLE**
>
> Navigating north from New Orleans   **Introduce process.**
>
> Mark Twain follows this process for his first trip as a cub pilot.   **Give background.**
>
> Step 1: Straighten out the boat.   **Explain steps.**
>
> Step 2: Stay close to the moored boats.
>
> Step 3: Pass Six-Mile, Nine-Mile, and Twelve-Mile points.
>
> Step 4: Cross the river when the calm water ends.

Option 2: Definition Analysis You can organize the details of a definition analysis in order of importance or impression.

> **EXAMPLE**
>
> A successful riverboat pilot must be a keen observer.   **Introduce term.**
>
> The riverboat pilot must observe the surface of the river, the landmarks along the shore, and signs of nature.   **General definition.**
>
> Quality 1: The surface can tell of rising water or hidden hazards.   **Explain features or qualities.**
>
> Quality 2: Landmarks tell where the boat is; pilot must recall what dangers to avoid at that point.
>
> Quality 3: The sky can give hints about what weather may be coming.

Option 3: Parts Analysis A parts analysis is organized as a listing of the subject's parts, with each explained.

> **EXAMPLE**
>
> Piloting a riverboat requires several skills.   **Introduce subject.**
>
> Part 1: recognize how weather might threaten the boat   **Explain parts.**
>
> Part 2: observe floating objects that could show a rising river; see ripples in the water surface that could indicate a hazard
>
> Part 3: use landmarks to know where boat is and where dangers lie

*For more information, see **Writing Workshop: Literary Analysis,** pages 804–811.*

6 Persuasive Writing

Persuasive writing allows you to use the power of language to inform and influence others. It includes speeches, persuasive essays, newspaper editorials, advertisements, and critical reviews.

> **RUBRIC: Standards for Writing**
>
> **Successful persuasive writing should**
>
> - hook the reader's attention with a strong introduction
> - state the issue and the writer's position
> - give opinions and support them with facts or reasons
> - have a reasonable and respectful tone
> - answer opposing views
> - use sound logic and effective language
> - conclude by summing up reasons or calling for action

*For more information, see **Writing Workshop: Persuasive Essay,** pages 276–283.*

6.1 KEY TECHNIQUES

Clarify Your Position What do you believe about the issue? Determine how you can express your opinion most clearly.

Know Your Audience Who will read your writing? Think about what your audience already knows and believes about the issue. Imagine any objections to your position that your audience might have. Determine what additional information they will need. Decide on the tone and approach that would be most effective.

Support Your Opinion Why do you feel the way you do about the issue? Use facts, statistics, examples, quotations, anecdotes, or expert opinions to support your view. Think of reasons that will convince your readers and evidence that can answer their objections.

Ways to Support Your Argument	
Statistics	facts that are stated in numbers
Examples	specific instances that explain points
Observations	events or situations you yourself have seen
Anecdotes	brief stories that illustrate points
Quotations	direct statements from authorities

*For more information, see **Identifying Faulty Reasoning**, page R22.*

Begin and End with a Bang How can you hook your readers and make a lasting impression? Think of a quotation, an anecdote, or a statistic that will catch your reader's attention and remain memorable. Create a strong summary or call to action with which you can conclude.

MODEL

Beginning

Stop before you call your doctor for medicine to cure that cold or ease that sore throat. You might be doing your body more harm than good by taking an antibiotic.

Conclusion

Listen to doctors when they suggest that antibiotics should be reserved for serious illness. Take the doctor's advice to drink lots of liquids and get bed rest instead of taking drugs for a less serious illness. Maybe humanity can win the battle with microbes by slowing their evolution into supermicrobes that resist antibiotics.

6.2 OPTIONS FOR ORGANIZATION

In a two-sided persuasive essay, you want to show the weaknesses of other opinions as you explain the strengths of your own.

Option 1: Reasons for Your Opinion

Introduction states issue and your position on it.
▼
Reason 1 with evidence and support
▼
Reason 2 with evidence and support
▼
Reason 3 with evidence and support
▼
Objections to whole argument
▼
Response to objections
▼
Conclusion includes restatement of your position and recommended action.

Option 2: Point-by-Point Basis

Introduction states issue and your position on it.
▼
Reason 1 with evidence and support
▼
Objections and responses for reason 1
▼
Reason 2 with evidence and support
▼
Objections and responses for reason 2
▼
Reason 3 with evidence and support
▼
Objections and responses for reason 3
▼
Conclusion includes restatement of your position and recommended action.

PRACTICE AND APPLY

ANSWERS

1. *Responses will vary. The letter should include a heading, inside address, salutation, body, and closing, with appropriate language, information, and format.*

2. *Responses will vary. The memo should include a heading and a body, with appropriate language, information, and format.*

7 Workplace and Technical Writing

Business writing is writing done in a workplace to support the work of a company or business. Several types of formats, such as memos, letters, e-mails, applications, and bylaws, have been developed to make communication easier.

> **RUBRIC: Standards for Writing**
>
> **Successful business writing should**
>
> - be courteous
> - use language that is geared to its audience
> - state the purpose clearly in the opening sentences or paragraph
> - have a formal tone and not contain slang, contractions, or sentence fragments
> - use precise words
> - present only essential information
> - present details in a logical order
> - conclude with a summary of important points

7.1 KEY TECHNIQUES

Think About Your Purpose Ask yourself why you are doing this writing. Do you want to promote yourself to a college admissions committee or a job interviewer? Do you want to order or complain about a product? Do you want to set up a meeting or respond to someone's ideas? Are you writing bylaws for an organization?

Identify Your Audience Determine who will read your writing. What background information will they need? What tone or language is appropriate?

Use a Pattern of Organization That Is Appropriate to the Content If you have to compare and contrast two products in a memo, for example, you can use the same compare-and-contrast organization that you would use in an essay.

Support Your Points What specific details might clarify your ideas? What reasons do you have for your statements?

Finish Strongly Determine the best way to sum up your statements. What is your main point? What action do you want the recipients to take?

Revise and Proofread Your Writing Just as you are graded on the quality of an essay you write for a class, you will be judged on the quality of your writing in the workplace.

7.2 MATCHING THE FORMAT TO THE OCCASION

E-mail messages, memos, and letters have similar purposes but are used in different situations. The chart shows how each format can be used.

Format	Occasion
Memo	Use to send correspondence **inside** the workplace only.
E-mail message	Use to send correspondence **inside or outside** the company.
Letter	Use to send correspondence **outside** the company.

TIP Memos are often sent as e-mail messages in the workplace. Remember that both require formal language and standard spelling, capitalization, and punctuation.

PRACTICE AND APPLY

Refer to the documents on page R41 to complete the following:

1. Draft a response to the letter. Then revise your letter as necessary according to the rubric at the beginning of this section. Make sure you have included the necessary information and have written in an appropriate tone. Proofread your letter for grammatical errors and spelling mistakes. Follow the format of the model and use appropriate spacing between elements.

2. Write a memo in response to the memo. Tell the recipient what actions you have taken. Follow the format of the model.

7.3 FORMATS

Business letters usually have a formal tone and a specific format as shown below. The key to writing a business letter is to get to the point as quickly as possible and to present your information clearly.

MODEL: BUSINESS LETTER

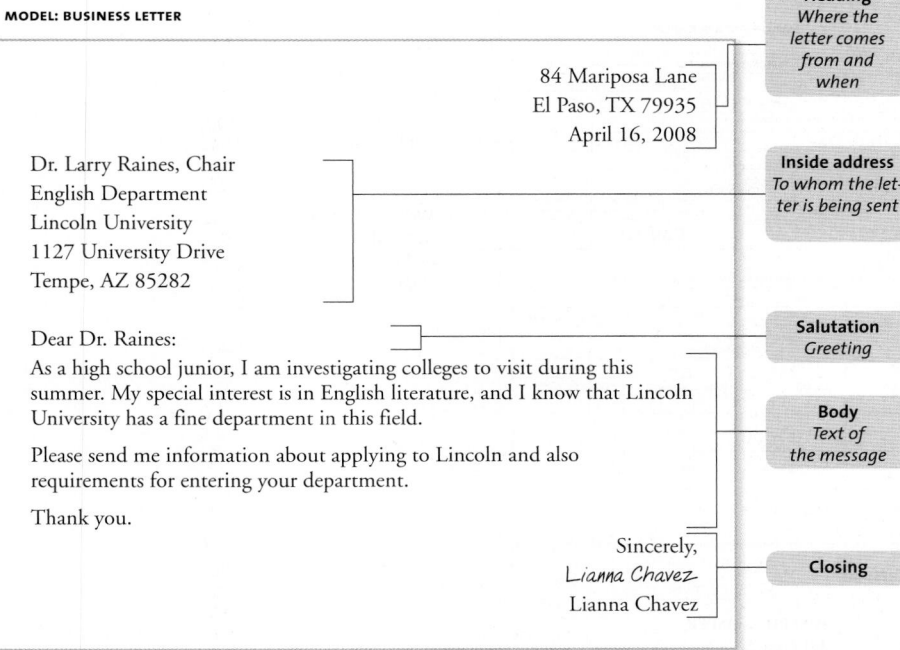

84 Mariposa Lane
El Paso, TX 79935
April 16, 2008

Dr. Larry Raines, Chair
English Department
Lincoln University
1127 University Drive
Tempe, AZ 85282

Dear Dr. Raines:

As a high school junior, I am investigating colleges to visit during this summer. My special interest is in English literature, and I know that Lincoln University has a fine department in this field.

Please send me information about applying to Lincoln and also requirements for entering your department.

Thank you.

Sincerely,
Lianna Chavez
Lianna Chavez

Heading
Where the letter comes from and when

Inside address
To whom the letter is being sent

Salutation
Greeting

Body
Text of the message

Closing

Memos are often used in workplaces as a way of conveying information in a direct and concise manner. They can be used to announce or summarize meetings and to request actions or specific information.

MODEL: MEMO

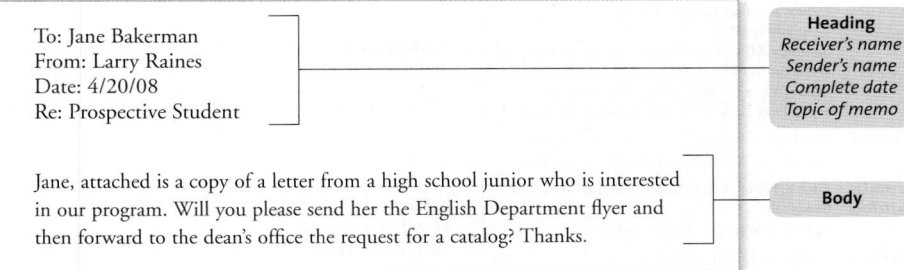

To: Jane Bakerman
From: Larry Raines
Date: 4/20/08
Re: Prospective Student

Jane, attached is a copy of a letter from a high school junior who is interested in our program. Will you please send her the English Department flyer and then forward to the dean's office the request for a catalog? Thanks.

Heading
*Receiver's name
Sender's name
Complete date
Topic of memo*

Body

TIP Don't forget to write the topic of your memo in the subject line. This will help the receiver determine the importance of your memo.

WRITING HANDBOOK **R41**

When you apply for a job, you may be asked to fill out an application form. Application forms vary, but most of them ask for similar kinds of information. If you are mailing your application, you may want to include a brief letter.

MODEL: JOB APPLICATION

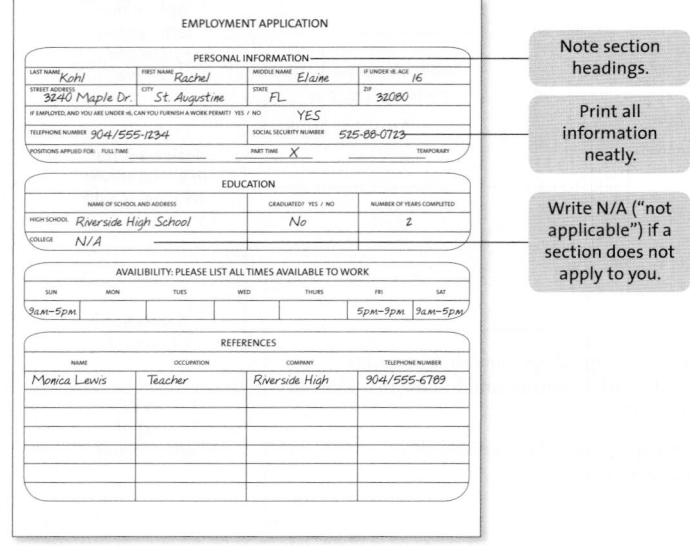

Note section headings.

Print all information neatly.

Write N/A ("not applicable") if a section does not apply to you.

MODEL: RÉSUMÉ

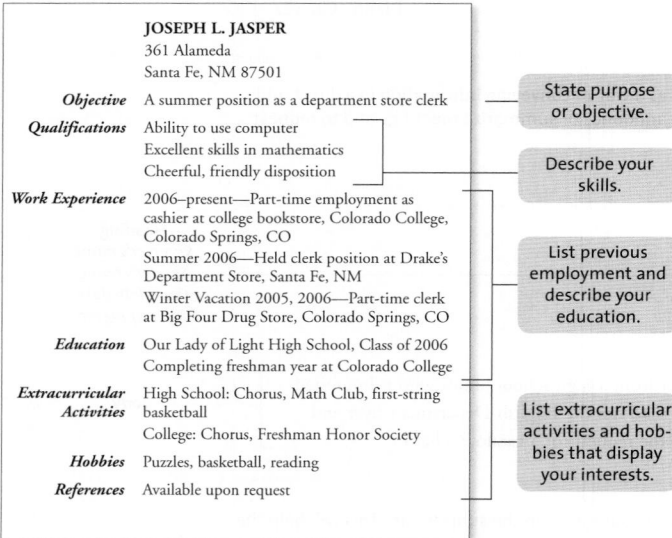

State purpose or objective.

Describe your skills.

List previous employment and describe your education.

List extracurricular activities and hobbies that display your interests.

Sometimes you may have to write technical documents, such as a list of procedures for conducting a meeting, a manual on rules of behavior, or the minutes of a meeting. These documents contain written descriptions of rules, regulations, and meetings and enable organizations and businesses to run smoothly. These bylaws for a poetry club include a description of the organization and information about how the club operates.

MODEL: BYLAWS DOCUMENT

Article I Name

SECTION 1. The name of this organization is the Free Verse Poets Society of North Shore High School.

Article II Purpose

SECTION 1. The purpose of this organization is to stimulate young developing poets, to create enthusiasm for poetry, to promote the scholarly study of poetry, and to inform the school and community about poetry.

Article III Membership Requirements

SECTION 1. To qualify for membership, a candidate must be a student at North Shore High School.

SECTION 2. Membership in Free Verse Poets Society is voluntary. However, all members are required to attend semimonthly meetings, participate in any club fundraisers, and assist in the quarterly publication of the club newsletter, *Plutonian Shore*.

Article IV Meetings

SECTION 1. Meetings will be held twice a month on a day designated by voting members. Meetings will be held in a classroom designated by the faculty advisor.

SECTION 2. A quorum shall consist of eight (8) members; at least two (2) student officers and the faculty advisor are required to be present at each meeting.

SECTION 3. All student officers are voting members of the Free Verse Poets Society; however, the faculty advisor may be called upon in the event of an evenly split vote.

Article V Officers

SECTION 1. This organization shall be governed by a faculty advisor and a panel of four (4) student officers: the president, vice-president, scribe, and treasurer. Each student officer will be elected at the start of the school year.

SECTION 2. For members to be eligible for election, they must have served one (1) year as a member in the Free Verse Poets Society. Freshmen are not eligible for election. Only seniors are eligible for the office of society president.

SECTION 3. The president will preside over regular and special meetings.

SECTION 4. The vice-president will guide activities of appointed committees.

SECTION 5. The scribe will record and distribute meeting minutes.

SECTION 6. The treasurer will be responsible for all money collected by the society.

PRACTICE AND APPLY

Refer to the documents on pages R42 and R43 to complete the following:

1. Visit a business and request an employment application for a job you would like to have. Make sure you understand what each question is asking before you begin to write. Fill out the application as neatly and completely as possible.

2. Write a set of bylaws for an organization that you already belong to or one that you would like to form. Follow the format of the document on page R43.

PRACTICE AND APPLY

ANSWERS

1. *Students' work should be legible, accurate, and complete.*

2. *Students' bylaws should follow the format shown.*

Good research involves using a variety of sources and materials. With an abundance of information at your fingertips, knowing where to go, how to access information, and how to record your findings are important skills and strategies.

CALIFORNIA

Included throughout this handbook: W1.6
Included in this handbook as indicated:
W1.7 (pgs. R48–R49)

WRITING TOOLS
For research tools and strategies, visit the **Research Center** at **ClassZone.com**.

1 Finding Sources

The **library** or **media center** and the **Internet** are the first places you will begin your research. Both the library and the Internet offer a wealth of resources, which include reference works, books, newspapers and periodicals, film, databases, catalogs, and other miscellaneous sources, such as music scores and maps.

1.1 REFERENCE WORKS

Reference works provide quick information that can help you refine or narrow your search. Reference works are roughly divided into two categories: general reference and specialized reference. Specialized reference works are focused on a particular field or area of study.

Reference Works	Examples
Encyclopedias—detailed information on nearly every subject, arranged alphabetically	*Encyclopaedia Britannica Encyclopedia.com Encyclopedia of Economics*
Dictionaries—word definitions, spellings, usage, pronunciations, and origins	*The American Heritage Dictionary Bartlett's Familiar Quotations*
Almanacs and Yearbooks—current facts and statistics	*World Almanac and Book of Facts*
Thesauri—lists of synonyms and antonyms	*Roget's International Thesaurus*
Biographical References—information on the lives of noteworthy people	*The Riverside Dictionary of Biography The International Who's Who*
Atlases—geographical and historical maps, charts, and graphics	*Rand McNally Atlas of the World*
Directories—names, addresses, and phone numbers of people and organizations	telephone books lists of business organizations, agencies, and publications
Indexes—alphabetical lists of newspaper and magazine articles	*Readers' Guide to Periodical Literature*

1.2 BOOKS

Nonfiction books provide in-depth information on specific topics. Your research may also require that you access fiction, poetry, or dramatic works. The following parts of a book will help you find information quickly and easily:

- **Title page**—a page that gives the book's name and the name of its author and publisher; usually the first full page of a book
- **Copyright page**—a page that gives the copyright date, or the date the book was published; usually located on the reverse side of the title page
- **Table of contents**—a list at the front of the book that gives the title of each chapter or section of the text and the page number on which it begins
- **Preface**—a short, preliminary section of a book in which the writer of the book briefly provides background information and, possibly, acknowledgments
- **Bibliography**—a list of related books and other materials used to write a text; usually placed at the end of the book
- **Glossary**—an alphabetized list of important and/or specialized words and their definitions; usually placed at the end of the book
- **Appendix**—a collection of additional materials that supply background or other related information on subject matter discussed in the main portion of the text; usually located at the end of the book
- **Index**—an alphabetized list of important topics, terms, and details covered in the book and the page numbers on which they can be found; located at the end of the book; useful for quickly finding specific information on a topic

*For more information, see **Choosing Reliable Books,** page 1277.*

Two basic systems are used to classify nonfiction books. Most high school and public libraries use the Dewey decimal system. University and research libraries generally use the Library of Congress system.

DEWEY DECIMAL SYSTEM

000–099	General works
100–199	Philosophy and psychology
200–299	Religion
300–399	Social science
400–499	Language
500–599	Natural sciences and mathematics
600–699	Technology (applied sciences)
700–799	Arts and recreation
800–899	Literature and rhetoric
900–999	Geography and history

LIBRARY OF CONGRESS SYSTEM

A	General works
B	Philosophy, psychology, religion
C	History
D	General history and history of Europe
E–F	American history
G	Geography, anthropology, recreation
H	Social sciences
J	Political science
K	Law
L	Education
M	Music
N	Fine arts
P	Language and literature
Q	Science
R	Medicine
S	Agriculture
T	Technology
U	Military science
V	Naval science
Z	Bibliography and library science

1.3 NEWSPAPERS AND PERIODICALS

Newspapers, magazines, and scholarly journals provide concise and current information on specific topics and the news of the day. Microforms are newspapers, periodicals, and reports stored on film (microfilm) or cards (microfiche) and viewable on special machines found at the library.

Types of Publications	Examples
Newspapers—published daily, weekly, or monthly; provide news reports, specialized features, and commentary; may be general or specialized	*New York Times* *Chicago Tribune* *Sacramento Bee*
Magazines—published monthly, quarterly, or at other intervals; provide news, articles on specific topics, and commentary; more in-depth than newspapers	*Newsweek* *Time* *Musician*
Journals—usually academic in scope; related to a specific field of study; highly specialized information	*Journal of Music Theory* *New England Journal of Medicine*

*For more information, see **Evaluating Newspapers and Periodicals,** page 1276.*

1.4 ELECTRONIC RESOURCES

Electronic resources include DVDs, videos, e-books, CD-ROMs, and audio resources. These resources may contain reference materials, movies, documentaries, television programs, books, music, speeches, textbooks, and various other content. While most documentaries, movies, and interviews are available on DVDs or CDs, you may want to directly access a film version. To quickly determine whether the piece is useful for your research, check the following:

- **Description or summary** of the piece—Does it contain the information you need, or is it otherwise relevant to your topic? Is it nonfiction or fiction?
- **Copyright date**—How current is the documentary or interview?
- **Producer** of the piece and its **participants**—Is the producer or creator reputable? Who is interviewed or featured?

PRACTICE AND APPLY

ANSWERS

1. *The quickest way to search a specific topic would be to use the index.*

2. *Depending on the topic, you would search newspapers, magazines, academic journals, or the Internet.*

3. *You might find a microfiche useful if you needed to look up information in out-of-date periodicals.*

1.5 DATABASES AND ONLINE CATALOGS

The library and Internet also offer large databases that allow you to search for articles on any number of topics. Often the library will subscribe to a database service, such as InfoTrac, Newsbank, or SIRS Researcher. The information on these databases is updated regularly.

Electronic catalogs have mostly replaced the card catalog system of book listings. Formerly filed in labeled drawers in libraries, listings can now be accessed from a library's Web site on the Internet.

1.6 OTHER RESOURCES

In addition to reference works found in the library or media center and on the Internet, you can get information from the following sources: corporate and nonprofit publications, lectures, correspondence, career guides, recordings, and television programming.

> #### PRACTICE AND APPLY
>
> 1. If you were looking through a nonfiction book on penguins, which part of the book would you search in order to find information on emperor penguins, a specific type of penguin?
>
> 2. If you wanted the most current information on a given topic, which source(s) would you search first?
>
> 3. Describe a situation in which you might find it useful to search microfiche.

1.7 WEB SOURCES

Whole libraries are on the Internet, as are thousands of other reliable and comprehensive sources for research. To conduct a search efficiently and find the best information for your topic, familiarize yourself with the following terms and procedures.

The main search tools for finding information on the Web are search engines, metasearch tools, and directories. In addition, there are virtual libraries and a host of other sites, such as newspaper archives, news associations, encyclopedias, the Library of Congress, and specialized databases.

Search engines—A search engine is a Web site that allows you to look for information on the World Wide Web. Examples include Google, Alltheweb, AltaVista, HotBot, and Go.com.

Metasearch tools—A metasearch tool is similar to a search engine, except that it simultaneously searches multiple search engines for the keywords you request. Examples include Dogpile, SurfWax, and Metacrawler.

Directories—Directories arrange Internet resources into subject categories and are useful when you are researching a general topic. Examples include Lycos, Galaxy, Yahoo!, Web Directory, and About.com.

Keyword searches—In a keyword search, you access a search engine and type in a phrase or term related to your subject. This allows you to retrieve Web sites and documents that have those keywords in them. Here are some tips for doing a keyword search:

- In the search box, type in a specific word or two that clearly identify your subject.
- When you want to find an exact phrase, or words in a certain order, such as *recording studio* (and not just *recording* or just *studio*), use quotation marks around the entire phrase. For instance, "recording studio" will provide results using those words in that order.
- If necessary, replace the end of a word with an asterisk. For example, the keyword *music** leads to sites that contain *music, musician,* and *musicianship.*

Boolean searches—A Boolean search lets you specify how the keywords in your search are related. This type of search allows you to refine, narrow, or expand your search so that your results are more focused on your topic needs. Use the following tips to conduct a Boolean search:

- For a search containing two or more words that do not need to be in a specific order, use the word AND between the words to indicate that the site or document should contain all the words specified. For example, *internship* AND *radio* will produce results containing both those words, but not in any particular order. For some search engines, you can use a plus sign instead of AND.
- The word OR broadens the search to include all documents that contain either word (*job* OR *career*).
- The word NOT—or, for some search engines, a minus sign—excludes unwanted terms from the search (*songwriting* NOT *commercials*).

Each Web site you encounter in your search will have a **URL** (uniform resource locator), which is its Web address. The abbreviation usually located at the end of the URL indicates the type and purpose of the Web site.

URL ABBREVIATIONS AND MEANINGS

.COM commercial—product information and sales; personal sites; some combinations of products and information, such as World Book Online

.EDU education—information about schools, courses, campus life, and research projects; students' and teachers' personal sites

.GOV United States government—official sites of the White House and of NASA, the FBI, and other government agencies and offices

.MIL United States military—official sites of the army, navy, air force, and marines, as well as of the Department of Defense and related agencies

.NET network—product information and sales

.ORG organization—charities, libraries, and other nonprofits; political parties

*For more information, see **Online Resources**, pages 1271–1273.*

1.8 YOUR OWN ORIGINAL DATA

Sometimes you will need information that you just can't find in books or online. A good way to get in-depth, firsthand information is by interviewing experts, conducting surveys, and recording data from your own observations, fieldwork, or experiments.

Interviews with experts—Whatever the subject of your research, look for people who have knowledge or experience in that field. For example, if you were researching shipwrecks on the Great Lakes, you might interview someone from the Great Lakes Maritime Society or a captain of a ship on the Great Lakes. Use the following tips when conducting an interview:

1. Plan your questions and rehearse what you will say.
2. During the interview, listen carefully and take notes. Ask permission if you want to record the interview.
3. Request clarification and ask follow-up questions when necessary.
4. After the interview, review your notes and summarize the conversation. If you recorded the conversation, you might want to transcribe it.
5. Identify strong statements you might want to quote directly.
6. Send a thank-you note to the interviewee.

Oral histories—For some kinds of presentations and papers, you may want to include an **oral history,** or a story of a person's experiences told in his or her own words. For example, if you were writing a paper on Native Americans and reservation life, you might want to include an oral history of someone who is experiencing that life and who knows how his or her tribe came to live on the reservation. To conduct an oral history, follow all the tips for conducting an interview.

Surveys—Surveys allow you to gather information from a broad range of people through the use of a **questionnaire.** For example, you may want to gather and compare people's opinions, preferences, or beliefs about a current news topic. Use the following tips to conduct a survey or to distribute a questionnaire:

1. Plan the survey. Choose whether you want to ask multiple-choice questions, yes/no questions, open-ended questions, true/false questions, or questions that refer to a rating scale. Prepare your questionnaire.
2. Determine the sample population, or group of people, you want to survey.
3. Administer the survey the same way to each person. You may ask people to respond in person, on the phone, or by e-mail, but your method should be the same for each, with the questions asked in the same manner and order.
4. Once the questionnaires have been completed, compile and interpret the responses. Was there a clear preference or opinion from the entire group? Do certain groups of people think one way while others think another? What conclusions can you draw from the results?
5. Summarize your results in writing; use charts or other graphic aids to provide a visual representation of the data.

Independent observation and field research—Field research and independent observation include any purposeful observations you make at a site or an event related to your topic. For example, you might visit a movie set to learn more about how movies are made and then record the activity you observed. For some research projects you may want to set up a **field study,** which is a systematic series of observations or a planned course of data collection. For some topics you might conduct experiments, as for a report in a science class.

2 Collecting Information

Once you have located your sources, you will need to sort through the information. To make it useful and manageable, you will want to take detailed notes, arrange your information in a logical and organized manner, and make sure your sources are reliable and credible.

2.1 TAKING NOTES

As you go through your sources, write down information that is relevant to your search.

Source cards—You will need to document the sources where you find your information or evidence so that you can credit the sources in your work. To create source cards, record on a separate index card all the information needed to identify each source you use in your research. Number each source card so that you can easily refer to it when you take notes and add documentation to your report, as in this example for a book.

> ⓵
>
> Ackerman, Diane. _A Natural History of the_
> _Senses_. New York: Vintage, 1990.

HERE'S HOW

MAKING SOURCE CARDS

Follow these guidelines when you make source cards:

- **Book** Write the author's or editor's complete name, the title, the location and name of the publisher, and the copyright date.
- **Magazine or Newspaper Article** Write the author's complete name (unless the article is unsigned), the title of the article, the name and date of the publication, and the page number(s) of the article.
- **Encyclopedia Article** Write the author's complete name (unless the article is unsigned), the title of the article, and the name and copyright date of the encyclopedia.
- **World Wide Web Site** Write the author's or editor's complete name (if available), the title of the document, publication information for any print version of it, the date of its electronic publication, the name of any institution or organization responsible for the site, the date when you accessed the site, and the document's address (in angle brackets).

Note cards—As you read your sources, write down all relevant facts, quotations, statistics, anecdotes, and examples on separate index cards, or **note cards.** When you're ready to draft your paper, you can arrange and organize the cards in different ways to present the information and then choose the best method of organization. Here is an example of a note card with an exact quotation from the Diane Ackerman book.

> _Insects and photoreception_
>
> "Bees can judge the angle at which light hits
> their photoreceptors, and therefore locate the
> position of the sun in the sky, even on a partly
> cloudy day" (265).

HERE'S HOW

TAKING NOTES

Follow these guidelines as you take your notes:

- **Use a separate index card** for each piece of information.
- **Write a heading** on each card, indicating the subject of the note.
- **Write the number of the corresponding source card** on each card.
- **Put direct quotations in quotation marks.**
- **Record the number of the page** where you found the material.

When recording information on note cards, you can use the following forms of **restatement** to avoid **plagiarism,** or presenting someone else's work as your own:

Paraphrase—When you paraphrase, you restate the writer's idea in your own words. Be sure to enclose in quotation marks any of the author's exact words that you include in a paraphrase.

Summary—When you summarize, you restate the main idea of the original, including key facts and statistics, but in a shorter version, usually about one-third the length of the original. A summary omits unnecessary details.

Quotation—When you use a writer's exact statement, you will need to place quotation marks around it. Be sure to copy the words exactly as the writer wrote them, including all punctuation. Use quotations for

- extremely important ideas that might be misrepresented by paraphrases
- clear and concise explanations
- ideas presented in unusually lively or vivid language

2.2 OUTLINING

Once you've arranged your note cards in a pattern of organization that is suitable for your topic, you can create a formal **outline** of how the information will be arranged in your report. An outline can be written in one of two ways: as a sentence outline or as a topic outline. The **sentence outline** contains entries written in sentence form; the **topic outline** contains only phrases or words that represent the ideas. With either choice, each main idea in the outline is designated by a Roman numeral. The subtopics that support the main ideas are designated with indented capital letters. The details that explain the subtopics are designated with numerals and lowercase letters.

MODEL: SENTENCE OUTLINE

Introduction: The human senses are varied and differ from those in animals.

I. Humans are believed to have five senses: sight, hearing, touch, taste, and smell.

   A. Aristotle, a Greek philosopher, first categorized the senses.

   B. Modern physics and physiology reclassified the senses.

II. Photoreceptors are those sense organs in living organisms that react to light.

   A. The human eye is a photoreceptor.

   B. Animal photoreception can be superior to that of humans.

     1. Insects have specialized eyes.

     2. Nocturnal animals can see in the dark.

     3. Some animals see the world in colors that are different from those perceived by humans.

MODEL: TOPIC OUTLINE

Introduction: The human senses are varied and differ from those in animals.

I. Five senses in humans

   A. First categorization of senses

   B. Modern reclassification of senses

II. Photoreception

   A. Human sight and photoreception

   B. Animal sight and photoreception

     1. Insects

     2. Nocturnal animals

     3. Animals vs. humans in perceiving colors

2.3 CHECKLIST FOR EVALUATING SOURCES

The information . . .

☑ is relevant to the topic you are researching

☑ is up-to-date (This point is especially important when researching time-sensitive topics in areas such as science, medicine, and sports.)

☑ is from an author who is qualified to write about the topic

☑ is from a trusted source that is updated or reviewed regularly

☑ makes the author's or institution's purpose for writing clear

☑ is written at the right level for your needs (For example, a children's book is probably too simplistic, while a scientific paper may be too complex.)

☑ has the level of detail you need—neither too general nor too specific

☑ can be verified in more than one source

3 Sharing Your Research

At last you have established your research goals, located sources of information, evaluated the materials, and taken notes on what you learned. Now you have a chance to share the results with people in your world—and even beyond. Here are some options you may choose to present your work:

- Give a speech to your classmates or to people in your community.
- Create a power presentation using desktop publishing software and share it with classmates, friends, or family members.
- Describe your research findings on your own Web site.
- Summarize the information in a newsletter or brochure.
- Share the results of your research in a formal research paper.

Grammar Handbook

Writing that has a lot of mistakes can confuse or even annoy a reader. A business letter with a punctuation error might lead to a miscommunication and delay a reply. A sentence fragment might lower your grade on an essay. Paying attention to grammar, punctuation, and capitalization rules can make your writing clearer and easier to read.

Included throughout this handbook: LC1.1

Included in this handbook as indicated: LC1.2 (pgs. R53–R55)

Quick Reference: Parts of Speech

PART OF SPEECH	FUNCTION	EXAMPLES
Noun	names a person, a place, a thing, an idea, a quality, or an action	
Common	serves as a general name, or a name common to an entire group	coyote, hunter, spear, bonfire
Proper	names a specific, one-of-a-kind person, place, or thing	Rainy Mountain, Virginia, Puritans
Singular	refers to a single person, place, thing, or idea	field, pony, child, man
Plural	refers to more than one person, place, thing, or idea	fields, ponies, children, men
Concrete	names something that can be perceived by the senses	lemon, shores, wind, canoe
Abstract	names something that cannot be perceived by the senses	fear, intelligence, honesty
Compound	expresses a single idea through a combination of two or more words	birthright, folk tale, Sky-World
Collective	refers to a group of people or things	species, army, flock
Possessive	shows who or what owns something	America's, Douglass's, men's, slaves'
Pronoun	takes the place of a noun or another pronoun	
Personal	refers to the person(s) making a statement, the person(s) being addressed, or the person(s) or thing(s) the statement is about	I, me, my, mine, we, us, our, ours, you, your, yours, she, he, it, her, him, hers, his, its, they, them, their, theirs
Reflexive	follows a verb or preposition and refers to a preceding noun or pronoun	myself, yourself, herself, himself, itself, ourselves, yourselves, themselves
Intensive	emphasizes a noun or another pronoun	(same as reflexives)
Demonstrative	points to one or more specific persons or things	this, that, these, those
Interrogative	signals a question	who, whom, whose, which, what
Indefinite	refers to one or more persons or things not specifically mentioned	both, all, most, many, anyone, everybody, several, none, some
Relative	introduces an adjective clause by relating it to a word in the clause	who, whom, whose, which, that

PART OF SPEECH	FUNCTION	EXAMPLES
Verb	expresses an action, a condition, or a state of being	
Action	tells what the subject does or did, physically or mentally	run, reaches, listened, consider, decides, dreamed
Linking	connects the subject to something that identifies or describes it	am, is, are, was, were, sound, taste, appear, feel, become, remain, seem
Auxiliary	precedes the main verb in a verb phrase	be, have, do, can, could, will, would, may, might
Transitive	directs the action toward someone or something; always has an object	The wind **snapped** the young tree in half.
Intransitive	does not direct the action toward someone or something; does not have an object	The young tree **snapped.**
Adjective	modifies a noun or pronoun	**frightened** man, **two** epics, **enough** time
Adverb	modifies a verb, an adjective, or another adverb	walked **out, really** funny, **far** away
Preposition	relates one word to another word	at, by, for, from, in, of, on, to, with
Conjunction	joins words or word groups	
Coordinating	joins words or word groups used the same way	and, but, or, for, so, yet, nor
Correlative	used as a pair to join words or word groups used the same way	both . . . and, either . . . or, neither . . . nor
Subordinating	introduces a clause that cannot stand by itself as a complete sentence	although, after, as, before, because, when, if, unless
Interjection	expresses emotion	whew, yikes, uh-oh

Quick Reference: The Sentence and Its Parts

The diagrams that follow will give you a brief review of the essentials of a sentence and some of its parts.

Thoreau's original cabin cost less than 30 dollars.

The **complete subject** includes all the words that identify the person, place, thing, or idea that the sentence is about.

The **complete predicate** includes all the words that tell or ask something about the subject.

cabin

cost

The **simple subject** tells exactly whom or what the sentence is about. It may be one word or a group of words, but it does not include modifiers.

The **simple predicate**, or **verb**, tells what the subject does or is. It may be one word or several, but it does not include modifiers.

Every word in a sentence is part of a complete subject or a complete predicate.

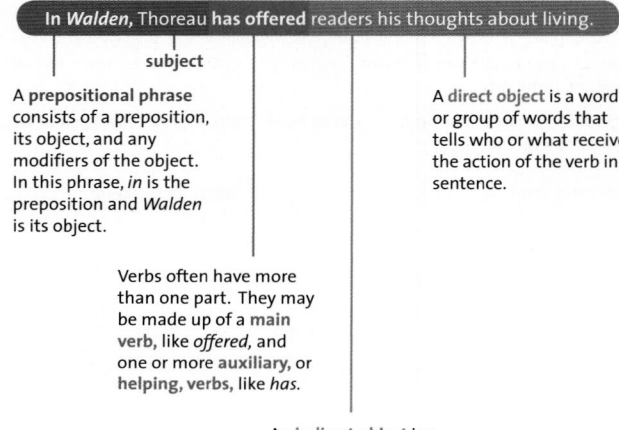

In *Walden*, Thoreau has offered readers his thoughts about living.

subject

A **prepositional phrase** consists of a preposition, its object, and any modifiers of the object. In this phrase, *in* is the preposition and *Walden* is its object.

A **direct object** is a word or group of words that tells who or what receives the action of the verb in a sentence.

Verbs often have more than one part. They may be made up of a **main verb**, like *offered*, and one or more **auxiliary**, or **helping**, **verbs**, like *has*.

An **indirect object** is a word or group of words that tells *to whom* or *for whom* or *to what* or *for what* about the verb. A sentence can have an indirect object only if it has a direct object. The indirect object always comes before the direct object in a sentence.

Quick Reference: Punctuation

MARK	FUNCTION	EXAMPLES
End Marks period, question mark, exclamation point	end a sentence	The games begin today. Who is your favorite contestant? What a play Jamie made!
period	follows an initial or abbreviation **Exception:** postal abbreviations of states	Prof. Ted Bakerman, D. H. Lawrence, Houghton Mifflin Co., P.M., A.D., oz., ft., Blvd., St. NE (Nebraska), NV (Nevada)
period	follows a number or letter in an outline	I. Volcanoes A. Central-vent 1. Shield
Comma	separates parts of a compound sentence	I had never disliked poetry, but now I really love it.
	separates items in a series	She is brave, loyal, and kind.
	separates adjectives of equal rank that modify the same noun	The slow, easy route is best.
	sets off a term of address	America, I love you. Come to the front, children.
	sets off a parenthetical expression	Hard workers, as you know, don't quit. I'm not a quitter, believe me.
	sets off an introductory word, phrase, or dependent clause	Yes, I forgot my key. At the beginning of the day, I feel fresh. While she was out, I was here. Having finished my chores, I went out.
	sets off a nonessential phrase or clause	Ed Pawn, the captain of the chess team, won. Ed Pawn, who is the captain, won. The two leading runners, sprinting toward the finish line, finished in a tie.
	sets off parts of dates and addresses	Send it by August 18, 2010, to Cherry Jubilee, Inc., 21 Vernona St., Oakland, Minnesota.
	follows the salutation and closing of a letter	Dear Jim, Sincerely yours,
	separates words to avoid confusion	By noon, time had run out. What the minister does, does matter. While cooking, Jim burned his hand.
Semicolon	separates items in a series if one or more items contain commas	We invited my sister, Jan; her friend, Don; my uncle Jack; and Mary Dodd.
	separates parts of a compound sentence that are not joined by a coordinating conjunction	The small books are on the top shelves; the large books are below. I dusted the books; however, I didn't wipe the shelves.
	separates parts of a compound sentence when the parts contain commas	After I ran out of money, I called my parents; but only my sister was home, unfortunately.

GRAMMAR HANDBOOK **R53**

For more help with punctuation, see

 GRAMMAR FOR WRITING
   pp. 222–263

MARK	FUNCTION	EXAMPLES
Colon	introduces a list	Those we wrote were the following: Dana, John, and Will.
	introduces a long quotation	Thomas Jefferson wrote: "We the people of the United States, in order to form a more perfect union...."
	follows the salutation of a business letter	Dear Ms. Williams: Dear Senator Wiley:
	separates certain numbers	1:28 P.M., Genesis 2:5
Dash	indicates an abrupt break in thought	I was thinking of my mother—who is arriving tomorrow—just as you walked in.
Parentheses	enclose less important material	Throughout her life (though some might think otherwise), she worked hard. The temperature on this July day (would you believe it?) is 65 degrees!
Hyphen	joins parts of a compound adjective before a noun	She lives in a first-floor apartment.
	joins parts of a compound with *all-*, *ex-*, *self-*, or *-elect*	The president-elect is a well-respected woman.
	joins parts of a compound number (to ninety-nine)	Today, I turn twenty-one.
	joins parts of a fraction	My cup is one-third full.
	joins a prefix to a word beginning with a capital letter	Life may have seemed simpler in pre-Civil War days. It's very chilly for mid-June.
	indicates that a word is divided at the end of a line	Did you know that school segrega-tion has been illegal since 1954?
Apostrophe	used with *s* to form the possessive of a noun or an indefinite pronoun	my friend's book, my friends' books, anyone's guess, somebody else's problem
	replaces one or more omitted letters in a contraction or numbers in a date	don't (omitted *o*), he'd (omitted *woul*), the class of '99 (omitted *19*)
	used with *s* to form the plural of a letter	I had two A's on my report card.
Quotation Marks	set off a speaker's exact words	Sara said, "I'm finally ready." "I'm ready," Sara said, "finally." Did Sara say, "I'm ready"? Sara said, "I'm ready!"
	set off the title of a story, an article, a short poem, an essay, a song, or a chapter	I liked Oates's "Hostage," Steinem's "Sisterhood," and Plath's "Mirror." Chapter II is titled "Our Gang's Dark Oath."
Ellipses	replace material omitted from a quotation	"We the people ... in order to form a more perfect union ...."
Italics	indicate the title of a book, a play, a magazine, a long poem, an opera, a film, or a TV series, or the names of ships, trains, and spacecraft	*The Scarlet Letter, The Crucible, Time, The Death of the Hired Man, West Side Story, Citizen Kane, The Spirit of St. Louis, The Best of Frank Sinatra, Lusitania*

Quick Reference: Capitalization

CATEGORY	EXAMPLES
People and Titles	
Names and initials of people	Emily Dickinson, T. S. Eliot
Titles used before or in place of names	Professor Holmes, Senator Long
Deities and members of religious groups	Jesus, Allah, Buddha, Zeus, Baptists, Roman Catholics
Names of ethnic and national groups	Hispanics, Jews, African Americans
Geographical Names	
Cities, states, countries, continents	New York, Maine, Haiti, Africa
Regions, bodies of water, mountains	the South, Lake Erie, Mount Katahdin
Geographic features, parks	Continental Divide, Everglades, Yellowstone
Streets and roads, planets	55 East Ninety-fifth Street, Maple Lane, Venus, Jupiter
Organizations, Events, Etc.	
Companies, organizations, teams	General Motors, Lions Club, Utah Jazz
Buildings, bridges, monuments	the Alamo, Golden Gate Bridge, Lincoln Memorial
Documents, awards	the Constitution, World Cup
Special named events	Super Bowl, World Series
Government bodies, historical periods and events	the Supreme Court, U.S. Senate, Harlem Renaissance, World War II
Days and months, holidays	Friday, May, Easter, Memorial Day
Specific cars, boats, trains, planes	Mustang, *Titanic*, *California Zephyr*
Proper Adjectives	
Adjectives formed from proper nouns	American League, French cooking, Emersonian period, Arctic waters
First Words and the Pronoun I	
First word in a sentence or quotation	This is it. He said, "Let's go."
First word of sentence in parentheses that is not within another sentence	The spelling rules are covered in another section. (Consult that section for more information.)
First words in the salutation and closing of a letter	Dear Madam, Very truly yours,
First word in each line of most poetry Personal pronoun *I*	Then am I A happy fly If I live Or if I die.
First word, last word, and all important words in a title	"The Fall of the House of Usher," *Incidents in the Life of a Slave Girl*

For more help with capitalization, see

 GRAMMAR FOR WRITING
pp. 200–221

For more help with pronouns, see

G GRAMMAR FOR WRITING
pp. 152–179

1 Nouns

A **noun** is a word used to name a person, a place, a thing, an idea, a quality, or an action. Nouns can be classified in several ways.

*For more information on different types of nouns, see **Quick Reference: Parts of Speech**, page R50.*

1.1 COMMON NOUNS

Common nouns are general names, common to entire groups.

> EXAMPLES: *writer, song, bravery*

1.2 PROPER NOUNS

Proper nouns name specific, one-of-a-kind things.

Common	Proper
writer, song, bravery, hunter	Mourning Dove, Mississippi, Granny

*For more information, see **Quick Reference: Capitalization**, page R55.*

1.3 SINGULAR AND PLURAL NOUNS

A noun may take a singular or a plural form, depending on whether it names a single person, place, thing, or idea or more than one. Make sure you use appropriate spellings when forming plurals.

Singular	Plural
church, lily, wife	churches, lilies, wives

*For more information, see **Forming Plural Nouns**, page R78.*

1.4 COMPOUND AND COLLECTIVE NOUNS

Compound nouns are formed from two or more words but express a single idea. They are written as single words, as separate words, or with hyphens. Use a dictionary to check the correct spelling of a compound noun.

> EXAMPLES: *birthright, folk tale, Sky-World*

Collective nouns are singular nouns that refer to groups of people or things.

> EXAMPLES: *army, flock, class, species*

1.5 POSSESSIVE NOUNS

A **possessive noun** shows who or what owns something.

> EXAMPLES: *Welty's, jury's, children's*

*For more information, see **Forming Possessives**, page R78.*

2 Pronouns

A **pronoun** is a word that is used in place of a noun or another pronoun. The word or word group to which the pronoun refers is called its **antecedent.**

2.1 PERSONAL PRONOUNS

Personal pronouns change their form to express person, number, gender, and case. The forms of these pronouns are shown in the following chart.

	Nominative	Objective	Possessive
Singular			
First person	I	me	my, mine
Second person	you	you	your, yours
Third person	she, he, it	her, him, it	her, hers, his, its
Plural			
First person	we	us	our, ours
Second person	you	you	your, yours
Third person	they	them	their, theirs

2.2 AGREEMENT WITH ANTECEDENT

Pronouns should agree with their antecedents in number, gender, and person.

If an antecedent is singular, use a singular pronoun.

> EXAMPLE: *Sarah laughed as her dog splashed in the lake.*

If an antecedent is plural, use a plural pronoun.

> EXAMPLES:
> *Sarah and Barbara took turns holding the leash as they walked the dog home.*
> *Andrew and Ryan finished the race before the rest of their teammates.*

The gender of a pronoun must be the same as the gender of its antecedent.

> EXAMPLES:
> *The little girl ran outside without tying her shoelaces.*
> *Daniel waved to his friends before boarding the plane.*

The person of the pronoun must be the same as the person of its antecedent. As the chart in Section 2.1 shows, a pronoun can be in first-, second-, or third-person form.

> EXAMPLE:
> *Those of you who like animals should consider getting your degree in veterinary science.*

GRAMMAR PRACTICE

Rewrite each sentence so that the underlined pronoun agrees with its antecedent.

1. *The World on the Turtle's Back* is a myth that tells about a pregnant woman and how <u>it</u> helped create the earth.

2. Many of the sea creatures and birds tried to retrieve the dirt at the bottom of the ocean, but they could not reach <u>him</u>.

3. The woman circles the earth with <u>their</u> daughter, helping the plants to grow.

4. Both of the twins molded clay animals and gave <u>it</u> life.

2.3 PRONOUN CASE

Personal pronouns change form to show how they function in sentences. Different functions are shown by different **cases.** The three cases are **nominative, objective,** and **possessive.** For examples of these pronouns, see the chart in Section 2.1.

A **nominative pronoun** is used as a subject or a predicate nominative in a sentence.

An **objective pronoun** is used as a direct object, an indirect object, or the object of a preposition.

```
SUBJECT      OBJECT      OBJECT OF PREPOSITION
  ↓            ↓            ↙
He explained it to me.
```

A **possessive pronoun** shows ownership. The pronouns *mine, yours, hers, his, its, ours,* and *theirs* can be used in place of nouns.

EXAMPLE: *These letters are yours.*

The pronouns *my, your, her, his, its, our,* and *their* are used before nouns.

EXAMPLE: *These are your letters.*

WATCH OUT! Many spelling errors can be avoided if you watch out for *its* and *their.* Don't confuse the possessive pronoun *its* with the contraction *it's,* meaning "it is" or "it has." The homonyms *they're* (a contraction of *they are*) and *there* ("in that place") are often mistakenly used for *their.*

TIP To decide which pronoun to use in a comparison, such as "He tells better tales than (I *or* me)," fill in the missing word(s): *He tells better tales than I* **tell.**

GRAMMAR PRACTICE

Replace the underlined words in each sentence with an appropriate pronoun and identify the pronoun as a nominative, objective, or possessive pronoun.

1. <u>Arthur Miller</u> was a playwright from New York.

2. *The Crucible* is one of <u>Arthur Miller's</u> most well-known plays.

3. <u>John Proctor and Reverend Parris</u> are two of the main characters.

4. Reverend Hale tries to convince <u>Rebecca Nurse and John Proctor</u> to falsely confess to practicing witchcraft.

5. <u>The Salem witch hunt</u> illustrates how the town's strict Christian principles indirectly caused the deaths of innocent villagers.

2.4 REFLEXIVE AND INTENSIVE PRONOUNS

These pronouns are formed by adding *-self* or *-selves* to certain personal pronouns. Their forms are the same, and they differ only in how they are used.

A **reflexive pronoun** follows a verb or preposition and reflects back on an earlier noun or pronoun.

EXAMPLES:
He threw himself forward.
Danielle mailed herself the package.

Intensive pronouns intensify or emphasize the nouns or pronouns to which they refer.

EXAMPLES:
The queen herself would have been amused.
I saw it myself.

WATCH OUT! Avoid using *hisself* or *theirselves.* Standard English does not include these forms.

NONSTANDARD: *He had painted hisself into a corner.*

STANDARD: *He had painted himself into a corner.*

2.5 DEMONSTRATIVE PRONOUNS

Demonstrative pronouns point out things and persons near and far.

	Singular	Plural
Near	this	these
Far	that	those

GRAMMAR PRACTICE
ANSWERS
1. *she*
2. *it*
3. *her*
4. *them*

GRAMMAR PRACTICE
ANSWERS
1. *He, nominative*
2. *his, possessive*
3. *They, nominative*
4. *them, objective*
5. *It, nominative*

GRAMMAR PRACTICE

ANSWERS

1. *who*
2. *who*
3. *Who*
4. *whose*

2.6 INDEFINITE PRONOUNS

Indefinite pronouns do not refer to specific persons or things and usually have no antecedents. The chart shows some commonly used indefinite pronouns.

Singular	Plural	Singular or Plural	
another	both	all	none
anybody	few	any	some
no one	many	more	most
neither	several		

TIP Indefinite pronouns that end in *one, body,* or *thing* are always singular.

> **INCORRECT:** *Does anybody think their hamburger is overcooked?*

> **CORRECT:** *Does anybody think his or her hamburger is overcooked?*

If the indefinite pronoun might refer to either a male or a female, *his or her* may be used to refer to it, or the sentence may be rewritten.

> **EXAMPLES:** *Everyone received his or her script.*
> *All the actors received their scripts.*

2.7 INTERROGATIVE PRONOUNS

An **interrogative pronoun** is used to ask a question. The interrogative pronouns are *who, whom, whose, which,* and *what.*

> **EXAMPLES:** *Whose backpack is on the kitchen table?*
> *Which dress do you prefer?*

TIP *Who* is used as a subject, *whom* as an object. To find out which pronoun you need to use in a question, change the question to a statement.

> **QUESTION:** *(Who/Whom) did you meet there?*
> **STATEMENT:** *You met (?) there.*

Since the verb has a subject (*you*), the needed word must be the object form, *whom.*

> **EXAMPLE:** *Whom did you meet there?*

WATCH OUT! A special problem arises when you use an interrupter, such as *do you think,* within a question.

> **EXAMPLE:** *(Who/Whom) do you believe is the more influential musician?*

If you eliminate the interrupter, it is clear that the word you need is *who.*

2.8 RELATIVE PRONOUNS

Relative pronouns relate, or connect, dependent (or subordinate) clauses to the words they modify in sentences. The relative pronouns are *that, what, whatever, which, whichever, who, whoever, whom, whomever,* and *whose.*

Sometimes short sentences with related ideas can be combined by using a relative pronoun.

> **SHORT SENTENCE:** *Mark Twain may be America's greatest humorist.*

> **RELATED SENTENCE:** *Mark Twain wrote* Huckleberry Finn.

> **COMBINED SENTENCE:** *Mark Twain, who wrote* Huckleberry Finn, *may be America's greatest humorist.*

GRAMMAR PRACTICE

Choose the appropriate interrogative or relative pronoun from the words in parentheses.

1. "The Notorious Jumping Frog" was written by Samuel Clemens, (who/whom) wrote under the pseudonym Mark Twain.

2. The story gained national fame for Mark Twain, (who/that) first published it in 1865.

3. (Who/Whom) do you think is funnier, Jim Smiley or the storyteller Simon Wheeler?

4. Smiley spent months educating his frog, (which/whose) fame as a jumper spread throughout the gold camps.

2.9 PRONOUN REFERENCE PROBLEMS

The referent of a pronoun should always be clear.

An **indefinite reference** occurs when the pronoun *it, you,* or *they* does not clearly refer to a specific antecedent.

> **UNCLEAR:** *In the review, it claimed the movie is well done.*

> **CLEAR:** *The review claimed the movie is well done.*

A **general reference** occurs when the pronoun *it, this, that, which,* or *such* is used to refer to a general idea rather than a specific antecedent.

> **UNCLEAR:** *Stella tutors students every day after school. This lets her help kids who are struggling with their schoolwork.*

> **CLEAR:** *Stella tutors students every day after school. Tutoring lets her help kids who are struggling with their schoolwork.*

Ambiguous means "having more than one possible meaning." An **ambiguous reference** occurs when a pronoun could refer to two or more antecedents.

UNCLEAR: *Stacey made Miranda a sandwich while she talked on the phone.*

CLEAR: *While Stacey talked on the phone, she made Miranda a sandwich.*

GRAMMAR PRACTICE

Rewrite the following sentences to correct indefinite, ambiguous, and general pronoun references.

1. In the poem "The Raven," it tells about a man who is grieving for his lover.

2. The raven refused to abandon its perch above the door. This frustrated the narrator.

3. The narrator told the raven that he thought he was a messenger from Lenore.

4. The raven always responded, "Nevermore." This frightened and confused the speaker.

3 Verbs

A **verb** is a word that expresses an action, a condition, or a state of being.

For more information, see Quick Reference: Parts of Speech, page R50.

3.1 ACTION VERBS

Action verbs express mental or physical activity.

EXAMPLE: *I walked to the store.*

3.2 LINKING VERBS

Linking verbs join subjects with words or phrases that rename or describe them.

EXAMPLE: *You are my friend.*

3.3 PRINCIPAL PARTS

Action and linking verbs typically have four principal parts, which are used to form verb tenses. The principal parts are the **present,** the **present participle,** the **past,** and the **past participle.**

Action verbs and some linking verbs also fall into two categories: regular and irregular. A **regular verb** is a verb that forms its past and past participle by adding -*ed* or -*d* to the present form.

Present	Present Participle	Past	Past Participle
perform	(is) performing	performed	(has) performed
hope	(is) hoping	hoped	(has) hoped
stop	(is) stopping	stopped	(has) stopped
marry	(is) marrying	married	(has) married

An **irregular verb** is a verb that forms its past and past participle in some other way than by adding -*ed* or -*d* to the present form.

Present	Present Participle	Past	Past Participle
bring	(is) bringing	brought	(has) brought
swim	(is) swimming	swam	(has) swum
steal	(is) stealing	stole	(has) stolen
grow	(is) growing	grew	(has) grown

3.4 VERB TENSE

The **tense** of a verb indicates the time of the action or state of being. An action or state of being can occur in the present, the past, or the future. There are six tenses, each expressing a different range of time.

The **present tense** expresses an action or state that is happening at the present time, occurs regularly, or is constant or generally true. Use the present part.

NOW: *That poet reads well.*

REGULAR: *I swim every day.*

GENERAL: *Time flies.*

The **past tense** expresses an action that began and ended in the past. Use the past part.

EXAMPLE: *The storyteller finished his tale.*

The **future tense** expresses an action or state that will occur. Use *shall* or *will* with the present part.

EXAMPLE: *They will attend the next festival.*

The **present perfect tense** expresses an action or state that (1) was completed at an indefinite time in the past or (2) began in the past and continues into the present. Use *have* or *has* with the past participle.

EXAMPLE: *Poetry has inspired readers throughout the ages.*

GRAMMAR PRACTICE

ANSWERS

Possible answers:

1. *The poem "The Raven" tells about a man grieving for his lover.*

2. *The raven refused to abandon its perch above the door. The raven's refusal frustrated the narrator.*

3. *The narrator told the raven that he thought the raven was a messenger from Lenore.*

4. *The raven always responded, "Nevermore." The raven's response frightened and confused the speaker.*

For more help with verbs, see

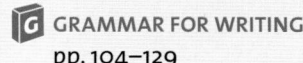 **GRAMMAR FOR WRITING**
pp. 104–129

GRAMMAR PRACTICE

ANSWERS

1. *is = present*

2. *ended = past*

   had lost = past perfect

3. *knew = past*

   pertains = present

   pertains > pertained

4. *will read = future*

   will apply = future

5. *accuse = present*

   knew = past

   knew > know

The **past perfect tense** expresses an action in the past that came before another action in the past. Use *had* with the past participle.

> **EXAMPLE:** *The witness had testified before the defendant confessed.*

The future perfect tense expresses an action in the future that will be completed before another action in the future. Use *shall have* or *will have* with the past participle.

> **EXAMPLE:** *They will have finished the novel before seeing the movie version of the tale.*

TIP The past-tense form of an irregular verb is not paired with an auxiliary verb, but the past-perfect-tense form of an irregular verb is always paired with an auxiliary verb.

> **INCORRECT:** *I have went to that restaurant before.*
>
> **INCORRECT:** *I gone to that restaurant before.*
>
> **CORRECT:** *I have gone to that restaurant before.*

3.5 PROGRESSIVE FORMS

The progressive forms of the six tenses show ongoing actions. Use forms of *be* with the present participles of verbs.

> **PRESENT PROGRESSIVE:** *She is rehearsing her lines.*
>
> **PAST PROGRESSIVE:** *She was rehearsing her lines.*
>
> **FUTURE PROGRESSIVE:** *She will be rehearsing her lines.*
>
> **PRESENT PERFECT PROGRESSIVE:** *She has been rehearsing her lines.*
>
> **PAST PERFECT PROGRESSIVE:** *She had been rehearsing her lines.*
>
> **FUTURE PERFECT PROGRESSIVE:** *She will have been rehearsing her lines.*

WATCH OUT! Do not shift from tense to tense needlessly. Watch out for these special cases:

- In most compound sentences and in sentences with compound predicates, keep the tenses the same.

  > **INCORRECT:** *Every morning they get up and went to work.*
  >
  > **CORRECT:** *Every morning they get up and go to work.*

- If one past action happened before another, indicate this with a shift in tense.

  > **INCORRECT:** *She thought she forgot her toothbrush.*
  >
  > **CORRECT:** *She thought she had forgotten her toothbrush.*

GRAMMAR PRACTICE

Identify the tense of the verb(s) in each of the following sentences. If you find an unnecessary tense shift, correct it.

1. The setting of *The Crucible* is the late 17th century in Salem, Massachusetts.

2. Before the witch trials ended, people had lost their ability to make objective judgments.

3. Playwright Arthur Miller knew that the play pertains to his own time.

4. People will read it far into the future, and many will apply its message to their own time.

5. In the play some accuse others of being witches, even though they knew the accusation was false.

3.6 ACTIVE AND PASSIVE VOICE

The voice of a verb tells whether its subject performs or receives the action expressed by the verb. When the subject performs the action, the verb is in the **active voice.** When the subject is the receiver of the action, the verb is in the **passive voice.**

Compare these two sentences:

> **ACTIVE:** *The Puritans did not celebrate Christmas.*
>
> **PASSIVE:** *Christmas was not celebrated by the Puritans.*

To form the passive voice, use a form of *be* with the past participle of the verb.

WATCH OUT! Use the passive voice sparingly. It can make writing awkward and less direct.

> **AWKWARD:** *The stories of hysterical witnesses were believed by gullible and fearful jurors.*
>
> **BETTER:** *Gullible and fearful jurors believed the stories of hysterical witnesses.*

There are occasions when you will choose to use the passive voice because

- you want to emphasize the receiver: *The king was shot.*
- the doer is unknown: *My books were stolen.*
- the doer is unimportant: *French is spoken here.*

For the five items below, identify the boldfaced verb phrase as active or passive.

1. *The Crucible* **has played** in theaters throughout the world.

2. It **was written** by Arthur Miller, one of America's greatest dramatists.

3. Miller **did** not **approve** of Reverend Parris's greed for gold.

4. **Has** the reputation of the minister **been maligned?**

4 Modifiers

Modifiers are words or groups of words that change or limit the meanings of other words. Adjectives and adverbs are common modifiers.

4.1 ADJECTIVES

Adjectives modify nouns and pronouns by telling which one, what kind, how many, or how much.

WHICH ONE: *this, that, these, those*

EXAMPLE: *That couch needs to be reupholstered.*

WHAT KIND: *large, unique, anxious, moldy*

EXAMPLE: *The anxious speaker shuffled through her notes.*

HOW MANY: *ten, many, several, every, each*

EXAMPLE: *Each child grabbed several candies from the bowl.*

HOW MUCH: *more, less, little*

EXAMPLE: *There was more snow on the ground in the morning.*

4.2 PREDICATE ADJECTIVES

Most adjectives come before the nouns they modify, as in the previous examples. A **predicate adjective,** however, follows a linking verb and describes the subject.

EXAMPLE: *My friends are very intelligent.*

Be especially careful to use adjectives (not adverbs) after such linking verbs as *look, feel, grow, taste,* and *smell.*

EXAMPLE: *The weather grows cold.*

4.3 ADVERBS

Adverbs modify verbs, adjectives, and other adverbs by telling where, when, how, or to what extent.

WHERE: *The children played outside.*

WHEN: *The author spoke yesterday.*

HOW: *We walked slowly behind the leader.*

TO WHAT EXTENT: *He worked very hard.*

Adverbs may occur in many places in sentences, both before and after the words they modify.

EXAMPLES: *Suddenly the wind shifted.*

The wind suddenly shifted.

The wind shifted suddenly.

4.4 ADJECTIVE OR ADVERB?

Many adverbs are formed by adding *-ly* to adjectives.

EXAMPLES: *sweet, sweetly; gentle, gently*

However, *-ly* added to a noun will usually yield an adjective.

EXAMPLES: *friend, friendly; woman, womanly*

4.5 COMPARISON OF MODIFIERS

Modifiers can be used to compare two or more things. The form of a modifier shows the degree of comparison. Both adjectives and adverbs have three forms: the **positive,** the **comparative,** and the **superlative**.

The **positive form** is used to describe individual things, groups, or actions.

EXAMPLES:

Stephen Crane was a great writer.

His descriptions are vivid.

The **comparative form** is used to compare two things, groups, or actions.

EXAMPLES:

I think that Stephen Crane was a greater writer than Jack London.

Crane's descriptions are more vivid.

The **superlative form** is used to compare more than two things, groups, or actions.

EXAMPLES:

I think that Crane was the greatest writer of his era.

Crane's descriptions are the most vivid I have ever read.

ANSWERS

1. *active*

2. *passive*

3. *active*

4. *passive*

For more help with modifiers, see

 GRAMMAR FOR WRITING
pp. 180–199

4.6 REGULAR COMPARISONS

Most one-syllable and some two-syllable adjectives and adverbs have comparatives and superlatives formed by adding -er and -est. All three-syllable and most two-syllable modifiers have comparatives and superlatives formed with *more* and *most*.

Modifier	Comparative	Superlative
tall	taller	tallest
kind	kinder	kindest
droopy	droopier	droopiest
expensive	more expensive	most expensive
wasteful	more wasteful	most wasteful

WATCH OUT! Note that spelling changes must sometimes be made to form the comparatives and superlatives of modifiers.

EXAMPLES:

friendly, friendlier (Change *y* to *i* and add the ending.)
sad, sadder (Double the final consonant and add the ending.)

4.7 IRREGULAR COMPARISONS

Some commonly used modifiers have irregular comparative and superlative forms. They are listed in the following chart.

Modifier	Comparative	Superlative
good	better	best
bad	worse	worst
far	farther *or* further	farthest *or* furthest
little	less *or* lesser	least
many	more	most
well	better	best
much	more	most

4.8 PROBLEMS WITH MODIFIERS

Study the tips that follow to avoid common mistakes:

Farther and Further Use *farther* for distances; use *further* for everything else.

Double Comparisons Make a comparison by using -er/ -est or by using *more/most*. Using -er with *more* or using -est with *most* is incorrect.

INCORRECT: *I like her more better than she likes me.*

CORRECT: *I like her better than she likes me.*

Illogical Comparisons An illogical or confusing comparison results when two unrelated things are compared or when something is compared with itself. The word *other* or the word *else* should be used in a comparison of an individual member to the rest of a group.

ILLOGICAL: *The narrator was more curious about the war than any student in his class.* (implies that the narrator isn't a student in the class)

LOGICAL: *The narrator was more curious about the war than any other student in his class.* (identifies that the narrator is a student)

Bad vs. Badly *Bad,* always an adjective, is used before a noun or after a linking verb. *Badly,* always an adverb, never modifies a noun. Be sure to use the right form after a linking verb.

INCORRECT: *Ed felt badly after his team lost.*

CORRECT: *Ed felt bad after his team lost.*

Good vs. Well *Good* is always an adjective. It is used before a noun or after a linking verb. *Well* is often an adverb meaning "expertly" or "properly." *Well* can also be used as an adjective after a linking verb when it means "in good health."

INCORRECT: *Helen writes very good.*

CORRECT: *Helen writes very well.*

CORRECT: *Yesterday I felt bad; today I feel well.*

Double Negatives If you add a negative word to a sentence that is already negative, the result will be an error known as a double negative. When using *not* or -n't with a verb, use *any-* words, such as *anybody* or *anything,* rather than *no-* words, such as *nobody* or *nothing,* later in the sentence.

INCORRECT: *I don't have no money.*

CORRECT: *I don't have any money.*

Using *hardly, barely,* or *scarcely* after a negative word is also incorrect.

INCORRECT: *They couldn't barely see two feet ahead.*

CORRECT: *They could barely see two feet ahead.*

Misplaced Modifiers Sometimes a modifier is placed so far away from the word it modifies that the intended meaning of the sentence is unclear. Prepositional phrases and participial phrases are often misplaced. Place modifiers as close as possible to the words they modify.

> MISPLACED: *The ranger explained how to find ducks in her office.* (The ducks were not in the ranger's office.)

> CLEARER: *In her office, the ranger explained how to find ducks.*

Dangling Modifiers Sometimes a modifier doesn't appear to modify any word in a sentence. Most dangling modifiers are participial phrases or infinitive phrases.

> DANGLING: *Coming home with groceries, our parrot said, "Hello!"*

> CLEARER: *Coming home with groceries, we heard our parrot say, "Hello!"*

GRAMMAR PRACTICE

Choose the correct word or words from each pair in parentheses.

1. Flannery O'Connor's story is (better/more better) than other stories I have read recently.

2. Mr. Shiftlet and Mrs. Crater (could/couldn't) hardly be less honest with each other.

3. Mr. Shiftlet says there isn't (any/no) broken thing on the farm that he can't fix.

4. He feels (good/well) about fixing the car.

5. Who do you think is the (stranger/strangest) person—Mr. Shiftlet or Mrs. Crater?

6. Mr. Shiftlet feels (bad/badly) about the rottenness of the world.

7. As Mr. Shiftlet drove on alone he felt (depresseder/more depressed) than ever.

8. Mr. Shiftlet didn't feel very (well/good) about being alone, so he picked up a hitchhiker.

9. One wonders how many other great stories Flannery O'Connor would have written had she lived (longer/more longer).

5 Prepositions, Conjunctions, and Interjections

5.1 PREPOSITIONS

A preposition is a word used to show the relationship between a noun or a pronoun and another word in the sentence.

Commonly Used Prepositions			
above	down	near	through
at	for	of	to
before	from	on	up
below	in	out	with
by	into	over	without

A preposition is always followed by a word or group of words that serves as its object. The preposition, its object, and modifiers of the object are called the **prepositional phrase.** In each example below, the prepositional phrase is highlighted and the object of the preposition is in boldface type.

> EXAMPLES:
> *The future of the entire* **kingdom** *is uncertain.*
> *We searched through the deepest* **woods.**

Prepositional phrases may be used as adjectives or as adverbs. The phrase in the first example is used as an adjective modifying the noun *future.* In the second example, the phrase is used as an adverb modifying the verb *searched.*

> WATCH OUT! Prepositional phrases must be as close as possible to the word they modify.

> MISPLACED: *We have clothes for leisurewear of many colors.*

> CLEARER: *We have clothes of many colors for leisurewear.*

5.2 CONJUNCTIONS

A conjunction is a word used to connect words, phrases, or sentences. There are three kinds of conjunctions: **coordinating conjunctions, correlative conjunctions,** and **subordinating conjunctions.**

Coordinating conjunctions connect words or word groups that have the same function in a sentence. They include *and, but, or, for, so, yet,* and *nor.*

Coordinating conjunctions can join nouns, pronouns, verbs, adjectives, adverbs, prepositional phrases, and clauses in a sentence.

GRAMMAR PRACTICE

ANSWERS

1. *better*
2. *could*
3. *any*
4. *good*
5. *stranger*
5. *bad*
7. *more depressed*
8. *good*
9. *longer*

For more help with the sentence and its parts, see

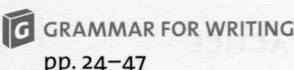 GRAMMAR FOR WRITING
pp. 24–47

These examples show coordinating conjunctions joining words of the same function:

EXAMPLES:

I have many friends but few enemies. (two noun objects)

We ran out the door and into the street. (two prepositional phrases)

They are pleasant yet seem aloof. (two predicates)

We have to go now, or we will be late. (two clauses)

Correlative conjunctions are similar to coordinating conjunctions. However, correlative conjunctions are always used in pairs.

Correlative Conjunctions		
both . . . and	neither . . . nor	whether . . . or
either . . . or	not only . . . but also	

Subordinating conjunctions introduce subordinate clauses—clauses that cannot stand by themselves as complete sentences. The subordinating conjunction shows how the subordinate clause relates to the rest of the sentence. The relationships include time, manner, place, cause, comparison, condition, and purpose.

Subordinating Conjunctions	
Time	*after, as, as long as, as soon as, before, since, until, when, whenever, while*
Manner	*as, as if*
Place	*where, wherever*
Cause	*because, since*
Comparison	*as, as much as, than*
Condition	*although, as long as, even if, even though, if, provided that, though, unless, while*
Purpose	*in order that, so that, that*

In the example below, the boldface word is the conjunction, and the highlighted words form a subordinate clause:

EXAMPLE: *Walt Whitman was a man of the people,* **although** *many did not appreciate his poems.*

Walt Whitman was a man of the people is an independent clause, because it can stand alone as a complete sentence. *Although many did not appreciate his poems* cannot stand alone as a complete sentence; it is thus a subordinate clause.

Conjunctive adverbs are used to connect clauses that can stand by themselves as sentences. Conjunctive adverbs include *also, besides, finally, however, moreover, nevertheless, otherwise,* and *then.*

EXAMPLE: *She loved the fall; however, she also enjoyed winter.*

5.3 INTERJECTIONS

Interjections are words used to show emotion, such as *wow* and *cool.* Interjections are usually set off from the rest of a sentence by a comma or by an exclamation mark.

EXAMPLE: *Thoreau lived in the woods by himself. Amazing!*

6 The Sentence and Its Parts

A **sentence** is a group of words used to express a complete thought. A complete sentence has a subject and a predicate.

*For more information, see **Quick Reference: The Sentence and Its Parts,** page R52.*

6.1 KINDS OF SENTENCES

There are four basic types of sentences.

Type	Definition	Example
Declarative	states a fact, a wish, an intent, or a feeling	I wrote an essay on "The Weary Blues" for class.
Interrogative	asks a question	Are you familiar with Langston Hughes?
Imperative	gives a command or direction	Read "The Weary Blues" aloud.
Exclamatory	expresses strong feeling or excitement	It sounds like a song!

6.2 COMPOUND SUBJECTS AND PREDICATES

A compound subject consists of two or more subjects that share the same verb. They are typically joined by the coordinating conjunction *and* or *or.*

EXAMPLE: *Courtney and Eric enjoy the theater.*

A compound predicate consists of two or more predicates that share the same subject. They too are typically joined by a coordinating conjunction, usually *and, but,* or *or.*

EXAMPLE: *The main character in "Winter Dreams" attended a prestigious university and became a successful businessman.*

6.3 COMPLEMENTS

A **complement** is a word or group of words that completes the meaning of the sentence. Some sentences contain only a subject and a verb. Most sentences, however, require additional words placed after the verb to complete the meaning of the sentence. There are three kinds of complements: direct objects, indirect objects, and subject complements.

Direct objects are words or word groups that receive the action of action verbs. A direct object answers the question *what* or *whom*.

> **EXAMPLES:**
>
> *The students asked many questions.* (Asked what?)
>
> *The teacher quickly answered the students.* (Answered whom?)

Indirect objects tell to whom or what or for whom or what the actions of verbs are performed. Indirect objects come before direct objects. In the examples that follow, the indirect objects are highlighted.

> **EXAMPLES:**
>
> My sister usually gave her *friends* good advice. (Gave to whom?)
>
> *Her brother sent the store a heavy package.* (Sent to what?)

Subject complements come after linking verbs and identify or describe the subjects. A subject complement that names or identifies a subject is called a **predicate nominative.** Predicate nominatives include **predicate nouns** and **predicate pronouns.**

> **EXAMPLES:**
>
> *My friends are very hard workers.*
>
> *The best writer in the class is she.*

A subject complement that describes a subject is called a **predicate adjective.**

> **EXAMPLE:** *The pianist appeared very energetic.*

7 Phrases

A **phrase** is a group of related words that does not contain a subject and a predicate but functions in a sentence as a single part of speech.

7.1 PREPOSITIONAL PHRASES

A **prepositional phrase** is a phrase that consists of a preposition, its object, and any modifiers of the object. Prepositional phrases that modify nouns or pronouns are called **adjective phrases.** Prepositional phrases that modify verbs, adjectives, or adverbs are **adverb phrases.**

> **ADJECTIVE PHRASE:** *The central character of the story is a villain.*
>
> **ADVERB PHRASE:** *He reveals his nature in the first scene.*

7.2 APPOSITIVES AND APPOSITIVE PHRASES

An **appositive** is a noun or pronoun that identifies or renames another noun or pronoun. An **appositive phrase** includes an appositive and modifiers of it.

An appositive can be either **essential** or **nonessential.** An **essential appositive** provides information that is needed to identify what is referred to by the preceding noun or pronoun.

> **EXAMPLE:** The Glass Menagerie *was written by playwright Tennessee Williams.*

A **nonessential appositive** adds extra information about a noun or pronoun whose meaning is already clear. Nonessential appositives and appositive phrases are set off with commas.

> **EXAMPLE:** *Williams uses Laura's glass menagerie, a collection of fragile animal figurines, to represent her relationship to reality.*

8 Verbals and Verbal Phrases

A **verbal** is a verb form that is used as a noun, an adjective, or an adverb. A **verbal phrase** consists of a verbal along with its modifiers and complements. There are three kinds of verbals: **infinitives, participles,** and **gerunds.**

8.1 INFINITIVES AND INFINITIVE PHRASES

An **infinitive** is a verb form that usually begins with *to* and functions as a noun, an adjective, or an adverb. An **infinitive phrase** consists of an infinitive plus its modifiers and complements. The examples that follow show several uses of infinitive phrases.

> **NOUN:** *To know her is my only desire.* (subject)
>
> *I'm planning to walk with you.* (direct object)
>
> *Her goal was to promote women's rights.* (predicate nominative)
>
> **ADJECTIVE:** *We saw his need to be loved.* (adjective modifying *need*)
>
> **ADVERB:** *She wrote to voice her opinions.* (adverb modifying *wrote*)

Because infinitives usually begin with *to*, it is usually easy to recognize them. However, sometimes *to* may be omitted.

> **EXAMPLE:** *Let no one dare [to] enter this shrine.*

For more help with verbals and verbal phrases, see

 GRAMMAR FOR WRITING
pp. 56–63

For more help with phrases, see

 GRAMMAR FOR WRITING
pp. 48–55

GRAMMAR PRACTICE

ANSWERS

1. *appositive phrase*
2. *infinitive phrase*
3. *participial phrase*
4. *appositive phrase*
5. *gerund phrase*

For more help with clauses, see

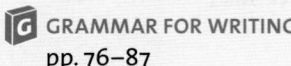 GRAMMAR FOR WRITING
pp. 76–87

8.2 PARTICIPLES AND PARTICIPIAL PHRASES

A **participle** is a verb form that functions as an adjective. Like adjectives, participles modify nouns and pronouns. Most participles are present-participle forms, ending in *-ing*, or past-participle forms ending in *-ed* or *-en*. In the examples that follow, the participles are highlighted:

MODIFYING A NOUN: *The jogging woman completed another lap on the track.*

MODIFYING A PRONOUN: *Bored, he began to doodle in the margins of his notebook.*

Participial phrases are participles with all their modifiers and complements.

MODIFYING A NOUN: *Changing tactics, the attorney questioned the witness.*

MODIFYING A PRONOUN: *Dismissed for the day, they filed out of the courtroom.*

8.3 DANGLING AND MISPLACED PARTICIPLES

A participle or participial phrase should be placed as close as possible to the word that it modifies. Otherwise the meaning of the sentence may not be clear.

MISPLACED: *The boys were looking for squirrels searching the trees.*

CLEARER: *The boys searching the trees were looking for squirrels.*

A participle or participial phrase that does not clearly modify anything in a sentence is called a **dangling participle.** A dangling participle causes confusion because it appears to modify a word that it cannot sensibly modify. Correct a dangling participle by providing a word for the participle to modify.

DANGLING: *Running like the wind, my hat fell off.* (The hat wasn't running.)

CLEARER: *Running like the wind, I lost my hat.*

8.4 GERUNDS AND GERUND PHRASES

A **gerund** is a verb form ending in *-ing* that functions as a noun. Gerunds may perform any function nouns perform.

SUBJECT: *Running is my favorite pastime.*

DIRECT OBJECT: *I truly love running.*

INDIRECT OBJECT: *You should give running a try.*

SUBJECT COMPLEMENT: *My deepest passion is running.*

OBJECT OF PREPOSITION: *Her love of running keeps her strong.*

Gerund phrases are gerunds with all their modifiers and complements.

SUBJECT: *Wishing on a star never got me far.*

OBJECT OF PREPOSITION: *I will finish before leaving the office.*

APPOSITIVE: *Her avocation, flying airplanes, finally led to full-time employment.*

GRAMMAR PRACTICE

Identify the underlined phrases as appositive phrases, infinitive phrases, participial phrases, or gerund phrases.

1. In "The Masque of the Red Death," Poe uses allegory, <u>a device representing abstract qualities.</u>

2. <u>To escape the plague,</u> Prince Prospero seals himself and his courtiers in a walled abbey.

3. <u>Feeling protected from the Red Death,</u> Prospero holds a lavish masquerade ball.

4. There suddenly appears in the last room a masked figure, <u>the Red Death in a ghastly shroud.</u>

5. <u>Killing the apparition</u> is impossible.

9 Clauses

A **clause** is a group of words that contains a subject and a verb. There are two kinds of clauses: independent clauses and subordinate clauses.

9.1 INDEPENDENT AND SUBORDINATE CLAUSES

An **independent clause** can stand alone as a sentence, as the word *independent* suggests.

INDEPENDENT CLAUSE: *Frederick Douglass was an eloquent speaker.*

A sentence may contain more than one independent clause.

EXAMPLE: *Frederick Douglass was an eloquent speaker, but he encountered a lot of opposition.*

In the preceding example, the coordinating conjunction *but* joins two independent clauses.

*For more information, see **Conjunctions,** page R63.*

A **subordinate clause** cannot stand alone as a sentence. It is subordinate to, or dependent on, an independent clause.

> **EXAMPLE:** *Although Frederick Douglass was a runaway slave, he frequently appeared in public to raise support for the abolitionist movement.*

The highlighted clause cannot stand by itself; it must be joined with an independent clause to form a complete sentence.

9.2 ADJECTIVE CLAUSES

An **adjective clause** is a subordinate clause used as an adjective. It usually follows the noun or pronoun it modifies. Adjective clauses are typically introduced by the relative pronoun *who, whom, whose, which,* or *that.*

> **EXAMPLES:** *Frederick Douglass wrote objectively about the whippings that Corey frequently gave him.*
>
> *The autobiographer whom I liked best was Frederick Douglass.*
>
> *He was a man who was determined to find freedom.*

*For more information, see **Relative Pronouns,** page R58.*

An adjective clause can be either essential or nonessential. An **essential adjective clause** provides information that is necessary to identify the preceding noun or pronoun.

> **EXAMPLE:** *The couch that we picked out will not be delivered for three weeks.*

A **nonessential adjective clause** adds additional information about a noun or pronoun whose meaning is already clear. Nonessential clauses are set off with commas.

> **EXAMPLE:** *Joel's grandmother, who was born in Italy, makes the best lasagna.*

> **TIP** The relative pronouns *whom, which,* and *that* may sometimes be omitted when they are objects in adjective clauses.
>
> **EXAMPLE:** *The autobiographer [whom] I liked best was Frederick Douglass.*

9.3 ADVERB CLAUSES

An **adverb clause** is a subordinate clause that is used to modify a verb, an adjective, or an adverb. It is introduced by a subordinating conjunction.

*For more information, see **Conjunctions,** page R63.*

Adverb clauses typically occur at the beginning or end of sentences.

> **MODIFYING A VERB:** *When we need you, we will call.*
>
> **MODIFYING AN ADVERB:** *I'll stay here where there is shelter from the rain.*
>
> **MODIFYING AN ADJECTIVE:** *Roman felt as good as he had ever felt.*

9.4 NOUN CLAUSES

A **noun clause** is a subordinate clause that is used as a noun. A noun clause may be used as a subject, a direct object, an indirect object, a predicate nominative, or the object of a preposition. Noun clauses are introduced either by pronouns, such as *that, what, who, whoever, which,* and *whose,* or by subordinating conjunctions, such as *how, when, where, why,* and *whether.*

*For more information, see **Conjunctions,** page R63.*

> **TIP** Because the same words may introduce adjective and noun clauses, you need to consider how a clause functions within its sentence. To determine if a clause is a noun clause, try substituting *something* or *someone* for the clause. If you can do it, it is probably a noun clause.
>
> **EXAMPLES:** *I know whose woods these are.*
>
> ("I know *something.*" The clause is a noun clause, direct object of the verb *know.*)
>
> *Give a copy to whoever wants one.* ("Give a copy to *someone.*" The clause is a noun clause, object of the preposition *to.*)

🔟 The Structure of Sentences

When classified by their structure, there are four kinds of sentences: simple, compound, complex, and compound-complex.

10.1 SIMPLE SENTENCES

A **simple sentence** is a sentence that has one independent clause and no subordinate clauses. Various parts of simple sentences may be compound, and simple sentences may contain grammatical structures such as appositive and verbal phrases.

> **EXAMPLES:**
>
> *Ambrose Bierce and Stephen Crane, two great American writers, both wrote during the latter half of the 19th century. (compound subject and an appositive)*
>
> *Crane, best known for writing fiction, also wrote great poetry. (participial phrase containing a gerund phrase)*

For more help with the structure of sentences, see

 GRAMMAR FOR WRITING
pp. 88–90

For more help with writing complete sentences, see

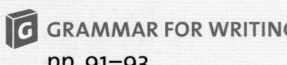 GRAMMAR FOR WRITING
pp. 91–93

10.2 COMPOUND SENTENCES

A **compound sentence** consists of two or more independent clauses. The clauses in compound sentences are joined with commas and coordinating conjunctions (*and, but, or, nor, yet, for, so*) or with semicolons. Like simple sentences, compound sentences do not contain any subordinate clauses.

> **EXAMPLES:**
>
> *I enjoyed the free pottery class, and I would like to go again.*
>
> *Carl Sandburg's "Chicago" seems to celebrate the youthful energy of a booming industrial city; however, the poem dwells on the negative impacts of growth.*

WATCH OUT! Do not confuse compound sentences with simple sentences that have compound parts.

> **EXAMPLE:** *The center fielder caught the ball and immediately threw it toward second base.* (Here *and* joins parts of a compound predicate, not a compound sentence.)

10.3 COMPLEX SENTENCES

A **complex sentence** consists of one independent clause and one or more subordinate clauses. Each subordinate clause can be used as a noun or as a modifier. If it is used as a modifier, a subordinate clause usually modifies a word in the independent clause, and the independent clause can stand alone. However, when a subordinate clause is a noun clause, it is a part of the independent clause; the two cannot be separated.

> **MODIFIER:** *One should not complain unless one has a better solution.*
>
> **NOUN CLAUSE:** *We sketched pictures of whoever we wished.* (The noun clause is the object of the preposition *of* and cannot be separated from the rest of the sentence.)

10.4 COMPOUND-COMPLEX SENTENCES

A **compound-complex sentence** contains two or more independent clauses and one or more subordinate clauses. Compound-complex sentences are, simply, both compound and complex. If you start with a compound sentence, all you need to do to form a compound-complex sentence is add a subordinate clause.

> **COMPOUND:** *All the students knew the answer, yet they were too shy to volunteer.*
>
> **COMPOUND-COMPLEX:** *All the students knew the answer that their teacher expected, yet they were too shy to volunteer.*

10.5 PARALLEL STRUCTURE

When you write sentences, make sure that coordinate parts are equivalent, or **parallel,** in structure.

> **NOT PARALLEL:** *Erin loved basketball and to play hockey.* (*Basketball* is a noun; *to play hockey* is a phrase.)
>
> **PARALLEL:** *Erin loved basketball and hockey.* (*Basketball* and *hockey* are both nouns.)
>
> **NOT PARALLEL:** *He wanted to rent an apartment, a new car, and traveling around the country.* (*To rent* is an infinitive, *car* is a noun, and *traveling* is a gerund.)
>
> **PARALLEL:** *He wanted to rent an apartment, to drive a new car, and to travel around the country.* (*To rent, to drive,* and *to travel* are all infinitives.)

11 Writing Complete Sentences

Remember, a sentence is a group of words that expresses a complete thought. In formal writing, try to avoid both sentence fragments and run-on sentences.

11.1 CORRECTING FRAGMENTS

A **sentence fragment** is a group of words that is only part of a sentence. It does not express a complete thought and may be confusing to a reader or listener. A sentence fragment may be lacking a subject, a predicate, or both.

> **FRAGMENT:** *Waited for the boat to arrive.* (no subject)
>
> **CORRECTED:** *We waited for the boat to arrive.*
>
> **FRAGMENT:** *People of various races, ages, and creeds.* (no predicate)
>
> **CORRECTED:** *People of various races, ages, and creeds gathered together.*
>
> **FRAGMENT:** *Near the old cottage.* (neither subject nor predicate)
>
> **CORRECTED:** *The burial ground is near the old cottage.*

In your writing, fragments may be a result of haste or incorrect punctuation. Sometimes fixing a fragment will be a matter of attaching it to a preceding or following sentence.

> **FRAGMENT:** *We saw the two girls. Waiting for the bus to arrive.*
>
> **CORRECTED:** *We saw the two girls waiting for the bus to arrive.*

11.2 CORRECTING RUN-ON SENTENCES

A **run-on sentence** is made up of two or more sentences written as though they were one. Some run-ons have no punctuation within them. Others may have only commas where conjunctions or stronger punctuation marks are necessary. Use your judgment in correcting run-on sentences, as you have choices. You can make a run-on two sentences if the thoughts are not closely connected. If the thoughts are closely related, you can keep the run-on as one sentence by adding a semicolon or a conjunction.

> **RUN-ON:** *We found a place for the picnic by a small pond it was three miles from the village.*
>
> **MAKE TWO SENTENCES:** *We found a place for the picnic by a small pond. It was three miles from the village.*
>
> **RUN-ON:** *We found a place for the picnic by a small pond it was perfect.*
>
> **USE A SEMICOLON:** *We found a place for the picnic by a small pond; it was perfect.*
>
> **ADD A CONJUNCTION:** *We found a place for the picnic by a small pond, and it was perfect.*

WATCH OUT! When you form compound sentences, make sure you use appropriate punctuation: a comma before a coordinating conjunction, a semicolon when there is no coordinating conjunction. A very common mistake is to use a comma alone instead of a comma and a conjunction. This error is called a **comma splice.**

> **INCORRECT:** *He finished the apprenticeship, he left the village.*
>
> **CORRECT:** *He finished the apprenticeship, and he left the village.*

GRAMMAR PRACTICE

Rewrite the following paragraph, correcting all fragments and run-ons.

The narrator in Charlotte Perkins Gilman's story "The Yellow Wallpaper" expects that her husband will laugh at her, that's an odd response, in my opinion. She could have lived more happily. If the relationship between her and her husband were an equal partnership. We can acknowledge that men and women may be different in some ways. Without believing that they are as different as this story suggests. The male character acts practical and "strong," the female character acts nervous and weak.

12 Subject-Verb Agreement

The subject and verb in a clause must agree in number. Agreement means that if the subject is singular, the verb is also singular, and if the subject is plural, the verb is also plural.

12.1 BASIC AGREEMENT

Fortunately, agreement between subjects and verbs in English is simple. Most verbs show the difference between singular and plural only in the third person of the present tense. In the present tense, the third-person singular form ends in *-s.*

Present-Tense Verb Forms	
Singular	**Plural**
I eat	we eat
you eat	you eat
she, he, it eats	they eat

12.2 AGREEMENT WITH *BE*

The verb *be* presents special problems in agreement, because this verb does not follow the usual verb patterns.

Forms of *Be*			
Present Tense		**Past Tense**	
Singular	**Plural**	**Singular**	**Plural**
I am	we are	I was	we were
you are	you are	you were	you were
she, he, it is	they are	she, he, it was	they were

12.3 WORDS BETWEEN SUBJECT AND VERB

A verb agrees only with its subject. When words come between a subject and a verb, ignore them when considering proper agreement. Identify the subject, and make sure the verb agrees with it.

> **EXAMPLES:**
>
> *A story in the newspapers tells about the 1890s.*
>
> *Dad as well as Mom reads the paper daily.*

For more help with subject-verb agreement, see

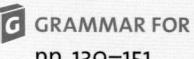 GRAMMAR FOR WRITING
pp. 130–151

GRAMMAR PRACTICE
ANSWERS

Possible answer: *The narrator in Charlotte Perkins Gilman's story "The Yellow Wallpaper" expects that her husband will laugh at her. That's an odd response, in my opinion. She could have lived more happily if the relationship between her and her husband were an equal partnership. We can acknowledge that men and women may be different in some ways without believing that they are as different as this story suggests. The male character acts practical and "strong"; the female character acts nervous and weak.*

12.4 AGREEMENT WITH COMPOUND SUBJECTS

Use plural verbs with most compound subjects joined by the word *and*.

> **EXAMPLE:** *My mother and her sisters call each other every Sunday.*

To confirm that you need a plural verb, you could substitute the plural pronoun *they* for *my mother and her sisters.*

If a compound subject is thought of as a unit, use a singular verb. Test this by substituting the singular pronoun *it*.

> **EXAMPLE:** *Liver and onions [it] is Robert's least favorite dish.*

Use a singular verb with a compound subject that is preceded by *each*, *every*, or *many a*.

> **EXAMPLE:** *Not every dog and cat at the shelter makes a good pet.*

When the parts of a compound subject are joined by *or*, *nor*, or the correlative conjunctions *either . . . or* or *neither . . . nor*, make the verb agree with the noun or pronoun nearest the verb.

> **EXAMPLES:**
> *Baseball or football is my favorite sport.*
> *Either my rabbits or my turtle was loose in my room.*
> *Neither Mrs. Howard nor her two sons were home at the time of the accident.*

12.5 PERSONAL PRONOUNS AS SUBJECTS

When using a personal pronoun as a subject, make sure to match it with the correct form of the verb *be*. (See the chart in Section 12.2.) Note especially that the pronoun *you* takes the forms *are* and *were*, regardless of whether it is singular or plural.

> **WATCH OUT!** *You is* and *you was* are nonstandard forms and should be avoided in writing and speaking. *We was* and *they was* are also forms to be avoided.
>
> **INCORRECT:** *You is facing the wrong direction.*
> **CORRECT:** *You are facing the wrong direction.*
> **INCORRECT:** *We was telling ghost stories.*
> **CORRECT:** *We were telling ghost stories.*

12.6 INDEFINITE PRONOUNS AS SUBJECTS

Some indefinite pronouns are always singular; some are always plural.

Singular Indefinite Pronouns			
another	either	neither	one
anybody	everybody	nobody	somebody
anyone	everyone	no one	someone
anything	everything	nothing	something
each	much		

> **EXAMPLES:**
> *Each of the writers was given an award.*
> *Somebody in the room upstairs is sleeping.*

Plural Indefinite Pronouns			
both	few	many	several

> **EXAMPLES:**
> *Many of the books in our library are not in circulation.*
> *Few have been returned recently.*

Still other indefinite pronouns may be either singular or plural.

Singular or Plural Indefinite Pronouns		
all	more	none
any	most	some

The number of the indefinite pronoun *any* or *none* often depends on the intended meaning.

> **EXAMPLES:**
> *Any of these topics has potential for a good article.* (any one topic)
> *Any of these topics have potential for good articles.* (all of the many topics)

The indefinite pronouns *all*, *some*, *more*, *most*, and *none* are singular when they refer to quantities or parts of things. They are plural when they refer to numbers of individual things. Context will usually give a clue.

> **EXAMPLES:**
> *All of the flour is gone.* (referring to a quantity)
> *All of the flowers are gone.* (referring to individual items)

12.7 INVERTED SENTENCES

Problems in agreement often occur in inverted sentences beginning with *here* or *there;* in questions beginning with *how, when, why, where,* or *what;* and in inverted sentences beginning with phrases. Identify the subject—wherever it is—before deciding on the verb.

EXAMPLES:

There clearly are far too many cooks in this kitchen.

What is the correct ingredient for this stew?

Far from the embroiled cooks stands the master chef.

GRAMMAR PRACTICE

Locate the subject of each clause in the sentences below. Then choose the correct verb.

1. Many poets have written great poetry, but few (is/are) as talented as Emily Dickinson.

2. There (is/are) many lines in her work that her readers (treasures/treasure).

3. Some of her readers (appreciates/appreciate) her use of dashes, while others (finds/find) it confusing.

4. Each of her poems (presents/present) an idea to think about.

5. What (is/are) the dominant vowel sound in the last four lines of "Much Madness is divinest Sense"?

6. The consonant that prevails in the same poem (seems/seem) to be *s.*

7. I can't decide whether the poem's sound or its ideas (is/are) more striking.

12.8 SENTENCES WITH PREDICATE NOMINATIVES

When a predicate nominative serves as a complement in a sentence, use a verb that agrees with the subject, not the complement.

EXAMPLES:

The hunting habits of the North American wolf are an example of how change in the environment affects animals. (The subject is the plural noun *habits*—not *wolf*—and it takes the plural verb *are.*)

An example of how change in the environment affects animals is seen in the hunting habits of the North American wolf. (The subject is the singular noun *example,* and it takes the singular verb *is seen.*)

12.9 *DON'T* AND *DOESN'T* AS AUXILIARY VERBS

The auxiliary verb *doesn't* is used with singular subjects and with the personal pronouns *she, he,* and *it.* The auxiliary verb *don't* is used with plural subjects and with the personal pronouns *I, we, you,* and *they.*

SINGULAR: *She doesn't have a costume for the rehearsal.*

Doesn't the doctor have an appointment Wednesday morning?

PLURAL: *They don't think they did very well on that math test.*

The cats don't need to be fed more than twice a day.

12.10 COLLECTIVE NOUNS AS SUBJECTS

Collective nouns are singular nouns that name groups of persons or things. *Team,* for example, is the collective name of a group of individuals. A collective noun takes a singular verb when the group acts as a single unit. It takes a plural verb when the members of the group act separately.

EXAMPLES:

Our team usually wins. (The team as a whole wins.)

Our team vote differently on most issues. (The individual members vote.)

12.11 RELATIVE PRONOUNS AS SUBJECTS

When the relative pronoun *who, which,* or *that* is used as a subject in an adjective clause, the verb in the clause must agree in number with the antecedent of the pronoun.

SINGULAR: *Have you selected one of the poems that is meaningful to you?*

The antecedent of the relative pronoun *that* is the singular *one;* therefore, *that* is singular and must take the singular verb *is.*

PLURAL: *The fairy tales, which have been collected from many different sources, are annotated.*

The antecedent of the relative pronoun *which* is the plural *fairy tales. Which* is plural, and it takes the plural verb *have been collected.*

GRAMMAR PRACTICE
ANSWERS

1. *few > are*
2. *lines > are*
   readers > treasure
3. *Some > appreciate*
   others > find
4. *Each > presents*
5. *sound > is*
6. *consonant > seems*
7. *sound or ideas > are*

Vocabulary and Spelling Handbook

The key to becoming an independent reader is to develop a toolkit of vocabulary strategies. By learning and practicing the strategies, you'll know what to do when you encounter unfamiliar words while reading. You'll also know how to refine the words you use for different situations—personal, school, and work.

Being a good speller is important when communicating your ideas in writing. Learning basic spelling rules and checking your spelling in a dictionary will help you spell words that you may not use frequently.

CALIFORNIA

Included in this handbook as indicated: **R1.1** (p. R74), **R1.2** (pgs. R73, R74), **R1.3** (p. R75), **LC1.2** (pgs. R76–R79)

WRITING TOOLS
Go to the **Writing Center** at **ClassZone.com** for interactive models, publishing ideas, and other support.

1 Using Context Clues

The context of a word is made up of the punctuation marks, words, sentences, and paragraphs that surround the word. A word's context can give you important clues about its meaning.

1.1 GENERAL CONTEXT

Sometimes you need to infer the meaning of an unfamiliar word by reading all the information in a passage.

I told my parents I wanted to quit playing the piano, but they told me to persevere anyway.

You can figure out from the context that *persevere* means "continue."

1.2 SPECIFIC CONTEXT CLUES

Sometimes writers help you understand the meanings of words by providing specific clues such as those shown in the chart.

1.3 IDIOMS, SLANG, AND FIGURATIVE LANGUAGE

Use context clues to figure out the meanings of idioms, figurative language, and slang.

An **idiom** is an expression whose overall meaning is different from the meaning of the individual words.

If you're going to buy a house with a garden, you'd better have a green thumb. (Green thumb means "ability to grow plants.")

Figurative language is language that communicates meaning beyond the literal meaning of the words. Note this example from "A Chip of Glass Ruby" by Nadine Gordimer:

There was the feeling, in the house, that he had wept and raged at her, that boulders of reproach had thundered down upon her absence, and yet he had said not one word. (Boulders of reproach had thundered down upon her absence means he was very angry that she was gone.)

Slang is informal language composed of made-up words and ordinary words that are used to mean something different from their meanings in formal English.

My parents freaked out when I told them that I went to the concert without their permission. (Freaked out means "became greatly distressed.")

Specific Context Clues		
Type of Clue	**Key Words/ Phrases**	**Example**
Definition or restatement of the meaning of the word	or, which is, that is, in other words, also known as, also called	*Perennials*—**plants that live for more than two years**—make up only one-third of the garden's exhibit.
Example following an unfamiliar word	such as, like, as if, for example, especially, including	Their new apartment was *arrayed* with many beautiful things, **such as a crystal lamp and a porcelain vase.**
Comparison with a more familiar word or concept	as, like, also, similar to, in the same way, likewise	The prairie grasses *undulated* in the wind **like the waves in the ocean.**
Contrast with a familiar word or experience	unlike, but, however, although, on the other hand, on the contrary	My dog is usually very **calm, unlike** our neighbor's dog, which is very *rowdy*.

For more information, see **Vocabulary Strategy: Context Clues,** pages 210 and 1000, and **Vocabulary Strategy: Idioms,** page 1200.

2 Analyzing Word Structure

Many words can be broken into smaller parts, such as base words, roots, prefixes, and suffixes.

2.1 BASE WORDS

A **base word** is a word part that by itself is also a word. Other words or word parts can be added to base words to form new words.

2.2 ROOTS

A **root** is a word part that contains the core meaning of the word. Many English words contain roots that come from older languages such as Greek, Latin, Old English (Anglo-Saxon), and Norse. Knowing the meaning of a word's root can help you determine the word's meaning.

Root	Meaning	Example
aster, astr (Greek)	star	asterisk
fic/ fac/ fec (Latin)	make, do	factory
spec/ spect/ spic (Latin)	look at, see, behold	spectator
ten (Latin)	stretch	tendon
derm/ derma (Greek)	skin	epidermis

*For more information, see **Vocabulary Strategy: Word Roots**, pages 86, 273, 326, 425, 472, 594, 686, 802, and 866.*

2.3 PREFIXES

A **prefix** is a word part attached to the beginning of a word. Most prefixes come from Greek, Latin, or Old English.

Prefix	Meaning	Example
un- (Old English)	not	unafraid
epi- (Greek)	upon, on, over	epicenter
syn- (Greek)	together, at the same time	synthesis
hexa- (Greek)	six	hexagram
geo- (Greek)	earth	geography
trans- (Latin)	across, beyond	transatlantic
dis- (Latin)	lack of, not	distrust
circum- (Latin)	around	circumvent
hemi- (Latin)	half	hemisphere

*For more information, see **Vocabulary Strategy: Prefixes**, pages 368, 390, 668, 736, and 1171.*

2.4 SUFFIXES

A **suffix** is a word part that appears at the end of a root or base word to form a new word. Some suffixes do not change word meaning. These suffixes are

- added to nouns to change the number of persons or objects
- added to verbs to change the tense
- added to modifiers to change the degree of comparison

Suffix	Meaning	Example
-s, -es	to change the number of a noun	trunk + s = trunks
-d, -ed, -ing	to change verb tense	sprinkle + d = sprinkled
-er, -est	to change the degree of comparison in modifiers	cold + er = colder icy + est = iciest

Other suffixes can be added to a root or base to change the word's meaning. These suffixes can also determine a word's part of speech.

Suffix	Meaning	Example
-ence	state or condition of	independence
-ous	full of	furious
-ate	to make	activate
-ly, -ily	manner	quickly

*For more information, see **Vocabulary Strategy: Suffixes**, pages 368 and 436.*

Strategies for Understanding Unfamiliar Words

- Look for any prefixes or suffixes. Remove them to isolate the base word or the root.

- See if you recognize any elements—prefix, suffix, root, or base—of the word. You may be able to guess its meaning by analyzing one or two elements.

- Consider the way the word is used in the sentence. Use the context and the word parts to make a logical guess about the word's meaning.

- Consult a dictionary to see whether you are correct.

Make inferences about the meanings of the following words from the fields of science and math. Consider what you have learned in this section about Greek, Latin, and Anglo-Saxon (Old English) word parts.

astronomy	efficacy	hexagonal
circumference	epidermis	spectrum
distend	geosciences	uncertainty

3 Understanding Word Origins

3.1 ETYMOLOGIES

Etymologies show the origin and historical development of a word. When you study a word's history and origin, you can find out when, where, and how the word came to be.

am•bas•sa•dor (ăm-băs′ə-dər, -dôr′) *n.* A diplomatic official of the highest rank appointed and accredited as representative in residence by one government or sovereign to another, usually for a specific length of time. [Middle English *ambassadour,* from Old French *ambassadeur,* from Medieval Latin *ambactia,* mission, from Latin *ambactus,* servant, ultimately of Celtic origin.]

com•mu•ni•ty (kə-myōō′nĭ-tē) *n., pl.* -**ties** A group of people living in the same locality and under the same government. [Middle English *communite,* citizenry, from Old French, from Latin *commūnitās,* fellowship, from *commūnis,* common.]

*For more information, see **Vocabulary Strategy: Etymologies**, pages 76, 253, and 1030.*

Trace the etymology of the words below, often used in the fields of history and political science.

diplomat	independence	legislature
government	justice	revolution
immigrant	laissez-faire	treaty

3.2 WORD FAMILIES

Words that have the same root make up a word family and have related meanings. The chart shows a common Greek and a common Latin root. Notice how the meanings of the example words are related to the meanings of their roots.

Latin Root	*med:* "middle"
English Words	**mediate** resolve or settle
	mediocre ordinary
	media² middle wall of a blood vessel
	medial toward the middle
	medium action midway between two extremes

Greek Root	*chron:* "time"
English Words	**chronicle** detailed narrative report
	chronic of long duration
	synchronize occur at same time
	anachronism out of proper order in time

*For more information, see **Vocabulary Strategy: Word Family**, page 1016.*

3.3 WORDS FROM CLASSICAL MYTHOLOGY

The English language includes many words from classical mythology. You can use your knowledge of these myths to understand the origins and meanings of these words. For example, *herculean task* refers to the strongman Hercules. Thus, *herculean task* probably means "a job that is large or difficult." The chart shows a few common words from mythology.

Greek	Roman	Norse
nemesis	insomnia	Thursday
atlas	fury	berserk
adonis	Saturday	rune
mentor	January	valkyrie

Look up the etymology of each word in the chart and locate the myth associated with it. Use the information from the myth to explain the origin and meaning of each word.

3.4 FOREIGN WORDS

The English language includes words from diverse languages, such as French, Dutch, Spanish, Italian, and Chinese. Many words stayed the way they were in their original language.

French	Dutch	Spanish	Italian
entree	maelstrom	rodeo	pasta
nouveau riche	trek	salsa	opera
potpourri	cookie	bronco	vendetta
tête-à-tête	snoop	tornado	grotto

*For more information, see **Vocabulary Strategy: Foreign Words,** pages 108 and 976.*

4 Synonyms and Antonyms

4.1 SYNONYMS

A **synonym** is a word with a meaning similar to that of another word. You can find synonyms in a thesaurus or a dictionary. In a dictionary, synonyms are often given as part of the definition of a word. The following word pairs are synonyms:

dry/arid   enthralled/fascinated   gaunt/thin

*For more information, see **Vocabulary Strategy: Synonyms,** page 119.*

4.2 ANTONYMS

An **antonym** is a word with a meaning opposite that of another word. The following word pairs are antonyms:

friend/enemy   absurd/logical

courteous/rude   languid/energetic

5 Denotation and Connotation

5.1 DENOTATION

A word's dictionary meaning is called its **denotation.** For example, the denotation of the word *rascal* is "an unethical, dishonest person."

5.2 CONNOTATION

The images or feelings you connect to a word add a finer shade of meaning, called **connotation.** The connation of a word goes beyond its basic dictionary definition. Writers use connotations of words to communicate positive or negative feelings.

Positive	Neutral	Negative
save	store	hoard
fragrance	smell	stench
display	show	flaunt

Make sure you understand the denotation and connotation of a word when you read it or use it in your writing.

*For more information, see **Vocabulary Strategy: Denotation and Connotation,** pages 127 and 754.*

6 Analogies

An **analogy** is a comparison between two things that are similar in some way but are otherwise dissimilar. Analogies are sometimes used in writing when unfamiliar subjects or ideas are explained in terms of familiar ones. Analogies often appear on tests as well, usually in a format like this:

TERRIER : DOG :: A) rat : fish
                    B) kitten : cat
                    C) trout : fish
                    D) fish : trout
                    E) poodle : collie

Follow these steps to determine the correct answer:

- Read the part in capital letters as "*bird* is to *fly* as . . ."

- Read the answer choices as "*rat* is to *fish*," "*kitten* is to *cat*," and so on.

- Ask yourself how the words *terrier* and *dog* are related. (A terrier is a type of dog.)

- Ask yourself which of the choices shows the same relationship. (A kitten is a kind of cat, but not in the same way that a terrier is a kind of dog. A kitten is a baby cat. A trout however, is a type of fish in the sense that a terrier is a type of dog. Therefore, the answer is C.)

*For more information, see **Vocabulary Strategy: Analogy,** page 1158.*

7 Homonyms and Homophones

7.1 HOMONYMS

Homonyms are words that have the same spelling and sound but have different origins and meanings.

I don't want to bore you with a story about how I had to bore through the living room wall.

Bore can mean "cause a person to lose interest," but an identically spelled word means "to drill a hole."

My dog likes to bark while it scratches the bark on the tree in the backyard.

Bark can mean "the sound made by a dog." However, another identically spelled word means "the outer covering of a tree." Each word has a different meaning and its own dictionary entry.

Sometimes only one of the meanings of two homonyms may be familiar to you. Use context clues to help you figure out the meaning of an unfamiliar word.

7.2 HOMOPHONES

Homophones are words that sound alike but have different meanings and spellings. The following homophones are frequently misused:

it's/its	they're/their/there
to/too/two	stationary/stationery

Many misused homophones are pronouns and contractions. Whenever you are unsure whether to write *your* or *you're* and *who's* or *whose*, ask yourself if you mean *you are* or *who is/has*. If you do, write the contraction. For other homophones, such as *scent* and *sent*, use the meaning of the word to help you decide which one to use.

8 Words with Multiple Meanings

Some words have acquired additional meanings over time that are based on the original meaning.

> **EXAMPLES:** *I was in a hurry so I jammed my clothes into the suitcase. Unfortunately, I jammed my finger in the process.*

These two uses of *jam* have different meanings, but both of them have the same origin. You will find all the meanings of *jam* listed in one entry in the dictionary.

9 Specialized Vocabulary

Specialized vocabulary is special terms suited to a particular field of study or work. For example, science, mathematics, and history all have their own technical or specialized vocabularies. To figure out specialized terms, you can use context clues and reference sources, such as dictionaries on specific subjects, atlases, or manuals.

*For more information, see **Vocabulary Strategy: Specialized Vocabulary,** pages 60, 242, 704, 786, and 960.*

10 Using Reference Sources

10.1 DICTIONARIES

A **general dictionary** will tell you not only a word's definitions but also its pronunciation, its parts of speech, and its history and origin. A **specialized dictionary** focuses on terms related to a particular field of study or work. Use a dictionary to check the spelling of any word you are unsure of in your English class and other subjects as well.

10.2 THESAURI

A **thesaurus** (plural, thesauri) is a dictionary of synonyms. A thesaurus can be helpful when you find yourself using the same modifiers over and over again.

10.3 SYNONYM FINDERS

A **synonym finder** is often included in word-processing software. It enables you to highlight a word and be shown a display of its synonyms.

10.4 GLOSSARIES

A **glossary** is a list of specialized terms and their definitions. It is often found in the back of textbooks and sometimes includes pronunciations. In fact, this textbook has three glossaries: the **Glossary of Literary Terms,** the **Glossary of Reading & Informational Terms,** and the **Glossary of Vocabulary in English & Spanish.** Use these glossaries to help you understand how terms are used in this textbook.

11 Spelling Rules

11.1 WORDS ENDING IN A SILENT *E*

Before adding a suffix beginning with a vowel or *y* to a word ending in a silent *e,* drop the *e* (with some exceptions).

> **amaze + -ing = amazing**
> **love + -able = lovable**
> **create + -ed = created**
> **nerve + -ous = nervous**

Exceptions: *change + -able = changeable; courage + -ous = courageous.*

When adding a suffix beginning with a consonant to a word ending in a silent *e,* keep the *e* (with some exceptions).

    late + -ly = lately
    spite + -ful = spiteful
    noise + -less = noiseless
    state + -ment = statement

Exceptions: *truly, argument, ninth, wholly, awful,* and others.

When a suffix beginning with *a* or *o* is added to a word with a final silent *e,* the final *e* is usually retained if it is preceded by a soft *c* or a soft *g.*

    bridge + -able = bridgeable
    peace + -able = peaceable
    outrage + -ous = outrageous
    advantage + -ous = advantageous

When a suffix beginning with a vowel is added to words ending in *ee* or *oe,* the final silent *e* is retained.

    agree + -ing = agreeing   **free + -ing = freeing**
    hoe + -ing = hoeing   **see + -ing = seeing**

11.2 WORDS ENDING IN Y

Before adding most suffixes to a word that ends in *y* preceded by a consonant, change the *y* to *i.*

    easy + -est = easiest
    crazy + -est = craziest
    silly + -ness = silliness
    marry + -age = marriage

Exceptions: *dryness, shyness,* and *slyness.*

However, when you add *-ing,* the *y* does not change.

    empty + -ed = emptied   but
    empty + -ing = emptying

When adding a suffix to a word that ends in *y* preceded by a vowel, the *y* usually does not change.

    play + -er = player
    employ + -ed = employed
    coy + -ness = coyness
    pay + -able = payable

11.3 WORDS ENDING IN A CONSONANT

In one-syllable words that end in one consonant preceded by one short vowel, double the final consonant before adding a suffix beginning with a vowel, such as *-ed* or *-ing.*

    dip + -ed = dipped   **set + -ing = setting**
    slim + -est = slimmest   **fit + -er = fitter**

The rule does not apply to words of one syllable that end in a consonant preceded by two vowels.

    feel + -ing = feeling   **peel + -ed = peeled**
    reap + -ed = reaped   **loot + -ed = looted**

In words of more than one syllable, double the final consonant when (**1**) the word ends with one consonant preceded by one vowel and (**2**) the word is accented on the last syllable.

    be•gin´   **per•mit´**   **re•fer´**

In the following examples, note that in the new words formed with suffixes, the accent remains on the same syllable:

    be•gin´ + -ing = be•gin´ ning = beginning
    per•mit´ + -ed = per•mit´ ted = permitted

In some words with more than one syllable, though the accent remains on the same syllable when a suffix is added, the final consonant is nevertheless not doubled, as in the following examples:

    tra´vel + -er = tra´vel•er = traveler
    mar´ket + -er = mar´ket•er = marketer

In the following examples, the accent does not remain on the same syllable; thus, the final consonant is not doubled:

    re•fer´ + -ence = ref´er•ence = reference
    con•fer´ + -ence = con´fer•ence = conference

11.4 PREFIXES AND SUFFIXES

When adding a prefix to a word, do not change the spelling of the base word. When a prefix creates a double letter, keep both letters.

    dis- + approve = disapprove
    re- + build = rebuild
    ir- + regular = irregular
    mis- + spell = misspell
    anti- + trust = antitrust
    il- + logical = illogical

When adding *-ly* to a word ending in *l,* keep both *l*'s, and when adding *-ness* to a word ending in *n,* keep both *n*'s.

    careful + -ly = carefully
    sudden + -ness = suddenness
    final + -ly = finally
    thin + -ness = thinness

11.5 FORMING PLURAL NOUNS

To form the plural of most nouns, just add -*s*.

prizes   dreams   circles   stations

For most singular nouns ending in *o*, add -*s*.

solos   halos   studios   photos   pianos

For a few nouns ending in *o*, add -*es*.

heroes   tomatoes   potatoes   echoes

When the singular noun ends in *s, sh, ch, x,* or *z*, add -*es*.

**waitresses   brushes   ditches
axes   buzzes**

When a singular noun ends in *y* with a consonant before it, change the *y* to *i* and add -*es*.

**army—armies   candy—candies
baby—babies   diary—diaries
ferry—ferries   conspiracy—conspiracies**

When a vowel (*a, e, i, o, u*) comes before the *y*, just add -*s*.

**boy—boys   way—ways
array—arrays   alloy—alloys
weekday—weekdays   jockey—jockeys**

For most nouns ending in *f* or *fe*, change the *f* to *v* and add -*es* or -*s*.

**life—lives   calf—calves   knife—knives
thief—thieves   shelf—shelves   loaf—loaves**

For some nouns ending in *f*, add -*s* to make the plural.

roofs   chiefs   reefs   beliefs

Some nouns have the same form for both singular and plural.

deer   sheep   moose   salmon   trout

For some nouns, the plural is formed in a special way.

**man—men   goose—geese
ox—oxen   woman—women
mouse—mice   child—children**

For a compound noun written as one word, form the plural by changing the last word in the compound to its plural form.

stepchild—stepchildren   firefly—fireflies

If a compound noun is written as a hyphenated word or as two separate words, change the most important word to the plural form.

**brother-in-law—brothers-in-law
life jacket—life jackets**

11.6 FORMING POSSESSIVES

If a noun is singular, add '*s*.

mother—my mother's car   Ross—Ross's desk
Exception: The *s* after the apostrophe is dropped after *Jesus', Moses',* and certain names in classical mythology (*Zeus'*). These possessive forms can be pronounced easily.

If a noun is plural and ends with *s*, just add an apostrophe.

**parents—my parents' car
the Santinis—the Santinis' house**

If a noun is plural but does not end in *s*, add '*s*.

**people—the people's choice
women—the women's coats**

11.7 SPECIAL SPELLING PROBLEMS

Only one English word ends in -*sede: supersede.* Three words end in -*ceed: exceed, proceed,* and *succeed.* All other verbs ending in the sound "seed" are spelled with -*cede.*

concede   precede   recede   secede

In words with *ie* or *ei,* when the sound is long *e* (as in *she*), the word is spelled *ie* except after *c* (with some exceptions).

i before *e*	thief	relieve	field
	piece	grieve	pier

except after *c*	conceit	perceive	ceiling
	receive	receipt	

Exceptions: *either, neither, weird, leisure, seize.*

12 Commonly Confused Words

WORDS	DEFINITIONS	EXAMPLES
accept/except	The verb *accept* means "to receive or believe"; *except* is usually a preposition meaning "excluding."	**Except** for some of the more extraordinary events, I can **accept** that the *Odyssey* recounts a real journey.
advice/advise	*Advise* is a verb; *advice* is a noun naming that which an *adviser* gives.	I **advise** you to take that job. Whom should I ask for **advice?**
affect/effect	As a verb, *affect* means "to influence." *Effect* as a verb means "to cause." If you want a noun, you will almost always want *effect*.	Did Circe's wine **affect** Odysseus' mind? It did **effect** a change in Odysseus' men. In fact, it had an **effect** on everyone else who drank it.
all ready/already	*All ready* is an adjective meaning "fully ready." *Already* is an adverb meaning "before or by this time."	He was **all ready** to go at noon. I have **already** seen that movie.
allusion/illusion	An *allusion* is an indirect reference to something. An *illusion* is a false picture or idea.	There are many **allusions** to the works of Homer in English literature. The world's apparent flatness is an **illusion.**
among/between	*Between* is used when you are speaking of only two things. *Among* is used for three or more.	**Between** *Hamlet* and *King Lear,* I prefer the latter. Emily Dickinson is **among** my favorite poets.
bring/take	*Bring* is used to denote motion toward a speaker or place. *Take* is used to denote motion away from such a person or place.	**Bring** the books over here, and I will **take** them to the library.
fewer/less	*Fewer* refers to the number of separate, countable units. *Less* refers to bulk quantity.	We have **less** literature and **fewer** selections in this year's curriculum.
leave/let	*Leave* means "to allow something to remain behind." *Let* means "to permit."	The librarian will **leave** some books on display but will not **let** us borrow any.
lie/lay	*Lie* means "to rest or recline." It does not take an object. *Lay* always takes an object.	Rover loves to **lie** in the sun. We always **lay** some bones next to him.
loose/lose	*Loose* (lo͞os) means "free, not restrained"; *lose* (lo͞oz) means "to misplace or fail to find."	Who turned the horses **loose?** I hope we won't **lose** any of them.
precede/proceed	*Precede* means "to go or come before." Use *proceed* for other meanings.	Emily Dickinson's poetry **precedes** that of Alice Walker. You may **proceed** to the next section of the test.
than/then	Use *than* in making comparisons; use *then* on all other occasions.	Who can say whether Amy Lowell is a better poet **than** Denise Levertov? I will read Lowell first, and **then** I will read Levertov.
their/there/they're	*Their* means "belonging to them." *There* means "in that place." *They're* is the contraction for "they are."	**There** is a movie playing at 9 P.M. **They're** going to see it with me. Sakara and Jessica drove away in **their** car after the movie.
two/too/to	*Two* is the number. *Too* is an adverb meaning "also" or "very." Use *to* before a verb or as a preposition.	Meg had **to** go **to** town, **too.** We had **too** much reading **to** do. **Two** chapters is **too** many.

Effective oral communication occurs when the audience understands a message the way the speaker intends it. Good speakers and listeners do more than just talk and hear. They use specific techniques to present their ideas effectively, and they are attentive and critical listeners.

Included in this handbook as indicated: LS1.4 (pgs. R82–R85), **LS1.6** (p. R82), **LS1.7** (p. R81), **LS1.8a** (p. R80), **LS1.8b** (p. R80), **LS1.8c** (pgs. R80, R82), **LS1.9** (pgs. R81–R82), **LS1.10** (p. R81), **LS1.11** (pgs. R82, R83, R84, R86–R87), **LS1.13** (pgs. R82–R83), **LS2.1abc** (p. R84), **LS2.3abcde** (p. R85), **LS2.5** (pgs. R84–R85)

1 Speech

In school, in business, and in community life, a speech is one of the most effective means of communicating.

1.1 AUDIENCE, PURPOSE, AND OCCASION

When developing and delivering a speech, your goal is to deliver a focused, coherent presentation that conveys your ideas clearly and relates to the background of your audience. By understanding your audience, you can tailor your speech to them appropriately and effectively.

- **Know Your Audience** What kind of group are you presenting to? Fellow classmates? A group of teachers? What are their interests and backgrounds? Understanding their different points of view can help you organize the information so that they understand and are interested in it.

- **Understand Your Purpose** Keep in mind your purpose for speaking. Are you trying to persuade the audience to do something? Perhaps you simply want to entertain them by sharing a story or experience. Your reason for giving the speech will guide you in organizing your thoughts and deciding on how to deliver it.

- **Know the Occasion** Are you speaking at a special event? Is it formal? Will others be giving speeches besides you? Knowing the type of occasion will help you tailor the language and length of your speech for the event.

1.2 PREPARING YOUR SPEECH

There are several approaches to preparing a speech. Your teacher may tell you which one to use.

- **Manuscript** Prepare a complete script of the speech in advance and use it to deliver the speech. Use for formal occasions, such as graduation speeches and political addresses, and to present technical or complicated information.

- **Memory** Prepare a written text in advance and then memorize it in order to deliver the speech word for word. Use for short speeches, as when introducing another speaker or accepting an award.

- **Extemporaneous** Prepare the speech and deliver it using an outline or notes. Use for informal situations, for persuasive messages, and to make a more personal connection with the audience.

1.3 DRAFTING YOUR SPEECH

If you are writing your speech beforehand, rather than working from notes, use these guidelines to help you:

- **Create a Unified Speech** Do this first by organizing your speech into paragraphs, each of which develops a single main idea. All the sentences in a paragraph should support the main idea of the paragraph, and all the paragraphs should support the main idea of the speech. Be sure that your speech has an introduction and a conclusion. Just as in a written product, use a pattern of organization that is appropriate to your subject and purpose.

- **Use Appropriate Language** The subject of your speech—and the way you choose to present it—should match your audience, your purpose, and the occasion. You can use informal language, such as slang, to share a story with your classmates. For a persuasive speech in front of a school assembly, use formal, standard American English. If you are giving an informative presentation, be sure to explain any terms that the audience may not be familiar with.

- **Provide Evidence** Include relevant facts, statistics, and incidents; quote experts to support your ideas and opinions. Elaborate—provide specific details, perhaps with visual or media displays—to clarify what you are saying.

- **Emphasize Important Points** To help your audience follow the main ideas and concepts of your speech, be sure to draw attention to important points. You can use rhyme, repetition, parallelism, and other rhetorical devices. You can also use figurative language for effect.

- **Use Precise Language** Use precise language to convey your ideas, and vary the structure and length of your sentences. You can keep the audience's attention with a word that elicits strong emotion. You can use a question or an interjection to make a personal connection with the audience.

- **Start Strong, Finish Strong** As you begin your speech, consider using a "hook"—an interesting question or statement meant to capture your audience's attention. At the end of the speech, restate your main ideas simply and clearly. Perhaps conclude with a powerful example or anecdote to reinforce your message.

- **Revise Your Speech** After you write your speech, revise, edit, and proofread it as you would a written report. Use a variety of sentence structures to achieve a natural rhythm. Check for correct subject-verb agreement and consistent verb tense. Correct run-on sentences and sentence fragments. Use parallel structure to emphasize ideas. Make sure you use complete sentences and correct punctuation and capitalization, even if no one else will see it. Your written speech should be clear and error-free.

1.4 DELIVERING YOUR SPEECH

Confidence is the key to a successful presentation. Use these techniques to help you prepare and present your speech:

Prepare

- **Review Your Information** Reread your notes and review any background research. You'll feel more confident during your speech.

- **Organize Your Notes** Some people prefer to include only key points. Others prefer the entire script. Write each main point, or each paragraph, of your speech on a separate numbered index card. Be sure to include your most important evidence and examples.

- **Plan Your Visual Aids and Sound Effects** If you are planning on using visual aids, such as slides, posters, charts, graphs, video clips, transparencies, or computer projections, now is the time to design your visual and sound elements and work them into your speech.

Practice

- **Rehearse** Rehearse your speech several times, possibly in front of a practice audience. Maintain good posture by standing with your shoulders back and your head up. If you are using visual aids, practice handling them. Adapt your rate of speaking, pitch, and tone of voice to your audience and setting. Glance at your notes to refresh your memory, but avoid reading them word for word. Your style of performance should express the purpose of your speech. Use the following chart to help you.

Purpose	Pace	Pitch	Tone
to persuade	fast but clear	even	urgent
to inform	using plenty of pauses	even	authoritative
to entertain	usually building to a "punch"	varied to create characters or drama	funny or dramatic

- **Use Audience Feedback** If you had a practice audience, ask them specific questions about your delivery: Did I use enough eye contact? Was my voice at the right volume? Did I stand straight, or did I slouch? Use the audience's comments to evaluate the effectiveness of your delivery and to set goals for future rehearsals.

- **Evaluate Your Performance** When you have finished each rehearsal, evaluate your performance. Did you pause to let an important point sink in, or use gestures for emphasis? Make a list of the aspects of your presentation that you will try to improve for your next rehearsal.

Present

- **Begin Your Speech** Try to look relaxed and smile.

- **Make Eye Contact** Try to make eye contact with as many audience members as possible. This will establish personal contact and help you determine if the audience understands your speech.

- **Remember to Pause** A slight pause after important points will provide emphasis and give your audience time to think about what you're saying.

- **Speak Clearly** Speak loud enough to be heard clearly, but not so loud that your voice is overwhelming. Use a conversational tone.

- **Maintain Good Posture** Stand up straight and avoid nervous movements that may distract the audience's attention from what you are saying.

- **Use Expressive Body Language** Use facial expressions to show your feelings toward your topic. Lean forward when you make an important point; move your hands and arms for emphasis. Use your body language to show your own style and reflect your personality.

- **Watch the Audience for Responses** If they start fidgeting or yawning, speak a little louder or get to your conclusion a little sooner. Use what you learn to decide what areas need improvement for future presentations.

- **Close your speech** As part of your closing remarks, be sure to thank your audience.

Respond to Questions

Depending on the content of your speech, your audience may have questions. Follow these steps to make sure that you answer questions in an appropriate manner:

- Think about what your audience may ask and prepare answers before your speech.

- Tell your audience at the beginning of your speech that you will take questions at the end. This helps avoid audience interruptions that may make your speech hard to follow.

- Call on audience members in the order in which they raise their hands.

- Repeat each question before you answer it to ensure that everyone has heard it. This step also gives you time to prepare your answer.

2 Different Types of Oral Presentations

2.1 INFORMATIVE SPEECH

When you deliver an informative speech, you give the audience new information, provide a better understanding of information, or enable the audience to use the information in a new way.

Use the following questions to evaluate your own presentation or that of a peer or a public figure.

Evaluate an Informative Speech

- Did the speaker have a specific, clearly focused topic?
- Did the speaker take the audience's previous knowledge into consideration?
- Did the speaker cite sources for the information?
- Did the speaker communicate the information objectively?
- Did the speaker explain technical terms?
- Did the speaker use visual aids effectively?
- Did the speaker anticipate and address any audience concerns or misunderstandings?
- Is the speech informative and accurate?

2.2 PERSUASIVE SPEECH

When you deliver a persuasive speech, you offer a thesis or clear statement on a subject, you provide relevant evidence to support your position, and you attempt to convince the audience to accept your point of view.

Use the following questions to evaluate the presentation of a peer or a public figure, or your own presentation.

*For more information, see **Speaking and Listening: Presenting a Persuasive Speech,** page 283.*

Evaluate a Persuasive Speech

- Did the speaker present a clear thesis or argument?
- Did the speaker anticipate and address audience concerns, biases, and counterarguments?
- Did the speaker use sound logic and reasoning in developing the argument?
- Did the speaker support the argument with valid evidence, examples, facts, expert opinions, and quotations?
- Did the speaker use rhetorical devices, such as emotional appeals, to support assertions?
- Were the speaker's voice, facial expressions, and gestures effective?
- Is your reaction to the speech similar to that of other audience members?
- Did you believe the speaker to be truthful and ethical?

2.3 DEBATE

A debate is a balanced argument covering both sides of an issue. In a debate, two teams compete to win the support of the audience. In a formal debate, two teams, each with two members, present their arguments on a given proposition or policy statement. One team argues for the proposition or statement, and the other argues against it. Each debater must consider the proposition closely and must research both sides of it.

Preparing for the Debate

In preparing for a debate, the debaters prepare a **brief,** an outline of the debate, accounting for the evidence and arguments of both sides of the **proposition** (topic). Debaters also prepare a **rebuttal,** a follow-up speech to support their arguments and counter the opposition's. Propositions are usually one of four types:

- **Proposition of fact**—determines whether a statement is true or false. An example is "Deforestation is ruining the rain forest."

- **Proposition of value**—determines the value of a person, place, or thing. An example is "Free trade will help small countries develop."

- **Proposition of problem**—determines whether a problem exists and whether it requires action.

- **Proposition of policy**—determines the action that will be taken. An example is "Students will provide tutoring services."

The two groups of debaters who argue a topic are called the **affirmative side** and the **negative side.** The affirmative side tries to convince the audience that the proposition should be accepted. The negative side argues against the proposition.

Use the following steps to prepare a brief:

- **Gather Information** Consult a variety of primary and secondary sources to gather the most reliable, up-to-date information about the proposition.

- **Identify Key Ideas** Sort out the important points and arrange them in order of importance.

- **List Arguments for and Against Each Key Idea** Look for strong arguments that support your side of the proposition and also note those that support your opponents' side.

- **Support Your Arguments** Find facts, quotations, expert opinions, and examples that support your arguments and counter your opponents'.

- **Write the Brief** Begin your brief with a statement of the proposition. Then list the arguments and evidence that support both sides of the proposition.

Planning the Rebuttal

The rebuttal is the opportunity to rebuild your case. Use the following steps to build a strong rebuttal:

- Listen to your opponents respectfully. Note the points you wish to overturn.

- Defend what the opposition has challenged.

- Cite weaknesses in their arguments, such as points they overlooked.

- Present counterarguments and supporting evidence.

- Offer your summary arguments. Restate and solidify your stance.

Use the following questions to evaluate a debate.

Evaluate a Team in a Debate

- Did the team prove that a significant problem does or does not exist? How thorough was the team's analysis of the problem?

- How did the team convince you that the proposition is or is not the best solution to the problem?

- How effectively did the team present reasons and evidence supporting the case?

- How effectively did the team refute and rebut arguments made by the opposing team?

- Did the speakers maintain eye contact and speak at an appropriate rate and volume?

- Did the speakers observe proper debate etiquette?

PRACTICE AND APPLY

View a political debate for a local, state, or national election. Use the preceding criteria to evaluate it.

2.4 NARRATIVE SPEECH

When you deliver a narrative speech, you tell a story or present a subject using a story-type format. A good narrative keeps an audience informed and entertained. It also allows you to deliver a message in a creative way.

Use the following questions to evaluate a speaker or your own presentation.

Evaluate a Narrative Speech

- Did the speaker choose a context that makes sense and contributes to a believable narrative?

- Did the speaker locate scenes and incidents in specific places?

- Does the plot flow well?

- Did the speaker use words that convey the appropriate mood and tone?

- Did the speaker use sensory details that allow the audience to experience the sights, sounds, and smells of a scene and the specific actions, gestures, and thoughts of the characters?

- Did the speaker use a range of narrative devices to keep the audience interested?

- Is your reaction to the presentation similar to that of other audience members?

2.5 REFLECTIVE SPEECH

In a reflective speech, you describe a personal experience and explore its significance. Use vivid description, visuals, and sound effects to re-create the experience for your audience and convey meaning.

Use the following questions to evaluate a speaker or your own presentation.

Evaluate a Reflective Speech

- Did the speaker describe an important experience in his or her life?
- Did the speaker use figurative language, sensory details, or other techniques to re-create the event for the audience?
- Did the speaker explain the significance of the event to the audience?
- Does the experience relate to a broader theme or a more general abstract idea about life?
- Did the speaker convey the message through one specific event or several related incidents?
- Did the speaker encourage the audience to think about the significance of the experience and apply it to their own lives?
- Was your reaction to the presentation similar to that of other audience members?

2.6 DESCRIPTIVE SPEECH

In a descriptive speech, you describe a subject with which you are personally familiar. A good description will enable your listeners to tell how you feel toward your subject.

Use the following questions to evaluate a speaker or your own presentation.

Evaluate a Descriptive Speech

- Did the speaker make clear his or her point of view toward the subject being described?
- Did the speaker use sensory details, figurative language, and factual details?
- Did the speaker use tone and pitch to emphasize important details?
- Did the speaker use facial expressions to emphasize his or her feelings toward the subject?
- Did the speaker change vantage points to help the audience see the subject from another position?
- Did the speaker change perspectives to show how someone else might feel toward the subject?

2.7 ORAL INTERPRETATION

When you perform an oral interpretation, you use appropriate vocal intonations, facial expressions, and gestures to bring a literature selection to life.

In an **oral reading,** you will present or read a poem, monologue, or passage from a literary selection, in which you assume the voice of a character, the narrator, or the speaker. An oral reading can also be a presentation of a dialogue between two or more characters, in which you, as the sole performer, take on all the roles.

Use the following techniques when giving an oral reading:

- **Speak Clearly** As you speak, pronounce your words clearly.
- **Control Your Volume** Make sure that you are loud enough to be heard, but do not shout.
- **Pace Yourself** Read at a moderate rate, but vary your pace if it seems appropriate to the emotions of the character or to the action you perform.
- **Vary Your Voice** Use a different voice for each character. Stress important words and phrases. Use your voice to express different emotions.

In a **dramatic reading,** several speakers participate in the reading of a play or some other work. Use the following techniques in your dramatic reading:

- **Prepare** Rehearse your material several times. Become familiar with the humorous and serious parts of the script. Develop a special voice that fits the personality of the character you portray.
- **Project** As you read your lines, aim your voice toward the back of the room to allow everyone to hear you.
- **Perform** React to the other characters as if you were hearing their lines for the first time. Deliver your own lines with the appropriate emotion. Use not only hand gestures and facial expressions but also other body movements to express your emotions.

*For more information, see **Speaking and Listening: Delivering an Oral Interpretation,** page 1079.*

Use the following questions to evaluate an artistic performance by a peer or a public presenter, a media presentation, or your own performance.

Evaluate an Oral Interpretation

- Did the speaker speak clearly, enunciating each word carefully?
- Did the speaker maintain eye contact with the audience?
- Did the speaker control his or her volume, projecting without shouting?
- Did the speaker vary the rate of speech appropriately to express emotion, mood, and action?
- Did the speaker use a different voice for each character?
- Did the speaker stress important words or phrases?
- Did the speaker's presentation allow you to identify and appreciate elements of the text such as character development, rhyme, imagery, and language?

PRACTICE AND APPLY

Develop an oral reading and present it to your class; evaluate the oral readings of your classmates, using the preceding criteria.

2.8 ORAL RESPONSE TO LITERATURE

An oral response to literature is a personal, analytical interpretation of a writer's story, novel, poem, or drama.

Use the following questions to evaluate a speaker or your own presentation.

Evaluate an Oral Response to Literature

- Did the speaker choose an interesting piece that he or she understands and feels strongly about?
- Did the speaker make a judgment that shows an understanding of significant ideas from the text?
- Did the speaker direct the audience to specific parts of the piece that support his or her ideas?
- Did the speaker identify and analyze the use of artistic elements such as imagery, figurative language, and character development?
- Did the speaker demonstrate an appreciation of the author's style?
- Did the speaker discuss any ambiguous or difficult passages and the impact of those passages on the audience?

PRACTICE AND APPLY

Listen as a classmate delivers an oral response to a selection you have read. Use the preceding criteria to evaluate the presentation.

3 Other Types of Communication

3.1 GROUP DISCUSSION

Successful groups assign a role to each member. These roles distribute responsibility among the members and help keep discussions focused.

Role	Responsibilities
Chairperson	• introduces topic • explains goal or purpose • participates in discussion and keeps it on track • helps resolve conflicts • helps group reach goal
Recorder	• takes notes on discussion • reports on suggestions and decisions • organizes and writes up notes • participates in discussion
Participants	• contribute relevant facts or ideas to discussion • respond constructively to one another's ideas • reach agreement or vote on final decision

3.2 INTERVIEWS

An **interview** is a formal type of conversation with a definite purpose and goal. To conduct a successful interview, use the following guidelines:

Prepare for the Interview

- Select your interviewee carefully. Identify who has the kind of knowledge and experience you are looking for.
- Set a time, a date, and a place. Ask permission to tape-record the interview.

- Learn all you can about the person you will interview or the topic you want information on.

- Prepare a list of questions. Create questions that encourage detailed responses instead of yes-or-no answers. Arrange your questions in order from most important to least important.

- Arrive on time with everything you need.

Conduct the Interview

- Ask your questions clearly and listen to the responses carefully. Give the person whom you are interviewing plenty of time to answer.

- Be flexible; follow up on any responses you find interesting.

- Avoid arguments; be tactful and polite.

- Even if you tape an interview, take notes on important points.

- Thank the person for the interview, and ask if you can call with any follow-up questions.

Follow Up on the Interview

- Summarize your notes or make a written copy of the tape recording as soon as possible.

- If any points are unclear or if information is missing, call and ask more questions while the person is still available.

- Select the most appropriate quotations to support your ideas.

- If possible, have the person you interviewed review your work to make sure you haven't misrepresented what he or she said.

- Send a thank-you note to the person in appreciation of his or her time and effort.

For more information, see **Speaking and Listening: Conducting an Interview,** *page 481.*

Evaluate an Interview

You can determine how effective your interview was by asking yourself these questions:

- Did you get the type of information you were looking for?

- Were your most important questions answered to your satisfaction?

- Were you able to keep the interviewee focused on the subject?

Responding to a Job Interview

In a job interview, you will be the person being interviewed. The person asking you questions will have several objectives in mind, and you will need to be prepared to respond in a professional manner. Keep these strategies in mind when you are being interviewed for employment:

- Prior to the interview, prepare a short list of questions relevant to the position.

- Respond honestly and effectively to each question, and use language that conveys sensitivity, maturity, and respect.

- Give responses that demonstrate knowledge of the subject or organization.

- Use active listening skills, as outlined in the next section.

4 Active Listening

Active listening is the process of receiving, interpreting, evaluating, and responding to a message. Whether you listen to a class discussion or a formal speech, use the following strategies to get as much as you can from the message.

Before Listening

- Learn what the topic is beforehand. You may need to read background information about the topic or learn technical terms in order to understand the speaker's message.

- Think about what you know or want to know about the topic.

- Have a pen and paper or a laptop computer to take notes.

- Establish a purpose for listening.

While Listening

- Focus your attention on the speaker.

- Listen for the speaker's purpose (usually stated at the beginning), which alerts you to main ideas.

- Listen for words or phrases that signal important points, such as *to begin with, in addition, most important, finally,* and *in conclusion.*

- Listen carefully for explanations of technical terms.

- Listen for ideas that are repeated for emphasis.

- Take notes. Write down only the most important points. Use an outline or list format to organize main ideas and supporting points.

- Note comparisons and contrasts, causes and effects, or problems and solutions.

- Note how the speaker uses word choice, voice pitch, posture, and gestures to convey meaning.

After Listening

- Ask relevant questions to clarify anything that was unclear or confusing.

- Review your notes to make sure you understand what was said.

- Summarize and paraphrase the speaker's ideas.

- You may also wish to compare your interpretation of the speech with the interpretations of others who listened to it.

4.1 CRITICAL LISTENING

Critical listening involves interpreting and analyzing a spoken message to judge its accuracy and reliability. Use these strategies as you listen to messages from advertisers, politicians, lecturers, and others:

- **Determine the Speaker's Purpose** Think about the background, viewpoint, and possible motives of the speaker. Separate facts from opinions. Listen carefully to details and evidence that a speaker uses to support the message.

- **Listen for the Main Idea** Figure out the speaker's main message before allowing yourself to be distracted by seemingly convincing facts and details.

- **Recognize the Use of Persuasive Techniques** Pay attention to a speaker's choice of words. Speakers may slant information to persuade you to buy a product or accept an idea. Persuasive devices such as inaccurate generalizations, either/or reasoning, and bandwagon or snob appeal may represent faulty reasoning and provide misleading information.

  *For more information, see **Persuasive Techniques,** page R20.*

- **Observe Verbal and Nonverbal Messages** A speaker's gestures, facial expressions, and tone of voice should reinforce the message. If they don't, you should question the speaker's sincerity and the reliability of his or her message.

- **Give Appropriate Feedback** An effective speaker looks for verbal and nonverbal cues from you, the listener, to gauge how the message is being received. For example, if you understand or agree with the message, you might nod your head. If possible, during or after a presentation, ask questions to clarify understanding.

4.2 VERBAL FEEDBACK

At times you will be asked to give direct feedback to a speaker. You may be asked to evaluate the way the speaker delivers the presentation as well as the content of the presentation.

Use the following questions to evaluate a speaker's delivery.

Evaluate Delivery

- Did the speaker articulate words clearly and distinctly?
- Did the speaker pronounce words correctly?
- Did the speaker vary his or her rate?
- Did the speaker's voice sound natural and not strained?
- Was the speaker's voice loud enough?

Use the following guidelines to give constructive suggestions for improvement on content.

Evaluate Content

Be Specific Don't make statements like "Your charts need work." Offer concrete suggestions, such as "Please make the type bigger so we can read the poster from the back of the room."

Discuss Only the Most Important Points Don't overload the speaker with too much feedback about too many details. Focus on important points, such as:

- Is the topic too advanced for the audience?
- Are the supporting details well organized?
- Is the conclusion weak?

Give Balanced Feedback Tell the speaker not only what didn't work but also what did work: "Consider dropping the last two slides, since you covered those points earlier. The first two slides got my attention."

Included throughout this handbook: LS1.1
Included in this handbook as indicated:
LS1.2 (p. R89), **LS1.3** (pgs. R90–R91, R94–R95), **LS1.14** (pgs. R90–R95)

WRITING TOOLS
Go to the **Writing Center** at **ClassZone.com** for interactive models, publishing ideas, and other support.

Every day you are exposed to hundreds of images and messages from television, radio, movies, newspapers, and the Internet. What is the effect of all this media? What do you need to know to be a smart media consumer? Being media literate means that you have the ability to think critically about media messages. It means that you are able to analyze and evaluate media messages and how they influence you and your world. To become media literate, you'll need the tools to study media messages.

1 Five Core Concepts in Media Literacy

from The Center for Media Literacy

The five core concepts of media literacy provide you with the basic ideas you can consider when examining media messages.

All media messages are "constructed." All media messages are made by someone. In fact, they are carefully thought out and researched and have attitudes and values built into them. Much of the information that you use to make sense of the world comes from the media. Therefore, it is important to know how media are put together so you can better understand the message it conveys.

Media messages are constructed using a creative language with its own rules. Each means of communication—whether it is film, television, newspapers, magazines, radio, or the Internet—has its own language and design. Therefore, the content of a message must use the language and design of the medium that conveys the message. Thus, the medium actually shapes the message. For example, a horror film may use music to heighten suspense, or a newspaper may use a big headline to signal the significance of a story. Understanding the language of each medium can increase your enjoyment of it as well as alert you to obvious and subtle influences.

Different people experience the same media messages differently. Personal factors such as age, education, and experience will affect the way a person responds to a media message. How many times has your interpretation of a film or book differed from that of a friend? Everyone interprets media messages through their own personal lens.

Media have embedded values and points of view. Media messages carry underlying values, which are purposely built into them by the creators of the message. For example, a commercial's main purpose may be to persuade you to buy something, but it also conveys the value of a particular lifestyle. Understanding not only the core message but also the embedded points of view will help you decide whether to accept or reject the message.

Most media messages are organized to gain profit and/or power. The creators of media messages often provide a commodity, such as information or entertainment, in order to make money. The bigger the audience, the higher the cost of advertising. Consequently, media outlets want to build large audiences in order to bring in more revenue from advertising. For example, a television network creates programming that appeals to the largest audience possible, and then uses the viewer ratings to attract more advertising dollars.

2 Media Basics

2.1 MESSAGE

When a film or TV show is created, it becomes a media product. Each media product is created to send a **message,** or an expression of belief or opinion, that serves a specific purpose. In order to understand the message, you will need to deconstruct it.

Deconstruction is the process of analyzing a media presentation. To analyze a media presentation you will need to look at its content, its purpose, the audience it's aimed at, and the techniques and elements that are used to create certain effects.

2.2 AUDIENCE

A **target audience** is a specific group of people that a product or presentation is aimed at. The members of a target audience usually share certain characteristics, such as age, gender, ethnic background, values, or lifestyle. For example, a target audience may be adults ages 40 to 60 who want to exercise and eat healthful foods.

Demographics are the characteristics of a population, including age, gender, profession, income, education, ethnicity, and geographic location. Media decision makers use demographics to shape their content to suit the needs and tastes of a target audience.

Nielsen ratings are the system used to track TV audiences and their viewing preferences. Nielsen Media Research, the company that provides this system, monitors TV viewing in a random sample of 5,000 U.S. households selected to represent the population as a whole.

2.3 PURPOSE

The **purpose,** or intent, of a media presentation is the reason it was made. Most media messages have more than one purpose, but each has a **core purpose.** To discover that purpose, think about why its creator paid for and produced the message. For example, an ad might entertain you with humor, but its core purpose is to persuade you to buy something.

2.4 TYPES AND GENRES OF MEDIA

The term *media* refers to television, newspapers, magazines, radio, movies, and the Internet. Each is a **medium,** or means for carrying information, entertainment, and advertisements to a large audience.

Each type of media has different characteristics, strengths, and weaknesses. Understanding how different types of media work and the role they play will help you become more informed about the choices you make in response to the media.

2.5 PRODUCERS AND CREATORS

People who control the media are known as **gatekeepers.** Gatekeepers decide what information to share with the public and the ways it will be presented. The following diagram gives some examples.

Who Controls the Media?

Media Owners		Media Products		Media Creators
TV networks	▶	Television	◀	Actors
Recording companies		Radio		Writers
Publishing companies		Magazines		Directors
		Movies		Webmasters
		Newspapers		
		Internet		

Media Sponsors
Clothing manufacturers
Fast-food restaurants
Department stores

Some forms of media are independently owned, while others are part of a corporate family. Some corporate families might own several different kinds of media. For example, a company may own three radio stations, five newspapers, a publishing company, and a small television station. Often a corporate "parent" decides the content for all of its holdings.

2.6 LAWS GOVERNING MEDIA

Four main laws and policies affect the content, delivery, and use of mass media.

The First Amendment to the Constitution forbids Congress to limit speech or the press.

Copyright law protects the rights of authors and other media creators against the unauthorized publishing, reproduction, and selling of their works.

Laws prohibit **censorship,** any attempt to suppress or control people's access to media messages.

Laws prohibit **libel,** the publication of false statements that damage a person's reputation.

2.7 INFLUENCE OF MEDIA

By sheer volume alone, media influences our very existence, values, opinions, and beliefs. Our environment is saturated with media messages from television, billboards, radio, newspapers, magazines, video games, and so on. Each of these media products is selling one message and conveying another—a message about values—in the subtext. For example, a car ad is meant to sell a car, but if you look closer, you will see that it is using a set of values, such as a luxurious lifestyle, to make the car attractive to the target audience. One message of the ad is that if you buy the car, you'll have the luxurious lifestyle. The other message is that the luxurious lifestyle is good and desirable. TV shows, movies, and news programs also convey subtexts of values and beliefs.

Media can also shape your opinions about the world. For example, news about crime shapes our understanding about how much and what type of crime is prevalent in the world around us. TV news items, talk show interviews, and commercials may shape our perception of a political candidate, a celebrity, an ethnic group, a country, or a region. As a consequence, our knowledge of someone or someplace may be completely based on the information we receive from the television or other media.

3 Film and TV

Films and television programs come in a variety of types. Films include comedies, dramas, documentaries, and animated features. Televison programs cover an even wider array, including dramas, sitcoms, talk shows, reality shows, newscasts, and so on. Producers of films and producers of television programs rely on many of the same elements to convey their messages. Among these elements are scripts, visual and sound elements, special effects, and editing.

3.1 SCRIPT AND WRITTEN ELEMENTS

The writer and editor craft a story for television or film using a script and storyboard. A **script** is the text or words of a film or television show. A **storyboard** is a device often used to plan the shooting of a film and to help the director envision and convey what the finished product will look like. It consists of a sequence of sketches showing what will appear in the film's shots, often with explanatory notes and dialogue written beside or underneath them as shown in the example.

*For more information, see **Speaking and Listening: Producing a Video Documentary,** page 605.*

Where is the cat?   I don't know. I haven't seen her.   Neither have I.

3.2 VISUAL ELEMENTS

Visual elements in film and television include camera shots, angles, and movements, as well as film components such as mise en scène, set design, props, and visual special effects.

A **camera shot** is a single, continuous view taken by a camera. **Camera angle** is the angle at which the camera is positioned during the recording of a shot or image. Each angle is carefully planned to create an effect. The following chart explains the different shots and angles.

Camera Shot/Angle	Effect
Establishing shot introduces viewers to the location of a scene, usually by presenting a wide view of an area	establishes the setting of a film
Close-up shot shows a detailed view of a person or an object	helps to create emotion and make viewers feel as if they know the character
Medium shot shows a view wider than a close-up but narrower than an establishing or long shot	shows part of an object or a character from the knees or waist up
Long shot is a wide view of a scene, showing the full figure(s) of a person or group and their surroundings	allows the viewer to see the "big picture" and shows the relationship between characters and the environment
Reaction shot shows someone reacting to something that occurred in a previous shot	allows the viewer to see how the subject feels in order to create empathy in the viewer
Low-angle shot looks up at an object or a person	makes a character, object, or scene appear more important or threatening
High-angle shot looks down on an object or a person	makes a character, object, or scene seem vulnerable or insignificant
Point-of-view (POV) shot shows a part of the story through a character's eyes	helps viewers identify with that character

Camera movement can create energy, reveal information, or establish a mood. The following chart shows some of the ways filmmakers move the camera to create an effect.

Camera Movement	Effect
Pan is a shot in which the camera scans a location from right to left or left to right	reveals information by showing a sweeping view of an area
Tracking shot is a shot in which the camera moves with the subject	establishes tension or creates a sense of drama
Zoom is the movement of the camera as it closes in on or moves farther away from the subject	captures action or draws the viewer's attention to detail

Mise en scène is a French term that refers to the arrangement of actors, props, and action on a film set. It is used to describe everything that can be seen in a frame, including the setting, lighting, visual composition, costumes, and action.

Framing is capturing people and objects within the "frame" of a screen or image. Framing is what the camera sees.

Composition is the arrangement of objects, characters, shapes, and colors within a frame and the relationship of the objects to one another.

3.3 SOUND ELEMENTS

Sound elements in film and television include music, voice-over, and sound effects.

Music may be used to set the mood and atmosphere in a scene. Music can have a powerful effect on the way viewers feel about a story. For example, fast-paced music helps viewers feel excited during an action scene.

Voice-over is the voice of the unseen commentator or narrator of a film, TV program, or commercial.

Sound effects are the sounds added to films, TV programs, and commercials during the editing process. Sound effects, such as laugh tracks or the sounds of punches in a fight scene, can create humor, emphasize a point, or contribute to the mood.

3.4 SPECIAL EFFECTS

Special effects include computer-generated animation, manipulated video images, and fast- or slow-motion sequences in films, TV programs, and commercials.

Animation on film involves the frame-by-frame photography of a series of drawings or objects. When these frames are projected—at a rate of 24 per second—the illusion of movement is achieved.

A **split screen** is a special-effects shot in which two or more separate images are shown in the same frame. One example is when two people, actually a distance apart, are shown talking to each other.

3.5 EDITING

Editing is the process of selecting and arranging shots in a sequence. The editor decides which scenes or shots to use, as well as the length of each shot, the number of shots, and their sequence. Editing establishes pace, mood, and a coherent story.

Cut is the transition from one shot to another. To create excitement, editors often use quick cuts, which are a series of short shots strung together.

Dissolve is a transitional device in which one scene fades into another.

Fade-in is a transitional device in which a white or black shot fades in to reveal the beginning of a new scene.

Fade-out is a transitional device in which a shot fades to darkness to end a scene.

Jump cut is an abrupt and jarring change from one shot to another. A jump cut shows a break in time or continuity.

Pace is the length of time each shot stays on the screen and the rhythm that is created by the transitions between shots. Short, quick cuts create a fast pace in a story. Long cuts slow down a story.

Parallel editing is a technique that cuts from one shot to another so as to suggest simultaneous action—often in different locations.

4 News

The **news** is information on events, people, and places in your community, your region, the nation, and the world. The news can be categorized by type, as shown in the chart.

Type	Description	Examples
Hard news	fact-based accounts of current events	local newspapers, newscasts, online wire services
Soft news	human-interest stories and other accounts that are less current or urgent than hard news	magazines and tabloid TV shows such as *Sports Illustrated, Access Hollywood*
News features	stories that elaborate on news reports	documentaries such as history reports on PBS
Commentary and opinion	essays and perspectives by experts, professionals, and media personalities	editorial pages, personal Web pages

4.1 CHOOSING THE NEWS

Newsworthiness is the significance of an event or action that makes it worthy of media reporting. Journalists and their editors usually weigh the following criteria in determining which stories should make the news:

Timeliness is the quality of being very current. Timely events usually take priority over previously reported events. For example, a car accident with fatalities will be timely on the day it occurs. Because of its timeliness it may be on the front page of a newspaper or the lead story on a newscast.

Widespread impact refers to the importance of an event and the number of people it could affect. The more widespread the impact of an event, the more likely it is to be newsworthy.

Proximity gauges the nearness of an event to a particular city, region, or country. People tend to be more interested in stories that take place locally and affect them directly.

Human interest is a quality of stories that cause readers or listeners to feel emotions such as happiness, anger, or sadness. People are interested in reading stories about other people.

Uniqueness refers to uncommon events or circumstances that are likely to be interesting to an audience.

Compelling video and **photographs** grab people's attention and stay in their minds.

4.2 REPORTING THE NEWS

While developing a news story, a journalist makes a variety of decisions about how to construct the story, such as what information to include and how to organize it. The following elements are commonly used in news stories:

5 *W*'s and *H* are the six questions reporters answer when writing news stories—*who, what, when, where, why,* and *how.* It is a journalist's job to answer these questions in any type of news report. These questions also serve as a structure for writing and editing a story.

Inverted pyramid is the means of organizing information according to importance. In the inverted pyramid diagram below, the most important information (the answers to the 5 *W*'s and *H*) appears at the top of the pyramid. The less important details appear at the bottom. Not all stories are reported using the inverted pyramid form. The style remains popular, however, because it enables a reader to get the essential information without reading the entire story. Notice the following example.

> About 2,000 people gathered at the Vietnam Veterans Memorial Wall on Friday in an antiwar demonstration.
>
> Demonstrators carried signs and sat peacefully as speakers from peace organizations around the world spoke on issues of ending the war.
>
> Speakers called for an immediate end to the war and urged citizens to voice their opinions to state officials and legislators.

Angle or slant is the point of view from which a story is written. Even an objective report must have an angle.

Consider these two headlines that describe a war demonstration.

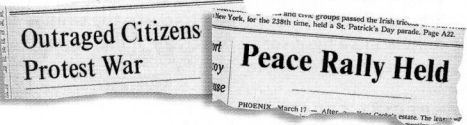

The first headline suggests that the article following it will be focused on the sentiment or mood of the crowd gathered to demonstrate against a war. The second headline suggests the article will be focused on the event.

Standards for News Reporting

The ideal of journalism is to present news in a way that is objective, accurate, and thorough. The best news stories contain the following elements:

- **Objectivity** The story takes a balanced point of view toward the issues; it is not biased, nor does it reflect a specific attitude or opinion.

- **Accuracy** The story presents factual information that can be verified.

- **Thoroughness** The story presents all sides of an issue; it includes background information, telling *who, what, when, where, why,* and *how.*

Balanced Versus Biased Reporting

Objectivity in news reporting can be measured by how balanced or biased the story is.

Balanced reporting represents all sides of an issue equally and fairly.

A balanced news story

- represents people and subjects in a neutral light

- treats all sides of an issue equally

- does not include inappropriate questions

- does not show stereotypes or prejudice toward people of a particular race, gender, age, religion, or other group

- does not leave out important background information that is needed to establish a context or perspective

Biased reporting is reporting in which one side is favored over another or in which the subject is unfairly represented. Biased reporting may show an overly negative view of a subject, or it may encourage racial, gender, or other stereotypes and prejudices. Sometimes biased reporting is apparent in the journalist's choice of sources.

Sources are the people interviewed for the news report, and also any written materials and documents the journalist used for background information. From each source, the journalist gets a different point of view. To decide whether news reporting is balanced or biased, you will need to pay attention to the sources. For a news story on a new medicinal drug, for instance, if the journalist's only source is a representative from the company that made the drug, the report may be biased. But if the journalist also includes the perspective of someone neutral, such as a scientist who is objectively studying the effects of drugs, the report may be more balanced. It is important to evaluate the **credibility,** or believability and trustworthiness, of both a source and the report itself. The following chart shows which sources are credible.

Sources for News Stories	
Credible Sources	**Weak Sources**
• experts in a field • people directly affected by the reported event (eyewitnesses) • published reports that are specifically mentioned or shown	• unnamed or anonymous sources • people who are not involved in the reported event (for example, people who heard about a story from a friend) • research, data, or reports that are not specifically named or are referred to only in vague terms (for example, "Research shows that …")

5 Advertising

Advertising is a sponsor's paid use of various media to promote products, services, or ideas. Some common forms of advertising are shown in the chart.

Type of Ad	Characteristics
Billboard	large outdoor advertising sign
Print ad	typically appears in magazines and newspapers; uses eye-catching graphics and persuasive copy
Flyer	print ad that is circulated by hand or mail
Infomercial	an extended ad on TV that usually includes detailed product information, demonstrations, and testimonials
Public service announcement	a message aired on radio or TV to promote ideas that are considered to be in the public interest
Political ad	broadcast on radio or TV to promote political candidates
Trailer	a short film promoting an upcoming movie, TV show, or video game

Marketing is the process of transferring products and services from producer to consumer. It involves determining the packaging and pricing of a product, how it will be promoted and advertised, and where it will be sold. One way companies market their products is by becoming media sponsors.

Sponsors pay for their products to be advertised. These companies hire advertising agencies to create and produce specific campaigns for their products. They then buy television or radio airtime or magazine, newspaper, or billboard space to feature ads where the target audience is sure to see them. Because selling time and space to advertisers generates much of the income the media need to function, the media need advertisers just as much as advertisers need the media.

Product placement is the intentional and identifiable featuring of brand-name products in movies, television shows, video games, and other media. The intention is to have viewers feel positive about a product because they see a favorite character using it. Another purpose may be to promote product recognition.

5.1 PERSUASIVE TECHNIQUES

Persuasive techniques are the methods used to convince an audience to buy a product or adopt an idea. Advertisers use a combination of visuals, sound, special effects, and words to persuade their target audience. Recognizing the following techniques can help you evaluate persuasive media messages and identify misleading information:

Emotional appeals use strong feelings rather than factual evidence to persuade consumers. An example of an emotional appeal that targets people's fear is a statement such as this: "Is your identity safe? Protect yourself with ProTech software."

Bandwagon appeal uses the argument that a person should believe or do something because "everyone else" does. These appeals take advantage of people's desire to be socially accepted. Purchasing a popular product seems less risky when many others also find it worthy to buy. An example of a bandwagon appeal is "More and more people are switching to Bright 'n' Fresh laundry detergent."

Slogans are memorable phrases used in advertising campaigns. Slogans substitute catchy phrases for factual information.

Logical appeals rely on logic and facts, appealing to a consumer's reason and his or her respect for authority. Two examples of logical appeals are expert opinions and product comparison.

Celebrity ads use one of the following two categories of spokesperson:

- **Celebrity authorities** are experts in a particular field. Advertisers hope that audiences will transfer the respect or admiration they have for the person to the product. For example, a famous chef may endorse a particular brand of cookware. The manufacturers of the cookware want you to think that it is a good product because a cooking expert wouldn't endorse poor-quality pots and pans.

- **Celebrity spokespeople** are famous people who endorse a product. Advertisers hope that audiences will associate the product with the celebrity.

Product comparison involves comparing a product with its competition. The competing product is portrayed as inferior. The intended effect is for people to question the quality of the competing product and to believe the featured product is superior.

6 Elements of Design

The design of a media message is just as important as the words are in conveying the message. Like words, visuals are used to persuade, inform, and entertain.

Graphics and images, such as charts, diagrams, maps, timelines, photographs, illustrations, cartoons, book covers, and symbols, present information that can be quickly and easily understood. The following basic elements are used to give meaning to visuals:

Color can be used to highlight important elements such as headlines and subheads. It can also create mood, because many colors have a strong emotional or psychological impact on the reader or viewer. For example, warm colors more readily draw the eye and are often associated with happiness and comfort. Cool colors are often associated with feelings of peace and contentment or sometimes sadness.

Lines—strokes or marks—can be thick or thin, long or short, and smooth or jagged. They can focus attention and create a feeling of depth. They can frame an object. They can also direct a viewer's eye or create a sense of motion.

Texture is the surface quality or appearance of an object. For example, an object's texture can be glossy, rough, wet, or shiny. Texture can be used to create contrast. It can also be used to make an image look "real." For example, a pattern on wrapping paper can create a feeling of depth even though the texture is only visual and cannot be felt.

Shape is the external outline of an object. Shapes can be used to symbolize living things or geometric objects. They can emphasize visual elements and add interest. Shapes can also symbolize ideas.

Notice how this photograph uses these design elements to convey a message.

In "reading" this visual image for its message, take note of the following:

- The **foreground image** in this photo is of an unhappy young woman with a plume of smoke rising from her head, indicating she is angry or unhappy—presumably with the situation depicted behind her. The **background images** include smokestacks spewing smoke into the environment. This would suggest that the message concerns her feelings about the environment.

- The **colors** orange and black suggest danger, the need to be alert, or a threatening situation. The colors in this scene indicate that the situation is threatening or dangerous.

- The smokestacks in the background are in silhouette and can only be defined by their **shape.** This suggestion of the image lends an air of mystery and foreboding to the message.

- The **lines** in this picture are primarily vertical (the smokestacks, the young woman, and the white smoke plume). The vertical lines draw your focus toward the top of the photo, where it centers on the crossed smoke plumes.

Considering all the design elements in this photograph, what is its message?

7 Evaluating Media Messages

Being able to respond critically to media images and messages will help you evaluate the reliability of the content and make informed decisions. Here are six questions to ask about any media message:

Who made—and who sponsored—this message, and for what purpose? The source of the message is a clue to its purpose. If the source of the message is a private company, that company may be trying to sell you a product. If the source is a government agency, that agency may be trying to promote a program or philosophy. To discover the purpose, think about why its creator paid for and produced the message.

Who is the target audience and how is the message specifically tailored to it? Think about the age group, ethnic group, gender, and/or profession the message is targeting. Decide how it relates to you.

What are the different techniques used to inform, persuade, entertain, and attract attention? Analyze the elements, such as humor, music, special effects, and graphics, that have been used to create the message. Think about how visual and sound effects, such as symbols, color, photographs, words, and music, support the purpose behind the message.

What messages are communicated (and/or implied) about certain people, places, events, behaviors, lifestyles, and so forth? The media try to influence who we are, what we believe in, how we view things, and what values we hold. Look or listen closely to determine whether certain types of behavior are being depicted and if judgments or values are communicated through those behaviors. What are the biases in the message?

How current, accurate, and credible is the information in this message? Think about the reputation of the source. Note the broadcast or publication date of the message and whether the message might change quickly. If a report or account is not supported by facts, authoritative sources, or eyewitness accounts, you should question the credibility of the message.

What is left out of this message that might be important to know? Think about what the message is asking you to believe. Also think about what questions come to mind as you watch, read, or listen to the message.

Applying Strategies to the SAT* and ACT

The test items in this section are modeled after test formats that are used on the SAT and ACT. The strategies presented here will help you prepare for these tests and others. This section offers general test-taking strategies and tips for answering multiple-choice items in critical reading and writing, as well as samples for impromptu writing and essay writing. For each test, read the tips in the margin. Then apply the tips to the practice items. You can also apply the tips to Assessment Practice tests in this book.

1 General Test-Taking Strategies

- Arrive on time and be prepared. Be sure to bring either sharpened pencils with erasers or pens—whichever you are told to bring.
- If you have any questions, ask them before the test begins. Make sure you understand the test procedures, the timing, and the rules.
- Read the test directions carefully. Look at the passages and questions to get an overview of what is expected.
- Tackle the questions one at a time rather than thinking about the whole test.
- Refer back to the reading selections as needed. For example, if a question asks about an author's attitude, you might have to reread a passage for clues.
- If you are not sure of your answer, make a logical guess. You can often arrive at the correct answer by reasoning and eliminating wrong answers.
- As you fill in answers on your answer sheet, make sure you match the number of each test item to the numbered space on the answer sheet.
- Don't look for patterns in the positions of correct choices.
- Only change an answer if you are sure your original choice is incorrect. If you do change an answer, erase your original choice neatly and thoroughly.
- Look for main ideas as you read passages. They are often stated at the beginning or the end of a paragraph. Sometimes the main idea is implied.
- Check your answers and reread your essay.

* SAT® is a registered trademark of the College Board, which was not involved in the production of, and does not endorse, this product.

2 Critical Reading

Most tests contain a critical reading section that measures your ability to read, understand, and interpret passages. The passages may be either fiction or nonfiction, and they can be 100 words or 500 to 850 words. They are drawn from literature, the humanities, social studies, and the natural sciences.

> **Directions:** Read the following passage. Base your answers to questions 1 and 2 on what is stated or implied in the passage.

PASSAGE

The chemical composition of diamond is extremely simple; like graphite it is composed of only one element: carbon. But the similarity ends there, for no two minerals could be more diverse. Diamond is hard, lustrous, and transparent; graphite is soft, dull, and opaque. Diamond has a specific gravity of 3.5, high for a nonmetallic mineral. Graphite's specific gravity is 2.2, extremely low for a metallic mineral. These strikingly different properties of the same element result from the way in which the carbon atoms are packed together. In diamond they are close together and held by strong electrical bonds, whereas in graphite they are far apart and have weak bonds.

Diamond is valued for its remarkable physical properties. It is harder and more resistant to abrasion than any other natural mineral; nothing can scratch it except another diamond. It is also insoluble in all acids and alkalis. Because of these resistant properties, the Greeks called the mineral *adamas,* meaning "invincible," and its present name derives from that.

—Cornelius Hurlbut, from *Minerals and Man*

---

❶ stem

1. The (main) idea of the first paragraph is that **❷**

choices

   (A) diamond and graphite consist of the same element but have different properties
   (B) the atoms in diamond and graphite are held together by electrical bonds
   (C) diamond is hard, lustrous, and transparent, while graphite is soft, dull, and opaque
   (D) diamond and graphite have a simple chemical composition consisting of one element
   (E) the specific gravity of diamond is high; graphite's specific gravity is low

2. The Greek word *adamas* is a fitting description of diamond's **❹**
   (A) international reputation
   (B) great value
   (C) jewelry applications **❺**
   (D) resistant properties
   (E) ancient lineage

Tips: Multiple Choice

A multiple-choice question consists of a stem and a set of choices. On some tests, there are four choices. On the SAT, there are five. The stem is usually in the form of a question or an incomplete sentence. One of the choices correctly answers the question or completes the sentence.

❶ Read the stem carefully and try to answer the question without looking at the choices.

❷ Pay attention to key words in the stem. They may direct you to the correct answer. Question 1 is looking for the *main* idea. Choices (B) through (E) focus on minor details.

❸ Read all the choices before deciding on the correct answer.

❹ Some questions ask you to interpret a word or a figure of speech. Question 2, for example, asks you to describe the character of a diamond based on the etymology of its name.

❺ After reading all of the choices, eliminate any that you know are incorrect. In question 2, you can safely eliminate choice (C) because this passage focuses on the scientific properties of diamond, not its uses.

Answers: 1. (A), **2.** (D)

Directions: Base your answers to questions 1 and 2 on the two passages below.

PASSAGE 1

❷

The president helps people make sense of politics. Congress is a tangle of committees, the bureaucracy is a maze of agencies. The president is one man ❸ trying to do a job—a picture much more understandable to the mass of people who find themselves in the same boat. Furthermore, he is the top man. He ought to know what is going on and set it right. So when the economy goes sour, or war drags on, or domestic violence erupts, the president is available to take the blame. Then when things go right, it seems the president must have had a hand in it.

—James David Barber, "The Presidential Character"

PASSAGE 2

No man or group at either end of Pennsylvania Avenue shares his peculiar ❷ status in our government and politics. That is why his services are in demand. By the same token, though, the obligations of all other men are different from his own. His Cabinet officers have departmental duties and constituents. His legislative leaders head Congressional parties, one in either House. His national ❹ party organization stands apart from his official family. His political allies in the states need not face Washington, or one another. The private groups that seek him out are not compelled to govern. And friends abroad are not compelled to run in our elections. Lacking his position and prerogatives, these men cannot regard his obligations as his own. They have their jobs to do; none is the same as his.

—Richard E. Neustadt, "Presidential Power"

❶ **1.** In Passage 1, what does the author mean when he says, "The president helps people make sense of politics"?

(A) The government is sponsoring political education classes for voters.

(B) People see the president in personal terms, as someone with a job to do.

(C) The White House has valuable information about the legislative process.

(D) Congress is an impenetrable maze of agencies and committees.

(E) Citizens have to think about international issues before they vote.

2. The authors of both passages would probably agree with which one of these statements about government? ❺

(A) It is difficult to penetrate the maze of government bureaucracies.

(B) Many elected officials are only concerned with local issues.

(C) Each president leaves an indelible imprint on the nation.

(D) Not everyone supports the president or his policies.

(E) The president holds a unique position in our political system.

Tips: Two Passages

Questions are sometimes based on a pair of related passages, which may have completely different views or may simply describe different aspects of the same subject. The two passages here discuss the role of the U.S. president.

❶ Before reading the passages, skim all the questions to see what information you will need.

❷ Find topic sentences and ask yourself whether the passages support or refute their topic sentences. In this case, both passages support their claims with examples and discussion.

❸ You can determine an author's attitude toward a subject by his or her choice of words. In passage 1, the words *tangle* and *maze* convey a subtle disapproval of government bureaucracies.

❹ Analyze supporting details. The author of passage 2 supports his claim that the president has unique responsibilities by contrasting his position with those of others.

❺ When working with two passages, look for related or contrasting ideas. To answer question 2, you have to find a common thread in the discussions of the presidency. Eliminate any answers that pertain to only one of the passages.

Answers: 1. (B), **2.** (E)

Directions: Read the following passage, taken from a novel published in 1900. Based on what is stated or implied in the passage, answer questions 1 through 5, which appear on the next page.

PASSAGE

❶ When Caroline Meeber boarded the afternoon train for Chicago, her total outfit consisted of a small trunk, a cheap imitation alligator-skin satchel, a small lunch in a paper box, and a yellow leather snap purse containing her ticket, a scrap of paper with her sister's address in Van Buren ❷
5 Street, and four dollars in money. It was in August, 1889. She was eighteen years of age, bright, timid, and full of the illusions of ignorance and youth. Whatever touch of regret at parting characterized her thoughts, it was certainly not for advantages now being given up. A gush of tears at her mother's farewell kiss, a touch in her throat when the cars clacked by the
10 flour mill where her father worked by the day, a pathetic sign as the familiar green environs of the village passed in review, and the threads which bound her so lightly to girlhood and home were irretrievably broken. ❸

To be sure, there was always the next station, where one might descend and return. There was the great city, bound more closely by these very
15 trains which came up daily. Columbia City was not so very far away, even once she was in Chicago. What, pray, is a few hours—a few hundred miles? She looked at the little slip bearing her sister's address and wondered. She gazed at the green landscape, now passing in swift review, until her swifter thoughts replaced its impression with vague conjectures of what Chicago
20 might be.

When a girl leaves her home at eighteen, she does one of two things. Either she falls into saving hands and becomes better, or she rapidly assumes the cosmopolitan standard of virtue and becomes worse. Of an intermediate balance, under the circumstances, there is no possibility. The city has its
25 cunning wiles, no less than the infinitely smaller and more human tempter. There are large forces which allure with all the soulfulness of expression possible in the most cultured human. The gleam of a thousand lights is often as effective as the persuasive light in a wooing and fascinating ❹ eye. Half of the undoing of the unsophisticated and natural mind is
30 accomplished by forces wholly superhuman. A blare of sound, a roar of life, ❸ a vast array of human hives, appeal to the astonished senses in equivocal terms. Without a counselor at hand to whisper cautious interpretations, what falsehoods may not these things breathe into the unguarded ear! Unrecognized for what they are, their beauty, like music, too often relaxes,
35 then weakens, then perverts the simpler human perceptions.

Tips: Reading Text

❶ Notice the characters who are presented in a passage. Be alert to details about their appearance, personality, or behavior.

❷ Identify the point of view from which the story is being told. In a first-person narrative, the narrator is a character in the story and uses the pronouns *I* and *me*. In a third-person narrative, the narrator is outside the story and uses the pronouns *he, she,* and *they.*

❸ Try to visualize the setting as you read, filling in details as they are presented. In this passage we see a young woman on a train headed for Chicago in 1889. She has left behind the "familiar green environs" of her home in the small town of Columbia City.

❹ Remember that a word can have several different meanings or subtle shades of meaning.

❺ Some test questions will ask you to interpret a figure of speech or an image. Try to understand why the author chose that particular image and what effect it achieves.

Answers: 1. (D), **2.** (B), **3.** (A), **4.** (C), **5.** (E)

1. The catalog of Caroline's belongings in lines 2–5 helps to
   (A) foreshadow her destiny
   (B) mock her appearance
   (C) create sympathy for her
   (D) convey her social status
   (E) portray her personality

2. What is implied about Caroline's life in the statement "Whatever touch of regret at parting characterized her thoughts, it was certainly not for advantages now being given up"?
   (A) It was hard for Caroline to leave behind the comforts of home.
   (B) Caroline's life at home offered few material benefits.
   (C) Caroline hated the life of poverty she led at home.
   (D) Moving to the city required a sacrifice on Caroline's part.
   (E) Once she left home, Caroline never looked back.

3. The description in lines 21–24 suggests that the city is a place that should be viewed with
   (A) distrust
   (B) respect
   (C) enthusiasm
   (D) contempt
   (E) nostalgia

4. The image of a tempter in lines 24–30 suggests the ❺
   (A) evils of human nature
   (B) simple beauty of music
   (C) corrupting influence of the city
   (D) vulnerable innocence of youth
   (E) pleasures of materialism

5. In line 29, "natural" most nearly means
   (A) normal
   (B) inborn
   (C) logical
   (D) real
   (E) naive

The critical reading section may feature sentence completion questions that test your knowledge of vocabulary. They may also measure your ability to figure out how different parts of a sentence logically fit together.

Directions: Choose the word or set of words that, when inserted, best fits the meaning of the complete sentence.

1. The investigator constructed a _____ of events to _____ the cause of the accident. ❶
   (A) chronology . . ascertain
   (B) timeline . . predict ❷
   (C) typology . . determine
   (D) collation . . understand
   (E) history . . prosecute

2. Russian author Alexander Solzhenitsyn tried to _____ government censorship by _____ some of his writings out of the country.
   (A) encircle . . translating
   (B) disrupt . . carrying
   (C) circumvent . . smuggling ❸
   (D) evade . . banishing
   (E) prevent . . propelling

3. Automakers can _____ the effects of global warming by reducing carbon-dioxide and other _____ emissions from cars and trucks. ❹
   (A) minimize . . natural
   (B) misuse . . harmful
   (C) correct . . excessive
   (D) mitigate . . toxic
   (E) relieve . . acute

4. Because they have a _____ appetite, bears will raid cabins, backpacks, and ❺ picnic areas in search of anything that smells of food. ❻
   (A) vicious
   (B) voracious
   (C) refined
   (D) notorious
   (E) selective

Tips: Sentence Completion

❶ When you are completing sentences with two words missing, think about which pair of suggested words fits both blanks.

❷ If one word in the answer choice is wrong, eliminate that choice from consideration. In sentence 1, *timeline* makes sense, but *predict* does not, because the accident occurred in the past.

❸ A prefix can help to unlock the meaning of a word. The Latin prefix *circum-* means "around." The writer was trying to circumvent, or go around, government censorship.

❹ Look for key words or phrases that link the ideas in a sentence. The word *by* introduces a phrase that explains how to do something—in this case, how to reduce global warming.

❺ Look for words that link the ideas in a sentence. The word *because* in sentence 4 signals a cause-and-effect relationship between appetite and behavior.

❻ If you don't know a word's meaning, look for clues within the sentence. For sentence 4, ask yourself: What sort of appetite would lead a bear to eat almost anything? An animal with a *refined* (C) or *selective* (E) appetite, for example, would choose only certain foods.

Answers: 1. (A), **2.** (C), **3.** (D), **4.** (B)

❸ Writing

The writing section of standardized tests measures your ability to express ideas clearly and correctly. You will be asked to identify errors in grammar and usage and to improve sentences and paragraphs.

> **Directions:** The following sentence contains either a single error or no error. If it does contains an error, select the underlined part that must be changed to make the sentence correct. If the sentence is correct as written, select answer choice (E).

1. <u>Neither</u> the Supreme Court <u>nor</u> the president <u>have</u> the power to create laws,
    (A)   (B)   (C) ❷

   because the Constitution <u>entrusts</u> that responsibility to Congresss alone. <u>No error</u>
                          (D) ❸   (E) ❶

> **Directions:** Determine if the underlined part of the following sentence needs improvement. If it does, select the best change presented. If the original phrasing is best, select answer (A).

2. Ancient Greeks believed in mythical <u>creatures, they combined</u> human and animal traits.
   - (A) creatures, they combined ❹
   - (B) creatures, and they combined
   - (C) creatures that combined ❺
   - (D) creatures, and which combined
   - (E) creatures such as could combine

> **Directions:** Following is an early draft of an essay. Read it and answer the question.

Controlling E-Waste

    (1) It is estimated that Americans generate about 2 million tons of technology-related trash each year. (2) Computer circuit boards, monitors, and printers are piling up in landfills. (3) They decay. (4) They can leak mercury and other toxic substances as a result of the decay. (5) Some public health officials think the U.S. should develop a federal law that requires technology companies to take back their used products and reduce the amount of hazardous material they use in manufacturing.

3. Which one of the following sentences combines sentences 3 and 4? ❻
   - (A) They can decay, also leaking mercury and other toxic substances.
   - (B) When they decay, they can leak mercury and other toxic substances.
   - (C) They decay; then they can leak mercury and other toxic substances.
   - (D) They decay, and thus leak mercury and other toxic substances.
   - (E) They can leak toxic substances such as mercury.

Tips: Grammar and Style

❶ Read the entire sentence or passage to grasp its overall meaning. Pay particular attention to any underlined portions.

❷ Watch for subject-verb agreement when using *neither...nor.* If both subjects are singular, the verb must be singular.

❸ Use prefixes to help you understand the meaning of words. The prefix *en-* in the word *entrust* means "in" or "within."

❹ Read through all of the choices before you decide which revision is best. In this case, answer (A) is *not* correct, because joining two independent clauses with only a comma creates a run-on sentence.

❺ Understand how to use *that* and *which. That* introduces an essential defining clause. *Which* introduces a nonessential clause. Use *which* if the clause can be omitted without changing the meaning of the sentence. Nonessential clauses are set off with commas.

❻ When combining sentences, think about how the ideas are related. Subordinating conjunctions such as *while, when, before, after,* and *until* express a relationship of time. *Because* and *since* indicate cause and effect.

Answers: 1. (C), **2.** (C), **3.** (B)

4 Essay

To determine how well you can develop and express ideas, many tests ask you to write an essay in response to an assignment, or prompt. The essay will represent a first draft and be scored based on the following criteria:

- **Focus** Establish a point of view in the opening paragraph.
- **Organization** Maintain a logical progression of ideas.
- **Support for Ideas** Use details and examples to develop an argument.
- **Style/Word Choice** Use words accurately and vary your sentences.
- **Grammar** Use Standard English and proofread for errors.

Think carefully about the issue presented in this quotation and the assignment below.

> Arts education and physical education both enjoy public support and help students grow and develop in many ways. In recent years, these programs have sometimes been marginalized or discontinued due to budget cuts or redirection of school resources. Sometimes schools have had to choose between these programs.

Assignment: If a school had to choose between funding its arts program and funding its physical education program, which option would you support? Plan and write an essay in which you develop your opinion on this issue. Support your position with specific reasons and examples taken from your studies and experience.

SAMPLE ESSAY

If I had to decide whether to cut arts or physical education programs from the curriculum, I would choose to save the arts. ❶

It's hard to cut physical education programs when our nation is struggling with an obesity epidemic. We all know that Americans don't get enough exercise. We drive everywhere, and we spend hours in front of the TV. But ❷ physical fitness is a medical and lifestyle issue, not an academic pursuit. Exercise and good nutrition require a personal, lifelong commitment, and that goes beyond what can be taught in a gym class.

The arts, on the other hand, are as much an academic pursuit as science, history, or literature. Acting in a play requires reading and interpreting a work of literature. Composing even a simple tune requires knowledge of harmony, rhythm, and timing. Painting and drawing require some understanding of the principles of light, color, and perspective. Whereas high school athletes often ❸ struggle with academics because of the demands of their sport, students in music and performing arts don't seem to experience those conflicting demands in the same way.

Arts education encourages students to be creative and to take risks. There are no right or wrong answers in art, so students who might not excel in other areas of academic life can gain respect through their music or dancing.

Music, painting, literature, dance, and theater not only enrich our lives but also stimulate us and teach us life lessons that a gym class never could. ❹

Tips: Writing an Essay

The SAT allows only 25 minutes for you to write an essay. Before you begin writing, take a few minutes to jot down the main points you want to make. Allow time to reread and proofread your essay before you hand it in.

❶ When you're writing a persuasive essay, state your point of view in the introduction. Be sure to keep your purpose in mind as you write.

❷ Take the opposing point of view into consideration and respond to it.

❸ Include concrete examples in the body of your essay to clarify your points and strengthen your arguments.

❹ Make sure your essay has a conclusion, even if it is just a single sentence. A conclusion pulls your ideas together and lets the reader know that you have finished.

❺ There will not be time to recopy your essay, so if you have to make a correction, do so neatly and legibly.

❻ You don't have to write a long essay. Length is less important than clarity of thought and correctness of expression. Your essay could range from 200 to 400 words.

Act An act is a major unit of action in a play, similar to a chapter in a book. Depending on their lengths, plays can have as many as five acts. Arthur Miller's play *The Crucible* has four acts.

See also **Drama; Scene.**

Allegory An allegory is a work with two levels of meaning, a literal one and a symbolic one. In such a work, most of the characters, objects, settings, and events represent abstract qualities. Personification is often used in traditional allegories. As in a fable or parable, the purpose of an allegory may be to convey truths about life, to teach religious or moral lessons, or to criticize social institutions.

Example: In Edgar Allan Poe's "The Masque of the Red Death," the main character Prospero, the sequence and the decorations of the rooms in the castle, and objects such as the ebony clock all have allegorical meaning.

See page 427.

Alliteration Alliteration is the repetition of consonant sounds at the beginnings of words. Poets use alliteration to impart a musical quality to their poems, to create mood, to reinforce meaning, to emphasize particular words, and to unify lines or stanzas. Note the examples of alliteration in the following line:

> Doubting, dreaming dreams no mortal ever dared to dream before.
>
> —Edgar Allan Poe, "The Raven"

See pages 437, 1237.

Allusion An allusion is an indirect reference to a person, place, event, or literary work with which the author believes the reader will be familiar.

Example: In "Speech in the Virginia Convention," Patrick Henry warns colonists not to be "betrayed with a kiss"— an allusion to the Apostle Judas, who betrayed Jesus by kissing him.

See pages 231, 902, 1145.

Ambiguity Ambiguity is a technique in which a word, phrase, or event has more than one meaning or can be interpreted in more than one way. Some writers deliberately create this effect to give richness and depth of meaning. T. S. Eliot and Robert Frost are two poets known for their use of ambiguity.

See pages 471, 897, 1015.

Analogy An analogy is a point-by-point comparison between two things for the purpose of clarifying the less familiar of the two subjects.

Example: In "My Dungeon Shook," James Baldwin draws an analogy between his nephew's probable reaction to seeing the stars shining while the sun is out and white people's reaction to black people moving out of their fixed places.

See pages 252, 272, 1157, 1197.

Anapest *See* **Meter.**

Anaphora Anaphora is a repetition of a word or words at the beginning of successive lines, clauses, or sentences.

> Blackness
> is a title,
> is a preoccupation,
> is a commitment . . .
>
> —Gwendolyn Brooks, "Primer for Blacks"

See pages 509, 1231.
See also **Repetition.**

Anecdote An anecdote is a brief story that focuses on a single episode or event in a person's life and that is used to illustrate a particular point.

Example: In "Straw into Gold," Sandra Cisneros provides an anecdote about the challenge she faced when ordered to make corn tortillas, a task she had never done before. This anecdote illustrates Cisneros's pluck in attempting the seemingly impossible.

See pages 371, 1223.

Antagonist An antagonist is usually the principal character in opposition to the **protagonist,** or hero of a narrative or drama. The antagonist can also be a force of nature.

Example: In "The Open Boat," the sea is the antagonist of the four shipwrecked men. Its powerful force is described in such detail that it seems like a character.

See pages 735, 937.
See also **Character; Protagonist.**

Antihero An antihero is a protagonist who has the qualities opposite to those of a hero; he or she may be insecure, ineffective, cowardly, sometimes dishonest or dishonorable, or—most often—a failure. A popular antihero in contemporary culture is the cartoon character Homer Simpson.

Aphorism An aphorism is a brief statement, usually one sentence long, that expresses a general principle or truth about life.

Example: Ralph Waldo Emerson's "Self-Reliance" is sprinkled with such memorable aphorisms as "A foolish consistency is the hobgoblin of little minds."
See pages 271, 361.

Archetype An archetype is a pattern in literature that is found in a variety of works from different cultures throughout the ages. An archetype can be a plot, a character, an image, or a setting. For example, the association of death and rebirth with winter and spring is an archetype common to many cultures.

Aside In drama, an aside is a short speech directed to the audience, or another character, that is not heard by the other characters on stage.
See also **Soliloquy.**

Assonance Assonance is the repetition of vowel sounds within words. Both poets and prose writers use assonance to impart a musical quality to their works, to create mood, to reinforce meaning, to emphasize particular words, and to unify lines, stanzas, or passages. Note examples of assonance in the following lines:

> Along the window-sill, the lipstick stubs
> Glittered in their steel shells.
> —Rita Dove, "Adolescence—III"

See also **Alliteration; Consonance; Rhyme.**

Atmosphere *See* **Mood.**

Audience Audience is the person or persons who are intended to read a piece of writing. The intended audience of a work determines its form, style, tone, and the details included. For example, Cabeza de Vaca's audience for *La Relación* was the king of Spain. Hence, *La Relación* took the form of a formal report with a patriotic tone that included details of the explorers' hardship and determination. Had the work been addressed to Cabeza de Vaca's wife, it would likely have been less formal and probably would have included details about his personal feelings.
See pages 69, 119, 1199.

Author's Purpose A writer usually writes for one or more of these purposes: to inform, to entertain, to express himself or herself, or to persuade readers to believe or do something. For example, the purpose of a news report is to inform; the purpose of an editorial is to persuade the readers or audience to do or believe something.
Examples: In *The Interesting Narrative of the Life of Olaudah Equiano,* the author's purpose is primarily to inform readers about the horrors that captured Africans endured in the holds of slave ships during the Middle Passage. Thoreau's purpose in "Civil Disobedience," on the other hand, is to persuade his audience to use nonviolent resistance to oppose unjust laws.
See pages 79, 371.

Author's Perspective An author's perspective is a unique combination of ideas, values, feelings, and beliefs that influences the way the writer looks at a topic. **Tone,** or attitude, often reveals an author's perspective. For example, Jonathan Edwards was a Puritan minister whose father and grandfather were also Puritan ministers; he began his theological training at age 12. His family upbringing, his beliefs, and the time and place in which he lived all contributed to the perspective found in *Sinners in the Hands of an Angry God.*
See pages 118, 395, 745.
See also **Author's Purpose; Tone.**

Autobiographical Essay *See* **Essay.**

Autobiography An autobiography is the story of a person's life written by that person. Generally written from the first-person point of view, autobiographies can vary in style from straightforward chronological accounts to impressionistic narratives.
Example: Both *Narrative of the Life of Frederick Douglass, an American Slave* and *Coming of Age in Mississippi* are autobiographies.
See pages 262, 536, 634.

Ballad A ballad is a narrative poem that was originally meant to be sung. Ballads often contain dialogue and repetition and suggest more than they actually state. Traditional **folk ballads,** composed by unknown authors and handed down orally, are written in four-line stanzas with regular rhythm and rhyme. A **literary ballad** is one that is modeled on the folk ballads but written by a single author—for example, Dudley Randall's "Ballad of Birmingham."
See page 1156.
See also **Narrative Poem; Rhyme; Rhythm.**

Biography A biography is a type of nonfiction in which a writer gives a factual account of someone else's life. Written in the third person, a biography may cover a person's entire life or focus on only an important part of it. The poet Carl Sandburg wrote an acclaimed six-volume biography of Abraham Lincoln. Modern biography includes a popular form called **fictionalized biography,** in which writers use their imaginations to re-create past conversations and to elaborate on some incidents.

Blank Verse A poem written in blank verse consists of unrhymed lines of iambic pentameter. In other words, each line of blank verse has five pairs of syllables. In most pairs, an unstressed syllable is followed by a stressed syllable. The most versatile of poetic forms, blank verse imitates the natural rhythms of English speech, as in the following lines:

> She ran | on tip | toe down | the dark | ened passage
> To meet | him in | the door | way with | the news
> And put | him on | his guard. | "Silas | is back."
> She pushed | him out | ward with | her through |
>   the door
> And shut | it aft | er her. | "Be kind," | she said.
>   —Robert Frost, "The Death of the Hired Man"

See pages 329, 903.
See also **Iambic Pentameter; Meter; Rhythm.**

Caesura A caesura is a pause or a break in a line of poetry. Poets use a caesura to emphasize the word or phrase that precedes it or to vary the rhythmical effects. In the following line, a caesura follows the word *die:*

> If we must die, let it not be like hogs
>   —Claude McKay, "If We Must Die"

Cast of Characters The cast of characters is a list of all the characters in a play, usually in the order of appearance. This list is found at the beginning of a script.
See page 133.

Catalog A catalog is a list of people, things, or attributes. This technique, found in epics and in the Bible, also characterizes Whitman's style, as seen in the beginning of this line:

> Kanuck, Tuckahoe, Congressman, Cuff, I give them the
> same, I receive them the same.
>   —Walt Whitman, "Song of Myself"

See page 509.

Character Characters are the people, and sometimes animals or other beings, who take part in the action of a story or novel. Events center on the lives of one or more characters, referred to as **main characters.** The other characters, called **minor characters,** interact with the main characters and help move the story along. In Kurt Vonnegut's story "Adam," Heinz Knechtmann is the main character, while the other expectant father, Mr. Sousa, is a minor character.

Characters may also be classified as either static or dynamic. **Static characters** tend to stay in a fixed position over the course of the story. They do not experience life-altering moments and seem to act the same, even though their situations may change. In contrast, **dynamic characters** evolve as individuals, learning from their experiences and growing emotionally.
See pages 693, 903, 937, 1123.
See also **Antagonist; Characterization; Foil; Motivation; Protagonist.**

Characterization Characterization refers to the techniques a writer uses to develop characters. There are four basic methods of characterization:

1. A writer may use physical description. In F. Scott Fitzgerald's "Winter Dreams," Judy Jones is described as follows:

> She wore a blue gingham dress, rimmed at throat and
> shoulders with a white edging that accentuated her
> tan. . . . She was arrestingly beautiful. The color in her
> cheeks was centered like the color in a picture—it was
> not a "high" color, but a sort of fluctuating and feverish
> warmth. . . .

2. The character's own actions, words, thoughts, and feelings might be presented. In Fitzgerald's story, after Judy Jones tries to revive the romance between herself and Dexter, she cries and says, "I'm more beautiful than anybody else, . . . why can't I be happy?"

3. The actions, words, thoughts, and feelings of other characters provide another means of developing a character. Mr. Sandwood, in Fitzgerald's story, exclaims about Judy Jones: "My God, she's good-looking!" To which Mr. Hedrick replies: "Good-looking! She always looks as if she wanted to be kissed! Turning those big cow-eyes on every calf in town!"

4. The narrator's own direct comments also serve to develop a character. The narrator of "Winter Dreams" says of Judy Jones:

> Whatever Judy wanted, she went after with the full pressure of her charm. There was no divergence of method, no jockeying for position or premeditation of effects—there was very little mental side to any of her affairs. She simply made men conscious to the highest degree of her physical loveliness.

See pages 667, 881, 1123.
See also **Character; Narrator.**

Chorus *In the theater of ancient Greece, the chorus was a group of actors who commented on the action of the play.* *Between scenes, the chorus sang and danced to musical accompaniment, giving insights into the message of the play. The chorus is often considered a kind of ideal spectator, representing the response of ordinary citizens to the tragic events that unfold. Certain dramatists have continued to employ this classical convention as a way of representing the views of the society being depicted.*
See also **Drama.**

Cliché A cliché is an overused expression that has lost its freshness, force, and appeal. The phrase "happy as a lark" is an example of a cliché.

Climax In a plot structure, the climax, or turning point, is the moment when the reader's interest and emotional intensity reach a peak. The climax usually occurs toward the end of a story and often results in a change in the characters or a solution to the conflict.
Example: In Edgar Allan Poe's "The Masque of the Red Death," the climax occurs when the Red Death arrives at the masked ball and is confronted by Prince Prospero. Shortly afterward, Prospero and all of his guests die.
See also **Falling Action; Plot; Rising Action; Resolution.**

Comedy A comedy is a dramatic work that is light and often humorous in tone, usually ending happily with a peaceful resolution of the main conflict. A comedy differs from a **farce** by having a more believable plot, more realistic characters, and less boisterous behavior.
See also **Drama; Farce.**

Comic Relief Comic relief consists of humorous scenes, incidents, or speeches that are included in a serious drama to provide a reduction in emotional intensity. Because it breaks the tension, comic relief allows an audience to prepare emotionally for events to come.

Complication A complication is an additional factor or problem introduced into the rising action of a story to make the conflict more difficult. Often, a plot complication makes it seem as though the main character is getting farther away from the thing he or she wants.

Conceit *See* **Extended Metaphor.**

Conflict A conflict is a struggle between opposing forces that is the basis of a story's plot. An **external conflict** pits a character against nature, society, or another character. An **internal conflict** is a conflict between opposing forces within a character.
Example: In "Coyote and the Buffalo," Coyote's struggle to keep Buffalo Bull from killing him is an external conflict, whereas Coyote's struggle to decide whether to kill and eat the buffalo cow is an internal conflict.
See pages 44, 735, 759, 1137.
See also **Antagonist; Plot.**

Connotation Connotation is the emotional response evoked by a word, in contrast to its denotation, which is its literal meaning. *Kitten,* for example, is defined as "a young cat." However, the word also suggests, or connotes, images of softness, warmth, and playfulness.

Consonance Consonance is the repetition of consonant sounds within and at the ends of words.

> Some late visitor entreating entrance at my chamber door.
> —Edgar Allan Poe, "The Raven"

See also **Alliteration; Assonance.**

Couplet *See* **Sonnet.**

Creation Myth *See* **Myth.**

Critical Essay *See* **Essay.**

Cultural Hero A cultural hero is a larger-than-life figure who reflects the values of a people. Rather than being the creation of a single writer, this kind of hero evolves from the telling of folk tales from one generation to the next. The role of the cultural hero is to provide a noble image that will inspire and guide the actions of all who share that culture.

Dactyl *See* **Meter.**

Denotation *See* **Connotation.**

Dénouement *See* **Falling Action.**

Description Description is writing that helps a reader to picture scenes, events, and characters. Effective description usually relies on imagery, figurative language, and precise diction, as in the following passage:

> I saw again the naked house on the prairie, black and grim as a wooden fortress; the black pond where I had learned to swim, its margin pitted with sun-dried cattle tracks; the rain gullied clay banks about the naked house, the four dwarf ash seedlings where the dishcloths were always hung to dry before the kitchen door.
> —Willa Cather, "A Wagner Matinee"

See pages 694, 711.
See also **Diction; Figurative Language; Imagery.**

Dialect A dialect is the distinct form of a language as it is spoken in one geographical area or by a particular social or ethnic group. A group's dialect is reflected in characteristic pronunciations, vocabulary, idioms, and grammatical constructions. When trying to reproduce a given dialect, writers often use unconventional spellings to suggest the way words actually sound. Writers use dialect to establish setting, to provide local color, and to develop characters. In the following passage, the use of dialect captures the sound and tang of frontier speech:

> And he had a little small bull-pup, that to look at him you'd think he warn't worth a cent but to set around and look ornery and lay for a chance to steal something.
> —Mark Twain,
> "The Notorious Jumping Frog of Calaveras County"

See pages 659, 1034.
See also **Local Color Realism.**

Dialogue Dialogue is conversation between two or more characters in either fiction or nonfiction. In drama, the story is told almost exclusively through dialogue, which moves the plot forward and reveals characters' motives.

See pages 650, 903, 1049.
See also **Drama.**

Diary A diary is a writer's personal day-to-day account of his or her experiences and impressions. Most diaries are private and not intended to be shared. Some, however, have been published because they are well written and provide useful perspectives on historical events or on the everyday life of particular eras. One important American diary found in this book is Mary Chesnut's diary of the Civil War.

Diction A writer's or speaker's choice of words is called diction. Diction includes both vocabulary (individual words) and syntax (the order or arrangement of words). Diction can be formal or informal, technical or common, abstract or concrete. In the following complex sentence, the diction is formal:

> When, however, the mass movement repudiates violence while moving resolutely toward its goal, its opponents are revealed as the instigators and practitioners of violence if it occurs.
> —Martin Luther King Jr., "Stride Toward Freedom"

See pages 255, 649, 1067.

Drama Drama is literature in which plot and character are developed through dialogue and action; in other words, drama is literature in play form. It is performed on stage and radio and in films and television. Most plays are divided into acts, with each act having an emotional peak, or climax, of its own. The acts sometimes are divided into scenes; each scene is limited to a single time and place. Most contemporary plays have two or three acts, although some have only one act.

See pages 128, 131, 1097.
See also **Act; Dialogue; Scene; Stage Directions.**

Dramatic Irony *See* **Irony.**

Dramatic Monologue A dramatic monologue is a lyric poem in which a speaker addresses a silent or absent listener in a moment of high intensity or deep emotion, as if engaged in private conversation. The speaker proceeds without interruption or argument, and the effect on the reader is that of hearing just one side of a conversation. This technique allows the poet to focus on the feelings, personality, and motivations of the speaker.

See also **Lyric Poetry; Soliloquy.**

Dynamic Character *See* **Character.**

Elegy An elegy is a poem written in tribute to a person, usually someone who has died recently. The tone of an elegy is usually formal and dignified.

Epic Poem An epic is a long narrative poem on a serious subject presented in an elevated or formal style. An epic traces the adventures of a hero whose actions consist of courageous, even superhuman, deeds, which often represent the ideals and values of a nation or race. Epics typically address universal issues, such as good and evil, life and death, and sin and redemption. Homer's *Iliad* and *Odyssey* are famous epics from western civilization. The *Ramayana* is an epic from India.

Epic Hero An epic hero is a larger-than-life figure who embodies the ideals of a nation or race. Epic heroes take part in dangerous adventures and accomplish great deeds. Many undertake long, difficult journeys and display great courage and superhuman strength.

Epithet An epithet is a brief descriptive phrase that points out traits associated with a particular person or thing.
Example: Carl Sandburg's "Chicago" begins with a series of epithets, such as "Hog Butcher for the World."

Essay An essay is a short work of nonfiction that deals with a single subject. Essays are often informal, loosely structured, and highly personal. They can be descriptive, informative, persuasive, narrative, or any combination of these. Amy Tan's personal essay "Mother Tongue" combines all of these qualities.

An **autobiographical essay** focuses on an aspect of a writer's life. Generally, writers of autobiographical essays use the first-person point of view, combining objective description with the expression of subjective feelings. Zora Neale Hurston's "How It Feels to Be Colored Me" is an example of an autobiographical essay.

See pages 371, 870, 1068, 1205.

Exaggeration *See* **Hyperbole.**

Experimental Poetry Poetry described as experimental is often full of surprises—unusual word order, invented forms, descriptions of ordinary objects, and other distinctive elements not found in traditional verse forms. William Carlos Williams belonged to a group of experimental poets known as the Imagists. Their poems contain sharp, clear images of striking beauty, similar to the ones found in haiku. E. E. Cummings's "anyone lived in a pretty how town" reflects his unique brand of poetic experimentation, such as altering the expected presentation of words.

See page 921.

Exposition Exposition is the part of a literary work that provides the background information necessary to understand characters and their actions. Typically found at the beginning of a work, the exposition introduces the characters, describes the setting, and summarizes significant events that took place before the action begins.
Example: In the exposition to "The Devil and Tom Walker," Washington Irving introduces the main characters—a miser and his wife—who dwell in a desolate house near a swamp and take wicked glee in hoarding things from each other.

See also **Plot; Rising Action.**

Expository Essay *See* **Essay.**

Extended Metaphor Like any metaphor, an extended metaphor is a comparison between two essentially unlike things that nevertheless have something in common. It does not contain the word *like* or *as*. An extended metaphor compares two things at some length and in various ways. Sometimes the comparison is carried throughout a paragraph, a stanza, or an entire selection. In the following stanza, notice the extended metaphor in which the speaker compares himself to a loom for God's use:

> Make me, O Lord, Thy spinning wheel complete.
> Thy holy word my distaff make for me.
> Make mine affections Thy swift flyers neat,
> And make my soul Thy holy spool to be.
> My conversation make to be Thy reel,
> And reel the yarn thereon spun of Thy wheel.
> —Edward Taylor, "Huswifery"

Like an extended metaphor, a **conceit** compares two apparently dissimilar things in several ways. The term usually implies a more elaborate, formal, and ingeniously clever comparison than the extended metaphor.

See pages 111, 857.

External Conflict *See* **Conflict.**

Eyewitness Account An eyewitness account is a firsthand report of an event written by someone who directly observed it or participated in it. As such, an eyewitness account is a primary source. Narrated from the first-person point of view, eyewitness accounts almost always include the following:

- objective facts about an event

- a chronological (time-order) pattern of organization

- vivid sensory details

- quotations from people who were present

- description of the writer's feelings and interpretations.

The excerpt from Anne Moody's autobiography, *Coming of Age in Mississippi*, is an eyewitness account of a sit-in in 1963.
See page 1181.
See also **Primary Source.**

Fable A fable is a brief tale that illustrates a clear, often directly stated, moral, or lesson. The characters in a fable are usually animals, but sometimes they are humans. The best-known fables—for example, "The Fox and the Crow" and "The Tortoise and the Hare" are those of Aesop, a Greek slave who lived about 600 B.C. Traditionally, fables are handed down from generation to generation as oral literature.

See also **Oral Literature.**

Falling Action In a plot structure, the falling action, or **resolution,** occurs after the climax to reveal the final outcome of events and to tie up any loose ends.

See also **Climax; Exposition; Plot; Rising Action.**

Farce A farce is a type of exaggerated comedy that features an absurd plot, ridiculous situations, and humorous dialogue. The main purpose of a farce is to keep an audience laughing. The characters are usually **stereotypes,** or simplified examples of different traits or qualities. Comic devices typically used in farces include mistaken identity, deception, wordplay—such as puns and double meanings— and exaggeration.

See also **Comedy; Stereotype.**

Fiction Fiction refers to works of prose that contain imaginary elements. Although fiction, like nonfiction, may be based on actual events and real people, it differs from nonfiction in that it is shaped primarily by the writer's imagination. For example, although Hemingway's "In Another Country" is based on autobiographical experiences, it cannot be classified as nonfiction because it is imbued with imaginary events and exaggeration in order to hold the reader's interest. The two major types of fiction are novels and short stories. The four basic elements of a work of fiction are **character, setting, plot,** and **theme.**

See also **Novel; Short Story.**

Figurative Language Figurative language is language that communicates ideas beyond the literal meaning of words. Figurative language can make descriptions and unfamiliar or difficult ideas easier to understand. Note the figurative language in this passage from "The Open Boat":

> A seat in this boat was not unlike a seat upon a bucking broncho, and, by the same token, a broncho is not much smaller. The craft pranced and reared, and plunged like an animal. As each wave came, and she rose for it, she seemed like a horse making at a fence outrageously high.
>
> —Stephen Crane, "The Open Boat"

The most common types of figurative language, called **figures of speech,** are **simile, metaphor, personification,** and **hyperbole.**

See pages 111, 525, 711, 853.
See also **Hyperbole; Metaphor; Personification; Simile.**

Figures of Speech *See* **Figurative Language.**

First-Person Point of View *See* **Point of View.**

Flashback A flashback is a scene that interrupts the action of a narrative to describe events that took place at an earlier time. It provides background helpful in understanding a character's present situation.

Example: William Faulkner's "A Rose for Emily" opens with Miss Emily's funeral, followed by a flashback that recounts how, when she was alive, Colonel Sartoris exempted her from paying taxes.

Foil A foil is a character whose traits contrast with those of another character. A writer might use a minor character as a foil to emphasize the positive traits of the main character.

Example: In Flannery O'Connor's "The Life You Save May Be Your Own," the innocent Lucynell Crater serves as a foil to the cunning, deceitful Mr. Shiftlet.

See page 1034.
See also **Character.**

Folk Tale A folk tale is a short, simple story that is handed down, usually by word of mouth, from generation to generation. Folk tales include legends, fairy tales, myths, and fables. Folk tales often teach family obligations or societal values. "Coyote and the Buffalo" is an Okanogan folk tale.

See also **Legend; Myth; Fable.**

Foot *See* **Meter.**

Foreshadowing Foreshadowing is a writer's use of hints or clues to indicate events that will occur in a story. Foreshadowing creates suspense and at the same time prepares the reader for what is to come.

Example: In Faulkner's "A Rose for Emily," the scene in which Miss Emily buys the rat poison foreshadows the death of Homer Barron.

See page 1020.

Form At its simplest, form refers to the physical arrangement of words in a poem—the length and placement of the lines and the grouping of lines into stanzas. The term can also be used to refer to other types of patterning in poetry—anything from rhythm and other sound patterns to the design of a traditional poetic type, such as a sonnet or dramatic monologue.

See also **Genre; Stanza.**

Frame Story A frame story exists when a story is told within a narrative setting, or "frame"; it creates a story within a story. This storytelling method has been used for over one thousand years and was employed in famous works such as *One Thousand and One Arabian Nights* and Geoffrey Chaucer's *The Canterbury Tales.* "The Notorious Jumping Frog of Calaveras County" by Mark Twain is also a frame story.

See page 667.

Free Verse Free verse is poetry that does not have regular patterns of rhyme and meter. The lines in free verse often flow more naturally than do rhymed, metrical lines and thus achieve a rhythm more like that of everyday human speech. Walt Whitman is generally credited with bringing free verse to American poetry.

> And you O my soul where you stand,
> Surrounded, detached, in measureless oceans of space,
> Ceaselessly musing, venturing, throwing, seeking
>   the spheres to connect them,
> Till the bridge you will need be form'd, till the
>   ductile anchor hold,
> Till the gossamer thread you fling catch
>   somewhere, O my soul.
>   —Walt Whitman, "The Noiseless Patient Spider"

See pages 509, 913.
See also **Meter; Rhyme.**

Genre Genre refers to the distinct types into which literary works can be grouped. The four main literary genres are fiction, poetry, nonfiction, and drama.

Gothic Literature Gothic literature is characterized by grotesque characters, bizarre situations, and violent events. Originating in Europe, gothic literature was a popular form of writing in the United States during the 19th century, especially in the hands of such notables as Edgar Allan Poe and Nathaniel Hawthorne. Interest in the gothic revived in the 20th century among southern writers such as William Faulkner and Flannery O'Connor.

See pages 403, 428, 1020.

Haiku Haiku is a form of Japanese poetry in which 17 syllables are arranged in three lines of 5, 7, and 5 syllables. The rules of haiku are strict. In addition to the syllabic count, the poet must create a clear picture that will evoke a strong emotional response in the reader. Nature is a particularly important source of inspiration for Japanese haiku poets, and details from nature are often the subjects of their poems.

Hero *See* **Cultural Hero; Tragic Hero.**

Historical Context The historical context of a literary work refers to the social conditions that inspired or influenced its creation. To understand and appreciate some works, the reader must relate them to particular events in history. For example, to understand fully Lincoln's "Gettysburg Address," the reader must imaginatively re-create the scene—Lincoln addressing a war-weary crowd on the very site where a horrific battle had recently been fought.

Example: Patrick Henry's "Speech in the Virginia Convention" was inspired by the British military buildup in the American colonies prior to the American Revolution; Martin Luther King's *Stride Toward Freedom* was inspired by the civil rights struggle of the 1950s to overturn segregation laws in the South.

See pages 69, 212, 226, 1161.

Historical Narratives Historical narratives are accounts of real-life historical experiences, given either by a person who experienced those events or by someone who has studied or observed them. Cabeza de Vaca's *La Relación,* William Bradford's *Of Plymouth Plantation,* and *The Interesting Narrative of the Life of Olaudah Equiano* all are historical narratives.

See pages 66, 70, 79, 89, 100.
See also **Primary Sources; Secondary Sources.**

Horror Fiction Horror fiction contains strange, mysterious, violent, and often supernatural events that create suspense and terror in the reader. Edgar Allan Poe is an author famous for his horror fiction.

Humor Humor is a term applied to a literary work whose purpose is to entertain and to evoke laughter—for example, Twain's "The Celebrated Jumping Frog of Calaveras County." In literature, there are three basic types of humor, all of which may involve exaggeration or irony. **Humor of situation,** which is derived from the plot of a work, usually involves exaggerated events or situational irony. **Humor of character** is often based on exaggerated personalities or on characters who fail to recognize their own flaws, a form of dramatic irony. **Humor of language** may include sarcasm, exaggeration, puns, or verbal irony, which occurs when what is said is not what is meant.

See pages 635, 1060, 1067.
See also **Comedy; Farce; Irony.**

GLOSSARY OF LITERARY TERMS   **R111**

Hyperbole Hyperbole is a figure of speech in which the truth is exaggerated for emphasis or for humorous effect. The expression "I'm so hungry I could eat a horse" is hyperbole. In the following passage, Dorothy Parker uses hyperbole to describe literary critics' love for a Hemingway novel:

> Ernest Hemingway wrote a novel called *The Sun Also Rises.* Promptly upon its publication, Ernest Hemingway was discovered, the Stars and Stripes were reverentially raised over him, eight hundred and forty-seven book reviewers formed themselves into the word "welcome," and the band played "Hail to the Chief" in three concurrent keys.
> —Dorothy Parker, "A Book of Great Short Stories"

See also **Understatement.**

Iamb *See Meter.*

Iambic Pentameter Iambic pentameter is a metrical pattern of five feet, or units, each of which is made up of two syllables, the first unstressed and the second stressed. Iambic pentameter is the most common meter used in English poetry; it is the meter used in blank verse and in the sonnet. The following lines are examples of iambic pentameter:

> So live, | that when | thy sum | mons comes | to join
> The innu | mera | ble car | avan, | which moves
> To that | myste | rious realm, | where each | shall take
> His cham | ber in | the si | lent halls | of death . . .
> —William Cullen Bryant, "Thanatopsis"

See pages 329, 903.
See also **Blank Verse; Meter; Sonnet.**

Idiom An idiom is a common figure of speech whose meaning is different from the literal meaning of its words. For example, the phrase "raining cats and dogs" does not literally mean that cats and dogs are falling from the sky; the expression means "raining heavily."

Imagery The descriptive words and phrases that a writer uses to re-create sensory experiences are called imagery. By appealing to the five senses, imagery helps a reader imagine exactly what the characters and experiences being described are like. In the following passage, the imagery lets the reader experience the miserliness of the main character and his wife:

> They lived in a forlorn-looking house that stood alone and had an air of starvation. A few straggling savin trees, emblems of sterility, grew near it; no smoke ever curled from its chimney. . . . A miserable horse, whose ribs were as articulate as the bars of a gridiron, stalked about a field, where a thin carpet of moss . . . tantalized and balked his hunger.
> —Washington Irving, "The Devil and Tom Walker"

The term *synesthesia* refers to imagery that appeals to one sense when another is being stimulated; for example, description of sounds in terms of colors, as in this passage:

> Music. The great blobs of purple and red emotion have not touched him.
> —Zora Neale Hurston, "How It Feels to Be Colored Me"

See page 860.
See also **Description; Kinesthetic Imagery.**

Imagists *See* **Experimental Poetry; Style.**

Interior Monologue *See* **Monologue; Stream of Consciousness.**

Internal Conflict *See* **Conflict.**

Inverted Syntax Inverted syntax is a reversal in the expected order of words.
Example: In the first line of "Upon the Burning of Our House," Anne Bradstreet writes "when rest I took" rather than "when I took rest."

Interview An interview is a conversation conducted by a writer or reporter in which facts or statements are elicited from another person, recorded, and then broadcast or published.

Irony Irony refers to a contrast between appearance and reality. **Situational irony** is a contrast between what is expected to happen and what actually does happen, as in the poem "Richard Cory," when a gentleman who is admired and envied commits suicide. **Dramatic irony** occurs when readers know more about a situation or a character in a story than the characters do. In Flannery O'Connor's "The Life You Save May Be Your Own," for example, readers find out that Mr. Shiftlet is a scoundrel before the other characters do. **Verbal irony** occurs when someone states one thing and means another, as in the following passage, when the narrator refers to honesty as an "incumbrance," or burden:

> Hicks was born honest, I without that incumbrance—so some people said.
> —Mark Twain, *The Autobiography of Mark Twain*

See pages 635, 882, 1033.

Kinesthetic Imagery Kinesthetic imagery re-creates the tension felt through muscles, tendons, or joints in the body. In the following passage, John Steinbeck uses kinesthetic imagery to describe a soldier's experience:

> This is how you feel after a few days of constant firing. Your skin feels thick and insensitive. There is a salty taste in your mouth. A hard, painful knot is in your stomach where the food is undigested. Your eyes do not pick up much detail and the sharp outlines of objects are slightly blurred. Everything looks a little unreal.
> —John Steinbeck, "Why Soldiers Don't Talk"

See page 1166.
See also **Imagery.**

Journal *See* **Diary.**

Legend A legend is a story passed down orally from generation to generation and popularly believed to have a historical basis. While some legends may be based on real people or situations, most of the events are either greatly exaggerated or fictitious. Like myths, legends may incorporate supernatural elements and magical deeds. But legends differ from myths in that they claim to be stories about real human beings and are often set in a particular time and place.

Limited Point of View *See* **Point of View.**

Line The line is the core unit of a poem. In poetry, line length is an essential element of the poem's meaning and rhythm. There are a variety of terms to describe the way a line of poetry ends or is connected to the next line. Line breaks, where a line of poetry ends, may coincide with grammatical units. However, a line break may also occur in the middle of a grammatical or syntactical unit, creating pauses or emphasis. Poets use a variety of line breaks to play with meaning, thus creating a wide range of effects.

Literary Criticism Literary criticism refers to writing that focuses on a literary work or a genre, describing some aspect of it, such as its origin, its characteristics, or its effects. Toni Morrison's "Thoughts on the African-American Novel" is an example of literary criticism.
See page 869.

Literary Letter A literary letter is a letter that has been published and read by a wider audience because it was written by a well-known public figure or provides information about the period in which it was written. Abigail Adams's "Letter to John Adams" is an example of a literary letter.
See pages 258, 1146, 1194.

Literary Nonfiction Literary nonfiction is nonfiction that is recognized as being of artistic value or that is about literature. Autobiographies, biographies, essays, and eloquent speeches typically fall into this category.

Local Color Realism Local color realism, especially popular in the late 18th century, is a style of writing that truthfully imitates ordinary life and brings a particular region alive by portraying the dialects, dress, mannerisms, customs, character types, and landscapes of that region. Mark Twain frequently uses local color realism in his writing for humorous effect.
See pages 660, 674.
See also **Dialect.**

Lyric Poem A lyric poem is a short poem in which a single speaker expresses thoughts and feelings. In a love lyric, a speaker expresses romantic love. In other lyrics, a speaker may meditate on nature or seek to resolve an emotional crisis. Anne Bradstreet's poem "To My Dear and Loving Husband" is a love lyric.

Magical Realism Magical realism is a style of writing that often includes exaggeration, unusual humor, magical and bizarre events, dreams that come true, and superstitions that prove warranted. Magical realism differs from pure fantasy in combining fantastic elements with realistic elements such as recognizable characters, believable dialogue, a true-to-life setting, a matter-of-fact tone, and a plot that sometimes contains historic events. This style characterizes some of the fiction of such influential South American writers as the late Jorge Luis Borges of Argentina and Gabriel García Márquez of Colombia.

Main Character *See* **Character.**

Memoir A memoir is a form of autobiographical writing in which a person recalls significant events and people in his or her life. Most memoirs share the following characteristics: (1) they usually are structured as narratives told by the writers themselves, using the first-person point of view; (2) although some names may be changed to protect privacy, memoirs are true accounts of actual events; (3) although basically personal, memoirs may deal with newsworthy events having a significance beyond the confines of the writer's life; (4) unlike strictly historical accounts, memoirs often include the writers' feelings and opinions about historical events, giving the reader insight into the impact of history on people's lives. N. Scott Momaday's *The Way to Rainy Mountain* is a memoir.

Metaphor A metaphor is a figure of speech that compares two things that have something in common. Unlike similes, metaphors do not use the words *like* or *as*, but make comparisons directly.

Example: Abigail Adams's statement "our country is . . . the first and greatest parent" is a metaphor.

See pages 111, 853, 918.
See also **Extended Metaphor; Figurative Language; Simile.**

Meter Meter is the repetition of a regular rhythmic unit in a line of poetry. Each unit, known as a **foot,** has one stressed syllable (indicated by a ´) and either one or two unstressed syllables (indicated by a �‿). The four basic types of metrical feet are the **iamb,** an unstressed syllable followed by a stressed syllable; the **trochee,** a stressed syllable followed by an unstressed syllable; the **anapest,** two unstressed syllables followed by a stressed syllable; and the **dactyl,** a stressed syllable followed by two unstressed syllables.

Two words are typically used to describe the meter of a line. The first word identifies the type of metrical foot—iambic, trochaic, anapestic, or dactylic—and the second word indicates the number of feet in a line: monometer (one foot), **dimeter** (two feet), **trimeter** (three feet), **tetrameter** (four feet), **pentameter** (five feet), **hexameter** (six feet), and so forth.

Examples: In "To My Dear and Loving Husband," by Anne Bradstreet, the meter is iambic pentameter, the most common form of meter in English poetry.

If ev | er man | were loved | by wife | then thee.

In the following lines from Henry Wadsworth Longfellow's "A Psalm of Life," the meter is trochaic tetrameter:

Tell me | not, in | mournful | numbers,
Life is | but an | empty | dream!—

See pages 335, 341, 847, 881.
See also **Rhythm; Scansion.**

Minor Character *See* **Character.**

Mise-en-Scène *Mise-en-scène* is a term from the French that refers to the various physical aspects of a dramatic presentation, such as lighting, costumes, scenery, makeup, and props.

Modernism Modernism was a literary movement that roughly spanned the time period between the two world wars, 1914–1945. Modernist works are characterized by a high degree of experimentation and spare, elliptical prose. Modernist characters are most often alienated people searching unsuccessfully for meaning and love in their lives. Katherine Ann Porter's "The Jilting of Granny Weatherall" is an example of modernist writing.

See page 894, 930, 990.

Monologue In a drama, the speech of a character who is alone on stage, voicing his or her thoughts, is known as a monologue. In a short story or a poem, the direct presentation of a character's unspoken thoughts is called an **interior monologue.** An interior monologue may jump back and forth between past and present, displaying thoughts, memories, and impressions just as they might occur in a person's mind.

See pages 111, 132.
See also **Stream of Consciousness.**

Mood Mood is the feeling or atmosphere that a writer creates for the reader. The writer's use of connotation, imagery, figurative language, sound and rhythm, and descriptive details all contribute to the mood. These elements help create a creepy, threatening mood in the following passage:

The swamp was thickly grown with great gloomy pines and hemlocks, . . . It was full of pits and quagmires, partly covered with weeds and mosses, where the green surface often betrayed the traveler into a gulf of black, smothering mud; . . .
—Washington Irving, "The Devil and Tom Walker"

See page 897.
See also **Connotation; Description; Diction; Figurative Language; Imagery; Style.**

Moral *See* **Fable.**

Motivation Motivation is the stated or implied reason behind a character's behavior. The grounds for a character's actions may not be obvious, but they should be comprehensible and consistent, in keeping with the character as developed by the writer.
See pages 403, 936, 1019.
See also **Character.**

Myth A myth is a traditional story, passed down through generations, that explains why the world is the way it is. Myths are essentially religious because they present supernatural events and beings and articulate the values and beliefs of a cultural group. A **creation myth** is a particular kind of myth that explains how the universe, the earth, and life on earth began. "The World on the Turtle's Back" is an Iroquois creation myth.
See page 33.

Narrative A narrative is any type of writing that is primarily concerned with relating an event or a series of events. A narrative can be imaginary, as is a short story or novel, or factual, as is a newspaper account or a work of history. The word *narration* can be used interchangeably with *narrative*, which comes from the Latin word meaning "tell."
See also **Fiction; Nonfiction; Novel; Plot; Short Story.**

Narrative Poem A narrative poem is a poem that tells a story using elements of character, setting, and plot to develop a theme. Edgar Allan Poe's "The Raven" is a narrative poem, as is Dudley Randall's "Ballad of Birmingham."
See pages 438, 903, 1156.
See also **Ballad.**

Narrator The narrator of a story is the character or voice that relates the story's events to the reader.
Example: The narrator of William Faulkner's "A Rose for Emily" is an unidentified citizen of Jefferson, Mississippi, Emily Grierson's hometown.
See pages 660, 1018.

Naturalism An offshoot of realism, naturalism was a literary movement that originated in France in the late 1800s. Like the realists, the naturalists sought to render common people and ordinary life accurately. However, the naturalists emphasized how instinct and environment affect human behavior. Strongly influenced by Charles Darwin's ideas, the naturalists believed that the fate of humans is determined by forces beyond individual control. Stephen Crane's story "The Open Boat" is an example of naturalism.
See pages 711, 745.

Nonfiction Nonfiction is writing about real people, places, and events. Unlike fiction, nonfiction is largely concerned with factual information, although the writer shapes the information according to his or her purpose and viewpoint. Biography, autobiography, and newspaper articles are examples of nonfiction.
See also **Autobiography; Biography; Essay.**

Novel A novel is an extended work of fiction. Like the short story, a novel is essentially the product of a writer's imagination. The most obvious difference between a novel and a short story is length. Because the novel is considerably longer, a novelist can develop a wider range of characters and a more complex plot.

Novella A novella is a work of fiction that is longer than a short story but shorter than a novel. A novella differs from a novel in that it concentrates on a limited cast of characters, a relatively short time span, and a single chain of events. The novella is an attempt to combine the compression of the short story with the development of a novel.

Octave *See* **Sonnet.**

Ode An ode is a complex lyric poem that develops a serious and dignified theme. Odes appeal to both the imagination and the intellect, and many commemorate events or praise people or elements of nature.

Off Rhyme *See* **Slant Rhyme.**

Omniscient Point of View *See* **Point of View.**

Onomatopoeia The word *onomatopoeia* literally means "name-making." It is the process of creating or using words that imitate sounds. The *buzz* of the bee, the *honk* of the car horn, the *peep* of the chick are all onomatopoetic, or echoic, words.
  Onomatopoeia as a literary technique goes beyond the use of simple echoic words. Writers, particularly poets, choose words whose sounds suggest their denotative and connotative meanings: for example, *whisper, kick, gargle, gnash,* and *clatter.*

Open Letter An open letter is addressed to a specific person but published for a wider readership.
Example: James Baldwin's "My Dungeon Shook" is an open letter addressed to his nephew but intended for the general public, particularly white Americans.
See pages 1146, 1194.

Oral Literature Oral literature is literature that is passed from one generation to another by performance or word of mouth. Folk tales, fables, myths, chants, and legends are part of the oral tradition of cultures throughout the world.
See pages 34, 44.
See also **Fable; Folk Tale; Legend; Myth.**

Oxymoron An oxymoron is a special kind of concise paradox that brings together two contradictory terms, such as "venomous love" or "sweet bitterness."

Parable A parable is a brief story that is meant to teach a lesson or illustrate a moral truth. A parable is more than a simple story, however. Each detail of the parable corresponds to some aspect of the problem or moral dilemma to which it is directed. The story of the prodigal son in the Bible is a classic parable. In *Walden*, Thoreau's parable of the strong and beautiful bug that emerges from an old table is meant to show that, similarly, new life can awaken in human beings despite the deadness of society.

Paradox A paradox is a statement that seems to contradict itself but may nevertheless suggest an important truth.
Example: In *Walden*, Henry David Thoreau writes the paradox "I am not as wise as the day I was born." The statement suggests that civilization erases a child's innate wisdom and spiritual awareness.

A special kind of paradox is the oxymoron, which brings together two contradictory terms, as in the phrases "wise fool" and "feather of lead."
See pages 372, 1192.

Parallel Plot A parallel plot is a particular type of plot in which two stories of equal importance are told simultaneously. The story moves back and forth between the two plots.

Parallelism Parallelism is the use of similar grammatical constructions to express ideas that are related or equal in importance. Note that in the following passage, Whitman begins the last three lines with the name of a type of tradesman, each followed by a gerund phrase beginning with *singing*:

> I hear America singing, the varied carols I hear,
> Those of mechanics, each one singing his as it should be blithe and strong,
> The carpenter singing his as he measures his plank or beam,
> The mason singing his as he makes ready for work, or leaves off work,
> —Walt Whitman, "I Hear America Singing"

This parallel construction creates a rolling rhythm and emphasizes the different types of people that comprise America.
See page 509.

Parody Parody is writing that imitates either the style or the subject matter of a literary work for the purpose of criticism, humorous effect, or flattering tribute.
See page 445.

Persona *See* **Speaker.**

Personal Essay *See* **Essay.**

Personification Personification is a figure of speech in which an object, animal, or idea is given human characteristics.
Example: In Emily Dickinson's poem "Because I could not stop for Death," death is personified as a gentleman of kindness and civility.
See pages 525, 712.

Persuasive Writing Persuasive writing is intended to convince a reader to adopt a particular opinion or to perform a certain action. Effective persuasion usually appeals to both the reason and the emotions of an audience. Patrick Henry, Jonathan Edwards, Martin Luther King Jr., and Malcolm X all use persuasion in their writing.
See pages 226, 245, 1157, 1193.

Petrarchan Sonnet *See* **Sonnet.**

Plot The plot is the sequence of actions and events in a literary work. Generally, plots are built around a **conflict**—a problem or struggle between two or more opposing forces. Plots usually progress through stages: exposition, rising action, climax, and falling action.

The **exposition** provides important background information and introduces the setting, characters, and conflict. During the **rising action,** the conflict becomes more intense and suspense builds as the main characters struggle to resolve their problem. The **climax** is the turning point in the plot when the outcome of the conflict becomes clear, usually resulting in a change in the characters or a solution to the conflict. After the climax, the **falling action** occurs and shows the effects of the climax. As the falling action begins, the suspense is over but the results of the decision or action that caused the climax are not yet fully worked out. The **resolution,** which often blends with the falling action, reveals the final outcome of events and ties up loose ends.
See pages 759, 1020.
See also **Climax; Conflict; Exposition; Falling Action; Rising Action.**

Poetry Poetry is language arranged in lines. Like other forms of literature, poetry attempts to re-create emotions and experiences. Poetry, however, is usually more condensed and suggestive than prose.

Poems often are divided into stanzas, or paragraph-like groups of lines. The stanzas in a poem may contain the same number of lines or may vary in length. Some poems have definite patterns of meter and rhyme. Others rely more on the sounds of words and less on fixed rhythms and rhyme schemes. The use of figurative language is also common in poetry.

The form and content of a poem combine to convey meaning. The way that a poem is arranged on the page, the impact of the images, the sounds of the words and phrases, and all the other details that make up a poem work together to help the reader grasp its central idea.

See pages 506, 839, 897, 1237.
See also **Experimental Poetry; Form; Free Verse; Meter; Rhyme; Rhythm; Stanza.**

Point of View Point of view refers to the narrative perspective from which events in a story or novel are told. In the **first-person point of view,** the narrator is a character in the work who tells everything in his or her own words and uses the pronouns *I, me,* and *my.* In the **third-person point of view,** events are related by a voice outside the action, not by one of the characters. A third-person narrator uses pronouns such as *he, she,* and *they.* In the **third-person omniscient point of view,** the narrator is an all-knowing, objective observer who stands outside the action and reports what different characters are thinking. Flannery O'Connor's "The Life You Save May Be Your Own" is told from the third-person omniscient point of view. In the **third-person limited point of view,** the narrator stands outside the action and focuses on one character's thoughts, observations, and feelings. Kate Chopin's "The Story of an Hour" is told from primarily the third-person limited point of view.

In the **second-person point of view,** rarely used, the narrator addresses the reader intimately as you. Much of John Steinbeck's essay "Why Soldiers Don't Talk" is narrated from the second-person point of view.

See pages 760, 1034, 1116.

Primary Sources Materials written or created by people who were present at events are called primary sources. Letters, diaries, speeches, autobiographies, and photographs are examples of primary sources, as are certain narrative accounts written by actual participants or observers.

See also **Secondary Sources.**

Prologue A prologue is an introductory scene in a drama.

Prop Prop, an abbreviation of *property,* refers to a physical object that is used in a stage production.

Example: In Arthur Miller's *The Crucible,* an important prop is the small rag doll that Mary Warren brings from the court and gives to Elizabeth Proctor.

Prose Generally, *prose* refers to all forms of written or spoken expression that are not in verse. The term, therefore, may be used to describe very different forms of writing— short stories as well as essays, for example.

Protagonist The protagonist is the main character in a work of literature, who is involved in the central conflict of the story. Usually, the protagonist changes after the central conflict reaches a climax. He or she may be a hero and is usually the one with whom the audience tends to identify. In Kurt Vonnegut's story "Adam," Heinz Knechtmann is the protagonist.

See page 1124.
See also **Antagonist; Character; Tragic Hero.**

Purpose *See* **Author's Purpose.**

Quatrain A quatrain is a four-line stanza, as in the following example:

> The snow had begun in the gloaming,
>   And busily all the night
> Had been heaping field and highway
>   With a silence deep and white.
>   —James Russell Lowell, "The First Snowfall"

See page 348.
See also **Poetry; Stanza.**

Realism As a general term, *realism* refers to any effort to offer an accurate and detailed portrayal of actual life. Thus, critics talk about Shakespeare's realistic portrayals of his characters and praise the medieval poet Chaucer for his realistic descriptions of people from different social classes.

More specifically, realism refers to a literary method developed in the 19th century. The realists based their writing on careful observations of contemporary life, often focusing on the middle or lower classes. They attempted to present life objectively and honestly, without the sentimentality or idealism that had colored earlier literature. Typically, realists developed their settings in great detail in an effort to re-create a specific time and place for the reader. Willa Cather, Kate Chopin, and Mark Twain are all considered realists.

See pages 660, 692, 760.
See also **Local-Color Realism; Naturalism.**

Recurring Theme *See Theme.*

Reflective Essay *See Essay.*

Refrain In poetry, a refrain is part of a stanza, consisting of one or more lines that are repeated regularly, sometimes with changes, often at the ends of succeeding stanzas. For example, in "The Raven," the line "Quoth the Raven, 'Nevermore'" is a refrain. Refrains are often found in ballads.

Regionalism Regionalism is a literary movement that arose from an effort to accurately represent the speech, manners, habits, history, folklore, and beliefs of people in specific geographic areas. Bret Harte's "The Outcasts of Poker Flat" is a famous example of American regionalist writing.

Repetition Repetition is a technique in which a sound, word, phrase, or line is repeated for emphasis or unity. Repetition often helps to reinforce meaning and create an appealing rhythm. The term includes specific devices associated with both prose and poetry, such as **alliteration** and **parallelism.**

See pages 225, 509, 839, 1193.
See also **Alliteration; Parallelism; Sound Devices.**

Resolution *See Falling Action.*

Rhetorical Devices *See* **Analogy; Repetition; Rhetorical Questions,** *Glossary of Reading and Informational Terms,* page R123.

Rhyme Rhyme is the occurrence of similar or identical sounds at the end of two or more words, such as *suite, heat,* and *complete.* Rhyme that occurs within a single line of poetry, as in the following example, is called **internal rhyme.**

> Ah, distinctly I <u>remember</u> it was in the bleak <u>December</u>;
> —Edgar Allan Poe, "The Raven"

When rhyme comes at the end of a line of poetry, it is called **end rhyme.** The pattern of end rhyme in a poem is called the **rhyme scheme** and is charted by assigning a letter, beginning with the letter *a,* to each line. Lines that rhyme are given the same letter. The rhyme scheme of the following stanza is *aabbcc:*

In silent night when rest I took	*a*
For sorrow near I did not look	*a*
I wakened was with thund'ring noise	*b*
And piteous shrieks of dreadful voice.	*b*
That fearful sound of "Fire!" and "Fire!"	*c*
Let no man know is my desire.	*c*

—Anne Bradstreet, "Upon the Burning of Our House"

See pages 335, 438, 847.
See also **Slant Rhyme.**

Rhyme Scheme *See* **Rhyme.**

Rhythm Rhythm refers to the pattern or flow of sound created by the arrangement of stressed and unstressed syllables, particularly in poetry. Some poems follow a regular pattern, or **meter,** of accented and unaccented syllables. Poets use rhythm to bring out the musical quality of language, to emphasize ideas, to create mood, and to reinforce subject matter.

See pages 839, 509.
See also **Meter.**

Rising Action Rising action is the stage of a plot in which the conflict develops and story events build toward a climax. During this stage, complications arise that make the conflict more intense. Tension grows as the characters struggle to resolve the conflict.

See pages 712, 759, 768.
See also **Plot.**

Romanticism Romanticism was a movement in the arts that flourished in Europe and America throughout much of the 19th century. Romantic writers glorified nature and celebrated individuality. Their treatment of subject was emotional rather than rational, intuitive rather than analytic. Washington Irving and Henry Wadsworth Longfellow were popular American romantic writers.

See pages 292, 312, 334, 342.

Sarcasm Sarcasm, a type of verbal irony, refers to a critical remark expressed in a statement in which literal meaning is the opposite of actual meaning. Sarcasm is mocking, and its intention is to hurt.

See also **Irony.**

Satire Satire is a literary technique in which foolish ideas or customs are ridiculed for the purpose of improving society. Satire may be gently witty, mildly abrasive, or bitterly critical. Short stories, poems, novels, essays, and plays all may be vehicles for satire.
Example: In "The Devil and Tom Walker," Irving satirizes various aspects of 18th-century New England life, including religious hypocrisy and the institution of marriage.

Scansion The process of determining meter is known as scansion. When you scan a line of poetry, you mark its stressed (´) and unstressed syllables (ˇ) in order to identify the rhythm.
See also **Meter.**

Scene In drama, a scene is a subdivision of an act. Each scene usually establishes a different time or place.
See also **Act; Drama.**

Scenery Scenery is a painted backdrop or other structures used to create the setting for a play.

Science Fiction Science fiction is prose writing that presents the possibilities of the past or the future, using known scientific data and theories as well as the creative imagination of the writer. Most science fiction comments on present-day society through the writer's fictional conception of a past or future society. Ray Bradbury and Kurt Vonnegut Jr. are two popular writers of science fiction.

Screenplay A screenplay is a play written for film.

Script The text of a play, film, or broadcast is called a script.

Secondary Sources Accounts written by people were not directly involved in or witnesses to an event are called secondary sources. A history textbook is an example of a secondary source.
See also **Primary Sources.**

Sensory Details Sensory details are words and phrases that appeal to the reader's senses of sight, hearing, touch, taste, and smell. For example, the sensory detail "a fine film of rain" appeals to the senses of sight and touch. Sensory details stimulate the reader to create images in his or her mind.
See also **Imagery.**

Sermon A sermon is a form of religious persuasion in which a speaker exhorts the audience to behave in a more spiritual and moral fashion. "Sinners in the Hands of an Angry God" is a sermon.

Setting The setting of a literary work refers to the time and place in which the action occurs. A story can be set in an imaginary place, such as an enchanted castle, or a real place, such as New York City or Tombstone, Arizona. The time can be the past, the present, or the future. In addition to time and place, setting can include the larger historical and cultural contexts that form the background for a narrative. Setting is one of the main elements in fiction and often plays an important role in what happens and why.
Example: Willa Cather's story "A Wagner Matinee" is set in Boston around the turn of the 20th century.
See pages 131, 660, 693, 1034.

Sestet *See* **Sonnet.**

Short Story A short story is a work of fiction that centers on a single idea and can be read in one sitting. Generally, a short story has one main conflict that involves the characters, keeps the story moving, and stimulates readers' interest.
See also **Fiction.**

Simile A simile is a figure of speech that compares two things that have something in common, using a word such as *like* or *as.*
Examples: Abigail Adams's statement "power and liberty are like heat and moisture" and Thoreau's statement "we live meanly, like ants" contain similes.
See pages 258, 372, 525.
See also **Figurative Language; Metaphor.**

Situational Irony *See* **Irony.**

Slant Rhyme Rhyme that is not exact but only approximate is known as slant rhyme, or **off rhyme,** as in the second and fourth lines below:

> I heard a Fly buzz—when I died—
> The Stillness in the Room
> Was like the Stillness in the Air—
> Between the Heaves of Storm—
>
> —Emily Dickinson,
> "I heard a Fly buzz—when I died—"

See page 525.
See also **Rhyme.**

Slave Narrative A slave narrative is an autobiographical account written by someone who endured the miseries of slavery. Olaudah Equiano's and Frederick Douglass's autobiographies are examples of slave narratives. These writers often use sensory details to re-create their experiences. For example, to re-create the horror of confinement in the hold of a slave ship, Equiano gives the reader such details as "the galling of the chains" and "the groans of the dying."

See pages 79, 537, 552.
See also **Autobiography.**

Soliloquy See **Monologue.**

Sonnet A sonnet is a 14-line lyric poem, commonly written in iambic pentameter. The **Petrarchan sonnet** consists of two parts. The first eight lines, called the octave, usually have the rhyme scheme *abbaabba*. In the last six lines, called the sestet, the rhyme scheme may be *cdecde, cdcdcd,* or another variation. The **octave** generally presents a problem or raises a question, and the *sestet* resolves or comments on the problem. James Weldon Johnson's "My City" is a Petrarchan sonnet. A **Shakespearean sonnet** is divided into three **quatrains** (groups of four lines) and a **couplet** (two rhyming lines). Its rhyme scheme is *abab cdcd efef gg.* The couplet usually expresses a response to the important issue developed in the three quatrains. Claude McKay's "If We Must Die" is a Shakespearean sonnet.

See page 847.
See also **Meter; Quatrain; Rhyme.**

Sound Devices See **Alliteration; Assonance; Consonance; Meter; Onomatopoeia; Repetition; Rhyme; Rhyme Scheme; Rhythm.**

Speaker The speaker of a poem, like the narrator of a story, is the voice that talks to the reader. In some poems, the speaker can be identified with the poet. In other poems, the poet invents a fictional character, or a persona, to play the role of the speaker. *Persona* is a Latin word meaning "actor's mask."

See pages 881, 839, 930.

Speech A speech is a talk or public address. The purpose of a speech may be to entertain, to explain, to persuade, to inspire, or any combination of these aims.

Stage Directions Stage directions are the playwright's instructions for the director, performers, and stage crew. Usually set in italics, they are located at the beginning of and throughout a script. Stage directions usually tell the time and place of the action and explain how characters move and speak. They also describe scenery, props, lighting, costumes, music, or sound effects.

See pages 128, 132.
See also **Drama.**

Stanza A stanza is a group of lines that form a unit in a poem. A stanza is usually characterized by a common pattern of meter, rhyme, and number of lines. Longfellow's "A Psalm of Life" is written in four-line stanzas. During the 20th century, poets experimented more freely with stanza form than did earlier poets, sometimes writing poems without any stanza breaks.

See page 335.

Static Character See **Character.**

Stereotype A stereotype is an over simplified image of a person, group, or institution. Sweeping generalizations about "all Southerners" or "every used-car dealer" are stereotypes. Simplified or stock characters in literature are often called stereotypes. Such characters do not usually demonstrate the complexities of real people.

Example: In Washington Irving's "The Devil and Tom Walker," Tom Walker's wife is a stereotype of a greedy and shrewish wife.

Stream of Consciousness Stream of consciousness is a technique that was developed by modernist writers to present the flow of a character's seemingly unconnected thoughts, responses, and sensations. The term was coined by American psychologist William James to characterize the unbroken flow of thought that occurs in the waking mind.

Example: In "The Love Song of J. Alfred Prufrock," T. S. Eliot uses this technique to reveal the jumble of thoughts that flow through Prufrock's mind.

See pages 929, 989.
See also **Modernism.**

Structure The structure of a literary work is the way in which it is put together—the arrangement of its parts. In poetry, structure refers to the arrangement of words and lines to produce a desired effect. A common structural unit in poetry is the stanza, of which there are numerous types. In prose, structure is the arrangement of larger units or parts of a selection. Paragraphs, for example, are a basic unit in prose, as are chapters in novels and acts in plays. The structure of a poem, short story, novel, play, or nonfiction selection usually emphasizes certain important aspects of content.

See pages 235, 329, 581.
See also **Form; Stanza.**

Style Style is the distinctive way in which a work of literature is written. Style refers not so much to what is said but how it is said. Word choice, sentence length, tone, imagery, and use of dialogue all contribute to a writer's style. A group of writers might exemplify common stylistic characteristics; for example, the Imagists of the early 20th century wrote in a style that employs compression and rich sensory images.

Example: E. E. Cummings's style is decidedly unconventional, breaking rules of capitalization, punctuation, diction, and syntax.

See pages 525, 537, 897, 969.

Surprise Ending A surprise ending is an unexpected plot twist at the end of a story.

Example: "The Story of an Hour" ends with a surprise when Mrs. Mallard drops dead after her husband, presumed to be dead, reappears.

See page 759.
See also **Irony.**

Suspense Suspense is the excitement or tension that readers feel as they become involved in a story and eagerly await the outcome.

Example: In Ambrose Bierce's "An Occurrence at Owl Creek Bridge," the suspense builds as the reader awaits the outcome of Peyton Farquhar's attempted escape from hanging at the hands of Union troops.

See page 582.
See also **Rising Action.**

Symbol A symbol is a person, place, or object that has a concrete meaning in itself and also stands for something beyond itself, such as an idea or feeling.

Example: In Gilman's "The Yellow Wallpaper," the wallpaper in the narrator's bedroom comes to symbolize her growing madness.

See pages 457, 768.

Synesthesia *See* **Imagery.**

Tall Tale A tall tale is a distinctively American type of humorous story characterized by exaggeration. Tall tales and practical jokes have similar kinds of humor. In both, someone gets fooled, to the amusement of the person or persons who know the truth, as in Twain's "The Notorious Jumping Frog of Calaveras County."

See page 659.
See also **Humor; Hyperbole.**

Theme A theme is an underlying message that a writer wants the reader to understand. It is a perception about life or human nature that the writer shares with the reader. In most cases, themes are not stated directly but must be inferred.

Example: One theme of "The Masque of the Red Death" could be stated, "No one, not even the wealthiest person, has the power to escape death."

Recurring themes are themes found in a variety of works. For example, authors from varying backgrounds might convey similar themes having to do with the importance of family values. **Universal themes** are themes that are found throughout the literature of all time periods.

See pages 429, 745, 756, 1002.

Third-Person Point of View *See* **Point of View.**

Title The title of a literary work introduces readers to the piece and usually reveals something about its subject or theme. Often, a poet uses the title to provide information necessary for understanding a poem.

Example: "A Worn Path," the title of Eudora Welty's short story, suggests the main character, Phoenix, herself: the path of her life is worn with age and struggle, and her life has centered on a single routine motivated by love.

See pages 760, 1004, 1232.

Tone Tone is a writer's attitude toward his or her subject. A writer can communicate tone through diction, choice of details, and direct statements of his or her position. Unlike mood, which refers to the emotional response of the reader to a work, tone reflects the feelings of the writer. To identify the tone of a work of literature, you might find it helpful to read the work aloud, as if giving a dramatic reading before an audience. The emotions that you convey in an oral reading should give you hints as to the tone of the work.

Example: Claude McKay's tone in "If We Must Die" is proud, defiant, and urgent.

See pages 509, 791, 850, 1060.
See also **Connotation; Diction; Mood; Style.**

Tragedy A tragedy is a dramatic work that presents the downfall of a dignified character who is involved in historically, morally, or socially significant events. The main character, or **tragic hero,** has a **tragic flaw,** a quality that leads to his or her destruction. The events in a tragic plot are set in motion by a decision that is often an error in judgment caused by the tragic flaw. Succeeding events are linked in a cause-and-effect relationship and lead inevitably to a disastrous conclusion, usually death. Arthur Miller's *The Crucible* could be classified as a tragedy.

Tragic Flaw *See* **Tragedy.**

Tragic Hero The ancient Greek philosopher Aristotle defined a tragic hero as a character whose basic goodness and superiority are marred by a tragic flaw that brings about or contributes to his or her downfall. The flaw may be poor judgment, pride, weakness, or an excess of an admirable quality. The tragic hero recognizes his or her own flaw and its consequences, but only after it is too late to change the course of events.

See also **Character.**

Traits *See* **Character.**

Transcendentalism The philosophy of transcendentalism, an American offshoot of German romanticism, was based on a belief that "transcendent forms" of truth exist beyond reason and experience. Ralph Waldo Emerson, the leader of the movement, asserted that every individual is capable of discovering this higher truth through intuition. Henry David Thoreau is another well-known transcendentalist writer.

See pages 361, 372, 382.
See also **Romanticism.**

Trickster Tale A trickster tale is a folk tale about an animal or person who engages in trickery, violence, and magic. Neither all good nor all bad, a trickster may be foolish yet clever, greedy yet helpful, immoral yet moral. "Coyote and the Buffalo" is a trickster tale.

See page 43.
See also **Folk Tale.**

Trochee *See* **Meter.**

Turning Point *See* **Climax.**

Understatement Understatement is a technique of creating emphasis by saying less than is actually or literally true. It is the opposite of **hyperbole,** or exaggeration. One of the primary devices of **irony,** understatement can be used to develop a humorous effect, to create satire, or to achieve a restrained tone.

Example: In "Letter to John Adams," Abigail Adams points out the tyranny of male power by gently saying, "I cannot say that I think you very generous to the ladies."

See also **Hyperbole; Irony.**

Unity of Effect When all elements of a story—plot, character, setting, imagery, and other other literary devices—work together to create a single effect, it is known as unity of effect. Edgar Allan Poe's "The Fall of the House of Usher" demonstrates the unity of effect.

See page 403.

Universal Theme *See* **Theme.**

Verbal Irony *See* **Irony.**

Voice The term *voice* refers to a writer's unique use of language that allows a reader to "hear" a human personality in his or her writing. The elements of style that determine a writer's voice include sentence structure, diction, and tone. For example, some writers are noted for their reliance on short, simple sentences, while others make use of long, complicated ones. Certain writers use concrete words, such as *lake* or *cold,* which name things that you can see, hear, feel, taste, or smell. Others prefer abstract terms such as *memory,* which name things that cannot be perceived with the senses. A writer's tone also leaves its imprint on his or her personal voice. The term can be applied to the narrator of a selection, as well as the writer.

See pages 649, 1059.
See also **Diction; Tone.**

Word Choice *See* **Diction.**

Glossary of Reading & Informational Terms

Almanac *See* **Reference Works.**

Analogy *See Glossary of Literary Terms, page R104.*

Appeals by Association Appeals by association imply that one will gain acceptance or prestige by taking the writer's position.
See also **Recognizing Persuasive Techniques**—*Reading Handbook, page R20.*

Appeal to Authority An appeal to authority calls upon experts or others who warrant respect.
See also **Recognizing Persuasive Techniques**—*Reading Handbook, page R20.*

Appeal to Reason *See* **Logical Appeal.**

Argument An argument is speech or writing that expresses a position on an issue or problem and supports it with reasons and evidence. An argument often takes into account other points of view, anticipating and answering objections that opponents of the position might raise.
See also **Claim; Counterargument; Evidence; General Principle.**

Assumption An assumption is an opinion or belief that is taken for granted. It can be about a specific situation, a person, or the world in general. Assumptions are often unstated.
See also **General Principle.**

Author's Message An author's message is the main idea or theme of a particular work.
See also **Main Idea; Theme,** *Glossary of Literary Terms, page R121.*

Author's Perspective *See Glossary of Literary Terms, page R105.*

Author's Position An author's position is his or her opinion on an issue or topic.
See also **Claim.**

Author's Purpose *See Glossary of Literary Terms, page R105.*

Autobiography *See Glossary of Literary Terms, page R105.*

Bias Bias is an inclination toward a particular judgment on a topic or issue. A writer often reveals a strongly positive or strongly negative opinion by presenting only one way of looking at an issue or by heavily weighting the evidence. Words with intensely positive or negative connotations are often a signal of a writer's bias.

Bibliography A bibliography is a list of books and other materials related to the topic of a text. Bibliographies can be good sources of works for further study on a subject.
See also **Works Consulted.**

Biography *See Glossary of Literary Terms, page R105.*

Business Correspondence Business correspondence includes all written business communications, such as business letters, e-mails, and memos. In general, business correspondence is brief, to the point, clear, courteous, and professional.

Cause and Effect A **cause** is an event or action that directly results in another event or action. An **effect** is the direct or logical outcome of an event or action. Basic **cause-and-effect relationships** include a single cause with a single effect, one cause with multiple effects, multiple causes with a single effect, and a chain of causes and effects. The concept of cause and effect also provides a way of organizing a piece of writing. It helps a writer show the relationships between events or ideas.
See also **False Cause**—*Reading Handbook, page R22.*

Chronological Order Chronological order is the arrangement of events in their order of occurrence. This type of organization is used in both fictional narratives and in historical writing, biography, and autobiography.

Claim In an argument, a claim is the writer's position on an issue or problem. Although an argument focuses on supporting one claim, a writer may make more than one claim in a work.

Clarify Clarifying is a reading strategy that helps a reader to understand or make clear what he or she is reading. Readers usually clarify by rereading, reading aloud, or discussing.

Classification Classification is a pattern of organization in which objects, ideas, or information is presented in groups, or classes, based on common characteristics.

Cliché A cliché is an overused expression. "Better late than never" and "hard as nails" are common examples. Good writers generally avoid clichés unless they are using them in dialogue to indicate something about characters' personalities.

Compare and Contrast To compare and contrast is to identify similarities and differences in two or more subjects. Compare-and-contrast organization can be used to structure a piece of writing, serving as a framework for examining the similarities and differences in two or more subjects.

Conclusion A conclusion is a statement of belief based on evidence, experience, and reasoning. A **valid conclusion** is a conclusion that logically follows from the facts or statements upon which it is based. A **deductive conclusion** is one that follows from a particular generalization or premise. An **inductive conclusion** is a broad conclusion or generalization that is reached by arguing from specific facts and examples.

Connect Connecting is a reader's process of relating the content of a text to his or her own knowledge and experience.

Consumer Documents Consumer documents are printed materials that accompany products and services. They are intended for the buyers or users of the products or services and usually provide information about use, care, operation, or assembly. Some common consumer documents are applications, contracts, warranties, manuals, instructions, package inserts, labels, brochures, and schedules.

Context Clues When you encounter an unfamiliar word, you can often use context clues as aids for understanding. Context clues are the words and phrases surrounding the word that provide hints about the word's meaning.

Counterargument A counterargument is an argument made to oppose another argument. A good argument anticipates opposing viewpoints and provides counterarguments to refute (disprove) or answer them.

Credibility *Credibility* refers to the believability or trustworthiness of a source and the information it contains.

Critical Review A critical review is an evaluation or critique by a reviewer or critic. Different types of reviews include film reviews, book reviews, music reviews, and art-show reviews.

Database A database is a collection of information that can be quickly and easily accessed and searched and from which information can be easily retrieved. It is frequently presented in an electronic format.

Debate A debate is an organized exchange of opinions on an issue. In academic settings, *debate* usually refers to a formal contest in which two opposing teams defend and attack a proposition.
See also **Argument; Debate**—*Speaking and Listening Handbook, pages R82–R83.*

Deductive Reasoning Deductive reasoning is a way of thinking that begins with a generalization, presents a specific situation, and then advances with facts and evidence to a logical conclusion. The following passage has a deductive argument imbedded in it: "All students in the drama class must attend the play on Thursday. Since Ava is in the class, she had better show up." This deductive argument can be broken down as follows: generalization—all students in the drama class must attend the play on Thursday; specific situation—Ava is a student in the drama class; conclusion—Ava must attend the play.
See also **Analyzing Logic and Reasoning**—*Reading Handbook, pages R20–R21.*

Dictionary *See* **Reference Works.**

Draw Conclusions To draw a conclusion is to make a judgment or arrive at a belief based on evidence, experience, and reasoning.

Editorial An editorial is an opinion piece that usually appears on the editorial page of a newspaper or as part of a news broadcast. The editorial section of a newspaper presents opinions rather than objective news reports.
See also **Op-Ed Piece.**

Either/Or Fallacy An either/or fallacy is a statement that suggests that there are only two possible ways to view a situation or only two options to choose from. In other words, it is a statement that falsely frames a dilemma, giving the impression that no options exist but the two presented—for example, "Either we stop the construction of a new airport, or the surrounding suburbs will become ghost towns."
See also **Identifying Faulty Reasoning**—*Reading Handbook, page R22.*

Emotional Appeals Emotional appeals are messages that evoke strong feelings—such as fear, pity, or vanity—in order to persuade instead of using facts and evidence to make a point. An **appeal to fear** is a message that taps into people's fear of losing their safety or security. An **appeal to pity** is a message that taps into people's sympathy and compassion for others to build support for an idea, a cause, or a proposed action. An **appeal to vanity** is a message that attempts to persuade by tapping into people's desire to feel good about themselves.
See also **Recognizing Persuasive Techniques**—*Reading Handbook, page R20.*

Encyclopedia *See* **Reference Works.**

Essay *See Glossary of Literary Terms, page R109.*

Ethical Appeals Ethical appeals establish a writer's credibility and trustworthiness with an audience. When a writer links a claim to a widely accepted value, for example, the writer not only gains moral support for that claim but also establishes a connection with readers.
See also **Recognizing Persuasive Techniques**—*Reading Handbook, page R20.*

Evaluate To evaluate is to examine something carefully and judge its value or worth. Evaluating is an important skill for gaining insight into what you read. A reader can evaluate the actions of a particular character, for example, or can form an opinion about the value of an entire work.

Evidence Evidence is the specific pieces of information that support a claim. Evidence can take the form of facts, quotations, examples, statistics, or personal experiences, among others.

Expository Essay *See* **Essay**, *Glossary of Literary Terms, page R109.*

Fact versus Opinion A **fact** is a statement that can be proved or verified. An **opinion,** on the other hand, is a statement that cannot be proved because it expresses a person's beliefs, feelings, or thoughts.
See also **Inference; Generalization.**

Fallacy A fallacy is an error in reasoning. Typically, a fallacy is based on an incorrect inference or a misuse of evidence. Some common logical fallacies are **circular reasoning, either/or fallacy, oversimplification, overgeneralization,** and **stereotyping.**
See also **Either/Or Fallacy; Logical Appeal; Overgeneralization; Identifying Faulty Reasoning**—*Reading Handbook, page R22.*

Faulty Reasoning *See* **Fallacy.**

Feature Article A feature article is a main article in a newspaper or a cover story in a magazine. A feature article is focused more on entertaining than informing. Features are lighter or more general than hard news and tend to be about human interest or lifestyles.

Functional Documents *See* **Consumer Documents; Workplace Documents.**

Generalization A generalization is a broad statement about a class or category of people, ideas, or things, based on a study of only some of its members.
See also **Overgeneralization.**

General Principle In an argument, a general principle is an assumption that links the support to the claim. If one does not accept the general principle as a truth, then the support is inadequate because it is beside the point.

Government Publications Government publications are documents produced by government organizations. Pamphlets, brochures, and reports are just some of the many forms these publications may take. Government publications can be good resources for a wide variety of topics.

Graphic Aid A graphic aid is a visual tool that is printed, handwritten, or drawn. Charts, diagrams, graphs, photographs, and maps can all be graphic aids.
See also **Graphic Aids**—*Reading Handbook, pages R5–R7.*

Graphic Organizer A graphic organizer is a visual illustration of a verbal statement that helps a reader understand a text. Charts, tables, webs, and diagrams can all be graphic organizers. Graphic organizers and graphic aids can look the same. However, graphic organizers and graphic aids do differ in how they are used. Graphic aids are the visual representations that people encounter when they read informational texts. Graphic organizers are visuals that people construct to help them understand texts or organize information.

Historical Documents Historical documents are writings that have played a significant role in human events or are themselves records of such events. The Declaration of Independence, for example, is a historical document.

How-To Book A how-to book is a book that is written to explain how to do something—usually an activity, a sport, or a household project.

Implied Main Idea *See* **Main Idea.**

Index The index of a book is an alphabetized list of important topics and details covered in the book and the page numbers on which they can be found. An index can be used to quickly find specific information about a topic.

Inductive Reasoning Inductive reasoning is the process of logical reasoning from observations, examples, and facts to a general conclusion or principle.
See also **Analyzing Logic and Reasoning**—*Reading Handbook, pages R20–R21.*

Inference An inference is a logical assumption that is based on observed facts and one's own knowledge and experience.

Informational Nonfiction Informational nonfiction is writing that provides factual information. It often explains ideas or teaches processes. Examples include news reports, science textbooks, software instructions, and lab reports.

Internet The Internet is a global, interconnected system of computer networks that allows for communication through e-mail, listservers, and the World Wide Web. The Internet connects computers and computer users throughout the world.

Journal A journal is a periodical publication issued by a legal, medical, or other professional organization. Alternatively, the term may be used to refer to a diary or daily record.

Literary Criticism *See Glossary of Literary Terms, page R113.*

Loaded Language Loaded language consists of words with strongly positive or negative connotations intended to influence a reader's or listener's attitude.

Logical Appeal A logical appeal relies on logic and facts, appealing to people's reasoning or intellect rather than to their values or emotions. Flawed logical appeals—that is, errors in reasoning—are considered logical fallacies.
See also **Fallacy.**

Logical Argument A logical argument is an argument in which the logical relationship between the support and the claim is sound.

Main Idea A main idea is the central or most important idea about a topic that a writer or speaker conveys. It can be the central idea of an entire work or of just a paragraph. Often, the main idea of a paragraph is expressed in a topic sentence. However, a main idea may just be implied, or suggested, by details. A main idea and supporting details can serve as a basic pattern of organization in a piece of writing, with the central idea about a topic being supported by details.

Make Inferences *See* **Inference.**

Monitor Monitoring is the strategy of checking your comprehension as you are reading and modifying the strategies you are using to suit your needs. Monitoring may include some or all of the following strategies: **questioning, clarifying, visualizing, predicting, connecting,** and **rereading.**

Narrative Nonfiction *See Glossary of Literary Terms, page R115.*

News Article A news article is a piece of writing that reports on a recent event. In newspapers, news articles are usually written in a concise manner to report the latest news, presenting the most important facts first and then more detailed information. In magazines, news articles are usually more elaborate than those in newspapers because they are written to provide both information and analysis. Also, news articles in magazines do not necessarily present the most important facts first.

Nonfiction *See Glossary of Literary Terms, page R115.*

Op-Ed Piece An op-ed piece is an opinion piece that usually appears opposite ("op") the editorial page of a newspaper. Unlike editorials, op-ed pieces are written and submitted by named writers.

Organization *See* **Pattern of Organization.**

Overgeneralization An overgeneralization is a generalization that is too broad. You can often recognize overgeneralizations by the appearance of words and phrases such as *all, everyone, every time, any, anything, no one,* and *none*. Consider, for example, this statement: "None of the sanitation workers in our city really care about keeping the environment clean." In all probability, there are many exceptions. The writer can't possibly know the feelings of every sanitation worker in the city.
See also **Identifying Faulty Reasoning**—*Reading Handbook, page R22.*

Overview An overview is a short summary of a story, a speech, or an essay. It orients the reader by providing a preview of the text to come.

Paraphrase Paraphrasing is the restating of information in one's own words.
See also **Summarize.**

Pattern of Organization A pattern of organization is a particular arrangement of ideas and information. Such a pattern may be used to organize an entire composition or a single paragraph within a longer work. The following are the most common patterns of organization: **cause-and-effect, chronological order, compare-and-contrast, classification, deductive, inductive, order of importance, problem-solution, sequential,** and **spatial.**
See also **Cause and Effect; Chronological Order; Classification; Compare and Contrast; Problem-Solution Order; Sequential Order; Patterns of Organization**—*Reading Handbook, pages R8–R12.*

Periodical A periodical is a publication that is issued at regular intervals of more than one day. For example, a periodical may be a weekly, monthly, or quarterly journal or magazine. Newspapers and other daily publications generally are not classified as periodicals.

Personal Essay *See* **Essay,** *Glossary of Literary Terms, page R116.*

Persuasion Persuasion is the art of swaying others' feelings, beliefs, or actions. Persuasion normally appeals to both the intellect and the emotions of readers. **Persuasive techniques** are the methods used to influence others to adopt certain opinions or beliefs or to act in certain ways. Types of persuasive techniques include emotional appeals, ethical appeals, logical appeals, and loaded language. When used properly, persuasive techniques can add depth to writing that's meant to persuade. Persuasive techniques can, however, be misused to cloud factual information, disguise poor reasoning, or unfairly exploit people's emotions in order to shape their opinions.

See also **Appeals by Association; Appeal to Authority; Emotional Appeals; Ethical Appeals; Loaded Language; Logical Appeal; Recognizing Persuasive Techniques—** *Reading Handbook, page R20.*

Predict Predicting is a reading strategy that involves using text clues to make a reasonable guess about what will happen next in a story.

Primary Source *See* **Sources.**

Prior Knowledge Prior knowledge is the knowledge a reader already possesses about a topic. This information might come from personal experiences, expert accounts, books, films, or other sources.

Problem-Solution Order Problem-solution order is a pattern of organization in which a problem is stated and analyzed and then one or more solutions are proposed and examined. Writers use words and phrases such as *propose, conclude, reason for, problem, answer,* and *solution* to connect ideas and details when writing about problems and solutions.

Propaganda Propaganda is a form of communication that may use distorted, false, or misleading information. It usually refers to manipulative political discourse.

Public Documents Public documents are documents that were written for the public to provide information that is of public interest or concern. They include government documents, speeches, signs, and rules and regulations. *See also* **Government Publications.**

Reference Works General reference works are sources that contain facts and background information on a wide range of subjects. More specific reference works contain in-depth information on a single subject. Most reference works are good sources of reliable information because they have been reviewed by experts. The following are some common reference works: **encyclopedias, dictionaries, thesauri, almanacs, atlases, chronologies, biographical dictionaries,** and **directories.**

Review *See* **Critical Review.**

Rhetorical Devices *See Glossary of Literary Terms, page R118.*

Rhetorical Questions Rhetorical questions are those that do not require a reply. Writers use them to suggest that their arguments make the answer obvious or self-evident.

Scanning Scanning is the process of searching through writing for a particular fact or piece of information. When you scan, your eyes sweep across a page, looking for key words that may lead you to the information you want.

Secondary Source *See* **Sources.**

Sequential Order A pattern of organization that shows the order in which events or actions occur is called sequential order. Writers typically use this pattern of organization to explain steps or stages in a process.

Setting a Purpose The process of establishing specific reasons for reading a text is called setting a purpose.

Sidebar A sidebar is additional information set in a box alongside or within a news or feature article. Popular magazines often make use of sidebar information.

Signal Words Signal words are words and phrases that indicate what is to come in a text. Readers can use signal words to discover a text's pattern of organization and to analyze the relationships among the ideas in the text.

Sources A source is anything that supplies information. **Primary sources** are materials written or created by people who were present at events, either as participants or as observers. Letters, diaries, autobiographies, speeches, and photographs are primary sources. **Secondary sources** are records of events that were created sometime after the events occurred; the writers were not directly involved or were not present when the events took place. Encyclopedias, textbooks, biographies, most newspaper and magazine articles, and books and articles that interpret or review research are secondary sources.

Spatial Order Spatial order is a pattern of organization that highlights the physical positions or relationships of details or objects. This pattern of organization is typically found in descriptive writing. Writers use words and phrases such as *on the left, to the right, here, over there, above, below, beyond, nearby,* and *in the distance* to indicate the arrangement of details.

Speech *See Glossary of Literary Terms, page R120.*

Stereotyping Stereotyping is a dangerous type of overgeneralization. Stereotypes are broad statements made about people on the basis of their gender, ethnicity, race, or political, social, professional, or religious group.

Summarize To summarize is to briefly retell, or encapsulate, the main ideas of a piece of writing in one's own words.
See also **Paraphrase.**

Support Support is any material that serves to prove a claim. In an argument, support typically consists of reasons and evidence. In persuasive texts and speeches, however, support may include appeals to the needs and values of the audience.
See also **General Principle.**

Supporting Detail *See* **Main Idea.**

Synthesize To synthesize information is to take individual pieces of information and combine them with other pieces of information and with prior knowledge or experience to gain a better understanding of a subject or to create a new product or idea.

Text Features Text features are design elements that indicate the organizational structure of a text and help make the key ideas and the supporting information understandable. Text features include headings, boldface type, italic type, bulleted or numbered lists, sidebars, and graphic aids such as charts, tables, timelines, illustrations, and photographs.

Thesaurus *See* **Reference Works.**

Thesis Statement In an argument, a thesis statement is an expression of the claim that the writer or speaker is trying to support. In an essay, a thesis statement is an expression, in one or two sentences, of the main idea or purpose of the piece of writing.

Topic Sentence The topic sentence of a paragraph states the paragraph's main idea. All other sentences in the paragraph provide supporting details.

Transcript A transcript is a written record of words originally spoken aloud.

Visualize Visualizing is the process of forming a mental picture based on written or spoken information.

Web Site A Web site is a collection of "pages" on the World Wide Web that is usually devoted to one specific subject. Pages are linked together and are accessed by clicking hyperlinks or menus, which send the user from page to page within the site. Web sites are created by companies, organizations, educational institutions, branches of the government, the military, and individuals.

Workplace Documents Workplace documents are materials that are produced or used within a work setting, usually to aid in the functioning of the workplace. They include job applications, office memos, training manuals, job descriptions, and sales reports.

Works Cited A list of works cited lists names of all the works a writer has referred to in his or her text. This list often includes not only books and articles but also nonprint sources.

Works Consulted A list of works consulted names all the works a writer consulted in order to create his or her text. It is not limited just to those works cited in the text.
See also **Bibliography.**

abdicate (ăb'dĭ-kāt') *v.* to give up responsibility for
   abdicar *v.* renunciar a una responsabilidad

aberration (ăb'ə-rā'shən) *n.* a disorder of the mind
   aberración *s.* desorden mental

abhor (ăb-hôr') *v.* to regard with disgust
   aborrecer *v.* detestar

abject (ăb'jĕkt') *adj.* low; contemptible; wretched
   abyecto *adj.* vil; despreciable; desgraciado

abominable (ə-bŏm'ə-nə-bəl) *adj.* thoroughly detestable
   abominable *adj.* totalmente detestable

acquiesce (ăk'wē-ĕs') *v.* to comply or give in
   consentir *v.* aceptar o ceder

adamant (ăd'ə-mənt) *adj.* immovable, especially in opposing something
   inflexible *adj.* inquebrantable, especialmente en oposición a algo

admonitory (ăd-mŏn'ĭ-tôr'ē) *adj.* warning
   admonitorio *adj.* que da una advertencia

affiliated (ə-fĭl'ē-āt-ĭd) *adj.* joined in close association **affiliate** *v.*
   afiliado *adj.* asociado **afiliar** *v.*

affinity (ə-fĭn'ĭ-tē) *n.* a kinship or likeness
   afinidad *s.* cercanía o semejanza

affluence (ăf'lōō-əns) *n.* wealth
   opulencia *s.* riqueza

alleviation (ə-lē'vē-ā'shən) *n.* relief
   alivio *s.* desahogo

ambiguity (ăm'bĭ-gyōō'ĭ-tē) *n.* unclearness; uncertainty
   ambigüedad *s.* vaguedad; incertidumbre

ameliorate (əmēl'yə-rāt') *v.* to improve
   mejorar *v.* aliviar

amethyst (ăm'ə-thĭst) *n.* purple or violet form of transparent quartz used as a gemstone
   amatista *s.* cuarzo transparente púrpura o violeta usado como piedra preciosa

amicable (ăm'ĭ-kə-bəl) *adj.* characterized by friendly goodwill
   amigable *adj.* caracterizado por buena voluntad

anarchy (ăn'ər-kē) *n.* condition of lawlessness and disorder, often due to lack of governmental authority
   anarquía *s.* desorden y confusión por falta de gobierno

anathema (ə-năth'ə-mə) *n.* a strong denunciation; a curse
   anatema *s.* fuerte rechazo; maldición

anomaly (ə-nŏm'ə-lē) *n.* departure from the normal rules
   anomalía *s.* desviación de las reglas normales

apathy (ăp'ə-thē) *n.* lack of feeling or interest
   apatía *s.* falta de sentimiento o de interés

appease (ə-pēz') *v.* to bring peace, quiet, or calm to; to soothe
   aplacar *v.* apaciguar; calmar; aquietar

arbitrary (är'bĭ-trĕr'ē) *adj.* based on unpredictable decisions rather than law
   arbitrario *adj.* que actúa basándose sólo en la voluntad o en el capricho y no sigue las leyes

ardor (är'dər) *n.* intense enthusiasm; passion
   ardor *s.* fuerte entusiasmo; pasión

artifice (är'tə-fĭs) *n.* a clever means to an end
   artificio *s.* estratagema; ardid

ascribe (ə-skrīb') *v.* to attribute to a specified cause or source
   adscribir *v.* atribuir a una causa o a una fuente

assign (ə-sīn') *n.* person to whom property is transferred in a will or other legal document
   beneficiario *s.* persona a la que transfiere propiedades un testamento u otro documento jurídico

attest (ə-tĕst') *v.* to affirm to be true; to be proof of
   atestiguar *v.* dar testimonio; certificar

avarice (ăv'ə-rĭs) *n.* immoderate desire for wealth; greed
   avaricia *s.* deseo desmedido de riqueza; codicia

aversion (ə-vûr'zhən) *n.* a strong dislike
   aversión *s.* fuerte desagrado

blasphemous (blăs'fə-məs) *adj.* disrespectful or offensive
   blasfemo *adj.* irrespetuoso u ofensivo

blatantly (blāt'nt-lē) *adv.* in an extremely obvious way; conspicuously
   descaradamente *adv.* abiertamente; patentemente

cabal (kə-băl') *n.* a group united in a secret plot
   cábala *s.* grupo unido en un complot secreto

callow (kăl'ō) *adj.* lacking adult experience; immature
   inmaduro *adj.* sin experiencia; inexperto

camaraderie (kä'mə-rä'də-rē) *n.* a spirit of friendly good-fellowship
   camaradería *s.* espíritu de amistad y compañerismo

cauterize (kô'tə-rīz') *v.* to burn or sear to destroy diseased tissue
   cauterizar *v.* quemar o chamuscar para destruir tejido dañado

cavorting (kə-vôr'tĭng) *adj.* prancing about in a playful manner **cavort** *v.*
   retozón *adj.* que hace cabriolas de modo juguetón
   retozar *v.*

celestial (sə-lĕs'chəl) *adj.* heavenly
   celestial *adj.* del cielo

censurer (sĕn'shər-ər) *n.* one who expresses strong disapproval or harsh criticism
   censor *s.* persona que expresa una fuerte desaprobación o crítica

cessation (sĕ-sā'shən) *n.* a coming to an end; a stopping
   cesación *s.* fin; terminación

circumvent (sûr'kəm-vĕnt') *v.* to avoid or get around by clever maneuvering
   circunvenir *v.* evitar o evadir con maniobras

citation (sī-tā'shən) *n.* formal statement of a soldier's achievements
   mención honorífica *s.* reconocimiento de los éxitos de un militar

coerce (kō-ûrs') *v.* to force
   coaccionar *v.* obligar

cognizant (kŏg'nĭ-zənt) *adj.* aware
   enterado *adj.* informado

commiseration (kə-mĭz'ə-rā'shən) *n.* a feeling of sympathy or pity
   conmiseración *s.* sentimiento de compasión

comport (kəm-pôrt') *v.* to agree
   concordar *v.* estar de acuerdo

conciliatory (kən-sĭl'ē-ə-tôr'ē) *adj.* showing goodwill to end an argument
   conciliador *adj.* que busca un acuerdo

congenial (kən-jēn'yəl) *adj.* suited to one's needs or nature; agreeable
   compatible *adj.* que concuerda con las necesidades o la naturaleza de uno; concorde

conjecture (kən-jĕk'chər) *v.* to guess
   conjeturar *v.* suponer

consternation (kŏn'stər-nā'shən) *n.* a state of paralyzing dismay; fear
   consternación *s.* estado de gran intranquilidad; temor

constitute (kŏn'stĭ-tōōt') *v.* to amount to; equal
   constituir *v.* equivaler; formar

contentious (kən-tĕn'shəs) *adj.* quarrelsome
   discutidor *adj.* pendenciero

contrive (kən-trīv') *v.* to plan skillfully; to design
   ingeniarse *v.* maquinar; inventar

convolution (kŏn'və-lōō'shən) *n.* a form or shape that is folded into curved, complicated windings
   circunvolución *s.* repliegue; enroscadura; enrollamiento

copious (kō'pē-əs) *adj.* in large amounts; abundant
   copioso *adj.* en gran cantidad; abundante

corroborate (kə-rŏb'ə-rāt') *v.* to support with evidence
   corroborar *v.* comprobar con evidencia

cosmic (kŏz'mĭk) *adj.* of, or belonging to, the universe
   cósmico *adj.* relativo al universo

countenance (koun'tə-nəns) *n.* appearance, especially the expression of the face
   semblante *s.* apariencia, especialmente la expresión de la cara

credulity (krĭ-dōō'lĭ-tē) *n.* an inclination to believe too readily
   credulidad *s.* facilidad para creer

dastardly (dăs'tərd-lē) *adj.* characterized by underhandedness or treachery
   miserable *adj.* solapado o traidor

dearth (dûrth) *n.* lack
   escasez *s.* carencia

decorum (dĭ-kôr'əm) *n.* good taste in conduct or appearance
  decoro *s.* buen gusto en la conducta y la apariencia

deference (dĕf'ər-əns) *n.* respect and honor due to a superior or elder
  deferencia *s.* respeto y honor que se debe a un superior o mayor

deliberately (dĭ-lĭb'ər-ĭt-lē) *adv.* in an unhurried and thoughtful manner
  deliberadamente *adv.* pausadamente

deliverance (dĭ-lĭv'ər-əns) *n.* rescue from danger
  salvación *s.* rescate de un peligro

demeanor (dĭ-mē'nər) *n.* behavior
  comportamiento *s.* conducta

depose (dĭ-pōz') *v.* to remove from rule
  deponer *v.* destituir del gobierno

deposition (dĕp'ə-zĭsh'ən) *n.* a written statement by a witness
  deposición *s.* testimonio escrito de un testigo

derision (dĭ-rĭzh'ən) *n.* harsh ridicule or mockery; scorn
  irrisión *s.* mofa o ridículo; escarnio

despotism (dĕs'pə-tĭz'əm) *n.* government by a ruler with unlimited power
  despotismo *s.* gobierno de poder ilimitado

detached (dĭ-tăcht') *adj.* reserved; aloof **detach** *v.*
  alejado *adj.* reservado; distante **alejarse** *v.*

dilapidated (dĭ-lăp'ĭ-dā'tĭd) *adj.* in a state of disrepair; rundown **dilapidate** *v.*
  dilapidado *adj.* en ruinas; desmantelado **dilapidar** *v.*

disapprobation (dĭs-ăp'rə-bā'shən) *n.* disapproval
  desaprobación *s.* censura

discern (dĭ-sûrn') *v.* to perceive or recognize something
  discernir *v.* percibir o reconocer algo

dissembling (dĭ-sĕm'blĭng) *n.* disguising the truth about something **dissemble** *v.*
  disimulación *s.* encubrimiento de la verdad **disimular** *v.*

dominion (də-mĭn'yən) *n.* control; authority over
  dominio *s.* control; soberanía

dwindle (dwĭn'dl) *v.* to become steadily less; to shrink
  menguar *v.* disminuirse poco a poco; encogerse

effrontery (ĭ-frŭn'tə-rē) *n.* disrespectful and insulting boldness
  insolencia *s.* desvergüenza y descaro

embody (ĕm-bŏd'ē) *v.* to represent in human form
  encarnar *v.* representar en forma humana

embroidered (ĕm'broi'dərd) *adj.* decorated with stitched designs **embroider** *v.*
  bordado *adj.* decorado con cosidos en relieve **bordar** *v.*

encroach (ĕn-krōch') *v.* to take over the possessions or rights of another
  invadir *v.* usurpar las posesiones o los derechos de otro

enmity (ĕn'mĭ-tē) *n.* hostility; hatred
  enemistad *s.* hostilidad; odio

enterprising (ĕn'tər-prī'zĭng) *adj.* possessing imagination and initiative
  emprendedor *adj.* que demuestra imaginación e iniciativa

entreaty (ĕn-trē'tē) *n.* plea
  súplica *s.* petición

epithet (ĕp'ə-thĕt') *n.* an abusive word or phrase
  epíteto *s.* palabra o frase insultante

equanimity (ē'kwə-nĭm'ĭ-tē) *n.* evenness of temper, especially under stress
  ecuanimidad *s.* serenidad y equilibrio, especialmente bajo presión

equivocal (ĭ-kwĭv'ə-kəl) *adj.* ambiguous
  equívoco *adj.* ambiguo

eradicate (ĭ-răd'ĭ-kāt') *v.* to destroy completely
  erradicar *v.* destruir por completo

esteem (ĭ-stēm') *v.* to set a high value on
  estimar *v.* dar mucho valor

estrangement (ĭ-strānj'-mənt) *n.* separation; alienation
  extrañamiento *s.* separación; desavenencia

excruciatingly (ĭk-skrōō'shē-ā'tĭng-lē) *adv.* in a way that causes great pain or distress
  dolorosamente *adv.* de modo que causa mucho dolor o angustia

exhilaration (ĭg-zĭl'ə-rā'shən) *n.* a feeling of high spirits or lively joy
  regocijo *s.* alborozo y gran alegría

expatriated (ĕk-spā′trē-ā′tĭd) *adj.* sent out of a country or area; banished **expatriate** *v.*
  expatriado *adj.* exiliado; desterrado **expatriar** *v.*

extenuate (ĭk-stĕn′yōō-āt′) *v.* to lessen the seriousness of, especially by providing partial excuses
  atenuar *v.* reducir la gravedad, especialmente dando excusas parciales

extenuating (ĭk-stĕn′yōō-āt′ĭng) *adj.* lessening the severity of **extenuate** *v.*
  atenuante *adj.* que reduce la gravedad **atenuar** *v.*

exultingly (ĭg-zult′ĭng-lē) *adv.* joyfully
  jubilosamente *adv.* con júbilo

fatuity (fə-tōō′ĭ-tē) *n.* something foolish or stupid
  fatuidad *s.* simpleza o estupidez

feigned (fānd) *adj.* not real; pretended **feign** *v.*
  fingido *adj.* irrea; ficticio **fingir** *v.*

felicity (fĭ-lĭs′ĭ-tē) *n.* great happiness
  felicidad *s.* dicha

flamboyant (flăm-boi′ənt) *adj.* marked by strikingly elaborate or colorful display
  flameante *adj.* llamativo; ostentoso; extravagante

flux (flŭks) *n.* change
  flujo *s.* fluctuación; cambio

garrulous (găr′ə-ləs) *adj.* extremely talkative
  locuaz *adj.* que habla mucho

glib (glĭb) *adj.* showing little thought, preparation, or concern
  simplista *adj.* que demuestra poca reflexión, preparación o interés

gullible (gŭl′ə-bəl) *adj.* easily deceived or tricked
  crédulo *adj.* que se deja engañar

harassing (hə-răs′ĭng) *adj.* persistently annoying **harass** *v.*
  molesto *adj.* que fastidia todo el tiempo **molestar** *v.*

harry (hăr′ē) *v.* to torment, often by constant attack
  hostilizar *v.* acosar con ataques constantes

imbued (ĭm-byōōd′) *adj.* deeply influenced by **imbue** *v.*
  imbuido *adj.* profundamente influenciado **imbuir** *v.*

immaculate (ĭ-măk′yə-lĭt) *adj.* without stain; pure
  inmaculado *adj.* sin mancha; puro

impede (ĭm-pēd′) *v.* to interfere with or slow the progress of
  impedir *v.* obstruir; dificultar

impel (ĭm-pĕl′) *v.* to drive forward; force
  impeler *v.* impulsar; obligar

impending (ĭm-pĕn′dĭng) *adj.* to be about to occur **impend** *v.*
  amenazante *adj.* a punto de ocurrir **amenazar** *v.*

imperceptible (ĭm′pər-sĕp′tə-bəl) *adj.* extremely slight; barely noticeable
  imperceptible *adj.* tenue; que casi no se nota

impertinent (ĭm-pûr′tn-ənt) *adj.* rude; ill-mannered
  impertinente *adj.* grosero; mal educado

imperviousness (ĭm-pûr′vē-əs-nəs) *n.* condition of not being able to be affected or disturbed
  imperturbabilidad *s.* imposibilidad de ser afectado o perturbado

impetuous (ĭm-pĕch′ōō-əs) *adj.* acting with sudden or rash energy; hasty
  impetuoso *adj.* que actúa de forma precipitada o irreflexiva; impulsivo

implacable (ĭm-plăk′ə-bəl) *adj.* impossible to satisfy
  implacable *adj.* que no se puede aplacar

importune (ĭm′pôr-tōōn′) *v.* to ask urgently or repeatedly; to annoy or trouble
  importunar *v.* preguntar con urgencia e insistencia; molestar

incense (ĭn-sĕns′) *v.* to cause to be extremely angry
  exasperar *v.* encolerizar; enfurecer

incorrigible (ĭn-kôr′ĭ-jə-bəl) *adj.* incapable of being reformed or corrected
  incorregible *adj.* que no se puede reformar o corregir

indifferent (ĭn-dĭf′ər-ənt) *adj.* having no particular interest
  indiferente *adj.* sin interés

induce (ĭn-dōōs′) *v.* to succeed in persuading someone to do something
  inducir *v.* persuadir; causar; producir

industry (ĭn′də-strē) *n.* hard work; diligence
  aplicación *s.* diligencia; laboriosidad

ineffable (ĭn-ĕf′ə-bəl) *adj.* beyond description; inexpressible
  inefable *adj.* que no se puede describir; inexpresable

inexorable (ĭn-ĕk′sər-ə-bəl) *adj.* relentless
   inexorable *adj.* implacable

inextricable (ĭn-ĕk′strĭ-kə-bəl) *adj.* incapable of being disentangled or untied
   inextricable *adj.* que no se puede descifrar o desenmarañar

infamous (ĭn′fə-məs) *adj.* having a very bad reputation; disgraceful
   infame *adj.* de mala reputación; vergonzoso

infidel (ĭn′fĭ-dəl) *n.* a person with no religious beliefs
   infiel *s.* el que no tiene creencias religiosas

ingenuously (ĭn-jĕn′yōō-əs-lē) *adv.* in a manner showing childlike innocence or simplicity
   ingenuamente *adv.* con candidez infantil

ingratiate (ĭn-grā′shē-āt′) *v.* to gain another's favor by deliberate effort
   congraciar *v.* conseguir aprobación o afecto con un esfuerzo deliberado

inherently (ĭn-hîr′ənt-lē) *adv.* related to part of something's inmost nature
   inherentemente *adv.* intrínsecamente

iniquity (ĭ-nĭk′wĭ-tē) *n.* wickedness
   iniquidad *s.* maldad

inordinate (ĭn-ôr′dn-ĭt) *adj.* exceeding reasonable limits; excessive
   excesivo *adj.* que sobrepasa los límites razonables; inmoderado

insidious (ĭn-sĭd′ē-əs) *adj.* treacherous
   insidioso *adj.* traidor

insipid (ĭn-sĭp′ĭd) *adj.* lacking in flavor; bland
   insípido *adj.* sin sabor; desabrido

interim (ĭn′tər-ĭm) *n.* period in between; interval
   ínterin *s.* intermedio; intervalo

interminable (ĭn-tûr′mə-nə-bol) *adj.* endless
   interminable *adj.* sin fin

interrogation (ĭn-tĕr′ə-gā′shən) *n.* a questioning
   interrogación *s.* averiguación

inundate (ĭn′ŭn-dāt′) *v.* to cover with water; to overwhelm
   inundar *v.* cubrir de agua; anegar

invincible (ĭn-vĭn′sə-bəl) *adj.* unbeatable
   invencible *adj.* inconquistable

inviolate (ĭn-vī′ə-lĭt) *adj.* not violated; intact
   inviolado *adj.* íntegro; intacto

jocular (jŏk′yə-lər) *adj.* humorous
   jocoso *adj.* chistoso

latent (lāt′nt) *adj.* existing in a hidden form
   latente *adj.* que existe en forma oculta

limber (lĭm′bər) *adj.* bending or moving easily; supple
   flexible *adj.* que se dobla o se mueve con facilidad; ágil

locomotion (lō′kə-mō′shən) *n.* the power to move from place to place
   locomoción *s.* movimiento de un lugar a otro

ludicrous (lōō′dĭ-krəs) *adj.* laughably absurd; ridiculous
   absurdo *adj.* risible; ridículo

lurch (lûrch) *v.* to lean or roll suddenly to one side; to stagger
   bambolearse *v.* dar banzados; tambalearse

lurid (lŏōr′ĭd) *adj.* shocking; gruesome
   escabroso *adj.* chocante; espeluznante

luxuriant (lŭg-zhŏōr′ē-ənt) *adj.* characterized by abundant growth
   frondoso *adj.* que tiene mucha vegetación

malign (mə-līn′) *adj.* evil; harmful
   maligno *adj.* malo; dañino

martial (mär′shəl) *adj.* warlike
   marcial *adj.* bélico

maudlin (môd′lĭn) *adj.* excessively sentimental
   sensiblero *adj.* sentimental en exceso

mediocrity (mē′dē-ŏk′rĭ-tē) *n.* lack of quality or excellence
   mediocridad *s.* poca calidad o mérito

meditative (mĕd′i-tā′tĭv) *adj.* engaged in serious thought or reflection
   meditabundo *adj.* que medita o reflexiona en silencio

melancholy (mĕl′ən-kŏl′ē) *adj.* gloomy; sad
   melancólico *adj.* triste; lúgubre

mercenary (mûr′sə-nĕr′ē) *n.* a professional soldier hired to fight in a foreign army
   mercenario *s.* soldado profesional contratado para pelear en un ejército extranjero

militant (mĭl′i-tənt) *adj.* aggressively active, especially for a cause
  militante *adj.* que apoya enérgicamente una causa

minutest (mī-nōō′tĭst) *adj.* smallest; most precise
  el más diminuto *adj.* el más pequeño; minucioso

miscellany (mĭs′ə-lā′nē) *n.* a mixture of various things
  miscelánea *s.* mezcla de cosas

misconstrued (mĭs′kən-strōōd′) *adj.* misunderstood; misinterpreted **misconstrue** *v.*
  malinterpretado *adj.* mal entendido **malinterpretar** *v.*

misgiving (mĭs-gĭv′ĭng) *n.* a feeling of doubt, mistrust, or uncertainty
  recelo *s.* sentimiento de duda, desconfianza o temor

mitigation (mĭt-ĭ-gā′shən) *n.* lessening of something that causes suffering
  mitigación *s.* moderación de algo que causa sufrimiento

mollify (mŏl′ə-fī′) *v.* to soothe; to reduce in intensity
  aplacar *v.* calmar; apaciguar

moratorium (môr′a-tôr′ē-əm) *n.* temporary stoppage or waiting period
  moratoria *s.* aplazamiento; período de espera

motley (mŏt′lē) *adj.* composed of diverse, often mismatched elements
  abigarrado *adj.* formado por elementos diversos y dispares

multifariously (mŭl′tə-fâr′ē-əs-lē) *adv.* in many and various ways
  variadamente *adv.* de modos muy variados

mundane (mŭn-dān′) *adj.* characteristic of or concerned with the ordinary
  mundano *adj.* que se preocupa de lo ordinario

myriad (mîr′ē-əd) *adj.* exceedingly numerous
  innumerable *adj.* en excesiva cantidad

nettled (nĕt′əld) *adj.* irritated; annoyed **nettle** *v.*
  irritado *adj.* molesto; picado **irritar** *v.*

nocturnal (nŏk-tûr′nəl) *adj.* occurring at night
  nocturno *adj.* que ocurre por la noche

nominal (nŏm′ə-nəl) *adj.* in name but not in reality
  nominal *adj.* de palabra pero no de hecho

nonconformist (nŏn′kən-fôr′mĭst) *n.* one who does not follow generally accepted beliefs, customs, or practices
  inconformista *s.* el que no sigue las creencias, costumbres y prácticas acostumbradas

obstinate (ob′stə-nĭt) *adj.* hard to control or treat
  obstinado *adj.* terco; porfiado

obstreperous (ŏb-strĕp′ər-əs) *adj.* very noisy and unruly
  estrepitoso *adj.* ruidoso y revoltoso

occult (ə-kŭlt′) *adj.* secret or hidden from view
  oculto *adj.* secreto o escondido

opaque (ō-pāk′) *adj.* not allowing light to pass through
  opaco *adj.* que no deja pasar la luz

opprobrious (ə-prō′brē-əs) *adj.* scornful; derogatory
  oprobioso *adj.* despectivo; derogatorio

oscillation (ŏs′ə-lā′shən) *n.* the action of swinging back and forth
  oscilación *s.* movimiento alternativo de un lado hacia otro

ostentation (ŏs′tĕn-tā′shən) *n.* display meant to impress others; boastful showiness
  ostentación *s.* exhibición que se hace para impresionar; alarde

ostentatious (ŏs′tĕn-tā′shəs) *adj.* loud; overdone
  ostentoso *adj.* pretencioso; aparatoso

overture (ō′vər-chōōr′) *n.* the orchestral introduction to a musical dramatic work
  obertura *s.* pieza instrumental con que empieza una obra musical extensa

paradoxical (păr′ə-dŏks′-ĭ-kəl) *adj.* self-contradictory
  paradójico *adj.* que encierra una contradicción

pariah (pə-rī′ə) *n.* an outcast, someone or something looked down on by others
  paria *s.* persona a la que se considera inferior

patent (păt′nt) *adj.* obvious; apparent
  patente *adj.* obvio; aparente

patrimony (păt′rə-mō′nē) *n.* estate or money inherited from ancestors
  patrimonio *s.* propiedades o dinero heredados de los antepasados

perfidy (pûr′fĭ-dē) *n.* treachery
  perfidia *s.* traición

persecution (pûr'sĭ-kyōō'shən) *n.* the act or practice of oppressing or harassing with ill-treatment, especially because of race, religion, gender, or beliefs
　　persecución *s.* acoso con malos tratos, castigos y penas, especialmente por motivo de raza, religión, género o creencias

pertinacity (pûr'tn-ăs'ĭ-tē) *n.* stubbornness; persistence
　　pertinacia *s.* terquedad; persistencia

perturbation (pûr'tər-bā'shən) *n.* disturbance of the emotions; agitation; uneasiness
　　perturbación *s.* alteración de las emociones; agitación; inquietud

pervade (pər-vād') *v.* to spread through every part of
　　penetrar *v.* infiltrarse en todas las partes

pestilential (pĕs'tə-lĕn'shəl) *adj.* deadly; poisonous
　　pestilente *adj.* mortal; venenoso

petulance (pĕch'ə-lənsĕ) *n.* ill temper; annoyance
　　malhumor *s.* mal genio; disgusto

pigmentation (pĭg'mən-tā'shən) *n.* coloring
　　pigmentación *s.* coloración

pillage (pĭl'ĭj) *n.* the act of looting or plundering by force
　　pillaje *s.* saqueo o rapiña a la fuerza

plague (plāg) *v.* to annoy; harass
　　fastidiar *v.* molestar; acosar

poignant (poin'yənt) *adj.* physically or mentally painful
　　punzante *adj.* que causa dolor físico o mental

portend (pôr-tĕnd') *v.* to serve as an omen of; to signify
　　augurar *v.* presagiar; significar

precarious (prĭ-kâr'ē-əs) *adj.* risky; uncertain
　　precario *adj.* arriesgado; inseguro

precipitate (prĭ-sĭp'ĭ-tāt') *v.* to bring about, especially abruptly
　　precipitar *v.* causar, especialmente de repente

predecessor (prĕd'ĭ-sĕs'ər) *n.* person who precedes or comes before
　　predecesor *s.* persona que precede o viene antes

preeminently (prē-ĕm'ə-nənt-lē) *adv.* above all; most importantly
　　preeminentemente *adv.* por encima de todo; sobre todo

presaging (prĕs'ĭj-ĭng) *adj.* predicting **presage** *v.*
　　presagioso *adj.* que anuncia o presagia **presagiar** *v.*

prescience (prĕsh'əns) *n.* knowledge of events before they occur
　　presciencia *s.* conocimiento de un suceso antes de que ocurra

preternatural (prē'tər-năch'ər-əl) *adj.* supernatural
　　preternatural *adj.* sobrenatural

procure (prō-kyŏŏr') *v.* to get by special effort; to obtain
　　adquirir *v.* conseguir con un esfuerzo especial; obtener

profusion (prə-fyōō'zhən) *n.* abundance; lavishness
　　profusión *s.* abundancia; esplendidez

propitious (prə-pĭsh'əs) *adj.* helpful or advantageous; favorable
　　propicio *adj.* benéfico; favorable

propriety (prə-prī'ĭ-tē) *n.* the quality of being proper; appropriateness
　　corrección *s.* decoro; idoneidad

providence (prŏv'ĭ-dəns) *n.* an instance of divine care
　　providencia *s.* ayuda divina

prudent (prōōd'nt) *adj.* showing caution or good judgment
　　prudente *adj.* que actúa con moderación y cautela

querulous (kwĕr'ə-ləs) *adj.* complaining
　　quejumbroso *adj.* quejicoso

rabid (răb'ĭd) *adj.* unreasonably extreme; fanatical
　　rabioso *adj.* inmoderamente extremo; fanático

radiation (rā'dē-ā'shən) *n.* movement of lines or rays from a center point
　　radiación *s.* movimiento de líneas o rayos desde un punto central

raiment (rā'ment) *n.* clothing; garments
　　vestimenta *s.* ropa; indumentaria

rapt (răpt) *adj.* deeply moved, delighted, or absorbed
　　arrebatado *adj.* profundamente conmovido, extasiado o absorto

rectitude (rĕk'tĭ-tōōd') *n.* morally correct behavior or thinking
　　rectitud *s.* conducta o pensamiento justo en el sentido moral

recurrent (rĭ-kûr′ənt) *adj.* occurring time after time
    recurrente *adj.* que se repite una y otra vez

redress (rĭ-drĕs′) *n.* the correction of a wrong; compensation
    remedio *s.* reparación de un daño; compensación

relinquish (rĭ-lĭng′kwĭsh) *v.* to withdraw from; to give up
    abandonar *v.* renunciar a; ceder

remonstrate (rĭ-mŏn′strāt) *v.* to object; to protest strongly
    protestar *v.* reclamar; oponerse fuertemente

rendezvous (rän′dā-vōō) *n.* a gathering place
    lugar de reunión *s.* punto de encuentro

replenish (rĭ-plĕn′ĭsh) *v.* to fill up again
    reabastecer *v.* volver a llenar

repudiate (rĭ-pyōō′dē-āt) *v.* to reject or renounce
    repudiar *v.* rechazar o renunciar

repulse (rĭ-pŭls′) *v.* to drive back by force
    rechazar *v.* hacer retroceder a la fuerza

resign (rĭ-zīn′) *v.* to submit or adapt oneself quietly without complaint
    resignarse *v.* someterse o adaptarse sin queja

respite (rĕs′pĭt) *n.* a period of rest or relief
    respiro *s.* período de descanso o de alivio

retaliating (rĭ-tăl′ē-āt′ĭng) *n.* taking revenge **retaliate** *v.*
    vengador *s.* el que toma venganza **vengarse** *v.*

retinue (rĕt′n-ōō′) *n.* a group of attendants or followers
    séquito *s.* grupo de ayudantes o seguidores

retrospective (rĕt′rə-spĕk′tĭv) *adj.* looking back into the past
    retrospectivo *adj.* que mira al pasado

reverie (rĕv′ə-rē) *n.* daydream
    ensueño *s.* arrobamiento

scintillating (sĭn′tl-āt-ĭng) *adj.* sparkling **scintillate** *v.*
    centelleante *adj.* chispeante **centellear** *v.*

scruple (skrōō′pəl) *n.* feeling of uneasiness or guilt that keeps a person from doing something
    escrúpulo *s.* sentimiento de duda o de culpa que impide hacer algo

slovenly (slŭv′ən-lē) *adj.* untidy in personal appearance
    desaliñado *adj.* descuidado en la apariencia personal

solace (sŏl′ĭs) *n.* comfort in sorrow or distress
    solaz *s.* consuelo en el dolor o angustia

solstice (sŏl′stĭs) *n.* either of two days of the year when the sun is farthest from the celestial equator; the summer solstice is the longest day of the year, and the winter solstice is the shortest.
    solsticio *s.* uno de los dos días en que el Sol está más lejos del ecuador; el solsticio de verano es el día más largo del año y el solsticio de invierno es el más corto.

somnambulant (sŏm-năm′byə-lənt) *adj.* sleepwalking
    sonámbulo *adj.* que camina dormido

sordid (sôr′dĭd) *adj.* wretched; dirty; morally degraded
    sórdido *adj.* vil; sucio; indecente

speculating (spĕk′yə-lā′tĭng) *n.* engaging in risky business transactions on the chance of a quick or considerable profit
    especulación *s.* operaciones comerciales arriesgadas con la esperanza de obtener una ganancia rápida o considerable

subjugation (sŭb′jə-gā′shən) *n.* control by conquering
    subyugación *s.* sometimiento por la fuerza

subservient (səb-sûr′vē-ənt) *adj.* acting like a servant
    servil *adj.* que actúa como un sirviente

substantive (sŭb′stən-tĭv) *adj.* significant; with a strong basis
    sustantivo *adj.* importante, fundamental o esencial

succumb (sə-kŭm′) *v.* to give in, especially to overpowering force or strength
    sucumbir *v.* rendirse, especialmente a una fuerza mayor

summarily (sə-mĕr′ə-lē) *adv.* quickly and without ceremony
    sumariamente *adv.* rápidamente y sin ceremonia

supinely (sōō-pīn′lē) *adv.* in a manner with the face upward
    en posición supina *adv.* boca arriba

surfeit (sûr′fĭt) *n.* a fullness beyond the point of satisfaction
    hartura *s.* saciedad más allá del punto de satisfacción

synthesis (sĭn′thĭ-sĭs) *n.* union of parts or elements into a whole
    síntesis *s.* composición de un todo por la unión de sus partes

tableau (tăb′lō′) *n.* dramatic scene or picture
    cuadro *s.* escena dramática

tacitly (tăs'ĭt-lē) *adj.* silently
   tácitamente *adv.* silenciosamente

tarry (tăr'ē) *v.* to delay
   demorar *v.* tardar

temerity (tə-mĕr'ĭ-tē) *n.* foolish boldness
   temeridad *s.* imprudencia

temperament (tĕm'prə-mənt) *n.* characteristic mode of emotional response
   temperamento *s.* modo característico de respuesta emocional

tender (tĕn'dər) *v.* to offer formally
   ofrecer *v.* presentar de modo formal

tentatively (tĕn'tə-tĭv-lē) *adv.* in a hesitant or uncertain manner
   tentativamente *adv.* de modo provisional o cauteloso

tenuous (tĕn'yōō-əs) *adj.* having little substance or strength; flimsy
   tenue *adj.* débil o delicado; endeble

tranquil (trăng'kwəl) *adj.* undisturbed; peaceful
   tranquilo *adj.* quieto; sereno

transgress (trăns-grĕs') *v.* to violate a command or law
   transgredir *v.* quebrantar una orden o una ley

tremulous (trĕm'yə-ləs) *adj.* trembling; quivering
   trémulo *adj.* tembloroso

trepidation (trĕp'ĭ-dā'shən) *n.* alarm or dread
   inquietud *s.* alarma o miedo

truculent (trŭk'yə-lənt) *adj.* eager for a fight; fierce
   belicoso *adj.* agresivo; feroz

tyranny (tĭr'ə-nē) *n.* cruel and oppressive government or rule
   tiranía *s.* gobierno cruel y opresivo

unalienable (ŭn-āl'yə-nə-bəl) *adj.* not to be taken away (Today the usual form is *inalienable*.)
   inalienable *adj.* que no se puede quitar

unassailable (ŭn'ə-sā'lə-bəl) *adj.* impossible to dispute or disprove
   inexpugnable *adj.* que no se puede refutar

undulating (ŭn'jə-lā'tĭng) *adj.* appearing to move in waves undulate v.
   ondulado *adj.* con movimiento de olas ondular v.

unremitting (ŭn'rĭ-mĭt'ĭng) *adj.* constant; never stopping
   perseverante *adj.* constante; incansable

usurer (yōō'zhər-ər) *n.* one who lends money, at interest, especially at an unusually or unlawfully high rate of interest
   usurero *s.* persona que presta dinero al interés, especialmente a una tasa muy alta o ilegal

usurpation (yōō'sər-pā'shən) *n.* the act of wrongfully taking over a right or power that belongs to someone else
   usurpación *s.* apropiación indebida de un derecho o poder que pertenece a otro

vagary (vā'gə-rē) *n.* strange idea
   capricho *s.* rareza

veritable (vĕr'ĭ-tə-bəl) *adj.* true; not unreal or imaginary
   verdadero *adj.* real; auténtico

vigilant (vĭj'ə-lənt) *adj.* alert; watchful
   vigilante *adj.* alerta; atento

virulent (vîr'yə-lənt) *adj.* extremely poisonous or harmful
   virulento *adj.* sumamente venenoso o dañino

vituperative (vī-tōō'pər-ə-tĭv) *adj.* abusively critical
   injurioso *adj.* que critica de modo ofensivo

whet (hwĕt) *adj.* sharpened whet v.
   afilado *adj.* agudo afilar v.

wrangling (răng'glĭng) *adj.* arguing noisily wrangle v.
   discutidor *adj.* que disputa en voz alta discutir v.

zealous (zĕl'əs) *adj.* eager and enthusiastic
   fervoroso *adj.* dedicado y entusiasta

Pronunciation Key

Symbol	Examples		Symbol	Examples		Symbol	Examples
ă	at, gas		m	man, seem		v	van, save
ā	ape, day		n	night, mitten		w	web, twice
ä	father, barn		ng	sing, hanger		y	yard, lawyer
âr	fair, dare		ŏ	odd, not		z	zoo, reason
b	bell, table		ō	open, road, grow		zh	treasure, garage
ch	chin, lunch		ô	awful, bought, horse		ə	awake, even, pencil,
d	dig, bored		oi	coin, boy			pilot, focus
ĕ	egg, ten		ŏŏ	look, full		ər	perform, letter
ē	evil, see, meal		ōō	root, glue, through			
f	fall, laugh, phrase		ou	out, cow			**Sounds in Foreign Words**
g	gold, big		p	pig, cap		KH	*German* i**ch**, au**ch**;
h	hit, inhale		r	rose, star			*Scottish* lo**ch**
hw	white, everywhere		s	sit, face		N	*French* e**n**tre, bo**n**, fi**n**
ĭ	inch, fit		sh	she, mash		œ	*French* f**eu**, c**œu**r;
ī	idle, my, tried		t	tap, hopped			*German* sch**ö**n
îr	dear, here		th	thing, with		ü	*French* **u**tile, r**u**e;
j	jar, gem, badge		*th*	then, other			*German* gr**ü**n
k	keep, cat, luck		ŭ	up, nut			
l	load, rattle		ûr	fur, earn, bird, worm			

Stress Marks

ˈ This mark indicates that the preceding syllable receives the primary stress. For example, in the word *language*, the first syllable is stressed: lăngˈgwĭj.

ˌ This mark is used only in words in which more than one syllable is stressed. It indicates that the preceding syllable is stressed, but somewhat more weakly than the syllable receiving the primary stress. In the word *literature*, for example, the first syllable receives the primary stress, and the last syllable receives a weaker stress: lĭtˈər-ə-chŏŏrˌ.

Adapted from *The American Heritage Dictionary of the English Language,* fourth edition. Copyright © 2000 by Houghton Mifflin Company. Used with the permission of Houghton Mifflin Company.

Index of Skills

audience, 568
authors' beliefs, 1161–1170
authors' perspectives, 865
characters, 175, 261, 325, 647, 764, 887
diction, 893, 918
expressions of naturalism, 753
forms, 568, 743
imagery, 443
literary works, 41, 85, 117, 126, 658
mood, 1241
poetry, 339, 1231–1235
roles, 1212
style, 1199
texts, 241, 380, 393, 400, 451, 523, 534, 558, 691, 885,
    1070, 1120, 1135, 1142, 1157, 1190
tone, 893
voice, 1229
writers, 893
Comparison-and-contrast organization, 1076, R11–R12, R35–
    R36. *See also* Analogies; Arguments.
    point-by-point, 1076, R11, R35
    signal words for, R11
    subject-by-subject, 1076, R11, R36
Comparison-contrast essay, 1072–1079
    key traits, 1072
    options for organization, 1076
    rubric for, 1078, R35
Complements, R65
Complex sentences, 243, 284, R68
    understanding, 403–424
Compound-complex sentences, 240, 243, 284, R68
Compound sentences, R68
Comprehension. *See* Assessment; Reading skills and strategies.
Conclusions
    of an argument, 223, 235
    about characters, 131–159, 195
    deductive, R21
    drawing, 49, 59, 117, 126, 241, 272, 443, 530, 548, 558,
        658, 910, 1131, 1221, 1229, R124
    inductive, R20
    kinds of, R31
    about poetry, 339
    about point of view, 424
    about tone, 332
Conflict, 44, R107
    analysis of, 548, 735, 1137–1142
    external, 551, 759, 1137
    internal, 551, 759
    in narrative writing, 551
    plot and, 759–764, 812
    resolution of, 759
    suspense and, 551

Conjunctions
    coordinating, 666, 669, 951, 961, 994, 1001, R51, R63
    correlative, R51, R63
    run-on sentences and, R69
    subordinating, R51, R63
Connecting, 212–217, 220, 271, 381, 445, 518, 533, 560, 570,
    646, 738–743, 784, 980, 1014, 1156, 1189
    literature, history, and culture, 28–29, 306–307, 502–503,
        628–629, 834–835, 1102–1103
Connotation, 754, 812, R75, R107. *See also* Denotation.
Consonance, 1237–1241, R107
Consumer documents, R15, R124. *See also* Business writing;
    Workplace and technical writing; Workplace documents.
Content-area vocabulary. *See* Academic vocabulary; Specialized
    vocabulary.
Context clues, 427, 606, R124. *See also* Vocabulary, in context.
    general, R72
    specific, R72
    word roots and, R73
Contractions, 1213
Conventions
    dramatic, 128–129, 131, 159, 160, 175, 176, 195, 197, 209
    grammatical. *See* Grammar.
Copyright page, R44
Counterarguments, 223, 235–241, 1145–1157, 1172–1175,
    R19, R124
Creation myths, 33–41, 323, R115
Credibility, 1281, R124
Crisis. *See* Climax.
Critical analysis
    analyzing author's perspective, 575
    analyzing author's purpose, 575
    analyzing essays, 389
    analyzing photographs, 987
    analyzing primary sources, 575, 743
    analyzing tone, 987
    argument in, 1175
    deductive reasoning, R21
    evaluation, 217, 389, 987
    examining general principles, 1175
    interpreting paradox, 389
    making judgments, 389
    text features, 743
Critical listening, R87
Critical reading. *See* Reading skills and strategies; Test-taking
    strategies.
Critical thinking. *See* Critical analysis; Reading skills and strategies.
Criticism. *See* Literary criticism.
Cultural characteristics
    analysis of, 99–108, 457–471
Cultural context
    analysis of, 85, 753, 1215–1221

tragedy, 128

types of characters, 131. *See also* Character types.

verbal irony, 635

Dramatic irony, 175, 635, 735, 759, 1033, 1044, R112–R113

Dramatic monologue, 929, R108

Drawing conclusions. *See* Conclusions.

E

Editing, of film and video, 605, 1177, R91. *See also* Camera shots in film and video; Media elements and techniques.

cut, R91

dissolve, R91

fade-in, R91

fade-out, R91

jump cut, R91

montage, 597

pace, R91

parallel editing, R91

Editing, of writing. *See* Revising and editing.

Effect. *See also* Cause-and-effect organization.

unity of, 403–424

Either/or fallacy, R22, R124

Elaboration, R31

Electronic media. *See also* Multimedia presentations; References; Research.

Internet, 1271–1275

Electronic sources. *See* References; Sources.

Electronic texts, strategies for reading, R18

Elements of design, R94

Ellipses, 1078, R54

Emotional appeals, 119–126, 223, 245, R20, R94, R124

Encyclopedia, 1269, R44, R124. *See also* References.

End marks, 480, R53

English sonnet. *See* Shakespearean sonnet.

Enjambment, 329, 330, 507

Essay questions in assessment. *See* Assessment; Writing for assessment.

Essays, literary, 244, 360, 365, 370, 382, 394, 450, 518, 784, 858, 868, 1066, 1114, 1172, 1192, 1204, 1214, 1222, R109

analysis of, 358–359, 371–380, 389

personal, 1204, 1214, 1222

persuasive, 244

reflective, 360, 372, 1045

Essays, writing

analytical, 109, 333, 535, 755, 804, 911, R37–R38

autobiographical, 867, R109

cause-effect, R36

comparison-contrast, 65, 1072, R35–R36

descriptive, 61, 595, 1213, R32–R33

expository, 211, 217, 221, 473, 803, 875, 987, R35

interpretive, 755

persuasive, 275, 276–282, R38

problem-solution, 1248–1254, R37

reflective, 474–480

Etymologies, 76, 1030, 1080, R74. *See also* Word origins.

Evaluation

of ideas, 371–380

Everyday texts. *See* Consumer documents; Workplace documents.

Evidence, 223, 235—241, 1145–1157, 1172–1175, R19, R23, R39. *See also* Arguments; Support.

bias in, R23

deductive reasoning and, R21

evaluating, R23

inductive reasoning and, R20

Exclamation points, R53

Exclamatory sentences, 233, R64

Experimental poetry, 921, R109

Explanatory writing. *See* Expository writing.

Exposition. *See* Plot.

Expository essay, 211, 221, 473, 803, 875, 987, R35

Expository texts. *See* Nonfiction.

Expository writing, 987, R35–R38

analysis, 109, 211, 221, 473, 804–810, 875, R37–R38

book review, 1065

cause-effect, R36

comparison-contrast, 65, 803, 987, 1072–1079, R35–R36

eyewitness report, 1191

options for organization, R35–R38

problem-solution, 1248–1254, R37

research papers, 1284–1301

Expressive writing. *See* Narrative writing.

Extended metaphors, 111, 857, R109

Eye contact, in speeches, 283, R81

Eyewitness account, 1181–1190, R109

F

Facial expression, in speeches, 283, R81

Facts, versus opinions, R125

Fallacies, 282, R22–R23, R125

circular reasoning, 282, R22

either/or fallacy, 282, R22, R124

evading the issue, R22

false analogy, R22

false cause, 282, R22

hasty generalization, R22

name-calling, R22

non-sequitur, R22

overgeneralization, 282, R22

oversimplification, R22

stereotyping, 62–64, R22, R128

Falling action. *See* Plot.

Faulty reasoning. *See* Fallacies.

Fear, appeals to. *See* Emotional appeals.

Feedback. *See* Peer response.

Fiction, types of, R110. *See also* Folk literature.
    horror fiction, R111
    novellas, 788, R115
    novels, 452, 454, 578, 580, 688, 670, 812, 962, 978, R115
    science fiction, 1093, R119
    short stories, 310, 402, 427, 456, 580, 596, 658, 692, 710, 744, 758, 766, 790, 936, 968, 988, 1002, 1018, 1080, 1032, 1112, 1134, R119

Figurative language, 347, 371, 525, 606, 711, 1065, R72, R110
    analysis of, 111–117, 356, 1015
    distinguishing from literal meaning, 853–857
    extended metaphor, 111, 857, R109
    hyperbole, 111, 649, 659, 667, R112
    metaphor, 111, 853, R114
    onomatopoeia, 437
    paradox, 389, 534, 1193
    personification, 111, 427, 679, 687, R116
    in poetry, 347, 525

Figures of speech. *See* Figurative language.

Film reviews, 220

Films, 63, 218, 596, R90–R91. *See also* Camera shots in film and video; Editing, of film and video; Media elements and techniques.
    documentaries, 876–877
    editing. *See* Editing, of film and video.
    film clips, 63, 218, 596
    point of view in, 596–597
    script and written elements, 605, R90
    sound elements, R90
    special effects, R91
    storyboard, 605, R90
    visual elements in, R90. *See also* Camera shots in film and video; Media elements and techniques.

Firsthand and expressive writing. *See* Narrative writing.

First-person point of view. *See* Point of view.

Flashbacks, 596, 989, 1019–1029, 1106, 1137, R34, R110

Foils (character), 129, 131, 195, 1034, R110

Folk literature, 32, 42
    strategies for reading, 33–41

Foreign words in English, R75

Foreshadowing, 759–769, 1019–1029, R110

Form, in poetry, 329–332, 506–507, 509–519, 525, 847–851, 903–934, R2, R111. *See also* Poetic forms; Stanza.

Formatting
    research paper, 1301
    workplace documents, R40–R43
    works cited, 1298–1299

Forms of writing. *See* Writing skills and strategies.

Fragments. *See* Sentence fragments.

Frame story, 667, 1137, R111

Free verse, 507, 509–519, 606, 913, R111

Freewriting. *See* Quickwriting.

G

Generalizations, R125
    deductive reasoning, R21
    hasty, R22
    inductive reasoning, R20
    making, 548, 1221
    overgeneralization, R22

General principle, in argument, 1172–1175, R20–R21, R24, R125

Genre, R111. *See also* Drama; Fiction, types of; Informational texts; Media genres and types; Nonfiction, types of; Poetic forms.

Gerunds and gerund phrases, 727, 737, 812, R66

Gestures, in speeches, 283, R81

Glittering generality, R20

Glossaries, R14, R44, R76

Gothic literature, 403, 428, 1020, R111

Grammar, R50–R69. *See also* specific grammar concepts.
    assessment practice, 289, 486–487, 611, 817, 1085, 1261
    style and, 77, 87, 211, 233, 243, 327, 369, 391, 426, 444, 549, 559, 569, 669, 687, 737, 765, 787, 867, 911, 919, 961, 977, 1001, 1017, 1031, 1057, 1065, 1121, 1159, 1191, 1213

Graphic aids, R5–R7, R125
    charts, R6
    diagrams, R6
    graphs, R5
    maps, R6
    tables, R6

Graphic organizers, R125
    charts, 33, 43, 51, 75, 79, 119, 131, 212, 225, 235, 245, 252, 255, 263, 272, 311, 329, 332, 341, 345, 347, 361, 367, 380, 389, 395, 435, 509, 525, 534, 537, 548, 563, 570, 581, 635, 658, 693, 705, 745, 839, 853, 857, 859, 869, 903, 913, 929, 937, 975, 999, 1019, 1033, 1059, 1067, 1181, 1193, 1142, 1223, 1237, 1241, 1243
    compare and contrast, 117, 126, 325, 443, 519, 568, 647, 743, 865, 1142, 1161, 1229, 1231
    concept maps, 457
    diagrams, 534
    story maps or story graphs, 1255
    timelines, 989
    Venn diagrams, 41, 339, 753, 764
    webs, 159, 551, 736, 802

Greek word parts, R74 . *See also* Word roots.

Group discussion, 16, 30, 31, 69, 30, 69, 99, 225, 255, 294, 308, 311, 473, 492, 504, 509, 551, 581, 616, 635, 659, 693, 711, 839, 881, 969, 1003, 1019, 1049, 1067, 1091, 1105, 1123 1145, 1181, 1215, R85

H

Hasty generalizations, R22

Headlines, 738–743, 811, 1177–1178, R3–R4, R88, R92, R94

Hierarchical organization. *See* Order of importance.

Historical context of literature, R111

    analysis of, 69–75, 96, 284, 568, 1123–1131, 1161–1169, 1256

    influence of, 32, 44, 52, 70, 80, 90, 118, 120, 224, 226, 234, 244, 246, 254, 262, 312, 382, 392, 396, 564, 578, 650, 674, 694, 760, 846, 860, 888, 1050, 1138, 1144, 1216

    recognizing, 52, 894–895

    understanding, 68, 80, 90, 133, 212–217, 226, 246, 256, 566, 636, 670, 688, 712, 746, 792, 978, 1004, 1068, 1214

Historical documents, 234, 284, 566, R125

Historical narratives, 66–67, 68, 78, 88, 98, 100, 284, 536, 550, R111

Homographs, 648

Homonyms, R75–R76

Homophones, R76

Humor, 635, 1060, 1067, R111. *See also* Comedy; Parody; Understatement.

    analysis of, 658

Hyperbole, 111, 649, 659, R112

    analysis of, 667

Hyphens, R54

I

Iamb, 341. *See also* Blank verse; Iambic pentameter; Sonnet.

Iambic pentameter, 329, 903, R112. *See also* Blank verse; Sonnet.

Ideas. *See also* Main ideas.

    evaluating, 332, 356, 367, 371–380, 389, 927, 1256

    identifying, 859–865, 1193–1199, 1256

    tracing the development of, 1243–1246

    for writing, R26

Idioms, 1256, R72, R112

Illustrations

    analysis of, 447

Imagery, 860, R112

    analysis of, 311–325, 443, 711–735, 764, 857, 959, 1080, 1115–1121, 1131, 1166, 1241, 1243–1246

    kinesthetic, 1166

    in literary journalism, 1046

    in poetry, 347, 519, 525

Imagism, 913–918

Imperative sentences, 228, 233, 444

Indefinite pronouns, R58

Independent (main) clauses, R66

Independent observation, R47

Independent reading

    ideas for, 290–291, 488–489, 612–613, 818–819, 1086–1087, 1262–1263

Indexes, 1269, 1270, 1274, 1277, R44, R125. *See also* References.

Indirect objects, R65

Inductive reasoning, R20–R21, R125

Inferences, making, 195, 241, 380, 435, 534, 593, 703, 812, 840, 865, 910, 913–918, 1080, 1131, 1221, 1229, R125

    about authors, 263–272

    about characters, 667, 969–975

    about historical context, 96

    about poetry, 341–345, 356, 437–443

Infinitives and infinitive phrases, 911, 1080, R65

Informal language 859, 1208, 1213, R72, R80. *See also* Slang.

Informal speech, 221

Information. *See* Electronic media; Informational texts; Reading for information; References; Sources.

Informational texts, 212, 214, 274, 381, 738, 740, 741, 1256, R3–R18, R126. *See also* Nonfiction; Public documents; Reading for information.

    forms, R13–R18

    patterns of organization, R8–R12

    text features, R3–R7

Informative articles. *See* News articles; Reading for information.

Interjections, R51, R64

Internal conflict, 551, 759, 1137

Internal rhyme, 437, 482

Internet, 1271–1275, R46. *See also* Electronic media; References; Web sites.

Interrogative sentences, 228, 233, 391, R64

Interviews, R112

    conducting, 51, 481, R47, R86

    evaluating, R86

    following up on, R86

    oral histories, R47

    preparing for, 481

    as research source, 1269, R47

    responding to, R86

Intransitive verbs, R51

Introductions, R28

Inverted sentences, 211, R71

Inverted syntax, 111–117, R112

Irony, 175, 325, 471, 635–647, 882, 1033–1044, 1080, R112–R113

    dramatic, 175, 635, 735, 759, 1033, 1044, R112–R113

    situational, 635, 759, 1033, R112, R119

    verbal, 195, 471, 635, 719, R111, R113, R118

Issues

    evading, as logical fallacy, R22

Italics, R54.

M

Peer response, 282, 480, 604, 810, 1077, 1303, R28
Performing arts. *See* Drama.
Periodicals, R45
    evaluating, as source, 1276
Periods (punctuation), R53
Personal essay, 1205–1212
Personification, 111, 427, 679, 687, 893, 1246, R116
Perspective. *See also* Point of view.
    author's, 67, 118, 395–400, 568, 575, 647, 685, 745–753,
        845, 869–874, 1190, 1212, R105
    in autobiography, 263
    in journalism, 1047
    in painting, 707
Persuasion. *See* Persuasive techniques.
Persuasive speeches
    reading, 225–231
Persuasive techniques, 222–223, 231, 245–252, 284, 965–967,
        1157, R20, R23. See also Appeals; Arguments.
    in advertising, 964–967, R94
    appeals by association, 245, 964–966, R20
    appeals to authority, 245
    appeals to loyalty, R20
    appeals to pity, fear, or vanity, 119, R20
    bandwagon appeals, R20, R94
    celebrity ads, R94
    emotional appeals, 223, 245, R20, R94
    ethical appeals, 223, 245
    evidence, R23
    glittering generalities, R20
    loaded language, R23
    logical appeal, 222, R94
    product comparisons, R94
    propaganda, R23
    purr words, 965
    slogans, 965, R94
    snob appeal, R20
    testimonial, R20
    transfer, 965, R20
Persuasive texts, 224, 244, 1192, R116.
    strategies for reading, R19–R24
Persuasive writing, R38–R39. *See also* Arguments.
    arguments, 1031, 1159
    editorial, 1201
    essays, 276–282, 1121
    key techniques, R39
    key traits, 276, 1031
    letter, 275
    options for organization, 280, R39
    rhetorical devices for, 233
    rubric for, 282, R38
    speeches, 233

Photographs
    analysis of, 707, 709, 980–987
    as primary sources, 980–987
Phrases
    adjective, 482, R65
    adverb, 83, 87, R65
    appositive, R65
    gerund, 727, 737, 812, R66
    infinitive, 911, R65
    participial, 407, 426, 482, 1017, R66
    prepositional, 74, 77, 284, 1078, R65
    verbal, 407, 426, 482, 727, 737, 812, 911, 1017, R65, R66
Plagiarism, 1279–1280. *See also* Works cited.
Planned drafting, R26
Plays. *See* Drama.
Plot, 759–764, R116–R117
    climax of, 128, 759, R2, R107
    conflict and, 759–764, 812
    in drama, 128
    exposition, 128, R2, R109
    falling action, 128, R2, R110
    foreshadowing and, 759
    in narrative poetry, 903
    resolution, 128, 759, R2, R110
    rising action, 128, R2, R118
    stages of, 128, R2, R116–R117
Poetic devices and elements. *See also* Poetic forms.
    alliteration, 437, 482, 1237–1241, R104
    assonance, 1237–1241, R105
    couplet, 847, R120
    enjambment, 329, 330, 507
    extended metaphor, 111, 857, R109
    figurative language, 347, 371, 525, 606, 711, 1065, R72,
        R110
    form, 329–332, 506–507, 509–519, 525, 847–851, 903–
        934, R2, R111
    hyperbole, 111, 649, 659, R112
    imagery, 347, 519, 525
    internal rhyme, 437, 482
    line breaks, 903, 918
    lines, 506–507, R113
    metaphor, 111, 339, 451, 853, 918, R114
    meter, 335, 341–345, 347, 482, 506–507, 847, 881, R114
    mood, 347–356
    onomatopoeia, 437, 482, R115
    personification, 111, 427, 679, 687, 893, 1246, R116
    quatrain, 348, 525, R117
    refrain, 839, R118
    repetition, 339, 437, 482, 509, 606, 711, 839–845, 994,
        1001
    rhyme, 335–339, 347, 437, 847, 902, R118
    rhyme scheme, 335–339

Page numbers that appear in italics refer to biographical information.

ACKNOWLEDGMENTS

UNIT 1

American Anthropological Association: "The World on the Turtle's Back," from *The Great Tree and the Longhouse: The Culture of the Iroquois* (pp. 12–19) by Hazel W. Hertzberg. Copyright © 1966 American Anthropological Association. Reproduced by permission of the American Anthropological Association. Not for sale or further reproduction.

University of Nebraska Press: "Coyote and the Buffalo," from *Coyote Stories* by Mourning Dove. Collected in *Masterpieces of American Indian Literature.* Published by the University of Nebraska Press. Reprinted by permission.

N. Scott Momaday: Excerpt from *The Way to Rainy Mountain* by N. Scott Momaday. Copyright © N. Scott Momaday. Reprinted by permission of the author.

Scribner: From *Cabeza De Vaca's Adventures in the Unknown Interior of America,* translated and annotated by Cyclone Covey. Copyright © 1961 Macmillan Publishing Company. Reprinted with the permission of Scribner, an imprint of Simon & Schuster Adult Publishing Group.

University of North Carolina Press: From *The Complete Works of Captain John Smith, 1580–1631,* edited by Philip L. Barbour, with a foreword by Thad W. Tate. Published for the Omohundro Institute of Early American History and Culture. Copyright © 1986 by the University of North Carolina Press. Used by permission of the publisher.

Alfred A. Knopf: Excerpts from *Of Plymouth Plantation, 1620–1647* by William Bradford, edited by Samuel Eliot Morison. Copyright 1952 by Samuel Eliot Morison and renewed 1980 by Emily M. Beck. Used by permission of Alfred A. Knopf, a division of Random House, Inc. For on-line information about other Random House, Inc., books and authors, see the Internet Web site at http://www.randomhouse.com.

Viking Penguin: *The Crucible* by Arthur Miller. Copyright 1952, 1953, 1954, renewed © 1980, 1981, 1982 by Arthur Miller. Used by permission of Viking Penguin, a division of Penguin Group (USA) Inc.

Thirteen/WNET New York: "McCarthyism." Courtesy Thirteen/WNET New York.

New York Times: From "The Demons of Salem, With Us Still" by Victor Navasky, the *New York Times,* September 8, 1996. Copyright © 1996 by the New York Times Co. Reprinted with permission.

Grove/Atlantic: Excerpt from *Timebends* by Arthur Miller. Copyright © 1987 by Arthur Miller. Used by permission of Grove/Atlantic, Inc.

Rolling Stone: From "The Crucible (film review)" by Peter Travers, *Rolling Stone,* December 12, 1996. © Rolling Stone LLC 1996. All rights reserved. Reprinted by permission.

U.S. News & World Report: "50 Ways to Fix Your Life" by Carolyn Kleiner Butler, *U.S. News & World Report,* January 3, 2005. Copyright © 2005 U.S. News & World Report, L.P. Reprinted with permission.

UNIT 2

Cynthia G. La Ferle: From "Thoreau Still Beckons, if I Can Take My Laptop" by Cynthia G. La Ferle, the *Christian Science Monitor,* October 3, 1997. Copyright © 1997 by Cynthia G. La Ferle. Reprinted by permission of the author.

Navajivan Trust: Excerpt from "Readiness for Satyagraha" by Mahatma Gandhi, from *The Essential Writings of Mahatma Gandhi,* edited by Raghavan Iyer. Published by Oxford University Press. Reprinted by permission of the Navajivan Trust.

Stephen King: Excerpt from *Danse Macabre* by Stephen King. Copyright © Stephen King. All rights reserved. Reprinted with permission.

UNIT 3

Harvard University Press: Excerpt from "My life closed twice before its close—" by Emily Dickinson. Reprinted by permission of the publishers and the Trustees of Amherst College from *The Poems of Emily Dickinson,* Thomas H. Johnson, ed., Cambridge, Mass.: The Belknap Press of Harvard University Press, Copyright 1951, 1955, 1979, 1983 by the President and Fellows of Harvard College.

Agencia Literaria Carmen Balcells and Didier Tisdel Jaén: "Ode to Walt Whitman" by Pablo Neruda, translated by Didier Tisdel Jaén. Published in *Nuevas odas elementales* and *Homage to Walt Whitman: A Collection of Poems from the Spanish.* © Fundación Pablo Neruda, 1956. Translation copyright © Didier Tisdel Jaén. Used by permission of Agencia Literaria Carmen Balcells, S. A., and Didier Tisdel Jaén.

Harvard University Press: "Because I could not stop for Death—" by Emily Dickinson. Reprinted by permission of the publishers and the Trustees of Amherst College from *The Poems of Emily Dickinson,* Thomas H. Johnson, ed., Cambridge, Mass.: The Belknap Press of Harvard University Press, Copyright © 1951, 1955, 1979 by the President and Fellows of Harvard College.

"Success is counted sweetest" by Emily Dickinson. Reprinted by permission of the publishers and the Trustees of Amherst College from *The Poems of Emily Dickinson,* Thomas H. Johnson, ed., Cambridge, Mass.: The Belknap Press of Harvard University Press, Copyright © 1951, 1955, 1979, 1983 by the President and Fellows of Harvard College.

"Much Madness is divinest Sense—" by Emily Dickinson. Reprinted by permission of the publishers and the Trustees of Amherst College from *The Poems of Emily Dickinson,* Thomas H. Johnson, ed., Cambridge, Mass.: The Belknap Press of Harvard University Press, Copyright © 1951, 1955, 1979, 1983 by the President and Fellows of Harvard College.

"My life closed twice before its close—" by Emily Dickinson. Reprinted by permission of the publishers and the Trustees of Amherst College from *The Poems of Emily Dickinson,* Thomas H. Johnson, ed., Cambridge, Mass.: The Belknap Press of Harvard University Press, Copyright © 1951, 1955, 1979, 1983 by the President and Fellows of Harvard College.

"The Soul selects her own Society" by Emily Dickinson. Reprinted by permission of the publishers and the Trustees of Amherst College from *The Poems of Emily Dickinson,* Thomas H. Johnson, ed., Cambridge, Mass.: The Belknap Press of Harvard University Press, Copyright 1951, 1955, 1979, 1983 by the President and Fellows of Harvard College.

"I heard a Fly buzz—when I died—" by Emily Dickinson. Reprinted by permission of the publishers and the Trustees of Amherst College from *The Poems of Emily Dickinson,* Thomas H. Johnson, ed., Cambridge, Mass.: The Belknap Press of Harvard University Press, Copyright © 1951, 1955, 1979 by the President and Fellows of Harvard College.

"My Life had stood—a Loaded Gun—" by Emily Dickinson. Reprinted by permission of the publishers and the Trustees of Amherst College from *The Poems of Emily Dickinson,* Thomas H. Johnson, ed., Cambridge, Mass.: The Belknap Press of Harvard University Press, Copyright © 1951, 1955, 1979, 1983 by the President and Fellows of Harvard College.

"Letter to Thomas Wentworth Higginson, April 16, 1862" by Emily Dickinson. Reprinted by permission of the publishers from *Letters of Emily Dickinson,* Thomas H. Johnson, ed., Cambridge, Mass.: The Belknap Press of Harvard University Press, Copyright © 1958, 1986, The President and Fellows of Harvard College; 1914, 1924, 1932, 1942 by Martha Dickinson Bianchi; 1952 by Alfred Leete Hampson; 1960 by Mary L. Hampson.

Scribner: "Letter to His Son, January 1861," by Robert E. Lee, from *R.E. Lee: A Biography* by Douglas Southall Freeman. Copyright © 1934, 1935 by Charles Scribner's Sons; copyright renewed © 1962, 1963 by Inez Goddin Freeman. Reprinted with the permission of Scribner, an imprint of Simon & Schuster Adult Publishing Group.

Thunder's Mouth Press: From "Letter, July 14, 1861, by Sullivan Ballou, from the book *For Love & Liberty: The Untold Civil War Story of Major Sullivan Ballou & His Famous Love Letter* by Robin Young. Copyright © 2003. Appears by permission of the publisher, Thunder's Mouth Press, A Division of Avalon Publishing Group.

UNIT 4

HarperCollins Publishers: From *The Autobiography of Mark Twain,* edited by Charles Neider. Copyright © 1917, 1940, 1958, 1959 by the Mark Twain Company, renewed 1987. Copyright 1924, 1945, 1952 by Clara Clemens Samossoud. Copyright © 1959 by Charles Neider, renewed 1987. Reprinted by permission of HarperCollins Publishers.

Viking Penguin: "Sumus Quod Sumus," from *Lake Wobegone Days* by Garrison Keillor. Copyright © 1985 by Garrison Keillor. Used by permission of Viking Penguin, a division of Penguin Group (USA) Inc.

UNIT 5

Alfred A. Knopf and Harold Ober Associates: "Harlem," from *The Collected Poems of Langston Hughes* by Langston Hughes. Copyright © 1994 by the Estate of Langston Hughes. Used by permission of Alfred A. Knopf, a division of Random House, Inc., and Harold Ober Associates Incorporated.

"The Negro Speaks of Rivers," from *The Collected Poems of Langston Hughes* by Langston Hughes. Copyright © 1994 by the Estate of Langston Hughes. Used by permission of Alfred A. Knopf, a division of Random House, Inc., and Harold Ober Associates Incorporated.

"I, Too," from *The Collected Poems of Langston Hughes* by Langston Hughes. Copyright © 1994 by the Estate of Langston Hughes. Used by permission of Alfred A. Knopf, a division of Random House, Inc., and Harold Ober Associates Incorporated.

"The Weary Blues," from *The Collected Poems of Langston Hughes* by Langston Hughes. Copyright © 1994 by the Estate of Langston Hughes. Used by permission of Alfred A. Knopf, a division of Random House, Inc., and Harold Ober Associates Incorporated.

Viking Penguin: "My City," from *Saint Peter Relates an Incident* by James Weldon Johnson. Copyright 1935 by James Weldon Johnson, © renewed 1963 by Grace Nail Johnson. Used by permission of Viking Penguin, a division of Penguin Group (USA) Inc.

Schomburg Center for Research in Black Culture: "If We Must Die" by Claude McKay. Courtesy of the Literary Representative for the Works of Claude McKay, Schomburg Center for Research in Black Culture, the New York Public Library, Astor, Lenox and Tilden Foundations.

GRM Associates: "Any Human to Another," from *The Medea and Some Poems* by Countee Cullen. Copyright 1936 by Harper and Brothers, copyright © renewed 1963 by Ida M. Cullen. Reprinted by permission of GRM Associates, Inc.

Liveright Publishing Corporation: "Storm Ending," from *Cane* by Jean Toomer. Copyright 1923 by Boni & Liveright, renewed 1951 by Jean Toomer. Used by permission of Liveright Publishing Corporation.

Harold Ober Associates: "A Black Man Talks of Reaping," from *Personals* by Arna Bontemps. Copyright © 1963 by Arna Bontemps. Reprinted by permission of Harold Ober Associates Incorporated.

Victoria Sanders & Associates: "How It Feels to Be Colored Me" by Zora Neale Hurston. Used with the permission of the Zora Neale Hurston Trust.

Doubleday: "Thoughts on the African-American Novel" by Toni Morrison, from *Black Women Writers,* edited by Mari Evans. Copyright © 1983 by Mari Evans. Used by permission of Doubleday, a division of Random House, Inc.

Harcourt: "Chicago," and "Grass," from *Chicago Poems* by Carl Sandburg. Copyright 1916 by Holt, Rinehart and Winston and renewed 1944 by Carl Sandburg. Reprinted by permission of Harcourt, Inc. This material may not be reproduced in any form or by any means without the prior written permission of the publisher.

Henry Holt and Company: "Acquainted with the Night" by Robert Frost, from *The Poetry of Robert Frost,* edited by Edward Connery Lathem. Copyright 1928, 1930, © 1969 by Henry Holt and , copyright 1944, 1951, 1956, 1958 by Robert Frost, copyright © 1967 by Lesley Frost Ballantine. Reprinted by permission of Henry Holt and Company, LLC.

"Nothing Gold Can Stay" by Robert Frost, from *The Poetry of Robert Frost,* edited by Edward Connery Lathem. Copyright 1928, 1930, 1969 by Henry Holt and , copyright 1944, 1951, 1956, 1958 by Robert Frost, copyright © 1967 by Lesley Frost Ballantine. Reprinted by permission of Henry Holt and Company, LLC.

"Out, Out—" by Robert Frost, from *The Poetry of Robert Frost,* edited by Edward Connery Lathem. Copyright 1928, 1930, 1969 by Henry Holt and , copyright 1944, 1951, 1956, 1958 by Robert Frost, copyright © 1967 by Lesley Frost Ballantine. Reprinted by permission of Henry Holt and Company, LLC.

"The Death of the Hired Man" by Robert Frost, from *The Poetry of Robert Frost,* edited by Edward Connery Lathem. Copyright 1928, 1930, 1969 by Henry Holt and , copyright 1944, 1951, 1956, 1958 by Robert Frost, copyright © 1967 by Lesley Frost Ballantine. Reprinted by permission of Henry Holt and Company, LLC.

New Directions Publishing Corporation: "Helen," from *Collected Poems, 1912–1944* by HD (Hilda Doolittle). Copyright © 1982 by the Estate of Hilda Doolittle. Reprinted by permission of New Directions Publishing Corp.

"In a Station of the Metro," from *Personae* by Ezra Pound. Copyright © 1926 by Ezra Pound. Reprinted by permission of New Directions Publishing Corp.

"Spring and All, Section I," and "This is Just to Say," from *Collected Poems, 1909–1939, Volume I* by William Carlos Williams. Copyright © 1938 by New Directions Publishing Corp. Reprinted by permission of New Directions Publishing Corp.

Liveright Publishing Corporation: "anyone lived in a pretty how town," from *Complete Poems: 1904–1962* by E. E. Cummings, edited by George J. Firmage. Copyright 1940, © 1968, 1991 by the Trustees for the E. E. Cummings Trust. Used by permission of Liveright Publishing Corporation. This selection may not be reproduced, stored in a retrieval system, or transmitted in any form or by any means without the prior written permission of the publisher. For more information about W. W. Norton/Liveright titles, please visit www.wwnorton.com.

Scribner: "Poetry," from *The Collected Poems of Marianne Moore* by Marianne Moore. Copyright © 1935 by Marianne Moore, copyright renewed © 1963 by Marianne Moore and T. S. Eliot. Reprinted with the permission of Scribner, an imprint of Simon & Schuster Adult Publishing Group.

Elizabeth Barnett, Literary Executor: "Recuerdo" by Edna St. Vincent Millay. From *Collected Poems,* HarperCollins. Copyright © 1922, 1950 by Edna St. Vincent Millay. All rights reserved. Used by permission of Elizabeth Barnett, Literary Executor.

Faber and Faber: "The Love Song of J. Alfred Prufrock," from *Collected Poems, 1909–1962* by T. S. Eliot. Reprinted by permission of Faber and Faber Limited.

Scribner: From *The Great Gatsby* by F. Scott Fitzgerald. Copyright 1925 by Charles Scribner's Sons. Copyright renewed 1953 by Frances Scott Fitzgerald Lanahan. Reprinted with permission of Scribner, an imprint of Simon & Schuster Adult Publishing Group.

"In Another Country," from *Men Without Women* by Ernest Hemingway. Copyright 1927 Charles Scribner's Sons. Copyright renewed 1955 by Ernest Hemingway. Reprinted with permission of Scribner, an imprint of Simon & Schuster Adult Publishing Group.

Viking Penguin: From *The Grapes of Wrath* by John Steinbeck. Copyright 1939, renewed © 1967 by John Steinbeck. Used by permission of Viking Penguin, a division of Penguin Group (USA) Inc.

Time Inc.: "The Grapes of Wrath: Photo Essay," *Life,* 5 June 1939. Copyright 1939 Time Inc. Reprinted with permission.

Harcourt: "The Jilting of Granny Weatherall," from *Flowering Judas and Other Stories* by Katherine Anne Porter. Copyright 1930 and renewed 1958 by Katherine Anne Porter. Reprinted by permission of Harcourt, Inc. This material may not be reproduced in any form or by any means without prior written permission of the publisher.

"A Worn Path," from *A Curtain of Green and Other Stories* by Eudora Welty. Copyright 1941 and renewed 1969 by Eudora Welty. Reprinted by permission of Harcourt, Inc. This material may not be reproduced in any form or by any means without prior written permission of the publisher.

Harvard University Press: Reprinted by permission of the publisher from *One Writer's Beginnings* by Eudora Welty, pp. 99–100, Cambridge, Mass: Harvard Universiry Press, Copyright © 1983, 1984 by Eudora Welty.

Random House: "A Rose for Emily," from *Collected Stories of William Faulkner* by William Faulkner. Copyright 1930 and renewed 1958 by William Faulkner. Used by permission of Random House, Inc.

Harcourt: "The Life You Save May Be Your Own," from *A Good Man Is Hard to Find and Other Stories* by Flannery O'Connor. Copyright 1953 by Flannery O'Connor and renewed 1981 by Regina O'Connor. Reprinted by permission of Harcourt, Inc. This material may not be reproduced in any form or by any means without prior written permission of the publisher.

Scribner: "A New Kind of War" by Ernest Hemingway, from *By-Line: Ernest Hemingway,* edited by William White. Copyright 1937 by New York Times and North American Newspaper Alliance, Inc. Copyright © renewed 1965 by Mary Hemingway, By-Line Ernest Hemingway, Inc., and the New York Times Company.

Viking Penguin: "A Book of Great Short Stories," from *The Portable Dorothy Parker* by Dorothy Parker, edited by Brendan Gill. Copyright 1927, renewed © 1955 by Dorothy Parker. Used by permission of Viking Penguin, a division of Penguin Group (USA) Inc.

Allene White: "The Duty of Writers," from *One Man's Meat* by E. B. White. Copyright 1939 by E. B. White. Reprinted by permission of Allene White.

UNIT 6

Barbara Hogenson Agency: From *Our Town* by Thornton Wilder. Copyright © 1938 The Thornton Wilder Family, LLC. Reprinted by permission of the Barbara Hogenson Agency.

Georges Borchardt: From *The Glass Menagerie* by Tennessee Williams. Copyright © 1945 by the University of the South and Edwin D. Williams. Reprinted by permission of Georges Borchardt, Inc.

Viking Penguin: From *Death of a Salesman* by Arthur Miller. Copyright 1949, renewed © 1977 by Arthur Miller. Used by permission of Viking Penguin, a division of Penguin Group (USA) Inc.

Random House: From *A Raisin in the Sun* by Lorraine Hansberry. Copyright © 1958 by Robert Nemiroff, as an unpublished work. Copyright © 1959, 1966, 1984 by Robert Nemiroff. Copyright renewed 1986, 1987 by Robert Nemiroff. Used by permission of Random House, Inc.

Viking Penguin: "Symptoms," from *Once There Was a War* by John Steinbeck. Copyright 1943, 1958 by John Steinbeck. Renewed © 1971 by Elaine Steinbeck, John Steinbeck IV, and Thomas Steinbeck. Used by permission of Viking Penguin, a division of Penguin Group (USA) Inc.

Farrar, Straus and Giroux: "The Death of the Ball Turret Gunner," from *The Complete Poems* by Randall Jarrell. Copyright © 1969, renewed 1997 by Mary von S. Jarrell. Reprinted by permission of Farrar, Straus and Giroux, LLC. Caution: Users are warned that this work is protected under copyright laws and downloading is strictly prohibited. The right to reproduce or transfer the work via any medium must be secured with Farrar, Straus and Giroux, LLC.

Dell Publishing: "Adam," from *Welcome to the Monkey House* by Kurt Vonnegut Jr. Copyright 1954 by Kurt Vonnegut Jr. Used by permission of Dell Publishing, a division of Random House, Inc.

Viking Penguin: From *If This Is a Man (Survival in Auschwitz)* by Primo Levi, translated by Stuart Woolf. Translation copyright © 1959 by Orion Press Inc., © 1958 by Guilio Einaudi editore SpA. Used by permission of Viking Penguin, a division of Penguin Group (USA) Inc.

Houghton Mifflin Company/Seymour Lawrence: "Ambush," from *The Things They Carried* by Tim O'Brien. Copyright © 1990 by Tim O'Brien. Reprinted by permission of Houghton Mifflin Company/Seymour Lawrence. All rights reserved.

Writers House: "Letter from Birmingham Jail" by Martin Luther King Jr. Copyright 1963 Martin Luther King Jr., copyright renewed 1991 Coretta Scott King. Reprinted by arrangement with the Estate of Martin Luther King Jr., c/o Writers House as agent for the proprietor New York, NY.

Broadside Press: "Ballad of Birmingham," from *Cities Burning* by Dudley Randall. By permission of Broadside Press.

Writers House: From *Stride Toward Freedom* by Martin Luther King Jr. Copyright 1958 Martin Luther King Jr., copyright renewed 1986 Coretta Scott King. Reprinted by arrangement with the Estate of Martin Luther King Jr., c/o Writers House as agent for the proprietor New York, NY.

Pathfinder Press: "Necessary to Protect Ourselves" by Malcolm X, from *Malcolm X: The Last Speeches,* edited by Bruce Perry. Copyright © 1989 Betty Shabazz, Bruce Perry, Pathfinder Press. All rights reserved. Reprinted by permission of Pathfinder Press.

Doubleday: Excerpt from *Coming of Age in Mississippi* by Anne Moody. Copyright © 1968 by Anne Moody. Used by permission of Doubleday, a division of Random House, Inc. For online information about other Random House, Inc., books and authors, see the Internet Web site at http://www.randomhouse.com.

HarperCollins Publishers: "Revolutionary Dreams," from *The Women and the Men* by Nikki Giovanni. Copyright © 1971, 1974, 1975 by Nikki Giovanni. Reprinted by permission of HarperCollins Publishers.

James Baldwin Estate: "My Dungeon Shook: Letter to My Nephew on the One Hundredth Anniversary of the Emancipation" by James Baldwin. Copyright © 1962 by James Baldwin. Copyright renewed. Originally published in *The Progressive.* Collected in *The Fire Next Time,* published by Vintage Books. Reprinted by arrangement with the James Baldwin Estate.

Sandra Dijkstra Literary Agency: "Mother Tongue" by Amy Tan. Copyright © 1990 by Amy Tan. First appeared in *The Threepenny Review.* Reprinted by permission of the author and the Sandra Dijkstra Literary Agency.

Harcourt: Excerpt from "In Search of Our Mothers' Gardens," in *In Search of Our Mothers' Gardens: Womanist Prose* by Alice Walker. Copyright © 1974 by Alice Walker. Reprinted by permission of Harcourt, Inc.

"Women," from *Revolutionary Petunias & Other Poems* by Alice Walker. Copyright © 1970 and renewed 1998 by Alice Walker. Reprinted by permission of Harcourt, Inc. This material may not be reproduced in any form or by any means without prior written permission of the publisher.

Susan Bergholz Literary Services: "Straw Into Gold" by Sandra Cisneros. Copyright © 1987 by Sandra Cisneros. First published in the *Texas Observer,* September 1987. Reprinted by permission of Susan Bergholz Literary Services, New York. All rights reserved.

Brooks Permissions: "Life for My Child Is Simple," and "Primer for Blacks" by Gwendolyn Brooks. Reprinted by consent of Brooks Permissions.

Rita Dove: "Adolescence–III," from *The Yellow House on the Corner* by Rita Dove. Carnegie Mellon University Press. Copyright © 1980 by Rita Dove. Reprinted by permission of the author.

"Testimonial," from *On the Bus with Rosa Parks* by Rita Dove. W. W. Norton and Company. First published in *Poetry* magazine, January 1998. Copyright © 1999 by Rita Dove. Reprinted by permission of the author.

University of Pittsburgh Press: "Forgetfulness," and "The Man in the Moon," from *Questions About Angels* by Billy Collins. Copyright © 1991, Billy Collins. Reprinted by permission of the University of Pittsburgh Press.

UNIT 7

Los Angeles Times: From " 'Grapes of Wrath' Author Guards Self From Threats at Moody Gulch" by Tom Cameron, *Los Angeles Times,* July 9, 1939. Copyright ©, 1939, *Los Angeles Times.* Reprinted with permission.

STUDENT RESOURCE BANK

R5: Excerpt from "History of the National Weather Service," from the Random House Web site (http://www.randomhouse.com/features/isaacsstorm/science/history.html). Copyright © 1999 by Random House, Inc. Used by permission of Random House, Inc.

R13: Adapted from "Katrina's South American Sister," from *Best Friends Magazine,* November/December 2005. Copyright © 2005 by Best Friends Animal Society. Adapted with permission.

R74: word definition: ambasador. Copyright © 2006 by Houghton Mifflin Company. Reproduced by permission from *The American Heritage Dictionary of the English Language, Fourth Edition.*

R74: word definition: community. Copyright © 2006 by Houghton Mifflin Company. Reproduced by permission from *The American Heritage Dictionary of the English Language, Fourth Edition.*

ART CREDITS

CONSULTANTS

Title page © Brand X Pictures; Photo © Duane McCubrey; Photo © Mark Schmidt; Photo © Bruce Forrester; Photo © McDougal Littell; Photo © Howard Gollub; Photo © Tamra Stallings; Photo © Mark Schmidt; Photo © Robert J. Marzano; Photo © McDougal Littell; Photo © Dawson & Associates Photography; Photo © Gitchell's Studio; Photo © Michael Romeo; Photo © Monica Ani; Photo © William McBride; Photo © Bill Caldwell; Photo © Gabriel Pauluzzi; Photo © Steven Scheffler. **California Teacher Advisory Panel** McDougal Littell In-House Art except *Jordana Benone* © Lifetouch School Portraits/Lifetouch National School Studios; *Linda Valdez* Photo by Linda Valdez; *Lynda Zimmerman* Photo by Lynda Zimmerman.

TABLE OF CONTENTS

Unit 1 verso *left, right* The Granger Collection, New York; **recto** © PunchStock; **Unit 2 verso** *left* © Gary Kelley, 1996; *right* © Gail Mooney/Masterfile; **recto** © PunchStock; **Unit 3 verso** *left* The Granger Collection, New York; *right* © Martin Rogers/Getty Images; **recto** © PunchStock; **Unit 4 verso** *left* © Bettmann/Corbis; *right* © Juniors Bildarchiv/age fotostock america, inc; **recto** © PunchStock; **Unit 5 verso** *left, Autoportrait* (1925), Tamara De Lempicka. Oil on wood, 35 cm × 26 cm. Private collection. © 2007 Artists Rights Society (ARS), New York/ADAGP, Paris; *right, The Cotton Club in Harlem, New York* (1930). Black and white photograph. Private collection. © Bridgeman Art Library; **recto** © PunchStock; **Unit 6 verso** *left, Thinking* (1990), Carlton Murrell. Oil on board. Private collection. © Bridgeman Art Library; *right* The Granger Collection, New York; **recto** © PunchStock; **Unit 7** *left* Cover of *The Grapes of Wrath* by John Steinbeck. © 1939 by John Steinbeck. Reprinted by permission of Penguin Books, a division of the Penguin Group (USA), Inc., 375 Hudson Street, New York, New York 10014. All rights reserved.; Cover photo: The Granger Collection, New York; *right* © Design Pics, Inc./Alamy Images; *inset right* © Bettmann/Corbis; **CA40** Pixtal/Punchstock.

INTRODUCTORY UNIT

xxxvi *top* The Granger Collection, New York; *center* © Images.com/Corbis; *bottom* Library of Congress; **1** *top left, Kindred Spirits* (1849), Asher Brown Durand. © Francis G. Mayer/Corbis; *top right* © Bettmann/Corbis; *bottom* © 20th Century Fox Film Corp. All rights reserved/Courtesy The Everett Collection; **2** *left, The Mayflower in Plymouth Harbor* (1882), William Formby Halsall. © Pilgrim Hall Museum, Plymouth, Massachusetts; *right* Library of Congress; **3** *left* © Reza Estakhrian/Getty Images; *right* © James P. Blair/National Geographic Image Collection; **4** *left to right* © Bettmann/Corbis; © Richard T. Nowitz/Corbis; *The Bloody Massacre perpetrated in...Boston on March 5th, 1770* (1770), Paul Revere. Colored engraving. Private collection. © Art Resource, New York; © Gary Kelley, 1996; *Wanderer Above a Sea of Fog* (1817), Casper David Friedrich. Oil on canvas, 94.8 cm × 74.8 cm. Inv.: 5161. On permanent loan from the Foundation for the Promotion of the Hamburg Art Collections. Hamburger Kunsthalle, Hamburg, Germany. Photo by Elke Walford. © Bildarchiv Preussischer Kulturbesitz/Art Resource, New York; **5** *left to right* © New York Public Library, Schomburg Center; Library of Congress; © Hulton-Deutsch Collection/Corbis; *Street Shadows* (1959), Jacob Lawrence. Egg tempera on hardboard, 24″ × 30″. Private collection, New York. Photograph courtesy of Gwendolyn Knight Lawrence/Art Resource, New York. © 2007 The Jacob and Gwendolyn Lawrence Foundation, Seattle/Artists Rights Society (ARS), New York; *The Green Machine* (1977), Frank Dahmer. Screenprint on paper, 13½″ × 17¼″. © National Vietnam Veterans Art Museum; **6** *Top to bottom* Cover of *The Great Gatsby* by F. Scott Fitzgerald. © 1980 by Charles Scribner's Sons. Reprinted by permission of Simon & Schuster, New York, Cover photo: The Granger Collection, New York; © Historical Picture Archive/Corbis; © Culver Pictures/The Art Archive; *Autoportrait* (about 1925), Tamara de Lempicka. Oil on wood, 35 cm × 26 cm. Private collection. © 2007 Artists Rights Society (ARS), New York/ADAGP, Paris; **8** © Culver Pictures/The Art Archive; **10** *top left* © Time & Life Images/Getty Images; *top right* © Eve Arnold/Magnum Photos; *center* © Randy Faris/Corbis; *bottom* © 20th Century Fox Film Corp. All rights reserved/Courtesy The Everett Collection.

UNIT 1

15 *top* © Manuscripts, Archives and Special Collections, Washington State University Libraries, Neg No. 89–052; *bottom* The Granger Collection, New York; **16** *left, Mandan Offering the Buffalo Skull.* Edward S. Curtis Collection. © McCormick Library of Special Collections, Northwestern University Library; *right, Arrival of the English in Virginia* (1585–1588), Theodore de Bry. From *Admiranta Narratio,* page 47. Engraving. Service Historique de la Marine, Vincennes, France. Photo © Giraudon/Art Resource, New York; **17** *left, Fire, allegory* (1566), Giuseppe Arcimboldo. Painted for Emperor Maximilian II. Limewood, 66.5 cm × 51 cm. Inv 1585. Kunsthistorisches Museum, Vienna. Photo © Erich Lessing/Art Resource, New York; *right* Library of Congress; **20** *top, bottom* The Granger Collection, New York; **24** © Richard T. Nowitz/Corbis; **25** The Granger Collection, New York; **27** *George Washington (Vaughn Portrait)* (1795), Gilbert Stuart. Oil on canvas, 28¾″ × 23¾″, Andrew W. Mellon Collection. © 2005 Board of Trustees, National Gallery of Art, Washington D.C.; **28** *top left* Library of Congress; *center left, Whaler off the Vineyard-Outward Bound* (1859), William Bradford. Oil on Fiberboard, 16″ × 24″. Smithsonian American Art Museum, Washington, D.C. © Smithsonian American Art Museum, Washington, D.C./Art Resource, New York; *bottom left* © Mary Evans Picture Library; *right* The Granger Collection, New York; **29** *top left* The Granger Collection, New York; *center left, bottom left* © North Wind/North Wind Picture Archives; **29** *top right* The Granger Collection, New York; *bottom right* Courtesy, American Antiquarian Society; **30** © Bruce Davidson/Magnum Photos, Courtesy of Toyota; **31** *top* © National Geographic/Getty Images; *bottom* AP/Wide World Photos; **32** *top* © North Wind/North Wind Picture Archives; *bottom* Fourteen foot Abnaki style birchbark canoe. © Henri Vaillancourt; **33** © ESA/PLI/Corbis; **42** *top* © Manuscripts, Archives and Special Collections, Washington State University Libraries, Neg No. 89–052; *bottom* © Don Pitcher/Stock Boston; **43** © The Road Runner show, Wile E. Coyote, Road Runner, 1966–1973/The Everett Collection; **50** *top* © N. Scott Momaday/Royce Carlton, Inc.; *bottom* © Sharon Maritz/Age Fotostock America, Inc.; **51** © David Alan Harvey/Magnum Photos; **53** Library of Congress; **61** The Granger Collection, New York; **62** *background* © Nick Koudis/Photodisc

Green/Getty Images; *left* © NMPFT/SSPL/The Image Works, Inc.; *inset* © 2005 Peter Fasciano and Chuck Pharis Video; **63** *top to bottom* Footage for *Stagecoach* provided by Castle Hill Productions, Inc.; © 2003 Classic Media, Inc., Lone Ranger ™ and associated character names and images are trademarks of Classic Media, Inc. All rights reserved. Footage for *Stagecoach* provided by Castle Hill Productions, Inc.; Excerpts and Photography from *Smoke Signals* provided courtesy of Miramax Films. All rights reserved; **64** *top left* Excerpts and Photography from *Smoke Signals* provided courtesy of Miramax Films. All rights reserved; *bottom left* © 2003 Classic Media, Inc., Lone Ranger™ and associated character names and images are trademarks of Classic Media, Inc. All rights reserved; *background* © United Artists/The Kobal Collection. Footage for *Stagecoach* provided by Castle Hill Productions, Inc.; **67** Library of Congress; **68** *top* Courtesy of the Ministry of Post, Spain; *bottom* © GoodShoot/SuperStock; **69** Illustration by Tom McNeely; **78** *top, bottom* The Granger Collection, New York; **88** *top* The Granger Collection, New York; *bottom* © Richard T. Nowitz/Corbis; **91** *Arrival of the English in Virginia* (1585–1588), Theodore de Bry. From *Admiranta Narratio*, page 47. Engraving. Service Historique de la Marine, Vincennes, France. Photo © Giraudon/Art Resource, New York; **93** © Getty Images; **98** *top* Culver Pictures; *bottom* © Raymond Forbes/Age Fotostock America, Inc.; **99, 102, 109** The Granger Collection, New York; **110** *top, Portrait of Anne Bradstreet,* LaDonna Gulley Warrick; *center* © Image Farm, Inc.; *bottom* © Jerry and Marcy Monkman/EcoPhotography; **111** © Pete Turner/Getty Images; **113** *Sampler* (1796), Abigail Gould. Linen plain weave embroidered with silk and wool, 25 cm. × 30 cm. Gift of Miss Jeannette Woodward 41.253. Museum of Fine Arts, Boston; **114** detail of *Silk-On-Linen Needlework Sampler* (1822). Relief Shumway. Hardwick, Massachusetts. © Christie's Images Ltd.; **116** *Needlework Sampler* (1774), Alice Mather. Norwich, Connecticut/Christie's Images Ltd.; **118** *background* © PhotoDisc; *top* The Granger Collection, New York; **119** © Comstock Images/Alamy Images; **128** The Granger Collection, New York/Courtesy of Al Hirschfeld Theatre; **130** *top* © Getty Images; *bottom left* © Stockdisc/Getty Images; *bottom* © Brand X Pictures/Jupiterimages; **131** © 20th Century Fox Film Corp. All rights reserved/Courtesy The Everett Collection; **132–133** *top* © 1996 Photofest; **135, 139** © 20th Century Fox Film Corp. All rights reserved/Courtesy The Everett Collection; **143** © 1996 Photofest; **149** *top, bottom* © 20th Century Fox Film Corp. All rights reserved/Courtesy The Everett Collection; **151** © Twentieth Century Film Corp./Photofest; **161** © 20th Century Fox Film Corp. All rights reserved/Courtesy The Everett Collection; **168** © 1996 Photofest; **176, 185** © 20th Century Fox Film Corp. All rights reserved/Courtesy The Everett Collection; **193** *top* © Robbie Jack/Corbis; **193** *bottom* © 20th Century Fox Film Corp. All rights reserved. Courtesy The Everett Collection; **197** © 20th Century Fox/The Kobal Collection; **205** © 20th Century Fox Film Corp. All rights reserved/Courtesy The Everett Collection; **212** © 1996 Photofest; **213** © Bettmann/Corbis; **214** *top* The New York Times Company; *bottom* © Bettmann/Corbis; **216** AP/Wide World Photos; **218** *top* © Barry Wetcher/20th Century Fox/The Kobal Collection; *bottom* © Romilly Lockyer/Getty Images; **220** AP/Wide World Photos; **222** © akg-images; **224** *top* The Granger Collection, New York; *bottom* © David Muench/Corbis; **234** *top, Thomas Jefferson* (1805), Gilbert Stuart. Oil on panel, 36⅛″ × 21″. National Portrait Gallery, Smithsonian Institution, Washington, D.C.: gift of the Regents of the Smithsonian Institution, the Thomas Jefferson Memorial Foundation, and the Enid and Crosby Kemper Foundation; owned jointly with Monticello. Photo © National Portrait Gallery, Smithsonian Institution/Art Resource, New York; *bottom* © Pat and Chuck Blackley;

235 The Granger Collection, New York; **237** Library of Congress; **239** The Granger Collection, New York; **244** *top* The Granger Collection, New York; *bottom* © Joseph Sohm/Visions of America/Corbis; **245, 249** The Granger Collection, New York; **254** *top* Library of Congress; *center* The Granger Collection, New York; *bottom* © Brand X Pictures/Alamy Images; **255** © Mark Sykes/Alamy Images; **257** The Granger Collection, New York; **259** *top, Abigail Smith Adams* (about 1766), Benjamin Blyth. Pastel on paper, 57.3 × 44.8 cm.© Massachusetts Historical Society, Boston/Bridgeman Art Library; *bottom, John Adams* (1766), Benjamin Blyth. Pastel on paper, 57.3 cm × 44.8 cm. © Massachusetts Historical Society, Boston, Massachusetts/Bridgeman Art Library; *frames,* © Image Farm, Inc.; *background* Courtesy of Adelphi Paper Hangings and the Colonial Williamsburg Foundation; **262** *top, Portrait of Benjamin Franklin* (about 1785), Joseph Siffred Duplessis. Oil on canvas, 72.4 cm × 59.6 cm. National Portrait Gallery, Smithsonian Institution, Washington, D.C. Photo © National Portrait Gallery, Smithsonian Institution/Art Resource, New York; *bottom* Library of Congress; **263** © Erik Dreyer/Getty Images; **270** © Bettmann/Corbis; **271** © Mike Caplanis/Luminary Graphics; **275** The Granger Collection, New York; **276, 282** © Craig Aurness/Corbis; **283** © Michael Newman/PhotoEdit; **290–291** © PunchStock.

UNIT 2

293 *top, Nathaniel Hawthorne* (1840), Charles Osgood. Oil on canvas. © Peabody Essex Museum, Salem, Massachusetts/Bridgeman Art Library; *bottom* The Granger Collection, New York; **294** *left, Lackawanna Valley* (1855), George Inness. Oil on canvas. The Granger Collection, New York; *right* The Granger Collection, New York; **295** *left* © Bettmann/Corbis; *right, Kindred Spirits* (1849), Asher Brown Durand. © Francis G. Mayer/Corbis; **296** Detail of *Summer Afternoon On the Hudson* (1852), Jasper Francis Crospey. © Christie's Images/Corbis; **298** © The British Museum/HIP/The Image Works, Inc.; **299** The Granger Collection, New York; **301** *right, left* Public Domain; *center* The Granger Collection, New York; Photo of all by Sharon Hoogstraten; **302** © Mary Evans Picture Library; **303** © Kim Grant/Lonely Planet Images; **306** *top left* Public Domain, Photo by Sharon Hoogstraten; *top right* Manuscripts, Archives and Rare Books Division, Schomburg Cener for Research in Black Culture, The New York Public Library, Astor, Lenox and Tilden Foundations; *center left, Map of the United States of America* (1816), John Melish. Map division. Astor, Lenox and Tilden Foundations. © New York Public Library/Art Resource, New York; *center right, USS Constitution in Action with HMS Guerriere, 19 August, 1812,* Michele Felice Corne © Francis G. Mayer/Corbis; *bottom* The Granger Collection, New York; **307** *top center* Public Domain, Photo by Sharon Hoogstraten; *top right* © Bettmann/Corbis; *center left, frame* © 1996 Image Farm, Inc. All rights reserved.; *center left, photo* © Bettmann/Corbis; *center* Courtesy of the California History Room, California State Library, Sacramento, California; *center right* Photo by Beth Reitmeyer; *bottom* The Granger Collection, New York; **308** © James P. Blair/National Geographic Image Collection; **309** *top* Pages from *Graphic Classics: Edgar Allan Poe* edited by Tom Pomplun. *The Tell-Tale Heart* adapted and illustrated by Rick Geary. Used by permission of Eureka Productions, Mount Horeb, Wisconsin; *bottom* © Lucasfilm, Ltd/Paramount/The Kobal Collection; **310** *top* © Historic Hudson Valley, Tarrytown, New York; *bottom* © Jodi Cobb/National Geographic Image Collection; **311** © Stockbyte/Getty Images; **328** *top* The Granger Collection, New York; *bottom* © Darrell Gulin/Corbis; **329** © Kirsty McLaren/Getty Images; **333** *Forest Landscape* (1800s), Asher Brown Durand. Oil on canvas, 76.2 cm × 66 cm.

© Brooklyn Museum of Art/Bridgeman Art Library; **334** *top* © Stock Montage; *bottom* AP/Wide World Photos; **335** © Tommy Flynn/Getty Images; **340** *top* The Granger Collection, New York; *bottom* © Corbis; **341** © C Squared Studios/Getty Images; **343** © iconsight/Alamy Images; **344** © David Zimmerman/Corbis; **346** *top* The Granger Collection, New York; *center* Library of Congress; *bottom* © Joseph Sohm/Stock Connection; **349** © Reynolds Stock Photo; **355** © Swerve/Alamy Images; **357** © North Wind/North Wind Picture Archives; **358** © Judith Jango-Cohen; **360** *top* © Bettmann/Corbis; *bottom* © Michele Burgess/ SuperStock; **361** Photograph by Jay Fechtman; **363** *Wanderer Above a Sea of Fog* (1817), Casper David Friedrich. Oil on canvas, 94.8 cm × 74.8 cm. Inv.: 5161 On permanent loan from the Foundation for the Promotion of the Hamburg Art Collections. Hamburger Kunsthalle, Hamburg, Germany. Photo by Elke Walford. © Bildarchiv Preussischer Kulturbesitz/ Art Resource, New York; **370** *top* Detail of *Henry David Thoreau* (1856), Benjamin D. Maxham. Daguerreotype, 6.3 cm x 4.7 cm. National Portrait Gallery, Smithsonian Institution, Washington, DC. © National Portrait Gallery, Smithsonian Institution/Art Resource, New York; *bottom* © age fotostock/SuperStock; **371** © Duane Lofton/Painet Inc.; **373** © Gail Mooney/Masterfile; **376** *top* © Corbis; *bottom* © David Muench/ Corbis; **377** *top* © RubberBall Productions/Getty Images; *bottom* © Arthur Morris/Corbis; **383** © Lynsey Addario/Corbis; **386** *left* © Underwood & Underwood/Corbis; *right* © Bettmann/Corbis; **386–387** *top on 2 pages* © Bettmann/Corbis; **387** *left* © Wally McNamee/Corbis; *right* © Reuters/Corbis; **393** Max Desfor/AP/Wide World Photos; **394** *top* © Brown Brothers, Sterling, PA; *bottom* © Corbis; **401** © Howard Kingsnorth/Getty Images; **402** *top* © Bettmann/ Corbis; *bottom* © Lake County Museum/Corbis; **403** © Bertrand Demée/Getty Images; **429** Cloister (1370–1410), Gloucester Cathedral, Gloucestershire, United Kingdom © Bridgeman Art Library; **429** *top left* © Bill Ross/Corbis; **430** *background* © Roger Wright/Getty Images; *left* © PNC/Getty Images; **437** © Michael Llewellyn/Getty Images; **439** *Raven* (1996) © Keith Carter Photographs; **445** © Illustration Works; **446** Gargoyles. Notre Dame, Paris. Photo © Vanni/Art Resource, New York; **447** © Arthur Rackham/Mary Evans Picture Library; **448** *left* © Arthur Rackham/Mary Evans Picture Library; *bottom* © Tim Flach/Getty Images; **451** © David Elliott/Getty Images; **452–453** © PictureQuest; **452** *top* © Les Cunliffe/Age Fotostock America, Inc.; *bottom* The Granger Collection, New York; **453** © Mary Evans Picture Library/The Image Works, Inc.; **454** *top* © Les Cunliffe/Age Fotostock America, Inc.; *center* *Portrait of Nathaniel Hawthorne* (about 1862), Emanuel Gottlieb Leutze. National Portrait Gallery, Smithsonian Institution, Washington D.C. Photo © National Portrait Gallery, Smithsonian Institution/Art Resource, New York; *bottom* PBS/Courtesy of Photofest; **454–455** © PhotoDisc; **455** Cover illustration by Troy Thomas © McDougal Littell; **456** *top* National Archives; *bottom* © S. Solum/Photolink/Getty Images; **457** © Carlos Dominguez/Corbis; **462** *The Last Halt: Stop of Hooker's Band in East Hartford before Crossing River* (1939), Alton S. Tobey. Study for East Hartford, Connecticut Postal Office. Oil on fiberboard, 26″ × 44 1/8″ . Transfer from General Services Administration. © Smithsonian American Art Museum, Washington, D.C./Art Resource/New York www. altontobey.org; **473** © Gary Kelley, 1996; **474, 480** © Joseph Sohm; ChromoSohm Inc./Corbis; **481** *left* © David Young-Wolff/PhotoEdit; *right* © Getty Images; **488–489** © PunchStock.

UNIT 3

491 *top* © Getty Images; *bottom, Union Soldiers Fighting in the Field,* Albert Bierstadt. Photo © Geoffrey Clements/Corbis; **492** *left* © Corbis; *right* The Granger Collection, New York; **493** *left* The Granger Collection, New York; *right* © Mort Künstler, Inc.; **496** The Granger Collection, New York; **498** *top* © Mary Evans Picture Library/The Image Works, Inc.; *frame* © Image Farm, Inc.; *bottom, The Laughing Philosopher* (1887), George C. Cox. Photograph. © Museum of the City of New York/Bridgeman Art Library; *frame* © Image Farm, Inc.; **499** © Tom Gauld/Heart USA Inc.; **500** The Granger Collection, New York; **501** *Prisoners from the Front* (1866), Winslow Homer. Oil on canvas, 24″ × 38″. The Metropolitan Museum of Art, Gift of Mrs. Frank B. Porter, 1922 (22.207). Photo © 1995 The Metropolitan Museum of Art, New York/Art Resource, New York; **502** *top* Public Domain; *left* The Granger Collection, New York; *right* © Corbis; *bottom* The Granger Collection, New York; **503** *top left, The Gettysburg Address, 1863,* Jean Leon Jerome Ferris. Private collection. Photo © Bridgeman Art Library; *top right* © Bettmann/Corbis; *center left, center right* The Granger Collection, New York; *bottom* © Araldo de Luca/Corbis; **504** © Corbis Sygma; **505** *top left* © Blue Man Productions, Inc.; *top right* The Granger Collection, New York; *center left* © Reuters/Corbis; *center right* AP/Wide World Photos; *bottom left* © Mitchell Gerber/Corbis *bottom center* © Flip Schulke/ Corbis; *bottom right* AP/Wide World Photos; **506** *Walt Whitman inciting the bird of freedom to soar* (1904), Max Beerbohm. Engraving. From *The Poets Corner* published by William Heinemann. © Central Saint Martins College of Art and Design, London/Bridgeman Art Library; **508** *top* National Archives; *bottom* © Fabio Cardoso/zefa/Corbis; **509** © Ken Fisher/Getty Images; **518** © PhotoDisc; **520** © Michael Powers/Veer; **521** © Laurent Bessol/Getty Images; **522** © Thomas Hoepker/Magnum Photos; **523** © Photodisc; **524** *top* The Granger Collection, New York; *bottom* © Gail Mooney/Masterfile; **525** © Photodisc/Veer; **527** © Carl Rosenstein/Getty Images; **528** © Martin Rogers/Getty Images; **529** © Nick Koudis/Getty Images; **530** © Todd Gipstein/Corbis; **531** © Dr. Dennis Kunkel/Getty Images; **532** © Jeremy Woodhouse/Getty Images; **533** *top* © ShutterStock; *center, bottom* © Artbeats; **535** © Mike Caplanis/Luminarygraphics.com; **536** *top* © Chester County Historical Society, West Chester, Pennsylvania; *bottom* © William Manning/Corbis; **540** *The Life of Harriet Tubman, #9* (1940), Jacob Lawrence. Casein tempera on hardboard, 12″ × 17 7/8″. Hampton University Museum. Photo courtesy of Gwendolyn Knight Lawrence/ Art Resource, New York. © 2007 The Jacob and Gwendolyn Lawrence Foundation, Seattle/Artists Rights Society (ARS), New York; **550** *top, Harriet Jacobs,* 1894, Cabinet photograph by Gilbert Studios, Washington, D.C. Gold toned albumin print; *bottom* © Bettmann/Corbis; **553** © New York Public Library, Schomburg Center; **555** Photographic History Collection, National Museum of American History, Smithsonian Institution, Washington, D.C.; **560–561** © Map Division, New York Public Library, Astor, Lenox and Tilden Foundations; **562** *top* Library of Congress; *bottom* © Joseph Sohm/ChromoSohm Inc./Corbis; **566** National Archives; **570** © Reza Estakhrian/Getty Images; **571–580** *bottom* © Photodisc; **571** *center* © Artbeats; *bottom right* The Granger Collection, New York; *frame* © Image Farm, Inc.; **572** *top left* United States Army Military History Institute; *frame* © Image Farm, Inc.; *top right* © Getty Images; *center* © Artbeats; **573** *center* © Artbeats; *bottom left* © David Toase/Getty Images; *bottom right, Mary Boykin Chesnut* (1856), Samuel S. Osgood. Oil on canvas adhered to masonite, 48″ × 30″ with frame. © Private Collection/Art Resource, New York; **574** *top left* The Granger Collection,

New York; *frame* © Image Farm, Inc.; *center* © Artbeats; **576** The Granger Collection, New York; **578–579** *Battle of Nashville,* Howard Pyle. © Minnesota Historical Society/Corbis; **578** *top* © Les Cunliffe/Age Fotostock America, Inc.; *bottom* © Alderman Library/University of Virginia; **579** Public Domain; **580** *top* © Bettmann/Corbis; *bottom* © Corbis; **581** © Nonstock/Jupiter Images; **583** © Stephen Graham/Owl Creek Productions; **584** © Peter L. Chapman/Index Stock Imagery, Inc.; **587** © Ionpost/Owl Creek Productions; **589** © Stephen Frink/Getty Images; **591** © Mike Zens/Corbis; **595** *Lincoln at Gettysburg II* (1939–1942), William H. Johnson. Gouache and pen and ink on paper, 19¾" × 17¹/₁₆". Gift of the Harmon Foundation. Smithsonian American Art Museum, Washington, D.C. © Smithsonian American Art Museum, Washington, D.C./Art Resource, New York; **596** *top* © Stephen Graham/Owl Creek Productions; *bottom* Clip courtesy of Owl Creek Production, L.L.C. www.owlcreekproductions.com; **598, 604** © Daryl Benson/Masterfile; **605** © Paul Edmondson/Corbis; **612–613** © PunchStock.

UNIT 4

615 *top, Willa Cather* (1923–1924), Nicholai Fechin. Oil on canvas. University of Nebraska Library. Gift of Dr. Philip L. and Helen Cather Southwick through University of Nebraska Foundation. Lincoln, Nebraska; *bottom, The Jolly Flatboatmen* (1877–1878), George Caleb Bingham. Oil on canvas, 26¹/₁₆" × 36³/₈". Daniel J. Terra Acquisition Endowment Fund, 1992.15. Terra Foundation for American Art, Chicago. © Terra Foundation for American Art, Chicago/Art Resource, New York; **616** *left, Family and their Dugout* (1870s), Anonymous. Photo 11" × 14". Near McCook Nebraska. © Nebraska State Historical Society, Lincoln, Nebraska; *right* © Joel Sartore/National Geographic Image Collection; **617** *left, A Sketch of a Faraway Look,* Herman Jean Joseph Richir. Bonhams, London. © Bridgeman Art Library/SuperStock © 2007 Artists Rights Society (ARS), New York/ADAGP, Paris; *right* © Corbis; **620** *The Hatch Family* (1871), Eastman Johnson. Oil on canvas, 48" × 73 3/8". The Metropolitan Museum of Art, Gift of Frederic H. Hatch, 1926 (26.97). Photo © 1999 The Metropolitan Museum of Art/Art Resource, New York; **622** The Newberry Library, Chicago, **623** Photo Courtesy of the South Dakota State Historical Society, State Archives; **624–625** © Juniors Bildarchiv/age fotostock america, inc; **626** © Bettman/Corbis; **627** *In the Garden* (1904), Mary Stevenson Cassatt. Pastel on paper, 66 cm. × 81.3 cm. © The Detroit Institute of Arts/Bridgeman Art Library; **628** *top left* © Comstock/Superstock; *top center* © Harry Taylor/Dorling Kindersley; *top right* © Bettmann/Corbis; *center left* © Time & Life Pictures/Getty Images; *center right* © Corbis; *bottom* © Images.com/Corbis; **629** *top* © Bettmann/Corbis *center;* © Corbis; *bottom* Royal biscuit. Biscuit label by Carr & Co. (CT13673A). Victoria and Albert Museum, London. © Victoria and Albert Museum, London/Art Resource, New York; **630** © Scimitar/The Kobal Collection; **631** *top* © 2004 Getty Images; *bottom* © Layne Kennedy/Corbis; **632** © Bettmann/Corbis; **633** The Granger Collection, New York; **634** *top* Library of Congress; *bottom* © Stephen Alvarez/National Geographic Image Collection; **635** © Design Pics Inc./Alamy; **637** Library of Congress; **639** *Levitation* © Scala/Art Resource, New York; **641** Library of Congress; **646** © Mike Caplains/www.luminarygraphics.com; **649** © Steve Bloom/Getty Images; **651** *background* Library of Congress; *inset* The Granger Collection, New York; *frame* © 1996 Image Farm, Inc. All rights reserved; **653** *left* © Mary Evans Picture Library/The Image Works, Inc.; *right* © The Mariners' Museum, Newport, Virginia; **659** © Rubberball/Age Fotostock America, Inc.; **661, 665, 666** The Granger Collection, New York; **670** *top* © Les Cunliffe/Age Fotostock America, Inc.; *bottom* ©

Corbis; **670–671** © Kevin Horan/Getty Images; **671** Cover of the original *The Adventures of Huckleberry Finn* by Mark Twain © 1885. Illustrated by E.W. Kemble/The Granger Collection, New York; **672** *top* © Brown Brothers, Sterling, Pennsylvania; *bottom* © Thomas Morse/PlaceStockPhoto.com; **673** © G. Brad Lewis/Getty Images; **678** © Bill Manns/The Art Archive; **682–683** Library of Congress; **684** Public Domain; **689** © Corbis; **692** *top* © Willa Cather Pioneer Memorial Collection/Nebraska State Historical Society; *bottom* © Age Fotostock/SuperStock; **693** © Terry Evans Photography; **695** *Old Souvenirs* (about 1881-1901), John F. Peto. Oil on canvas, 26 ¾" × 22". The Metropolitan Museum of Art, Bequest of Oliver Burr Jennings, 1968 (68.205.3) Photo © 1983 The Metropolitan Museum of Art, New York/Art Resource, New York; **705** Library of Congress; **706** © Hulton-Deutsch/Corbis; **707** *left* © Geoffrey Clements/Corbis; *right* © Corbis; **708** *top left, Castle Geyser and Firehole Basin (1871),* William Henry Jackson. Courtesy National Park Service, Yellowstone National Park, *YELL 36193;* (1871), William Henry Jackson. Courtesy Department of the Interior, Yellowstone National Park/National Park Service; *bottom left, The Castle Geyser, Firehole Basin* (1872), Thomas Moran. 7¹/₂" × 11" The Gilcrease Musem, Tulsa, Oklahoma. 0226.1363. © The Gilcrease Museum; *background* © Bill Ross/Corbis; **710** *top* The Granger Collection, New York; *bottom* © Nicole Duplaix/National Geographic Image Collection; **711** © Eric Nguyen/Jim Reed Photography/Corbis; **718–719** *The Much Resounding Sea* (1884), Thomas Moran. Oil on canvas, 25 ³/₁₆" x 62 ⁵/₁₆". Gift of the Avalon Foundation. Image © 2006 Board of Trustees, National Gallery of Art, Washington, D.C.; **738** Image manipulated German shipwreck survivors, Achille Beltrame. Engraving in Italian newspaper *La Domenica del Corriere,* February, 1941 Photo © Dagli Orti/The Art Archive; **739** Public Domain; **740** Library of Congress, Rare Book and Special Collections Division; **741** *top* Library of Congress, Rare Book and Special Collections Division; *bottom* © Bettmann/Corbis; **742** Library of Congress, Rare Book and Special Collections Division; **744** *top* © Underwood & Underwood/Corbis; *bottom* © Allen Prier/Panoramic Images/NGSImages.com; **745** © David McLain/Aurora Photos; **747** © Werner Forman/akg-images; **751** © Alamy Images; **755** © Joel Sartore/National Geographic Image Collection; **756** © Hulton-Deutsch Collection/Corbis; **758** *top* The Granger Collection, New York; *bottom* © Lee Foster/Lonely Planet Images; **761** *A Sketch of a Faraway Look,* Herman Jean Joseph Richir. Bonhams, London. © 2007 Artists Rights Society (ARS), New York/ADAGP, Paris ; **766** *top* © Brown Brothers, Sterling, PA; *bottom* © Getty Images; **767** © T. Kruesselmann/T.Hemmings/Espressokiss/zefa/Corbis; **784** Public Domain; **788** *top* © Les Cunliffe/Age Fotostock America, Inc.; *bottom* The Granger Collection, New York; **788–789** © John Churchman/Veer; **789** © McDougal Littell; **790** © Bettmann/Corbis; **791** © Gallery Stock Limited; **803** © 2005 Getty Images; **804, 810** © Richard Sisk/Jupiter Images; **811** *left* © Michael Newman/PhotoEdit; *right* © Lionel Isy-Schwart/Getty Images; **816–817** © PunchStock.

UNIT 5

821 *top* The Granger Collection, New York; *bottom, The Bicycle Race* (1912), Lyonel Feininger. Oil on canvas, 31⁵/₈" x 39¹/₂". Collection of Mr. and Mrs. Paul Mellon. © 2007 National Gallery of Art, Washington, D.C. © 2007 Artists Rights Society (ARS), New York/VG Bild-Kunst, Bonn; **822** *left, The Shelton with Sunspots* (1926), Georgia O'Keeffe. Oil on canvas, 123.1 cm × 76.8 cm. The Art Institute of Chicago, gift of Leigh B. Block (1985.206). © 1994 The Art Institute of Chicago, all rights reserved. © 2007 The Georgia O'Keeffe Museum/

UNIT 6

1089 *left, Man in Red* (2003), Diana Ong. Computer graphics. © Purestock/SuperStock; *right* © Gene Blevins/Corbis; **1090** *left* © K.J. Historical/Corbis; *right* © Bettmann/Corbis; **1091** *left, Incredibles Las Cosas Q'Se Ven, 2001* Mural at Ashland Avenue and 19th Street in Chicago. © Jeffrey Zimmermann; *right* © Josef Scaylea/Corbis; **1092** Digital image © 1996 Corbis; Original image courtesy of NASA/Corbis; **1094** © Jacques Langevin/Corbis Sygma; **1095** © Elliott Erwitt/Magnum Photos; **1096** © Josef Scaylea/Corbis; **1097** © Warner Brothers/Getty Images; **1099** *left* © Wally McNamee/Corbis; *right* © K.J. Historical/Corbis; **1100** AP/Wide World Photos; **1101** *White Cloud Over Purple* (1957), Mark Rothko. Oil on canvas, 143 cm × 138 cm. © Private collection/Bridgeman Art Library. © 2007 Kate Rothko Prizel and Christopher Rothko/Artists Rights Society (ARS), New York.; **1102** *top* Associated Press; *center left* The Granger Collection, New York; *center right* © Bettmann/Corbis; *bottom* © Getty Images; **1103** *top left* Photograph by Carmine Fantasia/McDougall Littell; *top right* © Getty Images; *center left* © AFP/Getty Images; *center right* © NOAA/Corbis; *bottom* Central Intelligence Agency; **1104** © Corbis; **1105** *top* © Google; *bottom* © Steven Hunt/Getty Images; **1106** *top* © Les Cunliffe/Age Fotostock America, Inc.; *center* AP/Wide World Photos; *bottom* Showtime/Coutesy of Photofest; **1106–1107** © Corbis; **1107** Cover of *Our Town* by Thornton Wilder. © 1938, 1957 by Thornton Wilder. Cover illustration © William Low. Reprinted by permission of Harper Perennial, a Division of Harper Collins Publishers; **1108** *top* © Les Cunliffe/Age Fotostock America, Inc.; *center* © Bettmann/Corbis; *bottom* © ArenaPal/Topham/The Image Works, Inc.; **1109** © Playbill/Photofest; **1110** *top* © Les Cunliffe/Age Fotostock America, Inc.; *center* © Bettmann/Corbis; *bottom* Marilyn Kingwill/ArenaPAL © ArenaPAL/Topham/The Image Works, Inc.; **1110–1111** © Angela Cappetta/Getty Images; **1111** The Granger Collection, New York; **1112** *top* © Les Cunliffe/Age Fotostock America, Inc.; *center* © Bettmann/Corbis; *bottom* © Joan Marcus; **1112–1113** © PhotoDisc, Inc.; **1113** © McDougal Littell; **1114** *top* National Archives; *center* AP/Wide World Photos; *bottom* Courtesy of Franklin D. Roosevelt Presidential Library and Museum; **1115** © Todd Gipstein/Corbis; **1117** © Bettmann/Corbis; **1119** © Time Life Pictures/Getty Images; **1122** *top* © Marko Shark/Corbis; *bottom* © Bettmann/Corbis; **1133** © Michael St. Maur Sheil/Corbis; **1134** © Bruno Barbey/Magnum Photos; **1136** *top* © Marilyn Knapp Litt; *bottom* © Olivier Martel/Corbis; **1137** © Bernard Annebicque/Corbis; **1143** © Time & Life Pictures/Getty Images; **1144** *top* © Time & Life Images/Getty Images; *bottom* © Bob Adelman/Magnum Photos; **1145** © Bob Adelman/Magnum Photos; **1147** © Bettmann/Corbis; **1152** © Bob Adelman/Magnum Photos; **1156** Dave King © Dorling Kindersley; **1160** *top* © Bettmann/Corbis; *center* © Time & Life Images/Getty Images; *bottom* © Michael S. Yamashita/Corbis; **1161** AP/Wide World Photos; **1163** © Bob Adelman/Magnum Photos; **1167** © Eve Arnold/Magnum Photos; **1168** © James Nubile/The Image Works, Inc.; **1172** *top* © Bob Adelman/Magnum Photos; *bottom* © Eve Arnold/Magnum Photos; **1173** *left* © Bettmann/Corbis; *right* © Flip Schulke/Corbis; **1176** © Paul Fusco/Magnum Photos; **1177** *top* © Courtesy of CBS News Archives; *bottom* © Richard Thornton/ShutterStock; **1178** *top* © Courtesy of CBS News Archives; *bottom* © Owen Franken/Corbis; **1180** *top* Courtesy of Bantam Doubleday Dell; *bottom* © New York Times Agency; **1181** © Greenblatt Bill/Corbis Sygma; **1183** © Bettmann/Corbis; **1187** © Bettmann/Corbis; **1192** *top* © Bettmann/Corbis; *bottom* © Corbis; **1201** © Najlah Feanny/Corbis Saba; **1202** *top* AP/Wide World Photos; *center* © Christopher Felver/Corbis; *bottom* © Bassouls Sophie/Corbis; **1204** *top* © Getty Images; *bottom* © Alex Mares-Manton/Getty Images; **1205** © E. Streichan/zefa/Corbis; **1207** *Apple* (1983), Andy Warhol. Synthetic polymer paint and silkscreen ink on canvas, 14″ × 11″. © The Andy Warhol Foundation for the Visual Arts/Artists Rights Society (ARS), New York © The Andy Warhol Foundation, Inc./Art Resource, New York. Courtesy Ronald Feldman Fine Arts, New York; **1214** *top* © Getty Images; *bottom, Crazy Patchwork* Quilt (1875), unknown artist. Smithsonian Institution, Washington, D.C. © Bridgeman Art Library; **1215** © Botanica/Jupiter Images; **1222** *top* © Gene Blevins/Corbis; *bottom* © Randy Faris/Corbis; **1223** © Angelo Cavalli/Getty Images; **1225** *Making Tortillas* (1926), Diego Rivera. University of California, San Francisco. © Bridgeman Art Library © 2008 Banco de México Diego Rivera & Frida Kahlo Museums Trust. Av. Cinco de Mayo No. 2, Col. Centro, Del. Cuauhtémoc 06059, Mexico, D.F.; **1230** *top* Photo © Nancy E. Crampton; *bottom* © Getty Images; **1232** © Eli Reed/Magnum Photos; **1236** *top* © Photograph of Rita Dove by Fred Viebahn; *bottom left* Courtesy of Pulitzer.org; *bottom background* © Jean-Claude Marlaud/Getty Images; **1237** © Photodisc Photography/Veer; **1238** © Ernest Crichlow Estate; **1242** *top* © Christopher Felver/Corbis; *bottom* © Alan Schein Photography/Corbis; **1243** © Randy Faris/Corbis; **1244** © Arthur Morris/Corbis; **1248, 1254** © J. David Andrews/Masterfile; **1255** © Phil Boorman/Getty Images; **1262–1263** © PunchStock.

UNIT 7

1265 *top* © Design Pics, Inc./Alamy Images; *top* inset © Bettmann/Corbis; *bottom* Photographer Dorothea Lange, 1935/Library of Congress; **1266** *left* © Bettmann/Corbis; *right* © Steven Hunt/Getty Images; **1267** *left* The Granger Collection, New York; *right* © NOAA/Corbis; **1270** *left* © Science Museum/SSPL/The Image Works, Inc.; *right inset* Public Domain; *right* © Jupiterimages; **1271** Reproduced with permission of Overture Inc. 2006 by Overture Inc. Alltheweb and the Alltheweb logo are trademarks of Overture Inc.; **1275** *Audience in recreation hall, Tulare Migrant Camp, Visalia, California* (1940). Photo by Arthur Rothstein. Voices From the Dust Bowl website. Courtesy of the American Folklife Center, Library of Congress; **1276** © Los Angeles Times. Reprinted with permission; **1281** *top* Library of Congress; *center* © United Nations; *bottom* NASA; **1284, 1301** © Jason Ernst/Age Fotostock America, Inc.; **1302** *left* © Bettmann/Corbis; *right* © Michael Newman/PhotoEdit; **1303** © Time Life Pictures/Getty Images.

STUDENT RESOURCE BANK

R03 National Archives; **R13** AP/Wide World Photos; **R14** © Bettmann/Corbis; **R16** Transportation Security Administration /U.S. Department of Homeland Security; **R18** *top* Museum of the American west, Autry National Center, Los Angeles; *bottom* © Denver Public Library, Western History Collection. Photographer Underwood & Underwood. Call number F46503. Denver, Colorado; **R95** *foreground, top* © Photodisc; *background* © Alain Evrard/Getty Images.

BACK COVER

© Brand X Pictures.